BIG MONKEY'S
COMPACT DISC PRICE GUIDE

A CD Collector's Handbook
By Rick Colon

ISBN   0-9761718-0-5
Library of Congress Control Number: 2004097071

Preface

I have been collecting music since around the late 1960s/1970s when I heard drifting from my brother Carlos's room all kinds of exciting music such as The Beatles, The Kinks, The Who, Santana and The Velvet Underground. I have been selling cds, videos, and dvds under the name Big Monkey Cds and Videos on Ebay where I have been a Powerseller with over 5,000 positives and no negatives and no "bought positives".

I started listening to music on the radio before models and actresses became musicians. Musicians could actually sing and play instruments. DJs selected the music on the radio and instinctively knew good music. Record executives did not pick out the music. It was not put on programmable tapes. There was not any sampling music because people could actually compose their own songs. I say all of this because you are going to notice there are some bands missing from this guide. Some bands, which are not included, will be in my next compact disc guide. For example, I will have more Pop, Punk, Soul, Rhythm and Blues, Jazz, and Country bands. Some bands, however, will not be there, since some of the later bands people are not collecting, because they do not have spontaneity, creativity, or longevity.

This price guide was designed for people who collect cds. So the information contained is what a collector would want to know: artist, title, format, label, catalog number (to order the cd if it is in print), country, year released and current value (what it is worth). Of course somebody may sell a cd for much less or much more than it is worth, but these prices are based on my thirty years of experience in the business.

What makes a compact disc collectible? A number of things make a cd collectible: supply and demand, whether it is a limited numbered edition, or whether the item is cut out (no longer available in stores). Other factors influencing the price of a cd are: whether it is a limited Japanese run, or if it is a gold cd. Additionally, if it is a promo (promotional cd), which is made to be played in stores selling cds or on the radio, such as Westwood One and King Biscuit live cds; they are also collectible. Also, a cd could be collectible because the cd is with the original longbox, which helped sell the cd in stores, or the cd could be a first issue, such as the Cross cds or The Beatles Abbey Road Japan cd.

Supply and demand makes a cd rise or fall in value. If a cd is by James Taylor and widely available in the United States it will not be worth as much as the first Judee Sill cd made in limited numbers by Rhino Handmade. If a cd is numbered and limited it is more rare than a cd widely distributed, still in print, and available in stores everywhere.

Why would a company such as Rhino Handmade make only 3,000 copies of the Judee Sill cd? Several factors probably determined Rhino's decision to issue this cd in limited quantities. First, it has ten bonus tracks, of which 3 are demos (songs recorded for record executives to hear), and 7 are live tracks. Another factor probably influenced Rhino's decision, which was that Judee was the first artist signed to Asylum by David Geffen. Other factors could have been that one song was produced by Graham Nash of The Hollies and Crosby, Stills, Nash And Young fame, and that Judee was considered to be a female Brian Wilson. These factors plus the fact that the cd is limited makes this cd collectible.

Japanese cds as a whole are worth more than their American or European counterparts because the Japanese make better quality cds. They will also release cds that are not available elsewhere like God Bless Tiny Tim by Tiny Tim. They have better sound quality and sometimes bonus tracks not available anywhere else. Some Japanese Mini Lp Cds, (small cd versions of the orginal Lp versions) go for huge prices. For example, The Emerson, Lake And Palmer Works and Welcome Back My Friends Mini Lps are fetching between $400 and $500 respectively because they were made in such limited quantities. Mini Lps, however, are not really good investments because they keep reissuing them and then the price drops as a result of supply and demand. However, they are wonderful to collect for the music and the goodies inside. For example, the early Rick Wakeman albums are available in Mini Lp Cd. The Journey To The Centre Of The Earth has the original inside booklet that came with the album version.

Gold cd versions have become quite popular. Mobile Fidelity Cds or MFSL cds and DCC Gold Cds and Sony Mastersound Gold Cds are all popular cds. There are also gold cds put out by Japan and Australia that are quite popular. For those of you who are not aware of this, Mobile Fidelity is still in business and cds are being sold at www.amusicdirect.com. They have just released John Lennon's Imagine and Plastic Ono Band. They also have released The Kinks Low Budget and Everybody's In Showbiz. The sound quality is quite good on gold cds and some such as Stand Up by Jethro Tull have the original artwork that made the album so unforgettable. There are some cheaply made gold cds, but the gold cds that I mentioned earlier are the best ones to buy for sound quality.

Promos (Promotional cds) are rare because they are made only for stores, or the radio, to promote an artist. They are extremely limited in nature. The European ones are more limited than the American ones, because Europe has fewer stores and radio stations. The labels sometimes put out live or greatest hits compilations to promote their artists that they do not release to the public. For example, there is a Midnight Oil promo compilation called Best Of The B-Sides. Westwood One live cds and

King Biscuit live cds are made by these labels to promote artists for the radio. There are only a few hundred made. Many of these concerts are never released to the public. These are legitimate releases made to promote the artists live for the radio. I do not list bootlegs (illegitimate releases) in my book. Bootlegs are releases that are not put out by legitimate labels or by the artists. The artist does receive any royalties from bootlegs, therefore artists become upset when people sell these illegitimate releases.

A Long Time ago cds were released with longboxes. These boxes were made so that people could look at the cd more easily while shopping in a store. Most people would buy the cd and immediately tear up the longboxes, and throw them away. Therefore longboxes have become hard to find. People may pay a high price to have the cd in the original longbox. If it is sealed, they may pay even more.

Sometimes a first issue cd is worth more than a later version of the same cd if it is unique. A case in point is the legendary Abbey Road Japanese release by The Beatles. This cd was released years before the American release so it is technically the first release of a Beatles cd. It sells for over $400 sealed.

Where do you go to get these cds? The best and cheapest place is pawn shops. They are inexpensive but many times, they are scratched. The next best place to buy a cd is used cd stores. They cost a little more but they are usually in better condition. The last place to buy a cd is on the Internet, but you will usually pay what the cd is actually worth, so it will cost more than the other places.

When you want to sell a cd, the Internet is best, because you will receive the actual worth of the cd. The used cd store will pay less, and the pawn shop even less than the used cd store.

What cds will go up in value in the future? The safest bets are Rhino Handmade cds available at www.rhino.com because these cds are extremely limited and very popular. Some Japanese cds, which are popular, will go up in value if they are not released elsewhere in the world. Other cds which will increase in value are some Mini Lp Cds. For example: Works and Welcome Back My Friends by Emerson, Lake And Palmer will probably increase in value. However, if these Mini Lp's are reissued, the price will go down. I also think that Westwood One live promos and King Biscuit live promos that are not released to the general public will go up in value.

If you want to contact me and say something positive I am available at bigmonkcd@aol.com also, my webpage is located at www.bigmonkeycdsandvideos.com. I will not answer negative email. If there is some group you would like me to add in the future, let me know. If you have some additional information, such as what you paid for a cd on the Internet, which is out of print, let me know all of the information on the cd including artist, title, format, label, catalog number, country, year released and current value and I will put it in the next guide. I realize that there are great bands that are not listed and I hope to rectify this in the future.

Acknowledgments

I would like to thank the following people for their help, support and inspiration: Kathleen Pool-Colon, Dr. and Mrs. Wildo D. Colon, Sylvia Colon, Carlos Colon, Linda Colon, Gloria Colon, Larry Fertitta, Randall Frierson, Hal Gatti, Mike Hughes, Jeff Lambing, John McLeaish, Don Meyers, Byron Pliler, Jason Pliler, David Seanor and Bill Sellers.

Randall "Randar" Frierson owns Groove Entertainment Records based in Garland, Texas, a Dallas suburb. I highly recommend him for import and hard to find cds in print.

Jason Pliler formatted the book into Adobe Pagemaker, completed page layout, and prepared the book to be published. Jason has a t-shirt business and can be reached at pax00@hotmail.com or at www.americanfilth.com.

# #

	Artist	Title	Format	Label	Catalog No	Country	Released	Value
A	10,000 Maniacs	Blind Man's Zoo	CD	Elektra	9-60815-2	U.S.A.	1989	6.99
	10,000 Maniacs	Hope Chest (Fredonia Recordings)	CD	Elektra	9-60962-2	U.S.A.	1990	8.99
	10,000 Maniacs	In My Tribe (With Peace Train)	CD	Elektra	9-60738-2	U.S.A.	1987	15.99
	10,000 Maniacs	Our Time In Eden	CD	Elektra	9-61385-2	U.S.A.	1992	6.99
	10,000 Maniacs	Trouble Me (3"/Elephant Pack)	CD Single	Elektra	EKR93CDX	England	1986	29.99
	10,000 Maniacs	Wishing Chair	CD	Elektra	9-60428-2	U.S.A.	1987	5.99
	10cc	10 Out Of 10	CD	Mercury	800-039-2	Germany	1981	53.99
	10cc	10cc/Sheet Music + 1	CD	DCC	DZS-053	U.S.A.	1990	13.99
	10cc	Alive - The Very Best Of	CD	Creative Man	CMD-010	U.S.A.	1996	7.99
	10cc	Hits	CD	Laserlight	15-193	Germany	1991	7.99
	10cc	KBFH Presents 10 CC	CD	King Biscuit	70710-88003-2	U.S.A.	1995	7.99
	10cc	Orig S.T. (DCC Gold Cd) (No Tray Art)	CD	DCC	GZS-1083	U.S.A.	1975	74.99
	10cc	The Orig S.T. (MFSL Gold Cd)	CD	Mobile Fidelity	UDCD-729	U.S.A.	1975	39.99
	10cc /Godley/Creme	Birds Of Prey	CD	Polydor K.K.	POCP-2080	Japan	1991	67.99
	10cc /Godley/Creme	Freeze Frame	CD	Polydor	POCP-2078	Japan	1991	11.99
	10cc /Godley/Creme	Freeze Frame	CD	PolyGram	831-555-2	Germany	1979	10.99
	10cc /Godley/Creme	Goodbye Blue Sky	CD	Polydor	P32P-20151	Japan	1988	13.99
	10cc /Godley/Creme	Images	CD	Karussell	550-007-2	Australia	1993	11.99
	10cc /Godley/Creme	Ismism	CD	Polydor	POCP-2079	Japan	1993	199.99
	10cc /Godley/Creme	L/Freeze Frame	CD	One Way	314-549-275-2	England	2000	11.99
	12 Rods	Separation Anxieties	CD	V2	63881-27070-2	U.S.A.	2000	8.99
	13th Floor Elevators	Best Of	CD	Nectar Masters	NTMCD516	England	1995	11.99
	13th Floor Elevators	Best Of; Manicure Your Mind	CD	M.I.L.	ESP3034	U.S.A.	1998	13.99
	13th Floor Elevators	Bull Of The Woods	CD	Spalax	SPA-14886	France	1969	9.99
	13th Floor Elevators	Bull Of The Woods	CD	Decal	CD-LIKM-004	France	1991	7.99
	13th Floor Elevators	Easter Everywhere	CD	Spalax	14888	France	1996	11.99
	13th Floor Elevators	Easter Everywhere	CD	Decal	CD-LIKM-002	France	1991	8.99
	13th Floor Elevators	Easter Everywhere (Ltd 1500)	Mini Lp	Sunspots	SPOT-522-CD	Italy	2002	18.99
	13th Floor Elevators	Easter Everywhere / Bull Woods	CD	Decal	CD-CHARLY-150	France	1988	19.99
	13th Floor Elevators	Elevator Live	CD	Decal	CD-LIKM-003	England	1991	8.99
	13th Floor Elevators	Grackle Debacle	CD	Spalax	CD14596	France	2002	19.99
	13th Floor Elevators	His Eye Is On The Pyramid	2CD	Snapper	SMD-CD-190	England	1999	19.99
	13th Floor Elevators	Levitation	CD	Magnum	CDTB-147	England	1994	8.99
	13th Floor Elevators	Live (Ltd 1500)	Mini Lp	Sunspots	SPOT-541-CD	Italy	2003	18.99
	13th Floor Elevators	Out Of Order/Live...	CD	Magnum	MACD-034	England	1994	6.99
	13th Floor Elevators	Psychedelic Sounds/Elevators Live!	CD	Decal	CD-CHARLY-159	France	1988	12.99
	13th Floor Elevators	The Masters	CD	Eagle	EAB-CD-069	EC	1997	14.99
	13th Floor Elevators	The Psychedelic Sound Of	CD	Decal	CD-LIKM-001	France	1991	9.99
	13th Floor Elevators	The Psychedelic Sounds Of...	CD	Spalax	14819	France	1996	11.99
	13th Floor Elevators	The Psychedelic Sounds...(Ltd 1500)	Mini Lp	Sunspots	SPOT-501-CD	Italy	2002	18.99
	13th Floor Elevators	The Psychedelic World Of (Box Set)	3CD	Charly	SANJ-709	England	2002	30.99
	13th Floor Elevators	The Reunion Concert	CD	Magnum	MM-075	England	2001	19.99
	13th Floor Elevators	Through The Rhythm	CD	M.I.L.	MIL-3042	U.S.A.	1998	8.99
	13th Floor Elevators	Unlock The Secret	CD	Spalax	CD14600	France	2002	19.99
	13th Floor Elevators	Up On The 13th Floor	CD	Dressed To Kill	METRO381	England	2000	8.99
	1910 Fruitgum Company	The Best Of: Simon Says	CD	Buddah	74465-99799-2	U.S.A.	2001	11.99
	2 Skinnee J's	Supermercado	CD	Capricorn	314-536-892-2	U.S.A.	1998	6.99
	30 Odd Foot Of Grunts/Crowe	Interviews/3 Live (DJ) Russell Crowe	CD	Artemis	751103-2	U.S.A.	2001	173.99
	311	311	CD	Capricorn	9-42041-2	U.S.A.	1995	6.99
	311	Evolver	CD	Volcano	53714-2	U.S.A.	2003	8.99
	311	From Chaos	CD	Volcano	32184-2	U.S.A.	2001	8.99
	311	Grassroots	CD	Capricorn	9-42026-2	U.S.A.	1994	4.99
	311	Grassroots (Clean)	CD	Capricorn	314-532-528-2	U.S.A.	1996	5.99

Artist	Title	Format	Label	Catalog No	Country	Released	Value
311	Live !	CD	Capricorn	314-538-263-2	U.S.A.	1998	6.99
311	Live ! (Clean)	CD	Capricorn	314-538-344-2	U.S.A.	1998	5.99
311	Music	CD	Capricorn	9-42008-2	U.S.A.	1994	6.99
311	Soundsystem	CD	Capricorn	314-564-645-2	U.S.A.	1999	8.99
311	Transistor	CD	Capricorn	314-536-181-2	U.S.A.	1997	6.99
311	Transistor (Clean)	CD	Capricorn	314-536-182-2	U.S.A.	1997	5.99
38 Special	Anthology	2CD	Hip O	069-490-652-2	U.S.A.	2001	19.99
38 Special	Bone Against Steel	CD	Capitol	86345	U.S.A.	1991	8.99
38 Special	Flashback (Best Of)	CD	A&M	CD-3910	U.S.A.	1987	9.99
38 Special	Live At Sturgis	CD	CMC INT.	06076-86281-2	U.S.A.	1999	9.99
38 Special	Resolution	CD	Razor & Tie	RT-2829-2	U.S.A.	1997	8.99
38 Special	Rock 'N' Roll Strategy	CD	A&M	CD-5218	U.S.A.	1988	7.99
38 Special	Self Titled	CD	Lemon	CDLEM11	England	2003	19.99
38 Special	Self Titled	CD	A&M	CD-3164	U.S.A.	1990	28.99
38 Special	Special Delivery	CD	A&M	75021-3165-2	U.S.A.	1978	46.99
38 Special	Special Forces	CD	A&M	CD-3299	U.S.A.	1988	12.99
38 Special	Special Forces	CD	Pony Canyon	D32Y3068	Japan	1987	13.99
38 Special	Strength In Numbers	CD	A&M	CD-5115	U.S.A.	1987	12.99
38 Special	The Hard Way	CD	MCA	MCAD-10203	U.S.A.	1991	12.99
38 Special	Tour De Force	CD	A&M	CD-3310	U.S.A.	1988	11.99
38 Special	Wild-Eyed Southern Boys	CD	A&M	CD-3298	U.S.A.	1988	12.99
4 Non Blondes	Bigger, Better, Faster, More?	CD	Interscope	92112-2	U.S.A.	1992	7.99
400 Blows	Look	CD	Line	TCCD-9.00534-0	Germany	1988	3.99
5th Dimension	Fifth Dimension - The Definitive Coll.	2CD	Arista	07822-18961-2	U.S.A.	1997	19.99
5th Dimension	In The House	CD	Columbia	CK-64375	U.S.A.	1995	7.99
5th Dimension	Portrait + 1	CD	Buddha	74465-99664-2	U.S.A.	2000	8.99
5th Dimension	Stoned Soul Picnic + 1	CD	Buddha	74465-99663-2	U.S.A.	2000	8.99
5th Dimension	The Age Of Aquarius + 1	CD	Buddah	74465-99666-2	U.S.A.	2000	8.99
5th Dimension	The Magic Garden	CD	Buddah	74465-99667-2	U.S.A.	2000	8.99
5th Dimension	Up, Up And Away + 3	CD	Buddah	74465-99665-2	U.S.A.	2000	8.99

A

Artist	Title	Format	Label	Catalog No	Country	Released	Value
A Flock of Seagulls	A Flock Of Seagulls	CD	Jive	1007-2-J	U.S.A.	1982	34.99
Aaron, Lee	Baby Go Round	CD Single	Koch	342-462	Germany	1995	12.99
Aaron, Lee	Bodyrock	CD	Attic	ACD-1257	Canada	1989	9.99
Aaron, Lee	Bodyrock	CD	Metronome	841-387-2	Germany	1989	9.99
Aaron, Lee	Call Of The Wild	CD	Attic	ACD-1212	Canada	1985	15.99
Aaron, Lee	Call Of The Wild + 1	CD	10 Records	DIXCD-46	England	1988	14.99
Aaron, Lee	Emotional Rain	CD	Hip Chic	78871-7000-2	Canada	1994	10.99
Aaron, Lee	Emotional Rain + 2	CD	No Bull	341-952	Germany	1995	10.99
Aaron, Lee	Lee Aaron	CD	10 Records	DIXCD-49	England	1987	9.99
Aaron, Lee	Lee Aaron/Metal Queen	CD	Attic	ACD-24104	Canada	1989	7.99
Aaron, Lee	Metal Queen	CD	Metronome	841-674-2	Germany	1984	14.99
Aaron, Lee	Metal Queen	CD	10 Records	DIXCD-47	England	1987	14.99
Aaron, Lee	Metal Queen	CD	Roadrunner	RR-349861	Holland	1985	14.99
Aaron, Lee	Metal Queen	CD	Attic	ACBD-1188	Canada	1984	14.99
Aaron, Lee	Powerline: The Best Of	CD	Attic	ACD-1369	Canada	1992	11.99
Aaron, Lee	Self Titled	CD	Attic	ACD-1231	Canada	1987	9.99
Aaron, Lee	Self Titled	CD	Metronome	841-675-2	Germany	1984	16.99
Aaron, Lee	Self Titled	CD	10 Records	258-206-222	Germany	1987	9.99
Aaron, Lee	Self Titled	CD	Attic	ACD-1193	Canada	1984	14.99
Aaron, Lee	Self Titled	CD	Roadrunner	RR-349842	Holland	1985	16.99

A	Artist	Title	Format	Label	Catalog No	Country	Released	Value
	Aaron, Lee	Sex With Love	CD Single	Metronome	865089-2	Germany	1991	12.99
	Aaron, Lee	Shakin´ Down The Odds Of Love (DJ)	CD Single	Hip Chic	LEEAARONC	Canada	1994	12.99
	Aaron, Lee	Some Girls Do	CD	Metronome	511-487-2	Germany	1991	9.99
	Aaron, Lee	Some Girls Do	CD	Attic	ACD-1322	Canada	1991	9.99
	Aaron, Lee	Superbitch	CD Single	Koch	33216-2	Germany	1996	12.99
	Aaron, Lee	The Best Of	CD	Edel	ATT-7200-2	Germany	1992	11.99
	Aaron, Lee /2 Preciious	Self Titled	CD	No Bull	33215-2	Germany	1996	6.99
	Aaron, Lee/ 2 Preciious	Self Titled	CD	Spastic Plastic Corp	0-77078-60032-6	Canada	1996	6.99
	Aaron, Lee/Project	Self Titled	CD	Metronome	841-625-2	Germany	1984	14.99
	Aaron, Lee/Swingin' Barflies	Slick Chick	CD	Barking Dog	BDM-007	Canada	2000	11.99
	Abba	Abba + 2	CD	Polar Music	314-549-960-2	U.S.A.	2001	8.99
	Abba	Arrival + 2	CD	Polar Music	314-549-961-2	U.S.A.	2001	8.99
	Abba	Best Of	CD	RCA	SPCD-1039	Australia	1975	8.99
	Abba	Definitive Collection Box (38 Pg Bklt)	2CD	Universal	549-974-2	Taiwan	2001	21.99
	Abba	Gold Greatest Hits (Gold Cd)	CD	Polar Music	517-007-2	Japan	2002	44.99
	Abba	Greatest Hits (Orig. Cover)	CD	Atlantic	19114-2	U.S.A.	1986	24.99
	Abba	Greatest Hits, Vol. 2 (Orig. Cover)	CD	Atlantic	16009-2	U.S.A.	1986	24.99
	Abba	Oro - Grandes Exitos	CD	Polydor	314-519-955-2	U.S.A.	1992	10.99
	Abba	Ring Ring + 3	CD	Polar Music	314-549-958-2	U.S.A.	2001	8.99
	Abba	Super Trouper + 2	CD	Polar Music	314-549-964-2	U.S.A.	2001	8.99
	Abba	The Album + 1	CD	Polar Music	314-549-962-2	U.S.A.	2001	8.99
	Abba	The Very Best Of (Musikladen)	2CD	Polydor	839-535-2	Germany	1990	56.99
	Abba	The Visitors + 4	CD	Polar Music	314-549-965-2	U.S.A.	2001	8.99
	Abba	Voulez-Vous + 3	CD	Polar Music	314-549-963-2	U.S.A.	2001	8.99
	Abba	Waterloo (Mega Medley)	CD Single	Polydor	561-494-2	Germany	1999	5.99
	Abba	Waterloo + 3	CD	Polar Music	314-543-959-2	U.S.A.	2001	8.99
	Abba/Agnetha & Frida	The Voice Of Abba	CD	Polydor	550-212-2	France	1994	6.99
	Abba/Frida	Shine	CD	Polar Music	823-580-2	England	1984	11.99
	Abba/Frida	Something's Going On	CD	Polydor	42280-0102-2	U.S.A.	1982	13.99
	ABC	Lexicon Of Love + 6	CD	Mercury	514942-2	England	1996	11.99
	ABC	The Remix Collection	CD	Connoisseur	VSOP-CD-182	England	1995	18.99
	Abrahams, Mick	Mick Abrahams	CD	BGO	BGOCD95	England	1992	13.99
	Abrahams, Mick	Mick's Back	CD	Indigo	IGOXCD-501	England	1996	13.99
	Abrahams, Mick	See My Way	CD	A New Day	AND-CD46	England	2000	13.99
	Abrahams, Mick Band	Live In Madrid	CD	Indigo	IGOCD-2065	England	1997	13.99
	Abraxas Pool	Abraxas Pool (Shrieve, Schon, Rolie)	CD	Miramar	09006-23082-2	U.S.A.	1997	4.99
	Abraxas Pool	Singles# 1 (DJ) (Shrieve, Schon, Rolie)	CD	Miramar	09006-23087-2	U.S.A.	1997	4.99
	AC/DC	'74 Jailbreak	CD	Atlantic	80178-2	U.S.A.	1987	6.99
	AC/DC	Back In Black	CD	Atlantic	92418-2	U.S.A.	1980	6.99
	AC/DC	Ballbreaker	CD	East West	61780-2	U.S.A.	1995	7.99
	AC/DC	Blow Up Your Video	CD	Atlantic	81828-2	U.S.A.	1988	7.99
	AC/DC	Bonfire (Promo Sampler)	CD	East West	PRCD-9941-2	U.S.A.	1997	13.99
	AC/DC	Cover You In Oil (Shaped)	CD Single	East West	7599-64289-2	Germany	1996	29.99
	AC/DC	Dirty Deeds Done Dirt Cheap	CD	Elektra	92414-2	U.S.A.	1976	6.99
	AC/DC	Dirty Eyes (Promo)	CD Single	East West	PRCD-9937-2	U.S.A.	1997	7.99
	AC/DC	Flick Of The Switch	CD	Atlantic	80100-2	U.S.A.	1987	7.99
	AC/DC	Fly On The Wall	CD	Atlantic	81263-2	U.S.A.	1987	7.99
	AC/DC	For Those About To Rock	CD	Elektra	92412-2	U.S.A.	1994	6.99
	AC/DC	High Voltage	CD	Atlantic	92413-2	U.S.A.	1994	6.99
	AC/DC	Highway To Hell	CD	Elektra	92419-2	U.S.A.	1979	6.99
	AC/DC	If You Want Blood You've Got It	CD	Atco	92447-2	U.S.A.	1994	6.99
	AC/DC	In The 20th Century Box Set	19CD	East West	7559-62589-2	Germany	2000	229.99
	AC/DC	Let There Be Rock	CD	Elektra	92445-2	U.S.A.	1977	6.99
	AC/DC	Live	CD	Atlantic	92215-2	U.S.A.	1992	7.99
	AC/DC	Live (Special Collector's Edition)	CD	Atlantic	92212-2	U.S.A.	1992	11.99
	AC/DC	Meltdown Summer Sampler (Promo)	CD	East West	PRCD-7453-2	U.S.A.	2000	7.99
	AC/DC	Powerage	CD	Atco	92446-2	U.S.A.	1994	7.99
	AC/DC	Razor's Edge	CD	Atlantic	91413-2	U.S.A.	1990	6.99

Artist	Title	Format	Label	Catalog No	Country	Released	Value
AC/DC	Stiff Upper Lip	CD	East West	62494-2	U.S.A.	2000	6.99
AC/DC	T.N.T.	CD	EMI	4770832	Australia	1995	18.99
AC/DC	Who Made Who	CD	Atlantic	81650-2	U.S.A.	1987	6.99
AC/DC/Box Set	Bonfire (Poster/Keychain/Pick/Sticker)	5CD	East West	62119-2	U.S.A.	1997	29.99
AC/DC/Fraternity/Bon Scott	Early Years 1967-72	CD	See For Miles	SEE-CD247	England	1988	9.99
AC/DC/Fraternity/Bon Scott	Fraternity - Complete + 8 (71-72)	2CD	Raven	RVCD-56	Australia	1996	28.99
Acadium	Breathe Awhile + 2	CD	Akarma	AK-239-CD	Italy	2003	14.99
Accept	A Compilation Of The Best	CD	Portrait	RK-40265	U.S.A.	1986	7.99
Accept	All Areas Worldwide Live	2CD	BMG	GUN-536452	Germany	1997	16.99
Accept	Balls To The Wall	CD	Portrait	RK-39241	U.S.A.	1984	11.99
Accept	Balls To The Wall + 2	CD	Sony	SK-85756	U.S.A.	2001	8.99
Accept	Breaker	CD	SPV	SPV085-57262CD	Germany	2002	8.99
Accept	Classics, Rocks 'N' Ballads	CD	Ariola	74321-77407-2	Germany	2000	12.99
Accept	Collection	CD	Castle	CCSCD311	England	1992	8.99
Accept	Death Row	CD	RCA	74321-23016-2	Holland	1999	8.99
Accept	Death Row + 1	CD	Victor Ent.	VICP-5435	Japan	1994	13.99
Accept	Eat The Heat	CD	Epic	EK-44368	U.S.A.	1989	8.99
Accept	Eat The Heat + 1	CD	RCA	74321-93211-2-1	Holland	2002	16.99
Accept	Hot & Slow	CD	BMG	74321-77407-2-6	Holland	2000	12.99
Accept	Hungry Years	CD	Castle	CLACD405	England	1995	8.99
Accept	I'm A Rebel	CD	SPV	SPV085-57272CD	Germany	2001	8.99
Accept	I'm A Rebel/Breaker	CD	SPV	SPV310-57490	Germany	2003	9.99
Accept	Metal Heart	CD	Sony	25.8P-5241	Japan	1985	24.99
Accept	Metal Heart	CD	Portrait	RK-39974	U.S.A.	1985	9.99
Accept	Metal Heart +1	CD	RCA	74321-93213-2-9	Holland	2002	16.99
Accept	Metal Masters	CD	Brain	827-742-2	Germany	1985	9.99
Accept	No Substitutes	CD	Sony	A-22627	U.S.A.	1995	8.99
Accept	Objection Overruled	CD	RCA	74321-12466-2	Holland	1996	9.99
Accept	Objection Overruled + 1	CD	Victor Ent.	VICP-5210	Japan	1993	26.99
Accept	Predator	CD	RCA	74321-33570-2	Holland	1999	10.99
Accept	Predator (W/ Bonus)	CD	Victor Ent.	VICP-5673	Japan	1997	27.99
Accept	Restless & Wild	CD	Sony	ESCA-5350	Japan	1991	18.99
Accept	Restless & Wild	CD	Portrait	RK-39213	U.S.A.	1983	11.99
Accept	Restless And Best	CD	BMG	521-962-2	England	2000	8.99
Accept	Rich And Famous (Only 6000)	CD Single	Drakkar	21952722	Germany	2002	7.99
Accept	Russian Roulette	CD	Sony	25.8P-5242	Japan	1986	24.99
Accept	Russian Roulette	CD	Portrait	RK-40354	U.S.A.	1986	11.99
Accept	Russian Roulette + 1	CD	RCA	74321-93212-2-0	Holland	2002	16.99
Accept	Self Titled	CD	SPV	SPV085-57252CD	Germany	2001	13.99
Accept	Self Titled/Restless & Wild	CD	SPV	SPV310-57480	Germany	2003	9.99
Accept	Staying A Life	2CD	Sony	ESCA-5169/70	Japan	1991	34.99
Accept	Staying A Life	2CD	RCA	ND74720	Holland	1990	24.99
Accept	Staying A Life	CD	Columbia	EK-46944	U.S.A.	1990	12.99
Accept	Steel Glove	CD	Castle	CCSCD422	England	1996	12.99
Accept	The Final Chapter (Live)	2CD	CMC INT.	06076-86232-2	U.S.A.	1998	10.99
Ace Of Base	Da Capo + 2	CD	Virgin	VJCP-68475	Japan	2003	38.99
Ackles, David	American Gothic (Prod/Bernie Taupin)	CD	Elektra	7599-61597-2	Germany	1993	19.99
Ackles, David	American Gothic (Prod/Bernie Taupin)	CD	Collector's Choice	CCM-312	U.S.A.	2003	11.99
Ackles, David	Subway To The Country	CD	Elektra	7599-61596-2	Germany	1993	19.99
Ackles, David	Subway To The Country	CD	Collector's Choice	CCM-313	U.S.A.	2003	11.99
Ackles, David/Rhinoceros	Self Titled	CD	Collector's Choice	CCM-311	U.S.A.	2003	11.99
Ackles, David/Rhinoceros	Self Titled	CD	Elektra	7559-61595-2	Germany	1993	19.99
Adam Ant	Manners & Physique	CD	Warner Bros.	WMC5-31	Japan	1990	11.99
Adam Ant	Manners & Physique	CD	MCA	MCAD-6315	U.S.A.	1985	7.99
Adam Ant	Strip	CD	CBS	CDCO3-25705	U.S.A.	1984	21.99
Adam/The Ants	Dirk Wears White Socks	CD	Columbia	EK-38698	U.S.A.	1992	33.99
Adam/The Ants	Kings Of The Wild Frontier	CD	Epic	EK-37033	U.S.A.	1980	10.99
Adam/The Ants	Prince Charming	CD	Epic	EK-37615	U.S.A.	1981	10.99

A	Artist	Title	Format	Label	Catalog No	Country	Released	Value
	Adams, Bryan	Hits On Fire	2CD	Pony Canyon	D50Y-3205	Japan	1986	44.99
	Adams, Bryan	Into The Fire	CD	A&M	CD-3907	U.S.A.	1987	6.99
	Adams, Bryan	Let's Make It.. Box Set (4 Cards)	CD	A&M	581-867-2	England	1996	24.99
	Adams, Bryan	Reckless (MFSL Gold Cd)	CD	Mobile Fidelity	UDCD-544	U.S.A.	1984	21.99
	Adams, Don	Get Smart	CD	Raven	RVCD-61	Australia	1996	19.99
	Addrisi Brothers	Never My Love (Lost Album Sessions)	CD	Varese	302-066-250-2	U.S.A.	2001	11.99
	Adler Band, Danny	The Roogalator Years	CD	Line	LICD-9.00705-0	Germany	1990	9.99
	Adler, Danny	Early Danny Adler	CD	Line	LICD-9.00725-0	Germany	1990	9.99
	Adler, Danny	Funky Afternoon	CD	Line	LICD-9.00914-0	Germany	1989	9.99
	Adler, Danny	Hometowns & High Iron	CD	Line	LICD-9.00913-0	Germany	1989	9.99
	Adler, Danny	Hubcap Heaven	CD	Line	LICD-9.00910-0	Germany	1989	9.99
	Adler, Danny	Mackinaw City	CD	Line	LICD-9.00911-0	Germany	1989	9.99
	Adler, Danny	Night Shift	CD	Line	LICD-9.00912-0	Germany	1989	9.99
	Adler, Danny/Band	Danny Adler Band	CD	Line	LICD-9.00593-0	Germany	1988	9.99
	Adler, Danny/Band	Live	CD	Line	LICD-9.00561-0	Germany	1988	9.99
	Adler,Danny	Gusha Gusha Music	CD	Line	LICD-9.00290-0	Germany	1990	9.99
	Aerosmith	A Little South Of Sanity	2CD	Geffen	25221-2	U.S.A.	1998	9.99
	Aerosmith	A Little South Of Sanity (Clean	2CD	Geffen	25308-2	U.S.A.	1998	10.99
	Aerosmith	Big 10" (Promo)	CD	Columbia	CSK-4236	U.S.A.	1991	7.99
	Aerosmith	Big Ones	CD	Geffen	GEFD-24716	U.S.A.	1994	6.99
	Aerosmith	Box Of Fire	13 CD	Columbia	CK-66687	U.S.A.	1995	59.99
	Aerosmith	Classics Live	CD	Columbia	CK-57369	U.S.A.	1993	6.99
	Aerosmith	Classics Live!	CD	Columbia	CK-40329	U.S.A.	1986	6.99
	Aerosmith	Classics Live! II	CD	Columbia	CK-40855	U.S.A.	1987	8.99
	Aerosmith	Done With Mirrors	CD	Geffen	9-24091-2	U.S.A.	1985	6.99
	Aerosmith	Draw The Line	CD	Columbia	CK-34856	U.S.A.	1977	8.99
	Aerosmith	Fly Away From Here	CD Single	Columbia	671330-2	Australia	2001	9.99
	Aerosmith	Gems	CD	Columbia	CK-44487	U.S.A.	1988	7.99
	Aerosmith	Get A Grip	CD	Geffen	GEFD-24455	U.S.A.	1993	6.99
	Aerosmith	Get Your Wings	CD	Columbia	CK-32847	U.S.A.	1974	9.99
	Aerosmith	Girls Of Summer	CD Single	Sony	672771-2	Germany	2002	9.99
	Aerosmith	Greatest Hits	CD	Columbia	CK-57367	U.S.A.	1980	8.99
	Aerosmith	Greatest Hits 1973-1988 + 2	CD	Columbia	487350-2	Australia	1997	11.99
	Aerosmith	Hole In My Soul	CD Single	Epic	664501-2	England	1997	4.99
	Aerosmith	Hole In My Soul	CD Single	Epic	664502-5	England	1997	4.99
	Aerosmith	Just Push Play	CD	Columbia	CK-62088	U.S.A.	2001	9.99
	Aerosmith	Just Push Play + 6 (Bonus Disc)	2CD	Sony	SICP-87-8	Japan	2001	34.99
	Aerosmith	Live Bootleg	CD	Columbia	CK-53045	U.S.A.	1978	9.99
	Aerosmith	Night In The Ruts	CD	Columbia	CK-36050	U.S.A.	1979	8.99
	Aerosmith	Nine Lives	CD	Columbia	CK-67547	U.S.A.	1997	7.99
	Aerosmith	Nine Lives (Clean)	CD	Columbia	CK-67994	U.S.A.	1997	6.99
	Aerosmith	Nine Lives + 4 (Bonus Disc)	2CD	Columbia	485020-2	Australia	1998	14.99
	Aerosmith	O Yeah! - Ultimate Aerosmith Hits	CD	Columbia	C2K-86700	U.S.A.	2002	14.99
	Aerosmith	O, Yeah! Ultimate Aerosmith Hits	2CD	Sony	SCIP-170-1	Japan	2002	19.99
	Aerosmith	Pandora's Box	3CD	Sony	SK-86567	U.S.A.	2002	24.99
	Aerosmith	Pandora's Box (Box Set)	3CD	Columbia	C3K-46209	U.S.A.	1991	19.99
	Aerosmith	Permanent Vacation (Remastered)	CD	Universal	493096-2	England	2001	8.99
	Aerosmith	Pink	CD Single	Columbia	CDL-664872-2	Austria	1997	5.99
	Aerosmith	Pump (Ltd. Ed. Black)	CD	Universal	2-24269	U.S.A.	1989	23.99
	Aerosmith	Pump (Remastered)	CD	Geffen	493097-2	England	1989	8.99
	Aerosmith	Rock In A Hard Place	CD	Columbia	CK-44487	U.S.A.	1982	9.99
	Aerosmith	Rocks	CD	Columbia	CK-34165	U.S.A.	1976	8.99
	Aerosmith	Self Titled	CD	Columbia	CK-32005	U.S.A.	1973	8.99
	Aerosmith	Talk This Way	CD	Baktabak	CBAK-4032	England	1992	9.99
	Aerosmith	Toys In Attic (Mastersound Gold Cd)	CD	Columbia	CK-64401	U.S.A.	1975	29.99
	Aerosmith	Toys In The Attic	CD	Columbia	CK-57362	U.S.A.	1993	7.99
	Aerosmith	Toys In The Attic	CD	Columbia	CK-33479	U.S.A.	1975	7.99
	Aerosmith	Young Lust: The Anthology	2CD	Geffen	493119-2	U.S.A.	2001	13.99

Artist	Title	Format	Label	Catalog No	Country	Released	Value
Aerosmith/W/Sticker/Cert.	Pandora's Toys Box (W/Button/Patch)	CD	Columbia	CK-476952	U.S.A.	1995	27.99
Aerosmith/Whitford/St Holmes	Self Titled	CD	Columbia	CK-66986	U.S.A.	1981	19.99
Affinity	1971 - 1972	CD	Angel Air	SJPCD145	England	2003	14.99
Affinity	If You Live	CD	Akarma	AK-215	Italy	2002	14.99
Affinity	Live Instrumentals	CD	Angel Air	SJPCD135	England	2003	14.99
Affinity	Self Titled + 2	CD	Repertoire	REP-4349-WP	Germany	2002	15.99
Affinity	Self Titled+ 8	CD	Angel Air	SJPCD111	England	2002	19.99
Affinity/Linda Hoyle	Pieces Of Me	CD	Akarma	AK-220	Italy	2003	14.99
Affinity/Linda Hoyle	Pieces Of Me	CD	Angel Air	SJPCD117	England	2002	17.99
Affinity/Linda Hoyle	Pieces Of Me	CD	Repertoire	REP-4473-WP	Germany	1995	16.99
Afrika-Bambaataa	Planet Rock	CD	Sony	32DP-692	Japan	1987	34.99
Afrika-Bambaataa	The 12" Mixes + 3 (Acappella)	CD	ZYX	10003-2	Germany	2001	9.99
Afrika-Bambaataa/Family	Beware (The Funk Is Everywhere)	CD	Sony	SRCS-6303	Japan	1986	28.99
Afro Celt Sound System	Release Remixes	CD	Real World	72438-38746-2-0	U.S.A.	2000	7.99
Afro Celt Sound System	Volume 1 Sound Magic	CD	Real World	0170-4-62359-2-1	U.S.A.	1996	7.99
Afro Celt Sound System	Volume 2 : Release	CD	Realworld	7243-8-47324-2-4	U.S.A.	1999	8.99
Afro Celt Sound System	Volume 3: Further In Time (Bonus Cd)	2CD	Real World	7243-8-10622-0-3	U.S.A.	2001	12.99
Afro Celt Sound System	When You're Falling (W/Peter Gabriel)	CD Single	Virgin	7243-8-97859-0-6	Holland	2001	8.99
Age Of Chance	Mecca	CD	Charisma	2-91366	U.S.A.	1989	5.99
Aguilera, Christina	My Kind Of Christmas	CD	RCA	07863-69343-2	U.S.A.	2000	5.99
a-ha	Road Club	CD Single	Warner Bros.	25P2-2131	Japan	1988	44.99
a-ha	Scoundrel Club	CD	Polydor	28XD-712	Japan	1987	19.99
Aiken, Clay	Invisible (Promo)	CD Single	RCA	RDJ566002RE1	U.S.A.	2003	156.99
Aiken, Clay	The Way (Promo)	CD Single	RCA	RDJ-59353-2	U.S.A.	2004	22.99
Air	10,000 Hz Legend	CD	Astralwerks	ASW-10332-2	U.S.A.	2001	9.99
Air	Everybody Hertz	CD Single	Astralwerks	ASW-11833-CD	U.S.A.	2002	7.99
Air	Playground Love - The Virgin Suicides	CD Single	Astralwerks	724389657326	U.S.A.	2000	5.99
Air	Premiers Symptomes	CD	Toshiba-EMI	VJCP-61029	Japan	1999	19.99
Air	Sexy Boy	CD Single	Caroline	CAR-6645-2	U.S.A.	1998	5.99
Air	The Virgin Suicides	CD	Astralwerks	7243-8488482-6	U.S.A.	2000	9.99
Air /Alessandro Baricco	City Reading (Tre Storie Western)	CD	Astralwerks	ASW-81871	U.S.A.	2003	7.99
Air Miami	Me. Me. Me	CD	4AD	9-46000-2	U.S.A.	1995	9.99
Air Supply	Greatest Hits	CD	Arista	07822-14611-2	U.S.A.	1999	8.99
Air Supply	Hearts In Motion	CD	Nippon Phonogram	32RD-53	Japan	1986	55.99
Air Supply	Heats In Motion	CD	Arista	ARCD-8426	U.S.A.	1986	54.99
Air Supply	Life Support	CD	EMI	7243-8-32368-2-4	Australia	1994	24.99
Air Supply	Self Titled	CD	BMG	BVCA-7324	Japan	1995	19.99
Air Supply/Russell Hitchcock	Self Titled	CD	Arista	ARCD-8456	U.S.A.	1988	20.99
Airplay	Self Titled	CD	BMG Victor	BVCP-7378	Japan	1980	24.99
Alabama	The Essential	CD	RCA	67621-2	U.S.A.	1998	6.99
Alarm, The	20th Ann. Coll EP (W/Int/2 Acoustic)	CD	21st Century	21C031	England	2001	8.99
Alarm, The	Close	CD Single	21st Century	21CS002A	England	2003	8.99
Alarm, The	Declaration + 10	CD	21st Century	21C011	England	2001	14.99
Alarm, The	Electric Folklore: Live + 8	CD	21st Century	21C014	England	2001	14.99
Alarm, The	Eponymous	CD	21st Century	21C010	England	2001	14.99
Alarm, The	Eye Of A Hurricane + 11	CD	21st Century	21C013	England	2001	14.99
Alarm, The	Newid	CD	Victor Ent.	VICP-26	Japan	1989	19.99
Alarm, The	Raw	CD	21st Century	21C016	England	2001	14.99
Alarm, The	Standards	CD	I.R.S.	X2-13056	U.S.A.	1990	8.99
Alarm, The	Strength + 7	CD	21st Century	21C012	England	2001	14.99
Alarm, The	The Change + 3	CD	21st Century	21C015	England	2001	14.99
Alarm, The/2 Cd/1 DVD	Sound And The Fury Live '81-'91	3CD	Shakedown	SHAKEBX-112Z	England	2003	31.99
Alberto/Lost Trios Paranoias	Italians From Outerspace	CD	Line	TACD-9.00776-0	Germany	1989	7.99
Alberto/Lost Trios Paranoias	Same	CD	Line	TACD-9.00554-0	Germany	1988	7.99
Alberto/Lost Trios Paranoias	Skite	CD	Line	TACD-9.00779-0	Germany	1989	7.99
Alemao	Bem Brasileiro	CD	Line	RICD-9.00833-0	Germany	1989	4.99
Alessi Brothers	Alessi	CD	A&M	UICY-3346	Japan	1976	29.99
Alessi Brothers	All For A Reason	CD	A&M	UICY-3347	Japan	1977	20.99

	Artist	Title	Format	Label	Catalog No	Country	Released	Value
A	Alessi Brothers	Driftin'	CD	A&M	UICY-3348	Japan	1978	34.99
	Alessi Brothers	Long Time Friends	CD	Warner Bros.	WPCR-10543	Japan	1982	29.99
	Alessi Brothers	Words And Music	CD	A&M	UICY-3349	Japan	1979	34.99
	Alexander, Willie/VU	Loco Live 1976 + Single Rare Trks	CD	Captain Trip	CTCD-342	Japan	1976	29.99
	Alexander, Willie/VU	Solo Loco Redux + 1	CD	Captain Trip	CTCD-410	Japan	1981	29.99
	Alice in Chains	Bank Heist (Promo Box Set Sampler)	CD	Sony	CSK-46417	U.S.A.	1999	19.99
	Alice in Chains	Jar Of Flies (Bonus Cd Rom Disc)	2CD	Columbia	CKR-66893	U.S.A.	1993	15.99
	Alice in Chains	Music Bank Box Set	4CD	Columbia	CXK-69580	U.S.A.	1999	35.99
	Alice in Chains	The Nona Tapes	CD Single	Columbia	CSK-442551	U.S.A.	1999	11.99
	Alien	Live In Stockholm 1990	CD	Avalon	MICP-10225	Japan	2001	44.99
	All Star Tribute	What's Going On?	CD	Columbia	CK-86199	U.S.A.	2001	9.99
	Allan, Davie/The Arrows	The Wild Angels S.T.	CD	Curb	D2-77607	U.S.A.	1993	34.99
	Allan, Laura	Hold On To Your Dreams	CD	Skyline	ST-00001	U.S.A.	1996	6.99
	Allen & Allen	Christmas Like Never Before	CD	CGI	51416-1150-2	U.S.A.	1995	2.99
	Allen, Daevid	Bananamoon	CD	Spalax	14945	France	1995	15.99
	Allen, Daevid	Death/Rock And Roll/Even More	CD	Voiceprint	VP114CD	England	1991	11.99
	Allen, Daevid	Divided Alien Clockwork Band; 1980	CD	Blueprint	BP269CD	England	1998	14.99
	Allen, Daevid	Dividedalienplaybax80	CD	Spalax	14837	France	1995	15.99
	Allen, Daevid	Dreaming A Dream	CD	GAS	AGASCD-007	England	1995	7.99
	Allen, Daevid	Eat Me Baby I'm A Jelly Bean	CD	GAS	AGASCD-016	England	1998	10.99
	Allen, Daevid	El Alin's New Wave	CD	Decal	CD-LIKM-73	England	1991	19.99
	Allen, Daevid	Good Morning	CD	Caroline	CAROL-1804-2	U.S.A.	1991	11.99
	Allen, Daevid	Je Ne Fum' Pas Des Bananes	CD	Legend	LM9013	France	1993	19.99
	Allen, Daevid	Microcosmic Allen	CD	No Meat Prod.	CD001	England	2000	14.99
	Allen, Daevid	Money Doesn't Make It	CD	InnerSPACE	7707	England	1999	14.99
	Allen, Daevid	N'esiste Pas	CD	Spalax	14817	France	1996	15.99
	Allen, Daevid	Now Is The Happiest Time...	CD	Spalax	14825	France	1995	15.99
	Allen, Daevid	Seven Drones	CD	Voiceprint	VP102CD	England	1991	11.99
	Allen, Daevid	The Austalian Years	CD	Voiceprint	VP101CD	England	1990	11.99
	Allen, Daevid	Twelve Selves	CD	Voiceprint	VP111CD	England	1993	11.99
	Allen, Daevid	Uglymusic.4.Monica	CD	Weed	7912	England	2003	14.99
	Allen, Daevid	University Of Errors 2 e²x10=tenure	CD	InnerSPACE	7715	England	2000	14.99
	Allen, Daevid	Voiceprint Radio Sessions (Promo)	CD	Voiceprint	VPRO12CD	England	1994	24.99
	Allen, Daevid/H Williamson	Stroking The Tail Of A Bird + 1	CD	Voiceprint	VP207CD	England	2000	11.99
	Allen, Daevid/H Williamson	Twenty Two Meanings	CD	Gliss	CD005	England	1999	11.99
	Allen, Daevid/Kramer	Hit Men	CD	Shimmy Disc	5080	U.S.A.	1998	14.99
	Allen, Daevid/Kramer	Who's Afraid?	CD	Shimmy Disc	SHIMMY-060	U.S.A.	1992	14.99
	Allen, Daevid/Magick Bros.	Live At The Witchwood 1991	CD	Voiceprint	VP107CD	England	1992	11.99
	Allen, Daevid/Magick Bros.	Passed Normal Vol. 5 (Trial Headlines)	CD	Fot	FOT-PN5	England	1992	19.99
	Allen, Daevid/Planet Gong	Opium For The People-Alien...	CD	Spalax	14844	France	1996	15.99
	Allen, Daevid/Russell Hibbs	Nectans Glen	CD	Voiceprint	VP206CD	England	1999	11.99
	Allen, Daevid/Trio	Live	CD	Voiceprint	VP122CD	England	1993	11.99
	Allen, Debbie/Kashif	Special Look (W/Jesse Johnson)	CD	MCA	MCAD-6317	U.S.A.	1989	18.99
	Allen, Deborah	Let Me Be The First	CD	RCA	PCD1-5318	U.S.A.	1984	89.99
	Allison, Luther	Bad Love	CD Single	Line	TLCD-9.01297-0	Germany	1994	4.99
	Allison, Luther	Bad Love	CD	Line	RRCD-9.01295-0	Germany	1994	7.99
	Allison, Luther	Live 89 - Let's Try It Again	CD	Line	RRCD-9.01309-0	Germany	1994	7.99
	Allman, Duane	An Anthology	CD	Polydor	831-444-2	U.S.A.	1990	14.99
	Allman, Duane	An Anthology, Vol. 2	CD	Polydor	831-445-2	U.S.A.	1990	12.99
	Allman, Gregg	20th Century Masters: The Millennium	CD	Mercury	314-586-822-2	U.S.A.	2002	7.99
	Allman, Gregg	I'm No Angel	CD	Epic	EK-40531	U.S.A.	1990	6.99
	Allman, Gregg	Just Before The Bullets Fly	CD	Epic	EK-44033	U.S.A.	1990	6.99
	Allman, Gregg	Just Before The Bullets Fly	CD	Sony	25.8P-5086	Japan	1988	16.99
	Allman, Gregg	Laid Back	CD	Polydor	831-941-2	U.S.A.	2001	8.99
	Allman, Gregg	Laid Back	CD	Sony	25.8P-5074	Japan	1988	20.99
	Allman, Gregg	No Stranger To The Dark : Best Of	CD	Epic	EK-85742	U.S.A.	2002	8.99
	Allman, Gregg	One More Try: An Anthology	2CD	PolyGram	529-725-2	U.S.A.	1997	24.99
	Allman, Gregg	Playin' Up A Storm	CD	Polydor	831-942-2	U.S.A.	2001	8.99

Artist	Title	Format	Label	Catalog No	Country	Released	Value	A
Allman, Gregg	Searching For Simplicity	CD	550 Music	BK-67143	U.S.A.	1997	6.99	
Allman, Gregg	Searching For Simplicity (DJ Sampler)	CD Single	Sony	BSK-3435	U.S.A.	1997	5.99	
Allman, Gregg	The Gregg Allman Tour	CD	Polydor	422-831-940-2	U.S.A.	1974	9.99	
Allman-Brothers Band	20th Century Masters: The Millennium	CD	Polydor	314-547-899-2	U.S.A.	2000	7.99	
Allman-Brothers Band	A Decade Of Hits	CD	Polydor	314-511-156-2	U.S.A.	1991	7.99	
Allman-Brothers Band	All Live !	CD	Karussell	551-824-2	Germany	1996	7.99	
Allman-Brothers Band	Allman Brothers At Fillmore East	CD	Capricorn	314-531-260-2	U.S.A.	1997	8.99	
Allman-Brothers Band	Allman Brothers Band	CD	PolyGram	PHCR-4438	Japan	1997	24.99	
Allman-Brothers Band	American University W.D.C.	CD	Allman Bros.	NO. 1	U.S.A.	2003	19.99	
Allman-Brothers Band	American University W.D.C.	CD	Universal	UICE-1063	Japan	2003	29.99	
Allman-Brothers Band	An Evening With: First Set	CD	Epic	EK-48998	U.S.A.	1992	8.99	
Allman-Brothers Band	An Evening With: Second Set	CD	Epic	EK-66795	U.S.A.	1995	8.99	
Allman-Brothers Band	At Fillmore East + 6 Deluxe Ed.	2CD	Mercury	B0000401-02	U.S.A.	2003	19.99	
Allman-Brothers Band	At Filmore East (MFSL Gold Cd)	2CD	Mobile Fidelity	UDCD-2-558	U.S.A.	1971	69.99	
Allman-Brothers Band	Back Where It All Begins (Promo)	CD Single	Epic	ESK-6230	U.S.A.	1994	7.99	
Allman-Brothers Band	Bad Rain (Promo)	CD Single	Epic	ESK-4178	U.S.A.	1991	7.99	
Allman-Brothers Band	Beginnings	CD	Capricorn	314-531-259-2	U.S.A.	1997	8.99	
Allman-Brothers Band	Brothers And Sisters	CD	PolyGram	PHCR-4443	Japan	1997	24.99	
Allman-Brothers Band	Brothers And Sisters	CD	Capricorn	314-331-262-2	U.S.A.	1997	8.99	
Allman-Brothers Band	Brothers And Sisters (MFSL Gold Cd)	CD	Mobile Fidelity	UDCD-617	U.S.A.	1973	31.99	
Allman-Brothers Band	Brothers Of The Road	CD	BMG	BVCA-7319	Japan	1995	22.99	
Allman-Brothers Band	Brothers Of The Road	CD	Razor & Tie	RE-2132-2	U.S.A.	1997	8.99	
Allman-Brothers Band	Collection	CD	Polydor K.K.	POCP-2160	Japan	1992	29.99	
Allman-Brothers Band	Collection	CD	Castle	CCSCD327	England	1993	8.99	
Allman-Brothers Band	Decade Of Hits 1969 - 1979	CD	Polydor K.K.	POCP-2560	Japan	1999	24.99	
Allman-Brothers Band	Dreams (7 Track Promo Sampler)	CD	Polydor	CDP-71	U.S.A.	1989	19.99	
Allman-Brothers Band	Dreams Box Set	4CD	PolyGram	839-417-2	U.S.A.	1989	35.99	
Allman-Brothers Band	Dreams Box Set	4CD	Polydor K.K.	POCP-2595/8	Japan	1999	99.99	
Allman-Brothers Band	Eat A Peach	CD	Capricorn	314-531-261-2	U.S.A.	1997	8.99	
Allman-Brothers Band	Eat A Peach	CD	PolyGram	PHCR-4441	Japan	1997	29.99	
Allman-Brothers Band	Eat A Peach (MFSL Gold Cd)	CD	Mobile Fidelity	UDCD-513	U.S.A.	1973	49.99	
Allman-Brothers Band	End Of The Line (Promo)	CD Single	Epic	ESK-4094	U.S.A.	1991	7.99	
Allman-Brothers Band	Enlightened Rogues	CD	PolyGram	PHCR-4446	Japan	1997	24.99	
Allman-Brothers Band	Enlightened Rogues	CD	Capricorn	314-531-265-2	U.S.A.	1997	8.99	
Allman-Brothers Band	Fillmore Concerts	2CD	Polydor K.K.	POCP-2565/6	Japan	1999	39.99	
Allman-Brothers Band	Fillmore East, February 1970	CD	Grateful Dead	GDCD-4063	U.S.A.	1996	54.99	
Allman-Brothers Band	Firing Line (Promo)	CD Single	Sanctuary	SANDJ-85546-2	U.S.A.	2003	7.99	
Allman-Brothers Band	Good Clean Fun (Promo)	CD Single	Epic	ESK-2075	U.S.A.	1990	7.99	
Allman-Brothers Band	Hell & High Water: Best Arista Years	CD	Arista	07822-18724-2	U.S.A.	1994	8.99	
Allman-Brothers Band	High Cost Of Low Living (Promo)	CD Single	Sanctuary	SANDJ-85558-2	U.S.A.	2003	7.99	
Allman-Brothers Band	Hittin' The Note	CD	Sanctuary	06076-84599-2	U.S.A.	2003	8.99	
Allman-Brothers Band	Hittin' The Note	CD	Universal	UICE-1055	Japan	2000	29.99	
Allman-Brothers Band	Hittin' The Note (Promo)	CD Single	Sanctuary	SANSP-84599-2	U.S.A.	2003	7.99	
Allman-Brothers Band	Idlewind South	CD	Capricorn	314-531-258-2	U.S.A.	1997	8.99	
Allman-Brothers Band	Idlewind South	CD	PolyGram	PHCR-4439	Japan	1997	24.99	
Allman-Brothers Band	IRSA Sampler (Promo)	CD	Sony	DISP-002175	U.S.A.	1994	74.99	
Allman-Brothers Band	Legendary Hits	CD	PolyGram	314-520-285-2	U.S.A.	1994	6.99	
Allman-Brothers Band	Live At Atlanta Pop Festival 1970	2CD	Epic	MHCP-139/40	Japan	2000	39.99	
Allman-Brothers Band	Live At Fillmore	CD	PolyGram	PHCR-4440	Japan	1997	29.99	
Allman-Brothers Band	Live At Fillmore 1971	2CD	Polydor K.K.	POCP-1283/4	Japan	1993	39.99	
Allman-Brothers Band	Live At Ludlow Garage 1970	2CD	PolyGram	843-260-2	U.S.A.	1990	16.99	
Allman-Brothers Band	Live At Ludlow Garage 1971	2CD	Polydor K.K.	POCP-1908/9	Japan	1991	39.99	
Allman-Brothers Band	Live Atlanta International Pop Festival	2CD	Epic	E2K-86909	U.S.A.	2003	19.99	
Allman-Brothers Band	Madness Of The West	CD	BMG	74321-56961-2	England	1998	7.99	
Allman-Brothers Band	Martin Scorsese Presents	CD	Universal	UICY-1224	Japan	2000	29.99	
Allman-Brothers Band	Martin Scorsese Presents	CD	Mercury	B000580-02	U.S.A.	2003	7.99	
Allman-Brothers Band	Melissa (Promo)	CD Single	Epic	ESK-4609	U.S.A.	1992	9.99	
Allman-Brothers Band	Mycology	CD	Sony	ESCA-6878	Japan	1998	24.99	

	Artist	Title	Format	Label	Catalog No	Country	Released	Value
A								
	Allman-Brothers Band	Mycology An Anthology	CD	Sony	BK-68682-2	U.S.A.	1998	6.99
	Allman-Brothers Band	Mycology: An Anthology (Promo)	CD	550 Music	ABK-68682-S1	U.S.A.	1998	14.99
	Allman-Brothers Band	No One To Run With (Promo)	CD Single	Epic	ESK-6041	U.S.A.	1994	7.99
	Allman-Brothers Band	Nobody Knows (Promo)	CD Single	Epic	ESK-4333	U.S.A.	1991	7.99
	Allman-Brothers Band	Peakin' At The Beacon	CD	Epic	EK-85205	U.S.A.	2000	8.99
	Allman-Brothers Band	Reach For The Sky	CD	Capricorn	314-558-381-2	U.S.A.	1997	8.99
	Allman-Brothers Band	Reach For The Sky	CD	BMG	BVCA-7318	Japan	1995	22.99
	Allman-Brothers Band	Reach For The Sky	CD	Razor & Tie	RE-2131-2	U.S.A.	1997	8.99
	Allman-Brothers Band	Road Goes On Forever	2CD	Universal	UICY-1098/9	Japan	2000	39.99
	Allman-Brothers Band	S.U.N.Y. At Stonybrook 09/19/71	CD	Allman Bros.	NO. 2	U.S.A.	2003	19.99
	Allman-Brothers Band	Self Titled	CD	Capricorn	314-531-257-2	U.S.A.	1997	8.99
	Allman-Brothers Band	Seven Turns	CD	Epic	EK-46144	U.S.A.	1990	8.99
	Allman-Brothers Band	Seven Turns (Promo)	CD Single	Epic	ESK-2184	U.S.A.	1990	7.99
	Allman-Brothers Band	Shades Of Two Worlds	CD	Epic	EK-47877	U.S.A.	1991	14.99
	Allman-Brothers Band	Soulshine (Promo)	CD Single	Epic	ESK-6559	U.S.A.	1994	7.99
	Allman-Brothers Band	The ABB Years (Promo)	CD	Capricorn	CAPCD-3003	U.S.A.	1998	24.99
	Allman-Brothers Band	The Best Of The Allman Brothers Band	CD	Polydor	823-708-2	Canada	1981	7.99
	Allman-Brothers Band	The Fillmore Concerts	2CD	Polydor	314-517-294-2	U.S.A.	1992	19.99
	Allman-Brothers Band	The Road Goes On Forever + 13	2CD	Mercury	314-589-260-2	U.S.A.	2001	14.99
	Allman-Brothers Band	Universal Masters Collection	CD	PolyGram	PHCY-2006	Japan	2000	24.99
	Allman-Brothers Band	Where It All Begins	CD	Epic	EK-64232	U.S.A.	1994	8.99
	Allman-Brothers Band	Win, Lose Or Draw	CD	PolyGram	PHCR-4444	Japan	1997	24.99
	Allman-Brothers Band	Win, Lose Or Draw	CD	Capricorn	314-531-263-2	U.S.A.	1997	8.99
	Allman-Brothers Band	Wipe The Window...	CD	PolyGram	PHCR-4445	Japan	1997	24.99
	Allman-Brothers Band	Wipe Windows Check Oil Dollar Gas	CD	Capricorn	314-531-264-2	U.S.A.	1997	7.99
	Allman-Brothers Band/Leavell	Chuck Leavell - Forever Blue	CD	Terminus	163	U.S.A.	2001	9.99
	Allman-Brothers Band/Leavell	Chuck Leavell - What's In That Bag?	CD	Capricorn	314-534-943-2	U.S.A.	1998	9.99
	Allman-Brothers Band/Neel	Johnny Neel - Comin' Atcha... Live	CD	Big Mo	1027-2	U.S.A.	1995	9.99
	Allman-Brothers Band/Oteil	Oteil/Peacemakers - Family Secret	CD	Artists House	AH00002	U.S.A.	2002	9.99
	Allman-Brothers Band/Trucks	Frogwings - Croakin' At Toad's	CD	Flying Frog	003	U.S.A.	2001	9.99
	Almond, Marc	Jacques (Brel Songs)	CD	Some Bizarre	BREL-1-CD	England	1989	11.99
	Almond, Marc	Open All Night (Limited Ed)	2CD	Blue Star	5236302	France	1999	10.99
	Almond, Marc	Singles 1984-1987	CD	Virgin	CDFAITH-3	England	1987	7.99
	Almond, Marc	Tenement Symphony	CD	Sire	9-26764-2	U.S.A.	1991	8.99
	Alpert, Herb	Beyond	CD	A&M	D32Y-3041	Japan	1980	103.99
	Alpert, Herb	Blow Your Own Horn	CD	A&M	CD-4949	U.S.A.	1983	78.99
	Alpert, Herb	Bullish	CD	A&M	CD-5022	U.S.A.	1984	49.99
	Alpert, Herb	Classics, Vol. 20	CD	A&M	75021-2518-2	U.S.A.	1987	17.99
	Alpert, Herb	Colors	CD	Almo Sounds	AMSCD-80025	U.S.A.	1999	5.99
	Alpert, Herb	Definitive Hits	CD	A&M	069-490-886-2	U.S.A.	2001	15.99
	Alpert, Herb	Fandango	CD	A&M	75021-3731-2	U.S.A.	1982	99.99
	Alpert, Herb	Keep Your Eye On Me	CD	A&M	75021-5125-2	U.S.A.	1991	14.99
	Alpert, Herb	Magic Man	CD	A&M	CD-3728	U.S.A.	1981	53.99
	Alpert, Herb	Midnight Dance	CD	A&M	75021-5391-2	U.S.A.	1992	7.99
	Alpert, Herb	Midnight Sun	CD	A&M	75021-5391-2	U.S.A.	1992	6.99
	Alpert, Herb	My Abstract Heart	CD	A&M	75021-5273-2	U.S.A.	1989	6.99
	Alpert, Herb	North On South St.	CD	A&M	75021-5345-2	U.S.A.	1991	8.99
	Alpert, Herb	Passion Dance	CD	Almo Sounds	AMSD-80014	U.S.A.	1997	11.99
	Alpert, Herb	Passion Dance (Promo)	CD Single	Almo Sounds	PRO-CD-8021	U.S.A.	1997	4.99
	Alpert, Herb	Rise	CD	Pony Canyon	D18Y4101	Japan	1979	16.99
	Alpert, Herb	Rise	CD	A&M	75021-3274-2	U.S.A.	1979	29.99
	Alpert, Herb	Second Wind	CD	Almo Sounds	AMSD-80005	U.S.A.	1996	8.99
	Alpert, Herb	Under A Spanish Moon	CD	A&M	75021-5209-2	U.S.A.	1988	6.99
	Alpert, Herb	Under The Spanish Moon	CD	Pony Canyon	D32Y3244	Japan	1988	16.99
	Alpert, Herb	Wild Romance	CD	A&M	75021-5082-2	U.S.A.	1985	49.99
	Alpert, Herb/Hugh Masekla	Self Titled	CD	A&M	75021-0819-2	U.S.A.	1978	39.99
	Alpert, Herb/Tijuana Brass	Beat Of The Brass	CD	A&M	75021-3266-2	U.S.A.	1968	224.99
	Alpert, Herb/Tijuana Brass	Bullish	CD	A&M	CD-5022	U.S.A.	1984	153.99

Artist	Title	Format	Label	Catalog No	Country	Released	Value	A
Alpert, Herb/Tijuana Brass	Christmas Album	CD	A&M	CD-4166	U.S.A.	1968	53.99	
Alpert, Herb/Tijuana Brass	Classics, Vol. 1	CD	A&M	CD-2501	U.S.A.	1986	24.99	
Alpert, Herb/Tijuana Brass	Four Sider	CD	A&M	75021-6011-2	U.S.A.	1990	115.99	
Alpert, Herb/Tijuana Brass	Foursider	CD	A&M	75021-6011-2	U.S.A.	1973	35.99	
Alpert, Herb/Tijuana Brass	Going Places	CD	A&M	CD-3264	U.S.A.	1990	134.99	
Alpert, Herb/Tijuana Brass	Greatest Hits Volume 1	CD	A&M	CD-3267	U.S.A.	1970	14.99	
Alpert, Herb/Tijuana Brass	Greatest Hits Volume 2	CD	A&M	75021-3269-2	U.S.A.	1973	63.99	
Alpert, Herb/Tijuana Brass	S.R.O.	CD	Pony Canyon	D32Y3087	Japan	1986	409.99	
Alpert, Herb/Tijuana Brass	Solid Brass	CD	A&M	75021-3268-2	U.S.A.	1988	104.99	
Alpert, Herb/Tijuana Brass	South Of The Border	CD	A&M	CD-3263	U.S.A.	1990	209.99	
Alpert, Herb/Tijuana Brass	The Lonely Bull	CD	A&M	75021-3101-2	U.S.A.	1962	39.99	
Alpert, Herb/Tijuana Brass	Tijuana Brass, Vol. 2	CD	A&M	75021-3262-2	U.S.A.	1963	39.99	
Alpert, Herb/Tijuana Brass	What Now My Love	CD	A&M	CD-3265	U.S.A.	1990	136.99	
Alpert, Herb/Tijuana Brass	Whipped Cream & Other Delights	CD	A&M	75021-3157-2	U.S.A.	1965	59.99	
Alpert, Herb/Tijuana Brass	Whipped Cream And Other Delights	CD	Pony Canyon	POCM-1948	Japan	1996	79.99	
Alpha Centauri	Self Titled	CD	Peacemaker	PACE-005	Canada	1994	9.99	
Alta Moda	Alta - Moda	CD	Line	CUCD-9.00984-0	Germany	1990	4.99	
Alvin, Dave	Blackjack David	CD	HighTone	HCD-08091	U.S.A.	1998	12.99	
Alvin, Dave	Every Night About This Time	CD	Line	DECD-9.00334-0	Germany	1987	12.99	
Alvin, Dave	Interstate City	CD	HighTone	HCD-08074	U.S.A.	1996	9.99	
Alvin, Dave	Public Domain: Songs From...	CD	HighTone	HCD-08122	U.S.A.	2000	11.99	
Alvin, Dave/Guilty Men	Out In California	CD	HighTone	HCD-08144	U.S.A.	2002	12.99	
Amazing Rhythm Aces	1999 - Live In Switzerland	CD	Blue Buffalo	BUF-1	Germany	1999	14.99	
Amazing Rhythm Aces	Absolutely Live	CD	Icehouse	9437	U.S.A.	2000	14.99	
Amazing Rhythm Aces	Between You & Us	CD	Alchemy	PILOT-113	England	2001	10.99	
Amazing Rhythm Aces	Chock Full Of Country Goodness	CD	Valley	VE-15035	U.S.A.	1999	5.99	
Amazing Rhythm Aces	Concert Classics, Vol. 3	CD	Renaissance	RRCC00703	U.S.A.	1999	10.99	
Amazing Rhythm Aces	Full House: Aces High	CD	International Trash	ARA-12	U.S.A.	2002	21.99	
Amazing Rhythm Aces	How Do You Spell Rhythum?	CD	International Trash	ARA-151	Australia	2003	24.99	
Amazing Rhythm Aces	Out Of The Blue	CD	Valley	VE-15034	U.S.A.	1999	12.99	
Amazing Rhythm Aces	Ride Again, Vol. 1	CD	Breaker	1	Australia	1997	14.99	
Amazing Rhythm Aces	Self Titled	CD	Collector's Choice	CCM-1872	U.S.A.	2001	7.99	
Amazing Rhythm Aces	Stacked Deck/Too Stuffed To Jump	CD	Collector's Choice	CCM-1222	U.S.A.	2000	14.99	
Amazing Rhythm Aces	Toucan Do It / Burning The Ballroom..	CD	Collector's Choice	CCM-1232	U.S.A.	2000	14.99	
Ambrosia	Ambrosia	CD	Warner Bros.	WPCR-10479	Japan	1999	19.99	
Ambrosia	Life Beyond L.A.	CD	Warner Bros.	26870	U.S.A.	2000	8.99	
Ambrosia	One Eighty	CD	Warner Bros.	WPCR-10507	Japan	1999	24.99	
Ambrosia	One Eighty	CD	Warner Bros.	WPCP-4803	Japan	1992	13.99	
Ambrosia	Road Island	CD	Warner Bros.	WPCR-10508	Japan	1999	24.99	
Ambrosia	Self Titled	CD	Warner Bros.	9-47565-2	U.S.A.	1975	14.99	
Ambrosia	Somewhere I've Never...	CD	Warner Bros.	9-47566-2	U.S.A.	1976	8.99	
Ambrosia	The Essentials	CD	Rhino	R2-76058	U.S.A.	2002	7.99	
Amen Corner	Farewell To The Magnificent Seven	CD	Line	IDCD-9.00293-0	Germany	1988	4.99	
Amen Corner	National Welsh Coast Live	CD	Line	IDCD-9.00306-0	Germany	1988	4.99	
America	Alibi	CD	Magic	5201192	France	1999	12.99	
America	America	CD	Warner Bros.	2576-2	U.S.A.	1972	8.99	
America	America	2CD	EMI	13102	U.S.A.	1999	12.99	
America	America Live	CD	Warner Bros.	7599-26690-2	Germany	1977	14.99	
America	Encore: More Greatest Hits	CD	Rhino	R2-70529	U.S.A.	1991	6.99	
America	Harbor	CD	Warner Bros.	7599-26883-2	Germany	1977	17.99	
America	Hat Trick	CD	Warner Bros.	7599-26692-2	Germany	1973	14.99	
America	Hearts	CD	Warner Bros.	9362-45986-2	Germany	1975	14.99	
America	Hideaway	CD	Warner Bros.	7599-26691-2	Germany	1976	17.99	
America	Highway: 30 Years of America	3CD	Rhino	R2-79887	U.S.A.	2000	30.99	
America	History - America's Greatest Hits	CD	Warner Bros.	3110-2	U.S.A.	1975	11.99	
America	Holiday	CD	Warner Bros.	7599-27501-2	Holland	1974	17.99	
America	Holiday Harmony	CD	Rhino	R2-74498	U.S.A.	2002	10.99	
America	Homecoming	CD	Warner Bros.	2-2655	U.S.A.	1972	14.99	

A	Artist	Title	Format	Label	Catalog No	Country	Released	Value
	America	Homecoming (DVD Audio)	CD	Rhino	R2-74367	U.S.A.	2002	12.99
	America	Horse With No Name (Audio/Video)	2CD	Master Tone	MM5101	England	1995	35.99
	America	Hourglass	CD	American	AGCD-494	U.S.A.	1994	6.99
	America	Human Nature	CD	Oxygen	90004-2	U.S.A.	1998	6.99
	America	In Concert	CD	EMI	7-48414-2	Australia	1985	19.99
	America	In Concert	CD	EMI	7243-8-54201-2-2	England	1996	14.99
	America	In Concert (King Biscuit Flower Hour)	CD	King Biscuit	70710-88001-2	U.S.A.	1995	9.99
	America	Perspective	CD	Magic	5201182	France	1999	13.99
	America	Perspective (With Red Box)	CD	EMI	724357608626	Holland	2000	19.99
	America	Premium Gold Collection	CD	EMI	7243-8-37638-2-5	Germany	1996	14.99
	America	Silent Letter	CD	Magic	5201162	France	1999	14.99
	America	The Complete Greatest Hits	CD	Rhino	R2-74375	U.S.A.	2001	14.99
	America	The Definitive America	CD	Warner Bros.	8122735522	Australia	2001	17.99
	America	The Last Unicorn (Greatest)	2CD	EMI	23035	Germany	2003	19.99
	America	View From The Ground	CD	Magic	5201125	France	1999	14.99
	America	You Can Do Magic	CD	Disky	DC-864352	Holland	1996	9.99
	America	Your Move +3 (Jimmy Webb Songs)	CD	Magic	5201142	France	1999	14.99
	America/Beckley, Gerry	Like A Brother (R. Lamm, C. Wilson)	CD	Transparentmusic	500022	U.S.A.	2000	23.99
	America/Beckley, Gerry	Like A Brother + 3	CD	Victor Ent.	VICP-61387	Japan	2001	19.99
	America/Dan Peek	Doer Of The Word	CD	Cool Sound	COOL-004	Japan	1998	14.99
	America/Gerry Beckley	Go Man Go (Van Go Gan Remixes)	CD	Human Nature	160839-01	U.S.A.	2000	23.99
	America/Gerry Beckley	Van Go Gan	CD	Human Nature	151397-02	U.S.A.	1999	23.99
	America/Jimmy Webb	The Last Unicorn [O.S.T.]	CD	Virgin	7-86735-2	Holland	1982	28.99
	American Breed	Bend Me, Shape Me Best Of	CD	Varese	VSCD-5493	U.S.A.	1994	24.99
	Ammons, Angela	Angela Ammons	CD	Universal	440-014-348-2	U.S.A.	2001	6.99
	Amon Duul	Collapsing — Singvogel...	CD	Spalax	14949	France	1995	14.99
	Amon Duul	Disaster	CD	Spalax	14948	France	1995	10.99
	Amon Duul	Disaster (Unreleased 1st Lp Tracks)	CD	Captain Trip	CTCD-022	Japan	1969	13.99
	Amon Duul	Experimente	CD	Spalax	14842	France	1996	10.99
	Amon Duul	Experimente (All Unreleased)	CD	Captain Trip	CTCD-014	Japan	2000	11.99
	Amon Duul	Para Dieswärts Düül + 2	CD	Repertoire	REP-4678-WY	Germany	2002	6.99
	Amon Duul	Para Dieswarts...(W/ Singles Tracks)	CD	Captain Trip	CTCD-017	Japan	1970	11.99
	Amon Duul	Para Dieswarts...(W/Singles Tracks)	CD	Spalax	SPA-14946	France	1970	10.99
	Amon Duul	Psychedelic Underground	CD	Captain Trip	CTCD-021	Japan	1969	13.99
	Amon Duul	Psychedelic Underground	CD	Repertoire	REP-4616-WY	Germany	2002	12.99
	Amon Duul	Psychedelic Underground	CD	Spalax	SPA-14947	France	1969	10.99
	Amon Duul II	Carnival in Babylon	CD	Captain Trip	CTCD-033	Japan	1971	9.99
	Amon Duul II	Carnival in Babylon + 4	CD	Repertoire	REP-4986	Germany	2002	19.99
	Amon Duul II	Eternal Flashback	CD	Captain Trip	CTCD-041	Japan	2000	9.99
	Amon Duul II	Hijack	CD	Garden Of Delights	GOD-079	Germany	2003	14.99
	Amon Duul II	Kobe (Reconstruction)	CD	Captain Trip	CTCD-039	Japan	1995	9.99
	Amon Duul II	Lemmingmania	CD	Captain Trip	CTCD-037	Japan	1975	9.99
	Amon Duul II	Live In Concert	CD	Windsong	WINCD-027	England	1992	13.99
	Amon Duul II	Live in London	CD	Captain Trip	CTCD-035	Japan	1973	11.99
	Amon Duul II	Live in Tokyo (1996)	CD	Captain Trip	CTCD-047	Japan	1996	9.99
	Amon Duul II	Made In Germany (Full Album)	CD	Repertoire	REP-4631-WY	Germany	2002	27.99
	Amon Duul II	Nada Moonshine # (Reunion)	CD	Captain Trip	CTCD-038	Japan	1996	9.99
	Amon Duul II	Phallus Dei	CD	Captain Trip	CTCD-030	Japan	1969	13.99
	Amon Duul II	Phallus Dei + 4	CD	Repertoire	REP-4872	Germany	2003	13.99
	Amon Duul II	Surrounded By The Bars	CD	Spalax	SPA-14810	France	1993	10.99
	Amon Duul II	Tanz Der Lemminge	CD	Repertoire	REP-4915	Germany	2002	15.99
	Amon Duul II	Tanz Der Lemminge	CD	Captain Trip	CTCD-032	Japan	1970	9.99
	Amon Duul II	Utopia	CD	Spalax	SPA-14878	France	1972	9.99
	Amon Duul II	Viva la Trance	CD	Captain Trip	CTCD-036	Japan	1973	9.99
	Amon Duul II	Vive La Trance	CD	Mantra	MANTRA-062	France	1973	9.99
	Amon Duul II	Vive La Trance + 1	CD	Repertoire	REP-4988	Germany	2002	15.99
	Amon Duul II	Wolf City	CD	Repertoire	REP-4987	Germany	2002	10.99
	Amon Duul II	Wolf City	CD	Captain Trip	CTCD-034	Japan	1972	9.99

Artist	Title	Format	Label	Catalog No	Country	Released	Value
Amon Duul II	Yeti	CD	Mantra	MANTRA-010	France	1970	21.99
Amon Duul II	Yeti	CD	Captain Trip	CTCD-031	Japan	1970	9.99
Amon Duul II	Yeti + 2	CD	Repertoire	REP-4914	Germany	2003	18.99
Amon Duul II/Chris Karrer	Sufisticated	CD	Captain Trip	CTCD-084	Japan	2000	9.99
Amon Duul II/The Cha.-Cy.	(3") (Faust/Embryo)	CD Single	Captain Trip	CTCD-199	Japan	1999	8.99
Amon Duul UK	Fool Moon	CD	Spalax	SPA-14516	France	1989	10.99
Amon Duul UK	Hawk Meets Penguin	CD	Spalax	14848	France	1996	10.99
Amon Duul UK	Meetings With Menmachines	CD	Spalax	14820	France	1996	10.99
Amon Duul/J Case Version	Para Dieswarts...(W/Single Tracks)	CD	Spalax	SPA-14950	France	1970	15.99
Amos, Tori	Caught A Light Sneeze (Picture Label)	CD Single	East West	7567-85524-2	France	1996	63.99
Amos, Tori	China	CD Single	East West	A7531CD	Germany	1992	34.99
Amos, Tori	China	CD Single	Atlantic	7576-85905-2	Germany	1994	26.99
Amos, Tori	China	CD Single	East West	7567-85755-9	France	1993	54.99
Amos, Tori	Cornflake Girl (Promo)	CD Single	Atlantic	PRCD-5606	U.S.A.	1994	13.99
Amos, Tori	Crucify Ltd Box Set (W/4 Prints)	CD Single	East West	A7479CDX	Japan	1994	39.99
Amos, Tori	From The Choirgirl (Promo Sampler)	CD	Atlantic	PRCD-8520	U.S.A.	1998	7.99
Amos, Tori	God	CD Single	East West	A7251CD	England	1993	11.17
Amos, Tori	Holiday Greetings	CD	Atlantic	PRCD-6589-2	U.S.A.	1995	72.99
Amos, Tori	Little Drummer Boy (Promo)	CD Single	Atlantic	PRCD-5409	U.S.A.	1994	32.99
Amos, Tori	Little Earthquakes	CD	East West	WMC5-488	Japan	1992	43.99
Amos, Tori	Past The Mission (Cd 2)	CD Single	East West	A7257CD	Germany	1994	18.39
Amos, Tori	Precious Things (Promo)	CD Single	Atlantic	PRCD-4742-2	U.S.A.	1992	349.99
Amos, Tori	Retrospective: Benefit Rainn (DJ)	CD	Atlantic	PRCD-6999-2	U.S.A.	1997	93.99
Amos, Tori	Silent All These Years	CD	Atlantic	YZ-618CD	England	1992	29.99
Amos, Tori	Silent All These Years	CD Single	East West	A7433CDX	U.S.A.	1992	39.99
Amos, Tori	Silent All These Years (Promo)	CD Single	East West	A7433CD	Germany	1992	19.99
Amos, Tori	Strange Little Girl (Withdrawn Promo)	CD	Atlantic	PRCD-300630	U.S.A.	2001	19.99
Amos, Tori	Tea With A Waitress (Promo)	CD	Atlantic	PRCD-5498-2	U.S.A.	1994	30.99
Amos, Tori	Tea With A Waitress (Promo/Interview)	CD	Atlantic	PRCD-5498-2	U.S.A.	1994	34.99
Amos, Tori	Tracks Venus And Back (Promo)	CD	Atlantic	PRCD-9091	U.S.A.	1999	8.99
Amos, Tori	Y Kant Tori Read	CD	Atlantic	81845-2	U.S.A.	1988	313.99
Anderson, Ian	A Raft Of Penguins (Promo)	CD Single	Fuel 2000	IAN-01	U.S.A.	2003	59.99
Anderson, Ian	Divinities - Four Dances With God (DJ)	CD	EMI	DPRO-79992	U.S.A.	1995	19.99
Anderson, Ian	Divinities: Twelve Dances With God	CD	EMI	7243-5-55262-2-9	U.S.A.	1995	8.99
Anderson, Ian	Postcard Day Promo	CD Single	Fuel 2000	FLDPRO-1120	U.S.A.	2000	19.99
Anderson, Ian	Rupi's Dance	CD	Fuel 2000	302-061-328-2	U.S.A.	2003	8.99
Anderson, Ian	Secret Language Of Birds (Promo)	CD Single	Papilion	BTFLYPRO2	England	2000	19.99
Anderson, Ian	The Secret Language Of Birds	CD	Fuel 2000	302-061-053-2	U.S.A.	2000	8.99
Anderson, Ian	Walk Into Light	CD	BGO	BGOCD350	England	1997	17.99
Anderson, Jade	Dive Deeper (Promo January 29, 2002)	CD	Columbia	1297-2133-2737	U.S.A.	2002	9.99
Anderson, Jade	Sugar High	CD Single	Columbia	38K-79757	U.S.A.	2002	3.99
Anderson, Jade	Sugar High (Promo)	CD Single	Columbia	CSK-56791	U.S.A.	2002	6.99
Anderson, Jon	3 Ships	CD	Warner Bros.	WMC5-568	Japan	1987	104.99
Anderson, Jon	Angels Embrace	CD	Higher Octave	HOMCD-7080	U.S.A.	1995	6.99
Anderson, Jon	Best South America 1993 (W/ Video)	CD	Iron Clad Ent.	22346-1	England	1993	75.99
Anderson, Jon	Candle Song	CD Single	EMI	7243-8-81697-2-1	England	1992	5.99
Anderson, Jon	Change We Must	CD Single	EMI	7243-8-81696-2-2	England	1994	5.99
Anderson, Jon	Change We Must	CD	EMI	7243-5-55088-2-9	U.S.A.	1994	9.99
Anderson, Jon	Deseo	CD	Windham Hill	01934-11140-2	U.S.A.	1994	4.99
Anderson, Jon	Earth Mother Earth	CD	Ellipsis Arts	CD4160	U.S.A.	1997	7.99
Anderson, Jon	In The City Of Angels	CD	Sony	25DP-5021	Japan	1988	15.99
Anderson, Jon	In The City Of Angels	CD	Columbia	CK-40910	U.S.A.	1988	8.99
Anderson, Jon	Olias Of Sunhillow	CD	East West	AMCY-18	Japan	1990	15.99
Anderson, Jon	Song Of Seven	CD	East West	AMCY-24	Japan	1990	15.99
Anderson, Jon	The More You Know	CD	Eagle	EAGCD018	EC	1998	8.99
Anderson, Jon	The More You Know + 1	CD	Victor Ent.	VICP-60216	Japan	1998	11.99
Anderson, Jon	The Promise Ring	CD	Om Town	OMCD-3001	U.S.A.	1997	13.99
Anderson, Jon	Toltec	CD	High Street	72902-10346-2	U.S.A.	1996	8.99

	Artist	Title	Format	Label	Catalog No	Country	Released	Value
A	Anderson, Jon/C2THype	Close To The Hype	CD Single	Griffin	GCDAJ-153-2	Canada	1994	7.99
	Anderson, Jon/Deep Forest	Speed Deep	CD Single	BMG	72902-10340-2	EC	1995	5.99
	Anderson, Jon/T. Dream	Legend (O.S.T. W/Tangerine Dream)	CD	Varese	VSD-5645	U.S.A.	1985	29.99
	Anderson, Jon/Vangelis	Chronicles	CD	Spectrum	550-196-2	England	1994	11.99
	Anderson, Jon/Vangelis	Page Of Life - 3 + Change We Must	CD	OmTown	OMCD-45337	U.S.A.	1991	9.99
	Anderson, Jon/Vangelis	Page Of Life + 4 - Change We Must	CD	Arista	261-373	Germany	1991	19.99
	Anderson, Jon/Vangelis	Private Collection	CD	PolyGram	813-174-2	U.S.A.	1983	11.99
	Anderson, Jon/Vangelis	Short Stories	CD	PolyGram	800-027-2	U.S.A.	1980	11.99
	Anderson, Jon/Vangelis	The Friends Of Mr. Cairo (W/I'll Find...)	CD	PolyGram	800-021-2	U.S.A.	1981	9.99
	Anderson, Jon/Various Artists	Requiem For The Americas	CD	Enigma	7-7354-2	U.S.A.	1989	5.99
	Anderson, Jon/Various Artists	The Deseo Remixes	CD	High Street	WHCD-10338	U.S.A.	1995	3.99
	Anderson, Jon/Various Artists	The Holiday Collection, Vol. 3	CD	MCA	HAND-22117	U.S.A.	1993	4.99
	Anderson, Laurie	Beautiful Red Dress	CD Single	Warner Bros.	9-21592-2	U.S.A.	1990	5.99
	Anderson, Laurie	Big Science	CD	Warner Bros.	3674-2	U.S.A.	1982	9.99
	Anderson, Laurie	Bright Red	CD	Warner Bros.	9-45534-2	U.S.A.	1994	8.99
	Anderson, Laurie	Bright Red (Promo Sampler)	CD	Warner Bros.	PRO-CD-7260	U.S.A.	1994	9.99
	Anderson, Laurie	Home Of The Brave	CD	Warner Bros.	CD-25400	U.S.A.	1986	10.99
	Anderson, Laurie	In Our Sleep	CD Single	Warner Bros.	9-43515-2	U.S.A.	1995	6.99
	Anderson, Laurie	Life On A String	CD	Nonesuch	19539-2	U.S.A.	2001	9.99
	Anderson, Laurie	Mister Heartbreak	CD	Warner Bros.	CD-25077	Canada	1984	6.99
	Anderson, Laurie	Strange Angels	CD	Warner Bros.	9-25900-2	U.S.A.	1989	7.99
	Anderson, Laurie	Talk Normal: The Anthology	CD	Rhino	R2-76648	U.S.A.	2000	14.99
	Anderson, Laurie	The Ugly One With The Jewels	CD	Warner Bros.	9-45847-2	U.S.A.	1995	11.99
	Anderson, Laurie	United States Live	4CD	Warner Bros.	9-25192-2	U.S.A.	1984	50.99
	Anderson, Miller	Bright City (Savoy Brown/T. Rex)	CD	Repertoire	REP-4524-WP	Germany	1995	14.99
	Anderson, Miller	Celtic Moon (Savoy Brown/T. Rex)	CD	Inakustik	INAK-9046	Sweden	1998	14.99
	Andre Cymone/Prince	A.C.	CD	Columbia	FC-40037	U.S.A.	1985	85.99
	Andrews, Julie	A Joyous Christmas	CD	RCA	ATCD-2108-2	U.S.A.	1991	7.99
	Andrews, Julie	A Little Bit Of Broadway	CD	Columbia	CK-44375	U.S.A.	1988	7.99
	Andrews, Julie	Broadway/Music Of Richard Rodgers	CD	Philips	442-603-2	U.S.A.	1994	9.99
	Andrews, Julie	Broadway/Words Of Alan Jay Lerner	CD	Phillips	446-219-2	U.S.A.	1996	7.99
	Andrews, Julie	Broadway's Fair/Heartrending Ballads...	CD	Sony	480998-2	Spain	1995	19.99
	Andrews, Julie	Camelot (With Richard Burton)	CD	Sony	SK-60542	U.S.A.	1998	8.99
	Andrews, Julie	Christmas With Julie Andrews	CD	Columbia	JK-65940	U.S.A.	1999	7.99
	Andrews, Julie	Cinderella + 4 (Original T.V. Broadcast)	CD	Sony	SK-60889	U.S.A.	1999	13.99
	Andrews, Julie	Classic Julie Classic Broadway	CD	Decca	289-468-593-2	U.S.A.	2001	14.98
	Andrews, Julie	Love, Julie	CD	USA Music	USACD-539	Canada	1987	14.99
	Andrews, Julie	The Best Of	CD	Columbia	983-403-2	England	1994	7.99
	Andrews, Julie	The Best Of - Thoroughly Modern Julie	CD	Rhino	R2-72281	U.S.A.	1996	13.99
	Andrews, Julie	The Sound Of Music + 15 (35th Ann)	2CD	RCA	07863-67972-2	U.S.A.	1995	19.99
	Andrews, Julie	The Sounds Of Christmas	CD	Hallmark	620XPR9707	U.S.A.	1990	44.99
	Andrews, Julie	Victor/Victoria (Broadway Cast)	CD	Philips	446-919-2	U.S.A.	1995	12.99
	Andrews, Julie/Andre Previn	A Christmas Treasure	CD	RCA	3829-2-R	U.S.A.	1967	7.99
	Andrews, Julie/Andre Previn	Gr. Christmas Songs (A Xmas Treasure	CD	RCA	07863-67971-2	U.S.A.	2000	9.99
	Andrews, Julie/Ben Kingsley	The King And I	CD	Philips	438-007-2	U.S.A.	1992	7.99
	Andrews, Julie/Rex Harrison	My Fair Lady (Original Broadway Cast)	CD	Columbia	CK-5090	U.S.A.	1988	8.99
	Andrews, Julie/Rex Harrison	My Fair Lady + 1 (Original London Cast)	CD	Sony	SK-60539	U.S.A.	1998	12.99
	Angel	Anthology	CD	Mercury	314-512-431-2	U.S.A.	1992	13.99
	Angel	Helluva Band	CD	Mercury	314-510-956-2	U.S.A.	1994	16.99
	Angel	Live Without A Net	2CD	Polystar	PSCW-1093/4	Japan	1992	61.99
	Angel	On Earth As It..	CD	Mercury	314-510-957-2	U.S.A.	1994	51.99
	Angel	On Earth As It...	CD	Polystar	PSCW-1090	Japan	1992	48.99
	Angel	Self Titled	CD	Mercury	314-510-955-2	U.S.A.	1994	13.99
	Angel	Sinful	CD	Polystar	PSCW-1092	Japan	1992	42.99
	Angel	Sinful + 2	CD	PolyGram	7-314-510959-2-4	U.S.A.	1994	59.99
	Angel	White Hot	CD	Polystar	PSCW-1091	Japan	1992	15.99
	Animal Logic	Animal Logic 1	CD	IRS	IRSD-82020	U.S.A.	1989	8.99
	Animal Logic	Animal Logic II	CD	I.R.S.	X2-13106	U.S.A.	1991	8.99

Artist	Title	Format	Label	Catalog No	Country	Released	Value
Animal Logic	Someday We'll Understand (Live/DJ)	CD Single	I.R.S.	IRSD-018	U.S.A.	1989	24.99
Animals	Animal Tracks	CD	EMI	7243-4-98936-2-7	England	1999	14.99
Animals	Animalisms + 13	CD	Repertoire	REP-4772-WY	Germany	1999	17.99
Animals	Ark + 1	CD	Essential	ESM-CD-801	England	2000	14.99
Animals	Greatest Hits Live + 1	CD	Essential	ESM-CD-802	England	2000	19.99
Animals	Gunsight	CD	Akarma	AK-074	Italy	2002	14.99
Animals	Rarities	CD	Prestige	PRCDSP500	England	1992	7.99
Animals	Retrospective	CD	Abkco	93252	USA	2004	8.99
Animals	Taken Live!	CD	Fuel 2000	302-061-198-2	U.S.A.	2002	7.99
Animals	The Animals	CD	EMI	7243-8-56699-2-7	England	1997	19.99
Animals	The Best Of The Animals	CD	Abkco	43242	U.S.A.	1989	7.99
Animals	The Complete Animals	2CD	EMI	CDS-79-4613-2	Holland	1990	14.99
Animals	The Story Of The Animals	2CD	BR Music	BS-8112-2	Holland	1999	14.99
Animals, The Original	Before We Were....	CD	Repertoire	REP-4845	Germany	2000	11.99
Animals/Eric Burdon	Absolute Animals 1964 - 1968	CD	Raven	RVCD-178	U.S.A.	2003	19.99
Animetal	Animetal Marathon (W/Sticker)	CD	Sony	SRCL-3779	Japan	1997	14.99
Animotion	Obsession - Best Of	CD	Rebound	314-520-501-2	U.S.A.	1998	7.99
Animotion	Self Titled (1st)	CD	Mercury	822-580-2	U.S.A.	1985	14.99
Animotion	Self Titled (3rd)	CD	Polydor	837-314-2	U.S.A.	1988	6.99
Animotion	Strange Behavior	CD	Casablanca	826-691-2	U.S.A.	1986	6.99
Ann-Margret	And Here She Is...	CD	BMG	BVCJ-1012	Japan	1961	24.99
Ann-Margret	Let Me Entertain You	CD	RCA	66882-2	U.S.A.	1996	7.99
Any Trouble	Live At The Venue	CD	Line	LICD-9.00099-0	Germany	1988	7.99
Apache Dancers	War Stories	CD	Line	LICD—9.01374-0	Germany	1991	4.99
Apache Dancers	War Stories	CD	Line	WICD-9.51058-0	Germany	1991	4.99
Aphex Twin	Digeridoo	CD Single	R&S	RSUK12CD	England	1992	39.99
Aphrodite's Child	666	2CD	Vertigo	838-430-2	Germany	1971	15.99
Aphrodite's Child	Babylon The Great: An Intro	CD	Mercury	586-870-2	England	2002	19.99
Aphrodite's Child	Best of Aphrodite's Child	CD	Mercury	838-706-2	Germany	1990	11.99
Aphrodite's Child	The Complete Collection	2CD	Mercury	534-073-2	Germany	1996	24.99
Apollo 100	Golden Instrumental Hits	CD	Laserlight	15-174	Germany	1990	4.99
Apollonia	The Same Dream (Promo)	CD Single	Warner Bros.	PRO-CD-3573	U.S.A.	1988	4.99
Apollonia 6	Self Titled	CD	Warner Bros.	WPCP-3701	Japan	1984	254.99
Apple	An Apple A Day + 4	CD	Repertoire	REP-4366-WP	Germany	2002	12.99
Applejacks	Tell Me When	CD	Deram	820-968-2	U.S.A.	1990	51.99
April Wine	Animal Grace	CD	Capitol	S21-57638	U.S.A.	1984	9.99
April Wine	Attitude	CD	Unidisc Music	AGEK-2099	Canada	1993	6.99
April Wine	Electric Jewels	CD	Aquarius	Q2-6504	Canada	1973	12.99
April Wine	First Decade	CD	Aquarius	Q2-555	Canada	1994	10.99
April Wine	First Glance	CD	Capitol	CDP-7-48416-2	U.S.A.	1978	16.99
April Wine	Forever For Now	CD	Aquarius	Q2-6511	Canada	1976	12.99
April Wine	Frigate	CD	Flood Ross	L2 00109	Canada	1994	6.99
April Wine	Harder...Faster	CD	Capitol	CDP-7-46068-2	U.S.A.	1979	9.99
April Wine	King Biscuit Flower Hour	CD	King Biscuit	KBF-CD-88046	Canada	1999	14.99
April Wine	On Record	CD	Aquarius	Q2-6503	Canada	1974	13.99
April Wine	Oowatanite	CD	Aquarius	Q2-56402	Canada	1998	9.99
April Wine	Power Play	CD	Capitol	CDP-7-48417-2	U.S.A.	1982	15.99
April Wine	Self Titled	CD	Aquarius	Q2-6502	Canada	1972	13.99
April Wine	Stand Back	CD	Aquarius	Q2-6506	Canada	1975	14.99
April Wine	The Nature Of The Beast	CD	Capitol	CDP-7-46067-2	U.S.A.	1981	10.99
April Wine	The Whole World's Going Crazy	CD	Aquarius	Q2-6510	Canada	1976	14.99
April Wine	Walking Through Fire	CD	Aquarius	Q2-6540	Canada	1988	11.99
Aqua	Barbie Girl (Single)	CD Single	MCA	MCADM-55393	U.S.A.	1997	5.99
Aqua	Lollipop	CD Single	MCA	MCADS-55410	U.S.A.	1997	4.99
Arcangel	Self Titled	CD	Sony	ESCA-7756	Japan	1983	16.99
Ardley, Neil	Kaleidoscope Of Rainbows	CD	Line	LICD-9.00351-0	Germany	1988	7.99
Arena	Breakfast In Biarritz	CD	Verglas	VGCD021	England	2001	14.99
Arena	Breakfast In Biarritz	CD	SPV	087-41462DCD	Germany	2001	14.99

A	Artist	Title	Format	Label	Catalog No	Country	Released	Value
	Arena	Contagion	CD	SPV	SPV087-65062CD	Germany	2003	13.99
	Arena	Contagious EP	CD	SPV	SPV076-65742CD	Germany	2003	11.99
	Arena	Contagious EP	CD	Verglas	VGCD023	England	2003	11.99
	Arena	Contagium	CD	Verglas	VGCD025	England	2004	14.99
	Arena	Contagium	CD	SPV	SPV076-60502CD	Germany	2004	14.99
	Arena	Immortal ?	CD	SPV	SPV085-41172CD	Germany	2000	11.99
	Arena	Immortal ?	CD	Verglas	VGCD019	England	2000	11.99
	Arena	Pride	CD	Verglas	VGCD004	England	1996	13.99
	Arena	Pride	CD	SPV	SPV085-28222CD	Germany	1996	13.99
	Arena	Songs From The Lion's Cage	CD	Verglas	VGCD001	England	1995	11.99
	Arena	Songs From The Lion's Cage	CD	SPV	SPV084-15622CD	Germany	1995	11.99
	Arena	The Cry EP	CD	SPV	SPV076-28302CD	Germany	1997	9.99
	Arena	The Cry EP	CD	Verglas	VGCD005	England	1997	9.99
	Arena	The Visitor	CD	Verglas	VGCD012	England	1998	13.99
	Arena	The Visitor	CD	SPV	SPV085-28622CD	Germany	1998	13.99
	Arena	Welcome To The Stage	CD	Verglas	VGCD009	England	1997	9.99
	Arena	Welcome To The Stage	CD	SPV	SPV084-28582CD	Germany	1997	9.99
	Argent	Argent	CD	Line	CLCD-9.01005-L	Germany	1991	10.99
	Argent	Argent/Ring Of Hands	2CD	BGO	BGOCD480	England	2000	22.99
	Argent	Encore	CD	BGO	BGOCD588	England	2003	12.99
	Argent	Hold Your Head Up (The Best Of)	CD	Epic	EICP-7037	Japan	2002	24.99
	Argent	Nexus	CD	Epic	489442-2	England	1974	14.99
	Argent, Rod	Classically Speaking (Ltd 1,000)	CD	Red House	REDHOUSE-001	U.S.A.	1998	24.99
	Argent, Rod	Red House	CD	Relativity	88561-1039-2	U.S.A.	1991	7.99
	Argent/Unit 4 + 2	Concrete and Clay/Unit 4+2 (7 Bonus)	CD	Repertoire	REP-4191-WY	Germany	1994	9.99
	Argent/Unit 4 + 2	Singles A's & B's	CD	Repertoire	REP-5016	Germany	2003	9.99
	Arkenstone, David	Another Star In The Sky	CD	Narada	ND-62014-2	U.S.A.	1994	9.99
	Arkenstone, David	Carvan Of Light	CD	Narada	7243-8-49797-2-0	U.S.A.	2000	6.99
	Arkenstone, David	Chronicles	CD	Narada	ND-64007-2	U.S.A.	1993	7.99
	Arkenstone, David	Citizen Of The World	CD	Windham Hill	01934-11398-2	U.S.A.	1999	7.99
	Arkenstone, David	Citizen Of Time	CD	Narada	ND-62008	U.S.A.	1989	7.99
	Arkenstone, David	Enchantment: A Magical Christmas	CD	Narada	ND-62016	U.S.A.	1997	8.99
	Arkenstone, David	Eternal Champion	CD	Narada	7243-8-45446-2-1	U.S.A.	1998	8.99
	Arkenstone, David	Frontier (O.S.T.)	CD	Paras	PRC30052	U.S.A.	2001	8.99
	Arkenstone, David	In The Wake Of The Wind	CD	Narada	ND-64003	U.S.A.	1991	9.99
	Arkenstone, David	Quest Of The Dream Warrior	CD	Narada	ND-64008	U.S.A.	1995	7.99
	Arkenstone, David	Return Of The Guardians	CD	Narada	ND-64011	U.S.A.	1996	8.99
	Arkenstone, David	Robot Wars	CD	Moonstone	28096-5102-2	U.S.A.	1993	7.99
	Arkenstone, David	Selections From Caravan Of Light (DJ)	CD	Narada	70876-15258-2-3	U.S.A.	2000	9.99
	Arkenstone, David	Sketches From An American Journey	CD	Paras	PRC11252	U.S.A.	2002	8.99
	Arkenstone, David	Spirit Wind	CD	Windham Hill	01934-11215-2	U.S.A.	1997	8.99
	Arkenstone, David	The Celtic Book Of Days	CD	Windham Hill	01934-11246-2	U.S.A.	1998	7.99
	Arkenstone, David	Valley In The Clouds	CD	Narada	ND-62001	U.S.A.	1987	7.99
	Arkenstone, David	Visionary: Ultimate Narada Collection	2CD	Narada	7243-8-11627-2-9	U.S.A.	2002	13.99
	Arkenstone, David/A White	Island	CD	Narada	ND-53005	U.S.A.	1989	7.99
	Arkenstone, David/Kostia	The Spirit Of Olympia	CD	Narada	ND-CD-4006	U.S.A.	1992	7.99
	Armageddon/Keith Relf	Armageddon	CD	Repertoire	PMS-7089-WP	Germany	1998	19.99
	Armageddon/Keith Relf	Armageddon	CD	Polydor K.K.	POCM-1969	Japan	1994	35.99
	Armatrading, Joan	Back To The Night	CD	A&M	CD-3141	U.S.A.	1975	54.99
	Armatrading, Joan	Greatest Hits	CD	A&M	CD-0525	U.S.A.	1996	12.99
	Armatrading, Joan	Self Titled	CD	A&M	CD-3228	U.S.A.	1976	8.99
	Armatrading, Joan	The Key (I Love It When...)	CD	A&M	CD-3318	U.S.A.	1983	28.99
	Armatrading, Joan	To The Limit	CD	A&M	CD-4732	U.S.A.	1978	57.99
	Arnold, David	Die Another Day (O.S.T.)	CD	Warner Bros.	48348-2	U.S.A.	2002	8.99
	Arnold, David	James Bond Project - Shaken/Stirred	CD	Warner Bros.	3984-20738-2	England	1997	7.99
	Arnold, David	The World Is Not Enough (O.S.T.)	CD	MCA	088-112-101-2	U.S.A.	1999	7.99
	Arnold, David	Tomorrow Never Dies (O.S.T.)	CD	A&M	31454-0830-2	U.S.A.	1997	7.99
	Arnold, Malcolm	The Bridge On The River Kwai (O.S.T.)	CD	Sony	SRCS-7072	Japan	1992	24.99

Artist	Title	Format	Label	Catalog No	Country	Released	Value
Arnold, P.P.	The First Cut	CD	Line	INCD-9.00611-0	Germany	1988	22.99
Art Of Noise	Below The Waste	CD	China	839-404-2	Germany	1989	17.99
Artful Dodger	Honor Among Thieves	CD	Pendulum	PEG012	U.S.A.	1997	13.99
Artful Dodger	Honor Among Thieves	CD	Columbia	CK-34273	U.S.A.	1990	13.99
Artful Dodger	Self Titled	CD	Pendulum	PEG011	U.S.A.	1997	66.99
Arthur, Joseph	Come To Where I'm From	CD	Real World	7243-8-48982-2-9	U.S.A.	2000	8.99
Artwoods	Art Gallery + 14 (Ron Wood's Brother)	CD	Repertoire	REP-4533-WP	Germany	2001	10.99
Artwoods	Singles A's & B's (Ron Wood's Brother)	CD	Repertoire	REP-4887-WP	Germany	2001	14.99
Ash, Daniel	Coming Down (Deluxe Ed.)	CD	Beggars Banquet	3076-2-R	U.S.A.	1991	11.99
Ashley, Steve	Mysterious Ways	CD	Line	LICD-9.00696-0	Germany	1989	6.99
Ashley, Steve	Speedy Return	CD	Line	LHCD-9.00708-0	Germany	1989	6.99
Ashley, Steve	Stroll On	CD	Line	LICD-9.00354-0	Germany	1989	6.99
Ashton, Tony	Best Of (W/ Kim Gardner)	CD	Repertoire	REP-4835-WY	Germany	2002	19.99
Ashton, Tony	Big Red And Other Love Songs	CD Single	Repertoire	REP-8018-YN	Germany	1996	9.99
Ashton, Tony	Live In The Studio	CD	Repertoire	REP-4509- WY	Germany	1994	14.99
Ashton, Tony/Remo Four	Best Of Tommy Quickly/Remo Four	CD	See For Miles	SEE-CD-349	England	1992	9.99
Ashton, Tony/Remo Four	In The First Place (George Harrison)	CD Single	Pilar	PILAR01CD	England	1999	16.99
Ashton, Tony/Remo Four	Smile + 8	CD	Repertoire	REP-7034-WZ	Germany	1996	9.99
Ashton, Tony/Remo Four	The Pye Singles	CD	Repertoire	REP-4186-WZ	Germany	1991	12.99
Ashton/Gardner/Dyke	Let It Roll: Live On Stage, 1971	CD	Purple	PUR-307	England	2001	14.99
Ashton/Gardner/Dyke	Self Titled	CD	Line	LMCD-9.51136-Z	Germany	1991	6.99
Ashton/Gardner/Dyke	Self Titled + 4	CD	Repertoire	REP-4565-WY	Germany	1998	14.99
Ashton/Gardner/Dyke	The Last Rebel + 10	CD	Purple	PUR-309	England	2003	14.99
Ashton/Gardner/Dyke	What A Bloody Long Day Its Been	CD	Repertoire	REP-4457-WY	Germany	2002	14.99
Ashton/Gardner/Dyke	Worst Of	CD	Repertoire	REP-4458-WY	Germany	2002	14.99
Ashton/Lord	First Of The Big Bands	CD	Line	LICD-9.00119-0	Germany	1988	11.99
Asia	Alive In Hallowed Halls	CD	Zoom Club	ZCRCD50	England	2001	8.99
Asia	Alpha	CD	Geffen	4008-2	U.S.A.	1983	8.99
Asia	Anthologia	2CD	Geffen	069-493-254-2	U.S.A.	2002	16.99
Asia	Anthology	CD	Snapper	155192	U.S.A.	1997	10.99
Asia	Aqua	CD	Warner Bros.	WPCP-4754	Japan	1992	13.99
Asia	Aqua + 1	CD	Orignial Masters	SMMCD-521	England	1998	11.99
Asia	Archiva 1	CD	Pavement	76962-32262-2	England	1996	6.99
Asia	Archiva 2	CD	Resurgence	LV-105-CD	Austria	1996	6.99
Asia	Arena + 1	CD	Orignial Masters	SMMCD-522	England	1998	11.99
Asia	Aria + 1	CD	Orignial Masters	SMMCD-523	England	1998	11.99
Asia	Aria + 1	CD	Warner Bros.	WPCP-5830	Japan	1994	13.99
Asia	Asia	CD	Geffen	422-008-2	Germany	1982	11.99
Asia	Asia/Then And Now	CD	Geffen	9-24298-2	U.S.A.	1990	8.99
Asia	Astra	CD	MCA	MCAD-20851	U.S.A.	1985	9.99
Asia	Aura + 3	CD	Windstorm	670211-3003-2	U.S.A.	2001	11.99
Asia	Axioms	2CD	Snapper	TECI-38048-9	Japan	2001	19.99
Asia	Best Of	CD	DCC	CASS-70093-2	U.S.A.	1996	8.99
Asia	Classic	CD	Geffen	493-058-2	Holland	2001	15.99
Asia	Enso Kai - Live At Budokan, Tokyo	CD	Alchemy	PILOT87-NMC	Japan	2001	27.99
Asia	Live In Japan '84	CD	Alchemy	PILOT-87	England	2001	14.99
Asia	Live In Koln	2CD	Blueprint	BP254CD	EU	1997	14.99
Asia	Live In Moscow (With Kari-Anne)	CD	Rhino	R2-70377	U.S.A.	1991	9.99
Asia	Live In Moscow 1990 (Wildest Dreams)	CD	Eagle	EAMCD037	EC	1998	12.99
Asia	Live In Nottingham	CD	Blueprint	BP253CD	EU	1997	14.99
Asia	Live In Osaka	2CD	Blueprint	BP252CD	EU	1997	14.99
Asia	Live In Philadelphia	2CD	Blueprint	BP255CD	EU	1998	14.99
Asia	Quandra	4CD	Zoom Club	ZCRCD85BOX	England	2002	46.99
Asia	Rare	CD	Resurgence	LV106CD	England	1999	7.99
Asia	The Best Of Asia Live	2CD	Eagle	EDM-CD-110	Germany	2000	15.99
Asia	The Collection	CD	Connoisseur	VSOP-CD-285	England	2000	14.99
Asia	Very Best Asia: Heat Of Moment	CD	Geffen	069-490-554-2	U.S.A.	2000	8.99
Asleep At The Wheel	Collision Course / The Wheel	CD	Acadia	ACA-8023	England	2002	19.99

A	Artist	Title	Format	Label	Catalog No	Country	Released	Value
	Asleep At The Wheel	Texas Gold/Wheelin' And Dealin'	CD	Acadia	ACA-8022	England	2002	19.99
	Association	And Then...Along Comes... + 5	CD	Warner Bros.	WPCR-10074	Japan	1999	25.99
	Association	Birthday + 3	CD	Warner Bros.	WPCR-10077	Japan	1999	26.99
	Association	French 60's Ep & Sp Collection	CD	Magic	5230142	France	1999	11.99
	Association	Goodbye, Columbus	CD	Warner Bros.	WPCR-10195	Japan	1999	35.99
	Association	Greatest Hits	CD	Warner Bros.	WPCR-1243	Japan	1997	24.99
	Association	Insight Out + 2	CD	Warner Bros.	WPCR-10076	Japan	1999	54.99
	Association	Just The Right Sound	2CD	Rhino	R2-78303	U.S.A.	2002	19.99
	Association	Renaissance + 2	CD	Warner Bros.	WPCR-10075	Japan	1999	29.99
	Association	Stop Your Motor + 4	CD	Warner Bros.	WPCR-10198	Japan	1999	29.99
	Association	The Essentials	CD	Rhino	R2-76158	U.S.A.	2002	13.99
	Association	Waterbeds In Trinidad!	CD	SME	SRCD-9819	Japan	2001	22.99
	Astaire/Rogers	Fred Astaire/Ginger Rogers At RKO	2CD	Rhino	R2-72957	U.S.A.	1998	12.99
	Astley, Edwin	Music From The TV Series The Saint	CD	Razor & Tie	RE-2156-2	U.S.A.	1997	8.99
	Astley, Edwin	Music/TV Series Secret Agent	CD	Razor & Tie	RE-2151-2	U.S.A.	1997	8.99
	Atlanta Rhythm Section/ARS	20th Century Masters: The Millennium	CD	Universal	314-520-382-2	U.S.A.	1997	8.99
	Atlanta Rhythm Section/ARS	'96	CD	CMC INT.	CMC-8303 -2	U.S.A.	1996	8.99
	Atlanta Rhythm Section/ARS	A Rock 'N Roll Alternative	CD	Polydor	837-821-2	U.S.A.	1977	19.99
	Atlanta Rhythm Section/ARS	A Rock 'N Roll Alternative	CD	Polydor K.K.	POCP-2142	Japan	1976	24.99
	Atlanta Rhythm Section/ARS	Back Up Against The Wall	CD	MCA Victor	MVCM-21013	Japan	1973	24.99
	Atlanta Rhythm Section/ARS	Backtracks	CD	Renaissance	RRBT-0602	U.S.A.	1999	12.99
	Atlanta Rhythm Section/ARS	Best	CD	Polydor K.K.	POCP-2145	Japan	1992	24.99
	Atlanta Rhythm Section/ARS	Best Of	CD	Universal	UICY-1515	Japan	2000	24.99
	Atlanta Rhythm Section/ARS	Champagne Jam	CD	Polydor	829-662-2	U.S.A.	1978	14.99
	Atlanta Rhythm Section/ARS	Eufaula	CD	Alchemy	PILOT-178	England	2003	9.99
	Atlanta Rhythm Section/ARS	Eufaula	CD	Intersound	5095-9553-2	U.S.A.	1999	6.99
	Atlanta Rhythm Section/ARS	Greatest Hits	CD	BCI	40022	U.S.A.	2001	8.99
	Atlanta Rhythm Section/ARS	Live At The Savoy , N. Y. 10 - 27,1981	CD	Phoenix Gems	5001	U.S.A.	2000	9.99
	Atlanta Rhythm Section/ARS	Original Artist Hit List	CD	Intersound	5095-4813-2	U.S.A.	2003	7.99
	Atlanta Rhythm Section/ARS	Partly Plugged	CD	Alchemy	PILOT-185	England	2003	9.99
	Atlanta Rhythm Section/ARS	Partly Plugged	CD	Southern Tracks	STCD-0079	U.S.A.	1997	8.99
	Atlanta Rhythm Section/ARS	Quinella	CD	Columbia	CK-37550	U.S.A.	1981	14.99
	Atlanta Rhythm Section/ARS	Red Tape	CD	Malibu	MEL.CD.9002	U.S.A.	1999	19.99
	Atlanta Rhythm Section/ARS	Self Titled	CD	MCA Victor	MVCM-21012	Japan	1972	24.99
	Atlanta Rhythm Section/ARS	The Best Of	CD	Polydor	849-375-2	U.S.A.	1991	8.99
	Atlanta Rhythm Section/ARS	The Collection	CD	Connoisseur	VSOP-CD-343	England	2001	14.99
	Atlanta Rhythm Section/ARS	The Very Best Of	CD	Cleopatra	CLP-972-2	U.S.A.	2001	9.99
	Atlanta Rhythm Section/ARS	Truth In A Structured Form	CD	Columbia	ZK-45465	U.S.A.	1989	14.99
	Atlantis	Get On Board + 1	CD	Repertoire	REP-7018-WP	Germany	2002	14.99
	Atlantis	It's Getting Better	CD	Repertoire	REP-4337-WP	Germany	2002	14.99
	Atlantis	Live	CD	Repertoire	REP-7036-WP	Germany	2002	14.99
	Atlantis	Self Titled	CD	Repertoire	REP-4145-WP	Germany	2002	14.99
	Atomic Rooster	BBC Radio 1 in Concert	CD	Windsong	WINCD-042	England	1993	19.99
	Atomic Rooster	BBC Sessions '71	CD	HUX	HUX003	England	1998	14.99
	Atomic Rooster	Best Of Atomic Rooster, Vol. 1-2	2CD	Blueprint	BP4504CD	England	1999	22.99
	Atomic Rooster	Castle Masters Collection	CD	Castle	CMC-3018	England	1990	12.99
	Atomic Rooster	Death Walks Behind You	CD	Repertoire	REP-4069-WZ	Germany	2001	13.99
	Atomic Rooster	Devil's Answer: Live On The BBC	CD	HUX	HUX005	England	1998	14.99
	Atomic Rooster	First 10 Explosive Years, Vol. 2	CD	Angel Air	SJPCD086	England	2001	17.99
	Atomic Rooster	Headline News	CD	Voiceprint	VP171CD	England	2003	16.99
	Atomic Rooster	Heavy Soul: The Anthology	2CD	Sanctuary	06076-81134-2	U.S.A.	2002	19.99
	Atomic Rooster	Heavy Soul: The Anthology	2CD	Castle	CMDDD364	England	2002	19.99
	Atomic Rooster	Home To Roost	CD	Raw Power	RAWCD-027	England	1997	12.99
	Atomic Rooster	In Hearing Of + 1	CD	Repertoire	REP-4563-WZ	Germany	2001	13.99
	Atomic Rooster	In Satan's Name	2CD	Snapper	SMD-CD-128	England	1997	15.99
	Atomic Rooster	Live And Raw: 1970-1971	CD	Angel Air	SJPCD060	England	2000	19.99
	Atomic Rooster	Live At The Marquee	CD	Angel Air	SJPCD104	England	2002	17.99
	Atomic Rooster	Live In Germany '83	CD	Retrowerk	RETRK107	England	2000	17.99

Artist	Title	Format	Label	Catalog No	Country	Released	Value
Atomic Rooster	Made In England	CD	One Way	OW-30644	U.S.A.	1994	13.99
Atomic Rooster	Made In England + 2	CD	Repertoire	REP-4165-WZ	Germany	2001	13.99
Atomic Rooster	Made In England + 2	CD	Akarma	AK-177	Italy	2003	14.99
Atomic Rooster	Millenium Collection	2CD	Millenium	20.4039-MI	Germany	1999	19.99
Atomic Rooster	Nice 'N' Greasy	CD	Akarma	AK-178	Italy	2003	14.99
Atomic Rooster	Nice 'N' Greasy	CD	Repertoire	REP-4134-WZ	Germany	2002	13.99
Atomic Rooster	Nice 'N' Greasy (W/Bonus Tracks)	CD	One Way	OW-30645	U.S.A.	1994	15.99
Atomic Rooster	Rarities	CD	Angel Air	SJPCD069	England	2000	20.99
Atomic Rooster	Resurrection (S.T./Death/In H + 9)	3CD	Akarma	AK-167	Italy	2002	49.99
Atomic Rooster	Self Titled + 1	CD	Repertoire	REP-4135-WZ	Germany	2002	13.99
Atomic Rooster	Self Titled + 3	CD	Akarma	AK-277	Italy	1999	14.99
Atomic Rooster	Self Titled + 3	CD	Receiver	RRCD-277	England	2000	17.99
Atomic Rooster	The Best Of	CD	Laserlight	12-666	Germany	1996	7.99
Atomic Rooster	The Best Of	CD	Success	9352CD	EEC	1994	9.99
Atomic Rooster	The Best Of The Rest	CD	Action Replay	CDAR-1001	England	1989	10.99
Atomic Rooster	The Devil Hits Back	CD	Alchemy	PILOT-30	England	2001	11.99
Atomic Rooster	The First 10 Explosive Years	CD	Angel Air	SJPCD038	England	1998	17.99
Atomic Rooster	The Ultimate Chicken Meltdown	CD	Pearls From The Past	PFTP-AR1	Canada	2000	10.99
Atomic Rooster/Leaf Hound	Growers Of Mushroom	CD	Repertoire	REP-4485-WY	Germany	2002	11.99
Atomic Rooster/Leaf Hound	Growers Of Mushroom + 2	CD	See For Miles	SEE-CD-403	England	1995	14.99
Au Go-Go Singers/R Furay	They Call Us The... (Stephen Stills)	CD	Collector's Choice	CCM-0112-2	U.S.A.	1999	13.99
Au Pairs	Live In Berlin	CD	Line	LICD-9.00111-0	Germany	1988	11.99
Auger, Brian	Best Of 1968 - 1987	2CD	Disconforme	DISC1924CD	Andorra	2000	29.99
Auger, Brian	Best Of 1969 - 1975	CD	Toy's Factory	TFCK-87613	Japan	1999	39.99
Auger, Brian	Here And Now + 5	CD	Disconforme	DISC1919CD	Andorra	2000	12.99
Auger, Brian	Mod Years 1965 -1969 + 6 (UK Art)	CD	Disconforme	DISC1923CD	Andorra	2000	14.99
Auger, Brian	Mod Years 1965 -1969 + 6 (USA Art)	CD	Disconforme	DISC1922CD	Andorra	2000	14.99
Auger, Brian	Oblivion Express	CD	Disconforme	DISC1909CD	Andorra	2000	12.99
Auger, Brian	Planet Earth Calling	CD	Garland	010	England	1987	7.99
Auger, Brian	Search Party - Planet Earth C + 1	CD	Disconforme	DISC1918CD	Andorra	2000	12.99
Auger, Brian/Julie Driscoll	Open (UK Art)	CD	Disconforme	DISC1902CD	Andorra	2000	12.99
Auger, Brian/Julie Driscoll	Open (USA Art)	CD	Disconforme	DISC1901CD	Andorra	2000	12.99
Auger, Brian/Julie Driscoll	W/ Trinity - Streetnoise	CD	Disconforme	DISC1905CD	Andorra	2000	13.99
Auger, Brian/Julie Tippett	Encore	CD	One Way	OW-33637	U.S.A.	1996	39.99
Auger, Brian/Oblivion Express	A Better Land	CD	Disconforme	DISC1910CD	Andorra	2000	8.99
Auger, Brian/Oblivion Express	Auger Rhythms: B A's Musical History	2CD	Quicksilver	4028	U.S.A.	2003	20.99
Auger, Brian/Oblivion Express	Best Of 1970 - 1975	2CD	Disconforme	DISC1921CD	Andorra	2000	29.99
Auger, Brian/Oblivion Express	Closer To It! + 4 (UK Art)	CD	Disconforme	DISC1913CD	Andorra	2000	10.99
Auger, Brian/Oblivion Express	Closer To It! + 4 (USA Art)	CD	Disconforme	DISC1912CD	Andorra	2000	10.99
Auger, Brian/Oblivion Express	Complete Oblivion Express	2CD	One Way	OW-32186	U.S.A.	1995	19.99
Auger, Brian/Oblivion Express	Happiness Heartaches	CD	Wounded Bird	WOU-2981	U.S.A.	2003	14.99
Auger, Brian/Oblivion Express	Keys To The Heart	CD	Disconforme	DISC1920CD	Andorra	2000	8.99
Auger, Brian/Oblivion Express	Live Oblivion 1	CD	Disconforme	DISC1915CD	Andorra	2000	19.99
Auger, Brian/Oblivion Express	Live Oblivion 2 + 1	CD	Disconforme	DISC1916CD	Andorra	2000	19.99
Auger, Brian/Oblivion Express	Reinforcements	CD	Disconforme	DISC1917CD	Andorra	2000	12.99
Auger, Brian/Oblivion Express	Second Wind	CD	Disconforme	DISC1911CD	Andorra	2000	8.99
Auger, Brian/Oblivion Express	Straight Ahead + 1	CD	Disconforme	DISC1914CD	Andorra	2000	13.99
Auger, Brian/Oblivion Express	The Best Of	CD	One Way	OW-34500	U.S.A.	1997	14.99
Auger, Brian/Oblivion Express	The Best Of	2CD	PolyGram	314-529-496-2	England	1996	29.99
Auger, Brian/Oblivion Express	Voices Of Other Times	CD	Miramar	09006-23152-2	U.S.A.	2000	8.99
Auger, Brian/Peter York	Steaming	CD	INAK	CD-855	Germany	1986	19.99
Auger, Brian/Trinity	Befour + 2 (French Art)	CD	Disconforme	DISC1907CD	Andorra	2000	12.99
Auger, Brian/Trinity	Befour + 2 (UK Art)	CD	Disconforme	DISC1908CD	Andorra	2000	12.99
Auger, Brian/Trinity	Befour + 2 (USA Art)	CD	Disconforme	DISC1906CD	Andorra	2000	13.99
Auger, Brian/Trinity	Definitely What! .... + 1 (UK Art)	CD	Disconforme	DISC1904CD	Andorra	2000	12.99
Auger, Brian/Trinity	Definitely What!... + 1 (USA Art)	CD	Disconforme	DISC1903CD	Andorra	2000	12.99
Auger, Brian/Trinity	Jools (Julie Driscoll) & Brian	CD	One Way	OW-57578	U.S.A.	1992	10.99
Auger, Brian/Trinity	W/ Julie Driscoll: If Your Memory...	CD	Dressed To Kill	DTK-430	England	2001	8.99

Artist	Title	Format	Label	Catalog No	Country	Released	Value
Auger, Brian/Trinity	W/ Julie Driscoll; Season Of Witch	CD	PolyGram	847-228-2	England	1999	11.99
Austin, Patti	End Of A Rainbow	CD	CTI	KICJ-8331	Japan	1976	39.99
Autograph	Buzz	CD	Point	BNR-10225	U.S.A.	2003	17.99
Autograph	Loud And Clear	CD	RCA	5796-2-R	U.S.A.	1987	12.99
Autograph	Missing Pieces	CD	PMI	76962-32263-2	U.S.A.	1997	10.99
Autograph	Sign In Please	CD	RCA	PCD1-5423	U.S.A.	1984	13.99
Autograph	That's The Stuff	CD	RCA	PCD1-7009	U.S.A.	1985	32.99
Avalon, Frankie	25 All Time Greatest Hits	CD	Varese	302-066-304-2	U.S.A.	2002	7.99
Avalon, Frankie	New Recordings Of Old Favorites	CD	Unidisc Music	AGEK-2149	Canada	1994	7.99
Avalon, Frankie	Venus	CD	Unidisc Music	SPLK-7159	Canada	1994	11.99
Avalon, Frankie	Venus (Disco Version)	CD Single	Unidisc Music	SP5-1715	Canada	1996	11.99
Average White Band	Best Of	CD	Repertoire	REP-4454-WZ	Germany	1994	9.99
Axelrod, David	1968 to 1970 An Axelrod Anthology	CD	EMI	94052	France	2001	14.99
Axelrod, David	Anthology II	CD	EMI	EMI-7484CD	France	2002	10.99
Axelrod, David	Axelrod Chronicles (Heavy Axe +8)	CD	Fantasy	9685	U.S.A.	2000	8.99
Axelrod, David	Earth Rot	CD	EMI	7-24352-16092-1	France	2003	12.99
Axelrod, David	Requiem: The Holocaust	CD	EMI	532975	France	2002	6.99
Axelrod, David	Self Titled (Late 60's)	CD	Mo' Wax	MW-141-CD	England	2001	6.99
Axelrod, David	Song Of Innocence	CD	EMI	15882	France	2001	12.99
Axelrod, David	Songs of Experience	CD	EMI	521589	France	2001	13.99
Axelrod, David	The Big Country	CD	EMI	580677	France	2003	11.99
Axxis	Profile: (The Best Of)	CD	Toshiba-EMI	TOCP-8156	Japan	1994	19.99
Ayers, Kevin	Banana Productions: The Best Of	CD	EMI	0777-7-92618-2	England	1989	11.99
Ayers, Kevin	Bananamour + 4	CD	EMI	43512	England	2003	13.99
Ayers, Kevin	Joy Of A Toy + 6	CD	EMI	43522	England	2003	24.99
Ayers, Kevin	Odd Ditties + 1	CD	Toshiba-EMI	TOCP-65968	Japan	2002	29.99
Ayers, Kevin	Rainbow Takeaway	CD	BGO	BGOCD189	England	1993	19.99
Ayers, Kevin	Singing The Bruise - BBC Sessions	CD	Band Of Joy	BOJCD-019	England	1996	19.99
Ayers, Kevin	Sweet Deceiver	CD	BGO	BGOCD98	England	1992	10.99
Ayers, Kevin	That's What You Get Babe	CD	BGO	BGOCD190	England	1993	14.99
Ayers, Kevin	The Confessions Of Dr Dream...	CD	BGO	BGOCD86	England	1990	19.99
Ayers, Kevin	The Kevin Ayers Collection	CD	See For Miles	SEE-CD117	England	1990	19.99
Ayers, Kevin	Whatevershebringswesing + 4	CD	EMI	43542	England	2003	19.99
Ayers, Kevin	Yes We Have No Mananas...	CD	BGO	BGOCD143	England	1993	19.99
Ayers, Kevin/Archibald	Banana Follies	CD	HUX	HUX-007	England	1998	19.99
Ayers, Kevin/Brian Eno	Lady June's Linguistic Leprosy	CD	See For Miles	SEE-CD350	England	1992	19.99
Ayers, Kevin/Cale/Eno/Nico	June 1, 1974	CD	Polygram K.K.	PHCR-4854	Japan	1998	34.99
Ayers, Kevin/Whole World	Shooting At The Moon + 5	CD	EMI	43532	England	2003	19.99
Ayers, Kevin/Wizards Twiddly	Turn The Lights Down	CD	Market Square	MSMCD-105	England	1999	19.99

B

Artist	Title	Format	Label	Catalog No	Country	Released	Value
B.B. King	Deuces Wild	CD	MCA	MCAD-11711	U.S.A.	1997	7.99
B.B. King	Live At The Regal	CD	MCA	MCAD-11646	U.S.A.	1997	8.99
B.B. King	Live At The Regal (MFSL Gold Cd)	CD	Mobile Fidelity	UDCD-548	U.S.A.	1965	23.99
B.T.O.	20th Century Masters: The Millennium	CD	MCA	314-548-096-2	U.S.A.	2000	8.99
B.T.O.	Anthology	2CD	Mercury	7314-514-902-2	Netherland	1993	29.99
B.T.O.	Anthology	2CD	Mercury	514-902-2	Australia	1993	29.99
B.T.O.	Bachman-Turner Overdrive (1st Lp)	CD	Mercury	838-196-2	U.S.A.	1990	24.99
B.T.O.	Bachman-Turner Overdrive (Compleat)	CD	Sun	7027	U.S.A.	1996	8.99
B.T.O.	Four Wheel Drive	CD	Mercury	830-970-2	U.S.A.	1990	19.99
B.T.O.	Freeways	CD	Mercury	838-199-2	U.S.A.	1989	19.99
B.T.O.	Greatest & Latest	CD	Disky	64677	Holland	2001	13.99
B.T.O.	Greatest Hits	CD	Mercury	422-830-039-2-7	U.S.A.	1988	7.99

Artist	Title	Format	Label	Catalog No	Country	Released	Value
B.T.O.	Head On	CD	Mercury	838-197-2	U.S.A.	1989	17.99
B.T.O.	Head On + 1	CD	Repertoire	REP-1012-WZ	Germany	2003	23.99
B.T.O.	II	CD	Mercury	822-504-2	U.S.A.	1990	8.99
B.T.O.	King Biscuit Flower Hour	CD	King Biscuit	70710-88039-2	U.S.A.	1998	14.99
B.T.O.	Not Fragile	CD	Mercury	830-178-2	U.S.A.	1990	8.99
B.T.O.	Rock N' Roll Nights	CD	Mercury	838-201-2	U.S.A.	1990	19.99
B.T.O.	Street Action	CD	Mercury	838-200-2	U.S.A.	1990	13.99
B.T.O.	The Best Of	CD	PolyGram	550-421-2	England	1998	14.99
B.T.O.	The Best Of B.T.O. (So Far)	CD	Mercury	558-234-2	England	1998	10.99
B.T.O.	The Best Of: Live	CD	Curb	D2-77653	U.S.A.	1994	7.99
B.T.O.	The Collection	CD	PolyGram	544-429-2	England	2001	14.99
B.T.O./Brave Belt	Brave Belt (With Randy Bachman)	2CD	Bullseye	BLR-CD-4054	Canada	2001	16.99
B-52's	Bouncing Off the Satellites	CD	Warner Bros.	9-25504-2	U.S.A.	1986	8.99
B-52's	Cosmic Thing	CD	Reprise	9-25854-2	U.S.A.	1989	8.99
B-52's	Debbie	CD Single	Reprise	9362-44528-2	Germany	1998	8.99
B-52's	Good Stuff	CD	Reprise	9-26995-2	U.S.A.	1992	6.99
B-52's	Hallucinating Pluto	CD Single	Reprise	9-44520-2	U.S.A.	1998	5.99
B-52's	Love Shack	CD Single	Reprise	9-21318-2	U.S.A.	1989	4.99
B-52's	Meet The Flintstones (DJ/Clamshell)	CD Single	MCA	MAC5P-2998	U.S.A.	1994	29.99
B-52's	Nude On The Moon Box Set	2CD	Rhino	R2-78357	U.S.A.	2002	16.99
B-52's	Party Mix/Mesopotamia	CD	Warner Bros.	W2-26401	U.S.A.	1990	9.99
B-52's	Revolution Earth	CD Single	Reprise	9362-40715	U.S.A.	1992	8.99
B-52's	Roam	CD Single	Warner Bros.	9-21441-2	U.S.A.	1989	6.99
B-52's	Self Titled	CD	Warner Bros.	3355-2	U.S.A.	1979	6.99
B-52's	Tell It Like It-T-I-Is (Ltd With Lie Test)	CD Single	Warner Bros.	9362-40604-2	Germany	1992	7.99
B-52's	Time Capsule	CD	Reprise	9-46920-2	U.S.A.	1998	8.99
B-52's	Time Capsule Mega Mixes (Promo)	CD	Warner Bros.	PRO-CD-9332	U.S.A.	1998	8.99
B-52's	Whammy	CD	Warner Bros.	9-23819-2	U.S.A.	1983	7.99
B-52's	Wild Planet	CD	Warner Bros.	3471-2	U.S.A.	1980	9.99
Babe Ruth	First Base + 2	CD	Repertoire	REP-4554-WP	Germany	2001	10.99
Babe Ruth	First Base/Amar Cabellero	CD	BGO	BGOCD382	England	1998	12.99
Babe Ruth	Grand Slam: The Best Of	CD	EMI	7243-8-30449-2-4	England	1995	16.99
Babe Ruth	Self Titled	CD	One Way	OW-56845	U.S.A.	1993	9.99
Babe Ruth	Self Titled/Stealin' Home	CD	BGO	BGOCD491	England	2000	12.99
Baby Tuckoo	First Born	CD	Line	ALCD-9.00157-0	Germany	1988	3.99
Babyface	Jewels (Best Of Solar)	CD	Victor Ent.	VDP-1518	Japan	1989	34.99
Babys, The	Anthology + 7	CD	Chrysalis	7243-5-23106-2	U.S.A.	2000	9.99
Babys, The	Broken Heart	CD	Chrysalis	F2-21150	U.S.A.	1990	13.99
Babys, The	Concert Classics (Promo/Only 100)	CD	Renaissance	RRCC00718	U.S.A.	2002	10.99
Babys, The	Head First	CD	One Way	OW-28995-2	U.S.A.	1978	12.99
Babys, The	On The Edge	CD	One Way	OW-31333	U.S.A.	2001	12.99
Babys, The	Self Titled	CD	Chrysalis	F2-21129	U.S.A.	1990	13.99
Babys, The	Self Titled/Broken Heart	CD	One Way	OW-31510	U.S.A.	2001	13.99
Babys, The	The Very Best Babys Album	CD	EMI	539-144-2	England	2002	13.99
Babys, The	Union Jacks	CD	One Way	OW-31332-2	U.S.A.	1980	13.99
Babys, The	Valentine Babys	CD	Alchemy	PILOT-107	England	2001	12.99
Bacharach, Burt	A&M Journey Of	CD	Polydor K.K.	POCM-1535	Japan	1996	49.99
Bacharach, Burt	Arthur (O.S.T.)	CD	Warner Bros.	WPCR-3867	Japan	1988	24.99
Bacharach, Burt	Arthur 2 (O.S.T.)	CD	Pony Canyon	D28Y-3253	Japan	1988	19.99
Bacharach, Burt	Casino Royale (O.S.T.)	CD	Varese	VSD-5265	U.S.A.	1990	9.99
Bacharach, Burt	I'll Never Fall In Love Again	CD	Karussell	550-057-2	Germany	1993	8.99
Bacharach, Burt	Lounge Legends	CD	Universal	UNI-5021CD	Germany	2000	12.99
Bacharach, Burt	Make It Easy On Yourself	CD	Polydor	POCM-2012	Japan	1995	24.99
Bacharach, Burt	One Amazing Night	CD	N2K	N2K-10008	U.S.A.	1998	9.99
Bacharach, Burt	Plays His Hits + 2	CD	MCA Victor	MVCE-22001	Japan	1998	18.99
Bacharach, Burt	Selections From the Look Of Love	CD	Rhino	PRCD-7285	U.S.A.	1998	15.99
Bacharach, Burt	Self Titled	CD	Polydor	POCM-2013	Japan	1995	24.99
Bacharach, Burt	The Greatest Hits Of Burt Bacharach	CD	Dressed To Kill	METRO339	England	2000	7.99

Artist	Title	Format	Label	Catalog No	Country	Released	Value
Bacharach, Burt	The Look Of Love Box Set	3CD	Rhino	R2-75339	U.S.A.	1998	37.99
Bacharach, Burt	The Love Songs Of Burt Bacharach	CD	Hip O	HIPD-40166	U.S.A.	1999	7.99
Bacharach, Burt	Toledo	CD Single	Mercury	8709672	England	1998	5.99
Bacharach, Burt	What's New Pussycat? + 1 (O.S.T.)	CD	Rykodisc	RCD-10740	U.S.A.	1998	8.99
Bacharach, Burt	Woman (W/Carly Simon)	CD	Polydor	POCM-2056	Japan	1996	27.99
Bacharach, Burt/Hal David	Lost Horizon + 1 (O.S.T.)	CD	Razor & Tie	RE-2152-2	U.S.A.	1997	18.99
Bacharach, Burt/Hal David	Promises, Promises	CD	Rykodisc	RCD-10750	U.S.A.	1998	69.99
Bacharach, Burt/Herb Alpert	Bacharach/Alpert/Tijuana Brass	CD	Arc	T24P-0109	Japan	1996	34.99
Bachelet, Pierre	10 Ans De Bachelet	2CD	Avrep	PD-75-328	EU	1992	24.99
Bachelet, Pierre	Histoire D'O (Story Of O)	CD	Cam	CSE-081	Italy	1992	15.99
Bachelet, Pierre	La Scène	CD	Avrep	PD-74-927	France	1991	19.99
Bachelet, Pierre	La Ville Ainsi Soit-Il	CD	Avrep	74321-29693-2	France	1995	19.99
Bachelet, Pierre	Pierre Bachelet	CD	Avrep	PD-71499	France	1987	19.99
Bachelet, Pierre	Pierre Bachelet	CD	Avrep	PD-70732	France	1985	19.99
Bachelet, Pierre	Pierre Bachelet	CD	Avrep	74321-12162-2	France	1992	19.99
Bachelet, Pierre/Merve Roy	Emmanuelle 1 (O.S.T.)	CD	Edel	SIL-5058-2	Germany	1990	30.99
Bachelet, Pierre/Merve Roy	Emmanuelle 1 (O.S.T.)	CD	Warner Bros.	WPCP03858	Japan	1973	35.99
Bacon Brothers/Kevin Bacon	Getting There	CD	Bluxo	4041-2	U.S.A.	1999	6.99
Bad 4 Good	Refugee (D Cooksey Of Terminator 2)	CD	MMG Inc.	AMCY-452	Japan	1992	29.99
Bad Brains	I Against I	CD	Line	INCD-9.00231-0	Germany	1987	13.99
Bad Brains	Rock For Light	CD	Line	LICD-9.00113-0	Germany	1987	8.99
Bad Brains	Rock For Light/I Against I	2CD	Line	LICD-9.21176-S	Germany	1992	19.99
Bad Company	10 From 6	CD	Atlantic	81625-2	U.S.A.	1985	7.99
Bad Company	Burnin' Sky	CD	Swan Song	SS-8500-2	U.S.A.	1977	10.99
Bad Company	Company Of Strangers	CD	East West	61808-2	U.S.A.	1995	6.99
Bad Company	Dangerous Age	CD	Atco	A2-81884	U.S.A.	1988	7.99
Bad Company	Desolation Angels	CD	Swan Song	SS-8506-2	U.S.A.	1979	9.99
Bad Company	Fame And Fortune	CD	Atlantic	81684-2	U.S.A.	1986	8.99
Bad Company	Here Comes Trouble	CD	Atco	91759-2	U.S.A.	1992	6.99
Bad Company	Holy Water	CD	Atco	A2-91371	U.S.A.	1990	6.99
Bad Company	In Concert: Merchants Of Cool	CD	Sanctuary	06076-84549-2	U.S.A.	2002	6.99
Bad Company	Rough Diamonds	CD	Atlantic	7-92452-2	U.S.A.	1982	10.99
Bad Company	Run With The Pack	CD	Swan Song	SS-8503-2	U.S.A.	1976	9.99
Bad Company	Self Titled	CD	Swan Song	SS-8501-2	U.S.A.	1990	8.99
Bad Company	Stories Told And Untold	CD	East West	61976-2	U.S.A.	1996	6.99
Bad Company	Straight Shooter	CD	Swan Song	7567-92436-2	Australia	1974	7.99
Bad Company	Straight Shooter	CD	Swan Song	SS-8502-2	U.S.A.	1975	8.99
Bad Company	The 'Original' Bad Co Anthology	2CD	Elektra	62391-2	U.S.A.	1999	16.99
Bad Company	What You Hear....	CD	Atlantic	92307-2	U.S.A.	1993	11.99
Bad English	Backlash	CD	Sony	ESCA-5382	Japan	1991	24.99
Bad English	Backlash	CD	Epic	EK-46935	U.S.A.	1991	7.99
Bad English	Greatest Hits	CD	Epic	480543-2	Austria	1995	14.99
Bad English	Self Titled	CD	Polydor	25-8P-5259	Japan	1989	24.99
Bad English	Self Titled	CD	Epic	EK-45083	U.S.A.	1989	7.99
Bad Habitz	Dedicated To Thin Lizzy	CD	Vertigo	PHCR-1193	Japan	1993	24.99
Bad News Reunion	Just One Night	CD	Line	LICD-9.01334-0	Germany	1998	3.99
Bad News Reunion	Two Steps Forward	CD	Line	LICD-9.00660-0	Germany	1988	3.99
Badalamenti, Angelo	Twin Peaks - Fire Walk... (O.S.T.)	CD	Warner Bros.	9-45019-2	U.S.A.	1992	6.99
Badalamenti, Angelo	Twin Peaks (O.S.T.)	CD	Warner Bros.	9-26316-2	U.S.A.	1990	7.99
Badalamenti, Angelo	Twin Peaks (Promo/Picture Label)	CD	Warner Bros.	9-26316-2-DJ	U.S.A.	1990	24.99
Badfinger	Airwaves + 5	CD	Elektra	PPCD-52712	U.S.A.	1999	8.99
Badfinger	Ass + 1	CD	Toshiba-EMI	TOCP-50066	Japan	1996	75.99
Badfinger	Ass + 1	CD	EMI	7243-8-53899-2-4	England	1996	79.99
Badfinger	BBC In Concert	CD	Fuel 2000	302-061-048-2	U.S.A.	2000	9.99
Badfinger	Best Of	CD	Capitol	7243-8-30129-2-3	U.S.A.	1994	9.99
Badfinger	Best Of Volume II	CD	Rhino	R2-70978	U.S.A.	1989	9.99
Badfinger	Day After Day	CD	Rykodisc	RCD-10189	U.S.A.	1990	8.99
Badfinger	Head First	2CD	Snapper	SMA-DD-829	England	2000	13.99

Artist	Title	Format	Label	Catalog No	Country	Released	Value
Badfinger	If You Want It... (Ltd 1,000 Promo)	2CD	EMI	DIDX-6972	Japan	1990	16.99
Badfinger	Magic Christian Music + 2	CD	Capitol	CDP-7975792	U.S.A.	1991	12.99
Badfinger	No Dice + 5 (DCC Gold Cd)	CD	DCC	GZS-1095	U.S.A.	1992	24.99
Badfinger	Shine On	CD	Edsel	ED-CD-302	England	1974	19.99
Badfinger	Straight Up + 6 (DCC Gold Cd)	CD	DCC	GZS-1088	U.S.A.	1995	34.99
Badfinger	The Very Best Of Badfinger	CD	Capitol	72435-26974-2-7	U.S.A.	2000	10.99
Badfinger	Wish You Were Here	CD	Warner Bros.	7599-26540-2	Germany	1974	15.99
Badfinger/Iveys	Maybe Tomorrow + 4	CD	Capitol	CDP-7-98692-2	U.S.A.	1992	60.99
Badfinger/Joey Molland	The Pilgrim	CD	Rykodisc	RCD-10212	U.S.A.	1992	7.99
Badfinger/Mike Gibbons	A Place In Time	CD	Forbidden	FOR1962	U.S.A.	1997	8.99
Badfinger/Pete Ham	7 Park Avenue + 5	CD	Video Arts	VACK-1122	Japan	1997	19.99
Badfinger/Pete Ham	Golders Green + 2	CD	Video Arts	VACK-1164	Japan	1999	19.99
Badfinger/Tommy Evans	Over You (The Final Tracks)	CD	Gipsy	GIPSY-BF1CD	U.S.A.	1992	22.99
Badfinger/Various Artists	Come And Get it - Tribute Badfinger	CD	Copper	CPR-2181	U.S.A.	1996	16.99
Badlands/Jake E. Lee	Self Titled +1 (Ray Gillen/Eric Singer)	CD	Atlantic	AMCY-698	Japan	1989	24.99
Baez, Joan	20th Century Masters: The Millennium	CD	A&M	314-490-418-2	U.S.A.	1999	8.99
Baez, Joan	5 + 2	CD	Vanguard	79700-2	U.S.A.	2002	8.99
Baez, Joan	A&M Classics, Vol. 8	CD	A&M	CD-2506	U.S.A.	1987	7.99
Baez, Joan	Any Day Now	2CD	Vanguard	VCD-79306/7	U.S.A.	1968	13.99
Baez, Joan	Baez Sings Dylan (Any Day Now + 5)	CD	Vanguard	79512-2	U.S.A.	1998	8.99
Baez, Joan	Baptism: A Journey Through Time + 3	CD	Vanguard	79721-2	U.S.A.	2003	8.99
Baez, Joan	Best Hits	CD	King	KICP-2533	Japan	2002	28.99
Baez, Joan	Blessed Are	2CD	Vanguard	VCD-6570/1	U.S.A.	1971	13.99
Baez, Joan	Blowin' Away	CD	Sony	A-33969	U.S.A.	1977	8.99
Baez, Joan	Brothers In Arms	CD	Gold Castle	D2-71363	U.S.A.	1991	7.99
Baez, Joan	Carry It On (O.S.T.)	CD	Vanguard	VCD-79313	U.S.A.	1971	8.99
Baez, Joan	Come From The Shadows	CD	A&M	CD-3103	U.S.A.	1972	28.99
Baez, Joan	Complete A & M Sessions	4CD	A&M	B000082802	U.S.A.	2003	24.99
Baez, Joan	Dark Chords On A Big Guitar	CD	Koch	KOC-CD-8622	U.S.A.	2003	8.99
Baez, Joan	David's Album	CD	Vanguard	VCD-79308	U.S.A.	1969	8.99
Baez, Joan	Diamonds	CD	A&M	540-500-2	England	1996	7.99
Baez, Joan	Diamonds & Rust	CD	A&M	CD-3233	U.S.A.	1975	8.99
Baez, Joan	Diamonds & Rust (MFSL Gold Cd)	CD	Mobile Fidelity	UDCD-646	U.S.A.	1975	29.99
Baez, Joan	Diamonds & Rust In The Bullring	CD	Virgin	0777-7-87089-2-6	England	1989	8.99
Baez, Joan	Diamonds: Best Of The Vanguard Years	2CD	King	KICP-134/7	Japan	1991	49.99
Baez, Joan	Donna Donna: Best Of	CD	King	KICP-8501	Japan	1999	28.99
Baez, Joan	Essential: From The Heart Live	CD	A&M	POCM-1524	Japan	2002	28.99
Baez, Joan	Farewell Angelina	CD	King	KICP-3002	Japan	1998	28.99
Baez, Joan	Farewell Angelina + 3	CD	Vanguard	79701-2	U.S.A.	2002	8.99
Baez, Joan	From Every Stage	2CD	A&M	75021-6506-2	U.S.A.	1976	14.99
Baez, Joan	Gone From Danger	CD	Guardian	7243-8-59357-2-5	U.S.A.	1997	6.99
Baez, Joan	Gracias A La Vida	CD	A&M	393614-2	Germany	1974	28.99
Baez, Joan	Greatest Hits	CD	A&M	31454-0510-2	U.S.A.	1996	13.99
Baez, Joan	Gulf Winds	CD	A&M	394603-2	Germany	1976	28.99
Baez, Joan	Hits: Greatest & Others	CD	Vanguard	VMD-79332	U.S.A.	1973	8.99
Baez, Joan	Honest Lullaby	CD	Epic	EK-35766	U.S.A.	1979	8.99
Baez, Joan	In Concert (Part 1/2)	2CD	Vanguard	VCD-113/114	U.S.A.	1988	13.99
Baez, Joan	In Concert, Part 1 + 1	CD	Vanguard	79598-2	U.S.A.	2002	8.99
Baez, Joan	In Concert, Part 2 + 3	CD	Vanguard	79599-2	U.S.A.	2002	8.99
Baez, Joan	Joan + 2	CD	Vanguard	79720-2	U.S.A.	2003	8.99
Baez, Joan	Live	CD	Epic	50997-463390-2-9	Germany	1997	8.99
Baez, Joan	Live At Newport	CD	Vanguard	77015-2	U.S.A.	1996	8.99
Baez, Joan	Live At Newport 1963 - 1965	CD	King	KICP-3003	Japan	1998	28.99
Baez, Joan	Live Europe '83 (Children Of The 80's)	CD	Festival	D-19715	Australia	1993	15.99
Baez, Joan	No Woman, No Cry	CD	Laserlight	15-450	Germany	1992	5.99
Baez, Joan	Noel + 6	CD	Vanguard	79596-2	U.S.A.	2001	8.99
Baez, Joan	One Day At A Time	CD	Vanguard	VCD-79310	U.S.A.	1970	8.99
Baez, Joan	Play Me Backwards	CD	Virgin	0777-7-86458-2-5	England	1992	8.99

B

B

Artist	Title	Format	Label	Catalog No	Country	Released	Value
Baez, Joan	Rare, Live & Classic Box Set	3CD	Vanguard	125/27-2	U.S.A.	1993	25.99
Baez, Joan	Recently	CD	Virgin	0777-7-87090-2-2	England	1987	8.99
Baez, Joan	Ring Them Bells	CD	Guardian	7243-8-34989-2-5	U.S.A.	1995	6.99
Baez, Joan	Self Titled + 3	CD	Vanguard	79594-2	U.S.A.	2001	8.99
Baez, Joan	Self Titled + 9	CD	King	KICP-2514	Japan	1992	24.99
Baez, Joan	Speaking Of Dreams	CD	Virgin	0777-7-87091-2-1	England	1989	8.99
Baez, Joan	The Best Of	CD	A&M	CD-3234	U.S.A.	1977	7.99
Baez, Joan	The Best Of + 1	CD	Vanguard	505-2	U.S.A.	1995	8.99
Baez, Joan	The First 10 Years - 5	2CD	Vanguard	VCD-6560/1	U.S.A.	1970	13.99
Baez, Joan	The Joan Baez Ballad Book, Vol. 1	CD	Vanguard	VFCD-7107	England	1986	19.99
Baez, Joan	The Joan Baez Ballad Book, Vol. 2	CD	Vanguard	VFCD-7108	England	1986	19.99
Baez, Joan	The Joan Baez Country Music Album	2CD	Vanguard	VCD-105/6	U.S.A.	1979	13.99
Baez, Joan	Very Early Joan - 2	2CD	Vanguard	VCD-79446/7	U.S.A.	1982	13.99
Baez, Joan	Volume 2 + 3	CD	Vanguard	79595-2	U.S.A.	2001	8.99
Bai Bang	Cop To Con	CD	Zero	XRCN-1007	Japan	1991	24.99
Baker, Anita	Giving You The Best... (Gold Cd)	CD	Warner Bros.	43P2-0014	Japan	1988	41.99
Baker, Chet	In New York + 1 (DCC Gold Cd)	CD	DCC	GZS-1101	U.S.A.	1958	14.99
Baker, Ginger	Do What ..(A Force Lp's/Stratavarious)	2CD	PolyGram	314-558-542-2	U.S.A.	1998	24.99
Baker, Ginger	Horses And Trees	CD	Celluloid	CEL-NY-6126-D	U.S.A.	1986	8.99
Baker, Gurvitz Army	Hearts On Fire	CD	Repertoire	REP-4605-WZ	Germany	1996	15.99
Baker, Gurvitz Army	The Baker Gurvitz Army	CD	Repertoire	REP-4163-WZ	Germany	1991	15.99
Baker, Gurwitz Army	Elysian Encounter	CD	Repertoire	REP-4388-WP	Germany	1993	15.99
Baker, Gurvitz Army	Freedom (Audio/Video)	2CD	Master Tone	MM5102	England	1995	19.99
Baker-Gurvitz Army	The Collection	CD	Castle	06076-81174-2	England	2000	8.99
Bakerloo	Bakerloo + 2	CD	Repertoire	REP-4358-WP	Germany	2002	10.99
Bakerloo	Self Titled	CD	Akarma	AK-261	Italy	2003	10.99
Baldry, "Long" John	It Ain't Easy (Prod/E John/R Stewart)	CD	Line	LECD-9.01235-0	Germany	1992	74.99
Balin, Marty	Balince - Best Of	CD	Rhino	R2-70968	U.S.A.	1990	49.99
Balin, Marty	Better Generation	CD	GWE	GWE002	U.S.A.	1991	5.99
Balin, Marty	Freedom Flight	CD	Solid Discs	SLD-7005-2	U.S.A.	1997	5.99
Balin, Marty/Bodacious D.F.	Bodacious D.F.	CD	Acadia	ACA-8036	England	2002	19.99
Balin, Marty/Grootna	Grootna	CD	Acadia	ACA-8035	England	2002	19.99
Ballard, Russ	Anthology	CD	Alchemy	PILOT-104	England	2001	13.99
Ballard, Russ	At The Third Stroke	CD	Sony	ESCA-7868	Japan	2001	24.99
Ballard, Russ	At The Third Stroke	CD	Renaissance	RMED00120-2	U.S.A.	1998	13.99
Ballard, Russ	Self Titled	CD	Sony	ESCA-5301	Japan	1974	24.99
Ballard, Russ	Self Titled	CD	EMI	538-7-91663 2	Germany	1984	10.99
Ballard, Russ	Self Titled/The Fire Still Burns	CD	Renaissance	RMED00105-2	U.S.A.	1996	15.99
Ballard, Russ	Winning/And The Barnet Dogs	CD	Renaissance	RMED00122-2	U.S.A.	1996	13.99
Ballbusters	No Jerk'n Off	CD	D.I.L.L.I.G.A.F.	D-00012	U.S.A.	1992	11.99
Bambi Molesters/Peter Buck	In Sonic Bullets - 13 From The Hip	CD	Big Beat	CDWIKD-217	England	2001	6.99
Banco Del Mutuo Soccorso	Banco Del Mutuo Soccorso (Gold Cd)	CD	BMG	74321-76370-2	Italy	2002	16.99
Banco Del Mutuo Soccorso	Darwin (Gold Cd)	CD	BMG	74321-76371-2	Italy	2002	16.99
Banco Del Mutuo Soccorso	Io Sono Nato Libero (Gold Cd)	CD	BMG	74321-91788-2	Italy	2002	16.99
Band	Across Great Divide Box Set (Padded)	3CD	Capitol	0777-7-89563-2-5	U.S.A.	1994	20.99
Band	Best Of The Band Volume II	CD	Rhino	R2-75947	U.S.A.	1999	8.99
Band	Cahoots + 5	CD	Capitol	72435-25391-2-3	U.S.A.	2000	11.99
Band	Highlights/Bonus Tracks (Promo)	CD	Capitol	7086-10831-2-8	U.S.A.	2000	7.99
Band	Islands + 2	CD	Capitol	72435-25392-2-2	U.S.A.	2001	8.99
Band	Jubilation	CD	River North	51416-1420-2	U.S.A.	1998	6.99
Band, The AKA	Master Of The Game	CD	Bouvier	0-20197-0110-7-8	U.S.A.	1987	64.99
Band	Music From Big Pink (MFSL Gold Cd)	CD	Mobile Fidelity	UDCD-527	U.S.A.	1968	49.99
Band	Music From Big Pink + 9	CD	Capitol	72435-25390-2-4	U.S.A.	2000	8.99
Band	Rock of Ages + 10	2CD	Capitol	72435-30181-2-2	U.S.A.	2001	10.99
Band	Selections/Great Divide Box (Promo)	CD	Capitol	DPRO-79800	U.S.A.	1994	14.99
Band	Stage Fright (DCC Gold Cd)	CD	DCC	GZS-1061	U.S.A.	1994	44.99
Band	Stagefright + 4	CD	Capitol	72435-25395-2-9	U.S.A.	2000	8.99
Band	The Band + 7	CD	Capitol	72435-25389-2-8	U.S.A.	2000	8.99

Artist	Title	Format	Label	Catalog No	Country	Released	Value
Band	The Band's Greatest Hits	CD	Capitol	72435-24941-2-5	U.S.A.	2000	7.99
Band	The Last Waltz (DVD Audio)	CD	Rhino	R2-78260	U.S.A.	2002	20.99
Band	The Last Waltz Box Set	4CD	Rhino	R2-78278	U.S.A.	2002	40.99
Band	The Very Best Album Ever	CD	Capitol	7243-5-39149-2-9	Holland	2002	19.99
Band, Richard	Re-Animator/Bride Re-Animator (OST)	CD	Silva Screen	FILMCD-082	England	1987	14.99
Bang Tango	Psycho Cafe	CD	MCA	MCAD-6300	U.S.A.	1989	34.99
Banks, Tony	A Curious Feeling	CD	Virgin	CASCD1148	England	1979	13.99
Banks, Tony	Bankstatement	CD	Atlantic	7-82007-2	U.S.A.	1989	12.99
Banks, Tony	Soundtracks	CD	Virgin	CAS-CD-1173	England	1986	14.99
Banks, Tony	Still	CD	Giant	9-24441-2	U.S.A.	1991	7.99
Banks, Tony	Strictly Inc.	CD	Virgin	7243-8-40718-2-0	England	1995	14.99
Banks, Tony	The Fugitive	CD	Virgin	TBCD1	England	1983	13.99
Banks, Tony	Throwback (Promo)	CD Single	Atlantic	PR-2804-2	U.S.A.	1989	6.99
Banks, Tony/Tribute	Strictly Banks: A Serious...	CD	Strictly Banks	SBCD1	England	2000	14.99
Barbarians	Are You A Boy Or Are You A Girl? + 3	CD	Sundazed	SC-6153	U.S.A.	2000	8.99
Barbieri, Gato	Last Tango In Paris + Bonus Suite	CD	Rykodisc	RCD-10724	U.S.A.	1998	29.99
Barclay James Harvest	& Other Short Stories	CD	BGO	BGOCD160	England	1994	10.99
Barclay James Harvest	Alone We Fly	CD	Polydor	800-026-2	Germany	1994	13.99
Barclay James Harvest	And Other Short Stories + 6	CD	EMI	7243-538-407-2-3	England	2002	13.99
Barclay James Harvest	Another Arable Parable	CD	EMI	CDP-746-709-2	EU	1987	12.99
Barclay James Harvest	Au Naturel (Promo)	CD Single	Swallowtail	SWALLOW-5	England	2001	12.99
Barclay James Harvest	Baby J/Once Again/BJH/Other Stories	4CD	EMI	BARCLAY-1	EU	1996	39.99
Barclay James Harvest	Baby James Harvest + 10	CD	EMI	7243-538-408-2-2	England	2002	13.99
Barclay James Harvest	Baby James Harvest/Once Again	2CD	EMI	582-345-2	England	2003	19.99
Barclay James Harvest	Barclay James Harvest/Once Again	CD	One Way	S21-18456	U.S.A.	1995	8.99
Barclay James Harvest	BBC In Concert 1972 (Mono/Stereo)	2CD	EMI	7243-538-980-2-1	England	2002	14.99
Barclay James Harvest	BBC Live In Concert 1972 (Mono)	CD	EMI	538-404-2	England	2003	13.99
Barclay James Harvest	Berlin: Concert For The People (9 Trk)	CD	Polydor	800-026-2	England	1984	8.99
Barclay James Harvest	Best Of - Hits 4 Ever (Master Series)	CD	Polydor	543-450-(28)	Germany	2002	12.99
Barclay James Harvest	Caught In The Light	CD	Polydor	7314-5-19303-2-4	England	1993	8.99
Barclay James Harvest	Early Morning Onwards	CD	Brimstone	BRIM-001	England	1997	8.99
Barclay James Harvest	Endless Dream	CD	Connoisseur	VSOP-CD-228	England	1998	9.99
Barclay James Harvest	Everyone Is Everybody Else + 4	CD	PolyGram	665-401-2	England	2003	13.99
Barclay James Harvest	Eyes Of The Universe	CD	Polydor	821-591-2	Holland	1998	10.99
Barclay James Harvest	Face To Face	CD	Universal	831-483-2	England	2003	11.99
Barclay James Harvest	Glasnost	CD	Universal	835-590-2	England	2003	11.99
Barclay James Harvest	Gone To Earth + 5	CD	PolyGram	665-398-2	England	2003	13.99
Barclay James Harvest	Gone To/Eyes Universe/Turn Tide	3CD	Polydor	511-334-2	France	1992	24.99
Barclay James Harvest	Greatest Hits	CD	ACE	AMI-50011-2	U.S.A.	1998	8.99
Barclay James Harvest	It's My Life	CD Single	Koch	LC: 10014	Germany	2002	8.99
Barclay James Harvest	Live	CD	Connoisseur	VSOP-CD-164	England	1991	29.99
Barclay James Harvest	Live In Bonn, 30th October 2002	CD	Pure	219-0102-0022	England	2003	14.99
Barclay James Harvest	Live Tapes	2CD	Polydor	821-523-2	England	1993	19.99
Barclay James Harvest	Loving Is Easy - Best	CD	Zounds	CD-27200521	Germany	1993	7.99
Barclay James Harvest	Master Series	CD	Polydor	MMTCD-201	South Afric	1999	12.99
Barclay James Harvest	Master Series	CD	Polydor	547-275-2	EU	1999	10.99
Barclay James Harvest	Millennium Edition (Master Series)	CD	Universal	543-450-2	EU	2000	10.99
Barclay James Harvest	Mockingbird	CD	Disky	DC-867212	Holland	1997	9.99
Barclay James Harvest	Mockingbird	CD	Spectrum	544-493-2	England	2001	9.99
Barclay James Harvest	Mockingbird - The Best Of	CD	EMI	529-542-2	EU	2001	9.99
Barclay James Harvest	Mockingbird: The Early Years Best Of	CD	EMI	529-542-2	Holland	2003	8.99
Barclay James Harvest	Octoberon + 5	CD	PolyGram	665-399-2	England	2003	13.99
Barclay James Harvest	Once Again (Quadrophonic Mix)	CD	Brimstone	BRIM-002	England	1998	19.99
Barclay James Harvest	Once Again + 5	CD	EMI	7243-538-406-2-4	England	2002	13.99
Barclay James Harvest	Premium Gold	CD	EMI	8-53513-2	Germany	1996	10.99
Barclay James Harvest	Revival - Live 1999 Tour Edition + 4	2CD	Eagle	EDGTE120	Germany	2000	16.99
Barclay James Harvest	Revival: Live 1999	CD	Eagle	EAGCD120	Germany	2000	10.99
Barclay James Harvest	Revolution Days + 1	CD	Pure	219-0101-0012	England	2003	10.99

B

Artist	Title	Format	Label	Catalog No	Country	Released	Value
Barclay James Harvest	Rings Of Changes	CD	Polydor	811-638-2	England	1993	10.99
Barclay James Harvest	River Of Dreams	CD	Polydor	7314-5-37576-2	England	2001	12.99
Barclay James Harvest	River Of Dreams	CD Single	Polydor	50681327-01	Germany	1997	7.99
Barclay James Harvest	River Of Dreams	CD Single	Polydor	50657362-02	Germany	1997	7.99
Barclay James Harvest	Self Titled (Compilation)	CD	Hanyang	CTAT-3574	South Kore	1991	24.99
Barclay James Harvest	Self Titled/Once Again	CD	BGO	BGOCD152	England	1996	12.99
Barclay James Harvest	Sorcerers And Keepers	CD	Spectrum	550-029-2	EU	1993	7.99
Barclay James Harvest	Strangely Mixed (Promo)	CD Single	Swallowtail	SWALLOW-4	England	2000	12.99
Barclay James Harvest	The Best Of	CD	EMI	CTMCD-309	England	1997	12.99
Barclay James Harvest	The Best Of	CD	Polydor	511-932-2	EU	1992	10.99
Barclay James Harvest	The Best Of	CD	Polydor	513-587-2	England	1992	10.99
Barclay James Harvest	The Best Of	CD	Polystar	511-439-2	Germany	1991	10.99
Barclay James Harvest	The Best Of, Vol. 3	CD	Electrola	538-791-5132	Germany	1990	14.99
Barclay James Harvest	The Collection	CD	EMI	529-237-2	EU	2000	10.99
Barclay James Harvest	The Compact Story Of	CD	Polydor	825-895-2	EU	1985	10.99
Barclay James Harvest	The Harvest Years	2CD	EMI	CDEN-5014	EU	1991	14.99
Barclay James Harvest	The Origin Of Pieces (Promo)	CD Single	Swallowtail	SWALLOW-3	England	1999	12.99
Barclay James Harvest	Their First Album + 13	CD	EMI	7243-538-405-2-5	England	2002	13.99
Barclay James Harvest	Through The Eyes.../Revival	CD	Snapper	SMD-CD-388	England	2002	15.99
Barclay James Harvest	Time Honoured Ghosts + 1	CD	PolyGram	665-400-2	England	2003	13.99
Barclay James Harvest	Turn Of The Tide	CD	Polydor	800-013-2	England	1993	10.99
Barclay James Harvest	Twice As Much	2CD	EMI	0777-7-99479-2-8	Germany	1992	14.99
Barclay James Harvest	Victims Of Circumstance	CD	Universal	817-950-2	England	2003	11.99
Barclay James Harvest	Welcome To The Show	CD	Polydor	841-751-2	England	1990	9.99
Barclay James Harvest	Welcome To The Show (Sampler)	CD Single	Polydor	BJHCD-1	England	1990	24.99
Barclay James Harvest	Who Do We Think We Are	CD Single	Polydor	BJHDJ-1	England	1993	19.99
Barclay James Harvest	XII + 5	CD	PolyGram	665-571-2	England	2003	13.99
Barclay James Harvest/J Lees	John Lees - A Major Fancy	CD	Eagle	EAGCD107	Germany	1999	10.99
Barclay James Harvest/J Lees	Through The Eyes John Lees - Nexus	CD	Eagle	EAGCD120	Germany	2001	10.99
Barclay James Harvest/Wooly	Wooly Wolstenholme - Blk Box.. + 9	CD	Eclectic	ECLCD-1007	England	2004	14.99
Barclay James Harvest/Wooly	Wooly Woltenholme - Maestoso	CD	Brimstone	BRIM-003	England	2000	10.99
Bardens, Pete	Big Sky	CD	HTD	HTD-CD22	England	1994	19.99
Bardens, Pete	Further Than You Know	CD	Miramar	MPCD-2601	U.S.A.	1993	7.99
Bardens, Pete	Peter Bardens	CD	Line	TACD-9.00559-0	Germany	1988	29.99
Bardens, Pete	Seen One Earth	CD	Capitol	7-46868-2	U.S.A.	1987	19.99
Bardens, Pete	Speed Of Light	CD	Capitol	7-48967-2	U.S.A.	1988	19.99
Bardens, Pete	The Answer	CD	Line	TACD-9.00562-0	Germany	1988	25.99
Bardens, Pete	The Art Of Levitation	CD	Castle	CMRCD-378	England	2002	19.99
Bardens, Pete	Water Colors	CD	Miramar	09006-23010-2	U.S.A.	1991	8.99
Bardens, Pete Mirage	Speed Of Light Live	CD	Mooncrest	CRESTCD-058-Z	England	2000	19.99
Bar-Kays, The	Contagious	CD	Mercury	830-305-2	U.S.A.	1987	22.99
Barone, Richard	Between Heaven And Cello	CD	Line	LICD-9.01289-0	Germany	1994	7.99
Barone, Richard	Clouds Over Eden	CD	Line	LICD-9.01100-0	Germany	1992	5.99
Barone, Richard	Cool Blue Halo	CD	Line	LICD-9.00707-0	Germany	1989	24.99
Barone, Richard	Cry Baby Cry	CD Single	Line	LICD-9.00884-E	Germany	1989	4.99
Barone, Richard	Forbidden	CD Single	Line	LICD-9.01245-E	Germany	1992	4.99
Barone, Richard	Nobody Knows Me	CD Single	Line	LICD-9.01217-E	Germany	1992	4.99
Barone, Richard	Primal Cuts	CD Single	Line	LICD-9.01003-E	Germany	1990	4.99
Barone, Richard	Primal Dream	CD	Line	LICD-9.00955-0	Germany	1990	7.99
Barone, Richard	River To River	CD Single	Line	LICD-9.00963-E	Germany	1990	4.99
Barrabas	¡Soltad a Barrabas !	CD	Disconforme	DISC1994CD	Andorra	2000	11.99
Barrabas	Bestial	CD	Disconforme	DISC1997CD	Andorra	2000	11.99
Barrabas	Checkmate	CD	Disconforme	DISC1993CD	Andorra	2000	11.99
Barrabas	Deperately	CD	Disconforme	DISC1990CD	Andorra	2000	11.99
Arrabas	Forbidden	CD	Disconforme	DISC1995CD	Andorra	2000	11.99
Barrabas	Piel De Barrabas	CD	Disconforme	DISC1996CD	Andorra	2000	11.99
Barrabas	Power	CD	Disconforme	DISC1992CD	Andorra	2000	11.99
Barrabas	The Best Of 1971 - 1984	CD	Disconforme	DISC1989CD	Andorra	2000	12.99

Artist	Title	Format	Label	Catalog No	Country	Released	Value
Barrabas	Watch Out !	CD	Disconforme	DISC1988CD	Andorra	2000	11.99
Barrabas	Wild Safari (W/Woman)	CD	Disconforme	DISC1991CD	Andorra	2000	11.99
Barre, Martin/Jethro Tull	A Trick Of Memory	CD	ZYX	ZYX-20282-2	Germany	1994	16.99
Barre, Martin/Jethro Tull	The Meeting	CD	Imago	72787-23016-2	U.S.A.	1996	9.99
Barrett, Syd	Barrett	CD	EMI	7243-8-28907-2-0	England	1994	10.99
Barrett, Syd	Crazy Diamond Box Set	3CD	EMI	0777-7-81412-2-8	Holland	1993	35.99
Barrett, Syd	Madcap Laughs	CD	EMI	7243-8-28906-2-1	England	1994	10.99
Barrett, Syd	Octopus - The Best Of	CD	Cleopatra	CLEO-5771-2	U.S.A.	1992	12.99
Barrett, Syd	Opel	CD	EMI	7243-8-28908-2-9	England	1994	10.99
Barrett, Syd	Space Daze	CD	Cleopatra	CLEO-7916-2	U.S.A.	1994	8.99
Barrett, Syd	The Best Of - Wouldn't You Miss Me	CD	Capitol	7243-5-32320-2-3	U.S.A.	2001	14.99
Barrett, Syd	The Peel Seesions	CD	Strange Fruit	SFPSCD043	England	1995	14.99
Barris, Chuck	Confessions Of A Dangerous Singer	CD	Domo	73017-2	U.S.A.	2001	8.99
Barron, Ronnie	Blue Delicacies	CD	Line	STCD-9.00594-0	Germany	1989	4.99
Barry, John	A View To a Kill (O.S.T.)	CD	Toshiba-EMI	TOCP-8813	Japan	1985	24.99
Barry, John	A View To A Kill (O.S.T.)	CD	Toshiba-EMI	CP32-5076	Japan	1985	69.99
Barry, John	Across The Sea Of Time (O.S.T.)	CD	Epic	EK-67355	U.S.A.	1995	11.99
Barry, John	Beyondness Things (Rejected Score)	CD	London	289-460-009-2	U.S.A.	1998	8.99
Barry, John	Body Heat (O.S.T.)	CD	Varese	VSD-5951	U.S.A.	2002	12.99
Barry, John	Born Free	CD	Varese	302-066-084-2	U.S.A.	2000	7.99
Barry, John	Classic John Barry Vol 1	CD	Silva America	SSD-1033	U.S.A.	1992	10.99
Barry, John	Cry, The Beloved Country (O.S.T.)	CD	Epic	EK-67354	U.S.A.	1995	14.99
Barry, John	Dances With Wolves (Promo Sampler)	CD	Epic	ZSK-2248	U.S.A.	1991	14.99
Barry, John	Dances With Wolves + 6 (O.S.T.)	CD	Epic	EK-63555	U.S.A.	2004	8.99
Barry, John	Dances Wolves + 3 (Sony Gold Cd)	CD	Epic	ZK-66817	U.S.A.	1995	21.99
Barry, John	Deadfall + 2 (O.S.T.)	CD	Retrograde	FSM-80124-2	U.S.A.	1997	17.99
Barry, John	Diamonds Are Forever + 9 (O.S.T.)	CD	EMI	72435-41420-2-4	U.S.A.	2003	11.99
Barry, John	Ember Years - Vol 3	CD	Play It Again	PIA-101	England	1994	12.99
Barry, John	EMI Years 1957-1960, Vol 1	CD	EMI	0777-7-89416-2-0	England	1992	11.99
Barry, John	EMI Years Vol. 2 1961	CD	EMI	0777-7-89586-2-8	England	1993	11.99
Barry, John	EMI Years, Vol. 3 1962-1964	CD	EMI	7243-8-35046-2-6	England	1995	11.99
Barry, John	Enigma (O.S.T.)	CD	Decca	467-864-2	Germany	2001	20.99
Barry, John	Eternal Echoes (Rejected Score)	CD	Decca	466-765-2	Germany	2001	6.99
Barry, John	From Russia With Love (O.S.T.)	CD	EMI	7-95344-2	U.S.A.	1963	5.99
Barry, John	Game Of Death/Nightgames (O.S.T.)	CD	Silva Screen	FILMCD-123	EEC	1979	19.99
Barry, John	Goldfinger (O.S.T.)	CD	EMI	7-95345-2	U.S.A.	1963	5.99
Barry, John	Hammett (O.S.T.) (Ltd 3000)	CD	Prometheus	PCR-506	Belgium	2000	24.99
Barry, John	High Road China (Expanded) Promo	CD	Super Tracks	JBCD-01	U.S.A.	1983	31.99
Barry, John	High Road To China (Ltd 2000)	CD	SCSE	SCSE-CD-2	Australia	1983	32.99
Barry, John	High Road To China (O.S.T.)	CD	Southern Cross	SCCD-1030	England	1990	23.99
Barry, John	Jagged Edge (Ltd 1000)	CD	Varese	BCL-6001	U.S.A.	1985	89.99
Barry, John	King Kong (O.S.T.)	CD	Mask	MK-702	Italy	1976	19.99
Barry, John	King Rat (O.S.T.)	CD	Columbia	JK-57894	U.S.A.	1995	18.99
Barry, John	Lion In Winter (O.S.T.)	CD	Silva Screen	FILMCD353	England	2001	11.99
Barry, John	Lounge Legends	CD	Universal	UNI-5317CD	Germany	2000	17.99
Barry, John	Masquerade (O.S.T.) (Ltd 3000)	CD	Prometheus	PCR-514	Belgium	2002	28.99
Barry, John	Mercury Rising (O.S.T.)	CD	Varese	VSD-5925	U.S.A.	1998	14.99
Barry, John	Monte Walsh (O.S.T.) (Ltd 3000)	CD	Film Score Monthly	FSMVOL2/NO4	U.S.A.	1970	26.99
Barry, John	Moonraker (O.S.T.)	CD	EMI	7-90620-2	U.S.A.	1979	4.99
Barry, John	Moviola	CD	Epic	EK-52985	U.S.A.	1992	8.99
Barry, John	Moviola II - Action And Adventure	CD	Epic	EK-66401	U.S.A.	1995	8.99
Barry, John	My Life (O.S.T.)	CD	Epic	EK-57683	U.S.A.	1993	6.99
Barry, John	Octopussy + 3 (O.S.T.)	CD	Rykodisc	RCD-10705	U.S.A.	1997	5.99
Barry, John	On Her Majesty's Secret... + 10 (O.S.T.)	CD	EMI	72435-41419-2-8	U.S.A.	2003	10.99
Barry, John	Out Of Africa (O.S.T.)	CD	Silva America	SSD-1033	U.S.A.	1993	9.99
Barry, John	Out Of Africa (O.S.T.)	CD	MCA	MCAD-6158	U.S.A.	1986	12.99
Barry, John	Passion Flower Hotel (London Cast)	CD	Sony	SMK-66175	England	1994	44.99
Barry, John	Peggy Sue Got Married (O.S.T.)	CD	Varese	VSD47275	U.S.A.	1986	16.99

Artist	Title	Format	Label	Catalog No	Country	Released	Value
Barry, John	Raise The Titanic	CD	Silva America	SSD-1102	U.S.A.	1999	19.99
Barry, John	Robin And Marian	CD	Silva Screen	SSD-1133	U.S.A.	2001	14.99
Barry, John	Ruby Cairo (O.S.T.)	CD	Sony	SRCS-6618	Japan	1992	19.99
Barry, John	Somewhere In Time	CD	Varese	VSD-5911	U.S.A.	1998	9.99
Barry, John	Somewhere in Time (MCA Gold Cd)	CD	MCA	MCAD-10954	U.S.A.	1980	24.99
Barry, John	Sophia Loren In Rome	CD	Pendulum	PEG023	England	1964	16.99
Barry, John	Swept From The Sea	CD	London	458-793-2	U.S.A.	1997	17.99
Barry, John	The Beyondness Of Things	CD	London	289-460-009-2	U.S.A.	1998	5.99
Barry, John	The Chase (O.S.T.)	CD	Varese	VSD-5229	U.S.A.	1989	46.99
Barry, John	The Film Music Of	CD	Columbia	CK-44376	U.S.A.	1988	10.99
Barry, John	The Ipcress File (O.S.T.)	CD	MCA Victor	MVCM-22046	Japan	1995	56.99
Barry, John	The John Barry Collection	CD	Fat Boy	FATCD-418/1-4	England	1994	6.99
Barry, John	The Knack ... + 4 (O.S.T.)	CD	Rykodisc	RCD-10718	U.S.A.	1965	13.99
Barry, John	The Last Valley (O.S.T.)	CD	Silva Screen	FILMCD-355	England	2001	21.99
Barry, John	The Lion In Winter	CD	Varese	VSD-5217	U.S.A.	1988	19.99
Barry, John	The Living Daylights (O.S.T.)	CD	Rykodisc	RCD-10725	U.S.A.	1998	5.99
Barry, John	The Man With Golden Gun (O.S.T.)	CD	EMI	7-90619-2	U.S.A.	1974	5.99
Barry, John	The Music Of	CD	Columbia	983-379-2	England	1994	11.99
Barry, John	The Quiller Memorandum (O.S.T.)	CD	Varese	VSD-5218	U.S.A.	1988	99.99
Barry, John	The Quiller Memorandum (O.S.T.)	CD	Varese	VSD-5218	U.S.A.	1988	48.99
Barry, John	The Scarlet Letter (O.S.T.)	CD	Epic	EK-67431	U.S.A.	1995	8.99
Barry, John	The Specialist (Score)	CD	Epic	EK-66370	U.S.A.	1994	6.99
Barry, John	The Specialist (Various)	CD	Epic	EK-66384	U.S.A.	1994	6.99
Barry, John	The Whisperers + 4 (O.S.T.)	CD	Rykodisc	RCD-10720	U.S.A.	1998	8.99
Barry, John	The White Buffalo (O.S.T.) (Ltd 3000)	CD	Prometheus	PCR-518	Belgium	2003	24.95
Barry, John	ThunderBall + 6 (O.S.T.)	CD	EMI	72435-80589-2-5	U.S.A.	2003	10.99
Barry, John	Until September/Star Crash (O.S.T.)	CD	Silva Screen	FILMCD-085	England	1991	47.99
Barry, John	Walkabout (O.S.T.)	CD	Silva Screen	FILMCD-399	England	2000	12.99
Barry, John	You Only Live Twice + 7 (O.S.T.)	CD	EMI	72435-41418-2-9	U.S.A.	2003	17.99
Barry, John	Zulu (O.S.T.)	2CD	Silva America	SSD-1095	U.S.A.	1999	14.99
Barry, John/Annie Ross	Ember Years.- Vol 2	CD	Play It Again	PLAY-003	England	1992	12.99
Barry, John/Chad/Jeremy	The John Barry Collection	4CD	Fat Boy	FATCD-418	EEC	1994	19.99
Barry, John/Chet Baker	Playing By Heart (With Chris Botti)	CD	Decca	289-466-275-2	U.S.A.	1999	8.99
Barry, John/Don Black	The Don Black Songbook	CD	Play It Again	PLAY-005	England	1993	16.99
Barry, John/McKneely	Out Of Africa	CD	Varese	VSD-5816	U.S.A.	1997	7.99
Barry, John/Various Artists	Indecent Proposal (O.S.T./Not Score)	CD	MCA	MCAD-10795	U.S.A.	1993	5.99
Barry, John/Various Artists	The Golden Child (O.S.T.)	CD	Toshiba-EMI	CP32-5343	Japan	1986	63.99
Barry, John/Various Artists	The Hits & The Misses	2CD	Play It Again	PLAY-007	England	1998	12.99
Basia	The Best Remixes + 2	CD	Sony	ESCA-5164	Japan	1990	39.99
Basic Black	Self Titled	CD	Motown	MOTD-6307	U.S.A.	1990	24.99
Bassey, Shirley	La Mujer	CD	PolyGram	838-033-2	U.S.A.	1989	53.99
Bassey, Shirley	The Bond Collection (12 Bond Songs)	CD	Tring Int.	JHD115	EEC	1996	99.99
Bassey, Shirley	The Magic Is You (Very Best Of)	CD	BR Music	BX-404-2	Netherland	1992	10.99
Bassey, Shirley	The Remix Album + 3 (James Bond)	CD	Toshiba-EMI	TOCP-65658	Japan	2000	34.99
Baton Rouge	Self Titled	CD	Pony Canyon	PCCY-01242	Japan	1997	29.99
Bators, Stiv	Disconnected	CD	Line	LICD-9.00174-0	Germany	1987	7.99
Bators, Stiv	Disconnected	CD	Bomp	BCD-4043	U.S.A.	1993	6.99
Bators, Stiv	L.A. L.A.	CD	Bomp	BCD-4046	U.S.A.	1994	6.99
Baumann, Peter	Phase By Phase - Retrospective '76-'81	CD	Virgin	7243-8-41376-2-5	England	1996	24.99
Baumann, Peter	Repeat Repeat	CD	Virgin	CDV2214	England	1990	34.99
Baumann, Peter	Romance '76	CD	Virgin	CDV2069	England	1990	34.99
Baumann, Peter	Trans-Harmonic Night	CD	Virgin	CDV2124	England	1990	34.99
Baumann, Rainer	The Blue(s) Mood	2CD	Line	STCD-9.21148-S	Germany	1992	12.99
Bay City Rollers	Dedication + 4	CD	BMG	BVCA-7370	Japan	1995	26.99
Bay City Rollers	It's A Game + 1	CD	BMG	BVCA-2043	Japan	1977	36.99
Be Bop Deluxe	Air Age Anthology	2CD	EMI	7243-8-54730-2-9	Holland	1997	24.99
Be Bop Deluxe	Axe Victim + 3	CD	EMI	7947262	Holland	1990	19.99
Be Bop Deluxe	Live! In The Air Age	CD	One Way	OW-18465	U.S.A.	1995	91.99

B

Artist	Title	Format	Label	Catalog No	Country	Released	Value
Be Bop Deluxe	Modern Music + 3	CD	EMI	7947312	Holland	1990	19.99
Be Bop Deluxe	Sunburst Finish + 3	CD	EMI	79477272	Holland	1990	19.99
Be Bop Deluxe	Tramcar To Tomorrow	CD	HUX	HUX-009	England	1998	15.99
Be Bop Deluxe	Tremulous Antenna (BBC Recordings)	CD	HUX	HUX028	England	2002	15.99
Be Good Tanyas	Chinatown	CD	Nettwerk	0-6700-30304-2-7	U.S.A.	2003	15.99
Beach Boys	15 Big Ones/Love You	CD	Capitol	72435-27945-2-2	U.S.A.	2000	7.99
Beach Boys	Beach Boys Concert/ Live In London	CD	Capitol	72435-31861-2-8	U.S.A.	2001	8.99
Beach Boys	Beach Boys' Party/Stack-O-Tracks	CD	Capitol	72435-31641-2-6	U.S.A.	2001	8.99
Beach Boys	Best Of Beach Boys - Volume 2	CD	Capitol	8329102	Australia	1995	10.99
Beach Boys	Best Of The Beach Boys	CD	Capitol	D-123946	U.S.A.	1988	8.99
Beach Boys	California Dreamin'	CD	Disky	SI-853422	Holland	1998	10.99
Beach Boys	Carl And The Passions/Holland	2CD	Capitol	72435-25694-2-7	U.S.A.	2000	19.99
Beach Boys	Endless Harmony Soundtrack	CD	Capitol	72434-96391-2-6	U.S.A.	1998	8.99
Beach Boys	Endless Harmony (Promo)	2CD	Sony	XADP90017~18	Japan	1990	449.99
Beach Boys	Endless Summer (DCC Gold Cd)	CD	DCC	GZS-1076	U.S.A.	1995	49.99
Beach Boys	Essential - Perfect Harmony	CD	Capitol	72438-21680-2-7	U.S.A.	1998	11.99
Beach Boys	Friends & 20/20	CD	Capitol	72435-3138-2-2	U.S.A.	2001	8.99
Beach Boys	Good Timin': Knebworth, England 1980	CD	Eagle	ER-20002-2	U.S.A.	2003	9.99
Beach Boys	Good Vibrations	CD	Toshiba-EMI	TOCP-50135	U.S.A.	1997	14.99
Beach Boys	Good Vibrations: 30 Years Of Box Set	6CD	Toshiba-EMI	TOCP-8021/6	U.S.A.	1993	63.99
Beach Boys	Good Vibrations: 30 Years Of (Box Set)	5CD	Capitol	0777-7-81294-2-4	U.S.A.	1993	30.99
Beach Boys	Greatest Hits	CD	Hollywood	HCD-109	U.S.A.	1987	4.99
Beach Boys	Greatest Hits Vol 2	CD	Capitol	7243-5-20238-2-0	U.S.A.	1963	9.99
Beach Boys	Greatest Hits Vol 3	CD	Capitol	72435-24511-2-4	U.S.A.	2000	9.99
Beach Boys	Hawthorne, Ca	2CD	Capitol	72435-31583-2-3	U.S.A.	2001	10.99
Beach Boys	I Can Hear Music - Vocals/Carl Wilson	CD	Toshiba-EMI	TOCP-66035	Japan	2002	33.99
Beach Boys	In Concert	CD	Capitol	72435-25933-2-3	U.S.A.	2001	7.99
Beach Boys	Instrumental Hits	CD	Toshiba-EMI	TOCP-66033	Japan	2002	34.99
Beach Boys	Keepin' The Summer Alive/S.T.	CD	Capitol	72435-27948-2-9	U.S.A.	2000	8.99
Beach Boys	Little Deuce Coupe/ All Summer Long	CD	Capitol	72435-31516-2-1	U.S.A.	2001	8.99
Beach Boys	Lost & Found (1961-62)	CD	DCC	DZS-054	U.S.A.	1991	8.99
Beach Boys	M.I.U. Album - L.A. (Light Album)	CD	Capitol	72435-27950-2-4	U.S.A.	2000	8.99
Beach Boys	Made in U.S.A.	CD	Capitol	7-46324-2	U.S.A.	1986	8.99
Beach Boys	Pet Sound Sessions (Promo Sampler)	CD	Capitol	DPRO-11241	U.S.A.	1996	23.99
Beach Boys	Pet Sounds	CD	Toshiba-EMI	TOCP-66031	Japan	2002	28.99
Beach Boys	Pet Sounds (Mono/Stereo)	CD	Capitol	72435-26266-2-5	U.S.A.	2001	8.99
Beach Boys	Pet Sounds + 1 (DCC Gold Cd)	CD	DCC	GZS-1035	U.S.A.	1993	57.99
Beach Boys	Pet Sounds + 3	CD	Capitol	7-48421-2	U.S.A.	1990	8.99
Beach Boys	Pet Sounds Sessions Box Set	4CD	Capitol	7243-8-37662-2-2	U.S.A.	1996	37.99
Beach Boys	Rarities & Beach Boys' Medley	CD	Toshiba-EMI	TOCP-3329	Japan	1997	37.99
Beach Boys	Selections/Good Vibration Box (DJ)	CD	Capitol	DPRO-79728	U.S.A.	1993	23.99
Beach Boys	Self Titled (Early Greatest)	CD	CTA	R-180264	Japan	1990	24.99
Beach Boys	Smiley Smile & Wild Honey	CD	Capitol	72435-31862-2-7	U.S.A.	2001	8.99
Beach Boys	Sounds Of Summer	CD	Capitol	72435-82710-2-7	U.S.A.	2003	8.99
Beach Boys	Special 14 Track Cd (Promo Sampler)	CD	Capitol	DPRO-79168	U.S.A.	1990	13.99
Beach Boys	Spirit Of America (DCC Gold Cd)	CD	DCC	GZS-1089	U.S.A.	1996	53.99
Beach Boys	Still Cruisin'	CD	Capitol	7-96239-2	U.S.A.	1989	13.99
Beach Boys	Summer Crush: Songs We Love...	CD	Emi-Capitol	72435-33311-2-2	U.S.A.	2001	7.99
Beach Boys	Summer In Paradise	CD	Navarre	BBR-727-2	U.S.A.	1992	33.99
Beach Boys	Sunflower & Surf's Up	CD	Capitol	72435-25692-2-9	U.S.A.	2000	15.99
Beach Boys	Surfer Girl / Shut Down	CD	Capitol	72435-31515-2-2	U.S.A.	2001	8.99
Beach Boys	Surfin' Safari & Surfin' Usa	CD	Capitol	72435-31517-2-0	U.S.A.	2001	44.99
Beach Boys	Surfin U.S.A./S Girl (MFSL Gold Cd)	CD	Mobile Fidelity	UDCD-521	U.S.A.	1963	44.99
Beach Boys	Ten Years Of Harmony	2CD	Columbia	456670-2	U.S.A.	1981	19.99
Beach Boys	The Absolute Best Vol. 1	CD	Capitol	7-96195-2	U.S.A.	1991	7.99
Beach Boys	The Absolute Best Volume 2	CD	Capitol	7-96796-2	U.S.A.	1991	7.99
Beach Boys	The Dutch Singles Collection	CD	EMI	7243-4-96507-2-5	EU	1998	29.99
Beach Boys	The Greatest Hits Vol 1	CD	Capitol	7243-5-21860-2-0	U.S.A.	1999	9.99

B

Artist	Title	Format	Label	Catalog No	Country	Released	Value
Beach Boys	Today & Summer Days	CD	Capitol	72435-31639-2-1	U.S.A.	2001	8.99
Beach Boys	Ultimate Christmas	CD	Capitol	72434-95734-2-0	U.S.A.	1998	8.99
Beach Boys/Al Jardine	Family And Friends Live Las Vegas	CD	HEAR	HV100	U.S.A.	2001	14.99
Beach Boys/Al Jardine	PT Cruiser	CD Single	Cruiser	CO5555	U.S.A.	2003	29.99
Beach Boys/Brian Wilson	California Feelin' - Best Beach Boys	CD	Toshiba-EMI	TOCP-66030	Japan	2002	34.99
Beach Boys/Brian Wilson	The Brian Wilson Productions	CD	Toshiba-EMI	TOCP-66034	Japan	2002	36.99
Beach Boys/Bruce Johnston	Going Public	CD	Edsel	EDCD-697	England	2000	12.99
Beach Boys/Bruce Johnston	Surfers' Pajama Party	CD	Del-Fi	DFCD-71228-2	U.S.A.	1994	8.99
Beach Boys/Bruce Johnston	Surfin' 'Round The World + 3	CD	Sundazed	SC-6100	U.S.A.	1997	8.99
Beach Boys/John Stamos	Forever (Promo)	CD Single	Brother	PROCD-3	U.S.A.	1992	74.99
Beach Boys/Kathy Troccoli	I Can Hear Music	CD Single	MCA	80127-2	England	1991	10.99
Beach Boys/Mike Love	Catch A Wave (Promo Only 125)	CD	Malibu	MEL.CD.101	U.S.A.	1996	24.99
Beach Boys/Spring	Self Titled	CD	Rhino	R2-75762	U.S.A.	1972	64.99
Beach Boys/Spring	Self Titled	CD	Repertoire	REP-4472-WP	Germany	2002	64.99
Beach Boys/Spring	Spring Plus (American By Mistake)	CD	See For Miles	SEE-CD269	England	1972	64.99
Beach Boys/S. S. M. Kali	Apache Inca (W/Mike Love)	2CD	Captain Trip	CTCD-272/273	Japan	2000	29.99
Beach Boys/V. A.	Guess I'm Dumb: Songs Beach Boys	CD	Castle	CMRCD-295	England	2002	11.99
Beach Boys/V. A.	Starflower	CD	Medicine Park	MP103	U.S.A.	2001	6.99
Beach Boys/V. A.	The Beach Boys - Stars & Stripes Vol 1	CD	River North	51416-1205-2	U.S.A.	1996	10.99
Beatle Jazz	A Bite Of The Apple (Beatles Songs)	CD	Zebra Acoustic	ZA-44410-2	U.S.A.	2000	8.99
Beatles	1	CD	EMI	7243-5-29325-2-8	U.S.A.	2000	10.99
Beatles	1 (Gold Disc)	CD	EMI	2000-306	Taiwan	2000	15.99
Beatles	1 Soundbites (Promo)	CD	EMI	CDLRL042	U.S.A.	2000	129.99
Beatles	1962-1966 (Red)	2CD	Capitol	0777-7-97036-2-3	U.S.A.	1993	16.99
Beatles	1967-1970 (Blue)	2CD	Capitol	0777-7-97039-2-0	U.S.A.	1993	18.99
Beatles	A Hard Day's Night	CD	Toshiba-EMI	TOCP-51113	Japan	1998	20.99
Beatles	Abbey Road	CD	Toshiba-EMI	TOCP-51122	Japan	1998	26.99
Beatles	Abbey Road (1st Rel On Cd/Recalled)	CD	EMI Odeon	CP35-3016	Japan	1983	184.99
Beatles	All You Need Is Love (Promo)	CD Single	EMI	DPRO708612119	U.S.A.	1997	14.99
Beatles	Anth. Vol. 2 - Cd-Rom Press Kit (Promo)	CD	Capitol	1306-026-001D	U.S.A.	1996	249.99
Beatles	Anthology 1	2CD	EMI	7243-8-34445-2-6	U.S.A.	1995	13.99
Beatles	Anthology 1 (Promo Sampler)	CD	EMI	DPRO-10289	U.S.A.	1995	28.99
Beatles	Anthology 2	2CD	EMI	7243-8-34448-2-3	U.S.A.	1996	18.99
Beatles	Anthology 2 (Promo Sampler)	CD	EMI	DPRO-11200	U.S.A.	1996	21.99
Beatles	Anthology 3	2CD	EMI	7243-8-34451-2-7	U.S.A.	1996	18.99
Beatles	Anthology 3 (Promo Sampler)	CD	EMI	DPRO-11322	U.S.A.	1996	24.99
Beatles	Baby It's You	CD Single	EMI	7243-8-58349-2-9	U.S.A.	1995	8.99
Beatles	Baby It's You (Valentine Promo)	CD Single	Capitol	DPRO-79533	U.S.A.	1995	49.99
Beatles	Beatles For Sale	CD	Toshiba-EMI	TOCP-51114	Japan	1998	20.99
Beatles	Cd Singles Collection (22)	22 CD	Capitol	0777-7-15901-2-2	U.S.A.	1992	80.99
Beatles	Compact Disc EP Collection	15 CD	Capitol	C2-15852	U.S.A.	1988	80.99
Beatles	Complete Christmas Recordings (DJ)	CD	On The Radio	A12EO300A	U.S.A.	1990	149.99
Beatles	Denmark & Netherlands June 1964	CD	Jasrac	BS-2021	Japan	2000	29.99
Beatles	Free As A Bird	CD Single	EMI	7243-8-58497-2-5	U.S.A.	1995	9.99
Beatles	Hello Goodbye (Promo)	CD Single	EMI	DPRO708612120	U.S.A.	1997	14.99
Beatles	Help!	CD	Toshiba-EMI	TOCP-51115	Japan	1998	31.99
Beatles	Hey Jude (3" Mono)	CD Single	Toshiba-EMI	XP10-2068	Japan	1968	24.99
Beatles	In The Beginning	CD	Polydor	314-549-268-2	U.S.A.	2000	8.99
Beatles	Let It Be	CD	Toshiba-EMI	TOCP-51123	Japan	1998	26.99
Beatles	Let It Be... Naked (W/Bonus Cd)	2CD	Capitol	7243-5-95713-2-4	U.S.A.	2003	9.99
Beatles	Let It Be/You Know My... (3")	CD Single	Toshiba-EMI	XP10-2072	Japan	1970	20.99
Beatles	Live At The BBC	2CD	EMI	7243-8-31796-2-6	U.S.A.	1996	14.99
Beatles	Live At The BBC Promo Sampler	CD	EMI	CDPCSPDJ-7261	Holland	1994	24.99
Beatles	Magical Mystery Tour	CD	Toshiba-EMI	TOCP-51124	Japan	1998	31.99
Beatles	Past Masters Vol. 1	CD	Toshiba-EMI	TOCP-51125	Japan	1998	26.99
Beatles	Past Masters Vol. 2	CD	Toshiba-EMI	TOCP-51126	Japan	1998	26.99
Beatles	Penny Lane (Promo)	CD Single	EMI	DPRO708612118	U.S.A.	1997	14.99
Beatles	Please Please Me	CD	Toshiba-EMI	TOCP-51111	Japan	1998	20.99

Artist	Title	Format	Label	Catalog No	Country	Released	Value
Beatles	Real Love	CD Single	EMI	7243-8-58544-2-2	U.S.A.	1996	13.99
Beatles	Revolver	CD	Toshiba-EMI	TOCP-51117	Japan	1998	26.99
Beatles	Rockin' At The Star-Club	CD	Sony	A-22131	U.S.A.	1991	12.99
Beatles	Rubber Soul	CD	Toshiba-EMI	TOCP-51116	Japan	1998	23.99
Beatles	Selections Red And Blue Albums (DJ)	CD	EMI	DPRO-79286	U.S.A.	1993	26.99
Beatles	Sgt. Pepper's Lonely Hearts Club Band	CD	Toshiba-EMI	TOCP-51118	Japan	1998	23.99
Beatles	Talkology Vol. 1 (1964-65)	CD	Talkology	TY001	England	2000	5.99
Beatles	Talkology Vol. 2 (1966)	CD	Talkology	TY002	England	2000	5.99
Beatles	Talkology Vol. 3 (1966 Japan)	CD	Talkology	TY003	England	2000	5.99
Beatles	The Beatles Anthology ABC-TV	Cd Rom	Apple	508784-2	U.S.A.	1995	121.99
Beatles	The Best I (1962-64)	CD	TF	T-1818	Japan	1988	14.99
Beatles	The Best II (1964-66)	CD	TF	T-1819	Japan	1988	15.99
Beatles	Westwood 1/BBC Beatles (6 Cds)	6CD	Westwood 1	9320100A	U.S.A.	1990	154.99
Beatles	White Album	2CD	Toshiba-EMI	TOCP-51119-20	Japan	1998	41.99
Beatles	White Album (30th Ann.)	2CD	EMI	7243-4-96895-2-7	England	1998	43.99
Beatles	With The Beatles	CD	Toshiba-EMI	TOCP-51112	Japan	1998	18.99
Beatles	Yellow Submarine	CD	Toshiba-EMI	TOCP-51121	Japan	1998	25.99
Beatles	Yellow Submarine	CD	Capitol	7243-5-21481-2-7	U.S.A.	1999	11.99
Beatles/George Martin	Interview/Red/Blue Cd	CD	EMI	RNB1	England	1993	24.99
Beatles/George Martin	With Ken Townsend	CD	EMI	BCD-20	Japan	1992	35.99
Beatles/Sheridan, Tony	My Bonnie + 10	CD	Repertoire	REP-4964	Germany	2001	14.99
Beatles/Superpickers	Pickin' On The Beatles, Volume 2	CD	CMH	CD-8033	U.S.A.	1999	8.99
Beatles/Various Artists	All You Need Is Covers	2CD	Sequel	NEECD-309	England	1999	14.99
Beatles/Various Artists	Beatles On Panpipes	CD	Big Eye	BIG-4029-2	U.S.A.	2001	5.99
Beatles/Various Artists	Come Together/Guitar Tribute/Beatles	CD	NYC	NYC-6004-2	U.S.A.	1993	8.99
Beatles/Various Artists	Help!	2CD	Sanctuary	CMDDD260	England	2001	14.99
Beatles/Various Artists	Lost Songs	CD	Vitamin	CD-8503	U.S.A.	1999	13.99
Beatles/Various Artists	Motown Sings the Beatles	CD	Razor & Tie	RE-2031	U.S.A.	1994	11.99
Beatles/Various Artists	Ob La Di: Beatles Hits Reggae Style	CD	Castle	PIESD-040	England	1999	8.99
Beatles/White Album 30th	Promo Test Press (No #/Rel Date Stkr)	2CD	EMI	CDP-496-8952	England	1998	74.99
Beau Brummels	66	CD	Warner Bros.	WPCP-5251	Japan	1996	38.99
Beau Brummels	Best Of	CD	Rhino	R2-75779	U.S.A.	1987	7.99
Beau Brummels	From The Vaults	CD	One Way	OW-35141	U.S.A.	1999	7.99
Beau Brummels	The Beau Brummels Collection	CD	Line	IMCD-9.00604-0	Germany	1989	9.99
Beau Brummels	Triangle	CD	Warner Bros.	7599-26886-2	Germany	1967	10.99
Beau-Hunks	On To The Show! (Little Rascals)	CD	Koch	3-8705-2	U.S.A.	1995	24.99
Beau-Hunks	Play The Original Little Rascals Music	CD	Koch	3-8702-2	U.S.A.	1994	30.99
Beautiful People	If 60's Were 90's (J Hendrix Remixes)	CD	Continuum	ISBCD-2063	Canada	1994	7.99
Beaver/Krause	Gandharva/In A Wild Sanctuary	CD	Warner Bros.	9-45663-2	U.S.A.	1994	8.99
Beavis/Butt-Head/Promo	Babes/Beavus & Butt-Head/Toyland	CD	Reprise	PRO-CD-6533-R	U.S.A.	1993	13.99
Beck	Golden Feelings	CD	Sonic Enemy	002	U.S.A.	1999	99.99
Beck	Sampler (Promo)	CD	DGC	INTR-10820	U.S.A.	2002	5.99
Beck, Bogert & Appice	BBA Live	2CD	Sony	ESCA-5067/8	Japan	1973	38.99
Beck, Jeff	Beck-Ola / Cosa Nostra	CD	Epic	EK-66084	U.S.A.	2000	6.99
Beck, Jeff	Beckology Box Set	3CD	Epic	E3K-48661	U.S.A.	1991	25.99
Beck, Jeff	Beckology: The Sampler (Promo)	CD	Epic	ESK-4275	U.S.A.	1991	11.99
Beck, Jeff	Blow By Blow	CD	Epic	EK-85440	U.S.A.	2001	13.99
Beck, Jeff	Blow By Blow (MFSL Gold Cd)	CD	Mobile Fidelity	UDCD-727	U.S.A.	1975	34.99
Beck, Jeff	Blow By Blow (Sony Gold Cd)	CD	Columbia	EK-53442	U.S.A.	1993	24.99
Beck, Jeff	Jeff + 2 (W/Pick)	CD	Epic	EICP-195	Japan	2003	22.99
Beck, Jeff	There And Back	CD	Epic	EK-35684	U.S.A.	1980	7.99
Beck, Jeff	Truth	CD	Epic	EK-66085	U.S.A.	2000	9.99
Beck, Jeff	Truth & Beck-Ola	CD	EMI	7954692	England	1991	14.99
Beck, Jeff	W/Jan Hammer Group Live	CD	Epic	EK-34433	U.S.A.	1977	8.99
Beck, Jeff	Who Else!	CD	Epic	EK-67987	U.S.A.	1999	6.99
Beck, Jeff	Wired	CD	Epic	EK-85439	U.S.A.	2001	8.99
Beck, Jeff	Wired (MFSL Gold Cd)	CD	Mobile Fidelity	UDCD-531	U.S.A.	1976	40.99
Beck, Jeff	You Had It Coming	CD	Epic	EK-61625	U.S.A.	2001	10.99

Artist	Title	Format	Label	Catalog No	Country	Released	Value
Beck, Jeff Group	Rough And Ready	CD	Epic	EK-30973	U.S.A.	1971	8.99
Beck, Jeff/Jed Leiber	Frankie's House	CD	Epic	EK-53194	U.S.A.	1992	10.99
Beck, Jeff/Seal	Manic Depression (Promo)	CD Single	Reprise	PRO-CD-6614	U.S.A.	1993	12.99
Becker, Walter	11 Tracks Of Whack	CD	Giant	9-24579-2	U.S.A.	1994	8.99
Becker, Walter	Words + Music	CD	Giant	PRO-CD-7144	U.S.A.	1994	8.99
Becker/Fagen	The Early Years	CD	Line	LICD-9.00070-0	Germany	1987	6.99
Bedford, David	Great Equatorial	CD	Voiceprint	VP156CD	England	1994	7.99
Bedford, David	My Mother, My Sister And I	CD	Voiceprint	CPVP003CD	England	1999	11.99
Bedford, David	Nurses Song With Elephants	CD	Voiceprint	VP116CD	England	1993	13.99
Bedford, David	Rime Of The Ancient Mariner	CD	Virgin	7243-8-39539-2-9	England	1975	12.99
Bedford, David	Song Of The White Horse	CD	Voiceprint	VP110CD	Austria	1983	12.99
Bedford, David	The Odyssey	CD	Caroline	7243-8-39574-2-2	U.S.A.	1976	12.99
Bee Gees	2 Years On	CD	Polydor	833-785-2	U.S.A.	1971	8.99
Bee Gees	Best Of, Vol. 1	CD	Polydor	831-594-2	U.S.A.	1987	7.99
Bee Gees	Best Of, Vol. 2	CD	Polydor	831-960-2	U.S.A.	1990	7.99
Bee Gees	Children Of The World	CD	Polydor	823-658-2	U.S.A.	1994	8.99
Bee Gees	Claustrophobia	CD	Cleopatra	CLP-4052-2	U.S.A.	1998	7.99
Bee Gees	Cucumber Castle	CD	Polydor	833-783-2	U.S.A.	1997	8.99
Bee Gees	E.S.P.	CD	Warner Bros.	7599-25541-2	U.S.A.	1987	7.99
Bee Gees	Greatest	2CD	Polydor	800-071-2	U.S.A.	1987	12.99
Bee Gees	Here at Last...Bee Gees...Live	2CD	Polydor	833-791-2	U.S.A.	1990	14.99
Bee Gees	Here At Last...Bee Gees...Live!	2CD	Polydor	833-791-2	U.S.A.	1977	29.99
Bee Gees	High Civilization	CD	Warner Bros.	7599-26530-2	U.S.A.	1991	7.99
Bee Gees	History	CD	Polydor	P22W22024	Japan	1985	59.99
Bee Gees	Horizontal	CD	Polydor	833-659-2	U.S.A.	1990	8.99
Bee Gees	Idea	CD	Polydor	833-660-2	U.S.A.	1997	8.99
Bee Gees	Life In A Tin Can	CD	Polydor	833-788-2	U.S.A.	1997	8.99
Bee Gees	Living Eyes	CD	Polydor	POCP-2244	Japan	1987	114.99
Bee Gees	Living Eyes	CD	Polydor	P28W-25030	Japan	1981	99.99
Bee Gees	Living Eyes	CD	Polydor	813-642-2	U.S.A.	1993	44.99
Bee Gees	Main Course	CD	Polydor	833-790-2	U.S.A.	1991	8.99
Bee Gees	Melody (O.S.T.)	CD	Universal	UICY-3564	Japan	2002	29.99
Bee Gees	Mr. Natural	CD	Polydor	833-789-2	U.S.A.	1992	8.99
Bee Gees	Odessa	CD	Polydor	825-451-2	U.S.A.	1987	8.99
Bee Gees	One	CD	Warner Bros.	7599-25887-2	U.S.A.	1989	7.99
Bee Gees	One Night Only + 6	2CD	Polydor	547-120-2	England	1999	18.99
Bee Gees	Rare Collection	CD	Polydor	P22W22026	Japan	1989	24.99
Bee Gees	Size Isn't Everything	CD	Polydor	521-055-2	U.S.A.	1993	7.99
Bee Gees	Special Collection	CD	Jasrac	GRN-26	Japan	1990	42.99
Bee Gees	Spirits Having Flown	CD	Polydor	827-335-2	U.S.A.	1994	8.99
Bee Gees	Still Waters	CD	Polydor	537-302-2	U.S.A.	1997	8.99
Bee Gees	Tales From The Brothers Gibb	4CD	Polydor	843-911-2	U.S.A.	1990	34.99
Bee Gees	The Bee Gees 1st	CD	Polydor	POCP-2225	Japan	1992	39.99
Bee Gees	The Bee Gees 1st	CD	Rebound	314-520-279-2	U.S.A.	1995	8.99
Bee Gees	Their Greatest Hits The...(Xtra Cd)	3CD	Polydor	314-589-521-2	U.S.A.	2001	29.99
Bee Gees	This Is Where I Came In	CD	Universal	549-626-2	U.S.A.	2001	8.99
Bee Gees	To Whom It May Concern	CD	Polydor	833-787-2	U.S.A.	1992	8.99
Bee Gees	Trafalgar	CD	Polydor	833-786-2	U.S.A.	1990	8.99
Bee Gees	Trafalgar (MFSL Gold Cd)	CD	Mobile Fidelity	UDCD-680	U.S.A.	1971	24.99
Bee Gees/Barry Gibb	Hawks (O.S.T.)	CD	Polydor	837-264-2	Germany	1988	94.99
Bee Gees/Robin Gibb	How Old Are You?	CD	Polydor	810-896-2	Germany	1995	16.99
Bee Gees/Robin Gibb	Magnet	CD	SPV	SPV098-57147-2	Germany	2003	16.99
Bee Gees/Robin Gibb	Please	CD Single	SPV	055-71463	Germany	2002	4.99
Bee Gees/Robin Gibb	Robin's Reign	CD	Spectrum	847-914-2	Germany	1970	46.99
Bee Gees/Robin Gibb	Secret Agent	CD	Polydor	821-797-2	Germany	1984	84.99
Bee Gees/Robin Gibb	Wait Forever	CD Single	SPV	030-71613	Germany	2003	4.99
Beggars Opera	Act One + 2	CD	Repertoire	IMS-7041-WP	Germany	1995	19.99
Beggars Opera	Pathfinder	CD	Repertoire	IMS-7028-WP	Germany	1995	15.99

Artist	Title	Format	Label	Catalog No	Country	Released	Value
Beggars Opera	Pathfinder	CD	Line	LICD-9.00728-0	Germany	1989	15.99
Beggars Opera	Waters Of Change	CD	Repertoire	IMS-7029-WP	Germany	1995	21.99
Beggars Opera	Waters Of Change (Line Version)	CD	Line	LICD-9.00724-0	Germany	1989	21.99
Beirach/John Abercrombie	Emerald City	CD	Line	COCD-9.00522-0	Germany	1989	10.99
Belew, Adrian	Coming Attractions	CD	Thirsty Ear	THI-57082-2	U.S.A.	2000	8.99
Belew, Adrian	Here	CD	Caroline	CAROL-1748-2	U.S.A.	1994	6.99
Belew, Adrian	Inner Revolution	CD	Atlantic	7-82370-2	U.S.A.	1992	6.99
Belew, Adrian	Mr. Music Head	CD	Atlantic	7-81959-2	U.S.A.	1989	5.99
Belew, Adrian	Op Zop Too Wah Promo Sampler	CD	Caroline	CARCDPRO9614	U.S.A.	1996	12.99
Belew, Adrian	Salad Days	CD	Thirsty Ear	THI-57061.2	U.S.A.	2000	8.99
Belew, Adrian	The Guitar As Orchestra	CD	Adrian Belew	ABP-7522-2	U.S.A.	1995	15.99
Belew, Adrian	Young Lions	CD	Atlantic	7-82099-2	U.S.A.	1990	7.99
Bell, Maggie	Live At The Rainbow 1974	CD	Angel Air	SJPCD100	England	2001	14.99
Bell, Maggie	Queen Of The Night	CD	Repertoire	REP-4661-WY	Germany	1997	11.99
Belle Stars	The Very Best Of	CD	Repertoire	REP-4437-WY	Germany	1993	10.99
Belushi, Jim	36-22-36	CD	House Of Blues	51416-1334-2	U.S.A.	1998	4.99
Ben	Self Titled	CD	Repertoire	REP-4195-WP	Germany	1991	11.99
Ben Folds Five	Tiny Dancer (Promo)	CD Single	Epic	ESK-59298	U.S.A.	2002	14.99
Benatar, Pat	All Fired Up: The Very Best Of	2CD	Chrysalis	7243-8-31094-2-5	U.S.A.	1994	17.99
Benatar, Pat	Best Shots	CD	Toshiba-EMI	TOCP-5972	Japan	1990	19.99
Benatar, Pat	Best Shots (W/Bonus DVD)	2CD	Capitol	72435-93492-0-6	U.S.A.	2003	24.99
Benatar, Pat	Crimes Of Passion	CD	Chrysalis	CP32-5067	Japan	1986	19.99
Benatar, Pat	Eight-Fifteen-Eighty	CD	CMC INT.	06076-86256-2	U.S.A.	1998	6.99
Benatar, Pat	Eight-Fifteen-Eighty + 1	CD	Victor Ent.	VICP-60408	Japan	1998	29.99
Benatar, Pat	Go	CD	Belchassio	79743	U.S.A.	2003	12.99
Benatar, Pat	Gravity's Rainbow	CD	Chrysalis	72438-19829-2-1	U.S.A.	1993	8.99
Benatar, Pat	Greatest Hits Live	CD	King Biscuit	70710-88054-2	U.S.A.	1999	13.99
Benatar, Pat	In Heat Of.../ Crimes of Passion	CD	BGO	BGOCD418	England	1998	14.99
Benatar, Pat	In The Heat Of The Night	CD	Chrysalis	CP32-5066	Japan	1986	19.99
Benatar, Pat	In The Heat Of...(DCC Gold Cd)	CD	DCC	GZS-1056	U.S.A.	1994	19.99
Benatar, Pat	Innomorata	CD	CMC INT.	06076-86216-2	U.S.A.	1997	6.99
Benatar, Pat	Innomorata	CD	BMG Victor	BVCP-6064	Japan	1997	29.99
Benatar, Pat	Live From Earth	CD	Chrysalis	CP32-5070	Japan	1986	19.99
Benatar, Pat	Live From Earth	CD	Chrysalis	VK-41444	U.S.A.	1983	6.99
Benatar, Pat	Precious Time	CD	Chrysalis	CP32-5069	Japan	1986	19.99
Benatar, Pat	Precious Time / Get Nervous	CD	BGO	BGOCD427	England	1998	14.99
Benatar, Pat	Seven The Hard Way	CD	Chrysalis	CP32-5097	Japan	1987	19.99
Benatar, Pat	Synchronistic Wanderings	3CD	Chrysalis	72434-99803-2-7	U.S.A.	1999	19.99
Benatar, Pat	Tropico	CD	Chrysalis	CP32-5030	Japan	1984	19.99
Benatar, Pat	Tropico Seven / The Hard Way	CD	BGO	BGOCD433	England	1998	14.99
Benatar, Pat	True Love	CD	Toshiba-EMI	TOCP-6662	Japan	1991	15.99
Benatar, Pat	True Love	CD	Chrysalis	F2-21805	U.S.A.	1991	5.99
Benatar, Pat	Wide Awake In Dreamland	CD	Chrysalis	VK-41628	U.S.A.	1988	10.99
Benatar, Pat	Wide Awake In Dreamland	CD	Chrysalis	CP32-5623	Japan	1989	19.99
Benatar, Pat/Neil Giraldo	Live	CD	Gold Circle Ent.	GC-50024-2	U.S.A.	2001	8.99
Benedictine Monks	Chant (MFSL Gold Cd)	CD	Mobile Fidelity	UDCD-725	U.S.A.	1994	29.99
Bennett, Tony	Playing With My Friends	CD	Columbia	CK-85833	U.S.A.	2001	7.99
Benno, Marc	Lost In Austin	CD	Polydor	POCM-2095	Japan	1998	24.99
Benno, Marc	Minnows (W/Jesse Ed Davis)	CD	Polydor K.K.	POCM-2034	Japan	1971	24.99
Benno, Marc	Self Titled	CD	Polydor	POCM-2033	Japan	1970	34.99
Benoit, David/Vince Guaraldi	Here's To You Charlie Brown	CD	Verve	314-543-637-2	U.S.A.	2000	12.99
Benson, George	Breezin' + 3	CD	Rhino	R2-76713	U.S.A.	2001	6.99
Bern, Dan	Dan Bern	CD	Sony	OK-67644	U.S.A.	1997	11.99
Bern, Dan	Fifty Eggs	CD	Sony	OK-67870	U.S.A.	1998	6.99
Bern, Dan	New American Language	CD	Messenger	MSGR-09	U.S.A.	2001	10.99
Bern, Dan	Smartie Mine	2CD	Line	LICD-9.21368-0	Germany	1998	20.99
Bernard, James	The Devil Rides Out/She/Quartermass	CD	Silva	SSD-1059	U.S.A.	1996	8.99
Bernard, James	The Horror Of Dracula	CD	Silva	FILMCD-708	England	1992	8.99

B

Artist	Title	Format	Label	Catalog No	Country	Released	Value
Bernhard, Sandra/Tori Amos	Without You I'm Nothing	CD	Enigma	773369-2	U.S.A.	1989	14.99
Bernstein, Elmer	Movie & TV Themes (MFSL Silver Cd)	CD	Mobile Fidelity	MFCD-851	U.S.A.	1962	29.99
Bernstein, Elmer	Return Of The Magnificent 7 (O.S.T.)	CD	Rykodisc	RCD-10714	U.S.A.	1997	12.99
Bernstein, Elmer	Stars 'N' Bars (Rejected Score)	CD	Varese	VCL9101.8	U.S.A.	1991	114.99
Bernstein, Elmer	The Great Escape	CD	RCA	09026-63241-2	U.S.A.	1999	16.99
Bernstein, Elmer	The Great Escape (O.S.T.)	CD	Rykodisc	RCD-10711	U.S.A.	1997	21.99
Bernstein, Elmer	The Magnificent Seven	CD	RCA	09026-63240-2	U.S.A.	1999	9.99
Bernstein, Elmer	To Kill A Mockingbird	CD	Mainstream	MDCD-602	U.S.A.	1991	22.99
Bernstein, Elmer	To Kill A Mockingbird + 4	CD	Varese	VSD-5754	U.S.A.	1997	13.99
Berry, Chuck	In London/Fresh Berry's	CD	BGO	BGOCD395	England	1998	14.99
Berry, Chuck	Live At The Fillmore Auditorium + 2	CD	Rebound	314-520-203-2	U.S.A.	1994	10.99
Berry, Chuck	The Chess Box	3CD	MCA	07674-10801-2-0	U.S.A.	1988	39.99
Berry, Chuck	The Ep Collection	CD	See For Miles	SEE-CD320	England	1991	12.99
Berry, Chuck	The Great Twenty Eight	CD	MCA	CHD-92500	U.S.A.	1984	9.99
Berry, Chuck	The London Chuck Berry Sessions	CD	MCA	CHD-9295	U.S.A.	1989	8.99
Berry, Chuck	Two Great Guitars/Super Blues Band	CD	BGO	BGOCD334	England	1998	14.99
Berry, Chuck /Friends	Soundtrack Hail! Hail! Rock 'N' Roll	CD	MCA	MCAD-6217	U.S.A.	1987	14.99
Berry, Dave	Hostage To The Beat	CD	Line	BUCD-9.00543-0	Germany	1988	22.99
Betts, Dickey	Highway Call	CD	Polydor	P2OP-22029	Japan	1974	24.99
Betts, Dickey	Highway Call	CD	PolyGram	422-835-115-2	U.S.A.	2001	9.99
Betts, Dickey	Let's Get Together	CD	Free Falls	FFE-7017-2	U.S.A.	2001	8.99
Betts, Dickey/Band	Live (Promo)	CD	Epic	ESK-1396	U.S.A.	1988	52.99
Betts, Dickey/Band	Pattern Disruptive	CD	Epic	EK-44289	U.S.A.	1988	8.99
Betts, Dickey/Great Southern	Atlanta's Burning Down	CD	BMG	BVCA-7321	Japan	1995	39.99
Betts, Dickey/Great Southern	Atlanta's Burning Down	CD	Razor & Tie	RE-2142-2	U.S.A.	1997	24.99
Betts, Dickey/Great Southern	Dickey Betts & Great Southern	CD	Razor & Tie	RE-2141-2	U.S.A.	1997	24.99
Betts, Dickey/Great Southern	Dickey Betts & Great Southern	CD	BMG	BVCA-7320	Japan	1995	39.99
Betts, Dickey/Great Southern	Southern Rock Jam	CD	BMG	75517-46900-2	U.S.A.	2002	8.99
Beu Sisters	Decisions	CD	Virgin	7243-8-13305-2-4	U.S.A.	2002	7.99
Bicycle	Bicycle	CD	Capricorn	314-546-046-2	U.S.A.	1999	7.99
Bif-Naked	Another 5 Songs And A Poem	CD	Atlantic	CD-92914	U.S.A.	2000	14.99
Bif-Naked	Bif Naked	CD	Aquarius	Q2-578	Canada	1996	8.99
Bif-Naked	I Bificus	CD	Atlantic	83201-2	U.S.A.	1999	6.99
Bif-Naked	Okenspay Ordway 1	CD	Aquarius	Q2-00580	Canada	1997	14.99
Bif-Naked	Purge	CD	Atlantic	CD-83509	U.S.A.	2001	10.99
Big Audio Dynamite	No. 10, Upping St.	CD	Columbia	473697-2	U.S.A.	1987	8.99
Big Brother & The Holding Co.	Be A Brother	CD	Acadia	ACA-8026	England	2002	12.99
Big Brother & The Holding Co.	Do What You Love	CD	Mystic	MYS-CD-152	England	2000	12.99
Big Brother & The Holding Co.	How Hard It Is	CD	Acadia	ACA-8028	England	2002	12.99
Big Brother W/No Holding Co	S E Tour + 5 (Ernie Joseph/No Janis)	CD	Akarma	AK-036	Italy	1971	10.99
Big Country	BBC Live In Concert	CD	Windsong	WINCD-075	England	1995	14.99
Big Country	Best Of - Master Series	CD	Mercury	534-230-2	England	1997	8.99
Big Country	Brighton Rock	CD	Snapper	SRECD-703	England	1997	18.99
Big Country	Eclectic	CD	Transatlantic	TRA-CD-234	England	1996	11.99
Big Country	In A Big Country	CD	Karussell	550-897-2	Germany	1995	13.99
Big Country	King Biscuit Flower Hour Live	CD	King Biscuit	70710-88022-2	U.S.A.	1997	12.99
Big Country	Kings Of Emotion	2CD	Snapper	SMD-CD-101	England	1998	12.99
Big Country	Non!	CD	Castle	TRAX-1016	England	1995	5.99
Big Country	Peace In Our Time (Promo)	CD Single	Reprise	PRO-CD-3338	U.S.A.	1988	14.99
Big Country	Radio One Sessions	CD	Nighttracks	CDNT007	England	1994	9.99
Big Country	The Best Of Big Country	CD	Mercury	314-518-716-2	U.S.A.	1994	7.99
Big Country	The Collection 1982-1988	CD	Connoisseur	VSOP-CD-178	England	1993	13.99
Big Country	The Crossing + 5	CD	Mercury	314-548-117-2	U.S.A.	2002	12.99
Big Country	Through A Big Country: Greatest Hits	CD	Mercury	846-022-2	England	1990	9.99
Big Country	Under Cover	CD	Backtracks	BCTRK001	England	2000	14.99
Big Country	Without The Aid Of A Safety Net - Live	CD	Compulsion	7243-8-29848-2-5	England	1997	12.99
Big Star	#1 Record & Radio City/Third Album	2CD	Line	LICD-9.21172-S	Germany	1992	20.99
Big Star	#1 Record/Radio City	CD	Line	LICD-9.00465-0	Germany	1990	14.99

Artist	Title	Format	Label	Catalog No	Country	Released	Value
Big Star	#1 Record/Radio City	CD	Stax	FCD-606-025	U.S.A.	1992	14.99
Big Star	Big Star's Biggest	CD	Line	LICD-9.00509-0	Germany	1987	11.99
Big Star	Columbia	CD	Zoo Ent.	72445-11060-2	Canada	1993	6.99
Big Star	Live	CD	Rykodisc	RCD-10221	U.S.A.	1992	9.99
Big Star	Nobody Can Dance	CD	Norton	CED-265	U.S.A.	1999	9.99
Big Star	The Best Of Big Star	CD	Big Beat	CDWIKK-197	England	1999	12.99
Big Star	Third Album/Sisters Lovers	CD	Line	LICD-9.00492-0	Germany	1987	15.99
Big Star	Third-Sister Lovers	CD	Rykodisc	RCD-10220	U.S.A.	1992	11.99
Big Star /Alex Chilton Solo	Beale Street Green	CD	Sykodisc	SCD1022X	Germany	1997	28.99
Big Star/Chris Bell	I Am The Cosmos	CD	Rykodisc	RCD-10222	U.S.A.	1992	10.99
Bighorn	Self Titled	CD	Sony	SRCS-9464	Japan	1978	34.99
Billion Dollar Babies	Complete Battle Axe	3CD	Alchemy	PILOT-77	England	2001	55.99
Birthday Party/Nick Cave	Hits	CD	4AD	9-45087-2	U.S.A.	1992	10.99
Birthday Party/Nick Cave	Junkyard	CD	Thirsty Ear	THI-21317.2	U.S.A.	1997	9.99
Birthday Party/Nick Cave	Prayers On Fire	CD	Thirsty Ear	THI-21318.2	U.S.A.	1997	11.99
Bishop, Elvin	20th Century Masters: The Millennium	CD	Mercury	314-589-529-2	U.S.A.	2002	8.99
Bishop, Elvin	Ace In The Hole	CD	Alligator	ALCD-4833	U.S.A.	1995	7.99
Bishop, Elvin	Big Fun	CD	Alligator	ALCD-4767	U.S.A.	1988	7.99
Bishop, Elvin	Don't Let The Bossman Get You Down	CD	Alligator	ALCD-4791	U.S.A.	1991	7.99
Bishop, Elvin	Feel It !	CD	Sundazed	SC-6190	U.S.A.	2003	8.99
Bishop, Elvin	Hog Heaven	CD	Capricorn	314-538-136-2	U.S.A.	1978	8.99
Bishop, Elvin	Is You Is Or Is You Ain't My Baby	CD	Line	LICD-9.00253-0	Germany	1988	24.99
Bishop, Elvin	Juke Joint Jump	CD	Capricorn	314-558-015-2	U.S.A.	1999	14.99
Bishop, Elvin	KBFH Presents	CD	King Biscuit	88057	Canada	2001	8.99
Bishop, Elvin	Let It Flow	CD	Capricorn	314-534-622-2	U.S.A.	1998	14.99
Bishop, Elvin	Raisin' Hell	CD	Capricorn	314-558-395- 2	U.S.A.	1998	8.99
Bishop, Elvin	Rock My Soul + 1	CD	Sundazed	SC-6191	U.S.A.	2003	8.99
Bishop, Elvin	Struttin' My Stuff	CD	Capricorn	314-536-135- 2	U.S.A.	1997	24.99
Bishop, Elvin	Sure Feels Good; The Best Of	CD	Polydor	314-513-307-2	U.S.A.	1992	8.99
Bishop, Elvin	That's My Partner (Smokey Smothers)	CD	Alligator	ALCD-4874	U.S.A.	2000	8.99
Bishop, Elvin	The Best Of: Tulsa Shuffle	CD	Epic	EK-57630	U.S.A.	1994	8.99
Bishop, Elvin	The Elvin Bishop Group	CD	Sundazed	SC-6189	U.S.A.	2003	8.99
Bishop, Elvin	The Skin I'm In	CD	Alligator	ALCD-4859	U.S.A.	1998	7.99
Bishop, Stephen	Careless	CD	MCA	MCAD-10840	U.S.A.	1976	9.99
Bishop, Stephen	On And on (The Hits Of)	CD	MCA	MCAD-11035	U.S.A.	1994	9.99
Bishop, Stephen/PhilCollins	Bowling In Paris + 1	CD	Atlantic	A2-81970	U.S.A.	1989	10.99
Bjork	Joga - 3 CD/Video Box Set	3CD	One Little Indian	202TP7BOX	England	1997	36.99
Bjork	Joga/Bachelorette	CD	Polydor	POCP-7289	Japan	1997	34.99
Black Crowes	Grits 'N' Gravy (Promo Sampler)	CD	Def American	PRO-CD-7102	U.S.A.	1995	24.99
Black Earth	The Black Earth	CD	Line	CUCD-9.00989-0	Germany	1990	14.99
Black Happy	Friendly Dog Salad	CD	Capricorn	9-42045-2	U.S.A.	1995	4.99
Black Happy	Last Polka	CD	Capricorn	9-42046-2	U.S.A.	1995	4.99
Black Happy	Peg Head	CD	Capricorn	9-42044-2	U.S.A.	1995	4.99
Black 'N Blue	Anthology One: Demos	CD	Majestic Rock	766487101226	England	2003	18.99
Black 'N Blue	In Heat	CD	Majestic Rock	766482648344	England	2003	18.99
Black 'N Blue	In Heat	CD	Geffen	9-24180-2	U.S.A.	1988	26.99
Black 'N Blue	Nasty Nasty	CD	Geffen	M5-24111	U.S.A.	1986	79.99
Black 'N Blue	Nasty Nasty	CD	Majestic Rock	766482648245	England	2003	18.99
Black 'N Blue	One Night Only Live	CD	Eon	5961900013	U.S.A.	1998	13.99
Black 'N Blue	Self Titled	CD	Alfa	ALCB-3017	Japan	1984	39.99
Black 'N Blue	Self Titled	CD	Geffen	M5-24041	U.S.A.	1984	22.99
Black 'N Blue	Self Titled	CD	Majestic Rock	766482648047	England	2003	18.99
Black 'N Blue	Ultimate Collection	CD	Hip O	069493027-2	U.S.A.	2001	15.99
Black 'N Blue	Without Love	CD	Alfa	ALCB-3018	Japan	1985	63.99
Black 'N Blue	Without Love	CD	Majestic Rock	766482648146	England	2003	18.99
Black Oak Arkansas	Ain't Life Grand	CD	Wounded Bird	WOU-111	U.S.A.	2001	9.99
Black Oak Arkansas	Balls Of Fire	CD	Repertoire	REP-4551-WY	Germany	1998	13.99
Black Oak Arkansas	Black Oak Arkansas	CD	Wounded Bird	WOU-354	U.S.A.	2000	9.99

Artist	Title	Format	Label	Catalog No	Country	Released	Value
Black Oak Arkansas	Greatest Hits	CD	Purple Pyramid	CLP-0995-2	U.S.A.	2001	8.99
Black Oak Arkansas	High On The Hog	CD	Rhino	R2-72222	U.S.A.	1995	12.99
Black Oak Arkansas	Hot & Nasty - Greatest Hits	CD	Rhino	R2-71146	U.S.A.	1992	8.99
Black Oak Arkansas	If An Angel Came To See You...	CD	Wounded Bird	WOU-7008	U.S.A.	2000	9.99
Black Oak Arkansas	KBFH Presents Black Oak Arkansas	CD	King Biscuit	70710-88040-2	U.S.A.	1998	8.99
Black Oak Arkansas	Keep The Faith	CD	Wounded Bird	WOU-381	U.S.A.	2000	9.99
Black Oak Arkansas	Live ! Mutha	CD	Wounded Bird	WOU-128	U.S.A.	2001	9.99
Black Oak Arkansas	Raunch 'N' Roll Live	CD	Wounded Bird	WOU-7019	U.S.A.	2000	14.99
Black Oak Arkansas	Self Titled	CD	Repertoire	REP-4268-WY	Germany	1998	13.99
Black Oak Arkansas	Street Party	CD	Sequel	RSA-CD-829	England	1995	9.99
Black Oak Arkansas	The Wild Bunch	CD	Cleopatra	CLP0705-2	U.S.A.	1999	8.99
Black Sabbath	Black Box (8 Cd/DVD)	9 CD	Rhino	R2-73923	U.S.A.	2004	89.99
Black Sabbath	Black Mass - Germany 1970	CD	Alchemy	PILOT-49	England	1999	13.99
Black Sabbath	Born Again	CD	Vertigo	814-271-2	Germany	1987	8.99
Black Sabbath	Born Again	CD	Essential	ESMCD334	England	1996	9.99
Black Sabbath	Cross Purposes	CD	I.R.S.	0777-7-13222-2-8	U.S.A.	1994	8.99
Black Sabbath	Cross Purposes	CD	Toshiba-EMI	TOCP-8128	Japan	1994	24.99
Black Sabbath	Cross Purposes +1	CD	Toshiba-EMI	TOCP-8128	Japan	1994	39.99
Black Sabbath	Dehumanizer	CD	Reprise	9-26965-2	U.S.A.	1992	8.99
Black Sabbath	Dehumanizer	CD	I.R.S.	7-13155-2	Holland	1995	8.99
Black Sabbath	Dehumanizer + 1	CD	Toshiba-EMI	TOCP-7255	Japan	1992	24.99
Black Sabbath	Forbidden	CD	I.R.S.	7243-8-37532-2-2	U.S.A.	1995	6.99
Black Sabbath	Headless Cross	CD	I.R.S.	0777-7-13002-2-6	England	1992	9.99
Black Sabbath	Heaven And Hell	CD	Essential	ESM-CD-330	England	1999	9.99
Black Sabbath	Heaven And Hell	CD	Warner Bros.	3372-2	U.S.A.	1987	8.99
Black Sabbath	Heaven And Hell	CD	Victor Ent.	VICP-61285	Japan	2001	21.99
Black Sabbath	Live Evil	CD	Essential	ESM-CD-333	England	1996	14.99
Black Sabbath	Live Evil	2CD	Warner Bros.	9-23742-2	U.S.A.	1987	14.99
Black Sabbath	Master Of Reality	CD	Warner Bros.	2-2562	U.S.A.	1987	7.99
Black Sabbath	Master Of Reality	CD	Essential	ESMCD303	England	1996	9.99
Black Sabbath	Mob Rules	CD	Essential	ESM-CD-332	England	1996	9.99
Black Sabbath	Mob Rules	CD	Warner Bros.	3605-2	U.S.A.	1987	8.99
Black Sabbath	Never Say Die	CD	Warner Bros.	2-3186	U.S.A.	1988	8.99
Black Sabbath	Never Say Die	CD	Essential	ESMCD329	England	1996	9.99
Black Sabbath	Paranoid	CD	Essential	ESMCD302	England	1996	9.99
Black Sabbath	Paranoid	CD	Warner Bros.	2-3104	U.S.A.	1987	6.99
Black Sabbath	Past Lives	2CD	Sanctuary	06076-84561-2	England	2002	15.99
Black Sabbath	Reunion	2CD	Epic	E2K-69115	U.S.A.	1998	9.99
Black Sabbath	Sabatoge	CD	Warner Bros.	2822-2	U.S.A.	1988	8.99
Black Sabbath	Sabatoge	CD	Essential	ESMCD306	England	1996	9.99
Black Sabbath	Sabbath Bloody Sabbath	CD	Warner Bros.	2695-2	U.S.A.	1988	7.99
Black Sabbath	Sabbath Bloody Sabbath	CD	Essential	ESMCD305	England	1996	9.99
Black Sabbath	Sabbath Stones: Greatest Hits	CD	I.R.S.	7243-8-37532-2-2	U.S.A.	1996	8.99
Black Sabbath	Self Titled	CD	Essential	ESMCD301	England	1996	9.99
Black Sabbath	Self Titled	CD	Warner Bros.	1871-2	U.S.A.	1988	7.99
Black Sabbath	Seventh Star	CD	Essential	ESMCD335	England	1996	9.99
Black Sabbath	Seventh Star	CD	Vertigo	826-704-2	England	1986	8.99
Black Sabbath	Singles Box Set	6CD	Castle	CMKBX002	England	2000	19.99
Black Sabbath	Symptom Of The Universe: 1970-1978)	2CD	Rhino	R2-73772	U.S.A.	2002	17.99
Black Sabbath	Technical Ecstasy	CD	Warner Bros.	2969-2	U.S.A.	1988	6.99
Black Sabbath	Technical Ecstasy	CD	Essential	ESMCD328	England	1996	9.99
Black Sabbath	The Best Of	2CD	Raw Power	RAWDD145	England	2000	10.99
Black Sabbath	The Eternal Idol	CD	Essential	ESMCD336	England	1996	9.99
Black Sabbath	The Eternal Idol	CD	Warner Bros.	25548-2	U.S.A.	1987	8.99
Black Sabbath	TYR	CD	I.R.S.	EIRSACD1038	England	1990	8.99
Black Sabbath	Under Wheels Of Confusion Box Set	4CD	Essential	BSF-CD-419	England	1996	23.99
Black Sabbath	Volume 4	CD	Warner Bros.	2-2602	U.S.A.	1988	8.99
Black Sabbath	Volume 4	CD	Essential	ESMCD304	England	1996	10.99

Artist	Title	Format	Label	Catalog No	Country	Released	Value
Black Sabbath	We Sold Our Soul...	CD	Warner Bros.	2-2923	U.S.A.	1988	8.99
Black Sabbath	We Sold Our Soul... (Like Original LP)	2CD	Essential	ESMCD331	England	1996	10.99
Black Sabbath/Bill Ward	Ward One: Along The Way	CD	Chameleon	D2-74816	U.S.A.	1989	59.99
Black Widow	Come To The Sabbat: The Anthology	2CD	Sanctuary	CMEDD661	England	2003	14.99
Black Widow	II	CD	Castle	CLACD263	England	1993	11.99
Black Widow	III	CD	Repertoire	REP-4241-WZ	Germany	2002	11.99
Black Widow	IV	CD	Blueprint	BP4197CD	England	1999	11.99
Black Widow	Return To The Sabbath	CD	Blueprint	BP4397CD	England	1999	11.99
Black Widow	Sacrifice	CD	Repertoire	REP-4067-WZ	Germany	2002	11.99
Black Widow	Self Titled	CD	Repertoire	REP-4031-WZ	Germany	2002	11.99
Black, Frank	Black Session (Live Promo)	CD	4AD	SA3447	France	1994	13.99
Black, Frank	Cult Of Ray (W/Bonus Cd)	2CD	Dragnet	481647-9	Austria	1995	14.99
Black, Frank	Frank Black	CD	Elektra	9-61467-2	U.S.A.	1993	7.99
Black, Frank	Oddballs	CD	Failsafe	IFPI-6100	U.S.A.	2000	14.99
Black, Frank	Selections/Teenager Of Year Promo	CD	4AD	PRCD-9000-2	U.S.A.	1994	5.99
Black, Frank	Self Titled	CD	Hello Club	HEL-311	U.S.A.	1993	29.99
Black, Frank	Teenager Of The Year	CD	Elektra	61618-2	U.S.A.	1994	7.99
Black, Frank	The Cult Of Ray	CD	American	9-43070-2	U.S.A.	1995	6.99
Black, Frank	The Live EP	CD	Epic	663463-5	England	1996	8.99
Black, Frank/The Catholics	Black Letter Days	CD	Spin Art	SPART113	U.S.A.	2002	7.99
Black, Frank/The Catholics	Devil's Workshop	CD	Spin Art	SPART112	U.S.A.	2002	9.99
Black, Frank/The Catholics	Dog In The Sand	CD	What Are	IFPI-2F70	U.S.A.	2001	9.99
Black, Frank/The Catholics	Frank Black And The Catholics	CD	Spin Art	SPART67	U.S.A.	1998	6.99
Black, Frank/The Catholics	Pistolero	CD	Spin Art	SPART70	U.S.A.	1999	11.99
Black, Frank/The Catholics	Self Titled (W/Bonus Cd)	2CD	PIAS	370	England	1998	14.99
Blackfoot	After The Reign	CD	Wildcat	WLD-9206	U.S.A.	1995	13.99
Blackfoot	Flyin' High	CD	Collectables	COL-CD-6452	U.S.A.	2000	8.99
Blackfoot	Highway Song Live	CD	Wounded Bird	WOU-910	U.S.A.	2002	8.99
Blackfoot	King Biscuit Flower Hour Live	CD	King Biscuit	70710-88037-2	U.S.A.	1998	8.99
Blackfoot	Maurader	CD	Atlantic	32107-2	U.S.A.	1990	8.99
Blackfoot	Medicine Man	CD	Nalli	ANR-1991	U.S.A.	1990	19.99
Blackfoot	Rattlesnake Rock 'N' Roll: The Best Of	CD	Rhino	R2-71614	U.S.A.	1994	14.99
Blackfoot	Rick Medlocke & Blackfoot	CD	Wounded Bird	WOU-1743	U.S.A.	2003	8.99
Blackfoot	Siogo	CD	Wounded Bird	WOU-9080	U.S.A.	2002	8.99
Blackfoot	Strikes	CD	Atlantic	38112-2	U.S.A.	1990	8.99
Blackfoot	Tomcattin'	CD	Atlantic	32101-2	U.S.A.	1990	9.99
Blackfoot	Vertical Smiles	CD	Wounded Bird	WOU-218	U.S.A.	2002	9.99
Blackmore, Ritchie	Ghost Of A Rose + 1	CD	Pony Canyon	YCCY-00007	Japan	2003	13.99
Blackmore, Ritchie	Ritchie Blackmore Rock Profile (Vol 1)	CD	Connoisseur	RP-VSOP-CD-143	England	1989	22.99
Blackmore, Ritchie	Ritchie Blackmore Rock Profile (Vol 2)	CD	Connoisseur	RP-VSOP-CD-157	France	1991	22.99
Blackmore, Ritchie	Stranger In Us All +1	CD	BMG Victor	BVCP-862	Japan	1995	17.99
Blackmore, Ritchie/Night	Fires At Midnight + 1	CD	Pony Canyon	PCCY-01512	Japan	2001	14.99
Blackmore, Ritchie/Night	Home Again	CD	SPV	055-74423-CDS	Germany	2002	10.99
Blackmore, Ritchie/Night	Shadow Of The Moon	CD	Edel	0037552EDL	U.S.A.	1998	10.99
Blackmore, Ritchie/Rainbow	Stranger In Us All	CD	RCA	FUEL-BEA-51565	U.S.A.	1995	6.99
Blackstreet/Mya	Take Me There	CD Single	Interscope	IND-95619	EU	1998	1.99
Blackstreet/Mya	Take Me There (Promo)	CD Single	Interscope	INTSP-6474	U.S.A.	1998	2.99
Blades, Ruben/Lou Reed	Nothing But The Truth	CD	Elektra	9-60754-2	U.S.A.	1988	18.99
Blaine, Hal	Deuces, T's, Roadsters & Drums + 10	CD	Sundazed	SC-11101	U.S.A.	2001	7.99
Blaine, Hal	Drums! Drums! A Go Go	CD	Varese	VSD-5612	U.S.A.	1996	18.99
Blaine, Hal	Psychedelic Percussion	CD	Universal	UICY-3367	Japan	2002	29.99
Blake Babies	Slow Learner	CD	Line	UTCD-9.00861-L	Germany	1989	14.99
Blancmange	Happy Families	CD	London	810-123-2	U.S.A.	1987	106.99
Blancmange	Heaven Knows	CD	Elite	024CDP	England	1992	93.99
Blast, C. L.	I Wanna Get Down	CD	Line	TLCD-9.00407-0	Germany	1988	8.99
Blasters	American Music	CD	HighTone	HCD-8086	U.S.A.	1997	9.99
Blasters	Testament	2CD	Rhino	R2-78345	U.S.A.	2002	20.99
Blasters	The Blasters Collection	CD	Warner Bros.	9-26451-2	U.S.A.	1990	13.99

B

Artist	Title	Format	Label	Catalog No	Country	Released	Value
Blasters	Trouble Bound	CD	HighTone	HCD-8148	U.S.A.	2002	10.99
Blind Boys of Alabama	Spirit Of The Century	CD	Realworld	7243-8-50918-2-7	U.S.A.	2001	13.99
Blind Faith	Blind Faith - Deluxe Edition	2CD	Polydor	314-549-529-2	U.S.A.	2001	19.99
Blind Faith	Blind Faith (MFSL Gold Cd)	CD	Mobile Fidelity	UDCD-507	U.S.A.	1969	24.99
Blind Melon	Soup (Promo Special Edition)	CD	Capitol	7243-8-34815-2-3	U.S.A.	1995	9.99
Block, Rory	Ain't I A Woman	CD	Rounder	0-11661-3120-2-9	U.S.A.	1992	6.99
Block, Rory	Angel Of Mercy	CD	Rounder	0-11661-3126-2-3	U.S.A.	1995	6.99
Block, Rory	Best Blues & Originals	CD	Rounder	0-11661-1525-2-6	U.S.A.	1995	8.99
Block, Rory	Best Blues & Originals, Vol. 2	CD	Munich	MRMCD-43	Holland	1997	9.99
Block, Rory	Blue Horizon	CD	Rounder	0-11661-3073-2-2	U.S.A.	1989	8.99
Block, Rory	Color Me Wild	CD	Alacazam!	ALA-1003	U.S.A.	1990	6.99
Block, Rory	Confessions Of A Blues Singer	CD	Rounder	0-11661-3154-2-6	U.S.A.	1998	7.99
Block, Rory	Gone Woman Blues: C B Collection	CD	Rounder	0-11661-1575-2-1	U.S.A.	1997	14.99
Block, Rory	High Heeled Blues	CD	Rounder	0-11661-3061-2-7	U.S.A.	1989	8.99
Block, Rory	House Of Hearts	CD	Rounder	0-11661-3104-2-1	U.S.A.	1987	8.99
Block, Rory	I'm Every Woman	CD	Rounder	0-11661-3174-2-0	U.S.A.	2002	6.99
Block, Rory	I'm Every Woman (Promo)	CD	Rounder	1161-3174-2A	U.S.A.	2002	10.99
Block, Rory	I've Got A Rock in My Sock	CD	Rounder	0-11661-3097-2-2	U.S.A.	1989	7.99
Block, Rory	Last Fair Deal	CD	Telarc	CD-83593	U.S.A.	2003	9.99
Block, Rory	Mama's Blues	CD	Rounder	0-11661-3117-2-5	U.S.A.	1991	8.99
Block, Rory	Rhinestones & Steel Strings	CD	Rounder	0-11661-3085-2-7	U.S.A.	1990	8.99
Block, Rory	The Early Tapes 75/76	CD	Munich	MRMCD-1	Holland	1977	9.99
Block, Rory	Tornado	CD	Rounder	0-11661-3140-2-3	U.S.A.	1996	5.99
Block, Rory	Turning Point	CD	Munich	MRCD-145	Holland	1996	8.99
Block, Rory	When A Woman Gets The Blues	CD	Rounder	0-11661-3139-2-7	U.S.A.	1995	7.99
Block, Rory	Woman In (E) Motion (Live 1988)	CD	Tradition	TM-107	Germany	1995	14.99
Blodwyn Pig	Ahead Rings Out (Promo)	CD	BGO	BGOCD54(P)	England	1990	14.99
Blodwyn Pig	Getting To This	CD	BGO	BGOCD81	England	1990	10.99
Blodwyn Pig	Lies	CD	Angel Air	SJPCD058	EU	1993	8.99
Blodwyn Pig	Live - All Tore Down	CD	Indigo	IGOCD-2011	England	1994	15.99
Blodwyn Pig	The Modern Alchemist	CD	Indigo	IGOXCD-507	England	1997	9.99
Blonde on Blonde	Contrasts + 2	CD	Sanctuary	CMRCD257	England	2001	10.99
Blonde on Blonde	Rebirth	CD	Repertoire	REP-4239-WP	Germany	1993	9.99
Blonde on Blonde	Reflection On A Life	CD	Repertoire	REP-4308-WP	Germany	1993	9.99
Blondie	Autoamerican + 3	CD	Chrysalis	72435-33595-2-2	U.S.A.	2001	8.99
Blondie	Blonde And Beyond	CD	Chrysalis	0946-2-21990-2-7	U.S.A.	1993	6.99
Blondie	Blondie + 5	CD	Chrysalis	72435-33596-2-1	U.S.A.	2001	8.99
Blondie	Denis '88 Remix	CD Single	Chrysalis	CHS-CD-3328	England	1988	12.99
Blondie	Eat To The Beat + 4	CD	Chrysalis	72435-33597-2-0	U.S.A.	2001	8.99
Blondie	Greatest Hits	CD	Chrysalis	72435-42068-2-5	U.S.A.	2002	9.99
Blondie	Live + 1	CD	Beyond	BYADV-78066	U.S.A.	1999	7.99
Blondie	Maria	CD Single	Beyond	74321-64563-2	EU	1999	6.99
Blondie	Maria	CD Single	Beyond	74321-78040-2	U.S.A.	1998	6.99
Blondie	No Exit + 3	CD	Beyond	63985-78003-2	U.S.A.	1999	6.99
Blondie	Nothing Is Real But The Girl	CD Single	Beyond	74321-66947-2	Germany	1999	4.99
Blondie	Once More Into The Bleach	CD	Chrysalis	VK-41658	U.S.A.	1988	6.99
Blondie	Parallel Lines + 1 (DCC Gold Cd)	CD	DCC	GZS-1062	U.S.A.	1994	53.99
Blondie	Parallel Lines + 4	CD	Chrysalis	72435-33599-2-8	U.S.A.	2001	8.99
Blondie	Picture This Live	CD	Chrysalis	72438-21440-2-1	U.S.A.	1997	8.99
Blondie	Plastic Letters + 2	CD	Chrysalis	7243-8-30793-2-2	England	1994	9.99
Blondie	Plastic Letters + 4	CD	Chrysalis	72435-33598-2-9	U.S.A.	2001	8.99
Blondie	Rapture	CD Single	Chrysalis	7243-8-58277-2-3	U.S.A.	1994	7.99
Blondie	Remixed Remade Remodeled	CD	Chrysalis	F2-32748	U.S.A.	1995	6.99
Blondie	The Essestial Collection	CD	Chrysalis	7243-8-55731-2-5	Australia	1997	8.99
Blondie	The Hunter + 1	CD	Chrysalis	72435-33670-2-2	U.S.A.	2001	9.99
Blondie	The Platinum Collection	2CD	Chrysalis	F2-31101	U.S.A.	1994	15.99
Blondie	X-Offenders (Audio/Video)	2CD	Master Tone	MM5103	England	1995	24.99
Blondie/Debbie Harry	The Complete Picture	CD	Chrysalis	3218172	Australia	1991	14.99

Artist	Title	Format	Label	Catalog No	Country	Released	Value
Blood, Sweat & Tears	Blood, Sweat & Tears (MFSL Gold Cd)	CD	Mobile Fidelity	UDCD-559	U.S.A.	1968	49.99
Blood, Sweat & Tears	Blood, Sweat & Tears + 2	CD	Columbia	CK-63986	U.S.A.	2000	8.99
Blood, Sweat & Tears	Child Is Father To Man (MFSL Gold Cd)	CD	Mobile Fidelity	UDCD-742	U.S.A.	2000	39.99
Blood, Sweat & Tears	Child Is Father To Man + 6 (Sony Gold)	CD	Sony	CK-64214	U.S.A.	1994	22.99
Blood, Sweat & Tears	Live (1980)	CD	Rhino	R2-71287	U.S.A.	1994	10.99
Blood, Sweat & Tears	More Than Ever + 6	CD	JP	JPCD-2003143	Russia	1976	35.99
Blood, Sweat & Tears	New City + 4	CD	JP	JPCD-2003144	Russia	1975	44.99
Blood, Sweat & Tears	Nuclear Blues	CD	Rhino	R2-71922	U.S.A.	1995	9.99
Blood, Sweat & Tears	What Goes Up!	2CD	Columbia	C2K-64166	U.S.A.	1995	18.99
Bloodrock	2	CD	One Way	S21-18405	U.S.A.	1995	8.99
Bloodrock	2	CD	Repertoire	REP-4535-WY	Germany	2002	10.99
Bloodrock	3	CD	One Way	OW-19479	U.S.A.	1998	6.99
Bloodrock	Bloodrock 'N' Roll	CD	Capitol	7-91622-2	U.S.A.	1990	10.99
Bloodrock	Bloodrock U.S.A. + 1	CD	One Way	OW-19478	U.S.A.	1998	6.99
Bloodrock	Live	CD	One Way	OW-19480	U.S.A.	1998	8.99
Bloodrock	Self Titled	CD	Repertoire	REP-4534-WY	Germany	2002	9.99
Bloodrock	Self Titled	CD	One Way	OW-18404	U.S.A.	1995	7.99
Bloodrock	Triptych (Passage/Whirlwind T + 9)	2CD	One Way	OW-25437	U.S.A.	2000	14.99
Bloomfield, Mike	American Hero	CD	Thunderbolt	CDTB-009	England	1994	7.99
Bloomfield, Mike	Between A Hard Place...	CD	Magnum	MM-041	England	1999	7.99
Bloomfield, Mike	It's Not Killing Me	CD	Sony	SICP-8015	Japan	2002	24.99
Bloomfield, Mike	Living In The Fast Lane	CD	Line	LICD-9.00395-0	Germany	1988	7.99
Bloomfield, Mike/Al Kooper	The Live Adventures Of	2CD	Sony	SRCS-8302-3	Japan	1997	49.99
Bloomfield, Mike/M V Bunch	Casting Pearls (W/Gravenites/Dryden)	CD	Golden State	GSR9675	U.S.A.	1972	25.99
Bloomfield/Kooper	Fillmore East: Lost Concert 12/13/68	CD	Columbia	CK-85278	U.S.A.	2003	11.99
Bloomfield/Kooper/Stills	Super Session + 1 (Sony Gold Cd)	CD	Columbia	CK-64611	U.S.A.	1995	34.99
Bloomfield/Kooper/Stills	Super Session + 4	CD	Columbia	CK-63406	U.S.A.	2003	10.99
Blue Cheer	Hello Tokyo Bye Bye Osaka	CD	Captain Trip	CTCD-190	Japan	1999	14.99
Blue Cheer	Live & Unreleased	CD	Captain Trip	CTCD-023	Japan	1974	9.99
Blue Cheer	Live San Jose 1968 + More	CD	MCA	CTCD-026	Japan	1968	34.99
Blue Cheer	New! Improved!	CD	Line	LMCD-9.51077-Z	Germany	1991	11.99
Blue Cheer	New! Improved!	CD	Akarma	AK-016	U.S.A.	1999	13.99
Blue Cheer	New! Improved! + 2	CD	Repertoire	IMS-7025-WP	Germany	1994	13.99
Blue Cheer	Oh! Pleasant Hope	CD	Line	LMCD-9.51080-Z	Germany	1991	11.99
Blue Cheer	Oh! Pleasant Hope	Mini Lp	Akarma	AK-018	Italy	1999	14.99
Blue Cheer	Original Human Being	Mini Lp	Akarma	AK-150	Italy	1999	11.99
Blue Cheer	Outside Inside	CD	Line	LMCD-9.51076-X	Germany	1991	8.99
Blue Cheer	Outside Inside	CD	Repertoire	REP-7024-WP	Germany	1994	10.99
Blue Cheer	Outside Inside +1	Mini Lp	Akarma	AK-012	Italy	1999	11.99
Blue Cheer	Self Titled	CD	Line	LMCD-9.51078-Z	Germany	1991	11.99
Blue Cheer	Self Titled	Mini Lp	Akarma	AK-017	Italy	1999	13.99
Blue Cheer	The Original Huming Beeing	CD	Line	LMCD-9.51079-Z	Germany	1991	11.99
Blue Cheer	Vincebus Eruptum	CD	Line	LMCD-9.51075-Z	Germany	1991	10.99
Blue Cheer	Vincebus Eruptum	CD	Repertoire	IMS-7023-WP	Germany	1994	10.99
Blue Cheer	Vincebus Eruptum + 1	Mini Lp	Akarma	AK-011	Italy	1999	11.99
Blue Cheer/Dickie Peterson	Child of The Darkness	CD	Captain Trip	CTCD-077	Japan	1997	9.99
Blue Cheer/Dickie Peterson	Tramp	CD	Captain Trip	CTCD-162	Japan	1996	9.99
Blue Cheer/Jerre Peterson	Tumbleweed (W/Dickie Peterson)	CD	Captain Trip	CTCD-223	Japan	2000	7.99
Blue Cheer/Mr. Roger's N.	Radical Music For Docile Minds	CD	Captain Trip	CTCD-314	Japan	2000	9.99
Blue Cheer/Playground	And The Gods... (A D McDonald)	CD	Captain Trip	CTCD-310	Japan	2000	9.99
Blue Cheer/Playground	D-Evilution (A D McDonald)	CD	Captain Trip	CTCD-405	Japan	2000	9.99
Blue Cheer/Playground	Self Titled (Andrew Duck McDonald)	CD	Captain Trip	CTCD-309	Japan	2000	9.99
Blue Cheer/Randy Holden	Early Works '64-'66	CD	Captain Trip	CTCD-056	Japan	1966	16.99
Blue Cheer/Randy Holden	Guitar God	CD	Captain Trip	CTCD-028	Japan	2000	13.99
Blue Cheer/Randy Holden	Population II + 8	CD	Prog. Line	PL-523	Australia	2001	29.99
Blue Magoos	Kaleidescopic Compendium: Best Of	CD	Mercury	314-512-313-2	U.S.A.	1992	12.99
Blue Magoos	Psychedelic Lollipop	CD	Repertoire	REP-4194-WP	Germany	2002	12.99
Blue Magoos	Psychedelic Lollipop/Elec Comic Book	CD	Collectables	COL-CD-2730	U.S.A.	1999	8.99

B

Artist	Title	Format	Label	Catalog No	Country	Released	Value
Blue Murder	Nothin' But Trouble	CD	Geffen	GEFD-24419	U.S.A.	1993	11.99
Blue Murder	Screaming Blue Murder	CD	MCA Victor	MVCG-18507	Japan	1994	27.99
Blue Murder	Self Titled (W/Carmine Appice)	CD	MCA Victor	MVCG-18505	Japan	1989	16.99
Blue Murder	Self Titled (W/Carmine Appice)	CD	Geffen	9-24212-2	U.S.A.	1989	10.99
Blue Oyster Cult	A Long Day's Night	CD	Sanctuary	06076-86320-2	U.S.A.	2002	6.99
Blue Oyster Cult	Agents Of Fortune (MFSL Gold Cd)	CD	Mobile Fidelity	UDCD-697	U.S.A.	1976	29.99
Blue Oyster Cult	Agents Of Fortune + 4	CD	Columbia	CK-85479	U.S.A.	2001	8.99
Blue Oyster Cult	Agents Of Fortune + 4 (Promo)	CD	Columbia	ACK-85479	U.S.A.	2001	7.99
Blue Oyster Cult	Blue Oyster Cult + 4	CD	Columbia	CK-85482	U.S.A.	2001	10.99
Blue Oyster Cult	Blue Oyster Cult + 4 (Promo)	CD	Columbia	ACK-85482	U.S.A.	2001	7.99
Blue Oyster Cult	Career of Evil: The Metal Years	CD	Columbia	CK-44300	U.S.A.	1987	8.99
Blue Oyster Cult	Club Ninja	CD	Columbia	CK-39979	U.S.A.	1986	24.99
Blue Oyster Cult	Cult Classic	CD	Herald	HER-008-2	U.S.A.	1994	7.99
Blue Oyster Cult	Cultosaurus Erectus	CD	Columbia	CK-36550	U.S.A.	1980	9.99
Blue Oyster Cult	Don't Fear The Reaper: The Best Of	CD	Columbia	CK-65918	U.S.A.	1983	8.99
Blue Oyster Cult	Extraterrestrial Live	CD	Columbia	CK-37946	U.S.A.	1982	12.99
Blue Oyster Cult	Fire Of Unknown Origin	CD	Columbia	CK-37389	U.S.A.	1981	10.99
Blue Oyster Cult	Heaven Forbid	CD	CMC INT.	06076-86241-2	U.S.A.	1998	10.99
Blue Oyster Cult	Imaginos	CD	Columbia	CK-40618	U.S.A.	1990	17.99
Blue Oyster Cult	Live 1976	CD	Castle	CLACD-269	England	1992	14.99
Blue Oyster Cult	Live 1976	CD	Griffin	GCD-149-2	U.S.A.	1994	8.99
Blue Oyster Cult	Mirrors	CD	Columbia	CK-36009	U.S.A.	1979	11.99
Blue Oyster Cult	On Flame With Rock And Roll	CD	Sony	A-21566	U.S.A.	1990	6.99
Blue Oyster Cult	On Your Feet Or On Your Knees (Live)	CD	Columbia	CK-33371	U.S.A.	1979	16.99
Blue Oyster Cult	Secret Treaties + 4	CD	Columbia	CK-85480	U.S.A.	2001	11.99
Blue Oyster Cult	Some Enchanted Evening	CD	Columbia	CK-35563	U.S.A.	1978	9.99
Blue Oyster Cult	Spectres	CD	Columbia	CK-35019	U.S.A.	1977	12.99
Blue Oyster Cult	Super Hits	CD	Sony	SK-65638	U.S.A.	1998	9.99
Blue Oyster Cult	The Curse Of The Hidden Mirror	CD	CMC INT.	06076-86304-2	U.S.A.	2001	7.99
Blue Oyster Cult	The Essential	CD	Columbia	CK-89085	U.S.A.	2003	8.99
Blue Oyster Cult	The Revolution By Night	CD	Columbia	CK-38947	U.S.A.	1983	11.99
Blue Oyster Cult	Then And Now	CD	Sanctuary	06076-86338-2	U.S.A.	2003	7.99
Blue Oyster Cult	Tyranny And Mutation + 4	CD	Columbia	CK-85481	U.S.A.	2001	8.99
Blue Oyster Cult	Tyranny And Mutation + 4 (Promo)	CD	Columbia	AK-85481-S1	U.S.A.	2001	7.99
Blue Oyster Cult	Workshop Of The Telescopes	CD	Sony	C2K-64163	U.S.A.	1995	11.99
Blue Oyster Cult/V Artists	Bad Channels (O.S.T.)	CD	Moonstone	12936-2	U.S.A.	1992	9.99
Blue Zone UK/Lisa Stansfield	Big Thing	CD	Arista	ARCD-8522	U.S.A.	1987	13.99
Blue, David	Stories (W/Ry Cooder)	CD	Line	LECD-9.51059-0	Germany	1991	30.99
Blue-Point Underground/Neu!	In New York City (Neu!)	CD	Captain Trip	CTCD-161	Japan	2000	14.99
Blues Band	These Kind Of Blues	CD	Line	DACD-9.00160-0	Germany	1987	49.99
Blues Brothers	Best Of The Blues Brothers	CD	Atlantic	82790-2	U.S.A.	1981	9.99
Blues Brothers	Briefcase Full Of Blues	CD	Atlantic	82788-2	U.S.A.	1978	9.99
Blues Brothers	Made In America	CD	Atlantic	82789-2	U.S.A.	1980	6.99
Blues Brothers	Original Soundtrack Recording	CD	Atlantic	82787-2	U.S.A.	1980	11.99
Blues Brothers	The Blues Brothers Complete	2CD	Atlantic	7567-80840-2	Australia	1998	13.99
Blues Brothers	The Definitive Collection	CD	Atlantic	7-82428-2	U.S.A.	1992	8.99
Blues Brothers Band	Red, White, & Blues	CD	Atlantic	7-14206-2	U.S.A.	1992	8.99
Blues Brothers/Friends	Live From Chicago's House Of Blues	CD	House Of Blues	51416-1273-2	U.S.A.	1997	15.99
Blues Brothers/V. A.	Blues Brothers 2000 (O.S.T.)	CD	Universal	UD-53116	U.S.A.	1997	7.99
Blues Image	Open (W/Ride Captain Ride)	CD	Repertoire	REP-4375-WY	Germany	1970	39.99
Blues Image	Open (W/Ride Captain Ride)	CD	Sundazed	SC-6196	U.S.A.	2004	10.99
Blues 'N' Trouble	Blues Graffiti/Live And/Or Rare	2CD	Road Goes On	BNTDCD-011	England	2000	24.99
Blues 'N' Trouble	Blues'N'Trouble Live	CD	Line	INCD-9.00572-0	Germany	1988	13.99
Blues 'N' Trouble	First Trouble	CD	Line	INCD-9.00326-0	Germany	1989	19.99
Blues 'N' Trouble	First Trouble/No Minor Keys	2CD	Line	LICD-9.21211-S	Germany	1992	24.99
Blues 'N' Trouble	First Trouble/No Minor Keys + 8	2CD	Road Goes On	BNTDCD-010	England	2000	24.99
Blues 'N' Trouble	Hat Trick	CD	Line	INCD-9.00397-0	Germany	1987	13.99
Blues 'N' Trouble	Live - Bag Full Of Boogie	CD	Line	LICD-9.01287-0	Germany	1994	13.99

Artist	Title	Format	Label	Catalog No	Country	Released	Value
Blues 'N' Trouble	No Minor Keys	CD	Line	INCD-9.00227-0	Germany	1990	13.99
Blues 'N' Trouble	Poor Moon	CD	Line	LICD-9.01274-0	Germany	1992	13.99
Blues 'N' Trouble	With Friends Like These...	CD	Line	INCD-9.00901-0	Germany	1991	13.99
Blues Project	Projections	CD	Verve	827918-2	U.S.A.	1989	39.99
Blues Project	The Blues Project Anthology	2CD	Polydor	31452-9758-2	U.S.A.	1997	25.99
Blues-Traveler	1,000,000 People.. (Promo Sampler)	2CD	A&M	31454-8064-2	U.S.A.	1995	13.99
Blues-Traveler	Straight On Till Morning (DJ Int. Disc)	CD	A&M	AMSAD-00503	U.S.A.	1997	7.99
Blue-Swede	The Golden Classics Of	CD	Collectables	72438-19522-2-1	U.S.A.	1997	8.99
Blunstone, Colin	Echo Bridge	CD	Renaissance	RMED125CD	U.S.A.	1996	12.99
Blunstone, Colin	Ennismore	CD	Sony	ESCA-7877	Japan	2002	49.99
Blunstone, Colin	I Don't Believe In Miracles	CD	Epic	32192-2	Austria	1979	19.99
Blunstone, Colin	Journey	CD	Sony	EICP-7035	Japan	2002	29.99
Blunstone, Colin	Live At The BBC	CD	Windsong	WINCD-079	England	1995	20.99
Blunstone, Colin	One Year	CD	Sony	510-577-2	England	2002	8.99
Blunstone, Colin	One Year	CD	Sony	ESCA-7575	Japan	1999	49.99
Blunstone, Colin	Sings His Greatest Hits	CD	Essential	ESSCD-139	England	1991	14.99
Blunstone, Colin	The Best Of Colin Blunstone	CD	Sony	EICP-7036	Japan	2002	39.99
Blunstone, Colin	The Light Inside	CD	Blueprint	BP125CD	England	1998	16.99
Blunstone, Colin/Rod Argent	Out Of The Shadows	CD	Koch	KOC-CD-8470	U.S.A.	2003	8.99
Blunstone, Colin/Rod Argent	Out Of The Shadows + 2	CD	Victor Ent.	VICP-61637	Japan	2002	24.99
Blur	13	CD	Virgin	7243-4-99129-2-2	U.S.A.	1999	7.99
Blur	Blur (With Bonus Cd)	2CD	EMI	7243-8-21524-2-2	Australia	1997	34.99
Blur	Bustin' + Dronin' + 6 (W/Bonus Disc)	2CD	Toshiba-EMI	TOCP-50444-5	Japan	1998	14.99
Blur	M.O.R.	CD Single	Virgin	7243-8-38611-2-5	U.S.A.	1997	5.99
Blur	Music Is My Radar (Promo)	CD	Virgin	DPRO-15793	U.S.A.	2000	4.99
Blur	On Your Own/Popscene	CD Single	EMI	7243-8-85154-2-9	Australia	1997	8.99
Blur	Tender	CD Single	EMI	7243-8-86734-0-1	Australia	1999	5.99
Blur	Tender (Promo)	CD Single	Virgin	DPRO13689	U.S.A.	1999	4.99
Blur	The Best Of	2CD	Virgin	7243-8-50457-2-1	U.S.A.	2000	10.99
Blur	The Best Of... The Radio Show (DJ)	CD	Virgin	CDIN134	England	2000	9.99
Blur	The Special Collectors Edition	CD	Toshiba-EMI	TOCP-8395	Japan	1994	19.99
Blur/Pet Shop Boys	Girls & Boys	CD	SBK	7243-8-58155-2-2	U.S.A.	1994	6.99
Blurt	Pagan Strings	CD	Spalax	14988	France	1992	12.99
Blurt	Smoke Time	CD	Line	TBCD-9.00307-0	Germany	1987	8.99
Blurt	The Body That They Built	CD	Line	TBCD-9.005540-J	Germany	1988	8.99
Boals, Mark	Ignition	CD	Victor Ent.	VICP-60351	Japan	1998	24.99
Bob And Tom	Moterheads	CD	Big Mouth	DIDX-01383	U.S.A.	1992	86.99
Bobs	Too Many Santas!	CD	Rounder	CD-9060	U.S.A.	1996	10.99
Boettcher, Curt	California Music	CD	Poptones	MC5037CD	England	2001	24.99
Boettcher, Curt	Misty Mirage + 5	CD	Poptones	MC5007CD	England	2000	24.99
Boettcher, Curt	There's An Innocent Face	CD	Sundazed	SC-6184	U.S.A.	2002	8.99
Boettcher, Curt/Millennium	Begin	CD	Sony	SRCS-6107	Japan	1991	22.99
Bofill, Angela	Teaser	CD	BMG	BVCM-35041	Japan	1983	21.99
Bolan, Marc	Begining Of Doves (Hard On Love)	CD	Castle	CMRCD-491	England	2002	13.99
Bolan, Marc	Cat Black + 1	CD	Cleopatra	CLP-9803-2	U.S.A.	1997	7.99
Bolan, Marc	Misty Mist	CD	Receiver	MER003	England	1992	8.99
Bolan, Marc/Tribute	Great Jewish Music (W/S Lennon)	CD	Tzadik	TZ-7126	U.S.A.	2000	7.99
Bolin, Tommy	A Retrospective (Promo)	CD	Geffen	PRO-CD-3657	U.S.A.	1989	8.99
Bolin, Tommy	From The Archives Vol. 1	CD	Rhino	R2-72194	U.S.A.	1996	9.99
Bolin, Tommy	Private Eyes	CD	Columbia	CK-34329	U.S.A.	1976	12.99
Bolin, Tommy	Teaser	CD	Epic	468016-2	Germany	1975	16.99
Bon Jovi	7 Series Sampler: One Wild Night	CD	Island	000049902	U.S.A.	2003	11.99
Bon Jovi	7800 Degrees Fahrenheit	CD	Mercury	7314-538-088-2	U.S.A.	1999	10.99
Bon Jovi	7800 Degrees Fahrenheit + 6 Live	2CD	PolyGram	PHCR-90013/14	Japan	1998	49.99
Bon Jovi	Bon Jovi In Brazil Edicao Limitada	CD	PolyGram	842-172-2	Brazil	1989	76.99
Bon Jovi	Bounce	CD	Island	440-063-055-2	U.S.A.	2002	11.99
Bon Jovi	Cross Road	CD	Mercury	522-936-2	U.S.A.	1995	10.99
Bon Jovi	Cross Road + 6 (Live/Outtakes)	2CD	PolyGram	PHCR-90021/22	Japan	1998	49.99

B

Artist	Title	Format	Label	Catalog No	Country	Released	Value
Bon Jovi	Crush	CD	Island	314-542-474-2	U.S.A.	2000	9.99
Bon Jovi	Crush + 3	CD	PolyGram	548-172-2	England	2000	9.99
Bon Jovi	Crush + Live From Osaka	2CD	Universal	UICM-1005/6	Japan	2000	34.99
Bon Jovi	Exclusive Lmtd Edition Sampler (DJ)	CD	Mercury	BJLTDCD1	Germany	2001	14.99
Bon Jovi	Great Box Set	CD	Nippon Phonogram	PHCR-3007-3010	Japan	1991	86.99
Bon Jovi	Keep The Faith	CD	Mercury	7314-538-091-2	U.S.A.	1999	6.99
Bon Jovi	Keep The Faith (Spanish Version)	CD	Mercury	314-514-694-2	U.S.A.	1993	13.99
Bon Jovi	Keep The Faith + 2 (7 Tracks Live Cd)	2CD	PolyGram	PHCR-16003/4	Japan	1992	29.99
Bon Jovi	Keep The Faith + 9 Live	2CD	PolyGram	PHCR-90019/20	Japan	1998	49.99
Bon Jovi	Live	CD	Mercury	314-518-250-2	Australia	1987	19.99
Bon Jovi	Most Requested (Promo Sampler)	CD	Mercury	SACD-548	U.S.A.	1992	34.99
Bon Jovi	New Jersey	CD	Mercury	7314-530-090-2	U.S.A.	1999	9.99
Bon Jovi	New Jersey + 7 Live/Outtakes	2CD	PolyGram	PHCR-90017/18	Japan	1998	49.99
Bon Jovi	One Wild Night Live 1985-2001	CD	Island	314-548-684-2	U.S.A.	2001	7.99
Bon Jovi	Self Titled	CD	Mercury	7314-538-087-2	U.S.A.	1999	12.99
Bon Jovi	Self Titled (Target Cd/Demos/Live)	CD	Island	440-063-541-2	U.S.A.	2003	12.99
Bon Jovi	Self Titled + 7 Live	2CD	PolyGram	PHCR-90011/12	Japan	1998	49.99
Bon Jovi	Slippery When Wet	CD	Mercury	32PD-148	Japan	1986	44.99
Bon Jovi	Slippery When Wet	CD	Mercury	7314-538-089-2	U.S.A.	1999	12.99
Bon Jovi	Slippery When Wet (Banned Cover)	CD	Mercury	PHCR-4269	Japan	1986	30.99
Bon Jovi	Slippery When Wet + 7 Live/Outtakes	2CD	PolyGram	PHCR-90015/16	Japan	1998	49.99
Bon Jovi	The Distance	CD Single	Universal	UICL-5013	Japan	2002	12.99
Bon Jovi	These Days + 1	CD	Mercury	7314-538-036-2	U.S.A.	1998	11.99
Bon Jovi	These Days + 8 (Live/Outtakes)	2CD	PolyGram	PHCR-90023/24	Japan	1998	49.99
Bon Jovi	This Feels Right	CD	Island	000154002	U.S.A.	2003	8.99
Bon Jovi	Undiscovered Soul	CD	Mercury	314-536-972-2	U.S.A.	1998	11.99
Bon Jovi/Amp Kit/Pick/Video	Box 2 - Amplifier Version (W/Booklet)	5CD	Nippon Phonogram	PHCB-51	Japan	1996	89.99
Bon Jovi/Richie Sambora	Stranger In This Town	CD	PolyGram	314-510-652-2	U.S.A.	1991	11.99
Bon Jovi/Richie Sambora	Undiscovered Soul + 7 1998 Tour Ed.	2CD	PolyGram	PHCR-16029/30	Japan	1998	49.99
Bond, Graham	Holy Magick/We Put Our Magick...	CD	BGO	BGOCD483	England	2000	12.99
Bond, Graham/Jack Bruce	The Sound of 65/There's A.. (G Baker)	CD	BGO	BGOCD500	England	1999	12.99
Bonds, Gary 'U S'	Greatest Hits	CD	Line	BLCD-9.01037-2	Germany	1991	13.99
Bonds, Gary 'U S'	The Best Of (Prod/Bruce Springsteen)	CD	EMI	7243-8-37812-2-5	U.S.A.	1996	7.99
Bonds, Gary 'U S'	The School Of Rock 'N' Roll: Best Of	CD	Rhino	R2-70971	U.S.A.	1990	8.99
Bonds, Gary 'U S'	Twist Up Calypso	CD	Line	BLCD-9.00723-L	Germany	1989	13.99
Bonds, Gary 'US'	Quarter To Three	CD	Line	BLCD-9.00719-L	Germany	1989	13.99
Bonds, Gary 'US'	The Collection	CD	Line	IMCD-9.00715-0	Germany	1989	13.99
Bongos	Drums Along The Hudson	CD	Line	LICD-9.00770-0	Germany	1991	15.99
Bonzo-Dog-Band	Complete BBC Recordings	CD	Strange Fruit	SFRSCD108	England	2002	14.99
Bonzo-Dog-Band	Cornology (All 5 Lp's Plus Rarities)	3CD	EMI	0777-7-99596-2-4	England	1992	34.99
Bonzo-Dog-Band	Legs Larry Smith (Sings Mel Brooks)	CD Single	Sanctuary	CMZX236	England	2001	12.99
Bonzo-Dog-Band	Legs Larry Smith (Sings Mel Brooks)	CD Single	MSI	MSIF-3860	Japan	2001	15.99
Bonzo-Dog-Band	New Tricks	CD	Castle	CMRCD-199	England	2001	11.99
Bonzo-Dog-Band	Roger Ruskin Spear (Elec Shock + 5)	CD	DJC	DJC005	England	1998	29.99
Bonzo-Dog-Band	The History Of The Bonzos	2CD	BGO	BGOCD376	England	1997	30.99
Bonzo-Dog-Band	Viv Stanshell (Sir Henry/Ndidi's Kraal)	CD	Demon	VERB-CD-1	England	1992	14.99
Bonzo-Dog-Band	Viv Stanshell (Sir Henry/Rawlinson)	CD	Charisma	7243-8-40343-2-0	England	1995	14.99
Bonzo-Dog-Band	Viv Stanshell (Teddy Boys Don't Knit)	CD	Virgin	CASCD-1153	England	1991	14.99
Boomtown Rats/Bob Geldof	Fine Art Of Surfacing	CD	Columbia	CK-36248	U.S.A.	1990	54.99
Boomtown Rats/Bob Geldof	Mondo Bongo	CD	Columbia	CK-37062	U.S.A.	1981	44.99
Boomtown Rats/Bob Geldof	Tonic For The Troops	CD	Columbia	CK-35750	U.S.A.	1989	14.99
Boomtown Rats/Bob Geldof	V Deep	CD	Mercury	800-042-2	Germany	1982	59.99
Boone, Pat	No More Mr. Nice Guy	CD	Hip-O	HIPD-40025	U.S.A.	1997	8.99
Booth And the Bad Angel	Booth And The Bad Angel	CD	Mercury	314-526-852-2	U.S.A.	1996	14.99
Booth And the Bad Angel	Fall in Love With Me (Cd 1)	CD Single	Mercury	566-123-2	England	1998	8.99
Booth And the Bad Angel	Fall in Love With Me (Cd 2)	CD Single	Mercury	566-125-2	EEn	1998	8.99
Booth And the Bad Angel	I Believe (Cd1)	CD Single	Mercury	578-045-2	England	1996	8.99
Booth And the Bad Angel	I Believe (Cd2)	CD Single	Mercury	578-237-2	England	1996	8.99

Artist	Title	Format	Label	Catalog No	Country	Released	Value
Boston	Boston Self Titled (Sony Gold Cd)	CD	Columbia	EK-52856	U.S.A.	1993	34.99
Boston	Boston: Greatest Hits	CD	Epic	EK-67622	U.S.A.	1997	10.99
Boston	Corporate America	CD	Artemis	751142-2	U.S.A.	2002	13.99
Boston	Don't Look Back (Sony Gold Cd)	CD	Sony	EK-66404	U.S.A.	1978	39.99
Boston	Higher Power	CD Single	Epic	ESK-8070	U.S.A.	1997	7.99
Boston	I Need Your Love	CD Single	MCA	MCSTD-1983	England	1994	8.99
Boston	Star-Spangled Banner/4th July Reprise (	CD Single	Epic	5163-1	U.S.A.	1997	18.99
Boston	Third Stage (MFSL Gold Cd)	CD	Mobile Fidelity	UDCD-582	U.S.A.	1986	36.99
Boston	Walk On	CD	MCA	MCAD-10973	U.S.A.	1994	6.99
Boston	What's Your Name	CD Single	MCA	MCA5P-3127	U.S.A.	1994	4.99
Boston/Barry Goudreau	Barry Goudreau	CD	Razor & Tie	RE-2104-2	U.S.A.	1996	16.99
Boston/Orion The Hunter	Orion The Hunter	CD	Razor & Tie	RE-2073	U.S.A.	1984	19.99
Boston-Pops/Arthur Fiedler	An American Salute	CD	BMG	6806-2-RG	U.S.A.	1991	10.99
Boswell, Simon/Various Artists	Demons 2 (O.S.T.)	CD	Apollon	CATALOG	Japan	1987	103.99
Bottle Rockets	Nancy Sinatra (Promo)	CD Single	Mercury	9049-2A	U.S.A.	1999	8.99
Bottle Rockets	Self Titled	CD	East Side Digital	80772	U.S.A.	1992	19.99
Boublil, Alan/Schonberg, C M	Les Miserables (Japanese Cast)	2CD	Toshiba-EMI	TOCT-8377/78	Japan	1994	74.99
Bow Wow Wow	Aphrodisiac (Best Of Bow Wow Wow)	CD	Camden	74321-41967-2	EC	1996	9.99
Bow Wow Wow	Girl Bites Dog - Your Compact Disc Pet	CD	EMI	7243-8-27223-2-8	U.S.A.	1993	7.99
Bow Wow Wow	I Want Candy	CD	RCA	07863-54375-2	U.S.A.	1993	10.99
Bow Wow Wow	Live In Japan	CD	Receiver	RRCD-233	England	1997	8.99
Bow Wow Wow	See Jungle (Some Songs 12" Versions)	CD	Great Expectations	PIPCD-013	France	1982	18.95
Bow Wow Wow	See Jungle! See Jungle!	CD	One Way	OW-34502	U.S.A.	1981	14.99
Bow Wow Wow	The Best Of Bow Wow Wow	CD	RCA	BG2-66943	U.S.A.	1996	12.99
Bow Wow Wow	When The Going Gets Tough...	CD	One Way	OW-34503	U.S.A.	1983	8.99
Bow Wow Wow	Wild In The USA	CD	Cleopatra	CLP-0424-2	U.S.A.	1999	8.99
Bowie, David	1. Outside Version 2 + 6	2CD	Arista	74321-39600-2	Australia	1996	24.99
Bowie, David	1.Outside (Cardboard Version)	CD	Virgin	7243-8-40711-2-7	U.S.A.	1995	14.99
Bowie, David	17 Album Track Sampler (Promo)	CD	EMI	CDLRL015	England	1999	29.99
Bowie, David	1966	CD	PRT	PYC-6001	England	1987	11.99
Bowie, David	Aladdin Sane	CD	RCA	PD-83890	Germany	1985	25.99
Bowie, David	Aladdin Sane	CD	RCA	PCD1-4852	U.S.A.	1985	28.99
Bowie, David	Aladdin Sane	CD	Rykodisc	RCD-10135	U.S.A.	1990	14.99
Bowie, David	Aladdin Sane (30th Ann Ltd Edition)	2CD	EMI	7243-583012-2-9	U.S.A.	2003	17.99
Bowie, David	Aladdin Sane (Enhanced)	CD	Virgin	7243-521902-0-1	U.S.A.	1999	13.99
Bowie, David	All Saints (Coll.Instrumentals 1977-1999)	CD	Virgin	7243-5-33045-2-2	U.S.A.	1999	8.99
Bowie, David	All Saints (Promo)	2CD	Disque Americ	045H2-910	Canada	1993	215.99
Bowie, David	Bang Bang (Live Version) (Promo)	CD Single	Virgin	DPRO-31593	U.S.A.	1987	74.99
Bowie, David	Best Of + 9 (W/Bonus DVD)	2CD	Virgin	72435-95692-0-8	U.S.A.	2004	15.99
Bowie, David	Best Of Bowie	2CD	EMI	7243-5-41930-2-6	U.S.A.	2002	20.99
Bowie, David	Best of David Bowie 1969-1974	CD	Virgin	7243-8-21849-2-8	U.S.A.	1997	14.99
Bowie, David	Best Of David Bowie 1969-1974	CD	EMI	72438-21320-2-8	U.S.A.	1997	11.99
Bowie, David	Black Tie Premiere Interview Ed	2CD	Savage	SADJ-50043-2	U.S.A.	1993	17.99
Bowie, David	Black Tie White Noise (Remixes)	CD Single	Savage	74785-50045-2	U.S.A.	1993	8.99
Bowie, David	Black Tie White Noise + 2	CD	Savage	74785-50212-2	U.S.A.	1993	8.99
Bowie, David	Black Tie White Noise + 3 (Ltd Box)	CD	BMG	BVCA-612	Japan	1993	34.99
Bowie, David	Black Tie, White N (Bonus CD/DVD)	3CD	Virgin	7243-5-90967-0-4	U.S.A.	2003	19.99
Bowell, David	Bowie At Beeb (W/Live Bonus Cd)	3CD	EMI	7087-6-15778-2-2	U.S.A.	2000	22.99
Bowie, David	Bowie At The Beeb (DJ Sampler Box)	CD	EMI Records	BEEBPRO-6872	England	2000	28.99
Bowie, David	Bowie/Eno (Promo Sampler)	CD	Rykodisc	VRCD-0142	U.S.A.	1991	12.99
Bowie, David	Changesbowie (Rykodisc Gold Cd)	CD	Rykodisc	RCD-80171	U.S.A.	1990	43.99
Bowie, David	Changesonebowie	CD	RCA	PD-81732	Germany	1985	36.99
Bowie, David	Changesonebowie	CD	RCA	PCD1-1732	U.S.A.	1985	24.99
Bowie, David	Changestwobowie	CD	RCA	PCD1-4202	U.S.A.	1985	25.99
Bowie, David	Changestwobowie	CD	RCA	PD84202	Germany	1985	52.99
Bowie, David	Christiane F.	CD	Virgin	7243-5-33093-2-9	U.S.A.	2001	15.99
Bowie, David	Club Bowie (Remixes CD)	CD	Virgin	7243-5-96758-2-4	England	2003	14.99
Bowie, David	Club Bowie: Rare/Unrel. 12" Mixes	CD	EMI	VTCD591	England	2003	14.99

B

Artist	Title	Format	Label	Catalog No	Country	Released	Value
Bowie, David	Cool World (3")	CD Single	Warner Bros.	WPDP-6306	Japan	1992	18.99
Bowie, David	David Live + 3	2CD	Rykodisc	RCD-10138/39	U.S.A.	1990	49.99
Bowie, David	Dead Man Walking	CD Single	RCA	74321-47585-2	EU	1997	7.99
Bowie, David	Dead Man Walking (5 Remixes)	CD Single	BMG	74321-47614-2	Australia	1997	18.99
Bowie, David	Dead Man Walking (CD 1)	CD Single	Arista	74321-47480-2	EU	1997	8.99
Bowie, David	Dead Man Walking (Limited Edition)	CD Single	RCA	74321-47584-2	England	1997	12.99
Bowie, David	Dead Man Walking (Promo)	CD Single	Virgin	DPRO-11249	U.S.A.	1997	6.99
Bowie, David	Diamond Dogs	CD	RCA	PD-83889	Germany	1985	42.99
Bowie, David	Diamond Dogs	CD	RCA	PCD1-0576	U.S.A.	1985	26.99
Bowie, David	Diamond Dogs (Enhanced)	CD	Virgin	7243-521904-0-9	U.S.A.	1999	8.99
Bowie, David	Diamond Dogs + 2	CD	Rykodisc	RCD-10137	U.S.A.	1990	15.99
Bowie, David	Diamond Dogs + 8 Limited Ed.	2CD	Virgin	7243-5-77857-2-3	Holland	2004	15.99
Bowie, David	Early On (1964-1966) + 3	CD	Rhino	R2-70526	U.S.A.	1991	9.99
Bowie, David	Earthling	CD	Virgin	7243-8-42627-2-3	U.S.A.	1997	8.99
Bowie, David	Earthling In The City (Promo)	CD	AT&T	81165-01	U.S.A.	1997	8.99
Bowie, David	Everyone Says Hi	CD Single	Sony	6730761-2	Austria	2002	9.99
Bowie, David	Everyone Says Hi (CD 1)	CD Single	Columbia	673134-2	England	2002	4.99
Bowie, David	Everyone Says Hi (CD 2)	CD Single	Columbia	673134-5	England	2002	4.99
Bowie, David	Everyone Says Hi (CD 3)	CD Single	Columbia	673134-3	England	2002	4.99
Bowie, David	Everyone Says Hi (Promo)	CD Single	Sony	SAMPCS-0120001	Spain	2002	6.99
Bowie, David	Fame 90	CD Single	Rykodisc	RCD5-1018	U.S.A.	1990	8.99
Bowie, David	Fame And Fashion	CD	RCA	PD-84919	Germany	1985	28.99
Bowie, David	Fame And Fashion (Best Of RCA)	CD	RCA	PCD1-4919	U.S.A.	1984	16.99
Bowie, David	Golden Years	CD	RCA	PD84792	Germany	1985	55.99
Bowie, David	Golden Years	CD	RCA	PCD1-4792	U.S.A.	1985	28.99
Bowie, David	Hallo Spaceboy	CD Single	RCA	74321-35384-2	Germany	1996	6.99
Bowie, David	Heart's Filthy Lesson (Shaped)	CD Single	Arista	74321-31807-2	Germany	1995	29.99
Bowie, David	Heathen (With Bonus Cd)	CD	Columbia	CK-86656	U.S.A.	2002	11.99
Bowie, David	Heroes	CD	RCA	PD-83867	Germany	1985	36.99
Bowie, David	Heroes	CD	RCA	PCD1-2522	U.S.A.	1985	36.99
Bowie, David	Heroes (Enhanced)	CD	Virgin	7243-521908-0-5	U.S.A.	1999	9.99
Bowie, David	Heroes + 2 (Rykodisc Gold Cd)	CD	Rykodisc	RCD-80143	U.S.A.	1991	71.99
Bowie, David	High Tech Soul (Promo Sampler)	CD	Rykodisc	RCD-PRO-9016	U.S.A.	1990	24.99
Bowie, David	'Hours...'	CD	Victor Ent.	VJCP-68160	Japan	1999	29.99
Bowie, David	Hours... & Brilliant Minutes (Promo)	CD	EMI	CDPRO-1920	Canada	1999	49.99
Bowie, David	Hunky Dory	CD	RCA	PD84623	Germany	1985	25.99
Bowie, David	Hunky Dory	CD	RCA	PCD1-4623	U.S.A.	1985	29.99
Bowie, David	Hunky Dory (Enhanced)	CD	Virgin	7243-521899-0-8	U.S.A.	1999	15.99
Bowie, David	Hunky Dory + 4 (Rykodisc Gold Cd)	CD	Rykodisc	RCD-80133	U.S.A.	1990	33.99
Bowie, David	I Can't Read	CD Single	Velvel	VEL-CD4504	U.S.A.	1997	8.99
Bowie, David	I Dig Everything: The 1966 Pye Singles	3CD	Castle	ESBCD-765	England	1999	14.99
Bowie, David	I'm Afraid Of Americans	CD Single	Virgin	7243-8-38618-2-8	U.S.A.	1997	16.99
Bowie, David	I'm Afraid Of Americans	CD Single	Virgin	DPRO-12749	U.S.A.	1997	13.99
Bowie, David	Interview Picture Disc	CD	Baktabak	CBAK-4040	England	1990	9.99
Bowie, David	I've Been Waiting For You	CD Single	Sony	38K-00369	Canada	2002	9.99
Bowie, David	Jump Interactive Cd-Rom	Cd-Rom	Ion	76986-40004-2-8	U.S.A.	1994	23.99
Bowie, David	Jump They Say (Promo)	CD Single	Savage	SADJ-50039-2	U.S.A.	1993	7.99
Bowie, David	Jump They Say (Remixes)	CD Single	Savage	74785-50034-2	U.S.A.	1993	4.99
Bowie, David	KBFH April 10-16, 1989	CD	DIR Network	4TRO100B	U.S.A.	1989	69.99
Bowie, David	KBFH April 17-23, 1989	CD	DIR Network	4WL0200A	U.S.A.	1989	69.99
Bowie, David	Let's Dance (Enhanced)	CD	Virgin	7243-521896-0-1	U.S.A.	1999	12.99
Bowie, David	Let's Dance + 1	CD	Virgin	7243-8-40982-2-3	U.S.A.	1983	7.99
Bowie, David	Little Wonder	CD Single	Virgin	74321-45207-2	EU	1997	6.99
Bowie, David	Little Wonder	CD Single	Virgin	7243-838585-2-1	U.S.A.	1997	8.99
Bowie, David	Little Wonder	CD Single	Arista	74321-44777-2	EC	1997	8.99
Bowie, David	Little Wonder (Ltd. Edition)	CD Single	RCA	74321-45208-2	England	1997	8.99
Bowie, David	Little Wonder (Promo)	CD Single	RCA	LW-02	England	1997	10.99
Bowie, David	Little Wonder (Promo)	CD Single	RCA	LW02	England	1997	10.99

B

Artist	Title	Format	Label	Catalog No	Country	Released	Value
Bowie, David	Liveandwell.Com	2CD	Risky Folio	CD#1/#2/UL0001	U.S.A.	2000	53.99
Bowie, David	Lodger	CD	RCA	PD-84234	U.S.A.	1985	31.99
Bowie, David	Lodger	CD	RCA	PCD1-3254	U.S.A.	1985	17.99
Bowie, David	Lodger (Enhanced)	CD	Virgin	7243-521909-0-4	U.S.A.	1999	14.99
Bowie, David	Lodger + 2	CD	Rykodisc	RCD-10146	U.S.A.	1991	15.99
Bowie, David	Love You Till Tuesday	CD	Pickwick	PWKS-4131-P	England	1992	64.99
Bowie, David	Love You Till Tuesday (Promo)	CD	Deram	RCD-017-2	Spain	1984	39.99
Bowie, David	Low	CD	RCA	PD-83856	Germany	1985	22.99
Bowie, David	Low	CD	RCA	PCD1-2030	U.S.A.	1985	22.99
Bowie, David	Low (Enhanced)	CD	Virgin	7243-521907-0-6	U.S.A.	1999	14.99
Bowie, David	Low + 3 (Rykodisc Gold Cd)	CD	Rykodisc	RCD-80142	U.S.A.	1991	39.99
Bowie, David	Man Who Sold The World	CD	RCA	PCD1-4816	U.S.A.	1985	34.99
Bowie, David	Man Who Sold The World	CD	RCA	PD-84664	Germany	1985	34.99
Bowie, David	Miracle Goodnight	CD Single	Arista	74321-16226-2	England	1993	17.99
Bowie, David	Miracle Goodnight (Promo)	CD Single	Savage	SADJ-50048-2	U.S.A.	1993	14.99
Bowie, David	Never Let Me Down (Enhanced)	CD	Virgin	7243-521894-0-3	U.S.A.	1999	12.99
Bowie, David	Never Let Me Down (Remixes)	CD Single	EMI	DPRO-31352	England	1987	34.99
Bowie, David	Never Let Me Down + 3	CD	Virgin	7243-8-40986-2-9	U.S.A.	1987	8.99
Bowie, David	Outside + 1	CD	BMG	BVCA-679	Japan	1995	13.99
Bowie, David	Peter And The Wolf (Bowie Narrates)	CD	RCA	19026-60878-2	U.S.A.	1992	29.99
Bowie, David	Pin Ups	CD	RCA	PD-84653	Germany	1985	29.99
Bowie, David	Pin Ups	CD	RCA	PCD1-0291	U.S.A.	1985	32.99
Bowie, David	Pin Ups (Enhanced)	CD	Virgin	7243-521903-0-0	U.S.A.	1999	8.99
Bowie, David	Pin-Ups + 2	CD	Rykodisc	RCD-10136	U.S.A.	1990	14.99
Bowie, David	Rarest One Bowie + 6 (S Monica '72)	CD	Mecca	BLCY-1019	Japan	2001	14.99
Bowie, David	Reality (W/Bonus CD)	2CD	Columbia	CK-90660	U.S.A.	2003	34.99
Bowie, David	Rise And Fall Of..	CD	RCA	PCD1-4702	U.S.A.	1985	34.99
Bowie, David	Rise And Fall Of...	CD	RCA	R32P-1037	Japan	1985	32.99
Bowie, David	Rise And Fall...	CD	RCA	PD-84702	Germany	1985	34.99
Bowie, David	Santa Monica '72	CD	Golden Years	GY002	England	1994	54.99
Bowie, David	Scary Monsters	CD	RCA	PD-83647	Germany	1985	24.99
Bowie, David	Scary Monsters	CD	RCA	PCD1-3647	U.S.A.	1985	39.99
Bowie, David	Scary Monsters (& Super Creeps) (Enha	CD	Virgin	7243-521895-0-2	U.S.A.	1999	8.99
Bowie, David	Scary Monsters + 4	CD	Rykodisc	RCD-20147	U.S.A.	1992	14.99
Bowie, David	Selections Changes Bowie (Promo)	CD	EMI	BOW-90	England	1990	7.99
Bowie, David	Seven #1	CD Single	Virgin	7243-8-96928-2-2	England	2000	16.99
Bowie, David	Seven #2	CD Single	Virgin	7243-8-96928-0-8	England	2000	16.99
Bowie, David	Seven #3	CD Single	Virgin	7243-8-96929-2-1	England	2000	13.99
Bowie, David	Seven (Promo)	CD Single	Virgin	SEVENDPRO1	EU	2000	8.99
Bowie, David	Seven (Promo)	CD Single	Virgin	03098	England	2000	14.99
Bowie, David	Slow Burn	CD Single	Columbia	672744-2	Austria	2002	9.99
Bowie, David	Slowburn (Promo)	CD Single	Sony	SDCI-80035	Japan	2002	53.99
Bowie, David	Sound + Vision	CD	Rykodisc	RCD-PRO-0120-2	U.S.A.	1989	10.99
Bowie, David	Sound + Vision Box Set	4CD	Rykodisc	RCD90120/21/22	U.S.A.	1991	79.99
Bowie, David	Sound + Vision Catalogue Sampler #1	CD	Rykodisc	RCD-PRO-131-3	U.S.A.	1990	11.99
Bowie, David	Space Oddity	CD	RCA	PCD1-4813	U.S.A.	1985	25.99
Bowie, David	Space Oddity	CD	RCA	PD-84813	Germany	1985	36.99
Bowie, David	Space Oddity (Enhanced)	CD	Virgin	7243-521898-0-9	U.S.A.	1999	14.99
Bowie, David	Space Oddity + 3	CD	Rykodisc	RCD-10131	U.S.A.	1990	13.99
Bowie, David	Stage	2CD	RCA	PD89002(2)	Germany	1985	106.99
Bowie, David	Stage + 1	2CD	Rykodisc	RCD-10144/45	U.S.A.	1991	44.99
Bowie, David	Station To Station	CD	RCA	PD-81327	Germany	1985	28.99
Bowie, David	Station To Station	CD	RCA	PCD1-1327	U.S.A.	1985	25.99
Bowie, David	Station To Station (Enhanced)	CD	Virgin	7243-521906-0-7	U.S.A.	1999	16.99
Bowie, David	Station To Station + 2 (Rykodisc Gold)	CD	Rykodisc	RCD-80141	U.S.A.	1991	46.99
Bowie, David	Strangers When We Meet	CD Single	Virgin	7243-8-38530-2-1	U.S.A.	1995	7.99
Bowie, David	Strangers When We Meet (Promo)	CD Single	Virgin	DPRO-11062	U.S.A.	1995	4.99
Bowie, David	Survive (CD 1)	CD Single	Virgin	7243-8-96486-0-7	England	2000	5.99

B

Artist	Title	Format	Label	Catalog No	Country	Released	Value
Bowie, David	Survive (CD 2)	CD Single	Virgin	7243-8-96487-0-6	England	2000	6.99
Bowie, David	Telling Lies	CD Single	RCA	74321-39741-2	England	1996	7.99
Bowie, David	The Best Of David Bowie 1974-1979	CD	Virgin	7243-4-94300-0-6	U.S.A.	1998	14.99
Bowie, David	The Buddha Of Suburbia	CD	Virgin	7243-8-40988-2-7	U.S.A.	1993	21.99
Bowie, David	The Buddha Of Suburbia (Holographic)	CD Single	Arista	74321-18168-2	England	1993	11.99
Bowie, David	The Deram Anthology 1966-1968	CD	Deram	12284-1784-2	U.S.A.	1997	8.99
Bowie, David	The Heart's Filthy Lesson	CD Single	Virgin	7243-8-38518-2-9	U.S.A.	1995	14.99
Bowie, David	The Man Who Sold The World (Enhance	CD	Virgin	7243-521901-0-2	U.S.A.	1999	10.99
Bowie, David	The Man Who... + 4 (Gold)	CD	Rykodisc	RCD-80132	U.S.A.	1990	26.99
Bowie, David	The Outside (Promo Sampler)	CD	Virgin	DPRO-11008	U.S.A.	1995	13.99
Bowie, David	The Pretty Things Are Going To Hell	CD Single	Virgin	7243-8-96293-2-3	Australia	1999	11.99
Bowie, David	The Rise/Fall Ziggy Stardust + 5 (Gold)	CD	Rykodisc	RCD-80134	U.S.A.	1990	28.99
Bowie, David	The Singles 1969 - 1993 (Bonus Disc)	3CD	Rykodisc	RCD-10218/19+1	U.S.A.	1993	18.99
Bowie, David	Thursday's Child	CD Single	Virgin	VSCDX-1753	EU	1999	7.99
Bowie, David	Thursday's Child	CD Single	Virgin	7243-8-96265-2-0	England	1999	7.99
Bowie, David	Thursday's Child (Promo)	CD Single	Virgin	VSCDJ1753	England	1999	7.99
Bowie, David	Tin Machine (Enhanced)	CD	Virgin	7243-521910-0-0	U.S.A.	1999	6.99
Bowie, David	Tonight (Enhanced)	CD	Virgin	7243-521897-0-0	U.S.A.	1999	15.99
Bowie, David	Tonight + 3	CD	Virgin	7243-8-40983-2-2	U.S.A.	1984	18.99
Bowie, David	Westwood 1 # 97-26, 6 - 23, 1997	2CD	Westwood 1	CORPEO2XC	U.S.A.	1997	99.99
Bowie, David	Westwood 1 #99-23 Jun 5-6, 1999	2CD	Westwood 1	CO9923A	U.S.A.	1999	99.99
Bowie, David	Westwood 1 #99-42 Oct.11,1999	CD	Westwood 1	KH9942A	U.S.A.	1999	69.99
Bowie, David	Young Americans	CD	RCA	PD-80998	Germany	1985	23.99
Bowie, David	Young Americans	CD	RCA	PCD1-0998	U.S.A.	1985	21.99
Bowie, David	Young Americans (Enhanced)	CD	Virgin	7243-521905-0-8	U.S.A.	1999	9.99
Bowie, David	Young Americans + 3 (Ryko Gold Cd)	CD	Rykodisc	RCD-80140	U.S.A.	1991	34.99
Bowie, David	Ziggy Stardust (3")	CD Single	Arc	G-1	Japan	1990	24.99
Bowie, David	Ziggy Stardust (30th Anniversary Book	2CD	EMI	7243-5-39826-2-1	U.S.A.	2002	19.99
Bowie, David	Ziggy Stardust (Enhanced)	CD	Virgin	7243-521900-0-3	U.S.A.	1999	12.99
Bowie, David	Ziggy Stardust (Promo)	CD	Golden Years	GYCDS002	England	1994	8.99
Bowie, David	Ziggy Stardust The Motion Picture	CD	Rykodisc	RCD-40148	U.S.A.	1992	16.99
Bowie, David/2 Unrel Trks	BBC Sessions '69 - '72 (Aborted Box)	CD	NMC	NMCD0072	England	1996	109.99
Bowie, David/Adrian Belew	Pretty Pink Rose (Single)	CD Single	Atlantic	PRCD-3294-2	U.S.A.	1990	7.99
Bowie, David/Bing Crosby	Peace Earth/Little Drummer Boy (Enh.)	CD Single	Oglio	OGL-85001-2	U.S.A.	1999	16.99
Bowie, David/Dana Gillespie	Andy Warhol + 2	CD	Griffin	GCD-355-2	U.S.A.	1995	12.99
Bowie, David/Eugene Ormandy	Peter And The Wolf (Bowie Narrates)	CD	RCA	RD82743	Germany	1985	39.99
Bowie, David/Eugene Ormandy	Peter And The Wolf (Bowie Narrates)	CD	RCA	RCD1-2743	U.S.A.	1985	39.99
Bowie, David/Morrissey	Strangers When.../Boy Racer (DJ)	CD	BMG	SOLO-1	England	1995	131.99
Bowie, David/The Nixons	On The Edge # 95-48, 11 - 20, 1995	CD	Westwood 1	CO7PWO1XE	U.S.A.	1995	42.99
Bowie, David/Tin Machine	Oy Vey, Baby	CD	Victory	383-480-004-2	U.S.A.	1992	29.99
Bowie, David/Tin Machine	Radio Session (Live)	CD Single	Victor Ent.	VICP-15014	Japan	1992	13.99
Bowie, David/Tin Machine	Tin Machine 2 (4 Trk. Promo Sampler)	CD Single	Victory	828-272-1/4/2	U.S.A.	1991	13.99
Bowie, David/Tin Machine	Tin Machine II	CD	Victory	314-511-216-2	U.S.A.	1991	19.99
Bowie, David/Tin Machine	Under The God	CD Single	EMI	CDMT68	England	1989	6.99
Bowie, David/Tin Machine	You Belong To Me (Ltd.Tin Can)	CD Single	Victory	869-487-2	England	1991	16.99
Bowie, David/Tribute	Crash Course For The Ravers	CD	Undercover	UNCV0002	U.S.A.	1996	6.99
Bowie, David/V. A.	Goth Oddity - Tribute To David Bowie	CD	Cleopatra	CLP-0428-2	U.S.A.	1999	8.99
Bowie, David/V. A.	Shake Your Congas	CD	RCA	74321-39147-2	U.S.A.	1997	6.99
Bowie, David/Vs 808 State	Sound + Vision	CD	Tommy Boy	TBCD-510	U.S.A.	1991	6.99
Box of Frogs	Self Titled/Strange Land	CD	Renaissance	RMED00106-2	U.S.A.	1996	15.99
Box Tops	Cry Like A Baby + 5	CD	Sundazed	SC-6159	U.S.A.	2000	8.99
Box Tops	Dimensions + 5	CD	Sundazed	SC-6161	U.S.A.	2000	8.99
Box Tops	Nonstop + 5	CD	Sundazed	SC-6160	U.S.A.	2000	8.99
Box Tops	Soul Deep - Best Of The Box Tops	CD	Arista	07822-18937-2	U.S.A.	1996	8.99
Box Tops	The Letter/Neon Rainbow + 4	CD	Sundazed	SC-6158	U.S.A.	2000	8.99
Boxer	Below The Belt	CD	EMI	7243-8-44342	England	2000	45.99
Boxer	Bloodletting	CD	EMI	7243-8-44341-2	England	2000	24.99
Boy George	The Crying Game - The Remixes	CD Single	SBK	K2-19785	U.S.A.	1993	15.99

B

Artist	Title	Format	Label	Catalog No	Country	Released	Value
Boyle, Gary	Electriglide	CD	Line	LICD-9.00746-0	Germany	1989	15.99
Boyle, Gary	The Dancer	CD	Line	LICD-9.00103-0	Germany	1988	14.99
Bozzio, Tony Levin, Stevens	Black Light Syndrome	CD	Magna Carta	MA-9019-2	U.S.A.	1997	8.99
Bozzio, Tony Levin, Stevens	Situation Dangerous	CD	Magna Carta	MA-9049-2	U.S.A.	2000	10.99
Brady Bunch	Christmas With The Brady Bunch	CD	MCA	MCAD-20890	U.S.A.	1970	8.99
Brady Bunch	It's A Sunshine Day: The Best Of	CD	MCA	MCAD-10764	U.S.A.	1993	15.99
Brady Bunch	Meet The	CD	MCA	MCAD-11457	U.S.A.	1996	14.99
Brady Bunch	Phonographic Album	CD	MCA	MCAD-11458	U.S.A.	1996	13.99
Brady Bunch	The Kids From The	CD	MCA	MCAD-11456	U.S.A.	1996	13.99
Brady Bunch/Barry Williams	The Real Greg Brady	CD Single	Good Guy Ent.	6022570002-2	U.S.A.	2000	6.99
Brady Bunch/Barry Williams	The Real Johnny Bravo	CD	Good Guy Ent.	6022570001-2	U.S.A.	1999	6.99
Brady Bunch/Maureen McCormi	When You Get A Little Lonely	CD	Phantom Hill	55001	U.S.A.	1995	24.99
Brady, Paul	Full Moon	CD	Line	LICD-9.00020-0	Germany	1987	14.99
Bragg, Billy	Levi Stubbs' Tears	CD Single	Line	LICD-9.00966-E	Germany	1990	8.99
Bragg, Billy	Talking With The Taxman	CD	Line	LICD-9.00237-0	Germany	1987	11.99
Bragg, Billy	The Internationale	CD	Line	UTCD-9.00982-L	Germany	1990	9.99
Bragg, Billy	Workers Playtime	CD	Line	LICD-9.00663-0	Germany	1988	8.99
Bramblett, Randall	See Through Me	CD	Capricorn	314-558-635-2	U.S.A.	1998	6.99
Bramlett, Bonnie	I'm Still The Same	CD	Koch	AUD-CD-8154	U.S.A.	2002	14.99
Bramlett, Bonnie	It's Time	CD	Polydor K.K.	P20P-22025	Japan	1974	39.99
Bramlett, Bonnie	It's Time/Ladie's Choice	CD	Raven	RVD-172	Australia	2004	24.99
Bramlett, Bonnie	Lady's Choice	CD	Capricorn	314-536-131-2	U.S.A.	1997	40.99
Bramlett, Delaney	Mobius Strip	CD	Sony	SRCS-6353	Japan	1996	29.99
Bramlett, Delaney	Sweet Inspiration + 4	CD	Pryaid	YDCD-0081	Japan	2002	34.99
Bramlett, Delaney/Bonnie	Accept No Substitute	CD	Collector's Choice	CCM-283-2	U.S.A.	2002	12.99
Bramlett, Delaney/Bonnie	Best Of	CD	Rhino	R2-70777	U.S.A.	1990	9.99
Bramlett, Delaney/Bonnie	D & B Together	CD	Sony	SRCS-6350	Japan	1996	17.99
Bramlett, Delaney/Bonnie	D & B Together + 6	CD	Columbia	CK-85743	U.S.A.	2003	8.99
Bramlett, Delaney/Bonnie	Home	CD	Stax	CDSXE-029	U.S.A.	1969	8.99
Bramlett, Delaney/Bonnie	Motel Shot	CD	East West	AMCY-2765	Japan	1998	17.99
Bramlett, Delaney/Bonnie	On Tour With Eric Clapton	CD	East West	AMCY-2766	Japan	1998	29.99
Bramlett, Delaney/Bonnie	On Tour With Eric Clapton	CD	Atco	33326-2	U.S.A.	1970	8.99
Bramlett, Delaney/Bonnie	To Bonnie From Delaney	CD	East West	AMCY-2764	Japan	1998	13.99
Bram-Tchaikovsky	Strange Man, Changed Man	CD	Warner Bros.	WPCR-1764	Japan	1998	40.99
Brand X	{Missing Period}	CD	Pony Canyon	PCCY-01141	Japan	1997	34.99
Brand X	A History: 1976-1980	CD	Caroline	CAROL-1116-2	U.S.A.	1997	8.99
Brand X	Brand X Featuring Phil Collins	CD	Disky	VI-867242	Holland	1996	14.99
Brand X	Do They Hurt?	CD	Caroline	CAROL-1389-2	U.S.A.	1989	10.99
Brand X	Is There Anything About?	CD	Columbia	484437-2	Austria	1982	12.99
Brand X	Livestock	CD	Virgin	VJD-28203	Japan	1989	24.99
Brand X	Manifest Destiny	CD	Cleopatra	CLP-9940-2	U.S.A.	1997	8.99
Brand X	Masques	CD	Caroline	CAROL-1391-2	U.S.A.	1989	12.99
Brand X	Moroccan Roll	CD	Caroline	CAROL-1392-2	U.S.A.	1989	12.99
Brand X	Product	CD	Caroline	CAROL-1390-2	U.S.A.	1988	12.99
Brand X	The Plot Thins - A History Of Brand X	CD	Virgin	CDVM-9005	England	1992	12.99
Brand X	The X-Files	2CD	Outer Music	OM-1011	U.S.A.	1998	20.99
Brand X	Unorthodox Behaviour	CD	Caroline	CAROL-1387-2	U.S.A.	1989	14.99
Brand X	Xcommunication	CD	Ozone	OZ-001	U.S.A.	1992	14.99
Brand X	Xtrax	CD	Passport	PBCD-6054	U.S.A.	1986	24.99
Brandt, Ronnie	Dig A Little Deeper	CD	Line	LICD—9.01362-0	Germany	2000	8.99
Brandt, Ronnie	Rudy's Thread	CD	Line	LICD-9.01330-0	Germany	1998	8.99
Branigan, Laura	Branigan	CD	Atlantic	19289-2	U.S.A.	1982	9.99
Branigan, Laura	Branigan 2	CD	Atlantic	7-80052-2	U.S.A.	1983	14.99
Branigan, Laura	Hold Me	CD	Atlantic	7-81265-2	U.S.A.	1985	39.99
Branigan, Laura	Laura Branigan (CD Graphics)	CD	Atlantic	7-82086-2	U.S.A.	1990	9.99
Branigan, Laura	Never In A Million Years (Promo)	CD Single	Atlantic	PRCD-3355-2	U.S.A.	1990	6.99
Branigan, Laura	Over My Heart	CD	Atlantic	7-82489-2	U.S.A.	1993	9.99
Branigan, Laura	Self Control	CD	Atlantic	7-80147-2	U.S.A.	1984	13.99

B

Artist	Title	Format	Label	Catalog No	Country	Released	Value
Branigan, Laura	The Best Of Branigan	CD	Atlantic	82757-2	U.S.A.	1995	7.99
Branigan, Laura	The Best Of Laura Branigan	CD	MMG Inc.	AMCY-254	Japan	1991	13.99
Branigan, Laura	The Essentials	CD	Rhino	R2-76080	U.S.A.	2002	6.99
Branigan, Laura	The Very Best Of	CD	Atlantic	9548-31561-2	Germany	1992	26.99
Branigan, Laura	Touch + 1	CD	Atlantic	7-81747-2	U.S.A.	1987	10.99
Branigan, Laura/Various Artist	Baywatch (O.S.T.)	CD	Scotti Bros.	72392-75445-2	U.S.A.	1994	13.99
Brannen, John	Mystery Street	CD	Apache	D2-71650	U.S.A.	1988	19.99
Brannen, John	Scarecrow	CD	Corazong	2000012	Netherland	2000	14.99
Brannen, John	Self Titled	CD	PolyGram	514-436-2	England	1993	14.99
Brasil, Pau	Pindorama	CD	Line	BSCD-9.00755-0	Germany	1990	7.99
Braxton, Toni	Secrets (W/Bonus Best Buy Cd)	2CD	La Face	008-26020-2	U.S.A.	1996	34.99
Bread	Baby I'm-A Want You	CD	Elektra	75015-2	U.S.A.	1972	10.99
Bread	Best Of	CD	Rhino	R2-74311	U.S.A.	2001	16.99
Bread	Bread	CD	Rhino	R2-73502	U.S.A.	1995	11.99
Bread	Guitar Man	CD	Elektra	9-60918-2	U.S.A.	1972	13.99
Bread	Manna	CD	Rhino	R2-73504	U.S.A.	1995	13.99
Bread	On The Waters	CD	Rhino	R2-73503	U.S.A.	1995	64.99
Bread	Retrospective	2CD	Rhino	R2-73509	U.S.A.	1996	17.99
Bread/David Gates	Essentials	CD	Elektra	7559-61961-2	Germany	1996	10.99
Bread/David Gates	First	CD	Elektra	7559-60910-2	Germany	1973	22.99
Bread/David Gates	Goodbye Girl	CD	Warner Bros.	WPCP-4166	Japan	1993	41.99
Bread/David Gates	Goodbye Girl	CD	Warner Bros.	61172-2	Argentina	1977	16.99
Bread/David Gates	It Is Well (Christian Lp)	CD	Vectron	6349221842	U.S.A.	1997	8.99
Bread/Larry Knechtel	Urban Gypsy	CD	Capitol	7-94382-2	U.S.A.	1990	8.99
Breeders	Cannonball	CD Single	Elektra	66279-2	U.S.A.	1993	12.99
Breeders	Cannonball 4 Trk Ltd Ed Digipack	CD Single	4AD	SHOCK-CD-4013	Australia	1993	12.99
Breeders	Divine Hammer	CD Single	4AD	BAD-3017-CD	England	1993	9.99
Breeders	Divine Hammer 4 Trk Ltd Ed Digipack	CD Single	4AD	SHOCK-CD-4014	Australia	1993	12.99
Breeders	Last Splash	CD	Elektra	9-61508-2	U.S.A.	1993	9.99
Breeders	Saints	CD Single	4AD	76974-3018-2	Canada	1994	9.99
Breeders	Title TK	CD	Elektra	62766-2	U.S.A.	2002	8.99
Breeders/Amps	Pacer (Kim Deal Songs)	CD	4AD	61823-2	U.S.A.	1995	8.99
Breeders/Amps	Pacer (Kim Deal Songs)	CD	4AD	CTX035CD	Australia	1995	8.99
Breeders/Amps	Tipp City (Kim Deal Songs)	CD Single	4AD	CORX021CD	Australia	1995	7.99
Breeders/Kelley Deal	Go To The Sugar Altar	CD	Nice	NR6001	U.S.A.	1996	8.99
Breeders/Tanya Donelly	Lovesongs For...(T. Muses/Belly)	CD	Reprise	09362-46495-2-6	U.S.A.	1997	7.99
Bremner, Billy	A Good Week's Work	CD	Gadfly	243	U.S.A.	1998	10.99
Bremner, Billy	Bash + 5	CD	Gadfly	275	U.S.A.	2001	15.99
Bremner, Tony	Star Trek: Symphonic Suites Vol. 1	CD	Label X	LXCD-703	U.S.A.	1986	8.99
Bremner, Tony	Star Trek: Symphonic Suites Vol. 2	CD	Label X	LXCD-704	U.S.A.	1986	8.99
Brennan, Maire	Máire	CD	Atlantic	7-82421-2	U.S.A.	1992	9.99
Brennan, Maire	Misty Eyed Adventures	CD	Atlantic	82701-2	U.S.A.	1994	7.99
Brennan, Maire	Perfect Time	CD	Word Records	7019965601	U.S.A.	1998	11.99
Brennan, Maire	Whisper To The Wild Water	CD	Epic	EK-63659	U.S.A.	1999	8.99
Brennan/Doran	Henceforward	CD	Line	COCD-9.00871-0	Germany	1989	19.99
Brewer And Shipley	Archive Alive!	CD	Archive	ACH-80006	U.S.A.	1997	16.99
Brewer And Shipley	Shanghai	CD	Calf Creek	9502	U.S.A.	1995	26.99
Brewer And Shipley	Tarkio + 2	CD	Buddah	75517-49510	U.S.A.	1996	9.99
Brewer And Shipley	The Best Of Brewer & Shipley	CD	Buddah	74465-99811-2	U.S.A.	2001	11.99
Brewer, Spencer	Portraits	CD	Narada	ND-61017	U.S.A.	1987	6.99
Bricusse, Leslie	Doctor Dolittle (O.S.T.) W/R Harrison	CD	Phillips	314-534-500-2	U.S.A.	1997	19.99
Brightman, Sarah	Harem (Remixes)	CD Single	EMI	708761793123	England	2003	60.99
Brightman, Sarah	Special Sampler (Promo)	CD Single	EMI	PCD-2321	Japan	2000	149.99
Bril, Igor/ A S Soviet J Band	Live At Village Gate (MFSL Silver Cd)	CD	Mobile Fidelity	MFCD-861	U.S.A.	1989	17.99
Briley, Martin	One Night With A Stranger	CD	PolyGram	9-42281-03322-3	Germany	1983	207.99
Brinsley Schwartz	Original Golden Greats/15 Thoughts Of	CD	BGO	BGOCD476	England	2000	16.99
Brinsley Schwartz	Self Titled	CD	Repertoire	REP-4421-WY	Germany	1994	10.99
Brinsley Schwartz	Silver Pistol	CD	Edsel	ED-CD-190	England	1986	19.99

Artist	Title	Format	Label	Catalog No	Country	Released	Value
Brinsley Schwartz	The New Favourites Of	CD	Vivid	VSD-512	Japan	1974	21.99
Brinsley Schwarz	Brinsley Schwarz/Despite it All	CD	BGO	BGOCD239	England	1994	15.99
Brinsley Schwarz	Nervous On The Road/New Favs	CD	BGO	BGOCD289	England	1995	15.99
Brinsley Schwarz	Please Don't Ever Change	CD	Edsel	EDCD-237	England	1987	19.99
Brinsley Schwarz	Surrender To The Rhythm: The Best	CD	EMI	7-96746-2	England	1991	11.99
Brinsley Schwarz	The New Favourites Of + 4	CD	Repertoire	REP-4942	Germany	2001	13.99
Brinsley Schwarz	What Is So Funny About Peace...	CD	HUX	HUX-023	England	2001	11.99
Brion, Jon	Punch Drunk Love (O.S.T.)	CD	Nonesuch	79813-2	U.S.A.	2002	7.99
British Invasion All-Stars	Regression (Jim McCarty, Eddie Phillips)	CD	Line	OLCD-9.50909-X	Germany	1991	12.99
British Invasion All-Stars	United	CD	Line	OLCD-9.51105-X	Germany	1991	12.99
Bromberg, David	Self Titled	CD	Sony	SRCS-6284	Japan	1993	39.99
Brook, Michael	Albino Alligator (W/Michael Stipe/Flea)	CD	4AD	9-46504-2	U.S.A.	1997	11.99
Brook, Michael	Cobalt Blue	CD	4AD	9-45000-2	U.S.A.	1992	7.99
Brook, Michael	Hybrid (With Eno/Lanois)	CD	Editions EG	EEGCD-41	U.S.A.	1985	14.99
Brook, Michael	Live At The Aquarium	CD	4AD	9-45444-2	U.S.A.	1992	14.99
Brook, Michael	Shona	CD	Sine	SIN002	England	1995	14.99
Brook, Michael/Brian Eno	Hybrid (With Daniel Lanois)	CD	Editions EG	EEGCD-41	U.S.A.	1985	11.99
Brook, Michael/Pieter Nooten	Sleeps With The Fishes	CD	4AD	CAD710-CD	England	1987	16.99
Brooker, Gary	Echoes In The Night	CD	Line	INCD-9.00076-0	Germany	1988	19.99
Brooker, Gary	Lead Me To The Water	CD	Line	LICD-9.00015-0	Germany	1987	16.99
Brooker, Gary	Lead Me To The Water/Echoes Night	2CD	Line	LICD-9.21195-S	Germany	1992	19.99
Brooker, Gary	No More Fear Of Flying	CD	Line	LICD-9.00046-0	Germany	1988	13.99
Brooker, Gary	No More Fear Of Flying + 2	CD	Repertoire	REP-4659-WY	Germany	1997	12.99
Brooker, Gary	Within Our House	CD	Repertoire	REP-1660-WY	Germany	1997	12.99
Brooks, Mel	Producers (Orig. B. Cast) Nathan Lane	CD	Sony	SK-89646	U.S.A.	2001	12.99
Brooks, Mel/Carl Reiner	2000 Year Old Man In The Year 2000	CD	Rhino	R2-72944	U.S.A.	1997	14.99
Brooks, Ray/Full Force	Songs Within	CD	Line	TLCD-9.00412-0	Germany	1987	7.99
Brotherhood Of Man	Golden Classics	CD	Collectables	COL-0563	U.S.A.	1994	8.99
Brotherhood Of Man	Hits & Kisses	2CD	Recall	SMD-CD-440	England	2002	9.99
Brotherhood Of Man	Twenty Greatest Hits	CD	Repertoire	REP-4298-WZ	Germany	1996	10.99
Brothers Johnson	Winners	CD	Pony Canyon	D28Y-3241	Japan	1981	399.99
Broughton, Edgar/Band	Bandages	CD	Repertoire	REP-4201-WY	Germany	2001	24.99
Broughton, Edgar/Band	Chilly Morning Mama	CD	Receiver	RRCD-7262	England	1998	19.99
Broughton, Edgar/Band	Demons At The Beeb	CD	HUX	HUX-020	England	2000	14.99
Broughton, Edgar/Band	Edgar Broughton Band + 4	CD	Repertoire	REP-4409-WY	Germany	2003	12.99
Broughton, Edgar/Band	In Side Out + 4	CD	Repertoire	REP-4410-WY	Germany	2002	12.99
Broughton, Edgar/Band	Oora	CD	BGO	BGOCD114	England	2002	14.99
Broughton, Edgar/Band	Self Titled/In Side Out	CD	BGO	BGOCD179	England	1993	12.99
Broughton, Edgar/Band	Sing Brother Sing	CD	EMI	EMI-11952	England	2000	11.99
Broughton, Edgar/Band	Wasa Wasa	CD	BGO	BGOCD129	England	1999	14.99
Broussard, Trina	Inside My Love (Promo Unreleased Cd)	CD	Sony	CSK-41799	U.S.A.	1999	121.99
Brown Bottle Flu	In Between	CD	Line	LICD—9.01372-0	Germany	2001	14.99
Brown, Arthur	Chisholm In My Bosom	CD	Line	LICD-9.00344-0	Germany	1989	19.99
Brown, Arthur	Dance	CD	Line	LICD-9.00002-0	Germany	1989	13.99
Brown, Arthur	Dance/Chisholm In My Bosom	CD	See For Miles	SEE-CD431	England	1995	12.99
Brown, Arthur	Order From Chaos Live '93	CD	Voiceprint	VP144	England	1993	11.99
Brown, Arthur	Speak No Tech	CD	Voiceprint	VPCD124	England	1993	10.99
Brown, Arthur	The Crazy World Of Arthur Brown + 5	CD	Polydor	833-736-2	England	1991	18.99
Brown, Arthur/Kingdom Come	Journey	CD	Voiceprint	VP137CD	England	1993	39.99
Brown, James	40th Anniversary Collection	2CD	PolyGram	31453-3409-2	U.S.A.	1996	12.99
Brown, James	It's A New Day...	CD	Polydor	POCP-1856	Japan	1970	54.99
Brown, James	James Brown's Funky Christmas	CD	Polydor	P2-27988	U.S.A.	1995	7.99
Brown, James	Live at the Apollo Volume II	2CD	Polydor	314-549-884-2	U.S.A.	2001	13.99
Brown, James	Santa's Got a Brand New Bag	CD	Rhino	R2-70194	U.S.A.	1988	19.99
Brown, James	Star Time Box Set	4CD	Polydor	849-108-2	U.S.A.	1991	26.99
Brown, Julie	Trapped In The Body...	CD	Sire	25634-2	U.S.A.	1990	64.99
Brown, Keisa	Keisa	CD	Line	TLCD-9.00673-0	Germany	1988	13.99
Brown, Pete/Battered Ornamen	A Meal You Can.. (W/Bonus)	CD	Repertoire	REP-4406-WY	Germany	2000	12.99

B

Artist	Title	Format	Label	Catalog No	Country	Released	Value
Brown, Pete/Battered Ornamen	A Meal You Can/Mantle-Piece	2CD	BGO	BGOCD489	England	2001	22.99
Brown, Pete/Battered Ornamen	Mantle-Piece	CD	Repertoire	REP-4405-WY	Germany	2000	12.99
Brown, Pete/Graham Bond	Two Heads Are Better... (W/Bonus)	CD	Repertoire	REP-4271-WY	Germany	1972	12.99
Brown, Pete/Ian Lynn	Party In The Rain	CD	Mystic	MYSCD-133	England	1999	14.99
Brown, Pete/Phil Ryan	Ardours Of The Lost Rake	CD	Voiceprint	VP255CD	England	2003	19.99
Brown, Pete/Phil Ryan	Coals To Jerusalem	CD	Blueprint	BP146CD	England	2003	19.99
Brown, Pete/Phil Ryan	The Land That Cream Forgot	CD	Vintage	VIN8031-2	England	1996	11.99
Brown, Pete/Piblokto!	Thing May Come/Thousands On Raft	2CD	BGO	BGOCD522	England	2001	22.99
Brown, Pete/Piblokto!	Things May Come.. + 2	CD	Repertoire	REP-4407-WY	Germany	2000	12.99
Brown, Pete/Piblokto!	Thousands On A Raft + 2	CD	Repertoire	REP-4408-WY	Germany	2000	14.99
Browne, Duncan	Self Titled + 4	CD	EMI	35623	England	2002	17.99
Browne, Duncan	Streets Of Fire	CD	Line	TACD-9.00786-0	Germany	1989	34.99
Browne, Duncan	The Wild Places	CD	Line	TACD-9.00778-0	Germany	1989	12.99
Browne, Duncan	The Wild Places '91	CD Single	Line	LICD-9.01130-E	Germany	1991	12.99
Browne, Duncan	The Wild Places/Streets Of Fire	CD	Essential	ESMCD-883	England	1989	16.99
Browne, Jackson	History (Promo)	CD	Warner Bros.	PCS-205	Japan	1996	149.99
Browne, Jackson	Hold Out	CD	Elektra	5E-511-2	U.S.A.	1980	15.99
Browne, Jackson	I'm Alive	CD	Elektra	9-61524-2	U.S.A.	1993	7.99
Browne, Jackson	I'm The Cat	CD Single	Elektra	7559-66027-2	Germany	1996	7.99
Browne, Jackson	Late For The Sky (DCC Gold Cd)	CD	DCC	GZS-1036	U.S.A.	1993	39.99
Browne, Jackson	Lawyers In Love	CD	Elektra	9-60268-2	Canada	1983	10.99
Browne, Jackson	Looking East (Enhanced)	CD	Elektra	61906-2	U.S.A.	1996	6.99
Browne, Jackson	Radio Sampler (Promo)	CD	Elektra	PRCD18027-2A	U.S.A.	2002	27.99
Browne, Jackson	Retrospective/I'm Alive (Promo/Paper)	2CD	Elektra	PRCD-8551-2	U.S.A.	1994	64.99
Browne, Jackson	Retrospective/I'm Alive/Jewel Case	2CD	Elektra	PRCD-8851-2	U.S.A.	1992	49.99
Browne, Jackson	Running On Empty	CD	Elektra	6E-113-2	U.S.A.	1977	10.99
Browne, Jackson	Saturate Before Using	CD	Asylum	E2-5051	U.S.A.	1972	10.99
Browne, Jackson	The Naked Ride Home	CD	Elektra	62793-2	U.S.A.	2002	11.99
Browne, Jackson	The Next Voice That You Hear (Promo)	CD Single	Elektra	PRCD-9901-2	U.S.A.	1997	4.99
Browne, Jackson	The Next Voice You Hear	CD	Elektra	62111-2	U.S.A.	1997	8.99
Browne, Jackson	The Pretender (DCC Gold Cd)	CD	DCC	GZS-1047	U.S.A.	1993	34.99
Browne, Jackson	The Rebel Jesus (Promo)	CD Single	Elektra	PRCD-9956-2	U.S.A.	1997	13.99
Browne, Jackson	World In Motion	CD	Elektra	9-60830-2	U.S.A.	1989	4.99
Brubeck, Dave/Vince Guaraldi	Quiet As The Moon	CD	Music Masters	01612-65067-2	U.S.A.	1991	6.99
Bruce, Jack	A Question Of Time	CD	Epic	EK-45279	U.S.A.	1989	5.99
Bruce, Jack	Band Live '75 (W/Bonus Cd)	2CD	Polydor	065607-2	England	2003	13.99
Bruce, Jack	BBC Live In Concert	CD	Windsong	WINCD-076	England	1995	12.99
Bruce, Jack	BBM (With Ginger Baker/Gary Moore)	CD	Virgin	39728	England	1994	10.99
Bruce, Jack	Cities Of The Heart	2CD	CMP	CMP-CD-1004	Germany	1993	13.99
Bruce, Jack	Concert Classics	CD	Renaissance	RRCC00709	U.S.A.	1999	8.99
Bruce, Jack	Doing This.... On Ice!	2CD	Alchemy	PILOT25	England	2001	13.99
Bruce, Jack	Harmony Row + 5	CD	Polydor	065605-2	England	2003	14.99
Bruce, Jack	How's Tricks? + 2	CD	Polydor	065608-2	England	2003	10.99
Bruce, Jack	Inazuma Super Session Live	CD	Epic	460453-2	Japan	1987	54.99
Bruce, Jack	Jet Set Jewel	CD	Polydor	065609-2	England	2003	10.99
Bruce, Jack	Live On The Old Grey Whistle Test	CD	Strange Fruit	WHISCD-010	England	1998	19.99
Bruce, Jack	Monkjack	CD	CMP	CMP-CD-1010	Germany	1995	9.99
Bruce, Jack	Monkjack Sampler (Promo)	CD	CMP	CMPCD-1010P	Germany	1995	4.99
Bruce, Jack	Out Of The Storm + 5	CD	Polydor	065606-2	England	2003	11.99
Bruce, Jack	Shadows In The Air	CD	Victor Ent.	VICP-61453	Japan	2001	7.99
Bruce, Jack	Somethinels	CD	CMP	CD-1001	Germany	1993	8.99
Bruce, Jack	Songs For A Tailor + 4	CD	Polydor	065603-2	England	2003	15.99
Bruce, Jack	The Collector's Edition	CD	CMP	CMP-CD-1013	Germany	1996	19.99
Bruce, Jack	Things We Like + 1	CD	Polydor	065604-2	England	2003	11.99
Bruce, Jack	Willpower	CD	Polydor	42283-7806-2	U.S.A.	1989	15.99
Bruce, Jack/BBM	Around The Next Dream (G Baker)	CD	Toshiba-EMI	VJCP-25110	Japan	1994	14.99
Bruce, Jack/BBM	Around The Next Dream (G Baker)	CD	Toshiba-EMI	TOCP-53271	Japan	2002	24.99
Bruce, Jack/BBM	Around The Next Dream + 4	CD	Virgin	7243-5-83673-2-4	England	2003	17.99

B

Artist	Title	Format	Label	Catalog No	Country	Released	Value
Bruce, Jack/BBM	City Of Gold (Ginger Baker/G Moore)	CD Single	Virgin	DPRO-12687	U.S.A.	1994	9.99
Bruce, Lenny	Lenny Bruce Originals - Volume 1	CD	Fantasy	FCD-60-023	U.S.A.	1991	8.99
Bruce, Lenny	Lenny Bruce Originals - Volume 2	CD	Fantasy	FCD-60-024	U.S.A.	1991	8.99
Bruce, Michael	Halo Of Ice	CD	Alchemy	PILOT-131	England	2002	16.99
Bruce, Michael	In My Own Way - The Complete + 21	2CD	Alchemy	PILOT-114	England	2002	13.99
Bruce/Terry	Best Of	CD	Sundazed	SC-11052	U.S.A.	1998	8.99
Bruford, Bill	All Heaven Broke Loose	CD	Caroline	CAROL-2103-2	U.S.A.	1991	19.99
Bruford, Bill	Dig?	CD	Caroline	CAROL-1500-2	U.S.A.	1989	15.99
Bruford, Bill	Earthworks Live - Stamping Ground	CD	Caroline	7243-8-39476-2-1	England	1994	7.99
Bruford, Bill	Feels Good To Me	CD	Caroline	CAROL-1524-2	U.S.A.	1989	10.99
Bruford, Bill	Footloose And Fancy Free	2CD	Discipline Global	DGM-0201	U.S.A.	2002	13.99
Bruford, Bill	Gradually Going Tornado	CD	Caroline	CAROL-1526-2	U.S.A.	1989	12.99
Bruford, Bill	Master Strokes 1978 - 1985	CD	Virgin	0777-7-86779-2-5	Holland	1986	8.99
Bruford, Bill	One Of A Kind	CD	Caroline	CAROL-1525-2	U.S.A.	1989	12.99
Bruford, Bill	The Bruford Tapes	CD	Caroline	CAROL-1528-2	U.S.A.	1989	12.99
Bruford, Bill/Earthworks	A Part, And Yet Apart + 1	CD	Pony Canyon	PCCY-01381	Japan	1999	34.99
Bruford, Bill/Earthworks	Bill Bruford's Earthworks	CD	Caroline	CAROL-1523-2	U.S.A.	1989	8.99
Bruford, Bill/Earthworks	Heavenly Bodies	CD	Venture	7243-8-44289-2-1	Germany	1997	11.99
Bruford, Bill/Earthworks	The Sound Of Surprise + 1	CD	Pony Canyon	PCCY-01496	Japan	2001	34.99
Bruford, Bill/Patrick Moraz	Flags	CD	Caroline	CAROL-1565-2	U.S.A.	1989	44.99
Bruford, Bill/Towner/Gomez	If Summer Had Its Ghosts	CD	Discipline	DGM-9705	U.S.A.	1997	12.99
Bruford/Levin	Blue Nights	2CD	Pony Canyon	PCCY-01435	Japan	2000	34.99
Bruford/Levin	Bruford Levin Upper Extremities	CD	Discipline Global	DGM-9805	U.S.A.	1999	14.99
Brute	Nine High A Pallet	CD	Capricorn	9-42029-2	U.S.A.	1995	8.99
Bryars, Gavin	A Man In A Gambling Room	CD	Point	456-514-2	England	1997	12.99
Bryars, Gavin	After The Requiem	CD	ECM	ECM-1424	U.S.A.	1991	12.99
Bryars, Gavin	Allegrasco, Alaric	CD	Daphénéo	9810	U.S.A.	1998	11.99
Bryars, Gavin	Cadman Requiem	CD	Point	462-511-2	U.S.A.	1998	12.99
Bryars, Gavin	Farewell To Philosophy	CD	Point	454-126-2	U.S.A.	1996	14.99
Bryars, Gavin	Jesus' Blood Never Failed Me Yet	CD	Point	438-823-2	U.S.A.	1993	10.99
Bryars, Gavin	Sinking Titanic ('75 Vrsn)/Jesus' Blood..	CD	Virgin	7243-8-45970-2-3	England	1998	20.99
Bryars, Gavin	The Last Days	CD	Argo	448-175-2	U.S.A.	1995	14.99
Bryars, Gavin	The Sinking Of The Titanic	CD	Point	446-061-2	U.S.A.	1994	7.99
Bryars, Gavin	Three Viennese Dancers	CD	ECM	ECM-1323	U.S.A.	1986	19.99
Bryars, Gavin	Vita Nova	CD	ECM	1533-445-351-2	England	1994	7.99
Brynner, Yul/Deborah Kerr	The King And I (O.S.T.)	CD	Angel	0777-7-64693-2-4	U.S.A.	1993	11.99
Bubble Puppy	A Gathering Of Promises	CD	Sunspots	SPOT-531-CD	Italy	2003	13.99
Bubble Puppy	A Gathering Of Promises	CD	EVA	EVA-B41/642038	France	1994	11.99
Bucchino, John	Grateful: Songs Of (W/Jimmy Webb)	CD	RCA	09026-63594-2	U.S.A.	2000	7.99
Buck, Peter (R.E.M.)/Minus 5	The Lonesome Death Of Buck McCoy	CD	Hollywood	HT-62115-2	U.S.A.	1997	13.99
Buck, Peter/Mark Eitzel	West	CD	Warner Bros.	9-46602-2	U.S.A.	1997	4.99
Buck, Peter/Mark Eitzel	Words + Music	CD	Warner Bros.	PRO-CD-8783	U.S.A.	1997	4.99
Buckingham, Lindsey	Law And Order	CD	Warner Bros.	561-2	U.S.A.	1981	9.99
Buckingham, Lindsey	Out Of The Cradle	CD	Reprise	9-26182-2	U.S.A.	1992	9.99
Buckley, Jeff	Grace	CD	Columbia	4759282	England	1996	14.99
Buckley, Jeff	Grace	CD	Sony	CK-57528	U.S.A.	1994	9.99
Buckley, Jeff	Grace EP	CD Single	Sony	11663085	Austria	1996	12.99
Buckley, Jeff	Live At Sin-É	CD Single	Columbia	44K-77296	U.S.A.	1993	9.99
Buckley, Jeff	Live From The Bataclan	CD Single	Columbia	662155-2	Austria	1995	13.99
Buckley, Jeff	Sketches For My Sweetheart	2CD	Columbia	C2K-67228	U.S.A.	1998	16.99
Buckley, Jeff	The Grace EP	CD Single	Columbia	663085-2	Australia	1996	11.99
Buckley, Jeff	The Grace EP's	5CD	Columbia	XC5D501178	England	1996	28.99
Buckley, Tim	Blue Afternoon	CD	Rhino	R2-70356	U.S.A.	1991	49.99
Buckley, Tim	Dream Letter: Live in London	2CD	Rhino	R2-70361	U.S.A.	1991	7.99
Buckley, Tim	Greetings from L.A.	CD	Warner Bros.	27261	Germany	1998	10.99
Buckley, Tim	Happy Sad	CD	Asylum	74045	Germany	1975	12.99
Buckley, Tim	Honeyman	CD	Edsel	EDCD-450	England	1995	11.99
Buckley, Tim	Live At The Troubadour 1969	CD	Manifesto	PT3-40705	U.S.A.	1994	9.99

B

Artist	Title	Format	Label	Catalog No	Country	Released	Value
Buckley, Tim	Look At The Fool	CD	Enigma	7-73509-2	Canada	1974	8.99
Buckley, Tim	Lorca	CD	Asylum	61339-2	Germany	1970	16.99
Buckley, Tim	Morning Glory	CD	Band Of Joy	BOJCD-009	England	1995	7.99
Buckley, Tim	Morning Glory: The Anthology	2CD	Rhino	R2-76722	U.S.A.	2001	16.99
Buckley, Tim	Once I Was (Live)	CD	Varese	061056	U.S.A.	1999	8.99
Buckley, Tim	Peel Sessions	CD	Strange Fruit	8348	England	1995	13.99
Buckley, Tim	Sefronia	CD	Manifesto	40701	U.S.A.	1995	8.99
Buckley, Tim	Starsailor	CD	Rhino	R2-70360	U.S.A.	1991	103.99
Buckley, Tim	The Dream Belongs to Me (Rarities)	CD	Manifesto	MFO-40706	U.S.A.	2001	8.99
Buckley, Tim	Tim Buckley/Goodbye & Hello	CD	Warner Bros.	8122-73569-2	Germany	2001	15.99
Buckley, Tim	Works In Progress (Ltd. 7500)	CD	Rhino	RHM2-7705	U.S.A.	1999	19.99
Budd, Harold	Agua	CD	La Cooka Ratcha	LCVP151CD	England	2002	11.99
Budd, Harold	By The Dawn's Early Light	CD	Warner Bros.	9-26649-2	U.S.A.	1991	6.99
Budd, Harold	Fenceless Night (Unrel. Promo)	CD	PolyGram	PMP-018	U.S.A.	1998	19.99
Budd, Harold	Lovely Thunder	CD	Editions EG	EEGCD-46	U.S.A.	1986	11.99
Budd, Harold	Lovely Thunder	CD	Virgin	VJD-28045	Japan	1986	24.99
Budd, Harold	Luxa	CD	Gyroscope	6637	U.S.A.	1996	12.99
Budd, Harold	Music for 3 Pianos	CD	Gyroscope	6603	U.S.A.	1994	14.99
Budd, Harold	The Pavilion Of Dreams	CD	Editions EG	EEGCD30	U.S.A.	1978	15.99
Budd, Harold	The Room	CD	Atlantic	83382	U.S.A.	2000	9.99
Budd, Harold	The Serpent...\ Abandoned Cities	CD	All Saints	ASCD08	U.S.A.	1992	12.99
Budd, Harold	The White Arcades	CD	All Saints	ASCD03	England	1992	19.99
Budd, Harold	Walk into My Voice	CD	Materiali Sonori	9-79281-2	U.S.A.	1996	14.99
Budd, Harold/Brian Eno	Ambient 2: The Plateaux Of Mirror	CD	Editions EG	EEGCD-18	U.S.A.	1980	16.99
Budd, Harold/Brian Eno	The Pearl	CD	Editions EG	EEGCD-37	U.S.A.	1984	16.99
Budd, Harold/Cocteau Twins	The Moon And The Melodies	CD	4AD	CAD-611-CD	Germany	1986	7.99
Budd, Harold/Hector Zazou	Glyph	CD	Made To Measure	MTM-37	Austria	1995	12.99
Budd, Harold/Roger Eno	Marco Polo (With David Sylvain)	CD	Materiali Sonori	90069	U.S.A.	1996	19.99
Budd, Harold/Zeitgeist	She Is A Phantom	CD	New Albion	NA066CD	U.S.A.	1994	6.99
Budda-Bang!	Sonic Decayed (Ray Harryhausen Cyclo	CD	Propulsion	333-2	U.S.A.	1993	6.99
Budgie	Bandolier	CD	Repertoire	RR-4100-WZ	Germany	1990	9.99
Budgie	Best Of	CD	MCA	MCLD-19067	England	1975	15.99
Budgie	Budgie	CD	Repertoire	RR-4012-C	Germany	1989	20.99
Budgie	Definitive Anthology: An Ecstacy Of..	2CD	Repertoire	REP-4435-WO	Germany	1996	14.99
Budgie	Deliver Us From Evil	CD	Griffin	GCD-622-2	U.S.A.	1996	13.99
Budgie	If I Were Brittania I'd Waive The Rules	CD	Repertoire	REP-4372-WZ	Germany	1993	17.99
Budgie	Impeckable	CD	Repertoire	GEP-4371-WZ	Germany	1993	10.99
Budgie	In For The Kill	CD	Repertoire	REP-4027-WZ	Germany	1994	11.99
Budgie	Never Turn Your Back On A Friend	CD	Repertoire	REP-4013-WZ	Germany	1996	10.99
Budgie	Nightflight	CD	Griffin	GCD-623-2	U.S.A.	1996	11.99
Budgie	Power Supply + 4	CD	Griffin	GCD-624-2	U.S.A.	1996	12.99
Budgie	Six Ton Budgie Ornithology Vol. 1	CD	Axel Records	AXEL/VINTAP-2	England	1996	19.99
Budgie	Squawk	CD	Repertoire	REP-4026-WZ	Germany	1996	21.99
Budgie, Ex	Budgie & Beyond (Gold Cd)	CD	Vicious Sloth	VSC-002	Australia	1994	44.99
Buffalo Springfield	Box Set	4CD	Rhino	R2-74324	U.S.A.	2001	37.99
Buffalo Springfield	Buffalo Springfield (Mono/Stereo)	CD	Elektra	62080-2	U.S.A.	1997	9.99
Buffalo Springfield	Last Time Around	CD	Atco	7-90393-2	U.S.A.	1968	9.99
Buffalo Springfield	Retrospective - The Best Of	CD	Atco	7904172	Australia	1969	8.99
Buffalo Springfield	Selections/Box Set (Promo)	CD	Rhino	PRCD-400038	U.S.A.	2001	28.99
Buffalo Tom	A Retrospective (Promo)	CD	Polydor	PRSAD-00734	U.S.A.	1998	7.99
Buffalo Tom	Asides From Buffalo Tom	CD	Beggars Banquet	82028	U.S.A.	2000	13.99
Buffalo Tom	Besides: Coll B-Sides and Rarities	CD	Beggars Banquet	82033	U.S.A.	2002	10.99
Buffalo Tom	Big Red Letter Day	CD	Beggars Banquet	92292	U.S.A.	1993	8.99
Buffalo Tom	Birdbrain	CD	Beggars Banquet	2434-2-H13	U.S.A.	1990	9.99
Buffalo Tom	Buffalo Tom	CD	Beggars Banquet	92426-2	U.S.A.	1992	6.99
Buffalo Tom	I'm Allowed (Promo)	CD Single	Beggars Banquet	PRCD-5451-2	U.S.A.	1993	2.99
Buffalo Tom	I'm Allowed (Tri-Fold Digipk/4 Pstcrds)	CD Single	Beggars Banquet	BBQ-30CD	England	1993	14.99
Buffalo Tom	Let Me Come Over	CD	BMI	ALBA472	Japan	1991	10.99

Artist	Title	Format	Label	Catalog No	Country	Released	Value
Buffalo Tom	Rachael (Promo)	CD	Polydor	PRCDP-00711	U.S.A.	1998	2.99
Buffalo Tom	Sleepy Eyed	CD	Beggars Banquet	61782-2	U.S.A.	1995	5.99
Buffalo Tom	Smitten	CD	Beggars Banquet	BBOCD-205	U.S.A.	1998	6.99
Buffalo Tom	Sodajerk	CD Single	Beggars Banquet	PRCD-5214-2	U.S.A.	1993	4.99
Buffalo Tom	Tangerine	CD Single	Beggars Banquet	BBQ-64CD	England	1995	4.99
Buffalo Tom	Wiser	CD Single	Beggars Banquet	81329	U.S.A.	1998	1.99
Buffett, Jimmy	A White Sport Coat.... (MFSL Gold Cd)	CD	Mobile Fidelity	UDCD-746	U.S.A.	1973	34.99
Buffett, Jimmy	Changes/Lattitudes.... (MCA Gold Cd)	CD	MCA	MCAD-10951	U.S.A.	1977	19.99
Buffett, Jimmy	Rancho Deluxe	CD	Rykodisc	RCD-10709	U.S.A.	1997	13.99
Buffett, Jimmy	Son/Son Of A Sailor (MFSL Gold Cd)	CD	Mobile Fidelity	UDCD-713	U.S.A.	1978	39.99
Buffett, Jimmy	Songs You Know...(MCA Gold Cd)	CD	MCA	MCAD-11169	U.S.A.	1985	23.99
Buffett, Jimmy/Promo	Boats/Beaches/Bars/Ballads Sampler	CD	MCA	CD33-3031	U.S.A.	1992	14.99
Buggles	Adventures In Modern Recording + 3	CD	Flavour	TFCK-87577	Japan	1997	29.99
Buggles	The Age Of Plastic + 3	CD	Island	261-546-274-2	Holland	1980	18.99
Bullens, Cindy	Cindy Bullens	CD	MCA	MCAD-6320	U.S.A.	1989	11.99
Bullens, Cindy	Neverland	CD	Artemis	751090-25	U.S.A.	2001	7.99
Bullens, Cindy	Somewhere Between...	CD	Artemis	ART-1012	U.S.A.	1999	6.99
Bunker, Clive/Jethro Tull	Awakening	CD	A New Day	AND-CD-21	England	1998	11.99
Burdon, Eric	Animal's Spirit	CD	Avenue	74321-79967-2	EU	2000	9.99
Burdon, Eric	Best Of Eric Burdon & War	CD	Rhino	R2-71954	U.S.A.	1995	9.99
Burdon, Eric	Comeback + 17 (O.S.T.)	2CD	Alchemy	PILOT-81	England	2003	12.99
Burdon, Eric	Eric Burdon Sings Animals Hits (Gold)	CD	Avenue	ASR-10608-2	U.S.A.	1995	28.99
Burdon, Eric	Essential Eric Burdon/Animals	CD	Polydor	8434682	Australia	1990	8.99
Burdon, Eric	F#¢k Me...I Thought He Was Dead!!!	CD	One Way	OW-35132	U.S.A.	1999	7.99
Burdon, Eric	Roxy Live	CD	One Way	OW-35131	U.S.A.	1999	7.99
Burdon, Eric	The Comeback Soundtrack	CD	Line	LICD-9.00058-0	Germany	1987	8.99
Burdon, Eric	The Night	CD	One Way	OW-34528	U.S.A.	2001	7.99
Burdon, Eric	The Unreleased	CD	Blue Wave	117	U.S.A.	1992	12.99
Burdon, Eric	The Wicked Man	CD	GNP	GNPD-2194	U.S.A.	1994	8.99
Burdon, Eric/ Animals	Eric Is Here	CD	One Way	OW-31376	U.S.A.	1995	13.99
Burdon, Eric/ Animals	Roadrunners	CD	Raven	RVCD-11	Australia	1990	19.99
Burdon, Eric/ Animals	The Animals' Greatest Hits	CD	Prism Leisure	PLATCD-222	England	1997	7.99
Burdon, Eric/ Animals	The Best Of (1966-1968)	CD	Polydor	849-388-2	U.S.A.	1991	16.99
Burdon, Eric/ Animals	The Twain Shall Meet	CD	One Way	OW-30336	U.S.A.	1994	11.99
Burdon, Eric/ Animals	Winds Of Change	CD	One Way	OW-30335	U.S.A.	1994	19.99
Burdon, Eric/ Animals	Winds Of Change/Twain Shall Meet	2CD	BGO	BGOCD562	England	2002	22.99
Burdon, Eric/ Band	Sun Secrets/Stop	CD	Rhino	R2-71219	U.S.A.	1993	7.99
Burdon, Eric/ New Animals	Psychedelic World	CD	Edsel	EDCD-656	England	2001	14.99
Burdon, Eric/ War	Black-Man's Burdon	2CD	Rhino	R2-71193	U.S.A.	1993	24.99
Burdon, Eric/And Band	That's Live	CD	INAK	1704-2	Germany	1985	10.99
Burdon, Eric/Animals	Love Is	CD	One Way	OW-30338	U.S.A.	1994	32.99
Burdon, Eric/J. Whitherspoon	Black & White Blues	CD	ARG	74321-30748-2	EC	1995	19.99
Burdon, Eric/War	Declares War (Gold Disc)	CD	Avenue	ASR-10604-2	U.S.A.	1995	16.99
Burdon, Eric/War	Love Is All Around	CD	Rhino	R2-71218	U.S.A.	1993	9.99
Burgon, Geoffrey	Brideshead Revisited (MFSL Sliver Cd)	CD	Mobile Fidelity	MFCD-790	U.S.A.	1982	49.99
Burke, Keni	Changes	CD	BMG	BVCP-7433	Japan	1981	19.99
Burnett, Carol	Once Upon A... + 3 (Orig. B. Cast)	CD	MCA	MCAD-10768	U.S.A.	1993	19.99
Burnette, Billy	Coming Home	CD	Capricorn	9-42007-2	U.S.A.	1992	8.99
Burris, Warren	Warren Burris	CD	Line	TLCD-9.00518-0	Germany	1988	79.99
Burroughs, William S.	Break Through..(W/Ornette Coleman)	CD	Sub Rosa	SR-008-CD	Belgium	2001	16.99
Burroughs, William S.	Call Me Burroughs	CD	Rhino	R2-71848	U.S.A.	1995	8.99
Burroughs, William S.	Dead City Radio (With John Cale)	CD	Island	422-846-264-2	U.S.A.	1990	10.99
Burroughs, William S.	Naked Lunch (Spoken Word)	3CD	Warner Bros.	2-522206	U.S.A.	1995	87.99
Burroughs, William S.	Spare Ass Annie/Other Tales	CD	Island	162-535-003-2	U.S.A.	1993	12.99
Burroughs, William S/Gus Van	The Elvis Of Letters	CD Single	Tim/Kerr	91CD001	U.S.A.	1991	7.99
Bush, Kate	Aspects Of The Sensual World	CD Single	Columbia	44K-73174	U.S.A.	1990	8.99
Bush, Kate	Best Works 1978 - 1993 (Promo)	2CD	Toshiba-EMI	SPCD-1402/1403	Japan	1993	149.99
Bush, Kate	Eat The Music	CD Single	Columbia	44K-77165	U.S.A.	1993	8.99

Artist	Title	Format	Label	Catalog No	Country	Released	Value
Bush, Kate	Eat The Music (Promo)	CD	EMI	SPCD-1716	France	1993	34.99
Bush, Kate	Hounds Of Love + 6	CD	EMI	7243-5-25239-2-4	England	1997	18.99
Bush, Kate	Interview Picture Disc	CD	Baktabak	CBAK-4011	England	1990	9.99
Bush, Kate	Lionheart	CD	EMI	0777-7-46065-2-3	England	1978	9.99
Bush, Kate	Live Hammersmith CD/PAL Video	CD	EMI	7243-8-30065-2-6	England	1994	39.99
Bush, Kate	Never For Ever	CD	EMI	7463602	England	1980	9.99
Bush, Kate	Rubberband Girl	CD Single	Columbia	44K-77332	U.S.A.	1993	8.99
Bush, Kate	The Dreaming	CD	EMI	7463612	England	1982	9.99
Bush, Kate	The Kick Inside	CD	EMI	0777-7-46012-2-1	England	1978	9.99
Bush, Kate	The Red Shoes	CD	Columbia	CK-53737	U.S.A.	1993	8.99
Bush, Kate	The Sensual World	CD Single	EMI	CDEM-102	England	1989	8.99
Bush, Kate	The Sensual World	CD	EMI	7950-7-82	England	1989	12.99
Bush, Kate	The Whole Story	CD	EMI	7-46414-2	U.S.A.	1986	7.99
Bush, Kate	This Woman's Work (Promo)	CD Single	Columbia	CSK-2029	U.S.A.	1990	18.99
Bush, Kate	This Woman's Work 1	CD	EMI	7-95238-2	England	1990	28.99
Bush, Kate	This Woman's Work Box Set	8 CD	EMI	79-5237-2	England	1990	84.99
Bush, Kate	This Woman's Work II	CD	EMI	7-95239-2	England	1990	28.99
Butcher, Jon/Axis	Along The Axis	CD	Bear Tracks	BTCD-979-471	Germany	1994	18.99
Butcher, Jon/Axis	American Dream Live	CD	Disky	7243-5-64036-2-8	Holland	2001	9.99
Butcher, Jon/Axis	Electric Factory	CD	Blues Bureau	2036	U.S.A.	1996	9.99
Butcher, Jon/Axis	King Biscuit Flower Hour	CD	King Biscuit	70710-88045-2	Canada	1999	8.99
Butcher, Jon/Axis	Pictures From The Front	CD	Capitol	CDP-590238	U.S.A.	1989	8.99
Butcher, Jon/Axis	Positively The Blues	CD	Blues Bureau	2030	U.S.A.	1995	9.99
Butcher, Jon/Axis	The Best Of: Dreamers Would Ride	CD	Razor & Tie	82172-2	U.S.A.	1998	13.99
Butcher, Jon/Axis	Wishes	CD	Capitol	CDP-7-46772-2	U.S.A.	1987	19.99
Butterfield Blues Band	An Anthology; The Elektra Years	2CD	Elektra	62124-2	U.S.A.	1997	24.99
Butterfield Blues Band	In My Own Dream	CD	Wounded Bird	WOU-4025	England	2002	13.99
Butterfield Blues Band	Keep On Moving	CD	Wounded Bird	WOU-4053	U.S.A.	2002	10.99
Butterfield Blues Band	Sometimes I Feel Like Smilin'	CD	Wounded Bird	WOU-5013	U.S.A.	2002	10.99
Butterfield Blues Band	The Resurrection Of Pigboy Crabshaw	CD	Elektra	74015-2	U.S.A.	1989	8.99
Butterfield, Paul	An Offer You Can't Refuse	CD	M.I.L.	6115	U.S.A.	1999	12.99
Butterfield, Paul	Better Days	CD	Rhino	R2-70877	U.S.A.	1973	6.99
Butterfield, Paul	East-West	CD	Elektra	7315-2	U.S.A.	1990	8.99
Butterfield, Paul	East-West Live	CD	Winner	447	U.S.A.	1996	9.99
Butterfield, Paul	It All Comes Back	CD	Rhino	R2-70878	U.S.A.	1973	12.99
Butterfield, Paul	Legendary P B Rides Again	CD	Amherst	AMH-93305	U.S.A.	1986	14.99
Butterfield, Paul	Live At Winterland Ballroom '73	CD	Victor Ent.	VICP-60651	Japan	1999	34.99
Butterfield, Paul	Original Lost Elektra Sessions	CD	Rhino	R2-73505	U.S.A.	1995	12.99
Butterfield, Paul	Paul Butterfield Blues Band	CD	Elektra	7294-2	U.S.A.	1987	11.99
Butterfield, Paul	Paul Butterfield Blues Band/East West	2CD	Elektra	8122-73571-2	England	2001	21.99
Butterfield, Paul	Put In In Your Ear	CD	Repertoire	REP-4075-WZ	Germany	1991	24.99
Butterfield, Paul	Resurrection Of Pigboy Crabshaw	CD	Rhino	74015-2	U.S.A.	1989	10.99
Butterfield, Paul	Strawberry Jam Live 1966 - 1968	CD	Winner	446	U.S.A.	1995	12.99
Buzzcocks	A Different Kind Of Tension	CD	Nettwerk	30247	U.S.A.	2001	12.99
Buzzcocks	A Different Kind.../Parts 1, 2, 3	CD	I.R.S.	X2-13154	U.S.A.	1992	12.99
Buzzcocks	All Set	CD	I.R.S.	72438-36962-2-2	U.S.A.	1996	7.99
Buzzcocks	Another Music In Different Kitchen + 4	CD	EMI	7243-5-34405-2-7	England	2001	9.99
Buzzcocks	Chronology	CD	EMI	7243-8-57026-2-4	England	1997	10.99
Buzzcocks	Entertaining Friends: Live Hammersmith	CD	EMI	7987292	England	1992	8.99
Buzzcocks	Ever Fallen In Love? - The Best Of	CD	EMI	7243-5-3846-2-8	England	1996	12.99
Buzzcocks	French + 3 (US Version)	CD	I.R.S.	72438-36761-25	U.S.A.	1995	8.99
Buzzcocks	Innocent	CD Single	Essential	2025	England	1993	4.99
Buzzcocks	Lest We Forget	CD	ROIR	158	U.S.A.	1988	7.99
Buzzcocks	Live At The Roxy	CD	Absolutely Free	FREE-CD-002	England	1989	14.99
Buzzcocks	Live in Paris	CD Single	Castle	61259	England	2001	4.99
Buzzcocks	Live Tension (Ltd Only 1977)	CD	Alchemy	SJLTD-02	England	2002	11.99
Buzzcocks	Love Bites + 4	CD	EMI	7243-5-34404-2-8	England	2001	9.99
Buzzcocks	Love Bites/Another Music	CD	I.R.S.	28309	U.S.A.	1994	13.99

B

Artist	Title	Format	Label	Catalog No	Country	Released	Value
Buzzcocks	Many Parts	CD	Restless	7-72377	England	1988	19.99
Buzzcocks	Modern	2CD	EMI	7243-5-21767-0-0	England	1999	8.99
Buzzcocks	Noise Annoys (Ltd Only 1977)	CD	Alchemy	SJLTD-01	England	2002	14.99
Buzzcocks	Paris: Encore Du Pain	CD	Yeaah!	YEAAH-1	England	1999	7.99
Buzzcocks	Peel Sessions	CD Single	Strange Fruit	SFPS044	England	1989	5.99
Buzzcocks	Product	3CD	EMI	7243-8-32767-2-1	England	1995	30.99
Buzzcocks	Singles - Going Steady + 4	CD	EMI	7243-5-34442-2-8	Australia	2001	15.99
Buzzcocks	Small Songs.../Beating Hearts	2CD	Alchemy	PILOT-78	England	2001	10.99
Buzzcocks	The Archive Series - BBC Sessions	CD	EMI	7243-4-97771-2-5	England	1998	13.99
Buzzcocks	The Early Years	CD Single	Receiver	RRSCD3013	England	1990	6.99
Buzzcocks	The Fab Four	CD Single	EMI	CDEM-104	England	1989	8.99
Buzzcocks	The Fab Four	CD Single	EMI	20-3519-2	England	1989	10.99
Buzzcocks	Time's Up	CD	Mute	9121-2	Canada	2000	9.99
Buzzcocks	Total Pop	CD	Weird Systems	21	England	1987	19.99
Buzzcocks	Trade Test Transmission	CD	Essential	ESSCD-195	England	1993	12.99
Buzzcocks/Steve Diggle	Here's One I Made Earlier	CD	AX -S	AXS95CD002	England	1995	16.99
Buzzcocks/Steve Diggle	Secret Public Years: 1981-1989	CD	Anagram	74	England	2000	13.99
Buzzcocks/Steve Diggle	Some Reality + 1	CD	Delicious	DEL-112	England	2003	19.99
Byaela, Jane	On The Edge	CD	Line	SDCD-9.00437-0	Germany	1988	24.99
Byrds	12 Dimensions Box Set (W/Papers)	4CD	Columbia	497610-2	England	2000	24.99
Byrds	Back Pages Sampler (Promo)	CD	Columbia	CSK-2239	U.S.A.	1990	10.99
Byrds	Ballad Of Easy Rider + 7	CD	Columbia	CK-65114	U.S.A.	1997	6.99
Byrds	Byrdmaniax (Line Version)	CD	Line	CLCD-9.00930-0	Germany	1990	13.99
Byrds	Byrdmaniax + 3	CD	Columbia	CK-65848	U.S.A.	2000	8.99
Byrds	Byrds (1973 Reunion Album)	CD	Elektra	7559-60955-2	Germany	1990	14.99
Byrds	Byrds (Adv. Music Promo Sampler #1)	CD	Columbia	CSK-7912	U.S.A.	1996	8.99
Byrds	Byrds Black Box Set	4CD	Columbia	C4K-46773	U.S.A.	1990	28.99
Byrds	Dr. Byrds & Mr. Hyde + 5	CD	Columbia	CK-65113	U.S.A.	1997	9.99
Byrds	Farther Along + 3	CD	Columbia	CK-65849	U.S.A.	2000	10.99
Byrds	Fifth Dimension + 6	CD	Columbia	CK-64847	U.S.A.	1996	10.99
Byrds	Four Dimensions (Ltd Pic Promo)	CD	Columbia	656544-5	England	2000	7.99
Byrds	Full Flyte 1965-1970	CD	Raven	RVCD-10	Australia	1990	14.99
Byrds	In The Beginning	CD	Rhino	R2-70244	U.S.A.	1988	7.99
Byrds	Live At The Fillmore - February 1969	CD	Columbia	CK-65910	U.S.A.	2000	8.99
Byrds	Love That Never Dies (Promo)	CD Single	Columbia	CSK-2227	U.S.A.	1990	9.99
Byrds	Mr. Tambourine Man + 6	CD	Columbia	CK-64845	U.S.A.	1996	7.99
Byrds	Never Before (Stereo, Alternate Takes)	CD	Columbia	A21143	U.S.A.	1989	21.99
Byrds	Notorious Byrd Brothers + 6	CD	Columbia	CK-65151	U.S.A.	1999	9.99
Byrds	Play The Songs Of Bob Dylan	CD	Columbia	501946-2	England	2001	14.99
Byrds	Preflyte	CD	Poptones	MC5044CD	England	2001	12.99
Byrds	Premium Best	CD	Sony	SRCS-8593	Japan	1998	39.99
Byrds	Sweetheart Of The Rodeo + 28	2CD	Columbia	C2K-87189	U.S.A.	2003	14.99
Byrds	Sweetheart Of The Rodeo + 8	CD	Columbia	CK-65150	U.S.A.	1997	11.99
Byrds	The Byrds 20 Essential Tracks	CD	Columbia	CK-47884	U.S.A.	1992	8.99
Byrds	The Preflyte Sessions	2CD	Sundazed	SC-11116	U.S.A.	2001	19.99
Byrds	Turn Turn Turn + 7	CD	Columbia	CK-64846	U.S.A.	1996	10.99
Byrds	Untitled (MFSL Gold Cd)	CD	Mobile Fidelity	UDCD-722	U.S.A.	1970	34.99
Byrds	Untitled/Unissued	CD	Columbia	C2K-65847	U.S.A.	2000	15.99
Byrds	Younger Than Yesterday + 6	CD	Columbia	CK-64848	U.S.A.	1996	8.99
Byrds/Gene Parsons	Kindling	CD	Warner Bros.	WPCR-10656	Japan	2000	29.99
Byrds/Various Artists	Byrd Parts (Solo/Together Compilation)	CD	Raven	RVCD-77	Australia	1998	20.99
Byrds/Various Artists	Byrd Parts 2	CD	Raven	RVCD-165	Australia	2003	20.99
Byrne, David	Angels (Promo)	CD Single	Warner Bros.	PRO-CD-6965	U.S.A.	1994	9.99
Byrne, David	Complete Score/C Wheel (W/Eno)	CD	Sire	3645-2	U.S.A.	1981	8.99
Byrne, David	David Byrne	CD	Warner Bros.	9-45558-2	U.S.A.	1994	8.99
Byrne, David	Feelings	CD	Warner Bros.	9-46605-2	U.S.A.	1997	7.99
Byrne, David	Look Into Eyeball (With Slipcover)	CD	Virgin	7243-8-50924-2-8	U.S.A.	2001	11.99
Byrne, David	Rei Momo	CD	Warner Bros.	W2-25990	U.S.A.	1989	6.99

Artist	Title	Format	Label	Catalog No	Country	Released	Value
Byrne, David	Self Titled Cd W/Book	CD	Sire	2-45666	U.S.A.	1994	24.99
Byrne, David	The Forest	CD	Warner Bros.	W2-26584	U.S.A.	1991	5.99
Byrne, David	Uh-Oh	CD	Warner Bros.	W2-26799	U.S.A.	1992	8.99
Byrne, David/Brian Eno	My Life In Bush Of Ghosts (W/ Qu'ran)	CD	Sire	6093-2	U.S.A.	1981	10.99

C

Artist	Title	Format	Label	Catalog No	Country	Released	Value
C*nts	Midnight Party (Lmt. 1000)	CD	Disturbing	31252	U.S.A.	1993	7.99
C.C.Revival	Bayou Country	CD	Fantasy	FCD-8387-2	U.S.A.	2000	13.99
C.C.Revival	Bayou Country (DCC Gold Cd)	CD	DCC	GZS-1038	U.S.A.	1993	34.99
C.C.Revival	CCR Box Set (Fake Wood Like)	6CD	Fantasy	6CCRCD-4434-2	U.S.A.	2001	58.99
C.C.Revival	Chronicle Volume 2 (Fantasy Gold Cd)	CD	Fantasy	CCGCD-23-2	U.S.A.	1995	22.99
C.C.Revival	Chronicle, Volume I (Fantasy Gold Cd)	CD	Fantasy	CCGCD-22-2	U.S.A.	1995	22.99
C.C.Revival	Cosmo's Factory	CD	Fantasy	FCD-8402-2	U.S.A.	2000	7.99
C.C.Revival	Cosmo's Factory (DCC Gold Cd)	CD	DCC	GZS-1031	U.S.A.	1994	25.99
C.C.Revival	Creedence Clearwater Revival	CD	Fantasy	FCD-8382-2	U.S.A.	2000	14.99
C.C.Revival	Green River (DCC Gold Cd)	CD	DCC	GZS-1064	U.S.A.	1993	14.99
C.C.Revival	Keep On Chooglin'	2CD	Fantasy	TVD98013	Australia	1995	20.99
C.C.Revival	Mardi Gras	CD	Fantasy	FCD-9404-2	U.S.A.	2000	11.99
C.C.Revival	Pendulum (DCC Gold Cd)	CD	DCC	GZS-1097	U.S.A.	1994	14.99
C.C.Revival	The CCR Mix	CD Single	Fantasy	ZYX-8659-5	Germany	1998	14.99
C.C.Revival	Willy And the Poor Boys	CD	Fantasy	FCD-8397-2	U.S.A.	2000	6.99
C.C.Revival	Willy And the Poor Boys (DCC Gold Cd)	CD	DCC	GZS-1010	U.S.A.	1994	39.99
C.C.Revival/Revisited	Recollection	2CD	Fuel 2000	FLD2-1015	U.S.A.	1998	6.99
Cabaret Voltaire	1974 - 76	CD	Mute	CABS15CD	England	1993	13.99
Cabaret Voltaire	2 X 45	CD	Mute	CABS9CD	England	1993	14.99
Cabaret Voltaire	8 Crépuscule Tracks	CD	Giant	GRI-6009-2	U.S.A.	1988	14.99
Cabaret Voltaire	Body And Soul	CD	Victor Ent.	VICP-5057	Japan	1991	24.99
Cabaret Voltaire	Body And Soul + 2	CD	Crepuscle	TWI-944-2	Austria	1991	13.99
Cabaret Voltaire	Code + 2	CD	Parlophone	CDPCS-7312	England	1987	45.99
Cabaret Voltaire	Colours EP	CD Single	Mute	9-61196-2	U.S.A.	1991	7.99
Cabaret Voltaire	Conform To Deform '82/'90	3CD	EMI	CVBOX1	England	2002	24.99
Cabaret Voltaire	Drinking Gasoline	CD Single	Virgin	CVMCD-1	England	1991	14.99
Cabaret Voltaire	Easy Life	CD Single	Parlophone	CDR-6261	England	1990	6.99
Cabaret Voltaire	Groovy, Laidback And Nasty + 1	CD	Parlophone	CDPCS-7338	England	1990	43.99
Cabaret Voltaire	Hai ! (Live In Japan)	CD	Mute	CABS11CD	England	1993	10.99
Cabaret Voltaire	Here To Go	CD Single	Parlophone	CDR-6166	England	1987	18.99
Cabaret Voltaire	Hypnotised	CD Single	Parlophone	CDR-6227	England	1989	8.99
Cabaret Voltaire	I Want You: Western Re-Works '92	CD Single	Virgin	CVCDT-6	England	1992	7.99
Cabaret Voltaire	International Language	CD	Instinct	INS-264-2	U.S.A.	1993	14.99
Cabaret Voltaire	Johnny Yesno (O.S.T.)	CD	Mute	CABS10CD	England	1993	8.99
Cabaret Voltaire	Keep On	CD Single	Parlophone	CDR-6250	England	1989	7.99
Cabaret Voltaire	Listen Up With	2CD	Mute	CABS5CD	England	1993	13.99
Cabaret Voltaire	Live At The Hacienda '83/'86	2CD	Cherry Red	CDMRED220	England	2003	19.99
Cabaret Voltaire	Live At The Lyceum	CD	Mute	CABS13CD	England	1993	8.99
Cabaret Voltaire	Live at the YMCA (27-10-79)	CD	Mute	CABS4CD	England	1993	9.99
Cabaret Voltaire	Methodology '74-'78 Attic Tapes	3CD	Mute	CABS17CD	England	2003	23.99
Cabaret Voltaire	Micro Phonies + 2	CD	Virgin	CVCD-2	England	1992	9.99
Cabaret Voltaire	Mix-Up	CD	Mute	CABS8CD	England	1993	7.99
Cabaret Voltaire	Nag Nag Nag	CD Single	Novamute	NOMU-103-CD	England	2002	6.99
Cabaret Voltaire	Nag Nag Nag	CD Single	Mute	CABS1CD	England	1990	6.99
Cabaret Voltaire	Orig. Sound Sheffield: Best Of '78/'82	CD	Mute	CABS16CD	England	2002	7.99
Cabaret Voltaire	Percussion Force + 3	CD Single	Crepuscle	TWI-951-2	Austria	1991	7.99
Cabaret Voltaire	Plasticity	CD	Instinct	INS-255-2	U.S.A.	1993	14.99

Artist	Title	Format	Label	Catalog No	Country	Released	Value
Cabaret Voltaire	Radiation: BBC Recordings '84 - '86	CD	Alchemy	PILOT-39	England	2003	10.99
Cabaret Voltaire	Red Mecca	CD	Mute	CABS3CD	England	1993	11.99
Cabaret Voltaire	Remixed	CD	EMI	7243-5-32573-2-3	England	2001	18.99
Cabaret Voltaire	Technology: W. Re-Works '92 + 2	CD	Virgin	CVCD-4	England	1992	9.99
Cabaret Voltaire	Technology: Western Re-Works 1992	CD	Caroline	CAROL-1875-2	U.S.A.	1992	9.99
Cabaret Voltaire	The Conversation	2CD	Instinct	INS-273-2	U.S.A.	1993	19.99
Cabaret Voltaire	The Covenant, The Sword...	CD	Virgin	CVCD-3	England	1985	11.99
Cabaret Voltaire	The Covenant, The Sword... + 2	CD	Caroline	CAROL-1331-2	U.S.A.	1985	11.99
Cabaret Voltaire	The Crackdown + 4	CD	Virgin	CVCD-1	England	1986	11.99
Cabaret Voltaire	The Drain Train/Pressure Company	CD	Mute	CABS14CD	England	1993	14.99
Cabaret Voltaire	The Golden Moments Of	CD	Rough Trade	RUF-CD-6001	England	1987	19.99
Cabaret Voltaire	The Living Legends	CD	Mute	CABS6CD	England	1993	11.99
Cabaret Voltaire	The Voice of America	CD	Mute	CABS2CD	England	1993	13.99
Cabaret Voltaire	Three Mantras	CD	Mute	CABS7CD	England	1993	11.99
Cabaret Voltaire	What Is Real	CD Single	Crepuscle	TWI-948-2	Austria	1991	8.99
Cabaret Voltaire/Chris Watson	Hafler Trio - A Bag Of Cats	CD	Touch	SPL-1	England	1992	9.99
Cabaret Voltaire/Chris Watson	Hafler Trio - A Small Child Dreams...	CD Single	Important	IMPREC-012	U.S.A.	2003	11.99
Cabaret Voltaire/Chris Watson	Hafler Trio - A Thirsty Fish	CD	Mute	KUT6CD	England	1995	10.99
Cabaret Voltaire/Chris Watson	Hafler Trio - All That Rises Must...	CD	Mute	KUT5CD	England	1995	11.99
Cabaret Voltaire/Chris Watson	Hafler Trio - Bang! An Open Letter	CD	Mute	KUT1CD	England	1995	16.99
Cabaret Voltaire/Chris Watson	Hafler Trio - Bootleg	CD	Ash Int.	ASH-1.3	U.S.A.	1995	21.99
Cabaret Voltaire/Chris Watson	Hafler Trio - Dislocation	CD	Staalplaat	STCD-003	Netherland	1990	17.99
Cabaret Voltaire/Chris Watson	Hafler Trio - F*ck	CD	Touch	TONE-3	England	1992	21.99
Cabaret Voltaire/Chris Watson	Hafler Trio - Four Ways Of Saying Five	CD	Mute	KUT4CD	England	1995	10.99
Cabaret Voltaire/Chris Watson	Hafler Trio - Hljodmynd	CD	Die Stadt	DS-01	Germany	2000	29.99
Cabaret Voltaire/Chris Watson	Hafler Trio - How To Reform Mankind	CD	Touch	TONE-24	England	1993	21.99
Cabaret Voltaire/Chris Watson	Hafler Trio - Ingotum Per Ignotius	CD	Touch	TONE-11	England	1989	21.99
Cabaret Voltaire/Chris Watson	Hafler Trio - Intoutof	CD	Mute	KUT14CD	England	1995	12.99
Cabaret Voltaire/Chris Watson	Hafler Trio - Kill The King	CD	Staalplaat	STCD-013	Netherland	1991	19.99
Cabaret Voltaire/Chris Watson	Hafler Trio - Master Of Money	CD	Touch	TONE-18	England	1997	21.99
Cabaret Voltaire/Chris Watson	Hafler Trio - Masturbatorium	CD	Touch	TONE-1	England	1991	21.99
Cabaret Voltaire/Chris Watson	Hafler Trio - No Man Put Asunder...	CD	Die Stadt	DS-57	Germany	2003	24.99
Cabaret Voltaire/Chris Watson	Hafler Trio - Normally	2CD	Soleilmoon	SOL093CD	U.S.A.	2003	14.99
Cabaret Voltaire/Chris Watson	Hafler Trio - One Dozen....	CD	Sub Rosa	SR-071-CD	Belgium	1994	21.99
Cabaret Voltaire/Chris Watson	Hafler Trio - Redintergrate 1, 2, 3	CD	Staalplaat	STCD-014	Netherland	1991	19.99
Cabaret Voltaire/Chris Watson	Hafler Trio - Resurrection Live Sweden	CD	Touch	TONE-22	England	1997	14.99
Cabaret Voltaire/Chris Watson	Hafler Trio - Seven Hours Sleep	CD	Mute	KUT3CD	England	1995	13.99
Cabaret Voltaire/Chris Watson	Hafler Trio - Walk Gently Through...	CD	Mute	KUT2CD	England	1995	10.99
Cabaret Voltaire/Chris Watson	Hafler Trio - Whistling About Chickens	2CD	Fire Inc.	F-10	Netherland	2002	18.99
Cabaret Voltaire/Chris Watson	Hafler Trio Play The Hafler Trio	CD	Staalplaat	STCD-031	Netherland	1991	19.99
Cabaret Voltaire/Chris Watson	Outside The Circle Of Fire	CD	Touch	TONE-37	England	1998	22.99
Cabaret Voltaire/Chris Watson	Stepping Into The Dark	CD	Touch	TONE-27	England	1996	22.99
Cabaret Voltaire/Chris Watson	Weather Report	CD	Touch	TONE-47	England	2003	22.99
Cabaret Voltaire/R Kirk/Barrat	Sweet Exorcist - CCCD	CD	Warp	WARPCD1	England	1990	25.99
Cabaret Voltaire/Richard Kirk	Agents With False Memories	CD	Ash Int.	ASH-3.1	U.S.A.	1996	16.99
Cabaret Voltaire/Richard Kirk	Al Jabr - One Million And Three (Prod.)	CD	Alphaphone	ALPHACD5	England	1999	19.99
Cabaret Voltaire/Richard Kirk	Alphaphone, Vol. 1: Step, Write, Run	2CD	Touch	TONE-6	England	1996	29.99
Cabaret Voltaire/Richard Kirk	Biochemical Dread - Bush Doctrine	CD	c0c0s0l1dc1t1	CSC006	England	2003	19.99
Cabaret Voltaire/Richard Kirk	Black Jesus Voice	CD	Mute	KIRK3CD	England	1995	13.99
Cabaret Voltaire/Richard Kirk	Blacworld - Subduing Demons ...	CD	Alphaphone	ALPHACD7	England	2001	21.99
Cabaret Voltaire/Richard Kirk	Dark Magus - Night Watchman	CD	Alphaphone	ALPHACD3	England	1997	21.99
Cabaret Voltaire/Richard Kirk	Darkness At Noon	CD	Touch	TONE-41	England	1999	21.99
Cabaret Voltaire/Richard Kirk	Digital Lifeforms	CD	Touch	TONE-21	England	1993	21.99
Cabaret Voltaire/Richard Kirk	Digital Terrestrials - Aural Illusions	CD	Die Stadt	DS-41	Germany	2001	19.99
Cabaret Voltaire/Richard Kirk	Disposable Half Truths	CD	Mute	KIRK-1-CD	England	1992	15.99
Cabaret Voltaire/Richard Kirk	Electronic Eye - Closed Circuit	2CD	Beyond	RBACD-8	England	1994	21.99
Cabaret Voltaire/Richard Kirk	Electronic Eye - Neurometrik	CD	Alphaphone	ALPHACD6	England	2000	21.99
Cabaret Voltaire/Richard Kirk	Electronic Eye - The Idea Of Justice	CD	Beyond	RBADCD-14	England	1995	13.99

C

Artist	Title	Format	Label	Catalog No	Country	Released	Value
Cabaret Voltaire/Richard Kirk	Hoodoo Talk (W/Peter Hope)	CD	Mute	KIRK5CD	England	1995	17.99
Cabaret Voltaire/Richard Kirk	Intone Unreleased Projects 1996/2000	CD	Intone	INTONECD03	England	2003	21.99
Cabaret Voltaire/Richard Kirk	Loopstatic	CD	Touch	TONE-12	England	2000	13.99
Cabaret Voltaire/Richard Kirk	Nitrogen - Intoxica	2CD	Alphaphone	ALPHACD1	England	1996	24.99
Cabaret Voltaire/Richard Kirk	Orchestral Terrestrial - Here/Elsewhere	CD	Die Stadt	DS-40	Germany	2001	19.99
Cabaret Voltaire/Richard Kirk	Sandoz - Afrocentris	CD	Intone	INTONECD01	England	2002	19.99
Cabaret Voltaire/Richard Kirk	Sandoz - Dark Continent	CD	Touch	TONE-4	England	1996	19.99
Cabaret Voltaire/Richard Kirk	Sandoz - Every Man Got Dreaming	CD	Touch	TONE-28	England	1995	7.99
Cabaret Voltaire/Richard Kirk	Sandoz - God Bless The Conspiracy	CD	Alphaphone	ALPHACD2	England	1997	14.99
Cabaret Voltaire/Richard Kirk	Sandoz - In Chant To Jah	CD	Touch	TONE-10	England	1998	18.99
Cabaret Voltaire/Richard Kirk	Sandoz - Intensely Radioactive	CD	Touch	TONE-23	England	1994	18.99
Cabaret Voltaire/Richard Kirk	Sweet Exorcist - Spirit Guide/L Tech	CD	Touch	TONE-33	England	1994	19.99
Cabaret Voltaire/Richard Kirk	The Number Of Magic	CD	TVT	TVT-7233CD	U.S.A.	1995	10.99
Cabaret Voltaire/Richard Kirk	Time High Fiction	2CD	Mute	KIRK2CD	England	1995	24.99
Cabaret Voltaire/Richard Kirk	Trafficante - Is This Now?	CD	Alphaphone	ALPHACD4	England	1998	22.99
Cabaret Voltaire/Richard Kirk	Twat: The War Against Terror	CD	Intone	INTONECD02	England	2003	21.99
Cabaret Voltaire/Richard Kirk	Ugly Spirit	CD	Mute	KIRK4CD	England	1995	10.99
Cabaret Voltaire/Richard Kirk	Virtual State	CD	TVT	TVT-7218CD	U.S.A.	1994	12.99
Cabaret Voltaire/S Mallinder	Pow-Wow Plus + 4	CD	Mute	MAL-1-CD	England	1992	24.99
Cactus	Cactology	CD	Rhino	R2-72411	U.S.A.	1996	19.99
Cactus	Cactus	CD	Atlantic	7567-80290-2	Germany	1977	18.99
Cactus	'OL 'N' Sweaty	CD	Atlantic	7567-80764-2	Germany	1998	23.99
Cactus	One Way...Or Another	CD	Line	LECD-9.01015-0	Germany	1991	16.99
Cactus	Restrictions	CD	Repertoire	REP-4131-WZ	Germany	2002	29.99
Cadbury, Dik	About Time	CD	Choice Of Music	200-102-2	Germany	2000	9.99
Cafferty, John/Beaver Brown	Eddie/Cruisers II - Eddie Lives (O.S.T.)	CD	Pony Canyon	PCCY-00001	Japan	1989	24.99
Cafferty, John/Beaver Brown	Eddie/The Cruisers (O.S.T.)	CD	Volcano	32001-2	U.S.A.	1983	9.99
Cafferty, John/Beaver Brown	Eddie/The Cruisers: Unreleased Tapes	CD	Scotti Bros.	72392-75231-2	U.S.A.	1991	13.99
Cafferty, John/Beaver Brown	Roadhouse	CD	Scotti Bros.	ZK-40980	U.S.A.	1988	8.99
Cafferty, John/Beaver Brown	Roadhouse	CD	Canyon	D32Y-0182	Japan	1988	14.99
Cafferty, John/Beaver Brown	Tough All Over	CD	Scotti Bros.	72392-75410-2	U.S.A.	1993	19.99
Cafferty, John/Beaver Brown	Tough All Over	CD	Pony Canyon	D32Y-0034	Japan	1985	20.99
Cage, John	25 Year Retrospective Concert	3CD	Wergo	WER-6247-2	Germany	1992	44.99
Cage, John	Atlas Eclipticalis & Winter Music/103	4CD	Asphodel	ASPH-2000	U.S.A.	2000	22.99
Cage, John	Birdcage	CD	Electronic Music	EMF-013	U.S.A.	2000	14.99
Cage, John	Cage Performs Cage: The Text Pieces I	2CD	Mode	MODE-84/85	U.S.A.	1999	19.99
Cage, John	Cheap Imitation	CD	Ampersand	AMPERE-03	U.S.A.	1999	11.99
Cage, John	Credo In US... More Works...	CD	Wergo	WER-6651-2	Germany	2001	19.99
Cage, John	Diary: How to Improve the World	CD	Wergo	WER-6912-2	Germany	2000	19.99
Cage, John	Empty Words (Parte III)	2CD	Ampersand	AMPERE-06	U.S.A.	2000	15.99
Cage, John	Etudes Australes	3CD	Wergo	WER-6152-2	Germany	1992	34.99
Cage, John	Europeras 3 & 4	2CD	Mode	MODE-38/39	U.S.A.	1995	59.99
Cage, John	Four Walls	CD	Long Arms	CDLA-02048	Russia	2002	9.99
Cage, John	Freeman Etudes, Books 3 & 4	CD	Mode	MODE-37	U.S.A.	1994	16.99
Cage, John	Joyce, Duchamp, Satie: An Alphabet	2CD	Wergo	WER-6310-2	Germany	2003	24.99
Cage, John	Music For Keyboard 1935-1948	2CD	Sony	SICC-76/7	Japan	2003	49.99
Cage, John	Music For Merce Cunningham	CD	Mode	MODE-24	U.S.A.	1991	19.99
Cage, John	Music of Changes	CD	Wergo	WER-60099-50	Germany	1988	15.99
Cage, John	Music Of Changes	CD	Lovely Music	LCD-2053	U.S.A.	1998	19.99
Cage, John	Number Pieces	CD	Mode	MODE-44	U.S.A.	1995	19.99
Cage, John	Roaratorio	2CD	Mode	MODE-28/29	U.S.A.	1992	12.99
Cage, John	Sonata XIII/Music For Marcel ...	CD	Wergo	WER-6074-2	Germany	1991	19.99
Cage, John	The Choral Works	CD	Mode	MODE-71	U.S.A.	1998	19.99
Cage, John	The Complete String Quartets Volume 1	CD	Mode	MODE-17	U.S.A.	1989	15.99
Cage, John	The Number Pieces 2	CD	Mode	MODE-75	U.S.A.	1999	15.99
Cage, John	The Orchestral Works 3	CD	Mode	MODE-108	U.S.A.	2002	15.99
Cage, John	The Orchestral Works, 2	CD	Mode	MODE-86	U.S.A.	2000	15.99
Cage, John	The Piano Concertos	CD	Mode	MODE-57	U.S.A.	1997	16.99

Artist	Title	Format	Label	Catalog No	Country	Released	Value
Cage, John	The Piano Works 2	CD	Mode	MODE-50	U.S.A.	1996	15.99
Cage, John	The Piano Works 3	CD	Mode	MODE-63	U.S.A.	1998	15.99
Cage, John	The Piano Works I	CD	Mode	MODE-47	U.S.A.	1995	15.99
Cage, John	The Works for Piano 4	CD	Mode	MODE-106	U.S.A.	2002	19.99
Cage, John	The Works For Saxophone I	CD	Mode	MODE-104	U.S.A.	2002	14.99
Cage, John	The Works For Violin 4	CD	Mode	MODE-100	U.S.A.	2001	14.99
Cage, John	The Works For Violin 5	CD	Mode	MODE-118	U.S.A.	2003	15.99
Cage, John	The Works For Violin, Vol. 3	CD	Mode	MODE-88	U.S.A.	2000	14.99
Cage, John	Variations II	CD	Wergo	WER-6636-2	Germany	1999	14.99
Cage, John	Works For Percussion	CD	Wergo	WER-6203-2	Germany	1991	15.99
Cage, John	Works For Piano, Toy Piano	CD	Wergo	WER-6158-2	Germany	1991	14.99
Cage, John	Works Piano & Prepared Piano Vol I	CD	Wergo	WER-60151-50	Germany	1988	13.99
Cage, John/David Tudor	Indeterminacy	2CD	Smithsonian	SF-40804/5	U.S.A.	1992	24.99
Cage, John/Hosokawa	Two 4th Power	CD	Wergo	WER-6617-2	Germany	1997	14.99
Cage, John/Jack Bruce	The Works For Piano 5	CD	Mode	MODE-123	U.S.A.	2003	14.99
Cage, John/K Patchen	The City Wears A Slouch...	CD	Cortical Foundation	CORTI-14	U.S.A.	1942	26.99
Cage, John/Leandre	Wonderful Widow ...	CD	Montaigne	MO-782121	France	2000	14.99
Cage, John/Leandre	Wonderful Widow Of ...	CD	Montaigne	MO-782076	France	1996	14.99
Cage, John/Sofia G.	One8	CD	Wergo	WER-6288-2	Germany	1996	14.99
Cake	Fashion Nugget	CD	Capricorn	314-532-867-2	U.S.A.	1996	8.99
Cake	Motorcade Of Generosity	CD	Capricorn	9-42035-2	U.S.A.	1995	8.99
Cake	Prolonging The Magic	CD	Capricorn	314-538-092-2	U.S.A.	1998	8.99
Cake	Prolonging The Magic (Clean)	CD	Capricorn	314-538-114-2	U.S.A.	1998	7.99
Cale, J J	20th Century Masters: The Millennium	CD	Mercury	314-586-761-2	U.S.A.	2002	8.99
Cale, J J	5	CD	Mercury	810-313-2	U.S.A.	1979	8.99
Cale, J J	8	CD	Mercury	811-152-2	U.S.A.	1983	14.99
Cale, J J	Anyway The Wind Blows: The Anth.	2CD	Mercury	314-532-901-2	U.S.A.	1997	24.99
Cale, J J	Closer To You	CD	Virgin	7243-8-39610-2	U.S.A.	1994	8.99
Cale, J J	Grasshopper	CD	Mercury	800-038-2	U.S.A.	1982	8.99
Cale, J J	Guitar Man	CD	Virgin	7243-8-41480-2	U.S.A.	1996	8.99
Cale, J J	Live	CD	Narada	7243-8-50642-2	U.S.A.	2001	8.99
Cale, J J	Naturally	CD	Mercury	830-042-2	U.S.A.	1972	8.99
Cale, J J	Number 10	CD	Silvertone	41506-2	U.S.A.	1992	8.99
Cale, J J	Okie	CD	Mercury	842-102-2	U.S.A.	1974	8.99
Cale, J J	Really	CD	Mercury	810-314-2	U.S.A.	1972	8.99
Cale, J J	Shades	CD	Mercury	800-105-2	U.S.A.	1980	14.99
Cale, J J	Special Edition	CD	Mercury	818-633-2	U.S.A.	1984	8.99
Cale, J J	The Very Best Of	CD	Mercury	314-534-754-2	U.S.A.	1998	8.99
Cale, J J	To Tulsa And Back	CD	Sanctuary	06076-84687-2	U.S.A.	2004	8.99
Cale, J J	Travel Log	CD	Silvertone	1306-2-J13	U.S.A.	1990	8.99
Cale, J J	Troubadour	CD	Mercury	810-001-2	U.S.A.	1976	8.99
Cale, J J/Leathercoated Minds	A Trip Down the Sunset Strip	CD	Captain Trip	CTCD-370	Japan	1967	19.99
Cale, John	5 Track EP (Promo Diff Cover)	CD	EMI	CDEMDJ621	England	2003	10.99
Cale, John	5 Tracks (EP)	CD	EMI	7243-552190-22	England	2003	11.99
Cale, John	Antartida	CD	Crepuscle	TWI-1008	Austria	1995	12.99
Cale, John	Artificial Intelligence	CD	Beggars Banquet	BBL-68CD	England	1985	12.99
Cale, John	Close Watch - An Introduction To	CD	Island	524-642-2	Germany	1999	12.99
Cale, John	Dream Interpretation	CD	Table Of Elements	TOE-CD-79	U.S.A.	2000	17.99
Cale, John	Dream Interpretation	CD	Captain Trip	CTCD-424	Japan	1969	14.99
Cale, John	Eat/Kiss - Music Films Of Andy Warhol	CD	Hannibal	HNCD-1407	U.S.A.	1997	11.99
Cale, John	Even Cowgirls Get The Blues	CD	Dance Teria	DANCD113	France	1991	14.99
Cale, John	Fear	CD	Island	262-046	Germany	1974	14.99
Cale, John	Fragments Of A Rainy Season	CD	Hannibal	HNCD-1372	U.S.A.	1992	9.99
Cale, John	Guts	CD	Island	846-065-2	France	1977	11.99
Cale, John	Helen Of Troy	CD	Island	522-116-2	Germany	1977	12.99
Cale, John	Hobosapiens	CD	EMI	593909-2	EU	2003	14.99
Cale, John	Hobosapiens (Promo Advance)	CD	EMI	HOBODJ001	England	2003	14.99
Cale, John	Honi Soit...	CD	A&M	394-849-2	Germany	1981	29.99

Artist	Title	Format	Label	Catalog No	Country	Released	Value
Cale, John	La Naissance De L'Amour	CD	Crepuscle	TWI-954-2	Austria	1993	14.99
Cale, John	Le Vent De La Nuit	CD	Crepuscle	TWI-1083	Austria	1999	14.99
Cale, John	More Fragments (Promo Sampler)	CD Single	Sacem	593119	France	1992	24.99
Cale, John	Music For A New Society	CD	Rhino	R2-71743	U.S.A.	1993	13.99
Cale, John	Nico, The Ballet	CD	Detour	3984-22122-2	Germany	1998	9.99
Cale, John	N'oublie Pas Que Tu Vas Mourir	CD	Crepuscle	TWI-1028	Austria	1995	19.99
Cale, John	Paris 1919	CD	Reprise	2131-2	U.S.A.	1973	15.99
Cale, John	Paris S'eveille (Booker T. By The V. U.)	CD	Delabel	DE-030934	France	1991	14.99
Cale, John	Sabotage (Live) + 4	CD	Diesel Motor	MOTORCD1002	England	1999	8.99
Cale, John	Seducing Down The Door: Collection	2CD	Rhino	R2-71685	U.S.A.	1994	19.99
Cale, John	Slow Dazzle	CD	Island	CID-9317	England	1975	12.99
Cale, John	Stainless Gamelan	CD	Table Of Elements	TOE-CD-80	U.S.A.	2000	17.99
Cale, John	Stainless Gamelan	CD	Captain Trip	CTCD-425	Japan	2000	14.99
Cale, John	Sun Blindness Music	CD	Table Of Elements	TOE-CD-75	U.S.A.	2000	17.99
Cale, John	Sun Blindness Music	CD	Captain Trip	CTCD-375	Japan	1965	14.99
Cale, John	The Academy In Peril	CD	Reprise	2079-2	U.S.A.	1972	29.99
Cale, John	The Island Years	2CD	Island	314-524-235-2	U.S.A.	1996	21.99
Cale, John	The Unknown	CD	Crepuscle	TWI-1023	Austria	1999	14.99
Cale, John	Vintage Violence + 2	CD	Columbia	CK-65935	U.S.A.	2001	8.99
Cale, John	Walking On Locusts	CD	Hannibal	HNCD-1395	U.S.A.	1996	13.99
Cale, John	Words For The Dying	CD	Warner Bros.	9-26024-2	U.S.A.	1989	8.99
Cale, John/ Angus Maclise	A Inside the Dream Syndicate Vol 1	CD	Captain Trip	CTCD-376	Japan	1965	14.99
Cale, John/ Angus Maclise	Inside The Dream Syndicate - Volume I	CD	Table Of Elements	TOE-CD-74	U.S.A.	2000	17.99
Cale, John/Bob Neuwirth	Last Day On Earth	CD	MCA	MCAD-11037	U.S.A.	1994	8.99
Cale, John/Terry Riley	Church Of Anthrax	CD	Columbia	COL-474604-2	Holland	1970	11.99
Cale, John/Various Artists	Somewhere In The City	CD	Velvel	63467-79717-2	U.S.A.	1998	7.99
California Executives	Dancing And Romancing	CD	Line	TLCD-9.00584-0	Germany	1988	229.99
California, Randy	Blues From The Soul	2CD	Acadia	ACAD-8047	England	2003	19.99
California, Randy	Euro-American	CD	Line	LICD-9.01346-0	Germany	1997	15.99
California, Randy	Euro-American	CD	Line	LICD-9.00041-0	Germany	1988	15.99
California, Randy	Euro-American/Shattered Dreams	2CD	Line	LICD-9.21173-S	Germany	1992	29.99
California, Randy	Kapt. Kopter/Fabulous Twirly Birds + 3	CD	Columbia	487579-2	Austria	1972	14.99
California, Randy	Restless + 7	CD	Acadia	ACA-8064	England	2003	12.99
California, Randy	Shattered Dreams	CD	Line	LICD-9.00197-0	Germany	1987	16.99
California, Randy	Shattered Dreams	CD	Line	LICD-9.01314-0	Germany	1997	16.99
California-Guitar-Trio	A Christmas Album	CD	Inside Out	6-93723-65422-5	Germany	2002	14.99
California-Guitar-Trio	Cg3+2 (With Tony Levin)	CD	Inside Out	6-93723-65242-9	Germany	2002	19.99
California-Guitar-Trio	Invitation	CD	Discipline Global	DGM-9501	England	1994	14.99
California-Guitar-Trio	Pathways	CD	Discipline Global	DGM-9803	England	1998	9.99
California-Guitar-Trio	Rocks The West	CD	Discipline Global	DGM-0003	England	2000	8.99
California-Guitar-Trio	The First Decade	CD	Inside Out	6-93723-65802-5	Germany	2003	8.99
California-Guitar-Trio	Yamanashi Blues	CD	Discipline Global	DGM-9301	England	1994	21.99
Call	20th Century Masters: The Millennium	CD	Hip O	314-560-825-2	U.S.A.	2000	11.99
Cama de Gato	Cama De Gato	CD	Line	RICD-9.00524-0	Germany	1988	14.99
Camel	A Live Record + 5	2CD	Decca	8829282	England	2002	16.99
Camel	A Nod And A Wink + 1	CD	Pony Canyon	PCCY-01599	Japan	2002	15.99
Camel	Breathless	CD	Deram	820-726-2	Germany	1992	15.99
Camel	Camel +3	CD	MCA	8829252	England	2002	11.99
Camel	Coming Of Age	2CD	Camel Productions	CP-008CD	U.S.A.	1998	23.99
Camel	Dust And Dreams	CD	Camel Productions	CP-001CD	U.S.A.	1991	14.99
Camel	Echoes	2CD	Deram	844-340-2	U.S.A.	1993	23.99
Camel	Gods Of Light	CD	Camel Productions	CP-010CD	U.S.A.	2000	10.99
Camel	Harbour Of Tears	CD	Camel Productions	CP-006CD	U.S.A.	1996	10.99
Camel	I Can See Your House From Here	CD	Deram	820-614-2	England	1990	19.99
Camel	Lunar Sea - An Anthology 1973-1985	2CD	Decca	8829952	Germany	2001	18.99
Camel	Master Series	CD	Deram	844-011-2	England	1997	13.99
Camel	Mirage + 4	CD	Deram	8829292	England	2002	13.99
Camel	Moonmadness + 6	CD	Decca	8829312	England	2002	13.99

Artist	Title	Format	Label	Catalog No	Country	Released	Value
Camel	Music Inspired The Snow Goose + 6	CD	Decca	8829302	England	2002	17.99
Camel	Never Let Go	2CD	Camel Productions	CP-004CD	U.S.A.	1993	16.99
Camel	Nude	CD	Deram	810-880-2	Germany	1983	15.99
Camel	On The Road 1972	CD	Camel Productions	CP-003CD	U.S.A.	1992	7.99
Camel	On The Road 1981	CD	Camel Productions	CP-007CD	U.S.A.	1997	10.99
Camel	On The Road 1982	CD	Camel Productions	CP-005CD	U.S.A.	1994	10.99
Camel	Pressure Points - Camel Live	CD	London	820-166-2	U.S.A.	1984	11.99
Camel	Rain Dances + 1	CD	Deram	820-725-2	U.S.A.	1991	17.99
Camel	Rajaz	CD	Camel Productions	74129-90009-2-9	U.S.A.	1999	13.99
Camel	Stationary Traveller	CD	Decca	820-020-2	England	1984	12.99
Camel	The Paris Collection	CD	Camel Productions	CP-011CD	U.S.A.	2001	13.99
Camel	The Single Factor	CD	Deram	800-081-2	Germany	1994	17.99
Cameo	Alligator Woman	CD	Polydor	PHCR-6083	Japan	1982	69.99
Cameo	Feel Me	CD	Nippon Columbia	PHCR-6081	Japan	1980	84.99
Cameo	Knights Of The Soundtable	CD	PolyGram	PHCR-6082	Japan	1981	34.99
Cameo	Style	CD	Polydor	PHCR-6084	Japan	1983	59.99
Campbell, Glen	The Very Best Of	CD	Capitol	CDP-546483	U.S.A.	1987	8.99
Campbell, Glen	The Very Best Of	CD	Capitol	72435-41816-2-7	U.S.A.	2003	8.99
Campbell, Glen/Jimmy Webb	Reunited With Jimmy Webb	CD	Raven	RVCD-95	Australia	1999	10.99
Can	Anthology - 25 Years	2CD	Mute/Spoon	9063-2	Austria	1998	11.99
Can	Delay 1968	CD	Spoon	SPOON-9062	England	2002	13.99
Can	Ege Bamyasi	CD	Spoon	SPOON-9056	England	2002	8.99
Can	Future Days	CD	Spoon	SPOON-9055	England	2002	11.99
Can	Monster Movie	CD	Spoon	SPOON-9057	England	2003	12.99
Can	Sacrilege	2CD	Mute	MUTE-9033-2	Canada	1997	11.99
Can	Soon Over Babaluma	CD	Spoon	SPOON-9065	England	2003	15.99
Can	Soundtracks	CD	Spoon	SPOON-9061	England	2003	14.99
Can	Tago Mago	CD	Spoon	SPOON-9054	England	2002	11.99
Can	Unlimited Editon	CD	Spoon	SPOON-1072	England	2003	7.99
Canned-Heat	'70 Concert - Live In Europe	CD	Magic	3930171	France	2002	18.99
Canned-Heat	Boogie With Canned Heat + 6	CD	Magic	4980302	France	1999	18.99
Canned-Heat	Canned Heat Blues Band	CD	Canned Heat	51416-1416-2	U.S.A.	1998	9.99
Canned-Heat	Far Out	2CD	Akarma	AJ-115/2	Italy	2000	18.99
Canned-Heat	Future Blues + 5	CD	Magic	3930170	France	2002	13.99
Canned-Heat	Hallelujah	CD	See For Miles	SEE-CD248	England	1969	16.99
Canned-Heat	Hallelujah + 4	CD	Magic	3930087	France	2001	18.99
Canned-Heat	Historical Figures/Ancient Heads + 1	CD	Magic	3930233	France	2002	10.99
Canned-Heat	Human Condition	CD	AIM	AIM-1071-CD	Australia	2002	11.99
Canned-Heat	KBFH- In Concert	CD	King Biscuit	70710-88005-2-4	U.S.A.	1995	10.99
Canned-Heat	Let's Work Together	3CD	Goldies	GLD-25439-2	Portugal	2001	19.99
Canned-Heat	Live At Topanga Corral + Vintage	Mini Lp	Akarma	AK003/5	Italy	1970	9.99
Canned-Heat	Living The Blues	2 Mini Lp	Akarma	AK-051/2	Italy	1999	16.99
Canned-Heat	The New Age	CD	BGO	BGOCD85	England	1990	14.99
Canned-Heat	The Ties That Bind	CD	Archive	ACH-80002	U.S.A.	1997	5.99
Canned-Heat/J L Hooker	Hooker 'N' Heat (MFSL Gold Cd)	2CD	Mobile Fidelity	UDCD-2-676	U.S.A.	1970	69.99
Canned-Heat/J L Hooker	Hooker N' Heat + 2	2CD	Magic	3930232	France	2002	21.99
Canned-Heat/Memphis Slim	Memphis Heat	CD	Verve	519-725-2	U.S.A.	1993	9.99
Capaldi, Jim	Let The Thunder Cry	CD	Purple Pyramid	CLP-0791-2	U.S.A.	1999	8.99
Capaldi, Jim	Living On The Outside	CD	SPV	SPV085-72512CD	Germany	2001	10.99
Capaldi, Jim	Living On The Outside	CD	Pyramid	024-691-018-2	U.S.A.	2003	8.99
Capaldi, Jim	Oh How We Danced	CD	Edsel	EDCD-502	England	1996	35.99
Capaldi, Jim	Short Cut Draw Blood	CD	Edsel	EDCD-504	England	1996	14.99
Capaldi, Jim	Some Come Running	CD	Island	91024-2	U.S.A.	1988	6.99
Capaldi, Jim	Whale Meat Again	CD	Edsel	EDCD-503	England	1996	14.99
Captain Beyond	Captain Beyond	CD	Polydor K.K.	P33P-25051	Japan	1990	13.99
Captain Beyond	Captain Beyond	CD	Capricorn	314-536-107- 2	U.S.A.	1997	8.99
Captain Beyond	Dawn Explosion	CD	One Way	OW-33639	U.S.A.	1997	16.99
Captain Beyond	Sufficiently Breathless	CD	Polydor K.K.	POCP-1827	Japan	1990	13.99

Artist	Title	Format	Label	Catalog No	Country	Released	Value
Captain Beyond	Sufficiently Breathless	CD	Capricorn	314-558-380-2	U.S.A.	1998	8.99
Captain-Beefheart	A Carrot Is As Close As A Rabbit...	CD	Virgin	0777-7-88303-2-0	England	1993	13.99
Captain-Beefheart	At His Best	CD	Buddah	SCD-4922	U.S.A.	1989	8.99
Captain-Beefheart	Blue Jeans And Moonbeams	CD	Virgin	CDV-2023	England	1974	10.99
Captain-Beefheart	Doc At Radar Station	CD	Virgin	71362	England	1980	11.99
Captain-Beefheart	Doc At The Radar Station	CD	Caroline	CAROL-1824-2	U.S.A.	1986	13.99
Captain-Beefheart	Dust Blows Forward - Anthology	2CD	Rhino	R2-75863	U.S.A.	1999	34.99
Captain-Beefheart	Dust Sucker	CD	Ozit Morpheus	BF6003	England	2002	18.99
Captain-Beefheart	I May Be Hungry But I Sure Ain't Weird	CD	Sequel	NEX-CD-215	England	1992	10.99
Captain-Beefheart	I'm Going to Do What I Wanna Do	2CD	Rhino	RHM2-7741	U.S.A.	2000	25.99
Captain-Beefheart	Legendary A & M Sessions	CD	Edsel	BLIMPCD902	England	1986	11.99
Captain-Beefheart	Lick My Decals Off, Baby	CD	Enigma	773394-2	Canada	1989	64.99
Captain-Beefheart	London 1974	CD	Movie Play Gold	MPG-74025	Portugal	1993	8.99
Captain-Beefheart	Mersey Trout (Live in Liverpool1980)	CD	Ozit Morpheus	BF-4003	England	2001	18.99
Captain-Beefheart	Mirror Man Sessions (Bonus Tracks)	CD	Buddah	91742	Germany	1999	8.99
Captain-Beefheart	Safe As Milk + 7	CD	Buddah	7446599605-2	U.S.A.	1999	8.99
Captain-Beefheart	Safe As Milk + 7	CD	Buddah	91752	Germany	1999	8.99
Captain-Beefheart	Safe As Milk + 9	CD	One Way	OW-29088	U.S.A.	1970	8.99
Captain-Beefheart	Shiny Beast (Bat Chain Puller)	CD	Rhino	R2-70365	U.S.A.	1979	17.99
Captain-Beefheart	Shiny Beast (Bat Chain Puller)	CD	Warner Bros.	WPCP-5741	Japan	1993	19.99
Captain-Beefheart	Spotlight Kid /Clear Spot	CD	Reprise	7599-26249-2	Germany	1972	16.99
Captain-Beefheart	Strictly Personal	CD	EMI	7243-8-29654-2-8	Holland	1994	13.99
Captain-Beefheart	The Best Beefheart (Pair)	CD	RCA	PCD-2-1232	U.S.A.	1987	13.99
Captain-Beefheart	The Mirror Man Sessions	CD	Buddah	7446599606-2	U.S.A.	1999	11.99
Captain-Beefheart	Trout Mask Replica	CD	Reprise	2027-2	U.S.A.	1970	9.99
Captain-Beefheart	Unconditionally Guaranteed	CD	Virgin	CDV-2015	England	1987	11.99
Captain-Beefheart/Magic Band	Grow Fins [Rarities 1965-1982] Box Set	5CD	Revenant	RVN-210	England	1999	49.99
Captain-Beefheart/Magic Band	Magnetic Hands UK 72-80 (Ltd 500)	CD	Viper	CD011	England	2002	22.99
Captain-Beefheart/Magic Band	Railroadism Live USA 72 - 81 (Ltd 500)	CD	Viper	CD015	England	2003	19.99
Cara, Irene	Anyone Can See	CD	Unidisc Music	SPLK-7298	Canada	1997	16.99
Cara, Irene	Carasmatic	CD	Elektra	60724-2	U.S.A.	1987	29.99
Cara, Irene	What A Feelin'	CD	Unidisc Music	SPLK-7299	Canada	1997	16.99
Caravan	All Over You...Too	CD	HTD	HTDCD-102	England	1999	13.99
Caravan	BBC Radio 1 Live In Concert	CD	Strange Fruit	SFRSCD058	England	1998	13.99
Caravan	Blind Dog At St. Dunstans'	CD	Repertoire	REP-4501-WY	Germany	1994	12.99
Caravan	Caravan + 1	CD	Decca	8829522	EU	2002	12.99
Caravan	Caravan Live Fairfield Halls, 1974	CD	Decca	8829022	England	2002	12.99
Caravan	Cool Water	CD	Classic Rock	CRP1007	England	2002	9.99
Caravan	Cunning Stunts + 3	CD	Deram	8829812	England	2001	14.99
Caravan	Ether Way	CD	HUX	HUX-013	England	1998	8.99
Caravan	For Girls Who Grow Plump In Night + 5	CD	Decca	8829802	England	2001	13.99
Caravan	Green Bottles For Marjorie	CD	Caravan	CARAV-001	England	2002	16.99
Caravan	If I Could Do It All Over Again... + 4	CD	Decca	8829682	England	2000	15.99
Caravan	In Concert (With Bonus DVD)	2CD	Classic Rock	CRP0956	England	2002	16.99
Caravan	In The Land Of Grey And Pink	CD	Deram	8829832	England	2001	13.99
Caravan	Live At The Fairfield Halls, 1974	CD	Universal	UICY-3517	Japan	2002	24.99
Caravan	New Symphonia + 4 - Full Concert	CD	Decca	8829692	England	2001	12.99
Caravan	Songs for Oblivion Fishermen	CD	HUX	HUX-002	England	1998	10.99
Caravan	Surprise Supplies	CD	HTD	HTDCD96	England	2002	11.99
Caravan	The Battle Of Hastings	CD	HTD	TRACD-311	England	1999	12.99
Caravan	The Canterbury Collection	CD	Kingdom	CDKVL9028	England	1986	10.99
Caravan	The HTD Years	CD	HTD	HTD-CD114	England	2000	15.99
Caravan	The Show Of Our Lives	CD	Mooncrest	CRESTCD-036-Z	England	1998	8.99
Caravan	Waterloo Lily + 4	CD	Deram	8829822	England	2001	13.99
Caravan	Where But For Caravan Would I?	2CD	Decca	524-755-2	England	2000	13.99
Caravan/Dave Sinclair	Before A Word Is Said	CD	Blueprint	BP130CD	England	2001	16.99
Caravan/Dave Sinclair	Moon Over Man	CD	Blueprint	BP119CD	England	2001	16.99
Caravan/Richard Sinclair	An Evening Of Magic	2CD	HTD	HTD-CD17	England	1993	29.99

Artist	Title	Format	Label	Catalog No	Country	Released	Value
Caravan/Richard Sinclair	Caravan Of Dreams	CD	Pony Canyon	PCCY-00343	Japan	1992	39.99
Caravan/Richard Sinclair	Caravan Of Dreams	CD	HTD	HTD-CD7	England	1992	8.99
Caravan/Richard Sinclair	R.S.V.P.	CD	Sinclair Songs	R.S.S.-CD001	England	1994	11.99
Carey, Mariah	Anytime You Need A Friend (Remixes)	CD Single	Columbia	660541-2	Australia	1994	94.99
Carey, Mariah	Boy (I Need You) Promo	CD Single	Island	CDPROMC0203	Australia	2002	44.99
Carey, Mariah	Fantasy (Promo/Remixes)	CD Single	Columbia	PRCD-96518	Mexico	1995	104.99
Carey, Mariah	Hero (Live)	CD Single	Sony	SRCS-6969	Japan	1993	36.99
Carey, Mariah	I Don't Wanna Cry (3")	CD Single	Sony	SRDS-8187	Japan	1990	74.99
Carey, Mariah	If It's Over (3")	CD Single	Sony	SRDS-8249	Japan	1991	35.99
Carey, Mariah	Love & Dream (Promo)	CD	Sony	XACS-90032	Japan	2001	172.99
Carey, Mariah	Love Takes Time (3")	CD Single	Sony	CSDS-8166	Japan	1990	54.99
Carey, Mariah	Mi Todo (My All) - Dance Mixes (DJ)	CD Single	Sony	PRCD-97427	Mexico	1998	64.99
Carey, Mariah	Mi Todo/Butterfly Latin Remixes	CD Single	Sony	CDMIX658685A	Mexico	1998	49.99
Carey, Mariah	Miss You Most (At Christmas Time) DJ	CD Single	Columbia	CSK-6647	U.S.A.	1994	203.99
Carey, Mariah	Reflections (Care Enough)	CD Single	Virgin	XDCS-93489	Japan	2001	90.99
Carey, Mariah	Self Titled (W/Samp-306 Live/Int Cd)	2CD	Columbia	466815-9	Australia	1991	131.99
Carey, Mariah	Self Titled + 11	CD	Sony	466815-9	Australia	1991	269.99
Carey, Mariah	Self Titled Christmas Sampler (Promo)	CD	Sony	XACS90023	Japan	1994	299.99
Carey, Mariah	Someday (3")	CD Single	Sony	CSDS-8176	Japan	1990	45.99
Carey, Mariah	Take A Look... (Promo)	CD Single	Sony	SAMPCS-8753	France	2000	94.99
Carey, Mariah	The One (Promo)	CD Single	Island	ISLR15774-2	U.S.A.	2003	29.99
Carey, Mariah	There's Got To Be...	CD Single	Columbia	656931-5	Australia	1991	89.99
Carey, Mariah	Underneath The Stars (Promo)	CD Single	Columbia	CSK-8776	U.S.A.	1996	174.99
Carey, Mariah	Vision Of Love (3")	CD Single	Sony	CSDS-8156	Japan	1990	44.99
Carlin, George	Back In Town	CD	Atlantic	92728-2	U.S.A.	1996	6.99
Carlin, George	Classic Gold	2CD	Atlantic	7-92219-2	U.S.A.	1992	12.99
Carlin, George	Little David Years 1971- 1977	7CD	Atlantic	92853-2	U.S.A.	1999	49.99
Carlin, George	You Are All Diseased	CD	Atlantic	92828-2	U.S.A.	1999	11.99
Carlisle, Belinda	(We Want) The Same Thing	CD Single	Virgin	VSCDP-1291	Japan	1990	7.99
Carlisle, Belinda	A Woman And A Man	CD	Ark21	61868-10010-2-7	U.S.A.	1996	9.99
Carlisle, Belinda	Belinda	CD	I.R.S.	IRSD-5741	U.S.A.	1986	7.99
Carlisle, Belinda	Heaven On Earth	CD	MCA	MCAD-42080	U.S.A.	1989	7.99
Carlisle, Belinda	Her Greatest Hits	CD	MCA	MCAD-10606	U.S.A.	1992	5.99
Carlisle, Belinda	Live Your Life Be Free	CD	MCA	MCAD-10446	U.S.A.	1991	6.99
Carlisle, Belinda	Real	CD	Virgin	7243-8-39102-2-9	U.S.A.	1993	6.99
Carlisle, Belinda	Runaway Horses	CD	MCA	MCAD-6339	U.S.A.	1989	7.99
Carlisle, Belinda	The Greatest Hits + 10 (Bonus Cd)	2CD	Virgin	7243-8-48470-2-9	Holland	1999	19.99
Carlos, João/Brasil	Jazz Brasil	CD	Line	BSCD-9.00756-0	Germany	1990	19.99
Carmen	Dancing On A Cold Wind	CD	Line	LICD-9.00601-0	Germany	1988	16.99
Carmen	Fandangos In Space	CD	Line	COCD-9.00598-0	Germany	1988	18.99
Carmen	Fandangos In Space/Dancing On A...	2CD	Line	LICD-9.21150-S	Germany	1992	29.99
Carmen	The Gypsies	CD	Line	LICD-9.00658-0	Germany	1989	22.99
Carmen, Eric	All By Myself (3")	CD Single	Arista	CD3-3021	U.S.A.	1988	19.99
Carmen, Eric	All By Myself (Soarer T.V. Promo)	CD Single	BMG	BVDA-25	Japan	1991	21.99
Carmen, Eric	Almost Paradise (Promo)	CD Single	RCA	RCA-9660-2-R	U.S.A.	1989	19.99
Carmen, Eric	Almost Paradise (Promo/Red)	CD Single	RCA	RCA-8917-7-R	U.S.A.	1989	19.99
Carmen, Eric	Best Of	CD	Arista	32RD-58	Japan	1985	27.99
Carmen, Eric	Best Of + 1	CD	Arista	ARCD-8548	U.S.A.	1988	9.99
Carmen, Eric	Best Selection	CD	BMG	BVCA-2611	Japan	1996	29.99
Carmen, Eric	Boats Against The Current	CD	BMG	BVCM-7320	Japan	1997	29.99
Carmen, Eric	Cartoon World (Promo)	CD Single	Pioneer	LPR-282	Japan	1998	14.99
Carmen, Eric	Change Of Heart	CD	BMG	BVCM-7321	Japan	1997	29.99
Carmen, Eric	Eric Carmen CD	CD	Geffen	GEBBD-24042	U.S.A.	1997	12.99
Carmen, Eric	Hungry Eyes	CD	RCA	PD-49594	Germany	1987	14.99
Carmen, Eric	I Was B...(DJ Heart Shaped Red Vrsn)	CD Single	Rhino	PRCD-400001	U.S.A.	2000	19.99
Carmen, Eric	I Was Born To Love You	CD Single	Pioneer	PICP-0022	Japan	1997	12.99
Carmen, Eric	I Was Born To Love You	CD	Rhino	R2-79792	U.S.A.	2000	11.99
Carmen, Eric	I Was Born To Love You (Promo)	CD Single	Pioneer	LPR-253	Japan	1997	14.99

Artist	Title	Format	Label	Catalog No	Country	Released	Value
Carmen, Eric	I Was Born... (Promo Heart Shaped)	CD Single	Rhino	PRCD-400001	U.S.A.	2000	14.99
Carmen, Eric	Make Me Lose Control	CD Single	Arista	AS1-9686	U.S.A.	1988	11.99
Carmen, Eric	My Heart Stops	CD Single	Arista	ASCD-2264	U.S.A.	1991	12.99
Carmen, Eric	Scott Muni's Ticket To Ride (DJ Int)	CD	DIR Network	DIR-5-16-88	U.S.A.	1988	29.99
Carmen, Eric	Self Titled	CD	BMG	BVCA-2351	Japan	1995	29.99
Carmen, Eric	Self Titled + 2	CD	Rhino	R2-71141	U.S.A.	1991	12.99
Carmen, Eric	Someone That ...	CD Single	Pioneer	PICP-0023	Japan	1998	12.99
Carmen, Eric	Someone That...(Promo)	CD Single	Pioneer	LPR-277	Japan	1998	14.99
Carmen, Eric	Songs From Winter Dreams (Promo)	CD	Pioneer	LPR-271	Japan	1997	34.99
Carmen, Eric	The Best Of	CD	BMG	BVCM-37337	Japan	2002	32.99
Carmen, Eric	The Best Of	CD	BMG	BVCM-37018	Japan	1998	29.99
Carmen, Eric	Tonight You're Mine	CD	BMG	BVCM-7322	Japan	1997	29.99
Carmen, Eric	Winter Dreams	CD	Pioneer	PICP-1152	Japan	1998	29.99
Carnes, Kim	Checking Out The Ghosts	CD	Teichiku	TECP-28767	Japan	1991	49.99
Carnes, Kim	Lighthouse	CD	Toshiba-EMI	CP32-5150	Japan	1986	45.99
Carnes, Kim	Mistaken Identity	CD	EMI	D-102349	U.S.A.	1981	12.99
Carpenter, John	Escape From New York + 6 (O.S.T.)	CD	Silva	SSD-1110	U.S.A.	2000	12.99
Carpenters	Anthology Box Set	4CD	Pony Canyon	PCCY-10023	Japan	1989	53.99
Carpenters	As Time Goes By	CD	Victor Ent.	UICY-1060	Japan	2001	39.99
Carpenters	Best Of Best + Karaoke	2CD	Pony Canyon	PCCY-10293	Japan	1992	89.99
Carpenters	Box - 35th Ann. Memorial Coll. Ed.	13 CD	Universal	UICY-9345	Japan	2003	359.99
Carpenters	From The Top	4CD	A&M	7-31454-000-2	U.S.A.	1991	33.99
Carpenters	Singles (1969-1981)	CD	A&M	CD-0456	U.S.A.	1999	9.99
Carpenters	Song For You (MFSL Gold/No UCDC)	CD	Mobile Fidelity	UDCD-525	U.S.A.	1972	29.99
Carpenters	Their Greatest Hits (Gold Cd)	CD	A&M	397048-2	Germany	1990	37.99
Carpenters	Yesterday Once More	2CD	A&M	75021-6601-2	U.S.A.	1987	14.99
Carpenters/Numbered	The Compact Disc Collection Box Set	12 CD	A&M	CARCD12	England	1990	154.99
Carr, Ian	Belladonna	CD	Line	LMCD-9.00744-0	Germany	1990	18.99
Carrack, Paul	Beautiful World	CD	Ark	61868-10024-2-0	U.S.A.	1997	6.99
Carrack, Paul	Blue Views	CD	Ark	61868-10007-2-3	U.S.A.	1995	7.99
Carrack, Paul	Groove Approved	CD	Chrysalis	F2-21709	U.S.A.	1989	5.99
Carrack, Paul	Groovin	CD	Carrack-UK	PCARCD3	England	2001	15.99
Carrack, Paul	One Good Reason	CD	Chrysalis	VK-41578	U.S.A.	1987	8.99
Carrack, Paul	SatisfyMySoul + 4	CD	Gold Circle	GI-67500-2	Holland	2001	19.99
Carrack, Paul	Suburban Voodoo	CD	Columbia	EK-38161	U.S.A.	1982	24.99
Carrack, Paul	Twenty-One Good Reasons	CD	Chrysalis	527221	U.S.A.	1994	11.99
Carrack, Paul/B. B. King	Satisfy My Soul	CD Single	Gold Circle	CDPCAR100	EU	2001	6.99
Carrasco, Joe "King"	Anthology	CD	One Way	MCAD-22157	U.S.A.	1983	8.99
Carrasco, Joe "King"	Bordertown	CD	New Rose	R.040C.D.	France	1985	14.99
Carrasco, Joe "King"	Royal, Loyal & Live	CD	RiosRoyalTexacali	RTA-CD-001	U.S.A.	1989	14.99
Carrasco, Joe "King"	Tales From The Crypt + 1	CD	ROIR	RUSCD8268	U.S.A.	2000	15.99
Carroll, Jim	Pools Of Mercury	CD	Mercury	314-538-113-2	U.S.A.	1998	11.99
Carroll, Jim	Praying Mantis	CD	Giant	9-24435-2	U.S.A.	1991	7.99
Carroll, Jim	Runaway Ep	CD Single	Kill Rock Stars	KRS367	U.S.A.	2000	7.99
Carroll, Jim Band	A World Without Gravity - The Best Of...	CD	Rhino	R2-71290	U.S.A.	1993	13.99
Carroll, Jim Band	Catholic Boy	CD	Atco	38132-2	U.S.A.	1980	14.99
Carroll, Jim Band	I Write Your Name	CD	Atlantic	80123-2	U.S.A.	1983	8.99
Carroll, Jim Band	People Who Died (Promo)	CD Single	Island	PRCD-6949-2	U.S.A.	1995	9.99
Cars	Anthology - Just What I Needed	2CD	Rhino	R2-73506	U.S.A.	1995	13.99
Cars	Candy-O	CD	Elektra	5E-507-2	U.S.A.	1979	8.99
Cars	Complete Greatest Hits	CD	Rhino	R2-78288	U.S.A.	2002	10.99
Cars	Door To Door	CD	Elektra	60747-2	U.S.A.	1987	5.99
Cars	Heartbeat City	CD	Elektra	9-60296-2	U.S.A.	1984	8.99
Cars	Panorama	CD	Elektra	5E-514-2	U.S.A.	1980	9.99
Cars	Shake It Up	CD	Elektra	567-2	U.S.A.	1981	6.99
Cars	The Cars (DCC Gold Cd)	CD	DCC	GZS-1032	U.S.A.	1993	25.99
Cars	The Cars + 14 Deluxe Edition	2CD	Rhino	R2-75700	U.S.A.	1999	16.99
Cars	The Cars Greatest Hits (DCC Gold Cd)	CD	DCC	GZS-1123	U.S.A.	1994	39.99

Artist	Title	Format	Label	Catalog No	Country	Released	Value
Cars	Westwood One Show#00-14	2CD	Westwood 1	PO85561133	U.S.A.	2000	59.99
Carter, Betty	Now It's My Turn	CD	Roulette	RCD-59066	Canada	1988	156.99
Carter, Carlene	C'est C Bon	CD	Razor And Tie	RE-2075	U.S.A.	1995	10.99
Carter, Carlene	Hindsight 20/20	CD	Giant	9-24655-2	U.S.A.	1996	5.99
Carter, Carlene	Musical Shapes / Blue Nun	CD	Demon	FIEND-CD-703	France	1991	25.99
Casanova	Heroes	CD	Bareknuckle	AVCB-66069	Japan	1999	24.99
Cash, Johnny	20th Century Masters: The Millennium	CD	Mercury	088-170-217-2-0	U.S.A.	2002	8.99
Cash, Johnny	All Aboard The Blue Train + 6	CD	Varese	302-066-487-2	U.S.A.	2003	8.99
Cash, Johnny	American III: Solitary Man	CD	American	CK-69691	U.S.A.	2000	14.99
Cash, Johnny	American IV: The Man.. + 1	CD	Universal	04400-77356-2-6	England	2003	10.99
Cash, Johnny	American Recordings	CD	American	9-45520-2	U.S.A.	1994	9.99
Cash, Johnny	At Folsum Prison (Complete) + 3	CD	Columbia	CK-65955	U.S.A.	2002	8.99
Cash, Johnny	At San Quentin + 6 (Complete Concert)	CD	Columbia	CK-66017	U.S.A.	2000	8.99
Cash, Johnny	Bitter Tears	CD	Columbia	CK-66507	U.S.A.	1995	8.99
Cash, Johnny	Blood Sweat And Tears	CD	Columbia	CK-66508	U.S.A.	1995	12.99
Cash, Johnny	Boom Chicka Boom + 1	CD	Mercury	842-155-2	U.S.A.	2003	8.99
Cash, Johnny	Cash Sings Cash	CD	Varese	302-066-537-2	U.S.A.	2004	8.99
Cash, Johnny	Christmas With	CD	Columbia	CK-90701	U.S.A.	2003	8.99
Cash, Johnny	Classic Cash	CD	Mercury	834-526-2	U.S.A.	1988	10.99
Cash, Johnny	Classic Cash: Hall Of Fame Series	CD	Mercury	834-526-2	U.S.A.	1987	10.99
Cash, Johnny	Classic Christmas	CD	Columbia	A-20726	U.S.A.	1989	7.99
Cash, Johnny	Come Along And Ride This Train	4CD	Bear Family	BCD-15563-DH	Germany	1991	89.99
Cash, Johnny	Country Christmas	CD	Laserlight	15-417	Germany	1991	5.99
Cash, Johnny	Essential Johnny Cash 1955-1983	3CD	Columbia	C3K-47991	U.S.A.	1992	31.99
Cash, Johnny	Get Rhythm/Story Trains And Rivers	CD	Collectables	COL-CD-6427	U.S.A.	1999	8.99
Cash, Johnny	God	CD	Columbia	CK-65545	U.S.A.	2000	8.99
Cash, Johnny	Gospel Coll. (Hymns From /Hymns By)	CD	Columbia	CK-48952	U.S.A.	1992	8.99
Cash, Johnny	Greatest ! + 4	CD	Varese	302-066-442-2	U.S.A.	2003	8.99
Cash, Johnny	Hymns By Johnny Cash + 1	CD	Columbia	CK-86331	U.S.A.	2002	8.99
Cash, Johnny	Hymns By/Sings Precious Memories	CD	S&P	7393430-701-2-7	U.S.A.	2000	14.99
Cash, Johnny	I Would Like To See You Again	CD	DCC	DZS-192	U.S.A.	2000	12.99
Cash, Johnny	Is Coming To Town	CD	Mercury	832-031-2	U.S.A.	1987	8.99
Cash, Johnny	Johnny 99	CD	Koch	KOC-CD-7980	U.S.A.	1999	8.99
Cash, Johnny	Legend At His.. Box (W/300 Pg. Book)	2CD	Collectables	310050	U.S.A.	2000	29.99
Cash, Johnny	Louisiana Hayride	CD	Scena	CD270506	U.S.A.	2003	13.99
Cash, Johnny	Love	CD	Columbia	CK-65544	U.S.A.	2000	8.99
Cash, Johnny	Love God Murder Box Set	3CD	Columbia	K-63809-S1	U.S.A.	2000	19.99
Cash, Johnny	Man In Black, Volume 1	5CD	Bear Family	BCD-15517-EH	Germany	1990	84.99
Cash, Johnny	Man In Black, Volume 2	5CD	Bear Family	BCD-15562-EH	Germany	1991	84.99
Cash, Johnny	Man In Black, Volume 3 (1963-1969)	6CD	Bear Family	BCD-15588-FI	Germany	1996	99.99
Cash, Johnny	Murder	CD	Columbia	CK-65543	U.S.A.	2000	8.99
Cash, Johnny	Mystery Of Life + 1	CD	Universal	04400-69089-2-2	England	2003	10.99
Cash, Johnny	Now Here's Johnny Cash + 5	CD	Varese	302-066-468-2	U.S.A.	2003	8.99
Cash, Johnny	Now, There Was A Song !	CD	Columbia	CK-66506	U.S.A.	1995	11.99
Cash, Johnny	Orange Blossom Special + 3	CD	Columbia	CK-86329	U.S.A.	2002	8.99
Cash, Johnny	Original Golden Hits, Vol. 1-2	CD	Collectables	COL-CD-6425	U.S.A.	1999	8.99
Cash, Johnny	Original Sun Sound + 6	CD	Varese	302-066-488-2	U.S.A.	2003	8.99
Cash, Johnny	Ragged Old Flag	CD	Columbia	CK-86261	U.S.A.	2001	8.99
Cash, Johnny	Ride This Train + 4	CD	Columbia	CK-86332	U.S.A.	2002	9.99
Cash, Johnny	Ring of Fire: The Best Of	CD	Columbia	CK-66890	U.S.A.	1995	8.99
Cash, Johnny	Rockabilly Blues	CD	Koch	KOC-CD-7979	U.S.A.	1999	8.99
Cash, Johnny	Showtime/Original Golden Hits, Vol. 3	CD	Collectables	COL-CD-6433	U.S.A.	1999	8.99
Cash, Johnny	Silver + 2	CD	Columbia	CK-86791	U.S.A.	2002	8.99
Cash, Johnny	Singing Story Teller/Rough Cut...	CD	Collectables	COL-CD-6431	U.S.A.	1999	8.99
Cash, Johnny	Sings Ballads Of The True West + 2	CD	Columbia	CK-86789	U.S.A.	2002	10.99
Cash, Johnny	Sings I Walk.../Sings Folsom Prison B	CD	Collectables	COL-CD-6437	U.S.A.	1999	8.99
Cash, Johnny	Sings the Greatest Hits/The Blue Train	CD	Collectables	COL-CD-6438	U.S.A.	1999	8.99
Cash, Johnny	Sings The Songs That Made Him + 4	CD	Varese	302-066-441-2	U.S.A.	2003	8.99

C

Artist	Title	Format	Label	Catalog No	Country	Released	Value
Cash, Johnny	Songs Of Our Soil + 2	CD	Columbia	CK-86792	U.S.A.	2002	8.99
Cash, Johnny	Sunday Down South/Sings Hank W	CD	Collectables	COL-CD-6432	U.S.A.	1999	8.99
Cash, Johnny	Sunday Morning Coming Down	CD	DCC	DZS-173	U.S.A.	2000	12.99
Cash, Johnny	The E.P. Collection	CD	See For Miles	SEE-CD-719	England	2000	14.99
Cash, Johnny	The Fabulous + 6	CD	Columbia	CK-86333	U.S.A.	2002	12.99
Cash, Johnny	The Holy Land	CD	Harmony	1786-2	U.S.A.	1999	10.99
Cash, Johnny	The Mercury Years	CD	Mercury	544-326-2	England	2000	8.99
Cash, Johnny	The Mystery Of Life	CD	Mercury	848-051-2	U.S.A.	1991	8.99
Cash, Johnny	The Sun Years	CD	Rhino	R2-70950	U.S.A.	1990	8.99
Cash, Johnny	The Very Best Of, Vol. 1	CD	Collectables	COL-CD-6146	U.S.A.	2000	8.99
Cash, Johnny	The Very Best Of, Vol. 2	CD	Collectables	COL-CD-6147	U.S.A.	2000	8.99
Cash, Johnny	Thirteen (Promo)	CD Single	American	PRO-CD-7433	U.S.A.	1995	8.99
Cash, Johnny	Unchained	CD	American	74321-39742-2	U.S.A.	1996	9.99
Cash, Johnny	Up Through the Years, 1955-1957	CD	Bear Family	BCD-15247-AH	Germany	1986	14.99
Cash, Johnny	Very Best Of: I Walk The Line	CD	Collectables	COL-CD-6010	U.S.A.	1999	8.99
Cash, Johnny	VH1 Storytellers	CD	Columbia	CK-69416	U.S.A.	1998	8.99
Cash, Johnny	Wanted Man	CD	Mercury	314-522-709-2	U.S.A.	1994	8.99
Cash, Johnny	Water From The Wells Of Home + 1	CD	Rebound	314-520-510-2	U.S.A.	2003	10.99
Cash, Johnny	With His Hot & Blue Guitar + 5	CD	Varese	302-066-369-2	U.S.A.	2002	8.99
Cash, Johnny/1 Of 3,000	Solitary Man Interview W/Tim Robbins	CD	American	DIDP-102319	U.S.A.	2000	9.99
Cash, Johnny/Carl Perkins	I Walk The Line/Little Fauss + 5	CD	Bear Family	BCD-16130-AH	Germany	1999	19.99
Cash, Johnny/Family	Christmas	CD	Columbia	A-24083	U.S.A.	1999	11.99
Cash, Johnny/Gordon Terry	Lotta, Lotta Women	CD	Bear Family	BCD-15881-AH	Germany	1995	18.99
Cash, Johnny/June Carter	Carryin' On + 2	CD	Columbia	CK-86088	U.S.A.	2002	8.99
Cash, Johnny/June Carter	Return To The Promised Land	CD	Renaissance	RMED-00235-2	U.S.A.	2000	14.99
Cash, Johnny/Linda Ronstadt	Concert: Behind Prison Walls '76	CD	Eagle	EAGCD269	England	2003	14.99
Cash, Johnny/Perkins/Lewis	The Survivors (Carl/Jerry Lee)	CD	Razor & Tie	RE-2077	U.S.A.	1995	14.99
Cash, Johnny/Tennessee Two	Complete Original Sun Singles	2CD	Varese	302-066-056-2	U.S.A.	1999	14.99
Cash, Johnny/Tennessee Two	Essential Sun Hits	CD	Varese	302-066-332-2	U.S.A.	2002	8.99
Cash, Johnny/Tennessee Two	Road Less Traveled	CD	Varese	302-066-214-2	U.S.A.	2001	8.99
Cash, Johnny/W Jennings	Heroes (W/Waylon Jennings)	CD	Razor & Tie	RE-2078-2	U.S.A.	1995	19.99
Cash, June Carter	Louisiana Hayride	CD	Scena	CD270708	U.S.A.	2003	11.99
Cash, June Carter	Press On	CD	Dualtone	1130	U.S.A.	1999	8.99
Cash, June Carter	Wildwood Flower	CD	Dualtone	1142	U.S.A.	2003	9.99
Cash, June Carter/Johnny	It's All... (App. Pride/Children's Lp) + 7	CD	Bear Family	BCD-16132-AR	Germany	1999	19.99
Cassidy, David	Romance	CD	Arista	610454-222	Germany	1985	146.99
Cathy Dennis/Ray Davies	Am I The Kinda Girl (W/Andy Partridge)	CD	Polydor	533-151-2	Germany	1996	11.99
Caught In The Act	Heat Of Emotion + 4	CD	Toshiba-EMI	TOCP-50778	Japan	1999	29.99
Caught In The Act	Relapse Of Reason + 4	CD	Toshiba-EMI	TOCP-50777	Japan	1999	29.99
Cave, Nick/Bad Seeds	No More Shall We Part	CD	Reprise	9-48039-2	U.S.A.	2001	11.99
Cave, Nick/Bad Seeds	Radio Sessions (Promo)	CD Single	Reprise	1007-2126-0373	U.S.A.	2001	15.99
Cave, Nick/Bad Seeds	Secret Life/Love Song (Cd W/Book)	CD	King Mob	1-902670-07-8	England	1998	20.99
Centaur	Power World	CD	Teichiku	TECX-25772	Japan	1994	19.99
Cetera, Peter/Chicago	Self Titled	CD	Warner Bros.	WPCP-3476	Japan	1990	49.99
Chad/Jeremy	Of Cabbages And Kings + 6	CD	Sundazed	SC-11118	U.S.A.	2002	15.99
Chad/Jeremy	Sing For You/Second Album + 5	CD	Repertoire	REP-4286-WY	Germany	1992	11.99
Chad/Jeremy	Yesterday's Gone	CD	A&M	DE2-41012	Canada	1964	8.99
Chairmen-Of-The-Board	Any Other Business	2CD	Sequel	NEECD-301	England	1999	19.99
Chairmen-Of-The-Board	Bittersweet/Skin I'm In	CD	Sequel	NEMCD-983	England	1999	11.99
Chairmen-Of-The-Board	Chairmen Of The Board/In Session	CD	Sequel	NEMCD-982	England	1999	11.99
Chairmen-Of-The-Board	Everything's Tuesday: The Best Of	CD	Castle	CMRCD-045	England	2000	11.99
Chambers Brothers	Now/People Get Ready	CD	Repertoire	REP-4734-WY	Germany	1999	14.99
Chambers Brothers	Time Has Come: Best Of	CD	Columbia	CK-65036	U.S.A.	1996	8.99
Champs	Everybody's Rockin'	CD	Line	BLCD-9.00382-L	Germany	1989	24.99
Champs	Go, Champs, Go!	CD	Line	BLCD-9.00380-L	Germany	1989	24.99
Champs	The Champs Collection	CD	Line	IMCD-9.00597-0	Germany	1989	11.99
Champs	The Champs Collection	CD	Line	BLCD-9.01040-L	Germany	1991	11.99
Chance, James	Christmas With Satan (3")	CD Single	Tiger Style	TS-038	U.S.A.	2002	4.99

Artist	Title	Format	Label	Catalog No	Country	Released	Value
Chance, James	Live in New York	CD	ROIR	RUSCD8267	U.S.A.	2000	10.99
Chance, James/Contortions	Buy The Contortions	CD	Infinite Zero	9-43048-2	U.S.A.	1995	11.99
Chance, James/Contortions	Irresistible Impulse (1st 4 Lps + More)	3CD	Tiger Style	TS-37	U.S.A.	2003	39.99
Chance, James/Contortions	Live In New York	CD	ROIR	ROI100	U.S.A.	1992	19.99
Chance, James/Contortions	Lost Chance (Live)	CD	ROIR	RUSCD8214	U.S.A.	1995	10.99
Chance, James/Contortions	Soul Exorcism	CD	ROIR	ROI191	U.S.A.	1992	14.99
Chance, James/Contortions	White Cannibal (Live)	CD	ROIR	RUSCD8267	U.S.A.	2000	10.99
Chance, James/White	Off White	CD	Infinite Zero	9-43033-2	U.S.A.	1995	11.99
Chandra, Sheila	The Zen Kiss	CD	Caroline	CAROL-2342-2	U.S.A.	1994	8.99
Channel Light Vessel	Automatic	CD	Gyroscope	GYR-6607-2	U.S.A.	1994	9.99
Channel Light Vessel	Automatic + 2	CD	Polydor	POCP-1430	Japan	1994	45.99
Channel Light Vessel	Excellent Spirits	CD	Gyroscope	GYR-6634-2	U.S.A.	1996	9.99
Channel Light Vessel	Excellent Spirits + 2	CD	Polydor	POCP-7152	Japan	1996	45.99
Chantays, The	Two Sides Of/Pipeline	CD	Repertoire	REP-4114-WZ	Germany	2002	12.99
Chapin, Harry	Bottom Line Encore Collection	2CD	Bottom Line	63440-47401-2	U.S.A.	1998	13.99
Chapin, Harry	Dance Band on the Titanic	CD	Elektra	9-60549-2	U.S.A.	1977	17.99
Chapin, Harry	Gold Medallion Collection	2CD	Elektra	9-60773-2	U.S.A.	1988	15.99
Chapin, Harry	Greatest Stories Live	CD	Elektra	6003-2	U.S.A.	1976	13.99
Chapin, Harry	On the Road to Kingdom Come	CD	Elektra	9-60613-2	U.S.A.	1976	8.99
Chapin, Harry	Story Of A Life Box Set	3CD	Rhino	R2-75875	U.S.A.	1999	33.99
Chapin, Harry	The Essentials	CD	Rhino	R2-76061	U.S.A.	2002	12.99
Chapin, Harry	Verities & Balderdash	CD	Elektra	1012-2	U.S.A.	1974	8.99
Chapin, Harry	VH1:Behind the Music	CD	Rhino	R2-74344	U.S.A.	2001	11.99
Chapin, Harry/V. A.	Harry Chapin Tribute	CD	Relativity Records	88561-1047-2	U.S.A.	1990	36.99
Chapman, Marshall	Dirty Linen	CD	Line	LICD-9.00309-0	Germany	1988	10.99
Chapman, Roger	A Turn Unstoned?	CD	SPV	SPV23018952CD	Germany	2002	9.99
Chapman, Roger	Before Your Very Eyes	CD	Thunderbolt	CDTB-183	England	1997	12.99
Chapman, Roger	Chappo	CD	Castle	CLACD-299	England	1993	8.99
Chapman, Roger	Chappo/Live In Hamburg	CD	Mystic	MYS-CD-179	England	2004	9.99
Chapman, Roger	Family/Friends (First 1000/Bonus Cd)	5CD	Mystic	MYS-CD-161	England	2003	74.99
Chapman, Roger	He Was She Was You Was We Was	CD	Castle	CLACD-373	England	1993	14.99
Chapman, Roger	Hybrid And Lowdown	CD	Mystic	MYS-CD-181	England	2004	7.99
Chapman, Roger	Hyenas Only Laugh For Fun	CD	Castle	CLACD-305	England	1993	7.99
Chapman, Roger	In My Own Time (Live)	CD	SPV	SPV08529532CD	Germany	2003	14.99
Chapman, Roger	Kiss My Soul	CD	Castle	CMRCD182	England	2001	7.99
Chapman, Roger	Live In Berlin	CD	Castle	CLACD-313	England	1993	7.99
Chapman, Roger	Mail Order Magic	CD	Castle	CLACD-301	England	1993	7.99
Chapman, Roger	Mango Crazy	CD	Castle	CLACD-304	England	1993	7.99
Chapman, Roger	Moth To A Flame	CD	Thunderbolt	CDTB-217	England	2001	12.99
Chapman, Roger	Riff Burglars	2CD	Mystic	MYS-CD-165	England	2003	19.99
Chapman, Roger	Rollin' And Tumblin'	CD	Mystic	MYS-CD-146	England	2001	9.99
Chapman, Roger	Techno Prisoners	CD	Castle	CLACD-371	England	1993	7.99
Chapman, Roger	Techno Prisoners + 5	CD	Mystic	MYS-CD-168	England	2004	7.99
Chapman, Roger	The Shadow Knows	CD	Castle	CLACD-370	England	1993	7.99
Chapman, Roger	The Shadow Knows + 4 (Berlin EP)	CD	Mystic	MYS-CD-167	England	2004	9.99
Chapman, Roger	Under No Obligation	CD	Mystic	MYS-CD-180	England	2004	7.99
Chapman, Roger	Walking The Cat	CD	Castle	CLACD-372	England	1993	7.99
Chapman, Roger	Zipper	CD	Castle	CLACD-314	England	1993	7.99
Chapman, Roger/The Shortlist	Live In Germany	CD	Castle	CLACD-320	England	1993	7.99
Chaquico, Craig	A Thousand Pictures	CD	Higher Octave	HOMCD-7084	U.S.A.	1996	8.99
Chaquico, Craig	Acoustic Highway	CD	Higher Octave	HOMCD-7050	U.S.A.	1993	8.99
Chaquico, Craig	Acoustic Planet	CD	Higher Octave	HOMCD-7070	U.S.A.	1994	8.99
Chaquico, Craig	Four Corners	CD	Higher Octave	HOMCD-47498	U.S.A.	1999	8.99
Chaquico, Craig	Once In A Blue Universe	CD	Higher Octave	HOMCD-44638	U.S.A.	1997	8.99
Chaquico, Craig	Panorama: The Best Of	CD	Higher Octave	HOMCD-49272	U.S.A.	2000	8.99
Chaquico, Craig	Shadow And Light	CD	Higher Octave	7243-8-12142-2-0	U.S.A.	2002	8.99
Characters	Act 1	CD	Line	FBCD-9.00442-0	Germany	1988	29.99
Charade	Self Titled	CD	Bareknuckle	AVCB-66038	Japan	1998	29.99

C

Artist	Title	Format	Label	Catalog No	Country	Released	Value
Charlene	Used To Be (W/Stevie Wonder)	CD	RCA Victor	R32M-1056	Japan	1982	19.99
Charles, Ray	Spirit Of Christmas, The	CD	Columbia	CK-40125	U.S.A.	1976	6.99
Charlie	Fight Dirty/Good Morning America	CD	Renaissance	RMED00154-2	U.S.A.	1996	13.99
Charlie	Lines	CD	Renaissance	RMED00151-2	U.S.A.	1996	45.99
Charlie	No Second Chance	CD	Renaissance	REMD00167-2	U.S.A.	1996	44.99
Charlie	The Best Of	CD	Renaissance	RMED00150-2	U.S.A.	2000	10.99
Chas/Dave	One Fing'n'anuvver	CD	Line	RTCD-9.01144-0	Germany	1992	8.99
Chase	Chase	CD	Sony	ESCA-7576	Japan	1997	29.99
Chase	In Pursuit	CD	Salt Inc.	52002	U.S.A.	1993	8.99
Chastain	Acoutic Visions	CD	Leviathan	199812	U.S.A.	1998	12.99
Chastain	Elegant Seduction	CD	Leviathan	19911-2	U.S.A.	1991	12.99
Chastain	For Those Who Dare	CD	Roadrunner	RCD9398	Germany	1990	14.99
Chastain	Guitar Master	CD	Leviathan	20020-2	U.S.A.	2002	12.99
Chastain	Guitar Masters 2002	CD	Leviathan	20022-2	U.S.A.	2002	12.99
Chastain	In Dementia	CD	Massacre	MASSCD122	England	1997	8.99
Chastain	Instrumental Variations	CD	Leviathan	19872-2	U.S.A.	1995	7.99
Chastain	Live! Wild & Truly Diminished!	CD	Leviathan	199212	U.S.A.	1992	12.99
Chastain	Movements Thru Time	CD	Leviathan	199252	U.S.A.	1992	8.99
Chastain	Mystery Of Illusion	CD	Road Racer	RO9742-2	Germany	1990	24.99
Chastain	Next Planet Please	CD	Leviathan	19941-2	U.S.A.	1994	12.99
Chastain	Rock Solid Guitar	CD	Leviathan	20012-2	U.S.A.	2001	11.99
Chastain	Ruler Of The Wasteland	CD	Fems/Apollon	APCY-8035	Japan	1990	96.99
Chastain	Sick Society	CD	Massacre	MASSCD076	England	1995	7.99
Chastain	Sick Society	CD	Leviathan	19952-2	U.S.A.	1995	8.99
Chastain	The 7th Of Never	CD	Leviathan	19871-2	U.S.A.	2001	8.99
Chastain	The 7th Of Never	CD	Massacre	MASSCD077	England	1995	7.99
Chastain	Voice Of The Cult	CD	Leviathan	19881-2	U.S.A.	1994	12.99
Chastain	Within The Heat	CD	Roadrunner	RCD9484	Germany	1989	11.99
Chastain/Cinn Improv Grp	17th Cent. R(4871032523791-174961)	CD	Diginet	4871032523791-1	U.S.A.	2002	9.99
Chastain/Cinn Improv Grp	Aberration (8983951179-87077)	CD	Diginet	8983951179-8707	U.S.A.	2001	9.99
Chastain/Cinn Improv Grp	Freeform Free For All	CD	Fems/Apollon	APCY-8339	Japan	1996	34.99
Chastain/Cinn Improv Grp	Inner Fire (6981001290991-148974)	CD	Diginet	6981001290991-1	U.S.A.	2001	9.99
Chastain/Cinn Improv Grp	Paragon (4871032523791-225798)	CD	Diginet	4871032523791-2	U.S.A.	2002	9.99
Chastain/Cinn Improv Grp	Zfunkdabunk (60996297299-123633)	CD	Diginet	60996297299-123	U.S.A.	2001	9.99
Chastain/CJSS	2-4-1	CD	Leviathan	19991-2	U.S.A.	1999	12.99
Chastain/CJSS	Best Of	CD	Fems/Apollon	APCY-8232	Japan	1995	39.99
Chastain/CJSS	Embriyonic Anim. (8983951179-91953)	CD	Diginet	8983951179-9195	U.S.A.	2001	9.99
Chastain/CJSS	Kings Of The World	CD	Pavement	PVMT-32352	England	2000	8.99
Chastain/CJSS	Praise The Loud	CD	Fems/Apollon	APCY-8232	Japan	1995	34.99
Chastain/CJSS	Retrospect	CD	Black Dragon	BDCD-044	Germany	1990	14.99
Chastain/CJSS	Sands/Time (609996297299-101520)	CD	Diginet	609996297299-10	U.S.A.	2001	9.99
Chastain/CJSS	World Gone Mad	CD	Fems/Apollon	APCY-8232	Japan	1996	34.99
Chastain/D-Daze	A New Day (8983951179-79272)	CD	Diginet	8983951179-7927	U.S.A.	2001	9.99
Chastain/Georgia Blues Dawgs	Hard Times (8983951179-85098)	CD	Diginet	8983951179-8509	U.S.A.	2001	9.99
Chastain/Leather Leone	Shock Waves	CD	Roadrunner	RCD-9463	Germany	1989	15.99
Chastain/Masahiro Chono	Overtune Toward 21st Century	CD Single	Teichiku	TECX-20900	Japan	1995	21.99
Chastain/Mike Haid	Strength Of B (609996297299-84505)	CD	Diginet	609996297299-84	U.S.A.	2001	9.99
Chastain/No Voices	Instatreasures (8983951179-81598)	CD	Diginet	8983951179-8159	U.S.A.	2001	9.99
Chastain/Riffology	7 Year Itch (487103253791-193913)	CD	Diginet	487103253791-19	U.S.A.	2002	9.99
Chastain/Riffology	Wicked Riffs (8983951179-83144)	CD	Diginet	8983951179-8314	U.S.A.	2001	9.99
Chastain/Ruud Cooth	Aftermath (4871032523791-198532)	CD	Diginet	4871032523791-1	U.S.A.	2002	9.99
Chastain/Ruud Cooth	Trouble (4871032523791-164720)	CD	Diginet	4871032523791-1	U.S.A.	2002	9.99
Chastain/Southern Gentlemen	Exotic D B (59915941718403-23474)	CD	Diginet	59915941718403-	U.S.A.	1999	9.99
Chastain/Spike!	Forum Sessions (8983951179-95029)	CD	Diginet	8983951179-9502	U.S.A.	2001	9.99
Chastain/Spike!	Price/Pleasure (609996297299-122707)	CD	Diginet	609996297299-12	U.S.A.	2001	9.99
Chastain/Zanister	Fear No Man	CD	Leviathan	20011	U.S.A.	2001	12.99
Chastain/Zanister	Symphonica Millennia	CD	Helre Du	HELLIO802	Germany	2001	12.99
Cheap Trick	All Shook Up	CD	Epic	EK-36498	U.S.A.	1990	11.99

C

Artist	Title	Format	Label	Catalog No	Country	Released	Value
Cheap Trick	At Budokan (MFSL Gold Cd)	CD	Mobile Fidelity	UDCD-709	U.S.A.	1979	14.99
Cheap Trick	At Budokan: the Complete Concert	2CD	Epic	E2K-65527	U.S.A.	1998	14.99
Cheap Trick	Busted	CD	Epic	EK-46013	U.S.A.	1991	10.99
Cheap Trick	Busted + 1	CD	Sony	ESCA-5130	Japan	1990	19.99
Cheap Trick	Cheap Trick (W/Bonus Cd)	2CD	Red Ant	RA002-2	U.S.A.	1997	5.99
Cheap Trick	Dream Police	CD	Epic	EK-35773	U.S.A.	1990	13.99
Cheap Trick	Gift (Christmas)	CD Single	Not Cool	75449	U.S.A.	1996	38.99
Cheap Trick	Heaven Tonight + 2	CD	Epic	EK-65648	U.S.A.	1998	9.99
Cheap Trick	In Color + 5	CD	Epic	EK-65573	U.S.A.	1998	10.99
Cheap Trick	Music For Hangovers	CD	Victor Ent.	VICP-60626	Japan	1999	13.99
Cheap Trick	Music For Hangovers	CD	Cheap Trick	20001	U.S.A.	1999	7.99
Cheap Trick	Next Positon Please	CD	Epic	EK-38794	U.S.A.	1990	11.99
Cheap Trick	One On One	CD	Epic	EK-38021	U.S.A.	1990	11.99
Cheap Trick	Self Titled + 2	CD	Victor Ent.	VICP-5828	Japan	1997	24.99
Cheap Trick	Self Titled + 5 (1977)	CD	Epic	EK-65572	U.S.A.	1998	8.99
Cheap Trick	Sex America Box Set	4CD	Epic	E4K-64938	U.S.A.	1996	27.99
Cheap Trick	Silver	2CD	Victor Ent.	VICP-61444	Japan	2001	34.99
Cheap Trick	Special One +1	CD	Victor Ent.	VICP-62179	Japan	2003	29.99
Cheap Trick	Special One (W/Bonus DVD)	2CD	Big 3	80498-36333-2-9	U.S.A.	2003	14.99
Cheap Trick	Stading On The Edge	CD	Epic	EK-39592	U.S.A.	1985	32.99
Cheap Trick	The Authorized Greatest Hits	CD	Epic	EK-66015	U.S.A.	2000	8.99
Cheap Trick	The Doctor	CD	Epic	EK-40405	U.S.A.	1986	51.99
Cheap Trick	The Greatest Hits	CD	Epic	EK-86473	U.S.A.	2002	8.99
Cheap Trick	Woke Up ... (Promo Trick Box)	CD	Warner Bros.	9-45425-2	U.S.A.	1994	49.99
Cheap Trick	Woke Up With A Monster	CD	Warner Bros.	9-45425-2	U.S.A.	1994	7.99
Cheap Trick	Woke Up With A Monster + 1	CD	Warner Bros.	WPCP-5772	Japan	1994	19.99
Cheap Trick	You Can Have Sex in America... (DJ)	CD	Epic	ESK-8110	U.S.A.	1996	13.99
Cheap Trick/Fuse	Self Titled (W/Rick/Tom)	CD	Sony	ESCA-7624	Japan	1991	29.99
Checker, Chubby/Only 500	All The Hits (Sings In Eng/Spa/Ger)	CD	Marginal	MAR-020	EEC	1996	53.99
Cheech & Chong	Big Bambu	CD	Warner Bros.	3251-2	U.S.A.	1978	6.99
Cheech & Chong	Cheech & Chong	CD	Warner Bros.	9-3520-2	U.S.A.	1978	6.99
Cheech & Chong	Greatest Hit	CD	Warner Bros.	3614-2	U.S.A.	1981	8.99
Cheech & Chong	Los Cochinos	CD	Warner Bros.	3252-2	U.S.A.	1973	6.99
Cheech & Chong	Sleeping Beauty	CD	Warner Bros.	3254-2	U.S.A.	1976	49.99
Cheech & Chong	Wedding Album	CD	Warner Bros.	3253-2	U.S.A.	1974	6.99
Cheech & Chong	Where There's Smoke There's...	2CD	Rhino	R2-74265	U.S.A.	2002	14.99
Cheech & Chong/Cheech Marin	My Name Is Cheech: School Bus Driver	CD	Rincon	74041-70508-2	U.S.A.	1992	6.99
Cher	20th Century Masters: The Millennium	CD	MCA	314-112-154-2	U.S.A.	2000	7.99
Cher	20th Century Masters: The Millennium	CD	Hip O	000051402	U.S.A.	2004	7.99
Cher	3614 Jackson High + 12 (Ltd. 4500)	CD	Rhino	RHM2-7733	U.S.A.	2000	26.99
Cher	Absolutely The Best, Vol. 1	CD	Fuel 2000	302-061-261-2	U.S.A.	2002	8.99
Cher	Bang Bang...The Best of	CD	EMI	E2-92773	U.S.A.	1990	8.99
Cher	Behind the Door: 1964-1974	CD	Raven	RVCD-108	Australia	2000	9.99
Cher	Believe	CD	Warner Bros.	47121-2	U.S.A.	1998	7.99
Cher	Black Rose	CD	Spectrum	552-747-2	England	1999	9.99
Cher	Cher	CD	Geffen	24164-2	U.S.A.	1996	7.99
Cher	Essential	CD	Hip O	314-585-499-2	U.S.A.	2001	8.99
Cher	Greatest Hits: 1965-1992	CD	Geffen	GED-24439	England	1999	11.99
Cher	Gypsys, Tramps & Thieves	CD	Movie Play	MP-74017	U.S.A.	1997	7.99
Cher	Half Breed	CD	MCA	MCAD-20210	U.S.A.	1973	7.99
Cher	Heart Of Stone	CD	Geffen	24239-2	U.S.A.	1989	7.99
Cher	I Paralyze	CD	Columbia	CK-38096	U.S.A.	1989	8.99
Cher	If I Could Turn Back Time: Greatest	CD	Geffen	24509-2	U.S.A.	1999	7.99
Cher	It's A Man's World	CD	Warner Bros.	9-46179-2	U.S.A.	1996	7.99
Cher	Live: The Farewell Tour	CD	Rhino	R2-73953	U.S.A.	2003	8.99
Cher	Living Proof	CD	Warner Bros.	47619-2	U.S.A.	2002	7.99
Cher	Love Hurts	CD	Geffen	GEFD-24421	U.S.A.	1991	7.99
Cher	Love Hurts (Wooden Box W/Cards)	CD	Geffen	GEFD-24421	U.S.A.	1999	32.99

C

Artist	Title	Format	Label	Catalog No	Country	Released	Value
Cher	Not.Com.mercial	CD	Isis	0119010102	U.S.A.	2000	24.99
Cher	Outrageous	CD	PolyGram	838-644-2	U.S.A.	1994	11.99
Cher	Take Me Home / Prisoner	CD	Casablanca	550-0382	Australia	1990	16.99
Cher	Take Me Home + 1	CD	Rebound	314-520-541-2	U.S.A.	2003	7.99
Cher	The Story: '64-'72 (W/Bonus Cd Rom)	2CD	EMI	7243-5-76141-0-8	England	2000	14.99
Cher	The Very Best Of	CD	Rhino	R2-73852	U.S.A.	2003	11.99
Cher	The Way Of Love	2CD	MCA	560209-2	U.S.A.	2000	16.99
Cher/Beavis & Butt-Head	I Got You Babe (Picture Label)	CD	Geffen	GFSTD-64	England	1993	7.99
Cher/Sonny And Cher	All I Ever Need Is You	CD	MCA	MCAD-22025	U.S.A.	1972	9.99
Cher/Sonny And Cher	All I Ever Need: Kapp/MCA Anthology	CD	MCA	MCAD-11300	U.S.A.	1996	9.99
Cher/Sonny And Cher	Good Times (O.S.T.)	CD	Sundazed	OW-35140	U.S.A.	2000	7.99
Cher/Sonny And Cher	Greatest Hits	CD	MCA	MCAD-11745	U.S.A.	1998	7.99
Cher/Sonny And Cher	I Got You Babe	CD	Rhino	R2-71233	U.S.A.	1993	8.99
Cher/Sonny And Cher	In Case You're In Love + 3	CD	Sundazed	SC-6141	U.S.A.	1998	8.99
Cher/Sonny And Cher	Live In Las Vegas, Vol. 2	CD	MCA	MCAD8004-2	U.S.A.	1974	34.99
Cher/Sonny And Cher	Look At Us + 3	CD	Sundazed	SC-6139	U.S.A.	1998	7.99
Cher/Sonny And Cher	Singles +	2CD	BR Music	BS-8124-2	Holland	2002	14.99
Cher/Sonny And Cher	The Beat Goes On	CD	Atlantic	7567-80801-2	Germany	1998	12.99
Cher/Sonny And Cher	The Best Of: The Beat Goes On	CD	Rhino	R2-76012	U.S.A.	1993	8.99
Cher/Sonny And Cher	The Essentials	CD	Rhino	R2-76155	U.S.A.	2002	8.99
Cher/Sonny And Cher	The Wonderous World Of + 3	CD	Sundazed	SC-6140	U.S.A.	1998	7.99
Cher/Sonny Bono	Inner Views + 11 (Ltd. 1500)	CD	Rhino	RHM2-7704	U.S.A.	2000	17.99
Chesney, Kenny	In My Wildest Dreams	CD	Capricorn	9-42023-2	U.S.A.	1993	94.99
Chesnutt, Vic	The Salesman & Bernadette	CD	Capricorn	314-538-239-2	U.S.A.	1998	12.99
Chic	Believer	CD	Atlantic	80107-2	U.S.A.	1987	38.99
Chic	Tongue In Chic	CD	Warner Bros.	AMCY-180	Japan	1982	36.99
Chicago	25 Years of Gold	CD	Liberation	MUSH32049-2	Australia	1995	21.99
Chicago	Chicago - Greatest Hits 1982-1989	CD	Reprise	9-26080-2	U.S.A.	1989	7.99
Chicago	Chicago II	CD	Rhino	R2-76172	U.S.A.	2002	16.99
Chicago	Chicago III	CD	Rhino	R2-76173	U.S.A.	2002	15.99
Chicago	Chicago in Concert	CD	Castle	PIESD-072	England	1998	8.99
Chicago	Chicago Live XXVI	CD	Chicago	CRD-3026	U.S.A.	1999	8.99
Chicago	Chicago The Masters (Live)	CD	Eagle	EAB-CD-088	EC	1998	9.99
Chicago	Chicago Transit A..(Sony Gold Cd)	CD	Columbia	CK-57186	U.S.A.	1969	65.99
Chicago	Chicago Transit Authority	CD	Rhino	R2-76171	U.S.A.	2002	14.99
Chicago	Chicago Transit Authority (1st Pressing)	2CD	Columbia	C2K-00008	U.S.A.	1983	19.99
Chicago	Chicago V +3	CD	Rhino	R2-76175	U.S.A.	2002	10.99
Chicago	Chicago VI +2	CD	Rhino	R2-76176	U.S.A.	2002	13.99
Chicago	Chicago XVIII	CD	Warner Bros.	7599255092	Australia	1986	8.99
Chicago	Greatest Hits. Vol. 2	CD	Columbia	CK-37682	U.S.A.	1981	7.99
Chicago	Group Portrait	4CD	Chicago	CRD-3018	U.S.A.	1989	23.99
Chicago	Hot Streets + 1	CD	Rhino	R2-76181	U.S.A.	2002	13.99
Chicago	Live in Japan	2CD	Chicago	CRD-3030	U.S.A.	1981	67.99
Chicago	Selectons From Chicago The Box (DJ)	CD	Rhino	PRCD-400089	U.S.A.	2003	24.99
Chicago	The Very Best of Chicago	2CD	Rhino	R2-76170	U.S.A.	2002	16.99
Chicago	VII + 1	CD	Rhino	R2-76177	U.S.A.	2002	9.99
Chicago	VIII + 3	CD	Rhino	R2-76178	U.S.A.	2002	12.99
Chicago	X + 2	CD	Rhino	R2-76179	U.S.A.	2003	9.99
Chicago	XI + 2	CD	Rhino	R2-76180	U.S.A.	2003	9.99
Chicago	XIII + 2	CD	Rhino	R2-76182	U.S.A.	2002	9.99
Chicago	XIV + 3	CD	Rhino	R2-76183	U.S.A.	2002	11.99
Chicago	XVI: The Live Album	CD	Nippon Crown	CRCL-80010	Japan	1999	24.99
Chicago	XXV: The Christmas Album	CD	Chicago	CRD-3035	U.S.A.	1999	9.99
Chicago/Bill Champlin	Burn Down The Night	CD	Bandai Visual	BCCA-22	Japan	1992	24.99
Chicago/Bill Champlin	He Started To Sing	CD	Polystar	PSCW-5341	Japan	1995	30.99
Chicago/Bill Champlin	Mayday (Live)	CD	Champlin	CR001	U.S.A.	1996	7.99
Chicago/Bill Champlin	No Wasted Moments	CD	Warner Bros.	WPCP-3645	Japan	1990	19.99
Chicago/Bill Champlin	Single (D Hall/Toto/M McDonald)	CD	Sony	ESCA-5300	U.S.A.	2002	24.99

C

Artist	Title	Format	Label	Catalog No	Country	Released	Value
Chicago/Bill Champlin	Through It All	CD	Polystar	PSCW-5080	Japan	1994	30.99
Chicago/Peter Cetera	Self Titled	CD	Warner Bros.	WPCP-1160	Japan	1988	43.99
Chicago/Robert Lamm	Life Is Good In My Neighborhood	CD	Warner Bros.	WPCP-5519	Japan	1993	34.99
Chicken Shack	40 Blue Fingers... (Christine McVie)	CD	Columbia	477347-2	England	1995	13.99
Chicken Shack	O.K. Ken? (Christine McVie)	CD	BGO	BGOCD186	England	1994	22.99
Chickens, Frank	Club Monkey	CD	Line	FECD-9.00706-0	Germany	1988	14.99
Chickens, Frank	Get Chickenized	CD	Line	FECD-9.00399-0	Germany	1987	14.99
Chieftains	Best Of The Claddagh Years	CD	Atlantic	83224-2	U.S.A.	1999	8.99
Chieftains	Santiago	CD	RCA	09026-68602-2	U.S.A.	1996	9.99
Chieftains	Tears Of Stone	CD	RCA	09026-68968-2	U.S.A.	1999	9.99
Chieftains	The Bells Of Dublin	CD	RCA	09026-60824-2	U.S.A.	1991	7.99
Chieftains	The Celtic Harp	CD	RCA	09026-61490-2	U.S.A.	1993	8.99
Chieftains	The Chieftains 1	CD	Claddagh	CC7CD	U.S.A.	1999	9.99
Chieftains	The Chieftains 2	CD	Claddagh	CC7CD	U.S.A.	1999	9.99
Chieftains	The Chieftains 3	CD	Claddagh	CC10CD	U.S.A.	1999	10.99
Chieftains	The Chieftains 4	CD	Claddagh	CC14CD	U.S.A.	1999	15.99
Chieftains	The Chieftains 7	CD	Columbia	CK-86018	U.S.A.	2002	9.99
Chieftains	The Chieftains 8	CD	Columbia	CK-86019	U.S.A.	2002	9.99
Chieftains	The Chieftains 9: Boil Breakfast Early	CD	Columbia	CK-86016	U.S.A.	2002	5.99
Chieftains	The Long Black Veil	CD	RCA	09026-62702-2	U.S.A.	1995	8.99
Chieftains	The Wide World Over	CD	RCA	09026-63917-2	U.S.A.	2002	13.99
Chiffons	Greatest Hits	CD	Line	BLCD-9.01038-L	Germany	1991	9.99
Chi-Lites	Love Your Way Through	CD	Blues International	PCD-2417	Japan	1992	64.99
Chilliwack	Greatest Hits	CD	Solid Gold	VCK-80129	Canada	1983	20.99
Chilton, Alex	19 Years: A Collection Of Alex Chilton	CD	Rhino	R2-70780	U.S.A.	1991	7.99
Chilton, Alex	1970	CD	Ardent	7-1515-2	U.S.A.	1996	13.99
Chilton, Alex	A Man Called Destruction	CD	Line	RRCD-9.01312-0	Germany	1995	11.99
Chilton, Alex	A Man Called Destruction	CD	Ardent	7-1507-2	U.S.A.	1995	11.99
Chilton, Alex	Bach's Bottom (Line Version)	CD	Line	9.00091	Germany	1980	9.99
Chilton, Alex	Bach's Bottom + 4 (Razor/Tie Version)	CD	Razor & Tie	RE-2010	U.S.A.	1993	12.99
Chilton, Alex	Cliches	CD	New Rose	422481	France	1993	13.99
Chilton, Alex	FC 98 Cd	CD	New Rose	FC-98-CD	France	1991	13.99
Chilton, Alex	Feudalist Tarts/No Sex	CD	Razor & Tie	RE-2032	U.S.A.	1994	14.99
Chilton, Alex	High Priest/Black List + 4	CD	Razor & Tie	RE-2033	U.S.A.	1994	14.99
Chilton, Alex	Like Flies On Sherbert	CD	Line	LICD-9.00486-0	Germany	1991	11.99
Chilton, Alex	Live In London	CD	Line	LICD-9.00139-0	Germany	1987	11.99
Chilton, Alex	Live In London	CD	Fuel	BEA-51561	U.S.A.	1980	11.99
Chilton, Alex	Set	CD	Bar/None	AHAON-110	U.S.A.	1999	9.99
Chilton, Alex	Stuff	CD	New Rose	ROSE-68-CD	France	1985	22.99
Chisholm, Melodye	Love Power	CD Single	Line	PRCD-9.01240-E	Germany	1992	6.99
Chocolate Watch Band	44	CD	Big Beat	CDWIKD25	England	1990	14.99
Chocolate Watch Band	At The Love-In: Live	CD	ROIR	RUSCD8272	U.S.A.	2001	14.99
Chocolate Watch Band	Get Away	CD	Orchard	3716	U.S.A.	2000	11.99
Chocolate Watch Band	Inner Mystique/One Step Beyond	CD	Big Beat	CDWIKD-111	England	2002	14.99
Chocolate Watch Band	No Way Out + 3	CD	Sundazed	SC-6023	U.S.A.	1994	11.99
Chocolate Watch Band	No Way Out + 8	CD	Big Beat	CDWIKD-118	England	2002	18.99
Chocolate Watch Band	One Step Beyond + 4	CD	Sundazed	SC-6025	U.S.A.	1994	11.99
Chocolate Watch Band	The Best Of	CD	Rhino	R2-70108	U.S.A.	1983	21.99
Chocolate Watch Band	The Inner Mystique + 4	CD	Sundazed	SC-6024	U.S.A.	1994	11.99
Chopper-One	A Punk Named Josh (Promo)	CD Single	Restless	RPRO-123	U.S.A.	1998	5.99
Chordettes	Greatest Hits	CD	Line	BLCD-9.01036-L	Germany	1991	10.99
Christian, Neil/Jimmy Page	1962 - 1973 (W/Ritchie Blackmore)	CD	See For Miles	SEE-CD-342	England	1992	24.99
Christian, Neil/Jimmy Page	That's Nice (Same As See For Miles)	CD	Castle	CMRCD824	England	2003	14.99
Christie, Lou	EnLightnin'ment: The Best Of	CD	Rhino	R2-70246	U.S.A.	1988	13.99
Church, Charlotte	Enchantment	CD	Columbia	CK-89710	U.S.A.	2002	10.99
Church, Charlotte	Voice Of An Angel	CD	Sony	SK-60957	U.S.A.	1998	8.99
Church, The	Life Before Starfish (Promo Sampler)	CD	Arista	APCD-9724	U.S.A.	1988	44.99
Church, The	Sometime Anywhere (Promo/W/Box)	2CD	Arista	18729-2	U.S.A.	1994	24.99

Artist	Title	Format	Label	Catalog No	Country	Released	Value
Ciani, Suzanne	Dream Suite	CD	Seventh Wave	SWP-7001-2	U.S.A.	1994	7.99
Ciani, Suzanne	History Of My Heart	CD	Private	2058-2-P	U.S.A.	1989	5.99
Ciani, Suzanne	Hotel Luna	CD	Private	01005-82090-2	U.S.A.	1991	7.99
Ciani, Suzanne	Meditations For Dreams...	CD	Seventh Wave	SWP-7008-2	U.S.A.	2002	11.99
Ciani, Suzanne	Neverland	CD	Private	2036-2-P	U.S.A.	1988	7.99
Ciani, Suzanne	Pianissimo	CD	Private	2073-2-P	U.S.A.	1990	10.99
Ciani, Suzanne	Pianissimo II	CD	Seventh Wave	SWP-7004-2	U.S.A.	1996	8.99
Ciani, Suzanne	Pianissimo III	CD	Seventh Wave	SWP-7007-2	U.S.A.	2001	8.99
Ciani, Suzanne	Private Music Of Suzanne Ciani	CD	Private	01005-82103-2	U.S.A.	1992	14.99
Ciani, Suzanne	Pure Romance	CD	Seventh Wave	SWP-7009-2	U.S.A.	2003	9.99
Ciani, Suzanne	Seven Waves	CD	Seventh Wave	SWP-7002-2	U.S.A.	1995	6.99
Ciani, Suzanne	Suzanne Ciani And The Wave Live!	CD	Seventh Wave	SWP-7005-2	U.S.A.	1997	6.99
Ciani, Suzanne	The Velocity Of Love	CD	Seventh Wave	SWP-7003-2	U.S.A.	1995	9.99
Ciani, Suzanne	Turning	CD	Seventh Wave	SWP-7006-2	U.S.A.	1999	8.99
Cielo y Tierra/Jon Anderson	Heaven & Earth	CD	East West	61948-2	U.S.A.	1996	6.99
Cinderella	20th Century Masters: The Millennium	CD	Mercury	314-542-850-2	U.S.A.	2000	8.99
Cinderella	Bad Attitude 1986-1994	CD	Connoisseur	VSOP-CD-251	England	1998	13.99
Cinderella	Don't Know What You (Gold Video Cd)	CD	Mercury	870-734-2	U.S.A.	1988	24.99
Cinderella	Heartbreak Station	CD	Mercury	848-018-2	U.S.A.	1990	7.99
Cinderella	In Concert	CD	Cleopatra	CLP-01372-2	U.S.A.	2004	8.99
Cinderella	Key Club (Live Greatest Hits)	CD	Cleopatra	CLP-0593-2	U.S.A.	1999	13.99
Cinderella	Live Train To Heartbreak Station	CD	Nippon Phonogram	PHCR-3014	Japan	1991	14.99
Cinderella	Long Cold Winter	CD	Mercury	834-612-4	U.S.A.	1988	8.99
Cinderella	Night Songs	CD	Mercury	830-076-4	U.S.A.	1986	9.99
Cinderella	Once Upon A Time	CD	Mercury	314-534-775-2	U.S.A.	1997	8.99
Cinderella	Shelter Me	CD Single	Nippon Phonogram	PHCR-8007	Japan	1990	19.99
Cinderella	Still Climbing	CD	Nippon Phonogram	PHCR-1266	Japan	1994	14.99
Cinderella	Still Climbing	CD	Mercury	522-947-2	England	1994	8.99
Cinderella	The Collection	CD	Connoisseur	VSOP-CD-335	England	2001	11.99
Cipollina, John	Raven	CD	Line	LICD-9.00053-0	Germany	1988	10.99
Circle Jerks	Golden Shower Of Hits	CD	Rhino	R2-71088	U.S.A.	1983	9.99
Circus Of Power	Self Titled	CD	RCA	R32P-1180	Japan	1989	29.99
Cities	Annihilation Absolute	CD	Enigma	32XB-156	Japan	1999	154.99
City Boy	Anthology	CD	Alchemy	PILOT-105	England	2002	12.99
City Boy	Heads Are Rolling	CD	Bear Tracks	BTCD-979420-AH	Germany	1991	22.99
City Boy	Self Titled	CD	Bear Tracks	BTCD-979415-2	Germany	1991	11.99
City Boy	Self Titled/Dinner At The Ritz	2CD	Renaissance	RMED-00216	U.S.A.	1998	19.99
City Boy	The Day The Earth Caught Fire	CD	Bear Tracks	BTCD-979419-AH	Germany	1991	12.99
City Boy	Young Men Gone West/Book Early	2CD	Renaissance	RMED-00217	U.S.A.	1998	15.99
Clannad	A Magical Gathering - Clannad Anth.	2CD	Rhino	R2-78255	U.S.A.	2002	13.99
Clannad	An Diolaim	CD	Music Club	50063	U.S.A.	1998	8.99
Clannad	Anam	CD	Atlantic	7-82409-2	U.S.A.	1992	6.99
Clannad	Atlantic Realm	CD	RCA	74321-31867-2	EC	1996	9.99
Clannad	Banba	CD	RCA	7-82503-2	U.S.A.	1993	8.99
Clannad	Celtic Collection	CD	Camden	74321-67453-2	EU	1999	12.99
Clannad	Clannad 2	CD	Shanachie	79007	England	1988	9.99
Clannad	Clannad In Concert	CD	Shanachie	79030	England	1987	9.99
Clannad	Crann Ull	CD	Intercord	INT-860.153	Germany	1980	7.99
Clannad	Dúlamán	CD	Shanachie	79008	England	1988	9.99
Clannad	Fuaim	CD	Atlantic	7-82481-2	U.S.A.	1982	9.99
Clannad	Greatest Hits	CD	RCA	07863-67878-2	U.S.A.	2000	6.99
Clannad	In Fortune's Hand	CD Single	RCA	PD-43972	England	1990	5.99
Clannad	Landmarks	CD	RCA	83083-2	U.S.A.	1998	8.99
Clannad	Legend	CD	RCA	PD70188	England	1984	12.99
Clannad	Lore + 6 (Bonus Cd)	2CD	RCA	74321-35975-2	England	1996	11.99
Clannad	Macalla	CD	RCA	PCD1-8063	U.S.A.	1985	12.99
Clannad	Magic Elements - The Best Of Clannad	CD	RCA	74321-62182-2	EU	1998	7.99
Clannad	Magical Ring	CD	RCA	ND71473	England	1983	11.99

Artist	Title	Format	Label	Catalog No	Country	Released	Value
Clannad	Past Present	CD	RCA	9912-2-R	U.S.A.	1989	6.99
Clannad	Rogha: The Best Of Clannad	CD	RCA	07863-66978-2	U.S.A.	1997	7.99
Clannad	Sirius	CD	RCA	6846-2-R	England	1988	10.99
Clannad	Sirius Cd Sampler	CD Single	RCA	SIRIUS-1	England	1988	9.99
Clannad	The Angel And the Soldier Boy	CD	RCA	PD-74328	England	1989	18.99
Clannad	The Celtic Voice	CD	Erin	ER-15089	U.S.A.	1999	11.99
Clannad	The Collection	CD	Ktel	CD-215	England	1987	8.99
Clannad	The Family Tree Sampler (Promo)	CD	Atlantic	PRCD-4945-2	U.S.A.	1993	7.99
Clannad	The Ultimate Collection	CD	RCA	74321-48674-2	England	1997	9.99
Clannad	Themes	CD	Atlantic	82737-2	U.S.A.	1995	5.99
Clapton, Eric	(I) Get Lost	CD Single	Warner Bros.	WPCR-10629	Japan	2000	17.99
Clapton, Eric	(I) Get Lost	CD Single	Reprise	9362-44809-2	Germany	2000	14.99
Clapton, Eric	(I) Get Lost (Promo)	CD Single	Warner Bros.	PRO-CD-4200	U.S.A.	1999	14.99
Clapton, Eric	24 Nights	2CD	Reprise	W2-26420	U.S.A.	1991	11.99
Clapton, Eric	461 Ocean Boulevard (MFSL Gold Cd)	CD	Mobile Fidelity	UDCD-594	U.S.A.	1974	25.99
Clapton, Eric	August	CD	Warner Bros.	9-25476-2	U.S.A.	2000	7.99
Clapton, Eric	Backless (MFSL Gold Cd)	CD	Mobile Fidelity	UDCD-653	U.S.A.	1978	29.99
Clapton, Eric	Blues (Promo Sampler)	CD	Polydor	CAT5P-001	U.S.A.	1999	28.99
Clapton, Eric	Box 1983 - 1994	7 CD	Warner Bros.	WPCR-1111/17	Japan	1999	61.99
Clapton, Eric	Change The World	CD Single	Reprise	2-17621	U.S.A.	1996	8.99
Clapton, Eric	Clapton Cronicles (Gold Cd/3 Song Cd)	2CD	Reprise	WPCR-10738	Japan	1999	39.99
Clapton, Eric	Crossroads Box Set	4CD	Polydor	835-261-2	U.S.A.	1988	29.99
Clapton, Eric	Crossroads Volume 2 Box Set	4CD	Polydor	529-305-2	U.S.A.	1996	24.99
Clapton, Eric	Eric Clapton (MFSL Gold Cd)	CD	Mobile Fidelity	UDCD-639	U.S.A.	1970	22.99
Clapton, Eric	Eric Clapton Blues	2CD	Polydor	314-547-178-2	U.S.A.	1999	14.99
Clapton, Eric	Eric Clapton's Rainbow Concert + 8	CD	Polydor	31452-7472-2	U.S.A.	1995	11.99
Clapton, Eric	From The Cradle	CD	Reprise	9-45735-2	U.S.A.	1994	7.99
Clapton, Eric	Get Plugged In (Promo Sampler)	CD	Polydor	PCD-301	Canada	1993	41.99
Clapton, Eric	I Ain't Gonna Stand For It	CD Single	Reprise	9362-44987-2	Germany	2001	6.99
Clapton, Eric	It Hurts Me Too	CD Single	Warner Bros.	WPCR-440	Japan	1995	14.99
Clapton, Eric	Just One Night (MFSL Gold Cd)	2CD	Mobile Fidelity	UDCD-2-608	U.S.A.	1980	24.99
Clapton, Eric	Martin Scorsese Presents	CD	Polydor	B0000796-02	U.S.A.	2003	8.99
Clapton, Eric	Me And Mr. Johnson	CD	Reprise	48423-2	U.S.A.	2004	8.99
Clapton, Eric	Money And Cigarettes	CD	Warner Bros.	9-47734-2	U.S.A.	2000	8.99
Clapton, Eric	My Father's Eyes (Promo)	CD Single	Reprise	PRO-CD-9170	U.S.A.	1998	6.99
Clapton, Eric	Pilgrim + 1	CD	Reprise	WPCR-1400	Japan	1998	34.99
Clapton, Eric	Reptile + 1	CD	Reprise	WPCR-11100	Japan	2001	24.99
Clapton, Eric	Selection The Best Of (Chronicles)	CD	Warner Bros.	SAM0189	England	1999	12.99
Clapton, Eric	Selections From Crossroads 2 (Promo)	CD	Polydor	PRSAD-000182	U.S.A.	1996	14.99
Clapton, Eric	Selections/Rainbow Concert (Promo)	CD	Polydor	PRSAD00002	U.S.A.	1995	8.99
Clapton, Eric	Slowhand (MFSL Gold Cd)	CD	Mobile Fidelity	UDCD-553	U.S.A.	1977	29.99
Clapton, Eric	Stone Free (Hendirx Tribute Promo)	CD Single	Reprise	PRO-CD-6672	U.S.A.	1993	24.99
Clapton, Eric	The Blues Years	CD	Castle	SELCD-565	England	1999	7.99
Clapton, Eric	The Cream Of Clapton	CD	PolyGram	31452-7116-2	U.S.A.	1995	7.99
Clapton, Eric	Time Pieces - The Best Of Eric Clapton	CD	Polydor	800-014-2	U.S.A.	1982	6.99
Clapton, Eric	Timepieces Vol. II Live In The 70's	CD	Polydor	811-835-2	U.S.A.	1983	7.99
Clapton, Eric	Tore Down (Promo)	CD Single	Reprise	PRO-CD-7150	U.S.A.	1994	4.99
Clapton, Eric	Unplugged	CD	Reprise	9-45024-2	U.S.A.	1992	6.99
Clapton, Eric	Wonderful Tonight	CD Single	Warner Bros.	9362-40257-2	Germany	1991	7.99
Clapton, Eric/B.B. King	Riding With The King	CD	Warner Bros.	9-47612-2	U.S.A.	2000	9.99
Clapton, Eric/T.D.F.	Retail Therapy (W/Simon Climie)	CD	Reprise	9-46489-2	U.S.A.	1997	12.99
Clark, Dave/Five	The History Of	2CD	Hollywood	HR-61482-2	U.S.A.	1993	55.99
Clark, Gene	American Dreamer 1964-1974	CD	Raven	RVCD-21	Australia	1992	14.99
Clark, Gene	Echoes (With Gosdin Brothers + 9)	CD	Columbia	CK48523	U.S.A.	1991	9.99
Clark, Gene	Firebyrd	CD	Hudson Canyon	HCR8649	U.S.A.	1994	7.99
Clark, Gene	Flying High	2CD	A&M	540-725-2	Germany	1998	19.99
Clark, Gene	Gypsy Angel: Demos 1983-1990	CD	Evangeline	GEL-4030	England	2001	11.99
Clark, Gene	No Other	CD	Collector's Choice	CCM-314	U.S.A.	2003	6.99

C

C

Artist	Title	Format	Label	Catalog No	Country	Released	Value
Clark, Gene	No Other	CD	Line	LECD-9.00889-0	Germany	1989	13.99
Clark, Gene	No Other	CD	East West	AMCY-6066	Japan	1999	24.99
Clark, Gene	Roadmaster	CD	Demon	ED-CD-198	England	1986	19.99
Clark, Gene	Two Sides To Every Story	CD	Polydor	835-739-2	U.S.A.	1977	24.99
Clark, Gene	Two Sides To Every Story	CD	Polydor	835-793-2	Germany	1977	146.99
Clark, Gene	White Light	CD	Polygram K.K.	POCM-2094	Japan	1998	24.99
Clark, Gene	White Light + 5	CD	A&M	493-209-2	England	2002	15.99
Clark, Gene/Carla Olson	Silhouetted In Light Live In Concert + 1	CD	Pan Fish Records	CRCL-7514	Japan	1997	25.99
Clark, Gene/Doug Dillard	F Exhibition/Through The.. (MFSL Cd)	CD	Mobile Fidelity	MFCD-791	U.S.A.	1969	34.99
Clark, Gene/Doug Dillard	The Fant. Exhibition/Through The..	CD	A&M	540-975-2	Germany	1998	19.99
Clark, Gene/Gosdin Bros	Gene Clark/Gosdin Brothers	CD	Edsel	EDCD-529	England	1997	14.99
Clark, Guy	Old Friends	CD	Line	LICD-9.00721-0	Germany	1989	11.99
Clark, Guy	The Essential Guy Clark (Gold Cd)	CD	Audiophile Legends	APH-102.818	Germany	2001	14.99
Clark, Mick	Steel & Fire	CD	Line	STCD-9.00797-0	Germany	1989	14.99
Clark, Petula	Downtown + 3	CD	Sequel	NEBCD-661	England	1993	8.99
Clark, Petula	I Know A Place + 4	CD	Sequel	NEBCD-660	England	1994	8.99
Clark, Petula	Just Pet + 2	CD	Sequel	NEBCD-902	England	1996	8.99
Clark, Petula	Meet Me In Battlesea Park Box Set	6CD	Fabulus	FBUBX001	England	2002	49.99
Clark, Petula	Portrait Of Petula + 4	CD	Sequel	NEBCD-659	England	1994	9.99
Clark, Petula	The International Collection Box Set	4CD	Bear Family	BCD-16212-DI	Germany	1998	44.99
Clark, Petula	The Pye Years - Volume Two	CD	RPM	RPM-159	England	1996	17.99
Clark, Petula	The Ultimate Collection	2CD	Sanctuary	SANDD111	England	2002	12.99
Clarke, John Cooper	Disguise In Love	CD	Epic	480530-2	England	1978	11.99
Clarke, John Cooper	Snap, Crackle & Bop	CD	Epic	477380-2	England	2003	20.99
Clarke, John Cooper	Very Best Of John Cooper Clarke	CD	Epic	506343-2	England	2002	19.99
Clash	1977 Revisited	CD	Relativity	88561-1036-2	U.S.A.	1990	13.99
Clash	Clash On Broadway Box Set	3CD	Epic	E3K-46991	U.S.A.	1991	24.99
Clash	Clash On Broadway: The Trailer (DJ)	CD	Epic	ESK-4274	U.S.A.	1991	19.99
Clash	Combat Rock	CD	Epic	EK-63896	U.S.A.	1999	7.99
Clash	Cut The Crap	CD	Epic	EK-66419	U.S.A.	1985	14.99
Clash	Give 'Em Enough Rope	CD	Epic	EK-63884	U.S.A.	1999	8.99
Clash	Live: From Here to Eternity	CD	Epic	EK-65747	U.S.A.	1999	7.99
Clash	London Calling	CD	Epic	EK-63885	U.S.A.	1999	10.99
Clash	Return To Brixton	CD Single	Epic	49K-73516	U.S.A.	1990	8.99
Clash	Return To Brixton	CD Single	CBS	656072-2	Australia	1990	14.99
Clash	Rockers Galore (Promo)	CD	Epic	ESK-47144	U.S.A.	1999	11.99
Clash	Sandinista!	2CD	Epic	E2K-63888	U.S.A.	1999	16.99
Clash	Story Of The Clash, Volume 1	2CD	Epic	E2K-63892	U.S.A.	1999	10.99
Clash	Super Black Market Clash	CD	Epic	EK-53191	U.S.A.	1993	9.99
Clash	The Clash (U.K. Version)	CD	Epic	EK-63883	U.S.A.	1999	9.99
Clash	The Clash (U.S. Version)	CD	Epic	EK-63882	U.S.A.	1999	9.99
Clash	The Clash Story +7	CD	Sonic Book	SONIC-BOOK-15	Italy	1999	9.99
Clash	The Singles	CD	Epic	EK-63886	U.S.A.	1991	9.99
Clash	The Trailer Cd Sampler (Promo)	CD	Epic	ESK-4274	U.S.A.	1991	14.99
Clash/Various Artists	Burning London The Clash Tribute	CD	Epic	EK-69106	U.S.A.	1999	9.99
Classics IV	Atomspherics 1966 - 1975	CD	Raven	RVCD-134	Australia	2002	16.99
Clayton, Willie	Forever	CD	Line	TLCD-9.00627-0	Germany	1988	18.99
Clayton-Thomas, David	David Clayton-Thomas/Tequila Sunrise	CD	Edsel	EDCD-722	England	1972	27.99
Clea/McLeod	Beyond Our Means	CD	Line	UTCD-9.00969-L	Germany	1990	12.99
Clear Blue Sky	Self Titled (Roger Dean Art)	CD	Repertoire	REP-4110-WP	Germany	2002	17.99
Clearlight	Clearlight + 1	CD	Collector's Choice	CCM-271-2	U.S.A.	2002	13.99
Clearlight Symphony	Les Contes Du Singe Fou	CD	Spalax	14594	France	1976	17.99
Clearlight Symphony	Self Titled	CD	Spalax	14592	France	1975	17.99
Clemons, Clarence	A Night With Mr. C	CD	Tristar	35401	U.S.A.	1996	6.99
Clemons, Clarence	Aja & The Big Man - Get It On	CD	D.M.L. Music	DMCR-25001	Japan	1995	14.99
Clemons, Clarence	Hero	CD	Columbia	SRCS-6479	Japan	1997	7.99
Clemons, Clarence	Live in Asbury Park	CD	Valley	VE-15165	U.S.A.	2002	7.99
Clemons, Clarence	Peacemaker	CD	Zoo Ent.	72445-11103-2	U.S.A.	1995	7.99

Artist	Title	Format	Label	Catalog No	Country	Released	Value
Clemons, Clarence	Rescue	CD	Tristar	35406	U.S.A.	1996	6.99
Clemons, Clarence	Rescue/Hero	CD	Collectables	COL-CD-6880	U.S.A.	2001	8.99
Cliff, Jimmy	Breakout	CD	Line	LICD-9.01109-0	Germany	1992	19.99
Cliff, Jimmy	Cool Runnings (Promo)	CD Single	Columbia	OSK-77207	U.S.A.	1993	7.99
Cliff, Jimmy	I'm A Winner	CD Single	Line	LICD-9.01246-E	Germany	1992	4.99
Cliff, Jimmy	The Harder They Come (O.S.T.)	CD	Island	314-586-158-2	U.S.A.	2001	15.99
Climax Blues Band	25 Years 1968-1993	2CD	Repertoire	REP-4310-WO	Germany	1994	19.99
Climax Blues Band	A Lot Of Bottle + 1	CD	Plum	1409-2	U.S.A.	1998	13.99
Climax Blues Band	A Lot Of Bottle + 1	CD	Repertoire	REP-4046-WZ	Germany	2002	13.99
Climax Blues Band	Blues Apostles	4CD	Akarma	AKCD-1444	Italy	2003	44.99
Climax Blues Band	Blues From The Attic	CD	Griffin	GCD-170-2	U.S.A.	1995	14.99
Climax Blues Band	Collection '77 - '83	CD	Virgin	0777-7-87928-2-6	England	1992	11.99
Climax Blues Band	Couldn't Get It Right	CD	Repertoire	REP-4802-WZ	Germany	2002	14.99
Climax Blues Band	Couldn't Get It Right...Plus	CD	See For Miles	SEE-CD222	England	1989	19.99
Climax Blues Band	FM/Live	CD	Plum	1408-2	U.S.A.	1998	14.99
Climax Blues Band	FM/Live	CD	Akarma	AKCD-138	Italy	2001	14.99
Climax Blues Band	FM/Live (W/Bonus Tracks)	CD	See For Miles	SEE-CD279	England	1989	29.99
Climax Blues Band	Gold Plated	CD	Repertoire	REP-4142-WY	Germany	2002	14.99
Climax Blues Band	Gold Plated	CD	See For Miles	SEE-CD670	England	1998	14.99
Climax Blues Band	Gold Plated + 2	CD	Plum	1412-2	U.S.A.	1998	19.99
Climax Blues Band	Got It Right: Best Of	CD	Plum	1423-2	U.S.A.	1999	14.99
Climax Blues Band	Harvest Years 1969-1972	CD	See For Miles	SEE-CD316	England	1998	11.99
Climax Blues Band	Plays On	CD	Repertoire	REP-4077-WZ	Germany	2002	14.99
Climax Blues Band	Plays On	CD	Plum	1402-2	U.S.A.	1998	14.99
Climax Blues Band	Rich Man + 1	CD	Plum	1414-2	U.S.A.	1998	14.99
Climax Blues Band	Rich Man + 1	CD	Repertoire	REP-4045-WZ	Germany	2002	14.99
Climax Blues Band	Rock & Pop Legends	CD	Disky	DC-863672	Holland	1996	9.99
Climax Blues Band	Sense Of Direction + 1	CD	Plum	1415-2	U.S.A.	1998	14.99
Climax Blues Band	Stamp Album	CD	Plum	1411-2	U.S.A.	1998	14.99
Climax Blues Band	Stamp Album	CD	Repertoire	REP-4719-WZ	Germany	2002	14.99
Climax Blues Band	The Climax Chicago Blues Band	CD	Repertoire	REP-4078-WZ	Germany	2002	14.99
Climax Blues Band	The Climax Chicago Blues Band	CD	Plum	1401-2	U.S.A.	1998	14.99
Climax Blues Band	Tightly Knit	CD	Repertoire	REP-4079-WZ	Germany	2002	14.99
Climax Blues Band	Tightly Knit + 1	CD	Plum	1410-2	U.S.A.	1998	14.99
Clouds	Scrapbook/Watercolour Days	CD	BGO	BGOCD317	England	1996	14.99
Cluster	Cluster II	CD	Spalax	14864	France	1996	17.99
Cluster	Live in Japan 1996	CD	Captain Trip	CTCD-055	Japan	1996	19.99
Cluster	Zuckerzeit	CD	Spalax	14865	France	1996	12.99
Cluster/Kluster	Klopfzeichen + 1	CD	Captain Trip	CTCD-128	Japan	1970	19.99
Cluster/Kluster	Zwei-Osterei + 1	CD	Captain Trip	CTCD-129	Japan	1970	10.99
Coal Porters, The	Chris Hillman Tribute Concerts	CD	Prima	SID013	England	2001	10.99
Cobain, Kurt/W.S. Burroughs	The "Priest" They Called Him	CD	Tim/Kerr	TK92CD044	U.S.A.	1992	9.99
Cobham, Billy	Spectrum	CD	Atlantic	8122-73519-2	Germany	1973	12.99
Cochise	Cochise	CD	Spiral	SCD-933	England	2002	18.99
Cochise	So Far	CD	Spiral	SCD-935	England	2002	18.99
Cochise	Swallow Tales	CD	Spiral	SCD-934	England	2002	18.99
Cockburn, Bruce	Listen For The Laugh (Promo)	CD	Columbia	CSK-5671	U.S.A.	1994	4.99
Cocker, Joe	Across From Midnight	CD	CMC INT.	06076-86245-2	U.S.A.	1998	5.99
Cocker, Joe	Across From Midnight (Adv. Promo Cd)	CD	CMC INT.	CMC-SP-86245-2	U.S.A.	1998	11.99
Cocker, Joe	Civilized Man	CD	EMI	0777-7-46038-2	Germany	1992	9.99
Cocker, Joe	Cocker	CD	Capitol	7243-8-19825-2	U.S.A.	1995	6.99
Cocker, Joe	Connoisseur's Cocker	CD	Raven	RVCD-16	Australia	1997	10.99
Cocker, Joe	Greatest Love Songs	CD	Hip O	HIPD-69887	U.S.A.	2003	7.99
Cocker, Joe	Have A Little Faith	CD	EMI	7243-8-29792-2-7	Holland	1994	8.99
Cocker, Joe	Have A Little Faith (CD 1)	CD Single	Capital	7243-8-82112-2-2	England	1995	5.99
Cocker, Joe	I Can Stand A Little Rain	CD	Rebound	314-520-237-2	U.S.A.	1995	7.99
Cocker, Joe	Jamaica Say You Will	CD	A&M	394-529-2	Germany	1998	9.99
Cocker, Joe	Joe Cocker! + 2	CD	A&M	096-490-420-2	U.S.A.	1999	9.99

Artist	Title	Format	Label	Catalog No	Country	Released	Value
Cocker, Joe	Let The Healing Begin	CD Single	Capitol	7243-8-81872-2-0	England	1994	4.99
Cocker, Joe	Live !	CD	Capitol	0777-7-93416-2	U.S.A.	1990	7.99
Cocker, Joe	Live In L.A.	CD	Castle	CLACD-189	England	1992	7.99
Cocker, Joe	Long Voyage Home Sampler (Promo)	CD	A&M	AMSAD-00042	U.S.A.	1995	14.99
Cocker, Joe	Luxury You Can Afford	CD	Asylum	7559-60821-2	Germany	1996	9.99
Cocker, Joe	Mad Dogs And Englishmen	CD	A&M	069-490-449-2	U.S.A.	1999	8.99
Cocker, Joe	Mad Dogs/English.. (MFSL Gold Cd)	CD	Mobile Fidelity	UDCD-736	U.S.A.	1970	42.99
Cocker, Joe	Mad Dogs/English.. (MFSL Silver Cd)	2CD	Mobile Fidelity	MFCD-2-824-1/2	U.S.A.	1970	31.99
Cocker, Joe	Night Calls	CD	Capitol	0777-7-97801-2	U.S.A.	1992	7.99
Cocker, Joe	No Ordinary World	CD	Red Ink	76692-13601-2	U.S.A.	2000	7.99
Cocker, Joe	One Night Of Sin	CD	Capitol	0777-7-92861-2	U.S.A.	1992	7.99
Cocker, Joe	Organic	CD	EMI	7243-8-53647-2-3	Holland	1996	8.99
Cocker, Joe	Respect Yourself	CD	Red Ink	76692-59480-2	U.S.A.	2002	7.99
Cocker, Joe	Respect Yourself Aussie Tour Ed. + 2	CD	EMI	542-204-2	Australia	2002	8.99
Cocker, Joe	Sheffield Steel (MFSL Gold Cd)	CD	Mobile Fidelity	UDCD-631	U.S.A.	1982	19.99
Cocker, Joe	Sheffield Steel + 4	CD	Island	044-063-152-2	U.S.A.	2002	8.99
Cocker, Joe	Stingray	CD	A&M	394-574-2	Germany	1994	9.99
Cocker, Joe	Super Hits	CD	550 Music	07464-66063-2	U.S.A.	2000	7.99
Cocker, Joe	The Anthology	2CD	A&M	069-490-390-2	U.S.A.	1999	12.99
Cocker, Joe	The Long Voyage Home Box Set	4CD	A&M	31454-0236-2	U.S.A.	1995	24.99
Cocker, Joe	Unchain My Heart	CD	EMI	0777-7-48285-2-9	Germany	1993	8.99
Cocker, Joe	Vance Arnold And The Avengers '63	CD	Voiceprint	VP214CD	England	2000	12.99
Cocker, Joe	When The Night Comes	CD Single	Capitol	20-3375-2	England	1989	9.99
Cocker, Joe	With A Little Help From My Friends + 2	CD	A&M	069-490-419-2	U.S.A.	1999	8.99
Cocker, Joe/Grease Band	On Air	CD	Strange Fruit	SFRSCD-036	England	1997	24.99
Cocteau Twins	Cd Single Box Set	10 CD	Capitol	C2-15788	U.S.A.	1991	49.99
Cocteau Twins	Collector Disc Q104	CD	Capitol	DPRO-79354	U.S.A.	1994	161.99
Cocteau Twins	Tishbite	CD Single	Fontana	0-42285-28032-6	U.S.A.	1996	18.99
Cohen, Leonard	Death Of A Ladies Man (Phil Spector)	CD	Columbia	07464-44286-2	U.S.A.	1977	8.99
Cohen, Leonard	Field Commander Cohen: Tour Of 1979	CD	Columbia	CK-66210	U.S.A.	2001	8.99
Cohen, Leonard	I'm Your Fan	CD	Columbia	CK-44191	U.S.A.	1988	6.99
Cohen, Leonard	Live	CD	Columbia	CK-66327	U.S.A.	1994	8.99
Cohen, Leonard	Live Songs	CD	Sony	484454-2	England	1997	8.99
Cohen, Leonard	More Best Of	CD	Columbia	CK-68636	U.S.A.	1997	8.99
Cohen, Leonard	New Skin For The Old Ceremony	CD	Columbia	CK-66952	U.S.A.	1995	8.99
Cohen, Leonard	Recent Songs	CD	Columbia	CK-36264	U.S.A.	1979	6.99
Cohen, Leonard	Songs From A Room	CD	Columbia	CK-9767	U.S.A.	1990	6.99
Cohen, Leonard	Songs Of Love And Hate	CD	Columbia	CK-66951	U.S.A.	1995	8.99
Cohen, Leonard	Ten New Songs	CD	Columbia	CK-85953	U.S.A.	2001	6.99
Cohen, Leonard	The Best Of	CD	Columbia	CK-34077	U.S.A.	1977	5.99
Cohen, Leonard	The Essential	2CD	Columbia	C2K-86884	U.S.A.	2002	13.99
Cohen, Leonard	The Future	CD	Columbia	CK-53226	U.S.A.	1992	6.99
Cohen, Leonard	The Songs Of	CD	Columbia	CK-9533	U.S.A.	1990	6.99
Cohen, Leonard	Various Positions	CD	Columbia	CK-66950	U.S.A.	1995	8.99
Cohen, Leonard/Tribute	More Fans (Promo Sampler)	CD Single	Columbia	SAMP-CD-1546	France	1990	44.99
Colbert, Robert	Dark Shadows - 30th Ann. Collection	CD	Varese	VSD-5702	U.S.A.	1996	10.99
Colbert, Robert	Dark Shadows - House Of/Night Of	CD	Rhino	R2-72401	U.S.A.	1990	19.99
Colbert, Robert	Dark Shadows - Volume 1	CD	Media Sounds	CD8100	U.S.A.	1990	24.99
Colbert, Robert	Dark Shadows - Volume 2	CD	Media Sounds	CD8101	U.S.A.	1990	24.99
Colbert, Robert	Dark Shadows - Volume 3	CD	Media Sounds	CD8102	U.S.A.	1990	24.99
Colbert, Robert	Dark Shadows - Volume 4	CD	Media Sounds	CD8103	U.S.A.	1990	24.99
Colbert, Robert	Dark Shadows (O.S.T.) + 2 Deluxe Ed	CD	Varese	302-066-066-2	U.S.A.	1999	14.99
Colbert, Robert	The Night Stalker And Other...	CD	Varese	302-066-156-2	U.S.A.	2000	10.99
Cold Blood/Lydia Pense	First Taste Of Sin	CD	Collectables	COL-CD-6155	U.S.A.	2002	9.99
Cold Blood/Lydia Pense	Lydia	CD	Warner Bros.	WPCP-3689	Japan	1974	19.99
Cold Blood/Lydia Pense	Lydia	CD	Collectables	COL-CD-6387	U.S.A.	2004	9.99
Cold Blood/Lydia Pense	Self Titled/Sisyphus	CD	Collectables	COL-CD-6813	U.S.A.	2002	10.99
Cold Blood/Lydia Pense	The Best Of	CD	GNP	GNPD-2238	U.S.A.	1995	11.99

C

Artist	Title	Format	Label	Catalog No	Country	Released	Value
Cold Blood/Lydia Pense	Thriller	CD	Warner Bros.	WPCP-3688	Japan	1973	74.99
Cold Blood/Lydia Pense	Vintage Blood: Live! 1973	CD	Dig Music	104	U.S.A.	2001	9.99
Cold Chisel	Breakfast At Sweethearts	CD	Line	MLCD-9.00152-L	Germany	1989	9.99
Cold Chisel	Cold Chisel	CD	Line	MLCD-9.00155-L	Germany	1990	9.99
Cold Chisel	East	CD	Line	LICD-9.00148-L	Germany	1991	19.99
Cold Chisel	Swingshift	CD	Line	LICD-9.00416-0	Germany	1987	14.99
Cold Chisel/Jimmy Barnes	Jimmy Barnes (Self Titled)	CD	Lemon	CDLEM12	England	2003	14.99
Coldplay	Mince Spies (Promo)	CD Single	EMI	COLDXMAS-01	England	2000	169.99
Cole, Nat King	The Christmas Song	CD	Capitol	7-46318-2	U.S.A.	1986	7.99
Cole, Natalie	Thankful	CD	One Way	OW-19084	U.S.A.	1996	56.99
Cole, Paula	Harbinger	CD	Imago	9-46041-2	U.S.A.	1994	5.99
Cole, Paula	I Don't Want To Wait	CD Single	Warner Bros.	9362439402	Australia	1994	5.99
Cole, Paula	This Fire	CD	Warner Bros.	9-46424-2	U.S.A.	1996	7.99
Cole, Paula Band	Amen	CD	Imago	9-47490-2	U.S.A.	1999	9.99
Collectors	Grass And Wild Strawberries	CD	Line	LECD-9.01013-0	Germany	1990	29.99
Collectors	The Collectors	CD	Line	LECD-9.01009-0	Germany	1991	29.99
Collins, Judy	3 & 4 (W/Jim (Roger) McGuinn)	CD	Wildflower	1301	U.S.A.	2004	12.99
Collins, Judy	All On A Wintry Night	CD	Wildflower	1297	U.S.A.	2000	12.99
Collins, Judy	Baby's Bedtime	CD	Lightyear	5102-2-LR12	U.S.A.	1990	8.99
Collins, Judy	Baby's Morningtime	CD	Lightyear	75002	U.S.A.	1990	8.99
Collins, Judy	Both Sides Now	CD	Intersound	3718	U.S.A.	1998	8.99
Collins, Judy	Bread And Roses	CD	Elektra	2-1076	U.S.A.	1990	81.99
Collins, Judy	Christmas At The Biltmore Estate	CD	Elektra	62120-2	U.S.A.	1997	6.99
Collins, Judy	Classic Broadway	CD	Intersound	3752	U.S.A.	1999	5.99
Collins, Judy	Colors Of The Day (DCC Gold Cd)	CD	DCC	GZS-1130	U.S.A.	1994	30.99
Collins, Judy	Come Rejoice!: A Judy Collins Christmas	CD	Rhino	R2-79085	U.S.A.	1994	6.99
Collins, Judy	Fifth Album	CD	Elektra	7300-2	U.S.A.	1990	9.99
Collins, Judy	Fires Of Eden	CD	Columbia	CK-46102	U.S.A.	1990	12.99
Collins, Judy	Forever: An Anthology	2CD	Elektra	62104-2	U.S.A.	1997	18.99
Collins, Judy	Hard Times For Lovers	CD	Elektra	171-2	U.S.A.	1990	7.99
Collins, Judy	Home Again	CD	Elektra	60304-2	U.S.A.	1990	24.99
Collins, Judy	In My Life	CD	Elektra	74027-2	U.S.A.	1990	9.99
Collins, Judy	Judith	CD	Elektra	2-111	U.S.A.	1990	8.99
Collins, Judy	Judy Sings Dylan...Just Like a Woman	CD	Geffen	GEFD-24612	U.S.A.	1993	7.99
Collins, Judy	Live At Newport, 1959-1966	CD	Vanguard	VMD-77013	U.S.A.	1994	8.99
Collins, Judy	Live At Wolf Trap	CD	Wildflower	1298	U.S.A.	2000	12.99
Collins, Judy	Living	CD	Elektra	75014-2	U.S.A.	1990	9.99
Collins, Judy	Maid Constant S./Golden Apples Sun	CD	Wildflower	1299	U.S.A.	2004	12.99
Collins, Judy	Recollections: The Best Of	CD	Elektra	61350-2	U.S.A.	1969	8.99
Collins, Judy	Running For My Life	CD	Elektra	253-2	U.S.A.	1990	29.99
Collins, Judy	Sanity And Grace	CD	Gold Castle	D2-71318	U.S.A.	1989	12.99
Collins, Judy	Shameless	CD	Mesa	7567-92584-2	U.S.A.	1994	6.99
Collins, Judy	The Times Of Our Lives	CD	Elektra	60001-2	U.S.A.	1990	7.99
Collins, Judy	The Very Best Of	CD	Rhino	R2-74374	U.S.A.	2001	7.99
Collins, Judy	True Stories And Other Dreams	CD	Elektra	75053-2	U.S.A.	1990	7.99
Collins, Judy	Trust Your Heart	CD	Gold Castle	D2-71302	U.S.A.	1988	12.99
Collins, Judy	Voices (Includes Songbook/Memoir)	CD	Clarkson Potter	4586370092	U.S.A.	1995	10.99
Collins, Judy	Whales & Nightingales	CD	Elektra	75010-2	U.S.A.	1990	7.99
Collins, Judy	Who Knows Where The Time Goes	CD	Elektra	74033-2	U.S.A.	1990	8.99
Collins, Judy	Wildflowers	CD	Elektra	74012-2	U.S.A.	1990	7.99
Collins, Judy	Wind Beneath My Wings	CD	Laserlight	15451	Germany	1992	4.99
Collins, Phil	12" Ers	CD	Atlantic	7-81847-2	U.S.A.	1987	6.99
Collins, Phil	Both Sides (Gold Cd)	CD	Warner Bros.	4509-93757-2	Australia	1993	19.99
Collins, Phil	Both Sides Of The Story	CD Single	Atlantic	2-85714	U.S.A.	1993	14.99
Collins, Phil	But Seriously	CD	Atlantic	82050-2	U.S.A.	1989	6.99
Collins, Phil	Dance Into The Light	CD	Atlantic	82949-2	U.S.A.	1996	5.99
Collins, Phil	Don't Lose That Number	CD Single	Atlantic	WPCR-2063	Japan	1985	34.99
Collins, Phil	Face Value (Atlantic Gold Cd)	CD	Atlantic	82520-2	U.S.A.	1993	74.99

Artist	Title	Format	Label	Catalog No	Country	Released	Value
Collins, Phil	Hello I Must Be Going	CD	Warner Bros.	A2-80035	U.S.A.	1982	6.99
Collins, Phil	Hits (Gold Cd)	CD	Warner Bros.	001-038-475	Taiwan	2001	34.99
Collins, Phil	I Wish It Would Rain Down	CD Single	Atlantic	84879-2	U.S.A.	1993	4.99
Collins, Phil	King Biscuit 11/9 To 11/15 1998	CD	DIR Network	C177AO1XC	U.S.A.	1998	34.99
Collins, Phil	No Jacket Required	CD	Atlantic	7-81240-2	U.S.A.	1985	6.99
Collins, Phil	Serious Hits ... Live!	CD	Atlantic	7-82157-2	U.S.A.	1990	7.99
Collins, Phil	Son Of A Man (German Promo)	CD Single	Walt Disney	0108116DNYP	Germany	1999	14.99
Collins, Phil	Testify	CD	Atlantic	83563-2	U.S.A.	2002	11.99
Collins, Phil	Wear My Hat	CD Single	Face Value	0630-19073-2	Germany	1997	29.99
Collins, Phil Big Band	Hot Night In Paris	CD	Atlantic	3984-27221-2	U.S.A.	1999	7.99
Collins, Phil/I. Din	Live From The Board (Gold Cd)	CD Single	Warner Bros.	4509-99789-2	Australia	1995	19.99
Collum, Bob	Low Rent Romeo	CD	Line	LICD—9.01361-0	Germany	2000	17.99
Collum, Bob	More Tragic Songs Of Life	CD	Line	LICD-9.01325-0	Germany	1998	14.99
Colosseum	Daughter of Time	CD	Essential	ESMCD644	England	1998	10.99
Colosseum	Live + 1	CD	Essential	ESMCD-641	England	1998	7.99
Colosseum	Milestones	2CD	Castle	CMDDD075	England	2000	24.99
Colosseum	The Valentyne Suite	CD	Essential	ESMCD-642	England	1998	10.99
Colosseum	Those Who Are About...	CD	Essential	ESMCD-643	England	1998	7.99
Colosseum /Bakerloo	Bakerloo + 2	CD	Repertoire	REP-4870-WP	Germany	2002	17.99
Colosseum II	Electric Savage	CD	One Way	OW-22081	U.S.A.	1993	8.99
Colosseum II	Electric Savage	CD	MCA Victor	MVCM-21054	Japan	1992	59.99
Colosseum II	Strange New Flesh	CD	Victor Ent.	VICP-2087	Japan	1993	59.99
Colosseum II	Strange New Flesh	CD	Castle	CLACD-104	England	1992	8.99
Colosseum II	War Dance	CD	One Way	OW-22082	U.S.A.	1993	8.99
Colosseum II	War Dance	CD	MCA Victor	MVCM-21055	Japan	1992	89.99
Colourbox	Best Of '82/'87	CD	4AD	GAD-2107-CD	U.S.A.	2001	11.99
Coltrane, John	A Love Supreme	CD	Impulse!	B0000610-02	U.S.A.	2003	8.99
Coltrane, John	My Favorite Things + 2	CD	Rhino	R2-75204	U.S.A.	1998	13.99
Coltrane, John	Selections Classic Quartet (Promo)	CD	Impulse!	IMPD-8898	U.S.A.	1998	9.99
Coming Up Roses	I Said Ballroom	CD	Line	UTCD-9.00860-L	Germany	1989	34.99
Commander Cody	Let's Rock	CD	Line	LICD-9.00277-0	Germany	1991	9.99
Commander Cody	Let's Rock	CD	Line	LICD—9.01355-0	Germany	1997	9.99
Commander Cody Band	Lose It Tonight	CD	Line	LICD-9.01349-0	Germany	1997	11.99
Commander Cody Band	Lose It Tonight	CD	Line	LICD-9.00054-0	Germany	1988	11.99
Commander Cody Band	Lose It Tonight/Let's Rock	2CD	Line	LICD-9.21213-S	Germany	1992	16.99
Commander Cody/LPA	Country Casanova	CD	MCA	MCAD-661	U.S.A.	1973	33.99
Commander Cody/LPA	Hot Licks, Cold Steel/Truckers Favs	CD	MCA	MCAD-31186	U.S.A.	1988	54.99
Commander Cody/LPA	Live From Deep In Heart Of Texas	CD	MCA	MCAD-659	U.S.A.	1974	29.99
Commander Cody/LPA	Lost In The Ozone	CD	MCA	MCAD-31185	U.S.A.	1988	8.99
Conception Corporation	Complete Conception (Ltd. 3500)	2CD	Rhino	RHM2-7728	U.S.A.	2000	29.99
Coney Hatch	Best Of 3	CD	Anthem	ANBD1065	Canada	1997	12.99
Coney Hatch	Friction	CD	Anthem	ANBD1070	Canada	1996	10.99
Coney Hatch	Self Titled	CD	Anthem	ANBD1037	Canada	1996	10.99
Conley, Earl Thomas	Treadin' Water	CD	RCA	PCD1-5175	U.S.A.	1990	54.99
Conniff, Ray	Say You, Say Me	CD	Sony	32DP-590	Japan	1986	89.99
Connor, Joanna	Believe It!	CD	Line	STCD-9.00772-0	Germany	1991	13.99
Connor, Joanna	Slipping Away	CD Single	Line	TLCD-9.01311-0	Germany	1995	5.99
Connor, Joanna/Band	Rock And Roll Gypsy	CD	Line	RRCD-9.01315-0	Germany	1995	8.99
Connors, Bill	Assembler	CD	Line	COCD-9.00519-0	Germany	1989	11.99
Connors, Bill	Double Up	CD	Line	COCD-9.00826-0	Germany	1990	11.99
Connors, Bill	Step It	CD	Line	COCD-9.00818-0	Germany	1990	11.99
Conrad, Tony	Early Minimalism: Volume One	4CD	Table Of Elements	TABLE-33	U.S.A.	1997	39.99
Conrad, Tony	Fantastic Glissando	CD	Table Of Elements	TABLE-82	U.S.A.	2003	29.99
Conrad, Tony	Slapping Pythagoras	CD	Table Of Elements	TABLE-23	U.S.A.	1995	17.99
Conrad, Tony/Faust	Outside The Dream Syndicate	2CD	Table Of Elements	TABLE-03	U.S.A.	2003	12.99
Conrads	Walk On!	CD	Line	LICD—9.01381-0	Germany	2001	17.99
Conrads	Way Back Home	CD	Line	LICD—9.01369-0	Germany	2000	17.99
Conti, Bill	For Your Eyes Only (O.S.T.)	CD	Rykodisc	RCD-10751	U.S.A.	2000	13.99

Artist	Title	Format	Label	Catalog No	Country	Released	Value
Continental Drifters	Better Day	CD	Razor & Tie	79301828644-2	U.S.A.	2001	7.99
Continental Drifters	Continental Drifters	CD	Razor & Tie	7930182221-2	U.S.A.	2000	9.99
Contours	Do You Love Me	CD	Motown	3746354152	U.S.A.	1988	13.99
Controllers	Clear View	CD	Malaco	MCD-7485	U.S.A.	1997	25.99
Controllers	The Timeless Soul Collection	CD	Line	TLCD-9.00467-0	Germany	1987	24.99
Controllers	Timeless Soul Collection Volume 2	CD	Line	TLCD-9.00687-0	Germany	1988	24.99
Convertino, Michael	The Hidden (O.S.T.)	CD	Varese	VCD-47349	U.S.A.	1987	54.99
Cooder, Ry	Boomer's Story	CD	Reprise	9-26398-2	U.S.A.	1972	12.99
Cooder, Ry	Bop Till You Drop	CD	Warner Bros.	3358-2	U.S.A.	1979	11.99
Cooder, Ry	Geronimo; An Am. Legend (O.S.T.)	CD	Columbia	CK-57760	U.S.A.	1993	13.99
Cooder, Ry	Into The Purple Valley	CD	Reprise	2052-2	U.S.A.	1972	8.99
Cooder, Ry	Jazz	CD	Warner Bros.	3197-2	U.S.A.	1978	11.99
Cooder, Ry	Johnny Handsome (O.S.T.)	CD	Warner Bros.	9-25996-2	U.S.A.	1989	7.99
Cooder, Ry	Ry Cooder	CD	Reprise	6402-2	U.S.A.	1970	12.99
Cooder, Ry	Trespass (O.S.T.)	CD	Sire	9-45220-2	U.S.A.	1993	8.99
Cooder, Ry/Ibrahim Ferrer	Buena Vista Social Club	CD	World Circuit	79478-2	U.S.A.	1997	9.99
Cooder, Ry/V.M. Bhatt	A Meeting By The River	CD	Water Lily	WLA-CS-29-CD	U.S.A.	1993	11.99
Cook, Peter	Over At Rainbow's	2CD	Proper Pairs	PVCD108	England	2002	14.99
Cooke, Sam	SAR Records Story Sampler (Promo)	CD	Abkco	PRO-2193	U.S.A.	1994	19.99
Cooke, Sam	The Man And His Music	CD	RCA	PCD1-7127	U.S.A.	1986	15.99
Coolidge, Rita	Dancing With An Angel	CD	Alfa	ALCB-298	Japan	1991	14.99
Coolidge, Rita	Satisfied	CD	Pony Canyon	D18Y4120	Japan	1979	158.99
Coolio (Ft L.V)	Gangsta's Paradise	CD Single	MCA	MCAD5-55104	U.S.A.	1995	6.99
Cooper, Alice	A Fistful Of Alice + Cd Single (Promo)	2CD	Guardian	7243-8-33080-2-6	U.S.A.	1997	14.99
Cooper, Alice	Alice Cooper's Greatest Hits	CD	Warner Bros.	7599-27330-2	Australia	1974	7.99
Cooper, Alice	Bed Of Nails	CD Single	Columbia	655318-2	England	1989	12.99
Cooper, Alice	Billion Dollar Babies (DVD Audio)	CD	Rhino	R2-76663	U.S.A.	2002	15.99
Cooper, Alice	Billion Dollar Babies + 14 (Bonus Cd)	2CD	Rhino	R2-79791	U.S.A.	2001	13.99
Cooper, Alice	Brutal Planet + 1	CD	Polydor K.K.	POCP-7492	Japan	2000	14.99
Cooper, Alice	Constrictor	CD	MCA	MCAD-5761	U.S.A.	1987	9.99
Cooper, Alice	Dada	CD	Warner Bros.	7599-23969-2	Germany	1982	10.99
Cooper, Alice	Dragon Town (Ltd. W/Bonus Cd)	2CD	Spitfire	SPT-15089-2	U.S.A.	2002	18.98
Cooper, Alice	Easy Action	CD	Rhino	R2-70350	U.S.A.	1989	25.99
Cooper, Alice	Flush The Fashion	CD	Warner Bros.	7599-26229-2	Germany	1980	15.99
Cooper, Alice	From The Inside	CD	Warner Bros.	7599-26064-2	Germany	1978	15.99
Cooper, Alice	Goes To Hell	CD	Warner Bros.	2896-2	U.S.A.	1976	8.99
Cooper, Alice	Hey Stoopid	CD	Epic	EK-46786	U.S.A.	1991	9.99
Cooper, Alice	Killer	CD	Warner Bros.	2567-2	U.S.A.	1971	10.99
Cooper, Alice	Lace And Whiskey	CD	Warner Bros.	7599-26227-2	Germany	1977	15.99
Cooper, Alice	Life And Crimes Of Box Set	4CD	Rhino	R2-75680	U.S.A.	1999	27.99
Cooper, Alice	Live Alice Cooper Show	CD	Warner Bros.	3138-2	U.S.A.	1977	7.99
Cooper, Alice	Live At The Whiskey A Go Go 1969	CD	Rhino	R2-70369-2	U.S.A.	1992	10.99
Cooper, Alice	Lost In America	CD Single	Epic	660347-2	Germany	1994	7.99
Cooper, Alice	Love It To Death	CD	Warner Bros.	1883-2	U.S.A.	1971	11.99
Cooper, Alice	Mascara & Monsters	CD	Rhino	R2-75806	U.S.A.	2001	8.99
Cooper, Alice	Muscle Of Love	CD	Warner Bros.	7599-26226-2	Germany	1973	15.99
Cooper, Alice	Nobody Likes... Alice Cooper Live	CD	Going For A Song	GFS071	England	1999	9.99
Cooper, Alice	Poison	CD Single	CBS	655061-2	England	1989	11.99
Cooper, Alice	Presents Stoopid News (Promo)	CD	Epic	ESK-4161	U.S.A.	1991	19.99
Cooper, Alice	Pretties for You	CD	Enigma	7-73362-2	U.S.A.	1989	25.99
Cooper, Alice	Prince Of Darkness	CD	MCA Victor	MVCM-18534	Japan	1989	18.99
Cooper, Alice	Prince Of Darkness	CD	MCA	MCAD-42315	U.S.A.	1989	4.99
Cooper, Alice	Raise Your Fist And Yell	CD	MCA	MCAD-42091	U.S.A.	1987	13.99
Cooper, Alice	School's Out	CD	Warner Bros.	2623-2	U.S.A.	1972	6.99
Cooper, Alice	Slack Alice Live In Toronto 1969	CD	Universal	YEAAH-53	England	1996	11.99
Cooper, Alice	Special Forces	CD	Warner Bros.	7599-26230-2	U.S.A.	1981	15.99
Cooper, Alice	The Essentials	CD	Rhino	R2-76044	U.S.A.	2002	8.99
Cooper, Alice	The Eyes Of	CD	Eagle	ER-20028-2	U.S.A.	2003	12.99

Artist	Title	Format	Label	Catalog No	Country	Released	Value
Cooper, Alice	The Last Temptation	CD	Epic	EK-52771	U.S.A.	1994	10.99
Cooper, Alice	Trash	CD	Epic	EK-45137	U.S.A.	1991	8.99
Cooper, Alice	Welcome To My Nightmare + 3	CD	Rhino	R2-74383	U.S.A.	2002	11.99
Cooper, Alice	Welcome To Nightmare (DVD Audio)	CD	Rhino	R2-76785	U.S.A.	2002	15.99
Cooper, Alice	Zipper Catches Skin	CD	Warner Bros.	7599-23719-2	Germany	1982	14.99
Cooper, Alice/Winger	In The Heart Of The Young	CD	Atlantic	82103-2	U.S.A.	1990	7.99
Cooper, Alice/Winger	Pull	CD	Atlantic	82485-2	U.S.A.	1993	8.99
Cooper, Alice/Winger	Self Titled	CD	Atlantic	81867-2	U.S.A.	1988	5.99
Cooper, Alice/Winger	Very Best Of	CD	Rhino	R2-78396	U.S.A.	2001	9.99
Cooper, D. C.	Self Titled	CD	Victor Ent.	VICP-60522	Japan	1998	16.99
Cooper, Lindsay	Schrodinger's Cat	CD	Line	FECD-9.01093-0	Germany	1991	29.99
Copeland, S./Klark Kent	Kollected Works	CD	I.R.S.	7243-8-29690-2-0	U.S.A.	1995	56.99
Copeland, Stewart	Talk Radio/Wall Street	CD	Varese	VSD-5459	U.S.A.	1997	23.99
Copeland, Stewart	The Equalizer & Other Cliff Hangers	CD	I.R.S.	IRSD-42099	U.S.A.	1988	19.99
Copeland, Stewart	The Leopard Son	CD	Ark 21	7243854570-2-9	U.S.A.	1996	9.99
Copeland, Stewart	The Rhythmatist	CD	A&M	CD-5084	U.S.A.	1985	65.99
Copperhead/John Cippolina	Copperhead	CD	Acadia	ACA-8005	England	2001	11.99
Corgan, Billy/S.Pumpkins	Stigmata Interview (Promo)	CD	Virgin	DPRO-14384	U.S.A.	1999	5.99
Corley, Al/Dynasty	Square Rooms	CD	Mercury	822-316-2	Germany	1984	10.99
Corrs	Best Of Sampler Cd (Promo)	CD	Lava	ASCD-279	Japan	1999	354.99
Corrs	The Corrs Live (Promo)	CD	Atlantic	PRCD-390	Germany	1996	92.99
Corrs/Bono Of U2	When The Stars Go Blue (Promo)	CD	Atlantic	PRCD-30082	U.S.A.	2002	7.99
Cosby, Bill	"Oh, Baby"	CD	Geffen	GEFD-24428	U.S.A.	1991	5.99
Cosby, Bill	Bill Cosby Is A Very Funny Fellow...	CD	Warner Bros.	1518-2	U.S.A.	1963	13.99
Cosby, Bill	Fat Albert	CD	Laugh.com	LGH1110	U.S.A.	2002	9.99
Cosby, Bill	I Started Out As A Child	CD	Warner Bros.	1567-2	U.S.A.	1964	12.99
Cosby, Bill	Revenge	CD	Warner Bros.	1691-2	U.S.A.	1967	14.99
Cosby, Bill	To Russell, My Brother...	CD	Warner Bros.	9-1734-2	U.S.A.	1968	14.99
Cosby, Bill	When I Was A Kid	CD	Laugh.com	LGH1127	U.S.A.	2002	9.99
Cosby, Bill	Why Is There Air?	CD	Warner Bros.	1606-2	U.S.A.	1965	13.99
Cosby, Bill	Wonderfulness	CD	Warner Bros.	1634-2	U.S.A.	1966	14.99
Costello, Elvis	13 Steps Lead Down	CD Single	Warner Bros.	9362-41556-2	Germany	1994	5.99
Costello, Elvis	2 1/2 Years Box Set	4CD	Rykodisc	RCD-90271/74	U.S.A.	1993	44.99
Costello, Elvis	45	CD Single	Mercury	0639152	England	2002	8.99
Costello, Elvis	45 (Promo)	CD Single	Mercury	EC45CJ1	England	2002	7.99
Costello, Elvis	A Taste Of Extreme Honey (Promo)	CD	Warner Bros.	PRO-CD-9076	U.S.A.	1990	12.99
Costello, Elvis	An Overview Disc (Promo Interview)	CD	Rykodisc	RCD-20282+1	U.S.A.	1995	8.99
Costello, Elvis	Baby Plays Around (3")	CD Single	Warner Bros.	W2949CD	England	1989	9.99
Costello, Elvis	Brutal Youth + 15 (Bonus Cd)	2CD	Rhino	R2-78390	U.S.A.	2002	15.99
Costello, Elvis	Costello & Nieve Box Set	5CD	Warner Bros.	9-46469-2	U.S.A.	1996	104.99
Costello, Elvis	Extreme Honey - Best Warner Bros.	CD	Warner Bros.	9-46801-2	U.S.A.	1997	6.99
Costello, Elvis	Get Happy! & Trust (Promo/B & W)	2CD	Rykodisk	VPRCD-275/76	U.S.A.	1994	49.99
Costello, Elvis	God Give Me... (Live Letterman DJ)	CD Single	Reprise	PRO-CD-9229-R	U.S.A.	1997	4.99
Costello, Elvis	King Of America + 11 (Live Bonus Cd)	2CD	Rykodisc	RCD-20281	U.S.A.	1995	19.99
Costello, Elvis	King of America + 5 (Gold Disc Cd)	CD	Rykodisc	RCD-80281	U.S.A.	1995	39.99
Costello, Elvis	Kojak Variety + 2 (W/Paper, Ltd 200)	CD	Warner Bros.	9-45903-2	U.S.A.	1995	109.99
Costello, Elvis	Let Him Dangle Plus ... (Promo)	CD	Warner Bros.	PRO-CD-3720	U.S.A.	1989	8.99
Costello, Elvis	Magic & Malice (Promo)	CD	Warner Bros.	PRO-CD-7748	U.S.A.	1990	8.99
Costello, Elvis	Mighty Like A Rose (Leatherbound Ed)	CD	Warner Bros.	9-26593-2	U.S.A.	1991	18.99
Costello, Elvis	Mighty Like A.. + 17 (W/Bonus Cd)	2CD	Rhino	R2-78189	U.S.A.	2002	14.99
Costello, Elvis	Punch The /Goodbye... (DJ W/Pin)	CD	Rykodisc	RCD-20279-ADV	Canada	1995	19.99
Costello, Elvis	She (Notting Hill/Promo)	CD Single	Island	314-546-196-2/4	U.S.A.	1999	8.99
Costello, Elvis	Smile	CD Single	Victor Ent.	UICL-5007	Japan	2002	12.99
Costello, Elvis	Spike (Advanced Diff. Cover Digipack)	CD	Warner Bros.	PRO-CD-3426	U.S.A.	1989	13.99
Costello, Elvis	Spike + 17 (Bonus Cd)	2CD	Rhino	R2-74286	U.S.A.	2001	14.99
Costello, Elvis	Sulky Girl	CD Single	Warner Bros.	9362-41439-2	Germany	1994	5.99
Costello, Elvis	Sunday Times CD	CD	Mercury	ELVIS-04-6	England	2002	6.99
Costello, Elvis	Sunday Times EP (Promo)	CD Single	Warner Bros.	ELVIS04	England	2002	4.99

Artist	Title	Format	Label	Catalog No	Country	Released	Value
Costello, Elvis	Taking Liberties (Rare Compilation)	CD	Columbia	CK-36839	U.S.A.	1980	19.99
Costello, Elvis	Tear Off Your Own Head	CD Single	Island	582-889-2	Holland	2002	6.99
Costello, Elvis	The Very Best Of Elvis Costello	CD	Rhino	R2-76652	U.S.A.	2001	16.99
Costello, Elvis	Veronica (3 ") Promo	CD Single	Warner Bros.	921156-2	Germany	1989	13.99
Costello, Elvis	Very Best Of	CD	Rykodisc	RCD-40283	U.S.A.	1994	11.99
Costello, Elvis	When I Was Cruel	CD	Victor Ent.	UICL-1017	Japan	2002	34.99
Costello, Elvis	When I Was Cruel (Advance Cd)	CD	Island	ILSF-15487-2	U.S.A.	2002	8.99
Costello, Elvis	When I was Cruel + 9	2CD	Mercury	063-894-2	England	2002	19.99
Costello, Elvis	Words And Music (Promo)	CD	Warner Bros.	PRO-CD-6955	U.S.A.	1994	13.99
Costello, Elvis/Anne Otter	For The Stars	CD	Deutsche	289-469-530-2	U.S.A.	2001	7.99
Costello, Elvis/Attractions	10 Bloody Marys/10 How's Fathers	CD	Demon	FIEND-CD27	England	1984	34.99
Costello, Elvis/Attractions	18 Song..(DJ/Almost/Imperial/Mighty)	CD	Rhino	PRCD-400057	U.S.A.	2003	15.99
Costello, Elvis/Attractions	2 1/2 Years In 31 Minutes (Promo)	CD	Rykodisc	VRCD-0271	U.S.A.	1993	8.99
Costello, Elvis/Attractions	All This Useless Beauty (Cd 4)	CD Single	Warner Bros.	9362-43747-2	Germany	1996	8.99
Costello, Elvis/Attractions	All This Useless...+ 17 (Bonus Cd)	2CD	Rhino	R2-74284	U.S.A.	2001	13.99
Costello, Elvis/Attractions	Almost Blue + 11	CD	Rykodisc	RCD-20277	U.S.A.	1994	14.99
Costello, Elvis/Attractions	Almost Blue/Imp Bedroom (DJ W/Pin)	2CD	Rykodisc	RCD-20277/8-ADV	Canada	1994	39.99
Costello, Elvis/Attractions	Armed Forces + 17 (W/Bonus Cd)	2CD	Rhino	R2-78190	U.S.A.	2002	20.99
Costello, Elvis/Attractions	Blood & Chocolate (Line Version)	CD	Line	IPCD-9.00200-0	Germany	1986	8.99
Costello, Elvis/Attractions	Blood & Chocolate + 15 (Bonus Cd)	2CD	Rhino	R2-78355	U.S.A.	2002	14.99
Costello, Elvis/Attractions	Blood/Chocolate + 6 (1 Not On Rhino)	CD	Rykodisc	RCD-20282	U.S.A.	1919	13.99
Costello, Elvis/Attractions	Distorted Angel (Cd 3)	CD Single	Warner Bros.	9362-43746-2	Germany	1996	8.99
Costello, Elvis/Attractions	Get Happy + 30	CD	Rhino	R2-73908	U.S.A.	2003	14.99
Costello, Elvis/Attractions	Get Happy!! + 10	CD	Rykodisc	RCD-20275	U.S.A.	1980	29.99
Costello, Elvis/Attractions	Get Happy/Trust (Promo W/Pin)	2CD	Rykodisc	RCD20275/6ADV	Canada	1994	27.99
Costello, Elvis/Attractions	Girls Girls Girls	2CD	Columbia	C2K-46897	U.S.A.	1989	8.99
Costello, Elvis/Attractions	Goodbye Cruel World + 9	CD	Rykodisc	RCD-20280	U.S.A.	1995	13.99
Costello, Elvis/Attractions	Highlights Almost Blue And...(Promo)	CD	Demon	ECPROMO-2	England	1994	12.99
Costello, Elvis/Attractions	Imperial Bedroom + 11 (Rykodisc Gold)	CD	Rykodisc	RCD-80278	U.S.A.	1994	35.99
Costello, Elvis/Attractions	Imperial Bedroom + 23 (W/Bonus Cd)	2CD	Rhino	R2-78188	U.S.A.	2002	14.99
Costello, Elvis/Attractions	KBFH May 27 - June 2, 1991	CD	DIR Network	A3FC0200C	U.S.A.	1991	89.99
Costello, Elvis/Attractions	Little Atoms (Cd 1)	CD Single	Warner Bros.	9362-43744-2	Germany	1996	8.99
Costello, Elvis/Attractions	Other End Of The Telescope (Cd 2)	CD Single	Warner Bros.	9362-43745-2	Germany	1996	8.99
Costello, Elvis/Attractions	Out Of Our Idiot	CD	Demon	FIEND-CD-67	England	1987	11.99
Costello, Elvis/Attractions	Punch The Clock + 26 (W/Bonus CD)	2CD	Rhino	R2-73910	U.S.A.	2003	14.99
Costello, Elvis/Attractions	Punch The Clock + 7	CD	Rykodisc	RCD-20279	U.S.A.	1995	16.99
Costello, Elvis/Attractions	Punch The World (Promo)	CD	Rykodisc	VRCD—0279/80	Canada	1995	13.99
Costello, Elvis/Attractions	Re-Examine (Promo Sampler)	CD	Rhino	PRCD-400043	U.S.A.	2001	14.99
Costello, Elvis/Attractions	Singles, Volume 1	12CD	Edsel	ELVISBOX-101	England	2003	39.99
Costello, Elvis/Attractions	Singles, Volume 2	12CD	Edsel	ELVISBOX-102	England	2003	39.99
Costello, Elvis/Attractions	Singles, Volume 3	11CD	Edsel	ELVISBOX-103	England	2003	39.99
Costello, Elvis/Attractions	Trust + 17 (W/Bonus CD)	2CD	Rhino	R2-73909	U.S.A.	2003	14.99
Costello, Elvis/Attractions	Trust + 9	CD	Rykodisc	RCD-20276	U.S.A.	1994	16.99
Costello, Elvis/Attractions	Undeniable Attraction(S) (Promo)	CD	Rhino	PRCD-400054	U.S.A.	2002	14.99
Costello, Elvis/Attractions	You Bowed Down	CD Single	Warner Bros.	9-43777-2	U.S.A.	1996	4.99
Costello, Elvis/Attractions	You Tripped At Every Step	CD Single	Warner Bros.	9362-41666-2	Germany	1994	10.99
Costello, Elvis/B Bacharach	Because It's A Lonely World (Int. With)	CD	Mercury	MECD-181	U.S.A.	1998	31.99
Costello, Elvis/B. Quartet	Excerpts Juliet Letters (Promo)	CD	Warner Bros.	PRO-CD-6018	U.S.A.	1993	5.99
Costello, Elvis/B. Quartet	Live At New York Town Hall (Promo)	CD	Warner Bros.	PRO-CD-6480	U.S.A.	1993	30.99
Costello, Elvis/B. Quartet	The Juliet Letters	CD	Warner Bros.	9-45180-2	U.S.A.	1993	8.99
Costello, Elvis/Bacharach	Gold Give Me Strength (Promo)	CD Single	MCA	MCA5P-3835	U.S.A.	1996	9.99
Costello, Elvis/Bacharach	Painted From Memory + 5 (Bonus Cd)	2CD	Universal	PHCR-4084/5	Japan	1999	39.99
Costello, Elvis/Bill Frisell	Deep Dead Blue - Live 25 June 25	CD	Warner Bros.	9362-46073-2	Germany	1995	10.99
Costello, Elvis/Bill Frisell	The Sweetest Punch	CD	Decca	314-559-865-2	U.S.A.	1999	8.99
Costello, Elvis/Imposters	Cruel Smile	CD	Island	440-063-388-2	U.S.A.	2002	8.99
Costello, Elvis/R Harvey	G.B.H.: Orig Music Channel 4 Series	CD	Rykodisc	RCD-20284	Canada	1991	8.99
Costello, Elvis/R Harvey	Jake's Progress O.S.T.	CD	Demon	DSCD-14	England	1995	5.99
Costello, Elvis/Tony Bennett	They Can't Take That Away From Me	CD Single	Columbia	660831-1	Germany	1994	19.99

C

Artist	Title	Format	Label	Catalog No	Country	Released	Value
Costello, Elvis/V. A.	Bespoke...Elvis Costello Tribute	CD	Rhino	R2-75273	U.S.A.	1998	19.99
Costello, Elvis/W. James	Now Ain't The Time For Your Tears	CD	DGC	DGCD-24507	U.S.A.	1993	6.99
Cotton, James	Live At Antone's Nightclub	CD	Line	ANCD-9.00615-0	Germany	1988	19.99
Cotton, Josey	Frightened By Nightingales	CD	Roxco	RXR-500	U.S.A.	1995	12.99
Count Five	Psychotic Revelation + 6	CD	Big Beat	CDWIKD-230	England	2003	14.99
Counting Crows	August And Everything... (MFSL Gold)	CD	Mobile Fidelity	UDCD-664	U.S.A.	1996	34.99
Counting Crows	Face The Promised Land/1000	CD	Potato Dog	7-62187-34086-4	U.S.A.	1999	53.99
County, Jayne	Deviation	CD	Royalty	ROI-105	U.S.A.	1995	8.99
County, Jayne	Goddess Of Wet Dreams	CD	ESP Disk	ESP-2002-2	Germany	1993	20.99
County, Jayne	Let Your Backbone Slip	CD	RPM	RPM-145	England	1995	14.99
County, Jayne	Rock 'N Roll Cleopatra	CD	Royalty	ROY872012	U.S.A.	1993	15.99
Courage, Alexander	Star Trek: Orig TV Soundtrack Vol. 2	CD	GNP	GNPD-8025	U.S.A.	1991	12.99
Courage, Alexander	Star Trek: Orig TV Soundtrack Vol. 3	CD	GNP	GNPD-8030	U.S.A.	1991	12.99
Courage, Alexander	Star Trek; Orig TV Soundtrack Vol. 1	CD	GNP	GNPD-8006	U.S.A.	1985	12.99
Coverdale/Page	Coverdale/Page	CD	Geffen	GEFD-24487	U.S.A.	1993	8.99
Coverdale/Page	Take Me For A Little While (Promo)	CD Single	Geffen	PRO-CD-4535	U.S.A.	1993	4.99
Covington, Julie	Self Titled + 2	CD	See For Miles	SEE-CD718	England	2000	19.99
Covington, Julie	The Beautiful Changes + 2	CD	See For Miles	SEE-CD687	England	1999	19.99
Cowboy Junkies	'Neath Your Covers Pt. 1	CD Single	Zoe	6-01143-2005-2-6	U.S.A.	2004	4.99
Cowboy/Chuck Leavell	A Different Time: A Best Of	CD	Polydor	314-519604-2	U.S.A.	1993	28.99
Cowboy/Chuck Leavell	Reach For The Sky	CD	Capricorn	314-558-381-2	U.S.A.	1998	5.99
Cowsills	28 Great Songs (1st 2 Lp's + 5 Bonus)	CD	Cowchip	20372-2	EEC	1988	29.99
Cowsills	Captain Sad Ship Fools/II x II + 4	CD	Cowchip	LP34-2	EEC	1988	24.99
Cowsills	Cowsills + 2	CD	Razor & Tie	RE-2037	U.S.A.	1994	16.99
Cowsills	The Cowsills In Concert + 4 (Milk EP)	CD	Razor & Tie	RE-2038	U.S.A.	1994	39.99
Cowsills	The Rain, The Park & Other Things	CD	Karussell	551-311-2	Australia	1990	14.99
Coyne, Kevin	M Head/Feet (W/Andy Summers)	CD	Virgin	CDV2033	England	1991	25.99
Coyne, Kevin	Sugar Candy Taxi	CD	PolyGram	51416-147-2	U.S.A.	1999	5.99
Coyne, Kevin	The Peel Sessions	CD	Strange Fruit	SFRCD-112	England	1990	9.99
Coyne, Kevin/Band	Stumbling Onto Paradise	CD	Line	LICD-9.00438-0	Germany	1987	21.99
CPR	CPR	CD	Samson	GC0145	U.S.A.	1998	7.99
CPR	Just Like Gravity	CD	Gold Circle	GC-20002-2	U.S.A.	2001	11.99
CPR	Live At The Wiltern	2CD	Samson	GC-0148	U.S.A.	1998	13.99
Crack the Sky	Dog City	CD	Grudge	4520-2-F	U.S.A.	1990	11.99
Cranberries	Bury The Hatchet (W/Bonus Cd)	2CD	Island	314-524-611-2	U.S.A.	1999	15.99
Cranberries	Doors And Windows (Cd Rom)	CD Single	Phillips	3106910302	U.S.A.	1995	10.99
Cranberries	For The Faithful Departed Sampler (DJ)	CD	Island	TTFD1	England	2002	49.99
Cranberries	Free To Decide Single	CD Single	Island	854-705-2	England	1996	4.99
Cranberries	Promises (CD 2)	CD Single	Island	572-593-2	England	1999	5.99
Cranberries	Salvation (Promo)	CD Single	Island	PRCD-7201-2	U.S.A.	1996	5.99
Cranberries	Zombie	CD Single	Island	854110-2	England	1994	7.99
Crash Test Dummies	The Ballad Of Peter Pumkinhead	CD Single	RCA	74321-27677-2	England	1994	5.99
Crawdaddys	Mystic Crawdaddys	CD	Line	WICD-9.00838-0	Germany	1989	24.99
Crawford, Johnny	Best Of Johnny Crawford	CD	Del-Fi	DFCD-71220	U.S.A.	1994	16.99
Crazy Elephant	S.T. (W/Gimme Gimme Good Lovin')	CD	Rock In Beat	36	Germany	2000	54.99
Crazy Horse	Crazy Horse	CD	Reprise	6438-2	U.S.A.	1971	14.99
Crazy Horse	Crazy Horse At Crooked Lake	CD	Sony	ESCA-7853	Japan	2001	13.99
Crazy Horse	Crazy Moon	CD	Raven	RVCD-66	Australia	1997	19.99
Crazy Horse	Le Meilleur De	CD	Spiral	495254-2	France	2001	10.99
Crazy Horse	Left For Dead (Promo)	CD	Sisapa	9CP0100B	U.S.A.	1990	8.99
Crazy Horse	Loose	CD	Warner Bros.	WPCR-2127	Japan	1998	27.99
Crazy Horse/Rockets	The Rockets	CD	Varese	302-066-269-2	U.S.A.	1968	13.99
Cream	Disraeli Gears (M/Stereo MFSL Gold)	CD	Mobile Fidelity	UDCD-562	U.S.A.	1967	32.99
Cream	Fresh Cream + 3 (DCC Gold Cd)	CD	DCC	GZS-1022	U.S.A.	1992	28.99
Cream	Fresh Live Cream (Cd Rom)	2CD	Castle	CMMDD-107	England	1993	34.99
Cream	Goodbye (MFSL Gold Cd)	CD	Mobile Fidelity	UDCD-681	U.S.A.	1969	27.99
Cream	Live Cream Vol. 1 & 2 (MFSL Gold Cd)	2CD	Mobile Fidelity	UDCD-2-625	U.S.A.	1972	43.99
Cream	The Very Best Of Cream	CD	Polydor	31452-3752-2	U.S.A.	1995	7.99

Artist	Title	Format	Label	Catalog No	Country	Released	Value
Cream	Those Were The Days Box Set	4CD	Polydor	31453-9000-2	U.S.A.	1997	41.99
Cream	Those Were... (Promo Sampler)	CD	Polydor	PRSAD-00553	U.S.A.	1997	24.99
Cream	Wheels Of Fire + 1 (DCC Gold Cd)	2CD	DCC	GZS(2)-1020	U.S.A.	1992	48.99
Creation	The Creation Collection	CD	Line	IMCD-9.00497-0	Germany	1987	19.99
Creatures	2nd Floor	CD Single	Sioux	SIOUX-3CD	England	1998	6.99
Creatures	A Bestiary Of	CD	Polydor	533677-2	Germany	1997	16.99
Creatures	Anima Animus	CD	Instinct	EX-413-2	U.S.A.	1999	10.99
Creatures	Anima Animus Tour 1999 (Promo)	CD	Sioux	SIOUX-8CD	England	1999	21.99
Creatures	Boomerang	CD	Geffen	9-24275-2	U.S.A.	1989	11.99
Creatures	Hybrids	CD	Instinct	INS-433-2	U.S.A.	1999	8.99
Creatures	Prettiest Thing	CD Single	Sioux	SIOUX-9CD	England	1999	6.99
Creatures	Say	CD Single	Sioux	SIOUX-6CDX	England	1999	10.99
Creatures	Sequins In The Sun	CD	Sioux	SIOUX11CDX	England	2000	19.99
Creatures	U.S. Retrace	CD	Instinct	INS-516-2	U.S.A.	2000	8.99
Creed	What If (Scream 3 Movie Promo)	CD Single	Wind Up	PROA-13056-2	U.S.A.	1999	6.99
Crematory	Illusions	CD	Teichiku	TECW-25111	Japan	1995	59.99
Crenshaw, Marshall	#447	CD	Razor & Tie	7930182844-2	U.S.A.	1999	9.99
Crenshaw, Marshall	Downtown	CD	Warner Bros.	9-25319-2	U.S.A.	1985	13.99
Crenshaw, Marshall	Field Day	CD	Warner Bros.	9-23873-2	U.S.A.	1983	10.99
Crenshaw, Marshall	Good Evening	CD	Warner Bros.	9-25908-2	U.S.A.	1989	12.99
Crenshaw, Marshall	I've Suffered For My Art...	CD	King Biscuit	KB-88059	U.S.A.	2001	7.99
Crenshaw, Marshall	Life's Too Short	CD	MCA	MCAD-10223	U.S.A.	1991	9.99
Crenshaw, Marshall	Live...My Truck Is My Home	CD	Razor & Tie	RT-2815	U.S.A.	1994	7.99
Crenshaw, Marshall	Marsall Crenshaw + 9	CD	Rhino	R2-79916	U.S.A.	2000	14.99
Crenshaw, Marshall	Mary Jean And 9 Others	CD	Warner Bros.	9-25583-2	U.S.A.	1987	22.99
Crenshaw, Marshall	Miracle Of Science + 2	CD	Pioneer	PICP-1150	Japan	1996	24.99
Crenshaw, Marshall	The 9 Volt Years	CD	Razor & Tie	7930182838-2	U.S.A.	1998	13.99
Crenshaw, Marshall	This Is Easy (Best Of)	CD	Rhino	R2-79915	U.S.A.	2000	11.99
Cressida	Asylum	CD	Repertoire	REP-4105-WP	Germany	2001	19.99
Cressida	Self Titled	CD	Repertoire	REP-4299-WP	Germany	2002	19.99
Crewe, Bob	Barbarella (O.S.T.)	CD	Harkit	HRKCD-8004	England	2002	23.99
Critters	Anthology: Complete Kapp Recordings 1	CD	MCA	MCAD-22126	U.S.A.	1994	39.99
Critters	Younger Girl + 7	CD	MCA Victor	MVCE-22012	Japan	1997	39.99
Croce, Jim	24 Karat Gold/Bottle (DCC Gold Cd)	CD	DCC	GZS-1060	U.S.A.	1994	58.99
Croce, Jim	Down The Highway	CD	Essential	ESM-CD-698	England	1999	11.99
Croce, Jim	Jim Croce 50th Anniversary Collection	2CD	Saja	7-92205-2	U.S.A.	1992	18.99
Croce, Jim	Jim Croce Live - The Final Tour	CD	Essential	ESM-CD-700	England	1999	7.99
Croce, Jim	Jim Croce: The Definitive Collection	2CD	Essential	ESACD-781	England	1999	23.99
Croce, Jim	Photographs & Memories	CD	Essential	ESM-CD-699	England	1999	9.99
Croce, Jim	Time In A Bottle	CD	Essential	ESM-CD-697	England	1999	11.99
Croce, Jim	VH1: Behind The Music	CD	Rhino	R2-74331	U.S.A.	2001	8.99
Croce, Jim	Words & Music (DCC Gold Cd)	CD	DCC	GZS-1134	U.S.A.	1999	14.99
Croce, Jim/Ingrid	Croce	CD	One Way	72435-20667-2-8	U.S.A.	1999	7.99
Crofts, Dash/Baha'i Chorale	Songs Of The Ancient Beauty	CD	Water	WMCD001	U.S.A.	1992	24.99
Cropper, Steve	With A Little Help From My Friends	CD	ZYX	SCD24-855-2	France	2002	14.99
Cropper, Steve	With A Little Help... (MFSL Silver Cd)	CD	Mobile Fidelity	MFCD-837	U.S.A.	1969	44.99
Crosby & Nash	Another Stoney Evening	CD	Grateful Dead	GDCD-4057	U.S.A.	1997	11.99
Crosby & Nash	Live	CD	MCA	088-112-052-2	U.S.A.	2000	8.99
Crosby & Nash	Whistling Down The Wire	CD	MCA	088-112-032-2	U.S.A.	2000	11.99
Crosby & Nash	Wind On The Water	CD	MCA	088-112-043-2	U.S.A.	2000	10.99
Crosby & Nash	Wind/The Water + 3 (Special Edition)	CD	Eureka	EURCD-409	England	2001	13.99
Crosby, David	Drive My Car	CD Single	A&M	CD17701	U.S.A.	1989	7.99
Crosby, David	If I Could Only Remember My Name....	CD	Atlantic	7203-2	U.S.A.	1971	11.99
Crosby, David	It's All Coming Back To Me	CD	A&M	AMCY-793	Japan	1994	13.99
Crosby, David	It's All Coming Back To Me Now...	CD	Atlantic	82620-2	U.S.A.	1994	8.99
Crosby, David	King Biscuit Flower Hour	CD	King Biscuit	70710-88007-2	U.S.A.	1996	12.99
Crosby, David	Oh Yes I Can	CD	A&M	CD-5232	U.S.A.	1989	5.99
Crosby, David	Thousand Roads	CD	Atlantic	7-82484-2	U.S.A.	1993	5.99

Artist	Title	Format	Label	Catalog No	Country	Released	Value
Crosby, David/Phil Collins	Hero	CD Single	Atlantic	7567-85757-2	Germany	1991	7.99
Crosby, Stills & Nash	After The Storm	CD	Atlantic	82654-2	U.S.A.	1994	6.99
Crosby, Stills & Nash	Allies	CD	Atlantic	7-80075-2	Germany	1983	75.99
Crosby, Stills & Nash	Crosby Stills & Nash (Atlantic Gold Cd)	CD	Atlantic	82522-2	U.S.A.	1993	64.99
Crosby, Stills & Nash	CSN	CD	Atlantic	82650-2	U.S.A.	1977	9.99
Crosby, Stills & Nash	CSN Box Set	4CD	Atlantic	7-82319-2	U.S.A.	1991	33.99
Crosby, Stills & Nash	CSN Boxed Set Sampler	CD	Atlantic	PRCD-4283-2	U.S.A.	1991	24.99
Crosby, Stills & Nash	Daylight Again	CD	Atlantic	82672-2	U.S.A.	1982	11.99
Crosby, Stills & Nash	Live It Up	CD	Atlantic	7-82107-2	U.S.A.	1990	5.99
Crosby, Stills, Nash And Young	Deja Vu	CD	East West	AMCY-4001	Japan	1970	36.99
Crosby, Stills, Nash/Young	American Dream	CD	Atlantic	7-81888-2	U.S.A.	1988	12.99
Crosby, Stills, Nash/Young	American Dream (Ltd Hrdbck Promo)	CD	Atlantic	PR-2552-2	U.S.A.	1988	153.99
Crosby, Stills, Nash/Young	Deja Vu	CD	Atlantic	82649-2	U.S.A.	1970	11.99
Crosby, Stills, Nash/Young	Four Way Street	2CD	Atlantic	7-82408-2	U.S.A.	1992	28.99
Crosby, Stills, Nash/Young	Heartland/Stand And Be Counted (DJ)	CD Single	Reprise	PRO-CD-100036	U.S.A.	1999	6.99
Crosby, Stills, Nash/Young	Looking Forward	CD	Reprise	9-47436-2	U.S.A.	1999	8.99
Crosby, Stills, Nash/Young	No Tears Left (Promo)	CD Single	Reprise	PRO-CD-9986	U.S.A.	1999	6.99
Crosby, Stills, Nash/Young	So Far	CD	Atlantic	82648-2	U.S.A.	1974	11.99
Cross, Christopher	Another Page	CD	Warner Bros.	9-23757-2	U.S.A.	1983	10.99
Cross, Christopher	Back Of My Mind	CD	Reprise	9-25685-2	U.S.A.	1988	15.99
Cross, Christopher	Christopher Cross	CD	Warner Bros.	7599233832	Australia	1979	8.99
Cross, Christopher	Every Turn Of The World	CD	Warner Bros.	WPCR-1186	Japan	1985	19.99
Cross, Christopher	Red Room	CD	CMC INT.	06076-86290-2	U.S.A.	2000	6.99
Cross, Christopher	Rendezvous	CD	Ariola	74321-10291-2	Germany	1992	12.99
Cross, Christopher	Rendezvous	CD	Polystar	PSCW-1072	Japan	1991	24.99
Cross, Christopher	Ride Like The Wind Remixes 2001	CD Single	Rhino	8122-77010-2	U.S.A.	2001	8.99
Cross, Christopher	Ride Like The Wind: Best Of	CD	Warner Bros.	3548-30656-2	Germany	1998	13.99
Cross, Christopher	The Definitive Christopher Cross	CD	Warner Bros.	8122735542	Australia	2001	12.99
Cross, Christopher	The Very Best Of Christopher Cross	CD	Rhino	R2-78335	U.S.A.	2002	13.99
Cross, Christopher	Walking In Avalon (R Room/Concert)	2CD	CMC INT.	06076-86248-2	U.S.A.	1998	9.99
Cross, Christopher	Window	CD	Priority	P2-53960	U.S.A.	1995	9.99
Crow, Sheryl	Anything But Down	CD Single	A&M	582-827-2	England	1998	7.99
Crow, Sheryl	C'mon C'mon + 2	CD	A&M	493-262-2	England	2002	21.99
Crow, Sheryl	C'mon C'mon + 6 (Japanese Tour Ed.)	2CD	Victor Ent.	UICA-9002/3	Japan	2002	37.99
Crow, Sheryl	If It Makes You Happy	CD Single	A&M	31458-1874-2	U.S.A.	1996	5.99
Crow, Sheryl	If It Makes You Happy	CD Single	A&M	31458-1875-2	U.S.A.	1996	6.99
Crow, Sheryl	Live At Budokan	CD	Universal	UICA-1012	Japan	2003	32.99
Crow, Sheryl	Live From Central Park	CD	A&M	069490574-2	England	1999	8.99
Crow, Sheryl	Sheryl Crow + 1	CD	Polygram K.K.	POCM-1200	Japan	1996	34.99
Crow, Sheryl	Sheryl Crow + 6 (Special Edition)	2CD	PolyGram	540-719-2	Germany	1996	17.99
Crow, Sheryl	Sheryl Crow On Sheryl Crow: The Int.	CD	A&M	AMSAD-00281	U.S.A.	1996	19.99
Crow, Sheryl	Soak Up The Sun	CD Single	A&M	497-705-2	England	2002	9.99
Crow, Sheryl	Soak Up The Sun	CD Single	A&M	497-688-2	Germany	2002	9.99
Crow, Sheryl	Steve McQueen	CD Single	A&M	497-742-2	England	2002	8.99
Crow, Sheryl	Strong Enough	CD Single	A&M	31458-0866-2	U.S.A.	1994	6.99
Crow, Sheryl	Strong Enough (Promo)	CD Single	A&M	31458-8407-2	U.S.A.	1993	10.99
Crow, Sheryl	Sweet Child O' Mine	CD Single	A&M	CSK-42160	U.S.A.	1999	5.99
Crow, Sheryl	The Globe Sessions	CD	A&M	06949-0404-2	U.S.A.	1999	7.99
Crow, Sheryl	The Globe Sessions (DTS)	CD	A&M	6928601076-2-5	U.S.A.	2001	11.99
Crow, Sheryl	The Globe Sessions + 6 (Tour Edition)	2CD	A&M	541-025-2	England	1999	19.99
Crow, Sheryl	There Goes The Neighborhood	CD Single	A&M	582-807-2	England	1998	6.99
Crow, Sheryl	There Goes The Neighborhood	CD Single	A&M	582-809-2	England	1998	6.99
Crow, Sheryl	Tuesday Music Club (Bonus Live Cd)	2CD	PolyGram	POCM-1054	Japan	1995	59.99
Crow, Sheryl	Tuesday Night Music Club	CD	A&M	31454-0126-2	U.S.A.	1993	7.99
Crow, Sheryl	What I Can Do for You (With Calendar)	CD Single	A&M	581-229-2	England	1995	24.99
Crow, Sheryl/Spiral Book	Tuesday Night Music Club (Promo)	CD	A&M	31458-401262	U.S.A.	1994	44.99
Crowded House	Afterglow	CD	Capitol	7243-5-23722-2-5	U.S.A.	2000	7.99
Crowded House	Afterglow (W/Bonus Int. Cd)	2CD	EMI	7243-524804-2-5	Canada	1999	9.99

Artist	Title	Format	Label	Catalog No	Country	Released	Value
Crowded House	Crowded House	CD	Capitol	7-46693-2	U.S.A.	1987	8.99
Crowded House	Distant Sun	CD Single	Capitol	7243-8-58136-2-7	U.S.A.	1994	4.99
Crowded House	Instinct	CD Single	Capitol	7243-8-83448-2-1	Australia	1996	4.99
Crowded House	Live At The Town... (Promo)	2CD	Capitol	CH1	England	1992	164.99
Crowded House	Locked Out (Promo)	CD Single	Capitol	DPRO-79297	U.S.A.	1993	4.99
Crowded House	Pineapple Head	CD Single	Capitol	7243-8-81647-2-6	England	1993	4.99
Crowded House	Recurring Dream + Live Disc	2CD	Capitol	7243-8-522482-9	Holland	1996	23.99
Crowded House	Temple Of Low Men	CD	Capitol	548763	U.S.A.	1988	6.99
Crowded House	Together Alone	CD	Capitol	527048	U.S.A.	1993	6.99
Crowded House	Woodface (Ltd Ed Fold Out Promo)	CD	Capitol	DPRO-79759	U.S.A.	1991	39.99
Cruise, Julee	The Art Of Being A Girl	CD	Water Music	302-060-282-2	U.S.A.	2002	9.99
Cruise, Julee	The Voice Of Love	CD	Warner Bros.	9-45390-2	U.S.A.	1993	6.99
Crumb, Robert	Presents Hot Women Singers	CD	Kein	KEIN-23284-CD	Switzerlan	2000	11.99
Cuccurullo, Warren	Machine Language	CD	Imago	72787-24001-2	U.S.A.	1997	8.99
Cuccurullo, Warren	Road Rage	CD	One Way	OW-35182	U.S.A.	2001	7.99
Cuccurullo, Warren	Thanks To Frank (Live)	CD	Imago	72787-23002-2	U.S.A.	1996	13.99
Cuccurullo, Warren	The Blue	CD	One Way	OW-35181	U.S.A.	2001	7.99
Cuccurullo, Warren	Trance Formed	CD	One Way	OW-35193	U.S.A.	2003	7.99
Cult	Best Of Rare Cult	CD	Atlantic	82029-2	U.S.A.	2000	9.99
Cult	Beyond Good And Evil	CD	Atlantic	83440-2	U.S.A.	2001	6.99
Cult	Ceremony	CD	Sire	9-26673-2	U.S.A.	1991	7.99
Cult	Dreamtime	CD	Beggars Banquet	BBL-57CD	England	1984	7.99
Cult	Electric	CD	Sire	9-25555-2	U.S.A.	1987	8.99
Cult	High Octane Cult	CD	Sire	9-46047-2	U.S.A.	1996	9.99
Cult	Love	CD	Sire	9-25359-2	U.S.A.	1985	9.99
Cult	Pure Cult	CD	Beggars Banquet	314-514-213-2	U.S.A.	1993	11.99
Cult	Rare Cult Box Set	6CD	Beggars Banquet	RCBOX1CD	England	2000	159.99
Cult	Self Titled	CD	Sire	9-45673-2	U.S.A.	1994	17.99
Cult	Sonic Temple	CD	Sire	9-25872-2	U.S.A.	1989	10.99
Culture Club	Kissing To Be Clever	CD	Virgin	0777-7-86179-2-1	U.S.A.	1982	9.99
Culture Club	The 12" Collection Plus	CD	Caroline	CAROL-1115-2	U.S.A.	1997	8.99
Culture Club	VH1 Story Tellers	2CD	Virgin	7243-8-46191-2-1	U.S.A.	1998	11.99
Culture Club	Your Kisses Are Charity (Cd 1)	CD Single	Virgin	7243-8-96058-2-2	England	1999	6.99
Cure	Bloodflowers	CD	Elektra	62236-2	U.S.A.	2000	7.99
Cure	Boys Don't Cry	CD	Elektra	9-60786-2	U.S.A.	1979	13.99
Cure	Close to Me	CD Single	Elektra	9-66582-2	U.S.A.	1990	9.25
Cure	Concert - The Cure Live	CD	Fiction	823-682-2	Germany	1984	13.99
Cure	Cut Here	CD Single	Fiction	587389-2	England	2001	9.99
Cure	Disintegration	CD	Elektra	9-60855-2	U.S.A.	1989	9.99
Cure	Entreat	CD	Polydor K.K.	POCP-9018	Japan	1991	21.99
Cure	Entreat (Live Wembley 1989)	CD	Polydor K.K.	POCP-9018	Japan	1991	44.99
Cure	Faith	CD	Elektra	9-60783-2	U.S.A.	1981	10.99
Cure	Fascination Street	CD Single	Elektra	9-66702-2	U.S.A.	1989	7.99
Cure	Friday (I'm In Love)	CD Single	Elektra	66146-2	U.S.A.	1992	5.99
Cure	Friday (I'm In Love) Promo	CD Single	Elektra	PRCD-8578-2	U.S.A.	1992	14.99
Cure	Galore: the Singles 1987-1997	CD	Fiction	62117-2	U.S.A.	1997	7.99
Cure	Greatest Hits + 18 (Bonus Cd)	2CD	Elektra	62725-2	U.S.A.	2001	14.99
Cure	Happily Ever After (17 Seconds/Faith)	CD	A&M	CD-6020	U.S.A.	1981	84.99
Cure	High	CD Single	Elektra	CD-66437	U.S.A.	1992	7.99
Cure	Japanese Whispers	CD	Ficiton	817-470-2	Germany	1983	20.99
Cure	Join Dots: B-sides/Rarities, 1978-2001	4CD	Rhino	R2-78043	U.S.A.	2004	41.99
Cure	Just Like Heaven (NTSC)	CDV	Elektra	64002-2	U.S.A.	1987	149.99
Cure	Kiss Me, Kiss Me, Kiss Me	CD	Elektra	9-60737-2	U.S.A.	1987	8.99
Cure	Love Song	CD Single	Elektra	9-66687-2	U.S.A.	1989	7.99
Cure	Lovesong (PAL)	CDV	Ficiton	081-398-2	England	1989	99.99
Cure	Lullaby	CD Single	Elektra	9-66664-2	U.S.A.	1993	6.99
Cure	Mint Car	CD Single	Ficiton	576-969-2	England	1996	7.99
Cure	Mint Car	CD Single	Ficiton	576-967-2	England	1996	7.99

Artist	Title	Format	Label	Catalog No	Country	Released	Value
Cure	Mint Car (Promo)	CD Single	Elektra	PRCD-9572-2	U.S.A.	1996	4.99
Cure	Mixed Up	CD	Elektra	9-60978-2	U.S.A.	1990	7.99
Cure	Never Enough	CD Single	Elektra	9-66604-2	U.S.A.	1990	6.99
Cure	Never Enough (3")	CD Single	Polydor	PODP-6005	Japan	1990	53.99
Cure	Paris	CD	Elektra	9-61552-2	U.S.A.	1993	6.99
Cure	Parispro (Promo)	CD Single	Ficiton	PARISPRO1	England	1993	18.99
Cure	Pictures of You	CD Single	Elektra	9-66639-2	U.S.A.	1990	7.99
Cure	Pornography	CD	Elektra	9-60785-2	U.S.A.	1982	10.99
Cure	Promo Sampler	CD	Elektra	CURE-1	Canada	1992	249.99
Cure	Seventeen Seconds	CD	Elektra	9-60784-2	U.S.A.	1980	11.99
Cure	Show (With Sideshow Ep)	2CD	Fiction	519-951-2	Germany	1996	14.99
Cure	Sideshow	CD Single	Elektra	66275-2	U.S.A.	1993	6.99
Cure	Staring At The Sea Singles 1979-1985	CD	Polydor K.K.	POCP-1880	Japan	1986	34.99
Cure	Strange Attraction	CD Single	Elektra	63999-2	U.S.A.	1996	13.99
Cure	The 13th (Promo)	CD Single	Elektra	PRCD-9523-2	U.S.A.	1996	14.99
Cure	The Head On The Door	CD	Elektra	9-60435-2	U.S.A.	1985	9.99
Cure	The Peel Sessions	CD	Strange Fruit	DE18341-2	England	1988	10.99
Cure	The Top	CD	Fiction	821-136-2	Germany	1984	18.99
Cure	Three Imaginary Boys	CD	Fiction	827-686-2	Germany	1979	13.99
Cure	Three Imaginary Boys	CD	Polydor K.K.	POCP-1871	Japan	1990	30.99
Cure	Wild Mood Swings + 1	CD	Polydor K.K.	POCP-7130	Japan	1996	20.99
Cure	Wish	CD	Elektra	9-61309-2	U.S.A.	1992	9.99
Cure	Wish	CD	Polydor	POCP-1190	Japan	1992	34.99
Currie, Billy/Steve Howe	Transportation	CD	I.R.S.	IRSD-42239	U.S.A.	1988	19.99
Currie, Cherie/Marie	Messin' With The Boys	CD	Renaissance	RMED00189-2	U.S.A.	1997	13.99
Currie, Cherie/Marie	Young And Wild	CD	Raven	RVCD-60	Australia	1998	14.99
Curry, Mini	100%	CD	Line	TLCD-9.00473-0	Germany	1987	24.99
Curry, Tim/Rocky Horror	The Best Of Tim Curry	CD	A&M	CD5269	U.S.A.	1981	49.99
Curry, Tyrone	Tyrone Curry	CD	Line	TLCD-9.00478-0	Germany	1987	24.99
Curtis, T.C.	Step By Step	CD	Line	TLCD-9.00828-0	Germany	1989	149.99
Curved Air	Air Conditioning	CD	Line	LECD-9.01023-0	Germany	1990	14.99
Curved Air	Air Conditoning	CD	Collector's Choice	CCM-148	U.S.A.	2000	7.99
Curved Air	Airborne	CD	Repertoire	REP-4493-WY	Germany	1994	12.99
Curved Air	Alive 1990	CD	Mystic	MYS-CD-141	England	2000	17.99
Curved Air	Live	CD	Repertoire	REP-4514-WY	Germany	1997	12.99
Curved Air	Live At The BBC	CD	Band Of Joy	BOJCD-014	England	1996	14.99
Curved Air	Love Child	CD	Snapper	SMMCD-609	England	1990	10.99
Curved Air	Masters From The Vaults	CD	Intense	INT1113	England	2002	14.99
Curved Air	Midnight Wire	CD	Repertoire	REP-4499-WY	Germany	1997	12.99
Curved Air	On Air	CD	Strange Fruit	SFRSCD022	England	1997	14.99
Curved Air	Phantasmagoria	CD	Collector's Choice	CCM-160	U.S.A.	2001	7.99
Curved Air	Second Album	CD	Collector's Choice	CCM-159	U.S.A.	2001	7.99
Cussick, Ian	A Bridge To Far	CD Single	Line	NFCD-9.01227-E	Germany	1992	4.99
Cussick, Ian	A Bridge Too Far	CD	Line	LICD-9.01337-0	Germany	1996	13.99
Cussick, Ian	Forever	CD	Line	LICD-9.01112-0	Germany	1991	12.99
Cussick, Ian	Live In The Fabrik In Hamburg	CD	Line	LICD-9.01305-0	Germany	1995	11.99
Cussick, Ian	Love Is The System	CD	Line	LICD-9.00689-0	Germany	1989	9.99
Cussick, Ian	Love Is The System	CD Single	Line	LICD-9.00874-E	Germany	1989	4.99
Cussick, Ian	Necromancer	CD	Line	NFCD-9.01283-0	Germany	1993	9.99
Cussick, Ian	Runaway Train	CD Single	Line	LICD-9.01131-E	Germany	1991	12.99
Cussick, Ian	The Voice From Scotland - Live	CD	Line	LICD-9.00935-0	Germany	1990	11.99
Cussick, Ian	Treasure Island	CD	Line	LICD-9.00684-0	Germany	1989	9.99
Cutler, Mark/Lexington 1-2-5	Mark Cutler And Lexington 1-2-5	CD	Line	LICD—9.01359-0	Germany	2000	14.99
Cyrkle	Neon	CD	Sony	SRCS-6452	Japan	1995	14.99
Cyrkle	The Minx (O.S.T.) + 8	CD	Sundazed	SC-11106	U.S.A.	2003	14.99
Czukay, Holger	Good Morning Story	CD	Tone Casualties	TCCD-9944	U.S.A.	1999	9.99
Czukay, Holger	La Luna	CD	Tone Casualties	TCCD-9945	U.S.A.	2000	6.99
Czukay, Holger/Dr. Walker	Clash	2CD	Tone Casualties	TCCD-9830	U.S.A.	1998	14.99

C

Artist	Title	Format	Label	Catalog No	Country	Released	Value
Czukay, Holger/U-She	The New Millennium	CD	Funfundvierzig	FUN-132-CD	Germany	2003	19.99

D

Artist	Title	Format	Label	Catalog No	Country	Released	Value
D.A.F.	Die Kleinen Und Die Bösen	CD	Line	DKCD-9.00847-0	Germany	1990	9.99
Dada	Dada	CD	Line	LECD-9.01014-0	Germany	1991	9.99
Dada, Sonia	Day At The Beach	CD	Capricorn	9-42037-2	U.S.A.	1995	7.99
Dada, Sonia	Self Titled	CD	Capricorn	9-42033-2	U.S.A.	1995	7.99
Dagradi, Tony	Dreams Of Love	CD	Line	COCD-9.00798-0	Germany	1989	14.99
Dagradi, Tony/Trio	Images From The Floating World	CD	Line	COCD-9.00727-0	Germany	1991	14.99
Daily, E. G.	Wild Child	CD	Pony Canyon	D32Y-3015	Japan	1987	79.99
Dali's Car	The Waking Hour	CD	Paradox	DOXCD1	Germany	1984	12.99
D'Alma	D'Alma	CD	Line	RICD-9.00832-0	Germany	1989	11.99
Dalton, Lacy J.	16th Avenue	CD	Columbia	CK-37975	U.S.A.	1982	55.99
Daltrey, Roger	Anthology	CD	Repertoire	REP-4670-WY	Germany	1998	14.99
Daltrey, Roger	Can't Wait To See The Movie	CD	EMI	DIXCD-54	England	1987	8.99
Daltrey, Roger	Celebration Music Townshend/Who	CD	Continuum	COND-19402	U.S.A.	1991	5.99
Daltrey, Roger	Celebration/Music Pete T./Who (Adv.)	CD	Continuum	19402	U.S.A.	1991	6.99
Daltrey, Roger	Daltrey + 1	CD	Repertoire	REP-4636-WY	Germany	1998	17.99
Daltrey, Roger	Martyrs & Madmen: The Best Of	CD	Rhino	R2-72846	U.S.A.	1997	6.99
Daltrey, Roger	McVicar	CD	PolyGram	527-341-2	England	1973	20.99
Daltrey, Roger	One Of The Boys + 3	CD	Repertoire	REP-4643-WY	Germany	1998	14.99
Daltrey, Roger	Pinball Wizard (Promo)	CD Single	Continuum	12402	U.S.A.	1991	14.99
Daltrey, Roger	Ride A Rock Horse	CD	Repertoire	REP-4642-WY	Germany	1998	14.99
Daltrey, Roger	Rocks In The Head	CD	Atlantic	82359-2	U.S.A.	1992	5.99
Daltrey, Roger	Under A Raging Moon +1	CD	Reprise	2295	U.S.A.	1985	9.99
Damian, Michael	Dreams Of Summer	CD	Pony Canyon	PCCY-10223	Japan	1991	24.99
Damian, Michael	Love Is A Mystery	CD	Alfa	25B2-83	Japan	1984	29.99
Damian, Michael	Self Titled	CD	Alfa	25B2-84	Japan	1986	29.99
Damian, Michael	Where Do We Go From Here	CD	Cypress	29B2-54	Japan	1989	29.99
Damned	Damned But Not Forgotten	CD	Dojo	DOJOCD-21	England	1986	10.99
Damned	Damned Damned Damned	CD	Castle	CMFCD505	England	2002	14.99
Damned	Final Damnation	CD	Restless	7-72385-2	Canada	1989	12.99
Damned	Grave Disorder	CD	Nitro	15844-2	U.S.A.	2001	8.99
Damned	I'm Alright Jack & The Beanstalk + 4	CD	Castle	CMRCD-543	England	1996	10.99
Damned	Music For Pleasure	CD	Demon	FIEND-CD-108	England	1977	7.99
Damned	Music For Pleasure + 3	CD	Castle	CMFCD506	England	2002	11.99
Damned	Sessions Of The Damned	CD	Fuel 2000	302-061-063-2	U.S.A.	2000	12.99
Damned	Smash It Up - Anthology 1976 - 1987	2CD	Castle	CMEDD476	England	2002	12.99
Damned	Tales From the Damned	CD	Cleopatra	RR-9337-2	U.S.A.	1980	14.99
Damned	The Best of the Damned	CD	Cleopatra	CLEO-7139-2	U.S.A.	1993	12.99
Damned	The Black Album	CD	Big Beat	CDWIK-906	EEC	1982	14.99
Damned	The Peel Sessions	CD Single	Strange Fruit	SFPSCD012	England	1988	10.99
Damned	The Radio One Sessions	CD	Nighttracks	CDNT011	England	1996	12.99
Damned Nation	Grand Design	CD	Z Records	ZR1997028	England	2000	26.99
Damned Nation	Just What The Doctor Ordered	CD	Pony Canyon	PCCY-00773	Japan	1995	24.99
Damned Nation	Road Of Desire	CD	Z Records	ZR1997014	England	1999	8.99
Danger	Who Do You Love	CD Single	Line	PRCD-9.01241-E	Germany	1992	5.99
Dangerous Toys	Greatest Hits Live: Vitamins...	CD	Cleopatra	CLP-0743-2	U.S.A.	1999	9.99
Dangerous Toys	Hellacious Acres	CD	Columbia	CK-46754	U.S.A.	1991	8.99
Dangerous Toys	Pissed	CD	Cleopatra	CLP-0502-2	U.S.A.	1999	8.99
Dangerous Toys	Self Titled	CD	Columbia	CK-45031	U.S.A.	1989	11.99

Artist	Title	Format	Label	Catalog No	Country	Released	Value
Dangerous Toys	The R*tist 4*merly Known As	CD	Cleopatra	CLP-0503-2	U.S.A.	1999	7.99
Daniels, Charlie/ Band	Super Hits	CD	Sony	EK-64182	U.S.A.	1993	5.99
Danko, Rick	Live On Breeze Hill/Times Like These	2CD	Breeze Hill	YDCD-0071/2	Japan	2001	39.99
Danko, Rick	Rick Danko	CD	Edsel	EDCD-650	England	2000	28.99
Danko, Rick/The Band	Danko/Fjeld/Andersen - 1 More Shot	2CD	Appleseed	APR-CD-1062	U.S.A.	2002	12.99
Danna, Mychael	Exotica (O.S.T.)	CD	Varese	VSD-5543	U.S.A.	1994	7.99
Danzig	4	CD	Universal	7314-586956-2	U.S.A.	2002	8.99
Danzig	6:66 Satan's Child	CD	E-Magine	673976-1005-2	U.S.A.	1999	8.99
Danzig	777:I Luciferi	CD	Spitfire	SPT-15204-2	U.S.A.	2002	8.99
Danzig	Black Aria	CD	E-Magine	673976-1013-2	U.S.A.	2000	8.99
Danzig	Blackacidevil	CD	E-Magine	673976-1011-2	U.S.A.	2000	8.99
Danzig	II: Lucifuge	CD	Universal	7314-586954-2	U.S.A.	2002	8.99
Danzig	III: How The Gods Kill	CD	Universal	7314-586955-2	U.S.A.	2002	8.99
Danzig	Live On The Black Hand Side	CD	Restless	7-73750-2	U.S.A.	2001	8.99
Danzig	Sacrifice	CD Single	E-Magine	673976-1012-2	U.S.A.	2000	5.99
Danzig	Self Titled	CD	Universal	7314-586953-2	U.S.A.	2002	8.99
Danzig	Thrall: Demonsweatlive + 1	CD	Universal	7314-586957-2	U.S.A.	2002	8.99
Darin, Bobby	If I Were A Carpenter	CD	Karussell	550-410-2	Australia	1996	9.99
Darin, Bobby	Live At The Desert Inn	CD	Motown	37463-6227-2	U.S.A.	1992	53.99
Dark Star	Graceadelica (CD 1)	CD Single	EMI	7243-8879250-2-9	England	1999	6.99
Dark Star	Graceadelica (CD 2)	CD Single	EMI	7243-8879926-2-2	England	1999	6.99
Dark Star	Self Titled + 6	CD	Pony Canyon	PCCY-00495	Japan	1993	49.99
Darren, James	This One's From The Heart	CD	Concord	CCD-4868-2	England	1999	11.99
Darvill, Martin/Friends	The Greatest Show On Earth	CD	Blueprint	BP4651CD	England	2000	11.99
David, Marcus	Greatest Hits	CD	Line	LICD-9.00757-L	Germany	1991	5.99
Davies, Dave	Afl1-3603 + 1	CD	BMG	74321-87401-2	Japan	2001	24.99
Davies, Dave	AFL1-3603/Glamour	CD	BGO	BGOCD587	England	2003	15.99
Davies, Dave	Anthology - Unfinished Business	2CD	Essential	ESS-CD-584	England	1998	21.99
Davies, Dave	Bug + 3 (Live/Female On Cover Version)	CD	Angel Air	SJPCD179	England	2004	11.99
Davies, Dave	Bugged...Live !	CD	Meta Media	MM005	U.S.A.	2002	14.99
Davies, Dave	Dave Davies + Glamour	CD	Demon	MAUCD-617	England	1992	17.99
Davies, Dave	Dave Davies Unfinished Business	2CD	Velvel	63467-79718-2	U.S.A.	1999	12.99
Davies, Dave	Fortis Green	CD	Meta Media	MM02	England	1999	14.99
Davies, Dave	Fragile	CD	Meta Media	MM04	England	2001	14.99
Davies, Dave	Live Solo At Marian College	CD	Meta Media	MM03	England	2000	14.99
Davies, Dave	Rock Bottom Live At The Bottom Line	CD	Koch	KOC-CD-8087	U.S.A.	2000	9.99
Davies, Dave	The Album That Never Was + 12	Mini Lp	Victor Ent.	VICP-61816	Japan	2002	29.99
Davies, Dave	Transformation Live Alexander Theatre	CD	Meta Media	MM006	U.S.A.	2003	14.99
Davies, Dave	Unfinished Business (Solo Kron. Promo)	CD	Velvel	CDPRO-014	U.S.A.	1997	49.99
Davies, Dave/Crystal Radio	Purusha And The Spiritual Planet	CD	Meta Media	MM01	England	1998	14.99
Davies, Dave/J. Carpenter	In The Mouth Of Madness	CD	DRG	12611	U.S.A.	1995	14.99
Davies, Dave/J. Carpenter	Village Of The Damned O.S.T.	CD	Varese	VSD-5629	U.S.A.	1995	19.99
Davies, Debbie	Love The Game	CD	Shanachie	9030	U.S.A.	2001	9.99
Davies, Ray	The Storyteller	CD	EMI	7243-4-94168-2-6	U.S.A.	1998	12.99
Davis, Carl/Royal P. Orch.	Conducts James Bond Themes	CD	Trumpets Of Joy	204510-201	Germany	2000	4.99
Davis, Jesse	Jesse Davis	CD	East West	AMCY-2583	Japan	1998	34.99
Davis, Jesse	Jesse Davis	CD	Line	LECD-9.00943-0	Germany	1990	19.99
Davis, Jesse	Keep Me Commin'	CD	East West	AMCY-2584	Japan	1998	29.99
Davis, Jesse	Ululu	CD	Sony	ESCA-7523	Japan	1994	29.99
Davis, Miles	Get Up With It - Part 1	CD	Line	CLCD-9.00927-L	Germany	1991	7.99
Davis, Miles	Get Up With It - Part 2	CD	Line	CLCD-9.00928-L	Germany	1991	7.99
Davis, Miles	Get Up With It (Pt 1/2)	2CD	Line	CLCD-9.21155-S	Germany	1991	13.99
Davis, Miles	Kind of Blue + 1	CD	Columbia	CK-64935	U.S.A.	1997	8.99
Davis, Miles	The Alternative (Promo)	CD	Columbia	CSK-16729-S1	U.S.A.	2001	13.99
Davis, Miles	The Essential	2CD	Columbia	C2K-85475	U.S.A.	2001	15.99
Davis, Spencer/Group	Eight Gigs A Week	2CD	Island	524-180-2	England	1996	18.99
Davis, Spencer/Group	Funky + 11	CD	One Way	OW-34529	U.S.A.	1969	12.99
Davis, Spencer/Group	Gimme Some Lovin' + 8	CD	Sundazed	SC-11103	U.S.A.	2001	12.99

Artist	Title	Format	Label	Catalog No	Country	Released	Value
Davis, Spencer/Group	Gluggo + 6	CD	Repertoire	REP-4683-WY	Germany	1997	12.99
Davis, Spencer/Group	I'm A Man + 8	CD	Sundazed	SC-11104	U.S.A.	2001	8.99
Davis, Spencer/Group	Living In A Back Street = 12	CD	Repertoire	REP-4682-WY	Germany	1997	12.99
Davis, Spencer/Group	Mojo Rhythms & Midnight Blues Vol.2	CD	RPM	RPM-216	England	2000	14.99
Davis, Spencer/Group	The Masters: With Their... (Gold Disc)	2CD	Purple Pyramid	CLP-0624-2	U.S.A.	1999	24.99
Davis, Spencer/Group	Time Seller (With Their.../Documentary)	2CD	RPM	RPM-508	England	2002	12.99
Davis, Tyrone	The Timeless Soul Collection	CD	Line	TLCD-9.00470-0	Germany	1987	31.99
Dawson, Julian	As Real As Disneyland	CD	PolyGram	831-607-2	Germany	1987	14.99
Dawson, Julian	Fragile As China	CD	Ariola	261.719	Germany	1997	12.99
Dawson, Julian	Headlines	CD	Ariola	13005.2	Germany	1993	12.99
Dawson, Julian	Hillbilly Zen	CD	Fledg'ling	FLED-3032	England	2002	14.99
Dawson, Julian	How Human Hearts Behave	CD	Ariola	19078.2	Germany	1994	11.99
Dawson, Julian	June Honeymoon Live (Promo)	CD	Ariola	11898.2	Germany	1992	24.99
Dawson, Julian	Live On The Radio	CD	Watermelon	CD-1003	U.S.A.	1989	14.99
Dawson, Julian	Luckiest Man In The Western World	CD	PolyGram	837-422-2	Germany	1988	19.99
Dawson, Julian	Move Over Darling	CD	SPV	SPV085-29032CD	Germany	2003	7.99
Dawson, Julian	Never Mind The Ballads	CD	BMG	34192.2	Germany	1996	9.99
Dawson, Julian	Spark	CD	Gadfly	247	U.S.A.	1999	11.99
Dawson, Julian	Steal That Beat (Lost Album)	CD	Hypertension	0161-HYP	England	1996	7.99
Dawson, Julian	Sunday Into Saturday Night	CD Single	BMG	14652-2	Germany	1993	5.99
Dawson, Julian	Travel On	CD	Watermelon	CD-1043	U.S.A.	1995	7.99
Dawson, Julian	Under The Sun	CD	Gadfly	258	U.S.A.	1999	8.99
Dawson, Julian	Under The Sun	CD	Fledg'ling	FLED-3025	England	1999	8.99
Day, Doris	It's Magic (1947-50) Box Set	6CD	Bear Family	BCD-15609-FK	Germany	1993	89.99
Day, Doris	Move Over Darling (1960-67) Box Set	8 CD	Bear Family	BCD-15800-HK	Germany	1997	101.99
Day, Doris	Pillow Talk Box Set	CD	Bear Family	BCD-15-913-BI	Germany	1996	44.99
Day, Doris	Que Sera (1956-59) Box Set	5CD	Bear Family	BCD-15797-EK	Germany	1996	92.99
Day, Doris	Secret Love (1951-55) Box Set	5CD	Bear Family	BCD-15746-EK	Germany	1995	89.99
Db's	Like This + 1	CD	Rhino	R2-70891	U.S.A.	1984	34.99
Db's	Neverland	CD	Line	LICD—9.01354-0	Germany	1999	14.99
Db's	Neverland (Stands/Repercussion + 2)	CD	Line	9.01354	Germany	1999	14.99
Db's	Paris Avenue	CD	Monkey Hill	MON-6122-2	U.S.A.	1994	7.99
Db's	Repercussion	CD	Line	LICD-9.01344-0	Germany	1997	9.99
Db's	Repercussion	CD	Line	9.01344	Germany	1997	9.99
Db's	Ride The Wild Tomtom	CD	Rhino	R2-71299	U.S.A.	1993	10.99
Db's	Stands For Decibels	CD	Line	LICD-9.01339-0	Germany	1997	9.99
Db's	Stands For Decibels	CD	Line	9.01339	Germany	1997	9.99
Db's	Stands For Decibels/Repercussion	2CD	Line	LICD-9.21191-S	Germany	1992	15.99
Db's	Stands For Decibels/Repercussion + 2	CD	Collector's Choice	CCM-250-2	U.S.A.	2001	9.99
Db's	The Sound Of Music	CD	I.R.S.	IRSD-42055	U.S.A.	1987	34.99
Db's/Holsapple/Stamey	Mavericks	CD	Rhino	R2-70795	U.S.A.	1991	6.99
Db's/Let's Active	Alaska (W/Chris Stamey/Mitch Easter)	CD	Hello Club	HEL-55	U.S.A.	1995	29.99
Db's/Peter Holsapple	Out Of My Way	CD	Monkey Hill	MON-8135-2	U.S.A.	1995	7.99
Db's/Will Rigby	Laura Cantrell (Will Plays Drums)	CD	Hello Club	HEL-67	U.S.A.	1996	19.99
Db's/Will Rigby	Will Rigby (W/Pete Holsapple)	CD	Hello Club	HEL-64	U.S.A.	1996	29.99
DCC Compact Classics	24 Karat Gold Disc Sampler	CD	DCC	GZS-PRO-1	U.S.A.	1993	149.99
De Young, Dennis	10 On Broadway	CD	A&M	9-82625-2	U.S.A.	1994	10.99
De Young, Dennis	Back To The World	CD	A&M	CD-5109	U.S.A.	1986	22.99
De Young, Dennis	Boomchild	CD	Warner Bros.	25P2-2137	Japan	1988	29.99
De Young, Dennis	Boomchild	CD	MCA	MCAD-42162	U.S.A.	1988	15.99
De Young, Dennis	Desert Moon	CD	A&M	395-006-2	Germany	1984	29.99
De Young, Dennis	The Best	CD	A&M	540-057-2	Taiwan	1992	14.99
De Young, Dennis	The Ulimate Collection	CD	Hip O	314-545-236-2	U.S.A.	1999	17.99
Deacon Blue	Whatever You Say, Say Nothing	CD	Columbia	OK-53755	U.S.A.	1993	7.99
Dead Bang	Dancin' On The Edge	CD	Victor Ent.	VICP-5481	Japan	1994	19.99
Dead Boys	Liver Than You'll Ever Be	CD	Alchemy	PILOT-112	England	2002	11.99
Dead Boys	Night Of The Living Dead Boys	CD	Bomp	BCD4017	U.S.A.	1999	12.99
Dead Boys	Night Of The Living Dead Boys	CD	Line	LICD-9.00220-0	Germany	1987	12.99

D

Artist	Title	Format	Label	Catalog No	Country	Released	Value
Dead Boys	We Have Come For Your Children	CD	Sire	7599-26054-2	Germany	1978	14.99
Dead Boys	Young Loud and Snotty	CD	Sire	9-26981-2	U.S.A.	1992	16.99
Dead Boys/Stiv Bators	Stiv Bators/Night Of Living Dead Boys	CD	Revenge	MIG-16/18	France	1981	16.99
Dead Can Dance	1981-1998 [Boxed Set W/DVD]	3CD	Rhino	R2-78359	U.S.A.	2001	59.99
Dead Famous People	Dead Famous People	CD	Line	UTCD-9.00862-L	Germany	1989	40.99
Dead Kennedys	Fresh Fruit For Rotting Vegetables + 6	2CD	Cherry Red	CDSBRED-155	England	1981	22.99
Dead Or Alive	Hit & Run Lover (Promo)	CD Single	Avex	AVCS-10337	Japan	2000	99.99
Dead Or Alive	Rip It Up (Nonstop Remix)	CD Single	Epic	32-8P-225	Japan	1987	36.99
Dead-Kennedys	Bedtime for Democracy	CD	Manifesto	MFD-42903	U.S.A.	1987	9.99
Dead-Kennedys	Frankenchrist	CD	Alternative Tentacles	VIRUS-45CD	U.S.A.	1985	14.99
Dead-Kennedys	Plastic Surgery Disasters/In God...	CD	Manifesto	MFD-42901	U.S.A.	1982	12.99
Deaf School	2nd Honeymoon	CD	Wizard	EVA-5001	Japan	1989	29.99
Deaf School	Don't Stop The World	CD	Wizard	EVA-5002	Japan	1989	29.99
Deaf School	English Boys, Working Girls	CD	Wizard	EVA-5003	Japan	1990	29.99
Deaf School	Second Coming	CD	Demon	FIEND-CD-135	England	1988	9.99
Dean, Michael	Living Vicariously/Michael Dean	CD	Direct Hit	DH-306	U.S.A.	1999	7.99
Death-In-Vegas	Dead Elvis	CD	Time Bomb	70930-43511-2	U.S.A.	1997	7.99
Death-In-Vegas/Iggy Pop	The Contino Sessions (With Iggy Pop)	CD	Deconstruction	70930-43521-2	U.S.A.	1999	8.99
Decameron	Third Light	CD	Line	TACD-9.00752-0	Germany	1989	10.99
Decameron	Tomorrow's Pantomime	CD	Line	TACD-9.00775-0	Germany	1989	14.99
December People	Sounds Like Christmas	CD	Magna Carta	MA-9025-2	U.S.A.	2001	8.99
Dedilhadas, Cordas	Cordas Dedilhadas De Pernambuco	CD	Line	RICD-9.00835-0	Germany	1989	13.99
Deep Feeling	Self Titled	CD	Nippon Phonogram	PHCR-4205	Japan	1994	35.99
Deep Forest/Peter Gabriel	While The Earth Sleeps	CD Single	Columbia	662821-2	Austria	1995	11.99
Deep Purple	1420 Beachwood Dr.	CD	Purple	PUR-201	England	2000	19.99
Deep Purple	24 Carat	CD	Warner Bros.	WPCR-870	Japan	1996	24.99
Deep Purple	24 Carat Purple	CD	EMI	7243-534692-2-1	England	2001	8.99
Deep Purple	30: Very Best Of	2CD	EMI	7243-4-96808-2-1	England	1998	13.99
Deep Purple	30: Very Best Of - Sp Collectors Ed	2CD	Warner Bros.	WPCR-10045/6	Japan	1998	34.99
Deep Purple	4 Track CD Sampler (Promo)	CD	BMG	DP001	EU	1993	32.99
Deep Purple	Abandon	CD	CMC INT.	06076-86250-2	U.S.A.	1998	10.99
Deep Purple	Abandon	CD	Teichiku	TECW25754	Japan	1998	13.99
Deep Purple	And Friends	2CD	Snapper	SMD-CD-475	England	2003	12.99
Deep Purple	Anthology	2CD	EMI	0777-7-96129-2-5	Germany	1991	14.99
Deep Purple	Anthology	2CD	Warner Bros.	WPCR-2113/4	Japan	1991	29.99
Deep Purple	Archive Alive	2CD	Archive	ACH-80003	U.S.A.	1999	14.99
Deep Purple	Bananas	CD	Sanctuary	06076-86351	U.S.A.	2003	8.99
Deep Purple	Bananas	CD	Toshiba-EMI	TOCP-66216	Japan	2003	24.99
Deep Purple	Bananas	CD	EMI	7243-5-91048-2-9	Germany	2003	8.99
Deep Purple	Bananas (Acetate Promo)	CD	Capitol	07243-5910492-8	England	2003	19.99
Deep Purple	Black Night	CD Single	Warner Bros.	WPCR-1583	Japan	1997	12.99
Deep Purple	Book Of Taliesyn	CD	Teichiku	TECW-21865	Japan	1999	24.99
Deep Purple	Book Of Taliesyn + 5	Mini Lp	Purple	VPCK-85321	Japan	2003	19.99
Deep Purple	Burn	CD	Warner Bros.	WPCR-872	Japan	1996	24.99
Deep Purple	Burn	CD	Warner Bros.	2-2766	U.S.A.	1987	16.99
Deep Purple	Burn (Gold Cd)	CD	Warner Bros.	WPCR-10194	Japan	1999	24.99
Deep Purple	California Jam 1974	Mini Lp	Purple	VPCK-85318	Japan	2003	24.99
Deep Purple	California Jamming (Live At The C J)	CD	EMI	7243-8-38334-2-9	England	1996	8.99
Deep Purple	Child In Time	CD	Karussell	551-339-2	Germany	1998	7.99
Deep Purple	Come Hell Or High Water	CD	Varese	VSD-1011	U.S.A.	1994	10.99
Deep Purple	Come Hell Or High Water + 3	CD	BMG Victor	BVCP-7478	Japan	1997	24.99
Deep Purple	Come Taste The Band	CD	EMI	7-94032-2	England	1990	16.99
Deep Purple	Come Taste The Band	CD	Warner Bros.	WPCR-874	Japan	1996	24.99
Deep Purple	Concerto for Group and Orchestra	CD	Warner Bros.	WPCR-864	Japan	1996	24.99
Deep Purple	Days May Come & Days May Go	CD	Purple	PUR-303DJ	England	2000	9.99
Deep Purple	Days May Come And Days May Go	Mini Lp	Purple	VPCK-85324	Japan	2003	24.99
Deep Purple	Deep Purple + 5	CD	EMI	7243-5-21597-2-7	EU	2000	10.99
Deep Purple	Fireball	CD Single	Warner Bros.	WPCR-1585	Japan	1997	12.99

D

Artist	Title	Format	Label	Catalog No	Country	Released	Value
Deep Purple	Fireball	CD	Warner Bros.	WPCR-866	Japan	1996	24.99
Deep Purple	Fireball (Gold Cd)	CD	Warner Bros.	WPCR-10191	Japan	1999	24.99
Deep Purple	Fireball + 9	CD	Rhino	R2-75651	U.S.A.	1996	18.99
Deep Purple	Gemini Suite Live	CD	Teichiku	TECX-23982	Japan	1996	25.99
Deep Purple	Gemini Suite Live	CD	Purple	PUR-204	England	1998	12.99
Deep Purple	Gemini Suite Live	Mini Lp	Purple	VPCK-85319	Japan	2003	24.99
Deep Purple	Highway Star	CD Single	Warner Bros.	WPCR-1587	Japan	1996	12.99
Deep Purple	Highway Star (3")	CD Single	Warner Bros.	WPDP-6342	Japan	1993	12.99
Deep Purple	House Of Blue Light	CD	Polydor	POCP-2646	Japan	1999	24.99
Deep Purple	House Of Blue Light	CD	Mercury	3145-46162-2	U.S.A.	1999	9.99
Deep Purple	In Absence Of Pink (Knebworth '85)	2CD	Connoisseur	DP-VSOP-CD-163	England	1991	19.99
Deep Purple	In Concert	2CD	Teichiku	TECX-28867/8	Japan	1999	39.99
Deep Purple	In Concert	2 Mini Lp	Purple	VPCK-85316	Japan	2003	29.99
Deep Purple	In Concert (Gold Cd)	2CD	Teichiku	TECP-50175-6	Japan	1990	159.99
Deep Purple	In Concert (Potrait LP)	CD	Rhino	R2-38050	U.S.A.	1981	14.99
Deep Purple	In Concert + 2	2CD	Spitfire	SPT-15069-2	U.S.A.	2001	15.99
Deep Purple	In Profile	CD	EMI	7234-4-95635-2-0	England	2000	7.99
Deep Purple	In Rock	CD	Warner Bros.	WPCR-865	Japan	1996	24.99
Deep Purple	In Rock (Gold Cd)	CD	Warner Bros.	WPCR-10190	Japan	1999	24.99
Deep Purple	In Rock + 12 (25th Anniversary Edition)	2CD	EMI	7243-8-34019-2-5	Germany	1995	15.99
Deep Purple	Inglewood: Live at the Forum	CD	Sonic Zoom	PUR-205	England	2002	13.99
Deep Purple	Interview Cd (Promo)	CD	EMI	CDP-519-973	Holland	1998	19.99
Deep Purple	Just Might Take Your Life	CD	Sonic Zoom	PUR-208	England	2002	9.99
Deep Purple	KBFH: In Concert + 4	2CD	King Biscuit	70710-88002-2-7	U.S.A.	1995	17.99
Deep Purple	Kneel And Pray	CD	Sonic Zoom	PUR-207	England	2002	12.99
Deep Purple	Lady Double Dealer	CD Single	Warner Bros.	WPCR-1591	Japan	1997	12.99
Deep Purple	Last Concert In Japan	CD	Warner Bros.	WPCR-876	Japan	1996	24.99
Deep Purple	Listen, Learn, Read On Box Set	6CD	EMI	7243-5-40973-2-4	Germany	2002	49.99
Deep Purple	Live & Rare (Scandanavian Nights)	2CD	Relativity	88561-1136-2	U.S.A.	1992	12.99
Deep Purple	Live At Royal Albert Hall	CD	Eagle	6-70211-5068-2	U.S.A.	1999	9.99
Deep Purple	Live At Royal Albert Hall	2CD	Polydor	POCP-7445/6	Japan	1999	34.99
Deep Purple	Live At The California Jam	CD	BMG	71278-60025-2	U.S.A.	1996	21.99
Deep Purple	Live At The California Jam	CD	Teichiku	TECW-25318	Japan	1996	24.99
Deep Purple	Live At The Olympia	2CD	EMI	7243-85798-2-2	England	1997	14.99
Deep Purple	Live At The Olympia '96	2CD	Teichiku	TECW-35568/9	Japan	1997	34.99
Deep Purple	Live At The Olympia '96	2CD	EMI	7243-8-57982-2-1	Holland	1997	18.99
Deep Purple	Live In Calif/Long Beach Arena 1976	2 Mini Lp	Purple	VPCK-85327	Japan	2003	29.99
Deep Purple	Live In Denmark '72	CD	Sonic Zoom	PUR-203	England	2002	17.99
Deep Purple	Live In Denmark '72	2 Mini Lp	Purple	VPCK-85317	Japan	2003	29.99
Deep Purple	Live In Japan	CD	Warner Bros.	WPCR-868	Japan	1996	24.99
Deep Purple	Live In Japan	3CD	Warner Bros.	WPCR-677/8/9	Japan	1996	47.99
Deep Purple	Live In Japan (Gold Cd)	CD	Warner Bros.	WPCR-10193	Japan	1999	24.99
Deep Purple	Live In Japan: 21st Ann Collectors	3CD	EMI	7243-8-27726-2-0	Holland	1993	39.99
Deep Purple	Live In London	CD	Teichiku	TECP-30170	Japan	1990	17.99
Deep Purple	Live In London 1974	2 Mini Lp	Purple	VPCK-85325	Japan	2003	29.99
Deep Purple	Live In Stockholm 1970	2 Mini Lp	Purple	VPCK-85323	Japan	2003	29.99
Deep Purple	Machine Head	DVD Aud	Rhino	R2-76664	U.S.A.	2002	14.99
Deep Purple	Machine Head	CD	Warner Bros.	WPCR-867	Japan	1996	24.99
Deep Purple	Machine Head - 25th Ann. Ed. + 8	2CD	Rhino	R2-75622	U.S.A.	1998	15.99
Deep Purple	Machine Head (Gold Cd)	CD	Warner Bros.	WPCR-10192	Japan	1999	24.99
Deep Purple	Made In Europe	CD	Warner Bros.	WPCR-875	Japan	1996	24.99
Deep Purple	Made In Europe	CD	EMI	CDP-7-93796-2	England	1990	8.99
Deep Purple	Made In Japan	2CD	Warner Bros.	WPCR-1578/9	Japan	1997	39.99
Deep Purple	Made In Japan (DCC Gold Cd)	CD	DCC	GZS-1120	U.S.A.	1996	49.99
Deep Purple	Made In Japan + 3 (Encores)	2CD	EMI	7243-8-57864-2-6	Holland	1998	11.99
Deep Purple	Mark III - The Final Concerts	2CD	Teichiku	TECX-35234-5	Japan	1990	39.99
Deep Purple	Never Before	CD Single	Warner Bros.	WPCR-1586	Japan	1997	12.99
Deep Purple	New Live & Rare	CD	Sonic Zoom	PUR-209	England	2003	9.99

D

Artist	Title	Format	Label	Catalog No	Country	Released	Value
Deep Purple	New, Live & Rare	CD	Teichiku	TECX-20509	Japan	2001	24.99
Deep Purple	New, Live & Rare - Bootleg Coll. '84-'00	12 CD	Thompson Thames	DPBSCD001	Australia	2001	89.99
Deep Purple	Nobody's Perfect + 3	2CD	Mercury	3145-46128-2	U.S.A.	1999	10.99
Deep Purple	On The Wings Of A Russian Foxbat	2CD	Teichiku	TECX-35042-3	Japan	1990	29.99
Deep Purple	Perfect Strangers + 2	CD	Polydor	POCP-2645	Japan	1999	24.99
Deep Purple	Perfect Strangers + 2	CD	Mercury	3145-46045-2	U.S.A.	1999	10.99
Deep Purple	Perfect Strangers + 3	2CD	Polydor	POCP-2649/50	Japan	2000	34.99
Deep Purple	Perk And Tit	CD	Sonic Zoom	PUR-206	England	2002	17.99
Deep Purple	Powerhouse	CD	Warner Bros.	WPCR-871	Japan	1996	24.99
Deep Purple	Purpendicular	CD	BMG Victor	BVCM-35013	Japan	1999	29.99
Deep Purple	Purpendicular	CD	CMC INT.	CMC-1001-2	U.S.A.	1996	8.99
Deep Purple	Purpendicular (Promo)	CD	BMG	DP-001	England	1996	49.99
Deep Purple	Purpendicular + 1	CD	BMG Victor	BVCP-913	Japan	1996	24.99
Deep Purple	Purple Passages (Best Of 1st 4 Lps)	CD	Warner Bros.	WPCP-5696	Japan	1972	29.99
Deep Purple	Purplexed	CD	BMG Victor	BVCM-31015	Japan	1998	24.99
Deep Purple	Scandanavian Nights	2CD	Teichiku	TECX-30919-20	Japan	1990	39.99
Deep Purple	Scandanavian Nights	2CD	Spitfire	SPT-15066-2	U.S.A.	2001	13.99
Deep Purple	Scandinavian Nights	2CD	Connoisseur	DP-VSOP-CD125	England	1972	11.99
Deep Purple	Self Titled	CD	Warner Bros.	WPCR-863	Japan	1996	24.99
Deep Purple	Self Titled (3rd Lp)	CD	Teichiku	TECW-21866	Japan	1999	24.99
Deep Purple	Self Titled + 5	Mini Lp	Purple	VPCK-85322	Japan	2003	19.99
Deep Purple	Shades 1968-1998 Box Set	4CD	Rhino	R2-75566	U.S.A.	1999	29.99
Deep Purple	Shades Of	CD	Teichiku	TECW-21864	Japan	1999	24.99
Deep Purple	Shades Of + 5	Mini Lp	Purple	VPCK-85320	Japan	2003	19.99
Deep Purple	Shades Of Deep Purple + 5	CD	EMI	7243-4-98336-2-3	EU	2000	12.99
Deep Purple	Singles A's & B's	CD	Warner Bros.	WPCR-2115	Japan	1993	24.99
Deep Purple	Slaves & Masters	CD	RCA	2421-2-R	U.S.A.	1990	10.99
Deep Purple	Slaves & Masters	CD	BMG Victor	BVCM-35012	Japan	1999	12.99
Deep Purple	Slaves & Masters	CD	BMG	74321-87192-1	Germany	2000	8.99
Deep Purple	Space Vols 1 & 2 (H Bomb)	2CD	Sonic Zoom	PUR-202	England	2001	10.99
Deep Purple	Special Gold Edition Box Set	2CD	EMI	EKPD-0733	Korea	1998	34.99
Deep Purple	Stormbringer	CD	EMI	0777-7-91084-2-8	England	1974	15.99
Deep Purple	Stormbringer	CD	Warner Bros.	WPCR-873	Japan	1996	24.99
Deep Purple	Strange Kind Of Woman	CD Single	Warner Bros.	WPCR-1584	Japan	1997	12.99
Deep Purple	The Battle Rages On..	CD	Giant	9-24517-2	U.S.A.	1993	7.99
Deep Purple	The Battle Rages On..	CD	BMG Victor	BVCP-7419	Japan	1995	29.99
Deep Purple	The Battle Rages On...(Pink/Promo)	CD	Giant	2-24517-A	U.S.A.	1993	24.99
Deep Purple	The Book Of Taliesyn + 5	CD	EMI	7243-5-21608-2-2	EU	2000	16.99
Deep Purple	The Deep Purple Family Album	CD	Connoisseur	RP-VSOP-CD-187	England	1993	8.99
Deep Purple	The Gemini Suite - Live (Gold Cd)	CD	Purple Pyramid	CLP-0234-2	U.S.A.	1998	14.99
Deep Purple	The Very Best	CD	Rhino	R3-79799	U.S.A.	2000	7.99
Deep Purple	This Time Around - Live Tokyo (Ltd Ed)	2CD	Purple	PUR-321IDLES	England	2001	24.99
Deep Purple	This Time Around Live In Tokyo 75	2 Mini Lp	Purple	VPCK-85326	Japan	2003	29.99
Deep Purple	Total Abandon - Live In Australia '99	2CD	Thompson Thames	DPTA-20-4-99	England	2001	18.99
Deep Purple	Total Abandon - Live In Australia '99	2CD	Thompson Thames	9-327066-000029	Australia	2000	18.99
Deep Purple	Under The Gun	CD	Spectrum	544-204-2	England	2001	8.99
Deep Purple	When We Rock...	CD	Warner Bros.	WPCR-877	Japan	1996	24.99
Deep Purple	Who Do We Think We Are	CD	Warner Bros.	WPCR-869	Japan	1996	24.99
Deep Purple	Who Do We Think We Are + 7	CD	EMI	7243-5-21607-2-3	EU	2000	12.99
Deep Purple	Who Do We Think We Are + 7	CD	Warner Bros.	WPCR-10885	Japan	2001	24.99
Deep Purple	Who Do We Think We Are + 7	CD	Rhino	R2-75652	U.S.A.	2002	13.99
Deep Purple	Woman From Tokyo	CD Single	Warner Bros.	WPCR-1588	Japan	1997	12.99
Deep Purple	You Keep On Moving	CD Single	Warner Bros.	WPCR-1592	Japan	1997	12.99
Deep Purple/Bernie Marsden	Alaska: Live Baked Alaska	CD	Zoom Club	ZCRCD46	England	2002	10.99
Deep Purple/Bernie Marsden	Alaska: The Bronze Years	CD	Castle	82310-72003-2-2	U.S.A.	2000	10.99
Deep Purple/Bernie Marsden	And About Time Too (W/Bonus)	CD	Purple	PUR-313	England	1999	11.99
Deep Purple/Bernie Marsden	Blues & Green	CD	Castle	CLACD-181	England	2001	11.99
Deep Purple/Bernie Marsden	Look At Me Now (W/Bonus)	CD	RPM	RPM-153	England	1996	11.99

Artist	Title	Format	Label	Catalog No	Country	Released	Value
Deep Purple/Bernie Marsden	The Friday Rock Sessions	CD	Raw Fruit	FRSCD007	England	1992	14.99
Deep Purple/Malcolm Arnold	Concerto For Group And Orchestra + 5	2CD	Harvest	07243-541006-2-8	England	2002	12.99
Deep Purple/Malcolm Arnold	Concerto For Group And Orchestra + 5	DVD Aud	Rhino	R2-73927	U.S.A.	2003	14.99
Def Leppard	Adrenalize	CD	Mercury	314-512-185-2	U.S.A.	1992	8.99
Def Leppard	Euphoria	CD	Mercury	314-546-212-2	U.S.A.	1999	8.99
Def Leppard	High 'N' Dry	CD	Mercury	818-836-2	U.S.A.	1990	8.99
Def Leppard	Hysteria	CD	Mercury	830-675-2	U.S.A.	1990	8.99
Def Leppard	On Through The Night	CD	Mercury	822-533-2	U.S.A.	1990	8.99
Def Leppard	Pyromania	CD	Mercury	810-308-2	U.S.A.	1990	8.99
Def Leppard	Pyromania (MFSL Gold)	CD	Mobile Fidelity	UDCD-520	U.S.A.	1983	34.99
Def Leppard	Retro-Active	CD	Mercury	314-518-305-2	U.S.A.	1993	8.99
Def Leppard	Rock Vault	2CD	Mercury	MECD-1008-2	U.S.A.	1999	16.99
Def Leppard	Slang	CD	Mercury	314-532-486-2	U.S.A.	1996	8.99
Def Leppard	Vault	CD	Mercury	314-528-815-2	U.S.A.	1995	8.99
Def Leppard	X	CD	Island	440-063-121-2	U.S.A.	2002	9.99
Delmoni, Arturo	Songs My Mother...(MFSL Aluminum)	CD	Mobile Fidelity	MFCD-687	U.S.A.	1990	55.99
Denaro	Denaro	CD	Line	LICD-9.01279-0	Germany	1992	10.99
Denny, Sandy	"Listen Listen" An Introduction To	CD	Island	IMCD-253	England	1999	11.99
Denny, Sandy	20th Century Masters: The Millennium	CD	A&M	440-063-314-2	U.S.A.	2002	8.99
Denny, Sandy	BBC Sessions: '71 - '73 (Withdrawn)	CD	Strange Fruit	SFRSCD006	England	1997	109.99
Denny, Sandy	Gold Dust: Live At The Royalty	CD	Island	IMCD-252	England	1998	8.99
Denny, Sandy	Like An Old Fashioned Waltz	CD	Hannibal	HNCD-4425	U.S.A.	1991	67.99
Denny, Sandy	No More Sad Refrains: The Anth.	2CD	A&M	314542-747-2	U.S.A.	2000	12.99
Denny, Sandy	No More Sad Refrains: The Anth.	2CD	Island	CRNCD7	England	2000	14.99
Denny, Sandy	Rendezvous	CD	Hannibal	HNCD-4423	U.S.A.	1991	24.99
Denny, Sandy	Sandy	CD	Island	IMCD-132	England	1972	14.99
Denny, Sandy	Sandy Denny (The Original)	CD	Disky	SI-905319	Holland	2003	9.99
Denny, Sandy	The Best	CD	Hannibal	HNCD-1328	U.S.A.	1987	10.99
Denny, Sandy	The Best Of	CD	Island	IMCD-217	England	1996	12.99
Denny, Sandy	The North Star Grassman/Ravens	CD	Hannibal	HNCD-4429	U.S.A.	1987	16.99
Denny, Sandy	The Original Sandy Denny	CD	Mooncrest	CRESTCD-002	England	1991	12.99
Denny, Sandy	Who Knows Where The Time Goes	3CD	Hannibal	HNCD-5301	U.S.A.	1985	38.99
Denny, Sandy/Fotheringay	Fotheringay	CD	Hannibal	HNCD-4426	U.S.A.	1991	24.99
Denny, Sandy/Ian Matthews	No Grey Faith... Song Of	CD	Perfect Pitch	PP007	England	2000	24.99
Denny, Sandy/Strawbs	Sandy Denny And The Strawbs	CD	Hannibal	HNCD-1361	U.S.A.	1991	24.99
Denny, Sandy/T. Lucas	The Attic Tracks 1972-1984	CD	Raven	RVCD-46	Australia	1995	13.99
Denver, John	Aerie	CD	BMG	BVCP-7490	Japan	1997	27.99
Denver, John	An Evening With John Denver + 6	2CD	RCA	07863-69353-2	U.S.A.	2001	20.99
Denver, John	The Country Roads Collection Box Set	4CD	RCA	07863-67437-2	U.S.A.	1997	43.99
Denver, John	The Rocky Mountain Collection	2CD	RCA	07863-66837-2	U.S.A.	1996	14.99
Depeche Mode	A Broken Frame	CD	Warner Bros.	18P2-2676	Japan	1989	35.99
Depeche Mode	Barrel Of A Gun	CD Single	Reprise	9-43828-2	U.S.A.	1997	5.99
Depeche Mode	Barrel Of A Gun (Promo)	CD Single	Reprise	PRO-CD-8600	U.S.A.	1997	19.99
Depeche Mode	Behind The Wheel (Remixes)	CD	Sire	PRO-CD-2953	U.S.A.	1987	91.99
Depeche Mode	Black Celebration	CD	Alfa	ALCB-64	Japan	1990	105.99
Depeche Mode	Blasphemous Rumours	CD Single	Reprise	9-40300-2	U.S.A.	1991	5.99
Depeche Mode	Condemnation	CD	Alfa	ALCB-848	Japan	1993	35.99
Depeche Mode	Enjoy The Silence (3")	CD Single	Alfa	ALDB-19	Japan	1990	89.99
Depeche Mode	Enjoy The Silence (Promo)	CD Single	Alfa	Y12-3B	Japan	1990	44.99
Depeche Mode	Exciter	CD	Reprise	9-47960-2	U.S.A.	2001	8.99
Depeche Mode	Exciter (Watermarked Cdr/Promo)	CD	Reprise	2-47960	U.S.A.	2001	34.99
Depeche Mode	For The Masses:Tribute	CD	1500	31454-0919-2	U.S.A.	1998	12.99
Depeche Mode	I Feel You (Maxi-Single) Black Cover	CD Single	Sire	9-40784-2	U.S.A.	1993	6.99
Depeche Mode	I Feel You (Silver Cover)	CD Single	Sire	9-40767-2	U.S.A.	1993	6.99
Depeche Mode	It's No Good (2)	CD Single	Mute	LCD-BONG-26.	England	1997	4.99
Depeche Mode	Music For the Masses	CD	Mute	32XB-195	Japan	1987	36.99
Depeche Mode	Music For The Masses (Promo)	CD	Mute	CDSTUMM-47	England	1987	14.99
Depeche Mode	Never Let Me Down Again	CD Single	Sire	9-40329-2	U.S.A.	1991	6.99

D

Artist	Title	Format	Label	Catalog No	Country	Released	Value
Depeche Mode	Only When I Loose Myself (Green)	CD Single	Mute	XLCDBONG29	England	1998	7.99
Depeche Mode	Only When I Lose Myself (Silver)	CD Single	Mute	LCDBONG29	England	1998	7.99
Depeche Mode	Only When I Lose Myself (Yellow)	CD Single	Mute	CDBONG29	England	1998	7.99
Depeche Mode	Personal Jesus	CD Single	Sire	9-21328-2	U.S.A.	1989	10.99
Depeche Mode	Policy Of Truth	CD Single	Sire	9-21534-2	U.S.A.	1990	7.99
Depeche Mode	Pro-CD-5192 (Selections DJ/Box 1/2)	CD	Reprise	PRO-CD-5192	U.S.A.	1998	23.99
Depeche Mode	Pro-CD-5242 (Selections Promo Box 3)	CD	Reprise	PRO-CD-5242	U.S.A.	1998	23.99
Depeche Mode	Singles 1986-1998 (W/Bonus Cd)	3CD	Reprise	9-47110-2	U.S.A.	1998	30.99
Depeche Mode	Some Great Reward	CD	Alfa	ALCB-63	Japan	1990	105.99
Depeche Mode	Songs Of Faith And Devotion	CD	Sire	9-45243-2	U.S.A.	1993	6.99
Depeche Mode	Songs Of Faith And Devotion (Live)	CD	Alfa	ALCB-892	Japan	1993	60.99
Depeche Mode	Songs Of Faith And Devotion Live	CD	Sire	9-45505-2	U.S.A.	1993	5.99
Depeche Mode	Speak & Spell	CD	Warner Bros.	18P2-2675	Japan	1989	26.99
Depeche Mode	Summer Tour '94 Cd Sampler	CD	Sire	PRO-CD-6950	U.S.A.	1994	169.99
Depeche Mode	The Singles 81>85	CD	Reprise	9-47298-2	U.S.A.	1985	7.99
Depeche Mode	Violater + 8	2CD	Alfa	ALCB-33	Japan	1990	199.99
Depeche Mode	X 1 (Ltd Ed) Box Set	4CD	Alfa	ALCB-201-4	Japan	1991	139.99
Depeche Mode	X 2 (Ltd Ed) Box Set	4CD	Alfa	ALCB-205-8	Japan	1991	86.99
Der KFC	...Letzte Hoffnung	CD	Line	DKCD-9.00883-0	Germany	1990	14.99
Der KFC	Knülle Im Politbüro	CD	Line	DKCD-9.00949-0	Germany	1990	14.99
Derek And the Dominos	In Concert (MFSL Gold Cd)	2CD	Mobile Fidelity	UDCD-2-660	U.S.A.	1973	41.99
Derek And the Dominos	Layla & Other... (MFSL Gold Cd)	CD	Mobile Fidelity	UDCD-585	U.S.A.	1970	49.99
Derek And the Dominos	Live At The Fillmore	2CD	PolyGram	314-521-682-2	U.S.A.	1994	10.99
Derek And the Dominos	The Layla Sessions Box Set	3CD	Polydor	847-083-2	U.S.A.	1990	29.99
Derringer, Rick	All American Boy	CD	Blue Sky	ZK-32481	U.S.A.	1990	8.99
Derringer, Rick	All American Boy/Spring Fever	CD	BGO	BGOCD549	England	2002	13.99
Derringer, Rick	Archive Alive	CD	Archive	ACH-80012	U.S.A.	1997	8.99
Derringer, Rick	Back To The Blues	CD	Shrapnel	BB-2008-2	U.S.A.	1993	8.99
Derringer, Rick	Blues Deluxe	CD	Shrapnel	BB-2039-2	U.S.A.	1998	8.99
Derringer, Rick	Derringer	CD	Blue Sky	ZK-34181	U.S.A.	1976	7.99
Derringer, Rick	Derringer/Sweet Evil	CD	BGO	BGOCD586	England	2004	13.99
Derringer, Rick	Electra Blues	CD	Shrapnel	BB-2023-2	U.S.A.	1994	8.99
Derringer, Rick	Free Ride	CD	Beyond	398-578-284-2	U.S.A.	2002	7.99
Derringer, Rick	Greatest And Latest	CD	Purple Pyramid	CLP-1305-2	U.S.A.	2003	7.99
Derringer, Rick	Guitars And Women + 2	CD	Razor & Tie	82170-2	U.S.A.	1998	7.99
Derringer, Rick	Jackhammer Blues	CD	Shrapnel	BB-2043-2	U.S.A.	2000	9.99
Derringer, Rick	Live Paradise Theater July 7, 1978	CD	Phoenix Rising	4004	U.S.A.	2000	8.99
Derringer, Rick	Rick Derringer & Friends (Ian Hunter)	CD	King Biscuit	KBD-88036	U.S.A.	1998	12.99
Derringer, Rick	Rock & Roll Hoochie Coo: The Best Of	CD	Epic	EK-57166	U.S.A.	1996	8.99
Derringer, Rick	Spring Fever	CD	Sony	SICP-8012	U.S.A.	2002	20.99
Derringer, Rick	Tend The Fire	CD	Code Blue	AMCE-2061	Japan	1996	28.99
Derringer, Rick/DBA	DBA (W/Tim Bogert/Carmen Appice)	CD	SPV	SPV08572202CD	Germany	2000	12.99
Des Barres, Michael	Somebody Up There Likes Me	CD	Victor Ent.	VDP-1126	Japan	1986	34.99
DeShannon, Jackie	Dancer/Quick Touches	CD	Line	LICD-9.00495-0	Germany	1989	41.99
Deviants	#3	CD	Captain Trip	CTCD-061	Japan	1969	12.99
Deviants	Barbarian Princes	CD	Captain Trip	CTCD-189	Japan	1999	14.99
Deviants	Disposable	CD	Captain Trip	CTCD-042	Japan	1968	14.99
Deviants	Dr. Crow	CD	Track	TRK-1020CD	England	2000	9.99
Deviants	Have Left The Planet	CD	Captain Trip	CTCD-163	Japan	1999	12.99
Deviants	Human Garbage (Live '84)	CD	Captain Trip	CTCD-092	Japan	1984	11.99
Deviants	Ptooff! (Limited 1000)	CD	Captain Trip	CTCD-311	Japan	2000	12.99
Deviants	The Deviants	CD	Line	TACD-9.00619-0	Germany	1988	12.99
Deviants/IXVI	Eating Jello With A Heated Folk	CD	Captain Trip	CTCD-355	Japan	1996	11.99
Deviants/Mick Farren	Fragments of Broken Probes	CD	Captain Trip	CTCD-046	Japan	1992	12.99
Deviants/Mick Farren	Mona The Carnovorous Circus	CD	Captain Trip	CTCD-175	Japan	1969	11.99
Deviants/Mick Farren	Mona The Carnovorous Circus	CD	Line	TACD-9.00620-0	Germany	1988	14.99
Deviants/Mick Farren	Vampires Stole My Lunch Money	CD	Captain Trip	CTCD-103	Japan	1978	12.99
Deviants/Mick Farren	Vampires Stole My Lunch Money	CD	Line	TACD-9.00628-0	Germany	1988	14.99

D

Artist	Title	Format	Label	Catalog No	Country	Released	Value
DeVille, Mink	Cabretta/Return To Magenta	CD	Raven	RVCD-59	Australia	1997	13.99
DeVille, Mink	Cadillac Walk: Mink DeVille Collection	CD	EMI	535016-2	England	2001	10.99
DeVille, Mink	Coup de Grace/Where Angels Fear To T	CD	Raven	RVCD-75	Australia	1998	13.99
DeVille, Mink	La Chat Bleu + 10	CD	Raven	RVCD-131	Australia	2003	13.99
DeVille, Mink	Savoir Faire	CD	Capitol	0777-7-48854-2-3	Netherland	1981	11.99
DeVille, Mink	Spanish Stroll 1977-1987	CD	Raven	RVCD-32	Australia	1997	13.99
DeVille, Mink	Sportin' Life	CD	Polydor	825-776-2	Germany	1985	18.99
DeVille, Mink/Chet Atkins	Miracle + 3 (Prod By Mark Knopfler)	CD	Raven	RVCD-41	Australia	1997	13.99
DeVille, Mink/Willy	Backstreets Of Desire	CD	Rhino	R2-71686	U.S.A.	1994	14.99
DeVille, Mink/Willy	Best Of	CD	CNR Music	2004-475	Netherland	1999	10.99
DeVille, Mink/Willy	Big Easy Fantasy	CD	Wotre	WMD-122151	France	1996	10.99
DeVille, Mink/Willy	Horse Of A Different Color		East West	3984-26690-2	Germany	2001	10.99
DeVille, Mink/Willy	Les Inoubliables De Willy Deville	CD	Worte	WMD-592016	France	1995	10.99
DeVille, Mink/Willy	Live	CD	Worte	WMD-592254	France	2001	11.99
DeVille, Mink/Willy	Live Greatest Hits: '76 - '93	CD	East West	7243-8-94620-2-9	Germany	1997	10.99
DeVille, Mink/Willy	Loup Garou	CD	East West	0630-12456-2	Germany	1996	10.99
DeVille, Mink/Willy	Love & Emotion: The Atlantic Years	CD	Atlantic	7567-82958-2	Germany	2001	10.99
DeVille, Mink/Willy	Victory Mixture (W/Dr. John/A Toussaint	CD	Blue Moon	PG1003	England	2003	10.99
DeVille, Mink/Willy/Acou Trio	Live In Berlin	2CD	Eagle	EDG-CD-243	Germany	2003	14.99
Devils, The/Duran Duran	Dark Circles	CD	Fullfill	TPCD007	England	2002	14.99
Devils, The/Duran Duran	Dark Circles + 1	CD	Cutting Edge	CTCR-18062	Japan	2003	29.99
Devils, The/Duran Duran	How I Learned To Stop...	CD	In At The Deep End	IATDE-010	England	2003	14.99
DeVito, Karla	Is This A Cool World... + 30 Min. Int.	CD	Renaissance	RMED00108-2	U.S.A.	1996	13.99
Devo	Adventures Of The Smart Patrol	CD	Discovery	77034	U.S.A.	1996	8.99
Devo	Duty Now.../New Traditionalists	CD	Virgin	0777-7-86995-2-1	England	1993	16.99
Devo	E-Z Listening Disc	CD	Rykodisc	RCD-20031	U.S.A.	1987	17.99
Devo	Greatest Hits	CD	Warner Bros.	9-26449-2	U.S.A.	1990	7.99
Devo	Greatest Misses	CD	Warner Bros.	9-26450-2	U.S.A.	1990	8.99
Devo	Harcore Vol. 2	CD	Rykodisc	RCD-20208	U.S.A.	1991	24.99
Devo	Hardcore Vol. 1	CD	Rykodisc	RCD-10188	U.S.A.	1990	24.99
Devo	Live (Ltd. Ed.)	CD	Rhino	RHM2-7708	U.S.A.	1999	24.99
Devo	Live: The Mongoloid Years	CD	Rykodisc	RCD-20209	U.S.A.	1992	24.99
Devo	Oh No It's Devo / Freedom Of Choice	CD	Virgin	0777-7-86997-2-9	England	1993	16.99
Devo	Oh No! It's Devo + 6	CD	Infinite Zero	9-43204-2	U.S.A.	1995	23.99
Devo	Pioneers Who Got Scalped (Anthology)	2CD	Rhino	R2-75967	U.S.A.	2000	16.99
Devo	Post Post-Modern Man	CD Single	Enigma	7-75551-2	U.S.A.	1990	5.99
Devo	Q: Are We Not Men?...\ Devo Live	CD	Virgin	0777-7-86996-2-0	England	1993	19.99
Devo	Recombo DNA (Limited To 5000)	2CD	Rhino	RHM2-7718	U.S.A.	2000	39.99
Devo	Shout + 1	CD	Infinite Zero	9-43094-2	U.S.A.	1996	49.99
Devo	Smoothnoodlemaps	CD	Enigma	7-73526-2	U.S.A.	1990	8.99
Devo	The Essentials	CD	Rhino	R2-76037	U.S.A.	2002	11.99
Devo	Total Devo	CD	Restless	7-72756-2	U.S.A.	1988	12.99
Devoto, Howard	Jerky Versions 0f The Dream	CD	Virgin	CDV-2272	U.S.A.	1983	89.99
Diamond Head	Borrowed Time	CD	Warner Bros.	18P2-2746	Japan	1989	24.99
Diamond, Neil	Glory Road - 1968 To 1972	2CD	MCA	MCAD2-10502	U.S.A.	1992	11.99
Diamond, Neil	Greatest Hits 1966-1992	2CD	Columbia	C2K-52703	U.S.A.	1995	14.99
Diamond, Neil	His 12 Greatest Hits (Gold Cd)	CD	MCA	MCAD-10955	U.S.A.	1974	24.99
Diamond, Neil	Hot August Night (MFSL Gold Disc)	2CD	Mobile Fidelity	UDCD-2-584	U.S.A.	1972	84.99
Diamond, Neil	In My Lifetime Box Set	3CD	Columbia	C3K-65013	U.S.A.	1996	22.99
Diamond, Neil	Play Me: Complete UNI St. Recordings	2CD	MCA	088-112-824-2	U.S.A.	2002	17.99
Diamond, Neil	The Essential Neil Diamond	2CD	Columbia	C2K-85681	U.S.A.	2001	13.99
Diamond, Neil	The Neil Diamond Collection	CD	MCA	088-112-119-2	U.S.A.	1999	8.99
Dickies	Dawn Of The Dickies + 2	CD	Captain Oi	AHOY-CD-150	England	2001	12.99
Dickies	Incredible Shrinking Dickies + 6	CD	Captain Oi	AHOY-CD-149	England	2001	19.99
Dickies	Killer Klowns From Outer Space	CD	Enigma	D2-73322	U.S.A.	1988	11.99
Dickies	Road Kill	CD Single	Triple X	51149-2	U.S.A.	1993	7.99
Dickies	Second Coming	CD	Enigma	7-73289-2	U.S.A.	1989	7.99
Dictators	Bloodbrothers	CD	Dictators	DFFD-001	U.S.A.	1998	11.99

D

Artist	Title	Format	Label	Catalog No	Country	Released	Value
Dictators	D.F.F.D.	CD	Dictators	DFFD-002	U.S.A.	2001	9.99
Dictators	Go Girl Crazy	CD	Au-Go-Go	ANDA-105-CD	Australia	1975	9.99
Dictators	Manifest Destiny	CD	East West	AMCY-10073	Japan	2002	24.99
Dictators	New York New York (F*&K'em + 3)	CD	ROIR	RUSCD8247	U.S.A.	1998	8.99
Diddley, Bo	The London Bo Diddley Sessions	CD	MCA	CHD-9296	U.S.A.	1989	6.99
Die Engel Des Herrn/Neu!	Live! As; Hippie Punks	CD	Captain Trip	CTCD-012	Japan	1993	9.99
Die Engel Des Herrn/Neu!	Self Titled	CD	Captain Trip	CTCD-008	Japan	2000	9.99
Die Krupps	Foundation	CD	Captain Trip	CTCD-057	Japan	1981	14.99
Die Radierer	Eisbaren Und Zitronen	CD	Line	DKCD-9.51055-0	Germany	1991	14.99
Die With Dignity/La! Neu?	Kraut? (Dinger's Family)	CD	Captain Trip	CTCD-098	Japan	2000	19.99
Die Zimmermänner	1001 Wege Sex Zu Machen...	CD	Line	DKCD-9.51051-0	Germany	1991	14.99
Diesel Park West	All The Myths...	CD Single	Food	CDFOOD17	England	1989	7.99
Diesel Park West	Boy On Top (Ltd/4 Prints)	CD Single	Food	CDFOOD36	England	1992	18.99
Diesel Park West	Boy On Top...	CD Single	Food	CDFOOD36	England	1992	7.99
Diesel Park West	Cat Still Scratching	CD Single	Demon	DERV2CD	England	1993	7.99
Diesel Park West	Decency	CD	Food	FOODCD7	England	1992	24.99
Diesel Park West	Fall To Love	CD Single	Food	CDFOOD35	England	1992	6.99
Diesel Park West	Fall To Love (Ltd)	CD Single	Food	CDFOODS35	England	1992	10.99
Diesel Park West	Flipped	CD	Food	CDDPW1001	England	1990	24.99
Diesel Park West	Food X-Mas EP	CD Single	Food	CDFOOD23	England	1989	14.99
Diesel Park West	FreakGene	CD	Permanent	PERMCD29	England	1995	24.99
Diesel Park West	God Only Knows (CD 1)	CD Single	Food	CDFOODS39	England	1992	10.99
Diesel Park West	God Only Knows (CD 2)	CD Single	Food	CDFOOD39	England	1992	6.99
Diesel Park West	Jackie Is Still Sad	CD Single	Food	CDFOOD15	England	1988	9.99
Diesel Park West	Left Hand Band: The Very Best Of	CD	Chrysalis	CDCHRM105	England	1997	19.99
Diesel Park West	Like Princes Do	CD Single	Food	CDFOOD19	England	1989	9.99
Diesel Park West	Love It !	CD Single	Thunderbird	CSA-008	England	1998	7.99
Diesel Park West	Shakespeare Alabama + 2	CD	Food	FOODCD2	England	1989	24.99
Diesel Park West	Six Days To Juju	CD Single	Demon	DERVCD1	England	1993	7.99
Diesel Park West	Thought For Food	CD	Hypertension	0199-HYP	England	2000	14.99
Diesel Park West	Vs. Corporate Waltz	CD	Demon	FIEND-CD-747	England	1993	21.99
Diesel Park West	When The Hoodoo	CD Single	Food	CDFOOD20	England	1989	8.99
Diesel Park West/John Butler	So Real	CD	Source One	211	England	1997	8.99
Diesel Park West/John Butler	The Loyal Serpent	CD	Chrysalis	CDCHR-6128	England	1997	8.99
Diesel Park West/John Butler	Worthless B*stard Rock	CD	Mystic	MYS-CD-145	England	2003	14.99
Diesel Park West/MOBY1	Hip Replacement	CD	Thunderbird	CSA-115	England	1998	34.99
Diesel Park West/MOBY1	Hip Replacement Ltd Ed (S Al Demos)	CD	Thunderbird	CSA-115LE	England	1998	44.99
Dinger, Klaus/Dusseldorf/Neu!	Neondian	CD	Captain Trip	CTCD-016	Japan	1985	12.99
Dinger, Thomas/1-A Dusseldorf	D.J.F. (Lmtd 1000)	CD	Captain Trip	CTCD-251	Japan	2000	9.99
Dinger, Thomas/1-A Dusseldorf	Fettleber	CD	Captain Trip	CTCD-160	Japan	2000	9.99
Dinger, Thomas/1-A Dusseldorf	Konigreich Bilk	CD	Captain Trip	CTCD-201	Japan	2000	9.99
Dinger, Thomas/1-A Dusseldorf	Live (Lmtd 1000)	CD	Captain Trip	CTCD-305	Japan	2000	9.99
Dinger, Thomas/Neu!	Fur Mich + 2	CD	Captain Trip	CTCD-078	Japan	1982	16.99
Dinosaurs/Barry Melton	Dinosaurs (J Cippolina, M Saunders)	CD	Line	LICD-9.00661-0	Germany	1988	18.99
Dio	Angry Machines	CD	Spitfire	SPT-5021-2	U.S.A.	2000	7.99
Dio	Angry Machines	CD	Mayhem	11104-2	England	1996	10.99
Dio	Angry Machines + 1	CD	Polygram K.K.	PHCR-1467	Japan	1996	27.99
Dio	Born On The Sun (Promo)	CD Single	Reprise	PRO-CD-4360	U.S.A.	1990	5.99
Dio	Diamonds: The Best Of	CD	Vertigo	512-206-2	England	1992	13.99
Dio	Diamonds: The Best Of	CD	Universal	UICY-2571	Japan	2002	24.99
Dio	Dream Evil	CD	Warner Bros.	25612-2	U.S.A.	1987	7.99
Dio	Dream Evil	CD	Universal	UICY-3730	Japan	2002	23.99
Dio	Dream Evil	CD	Vertigo	832-530-2	Germany	1987	11.99
Dio	Evil Collection: The Very Best Of	CD	Mercury	7314-586-660-2	Germany	2002	12.99
Dio	Evilution (Promo)	CD Single	Reprise	PRO-CD-6760	U.S.A.	1994	5.99
Dio	Evilution (Promo)	CD Single	Reprise	PRO-CD-6855	U.S.A.	1994	5.99
Dio	Excerpts From Lock Up ... (DJ)	CD	Vertigo	DIOCD-1	England	1990	15.99
Dio	Hey Angel	CD Single	Vertigo	DIOCD-9	England	1990	7.99

D

Artist	Title	Format	Label	Catalog No	Country	Released	Value
Dio	Hey Angel (Promo)	CD Single	Reprise	PRO-CD-4476	U.S.A.	1990	5.99
Dio	Holy Diver	CD	Warner Bros.	9-23836-2	U.S.A.	1983	11.99
Dio	Holy Diver	CD	Universal	UICY-3727	Japan	2002	23.99
Dio	Inferno - Last In Live	CD	Mayhem	11115-2	England	1998	13.99
Dio	Inferno: The Last In Live	2CD	Spitfire	SPT-5022-2	U.S.A.	2000	16.99
Dio	Inferno: The Last In Live (W/Bonus)	2CD	Teichiku	TECW-35704~5	Japan	1998	34.99
Dio	Intermission	CD	Vertigo	PHCR-4126	Japan	1995	23.99
Dio	Intermission	CD	Vertigo	830-078-2	Germany	1992	16.99
Dio	Jesus, Mary/Holy Ghost (Promo)	CD Single	Reprise	PRO-CD-6914	U.S.A.	1994	5.99
Dio	Killing The Dragon	CD	Spitfire	SPT-15199-2	U.S.A.	2002	12.99
Dio	Killing The Dragon	CD	Victor Ent.	VCP-61916	Japan	2002	23.99
Dio	Lock Up The Wolves	CD	Reprise	9-26212-2	U.S.A.	1990	10.99
Dio	Lock Up The Wolves	CD	Vertigo	PHCR-4124	Japan	1995	23.99
Dio	Magica	CD	Spitfire	6-70211-5020-2	U.S.A.	2000	13.99
Dio	Magica + 1	CD	Polydor	POCP-7465	Japan	2000	23.99
Dio	Sacred Heart	CD	Universal	UICY-3729	Japan	2002	23.99
Dio	Sacred Heart	CD	Warner Bros.	25292-2	U.S.A.	1985	10.99
Dio	Stand Up And Shout: The Ant	2CD	Rhino	R2-73855	U.S.A.	2003	12.99
Dio	Strange Highways	CD	Reprise	45527-2	U.S.A.	1993	7.99
Dio	Strange Highways	CD	Vertigo	PHCR-4298	Japan	1996	23.99
Dio	Strange Highways	CD	Vertigo	518-486-2	England	1993	7.99
Dio	The Anthology Vol. 1	CD	Connoisseur	VSOP-CD-245	England	1997	12.99
Dio	The Anthology Vol. 2	CD	Connoisseur	VSOP-CD-338	England	2001	12.99
Dio	The Last In Line	CD	Universal	UICY-3728	Japan	2002	23.99
Dio	The Last In Line	CD	Warner Bros.	9-25100-2	U.S.A.	1984	10.99
Dio	The Master Series	CD	PolyGram	538-068-2	Germany	1998	9.99
Dio	Very Beast Of	CD	Rhino	R2-79983	U.S.A.	2001	7.99
Dio	Wild One (Promo)	CD Single	Reprise	PRO-CD-4080	U.S.A.	1990	5.99
Dion	Alone With Dion	CD	Line	BLCD-9.00801-L	Germany	1990	6.99
Dion	Best Of The Gospel Years	CD	ACE	CDCH-644	England	1997	12.99
Dion	Born To Be With You/ Streetheart + 1	CD	ACE	CDCHD-793	England	2001	18.99
Dion	Bronx Blues: (1962-1965)	CD	Columbia	CGK-46972	U.S.A.	1991	13.99
Dion	Greatest Hits	CD	Line	BLCD-9.01039-L	Germany	1991	9.99
Dion	Love Came To Me	CD	Line	BLCD-9.00773-L	Germany	1990	6.99
Dion	Return Of The Wanderer/Fire In..	CD	ACE	CDCH-936	England	1990	14.99
Dion	Rock N' Roll Christmas	CD	Right Stuff	0777-7-66718-2-6	U.S.A.	1993	7.99
Dion	Runaround Sue	CD	Line	BLCD-9.00973-L	Germany	1990	7.99
Dion	Runaround Sue: The Best	CD	ACE	CDCH-915	England	1988	10.99
Dion	Sanctuary/Suite For Late Summer + 3	CD	ACE	CDCHD-792	England	2001	17.99
Dion	Sit Down.../You're Not Alone + 1	CD	ACE	CDCHD-791	England	2001	17.99
Dion	The Road I'm On - A Retrospective	2CD	Columbia	C2K-64889	U.S.A.	1997	13.99
Dion	Yo Frankie	CD	Arista	ARCD-8549	U.S.A.	1989	6.99
Dion	Yo Frankie - Hall Of Fame DJ Sampler	CD Single	Arista	ASCD-9815	U.S.A.	1989	12.99
Dion /The Belmonts	Greatest Hits	CD	Line	BLCD-9.01033-L	Germany	1991	9.99
Dion /The Belmonts	Lovers Who Wander	CD	Line	BLCD-9.00758-L	Germany	1990	6.99
Dion /The Belmonts	Lovers Who Wander / So Why Didn't...	CD	ACE	CDCH-943	England	1998	12.99
Dion /The Belmonts	Presenting Dion And The Belmonts	CD	Line	BLCD-9.00981-L	Germany	1990	9.99
Dion /The Belmonts	Runaround Sue/Best Of The Rest	CD	ACE	CDCH-915	England	1998	14.99
Dion /The Belmonts	Wish Upon A Star	CD	Line	BLCD-9.00726-L	Germany	1990	6.99
Dion /The Belmonts	Wish Upon A Star/Alone With	CD	ACE	CDCH-945	England	1998	14.99
Dion, Celine	All The Way... A Decade Of Song	CD	Epic	EK-63760	U.S.A.	1999	8.99
Dion, Celine	Celine Dion	CD	Epic	EK-52473	U.S.A.	1992	6.99
Dion, Celine	Falling Into You	CD	Epic	BK-67541	U.S.A.	1996	8.99
Dion, Celine	It's All Coming Back To Me Now	CD Single	Columbia	663616-2	Austria	1996	5.99
Dion, Celine	Let's Talk About Love	CD	Epic	BK-68861	U.S.A.	1997	6.99
Dion, Celine	Only One Road	CD Single	Columbia	661450-2	Austria	1994	5.99
Dion, Celine	S'il Suffisait D'aimer	CD	Epic	BK-69679	U.S.A.	1998	9.99
Dion, Celine	The Colour Of My Love	CD	Epic	BK-57555	U.S.A.	1993	6.99

Artist	Title	Format	Label	Catalog No	Country	Released	Value
Dion, Celine	These Are Special Times (Xmas Cd)	CD	550 Music	BK-69523	U.S.A.	1998	8.99
Dion, Celine	Unison	CD	Epic	EK-46893	U.S.A.	1990	7.99
Dire Straits	Alchemy	2CD	Warner Bros.	9-25085-2	U.S.A.	1984	21.99
Dire Straits	Brothers Arms (1st Single/Only 20000)	CD Single	Vertigo	884-285-2	U.S.A.	1985	105.99
Dire Straits	Brothers In Arms	CD	Warner Bros.	9-47773-2	U.S.A.	2000	8.99
Dire Straits	Dire Straits	CD	Warner Bros.	9-47769-2	U.S.A.	2000	7.99
Dire Straits	Heavy Fuel (Hamburger)	CD Single	Vertigo	DSHAM-17	England	1991	14.99
Dire Straits	Live At The BBC	CD	Warner Bros.	9-460532-2	U.S.A.	1995	10.99
Dire Straits	Love Over Gold	CD	Warner Bros.	9-47772-2	U.S.A.	2000	8.99
Dire Straits	Making Movies	CD	Warner Bros.	9-47771-2	U.S.A.	2000	11.99
Dire Straits	On Every Street	CD	Warner Bros.	9-26680-2	U.S.A.	1991	7.99
Dire Straits	On The Night (Promo Sampler)	CD	Vertigo	SAMPLER-OTN1	Germany	1993	14.99
Dire Straits	Sultans of Swing + 7 (Limited Edition)	2CD	Vertigo	538-003-2	U.S.A.	1998	14.99
Dire-Straits	On The Night (Live)	CD	Warner Bros.	9-45259-2	U.S.A.	1993	7.99
Disney	Aladdin And The King Of Thieves	CD	Walt Disney	60924-7	U.S.A.	1996	5.99
Disney	Gumby (J Richman/Flo & Eddie)	CD	Buena Vista	CD-017	U.S.A.	1989	24.99
Disney	Stay Awake (Interp/Disney Songs)	CD	A&M	CD-3918	U.S.A.	1988	11.99
Disney/Alan Menken	Aladdin	CD	Walt Disney	CD-60846	U.S.A.	1992	7.99
Disney/Alan Menken	Beauty and the Beast	CD	Walt Disney	60618-2	U.S.A.	1991	11.99
Disney/Alan Menken	Beauty And The Beast (Pic Label)	CD	Walt Disney	60861-7	U.S.A.	1994	11.99
Disney/Alan Menken	El Jorobado De Neote Dame (Spanish)	CD	Walt Disney	67893-7	U.S.A.	1996	7.99
Disney/Alan Menken	Hunchback Of... (Picture Label Cd)	CD	Walt Disney	60893-7	U.S.A.	1996	11.99
Disney/Alan Menken	Pocahontas (Musicland Pic Cd)	CD	Walt Disney	60874-7	U.S.A.	1995	11.99
Disney/Alan Menken	The Little Mermaid	CD	Walt Disney	CD-018	U.S.A.	1989	15.99
Disney/All-4-One	Someday	CD Single	Walt Disney	HR-64012-2	U.S.A.	1996	4.99
Disney/Billy Joel	Oliver & Company	CD	Walt Disney	60890-7	U.S.A.	1995	7.99
Disney/Bruce Broughton	The Rescuers Down Under (O.S.T.)	CD	Walt Disney	60613-2	U.S.A.	1991	8.99
Disney/Churchill, Morey	Bambi	CD	Walt Disney	60880-7	U.S.A.	1996	9.99
Disney/Churchill, Morey	Snow White And The Seven Dwarfs	CD	Walt Disney	60850-7	U.S.A.	1993	11.99
Disney/Danny Elfman	Flubber (O.S.T.)	CD	Walt Disney	60952-7	U.S.A.	1997	6.99
Disney/Elton John, Tim Rice	Can You Feel The Love Tonight	CD Single	Hollywood	HR-64543-2	U.S.A.	1994	5.99
Disney/Elton John, Tim Rice	Can You Feel... (Promo Picture Label)	CD Single	Hollywood	PRCD-10441-2	U.S.A.	1994	12.99
Disney/Elton John, Tim Rice	Circle Of Life (Promo Picture)	CD Single	Hollywood	PRCD-10448-2	U.S.A.	1994	14.99
Disney/Elton John, Tim Rice	Lion King (Orig. B. Cast Picture Cd)	CD	Walt Disney	60802-7	U.S.A.	1997	16.99
Disney/Elton John, Tim Rice	The Lion King (Picture Label Cd)	CD	Walt Disney	60858-7	U.S.A.	1994	19.99
Disney/Fain, Cahn	Peter Pan + 2	CD	Walt Disney	60958-7	U.S.A.	1997	12.99
Disney/Harline, Smith	Pinocchio	CD	Walt Disney	60845-2	U.S.A.	1992	9.99
Disney/Hayley Mills	Let's Get Together	CD	Walt Disney	60407-7	U.S.A.	1998	16.99
Disney/Jennifer Rush	Colors/Wind (German/Pocahontas)	CD Single	Polydor	577-517-2	Germany	1995	14.99
Disney/Julie Andrews	Mary Poppins + 1	CD	Walt Disney	60615-7	U.S.A.	1997	15.99
Disney/K Mart	101 Dalmatians Picture CD Sampler	CD Single	Walt Disney	60382-7	U.S.A.	1997	7.99
Disney/Kathie Lee Gifford	Pooh's Grand Adventure	CD	Walt Disney	60619-7	U.S.A.	1997	7.99
Disney/Lea Salonga	Mulan (Picture Label Cd)	CD	Walt Disney	60631-7	U.S.A.	1998	12.99
Disney/Lebo M	Rhythm Of The Pride Lands	CD	Walt Disney	60871-7	U.S.A.	1995	7.99
Disney/Mannheim Steamroller	Meets The Mouse (Adv Disney Cd)	CD	Walt Disney	1023897	U.S.A.	1998	10.99
Disney/Maxi Priest	It Starts In The Heart (Jungle 2 Jungle)	CD Single	Walt Disney	03MS29400	U.S.A.	1997	2.99
Disney/McDonalds	Buddy Songs, Vol. 1	CD	Walt Disney	60374-7	U.S.A.	1996	7.99
Disney/McDonalds	Hero Songs, Vol. 3	CD	Walt Disney	60376-7	U.S.A.	1996	7.99
Disney/McDonalds	Rascal Songs, Vol. 2	CD	Walt Disney	60375-7	U.S.A.	1996	7.99
Disney/Michael Kamen	101 Dalmnations (O.S.T./G Close)	CD	Walt Disney	60911-7	U.S.A.	1996	7.99
Disney/Phil Collins	Strangers Like Me	CD Single	Walt Disney	D12187	Australia	1999	14.99
Disney/Phil Collins	Tarzan (Canadian O.S.T.)	CD	Walt Disney	DIS626457	Canada	1999	9.99
Disney/Phil Collins	Tarzan (German Enhanced O.S.T.)	CD	Edel	0105282DNY	Germany	1999	14.99
Disney/Phil Collins	Tarzan (Holographic Numbered Cd)	CD	Walt Disney	60020-7	U.S.A.	1999	9.99
Disney/Phil Collins	Tarzan (Italian O.S.T.)	CD	Sony	WDR-496492-2	Italy	1999	12.99
Disney/Phil Collins	Tarzan (O.S.T.)	CD	Walt Disney	60645-7	U.S.A.	1998	8.99
Disney/Phil Collins	Tarzan (Spanish O.S.T.)	CD	Walt Disney	67645-7	Spain	1999	15.99
Disney/Phil Collins	Tarzan (Taiwan With Bonus VCD)	2CD	Rock	20113	Taiwan	1998	19.99

D

Artist	Title	Format	Label	Catalog No	Country	Released	Value
Disney/Phil Collins	Two Worlds	CD Single	Avex	AVCW-12011	Japan	1999	46.99
Disney/Phil Collins	You'll Be In My Heart	CD Single	Avex	AVCW-12003	Japan	1999	46.99
Disney/Phil Collins	You'll Be In My Heart (Academy Cd)	CD Single	GKS Ent.	15917	U.S.A.	1999	49.99
Disney/Phil Collins	You'll Be in My Heart (Pic Disc)	CD	Walt Disney	60021-7	U.S.A.	1999	9.99
Disney/Phil Collins/M Mancina	Tarzan (Special Pop Up Edition)	CD	Disney	D24120	U.S.A.	1998	14.99
Disney/Pioneer Promo	Selections From Fantasia... (Promo Cd)	CD	Walt Disney	PR-CD1	U.S.A.	1990	49.99
Disney/Randy Edelman	Tall Tale (O.S.T.)	CD	Walt Disney	60867-7	U.S.A.	1995	13.99
Disney/Randy Newman	James/Giant Peach (Picture Label Cd)	CD	Walt Disney	60905-7	U.S.A.	1996	13.99
Disney/Sherman Brothers	Bedknobs and Broomsticks + 3 (O.S.T)	CD	Buena Vista	60784-7	U.S.A.	2002	8.99
Disney/Sherman Brothers	The Happiest Millionaire + 2 (O.S.T.)	CD	Buena Vista	60781-7	U.S.A.	2002	16.99
Disney/Sherman Brothers	The Jungle Book	CD	Walt Disney	60950-7	U.S.A.	1997	11.99
Disney/Sinbad	First Kid (O.S.T.)	CD	Walt Disney	60923-7	U.S.A.	1996	5.99
Disney/Stephen Endelman	Tom And Huck	CD	Walt Disney	60892-7	U.S.A.	1995	8.99
Disney/Sting	Emperor's New Groove (Academy Cd)	CD Single	Walt Disney	WDR-03MS36500	U.S.A.	2000	49.99
Disney/Sting	The Emperor's New Groove	CD	Walt Disney	60689-7	U.S.A.	2000	11.99
Disney/Various Artists	101 Dalmatians + 1	CD	Walt Disney	60654-7	U.S.A.	1998	8.99
Disney/Various Artists	75 Years Music And Memories Box Set	3CD	Walt Disney	70983-2	U.S.A.	1998	34.99
Disney/Various Artists	And The Winner Is...	CD	Walt Disney	60873-2	U.S.A.	1994	6.99
Disney/Various Artists	Classic Disney Collection Box Set	5CD	Walt Disney	70900-2	U.S.A.	1997	33.99
Disney/Various Artists	Dear Heart (Romantic Songs)	CD	Walt Disney	60042-7	U.S.A.	1991	6.99
Disney/Various Artists	Disney On Broadway (Promo)	CD	Walt Disney	60752-7	U.S.A.	2001	5.99
Disney/Various Artists	Disney Wonderful Christmas	CD	Avex	AVCW-12247	Japan	2001	19.99
Disney/Various Artists	Disney's Greatest Pop Hits	CD	Walt Disney	60637-2	U.S.A.	1998	12.99
Disney/Various Artists	For Our Children (Dylan, B. Wilson)	CD	Walt Disney	60616-2	U.S.A.	1991	22.99
Disney/Various Artists	Off/Album/Disneyland/Disney World	CD	Walt Disney	60820-2	U.S.A.	1991	49.99
Disney/Various Artists	Take A Song Along	CD	Walt Disney	60490-7	U.S.A.	1999	6.99
Disney/Various Artists	The Music Behind The Magic Box Set	4CD	Walt Disney	60014-7	U.S.A.	1994	19.99
Disney/Various Artists	The Music Of Disney Box Set	3CD	Walt Disney	60957-2	U.S.A.	1992	33.99
Disney/Various Artists	Tokyo Disneyland Xmas Fantasy 2001	CD	Avex	AVCW-12248	Japan	2001	19.99
Disney/Various Artists	Walt Disney Sampler '95 (Promo)	CD Single	Walt Disney	B50905-09	U.S.A.	1995	8.99
Dissidenten	Live In New York	CD	Line	OLCD-9.51094-X	Germany	1991	12.99
Distance, The	Self Titled	CD	Victor Ent.	VICP-60191	Japan	1997	23.99
Divine Comedy	Divine Selection (Promo)	CD	Sony	XDCS93277	Japan	1996	24.99
Divine/Pretty Flamingos Fame	The Best Of	CD	Hot Prod.	16	Canada	1991	14.99
Dixie Chicks	Little Ol' Cowgirl	CD	Crystal Clear	CCR9250	U.S.A.	1994	79.99
Dixie Chicks	Shouldn't A Told You That	CD	Crystal Clear	CCR9369	U.S.A.	1993	44.99
Dixie Dregs	Bring 'Em Back Alive	CD	Capricorn	9-42005-2	U.S.A.	1992	7.99
Dixie Dregs	California Screamin'	CD	Zebra	ZD-44021-2	U.S.A.	2000	9.99
Dixie Dregs	Dregs Of The Earth	CD	Arista	ARCD-8116	U.S.A.	1980	9.99
Dixie Dregs	Free Fall	CD	Capricorn	CPN-0189	U.S.A.	1977	9.99
Dixie Dregs	Full Circle	CD	Capricorn	42021-2	U.S.A.	1994	7.99
Dixie Dregs	Industry Standard	CD	BMG Victor	BVCA-2055	Japan	1982	55.99
Dixie Dregs	KBFH Presents	CD	King Biscuit	70710-88031-2	Canada	1997	8.99
Dixie Dregs	Night Of The Living Dregs	CD	Capricorn	CPN-0216	U.S.A.	1979	8.99
Dixie Dregs	The Best Of: Divided We Stand	CD	Arista	ARCD-8608	U.S.A.	1989	8.99
Dixie Dregs	The Great Spectacular	CD	Dregs	DRG-0197	U.S.A.	1995	55.99
Dixie Dregs	Unsung Heroes	CD	BMG Victor	BVCA-7334	Japan	1981	28.99
Dixie Dregs	Unsung Heroes	CD	Arista	ARCD-8120	U.S.A.	1981	8.99
Dixie Dregs	What If	CD	Capricorn	CPN-0203	U.S.A.	1978	8.99
Dixie Dregs/Andy West	Rama 1	CD	Magna Carta	MA-9061-2	U.S.A.	2002	7.99
Dixie Dregs/T. Lavitz	From The West	CD	Passport	PJCD-88026	U.S.A.	1987	29.99
Dixie Dregs/T. Lavitz	Gossip	CD	Wildcat	WLD-9220	U.S.A.	1996	11.99
Dixie Dregs/T. Lavitz	Jazz Is Dead - Blue Light Rain	CD	Zebra	ZD-44009-2	U.S.A.	1998	9.99
Dixie Dregs/T. Lavitz	Jazz Is Dead - Great Sky River	CD	Zebra	ZD-44023-2	U.S.A.	2001	9.99
Dixie Dregs/T. Lavitz	Jazz Is Dead - Laughing Water	CD	Zebra	ZD-44019-2	U.S.A.	1999	9.99
Dixie Dregs/T. Lavitz	Mood Swing	CD	Nova	9134-2	U.S.A.	1992	7.99
Dixie Dregs/T. Lavitz	Storytime	CD	Passport	PJCD-88012	U.S.A.	1986	14.99
Dixie Dregs/T. Lavitz	T. Lavitz And The Bad Habitz	CD	Enigma	7-73512-2	U.S.A.	1990	19.99

D

Artist	Title	Format	Label	Catalog No	Country	Released	Value
Dizzy Mizz Lizzy	Self Titled	CD	Toshiba-EMI	TOCP-8460	Japan	1994	19.99
Do Monte, Heraldo	Cordas Vivas	CD	Line	RICD-9.00574-0	Germany	1988	9.99
Doctor's Children	King Buffalo	CD	Line	URCD-9.00322-0	Germany	1987	24.99
Doheny, Ned	Best Collection	CD	Polystar	PSCW-5313	Japan	1995	25.99
Doheny, Ned	Between Two Worlds	CD	Polystar	PSCW-5030	Japan	1993	23.99
Doheny, Ned	Hard Candy (Eagles/Linda Ronstadt)	CD	Sony	25DP-5528	Japan	1988	21.99
Doheny, Ned	Life After Romance	CD	Polystar	P33R-25004	Japan	1988	26.99
Doheny, Ned	Life After Romance	CD	Pony Canyon	YDCD-0012	Japan	1988	26.99
Doheny, Ned	Love Like Ours	CD	Polystar	PSCW-1007	Japan	1991	22.99
Doheny, Ned	Postcards From Hollywood	CD	Polystar	PSCW-1066	Japan	1991	22.99
Doheny, Ned	Prone	CD	Sony	25DP-5529	U.S.A.	1988	20.99
Doheny, Ned	Self Titled	CD	Warner Bros.	18P2-2770	Japan	1989	34.99
Dokken	Back For The Attack	CD	Elektra	7559-60735-2	Germany	1987	9.99
Dokken	Back In The Streets	CD	Repertoire	REP-4005-WG	Germany	2001	16.99
Dokken	Beast From The East	CD	Elektra	9-60823-2	U.S.A.	1988	13.99
Dokken	Breaking The Chains	CD	Elektra	9-60290-2	U.S.A.	1983	13.99
Dokken	Dokken (Limited Edition)	CD	Victor Ent.	VICP-8140	Japan	1994	24.99
Dokken	Dysfunctional	CD	Columbia	CK-67075	U.S.A.	1995	7.99
Dokken	Dysfunctional + 1	CD	Victor Ent.	VICP-5579	Japan	1995	21.99
Dokken	Erase The Slate	CD	CMC INT.	06076-86274-2	U.S.A.	1999	9.99
Dokken	Erase The State	CD	Polygram K.K.	PHCW-1034	Japan	1999	16.99
Dokken	Japan Live '95	CD	CMC INT.	06076-86331-2	U.S.A.	2003	8.99
Dokken	Live From The Sun	CD	Mercury	PHCW-1071	Japan	2000	34.99
Dokken	Live From The Sun	CD	CMC INT.	06076-86285-2	U.S.A.	2000	9.99
Dokken	Long Way Home + 2	CD	Universal	UICE-1024	Japan	2002	12.99
Dokken	One Live Night	CD	CMC INT.	06076-86206-2	U.S.A.	1996	8.99
Dokken	One Live Night	CD	Victor Ent.	VICPS-85514	Japan	1995	10.99
Dokken	Self Titled	CD	Victor Ent.	VICP-5479	Japan	1994	59.99
Dokken	Shadowlife	CD	CMC INT.	06076-86210-2	U.S.A.	1997	9.99
Dokken	Shadowlife + 2	CD	Victor Ent.	VICP-5839	Japan	1997	19.99
Dokken	The Best Of	CD	Warner Bros.	WPCR-13	Japan	1994	11.99
Dokken	The Very Best Of	CD	Rhino	R2-75834	U.S.A.	1999	9.99
Dokken	Then & Now	CD	Sanctuary	06076-86325-2	U.S.A.	2002	8.99
Dokken	Tooth And Nail	CD	Elektra	32XD-302	Japan	1984	38.99
Dokken	Tooth And Nail	CD	Elektra	9-60376-2	U.S.A.	1984	10.99
Dokken	Under Lock And Key	CD	Elektra	9-60458-2	U.S.A.	1985	9.99
Dokken	Very Best Of	CD	Rhino	R2-75834	U.S.A.	1999	9.99
Dokken, Don	Up From The Ashes	CD	Geffen	9-24301-2	U.S.A.	1990	9.99
Dolan, Terry	Acoustic Rangers	CD	Line	SDCD-9.00453-0	Germany	1987	14.99
Doldinger, Klaus	The Neverending Story (Score Only)	CD	Warner Bros.	2292-50396-2	Germany	1984	29.99
Doldinger, Klaus/ G. Moroder	The Neverending Story (O.S.T.)	CD	EMI	7-92708-2	U.S.A.	1984	15.99
Donnas	Am. Teenage Rock 'N' Roll Machine	CD	Lookout	LK-191	U.S.A.	1998	12.99
Donnas	Get Skintight	CD	Network	NXCA-00007	Japan	2000	24.99
Donnas	Self Titled	CD	Lookout	LK-201	U.S.A.	1998	12.99
Donnas	Spend The Night (W/Bonus DVD)	2CD	Atlantic	83567-2	U.S.A.	2002	23.99
Donnas	The Donnas Turn 21	CD	Network	NXCA-00018	Japan	2001	24.99
Donovan	A Gift From A Flower To A Garden	CD	Collector's Choice	CCM-144-2	U.S.A.	2000	13.99
Donovan	A Gift From A Flower To A Garden	CD	BGO	BGOCD194	England	1993	14.99
Donovan	Atlantis Calling + 11	CD	Rock Cartoon	RCAR-102-5212	Germany	1999	11.99
Donovan	Barabajagal	CD	Epic	EK-26481	U.S.A.	1968	8.99
Donovan	Catch The Wind	CD	Castle	PIESD-191	England	2000	9.99
Donovan	Classics Live (Gurdy M/Harrison Verse)	CD	Permanent	PERM-CD-2	England	1990	18.99
Donovan	Cosmic Wheels	CD	Epic	477378-2	England	1995	11.99
Donovan	Donovan	CD	BGO	BGOCD375	England	1998	13.99
Donovan	Essence To Essence	CD	Epic	489443-2	England	1973	12.99
Donovan	Fairytale + 6	CD	Castle	CMRCD360	England	2001	11.99
Donovan	Golden Hits	CD	Cleopatra	CLP-0852-2	U.S.A.	2000	6.99
Donovan	Golden Hits (Lady Of The Stars)	CD	Music Masters	MACD-61075-2	Holland	1996	7.99

Artist	Title	Format	Label	Catalog No	Country	Released	Value
Donovan	Greatest Hits - Live Vancouver	CD	Varese	302-066-259-2	U.S.A.	2001	7.99
Donovan	Greatest Hits + 4	CD	Epic	EK-65730	U.S.A.	1999	9.99
Donovan	HMS Donovan	CD	BGO	BGOCD372	England	1997	21.99
Donovan	Hurdy Gurdy Man	CD	Epic	EK-26420	U.S.A.	1968	8.99
Donovan	Hurdy Gurdy Man (DJ/Harrison Verse)	CD Single	Great N Arts	610007-CDPRO	U.S.A.	1990	12.99
Donovan	In Concert	CD	BGO	BGOCD90	England	1993	11.99
Donovan	Love Is Hot Truth Is Molten 19	CD	Raven	RVCD-68	Australia	1998	12.99
Donovan	Mellow	2CD	Recall	SMD-CD-158	England	1997	14.99
Donovan	Mellow Yellow	CD	Epic	474605-2	Holland	2002	11.99
Donovan	Mellow Yellow/Wear Your Love...	CD	Collectables	CCM-6644	U.S.A.	2001	8.99
Donovan	Neutronica (W/Bonus)	CD	Alchemy	PILOT-89	England	2001	14.99
Donovan	Open Road	CD	Repertoire	REP-4880	Germany	2000	25.99
Donovan	Peace And Love Songs	CD	Collectables	CCM-9342	U.S.A.	2003	6.99
Donovan	Pied Piper	CD	Rhino	R2-78290	U.S.A.	2002	8.99
Donovan	Rising (H Gurdy Man/Harrison Verse)	CD	Great N Arts	GNA-61007-002	U.S.A.	1990	24.99
Donovan	Rising Again	CD	Alchemy	PILOT-59	England	2000	11.99
Donovan	Summer Day Reflection Songs	2CD	Castle	06076-81100-2	England	2001	19.99
Donovan	Sunshine Superman	CD	BGO	BGOCD68	England	1990	8.99
Donovan	Sunshine Superman	CD	Epic	EK-26217	U.S.A.	1966	10.99
Donovan	Sunshine Superman (Lady Of T Stars)	CD	Charly	CDCD-1206	England	1994	8.99
Donovan	Sunshine Superman: Very Best Of	CD	EMI	540-777-2	England	2002	8.99
Donovan	Sunshine Troubador (Lady Of T Stars)	CD	Hallmark	30501-2	England	1996	8.99
Donovan	Super Hits	CD	Sony	SK-61053	U.S.A.	2000	7.99
Donovan	Sutras	CD	American	9-43075-2	U.S.A.	1996	9.99
Donovan	Till I See You... (Lady Of The Stars)	CD	Success	22534CD	EEC	1994	8.99
Donovan	Troubadour The Definitive Collection	2CD	Epic	E2K-46986	U.S.A.	1992	16.99
Donovan	Very Best Of: The Early Years	CD	Sanctuary	06076-81184-2	U.S.A.	2002	8.99
Donovan	What's Bin Did And What's Bin Hid + 4	CD	Castle	CMRCD-361	England	2001	11.99
Doobie Brothers	Best Of The Doobie Brothers Live	CD	Columbia	JK-65281	U.S.A.	1999	8.99
Doobie Brothers	Best Of The Doobies (DCC Gold Cd)	CD	DCC	GZS-1121	U.S.A.	1994	41.99
Doobie Brothers	Best Of The Doobies Vol 2	CD	Warner Bros.	7599236122	Australia	1981	7.99
Doobie Brothers	Doobie's Choice	CD	Rhino	R2-78298	U.S.A.	2003	8.99
Doobie Brothers	Greatest Hits	CD	Rhino	R2-74386	U.S.A.	2001	12.99
Doobie Brothers	Long Train Runnin' Box Set	4CD	Rhino	R2-75876	U.S.A.	1999	33.99
Doobie Brothers	Minute By Minute	CD	Warner Bros.	3193-2	U.S.A.	1978	6.99
Doobie Brothers	One Step Closer	CD	Warner Bros.	9-26628-2	U.S.A.	1980	7.99
Doobie Brothers	One Step Closer	CD	Warner Bros.	WPCP-3168	Japan	1980	24.99
Doobie Brothers	Sibling Rivalry	CD	Rhino	R2-75809	U.S.A.	2000	8.99
Doobie Brothers	Takin' It To The Streets	CD	Warner Bros.	2899-2	U.S.A.	1976	10.99
Doobie Brothers	The Captain And Me	CD	Warner Bros.	2694-2	U.S.A.	1973	7.99
Doobie Brothers	The Captain And Me (DVD Audio)	CD	Rhino	R2-78347	U.S.A.	2002	14.99
Doobie Brothers	The Doobie Brothers	CD	Warner Bros.	2-1919	U.S.A.	1971	10.99
Doobie Brothers	Toulouse Street	CD	Warner Bros.	246183	Australia	1972	10.99
Doobie Brothers	What Were Once Vices Are Now Habits	CD	Warner Bros.	2750-2	U.S.A.	1974	13.99
Doobie Brothers/P Simmons	Patrick Simmons - Arcade	CD	Warner Bros.	WPCP-4154	Japan	1991	104.99
Doobie Brothers/T Johnston	Everything You've Heard Is True	CD	Warner Bros.	WPCP-4613	Japan	1979	104.99
Doors	Absolutely Live	CD	Elektra	61972-2	U.S.A.	1996	9.99
Doors	Alive She Cried	CD	Elektra	9-60269-2	U.S.A.	1983	11.99
Doors	Backstage Dangerous: Prvt. Rehearsal	2CD	Rhino	RHM2-7908	U.S.A.	2000	34.99
Doors	Best of the Doors (W/Bonus CD)	2CD	Elektra	7599-62569-2	Germany	2000	19.99
Doors	Break On Through (Promo)	CD Single	Elektra	PRCD-8314-2	U.S.A.	1991	6.99
Doors	Bright Midnight Sampler	CD	Rhino	R2-78330	U.S.A.	2000	12.99
Doors	Complete Studio Recordings Box Set	7 CD	Elektra	62434-2	U.S.A.	1999	69.99
Doors	Doors Live Black Box Set	4CD	Elektra	62123-2	U.S.A.	1997	34.99
Doors	Essential Rarities	CD	Elektra	62530-2	U.S.A.	2000	11.99
Doors	Greatest Hits	CD	Elektra	61996-2	U.S.A.	1996	8.99
Doors	In Concert	2CD	Elektra	9-61082-2	U.S.A.	1991	11.99
Doors	L.A. Woman (DCC Gold Cd)	CD	DCC	GZS-1034	U.S.A.	1993	29.99

Artist	Title	Format	Label	Catalog No	Country	Released	Value
Doors	Live At The Aquarius: The 2nd Show	2CD	Rhino	RHM2-7907	U.S.A.	2000	34.99
Doors	Live At The Aquarius: The First	2CD	Rhino	RHM2-7906	U.S.A.	2000	34.99
Doors	Live At The Hollywood Bowl	CD	Elektra	9-60741-2	U.S.A.	1987	11.99
Doors	Live In Detroit	2CD	Rhino	RHM2-7902	U.S.A.	2000	24.99
Doors	Live In Hollywood	CD	Elektra	755-62733-2	Germany	2002	11.99
Doors	Live In Hollywood: Highlights Aquarius	CD	Rhino	RHM2-7905	U.S.A.	2000	14.99
Doors	Lost Interview Tapes Vol. 1	CD	Rhino	RHM2-7904	U.S.A.	2000	11.99
Doors	Lost Interview Tapes Vol. 2	CD	Rhino	RHM2-7909	U.S.A.	2000	11.99
Doors	Morrison Hotel	CD	Elektra	75007-2	U.S.A.	1970	11.99
Doors	No One Here Gets Out Alive	4CD	Rhino	RHM2-7903	U.S.A.	2000	49.99
Doors	Strange Days (DCC Gold Cd)	CD	DCC	GZS-1026	U.S.A.	1993	35.99
Doors	Super Selection	CD	Echo Industry	AVC-305	Japan	1988	14.99
Doors	The Doors - Promo Box Set Sampler	CD	Elektra	PRCD-9920-2	U.S.A.	1997	11.99
Doors	The Doors (DCC Gold Cd)	CD	DCC	GZS-1023	U.S.A.	1993	35.99
Doors	The Doors Box Set - Part 1	2CD	Elektra	7559-62295-2	Germany	1998	29.99
Doors	The Doors Box Set - Part 2	2CD	Elektra	7559-62296-2	U.S.A.	1998	29.99
Doors	The Doors Box Set (Promo) Case Set	4CD	Elektra	PRCD-9921-2	U.S.A.	1997	39.99
Doors	The Soft Parade	CD	Elektra	7599750052	Australia	1969	9.99
Doors	The Very Best Of The Doors	CD	Rhino	R2-78376	U.S.A.	2001	13.99
Doors	Waiting For The Sun (DCC Gold Cd)	CD	DCC	GZS-1045	U.S.A.	1993	35.99
Doors	Westwood 1 # 00-28, 7, 8/9, 2000	2CD	Westwood 1	CO0028-062600	U.S.A.	2000	89.99
Doors/Danny Sugarman	No One Here Gets Out Alive	CD	Warner Bros.	2-523024	U.S.A.	1995	14.99
Doors/Jim Morrison	An American Prayer	CD	Elektra	61812-2	U.S.A.	1995	8.99
Doors/Ray Manzarek	The Doors Myth And Reality	2CD	Monster Sounds Ent.	MSE-1018	U.S.A.	1996	10.99
Doors/Ray Manzarek	The Golden Scarab	CD	Mercury	314-512-445-2	U.S.A.	1992	24.99
Doors/Ray Manzarek/D Read	Freshly Dug	CD	Ozit	OZITCD-0051	England	1999	8.99
Doors/Various Artists	Stoned Immaculate - Music/The Doors	CD	Elektra	62475-2	U.S.A.	2000	7.99
Downes, Geoffrey	Evolution	CD	Blueprint	BP215CD	Austria	1996	10.99
Downes, Geoffrey	Vox Humana	CD	Blueprint	BP214CD	Austria	1995	12.99
Downes, Geoffrey/NDO	The Light Programme	CD	Blueprint	BP216CD	England	1996	23.99
Downes, Geoffrey/NDO	The World Service	CD	Blueprint	BP331CD	England	1999	10.99
Downey, Roma/Phil Coulter	Healing Angel	CD	RCA	09026-63551-2	U.S.A.	1999	6.99
Downliners Sect	Savage Return	CD	Line	OLCD-9.51124-X	Germany	1991	9.99
Download	Furnace	CD	Cleopatra	CLEO-9644-2	U.S.A.	1995	11.99
Download	Sidewinder Ep (Promo)	CD	Nettwerk	NTCDPRO-9609	U.S.A.	1996	14.99
Download	The Eyes Of Stanley Pain (Adv Cd)	CD	Nettwerk	0-6700-30101-2-1	U.S.A.	1996	14.99
Doyle, Patrick	Exit To Eden (O.S.T.)	CD	Varese	VSD-5553	U.S.A.	1994	7.99
Doyle, Patrick	Great Expectations-The Score	CD	Atlantic	83063-2	U.S.A.	1997	13.99
Dr Feelgood	Brilleaux	CD	Line	LICD-9.00819-0	Germany	1990	15.99
Dr Feelgood	Brilleaux	CD	Nippon Crown	CRCL-7003	Japan	1990	19.99
Dr Feelgood	Doctor's Orders	CD	Line	LICD-9.00044-0	Germany	1988	14.99
Dr Feelgood	Fast Women Slow Horses	CD	Line	LICD-9.00062-0	Germany	1988	15.99
Dr Feelgood	Live In London	CD	Line	LICD-9.00975-0	Germany	1990	14.99
Dr Feelgood	Mad Man Blues	CD	Line	LICD-9.00971-0	Germany	1990	15.99
Dr Hook/Medicine Show	20 Great Love Songs	CD	Disky	724348-66622-2	Holland	1996	11.99
Dr Hook/Medicine Show	A Couple More Years	CD	Disky	871153-90520-41	Holland	2002	8.99
Dr Hook/Medicine Show	A Little Bit More	CD	PolyGram	839-263-2	U.S.A.	1990	8.99
Dr Hook/Medicine Show	Bankrupt	CD	EMI	7243-8-29573-2-4	Australia	1995	5.99
Dr Hook/Medicine Show	Best Of The 70's	CD	Disky	724389-90342-3	Holland	2000	7.99
Dr Hook/Medicine Show	Classic Masters	CD	Capitol	7243-5-38396-2-8	U.S.A.	2002	8.99
Dr Hook/Medicine Show	Collection	CD	EMI	724381-44652-2	Australia	1997	11.99
Dr Hook/Medicine Show	Concert Classics (Promo/Only 100)	CD	Renaissance	RRCC00719	U.S.A.	2002	12.99
Dr Hook/Medicine Show	Countryside	CD	Ktel	022775-31812-8	U.S.A.	1995	14.99
Dr Hook/Medicine Show	Definitive Collection	CD	EMI	724358-25392-4	Australia	2003	14.99
Dr Hook/Medicine Show	Greatest Hits	CD	Sony	50997-472420-2-1	Germany	1995	9.99
Dr Hook/Medicine Show	Greatest Hits (And More)	CD	Capitol	CDP-7-46620-2	U.S.A.	1987	6.99
Dr Hook/Medicine Show	I Got Stoned & I Missed It	CD	Raven	RVCD-161	Australia	2003	12.99
Dr Hook/Medicine Show	Live In Denver	CD	Brilliant	871227-33308-60	Holland	2002	9.99

Artist	Title	Format	Label	Catalog No	Country	Released	Value
Dr Hook/Medicine Show	Love Songs	CD	EMI	7243-497-943-2-0	England	1999	7.99
Dr Hook/Medicine Show	Making Love & Music (1976-79)	CD	EMI	0777-7-89072-2-0	England	1995	8.99
Dr Hook/Medicine Show	On The Run 1976	CD	Alchemy	PILOT-116	England	2001	12.99
Dr Hook/Medicine Show	Original Gold	CD	Disky	724348-57682-8	Holland	1999	13.99
Dr Hook/Medicine Show	Our Swedish Collection	CD	Capitol	724349-88292-8	Sweden	2001	19.99
Dr Hook/Medicine Show	Players In The Dark	CD	Mercury	800-054-2	Germany	1982	29.99
Dr Hook/Medicine Show	Pleasure & Pain	CD	EMI	7243-8-38209-2-4	Australia	1996	7.99
Dr Hook/Medicine Show	Pleasure And Pain Box Set	3CD	EMI	7243-8-53780-2-7	Holland	1996	34.99
Dr Hook/Medicine Show	Premium Gold Collection	CD	EMI	724383-75802-9	Holland	1996	7.99
Dr Hook/Medicine Show	Revisited	CD	Columbia	CK-34147	U.S.A.	1987	8.99
Dr Hook/Medicine Show	Rx	CD	Sony	079892-76362-1	U.S.A.	1996	7.99
Dr Hook/Medicine Show	Self Titled	CD	Columbia	CK-30898	U.S.A.	1992	7.99
Dr Hook/Medicine Show	Sharing The Night Together	CD	EMI	0777-7-572-422-6	England	2000	8.99
Dr Hook/Medicine Show	Singles	CD	BR Music	871208-90529-25	Holland	2000	9.99
Dr Hook/Medicine Show	Sloppy Seconds	CD	Columbia	CK-31622	U.S.A.	1989	7.99
Dr Hook/Medicine Show	Sometimes You Win	CD	EMI	793515-42022-6	Netherland	2001	12.99
Dr Hook/Medicine Show	Super Hits	CD	Sony	SK-85876	U.S.A.	2001	6.99
Dr Hook/Medicine Show	Take The Bait	CD	Karussell	550-055-2	Germany	1993	11.99
Dr Hook/Medicine Show	The Essential	CD	Epic	EK-86813-2	U.S.A.	2003	8.99
Dr Hook/Medicine Show	Vintage Years	3CD	EMI	7243-593-822-2-7	England	2003	34.99
Dr Hook/Medicine Show	When You're In Love...	CD	Disky	724348-64292-9	Holland	1998	7.99
Dr Hook/Medicine Show/Solo	D. Locoirriere - Out Of The Dark	CD	Track	TRK-1001CD	England	2001	39.99
Dr Hook/Medicine Show/Solo	D. Locorriere - Running W/ Sissors	CD	CNR Music	CNR-1382	Netherland	1996	42.99
Dr John	Afterglow	CD	Blue Thumb	BTD-7000	U.S.A.	1995	8.99
Dr John	Anutha Zone	CD	Virgin	495-490-2	England	1998	7.99
Dr John	Babylon	CD	Wounded Bird	WOU-270	U.S.A.	2002	9.99
Dr John	Babylon	CD	Atco	80438	Germany	1969	7.99
Dr John	City Lights	CD	Acadia	ACA-8060	England	2003	14.99
Dr John	Creole Moon	CD	Blue Note	7243-5-34591-2-3	U.S.A.	2001	9.99
Dr John	Cut Me While I'm Hot: 60's Sessions	CD	Thunderbolt	CDTB-158	England	1995	19.99
Dr John	Desitively Bonnaroo	CD	Atco	7567-80441-2	Germany	1993	9.99
Dr John	Diggin' (Cut Me While I'm Hot/Pair)	CD	RCA	PDC-2-1263	U.S.A.	1990	19.99
Dr John	Dr John/His New Orleans...	CD	Diablo	DIAB-8015	England	1999	11.99
Dr John	Dr. John/His New Orleans..	CD	ACE	ACE2020	U.S.A.	1990	7.99
Dr John	Duke Elegant	CD	Blue Note	7243-5-23220-2-2	U.S.A.	2000	8.99
Dr John	Essential Recordings	CD	Cleopatra	CLP-0968-2	U.S.A.	2001	11.99
Dr John	Funky New Orleans	CD	Metro	METRCD002	England	2000	8.99
Dr John	Goin' Back To New Orleans	CD	Warner Bros.	26940-2	U.S.A.	1992	9.99
Dr John	Gumbo	CD	Atco	7567-80398-2	Germany	1993	7.99
Dr John	Gumbo/In The Right Place (Gold Cd)	CD	Mobile Fidelity	UDCD-619	U.S.A.	1973	39.99
Dr John	Hollywood Be Thy Name	CD	BGO	BGOCD62	England	1990	9.99
Dr John	Hoodoo: The Collection	CD	Music Club	50142	U.S.A.	2000	8.99
Dr John	In A Sentimental Mood	CD	Warner Bros.	25889-2	U.S.A.	1988	7.99
Dr John	In The Right Place	CD	Atco	7567-80360-2	Germany	1993	8.99
Dr John	Loser For You Baby	CD	Thunderbolt	CDTB-066	England	2002	14.99
Dr John	Mos' Scocious: Anthology	2CD	Rhino	R2-71450	U.S.A.	1993	24.99
Dr John	Next Hex: The Nashville Session '74	CD	Cleopatra	CLP-0713-2	U.S.A.	1999	9.99
Dr John	On A Mardi Gras Day	CD	Great Southern	11024	U.S.A.	1994	14.99
Dr John	Plays Mac Rebbenack	CD	Classic	DAD-1023	U.S.A.	1998	11.99
Dr John	Plays Mac Rebbenack + 4	CD	Clean Cuts	CCD720	U.S.A.	2002	13.99
Dr John	Remedies	CD	Wounded Bird	WOU-316	U.S.A.	2002	9.99
Dr John	Such A Night! Live In London	CD	Making Waves	107	England	1988	19.99
Dr John	Tango Palace	CD	Acadia	ACA-8061	England	2003	14.99
Dr John	Television	CD	GRP	MGD-4024	U.S.A.	1994	7.99
Dr John	The Brightest Smile In Town	CD	Classic	DAD-1017	U.S.A.	1998	19.99
Dr John	The Essentials	CD	Rhino	R2-76068	U.S.A.	2002	8.99
Dr John	The Night Tripper: Gris-Gris	CD	Collector's Choice	CCM-131-2	U.S.A.	2000	15.99
Dr John	The Night Tripper: Gris-Gris	CD	East West	AMCY-3167	Japan	1968	14.99

D

Artist	Title	Format	Label	Catalog No	Country	Released	Value
Dr John	The Night Tripper: Gris-Gris	CD	Repertoire	REP-4130-WZ	Germany	2002	14.99
Dr John	The Rebennack Chronicles, Vol. 1	CD	Skinji Brim	9317	U.S.A.	2003	19.99
Dr John	The Sun, Moon & Herbs	CD	Wounded Bird	WOU-362	U.S.A.	2002	9.99
Dr John	The Ultimate	CD	Warner Bros.	27612-2	U.S.A.	1987	8.99
Dr John	The Very Best Of	CD	Rhino	R2-71924	U.S.A.	1995	8.99
Dr John	Trippin' Live	CD	Surefire	60150-13047-2	U.S.A.	1997	7.99
Dr John	Woman Is The Root Of All Evil	CD	Movie Play	MP-74069	U.S.A.	2001	13.99
Dr John	Zu Zu Man	CD	Thunderbolt	CDTB-069	England	2002	7.99
Dr Strangely Strange	Alternative Medicine (Gary Moore)	CD	Big Beat	CDWIKD-177	England	1997	19.99
Dr Strangely Strange	Heavy Pettin'	CD	Repertoire	REP-4273-WP	Germany	2002	19.99
Dr Strangely Strange	Kip Of The Serenes	CD	Island	510-949-2	England	1976	19.99
Dr Who	Music From The Tenth Planet	CD	Ochre	OCH-050	England	1966	19.99
Dragonfly	Almost Abandoned	CD	Line	RTCD-9.01179-0	Germany	1992	17.99
Drake, Nick	Fruit Tree Box Set	4CD	Rykodisc	HNCD-5402	U.S.A.	1986	94.99
Drake, Nick	Sweet Suggestions Of The Pink Moon	CD	Sonic Book	SONIC-BOOK-20	Italy	1999	16.99
Dread Zeppelin	5,000,000*	CD	I.R.S.	X2-13099	U.S.A.	1991	9.99
Dread Zeppelin	Un - Led -Ed	CD	I.R.S.	IRSD-82048	U.S.A.	1990	8.99
Dream Academy	A Different Kind Of... (DJ Picture Cd)	CD	Reprise	9-26307-2	U.S.A.	1990	18.99
Dream Academy	Angel Of Mercy	CD Single	Reprise	9362-40166-2	England	1990	9.99
Dream Academy	Angel Of Mercy (Promo)	CD Single	Reprise	PRO-CD-4892	U.S.A.	1990	14.99
Dream Academy	Love	CD Single	Reprise	9-21738-2	U.S.A.	1990	19.99
Dream Academy	Remembrance Days	CD	Warner Bros.	9-25625-2	U.S.A.	1987	6.99
Dream Academy	Somewhere In The Sun (Best Of)	CD	Warner Bros.	WPCR-10571	Japan	1999	39.99
Dream Academy	The Dream Academy	CD	Warner Bros.	9-25265-2	U.S.A.	1985	15.99
Dream Syndicate	3 & 1/2: Lost Tapes	CD	Atavistic	ALP65	U.S.A.	1996	11.99
Dream Syndicate	Medicine Show	CD	A&M	CD-4990	U.S.A.	1984	79.99
Dream Syndicate	Out Of The Grey + 6	CD	Atavistic	ALP66CD	U.S.A.	1997	8.99
Dream Syndicate	Tell Me When It's Over: The Best Of	CD	Rhino	R2-70373	U.S.A.	1992	14.99
Dream Syndicate	The Days Of Wine And Roses + 8	CD	Rhino	R2-79937	U.S.A.	2001	14.99
Dream Theater	4 Degrees Of Radio Edits (Int Fan Club)	CD	Dream Theater	DTIFC-006	England	2001	44.99
Dream Theater	A Change Of Seasons	CD	East West	61842-2	U.S.A.	1995	10.99
Dream Theater	Afterlife	CD Single	MCA	CD-45-17783	U.S.A.	1989	92.99
Dream Theater	Awake	CD	East West	90126-2	U.S.A.	1994	8.99
Dream Theater	Awake (W/3" CD)	2CD	East West	AMCY-750	Japan	1994	69.99
Dream Theater	Cleaning Out The Closet (Int Fan Club)	CD	Dream Theater	DTIFC-004	England	1999	53.99
Dream Theater	Falling Into Infinity	CD	East West	AMCY-2315	Japan	1997	34.99
Dream Theater	Falling Into Infinity	CD	East West	7559-62060-2	U.S.A.	1997	10.99
Dream Theater	Images And Words	CD	Atco	7-92148-2	U.S.A.	1992	10.99
Dream Theater	Live At The Marquee	CD	Warner Bros.	7567-92286-2	Germany	1993	11.99
Dream Theater	Live Scenes From New York	2CD	East West	62661-2	U.S.A.	2001	26.99
Dream Theater	Making Of Falling/Infinity (Int Fan Club)	CD	Dream Theater	DTIFC-002	England	1997	104.99
Dream Theater	Once In A Livetime	2CD	East West	62308-2	U.S.A.	1998	14.99
Dream Theater	Once/Livetime Outtakes (Int Fan Club)	CD	Dream Theater	DTIFC-003	England	1998	104.99
Dream Theater	R Scott's Show (F Club) Sign Gold/#rd	CD	Dream Theater	DTIFC-001	England	1996	132.99
Dream Theater	Scenes From A Memory	CD	East West	7559-62448-2	U.S.A.	1999	10.99
Dream Theater	Scenes From World Tour (Int Fan Club)	CD	Dream Theater	DTIFC-005	England	2000	53.99
Dream Theater	Six Degrees Of Inner Turbulence	CD	East West	62742-2	U.S.A.	2002	14.99
Dream Theater	Six Degrees Of Turbulence + 1	2CD	Warner Bros.	AMCY-7311~2	Japan	2002	43.99
Dream Theater	Taste The Memory (Int Fan Club)	CD	Dream Theater	DTIFC-007	England	2002	44.99
Dream Theater	Train Of Thought	CD	East West	62891-2	U.S.A.	2003	8.99
Dream Theater	When Dream And Day Unite	CD	MCA	MCD42259	France	1989	12.99
Dream Theater	When Dream And Day Unite	CD	One Way	OW-35188	U.S.A.	1996	7.99
Driscoll, Julie	1969 - 1971	CD	Disconforme	DISC1966CD	Andorra	2001	12.99
Driscoll, Julie/Tippetts	Sunset Glow	CD	Disconforme	DISC1967CD	Andorra	2001	12.99
Druid	Toward the Sun/Fluid Druid	2CD	BGO	BGOCD285	England	2002	15.99
Dubliners	Anthology	CD	Line	TACD-9.00792-0	Germany	1989	12.99
Ducks Deluxe	All Too Much	CD	P-Vine	PVCP-8729	Japan	1998	17.99
Ducks Deluxe	Ducks Deluxe/Taxi To Terminal Zone	2CD	BGO	BGOCD539	England	2001	13.99

Artist	Title	Format	Label	Catalog No	Country	Released	Value
Ducks Deluxe/Various Artists	Heroes/P Rock (3 Live Farewell Gig)	CD	Magnum	MM-154	England	1994	19.99
Dudek, Irek	A New Vision Of Blues...	CD	Line	RRCD-9.01299-0	Germany	1994	12.99
Dudek, Les	Self Titled	CD	Sony	SRCS6187	Japan	1976	81.99
Dudley, Anne	The 10th Kingdom (O.S.T.)	CD	Varese	302-066-115-2	U.S.A.	2000	11.99
Duke, George	Dream On	CD	Epic	EK-37532	U.S.A.	1982	8.99
Duke, George	Self Titled	CD	Elektra	9-60480-2	U.S.A.	1986	53.99
Duke, George	Thief In The Night	CD	Elektra	WPCP-3572	Japan	1995	24.99
Dumptruck	D Is For	CD	Big Time	6002-2-B	U.S.A.	1983	13.99
Dumptruck	Days Of Fear	CD	Unclean	10030	U.S.A.	1995	4.99
Dumptruck	For The Country	CD	Big Time	6051-2-B	U.S.A.	1987	8.99
Dumptruck	Lemmings Travel To The Sea	2CD	Devil In The Woods	37	U.S.A.	2001	13.99
Dumptruck	Positively Dumptruck	CD	Big Time	6004-2-B	U.S.A.	1986	13.99
Dumptruck	Terminal	CD	Devil In The Woods	24	U.S.A.	2000	10.99
Duofel	As Cores Do Brasil	CD	Line	CUCD-9.00998-0	Germany	1990	12.99
Du-Prez, John	A Fish Called Wanda	CD	Little Major	SSLM-SL5147-2	U.S.A.	1988	13.99
Duran Duran	4 Ep's (Nite/Carnival/Tiger/Strange)	2CD	Toshiba-EMI	TOCP-6707~8	Japan	1991	84.99
Duran Duran	Arena	CD	Toshiba-EMI	TOCP-6753	Japan	1984	39.99
Duran Duran	Arena	CD	Capitol	7243-819818-2	U.S.A.	1995	7.99
Duran Duran	Arena + 2	CD	EMI	7243-578085-2-1	England	2004	10.99
Duran Duran	Big Thing	CD	Toshiba-EMI	TOCP-3301	Japan	1988	18.99
Duran Duran	Big Thing	CD	Capitol	0777-7-89834-2	U.S.A.	2000	7.99
Duran Duran	Big Thing + 5 (Bonus Cd)	2CD	EMI Odeon	CP15-5769-70	Japan	1988	66.99
Duran Duran	Complete Tour (ESD-DD03-Complete)	14 CD	Music.Com	ESD-DD03-COMP	U.S.A.	2003	159.99
Duran Duran	Costa Mesa, Ca. July 16, 2003	2CD	Music.Com	ES-DD03-0716	U.S.A.	2003	24.99
Duran Duran	Essential [Night Versions] (Bonus Cd)	2CD	EMI	72434-93922-0-5	U.S.A.	1998	35.99
Duran Duran	Fukuoka, Japan July 08, 2003	2CD	Music.Com	ES-DD03-0708	U.S.A.	2003	24.99
Duran Duran	Greatest	CD	Capitol	7243-496239-2-7	U.S.A.	1998	5.99
Duran Duran	Las Vegas, Nv. July 17, 2003	2CD	Music.Com	ES-DD03-0717	U.S.A.	2003	24.99
Duran Duran	Liberty	CD	Capitol	0777-7-94292-2	U.S.A.	1996	8.99
Duran Duran	Liberty + 3 (W/Bonus Cd)	2CD	Toshiba-EMI	TOCP-6265	Japan	1990	49.99
Duran Duran	Medazzaland	CD	Capitol	7243-8-33876-2-5	U.S.A.	1997	7.99
Duran Duran	Medazzaland + 1	CD	Virgin	VJCP25317	Japan	1998	21.99
Duran Duran	Nagoya, Japan July 10, 2003	2CD	Music.Com	ES-DD03-0710	U.S.A.	2003	24.99
Duran Duran	Notorious	CD	Capitol	07777464152	U.S.A.	1993	9.99
Duran Duran	Original Gold	2CD	Disky	HR-857722	Holland	2000	13.99
Duran Duran	Osaka, Japan July 07, 2003	2CD	Music.Com	ES-DD03-0707	U.S.A.	2002	24.99
Duran Duran	Pop Trash	CD	Hollywood	HR-62266-2	U.S.A.	2000	5.99
Duran Duran	Pop Trash + 2	CD	Avex	AVCW-13011	Japan	2000	29.99
Duran Duran	Rio + 3	CD	Capitol	7243-529924-0	U.S.A.	2001	8.99
Duran Duran	Sampler (Promo)	CD	Virgin	PCD-0888	Japan	1997	249.99
Duran Duran	Self Titled + 1	Mini Lp	Capitol	7243-584380-2	U.S.A.	2003	9.99
Duran Duran	Self Titled + 1	CD	Capitol	7243-584809-2	U.S.A.	2003	8.99
Duran Duran	Self Titled + 1	CD	Toshiba-EMI	TOCP-3012	Japan	1995	20.99
Duran Duran	Seven & The Ragged Tiger	CD	Capitol	7243-584811-2	U.S.A.	2003	8.99
Duran Duran	Seven & The Ragged Tiger	CD	Capitol	7243-584382-2	U.S.A.	2003	9.99
Duran Duran	Strange Behaviour	2CD	EMI	7243-4-93972-2-4	England	1999	28.99
Duran Duran	Thank You	CD	Capitol	7243-829419-2	U.S.A.	1995	5.99
Duran Duran	Thank You (W/Bonus Cd)	2CD	EMI	7243-8-32943-2-9	Holland	1995	29.99
Duran Duran	Thank You + 2	CD	Toshiba-EMI	TOCP-8195	Japan	1995	18.99
Duran Duran	The Reflex	CD Single	Capitol	C2-15712	U.S.A.	1991	14.99
Duran Duran	The Singles '81 - '85	13 CD	EMI	7243-551728-2	England	2003	38.99
Duran Duran	The Wedding Album	CD	Parlophone	0777-7-98876-2-0	England	1993	7.99
Duran Duran	The Wedding Album + 1	CD	Toshiba-EMI	TOCP-7230	Japan	1993	18.99
Duran Duran	Tokyo, Japan July 11, 2003	2CD	Music.Com	ES-DD03-0711	U.S.A.	2003	24.99
Duran Duran	Tokyo, Japan July 12, 2003	2CD	Music.Com	ES-DD03-0712	U.S.A.	2003	24.99
Duran Duran	Tokyo, Japan July 12, 2003	2CD	Music.Com	ES-DD03-0712	U.S.A.	2003	24.99
Duran Duran/N Outsiders	Neurotic Outsiders	CD	Warner Bros.	WPCR-798	Japan	1996	29.99
Duran Duran/N Outsiders	Neurotic Outsiders	CD	Warner Bros.	46290-2	U.S.A.	1996	9.99

D

D

Artist	Title	Format	Label	Catalog No	Country	Released	Value
Durutti Column	Box Set (1st 4 Albums)	4CD	Factory	FACD224	Japan	1988	99.99
Durutti Column	Domo Arigato (Live In Japan)	CD	Factory	FACD144	Japan	1985	24.99
Dury, Ian/Blockheads	Do It Yourself + 7	CD	Repertoire	REP-4547-WY	Germany	1996	13.99
Dury, Ian/Blockheads	Laughter + 1	CD	Hit	AHLCD-59	England	1998	15.99
Dury, Ian/Blockheads	Mr Love Pants	CD	Ronnie Harris	DUR1	England	1998	16.99
Dury, Ian/Blockheads	New Boots And Panties + 5	CD	Repertoire	REP-4546-WY	Germany	1996	15.99
Dury, Ian/Blockheads	Reasons To Be Cheerful	2CD	Repertoire	REP-4592-WO	Germany	1996	19.99
Dury, Ian/Blockheads	Sex & Drugs & Rock & Roll - Best Of	CD	Rhino	R2-70270	U.S.A.	1992	8.99
Dury, Ian/Blockheads	Straight From The Desk	CD	Bloxlive	BLOXLIVE001	Japan	2001	34.99
Dury, Ian/Blockheads	Ten More Turnips From The Tip	CD	Ronnie Harris	DUR2	England	2002	12.99
Dury, Ian/Blockheads	The Best Of Ian Dury	CD	Repertoire	REP-4507-WG	Germany	1995	14.99
Dury/Kilburn & High-Roads	Handsome + 4	CD	Essential	ESM-CD-775	England	1999	11.99
Dust	First Album	CD	Repertoire	REP-4022-WZ	Germany	2001	10.99
Dust	Hard Attack	CD	Repertoire	REP-4030-WZ	Germany	2001	10.99
Dutch Royal Military Band	The Lord Of The Rings	CD	Ottavo	OTR-C18924	Holland	1989	8.99
Dylan, Bob	(A Fool Such As I)	CD	Sony	SRCS-6163	Japan	1991	117.99
Dylan, Bob	4 Songs/Love And Theft (Promo)	CD	Columbia	CSK-32657	U.S.A.	2001	24.99
Dylan, Bob	Another Side Of	CD	Columbia	CH-90327	U.S.A.	2003	11.99
Dylan, Bob	Another Side Of Bob Dylan	CD	Columbia	465033-2	Australia	1964	8.99
Dylan, Bob	At Budokan	2CD	Columbia	C2K-36067	U.S.A.	1978	19.99
Dylan, Bob	Biograph (Small Size Super Bit Map)	3CD	Columbia	C3K-65298	U.S.A.	2002	18.99
Dylan, Bob	Blonde On Blonde	2CD	Columbia	CH-90325	U.S.A.	2003	11.99
Dylan, Bob	Blonde On Blonde (Sony Gold Cd)	CD	Columbia	CK-53016	U.S.A.	1966	26.99
Dylan, Bob	Blood On The Tracks	CD	Columbia	CH-90323	U.S.A.	2003	12.99
Dylan, Bob	Blood On The Tracks (20 Bit Rem)	Mini Lp	Columbia	4953202000	England	1975	24.99
Dylan, Bob	Bob Dylan	CD	Columbia	462835-2	Australia	1967	10.99
Dylan, Bob	Bootleg Series, Vol. 6: Live 1964	2CD	Columbia	C2K-86882	U.S.A.	2004	16.99
Dylan, Bob	Bringing It All Back Home	CD	Columbia	CH-90326	U.S.A.	2003	11.99
Dylan, Bob	Desire	CD	Columbia	CH-90318	U.S.A.	2003	11.99
Dylan, Bob	Dylan (A Fool Such As I)	CD	Columbia	CD-32286	Austria	1973	99.99
Dylan, Bob	Dylan 'N' Rock (Promo Sampler)	2CD	Columbia	XCDS-93111-2	Japan	1994	749.99
Dylan, Bob	Empire Burlesque	CD	Columbia	CK-40110	U.S.A.	1985	8.99
Dylan, Bob	Forever Young (Promo Sampler)	CD	Columbia	SAMPCD1224	U.S.A.	1988	129.99
Dylan, Bob	Forever Young (Promo)	CD	Columbia	XPCD-116	England	1990	74.99
Dylan, Bob	Good As I Been To You	CD	Columbia	CK-53200	U.S.A.	1992	8.99
Dylan, Bob	Good As I've Been To You DJ Sampler	CD	Columbia	CSK-4857	U.S.A.	1992	20.99
Dylan, Bob	Greatest Hits	CD	Columbia	CK-65975	U.S.A.	1999	7.99
Dylan, Bob	Greatest Hits (Columbia Gold Cd)	CD	Columbia	460907-9	Germany	1967	21.99
Dylan, Bob	Greatest Hits Vol. 1,2,3 + EP Box Set	5CD	Columbia	C5K-86024	Australia	1999	33.99
Dylan, Bob	Greatest Hits Vol. 2	2CD	Columbia	C2K-65976	U.S.A.	1999	12.99
Dylan, Bob	Greatest Hits, Vol 3, Cd Plus	3CD	Columbia	CXR-67324	U.S.A.	1994	21.99
Dylan, Bob	Hard Rain	CD	Columbia	CK-34349	U.S.A.	1988	8.99
Dylan, Bob	Highway 61 Revisited (DCC Gold Cd)	CD	DCC	GZS-1021	U.S.A.	1993	39.99
Dylan, Bob	Highway 61 Revisited (Mono)	CD	Sony	5060552	Austria	1965	19.99
Dylan, Bob	Highway 61 Revisitied	CD	Columbia	CH-90324	U.S.A.	2003	11.99
Dylan, Bob	Infidels	CD	Columbia	CH-90317	U.S.A.	2003	11.99
Dylan, Bob	John Wesley Harding	CD	Columbia	CH-90320	U.S.A.	2003	11.99
Dylan, Bob	Knocked Out Loaded	CD	Columbia	CK-40439	U.S.A.	1986	10.99
Dylan, Bob	Le Sampler (Fr. Promo)	CD	Sony	SAMPCD4609-2	France	1997	32.99
Dylan, Bob	Live & Rare, Vol. 1 (Promo)	CD Single	Columbia	CDNEK-1570	Canada	2000	14.99
Dylan, Bob	Live & Rare, Vol. 2 (Promo)	CD	Columbia	CDNEK-1625	Canada	2002	14.99
Dylan, Bob	Live 1961-2000	CD	Sony	SRCS-2438	Japan	2001	19.99
Dylan, Bob	Live 1966 (Royal Albert Hall)	2CD	Columbia	C2K-65759	U.S.A.	1998	16.99
Dylan, Bob	Live 1975 - Rolling Thunder R/DVD	2CD	Columbia	C2K-87047	U.S.A.	2002	16.99
Dylan, Bob	Live 96 (Promo 1 Of 5000)	CD	Columbia	CSK-3818	U.S.A.	1997	14.99
Dylan, Bob	Love & Theft + 2 (Bonus Cd)	2CD	Columbia	CK-86076	U.S.A.	2001	13.99
Dylan, Bob	Love And Theft	CD	Columbia	CH-90340	U.S.A.	2003	10.99
Dylan, Bob	Love Sick (Promo)	CD Single	Columbia	CSK-3467	U.S.A.	1997	19.99

Artist	Title	Format	Label	Catalog No	Country	Released	Value
Dylan, Bob	Love Sick Cd 1	CD Single	Columbia	665997-2	Austria	1998	12.99
Dylan, Bob	Love Sick Cd 2	CD Single	Columbia	665997-5	Sweden	1998	12.99
Dylan, Bob	Masterpieces	CD	Columbia	462448-9	Australia	1991	24.99
Dylan, Bob	Million Miles Live '97-'99 (DJ)	CD	Columbia	CSK-41473	U.S.A.	1999	9.99
Dylan, Bob	MTV Unplugged + 1	CD	Columbia	478374-2	England	1995	59.99
Dylan, Bob	Music & Words 1998-1963 (Promo)	CD	Columbia	CSK-6226	U.S.A.	1998	11.99
Dylan, Bob	Nashville Skyline	CD	Columbia	CH-90319	U.S.A.	2003	10.99
Dylan, Bob	New Morning	CD	Columbia	CK-30290	U.S.A.	1970	8.99
Dylan, Bob	Not Dark Yet	CD Single	Columbia	COL-665443-2	Austria	1997	20.99
Dylan, Bob	Not Dark Yet - Dylan Alive Vol. 2	CD Single	Sony	SRCS-8914	Japan	1998	22.99
Dylan, Bob	Oh Mercy	CD	Columbia	CH-90316	U.S.A.	2003	10.99
Dylan, Bob	Pat Garrett & Billy The Kid	CD	Columbia	CK-32460	U.S.A.	1973	10.99
Dylan, Bob	Planet Waves	CD	Columbia	CH-90339	U.S.A.	2003	10.99
Dylan, Bob	Real Live	CD	Columbia	CK-39944	U.S.A.	1984	10.99
Dylan, Bob	Sampler (Promo)	CD	Columbia	SAMPCD1158	Germany	1987	164.99
Dylan, Bob	Saved	CD	Columbia	CK-36553	U.S.A.	1980	10.99
Dylan, Bob	Self Portrait	CD	Columbia	CK-30050	U.S.A.	1970	7.99
Dylan, Bob	Shot Of Love	CD	Columbia	CK-37496	U.S.A.	1981	10.99
Dylan, Bob	Slow Train Coming	CD	Columbia	CH-90322	U.S.A.	2003	10.99
Dylan, Bob	Street Legal	CD	Columbia	CH-90338	U.S.A.	2003	10.99
Dylan, Bob	Street Legal (Orig. Don Devito Remix)	CD	Columbia	CK-35453	U.S.A.	1978	8.99
Dylan, Bob	The Best Of	CD	Columbia	487924-2	Australia	1997	12.99
Dylan, Bob	The Best Of Vol. 2 + 2 (Bonus Cd)	2CD	Columbia	498361-9	Australia	2000	19.99
Dylan, Bob	The Bootleg Series (Promo Sampler)	CD	Columbia	CSK-3081	U.S.A.	1991	14.99
Dylan, Bob	The Essential Bob Dylan	2CD	Columbia	C2K-85168	U.S.A.	2000	18.99
Dylan, Bob	The Freewheelin' Bob Dylan	CD	Columbia	CH-90321	U.S.A.	2003	11.99
Dylan, Bob	The Times They Are A-Changin'	CD	Columbia	CK-8905	U.S.A.	1964	8.99
Dylan, Bob	The Ultimate Collection	2CD	Columbia	5031339000	Germany	2001	21.99
Dylan, Bob	Things Have Changed (Promo)	CD Single	Columbia	CSK-46489	U.S.A.	2000	10.99
Dylan, Bob	Things Have...Dylan Alive Vol.3	CD Single	Sony	SRCS-2306	Japan	2000	22.99
Dylan, Bob	Time Out Of Mind	CD	Columbia	CK-68556	U.S.A.	1997	8.99
Dylan, Bob	Time Out Of Mind (4 Trk DJ Sampler)	CD	Columbia	CSK-2926	U.S.A.	1997	19.99
Dylan, Bob	Unplugged (Recalled/W/Love Zero)	CD	Sony	SRCS-7176	Japan	1995	249.99
Dylan, Bob	World Gone Wrong	CD	Columbia	CK-57590	U.S.A.	1993	5.99
Dylan, Bob/Funkstar De Luxe	All Along The Watchtower (Maxi)	CD Single	Hypnotic	012805-6	Germany	2001	5.99
Dylan, Bob/Grateful Dead	Dylan And The Dead	CD	Columbia	CK-45056	U.S.A.	1988	9.99
Dylan, Bob/The Band	Before The Flood	2CD	Columbia	C2K-37661	U.S.A.	1974	14.99
Dylan, Bob/The Band	The Basement Tapes	2CD	Columbia	C2K-33682	U.S.A.	1975	14.99
Dylan, Bob/Various Artists	I Shall Be Unreleased: Songs	CD	Rhino	R2-70518	U.S.A.	1991	29.99
Dylan, Bob/Various Artists	Uncut - Hard Rain Vol.1 (W/Magazine)	CD	Uncut	UNCUT-2002-05	U.S.A.	2002	19.99
Dylan, Bob/Various Artists	Uncut - Hard Rain Vol.2 (W/Magazine)	CD	Uncut	UNCUT-2002-06	U.S.A.	2002	19.99

E

E.L.O.	Alright (Promo)	CD	Epic	ESK-16520	U.S.A.	2001	7.99
E.L.O.	Definitive Collection + 8 (Bonus Cd)	2CD	Epic	472421-9	Holland	1992	14.99
E.L.O.	Discovery (Sony Gold Disc)	CD	Sony	ZK-64646	U.S.A.	1979	21.99
E.L.O.	Discovery + 3	CD	Epic	EK-85420	U.S.A.	2001	8.99
E.L.O.	Discovery + 3 (Adv. Cd)	CD	Epic	AEK-85420-S1	U.S.A.	2001	10.99
E.L.O.	Eldorado - Symphony By + 2 (Adv. Cd)	CD	Epic	AEK-85419-S1	U.S.A.	2002	10.99
E.L.O.	Eldorado (DCC Gold Disc)	CD	DCC	GZS-1041	U.S.A.	1993	55.99
E.L.O.	Eldorado + 2	CD	Epic	EK-85419	U.S.A.	2001	8.99
E.L.O.	Face the Music (Sony Gold Cd)	CD	Epic	ZK-57184	U.S.A.	1973	37.99
E.L.O.	First Light Series Vol. 2	CD	Toshiba-EMI	TOCP-65956	Japan	2001	28.99

Artist	Title	Format	Label	Catalog No	Country	Released	Value
E.L.O.	First Light Series Vol.1 + 2	CD	Toshiba-EMI	TOCP-65955	Japan	2002	28.99
E.L.O.	Flashback Box Set	3CD	Epic	E3K-85123	U.S.A.	2001	25.99
E.L.O.	Friends And Relatives	2CD	Eagle	EDL-EAG-176-2	EC	2000	24.99
E.L.O.	Greatest Hits Live, Part II	CD	BMG	44844-2	U.S.A.	1998	8.99
E.L.O.	Live At Winterland 1976	CD	Eagle	EAMCD0038	England	1998	7.99
E.L.O.	Secret Messages + 3	CD	Epic	EK-85424	U.S.A.	2001	9.99
E.L.O.	Strange Magic The Best Of E.L.O.	2CD	Epic	Z2K-64157	U.S.A.	1995	14.99
E.L.O.	Time + 3 (Adv. Cd)	CD	Epic	AEK-85421-S1	U.S.A.	2002	10.99
E.L.O.	Zoom + 1	CD	Sony	SRCS-2466	Japan	2001	24.99
E.L.O. / II	Electric Light Orchestra Part Two	CD	Scotti Bros.	72392-75222-2	U.S.A.	1990	14.99
E.L.O. / II	Moment Of Truth	CD	Curb	D2-77692	U.S.A.	1994	4.99
E.L.O. / II	One Night - Live in Australia	CD	CMC INT.	06076-86215-2	U.S.A.	1997	8.99
E.L.O. / Jeff Lynne	Lift Me Up	CD Single	Reprise	W9795CD	England	1990	44.99
E.L.O. /Jeff Lynne	Armchair Theatre	CD	Reprise	9-26184-2	U.S.A.	1990	10.99
E.L.O. /Jeff Lynne	Interview Disc Zoom (Promo Cd)	CD	Epic	DIDP-104898	U.S.A.	2001	14.99
E.L.O. /The Move/Co.	E.L.O./The Move/Co. - Premium Gold	CD	EMI	7243-5-22850-2-0	Germany	1999	13.99
Eagles	1994 Tour Collection (Promo Sampler)	CD	Elektra	PRCD-8983-2	U.S.A.	1994	9.99
Eagles	Eagles	CD	Asylum	7559606232	Australia	1972	8.99
Eagles	Get Over It	CD Single	BMG	72064-21945-2-2	Germany	1994	5.99
Eagles	Get Over It (Promo)	CD	Geffen	PRO-CD-4679	U.S.A.	1994	6.99
Eagles	Hell Freezes Over	CD	Geffen	GEFD-24725	U.S.A.	1994	9.99
Eagles	Hell Freezes Over (Gold Cd)	CD	Geffen	GED-24928	U.S.A.	1994	35.99
Eagles	Hole In The World (W/Bonus DVD)	CD Single	Eagles	70011	U.S.A.	2003	11.99
Eagles	Hotel California (DCC Gold CD)	CD	DCC	GZS-1024	U.S.A.	1993	39.99
Eagles	Live	2CD	Elektra	705-2	U.S.A.	1980	10.99
Eagles	Love Will Keep Us Alive	CD Single	Geffen	GED-21980	Australia	1995	9.99
Eagles	On The Border	CD	Asylum	7559605952	Australia	1974	8.99
Eagles	One Of These Nights	CD	Asylum	7E-1039-2	U.S.A.	1975	9.99
Eagles	Selected Works 1972 - 1999	4CD	Elektra	62575-2	U.S.A.	2000	34.99
Eagles	The Long Run	CD	Elektra	7559605602	Australia	1979	6.99
Eagles	The Very Best Of	2CD	Rhino	R2-73971	U.S.A.	2003	19.99
Eagles	The Very Best Of The Eagles	CD	Elektra	9548-32375-2	Germany	1994	14.99
Eagles	Their Greatest Hits (DCC Gold CD)	CD	Elektra	GZS-1039	U.S.A.	1993	28.99
Eagles/Bernie Leadon	Natural Progressions	CD	Wounded Bird	WOU-1107	U.S.A.	2002	15.99
Eagles/Don Felder	Airborne	CD	Wounded Bird	WOU-6295	U.S.A.	2002	13.99
Eagles/Don Felder	Airborne	CD	Elektra	755-960295-2	Germany	1996	11.99
Eagles/Randy Meisner	Meisner, (Billy) Swan & (Charlie) Rich	CD	Rev-Ola	CDREV12	England	2002	17.99
Eagles/Randy Meisner	One More Song	CD	Epic	EK-36748	U.S.A.	1991	43.99
Eagles/Randy Meisner	Randy Meisner	CD	Wounded Bird	WOU-140	U.S.A.	2002	14.99
Earl, Ronnie	I Like It When It Rains	CD	Line	ANCD-9.00448-0	Germany	1988	14.99
Earth Opera/Dave Grisman	Earth Opera	CD	Wounded Bird	WOU-4016	U.S.A.	2001	13.99
Earth Opera/John Cale	The Great American Eagle Tragedy	CD	Wounded Bird	WOU-4038	U.S.A.	2001	9.99
Earth Wind & Fire	Expanded Edition Sampler	CD	Columbia	CSK-42237	U.S.A.	1999	14.99
Earth Wind & Fire/Philip Bailey	The Wonders Of His Love	CD	Myrrh	1181	U.S.A.	1984	20.99
Earthquake	8.5	CD	Line	BECD-9.00476-0	Germany	1987	24.99
Earthquake	Levelled	CD	Line	BECD-9.00481-0	Germany	1987	24.99
Earthquake	Rocking The World	CD	Line	BECD-9.00468-0	Germany	1987	24.99
Earthquake	Sittin' In The Middle Of Madness	CD	Essential	ESM-CD-869	England	2000	12.99
Earthshaker	Fugitive	CD	King	KICS-2862	Japan	1999	24.99
Earthshaker	Midnight Flight	CD	King	KICS-2803	Japan	1999	24.99
Earthshaker	Passion	CD	King	KICS-2864	Japan	1999	49.99
Earthshaker	The Best Of 1987-1992	CD	Toshiba-EMI	TOCT-6646	Japan	1992	25.99
East Of Eden	A New Leaf	CD	Prog. Line	PL-566	Australia	2002	16.99
East Of Eden	Armadillo	CD	Talking Elephant	TECD-015	England	2000	16.99
East Of Eden	Jig-A-Jig	CD	Repertoire	REP-7073-WP	Germany	2002	19.99
East Of Eden	Kalipse	CD	Transatlantic	TRACD-303	England	1997	8.99
East Of Eden	Mercator Projected	CD	Repertoire	REP-7040-WP	Germany	2002	19.99
East Of Eden	Self Titled	CD	Repertoire	REP-4877-DG	Germany	2001	19.99

E

Artist	Title	Format	Label	Catalog No	Country	Released	Value
Easton, Elliot	Change No Change + 5	CD	Rhino	R2-73514	U.S.A.	1996	37.99
Easton, Sheena	The Most Of Sheena Easton	CD	EMI	8140482	Australia	1992	12.99
Easton, Sheena	You Could Have Been With Me + 3	CD	One Way	72435-23536-2-0	U.S.A.	2000	15.99
Easybeats	Easy + 8	CD	Repertoire	REP-4284-WY	Germany	1992	13.99
Easybeats	Friday On My Mind + 6	CD	Repertoire	RE-4162-WY	Germany	1992	19.99
Easybeats	Friday On My Mind/Falling Off The..	CD	Collectables	COL-CD-2848	U.S.A.	2002	12.99
Easybeats	Friends + 11	CD	Repertoire	REP-4278-WY	Germany	2002	15.99
Easybeats	It's 2 Easy + 11	CD	Repertoire	REP-4302-WY	Germany	1993	15.99
Easybeats	Live - Studio And Stage	CD	Raven	RVCD-40	Australia	1995	15.99
Easybeats	The Best Of	CD	Repertoire	REP-4542-WG	Germany	1995	12.99
Easybeats	The Definitive Collection	2CD	Repertoire	REP-4505-WO	Germany	1996	15.99
Easybeats	The Easybeats Collection	CD	Line	IMCD-9.00823-0	Germany	1989	24.99
Easybeats	The Shame Just Drained + 9	CD	Repertoire	REP-4304-WY	Germany	1993	13.99
Easybeats	The Very Best Of	CD	Varese	302-066-437-2	U.S.A.	2002	9.99
Easybeats	Vigil + 8	CD	Repertoire	REP-4240-WY	Germany	1992	13.99
Easybeats	Volume 3 + 11	CD	Repertoire	REP-4303-WY	Germany	1993	13.99
Echo & The Bunnymen	Ballyhoo: The Best Of	CD	Korova	070630-19103-2-0	England	1997	14.99
Echo & The Bunnymen	BBC Radio 1 Live In Concert	CD	Windsong	WINCD-006	England	1988	19.99
Echo & The Bunnymen	Crocodiles + 10	CD	Rhino	082564-61161-2-6	U.S.A.	2004	8.99
Echo & The Bunnymen	Crystal Days 1979-1999 [Boxed Set]	4CD	Rhino	R2-74263	U.S.A.	2001	37.99
Echo & The Bunnymen	Evergreen + 4 (W/Bonus CD)	2CD	PolyGram	3984-29642-2	England	2000	19.99
Echo & The Bunnymen	Flowers	CD	Cooking Vinyl	COOK-CD-208	England	2001	9.99
Echo & The Bunnymen	Heaven Up Here + 5	CD	Rhino	082564-61162-2-5	U.S.A.	2004	8.99
Echo & The Bunnymen	Live In Liverpool	CD	Cooking Vinyl	COOK-CD-223	England	2002	9.99
Echo & The Bunnymen	Ocean Rain + 8	CD	Rhino	082564-61165-2-2	U.S.A.	2004	8.99
Echo & The Bunnymen	Porcupine + 7	CD	Rhino	082564-61163-2-4	U.S.A.	2004	8.99
Echo & The Bunnymen	Reverberation (No Ian McCulloch)	CD	Sire	26388-2	U.S.A.	1990	7.99
Echo & The Bunnymen	Self Titled + 7	CD	Rhino	082564-61164-2-3	U.S.A.	2004	8.99
Echo & The Bunnymen	Songs To Learn & Sing	CD	Warner Bros.	WMC5-58	Japan	1985	29.99
Echo & The Bunnymen	Songs To Learn And Sing	CD	Sire	25360-2	U.S.A.	1987	5.99
Echo City	Gramophone	CD	Line	DACD-9.00336-0	Germany	1987	12.99
Echoe Band	The Echoe Band: 1965-1969	CD	Gear Fab	GF-195	U.S.A.	2003	18.99
Eddie/The Hot Rods	Thriller + 3	CD	Captain Oi	AHOY-CD-192	England	2002	13.99
Eddie/The Hotrods	Doing Anything They Wanna Do	CD	Anagram	CDMGRAM-108	England	1996	12.99
Eddie/The Hotrods	Teenage Depression + 12	CD	Captain Oi	AHOY-CD-132	England	2000	15.99
Eddie/The Hotrods	The Best (The End of the Beginning)	CD	Island	IMCD-156	France	1993	8.99
Eddy, Duane	Greatest Hits	CD	Line	BLCD-9.01034-L	Germany	1991	8.99
Eddy, Nelson	Greatest Hits	CD	Sony	A-24298	U.S.A.	1988	7.99
Eddy, Nelson	Oklahoma!	CD	Sony	SK-53326	U.S.A.	1993	8.99
Eddy, Nelson	Operatic Arias And Concert Songs	CD	Pearl	GEM-0092	England	2000	8.99
Edith	....A Space Between Ever And Never....	CD	Progressive	PRO-003	Canada	1991	9.99
Edmunds, Dave	A Pile Of Rock Live	CD	Castle	06076-81107-2	England	2001	7.99
Edmunds, Dave	Anthology (1968-1990)	2CD	Rhino	R2-71191	U.S.A.	1993	20.99
Edmunds, Dave	Best Of	CD	Arista	74321-12540-2	Germany	1993	12.99
Edmunds, Dave	Chronicles (1968-84)	CD	Connoisseur	VSOP-CD-209	England	1994	45.99
Edmunds, Dave	Chutes And Ladders (Promo Sampler)	CD	Rhino	PRCD-7067	U.S.A.	1994	9.99
Edmunds, Dave	Closer To The Flame	CD	Capitol	7-90372-2	U.S.A.	1990	6.99
Edmunds, Dave	D.E.7th / Information	CD	BGO	BGOCD545	England	2002	13.99
Edmunds, Dave	From Small Things: Best Of	CD	Columbia	CK-90278	U.S.A.	2004	8.99
Edmunds, Dave	Get It	CD	Swan Song	8418-2	U.S.A.	1977	14.99
Edmunds, Dave	Interview: Plugged In (Promo)	CD	Rhino	PRCD-7075	U.S.A.	1994	7.99
Edmunds, Dave	Live King Biscuit	CD	King Biscuit	70710-88048-2	U.S.A.	1999	13.99
Edmunds, Dave	Plugged In	CD	Rhino	R271770	U.S.A.	1994	7.99
Edmunds, Dave	Repeat When Necessary	CD	Swan Song	7567-90337-2	Germany	1979	17.99
Edmunds, Dave	Riff Raff/I Hear You Rockin' (Live)	CD	BGO	BGOCD559	England	2002	14.99
Edmunds, Dave	Rockin'	CD	Camden	74321-45192-2	England	1997	9.99
Edmunds, Dave	Rockpile + 6	CD	Repertoire	REP-4966	Germany	2001	14.99
Edmunds, Dave	Subtle As A Flying Mallet	CD	RCA	74321-12850-2	Germany	1976	9.99

E

Artist	Title	Format	Label	Catalog No	Country	Released	Value
Edmunds, Dave	The Best Of Dave Edmunds	CD	Swan Song	8510-2	U.S.A.	1981	9.99
Edmunds, Dave	Tracks On Wax 4	CD	Swan Song	8505-2	U.S.A.	1978	23.99
Edmunds, Dave	Twangin'	CD	Swan Song	7-16034-2	U.S.A.	1981	10.99
Edwards, Mark	Code Of Honor	CD	Metal Blade	PHCR-16162	Japan	1985	39.99
Egan, Walter	Apocalypso Now	CD	Gaff	1128	U.S.A.	2002	8.99
Egan, Walter	Hi-Fi/The Last Stroll	CD	Bear Family	BTCD-979413	Germany	1991	16.99
Egan, Walter	Mad Dog (Lost Album + 5)	CD	Red Steel	RMCCD9217	England	2001	14.99
Egan, Walter	The Lost Album	CD	Renaissance	RMED00236-2	U.S.A.	2000	9.99
Egan, Walter	The Meaning Of Live ('78 -'79)	CD	Red Steel	RMCCD9225	England	2002	14.99
Egan, Walter	Walternative	CD	WE	13	U.S.A.	1999	14.99
Egan, Walter/Fleetwood Mac	Not Shy (Buckingham/Nicks)	CD	Razor & Tie	RE-2027-2	U.S.A.	1993	74.99
Egg	Self Titled	CD	Polydor	POCD-1843	Japan	1991	38.99
Egg	The Civil Surface	CD	Caroline	CAROL-1814-2	U.S.A.	1992	24.99
Egg	The Civil Surface	CD	Charisma	CACD-1510	England	1990	24.99
Egg	The Polite Force	CD	Polydor	POCD-1844	Japan	1971	32.99
Eidelman, Cliff	Star Trek VI: Undiscovered Country	CD	MCA	MCAD-10512	U.S.A.	1991	8.99
El Debarge	Self Titled	CD	BMG	R32M-1011	Japan	1986	40.99
Elbow	Asleep In The Back	CD	V2	63881-27116-2	U.S.A.	2000	8.99
Electric Flag	A Long Time Comin'	CD	Columbia	CK-9597	U.S.A.	1968	15.99
Electric Flag	An American Music Band	CD	Columbia	A-21615	U.S.A.	1990	11.99
Electric Flag	I Found Out	CD	Dressed To Kill	METRO472	England	2000	14.99
Electric Flag	Live	CD	Get Back	GET-520	England	1998	12.99
Electric Flag	The Band Kept Playing	CD	Wounded Bird	WOU-8112	U.S.A.	2002	12.99
Electric Flag	Trip O.S.T.	CD	Curb Records	D2-77863	U.S.A.	1996	13.99
Electric Prunes	Artifact (Gold Cd)	CD	Prunetwang	8-69696-9	U.S.A.	2001	49.99
Electric Prunes	I Had Too Much To Dream + 2	CD	Collector's Choice	CCM-132	U.S.A.	2000	10.99
Electric Prunes	I Had Too Much To Dream + 2	CD	Rhino	R2-7520	U.S.A.	2000	13.99
Electric Prunes	Long Day's Flight	CD	Edsel	EDCD-179	England	1986	12.99
Electric Prunes	Lost Dreams	CD	Birdman	BMR-022	Australia	2001	11.99
Electric Prunes	Mass In F Minor	CD	Line	LECD-9.00888-0	Germany	1990	7.99
Electric Prunes	Mass in F Minor + 2	CD	Collector's Choice	CCM-134	U.S.A.	2000	10.99
Electric Prunes	Mass In F Minor + 2	CD	Rhino	R2-7519	U.S.A.	2000	13.99
Electric Prunes	Stockholm '67	CD	Birdman	BMR-039	Australia	1997	12.99
Electric Prunes	Underground + 2	CD	Collector's Choice	CCM-133	U.S.A.	2000	10.99
Electric Prunes	Underground + 2	CD	Rhino	R2-7518	U.S.A.	2000	13.99
Electric Prunes/Sanctions	Then Came The E Prunes (Jim/Lords)	CD	Prunetwang	EP007-CD	U.S.A.	2001	18.99
Elegant Punk	Avant-Pop	CD	Warner Bros.	WPCL-737	Japan	1993	24.99
Eleven Bloody Men	Eleven Bloody Men	CD	Line	LICD-9.01263-0	Germany	1992	15.99
Eleven Bloody Men	Eleven Bloody Men	CD	Line	BECD-9.00589-0	Germany	1988	15.99
Elf	Carolina Country Ball	CD	Line	LICD-9.00115-0	Germany	1991	19.99
Elf	Corolina Country Ball	CD	Connoisseur	VSOP-CD-167	England	1991	19.99
Elf	Elf	CD	Epic	EK-31789	U.S.A.	1972	11.99
Elfman, Danny	A Civil Action (O.S.T.)	CD	Hollywood	HR-62158-2	U.S.A.	1998	7.99
Elfman, Danny	A Simple Plan (O.S.T.)	CD	Compass III	COM-0105	U.S.A.	1999	16.99
Elfman, Danny	Article 99 (O.S.T.)	CD	Varese	VSD-5352	U.S.A.	1992	24.99
Elfman, Danny	Batman (O.S.T.)	CD	Warner Bros.	25977-2	U.S.A.	1989	10.99
Elfman, Danny	Batman Returns (O.S.T.)	CD	Warner Bros.	26972-2	U.S.A.	1992	9.99
Elfman, Danny	Beetlejuice (O.S.T.)	CD	Geffen	24202-2	U.S.A.	1988	12.99
Elfman, Danny	Big Top Pee-Wee (O.S.T.)	CD	Pendulum	PEG016	U.S.A.	1988	11.99
Elfman, Danny	Darkman (O.S.T.)	CD	MCA	MCAD-10094	U.S.A.	1990	14.99
Elfman, Danny	Dick Tracy (Score)	CD	Warner Bros.	26264-2	U.S.A.	1990	8.99
Elfman, Danny	Dolores Claiborne (O.S.T.)	CD	Varese	VSD-5602	U.S.A.	1995	12.99
Elfman, Danny	Edward Sissorhands (O.S.T.)	CD	MCA	MCAD-10133	U.S.A.	1990	9.99
Elfman, Danny	Extreme Measures (O.S.T.)	CD	Varese	VCD-5767	U.S.A.	1996	9.99
Elfman, Danny	Instinct (O.S.T.)	CD	Varese	VSD-6041	U.S.A.	1999	7.99
Elfman, Danny	Mars Attacks (O.S.T.)	CD	Atlantic	82992-2	U.S.A.	1997	14.99
Elfman, Danny	Midnight Run (O.S.T.)	CD	MCA	MCAD-6250	U.S.A.	1988	39.99
Elfman, Danny	Mission Impossible (Score)	CD	Point	454-525-2	U.S.A.	1996	8.99

E

Artist	Title	Format	Label	Catalog No	Country	Released	Value
Elfman, Danny	Music/Darkened Theatre - Vol. 1	CD	MCA	MCAD-10065	U.S.A.	1990	8.99
Elfman, Danny	Music/Darkened Theatre - Vol. 2	2CD	MCA	MCAD2-11550	U.S.A.	1996	21.99
Elfman, Danny	Nightbreed + 1 (O.S.T.)	CD	MCA	MCAD8037	U.S.A.	1990	24.99
Elfman, Danny	Pee Wee's Big Adventure/Back To Scho	CD	Varese	VCD-47281	U.S.A.	1986	22.99
Elfman, Danny	Planet Of The Apes (O.S.T.)	CD	Sony	SK-89666	U.S.A.	2001	8.99
Elfman, Danny	Proof Of Life (O.S.T.)	CD	Varese	302-066-208-2	U.S.A.	2000	8.99
Elfman, Danny	Red Dragon (O.S.T.)	CD	Decca	289-473-248-2	U.S.A.	2002	8.99
Elfman, Danny	Sleepy Hollow (O.S.T.)	CD	Hollywood	HR-16226-2	U.S.A.	1999	11.99
Elfman, Danny	So Lo	CD	MCA	MCAD-25051	U.S.A.	1984	30.99
Elfman, Danny	The Frightneners (O.S.T.)	CD	MCA	MCAD-11469	U.S.A.	1996	9.99
Elfman, Danny	The Hulk (O.S.T.)	CD	Decca	B000063302	U.S.A.	2003	8.99
Elfman, Danny	The Nightmare Before Xmas (O.S.T.)	CD	Walt Disney	60855-7	U.S.A.	1993	9.99
Elfman, Danny	Wisdom (O.S.T.)	CD	Varese	VS-5209	U.S.A.	1988	28.99
Elfman, Danny/John Debeny	Spy Kids (O.S.T.)	CD	Chapter III Classics	66760-30002-2-8	U.S.A.	2001	14.99
Elfman, Danny/Oingo Boingo	Forbidden Zone (O.S.T.)	CD	Varese	VSD-5268	U.S.A.	1990	28.99
Elias, Eliane	Fantasia	CD	Blue Note	596146	U.S.A.	1992	7.99
Elias, Eliane	Plays Jobim	CD	Blue Note	7-93089-2	U.S.A.	1990	11.99
Elias, Eliane	Solos And Duets With Herbie Hancock	CD	Blue Note	7243-8-32073-2-9	U.S.A.	1995	29.99
Elias, Eliane	The Best Of Eliane Elias On Denon	CD	Denon	DC-8592	Japan	1995	14.99
Elias, Eliane	The Three Americas	CD	Blue Note	7243-8-53328-2-1	U.S.A.	1997	6.99
Elliot, Mama Cass	Bubble Gum, Lemonade & ...	CD	Victor Ent.	UICY-3362	Japan	2002	24.99
Elliot, Mama Cass	Cass Elliot	CD	BMG	74321-78825-2	Japan	2000	24.99
Elliot, Mama Cass	Don't Call Me Mama Anymore (Live)	CD	One Way	OW-71000	U.S.A.	2000	8.99
Elliot, Mama Cass	Dream A Little Dream	CD	Victor Ent.	UICY-3304	Japan	2001	24.99
Elliot, Mama Cass	Dream A Little Dream (Collection)	CD	MCA	MCAD-11523	U.S.A.	1997	8.99
Elliott, Ron	The Candlestickmaker	CD	Line	LECD-9.00944-0	Germany	1990	11.99
Ellis, Lauren	Push The River	CD	Line	LICD—9.01371-0	Germany	2000	4.99
Ellison, Lorraine	Stay With Me	CD	Line	LECD-9.01011-0	Germany	1991	39.99
Ellwood, William	Openings	CD	Narada	ND-61010	U.S.A.	1986	9.99
Eloy	Best Of Vol. 1: '72 - '75	CD	EMI	7243-8-28116-2-6	Holland	1994	10.99
Eloy	Best Of Vol. 1: '72 - '75 (Diff. Cvr.)	CD	Griffin	GCD-587-2	U.S.A.	1996	12.99
Eloy	Best Of Vol. 2: 1976 - 1979	CD	EMI	7243-8-37045-2-1	Holland	1996	10.99
Eloy	Childhood Memories	CD Single	SPV	055-48213	Germany	1994	4.99
Eloy	Chronicles Vol. 1 (Re-Recorded Mixes)	CD	SPV	SPV084-48182CD	Germany	1993	9.99
Eloy	Chronicles Vol. 1/2	2CD	SPV	SPV310-48220CD	Germany	2001	24.99
Eloy	Chronicles Vol. 2 (Re-Recorded Mixes)	CD	SPV	SPV084-48192CD	Germany	1994	9.99
Eloy	Chronicles, Vol. 1	CD	Victor Ent.	VICP-5410	Japan	1994	29.99
Eloy	Chronicles, Vol. 2	CD	Victor Ent.	VICP-5510	Japan	1994	29.99
Eloy	Colours	CD	EMI	538-7-92499-2	EEC	1980	10.99
Eloy	Dawn	CD	EMI	538-7-91129-2	EEC	1976	10.99
Eloy	Destination	CD	SPV	SPV084-48082CD	Germany	1992	9.99
Eloy	Destination	CD	Victor Ent.	VICP-5336	Japan	1993	29.99
Eloy	Eloy Live	CD	EMI	538-7-48503-2	EEC	1978	10.99
Eloy	Fire And Ice	CD Single	SPV	055-48093	Germany	1992	4.99
Eloy	Floating + 3	CD	EMI	7243-5-22686-2-7	Holland	2001	10.99
Eloy	Generation Of Innocence	CD Single	SPV	084-48202-P	Germany	1994	4.99
Eloy	Inside + 2	CD	EMI	7243-5-22681-2-2	Holland	2001	10.99
Eloy	Metromania	CD	EMI	538-7-92502-2	EEC	1984	10.99
Eloy	Ocean	CD	EMI	538-7-92020-2	EEC	1977	10.99
Eloy	Ocean 2 - The Answer	CD	BMG	74321-61259-2	Germany	1998	15.99
Eloy	Performance	CD	EMI	538-7-92501-2	EEC	1983	10.99
Eloy	Planets	CD	EMI	538-7-92500-2	EEC	1981	10.99
Eloy	Power And The Passion + 1	CD	EMI	7243-5-22760-2-8	Holland	2001	10.99
Eloy	Ra	CD	Victor Ent.	VICP-5335	Japan	1993	29.99
Eloy	Ra	CD	SPV	SPV085-48022CD	Germany	1998	9.99
Eloy	Ra (Different Cover/600 Only)	CD	SPV	MS-1058/85-4802	Germany	1988	29.99
Eloy	Rarities	CD	EMI	538-7-96721-2	EEC	1991	10.99
Eloy	Self Titled (1st Lp)	CD	Phillips	838-821-2	Germany	1971	10.99

E

Artist	Title	Format	Label	Catalog No	Country	Released	Value
Eloy	Self Titled (1st/W/ Bonus Int. Cd/Trks)	2CD	Second Battle	SB010	Germany	1998	19.99
Eloy	Silent Cries And Mighty Echoes	CD	EMI	538-7-92021-2	EEC	1979	10.99
Eloy	The Answer	CD Single	BMG	74321-62565-2	Germany	1998	8.99
Eloy	The Tides Return Forever	CD	SPV	SPV084-48202CD	Germany	1994	9.99
Eloy	The Tides Return Forever	CD	Victor Ent.	VICP-5569	Japan	1994	29.99
Eloy	Time To Turn	CD	EMI	538-7-48487-2	EEC	1982	11.99
Eloy	Timeless Passages	2CD	EMI	7243-5-82464-2-1	Holland	2003	19.99
Embryo	Africa	CD	Materiali Sonori	MASOCD-90022	Italy	1992	14.99
Embryo	Anthology (Every Day Ok 1970- 1979)	CD	Materiali Sonori	MASO-12	Italy	1992	14.99
Embryo	Apo - Calypso + 2	CD	Disconforme	DISC1933CD	Andorra	1999	10.99
Embryo	Bad Heads And Bad Cats + 1	CD	Disconforme	DISC1932CD	Andorra	1999	10.99
Embryo	Bremen 1971	CD	Garden O D	GOD-084	Germany	2003	19.99
Embryo	Embryo's Rache + 2	CD	Materiali Sonori	MASOCD-90050	Italy	1994	15.99
Embryo	Embryos Reise	CD	Schneeball	1652042	Germany	1994	13.99
Embryo	Father, Son And Holy Ghosts	CD	Disconforme	DISC1935CD	Andorra	1999	13.99
Embryo	Father, Son And Holy Ghosts + 1	CD	Garden O D	GOD-92	Germany	2003	14.99
Embryo	For Eva (W/Mal Waldron)	CD	Disconforme	DISC1939CD	Andorra	1999	10.99
Embryo	Hallo Mik	CD	Schneeball	24462-5	Germany	2003	14.99
Embryo	Ibn Battuta	CD	Schneeball	3052-2	Germany	1994	14.99
Embryo	Into The Light	CD	Materiali Sonori	MASOCD-90116	Italy	1999	14.99
Embryo	Invisible Documents ('74 Live)	2CD	Disconforme	DISC1931CD	Andorra	1999	24.99
Embryo	La Blama Sporozzi + 2	2CD	Disconforme	DISC1934CD	Andorra	1999	14.99
Embryo	Life Live '80 (W/Charlie Mariano)	CD	Disconforme	DISC1940CD	Andorra	2001	10.99
Embryo	Live Casablanca Tour '98	CD	Schneeball	8536-2	Germany	1999	14.99
Embryo	Live In Berlin	CD	United One	U1CD-2015-2	Germany	1998	17.99
Embryo	Live Vol. 1 2000	CD	Schneeball	9753-2	Germany	2001	14.99
Embryo	Live Vol. 1 2001	CD	Schneeball	0835-2	Germany	2001	14.99
Embryo	Ni Hau	CD	Schneeball	3062-2	Germany	1996	17.99
Embryo	One Night At Joan Miro Foundation	2CD	Disconforme	DISC1938CD	Andorra	2000	14.99
Embryo	Opal + 2	CD	Materiali Sonori	MASOCD-90012	Italy	1990	10.99
Embryo	Rocksession	CD	Repertoire	PMS-7077-WP	Germany	1998	15.99
Embryo	Steig Aus	CD	Repertoire	PMS-7078 -WP	Germany	1998	15.99
Embryo	Surfin'	CD	Disconforme	DISC1937CD	Andorra	1999	14.99
Embryo	Turn Peace + 1	CD	Schneeball	01045-26	Germany	1989	16.99
Embryo	W/ Yoruba Dun Dun Orchester + 2	CD	Schneeball	CD26	Germany	1989	16.99
Embryo	We Keep On + 2	CD	Disconforme	DISC1936CD	Andorra	1999	14.99
Embryo	Zack Glück	CD	Materiali Sonori	MASOCD-90038	Italy	1992	15.99
Emerson, Keith	Changing States	CD	AMP	AMP-CD-026	England	1995	16.99
Emerson, Keith	Honky	CD	Gunslinger	GSR-612000	U.S.A.	2000	11.99
Emerson, Keith	Inferno + 1	CD	Cinevox	CD-MDF-306	Italy	1997	20.99
Emerson, Keith	La Chiesa (Demon 3) O.S.T.	CD	Cinevox	JIM-0105	Japan	1992	16.99
Emerson, Keith	La Chiesa + 4 (Demon 3) O.S.T.	CD	Cinevox	CD-MDF-329	Italy	1997	11.99
Emerson, Keith	Murderock	CD	Jimco	JIM-0014	Japan	1997	18.99
Emerson, Keith	Murderock + 4	CD	Cinevox	CD-MDF-345	Italy	1997	11.99
Emerson, Keith	Nighthawks	CD	Net Event	A-128022	England	2002	11.99
Emerson, Keith	The Christmas Album	CD	Gunslinger	GSR-0472999	U.S.A.	1999	11.99
Emerson, Lake & Palmer	Black Moon	CD	Castle	CMRCD-227	England	2001	11.99
Emerson, Lake & Palmer	Brain Salad Surgery (DVD Audio)	CD	Rhino	R2-75980	U.S.A.	2000	15.99
Emerson, Lake & Palmer	Brain Salad Surgery + 1	CD	Rhino	R2-72459	U.S.A.	1996	9.99
Emerson, Lake & Palmer	Brain Salad Surgery + 3	CD	Castle	CMRCD-201	England	2001	11.99
Emerson, Lake & Palmer	Emerson Lake & Palmer	CD	Castle	CMRCD-165	England	2001	11.99
Emerson, Lake & Palmer	Fanfare For The Common Man	2CD	Castle	CMEDD110	England	2001	21.99
Emerson, Lake & Palmer	I Believe In Father Christmas Ep	CD Single	Rhino	R2-72242	U.S.A.	1995	14.99
Emerson, Lake & Palmer	In The Hot Seat + 1	CD	Victor Ent.	VICP-60646	Japan	1999	24.99
Emerson, Lake & Palmer	King Biscuit Flower Hour	2CD	King Biscuit	88025-2	U.S.A.	1997	19.99
Emerson, Lake & Palmer	Live At The Isle Of Wight Festival	CD	Victor Ent.	VICP-60443	Japan	1998	24.99
Emerson, Lake & Palmer	Live At The Royal Albert Hall	CD	Castle	CMRCD-228	England	2001	9.99
Emerson, Lake & Palmer	Live In Poland	CD	Metal Mind	PROG-CD-0060	England	1997	8.99

E

Artist	Title	Format	Label	Catalog No	Country	Released	Value
Emerson, Lake & Palmer	Love Beach + 3	CD	Castle	CMRCD-226	England	2001	11.99
Emerson, Lake & Palmer	Manticore Vaults Vol. 1 Box Set	7 CD	Castle	CMXBX-309	England	2001	39.99
Emerson, Lake & Palmer	Manticore Vaults Vol. 2 Box Set	8 CD	Castle	CMXBX-330	England	2001	39.99
Emerson, Lake & Palmer	Manticore Vaults Vol. 3 Box Set	5CD	Castle	CMYBX-524	England	2002	34.99
Emerson, Lake & Palmer	Pictures At An Exhibition + 1	CD	Castle	CMRCD-167	England	2001	11.99
Emerson, Lake & Palmer	Return Of The Manticore (DJ Sampler)	CD	Victory	SACD-757	U.S.A.	1993	7.99
Emerson, Lake & Palmer	Return Of The Manticore Box Set	4CD	Victory	383-484-004-2	U.S.A.	1993	23.99
Emerson, Lake & Palmer	Re-Works	3CD	Alchemy	PILOT-145	England	2003	19.99
Emerson, Lake & Palmer	Tarkus	CD	Castle	CMRCD-166	England	2001	9.99
Emerson, Lake & Palmer	Tarkus (MFSL Gold Cd)	CD	Mobile Fidelity	UDCD-598	U.S.A.	1971	28.99
Emerson, Lake & Palmer	The Atlantic Years	2CD	Atlantic	7-82403-2	U.S.A.	1992	19.99
Emerson, Lake & Palmer	Then & Now	2CD	Eagle	ENT.1001-2	U.S.A.	1998	19.99
Emerson, Lake & Palmer	Trilogy (MFSL Gold Cd)	CD	Mobile Fidelity	UDCD-621	U.S.A.	1972	24.99
Emerson, Lake & Palmer	Trilogy + 1	CD	Castle	CMRCD-200	England	2001	11.99
Emerson, Lake & Palmer	Welcome Back My Friends...	2CD	Castle	CMDDD202	England	2001	16.99
Emerson, Lake & Palmer	Works Live	2CD	Castle	CMDDD229	England	2001	16.99
Emerson, Lake & Palmer	Works Volume 2 + 3	CD	Castle	CMRCD-225	England	2001	11.99
Emerson, Lake & Palmer	Works, Volume 1 + 3	2CD	Castle	CMDDD224	England	2001	16.99
Emerson, Lake & Palmer/3	...To The Power Of Three	CD	Geffen	924-181-2	U.S.A.	1988	8.99
England	Garden Shed (Like Gabriel Genesis)	CD	Edison	ERC-32004	Japan	1977	44.99
England Dan/John Ford Coley	Best Of	CD	Atlantic	76018-2	U.S.A.	1979	7.99
England Dan/John Ford Coley	Dr.Heckle And Mr.Jive (Dan Seals)	CD	East West	AMCY-6143	Japan	2000	27.99
England Dan/John Ford Coley	Nights Are Forever (Dan Seals)	CD	East West	AMCY-6142	Japan	2000	27.99
England Dan/John Ford Coley	The Essentials	CD	Rhino	R2-76056	U.S.A.	2003	8.99
England Dan/John Ford Coley	The Very Best Of	CD	Rhino	R2-72568	U.S.A.	1996	8.99
Eno, Brian	A Year (Bonus Cd Of Year Of ...Book)	CD Single	Opal	259441-0101	France	1998	56.99
Eno, Brian	Ali Click	CD Single	Warner Bros.	9-40650-2	U.S.A.	1992	9.99
Eno, Brian	Ambient 1: Music For Airports	CD	Editions EG	EEGCD-17	U.S.A.	1978	8.99
Eno, Brian	Ambient 4: On Land	CD	Editions EG	EEGCD-20	U.S.A.	1982	12.99
Eno, Brian	Another Green World	CD	Toshiba-EMI	VJCP-23194	Japan	1993	24.99
Eno, Brian	Apollo Atmospheres & Soundtracks	CD	Editions EG	EGCD-53	U.S.A.	1983	11.99
Eno, Brian	Before And After Science	CD	Editions EG	EGCD-32	U.S.A.	1977	14.99
Eno, Brian	Before And After Science	CD	Toshiba-EMI	VJCP-23195	Japan	1993	24.99
Eno, Brian	Bell Studies/Clock Of The Long Now	CD	Opal	OPALCD2	England	2003	14.99
Eno, Brian	Compact Forest Proposal	CD	Opal	921143052D18	England	2001	19.99
Eno, Brian	Desert Island Selection	CD	Editions EG	EGCD-65	U.S.A.	1986	11.99
Eno, Brian	Discreet Music	CD	Editions EG	EEGCD-23	U.S.A.	1975	11.99
Eno, Brian	Eno 1 (Instrumental Box)	3CD	Virgin	7243-8-39110-2-8	England	1993	136.99
Eno, Brian	Eno 2 (Vocal Box)	3CD	Virgin	7243-8-39114-2-4	England	1993	80.99
Eno, Brian	Eno Sampler (Promo) (No Tray Art)	CD	Virgin	DPRO-14130	U.S.A.	1994	24.99
Eno, Brian	Extracts From Music For White Cube	CD	Opal	10465231-01	England	1997	109.99
Eno, Brian	Fractal Zoom	CD Single	Warner Bros.	9-40539-2	U.S.A.	1992	6.99
Eno, Brian	Fractal Zoom	CD Single	Warner Bros.	9362-40496-2	Germany	1992	6.99
Eno, Brian	Here Come The Warm Jets	CD	Editions EG	EGCD-11	U.S.A.	1973	12.99
Eno, Brian	Here Come The Warm Jets	CD	Toshiba-EMI	VJCP-23193	Japan	1993	24.99
Eno, Brian	I Dormienti	CD	Opal	0899-0829B23	England	1999	19.99
Eno, Brian	Kite Stories	CD	Opal	009994155B18	England	1999	19.99
Eno, Brian	Lightness: Music For Marble Palace	CD	Opal	10494881-01	England	1997	19.99
Eno, Brian	Music For Civic Recovery Centre	CD	Opal	846.780.000.000	England	2000	19.99
Eno, Brian	Music For Films	CD	Editions EG	EEGCD-5	U.S.A.	1978	13.99
Eno, Brian	Neroli	CD	Caroline	CAROL-6600-2	U.S.A.	1993	12.99
Eno, Brian	Nerve Net	CD	Warner Bros.	9-45033-2	U.S.A.	1992	7.99
Eno, Brian	Nerve Net Sampler (Promo)	CD	Warner Bros.	PRO-CD-5886	U.S.A.	1990	9.99
Eno, Brian	Sonora Portraits (With Book)	CD	Auditorium Edizioni	1295701102	Italy	1999	14.99
Eno, Brian	Taking Tiger Mountain (By Strategy)	CD	Editions EG	EGCD-17	U.S.A.	1974	11.99
Eno, Brian	Textures	CD	Standard Music Lib.	ESL-003-CD	England	1999	449.99
Eno, Brian	The Drop (With 3" Bonus Cd)	2CD	For Life	FLCP-1005	Japan	1997	28.99
Eno, Brian	The Shutov Assembly	CD	Warner Bros.	9-45010-2	U.S.A.	1992	8.99

E

Artist	Title	Format	Label	Catalog No	Country	Released	Value
Eno, Brian	Thursday Afternoon	CD	Editions EG	EGCD-64	U.S.A.	1985	13.99
Eno, Brian	UK Brian Eno (Music Publishing Promo)	CD	BMG	BMG-PUB038	England	2003	79.99
Eno, Brian/Cluster	Cluster & Eno	CD	Sky	SKY-CD-3010	Germany	1977	32.99
Eno, Brian/Derek Jarman	Blue	CD	Elektra	79337-2	U.S.A.	1993	14.99
Eno, Brian/Harmonia 76	Tracks & Traces	CD	Rykodisc	RCD-10428	U.S.A.	1997	20.39
Eno, Brian/J. Peter Schwalm	Drawn From Life	CD	Virgin	7243-8-10148-20	England	2001	11.99
Eno, Brian/Jah Wobble	Spinner	CD	Gyroscope	GYR-6614-2	U.S.A.	1995	9.99
Eno, Brian/John Cale	Been There Done That (Promo)	CD Single	Warner Bros.	PRO-CD-4493	U.S.A.	1990	19.99
Eno, Brian/John Cale	One Word	CD Single	Warner Bros.	9-40001-2	U.S.A.	1991	10.99
Eno, Brian/John Cale	One Word (Grandfather's H/Palanquin)	CD Single	Land	LANDHO4	England	1990	53.99
Eno, Brian/John Cale	Words/Music Wrong Way Up (Promo)	CD	Warner Bros.	PRO-CD-4691	U.S.A.	1991	14.99
Eno, Brian/John Cale	Wrong Way Up	CD	Warner Bros.	9-26421-2	U.S.A.	1990	11.99
Eno, Brian/John Cale	Wrong Way Up	CD	All Saints	ASCD12	England	1995	7.99
Eno, Brian/John Paul Jones	Music For Films III	CD	Warner Bros.	9-25769-2	U.S.A.	1988	11.99
Eno, Brian/Peter Schwalm	Reigakusya (Ltd Holographic)	2CD	Victor Ent.	VICP-60980-1	Japan	2000	54.99
Eno, Brian/Peter Sinfield	From Ibiza (1st Ed. Land Clear/Cd)	CD	Tecval	CMDS-1059	Switzerlan	1979	21.99
Eno, Brian/Peter Sinfield	In A Land Of Clear Colours (2nd Ed)	CD	Voiceprint	VP151CD	England	1993	14.99
Eno, Brian/Robert Fripp	Headcandy Win Cd-Rom/W Unrel.Cd	Cd-Rom	Ion	76896-40067-2	U.S.A.	1994	34.99
Eno, Brian/Robert Fripp	The Essential Fripp And Eno + 4 Unrel.	CD	Caroline	CAROL-1886-2	U.S.A.	1994	12.99
Eno, Brian/Roger Eno	18 Keyboard Pieces/H.F. Micheelsen	CD	Opal	OPALCD1	England	2002	31.99
Eno, Roger	Between Tides	CD	All Saints	ASCD01	England	1992	8.99
Eno, Roger	Flatlands	CD	All Saints	ASCD-36	U.S.A.	1998	11.99
Eno, Roger	Islands	CD	La Cooka Ratcha	LCVP103CD	England	2000	8.99
Eno, Roger	Lost In Translation	CD	All Saints	ASCD18	England	1994	8.99
Eno, Roger	Music Neglected English Composers	CD	Resurgence	RES126CD	Austria	1997	14.99
Eno, Roger	Swimming	CD	All Saints	ASCD-28	England	1996	9.99
Eno, Roger	The Long Walk	2CD	La Cooka Ratcha	LCVP116CD	England	2000	14.99
Eno, Roger	The Nightgarden	CD	La Cooka Ratcha	LCVP104CD	England	1999	10.99
Eno, Roger/Brian Eno	Voices	CD	Editions EG	EEGCD-42	U.S.A.	1985	9.99
Eno, Roger/Kate St.John	The Familiar	CD	Caroline	CAROL-6601-2	U.S.A.	1992	10.99
Eno, Roger/Kate St.John	The Familiar	CD	All Saints	FLCP-1014	Japan	1992	10.99
Eno, Roger/Lol Hammond	Damage	2CD	All Saints	ASCD-37	England	1999	15.99
Eno, Roger/Peter Hammill	The Appointed Hour	CD	Fie!	FIE-9120	England	1999	13.99
Eno/Moebius/Roedelius	After The Heat	CD	Gyroscope	GYR-6621-2	U.S.A.	1977	25.99
Eno/Moebius/Roedelius/Plank	Begegnungen	CD	Gyroscope	GYR-6622-2	U.S.A.	1977	14.99
Eno/Moebius/Roedelius/Plank	Begegnungen II	CD	Gyroscope	GYR-6622-2	U.S.A.	1977	14.99
Entombed	Wolverine Blues (W/Comic Book)	CD	Columbia	CK-57742-S1	U.S.A.	1994	14.99
Entwistle, John	Anthology	CD	Repertoire	REP-4600-WY	Germany	1996	15.99
Entwistle, John	King Biscuit Flower Hour (Live)	CD	King Biscuit	70710-88030-2	U.S.A.	1997	11.99
Entwistle, John	Rigor Mortis Sets In	CD	Repertoire	REP-4621-WY	Germany	1997	15.99
Entwistle, John	Smash Your Head Against..+ 2	CD	Sundazed	SC-6116	U.S.A.	1997	12.99
Entwistle, John	The Rock	CD	Repertoire	REP-4696-WY	Germany	1996	11.99
Entwistle, John	Thunderfingers: The Best	CD	Rhino	R2-75270	U.S.A.	1996	14.99
Entwistle, John	Too Late The Hero	CD	Repertoire	REP-4634-WY	Germany	1997	12.99
Entwistle, John	Whistle Rhymes	CD	Repertoire	REP-4618-WY	Germany	1996	13.99
Entwistle, John/Band	Left For Live	CD	J-Bird	JBD-80286-2	U.S.A.	1999	8.99
Entwistle, John/Ox	Mad Dog	CD	Repertoire	REP-4629-WY	Germany	1997	12.99
Enuff Znuff	10 + 2	CD	Pony Canyon	PCCY-01445	Japan	2000	19.99
Enya	A Box Of Dreams	3CD	Warner Bros.	3984-21333-2	England	1997	54.99
Enya	A Day Without Rain	CD	Reprise	9-47426-2	U.S.A.	2000	9.99
Enya	Enya (1st Version - Same/The Celts)	CD	Atlantic	7-81842-2	U.S.A.	1986	17.99
Enya	Oiche Chiun	CD Single	Reprise	9-40660-2	U.S.A.	1988	4.99
Enya	Only If...	CD Single	Reprise	9-17266-2	U.S.A.	1997	8.99
Enya	Only Time/The Collection/Sampler (DJ)	CD	Warner Bros.	PRO-3645	England	2002	14.99
Enya	Only Time: The Collection	4CD	Warner Bros.	80927-49211-2	U.S.A.	2002	34.99
Enya	Orinoco Flow	CD Single	Warner Bros.	WPCR-1146	Japan	1997	7.99
Enya	Paint The Sky (Gold Cd)	CD	Warner Bros.	WPCR-2345	Japan	1997	24.99
Enya	Paint The Sky With Stars: Best Of	CD	Reprise	9-46835-2	U.S.A.	1997	7.99

E

Artist	Title	Format	Label	Catalog No	Country	Released	Value
Enya	Shepherd Moons	CD	Reprise	9-26775-2	U.S.A.	1988	8.99
Enya	Special Sampler (Promo)	CD	Warner Bros.	PCS-594	Japan	2002	149.99
Enya	Storms In Africa	CD Single	Warner Bros.	16P2-2877	Japan	1989	22.99
Enya	The Celts	CD	Reprise	9-45081-2	U.S.A.	1986	8.99
Enya	The Celts (Gold Cd)	CD	Warner Bros.	WPCR-10090	Japan	1999	206.99
Enya	The Frog Prince	CD	Spectrum	551-099-2	Germany	1985	5.99
Enya	The Memory Of Trees	CD	Reprise	9-46106-2	U.S.A.	1995	9.99
Enya	Themes Calmi Cuori Appassionati	CD	Warner Bros.	WPCR-11006	Japan	2001	6.99
Enya	Watermark	CD	Reprise	9-26774-2	U.S.A.	1988	9.99
Enya	Wild Child	CD Single	Warner Bros.	8573873782	England	2001	8.99
Erasure	The Other Sampler (Promo)	CD	Mute	MUSDJ-133-2	U.S.A.	2003	47.99
Erickson, Roky	I Think Of Demons	CD	Edsel	EDCD-528	England	1997	13.99
Erickson, Roky	You're Gonna Miss Me-Best Of	CD	Restless	7-72532-2	U.S.A.	1991	13.99
Erickson, Roky/13th Floor E.	All That May Do My Rhyme	CD	Trance	TR-33CD	U.S.A.	1995	8.99
Erickson, Roky/Aliens	The Evil One + 5	CD	Sympathy For The	SFTRI-685-CD	U.S.A.	2002	9.99
Erickson, Roky/Nervebreakers	Live In Dallas	CD	New Rose	422404	France	1992	19.99
Erickson, Roky/Various Artists	Where The Pyramyd Meets The Eye	CD	Sire	9-26422-2	U.S.A.	1990	5.99
Essex, David	Gold Collection	CD	Columbia	471015-2	France	1992	12.99
Essex, David	Here We Are All Together	CD	Lamplight	LAMP-23-CD	England	1998	8.99
Essex, David	Living In England	CD	Lamplight	CIR-1002-2	England	1995	5.99
Essex, David	Rock On	CD	Columbia	CK-32560	U.S.A.	1973	5.99
Estefan, Gloria	I Wish You (Promo)	CD Single	Epic	ESK-58373	U.S.A.	2003	14.99
Eternal Flame	Desire + 2	CD	Dreamchaser	SCCD-8	Japan	1998	29.99
Eurythmics	17 Again (Disc 1)	CD Single	RCA	74321-72626-2	England	1999	7.99
Eurythmics	17 Again (Disc 2)	CD	RCA	74321-72672-2	England	1999	7.99
Eurythmics	1984 (For The Love Of Big Brother)	CD	RCA	PCD1-5371	U.S.A.	1984	8.99
Eurythmics	Be Yourself Tonight	CD	RCA	PCD1-5429	U.S.A.	1985	8.99
Eurythmics	Eurythmics - Sampled Live 1983-1989	CD	RCA	KCDP-51191	Canada	1993	31.99
Eurythmics	Greatest Hits	CD	RCA	ARCD-8680	U.S.A.	1992	8.99
Eurythmics	Greatest Hits + 4	CD	BMG	061921-0610-2-0	Canada	1998	12.99
Eurythmics	In The Garden	CD	RCA	07863-65134-2	U.S.A.	1991	8.99
Eurythmics	Live 1983-1989	2CD	Arista	07822-17704-2	U.S.A.	1993	15.99
Eurythmics	Peace	CD	Arista	07822-14617-2	U.S.A.	1999	8.99
Eurythmics	Revenge	CD	RCA	PCD1-5847	U.S.A.	1986	8.99
Eurythmics	Rough And Tough At The Roxy (DJ)	CD	RCA	5629-2-RDJ	U.S.A.	1986	74.99
Eurythmics	Savage	CD	RCA	6794-2-R	U.S.A.	1987	8.99
Eurythmics	Sweet Dreams (Are Made Of This)	CD	RCA	PCD1-4681	U.S.A.	1982	8.99
Eurythmics	Touch	CD	RCA	PCD1-4917	U.S.A.	1983	8.99
Eurythmics	Touch Dance: Remix Collection	CD	BMG	ND-75151	England	1992	10.99
Eurythmics	We Too Are One	CD	Arista	ARCD-8606	U.S.A.	1989	8.99
Evanescence	Fallin' + 1 (W/Bonus DVD)	2CD	Sony	EICP-240-241	Japan	2003	55.99
Even Dozen Jug Band	Even Dozen Jug Band (J. Sebastian)	CD	Collector's Choice	CCM-263-2	U.S.A.	2002	14.99
Everclear	For College Radio Only	CD	Capitol	DPRO-12099	U.S.A.	1997	24.99
Everly Brothers	All They Had To Do Is Dream	CD	Carlton Sounds	30360-00832	England	1997	7.99
Everly Brothers	Born Yesterday	CD	Mercury	836-142-2	U.S.A.	1985	14.99
Everly Brothers	Brothers In Rhythm	2CD	Snapper	SMD-CD-179	England	1998	12.99
Everly Brothers	EB 84	CD	Mercury	822-431-2	U.S.A.	1984	14.99
Everly Brothers	Everly Brothers' Best (DCC Gold Cd)	CD	DCC	GZS-1141	U.S.A.	2000	19.99
Everly Brothers	Everly Country	CD	Connoisseur	VSOP-CD-237	England	1997	12.99
Everly Brothers	Greatest Hits	CD	Line	BLCD-9.01032-L	Germany	1991	11.99
Everly Brothers	Greatest Love Songs, Vol. 1	CD	Prism Leisure	PLATCD-168	England	1996	8.99
Everly Brothers	Greatest Love Songs, Vol. 2	CD	Prism Leisure	PLATCD-169	England	1997	8.99
Everly Brothers	Greatest Recordings	CD	ACE	CDCH-903	England	1986	11.99
Everly Brothers	Heartaches & Harmonies [Boxed Set]	4CD	Rhino	R2-71779	U.S.A.	1994	34.99
Everly Brothers	Hightlights Reunion Concert	CD	QED	QED-304	EEC	1998	10.99
Everly Brothers	I Grandi Del Rock	CD	RCA	74321-13522-2	Italy	1993	9.99
Everly Brothers	Nice Guys	CD	Magnum Force	CDMF-1028	England	1988	14.99
Everly Brothers	Original British Singles	CD	ACE	CDCHM-544	England	1994	11.99

E

Artist	Title	Format	Label	Catalog No	Country	Released	Value
Everly Brothers	Pass The Chicken And Listen	CD	Edsel	ED-CD-319	England	1991	14.99
Everly Brothers	Rare Solo Classics	CD	Curb	CURCD-068	England	1999	8.99
Everly Brothers	Reunion At The Albert Hall	2CD	Castle	PIEDD-230	England	2000	8.99
Everly Brothers	Self Titled (Cadence)/Fab. Style Of	CD	ACE	CDCH-932	England	1990	11.99
Everly Brothers	Sing Great Country Hits	CD	Connoisseur	VSOP-CD-237	England	1997	12.99
Everly Brothers	Songs Our Daddy Taught Us	CD	Line	BLCD-9.00965-L	Germany	1990	11.99
Everly Brothers	Songs Our Daddy Taught Us	CD	ACE	029667107525	U.S.A.	1995	11.99
Everly Brothers	Songs Our Daddy Taught Us	CD	Rhino	R2-70212	U.S.A.	1990	11.99
Everly Brothers	Songs Our Daddy Taught Us	CD	ACE	CDCHM-75	England	1990	11.99
Everly Brothers	Stories We Could Tell	CD	RCA	74321-432552	EEC	1996	9.99
Everly Brothers	Susie Q	CD	ACE	CDMF-052	England	1987	11.99
Everly Brothers	The Best Of: 1957 - 1960	CD	Music Club	MCCD-209	EEC	1995	10.99
Everly Brothers	The Best Of: 1957 - 1960 (W/Box)	CD	Music Club	MCCDSE-209	EEC	1996	12.99
Everly Brothers	The E.P. Collection	CD	See For Miles	SEE-CD-482	England	1997	14.99
Everly Brothers	The Everly Brothers	CD	Line	BLCD-9.00954-L	Germany	1990	11.99
Everly Brothers	The Everly Brothers (Cadence)	CD	Rhino	R2-70211	U.S.A.	1990	8.99
Everly Brothers	The Fabulous Style Of	CD	Rhino	R2-70213	U.S.A.	1990	11.99
Everly Brothers	The Fabulous Style Of...	CD	Line	BLCD-9.00961-L	Germany	1990	11.99
Everly Brothers	The Masters (20 Classic Tracks)	CD	Eagle	EAB-CD-032	EEC	1997	10.99
Everly Brothers	The Mercury Years	CD	Mercury	314-514-905-2	U.S.A.	1993	9.99
Everly Brothers	The Very Best Of	CD	Crimson	CRIMCD-65	England	1997	7.99
Everly Brothers	Two Yanks In England	CD	Demon	FIEND-CD-297	England	1989	19.99
Everly, Don	Brother Jukebox	CD	Oh Boy	OBR-412	U.S.A.	2002	14.99
Everly, Don	Brother Jukebox	CD	Sundown	CDSD-002	England	1994	11.99
Everly, Phil	London Sessions (Nothing Too/Mystic)	CD	Sequel	NEX-CD-164	England	1991	19.99
Everly, Phil	Louise	CD	Magnum Force	CDMF-053	England	1994	19.99
Everly, Phil	Self Titled	CD	BGO	BGOCD199	England	1993	14.99
Everly, Phil	The Solo Years	CD	Castle	SELCD-545	England	1998	6.99
Every Mother's Son	Come On Down To My Boat (Best Of)	CD	Collectables	COL-CD-5867	U.S.A.	1997	9.99
Everything	Labrador	CD	Capricorn	9-42036-2	U.S.A.	1995	8.99
Everything But the Girl	Acoustic	CD	Atlantic	7-82395-2	U.S.A.	1992	9.99
Everything But the Girl	Amplified Heart	CD	Atlantic	82605-2	U.S.A.	1994	7.99
Everything But the Girl	Before Today	CD Single	Atlantic	2-84871	U.S.A.	1996	4.99
Everything But the Girl	Eden	CD	Blanco Y Negro	2292-40395-2	France	1985	12.99
Everything But the Girl	Home Movies (The Best Of)	CD	Blanco Y Negro	4509-92319-2	Germany	1993	11.99
Everything But the Girl	Love Not Money + 2	CD	Sire	9-25274-2	U.S.A.	1985	9.99
Everything But the Girl	Missing	CD Single	Atlantic	85620-2	U.S.A.	1994	7.99
Everything But the Girl	The Best Of Everything But The Girl	CD	Blanco Y Negro	0630-16637-2	France	1993	9.99
Everything But the Girl	The Language Of Life	CD	Atlantic	7-82057-2	U.S.A.	1990	6.99
Everything But the Girl	Walking Wounded	CD	Atlantic	82912-2	U.S.A.	1996	12.99
Explorers Club	Raising The Mammoth	CD	Magna Carta	MA-9046-2	U.S.A.	2002	24.99
Explorers Club/Steve Howe	Age Of Impact	CD	Magna Carta	MA-9021-2	U.S.A.	1998	8.99
Express	Ich Tarzan Du Jane	CD Single	ZYX	ZYX-7258-2	Germany	2000	14.99
Eye To Eye/Donald Fagen	Shakespeare Stole My Baby	CD	Warner Bros.	WPCR-10563	Japan	1999	23.99
Eye To Eye/Toto	S.T./Shakespeare Stole My Baby	CD	Wounded Bird	WOU-3570	U.S.A.	2002	14.99
Eyes Adrift	S.T. (Meat Puppets, Nirvana, Sublime)	CD	Spin Art	SPART-115	U.S.A.	2002	9.99
Ezo	Fire Fire	CD	Victor Ent.	VICL-2080	Japan	1991	22.99
Ezo	Self Titled	CD	Victor Ent.	VICL-2072	Japan	1991	22.99

F

Artist	Title	Format	Label	Catalog No	Country	Released	Value
Fabulous Poodles	His Masters Choice	CD	Sequel	NEM-CD-697	England	1995	11.99
Fabulous Thunderbirds	Butt Rockin' + 3	CD	Benchmark	CD8004	U.S.A.	2001	10.99
Fabulous Thunderbirds	Butt Rockin'/T-Bird Rhythm	CD	BGO	BGOCD193	England	1996	14.99

Artist	Title	Format	Label	Catalog No	Country	Released	Value
Fabulous Thunderbirds	Different Tacos (Rarities 1st 4 Lps)	CD	Country Town	CTM-3006	U.S.A.	1996	14.99
Fabulous Thunderbirds	Girls Go Wild (Self Titled 1st Lp + 3)	CD	Benchmark	CD8002	U.S.A.	2001	10.99
Fabulous Thunderbirds	High Water	CD	High Street	72902-10357-2	U.S.A.	1997	9.99
Fabulous Thunderbirds	Hot Number	CD	Columbia	ZK-40818	U.S.A.	1987	7.99
Fabulous Thunderbirds	Hot Number	CD	Sony	SRCS-6423	Japan	1995	24.99
Fabulous Thunderbirds	Hot Stuff-The Greatest Hits	CD	Epic	ZK-53007	U.S.A.	1992	9.99
Fabulous Thunderbirds	Live	CD	CMC INT.	06076-86315-2	U.S.A.	2001	8.99
Fabulous Thunderbirds	Live	CD	Sanctuary	SANCD116	England	2002	9.99
Fabulous Thunderbirds	Powerful Stuff	CD	Columbia	ZK-45094	U.S.A.	1989	6.99
Fabulous Thunderbirds	Powerful Stuff	CD	Sony	SRCS-6424	Japan	1995	24.99
Fabulous Thunderbirds	Roll Of The Dice	CD	Private	1005-82130-2	U.S.A.	1995	8.99
Fabulous Thunderbirds	Roll Of The Dice	CD	BMG Victor	BVCP-882	Japan	1995	24.99
Fabulous Thunderbirds	Self Titled/What's The Word	CD	BGO	BGOCD192	England	1996	29.99
Fabulous Thunderbirds	Tacos Deluxe	CD	Benchmark	CD8006	U.S.A.	2003	10.99
Fabulous Thunderbirds	T-Bird Rhythm	CD	Benchmark	CD8005	U.S.A.	2001	10.99
Fabulous Thunderbirds	The Essential (Chrysalis Lps Best Of)	CD	Chrysalis	F2-21851	U.S.A.	1991	8.99
Fabulous Thunderbirds	Tuff Enuff	CD	Columbia	ZK-40304	U.S.A.	1986	8.99
Fabulous Thunderbirds	Tuff Enuff	CD	Sony	SRCS-6422	Japan	1995	24.99
Fabulous Thunderbirds	Walk That Walk, Talk That Talk	CD	Epic	ZK-47878	U.S.A.	1991	12.99
Fabulous Thunderbirds	What's The Word + 4	CD	Benchmark	CD8003	U.S.A.	2001	10.99
Fabulous Thunderbirds	Wrap It Up	CD	Sony	A-24202	U.S.A.	1993	7.99
Faces	A Nod Is As Good As A Wink...	CD	Warner Bros.	2574-2	U.S.A.	1971	6.99
Faces	Best Of Faces: Good Boys...	CD	Rhino	R2-75830	U.S.A.	1999	10.99
Faces	Long Player	CD	Warner Bros.	1892-2	U.S.A.	1971	8.99
Faces	Ooh La La	CD	Warner Bros.	2665-2	U.S.A.	1973	8.99
Fagen, Donald	Century's End (3")	CD Single	Warner Bros.	W7972CD	England	1993	27.99
Fagen, Donald	Kamakiriad	CD	Warner Bros.	9-45230-2	U.S.A.	1993	6.99
Fagen, Donald	Kamakiriad (Promo Gold Cd)	CD	Reprise	9-45230-DJ	U.S.A.	1993	39.99
Fagen, Donald	New Frontier (CD Video)	CDV	Warner Bros.	9-25679-2	U.S.A.	1982	12.99
Fagen, Donald	The Nightfly	CD	Warner Bros.	9-23696-2	U.S.A.	1982	8.99
Fagen, Donald	The Nightfly (DVD Audio)	CD	Rhino	R2-78138	U.S.A.	2003	14.99
Fagen, Donald	The Nightfly (Pioneer Gold Cd)	CD	Warner Bros.	43XD-2003	Japan	1982	311.99
Fagen, Donald	Tomorrow's Girls	CD Single	Warner Bros.	918502-2	U.S.A.	1993	13.99
Fagen, Donald	Tomorrow's Girls (3")	CD Single	Warner Bros.	WPDP-6320	Japan	1993	19.99
Fagen, Donald	Tomorrows Girl's EP	CD Single	Warner Bros.	WPCP-5503	Japan	1993	10.99
Fagen, Donald	Trans-Island Skyway	CD Single	Warner Bros.	9362-41062-2	England	1993	16.99
Fagen, Donald	Trans-Island Skyway (3")	CD Single	Warner Bros.	WPDP-6332	Japan	1993	19.99
Fagen, Donald	Words & Music	CD	Reprise	PRO-CD-6461-R	U.S.A.	1993	9.99
Fahey, John	After The Ball	CD	Collector's Choice	CCM-213	U.S.A.	2001	9.99
Fahey, John	America (Complete Version)	CD	Takoma	TAKCD-8903	U.S.A.	1998	10.99
Fahey, John	Best Of John Fahey 1959 - 1977 + 3	2CD	Takoma	TAKCD-8915	U.S.A.	2002	15.99
Fahey, John	Best Of, Vol. 2: 1964-1983	CD	Takoma	TAKCD-8916	U.S.A.	2002	10.99
Fahey, John	Best Vanguard (Y Princess/All Requia)	2CD	Vanguard	VMD-79523	U.S.A.	1999	12.99
Fahey, John	Blind Joe Death (Re-Recorded Stereo)	CD	Takoma	TAKCD-1002	U.S.A.	1996	12.99
Fahey, John	Christmas Album	CD	Burnside	BCD-0004-2	U.S.A.	1994	9.99
Fahey, John	Christmas Guitar, Vol. 1	CD	Varrick	CD-VR-002	U.S.A.	2000	9.99
Fahey, John	Christmas With John Fahey, Vol. 2	CD	Takoma	CDP-72745	U.S.A.	1975	9.99
Fahey, John	City Of Refuge	CD	PolyGram	830-127-2	Germany	1997	7.99
Fahey, John	Dance Of Death/Other Plantation + 4	CD	Takoma	TAKCD-8909	U.S.A.	1999	10.99
Fahey, John	Days Have Gone By	CD	Takoma	TAKCD-6509	U.S.A.	2001	9.99
Fahey, John	Death Chants...('63 / '67 Versions)	CD	Takoma	TAKCD-8908	U.S.A.	1999	11.99
Fahey, John	Essential (Yellow Princess/Requia - 1)	2CD	Vanguard	VMD-55/56	U.S.A.	1993	14.99
Fahey, John	Fare Forward Voyagers	CD	Shanachie	SHANCD-99005	England	1992	29.99
Fahey, John	Georgia Stomps...	CD	Table Of Elements	TOE-CD-38	U.S.A.	1998	14.99
Fahey, John	God, Time & Casuality	CD	Shanachie	SHANCD-97006	England	1990	10.99
Fahey, John	Great San Bernardino Birthday Party	CD	Takoma	TAKCD-6508	U.S.A.	2000	10.99
Fahey, John	Hitomi	CD	LivHouse	LIV-001CD	EU	2000	17.99
Fahey, John	I Remember Blind Joe Death	CD	Varrick	CD-VR-028	U.S.A.	1987	9.99

F

Artist	Title	Format	Label	Catalog No	Country	Released	Value
Fahey, John	Legend Of Blind Joe Death	CD	Takoma	TAKCD-8901	U.S.A.	1996	10.99
Fahey, John	Let Go	CD	Varrick	CD-VR-008	U.S.A.	1997	9.99
Fahey, John	Live In Tasmania	CD	Takoma	CDP-72789	U.S.A.	1981	29.99
Fahey, John	Of Rivers And Religion	CD	Collector's Choice	CCM-212	U.S.A.	2001	9.99
Fahey, John	Old Girlfriends...	CD	Varrick	CD-VR-031	U.S.A.	1992	9.99
Fahey, John	Olf Fashioned Love	CD	Takoma	TAKCD-6511	U.S.A.	2003	11.99
Fahey, John	Railroad	CD	Shanachie	SHANCD-99003	England	1992	29.99
Fahey, John	Rain Forests Oceans & Other Themes	CD	Varrick	CD-VR-019	U.S.A.	1990	9.99
Fahey, John	Red Cross	CD	Revenant	RVN-104	England	2003	14.99
Fahey, John	Requia And Other Guitar...	CD	Vanguard	VMD-79259	U.S.A.	1997	10.99
Fahey, John	Return of the Repressed: Anthology	2CD	Rhino	R2-71737	U.S.A.	1994	24.99
Fahey, John	The Epiphany Of Glenn Jones	CD	Thirsty Ear	THI-57037.2	U.S.A.	1997	9.99
Fahey, John	The New Possibility: Christmas Album	CD	Takoma	TAKCD-8912	U.S.A.	2000	10.99
Fahey, John	The Voice Of The Turtle	CD	Takoma	TAKCD-6501	U.S.A.	1996	10.99
Fahey, John	Transfiguration Of Blind Joe Death	CD	Takoma	TAKCD-6504	U.S.A.	1998	10.99
Fahey, John	Trio Vol. 1	CD	Jazzoo	ZJ01	U.S.A.	2002	9.99
Fahey, John	Visits Washington D.C.	CD	Takoma	CDP-72769	U.S.A.	1980	29.99
Fahey, John	Womblife	CD	Table Of Elements	TOE-CD-37	U.S.A.	1997	22.99
Fahey, John	Yellow Princess (Complete Version)	CD	Vanguard	VMD-79293	U.S.A.	2001	14.99
Fahey, John/Terry Robb	Popular Songs Christmas/New Year's	CD	Varrick	CD-VR-012	U.S.A.	1990	9.99
Fair Warning	A Decade Of	2CD	Avalon	MICP-10275	Japan	2001	24.99
Fair Warning	Angels Of Heaven	CD Single	Zero	XRCN-1288	Japan	1996	9.99
Fair Warning	Early Warnings '92-'95	CD	Warner Bros.	WPCR-1927	Japan	1997	16.99
Fair Warning	Four	CD	Frontiers	FR-CD-050	Italy	2000	14.99
Fair Warning	Go!	CD Single	Zero	XRCN-1292	Japan	1997	15.99
Fair Warning	Heart On The Run	CD Single	Avalon	MICP-40001	Japan	2000	9.99
Fair Warning	In The Ghetto	CD Single	Warner Bros.	WMC5-590	Japan	1993	15.99
Fair Warning	Live And More	CD	Zero	XRCN-2032-3	Japan	1998	17.99
Fair Warning	Live And More (W/Bonus)	2CD	Frontiers	FR-CD-054	Italy	2000	24.99
Fair Warning	Live At Home	CD	Warner Bros.	WPCR-405	Japan	1995	22.99
Fair Warning	Live In Japan	CD	Warner Bros.	WMC5-677	Japan	1993	21.99
Fair Warning	Rainmaker	CD	WEA	0630-10336-2	Germany	1995	17.99
Fair Warning	Rainmaker + 2	CD	Warner Bros.	WPCR-220	Japan	1995	22.99
Fair Warning	Save Me	CD Single	Zero	XRCN-1298	Japan	1997	14.99
Fair Warning	Self Titled	CD	WEA	9031-77043-2	Germany	1992	22.99
Fair Warning	Still I Believe	CD Single	Avalon	MICP-10182	Japan	2000	14.99
Fairport Convention	20th Century Masters: The Millennium	CD	A&M	069-493-308-2	U.S.A.	2002	8.99
Fairport Convention	25th Anniversary Concert	2CD	Woodworm	WRDCD-022	England	1993	24.99
Fairport Convention	25th Anniversary Concert	2CD	Festival	D46031	Australia	1996	24.99
Fairport Convention	Across The Decades	2CD	Snapper	SMD-CD-484	England	2003	12.99
Fairport Convention	Angel Delight	CD	Island	514-631-2	England	1971	11.99
Fairport Convention	Archive	CD	Rialto	RMCD-231Z	England	2001	11.99
Fairport Convention	AT2/The Boot	4CD	Woodworm	WR4CD-034	England	2000	49.99
Fairport Convention	Babbacombe Lee	CD	Island	512-755-2	England	1971	12.99
Fairport Convention	Before The Moon	2CD	Alchemy	PILOT-133	England	2002	14.99
Fairport Convention	Bonny Bunch Roses/Tipplers Tale	CD	Vertigo	512-988-2	England	1992	34.99
Fairport Convention	Close To The Wind	CD	Mooncrest	CRESTCD-035	England	1998	12.99
Fairport Convention	Close To The Wind	DVD Aud	Silverline	288086-9	U.S.A.	2002	14.99
Fairport Convention	Cropredy (30th Ann Concert)	3CD	Castle	CMETD-815	England	2003	24.99
Fairport Convention	Cropredy 2002: Another Gig..	2CD	Woodworm	WR2CD-039	England	2002	24.99
Fairport Convention	Cropredy 98	CD	Woodworm	WRCD-031	England	1999	10.99
Fairport Convention	Cropredy Box (30th Ann Concert)	3CD	Woodworm	WR3CD026	England	1998	24.99
Fairport Convention	Encore Encore (Farewell, Farewell + 3)	CD	Folkprint	FP001CD	England	1997	7.99
Fairport Convention	Encore, Encore (Farewell, Farewell + 3)	CD	Eagle	EAMCD-083	England	1999	7.99
Fairport Convention	Festival Copredy 2002 (Another Gig)	2CD	Talking Elephant	TECD-054	England	2003	19.99
Fairport Convention	Fiddlestix (Best Of 1972-84)	CD	Raven	RVCD-47	Australia	1998	12.99
Fairport Convention	From Cropredy To Portmeirion	CD	Talking Elephant	TECD-042	England	2002	12.99
Fairport Convention	Full House + 4	CD	Island	586-375-2	Germany	2001	11.99

Artist	Title	Format	Label	Catalog No	Country	Released	Value
Fairport Convention	Full House + 4	Mini Lp	Universal	UICY-9322	Japan	2003	22.99
Fairport Convention	Gladys' Leap (W/Expletive Delighted)	2CD	Folkprint	FP002CD	EU	1997	12.99
Fairport Convention	Gladys' Leap + 3	CD	Talking Elephant	TECD-034	England	2001	11.99
Fairport Convention	Gottle O' Geer	CD	Island	546-420-2	England	1999	13.99
Fairport Convention	Heritage	CD	Disky	SI-905323	Holland	2003	8.99
Fairport Convention	Heyday BBC Radio Sessions	CD	MIDI	MDC6-1141	Japan	1991	24.99
Fairport Convention	Heyday BBC Radio Sessions + 8	Mini Lp	Universal	UICY-9324	Japan	2003	22.99
Fairport Convention	Heyday BBC Radio Sessions+ 8	CD	Island	586-542-2	England	2002	9.99
Fairport Convention	House Full Live La Troubadour	CD	MIDI	MDC6-1110	Japan	1990	24.99
Fairport Convention	House Full: Live At La Troubadour + 2	Mini Lp	Universal	UICY-9323	Japan	2003	22.99
Fairport Convention	House Full: Live La Troubadour + 2	CD	Island	586-376-2	Germany	2001	15.99
Fairport Convention	In Real Time Live '87	CD	Island	846-559-2	England	1990	9.99
Fairport Convention	Jewel In The Crown	CD	Green Linnet	GLCD-3103	U.S.A.	1995	7.99
Fairport Convention	Jewel In The Crown	CD	Woodworm	WRCD-023	England	1995	8.99
Fairport Convention	Kind Fortune	2CD	Snapper	SMD-CD-214	England	2000	12.99
Fairport Convention	Leige And Leaf + 2	Mini Lp	Universal	UICY-9321	Japan	2003	22.99
Fairport Convention	Liege & Lief + 2	CD	Island	IMCD-291	EU	2002	13.99
Fairport Convention	Liege And Leaf	CD	Polystar	P32D-25006	Japan	1987	19.99
Fairport Convention	Liege And Leaf	CD	Polystar	PSCD-1126	Japan	1991	24.99
Fairport Convention	Live At Open Air Germany 1999	CD	Think Prog.	No Number	Germany	2000	15.99
Fairport Convention	Live Convention	CD	Island	842-812-2	England	1990	12.99
Fairport Convention	Live Convention	CD	Polystar	PSCD-1127	Japan	1991	24.99
Fairport Convention	Meet Me On The Ledge '67 - '75	2CD	A&M	314-564-68702	U.S.A.	1999	15.99
Fairport Convention	Meet Me On The Ledge '67 - '75	2CD	Island	564-687-2	England	1999	15.99
Fairport Convention	Moat On The Ledge - Live Broughton	CD	Talking Elephant	TECD-052	England	2003	12.99
Fairport Convention	Nine	CD	Island	512-756-2	England	1992	12.99
Fairport Convention	Old New Borrowed Blue	CD	Woodworm	WRCD-024	England	1996	14.99
Fairport Convention	Old New Borrowed Blue (Different Art)	CD	Green Linnet	GLCD-3114	U.S.A.	1996	14.99
Fairport Convention	Proclaimers - This Is The Story	CD	Nettwerk	30192	U.S.A.	2001	8.99
Fairport Convention	Proclaimers: Born Innocent	CD	Persevere	PERSRECCD09	England	2003	10.99
Fairport Convention	Proclaimers: Hit The Highway	CD	Nettwerk	30190	U.S.A.	2001	8.99
Fairport Convention	Proclaimers: Persevere	CD	Nettwerk	30193	U.S.A.	2001	9.99
Fairport Convention	Proclaimers: Sunshine On Leith + 4	CD	Nettwerk	30191	U.S.A.	2001	6.99
Fairport Convention	Proclaimers: The Best Of	CD	Capitol	38682	England	2002	12.99
Fairport Convention	Proclaimers: There's A Touch	CD Single	Nettwerk	33124	U.S.A.	2001	3.99
Fairport Convention	Red & Gold + 1	CD	HTD	HTD-CD-47	England	1995	7.99
Fairport Convention	Red & Gold + 1	CD	Talking Elephant	TECD-014	England	2001	7.99
Fairport Convention	Rhythm Of The Times	CD	Pickwick	751062	England	2003	8.99
Fairport Convention	Rhythm Of The Times	CD	Delta	47-002	England	1999	8.99
Fairport Convention	Rising For The Moon	CD	Island	512-757-2	England	1992	14.99
Fairport Convention	Rose/B Lee/Nine/Rising Moon	4CD	Island	512-753-2	England	1992	34.99
Fairport Convention	Rosie	CD	Island	512-754-2	England	1992	8.99
Fairport Convention	Scrum-Half Bricking (500/B Rugby)	CD	Front Row	BRUFC-01	England	2003	24.99
Fairport Convention	Self Titled	CD	Polydor	POCP-2085	Japan	1991	24.99
Fairport Convention	Self Titled +4	Mini Lp	Island	UICY-9318	Japan	2003	22.99
Fairport Convention	Self Titled + 4	CD	Island	068-291-2	England	2003	11.99
Fairport Convention	Shines Like Gold	CD	Eureka	EURCD-406	England	1999	8.99
Fairport Convention	Shines Like Gold	CD	Eureka	EURCD406	England	1999	8.99
Fairport Convention	Shines Like Gold (Special Edition)	3CD	Eureka	EURBOX1	England	2003	39.99
Fairport Convention	Some Of Our Yesterdays '85-'95	2CD	Castle	CMDDD-367	England	2001	12.99
Fairport Convention	The Airing Cupboard Tapes '71-'74 + 4	CD	Talking Elephant	TECD-046	England	2002	12.99
Fairport Convention	The Fairport Connection (MVC Promo)	CD	Island	FAIRCONN-001	England	2003	13.99
Fairport Convention	The Five Seasons + 1	CD	HTD	HTD-CD-48	England	1995	9.99
Fairport Convention	The Five Seasons + 1	CD	Talking Elephant	TECD-019	England	2001	9.99
Fairport Convention	The History Of	CD	Island	PHCR-4848	Japan	1998	24.99
Fairport Convention	The History Of	CD	Island	846-083-2	England	1991	11.99
Fairport Convention	The History Of	CD	Polystar	PSCD-1130	Japan	1991	19.99
Fairport Convention	The History Of	CD	Polystar	P40D-25046	Japan	1988	19.99

F

Artist	Title	Format	Label	Catalog No	Country	Released	Value
Fairport Convention	The Other Boot/The Third Leg	3CD	Woodworm	WR3CD-037	England	2003	34.99
Fairport Convention	The Wood And The Wire	CD	Woodworm	WRCD-033	England	1999	10.99
Fairport Convention	The Woodworm Years + 2	CD	Voiceprint	VPJ-062	Japan	1998	24.99
Fairport Convention	The Woodworm Years + 2	CD	Folkprint	FP003CD	England	1998	9.99
Fairport Convention	Then & Now 1982 - 1996 The Best Of	CD	Metro	METRCD076	England	2002	9.99
Fairport Convention	Then & Now 1982-1996: (Best Of)	CD	Metro	METRCD076	England	2002	6.99
Fairport Convention	Tipplers Tales	CD	BGO	BGOCD72	England	1989	29.99
Fairport Convention	Unconventional Box Set	4CD	Free Reed	FRQCD-35	England	2002	65.99
Fairport Convention	Unhalfbricking	CD	Polystar	P32D-25025	Japan	1987	24.99
Fairport Convention	Unhalfbricking	CD	Polystar	PSCD-1125	Japan	1991	24.99
Fairport Convention	Unhalfbricking + 2	CD	Island	063-596-2	EU	2003	12.99
Fairport Convention	Unhalfbricking + 3	Mini Lp	Universal	UICY-9320	Japan	2003	22.99
Fairport Convention	What We Did On Our Holidays	CD	Polystar	PSCD-1125	Japan	1991	24.99
Fairport Convention	What We Did On Our Holidays	CD	Polystar	P32D-20025	Japan	1987	24.99
Fairport Convention	What We Did On Our Holidays + 3	CD	Island	063-597-2	EU	2003	11.99
Fairport Convention	What We Did On Our Holidays + 3	Mini Lp	Universal	UICY-9319	Japan	2003	22.99
Fairport Convention	What We Did.. An Introduction To	CD	Island	564-772-2	England	1999	11.99
Fairport Convention	Who Knows Where The Time Goes	CD	Woodworm	WRCD-025	England	1997	8.99
Fairport Convention	Wishfulness Waltz	CD	Mooncrest	CRESTCD-048-Z	England	2000	12.99
Fairport Convention	XXXV : '67-'02 The 35th Ann. Album	CD	Woodworm	WRCD-038	England	2001	8.99
Fairport Convention/Allcock	Maart	CD	Woodworm	WRDCD-012	England	1990	12.99
Fairport Convention/C Lelslie	Chris Leslie/Beryl Marriott - The Gift	CD	Beautiful Jo	BEJOCD5	England	1995	18.99
Fairport Convention/D Pegg	Birthday Party	CD	Woodworm	WRDCD-027	England	1998	14.99
Fairport Convention/D Pegg	The Cocktail Cowboy...	CD	Resurgent	4311	U.S.A.	1998	14.99
Fairport Convention/Donahue	Brief Encounters (W/Doug Morter)	CD	Funfundvierzig	FUN-005-CD	Germany	1989	29.99
Fairport Convention/Donahue	Hellecasters - Escape From H	CD	Pharoah	7002	England	1997	14.99
Fairport Convention/Donahue	Hellecasters - Hell 3: New Axes..	CD	Pharoah	7003	England	1997	14.99
Fairport Convention/Donahue	Hellecasters - The Return Of	CD	Pharoah	7001	England	1993	14.99
Fairport Convention/Donahue	Hellecasters: E Listening Vol. 1	CD	HighTone	HCD-8146	U.S.A.	2001	14.99
Fairport Convention/Donahue	Neck Of The Wood	CD	Road Goes On	RGFCD011	England	1992	49.99
Fairport Convention/Donahue	Telecasting Recast	CD	Pharoah	7004	England	1999	14.99
Fairport Convention/Hutchings	A Word In Your Ear Plus + 9	CD	Talking Elephant	TECD047	England	2002	16.99
Fairport Convention/Hutchings	Albion Band '89: Give Me A Saddle...	CD	Topic	TSCD454	England	1989	9.99
Fairport Convention/Hutchings	Albion Band: 1990	CD	Topic	TSCD457	England	1990	13.99
Fairport Convention/Hutchings	Albion Band: A Christmas Present From	CD	Making Waves	SPINCD131	England	1999	18.99
Fairport Convention/Hutchings	Albion Band: Acoustic Years 1993-97	CD	HTD	HTD-CD-74	England	1997	8.99
Fairport Convention/Hutchings	Albion Band: Acousticity	CD	HTD	HTD-CD-13	England	1993	7.99
Fairport Convention/Hutchings	Albion Band: Albion Heart	CD	HTD	HTD-CD-30	England	1995	7.99
Fairport Convention/Hutchings	Albion Band: Albion Heart (Comp Vrsn)	CD	Delta	Delta-47011	England	1999	9.99
Fairport Convention/Hutchings	Albion Band: Along the Downs	CD	Mooncrest	CRESTCD-005	England	2000	14.99
Fairport Convention/Hutchings	Albion Band: Along The Pilgrims Way	CD	Mooncrest	CRESTCD-028	England	1998	11.99
Fairport Convention/Hutchings	Albion Band: An Evening With	CD	Talking Elephant	TECD041	England	2002	14.99
Fairport Convention/Hutchings	Albion Band: BBC Radio One	CD	Windsong	WINCD-041	England	1993	19.99
Fairport Convention/Hutchings	Albion Band: BBC Sessions	CD	Strange Fruit	SFRSCD050	England	1998	19.99
Fairport Convention/Hutchings	Albion Band: Before Us Stands...	CD	HTD	HTD-CD-90	England	1999	8.99
Fairport Convention/Hutchings	Albion Band: Cambridge Folk Festival	CD	Strange Fruit	CAFECD002	England	1998	11.99
Fairport Convention/Hutchings	Albion Band: Captured	CD	HTD	HTD-CD-19	England	1994	14.99
Fairport Convention/Hutchings	Albion Band: Christmas Album	CD	HTD	HTD-CD-105	England	1999	8.99
Fairport Convention/Hutchings	Albion Band: Collection	CD	Mooncrest	CRESTCD-030	England	1998	9.99
Fairport Convention/Hutchings	Albion Band: Demi Paradise	CD	HTD	HTD-CD-54	England	1996	7.99
Fairport Convention/Hutchings	Albion Band: Happy Accident	CD	HTD	HTD-CD-82	England	1998	7.99
Fairport Convention/Hutchings	Albion Band: I Got New Shoes	CD	Making Waves	SPINCD132	England	1988	18.99
Fairport Convention/Hutchings	Albion Band: Lark Rise To Candleford	CD	Virgin	CDSCD-4020	England	1991	39.99
Fairport Convention/Hutchings	Albion Band: No Surrender	2CD	Snapper	SMD-CD-485	England	2003	14.99
Fairport Convention/Hutchings	Albion Band: Prospect Before Us +2	CD	Hannibal	HNCD-1403	U.S.A.	1993	9.99
Fairport Convention/Hutchings	Albion Band: Ridgerangers (TV)	CD	HTD	HTD-CD-103	England	1999	14.99
Fairport Convention/Hutchings	Albion Band: Rise Up Like Sun + 4	CD	Fledg'ling	FLED-3040	England	2003	14.99
Fairport Convention/Hutchings	Albion Band: Road Movies	CD	Topic	TSCD523	England	2001	7.99

F

Artist	Title	Format	Label	Catalog No	Country	Released	Value
Fairport Convention/Hutchings	Albion Band: Sella Maris	CD	Making Waves	SPINCD130	England	1987	18.99
Fairport Convention/Hutchings	Albion Band: Songs/Shows Vol. 1/2	2CD	Road Goes On	RGFCD006	England	1992	14.99
Fairport Convention/Hutchings	Albion Band: The Best Of 89/80	CD	HTD	HTD-CD-87	England	1998	11.99
Fairport Convention/Hutchings	Albion Band: The HTD Years	CD	HTD	HTD-CD-116	England	2000	14.99
Fairport Convention/Hutchings	Albion Band: Under The Rose	CD	Making Waves	SPINCD110	England	1996	18.99
Fairport Convention/Hutchings	Albion Band: Wild Side Of Town	CD	Celtic Music	CMCD-042	England	1987	18.99
Fairport Convention/Hutchings	Albion Band: Wings	CD	HTD	HTD-SC-1	England	1998	7.99
Fairport Convention/Hutchings	Albion Christmas Band: Albion X-Mas	CD	Talking Elephant	TECD060	England	2003	12.99
Fairport Convention/Hutchings	Albion Country Band: Battle/Field	CD	BGO	BGOCD354	England	1997	18.99
Fairport Convention/Hutchings	All Stars: As You Like It	CD	Making Waves	SPINCD135	England	1988	18.99
Fairport Convention/Hutchings	All Stars: By Glouchester Docks.. + 3	CD	Road Goes On	AHCD-005	England	1992	14.99
Fairport Convention/Hutchings	An Albion Journey	CD	Hannibal	HNCD4802	U.S.A.	1988	9.99
Fairport Convention/Hutchings	An Hour With Cecil Sharp	CD	Damnbuster	DAMCD014	England	2000	18.99
Fairport Convention/Hutchings	B Beat Combo: Batter P/John Keats	CD	HTD	HTD-CD-62	England	1996	28.99
Fairport Convention/Hutchings	B Beat Combo: Twangin' n' A-Traddin'	CD	HTD	HTD-CD-25	England	1994	12.99
Fairport Convention/Hutchings	Crab Wars As Remembered, Vol. 1	CD	Damnbuster	DAMCD017	England	1994	18.99
Fairport Convention/Hutchings	Crab Wars As Remembered, Vol. 2	CD	Damnbuster	DAMCD020	England	1994	18.99
Fairport Convention/Hutchings	Crab Wars As Remembered, Vol. 3	CD	Damnbuster	DAMCD023	England	1994	18.99
Fairport Convention/Hutchings	Folk Your Way To Fitness	CD	HTD	HTD-CD-75	England	1997	7.99
Fairport Convention/Hutchings	Grandson Of Morris On	CD	Talking Elephant	TECD038	England	2002	12.99
Fairport Convention/Hutchings	Human Nature	CD	Talking Elephant	TECD053	England	2003	17.99
Fairport Convention/Hutchings	Judy Dunlop - Stay With Me	CD	Road Goes On	RGFCD008	England	1992	19.99
Fairport Convention/Hutchings	Kickin' Up The Sawdust	CD	BGO	BGOCD244	England	1994	10.99
Fairport Convention/Hutchings	Morris On	CD	Hannibal	HNCD-4406	U.S.A.	1987	17.99
Fairport Convention/Hutchings	Prospect Before Us	CD	BGO	BGOCD486	England	2000	12.99
Fairport Convention/Hutchings	Rattlebone & Ploughjack	CD	BGO	BGOCD353	England	1997	14.99
Fairport Convention/Hutchings	Ridgeriders In Concert	CD	Talking Elephant	TECD035	England	2001	17.99
Fairport Convention/Hutchings	Son Of Morris On + 2	CD	Talking Elephant	TECD051	England	2003	15.99
Fairport Convention/Hutchings	Street Cries	CD	Topic	TSCD535	England	2001	12.99
Fairport Convention/Hutchings	The Compleat Dancing Master	CD	Fledg'ling	FLED-3038	England	2002	24.99
Fairport Convention/Hutchings	The Etchingham Steam Band	CD	Fledg'ling	FLED-3002	England	1995	9.99
Fairport Convention/Hutchings	The Guv'nor, Vol. 1 (Sandy Denny)	CD	HTD	HTD-CD-23	England	1994	9.99
Fairport Convention/Hutchings	The Guv'nor, Vol. 2 (Sandy Denny)	CD	HTD	HTD-CD-29	England	1995	9.99
Fairport Convention/Hutchings	The Guv'nor, Vol. 3 (Sandy Denny)	CD	HTD	HTD-CD-28	England	1995	9.99
Fairport Convention/Hutchings	The Guv'nor, Vol. 4 (Sandy Denny)	CD	HTD	HTD-CD-66	England	1996	9.99
Fairport Convention/Hutchings	The Guv'nor, Vol. 5 (Sandy Denny)	CD	Talking Elephant	TECD037	England	2002	12.99
Fairport Convention/Hutchings	The Guv'nor's Big Birthday Bash	CD	Talking Elephant	TECD033	England	2003	16.99
Fairport Convention/Rowland	Phar Lap/Zeus And Roxanne	CD	Percepto	PERCEPTO-004	England	2001	18.99
Fairport Convention/S Nichol	Before Y Time/Consonant P Carol	2CD	Resurgent	4259	U.S.A.	1998	15.99
Fairport Convention/Swarbrick	Swarb Aid	CD	Woodworm	WRCD-032	England	1999	14.99
Fairport Convention/T Lucas	Eclection	CD	Collector's Choice	CCM-233-2	U.S.A.	2002	16.99
Faith No More	Epic	CD Single	Polydor	POCD-1021	Japan	1990	15.99
Faithfull, Marianne	20th Century Blues	CD	RCA	74321-38656-2	U.S.A.	1996	7.99
Faithfull, Marianne	A Child's Adventure	CD	Island	7-90066-2	U.S.A.	1983	11.99
Faithfull, Marianne	A Secret Life (W/Angelo Badalamenti)	CD	Island	314-524-096-2	U.S.A.	1994	9.99
Faithfull, Marianne	A Stranger On Earth - An Intro	CD	Decca	585-152-2	England	2001	14.99
Faithfull, Marianne	B English/S Weather (MFSL Gold)	CD	Mobile Fidelity	UDCD-640	U.S.A.	1987	24.99
Faithfull, Marianne	Blazing Away	CD	Island	842-794-2	U.S.A.	1990	7.99
Faithfull, Marianne	Come My Way + 4	CD	Victor Ent.	UICY-3296	Japan	2002	24.99
Faithfull, Marianne	Dangerous Acquaintances	CD	Island	842-483-2	France	1981	9.99
Faithfull, Marianne	Faithless	CD	Line	GACD-9.00545-0	Germany	1988	7.99
Faithfull, Marianne	Faithless	CD	Sanctuary	06076-81118-2	U.S.A.	2001	8.99
Faithfull, Marianne	Greatest Hits	CD	Abkco	CD-547	U.S.A.	1987	10.99
Faithfull, Marianne	Kissin' Time	CD	EMI	7243-8-12009-2-6	England	2002	9.99
Faithfull, Marianne	Kissin' Time + 2	CD	Virgin	VJCP-68370	Japan	2002	13.99
Faithfull, Marianne	Love In A Mist + 3	CD	Victor Ent.	UICY-3299	Japan	2002	24.99
Faithfull, Marianne	Marianne Faithfull + 6	CD	Victor Ent.	UICY-3297	Japan	2002	24.99
Faithfull, Marianne	North Country Maid + 3	CD	Victor Ent.	UICY-3298	Japan	2002	24.99

Artist	Title	Format	Label	Catalog No	Country	Released	Value
Faithfull, Marianne	Rich Kid Blues	CD	Diablo	DIAB-8043	England	2002	11.99
Faithfull, Marianne	Seven Deadly Sins	CD	RCA	74321-60119-2	U.S.A.	1998	8.99
Faithfull, Marianne	Sex With Strangers	CD Single	Virgin	724354620621	Holland	2002	7.99
Faithfull, Marianne	Sex With Strangers (Promo)	CD	Virgin	HUTCDP147	England	2002	14.99
Faithfull, Marianne	Strange Weather	CD	Island	842-593-2	U.S.A.	1987	7.99
Faithfull, Marianne	Vagabond Ways	CD	Instinct	INS-515-2	U.S.A.	2000	9.99
Falco	Remix Hit Collection	CD	Sire	9-26796-2	U.S.A.	1991	11.99
Falco	Rock Me Amadeus - Remix 1991	CD Single	East West	9031-75223-2	Germany	1991	14.99
Falco	The Hit Singles + 3	CD	East West	3984-23479-2	Germany	1999	17.99
Falcon	Chartscraper	CD	Teichiku	TECW-25322	Japan	1996	24.99
Falcon, Rose/Billy Falcon	Breakable (Promo)	CD	Columbia	CSK-56850	U.S.A.	2002	10.99
Falkner, Jason	Can You Still Feel ?	CD	Elektra	62205-2	U.S.A.	1999	8.99
Falkner, Jason	Everyone Says It's On	2CD	Air Mail	AIRCD-026/7	Japan	2001	39.99
Falkner, Jason	I Live	CD Single	Elektra	7559642262	Australia	1997	4.99
Fall	Backdrop	CD	Cog Sinister	COG-127-CD	England	2001	7.99
Fall	Code:Selfish + 2	CD	Cog Sinister	COG-133-CD	England	2002	7.99
Fall	Dragnet + 6	CD	Cog Sinister	COG-113-CD	England	2002	8.99
Fall	Early Fall 77-79	CD	Cog Sinister	COG-123-CD	England	2001	9.99
Fall	Fall In A Hole	2CD	Cog Sinister	COG-137-CD	England	2003	12.99
Fall	Grotesque	CD	Cog Sinister	COG-106-CD	England	1998	10.99
Fall	Hex Enduction Hour	CD	Line	LICD-9.00126-0	Germany	1988	13.99
Fall	I Am As Pure As Oranji	CD	Alchemy	PILOT-61	England	2000	12.99
Fall	Live 1977	CD	Cog Sinister	COG-114-CD	England	1999	9.99
Fall	Live in Liverpool '78	CD	Cog Sinister	COG-118-CD	England	2001	9.99
Fall	Live In Zagreb	CD	Cog Sinister	COG-109-CD	England	2002	9.99
Fall	Perverted By Language	CD	Line	LICD-9.00116-0	Germany	1988	13.99
Fall	Reykjavik [Austurbæjarbió]	CD	Cog Sinister	COG-125-CD	England	2001	9.99
Fall	Room To Live (W/Live EP)	2CD	Cog Sinister	COG-105-CD	England	1998	12.99
Fall	Shift-Work + 2	CD	Cog Sinister	COG-134-CD	England	2002	7.99
Family	A Song For Me	CD	Line	MLCD-9.00805-L	Germany	1989	13.99
Family	A Song For Me + 6	CD	Mystic	MYSCD170	England	2003	11.99
Family	A Song For Me/Anyway	2CD	Line	LICD-9.21190-S	Germany	1992	16.99
Family	Anyway	CD	Line	MLCD-9.00814-L	Germany	1989	28.99
Family	Anyway + 3	CD	Mystic	MYSCD171	England	2003	11.99
Family	Bandstand + 2	CD	Line	MLCD-9.00821-L	Germany	1989	19.99
Family	Bandstand + 4	CD	Mystic	MYSCD173	England	2003	10.99
Family	BBC Radio One Live In Concert	CD	Windsong	WINCD-001	England	1992	13.99
Family	Entertainment	CD	Pucker Ent.	PUC702	England	2003	17.99
Family	Fearless	CD	Line	MLCD-9.00816-L	Germany	1989	17.99
Family	Fearless + 4	CD	Mystic	MYSCD172	England	2003	11.99
Family	It's Only A Movie	CD	Line	MLCD-9.00824-L	Germany	1989	9.99
Family	It's Only A Movie + 5	CD	Mystic	MYSCD174	England	2003	11.99
Family	Live	CD	Mystic	MYSCD176	England	2003	11.99
Family	Masters From The Vaults	CD	Classic Rock	CRP1115	England	2003	10.99
Family	Music Doll's/Family Ent.(Hrdbk) + 2	CD	See For Miles	SFM-1968	England	1999	44.99
Family	Singles A's & B's	CD	Castle	CCSCD-354	England	1994	9.99
Family	The Best Of Family	CD	Line	CRCD-9.01238-H	Germany	1993	11.99
Family	The Peel Sessions	CD	Strange Fruit	DEI8333-2	England	1988	5.99
Family /Streetwalkers	BBC Radio One In Concert	CD	Windsong	WINCD-061	England	1994	14.99
Family /Streetwalkers	Red Card + 1	CD	Repertoire	REP-4147-WP	Germany	2002	12.99
Family, The	Self Titled (Prince Related)	CD	Warner Bros.	WPCP-3646	Japan	1985	103.99
Family, The	Self Titled (Prince Related)	CD	Paisley Park	7599-25322-2	Germany	1985	163.99
Fankhauser, M/Fapardokly	Fapardokly	CD	Sundazed	SC6059	U.S.A.	1995	12.99
Fankhauser, Merrell	California Live (W/Nicky Hopkins)	CD	Legend	LM9007	France	1991	29.99
Fankhauser, Merrell	Flying To Machu Picchu	CD	Legend	LM9002	France	1992	17.99
Fankhauser, Merrell	Goin' Back To Delta	CD	Captain Trip	CTCD224	Japan	2000	19.99
Fankhauser, Merrell	Jungle Lo Lo Band	CD	Legend	LM9015	France	1995	17.99
Fankhauser, Merrell	Maui + 8	CD	Subliminal Sound	SUBMXCD-3	Sweden	1998	14.99

F

Artist	Title	Format	Label	Catalog No	Country	Released	Value
Fankhauser, Merrell	Maui + 8	CD	Captain Trip	CTCD-183	Japan	1975	14.99
Fankhauser, Merrell	MU (Los Angeles, '71/Hawaii, '74)	2CD	Sundazed	SC-11037	U.S.A.	1997	15.99
Fankhauser, Merrell	On The Blue Road	CD	D-Town	DCD7	U.S.A.	1995	9.99
Fankhauser, Merrell	The Man From MU	CD	Horizons	HZ003	Italy	2001	14.99
Fankhauser, Merrell	Things + 3 (With H.M.S. Bounty)	CD	Sundazed	SC-6094	U.S.A.	1997	10.99
Fankhauser, Merrell/Cippolina	Doctor Fankhauser	CD	Legend	LM9010	France	1992	12.99
Fankhauser, Merrell/Exiles	Desert Island Treasures	CD	Dionysus	BA1116	U.S.A.	1997	10.99
Fankhauser, Merrell/Exiles	The Early Years 1964-1967 (LP + 4)	CD	Legend	LM9006	France	1994	17.99
Fankhauser, Merrell/H.Band	Visitor From The Year 2000 AD	CD	American Sound	AS-1	U.S.A.	1999	14.99
Fankhauser, Merrell/Impacts	Eternal Surf	CD	Gee Dee	GD270126-2	Germany	1997	19.99
Fankhauser, Merrell/Impacts	Sex Wax & Surf	CD	Captain Trip	CTCD198	Japan	1998	14.99
Fankhauser, Merrell/Mu	MU Compilation	CD	Sundazed	SC11037	U.S.A.	1997	11.99
Fankhauser, Merrell/Mu	Return To Mu (Ed Cassidy, J Ferguson)	CD	Sundazed	SC-11088	U.S.A.	2003	13.99
Fankhauser, Merrell/Mu	Return To Mu (Ed Cassidy/J Ferguson)	CD	Captain Trip	CTCD237	Japan	2000	13.99
Fankhauser, Merrell/Mu	The Last Album (Bonus Tracks)	CD	Akarma	AK-258-CD	Italy	2003	14.99
Fankhauser, Merrell/Yoriko	Tropical Heat	CD	Captain Trip	CTCD409	Japan	2003	14.99
Fankhauser-Cassidy Band	Further On Up The Road	2 Mini Lp	Akarma	AK-099/2	Italy	2000	24.99
Fanny	1st Time/L Time: Reprise (Ltd 5000)	4CD	Rhino	RHM2-7734	U.S.A.	2000	79.99
Fantastic Four	Best Of	CD	Motown	MOTD-5464	U.S.A.	1991	50.99
Farlowe, Chris	14 Things To Think About +12	CD	Repertoire	REP-4280-WY	Germany	1993	18.99
Farlowe, Chris	24 Things To Think About	CD	Victor Ent.	VICP-61207	Japan	2000	24.99
Farlowe, Chris	BBC In Concert	CD	Windsong	WINCD-081	England	1995	18.99
Farlowe, Chris	Born Again	CD	Line	DACD-9.00183-0	Germany	1987	9.99
Farlowe, Chris	Dig The Buzz -first Recordings '62-'65	CD	MSI	MSIF-3889	Japan	2000	24.99
Farlowe, Chris	Don't Walk Away	CD Single	Line	LICD-9.01251-E	Germany	1992	8.99
Farlowe, Chris	Farlowe That!	CD	Delicious	DEL116	England	2003	14.99
Farlowe, Chris	Glory Bound	CD	Delicious	DEL103	England	2000	14.99
Farlowe, Chris	Greatest Hits	2CD	Castle	CMDDD213	England	2001	16.99
Farlowe, Chris	Hits	CD	Repertoire	REP-4834	Germany	2002	16.99
Farlowe, Chris	I'm The Greatest (W/Mick Jagger)	CD	See For Miles	SEE-CD-396	England	1998	27.99
Farlowe, Chris	I'm The Greatest (W/Mick Jagger)	CD	MSI	MSIF-7185	Japan	1998	32.99
Farlowe, Chris	Live In Hamburg, The Live EP	CD	Line	DACD-9.00602-L	Germany	1988	24.99
Farlowe, Chris	Lonesome Road	CD	Indigo	IGOXCD-500	England	1996	10.99
Farlowe, Chris	Mr. Soulful	CD	Castle	SHCD-156	England	1987	14.99
Farlowe, Chris	Out Of Time: The Immediate Anthology	2CD	Sequel	NEECD-310	England	2000	14.99
Farlowe, Chris	The Art Of + 11	CD	Repertoire	REP-4292-WY	Germany	1993	18.99
Farlowe, Chris	The Chris Farlowe Collection	CD	Line	IDCD-9.00506-0	Germany	1988	13.99
Farlowe, Chris	The Very Best Of	CD	BMG	74321-96050-2	England	2002	8.99
Farlowe, Chris	The Voice	CD	Delicious	DEL106	England	2001	14.99
Farlowe, Chris	The Voice	CD	Citadel	CIT4CD	England	2000	12.99
Farlowe, Chris	Waiting In The Wings	CD	Line	LICD-9.01200-0	Germany	1992	12.99
Farlowe, Chris	Waiting In The Wings	CD	Delicious	DEL109	England	2002	14.99
Farlowe, Chris/Roy Herrington	Live In Berlin	CD	Delicious	DEL104	England	2002	14.99
Farlowe, Chris/Thunderbirds	Out Of The Blue	CD	Line	DACD-9.00078-0	Germany	1987	24.99
Farlowe, Chris/Thunderbirds	Out Of The Blue/Born Again	2CD	Line	LICD-9.21189-S	Germany	1992	24.99
Fastway	All Fired Up	CD	Columbia	CK-39373	U.S.A.	1984	25.99
Fastway	Bad Bad Girls	CD	Enigma	7-73582-2	U.S.A.	1990	11.99
Fastway	Bad Bad Girls	CD Single	Legacy	LGYC104	Sweden	1990	15.99
Fastway	Collection	CD	Connoisseur	VSOP-CD-318	England	2000	12.99
Fastway	On Target	CD	Griffin	GCD-287-2	England	1994	13.99
Fastway	On Target	CD	Enigma	7-75411-2	U.S.A.	1989	10.99
Fastway	On Target (Reworked)	CD	Receiver	RRCD-2612	England	1998	12.99
Fastway	On Target/Bad Bad Girls	CD	Dojo	LOMA-CD-6	France	1990	29.99
Fastway	Say What You Will: Live	CD	Receiver	RRCD-147	England	1991	29.99
Fastway	Self Titled	CD	Columbia	CK-38662	U.S.A.	1983	14.99
Fastway	Self Titled/All Fired Up	CD	BGO	BGOCD484	England	2000	13.99
Fastway	The World Waits For You	CD	Columbia	CK-40549	U.S.A.	1987	34.99
Fastway	Trick Or Treat	CD	Columbia	CK-40549	U.S.A.	1987	12.99

F

Artist	Title	Format	Label	Catalog No	Country	Released	Value
Fastway	Waiting For The Roar	CD	Columbia	CK-40268	U.S.A.	1985	39.99
Fastway	Waiting For The Roar	CD	Columbia	CK-40268	U.S.A.	1986	38.99
Fat Boys, The	Self Titled	CD	Sutra	SCD-1015	U.S.A.	1984	60.99
Fat Mattress	Black Sheep Of The Family (Anthology)	2CD	Essential	ESMCD-865	England	2000	12.99
Fat Mattress	Fat Mattress + 5	CD	Sequel	1019-2	U.S.A.	1992	18.99
Fatala	Gongoma Times	CD	Caroline	CAROL-2331-2	U.S.A.	1993	10.99
Faust	BBC Sessions Plus	CD	Recommeded	RER-F5	England	2001	14.99
Faust	Edinburgh 1997	CD	Klangbad	KLANG-F2	Germany	1997	14.99
Faust	Faust	Mini Lp	Universal	UICY-9259	Japan	2002	29.99
Faust	Faust / So Far	CD	Collector's Choice	CCM-179-2	U.S.A.	2000	13.99
Faust	Freispiel	CD	Klangbad	FRR-1992	EC	2002	12.99
Faust	IV	CD	Caroline	CAR-1885	U.S.A.	1992	10.99
Faust	Patchwork 1971-2002	CD	Staubgold	STAUB-37-CD	Germany	2003	17.99
Faust	Ravvivando	CD	Klangbad	KLANG-36002	Germany	1999	9.99
Faust	Ravvivando (Remixed By Soft Cell)	CD Single	Klangbad	KLANG-62832	Germany	1999	9.99
Faust	Seventy One Minutes Of...	CD	Recommeded	RER-F1CD	England	1996	12.99
Faust	So Far	Mini Lp	Universal	UICY-9260	Japan	2002	29.99
Faust	Tapes	CD	Recommeded	RER-F2CD	England	1995	22.99
Faust	The Land Of Ukko & Rauni	2CD	Captain Trip	CTCD-289/290	Japan	2000	23.99
Faust	Wumme Years: 1970-1973	5CD	Recommeded	RER-FB1	England	2000	74.99
Faust	You Know FaUSt	CD	Recommeded	RER-F4	England	1997	12.99
Fear	Have Another Beer With Fear	CD	Hall Of Records	HOR1101	U.S.A.	2000	10.99
Fear	The Record + 1	CD	Rhino	R2-79941	U.S.A.	2001	19.99
Feelies	Crazy Rhythms (Line Version)	CD	Line	LICD-9.00168-0	Germany	1987	22.99
Feelies	Crazy Rhythms + 1	CD	A&M	75021-5319-2	U.S.A.	1990	22.99
Feelies	Only Life	CD	A&M	CD-5214	U.S.A.	1988	18.99
Feelies	The Good Earth	CD	Twin Tone	TTC-8673-2	U.S.A.	1986	29.99
Feelies	The Good Earth (Line Version)	CD	Line	LICD-9.00428-0	Germany	1987	29.99
Ferenzik	Devil's Playground	CD	Rraxxo	100020-C	Canada	1995	7.99
Ferenzik	Wheel Of Nesh	CD	Rraxxo	100030-C	Canada	1997	7.99
Ferenzik	Wild Man Of Borneo	CD	Rraxxo	10010-C	Canada	1990	7.99
Ferenzik	Zero Points For Zeus	CD	Rraxxo	10010-C	Canada	2000	7.99
Ferrer, Ibrahim	Buena Vista Social Club Presents	CD	World Circuit	79532-2	U.S.A.	1999	14.99
Ferry, Bryan	Another Time, Another Place	CD	EMI	7243-8-47600-2-1	Germany	1999	8.99
Ferry, Bryan	As Time Goes By	CD	Virgin	848271-2	EU	1999	9.99
Ferry, Bryan	Bete Noir	CD	EMI	7243-8-47710-2-7	Germany	1999	7.99
Ferry, Bryan	Boys And Girls	CD	EMI	7243-8-47722-2-2	Germany	1999	7.99
Ferry, Bryan	Frantic	SACD	EMI	7243-8-12138-2-7	Germany	2002	14.99
Ferry, Bryan	Frantic	CD	Virgin	7243-8119842-1	Holland	2002	10.99
Ferry, Bryan	Frantic (Adv. DJ/Different Cvr/Pic Cd)	CD	Virgin	7087-6-16838-2-0	U.S.A.	2002	13.99
Ferry, Bryan	Girl Of My Best Friend	CD	Toshiba-EMI	VJCP-20012	Japan	1993	30.99
Ferry, Bryan	Goddess Of Love	CD Single	Virgin	7243-5-46449-2-4	England	2002	5.99
Ferry, Bryan	In Your Mind	CD	EMI	7243-8-47604-2-7	Germany	1999	8.99
Ferry, Bryan	Interview (Promo)	CD	Virgin	DPRO-12699	U.S.A.	1994	9.99
Ferry, Bryan	It's All Over Now Baby Blue	CD Single	Virgin	7243-5-46420-2-9	Germany	2002	5.99
Ferry, Bryan	Let's Stick Together	CD	EMI	7243-8-47602-2-9	Germany	1999	8.99
Ferry, Bryan	Mamouna	CD	EMI	7243-8-47715-2-2	Germany	1999	7.99
Ferry, Bryan	Mamouna + 2	CD	Toshiba-EMI	VJCP-25133	Japan	1994	22.99
Ferry, Bryan	Mamouna EP	CD Single	Virgin	V25H-38458	U.S.A.	1994	10.99
Ferry, Bryan	One Way Love	CD Single	Virgin	7243-5-46652-2-6	England	2002	9.99
Ferry, Bryan	Slave To Love: Best Of The Ballads	CD	Virgin	7243-8-49585-2-7	U.S.A.	2000	9.99
Ferry, Bryan	Taxi	CD	EMI	7243-8-47712-2-5	Germany	1999	8.99
Ferry, Bryan	The Archive & Live Collection	3CD	Virgin	7243-8-91939-2-3	England	1993	54.99
Ferry, Bryan	The Bride Stipped Bare	CD	EMI	7243-8-47606-2-5	Germany	1999	8.99
Ferry, Bryan	The Right Stuff	CD Single	Virgin	CDEP-8	England	1987	6.99
Ferry, Bryan	These Foolish Things	CD	EMI	7243-8-47598-2-7	Germany	1999	8.99
Ferry, Bryan	Tokyo Joe	CD Single	Virgin	VJCP-50133	Japan	1997	18.99
Ferry, Bryan	Will You Love Me Tomorrow	CD Single	Reprise	9-40949-2	U.S.A.	1993	5.99

F

Artist	Title	Format	Label	Catalog No	Country	Released	Value
Ferry, Bryan	Will You Love Me Tomorrow	CD Single	Virgin	7243-5-91938-2-4	England	1993	5.99
Fever Tree	Creation/For Sale	CD	TRC	TRC-050	Germany	1994	24.99
Fever Tree	Filigree & Shadow (1st Lp + Rarities)	CD	Spalax	14595	France	2002	14.99
Fever Tree	San Francisco Girls (Self Titled + 7)	CD	Gear Fab	GF-199	U.S.A.	2003	11.99
Fever Tree	San Francisco Girls: The Best Of	CD	Era	5015-2	U.S.A.	1992	21.99
Fever Tree	Self Titled/Another Time, Another..	CD	See For Miles	SEE-CD364	England	1997	18.99
Fiction Factory	Another Story	CD	Line	LICD-9.00077-0	Germany	1987	74.99
Fiddler, John	The Big Buffalo	CD	Angel Air	SJPCD048	EU	2000	12.99
Fiedel, Brad	Blink (O.S.T.)	CD	Milan	73138-35659-2	U.S.A.	1994	9.99
Fiedel, Brad	The Terminator O.S.T. (Jay Ferguson)	CD	DCC	DZS-058	U.S.A.	1984	26.99
Fiedel, Brad/Ian Hunter	Fright Night (Red/Black Case) O.S.T.	CD	CBS	SZ-40087	U.S.A.	1985	133.99
Fielding, Jerry	Wild Bunch (O.S.T./Mono/Complete)	CD	Screen Archives	SC-3-JF	U.S.A.	1993	19.99
Figgs, The	Badger	CD Single	Hearbox	HB0003-2	U.S.A.	2001	7.99
Figgs, The	Banda Macho	CD	Capitol	7243-8-36687-2-4	U.S.A.	1996	3.99
Figgs, The	Hi-Fi Dropouts	CD Single	Imago	72787-25081-2	U.S.A.	1994	6.99
Figgs, The	Low-Fi At Society High	CD	Imago	72787-21042-2	U.S.A.	1994	3.99
Fiji Mariners, The	Self Titled	CD	Capricorn	314-558-555-2	U.S.A.	1998	8.99
Finn, Neil	Neil Finn/C House/Split Enz (DJ)	CD	Sony	NF-12345	U.S.A.	1998	24.99
Finn, Neil	One All (Diff.Trk Order Than One Nil)	CD	Nettwerk	0-6700-30265-2-9	U.S.A.	2002	9.99
Finn, Neil	One Nil	CD	EMI	7243-532039-2-4	EU	2001	8.99
Finn, Neil	She Will Have Her Way	CD Single	Parlophone	7243-8-85646-2-5	England	1998	4.99
Finn, Neil	Try Whistling This	CD	Parlophone	OK-69372	U.S.A.	1998	7.99
Finn, Neil/Friends	7 Worlds Collide - Live At St. James	CD	Parlophone	7243-536645-2-7	Germany	2002	8.99
Finn, Neil/Tim	Finn Brothers	CD	EMI	7243-8-35632-2-7	Australia	1995	19.99
Finn, Tim	Before & After	CD	Capitol	0777-7-94904-2-4	U.S.A.	1993	13.99
Finn, Tim	Big Canoe + 2	CD	Virgin	CDV-2369	Germany	1986	18.99
Finn, Tim	Escapade	CD	Mushroom	MUSH32426.2	Australia	1994	9.99
Finn, Tim	Feeding The Gods	CD	What Are	PERISCOPE-002	U.S.A.	2001	11.99
Finn, Tim	Say It Is So	CD	What Are	WAR-60039-2	U.S.A.	2000	5.99
Finn, Tim	Steel City	CD Single	Columbia	665483.2	Australia	1997	9.99
Finn, Tim	Tim Finn	CD	Capitol	7-48735-2	U.S.A.	1989	9.99
Finn, Tim	What You've Done (EP)	CD	Periscope	550160-0	Australia	2001	10.99
Finn, Tim/B.Runga/D.Dobbyn	Together In Concert : Live	CD	Epic	5011402000	Australia	2000	15.99
Firefall	Firefall	CD	Line	LECD-9.00893-0	Germany	1989	10.99
Firefall	Greatest Hits	CD	Rhino	R2-71055	U.S.A.	1992	11.99
Firefall	Self Titled (1st Lp)	CD	Rhino	R2-70379	U.S.A.	1990	8.99
Firefall	The Essentials	CD	Rhino	R2-76047	U.S.A.	2002	8.99
Firehouse	Hold Your Fire + 1	CD	Sony	ESCA-5612	Japan	1992	29.99
Firehouse	Love Of A Lifetime	CD Single	Sony	ESCA-5508	Japan	1991	15.99
Firehouse	Prime Time	CD	Pony Canyon	PCCY-01673	Japan	2003	29.99
Firehouse	The Best Of	CD	Sony	CPK-1918	Japan	1998	29.99
Firesign Theatre	Back/The Shadows (MFSL 2 CDs)	CD	Mobile Fidelity	MFCD-2-747	U.S.A.	1994	39.99
Firesign Theatre	Boom Dot Bust	CD	Rhino	R2-75983	U.S.A.	1999	8.99
Firesign Theatre	Dear Friends (MFSL Silver Cd)	CD	Mobile Fidelity	MFCD-758	U.S.A.	1972	19.99
Firesign Theatre	Don't Crush That..(MFSL Silver Cd)	CD	Mobile Fidelity	MFCD-880	U.S.A.	1970	19.99
Firesign Theatre	Fighting Clowns (MFSL Silver Cd)	CD	Mobile Fidelity	MFCD-748	U.S.A.	1980	34.99
Firesign Theatre	How Can You Be... (MFSL Silver Cd)	CD	Mobile Fidelity	MFCD-834	U.S.A.	1969	34.99
Firesign Theatre	I Think We're All..(MFSL Silver Cd)	CD	Mobile Fidelity	MFCD-785	U.S.A.	1971	11.99
Firesign Theatre	In The Next World...	CD	Laugh.com	LGH-1078	U.S.A.	2001	9.99
Firesign Theatre	Not Insane	CD	Laugh.com	LGH-1075	U.S.A.	2001	9.99
Firesign Theatre	Tale Of The Giant Rat Of Sumatra	CD	Laugh.com	LGH-1075	U.S.A.	2001	9.99
Firesign Theatre	Waiting For The...(MFSL Silver Cd)	CD	Mobile Fidelity	MFCD-762	U.S.A.	1968	19.99
Firm	Mean Business	CD	Atlantic	7-81628-2	U.S.A.	1986	12.99
Firm	The Firm	CD	Atlantic	7-81239-2	U.S.A.	1985	10.99
Fitzgerald, Ella	The Cole Porter Songbook	2CD	Verve	314-537-257-2	U.S.A.	1997	11.99
Five Day Week Straw People	Five Day Week Straw People + 9	CD	Akarma	AK-218-CD	Italy	2002	14.99
Fixx	Calm Animals	CD	Rainman	RMCD101	U.S.A.	2003	8.99
Fixx	Happy Landings And Lost Tracks	CD	Rainman	RMCD102	U.S.A.	2003	8.99

F

Artist	Title	Format	Label	Catalog No	Country	Released	Value
Fixx	Real Time Stood Still: Gr. Hits Live	CD	Rainman	RMCD103	U.S.A.	2003	8.99
Fixx	Shuttered Room + 2	CD	Rainman	RMCD104	U.S.A.	2003	8.99
Fixx	Want That Life	CD	Rainman	RMCD116	U.S.A.	2003	8.99
Flack, Roberta	First Take	CD	Atlantic	82792-2	U.S.A.	1969	8.99
Flack, Roberta/D. Hathaway	Roberta Flack & Donny Hathaway	CD	Atlantic	82794-2	U.S.A.	1972	11.99
Flacke, Ray	Untitled Island	CD	Line	INCD-9.01149-0	Germany	1991	22.99
Flaherty/Ahrens/Newman	Anastasia + 1	CD	Atlantic	83053-2	U.S.A.	1997	8.99
Flamin' Groovies	A Bucket Of Brains	CD	EMI	7243-8-32144-2-6	U.S.A.	1995	12.99
Flamin' Groovies	A Collection of Rare Demos...	CD	Marilyn	USMCD1020	U.S.A.	1993	18.99
Flamin' Groovies	Absolutely The Best	CD	Fuel 2000	FLD1035	U.S.A.	1999	6.99
Flamin' Groovies	Backtracks	CD	Renaissance	CRANCH-17	U.S.A.	1999	6.99
Flamin' Groovies	Best Of-Oldies But Groovies	CD	AIM	AIM-2001-CD	Australia	1996	11.99
Flamin' Groovies	California Born And Bred	CD	Norton	CED-243	U.S.A.	1995	10.99
Flamin' Groovies	Flamingo + 6	CD	Big Beat	CDWIK-925	England	1990	10.99
Flamin' Groovies	Flamingo/Teenage Head	CD	Teichiku	28CP-23	Japan	1988	29.99
Flamin' Groovies	Groove In	CD	Revenge	EV-300	France	1988	10.99
Flamin' Groovies	Groovies Greatest Grooves	CD	Warner Bros.	WPCR-1706	Japan	1997	49.99
Flamin' Groovies	In Person!!!	CD	Norton	CED-255	U.S.A.	1997	11.99
Flamin' Groovies	Jumpin' In The Night	CD	Warner Bros.	WPCR-1709	Japan	1997	48.99
Flamin' Groovies	Live 68/70	CD	New Rose	EVA-B17	France	1992	19.99
Flamin' Groovies	Live At The Festival Of The Sun	CD	AIM	AIM-1051	Australia	1994	9.99
Flamin' Groovies	Now	CD	Warner Bros.	WPCR-1708	Japan	1997	63.99
Flamin' Groovies	One Night Stand	CD	AIM	AIM-1008	Australia	1992	9.99
Flamin' Groovies	Rock Juice	CD	National	NAT-030-2	U.S.A.	1992	9.99
Flamin' Groovies	Shake Some Action	CD	AIM	AIM-1017/CD	Australia	1976	11.99
Flamin' Groovies	Shake Some Action With The	2CD	Dressed To Kill	AOP164	England	1999	15.99
Flamin' Groovies	Sixteen Tunes	CD	Skydog	62-247-2	France	1982	13.99
Flamin' Groovies	Step Up	CD	AIM	AIM-1030-CD	Australia	1996	9.99
Flamin' Groovies	Still Shakin'	CD	Unidisc Productions	BDK-5683	Canada	1992	9.99
Flamin' Groovies	Supernazz + 4	CD	Sundazed	SC-6130	U.S.A.	2000	5.99
Flamin' Groovies	Supersneakers	CD	Sundazed	SC-6077	U.S.A.	1996	8.99
Flamin' Groovies	Teenage Head + 5	CD	Big Beat	CDWIK-926	England	1990	10.99
Flamin' Groovies	Teenage Head + 7	CD	Buddah	7446599627-2	U.S.A.	1999	8.99
Flamin' Groovies	The Flamin' Groovies	2CD	Snapper	SNAF-830-CD	England	2002	19.99
Flamin' Groovies	The Flamin' Groovies Collection	2CD	Purple Flame	PF-2057	England	2000	19.99
Fleetwood Mac	25 Years The Chain (Box Set)	4CD	Warner Bros.	9362-45129-2	Germany	1992	44.99
Fleetwood Mac	Bare Trees	CD	Reprise	2278-2	U.S.A.	1972	8.99
Fleetwood Mac	Behind The Mask	CD	Warner Bros.	9-26111-2	U.S.A.	1990	8.99
Fleetwood Mac	Behind The Mask (Deluxe Box)	CD	Reprise	9-26206-2	U.S.A.	1990	29.99
Fleetwood Mac	Blue Horizon Sessions '67-'69 Box Set	6CD	Sire	73003-2	U.S.A.	1999	29.99
Fleetwood Mac	English Rose	CD	Sony	ESCA-5421	Japan	1991	24.99
Fleetwood Mac	Fleetwood Mac	CD	Warner Bros.	2281-2	U.S.A.	1977	11.99
Fleetwood Mac	Future Games	CD	Reprise	6465-2	U.S.A.	1971	8.99
Fleetwood Mac	Greatest Hits	CD	Reprise	9-25801-2	U.S.A.	1988	9.99
Fleetwood Mac	Greatest Hits	CD	Columbia	460704-2	England	1989	9.99
Fleetwood Mac	Heroes Are Hard To Find	CD	Reprise	2196-2	U.S.A.	1974	7.99
Fleetwood Mac	In Chicago 1969 + 2	2CD	Sire	9-45283-2	U.S.A.	1994	19.99
Fleetwood Mac	Jumping At The Shadows (Live)	2CD	Indigo	IGOXDCD2507	England	2002	19.99
Fleetwood Mac	Kiln House	CD	Reprise	6408-2	U.S.A.	1970	17.99
Fleetwood Mac	Live	2CD	Warner Bros.	3500-2	U.S.A.	1980	15.99
Fleetwood Mac	Live	2CD	Warner Bros.	3500-2	U.S.A.	1980	18.99
Fleetwood Mac	Live At The BBC	2CD	Castle	CASTLE-114-2	England	1995	11.99
Fleetwood Mac	Live At The Boston Tea Party, Vol 1	CD	Snapper	636551612227	U.S.A.	2003	7.99
Fleetwood Mac	Live At The Boston Tea Party, Vol 2	CD	Snapper	636551612722	U.S.A.	2003	7.99
Fleetwood Mac	Live At The Boston Tea Party, Vol. 3	CD	Snapper	636551613026	U.S.A.	2003	7.99
Fleetwood Mac	Live At The Marquee, 1967	CD	BMG	6076-80208-2	U.S.A.	2001	7.99
Fleetwood Mac	Live In Boston	CD	Line	IMCD-9.00129-0	Germany	1987	9.99
Fleetwood Mac	London Live '68	CD	Magnum	MACD-1038	England	1985	5.99

F

Artist	Title	Format	Label	Catalog No	Country	Released	Value
Fleetwood Mac	Madison Blues Live	CD	Castle	MAC-CD-187	England	1994	7.99
Fleetwood Mac	Mirage	CD	Warner Bros.	23607-2	Australia	1982	8.99
Fleetwood Mac	Mystery To Me	CD	Reprise	25982-2	U.S.A.	1973	11.99
Fleetwood Mac	Penguin	CD	Reprise	2138-2	U.S.A.	1973	8.99
Fleetwood Mac	Rumours	CD	Warner Bros.	3010-2	U.S.A.	1977	9.99
Fleetwood Mac	Selections From 25 Years The Chain	2CD	Warner Bros.	9362-45188-2	Australia	1992	13.99
Fleetwood Mac	Shrine '69 (Live)	CD	Rykodisc	RCD-10424	U.S.A.	1999	8.99
Fleetwood Mac	Silver Springs	CD Single	Reprise	PRO-CD-8900	U.S.A.	1997	8.99
Fleetwood Mac	Tango In The Night	CD	Warner Bros.	9-25471-2	U.S.A.	1987	8.99
Fleetwood Mac	The Chain (Promo Sampler)	CD	Warner Bros.	PRO-CD-5905	U.S.A.	1992	14.99
Fleetwood Mac	The Chain (Promo)	CD Single	Reprise	PRO-CD-9055-R	U.S.A.	1997	8.99
Fleetwood Mac	The Dance	CD	Reprise	9-46702-2	U.S.A.	1997	7.99
Fleetwood Mac	The Early Years	CD	Essex Entertainment	SCD-4918	U.S.A.	1988	7.99
Fleetwood Mac	The Original + 4	CD	Snapper	156072	U.S.A.	2000	9.99
Fleetwood Mac	The Pious Bird Of Good Omen	CD	Columbia	480524-2	England	1969	9.99
Fleetwood Mac	The Very Best Of Fleetwood Mac	2CD	Reprise	R2-73775	U.S.A.	2002	19.99
Fleetwood Mac	Then Play On	CD	Reprise	7599-27448-2	Australia	1970	10.99
Fleetwood Mac	Time	CD	Warner Bros.	9-45920-2	U.S.A.	1995	6.99
Fleetwood Mac	Tour 97 (Promo Cd)	2CD	Best Buy	R71508-03-A	U.S.A.	1997	14.99
Fleetwood Mac	Tusk	CD	Warner Bros.	3350-2	U.S.A.	1990	9.99
Fleetwood Mac/John McVie	Gotta Band (With Lola Thomas)	CD	Warner Bros.	9-26909-2	U.S.A.	1992	5.99
Fleetwood Mac/M Fleetwood	The Visitor (W/G Harrison/P Green)	CD	Great Expectations	PIPCD-020	France	1981	83.99
Fleetwood Mac/Various Artists	Tribute: Blues Yrs (3 Groundhog Trks)	CD	Blue Flame	BFCD002	Italy	2002	14.99
Fleshtones	Vs. Reality	CD	Emergo	EM-34-9634	Germany	1987	53.99
Flex	The Silent Death Of Dreams	CD	Line	IPCD-9.00677-0	Germany	1988	9.99
Flock	Dinosaur Swamp	CD	One Way	A-26658	U.S.A.	1996	9.99
Flock	The Best Of The Flock	CD	Columbia	CK-53440	U.S.A.	1993	10.99
Flock	The Flock	CD	One Way	A-26657	U.S.A.	1996	9.99
Flores, Rosie	Rockabilly Filly	CD	HighTone	HCD-8067	Canada	1995	7.99
Flower Kings, The	Alive On Planet Earth	2CD	SPV	089-31862DCD	Germany	2000	8.99
Flower Kings, The	Alive On Planet Earth	2CD	Inside Out	IOMCD054	U.S.A.	2000	8.99
Flower Kings, The	Back In The World Of Adventures	CD	SPV	SPV085-31812CD	Germany	1995	10.99
Flower Kings, The	Back In The World Of Adventures	CD	Inside Out	IOMCD051	U.S.A.	1995	10.99
Flower Kings, The	Flower Power	2CD	SPV	SPV092-31762CD	Germany	1999	16.99
Flower Kings, The	Flower Power	2CD	Inside Out	IOMCD046	U.S.A.	1999	16.99
Flower Kings, The	Flower Power + 4	2CD	Avalon	MICP-90001	Japan	1999	22.99
Flower Kings, The	Meet The Flower Kings	2CD	SPV	089-60462DCD	Germany	2003	14.99
Flower Kings, The	Meet The Flower Kings	2CD	Inside Out	IOMCD142	U.S.A.	2003	14.99
Flower Kings, The	Meet The Flower Kings (2 CD/2 DVD)	4CD	Inside Out	IOMLTDDVD005	U.S.A.	2003	39.99
Flower Kings, The	Meet The Flower Kings (2 CD/2 DVD)	4CD	SPV	556-60468DVD	Germany	2003	39.99
Flower Kings, The	Retropolis	CD	Inside Out	IOMCD050	U.S.A.	1996	9.99
Flower Kings, The	Retropolis	CD	Inside Out	SPV085-31802CD	Germany	1996	9.99
Flower Kings, The	Scanning The Greenhouse + 1	CD	Avalon	MICP-10076	Japan	1998	24.99
Flower Kings, The	Space Revolver	CD	SPV	SPV085-41222CD	Germany	2000	8.99
Flower Kings, The	Space Revolver (Ltd Ed.)	CD	Inside Out	IOMCD062	U.S.A.	2000	24.99
Flower Kings, The	Space Revolver (Ltd Ed.)	CD	SPV	SPV087-41220CD	Germany	2000	24.99
Flower Kings, The	Space Revolver + 5 (W/Bonus Cd)	2CD	Avalon	MICP-90004	Japan	2000	24.99
Flower Kings, The	Stardust We Are	2CD	SPV	SPV092-31782CD	Germany	1997	10.99
Flower Kings, The	Stardust We Are	2CD	Inside Out	IOMCD048	U.S.A.	1997	10.99
Flower Kings, The	The Rainmaker	CD	SPV	SPV085-41672CD	Germany	2001	12.99
Flower Kings, The	The Rainmaker	CD	Inside Out	IOMCD085	U.S.A.	2001	12.99
Flower Kings, The	The Rainmaker (Ltd. Ed.)	CD	Inside Out	IOMLTDCD085	U.S.A.	2001	19.99
Flower Kings, The	The Rainmaker + 1 (Ltd. Ed.)	CD	SPV	088-41670DCD	Germany	2001	19.99
Flower Kings, The	Unfold The Future	2CD	Inside Out	IOMCD112	U.S.A.	2002	15.99
Flower Kings, The	Unfold The Future	2CD	SPV	089-65392DCD	Germany	2002	15.99
Flower Kings, The	Unfold The Future +1 (Ltd. Ed.)	2CD	SPV	092-65390DCD	Germany	2002	18.99
Flower Kings, The	Unfold The Future (Ltd. Ed.)	2CD	Inside Out	IOMLTDCD112	U.S.A.	2002	18.99
Flower Pot Men	Let's Go To San Francisco	CD	Repertoire	REP-4344-WZ	Germany	2002	10.99

F

Artist	Title	Format	Label	Catalog No	Country	Released	Value
Flower Pot Men	Peace Album: Past Imperfect	CD	Repertoire	REP-4883-WZ	Germany	2002	10.99
Flower Pot Men/Ivy League	Major League: Collectors' Ivy League	2CD	Sequel	NEECD-289	England	1998	24.99
Flying Burrito Brothers	Back To Sweetheart Of Rodeo	2CD	Appaloosa	CDSD-502	England	1996	29.99
Flying Burrito Brothers	Best Of Flying Burrito Brothers	CD	Relix	RRCD2069	U.S.A.	1995	7.99
Flying Burrito Brothers	Bicentennial Burritos '76	CD	Relix	RRCD2098	U.S.A.	1999	8.99
Flying Burrito Brothers	Cabin Fever	CD	Relix	RRCD-2008	U.S.A.	1989	7.99
Flying Burrito Brothers	Close Encounters To The West Coast	CD	Relix	RRCD2044	U.S.A.	1991	7.99
Flying Burrito Brothers	Dim Lights, Thick Smoke..	CD	Edsel	EDCD-197	England	1987	19.99
Flying Burrito Brothers	Eye Of A Hurricane	CD	One Way	OW-30330	U.S.A.	1994	6.99
Flying Burrito Brothers	Flying Again	CD	Line	CLCD-9.00931-0	Germany	1990	29.99
Flying Burrito Brothers	Honky Tonkin'	CD	One Way	ONE35186	U.S.A.	2001	8.99
Flying Burrito Brothers	In Concert	CD	All At Once	HP-93422	Germany	1994	7.99
Flying Burrito Brothers	Live From Europe	CD	Relix	RRCD-2022	U.S.A.	1986	8.99
Flying Burrito Brothers	Out Of The Blue	2CD	A&M	540-408-2	Germany	1996	12.99
Flying Burrito Brothers	Sin City	CD	Relix	RRCD2052	U.S.A.	1995	7.99
Flying Burrito Brothers	Sin City - The Very Best Of	CD	A&M	069493-264-2	U.S.A.	2002	12.99
Flying Burrito Brothers	Sons Of The Golden West	CD	Arista	GDCD4065	U.S.A.	1999	7.99
Flying Burrito Brothers	Southern Tracks	CD	Voodoo	VD-103	France	1990	14.99
Flying Burrito Brothers	The Flying Burrito Bros	CD	Mobile Fidelity	MFCD-772	U.S.A.	1971	99.99
Flying Burrito Brothers	The Guilded Palace Of Sin/B Deluxe	CD	A&M	540-704-2	Germany	1997	11.99
Flying Burrito Brothers	Too Much Honky Tonkin'	CD	Country Stars	CTS-55439	Germany	1996	7.99
FM	Aphrodesiac	CD	Music For Nations	CDMFN-141	France	1992	13.99
FM	Closer To Heaven	CD	Alfa	ALCB-804	Japan	1993	27.99
FM	Dead Man's Shoes	CD	Raw Power	RAW-CD-107	England	1995	10.99
FM	Indiscreet	CD	Columbia	CD-PRT-26827	England	1986	27.99
FM	Live Acoustical Intercourse	CD	Alfa	ALCB-748	Japan	1992	21.99
FM	Long Time No See	2CD	Essential	ESM-086	England	2003	24.99
FM	No Electricity Requiered (W/Bonus)	2CD	Music For Nations	CDMFN-155	France	1993	13.99
FM	Only The Strong	CD	Connoisseur	VSOP-CD-203	England	1994	9.99
FM	Paraphernalia	2CD	Alfa	ALCB-3140~41	Japan	1996	49.99
FM	Takin' It To The Street	CD	Music For Nations	CDMFN-119	France	1991	11.99
FM	Tough It Out	CD	Epic	EK-45308	U.S.A.	1988	18.99
FM/Nash The Slash	Black Noise	CD	One Way	OW-33651	U.S.A.	1993	10.99
FM/Nash The Slash	Retroactive	CD	Now See Hear	NSHSD1194	Canada	1995	12.99
FM/Nash The Slash	Tonight + 5	CD	Duke Street	DSBBD-31042	Canada	1987	8.99
Focus	3	CD	Red Bullet	RB-66.189	Holland	2001	11.99
Focus	8	CD	Musea	FGBG-4472.AR	France	2002	14.99
Focus	At The Rainbow	CD	Red Bullet	RB-66.190	Holland	2001	9.99
Focus	Focus Con Proby	CD	EMI	CDM-7-48339-2	Holland	1998	24.99
Focus	Hamburger Concerto	CD	Red Bullet	RB-66.191	Holland	2001	9.99
Focus	Hocus Pocus - The Best Of Focus	CD	Red Bullet	RB-66.194	Holland	1993	14.99
Focus	In And Out Of Focus	CD	Red Bullet	RB-66.187	Holland	2001	15.99
Focus	Live In America	CD	Classic Rock	CRP1090	England	2003	12.99
Focus	Masters From The Vaults	CD	Classic Rock	CRP1112	England	2003	11.99
Focus	Mother Focus	CD	Red Bullet	RB-66.192	Holland	2001	9.99
Focus	Moving Waves	CD	Red Bullet	RB-66.188	Holland	2001	15.99
Focus	Ship Of Memories	CD	Red Bullet	RB-66.193	Holland	2001	9.99
Focus/Akkerman/Van Leer	Focus: Jan Akkerman/Thijs Van Leer	CD	Vertigo	824-524-2	Germany	1985	19.99
Focus/Jan Akkerman	10,000 Clowns On A Rainy Day	2CD	Patio	P.M.97002	Netherland	1997	29.99
Focus/Jan Akkerman	A Talent's Profile	CD	EMI	CDP-7-90630-2	England	1988	12.99
Focus/Jan Akkerman	Aranjuez	CD	Columbia	CDCBS26612	Sweden	1985	11.99
Focus/Jan Akkerman	Blues Hearts	CD	EMI	7243-8-31091-2-8	Holland	1994	19.99
Focus/Jan Akkerman	Brainbox - To You	CD	EMI	CDM-7-90609-2	Holland	1988	12.99
Focus/Jan Akkerman	Brainbox - Very Best Album Ever	CD	EMI	7243-5-39979-2-2	Holland	2002	14.99
Focus/Jan Akkerman	Brainbox + 5	CD	Pseudonym	CDP1033-DD	Holland	1996	14.99
Focus/Jan Akkerman	C.U.	CD	Coast To Coast	CTC2990448	Holland	2004	19.99
Focus/Jan Akkerman	Can't Stand Noise + 4	CD	Inakustik	INAK11001CD	Germany	1983	9.99
Focus/Jan Akkerman	Collage	CD	Sony	50997-494759-2-2	Holland	2002	8.99

F

Artist	Title	Format	Label	Catalog No	Country	Released	Value
Focus/Jan Akkerman	Eli (W/Kaz Lux)	CD	WEA	002292-42361-2-9	Germany	1995	11.99
Focus/Jan Akkerman	Focus In Time + 1	CD	Avalon	MICY-1042	Japan	1996	34.99
Focus/Jan Akkerman	From The Basement + 8	CD	HUX	HUX-012	England	1998	12.99
Focus/Jan Akkerman	Heartware + 8	CD	HUX	HUX-016	England	1998	12.99
Focus/Jan Akkerman	LIVE (Montreux Jazz Festival, 1978)	CD	Psuedonym	CDP-1034-DD	Holland	1998	11.99
Focus/Jan Akkerman	Live (W/Joachim Kuhn)	CD	Inakustik	INAK868CD	Germany	2000	14.99
Focus/Jan Akkerman	Live At Alexander's	CD	Akkernet	02	Netherland	1999	19.99
Focus/Jan Akkerman	Live At The Priory	CD	Akkernet	01	Netherland	1998	19.99
Focus/Jan Akkerman	Oil In The Family	CD	Red Bullet	RB-66.140	Holland	1998	10.99
Focus/Jan Akkerman	Passion	CD	Roadrunner	RR-8577-2	England	1999	18.99
Focus/Jan Akkerman	Pleasure Point + 12	CD	HUX	HUX-011	England	1998	12.99
Focus/Jan Akkerman	Profile	CD	BGO	BGOCD490	England	2000	15.99
Focus/Jan Akkerman	Puccini's Cafe	CD	EMI	0777-7-89192-2-3	Holland	1993	11.99
Focus/Jan Akkerman	Self Titled	CD	WEA	002292-42360-2-0	Germany	1995	10.99
Focus/Jan Akkerman	Tabernakel	CD	Wounded Bird	WOU-7032	U.S.A.	2001	9.99
Focus/Jan Akkerman	The Complete Guitarist	CD	Charly	CPCD-8204	England	1996	11.99
Focus/Jan Akkerman	The Guitar Player	CD	Charly	RM-1507	England	1996	24.99
Focus/Jan Akkerman	The Noise Of Art	CD	I.R.S.	IRSD-82041	U.S.A.	1990	49.99
Fogelberg, Dan	Captured Angel	CD	Epic	EK-33499	U.S.A.	1975	8.99
Fogelberg, Dan	Exiles	CD	Epic	EK-40271	U.S.A.	1987	8.99
Fogelberg, Dan	Greatest Hits	CD	Epic	EK-38308	U.S.A.	1982	9.99
Fogelberg, Dan	Greetings From The West	2CD	Epic	E2K-48625	U.S.A.	1991	13.99
Fogelberg, Dan	High Country Snows	CD	Epic	EK-39616	U.S.A.	1985	7.99
Fogelberg, Dan	Home Free	CD	Columbia	CK-31751	U.S.A.	1972	7.99
Fogelberg, Dan	Nether Lands	CD	Epic	EK-34185	U.S.A.	1977	7.99
Fogelberg, Dan	Phoenix	CD	Epic	EK-35634	U.S.A.	1979	7.99
Fogelberg, Dan	Portrait: The Music Of: 1972-1997	4CD	Epic	E4K-67949	U.S.A.	1997	38.99
Fogelberg, Dan	Promises	CD	Sony	A-28450	U.S.A.	1997	7.99
Fogelberg, Dan	River Of Souls	CD	Epic	EK-46934	U.S.A.	1993	8.99
Fogelberg, Dan	Souvenirs	CD	Epic	EK-33137	U.S.A.	1974	11.99
Fogelberg, Dan	The Essential	CD	Epic	EK-89066	U.S.A.	2003	8.99
Fogelberg, Dan	The Innocent Age	2CD	Epic	E2K-37393	U.S.A.	1981	11.99
Fogelberg, Dan	The Very Best Of	CD	Epic	EK-85280	U.S.A.	2000	8.99
Fogelberg, Dan	The Wild Places	CD	Epic	EK-45059	U.S.A.	1990	7.99
Fogelberg, Dan	Windows And Walls	CD	Epic	EK-39004	U.S.A.	1984	7.99
Fogelberg, Dan/Fools Gold	Mr Lucky	CD	SME	SRCS-9829	Japan	1977	24.99
Fogelberg, Dan/Fools Gold	Self Titled (W/J Walsh/D Felder/Toto)	CD	BMG	BVCA-7330	Japan	1976	24.99
Fogelberg, Dan/Tim Weisberg	No Resemblance Whatsoever	CD	Giant	9-24626-2	U.S.A.	1995	7.99
Fogelberg, Dan/Tim Weisberg	Twin Sons Of Different Mothers	CD	Epic	EK-35339	U.S.A.	1978	7.99
Fogerty, John	Almost Saturday Night (Promo)	CD Single	Reprise	PRO-CD-9376	U.S.A.	1998	5.99
Fogerty, John	Bad Bad Boy (Promo)	CD Single	Warner Bros.	PRO-CD-9138-R	U.S.A.	1997	5.99
Fogerty, John	Blue Boy (Promo)	CD Single	Warner Bros.	PRO-CD-8943	U.S.A.	1997	5.99
Fogerty, John	Blue Moon Swamp	CD	Warner Bros.	9-45426-2	U.S.A.	1997	7.99
Fogerty, John	Blue Moon Swamp (Adv. Promo Copy)	CD	Warner Bros.	2-45426-AB	U.S.A.	1997	9.99
Fogerty, John	Centerfield (Altered Vanz Version)	CD	Warner Bros.	0044-50306-2	U.S.A.	1985	8.99
Fogerty, John	Centerfield (Altered Version Vanz)	CD	Warner Bros.	9-25203-2	U.S.A.	1985	9.99
Fogerty, John	Centerfield (W/Zans Kant Danz)	CD	Warner Bros.	9-25203-2	U.S.A.	1985	64.99
Fogerty, John	Centerfield (W/Zans Kant Danz)	CD	Bellaphon	290-07-085	Germany	1985	64.99
Fogerty, John	Eye Of The Zombie	CD	Dreamworks	0044-50307-2	U.S.A.	1986	9.99
Fogerty, John	John Fogerty	CD	Fantasy	CDFA-507	England	1975	12.99
Fogerty, John	Premonition (Advance Copy)	CD	Reprise	2-46908-AB	U.S.A.	1998	9.99
Fogerty, John	The Blue Ridge Rangers	CD	Fantasy	FCD-4502-2	U.S.A.	1991	7.99
Fogerty, John	Walking In A Hurricane (Promo)	CD Single	Warner Bros.	PRO-CD-8766	U.S.A.	1997	5.99
Fogerty, Tom	Deal it Out/Precious Gems	CD	Fantasy	FCD-9611-2	Germany	1999	15.99
Fogerty, Tom	The Very Best Of	CD	Varese	VSD-6030	U.S.A.	1999	9.99
Fogerty, Tom	Tom Fogerty / Exalibur + 1	CD	Fantasy	FCD-9407-2	Germany	1999	13.99
Fogerty, Tom	Zephyr National & Myopia	CD	Fantasy	FCD-9448-2	Germany	1999	13.99
Fogerty, Tom/Ruby	Precious Gems	CD	Line	MLCD-9.00018-L	Germany	1990	9.99

F

Artist	Title	Format	Label	Catalog No	Country	Released	Value
Fogerty, Tom/Sidekicks	Rainbow Carousel	CD	Line	LICD-9.01162-0	Germany	1992	18.99
Foghat	Best Of	CD	Rhino	R2-70088	U.S.A.	1990	10.99
Foghat	Energized	CD	Rhino	R2-70883	U.S.A.	1974	9.99
Foghat	Foghat (1st Lp)	CD	Rhino	R2-70887	U.S.A.	1972	8.99
Foghat	Foghat (Aka Rock And Roll)	CD	Rhino	R2-70890	U.S.A.	1973	9.99
Foghat	Fool For The City	CD	Rhino	R2-70882	U.S.A.	1975	8.99
Foghat	Live	CD	Rhino	R2-70884	U.S.A.	1977	8.99
Foghat	Night Shift	CD	Rhino	R2-70888	U.S.A.	1976	8.99
Foghat	Rock And Roll Outlaws	CD	Rhino	R2-70889	U.S.A.	1974	9.99
Foghat	Stone Blue	CD	Rhino	R2-70881	U.S.A.	1978	6.99
Foghat	The Essentials	CD	Rhino	R2-76055	U.S.A.	2002	8.99
Foley, Ellen	Night Out	CD	Epic	CD32588	Germany	1979	59.99
Foley, Ellen	Spirit Of St. Louis	CD	Epic	494979-2	England	1981	12.99
Foley, Ellen	The Very Best Of Ellen Foley	CD	Columbia	471842-2	Germany	1992	22.99
Foley, Ellen/The Clash	Spirit Of St. Louis	CD	Sony	EICP-7038	Japan	2002	29.99
Folk, Robert	The Toy Soldiers O.S.T.	CD	Intrada	MAF-7015D	U.S.A.	1991	54.99
Fool's Process	Self Titled	CD	Capricorn	314-534-659-2	U.S.A.	1997	7.99
Forcefield	Forcefield II: The Talisman	CD	President	PCOM-1095	England	1988	22.99
Forcefield	Forcefield II: The Talisman	CD	Griffin	GCD-115-2	U.S.A.	1993	13.99
Forcefield	Forcefield III: To Oz & Back	CD	Griffin	GCD-133-2	U.S.A.	1994	13.99
Forcefield	Forcefield IV: Let The Wild Run Free	CD	Griffin	GCD-116-2	U.S.A.	1993	13.99
Forcefield	Instrumentals	CD	Griffin	GCD-121-2	U.S.A.	1993	12.99
Forcefield	Self Titled	CD	President	PCOM-1088	England	1987	12.99
Forcefield	Self Titled	CD	Griffin	GCD-134-2	U.S.A.	1995	14.99
Ford, Lita	Black	CD	ZYX	20330-2	Germany	1995	11.99
Ford, Lita	Dancin' On The Edge	CD	Mercury	818-864-2	U.S.A.	1984	14.99
Ford, Lita	Dangerous Curves	CD	Spitfire	SPT-15201-2	U.S.A.	2001	8.99
Ford, Lita	Dangerous Curves	CD	BMG Victor	BVCP-171	Japan	1991	29.99
Ford, Lita	Greatest Hits	CD	RCA	7863-66199-2	U.S.A.	1993	9.99
Ford, Lita	Greatest Hits Live!	CD	Cleopatra	CLP-0804-2	U.S.A.	2000	7.99
Ford, Lita	Interview (Pic Cd)	CD	Baktabak	CBAK-4020	England	1995	7.99
Ford, Lita	Lita	CD	RCA	6397-2-R	U.S.A.	1988	14.99
Ford, Lita	Out For Blood	CD	Mercury	810-331-2	U.S.A.	1983	19.99
Ford, Lita	Stiletto	CD	Spitfire	SPT-15202-2	U.S.A.	2001	7.99
Ford, Lita	The Best Of	CD	Dreamland	66037-2	U.S.A.	1992	8.99
Ford, Lita	The Best Of	CD	BMG	BVCP-224	Japan	1992	29.99
Ford, Lita/Ozzy Osbourne	Close My Eyes Forever	CD Single	BMG	R10D-119	Japan	1989	14.99
Foreigner	4 (DVD Audio)	CD	Rhino	R2-74366	U.S.A.	2001	14.99
Foreigner	4 + 2	CD	Rhino	R2-78275	U.S.A.	2002	11.99
Foreigner	Agent Provocateur	CD	Atlantic	82796-2	U.S.A.	1995	8.99
Foreigner	All I Need To Know (Promo)	CD Single	Rhythm Safari	DPRO-50890	U.S.A.	1995	5.99
Foreigner	Complete Greatest Hits	CD	Rhino	R2-78266	U.S.A.	2002	9.99
Foreigner	Double Vision + 2	CD	Rhino	R2-78187	U.S.A.	2002	9.99
Foreigner	Foreigner + 4	CD	Rhino	R2-74270	U.S.A.	2002	9.99
Foreigner	Head Games + 1	CD	Rhino	R2-78198	U.S.A.	2002	9.99
Foreigner	Inside Information	CD	Atlantic	A2-81808	U.S.A.	1987	8.99
Foreigner	Jukebox Heroes: The Anthology	2CD	Rhino	R2-79884	U.S.A.	2000	14.99
Foreigner	Live	CD	Atlantic	82525-2	U.S.A.	1993	8.99
Foreigner	Low Down/Dirty Promo Stereo Box	CD Single	Atlantic	PRCD-3999-2	U.S.A.	1991	32.99
Foreigner	Media America Radio/Up Close (DJ)	2CD	Neer Perfect	3R50100B	U.S.A.	1988	44.99
Foreigner	Mr. Moonlight	CD	Rhythm Safari	P2-53961	U.S.A.	1994	8.99
Foreigner	Mr. Moonlight + 1	CD	BMG Victor	BVCA-648	Japan	1994	29.99
Foreigner	Records	CD	Atlantic	82800-2	U.S.A.	1982	7.99
Foreigner	Self Titled (1s Lp DVD Audio)	CD	Rhino	R2-76665	U.S.A.	2001	14.99
Foreigner	The Best Of Ballads	CD	East West	AMCY-2963	Japan	1998	39.99
Foreigner	The Definitive	CD	Rhino	8122735962	Australia	2002	14.99
Foreigner	The Platinum Collection	CD	Warner Bros.	7567809492	Australia	1999	12.99
Foreigner	The Very Best And Beyond	CD	Atlantic	7-89999-2	U.S.A.	1992	7.99

F

Artist	Title	Format	Label	Catalog No	Country	Released	Value
Foreigner	Unusual Heat (W/O Lou Gramm)	CD	Atlantic	A2-82299	U.S.A.	1991	6.99
Foreigner	Westwood 1 # 95-17 (4-17-95)	2CD	Westwood 1	C02NF010D	U.S.A.	1995	59.99
Foreigner	White Lie	CD Single	Arista	74321-23286-2-2	England	1994	4.99
Foreigner/Lou Gramm	Foreigner In A Strange Land	CD	Magnum	CDTB-065	England	1995	10.99
Foreigner/Lou Gramm	Long Hard Look	CD	Atlantic	7-81915-2	U.S.A.	1989	9.99
Foreigner/Lou Gramm	Mystic Foreigner	CD	Rough Trade	RTD-397.0031.2	Germany	1997	25.99
Foreigner/Lou Gramm	Ready Or Not	CD	Atlantic	7-81728-2	U.S.A.	1987	9.99
Foreigner/Mick Jones	Mick Jones	CD	Atlantic	7-81991-2	U.S.A.	1989	8.99
Foreigner/Shadow King	Shadow King (With Lou Gramm)	CD	Atlantic	7-82324-2	U.S.A.	1991	8.99
Forest	Self Titled/Full Circle	CD	BGO	BGOCD236	England	1994	13.99
Foster, David	The Best Of Me (MFSL Silver Cd)	CD	Mobile Fidelity	MFCD-810	U.S.A.	1985	20.99
Foundations, The	Baby Now That I've Found You	2CD	Sequel	NEECD-300	England	1998	12.99
Foundations, The	The Very Best Of	CD	Sanctuary	06076-81170-2	U.S.A.	2002	8.99
Four Seasons	25th Anniversary Collection	3CD	Rhino	RNRD-72998-2	U.S.A.	1988	40.99
Four Seasons	Greatest Hits Vol. 1	CD	Rhino	R2-70594	U.S.A.	1991	7.99
Four Seasons	Greatest Hits Vol. 2	CD	Rhino	R2-70595	U.S.A.	1991	7.99
Four Seasons	In Season: Anthology	2CD	Rhino	R2-74266	U.S.A.	2001	19.99
Four Seasons	Off Seasons: Criminally Ignored Sides	CD	Rhino	R2-74267	U.S.A.	2001	14.99
Four Seasons	Very Best Of	CD	Rhino	R2-74494	U.S.A.	2003	9.99
Four Tops/Smokey Robinson	Indestructible	CD Single	Arista	661-510-2	Germany	1988	12.99
Fourplay/Bob James	4	CD	Warner Bros.	9-46921-2	U.S.A.	1998	7.99
Fourplay/Bob James	Between The Sheets	CD	Warner Bros.	9-45340-2	U.S.A.	1993	8.99
Fourplay/Bob James	Elixir	CD	Warner Bros.	9-45922-2	U.S.A.	1994	6.99
Fourplay/Bob James	Fourplay	CD	Warner Bros.	9-26656-2	U.S.A.	1991	9.99
Fourplay/Bob James	Heartfelt	CD	Bluebird	63916	U.S.A.	2002	9.99
Fourplay/Bob James	Snowbound (Xmas Cd)	CD	Warner Bros.	9-47504-2	U.S.A.	1999	9.99
Fourplay/Bob James	The Best Of Fourplay	CD	Warner Bros.	9-46661-2	U.S.A.	1997	11.99
Fourplay/Bob James	Yes, Please	CD	Warner Bros.	9-47694-2	U.S.A.	2000	9.99
Fowley, Kim	Born to be Wild	CD	Ascension	ANCD-015	Australia	1968	14.99
Fowley, Kim	Michigan Babylon	CD	Detroit Electric	DE-02	U.S.A.	2000	15.99
Fowley, Kim	Outrageous	CD	Ascension	ANCD-016	Australia	1969	14.99
Fowley, Kim	The Day the Earth Stood Still	CD	Spalax	14260	France	1970	24.99
Foxx, Jamie	Peep This	CD	RCA	66436-2	U.S.A.	1994	43.99
Foxx, John	In Mysterious Ways + 3	CD	Edsel	EDCD-705	England	2001	16.99
Foxx, John	Metamatic + 6	CD	Virgin	0777-7-87822-2-3	Germany	1993	17.99
Foxx, John	The Garden + 5	CD	Edsel	EDCD-703	England	2001	16.99
Foxx, John	The Golden Section	CD	Virgin	VJCP-23198	Japan	1983	53.99
Foxx, John	The Golden Section + 6	CD	Edsel	EDCD-704	England	2001	16.99
Foxx, John/Louis Gordon	Crash And Burn	CD	Metamatic	META005CD	England	2003	16.99
Foxx, John/Louis Gordon	Shifting City	CD	Metamatic	META-0002CD	England	1995	16.99
Foxx, John/Louis Gordon	The Pleasures Of Electricity	CD	Metamatic	META-0004CD	England	2001	16.99
Frampton, Peter	Anthology: History Peter Frampton	CD	A&M	069-490-825-2	U.S.A.	2001	8.99
Frampton, Peter	Frampton	CD	A&M	CD-4512	U.S.A.	2000	7.99
Frampton, Peter	Frampton Comes Alive! (Del Ed.) + 4	2CD	A&M	069-490-561-2	U.S.A.	2001	15.99
Frampton, Peter	Frampton Comes Alive! (MFSL Gold)	2CD	Mobile Fidelity	UDCD-2-678	U.S.A.	1976	73.99
Frampton, Peter	Frampton's Camel	CD	A&M	069-490-715-2	U.S.A.	2000	9.99
Frampton, Peter	I'm In You	CD	A&M	069-490-714-2	U.S.A.	2000	8.99
Frampton, Peter	Peter Frampton	CD	Relativity	88561-4192-2	U.S.A.	1994	8.99
Frampton, Peter	Something's Happening	CD	A&M	069-490-730-2	U.S.A.	2000	8.99
Frampton, Peter	When All The Pieces Fit	CD	Atlantic	7-82030-2	U.S.A.	1989	9.99
Frampton, Peter/The Herd	Paradise And Underworld	CD	Repertoire	REP-4257-WG	Germany	1992	12.99
Franke, Christopher	Babylon 5	CD	Sonic Images	SI-8502-2	U.S.A.	1995	5.99
Franke, Christopher	Babylon 5: And The Rock Cried...	CD	Sonic Images	SI-0320-2	U.S.A.	1998	17.99
Franke, Christopher	Babylon 5: Chrysalis	CD	Sonic Images	SI-1112-2	U.S.A.	1998	17.99
Franke, Christopher	Babylon 5: Darkness Ascending	CD	Sonic Images	SI-0516-2	U.S.A.	1999	17.99
Franke, Christopher	Babylon 5: Endgame	CD	Sonic Images	SI-1420-2	U.S.A.	1998	17.99
Franke, Christopher	Babylon 5: Fall Of The Night	CD	Sonic Images	SI-1222-2	U.S.A.	1998	17.99
Franke, Christopher	Babylon 5: Falling Towards Apotheosis	CD	Sonic Images	SI-0404-2	U.S.A.	1999	17.99

F

Artist	Title	Format	Label	Catalog No	Country	Released	Value
Franke, Christopher	Babylon 5: In The Beginning	CD	Sonic Images	SI-8812-2	U.S.A.	1998	17.99
Franke, Christopher	Babylon 5: Interludes/Examinations	CD	Sonic Images	SI-1315-2	U.S.A.	1998	17.99
Franke, Christopher	Babylon 5: Into The Fire	CD	Sonic Images	SI-1406-2	U.S.A.	1998	17.99
Franke, Christopher	Babylon 5: Late Delivery	CD	Sonic Images	SI-0312-2	U.S.A.	1997	17.99
Franke, Christopher	Babylon 5: Lines Of Communication	CD	Sonic Images	SI-1411-2	U.S.A.	1998	17.99
Franke, Christopher	Babylon 5: Long Night	CD	Sonic Images	SI-1405-2	U.S.A.	1998	17.99
Franke, Christopher	Babylon 5: Messages From Earth	CD	Sonic Images	SI-8602-2	U.S.A.	1997	17.99
Franke, Christopher	Babylon 5: No Retreat, No Surrender	CD	Sonic Images	SI-1415-2	U.S.A.	1998	17.99
Franke, Christopher	Babylon 5: Objects At Rest	CD	Sonic Images	SI-0522-2	U.S.A.	1999	17.99
Franke, Christopher	Babylon 5: Ragged Edge	CD	Sonic Images	SI-1513-2	U.S.A.	1998	17.99
Franke, Christopher	Babylon 5: Severed Dreams	CD	Sonic Images	SI-0310-2	U.S.A.	1997	17.99
Franke, Christopher	Babylon 5: Shadow Dancing	CD	Sonic Images	SI-0321-2	U.S.A.	1997	17.99
Franke, Christopher	Babylon 5: Sleeping In Light	CD	Sonic Images	SI-0523-2	U.S.A.	1999	17.99
Franke, Christopher	Babylon 5: The Coming Of Shadows	CD	Sonic Images	SI-1209-2	U.S.A.	1998	17.99
Franke, Christopher	Babylon 5: The Face Of The Enemy	CD	Sonic Images	SI-1417-2	U.S.A.	1998	17.99
Franke, Christopher	Babylon 5: The River Of Souls	CD	Sonic Images	SI-8907-2	U.S.A.	1999	17.99
Franke, Christopher	Babylon 5: Thirdspace	CD	Sonic Images	SI-8900-2	U.S.A.	1999	17.99
Franke, Christopher	Babylon 5: Walkabout	CD	Sonic Images	SI-0318-2	U.S.A.	1997	17.99
Franke, Christopher	Babylon 5: War Without End, Vol. 1	CD	Sonic Images	SI-1316-2	U.S.A.	1998	17.99
Franke, Christopher	Babylon 5: War Without End, Vol. 2	CD	Sonic Images	SI-1317-2	U.S.A.	1998	17.99
Franke, Christopher	Babylon 5: Whatever...Mr. Garibaldi	CD	Sonic Images	SI-1402-2	U.S.A.	1998	17.99
Franke, Christopher	Babylon 5: Z'Ha'Dum	CD	Sonic Images	SI-0322-2	U.S.A.	1997	17.99
Franke, Christopher	Bridge To Eternity	CD Single	Sonic Images	37-392-414	Germany	1996	24.99
Franke, Christopher	Enchanting Nature	CD	Earth Tone	ET-7401-2	U.S.A.	1994	8.99
Franke, Christopher	Epic	CD	Earth Tone	ET-7907-2	U.S.A.	1999	8.99
Franke, Christopher	Klemania	CD	Sonic Images	SI-8504-2	U.S.A.	1995	8.99
Franke, Christopher	La Prophetie Des Andes	CD	Priority	842724-2	France	1996	24.99
Franke, Christopher	McBain (O.S.T.)	CD	Sonic Images	SI-5011-2	U.S.A.	1993	17.99
Franke, Christopher	Morhing Space: The Singles	CD Single	Sonic Images	SI-8504-2-R	U.S.A.	1995	24.99
Franke, Christopher	New Music For Films, Vol. 1	CD	Varese	VSD-5393	U.S.A.	1993	17.99
Franke, Christopher	New Music For Films, Vol. 2	CD	Sonic Images	SI-4906-2	U.S.A.	2000	10.99
Franke, Christopher	Night Of The Running Man	CD	Super Tracks	STCD-500	U.S.A.	1995	13.99
Franke, Christopher	Pacific Blue	CD	Bellaphon	290.25.008	Germany	1997	7.99
Franke, Christopher	Pacific Coast Highway	CD	Private	01005-82094-2	U.S.A.	1991	5.99
Franke, Christopher	Perry Rhodan (O.S.T.) Pax Terra	CD	Sonic Images	37-362-423	Germany	1996	11.99
Franke, Christopher	Raven (O.S.T.)	CD	Sonic Images	SI-8112-2	U.S.A.	1996	32.99
Franke, Christopher	Self Titled	CD	Sonic Images	SI-8402-2	U.S.A.	1995	17.99
Franke, Christopher	Tenchi The Movie +3	CD	Pioneer	PIO-CD-5176-2	U.S.A.	2002	36.99
Franke, Christopher	The Best Of Babylon 5	CD	Sonic Images	SI-8931-2	U.S.A.	2001	17.99
Franke, Christopher	The Calling (O.S.T.)	CD	Edel	0121572ERE	Germany	2000	10.99
Franke, Christopher	The Celestine Prophecy	CD	Priority	841893-2	Netherland	1996	24.99
Franke, Christopher	The London Concert	CD	Varese	VSD-5399	U.S.A.	1992	7.99
Franke, Christopher	The Tommyknockers (O.S.T.)	CD	Sonic Images	SI-8901-2	U.S.A.	1999	17.99
Franke, Christopher	Transformation Of Mind	CD	Earth Tone	ET-7704-2	U.S.A.	1997	18.99
Franke, Christopher	Universal Soldier (O.S.T.)	CD	Varese	VSD-5373	U.S.A.	1995	8.99
Franklin, Aretha	I Never Loved A Man... (MFSL Gold)	CD	Mobile Fidelity	UDCD-574	U.S.A.	1967	29.99
Franklin, Aretha	Lady Soul/Aretha Now (MFSL Gold)	CD	Mobile Fidelity	UDCD-623	U.S.A.	1968	32.99
Franklin, Aretha	Live At The Fillmore (MFSL Silver CD)	CD	Mobile Fidelity	MFCD-820	U.S.A.	1971	40.99
Freak Of Nature	Gathering Of Freaks	CD	Victor Ent.	VICP-5462	Japan	1994	39.99
Freak Of Nature	Self Titled	CD	Victor Ent.	VICP-5242	Japan	1993	29.99
Fred, John/The Playboys	Judy In Disguise With Glasses	CD	Repertoire	REP-4153-WZ	Germany	1991	19.99
Fred, John/The Playboys	The History Of	CD	Paula	PCD-9000	U.S.A.	1991	19.99
Free	20th Century Masters: The Millennium	CD	Universal	314-490-735-2	U.S.A.	2002	8.99
Free	All Right Now	CD	Karussell	544-167-2	Germany	2001	8.99
Free	An Introduction To (No Allright Now)	CD	Island	524-555-2	Holland	1999	11.99
Free	At Last + 4	CD	Universal	586-229-2	England	2002	11.99
Free	Fire And Water + 5	CD	Universal	586-227-2	England	2003	11.99
Free	Heartbreaker + 6	CD	Universal	586-230-2	England	2002	11.99

F

Artist	Title	Format	Label	Catalog No	Country	Released	Value
Free	Highway + 6	CD	Universal	586-226-2	England	2002	11.99
Free	Live + 3	CD	Universal	586-228-2	England	2002	11.99
Free	Molten Gold: The Anthology	2CD	A&M	31451-8456-2	U.S.A.	1993	14.99
Free	Self Titled + 10	CD	Universal	586-225-2	England	2002	11.99
Free	Songs Of Yesterday	5CD	Island	542-499-2	England	2000	39.99
Free	The Best	CD	A&M	75021-3663-2	U.S.A.	1990	8.99
Free	The Free Story	CD	PolyGram	842-343-2	Holland	2001	8.99
Free	The Universal Masters Collection	CD	Universal	586-315-2	Germany	2001	12.99
Free	Tons Of Sobs + 8	CD	Universal	586-149-2	England	2003	11.99
Free/Back Street Crawler	Second Street	CD	Repertoire	REP-4376-WY	Germany	1997	11.99
Free/Back Street Crawler	The Band Plays On	CD	Repertoire	REP-4265-WY	Germany	1997	11.99
Free/Crawler	Crawler (No Paul Kossoff)	CD	Sony	ESCA-5539	Japan	1977	94.99
Free/Paul Kossoff	Best Of	CD	Track	TRA-1034CD	England	2003	11.99
Free/Paul Kossoff	Blue Blue Soul	CD	Music Club	50022	U.S.A.	1997	8.99
Free/Paul Kossoff	Croyden, June 15th 1971 Live!	CD	Repertoire	REP-4530-WY	Germany	1995	18.99
Free/Paul Kossoff	Koss	CD	Castle	CLACD127	England	1992	19.99
Free/Paul Kossoff	Kossoff/Kirke/Tetsu/Rabbit	CD	Polygram K.K.	PHCR-4810	Japan	1997	29.99
Freedom/Procol Harum	Black On White	CD	Angel Air	SJPCD028	England	1999	14.99
Freedom/Procol Harum	Freedom At Last/Through The Years	2CD	Angel Air	SJPCD027	England	1999	22.99
Freedom/Procol Harum	Is More Than A Word	CD	Angel Air	SJPCD073	England	2000	8.99
Freedom/Procol Harum	Is More Than A Word	CD	Akarma	AK-219	Italy	2003	8.99
Freedom/Procol Harum	Self Titled	CD	Angel Air	SJPCD063	England	2000	8.99
Freedom/Procol Harum	Through The Years	CD	Akarma	AK-222	Italy	2003	8.99
Freeman, Danny	Blues Cruise	CD	Line	STCD-9.00535-0	Germany	1988	24.99
Freeman, Danny	Out Of The Blue	CD	Line	STCD-9.00537-0	Germany	1988	24.99
Fresh Aire/Chip Davis	Sunday Morning Coffee	CD	American	AGCD100	U.S.A.	1991	8.99
Fresh Bush/Invisible Man	Hard Times (President Bush)	CD	I.R.S.	DPRO-67104	U.S.A.	1992	7.99
Frey, Glenn	Live	CD	MCA	MCAD-10826	U.S.A.	1993	7.99
Frey, Glenn	Livin' Right (Promo Remix)	CD Single	MCA	CD45-17762	U.S.A.	1989	7.99
Frey, Glenn	No Fun Aloud	CD	Elektra	60129-2	U.S.A.	1982	8.99
Frey, Glenn	Solo Collection	CD	MCA	MCAD-11227	U.S.A.	1995	8.99
Frey, Glenn	Solo Collection + 1	CD	Victor Ent.	UICY-2582	Japan	2002	29.99
Frey, Glenn	Soul Searchin'	CD	MCA	MCAD-6239	U.S.A.	1988	7.99
Frey, Glenn	Strange Weather	CD	MCA	MCAD-10599	U.S.A.	1992	5.99
Frey, Glenn	Strange Weather - Live/Dublin (DJ CD)	CD	MCA	MCA3P-2469	U.S.A.	1992	24.99
Frey, Glenn	The Allnighter	CD	MCA	MCAD-5501	U.S.A.	1984	8.99
Frey, Glenn	The Best Of	CD	MCA	112-497-2	Holland	2001	17.99
Frijid Pink	Defrosted + 4	CD	Repertoire	REP-4172-WZ	Germany	2002	11.99
Frijid Pink	Earth Omen + 2	CD	Repertoire	REP-4465-WT	Germany	2001	11.99
Frijid Pink	Hibernated Box Set	3CD	Akarma	AK-216/3	Italy	2002	44.99
Frijid Pink	Self Titled + 2	CD	Repertoire	REP-4156-WZ	Germany	1998	11.99
Fripp, Robert	1999 Soundscapes Live In Argentina	CD	Discipline Global	DGM-9402-2	U.S.A.	1994	16.99
Fripp, Robert	Blessing/Tears: Soundscapes, Vol. 2	CD	Discipline Global	DGM-9506	England	1995	11.99
Fripp, Robert	Exposure	CD	Editions EG	EEGCD-41	U.S.A.	1979	9.99
Fripp, Robert	God Save The King	CD	Editions EG	EEGCD-9	U.S.A.	1985	9.99
Fripp, Robert	Let The Power Fall	CD	Editions EG	EEGCD-10	U.S.A.	1981	7.99
Fripp, Robert	November Suite: Live Greenpark	CD	Discipline Global	DGM-9701	England	1997	9.99
Fripp, Robert	Pie Jesu	CD Single	Discipline Global	DGM-9704	England	1997	5.99
Fripp, Robert	Radiophonics: Soundscapes, Vol. 1	CD	Discipline Global	DGM-9505	U.S.A.	1996	9.99
Fripp, Robert	That Which P: Soundscapes Vol. 3	CD	Discipline Global	DGM-9701	England	1996	9.99
Fripp, Robert	The Gates Of Paradise, Vol. 1	CD	Discipline Global	DGM-9608	England	1997	8.99
Fripp, Robert	The Gates Of Paradise, Vol. 1 (Ltd Ed)	CD	Discipline Global	DGM-9608A	England	1997	14.99
Fripp, Robert/Brian Eno	Evening Star	CD	Editions EG	EEGCD-3	U.S.A.	1989	10.99
Fripp, Robert/Brian Eno	No Pussyfooting	CD	Editions EG	EEGCD-2	U.S.A.	1989	10.99
Fripp, Robert/Jeffrey Fayman	A Temple In The Clouds	CD	Projekt	104	U.S.A.	2000	9.99
Fripp, Robert/League Of C	And The League/Crafty Guitarists Live	CD	Editions EG	EEGCD-43	U.S.A.	1986	14.99
Fripp, Robert/League Of C	Intergalactic Boogie Express	CD	Discipline Global	DGM-9502	England	1995	12.99
Fripp, Robert/League Of C	Show Of Hands	CD	Editions EG	EEG-2102-2	U.S.A.	1991	8.99

F

Artist	Title	Format	Label	Catalog No	Country	Released	Value
Fripp, Robert/League Of G	Thang Thrang Gozinbulx	CD	Discipline Global	DGM-9602	U.S.A.	1996	13.99
Fripp, Robert/Rieflin/Gunn	Repercussions Of Angelic Behavior	CD	First World	FWD-99.06	England	1999	11.99
Fripp, Robert/Trey Gunn	String Quartet	CD	Discipline Global	DGM-9303	England	1993	11.99
Fripp/Giles,Giles And	Brondesbury Tapes (1968)	CD	Mister E	MRE-001CD	U.S.A.	1968	16.99
Fripp/Giles,Giles And	The Brondesbury Tapes	CD	Voiceprint	VP235CD	England	2001	16.99
Frith, Fred	Allies	CD	RecRec	RECDEC-70	Switzerlan	1996	14.99
Frith, Fred	Clearing	CD	Tzadik	TZ-7605	U.S.A.	2001	11.99
Frith, Fred	Eye To Ear	CD	Tzadik	TZ-7503	U.S.A.	1997	11.99
Frith, Fred	Freedom In Fragments	CD	Tzadik	TZ-7076	U.S.A.	2002	12.99
Frith, Fred	Gravity	CD	Recommded	ReR-FRED	England	2003	15.99
Frith, Fred	Gravity + 6	CD	East Side Digital	80452	U.S.A.	1990	15.99
Frith, Fred	Guitar Solos	CD	Recommded	ReR-FRO-02	England	1991	15.99
Frith, Fred	Helter Skelter	CD	RecRec	RECDEC-40	Switzerlan	1993	14.99
Frith, Fred	Keep The Dog Live	2CD	Recommded	ReR-FRA-03	England	2003	24.99
Frith, Fred	Pacifica (1993-95)	CD	Tzadik	TZ-7034	U.S.A.	1998	11.99
Frith, Fred	Prints	CD	Recommded	ReR-FRA-02	England	2002	14.99
Frith, Fred	Speechless + 5	CD	Recommded	ReR-FRO-04	England	2003	14.99
Frith, Fred	Step Across The Border	CD	RecRec	RECDEC-30	Switzerlan	1990	14.99
Frith, Fred	Step Across The Border	CD	Recommded	ReR-FRO-03	England	2003	14.99
Frith, Fred	Stone, Brick, Glass...	2CD	I Dischi Di Angelica	IDA014	Italy	1999	34.99
Frith, Fred	The Previous Evening	CD	Recommded	RER-FF1	England	1997	11.99
Frith, Fred	The Technology Of Tears	CD	RecRec	RECDEC-20	Switzerlan	1988	10.99
Frith, Fred	Top Of His Head	CD	Made To Measure	MTM-21-CD	Belgium	1995	14.99
Frith, Fred/Bourne/Oswald	Dearness	CD	Spool	SPL-116	Canada	2002	14.99
Frith, Fred/Chris Cutler	Two Gentlemen In Verona	CD	Recommded	RER-CCFF3	England	1999	12.99
Frith, Fred/Chris Cutler	Volume 2. Live in Trondheim...	CD	Recommded	RER-CCFF2CD	England	1994	14.99
Frith, Fred/Dresser/Mori	Later	CD	Victo	VICTO-070	Canada	2000	15.99
Frith, Fred/Drouet/Sclavis	I Dream Of You Jumping	CD	Victo	VICTO-072	Canada	2001	15.99
Frith, Fred/E Modern	Traffic Continues	CD	Winter/Winter	910044-2	Germany	2000	14.99
Frith, Fred/Et Al	Oasis	CD	Mills College	CD-004	U.S.A.	2001	14.99
Frith, Fred/Ferdinand	Dropera	CD	RecRec	RECDEC-32	Switzerlan	1991	14.99
Frith, Fred/Guitar Quartet	Ayaya Moses	CD	Ambiances	AM-051	Canada	1997	11.99
Frith, Fred/Henry Kaiser	Friends & Enemies	2CD	Cuneiform	CUNE-117/18	U.S.A.	1999	19.99
Frith, Fred/Hideki/Mori	Death Ambient	CD	Tzadik	TZ-7207	U.S.A.	1996	11.99
Frith, Fred/Hodgkinson	Live Improvisations	CD	Woof	WOOF-013	England	1992	16.99
Frith, Fred/John Zorn	Art Of Memory	CD	Incus	INCUS-CD20	England	1994	14.99
Frith, Fred/Maybe Monday	Digital Wildlife	CD	Winter/Winter	910-071-2	Germany	2002	13.99
Frith, Fred/R Lussier	Nous Autres	CD	Victo	VICTO-001	Canada	1995	15.99
Fritsch, Eloy	Space Music	CD	Dreaming	DR-8404.AR	France	1998	12.99
Froese, Edgar	Ages	CD	Virgin	CDOVD480	England	1997	11.99
Froese, Edgar	Ambient Highway, Vol. 1	CD	TDI	TDP003CD	EU	2003	12.99
Froese, Edgar	Ambient Highway, Vol. 2	CD	TDI	TDP004CD	EU	2003	12.99
Froese, Edgar	Ambient Highway, Vol. 3	CD	TDI	TDPCD005	EU	2003	12.99
Froese, Edgar	Ambient Highway, Vol. 4	CD	TDI	TDP006CD	EU	2003	12.99
Froese, Edgar	Aqua	CD	Virgin	0777-7-87214-2-0	Germany	1974	13.99
Froese, Edgar	Beyond The Storm	2CD	Virgin	7243-8-40104-2-3	Holland	1995	21.99
Froese, Edgar	Epsilon In Malaysian Pale	CD	Caroline	CAROL-1625-2	U.S.A.	1990	24.99
Froese, Edgar	Introduction To The Ambient Highway	CD	TDI	TDPCD002	EU	2003	19.99
Froese, Edgar	Kamikaze (O.S.T.)	CD	Caroline	CAROL-1626-2	U.S.A.	1990	24.99
Froese, Edgar	Pinnacles	CD	Caroline	CAROL-1627-2	U.S.A.	1990	29.99
Froese, Edgar	Stuntman	CD	Virgin	CDV-2139	England	1979	11.99
Frontiere, Dominic	The Outer Limits (O.TV.S.T.)	CD	GNP	GNPD-8032	U.S.A.	1993	12.99
Fruitcake	One More Slice	CD	Cyclops	CYCL-057	England	1993	14.99
Frumpy	2	CD	Repertoire	REP-4339-WP	Germany	2002	13.99
Frumpy	All Will Be Changed + 2	CD	Repertoire	REP-4146-WP	Germany	2002	13.99
Frumpy	Best Of	CD	Universal	536-216-2	England	2003	12.99
Frumpy	By The Way	CD	Repertoire	IMS-7019-WP	Germany	2002	12.99
Frumpy	Frumpy: Live Ninety-Five	CD	SPV	SPV084-89892CD	Germany	2003	9.99

F

Artist	Title	Format	Label	Catalog No	Country	Released	Value
Frumpy	Live	2CD	Repertoire	IMS-7035-WL	Germany	2002	15.99
Fugs	Electromagnetic... (Reprise Lps)	3CD	Rhino	RHM2-7759	U.S.A.	2001	64.99
Fugs	First Album + 10	CD	ACE	CDWIKD-119	England	1993	11.99
Fugs	Live From The 60s	CD	ACE	CDWIKD-125	Germany	1994	13.99
Fugs	No More Slavery + 5	CD	ACE	CDWIKD-145	England	1996	13.99
Fugs	Real Woodstock Festival	2CD	ACE	CDWIK2-160	England	1995	16.99
Fugs	Refuse To Be Burnt Out + 2	CD	ACE	CDWIKD-139	England	1995	13.99
Fugs	Second Album + 5	CD	ACE	CDWIKD-121	England	1993	11.99
Fugs	Songs From A Portable Forest	CD	Gazell	GPCD-2003	U.S.A.	1990	15.99
Fugs/Ed Sanders	American Bard	CD	Olufsen	DOCD-5324	Austria	1996	14.99
Fugs/Ed Sanders	Songs In Ancient Greek + 1	CD	Olufsen	DOCD-5073	Austria	1988	14.99
Fugs/Peter Stampfel	Peter Stampfel (Holy Modal Rounders)	CD	Hello Club	HEL-45	U.S.A.	1994	29.99
Fugs/Tuli Kupferberg	No Deposit, No Return/Tuli & Friends	CD	Shimmy Disc	SDE-9133/CD	Holland	1993	9.99
Full Force	Get Busy 1 Time	CD	Sony	25DP-5465	Japan	1988	54.99
Fuzzbubble	Demos, Out-Takes & Rarities	CD	Not Lame	NLL-014	U.S.A.	2002	13.99
Fuzzy Duck	Self Titled + 4	CD	Repertoire	REP-4352-WP	Germany	2002	14.99
Fygi, Laura	Bewitched	CD	Verve	314-514-724-2	U.S.A.	1993	9.99

G

Artist	Title	Format	Label	Catalog No	Country	Released	Value
Gabrels, Reeves	The Sacred Squall Of Now	CD	Upstart	UPSTART-020	U.S.A.	1995	5.99
Gabrels, Reeves	Ulysses (Della Notte)	CD	E-Magine	EMA-61050-2	U.S.A.	2000	5.99
Gabriel, Peter	06/07/03 - MOUNTAIN VIEW, CA	2CD	Music.Com	ES-PG03-0607	U.S.A.	2003	24.99
Gabriel, Peter	06/08/03 - IRVINE, CA	2CD	Music.Com	ES-PG03-0608	U.S.A.	2003	24.99
Gabriel, Peter	06/11/03 - DALLAS, TX	2CD	Music.Com	ES-PG03-0611	U.S.A.	2003	24.99
Gabriel, Peter	06/12/03 - HOUSTON, TX	2CD	Music.Com	ES-PG03-0612	U.S.A.	2003	24.99
Gabriel, Peter	06/14/03 - WEST PALM BEACH, FL	2CD	Music.Com	ES-PG03-0614	U.S.A.	2003	24.99
Gabriel, Peter	06/16/03 - ATLANTA, GA	2CD	Music.Com	ES-PG03-0616	U.S.A.	2003	24.99
Gabriel, Peter	06/18/03 - MANSFIELD, MA	2CD	Music.Com	ES-PG03-0618	U.S.A.	2003	24.99
Gabriel, Peter	06/20/03 - HOLMDEL, NJ	2CD	Music.Com	ES-PG03-0620	U.S.A.	2003	24.99
Gabriel, Peter	06/21/03 - CAMDEN, NJ	2CD	Music.Com	ES-PG03-0621	U.S.A.	2003	24.99
Gabriel, Peter	06/22/03 - BRISTOW, VA	2CD	Music.Com	ES-PG03-0622	U.S.A.	2003	24.99
Gabriel, Peter	06/24/03 - WANTAGH, NY	2CD	Music.Com	ES-PG03-0624	U.S.A.	2003	24.99
Gabriel, Peter	06/26/03 - MILWAUKEE, WI	2CD	Music.Com	ES-PG03-0626	U.S.A.	2003	24.99
Gabriel, Peter	06/28/03 - TINLEY PARK, IL	2CD	Music.Com	ES-PG03-0628	U.S.A.	2003	24.99
Gabriel, Peter	06/29/03 - CLARKSTON, MI	2CD	Music.Com	ES-PG03-0629	U.S.A.	2003	24.99
Gabriel, Peter	07/01/03 - COLUMBUS, OH	2CD	Music.Com	ES-PG03-0701	U.S.A.	2003	24.99
Gabriel, Peter	07/02/03 - NOBLESVILLE, IN	2CD	Music.Com	ES-PG03-0702	U.S.A.	2003	24.99
Gabriel, Peter	07/04/03 - TORONTO, ON	2CD	Music.Com	ES-PG03-0704	U.S.A.	2003	24.99
Gabriel, Peter	07/05/03 - LONDON, ON	2CD	Music.Com	ES-PG03-0705	U.S.A.	2003	24.99
Gabriel, Peter	07/06/03 - MONTREAL, QC	2CD	Music.Com	ES-PG03-0706	U.S.A.	2003	24.99
Gabriel, Peter	Before US: A Brief History (Promo)	CD	Geffen	PRO-CD-4412	U.S.A.	1992	49.99
Gabriel, Peter	Biko	CD Single	Virgin	CDPGS-612	Germany	1987	12.99
Gabriel, Peter	Birdy (Ltd Numbered)	CD	Geffen	069-493-283-2	U.S.A.	2002	11.99
Gabriel, Peter	Blood Of Eden	CD Single	Virgin	PGSDX-9	England	1993	8.99
Gabriel, Peter	Deutsches Album (German Security)	CD	Virgin	0777-7-87220-2-1	Holland	1987	18.99
Gabriel, Peter	Digging In The Dirt	CD Single	Geffen	GEFDM-21816	U.S.A.	1992	7.99
Gabriel, Peter	Digging In The Dirt (Digipack)	CD Single	Virgin	7243-8-90008-2-5	England	1992	11.99
Gabriel, Peter	Digging In The Dirt (Leatherbound Box)	CD Single	Virgin	7243-8-90007-2-6	England	1992	14.99
Gabriel, Peter	Ein Deutsches Album (German 3rd LP)	CD	Virgin	0777-7-86767-2-0	Holland	1987	18.99
Gabriel, Peter	Encore Collectors Box (19 Shows/Bklt)	38CD	Music.Com	ESD-PG03-CB	U.S.A.	2003	474.99
Gabriel, Peter	Eve Cd-Rom	Cd-Rom	Realworld	71143-67004-5-6	England	1996	23.99
Gabriel, Peter	From Us To You... (Promo)	CD	Album Network	H6HXO300C	U.S.A.	1992	13.99
Gabriel, Peter	Hit	2CD	Geffen	B00011486-02	U.S.A.	2003	14.99

Artist	Title	Format	Label	Catalog No	Country	Released	Value
Gabriel, Peter	Long Walk Home (Rabbit Proof Fence)	CD	Realworld	PGCD10	Australia	2002	11.99
Gabriel, Peter	Lovetown	CD Single	Epic	660480-2	England	1993	9.99
Gabriel, Peter	Me / The Peter Gabriel Interview	CD	Baktabak	CBAK-4072	England	1993	10.99
Gabriel, Peter	Ovo The Millenium Show (Story/Ovo)	2CD	Real World	RWPG01/O2	England	2000	29.99
Gabriel, Peter	Passion (Ltd Numbered)	CD	Geffen	069-493-285-2	U.S.A.	2002	11.99
Gabriel, Peter	Peter Gabriel 1 (Ltd Numbered)	CD	Geffen	069-493-301-2	U.S.A.	2002	11.99
Gabriel, Peter	Peter Gabriel 2 (Ltd Numbered)	CD	Geffen	069-493-302-2	U.S.A.	2002	11.99
Gabriel, Peter	Peter Gabriel 3 (Ltd Numbered)	CD	Geffen	069-493-279-2	U.S.A.	2002	13.99
Gabriel, Peter	Plays Live - Highlights (Ltd Numbered)	CD	Geffen	069-493-282-2	U.S.A.	2002	17.99
Gabriel, Peter	Plays Live (Highlights + 6)	2CD	Geffen	GEFD2-25319	U.S.A.	1983	18.99
Gabriel, Peter	Remaster Sampler (Promo)	CD	Geffen	CATF-05033-2	U.S.A.	2002	12.99
Gabriel, Peter	Revisited	CD	Atlantic	82429-2	U.S.A.	1992	5.99
Gabriel, Peter	Secret World (In-Store Promo Sampler)	CD	Geffen	PRO-CD-4678	U.S.A.	1994	14.99
Gabriel, Peter	Secret World Live	2CD	Geffen	GEFD2-24722	U.S.A.	1994	20.99
Gabriel, Peter	Security (Ltd Numbered)	CD	Geffen	069-493-280-2	U.S.A.	2002	11.99
Gabriel, Peter	Shaking The Tree (Ltd Numbered)	CD	Geffen	069-493-286-2	U.S.A.	2002	12.99
Gabriel, Peter	Sledgehammer	CD Single	Virgin	CDF-4	England	1986	11.99
Gabriel, Peter	So (Ltd Numbered)	CD	Geffen	069-493-284-2	U.S.A.	2002	16.99
Gabriel, Peter	So (Original Trk Listing)	CD	Geffen	9-24088-2	U.S.A.	1986	9.99
Gabriel, Peter	Solsbury Hill	CD Single	Virgin	CDF-33	Germany	1983	13.99
Gabriel, Peter	Steam	CD Single	Geffen	GEFDM-21820	U.S.A.	1992	5.99
Gabriel, Peter	Steam (Black Side Of House Box)	CD	Virgin	7243-8-91033-2-8	England	1992	19.99
Gabriel, Peter	The Barry Williams Show	CD Single	Virgin	7243-5-46740-20	England	2002	9.99
Gabriel, Peter	Up (Promo W/ 2 Different Tracks)	CD	Virgin	PGCDJ11	England	2002	59.99
Gabriel, Peter	Up (Radio Interview)	CD	Virgin	PGCDIV11	England	2002	33.99
Gabriel, Peter	Up + 3	2CD	Virgin	VJCP-58450.51	Japan	2002	37.99
Gabriel, Peter	Us (Ltd Numbered)	CD	Geffen	069-493-287-2	U.S.A.	2002	16.99
Gabriel, Peter	Xplora 1 Peter Gabriel's Secret World	Cd-Rom	Realworld	04042-11505-6-4	U.S.A.	1994	44.99
Gabriel, Peter/ W/Autograph	Deluxe Road Case (19 Shows/Bklt)	38CD	Music.Com	ESD-PG03-RC	U.S.A.	2003	749.99
Gabriel, Peter/A R Orchestra	American Rock Orchestra Dream/Red	CD	Koch	KOC-CD-8080	U.S.A.	2001	8.99
Gabriel, Peter/Afro Celt S. S.	When You're Falling	CD Single	Real World	RWSCD114	EU	2001	10.99
Gaines, Jeffrey	Always Be	CD	Artemis	751-071-2	U.S.A.	2001	5.99
Gaines, Jeffrey	Toward The Sun	CD	Artemis	751152-2	U.S.A.	2003	5.99
Gainsbourg, Serge	Aux Armes Et Caetera	CD	Universal	UNI-8433CD	France	2001	14.99
Gainsbourg, Serge	Confidentiel	CD	Universal	UNI-8610CD	France	2001	17.99
Gainsbourg, Serge	Du Chant À La Lune	CD	Universal	UNI-8606CD	France	2001	15.99
Gainsbourg, Serge	Gainsbourg Percussions	CD	Universal	UNI-8426CD	France	2001	17.99
Gainsbourg, Serge	Histoire De Melody Nelson	CD	Universal	UNI-8429CD	France	2001	17.99
Gainsbourg, Serge	Initials B.B	CD	Universal	UNI-8612CD	France	2001	10.99
Gainsbourg, Serge	L'étonnant Serge Gainsbourg No. 3	CD	Universal	UNI-8423CD	France	2001	15.99
Gainsbourg, Serge	L'Homme À La Tete De Chou	CD	Universal	UNI-8432CD	France	2001	14.99
Gainsbourg, Serge	Love On The Beat	CD	Universal	UNI-8611CD	France	2001	10.99
Gainsbourg, Serge	Mauvaises Nouvelles Des Étoiles	CD	Universal	UNI-8444CD	France	2001	17.99
Gainsbourg, Serge	N°2	CD	Universal	UNI-8608CD	France	2001	14.99
Gainsbourg, Serge	N°2 + 4	CD	Universal	UNI-8422CD	France	2003	17.99
Gainsbourg, Serge	N°4	CD	Universal	UNI-8609CD	France	2001	14.99
Gainsbourg, Serge	Rock Around The Bunker	CD	Universal	UNI-8431CD	France	2001	14.99
Gainsbourg, Serge	Vu De L'exterieur	CD	Universal	UNI-8430CD	France	2001	12.99
Gainsbourg, Serge	You're Under Arrest	CD	Universal	UNI-8437CD	France	2001	10.99
Galactic	Coolin' Off	CD	Capricorn	314-558-521-2	U.S.A.	1998	7.99
Galactic	Crazyhorse Mongoose	CD	Capricorn	314-558-842-2	U.S.A.	1998	5.99
Galadriel	Self Titled	CD	Akarma	AK-158-CD	Italy	1999	12.99
Gallant, Joe/Illuminati	Music Grateful Dead & Beyond Vol. 1	CD	Relix	RRCD2085	U.S.A.	1997	7.99
Gallant, Joe/Illuminati	Music Grateful Dead & Beyond Vol. 2	CD	Relix	RRCD2092	U.S.A.	1997	7.99
Gamma	1	CD	Wounded Bird	WOU-6219	U.S.A.	2002	10.99
Gamma	2	CD	Wounded Bird	WOU-6288	U.S.A.	2002	10.99
Gamma	3	CD	Wounded Bird	WOU-6634	U.S.A.	2002	10.99
Gamma	Best Of	CD	GNP	GNPD-2208	U.S.A.	1992	10.99

G

Artist	Title	Format	Label	Catalog No	Country	Released	Value
Gamma	Concert Classics (Promo/100)	CD	Renaissance	RRCC00716	U.S.A.	1999	13.99
Gandalf	Gandalf	CD	See For Miles	SEE-CD326	England	1991	13.99
Gandalf	Magic Theatre	CD	Warner Bros.	2292-40293-2	Austria	1983	11.99
Gandalf	To Another Horizon	CD	Warner Bros.	2292-40074-2	Germany	1983	11.99
Gandalf/Steve Hackett	Gallery Of Dreams	CD	Columbia	481488-2	Netherland	1992	34.99
Gap Band, The	8	CD	Total Exp	FD-89992	Germany	1985	61.99
Garbage	The World Is Not Enough	CD Single	MGM	155-672-2	EU	1999	10.99
Garcia, Jerry	Compliments	CD	Grateful Dead	GDCD40092	U.S.A.	1990	13.99
Garcia, Jerry	Compliments (Line Version)	CD	Line	GDCD-9.00644-0	Germany	1989	11.99
Garcia, Jerry	Garcia	CD	Grateful Dead	GDCD4003	U.S.A.	1988	9.99
Garcia, Jerry	Garcia (Line Version)	CD	Line	GDCD-9.00656-0	Germany	1989	11.99
Garcia, Jerry	Reflections	CD	Grateful Dead	GDCD40082	U.S.A.	1990	9.99
Garcia, Jerry	Reflections (Line Version)	CD	Line	GDCD-9.00651-0	Germany	1989	11.99
Garcia, Jerry	Run For The Roses	CD	Arista	ARCD-8557	U.S.A.	1982	8.99
Garcia, Jerry Band	Cats Under The Stars	CD	Arista	ARCD-8535	U.S.A.	1978	24.99
Garcia, Jerry Band	Don't Let Go	2CD	Grateful Dead	GDCD4078	U.S.A.	2001	19.99
Garcia, Jerry Band	How Sweet it Is	CD	Grateful Dead	GDCD4051	U.S.A.	1997	9.99
Garcia, Jerry Band	Jerry Garcia Band	2CD	Arista	ARCD-8690	U.S.A.	1991	12.99
Garcia, Jerry Band	Shining Star	2CD	Grateful Dead	GDCD4079	U.S.A.	2001	19.99
Garcia, Jerry/Acoustic Band	Almost Acoustic (Line Version)	CD	Line	GDCD-9.00648-0	Germany	1989	11.99
Garcia, Jerry/D. Grisman	Been All Around The World	CD	Acoustic Disc	ACD-57	U.S.A.	2004	8.99
Garcia, Jerry/D. Grisman	Jerry Garcia & David Grisman	CD	Acoustic Disc	ACD-2	U.S.A.	1991	9.99
Garcia, Jerry/D. Grisman	Not For Kids Only	CD	Acoustic Disc	ACD-9	U.S.A.	1993	11.99
Garcia, Jerry/D. Grisman	Old & In The Way	CD	Rykodisc	RCD-10009	U.S.A.	1986	8.99
Garcia, Jerry/D. Grisman	Old And In The Way (Line Version)	CD	Line	GDCD-9.00652-0	Germany	1989	11.99
Garcia, Jerry/D. Grisman	Shady Grove	CD	Acoustic Disc	ACD-21	U.S.A.	1996	12.99
Garcia, Jerry/D. Grisman	So What	CD	Acoustic Disc	ACD-33	U.S.A.	1998	13.99
Garcia, Jerry/H. Wales	Hooteroll?	CD	Rykodisc	RCD-10052	U.S.A.	1987	9.99
Garcia, Jerry/Rice/Grisman	The Pizza Tapes	CD	Accoustic Disc	ACD-41	U.S.A.	2000	11.99
Garcia, Russell	Time Machine/Atlantis, Lost...(O.S.T.)	CD	GNP	GNPD8008	U.S.A.	1987	12.99
Garfunkel, Art	Breakaway	CD	Columbia	CK-33700	U.S.A.	1975	8.99
Garfunkel, Art/Sharp & M.	Everything Waits To Be Noticed	CD	EMI	7243-5-40990-2-1	U.S.A.	2002	8.99
Gatton, Danny	Hot Rod Guitar: The Anthology	2CD	Rhino	R2-75691	U.S.A.	1999	24.99
Gatton, Danny	Runnin' Wild: Renegade Yrs '81 - '88	4CD	Renegade	RENCDX-430A	U.S.A.	2002	119.99
Gaye, Marvin	Collection Box Set	4CD	Motown	MOTD4-6311	U.S.A.	1990	36.99
Gaye, Marvin	The Master 1961-1984 Box Set	4CD	Motown	31453-0492-2	U.S.A.	1995	43.99
Gaye, Marvin	What's Going On	CD	Motown	31453-0022-2	U.S.A.	1994	8.99
Gaye, Marvin	What's Going On + 26 (Deluxe Edition)	2CD	Motown	440-013-404-2	U.S.A.	2001	14.99
Gaynor, Gloria	I Will Survive (Phil Kelsey Remix)	CD Single	Polydor	PZCD-270	England	1993	11.99
Gaynor, Mitzi/Rossano Brazzi	South Pacific (O.S.T.)	CD	RCA	07863-67977-2	U.S.A.	2000	10.99
Geller, Uri	Self Titled (W/Del Newman)	CD	Forkbender	FORK-1-CD	England	1973	11.99
Generation X	BBC Live At Paris Theatre '78 & '81	CD	EMI	7243-4-99402-2-2	England	1999	11.99
Generation X	Generation X + 5	CD	EMI	7243-5-38936-2-0	England	2002	11.99
Generation X	Perfect Hits 1975-1981	CD	Chrysalis	F2-21862	U.S.A.	1991	7.99
Generation X	The Idol Generation	CD	Castle	ACDCD-011	Australia	1981	8.99
Generation X	Valley Of The Dolls + 2	CD	EMI	7243-5-38935-2-1	England	2002	11.99
Genesis	2 Songs/The Longs + Interview (DJ)	CD Single	Atlantic	PRCD-4997	U.S.A.	1993	12.99
Genesis	Abacab	CD	Atlantic	82693-2	U.S.A.	1994	7.99
Genesis	Abacab (Atlantic Gold Cd)	CD	Atlantic	82521-2	U.S.A.	1993	101.99
Genesis	And Then There Were Three	CD	Atlantic	82691-2	U.S.A.	1994	8.99
Genesis	Archive Vol. 1 (Promo Sampler)	CD	Atlantic	PRCD-8583	U.S.A.	1998	18.99
Genesis	Archives, Vol. 1: 1967-1975 Box Set	4CD	Virgin	82858-2	U.S.A.	1998	43.99
Genesis	Archives, Vol. 2: 1976-1992 Box Set	3CD	Virgin	7243-85034329	England	2000	19.99
Genesis	Calling All Stations	CD	Atlantic	83037-2	U.S.A.	1997	5.99
Genesis	Calling All Stations (Adv. Promo)	CD	Virgin	83037-2P	U.S.A.	1997	7.99
Genesis	Calling All Stations (DJ/Album Sampler)	CD	Virgin	GENCDJ6	England	1997	11.99
Genesis	Congo	CD Single	Virgin	7243-8-94520-2-0	Holland	1997	11.99
Genesis	Congo (Promo)	CD Single	Atlantic	PRCD-8202-2	U.S.A.	1997	9.99

G

Artist	Title	Format	Label	Catalog No	Country	Released	Value
Genesis	Duke	CD	Atlantic	82692-2	U.S.A.	1994	8.99
Genesis	Foxtrot	CD	Atlantic	8267492	U.S.A.	1994	9.99
Genesis	From Genesis To Revelation + 10	2CD	Snapper	142952	U.S.A.	2000	12.99
Genesis	Genesis (Self Titled)	CD	Atlantic	80116-2	U.S.A.	1983	6.99
Genesis	Genesis Archive '67 - '75: (Promo Int.)	2CD	Virgin	IVCDJBOX6	EU	1998	49.99
Genesis	Genesis Revelation (Gold Cd W/Prints)	CD	Griffin	MCCDSE-133	England	1996	24.99
Genesis	I Can't Dance	CD Single	Atlantic	85906-2	U.S.A.	1991	11.99
Genesis	In The Studio: Abacab Sept. 9,1996	CD	Album Network	147156-2	U.S.A.	1996	29.99
Genesis	Interview	CD	Baktabak	CBAK-4028	England	1990	9.99
Genesis	Invisible Touch	CD	Atlantic	81641-2	U.S.A.	1986	7.99
Genesis	Lamb Lies Down On Broadway	2CD	Atlantic	82677-2	U.S.A.	1994	14.99
Genesis	Land Of Confusion	CD Single	Virgin	SNEG-3-12	England	1986	13.99
Genesis	Live	CD	Atlantic	82676-2	U.S.A.	1994	10.99
Genesis	Live The Way...2 Cd Spec. Ed.	CD	Virgin	7243-8-45571-2-6	England	1998	14.99
Genesis	Live: Way We Walk, Vol. 1 (Shorts)	CD	Atlantic	82452-2	U.S.A.	1992	7.99
Genesis	Live: Way We Walk, Vol. 2 (Longs)	CD	Atlantic	82461-2	U.S.A.	1993	7.99
Genesis	No Son Of Mine	CD Single	Virgin	GENDG-6	England	1991	7.99
Genesis	Not About Us (CD 1)	CD Single	Virgin	7243-8-94918-2-1	EU	1998	7.99
Genesis	Not About Us (CD 2)	CD Single	Virgin	7243-8-94909-2-3	EU	1998	7.99
Genesis	Nursery Chryme	CD	Atlantic	82673-2	U.S.A.	1994	10.99
Genesis	Seconds Out	2CD	Atlantic	82689-2	U.S.A.	1994	13.99
Genesis	Selling England By The Pound	CD	Atlantic	82675-2	U.S.A.	1994	10.99
Genesis	Shipwrecked (CD 1)	CD Single	Virgin	7243-8-94703-2-1	England	1997	5.99
Genesis	Shipwrecked (CD 2)	CD Single	Virgin	7243-8-94702-2-2	England	1997	5.99
Genesis	Spot The Pigeon	CD Single	Atlantic	CDF-40	England	1977	19.99
Genesis	Tell Me Why (CD 2)	CD Single	Virgin	GENDX-11	England	1991	16.99
Genesis	Tell Me Why (Disc 1)	CD	Virgin	GENDG-11	England	1993	8.99
Genesis	The Carpet Crawlers 1999	CD Single	Virgin	7243-8-96420-25	EU	1999	9.99
Genesis	The Dividing Line (Promo)	CD Single	Atlantic	PRCD-8342	U.S.A.	1997	7.99
Genesis	Three Sides Live	2CD	Atlantic	82694-2	U.S.A.	1994	13.99
Genesis	Three Sides Live (No Hackett)	2CD	Atlantic	CD-2000	Canada	1981	23.99
Genesis	Tonight, Tonight, Tonight	CD Single	Virgin	DRAW-412	England	1987	9.99
Genesis	Trespass	CD	Virgin	7243-8-39773-2-1	England	1994	12.99
Genesis	Trick Of The Tail	CD	Atlantic	82688-2	U.S.A.	1994	8.99
Genesis	Turn It On Again - The Hits	CD	Atlantic	83544-2	U.S.A.	1999	11.99
Genesis	We Can't Dance	CD	Atlantic	82344-2	U.S.A.	1991	5.99
Genesis	Westwood 1 # 00-35, 8-26/27, 2000	2CD	Westwood 1	CO0035-A-081500	U.S.A.	2000	89.99
Genesis	Wind And Wuthering	CD	Atlantic	82690-2	U.S.A.	1994	7.99
Genesis/Guddal Matte	Genesis For 2 Grand Pianos	CD	NCB	01-43N	Norway	2000	14.99
Genesis/Palmer	We Know What We Like (Orchestral)	CD	RCA	6242-2-RC	U.S.A.	1987	24.99
Genesis/Solo	It's Only Knock/Knowall (Ger. Fan Cd)	CD	It	IT-2001	Germany	2001	34.99
Genesis/Thomas/Gunn	Giants Dance (Orig. Members Genesis)	CD	Blueprint	BP223CD	Austria	1996	12.99
Genesis/Various Artists	A Tribute To Genesis	CD	Cleopatra	CLP-1183-2	U.S.A.	2002	14.99
Genesis/Various Artists	Supper's Ready	CD	Magna Carta	MA-9004-2	U.S.A.	1995	14.99
Genesis/Various Artists	The Fox Lies Down: A Tribute	CD	Cleopatra	CLP-0287-2	U.S.A.	1998	14.99
Genesis/Various Artists	The River Of Constant Change	2CD	Mellow	MMP-270	Italy	1995	19.99
Gentle Giant	Acquiring The Taste	CD	Vertigo	842-917-2	U.S.A.	1971	10.99
Gentle Giant	Acquiring The Taste (Line Version)	CD	Line	LICD-9.00726-0	Germany	1989	10.99
Gentle Giant	Edge Of Twilight	2CD	Vertigo	534-101-2	Germany	1996	12.99
Gentle Giant	Free Hand/Interview	CD	BGO	BGOCD421	England	1998	17.99
Gentle Giant	Gentle Giant	CD	Line	LICD-9.00722-0	Germany	1989	13.99
Gentle Giant	In A Glass House + 2	Mini Lp	Alucard	ALU-GG-02	England	2000	19.99
Gentle Giant	In A Palesport House	CD	Glass House	GLASS102CD	England	2000	11.99
Gentle Giant	Interview In Concert	CD	Glass House	GLASS103CD	England	2000	18.99
Gentle Giant	King Biscuit Flower Hour	CD	King Biscuit	70710-88035-2	U.S.A.	1998	8.99
Gentle Giant	Live - Rome 1974	CD	Glass House	GLASS101CD	England	2000	13.99
Gentle Giant	Live (Playing the Fool) / Civilian	2CD	BGO	BGOCD435	England	1999	15.99
Gentle Giant	Octopus	CD	Line	LICD-9.00736-0	Germany	1989	13.99

G

Artist	Title	Format	Label	Catalog No	Country	Released	Value
Gentle Giant	Octopus	CD	Repertoire	IMS-7032-WP	Germany	1995	10.99
Gentle Giant	Self Titled	CD	Repertoire	IMS-7031-WP	Germany	1995	10.99
Gentle Giant	The Last Steps	CD	Red Steel	RMC-CD-0205	England	1996	16.99
Gentle Giant	The Missing Piece/Giant For A Day	CD	BGO	BGOCD431	England	1999	16.99
Gentle Giant	The Power And The Glory	CD	Capitol	07777-91849-2-7	Canada	1989	9.99
Gentle Giant	Three Friends	CD	Line	LICD-9.00730-0	Germany	1989	15.99
Gentle Giant	Totally Out of the Woods	2CD	HUX	HUX018	England	2000	21.99
Gentle Giant	Under Construction Box Set	2CD	Alucard	ALU-GG-01	England	1997	34.99
Gentle Soul	Self Titled + 9	CD	Sundazed	SC-11123	U.S.A.	2003	10.99
Geordie	No Good Woman + 2 (No B Johnson)	CD	Landmark	15014-2	England	2001	11.99
Geordie	No Sweat (No Brian Johnson)	CD	Navarre	72182	U.S.A.	2002	8.99
Geordie/Brian Johnson	A Band From Geordieland	CD	Repertoire	REP-4515-WY	Germany	1998	12.99
Geordie/Brian Johnson	Don't Be Fooled By The Name	CD	Repertoire	REP-4124-WZ	Germany	2002	11.99
Geordie/Brian Johnson	Hope You Like It	CD	Repertoire	REP-4033-WZ	Germany	2002	11.99
Georgia Satellites	The Essentials	CD	Rhino	R2-76051	U.S.A.	2002	8.99
Germs	(MIA) The Complete Anthology	CD	Rhino	R2-79954	U.S.A.	2002	14.99
Geronimo Black	Self Titled + 1	CD	One Way	OW-22114	U.S.A.	1994	9.99
Gerry & the Pacemakers	Ferry Cross The Mersey + 14	CD	Repertoire	REP-4423—WY	Germany	1994	12.99
Gerry & the Pacemakers	How Do You Like It? + 10	CD	Repertoire	REP-4422-WY	Germany	1994	12.99
Gerry/Pacemakers	How Do You Like It?/Ferry Across...	CD	EMI	7243-5-38847-2-7	Holland	2002	14.99
Gerry/The Pacemakers	Gerry Cross The Mersey	CD	Razor & Tie	RE-2084-2	U.S.A.	1995	9.99
Getz, Stan	Bossa Nova	CD	PolyGram	314-529-904-2	U.S.A.	1996	10.99
Getz, Stan	Jazz Masters 8	CD	Verve	314-519-823-2	U.S.A.	1994	9.99
Getz, Stan	Serenity	CD	PolyGram	838-770-2	U.S.A.	1991	10.99
Getz, Stan/Gilberto	Getz/Gilberto (MFSL Gold Cd)	CD	Mobile Fidelity	UDCD-607	U.S.A.	1964	29.99
Getz, Stan/Joao Gilberto	Getz/Gilberto	CD	Verve	314-521-41-2	U.S.A.	1997	11.99
Giacchino, Michael/N Sinfonia	L World Jurassic Park (Playstation/ST)	CD	Sonic Images	SID-8803	U.S.A.	1998	11.99
Giant	It Takes Two + Giant Live	CD Single	Pony Canyon	PCCY-10145	Japan	1990	24.99
Gibbons, Steve/Band	Any Road Up/Rollin' On	2CD	Road Goes On	RGFCD035	England	1996	34.99
Gibbons, Steve/Band	Caught In The Act - Live	CD	Repertoire	REP-4048-WZ	Germany	2002	15.99
Gibbons, Steve/Band	Caught In The Act/On The Loose	2CD	Road Goes On	SGDCD050	England	2003	34.99
Gibbons, Steve/Band	Down In The Bunker	CD	Repertoire	REP-4047-WZ	Germany	2002	15.99
Gibbons, Steve/Band	Down In The Bunker	CD	Road Goes On	RGFCD044	England	2000	15.99
Gibbons, Steve/Band	Dylan Project: Live At Cropredy '99	CD	Woodworm	WRCD-029	England	1998	14.99
Gibbons, Steve/Band	From Birmingham To Memphis	CD	Linn	AKD-19	England	1992	24.99
Gibbons, Steve/Band	Live At The Robin '98	CD	Reckless	REC-1	England	1998	14.99
Gibbons, Steve/Band	Maintaining Radio Silence	CD	Road Goes On	SGCD-043	England	1998	19.99
Gibbons, Steve/Band	On The Loose	CD	Magnum Force	CDMF-041	England	1991	12.99
Gibbons, Steve/Band	Riding Out The Dark	CD	SPV	SPV084-88292CD	Germany	1990	12.99
Gibbons, Steve/Band	Short Stories/Stained Glass	2CD	Road Goes On	RGFCD048	England	2002	34.99
Giddens, Jerry	Livin' Ain't Easy	CD	Line	SDCD-9.00701-0	Germany	1989	6.99
Gilberto, Astrud	Finest Hour	CD	Verve	314-520-790-2	U.S.A.	2001	9.99
Gilberto, Astrud	Jazz Masters 9	CD	PolyGram	314-519-824-2	U.S.A.	1993	5.99
Gilberto, Astrud	Talkin' Verve	CD	Verve	314-539-675-2	U.S.A.	1998	9.99
Gilberto, Astrud	The Silver Collection	CD	Verve	823-451-2	Germany	1970	8.99
Gilberto, João	The Legendary Joao Gilberto	CD	World Pacific	7-93891-2	U.S.A.	1990	17.99
Gilgamesh	Another Fine Tune ...	CD	Spalax	14838	France	2000	14.99
Gilgamesh	Arriving Twice	CD	Cuneiform	CUNE-140	U.S.A.	2000	10.99
Gilgamesh	Self Titled	CD	Virgin	VJCP-2534	Japan	1990	19.99
Gillan, Ian	Accidentally On Purpose (W/Bonus)	CD	Virgin	CDV-2498	England	1988	10.99
Gillan, Ian	Born Again	CD	Essential	ESM-CD-334	England	1996	9.99
Gillan, Ian	Cherkazoo And Other Stories...	CD	Line	OLCD-9.51231-Z	Germany	1992	12.99
Gillan, Ian	Cherkazoo And Other Stories...	CD	Eagle	EAMCD052	England	1999	12.99
Gillan, Ian	Clear Air Turbulence	CD	Eagle	EAMCD047	England	1998	9.99
Gillan, Ian	Double Trouble (W/Bonus)	CD	Virgin	CDVM-3506	England	1989	9.99
Gillan, Ian	Dreamcatcher	CD	Ark 21	7243-8-21246-2-7	England	1997	8.99
Gillan, Ian	Dreamcatcher + 2	CD	Teichiku	TOCP-50315	Japan	1992	25.99
Gillan, Ian	Future Shock (W/Bonus)	CD	Virgin	CDVM-2196	England	1988	22.99

G

Artist	Title	Format	Label	Catalog No	Country	Released	Value
Gillan, Ian	Garth Rockett/The Moonshiners	CD	Purple	PUR-324	England	2000	22.99
Gillan, Ian	Glory Road (W Bonus)	CD	Virgin	CDVM-2171	England	1988	9.99
Gillan, Ian	Ian Gillian (W/Bonus DVD)	CD	Classic Rock	CRP0966	England	2002	14.99
Gillan, Ian	Japanese Album	CD	Purple	PUR-306	England	2000	10.99
Gillan, Ian	Live At Budokan Vol. 1/2	2CD	Virgin	CDVM-3507	England	1989	22.99
Gillan, Ian	Live At Reading '80	CD	Raw Fruit	FRSCD002	England	1990	15.99
Gillan, Ian	Magic (W/Bonus)	CD	Virgin	CDVM-2238	England	1988	9.99
Gillan, Ian	Mr. Universe (W/Bonus)	CD	Virgin	CDVM-2589	England	1989	9.99
Gillan, Ian	Naked Thunder	CD	Blueprint	BP4108CD	England	1998	14.99
Gillan, Ian	Rock Profile	CD	Connoisseur	VSOP-CD-214	England	1995	15.99
Gillan, Ian	Scarabus	CD	Eagle	EAMCD049	England	1998	9.99
Gillan, Ian	The BBC Tapes Vol. 1	CD	Purple	PUR-319	England	1997	14.99
Gillan, Ian	The BBC Tapes Vol. 2	CD	Purple	PUR-320	England	1997	14.99
Gillan, Ian	The Gillan Tapes Vol. 1	CD	Angel Air	SJPCD-004	England	1997	10.99
Gillan, Ian	The Japanese Album (Diff Contents)	CD	RPM	RPM-113	England	1993	10.99
Gillan, Ian	The Rockfiled Mixes	CD	Angel Air	SJPCD-007	England	1997	14.99
Gillan, Ian	The Very Best Of	CD	Music Club	MCCD-032	England	1991	7.99
Gillan, Ian	Toolbox	CD	Eagle	EAMCD051	England	1998	9.99
Gillan, Ian	Trouble - The Best Of	CD	Virgin	VVIPD-113	England	1991	11.99
Gillan, Ian	What I Did On My Vacation	CD	Virgin	DIXD-CD-39	England	1986	10.99
Gillan, Ian/Band	Child In Time	CD	Virgin	CDVM-2606	England	1989	9.99
Gillan, Ian/Band	Live At The Rainbow	CD	Angel Air	SJPCD017	England	1998	14.99
Gillan, Ian/Javelins	Raving With	CD	Purple	PUR-311	England	2000	14.99
Gillan, Ian/Javelins	Solo Agency (DJ/Diff Insert/P Wallet)	CD	RPM	RPM-132	England	2001	19.99
Gillan, Ian/Ray Slijngaard	Smoke On The Water (Club Remix)	CD Single	Victor Ent.	VICP-35001	Japan	1998	24.99
Gillan, Ian/Ray Slijngaard	Smoke On The Water: Rock 'N' Rap	CD	Victor Ent.	VICP-60192	Japan	1998	29.99
Gillan, Ian/Roger Glover	The Complete Episode Six	CD	Collectables	COL-CD-0567	U.S.A.	1994	6.99
Gillan, Ian/Roger Glover	The Complete Episode Six	CD	Sequel	NEX-CD-156	England	1991	9.99
Gillan, Ian/Roger Glover	The Episode/Live At The BBC	CD	Purple	PUR-318	England	1999	14.99
Gilmour, Dave	About Face	CD	Columbia	CK-39296	U.S.A.	1984	9.99
Gilmour, Dave	David Gilmour	CD	Columbia	CK-35388	U.S.A.	1978	9.99
Giltrap, Gordon	Gordon Giltrap/Portrait	CD	Essential	ESM-CD-326	England	1997	9.99
Gin On The Rocks	Coolest Groove	CD	Teichiku	TECP-25591	Japan	1990	9.99
Ginsberg, Allen	New York Blues: Rags...	CD	Locust	LOCUST-12	U.S.A.	2002	9.99
Ginsberg, Allen/Corso	3 Angels (W/Orlovsky)	CD	BBE	BGSW-001-CD	England	1992	14.99
Girls, The/70's Punk	Live at the Rathskeller: 5/17/79	CD	Abaton Book	ABA-007CD	U.S.A.	2002	12.99
Girlschool	Anthology	2CD	Castle	CMDDD014	England	2000	14.99
Girlschool	C'mon Let's Go	CD	Castle	CMACD-149	England	1991	7.99
Girlschool	Collection	2CD	Sanctuary	06076-81116-2	U.S.A.	2001	13.99
Girlschool	Demolition/Hit And Run	CD	Dojo	LOMA-CD-1	France	1991	24.99
Girlschool	Emergency (Demolition/Hit & Run + 6)	2CD	Snapper	SMD-CD-126	England	1997	12.99
Girlschool	From The Vaults	CD	Sequel	NEM-CD-642	EEC	1994	9.99
Girlschool	Girlschool/Live	2CD	Powerage	PRAGE013DCD	England	2002	14.99
Girlschool	King Biscuit Flower Hour Presents	CD	King Biscuit	70710-88032-2	U.S.A.	1997	8.99
Girlschool	Live	CD	Communique	CMGCDO13	England	1995	12.99
Girlschool	Nightmare At Maple Cross/Take A Bite	CD	Dojo	LOMA-CD-8	France	1991	24.99
Girlschool	Nightmare At Maple.../Take A Bite	CD	Teichiku	TECP-25645	Japan	1999	39.99
Girlschool	Not That Innocent	CD	Communique	CMGCD024	England	2002	13.99
Girlschool	Race With The Devil	CD	Receiver	RRCD254	England	1998	8.99
Girlschool	Race With The Devil	CD	Disky	SI-794122	Holland	2002	8.99
Girlschool	Screaming Blue Murder/Play Dirty	CD	Dojo	LOMA-CD-4	France	1991	24.99
Girlschool	Self Titled	CD	Griffin	GCD-455-2	U.S.A.	1995	7.99
Girlschool	Take A Bite	CD	Enigma	7-75406-2	U.S.A.	1989	12.99
Girlschool	The Collection	2CD	Castle	CMDDD014	England	2000	13.99
Girlschool	The Collection	CD	Castle	CCSCD314	England	1991	9.99
Girlschool	The Very Best Of	CD	Sanctuary	06076-81162-2	U.S.A.	2002	8.99
Giuffria	Self Titled	CD	MCA Victor	MVCM-21064	Japan	1992	18.99
Giuffria	Silk And Steel	CD	MCA	MCAD-5742	U.S.A.	1986	25.99

G

Artist	Title	Format	Label	Catalog No	Country	Released	Value
Glass Harp/Phil Keaggy	Glass Harp	CD	Line	LCCD-9.01253-0	Germany	1993	24.99
Glass Harp/Phil Keaggy	It Makes Me Glad	CD	Line	LICD-9.01255-0	Germany	1993	24.99
Glass Harp/Phil Keaggy	Synergy	CD	Line	LICD-9.01254-0	Germany	1993	24.99
Glass, Phillip	1000 Airplanes On The Roof	CD	Virgin	7-91065-2	U.S.A.	1989	9.99
Glass, Phillip	A Descent Into The Maelström	CD	Orange Mountain	0005	U.S.A.	2002	12.99
Glass, Phillip	Dance Nos. 1 - 5	2CD	Columbia	M2K-44765	U.S.A.	1988	22.99
Glass, Phillip	Dancepieces	CD	Columbia	MK-39539	U.S.A.	1987	6.99
Glass, Phillip	Dracula	CD	Nonesuch	79542-2	U.S.A.	1999	12.99
Glass, Phillip	Einstein On The Beach	3CD	Nonesuch	79323-2	U.S.A.	1993	27.99
Glass, Phillip	Glassworks	CD	Columbia	MK-37265	U.S.A.	1982	8.99
Glass, Phillip	Heroes Symphony	CD	Point	454-388-2	U.S.A.	1996	11.99
Glass, Phillip	Kundun	CD	Nonesuch	79460-2	U.S.A.	1998	8.99
Glass, Phillip	Low Symphony	CD	Point	438-150-2	U.S.A.	1993	11.99
Glass, Phillip	North Star	CD	Virgin	CDV-2085	England	1977	10.99
Glass, Phillip	Symphony No. 3	CD	Nonesuch	79581-2	U.S.A.	1996	9.99
Glass, Phillip/F. M. Suso	Music From The Screens	CD	Point	432-966-2	U.S.A.	1992	14.99
Glenn, Karen	Deja Voodoo	CD	Pink Noise	CR70004	U.S.A.	1995	8.99
Glitter, Gary	20 Greatest Hits	CD	Repertoire	REP-4229-WG	Germany	2001	14.99
Glitter, Gary	Rock And Roll: Greatest Hits	CD	Rhino	R2-75201	U.S.A.	1995	6.99
Glitter, Gary	The Glam Years	2CD	Repertoire	REP-4430-WO	Germany	1995	34.99
Glitter, Gary	Ultimate Gary Glitter, The	2CD	Snapper	GGCD-01	England	1997	11.99
Glory	Positive Buoyant	CD	Victor Ent.	VICP-5251	Japan	1993	24.99
Glory	Wintergreen	CD	Victor Ent.	VICP-60290	Japan	1998	24.99
Glove	Blue Sunshine	CD	Polydor	815-019-2	England	1990	13.99
Glover, Dana	Testimony	CD	Dreamworks	0044-50299-2	U.S.A.	2002	8.99
Glover, Roger	Elements/The Mask	CD	Connoisseur	VSOP-CD-183	England	1995	24.99
Glover, Roger/Guests	The Butterfly Ball	CD	Line	LICD-9.00013-0	Germany	1987	9.99
Glover, Roger/Guests	The Butterfly Ball (Enhanced)	CD	Connoisseur	EVSOP-CD-265	England	1999	12.99
Glover, Roger/Guests	The Butterfly Ball + 2	CD	Spitfire	SPT-15157-2	U.S.A.	2001	9.99
Glover, Roger/Guests	The Butterfly Ball + 9	CD	Repertoire	REP-4567-WY	Germany	1995	12.99
Glover, Roger/Guilty Party	Snapshot	CD	Red Ink	7669-2-23630-2-8	U.S.A.	2002	7.99
Go-Betweens	'78 'til 79: The Lost Album	CD	Jetset	TWA-19-CD	U.S.A.	1979	19.99
Godsmack	All Wound Up	CD	EK	7-94473-50102-4	U.S.A.	1998	79.99
Godz	2	CD	ESP	ESPCD-1047	Netherland	2003	12.99
Godz	Alien	CD	ESP	ESPCD3008	Netherland	1993	19.99
Godz	Contact High With The Godz	CD	ESP	ESPCD-1037	Netherland	2003	12.99
Godz	Godz Bless America	CD	ESP	ESPCD3019	Netherland	1993	19.99
Godz	Godzhunheit	CD	ESP	ESPCD2017	Netherland	1993	19.99
Godz	The Godz Greatest Hits Live	CD	High Chief	7-03026-10027-7	U.S.A.	1995	8.99
Godz	The Third Testament	CD	ESP	ESPCD-1077	Italy	2003	9.99
Godz/Casablanca	Power Rock From USA (Ist Lp + 7 2nd)	CD	Black Rose	BR-115	Sweden	2001	24.99
Goffin, Louise	Sometimes A Circle	CD	Dreamworks	0044-50290-2	U.S.A.	2002	6.99
Go-Go's	Beauty And The Beat	CD	I.R.S.	44797-5021-2	U.S.A.	1981	8.99
Go-Go's	God Bless The Go-Go's	CD	Teichiku	TECI-24062	Japan	2001	29.99
Go-Go's	Good Girl	CD Single	I.R.S.	58347	U.S.A.	1995	21.99
Go-Go's	Greatest Hits	CD	I.R.S.	44797-0059-2	U.S.A.	1990	8.99
Go-Go's	Return To The Valley Of The Go-Go's	2CD	I.R.S.	7243-8-29694-2-6	U.S.A.	1994	16.99
Go-Go's	Self Titled (3")	CD Single	I.R.S.	CC31013	U.S.A.	1988	10.99
Go-Go's	Talk Show	CD	I.R.S.	069-490-389-2	U.S.A.	1984	8.99
Go-Go's	The Whole World Lost Its Head	CD Single	I.R.S.	7243-8-58290-2-4	U.S.A.	1994	8.99
Go-Go's	Vacation	CD	A&M	069-490-388-2	U.S.A.	1982	8.99
Go-Go's/Gina Schock	House Of Schock	CD	Capitol	CDP-7-46925-2	U.S.A.	1988	34.99
Gold, Andrew	Thank You For Being A Friend: Best Of	CD	Rhino	R2-73511	U.S.A.	1997	8.99
Gold, Andrew	What's Wrong With This Picture?	CD	Warner Bros.	WPCR-4150	Japan	1976	34.99
Golden Dawn	A Power Plant	CD	Sunspots	SPOT-513-CD	Italy	2002	11.99
Golden Earring	2nd Live	2CD	Red Bullet	RB-66.214	Netherland	2001	13.99
Golden Earring	Bloody Buccaneers	CD	Columbia	468-093-2	Netherland	2001	9.99
Golden Earring	Contraband	CD	Red Bullet	RB-66.209	Netherland	2001	9.99

G

Artist	Title	Format	Label	Catalog No	Country	Released	Value
Golden Earring	Cut	CD	Red Bullet	RB-66.215	Netherland	2001	9.99
Golden Earring	Devil Made Us Do It: 35 Years	4CD	Universal	7314-549149-2-5	Netherland	2000	74.99
Golden Earring	Devil Made Us Do It: 35 Years	2CD	Universal	7314-549154-2-7	Netherland	2000	24.99
Golden Earring	Eight Miles High	CD	Red Bullet	RB-66.202	Netherland	2001	9.99
Golden Earring	Face It	CD	Columbia	477-650-2	Netherland	1994	9.99
Golden Earring	Grab It For A Second	CD	Red Bullet	RB-66.211	Netherland	2001	9.99
Golden Earring	Just Earring + 6	CD	Rotation	064-442-2	Netherland	2002	9.99
Golden Earring	Keeper Of The Flame	CD	Red Bullet	RB-66.220	Netherland	2001	9.99
Golden Earring	Last Blast Of The Century	2CD	CNR Music	2004-480	Netherland	1999	24.99
Golden Earring	Live	2CD	Red Bullet	RB-66.210	Netherland	2001	13.99
Golden Earring	Love Sweat	CD	Columbia	481-112-2	Netherland	1995	9.99
Golden Earring	Milbrook USA (W/Bonus DVD)	2CD	Universal	0440-067-598-0-7	Netherland	2003	24.99
Golden Earring	Miracle Mirror	CD	Polydor	843-135-2	Netherland	1994	9.99
Golden Earring	Moontan	CD	Red Bullet	RB-66.206	Netherland	2001	9.99
Golden Earring	Moontan + 6	CD	MCA	MCD-21359	U.S.A.	2002	9.99
Golden Earring	N.E.W.S.	CD	Red Bullet	RB-66.216	Netherland	2001	9.99
Golden Earring	Naked II	CD	CNR Music	2003-447	Netherland	1997	9.99
Golden Earring	No Promises... No Debts	CD	Red Bullet	RB-66.212	Netherland	2001	9.99
Golden Earring	On The Double	CD	Red Bullet	RB-66.201	Netherland	2001	9.99
Golden Earring	Paradise In Distress	CD	CNR Music	2003-885	Netherland	1999	9.99
Golden Earring	Prisoner Of The Night	CD	Red Bullet	RB-66.213	Netherland	2001	9.99
Golden Earring	Self Titled	CD	Red Bullet	RB-66.203	Netherland	2001	9.99
Golden Earring	Seven Tears	CD	Red Bullet	RB-66.204	Netherland	2001	9.99
Golden Earring	Something Heavy Going Down	CD	Red Bullet	RB-66.217	Netherland	2001	9.99
Golden Earring	Switch	CD	Red Bullet	RB-66.207	Netherland	2001	9.99
Golden Earring	The Complete Naked Truth	2CD	Columbia	472-619-3	Netherland	1998	26.99
Golden Earring	The Continuing Story Of Radar Love	CD	MCA	MCAD-6355	U.S.A.	1989	7.99
Golden Earring	The Hole	CD	Red Bullet	RB-66.218	Netherland	2001	9.99
Golden Earring	The Red Bullet Years	20 CD	Red Bullet	RB-66.200	Netherland	2002	244.99
Golden Earring	To The Hilt	CD	Red Bullet	RB-66.208	Netherland	2001	9.99
Golden Earring	Together	CD	Red Bullet	RB-66.205	Netherland	2001	9.99
Golden Earring	Winter Harvest	CD	Polydor	843-134-2	Netherland	1990	34.99
Golden Palominos	No Thought, No Breath.... Remix Ep	CD	Restless	7-72790-2	U.S.A.	1995	8.99
Goldenberg, Billy/Pierce Brosna	Around The World In 80 Days (O.S.T.)	CD	Cinedisc	CDC-1009	U.S.A.	1989	12.99
Goldsmith, Jerry	Alien (O.S.T.)	CD	Silva	FILMCD-003	England	1988	59.99
Goldsmith, Jerry	Insurrection (O.S.T.)	CD	GNP	GNP-8059	U.S.A.	1998	10.99
Goldsmith, Jerry	Planet Of The Apes + 9 (O.S.T.)	CD	Varese	VSD-5848	U.S.A.	1997	10.99
Goldsmith, Jerry	Poltergeist II: The Other Side + 8	CD	Intrada	VJF-5002D	U.S.A.	1993	22.99
Goldsmith, Jerry	Psycho II (2) O.S.T.	CD	Varese	VSD-5252	U.S.A.	1990	59.99
Goldsmith, Jerry	Raggedy Man (O.S.T.) 1500 Only	CD	Varese	VCL-9101.7	U.S.A.	1991	139.99
Goldsmith, Jerry	Rambo First Blood II (O.S.T.)	CD	Varese	VCD-47234	U.S.A.	1985	18.99
Goldsmith, Jerry	Rent-A-Cop (O.S.T.)	CD	Intrada	MAF-7002D	U.S.A.	1987	64.99
Goldsmith, Jerry	Stagecoach/Trouble W Angels (OST)	CD	Mainstream	MDCD-608	Japan	1991	22.99
Goldsmith, Jerry	Star Trek V: The Final Frontier (O.S.T.)	CD	Epic	EK-45267	U.S.A.	1989	12.99
Goldsmith, Jerry	Star Trek: First Contact (W/Magnet)	CD	GNP	GNP-8052	U.S.A.	1996	10.99
Goldsmith, Jerry	Star Trek: M Picture+ 8 /Inside S.T.	2CD	Columbia	C2K-66134	U.S.A.	1998	24.99
Goldsmith, Jerry	Supergirl + 11	CD	Silva	SSD-1025	U.S.A.	1993	20.99
Goldsmith, Jerry	The Ghost And The Darkness (O.S.T.)	CD	Hollywood	HR-62089-2	U.S.A.	1996	39.99
Goldsmith, Jerry	Total Recall (O.S.T.)	CD	Varese	VSD-5267	U.S.A.	1990	14.99
Goldsmith, Jerry	Warlock (O.S.T.)	CD	Intrada	MAF-7003D	U.S.A.	1989	41.99
Goldsmith, Jerry/HSOO	Rambo III (O.S.T.)	CD	Intrada	RVF-6006D	U.S.A.	1989	22.99
Gomm, Ian	Come On	CD	Line	LICD-9.01335-0	Germany	1997	12.99
Gomm, Ian	Rock 'N' Roll Heart	CD	Gommsongs	GOMCD1	England	2002	12.99
Gomm, Ian	Summer Holiday!	CD	Line	ALCD-9.00127-0	Germany	1987	22.99
Gomm, Ian	The Village Voice	CD	Line	ALCD-9.00016-0	Germany	1988	12.99
Gomm, Ian	What A Blow	CD	Line	ALCD-9.00033-0	Germany	1988	12.99
Gomm, Ian	What Makes A Man A...	CD	Line	ALCD-9.00235-0	Germany	1991	12.99
Gong	25th Birthday Party (Oct 8/9, 1994)	2CD	Voiceprint	VPGAS101CD	England	1995	18.99

G

Artist	Title	Format	Label	Catalog No	Country	Released	Value
Gong	Absolutely The Best Of Gong	2CD	Fuel 2000	302-061-171-2	U.S.A.	2001	12.99
Gong	Acid Motherhood	CD	Voiceprint	VP311CD	England	2004	12.99
Gong	Angel's Egg (R Gnome Invisible Pt.2)	CD	Spalax	14833	France	1996	10.99
Gong	Angel's Egg (R Gnome Invisible Pt.2)	CD	Caroline	CAROL-1662-2	U.S.A.	1973	9.99
Gong	Bedrock In Concert (CD W/DVD)	2CD	Classic Rock	CRP0964	England	2002	19.99
Gong	Best Of	CD	Summit	SUMCD 4117	France	1997	9.99
Gong	Best Of	CD	Mantra	MANTRA-111	France	1997	9.99
Gong	Camembert Eclectique	CD	GAS	AGASCD-001	England	1994	10.99
Gong	Camembert Electrique	CD	Spalax	14826	France	1996	10.99
Gong	Continental Circus + 2	CD	Giacomo	777	France	1994	24.99
Gong	Downwind	CD	Arista	251-138	Germany	1992	17.99
Gong	Expresso II	CD	Caroline	CAROL-1659-2	U.S.A.	1990	10.99
Gong	Family Jewels	2CD	GAS	AGASCD008	England	1998	74.99
Gong	Flying Tepot	CD	Spalax	14828	France	1996	10.99
Gong	From Here To Eternitea	2CD	Recall	SMD-CD-366	England	2002	12.99
Gong	Full Circle Live 1988	CD	Musea	FGBG-4388.AR	France	2001	12.99
Gong	Gazeuse! (Expresso)	CD	Virgin	0777-7-87238-2-0	Holland	1989	12.99
Gong	Glastonbury Fayre 1971	CD	GAS	GAS-ARC CD001	England	2002	22.99
Gong	Gong Est Mort, Vive Gong!	CD	Celluloid	66915-2	Holland	1992	9.99
Gong	Gong Family Box Set	4CD	Cleopatra	CLP-0580-2	U.S.A.	1999	34.99
Gong	Live 2 Infinitea	CD	Snapper	SMA-CD-834	England	2000	11.99
Gong	Live 2 Infinity	CD	Snapper	SMACD836	England	2000	11.99
Gong	Live At Sheffield '74	CD	Mantra	MANTRA-042	France	1990	10.99
Gong	Live Au Bataclan '73	CD	Mantra	MANTRA-025	France	1990	10.99
Gong	Live Etc.	CD	Virgin	CDVM 3501	England	1977	10.99
Gong	Live In Nottingham	CD	Classic Rock	CRP1058	England	2003	12.99
Gong	Live On TV 1990	CD	Code 90	NINETY-1	France	1993	14.99
Gong	Magick Brother	CD	Spalax	14812	France	1996	11.99
Gong	Magick Brother, Mystic Sister	CD	Spalax	14812	France	1996	12.99
Gong	OK Friends 2001 Tour	CD	GAS	AGASCD017	England	2003	12.99
Gong	Other Side Of The Sky	2CD	Snapper	SMCD-189	England	1999	12.99
Gong	Radio Gnome Trilogy Box Set	3CD	Spalax	14707	France	1995	44.99
Gong	Shamal	CD	Caroline	CAROL-1663-2	U.S.A.	1989	15.99
Gong	Shapeshifter	CD	Celluloid	66914-2	Holland	1992	10.99
Gong	The Best Of	CD	Nectar Masters	NTMCD517	England	1996	9.99
Gong	The History & Mystery Of Planet Gong	CD	Spalax	14518	France	1991	9.99
Gong	The History And Mystery Of	2CD	Alchemy	PILOT-67	England	2001	12.99
Gong	The Peel Sessions	CD	Strange Fruit	SFRCD137	England	1995	14.99
Gong	The Very Best Of Gong	CD	Summit	SUMCD-4117	France	1997	9.99
Gong	Wingful Of Eyes	CD	Virgin	7243-8-41377-2-4	England	1986	9.99
Gong	Would You Like Some Tea?	CD	Think Prog.	TPCD-1.807.030	Germany	1998	12.99
Gong	You	CD	Spalax	14834	France	1996	10.99
Gong	You Remixed Phase 1 & 2	2CD	Gliss	CD001	England	1997	15.99
Gong	You Remixed Phase 1.5	CD	Pony Canyon	PCCY-01145	Japan	1997	29.99
Gong	Zero To Infinity	CD	Snapper	SMA-CD-824	England	2000	20.99
Gong/Brainville	The Children's Crusade	CD	Shimmy Disc	5096	U.S.A.	1999	12.99
Gong/Daevid Allen	The World of Daevid Allen and Gong	3CD	Snapper	SNAJ725CD	England	1997	29.99
Gong/Dashiell Hedayat	Obsolete	CD	Mantra	MANTRA-075	England	1971	24.99
Gong/Didier Malherbe	Bloom	CD	Voiceprint	VP218CD	England	2003	14.99
Gong/Didier Malherbe	Faton Bloom	CD	Voiceprint	VP218CD	England	2003	14.99
Gong/Didier Malherbe	Fetish	CD	Mantra	COM-6031	France	1990	15.99
Gong/Didier Malherbe	Fluvius	CD	Tangram	852-492	Germany	1994	29.99
Gong/Didier Malherbe	Hadouk (W/Loy Ehrlich)	CD	Zebra Acoustic	ZA-44409-2	U.S.A.	1996	12.99
Gong/Didier Malherbe	Live New Morning (W/Bensusan)	CD	Zebra Acoustic	ZA-44401-2	U.S.A.	1997	12.99
Arng/Didier Malherbe	Now - Hadouk Trio	CD	Celluloid	67039-2	Holland	2002	14.99
Gong/Didier Malherbe	Shamanimal - Hadouk Trio	CD	Celluloid	67015-2	Holland	1999	14.99
Gong/Didier Malherbe	Zeff	CD	Tangram	842-620	Germany	1992	29.99
Gong/Global Family	How To Nuke The Eiffel Tower	CD	Voiceprint	VPGASCD102	England	1995	12.99

G

Artist	Title	Format	Label	Catalog No	Country	Released	Value
Gong/Gongmaison	Glastonbury Festival 89	CD	GAS	AGASCD-004	England	1995	14.99
Gong/Gongmaison	Gong Maison	CD	Demi Monde	DMCD-1022	England	1989	12.99
Gong/Gongzilla	East Village Sessions	CD	Lolo	017-2	U.S.A.	2003	14.99
Gong/Gongzilla	Live!	CD	Lolo	016-2	U.S.A.	2003	14.99
Gong/Gongzilla	Suffer	CD	Lolo	003-2	U.S.A.	1995	14.99
Gong/Gongzilla	Thrive	CD	Lolo	010-2	U.S.A.	1996	14.99
Gong/Invisible Opera Co.Tibet	Glissando Spirit (No Gong On This Lp)	CD	Voiceprint	VP147CD	England	1996	12.99
Gong/Invisible Opera Co.Tibet	Invisible Opera Company Of Tibet	CD	Voiceprint	VP106CD	England	1987	11.99
Gong/Invisible Opera Co.Tibet	Jewel In The Lotus	CD	GAS	AGASCD-006	England	1996	14.99
Gong/New York Gong	About Time	CD	Spalax	14832	France	1994	12.99
Gong/Paragong	Live '73	CD	GAS	AGASCD-002	England	1995	14.99
Gong/Pierre Moerlen	Breakthrough	CD	Arc	EUCD-1053	England	1986	29.99
Gong/Pierre Moerlen	Full Circle Live 1988	CD	Outer Music	OM-1006	U.S.A.	1998	22.99
Gong/Pierre Moerlen	Second Wind	CD	Line	LICD-9.00698-0	Germany	1988	29.99
Gong/Pierre Moerlen	Time Is The Key	CD	Arista	251-183	Germany	1992	19.99
Gong/Pip Pyle	7 Year Itch	CD	Voiceprint	VP198-CD	England	1998	12.99
Gong/Pip Pyle	Equipe Out	CD	Voiceprint	VP213CD	England	2000	12.99
Gong/Planet Gong	Floating Anarchy 1977	CD	Spalax	14829	France	1995	10.99
Gong/Planet Gong	Live Floating Anarchy 1991	CD	GAS	AGASCD-003	England	1995	14.99
Gong/Steve Hillage	Arzachel (W/S Hillage/Egg Members)	Mini Lp	Akarma	AK-184-CD	Italy	2001	19.99
Gong/Tim Blake	Blake's New Jerusalem	CD	Voiceprint	VP212CD	England	2000	12.99
Gong/Tim Blake	Caldea Music II	CD	Synergy	SRCD55303	Andorra	2003	19.99
Gong/Tim Blake	Crystal Machine	CD	Voiceprint	VP211CD	England	2000	10.99
Gong/Tim Blake	Magick	CD	Voiceprint	VP210CD	England	2000	12.99
Gong/Tim Blake	The Tide Of The Century	CD	Blueprint	BP340CD	England	2003	11.99
Goo Goo Dolls	First Release	CD	Metal Blade	CAROL-2211-2	U.S.A.	1994	60.99
Good Rats, The	Birth Comes To Us All	CD	Fireball	5304	U.S.A.	1995	10.99
Good Rats, The	From Rats To Riches	CD	Fireball	6252	U.S.A.	1995	10.99
Good Rats, The	Great American Music	CD	Uncle Rat	4	U.S.A.	1999	12.99
Good Rats, The	Live At Last	CD	Uncle Rat	2	U.S.A.	1997	12.99
Good Rats, The	Rat City In Blue	CD	Uncle Rat	8	U.S.A.	1999	12.99
Good Rats, The	Self Titled + 1	CD	One Way	OW-22121	U.S.A.	1994	11.99
Good Rats, The	Tasty	CD	Uncle Rat	3	U.S.A.	1997	12.99
Good Rats, The	Tasty Seconds	CD	Uncle Rat	1	U.S.A.	1997	12.99
Goodwin, Ron/3 Symp. Suites	Miss Marple/Lancelot/Force 10	CD	Label X	LXE-706	Germany	1992	19.99
Gordian Knot	Emergent	CD	Sensory	SR-3016	U.S.A.	2003	10.99
Gordian Knot	Self Titled	CD	Sensory	SR-3005	U.S.A.	1999	10.99
Gore, Leslie	Sunshine, Lollipops...Best Of	CD	Rhino	R2-75325	U.S.A.	1998	8.99
Gore, Michael	Terms Of Endearment (O.S.T.)	CD	Capitol	CDP-746076-2	U.S.A.	1989	79.99
Goulet, Robert	Greatest Hits	CD	Columbia	CK-9815	U.S.A.	1988	7.99
Govi	Andalusian Nights	CD	Higher Octave	HOMCD-46930	U.S.A.	1999	10.99
Govi	Cuchama	CD	Real Music	RM-0791	U.S.A.	1993	10.99
Govi	Guitar Odyssey	CD	Real Music	RM0802	U.S.A.	1997	10.99
Govi	No Strings Attached	CD	Real Music	RM0811	U.S.A.	1999	10.99
Govi	Passion & Grace	CD	Real Music	RM0793	U.S.A.	1995	10.99
Govi	Seventh Heaven	CD	Higher Octave	HOMCD-49424	U.S.A.	2000	12.99
Govi	Sky High	CD	Real Music	RM-0783	U.S.A.	1988	10.99
Gov't Mule	A Dose Of The Mule (Promo)	CD	Capricorn	CPC-0313	U.S.A.	1997	5.99
Gov't Mule	A Piece Of The Ass (Promo)	CD Single	Relativity	RPROCD-0391	U.S.A.	1995	5.99
Gov't Mule	Bad Little Doggie (Promo)	CD Single	Capricorn	CAPCP-2042	U.S.A.	1999	5.99
Gov't Mule	Blind Man In The Dark (Promo)	CD Single	Capricorn	MECP-375	U.S.A.	1998	5.99
Gov't Mule	Deep End, Vol. 1 (W/H T/Bonus CD)	2CD	ATO	79102-21502-2	U.S.A.	2001	29.99
Gov't Mule	Deepest End: Live Concert (CD/DVD)	2CD	Evangeline	GELD-4070	England	2003	19.99
Gov't Mule	Deepest End: Live Concert (CD/DVD)	2CD	ATO	79102-21517-2	U.S.A.	2003	19.99
Gov't Mule	Dose	CD	Capricorn	314-536-504-2	U.S.A.	2001	9.99
Gov't Mule	Drivin' Rain (Promo)	CD Single	ATO	ATOR-0012	U.S.A.	2002	5.99
Gov't Mule	Fallen Down (Promo)	CD Single	Capricorn	CAPCP-2048	U.S.A.	2000	5.99
Gov't Mule	Life Before Insanity	CD	Capricorn	314-546-489-2	U.S.A.	1998	9.99

G

Artist	Title	Format	Label	Catalog No	Country	Released	Value
Gov't Mule	Life Before Insanity (Promo)	CD	Universal	UMCF-4011-2	Canada	1999	5.99
Gov't Mule	Life On The Outside (Promo)	CD Single	ATO	ATOR-0007	U.S.A.	2001	5.99
Gov't Mule	Live At Roseland Ballroom	CD	Foundation	720907-1301-2	U.S.A.	1996	10.99
Gov't Mule	Live.. With A Little Help (Collector's Ed.)	CD	Capricorn	314-546-694-2	U.S.A.	1999	12.99
Gov't Mule	Live... With A Little Help..., Vol. 2	CD	Evangeline	GEL-4058	England	2002	14.99
Gov't Mule	Live...With A Little Help...	2CD	Capricorn	314-538-958-2	U.S.A.	1999	9.99
Gov't Mule	Self Titled	CD	Relativity	88561-1515-2	U.S.A.	1995	7.99
Gov't Mule	She Said, She Said (Promo)	CD Single	Capricorn	CAPCD-2002	U.S.A.	1998	5.99
Gov't Mule	Soulshine (Promo)	CD Single	Capricorn	CAPCP-2038	U.S.A.	1999	5.99
Gov't Mule	Soulshine (Promo)	CD Single	ATO	ATOR-0008	U.S.A.	2002	5.99
Gov't Mule	The Deep End, Vol. 1 (Adv. Promo)	CD	ATO	ATO-A0003	U.S.A.	2001	9.99
Gov't Mule	The Deep End, Vol. 2 (Adv. Promo)	CD	ATO	ATO-0006	U.S.A.	2002	9.99
Gov't Mule	The Deep End, Vol. 2 (W/Bonus CD)	2CD	ATO	79102-21507-2	U.S.A.	2002	29.99
Gov't Mule	Thorazine Shuffle (Promo)	CD Single	Capricorn	CAPCP-2013	U.S.A.	1998	5.99
Gov't Mule/Warren Haynes	I'll Be The One (Promo)	CD Single	Megaforce	CDP-962	U.S.A.	1993	7.99
Gov't Mule/Warren Haynes	Tales Of Ordinary Madness	CD	Megaforce	020286-1971-2-6	U.S.A.	1993	8.99
Gov't Mule/Warren Haynes	The Lone EP	CD	ATO	79102-21511-2	U.S.A.	2003	14.99
Gov't Mule/Warren Haynes	Wintertime Blues: 11th Annual...	CD	Evil Teen	6-51751-0017-2	U.S.A.	2000	14.99
Gpx-Cyber-Formula	Pictureland II	CD	Datam Polystar	DPCX-5034	Japan	1994	39.99
Gracious	Self Titled	CD	Repertoire	REP-4060-WP	Germany	2001	14.99
Gracious	Self Titled/This Is	CD	BGO	BGOCD256	England	2002	19.99
Graham, Larry	One In A Million You	CD	Warner Bros.	WPCR-1821	Japan	1980	54.99
Graham, Larry/George Duke	Sooner Or Later	CD	Warner Bros.	WPCR-1823	Japan	1982	44.99
Grainer, Ron	Doctor Who: Variations On A Theme	CD Single	Silva Screen	FILMCD-706	England	1991	13.99
Grainer, Ron	The Prisoner - Vol. 1 (O.S.T.)	CD	Silva Screen	FILMCD-042	England	1989	14.99
Grainer, Ron	The Prisoner - Vol. 2 (O.S.T.)	CD	Silva Screen	FILMCD-084	England	1991	14.99
Grainer, Ron	The Prisoner - Vol. 3 (O.S.T.)	CD	Silva Screen	FILMCD-126	England	1992	14.99
Grainer, Ron	The Prisoner (Promo)	CD Single	Bonfoniso	NRIC-112-CD	England	1990	119.99
Grainer, Ron	The Prisoner File #1	CD	Silva Screen	FILMCD-601	England	2002	14.99
Grainer, Ron	The Prisoner File #2	CD	Silva Screen	FILMCD-602	England	2002	14.99
Grainer, Ron	The Prisoner File #3	CD	Silva Screen	FILMCD-603	England	2002	14.99
Grainer, Ron/FAB/MC No 6	The Prisoner	CD Single	Telstar	FAB-CD6	England	1990	59.99
Grand Funk Railroad	All The Girls In The World Beware !!	CD	Capitol	72435-80532-2	U.S.A.	2003	8.99
Grand Funk Railroad	Best Of...	CD	Capitol	7-90608-2	U.S.A.	1991	9.99
Grand Funk Railroad	Born To Die + 2	CD	Capitol	72435-80498-2	U.S.A.	2003	8.99
Grand Funk Railroad	Caught In The Act Live	CD	Capitol	72435-80592-2	U.S.A.	2003	8.99
Grand Funk Railroad	Classic Masters	CD	Capitol	72435-39857-2	U.S.A.	2002	8.99
Grand Funk Railroad	Closer To Home + 4	CD	Capitol	72435-39380-2-4	U.S.A.	2002	9.99
Grand Funk Railroad	Collection	CD	Castle	CCSCD332	England	1993	8.99
Grand Funk Railroad	E Pluribus Funk + 4	CD	Capitol	72435-41724-2	U.S.A.	2002	8.99
Grand Funk Railroad	Good Singin', Good Playin' (F Zappa)	CD	Hip O	HIPD-40144	U.S.A.	1999	8.99
Grand Funk Railroad	Grand Funk +2	CD	Capitol	72435-39381-2-3	U.S.A.	2002	9.99
Grand Funk Railroad	Heavy Hitters	CD	Capitol	S21-57244	U.S.A.	1995	7.99
Grand Funk Railroad	Hits	CD	Capitol	C2-46623	U.S.A.	1990	7.99
Grand Funk Railroad	Live Album (W/Poster)	2CD	EMI	72435-76239-2-6	Holland	2003	18.99
Grand Funk Railroad	Live Album + Bonus Tracks	CD	Capitol	72435-39326-2-6	U.S.A.	2002	8.99
Grand Funk Railroad	Live Bosnia	2CD	Capitol	72438-21935-2-4	U.S.A.	1997	24.99
Grand Funk Railroad	Live The 1971 Tour	CD	Capitol	72435-39501-2-5	U.S.A.	2002	7.99
Grand Funk Railroad	Lives	CD	Lissmark	6346	U.S.A.	2001	10.99
Grand Funk Railroad	More Of The Best + 3	CD	Rhino	R2-70530	U.S.A.	1991	7.99
Grand Funk Railroad	On Time	CD	Capitol	CP21-6037	Japan	1969	8.99
Grand Funk Railroad	On Time + 2	CD	Capitol	72435-39502-2-4	U.S.A.	2002	11.99
Grand Funk Railroad	Phoenix + 1	CD	Capitol	72435-41723-2	U.S.A.	2002	8.99
Grand Funk Railroad	Radio Promo Sampler	CD	Capitol	70876-12117-2-6	U.S.A.	1997	10.99
Grand Funk Railroad	Rock Champions	CD	EMI	72435-76380-2-9	Holland	2001	9.99
Grand Funk Railroad	Shinin' On + 2	CD	Capitol	72435-80531-2	U.S.A.	2003	8.99
Grand Funk Railroad	Survival + 5	CD	Capitol	72435-41725-2	U.S.A.	2002	8.99
Grand Funk Railroad	The Best Of	CD	Capitol	S21-56668	U.S.A.	1995	7.99

G

Artist	Title	Format	Label	Catalog No	Country	Released	Value
Grand Funk Railroad	The Best Of	CD	Toshiba-EMI	TOCP-50119	Japan	1999	29.99
Grand Funk Railroad	Thirty Years Of Funk (1969 - 1999)	3CD	Capitol	72434-99523-2	U.S.A.	1999	24.99
Grand Funk Railroad	Thirty Years Of Funk (Promo)	CD	Capitol	72434-99526	U.S.A.	1999	19.99
Grand Funk Railroad	Trunk Full Funk (1st 4/Able Hold Rest)	4CD	Capitol	72435-41422-2	U.S.A.	2002	49.99
Grand Funk Railroad	Very Best Album Ever	CD	EMI	72435-35974-2-9	Holland	2001	10.99
Grand Funk Railroad	We're An American Band + 4	CD	Capitol	72435-41726-2	U.S.A.	2002	8.99
Grand Funk Railroad	What's Funk ?	CD	Lissmark	6347	U.S.A.	2001	10.99
Grand Funk/Mark Farner	Heirlooms Complete Atlantic (1st 2 Lps)	CD	Lissmark	6345	U.S.A.	2000	10.99
Grand Funk/Mark Farner	Just Another.../Some Kind Of..	CD	KMG	KMGD8656	U.S.A.	1998	8.99
Grand Funk/Mark Farner	Live! N'rG	CD	Lissmark	1051	U.S.A.	2003	10.99
Grand Funk/Mark Farner	Wake Up/Closer To Home	CD	KMG	KMGD8951	U.S.A.	2000	8.99
Grand Prix	Samurai	CD	Toshiba-EMI	TOCP-8086	Japan	1993	24.99
Grant, Amy	A Christmas Album	CD	RCA	07863-66259-2	U.S.A.	1983	8.99
Grant, Amy	A Christmas To Remember	CD	A&M	0694904622	U.S.A.	1999	6.99
Grant, Amy	Age To Age	CD	RCA	07863-66255-2	U.S.A.	1982	8.99
Grant, Amy	Amy Grant	CD	RCA	07863-66260-2	U.S.A.	1977	8.99
Grant, Amy	Behind The Eyes	CD	A&M	31454-0760-2	U.S.A.	1997	5.99
Grant, Amy	Heart In Motion	CD	Myrrh	7016907619	U.S.A.	1991	5.99
Grant, Amy	Home For Christmas	CD	A&M	31454-0001-2	U.S.A.	1992	6.99
Grant, Amy	House Of Love	CD	A&M	31454-0230-2	U.S.A.	1994	6.99
Grant, Amy	In Concert Volume One	CD	RCA	07863-66263-2	U.S.A.	1981	7.99
Grant, Amy	In Concert Volume Two	CD	RCA	07863-66264-2	U.S.A.	1981	7.99
Grant, Amy	Lead Me On	CD	A&M	CD-5199	U.S.A.	1988	8.99
Grant, Amy	Lead Me On (Promo Signed Gold Cd)	CD	Myrrh	9016656472	U.S.A.	1988	79.99
Grant, Amy	Legacy... Hymns (Bonus DVD)	2CD	Word	0694933160	U.S.A.	2002	11.99
Grant, Amy	My Father's Eyes	CD	RCA	07863-66261-2	U.S.A.	1979	9.99
Grant, Amy	Never Alone	CD	RCA	07863-66262-2	U.S.A.	1980	7.99
Grant, Amy	Straight Ahead	CD	RCA	07863-66256-2	U.S.A.	1984	9.99
Grant, Amy	Takes A Little Time	CD Single	Myrrh	701703161X	U.S.A.	1997	8.99
Grant, Amy	The Collection	CD	RCA	07863-66258-2	U.S.A.	1993	9.99
Grant, Amy	Unguarded	CD	Myrrh	7-01-680627-8	U.S.A.	1985	9.99
Grapefruit	Around Grapefruit + 1	CD	Repertoire	REP-4363-WP	Germany	2001	11.99
Grapefruit	Deep Water + 2	CD	Repertoire	REP-4364-WP	Germany	2002	11.99
Grapow, Roland	The Four Seasons Of Life	CD	Victor Ent.	SRCD-2356	Japan	1997	34.99
Grass Roots, The	Let's Live For Today/Feelings	CD	Repertoire	REP-4594-WY	Germany	1996	12.99
Grass Roots, The	The Grass Roots All Time Greatest Hits	CD	MCA	MCAD-11467	U.S.A.	1996	8.99
Grass Roots, The	The Grass Roots Greatest Hits Vol. 1	CD	MCA	MCAD-31132	U.S.A.	1987	11.99
Grass Roots, The	The Grass Roots Greatest Hits Vol. 2	CD	MCA	MCAD-31133	U.S.A.	1987	11.99
Grateful Dead	Academy Of Music (Promo)	CD	Grateful Dead	GDCD225S	U.S.A.	2004	8.99
Grateful Dead	American Beauty (DVD Audio)	CD	Rhino	R2-74385	U.S.A.	2001	14.99
Grateful Dead	American Beauty + 6	CD	Rhino	R2-74397	U.S.A.	2003	10.99
Grateful Dead	Anthem Of The Sun + 3	CD	Rhino	R2-74393	U.S.A.	2003	10.99
Grateful Dead	Aoxomoxoa + 4	CD	Rhino	R2-74394	U.S.A.	2003	10.99
Grateful Dead	Arista Years 1977-1995 (DJ Sampler)	CD	Arista	01096-18934-2	U.S.A.	1996	14.99
Grateful Dead	Best Of Skeletons From The Closet	CD	Warner Bros.	2764-2	U.S.A.	1974	6.99
Grateful Dead	Birth Of The Dead	2CD	Rhino	R2-74391	U.S.A.	2003	14.99
Grateful Dead	Blues For Allah	CD	Grateful Dead	GDCD4001	U.S.A.	1975	14.99
Grateful Dead	Blues For Allah (Line Version)	CD	Line	GDCD-9.00650-0	Germany	1989	10.99
Grateful Dead	Built To Last	CD	Arista	ARCD-8575	U.S.A.	1989	6.99
Grateful Dead	Dead In A Deck (Built Pic Cd W/Cards)	CD	Arista	ARCD-8575-DL	U.S.A.	1989	24.99
Grateful Dead	Dead Set	CD	Arista	A2CD-8522	U.S.A.	1987	8.99
Grateful Dead	Dick's Picks 7 - 12 (Promo Sampler)	CD	Grateful Dead	ASCD-3559	U.S.A.	1998	14.99
Grateful Dead	Dick's Pick's Vol. 1	2CD	Grateful Dead	GDCD-4019	England	1993	13.99
Grateful Dead	Dick's Picks Vol. 10	3CD	Greatful Dead	GDCD-4030	England	1998	19.99
Grateful Dead	Dick's Picks Vol. 11	3CD	Labelful Dead	GDCD-4031	England	1998	22.99
Grateful Dead	Dick's Picks Vol. 12	3CD	Grateful Dead	GDCD-4032	England	1998	18.99
Grateful Dead	Dick's Picks Vol. 13	3CD	Grateful Dead	GDCD-4033	England	1999	18.99
Grateful Dead	Dick's Picks Vol. 14	4CD	Grateful Dead	GDCD-4034	England	1999	24.99

Artist	Title	Format	Label	Catalog No	Country	Released	Value
Grateful Dead	Dick's Picks Vol. 15	3CD	Grateful Dead	GDCD-4035	England	1999	19.99
Grateful Dead	Dick's Picks Vol. 16	3CD	Grateful Dead	GDCD-4036	England	2000	18.99
Grateful Dead	Dick's Picks Vol. 17	3CD	Grateful Dead	GDCD-4037	England	2000	19.99
Grateful Dead	Dick's Picks Vol. 18	3CD	Grateful Dead	GDCD-4038	England	2000	18.99
Grateful Dead	Dick's Picks Vol. 19	3CD	Grateful Dead	GDCD-4039	England	2000	18.99
Grateful Dead	Dicks Picks Vol. 2	CD	Grateful Dead	GDCD-4020	England	1995	9.99
Grateful Dead	Dick's Picks Vol. 20	4CD	Grateful Dead	GDCD-4040	England	2001	22.99
Grateful Dead	Dick's Picks Vol. 21	3CD	Grateful Dead	GDCD-4041	England	2001	19.99
Grateful Dead	Dick's Picks Vol. 22	2CD	Grateful Dead	GDCD-4042	England	2001	14.99
Grateful Dead	Dick's Picks Vol. 23	3CD	Grateful Dead	GDCD-4043	England	2001	19.99
Grateful Dead	Dick's Picks Vol. 24	2CD	Grateful Dead	GDCD-4044	England	2002	14.99
Grateful Dead	Dick's Picks Vol. 3	2CD	Grateful Dead	GDCD2-4022	England	1995	14.99
Grateful Dead	Dick's Picks Vol. 4	3CD	Grateful Dead	GDCD3-4023	England	1996	18.99
Grateful Dead	Dick's Picks Vol. 5	3CD	Greatfull Dead	GDCD3-4025	England	1995	14.99
Grateful Dead	Dick's Picks Vol. 6	3CD	Grateful Dead	GDCD3-4026	England	1996	18.99
Grateful Dead	Dick's Picks Vol. 7	3CD	Grateful Dead	GDCD3-4027	England	1997	14.99
Grateful Dead	Dick's Picks Vol. 8	3CD	Grateful Dead	GDCD3-4028	England	1997	19.99
Grateful Dead	Dick's Picks Vol. 9	3CD	Grateful Dead	GDCD-4029	England	1997	19.99
Grateful Dead	Dick's Picks, Vol. 25	4CD	Grateful Dead	GDCD-4045	U.S.A.	2002	22.99
Grateful Dead	Dick's Picks, Vol. 26	2CD	Grateful Dead	GDCD-4046	U.S.A.	2002	14.99
Grateful Dead	Dick's Picks, Vol. 27	3CD	Grateful Dead	GDCD-4047	U.S.A.	2003	18.99
Grateful Dead	Dick's Picks, Vol. 28	4CD	Grateful Dead	GDCD-4048	U.S.A.	2003	24.99
Grateful Dead	Dick's Picks, Vol. 29	6CD	Grateful Dead	GDCD-4049	U.S.A.	2003	29.99
Grateful Dead	Dick's Picks, Vol. 30	4CD	Grateful Dead	DECD216	U.S.A.	2003	24.99
Grateful Dead	Dick's Picks, Vol. 31	4CD	Grateful Dead	DECD222	U.S.A.	2004	24.99
Grateful Dead	Dozin' At The Knick	3CD	Grateful Dead	GDCD-4025	U.S.A.	1996	16.99
Grateful Dead	Europe '72 + 7	2CD	Rhino	R2-74399	U.S.A.	2003	12.99
Grateful Dead	Fallout From The Phil Zone	2CD	Grateful Dead	GDCD-4052	U.S.A.	1997	19.99
Grateful Dead	Fillmore East 2/11/69	2CD	Grateful Dead	GDCD-4054	U.S.A.	1997	18.99
Grateful Dead	For The Faithful (Pair Lps/Reckoning)	CD	Arista	ARPDL2-1053	U.S.A.	1981	12.99
Grateful Dead	From The Mars Hotel	CD	Arista	GDCD4007	U.S.A.	1989	8.99
Grateful Dead	From The Mars Hotel (Line Version)	CD	Line	GDCD-9.00646-0	Germany	1989	10.99
Grateful Dead	From The Mars Hotel (MFSL Silver Cd)	CD	Mobile Fidelity	MFCD-830	U.S.A.	1974	21.99
Grateful Dead	From The Mars Hotel (Picture Cd)	CD	Grateful Dead	GDPD-4007	England	1974	29.99
Grateful Dead	Go To Heaven	CD	Arista	ARCD-8181	U.S.A.	1980	6.99
Grateful Dead	Golden Road 1965-1973 Box Set	12 CD	Rhino	R2-74401	U.S.A.	2001	59.99
Grateful Dead	Grateful Dead (Skull & Roses) + 2	CD	Rhino	R2-74398	U.S.A.	2003	10.99
Grateful Dead	Grateful Dead Documentary (Promo)	2CD	Grateful Dead	GDCD40831/2	U.S.A.	2001	24.99
Grateful Dead	Grayfolded	2CD	Snapper	SMD-CD-215	EU	1999	9.99
Grateful Dead	History Dead Vol. 1 (Bear's Choice) + 4	CD	Rhino	R2-74400	U.S.A.	2003	10.99
Grateful Dead	Hundred Year Hall	2CD	Arista	GDCD-40202	U.S.A.	1995	10.99
Grateful Dead	Hundred Year Hall (Line Version)	2CD	Line	GDCD-9.21318-0	Germany	1995	19.99
Grateful Dead	In The Dark	CD	Arista	ARCD-8452	U.S.A.	1987	6.99
Grateful Dead	Infrared Roses	CD	Grateful Dead	GDCD-40142	U.S.A.	1991	19.99
Grateful Dead	Infrared Roses (Line Version)	CD	Line	GDCD-9.01139-0	Germany	1991	24.99
Grateful Dead	Ladies And Gentlemen...	4CD	Grateful Dead	GDCD-4075	U.S.A.	2000	34.99
Grateful Dead	Live Dead	CD	Rhino	R2-74395	U.S.A.	2003	10.99
Grateful Dead	New Year's Eve At Winterland (Promo)	CD	Grateful Dead	GDCD4091	U.S.A.	2003	14.99
Grateful Dead	One From the Vault	2CD	Grateful Dead	GDCD40132	U.S.A.	1991	12.99
Grateful Dead	One From The Vault - 1 (Line Version)	CD	Line	GDCD-9.01095-L	Germany	1991	10.99
Grateful Dead	One From The Vault - 2 (Line Version)	CD	Line	GDCD-9.01096-L	Germany	1991	10.99
Grateful Dead	One From The Vault (Line Version)	2CD	Line	GDCD-9.21157-S	Germany	1991	19.99
Grateful Dead	Postcards Of The Hanging	2CD	Grateful Dead	GDCD-4069	U.S.A.	2002	14.99
Grateful Dead	Reckoning	CD	Arista	A2CD-8523	U.S.A.	1980	8.99
Artful Dead	Rockin' The Rhein With The	3CD	Rhino	R2-78921	U.S.A.	2004	14.99
Grateful Dead	Selections From Golden Road	CD	Rhino	PRCD-400046	U.S.A.	2001	16.99
Grateful Dead	Shakedown Street	CD	Arista	ARCD-8228	U.S.A.	1978	8.99
Grateful Dead	So Many Roads (1965-1995) (Box Set)	5CD	Grateful Dead	GDCD-4066	U.S.A.	1999	38.99

G

Artist	Title	Format	Label	Catalog No	Country	Released	Value
Grateful Dead	So Many Roads Promo Sampler	CD	Grateful Dead	GDPCD-3740	U.S.A.	1999	14.99
Grateful Dead	Stayin' Alive (Limited Numbered)	CD	Line	GDCD-9.00750-E	Germany	1989	499.99
Grateful Dead	Steal Your Face	2CD	Grateful Dead	GDCD4006	U.S.A.	1989	16.99
Grateful Dead	Steal Your Face - Vol. 1 (Line Version)	CD	Line	GDCD-9.00654-0	Germany	1989	10.99
Grateful Dead	Steal Your Face - Vol. 2 (Line Version)	CD	Line	GDCD-9.00655-0	Germany	1989	10.99
Grateful Dead	Steal Your Face (Line Version)	2CD	Line	GDCD-9.21154-S	Germany	1991	19.99
Grateful Dead	Steppin' Out England '72	4CD	Arista	GDCD4084	U.S.A.	2002	24.99
Grateful Dead	Steppin' Out England '72 (DJ Sampler)	CD	Arista	GDPCD4084	U.S.A.	2002	14.99
Grateful Dead	Still Truckin'	CD	Baktabak	CBAK-4039	England	1992	5.99
Grateful Dead	Telltales	CD	Telltales	TEL-06	England	1990	8.99
Grateful Dead	Terrapin Station	CD	Arista	ARCD-8065	U.S.A.	1977	7.99
Grateful Dead	Terrapin Station Box Set (W/Cover)	3CD	Grateful Dead	GDCD-4055	U.S.A.	1997	31.99
Grateful Dead	The Arista Years	2CD	Arista	07822-18954-2	U.S.A.	1996	16.99
Grateful Dead	The Closing Of Winterland	4CD	Grateful Dead	GDCD4090	U.S.A.	2003	22.99
Grateful Dead	The Grateful Dead + 6	CD	Rhino	R2-74392	U.S.A.	2003	10.99
Grateful Dead	The Very Best Of	2CD	Rhino	R2-73899	U.S.A.	2003	13.99
Grateful Dead	Trouble Ahead, Trouble Behind	CD	Yeaah!	YEAAH3	England	1971	10.99
Grateful Dead	Two From the Vault	2CD	Grateful Dead	GDCD40162	U.S.A.	1992	11.99
Grateful Dead	Two From The Vault (Line Version)	2CD	Line	GDCD-9.21210-S	Germany	1992	19.99
Grateful Dead	View From the Vault III	3CD	Grateful Dead	GDCD-4087	U.S.A.	2002	23.99
Grateful Dead	Wake Of The Flood (Line Version)	CD	Line	GDCD-9.00643-0	Germany	1989	10.99
Grateful Dead	Wake Of The Flood (Picture Cd)	CD	Grateful Dead	GDPD-4002	England	1973	29.99
Grateful Dead	What A Long Strange Trip It's Been	2CD	Warner Bros.	3091-2	U.S.A.	1989	11.99
Grateful Dead	Without A Net	2CD	Arista	ACD2-8634	U.S.A.	1990	9.99
Grateful Dead	Without A Net (Clown Pic 2 Cd Promo)	CD	Arista	ACD2-8634-DL	U.S.A.	1990	29.99
Grateful Dead	Workingman's Dead (DVD Audio)	CD	Rhino	R2-78356	U.S.A.	2001	14.99
Grateful Dead	Workingman's Dead + 7	CD	Rhino	R2-74396	U.S.A.	2003	10.99
Grateful Dead/Best Buy	A Glimpse Of The Vault (Promo)	CD	Grateful Dead	07822-13267-2	U.S.A.	1996	24.99
Grateful Dead/Rock Scully	Living With The Dead	2CD	Time Warner	2-523717	U.S.A.	1995	8.99
Grauzone	Grauzone	CD	Line	DKCD-9.01004-0	Germany	1990	24.99
Grave Digger	The Reaper	CD	BMG	BVCP-705	Japan	1994	24.99
Grave Digger	Witch Hunter/War Games	CD	Victor Ent.	VICP-8130	Japan	1994	49.99
Gravenites, Nick	Bluestar	CD	Line	LICD-9.00050-0	Germany	1988	24.99
Gravenites, Nick/M. Bloomfield	My Labors + 3 (Live 1969)	CD	Acadia	ACA-8010	England	2001	16.99
Gravenites/Cipollina Band	Monkey Medicine	CD	Line	LICD-9.00144-0	Germany	1988	24.99
Gravy Train	Ballad Of A Peaceful Man	CD	Repertoire	REP-4122-WP	Germany	2002	12.99
Gravy Train	Second Birth	CD	Castle	NEM612	England	1994	14.99
Gravy Train	Self Titled	CD	Repertoire	REP-4063-WP	Germany	2002	12.99
Gravy Train	Staircase To The Day	CD	Repertoire	REP-4133-WP	Germany	2002	12.99
Gray, Dobie	Ultimate Collection	CD	Hip O	314-541-490-2	U.S.A.	2001	9.99
Grease Band	Grease Band/Amazing Grease	CD	Line	LICD-9.01101-0	Germany	1991	19.99
Great White	A Shot In The Dark + 1	CD	Toshiba-EMI	CP32-5566	Japan	1987	41.99
Great White	Blue EP	CD Single	Toshiba-EMI	TOCP-6876	Japan	1991	26.99
Great White	BURRN! Presents Best	CD	Toshiba-EMI	TOCP-50499	Japan	1998	29.99
Great White	Can't Get There From Here	CD	Portrait	VK-69547	U.S.A.	1999	7.99
Great White	Can't Get There From Here + 1	CD	Victor Ent.	VICP-60628	Japan	1999	29.99
Great White	Gallery + 2	CD	Axe Killer	305-006-2	France	1999	19.99
Great White	Great Zeppelin (Led Zep Tribute)	CD	Victor Ent.	VICP-60660	Japan	1999	24.99
Great White	Great Zeppelin (Led Zep Tribute)	CD	Cleopatra	CLP-0504-2	U.S.A.	1999	12.99
Great White	Hooked	CD	Capitol	7243-4-98290-2-2	U.S.A.	1991	12.99
Great White	Hooked (Banned Cover)	CD	Toshiba-EMI	TOCP-6964	Japan	1991	55.99
Great White	Hooked (Banned/Back Booklet Lady)	CD	Capitol	CDP-7-95330-2	U.S.A.	1991	14.99
Great White	Hooked (Banned/Back Cover Fin)	CD	Capitol	C2-96243	U.S.A.	1991	14.99
Great White	Hooked + 11 Live In New York	2CD	Toshiba-EMI	TOCP-6964/65	Japan	1991	99.99
Great White	Latest & Greatest	CD	Portrait	VK-69878	U.S.A.	2000	7.99
Great White	Let It Rock	CD	Imago	72787-23005-2	U.S.A.	1999	12.99
Great White	Let It Rock + 1	CD	BMG Victor	VICP-5680	Japan	1996	24.99
Great White	Live In London	CD	Toshiba-EMI	TOCP-6147	Japan	1991	39.99

Artist	Title	Format	Label	Catalog No	Country	Released	Value
Great White	Once Bitten	CD	Capitol	CDP-7-46910-2	U.S.A.	1987	8.99
Great White	Once Bitten	CD	Toshiba-EMI	TOCP-6539	Japan	1990	24.99
Great White	Once Bitten (Different Save Your Love)	CD	EMI	7243-5-24576-2	EU	2000	9.99
Great White	Psycho City	CD	Capitol	0777-7-98835-2-3	U.S.A.	1992	14.99
Great White	Psycho City + 1	CD	Pony Canyon	PCCY-00372	Japan	1992	19.99
Great White	Psycho City + 4	CD	Axe Killer	305-332-2	France	1999	19.99
Great White	Recover	CD	Cleopatra	CLP-1187-2	U.S.A.	2002	12.99
Great White	Recovery Live!	CD	Toshiba-EMI	TOCP-7066	U.S.A.	1992	29.99
Great White	Recovery Live!/On Your Knees	CD	Enigma	D2-73295	Canada	1987	25.99
Great White	Rock Me	CD	Disky	DC-881862	Holland	1995	12.99
Great White	Sail Away	2CD	Zoo Ent.	72445-11080-2	U.S.A.	1994	12.99
Great White	Sail Away + 2	2CD	BMG Victor	BVCP-2811/12	Japan	1994	24.99
Great White	Self Titled	CD	Toshiba-EMI	EYS-81643	Japan	1984	39.99
Great White	Self Titled	CD	Capitol	CDP-7-48953-2	U.S.A.	1984	10.99
Great White	Shot In The Dark	CD	Razor & Tie	RE-2110-2	U.S.A.	1996	14.99
Great White	Shot In The Dark (Original Release)	CD	Telegraph	GWD90540	U.S.A.	1986	29.99
Great White	Shot In The Dark (Re-Recorded)	CD	Capitol	CDP-7-48466-2	U.S.A.	1986	13.99
Great White	Stage	CD	BMG Victor	BVCP-896	Japan	1995	17.99
Great White	Stage	CD	Zoo Ent.	72445-11121-2	U.S.A.	1996	12.99
Great White	Stage + 2	2CD	BMG Victor	BVCP-2813/14	Japan	1995	39.99
Great White	Stick It + 5	CD	Axe Killer	304-677-2	France	1999	14.99
Great White	The Best Of	CD	EMI	7243-5-23522-2-7	U.S.A.	2000	8.99
Great White	The Best: 1986-1992	CD	Capitol	7243-8-27185-2	U.S.A.	1993	7.99
Great White	Twice Shy	CD	Capitol	CDP-7-93636-2	U.S.A.	1989	10.99
Great White	Twice Shy + 2	CD	Toshiba-EMI	CP32-5849	Japan	1989	24.99
Great White	Twice Shy +2 / Live At Marquee (2CD)	2CD	Capitol	CDP-7936362	Germany	1989	99.99
Great White/W/Cassette	Hooked Promo Box (W/Net/S Tooth)	CD	Capitol	CDP-7-95330-2	U.S.A.	1991	49.99
Greatest Show On Earth	Horizons	CD	Repertoire	REP-4484-WP	Germany	2002	12.99
Greatest Show On Earth	Horizons/The Going's Easy	CD	See For Miles	SEE-CD-473	England	1997	16.99
Greatest Show On Earth	The Going's Easy + 1	CD	Repertoire	REP-4483-WP	Germany	2002	12.99
Green Jello	Cereal Killer Soundtrack	CD	Zoo	72445-11038-2	U.S.A.	1992	8.99
Green, Garland	Jealous Kind Of Fella	CD	Varese	VSD-5611	U.S.A.	1995	8.99
Green, Peter	A Case For The Blues	CD	Versailles	478341-2	Austria	1993	8.99
Green, Peter	A Fool No More	CD	Armoury	ARMCD047	Germany	2001	8.99
Green, Peter	Bandit	CD	Milan	74321-47464-2	U.S.A.	1997	8.99
Green, Peter	Blue Guitar	CD	Rhino	RNCD-1003	Germany	1991	11.99
Green, Peter	Blues By Green	CD	Fuel 2000	302-061-307-2	U.S.A.	2003	8.99
Green, Peter	Blues For Dhyana	CD	Culture Press	1009	France	1998	8.99
Green, Peter	Collection	CD	Fuel 2000	302-061-118-2	U.S.A.	2001	8.99
Green, Peter	Green & Guitar - Best Of Peter Green	CD	Music Club	MCCD-244	EU	1996	11.99
Green, Peter	Green & Guitar: Best Of 1977-1981	CD	Music Club	50001	U.S.A.	1996	9.99
Green, Peter	In The Skies	CD	Laserlight	21-064	Germany	1998	10.99
Green, Peter	In The Skies	CD	Rhino	RNCD-1001	Germany	1991	10.99
Green, Peter	Into The Skies (W/Box)	CD	EMI	576-028-2	EU	2001	16.99
Green, Peter	Kolors	CD	Rhino	RNCD-1005	Germany	1992	17.99
Green, Peter	Legend	CD	Rhino	RNCD-1009	Germany	1998	10.99
Green, Peter	Little Dreamer	CD	Rhino	RNCD-1002	England	1991	10.99
Green, Peter	MacBeth: An Original Score	CD	Rephlex	80714	England	2001	8.99
Green, Peter	The End Of The Game	CD	Warner Bros.	7599-26758-2	Germany	1979	8.99
Green, Peter	The Peter Green Collection 1978-1983	CD	Fuel 2000	302-061-118-2	U.S.A.	2001	13.99
Green, Peter	Watcha Gonna Do?	CD	Rhino	RNCD-1006	Germany	1998	10.99
Green, Peter	White Sky	CD	Rhino	RNCD-1004	Germany	1998	10.99
Green, Peter/Mick	Green's Blues	CD	M.I.L.	6103	U.S.A.	1998	9.99
Green, Peter/Splinter Group	Destiny Road	CD	Snapper	128172	U.S.A.	1999	8.99
Green, Peter/Splinter Group	Destiny Road	CD	Snapper	SMMCD-631	England	1999	8.99
Green, Peter/Splinter Group	Hot Foot Powder	CD	Snapper	SMA-CD-828	England	2000	8.99
Green, Peter/Splinter Group	Me And The Devil (Limited Numbered)	3CD	Snapper	SMB-CD-844	England	2001	39.99
Green, Peter/Splinter Group	Peter Green Splinter Group	CD	Snapper	155902	U.S.A.	1997	8.99

G

Artist	Title	Format	Label	Catalog No	Country	Released	Value
Green, Peter/Splinter Group	Reaching The Cold 100	CD	Eagle	82699-20004-2-8	England	2003	9.99
Green, Peter/Splinter Group	Soho Live At Ronnie Scotts	2CD	Snapper	SMD-CD-327	U.S.A.	2001	15.99
Green, Peter/Splinter Group	Splinter Group/Destiny Road	2CD	Snapper	SMD-CD-466	England	2003	15.99
Green, Peter/Splinter Group	The Best Of	2CD	Snapper	SMA-DD-849	U.S.A.	2002	15.99
Green, Peter/Splinter Group	The Clown	CD	Culture Press	1029	France	2001	9.99
Green, Peter/Splinter Group	The Robert Johnson Songbook	CD	Snapper	636551614122	U.S.A.	2003	9.99
Green, Peter/Splinter Group	Time Traders	CD	Spitfire	6-70211-3006-2-8	U.S.A.	2001	9.99
Green, Peter/Splinter Group	Time Traders	CD	Eagle	EAGCD-193	England	2001	9.99
Green, Peter/Tribute	Peter Green Songbook	2CD	Seagull	111101-307	Germany	2000	15.99
Greenbaum, Norman	Petaluma	CD	Edsel	EDCD-544	England	1997	12.99
Greenbaum, Norman	Spirit In The Sky + 1	CD	Varese	302-066-229-2	U.S.A.	2001	9.99
Greenbaum, Norman	The Best Of Spirit In The Sky	CD	Repertoire	REP-4677-WY	Germany	1997	14.99
Greenhaw, Art	Lugosi: Hollywood's Dracula	CD	McWhorter	156073-W1	U.S.A.	1997	8.99
Greenslade	Bedside Manners Are Extra	CD	Warner Bros.	7599-26866-2	Germany	1973	14.99
Greenslade	Greenslade	CD	Warner Bros.	WPCP-4794	Japan	1992	16.99
Greenslade	Large Afternoon	CD	Mystic	MYS-CD-142	England	2001	10.99
Greenslade	Live	CD	Mystic	MYS-CD-136	England	1999	13.99
Greenslade	Live 2001 (The Full Ed.)	CD	Belle Antique	GSLCD01	Japan	2002	18.99
Greenslade, Dave	From The Discworld	CD	Virgin	7243-8-39512-2-2	Holland	1994	10.99
Greenslade, Dave	Going South	CD	Mystic	MYS-CD-137	England	1999	12.99
Greenslade/Woodroffe	The Pentateuch Of The Cosmogony	CD	BGO	BGOCD170	England	1994	34.99
Greenwich, Ellie	Composes.../ Let it Be Written...	CD	Raven	RVCD-84	Australia	1999	13.99
Gregson, Clive/C Collister	A Change In The Weather	CD	Line	FBCD-9.00848-0	Germany	1989	10.99
Greyhound Soul	Alma De Galgo	CD	Line	LICD—9.01382-0	Germany	2001	10.99
Greyhound Soul	Freaks	CD	Line	LICD—9.01365-0	Germany	2000	10.99
Griffith, Andy	Just As I Am	CD	Sony	A-26709	U.S.A.	1996	6.99
Griffith, Andy	Sings Favorite Old-Time Songs	CD	Capitol	S21-18938	U.S.A.	1996	8.99
Griffith, Andy/TV Show Songs	Song, Theme Andy Griffith Show	CD	Capitol	72435-23246-2-0	U.S.A.	2000	8.99
Grimes, Carol	Daydreams & Danger	CD	Line	INCD-9.00539-0	Germany	1988	13.99
Grimes, Carol	Eyes Wide Open	CD	Line	INCD-9.00329-0	Germany	1987	13.99
Grimes, Carol	Heart In My Hands	CD Single	Line	INCD-9.00820-E	Germany	1989	4.99
Grimes, Carol	Why Don't They Dance	CD	Line	INCD-9.00668-0	Germany	1989	13.99
Grisman, David	Hot Dawg (MFSL Gold Cd)	CD	Mobile Fidelity	UDCD-506	U.S.A.	1979	99.99
Grobschnitt	Self Titled	CD	Repertoire	PMS-7093	Germany	1972	12.99
Grobschnitt	Solar Music-Live	CD	Repertoire	PMS-7096	Germany	1978	12.99
Groovegrass Boyz/B Collins	Groovegrass 101 (Wiesman/Watson)	CD	Reprise	9-47238-2	U.S.A.	1998	7.99
Grossman, Stefan	Hot Dogs	CD	Line Records	TACD-9.01237-0	Germany	1993	14.99
Groundhogs	3744 James Road The HTD Ant.	2CD	Castle	CMDDD277	England	2001	17.99
Groundhogs	Back Against The Wall	CD	Thunderbolt	CDTB-111	England	2002	9.99
Groundhogs	Back Against The Wall	CD	Demi Monde	CDTL-005	England	1987	8.99
Groundhogs	Back Against The Wall	2CD	Alchemy	PILOT-84	England	2001	19.99
Groundhogs	BBC Radio 1 Live In Concert	CD	Strange Fruit	SFRSCD106	U.S.A.	2002	14.99
Groundhogs	BBC Radio One. Live In Concert	CD	Windsong	WINCD-064	England	1994	14.99
Groundhogs	Best 1969-72	CD	One Way	OW-18201	U.S.A.	1995	8.99
Groundhogs	Best 1969-72	CD	EMI	CDP-7-90434-2	England	1990	7.99
Groundhogs	Black Diamond/Crosscut Saw	CD	BGO	BGOCD131	England	1994	13.99
Groundhogs	Blues Obituary	CD	BGO	BGOCD6	England	2002	13.99
Groundhogs	Checkin' It Out	CD	Sequel	NEB-CD-850	England	1996	8.99
Groundhogs	Classic Album Cuts 1968-1976	CD	Document	CSAP-CD-112	England	1992	7.99
Groundhogs	Classic Recordings From The 70's	CD	Mooncrest	CRESTCD-049	England	2000	8.99
Groundhogs	Eccentric Man: Live At The Marquee	CD	Prism Leisure	PLATCD-243	England	1993	7.99
Groundhogs	Extremely Live	CD	SPM	SPMCD002	Germany	1988	14.99
Groundhogs	Extremely Live (Hogs Road/Less Trks)	CD	Demi Monde	CDTL-008	England	1988	14.99
Groundhogs	Groundhog Blues	CD	Delta	CD6189	England	1999	8.99
Aroundhogs	Groundhog Night Live	2CD	HTD	HTD-CD-12	England	1993	14.99
Groundhogs	Groundhog Night...Groundhog Live	CD	Griffin	GCD-169-2	U.S.A.	1995	7.99
Groundhogs	Hoggin' The Stage	CD	Receiver	RRCD-207	England	1995	15.99
Groundhogs	Hogs In Wolfs Clothing	CD	HTD	HTD-CD-81	England	1998	7.99

Artist	Title	Format	Label	Catalog No	Country	Released	Value
Groundhogs	Hogs On The Road	CD	Thunderbolt	CDTB-114	England	2002	9.99
Groundhogs	Hogwash + 4	CD	BGO	BGOCD44	England	1996	13.99
Groundhogs	Live At Leeds	CD	Akarma	AK-10	Italy	2003	10.99
Groundhogs	Live At Leeds	CD	EMI	535-554-2	England	2002	10.99
Groundhogs	Live At The Astoria	CD	Talking Elephant	TECD026	England	2001	11.99
Groundhogs	Muddy Waters Songbook	CD	HTD	HTD-CD-91	England	1999	8.99
Groundhogs	Muddy Waters Songbook	CD	Castle	82310-72073-2-1	U.S.A.	1999	8.99
Groundhogs	No Surrender	CD	Magnum	MACD-008	U.S.A.	1995	7.99
Groundhogs	No Surrender	CD	Transatlantic	TRA-CD-328	England	2000	8.99
Groundhogs	No Surrender: Razor's Edge Tour '85	CD	HTD	HTD-CD-86	England	1998	7.99
Groundhogs	On Air - 1970-72	CD	Strange Fruit	SFRSCD053	England	1998	14.99
Groundhogs	Razor's Edge	CD	Blueprint	BP270CD	England	2003	12.99
Groundhogs	Scratching The Surface +4	CD	BGO	BGOCD15	England	2002	13.99
Groundhogs	Scratching/Blues O/Thank C/Split	4CD	EMI	7243-8-34907-2-1	England	1996	34.99
Groundhogs	Solid	CD	Castle	CLACD-266	England	1992	8.99
Groundhogs	Solid	CD	Talking Elephant	TECD025	England	2001	11.99
Groundhogs	Solid +1	CD	Repertoire	REP-4307-WY	Germany	1993	13.99
Groundhogs	Split	CD	Akarma	AK-41	Italy	2003	13.99
Groundhogs	Split	CD	BGO	BGOCD76	England	1996	13.99
Groundhogs	Thank Christ For The Bomb	CD	BGO	BGOCD67	England	1994	13.99
Groundhogs	Thank Christ For The Bomb	CD	Akarma	AK-40	Italy	2003	13.99
Groundhogs	The Best Of	CD	EMI	7243-8-55504-2-3	U.S.A.	1999	8.99
Groundhogs	The HTD Years	CD	HTD	HTD-CD-115	England	2000	14.99
Groundhogs	The Lost Tapes, Vol. 1	CD	Blue Flame	BFBL-004	Italy	2003	17.99
Groundhogs	The Lost Tapes, Vol. 2	CD	Blue Flame	BFBL-005	Italy	2003	17.99
Groundhogs	The Masters: Groundhogs Live!	CD	Eagle	EAB-CD-087	England	2000	7.99
Groundhogs	Who Said Cherry Red?	CD	Indigo	IGOCD-2058	England	1996	8.99
Groundhogs	Who Will Save The World?	CD	BGO	BGOCD77	England	1994	13.99
Groundhogs/John Dummer	John Dummer Band: Nine By Nine + 2	CD	Sanctuary	06076-81270-2	U.S.A.	2003	13.99
Groundhogs/John Lee Hooker	The 1965 London Sessions	CD	Sequel	NEB-CD-657	England	1993	14.99
Groundhogs/Tony McPhee	A Carol For All God's Creatures	CD Single	Loose	LSECDS-30	England	1996	4.99
Groundhogs/Tony McPhee	Bleaching The Blues	CD	HTD	HTD-CD-72	England	1997	7.99
Groundhogs/Tony McPhee	Foolish Pride	CD	HTD	HTD-CD-10	England	1993	7.99
Groundhogs/Tony McPhee	Herbal Mixtures: Please Leave...	CD	Distortions	D-1012	England	1996	12.99
Groundhogs/Tony McPhee	Me And The Devil/Asked For Water..	CD	BGO	BGOCD332	England	1998	14.99
Groundhogs/Tony McPhee	Slide TS Slide	CD	HTD	HTD-CD-26	England	1994	7.99
Groundhogs/Tony McPhee	The Blues & The Beast	CD	Nibelung	Nr. 23013-222	Germany	1991	12.99
Groundhogs/Tony McPhee	Two Sides Of	CD	Castle	CLACD-267	England	1994	14.99
Groundhogs/Various Artists	Best Of A.O.G. (2 Unreleased McPhee)	CD	HTD	HTD-CD-20	England	1994	8.99
Group 87	Group 87 (O'Hearn, Bozzio, Isham)	CD	One Way	OW-32336	U.S.A.	1980	8.99
Gruppo Sportivo	10 Mistakes/Buddy Odor Is A Gas!	CD	Psuedonym	CDP-1067-DD	Holland	2000	11.99
Gruppo Sportivo	Back To 19 Mistakes	CD	Ariola	258.848	Holland	1988	11.99
Gruppo Sportivo	Back To '78 / Copy Copy	CD	Pseudonym	CDP-1068-DD	Holland	2000	11.99
Gruppo Sportivo	Hey Girl	CD	Disky	DC-854242	Holland	1999	7.99
Gruppo Sportivo	I Don't Think So/Click Here	CD Single	Pseudonym	CDSP-1072-DD	Holland	2000	5.99
Gruppo Sportivo	Married With Singles	CD	Pseudonym	CDP-1070-DD	Holland	2000	12.99
Gruppo Sportivo	Pop! Goes the Brain / Design Moderne	CD	Pseudonym	CDP-1069-DD	Holland	2000	11.99
Gruppo Sportivo	Repeatlemania	CD Single	Van	997011-3	U.S.A.	1992	7.99
Gruppo Sportivo	Second Life + 5 (Bonus Cd)	2CD	Amsterdamned	70006-2	Holland	1997	14.99
Gruppo Sportivo	Sing Sing	CD	Van	74321-18410-2	Holland	1994	14.99
Gruppo Sportivo	Sucker Of The Century	CD	Jaws	JAWS-557-2	Holland	1990	22.99
Gruppo Sportivo	Young & Out	2CD	Van	997011-2	Holland	1992	19.99
Gruppo Sportivo/Hans V.	Commercial Break	CD	Van	307.2180.2	Holland	1994	14.99
Gryphon	About As Curious As It Can Be	CD	HUX	HUX-027	England	2002	13.99
Gryphon	Gryphon/Midnight Mushrumps	CD	Essential	ESMCD356	U.S.A.	1996	17.99
Gryphon	Red Queen to Gryphon../Raindance	CD	Essential	ESMCD-460	England	1997	17.99
Gryphon	The Collection	CD	Griffin	GCD-454-2	U.S.A.	1995	14.99
Gryphon	Treason	CD	C-Five	C5CD-602	England	1993	24.99

G

Artist	Title	Format	Label	Catalog No	Country	Released	Value
GTR	GTR	CD	One Way	DRC12968	U.S.A.	1986	13.99
GTR	King Biscuit Flower Hour Live	CD	King Biscuit	70710-88021-2	U.S.A.	1997	9.99
GTR/Max Bacon	From The Banks Of The River Irwell	CD	Blueprint	BP353CD	Austria	2002	19.99
GTR/Max Bacon	The Higher You Climb	CD	Now + Then	NTHEN23	England	1995	30.99
Guadalcanal Diary	2 X 4	CD	Elektra	60752-2	U.S.A.	1987	25.99
Guaraldi, Vince/Trio	A Boy Named Charlie Brown	CD	Fantasy	FCD-8430-2	U.S.A.	1989	8.99
Guaraldi, Vince/Trio	A Charlie Brown Christmas	CD	Fantasy	FCD-8431-2	U.S.A.	1988	8.99
Guaraldi, Vince/Trio	Charlie Brown's Holiday Hits	CD	Fantasy	FCD-9682-2	U.S.A.	1998	12.99
Guaraldi, Vince/Trio	Greatest Hits	CD	Fantasy	FCD-7706-2	U.S.A.	1989	8.99
Guaraldi, Vince/Trio	Oh, Good Grief!	CD	Warner Bros.	1747-2	U.S.A.	1968	8.99
Guem	O Universo Ritmico De Guem	CD	Line	RICD-9.00834-0	Germany	1989	24.99
Guess Who	# 10	CD	RCA	061921-0621-2	Canada	1998	12.99
Guess Who	All This For A Song	CD	Unidisc Music	UBK-4133	Canada	1979	10.99
Guess Who	American Woman + 1	CD	Buddha	74465-99734-2	U.S.A.	2000	8.99
Guess Who	Anthology	2CD	Buddah	82876-54850-2	U.S.A.	2003	18.99
Guess Who	Canned Wheat + 2	CD	Buddah	74465-99763-2	U.S.A.	2000	8.99
Guess Who	Greatest Hits	CD	RCA	07863-67774-2	U.S.A.	1999	8.99
Guess Who	Guess Who's Back?	CD	Unidisc Music	UBK-4132	Canada	2001	10.99
Guess Who	Hey Ho What You Do To Me!	CD	Legend	L-00011	Canada	1997	12.99
Guess Who	I Grandi Del Rock	CD	RCA	74321-13533-2	U.S.A.	1993	10.99
Guess Who	It's Time	CD	Legend	L-00012	Canada	1997	12.99
Guess Who	Liberty	CD	Aquarius	6027-00574-2-5	Canada	1994	8.99
Guess Who	Liberty	CD	Aquarius	Q2-06027	Canada	1998	10.99
Guess Who	Live At The Paramount + 6	CD	Buddah	74465-99753-2	U.S.A.	2000	8.99
Guess Who	Lonely One	CD	Intersound	9158	U.S.A.	1995	12.99
Guess Who	No Strings Attached	CD	SST	SSTCD-265	U.S.A.	1989	19.99
Guess Who	Road Food	CD	RCA	078635-0405-2	Canada	1998	12.99
Guess Who	Rockin'	CD	RCA	061921-0532-2	Canada	1998	12.99
Guess Who	Runnin' Back Thru Canada	2CD	RCA	74321-81182-2	Canada	2001	14.99
Guess Who	Shakin' All Over	CD	Legend	L-00010	Canada	1997	12.99
Guess Who	Shakin' All Over (Vintage Rar. 63/67)	CD	Sundazed	SC-11113	U.S.A.	2001	8.99
Guess Who	Share The Land + 2	CD	Buddah	74465-99762-2	U.S.A.	2000	8.99
Guess Who	So Long Bannatyne	CD	RCA	061921-0615-2	Canada	1998	12.99
Guess Who	The Best Of	CD	RCA	3662-2-R	U.S.A.	1971	7.99
Guess Who	The Best Of Volume 2	CD	RCA	CCD-7066	Canada	1998	12.99
Guess Who	The Guess Who Collection	2CD	RCA	BG2-61077	U.S.A.	1988	13.99
Guess Who	The Spirit Lives On (Enhanced CD)	CD	J-Bird	6-1476-80206-2	U.S.A.	1998	7.99
Guess Who	The Ultimate Collection	3CD	RCA	07863-67300-2	U.S.A.	1997	19.99
Guess Who	The Way They Were +2	CD	Magic	30047	France	2001	14.99
Guess Who	This Time Long Ago	2CD	Legend	L-00013	Canada	1997	14.99
Guess Who	Track Record	2CD	RCA	KCD2-7115	U.S.A.	1991	13.99
Guess Who	Wheatfield Soul	CD	RCA	4141-2-R	U.S.A.	1968	12.99
Guess Who/Burton Cummings	Burton Cummings + 1	CD	Epic	EK-65972	U.S.A.	2000	9.99
Guess Who/Burton Cummings	Dream Of A Child + 2	CD	Epic	EK-65970	U.S.A.	2000	9.99
Guess Who/Burton Cummings	My Own Way To Rock + 2	CD	Epic	EK-65969	U.S.A.	2000	9.99
Guess Who/Burton Cummings	Up Close And Alone	CD	Hip O	HIPD-40067	U.S.A.	1997	7.99
Guess Who/Burton Cummings	Woman Love + 2	CD	Epic	EK-65971	U.S.A.	2000	9.99
Gunn, Trey	One Thousand Years	CD	Discipline	DR-9302-2	U.S.A.	1993	8.99
Gunn, Trey Band	Live Encounter	CD	First World	0113	U.S.A.	2001	11.99
Gunn, Trey Band	The Joy Of Molybdenum	CD	Discipline Global	DGM0001	U.S.A.	2000	11.99
Guns 'N Roses	Ain't It Fun	CD	Geffen	GFSTD-62	England	1993	5.99
Guns 'N Roses	Appetite For Destruction	CD	Geffen	9-24148-2	U.S.A.	1987	8.99
Guns 'N Roses	Appetite For Destruction	CD	MCA Victor	MVCG-19304	Japan	1987	29.99
Guns 'N Roses	Appetite For Destruction (Edited)	CD	Geffen	9-24211-2	U.S.A.	1987	7.99
Guns 'N Roses	Appetite For Destruction (MFSL Gold)	CD	Mobile Fidelity	UDCD-699	U.S.A.	1997	54.99
Guns 'N Roses	Dead Horse	CD Single	Geffen	PRO-CD-4511	U.S.A.	1993	19.99
Guns 'N Roses	Dead Horse (Promo)	CD Single	Geffen	PRO-CD-4511	U.S.A.	1993	14.99
Guns 'N Roses	Don't Cry (Promo)	CD Single	Geffen	MVDG-1	Japan	1991	24.99

G

Artist	Title	Format	Label	Catalog No	Country	Released	Value
Guns 'N Roses	Don't Cry (Promo)	CD Single	Geffen	PRO-CD-4232	Japan	1991	14.99
Guns 'N Roses	Estranged (Promo)	CD Single	Geffen	PRO-CD-4497	U.S.A.	1993	14.99
Guns 'N Roses	Explosive In Store Play (Promo)	CD	Geffen	PRO-CD-4602	U.S.A.	1994	24.99
Guns 'N Roses	G 'N R Lies	CD	Geffen	9-24198-2	U.S.A.	1988	13.99
Guns 'N Roses	G 'N R Lies	CD	MCA Victor	MVCG-19305	Japan	1988	29.99
Guns 'N Roses	G 'N R Lies (MFSL Gold)	CD	Mobile Fidelity	UDCD-748	U.S.A.	1988	24.99
Guns 'N Roses	Garden Of Eden (Promo)	CD Single	Geffen	PRO-CD-4366	U.S.A.	1991	49.99
Guns 'N Roses	Greatest Hits (Promo Sampler)	CD	Geffen	GNRCDP1	England	2004	29.99
Guns 'N Roses	Knockin' On Heaven's Door (Promo)	CD Single	Geffen	PRO-CD-4140	U.S.A.	1990	24.99
Guns 'N Roses	Live And Let Die (Promo)	CD Single	Geffen	PRO-CD-4352	U.S.A.	1991	7.99
Guns 'N Roses	Live And Let Die (Promo)	CD Single	Geffen	MVDG-6	Japan	1991	24.99
Guns 'N Roses	Live Era '87-'93 (Promo Sampler)	CD	Interscope	INT5P-6734	U.S.A.	1999	9.99
Guns 'N Roses	Live Era '87-'93 (W/Bonus)	2CD	MCA Victor	MVCF-30005/6	Japan	1999	44.99
Guns 'N Roses	Live Era: '87-'93	2CD	Geffen	06069-490514-2-6	U.S.A.	1999	9.99
Guns 'N Roses	Live Era: '87-'93 [Clean]	2CD	Interscope	6069-490551-2	U.S.A.	1999	8.99
Guns 'N Roses	Nightrain (Promo)	CD Single	Geffen	PRO-CD-3625	U.S.A.	1987	19.99
Guns 'N Roses	November Rain (Promo)	CD Single	Geffen	PRO-CD-4387	U.S.A.	1992	12.99
Guns 'N Roses	On Tour Now !!	CD	Geffen	PRO-CD-4441	U.S.A.	1991	24.99
Guns 'N Roses	Patience (Promo)	CD Single	Geffen	PRO-CD-3437	U.S.A.	1988	24.99
Guns 'N Roses	Selections/Use Your Illusion 1/2 (DJ)	CD	Geffen	PRO-CD-4328	U.S.A.	2000	24.99
Guns 'N Roses	Since I Don't Have You (Promo)	CD Single	Geffen	PRO-CD-4610	U.S.A.	1993	7.99
Guns 'N Roses	Sweet Child O' Mine (Promo)	CD Single	Geffen	PRO-CD-3147	U.S.A.	1987	49.99
Guns 'N Roses	Sympathy For The Devil	CD Single	MCA Victor	MVCG-10001	Japan	1994	5.99
Guns 'N Roses	The Spaghetti Incident ?	CD	Geffen	GEFD-24617	U.S.A.	1993	6.99
Guns 'N Roses	The Spaghetti Incident?	CD	MCA Victor	MVCG-19306	Japan	1997	29.99
Guns 'N Roses	Use You Illusion I	CD	Geffen	GEFD-24415	U.S.A.	1991	9.99
Guns 'N Roses	Use You Illusion I	CD	MCA Victor	MVCG-43	Japan	1991	29.99
Guns 'N Roses	Use Your Illusion (Best Of 1/2)	CD	Geffen	7206-4-24463-2	U.S.A.	2002	8.99
Guns 'N Roses	Use Your Illusion I (MFSL Gold)	CD	Mobile Fidelity	UDCD-711	U.S.A.	1997	54.99
Guns 'N Roses	Use Your Illusion II	CD	MCA Victor	MVCG-44	Japan	1991	29.99
Guns 'N Roses	Use Your Illusion II	CD	Geffen	GEFD-24420	U.S.A.	1991	9.99
Guns 'N Roses	Use Your Illusion II (MFSL Gold)	CD	Mobile Fidelity	UDCD-712	U.S.A.	1997	54.99
Guns 'N Roses	Welcome To The Jungle (Promo)	CD Single	Geffen	PRO-CD-2668	U.S.A.	1987	39.99
Guns 'N Roses	Yesterdays (Promo)	CD Single	Geffen	PRO-CD-4470	U.S.A.	1992	14.99
Guns 'N Roses/Duff McKagan	Believe In Me	CD	Geffen	GEFD-24605	U.S.A.	1993	8.99
Guns 'N Roses/Izzy Stradlin	117 Degrees	CD	Geffen	25202-2	U.S.A.	1998	5.99
Guns 'N Roses/Izzy Stradlin	117 Degrees	CD	Geffen	GEFD25202	Australia	1998	9.99
Guns 'N Roses/Izzy Stradlin	117 Degrees + 2	CD	MCA Victor	MVCF-24027	Japan	1998	34.99
Guns 'N Roses/Izzy Stradlin	And The Ju Ju Hounds	CD	Geffen	GEFD-24490	U.S.A.	1992	7.99
Guns 'N Roses/Izzy Stradlin	On Down The Road	CD	Victor Ent.	VICP-61913	Japan	2002	29.99
Guns 'N Roses/Izzy Stradlin	Pressure Drop	CD Single	Geffen	GFSTD25	England	1993	6.99
Guns 'N Roses/Izzy Stradlin	Ride On	CD	MCA Victor	MVCL-24020	Japan	1999	29.99
Guns 'N Roses/Izzy Stradlin	River	CD	Victor Ent.	VICP-61366	Japan	2000	34.99
Guns 'N Roses/Izzy Stradlin	River	CD	Sanctuary	SANCD076	England	2001	9.99
Gurvitz, Adrian	Acoustic Heart	CD	Playfull	10011-2	U.S.A.	1999	8.99
Gurvitz, Adrian	Classic + 1	CD	EMI	5251362	France	2000	22.99
Gurvitz, Adrian/3 Man Army	A Third Of A Lifetime + 3	CD	Repertoire	RR-4071-WZ	Germany	1990	11.99
Gurvitz, Adrian/Gun	Gun + 4	CD	Repertoire	REP-4840-WZ	Germany	2000	13.99
Gurvitz, Adrian/Gun	Gunsight + 3	CD	Repertoire	REP-4841-WZ	Germany	2000	13.99
Guthrie, Arlo	Alice's Restuarant	CD	Reprise	6267-2	U.S.A.	1967	7.99
Guthrie, Arlo	Alice's Restuarant Revisited	CD	Koch	KOC-CD-7959	U.S.A.	1996	8.99
Guthrie, Arlo	Amigo	CD	Koch	KOC-CD-7954	U.S.A.	1998	8.99
Guthrie, Arlo	Arlo Guthrie	CD	Koch	KOC-CD-7953	U.S.A.	1997	8.99
Guthrie, Arlo	Power Of Love	CD	Rising Son	RSR-CD-3558	U.S.A.	1981	19.99
Aruthrie, Arlo	Running Down The Road	CD	Koch	KOC-CD-7949	U.S.A.	1997	8.99
Guthrie, Arlo	Someday	CD	Rising Son	RSR-CD-0001	U.S.A.	1986	19.99
Guthrie, Joady	Spys On Wall St	CD	Line	RBCD-9.00585-0	Germany	1989	12.99
Guy, Buddy/Junior Wells	Drinkin' TNT (B Wyman, Dallas Taylor)	CD	Blind Pig	BP71182	U.S.A.	1988	11.99

G

Artist	Title	Format	Label	Catalog No	Country	Released	Value

H

Artist	Title	Format	Label	Catalog No	Country	Released	Value
H.P. Lovecraft	Two Classic Albums From	CD	Collector's Choice	CCM-139-2	U.S.A.	2000	13.99
Hackett, Steve	A Midsummer Night's Dream	CD	Angel	7243-5-56348-2-5	U.S.A.	1997	8.99
Hackett, Steve	Bay Of Kings + 20 MP3's	CD	Camino	CAMCD08	England	1983	8.99
Hackett, Steve	Blues With A... + 20 Bonus MP3's	CD	Camino	CAMCD13	England	1994	8.99
Hackett, Steve	Cured	CD	Caroline	CAROL-1858-2	U.S.A.	1981	8.99
Hackett, Steve	Darktown + 2	CD	Mercury	PHCW-1027	Japan	1999	29.99
Hackett, Steve	Defector	CD	Charisma	VDSCD-4018	England	1989	8.99
Hackett, Steve	Feedback 86	CD	Camino	CAMCD21	England	2000	8.99
Hackett, Steve	Genesis Files	2CD	Snapper	SMD-CD-382	England	2002	17.99
Hackett, Steve	Guitar Noir + 5	CD	Camino	CAMCD12	England	1993	8.99
Hackett, Steve	Highly Strung	CD	Charisma	HACKCD1	England	1989	8.99
Hackett, Steve	Live Archive (Box Set)	5CD	Camino	10MCD-090	England	2001	39.99
Hackett, Steve	Momentum	CD	Herald	HER-009	U.S.A.	1994	8.99
Hackett, Steve	Please Don't Touch	CD	Caroline	CAROL-1861-2	U.S.A.	1978	8.99
Hackett, Steve	Spectral Mornings	CD	Charisma	CDSCD4017	England	1989	9.99
Hackett, Steve	The Tokyo Tapes	CD	Camino	1-5567-2	England	1999	24.99
Hackett, Steve	The Unauthorised Biography	CD	Virgin	CDVM-9014	England	1992	12.99
Hackett, Steve	There Are Many Sides To The Night	CD	Camino	CAMCD14	England	1994	9.99
Hackett, Steve	Till We Have Faces + 20 Bonus MP3's	CD	Camino	CAMCD09	England	1984	8.99
Hackett, Steve	Time Lapse + 20 Bonus MP3's	CD	Camino	CAMCD11	England	1990	10.99
Hackett, Steve	Voyage Of The Acolyte	CD	Caroline	CAROL-1863-2	U.S.A.	1975	10.99
Hackett, Steve	Watcher Of Skies Genesis Revisited	CD	Guardian	7243-8-21943-2-3	U.S.A.	1996	10.99
Hackett, Steve/John H.	Sketches Of Satie	CD	Camino	CAMCD20	England	2000	12.99
Hagar, Sammy	36 All-Time Greatest Hits	3CD	EMI	72435-21097-2-2	U.S.A.	1999	19.99
Hagar, Sammy	All Night Long	CD	One Way	72438-19094-23	U.S.A.	1996	13.99
Hagar, Sammy	Both Sides Now (Promo)	CD Single	Track Factory	TRK5P-90091	U.S.A.	1997	5.99
Hagar, Sammy	Classic Masters	CD	Capitol	7243-5-41798-2-2	U.S.A.	2002	8.99
Hagar, Sammy	Danger Zone	CD	Toshiba-EMI	TOCP-7516	Japan	1992	14.99
Hagar, Sammy	Danger Zone	CD	BGO	BGOCD281	England	1995	11.99
Hagar, Sammy	Deeper Kinder Love (Promo)	CD Single	Beyond	BYDJ-78174-2	U.S.A.	2000	5.99
Hagar, Sammy	Give To Live (Promo)	CD Single	Geffen	PRO-CD-2750	U.S.A.	1987	9.99
Hagar, Sammy	Greatest Hits Live	CD	EMI	72435-36820-2-6	U.S.A.	2002	5.99
Hagar, Sammy	Hallelujah (Promo)	CD Single	Sanctuary	SANDJ-85553-2	U.S.A.	2003	13.99
Hagar, Sammy	High Hopes	CD Single	Geffen	PRO-CD-4616	U.S.A.	1994	5.99
Hagar, Sammy	I Can't Drive 65	CD Single	Hybrid	PRCD-300709	U.S.A.	2001	24.99
Hagar, Sammy	I Never Said Goodbye	CD	Geffen	9-24144-2	Germany	1987	13.99
Hagar, Sammy	Kama (Promo)	CD Single	Track Factory	TRK5P-4095	Taiwan	1997	15.99
Hagar, Sammy	Let Sally Drive	CD Single	Beyond	BYDJ-78173-2	U.S.A.	2000	5.99
Hagar, Sammy	Little White Lies	CD Single	Track Factory	TRD-49036	EU	1997	7.99
Hagar, Sammy	Little White Lies	CD Single	MCA Victor	MVCE-9002	Japan	1997	14.99
Hagar, Sammy	Little White Lies (Promo)	CD Single	Track Factory	TRK5P-3964	U.S.A.	1997	5.99
Hagar, Sammy	Live 1980	CD	Capitol	CDP-7-48432-2	U.S.A.	1983	14.99
Hagar, Sammy	Live 1980 + 1	CD	One Way	72438-19093-24	U.S.A.	1996	15.99
Hagar, Sammy	Live And Raw In Cabo (Promo)	CD Single	Beyond	BYDJ-78166-2	U.S.A.	2000	9.99
Hagar, Sammy	Live And Raw In Cabo (Promo)	CD Single	Beyond	BYDJ-78167-2	U.S.A.	2000	9.99
Hagar, Sammy	Live From St. Louis (Limited Ed/Promo)	CD	Sanctuary	SANDJ-85568-2	U.S.A.	2003	24.99
Hagar, Sammy	Live Hallelujah	CD	Sanctuary	06076-84608-2	U.S.A.	2003	15.99
Hagar, Sammy	Live In Cabo (Best Buy/Promo)	CD Single	Track Factory	TRK5P-4368	U.S.A.	1999	13.99
Hagar, Sammy	Live: Loud And Clear	CD	BGO	BGOCD149	England	1992	12.99
Hagar, Sammy	Looking Back	CD	Geffen	32XD-563	Japan	1986	40.99
Hagar, Sammy	Marching To Mars	CD	Track Factory	TRD-11627	EU	1997	9.99
Hagar, Sammy	Marching To Mars (Promo)	CD Single	Track Factory	TRK5P-4011	U.S.A.	1997	5.99

Artist	Title	Format	Label	Catalog No	Country	Released	Value
Hagar, Sammy	Marching To Mars + 2	CD	MCA Victor	MVCE-240-10	Japan	1997	21.99
Hagar, Sammy	Mas Tequila (Promo)	CD Single	Track Factory	TRK5P-4304	U.S.A.	1999	5.99
Hagar, Sammy	Mas Tequila (Promo)	CD Single	MCA	155-582-2	EU	1999	7.99
Hagar, Sammy	Masters Of Rock	CD	EMI	7243-5-34694-2-9	EU	2001	12.99
Hagar, Sammy	Musical Chairs	CD	BGO	BGOCD201	England	1996	13.99
Hagar, Sammy	Musical Chairs	CD	Toshiba-EMI	TOCP-8343	Japan	1996	14.99
Hagar, Sammy	Musical Chairs	CD	One Way	72438-19091-26	U.S.A.	1996	13.99
Hagar, Sammy	Nine On A Ten Scale	CD	One Way	72438-19095-22	U.S.A.	1996	13.99
Hagar, Sammy	Nine On A Ten Scale	CD	Repertoire	REP-4869	Germany	2000	13.99
Hagar, Sammy	Nine On A Ten Scale	CD	BGO	BGOCD182	England	1993	13.99
Hagar, Sammy	Not 4 Sale (W/O T-Shirt)	CD	33rd Street	33RD-ST-3315	U.S.A.	2002	9.99
Hagar, Sammy	Not 4 Sale (W/T-Shirt)	CD	33rd Street	33RD-ST-3315	U.S.A.	2002	39.99
Hagar, Sammy	On The Other Hand (Promo)	CD Single	Track Factory	TRK5P-4158	U.S.A.	1998	7.99
Hagar, Sammy	Red Hot Live	CD	Capitol	CDL-57245	Canada	1989	9.99
Hagar, Sammy	Red Voodoo	CD	Track Factory	TRKD-118727	EU	1999	12.99
Hagar, Sammy	Red Voodoo (Advance Promo)	CD	MCA	GEFD-24702DJ	U.S.A.	1999	14.99
Hagar, Sammy	Red Voodoo + 1	CD	MCA Victor	MVCE-24135	Japan	1999	14.99
Hagar, Sammy	Rematch And More	CD	Capitol	CDP-7-46471-2	U.S.A.	1987	24.99
Hagar, Sammy	Right On Right (Promo)	CD Single	Track Factory	TRK5P-4407	U.S.A.	1999	8.99
Hagar, Sammy	Sammy Hagar Returns Home (DJ)	CD	Geffen	PRO-CD-2832	U.S.A.	1987	14.99
Hagar, Sammy	Sammy/Wabo's Live Hallelujah	CD	Sanctuary	MISCD026	EU	2003	18.99
Hagar, Sammy	Sammy/Wabo's Live Hallelujah (DJ)	CD	Sanctuary	MISPRO26	England	2003	24.99
Hagar, Sammy	Sammy/Webo's Live Hallelujah (DJ)	CD	Sanctuary	SANSP-84608-2	U.S.A.	2003	19.99
Hagar, Sammy	Self Tited (Red Album) + 1	CD	One Way	72438-19096-21	U.S.A.	1996	14.99
Hagar, Sammy	Self Titled (Red Album)	CD	BGO	BGOCD181	England	1993	13.99
Hagar, Sammy	Serious Juju	CD Single	Beyond	63985-78160-2	U.S.A.	2000	5.99
Hagar, Sammy	Serious Juju (Promo)	CD Single	Beyond	BYDJ-78154-2	U.S.A.	2000	5.99
Hagar, Sammy	Shag (Promo)	CD Single	Track Factory	TRK5P-4367	U.S.A.	1999	5.99
Hagar, Sammy	Standing Hampton	CD	Geffen	GEFD-02006	Germany	1981	12.99
Hagar, Sammy	Street Machine	CD	Capitol	CDP-748433-2	U.S.A.	1979	10.99
Hagar, Sammy	Ten 13	CD	Beyond	63985-78110-2	U.S.A.	2000	6.99
Hagar, Sammy	The Anthology	CD	Connoisseur	VSOP-CD-207	England	1994	7.99
Hagar, Sammy	The Best Of	CD	EMI	72435-21097-2-2	U.S.A.	1999	8.99
Hagar, Sammy	The Best Of	CD	Disky	DC-881622	Holland	1995	8.99
Hagar, Sammy	The Best Of	CD	Capitol	0777-7-80262-2-8	Holland	1992	9.99
Hagar, Sammy	Three Lock Box	CD	Geffen	2021-1	U.S.A.	1982	8.99
Hagar, Sammy	Three Lock Box	CD	MCA Victor	MVCG-21005	Japan	1982	14.99
Hagar, Sammy	Turn Up The Music	CD	Capitol	S21-56748	U.S.A.	1993	7.99
Hagar, Sammy	Unboxed	CD	Geffen	GED24702	France	1994	8.99
Hagar, Sammy	Unboxed (Promo)	CD	Geffen	GEFD-24702DJ	U.S.A.	1994	12.99
Hagar, Sammy	VOA (Voice Of America)	CD	Geffen	24043-2	U.S.A.	1984	11.99
Hagar, Sammy	VOA (Voice Of America)	CD	MCA Victor	MVCG-21006	Japan	1984	14.99
Hagar, Sammy/HSAS	Through The Fire	CD	Geffen	4023	U.S.A.	1984	9.99
Hagen, Earle	The Andy Griffith Show (Songs From)	CD	Capitol	72435-23246-2-0	U.S.A.	2000	11.99
Haggard, Merle	A Friend In California	CD	Epic	EK-40286	U.S.A.	1986	54.99
Haggard, Merle	Amber Waves Of Grain	CD	Epic	EK-40224	U.S.A.	1985	74.99
Haggard, Merle	Back To The Barrooms	CD	MCA	MCAD-31009	U.S.A.	1980	53.99
Haggard, Merle	Going Where The Lonely Go	CD	Epic	EK-38092	U.S.A.	1990	38.99
Haggard, Merle	Kern River	CD	Epic	EK-39602	U.S.A.	1985	99.99
Haggard, Merle	Ramblin' Fever	CD	MCA	MCAD-1643	U.S.A.	1977	53.99
Haggard, Merle/The Strangers	I'm A Lonesome Fugitive/Mama Tried	CD	BGO	BGOCD328	England	1996	13.99
Hairston, Curtis/B.B.&Q.Band	Self Titled	CD	Atlantic	AMCY-2592	Japan	1986	89.99
Hakmoun, Hassan/Zahar	Trance	CD	Caroline	CAROL-2334-2	U.S.A.	1993	10.99
Halford, Rob/Trent Reznor	Voyeurs	CD	Interscope	INTD-90155	U.S.A.	1998	6.99
Halford/Judas Priest	Live Insurrection + 1	2CD	Victor	VIZP-7	Japan	2001	14.99
Hall & Oates	12 Inch Collection Vol. 1	Mini Lp	BMG Victor	BVCM-37396	Japan	2003	24.99
Hall & Oates	12 Inch Collection Vol. 2	Mini Lp	BMG Victor	BVCM-37438	Japan	2003	24.99
Hall & Oates	Abandoned Lucheonette	CD	Atlantic	SD-19139	U.S.A.	1973	9.99

H

Artist	Title	Format	Label	Catalog No	Country	Released	Value
Hall & Oates	Along The Red Ledge	CD	RCA	07863-66939-2	U.S.A.	1996	14.99
Hall & Oates	Atlantic Collection	CD	Rhino	R2-72205	U.S.A.	1996	9.99
Hall & Oates	Backtracks	CD	Renaissance	RRBT00607	U.S.A.	1999	12.99
Hall & Oates	Beauty On A Back Street	CD	RCA	07863-66938-2	U.S.A.	1996	14.99
Hall & Oates	Best Of-Starting All Over Again	2CD	RCA	74321-52491-2	Germany	1997	21.99
Hall & Oates	Big Bam Boom	CD	RCA	07863-66937-2	U.S.A.	1996	8.99
Hall & Oates	Bigger Than The Both Of Us	CD	RCA	1467-2-R	U.S.A.	1981	13.99
Hall & Oates	Change Of Season + 1	Mini Lp	BMG Victor	BVCM-37299	Japan	2002	24.99
Hall & Oates	Collection	CD	BMG	74321-87021-2	Australia	2001	12.99
Hall & Oates	Daryl Hall And John Oates +2	CD	Buddah	74465-99754-2	U.S.A.	2000	9.99
Hall & Oates	Do It For Love	CD	U-Watch	8269-480100-2-0	U.S.A.	2003	9.99
Hall & Oates	Do It For Love + 1	CD	Victor Ent.	VICP-62198	Japan	2003	29.99
Hall & Oates	Ecstasy On The Edge	CD	Alchemy	PILOT-124	England	2001	11.99
Hall & Oates	Greatest Hits Live	CD	RCA	07863-68094-2	U.S.A.	2001	10.99
Hall & Oates	H20	CD	RCA	PCD1-4383	U.S.A.	1982	7.99
Hall & Oates	H2O	Mini Lp	BMG Victor	BVCM-37294	Japan	2002	24.99
Hall & Oates	Legendary	3CD	BMG	74321-91303-2	Australia	2003	15.99
Hall & Oates	Live At Apollo (Medley Split Into 4 Trks)	Mini Lp	BMG	BVCM-37297	Japan	2002	24.99
Hall & Oates	Live In Concert (WQED)	CD	Push	PSHJC-90203-2	U.S.A.	1998	29.99
Hall & Oates	Marigold Sky + 1	CD	BMG Victor	BVCN-712	Japan	1997	29.99
Hall & Oates	Marigold Sky + 1	CD	Eagle	EAGCD011	Germany	1997	10.99
Hall & Oates	No Goodbye	CD	MMG Inc.	AMCY-185	Japan	1990	91.99
Hall & Oates	Past Times Behind (MFSL Silver Cd)	CD	Mobile Fidelity	MFCD-879	U.S.A.	1986	109.99
Hall & Oates	Promise Ain't Enough	CD Single	Eagle	EAGXSO11	England	1997	10.99
Hall & Oates	Really Smokin'	CD	Thunderbolt	CDTB-122	England	1993	8.99
Hall & Oates	Rich Girl	CD	BMG	74321-62803-2	England	1998	10.99
Hall & Oates	Rock 'N' Soul, Pt. 1: Greatest Hits	CD	RCA	PCD1-4858	U.S.A.	1983	8.99
Hall & Oates	Rock 'N' Soul, Pt. 1: Greatest Hits	Mini Lp	BMG Victor	BVCM-37295	Japan	2002	24.99
Hall & Oates	Romeo Is Bleeding	CD Single	Eagle	EAGXB011	England	1998	10.99
Hall & Oates	Sara Smile (Audio/Video)	2CD	Master Tone	MM511	England	1995	24.99
Hall & Oates	The Ballads Collection	CD	RCA	07863-69390-2	U.S.A.	2001	8.99
Hall & Oates	The Best Of Times: Greatest Hits	CD	BMG Victor	BVCA-679	Japan	1995	24.99
Hall & Oates	The Best Of: Looking Back	CD	BMG	PD-90388	Germany	1991	8.99
Hall & Oates	The Sky Is Falling	CD Single	Eagle	EAGXAO11	England	1998	10.99
Hall & Oates	The Very Best Of	CD	RCA	07863-69319-2	U.S.A.	2001	9.99
Hall & Oates	VH-1 Behind The Music: Collection	CD	RCA	07863-65105-2	England	2002	8.99
Hall & Oates	Voices (MFSL Silver Cd)	CD	Mobile Fidelity	UDCD-530	U.S.A.	1980	29.99
Hall & Oates	War Babies	CD	Atlantic	7567-80779-2	Germany	1998	24.99
Hall & Oates	Whole Oats	CD	Atlantic	SD-7242-2	U.S.A.	1972	24.99
Hall & Oates	Whole Oats	CD	MMG Inc.	AMCY-182	Japan	1990	29.99
Hall & Oates	X-Static +2	CD	Buddah	74465-99755-2	U.S.A.	2000	9.99
Hall & Oates/Chicago	1998 Tour Collector's 2 Cd Set	2CD	Best Buy	2374	U.S.A.	1998	29.99
Hall & Oates/Daryl Hall	3 Hearts/Happy Ending Machine	CD	RCA	PCD1-7196	U.S.A.	1986	11.99
Hall & Oates/Daryl Hall	3 Hearts/Happy Ending Machine	Mini Lp	BMG Victor	BVCM-37301	Japan	2002	24.99
Hall & Oates/Daryl Hall	Can't Stop Dreaming	CD	BMG Victor	BVCP-994	Japan	1996	29.99
Hall & Oates/Daryl Hall	Sacred Songs + 2	CD	Buddah	74465-99604-2	U.S.A.	1999	12.99
Hall & Oates/Daryl Hall	Soul Alone	CD	Epic	EK-53937	U.S.A.	1993	11.99
Hall & Oates/Gulliver	Self Titled (Daryl Hall's First Group)	CD	Collector's Choice	CCM-310-2	U.S.A.	2003	9.99
Hall & Oates/John Oates	All Good People (Phunk Shui + 1)	CD	Liquid 8	12130	U.S.A.	2003	10.99
Hall & Oates/John Oates	Phunk Shui	CD	Beyond	398-578-283-2	U.S.A.	2002	9.99
Hall & Oates/John Oates	Phunk Shui + 1	CD	Teichiku	TECI-24127	Japan	2002	20.99
Hall & Oates/John Oates	Phunk Shui + 3	CD	Phunk Shui	480400	U.S.A.	2003	15.99
Hall, Lani	A & M Classics	CD	Pony Canyon	D32Y3512	Japan	1987	54.99
Halliday, Toni/Curve	Woman In Mind	CD Single	Anxious	013	U.S.A.	1989	207.99
Hamill, Claire	Abracadabra	CD	Blueprint	BP305CD	England	2001	14.99
Hamill, Claire	Love In The Afternoon	CD	Blueprint	BP307CD	England	1999	14.99
Hamill, Claire	October + 1	CD	Blueprint	BP238CD	EU	1997	24.99
Hamill, Claire	Stage Door Johnnies	CD	Blueprint	BP302CD	England	2003	29.99

H

Artist	Title	Format	Label	Catalog No	Country	Released	Value
Hamill, Claire	Summer + 4 (Bonus Cd)	2CD	Blueprint	BP277CD	EU	1998	19.99
Hamill, Claire	Touchpaper	CD	Voiceprint	VP306CD	England	2000	14.99
Hamill, Claire	Voices	CD	Blueprint	BP308CD	England	2001	20.99
Hamlisch, Marvin	The Spy Who Loved Me (O.S.T.)	CD	EMI	7-96211-2	U.S.A.	1977	8.99
Hammer, Jan	Drive (With Jeff Beck)	CD	Miramar	09006-23044-2	U.S.A.	1994	14.99
Hammer, Jan	Escape From Television	CD	MCA	MCAD-42103	U.S.A.	1987	7.99
Hammer, Jan	Miami Vice-The Complete Collection	2CD	One Way	35185	U.S.A.	2002	16.99
Hammer, Jan	Snapshots 1.2	CD	One Way	OW-35171	U.S.A.	2000	5.99
Hammer, Jan/James Young	City Slicker	CD	Line	FBCD-9.00239-0	Germany	1987	16.99
Hammerhead	Heart Made Of Steel	CD	Pseudonym	CDP-1065-DD	Holland	2000	14.99
Hammill, Peter	A Black Box	CD	Caroline	CAROL-1690-2	U.S.A.	1990	9.99
Hammill, Peter	A Black Box	CD	Virgin	CDOVD-140	England	1983	9.99
Hammill, Peter	After The Show: A Collection	CD	Virgin	CDOVD-460	England	1996	14.99
Hammill, Peter	And Close As This	CD	Line	DACD-9.00254-0	Germany	1987	11.99
Hammill, Peter	And Close As This	CD	Virgin	CDV-2409	England	1986	11.99
Hammill, Peter	Chameleon In...	CD	Virgin	CASCD-1067	England	1973	8.99
Hammill, Peter	Chameleon In....	CD	Caroline	CAROL-1691-2	U.S.A.	1990	8.99
Hammill, Peter	Clutch	CD	Fie!	FIE-9127	England	2002	11.99
Hammill, Peter	Enter K	CD	Fie!	FIE-9101	England	1992	10.99
Hammill, Peter	Everyone You Hold	CD	Discipline Global	DGM-9117	U.S.A.	1997	8.99
Hammill, Peter	Everyone You Hold	CD	Fie!	FIE-9117	England	1997	10.99
Hammill, Peter	Fall Of The House Of Usher	CD	Fie!	FIE-9121	England	1999	17.99
Hammill, Peter	Fireships	CD	Fie!	FIE-9103	England	1992	10.99
Hammill, Peter	Fix On The Mix	CD Single	Golden Hind	CD-GH-70072	Germany	1994	10.99
Hammill, Peter	Fool's Mate	CD	Virgin	CASCD-1037	England	1971	8.99
Hammill, Peter	Fool's Mate	CD	Caroline	CAROL-1697-2	U.S.A.	1990	8.99
Hammill, Peter	Fool's Mate/In Camera	2CD	Virgin	581-7482	England	2003	14.99
Hammill, Peter	In A Foreign Town	CD	Line	DACD-9.00685-0	Germany	1988	13.99
Hammill, Peter	In A Foreign Town	CD	Fie!	FIE-9108	England	1994	11.99
Hammill, Peter	In Camera	CD	Caroline	CAROL-1629-2	U.S.A.	1990	8.99
Hammill, Peter	In Camera	CD	Virgin	CASCD-1089	England	1974	18.99
Hammill, Peter	Loops & Reels	CD	Fie!	FIE-9105	England	1993	9.99
Hammill, Peter	Margin + Live	2CD	Fie!	FIE-9125	England	2001	14.99
Hammill, Peter	Nadir's Big Chance	CD	Caroline	CAROL-1630-2	U.S.A.	1990	8.99
Hammill, Peter	Nadir's Big Chance	CD	Virgin	CASCD-1099	England	1975	8.99
Hammill, Peter	None Of Above	CD	Fie!	FIE-9122	England	2000	17.99
Hammill, Peter	Offensichtlich Goldfish	CD	Golden Hind	CD-GH-70112	Germany	1999	12.99
Hammill, Peter	Out Of Water	CD	Enigma	73540-2	U.S.A.	1990	12.99
Hammill, Peter	Out Of Water	CD	Fie!	FIE-9109	England	1994	10.99
Hammill, Peter	Over	CD	Caroline	CAROL-1849-2	U.S.A.	1991	9.99
Hammill, Peter	Over	CD	Virgin	CASCD-1125	England	1977	9.99
Hammill, Peter	Past Go - Collected	CD	Fie!	FIE-9112	England	1996	8.99
Hammill, Peter	Patience	CD	Fie!	FIE-9102	England	1992	10.99
Hammill, Peter	Ph7	CD	Caroline	CAROL-1696-2	U.S.A.	1990	9.99
Hammill, Peter	Ph7	CD	Virgin	CASCD-1146	England	1979	9.99
Hammill, Peter	Roaring Forties	CD	Fie!	FIE-9107	England	1994	10.99
Hammill, Peter	Room Temperature	2CD	Fie!	FIE-9110	England	1995	13.99
Hammill, Peter	Room Temperature: Live	CD	Enigma	72560-2	U.S.A.	1993	12.99
Hammill, Peter	Sitting Targets	CD	Caroline	CAROL-1695-2	U.S.A.	1990	7.99
Hammill, Peter	Sitting Targets	CD	Virgin	CDV-2203	England	1981	7.99
Hammill, Peter	Skin	CD	Line	DACD-9.00145-0	Germany	1987	11.99
Hammill, Peter	Skin	CD	Virgin	CDOVD-344	England	1986	11.99
Hammill, Peter	Sonix	CD	Fie!	FIE-9114	England	1996	10.99
Hammill, Peter	The Calm (After The Storm)	CD	Virgin	CDVM-9017	England	1993	10.99
Hammill, Peter	The Future Now	CD	Caroline	CAROL-1694-2	U.S.A.	1990	8.99
Hammill, Peter	The Future Now	CD	Virgin	CASCD-1137	England	1978	8.99
Hammill, Peter	The Love Songs	CD	Caroline	CAROL-1692-2	U.S.A.	1990	9.99
Hammill, Peter	The Love Songs	CD	Virgin	CASCD-1166	England	1984	9.99

H

Artist	Title	Format	Label	Catalog No	Country	Released	Value
Hammill, Peter	The Margin/Live	CD	Line	DACD-9.00579-0	Germany	1988	13.99
Hammill, Peter	The Noise	CD	Fie!	FIE-9104	England	1993	10.99
Hammill, Peter	The Peel Sessions	CD	Strange Fruit	SFRCD136	England	1995	14.99
Hammill, Peter	The Silent Corner...	CD	Caroline	CAROL-1693-2	U.S.A.	1990	9.99
Hammill, Peter	The Silent Corner...	CD	Virgin	CASCD-1083	England	1974	9.99
Hammill, Peter	The Storm (Before The Calm)	CD	Virgin	CDVM-9018	England	1993	7.99
Hammill, Peter	The Thin Man Sings Ballads	CD	Fie!	FIE-9126	England	2001	9.99
Hammill, Peter	There Goes The Daylight	CD	Fie!	FIE-9106	England	1993	10.99
Hammill, Peter	This	CD	Fie!	FIE-9118	England	1998	10.99
Hammill, Peter	Tides (Live)	CD	Sine	SIN006	England	1996	12.99
Hammill, Peter	Typical (Solo Performances)	2CD	Fie!	FIE-9119	England	1999	15.99
Hammill, Peter	What Now?	CD	Fie!	FIE-9123	England	2001	10.99
Hammill, Peter	X My Heart	CD	Discipline Global	DGM-9111	U.S.A.	1996	7.99
Hammill, Peter	X My Heart	CD	Fie!	FIE-9111	England	1996	17.99
Hammill, Peter/Guy Evans	Spur Of The Moment	CD	Line	DACD-9.00564-0	Germany	1988	10.99
Hammill, Peter/Guy Evans	The Union Chapel Concert	2CD	Fie!	FIE-9115	England	1997	19.99
Hammill, Peter/Sonix	Unsung	CD	Fie!	FIE-9124	England	2001	17.99
Hammond, Albert	Songsmith + 2	CD	Sony	A-22036	U.S.A.	1990	6.99
Hammond, John	Bluesman!	Mini Lp	Comet	UV-054	U.S.A.	2002	11.99
Hammond, John	Sooner Or Later	CD	Water	WATER-105	U.S.A.	2002	10.99
Hammond, John	Southern Fried (W/Duane Allman)	CD	Water	WATER-106	U.S.A.	2003	10.99
Hampton, Col. Bruce/A R U	And The Aquarium Rescue Unit	CD	Capricorn	9-42000-2	U.S.A.	1992	7.99
Hampton, Col. Bruce/A R U	Mirrors Of Embarrassment	CD	Capricorn	9-42016-2	U.S.A.	1993	7.99
Hanoi Rocks	A Day Late, A Dollar Short (Box/Pin)	CD Single	Victor Ent.	VIZP- 21	Japan	2003	24.99
Hanoi Rocks	All Those Glamourous Years	CD	Mercury	PHCR-1484	Japan	1996	24.99
Hanoi Rocks	All Those Wasted Years	CD	Sanctuary	CMRCD186	England	2001	8.99
Hanoi Rocks	All Those Wasted Years	CD	Mercury	33PD-443	Japan	1985	24.99
Hanoi Rocks	All Those Wasted Years	CD	Geffen	9-24266-2	U.S.A.	1991	8.99
Hanoi Rocks	Back To Mystery City	CD	Mercury	23PD-108	Japan	1983	24.99
Hanoi Rocks	Back To Mystery City	CD	Sanctuary	CMRCD125	England	2001	8.99
Hanoi Rocks	Back To Mystery City	CD	Geffen	9-24265-2	U.S.A.	1989	7.99
Hanoi Rocks	Bangkok Shocks, Saigon Shakes	CD	Sanctuary	CMRCD124	England	2001	8.99
Hanoi Rocks	Bangkok Shocks, Saigon Shakes	CD	Geffen	9-24262-2	U.S.A.	1989	8.99
Hanoi Rocks	Bangkok Shocks, Saigon Shakes + 6	CD	Johanna	JHNCD-2037	Finland	1997	10.99
Hanoi Rocks	Bangkok Shocks... (Different Cover)	CD	Mercury	PHCR-4162	Japan	1996	24.99
Hanoi Rocks	Box Set	4CD	Johanna	JHNCD-2524	Finland	2001	39.99
Hanoi Rocks	Decadent Dangerous Delicious	2CD	Essential	ESACD882	England	2000	14.99
Hanoi Rocks	Dim Sum Ep (Promo)	CD Single	Geffen	PRO-CD-3738	U.S.A.	1989	14.99
Hanoi Rocks	In My Darkest Moment	CD Single	Akashic Rocks	ARCDS-002	Finland	2002	12.99
Hanoi Rocks	Lean On Me	CD	Lick	LIC-CD-11	England	1992	17.99
Hanoi Rocks	Lean On Me	CD	Sanctuary	CMRCD187	England	2001	8.99
Hanoi Rocks	Lean On Me	CD	Mercury	PHCR-5001	Japan	1992	24.99
Hanoi Rocks	Million Miles Away	CD	Mercury	32PD-130	Japan	1985	25.99
Hanoi Rocks	Oriental Beat	CD	Sanctuary	CMRCD185	England	2001	8.99
Hanoi Rocks	Oriental Beat	CD	Geffen	9-24263-2	U.S.A.	1989	9.99
Hanoi Rocks	Oriental Beat + 5	CD	Johanna	JHNCD-2063	Finland	1997	10.99
Hanoi Rocks	People Like Me	CD Single	Victor Ent.	VICP- 62090	Japan	2002	15.99
Hanoi Rocks	People Like Me (Gold CD)	CD Single	Akashic Rocks	ARCDS-001	Finland	2002	17.99
Hanoi Rocks	People Like Me (Promo)	CD Single	Akashic Rocks	ARPRCD-001	Finland	2002	12.99
Hanoi Rocks	Self Destruction Blues	CD	Mercury	23PD-107	Japan	1982	24.99
Hanoi Rocks	Self Destruction Blues	CD	Sanctuary	CMRCD126	England	2001	8.99
Hanoi Rocks	Self Destruction Blues	CD	Geffen	9-24264-2	U.S.A.	1989	8.99
Hanoi Rocks	Story	CD	Mercury	PPD-3086	Japan	1990	44.99
Hanoi Rocks	Strange Boys Play Weird Openings	4CD	Mercury	PHCR 3109~12	Japan	1991	54.99
Hanoi Rocks	The Best Of	CD	Lick	LIC-CD8	England	1985	13.99
Hanoi Rocks	The Collection	CD	AAB	AABCD-4	Finland	1989	11.99
Hanoi Rocks	Tracks From A Broken Dream	CD	Nippon Phonogram	PHCR-2	Japan	1990	29.99
Hanoi Rocks	Tracks From A Broken Dream	CD	Lick	LIC-CD-10	England	1990	19.99

H

Artist	Title	Format	Label	Catalog No	Country	Released	Value
Hanoi Rocks	Twelve Shots On The Rocks	CD	Victor Ent.	VICP- 62120	Japan	2002	21.99
Hanoi Rocks	Twelve Shots On The Rocks (Promo)	CD	Liquor/Poker	6002-2	U.S.A.	2003	9.99
Hanoi Rocks	Twelve Shots On The Rocks + 1	CD	Seoul	SRCD-2639	Korea	2003	21.99
Hanoi Rocks	Two Steps From The Move	CD	Mercury	23PD-109	Japan	1984	24.99
Hanoi Rocks	Two Steps From The Move + 8	CD	Columbia	471-417-2	England	1984	14.99
Hanoi Rocks	Two Steps From... (Ian Hunter)	CD	Epic	EK-39614	U.S.A.	1984	11.99
Hanoi Rocks	Up Around The Bend: Def. Coll.	2CD	Sanctuary	SMEDD002	England	2004	14.99
Hanoi Rocks	Up Around the Bend: Super Best	CD	Mercury	PPD-1044	Japan	1985	8.99
Hanoi Rocks/Andy McCoy	Aspects Of	2CD	Polarvox	WISHCD-50	Finland	1995	44.99
Hanoi Rocks/Andy McCoy	Briard (W/ Pete Malmi)	CD Single	BMG	74321-41760-2	Finland	1996	24.99
Hanoi Rocks/Andy McCoy	Building On Tradition	CD	Avex	AVCM-65008	Japan	1995	24.99
Hanoi Rocks/Andy McCoy	Building On Tradition	CD	AMT	AMTCD-2069	Finland	1995	14.99
Hanoi Rocks/Andy McCoy	Building On Tradition	CD	Revenge	MIG-59	France	1996	14.99
Hanoi Rocks/Andy McCoy	F*ck The Army (W/Pete Malmi)	CD Single	BMG	74321-41777-2	Finland	1996	24.99
Hanoi Rocks/Andy McCoy	Foxfield Junction (No Pic Sleeve/DJ)	CD Single	AMT	AMTPROMO-215	Finland	1995	24.99
Hanoi Rocks/Andy McCoy	Let It Rock	CD Single	AMT	AMTXCD-218	Finland	1995	24.99
Hanoi Rocks/Andy McCoy	R' N' R Memorabilia - Best Solo Tracks	CD	Capitol	7243-5-91591-2-6	Finland	2003	34.99
Hanoi Rocks/Andy McCoy	Strung Out (No Picture Sleeve)	CD Single	AMT	AMTXCD-214	Finland	1995	24.99
Hanoi Rocks/Andy McCoy	The Real McCoy (O.S.T.)	CD	Megamania	1000-121072	Finland	1999	34.99
Hanoi Rocks/Andy McCoy	Too Far Gone (3")	CD Single	H.I.T. Ave.	10GD-5017	Japan	1988	24.99
Hanoi Rocks/Andy McCoy	Too Much Ain't Enough	CD	H.I.T. Ave.	32GD-7016	Japan	1988	24.99
Hanoi Rocks/Andy McCoy	Too Much Ain't Enough	CD	Amulet	WISHCD6	Finland	1988	24.99
Hanoi Rocks/Andy McCoy	Too Much Ain't Enough (3")	CD Single	H.I.T. Ave.	10GD-5021	Japan	1988	24.99
Hanoi Rocks/Cherry Bombz	Coming Down Slow + 2	CD	High Dragon	HD-CD-201	France	1987	34.99
Hanoi Rocks/Cherry Bombz	House Of Ecstasy	CD	Nippon Phonogram	PHCR-4222	Japan	1986	44.99
Hanoi Rocks/Michael Monroe	Dead, Jail Or Rock 'N' Roll	CD Single	Mercury	876-193-2	Germany	1989	5.99
Hanoi Rocks/Michael Monroe	Dead, Jail Or Rock 'N' Roll (3")	CD Single	Mercury	PPDS-15	Japan	1989	24.99
Hanoi Rocks/Michael Monroe	Demolition 23	CD	Renagade Nations	PHCR-1260	Japan	1994	24.99
Hanoi Rocks/Michael Monroe	Demolition 23	CD	Music For Nations	CDMFN-176	England	1995	14.99
Hanoi Rocks/Michael Monroe	Demolition 23 - Nothin's Allright (3")	CD Single	Renagade Nations	PHDR-907	Japan	1994	24.99
Hanoi Rocks/Michael Monroe	Jerusalem Slim	CD	Mercury	514-680-2	Germany	1992	24.99
Hanoi Rocks/Michael Monroe	Life Gets You Dirty	CD	Nippon Crown	CRCL-4735	Japan	1995	24.99
Hanoi Rocks/Michael Monroe	Life Gets You Dirty	CD	SPV	SPV085-21522CD	Germany	1999	11.99
Hanoi Rocks/Michael Monroe	Magic Carpet Ride (W/ Slash) 3" Cd	CD Single	Warner Bros.	WPDP-6336	Japan	1993	24.99
Hanoi Rocks/Michael Monroe	Magic Carpet Ride (W/ Slash) Promo	CD Single	Warner Bros.	PRO-CD-6391	U.S.A.	1993	7.99
Hanoi Rocks/Michael Monroe	Man With No Eyes	CD Single	Vertigo	VERCD46	England	1990	12.99
Hanoi Rocks/Michael Monroe	Man With No Eyes	CD Single	Mercury	876-739-2	Germany	1990	12.99
Hanoi Rocks/Michael Monroe	Man With No Eyes (3")	CD Single	Mercury	PHDR-4	Japan	1990	24.99
Hanoi Rocks/Michael Monroe	Man With No Eyes (Promo)	CD Single	Mercury	CDP-193	U.S.A.	1989	7.99
Hanoi Rocks/Michael Monroe	Nights Are So Long	CD	Mercury	PHCR-4521	Japan	1997	34.99
Hanoi Rocks/Michael Monroe	Not Fakin' It	CD	Lemon	CDLEM10	England	2003	10.99
Hanoi Rocks/Michael Monroe	Not Fakin' It	CD	Mercury	838-627-2	U.S.A.	1989	10.99
Hanoi Rocks/Michael Monroe	Not Fakin' It	CD	Nippon Phonogram	PPD-1045	Japan	1989	16.99
Hanoi Rocks/Michael Monroe	Not Fakin' It (Promo Sampler)	CD	Mercury	CDP-107	U.S.A.	1989	14.99
Hanoi Rocks/Michael Monroe	Peace Of Mind	CD	Dead Line	CLP-0830-2	U.S.A.	2000	6.99
Hanoi Rocks/Michael Monroe	Peace Of Mind	CD	Mercury	PHCR-1457	Japan	1998	24.99
Hanoi Rocks/Michael Monroe	She's No Angel (3")	CD Single	Mercury	PPDS-20	Japan	1989	24.99
Hanoi Rocks/Michael Monroe	Stranded	CD Single	Ranch	RANCH-03	Finland	2003	24.99
Hanoi Rocks/Michael Monroe	Take Them And Break Them EP	CD Single	Nippon Crown	CRCL-4804	Japan	2002	24.99
Hanoi Rocks/Michael Monroe	Whatcha Want	CD	Nippon Crown	CRCL-4812	Japan	2003	29.99
Hanoi Rocks/Michael Monroe	Whatcha Want (Promo/Slipcase)	CD	SPV	085-7473-2-P	Germany	2002	19.99
Hanoi Rocks/Michael Monroe	While You Were Looking At Me	CD Single	Mercury	CDP-224	U.S.A.	1990	12.99
Hanoi Rocks/Monroe/McCoy	Yahoo! (W/Nasty Suicide/Sam Yaffa)	CD	Yahoo	YAHOOCD-2	Finland	1988	34.99
Hanoi Rocks/Shooting Gallery	House Of Ecstasy (Promo)	CD Single	Mercury	CDP-648	U.S.A.	1992	7.99
Hanoi Rocks/Shooting Gallery	Self Titled	CD	Nippon Phonogram	PHCR-1167	Japan	1992	16.99
Hanoi Rocks/Shooting Gallery	Self Titled	CD	Mercury	314-512-184-2	Canada	1992	7.99
Hanoi Rocks/Shooting Gallery	Self Titled (Promo)	CD	Mercury	SACD-479	U.S.A.	1992	9.99
Hanoi Rocks/Shooting Gallery	Teenage Breakdown (Promo)	CD Single	Mercury	CDP-713	U.S.A.	1992	7.99

H

Artist	Title	Format	Label	Catalog No	Country	Released	Value
Hanoi Rocks/Suicide Twins	Silver Missles And The Nightengales	CD	Essential	ESM-CD-276	England	1995	8.99
Hansson, Bo	Attic Thoughts	CD	Silence	SRSCD-3625	Sweden	1995	12.99
Hansson, Bo	Lord Of The Rings + 1	CD	Virgin	07243-812061-2-6	England	2002	11.99
Hansson, Bo	Lord Of The Rings + 1	CD	Silence	SRSCD-3600	Sweden	2001	12.99
Hansson, Bo	Lord Of The Rings + 11 (Extended)	CD	Nota Blu	NOTABLU936161	EEC	1993	22.99
Hansson, Bo	Magicians Hat + 2	CD	Silence	SRSCD-3615	Sweden	2002	12.99
Hansson, Bo/Karlsson	Hansson & Karlsson	CD	Polydor	557-279-2	Germany	1998	12.99
Hansson, Jonas	Classica	CD	Marquee	MICY-1120	Japan	1999	27.99
Hansson, Jonas	No. 1	CD	Apollon	APCY-8172	Japan	1994	27.99
Happy The Man	Live	CD	Cuneiform	CUNE-55014	U.S.A.	1999	15.99
Happy The Man	3rd "Better Late..."	CD	Cuneiform	55001	U.S.A.	1990	12.99
Happy The Man	Beginnings	CD	Cuneiform	55003	U.S.A.	1990	12.99
Happy The Man	Crafty Hands	CD	BMG Victor	ERC-32006	Japan	1988	29.99
Happy The Man	Death's Crown	CD	Cuneiform	55015	U.S.A.	1999	12.99
Happy The Man	Happy The Man	CD	BMG Victor	ERC-32005	Japan	1988	29.99
Happy The Man	Live	CD	Linden	LM-2021	U.S.A.	1994	12.99
Happy The Man	Retrospective	CD	East Side Digital	ESD80292	U.S.A.	1989	19.99
Hapshash/Coloured Coat	Feat. Human Host/Heavy Metal Kids	CD	Repertoire	REP-4404-WY	Germany	2002	14.99
Hapshash/Coloured Coat	Feat. Human Host/Heavy Metal Kids	CD	Akarma	AKCD-204	Italy	2003	14.99
Hapshash/Coloured Coat	Western Flier	CD	Repertoire	REP-4415-WY	Germany	2002	19.99
Hard Stuff	Bolex Dementia	CD	Line	LICD-9.00385-0	Germany	1988	14.99
Hard Stuff	Bulletproof	CD	Line	LICD-9.00381-0	Germany	1990	16.99
Hardin & York	Best Of Hardin & York: Listen Everyone	CD	Purple	PUR-323	England	2000	17.99
Hardin & York	For The World	CD	Repertoire	REP-4489-WY	Germany	2002	14.99
Hardin & York	Live	CD	Repertoire	REP-4459-WY	Germany	2002	14.99
Hardin & York	Live At The Marquee	CD	RPM	RPM-135	England	1995	11.99
Hardin & York	Live In The 70's	CD	Angel Air	SJPCD016	England	1998	14.99
Hardin & York	Still A Few Pages Left...	CD	RPM	RPM-106	England	1995	19.99
Hardin & York	The World's Smallest Bighand	CD	Repertoire	REP-4482-WY	Germany	2002	14.99
Hardin & York	Tomorrow Today	CD	Repertoire	REP-4481-WY	Germany	2002	14.99
Hardin, Eddie	Wind In The Willows	CD	Purple	PUR-327	England	2002	17.99
Hardin, Eddie	Wind In The Willows Live	CD	Angel Air	SJPCD019	England	1998	12.99
Hardin, Eddie	With Charlie McCraken	CD	Repertoire	REP-4452-WY	Germany	2002	10.99
Hardin, Eddie	Wizard's Convention	2CD	Cleopatra	CLP-0700-2	U.S.A.	1999	19.99
Hardin, Eddie	Wizard's Convention + 2	CD	Purple	PUR-316	England	2003	14.99
Hardin, Eddie	Wizard's Convention + 21	2CD	Eagle	EDM-CD-080	Germany	1999	19.99
Hardin, Eddie	Wizard's Convention + 6	CD	Repertoire	REP-4474-WY	Germany	1994	14.99
Hardin, Eddie	Wizard's Convention, Vol. 2	CD	Resurgent	4153	U.S.A.	1997	14.99
Hardin, Eddie	You Can't Teach An Old Dog...	CD	Repertoire	REP-4464-WY	Germany	1994	29.99
Hardin, Tim	1 / 2	CD	Repertoire	IMS-7030-WP	Germany	1995	19.99
Hardin, Tim	20th Century Masters: The Millennium	CD	Universal	314-016-405-2	U.S.A.	2002	8.99
Hardin, Tim	3 (Live In Concert)	CD	Line	LMCD-9.51073-Z	Germany	1991	24.99
Hardin, Tim	3 Live In Concert + 3	CD	PolyGram	314-527-448-2	U.S.A.	1995	24.99
Hardin, Tim	Bird On A Wire	CD	Columbia	CK-30551	U.S.A.	1989	14.99
Hardin, Tim	Black Sheep Boy: An Introduction To	CD	Polydor	589-812-2	England	2002	11.99
Hardin, Tim	Hang On To A Dream: Verve Records	2CD	Polydor	314-521-583-2	U.S.A.	1994	24.99
Hardin, Tim	Nine	CD	See For Miles	SEE-CD-335	England	1994	14.99
Hardin, Tim	Reason To Believe: Best Of	CD	Polydor	833-954-2	U.S.A.	1987	9.99
Hardin, Tim	Simple Songs	CD	Columbia	CK-64858	U.S.A.	1996	14.99
Hardin, Tim	Suite For Susan.../Bird On A Wire	CD	BGO	BGOCD470	England	2000	14.99
Hardin, Tim	The Essential 1963 - 1980	CD	Raven	RVCD-104	Australia	2000	12.99
Hardin, Tim	The Homecoming Concert	CD	Line	LICD-9.00040-0	Germany	1987	24.99
Hardin, Tim	This Is	CD	Atlantic	80780-2	U.S.A.	1998	11.99
Hardin, Tim	Tim Hardin - 1	CD	Line	LMCD-9.51113-Z	Germany	1991	24.99
Ardin, Tim	Tim Hardin - 2	CD	Line	LMCD-9.51069-Z	Germany	1991	24.99
Hardin, Tim	Tim Hardin - 4	CD	Line	LICD-9.51091-Z	Germany	1991	24.99
Harlequin	Love Crimes	CD	Sony	SRCS-9462	Japan	1980	17.99
Harley, Steve	Live At The BBC	CD	Strange Fruit	SFRSCD-056	England	1998	14.99

H

Artist	Title	Format	Label	Catalog No	Country	Released	Value
Harmonia/Neu!	Deluxe (W/Cluster)	CD	Polydor	POCP-2388	Japan	1975	21.99
Harmonia/Neu!	Musik Von Harmonia (W/Cluster)	CD	Polydor	POCP-2387	Japan	1974	24.99
Harper, Roy	An Introduction To	CD	Science Fiction	HUCD017	Austria	1994	12.99
Harper, Roy	Born In Captivity	CD	Line	OLCD-9.51041-X	Germany	1991	14.99
Harper, Roy	Born In Captivity/Work Of Heart	CD	Science Fiction	HUCD008	England	1995	14.99
Harper, Roy	Bullinamingvase	CD	Science Fiction	HUCD021	Austria	1996	12.99
Harper, Roy	Burn The World Live/Studio	CD	Line	OLCD-9.51047-X	Germany	1991	10.99
Harper, Roy	Come Out Fighting Ghengis Smith	CD	Line	OLCD-9.51054-X	Germany	1991	14.99
Harper, Roy	Commercial Breaks	CD	Science Fiction	HUCD016	Austria	1994	12.99
Harper, Roy	Death Or Glory	CD	Hypertension	HYCD-200-127	Germany	1992	12.99
Harper, Roy	Death Or Glory?	CD	Awareness	AWPD-037	U.S.A.	1992	12.99
Harper, Roy	Descendants Of Smith	CD	EMI	CDP-7-90139-2	England	1988	15.99
Harper, Roy	East Of The Sun	CD	Science Fiction	HUCD034	England	2001	12.99
Harper, Roy	Flashes From The Archives Of Oblivion	CD	Line	OLCD-9.51049-X	Germany	1991	12.99
Harper, Roy	Flat Baroque And Beserk	CD	Science Fiction	HUCD003	Austria	1994	12.99
Harper, Roy	Folkjokeopus	CD	Line	OLCD-9.51043-X	Germany	1991	12.99
Harper, Roy	Gardens Of Uranium/Decendants Of S	CD	Science Fiction	HUCD014	Austria	1994	11.99
Harper, Roy	Hats Off	CD	Right Stuff	7243-5-27640-2-0	U.S.A.	2001	10.99
Harper, Roy	Hats Off	CD	Right Stuff	7243-5-27640-2	U.S.A.	2001	10.99
Harper, Roy	HQ	CD	Science Fiction	HUCD019	Austria	1995	12.99
Harper, Roy	In Between Every Line	CD	Science Fiction	HUCD018	Austria	1994	10.99
Harper, Roy	Legend	CD	Tring Int.	JHD064	EEC	1995	8.99
Harper, Roy	Lifemask	CD	Line	OLCD-9.51044-X	Germany	1991	12.99
Harper, Roy	Live At Les Cousins	CD	Blueprint	BP220CD	England	1996	12.99
Harper, Roy	Loony On The Bus	CD	Line	OLCD-9.51045-X	Germany	1991	24.99
Harper, Roy	Once	CD	Awareness	X2-13078	U.S.A.	1990	8.99
Harper, Roy	Once	CD	Line	LICD-9.00892-0	Germany	1990	12.99
Harper, Roy	Poems, Speeches, Thoughts/Doodles	CD	Science Fiction	HUCD029	EU	1997	12.99
Harper, Roy	Return Of The Sophisticated Beggar	CD	Mooncrest	CRESTCD027	England	1997	12.99
Harper, Roy	Royal Festival Hall London 6-10-2001	2CD	Science Fiction	HUCD035	England	2001	24.99
Harper, Roy	Sophisticated Beggar	CD	Magnum	CDSD-051	England	2002	12.99
Harper, Roy	Stormcock	CD	Line	OLCD-9.51048-X	Germany	1991	12.99
Harper, Roy	Stormcock	CD	Science Fiction	HUCD004	EU	1994	12.99
Harper, Roy	The BBC Tapes, Vol. 1	CD	Science Fiction	HUCD022	EU	1997	12.99
Harper, Roy	The BBC Tapes, Vol. 2	CD	Science Fiction	HUCD023	EU	1997	12.99
Harper, Roy	The BBC Tapes, Vol. 3	CD	Science Fiction	HUCD024	EU	1997	12.99
Harper, Roy	The BBC Tapes, Vol. 4	CD	Science Fiction	HUCD025	EU	1997	12.99
Harper, Roy	The BBC Tapes, Vol. 5	CD	Science Fiction	HUCD026	EU	1997	12.99
Harper, Roy	The BBC Tapes, Vol. 6	CD	Science Fiction	HUCD027	EU	1997	12.99
Harper, Roy	The Dream Society	CD	Science Fiction	HUCD030	EU	1998	12.99
Harper, Roy	The Green Man	CD	Science Fiction	HUCD033	England	2000	12.99
Harper, Roy	The Unknown Soldier	CD	Science Fiction	HUCD031	England	1999	12.99
Harper, Roy	Unhinged	CD	Science Fiction	HUCD020	Austria	1995	12.99
Harper, Roy	Valentine + 3	CD	Line	OLCD-9.51046-X	Germany	1991	12.99
Harper, Roy	Work Of Heart	CD	Line	OLCD-9.51042-X	Germany	1991	19.99
Harris, Eddie/Yes/Jeff Beck	In The U.K. (With S Winwood/ Is It In)	CD	Collectables	COL-CD-6241	U.S.A.	1999	10.99
Harris, Emmylou	Portraits Box Set	3CD	Reprise	9-45308-2	U.S.A.	1996	22.99
Harris, Richard	Camelot	CD	Warner Bros.	3102-2	U.S.A.	1967	8.99
Harris, Richard	Camelot (Orig. 1982 London Cast)	CD	Jay	CDJAY-1295	U.S.A.	1989	22.99
Harris, Richard	Webb Sessions (Tramp Shining + 9)	CD	Raven	RVCD-52	Australia	1995	12.99
Harris, Sam	Sam-I-Am	CD	Motown	B20D-61039	Japan	1989	25.99
Harris, Sugarcane	Sugarcane	CD	Acadia	ACA8024	England	2002	11.99
Harrison, George	A Conversation With George Harrison	CD	Capitol	7087-6-15950-2-4	U.S.A.	2001	14.99
Harrison, George	All Things Must Pass + 5	2CD	Capitol	7243-5-30474-2-9	U.S.A.	2001	18.99
Harrison, George	All Things Must Pass Promo Sampler	CD	Capitol	7087-6-13912-2-4	U.S.A.	2001	10.99
Harrison, George	Best Of Dark Horse 1976-1989	CD	Warner Bros.	9-25726-2	U.S.A.	1989	20.99
Harrison, George	Chant And Be Happy! + 1	CD	XXI	XXI-CD-2-2130	Canada	1991	14.99
Harrison, George	Cloud Nine (Promo Pic Disc)	CD	Warner Bros.	9-25643-2	U.S.A.	1987	23.99

Artist	Title	Format	Label	Catalog No	Country	Released	Value
Harrison, George	Cloud Nine + 2	CD	Capitol	7243-5-94090-2-3	U.S.A.	2004	9.99
Harrison, George	Dark Horse	CD	Capitol	7-98079-2	U.S.A.	1991	13.99
Harrison, George	Dark Horse '76 - '92 Box (7 Cd/DVD)	8 CD	Capitol	7243-5-97051-0-1	U.S.A.	2004	64.99
Harrison, George	Dark Horse Catalogue Box (7 Cd/DVD)	8 CD	Parlophone	7243-5-94085-2-1	England	2004	64.99
Harrison, George	Dark Horse Yrs '76 - '92 (DJ/Sampler)	CD	Parlophone	DARKH-002	England	2004	24.99
Harrison, George	Electronic Sound	CD	EMI	7243-8-55239-2-2	England	1996	15.99
Harrison, George	Extra Texture	CD	Capitol	7-98080-2	U.S.A.	1991	14.99
Harrison, George	George Harrison + 1	CD	Capitol	7243-5-94087-2-9	U.S.A.	2004	9.99
Harrison, George	Gone Troppo + 1	CD	Capitol	7243-5-94089-2-7	U.S.A.	2004	9.99
Harrison, George	Live In Japan	2 SACD	Capitol	7243-5-94665-2-1	U.S.A.	2004	16.99
Harrison, George	Live In Japan (Promo Sampler)	CD	Warner Bros.	PRO-CD-5555	U.S.A.	1992	24.99
Harrison, George	Living In The Material World	CD	Capitol	7-94110-2	U.S.A.	1991	12.99
Harrison, George	Maximum George Harrison	CD	Chrome Dreams	ABCD107	England	2002	9.99
Harrison, George	My Sweet Lord (Misspelled Rord)	CD Single	Toshiba-EMI	TOCP-40153	Japan	2002	174.99
Harrison, George	My Sweet Lord (Single)	CD	Capitol	7243-5-50438-2-5	U.S.A.	2002	7.99
Harrison, George	Somewhere In England + 1	CD	Capitol	7243-5-94088-2-8	U.S.A.	2004	9.99
Harrison, George	Thirty Three & 1/3 + 1	CD	Capitol	7243-5-94086-2-0	U.S.A.	2004	9.99
Harrison, George	This Is Love (Promo)	CD Single	Parlophone	DARKH-001	England	2004	11.99
Harrison, George	This Is Love (Promo/Japanese Pkging)	CD Single	Warner Bros.	PRO-CD-3068	U.S.A.	1987	15.99
Harrison, George	Wonderwall Music	CD	Capitol	7-98706-2	U.S.A.	1992	28.99
Harrison, George/Friends	The Concert For Bangla Desh	2CD	Capitol	7-93265-2	U.S.A.	1971	19.99
Harrison, George/Steve Wood	Everest (O.S.T.)	CD	Ark21	61868-10026-2-8	U.S.A.	1998	8.99
Harrison, George/V.A.	Concert For George (O.S.T.)	2CD	Rhino	R2-74546	U.S.A.	2003	16.99
Harrison, Jerry/Casual Gods	Casual Gods	CD	Sire	W2-25663	U.S.A.	1988	5.99
Harrison, Jerry/Casual Gods	Rev It Up	CD Single	Sire	PRO-CD-2941	U.S.A.	1988	4.99
Harrison, Jerry/Casual Gods	Walk On Water	CD	Sire	9-25943-2	U.S.A.	1990	7.99
Harry, Debbie	Collection	CD	Disky	DC-888402	Holland	1997	7.99
Harry, Debbie	Debravation	CD	Sire	9-45303-2	U.S.A.	1993	7.99
Harry, Debbie	Def, Dumb, & Blonde	CD	Sire	9-25938-2	U.S.A.	1989	5.99
Harry, Debbie	Kookoo + 1	CD	Razor & Tie	7930182184-2	U.S.A.	1999	10.99
Harry, Debbie	Rock Bird	CD	Geffen	9-24123-2	U.S.A.	1986	10.99
Harry, Debbie	Sweet And Low	CD Single	Sire	9-21492-2	U.S.A.	1989	14.99
Hart, Corey	Spot You In A Coalmine	CD	Toshiba-EMI	CP20-5734	Japan	1988	13.99
Hart, Corey	Young Man Running	CD	Toshiba-EMI	CP32-5653	Japan	1988	12.99
Hart, Mickey	At The Edge	CD	Rykodisc	RCD-10124	U.S.A.	1990	7.99
Hart, Mickey	Mickey Hart's Mystery Box (Adv. Copy)	CD	Rykodisc	RCD-10338-ADV	U.S.A.	1996	19.99
Hart, Mickey	Planet Drum (Gold)	CD	Rykodisc	RCD-80206	U.S.A.	1994	18.99
Hart, Mickey	Rolling Thunder	CD	Grateful Dead	GDCD40112	U.S.A.	1990	9.99
Hart, Mickey	Rolling Thunder (Line Version)	CD	Line	GDCD-9.00647-0	Germany	1989	9.99
Hart, Mickey	Spirit Into Sound	CD	Grateful Dead	GDCD-4071	U.S.A.	1999	10.99
Hart, Mickey/Airto/Purim	Dafos (Gold)	CD	Rykodisc	RCD-80108	U.S.A.	1994	44.99
Hart, Mickey/Planet Drum	Supralingua (W/Bonus Cd)	2CD	Rykodisc	RCD-10396	U.S.A.	1998	14.99
Hart, Mickey/Rhythm Devils	The Apocalypse Now Sessions	CD	Rykodisc	RCD-10109	U.S.A.	1989	16.99
Hart/Wolfe/Hemmings	Yamantaka + 3	CD	Celestial Harmonies	13003-2	Germany	1991	10.99
Hartman, Dan/Denise Lopez	The Love You Take (Scrooged Promo)	CD Single	A&M	CD-17668	U.S.A.	1988	4.99
Haslam, Annie	A New Life	CD Single	One Way	PRO-102	U.S.A.	1996	19.99
Haslam, Annie	Annie Haslam	CD	Sony	ESCA-7859	Japan	2001	29.99
Haslam, Annie	Annie Haslam (Promo)	CD	Apollon	X401CD17	Japan	1994	39.99
Haslam, Annie	Annie In Wonderland	Mini Lp	Warner Bros.	WPCR-10884	Japan	2001	54.99
Haslam, Annie	Annie In Wonderland	CD	Warner Bros.	7599-26515-2	Germany	1996	29.99
Haslam, Annie	Annie In Wonderland	CD	Warner Bros.	WPCR-1449	Japan	1997	54.99
Haslam, Annie	Blessing In Disguise	CD	One Way	OW-31450	U.S.A.	1996	8.99
Haslam, Annie	Blessing In Disguise (Promo)	CD	One Way	PRO-101	U.S.A.	1994	14.99
Haslam, Annie	In Another Life	CD Single	One Way	PRO-103	U.S.A.	1996	19.99
Aslam, Annie	It Snows In Heaven Too	CD	White Dove	WD-000-03	U.S.A.	2000	14.99
Haslam, Annie	Live Under Brazilian Skies + 1	CD	Mercury	PHCW-1028	Japan	1999	24.99
Haslam, Annie	One Enchanted Evening	CD	White Dove	WD-00-004	U.S.A.	2002	14.99
Haslam, Annie	Still Life	CD	One Way	OW-32190	U.S.A.	1985	15.99

H

Artist	Title	Format	Label	Catalog No	Country	Released	Value
Haslam, Annie	The Angels Cry (Promo)	CD Single	Epic	ESK-73219	U.S.A.	1989	19.99
Haslam, Annie	The Dawn Of Ananda	CD	White Dove	WD-000-02	U.S.A.	2000	14.99
Haslam, Annie/Akio Dobashi	Diving For Pearls	CD Single	Virgin	VJDP-10148	Japan	1991	24.99
Haslam, Annie/Akio Dobashi	Fox (W/Six Days And Seven Nights)	CD	Apollon	APCY-8210	Japan	1994	39.99
Haslinger, Paul	Future Primitive	CD	Wildcat	WLD-9211-2	U.S.A.	1994	22.99
Haslinger, Paul	Planetary Traveler (W/Bonus Cd Rom)	2CD	Third Planet	3000	U.S.A.	1998	14.99
Haslinger, Paul	The Score	CD	RGB	RGB-506-2	U.S.A.	1999	7.99
Haslinger, Paul	World Without Rules	CD	RGB	RGB-504-2	U.S.A.	1996	7.99
Haslinger, Paul/Coma Virus	Hidden (W/David Torn)	CD	Side Affects	DFX-027	U.S.A.	1997	8.99
Hassell, Jon	4th World Vol. 2: D Theory/Malaya	CD	Editions EG	EEGCD-13	U.S.A.	1981	14.99
Hassell, Jon	Aka - Darbari - Java - Magic Realism	CD	Editions EG	EEGCD-31	U.S.A.	1983	12.99
Hassell, Jon	Aka - Darbari - Java - Magic Realism	CD	Virgin	VJCP-2507	Japan	1990	39.99
Hassell, Jon	City: Works Of Fiction	CD	Warner Bros.	9-26153-2	U.S.A.	1990	9.99
Hassell, Jon	Earthquake Island	CD	Tomato	2696122	Holland	1989	12.99
Hassell, Jon	Fascinoma	CD	Water Lily	70	U.S.A.	1999	11.99
Hassell, Jon	Hollow Bamboo	CD	Water Lily	71	U.S.A.	2002	11.99
Hassell, Jon	Magic Realism	CD	Caroline	CAROL-1572-2	U.S.A.	1983	14.99
Hassell, Jon	Personals/G-Spot	CD Single	Warner Bros.	41574	Germany	1994	5.99
Hassell, Jon	Power Spot (With Brian Eno)	CD	ECM	78118-21327-2	U.S.A.	1986	11.99
Hassell, Jon	Sulla Strada	CD	Materiali Sonori	90066	U.S.A.	1995	15.99
Hassell, Jon	Vernal Equinox	CD	Lovely M	LCD-1021	U.S.A.	1993	12.99
Hassell, Jon	Voiceprint (Blind from the Facts)	CD Single	Opal	41178	Germany	1990	8.99
Hassell, Jon	Voiceprint (Blind from the Facts)	CD Single	Opal	PRO-A-4301	U.S.A.	1993	6.99
Hassell, Jon/Blue Screen	Dressing For Pleasure	CD	Warner Bros.	9-45523-2	U.S.A.	1994	8.99
Hassell, Jon/Blue Screen	Dressing For Pleasure Sampler (Promo)	CD	Warner Bros.	PRO-CD-6951	U.S.A.	1994	8.99
Hassell, Jon/Brian Eno	4th World Vol. 1: Possible Musics	CD	Editions EG	EEGCD-7	U.S.A.	1980	15.99
Hassell, Jon/Brian Eno	The Surgeon Of The Nightsky	CD	Capitol	CDP-7-46880 2	U.S.A.	1987	16.99
Hassell, Jon/Farafina	Flash Of The Spirit	CD	Intuition	566-7-91186-2	Germany	1988	24.99
Hatfield And the North	Live 1990	CD	Code 90	NINETY-6	England	1993	15.99
Hatfield And the North	Self Titled	CD	Virgin	CDV-2008	Holland	1973	10.99
Hatfield And the North	The Rotters' Club	CD	Virgin	CDV2030	Holland	1975	10.99
Havens, Richie	Mixed Bag	CD	Polydor	835-210-2	U.S.A.	1967	14.99
Havens, Richie	Stonehenge	CD	Evangeline	GEL-4054	England	2001	12.99
Hawkins, Ronnie	The Ep Collection (With The Band)	CD	See For Miles	SEE-CD735	England	2002	19.99
Hawkins, Ronnie/Hawks	Best Of	CD	Rhino	R2-70966	U.S.A.	1990	8.99
Hawkins, Screamin' Jay	Somethin' Funny Goin' On	CD	Bizarre	BP-40105-2	U.S.A.	1994	9.99
Hawkwind	1999 Party: Chicago 1974 (W/Poster)	2CD	EMI	HAWKS-6	England	1997	17.99
Hawkwind	25 Years On (Box Set)	4CD	Griffin	GCD-299-2	U.S.A.	1994	39.99
Hawkwind	25 Years On 1970-1973	CD	Griffin	GCD-295-2	U.S.A.	1994	12.99
Hawkwind	25 Years On 1973-1977	CD	Griffin	GCD-296-2	U.S.A.	1994	12.99
Hawkwind	25 Years On 1977-1986	CD	Griffin	GCD-297-2	U.S.A.	1994	12.99
Hawkwind	25 Years On 1987-1994	CD	Griffin	GCD-298-2	U.S.A.	1994	12.99
Hawkwind	A Anarchists (PRX5/No High Rise)	2CD	Snapper	SMD-CD-121	England	1997	13.99
Hawkwind	Acid Daze - The History Of	2CD	Receiver	RRDCD1X	England	1990	17.99
Hawkwind	Acid Daze Volume 1	CD	Receiver	RRCD-125	England	1993	8.99
Hawkwind	Acid Daze Volume 1	CD	Receiver	WM-052159	France	1993	8.99
Hawkwind	Acid Daze Volume 1	CD	Trojan	876545	Germany	1993	8.99
Hawkwind	Acid Daze Volume 2	CD	Receiver	WM-052160	France	1993	8.99
Hawkwind	Acid Daze Volume 2	CD	Trojan	876546	Germany	1993	8.99
Hawkwind	Acid Daze Volume 2	CD	Receiver	RRCD-126	England	1993	8.99
Hawkwind	Acid Daze Volume 3 + 1	CD	Receiver	RRCD-127	England	1993	8.99
Hawkwind	Acid Daze Volume 3 + 1	CD	Receiver	WM-052188	France	1993	8.99
Hawkwind	Alien4	CD	Rough Trade	375.4118.2	Germany	1995	19.99
Hawkwind	Alien4	CD	EBS	EBSCD-118	England	1996	19.99
Hawkwind	Alien4 (Digipack)	CD	EBS	EBSSCD-118	England	1995	19.99
Hawkwind	Anthology (Box Set)	3CD	Essential	ESBCD-168	England	1991	34.99
Hawkwind	Anthology 1967-1982	2CD	Essential	ESD-CD-664	England	1998	12.99
Hawkwind	Anthology Volume 1 + 1	CD	Samrai	SAMRCD-038	England	1986	9.99

H

Artist	Title	Format	Label	Catalog No	Country	Released	Value
Hawkwind	Anthology Volume 2 + 4	CD	Samrai	SAMRCD-039	England	1986	9.99
Hawkwind	Area S4	CD	Emergency	EBCD-107	England	1995	16.99
Hawkwind	Area S4	CD Single	Emergency	EBCD-107	U.S.A.	1995	14.99
Hawkwind	Astounding Sounds Amazing Music	CD	Virgin	7-87269-2	France	1989	34.99
Hawkwind	Astounding Sounds Amazing Music	CD	Virgin	CDSCD-4004	England	1989	34.99
Hawkwind	Astounding Sounds Amazing Music	CD	Virgin	885239	Germany	1989	34.99
Hawkwind	Astounding Sounds Amazing Music + 3	CD	Griffin	GCD-483-2	U.S.A.	1996	49.99
Hawkwind	Astounding Sounds Amazing... Box Set	CD	Griffin	GCD-345-0	U.S.A.	1996	69.99
Hawkwind	Atomhenge 76 (Live)	2CD	Voiceprint	HAWKVP5CD	England	2000	21.99
Hawkwind	BBC Radio 1 live in Concert	CD	Windsong	WINCD-007	England	1991	19.99
Hawkwind	BBC Radio 1 live in Concert	CD	Windsong	60.0007.2	Germany	1991	19.99
Hawkwind	BBC Radio 1 live in Concert	CD	ROIR	ROI-60007	U.S.A.	1992	19.99
Hawkwind	BBC Radio 1 live in Concert	CD	Windsong	MSIF-3099	Japan	1992	19.99
Hawkwind	BBC Radio 1 live in Concert	CD	Wotre	WMD-292459	France	1994	19.99
Hawkwind	Best Of & The Rest: Live	CD	Trojan	884538	Germany	1990	8.99
Hawkwind	Best Of & The Rest: Live	CD	Action Replay	CDAR-1018	England	1990	8.99
Hawkwind	Best Of: Friends & Relations	CD	Flicknife	SHARP-1724-CD	England	1988	9.99
Hawkwind	Best Of: Friends & Relations	CD	Emporio	EMPRCD-547	England	1994	9.99
Hawkwind	Best Of: Friends & Relations	CD	Anagram	CDMGRAM-61	England	1993	9.99
Hawkwind	Best Of: Friends & Relations	CD	Griffin	GCD-535-2	U.S.A.	1995	9.99
Hawkwind	Best Of: Friends & Relations	CD	Cherry Red	987.161	Germany	1993	9.99
Hawkwind	Bring Me The Head ... (Digipack)	CD	Spalax	14846	France	1996	19.99
Hawkwind	Bring Me The Head Of Yuri Gagarin	CD	Magnum	MACD-040	U.S.A.	1996	19.99
Hawkwind	Bring Me The Head Of Yuri Gagarin	CD	Thunderbolt	CDTB-101	England	1993	19.99
Hawkwind	Bring Me The Head Of Yuri Gagarin	CD	Decal	CDCHARLY-40	England	1986	19.99
Hawkwind	British Tribal Music	CD	Start	STFCD-2	England	1987	34.99
Hawkwind	British Tribal Music	CD	Galaxy	GLX 9046	Germany	1987	34.99
Hawkwind	California Brainstorm	CD	Iloki	ILCD-1014	U.S.A.	1992	8.99
Hawkwind	California Brainstorm + 1 (W/Book)	CD	SPV	SPV999-15452CD	Germany	1994	44.99
Hawkwind	California Brainstorm + 1 (W/Book)	CD	Cyclops	CYCL-015	England	1994	44.99
Hawkwind	Castle Masters Collection	CD	Castle	CMC-3002	Germany	1993	14.99
Hawkwind	Choose Your Masques + 2	CD	Emergency	EBSCD-124	England	1996	24.99
Hawkwind	Choose Your Masques + 2	CD	Griffin	GCD-613-2	U.S.A.	1996	24.99
Hawkwind	Church Of Hawkwind + 3	CD	Griffin	GN-0932-2	U.S.A.	1994	14.99
Hawkwind	Church Of Hawkwind + 3	CD	Dojo	DOJOCD-86	England	1994	14.99
Hawkwind	Church Of Hawkwind + 3	CD	Sound	SOL-3010.862	Germany	1994	14.99
Hawkwind	Collector Series Vol 1 : Complete 79	2CD	Voiceprint	HAWKVP4CD	England	2000	22.99
Hawkwind	Collector Series Vol 2 : Live 1982	2CD	Voiceprint	HAWKVP3CD	England	1999	22.99
Hawkwind	Cosmic Travellers: Friends/R Vol 6	CD	Anagram	CDMGRAM-105	England	1996	18.99
Hawkwind	Dawn of Hawkwind	CD	Voiceprint	VPJ-105	Japan	1999	14.99
Hawkwind	Dawn of Hawkwind	CD	Blueprint	BP309CD	England	1999	14.99
Hawkwind	Decide Your Future E.P	CD Single	Griffin	GCDHA-120-2	U.S.A.	1994	9.99
Hawkwind	Decide Your Future E.P	CD Single	4 Real	4R2CD	England	1993	9.99
Hawkwind	Decide Your Future E.P	CD Single	Emergency	EBCD-108	England	1995	9.99
Hawkwind	Decide Your Future E.P	CD Single	Emergency	EBCD-108	England	1995	8.99
Hawkwind	Decide Your Future E.P	CD Single	Griffin	GCDHA-120-2	U.S.A.	1994	8.99
Hawkwind	Decide Your Future E.P	CD Single	4 Real	4R2CD	England	1993	8.99
Hawkwind	Distant Horizons	CD	Emergency	EBSCD-139	England	1997	37.99
Hawkwind	Doremi Fasol Latido	CD	One Way	CDLL-57475	U.S.A.	1991	8.99
Hawkwind	Doremi Fasol Latido + 1	CD	Toshiba-EMI	TOCP-7362	Japan	1992	39.99
Hawkwind	Doremi Fasol Latido + 2	CD	EMI	7243-8-37554-2-4	England	2001	15.99
Hawkwind	Early Daze [Best Of..]	CD	Thunderbolt	CDTB-044	England	1987	24.99
Hawkwind	Electric Tepee	CD	Dojo	DOJOCD-244	England	1995	8.99
Hawkwind	Electric Tepee	CD	Musidisc	11049-2	France	1992	8.99
Hawkwind	Electric Tepee	CD	Griffin	GN-0931-2	U.S.A.	1995	8.99
Hawkwind	Electric Tepee	CD	Sound	SOL-3012.442	Germany	1995	8.99
Hawkwind	Electric Tepee	CD	Essential	ESSCD-181	England	1992	8.99
Hawkwind	Elf And The Hawk + 3	CD	Black Widow	BWRCD-026-2	Italy	1999	14.99

H

Artist	Title	Format	Label	Catalog No	Country	Released	Value
Hawkwind	Entire And Infinite ... (No I C Reprise)	4CD	Dressed To Kill	REDTK98	England	1999	17.99
Hawkwind	Epoch Eclipse: 30 Year Anthology	3CD	EMI	521751-2	England	1999	29.99
Hawkwind	Epoche Eclipse: Ultimate Best Of	CD	EMI	521747-2	England	1999	13.99
Hawkwind	Family Box (Limited)	4CD	Hypnotic	CLP0686-2	U.S.A.	2000	24.99
Hawkwind	Friends & Relations : The Rarities	CD	Griffin	GCD-523-2	U.S.A.	1995	13.99
Hawkwind	Friends & Relations : The Rarities	CD	Anagram	CDMGRAM-91	England	1995	13.99
Hawkwind	Friends/Relations: Best Of + Rarities	CD	Anagram	CDMGRAM-152	England	2001	14.99
Hawkwind	Gimme Shelter Rock	CD Single	EMI	CDORDER-R1	England	1993	12.99
Hawkwind	Golden Void 1969-1979 (Gold Cds)	2CD	Purple Pyramid	CLP-0471-2	U.S.A.	1999	14.99
Hawkwind	Hall Of The Mountain Grill	CD	Fame	CDFA-3133	England	1989	9.99
Hawkwind	Hall Of The Mountain Grill	CD	One Way	S21-47660	U.S.A.	1992	9.99
Hawkwind	Hall Of The Mountain Grill	CD	EMI	432053-2	Australia	1996	9.99
Hawkwind	Hall Of The Mountain Grill + 5	CD	EMI	7243-5-30035-2-4	England	2001	16.99
Hawkwind	Hawklords : 25 Years On	CD	Virgin	CDSCD-4014	England	1989	114.99
Hawkwind	Hawkwind Coll. (Yuri + 1/S Ritual 2)	2CD	Dressed To Kill	TOPAK515	England	2001	18.99
Hawkwind	Hawkwind Family Tree	CD	Voiceprint	HAWKVP13CD	England	2000	14.99
Hawkwind	In The Beginning	CD	Charly	CDCD-1131	England	1994	5.99
Hawkwind	In Your Area	CD	Voiceprint	HAWKVP17CD	England	2000	11.99
Hawkwind	In Your Area	CD	Griffin	GCD-740-2	U.S.A.	1999	11.99
Hawkwind	Independent Days Volumes 1/2 + 2	CD	Griffin	GCD-497-2	U.S.A.	1995	12.99
Hawkwind	Independent Days Volumes 1/2 + 2	CD	Cherry Red	997.040	Germany	1995	12.99
Hawkwind	Independent Days Volumes 1/2 + 2	CD	Anagram	CDMGRAM-94	England	1995	12.99
Hawkwind	Ironstrike : 14 Rock Hard Hits	CD	Avanti	ISTCD-004	U.S.A.	1989	11.99
Hawkwind	It Is the Business...	CD	Musidisc	11220-2	France	1993	10.99
Hawkwind	It Is the Business...	CD	Essential	ESSCD-196	England	1993	10.99
Hawkwind	It Is the Business...	CD	Essential	ESMCD-196	England	1996	10.99
Hawkwind	It Is the Business...	CD	Griffin	GCDHA-161-2	U.S.A.	1994	10.99
Hawkwind	It Is the Business... (Hrdbk Cover)	CD	Essential	ESMCD-740	England	1999	24.99
Hawkwind	Levitation	CD	Essential	ESMCD-736	England	1999	13.99
Hawkwind	Levitation	CD	Castle	CLACD-129	England	1987	13.99
Hawkwind	Levitation : Hawkwind Live '79	CD	Castle	TFO-17-1/2	U.S.A.	1988	13.99
Hawkwind	Levitation : Hawkwind Live '79	CD	Teichiku	TECP-18018	Japan	1988	34.99
Hawkwind	Levitation + 1	CD	Griffin	GCD-230-2	U.S.A.	1994	14.99
Hawkwind	Live	CD	Brilliant	BT-33032	England	2000	11.99
Hawkwind	Live & Rare: Onward Flies The Bird	CD	Emporio	EMPRCD-710	England	1997	8.99
Hawkwind	Live 1970 1972	CD	Pegasus	PEG-CD-197	England	1999	9.99
Hawkwind	Live 1990	CD	Voiceprint	HAWKVP12CD	England	2001	14.99
Hawkwind	Live '79/Levitation/Space Bandits Box	3CD	Castle	CLA-BX-911	England	1992	29.99
Hawkwind	Live At Glastonbury 1990	CD	Voiceprint	HAWKVP1CD	England	1999	14.99
Hawkwind	Live Chronicles	CD	Castle	CCSCD-321	England	1992	16.99
Hawkwind	Live Chronicles + 6	2CD	Griffin	GCDHA-0136-2	U.S.A.	1994	13.99
Hawkwind	Live Chronicles Bonus Collection	2CD	Castle	CCSCD-829	England	1998	19.99
Hawkwind	Live Seventy Nine	CD	Griffin	GCD-229-2	U.S.A.	1994	10.99
Hawkwind	Live Seventy Nine	CD	Essential	ESMCD-735	England	1999	10.99
Hawkwind	Live Seventy Nine	CD	Castle	CLACD-243	England	1992	10.99
Hawkwind	Live Space 1990: N Ending (W/Book)	CD	Sonic Book	SCONC-019	Italy	1991	39.99
Hawkwind	Lord Of Light	CD	Cleopatra	CLEO-5773-2	U.S.A.	1993	7.99
Hawkwind	Love In Space	2CD	Emergency	EBSSCD-120	England	1996	29.99
Hawkwind	Love In Space E.P	CD Single	Emergency	EBCD-106	England	1997	10.99
Hawkwind	Love In Space E.P (Promo)	CD Single	Emergency	EBCD-106-Demo	England	1997	14.99
Hawkwind	Master Of The Universe	CD	Laserlight	21-059	Germany	1999	8.99
Hawkwind	Master Of The Universe	CD	Pulse	PLSCD-207	England	1997	10.99
Hawkwind	Master Of The Universe	CD	Pulse	PLSCD-207	England	2001	10.99
Hawkwind	Masters Of Rock	CD	EMI	5-37765-2	England	2002	12.99
Hawkwind	Masters Of The Universe	CD	Magnum	MACD-028	U.S.A.	1996	10.99
Hawkwind	Masters Of The Universe	CD	Thunderbolt	CDTB-105	England	1992	10.99
Hawkwind	Masters Of The Universe	CD	Magnum	HD-2032	Korea	1999	10.99
Hawkwind	Masters Of The Universe	CD	Marble Arch	CMACD-129	England	1991	10.99

H

Artist	Title	Format	Label	Catalog No	Country	Released	Value
Hawkwind	Masters Of The Universe	CD	Fame	CDFA-3220	England	1989	10.99
Hawkwind	Masters Of The Universe	CD	Spalax	14972	France	1996	10.99
Hawkwind	Mighty Hawkwind Classics 1980-1985	CD	Griffin	GCD-496-2	U.S.A.	1995	8.99
Hawkwind	Mighty Hawkwind Classics 1980-1985	CD	Cherry Red	987.153	Germany	1992	8.99
Hawkwind	Mighty Hawkwind Classics 1980-1985	CD	Anagram	CDMGRAM-53	England	1992	8.99
Hawkwind	Night Of The Hawk + 3	CD	Powerhouse	POWCD-5502	England	1989	39.99
Hawkwind	Night Of The Hawk + 3	CD	Aris	885239	Germany	1989	39.99
Hawkwind	Night Riding	CD	Knight	KNCD-10017	England	1990	12.99
Hawkwind	Out & Intake + 2	CD	Sound	SOL-3011.532	Germany	1994	7.99
Hawkwind	Out & Intake + 2	CD	Dojo	DOJOCD-153	England	1994	7.99
Hawkwind	Out & Intake + 2	CD	Griffin	GN-03922-2	U.S.A.	1992	7.99
Hawkwind	Out & Intake + 2	CD	Flicknife	SHARP-040CD	England	1987	7.99
Hawkwind	Palace Springs	CD	GWR	GWCD-104	England	1991	7.99
Hawkwind	Palace Springs	CD	Road Racer	RR-93032	Holland	1991	7.99
Hawkwind	Palace Springs	CD	Castle	CLACD-303	England	1992	7.99
Hawkwind	Palace Springs	CD	Road Racer	RRD-9303	U.S.A.	1991	7.99
Hawkwind	Palace Springs (Hrdbk)	CD	Essential	ESMCD-739	England	1999	34.99
Hawkwind	Psy. Warlords (Cloth Slv/Badge/Photo)	CD	Semaphore	57412	Germany	1992	22.99
Hawkwind	Psy. Warlords (Cloth Slv/Badge/Photo)	CD	Cleopatra	CLEO-5741-2	U.S.A.	1992	22.99
Hawkwind	PXR5	CD	Virgin	CDSCD-4016	England	1989	49.99
Hawkwind	Quark Strangeness & Charm	CD	Griffin	GCDHA-162-2	U.S.A.	1995	24.99
Hawkwind	Quark Strangeness & Charm	CD	Virgin	CDSCD-4008	England	1989	49.99
Hawkwind	Quark Strangeness & Charm	CD	Virgin	7-87271-2	Germany	1989	49.99
Hawkwind	Quark Strangeness & Charm	CD	Griffin	GCD-370-0	U.S.A.	1995	24.99
Hawkwind	Quark Strangeness & Charm E.P	CD Single	Griffin	GCD-312-2	U.S.A.	1994	9.99
Hawkwind	Quark Strangeness & Charm E.P	CD Single	Emergency	EBCD-110	England	1994	14.99
Hawkwind	Ridicule	CD	Obsession	EFA-75191	Germany	1990	8.99
Hawkwind	Ridicule	CD	New Rose	NR-761	France	1990	8.99
Hawkwind	Ridicule	CD	Obsession	OBCESSCD-1	England	1990	8.99
Hawkwind	Self Titled	CD	One Way	S21-57658	U.S.A.	1992	11.99
Hawkwind	Self Titled	CD	Repertoire	REP-4403-WY	Germany	1994	11.99
Hawkwind	Self Titled + 4	CD	EMI	HAWKS-1	England	1996	12.99
Hawkwind	Silver Machine	CD	Legend	WZ-90144	Germany	1994	7.99
Hawkwind	Silver Machine	CD	Spectrum	550-764-2	Germany	1995	7.99
Hawkwind	Silver Machine	CD	Hallmark	HALMCD-1125	England	2001	7.99
Hawkwind	Silver Machine	CD	Hallmark	308412	England	1998	7.99
Hawkwind	Silver Machine - Live	CD	Planet	PML-1075	England	2001	7.99
Hawkwind	Silver Machine (Promo)	CD Single	Eclipse	DECLIPSE-1999	England	1999	16.99
Hawkwind	Sonic Attack + 1	CD	Griffin	GCD-612-2	U.S.A.	1996	42.99
Hawkwind	Sonic Attack + 1	CD	Emergency	EBSCD-123	England	1996	42.99
Hawkwind	Sonic Boom Killers A's/B's '70 To '80	CD	Repertoire	REP-4676-WY	Germany	2003	15.99
Hawkwind	Space Bandits	CD	Teichiku	TECP-25662	Japan	1990	39.99
Hawkwind	Space Bandits	CD	Essential	ESMCD-738	England	1999	8.99
Hawkwind	Space Bandits	CD	GWR	GWCD-103	England	1990	8.99
Hawkwind	Space Bandits	CD	Castle	CLACD-282	England	1992	8.99
Hawkwind	Space Bandits	CD	Road Racer	RR-9347	U.S.A.	1990	8.99
Hawkwind	Space Bandits	CD	Road Racer	7-9347-2	France	1990	8.99
Hawkwind	Space is Deep	CD	Receiver	RRCD-206	England	1995	8.99
Hawkwind	Space Ritual + 3	2CD	EMI	7243-5-30032-2-7	England	2001	17.99
Hawkwind	Space Ritual Alive	CD	One Way	S22-57659	U.S.A.	1992	12.99
Hawkwind	Space Ritual Volume 2	CD	Cd Label	CDTL-003	England	1987	8.99
Hawkwind	Space Ritual Volume 2	CD	Spalax	14520	France	1997	8.99
Hawkwind	Space Ritual Volume 2	CD	Thunderbolt	CDTB-099	England	1991	8.99
Hawkwind	Space Ritual Volume 2	CD	Magnum	MACD-023	U.S.A.	1995	8.99
Hawkwind	Spacebrock	CD	Voiceprint	HAWKVP18CD	England	2000	9.99
Hawkwind	Spirit Of The Age	CD	Virgin	COM-CD8	England	1988	12.99
Hawkwind	Spirit Of The Age	CD	Elite	ELITE-021-CD	England	1991	12.99
Hawkwind	Spirit Of The Age Solstice Remixes	CD Single	Emergency	EBCD-109	England	1995	12.99

H

Artist	Title	Format	Label	Catalog No	Country	Released	Value
Hawkwind	Spirit Of The Age Solstice Remixes	CD Single	Griffin	GCD-343-2	U.S.A.	1995	12.99
Hawkwind	Spirit Of The Age Solstice Remixes	CD Single	4 Real	4R1CD	England	1993	12.99
Hawkwind	Spirit Of The Age Solstice Remixes	CD Single	Emergency	EBCD-109	England	1995	18.99
Hawkwind	Spirit Of The Age Solstice Remixes	CD Single	Griffin	GCD-343-2	U.S.A.	1995	18.99
Hawkwind	Spirit Of The Age Solstice Remixes	CD Single	4 Real	4R1CD	England	1993	18.99
Hawkwind	Stasis: UA Years 1971-1975 + 4	CD	EMI	7-46694-2	Germany	1990	10.99
Hawkwind	Stasis: UA Years 1971-1975 + 4	CD	One Way	S21-17607	U.S.A.	1994	10.99
Hawkwind	Stasis: UA Years 1971-1975 + 4	CD	Fame	CDFA-3267	England	1992	10.99
Hawkwind	Stasis: UA Years 1971-1975 + 4	CD	EMI	CZ-297	England	1990	10.99
Hawkwind	Tales From Atomhenge	CD	Virgin	263-219	Germany	1992	17.99
Hawkwind	Tales From Atomhenge	CD	Virgin	PM-500	France	1992	17.99
Hawkwind	Tales From Atomhenge	CD	Virgin	CDVM-9008	England	1992	17.99
Hawkwind	The Best Of	CD	Wotre	WMD-292460	France	1994	8.99
Hawkwind	The Best Of	CD	Castle	MATCD-293	England	1994	8.99
Hawkwind	The Business Trip Live	CD	Emergency	EBSCD-111	England	1994	8.99
Hawkwind	The Business Trip Live	CD	Griffin	GCD-280-2	U.S.A.	1994	8.99
Hawkwind	The Business Trip Live	CD	PIAS	990.350	Germany	1994	8.99
Hawkwind	The Business Trip Live (Digipack)	CD	Emergency	EBSSCD-111	England	1994	8.99
Hawkwind	The Business Trip Live (Digipack)	CD	Griffin	GCD-279-2	U.S.A.	1994	8.99
Hawkwind	The Business Trip Live (Digipack)	CD	PIAS	375.4114.2	Germany	1994	8.99
Hawkwind	The Chronicle of the Black Sword	CD	Sound	SOL-3010.722	Germany	1992	24.99
Hawkwind	The Chronicle of the Black Sword + 2	CD	Dojo	DOJOCD-72	England	1992	29.99
Hawkwind	The Chronicle of the Black Sword + 2	CD	Griffin	GCDHA-0142-2	U.S.A.	1994	29.99
Hawkwind	The Chronicle of the Black Sword + 3	CD	Flicknife	SHARP-033D	England	1986	29.99
Hawkwind	The Collection	CD	Castle	CCSCD-148	England	1986	8.99
Hawkwind	The Collection	CD	Sound	SOL-2873.148	Germany	1986	8.99
Hawkwind	The Friday Rock Show Sessions	CD	Raw Fruit	FRSCD005	England	1992	25.99
Hawkwind	The Friday Rock Show Sessions	CD	Raw Fruit	321.5005.2	Germany	1992	25.99
Hawkwind	The Hawklords Live	CD	Dojo	DOJOCD-71	England	1992	29.99
Hawkwind	The Hawklords Live	CD	Sound	SOL-3010.712	Germany	1992	29.99
Hawkwind	The Hawklords Live	CD	Griffin	GN-03921-2	U.S.A.	1992	29.99
Hawkwind	The Masters	CD	Eagle	EABCD-084	England	1998	12.99
Hawkwind	The Stonehenge Collection	2CD	Cleopatra	CLP-0850-2	U.S.A.	2000	12.99
Hawkwind	The Text Of Festival	CD	Thunderbolt	CDTB-068	England	1993	19.99
Hawkwind	The Text Of Festival	CD	Thunderbolt	CDTB-2.068	England	1988	19.99
Hawkwind	The Xenon Codex	CD	GWR	GWCD-26	England	1988	12.99
Hawkwind	The Xenon Codex	CD	Enigma	7-75407-2	U.S.A.	1989	12.99
Hawkwind	The Xenon Codex	CD	Teichiku	TECP-25663	Japan	1990	12.99
Hawkwind	The Xenon Codex	CD	Castle	CLACD-281	England	1992	12.99
Hawkwind	The Xenon Codex (Hrdbk)	CD	Essential	ESMCD-737	England	1999	34.99
Hawkwind	This Is Hawkwind Do Not Panic	CD	Griffin	GCDHA-163-2	U.S.A.	1994	8.99
Hawkwind	This Is Hawkwind Do Not Panic	CD	Cherry Red	897.154	Germany	1992	8.99
Hawkwind	This Is Hawkwind Do Not Panic	CD	Anagram	CDMGRAM-54	England	1992	8.99
Hawkwind	Thrilling Hawkwind Adventures	CD	Griffin	GCD840-2	U.S.A.	2000	11.99
Hawkwind	Travellers Aid Trust	CD	Anagram	CDMGRAM-56	England	1992	20.99
Hawkwind	Travellers Aid Trust (Trk Sugar Cubes)	CD	Flicknife	CDSHARP-2045	England	1988	20.99
Hawkwind	Undisclosed Files Addendum	CD	Emergency	EBSCD-114	England	1995	13.99
Hawkwind	Undisclosed Files Addendum	CD	PIAS	375.4114.2	Germany	1995	13.99
Hawkwind	Undisclosed Files... (Metal Ltd 500)	CD	Griffin	GCD-372-2	U.S.A.	1995	49.99
Hawkwind	Warrior On The Edge Of Time	CD	Sound	SOL-3010.942	Germany	1992	72.99
Hawkwind	Warrior On The Edge Of Time + 1	CD	Dojo	DOJOCD-84	England	1992	72.99
Hawkwind	Warrior On The Edge Of..(W/Book)	CD	Griffin	55421-3931-2	U.S.A.	1993	81.99
Hawkwind	Weird Tapes No 1	CD	Voiceprint	HAWKVP6CD	England	2000	17.99
Hawkwind	Weird Tapes No 2	CD	Voiceprint	HAWKVP7CD	England	2000	17.99
Hawkwind	Weird Tapes No 3	CD	Voiceprint	HAWKVP8CD	England	2000	17.99
Hawkwind	Weird Tapes No 4	CD	Voiceprint	HAWKVP9CD	England	2000	17.99
Hawkwind	Weird Tapes No 5	CD	Voiceprint	HAWKVP10CD	England	2000	17.99
Hawkwind	Weird Tapes No 6	CD	Voiceprint	HAWKVP??CD	England	2000	17.99

H

Artist	Title	Format	Label	Catalog No	Country	Released	Value
Hawkwind	Weird Tapes No 7	CD	Voiceprint	HAWKVP14CD	England	2000	17.99
Hawkwind	Welcome To The Future Box Set	4CD	Dressed To Kill	CLP0220-2	England	1998	17.99
Hawkwind	White Zone	CD	Griffin	GCD-376-2	U.S.A.	1995	8.99
Hawkwind	White Zone	CD	Emergency	EBSSCD-113	England	1995	8.99
Hawkwind	X In Search of Space	CD	Toshiba-EMI	TOCP-6830	Japan	1992	39.99
Hawkwind	X In Search of Space	CD	Toshiba-EMI	TOCP-6798	Japan	1991	39.99
Hawkwind	X In Search of Space	CD	Fame	CDFA-3192	England	1989	9.99
Hawkwind	X In Search of Space	CD	One Way	CDLL-57474	U.S.A.	1991	9.99
Hawkwind	X In Search Of Space + 2	CD	EMI	7243-8-37553-2-5	England	2001	17.99
Hawkwind	Year 2000:C Hawkwind Vol. 1	2CD	Alchemy	PILOT-33	England	1999	12.99
Hawkwind	Year 2000:C Hawkwind Vol. 2	CD	Alchemy	PILOT-64	England	2000	9.99
Hawkwind	YR 2000: C HW Vol. 1 Cd 1 (DJ)	CD	Alchemy	PILOT-33-ONE	England	1999	8.99
Hawkwind	YR 2000: C HW Vol. 1 Cd 2 (DJ)	CD	Alchemy	PILOT-33-TWO	England	1999	8.99
Hawkwind	Yule Ritual Live At The Astoria	2CD	Voiceprint	HAWKVP19CD	England	2001	15.99
Hawkwind	Zones	CD	Griffin	GCDHA-164-2	U.S.A.	1994	7.99
Hawkwind	Zones	CD	Cherry Red	987.199	Germany	1992	7.99
Hawkwind	Zones	CD	Anagram	CDMGRAM-57	England	1992	7.99
Hawkwind	Zones/Do Not Panic	2CD	Anagram	CDM-GRAM-160	England	2002	16.99
Hawkwind	Zones/Stonehenge	CD	Flicknife	SHARP-1422CD	England	1988	21.99
Hawkwind /Box Set/Int Cd	Off. Pic Log Bk (Insert Sh/Badge)	3CD	Flicknife	HWBOX-01	England	1987	49.99
Hawkwind/Adrian Shaw	Displaced Person	CD	Woronzow	WOO-29CD	England	1997	12.99
Hawkwind/Adrian Shaw	Head Cleaner	CD	Woronzow	WOO-32CD	England	1999	10.99
Hawkwind/Adrian Shaw	Tea for the Hydra	CD	Woronzow	WOO-27CD	England	1996	19.99
Hawkwind/Alan Davey	Bedouin	CD	Emergency	EBSCD-133	England	1997	18.99
Hawkwind/Alan Davey	Captured Rotation	CD	Emergency	EBSSCD-122	England	1996	20.99
Hawkwind/Alan Davey	Chaos Delight	CD	Black Widow	BWRCD-033-2	Italy	2000	29.99
Hawkwind/D Thompson	Tribal Drums	Cd Rom	D Thompson	DT-001	England	1999	29.99
Hawkwind/Dave Brock	& The Agents of Chaos	CD	Flicknife	SHARP-1842	England	1989	15.99
Hawkwind/Dave Brock	Earthed To The Ground	CD	Flicknife	SHARP-018	England	1984	15.99
Hawkwind/Dave Brock	Memos and Demos	CD	Voiceprint	HAWKVP20CD	England	2001	19.99
Hawkwind/Dave Brock	Strange Trips & Pipe Dreams	CD	Emergency	EBSSCD-116	England	1995	11.99
Hawkwind/Dave Brock	Strange Trips & Pipe Dreams	CD	Griffin	GCD-515-2	U.S.A.	1995	11.99
Hawkwind/H Bainbridge	Interstellar Chaos	CD	Taste	TASTE-40-CD	England	1993	24.99
Hawkwind/H Bainbridge	Red Shift	CD	Taste	TASTE-65-CD	England	1996	24.99
Hawkwind/H L Langton	Chain Reaction	CD	Allegro	LLG-CD777	England	2000	12.99
Hawkwind/H L Langton	Elegy	CD	Allegro	LLG-CD712	England	1991	12.99
Hawkwind/H L Langton	On the Move	CD	BMA	BMA-C-0318-S	England	1997	9.99
Hawkwind/H L Langton	River Run	CD	Allegro	LLG-CD6	England	1994	14.99
Hawkwind/High Tide	A Fierce Nature (SPM-WWR-CD-012)	CD	World Wide	WWR-CD-0012	England	1990	10.99
Hawkwind/High Tide	Ancient Gates (SPM-WWR-CD-007)	CD	World Wide	WWR-CD-007	England	1990	10.99
Hawkwind/High Tide	Interesting Times + 2	CD	Akarma	AK-091	Italy	1999	18.99
Hawkwind/High Tide	Precious Cargo	CD	Akarma	AK-002	Italy	1999	18.99
Hawkwind/High Tide	Sea Shanties	CD	Toshiba-EMI	TOCP-7801	Japan	1993	39.99
Hawkwind/High Tide	Sea Shanties/High Tide	CD	Liberty	7243-8-29711-2-2	U.S.A.	1994	29.99
Hawkwind/High Tide	Self Titled	CD	Toshiba-EMI	TOCP-7802	Japan	1993	39.99
Hawkwind/High Tide	The Flood (SPM-WWR-CD-0005)	CD	World Wide	WWR-CD-0005	England	1990	10.99
Hawkwind/High Tide	The Reason ..(SPM-WWR-CD-0024)	CD	World Wide	WWR-CD-0024	England	1990	10.99
Hawkwind/High Tide	Tony Hill - Inexactness	CD	Rubric	RUB-27	England	2001	7.99
Hawkwind/Inner City Unit	New Anatomy	CD	Thunderbolt	CDTB-096	England	1993	21.99
Hawkwind/Inner City Unit	New Anatomy	CD	Spalax	14845	France	1996	21.99
Hawkwind/Inner City Unit	Pass Out + 8 (Released Ltd Twice)	CD	Oldhitz	CD-OLD-001	England	1990	21.99
Hawkwind/M Moorcock	New World's Fair Box + 4 (W/Book)	CD	Griffin	GCD-332-0	U.S.A.	1995	24.99
Hawkwind/M Moorcock	The New World's Fair + 4	CD	Dojo	DOJOCD-88	England	1995	19.99
Hawkwind/Nik Turner	Live Deeply Vale Free Festival 1978	CD	Ozit	OZITCD-0053	England	2000	22.99
Hawkwind/Nik Turner	Past Or Future ?	CD	Cleopatra	CLP-9685-2	U.S.A.	1996	11.99
Hawkwind/Nik Turner	Prophets Of Time	CD	Cleopatra	CLEO-6908-2	U.S.A.	1994	11.99
Hawkwind/Nik Turner	Sonic Attack 2001	CD	Dossier	DCD-9080	Germany	1996	11.99
Hawkwind/Nik Turner	Space Ritual 1994 Live	2CD	Cleopatra	CLEO-9506-2	U.S.A.	1995	22.99

H

Artist	Title	Format	Label	Catalog No	Country	Released	Value
Hawkwind/Nik Turner	Space Ritual Live	2CD	Captain Trip	CTCD-018/19	Japan	1994	24.99
Hawkwind/Nik Turner	Sphynx	CD	Cleopatra	CLEO-2135-2	England	1993	14.99
Hawkwind/Nik Turner	Sphynx Xitintoday	CD	Emergency	NIKTCD-333	England	1997	126.99
Hawkwind/Robert Calvert	At The Queen Elizabeth Hall	CD	BGO	BGOCD187	England	1992	19.99
Hawkwind/Robert Calvert	Blueprints From The Cellar	CD	BGO	BGOCD135	England	1992	14.99
Hawkwind/Robert Calvert	Captain Lockheed/The Starfighters	CD	BGO	BGOCD5	England	1987	19.99
Hawkwind/Robert Calvert	Freq + 2	CD	Cleopatra	CLEO-9467-2	U.S.A.	1994	13.99
Hawkwind/Robert Calvert	Freq Revisited + 2	CD	Anagram	CDMGRAM55	England	1992	13.99
Hawkwind/Robert Calvert	Hype	CD	See For Miles	SEE-CD278	England	1989	18.99
Hawkwind/Robert Calvert	Lucky Leif And The Longships	CD	BGO	BGOCD2	England	1987	19.99
Hawkwind/Robert Calvert	Revenge	CD	Blueprint	BP320CD	England	1999	12.99
Hawkwind/Robert Calvert	Test-Tube Conceived	CD	Thunderbolt	CDTB-113	England	1992	14.99
Hawkwind/Robert Calvert	Test-Tube Conceived (Black/L Purple)	CD	Cd Label	CDTL-007	England	1987	14.99
Hawkwind/Simon House	Yassasim	CD	Emergency	EBSSCD-115	England	1995	9.99
Hawkwind/Simon House	Yassasim	CD	Griffin	GCD-517-2	U.S.A.	1995	9.99
Hawkwind/Simon House	Yassasim	CD	Griffin	GCD-494-2	U.S.A.	1995	9.99
Hawkwind/Tim Blake	Blake's New Jerusalem	CD	Mantra	MANTRA-068	France	1992	12.99
Hawkwind/Tim Blake	Crystal Machine	CD	Mantra	MANTRA-067	France	1992	12.99
Hawkwind/Tim Blake	Magick	CD	Mantra	MANTRA-069	France	1992	14.99
Hawkwind/Tim Blake	Magick	CD	Voiceprint	VP105CD	England	1991	14.99
Hawkwind/Various Artists	Emergency Broadacst System Samples	CD	Emergency	EBSCD-119	England	1996	16.99
Hawkwind/Various Artists	Nik Turner/Travellers of Space (DJ)	CD	Cleopatra	CLEO-PRO-2	U.S.A.	1996	10.99
Hayes, David	Born Heroes	CD	Line	LICD-9.01290-0	Germany	1993	7.99
Hayes, Issac	Chocolate Salty Balls	CD Single	Columbia	666798-2	Germany	1998	7.99
Hayes-Springer Brotherhood	Sneaker Waves	CD	Line	RBCD-9.00491-0	Germany	1987	7.99
Hayride	Elfin Magic	CD	Capricorn	9-42032-2	U.S.A.	1995	6.99
Hayward, Justin	Classic Blue	CD	Griffin	GCD-221-2	U.S.A.	1994	15.99
Hayward, Justin	Live In San Capistrano	CD	Nightwood	305829	U.S.A.	1998	24.99
Hayward, Justin	Moving Mountains + 1	CD	Anchor	ANZ-701	U.S.A.	1989	37.99
Hayward, Justin	Night Flight	CD	PolyGram	820-555-2	U.S.A.	1989	18.99
Hayward, Justin	Songwriter + 2	CD	Decca	820-492-2	Germany	1987	15.99
Hayward, Justin	The View From The Hill	CD	CMC INT.	0607686202-2	U.S.A.	1996	9.99
Hayward, Justin	The Way Of The World	CD Single	CMC INT.	CMC-DJ-87201-2	U.S.A.	1996	7.99
Hayward, Justin/Alice Cooper	Flash Fearless/Zorg Women Pts 5/6	CD	RPM	RPM-147	England	1995	14.99
Hayward, Justin/Friends	Classic Moody Blues Hits	CD	Mausoleum	71278-60030-2	U.S.A.	1996	11.99
Hayward, Justin/Friends	Classic Moody Blues Hits + 4	CD	Isba	ISB-CD-5047	Canada	1994	19.99
Hayward, Justin/John Lodge	Blue Jays + 1	CD	PolyGram	820-491-2	U.S.A.	1987	10.99
Hazelwood, Lee	For Every Solution ...	CD	City Slang	CITY-20194CD	Germany	2003	9.99
Hazelwood, Lee	Lounge Legends	CD	Polydor	UNI-9882CD	Germany	2002	10.99
Head East	Choice Of Weapons	CD	Dark Heart	DKH-2001-CD	U.S.A.	1988	13.99
Head East	Live On Stage	CD	A&M	069-470-756-2	U.S.A.	2000	9.99
Head Hands & Feet	Home From Home (The Mersey Lps)	CD	See For Miles	SEE-CD-633	England	1996	9.99
Head Hands & Feet	Old Soldiers Never Die	CD	Repertoire	RE-4266-WY	Germany	1994	12.99
Head Hands & Feet	Self Titled	CD	See For Miles	SEE-CD-458	England	1998	9.99
Head Hands & Feet	Tracks Plus (+ 2)	CD	See For Miles	SEE-CD-459	England	1996	9.99
Heads Or Tales	Eternity Becomes A Lie	CD	Victor Ent.	VICP-5661	Japan	1995	12.99
Heart	Bad Animals	CD	Capitol	7-46676-2	U.S.A.	1987	6.99
Heart	Bebe Le Strange	CD	Epic	EK-36371	U.S.A.	1980	7.99
Heart	Brigade	CD	Capitol	591820	U.S.A.	1990	6.99
Heart	Desire Walks On	CD	Capitol	0777-7-99627-2-3	U.S.A.	1993	6.99
Heart	Desire Walks On + 2	CD	Toshiba-EMI	TOCP-53018	Japan	1999	22.99
Heart	Dog & Butterfly	CD	Columbia	RK-35555	U.S.A.	1990	7.99
Heart	Dreamboat Annie (DCC Gold Cd)	CD	DCC	GZS-1058	U.S.A.	1994	63.99
Heart	Greatest Hits	CD	Epic	EK-69015	U.S.A.	1998	6.99
Heart	Heart (MFSL Gold Cd)	CD	Mobile Fidelity	UDCD-597	U.S.A.	1986	27.99
Heart	Heart Greatest Hits 1985-1995	CD	Capitol	72435-26803-2-0	U.S.A.	2000	6.99
Heart	Little Queen	CD	Columbia	RK-34799	U.S.A.	1977	7.99
Heart	Magazine	CD	Capitol	S21-18322	U.S.A.	1995	7.99

H

Page: 174

Artist	Title	Format	Label	Catalog No	Country	Released	Value
Heart	Passionworks	CD	Epic	EK-38800	U.S.A.	1983	7.99
Heart	Private Audition	CD	Epic	EK-38049	U.S.A.	1986	13.99
Heart	Rock The House Live!	CD	Capitol	C2-95797	U.S.A.	1991	6.99
Heart	The Road Home + 1	CD	Toshiba-EMI	TOCP-53019	Japan	1999	11.99
Hecht, Daniel	Willow	CD	Windham Hill	WD-1013	U.S.A.	1980	12.99
Hefti, Neal	Batman (Original Television S.T.)	CD	Casablanca	834-908-2	U.S.A.	1989	29.99
Hefti, Neal	Batman Theme (Whole 1st Lp)	CD	RCA	3573-2-R	U.S.A.	1989	8.99
Hefti, Neal	Batman Theme/19 Bat Songs (2 Lp's)	CD	Razor & Tie	RE-2153-2	U.S.A.	1997	10.99
Helicon	Self Titled	CD	Victor Ent.	VICP-5240	Japan	1993	16.99
Helix	B Sides	CD	Griffin	GCD-6237-2	U.S.A.	2002	11.99
Helix	Back For Another Taste	CD	Castle	CLACD-346	England	1993	10.99
Helix	Breaking Loose	CD	H/S	781	U.S.A.	1999	13.99
Helix	Half Alive	CD	De Rock	DERCD-9012	U.S.A.	1998	8.99
Helix	Helix	CD	Toshiba-EMI	TOCP-8082	Japan	1993	29.99
Helix	It's A Business Doing Pleasure	CD	Aquarius	Q21H-570	Canada	1993	12.99
Helix	Long Way To Heaven	CD	Capitol	0777-7-12411-2	Canada	1985	18.99
Helix	No Rest For The Wicked	CD	Griffin	GCD-791-2	U.S.A.	2000	17.99
Helix	Over 60 Minutes With	CD	Capitol	C21Y-93571	Canada	1990	13.99
Helix	The Best of Helix: Deep Cuts	CD	Razor & Tie	79301-82187-2	U.S.A.	1999	13.99
Helix	Walkin' On The Razor's Edge	CD	Capitol	72435-24699-2	U.S.A.	2002	29.99
Helix	White Lace And Black Leather	CD	H/S	782	U.S.A.	1999	12.99
Helix	Wild In The Streets	CD	Griffin	GCD-1006	U.S.A.	2002	24.99
Helix/Brian Vollmer	When Pigs Fly	CD	Griffin	GCD-2575-2	U.S.A.	2002	9.99
Helix/Cherry St.	Buster Cherry	CD	Perris	PER0003-2	Canada	1999	12.99
Helix/Cherry St.	Squeeze It Dry	CD	JRS	7-3333-35832-2	U.S.A.	1993	21.99
Helix/Cherry St.	X-Rated	CD	Perris	PER0073-2	Canada	2001	13.99
Hell, Richard	Time	2CD	Matador	OLE-530-2	U.S.A.	2002	13.99
Hell, Richard/Voidoids	Blank Generation	CD	Sire	9-26137-2	U.S.A.	1990	12.99
Hell, Richard/Voidoids	Destiny Street	CD	Line	LICD-9.00100-0	Germany	1987	11.99
Helloise	Cosmogony + 9	CD	Belle Antique	CDP-1035-DD	Japan	1985	15.99
Helloween	Pumpkin Box	4CD	Victor Ent.	VICP-60184-87	Japan	1998	49.99
Helloween	Rabbit Don't Come Easy + 1	CD	Victor Ent.	VICP-62323	Japan	2003	29.99
Helm, Levon	American Son	CD	Victor Entertainment	UICY-3352	Japan	2002	19.99
Helm, Levon	Levon Helm (MFSL Silver Cd)	CD	Mobile Fidelity	MFCD-759	U.S.A.	1978	68.99
Helm, Levon	The Rco All-Stars (MFSL Silver Cd)	CD	Mobile Fidelity	MFCD-761	U.S.A.	1977	29.99
Helm, Levon	The Ties That Bind (Best Of '75 - '96)	CD	Raven	RVCD-87	Australia	1999	9.99
Help Yourself	Self Titled/Beware The Shadow	CD	BGO	BGOCD385	England	2002	13.99
Help Yourself	Strange Affair/K Whaley/Happy Days	2CD	BGO	BGOCD452	England	1999	17.99
Hendrix, Jimi	(Last Concert With) Experience	2CD	Sunspots	SPOT-516-CD	Italy	2002	14.99
Hendrix, Jimi	Albert Hall Experience + 3	2CD	Snapper	SNAF-822-CD	England	2001	15.99
Hendrix, Jimi	Are You Experienced? + 7	CD	MCA	MCAD-11602	U.S.A.	1997	7.99
Hendrix, Jimi	Axis Bold As Love	CD	Polydor	P33P-25023	Japan	1967	35.99
Hendrix, Jimi	Axis: Bold as Love	CD	MCA	MCAD-11601	U.S.A.	1997	9.99
Hendrix, Jimi	Band Of Gypsys	CD	Capitol	72434-93446-2-4	U.S.A.	1997	8.99
Hendrix, Jimi	Band Of Gypsys (Mini Lp Numbered)	CD	Capitol	DPRO-79534	U.S.A.	1970	11.99
Hendrix, Jimi	Band Of Gypsys (Puppet Version)	CD	Polydor	P20P-22006	Japan	1970	57.99
Hendrix, Jimi	BBC Sessions	2CD	MCA	MCAD2-11742	U.S.A.	1998	16.99
Hendrix, Jimi	BBC Sessions (Promo Sampler)	CD	MCA	MCA5P-4167	U.S.A.	1998	14.99
Hendrix, Jimi	Blues	CD	MCA	MCAD-11060	U.S.A.	1994	10.99
Hendrix, Jimi	Box Set 8 Song Promo Sampler	CD	MCA	MCAR-25121-2	U.S.A.	2000	9.99
Hendrix, Jimi	Concerts	CD	Polydor	P33P-25038	Japan	1987	44.99
Hendrix, Jimi	Crash Landing	CD	Polydor	847-263-2	U.S.A.	1975	41.99
Hendrix, Jimi	Crosstown Conversation	CD	Baktabak	CBAK-4082	England	1994	8.99
Hendrix, Jimi	Cry Of Love	CD	Reprise	2034-2	U.S.A.	1971	14.99
Hendrix, Jimi	Day Tripper (3" Cd)	CD	Rykodisc	RCD3-1008	U.S.A.	1988	5.99
Hendrix, Jimi	Electric Ladyland	CD	MCA	MCAD-11600	U.S.A.	1997	8.99
Hendrix, Jimi	Electric Ladyland (Nude Girls Cover)	2CD	Polydor	823-359-2	Germany	1968	46.99
Hendrix, Jimi	Essential Jimi Hendrix, Vol. 1/2	2CD	Reprise	9-26035-2	U.S.A.	1989	19.99

Artist	Title	Format	Label	Catalog No	Country	Released	Value
Hendrix, Jimi	Experience Hendrix	CD	MCA	MCAD-11671	U.S.A.	1997	8.99
Hendrix, Jimi	Experience Hendrix + 8 (Bonus Cd)	2CD	MCA	112-383-2	EEC	2000	25.99
Hendrix, Jimi	First Rays Of The New Rising Sun	CD	MCA	MCAD-11599	U.S.A.	1997	13.99
Hendrix, Jimi	In the West	CD	Polydor	831-312-2	Germany	1988	55.99
Hendrix, Jimi	Jimi Hendrix (Compact Disc + Cd Rom)	CD	Weton W	WWCDR006	Holland	2001	8.99
Hendrix, Jimi	Jimi Hendrix Experience Box Set (Felt)	4CD	MCA	088-112-317-2	U.S.A.	2000	43.99
Hendrix, Jimi	Jimi Plays Monterey	CD	Reprise	CD-25358	Canada	1986	34.99
Hendrix, Jimi	Kiss The Sky (Best Of)	CD	Reprise	9-25119-2	U.S.A.	1984	10.99
Hendrix, Jimi	Lifelines Box Set	4CD	Reprise	9-26435-2	U.S.A.	1990	54.99
Hendrix, Jimi	Live At Berkeley	CD	Universal	B0001102-02	U.S.A.	2003	8.99
Hendrix, Jimi	Live At Fillmore East (Promo Sampler)	CD	MCA	MCA5P-4319	U.S.A.	1999	9.99
Hendrix, Jimi	Live At The Filmore East	2CD	MCA	MCAD2-11931	U.S.A.	1999	18.99
Hendrix, Jimi	Live At Winterland	CD	Polydor	P33P-20119	Japan	1989	44.99
Hendrix, Jimi	Live At Winterland (Gold/Diff Booklet)	CD	Rykodisc	RCD-80038	U.S.A.	1992	64.99
Hendrix, Jimi	Live At Winterland (Picture Cd)	CD	Polydor	847 238-2	Australia	1987	23.99
Hendrix, Jimi	Live At Winterland Box Set (W T-Shirt)	2CD	Rykodisc	RCD-90038	U.S.A.	1992	69.99
Hendrix, Jimi	Live At Woodstock	2CD	MCA	MCAD2-11987	U.S.A.	1999	15.99
Hendrix, Jimi	Live/Isle of Wight '70	CD	Polydor	847-236-2	Australia	1991	13.99
Hendrix, Jimi	Martin Scorsese Presents	CD	Universal	B0000698-02	U.S.A.	2003	8.99
Hendrix, Jimi	Merry Christmas And Happy New Year	CD Single	MCA	088-155-651-2	U.S.A.	1999	6.99
Hendrix, Jimi	Midnight Lightning	CD	Polydor K.K.	P33P-25025	Japan	1989	67.99
Hendrix, Jimi	Radio One	CD	Rykodisc	RCD-20078	U.S.A.	1988	9.99
Hendrix, Jimi	Smash Hits (12 Song Version)	CD	MCA	088-112-984-2	U.S.A.	2002	8.99
Hendrix, Jimi	Smash Hits (Cd+C)	CD	Reprise	2276-2	U.S.A.	1972	6.99
Hendrix, Jimi	South Saturn Delta	CD	MCA	MCAD-11684	U.S.A.	1997	7.99
Hendrix, Jimi	Stages Box Set	4CD	Reprise	9-26732-2	U.S.A.	1991	157.99
Hendrix, Jimi	The Jimi Hendrix Concerts	CD	Reprise	9-22306-2	U.S.A.	1989	38.99
Hendrix, Jimi	The Ultimate Experience	CD	MCA	MCAD-10829	U.S.A.	1993	4.99
Hendrix, Jimi	Unistar Showcase Rock 1-14/16/93	2CD	Unistar	HL860100A	U.S.A.	1993	89.99
Hendrix, Jimi	Voodoo Child + 1	2CD	Universal	170-322-2	England	2001	13.99
Hendrix, Jimi	Voodoo Soup	CD	MCA	MCAD-11236	U.S.A.	1995	9.99
Hendrix, Jimi	War Heroes	CD	Polydor	847-262-2	Germany	1988	44.99
Hendrix, Jimi	War Heroes	CD	Polydor	813-573-2	Germany	1988	44.99
Hendrix, Jimi/Cat Mother	A.N. Newsboys - Street Giveth	CD	Polydor	31453-7616-2	U.S.A.	1969	29.99
Hendrix, Jimi/Eire Apparent	Sunrise + 1	CD	One Way	OW-27734	U.S.A.	1993	11.99
Hendrix, Jimi/Promo	Between The Lines Lifelines Sampler	CD	Reprise	PRO-CD-4541	U.S.A.	1990	23.99
Hendrix, Jimi/Various Artists	Here It Is, The Music (DJ) W/ Fire Live	CD	Rykodisc	CDK-00099	U.S.A.	1988	7.99
Henley, Don	Actual Miles	CD	Geffen	GEFD-24834	U.S.A.	1995	9.99
Henley, Don	Building The Perfect..(MFSL Gold)	CD	Mobile Fidelity	UDCD-705	U.S.A.	1984	29.99
Henley, Don	End Of The Innocence (Clothbound)	CD	Geffen	2-24217	U.S.A.	1989	19.99
Henley, Don	End Of The Innocence (MFSL Gold)	CD	Mobile Fidelity	UDCD-721	U.S.A.	1989	27.99
Henley, Don	I Can't Stand Still	CD	Asylum	9-60048-2	U.S.A.	1982	7.99
Henley, Don	In The Studio (End Of Innocence)	CD	Album Network	5TX0100A	U.S.A.	1989	34.99
Henley, Don	Inside Job	CD	Warner Bros.	9-47083-2	U.S.A.	2000	8.99
Henley, Don	New York Minute (3" Single)	CD	Geffen	GEF-66CD	U.S.A.	1989	13.99
Henley, Don	Through Your Hands (Promo)	CD Single	Revolution	PRO-CD-8576-R	U.S.A.	1996	7.99
Henry Cow	In Praise Of (500 JPN/32 UK)	Mini Lp	Recommeded	HCSPECIALED4	England	2002	13.99
Henry Cow	In Praise Of Learning (Original Mix)	CD	Recommeded	ReR-HC3	England	2002	13.99
Henry Cow	In Praise Of... (Inferior S W/Bon Trks)	CD	East Side Digital	80502	U.S.A.	1991	13.99
Henry Cow	Legend (500 JPN/32 UK)	Mini Lp	Recommeded	HCSPECIALED2	England	2002	18.99
Henry Cow	Legend (Inferior Sound W/Bon Trks)	CD	East Side Digital	80482	U.S.A.	1991	14.99
Henry Cow	Special Editon Box (500 JPN/32 UK)	Mini Lp	Recommeded	HCSPECIALED1	England	2002	69.99
Henry Cow	Unrest (500 JPN/32 UK)	Mini Lp	Recommeded	HCSPECIALED3	England	2002	18.99
Henry Cow	Unrest (Remastered)	CD	Recommeded	ReR-HC2	England	2002	19.99
Henry Cow	Unrest (W/Inferior Sound)	CD	East Side Digital	80492	U.S.A.	1991	14.99
Henry Cow	Western Culture	CD	East Side Digital	ESD-80852	U.S.A.	1991	14.99
Henry Cow	Western Culture (500 JPN/32 UK)	Mini Lp	Recommeded	HCSPECIALED5	England	2002	18.99
Henry Cow	Western Culture + 3	CD	Recommeded	ReR-HC4	England	2002	19.99

Artist	Title	Format	Label	Catalog No	Country	Released	Value
Henry Cow/Robert Wyatt	Concerts (W/Greasy Truckers Side)	2CD	East Side Digital	ESD-80822/32	U.S.A.	1995	29.99
Herman, Woody	Giant Steps	CD	Fantasy	OJCCD-334-2	U.S.A.	1994	9.99
Herman, Woody	Keep On Keepin' On: 1968-1970	CD	Chess	GRD-818	U.S.A.	1998	14.99
Herman's Hermits	Blaze + 12	CD	Repertoire	REP-4850	Germany	2001	11.99
Herman's Hermits	Herman's Hermits/Both Sides Of	CD	EMI	7243-5-38849-2-5	England	2002	11.99
Herman's Hermits	Mrs. Brown You've Got... +13	CD	Repertoire	REP-4424-WY	Germany	1994	11.99
Herman's Hermits	No Milk Today + 7	CD	Magic	4977642	France	1998	11.99
Herman's Hermits	The Hermhits	Mini Lp	Akarma	AK-196	Italy	2003	14.99
Herman's Hermits	Their Greatest Hits	CD	Abkco	42272	U.S.A.	1987	7.99
Herman's Hermits	There's A Kind of Hush... + 11	CD	Repertoire	REP-4849	Germany	2001	11.99
Heron, Mike	Mike Heron's Reputation	CD	Unique Gravity	UGCD-5606	Austria	1975	19.99
Herrmann, Bernard	A History of Hitchcock Dial M Murder	CD	Silva	SSD-1030	U.S.A.	1993	11.99
Herrmann, Bernard	Alfred Hitchcock's Film Music	CD	Milan	CD-CH022	Switzerlan	1986	12.99
Herrmann, Bernard	Anna And The King Of Siam	CD	Varese	302-066-091-2	U.S.A.	2000	14.99
Herrmann, Bernard	Anth. Vol. 1: Magnificent Ambersons	CD	Preamble	PRCD-1783	U.S.A.	1990	12.99
Herrmann, Bernard	Anth. Vol. 2: Citizen Kane	CD	Preamble	PRCD-1788	U.S.A.	1991	12.99
Herrmann, Bernard	Anth. Vol. 3: The Inquirer	CD	Preamble	PRCD-1789	U.S.A.	1992	12.99
Herrmann, Bernard	Battle Of Neretva	CD	Southern Cross	SCCD-5005	Australia	1987	24.99
Herrmann, Bernard	Beneath The 12-Mile Reef	CD	Film Score Monthly	FSMVOL3/NO10	U.S.A.	1953	24.99
Herrmann, Bernard	Bernard Herrmann At The Movies	CD	Label X	ATM-CD-2003	EEC	1996	19.99
Herrmann, Bernard	Cape Fear	CD	MCA	MCAD-10463	U.S.A.	1991	29.99
Herrmann, Bernard	Citizen Kane	CD	Varese	302-065-806-2	U.S.A.	1999	11.99
Herrmann, Bernard	Citizen Kane - The Essential B.H. Film...	2CD	Silva	SSD-1093	U.S.A.	1999	19.99
Herrmann, Bernard	Citizen Kane/Conducts Great Film...+ 2	CD	Polydor K.K.	POCL-3687	Japan	1994	49.99
Herrmann, Bernard	Citizen Kane/Magnificent Ambersons	CD	Disconforme	SFCD33553	Andorra	2000	11.99
Herrmann, Bernard	Citizen Kane: Classic Film Scores Of	CD	RCA	0707-2-RG	U.S.A.	1974	12.99
Herrmann, Bernard	Citzen Kane + 3	CD	London	417-852-2	U.S.A.	1988	11.99
Herrmann, Bernard	Classic Fantasy Film Scores	CD	Cloud Nine	ANC-7014	England	1988	33.99
Herrmann, Bernard	Classic Jazz	CD	London	444-785-2	U.S.A.	1996	10.99
Herrmann, Bernard	Concerto Macabre	CD	Koch	3-7609-2	U.S.A.	1996	10.99
Herrmann, Bernard	Day the Earth Stood.. (Gold 2 Ex.Trks)	CD	Fox	8739-02	U.S.A.	1995	81.99
Herrmann, Bernard	Devil Daniel Webster/Currier And Ives	CD	Koch	3-7224-2-H1	U.S.A.	1994	10.99
Herrmann, Bernard	Echoes Quartet Ect...	CD	Unicorn	UKCD-2069	England	1994	14.99
Herrmann, Bernard	Erik Satie & Darius Milhaud	CD	London	443-897-2	Germany	1996	10.99
Herrmann, Bernard	Fahrenheit 451	CD	Varese	VSD-5551	U.S.A.	1995	11.99
Herrmann, Bernard	Fantasy Film World Of (MFSL Gold Cd)	CD	Mobile Fidelity	UDCD-656	U.S.A.	1974	22.99
Herrmann, Bernard	Film Fantasy	CD	London	421-266-2	U.S.A.	1989	10.99
Herrmann, Bernard	From Welles And Hitchcock...	CD	Victor Enter.	VICP-8099	Japan	1993	34.99
Herrmann, Bernard	Garden Of Evil	CD	Marco Polo	8.223841	Germany	1998	14.99
Herrmann, Bernard	Great British Film Music	CD	London	448-954-2	Germany	1996	10.99
Herrmann, Bernard	Great Film Music + 13	CD	London	443-899-2	Germany	1996	10.99
Herrmann, Bernard	Great Hitchcock Movie Thrillers	CD	London	436-797-2	U.S.A.	1992	11.99
Herrmann, Bernard	Herrmann At Fox, Vol. 1	CD	Varese	302-066-052-2	U.S.A.	1999	14.99
Herrmann, Bernard	Herrmann At Fox, Vol. 2	CD	Varese	302-066-053-2	U.S.A.	1999	14.99
Herrmann, Bernard	Herrmann/Hitchcock: P Terror	CD	Silva	STD-5005	U.S.A.	1996	11.99
Herrmann, Bernard	Hitchcock 100 Years (HDCD)	CD	Milan	73138-35884-2	U.S.A.	1999	11.99
Herrmann, Bernard	Hitchcock Pres. (Unrel. Torn Curtain)	CD	Hip O	HIPD-64661	U.S.A.	1999	11.99
Herrmann, Bernard	It's Alive 2	CD	Silva Screen	FILMCD-074	U.S.A.	1990	23.99
Herrmann, Bernard	Jane Eyre	CD	Marco Polo	8.223535	Germany	1994	14.99
Herrmann, Bernard	Jason And The Argonauts	CD	Intrada	MAF7083	U.S.A.	1999	23.99
Herrmann, Bernard	Journey Center Of The Earth S.T.	CD	Varese	VSD-5849	U.S.A.	1997	11.99
Herrmann, Bernard	Joy In The Morning	CD	Film Score Monthly	FSMVOL5/NO3	U.S.A.	1965	24.99
Herrmann, Bernard	M Film Concert Series (London Lp's)	4CD	Masters Film	SRS-2005/8	Canada	1989	132.99
Herrmann, Bernard	Marnie	CD	Varese	302-066-094-2	U.S.A.	2000	11.99
Arrtmann, Bernard	Moby Dick/For The Fallen	CD	Unicorn	UKCD-2061	England	1993	14.99
Herrmann, Bernard	Music From Great Film Classics + 19	CD	London	448-948-2	Germany	1996	10.99
Herrmann, Bernard	Music From The Great Hitchcock Films	CD	Polydor K.K.	POCL-3686	Japan	1994	49.99
Herrmann, Bernard	Music Great Film Classics (MFSL Gold)	CD	Mobile Fidelity	UDCD-701	U.S.A.	1971	17.99

H

Artist	Title	Format	Label	Catalog No	Country	Released	Value
Herrmann, Bernard	Mysterious Film World (MFSL Gold Cd)	CD	Mobile Fidelity	UDCD-692	U.S.A.	1975	22.99
Herrmann, Bernard	Mysterious Island	CD	Cloud Nine	ACN-7017	England	1993	32.99
Herrmann, Bernard	Night Digger	CD	Label X	LXCD-12	Australia	1994	24.99
Herrmann, Bernard	North By Northwest	CD	Varese	VCD-47205	U.S.A.	1980	11.99
Herrmann, Bernard	North By Northwest	CD	Unicorn	UKCD-2040	England	1990	14.99
Herrmann, Bernard	North By Northwest + 38	CD	Rhino	R2-72101	U.S.A.	1995	12.99
Herrmann, Bernard	On Dangerous Ground	CD	Film Score Monthly	VOL6/NO16	U.S.A.	2003	24.99
Herrmann, Bernard	Orson Welles At The Movies	CD	Label X	ATM-CD-2008	Australia	1996	19.99
Herrmann, Bernard	Psycho	CD	Unicorn	UKCD-2021	England	1989	8.99
Herrmann, Bernard	Psycho	CD	Varese	VSD-5765	U.S.A.	1997	11.99
Herrmann, Bernard	Psycho/North By Northwest	CD	Unicorn	UKCD-2080	England	1996	14.99
Herrmann, Bernard	Sisters	CD	Southern Cross	SCCD-903	U.S.A.	1985	23.99
Herrmann, Bernard	Symphony No. 21/No. 2/Music Hamlet	CD	Unicorn	UKCD-2066	England	1994	24.99
Herrmann, Bernard	Symphony/The Fantasticks	CD	Unicorn	UKCD-2063	England	1993	14.99
Herrmann, Bernard	Taxi Driver	CD	Varese	VSD-5279	U.S.A.	1986	8.99
Herrmann, Bernard	Taxi Driver + 7	CD	Arista	07822-19005-2	U.S.A.	1998	8.99
Herrmann, Bernard	The 3 Worlds Of Gulliver	CD	Cloud Nine	ACN-7018	England	1993	33.99
Herrmann, Bernard	The 7th Voyage Of Sinbad	CD	Varese	VSD-5961	U.S.A.	1998	11.99
Herrmann, Bernard	The 7th Voyage Of Sinbad	CD	Varese	VCD47256	U.S.A.	1980	11.99
Herrmann, Bernard	The CBS Years, Vol. 1	CD	Prometheus	PCD-152	Belgium	2003	14.99
Herrmann, Bernard	The CBS Years, Vol. 2	CD	Prometheus	PCD-153	Belgium	2003	14.99
Herrmann, Bernard	The Day the Earth Stood Still	CD	Fox	07822-11010-2	U.S.A.	1993	11.99
Herrmann, Bernard	The Film Scores (SBM)	CD	Sony	SK-62700	U.S.A.	1996	15.99
Herrmann, Bernard	The Ghost And Mrs. Muir	CD	Disconforme	SFCD33508	Andorra	1999	11.99
Herrmann, Bernard	The Ghost And Mrs. Muir O.S.T. + 21	CD	Varese	VSD-5850	U.S.A.	1997	11.99
Herrmann, Bernard	The Ghost Mrs. Muir (Short Version)	CD	Varese	VCD-47254	U.S.A.	1985	21.99
Herrmann, Bernard	The Great Hitchcock Movie Thrillers	CD	London	443-895-2	Germany	1996	11.99
Herrmann, Bernard	The Kentuckian	CD	Preamble	PRCD-1777	U.S.A.	1987	12.99
Herrmann, Bernard	The Snows Of Kilimanjaro/5 Fingers	CD	Marco Polo	8.225168	Canada	2001	19.99
Herrmann, Bernard	The Three Worlds Of Gulliver	CD	Varese	302-066-162-2	U.S.A.	2001	14.99
Herrmann, Bernard	The Trouble With Harry	CD	Varese	VSD-5971	U.S.A.	1998	11.99
Herrmann, Bernard	The Twilight Zone	2CD	Varese	302-066-087-2	U.S.A.	1999	18.99
Herrmann, Bernard	To Catch a Thief: History of Hitchcock II	CD	Silva	SSD-1045	U.S.A.	1995	11.99
Herrmann, Bernard	Torn Curtain	CD	Silva	SSD-1051	U.S.A.	1995	11.99
Herrmann, Bernard	Torn Curtain (The Unused Score)	CD	Varese	VSD-5817	U.S.A.	1998	10.99
Herrmann, Bernard	Twilight Zone 40th Ann. Collection	4CD	Silva	STD-2000	U.S.A.	1999	44.99
Herrmann, Bernard	Vertigo	CD	Varese	VSD-5600	U.S.A.	1995	14.99
Herrmann, Bernard	Vertigo	CD	Mercury	422-106-2	U.S.A.	1986	11.99
Herrmann, Bernard	Vertigo + 9	CD	Varese	VSD-5759	U.S.A.	1996	11.99
Herrmann, Bernard	Warsaw Concerto	CD	London	421-261-2	U.S.A.	1988	10.99
Herrmann, Bernard	Welles Raises Kane	CD	Unicorn	UKCD-2065	England	1994	14.99
Herrmann, Bernard	Wuthering Heights	3CD	Unicorn	UKCD2050/51/52	England	1992	49.99
Herrmann, Bernard/Alex North	Jane Eyre/A Streetcar Named Desire	CD	Disconforme	SFCD33519	Andorra	1999	11.99
Herrmann, Bernard/D Elfman	Psycho (O.S.T.)	CD	Virgin	7243-8-47657-2-9	U.S.A.	1998	8.99
Herrmann, Bernard/McNeely	The Day The Earth Stood Still	CD	Varese	302-066-314-2	U.S.A.	2003	11.99
Herrmann, Bernard/Newman	The Egyptian	CD	Marco Polo	8.225078	Canada	1999	21.99
Herrmann, Bernard/Raff	Symphony No. 5, Op. 177 "Lenore"	CD	Unicorn	UKCD-2031	England	1990	14.99
Herrmann, Bernard/Rozsa	Great Shakespeare Films	CD	London	421-268-2	U.S.A.	1989	10.99
Herrmann, Bernard/Satie	Gymnopedies	CD	London	421-395-2	U.S.A.	1989	10.99
Herrmann, Bernard/Stokowski	Ives Symphony 2	CD	London	433-017-2	U.S.A.	1991	10.99
Herrmann/Bernstein	View Pompey's Head/Blue Denim	CD	Film Score Monthly	FSMVOL4/NO15	U.S.A.	1959	33.99
Herrmann/Black	The Four Faces Of Jazz (MFSL Gold)	CD	Mobile Fidelity	UDCD-672	U.S.A.	1973	18.99
Herrmann/Gershwin	Gershwin Orchestral Works	CD	Karussell	450-062-2	EC	1993	8.99
Herrmann/Moss/Korngold	Classical Hollywood	CD	Bay Cities	BCD-1014	U.S.A.	1990	14.99
Herrmann/Newman	The Egyptian	CD	Varese	VSD-5258	U.S.A.	1990	11.99
Herrmann/Newman	The Egyptian + 13	CD	Film Score Monthly	FSMVOL4/NO5	U.S.A.	1954	24.99
Herrmann/Newman/Steiner	Celebrating The Classics	CD	Themes&Variations	T&V-0001	U.S.A.	1999	14.99
Herrmann/Orson Welles	War Of The Worlds - Uncut Broadcast	CD	Metacom	RM#7400300	U.S.A.	1967	8.99

H

Artist	Title	Format	Label	Catalog No	Country	Released	Value
Herrmann/Porter/Ives	Chamber Music Northwest	CD	Delos	DE-3088	U.S.A.	1991	14.99
Herrmann/Raskin	Classics Series 1: Laura/Jane Eyre	CD	Fox	07822-11006-2	U.S.A.	1993	11.99
Herrmann/Rozsa/Waxman	Herrmann/Waxman/Rozsa/Jackson	CD	Koch	3-7152-2-H1	U.S.A.	1992	11.99
Herrmann/Schifrin	Alfred Hitchcock, Master of Mayhem	CD	Intersound	CDS-524	U.S.A.	1990	14.99
Herrmann/Schuman	Herrmann: Symphony No. 1	CD	Koch	3-7135-2-H1	U.S.A.	1992	14.99
Herrmann/Shire/Gold	Classical Hollywood II	CD	Bay Cities	BCD-1021	U.S.A.	1991	14.99
Herrmann/Waxman/North	The Paradine Case	CD	Koch	3-7225-2-H1	U.S.A.	1995	11.99
Hester, Carolyn	A Tom Paxton Tribute	CD	Road Goes On	CHCD-047	England	1999	16.99
Hester, Carolyn	At Town Hall	CD	Bear Family	BCD-15520	Germany	1990	19.99
Hester, Carolyn	Dear Companion	2CD	Bear Family	BCD-15701	Germany	1995	34.99
Hester, Carolyn	From These Hills	CD	Road Goes On	RGFCD033	England	1996	16.99
Hester, Carolyn	Texas Songbird	CD	Road Goes On	RGFCD-019	England	1996	15.99
Hester, Carolyn	The Traditional Album + 4	CD	Road Goes On	RGFCD025	England	1995	14.99
Hester, Carolyn/Bob Dylan	Carolyn Hester + 2	CD	Columbia	CK-57310	U.S.A.	1977	12.99
Hewitt, Jennifer Love	Bare Naked	CD Single	Jive	9254182	Australia	2002	6.99
Hewitt, Jennifer Love	Bare Naked + 1	CD	Zomba	ZJCI-10101	Japan	2002	25.99
Hewitt, Jennifer Love	How Do I Deal	CD Single	Warner Bros.	4/2-47276	U.S.A.	1998	4.99
Hewitt, Jennifer Love	Jennifer Love Hewitt	CD	Atlantic	82934-2	U.S.A.	1996	8.99
Hewitt, Jennifer Love	Lets Go Bang	CD	Atlantic	82819-2	U.S.A.	1995	8.99
Hewitt, Jennifer Love	Love Songs	CD	Meldac	MECP-28003	Japan	1992	34.99
Hiatt, John	Bring The Family (MFSL Gold Cd)	CD	Mobile Fidelity	UDCD-603	U.S.A.	1987	29.99
Hiatt, John	Crossing Muddy Waters	CD	Sanctuary	SANCD003	England	2000	10.99
Hiatt, John	Greatest Hits	2CD	A&M	540-874-2	Holland	1998	12.99
Hiatt, John	Hangin' Around The Observatory	CD	Epic	EK-32688	U.S.A.	1974	12.99
Hiatt, John	I'll Never Get Over You	CD Single	Sanctuary	SANX102	Japan	2001	8.99
Hiatt, John	In-Store Play (Promo Sampler)	CD	A&M	31454-8034-2	U.S.A.	1993	19.99
Hiatt, John	Little Head	CD	Capitol	7243-8-54672-2-6	U.S.A.	1997	9.99
Hiatt, John	Living A Little, Laughing A..1974-85	CD	Raven	RVCD-50	Australia	1995	10.99
Hiatt, John	Overcoats	CD	Epic	EK-33190	U.S.A.	1975	19.99
Hiatt, John	Perfectly Good Guitar	CD	A&M	31451-0135-2	U.S.A.	1993	8.99
Hiatt, John	Perfectly Good Guitar (Promo/Crate)	CD	A&M	31454-0135-2	U.S.A.	1993	69.99
Hiatt, John	Riding With The King (MFSL Gold Cd)	CD	Mobile Fidelity	UDCD-704	U.S.A.	1983	19.99
Hiatt, John	Slow Turning (MFSL Gold Cd)	CD	Mobile Fidelity	UDCD-749	U.S.A.	1988	33.99
Hiatt, John	Slug Line/Two Bit Monsters	CD	BGO	BGOCD176	England	1993	14.99
Hiatt, John	Stolen Moments	CD	A&M	75021-5310-2	U.S.A.	1990	7.99
Hiatt, John	The Tiki Bar Is Open	CD	Sanctuary	SANCD096	England	2001	11.99
Hiatt, John	Walk On	CD	Capitol	7243-8-33416-2-7	U.S.A.	1995	8.99
Hiatt, John	Walk On (Promo Interview)	CD	Capitol	DPRO-10280	U.S.A.	1995	7.99
Hiatt, John	Warming Up To The Ice Age	CD	Geffen	9-24055-2	U.S.A.	1985	6.99
Hiatt, John	Warming Up To The Ice Age	CD	Lemon	CDLEM08	England	2003	8.99
Hiatt, John	Y'all Caught	CD	Geffen	9-24247-2	U.S.A.	1989	9.99
Hicks, Dan/Hot Licks	It Happened One Bite	CD	Warner Bros.	WPCR-10306	Japan	1999	19.99
Hicks, Dan/Hot Licks	It Happened One Bite + 9 (Ltd. 4500)	CD	Rhino	RHM2-7719	U.S.A.	2000	23.99
Hicks, Hinda	Everything To Me (Unreleased Cd)	CD	Universal	7-51654-81262-7	England	2000	64.99
Highwaymen/Kristofferson	Highwayman (Cash/Jennings/Nelson)	CD	Columbia	CK-40056	U.S.A.	1985	11.99
Highwaymen/Kristofferson	Higwayman 2 (Cash/Jennings/Nelson)	CD	Columbia	CK-45240	U.S.A.	1990	11.99
Highwaymen/Kristofferson	Road Goes..(Cash/Jennings/Nelson)	CD	Capitol	7423-8-28091-2	U.S.A.	1994	8.99
Hill, Benny	The Best Of	CD	Continuum	19206-2	U.S.A.	1992	6.99
Hillage, Steve	Fish Rising	CD	Virgin	0777-7-87277-2-9	Holland	1975	15.99
Hillage, Steve	L	CD	Virgin	7243-8-42981-2-5	England	1976	10.99
Hillage, Steve	Live Herald	CD	Caroline	CAROL-1671-2	U.S.A.	1990	11.99
Hillage, Steve	Rainbow Dome Musick	CD	Caroline	CAROL-1803-2	U.S.A.	1979	15.99
Hillage, Steve/Khan	Space Shanty	CD	Deram	844-008-2	England	1972	11.99
Hillman, Chris	Clear Sailin'	CD	Wounded Bird	WOU-1104	U.S.A.	2002	9.99
Hillman, Chris	Desert Rose	CD	Sugar Hill	SH-CD-3743	U.S.A.	1990	10.99
Hillman, Chris	Like A Hurricane	CD	Sugar Hill	SHCD-3878	U.S.A.	1998	9.99
Hillman, Chris	Morning Sky	CD	Sugar Hill	SH-CD-3729	U.S.A.	1982	10.99
Hillman, Chris	Slippin' Away	CD	Line	LECD-9.00941-0	Germany	1990	10.99

H

Artist	Title	Format	Label	Catalog No	Country	Released	Value
Hillman, Chris	Slippin' Away	CD	Wounded Bird	WOU-1062	U.S.A.	2002	10.99
Hillman, Chris/Herb Pederson	Bakersfield Bound	CD	Sugar Hill	SHCD-3850	U.S.A.	1996	11.99
Hillman, Chris/Hillmen	The Hillmen + 1	CD	Sugar Hill	SHCD-3719	U.S.A.	1995	10.99
Hillman/Pedersen/Rice/Rice	Out Of The Woodwork	CD	Rounder	CD-0390	U.S.A.	1997	11.99
Hillman/Pedersen/Rice/Rice	Rice, Rice, Hillman & Pedersen	CD	Rounder	11661-0450-2	U.S.A.	1999	11.99
Hillman/Pedersen/Rice/Rice	Running Wild	CD	Rounder	11661-0483-2	U.S.A.	2001	11.99
Hine, Rupert	Pick Up A Bone	CD	Line	LICD-9.00123-0	Germany	1991	18.99
Hine, Rupert	Unfinished Picture	CD	Line	LICD-9.00118-0	Germany	1988	10.99
Hinton, Eddie	Cry & Moan	CD	Bullseye Blues	CD-BB-9504	U.S.A.	1991	12.99
Hinton, Eddie	Dear Y'all: The Songwriting Sessions	CD	Zane	ZNCD 1016	England	2004	18.99
Hinton, Eddie	Hard Luck Guy	CD	Capricorn	314-538-655-2	U.S.A.	1999	19.99
Hinton, Eddie	Letters From Mississippi	CD	Line	INCD-9.00172-0	Germany	1987	24.99
Hinton, Eddie	Letters From Mississippi (MFSL Silver)	CD	Mobile Fidelity	MFCD-1-749	U.S.A.	1987	24.99
Hinton, Eddie	Very Blue Highway	CD	Bullseye Blues	CD-BB-9528	U.S.A.	1993	10.99
Hinton, Eddie	Very Extremely Dangerous	CD	Capricorn	314-536-111-2	U.S.A.	1997	10.99
Hisaishi, Joe	Nausicaa/Valley Of The Wind (O.S.T.)	CD	Tokuma	TKCA-70133	Japan	1993	11.99
Hitchcock, Robyn	Catalog Sampler (Promo)	CD	Rhino	PRCD-7083	U.S.A.	1994	21.99
Hitchcock, Robyn	Groovy Decay	CD	Line	ALCD-9.00008-0	Germany	1987	10.99
Hodgson, Roger	Hai Hai	CD	A&M	395-112-2	Germany	1987	8.99
Hodgson, Roger	Hungry	CD Single	Epic	6692152	Germany	2000	2.99
Hodgson, Roger	In The Eye Of The Storm	CD	A&M	395-004-2	France	1984	12.99
Hodgson, Roger	Open The Door	CD	Epic	4977392000	Holland	2000	10.99
Hodgson, Roger	Rites Of Passage	CD	Unichourd	UNIVP001CD	England	1997	9.99
Hole	Be A Man (Promo)	CD Single	Warner Bros.	PRCD-9166	U.S.A.	1999	5.99
Hole	Live Through This + 5 (Bonus Cd)	2CD	Geffen	GEFD-24631	Australia	1994	39.99
Hole	The First Sessions	CD	SympathyFTRI	SFTRI-53CD	U.S.A.	1990	8.99
Holland, Dozier, Holland	Why Can't We Be Lovers	2CD	Castle	CMDDD046	England	2000	21.99
Holland, Jools	Small World Big Band	CD	Rhino	R2-78264	U.S.A.	2001	10.99
Holland, Jools	The Maiden's Lament	CD Single	I.R.S.	EIRSCD-145	England	1990	10.99
Holland, Jools/Ray Davies	More Friends (Chrissie Hynde)	CD	Warner Bros.	R2-73884	U.S.A.	2002	12.99
Hollies	30th Anniversary Collection 1963-1993	3CD	EMI	0777-7-99917-2-3	U.S.A.	1993	29.99
Hollies	All The World Is Love	CD	BR Music	BR-146-2	Holland	1994	11.99
Hollies	Another Night + 7	CD	Magic	5244082	France	1999	11.99
Hollies	Archive Alive!	CD	Archive	ACH-80016	U.S.A.	1997	29.99
Hollies	At Abbey Road + 4 - 1973-1989	CD	EMI	7243-496434-2-0	England	1998	10.99
Hollies	Confessions Of The Mind	CD	BGO	BGOCD96	England	1990	13.99
Hollies	Dear Eloise / King Midas Reverse + 4	CD	Sundazed	SC-6123	U.S.A.	1997	16.99
Hollies	Distant Light	CD	Epic	EK-30958	U.S.A.	1972	13.99
Hollies	Evolution + 5	CD	Sundazed	SC-6122	U.S.A.	1999	9.99
Hollies	Hollies	CD	Epic	EK-32574	U.S.A.	1974	8.99
Hollies	Hollies Sing Hollies	CD	EMI	7243-5-20130-2-9	Germany	1999	13.99
Hollies	In The Hollies Style + 8	CD	Magic	5251272	France	2000	11.99
Hollies	Moving Finger + 4	CD	Sundazed	SC-6125	U.S.A.	1997	10.99
Hollies	Romany + 8	CD	Magic	4975782	France	1998	12.99
Hollies	Stay + 10	CD	Magic	5244122	France	1999	11.99
Hollies	The Hollies	CD	Toshiba-EMI	TOCP-7543	Japan	1993	29.99
Hollies	The Hollies Sing Dylan	CD	EMI	7243-5-20131-2-8	Holland	1999	14.99
Hollies	What Goes Around...+ 1	CD	Wounded Bird	WOU-8076	U.S.A.	2001	9.99
Hollies	Write On + 5	CD	Magic	5244142	France	1999	11.99
Holly, Buddy	Holly In The Hills/Giant	CD	BGO	BGOCD563	England	2002	14.99
Holly, Buddy	The Buddy Holly Collection	2CD	MCA	MCAD2-10883	U.S.A.	1993	19.99
Hollywood Fats Band	Hollywood Fats Band	CD	Line	STCD-9.00595-0	Germany	1991	24.99
Holmes Brothers	Jubilation	CD	Caroline	CAROL-2319-2	U.S.A.	1992	11.99
Holmes, Rupert	Mystery Of Edwin Drood	CD	Varese	VSD-5597	Japan	1986	50.99
Holy Modal Rounders	Good Taste Is Timeless	CD	Sundazed	SC-6208	U.S.A.	2003	11.99
Hondells/Glen Campbell	Self Titled/Little Honda (Gary Usher)	CD	Repertoire	REP-4397-WP	Germany	1994	29.99
Honeymoon Suite	Dreamland	CD	Frontiers	FR-CD-119	Italy	2002	13.99
Honeymoon Suite	Lemon Tongue + 2	CD	Griffin	GCD-3542-2	U.S.A.	2002	13.99

H

Artist	Title	Format	Label	Catalog No	Country	Released	Value
Honeymoon Suite	Monsters Under The Bed	CD	WEA	CD-75532	Canada	1991	10.99
Honeymoon Suite	Racing After Midnight	CD	WEA	CD-55445	Canada	1988	8.99
Honeymoon Suite	Self Titled	CD	Warner Bros.	9-25098-2	U.S.A.	1984	11.99
Honeymoon Suite	The Big Prize	CD	Warner Bros.	9-25293-2	U.S.A.	1985	11.99
Honeymoon Suite	The Singles	CD	WEA	CD-56979	Canada	1989	12.99
Honeyrods, The	Self Titled	CD	Capricorn	314-536-030-2	U.S.A.	1997	8.99
Honeys/Brian Wilson	The Honeys Collection	CD	Collectors Choice	72435-29850-2-9	U.S.A.	2001	23.99
Hooker, John Lee	The Healer	CD	Capricorn	314-538-689-2	U.S.A.	1999	9.99
Hooker, John Lee	The Healer (MFSL Gold Cd)	CD	Mobile Fidelity	UDCD-567	U.S.A.	1989	44.99
Hooker, John Lee/V. Artists	From Clarksdale To Heaven	CD	Eagle	EADCD228	Germany	2002	12.99
Hootie & the Blowfish	An Interview With Darius Rucker	CD	Baktabak	CBAK4065	England	1993	11.99
Hootie & the Blowfish	Musical Chairs Sales Promo Sampler	CD	Atlantic	PRCD-8667	U.S.A.	1998	8.99
Hootie & the Blowfish	Talking With (Promo)	CD	Atlantic	PRCD-6745-2	U.S.A.	1996	11.99
Hopkin, Mary	Earth Song	CD	Capitol	7-98695-2	U.S.A.	1992	29.99
Hopkin, Mary	Post Card + 3	CD	Capitol	7-97578-2	U.S.A.	1991	13.99
Hopkin, Mary	Spirit	CD	Trax	MODCD1045	England	1989	59.99
Hopkin, Mary	Those Were The Days (Greatest Hits)	CD	EMI	7243-8-30197-2-4	Holland	1995	19.99
Hopkins, Nicky	The Revolutionary Piano Of	CD	Columbia	478502-2	England	1966	11.99
Hopkins, Nicky	The Tin Man Was A Dreamer	CD	Columbia	480969-2	England	1973	11.99
Hopkins, Nicky	The Tin Man Was A Dreamer	CD	Sony	SRCS-6450	Japan	1973	24.99
Hopper, Hugh	1984	CD	Cuneiform	RUNE-104	U.S.A.	1998	13.99
Hopper, Hugh	Alive	CD	Blueprint	BP150CD	England	2003	14.99
Hopper, Hugh	Best Soft	CD	Mantra	MAN-105	France	2000	9.99
Hopper, Hugh	Hopper Tunity Box	CD	Culture Press	12842	France	1999	24.99
Hopper, Hugh	Improvisations/Mind In The Trees	CD	Voiceprint	VP1014CD	England	2003	14.99
Hopper, Hugh	Meccano Pelorus	CD	Cuneiform	55006	U.S.A.	1995	29.99
Hopper, Hugh	Parabolic Versions	CD	Voiceprint	VP209CD	England	2000	14.99
Hopper, Hugh/Alan Gowen	Bracknell - Bresse Improvisations	CD	Voiceprint	VP186CD	Austria	1996	14.99
Hopper, Hugh/Alan Gowen	Two Rainbows Daily	CD	Cuneiform	RUNE-77	U.S.A.	1995	12.99
Hopper, Hugh/Band	Carousel	CD	Cuneiform	RUNE-67	U.S.A.	1995	9.99
Hopper, Hugh/Frances Knight	The Swimmer	CD	Resurgence	RES215CD	U.S.A.	2001	15.99
Hopper, Hugh/Hughscore	Highspotparadox	CD	Tim/Kerr	TK109-2	U.S.A.	1997	12.99
Hopper, Hugh/Kramer	A Remark Hugh Made	CD	Shimmy Disc	SHIMMY-076	U.S.A.	1994	14.99
Hopper, Hugh/Kramer	Huge	CD	Blueprint	BP248CD	England	2003	14.99
Hopper, Hugh/Lisa S.Klossner	Cryptids	CD	Blueprint	BP337CD	U.S.A.	2000	14.99
Hopper, Hugh/Lisa S.Klossner	Different	CD	Blueprint	BP303CD	England	1997	14.99
Hopper, Hugh/Mark Hewins	Adreamor	CD	Impetus	IMP-19423	EU	1995	29.99
Hopper/Dean/Tippett/Gallivan	Cruel But Fair	CD	One Way	OW-31373	France	1996	14.99
Hopper/Dean/Tippett/Gallivan	Mercy Dash	CD	Culture Press	3012802	France	1996	10.99
Horner, James	An American Tail (O.S.T.)	CD	MCA	MCAD-39096	U.S.A.	1986	12.99
Horner, James	Apollo 13 (O.S.T. MCA Gold Cd)	CD	MCA	MCAD-11316	U.S.A.	1995	10.99
Horner, James	Dad (O.S.T.)	CD	MCA	MCAD-6359	U.S.A.	1989	37.99
Horner, James	Land Before Time (O.S.T.)	CD	MCA	MCAD-6266	U.S.A.	1988	24.99
Horner, James	Star Trek II: The Wrath Of Khan S.T.	CD	GNP	GNPD-8022	U.S.A.	1990	13.99
Horner, James	Star Trek III: Search For Spock S.T.	CD	GNP	GNPD-8023	U.S.A.	1990	14.99
Horner, James	The Pagemaster (O.S.T.)	CD	Fox	D7822-11019-2	U.S.A.	1994	13.99
Horner, James	The Pelican Brief (O.S.T.)	CD	Big Screen	9-24544-2	U.S.A.	1993	13.99
Horner, James	Thunderheart (O.S.T.)	CD	Intrada	MAF-7027D	U.S.A.	1992	18.99
Hornsby, Bruce/Range	Scenes From The Southside	CD	RCA	6686-2-R	U.S.A.	1988	8.99
Hornsby, Bruce/Range	The Way It Is	CD	RCA	PCD1-5904	U.S.A.	1986	9.99
Hot Tuna	America's Choice	CD	RCA	07863-66871-2	U.S.A.	1996	8.99
Hot Tuna	And Furthurmore...	CD	Grateful Dead	GDCD-4068	U.S.A.	1999	14.99
Hot Tuna	Burgers	CD	RCA	07863-66870-2	U.S.A.	1996	8.99
Hot Tuna	Classic Hot Tuna Acoustic	CD	Relix	RRCD2075	U.S.A.	1996	9.99
Hot Tuna	Classic Hot Tuna Electric	CD	Relix	RRCD2076	U.S.A.	1996	7.99
Hot Tuna	Double Dose	CD	Edsel	EDCD397	England	1994	29.99
Hot Tuna	First Pull Up, Then Pull Down	CD	RCA	07863-66873-2	U.S.A.	1996	10.99
Hot Tuna	Historic Hot Tuna	CD	Relix	RRCD-2011	U.S.A.	1984	10.99

H

Artist	Title	Format	Label	Catalog No	Country	Released	Value
Hot Tuna	Hoppkorv	CD	RCA	07863-66874-2	U.S.A.	1996	10.99
Hot Tuna	Hot Tuna	CD	RCA	07863-66872-2	U.S.A.	1996	8.99
Hot Tuna	Live At Sweetwater Vol. 1	CD	Relix	RRCD2058	U.S.A.	1992	10.99
Hot Tuna	Live At Sweetwater Vol. 2	CD	Relix	RRCD2062	U.S.A.	1993	10.99
Hot Tuna	Live In Japan	CD	Relix	RRCD-2093	U.S.A.	1997	11.99
Hot Tuna	Pair A Dice Found	CD	Epic	EK-46831	U.S.A.	1990	10.99
Hot Tuna	Platinum & Gold Collection	CD	RCA	82876-50899-2	U.S.A.	2003	8.99
Hot Tuna	Splashdown One	CD	Relix	RRCD2004	U.S.A.	1995	11.99
Hot Tuna	Splashdown Two	CD	Relix	RRCD2080	U.S.A.	1997	11.99
Hot Tuna	The Best Of Hot Tuna	2CD	RCA	07863-67692-2	U.S.A.	1998	21.99
Hot Tuna	The Phosphorescent Rat	CD	RCA	07863-67564-2	U.S.A.	1998	8.99
Hot Tuna	Trimmed And Burning	CD	Edsel	EDCD-396	England	1994	19.99
Hot Tuna	Yellow Fever	CD	RCA	74321-83501-2	Spain	2000	11.99
Hot Tuna	Yellow Fever	CD	BMG	74321-56015-2	Japan	1998	39.99
Hour Glass	Power Of Love + 6	CD	EMI	0777-7-98826-2-5	U.S.A.	1992	19.99
Hour Glass	The Hour Glass + 7	CD	EMI	0777-7-96059-2-7	U.S.A.	1992	19.99
Hour Glass	The Hour Glass/The Allman Brothers	CD	BGO	BGOCD536	England	2001	14.99
Houston, Whitney	Miracle (Promo)	CD Single	Arista	ASCD-2222	U.S.A.	1991	19.99
Houston, Whitney	Self Titled (Gold Cd)	CD	Nippon Columbia	ARCD-8212	Japan	1985	64.99
Houston, Whitney	The Bodyguard (Limited Edition)	CD	Arista	74321-16929-2	U.S.A.	1993	24.99
Houston, Whitney	The Preacher's Wife (Different Cover)	CD	BMG	BVCA-718	Japan	1996	84.99
Houston, Whitney	Whitney (Gold Cd)	CD	Nippon Columbia	ARCD-8405	Japan	1987	56.99
Howard, James Newton	The Man In The Moon (O.S.T.)	CD	Reprise	9-26763-2	U.S.A.	1991	12.99
Howard, Maxine	Blues Shoes With No Strings	CD	Line	STCD-9.00840-0	Germany	1989	8.99
Howard, Maxine	Fallin' Out Over The Blues	CD	Line	STCD-9.00599-0	Germany	1988	8.99
Howard, Maxine	Family Gospel Selection	CD	Line	STCD-9.01114-0	Germany	1991	8.99
Howe, Steve	Beginnings	CD	Atlantic	80319-2	U.S.A.	1975	9.99
Howe, Steve	Homebrew 1 & 2	2CD	Inside Out	6-93723-65192-7	Germany	1996	19.99
Howe, Steve	Homebrew Volume 1	CD	Herald	HER-014-2	U.S.A.	1996	11.99
Howe, Steve	Homebrew Volume 2	CD	Purple Pyramid	CLP-0841-2	U.S.A.	2000	15.99
Howe, Steve	Light Walls	2CD	Snapper	SMD-CD-480	England	2003	14.99
Howe, Steve	Live In America - Pulling Strings	CD	Flavour	FVCK-80105	Japan	2000	34.99
Howe, Steve	Mothballs (Gold Cd)	CD	Big Eye	BIG-4031-2	U.S.A.	1998	7.99
Howe, Steve	Natural Timbre	CD	Spitfire	SPT-15208-2	U.S.A.	2001	9.99
Howe, Steve	Not Necessarily Acoustic	CD	Herald	HER-012-2	U.S.A.	1994	12.99
Howe, Steve	Portraits Of Bob Dylan	CD	Victor Ent.	VICP-60785	Japan	2000	29.99
Howe, Steve	Pulling Strings	CD	Resurgence	RES132CD	EEC	1998	14.99
Howe, Steve	Quantum Guitar	CD	Resurgence	RES130CD	U.S.A.	1998	12.99
Howe, Steve	The Grand Scheme Of Things	CD	Acadia	ACA-8027	England	2002	9.99
Howe, Steve	The Steve Howe Album	CD	Atlantic	81559-2	U.S.A.	1979	9.99
Howe, Steve	Turbulence	CD	Acadia	ACA-8025	England	2002	8.99
Howe, Steve/Bodast	The Early Years	CD	C5	C5CD-528	France	1990	19.99
Howe, Steve/Martin Taylor	Masterpiece Guitars	CD	P 3 Music	M-006	England	2003	14.99
Howe, Steve/Paul Sutin	Seraphim	CD	CMC INT.	CMC-7504-2	U.S.A.	1995	11.99
Howe, Steve/Paul Sutin	Voyagers	CD	CMC INT.	CMC-7503-2	U.S.A.	1995	11.99
Howe, Steve/Tomorrow	50 Minute Technicolour Dream	CD	RPM	RPM-184	England	1998	13.99
Howe, Steve/Tomorrow	A Teenage Opera	CD	RPM	RPM-165	England	1996	12.99
Howe, Steve/Tomorrow	Live And Unreleased	CD	Purple Pyramid	CLP-0989-2	U.S.A.	2001	12.99
Howe, Steve/Tomorrow	Tomorrow + 12 Featuring Keith West	CD	EMI	7243-498819-2-1	EU	1999	18.99
Howlin' Wilf/Vee Jays	Blue Men Shake Your Hips	CD	Line	WFCD-9.00683-0	Germany	1989	12.99
Howlin' Wolf	The London Howlin' Wolf Sessions	CD	MCA	CHD-9297	U.S.A.	1989	10.99
Howlin' Wolf	The Real Folk Blues + 2 (MFSL Gold)	CD	Mobile Fidelity	UDCD-645	U.S.A.	1987	44.99
Howlin' Wolf/Eric Clapton	London Howlin' Wolf Sess. (MCA Gold)	CD	MCA	CHD-9351	U.S.A.	1974	26.99
Hudson, David	Night And Day	CD	Line	TLCD-9.00583-0	Germany	1988	17.99
Hughes, Glenn	Addiction	CD	Zero	XRCN-1280	Japan	1996	19.99
Hughes, Glenn	Addiction	CD	Zero	XRCN-1280	Japan	1996	11.99
Hughes, Glenn	Blues	CD	Shrapnel	RR-9088-2	U.S.A.	1992	10.99
Hughes, Glenn	Building The Machine	CD	SPV	SPV085-72372CD	Germany	2001	11.99

H

Artist	Title	Format	Label	Catalog No	Country	Released	Value
Hughes, Glenn	Burning Japan Live	CD	SPV	SPV084-18202CD	Germany	1995	10.99
Hughes, Glenn	Burning Japan Live + 4	CD	Shrapnel	SH-1082CD	U.S.A.	1995	11.99
Hughes, Glenn	Different Stages: The Best Of	CD	SPV	SPV315-74332CD	Germany	2002	10.99
Hughes, Glenn	Feel	CD	SPV	SPV082-89762CD	Germany	1995	9.99
Hughes, Glenn	Feel/Addiction	2CD	SPV	SPV310-29960	Germany	2000	24.99
Hughes, Glenn	From Now On...	CD	Roadrunner	RR-9007-2	Holland	1994	8.99
Hughes, Glenn	From the Archives, Vol. 1: I & P	CD	Resurgent	2040	U.S.A.	1998	14.99
Hughes, Glenn	HTP: 2	CD	Shrapnel	SH-1167CD	U.S.A.	2003	11.99
Hughes, Glenn	Play Me Out (Special Edition)	CD	RPM	RPM-149	England	1995	16.99
Hughes, Glenn	Return Of Crystal Karma	2CD	SPV	SPV085-2181A-D	Germany	2000	24.99
Hughes, Glenn	Songs In The Key Of Rock	CD	Frontiers	FR-CD-148D	Italy	2003	11.99
Hughes, Glenn	Songs In The Key Of Rock + 1	CD	Pony Canyon	PCCY-01650	Japan	2003	24.99
Hughes, Glenn	Talk About It	CD	Zero	XRCN-1293	Japan	1997	54.99
Hughes, Glenn	The Way It Is	CD	SPV	SPV085-21032CD	Germany	1999	8.99
Hughes, Glenn/Geoff Downes	The Work Tapes	CD	Blueprint	BP285CD	EU	1998	15.99
Hughes, Glenn/Pat Thrall	Hughes Thrall	CD	Epic	ZK-38116	U.S.A.	1991	8.99
Hughes, Glenn/Turner Project	HTP II	CD	MTM	068181	Germany	2003	11.99
Hughes, Glenn/Turner Project	Hughes Turner Project	CD	Pony Canyon	PCCY-01556	Japan	2002	39.99
Hughes, Glenn/Turner Project	Live In Tokyo	CD	Pony Canyon	PCCY-01598	Japan	2002	39.99
Hughes, Glenn/Voodoo Hill	Self Titled	CD	Perris	PER0081-2	Canada	2001	8.99
Hullaballoos	England's Newest S S/On Hullabaloo	CD	Collectables	COL-CD-6299	U.S.A.	2000	9.99
Hullaballoos	Self Titled/On Hullaballoos	CD	Repertoire	REP-4593-WY	Germany	1996	15.99
Human League	Crash	CD	A&M	CD-5129	U.S.A.	1986	8.99
Human League	Dare (Ltd Book Cd W/ Love/Dancing)	2CD	Virgin	7243-5-42365-2-1	England	2002	17.99
Human League	Dare + 2	CD	Caroline	CAROL-1114-2	U.S.A.	1983	8.99
Human League	Dare/Love And Dancing	CD	Caroline	CAR-80601	U.S.A.	2003	9.99
Human League	Love And Dancing	CD	A&M	CD-3209	U.S.A.	1988	13.99
Human League	Octopus	CD	East West	61788-2	U.S.A.	1995	8.99
Human League	Reproduction (Bonus Tracks)	CD	Caroline	CAR-80165	U.S.A.	2003	8.99
Human League	Romantic	CD	A&M	75021-5316-2	U.S.A.	1990	7.99
Human League	Secrets	CD	Ark 21	186-810-075-2	U.S.A.	2001	7.99
Human League	Tell Me When (Cd 1)	CD Single	East West	4509-98876-2	England	1994	5.99
Human League	Tell Me When (Cd 2)	CD Single	East West	4509-98878-2	England	1994	5.99
Human League	The Best Of The Human League	CD	Disky	VI-248232	Holland	1999	9.99
Human League	The Very Best Of The Human League	CD	Ark21	61868-10034-2-7	U.S.A.	1998	11.99
Human League	Travelogue + 8	CD	Caroline	CAR-80115	U.S.A.	2003	8.99
Human League/The Future	Golden Hour Of The Future (1977)	CD	Black Melody	MEL-004-CD	England	2002	19.99
Humble Pie	As Safe As Yesterday Is	CD	Line	IDCD-9.00296-0	Germany	1987	12.99
Humble Pie	As Safe As Yesterday Is + 2	CD	Repertoire	REP-4237-WY	Germany	1992	14.99
Humble Pie	Back On Track	CD	Sanctuary	SANCD106	England	2002	10.99
Humble Pie	Eat It	CD	Polydor K.K.	POCM-1889	Japan	1993	26.99
Humble Pie	Greatest Hits	CD	Woodford	WMCD-5527	Holland	1990	11.99
Humble Pie	Hot 'N' Nasty: The Anthology	2CD	A&M	31454-0164-2	U.S.A.	1994	14.99
Humble Pie	Humble Pie	CD	Polydor K.K.	POCM-1885	Japan	1993	65.99
Humble Pie	In Concert	CD	King Biscuit	70710-88015-2	U.S.A.	1995	14.99
Humble Pie	Live At The Whisky-A-Go-Go '69	CD	Castle	CMRCD-368	England	2001	9.99
Humble Pie	Performance - Rockin' The Filmore	CD	Polydor K.K.	POCM-1887	Japan	1993	24.99
Humble Pie	Rock On (MFSL Aluminum)	CD	Mobile Fidelity	MFCD-1-847	U.S.A.	1990	53.99
Humble Pie	Smokin'	CD	A&M	POCM-1888	Japan	1993	24.99
Humble Pie	Street Rats	CD	Pony Canyon	PCCY-10197	Japan	1991	79.99
Humble Pie	The Immediate Years	2CD	Snapper	SMD-CD-212	England	1999	10.99
Humble Pie	The Immediate Years Box Set	2CD	Charly	CDIMMBOX3	England	1995	14.99
Humble Pie	The Scrubbers Sessions	CD	Archive	ACH-80001	U.S.A.	1996	11.99
Humble Pie	Thunderbox	CD	Pony Canyon	D20Y-4026	Japan	1991	79.99
Humble Pie	Town And Country	CD	Line	MLCD-9.00303-L	Germany	1990	12.99
Humble Pie	Town And Country	CD	Repertoire	REP-4231-WY	Germany	1992	14.99
Humblebums	First Collection	CD	Line	TACD-9.00557-0	Germany	1988	24.99
Humblebums	S.T. Album (W/Gerry Rafferty)	CD	Line	TACD-9.00551-0	Germany	1988	19.99

Artist	Title	Format	Label	Catalog No	Country	Released	Value
Hungry Hearts	Hungry Hearts	CD	Line	OLCD-9.91262-Z	Germany	1992	9.99
Hunter, Ian	All American Alien Boy	CD	Columbia	491695-2	England	1976	10.99
Hunter, Ian	All Of The Good Ones Are Taken	CD	Columbia	474780-2	Austria	1983	29.99
Hunter, Ian	Dirty Laundry	CD	Norsk	IDCD-44	Norway	1995	13.99
Hunter, Ian	Ian Hunter	CD	Columbia	477359-2	England	1975	11.99
Hunter, Ian	M.I.A. (Bonus Cd)	2CD	Alchemy	PILOT-52	England	2000	16.99
Hunter, Ian	Michael Picasso	CD Single	Citadel	CIT-102CDS	England	1996	14.99
Hunter, Ian	Once Bitten Twice Shy	2CD	Columbia	C2K-61406	U.S.A.	2000	21.99
Hunter, Ian	Overnight Angels + 1	CD	Columbia	506063-2	England	1977	15.99
Hunter, Ian	Rant	CD	Fuel 2000	302-061-116-2	U.S.A.	2001	11.99
Hunter, Ian	Rant Ep	CD Single	Papillon	BTFLYS0017	England	2001	5.99
Hunter, Ian	Shades Of Ian Hunter	CD	Chrysalis	VK-41670	U.S.A.	1988	7.99
Hunter, Ian	Short Back N' Sides + 13 (Bonus Disc)	2CD	Chrysalis	7243-8-29552-2-1	England	1994	16.99
Hunter, Ian	The Artful Dodger	CD	Polydor	531-794-2	Norway	1996	25.99
Hunter, Ian	The Artful Dodger	CD Single	Citadel	CIT-101CDS	England	1996	10.99
Hunter, Ian	The Collection (Gold Cd)	CD	Castle	CCSCD-290	England	1991	14.99
Hunter, Ian	Welcome To The Club + 4	2CD	Chrysalis	7243-8-29557-2-6	England	1994	24.99
Hunter, Ian	You're Never Alone...	CD	Chrysalis	07243-5-21853-2-	England	1999	12.99
Hunter, Ian	Yui Orta + 2 (Pre-Bowie Ronson)	CD	Lemon	CDLEM06	England	2003	14.99
Hunter, Ian/ Felix Pappalardi	The Secret Sessions (Mick Ronson)	CD	Pet Rock	71278-60042-2	U.S.A.	1999	14.99
Hunter, Ian/Ronson Band	BBC Live In Concert	CD	Windsong	WINCD-078	England	1989	14.99
Hunter, Robert	A Box Of Rain	CD	Rykodisc	RCD-10214	U.S.A.	1991	7.99
Hunter, Robert	Promontory Rider	CD	Relix	RRCD-2002	U.S.A.	1989	7.99
Hunter, Robert	Rock Columbia	CD	Relix	RRCD2019	U.S.A.	1994	7.99
Hunter, Robert	Sentinel	CD	Rykodisc	RCD-20265	U.S.A.	1993	7.99
Hunter, Robert	Tales Of The Great Rum Runners	CD	Line	GDCD-9.00716-0	Germany	1989	11.99
Hunter, Robert	Tiger Rose (Line Version)	CD	Line	GDCD-9.00653-0	Germany	1989	10.99
Hurricane	Over The Edge	CD	Enigma	D2-73320	U.S.A.	1988	44.99
Hüsker Dü	8 Miles High Ep	CD	SST	SST-CD-270	U.S.A.	1990	8.99
Hüsker Dü	The Living End (Adv. Cd)	CD	Warner Bros.	2-45582-A	U.S.A.	1994	7.99
Husker Du/Grant Hart	Ecce Homo	CD	Rough Trade	RTD-30962	England	1995	64.99
Hutchence, Michael	A Straight Line (Promo Cd)	CD Single	V2	V2FJ-27630-2	U.S.A.	1999	4.99
Hydra	Hydra	CD	Capricorn	314-538-134- 2	U.S.A.	1998	11.99
Hydra	Land Of Money	CD	Capricorn	314-538-653-2	U.S.A.	1999	11.99

I

Artist	Title	Format	Label	Catalog No	Country	Released	Value
Ian, Janis	Present Company	CD	BGO	BGOCD165	England	1992	10.99
Ibert/Martin/Larsson	Ibert- Martin: Saxophone Concertos	CD	Line	CACD-9.01219-P	Germany	1992	12.99
Icon	Live Bootleg	CD	Epilogue Ent.	0-12053-2	U.S.A.	1999	20.99
Icon	Night Of Crime/E More Perfect Union	CD	Reborn Classics	RC-1014	Germany	1993	24.99
Icon	Night Of The Crime	CD	MSI	MSI-10755	Japan	1998	22.99
Icon	Self Titled	CD	MSI	MSI-10756	Japan	1998	22.99
Icon/Jerry Harrison	Right Between The Eyes	CD	Atlantic	82010-2	U.S.A.	1989	23.99
Ides of March	Ideology	CD	Sundazed	SC-11067	U.S.A.	2000	11.99
Ides of March	Vehicle + 3	CD	Magic	5234132	France	1996	28.99
Idle Strand	Blackberry Way/Cut And Run	CD	Line	LICD-9.01323-0	Germany	1995	6.99
Idle Strand	Blackberry Way/Cut And Run	CD	Line	BWCD-9.00702-0	Germany	1989	6.99
Idol, Billy	Billy Idol	CD	Chrysalis	32-1377-2	U.S.A.	1982	8.99
Idol, Billy	Charmed Life	CD	Chrysalis	F2-21735	U.S.A.	1990	5.99
Idol, Billy	Cyberpunk	CD	Chrysalis	526000	U.S.A.	1993	5.99
Idol, Billy	Don't Stop	CD	Chrysalis	F2-21729	U.S.A.	1983	9.99
Idol, Billy	Greatest Hits + 3 (Bonus Cd)	CD	Chrysalis	72435-36407-0-5	U.S.A.	2001	19.99
Idol, Billy	Heroin	CD Single	Chrysalis	F2-24832	U.S.A.	1993	14.99

Artist	Title	Format	Label	Catalog No	Country	Released	Value
Idol, Billy	Rebel Yell + 5 (Expanded Edition)	CD	Chrysalis	72435-20695-2-1	U.S.A.	1999	11.99
Idol, Billy	Shock To The System (Cd 1)	CD Single	EMI	0946-3-23995-2-6	England	1993	11.99
Idol, Billy	VH1 - Storytellers	CD	Capitol	72435-36919-2-9	U.S.A.	2001	6.99
Idol, Billy	Vital Idol	CD	Chrysalis	72435-32859-2-0	U.S.A.	2002	9.99
Idol, Billy	Whiplash Smile	CD	Chrysalis	VK-41514	U.S.A.	1986	7.99
IEM/Porcupine Tree	Have Come For Your Children	CD	Impress	IEM1-01-6	England	2001	72.99
Ifukube, Akira/Godzilla	Godzilla (O.S.T. 1954/Mono)	CD	Toshiba-EMI	TYCY-5345	Japan	1993	32.99
Ifukube, Akira/Godzilla	Godzilla Vs. Mecha-Godzilla (O.S.T.)	2CD	Toshiba-EMI	TYCY-5352/43	Japan	1993	28.99
Ifukube, Akira/Godzilla	History Of Godzilla Vol. 1	CD	Apollon	APCF-5096	Japan	1991	26.99
Ifukube, Akira/Godzilla	Perfect Collection Toho Vol.1	2CD	Future Land	LD25-5033/34	Japan	1987	35.99
Illusion	Enchanted Caress	CD	Line	OLCD-9.50968-X	Germany	1991	9.99
Impacts	Wipe Out (W/ Merrel Fankenhauser)	CD	Del-Fi	DFCD-71234-2	U.S.A.	1996	7.99
Impellitteri	Answer To The Master	CD	Victor Ent.	VICP-5420	Japan	1994	34.99
Impellitteri	Grin And Bear It	CD	Victor Ent.	VICP-5199	Japan	1993	29.99
Impellitteri	Screaming Symphony	CD	Victor Ent.	VICP-5729	Japan	1996	29.99
Impellitteri	Self Titled	CD	Sony	SRCS-8034	Japan	1987	34.99
Impellitteri	The Very Best Of	CD	Victor Ent.	VICP-62018	Japan	2002	29.99
Incredible String Band	5000 Spirits.../Hangman's Beautiful...	2CD	Collector's Choice	CCM-289	U.S.A.	2002	14.99
Incredible String Band	BBC Radio 1 Live in Concert	CD	Windsong	WINCD-033	England	1992	14.99
Incredible String Band	Be Glad For The Song...	CD	Edsel	EDCD-564	England	1998	19.99
Incredible String Band	Bloomsbury 2000 (Complete Reunion)	CD	Pig's Whisker	PWMD-5024	England	2001	14.99
Incredible String Band	Changing Horses/I Looked Up	2CD	Collector's Choice	CCM-291	U.S.A.	2002	14.99
Incredible String Band	Earthspan	CD	Edsel	EDCD-360	England	1994	19.99
Incredible String Band	First Girl I Loved	CD	Sanctuary	06076-80226-2	U.S.A.	2001	12.99
Incredible String Band	Hard Rope & Silken Twine	CD	Edsel	EDCD-368	England	1994	24.99
Incredible String Band	Here Till There Is There: An Intro	CD	PolyGram	7314-5-86196-2-8	England	2001	10.99
Incredible String Band	Heritage	CD	Disky	SI-905322	Holland	2003	8.99
Incredible String Band	Liquid Acrobat As Regards The Air	CD	Sepia-Tone	STONE-09-CD	U.S.A.	2002	11.99
Incredible String Band	No Ruinous Feud	CD	Edsel	EDCD-367	England	1994	19.99
Incredible String Band	On Air	CD	Strange Fruit	SFRSCD-034	England	1997	16.99
Incredible String Band	Self Titled	CD	Sepia-Tone	STONE-08-CD	U.S.A.	2002	11.99
Incredible String Band	The Chelsea Sessions 1967	CD	Sanctuary	06076-80225-2	England	2001	12.99
Incredible String Band	The Hannibal Sampler (Promo)	CD	Hannibal	VRCD-4437	U.S.A.	1994	24.99
Incredible String Band	U: Surreal Parable/Song And Dance	2CD	Collector's Choice	CCM-288	U.S.A.	2002	14.99
Incredible String Band	Wee Tam/The Big Huge	2CD	Collector's Choice	CCM-290	U.S.A.	2002	14.99
Incredible String Band/C.O.B.	Spirit Of Love	CD	BGO	BGOCD534	England	2001	17.99
Indian Summer	Self Titled	CD	Repertoire	REP-4357-WP	Germany	1993	15.99
Indigo Girls	Self Titled (Sony Gold Cd)	CD	Columbia	EK-66224	U.S.A.	1994	14.99
Insane Clown Posse	Juggalo Show The Complete Collection	8 CD	Psychopathic	PSY-10000	U.S.A.	2001	99.99
INXS	Best Of	CD	Rhino	R2-78251	U.S.A.	2002	9.99
INXS	Compilation (Promo)	CD	Atlantic	PRCD-3416-2	U.S.A.	1990	24.99
INXS	Kick + 4	CD	Rhino	R2-78204	U.S.A.	2002	12.99
INXS	Profiled (Promo)	CD	Atlantic	PRCD-3673-2	U.S.A.	1990	8.99
INXS	Shine Like It Does: Anthology ('79-'97)	2CD	Rhino	R2-74262	U.S.A.	2001	13.99
INXS	The Kick + 6 (Special Ed)	CD	Warner Bros.	22P2-2399	Japan	1989	40.99
INXS	Welcome To Wherever You Are + 5	CD	Rhino	R2-78206	U.S.A.	2002	10.99
INXS	X + 5	CD	Rhino	R2-78205	U.S.A.	2002	10.99
IQ	Are You Sitting Comfortably?	CD	Giant Elec Pea	GEPCD-1013	EU	1992	14.99
IQ	Ever	CD	Giant Elec Pea	GEPCD-1006	EU	1994	14.99
IQ	Forever Live	2CD	Giant Elec Pea	GEPCD-1016	EU	2000	19.99
IQ	Forever Live Box Set (W/Video)	2CD	Giant Elec Pea	GEPCDVBOX-1	EU	2000	44.99
IQ	J'ai Pollette D'arnu	CD	Giant Elec Pea	GEPCD-1001	EU	1991	14.99
IQ	Living Proof	CD	Giant Elec Pea	GEPCD-1004	EU	1992	14.99
IQ	Nine In A Pond Is Here (Ltd Ed)	CD	MSI	CDMS1049	France	1989	24.99
IQ	Nomzamo + 3	CD	Giant Elec Pea	GEPCD-1012	EU	1992	15.99
IQ	Seven Stories Into '98 (Old/New Ver.)	2CD	Giant Elec Pea	MIMP-0001	EU	1998	29.99
IQ	Subterranea	2CD	Giant Elec Pea	GEPCD-1021	EU	1998	29.99
IQ	Subterranea (The Concert)	2CD	Giant Elec Pea	GEPCD-1027	EU	2000	24.99

Artist	Title	Format	Label	Catalog No	Country	Released	Value
IQ	Tales From The Lush Attic + 1	CD	Giant Elec Pea	GEPCD-1010	EU	1992	15.99
IQ	The Lost Attic	CD	Giant Elec Pea	GEPCD-1024	EU	2000	14.99
IQ	The Seventh House	CD	Giant Elec Pea	GEPCD-1028	EU	2001	14.99
IQ	The Wake	CD	Giant Elec Pea	GEPCD-1011	EU	1992	16.99
Iron Butterfly	Ball	CD	Collector´s Choice	CCM-088-2	U.S.A.	1999	11.99
Iron Butterfly	Ball.	CD	Line	LECD-9.00950-0	Germany	1990	8.99
Iron Butterfly	Heavy	CD	Rhino	R2-71521	U.S.A.	1993	9.99
Iron Butterfly	Heavy	CD	Repertoire	REP-4128-WZ	Germany	2002	14.99
Iron Butterfly	In-A-Gadda-Da-Vida + 2 (Deluxe)	CD	Rhino	R2-72196	U.S.A.	1995	24.99
Iron Butterfly	In-A-Gadda-Da-Vida + 2 (MFSL Gold)	CD	Mobile Fidelity	UDCD-675	U.S.A.	1968	49.99
Iron Butterfly	Light And Heavy	CD	Rhino	R2-71186	U.S.A.	1993	9.99
Iron Butterfly	Live	CD	Rhino	R2-71166	U.S.A.	1993	9.99
Iron Butterfly	Metamorphosis	CD	Rhino	R2-71522	U.S.A.	1993	9.99
Iron Butterfly	Scorching Beauty	CD	Repertoire	REP-4558-WY	Germany	1995	14.99
Iron City Houserockers	Pumping Iron & Sweating..(Best Of)	CD	Rhino	R2-70375	U.S.A.	1992	14.99
Iron Maiden	17 Numbers By The Beast (Promo)	CD	Columbia	CSK-56740	U.S.A.	2002	49.99
Iron Maiden	A Real Dead One (Enhanced)	Mini Lp	Columbia	CBS-86036	U.S.A.	2000	10.99
Iron Maiden	A Real Live Dead One (Enhanced)	2CD	Columbia	CK-86219	U.S.A.	2002	19.99
Iron Maiden	A Real Live One (Enhanced)	Mini Lp	Columbia	CBS-86035	U.S.A.	2002	10.99
Iron Maiden	Be Quick Or Be Dead (Promo)	CD Single	Epic	ESK-4551	U.S.A.	1992	24.99
Iron Maiden	Be Quick Or Be Dead (Promo)	CD	EMI	SPCD1585	France	1992	39.99
Iron Maiden	Best Of The Beast + 7 (Bonus Cd)	2CD	EMI	CDEMS-1097	England	1996	49.99
Iron Maiden	Brave New World	CD	Columbia	CK-62208	U.S.A.	2000	8.99
Iron Maiden	Brave New World (Promo Sampler)	CD	EMI	CDBNWDJ-001	England	2000	49.99
Iron Maiden	Bring Your Daughter.. (Promo)	CD Single	Epic	ESK-4007	U.S.A.	1991	49.99
Iron Maiden	Dance Of Death	CD	Toshiba-EMI	TOCP-66212	Japan	2003	29.99
Iron Maiden	Dance Of Death	CD	Columbia	CK-89061	U.S.A.	2003	8.99
Iron Maiden	Dance Of Death (Promo Sampler)	CD	EMI	DODUKDJ001	England	2003	29.99
Iron Maiden	Ed Hunter	3CD	Columbia	C3K-63726	U.S.A.	1999	15.99
Iron Maiden	Ed Hunter (Promo/Cd Rom)	Cd-Rom	EMI	EDHUNTER666	England	1999	12.99
Iron Maiden	Eddie's Archive (Promo Sampler)	CD	EMI	CDSP-255	England	2002	49.99
Iron Maiden	Eddie's Archive (Promo Sampler)	CD	Columbia	CSK-59260	U.S.A.	2002	59.99
Iron Maiden	Eddie's Archive Box Set	6CD	Columbia	69699-86907-2	U.S.A.	2002	64.99
Iron Maiden	Edward The Great	CD	EMI	7243-5-43103-2-4	Argentina	2003	12.99
Iron Maiden	Edward The Great	CD	Columbia	69699-86969-2	U.S.A.	2002	8.99
Iron Maiden	Edward The Great (Promo Sampler)	CD	EMI	EDDIE001	England	2002	29.99
Iron Maiden	Fear Of The Dark (Bonus Cd/Pic Cds)	2CD	Castle	CASTLE-111-2	U.S.A.	1995	20.99
Iron Maiden	Fear Of The Dark (Enhanced)	CD	Columbia	CK-86217	U.S.A.	2002	8.99
Iron Maiden	Fear Of The Dark + 7 (W/Bonus Cd)	2CD	EMI	CDEM-1579	England	1995	20.99
Iron Maiden	First Ten Years Box Set	10CD	Toshiba-EMI	TOCP-6181~90	Japan	1991	219.99
Iron Maiden	Holy Smoke (Promo)	CD Single	Epic	ESK-2194	U.S.A.	1996	29.99
Iron Maiden	Killers (1st Pressing/Poster)	CD	EMI Odeon	CP32-5107	Japan	1980	64.99
Iron Maiden	Killers (Enhanced)	CD	Columbia	CK-86209	U.S.A.	2002	8.99
Iron Maiden	Killers + 8 (Bonus Cd/Pic Cds)	2CD	Castle	CASTLE-103-2	U.S.A.	1995	36.99
Iron Maiden	Killers + 8 (Pic Cds W/Bonus Cd)	2CD	EMI	CDEM-1571	England	1995	36.99
Iron Maiden	Live After Death (Enhanced)	CD	Columbia	CK-86213	U.S.A.	2002	8.99
Iron Maiden	Live After Death + 3 (Bonus Cd)	2CD	Castle	CASTLE-107-2	U.S.A.	1995	20.99
Iron Maiden	Live After Death + 3 (W/Bonus Cd)	2CD	EMI	CDEM-1575	England	1995	20.99
Iron Maiden	Live At Donington 1992 (Enhanced)	2CD	Columbia	CK-86222	U.S.A.	2002	11.99
Iron Maiden	No More Lies (Special Edition)	CD Single	EMI	72435-48417-0-5	England	2004	16.99
Iron Maiden	No Prayer For Dying + 4 (Bonus Cd)	2CD	EMI	CDEM-1578	England	1995	20.99
Iron Maiden	No Prayer For Dying + 4 (Bonus Cd)	2CD	Castle	CASTLE-110-2	U.S.A.	1995	20.99
Iron Maiden	No Prayer For The Dying (Enhanced)	CD	Columbia	CK-86216	U.S.A.	2002	8.99
Iron Maiden	Number Of The Beast + 2 (Bonus Cd)	2CD	EMI	CDEM-1572	England	1995	36.99
Iron Maiden	Number Of The Beast + 2 (Bonus Cd)	2CD	Castle	CASTLE-104-2	U.S.A.	1995	36.99
Iron Maiden	Piece Of Mind (Enhanced)	CD	Columbia	CK-86211	U.S.A.	2002	8.99
Iron Maiden	Piece Of Mind + 2 (Pic Cds/Bonus Cd)	2CD	Castle	CASTLE-105-2	U.S.A.	1995	24.99
Iron Maiden	Piece Of Mind + 2 (W/Bonus Cd)	2CD	EMI	CDEM-1573	England	1995	24.99

Artist	Title	Format	Label	Catalog No	Country	Released	Value
Iron Maiden	Powerslave	CD	Toshiba-EMI	TOCP-6341	Japan	1984	40.99
Iron Maiden	Powerslave	CD	Columbia	CK-86212	U.S.A.	2002	8.99
Iron Maiden	Powerslave (Enhanced)	CD	Columbia	CK-86212	U.S.A.	2002	8.99
Iron Maiden	Powerslave + 4 (W/Bonus Cd)	2CD	EMI	CDEM-1574	England	1995	21.99
Iron Maiden	Powerslave + 4 (W/Bonus Cd)	2CD	Castle	CASTLE-106-2	England	1995	21.99
Iron Maiden	Rock In Rio	2CD	Toshiba-EMI	TOCP- 65948-9	Japan	2002	49.99
Iron Maiden	Rock In Rio	2CD	Columbia	C2K-86000	U.S.A.	2002	13.99
Iron Maiden	Run To The Hills	CD Single	EMI	CDEMS612	England	2002	7.99
Iron Maiden	Self Titled	CD	Toshiba-EMI	TOCP-6337	Japan	1980	58.99
Iron Maiden	Self Titled (Enchanced)	CD	Columbia	CK-86207	U.S.A.	2002	8.99
Iron Maiden	Self Titled + 3 (Bonus Cd/Pic Cds)	2CD	Castle	CASTLE-102-2	U.S.A.	1995	44.99
Iron Maiden	Self Titled + 3 (Pic Cds W/Bonus Cd)	2CD	EMI	CDEM-1570	England	1995	44.99
Iron Maiden	Seventh Son Of A.. + 9 (Bonus Cd)	2CD	Castle	CASTLE-109-2	U.S.A.	1995	26.99
Iron Maiden	Seventh Son Of A... + 9 (Bonus Cd)	2CD	EMI	CDEM-1577	England	1995	26.99
Iron Maiden	Seventh Son/Seventh Son (Enhan)	CD	Columbia	CK-86215	U.S.A.	2002	8.99
Iron Maiden	Somewhere In Time (Enhanced)	CD	Columbia	CK-86214	U.S.A.	2002	8.99
Iron Maiden	Somewhere In Time + 4 (Bonus Cd)	2CD	Castle	CASTLE-108-2	U.S.A.	1995	24.99
Iron Maiden	Somewhere In Time + 4 (Bonus Cd)	2CD	EMI	CDEM-1576	England	1995	24.99
Iron Maiden	The Number Of The Beast (Enhanced)	CD	Columbia	CK-86210	U.S.A.	2002	8.99
Iron Maiden	The Soundhouse Tapes (Promo)	CD	Columbia	CSK-56882	U.S.A.	2002	149.99
Iron Maiden	The X Factor (Enhanced)	CD	Columbia	CK-86223	U.S.A.	2002	8.99
Iron Maiden	The X Factor + 3 (W/Bonus Cd)	2CD	Toshiba-EMI	TOCP-8588	Japan	1995	29.99
Iron Maiden	Virtual X1	CD	Columbia	CK-86317	U.S.A.	2002	8.99
Iron Maiden	Virtual X1 + 2 (W/Bonus Cd)	2CD	Toshiba-EMI	TOCP-50440	Japan	1998	29.99
Iron Maiden/Bruce Dickinson	Accident Of Birth	CD	CMC INT.	06076-86217-2	U.S.A.	1997	9.99
Iron Maiden/Bruce Dickinson	Accident Of Birth + 1	CD	Victor Ent.	VICP-60002	Japan	1997	24.99
Iron Maiden/Bruce Dickinson	Alive In Studio A	2CD	Sanctuary	06076-86227-2	U.S.A.	1998	14.99
Iron Maiden/Bruce Dickinson	Alive In Studio A + 3	2CD	Victor Ent.	VICP-40149/50	Japan	1995	34.99
Iron Maiden/Bruce Dickinson	Back From The Edge	CD Single	Victor Ent.	VICP-15059	Japan	1996	10.99
Iron Maiden/Bruce Dickinson	Balls To Picasso	CD	Mercury	314-522-491-2	U.S.A.	1994	8.99
Iron Maiden/Bruce Dickinson	Balls To Picasso (W/Bonus)	CD	Victor Ent.	VICP-60024	Japan	1997	34.99
Iron Maiden/Bruce Dickinson	Best Of	CD	Victor Ent.	VICP-61579	Japan	2000	23.99
Iron Maiden/Bruce Dickinson	Best Of + 14 (W/Bonus CD)	2CD	Metal-Is	85225	England	2001	24.99
Iron Maiden/Bruce Dickinson	Chemical Wedding	CD	CMC INT.	06076-86259-2	U.S.A.	1998	9.99
Iron Maiden/Bruce Dickinson	Chemical Wedding + 1	CD	Victor Ent.	VICP-60468	Japan	1998	23.99
Iron Maiden/Bruce Dickinson	Killing Floor	CD Single	Victor Ent.	VICP-60467	Japan	1998	10.99
Iron Maiden/Bruce Dickinson	Live EP	CD Single	Victor Ent.	VICP-15074	Japan	1996	14.99
Iron Maiden/Bruce Dickinson	Man Of Sorrows	CD Single	Victor Ent.	VICP-60088	Japan	1997	10.99
Iron Maiden/Bruce Dickinson	Scream For Me Brazil '99 (Live)	CD	Sanctuary	06076-84527-2	U.S.A.	1999	8.99
Iron Maiden/Bruce Dickinson	Scream For Me Brazil '99 (Live)	CD	Victor Ent.	VICP-60861	Japan	1999	34.99
Iron Maiden/Bruce Dickinson	Skunkworks	CD	Sanctuary	06076-84517-2	U.S.A.	2002	9.99
Iron Maiden/Bruce Dickinson	Skunkworks	CD	Victor Ent.	VICP-5674	Japan	1996	39.99
Iron Maiden/Bruce Dickinson	Tattooed Millionaire (W/ Bonus)	CD	Victor Ent.	VICP-60023	Japan	1997	34.99
Iron Maiden/Bruce Dickinson	Tattooed Millionare	CD	EMI	CK-46139	U.S.A.	1990	9.99
Iron Maiden/Bruce Dickinson	Tattooed Millionare	CD	Sony	86464	Australia	2002	29.99
Iron Maiden/Bruce Dickinson	Tattooed Millionare + 5	CD	Sony	86464	Australia	2002	29.99
Iron Maiden/Samson	1993	CD	Magnum	CDTB-159	England	1996	10.99
Iron Maiden/Samson	Before The Storm + 6	CD	Molten Metal	MM53302-2	U.S.A.	2002	14.99
Iron Maiden/Samson	Burning Emotion: Best Of 1985 - 1990	CD	Magnum	CDTB-169	England	1995	8.99
Iron Maiden/Samson	Head On	CD	Repertoire	REP-4037-WZ	Germany	1989	10.99
Iron Maiden/Samson	Head On + 2	CD	Sanctuary	CMRCD188	England	2001	8.99
Iron Maiden/Samson	Head Tactics	CD	Toshiba-EMI	TOCP-7976	Japan	1993	14.99
Iron Maiden/Samson	Joint Forces + 1	CD	Repertoire	REP-4340-WZ	Germany	1995	10.99
Iron Maiden/Samson	Live At Reading	CD	Repertoire	REP-4040-WZ	Germany	1990	10.99
Iron Maiden/Samson	Live At Reading 1981 + 3	CD	Sanctuary	CMRCD-191	England	2001	11.99
Iron Maiden/Samson	Live At The Marquee	CD	Magnum	CDTB-157	England	1994	11.99
Iron Maiden/Samson	Live In London 2000 (CD/DVD)	2CD	Zoom Club	ZCRCD48	England	2001	15.99
Iron Maiden/Samson	Live: The Blues Nights	CD	Mystic	MYSCD-155	England	2002	14.99
Iron Maiden/Samson	Past, Present And Future	2CD	Zoom Club	ZCRCD18	England	1999	15.99
Iron Maiden/Samson	Pillars Of Rock	2CD	Connoisseur	VSOPCD151	England	1990	14.99

Artist	Title	Format	Label	Catalog No	Country	Released	Value
Iron Maiden/Samson	Refugee + 1	CD	Magnum	CDTB-163	England	1995	8.99
Iron Maiden/Samson	Riding With The Angels	2CD	Essential	CMEDD465	England	2002	14.99
Iron Maiden/Samson	Shock Tactics	CD	Repertoire	REP-4038-WZ	Germany	1989	10.99
Iron Maiden/Samson	Shock Tactics + 3	CD	Sanctuary	CMRCD190	England	2001	9.99
Iron Maiden/Samson	Survivors + 5	CD	Repertoire	REP-4039-WZ	Germany	1990	10.99
Iron Maiden/Samson	Survivors + 9	CD	Sanctuary	CMRCD188	England	2001	8.99
Iron Maiden/Samson	Test Of Time	CD	Delta	47-009	England	1999	11.99
Iron Maiden/Samson	Thank You And Goodnight	CD	Magnum	CDTB-160	England	1995	8.99
Iron Maiden/Samson	The BBC Sessions	CD	High Vaultage	HV-1006	Germany	1997	14.99
Iron Maiden/Samson	The Masters	2CD	Eagle	EDMCD-027	Germany	1998	15.99
Iron Maiden/Samson	There And Back	2CD	Zoom Club	ZCRCD57	England	2001	15.99
Iron Maiden/Tribute	Made In Tribute	CD	Toy's Factory	TFCK-87101	Japan	1997	39.99
Isley Brothers	Grand Slam	CD	Sony	SRCS-6124	U.S.A.	1981	44.99
Isley Brothers	Showdown	CD	Sony	SRCS-6467	Japan	1978	44.99
Isotope	Deep End	CD	Line	LICD-9.00410-0	Germany	1987	11.99
Isotope	Illusion	CD	Line	LICD-9.00402-0	Germany	1987	11.99
Isotope	Isotope	CD	Line	LICD-9.00405-0	Germany	1987	11.99
Issak, Chris/Bonus DVD	Always Got Tonight/Chris Issak Show	2CD	Reprise	PRO-100826	U.S.A.	2002	61.99
It's A Beautiful Day	Choice Quality Stuff...Anytime	CD	TRC	TRC-007	Germany	1990	35.99
It's A Beautiful Day	Creed Of Love	CD	Strawberry	SRCD-117	U.S.A.	1998	14.99
It's A Beautiful Day	Greatest Hits (Limited Pic Cd)	CD	TRC	TRC-051	Germany	1995	34.99
It's A Beautiful Day	It's a Beautiful Day	CD	San Francisco Soun	SFS-11790DA	U.S.A.	1969	21.99
It's A Beautiful Day	It's A Beautiful Day At Carnegie Hall	CD	Columbia	480970-2	Austria	1972	21.99
It's A Beautiful Day	It's a Beautiful Day/Marrying Maiden	CD	Columbia	494893-2	England	1999	24.99
It's A Beautiful Day	Marrying Maiden	CD	San Francisco Soun	SFS-04800	U.S.A.	1970	14.99
Ives, Burl	Have A Holly Jolly Christmas	CD	MCA	MCAD-25992	U.S.A.	1965	5.99
Ives, Burl	Rudolph The Red.... (Whole TV S.T.)	CD	MCA	MCAD-22177	U.S.A.	1969	5.99

J

Artist	Title	Format	Label	Catalog No	Country	Released	Value
J. Geils Band	Bloodshot	CD	Atlantic	7567-82801-2	U.S.A.	1995	8.99
J. Geils Band	Flashback: Best Of	CD	EMI	E2-46551	U.S.A.	1985	8.99
J. Geils Band	Freeze Frame	CD	EMI	7-46014-2	U.S.A.	1981	8.99
J. Geils Band	Freeze Frame	CD	BGO	BGOCD196	England	1995	12.99
J. Geils Band	Full House: Live	CD	Atlantic	7567-82803-2	U.S.A.	1995	8.99
J. Geils Band	Hotline	CD	Atlantic	SD-18147	U.S.A.	1990	16.99
J. Geils Band	Houseparty: Anthology	2CD	Rhino	R2-71164	U.S.A.	1992	29.99
J. Geils Band	Ladies Invited	CD	Atlantic	7567-81431-2	U.S.A.	1995	14.99
J. Geils Band	Live: Blow Your Face Out	CD	Rhino	R2-71278	U.S.A.	1993	8.99
J. Geils Band	Love Stinks	CD	EMI	7-92703-2	U.S.A.	1980	8.99
J. Geils Band	Love Stinks	CD	BGO	BGOCD254	England	1995	12.99
J. Geils Band	Monkey Island	CD	Atlantic	7567-82804-2	U.S.A.	1995	8.99
J. Geils Band	Nightmares.. And Other Tales...	CD	Atlantic	7567-82805-2	U.S.A.	1995	8.99
J. Geils Band	Sanctuary	CD	BGO	BGOCD262	England	1995	12.99
J. Geils Band	Sanctuary + 2	CD	Razor & Tie	RE-82173-2	U.S.A.	1998	12.99
J. Geils Band	Self Titled	CD	Atlantic	7567-82806-2	U.S.A.	1995	8.99
J. Geils Band	Showtime ! (Live)	CD	BGO	BGOCD264	England	1995	17.99
J. Geils Band	The Best Of	CD	Atlantic	19234-2	U.S.A.	1979	8.99
J. Geils Band	The Morning After	CD	Atlantic	7567-82807-2	U.S.A.	1995	8.99
Jacks	Super Session	CD	Toshiba-EMI	TOCT-10132	Japan	1998	28.99
Jacks	Vacant World	CD	Toshiba-EMI	TOCT-25104	Japan	1998	28.99
Jackson 5	Soulsation (25th Ann. Promo Sampler)	CD	Motown	37463-1347-2	U.S.A.	1995	12.99
Jackson 5	Soulsation Box Set	4CD	Motown	31453-0489-2	U.S.A.	1995	28.99
Jackson, Janet	1986/1996 Design Of A Decade + 2	CD	Polydor	POCM-9011	Japan	1995	84.99

Artist	Title	Format	Label	Catalog No	Country	Released	Value
Jackson, Janet	Alright Remix	CD Single	Pony Canyon	PCCY-10120	Japan	1990	53.99
Jackson, Janet	Come Back To Me (Remixes)	CD Single	Pony Canyon	PCCY-10131	Japan	1990	54.99
Jackson, Janet	Escapade Remix	CD Single	Pony Canyon	PCCY-10119	Japan	1990	53.99
Jackson, Janet	Love Will Never Do (Remixes)	CD Single	Pony Canyon	PCCY-10191	Japan	1990	64.99
Jackson, Janet	Miss You Much Remix	CD Single	Pony Canyon	PCCY-10083	Japan	1989	34.99
Jackson, Janet	More Control 12" Remix	CD Single	Pony Canyon	D22Y-3360	Japan	1989	34.99
Jackson, Janet	Rhythm Nation Remix	CD Single	Pony Canyon	PCCY-10084	Japan	1989	64.99
Jackson, Joe	(He's A) Shape In A Drape	CD Single	A&M	75021-2376-2	U.S.A.	1998	14.99
Jackson, Joe	Beat Crazy	CD	A&M	CD-3241	U.S.A.	1980	34.99
Jackson, Joe	Big World	CD	A&M	CD-6021	U.S.A.	1986	11.99
Jackson, Joe	Blaze Of Glory	CD	A&M	CD-5249	U.S.A.	1989	9.99
Jackson, Joe	Body And Soul	CD	A&M	CD-3286	U.S.A.	1984	10.99
Jackson, Joe	Greatest Hits	CD	A&M	31454-0524-2	U.S.A.	1996	7.99
Jackson, Joe	Heaven & Hell	CD	Sony	SK60273	U.S.A.	1997	9.99
Jackson, Joe	I'm The Man + 1	CD	A&M	069-493-089-2	U.S.A.	2001	8.99
Jackson, Joe	Jumpin' Jive	CD	A&M	31454-0991-2	U.S.A.	1998	8.99
Jackson, Joe	Laughter & Lust	CD	Virgin	2-91628	U.S.A.	1991	7.99
Jackson, Joe	Live 1980/86	2CD	A&M	75021-6706-2	U.S.A.	1988	12.99
Jackson, Joe	Look Sharp! + 2	CD	A&M	314-586-194-2	U.S.A.	2001	8.99
Jackson, Joe	Night And Day (Deluxe Edition)	2CD	A&M	80000701-02	U.S.A.	2003	16.99
Jackson, Joe	Night And Day (MFSL Gold Cd)	CD	Mobile Fidelity	UDCD-539	U.S.A.	1982	74.99
Jackson, Joe	Night And Day II	CD	Sony	SK-89261	U.S.A.	2000	9.99
Jackson, Joe	Night Music	CD	Virgin	7243-8-39880-2-0	U.S.A.	1994	5.99
Jackson, Joe	Oh Well	CD Single	Virgin	VUSCD-41	Austria	1991	90.99
Jackson, Joe	Steppin' Out The Best Of Joe Jackson	2CD	A&M	314-556-537-2	U.S.A.	2001	20.99
Jackson, Joe	Stepping Out	CD	A&M	397-052-2	Germany	1990	9.99
Jackson, Joe	Stranger Than Fiction	CD Single	Virgin	VUSCD-40	England	1991	7.99
Jackson, Joe	Summer In The City (Live In New York)	CD	Sony	SK-89237	U.S.A.	2000	7.99
Jackson, Joe	Symphony No. 1 (Black/Regular Cd)	CD	Sony	SK-64435	U.S.A.	1999	9.99
Jackson, Joe	The Collection	CD	Spectrum	544-513-2	England	2001	9.99
Jackson, Joe	This Is it	2CD	A&M	540-402-2	England	1997	21.99
Jackson, Joe	Tucker The Man And His Dream	CD	A&M	CD-3917	U.S.A.	1988	19.99
Jackson, Joe	Volume 4 (W/Live Bonus Disc)	2CD	Rykodisc	RCD-10638	U.S.A.	2003	13.99
Jackson, Joe	Will Power (MFSL Gold Cd)	CD	Mobile Fidelity	UDCD-503	U.S.A.	1987	104.99
Jackson, Joe/Blue/Yellow Cvr	Symphony No. 1 (Alternate Cover)	CD	Sony	SK-64435	U.S.A.	1999	12.99
Jackson, Michael	Dangerous (Ltd. Ed.)	CD	Epic	07464-48900-2	U.S.A.	1991	22.99
Jackson, Michael	Give In To Me (Promo)	CD Single	Epic	XPCD255	England	1993	149.99
Jackson, Michael	Gone Too Soon (Promo)	CD Single	Epic	ESK-5562	U.S.A.	1993	14.99
Jackson, Michael	Heal The World (Promo)	CD Single	Epic	ESK-74708	U.S.A.	1991	14.99
Jackson, Michael	History (Gold Cd)	2CD	Epic	E2K-59000	U.S.A.	1995	14.99
Jackson, Michael	Invincible Box Set (Grn. DJ Cd/VCD)	2CD	Columbia	CPK-2514	Korea	2001	204.99
Jackson, Michael	Jam (M Jordan W/Michael On Cvr/DJ)	CD Single	Epic	ESK-74333	U.S.A.	1992	89.99
Jackson, Michael	Off The Wall (Special Edition)	CD	Epic	EK-60070	U.S.A.	2001	13.99
Jackson, Michael	Scream	CD Single	Epic	49K-78001	U.S.A.	1995	4.99
Jackson, Michael	The History Of (Promo)	CD	Epic	QY/8P-90093	Japan	1995	174.99
Jackson, Michael	Thriller + 4 (Special Edition Gold Cd)	CD	Epic	EK-60073	U.S.A.	2001	14.99
Jackson, Michael	Who Is It (Promo)	CD Single	Epic	ESK-74406	U.S.A.	1992	10.99
Jackson, Michael/Only 6000	The Bad Mixes (Promo)	CD	Epic	ESK-1215MC	U.S.A.	1988	171.99
Jade	Mr. Joy	CD	Line	TLCD-9.00447-0	Germany	1988	24.99
Jade Warrior	At Peace	CD	Earthsounds	CDEASM001	England	1989	19.99
Jade Warrior	Breathing The Storm	CD	Line	OLCD-9.51062-Z	Germany	1992	12.99
Jade Warrior	Breathing The Storm	CD	Blueprint	BP342CD	England	2000	11.99
Jade Warrior	Distant Echoes	CD	Blueprint	BP343CD	England	2000	12.99
Jade Warrior	Eclipse	CD	Acme Deluxe	ADCD1021	England	1998	24.99
Jade Warrior	Elements: The Island Anthology	2CD	Island	524-139-2	England	1995	34.99
Jade Warrior	Fifth Element	CD	Background	HBG-123/10	England	1998	12.99
Jade Warrior	Jade Warrior	CD	Background	HBG-123/11	England	2000	12.99
Jade Warrior	Jade Warrior (Line Version)	CD	Line	LICD-9.00548-0	Germany	1988	12.99

J

Artist	Title	Format	Label	Catalog No	Country	Released	Value
Jade Warrior	Last Autumn's Dream	CD	Background	HBG-123/13	England	2000	12.99
Jade Warrior	Last Autumn's Dream (Line Version)	CD	Line	LICD-9.00563-0	Germany	1988	12.99
Jade Warrior	Released	CD	Background	HBG-123/12	England	2000	12.99
Jade Warrior	Released (Line Version)	CD	Line	LICD-9.00550-0	Germany	1988	12.99
Jaded Heart	Inside Out	CD	Zero	XRCN-1153	Japan	1994	34.99
Jagger, Chris	Atcha	CD	Griffin	GCD-258-2	U.S.A.	2001	9.99
Jagger, Chris	Channel Fever	CD	Blueprint	BP9186CD	England	2000	11.99
Jagger, Chris	Rock The Zydeco	CD	Curb	D2-77794	U.S.A.	1995	7.99
Jagger, Mick	Don't Tear Me Up (Promo)	CD Single	Atlantic	PRCD-5015-2	U.S.A.	1993	14.99
Jagger, Mick	God Gave Me Everything	CD Single	Virgin	7243-5-46067-2-4	U.S.A.	2001	7.99
Jagger, Mick	Goddess In The Doorway	CD	Virgin	7243-8-11288-2-4	U.S.A.	2001	7.99
Jagger, Mick	Out Of Focus (Promo)	CD Single	Atlantic	PRCD-5152-2	U.S.A.	1993	19.99
Jagger, Mick	Performance Soundtrack	CD	Warner Bros.	9-26400-2	U.S.A.	1970	24.99
Jagger, Mick	Primitive Cool	CD	Atlantic	82554-2	U.S.A.	1987	9.99
Jagger, Mick	She's The Boss	CD	Columbia	CK-39940	U.S.A.	1985	9.99
Jagger, Mick	She's The Boss	CD	Sony	32DP-213	Japan	1985	34.99
Jagger, Mick	Sweet Thing (Promo)	CD Single	Atlantic	PRCD-4929-2	U.S.A.	1993	15.99
Jagger, Mick	Sweet Thing (Promo)	CD Single	Atlantic	PRCD-4939-2	U.S.A.	1993	12.99
Jagger, Mick	Sweet Thing (Promo)	CD Single	Atlantic	PRCD-4900-2	U.S.A.	1993	15.99
Jagger, Mick	Visions Of Paradise	CD Single	Virgin	7243-5-46315-28	U.S.A.	2002	5.99
Jagger, Mick	Wandering Spirit	CD	Atlantic	7-82436-2	U.S.A.	1993	7.99
Jagger, Mick	Wandering Spirit (Promo/Interview)	CD	Atlantic	PRCD-5002-2	U.S.A.	1993	15.99
Jagger, Mick	Wired All Night (Promo)	CD Single	Atlantic	PRCD-5020-2	U.S.A.	1993	21.99
Jagger, Mick/Various Artists	Ned Kelly (O.S.T.)	CD	Rykodisc	RCD-10708	U.S.A.	1997	13.99
Jam, The	A Selection From The BBC (DJ)	CD	Polydor	JAMBBC1	England	2002	19.99
Jam, The	All Mod Cons	CD	Polydor	537-419-2	England	1997	8.99
Jam, The	All Mod Cons/S Affects (MFSL Gold)	CD	Mobile Fidelity	UDCD-673	U.S.A.	1980	24.99
Jam, The	At The BBC (W/Bonus Live Cd)	3CD	Polydor	5899382	England	2002	34.99
Jam, The	Beat Surrender	CD	Polydor	550-006-2	England	1993	5.99
Jam, The	Collection	CD	Polydor	31453-1493-2	U.S.A.	1996	10.99
Jam, The	Compact Snap	CD	Polydor	821-712-2	U.S.A.	1990	19.99
Jam, The	Dig The New Breed	CD	Polydor	810-041-2	U.S.A.	1982	17.99
Jam, The	Direction Reaction Creation Box Set	5CD	Polydor	537-143-2	England	1997	59.99
Jam, The	Direction Reaction... Box Sampler (DJ)	CD	Polydor	JAM1	England	1997	19.99
Jam, The	Extras	CD	Polydor	314-513-177-2	U.S.A.	1992	10.99
Jam, The	In The City	CD	Polydor	537-417-2	England	1997	7.99
Jam, The	Jam Covers (Promo Sampler)	CD	Polydor	SACD-491	U.S.A.	1992	29.99
Jam, The	Live Jam	CD	Polydor	519-867-2	England	1993	6.99
Jam, The	Setting Sons	CD	Polydor	537-420-2	England	1997	8.99
Jam, The	Singles 1977-1979 Box Set	9 CD	Polydor	587-610-2	England	2001	49.99
Jam, The	Singles 1980-1982 Box Set	9 CD	Polydor	587-620-2	England	2001	49.99
Jam, The	Sound Effects	CD	Polydor	537-421-2	England	1997	8.99
Jam, The	The Complete Jam (Promo Sampler)	CD Single	Universal	JAMPCD1	England	2002	19.99
Jam, The	The Gift	CD	Polydor	537-422-2	England	1997	10.99
Jam, The	The Peel Sessions	CD	Strange Fruit	SFPSCD080	England	1977	11.99
Jam, The	The Peel Sessions	CD	Strange Fruit	SFPSCD080	England	1996	13.99
Jam, The	The Sound Of The Jam + 5	CD	Polydor	589-781-2	England	2002	12.99
Jam, The	The Very Best Of	CD	Polydor	537-423-2	England	1997	9.99
Jam, The	This Is The Modern World	CD	Polydor	537-418-2	England	1997	7.99
Jam, The/Bruce Foxton	Touch Sensitive + 4	CD	Cherry Red	CDM-RED-192	England	2001	19.99
James	I Know What I'm Here For (Cd 1)	CD Single	Mercury	562-227-2	EU	1999	3.99
James	Laid	CD	Mercury	314-514-943-2	U.S.A.	1993	5.99
James	Runaground (Cd 1)	CD Single	Fontana	568-853-2	England	1998	7.99
James	Say Something	CD	Mercury	858-797-2	U.S.A.	1994	5.99
James	Seven (Promo)	CD Single	Fontana	CDP-702	U.S.A.	1992	3.99
James	She's A Star (Promo)	CD Single	Mercury	MECP-186	U.S.A.	1997	1.99
James	The Best Of James	CD	Mercury	536-898-2	U.S.A.	1998	8.99
James	Tomorrow (Promo)	CD Single	Mercury	MECP-253	U.S.A.	1997	7.99

J

Artist	Title	Format	Label	Catalog No	Country	Released	Value
James	Wah Wah	CD	Fontana	522-827-2	England	1994	7.99
James	Whiplash	CD	Mercury	314-534-354-2	U.S.A.	1997	5.99
James, Bob	Heads	CD	Warner Bros.	9-45968-2	U.S.A.	1977	6.99
James, Elmore	King Of The Slide Guitar	2CD	Capricorn	9-42006-2	U.S.A.	1992	34.99
James, Tommy	A Night In The Big City	CD	Aura	AU-3040	U.S.A.	1995	8.99
James, Tommy	Solo Years 1970 - 1981	CD	Rhino	R2-70735	U.S.A.	1991	29.99
James, Tommy/Shondells	Anthology	CD	Rhino	R2-70920	U.S.A.	1989	9.99
James, Tommy/Shondells	Crimson & Clover/Cellophane Symp	CD	Rhino	R2-70534	U.S.A.	1992	13.99
James, Tommy/Shondells	Hanky Panky/It's Only Love + 1	CD	Repertoire	REP-4425-WY	Germany	1994	13.99
James, Tommy/Shondells	It's A New Vibration (Anthology)	2CD	West Side	WESD-203	England	1997	19.99
James, Tommy/Shondells	The Essentials	CD	Rhino	R2-76039	U.S.A.	2002	8.99
James-Gang	Greatest Hits	CD	MCA	088-112-064-2	U.S.A.	2000	7.99
James-Gang	Live In Concert	CD	BGO	BGOCD120	England	1999	24.99
James-Gang	Live In Concert (MFSL Silver Cd)	CD	Mobile Fidelity	MFCD-789	U.S.A.	1971	49.99
James-Gang	Passin' Thru	CD	One Way	MCAD-22066	U.S.A.	1992	8.99
James-Gang	Rides Again	CD	MCA	088-112-283-2	U.S.A.	2000	9.99
James-Gang	The Best Of The James Gang	2CD	Repertoire	REP-4671-WR	Germany	1998	24.99
James-Gang	Thirds.	CD	MCA	088-112-022-2	U.S.A.	2000	8.99
James-Gang	Yer' Album	CD	MCA	088-112-282-2	U.S.A.	2000	8.99
Jamiroquai	Synkronized + 3 (W/Bonus Cd)	2CD	Sony	494517- 9	Australia	1999	15.99
Jan & Dean	Save For A Rainy Day + 13	CD	Sundazed	SC-11035	U.S.A.	1996	8.99
Jan & Dean	Take Brian Surfin'	CD	Toshiba-EMI	TOCP-66038	Japan	2002	32.99
Jan & Dean/Jan Berry	Second Wave	CD	One Way	OW-34524	U.S.A.	1997	11.99
Jane's Addiction	Classic Girl (Cd 2)	CD Single	Warner Bros.	9-40129-2	U.S.A.	1991	5.99
Jane's Addiction	Classic Girl (Promo)	CD Single	Warner Bros.	PRO-CD-4633	U.S.A.	1991	15.99
Jane's Addiction	Live And Rare	CD	Warner Bros.	WPCP-4450	Japan	1991	15.99
Jane's Addiction	Ritual De Lo Habitual (DJ/Novena Bklt)	CD	Warner Bros.	25993-DJ	U.S.A.	1990	103.99
Jane's Addiction	So What! (Promo)	CD Single	Warner Bros.	PRO-CD-9060	U.S.A.	1997	5.99
Jansch, Bert	Avocet	CD	Castle	CMQCD763	England	2003	8.99
Jansch, Bert	BBC Radio One In Concert	CD	Windsong	WINCD-039	England	1993	14.99
Jansch, Bert	Birthday Blues	CD	Castle	CMRCD334	England	2002	8.99
Jansch, Bert	Crimson Moon + 10 (W/Bonus Cd)	2CD	When!	WENCD211	England	2000	21.99
Jansch, Bert	Dazzling Stranger: The Anthology	2CD	Castle	CMEDD009	England	2002	15.99
Jansch, Bert	Down Under: Live In Australia	CD	Castle	CMRCD022	England	2001	8.99
Jansch, Bert	Edge Of A Dream	CD	Sanctuary	SANCD136	England	2002	8.99
Jansch, Bert	From The Outside + 3	CD	Castle	CMRCD170	England	2001	8.99
Jansch, Bert	Heartbreak	CD	Line	TACD-9.00791-0	Germany	1989	9.99
Jansch, Bert	Heartbreak	CD	Hannibal	HNCD1312	U.S.A.	1993	8.99
Jansch, Bert	It Don't Bother Me	CD	Castle	CMRCD-205	England	2002	8.99
Jansch, Bert	It Don't Bother Me + 4	CD	Demon	TDEMCD16	England	1994	19.99
Jansch, Bert	Jack Orion	CD	Castle	CMRCD-304	England	2002	8.99
Jansch, Bert	Jack Orion/Nicola	CD	Essential	ESMCD459	England	1997	11.99
Jansch, Bert	Leather Launderette	CD	Black Crow	CRO-218	England	1988	29.99
Jansch, Bert	Live At The 12 Bar	CD	Essential	ESMCD921	England	2000	8.99
Jansch, Bert	Moonshine	CD	Castle	CMRCD112	England	2001	8.99
Jansch, Bert	Nicola + 2	CD	Castle	CMRCD333	England	2002	8.99
Jansch, Bert	Nicola/Birthday Blues	CD	Demon	TDEMCD17	England	1994	19.99
Jansch, Bert	Rosemary Lane	CD	Line	TACD-9.00784-0	Germany	1989	9.99
Jansch, Bert	Rosemary Lane	CD	Castle	CMRCD335	England	2002	8.99
Jansch, Bert	Self Titled + 2	CD	Castle	CMRCD204	England	2001	8.99
Jansch, Bert	Self Titled/It Don't Bother Me Minus 2	CD	Essential	ESMCD407	England	1997	15.99
Jansch, Bert	Sketches + 1	CD	Temple	TP-035	England	1995	12.99
Jansch, Bert	The Best Of	CD	Shanachie	SHANCD-99004	U.S.A.	1992	8.99
Jansch, Bert	The Ornament Tree	CD	Castle	CMRCD111	England	2001	8.99
Jansch, Bert	The Toy Balloon	CD	Cooking Vinyl	COOK-CD-138	England	1998	8.99
Jansch, Bert	When The Circus Comes To Town	CD	Cooking Vinyl	COOK-CD-092	England	1995	11.99
Jansch, Bert	Young Man Blues: Glasgow '62 - '64	CD	Big Beat	CDWIKD182	England	1998	8.99
Jansch, Bert/Conundrum	Thirteen Down	CD	Kicking Mule	KMC3909	U.S.A.	1998	8.99

Artist	Title	Format	Label	Catalog No	Country	Released	Value
Jansch, Bert/John Renbourn	After The Dance	CD	Shanachie	SHANCD-99006	U.S.A.	1994	11.99
Jansch, Bert/John Renbourn	Bert And John	CD	Castle	CMRCD203	England	2002	11.99
Jansch, Bert/John Renbourn	Bert And John (W/Bonus Tracks)	CD	Wooded Hill	HILLCD-8	England	1998	11.99
Jansch, Bert/John Renbourn	Stepping Stones	CD	Vanguard	VMD-6506	U.S.A.	1995	24.99
Jansch, Bert/Loren Auerbach	After The Long Night	CD	Castle	CMRCD168	England	2002	8.99
Japan	Adolescent Sex	CD	Caroline	CAROL-1201-2	U.S.A.	1978	17.99
Japan	Exorcising Ghosts	CD	Virgin	VGDCD-3510	England	1984	13.99
Japan	Exorcising Ghosts (Complete Version)	2CD	Virgin	VJCP-36017	Japan	1984	43.99
Japan	Gentlemen Take Polaroids	CD	Caroline	CAROL-1829-2	U.S.A.	1984	6.99
Japan	In Vogue	CD	Camden	74321-39338-2	EC	1996	7.99
Japan	Obscure Alternatives	CD	Caroline	CAROL-1202-2	U.S.A.	1978	6.99
Japan	Oil On Canvas	CD	Caroline	CAROL-1832-2	U.S.A.	1984	10.99
Japan	Oil On Canvas (Complete Version)	2CD	Virgin	VJD-25009~10	Japan	1983	48.99
Japan	Quiet Life + 4	CD	Camden	74321-89582-2	Australia	2001	13.99
Japan	The Singles: Japan	2CD	BMG Victor	74321-39836-2	Japan	1996	44.99
Japan	Tin Drum	CD	Caroline	CAROL-1830-2	U.S.A.	1984	14.99
Japan/Jansen/Barbieri/Karn	Seed	CD	Medium	MPCD2	Austria	1994	16.99
Japan/Rain Tree Crow	Rain Tree Crow	CD	Virgin	0777-7-86252-2-3	England	1991	9.99
Japan/S Jansen/R Barbieri	Stories Across Borders	CD	Virgin	CDVE-908	Germany	1991	14.99
Jarre, Jean Michel	Equinoxe (MFSL Gold Cd)	CD	Mobile Fidelity	UDCD-647	U.S.A.	1978	59.99
Jarre, Jean Michel	Oxygene (MFSL Gold Cd)	CD	Mobile Fidelity	UDCD-613	U.S.A.	1976	15.99
Jarre, Maurice	Ghost	CD	Varese	VSD-5276	U.S.A.	1990	6.99
Jarre, Maurice	No Way Out (O.S.T.)	CD	Varese	VCD-47301	U.S.A.	1987	26.99
Jarre, Maurice	Tai-Pan (O.S.T.)	CD	Varese	VSD-47274	U.S.A.	1986	136.99
Jarre, Maurice/No Art	Sunchaser (Only 28/Rest Destroyed)	CD	Milan	38998-2	U.S.A.	1996	544.99
Jars Of Clay	Drummer Boy (Promo)	CD Single	Essential	JDJ-42431-2	U.S.A.	1996	8.99
Jars Of Clay	Flood	CD Single	Essential	01241-42375-2	U.S.A.	1996	3.99
Jars Of Clay	Flood (Promo)	CD Single	Essential	JDJ-42375-2	U.S.A.	1996	6.99
Jars Of Clay	If I Left The Zoo	CD	Essential	83061-0499-2	U.S.A.	1999	7.99
Jars Of Clay	Jar Of Gems + 14 (Bonus Cd)	2CD	Zomba	9221812	Singapore	2001	24.99
Jars Of Clay	Jars Of Clay (Platinum)	CD	Essential	CD-70010	U.S.A.	1995	14.99
Jars Of Clay	Little Drummer Boy	CD Single	Essential	ERCD-5622	U.S.A.	1995	5.99
Jars Of Clay	Much Afraid	CD	Essential	01241-41612-2	U.S.A.	1997	5.99
Jars Of Clay	The Eleventh Hour	CD	Essential	83061-0629-2	U.S.A.	2002	9.99
Jars Of Clay	The White Elephant Sessions (Promo)	CD	Essential	83061-0140-1	U.S.A.	2000	23.99
Jars Of Clay	Unforgetful You (Promo)	CD	Essential	JDJ-42630-2	U.S.A.	1999	5.99
Jazz Passengers	In Love	CD	High Street	72902-10328-2	U.S.A.	1994	19.99
Jazz Passengers	Individually Twisted	CD	32 Records	32007	U.S.A.	1996	14.99
Jazz Passengers/D. Harry	Live In Spain	CD	32 Jazz	32077	U.S.A.	1998	19.99
Jealous Girl	Twice Bitten	CD	Line	GACD-9.00637-0	Germany	1988	14.99
Jefferson Airplane	2400 Fulton Street	2CD	RCA	5724-2-R-P1/2	U.S.A.	1987	10.99
Jefferson Airplane	After Bathing At Baxter's	CD	RCA	07863-66798-2	U.S.A.	1996	7.99
Jefferson Airplane	Bark	CD	RCA	07863-66574-2	U.S.A.	1996	8.99
Jefferson Airplane	Bless Its Pointed Little Head + 3	CD	RCA	82876-61643-2	U.S.A.	2004	9.99
Jefferson Airplane	Cleared For Take Off	CD	Acrobat	ACMCD-4001	England	2003	14.99
Jefferson Airplane	Crown Of Creation (MFSL Gold Cd)	CD	Mobile Fidelity	UDCD-523	U.S.A.	1968	34.99
Jefferson Airplane	Crown Of Creation + 2	CD	RCA	74321-84788-2	Spain	2001	14.99
Jefferson Airplane	Early Flight	CD	RCA	07863-67419-2	U.S.A.	1997	11.99
Jefferson Airplane	Feed Your Head Live 67-69	CD	Prism Leisure	PLATCD-201	England	1996	6.99
Jefferson Airplane	Ignition Box (1st/Pillow/Baxter/Crown)	4CD	RCA	07863-68032-2	U.S.A.	2001	44.99
Jefferson Airplane	Jefferson Airplane	CD	Epic	EK-45271	U.S.A.	1989	6.99
Jefferson Airplane	Jefferson Airplane Loves You (Promo)	CD	RCA	RDJ-66113-2	U.S.A.	1992	14.99
Jefferson Airplane	Journey - The Best Of	CD	Camden	74321-40057-2	England	1996	11.99
Jefferson Airplane	Live At The Filmore East	CD	RCA	07863-67563-2	U.S.A.	1998	6.99
Jefferson Airplane	Live At The Monterey Festival	CD	Thunderbolt	CDTB-074	England	1995	11.99
Jefferson Airplane	Live In Monterey	CD	Park South	75766-70584-2-3	U.S.A.	2001	11.99
Jefferson Airplane	Long John Silver	CD	RCA	07863-66800-2	U.S.A.	1996	14.99
Jefferson Airplane	Love Songs	CD	RCA	07863-67900-2	U.S.A.	2000	8.99

Artist	Title	Format	Label	Catalog No	Country	Released	Value
Jefferson Airplane	Loves You Box Set	3CD	RCA	07863-61110-2	U.S.A.	1992	23.99
Jefferson Airplane	Platinum	CD	RCA	82876-51651-2	U.S.A.	2003	8.99
Jefferson Airplane	Somebody To Love (Gr. Hits)	CD	LT Series	LT-5049A	Germany	2001	6.99
Jefferson Airplane	Somebody To Love (Gr. Hits)	CD	Armoury	ARMCD016	Germany	2002	6.99
Jefferson Airplane	Somebody To Love (Live)	CD	Success	16257CD	EEC	1995	6.99
Jefferson Airplane	Surrealistic Pillow (S/M RCA Gold Cd)	CD	RCA	07863-66598-2	U.S.A.	1995	21.99
Jefferson Airplane	Surrealistic Pillow (Stereo/Mono)	CD	RCA	07863-68031-2	U.S.A.	2001	9.99
Jefferson Airplane	Surrealistic Pillow + 4	CD	RCA	74321-84791-2	Spain	2001	19.99
Jefferson Airplane	Surrealistic Pillow Ep (24 Bit)	CD Single	Magic	86.560	France	2002	9.99
Jefferson Airplane	Takes Off (Stereo/Mono)	CD	RCA	07863-66797-2	U.S.A.	1996	10.99
Jefferson Airplane	Takes Off + 4	CD	RCA	74321-84789-2	Spain	2001	14.99
Jefferson Airplane	The Best Of	CD	Camden	74321841022	England	2001	8.99
Jefferson Airplane	The Gold Collection (Gold Cd)	2CD	Retro	R2CD.40-49	EEC	1997	19.99
Jefferson Airplane	The Roar Of	CD	RCA	07863-68035-2	U.S.A.	2001	9.99
Jefferson Airplane	The Worst Of Jefferson Airplane	CD	RCA	07863-67420-2	U.S.A.	1997	6.99
Jefferson Airplane	Thirty Seconds Over Winterland	CD	RCA	0147-2-G	U.S.A.	1973	18.99
Jefferson Airplane	Volunteers + 5	CD	RCA	82876-61642-2	U.S.A.	2004	10.99
Jefferson Airplane	Volunteers (MFSL Gold Cd)	CD	Mobile Fidelity	UDCD-540	U.S.A.	1969	44.99
Jefferson Airplane	Volunteers + 6	CD	RCA	74321-78227-2	Spain	2001	10.99
Jefferson Airplane	We All Are One + 3	CD	Sonic Book	SONIC-BOOK-3	Italy	1999	22.99
Jefferson Airplane	White Rabbit (Live)	CD	Master Tone	AB-3019	England	1995	7.99
Jefferson Airplane/KBC Band	KBC Band	CD	Arista	ARCD-8440	U.S.A.	1986	9.99
Jefferson Airplane/P. Kantner	A Guide Through The Chaos	2CD	Monster Sounds Ent.	MSE-1017	U.S.A.	1996	11.99
Jefferson Airplane/P. Kantner	Rock And Roll Orchestra (Bonus CD)	2CD	CIA	NO #	U.S.A.	2004	19.99
Jefferson Airplane/Starship	Behind The Music Collection	CD	RCA	07863-67969-2	U.S.A.	2000	8.99
Jefferson Airplane/Starship	Greatest Hits (More Airplane Than S)	2CD	Double Platinum	DBP-102028	Holland	2001	19.99
Jefferson Airplane/Starship	Hits	2CD	RCA	07863-67705-2	U.S.A.	1998	14.99
Jefferson Starship	10-31-00 B. B. King Blues Club N.Y.	3CD	CIA	XM-01	U.S.A.	2002	19.99
Jefferson Starship	Across The Sea Of Suns	2CD	Zebra	ZD-44024-2	U.S.A.	2001	12.99
Jefferson Starship	Blows Against The Empire (Orig Mix)	CD	RCA	3868-2-R	U.S.A.	1970	11.99
Jefferson Starship	Blows Against The Empire (Remixed)	CD	RCA	07863-67440-2	U.S.A.	1997	11.99
Jefferson Starship	Deep Space/Virgin Sky	CD	Essential	ESMCD-493	England	1995	8.99
Jefferson Starship	Deep Space/Virgin Sky (DJ Sampler)	CD	Intersound	9151-A	U.S.A.	1995	12.99
Jefferson Starship	Dragonfly	CD	RCA	07863-66879-2	U.S.A.	1997	9.99
Jefferson Starship	Earth	CD	RCA	07863-66878-2	U.S.A.	1997	10.99
Jefferson Starship	Freedom At Point Zero	CD	RCA	07863-66877-2	U.S.A.	1997	14.99
Jefferson Starship	Gold	CD	RCA	07863-67560-2	U.S.A.	1998	9.99
Jefferson Starship	Greatest Hits Live At The Fillmore	CD	CMC INT.	06076-86278-2	U.S.A.	1999	9.99
Jefferson Starship	King Biscuit September 11 - 17, 1989	CD	DIR Network	69M0100A	U.S.A.	1989	38.99
Jefferson Starship	Let Me Fly (Promo)	CD Single	CMC INT.	CMCDJ-87293-2	U.S.A.	1999	6.99
Jefferson Starship	Miracles (Live Series)	CD	Intersound	72438-19412-2-5	U.S.A.	1997	5.99
Jefferson Starship	Modern Times	CD	BMG	74321-55505-2	Japan	1998	21.99
Jefferson Starship	Nuclear Furniture	CD	BMG	BVCM-7337	Japan	1984	32.99
Jefferson Starship	Nuclear Furniture	CD	BMG	PD-84921	Japan	1998	24.99
Jefferson Starship	Platinum & Gold Collection	CD	RCA	82876-50901-2	U.S.A.	2003	8.99
Jefferson Starship	Post 9/11 (11/02/01) Petaluma, Ca.	2CD	CIA	NO #	U.S.A.	2004	19.99
Jefferson Starship	Post 9/11 (11/10/01) Lancaster, PA	2CD	CIA	NO #	U.S.A.	2004	19.99
Jefferson Starship	Post 9/11 (11/13/01) Towson, MD	2CD	CIA	NO #	U.S.A.	2004	19.99
Jefferson Starship	Post 9/11 (11/19/01) Piermont, NJ	2CD	CIA	NO #	U.S.A.	2004	19.99
Jefferson Starship	Post 9/11 (9/19/01) Randolph, MA	2CD	CIA	NO #	U.S.A.	2004	19.99
Jefferson Starship	Post 9/11 (9/21-01) Seaside H, NJ	2CD	CIA	NO #	U.S.A.	2004	19.99
Jefferson Starship	Red Octopus (DCC Gold Cd)	CD	DCC	GZS-1110	U.S.A.	1997	14.99
Jefferson Starship	Spitfire	CD	RCA	07863-66876-2	U.S.A.	1997	19.99
Jefferson Starship	Starship Chronicle August 12 - 18, '96	CD	DIR Network	RAD-KB-96-33	U.S.A.	1996	38.99
Jefferson Starship	UK 2002 Tour Black Box	10CD	CIA	XM-03/09	U.S.A.	2002	109.99
Jefferson Starship	Vinoy, St. Petersburg, Fla. 11-11-2000	2CD	CIA	XM-02	U.S.A.	2002	19.99
Jefferson Starship	Windows Of Heaven + 1	CD	Victor Ent.	VICP-60627	Japan	1999	14.99
Jefferson Starship	Winds Of Change	CD	RCA	PCD1-4372	U.S.A.	1982	14.99

J

Artist	Title	Format	Label	Catalog No	Country	Released	Value
Jefferson Starship/5 Extra	Deeper Space/Extra Virgin Sky	2CD	Rainman	RMCD119	U.S.A.	2003	19.99
Jeffreys, Garland	And Grinder's Switch	CD	Vanguard	VMD-6550	U.S.A.	1970	24.99
Jeffreys, Garland	Don't Call Me Buckwheat	CD	RCA	07863-61112-2	U.S.A.	1991	5.99
Jeffreys, Garland	Escape Artist + 4	CD	Epic	EK-36983	U.S.A.	1981	8.99
Jeffreys, Garland	Matador And More...	CD	A&M	397-179-2	U.S.A.	1992	13.99
Jeffreys, Garland	Sexuality	CD Single	Logic	74321-48214-2	U.S.A.	1997	5.99
Jeffreys, Garland	The Answer (Promo)	CD Single	RCA	RDJ-62295-2	U.S.A.	1992	5.99
Jeffreys, Garland	Wild In The Streets (Best 1977-1983)	CD	Raven	RVCD-1242002	Australia	2002	10.99
Jeffreys, Garland	Wildlife Dictionary + 1	CD	BMG	74321-43849-2	Japan	1997	29.99
Jellyfish	Bellybutton + 6 Live	CD	Toshiba-EMI	VJCP-28175	Japan	1993	32.99
Jellyfish	Jellyfish Comes Alive (Promo)	CD	Charisma	PRCD-084	U.S.A.	1991	24.99
Jellyfish	Jellyfish Fan Club Box Set	4CD	Not Lame	NLA-007	U.S.A.	2002	129.99
Jellyfish	New Mistake	CD Single	Charisma	0777-7-12663-2-4	U.S.A.	1993	8.99
Jellyfish	Spilt Milk	CD	Toshiba-EMI	TOCP-53032	Japan	1999	29.99
Jenkins, Johnny	Blessed Blues	CD	Capricorn	314-532-565-2	U.S.A.	1996	24.99
Jenkins, Johnny	Ton-Ton Macoute ! + 2	CD	Capricorn	314-536-106-2	U.S.A.	1997	24.99
Jennings, Waylon	A Man Called Hoss	CD	MCA	MCAD-42038	U.S.A.	1987	54.99
Jensen, Jane	Comic Book Whore	CD	Interscope	INTD-90112	U.S.A.	1996	4.99
Jericho	Self Titled	CD	Repertoire	REP-4058-WZ	Germany	2002	14.99
Jericho Jones	Junkies, Monkeys and Donkeys + 5	CD	Repertoire	REP-4101-WZ	Germany	2002	14.99
Jesus/Mary Chain	Far Gone And Out	CD	Blanco Y Negro	9-40422-2	U.S.A.	1992	3.99
Jesus/Mary Chain	Hate Rock 'N' Roll	CD	American	9-43043-2	U.S.A.	1995	7.99
Jesus/Mary Chain	Munki	CD	Sub Pop	SPCD-426	U.S.A.	1998	10.99
Jethro Tull	20 Years Of Jethro Tull Box Set	3CD	Chrysalis	F2-21653	U.S.A.	1988	36.99
Jethro Tull	25th Ann. Box Set (Cigar)	4CD	Reprise	0946-3-26004-2-4	England	1993	69.99
Jethro Tull	A	CD	Chrysalis	F2-21301	U.S.A.	1980	13.99
Jethro Tull	A (W/Bonus DVD)	2CD	Chrysalis	72435-97103-0-3	U.S.A.	2004	19.99
Jethro Tull	A Classic Case (With David Palmer)	CD	RCA	09026-62510-2	U.S.A.	1985	6.99
Jethro Tull	A Jethro Tull Collection	CD	Disky	DC-878612	Netherlands	1997	6.99
Jethro Tull	A Little Light Music	CD	Chrysalis	0946-3-21954-2-5	U.S.A.	1992	9.99
Jethro Tull	A Passion Play (MFSL Gold Cd)	CD	Mobile Fidelity	UDCD-720	U.S.A.	1973	44.99
Jethro Tull	A Passion Play + 1	CD	Chrysalis	72435-81569-0-4	U.S.A.	2003	10.99
Jethro Tull	Aqualung (DCC Gold Cd)	CD	DCC	GZS-1105	U.S.A.	1997	56.99
Jethro Tull	Aqualung 25th Anniversary	CD	Chrysalis	7243-8-52213-2-3	England	1996	12.99
Jethro Tull	Bends Like A Willow	CD Single	Papillion	BTFLYS-001	England	1999	8.99
Jethro Tull	Benefit (Mini Lp)	CD	Chrysalis	7243-8-56081-2-4	Holland	1970	24.99
Jethro Tull	Benefit + 4	CD	Chrysalis	7243-5-35457-2-7	Holland	2001	10.99
Jethro Tull	Best Of Jethro Tull (Ann. Collection)	2CD	Chrysalis	0946-3-26015-2-0	U.S.A.	1993	15.99
Jethro Tull	Bursting Out	2CD	Chrysalis	72435-93396-2-7	U.S.A.	2004	12.99
Jethro Tull	Catfish Rising	CD	Chrysalis	F2-21863	U.S.A.	1991	10.99
Jethro Tull	Christmas Album	CD	Fuel 2000	302-061-340-2	U.S.A.	2003	8.99
Jethro Tull	Christmas Album	CD	Fuel 2000	302-061-340-2	U.S.A.	2003	16.99
Jethro Tull	Christmas Sampler (Promo)	CD	Chrysalis	DPRO-10421	U.S.A.	1995	16.99
Jethro Tull	Crest Of A Knave	CD	Chrysalis	VK-41590	U.S.A.	1987	6.99
Jethro Tull	Gift Of Roses/Xmas Song (2000 Vrsn)	CD Single	Fuel 2000	FLD333	U.S.A.	2000	24.99
Jethro Tull	Heavy Horses	CD	Chrysalis	F2-21175	U.S.A.	1978	11.99
Jethro Tull	Heavy Horses + 2	CD	Chrysalis	72435-83516-2-0	U.S.A.	2003	10.99
Jethro Tull	In Concert (BBC)	CD	Master Tone	8225	U.S.A.	1998	6.99
Jethro Tull	J-Tull Dot Com (Banned Cover)	CD	Roadrunner	RR-8615-2	England	1999	14.99
Jethro Tull	J-Tull Dot Com (Promo Alt. Version)	CD	Fuel 2000	FLDPRO-1102	U.S.A.	1999	29.99
Jethro Tull	J-Tull Dot Com (Promo)	CD Single	Fuel 2000	FLDPRO-1103	U.S.A.	1999	29.99
Jethro Tull	King Biscuit Flower Hour (3, 19, 1989)	CD	DIR Network	4M-40100B	U.S.A.	1989	49.99
Jethro Tull	Live - Bursting Out (Long Version)	2CD	Chrysalis	32-1201-2	England	1978	38.99
Jethro Tull	20 Years Of Jethro Tull Box Set	3CD	Chrysalis	F2-21653	U.S.A.	1988	36.99
Jethro Tull	25th Ann. Box Set (Cigar)	4CD	Reprise	0946-3-26004-2-4	England	1993	69.99
Jethro Tull	A	CD	Chrysalis	F2-21301	U.S.A.	1980	13.99
Jethro Tull	A (W/Bonus DVD)	2CD	Chrysalis	72435-97103-0-3	U.S.A.	2004	19.99
Jethro Tull	A Classic Case (With David Palmer)	CD	RCA	09026-62510-2	U.S.A.	1985	6.99

Artist	Title	Format	Label	Catalog No	Country	Released	Value
Jethro Tull	A Jethro Tull Collection	CD	Disky	DC-878612	Netherlands	1997	6.99
Jethro Tull	A Little Light Music	CD	Chrysalis	0946-3-21954-2-5	U.S.A.	1992	9.99
Jethro Tull	A Passion Play (MFSL Gold Cd)	CD	Mobile Fidelity	UDCD-720	U.S.A.	1973	44.99
Jethro Tull	A Passion Play + 1	CD	Chrysalis	72435-81569-0-4	U.S.A.	2003	10.99
Jethro Tull	Aqualung (DCC Gold Cd)	CD	DCC	GZS-1105	U.S.A.	1997	56.99
Jethro Tull	Aqualung 25th Anniversary	CD	Chrysalis	7243-8-52213-2-3	England	1996	12.99
Jethro Tull	Bends Like A Willow	CD Single	Papillion	BTFLYS-001	England	1999	8.99
Jethro Tull	Benefit (Mini Lp)	CD	Chrysalis	7243-8-56081-2-4	Holland	1970	24.99
Jethro Tull	Benefit + 4	CD	Chrysalis	7243-5-35457-2-7	Holland	2001	10.99
Jethro Tull	Best Of Jethro Tull (Ann. Collection)	2CD	Chrysalis	0946-3-26015-2-0	U.S.A.	1993	15.99
Jethro Tull	Bursting Out	2CD	Chrysalis	72435-93396-2-7	U.S.A.	2004	12.99
Jethro Tull	Catfish Rising	CD	Chrysalis	F2-21863	U.S.A.	1991	10.99
Jethro Tull	Christmas Album	CD	Fuel 2000	302-061-340-2	U.S.A.	2003	8.99
Jethro Tull	Christmas Album	CD	Fuel 2000	302-061-340-2	U.S.A.	2003	16.99
Jethro Tull	Christmas Sampler (Promo)	CD	Chrysalis	DPRO-10421	U.S.A.	1995	16.99
Jethro Tull	Crest Of A Knave	CD	Chrysalis	VK-41590	U.S.A.	1987	6.99
Jethro Tull	Gift Of Roses/Xmas Song (2000 Vrsn)	CD Single	Fuel 2000	FLD333	U.S.A.	2000	24.99
Jethro Tull	Heavy Horses	CD	Chrysalis	F2-21175	U.S.A.	1978	11.99
Jethro Tull	Heavy Horses + 2	CD	Chrysalis	72435-83516-2-0	U.S.A.	2003	10.99
Jethro Tull	In Concert (BBC)	CD	Master Tone	8225	U.S.A.	1998	6.99
Jethro Tull	J-Tull Dot Com (Banned Cover)	CD	Roadrunner	RR-8615-2	England	1999	14.99
Jethro Tull	J-Tull Dot Com (Promo Alt. Version)	CD	Fuel 2000	FLDPRO-1102	U.S.A.	1999	29.99
Jethro Tull	J-Tull Dot Com (Promo)	CD Single	Fuel 2000	FLDPRO-1103	U.S.A.	1999	29.99
Jethro Tull	King Biscuit Flower Hour (3, 19, 1989)	CD	DIR Network	4M-40100B	U.S.A.	1989	49.99
Jethro Tull	Live - Bursting Out (Long Version)	2CD	Chrysalis	32-1201-2	England	1978	38.99
Jethro Tull	Live At Hammersmith '84 (Gold Cd)	CD	Raw Fruit	FRSCD004	England	1990	42.99
Jethro Tull	Living In The Past	2 Mini LP	Toshiba-EMI	TOCP-67369	Japan	2004	44.99
Jethro Tull	Living In The Past (Cd 1)	CD Single	Chrysalis	0946-3-23970-2-7	England	1993	18.99
Jethro Tull	Living in the Past LP Ver.(MFSL Gold)	2CD	Mobile Fidelity	UDCD-2-708	U.S.A.	1972	74.99
Jethro Tull	Living With The Past	CD	Fuel 2000	302-061-199-2	U.S.A.	2002	10.99
Jethro Tull	M.U. - The Best Of	CD	Chrysalis	F2-21078	U.S.A.	1985	7.99
Jethro Tull	Minstrel In The Gallery	CD	Chrysalis	F2-21082	U.S.A.	1975	11.99
Jethro Tull	Minstrel In The Gallery + 5	CD	Chrysalis	72435-41572-2-6	U.S.A.	2002	10.99
Jethro Tull	Nightcap	2CD	Chrysalis	7243-8-28157-2-3	England	1993	14.99
Jethro Tull	Orig Masters (DCC Gold Cd) Long Ver.	CD	DCC	GZS-1126	U.S.A.	1998	84.99
Jethro Tull	Part Of The Machine	CD Single	Chrysalis	TUL-PCD-1	England	1988	13.99
Jethro Tull	Rattlesnake Trail (Promo)	CD Single	Chrysalis	DPRO-23457	U.S.A.	1989	37.99
Jethro Tull	Repeat - The Best Of Jethro Tull Vol.II	CD	Chrysalis	F2-21135	U.S.A.	1977	8.99
Jethro Tull	Rock Island	CD	Chrysalis	F2-21708	U.S.A.	1989	6.99
Jethro Tull	Rocks On The Road	CD Single	Chrysalis	F2-23818	U.S.A.	1991	24.99
Jethro Tull	Rocks On The Road (Part 2)	CD Single	Chrysalis	323858-2	England	1991	27.99
Jethro Tull	Roots To Branches	CD	Chrysalis	F2-35418	U.S.A.	1997	8.99
Jethro Tull	Said She Was A Dancer	CD Single	Chrysalis	TULLCD-4	England	1987	19.99
Jethro Tull	Songs From The Wood (MFSL Gold)	CD	Mobile Fidelity	UDCD-734	U.S.A.	1977	44.99
Jethro Tull	Songs From The Wood + 2	CD	Chrysalis	72435-81570-2-4	U.S.A.	2003	10.99
Jethro Tull	Stand Up (MFSL Gold Cd)	CD	Mobile Fidelity	UDCD-524	U.S.A.	1969	49.99
Jethro Tull	Stand Up + 4	CD	Chrysalis	7243-5-35458-2-6	Holland	2001	13.99
Jethro Tull	Stormwatch	CD	Chrysalis	F2-21238	U.S.A.	1979	13.99
Jethro Tull	Stormwatch + 4	CD	Chrysalis	72435-96573-2-5	U.S.A.	2004	10.99
Jethro Tull	The Broadsword And The Beast	CD	Chrysalis	F2-21380	U.S.A.	1982	10.99
Jethro Tull	The Very Best Of	CD	Chrysalis	72435-32614-2-9	U.S.A.	2001	7.99
Jethro Tull	Thick As A Brick (MFSL Gold Cd)	CD	Mobile Fidelity	UDCD-510	U.S.A.	1972	42.99
Jethro Tull	Thick As A Brick 25th Anniversary	CD	Chrysalis	7243-8-57705-2-4	U.S.A.	1997	12.99
Jethro Tull	This Was + 3	CD	Chrysalis	7243-5-35459-2-5	Holland	2001	12.99
Jethro Tull	Through The Years	CD	EMI	7243-8-55505-2-2	Australia	1997	9.99
Jethro Tull	To Cry You A Song (Tribute)	CD	Magna Carta	MA-9009-2	U.S.A.	1996	19.99
Jethro Tull	Too Old To Rock 'N' Roll...	CD	Chrysalis	VK-41111	U.S.A.	1976	6.99
Jethro Tull	Too Old To Rock 'N Roll...+ 2	CD	Chrysalis	72435-41573-2-5	U.S.A.	2002	10.99

Artist	Title	Format	Label	Catalog No	Country	Released	Value
Jethro Tull	Ult. Box (CD/Lyric Book/Pic Lp/Video)	CD	EMI	7-900510-00516	England	1996	99.99
Jethro Tull	Under Wraps	CD	Chrysalis	VK-41461	U.S.A.	1984	11.99
Jethro Tull	War Child (MFSL Gold Cd)	CD	Mobile Fidelity	UDCD-745	U.S.A.	1974	39.99
Jethro Tull	War Child +7	CD	Chrysalis	72435-41571-2-7	U.S.A.	2002	10.99
Jethro Tull	Westwood 1 # 00-44, 10 28/29, 2000	2CD	Westwood 1	CO000-4-101800	U.S.A.	2000	59.99
Jett, Joan/Blackhearts	Album +3	CD	Blackheart	JJ-757	U.S.A.	1992	24.99
Jett, Joan/Blackhearts	Bad Reputation + 5	CD	Sony	486505-2	Germany	1996	38.99
Jett, Joan/Blackhearts	Fetish	CD	Blackheart	483-376-969-2	U.S.A.	1999	13.99
Jett, Joan/Blackhearts	Fit To Be Tied - Greatest Hits	CD	Mercury	314-536-440-2	U.S.A.	1997	15.99
Jett, Joan/Blackhearts	Glorious Results Of A Misspent Youth	CD	Victor Ent.	VICP-5176	Japan	1992	31.99
Jett, Joan/Blackhearts	Glorious Results/Misspent Youth + 4	CD	Blackheart	JJ767	U.S.A.	1992	24.99
Jett, Joan/Blackhearts	Go Home (Promo)	CD Single	Warner Bros.	PRO-CD-6934	U.S.A.	1990	6.99
Jett, Joan/Blackhearts	Good Music	CD	Columbia	ZK-40544	U.S.A.	1986	9.99
Jett, Joan/Blackhearts	I Love Rock & Roll + 3	CD	Blackheart	JJ747	U.S.A.	1992	12.99
Jett, Joan/Blackhearts	Naked	CD	Victor Ent.	VICP-62690	Japan	2004	24.99
Jett, Joan/Blackhearts	Notorious	CD	Columbia	ZK-47488	U.S.A.	1991	8.99
Jett, Joan/Blackhearts	Pure And Simple	CD	Warner Bros.	9-45567-2	U.S.A.	1994	7.99
Jett, Joan/Blackhearts	The Hit List	CD	Columbia	ZK-45473	U.S.A.	1990	7.99
Jett, Joan/Blackhearts	Up Your Alley	CD	Blackheart	ZK-44146	U.S.A.	1988	9.99
Jewel	A Christmas Card (Promo)	CD Single	Atlantic	PRCD-8326-2	U.S.A.	1997	44.99
Jewel	A Christmas CD (Promo)	CD Single	Atlantic	PRCD-8326-2	U.S.A.	1997	39.99
Jewel	Break Me (Promo)	CD Single	Atlantic	PRCD-300804	U.S.A.	2002	19.99
Jewel	Break Me (Promo)	CD Single	Atlantic	PRO-3199	Germany	2002	9.99
Jewel	Down So Long (Promo)	CD Single	Atlantic	PRCD-8819	U.S.A.	1999	14.99
Jewel	Foolish Games (Promo)	CD Single	East West	PRCD-8141	U.S.A.	1997	8.99
Jewel	Free Sampler (Promo)	CD	Atlantic	JEWEL-1	Germany	1997	11.99
Jewel	Hands (Promo)	CD Single	Atlantic	PRCD-8703	U.S.A.	1998	64.99
Jewel	Jewel Interviews & Answers (Promo)	CD	Atlantic	PRCD-8939	U.S.A.	1999	34.99
Jewel	Joy - Holiday Collection 5-Song (DJ)	CD	Atlantic	CD-ACETATE	U.S.A.	1999	34.99
Jewel	Jupiter (Promo)	CD Single	Atlantic	PRCD-8952	U.S.A.	1999	12.99
Jewel	Save The Linoleum (Promo)	CD Single	Atlantic	PRCD-5999-2	U.S.A.	1994	84.99
Jewel	Standing Still (Promo)	CD Single	Atlantic	AT0123CDDJ	England	2001	9.99
Jewel	Standing Still (Promo)	CD Single	Atlantic	PRCD-300606	U.S.A.	2001	12.99
Jewel	This Way - Snippets	CD	Atlantic	PRO-2972	Germany	2002	9.99
Jewel	What's Simple Is True (Promo)	CD Single	Atlantic	PRCD-9044	U.S.A.	1998	14.99
Jewel	Who Will Save Your Soul (DJ)	CD Single	East West	PRCD-6585	U.S.A.	1996	19.99
Jewel	Who Will Save Your Soul (Promo)	CD Single	East West	PRCD-5998-2	U.S.A.	1995	24.99
Jewel	Who Will Save../91X Interview	CD Single	Atlantic	PRCD-6146-2	U.S.A.	1995	64.99
Jewel	You Were Meant For Me (Promo)	CD Single	Atlantic	PRCD-6888	U.S.A.	1996	19.99
Jewel	You Were Meant...(Phyllis Barnabee)	CD Single	East West	PRCD-6416-2	U.S.A.	1995	89.99
Jingle-Cats	Here Comes Santa Claws	CD	Jingle Cats	41229-2	U.S.A.	1994	6.99
Jingle-Cats	Meowy Christmas	CD	Jingle Cats	9-41226-2	U.S.A.	1993	6.99
Jingle-Dogs	Jingle Dogs - Christmas Unleashed	CD	Jingle Cats	JCCD01231	U.S.A.	1995	6.99
Jngr/Parker	Off The Peg	CD	Line	UTCD-9.00812-L	Germany	1989	19.99
Jo Jo Gunne/Jay Ferguson	Asylum: J J Gunne/Bite Down Hard + 3	CD	Rhino	RHM2-7722	U.S.A.	2000	24.99
Jo Jo Gunne/Jay Ferguson	Asylum: Jumpin' The/So ...Where's + 2	CD	Rhino	RHM2-7723	U.S.A.	2002	34.99
Jobim, Antonio Carlos	Antonio Carlos Jobim	CD	Warner Bros.	9-46114-2	U.S.A.	1995	10.99
Jobim, Antonio Carlos	Compact Jazz	CD	Verve	843-273-2	U.S.A.	1997	7.99
Jobim, Antonio Carlos	Finest Hour	CD	Verve	069-490-669-2	U.S.A.	2000	14.99
Jobim, Antonio Carlos	Jazz Masters 13	CD	Verve	314-516-409-2	U.S.A.	1994	6.99
Jobim, Antonio Carlos	Jazz 'Round Midnight	CD	Verve	314-539-677-2	U.S.A.	1998	12.99
Jobim, Antonio Carlos	Jobim Encontro Piazzolla	CD	West Wind	WW-2209	Germany	1991	12.99
Jobim, Antonio Carlos	Quiet Now Nights Of Quiet Stars	CD	Verve	314-559-733-2	U.S.A.	1999	7.99
Jobim, Antonio Carlos	Stone Flower	CD	Epic	ZK-45480	U.S.A.	1990	9.99
Jobim, Antonio Carlos	Terra Brasilis	CD	Warner Bros.	2-3409	U.S.A.	1980	8.99
Jobim, Antonio Carlos	The Composer Of Desafinado Plays	CD	Verve	314-521-431-2	U.S.A.	1990	12.99
Jobim, Antonio Carlos	The Man From Ipanema	3CD	Verve	314-525-880-2	U.S.A.	1995	34.99
Jobim, Antonio Carlos	Urubu	CD	Warner Bros.	2928-2	U.S.A.	1976	9.99

J

Artist	Title	Format	Label	Catalog No	Country	Released	Value
Jobim, Antonio Carlos	Wave	CD	A&M	CD-0812	U.S.A.	1988	9.99
Jobim, Tom	A Arte De Tom Jobim	CD	PolyGram	836-253-2	U.S.A.	1988	24.99
Jobson, Eddie	Theme Of Secrets	CD	Private Music	2005-2-P	U.S.A.	1985	24.99
Jobson, Eddie/Zinc	The Green Album	CD	One Way	S21-56846	U.S.A.	1992	29.99
Jody Grind	Far Canal	CD	Line	TACD-9.00631-0	Germany	1988	9.99
Joel, Billy	2000 Years - The Millennium Concert	2CD	Columbia	C2K-63792	U.S.A.	2000	12.99
Joel, Billy	52nd Street	CD	Columbia	CK-69385	U.S.A.	1998	7.99
Joel, Billy	52nd Street (Sony Gold Cd)	CD	Columbia	CK-52858	U.S.A.	1993	32.99
Joel, Billy	An Innocent Man	CD	Columbia	CK-69389	U.S.A.	1998	6.99
Joel, Billy	Cold Spring Harbor	CD	Columbia	CK-69390	U.S.A.	1998	6.99
Joel, Billy	Complete Gr. Hits Collection Box Set	4CD	Columbia	CXK-68007	U.S.A.	1997	19.99
Joel, Billy	Early Years Vol. 1	CD	Rock & Melody	3445.2116-2	England	1999	6.99
Joel, Billy	Early Years Vol.2	CD	Rock & Melody	3445.2117-2	England	1999	6.99
Joel, Billy	Essential Billy Joel	2CD	Columbia	C2K-86005	U.S.A.	2001	14.99
Joel, Billy	Fantasies & Delusions	CD	Sony	CK-85397	U.S.A.	2001	5.99
Joel, Billy	Glass Houses	CD	Columbia	CK-69386	U.S.A.	1998	8.99
Joel, Billy	Greatest Hits Vol. I & II	CD	Columbia	C2K-69391	U.S.A.	1998	14.99
Joel, Billy	Greatest Hits Volume III	CD	Columbia	CK-67647	U.S.A.	1997	8.99
Joel, Billy	Kohept	CD	Columbia	CK-69393	U.S.A.	1998	8.99
Joel, Billy	Path To The River Of Dreams (Promo)	CD	Sony	CDNK-874	Canada	1993	14.99
Joel, Billy	Piano Man	CD	Columbia	CK-69381	U.S.A.	1998	6.99
Joel, Billy	Remastered (Promo Sampler)	CD	Columbia	CSK-41485	U.S.A.	1998	17.99
Joel, Billy	River Of Dreams	CD	Columbia	CK-69395	U.S.A.	1998	6.99
Joel, Billy	Songs In The Attic	CD	Columbia	CK-69387	U.S.A.	1998	6.99
Joel, Billy	Storm Front	CD	Columbia	CK-69394	U.S.A.	1998	6.99
Joel, Billy	Storm Front Tour Cd (Promo)	CD	Columbia	CSK-2127	U.S.A.	1990	34.99
Joel, Billy	Streetlife Serenade	CD	Columbia	CK-69382	U.S.A.	1998	6.99
Joel, Billy	The Bridge	CD	Columbia	CK-69392	U.S.A.	1998	7.99
Joel, Billy	The Millenium Concert (Promo Sampler)	CD	Columbia	CSK-12694	U.S.A.	2000	14.99
Joel, Billy	The Nylon Curtain	CD	Columbia	CK-69388	U.S.A.	1998	7.99
Joel, Billy	The Stranger	CD	Columbia	CK-69384	U.S.A.	1998	6.99
Joel, Billy	Turnstiles	CD	Columbia	CK-69383	U.S.A.	1998	6.99
Joel, Billy	Words Without Music (Promo)	CD	Sony	CSK-54920	U.S.A.	2001	9.99
Joel, Billy/Atilla/Hassles	Rollin' Home	CD	Solid Rock	4211	U.S.A.	1969	14.99
Johansen, David	And The Harry Smiths	CD	Chesky	JD196	U.S.A.	2000	13.99
Johansen, David	Crucial Music	CD	Relativity	88561-1033-2	U.S.A.	1990	8.99
Johansen, David	David Johansen + 1	CD	Razor & Tie	RE-1990	U.S.A.	1992	51.99
Johansen, David	From Pumps To Pompadour	CD	Rhino	R2-71877	U.S.A.	1999	8.99
Johansen, David	Here Comes The Night + 1	CD	Razor & Tie	RE-1993	U.S.A.	1992	11.99
Johansen, David	In Style	CD	Razor & Tie	RE-1989	U.S.A.	1992	13.99
Johansen, David	Live	CD	Epic	ZK-53218	U.S.A.	1993	19.99
Johansen, David	Live It Up	CD	Razor & Tie	RE-1994	U.S.A.	1992	14.99
Johansen, David	Looking Good	CD	Sony	A-28063	U.S.A.	1996	8.99
Johansen, David	Sweet Revenge + 3	CD	Maximum	MAX-9001	U.S.A.	1997	13.99
Johansen, David/Syl Sylvain	Tokyo Dolls Live	CD	Teichiku	TECP-25235	Japan	1990	34.99
John Rutter/C. Singers	Brother Sun, Sister Moon	CD	American	AGCD588	U.S.A.	1988	12.99
John Wesley Harding	Collected Stories 1990 - 1991 (Book)	CD	Sire	PRO-CD-4698	U.S.A.	1991	24.99
John Wesley Harding	New Deal	CD	Line	LICD-9.01316-0	Germany	1996	11.99
John, Elton	16 Legendary Covers From 1969/1970	CD	Purple Pyramid	CLP-0237-2	U.S.A.	1998	6.99
John, Elton	17-11-70	CD	Rocket	314-528-165-2	U.S.A.	1995	9.99
John, Elton	A Single Man	CD	Mercury	314-558-4742	U.S.A.	1998	7.99
John, Elton	Blue Moves	2CD	MCA	MCAD2-11667	U.S.A.	1997	15.99
John, Elton	Breaking Hearts	CD	MCA	MCAD-10501	U.S.A.	1983	8.99
John, Elton	Candle In The Wind 97	CD Single	Rocket	31456-8108-2	U.S.A.	1997	4.99
John, Elton	Captain Fantastic...	CD	Rocket	314-528-160-2	U.S.A.	1995	9.99
John, Elton	Caribou	CD	Rocket	314-528-158-2	U.S.A.	1995	9.99
John, Elton	Celebrating Elton John's 50th Birthday	CD	Rocket	RKSAD-00415	U.S.A.	1997	24.99
John, Elton	Don't Shoot Me I'm Only...	CD	Rocket	314-528-154-2	U.S.A.	1995	9.99

J

Artist	Title	Format	Label	Catalog No	Country	Released	Value
John, Elton	Duets	CD	MCA	MCAD-10926	U.S.A.	1993	7.99
John, Elton	Elton John	CD	Rocket	314-528-156-2	U.S.A.	1995	9.99
John, Elton	Empty Sky	CD	Rocket	314-528-1157-2	U.S.A.	1995	7.99
John, Elton	Excerpts From To Be...(Promo)	CD	MCA	MCAD-9070	Canada	1990	154.99
John, Elton	Goodbye Yellow Brick R (MFSL Gold)	CD	Mobile Fidelity	UDCD-526	U.S.A.	1973	46.99
John, Elton	Goodbye Yellow Brick Road	CD	Rocket	314-528-159-2	U.S.A.	1995	9.99
John, Elton	Great Box/20Th Anniversary Special	4CD	Nippon Columbia	PHCR-3133-36	Japan	1991	153.99
John, Elton	Greatest Hits (DCC Gold Cd)	CD	DCC	GZS-1071	U.S.A.	1994	41.99
John, Elton	Greatest Hits 1970 - 2002 (Promo)	CD	Universal	ELTON2002-3	Spain	2002	49.99
John, Elton	Greatests Hits Vol. II	CD	Polydor	314-512-533-2	U.S.A.	1992	7.99
John, Elton	Here And There	2CD	Rocket	314-528-164-2	U.S.A.	1995	9.99
John, Elton	Honky Chateau	CD	Rocket	314-528-162-2	U.S.A.	1995	9.99
John, Elton	Honky Chateau (MFSL Gold Cd)	CD	Mobile Fidelity	UDCD-536	U.S.A.	1972	33.99
John, Elton	I Want Love	CD	Mercury	5887092	Australia	2001	12.99
John, Elton	Ice On Fire	CD	Mercury	314-558-476-2	U.S.A.	1998	7.99
John, Elton	Jump Up	CD	Rocket	0800-037-2	Germany	1982	10.99
John, Elton	Lady Samantha	CD	DJM	832-019-2	England	1974	12.99
John, Elton	Leather Jackets	CD	MCA	MCAD-10498	U.S.A.	1986	8.99
John, Elton	Live In Australia	CD	Mercury	314-558-477-2	U.S.A.	1987	8.99
John, Elton	Made In England	CD Single	Rocket	422-852-173-2	U.S.A.	1995	9.99
John, Elton	Made In England	CD Single	Rocket	422-852-093-2	U.S.A.	1995	9.99
John, Elton	Made In England	CD	Mercury	526-915-2	U.S.A.	1995	6.99
John, Elton	Madman Across The Water	CD	Rocket	314-528-161-2	U.S.A.	1995	10.99
John, Elton	Madman Across The Water (Promo)	CD Single	Polydor	CDP-819	U.S.A.	1992	19.99
John, Elton	Madman Across Water (MFSL Gold)	CD	Mobile Fidelity	UDCD-516	U.S.A.	1971	60.99
John, Elton	Music Reach Out (Song For Guy) DJ	CD	Mercury	EJCCM02	England	2002	169.99
John, Elton	One Night Only - The Greatest Hits	CD	Universal	440-013-050-2	U.S.A.	2000	6.99
John, Elton	Original Sin	CD Single	Mercury	588-999-2	England	2001	7.99
John, Elton	Original Sin	CD Single	Mercury	582-850-2	England	2001	7.99
John, Elton	Original Sin (Promo)	CD	Universal	UNIR-20782-2	U.S.A.	2001	9.99
John, Elton	Pickin' On Elton John	CD	CMH	CD-8599	U.S.A.	2001	8.99
John, Elton	Please (Cd 1)	CD Single	Mercury	852-685-2	England	1995	4.99
John, Elton	Please (Cd 2)	CD Single	Mercury	852-687-2	England	1995	4.99
John, Elton	Prologue	CD	Dolphin	BLCK-86014	Japan	1998	26.99
John, Elton	Rare Masters	2CD	Polydor	314-514-138-2	U.S.A.	1992	15.99
John, Elton	Reg Strikes Back	CD	Mercury	558-478-2	Germany	1998	7.99
John, Elton	Rock Of The Westies	CD	Rocket	314-532-432-2	U.S.A.	1995	8.99
John, Elton	Runaway Train (Promo)	CD Single	MCA	MCA5P-2305	U.S.A.	1992	10.99
John, Elton	Sleeping With The Past	CD	Mercury	314-558-479-2	U.S.A.	1998	5.99
John, Elton	Songs From West Coast (Bonus Cd)	2CD	Rocket	063-087-0	England	2001	13.99
John, Elton	The Big Picture	CD	Rocket	536-266-2	England	1997	5.99
John, Elton	The Complete Thom Bell Sessions	CD	MCA	MCAD-39115	U.S.A.	1989	7.99
John, Elton	The Fox	CD	MCA	MCAD-10497	U.S.A.	1981	11.99
John, Elton	The Muse	CD	PolyGram	PHCW-1712	Japan	2000	39.99
John, Elton	The One	CD	Mercury	314-558-480-2	U.S.A.	1998	6.99
John, Elton	The Very Best Of Elton John	2CD	Phonogram	846947-2	Australia	1996	15.99
John, Elton	To Be Continued... Box Set	4CD	MCA	MCAD4-10110	U.S.A.	1990	61.99
John, Elton	Too Low For Zero	CD	Mercury	558-475-2	U.S.A.	1998	11.99
John, Elton	Tumbleweed Connection	CD	Rocket	314-528-155-2	U.S.A.	1995	10.99
John, Elton	Tumbleweed Connection (MFSL Gold)	CD	Mobile Fidelity	UDCD-543	U.S.A.	1970	33.99
John, Elton	Victim Of Love	CD	MCA	MCAD-22014	U.S.A.	1990	5.99
John, Elton	Westwood 1 # 01-15, 4 - 14/15,2001	2CD	Westwood 1	CO0115A040401	U.S.A.	2001	89.99
John, Elton	Written In The Stars	CD Single	Island	314-566-918-2	U.S.A.	1999	5.99
John, Elton/Bernie Taupin	Elton John/B Taupin (Publishing DJ)	2CD	PolyGram	PIP-CD-2002/2	U.S.A.	1990	70.99
John, Elton/Bernie Taupin	Two Rooms	CD	Polydor	845-750-2	U.S.A.	1991	6.99
John, Elton/LeAnn Rimes	Written In The Stars	CD Single	Mercury	572-577-2	England	2000	5.99
John, Elton/Tim Rice	Aida	CD	Buena Vista	60671-7	U.S.A.	2000	9.99
Johnny/The Roccos	Knee Deep In The Blues	CD	Line	STCD-9.00676-0	Germany	1988	14.99

Artist	Title	Format	Label	Catalog No	Country	Released	Value
John's-Children/Sparks	Music For The Herd Of Herring	CD	Captain Trip	CTCD-316	Japan	2000	14.99
Johnson, Brian/Geordie	Keep On Rocking!	CD	Anchor	ANZ-700	England	1989	12.99
Johnson, Don	Heartbeat + 6 (From Let It Roll)	CD	Razor & Tie	RE-82168	U.S.A.	1998	12.99
Johnson, Don	Let It Roll	CD	Epic	EK-40869	U.S.A.	1989	15.99
Johnson, Laurie	The Avengers	CD	Varese	VSD-5501	U.S.A.	1980	12.99
Johnson, Marv/Motown	More Marvin Johnson (Only 500)	CD	Marginal	MAR-069	EEC	1997	29.99
Johnson, Robert	King Delta Blues Singers (Sony Gold)	CD	Columbia	CK-52944	U.S.A.	1966	19.99
Johnson, Robert	King Of The Delta Blues Singers + 1	CD	Columbia	CK-65746	U.S.A.	1998	7.99
Johnson, Robert	The Complete Recordings Box Set	2CD	Sony	C2K-46222	U.S.A.	1990	19.99
Johnson, Ronnie	Give Them Enough Rope	CD	Line	OLCD-9.51097-X	Germany	1991	29.99
Johnson, Wilko	Barbed Wire Blues	CD	Line	INCD-9.00674-0	Germany	1988	24.99
Johnson, Wilko	Call It What You Want	CD	Line	INCD-9.00435-0	Germany	1988	24.99
Joi	One And One Is One	CD	Astralwerks	ASW-6253-2	U.S.A.	1999	8.99
Jones, Brian/Rolling Stones	Pipes Of Pan At Jajouka + 2	CD	Phillips	PHCP-1473	Japan	1995	44.99
Jones, Brian/Rolling Stones	The Pipes Of Pan At Jajouka	CD	Point	446-487-2	U.S.A.	1995	8.99
Jones, Charlie L.	Charlie L. Jones	CD	Line	TLCD-9.00493-0	Germany	1988	24.99
Jones, Freddy/Band	A Mile High Live	CD	Capricorn	314-538-688-2	U.S.A.	1999	19.99
Jones, Freddy/Band	Lucid	CD	Capricorn	314-536-192-2	U.S.A.	1997	14.99
Jones, Freddy/Band	North Avenue Wake Up Call	CD	Capricorn	9-42040-2	U.S.A.	1995	14.99
Jones, Freddy/Band	Self Titled	CD	Capricorn	9-42029-2	U.S.A.	1995	14.99
Jones, Freddy/Band	Waiting For The Night	CD	Capricorn	9-42022-2	U.S.A.	1994	14.99
Jones, Howard	The Essentials	CD	Rhino	R2-76038	U.S.A.	2002	8.99
Jones, Jill	Self Titled (Prince Related)	CD	Paisley Park	25575-2	U.S.A.	1987	59.99
Jones, John Paul	John Paul Jones	CD	Sony	A-28877	U.S.A.	1973	34.99
Jones, John Paul	Music From The Film Scream For Help	CD	East West	AMCY-2746	Japan	1998	64.99
Jones, John Paul	The Thunderthief	CD	Discipline Global	DGM0104	U.S.A.	2001	10.99
Jones, John Paul	Zooma	CD	Discipline Global	DGM9909	U.S.A.	1999	8.99
Jones, John Paul/D. Galas	Do You Take This Man?	CD Single	Mute	CD-MUTE-171	England	1994	8.99
Jones, John Paul/D. Galas	The Sporting Life	CD	Mute	MUTE-61672-2	U.S.A.	1994	11.99
Jones, Michael	Pianoscapes	CD	Narada	ND-61001	U.S.A.	1985	9.99
Jones, Norah	Come Away With Me	CD	Blue Note	7243-5-32088-2-0	U.S.A.	2002	10.99
Jones, Quincy	In The Heat.../They Call Me...(O.S.T.)	CD	Beyond	398-578-255-2	U.S.A.	2001	10.99
Jones, Quincy	Mellow Madness (W/Poster)	CD	A&M	UCCM-9159	Japan	1975	21.99
Jones, Quincy	Q: The Musical Biography Box Set	4CD	Rhino	R2-74363	U.S.A.	2001	99.99
Jones, Rickie Lee	Girl At Her Volcano	CD	Warner Bros.	WPCP-3710	Japan	1990	20.99
Jones, Rickie Lee	It's Like This + 2 (Bonus Cd)	CD	Artemis	751-056-2	U.S.A.	2000	14.99
Jones, Rickie Lee	Live At Red Rocks	CD	Artemis	751101-2	U.S.A.	2001	8.99
Jones, Rickie Lee	Naked Songs	CD	Reprise	9-45950-2	U.S.A.	1995	7.99
Jones, Rickie Lee	Pirates	CD	Warner Bros.	3432-2	U.S.A.	1981	6.99
Jones, Rickie Lee	Pop Pop	CD	Geffen	GEFD-24426	U.S.A.	1991	7.99
Jones, Rickie Lee	Rickie Lee Jones	CD	Warner Bros.	3296-2	U.S.A.	1979	10.99
Jones, Rickie Lee	The Magazine	CD	Warner Bros.	25117-2	U.S.A.	1984	6.99
Jones, Rickie Lee	Traffic From Paradise	CD	Geffen	GEFD-24602	U.S.A.	1993	6.99
Jones, Shirley	Silent Strength	CD	Diadem	7-90113-052-0	U.S.A.	1989	36.99
Jones, Shirley/G. MacRae	Carousel + 2 (O.S.T.)	CD	Angel	0777-7-64692-2-5	U.S.A.	1993	11.99
Jones, Shirley/G. MacRae	Oklahoma! + 11 (O.S.T.)	CD	Angel	7243-5-27350-2-0	U.S.A.	2001	14.99
Jones, Tom	Best Of	CD	Repertoire	REP-4508-WZ	Germany	1995	10.99
Jones, Tom	Hits & Duets	CD	Metro	METRCD033	England	2000	8.99
Jones, Tom	I (Who Have Nothing)/She's A Lady	CD	Repertoire	REP-4694-WY	Germany	1998	10.99
Jones, Tom	The Best Of... Tom Jones	CD	PolyGram	42284-4823-2	U.S.A.	1997	8.99
Jones, Tom	The Collection	3CD	Weton Wesgram B.V	KBOX3271	Holland	2000	19.99
Jones, Tom/Stereophonics	Mama Told Me Not To Come	CD Single	Gut	CKGUT-31	England	2000	5.99
Jones, Trevor/Buggles	Cleopatra	CD	CMR	CMR-1999-1	U.S.A.	1999	54.99
Jones, Trevor/Buggles	Gulliver's Travels	CD	RCA	09026-68475-2	U.S.A.	1996	18.99
Jones, Trevor/Buggles	Runaway Train (O.S.T.)	CD	Milan	CD-CH267	France	1986	69.99
Joplin, Janis	18 Essential Songs + 12 (Bonus Cd)	2CD	Columbia	CK67005.2	Australia	1997	19.99
Joplin, Janis	Box Of Pearls	5CD	Columbia	C5K-65937	U.S.A.	1999	28.99
Joplin, Janis	Farewell Song	CD	Columbia	CK-37569	U.S.A.	1982	7.99

J

Artist	Title	Format	Label	Catalog No	Country	Released	Value
Joplin, Janis	Greatest Hits (Sony Gold Cd)	CD	Columbia	032190-2	Austria	1973	16.99
Joplin, Janis	I Got Dem Ol' Kozmic Blues Again..	CD	Columbia	CK-65785	U.S.A.	1999	8.99
Joplin, Janis	In Concert	CD	Columbia	466838-2	Australia	1972	10.99
Joplin, Janis	Janis Box Set	3CD	Columbia	C3K-48845	U.S.A.	1993	19.99
Joplin, Janis	Janis Joplin's Greatest Hits + 2	CD	Columbia	CK-65869	U.S.A.	1999	7.99
Joplin, Janis	Love, Janis	CD	Columbia	CK-85730	U.S.A.	2001	7.99
Joplin, Janis	Six Sides Of Janis (Promo)	CD	Columbia	CSK-5223	U.S.A.	1993	11.99
Joplin, Janis/Big Brother	Cheaper Thrills	CD	Acadia	ACA-8001	England	2000	7.99
Joplin, Janis/Big Brother	Live At Winterland	CD	Columbia	CK-64869	U.S.A.	1998	10.99
Joplin, Janis/Big Brother	Live/San Fr '66 (Cheaper Thrills + 1)	CD	Varese	302-066-344-2	U.S.A.	2002	8.99
Joplin, Janis/Full Tilt Boogie	Pearl (Sony Gold Cd)	CD	Columbia	CK-53441	U.S.A.	1971	23.99
Joplin, Josh/Group	The Future That Was	CD	Artemis	751143-2	U.S.A.	2002	6.99
Josefus	Dead Box	3CD	Akarma	AK-235-CD	Italy	2003	44.99
Josie/Pussycats	Stop Look Listen: Capitol Records + 6	CD	Rhino	RHM2-7783	U.S.A.	2000	22.99
Journey	Arrival	CD	Columbia	CK-69864	U.S.A.	2001	7.99
Journey	Captured	CD	Columbia	CK-67721	U.S.A.	1996	7.99
Journey	Departure	CD	Columbia	CK-67727	U.S.A.	1996	7.99
Journey	Dream After Dream	CD	Sony	SRCS-6269	Japan	1980	25.99
Journey	Escape	CD	Columbia	CK-67722	U.S.A.	1996	7.99
Journey	Evolution	CD	Columbia	CK-67726	U.S.A.	1996	7.99
Journey	Frontiers	CD	Columbia	CK-67723	U.S.A.	1996	7.99
Journey	Greatest Hits	CD	Columbia	CK-44493	U.S.A.	1988	7.99
Journey	Greatest Hits Live	CD	Columbia	CK-69139	U.S.A.	1998	7.99
Journey	Infinity	CD	Columbia	CK-67725	U.S.A.	1996	7.99
Journey	Infinity (Sony Gold Cd)	CD	Columbia	CK-57207	U.S.A.	1986	24.99
Journey	Look Into The Future	CD	Columbia	CK-33904	U.S.A.	1976	7.99
Journey	Next	CD	Columbia	CK-34311	U.S.A.	1977	7.99
Journey	Raised On Radio	CD	Columbia	CK-67724	U.S.A.	1996	7.99
Journey	Red-13	CD	Journey	72410-19105-2	U.S.A.	2002	7.99
Journey	Self Titled	CD	Columbia	477-854 2	Germany	1995	7.99
Journey	Star Box Cd Sampler	CD	Sony	25DP-5204	Japan	1988	90.99
Journey	The Essential	2CD	Columbia	C2K-86080	U.S.A.	2001	14.99
Journey	Time3 (Time Cubed) Box Set	3CD	Columbia	C3K-48937	U.S.A.	1992	20.99
Journey	Trial By Fire	CD	Columbia	CK-67514	U.S.A.	1996	6.99
Journey	When You Love A Woman	CD Single	Columbia	38K-78428	U.S.A.	1998	4.99
Journey/Steve Perry	For The Love Of Strange Meds	CD	Columbia	477196-2	Australia	1995	6.99
Journey/Steve Perry	For The Love Of Strange Meds	CD	Columbia	CK-44287	U.S.A.	1994	5.99
Journey/Steve Perry	Greatest Hits + 5 Unreleased	CD	Sony	SK-69686	U.S.A.	1998	13.99
Journey/Steve Perry	Street Talk	CD	Sony	SK-67849	U.S.A.	1996	6.99
Joy Division	Closer	CD	London	7314-520015-2-8	England	1993	8.99
Joy Division	Complete BBC Recordings	CD	Strange Fruit	SFRSCD094	England	2000	14.99
Joy Division	Heart And Soul Box Set	4CD	London	3984-29040-2	England	1999	49.99
Joy Division	Heart And Soul Box Set	4CD	Rhino	R2-78406	U.S.A.	2001	49.99
Joy Division	Live From Preston 28th Feb 1980	CD	Factory	FACD260	Sweden	2003	10.99
Joy Division	Love Will Tear Us Apart	CD Single	PolyGram	422-850-129-2	Canada	1995	8.99
Joy Division	Permanent	CD	London	3984-28221-2	England	1999	8.99
Joy Division	Still	CD	London	7314-520017-2-6	England	1993	8.99
Joy Division	Substance	CD	London	3984-28224-2	England	1999	8.99
Joy Division	The Peel Sessions	CD Single	Strange Fruit	SFPSCD013	England	1988	14.99
Joy Division	Unknown Pleasures	CD	London	7314-520016-2-7	England	1993	8.99
Joy Division /T-Shirt/Poster	Ltd Ed Box Set (Preston/Les Bains)	3CD	Alchemy	REFRACTURBX1	England	2003	49.99
Joy Of Cooking	American Originals	CD	Capitol	99355	U.S.A.	1993	69.99
Joy Of Cooking	Self Titled	CD	Acadia	ACA-8050	England	2002	11.99
Judas Priest	98 Live Meltdown	2CD	CMC INT.	06076-86261-2	U.S.A.	1998	10.99
Judas Priest	98 Live Meltdown	2CD	Victor Ent.	VICP-61648/9	Japan	2000	34.99
Judas Priest	A Touch Of Evil (Promo)	CD Single	Columbia	CSK-2218	U.S.A.	1990	14.99
Judas Priest	British Steel +2	CD	Columbia	CK-85752	U.S.A.	2001	7.99
Judas Priest	British Steel + 2	CD	Sony	ESCA-7872	Japan	2000	24.99

Artist	Title	Format	Label	Catalog No	Country	Released	Value
Judas Priest	British Steel/P Of Entry/Screaming...	3CD	Columbia	C3K-65607	U.S.A.	1998	24.99
Judas Priest	Bullet Train (DJ/Tri-Fold Sleeve)	CD Single	SPV	80000128	Germany	1997	19.99
Judas Priest	Bullet Train (Promo)	CD Single	CMC INT.	CMCDJ-87232-2	U.S.A.	1997	15.99
Judas Priest	Bullet Train (Promo)	CD Single	SPV	80000131	Germany	1997	13.99
Judas Priest	Collection	CD	Castle	CCSCD213	England	1989	7.99
Judas Priest	Defenders Of The Faith + 2	CD	Columbia	CK-85438	U.S.A.	2001	8.99
Judas Priest	Defenders Of The Faith + 2	CD	Sony	ESCA-7875	Japan	2001	21.99
Judas Priest	Demolition	CD	Atlantic	83480-2	U.S.A.	2001	7.99
Judas Priest	Demolition +2	CD	SPV	SPV085-72422CD	Germany	2001	9.99
Judas Priest	Demolition (Adv Promo)	CD	Atlantic	2A-83480	U.S.A.	2001	24.99
Judas Priest	Demolition (Adv Promo)	CD	SPV	SPV085-72422-P	Germany	2001	29.99
Judas Priest	Demoliton (Clean)	CD	Atlantic	83508-2	U.S.A.	2001	7.99
Judas Priest	Demoliton + 1	CD	Victor Ent.	VICP-61349	Japan	2001	14.99
Judas Priest	Genocide (Rocka Rolla/Sad Wings)	2CD	Snapper	SMD-CD-273	England	2000	11.99
Judas Priest	Hell Bent For Leather + 2	CD	Columbia	CK-86181	U.S.A.	2001	8.99
Judas Priest	Hero Hero	CD	Line	LICD-9.00414-0	Germany	1987	8.99
Judas Priest	Hero Hero	CD	Koch	KOC-CD-8069	U.S.A.	2000	8.99
Judas Priest	Hero Hero	CD	Victor Ent.	VICP-61652	Japan	2000	24.99
Judas Priest	Johnny Be Goode !	CD Single	Atlantic	A9114CD	England	1988	9.99
Judas Priest	Jugulator	CD	CMC INT.	06076-86224-2	U.S.A.	1997	7.99
Judas Priest	Jugulator	CD	Zero	XRCN-2001	Japan	1997	34.99
Judas Priest	Jugulator (Adv Promo)	CD	SPV	SPV085-18782P	Germany	1997	29.99
Judas Priest	Jugulator (J Priest Tour Sticker Pic Slv)	CD	Victor Ent.	VICP-61647	Japan	2001	44.99
Judas Priest	Killing Machine + 2 (Hell Bent)	CD	Sony	EICP-7011	Japan	2000	19.99
Judas Priest	Live In London	2CD	SPV	SPV085-74262CD	England	2003	12.99
Judas Priest	Living After Midnight	CD	Columbia	487242-2	Australia	2003	9.99
Judas Priest	Ltd Ed Collector's Sampler (Promo)	CD	Sony	SAMPCD-11067	England	2002	18.99
Judas Priest	Metal Works '73 - '93	2CD	Sony	ESCA-5750	Japan	1992	69.99
Judas Priest	Metal Works '73-'93	2CD	Columbia	C2K-53932	U.S.A.	1993	10.99
Judas Priest	Painkiller + 2	CD	Sony	ESCA-5159	Japan	1990	14.99
Judas Priest	Painkiller + 2	CD	Epic	EICP-7045	Japan	2000	24.99
Judas Priest	Painkiller +2	CD	Columbia	CK-86382	U.S.A.	2002	7.99
Judas Priest	Point Of Entry + 2	CD	Columbia	CK-85436	U.S.A.	2001	7.99
Judas Priest	Priest In The East	CD	Sony	ESCA-7666	Japan	1997	24.99
Judas Priest	Priest Live & Rare	CD	Sony	ESCA-7713	Japan	1998	17.99
Judas Priest	Priest Live! + 3	2CD	Columbia	CK-86378	U.S.A.	2002	10.99
Judas Priest	Priest...Live! + 3	2CD	Epic	EICP-7042/3	Japan	2000	34.99
Judas Priest	Ram It Down	CD	Epic	25-8P-5024	Japan	1988	14.99
Judas Priest	Ram It Down + 2	CD	Columbia	CK-86381	U.S.A.	2002	7.99
Judas Priest	Ram It Down + 2	CD	Epic	EICP-7044	Japan	2000	24.99
Judas Priest	Rocka Rolla	Mini Lp	Teichiku	TECI-24073	Japan	2001	29.99
Judas Priest	Rocka Rolla	CD	Repertoire	REP-4305-WY	Germany	1993	14.99
Judas Priest	Rocka Rolla	CD	Victor Ent.	VICP-61650	Japan	2000	24.99
Judas Priest	Rocka Rolla (Demon Cover)	CD	Line	LICD-9.00101-0	Germany	1987	9.99
Judas Priest	Rocka Rolla + 1	CD	Koch	KOC-CD-8068	U.S.A.	2000	8.99
Judas Priest	Rocka Rolla/Sad Wings Of Destiny	2CD	Line	LICD-9.21214-S	Germany	1992	16.99
Judas Priest	Sad Wings Of Destiny	CD	Line	LICD-9.00112-0	Germany	1987	8.99
Judas Priest	Sad Wings Of Destiny	Mini Lp	Teichiku	TECI-24074	Japan	2001	29.99
Judas Priest	Sad Wings Of Destiny	CD	Repertoire	REP-4552-WY	Germany	2002	14.99
Judas Priest	Sad Wings Of Destiny	CD	Victor Ent.	VICP-61651	Japan	2000	24.99
Judas Priest	Screaming For Vengance + 2	CD	Columbia	CK-85435	U.S.A.	2001	7.99
Judas Priest	Sin After Sin + 2	CD	Columbia	CK-86183	U.S.A.	2001	7.99
Judas Priest	Sin After Sin + 2	CD	Epic	EICP-7009	Japan	2000	24.99
Judas Priest	Stained Glass + 2	CD	Columbia	CK-85434	U.S.A.	2001	7.99
Judas Priest	Stained Glass + 2	CD	Epic	EICP-7010	Japan	2000	24.99
Judas Priest	Starbox	CD	Sony	ESCA-5858	Japan	1992	74.99
Judas Priest	The Best Of	Mini Lp	Teichiku	TECI-24080	Japan	2000	29.99
Judas Priest	The Best Of	CD	Koch	KOC-CD-8071	U.S.A.	2001	8.99

J

Artist	Title	Format	Label	Catalog No	Country	Released	Value
Judas Priest	The Best Of: Living After...	CD	Columbia	CK-65180	U.S.A.	1998	8.99
Judas Priest	Turbo + 2	CD	Columbia	CK-85437	U.S.A.	2002	7.99
Judas Priest	Turbo + 2	CD	Epic	EICP-7041	Japan	2000	24.99
Judas Priest	Tyrant:The Original Masters	CD	Eureka	EURCD-481	England	1998	12.99
Judas Priest	Unleashed In The East + 4	CD	Columbia	CK-86182	U.S.A.	2001	7.99
Judas Priest	Unleashed In The East + 4	CD	Epic	EICP-7012	Japan	2000	24.99
Judas Priest/Eddie Money	Bullet Train (DJ/4 Trks Eddie Money)	CD Single	CMC INT.	CMCDJ87234-2	England	1997	14.99
Judas Priest/Glenn Tipton	Baptizm Of Fire	CD	Atlantic	7567-82974-2	U.S.A.	1997	8.99
Judas Priest/Holds All 12 Rem	Turbo/Live/Ram It/Painkiller Box Set	5CD	Columbia	C5K-86390	U.S.A.	2002	44.99
Jude	No One Is Really Beautiful	CD	Maverick	9-47087-2	U.S.A.	1998	5.99
Jude	You're So Hot I Love You (Promo)	CD Single	Maverick	5032	U.S.A.	1999	5.99
Juice On The Loose	Secret Life	CD	Line	LICD—9.01377-0	Germany	1987	14.99
Juice On The Loose	Secret Life	CD	Line	LICD-9.00504-0	Germany	1987	14.99
Juicy Lucy	Blue Thunder	CD	Outer Music	OM1001	England	1998	29.99
Juicy Lucy	Get A Whiff Of This	CD	Repertoire	REP-4428-WY	Germany	1993	11.99
Juicy Lucy	Here She Comes Again	CD	Navarre	72112	U.S.A.	1995	8.99
Juicy Lucy	Juicy Lucy	CD	Jamm	JR-5078	U.S.A.	1995	8.99
Juicy Lucy	Lie Back And Enoy It	CD	Repertoire	REP-4427-WY	Germany	1993	11.99
Juicy Lucy	Lie Back And.../Get A Whiff A This	CD	One Way	OW-34434	U.S.A.	1997	19.99
Juicy Lucy	Pieces + 1	CD	Repertoire	REP-4644-WY	Germany	1997	11.99
Juicy Lucy	Self Titled/Lie Back And...	CD	BGO	BGOCD279	England	1995	19.99
Juicy Lucy	Who Do You Love	CD	Castle	CMRCD-564	England	2002	11.99
Junior	"JI"	CD	Nippon Phonogram	PHCR-1095	Japan	1982	51.99
Jupp, Mickey	As The Yeahs Go By	CD	Line	LICD-9.01026-0	Germany	1991	18.99
Jupp, Mickey	Juppanese	CD	Line	LICD-9.00061-0	Germany	1987	15.99
Jupp, Mickey	Juppanese + 5	CD	Repertoire	REP-4441-WY	Germany	1994	18.99
Jupp, Mickey	Juppanese/Long Distance Romancer	2CD	Line	LICD-9.21188-S	Germany	1992	24.99
Jupp, Mickey	Legend (Red Boot)	CD	Repertoire	RR-4061-CX	Germany	1971	18.99
Jupp, Mickey	Long Distance Romancer	CD	Line	LICD-9.00003-0	Germany	1991	18.99
Jupp, Mickey	Oddities	CD	Line	LICD-9.00464-0	Germany	1987	18.99
Jupp, Mickey	Oxford	CD	Line	LICD-9.01343-0	Germany	1997	18.99
Jupp, Mickey	Oxford	CD	Line	COCD-9.00039-0	Germany	1987	18.99
Jupp, Mickey	Some People Can't Dance	CD	Line	LICD-9.00069-0	Germany	1987	18.99
Jupp, Mickey	X	CD	Line	LICD-9.00513-0	Germany	1988	18.99
Jupp, Mickey	You Say Rock	CD	Gazell	500-014-2	Sweden	1994	24.99

K

K

Artist	Title	Format	Label	Catalog No	Country	Released	Value
Kadukura, Satoshi	Windaria (O.S.T.)	CD	Victor Ent.	VICL-23074	Japan	1994	24.99
Kain	Reciclagem	CD	Line	RICD-9.00831-0	Germany	1989	6.99
Kaleidoscope	A Beacon From Mars	CD	Line	CLCD-9.01007-0	Germany	1991	13.99
Kaleidoscope	Bernice	CD	Edsel	EDCD-534	England	1997	10.99
Kaleidoscope	Dive Into Yesterday	CD	Mercury	534-003-2	Germany	1996	21.99
Kaleidoscope	Incredible!	CD	Edsel	EDCD-533	England	1997	10.99
Kaleidoscope	Infinite Colours...The Best Of	CD	Edsel	EDCD-698	England	2001	18.99
Kaleidoscope	Side Trips	CD	Line	CLCD-9.00925-0	Germany	1989	14.99
Kaleidoscope	Tangerine Dream	CD	Repertoire	PMS-7074-WP	Germany	1998	20.99
Kaleidoscope	White Faced Lady/From Home/Home	2CD	Alchemy	PILOT-56	England	2000	15.99
Kaleidoscope/Chris Darrow	A Southern California Drive	CD	Line	LICD-9.00236-0	Germany	1991	18.99
Kaleidoscope/Chris Darrow	Chris Darrow/Under My Own Disguise	CD	BGO	BGOCD513	England	2001	15.99
Kaleidoscope/Chris Darrow	Harem Girl	CD	Taxim	TX-2039-2	U.S.A.	1998	22.99
Kaleidoscope/Chris Darrow	Slide On In	CD	Taxim	TX-2058-2	U.S.A.	2002	22.99
Kaleidoscope/Fairfield Parlour	Home To Home	CD	Repertoire	REP-4144-WP	Germany	1994	24.99

Artist	Title	Format	Label	Catalog No	Country	Released	Value
Kanno, Yoko	Macross Plus Original Sound Track II	CD	JVC	JVC-1004-2	U.S.A.	1994	14.99
Kanno, Yoko	Macross Plus Original Soundtrack	CD	JVC	JVC-1004-2	U.S.A.	1994	14.99
Kansas	Always Never The Same	CD	River North	51416-1384-2	U.S.A.	1998	5.99
Kansas	Audio Visions	CD	Epic	ZK-66417	U.S.A.	1980	9.99
Kansas	Definitive Collection + 5 (Bonus CD)	2CD	Epic	EPC-487592-9	Holland	1997	12.99
Kansas	Drastic Measures	CD	Epic	ZK-66426	U.S.A.	1983	9.99
Kansas	Dust In The Wind	CD	Zounds	CD-27200309-B	Germany	1991	5.99
Kansas	Freaks Of Nature	CD	Intersound	9148	U.S.A.	1995	4.99
Kansas	In The Spirit Of Things	CD	MCA	MCAD-6254	U.S.A.	1988	5.99
Kansas	In The Spirit Of Things	CD	MCA	MCAD-6254	U.S.A.	1988	5.99
Kansas	Kansas	CD	Epic	ZK-32817	U.S.A.	1974	7.99
Kansas	Kansas [Boxed Set]	2CD	Epic	Z2K-47364	U.S.A.	1994	10.99
Kansas	Leftoverture + 2	CD	Epic	EK-85386	U.S.A.	2001	6.99
Kansas	Masque + 2	CD	Epic	EK-85654	U.S.A.	2001	9.99
Kansas	Monolith	CD	Epic	ZK-36008	U.S.A.	1979	7.99
Kansas	Point Of Know Return + 2	CD	Epic	EK-85387	U.S.A.	2002	6.99
Kansas	Power	CD	MCA	MCAD-5838	U.S.A.	1986	9.99
Kansas	Star Box	CD	Sony	SRCS-6901	Japan	1993	24.99
Kansas	The Best Of Kansas	CD	Epic	ZK-65690	U.S.A.	1999	8.99
Kansas	The Ultimate	2CD	Epic	E2K-86452	U.S.A.	2002	15.99
Kansas/Kerry Livgren	Collector's Sedition	CD	Numavox	0009	U.S.A.	2000	14.99
Kansas/Kerry Livgren	Odyssey Into The Mind'S Eye	CD	Numavox	0004	U.S.A.	1996	19.99
Kansas/Kerry Livgren	One Of Several Possible Musiks	CD	One Way	OW-32644	U.S.A.	1996	9.99
Kansas/Kerry Livgren	Prime Mover II	CD	Numavox	0005	U.S.A.	1998	18.99
Kansas/Kerry Livgren	Reconstructions (Reconstructed) + 3	CD	Numavox	0003	U.S.A.	1997	21.99
Kansas/Kerry Livgren	Seeds Of Change + 21 Minute Int.	CD	Renaissance	RMED00112-2	U.S.A.	1996	24.99
Kansas/Kerry Livgren	When Things Get Electric	CD	Numavox	0001	U.S.A.	1994	13.99
Kansas/Kerry Livgren/AD	Art Of The State	CD	Numavox	0002	U.S.A.	1998	12.99
Kansas/Kerry Livgren/AD	Live	CD	Numavox	0006	U.S.A.	1998	14.99
Kansas/Kerry Livgren/AD	Time Line + 24 Minute Interview	CD	Renaissance	RMED00101-2	U.S.A.	1996	15.99
Kansas/Steve Walsh	Glossolalia	CD	Magna Carta	MA-9043-2	U.S.A.	2000	8.99
Kansas/Walsh, Steve	Schemer-Dreamer	CD	Sony	SRCS-6296	Japan	1993	24.99
Karas, Anton	The Third Man (O.S.T.)	CD	Disconforme	SFCD33538	Andorra	1999	8.99
Karloff, Boris/A Hague	How The Grinch Stole Christmas	CD	PolyGram	314-528-438-2	U.S.A.	1995	6.99
Karloff, Boris/A Hague	How The Grinch.../Horton Hears A...	CD	Rhino	R2-75969	U.S.A.	1999	6.99
Karloff, Boris/Jean Arthur	Peter Pan - 1950 Broadway Cast	CD	Columbia	CK-4312	U.S.A.	1950	49.99
Karn, Mick	Bestial Cluster	CD	CMP	CMP-CD-1002	Germany	1993	9.99
Karn, Mick	Each Eye A Path	CD	Medium	MPCD12	England	2000	9.99
Karn, Mick	The Tooth Mother	CD	CMP	CMP-CD-1008	Germany	1995	9.99
Karniggels	Die Musik Zum Film	CD	Line	CICD-9.01194-0	Germany	1992	12.99
Kashif	Send Me Your Love	CD	Arista	ARCD-8205	U.S.A.	1984	106.99
Katrina/The Waves	Anthology	CD	One Way	OW-18200	U.S.A.	1986	8.99
Katrina/The Waves	Break Of Hearts	CD	Attic	ACD-1255	Canada	1989	16.99
Katrina/The Waves	Break Of Hearts	CD	Capitol	CDP-7-92649-2	U.S.A.	1989	16.99
Katrina/The Waves	Brown Eyed Son	CD Single	Line	ALCD-9.01137-E	Germany	1991	6.99
Katrina/The Waves	Roses (Compilation Edge/Turnaround)	CD	Polydor	3145-29761-2	Canada	1995	8.99
Katrina/The Waves	Self Titled/Waves	CD	BGO	BGOCD330	England	1996	14.99
Katrina/The Waves	The Original Recordings '83 - '84	CD	Bongo Beat	BB-1965-2	Canada	2003	17.99
Katrina/The Waves	Volume 2	CD	Total	1198	Canada	1995	16.99
Katrina/The Waves	Walk On Water	CD	Warner Bros.	0630-19837-2	England	1997	9.99
Katrina/The Waves	Walking On Sunshine: Gr Hits	CD	EMI	CDEMC-3766	England	1998	8.99
Kaukonen, Jorma	Barbeque King	CD	Acadia	ACA-8004	England	2001	12.99
Kaukonen, Jorma	Blue Country Heart	CD	Columbia	CK-86394	U.S.A.	2002	9.99
Kaukonen, Jorma	Jorma	CD	Acadia	ACA-8003	England	2001	11.99
Kaukonen, Jorma	Magic	CD	Relix	RRCD-2007	U.S.A.	1987	10.99
Kaukonen, Jorma	Too Hot To Handle	CD	Relix	RRCD-2012	U.S.A.	1984	10.99
Kaukonen, Jorma	Too Many Years...	CD	Relix	RRCD-2094	U.S.A.	1998	10.99
Kaukonen, Jorma	Unreleased W/Blue Country Heart	CD	Columbia	CSK-59878	U.S.A.	2002	12.99

K

Artist	Title	Format	Label	Catalog No	Country	Released	Value
Kaukonen, Jorma/Constanten	Embryonic Journey (Signed)	CD	Relix	RRCD-2067	U.S.A.	1995	14.99
Kaukonen, Jorma/T Hobson	Quah	CD	Relix	RRCD2027	U.S.A.	1997	10.99
Kaukonen, Jorma/Trio	Live - Feat M Falzarano/Pete Sears	CD	Relix	RRCD2110	U.S.A.	2000	14.99
Kaukonen, Jorman/T Hobson	Quah + 4	CD	RCA	07863-65139-2	U.S.A.	2003	13.99
Kayak	Close To The Fire + 2	CD	Avalon	MICP-10190	Japan	2000	26.99
Keen, Robert Earl	No Kinda Dancer	CD	Line	SDCD-9.00815-O	Germany	1989	12.99
Kell, Tom/J D Souther	One Sad Night (W/Bernie Leadon)	CD	Warner Bros.	9-26508-2	U.S.A.	1991	13.99
Kelly, Dave/Band	Heart Of The City	CD	Line	LICD-9.00324-0	Germany	1987	15.99
Kelly, Dave/Band	Resting My Bones	CD	Hypertension	HYP1209	England	2002	15.99
Kelly, Dave/Band	Self Titled	CD	BGO	BGOCD530	England	2002	19.99
Kelly, Dave/Band	Standing At The Crossroads	CD	Inakustik	INAK8807CD	Germany	1995	14.99
Kelly, Dave/Band	Survivors (W/Bob Hall)	CD	Appaloosa	AP-001	England	2000	12.99
Kelly, Dave/Band	When The Blues Come To Call	CD	Hypertension	HYCD200-141	England	1994	15.99
Kelly, Dave/Band	Willing	CD	Appaloosa	AP-003	England	1998	14.99
Kelly, David/Band	Mind In A Glass	CD	Line	LICD-9.00703-0	Germany	1988	15.99
Kelly, Jo Ann	Black Rat Swing	2CD	Castle	CMDDD596	England	2003	12.99
Kelly, Jo Ann	Fahey, Kelly, Mann, Miller, Seidler	Mini Lp	Air Mail	AIRAC-1022	Japan	2000	34.99
Kelly, Jo Ann	Jo Ann	CD	Line	STCD-9.00712-0	Germany	1989	24.99
Kelly, Jo Ann	Just Restless	CD	Appaloosa	AP-028	England	1994	15.99
Kelly, Jo Ann	Key To The Highway	CD	Mooncrest	CRESTCD037	England	1999	12.99
Kelly, Jo Ann	Self Titled	CD	BGO	BGOCD429	England	1999	19.99
Kelly, Jo Ann	Talkin' Low	CD	Mooncrest	CRESTCD045	England	2000	12.99
Kelly, Jo Ann	Tramp 1974	CD	Mooncrest	CRESTCD063	England	2001	12.99
Kelly, Jo Ann	Women In (E)motion Festival	CD	Tradition/Mod	T&M110	England	1995	15.99
Kendall, Elliot	Le Hot Show + 5 (Featuring Rubinoos)	CD	Shattered	SHA-015	U.S.A.	2000	8.99
Kennedy, Ray	Self Titled	CD	Sony	SRCS-6139	Japan	1980	34.99
Kennedys	Life Is Large	CD	Green Linnet	GLCD-2123	U.S.A.	1996	14.99
Kenny	Best Of	CD	Repertoire	REP-4510-WG	Germany	1994	12.99
Kenny G.	Kenny G	CD	Arista	ARCD-8036	U.S.A.	1982	6.99
Kenny-G	Breathless	CD	Arista	07822-18646-2	U.S.A.	1992	6.99
Kenny-G	Classics Key Of G (2 Diff. Covers)	CD	Arista	07822-19085-2	U.S.A.	1999	9.99
Kenny-G	Duotones	CD	Artista	ARCD-8496	U.S.A.	1986	7.99
Kenny-G	Faith - A Holiday Album	CD	Arista	07822-19090-2	U.S.A.	1999	7.99
Kenny-G	G Force	CD	Arista	ARCD-8192	U.S.A.	1983	6.99
Kenny-G	Gravity	CD	Arista	ARCD-8282	U.S.A.	1985	6.99
Kenny-G	Greatest Hits	CD	Artista	07822-18991-2	U.S.A.	1998	8.99
Kenny-G	Kenny G Live	CD	Arista	A2CD-8613	U.S.A.	1989	5.99
Kenny-G	Miracles/The Holiday Album	CD	Arista	07822-18767-2	U.S.A.	1994	6.99
Kenny-G	Silhouette	CD	Artista	ARCD-8457	U.S.A.	1988	5.99
Kenny-G	The Moment	CD	Arista	07822-18935-2	U.S.A.	1996	6.99
Kenton, Stan	A Merry Christmas + 1	CD	Capitol	CDP-7-94451-2	U.S.A.	1990	10.99
Kenton, Stan/June Christy	Road Show Vol 1 (Four Freshmen)	CD	Capitol	C2-96328	U.S.A.	1991	44.99
Kentucky Colonels	Livin' In The Past + 6 (J Garcia Intro.)	CD	Hollywood	HS-67003	U.S.A.	1997	9.99
Kerouac, Jack	Kicks Joy Darkness (Stipe, John Cale)	CD	Rykodisc	RCD-10329	U.S.A.	1997	7.99
Kershaw, Nik	The Riddle	CD	MCA	251-595-2	U.S.A.	1984	34.99
Kershaw, Nik	Works	CD	MCA	DMCF-3438	U.S.A.	1989	104.99
Ketcham, Charles	Music Four Alfred Hitchcock Films	CD	Varese	VCD-47225	U.S.A.	1985	29.99
Ketchum, Hal Michael	Threadbare Alibis	CD	Line	SDCD-9.00749-0	Germany	1989	29.99
Khan, Chaka	Come 2 My House	CD	BMG	BVCP-21026	Japan	1998	29.99
Khan, Chaka	Don't Talk 2 Strangers	CD Single	NPG	DPRO-13668	U.S.A.	1996	5.99
Khan, Chaka	Perfect Fit	CD Single	Warner Bros.	28XD-664	Japan	1992	34.99
Khan, Chaka	Self Titled	CD	Warner Bros.	WPCR-318	Japan	1982	33.99
Khan, Chaka	The Remix Project	CD	Warner Bros.	WPCP-5697	Japan	1993	19.99
Khan, N.F.A./M. Brook	Remixed: Star Rise	CD	Caroline	CAR-2369-2	U.S.A.	1997	7.99
Khan, Nusrat Fateh Ali	Mustt Mustt	CD	Real World	91630-2	U.S.A.	1990	10.99
Khan, Nusrat Fateh Ali	Shahen-Shah	CD	Caroline	CAROL-2302-2	U.S.A.	1989	7.99
Kick	Heartland	CD	Line	LICD-9.01202-0	Germany	1992	29.99
Kick	This Can't Be Love	CD Single	Line	LICD-9.01224-E	Germany	1992	17.99

K

Artist	Title	Format	Label	Catalog No	Country	Released	Value
Kid Bangham	Somebody's Got To Suffer	CD	Rainman	RMCD111	U.S.A.	2003	22.99
Kid Creole/Coconuts	Off The Coast Of Me + 5	CD	Rainman	RMCD117	U.S.A.	2003	10.99
Kid Creole/Coconuts	Too Cool To Conga	CD	Rainman	RMCD112	U.S.A.	2003	10.99
Kihn, Greg	Again	CD	Line	BECD-9.00472-0	Germany	1987	28.99
Kihn, Greg	All The Right Reasons	CD	Essential	ESM-CD-867	England	2000	14.99
Kihn, Greg	Citizen Kihn	CD	Line	BECD-9.00596-0	Germany	1988	63.99
Kihn, Greg	Greg Kihn	CD	Line	BECD-9.00469-0	Germany	1987	16.99
Kihn, Greg	Horror Show	CD	Clean Cuts	CCD716	U.S.A.	1996	7.99
Kihn, Greg	Khintagious	CD	Line	BECD-9.00505-0	Germany	1987	44.99
Kihn, Greg	Kihn Of Hearts	CD	Riot	FR-2001	U.S.A.	1992	16.99
Kihn, Greg	Kihnsolidation: The Best Of Greg Kihn	CD	Rhino	R2-70900	U.S.A.	1989	9.99
Kihn, Greg	Kihnspicuous Taste: The Best Of	2CD	Snapper	SMD-CD-116	England	1998	16.99
Kihn, Greg	King Biscuit Flower Hour	CD	King Biscuit	KBD-88004	U.S.A.	1996	8.99
Kihn, Greg	Love And Rock And Roll	CD	Line	BECD-9.00507-0	Germany	1987	23.99
Kihn, Greg	Unkihntrollable (Live)	CD	Rhino	R2-885986	U.S.A.	1990	7.99
Kihn, Greg Band	RocKihnRoll	CD	Line	BECD-9.00198-0	Germany	1987	89.99
Kihn, Greg/Band	Glass House Rock	CD	Line	BECD-9.00487-0	Germany	1987	69.99
Kihn, Greg/Band	Kihnspiracy	CD	Line	BECD-9.00502-0	Germany	1987	17.99
Kihn, Greg/Band	Kihntinued	CD	Line	BECD-9.00510-0	Germany	1987	19.99
Kihn, Greg/Band	Next Of Kihn	CD	Line	BECD-9.00479-0	Germany	1987	21.99
Kihn, Greg/Band	The Story So Far ...	CD	Line	BECD-9.00953-0	Germany	1990	14.99
Kihn, Greg/Band	With The Naked Eye	CD	Line	BECD-9.00482-0	Germany	1987	59.99
Killer Dwarfs	Big Deal + 8	CD	Collectables	COL-CD-6450	U.S.A.	2000	10.99
Killer Dwarfs	Dirty Weapons + 5	CD	Collectables	COL-CD-6451	U.S.A.	2000	10.99
Killer Dwarfs	Method To The Madness	CD	Epic	EK-47322	U.S.A.	1992	10.99
Killer Dwarfs	Reunion Of Scribes (Live 2001)	CD	Bullseye	BLP-CD-4067	Canada	2002	13.99
Killer Dwarfs	Self Titled	CD	Bullseye	BLP-CD-4022	Canada	2002	12.99
Killer Dwarfs	Stand Tall	CD	Grudge	GRD-0954	U.S.A.	1986	49.99
Killing Floor	Out Of Uranus	CD	Akarma	AK-232	Italy	2003	10.99
Killing Floor	Out Of Uranus	CD	Repertoire	REP-4367-WP	Germany	2002	10.99
Killing Floor	Rock The Blues	CD	See For Miles	SEE-CD-355	England	1992	13.99
Killing Floor	Self Titled	CD	Akarma	AK-212	Italy	2003	10.99
Killing Floor	Self Titled	CD	Repertoire	REP-4532-WP	Germany	2002	10.99
Kincade	The Best Of	CD	Repertoire	REP-4347-WG	Germany	2002	10.99
King Crimson	AAA Sampler (Promo)	CD	Virgin	DPRO-12722	U.S.A.	1995	14.99
King Crimson	Absent Lovers	2CD	Discipline Global	DGM9084	U.S.A.	1998	14.99
King Crimson	B'Boom	2CD	Discipline Global	DGM-9503	U.S.A.	1995	12.99
King Crimson	Beat	CD	Caroline	CAROL-1593-2	U.S.A.	2000	8.99
King Crimson	Beginner's Guide To King Crimson Club	CD	Discipline Global	DGM-0008	England	2000	13.99
King Crimson	Cirkus: A Young Person's Guide/Live	2CD	Discipline Global	CDVKCD-12	England	1999	24.99
King Crimson	Club # 1 Live At Marquee 1969	CD	Discipline Global	CLUB1	U.S.A.	1998	29.99
King Crimson	Club # 10 Live Central Park 1974	CD	Discipline Global	CLUB10	U.S.A.	2000	18.99
King Crimson	Club # 11 Live Mole's Club 1981	CD	Discipline Global	CLUB11	U.S.A.	2000	10.99
King Crimson	Club # 13 Nashville Rehersals 1997	CD	Discipline Global	CLUB13	U.S.A.	2000	16.99
King Crimson	Club # 14 Live At Plymouth 1971	2CD	Discipline Global	CLUB14	U.S.A.	2000	34.99
King Crimson	Club # 15 Live In Mainz 1974	CD	Discipline Global	CLUB15	U.S.A.	2001	23.99
King Crimson	Club # 16 Live In Berkeley 1982	CD	Discipline Global	CLUB16	U.S.A.	2001	26.99
King Crimson	Club # 18 Live In Detroit 1971	2CD	Discipline Global	CLUB18	U.S.A.	2001	25.99
King Crimson	Club # 19 Live In Nashville 2001	CD	Discipline Global	CLUB19	U.S.A.	2002	16.99
King Crimson	Club # 2 Live At Jacksonville 1972	CD	Discipline Global	CLUB2	U.S.A.	1998	18.99
King Crimson	Club # 20 Live At The Zoom Club	2CD	Discipline	CLUB20	U.S.A.	2002	17.99
King Crimson	Club # 21 Champaign - Urbana	CD	Discipline Global	CLUB21	U.S.A.	2002	14.99
King Crimson	Club # 23 Live In Orlando, FLA '72	2CD	Discipline Global	CLUB23	U.S.A.	2003	34.99
King Crimson	Club # 24 Live In Guildeford 1972	CD	Discipline Global	CLUB24	U.S.A.	2003	29.99
King Crimson	Club # 3 Beat Club Bremen 1972	CD	Discipline Global	CLUB3	U.S.A.	1999	37.99
King Crimson	Club # 4 Live Cap De'Agde 1982	CD	Discipline Global	CLUB4	U.S.A.	1999	14.99
King Crimson	Club # 5/6 On Broadway 1995	2CD	Discipline Global	CLUB5/6	U.S.A.	1999	17.99
King Crimson	Club # 8 VROOOM Sessions 1994	CD	Discipline Global	CLUB8	U.S.A.	1999	14.99

K

Artist	Title	Format	Label	Catalog No	Country	Released	Value
King Crimson	Club # 9 Live Summit Studios 1972	CD	Discipline Global	CLUB9	U.S.A.	2000	24.99
King Crimson	Club #12 Hyde Park July 5, 1969 + 2	CD	Discipline Global	CLUB-12	U.S.A.	2002	29.99
King Crimson	Collectors' King Crimson, Vol. 1	3CD	Pony Canyon	PCCY-01394	Japan	1999	84.99
King Crimson	Collectors' King Crimson, Vol. 2	3CD	Pony Canyon	PCCY-01440	Japan	2000	84.99
King Crimson	Collectors' King Crimson, Vol. 4	3CD	Pony Canyon	PCCY-01493	Japan	2001	84.99
King Crimson	Collectors' King Crimson, Vol. 5	3CD	Pony Canyon	PCCY-01539	Japan	2001	84.99
King Crimson	Collectors' King Crimson, Vol. 6	3CD	Pony Canyon	PCCY-01583	Japan	2002	84.99
King Crimson	Collectors' King Crimson, Vol. 7	4CD	Universal	UICE-1046/9	Japan	2003	84.99
King Crimson	Collectors' King Crimson, Vol.3	3CD	Pony Canyon	PCCY-01467	Japan	2000	84.99
King Crimson	Dinosaur	CD Single	Discipline Global	7243-8-38480-2-7	U.S.A.	1995	6.99
King Crimson	Dinosaur (Promo)	CD Single	Discipline Global	DPRO-12720	U.S.A.	1995	12.99
King Crimson	Discipline	CD	Caroline	CAROL-1592	U.S.A.	2000	8.99
King Crimson	Earthbound	Mini Lp	Caroline	PCCY-1515	Japan	2000	22.99
King Crimson	Epitaph Ltd Box Volumes 1 - 4	4CD	Discipline Global	DGM9607A/B/C/D	England	1997	89.99
King Crimson	Epitaph Volumes One & Two	2CD	Discipline Global	DGM9607A/B	U.S.A.	1997	22.99
King Crimson	Epitaph Volumes One & Two	2 Mini Lp	Pony Canyon	PCCY-01087	Japan	1997	34.99
King Crimson	Epitaph Volumes Three & Four	2 Mini Lp	Pony Canyon	PCCY-01180	Japan	1997	34.99
King Crimson	Epitaph Volumes Three & Four	2CD	Discipline Global	DGM9607C/D	U.S.A.	1997	34.99
King Crimson	Frame By Frame Box Set	4CD	Carol	1595-2	U.S.A.	1991	58.99
King Crimson	Happy With What ...	CD	Sanctuary	06076-84580-2	U.S.A.	2002	8.99
King Crimson	Happy With What...	CD	Sanctuary	SANCD123	England	2002	11.99
King Crimson	Heavy Construkction Live Europe '00	3CD	Discipline Global	DGM-0013	U.S.A.	2000	21.99
King Crimson	In The Court Of The Crimson King	CD	Caroline	CAROL-1502-2	U.S.A.	2000	8.99
King Crimson	In The Wake Of Poseidon	CD	Caroline	CAROL-1503-2	U.S.A.	2000	8.99
King Crimson	Islands	CD	Caroline	CAROL-1505-2	U.S.A.	2000	8.99
King Crimson	Ladies Of The Road Special Edition	2CD	Discipline Global	DGM-9706	England	2002	18.99
King Crimson	Lark's Tongue In Aspic	CD	Caroline	CAROL-1506	U.S.A.	2000	8.99
King Crimson	Level Five Ltd. Ed. Tour Cd	CD	Pony Canyon	PCCY-01576	Japan	2001	29.99
King Crimson	Lizard	CD	Caroline	CAROL-1504	U.S.A.	2000	8.99
King Crimson	People (Promo)	CD Single	Discipline Global	DPRO-12782	U.S.A.	1995	19.99
King Crimson	Red	CD	Caroline	CAROL-1508	U.S.A.	2000	8.99
King Crimson	Schizoid Man	CD Single	Pony Canyon	PCCY-01540	Japan	2001	29.99
King Crimson	Schizoid Man (5 Versions)	CD Single	Virgin	7243-8-93675-2-2	Holland	1996	5.99
King Crimson	Sex Sleep Eat Drink Dream	CD Single	Virgin	7243-8-38519-2	U.S.A.	1995	24.99
King Crimson	Shoganai (Happy With What..)	2CD	Universal	UICE-1027	Japan	2002	26.99
King Crimson	Sleepless - The Concise King Crimson	CD	Caroline	CAROL-1887-2	U.S.A.	1993	6.99
King Crimson	Starless And Bible Black	CD	Caroline	CAROL-1507-2	U.S.A.	2000	8.99
King Crimson	The Abbreviated King Crimson	CD	Caroline	CAROL-1467-2	U.S.A.	1991	7.99
King Crimson	The Compact King Crimson	CD	Caroline	CAROL-1509-2	U.S.A.	1988	8.99
King Crimson	The ConstruKction Of Light	CD	Virgin	7243-8-49261-2-0	U.S.A.	2000	9.99
King Crimson	The First Three (Picture CDs)	3CD	Virgin	TPAK-28	England	1993	44.99
King Crimson	The Great Deceiver Box Set	4CD	Carol	1597-2	U.S.A.	1992	57.99
King Crimson	The Night Watch	2CD	Pony Canyon	PCCY-01177	Japan	1997	44.99
King Crimson	The Night Watch	2CD	Discipline Global	DGM9707	U.S.A.	1997	12.99
King Crimson	The Power To Believe	CD	Sanctuary	SANCD-155	England	2003	13.99
King Crimson	Thrak	CD	Virgin	7243-8-40313-2-9	U.S.A.	1995	8.99
King Crimson	Thrak (Metal/Stkr/Prgrm/Butn/Gold)	CD	Discipline Global	KCCDX1	England	1995	18.99
King Crimson	Thrak Sampler (Promo)	CD	Virgin	KCPRO1	England	1995	9.99
King Crimson	Thrak: 30th Ann. Remaster Ltd. Ed.	CD	Virgin	CDVKCX13	England	2002	22.99
King Crimson	Thrakattak	CD	Discipline Global	DGM9604	U.S.A.	1996	11.99
King Crimson	Three Of A Perfect Pair	CD	Caroline	CAROL-1595-2	U.S.A.	2000	8.99
King Crimson	USA	Mini Lp	Pony Canyon	PCCY-01616	Japan	2000	22.99
King Crimson	VRoOM Vroom	2CD	Discipline Global	DGM0105	U.S.A.	2001	19.99
King Crimson	Vrooom	CD	Discipline	DR-9401-2	U.S.A.	1994	7.99
King Crimson	Young Person's Guide To King Crimson	2CD	Virgin	VJCP-3001-2	Japan	1990	115.99
King Crimson/Ffwd	Ffwd	CD	Inter-modo	INTA-001-CD	England	1994	29.99
King Crimson/ProjeKct Four	Club # 7 Proj 4 Live S Francisco '98	CD	Discipline Global	CLUB7	U.S.A.	2000	13.99
King Crimson/ProjeKct Four	West Coast Live	CD	Pony Canyon	PCCY-01386	Japan	1999	29.99

K

Artist	Title	Format	Label	Catalog No	Country	Released	Value
King Crimson/ProjeKct One	Club #22 Jazz Cafe Suite Dec '97	CD	Discipline Global	CLUB-22	U.S.A.	2003	16.99
King Crimson/ProjeKct One	Deception Thr. /Beg Guide/Projekct 1	CD	Discipline Global	DGM-9915	England	1999	13.99
King Crimson/ProjeKct One	Live At The Jazz Cafe	CD	Pony Canyon	PCCY-01319	Japan	1999	16.99
King Crimson/ProjeKct One	ProjeKct Box Set	4CD	Discipline Global	DGM-9913	U.S.A.	1998	26.99
King Crimson/ProjeKct Three	Masque	CD	Pony Canyon	PCCY-01404	Japan	1999	29.99
King Crimson/ProjeKct Two	Club # 17 Live In Northhampton 1998	CD	Discipline Global	CLUB17	U.S.A.	2001	16.99
King Crimson/ProjeKct Two	Live Groove	CD	Pony Canyon	PCCY-01320	Japan	1998	29.99
King Crimson/ProjeKct Two	Space Groove	2CD	Discipline Global	DGM-9801	England	1998	16.99
King Crimson/ProjeKct X	Heaven And Earth	CD	Discipline Global	DGM0005	England	2000	24.99
King, Carole	A Natural Woman: Ode Coll. ('68-'76)	2CD	Epic	E2K-65426	U.S.A.	1998	15.99
King, Carole	Brill Building Legends (Rare/Demos)	2CD	Repertoire	REP-5002	Germany	2003	14.99
King, Carole	City Streets (Leatherbound Promo)	CD	Capitol	7-90885-2	U.S.A.	1989	19.99
King, Carole	City Streets (W/Eric Clapton)	CD	Capitol	C2-90885	U.S.A.	1988	7.99
King, Carole	Colour Of Your Dreams	CD	Valley	VE-15078-CD	U.S.A.	1999	11.99
King, Carole	Cryin' In The Rain	2CD	Delta	63016	England	2002	11.99
King, Carole	Fantasy	CD	Epic	EK-34962	U.S.A.	1991	7.99
King, Carole	Goin' Back	CD	Sony	A-28556	U.S.A.	1997	7.99
King, Carole	Her Greatest Hits + 2	CD	Epic	EK-65846	U.S.A.	1999	8.99
King, Carole	In Concert	CD	Priority	P2-53878	U.S.A.	1994	7.99
King, Carole	In Concert	CD	Valley	VE-15080-CD	U.S.A.	1999	7.99
King, Carole	Love Makes The World	CD	Koch	KOC-CD-8346	U.S.A.	2001	7.99
King, Carole	Music	CD	Epic	EK-34949	U.S.A.	1991	8.99
King, Carole	Music/Fantasy	2CD	Sony	508-763-2	England	2002	15.99
King, Carole	Pearls/Time Gone By	CD	Valley	VE-15079-CD	U.S.A.	1999	10.99
King, Carole	Pearls: Songs Of Goffin And King	CD	Priority	P2-53879	U.S.A.	1994	8.99
King, Carole	Really Rosie	CD	Epic	EK-65744	U.S.A.	1999	8.99
King, Carole	Really Rosie/Her Gr. Hits/Tapestry	3CD	Epic	E3K-61564	U.S.A.	2000	24.99
King, Carole	Rhymes & Reasons	CD	Epic	EK-34950	U.S.A.	1991	7.99
King, Carole	Speeding Time	CD	Warner Bros.	7567-80118-2	Germany	1996	9.99
King, Carole	Super Hits	CD	Epic	EK-66066	U.S.A.	2000	5.99
King, Carole	Tapestry (Sony Gold Cd)	CD	Epic	EK-66226	U.S.A.	1971	27.99
King, Carole	Tapestry + 2	CD	Epic	EK-65850	U.S.A.	1999	8.99
King, Carole	The Carnegie Hall Concert	CD	Epic	EK-64942	U.S.A.	1996	9.99
King, Carole	The Early Years	CD	Hallmark	31198-2	England	2000	8.99
King, Carole	The Very Best Of	CD	Sony	496181	Australia	2001	15.99
King, Carole	Thoroughbred	CD	Epic	EK-34963	U.S.A.	1991	7.99
King, Carole	Time Gone By	CD	Priority	P2-53880	U.S.A.	1994	8.99
King, Carole	Wrap Around Joy	CD	Epic	EK-34953	U.S.A.	1991	7.99
King, Carole	Wrap Around Joy/Thoroughbred	2CD	Sony	508-764-2	England	2002	15.99
King, Carole	Writer	CD	Epic	EK-34944	U.S.A.	1991	8.99
King, Carole	Writer/Rhymes & Reasons	2CD	Sony	508-762-2	England	2002	15.99
King, Morgana	New Beginnings	CD	Line	LICD-9.00761-0	Germany	1990	18.99
Kingdom Come	Bad Image	CD	Warner Bros.	4509-93148-2	Germany	1993	14.99
Kingdom Come	Balladesque (The Best Of)	CD	Dogo Bros.	39035-423	Germany	1998	14.99
Kingdom Come	Hands Of Time	CD	Polydor	849-329-2	U.S.A.	1991	11.99
Kingdom Come	In Your Face	CD	Polydor	839-192-2	U.S.A.	1989	9.99
Kingdom Come	Independent	CD	Ulftone	UTCD-065	Germany	2003	12.99
Kingdom Come	Live And Unplugged	CD	Viceroy	35-450-425	Germany	1996	23.99
Kingdom Come	Master Seven	CD	Bellaphon	290.25.002	Germany	1997	10.99
Kingdom Come	Self Titled	CD	Polydor	835-368-2	U.S.A.	1988	12.99
Kingdom Come	Too	CD	Spitfire	SPT-CD-124	EU	2000	17.99
Kingdom Come	Twilight Cruiser	CD	Viceroy	33-008—423	Germany	1995	13.99
Kingfish	A Night In New York	CD	Relix	RRCD-2089	U.S.A.	1997	6.99
Kingfish	Alive In '85	CD	Relix	RRCD2016	U.S.A.	1991	5.99
Kingfish	Best Of Kingfish	CD	Relix	RRCD2084	U.S.A.	1996	4.99
Kingfish	King Biscuit Flower Hour Presents	2CD	King Biscuit	70710-88006-2	U.S.A.	1995	15.99
Kingfish	Kingfish (Line Version)	CD	Line	GDCD-9.00645-0	Germany	1989	9.99
Kingfish	Live At My Father's Place	CD	Relix	RRCD2089	U.S.A.	1997	8.99

K

Artist	Title	Format	Label	Catalog No	Country	Released	Value
Kingfish	Live'N'Kickin'	CD	Line	JECD-9.00857-0	Germany	1989	24.99
Kingfish	Sundown On The Forest	CD	Phoenix Rising	2001	U.S.A.	1998	9.99
Kingfish	Trident	CD	Line	JECD-9.00863-0	Germany	1989	24.99
Kingsmem	Live & Unreleased	CD	Jerden	JRCD-7004	U.S.A.	1992	17.99
Kingsmen	Best Of	CD	Rhino	R2-70745	U.S.A.	1989	8.99
Kingsmen	The Kingsmen In Person	CD	Sundazed	SC-6004	U.S.A.	1993	10.99
Kinks	25 Years - The Ultimate Collection	CD	PolyGram	842078-2	Canada	1989	17.99
Kinks	Arthur Or The Decline ... + 10	CD	Essential	ESM-CD-511	England	1998	11.99
Kinks	Available For Licensing...(Promo)	CD	Razor & Tie	RTS752	U.S.A.	1998	24.99
Kinks	BBC Sessions (Promo Sampler)	CD	Sanctuary	SANPRO10	England	2001	6.99
Kinks	Borders Comp. (Promo Unrel. Live Trk)	CD	Velvel	VELDJ78710-2	U.S.A.	1998	9.99
Kinks	Celluloid Heroes	CD	Velvel	VEL-CD-79734	U.S.A.	2001	8.99
Kinks	Come Dancing With (Best Of Diff. Trks)	CD	Arista	A2CD-8428	U.S.A.	1986	8.99
Kinks	Come Dancing With The Kinks	CD	Velvel	VEL-79733	U.S.A.	2000	8.99
Kinks	Did Ya	CD Single	Columbia	44K-74050	U.S.A.	1991	11.99
Kinks	Don't Forget To Dance	CD Single	Arista	74321-13816-2	Germany	1993	12.99
Kinks	Entertainment (Promo)	CD Single	MCA	CD45-18168	U.S.A.	1989	14.99
Kinks	EP Collection #1 (Red)	10 CD	Essential	ESFCD-667	England	1998	44.99
Kinks	EP Collection #2 (Blue)	10 CD	Essential	ESFCD-904	England	1998	44.99
Kinks	Everybody Is In Showbiz + 2	CD	Velvel	63467-79720-2	U.S.A.	1998	8.99
Kinks	Everybody's In ...(MFSL Gold) + 2	CD	Mobile Fidelity	UDSACD-2010	U.S.A.	2003	24.99
Kinks	Face To Face + 7	CD	Essential	ESM-CD-479	England	1998	11.99
Kinks	Give The People What They Want	CD	Velvel	63467-79730-2	U.S.A.	1999	8.99
Kinks	God Save The Kinks (2 Cd Promo)	CD	Essential	KINKS1	England	1998	17.99
Kinks	God Save The Kinks (Br. 10 Song DJ)	CD	Essential	KINKS2	England	1998	9.99
Kinks	God Save The Kinks (Pur.10 Song DJ)	CD	Essential	KINKS3	England	1998	9.99
Kinks	Hatred (Promo)	CD Single	Columbia	CSK-5076	U.S.A.	1993	12.99
Kinks	How Do I Get Close To You (Promo)	CD Single	MCA	CD45-17969	U.S.A.	1989	14.99
Kinks	Introspective	CD	Baktabak	CINT-5005	England	1991	8.99
Kinks	Kinda Kinks + 11	CD	Essential	ESM-CD-483	England	1998	11.99
Kinks	King Biscuit Flower Hour 1/29/01	CD	DIR Network	0159-2146-1840	U.S.A.	2001	49.99
Kinks	King Biscuit Flower Hour 11/1/87	CD	DIR Network	1LF0500A	U.S.A.	1987	49.99
Kinks	Kinks BBC Sessions 1964-1977	2CD	Sanctuary	06076-84504-2	England	2001	21.99
Kinks	Limited Edition Compilation #3	CD	Velvel	VELDJ798719-2	U.S.A.	1999	12.99
Kinks	Limited Edition Compilation 2 (Promo)	CD	Velvel	VELDJ78716-2	U.S.A.	1998	12.99
Kinks	Live At Kelvin Hall (Mono/Stereo)	CD	Essential	ESM-CD-508	England	1998	11.99
Kinks	Lmtd Ed. Comp 1 Unrel. Live Trk (DJ)	CD	Velvel	VELDJ78704-2	U.S.A.	1998	12.99
Kinks	Lost And Found (1986-89)	CD	MCA	MCAD-10338	U.S.A.	1991	7.99
Kinks	Low Budget (MFSL SACD Gold) + 3	CD	Mobile Fidelity	UDSACD-2008	U.S.A.	2003	24.99
Kinks	Low Budget + 3	CD	Velvel	63467-79727-2	U.S.A.	1999	8.99
Kinks	Misfits + 4	CD	Velvel	63467-79726-2	U.S.A.	1998	8.99
Kinks	Muswell Hillbillies + 2	CD	Velvel	63467-79719-2	U.S.A.	1998	8.99
Kinks	One For The Road (Enh. Live Disc + 1)	2CD	Velvel	63467-79728-2	U.S.A.	1999	11.99
Kinks	Only A Dream	CD Single	Columbia	6590201-2	Germany	1993	14.99
Kinks	Only A Dream (Promo)	CD Single	Columbia	659922-2	England	1993	9.99
Kinks	Only A Dream (Promo)	CD Single	Columbia	PRO-765	Austria	1993	19.99
Kinks	Part 1 Lola Versus Powerman... + 3	CD	Essential	ESM-CD-509	England	1998	11.99
Kinks	Percy + 5 (Mono)	CD	Essential	ESM-CD-510	England	1998	11.99
Kinks	Phobia	CD	Columbia	CK-48724	U.S.A.	1993	8.99
Kinks	Preservation Act 1 + 2	CD	Velvel	63467-79721-2	U.S.A.	1998	8.99
Kinks	Preservation Act 2 + 2	CD	Velvel	63467-79722-2	U.S.A.	1998	8.99
Kinks	Scattered (Promo)	CD Single	Columbia	CSK-74872	U.S.A.	1993	19.99
Kinks	Scattered (Promo)	CD Single	Columbia	658992-2	Austria	1993	9.99
Kinks	Schoolboys In Disgrace	CD	Velvel	63467-79724-2	U.S.A.	1998	8.99
Kinks	Sleepwalker + 5	CD	Velvel	63467-79725-2	U.S.A.	1998	8.99
Kinks	Soap Opera + 4	CD	Velvel	63467-79723-2	U.S.A.	1998	8.99
Kinks	Something Else By The Kinks + 8	CD	Essential	ESM-CD-480	England	1998	11.99
Kinks	State Of Confusion + 4	CD	Velvel	63467-79731-2	U.S.A.	1999	8.99

K

Artist	Title	Format	Label	Catalog No	Country	Released	Value
Kinks	The Archway Tavern Coll. (Fan Club)	CD	Castle	KINKFAN1	England	2001	29.99
Kinks	The Best And Kollektable Kinks	CD	Victor Ent.	VICP-5332	Japan	1993	39.99
Kinks	The Complete Collection (Gold Cd)	CD	Castle	CCSCD-300	England	1989	12.99
Kinks	The Days EP	CD Single	Castle	WEN-X-1016	England	1996	5.99
Kinks	The Greatest Hits I (1964 - 1970)	CD	Victor Ent.	VICP-61491	Japan	2001	34.99
Kinks	The Greatest Hits II (1971-1975)	CD	Victor Ent.	VICP-61492	Japan	2001	29.99
Kinks	The Greatest Hits III (1977-1984)	CD	Victor Ent.	VICP-61493	Japan	2001	29.99
Kinks	The Kink Kontroversy + 4	CD	Essential	ESM-CD-507	England	1998	11.99
Kinks	The Kink Kronikles	2CD	Reprise	6454-2	U.S.A.	1972	14.99
Kinks	The Kinks Live - The Road	CD	MCA	MCAD-42107	U.S.A.	1987	11.99
Kinks	The Kinks The Village Green + 47	3CD	Sanctuary	SMETD-102	EU	2004	19.99
Kinks	The Marble Arch Years Box Set	3CD	Sanctuary	CMGBX318	England	2001	29.99
Kinks	The Singles Collection	2CD	Essential	ESS-CD-592	England	1997	17.99
Kinks	The Ultimate Collection	2CD	Sanctuary	SANDD-109	England	2002	16.99
Kinks	Think Visual	CD	MCA	MCAD-5822	U.S.A.	1986	7.99
Kinks	To The Bone	2CD	Guardian	7243-8-37303-2-2	U.S.A.	1996	11.99
Kinks	To The Bone (1994 Version)	CD	Grapevine	KNKCD-1	England	1994	11.99
Kinks	To The Bone (Cd 2 Only, No Tray Art)	CD	Guardian	7243-8-37303-2-2	U.S.A.	1996	11.99
Kinks	To The Bone (Sampler/Holographic)	CD	Guardian	7087-6-10071-2-1	U.S.A.	1996	13.99
Kinks	UK Jive	CD	MCA	MCAD-6337	U.S.A.	1989	7.99
Kinks	Up Close (99-22) 5/24, 99	2CD	Media America	9922/23	U.S.A.	1999	69.99
Kinks	Waterloo Sunset '94 Ep	CD Single	Grapevine	KNKCD-2	England	1994	17.99
Kinks	Westwood 1 Show # 97-27 (6/30/97)	2CD	Westwood 1	CORW802XD	U.S.A.	1997	74.99
Kinks	Word Of Mouth + 2	CD	Velvel	63467-79732-2	U.S.A.	1999	8.99
Kinks	You Really Got Me + 12	CD	Essential	ESM-CD-482	England	1998	11.99
Kinks	You Really Got Me/Kinda Kinks (Gold)	CD	Mobile Fidelity	UDCD-679	U.S.A.	1965	24.99
Kinks/ELO	Westwood One June 19, 1995	CD	Westwood 1	CO44U010D	U.S.A.	1995	69.99
Kinks/Kast Off Kinks	The Archway EP (Fan Club Cd)	CD	Kinks Fan Club	OKFC-CDEP-1	England	2001	29.99
Kinks/Larry Page Orchestra	Kinky Music - Arranged By Ray Davies	CD	RPM	RPM-213	England	2000	14.99
Kinks/Mapleoak/Peter Quaife	Maple Oak + 2	CD	Elegy	E580/1	England	2000	24.99
Kinks/Michael Penn	King Biscuit October 22 - 28, 1990	CD	DIR Network	A0RF0100B	U.S.A.	1990	44.99
Kiske, Michael	Ready To Sacrifice (W/Sticker)	CD	Victor Ent.	VICP-60650	Japan	1999	19.99
Kiss	Alive II	2CD	Mercury	314-532-382-2	U.S.A.	1997	10.99
Kiss	Alive III	CD	Mercury	514-777-2	U.S.A.	1993	8.99
Kiss	Alive!	2CD	Mercury	314-532-377-2	U.S.A.	1997	10.99
Kiss	Animalize	CD	Mercury	822-495-2	U.S.A.	1998	8.99
Kiss	Asylum	CD	Mercury	826-099-2	U.S.A.	1998	8.99
Kiss	Box Set	5CD	Universal	586-561-2	U.S.A.	2001	42.99
Kiss	Carnival Of Souls	CD	Mercury	PHCR-1560	Japan	1997	15.99
Kiss	Carnival Of Souls - The Final Sessions	CD	Mercury	536-323-2	U.S.A.	1997	7.99
Kiss	Chikara	CD	Polystar	P30R-20008	Japan	1988	49.99
Kiss	Chikara (Best Of)	CD	Polystar	P30R-20008	Japan	1988	74.99
Kiss	Crazy Nights	CD	Mercury	832-626-2	U.S.A.	1998	8.99
Kiss	Crazy Nights	CD	Polystar	P33R-20006	Japan	1987	29.99
Kiss	Creatures Of The Night	CD	Mercury	532-391-2	U.S.A.	1997	8.99
Kiss	Definitive Kiss Collection (Suitcase)	5CD	Mercury	314-586-561-2	U.S.A.	2001	99.99
Kiss	Destroyer	CD	Mercury	314-532-378-2	U.S.A.	1997	8.99
Kiss	Double Platinum	CD	Mercury	314-532-383-2	U.S.A.	1978	8.99
Kiss	Dressed To Kill	CD	Mercury	314-532-376-2	U.S.A.	1997	8.99
Kiss	Dynasty	CD	Mercury	314-532-388-2	U.S.A.	1997	8.99
Kiss	First Kiss Last Licks (Promo Only 800)	CD	Mercury	PRO-792-1	U.S.A.	1990	89.99
Kiss	God Gave Rock And Roll To You..	CD Single	Interscope	PRCD-4076-2	U.S.A.	1991	12.99
Kiss	Greatest Hits	CD	Mercury	536-159-2	U.S.A.	1996	8.99
Kiss	Greatest Kiss	CD	Mercury	534-725-2	U.S.A.	1997	7.99
Kiss	Hot In The Shade	CD	Mercury	838-913-2	U.S.A.	1989	8.99
Kiss	Hotter Than Hell	CD	Mercury	314-532-375-2	U.S.A.	1997	8.99
Kiss	Kiss (Self Titled)	CD	Mercury	314-532-374-2	U.S.A.	1997	8.99
Kiss	Kiss Killers	CD	Mercury	512-758-2	Germany	1982	13.99

K

Artist	Title	Format	Label	Catalog No	Country	Released	Value
Kiss	Lick It Up	CD	Mercury	558-858-2	U.S.A.	1998	8.99
Kiss	Love Gun	CD	Mercury	314-532-381-2	U.S.A.	1997	8.99
Kiss	MTV Unplugged	CD	Mercury	528-950-2	U.S.A.	1996	7.99
Kiss	Music From "The Elder" (Lou Reed)	CD	Mercury	314-532-390-2	U.S.A.	1997	8.99
Kiss	New York Groove (W/You Wanted)	2CD	Mercury	MECP-120	U.S.A.	1996	79.99
Kiss	Psycho Circus	CD	Mercury	558-992-2	U.S.A.	1998	7.99
Kiss	Psycho Circus (Holographic Cover)	CD	Mercury	314-558-992-2	U.S.A.	1998	8.99
Kiss	Psycho Circus (Single)	CD	Mercury	566-465-2	Sweden	1998	5.99
Kiss	Psycho Circus Video Bonus CD Promo	CD	Mercury	MECP-449	U.S.A.	1998	13.99
Kiss	Revenge	CD	Mercury	848-037-2	U.S.A.	1992	7.99
Kiss	Rock And Roll Over	CD	Mercury	314-532-380-2	U.S.A.	1997	8.99
Kiss	Selected Tracks/Greatest Kiss (Promo)	CD	Mercury	578889-2	U.S.A.	1997	49.99
Kiss	Smashes, Thrashes & Hits	CD	Mercury	836-427-2	U.S.A.	1993	8.99
Kiss	The Very Best of Kiss	CD	Universal	063122	U.S.A.	2002	8.99
Kiss	Unmasked	CD	Mercury	314-532-389	U.S.A.	1997	9.99
Kiss/1st 4 CDs(1000 Only)	First Licks Promo (Gr Box/Red Sticker)	4CD	Mercury	846-766-2	U.S.A.	1990	149.99
Kiss/Ace Frehley	12 Picks	CD	Megaforce	020286-1976-2	U.S.A.	1997	8.99
Kiss/Ace Frehley	Ace Frehley	CD	Mercury	314-532-385-2	U.S.A.	1997	8.99
Kiss/Ace Frehley	Frehley's Comet	CD	Atlantic	81749-2	U.S.A.	1987	11.99
Kiss/Ace Frehley	Live + 1	CD	Atlantic	81826-2	U.S.A.	1990	12.99
Kiss/Ace Frehley	Loaded Deck (With Free Guitar Pick)	CD	Megaforce	02028619972	U.S.A.	1997	14.99
Kiss/Ace Frehley	Second Sighting	CD	Warner Bros.	25XD-1087	Japan	1988	19.99
Kiss/Ace Frehley	Second Sighting	CD	Atlantic	81862-2	U.S.A.	1990	10.99
Kiss/Ace Frehley	Trouble Walkin'	CD	Atlantic	82042-2	U.S.A.	1989	9.99
Kiss/Ace Frehley Tribute	Spacewalk + 2	CD	Victor Ent.	VICP-5679	Japan	1996	12.99
Kiss/Eric Carr	Rockology	CD	Spitfire	SPT-5099-2	U.S.A.	2000	13.99
Kiss/Gene Simmons	Gene Simmons	CD	Mercury	314-532-384-2	U.S.A.	1997	7.99
Kiss/Paul Stanley	Paul Stanley	CD	Mercury	314-532-387-2	U.S.A.	1997	8.99
Kiss/Peter Criss	Criss Cat	CD	Tony Nicole Tony	0004-2SE	U.S.A.	1993	11.99
Kiss/Peter Criss	Let Me Rock You	CD	Mercury	314-558-072-2	U.S.A.	1998	14.99
Kiss/Peter Criss	Out Of Control	CD	Mercury	314-558-071-2	U.S.A.	1998	14.99
Kiss/Peter Criss	Peter Criss	CD	Mercury	314-532-386-2	U.S.A.	1997	8.99
Kiss/Various Artists	Kiss My Ass: Classic Kiss Regrooved	CD	PolyGram	314-522-123-2	U.S.A.	1994	7.99
Kitaro	Best Of Kitaro	CD	Canyon	P3012	Japan	1985	9.99
Kitaro	Best Of Kitaro Vol. 2 (W/Soong Sisters)	2CD	Domo	72438-47110-2-3	U.S.A.	1999	10.99
Kitaro	Cirque Ingenieux	CD	Domo	71022-2	U.S.A.	1997	8.99
Kitaro	Gaia.Onbashira	CD	Domo	72438-45789-2-3	U.S.A.	1998	5.99
Kitaro	Heaven & Earth	CD	Geffen	GEFD-24614	U.S.A.	1993	13.99
Kitaro	India	CD	Geffen	9-24085-2	U.S.A.	1985	11.99
Kitaro	Kojiki	CD	Geffen	9-24255-2	U.S.A.	1990	7.99
Kitaro	Live In America	CD	Geffen	GEFD-24323	U.S.A.	1991	9.99
Kitaro	Mandala	CD	Domo	DOMO-71001	U.S.A.	1994	8.99
Kitaro	Peace On Earth	CD	Domo	71014-2	U.S.A.	1996	6.99
Kitaro	Silk Road	2CD	Kuckuck	12051-2	Germany	1981	24.99
Kitaro	Silk Road Suite	CD	Kuckuck	CD-065/66	Germany	1983	34.99
Kitaro	Six Musical Portraits	CD	Domo	70876-13222-2-4	U.S.A.	1998	7.99
Kitaro	Ten Years	2CD	Geffen	9-24207-2	U.S.A.	1988	10.99
Kitaro	Ten Years	2CD	Geffen	9-24207-2	U.S.A.	1988	10.99
Kitaro	Tenku	CD	Geffen	9-24112-2	U.S.A.	1986	5.99
Kitaro	The Light Of The Spirit	CD	Domo	DJCP-50010	Japan	1998	8.99
Kitaro	Toward The West	CD	Geffen	9-24094-2	U.S.A.	1985	18.99
Kitaro	Twin Best	2CD	Victor Ent.	VICL-41027~28	Japan	1998	44.99
Kitaro/Jon Anderson	Dream	CD	Domo	72438-48280-2-8	U.S.A.	1999	8.99
Kix	Blow My Fuse	CD	Atlantic	A2-81877	U.S.A.	1988	9.99
Kix	Cool Kids	CD	Atlantic	7-80056-2	U.S.A.	1990	12.99
Kix	Hot Wire	CD	East West	A2-91714-2	U.S.A.	1991	8.99
Kix	Live	CD	Atlantic	7-82499-2	U.S.A.	1993	14.99
Kix	Midnite Dynamite	CD	Atlantic	7-81267-2	U.S.A.	1990	14.99

Artist	Title	Format	Label	Catalog No	Country	Released	Value
Kix	Self Titled	CD	Atlantic	19307-2	U.S.A.	1990	11.99
Kix	Show Business	CD	CMC INT.	CMC-7303-2	U.S.A.	1995	9.99
Kix	The Essentials	CD	Rhino	R2-76048	U.S.A.	2002	8.99
Klaatu	Klaatu & Hope	CD	Collector´s Choice	72435-22335-2-6	U.S.A.	1999	15.99
KLF	The White Room	2CD	Arista	ARCD-8657	U.S.A.	1991	14.99
KLF/Red Army Choir	K Cera Cera	CD Single	NMC	KCC-1-2	Israel	1993	13.99
KLF/The Timelords	Doctorin' The Tardis	CD Single	TVT	TVT-4025-2	U.S.A.	1991	13.99
KLF/The Timelords	The History Of The Jams	CD	TVT	TVT-4040CD	U.S.A.	1988	10.99
Klingman, Moogy	Old Times, Good Times	CD	Moogy Music	TRBAZAAR.COM	U.S.A.	1999	8.99
Klingman, Moogy	The First Recordings (1970-1972)	CD	Moogy Music	TRBAZAAR.COM	U.S.A.	2000	8.99
Klingman, Moogy/B. Linhart	The Buzzy/Moogy Sessions	CD	Moogy Music	TRBAZAAR.COM	U.S.A.	2000	8.99
Klingman, Moogy/F. Parade	Take Your Place In The Freak Parade	CD	Moogy Music	TRBAZAAR.COM	U.S.A.	2001	8.99
Klingman, Moogy/R. Wright	Tomorrow's Hits Today!	CD	Moogy Music	TRBAZAAR.COM	U.S.A.	1999	8.99
Knack	... But The Little Girls Understand + 4	CD	Capitol	72435-38112-2-8	U.S.A.	2002	8.99
Knack	Get The Knack/But The Little Girls...	CD	BGO	BGOCD248	England	1994	19.99
Knack	Get The Knack+ 5	CD	Capitol	72435-38118-2-2	U.S.A.	2002	8.99
Knack	Normal As The Next Guy	CD	Smile	ID1156ZR	U.S.A.	2001	8.99
Knack	Proof: The Very Best Of	CD	Rhino	R2-75285	U.S.A.	1998	14.99
Knack	Retrospective	CD	Capitol	0777-7-80537-2-9	U.S.A.	1992	6.99
Knack	Round Trip + 5	CD	Capitol	72435-38110-2-0	U.S.A.	2002	8.99
Knack	Serious Fun + 4	CD	Charisma	72435-38111-2-9	U.S.A.	2002	8.99
Knack	Zoom + 1	CD	East West	AMCY-2798	Japan	1998	39.99
Knickerbockers	Lies + 4	CD	Sundazed	SC-6011	U.S.A.	1994	8.99
Knight, Frederick	The Timeless Soul Collection	CD	Line	TLCD-9.00471-0	Germany	1987	24.99
Knight, Gladys/The Pips	Everybody Needs Love	CD	Motown	MOTD-5126	U.S.A.	1986	89.99
Knight, Gladys/The Pips	Everybody Needs.../If I Were...	CD	Motown	R4CM-1014	U.S.A.	1986	61.99
Knight, Gladys/The Pips	Feelin' Bluesy	CD	Motown	37463-5467-2	U.S.A.	1968	81.99
Knight, Gladys/The Pips	Gladys Knight & The Pips Collection	CD	Buddah	74465-99726-2	U.S.A.	2000	8.99
Knight, Gladys/The Pips	Nitty Gritty	CD	Motown	MOTD-5148	U.S.A.	1969	84.99
Knight, Gladys/The Pips	Silk & Soul	CD	Motown	MOTD-5458	U.S.A.	1968	49.99
Knight, Gladys/The Pips	Visions	CD	Columbia	CK-38205	U.S.A.	1983	69.99
Knitters/X & Dave Alvin	Poor Little Creature In The Road	CD	Rhino	R2-79946	U.S.A.	1985	12.99
Knopfler, M/D Edmunds	The Booze Brothers By Brewers Droop	CD	Brilliant	BT-33011	EC	1999	13.99
Knopfler, Mark	A Shot At Glory	CD	Mercury	548127-2	England	2000	9.99
Knopfler, Mark	A Shot At Glory (O.S.T.)	CD	Warner Bros.	9-48324-2	U.S.A.	2000	9.99
Knopfler, Mark	Cal (O.S.T.)	CD	Mercury	822-769-2	U.S.A.	1984	8.99
Knopfler, Mark	Golden Heart	CD	Warner Bros.	9-46026-2	U.S.A.	1996	8.99
Knopfler, Mark	Last Exit To Brooklyn	CD	Warner Bros.	9-25986-2	U.S.A.	1989	8.99
Knopfler, Mark	Local Hero (O.S.T.)	CD	Warner Bros.	23827-2	U.S.A.	1988	14.99
Knopfler, Mark	Metroland (O.S.T.)	CD	Warner Bros.	47006-2	U.S.A.	1999	24.99
Knopfler, Mark	Sailing To Philadelphia	CD	Mercury	9-47753-2	U.S.A.	2000	7.99
Knopfler, Mark	Screenplaying	CD	Warner Bros.	9-45457-2	U.S.A.	1993	9.99
Knopfler, Mark	The Princess Bride (O.S.T.)	CD	Vertigo	832-864-2	Germany	1997	13.99
Knopfler, Mark	The Ragpicker's Dream + 5	2CD	Mercury	063-293-2	Australia	2002	15.99
Knopfler, Mark	Wag The Dog (O.S.T.)	CD	PolyGram	536-864-2	England	1998	12.99
Knopfler, Mark	What It Is	CD Single	Mercury	562-885-2	EU	2000	4.99
Knopfler, Mark	Words + Music (Promo)	CD	Warner Bros.	PRO-CD-8201	U.S.A.	1994	10.99
Koivistoinen, Eero	Picture In Three Colours	CD	Line	COCD-9.00515-0	Germany	1988	24.99
Koobas	Self Titled + 8	CD	BGO	BGOCD487	England	2002	21.99
Kooper, Al	Al's Big Deal	CD	Sony	SRCS-6472	Japan	1995	21.99
Kooper, Al	Easy Does It	CD	Sony	SRCS-6198	U.S.A.	1992	20.99
Kooper, Al	I Stand Alone	CD	Sony	SRCS-6196	Japan	1992	21.99
Kooper, Al	Kooper Session Super Session Vol.2	CD	Sony	SRCS-6195	Japan	1992	21.99
Kooper, Al	Naked Songs	CD	Sony	SRCS-9276	Japan	1997	16.99
Kooper, Al	Rare & Well Done (B/White Promo)	2CD	Columbia	AC2K-62153	U.S.A.	2001	18.99
Kooper, Al	ReKOOPERation	CD	Music Masters Inc.	01612-65107-2	U.S.A.	1994	7.99
Kooper, Al	Soul Of A Man	2CD	Music Masters Inc.	01612-65113-2	U.S.A.	1995	24.99
Kooper, Al	What Do All Of These...(Promo)	CD	Music Masters Inc.	DB145L0081880	U.S.A.	1994	10.99

K

Artist	Title	Format	Label	Catalog No	Country	Released	Value
Korner, Alexis	Accidentally New Orleans	CD	Line	TACD-9.00637-0	Germany	1988	18.99
Korner, Alexis	BBC Radio Sessions	CD	Music Club	MCCD-179	England	1995	14.99
Korner, Alexis	Blues Incorporated	CD	Line	TACD-9.00634-0	Germany	1988	18.99
Korner, Alexis	I Wonder Who?	CD	BGO	BGOCD136	England	2002	16.99
Korner, Alexis	Live In Paris	CD	Thunderbolt	CDTB-109	England	1997	14.99
Korner, Alexis	Me	CD	Essential	ESMCD807	England	1999	10.99
Korner, Alexis	New Generation Of Blues	CD	BGO	BGOCD102	England	1998	16.99
Korner, Alexis	On The Move	CD	Essential	ESMCD809	England	1997	10.99
Korner, Alexis	Red Hot From Alex (W/Cyril Davies)	CD	Sanctuary	06076-81273-2	U.S.A.	2003	9.99
Korner, Alexis	Sky High	CD	Indigo	IGOCD2012	England	1994	8.99
Korner, Alexis	Testament	CD	Thunderbolt	CDTB-026	England	1996	8.99
Korner, Alexis	The Lost Album	CD	Thunderbolt	CDTB-162	England	1996	19.99
Korner, Alexis	The Masters	CD	Eagle	EABCD092	Germany	1998	14.99
Korner, Alexis	The Party Album	CD	Essential	ESMCD805	England	1999	12.99
Korner, Alexis/Beefeaters	Meet You There	CD	Repertoire	REP-4440-WP	Germany	2001	12.99
Korner, Alexis/Blues Inc.	R&B From The Marquee (MFSL Gold)	CD	Mobile Fidelity	UDCD-657	U.S.A.	1962	16.99
Korner, Alexis/Charlie Watts	1961 - 1972 (Jack Bruce/Mel Collins)	CD	Castle	CCSCD150	England	1992	16.99
Korner, Alexis/Charlie Watts	Bootleg Him ! (Robert Plant/Cream)	CD	Essential	ESMCD806	England	1999	10.99
Korner, Alexis/Keith Richards	1972 - 1983 (E Clapton/P Frampton)	CD	Castle	CCSCD192	England	1992	16.99
Korner, Alexis/Keith Richards	Get Off My Cloud (Frampton/Hopkins)	CD	Sequel	NEX-CD-134	England	1996	9.99
Korner, Alexis/Rolling Stones	Musically Rich... And Famous (Clapton)	2CD	Castle	ESDCD653	England	1998	14.99
Korngold, Erich Wolfgang	The Film Music (DCC Gold Cd)	CD	DCC	GZS-1094	U.S.A.	1962	10.99
Kortchmar, Danny	Innuendo (Louise Goffin/Jim Keltner)	CD	Warner Bros.	WPCP-4162	Japan	1973	44.99
Kottke, Leo	1971-1976: Did You Hear Me?	CD	BGO	BGOCD362	England	1996	18.99
Kottke, Leo	6- and 12-String Guitar	CD	Takoma	TAKCD-6503	U.S.A.	2004	11.99
Kottke, Leo	A Shout Toward Noon	CD	Private	2007-2-P	U.S.A.	1989	8.99
Kottke, Leo	Anthology	2CD	Rhino	R2-72585	U.S.A.	1997	24.99
Kottke, Leo	Balance	CD	Chrysalis	VK-41234	U.S.A.	1979	14.99
Kottke, Leo	Balance	CD	BGO	BGOCD263	England	1995	16.99
Kottke, Leo	Best Of Capitol Years: '70 - '75	CD	Blue Note	7243-5-42312-2-3	U.S.A.	2003	9.99
Kottke, Leo	Best Of Chrysalis: '76 - '83	CD	Blue Note	7243-5-42313-2-2	U.S.A.	2003	9.99
Kottke, Leo	Burnt Lips	CD	BGO	BGOCD259	England	1996	16.99
Kottke, Leo	Burnt Lips	CD	Chrysalis	VK-41191	U.S.A.	1978	14.99
Kottke, Leo	Chewing Pine	CD	One Way	OW-18461	U.S.A.	1996	8.99
Kottke, Leo	Chewing Pine	CD	BGO	BGOCD148	England	1994	12.99
Kottke, Leo	Dreams And All That Stuff	CD	BGO	BGOCD132	England	1994	14.99
Kottke, Leo	Dreams And All That Stuff	CD	One Way	OW-18462	U.S.A.	1996	8.99
Kottke, Leo	Essential	CD	Chrysalis	F2-21852	U.S.A.	1991	14.99
Kottke, Leo	Great Big Boy	CD	Private	01005-82087-2	U.S.A.	1992	6.99
Kottke, Leo	Greenhouse	CD	BGO	BGOCD50	England	1993	12.99
Kottke, Leo	Greenhouse	CD	One Way	OW-18457	U.S.A.	1995	8.99
Kottke, Leo	Guitar Music	CD	BGO	BGOCD261	England	1995	16.99
Kottke, Leo	Guitar Music	CD	Chrysalis	VK-41328	U.S.A.	1981	14.99
Kottke, Leo	Hear The Wind Howl	CD	Disky	DC-868682	Holland	1997	8.99
Kottke, Leo	Ice Water	CD	BGO	BGOCD146	England	1994	12.99
Kottke, Leo	Ice Water	CD	One Way	OW-18458	U.S.A.	1996	8.99
Kottke, Leo	Leo Kottke/Peter Lang/John Fahey	CD	Takoma	CDP-72740	U.S.A.	1987	18.99
Kottke, Leo	Leo Live	CD	Private	01005-82132-2	U.S.A.	1995	12.99
Kottke, Leo	Live In Europe	CD	BGO	BGOCD265	England	1996	16.99
Kottke, Leo	Mudlark	CD	BGO	BGOCD101	England	1993	12.99
Kottke, Leo	Mudlark	CD	One Way	OW-18460	U.S.A.	1995	8.99
Kottke, Leo	My Father's Face	CD	Private	2050-2-P	U.S.A.	1989	8.99
Kottke, Leo	My Feet Are Smiling	CD	One Way	OW-18459	U.S.A.	1996	8.99
Kottke, Leo	My Feet Are Smiling	CD	BGO	BGOCD134	England	1994	12.99
Kattke, Leo	One Guitar, No Vocals	CD	Private	01005-82171-2	U.S.A.	1999	14.99
Kottke, Leo	Paul Bunyan (W/Jonathan Winters)	CD	BMG	74041-70780-2	U.S.A.	1990	14.99
Kottke, Leo	Paul Bunyan (W/Jonathan Winters)	CD	Windham Hill	WD-0717	U.S.A.	1990	14.99
Kottke, Leo	Peculiaroso	CD	Private	01005-82111-2	U.S.A.	1994	6.99

K

Artist	Title	Format	Label	Catalog No	Country	Released	Value
Kottke, Leo	Regards From Chuck Pink	CD	Private	2025-2-P	U.S.A.	1988	10.99
Kottke, Leo	Renfield's Laugh	CD	Private	01005-82087-2	U.S.A.	1999	8.99
Kottke, Leo	Self Titled	CD	Chrysalis	VK-41106	U.S.A.	1976	14.99
Kottke, Leo	Self Titled	CD	BGO	BGOCD257	England	1996	16.99
Kottke, Leo	Standing In My Shoes	CD	Private	01005-82146-2	U.S.A.	1997	12.99
Kottke, Leo	That's What	CD	Private	2068-2-P	U.S.A.	1990	10.99
Kottke, Leo	The Best	2CD	BGO	BGOCD277	England	2002	20.99
Kottke, Leo	Time Step	CD	Chrysalis	FV-41411	U.S.A.	1983	14.99
Kottke, Leo	Time Step	CD	BGO	BGOCD255	England	1995	16.99
Kottke, Leo/Mike Gordon	Clone (W/Mike Gordon Of Phish)	CD	Private	11662	U.S.A.	2002	8.99
Kraftwerk	Autobahn	CD	EMI	564-7-46153-2	Holland	1974	18.99
Kraftwerk	Autobahn 5 Trk Promo Sampler	CD Single	Toshiba-EMI	TOCP-50578	Japan	2000	49.99
Kraftwerk	Autobahn Tour	CD	Nippon Crown	CRCL-4035	Japan	1998	24.99
Kraftwerk	Computer World + 1	CD	Toshiba-EMI	TOCP-8974	Japan	1997	20.99
Kraftwerk	Computerwelt (Sung In German)	CD	EMI	564-7-46130-2	EU	1981	21.99
Kraftwerk	Die Mensch-Maschine (Sung German)	CD	EMI	564-7-46131-2	Germany	1978	21.99
Kraftwerk	Electric Cafe	CD	Capitol	9-25525-2	U.S.A.	1986	8.99
Kraftwerk	Expo 2000	CD Single	EMI	CDEM562	England	2000	10.99
Kraftwerk	Expo 2000 (Holographic Cover)	CD	EMI	7243-8-87984-2-6	Germany	1999	10.99
Kraftwerk	Expo 2000 (Promo)	CD Single	EMI	CDKLANG001	England	2000	12.99
Kraftwerk	Expo 2000 4 Trk. (Promo)	CD Single	Toshiba-EMI	TOCP-40135	Japan	2000	24.99
Kraftwerk	Expo 2000 Limited Edition	CD	EMI	EXPO2000GMBH	Germany	2000	12.99
Kraftwerk	Expo 2000 Remixes	CD Single	EMI	8896120	Germany	2000	12.99
Kraftwerk	Expo Remix	CD	Astralwerks	7243-8-38768-2-2	U.S.A.	2001	10.99
Kraftwerk	Radioactivity	CD	EMI	0777-7-46474-2-7	U.S.A.	1975	8.99
Kraftwerk	Radio-Aktivität (Sung In German)	CD	EMI	0777-7-46132-2-4	Germany	1975	21.99
Kraftwerk	Ralf & Florian	CD	Germanofon	941023	Germany	1973	17.99
Kraftwerk	The Man Machine	CD	Capitol	7-46039-2	U.S.A.	1978	10.99
Kraftwerk	The Mix	CD	Elektra	9-60869-2	U.S.A.	1991	8.99
Kraftwerk	The Mix	CD	EMI	7966712	Netherland	1991	8.99
Kraftwerk	The Mix (German)	CD	EMI	1C5687966502	Germany	1991	21.99
Kraftwerk	The Mix (Sung In German)	CD	Kling Klang	568-7-96650-2	Holland	1991	21.99
Kraftwerk	Tour De France	CD Single	EMI	7243-8-87421-0-8	Germany	1999	11.99
Kraftwerk	Tour De France 2003	CD	EMI	5917082	England	2003	16.99
Kraftwerk	Tour De France 2003	CD Single	EMI	CDEM626	England	2003	10.99
Kraftwerk	Tour De France 2003 (Ltd Ed.)	CD Single	Capitol	724355266026	France	2003	9.99
Kraftwerk	Trans Europa Express (Sung German)	CD	EMI	564-7-46133-2	EU	1977	21.99
Kraftwerk	Trans-Europe Express	CD	Capitol	0777-7-46473-2-8	U.S.A.	1977	8.99
Kraftwerk	Trans-Europe Express (EP)	CD Single	Capitol	C2-15620	U.S.A.	1990	29.99
Kraftwerk/Organisation	Tone Float + 1	CD	Crown	CR-0426	England	1996	18.99
Kraftwerk/Various	Trancewerk Express Vol II	CD	Cleopatra	CLP-9904-2	U.S.A.	1997	26.99
Kramer, Wayne	Citizen Wayne	CD	Epitaph	86488-2	U.S.A.	1997	7.99
Kramer, Wayne	Dangerous Madness	CD	Epitaph	86458-2	U.S.A.	1996	10.99
Kramer, Wayne	Death Tongue	CD	Progressive	PRO-023	U.S.A.	1991	15.99
Kramer, Wayne	Live At Dingwalls 1979	CD	Captain Trip	CTCD-260	Japan	1979	22.99
Kramer, Wayne	LLMF	CD	Epitaph	86539-2	U.S.A.	1998	11.99
Kramer, Wayne	The Hard Stuff +4	CD	Muscle Tone	MTR02	U.S.A.	2002	5.99
Kramer, Wayne/Pink Fairies	Cocaine Blues	CD	Total Energy	3028	U.S.A.	2000	21.99
Kramer, Wayne/Pink Fairies	Cocaine Blues	CD	Captain Trip	CTCD-348	Japan	1978	24.99
Krauss, Alison	Now That I've Found You	CD	Rounder	RCD-325	U.S.A.	1995	10.99
Kreidler/La! Neu?	Resport	CD	Captain Trip	CTCD-107	Japan	2000	11.99
Kreiger, Henry/Tom Eyen	Dreamgirls (Orig. Broadway Cast)	CD	Universal	2007-2	U.S.A.	1982	7.99
Kreyson	Crusaders	CD	Victor Ent.	VICP-5263	Japan	1993	34.99
Krieger, Robbie	Cinematix	CD	Oglio	OGL82009-2	U.S.A.	2000	14.99
Krieger, Robbie	No Habla	CD	I.R.S.	IRSD-82004	U.S.A.	1989	16.99
Krieger, Robbie	Robbie Krieger & Friends	CD	World Pacific	7-96101-2	U.S.A.	1991	18.99
Krieger, Robbie	Robby Krieger (MFSL Cafe Silver Cd)	CD	Mobile Fidelity	CAFE-CD-730	U.S.A.	1985	95.99
Krieger, Robbie	Versions/Robby Kriegger	CD	One Way	OW-33657	U.S.A.	1996	14.99

K

Artist	Title	Format	Label	Catalog No	Country	Released	Value
Krieger, Robbie Org.	Robby Krieger Org. RKO Live!	CD	One Way	OW-31371	U.S.A.	1995	12.99
Kristofferson, Kris	Singer/Songwriter	2CD	Sony	A2K48621	U.S.A.	1991	13.99
Krokus	Alive And Screamin'	CD	Spitfire	SPT-15132-2	U.S.A.	2000	14.99
Krokus	Change Of Address	CD	Ariola	74321-25868-2	Holland	1999	14.99
Krokus	Hardware	CD	Ariola	253.322	Germany	1998	13.99
Krokus	Headhunter	CD	Spitfire	SPT-15121-2	U.S.A.	2000	12.99
Krokus	Heart Attack	CD	Spitfire	SPT-15133-2	U.S.A.	2000	9.99
Krokus	Long Stick Goes Boom: The Anthology	CD	Castle	CMRCD-713	England	2003	14.99
Krokus	Metal Rendez-Vous	CD	Ariola	259.048	Germany	1998	15.99
Krokus	One Vice At A Time	CD	Ariola	254.400	Germany	1998	15.99
Krokus	Rock The Block	CD	Warner Bros.	0927-49735-2	Switzerlan	2003	15.99
Krokus	Round 13	CD	Angel Air	SJPCD031	England	1999	14.99
Krokus	Stampede	CD	Justin	JED-18	Canada	1991	14.99
Krokus	Stampede/To Rock Or Not To Be	CD	Angel Air	SJPCD042	England	1999	15.99
Krokus	Stayed Awake All Night: The Best Of	CD	Arista	ARCD-8607	U.S.A.	1989	8.99
Krokus	The Blitz	CD	Spitfire	SPT-15131-2	U.S.A.	2000	13.99
Krokus	The Definitive Collection	CD	Arista	ARCD-4638	U.S.A.	2000	8.99
Krokus	The Dirty Dozen (Very Best Of '79 - '83)	CD	Ariola	74321-13471-2	Germany	1993	12.99
Krokus	To Rock Or Not To Be	CD	Phonag	P-81100	Switzerlan	1995	11.99
Kunzel, Erich	Star Tracks	CD	Telarc	CD-80094	U.S.A.	1984	6.99
Kunzel, Erich	Symphonic Star Trek	CD	Telarc	CD-80383	U.S.A.	1996	6.99
Kursaal Flyers/Records	Chocs Away/Great Artiste	CD	On The Beach	FOAMCD-3	EU	1991	16.99
Kursaal Flyers/Records	Former Tour De Force...	CD	Line	WFCD-9.00682-0	Germany	1988	24.99
Kursaal Flyers/Records	Golden Mile/Five Live Kursaals	CD	Columbia	506-065-2	England	2002	16.99
Kursaal Flyers/Records	Hit Records: The Best Of	CD	On The Beach	FOAMCD-6	EU	2002	12.99
Kursaal Flyers/Records	In For A Spin	CD	Line	LICD-9.00067-0	Germany	1988	24.99

L

L

Artist	Title	Format	Label	Catalog No	Country	Released	Value
L. A. Guns	Live! Vampires	CD	Vertigo	PHCR-1160	Japan	1992	21.99
L.T.D.	Love Magic	CD	Pony Canyon	D32Y3590	Japan	1981	76.99
La Dusseldorf/Neu!	Individuellos (Bonus Tracks)	CD	Captain Trip	CTCD-066	Japan	2000	15.99
La Dusseldorf/Neu!	Self Titled	CD	Captain Trip	CTCD-064	Japan	2000	14.99
La Dusseldorf/Neu!	Viva	CD	Captain Trip	CTCD-065	Japan	2000	14.99
La! Neu?	Blue	CD	Captain Trip	CTCD-178	Japan	1986	22.99
La! Neu?	Cha Cha 2000:Live In Tokyo	2CD	Captain Trip	CTCD-100/101	Japan	1996	34.99
La! Neu?	Dusseldorf	CD	Captain Trip	CTCD-051	Japan	1996	22.99
La! Neu?	Gold Regen (Ma And Thomas Also)	CD	Captain Trip	CTCD-123	Japan	2000	22.99
La! Neu?	Live At Kunsthalle Dusseldorf	2CD	Captain Trip	CTCD-344/345	Japan	1998	34.99
La! Neu?	Live In Tokyo Vol. 2	2CD	Captain Trip	CTCD-176/177	Japan	1996	34.99
La! Neu?	Rembrant	CD	Captain Trip	CTCD-087	Japan	1998	22.99
La! Neu?	Zeeland (W/Klaus Dinger's Ma)	CD	Captain Trip	CTCD-086	Japan	2000	22.99
La! Neu?/Kraftwerk	Year Of The Tiger	CD	Captain Trip	CTCD-124	Japan	2000	22.99
Labrada, Gonzalo/Trio	Imagens Do Brasil	CD	Line	BSCD-9.00740-0	Germany	1990	12.99
La-Brea-Stompers	Funzo's Knuckle...(Daniel Clowes Art)	CD	DB	DB-159	U.S.A.	1993	6.99
Ladies Room	Lock And Key	CD	Sony	ESCB-1277	Japan	1992	29.99
LaFlamme, David	White Bird + Inside Out	CD	Line	LICD-9.01099-0	Germany	1991	14.99
LaFlamme, David/Linda	Workin' In The Gold Mine	CD	Davlin	CATD1-0627N	U.S.A.	2000	14.99
Lake, Greg	From The Beginning (Retrospective)	CD	Rhino	R2-72627	U.S.A.	1997	24.99
Lake, Greg	Greatest Hits Live	CD	King Biscuit	8267-8-40027-2-2	U.S.A.	2003	9.99
Lake, Greg	I Believe In Father Christmas	CD Single	Atlantic	7567-85786-2	Germany	1992	9.99
Lake, Greg	King Biscuit Flower Hour	CD	King Biscuit	7-07108-8010-2-6	U.S.A.	1995	9.99
Lake, Greg/Gary Moore	Greg Lake	CD	Zoom Club	ZCRCD42	England	2000	21.99
Lana Lane	Ballad Collection II	CD	Avalon	MICP-10214	Japan	2000	29.99

Artist	Title	Format	Label	Catalog No	Country	Released	Value
Lana Lane	Echoes From The Ocean	CD	Avalon	MICY-1106	Japan	1999	20.99
Land, Michael/George Lucas	Dig (O.S.T.) W/Bonus Cd Rom	2CD	Angel	7243-5-55567-2-1	U.S.A.	1996	5.99
Lane, Robin	Catbird Seat	CD	Ocean Music	OM-1002	U.S.A.	1995	4.99
Lane, Robin/Chartbusters	Self Titled	CD	Collector's Choice	CCM-308-2	U.S.A.	2003	8.99
Lane, Ronnie	April Fool	CD	Alchemy	PILOT-20	England	1999	11.99
Lane, Ronnie	Kuschty Rye - The Singles	CD	Alchemy	PILOT-19	England	1997	11.99
Lane, Ronnie	Rocket 69	2CD	Alchemy	PILOT-69	England	2001	14.99
Lang, Jonny	Missing Your Love (Promo)	CD Single	A&M	AMCDP-00514	U.S.A.	1997	8.99
Lang, Jonny	Still Rainin' (Promo)	CD Single	A&M	AMCDP-00763	U.S.A.	1996	5.99
Lang, Jonny/Big Bang	Smokin'	CD	Disque Americ	0JAT1<1195>	U.S.A.	1995	14.99
Lanois, Daniel	Acadie	CD	Warner Bros.	9-25969-2	U.S.A.	1989	24.99
Lanois, Daniel	For The Beauty Of Wynona	CD	Warner Bros.	9-45030-2	U.S.A.	1993	10.99
Lanois, Daniel	The Maker	CD Single	Opal	921-423-2	Germany	1989	10.99
Lanois, Daniel	The Messenger (Promo)	CD Single	Warner Bros.	PRO-CD-6316	U.S.A.	1990	13.99
Lanz, David	An Evening With David Lanz	CD	Narada	72438-47024-2-7	U.S.A.	1999	13.99
Lanz, David	Beloved: A David Lanz Collection	CD	Narada	ND-64009	U.S.A.	1999	12.99
Lanz, David	Cristofori's Dream	CD	Narada	72438-49663-2-0	U.S.A.	1999	7.99
Lanz, David	East Of The Moon	CD	Decca	289-466-967-2	U.S.A.	1999	5.99
Lanz, David	Return To The Heart	CD	Narada	CD-4005	U.S.A.	1991	10.99
Lanz, David	Sacred Road	CD	Narada	ND-64010	U.S.A.	1996	8.99
Lanz, David	Skyline Firedance: Orchestral Works	2CD	Narada	ND2-64001	U.S.A.	1990	14.99
Lanz, David	Songs From An English Garden	CD	Narada	72438-45447-2-0	U.S.A.	1998	11.99
Lanz, David/Paul Speer	Bridge Of Dreams	CD	Narada	ND-63024	U.S.A.	1993	8.99
Laraaji	Ambient 3: Days Of Radiance	CD	Editions EG	EEGCD-19	U.S.A.	1980	14.99
Laraaji/Audio Active	The Way Out Is The Way In	CD	All Saints	ASCD26	England	1995	9.99
Larry/The Movers	Best Intentions	CD	Line	LICD-9.01319-0	Germany	1995	14.99
Larson, Nicolette	Very Best Of	CD	Rhino	R2-75833	U.S.A.	1999	8.99
Last	L.A. Explosion	CD	Line	LICD-9.01134-0	Germany	1991	10.99
Last Poets	Best Of The Prime Time Rhyme Vol. 1	CD	On The One	L.P.1	France	1988	14.99
Last Poets	Best Of The Prime Time Rhyme Vol. 2	CD	On The One	SP-31CD	France	1988	14.99
Last Poets	Freedom Express	CD	Celluloid	CELD6172	Holland	1990	9.99
Last Poets	This Is Madness	CD	Sunspots	SPOT-512-CD	Italy	2002	11.99
Laswell, Bill	Filmtracks 2000	CD	Tzadik	TZ-7511	U.S.A.	2001	11.99
Laswell, Bill	Hashshisheen Soundtrack	CD	Sub Rosa	SR-154-CD	Belgium	2000	14.99
Laswell, Bill	Invisible Design	CD	Tzadik	TZ-7044	U.S.A.	1999	11.99
Laswell, Bill/Pete Namlook	Outland 3	CD	Ambient World	AW-027	Germany	1998	38.99
Lattisaw, Stacy	With You	CD	Cotillion	16049-2	U.S.A.	1990	14.99
Lauper, Cyndi	Hat Full Of Stars	CD	Epic	EK-52878	U.S.A.	1993	10.99
Lauper, Cyndi	Merry Christmas... Have A Nice Life	CD	Epic	EK-69611	U.S.A.	1998	8.99
Lauper, Cyndi	She's So Unusual + 3	CD	Epic	EK-62169	U.S.A.	2000	9.99
Lauper, Cyndi	Shine	CD	Oglio	OGL-82015-2	U.S.A.	2001	12.99
Lauper, Cyndi	Sisters Of Avalon	CD	Epic	EK-66433	U.S.A.	1996	8.99
Lauper, Cyndi	The Best Remixes	CD	Sony	ESCA-6628	Japan	1996	24.99
Lauper, Cyndi	Time After Time - Best Of (Gold Cd)	CD	Sony	501156-2	Germany	2000	12.99
Lauper, Cyndi	True Colors	CD	Epic	RK-40313	U.S.A.	1988	10.99
Lauper, Cyndi	Twelve Deadly Cyns...And Then Some	CD	Epic	EK-66100	U.S.A.	1994	8.99
Lawley, Linda	Linda Lawley	CD	Line	LICD-9.00800-0	Germany	1989	12.99
Lawley, Linda	Love Is Strange	CD Single	Line	LICD-9.00962-E	Germany	1990	3.99
Lazy Poker	Lazy Poker	CD	Line	FBCD-9.00972-0	Germany	1990	14.99
Leary, Timothy	Beyond Life (Legend Of A Mind '97)	CD	Mercury	314-534-216-2	U.S.A.	1997	13.99
Leary, Timothy	The Psychedelic Experience	CD	Locust	LOCUST-27	U.S.A.	2003	12.99
Leary, Timothy/Jimi Hendrix	Turn On, Tune In, Drop Out (Hendrix)	CD	Mercury	PERF-389CD	U.S.A.	1967	11.99
Leatherwolf	Self Titled	CD	Island	7-90660-2	U.S.A.	1987	29.99
Leatherwolf	Street Ready	CD	Island	7-91072-2	U.S.A.	1989	11.99
Leatherwolf	Wide Open	CD	Perris	PER0020-2	Canada	1999	11.99
Led Zeppelin	Baby Come On Home (Promo)	CD Single	Atlantic	PRCD-5255-2	U.S.A.	1993	19.99
Led Zeppelin	BBC Session In-Store Play (DJ)	CD	Atlantic	PRCD-8401-2	U.S.A.	1997	39.99
Led Zeppelin	BBC Sessions	2CD	Atlantic	83061-2	U.S.A.	1997	14.99

L

Artist	Title	Format	Label	Catalog No	Country	Released	Value
Led Zeppelin	Boxed Set 2 (Black Part 2 Crop Set)	2CD	Atlantic	82477-2	U.S.A.	1993	19.99
Led Zeppelin	Coda	CD	Atlantic	92444-2	U.S.A.	1994	8.99
Led Zeppelin	Communication Breakdown (Promo)	CD Single	Atlantic	PRCD-8402	U.S.A.	1997	14.99
Led Zeppelin	Complete Studio Recordings Box Set	10 CD	Atlantic	7-82526-2	U.S.A.	1993	99.99
Led Zeppelin	Girl I Love Enhanced Video (Promo)	CD Single	Atlantic	PRCD-8376-2	U.S.A.	1997	49.99
Led Zeppelin	Houses Of The Holy	CD	Atlantic	82638-2	U.S.A.	1994	9.99
Led Zeppelin	How The West Was Won	3CD	Atlantic	83587-2	U.S.A.	2003	21.99
Led Zeppelin	II	CD	Atlantic	82633-2	U.S.A.	1994	7.99
Led Zeppelin	III	CD	Atlantic	82678-2	U.S.A.	1994	8.99
Led Zeppelin	In Through The Out Door	CD	Atlantic	92443-2	U.S.A.	1994	9.99
Led Zeppelin	Interview Disc 2003 (Promo)	CD	Atlantic	PRCD-301150	U.S.A.	2003	29.99
Led Zeppelin	IV (Zoso)	CD	Atlantic	82638-2	U.S.A.	1994	12.99
Led Zeppelin	Led Zeppelin (Self Titled)	CD	Atlantic	82632-2	U.S.A.	1994	10.99
Led Zeppelin	Led Zeppelin Box Set (Crop)	4CD	Atlantic	7-82144-2	U.S.A.	1990	33.99
Led Zeppelin	Physical Graffiti	2CD	Atlantic	92442-2	U.S.A.	1994	14.99
Led Zeppelin	Presence	CD	Atlantic	92439-2	U.S.A.	1994	9.99
Led Zeppelin	Profiled (Promo Interviews)	CD	Atlantic	PRCD-3629-2	U.S.A.	1990	14.99
Led Zeppelin	Profiled/Selection Remasters (Promo)	2CD	Atlantic	LZ-PRO1-2	Australia	1990	249.99
Led Zeppelin	Rare Interviews	CD	Master Tone	8238	England	1997	5.99
Led Zeppelin	Remasters (Zeppelin Shaped Promo)	CD	Atlantic	CD-LZ1	England	1990	44.99
Led Zeppelin	Remasters Box Set	3CD	Atlantic	7-82371-2	U.S.A.	1990	19.99
Led Zeppelin	Remasters Sampler (Promo)	CD	Atlantic	95289-2	France	1990	49.99
Led Zeppelin	Sampler (How The West...) Promo	CD	Atlantic	PRCD-301140	U.S.A.	2003	39.99
Led Zeppelin	Sampler Originals Vs. Covers (Promo)	2CD	Atlantic	ASCD-94/95	Japan	1995	224.99
Led Zeppelin	Song Remains Same (Remastered)	2 Mini Lp	Warner Bros.	WPCR-11619-20	Japan	2003	34.99
Led Zeppelin	Special Sampler (Promo)	CD	East West	ASCD-112	Japan	1996	104.99
Led Zeppelin	Special Sampler (Promo)	CD	Atlantic	ASCD-112	Japan	1996	499.99
Led Zeppelin	The Best Of: Early Days	CD	Atlantic	83268-2	U.S.A.	1999	8.99
Led Zeppelin	The Best Of: Latter Days	CD	Atlantic	83278-2	U.S.A.	2000	8.99
Led Zeppelin	The Girl I Love/ L. Z. Medley (Promo)	CD	Atlantic	PRCD-8351	U.S.A.	1997	14.99
Led Zeppelin	Whole Lotta Love	CD Single	East West	AMCY-2403	Japan	1997	14.99
Led Zeppelin	Whole Lotta Love	CD Single	Atlantic	7567-84014-6	Germany	1997	8.99
Led Zeppelin	Whole Lotta Love (Gold)	CD Single	Atlantic	7567840142	Australia	1997	12.99
Led Zeppelin/Tribute	Encomium Sampler (DJ)	CD	Atlantic	PRCD-6117-2	U.S.A.	1995	9.99
Led Zeppelin/Tribute	Stairway To Heaven (Lou Gramm)	CD	Warner Bros.	3984-20149-2	Japan	1997	34.99
Led Zeppelin/W/Single	Stairway To Heaven (Promo Fold Out)	CD Single	Atlantic	PRCD-4424-2	U.S.A.	1992	124.99
LeDoux, Chris	Cowboys Ain't Easy To Love	CD	Capitol	CDP-7-97600-2	U.S.A.	1978	79.99
LeDoux, Chris	Life As A Rodeo Man	CD	Liberty	C2-96872	U.S.A.	1991	74.99
LeDoux, Chris	Old Cowboy Heroes	CD	Liberty	C2-97595	U.S.A.	1991	79.99
Lee Rocker/Big Blue	Atomic Boogie Hour	CD	Black Top	BT-1121	U.S.A.	1995	7.99
Lee Rocker/Big Blue	Lee Rocker's Big Blue	CD	Black Top	BT-1105	U.S.A.	1994	7.99
Lee, Albert	Black Claw/Country Fever	CD	Line	LICD-9.51057-0	Germany	1991	15.99
Lee, Albert	Head Hands & Feet - Old Soldiers..	CD	Repertoire	REP-4266-WY	Germany	1994	14.99
Lee, Albert	Heads Hands & Feet	CD	See For Miles	SEE-CD-458	England	1998	12.99
Lee, Albert	Heads Hands & Feet - Home From H	CD	See For Miles	SEE-CD-633	England	1996	13.99
Lee, Albert	Heads Hands & Feet - Tracks Plus + 2	CD	See For Miles	SEE-CD-459	England	1996	14.99
Lee, Alvin	Detroit Deisel	CD	Alfa	32XB-229	Japan	1986	29.99
Lee, Alvin	Freefall (W/George Harrison/Jon Lord)	CD	Rainman	RMCD106	U.S.A.	2003	14.99
Lee, Alvin	In Flight + 2	2CD	Rainman	RMCD107	U.S.A.	2003	14.99
Lee, Alvin	Let It Rock + 2	CD	Rainman	RMCD108	U.S.A.	2003	14.99
Lee, Alvin	Pump Iron	CD	Rainman	RMCD109	U.S.A.	2003	14.99
Lee, Alvin	RX 5 + 1	CD	Rainman	RMCD105	U.S.A.	2003	14.99
Leeds, Eric/Prince	Times Squared	CD	Paisley Park	9 27499-2	U.S.A.	1991	27.99
Left Banke	There's Gonna Be..(Complete Mercury)	CD	Mercury	848-095-2	U.S.A.	1992	39.99
Left Banke	Too	CD	Phonogram	PHCR-4236	Japan	1995	74.99
Left Banke	Too	CD	Line	LMCD-9.51167-Z	Germany	1992	17.99
Left Banke	Walk Away Renee / Pretty Ballerina	CD	Line	LMCD-9.51166-Z	Germany	1992	29.99
Left Banke	Walk Away Renee/Pretty Ballerina	CD	Phonogram	PHCR-4235	Japan	1995	104.99

L

Artist	Title	Format	Label	Catalog No	Country	Released	Value
Lehrer, Tom	Song & More Songs	CD	Rhino	R2-72776	U.S.A.	1997	16.99
Lehrer, Tom	The Remains Of Tom Lehrer	3CD	Rhino	R2-79831	U.S.A.	2000	42.99
Leigh, Mitch	Man Of La Mancha + 1 (1965 B. Cast)	CD	Decca	012-159-387-2	U.S.A.	2001	9.99
Lemon Pipers, The	The Best Of: Green Tambourine	CD	Buddah	74465-99798-2	U.S.A.	2001	8.99
Lemper, Ute	Punishing Kiss (W/Elvis Costello)	CD	Decca	289-466-473-2	U.S.A.	2000	7.99
Lennon, John	Anthology (Cloud Box Set)	4CD	Capitol	7243-8-30614-2-6	U.S.A.	1998	39.99
Lennon, John	Bedism	CD	Dressed To Kill	DRESS155	England	1980	8.99
Lennon, John	Excerpts From Anthology	CD	Capitol	7087-6-13507-2-2	U.S.A.	1998	18.99
Lennon, John	Howitis	CD	EMI	7087-6-13515-2-1	U.S.A.	1998	17.99
Lennon, John	Imagine (MFSL Gold)	CD	Mobile Fidelity	UDCD-759	U.S.A.	2003	24.99
Lennon, John	Imagine (O.S.T.)	CD	EMI	7-90803-2	U.S.A.	1988	8.99
Lennon, John	Imagine + 1	CD	EMI	7243-5-24858-2-6	U.S.A.	2000	8.99
Lennon, John	In His Life	CD	Master Tone	8048	Holland	1996	7.99
Lennon, John	Jealous Guy	CD Single	Parlophone	CDR-6199	England	1988	7.99
Lennon, John	John Lennon Collection Vol 1/2 Int.	2CD	Dressed To Kill	ONEPAK556/557	England	2000	14.99
Lennon, John	Lennon (Box Set)	4CD	Capitol	7-95221/4-2	U.S.A.	1990	34.99
Lennon, John	Lennon Legend (Gold Cd)	CD	Universal	2000-883-081	Taiwan	2000	19.99
Lennon, John	Live In New York	CD	EMI	546196	U.S.A.	1986	8.99
Lennon, John	Love (3" Cd)	CD	Toshiba-EMI	TODP-2555	Japan	1998	12.99
Lennon, John	Menlove Ave.	CD	EMI	7-46576-2	U.S.A.	1986	10.99
Lennon, John	Mind Games	CD	EMI	7-46769-2	U.S.A.	1973	8.99
Lennon, John	Plastic Ono Band - Live Toronto 1969	CD	EMI	0777-7-90428-2-1	U.S.A.	1995	15.99
Lennon, John	Shaved Fish (Orig Japanese Pressing)	CD	EMI	CDP-7-46642-2	Japan	1985	39.99
Lennon, John	Sometime In New York City	2CD	EMI	0777-7-93850-2-7	U.S.A.	1972	13.99
Lennon, John	Starting Over (Promo)	CD	EMI	7087-6-15670-2-1	U.S.A.	2000	13.99
Lennon, John	The John Lennon Collection	CD	EMI	7-91516-2	U.S.A.	1989	7.99
Lennon, John	The John Lennon Collection (DJ)	CD	Toshiba-EMI	SPCD-1	Japan	1989	126.99
Lennon, John	The Last Word (Interview)	CD	Baktabak	CBAK4014	England	1980	7.99
Lennon, John	Walls And Bridges	CD	EMI	7-46768-2	U.S.A.	1974	8.99
Lennon, John	Wonsaponatime	CD	EMI	7234-4-97639-2-0	U.S.A.	1998	8.99
Lennon, John/Yoko Ono	Double Fantasy (MFSL Gold Disc)	CD	Mobile Fidelity	UDCD-600	U.S.A.	1980	33.99
Lennon, John/Yoko Ono	Double Fantasy (Orig Pressing)	CD	Geffen	2001-2	U.S.A.	1984	7.99
Lennon, John/Yoko Ono	Double Fantasy + 3	CD	EMI	7243-5-28739-2-0	U.S.A.	2000	9.99
Lennon, John/Yoko Ono	Milk And Honey + 4	CD	Toshiba-EMI	TOCP-65535	Japan	2001	34.99
Lennon, John/Yoko Ono	Plastic Ono Band + 2	CD	EMI	7243-5-28740-2-6	U.S.A.	2000	12.99
Lennon, John/Yoko Ono	Plastic Ono Band + 2 (MFSL Gold)	CD	Mobile Fidelity	UDCD-760	U.S.A.	2003	24.99
Lennon, John/Yoko Ono	Unfinished Music No. 1 :Two Virgins	CD	Rock Classics	449818-2	Germany	1988	13.99
Lennon, John/Yoko Ono	Unfinished Music No. 1: 2 Virgins + 1	CD	Rykodisc	RCD-10411	U.S.A.	1997	8.99
Lennon, John/Yoko Ono	Unfinished Music No. 2: Life With + 2	CD	Rykodisc	RCD-10412	U.S.A.	1997	8.99
Lennon, John/Yoko Ono	Wedding Album + 3	CD	Rykodisc	RCD-10413	U.S.A.	1997	8.99
Lennon, Julian	Help Yourself	CD	Atlantic	7-82280-2	U.S.A.	1991	7.99
Lennon, Julian	Mr. Jordan	CD	Atlantic	7-81928-2	U.S.A.	1989	9.99
Lennon, Julian	Now You're In Heaven	CD Single	Atlantic	PR-2653-2	U.S.A.	1989	4.99
Lennon, Julian	Photograph Smile	CD	4tune Music	MFAR-44CD	England	1998	7.99
Lennon, Julian	The Secret Value Of Daydreaming	CD	Atlantic	7-81640-2	U.S.A.	1986	8.99
Lennon, Julian	Valotte	CD	Atlantic	7-80184-2	U.S.A.	1984	8.99
Lennon, Julian	VH1 Behind The Music	CD	Rhino	R2-74361	U.S.A.	2001	8.99
Lennon, Julian	You're The One	CD Single	Atlantic	PR-2741-2	U.S.A.	1989	4.99
Lennon, Sean	Half Horse/Half Musician	CD	Toshiba-EMI	TOCP-61010	Japan	1999	7.99
Lennon, Sean	Half Horse/Half Musician (Promo)	CD	Capitol	D-PRO-9005	U.S.A.	1999	13.99
Lennon, Sean	Into The Sun	CD	Grand Royal	7243-4-94551-2-2	U.S.A.	1998	7.99
Lennon, Sean/Cibo Matto	Stereo Type A	CD	Warner Bros.	9-47345-2	U.S.A.	1999	8.99
Lennon, Sean/Cibo Matto	Super Relax	CD	Warner Bros.	9-46478-2	U.S.A.	1997	14.99
Lennon, Sean/Cibo Matto	Viva! La Woman	CD	Warner Bros.	9-45989-2	U.S.A.	1996	9.99
Lennox, Annie	Bare	CD	J Records	82876-52350-2	U.S.A.	2003	8.99
Lennox, Annie	Bare (W/Bonus DVD)	2CD	J Records	82876-52072-2	U.S.A.	2003	21.99
Lennox, Annie	Diva	CD	Arista	07822-18704-2	U.S.A.	1992	5.99
Lennox, Annie	In-Store Sampler (Promo)	CD	Arista	ASCD-2873	U.S.A.	1995	24.99

L

Artist	Title	Format	Label	Catalog No	Country	Released	Value
Lennox, Annie	Medusa	CD	RCA	74321-25717-2	U.S.A.	1995	7.99
Lennox, Annie	Medusa/Live In Central Park (9 Trks)	2CD	BMG	73847-69527-2	U.S.A.	2001	12.99
Leonard, Scott/Bee Gees	My Favorite: The Bee Gees	CD	Sony	SRCS-8043	Japan	1996	45.99
Lerner/Lowe	Paint Your Wagon (O.S.T.)	CD	MCA	MCAD-37099	U.S.A.	1977	8.99
Le-Roux	So Fired Up	CD	RCA	JAC2000	Japan	1983	21.99
Le-Roux	Up	CD	Zoom Club	ZCRCD54	England	1980	17.99
Lesh, Phi/Friends	Mason's Children Promo	CD Single	Columbia	CSK-59828	U.S.A.	2002	3.99
Lesh, Phi/Friends	There And Back Again (W/Bonus Cd)	2CD	Columbia	CK-86624	U.S.A.	2002	19.99
Lesh, Phil/Friends	Highlights Volume 1	2CD	Arista	GDCD-4401	U.S.A.	1999	13.99
Let's Active	Big Plans For Everybody	CD	I.R.S.	IRSD-5703	U.S.A.	1986	29.99
Let's Active	Cypress/Afoot	CD	I.R.S.	CD-70056	U.S.A.	1989	18.99
Let's Active	Every Dog Has His Day	CD	I.R.S.	IRSD-42151	U.S.A.	1988	19.99
Levin, Pete/Danny Gottlieb	Masters In This Hall (New Age Xmas)	CD	Rhino	R2-79426	U.S.A.	1990	24.99
Levin, Tony	Pieces Of The Sun	CD	Narada	72438-11626-2-0	U.S.A.	2002	11.99
Levin, Tony	Waters Of Eden	CD	Narada	72438-49132-2-9	U.S.A.	2000	14.99
Levin, Tony	World Diary	CD	Pony Canyon	PCCY-00860	Japan	1995	34.99
Levin, Tony/Arista All Stars	Blue Montreux Vol. 1 & 2	CD	BMG Victor	BVCJ-37065/6	Japan	1999	99.99
Levin, Tony/Band	Double Expresso	2CD	Narada	PD2-42523	U.S.A.	2000	14.99
Levin, Tony/Liquid Tension E	Liquid Tension Experiment 1	CD	Magna Carta	MA-9023-2	U.S.A.	1998	8.99
Levin, Tony/Liquid Tension E	Liquid Tension Experiment 2	CD	Magna Carta	MA-9035-2	U.S.A.	1999	8.99
Levin, Tony/Marotta/Gorn	From The Caves Of The Iron Mountain	CD	Discipline Global	DGM-9706	England	1997	7.99
Levin, Tony/Spin 1ne 2wo	Spin 1ne 2wo (P Carrack/R Hine)	CD	Columbia	473-910-2	Italy	1993	29.99
Lewie, Jona	The Best Of Jona Lewie	CD	Metro	METRCD077	England	2002	9.99
Lewis, Bobby	Tossin' & Turnin'	CD	Line	BLCD-9.00323-L	Germany	1988	19.99
Lewis, Donna/Richard Marx	At The Beginning (Anastasia O.S.T.)	CD	Atlantic	2-84037	U.S.A.	1997	7.99
Lewis, Huey/Clover	Unavailable	CD	Lemon	CDLEM16	England	2003	12.99
Lewis, Huey/News	Fore!	CD	Disky	SI-859522	Holland	1986	8.99
Lewis, Huey/News	Four Chords & Several Years Ago	CD	Elektra	61500-2	U.S.A.	1994	7.99
Lewis, Huey/News	Hard At Play	CD	EMI	7-93355-2	U.S.A.	1991	7.99
Lewis, Huey/News	Huey Lewis & The News/Picture This	CD	BGO	BGOCD417	England	1998	16.99
Lewis, Huey/News	Plan B	CD	Silvertone	01241-41767-2	U.S.A.	2001	7.99
Lewis, Huey/News	Sports (Expanded) + 5	CD	Chrysalis	72435-20669-2-6	U.S.A.	1999	10.99
Lewis, Huey/News	Sports (MFSL Gold Cd)	CD	Mobile Fidelity	UDCD-509	U.S.A.	1983	38.99
Lewis, Huey/News	Sports/Small World.	CD	BGO	BGOCD432	England	1998	16.99
Lewis, Huey/News	The Only One	CD	Disky	DC-882822	Holland	1997	8.99
Lewis, Huey/News	Time Flies.. The Best Of	CD	Elektra	61977-2	U.S.A.	1996	8.99
Lewis, Jerry Lee	16 Thrillers From The Killer	CD	Varese	302-061-269-2	U.S.A.	2003	8.99
Lewis, Jerry Lee	25 All-Time Greatest Sun Recordings	CD	Varese	302-066-129-2	U.S.A.	2000	8.99
Lewis, Jerry Lee	All Killer, No Filler:The Anthology Of	2CD	Rhino	R2-71216	U.S.A.	1993	29.99
Lewis, Jerry Lee	Best Of Jerry Lee Lewis, Vol. 2	CD	Mercury	822-789-2	U.S.A.	1987	24.99
Lewis, Jerry Lee	Classic Box Set	8 CD	Bear Family	BCD-15420	Germany	1989	109.99
Lewis, Jerry Lee	Complete Palomino Club Recordings	2CD	Rhino	R2-70385	U.S.A.	1989	54.99
Lewis, Jerry Lee	Golden Hits Of	CD	Smash	826-251-2	U.S.A.	1987	14.99
Lewis, Jerry Lee	Heartbreak	CD	Rhino	R2-70697	U.S.A.	1992	14.99
Lewis, Jerry Lee	Honky Tonk Rock 'N' Roll Piano Man	CD	ACE	CDCHD-332	England	1991	15.99
Lewis, Jerry Lee	I Am What I Am	CD	MCA	MCAD-5478	U.S.A.	1984	24.99
Lewis, Jerry Lee	I'm On Fire	CD	Polydor	826-139-2	U.S.A.	1985	24.99
Lewis, Jerry Lee	Jerry Lee Lewis (Debut Album)	CD	Rhino	R2-70656	U.S.A.	1957	8.99
Lewis, Jerry Lee	Jerry Lee's Greatest (2nd Album)	CD	Rhino	R2-70657	U.S.A.	1961	8.99
Lewis, Jerry Lee	Killer: The Mercury Years	CD	Mercury	836-935-2	U.S.A.	1989	13.99
Lewis, Jerry Lee	Killer: Vol. 2 (1969 - 72)	CD	Mercury	836-938-2	U.S.A.	1989	13.99
Lewis, Jerry Lee	Killer: Vol.3 (1973 - 77)	CD	Mercury	836-941-2	U.S.A.	1989	13.99
Lewis, Jerry Lee	Live At The Star Club Hamburg	CD	Rhino	R2-70268	U.S.A.	1992	15.99
Lewis, Jerry Lee	Live At The Star Club, Hamburg + 1	CD	Bear Family	BCD-15467	Germany	1994	15.99
Lewis, Jerry Lee	Live At The Vapors Club	CD	ACE	CDCHD-326	England	1991	16.99
Lewis, Jerry Lee	Mercury Smashes/Rockin' Sessions	10 CD	Bear Family	BCD-15784	Germany	2000	147.99
Lewis, Jerry Lee	Mercury/Smash Years Recordings + 4	CD	Collectables	5694	U.S.A.	1996	8.99
Lewis, Jerry Lee	Milestone (Sun & Smash 1956-77)	CD	Rhino	R2-71499	U.S.A.	1989	14.99

L

Artist	Title	Format	Label	Catalog No	Country	Released	Value
Lewis, Jerry Lee	Monsters/Roots	CD	Collectables	6439	U.S.A.	1999	8.99
Lewis, Jerry Lee	My Fingers Do The Talkin'	CD	MCA	MCAD-5387	U.S.A.	1982	24.99
Lewis, Jerry Lee	Original Golden Hits, Vol. 1 - 2	CD	Collectables	6426	U.S.A.	1999	8.99
Lewis, Jerry Lee	Original Sun Greatest Hits Box Set	4CD	Rhino	R2-70255	U.S.A.	1989	49.99
Lewis, Jerry Lee	Original Sun's Greatest	CD	Rhino	R2-70255	U.S.A.	1983	10.99
Lewis, Jerry Lee	Pretty Much Country	CD	ACE	CDCHD-348	England	1992	13.99
Lewis, Jerry Lee	Rocket 88	CD	Rhino	R2-70698	U.S.A.	1992	14.99
Lewis, Jerry Lee	Rockin' My Life Away	CD	Warner Bros.	26689-2	U.S.A.	1991	12.99
Lewis, Jerry Lee	Rockin' Rhythm.../Golden Cream...	CD	Collectables	6428	U.S.A.	1999	8.99
Lewis, Jerry Lee	Rockin' The Blues: 25 Great Sun R	CD	Varese	302-066-384-2	U.S.A.	2002	8.99
Lewis, Jerry Lee	Southern Roots/Boogie Woogie C M	CD	Raven	RVCD-173	Australia	2004	12.99
Lewis, Jerry Lee	Taste Of Country/Ole Tyme Country M	CD	Collectables	6430	U.S.A.	1999	8.99
Lewis, Jerry Lee	The E.P. Collection, Vol. 1	CD	See For Miles	SEE-CD-307	England	1996	16.99
Lewis, Jerry Lee	The E.P. Collection, Vol. 2	CD	See For Miles	SEE-CD-397	England	1996	16.99
Lewis, Jerry Lee	The Ferriday Fireball	CD	Charly	CD-1	England	1986	19.99
Lewis, Jerry Lee	The Greatest Live Show On Earth	CD	Bear Family	BCD-15608	Germany	1991	18.99
Lewis, Jerry Lee	The Greatest Live Show On Earth	CD	Collectables	5694	U.S.A.	1997	8.99
Lewis, Jerry Lee	The Greatest Live Show On Earth	CD	Smash	830-528-2	U.S.A.	1987	18.99
Lewis, Jerry Lee	The Locust Years... Box Set	8 CD	Bear Family	BCD-15783	Germany	1994	109.99
Lewis, Jerry Lee	The Session	CD	Mercury	822-751-2	U.S.A.	1987	24.99
Lewis, Jerry Lee	Wild One: Rare Tracks From	CD	Rhino	R2-70899	U.S.A.	1989	22.99
Lewis, Jerry Lee	Would You Take Another Chance..	CD	Mercury	830-399-2	U.S.A.	1987	24.99
Lewis, Jerry Lee/Albert Lee	Session In London (Peter Frampton)	CD	PolyGram	822-751-2	U.S.A.	1973	49.99
Lewis, Ramsey	Goin' Latin	CD	MCA Victor	MVCJ-19030	Japan	1998	32.99
Lewis, Ramsey	Hang On Ramsey/Wade In The Water	CD	BGO	BGOCD396	England	1998	14.99
Lewis, Ramsey	Maiden Voyage (And More)	CD	Chess	GRD-804	U.S.A.	1994	12.99
Lewis, Ramsey	Priceless Jazz Collection (18)	CD	Chess	GRD-9898	U.S.A.	1998	8.99
Lewis, Ramsey	Ramsey Lewis Trio: In Person 1960-67	2CD	Chess	GRD2-814	U.S.A.	1998	19.99
Lewis, Ramsey	Routes	CD	Sony	SRCS-6427	Japan	1981	54.99
Lewis, Ramsey	Sun Goddess	CD	Columbia	CK-33194	U.S.A.	1974	7.99
Lewis, Ramsey	The In Crowd	CD	Argo	CDCD-1103	EEC	1990	8.99
Lewis, Ramsey/Trio	Sound Of Christmas	CD	Pilz	CD:44-5453-2	Germany	1991	12.99
Lewis, Ramsey/Trio	The In Crowd	CD	Chess	CHD-9185	U.S.A.	1990	12.99
Liberty Cage	Sleep Of The Just	CD	Line	LICD-9.01293-0	Germany	1994	12.99
Liebman, Dave	One Of A Kind	CD	Line	COCD-9.00887-0	Germany	1990	12.99
Lightfoot, Gordon	A Painter Passing Through	CD	Warner Bros.	9-46949-2	U.S.A.	1998	7.99
Lightfoot, Gordon	Cold On The Shoulder	CD	Reprise	9362-45688-2	Germany	1994	8.99
Lightfoot, Gordon	Complete Greatest Hits	CD	Rhino	R2-78287	U.S.A.	2002	12.99
Lightfoot, Gordon	Did She Mention/Back Here On E	CD	BGO	BGOCD167	England	1998	14.99
Lightfoot, Gordon	Did She Mention/Here On Earth	CD	Bear Family	BCD-15699	Germany	1994	14.99
Lightfoot, Gordon	Don Quixote	CD	Reprise	9362-45687-2	Germany	1994	9.99
Lightfoot, Gordon	Dream Street Rose	CD	Rhino	R2-78163	U.S.A.	2002	8.99
Lightfoot, Gordon	Early (Lightfoot !)/Sunday Concert	CD	BGO	BGOCD166	England	1998	14.99
Lightfoot, Gordon	East Of Midnight	CD	Warner Bros.	9-25482-2	U.S.A.	1987	8.99
Lightfoot, Gordon	Endless Wire	CD	Reprise	9362-45685-2	Germany	1994	8.99
Lightfoot, Gordon	Gord's Gold	CD	Reprise	2237-2	U.S.A.	1995	8.99
Lightfoot, Gordon	Gord's Gold, Vol. 2	CD	Warner Bros.	9-25784-2	U.S.A.	1988	10.99
Lightfoot, Gordon	If You Could Read My Mind (Stranger)	CD	Reprise	6392-2	U.S.A.	1987	8.99
Lightfoot, Gordon	Lightfoot !/The Way I Feel	CD	Bear Family	BCD-15576	Germany	1994	14.99
Lightfoot, Gordon	Old Dan's Records	CD	Rhino	R2-78162	U.S.A.	2002	8.99
Lightfoot, Gordon	Salute	CD	Rhino	R2-78165	U.S.A.	2002	8.99
Lightfoot, Gordon	Shadows	CD	Rhino	R2-78164	U.S.A.	2002	8.99
Lightfoot, Gordon	Songbook (Pair Lps)	CD	RCA	PCD-2-1081	U.S.A.	1985	13.99
Lightfoot, Gordon	Songbook [Boxed Set]	4CD	Rhino	R2-75802	U.S.A.	1999	49.99
Lightfoot, Gordon	Summer Side Of Life	CD	Reprise	9362-45686-2	Germany	1994	9.99
Lightfoot, Gordon	Summertime Dream	CD	Reprise	2246-2	U.S.A.	1976	7.99
Lightfoot, Gordon	Sunday Concert Plus + 1	CD	Bear Family	BCD-15691	Germany	1994	12.99
Lightfoot, Gordon	Sundown	CD	Reprise	2177-2	U.S.A.	1974	8.99

L

Artist	Title	Format	Label	Catalog No	Country	Released	Value
Lightfoot, Gordon	The Complete Greatest Hits	CD	Rhino	R2-78287	U.S.A.	2002	9.99
Lightfoot, Gordon	The United Artists Collection	2CD	EMI	E2-27015	U.S.A.	1995	12.99
Lightfoot, Gordon	The Way I Feel	CD	BGO	BGOCD296	England	1998	14.99
Lightfoot, Gordon	Waiting For You	CD	Warner Bros.	9-45208-2	U.S.A.	1993	9.99
Lil' Kim Feat. Phil Collins	In The Air Tonite	CD Single	Warner Bros.	8573-89707-5	Germany	2001	10.99
LiLiPUT	LiLiPUT	2CD	Kill Rock Stars	KRS-373	U.S.A.	2001	19.99
Lillian Axe	Fields Of Yesterday	CD	Z Records	ZR1997013	England	1999	19.99
Lillian Axe	Live 2002	2CD	Red/Gold Int.	RGI-2006	U.S.A.	2002	15.99
Lillian Axe	Love And War	CD	MCA	MCAD-6301	U.S.A.	1989	40.99
Lillian Axe	Out Of Darkness, Into Light (1987-89)	CD	I.R.S.	X2-13133	U.S.A.	1991	21.99
Lillian Axe	Poetic Justice	CD	I.R.S.	X2-13129	U.S.A.	1992	10.99
Lillian Axe	Psychoschizophrenia	CD	I.R.S.	0777-7-13198-2-2	U.S.A.	1993	13.99
Lillian Axe	Self Titled	CD	MCA	MCAD-42146	U.S.A.	1988	24.99
Lindisfarne	Amigos	CD	Castle	CLACD384	England	1993	7.99
Lindisfarne	Another Fine Mess Live	CD	Code 90	NINETY-5	France	1993	6.99
Lindisfarne	Anthology : Road To Kingdom Come	2CD	Essential	ESACD884	England	2000	11.99
Lindisfarne	Archive	CD	Rialto	RMCD-222Z	England	1998	19.99
Lindisfarne	Back And Fourth	CD	Essential	ESM-CD-811	England	1999	9.99
Lindisfarne	Back On The Tyne	2CD	Eagle	EDM-CD-131	Germany	2002	12.99
Lindisfarne	Blues From The Bothy	CD Single	River City	RCR-9702EP	England	1997	6.99
Lindisfarne	BT 3 (Buried Treasures, Vol. 3)	CD	Siren	SRNC202CD	England	2002	8.99
Lindisfarne	Buried Treasures, Vol. 1	CD	Virgin	0777-7-86596-2-4	England	2000	8.99
Lindisfarne	Buried Treasures, Vol. 2	CD	Virgin	0777-7-86597-2-3	England	2000	8.99
Lindisfarne	Buried Treasures, Vol. 3	CD	Blueprint	BP4776CD	England	2001	8.99
Lindisfarne	Caught In The Act	CD	Castle	CCSCD346	England	1992	8.99
Lindisfarne	City Songs: Live On The BBC	CD	Alchemy	PILOT-34	England	2001	11.99
Lindisfarne	Complete BBC Recordings 1971-1975	5CD	Alchemy	FOGBOX 1	England	2000	99.99
Lindisfarne	Cropredy Concert	CD	Mooncrest	CRESTCD-024	England	1997	11.99
Lindisfarne	Dance Your Life Away	CD	Castle	CLACD383	England	1993	6.99
Lindisfarne	Day Of The Jackal	CD Single	Essential	ESSX2026	England	1993	6.99
Lindisfarne	Dealer's Choice	CD	Alchemy	PILOT-36	England	1998	11.99
Lindisfarne	Dingly Dell + 1	CD	Castle	CASCD1057	England	1988	7.99
Lindisfarne	Elvis Lives On The Moon	CD	Essential	ESMCD391	England	2001	6.99
Lindisfarne	Fog On The Tyne + 2	Mini Lp	Toshiba-EMI	TOCP-67262	Japan	2000	33.99
Lindisfarne	Fog On The Tyne + 2	CD	Castle	CASCD1050	England	1988	7.99
Lindisfarne	Fog On The Tyne Classic And Live	CD	Metro	METRCD118	England	2003	7.99
Lindisfarne	Here Comes The Neighbourhood	CD	Park	PRKCD47	England	1998	6.99
Lindisfarne	Lady Eleanor	2CD	Snapper	SMD-CD-159	England	1998	11.99
Lindisfarne	Live	CD	Armoury	ARMCD025	Germany	2000	11.99
Lindisfarne	Live 1990	CD	Hannibal	HNCD-4406	England	1994	11.99
Lindisfarne	Live At The Cambridge Folk Festival	CD	Strange Fruit	CAFECD005	England	1999	14.99
Lindisfarne	Magic In The Air/Caught In The Act	2CD	Castle	CMDDD077	England	2000	16.99
Lindisfarne	Nicely Out Of Tune + 2	Mini Lp	Toshiba-EMI	TOCP-67261	Japan	2000	33.99
Lindisfarne	Nicely Out Of Tune + 2	CD	Castle	CASCD1025	England	1988	7.99
Lindisfarne	On Tap	CD	Essential	ESMCD399	England	1996	7.99
Lindisfarne	Other Side Of	CD	Mooncrest	CRESTCD-020	England	1996	6.99
Lindisfarne	Promenade	CD	Park	PRKCD60	England	2002	20.99
Lindisfarne	Run For Home Collected	CD	Music Club	MCCD305	England	1997	7.99
Lindisfarne	Self Titled	CD	Castle	PIESD166	England	1999	9.99
Lindisfarne	Sleepless Nights	CD	Castle	82310-72249-2-2	U.S.A.	1993	6.99
Lindisfarne	The Best 16 Classic Tracks	CD	Disky	VI-863012	Holland	1995	7.99
Lindisfarne	The Best Of 16 Classics	CD	Virgin	0777-7-87336-2-1	England	2003	9.99
Lindisfarne	The News	CD	Essential	ESMCD812	England	1999	10.99
Lindisfarne	The Peel Sessions	CD	Strange Fruit	SFPSCD059	England	1993	14.99
Ardisfarne	The Very Best Of	CD	EMI	592-585-2	England	2003	9.99
Lindisfarne	Time Gentlemen Please	CD	MWM	MWMCDSP60	England	2003	14.99
Lindisfarne	Untapped & Acoustic	CD	Park	PRKCD43	England	1999	20.99
Lindisfarne	We Can Make It	CD Single	Essential	ESSX2044	England	1995	5.99

L

Artist	Title	Format	Label	Catalog No	Country	Released	Value
Lindisfarne	We Can Swing Together	CD	Alchemy	PILOT-35	England	2001	11.99
Lindisfarne/Alan Hull	Back To Basics	CD	Mooncrest	CRESTCD-017	England	1994	14.99
Lindisfarne/Alan Hull	Pipedream	CD	Castle	CASCD1069	England	1990	10.99
Lindisfarne/Alan Hull	Squire	CD	Rhino	8122-73593-2	England	2002	14.99
Lindisfarne/Alan Hull	Statues And Liberties	CD	Transatlantic	TRA-CD-246	England	1997	21.99
Lindisfarne/Alan Hull	When The War Is Over	2CD	Alchemy	PILOT-37	England	2001	14.99
Lindisfarne/Rod Clements	One Track Mind +3	CD	Siren	SRNA409CD	England	2002	13.99
Lindisfarne/Rod Clements	Stamping Ground	CD	Market Square	MSMCD-107	England	2000	13.99
Lindley, David/El Rayo-X	El Rayo Live	CD	Warner Bros.	WPCP-3444	Japan	1990	22.99
Lindley, David/El Rayo-X	El Rayo-X	CD	Elektra	2-524	U.S.A.	1981	11.99
Lindley, David/El Rayo-X	Very Greasy	CD	Elektra	9-60768-2	U.S.A.	1995	9.99
Lindley, David/El Rayo-X	Win This Record	CD	Elektra	9-60178-2	U.S.A.	1982	9.99
Lindsay, Paul	Honey In The Stone	CD	Line	LICD—9.01366-0	Germany	2001	14.99
Line, Lorie	Heart And Soul	CD	Time Line	TLP-09CD	U.S.A.	1995	6.99
Line, Lorie	Lorie Line Live	CD	Time Line	TLP-12CD	U.S.A.	1996	9.99
Line, Lorie	Music From The Heart	CD	Time Line	TLP-11CD	U.S.A.	1997	8.99
Line, Lorie	Open House	CD	Time Line	TLP-14CD	U.S.A.	1997	6.99
Line, Lorie	Sharing The Season, Vol. 2 (Xmas Cd)	CD	Time Line	TLP-06-CD	U.S.A.	1993	8.99
Line, Lorie	Storyline	CD	Time Line	TLP02CD	U.S.A.	1990	6.99
Line, Lorie	The Silver Album (Xmas Cd)	CD	Time Line	TLP-18	U.S.A.	2000	6.99
Lion	Dangerous Attraction	CD	Pony Canyon	PCCY-00014	Japan	1987	43.99
Lion	Trouble In Angel City	CD	Grand Slamm	SLAMCD-5	U.S.A.	1989	20.99
Lionheart	Hot Tonight	CD	Sony	SRCS-6245	Japan	1984	33.99
Lipold, Gerhard	Mandala	CD	Line	IPCD-9.00759-0	Germany	1988	29.99
Litter	$100 Fine + 1	CD	Ktel	10002	U.S.A.	1991	14.99
Litter	Distortions + 7	CD	Arf! Arf!	AA-077	U.S.A.	1999	14.99
Litter	Emerge	CD	One Way	OW-22162	U.S.A.	1995	29.99
Litter	Live At The Mirage 1990	CD	Arf! Arf!	AA-079	U.S.A.	1998	14.99
Litter	Re-Emerge	CD	Arf! Arf!	AA-080	U.S.A.	1999	14.99
Little Angels	Big Bad World	CD Single	Polydor	POOP-20234	Japan	1989	19.99
Little Angels	Live At The Hammersmith Odeon	CD Single	Polydor	POCP-1127	Japan	1991	19.99
Little Angels	Young Gods + 3	CD	Polydor	POCP-1083	Japan	1991	44.99
Little Eden	Solitude Road	CD	Line	INCD-9.00839-0	Germany	1989	19.99
Little Feat	Ain't Had Fun Enough	CD	Zoo Ent.	72445-11097-2	U.S.A.	1995	8.99
Little Feat	As Time Goes By: The Very Best Of	CD	Warner Bros.	9548-32247-2	England	1994	21.99
Little Feat	Chinese Work Songs	CD	CMC INT.	06076-86295-2	U.S.A.	2000	8.99
Little Feat	Dixie Chicken	CD	Warner Bros.	2686-2	U.S.A.	1973	8.99
Little Feat	Down On The Farm	CD	Warner Bros.	3345-2	U.S.A.	1987	8.99
Little Feat	Down Upon The Suwannee River	2CD	Hot Tomato	HTR-0206	U.S.A.	2003	13.99
Little Feat	Extended Version	CD	BMG	75517456212	U.S.A.	2000	5.99
Little Feat	Feats Don't Fail Me Now	CD	Warner Bros.	2784-2	U.S.A.	1974	8.99
Little Feat	Highwire Act Live In St. Louis 2003	2CD	Hot Tomato	HTR-0210	U.S.A.	2003	13.99
Little Feat	Hotcakes And Outtakes: 30 Years Of	4CD	Rhino	R2-79912	U.S.A.	2000	52.99
Little Feat	Hoy-Hoy!	CD	Warner Bros.	3538-2	U.S.A.	1990	8.99
Little Feat	Kickin' It At The Barn	CD	Hot Tomato	HTR-0208	U.S.A.	2003	8.99
Little Feat	Late Night Truck Stop	2CD	Alchemy	PILOT-110	England	2001	18.99
Little Feat	Let It Roll	CD	Warner Bros.	25750-2	U.S.A.	1988	8.99
Little Feat	Little Feat	CD	Warner Bros.	1890-2	U.S.A.	1971	8.99
Little Feat	Live At Ram's Head	2CD	Hot Tomato	HTR-0205	U.S.A.	2002	13.99
Little Feat	Live From Neon Park	2CD	Zoo Ent.	72445-11129-2	U.S.A.	1996	18.99
Little Feat	Raw Tomatos, Volume 1	2CD	Hot Tomato	HTR-0203	U.S.A.	2002	13.99
Little Feat	Representing The Mambo	CD	Warner Bros.	26163-2	U.S.A.	1990	8.99
Little Feat	Ripe Tomatos, Vol. One	2CD	Hot Tomato	HTR-0204	U.S.A.	2002	13.99
Little Feat	Sailin' Shoes	CD	Warner Bros.	2600-2	U.S.A.	1972	8.99
Little Feat	Shake Me Up	CD	Morgan Creek	2959-20005-2	U.S.A.	1991	9.99
Little Feat	The Last Record Album	CD	Warner Bros.	2884-2	U.S.A.	1988	8.99
Little Feat	Time Loves a Hero	CD	Warner Bros.	3015-2	U.S.A.	1977	8.99
Little Feat	Under The Radar	CD	CMC INT.	06076-86253-2	U.S.A.	1998	7.99

Artist	Title	Format	Label	Catalog No	Country	Released	Value
Little Feat	Waiting For Columbus - Deluxe Edition	2CD	Rhino	R2-78274	U.S.A.	2002	18.99
Little Feat/Barrere & Tackett	Barrere & Tackett - Live North Cafe	CD	Relix	RRCD2115	U.S.A.	2001	7.99
Little Feat/Lowell George	Lightning Rod Man	CD	Rhino	R2-71563	U.S.A.	1993	8.99
Little Feat/Lowell George	Thanks I'll Eat It Here	CD	Warner Bros.	3194-2	U.S.A.	1979	8.99
Little Free Rock	Little Free Rock	CD	Line	TACD-9.00633-0	Germany	1988	19.99
Little River Band	Get Lucky	CD	MCA	2292-57164-2	U.S.A.	1990	11.99
Little River Band	Monsoon	CD	MCA	MCAD-42193	U.S.A.	1988	12.99
Little River Band	Reminiscing: 20th Ann Collection	2CD	Rhino	R2-71745	U.S.A.	1995	15.99
Little Village	Little Village	CD	Reprise	9-26713-2	U.S.A.	1992	9.99
Little-Richard	18 Greatest Hits	CD	Rhino	RNCD-75899	U.S.A.	1985	8.99
Little-Richard	Get Down With It: Okeh Sessions + 3	CD	Epic	EK-86668	U.S.A.	2004	8.99
Little-Richard	Good Golly Miss Molly	CD	SMS	SMS-01	England	1995	12.99
Little-Richard	Greatest Hits	CD	Prime Cuts	1330	England	1995	11.99
Little-Richard	Greatest Hits Recorded Live	CD	Epic	EK-40389	U.S.A.	1990	9.99
Little-Richard	Here's Little Richard	CD	P-Vine	PCD-1901	Japan	2003	44.99
Little-Richard	His Greatest Hits	CD	Vee-Jay	1124	U.S.A.	1964	9.99
Little-Richard	It's Real	CD	PolyGram	839-406-2	U.S.A.	1989	19.99
Little-Richard	Keep Knockin': The Best Of	CD	Repertoire	REP-4876	Germany	2002	15.99
Little-Richard	Rip It Up	CD	Chameleon	D2-74797	U.S.A.	1990	10.99
Little-Richard	Rocking With The Georgia Peach	2CD	Recall	SMD-CD-413	England	2002	12.99
Little-Richard	Self Titled (Specialty)	CD	Timeless Treasures	106	U.S.A.	1994	14.99
Little-Richard	Shag On Down By The Union Hall	CD	Specialty	SPCD-7063-2	U.S.A.	1992	8.99
Little-Richard	Shake It All About (Kids Record)	CD	Disney	60849-2	U.S.A.	1992	34.99
Little-Richard	Sings The Gospel	CD	Prime Cuts	2335	England	1996	9.99
Little-Richard	The Best Of The Vee Jay Years, Vol. 1	CD	Collectables	7247	U.S.A.	2000	9.99
Little-Richard	The Best Of The Vee Jay Years, Vol. 2	CD	Collectables	7248	U.S.A.	2000	9.99
Little-Richard	The E.P. Collection	CD	See For Miles	SEE-CD-366	England	1998	14.99
Little-Richard	The Explosive	CD	BGO	BGOCD368	England	2002	11.99
Little-Richard	The Formative Years 1951-53	CD	Bear Family	BCD-15448	Germany	1989	14.99
Little-Richard	The Georgia Peach	CD	Specialty	SPCD-7012-2	U.S.A.	1991	12.99
Little-Richard	The Specialty Box	3CD	Specialty	SPCD-8508-2	U.S.A.	1990	33.99
Little-Steven	Born Again Savage	CD	Renegade Nation	LS00199CD	U.S.A.	1999	8.99
Little-Steven	The Voice Of America	CD	Razor & Tie	RE-1984	U.S.A.	1984	84.99
Little-Steven/Disciples Of Soul	Men Without Women	CD	Razor & Tie	RE1981	U.S.A.	1991	11.99
Liverbirds	More Of	CD	Repertoire	IMS-7010-WP	Germany	1994	24.99
Liverbirds	Star - Club, Vol. 4	CD	Repertoire	IMS-7009-WP	Germany	1994	24.99
Living Earth	Living Earth	CD	Relix	RRCD-2033	U.S.A.	1988	8.99
Lizzy Borden	Deal With The Devil	CD	Metal Blade	3984-14343-2	U.S.A.	2000	11.99
Lizzy Borden	Love You To Pieces	CD	Metal Blade	3984-14089-2	U.S.A.	1995	11.99
Lizzy Borden	Love You To Pieces/Give 'Em the Axe	CD	Enigma	7-72113-2	U.S.A.	1990	16.99
Lizzy Borden	Master Of Disguise	CD	Metal Blade	3984-14067-2	U.S.A.	1994	9.99
Lizzy Borden	Menace To Society	CD	Enigma	3984-14090-2	U.S.A.	1995	10.99
Lizzy Borden	Terror Rising/Give 'Em The Axe	CD	Metal Blade	3984-14091-2	U.S.A.	1995	15.99
Lizzy Borden	The Best Of	CD	Metal Blade	3984-14052-2	England	1994	8.99
Lizzy Borden	The Murderess Metal Road Show	CD	Enigma	3984-14092-2	U.S.A.	1995	16.99
Lizzy Borden	Visual Lies + 4	CD	Metal Blade	3984-14428-2	U.S.A.	2002	11.99
Lockett, Pete/Network Sparks	From Around The World	CD	Arc	EUCD1742	England	2002	16.99
Lockett, Pete/Network Sparks	One (W/Bill Bruford)	CD	M.E.L.T. 2000	50-1001-2	England	2000	18.99
Loesser, Frank/Broadway	How To Succeed + 17 (Orig Brdwy)	CD	RCA	82876-56051-2	U.S.A.	2003	9.99
Loesser, Frank/Broadway	How/Succeed/Business...(Broderick)	CD	RCA	09026-68197-2	U.S.A.	1995	8.99
Loesser, Frank/Broadway	How/Succeed/Business...(R. Morse)	CD	RCA	60352-2-RG	U.S.A.	1961	7.99
Loesser, Frank/Movie	How/Succeed/Business (OST/Morse)	CD	Rykodisc	RCD-10728	U.S.A.	1998	29.99
Lofgren, Nils	Acoustic Live	CD	Demon	FIEND-CD-934	England	1998	11.99
Lofgren, Nils	Archive Alive!	CD	Connoisseur	NSP-CD-517	England	1997	7.99
Lofgren, Nils	Breakaway Angel	CD	Vision	1009	U.S.A.	2001	11.99
Lofgren, Nils	Code Of The Road	CD	Castle	CLACD-311	England	1993	11.99
Lofgren, Nils	Crooked Line (W/Bruce Springsteen)	CD	Rykodisc	RCD-10238	U.S.A.	1992	11.99
Lofgren, Nils	Cry Tough	CD	A&M	5409032	England	1976	36.99

L

Artist	Title	Format	Label	Catalog No	Country	Released	Value
Lofgren, Nils	Damaged Goods	CD	Pure	2230	U.S.A.	1995	7.99
Lofgren, Nils	Damaged Goods	CD	Essential	ESS-CD-337	England	1995	7.99
Lofgren, Nils	Drunken Driver	CD Single	Rykodisc	RCD5-1029	U.S.A.	1992	9.99
Lofgren, Nils	Every Breath (O.S.T.)	2CD	SPV	SPV087-89122CD	Holland	1994	12.99
Lofgren, Nils	Flip	CD	Sony	32DP-233	Japan	1986	27.99
Lofgren, Nils	Into The Night	CD	BMG	74321-59869-2	Germany	1998	9.99
Lofgren, Nils	Just A Little	CD Single	Rykodisc	RCD5-1026	U.S.A.	1992	7.99
Lofgren, Nils	Live On The Test	CD	Windsong	WHISCD-001	England	1993	14.99
Lofgren, Nils	Nils	CD	Bear Tracks	BTCD-979-421	Germany	1979	23.99
Lofgren, Nils	Nils Lofgren	CD	Rykodisc	RCD-10041	U.S.A.	1988	13.99
Lofgren, Nils	Nils Lofgren Band Live	2CD	Vision	1011	England	2003	19.99
Lofgren, Nils	Rare Tracks Collection	CD	Video Arts	VACK-2008	Japan	1994	32.99
Lofgren, Nils	Silver Lining	CD	Rykodisc	RCD-10170	U.S.A.	1991	7.99
Lofgren, Nils	Steal Your Heart	2CD	A&M	5404112	England	1996	19.99
Lofgren, Nils	Trouble's Back (W/Keith Don't Go)	CD	Rykodisc	RCD-51022	U.S.A.	1991	9.99
Lofgren, Nils	Valentine	CD Single	Castle	ESS-X-2002	England	1991	4.99
Lofgren, Nils	Wonderland	CD	MCA	MCA-001	Japan	1992	44.99
Lofgren, Nils/Grin	1+1	CD	Epic	ZK-31038	U.S.A.	1969	9.99
Lofgren, Nils/Grin	All Out	CD	Epic	477847-2	Holland	1972	9.99
Logan, Jack	Buzz Me In	CD	Capricorn	314-538-925-2	U.S.A.	1998	5.99
Loggins, Kenny	Alive	2CD	Columbia	C2K-36738	U.S.A.	1980	24.99
Loggins, Kenny	Back To Avalon	CD	Columbia	CK-40535	U.S.A.	1988	5.99
Loggins, Kenny	Celebrate M H/Nightwatch/Keep Fire	3CD	Columbia	C3K-65382	U.S.A.	1997	22.99
Loggins, Kenny	Celebrate Me Home	CD	Columbia	CK-34655	U.S.A.	1977	8.99
Loggins, Kenny	December (Christmas CD)	CD	Columbia	CK-69371	U.S.A.	1998	6.99
Loggins, Kenny	High Adventure	CD	Columbia	CK-34673	U.S.A.	1982	8.99
Loggins, Kenny	It's About Time	CD	All The Best	0001-2	U.S.A.	2003	10.99
Loggins, Kenny	Keep The Fire (W Stevie Nicks)	CD	Columbia	CK-36172	U.S.A.	1979	8.99
Loggins, Kenny	Leap Of Faith	CD	Columbia	CK-46140	U.S.A.	1991	6.99
Loggins, Kenny	More Songs From Pooh Corner	CD	Columbia	CK-63514	U.S.A.	2000	8.99
Loggins, Kenny	Nightwatch	CD	Columbia	CK-35387	U.S.A.	1978	8.99
Loggins, Kenny	Outside: From The Redwoods	CD	Columbia	CK-57391	U.S.A.	1993	6.99
Loggins, Kenny	Return To Pooh Corner	CD	Sony	LK-57674	U.S.A.	1994	5.99
Loggins, Kenny	The Essential (W/Messina)	2CD	Columbia	C2K-86282	U.S.A.	2002	18.99
Loggins, Kenny	The Unimaginable Life	CD	Columbia	CK-67865	U.S.A.	1997	6.99
Loggins, Kenny	Vox Humana	CD	Columbia	CK-39174	U.S.A.	1985	7.99
Loggins, Kenny	Yesterday, Today, Tomorrow: Gr. Hits	SACD	Columbia	SCD-67986	U.S.A.	1997	10.99
Loggins/Messina	Full Sail	CD	Columbia	CK-32540	U.S.A.	1973	7.99
Loggins/Messina	Full Sail (MFSL Gold Cd)	CD	Mobile Fidelity	UDCD-733	U.S.A.	1973	19.99
Loggins/Messina	Mother Lode	CD	Columbia	CK-33175	U.S.A.	1972	8.99
Loggins/Messina	Native Sons	CD	Columbia	CK-33578	U.S.A.	1976	9.99
Loggins/Messina	On Stage	2CD	Columbia	C2K-65488	U.S.A.	1998	17.99
Loggins/Messina	Self Titled	CD	Columbia	CK-31748	U.S.A.	1972	8.99
Loggins/Messina	Sittin' In	CD	Columbia	CK-64414	U.S.A.	1994	8.99
Loggins/Messina	Sittin' In (MFSL Silver Cd)	CD	Mobile Fidelity	MFCD-829	U.S.A.	1971	31.99
Loggins/Messina	Sittin' In (Sony Gold Cd)	CD	Columbia	CK-53815	U.S.A.	1972	27.99
Loggins/Messina	Sittin' In/Self Titled/Full Sail	3CD	Columbia	C3K-65383	U.S.A.	1997	22.99
Loggins/Messina	The Best Of Friends	CD	Columbia	CK-34388	U.S.A.	1992	5.99
Lomax, Jackie	Is This What You Want? + 5	CD	EMI	7975812	England	1991	59.99
London Pops Orchestra	Music Of Star Trek The First 30 Years...	CD	BCI	BCCD-305	U.S.A.	1993	5.99
London Symphony Orchestra	The British Invasion: Volume 1	CD	Telarc	CD-80472	U.S.A.	1997	5.99
London Symphony Orchestra	The British Invasion: Volume 2	CD	Telarc	CD-80478	U.S.A.	1998	5.99
London, Julie	Love Letters	CD	Toshiba-EMI	TOCJ-5377	Japan	1962	45.99
Lone Justice	Lone Justice	CD	Geffen	9-24060-2	U.S.A.	1985	8.99
Lonesome-Bob	Things Change	CD	LEAP	LCD-1103	U.S.A.	2002	8.99
Long Ryders, The	Anthology	2CD	PolyGram	558-280-2	U.S.A.	1998	53.99
Longet, Claudine	Run Wild, Run Free	CD	Polydor K.K.	POCM-1943	Japan	1994	34.99
Looking-Glass	Brandy (You're A Fine Girl) (Orig. LP)	CD	Sony	A-28454	U.S.A.	1998	6.99

L

Artist	Title	Format	Label	Catalog No	Country	Released	Value
Lopez, Jennifer	Ain't It Funny (Promo)	CD Single	Epic	ESK-32775	U.S.A.	2001	14.99
Lorber, Jeff/Fusion	Lift Off	CD	Arista	ARCD-8393	U.S.A.	1984	24.99
Lorber, Jeff/Fusion	Wizard Island	CD	Arista	ARCD-8081	U.S.A.	1980	24.99
Lord Sutch/Heavy Friends	Hands Of Jack The Ripper	CD	Line	LECD-9.01010-0	Germany	1991	23.99
Lord Sutch/Heavy Friends	Lord Sutch And Heavy Friends	CD	Line	LECD-9.00947-0	Germany	1990	23.99
Lord Sutch/Screaming	Midnight Man	CD	Raucous	RAUCD-070	England	2000	9.99
Lord Sutch/Screaming	Monster Rock	CD	Dominion	4322-2	U.S.A.	2000	9.99
Lord Sutch/Screaming	Rock And Horror	CD	ACE	029667106528	U.S.A.	1982	11.99
Lord, Jon	Before I Forget	CD	Purple	PUR-310	England	2001	11.99
Lord, Jon	Before I Forget (W/Bonus)	CD	RPM	RPM-126	England	1994	14.99
Lord, Jon	Gemini Suite	CD	Line	LICD-9.00122-0	Germany	1987	19.99
Lord, Jon	Live At The Basement	2CD	Point	BNR-50340	Germany	2003	11.99
Lord, Jon	Pictured Within	CD	EMI	493704-2	Germany	1999	11.99
Lord, Jon	Sarabande	CD	Line	LICD-9.00124-0	Germany	1987	11.99
Lord, Jon	Sarabande	CD	Spitfire	SPT-15077-2	U.S.A.	2001	8.99
Lord, Jon	Sarabande	CD	Purple	PUR-305	England	2000	11.99
Lord, Jon	Windows	CD	Line	MLCD-9.00113-L	Germany	1992	12.99
Lord, Jon	Windows	CD	Purple	PUR-322	England	2000	12.99
Lords Of Acid	Expand Your Head.Com	CD	Antler Subway	NR6047	U.S.A.	1999	6.99
Lords/New Church	Killer Lords + 7	CD	I.R.S.	0777-7-13178-28	Holland	1993	23.99
Lords/New Church	The Anthology	CD	Remedy	REM200206	France	2000	17.99
Lords/New Church	The Lords Of The New Church	CD	I.R.S.	CD-75029	U.S.A.	1982	11.99
Lords/New Church	The Lord's Prayer 1 + 17 (Bonus Cd)	2CD	Alchemy	PILOT-100	England	2002	14.99
Lords/New Church	The Lords Prayer 2 (W/Bonus Live Cd)	2CD	Alchemy	PILOT-126	England	2002	14.99
Los Lobos	By The Light Of The Moon	CD	Slash	9-25523-2	U.S.A.	1986	8.99
Los Lobos	Colossal Head	CD	Warner Bros.	46172-2	U.S.A.	1996	6.99
Los Lobos	Del Este de Los Angeles (Just Another..	CD	Hollywood	HR-62242-2	U.S.A.	2000	8.99
Los Lobos	El Cancionero: Mas Y Mas [Boxed Set]	4CD	Rhino	R2-76670	U.S.A.	2000	44.99
Los Lobos	Good Morning Aztlán (Gold Cd)	CD	Mobile Fidelity	UDSACD-2022	U.S.A.	2002	24.99
Los Lobos	Good Morning Aztlán (W/Bonus Cd)	2CD	Hollywood	HR-65518-2	U.S.A.	2002	15.99
Los Lobos	How Will The Wolf Survive?	CD	Slash	9-25177-2	U.S.A.	1984	8.99
Los Lobos	Just Another Band From East LA	2CD	Slash	45367-2	U.S.A.	1993	14.99
Los Lobos	Kiko	CD	Slash	9-26786-2	U.S.A.	1992	7.99
Los Lobos	La Pistola Y El Corazon	CD	Slash	9-25790-2	U.S.A.	1988	5.99
Los Lobos	Papa's Dream	CD	Music For Little	MLP-42562	U.S.A.	1995	7.99
Los Lobos	The Neighborhood	CD	Slash	9-26131-2	U.S.A.	1990	8.99
Los Lobos	The Ride	CD	Hollywood	HR-62443-2	U.S.A.	2004	8.99
Los Lobos	This Time	CD	Hollywood	HR-62185-2	U.S.A.	1998	6.99
Los Lobos	This Time (Gold CD)	CD	Mobile Fidelity	UDSACD-2024	U.S.A.	2004	24.99
Lost And Found	Everybody's Here	CD	Sunspots	SPOT-532-CD	Italy	2003	9.99
Lothar/The Hand People	Space Hymn (Complete Recordings)	CD	Acadia	ACA-8058	England	2003	14.99
Lothar/The Hand People	This Is It, Machines	CD	See For Miles	SEE-CD75	France	1991	11.99
Loudness	8186 Live	2CD	Warner Bros.	WPCV-10130/1	Japan	2000	34.99
Loudness	Best Album	CD	Nippon Columbia	COCP-31755	Japan	2000	22.99
Loudness	Best Songs Collection	2CD	Nippon Columbia	COCA-12651/2	Japan	1995	18.99
Loudness	Brand New Album	CD	Tokuma	TKCA-72403	Japan	2000	22.99
Loudness	Devil Soldier	CD	Nippon Columbia	COCA-11084	Japan	1994	19.99
Loudness	Disillusion (English Version)	CD	Nippon Columbia	COCA-12143	Japan	1994	21.99
Loudness	Disillusion (Japanese)	CD	Nippon Columbia	COCA-11124	Japan	1993	21.99
Loudness	Dragon	CD	BMG	BMCR-7027	Japan	1998	22.99
Loudness	Engine	CD	BMG	BMCR-7035	Japan	1999	22.99
Loudness	Eurobounds	CD	Nippon Columbia	COCP-31219	Japan	2001	17.99
Loudness	Ghetto Machine	CD	BMG	BMCR-7017	Japan	1997	16.99
Loudness	Ghetto Machine/Dragon	2CD	Dream Catcher	CRIDE-13	England	1999	17.99
Loudness	Heavy Metal Hippies	CD	Warner Bros.	WPCV-10172	Japan	2000	22.99
Loudness	Hurricane Eyes (English Version)	CD	Atco	07567-90619-2	U.S.A.	1987	13.99
Loudness	Hurricane Eyes (Japanese)	CD	Warner Bros.	WPCV-10133	Japan	2000	30.99
Loudness	Jealousy	CD	Warner Bros.	WPCV-10134	Japan	2000	18.99

L

Artist	Title	Format	Label	Catalog No	Country	Released	Value
Loudness	Lightning Strikes	CD	Atco	07567-90512-2-6	U.S.A.	1986	14.99
Loudness	Lightning Strikes	CD	Warner Bros.	WPCV-10129	Japan	2000	22.99
Loudness	Live-Loud-Alive: Loudness In Tokyo	2CD	Nippon Columbia	COCA-12144/5	Japan	1994	18.99
Loudness	Loud 'N' Rare	CD	Warner Bros.	WPCV-10135	Japan	2000	22.99
Loudness	Loud 'N' Raw	CD	Warner Bros.	WPCV-10173	Japan	2000	19.99
Loudness	Loudest	2CD	Warner Bros.	WPCL-556~7	Japan	1991	36.99
Loudness	Loudness	CD	Warner Bros.	WPCV-10170	Japan	1991	22.99
Loudness	Loudness Live 2002	CD	Tokuma	TKCA-72551	Japan	2000	22.99
Loudness	Masters Of Loudness	2CD	Warner Bros.	WPC6-8220~1	Japan	1996	29.99
Loudness	On The Prowl	CD	Warner Bros.	WPCV-10169	Japan	2000	22.99
Loudness	On The Prowl	CD	Wounded Bird	WOU-1637	U.S.A.	2003	10.99
Loudness	Once And For All	CD	Warner Bros.	WPCV-10171	Japan	2000	18.99
Loudness	Pandamonium	CD	Nippon Columbia	COCP-31683	Japan	2002	17.99
Loudness	Pandemonium	CD	Columbia	CK-31683	U.S.A.	2002	9.99
Loudness	Re-Masterpieces: The Best Of	CD	Columbia	CK-31755	U.S.A.	2002	11.99
Loudness	Shadows Of War	CD	Warner Bros.	WPCV-10128	Japan	2000	22.99
Loudness	Shadows/War (Lightning S/Japanese)	CD	Warner Bros.	WPCL-249	Japan	1986	22.99
Loudness	Soldier Of Fortune	CD	Warner Bros.	WPCV-10168	Japan	2000	30.99
Loudness	Soldier Of Fortune	CD	Atco	07567-91283-2	U.S.A.	1989	10.99
Loudness	Soldier's Just Came Back	CD	Nippon Columbia	COCP-31421	Japan	2000	22.99
Loudness	The Birthday Eve	CD	Nippon Columbia	COCA-11083	Japan	1993	15.99
Loudness	The Law Of Devil's Land	CD	Nippon Columbia	COCA-11123	Japan	1994	18.99
Loudness	The Very Best Of	CD	Nippon Columbia	COCA-14220	Japan	1997	21.99
Loudness	Thunder In The East	CD	Nippon Columbia	COCA-12146	Japan	1994	22.99
Loudness	Thunder In The East	CD	Wounded Bird	WOU-246	U.S.A.	2003	10.99
Loudness/Rinne Tensei	Spiritual Canoe	CD	Nippon Columbia	COCP-31280	Japan	2001	18.99
Louise, Tina	It's Time For Tina	CD	Oglio	OGL-81598-2	U.S.A.	1998	9.99
Louistine	Take Me On	CD	Line	TLCD-9.00355-0	Germany	1988	19.99
Love	Best Of	CD	Rhino	R2-73840	U.S.A.	2003	9.99
Love	Comes In Colours	CD	Raven	RVCD-29	Australia	1992	12.99
Love	Da Capo (Mono/Stereo + 1)	CD	Elektra	8122-73604-2	Germany	2002	12.99
Love	Electrically Speaking - Live + 4	CD	Yeaah!	YEAAH-49	England	2001	10.99
Love	False Start	CD	MCA	MCAD-22029	U.S.A.	1990	8.99
Love	Forever Changes (Orig. Abrupt Ending)	CD	Elektra	74013-2	U.S.A.	1967	8.99
Love	Forever Changes + 7	CD	Rhino	R2-76717	U.S.A.	2001	12.99
Love	Love - Mono/Stereo + 2	CD	Elektra	8122-73567-2	Germany	2001	14.99
Love	Love Story 1966-1972	2CD	Rhino	R2-78005	U.S.A.	1995	21.99
Love	Out Here	CD	MCA	MCAD-22030	U.S.A.	1990	19.99
Love	Out There	CD	Big Beat	CDWIKD-69	England	1990	13.99
Love	Studio/Live	CD	MCA	MCAD-22036	U.S.A.	1991	11.99
Love /Arthur Lee	S/T	CD	New Rose	ROSECD-288	France	1992	20.99
Love /Arthur Lee	The Forever Changes Concert	2CD	Snapper	SMA-CD-868	England	2003	15.99
Love /Arthur Lee	Vindicator + 5	CD	A&M	540-697-2	Germany	1997	35.99
Love /Arthur Lee/Shack	Live In Liverpool 1992	CD	Viper	CD-003	England	2000	12.99
Love Corporation	Dance Stance	CD	Creation	CRECD199	Austria	1997	15.99
Love Exchange, The	Self Titled + 6	CD	Sundazed	SC-6113	U.S.A.	2001	8.99
Love Sculpture	Blues Helping	CD	EMI	7234-4-99416-2-5	Holland	1999	17.99
Love Sculpture	Forms And Feelings	CD	EMI	538-7-48965-2	Germany	1999	12.99
Love Sculpture	Premium Gold Collection	CD	EMI	7243-5-26926-2-0	Germany	2000	11.99
Love Spit Love	Love Spit Love (With Bonus Cd Rom)	2CD	Alchemy	PILOT41	England	1994	19.99
Love Spit Love	Trysome Eatone	CD	Warner Bros.	9-46560-2	U.S.A.	1997	7.99
Loveless, Patti	Self Titled	CD	MCA	MCAD-5915	U.S.A.	1987	75.99
Lovemongers	Battle Of Evermore	CD Single	Capitol	0777-7-15953-2-5	U.S.A.	1992	16.99
Lovemongers	Kiss (Promo)	CD Single	Will	127609-1	U.S.A.	1998	16.99
Lovemongers	Lovemongers Christmas	Mini Lp	Teichiku	TECI-24079	Japan	2001	27.99
Lovemongers	Whirlygig	CD	Will	WILL048	U.S.A.	1997	12.99
Loverboy	Big Ones	CD	Columbia	CK-45411	U.S.A.	1989	8.99
Loverboy	Get Lucky	CD	Columbia	CK-37638	U.S.A.	1981	10.99

Artist	Title	Format	Label	Catalog No	Country	Released	Value
Loverboy	Keep It Up	CD	Columbia	CK-38703	U.S.A.	1983	16.99
Loverboy	Live, Loud And Loose	CD	Columbia	CK-62083	U.S.A.	2001	10.99
Loverboy	Loverboy Classics: Their Gr Hits	CD	Columbia	CK-66648	U.S.A.	1994	9.99
Loverboy	Lovin' Every Minute Of It	CD	Columbia	CK-39953	U.S.A.	1985	9.99
Loverboy	Self Titled	CD	Columbia	CK-36762	U.S.A.	1980	10.99
Loverboy	Super Hits	CD	Columbia	CK-65272	U.S.A.	1997	8.99
Loverboy	Temperature's Rising	CD	Sony	A-24191	U.S.A.	1994	5.99
Loverboy	VI	CD	CMC INT.	06076-86220-2	U.S.A.	1997	8.99
Loverboy	Wildside	CD	Columbia	CK-40893	U.S.A.	1987	6.99
Lovich, Lene	Flex	CD	Line	LICD-9.01071-0	Germany	1991	11.99
Lovich, Lene	Flex + 8	CD	Rhino	R2-70521	U.S.A.	1980	11.99
Lovich, Lene	March + 2	CD	Line	OLCD-9.91030-X	Germany	1991	11.99
Lovich, Lene	No Man's Land	CD	Line	LICD-9.01074-0	Germany	1991	11.99
Lovich, Lene	Stateless	CD	Line	LICD-9.01066-0	Germany	1991	11.99
Lovich, Lene	Stateless + 6	CD	Rhino	R2-70520	U.S.A.	1979	11.99
Lovich, Lene	Stateless/Flex	2CD	Line	LICD-9.21187-S	Germany	1992	19.99
Lovich, Lene	Wonderland	CD Single	Line	PACD-9.00870-E	Germany	1989	7.99
Lovin' Spoonful	19 Great Songs	CD	Movie Play	MP-74003	U.S.A.	1989	11.99
Lovin' Spoonful	Anthology	CD	Rhino	R2-70944	U.S.A.	1990	9.99
Lovin' Spoonful	Daydream + 5	CD	Buddah	74465-99731-2	U.S.A.	2002	8.99
Lovin' Spoonful	Do You Believe In Magic + 5	CD	Buddah	74465-99730-2	U.S.A.	2002	8.99
Lovin' Spoonful	Do You Believe In Magic/Hums	CD	RCA	75517-49500-2	U.S.A.	1995	8.99
Lovin' Spoonful	Everything Playing + 3	CD	Buddah	74465-99733-2	U.S.A.	2003	8.99
Lovin' Spoonful	Greatest hits	CD	Buddah	74465-99716-2	U.S.A.	2001	7.99
Lovin' Spoonful	Hums Of The + 6	CD	Buddah	74465-99732-2	U.S.A.	2003	8.99
Lovin' Spoonful	Live Hotel Seville (No John Sebastian)	CD	Varese	302-065-995-2	U.S.A.	1999	9.99
Lovin' Spoonful	What's Up Tiger Lily?/You're A Big Boy	CD	Razor & Tie	RE-2167-2	U.S.A.	1998	8.99
Lovin' Spoonful/Jerry Yester	Just Like The Big Time	CD	Pony Canyon	PCCY-00072	Japan	1990	55.99
Low Flying Aircraft	Low Flying Aircraft (D Cross/K Tippett)	CD	Line	COCD-9.00426-0	Germany	1987	24.99
Low Gods	Menagerie	CD	Line	TCCD-9.00614-J	Germany	1988	6.99
Lowe, Nick	16 All-Time Lowes	CD	Demon	FIEND-CD-20	England	1985	15.99
Lowe, Nick	Basher: The Best of Nick Lowe	CD	Columbia	CK-45313	U.S.A.	1989	9.99
Lowe, Nick	Dig My Mood	CD	Demon	UPSTART-038	U.S.A.	1998	12.99
Lowe, Nick	Jesus Of Cool	CD	Demon	FIEND-CD-131	England	1989	14.99
Lowe, Nick	Labour Of Lust	CD	Columbia	CK-36087	U.S.A.	1979	23.99
Lowe, Nick	Labour Of Lust	CD	Demon	FIEND-CD-182	U.S.A.	1990	14.99
Lowe, Nick	Nick Lowe & His Cowboy Outfit	CD	Demon	FIEND-CD-185	U.S.A.	1990	31.99
Lowe, Nick	Nick The Knife	CD	Demon	FIEND-CD-183	England	1990	15.99
Lowe, Nick	Nick The Knife	CD	Columbia	CK-37932	U.S.A.	1982	40.99
Lowe, Nick	Nicks Knack	CD	Demon	FIEND-CD-59	England	1986	34.99
Lowe, Nick	Party Of One + 2	CD	Upstart	UPSTART-029	U.S.A.	1995	7.99
Lowe, Nick	Pinker And Prouder Than Previous	CD	Demon	FIEND-CD-99	England	1988	21.99
Lowe, Nick	Poor Side Of Town	CD Single	Sound Circus	SCCDS-9	Japan	2001	16.99
Lowe, Nick	Pure Pop For Now People	CD	Columbia	CK-35329	U.S.A.	1978	39.99
Lowe, Nick	The Abominable Showman	CD	Demon	FIEND-CD-184	England	1990	26.99
Lowe, Nick	The Convincer	CD	Yep Roc	YEP2027	U.S.A.	2001	7.99
Lowe, Nick	The Doings Box Set	4CD	Demon	LOWE-50	England	1999	47.99
Lowe, Nick	The Impossible Bird	CD	Upstart	UPSTART-013	U.S.A.	1994	10.99
Lowe, Nick	The Wilderness Years	CD	Demon	FIEND-CD-203	England	1991	12.99
Lowe, Nick	True Love Travels On A Gravel Road	CD Single	Demon	NICK-A315	England	1994	10.99
Lowe, Nick	You Inspire Me	CD Single	Demon	VEXCD-17	England	1998	10.99
Lowe, Nick/Cowboy Outfit	The Rose Of England	CD	Demon	FIEND-CD-73	England	1988	39.99
Lowe, Nick/Impossible Birds	Live! On The Battlefield	CD Single	Upstart	UPSTART-021	U.S.A.	1995	7.99
Lucifer's Friend	Banquet	CD	Repertoire	REP-7017-WP	Germany	2002	11.99
Lucifer's Friend	Good Time Warrior	CD	Warner Bros.	WPCR-1719	Japan	1997	32.99
Lucifer's Friend	I'm Just A Rock 'N' Roll Singer	CD	Repertoire	REP-7042-WP	Germany	2002	14.99
Lucifer's Friend	Mean Machine	CD	Warner Bros.	WPCR-1721	Japan	1997	32.99
Lucifer's Friend	Mind Exploding	CD	Repertoire	REP-7085-WP	Germany	2002	11.99

Artist	Title	Format	Label	Catalog No	Country	Released	Value
Lucifer's Friend	Self Titled + 5	CD	Repertoire	REP-4059-WP	Germany	1998	15.99
Lucifer's Friend	Sneak Me In	CD	Warner Bros.	WPCR-1720	Japan	1997	32.99
Lucifer's Friend	Sumo Grip + 1	CD	Castle	ESMCD-489	England	1994	14.99
Lucifer's Friend	Where The Groupie Killed The Blues	CD	Repertoire	REP-4143-WP	Germany	2002	11.99
Lulu	Best Of	CD	Rhino	R2-71815	U.S.A.	1994	9.99
Lulu	Most Of Lulu/Lulu's Album	CD	EMI	7243-5-38850-2-1	England	2002	11.99
Lulu	The Man Who Sold The World	CD	Sequel	NEMCD423	England	1999	12.99
Lulu	Together	CD	Mercury	0630212	England	2002	11.99
Lulu/Mindbenders	To Sir, With Love (O.S.T.)	CD	Sin-Drome	SD-8935	U.S.A.	1999	25.99
Lunch, Lydia	13.13.	CD	Line	LICD-9.00096-0	Germany	1988	19.99
Lydon, John	Psycho's Path	CD	Virgin	7243-8-44209-2-5	U.S.A.	1997	8.99
Lydon, John/Time Zone	World Destruction (Afrika Bambaataa)	CD Single	Restless	7-72661-2	England	1984	11.99
Lyle-McGuinnes Band	Acting On Impulse	CD	Line	LICD-9.00182-0	Germany	1988	18.99
Lynn, Cheryl	Preppie	CD	Sony	SRCS-9018	Japan	1996	89.99
Lynn, Cheryl	Start Over	CD	EMI	7-46569-2	U.S.A.	1987	21.99
Lynx	Self Titled	CD	Dynamo Brazilie	DYN08	Brazil	1994	38.99
Lynyrd Skynyrd	20th Century Masters: The Millennium	CD	MCA	088-111-941-2	U.S.A.	1999	8.99
Lynyrd Skynyrd	All Time Greatest Hits	CD	MCA	088-112-229-2	U.S.A.	2000	7.99
Lynyrd Skynyrd	Box Set	3CD	MCA	MCAD3-10390	U.S.A.	1991	29.99
Lynyrd Skynyrd	Can't Take That Away	CD Single	Atlantic	7567-85761-2	U.S.A.	1993	10.99
Lynyrd Skynyrd	Christmas Time Again	CD	CMC INT.	06076-86298-2	U.S.A.	2000	6.99
Lynyrd Skynyrd	Comp. Muscle Shoals (First/Last + 8)	CD	MCA	088-111-888-2	U.S.A.	1998	10.99
Lynyrd Skynyrd	Comp. Muscle Shoals (First/Last + 8)	CD	MCA Victor	MVCE-24139	Japan	1999	29.99
Lynyrd Skynyrd	Double Trouble	CD	MCA	088-112-341-2	U.S.A.	2000	6.99
Lynyrd Skynyrd	Edge Of Forever	CD	CMC INT.	06076-86272-2	U.S.A.	1999	6.99
Lynyrd Skynyrd	Edge Of Forever +1	CD	Victor Ent.	VICP-60882	Japan	2001	29.99
Lynyrd Skynyrd	Endangered Species	CD	Capricorn	42028-2	U.S.A.	1994	18.99
Lynyrd Skynyrd	Endangered Species	CD	Capricorn	9-42028-2	U.S.A.	1994	8.99
Lynyrd Skynyrd	Essential	2CD	MCA	088-111-807-2	U.S.A.	1998	11.99
Lynyrd Skynyrd	Freebird: The Movie	CD	MCA	MCAD-11472	U.S.A.	1996	9.99
Lynyrd Skynyrd	Freebird: The Movie	CD	MCA Victor	MVCE-24052	Japan	1996	29.99
Lynyrd Skynyrd	Gimme Back My Bullets	CD	MCA Victor	MVCE-19304	Japan	1997	29.99
Lynyrd Skynyrd	Gimme Back My Bullets + 2	CD	MCA	088-112-023-2	U.S.A.	1999	8.99
Lynyrd Skynyrd	Gold & Platinum	2CD	MCA	MCAD2-6898	U.S.A.	1979	12.99
Lynyrd Skynyrd	Legend	CD	MCA	MCAD-42084	U.S.A.	1987	4.99
Lynyrd Skynyrd	Legend	CD	MCA Victor	MVCE-19306	Japan	1997	29.99
Lynyrd Skynyrd	Lynyrd Skynyrd 1991	CD	MCA	A2-82258	U.S.A.	1991	7.99
Lynyrd Skynyrd	Lynyrd Skynyrd 1991	CD	East West	AMCY-265	Japan	1991	22.99
Lynyrd Skynyrd	Lyve From Steel Town	CD	CMC INT.	06076-86247-2	U.S.A.	1998	8.99
Lynyrd Skynyrd	Lyve From Steel Town	2CD	Victor Ent.	VICP-60442/3	Japan	1998	49.99
Lynyrd Skynyrd	Mama's Song	CD Single	SPV	SPV055-71093	Germany	2000	10.99
Lynyrd Skynyrd	Nuthin' Fancy	CD	MCA Victor	MVCE-19303	Japan	1997	29.99
Lynyrd Skynyrd	Nuthin' Fancy + 2	CD	MCA	088-112-024-2	U.S.A.	1999	9.99
Lynyrd Skynyrd	Old Time Greats	2CD	Repertoire	REP-4637—WL	Germany	1997	19.99
Lynyrd Skynyrd	One More From The Road + 10	CD	MCA	088-112-657-2-4	U.S.A.	2001	16.99
Lynyrd Skynyrd	One More From The Road + 10	2CD	Universal	UICY-1094/5	Japan	2000	49.99
Lynyrd Skynyrd	Pronounced Leh-Nerd Skin-Nerd	CD	MCA Victor	MVCE-19301	Japan	1997	29.99
Lynyrd Skynyrd	Pronounced Leh-Nerd Skin-Nerd (Gold)	CD	MCA	MCAD-10953	U.S.A.	1973	29.99
Lynyrd Skynyrd	Pronounced Leh-Nerd Skin-Nerd + 5	CD	MCA	088-112-727-2	U.S.A.	2001	8.99
Lynyrd Skynyrd	Rock Masterpiece Collection	CD	MCA Victor	MVCM-20074	Japan	1997	29.99
Lynyrd Skynyrd	Second Helping	CD	MCA Victor	MVCE-19302	Japan	1997	29.99
Lynyrd Skynyrd	Second Helping (MFSL Gold Cd)	CD	Mobile Fidelity	UDCD-556	U.S.A.	1973	44.99
Lynyrd Skynyrd	Second Helping + 3	CD	MCA	088-111-648-2	U.S.A.	1999	9.99
Lynyrd Skynyrd	Skynyrd's Collectables	2CD	Universal	UICY-1047/8	Japan	2001	49.99
Lynyrd Skynyrd	Skynyrd's Innyrds	CD	MCA	MCAD-42293	U.S.A.	1990	6.99
Lynyrd Skynyrd	Skynyrd's Innyrds	CD	MCA Victor	MVCE-19307	Japan	1997	29.99
Lynyrd Skynyrd	Solo Flytes	CD	MCA	088-112-041-2	U.S.A.	1999	9.99
Lynyrd Skynyrd	Southern By The Grace...	CD	MCA	MCAD-8027	U.S.A.	1988	9.99

Artist	Title	Format	Label	Catalog No	Country	Released	Value
Lynyrd Skynyrd	Southern Knights - Live In The USA	CD	SPV	SPV087-44192	Germany	1996	8.99
Lynyrd Skynyrd	Street Survivors	CD	MCA Victor	MVCE-19305	Japan	1997	29.99
Lynyrd Skynyrd	Street Survivors (MCA Gold Cd)	CD	MCA	MCAD-11171	U.S.A.	1977	27.99
Lynyrd Skynyrd	Street Survivors + 3	CD	MCA	088-112-750-2	U.S.A.	2001	8.99
Lynyrd Skynyrd	Sweet Home Alabama	CD	BMG	74321-46311-2	U.S.A.	1997	8.99
Lynyrd Skynyrd	Talked Myself Into It	CD Single	CMC INT.	06076-87235-2	U.S.A.	1997	10.99
Lynyrd Skynyrd	The Best Of The Rest	CD	MCA	MCAD-31006	U.S.A.	1982	6.99
Lynyrd Skynyrd	The Collection	CD	Spectrum	544-451-2	EU	2000	9.99
Lynyrd Skynyrd	The Last Rebel	CD	MCA	7567-82447-2	U.S.A.	1993	7.99
Lynyrd Skynyrd	The Last Rebel	CD	East West	AMCY-511	Japan	1993	22.99
Lynyrd Skynyrd	Then And Now	CD	CMC INT.	06076-86293-2	U.S.A.	2000	8.99
Lynyrd Skynyrd	Thyrty (30th Anniversary Best Of)	2CD	MCA	088-113-227-2	U.S.A.	2003	14.99
Lynyrd Skynyrd	Turn It Up !	CD	Sanctuary	06076-86319-2	U.S.A.	2002	8.99
Lynyrd Skynyrd	Twenty	CD	CMC INT.	06076-86211-2	U.S.A.	1997	8.99
Lynyrd Skynyrd	Twenty/Edge Of Forever	2CD	SPV	SPV310-71260	Germany	2002	16.99
Lynyrd Skynyrd	Universal Masters	CD	Universal	UICY-1013	Japan	2000	29.99
Lynyrd Skynyrd	Vicious Cycle	CD	Sanctuary	06076-84610-2	U.S.A.	2003	13.99
Lynyrd Skynyrd	What's Your Name + 2	CD	MCA	MCAD-20401	U.S.A.	1997	6.99
Lynyrd Skynyrd/Allen Collins B	Allen Collins Band - Here, There...	CD	MCA	MCAD-31324	U.S.A.	1983	49.99

M

Artist	Title	Format	Label	Catalog No	Country	Released	Value
Maccoll, Kirsty	Electric Landlady	CD	Virgin	91688-2	U.S.A.	1991	6.99
Maccoll, Kirsty	Galore	CD	Virgin	7243-8-39982-27	Germany	1995	22.99
Maccoll, Kirsty	Kite	CD	Virgin	7243-8-27895-29	U.S.A.	1989	10.99
Maccoll, Kirsty	Mambo De La Luna (Cd 1)	CD Single	V2	VVR5010973	EU	1999	3.99
Maccoll, Kirsty	My Affair	CD Single	Virgin	VSCDG-1354	England	1991	9.99
Maccoll, Kirsty	The One And Only	CD	Metro	METRCD063	England	2001	10.99
Maccoll, Kirsty	Titanic Days	CD	I.R.S.	7243-8-27214-20	U.S.A.	1993	24.99
Maccoll, Kirsty	Titanic Days	CD	Warner Bros.	WMC5-693	Japan	1994	24.99
Maccoll, Kirsty	Tropical Brainstorm (16 Tracks, Video)	CD	Instinct	INS-557-2	U.S.A.	2001	8.99
Maccoll, Kirsty	Tropical Brainstorm + 2	CD	Sony	V2CI-71	Japan	2000	24.99
Maccoll, Kirsty	Walking Down Madison	CD Single	Virgin	VSCDG-1348	England	1991	7.99
MacDonald, Jeanette	Would You	CD	Mac/Eddy	JN132	U.S.A.	1994	10.99
MacDonald, Jeanette, N Eddy	San Francisco And Other...	CD	RCA	09026-60877-2	U.S.A.	1991	8.99
MacDonald, Jeanette/N Eddy	Ah, Sweet Mystery Of Life	CD	Pavillion	PAST-CD-7026	Germany	1993	19.99
MacDonald, Jeanette/N Eddy	Jeanette MacDonald And Nelson Eddy	CD	Again	LBACD-004	Brazil	2000	10.99
MacDonald, Jeanette/N Eddy	Love's Old Songs	CD	Master Song	503132	Australia	2000	7.99
MacDonald, Jeanette/N Eddy	Sweethearts	CD	RCA	DMC1-0876	U.S.A.	1989	6.99
MacDonald, Jeanette/N Eddy	When I'm Calling You	CD	ASV	CD-AJA-5124	England	1994	10.99
Machinations	Uptown	CD	Line	CUCD-9.00990-0	Germany	1990	25.99
Mack, Lonnie	Glad I'm In The Band	CD	Sundazed	SC-6192	U.S.A.	2003	8.99
Mack, Lonnie	Hills Of Indiana	CD	Sundazed	SC-6195	U.S.A.	2003	8.99
Mack, Lonnie	Whatever's Right	CD	Sundazed	SC-6193	U.S.A.	2003	8.99
Mackay, Andy	In Search Of Eddie Riff + 3	CD	Riff	CD002	England	1999	8.99
Mackay, Andy	Resolving Contradictions + 4	CD	Riff	CD001	England	1992	8.99
Mackay, Andy/Various Artists	Rock Follies + 1	CD	Virgin	7243-849231-2-9	England	2000	14.99
Mackay, Andy/Various Artists	Rock Follies Of '77 + 1	CD	Virgin	7243-849232-2-8	England	2000	14.99
Maclean, Bryan	Candy's Waltz	CD	Sundazed	SC-11076	U.S.A.	2000	10.99
Maclean, Bryan	Ifyoubelievein	CD	Sundazed	SC-11051	U.S.A.	1997	10.99
MacLeod, Doug/Band	54th And Vermont	CD	Line	STCD-9.00817-0	Germany	1989	24.99
Madhouse	16 (Prince Related)	CD	Paisley Park	9-25658-2	U.S.A.	1987	77.99
Madhouse	8 (Prince Related)	CD	Paisley Park	9-25545-2	U.S.A.	1987	106.99
Madison	Diamond Mistress	CD	Victor Ent.	VDP-1073	Japan	1986	34.99

Artist	Title	Format	Label	Catalog No	Country	Released	Value
Madness	Absolutely	CD	Virgin	72438-49264-2-7	England	1999	8.99
Madness	Keep Moving	CD	Virgin	72438-49267-2-4	England	2000	8.99
Madness	Keep Moving (W/Wings.../Sun And Rain)	CD	Geffen	GEFD4022	U.S.A.	1979	5.99
Madness	Mad Not Mad	CD	Virgin	72438-49268-2-3	England	2000	8.99
Madness	One Step Beyond	CD	Virgin	72438-49263-2-8	England	1999	8.99
Madness	Our House	CD	Virgin	72435-42695-2-3	England	2002	8.99
Madness	Seven	CD	Virgin	72438-49265-2-6	England	1999	8.99
Madness	The Lot (Remastered/All 24 Videos)	6CD	Virgin	7243-8-48074-0-5	England	1985	37.99
Madness	The Madness	CD	Virgin	0777-7-86914-2-6	England	1988	8.99
Madness	The Peel Sessions	CD	Strange Fruit	SFPSCD007	England	1988	9.99
Madness	The Rise And Fall Of	CD	Virgin	72438-49266-2-5	England	2000	8.99
Madness	Total Madness...The Very Best Of	CD	Geffen	GEFD-25145	U.S.A.	1997	5.99
Madness	Ultimate Collection	CD	Hip O	069-490-699-2	U.S.A.	2000	9.99
Madness	Universal Madness (Live)	CD	Golden Voice	44402-2	U.S.A.	1998	9.99
Madness	Wonderful	CD	Virgin	72438-48406-2-4	England	1999	8.99
Madonna	Amazing (Promo)	CD Single	Warner Bros.	PRO-2645	Germany	2000	39.99
Madonna	Amazing (Promo)	CD Single	Warner Bros.	SPO-82-W	Spain	2000	74.99
Madonna	American Pie	CD Single	Sire	9362448392	England	2000	5.99
Madonna	American Pie (Promo)	CD Single	Warner Bros.	PRO-A-100115	U.S.A.	2000	74.99
Madonna	American Pie (Promo)	CD Single	Warner Bros.	PCD-1275	Mexico	2000	23.99
Madonna	Another Suitcase...(Promo Cd)	CD Single	Warner Bros.	PRO-CD-4751-R	U.S.A.	1997	359.99
Madonna	Bad Girl (Promo)	CD Single	Sire	PRO-CD-5888	U.S.A.	1992	14.99
Madonna	Beautiful Stranger (Promo)	CD Single	Warner Bros.	PRO-1417	Germany	1999	13.99
Madonna	Bedtime Stories	CD	Sire	9-45767-2	U.S.A.	1994	7.99
Madonna	Bedtime Stories (Chap 2 Promo)	CD Single	Warner Bros.	PRO-CD-7600-R	U.S.A.	1994	299.99
Madonna	Bedtime Stories (Light Blue Felt Ed.)	CD	Maverick	9-45767-2	U.S.A.	1994	86.99
Madonna	Bedtime Stories (Ltd)	CD	Warner Bros.	9-45767-2	U.S.A.	1994	69.99
Madonna	Best Of 1983-1990 (Promo)	CD	Warner Bros.	PCS-44	Japan	1990	309.99
Madonna	Borderline	CD Single	Sire	7599-20218-2	Germany	1983	6.99
Madonna	Buenos Aires (Promo)	CD Single	Warner Bros.	PRCD-634	Germany	1997	149.99
Madonna	Buenos Aires (Promo)	CD Single	Warner Bros.	PRO-CD-8984-R	U.S.A.	1997	69.99
Madonna	Cd Single Collection (40 (3") Cds)	CD Single	Warner Bros.	WPDR-3100-39	Japan	1997	305.99
Madonna	Cosmic Climb	CD Single	Receiver	RRSCD3000	England	1993	8.99
Madonna	Crazy For You	CD Single	Sire	W0008CD	England	1991	4.99
Madonna	Dear Jesse (Pic Cd)	CD Single	Sire	921-452-2	England	1989	179.99
Madonna	Die Another Day (Promo)	CD Single	Warner Bros.	PRO-3599	Germany	2002	13.99
Madonna	Don't Cry For Me Argentina (Promo)	CD Single	Warner Bros.	PRCD-469	Germany	1997	34.99
Madonna	Don't Tell Me (Promo)	CD Single	Warner Bros.	PCD-1343	Mexico	2000	23.99
Madonna	Don't Tell Me (Promo)	CD Single	Warner Bros.	WPCR-10903	Japan	2000	39.99
Madonna	Don't Tell Me (Promo)	CD Single	Warner Bros.	PR2296	England	2000	34.99
Madonna	Don't Tell Me (Remixes)	CD Single	Warner Bros.	WPCR-10904	Japan	2001	34.99
Madonna	Erotica Remixes	CD	Warner Bros.	WPCP-5150	Japan	1992	24.99
Madonna	Evita (O.S.T.)	2CD	Warner Bros.	WPCR-1001/2	Japan	1997	28.99
Madonna	Evita (Selections Promo)	CD	Warner Bros.	PRCD440	England	1997	15.99
Madonna	Frozen Remixes	CD Single	Warner Bros.	WPCR-1846	Japan	1998	13.99
Madonna	Frozen Stereo MC Mix(Promo)	CD Single	Warner Bros.	PRO-CD-9254-R	U.S.A.	1998	34.99
Madonna	GHV 2 (Remixed)	CD Single	Warner Bros.	SP-199-W	Spain	2001	119.99
Madonna	GHV2 (Remixed Best Of '91-2001 DJ)	2CD	Warner Bros.	PRO-CD-100781	U.S.A.	2001	199.99
Madonna	Holiday (3")	CD Single	Warner Bros.	9211402	Germany	1989	19.99
Madonna	Holiday (Promo)	CD Single	Sire	SAM800	England	1983	154.99
Madonna	Hollywood (Withdrawn Promo)	CD Single	Warner Bros.	PCD-1608	Mexico	2003	88.99
Madonna	Human Nature (3")	CD Single	Warner Bros.	WPDR-3027	Japan	1995	29.99
Madonna	I'm Breathless (Promo)	CD	Warner Bros.	PCS-48	Japan	1990	206.99
Madonna	Into The Hollywood Groove (DJ)	CD Single	Warner Bros.	RRCG0301	U.S.A.	2003	74.99
Ardonna	Keep It Together (Mini Album)	CD Single	Larner Bros.	WPCP-3200	Japan	1990	38.99
Madonna	Like A Prayer (Promo Pic Disc)	CD	Sire	25844-2	U.S.A.	1989	44.99
Madonna	Like A Prayer (Promo)	CD	Warner Bros.	PCS-19	Japan	1989	499.99
Madonna	Like A Prayer (Promo)	CD	Warner Bros.	PCS-19	Japan	1989	273.99

Artist	Title	Format	Label	Catalog No	Country	Released	Value
Madonna	Like A Virgin (Blue Label/1st Pressing)	CD	Warner Bros.	9-25157-2	U.S.A.	1984	39.99
Madonna	Little Star (Promo)	CD Single	Warner Bros.	W459CDDJ	England	1998	154.99
Madonna	Live To Tell	CD Single	Sire	7599-20461-2	Germany	1986	5.99
Madonna	Love Don't Live Here... (Promo)	CD Single	Warner Bros.	PRO-CD-7934-R	U.S.A.	1996	19.99
Madonna	Lucky Star (3")	CD Single	Warner Bros.	7599-21139-2	Germany	1983	12.99
Madonna	Music	CD Single	Warner Bros.	9-16826-2	U.S.A.	2000	3.99
Madonna	Music (Promo)	CD Single	Warner Bros.	PCS-482	Japan	2000	103.99
Madonna	Music (Promo)	CD Single	Warner Bros.	PCS-471	Japan	2000	99.99
Madonna	Music (Remixes)	CD	Warner Bros.	WPCR-10902	Japan	2001	34.99
Madonna	Music Remixes (Promo)	CD Single	Warner Bros.	PCS-482	Japan	2000	249.99
Madonna	Nothing Really Matters (Promo)	CD	Warner Bros.	PRO-CD-9647	U.S.A.	1998	39.99
Madonna	One More Chance	CD Single	Warner Bros.	WO337CD	England	1996	9.99
Madonna	Papa Don't Preach (Gold)	CDV	Warner Bros.	24P6-0501	Japan	1988	77.99
Madonna	Rain	CD Single	Sire	9362-40997-2	England	1993	5.99
Madonna	Rain (EP)	CD Single	Warner Bros.	WPCP-5644	Japan	1993	18.99
Madonna	Rain (Promo)	CD Single	Warner Bros.	WPCP-5644	Japan	1993	39.99
Madonna	Ray Of Light (Promo)	CD Single	Warner Bros.	PRCD-1142	Germany	1999	54.99
Madonna	Ray Of Light (W/Words/Music Cd)	2CD	Warner Bros.	WPCR-10556/7	Japan	1999	43.99
Madonna	Remixed Prayers	CD Single	Warner Bros.	WPCR-1505	Japan	1989	18.99
Madonna	Royal Box Set (Promo)	CD	Sire	26464-2	U.S.A.	1990	39.99
Madonna	Secret (Remixes)	CD Single	Warner Bros.	WPCR-1513	Japan	1994	17.99
Madonna	Secrets (Promo)	CD Single	Sire	PRO-CD-7243-R	U.S.A.	1994	59.99
Madonna	Sex (W/Comic Book/Book)	CD	Warner Bros.	0224258	U.S.A.	1992	124.99
Madonna	Single Edits Of Album Remixes (Promo)	CD Single	Sire	PRO-CD-2892	U.S.A.	1987	94.99
Madonna	Something To Remember	CD	Warner Bros.	SR-46204-2	Mexico	1995	49.99
Madonna	Something To Remember	CD	Warner Bros.	46204-2	Argentina	1987	49.99
Madonna	Something To Remember	CD	Sire	9-46100-2	U.S.A.	1995	6.99
Madonna	Take A Bow	CD Single	Sire	9362-41874-2	England	1994	8.99
Madonna	Take A Bow	CD Single	Warner Bros.	9-41887-2	U.S.A.	1994	3.99
Madonna	Take A Bow Remixes	CD Single	Warner Bros.	WPCR-1514	Japan	1994	17.99
Madonna	True Blue (Gold Cd)	CD	Warner Bros.	43P2-0002	Japan	1996	97.99
Madonna	True Blue/Super Club Mix	CD Single	Warner Bros.	7599255332	Japan	1996	16.99
Madonna	What it Feels Like (Promo)	CD Single	Warner Bros.	PR2461	England	2001	19.99
Madonna	What It Feels Like (Promo)	CD Single	Warner Bros.	PRO-2522	Germany	2001	13.99
Madonna	What it Feels Like (Promo)	CD Single	Warner Bros.	PRO-2524	Germany	2001	43.99
Madonna	What it Feels Like (Promo)	CD Single	Warner Bros.	PCD-1378	Mexico	2001	23.99
Madonna	What it Feels Like Remixes (DJ)	CD Single	Warner Bros.	WPCR-10906	Japan	2001	34.99
Madonna	Words And Music (Promo)	CD	Warner Bros.	PRO-CD-9209	U.S.A.	1998	29.99
Madonna	You Can Dance (Gold Cd)	CD	Warner Bros.	43XD-2000	Japan	1987	92.99
Madonna	You Can Dance (Promo)	CD Single	Sire	PRO-CD-2892	U.S.A.	1987	84.99
Madonna	You Must Love Me	CD Single	Warner Bros.	2-17495	U.S.A.	1996	3.99
Madonna	You Must Love Me (Promo)	CD Single	Warner Bros.	PRO-6214	Germany	1996	21.99
Madonna	You'll See (Promo)	CD Single	Warner Bros.	WPCR-556	Japan	1995	182.99
Madonna	You'll See (Promo)	CD Single	Warner Bros.	PRO-CD-7900-R	U.S.A.	1999	12.99
Madonna/Numbered	Erotica (Special Tour Gold Cd)	CD	Maverick	9362-45031-2	Australia	1992	39.99
Magazine	BBC Radio One Live In Concert	CD	Windsong	WINCD-040	England	1993	28.99
Magazine	Magic, Murder And The Weather	CD	Virgin	0777-7-87346-2-8	England	1988	8.99
Magazine	Maybe It's Right To Be.. Box Set	3CD	Virgin	7243-8-49896-2-0	England	2000	34.99
Magazine	Play	CD	Virgin	0777-7-87347-2-7	England	1988	8.99
Magazine	Rays And Hail 1978- 1981	CD	Virgin	0777-7-87959-2-6	England	1993	8.99
Magazine	Real Life	CD	Caroline	CAROL-1808-2	U.S.A.	1991	8.99
Magazine	Scree	CD	Caroline	CAROL-1811-2	U.S.A.	1991	8.99
Magazine	Secondhand Daylight	CD	Caroline	CAROL-1809-2	U.S.A.	1991	8.99
Magazine	The Correct Use Of Soap	CD	Caroline	CAROL-1810-2	U.S.A.	1991	8.99
Magazine	Where The Power Is	CD	Virgin	7243-8-49895-2-1	U.S.A.	2000	14.99
Magma	1,001 Degrees Centigrade	CD	Seventh	REX-VI	France	1988	11.99
Magma	Attahk	CD	Seventh	REX-XIII	France	1989	11.99
Magma	BBC 1974 Londres	CD	Seventh	AKT-XIII	France	1999	14.99

M

Artist	Title	Format	Label	Catalog No	Country	Released	Value
Magma	Concert 1971 Bruxelles - Theatre 140	CD	Seventh	AKT-VIII	France	1996	24.99
Magma	Concert Bobino (Live)	CD	Seventh	AKT-V	France	1995	24.99
Magma	Floe Essi / Ektah	CD	Seventh	A-XXVI	France	1998	11.99
Magma	Hhai / Live + 1	2CD	Seventh	REX-X-XI	France	1989	29.99
Magma	Inedits	CD	Seventh	AKT-XIX	France	1989	14.99
Magma	Kobaia	2CD	Seventh	REX-IV-V	France	1988	29.99
Magma	Kohntarkosz	CD	Seventh	REX-VIII	France	1989	11.99
Magma	Kohntarkosz	CD	Pony Canyon	PCCY-10180	Japan	1991	22.99
Magma	Kompila	CD	Seventh	REX-XX	France	1997	11.99
Magma	Le Voix De Magma: Live Dournevez	CD	Seventh	AKT-I	France	1992	14.99
Magma	Les Genies Du Rock N°38	CD	Atlas	438	France	1993	14.99
Magma	Live	CD	Snapper	SNAP-008CD	England	2001	12.99
Magma	Mekanik Destruktiw Kommandoh	CD	Seventh	REX-VII	France	1989	11.99
Magma	Mekanik Destruktiw Kommandoh	CD	Pony Canyon	PCCY-10181	Japan	1991	34.99
Magma	Mekanik Kommandoh	CD	Seventh	REX-6Z	France	1989	11.99
Magma	Mekanik Zeuhl Wortz 1976	CD	Kisses Deluxe	KISS-39	France	1994	19.99
Magma	Merci	CD	Seventh	REX-III	France	1988	11.99
Magma	Mythes Et Legendes Volume I	CD	Seventh	REX-XIV	France	1989	14.99
Magma	Retrospektiw I & II (Live)	2CD	Seventh	REX-XVI-XVII	France	1989	19.99
Magma	Retrospektiw III (Live)	CD	Seventh	REX-XV	France	1989	11.99
Magma	Simples	CD	Seventh	REX-II	France	1998	14.99
Magma	Spiritual	2CD	Recall	SMD-CD-291	England	2002	12.99
Magma	Theatre du Taur - Toulouse 1975	CD	Seventh	AKT-IV	France	1996	11.99
Magma	Theusz Hamtaahk Trilogy	3CD	Seventh	AKT29-31	France	2001	54.99
Magma	Udu Wudu + 1	CD	Seventh	REX-XII	France	1989	11.99
Magma	Wurdah Itah - Tristan Et Iseult S. T.	CD	Seventh	REX-IX	France	1989	11.99
Magma/Benoit Widemann	Stress	CD	Musea	FBGB-4238.AR	France	2001	14.99
Magma/Benoit Widemann	Tsumami	CD	Musea	FBGR-4271.AR	France	2001	14.99
Magma/Christian Vander	65 !	CD	Seventh	AX	France	1993	14.99
Magma/Christian Vander	A Tous Les Enfants	CD	Seventh	AXIV	France	1994	14.99
Magma/Christian Vander	Korusz	2CD	Seventh	AKT-14/14L	France	2000	29.99
Magma/Christian Vander	Les Voyages De Christophe Colomb	CD	Seventh	AKT-III	France	1993	14.99
Magma/Christian Vander	Offering A Fiieh	CD	Seventh	AIX	France	1993	11.99
Magma/Christian Vander	Offering I & II	2CD	Seventh	AI-AII	France	1986	24.99
Magma/Christian Vander	Offering III & IV	2CD	Seventh	AV-AVI	France	1990	24.99
Magma/Christian Vander	Offering: Paris Teatre Dejazet 1987	CD	Seventh	AKT- XI	France	1998	14.99
Magma/Christian Vander	To Love	CD	Seventh	AIII	France	1988	19.99
Magma/Christian Vander Trio	Jour Apres Jour	CD	Seventh	AIV	France	1990	14.99
Magma/Michel Graillier	Dream Drops	CD	Universal	0134342	Netherland	2001	12.99
Magma/Michel Graillier	Fairly	CD	CDM	794881656226	Netherland	2002	17.99
Magma/Michel Graillier	Portrait in Black & White	CD	Quantum	6920	England	1995	14.99
Magma/Michel Graillier	Soft Talk	CD	Harmonia Mundi	SKE333014	France	2000	11.99
Magma/One Shot	Vendredi 13	CD	Soleilmoon	SOL006CD	U.S.A.	1999	17.99
Magma/Stella Vander	D'Epreuves D'Amour	CD	Seventh	A-VIII	France	1991	14.99
Magma/The Unnamables	Univeria Zekt (Part Of 4 CD Box)	4CD	Musea	FGBG-4086.AR	France	1993	54.99
Magna Carta	A Touch Of Class	CD	Talking Elephant	TECD043	England	2002	11.99
Magna Carta	Ages And Seasons	2CD	Recall	SMD-CD-481	England	2003	12.99
Magna Carta	Evergreen	CD	HTD	HTDCD113	England	2000	8.99
Magna Carta	Forever	CD	Mooncrest	CRESTCD-061	England	2000	11.99
Magna Carta	Gold Deluxe Edition	2CD	Retro	R2CD-4256	England	2003	12.99
Magna Carta	Heartlands	CD	Sound Products	SPHCD-7813	England	1992	29.99
Magna Carta	In Concert	CD	HTD	HTDCD-69	England	1996	8.99
Magna Carta	L Tierras (Sweet Deceiver/Northlands)	CD	Barsa Pr.	DK-860040	Italy	1996	21.99
Magna Carta	Live At The BBC	CD	Psuedonym	CDP-1022-DD	Holland	1995	12.99
Magna Carta	Live In Grassington	CD	HTD	HTD-CD-98	England	1999	8.99
Magna Carta	Lord Of The Ages	CD	Vertigo	846-448-2	Germany	1991	13.99
Magna Carta	Lord Of The Ages/Martin's Cafe	CD	Mercury	538-813-2	Germany	1999	11.99
Magna Carta	Midnight Blue + 1	CD	HTD	HTD-CD101	England	1999	8.99

M

Artist	Title	Format	Label	Catalog No	Country	Released	Value
Magna Carta	Milestones	2CD	Vertigo	526-156-2	Germany	1994	34.99
Magna Carta	Old Master & New Horizons	CD	Vertigo	510-660-2	Germany	1991	13.99
Magna Carta	One To One	CD	Tembo	TMBCD118	England	1988	29.99
Magna Carta	Rings Around The Moon	CD	HTD	HTDCD112	England	2000	8.99
Magna Carta	Seasons	CD	Vertigo	846-447-2	Germany	1991	13.99
Magna Carta	Seasons In The Tide	CD	Gold Circle Ent.	GI-67502-5	U.S.A.	2001	8.99
Magna Carta	Seasons/Songs From Wasties Orchard	CD	Mercury	538-812-2	Germany	1999	11.99
Magna Carta	Self Titled (Times Of Change)	CD	HTD	HTDCD68	England	1996	8.99
Magna Carta	Self Titled (Times Of Change) + 1	CD	Mercury	538-837-2	Germany	1999	11.99
Magna Carta	Songs For The Wasties Orchard	CD	Repertoire	REP-4447-WP	Germany	1994	14.99
Magna Carta	State Of The Art	CD	Hypertension	HYCD-200-144	England	1993	11.99
Magna Carta	State Of The Art	CD	Talking Elephant	TECD-032	England	2001	11.99
Magna Carta	State Of The Heart	CD	HTD	HTD-CD-99	England	1999	8.99
Magna Carta	Where To Now?	CD	Lost & Found	542-543-2	England	2000	21.99
Magna Carta/Chris Simpson	Listen To The Man	CD	Celtic Music	CMCD-019	England	1984	22.99
Magnus, Nick	Inhaling Green	CD	Centaur Discs	CENCD-017	Austria	1999	29.99
Mahal, Taj	Happy To Be Just ...(MFSL Aluminum)	CD	Mobile Fidelity	MFCD-1-765	U.S.A.	1991	49.99
Mahal, Taj	Recycling The Blues (MFSL Aluminum)	CD	Mobile Fidelity	MFCD-1-764	U.S.A.	1972	49.99
Mahal, Taj	Sing A Happy ... Warner Recordings	2CD	Rhino	RHM2-7749	U.S.A.	2000	39.99
Mahavishnu Orchestra	Apocalypse	CD	Columbia	CK-46111	U.S.A.	1990	8.99
Mahavishnu Orchestra	Between Nothingness And Eternity	CD	Columbia	CK-32766	U.S.A.	1990	8.99
Mahavishnu Orchestra	Birds of Fire	CD	Columbia	CK-66081	U.S.A.	2000	9.99
Mahavishnu Orchestra	Collection	CD	Griffin	GCD-314-2	England	1994	8.99
Mahavishnu Orchestra	Inner Mounting Flame	CD	Columbia	CK-65523	U.S.A.	1998	9.99
Mahavishnu Orchestra	Inner Mounting Flame (MFSL Gold Cd)	CD	Mobile Fidelity	UDCD-744	U.S.A.	1971	34.99
Mahavishnu Orchestra	Inner Worlds	CD	Columbia	CK-52923	U.S.A.	1990	8.99
Mahavishnu Orchestra	Mahavishnu	CD	Wounded Bird	WOU-5190	U.S.A.	2002	8.99
Mahavishnu Orchestra	The Lost Trident Sessions	CD	Columbia	CK-65959	U.S.A.	1999	9.99
Mahavishnu Orchestra	Visions Of The Emerald Beyond	CD	Columbia	CK-46867	U.S.A.	1991	8.99
Mahogany Rush	Child Novelty/Maxoom/S Universe	2CD	Big Beat	CDWKM2-149	England	1995	21.99
Mahogany Rush	Child Of The Novelty	CD	Repertoire	RR-4029-C	Germany	1989	24.99
Mahogany Rush	Dragonfly: The Best Of	CD	Razor & Tie	RE-2105-2	U.S.A.	1996	24.99
Mahogany Rush	IV	CD	Sony	SRCS-6244	Japan	1992	24.99
Mahogany Rush	Maxoom (Mispelled Mahagony)	CD	If 6 Was 9	BOD13	Germany	1994	14.99
Mahogany Rush	Strange Universe	CD	Repertoire	RR-4028-C	Germany	1989	24.99
Mahogany Rush	Tales Of The Unexpected	CD	Columbia	CK-35753	U.S.A.	1990	11.99
Mahogany Rush	What's Next	CD	Black Rose	BR-130	Sweden	1999	14.99
Mahogany Rush/Frank Marino	Double Live	2CD	SPV	7014401125	Germany	1992	12.99
Mahogany Rush/Frank Marino	Eye Of The Storm	CD	Just A Minute	MIN-003	U.S.A.	2001	12.99
Mahogany Rush/Frank Marino	From The Hip	CD	SPV	SPV084-88792CD	Germany	2001	8.99
Mahogany Rush/Frank Marino	Full Circle	CD	SPV	SPV22075892CD	Germany	1998	8.99
Mahogany Rush/Frank Marino	Juggernaut	CD	Black Rose	BR-129	Sweden	1998	14.99
Mahogany Rush/Frank Marino	Live	CD	Columbia	CK-35257	U.S.A.	1990	11.99
Mahogany Rush/Frank Marino	Stories Of A Hero	CD	Zounds	CD-27440040	Germany	2000	11.99
Mahogany Rush/Frank Marino	The Power Of Rock 'N' Roll	CD	Black Rose	BR-128	Sweden	2004	11.99
Mahogany Rush/Frank Marino	World Anthem	CD	Sony	564-374-2	Holland	1977	9.99
Malmsteen, Yngwie	Alchemy	CD	Pony Canyon	PCCY-01409	Japan	1999	24.99
Malmsteen, Yngwie	Alchemy	CD	Spitfire	SPT-15139-2	U.S.A.	2000	8.99
Malmsteen, Yngwie	Anthology 1994-1999	CD	Pony Canyon	PCCY-01446	Japan	2000	24.99
Malmsteen, Yngwie	Anthology 1994-1999	CD	Spitfire	SPT-15141-2	U.S.A.	2000	9.99
Malmsteen, Yngwie	Archive	8 CD	Pony Canyon	PCCY-01501	Japan	2001	299.99
Malmsteen, Yngwie	Attack + 1	CD	Pony Canyon	PCCY01582	Japan	2002	24.99
Malmsteen, Yngwie	Attack + 1	CD	Epic	RNK-75421	U.S.A.	2002	16.99
Malmsteen, Yngwie	Concerto Suite Live/Jpn Philharmonic	CD	Pony Canyon	PCCY-01551-2	Japan	2002	24.99
Malmsteen, Yngwie	Concerto Suite/Guitar/Orchestra Op. 1	CD	Spitfire	SPT-15138-2	U.S.A.	2000	9.99
Malmsteen, Yngwie	Double Live	2CD	Spitfire	SPT-15134-2	U.S.A.	2000	13.99
Malmsteen, Yngwie	Eclipse	CD	Polydor	843-361-2	U.S.A.	1990	13.99
Malmsteen, Yngwie	Facing The Animal	CD	Spitfire	SPT-15140-2	U.S.A.	2000	9.99

M

Artist	Title	Format	Label	Catalog No	Country	Released	Value
Malmsteen, Yngwie	Facing The Animal + 1	CD	Pony Canyon	PCCY-01154	Japan	1994	17.99
Malmsteen, Yngwie	Facing The Animal + 1	CD	Pony Canyon	PCCY-01154	Japan	1998	24.99
Malmsteen, Yngwie	Fire & Ice	CD	Elektra	61137-2	U.S.A.	1992	11.99
Malmsteen, Yngwie	Fire & Ice + 1	CD	Warner Bros.	AMCY-3084	Japan	2000	24.99
Malmsteen, Yngwie	Genesis	CD	Pony Canyon	PCCY-01627	Japan	2002	24.99
Malmsteen, Yngwie	I Can't Wait	CD	Pony Canyon	PCCY-00629	Japan	1994	22.99
Malmsteen, Yngwie	I Can't Wait EP	CD Single	Pony Canyon	PCCY-00629	Japan	1994	19.99
Malmsteen, Yngwie	Inspiration	CD	Spitfire	SPT-15137-2	U.S.A.	2000	12.99
Malmsteen, Yngwie	Inspiration + 1	CD	Pony Canyon	PCCY-01009	Japan	1996	24.99
Malmsteen, Yngwie	Live in Leningrad: Trial by Fire	CD	Polydor	839-726-2	U.S.A.	1989	10.99
Malmsteen, Yngwie	Live! + 3 (W/Bonus Cd)	3CD	Pony Canyon	PCCY-01277	Japan	1998	49.99
Malmsteen, Yngwie	Magnum Opus	CD	Spitfire	SPT-15136-2	U.S.A.	2000	14.99
Malmsteen, Yngwie	Marching Out	CD	Polydor	P33P-20002	Japan	1986	39.99
Malmsteen, Yngwie	Marching Out	CD	Polydor	825-733-2	U.S.A.	1985	15.99
Malmsteen, Yngwie	Odyssey	CD	Polydor	835-451-2	U.S.A.	1988	11.99
Malmsteen, Yngwie	Power And Glory (3" Cd/Takada)	CD Single	Pony Canyon	PCDY-00127	Japan	1994	18.99
Malmsteen, Yngwie	Rising Force	CD	Polydor	825-324-2	U.S.A.	1984	10.99
Malmsteen, Yngwie	The Collection	CD	Polydor	849-271-2	U.S.A.	1989	10.99
Malmsteen, Yngwie	The Seventh Sign	CD	Spitfire	SPT-15135-2	U.S.A.	2000	12.99
Malmsteen, Yngwie	Trilogy	CD	Polydor	831-073-2	U.S.A.	1986	11.99
Malmsteen, Yngwie	War To End All Wars + 1	CD	Spitfire	SPT-15171-2	U.S.A.	2000	9.99
Malmsteen, Yngwie	War To End All Wars + 2	CD	Pony Canyon	PCCY-1483	Japan	2001	24.99
Malmsteen, Yngwie	Young Person's Guide Classics, Vol. 1	CD	Pony Canyon	PCCY-00487	Japan	2000	29.99
Malmsteen, Yngwie	Young Person's Guide Classics, Vol. 2	CD	Pony Canyon	PCCY-00478	Japan	2000	29.99
Malmsteen, Yngwie/Alcatrazz	Dangerous Games	CD	Toshiba-EMI	TOCP-6854	Japan	1986	32.99
Malmsteen, Yngwie/Alcatrazz	Disturbing the Peace	CD	Toshiba-EMI	TOCP-6853	Japan	1985	19.99
Malmsteen, Yngwie/Alcatrazz	Live Sentence	CD	Grand Slamm	SLAMCD-12	U.S.A.	1984	16.99
Malmsteen, Yngwie/Alcatrazz	No Parole From Rock 'N Roll	CD	Grand Slamm	SLAMCD11	U.S.A.	1983	21.99
Malmsteen, Yngwie/Alcatrazz	The Best	CD	Renaissance	RMED00102	U.S.A.	1998	12.99
Malmsteen, Yngwie/Steeler	Self Titled (Malmsteen's 1st Band)	CD	Shrapnel	SH-1007CD	U.S.A.	1990	20.99
Malo	Celebration Box Set	4CD	Rhino	RHM2-7780	U.S.A.	2001	59.99
Malo	Malo	CD	Warner Bros.	2584-2	U.S.A.	1972	14.99
Malo	Malo (Line Version)	CD	Line	LECD-9.00896-0	Germany	1990	9.99
Malo	Senorita	CD	GNP	GNPD-2244	U.S.A.	1998	10.99
Malo	The Best Of Malo	CD	GNP/Crescendo	GNPD-2205	U.S.A.	1991	10.99
Malone, Michelle	Homegrown	CD	SBS	CD-SBS-004	U.S.A.	1999	8.99
Mama's Boys	Plug It In	CD	Line	ALCD-9.00136-0	Germany	1988	14.99
Mamas/Papas	All The Leaves Are Brown	2CD	MCA	088-112-653-2	U.S.A.	2001	19.99
Mamas/Papas	California Dreamin' The Best Of	CD	Victor Ent.	UICY-1120	Japan	2002	21.99
Mamas/Papas	Creeque Alley The History Of	2CD	MCA	MCAD2-10195	U.S.A.	1991	10.99
Mamas/Papas	Deliver/Papas & The Mamas + 1	CD	BGO	BGOCD462	England	1999	14.99
Mamas/Papas	Greatest Hits	CD	MCA	MCAD-11740	U.S.A.	1998	7.99
Mamas/Papas	Monterey International Pop Festival	CD	MCA	MCAD-22033	U.S.A.	1990	10.99
Mamas/Papas	People Like Us	CD	Victor Ent.	UICY-3365	Japan	2002	21.99
Mamas/Papas	The EP Collection	CD	See For Miles	SEE-CD333	France	1992	14.99
Mamas/Papas	The Great Mamas & Papas (Live 1982)	CD	Goldies	GLD-63109	Portugal	1997	10.99
Mamas/Papas/Denny Doherty	Watcha Gonna Do	CD	Victor Ent.	UICY-3361	Japan	2002	29.99
Mammoth	Self Titled	CD	Jive	1094-2-J	U.S.A.	1989	10.99
Mammoth	XXXL	CD	Angel Air	SJPCD006	England	1998	7.99
Man	1994 Official Bootleg	CD	Voiceprint	PNTVP109CD	England	1999	11.99
Man	1994 Official Bootleg	CD	Eagle	EAMCD066	Germany	1999	11.99
Man	2 Ozs. Plastic W/ A Hole in the Middle	CD	See For Miles	SEE-CD-273	England	1969	11.99
Man	2 Ozs. Plastic W/ A Hole in the Middle	CD	Repertoire	REP-4025-WZ	Germany	1996	11.99
Man	3 Decades Of Man: 70's, 80's, 90's	2CD	Eagle	EDMCD099	Germany	2000	14.99
Man	All's Well That Ends Well	CD	Eagle	EAMCD068	Germany	1999	11.99
Man	All's Well That Ends Well	CD	Voiceprint	PNTVP103CD	England	1999	11.99
Man	Back Into The Future	CD	BGO	BGOCD211	England	2002	12.99
Man	BBC Radio One Live In Concert	CD	Windsong	WINCD-045	England	1993	14.99

M

Artist	Title	Format	Label	Catalog No	Country	Released	Value
Man	Be Good To Yourself....	CD	BGO	BGOCD14	England	1996	12.99
Man	Call Down The Moon	CD	Griffin	GCD-480-2	U.S.A.	1995	8.99
Man	Call Down The Moon	CD	Voiceprint	PNTVP116CD	England	1998	11.99
Man	Dawn Of Man (USA/Diff. Track Order)	2CD	Recall	RXG-124	U.S.A.	1998	12.99
Man	Do You Like It Here..	CD	Voiceprint	PNTVP107CD	England	1999	11.99
Man	Do You Like It Here...	CD	Eagle	EAMCD077	Germany	1999	11.99
Man	Downtown Live	CD	Altrichter	AM-310559	Germany	2002	19.99
Man	Edangered Species	CD	Evangeline	GEL-4001	England	2000	9.99
Man	Friday The 13th	CD	Line	LICD-9.00071-0	Germany	1988	9.99
Man	Friday The 13th	CD	Voiceprint	PNTVP106	England	1999	11.99
Man	Friday The 13th	CD	Eagle	EAMCD062	Germany	1999	11.99
Man	Legal Bootleg Live '99	CD	Altrichter	AM-310556	Germany	2000	19.99
Man	Live 1998 Star Club	2CD	Krucker	38765/66-2	Germany	1998	14.99
Man	Live At Reading '83	CD	Raw Fruit	FRSCD010	England	1992	14.99
Man	Live At The Padget Rooms Penarth	CD	BGO	BGOCD365	England	2002	14.99
Man	Live At The Rainbow 1972	CD	Eagle	EAMCD060	Germany	1999	11.99
Man	Live In London 1975	CD	Voiceprint	PNTVP101CD	England	1998	11.99
Man	Live In London 1975	CD	Eagle	EAMCD061	Germany	1998	11.99
Man	Man (3rd Lp)	CD	Voiceprint	PNTVP117CD	England	1999	11.99
Man	Man (3rd LP) + 2	CD	Repertoire	REP-4969	Germany	2003	11.99
Man	Man Alive	2CD	Recall	SMD-CD-478	England	2003	12.99
Man	Many Are Called But Few Get Up	2CD	Receiver	RRDCD-312-Z	England	2001	14.99
Man	Maximum Darkness	CD	BGO	BGOCD43	England	1996	12.99
Man	Perfect Timing: The UA Years + 3	CD	EMI	CDEMS-1403	England	1991	14.99
Man	Rare (Singles/Studio)	CD	Voiceprint	PNTVP120CD	England	1999	14.99
Man	Revelation	CD	See For Miles	SEE-CD-274	England	1969	11.99
Man	Revelation	CD	Repertoire	REP-4024-WZ	Germany	1996	11.99
Man	Rhinos, Winos And Lunatics	CD	BGO	BGOCD208	England	2002	14.99
Man	Slow Motion	CD	BGO	BGOCD209	England	1996	12.99
Man	The 1999 Party Tour	CD	Voiceprint	PNTVP112CD	England	1998	11.99
Man	The 1999 Party Tour	CD	Eagle	EAMCD069	Germany	1998	11.99
Man	The Dawn Of Man	2CD	Recall	IVP30811	England	1997	12.99
Man	The Definitive Collection	2CD	Castle	CCSCD-832	England	1998	14.99
Man	The Early Years	CD	Dojo	EARL-D10	England	1993	7.99
Man	The Pye Collection	2CD	Essential	ESACD-917	England	2000	14.99
Man	The Twang Dynasty	CD	Voiceprint	PNTVP113CD	England	1998	11.99
Man	The Twang Dynasty	CD	Eagle	EAMCD065	England	1998	11.99
Man	The Welsh Connection	CD	Voiceprint	PNTVP102CD	England	1999	11.99
Man	The Welsh Connection	CD	Eagle	EAMCD063	Germany	1999	11.99
Man	To Live For To Die	CD	Eagle	EAMCD067	Germany	1999	11.99
Man	To Live For To Die	CD	Voiceprint	PNTVP108CD	England	1999	11.99
Man	Undrugged (1st 500 Diff. Song Order)	CD	Voiceprint	PNTVP121CD	England	2002	14.99
Man/Big Sleep	Bluebell Wood (Hugo Montes Label)	CD	Globe	HMP-CD-005	Germany	1971	24.99
Man/Deke Leonard	Before Your Very Eyes + 2	CD	Voiceprint	PNTVP114CD	England	2000	14.99
Man/Deke Leonard	Iceberg/Kamikaze	CD	BGO	BGOCD288	England	1996	19.99
Man/Deke Leonard	The Force- Force's First	CD	Line	LICD-9.00080-0	Germany	1989	9.99
Man/Deke Leonard	Unfinished Business	CD	Road Goes On	RGF-DL501	England	2002	14.99
Man/Hawkwind	Greasy Truckers Party	CD	Voiceprint	PNTVP104CD	England	1999	11.99
Man/Hawkwind	Greasy Truckers Party	CD	Eagle	EAMCD064	Germany	1999	11.99
Man/Help Yourself	S Affair/R Of Ken Whaley/Happy Days	2CD	BGO	BGOCD452	England	1999	19.99
Man/Help Yourself	Self Titled/Beware The Shadow	CD	BGO	BGOCD385	England	1999	19.99
Man/Jeff Jones	Ride	CD	Border	7115	England	1995	5.99
Man/Malcolm Morely	Lost And Found	CD	HUX	HUX034	England	2002	8.99
Man/Martin Ace	Flying Aces - Seashell	CD	Voiceprint	PNTVP122CD	England	2003	14.99
Man/Neutrons	Black Hole Star/Tales Bl. Cocoons + 1	CD	BGO	BGOCD598	England	2004	19.99
Man/The Bystanders	Birth Of Man	CD	See For Miles	SEE-CD-301	England	1990	29.99
Man/The Bystanders	Pattern People: The Pye Anthology	CD	Castle	82310-72211-2-9	U.S.A.	2002	12.99
Manchester, Melissa	Best Selection	CD	BMG Victor	BVCA-2609	Japan	1999	24.99

M

Artist	Title	Format	Label	Catalog No	Country	Released	Value
Manchester, Melissa	Better Days & Happy Endings	CD	BMG Victor	BVCA-7375	Japan	1999	49.99
Manchester, Melissa	Don't Cry Out Loud	CD	BMG Victor	BVCA-7376	Japan	1999	49.99
Manchester, Melissa	For The Working Girl	CD	BMG Victor	BVCA-7378	Japan	1999	49.99
Manchester, Melissa	Hey Rickey	CD	BMG Victor	BVCA-7379	Japan	1999	49.99
Manchester, Melissa	Melissa	CD	BMG Victor	BVCA-7374	Japan	1999	21.99
Manchester, Melissa	Melissa Manchester	CD	BMG Victor	BVCA-7377	Japan	1999	49.99
Manchester, Melissa	Singin'	CD	BMG Victor	BVCM-37276	Japan	2002	23.99
Manchester, Melissa	The Many Moods Of (Pair Cd)	CD	Arista	ARPCD2-1086	U.S.A.	1984	19.99
Mancini, Henry/Royal P Pops	Mancini Rocks The Pops	CD	Denon	CO-73078	Japan	1989	19.99
Mandalaband	The Eye Of Wendor (Justin Hayward)	CD	Line	OLCD-9.51232-Z	Germany	1992	14.99
Mandel, Harvey	Baby Batter	CD	Line	JACD-9.00793-0	Germany	1989	11.99
Mandel, Harvey	Baby Batter	CD	BGO	BGOCD252	England	1998	11.99
Mandel, Harvey	Baby Batter/The Snake	CD	Western Front	CD-1015	U.S.A.	1995	14.99
Mandel, Harvey	Baby Batter/The Snake	CD	Akarma	AK-75	Italy	2003	14.99
Mandel, Harvey	Cristo Redentor + 8	CD	Raven	RVCD163	Australia	2003	14.99
Mandel, Harvey	Emerald Triangle	CD	ESP	ESP-9701	U.S.A.	1998	12.99
Mandel, Harvey	Feel The Sound	CD	Line	JACD-9.00799-0	Germany	1989	11.99
Mandel, Harvey	Feel The Sound Of	CD	Repertoire	REP-4715	Germany	2002	12.99
Mandel, Harvey	Lick This	CD	ESP	ESP-6910	U.S.A.	2000	12.99
Mandel, Harvey	Planetary Warrior	CD	Lightyear	54215-2	U.S.A.	1997	8.99
Mandel, Harvey	Shangrenade	CD	Line	JACD-9.00802-0	Germany	1989	14.99
Mandel, Harvey	Shangrenade	CD	Repertoire	REP-4712	Germany	2002	14.99
Mandel, Harvey	Shangrenade	CD	BGO	BGOCD410	England	1998	14.99
Mandel, Harvey	Shangrenade/Feel The Sound	CD	Akarma	AK-166	Italy	2003	14.99
Mandel, Harvey	Snakes & Stripes	CD	Clarity	CDC-1014	U.S.A.	1995	11.99
Mandel, Harvey	The Mercury Years	2CD	Mercury	314-528-275-2	U.S.A.	1995	39.99
Mandel, Harvey	The Snake	CD	Line	JACD-9.00796-0	Germany	1989	18.99
Mandel, Harvey	The Snake	CD	Repertoire	REP-4711	Germany	2002	12.99
Mandel, Harvey	The Snake	CD	BGO	BGOCD398	England	1998	12.99
Mandel, Harvey	Twist City	CD	Western Front	CD-1002	U.S.A.	1994	14.99
Mandel, Harvey	West Coast Killaz	CD	ESP	ESP-6969	U.S.A.	2003	12.99
Mandel, Johnny	The Sandpipers (O.S.T.)	CD	Verve	31453-1229-2	U.S.A.	1996	45.99
Mandrake Root	Takes Of The Sacred	CD	Zero	XRCN-1172	Japan	1994	21.99
Mangione, Chuck	70 Miles Young	CD	A&M	CD-3237	U.S.A.	1978	29.99
Mangione, Chuck	Bellavia	CD	A&M	CD-3172	U.S.A.	1975	60.99
Mangione, Chuck	Feels So Good	CD	A&M	CD-3219	U.S.A.	1978	8.99
Mangione, Chuck	Main Squeeze	CD	A&M	CD-3220	U.S.A.	1976	59.99
Manhattan Transfer	Extensions (MFSL Gold Cd)	CD	Mobile Fidelity	UDCD-578	U.S.A.	1979	29.99
Manic Street Preachers	Manics DJ Copy (Best Of/Promo)	CD	Epic	QDCA-93182	Japan	1998	349.99
Manic Street Preachers	The Holy Bible	CD	Epic	477421-9	England	1994	49.99
Manifest Destiny	All Life All Minds	CD	Victor Ent.	VICP-5737	Japan	1996	44.99
Manilow, Barry	Manilow	CD	RCA	PCD1-7044	U.S.A.	1985	53.99
Manitoba'a Wild Kingdom	...And You? (The Dictators)	CD	MCA	MCAD-6367	U.S.A.	1990	7.99
Mann, Aimee	Bachelor No. 2	CD	V2	WR1015872	U.S.A.	1999	10.99
Mann, Aimee	I'm With Stupid	CD	DGC	DGCD-24951	U.S.A.	1995	9.99
Mann, Aimee	I'm With Stupid (Sp. Prepared DJ Cd)	CD	Geffen	PRO-CD-4843	U.S.A.	1995	13.99
Mann, Aimee	Lost In Space	CD	Super Ego	SE-007	U.S.A.	2002	11.99
Mann, Aimee	That's Just What You Are	CD Single	Imago	72787-25086-2	U.S.A.	1994	9.99
Mann, Aimee	Ultimate Collection	CD	Hip-O	314-524-760-2	U.S.A.	2000	9.99
Mann, Aimee	Whatever	CD	Imago	72787-21017-2	U.S.A.	1993	9.99
Mann, Barry	Who Put The Bomp In The....	CD	Marginal	MAR-007	EEC	1995	24.99
Mann, Billy	Billy Mann (Self Titled Album)	CD	DV8	31454-0365-2	U.S.A.	1995	5.99
Mann, Manfred	At Abbey Road	CD	EMI	7243-8-21136-2-1	England	1997	8.99
Mann, Manfred	BBC Sessions	CD	EMI	7243-4-97770-2-6	Holland	1998	12.99
Mann, Manfred	Manfred Mann Album / 5 Faces Of + 4	CD	EMI	E2-37067	U.S.A.	1996	18.99
Mann, Manfred	Soul Of Mann	CD	EMI	7243-4-98935-2-8	EU	1999	9.99
Mann, Manfred	The Best Of EMI Years	2CD	EMI	GCD-559-2	U.S.A.	1996	11.99
Mann, Manfred/Chapter 3	Volume One + 4	CD	Creature	MANN-001	Germany	1999	8.99

M

Artist	Title	Format	Label	Catalog No	Country	Released	Value
Mann, Manfred/Earth Band	Angel Station + 2	CD	Creature	MANN-011	Germany	1999	8.99
Mann, Manfred/Earth Band	Blindin'	CD	Music Club	MCCD-414	England	2000	8.99
Mann, Manfred/Earth Band	Criminal Tango + 4	CD	Creature	MANN-015	Germany	1999	8.99
Mann, Manfred/Earth Band	Glorified Magnified + 2	CD	Creature	MANN-004	Germany	1999	8.99
Mann, Manfred/Earth Band	Messin' + 2	CD	Creature	MANN-005	Germany	1998	8.99
Mann, Manfred/Earth Band	Nightingales & Bombers + 2	CD	Creature	MANN-008	Germany	1999	8.99
Mann, Manfred/Earth Band	On The Road	CD	Brilliant	BT-33085	Germany	2001	7.99
Mann, Manfred/Earth Band	Somewhere In Afrika + 5	CD	Creature	MANN-013	Germany	1999	8.99
Mann, Manfred/Earth Band	The Best Of	CD	Warner Bros.	9-46231-2	U.S.A.	1996	9.99
Mann, Manfred/Earth Band	The Good Earth + 3	CD	Creature	MANN-007	Germany	1998	8.99
Mann, Manfred/Earth Band	The Roaring Silence + 2	CD	Creature	MANN-009	Germany	1998	8.99
Mann, Manfred/Earth Band	Watch + 4	CD	Creature	MANN-010	Germany	1998	8.99
Mann, Manfred/Earth Band	Wired	CD	Alchemy	PILOT91	England	2001	9.99
Mann, Manfred/Earthband	Budapest Live + 3	CD	Creature	MANN-014	Germany	1999	8.99
Mann, Manfred/Earthband	Chance + 4	CD	Creature	MANN-012	Germany	1999	8.99
Mann, Manfred/Earthband	Masque + 4	CD	Creature	MANN-016	Germany	1999	8.99
Mann, Manfred/Plain Music	Plains Music	CD	Priority	CDL-57123	U.S.A.	1991	8.99
Mannheim Steamroller	Christmas Angel (Olivia Newton - John)	CD	American	AG-1998—2	U.S.A.	1998	7.99
Mannheim Steamroller	Classical Gas (W/Mason Williams)	CD	American	AG-800-2	U.S.A.	1987	9.99
Mannheim Steamroller	Fresh Aire V	CD	American	AG-5005-2	U.S.A.	1983	10.99
Manson, Marilyn	Smells Like Children	CD	Interscope	92641-2	U.S.A.	1995	8.99
Manuel, Richard/The Band	Whispering Pines/Live At....	CD	Pryaid	YDCD-0082	Japan	2002	39.99
Manzanera, Phil	A Million Reasons..(Souther Cross +4)	CD	Expression	EXVP1-CD	England	1997	8.99
Manzanera, Phil	Diamond Head + 1	CD	Expression	6043-88457-5-2	England	1999	10.99
Manzanera, Phil	Expression Records Sampler	CD	Expression	EXPCD20	England	2000	12.99
Manzanera, Phil	K-Scope +3	CD	Expression	7243-5263-10-25	England	2000	10.99
Manzanera, Phil	Manzanera Collection	2CD	Caroline	CAROL-1798-2	U.S.A.	1996	13.99
Manzanera, Phil	Primitive Guitars + 2	CD	Expression	7243-849275-23	England	2000	10.99
Manzanera, Phil	The Manzanera Archives: Rare One	CD	Expression	EXPCD21	England	2000	10.99
Manzanera, Phil	The Wasted Lands	CD	Expression	EXVP11-CD	England	1999	10.99
Manzanera, Phil	Vozero	CD	Expression	EXVP-12CD	England	1999	10.99
Manzanera, Phil/801	801 Latino	CD	Expression	EXPCD-24	England	2001	10.99
Manzanera, Phil/801	801 Live @ Hull	CD	Expression	EXPCD23	England	2000	10.99
Manzanera, Phil/801	801 Live + 2	CD	Expression	6043-88457-7-2	England	1999	10.99
Manzanera, Phil/801	Listen Now + 3	CD	Expression	7243-849276-22	England	2000	10.99
Manzanera, Phil/801	Live At Manchester University	CD	Expression	EXVP2CD	EU	1997	10.99
Manzanera, Phil/801	Manchester	CD	Expression	EXPCD25	England	2001	10.99
Manzanera, Phil/Quiet Sun	Mainstream	CD	Expression	6043-88457-6-2	England	1999	10.99
Manzanera/Mackay	Crack The Whip	CD	Relativity	88561-8263-2	U.S.A.	1988	10.99
Manzanera/Mackay	Live At The Palace	CD	Expression	EXVP3CD	EU	1997	10.99
Manzanera/Mackay	Manzanera/Mackay (The Explorers)	2CD	Expression	EXPCD26	England	2001	24.99
Manzanera/Mackay	Up In Smoke	CD	Relativity	88561-1010-2	U.S.A.	1989	10.99
Mara	Poetry And Motion	CD	Teichiku	TECX-25666	Japan	1994	32.99
Mardones, Benny	Bless A Brand New Angel	CD	Crave	HK69336	U.S.A.	1998	8.99
Mardones, Benny	Never Run Never Hide	CD	Polydor	839-582-2	U.S.A.	1980	39.99
Mardones, Benny	Self Titled	CD	Curb	D2-77292	U.S.A.	1989	13.99
Marillion	Afraid Of Sunlight + 9 (W/Bonus Cd)	2CD	Sanctuary	06076-84536-2	U.S.A.	2002	12.99
Marillion	Anorak In The UK: Live	CD	EMI	7243-5-38727-2-4	England	2002	11.99
Marillion	Anorak In The UK: Live + 8 (Bonus Cd)	2CD	Intact	080202	EU	2002	24.99
Marillion	Anoraknophobia	CD	CMC INT.	06076-84506-2	U.S.A.	2001	8.99
Marillion	Best Of Both Worlds	2CD	Sanctuary	06076-84538-2	U.S.A.	2002	14.99
Marillion	Brave + 11 (W/Bonus Cd)	2CD	Sanctuary	06076-84535-2	U.S.A.	2002	12.99
Marillion	B-Sides Themselves	CD	EMI	0777-7-48807-2-5	England	1988	15.99
Marillion	Clutching At Straws + 12 (Bonus Cd)	2CD	Sanctuary	06076-84534-2	U.S.A.	2002	12.99
Marillion	Essential Collection	CD	EMI	7243-8-53593-2-3	England	1996	10.99
Marillion	Fugazi + 7 (W/Bonus Cd)	2CD	Sanctuary	06076-84529-2	U.S.A.	2001	12.99
Marillion	Holidays In Eden + 14 (W/Bonus Cd)	2CD	Sanctuary	06076-84532-2	U.S.A.	2002	12.99
Marillion	Kayleigh: The Best Of	CD	Disky	DC-867182	Holland	1996	9.99

M

Artist	Title	Format	Label	Catalog No	Country	Released	Value
Marillion	Kayleigh: The Essential	CD	EMI	494564-2	England	1998	10.99
Marillion	Made Again + 19 (W/Bonus Cd)	2CD	Sanctuary	06076-81108-2	U.S.A.	2001	12.99
Marillion	Marillion.com	CD	Sanctuary	06076-84531-2	U.S.A.	1999	8.99
Marillion	Misplaced Childhood + 17 (Bonus Cd)	2CD	Sanctuary	06076-84530-2	U.S.A.	2001	12.99
Marillion	Radiation + 2	CD	Velvel	63467-79760-2	U.S.A.	1998	11.99
Marillion	Reel To Real + 1/Brief Encounter	2CD	Sanctuary	06076-84537-2	U.S.A.	2002	12.99
Marillion	Script/Jester's Tear + 7 (Bonus Cd)	2CD	Sanctuary	06076-84528-2	U.S.A.	2001	14.99
Marillion	Season's End + 9 (W/Bonus Cd)	2CD	Sanctuary	06076-84533-2	U.S.A.	2002	12.99
Marillion	Singles Box, Vol. 1: '82 - '88	12 CD	EMI	7243-8-88667-2-9	England	2000	49.99
Marillion	Singles Box, Vol. 2: '89 - '95	12 CD	EMI	7243-5-50821-2-1	England	2002	49.99
Marillion	Singles Coll. '82-'92 (Same/Six I.R.S.)	CD	EMI	CDEMD1033	England	1992	13.99
Marillion	Six Of One, Half-Dozen Of The Other	CD	I.R.S.	X2-13157	U.S.A.	1992	13.99
Marillion	Tales From The Engine Room	CD	Cleopatra	CLP0375CD	U.S.A.	2001	9.99
Marillion	Thieving Magpie	2CD	EMI	0777-7-91463-2-1	England	1988	19.99
Marillion	This Strange Engine + 2	CD	Pony Canyon	PCCY-01098	Japan	1997	24.99
Marillion	Warm Wet Circles	CD	Disky	SI-905232	Holland	2003	8.99
Marillion	Yin And Yang Radio Edits	CD	Dick Brothers	DDick13CDFAN	EEC	1995	49.99
Marillion/Fish	Derek Dick And His....	2CD	Chocolate Frog	CFVP003CD	England	2000	28.99
Marillion/Fish	Fellini Days + 9 (W/Bonus Issue 30 Cd)	2CD	Chocolate Frog	CFVP007CD	England	2001	18.99
Marillion/Fish	Fellini Nights	2CD	Chocolate Frog	CFVP014CD	England	2002	18.99
Marillion/Fish	Field Of Crows	CD	Chocolate Frog	CFVPO16CD	England	2003	10.99
Marillion/Fish	Fish Head Curry	2CD	Dick Brothers	DDICK18CD	England	1996	28.99
Marillion/Fish	For Whom The Bell Tolls	2CD	Chocolate Frog	CFVP002CD	England	2000	28.99
Marillion/Fish	Fortunes Of War	CD	Roadrunner	RR-8689-2	U.S.A.	1998	9.99
Marillion/Fish	Funny Farm Interview	CD	Dick Brothers	DDick15CD	England	1995	23.99
Marillion/Fish	Internal Exile + 3	CD	Roadrunner	RR-8683-2	England	1999	9.99
Marillion/Fish	Kettle Of Fish (1st 30,000/Bonus Cd)	2CD	Roadrunner	RR-8678-8	England	1998	21.99
Marillion/Fish	Krakow	2CD	Roadrunner	RR-8681-2	England	1998	19.99
Marillion/Fish	Live Acoustic Sessions	2CD	Chocolate Frog	CFVP006CD	England	2000	28.99
Marillion/Fish	Live At The Funny Farm	CD	Renaissance	RMED00136	U.S.A.	1996	12.99
Marillion/Fish	Mixed Company	2CD	Chocolate Frog	CFVP016CD	England	2003	28.99
Marillion/Fish	Pigpen's Birthday	2CD	Dick Brothers	DDICK16CD	England	1993	18.99
Marillion/Fish	Raingods With Zippos	CD	Roadrunner	RR-8677-2	England	1999	9.99
Marillion/Fish	Sashimi	2CD	Chocolate Frog	CFVP008CD	England	2001	28.99
Marillion/Fish	Songs From The Mirror + 1	CD	Roadrunner	RR-8682-2	England	1998	9.99
Marillion/Fish	Suits	CD	Roadrunner	RR-8686-2	England	1998	9.99
Marillion/Fish	Sunsets On Empire (Bonus Interview)	2CD	Dick Brothers	484-463-2	EU	1997	29.99
Marillion/Fish	Sunsets On Empire (Video Clip/Brother)	CD	Lightyear	54197-2	U.S.A.	1997	9.99
Marillion/Fish	Sunsets On Empire + 1	CD	Roadrunner	RR-8679-2	England	1998	9.99
Marillion/Fish	Sushi	2CD	Roadrunner	RR-8680-2	England	1998	19.99
Marillion/Fish	Tales From The Big Bus	2CD	Roadrunner	RR-8688-2	England	1998	21.99
Marillion/Fish	The Complete BBC Sessions	2CD	Blueprint	BP297CD	England	2001	28.99
Marillion/Fish	Toiling In The Reeperbahn	2CD	Chocolate Frog	CFVP001CD	England	2000	13.99
Marillion/Fish	Uncle Fish And The Crypt Creepers	2CD	Dick Brothers	DDICK17CD	England	1993	28.99
Marillion/Fish	Virgil In A Wilderness Of Mirrors + 5	CD	Roadrunner	RR-8687-2	England	1999	9.99
Marillion/Fish	Yang	CD	Chocolate Frog	CFVP005CD	England	2001	18.99
Marillion/Fish	Yin	CD	Chocolate Frog	CFVP004CD	England	2000	18.99
Marilyn Manson	Astonishing Panorama Of...(Promo)	CD Single	Nothing	INT5P-6723	U.S.A.	1999	7.99
Mark, Jon	A Celtic Story	CD	White Cloud	11002-2	Germany	1993	18.99
Mark, Jon	A Sunday In Autumn	CD	White Cloud	11003-2	Germany	1994	18.99
Mark, Jon	Alhambra (Gold Cd)	CD	Kuckuck	11100-2	Germany	1992	16.99
Mark, Jon	All The Best Of	CD	White Cloud	11027-2	Germany	1996	19.99
Mark, Jon	Asia Journey	CD	White Cloud	11009-2	Germany	1996	18.99
Mark, Jon	Hot Night	CD	Line	LICD-9.01129-0	Germany	1992	13.99
Mark, Jon	Hot Night	CD Single	Line	LICD-9.01132-E	Germany	1991	7.99
Mark, Jon	Land Of Merlin	CD	Kuckuck	11094-2	Germany	1992	12.99
Mark, Jon	Song For A Friend	CD	Line	LICD-9.00508-0	Germany	1988	13.99
Mark, Jon	The Lady And The Artist	CD	Line	LICD-9.00063-0	Germany	1987	13.99

M

Artist	Title	Format	Label	Catalog No	Country	Released	Value
Mark, Jon	The Standing Stones Of Callanish	CD	Kuckuck	11082-2	Germany	1988	12.99
Mark, Jon/David A. Clark	Leaving Of Ireland	CD	White Cloud	WH-CL-11035-2	Germany	1999	18.99
Mark/Almond	73	CD	Sony	SICP-8070	Japan	2002	29.99
Mark/Almond	Mark/Almond	CD	Line	LICD-9.00105-0	Germany	1987	12.99
Mark/Almond	Mark-Almond	CD	Universal	UICY-3328	Japan	2001	29.99
Mark/Almond	Mark-Almond '73	CD	Line	LICD-9.00514-0	Germany	1988	12.99
Mark/Almond	Mark-Almond I/Mark-Amond II	2CD	Line	LICD-9.21186-S	Germany	1992	19.99
Mark/Almond	Mark-Almond II	CD	Line	LICD-9.00517-0	Germany	1988	12.99
Mark/Almond	Mark-Almond II	CD	Universal	UICY-3329	Japan	2001	29.99
Mark/Almond	Nightmusic	CD	White Cloud	11026-2	U.S.A.	1996	18.99
Mark/Almond	Other Peoples Rooms	CD	Universal	UICY-3061	Japan	2000	29.99
Mark/Almond	Rising	CD	Line	LICD-9.00511-0	Germany	1988	12.99
Mark/Almond	Rising	CD	Sony	SICP-8069	Japan	2002	29.99
Mark/Almond	The Best Of Mark/Almond + 1	CD	Rhino	R2-70571	U.S.A.	1991	14.99
Mark/Almond	The Last And Live	CD	Line	LICD-9.00415-0	Germany	1987	15.99
Mark/Almond	To The Heart	CD	MCA	MCAD-22084	U.S.A.	1976	15.99
Mark/Almond	Tuesday In New York	CD	Line	LICD-9.00056-0	Germany	1987	15.99
Marley, Bob/The Wailers	Babylon By Bus	CD	Tuff Gong	314-548-900-2	U.S.A.	2001	7.99
Marley, Bob/The Wailers	Catch A Fire (MFSL Gold Cd)	CD	Mobile Fidelity	UDCD-654	U.S.A.	1973	24.99
Marley, Bob/The Wailers	Catch A Fire (Promo Sampler)	CD	Island	CATR-05017-2	U.S.A.	2001	11.99
Marley, Bob/The Wailers	Catch A Fire + 2	CD	Tuff Gong	314-548-893-2	U.S.A.	2001	7.99
Marley, Bob/The Wailers	Chant Down Babylon	CD	Tuff Gong	314-546-404-2	U.S.A.	1999	7.99
Marley, Bob/The Wailers	Confrontation + 1	CD	Tuff Gong	314-548-903-2	U.S.A.	2001	14.99
Marley, Bob/The Wailers	Exodus (MFSL Gold Cd)	CD	Mobile Fidelity	UDCD-628	U.S.A.	1977	24.99
Marley, Bob/The Wailers	Live! + 1	CD	Tuff Gong	314-548-896-2	U.S.A.	2001	7.99
Marley, Bob/The Wailers	Natural Mystic	CD	Tuff Gong	314-524-103-2	U.S.A.	1995	7.99
Marley, Bob/The Wailers	Rastaman Vibration + 1	CD	Tuff Gong	314-548-897-2	U.S.A.	2001	7.99
Marley, Bob/The Wailers	Songs Of Freedom Box Set	4CD	Island	314-514-432-2	U.S.A.	1999	37.99
Marley, Bob/The Wailers	Uprising + 2	CD	Tuff Gong	314-548-902-2	U.S.A.	2001	7.99
Marques/Leao	Comboio	CD	Line	RICD-9.00573-0	Germany	1988	24.99
Marriott, Steve	Marriott	CD	Polydor	POCM-1892	Japan	1993	56.99
Marriott, Steve	Marriott Alternative History	CD	Outlaw	OTR-1100016	England	1996	12.99
Marriott, Steve	Marriott And The All Stars	CD	Outlaw	OTR-1100017	England	1996	12.99
Marriott, Steve/All Stars	Pure Energy	CD	Outlaw	OTR-1100015	England	1996	12.99
Mars, Chris	75% Less Fat	CD	Island	162-888-004-2	U.S.A.	1993	8.99
Mars, Chris	Anonymous Botch	CD	Bar/None	AHAON-085	U.S.A.	1996	8.99
Mars, Chris	Horseshoes And Hand Grenades	CD	Island	314-513-198-2	U.S.A.	1992	8.99
Mars, Chris	Tenterhooks	CD	Bar/None	AHAON-052	U.S.A.	1995	5.99
Marsalis, Ellis	Piano In E / Solo Piano	CD	Line	COCD-9.01022-0	Germany	1991	13.99
Marsupilami	Arena	CD	Line	TACD-9.00741-0	Germany	1989	14.99
Marsupilami	Marsupilami	CD	Line	TACD-9.007370	Germany	1989	9.99
Martin, Eric	Soul Sessions - The Capitol Years + 1	CD	Toshiba-EMI	TOCP-50048	Japan	1996	39.99
Martin, George	In My Life	CD	Pony Canyon	PCCY-01179	Japan	1998	29.99
Martin, George	Live And Let Die (O.S.T.)	CD	EMI	7-90629-2	U.S.A.	1973	8.99
Martin, Marilyn	Self Titled (Of Separate Lives Fame)	CD	Warner Bros.	32XD-459	U.S.A.	1986	136.99
Martin, Skip/Dazz Band	For Women Only (Kool/Gang)	CD	P-Vine	PCD-3788	Japan	1995	32.99
Marvelettes	Self Titled/Sophisticated Soul	CD	Motown	MOTD-8055	U.S.A.	1977	33.99
Marx, Groucho	Here's Groucho	CD	MCA	MCAD-20847	U.S.A.	1995	7.99
Masked Marauders	Complete Deity Recordings (Ltd 2000)	CD	Rhino	RHM2-7746	U.S.A.	2000	21.99
Mason Proffit	Come & Gone	CD	Line	LECD-9.00897-0	Germany	1990	9.99
Mason, Dave	Alone Together (MFSL Gold Cd)	CD	Mobile Fidelity	UDCD-573	U.S.A.	1970	37.99
Mason, Dave	Certified Live	CD	Sony	SRCS-6182	Japan	1992	24.99
Mason, Dave	Dave Mason	CD	Sony	SRCS-6181	Japan	1992	24.99
Mason, Dave	Headkeeper	CD	MCA	MCAD-31326	U.S.A.	1972	12.99
Mason, Dave	It's Like You Never Left	CD	One Way	A-26077	U.S.A.	1995	8.99
Mason, Dave	Let It Flow	CD	Columbia	CK-34680	U.S.A.	1977	7.99
Mason, Dave	Mariposa De Oro	CD	Sony	SRCS-6365	Japan	1994	24.99
Mason, Dave	Old Crest On A New Wave	CD	Sony	SRCS-6366	Japan	1994	24.99

M

Artist	Title	Format	Label	Catalog No	Country	Released	Value
Mason, Dave	Show Me Some Affection	CD	Elite	ELITE010CD	England	1991	29.99
Mason, Dave	Some Assembly Required	CD	Chumley	CHD-00101	U.S.A.	1987	50.99
Mason, Dave	Split Coconut	CD	Sony	SRCS-6364	Japan	1994	24.99
Mason, Dave	The Best Of Dave Mason	CD	Columbia	CK-57165	U.S.A.	1995	6.99
Mason, Dave	Two Hearts	CD	MCA	MCAD-42086	U.S.A.	1987	6.99
Mason, Dave/Cass Elliot	Dave Mason & Cass Elliot	CD	MCA Victor	MVCM-21053	Japan	1992	29.99
Mason, Dave/Jim Capaldi	Live - The 40,000 HeadmenTour	CD	Castle	06076-81173-2	U.S.A.	2002	10.99
Mason, Nick	Fictitious Sports	CD	Columbia	A-75070	U.S.A.	1981	29.99
Mason, Nick/Rick Fenn	Profiles	CD	Columbia	CK-40142	U.S.A.	1985	13.99
Masquerade	Self Titled	CD	Zero	XRCN-1011	Japan	1992	19.99
Massey, Will T./Like J Cougar	Will T. Massey (Like Springsteen)	CD	MCA	MCAD-10185	U.S.A.	1991	6.99
Master P/Various Artists	Kenny's Dead	CD Single	Columbia	666965-2	Austria	1998	10.99
Matchbox 20	Hits (Promo)	CD	Warner Bros.	MBOX-2002	Canada	2002	29.99
Matching Mole	BBC Radio 1 Live In Concert	CD	Windsong	WINCD-063	England	1994	19.99
Matching Mole	Little Red Record	CD	Columbia	COL-471488-2	France	1972	12.99
Matching Mole	March	CD	Cuneiform	RUNE-172	U.S.A.	2002	11.99
Matching Mole	Self Titled	CD	Columbia	505478-2	Holland	2001	11.99
Matching Mole	Self Titled	CD	Sony	SMM-54782	England	2003	11.99
Matching Mole	Smoke Signals (Live)	CD	Cuneiform	RUNE-150	U.S.A.	2001	11.99
Matlock, Glen	My Little Philistine	CD Single	Creation	CRESCD229	England	1996	4.99
Matsuura, Yuki	S M Girls Saber Marionette J	CD	King Record	KICA-292	Japan	1996	24.99
Matthews Southern Comfort	First	CD	Line	LICD-9.01261-0	Germany	1993	18.99
Matthews Southern Comfort	Later That Same Year	CD	Line	LCCD-9.01264-0	Germany	1993	39.99
Matthews Southern Comfort	Scion	CD	Band Of Joy	BOJCD-007	England	1995	12.99
Matthews Southern Comfort	Second Spring	CD	Line	LCCD-9.01265-0	Germany	1993	18.99
Matthews Southern Comfort	Self Titled/Second Spring	CD	BGO	BGOCD313	England	1996	15.99
Matthews Southern Comfort	The Best Of	CD	MCA	MCAD-10519	U.S.A.	1992	19.99
Matthews, Dave/Band	Rapunzel (Promo)	CD Single	RCA	RDJ-65748-2	U.S.A.	1999	125.99
Matthews, Dave/Band	Recently	CD	Bama Rags	Bama-002	U.S.A.	1994	283.99
Matthews, Ian	Camouflage	CD	Perfect Pitch	PP004	England	1995	11.99
Matthews, Ian	Discreet Repeat	CD	Line	LICD-9.00560-0	Germany	1988	19.99
Matthews, Ian	Excerpts From Swine Lake	CD	Demon	FIEND-CD-942	England	1998	14.99
Matthews, Ian	Get It Back	CD Single	Line	LICD-9.01233-E	Germany	1992	7.99
Matthews, Ian	God Looked Down	CD	Watermelon	CD-1055	U.S.A.	1996	14.99
Matthews, Ian	If You Saw/Tigers Will Survive	CD	Vertigo	514-167-2	England	1993	24.99
Matthews, Ian	Journeys From Gospel Oak	CD	Line	LICD-9.00133-0	Germany	1988	19.99
Matthews, Ian	Journeys From Gospel Oak	CD	Mooncrest	CRESTCD-004	England	1995	14.99
Matthews, Ian	Live Alone (Notebook Series, Vol. 2)	CD	Line	OLCD-9.51141-Z	Germany	1993	14.99
Matthews, Ian	More Than A Song - Self Titled	CD	Perfect Pitch	PP010	England	2001	11.99
Matthews, Ian	Nights In Manhatten (And Points W)	CD	DCC	DZS-144	U.S.A.	1997	8.99
Matthews, Ian	Orphans & Outcasts, Vol. 1	CD	Dirty Linen	102	England	1993	19.99
Matthews, Ian	Orphans & Outcasts, Vol. 2	CD	Dirty Linen	104	England	1994	19.99
Matthews, Ian	Orphans & Outcasts, Vol. 3	CD	Perfect Pitch	PP005	England	1999	11.99
Matthews, Ian	Pure And Crooked	CD	Line	OLCD-9.91248-Z	Germany	1992	19.99
Matthews, Ian	Pure And Crooked + 5	CD	Watermelon	CD-1029	U.S.A.	1994	19.99
Matthews, Ian	Shook	CD	Line	LICD-9.00014-0	Germany	1987	15.99
Matthews, Ian	Siamese Friends	CD	Line	LICD-9.00150-0	Germany	1987	11.99
Matthews, Ian	Skeleton Keys	CD	Line	LICD-9.01182-0	Germany	1992	14.99
Matthews, Ian	Skeleton Keys	CD	Rhino	R2-79054	U.S.A.	1993	9.99
Matthews, Ian	Spot Of Interference	CD	Line	LICD-9.00060-0	Germany	1988	18.99
Matthews, Ian	Stealin' Home	CD	Line	LICD-9.00074-0	Germany	1987	21.99
Matthews, Ian	Stealin' Home/Siamese Friends	2CD	Line	LICD-9.21193-S	Germany	1992	34.99
Matthews, Ian	Such Is Life	CD	Road Goes On	RGFCD030	England	1996	14.99
Matthews, Ian	The Dark Ride	CD	Watermelon	CD-1025	U.S.A.	1995	14.99
Attthews, Ian	The Iain Adventure	CD	Perfect Pitch	PP008	England	2000	11.99
Matthews, Ian	The Seattle Years 1978 - 1984	CD	Varese	VSD-5738	U.S.A.	1996	8.99
Matthews, Ian	The Soul Of Many Places '72-'74	CD	Elektra	61457-2	U.S.A.	1993	12.99
Matthews, Ian	Tiniest Wham	CD	Perfect Pitch	PP006	England	2002	11.99

M

Artist	Title	Format	Label	Catalog No	Country	Released	Value
Matthews, Ian	Valley Hi/Some Days You Eat...	CD	Water	WATER-124	U.S.A.	2003	14.99
Matthews, Ian	Walking A Changing Line	CD	Windham Hill	WD-1070	U.S.A.	1988	9.99
Matthews, Ian	Witness: More Than A Song Live	CD	Turtle	TRSA-0013	U.S.A.	2003	11.99
Matthews, Ian/Elliott Murphy	Bootleg Series: The Cornish Pub	2CD	Blue Rose	BLUBS-002	Germany	2001	24.99
Matthews, Ian/Elliott Murphy	La Terre Commune 2001	CD	Eminent	EM-25070-2	Germany	2001	19.99
Matthews, Ian/Hamilton Pool	Return To Zero	CD	Watermelon	CD-1031	U.S.A.	1995	14.99
May Blitz	2nd Of May	CD	Line	LMCD-9.00747-0	Germany	1990	15.99
May Blitz	2nd Of May	CD	Repertoire	IMS-7027-WP	Germany	1995	15.99
May Blitz	May Blitz	CD	Line	LMCD-9.00742-0	Germany	1990	15.99
May Blitz	Self Titled	CD	Repertoire	IMS-7026-WP	Germany	1994	15.99
May Blitz	Self Titled/2nd Of May	CD	BGO	BGOCD153	England	1992	15.99
May East	Tabapora	CD	Line	RICD-9.00710-0	Germany	1988	12.99
May, Billy	Green Hornet (Orig. T.V. Soundtrack)	Mini Lp	Max Ent.	BLXL-1007-9	Japan	1999	20.99
May, Brian	Another World	CD	Hollywood	HR-62103-25	U.S.A.	1998	9.99
May, Brian	Another World	CD	Parlophone	494073-2	England	1998	12.99
May, Brian	Another World (Promo)	CD	Parlophone	CDPP057	England	1998	19.99
May, Brian	Another World + 2	CD	Toshiba-EMI	TOCP-50473	Japan	1998	29.99
May, Brian	Back To Light (Commemorative/Gold)	CD	Parlophone	CDPCSD-X123	England	1993	54.99
May, Brian	Back To The Light	CD	Parlophone	CDPCSD-123	England	1992	12.99
May, Brian	Back To The Light (CD 1/Boxed)	CD Single	Parlophone	CDR-6329	England	1992	14.99
May, Brian	Back To The Light (CD 2)	CD Single	Parlophone	CDRX-6329	England	1992	14.99
May, Brian	Back To The Light (DJ Sampler)	CD	Parlophone	MAYDJ-1	England	1992	29.99
May, Brian	Back To The Light (Promo)	CD Single	Parlophone	CDRDJ-6329	England	1992	24.99
May, Brian	Back To The Light + 1	CD	Hollywood	HR-61404-2	U.S.A.	1992	6.99
May, Brian	Back To The Light + 2	CD	Toshiba-EMI	TOCP-7235	Japan	1992	29.99
May, Brian	Driven By You	CD Single	Parlophone	CDR-6304	England	1991	9.99
May, Brian	Driven By You	CD Single	Hollywood	HR-64642	U.S.A.	1993	9.99
May, Brian	Driven By You (DJ/W/Compass Box)	CD Single	Hollywood	PRCD-10273-2	U.S.A.	1993	44.99
May, Brian	Driven By You (Promo)	CD Single	Parlophone	CDRDJ-6304	England	1991	24.99
May, Brian	Driven By You (Promo)	CD Single	Hollywood	PRCD-10322-2	U.S.A.	1993	14.99
May, Brian	Last Horizon (CD 1)	CD Single	Parlophone	CDR-6371	England	1993	7.99
May, Brian	Last Horizon (CD 2/Pop Up Slv)	CD Single	Parlophone	CDRS-6371	England	1993	12.99
May, Brian	Last Horizon (Promo)	CD Single	Parlophone	HORIZON-1	England	1993	24.99
May, Brian	Live At The Brixton Academy	CD	EMI	CDPCSD-150	England	1994	18.99
May, Brian	Resurrection (CD 1)	CD Single	Parlophone	CDR-6351	U.S.A.	1993	9.99
May, Brian	Resurrection (CD 2)	CD Single	Parlophone	CDRS-6351	England	1993	9.99
May, Brian	The Business	CD Single	Parlophone	CDR-6498	England	1998	7.99
May, Brian	The Business (Promo)	CD Single	Hollywood	PRCD-10828	U.S.A.	1998	9.99
May, Brian	The Business (Promo)	CD Single	Parlophone	CDRDJ-6498	England	1998	24.99
May, Brian	Too Much Love Will Kill You	CD Single	Toshiba-EMI	TOCP-7436	Japan	1992	34.99
May, Brian	Too Much Love Will Kill You (CD 1)	CD Single	Parlophone	CDR-6320	England	1992	7.99
May, Brian	Too Much Love Will Kill You (CD 2)	CD Single	Parlophone	CDRS-6320	England	1992	7.99
May, Brian	Too Much Love Will Kill You (DJ)	CD Single	Hollywood	PRCD-10342-2	U.S.A.	1993	12.99
May, Brian	Why Don't We Try Again	CD	Parlophone	CDR-6504	England	1998	9.99
May, Brian/Cozy Powell	Resurrection	CD Single	Toshiba-EMI	TOCP-8087	Japan	1993	29.99
May, Phil/Fallen Angels	Fallen Angels	CD	Line	BUCD-9.00542-0	Germany	1988	14.99
Mayall, John	A Banquet In Blues	CD	One Way	MCAD-22075	U.S.A.	1993	12.99
Mayall, John	A Hard Core Package	CD	One Way	MCAD-22071	U.S.A.	1993	12.99
Mayall, John	A Hard Core Package/Last British Blues	2CD	BGO	BGOCD493	England	2000	19.99
Mayall, John	A Sense Of Place	CD	Island	842-795-2	U.S.A.	1990	11.99
Mayall, John	Archive	CD	Rialto	RMCD-232Z	England	2001	12.99
Mayall, John	Archives To The Eighties + 5	CD	Polydor	837-127-2	U.S.A.	1989	15.99
Mayall, John	Back To The Roots + 4	2CD	Polydor	314-549-424-2	U.S.A.	2001	11.99
Mayall, John	Blue For You	CD	Dressed To Kill	DTK-385	England	2000	12.99
Mayall, John	Blues For The Lost Days	CD	Silvertone	ORECD-41605	U.S.A.	1997	8.99
Mayall, John	Blues From Laurel Canyon	CD	Deram	820-539-2	U.S.A.	1989	11.99
Mayall, John	Blues Power	2CD	Recall	SMD-CD-233	England	1999	12.99
Mayall, John	Crusade	CD	London	820-537-2	U.S.A.	1988	9.99

M

Artist	Title	Format	Label	Catalog No	Country	Released	Value
Mayall, John	Drivin' On: The ABC Years '75 - '82	CD	MCA	MCAD-11787	U.S.A.	1998	39.99
Mayall, John	Empty Rooms	CD	PolyGram	314-527-457-2	England	1996	10.99
Mayall, John	Jazz Blues Fusion	CD	Polydor	527-460-2	Germany	1996	8.99
Mayall, John	Live At The Marquee 1969	CD	Eagle	EAMCD070	England	1999	8.99
Mayall, John	London Blues 1964-1969	2CD	Deram	844-302-2	U.S.A.	1992	20.99
Mayall, John	Looking Back	CD	Deram	820-331-2	Germany	1990	12.99
Mayall, John	Lost And Gone	CD	Movie Play	MP-74070	U.S.A.	2001	10.99
Mayall, John	Lots Of People	CD	One Way	MCAD-22073	U.S.A.	1977	14.99
Mayall, John	Memories	CD	Polydor	527-459-2	England	1996	11.99
Mayall, John	New Year, New Band, New Company	CD	One Way	MCAD-22072	U.S.A.	1975	14.99
Mayall, John	New Year, New Band/Lots Of People	2CD	BGO	BGOCD492	England	2000	19.99
Mayall, John	Nightriding: John Mayall	CD	Knight	KNCD-10010	England	1988	15.99
Mayall, John	Padlock On The Blues	CD	Cleopatra	CLP0597-2	U.S.A.	1999	9.99
Mayall, John	Primal Solos	CD	London	820-320-2	U.S.A.	1977	10.99
Mayall, John	Roadshow Blues Band	CD	Thunderbolt	CDTB-060	England	1988	11.99
Mayall, John	Rock The Blues Tonight	CD	Indigo	IGOXDCD-102 X	England	1999	11.99
Mayall, John	Rockin' The Roadshow	2CD	Sanctuary	06076-81299-2	U.S.A.	2003	14.99
Mayall, John	Room To Move	2CD	PolyGram	314-517-291-2	U.S.A.	1992	14.99
Mayall, John	Silver Tones: The Best Of	CD	Silvertone	ORECD-41658	U.S.A.	1998	11.99
Mayall, John	Some Of My Best Friends Are Blues	CD	Decal	CD-LIK-1	England	1986	15.99
Mayall, John	Spinning Coin	CD	Silvertone	ORECD-41541	U.S.A.	1995	11.99
Mayall, John	The Blues Alone	CD	London	820-535-2	U.S.A.	1988	8.99
Mayall, John	The Blues Alone (MFSL Gold Cd)	CD	Mobile Fidelity	UDCD-662	U.S.A.	1967	16.99
Mayall, John	The Collection	CD	Castle	CCSCD-137	England	1986	12.99
Mayall, John	The Diary Of A Band, Vol. 1	CD	London	844-029-2	U.S.A.	1994	49.99
Mayall, John	The Diary Of A Band, Vol. 2	CD	Deram	844-030-2	U.S.A.	1994	49.99
Mayall, John	The Last Of The British Blues	CD	One Way	MCAD-22074	U.S.A.	1978	7.99
Mayall, John	The Last Of The British Blues	CD	One Way	MCAD-22074	U.S.A.	1993	12.99
Mayall, John	The Masters	2CD	Eagle	6-70211-5055-2	England	1999	14.99
Mayall, John	The Power Of The Blues	CD	Decal	CDCHARLEY-212	England	1990	15.99
Mayall, John	The Turning Point + 3	CD	Polydor	314-549-423-2	U.S.A.	2001	11.99
Mayall, John	Time Capsule (Powerhouse 4/B Synd.)	CD	Private Stash	STASHCD01	U.S.A.	2000	24.99
Mayall, John	Time Expired, Notice To Appear	CD	One Way	MCAD-22070	U.S.A.	1993	12.99
Mayall, John	Time Expired/A Banquet In Blues	2CD	BGO	BGOCD495	England	2000	19.99
Mayall, John	USA Union	CD	Polydor	314-527-458-2	England	1996	11.99
Mayall, John	Waiting For The Right Time	CD	Elite	ELITE-001	England	1991	24.99
Mayall, John	Wake Up Call	CD	Silvertone	ORECD-41518	U.S.A.	1993	11.99
Mayall, John/Bluesbreakers	70th Birthday Concert	2CD	Eagle	ER-20017-2	U.S.A.	2003	16.99
Mayall, John/Bluesbreakers	A Hard Road (P Green/McVie) + 22	2CD	Deram	B0001083-02	U.S.A.	2003	14.99
Mayall, John/Bluesbreakers	As It All Began: The Best Of	CD	Deram	42284-4785-2	U.S.A.	1997	13.99
Mayall, John/Bluesbreakers	Bare Wires	CD	Rebound	314-520-206-2	U.S.A.	1994	8.99
Mayall, John/Bluesbreakers	Behind The Iron Curtain	CD	GNP	GNPD-2184	U.S.A.	1991	14.99
Mayall, John/Bluesbreakers	Blues Forever	CD	Fuel 2000	302-061-287-2	U.S.A.	2003	8.99
Mayall, John/Bluesbreakers	Chicago Line	CD	Island	842-869-2	U.S.A.	1988	24.99
Mayall, John/Bluesbreakers	Cross Country Blues	CD	One Way	OW-30009	U.S.A.	1994	12.99
Mayall, John/Bluesbreakers	Plays Mayall	CD	London	820-536-2	England	1988	24.99
Mayall, John/Bluesbreakers	Return Of The Bluesbreakers + 3	CD	AIM	AIM-1004CD	Australia	1993	13.99
Mayall, John/Bluesbreakers	Stories	CD	Eagle	WK59669	U.S.A.	2002	11.99
Mayall, John/Bluesbreakers	Stories	CD	Red Ink	7669-2-59669-2-9	U.S.A.	2002	11.99
Mayall, John/Bluesbreakers	The 1982 Reunion Concert	CD	One Way	WO-30008	U.S.A.	1994	12.99
Mayall, John/Bluesbreakers	The 1982 Reunion Concert	CD	Repertoire	REP-4393-WY	Germany	1994	12.99
Mayall, John/Eric Clapton	Blues Breakers (MFSL Gold)	CD	Mobile Fidelity	UDCD-616	U.S.A.	1966	29.99
Mayall, John/Eric Clapton	Bluesbreakers + 12	CD	Universal	UICY-9169	Japan	2002	34.99
Mayall, John/Eric Clapton	Bluesbreakers + 2	CD	Universal	882-967-2	U.S.A.	2001	9.99
Mayall, John/Friends	Along For The Ride (Peter Green)	CD	Eagle	WK-18474	U.S.A.	2001	8.99
Mayall, John/Friends	Along For The Ride + 1	SACD	Audio Fidelity	AFZ-016	U.S.A.	2003	11.99
Mayer, John	Room For Squares (Orig Cd/Diff Mixes)	CD	Aware	AWA-110	U.S.A.	2001	64.99
Mazzy Star	Fade Into You	CD	Capitol	7243-8-58121-2-5	U.S.A.	1994	9.99

M

Artist	Title	Format	Label	Catalog No	Country	Released	Value
Mazzy Star	Fade Into You Plus Live Tracks (DJ)	CD	Capitol	DPRO-79401	U.S.A.	1994	12.99
Mazzy Star	She Hangs Brightly	CD	Capitol	7-96508-2	U.S.A.	1990	10.99
MC5	American Ruse	CD	Total Energy	NERCD-2001	U.S.A.	2001	6.99
MC5	Babes In Arms	CD	ROIR	RUSCD8236	U.S.A.	1998	13.99
MC5	Back In The U.S.A.	CD	Rhino	R2-71033	U.S.A.	1992	9.99
MC5	Black To Comm	CD	Receiver	RRCD-185	England	1994	15.99
MC5	High Time	CD	Rhino	R2-71034	U.S.A.	1992	9.99
MC5	Kick Out The Jams	CD	Warner Bros.	WPCP-4056	Japan	1969	29.99
MC5	Kick Out The Jams	CD	Elektra	9-60894-2	U.S.A.	1969	7.99
MC5	Live 1969-70	CD	Victor Ent.	VICP-61425	Japan	2001	29.99
MC5	Live Detroit 68/69	CD	Victor Ent.	VICP-61424	Japan	2001	29.99
MC5	Looking At You	CD	Receiver	RRCD-193	England	1994	7.99
MC5	Motor City Is Burning	CD	Essential	ESMCD-799	England	1999	12.99
MC5	Power Trip	CD	Alive	ALIVE005	U.S.A.	1998	15.99
MC5	The Big Bang! Best Of...	CD	Rhino	R2-79783	U.S.A.	2000	10.99
MC5	Thunder Express + 2	CD	Nippon Columbia	COCB-50320	Japan	2000	29.99
MC5	Thunder Express + 2	CD	Jungle	FREUD-CD-71	England	1999	12.99
McCallum, David	Music Is A ...(A Part Of Me/A Bit More)	CD	EMI	533-131-2	England	2001	15.99
McCallum, David	Open Channel D	CD	Rev-Ola	CREV043	England	1997	24.99
McCarthy, Dennis	Deep Space Nine : Emissary	CD	GNP	GNPD-8034	U.S.A.	1993	12.99
McCarthy, Dennis	Generations (O.S.T.)	CD	GNP	GNPD-8040	U.S.A.	1994	14.99
McCarthy, Dennis	Theme From Deep Space Nine	CD Single	GNP	GNPD-1401	U.S.A.	1993	8.99
McCartney, Linda	A Garland For Linda	CD	EMI Classics	7243-5-56961-2-0	U.S.A.	2000	9.99
McCartney, Linda	Wide Prairie	CD	Capitol	7243-4-97910-2-2	U.S.A.	1998	9.99
McCartney, Linda	Wide Prairie (Promo)	CD Single	EMI	CDR-DJ-6510	England	1998	13.99
McCartney, Paul	All The Best	CD	Capitol	7-48287-2	U.S.A.	1987	8.99
McCartney, Paul	All The Best (Gold Cd)	CD	Toshiba-EMI	TOCP-6117	Japan	1991	44.99
McCartney, Paul	Back In The U.S. Live 2002 + DVD	2CD	Capitol	7243-5-42318-2-7	U.S.A.	2002	23.99
McCartney, Paul	Choba B Cccp	CD	EMI	7976152	U.S.A.	1987	11.99
McCartney, Paul	Driving Rain	CD Single	Capitol	7087-6-15995-2-7	U.S.A.	2001	5.99
McCartney, Paul	Driving Rain	CD	Capitol	7243-5-35510-2-5	U.S.A.	2001	7.99
McCartney, Paul	Driving Rain (Promo Sampler)	CD	Capitol	7087-6-15995-2-7	U.S.A.	2001	11.99
McCartney, Paul	Flaming Pie	CD	Capitol	7243-8-56500-2-4	U.S.A.	1997	8.99
McCartney, Paul	Flaming Pies (DJ/W/Six Recipies)	CD	EMI	7243-8-56500-2-4	England	1997	39.99
McCartney, Paul	Flowers In The Dirt + 3	CD	EMI	0777-7-89138-2-5	England	1993	11.99
McCartney, Paul	Freedom	CD Single	Capitol	7243-5-50291-2-6	U.S.A.	2001	5.99
McCartney, Paul	Freedom (Promo)	CD Single	Capitol	7087-6-16903-2	U.S.A.	2002	11.99
McCartney, Paul	From A Lover To A Friend (Promo)	CD Single	Capitol	DPRO-15992-2	U.S.A.	2001	11.99
McCartney, Paul	Give My Regards To Broad Street + 2	CD	EMI	0777-7-89268-2-5	Holland	1993	15.99
McCartney, Paul	In Conversation	CD	Baktabak	CBAK-4063	England	1994	9.99
McCartney, Paul	Interview (Best Buy/Run Devil Bonus)	CD	Capitol	7243-5-23343-2	U.S.A.	1999	19.99
McCartney, Paul	Liverpool Oratorio	2CD	EMI Classics	7-54371-2	U.S.A.	1991	14.99
McCartney, Paul	McCartney	CD	EMI	0777-7-89239-2-3	England	1993	14.99
McCartney, Paul	McCartney (DCC Gold Cd)	CD	DCC	GZS-1029	U.S.A.	1993	39.99
McCartney, Paul	McCartney II + 3	CD	EMI	0777-7-89137-2-6	England	1993	8.99
McCartney, Paul	My Brave Face (Cancelled Promo)	CD	Capitol	CDP-7-15468-2	U.S.A.	1989	249.99
McCartney, Paul	My Brave Face (Promo)	CD Single	Capitol	DPRO-79592	U.S.A.	1989	12.99
McCartney, Paul	New World Sampler (Promo)	2CD	Capitol	DPRO-79671	U.S.A.	1993	64.99
McCartney, Paul	No Other Baby/Br Eyed H Man	CD Single	Parlophone	7243-8-87739-2-8	England	1999	9.99
McCartney, Paul	Off the Ground Complete Works	2CD	Capitol	7243-8-28227-2-1	Holland	1993	88.99
McCartney, Paul	Paul Is Live	CD	EMI	7243-8-27704-2-8	U.S.A.	1993	8.99
McCartney, Paul	Paul Is Live (Promo Sampler)	CD	Parlophone	PMLIVE-1	Germany	1993	39.99
McCartney, Paul	Press To Play + 2	CD	EMI	0777-7-89269-2-4	Germany	1993	13.99
McCartney, Paul	Run Devil Run	CD	Capitol	7243-5-22351-2-4	U.S.A.	1999	7.99
McCartney, Paul	Standing Stone	CD	EMI Classics	7243-5-56484-2-6	U.S.A.	1997	8.99
McCartney, Paul	The World Tonight	CD Single	EMI	7243-8-58650-2-2	U.S.A.	1997	8.99
McCartney, Paul	The World Tonight	CD Single	Capitol	7087-6-12034-2-4	U.S.A.	1997	8.99
McCartney, Paul	Tripping The Live Fantastic	2CD	Capitol	7-94778-2	U.S.A.	1990	25.99

M

Artist	Title	Format	Label	Catalog No	Country	Released	Value
McCartney, Paul	Tug Of War	CD	Capitol	0777-7-89266-2-7	England	1993	15.99
McCartney, Paul	Unplugged	CD	Toshiba-EMI	TOCP-6713	Japan	1991	11.99
McCartney, Paul	Vanilla Sky (Academy Promo)	CD Single	Warner Bros.	22856-1	U.S.A.	2001	174.99
McCartney, Paul	Young Boy (Disc 2)	CD Single	Parlophone	7243-8-83951-2-0	England	1997	8.99
McCartney, Paul/C. Aubut	Family Way (O.S.T.) Paul's Lp As Well	CD	XXI	XXI-CD-2-1468	U.S.A.	2003	19.99
McCartney, Paul/C. Aubut	The Family Way	CD	Phillips	314-528-922-2	U.S.A.	1995	9.99
McCartney, Paul/Crickets	T-Shirts	CD	Epic	EK-44446	U.S.A.	1988	14.99
McCartney, Paul/D Laine	Holly Days	CD	Magic	3930035	France	2000	19.99
McCartney, Paul/Fireman	Rushes	CD	EMI	7243-4-97055-2-4	England	1998	24.99
McCartney, Paul/Fireman	Strawberries Oceans Ships Forest	CD	Capitol	7243-8-27167-2-3	U.S.A.	1993	19.99
McCartney, Paul/G Nash	McGough/McGear (Hendrix/Bruce)	CD	EMI	CDP7-91877-2	England	1989	83.99
McCartney, Paul/Ginsberg	The Ballad Of The Skeletons	CD	Mercury	697-120-101-2	U.S.A.	1996	10.99
McCartney, Paul/Linda	Ram (DCC Gold Cd)	CD	DCC	GZS-1037	U.S.A.	1993	44.99
McCartney, Paul/Linda	Ram + 2	CD	EMI	0777-7-89139-2-4	Holland	1993	13.99
McCartney, Paul/M McGear	McGear + 1	CD	Rykodisc	RCD-10192	U.S.A.	1974	24.99
McCartney, Paul/M McGear	Woman	CD	Edsel	EDCD-507	England	1997	24.99
McCartney, Paul/Thrillington	Thrillington	CD	Regal Zonophone	7243-8-32145-2-5	England	1995	14.99
McCartney, Paul/V.A.	MPL's Treasury Of Songs... (Promo)	CD	MPL	MPLCD1-3	England	1993	149.99
McCartney, Paul/V.A.	Orig. Vrsns 4 Songs/"Run Devil Run"	CD	Capitol	7243-5-23426-2-4	U.S.A.	1999	12.99
McCartney, Paul/Wings	All My Trials (Single)	CD Single	EMI	CDR-6278	England	1990	11.99
McCartney, Paul/Wings	All Time Favorites (Promo)	2CD	Toshiba-EMI	SPCD-1330~31	Japan	1993	599.99
McCartney, Paul/Wings	At The Speed Of Sound + 3 (Gold Cd)	CD	DCC	GZS-1096	U.S.A.	1996	41.99
McCartney, Paul/Wings	Back To The Egg + 3	CD	EMI	0777-7-89136-2-7	England	1993	15.99
McCartney, Paul/Wings	Band On The Run + 2	CD	EMI	0777-7-89240-2-9	Holland	1993	13.99
McCartney, Paul/Wings	Band On The Run (25th Ann. Ed.)	2CD	Capitol	7243-4-99176-2-0	U.S.A.	1999	14.99
McCartney, Paul/Wings	Band On The Run (DCC Gold Cd)	CD	DCC	GZS-1030	U.S.A.	1993	49.99
McCartney, Paul/Wings	Best 16	CD	TF	T-2006	Japan	1988	28.99
McCartney, Paul/Wings	Flowers In The Dirt (W/Bonus Mix Cd)	2CD	Toshiba-EMI	TOCP-6118.19	Japan	1991	49.99
McCartney, Paul/Wings	In Siegen	CD	Collector's Friend	CFF-001	Germany	1999	12.99
McCartney, Paul/Wings	Liverpool Sound Collage	CD	Capitol	7243-5-28817-2-7	U.S.A.	2000	10.99
McCartney, Paul/Wings	London Town + 2	CD	EMI	0777-7-89265-2-8	England	1993	14.99
McCartney, Paul/Wings	MPL Collection (DJ Publishing Sampler)	5CD	Capitol	MPL96-1	U.S.A.	2000	599.99
McCartney, Paul/Wings	Oobu Joobu - Ecology	CD	Best Buy	00031-27850-6	U.S.A.	1997	8.99
McCartney, Paul/Wings	Paul McCartney Rocks (DJ Sampler)	CD	EMI	DPRO-79987	U.S.A.	1990	21.99
McCartney, Paul/Wings	Pipes Of Peace + 3	CD	EMI	0777-7-89267-2-6	England	1993	12.99
McCartney, Paul/Wings	Red Rose Speedway + 3	CD	Capitol	7-52026-2	U.S.A.	1973	12.99
McCartney, Paul/Wings	Red Rose Speedway + 4	CD	EMI	0777-7-89238-2-4	Canada	1993	17.99
McCartney, Paul/Wings	Red Rose Speedway + 4 (DCC Gold)	CD	DCC	GZS-1091	U.S.A.	1996	44.99
McCartney, Paul/Wings	The Paul McCartney Collection (Promo)	CD	Parlophone	CDPMCOLDJ-1	England	1993	24.99
McCartney, Paul/Wings	Venus And Mars + 3	CD	EMI	0777-7-89241-2-8	England	1993	13.99
McCartney, Paul/Wings	Venus And Mars + 3 (DCC Gold Cd)	CD	DCC	GZS-1067	U.S.A.	1994	44.99
McCartney, Paul/Wings	Wild Life + 4	CD	EMI	0777-7-89237-2-5	England	1993	13.99
McCartney, Paul/Wings	Wings At The Speed of Sound + 3	CD	EMI	0777-7-89140-2-0	Holland	1993	11.99
McCartney, Paul/Wings	Wings Greatest Hits	CD	EMI	0777-7-89317-2-0	Canada	1993	12.99
McCartney, Paul/Wings	Wings Over America	2CD	Capitol	7-46715-2	U.S.A.	1978	21.99
McCartney, Paul/Wings	Wingspan (Promo Sampler)	CD	Capitol	7087-6-15951-2-3	U.S.A.	2001	19.99
McCartney, Paul/Wings	Wingspan: History (Leatherbound Ed.)	CD	Capitol	7243-5-32948-2-3	U.S.A.	2001	29.99
McCartney, Paul/Wings	Wingspan-Hits/History	2CD	Toshiba-EMI	TOCP-65746+47	Japan	2001	44.99
McCartney, Paul/Wings	Working Classical	CD	EMI Classics	7243-5-56897-2-6	U.S.A.	1999	14.99
McCleod, Doug/Band	Woman In The Street	CD	Line	STCD-9.00444-0	Germany	1988	12.99
McCluskey Brothers	Wonderful Affair	CD	Line	LICD-9.01307-0	Germany	1996	12.99
McCord, Kent/One Way	I Cry	CD	P-Vine	PCD-1951	Japan	1994	37.99
McCoys	Best Of The McCoys	CD	Epic	480951-2	Austria	1995	21.99
McCoys	Hang On Sloopy/You Make Me Feel..	CD	Repertoire	REP-4294-WY	Germany	1993	24.99
McCullough, Henry	Cut	CD	Line	LICD-9.00342-0	Germany	1987	18.99
McCullough, Henry	Cut	CD	Line	LICD—9.01378-0	Germany	1987	18.99
McCullough, Henry	Get In The Hole Live	CD	Line	LICD-9.00686-0	Germany	1989	24.99
McCullough, Henry	Hell Of A Record	CD	Line	LICD—9.01376-0	Germany	1988	18.99

M

Artist	Title	Format	Label	Catalog No	Country	Released	Value
McCullough, Henry	Hell Of A Record	CD	Line	LICD-9.00072-0	Germany	1988	18.99
McDonald, Country Joe	A Reflection/Changing Times Box Set	4 Mini Lp	Akarma	AK/4VMD-171/4	Italy	2002	44.99
McDonald, Country Joe	Animal Tracks	CD	Line	RBCD-9.00301-0	Germany	1988	12.99
McDonald, Country Joe	Carry On	CD	Line	RBCD-9.01302-0	Germany	1994	12.99
McDonald, Country Joe	Child's Play	CD	Line	RBCD-9.00298-0	Germany	1988	12.99
McDonald, Country Joe	Child's Play	CD	One Way	OW-34431	U.S.A.	1983	8.99
McDonald, Country Joe	Classics	CD	Fantasy	FCD-7709-2	U.S.A.	1989	7.99
McDonald, Country Joe	Country Joe	CD	One Way	OW-30997	U.S.A.	1974	8.99
McDonald, Country Joe	Goodbye Blues	CD	Line	RBCD-9.0128-0	Germany	1993	12.99
McDonald, Country Joe	Incredible! Live!	CD	One Way	OW-30996	U.S.A.	1972	8.99
McDonald, Country Joe	Into The Fray	CD	Line	RBCD-9.00603-0	Germany	1988	12.99
McDonald, Country Joe	Into The Fray	CD	One Way	OW-31370	U.S.A.	1982	8.99
McDonald, Country Joe	Leisure Suite	CD	Line	RBCD-9.00317-0	Germany	1988	24.99
McDonald, Country Joe	Love Is A Fire	CD	Line	RBCD-9.01292-0	Germany	1993	12.99
McDonald, Country Joe	On My Own	CD	Line	RBCD-9.00305-0	Germany	1988	12.99
McDonald, Country Joe	On My Own	CD	One Way	OW-31372	U.S.A.	1980	8.99
McDonald, Country Joe	Paradise With An Ocean View	CD	Line	RBCD-9.01209-0	Germany	1992	24.99
McDonald, Country Joe	Paris Sessions	CD	One Way	OW-30999	U.S.A.	1973	8.99
McDonald, Country Joe	Peace On Earth	CD	Line	RBCD-9.00068-0	Germany	1988	12.99
McDonald, Country Joe	Peace On Earth	CD	One Way	OW-31369	U.S.A.	1984	8.99
McDonald, Country Joe	Rock 'N' Roll Music From Planet Earth	CD	Line	RBCD-9.01212-0	Germany	1992	19.99
McDonald, Country Joe	Superstitious Blues	CD	Line	RBCD-9.00942-0	Germany	1989	24.99
McDonald, Country Joe	Thinking Of Woody Guthrie	CD	Vanguard	VMD-6546	U.S.A.	1969	11.99
McDonald, Country Joe	Tonight I'm Singing Just For You	CD	One Way	OW-31000	U.S.A.	1970	8.99
McDonald, Country Joe	Vietnam Experience	CD	Line	RBCD-9.00418-0	Germany	1991	24.99
McDonald, Country Joe/Fish	C.J. Fish	CD	Vanguard	6555-2	U.S.A.	1970	12.99
McDonald, Country Joe/Fish	Collected Country Joe/Fish ('63-'70)	CD	Vanguard	VCD-111	U.S.A.	1987	20.99
McDonald, Country Joe/Fish	Collector's Items (The First Three EPs)	CD	Line	RBCD-9.01201-0	Germany	1992	34.99
McDonald, Country Joe/Fish	Electric Music For The Mind And Body	CD	Vanguard	79244-2	U.S.A.	1987	12.99
McDonald, Country Joe/Fish	Here We Go Again	CD	Vanguard	79299-2	U.S.A.	1969	14.99
McDonald, Country Joe/Fish	I-Feel-Like-I'm-Fixin'-To-Die Rag	CD	Vanguard	VMD-79266	U.S.A.	1988	14.99
McDonald, Country Joe/Fish	Live! Fillmore West 1969	CD	Vanguard	139/40-2	U.S.A.	1994	12.99
McDonald, Country Joe/Fish	Rag Baby Eps Box Set	CD	Akarma	AK-919	Italy	1965	19.99
McDonald, Country Joe/Fish	The Life And Times Of...	CD	Vanguard	VCD-27/28	U.S.A.	1981	12.99
McDonald, Country Joe/Fish	Together	CD	Vanguard	VMD-79277	U.S.A.	1968	12.99
McDonald, Ian	Drivers Eyes	CD	Camino	CAMCD18	England	1999	8.99
McDonald, Michael	In The Spirit (Christmas CD)	CD	MCA	088-170-230-2	U.S.A.	2001	7.99
McDonald, Michael	Very Best Of	CD	Rhino	R2-76649	U.S.A.	2001	9.99
McEntire, Reba	It's Your Call (Telephone Cd/Promo)	CD	MCA	MCA3P-10673	U.S.A.	1992	44.99
McGarrigle, Kate & Anna	Dancer With Bruised Knees	CD	Warner Bros.	7599-25958-2	Germany	1995	12.99
McGarrigle, Kate & Anna	Entre Lajeunesse...(French Album)	CD	Hannibal	HNCD-1302	U.S.A.	1992	39.99
McGarrigle, Kate & Anna	Heartbeats Accelerating	CD	Private	2070-2-P	U.S.A.	1990	15.99
McGarrigle, Kate & Anna	Love Over And Over	CD	PolyGram	422-841-101-2	Canada	1982	12.99
McGarrigle, Kate & Anna	Matapedia	CD	Hannibal	HCD-1394	U.S.A.	1996	12.99
McGarrigle, Kate & Anna	Self Titled	CD	Warner Bros.	9362-45677-2	Germany	1995	12.99
McGarrigle, Kate & Anna	The McGarrigle Hour	CD	Hannibal	HNCD-1417	U.S.A.	1998	17.99
McGarrigle, Kate & Anna	Vache Qui Pleure	CD	La Tribu	TRICD-7211	Canada	2003	19.99
McGoohan, Patrick/Goodman	On The Trail Of The Prisoner (Int. Cd)	CD	Keystone M	KMGCDS1160	England	2002	64.99
McGuinn, Clark & Hillman	3 Byrds Live In London	CD	Master Tone	8228	U.S.A.	1998	9.99
McGuinn, Clark & Hillman	City	CD	One Way	S21-18503	U.S.A.	1996	14.99
McGuinn, Clark & Hillman	McGuinn, Clark & Hillman	CD	Capitol	7-96355-2	U.S.A.	1979	17.99
McGuinn, Clark & Hillman	Self Titled	CD	Toshiba-EMI	TOCP-6387	Japan	1990	17.99
McGuinn, Clark & Hillman	Three Byrds Land In London	2CD	Strange Fruit	SFRSCD001	England	1997	34.99
McGuinn, Roger	Back From Rio	CD	Arista	ARCD-8648	U.S.A.	1990	7.99
McGuinn, Roger	Born To Rock 'N Roll	CD	Columbia	CK-47494	U.S.A.	1991	11.99
McGuinn, Roger	Born To Rock 'N Roll	CD	Edsel	EDCD-281	England	1988	11.99
McGuinn, Roger	Cardiff Rose	CD	Columbia	CK-34154	U.S.A.	1976	14.99
McGuinn, Roger	Live From Mars	CD	Hollywood	HR-62090-2	U.S.A.	1996	19.99

M

Artist	Title	Format	Label	Catalog No	Country	Released	Value
McGuinn, Roger	Peace On You + 1	CD	Sundazed	SC-6202-2	U.S.A.	2004	11.99
McGuinn, Roger	Self Titled + 2	CD	Sundazed	SC-6201-2	U.S.A.	2004	11.99
McGuinn, Roger	Treasures From The Folk Den	CD	Appleseed	APR-CD-1046	U.S.A.	2001	9.99
McGuire, Barry	Eve Of Destruction	CD	MCA	MCD-18227	Germany	1985	16.99
McKee, Maria	Life Is Sweet	CD	Geffen	GEFD-24819	U.S.A.	1996	8.99
McKee, Maria	Maria McKee	CD	Geffen	9-24229-2	U.S.A.	1989	8.99
McKee, Maria	You Gotta Sin To Get Saved	CD	Geffen	GEFD-24508	U.S.A.	1993	6.99
McKendree Spring	First	CD	Line	LICD-9.01256-0	Germany	1994	14.99
McKendree Spring	God Bless The Conspiracy	CD	Edsel	EDCD-497	England	1996	14.99
McKendree Spring	McKendree Spring 3	CD	Line	LICD-9.01258-0	Germany	1994	14.99
McKendree Spring	Second Thoughts	CD	Line	LICD-9.01257-0	Germany	1994	14.99
McKendree Spring	Spring Suite	CD	Line	LICD-9.01260-0	Germany	1993	14.99
McKendree Spring	Tracks	CD	Line	LICD-9.01259-0	Germany	1993	14.99
McKenzie, Scott	Stained Glass Reflections 1960-1970	CD	Raven	RVCD-115	Australia	2000	18.99
McLean, Don	American Pie (MFSL Gold Cd)	CD	Mobile Fidelity	UDCD-728	U.S.A.	1980	33.99
McLean, Don	American Pie + 2	CD	Capitol	72435-84279-2-9	U.S.A.	2003	8.99
McLean, Don	And I Love You So	CD	EMI	CDP-7934442	England	1989	11.99
McLean, Don	Believers + 1	CD	Hip O	HIPD-40060	U.S.A.	1997	8.99
McLean, Don	Best Of	CD	EMI	CDP-7-91476-2	U.S.A.	1988	6.99
McLean, Don	Chained Lightning + 1	CD	Hip O	HIPD-40061	U.S.A.	1997	8.99
McLean, Don	Christmas	CD	Curb	D2-77512	U.S.A.	1991	7.99
McLean, Don	Christmas Dreams	CD	Hip O	HIPD-40074	U.S.A.	1997	7.99
McLean, Don	Classics (Re-Recorded A Pie/Vincent)	CD	Curb	D2-77547	U.S.A.	1992	7.99
McLean, Don	Crying: The Most Beautiful Love Songs	CD	BR Music	BX417-2	Holland	1994	11.99
McLean, Don	Favorites And Rarities	2CD	EMI	0777-7-98603-2-6	U.S.A.	1992	13.99
McLean, Don	For The Memories Vol. 1/2 (He's G Y)	CD	Gold Castle	D2-71330	U.S.A.	1989	19.99
McLean, Don	For The Memories Vol. 1/2 (Rainbow)	2CD	Hip O	HIPD-40054	U.S.A.	1997	19.99
McLean, Don	Greatest Hits Live (Dominion)	2CD	Hip O	HIPD2-40033	U.S.A.	1997	12.99
McLean, Don	Greatest Hits Then & Now	CD	EMI	7-46586-2	U.S.A.	1987	8.99
McLean, Don	Headroom	CD	Curb	D2-77427	U.S.A.	1991	5.99
McLean, Don	Homeless Brother	CD	BGO	BGOCD247	England	1996	14.99
McLean, Don	Killing Us Softly	CD	Festival	TVD-93403	Australia	1994	11.99
McLean, Don	Love Tracks	CD	Capitol	CDP-7-48080-2	U.S.A.	1988	9.99
McLean, Don	Playin' Favorites	CD	BGO	BGOCD21	England	1996	14.99
McLean, Don	Prime Time + 1	CD	Hip O	HIPD-40055	U.S.A.	1997	8.99
McLean, Don	River Of Love	CD	Curb	D2-77791	U.S.A.	1995	11.99
McLean, Don	Self Titled	CD	BGO	BGOCD246	England	1996	14.99
McLean, Don	Sings Marty Robbins	CD	Madacy	1367	U.S.A.	2001	8.99
McLean, Don	Solo (Live)	CD	BGO	BGOCD300	England	1996	18.99
McLean, Don	Starry Starry Night	2CD	Madacy	1368	U.S.A.	2001	17.99
McLean, Don	Tapestry	CD	EMI	7243-8-53928-2-5	U.S.A.	1996	8.99
McLean, Don	Tapestry	CD	BGO	BGOCD232	England	1996	14.99
McLean, Don	The Don McLean Collection	CD	Music Club	MCCD438	U.S.A.	2000	10.99
McMurray, David	The Secret Life	CD	Line	TLCD-9.00830-0	Germany	1989	19.99
McNair, Barbara	You're Gonna Love (Only 500)	CD	Marginal	MAR-058	EEC	1997	23.99
McTell, Ralph	Streets Of London	CD	Line	TACD-9.00556-0	Germany	1988	8.99
McVie, Christine	Christine Mcvie	CD	Warner Bros.	WPCP-3410	Japan	1984	29.99
McVie, Christine (Perfect)	Christine Perfect	CD	Columbia	474700-2	Austria	1970	69.99
Mealticket	Take Away	CD	Line	TACD-9.00780-0	Germany	1989	12.99
Meat Loaf	Back From Hell! - The Very Best Of	CD	Columbia	475652-2	Germany	1993	18.99
Meat Loaf	Back Out Of Hell II (Deluxe Ed)	2CD	MCA	088-112-810-2	U.S.A.	2002	14.99
Meat Loaf	Bad Attitude	CD	Arista	07863-55454-2	U.S.A.	1984	9.99
Meat Loaf	Bat Out of Hell (Sony Gold Cd)	CD	Columbia	EK-57443	U.S.A.	1993	24.99
Meat Loaf	Bat Out Of Hell + 2	CD	Epic	EK-62171	U.S.A.	2001	8.99
Meat Loaf	Bat Out Of Hell II (Full Color Picture Cd)	CD	MCA	MCASD-10699	U.S.A.	1993	29.99
Meat Loaf	Bat Out Of Hell II (Wheel Box)	CD	MCA	MCAD-10971	U.S.A.	1993	29.99
Meat Loaf	Blind Before I Stop	CD	Atlantic	7-81698-2	U.S.A.	1986	10.99
Meat Loaf	CD Sampler (Promo)	CD	MCA	MCA3P-3562	U.S.A.	1995	19.99

M

Artist	Title	Format	Label	Catalog No	Country	Released	Value
Meat Loaf	Couldn't Have Said It... (W/Bonus Cd)	2CD	Polydor	076-118-2	U.S.A.	2003	15.99
Meat Loaf	Deadringer	CD	Epic	EK-36007	U.S.A.	1981	9.99
Meat Loaf	Definitive Collection + 4 (Bonus CD)	2CD	Epic	480567-9	Holland	1995	11.99
Meat Loaf	Hits Out Of Hell	CD	Epic	450447-2	England	1994	7.99
Meat Loaf	I'd Lie For You (And That's The Truth)	CD Single	Virgin	7243-8-93187-2-2	England	1995	8.99
Meat Loaf	I'd Lie For You...	CD Single	Virgin	7243-8-93188-2-1	England	1995	9.99
Meat Loaf	I'd Lie For You...	CD Single	MCA	MCADM-55135	U.S.A.	1995	5.99
Meat Loaf	Life Is A Lemon... (Promo)	CD Single	MCA	MCA5P-2883	U.S.A.	1993	12.99
Meat Loaf	Live Around The World (Limited Ed.)	2CD	Tommy Boy	TBCD-1187	U.S.A.	1996	13.99
Meat Loaf	Live At Wembley	CD	Arista	258-599	England	1987	14.99
Meat Loaf	Midnight At the Lost and Found	CD	Epic	EK-38444	U.S.A.	1983	9.99
Meat Loaf	Not A Dry Eye In The House	CD Single	MCA	MCADM-55177	U.S.A.	1996	5.99
Meat Loaf	Not A Dry Eye In The House	CD Single	Virgin	7243-8-93324-2-1	England	1996	8.99
Meat Loaf	Objects In The Rear View...	CD Single	Virgin	7243-8-92423-2-4	England	1994	8.99
Meat Loaf	Objects In The Rear View...	CD Single	Virgin	7243-8-92422-2-5	England	1994	8.99
Meat Loaf	Objects In The Rear View...	CD Single	MCA	MCADM-54858	U.S.A.	1994	5.99
Meat Loaf	Paradise By The Dashboard Light (DJ)	CD Single	MCA	MCA5P-2492	U.S.A.	1992	14.99
Meat Loaf	Prime Cuts	CD	Arista	260-363	Germany	1989	9.99
Meat Loaf	Rock And Roll Dreams...	CD Single	Virgin	7243-8-92234-2-2	Australia	1993	9.99
Meat Loaf	Rock And Roll Dreams....	CD Single	MCA	MCADM-54797	U.S.A.	1994	5.99
Meat Loaf	Twelve Inch Mixes	CD	Epic	450131-2	England	1993	12.99
Meat Loaf	Two Out Of Three Ain't Bad	CD	Sony	A-58144	U.S.A.	2002	6.99
Meat Loaf	Very Best Of Meat Loaf	2CD	Epic	E2K-69335	U.S.A.	2001	15.99
Meat Loaf	Welcome To The Neighbourhood	CD	MCA	MCAD-11341	U.S.A.	1995	6.99
Meat Loaf	Welcome To The Neighbourhood + 2	CD	Toshiba-EMI	VJCP-25199	Japan	1995	34.99
Meat Loaf/Various Artists	Meat Loaf And Friends (W/Bonus Cd)	CD	Epic	472419-2	Holland	1992	14.99
Meco	The Best Of Meco	CD	Casablanca	314-553-255-2	U.S.A.	1997	17.99
Medium Medium	Live In Holland	CD	Line	TCCD-9.00529-0	Germany	1988	24.99
Medium Medium	The Glitterhouse & Plus	CD	Line	TCCD-9.00577-0	Germany	1988	24.99
Meek, Joe/The Blue Men	I Hear A New World	CD	Line	OLCD-9.51161-X	Germany	1991	14.99
Megadeth	Capitol Punishment	CD	Capitol	7243-5-25916-2-6	U.S.A.	2000	8.99
Megadeth	Capitol Punishment + 1	CD	Toshiba-EMI	TOCP-8555	Japan	2000	21.99
Megadeth	Countdown To Extinction	CD	Capitol	CDP-7-98531-2	U.S.A.	1992	6.99
Megadeth	Countdown To Extinction + 2	CD	Toshiba-EMI	TOCP-7164	Japan	1992	19.99
Megadeth	Cryptic Warnings + 1	CD	Toshiba-EMI	TOCP-50211	Japan	1997	17.99
Megadeth	Cryptic Writings (W/Extra CD Promo)	CD Single	Capitol	7087-6-12053-2-9	U.S.A.	1997	24.99
Megadeth	Hidden Treasures + 4	CD	Toshiba-EMI	TOCP-8555	Japan	1995	21.99
Megadeth	Killing Is My Business... + 4	CD	Loud	9046-2	U.S.A.	2002	9.99
Megadeth	Live Trax	CD	Toshiba-EMI	TOCP-50355	Japan	1997	24.99
Megadeth	Megabox	4CD	Toshiba-EMI	TOCP-7591~95	Japan	1995	99.99
Megadeth	Peace Sells... But Who's Buying	CD	Capitol	CDP-7-46370-2	Holland	1986	7.99
Megadeth	Risk + 6 (W/Bonus Cd)	CD	EMI	5223360	EEC	1999	29.99
Megadeth	Rude Awakening	2CD	Sanctuary	06076-84544-2	U.S.A.	2002	14.99
Megadeth	Rude Awakening + 1	2CD	Victor Ent.	VICP-61754/55	Japan	2002	34.99
Megadeth	Rust In Peace	CD	Capitol	CDP-7-91935-2	England	1990	7.99
Megadeth	So Far, So Good... So What!	CD	Capitol	CDP-7-48148-2	England	1987	9.99
Megadeth	So Far, So Good...So What!	CD	Toshiba-EMI	TOCP-6752	Japan	1991	24.99
Megadeth	Still Alive.. And Well?	CD	Sanctuary	06076-84566-2	U.S.A.	2002	8.99
Megadeth	Still Alive..And Well?	CD	Victor Ent.	VICP-62129	Japan	2002	21.99
Megadeth	The World Needs A Hero	CD	Sanctuary	06076-84503-2	U.S.A.	2001	8.99
Megadeth	The World Needs A Hero (Clean)	CD	Sanctuary	06076-84505-2	U.S.A.	2001	8.99
Megadeth	The World Needs A Hero + 1	CD	Victor Ent.	VICP-61348	Japan	2001	21.99
Megadeth	Youthanasia	CD	Capitol	7243-8-29004-2-9	U.S.A.	1994	5.99
Megadeth	Youthanasia (Ltd. Ed. Box/W T-Shirt)	CD	Capitol	7243-8-30916-2-1	U.S.A.	1994	24.99
Megadeth	Youthanasia + 4	CD	Toshiba-EMI	TOCP-8397	Japan	1994	19.99
Mekons	Millionaire	CD	Quarterstick	QS23CD	Canada	1993	8.99
Melanie	(Unplugged And) Solo Powered - All The	2CD	Angel Air	SJPCD103	England	2002	24.99
Melanie	Affectionately Melanie	CD	Sequel	NEB-CD-662	England	1993	49.99

M

Artist	Title	Format	Label	Catalog No	Country	Released	Value
Melanie	Am I Real Or What ?	CD	Bellaphon	284-07-012	Germany	1991	34.99
Melanie	Antlers - Christmas For True Believers)	CD	Blue Moon	BMXCD-91180	U.S.A.	1996	8.99
Melanie	Ballroom Streets - 4	CD	Tomato	2696052	Holland	1989	14.99
Melanie	Ballroom Streets - 4	CD	Rhino	R2-71283	U.S.A.	1994	14.99
Melanie	Beautiful People (New Versions)	CD	Brilliant	BT-33023	England	1999	8.99
Melanie	Beautiful People: Greatest Hits	CD	Buddah	7446-599630-2	U.S.A.	1999	7.99
Melanie	Born To Be	CD	C-Five	C5CD-582	England	1992	34.99
Melanie	Brand New Key: Live 1975 (Audio/Video	2CD	Master Tone	MM5514	England	1995	24.99
Melanie	Candles In The Rain + 2	CD	Buddah	75517-49509-2	U.S.A.	1996	49.99
Melanie	Cowabonga - (German Copy Sounds Be	CD	Baierle	CD-572-61013-CY	Germany	1988	34.99
Melanie	Crazy Love	CD	Pyramid	8-0246-90213-2-5	U.S.A.	2002	8.99
Melanie	Crazy Love + 1	CD	Sound & Vision	SCCD-1006	EU	2002	9.99
Melanie	Four Sides Of	2CD	Buddah	BDK2-95005	Canada	1992	43.99
Melanie	Four Sides Of	2CD	Wooded Hill	HILLCD-10	England	1998	43.99
Melanie	Freedom Knows My Name + 5	CD	Lonestar	7-81402-1947-2-5	U.S.A.	1993	7.99
Melanie	Gather Me	CD	C-Five	C5CD-591	England	1992	34.99
Melanie	Her Greatest Hits: Live & New Box Set	2CD	Laserlight	24-337	Germany	1996	19.99
Melanie	Leftover Wine	CD	One Way	OW-27649	U.S.A.	1993	29.99
Melanie	Live At Carnegie Hall	2CD	Euro Trend	CD-152.388	Austria	1999	37.99
Melanie	Low Country	CD	Melanie	62342	U.S.A.	1997	74.99
Melanie	Melanie (1987)	CD	CNR Music	100.130	Netherland	1987	74.99
Melanie	Melanie On Air	CD	Strange Fruit	SFRSCD035	England	1997	21.99
Melanie	Moments From My Life (New Recordings	CD	Disky	SI-794002	Holland	2002	8.99
Melanie	Old Bitch Warrior + 3	CD	Creastars	74321-29357-2	EC	1995	24.99
Melanie	Precious Cargo	CD	Precious Cargo	PC-1947	U.S.A.	1991	24.99
Melanie	Recorded Live @ Borders 1999	CD	Des	DES00499	U.S.A.	2000	14.99
Melanie	Recorded Live @ Borders 1999	CD	Disky	SI-792272	Holland	2002	14.99
Melanie	Ring The Living Bell	2CD	Renagade N	RAMJ001	U.S.A.	1999	34.99
Melanie	Ruby Tuesday + 2 (New Versions)	CD	Planet Song	7028	England	2000	8.99
Melanie	Shine On: The Latest And Greatest	CD	Deshima	DES-497705-2	Germany	2000	14.99
Melanie	Silence Is King	CD	Hypertension	HYCD-200-130	England	1993	34.99
Melanie	Silver Anniversary (W/Count/If If/Taking)	2CD	Hypertension	HYCD-200-136	England	1993	44.99
Melanie	Silver Anniversary (W/Freedom/Candles	2CD	Dino	CNCD-1372	Holland	1993	44.99
Melanie	The Best Of + 4	CD	Rhino	R2-70991	U.S.A.	1990	9.99
Melanie	The Good Book	CD	C-Five	C5CD-597	England	1993	28.99
Melanie	These Nights	CD	Mango Gang	120647	U.S.A.	2001	8.99
Melanie	Unchained Melanie	CD	VTM Ent.	2347	U.S.A.	1996	74.99
Melanie	Victim Of The Moon	CD	Afterglow	31	U.S.A.	2002	11.99
Melanie C	I Turn To You	CD Single	Virgin	7243-8-97008-0-0	England	2000	7.99
Melanie C	I Turn To You (Promo UK)	CD Single	Virgin	VSCDJ1772	England	2000	7.99
Melanie C	If That Were Me	CD Single	Virgin	7243-8-97394-0-4	Australia	2000	12.99
Melanie C	If That Were Me	CD Single	Virgin	7243-8-972890-3	England	2000	8.99
Melanie C	Never Be The Same Again	CD Single	Virgin	DPRO-15704	U.S.A.	2000	7.99
Melanie C	Norther Star	CD Single	Virgin	7243-8-96388-0-6	England	1999	5.99
Melanie C	Norther Star (With 4 Postcards)	CD Single	Virgin	7243-8-96388-2-0	EU	1999	21.99
Melanie C	Northern Star + 2	CD	Virgin	7243-8-50064-2-5	England	2000	19.99
Melcher, Terry	Royal Flush	CD	BMG Victor	BVCM-37125	Japan	2000	29.99
Melcher, Terry	Terry Melcher	CD	Warner Bros.	WPCR-2321	Japan	1998	29.99
Meliah Rage	Solitary Solitude	CD	Epic	7464-46024-2	U.S.A.	1990	11.99
Mellencamp, John	American Fool	CD	Mercury	814-993-2	U.S.A.	1982	6.99
Mellencamp, John	Big Daddy	CD	Mercury	838-220-2	U.S.A.	1989	5.99
Mellencamp, John	Chestnut Street Incident	CD	Original Masters	513	U.S.A.	1998	8.99
Mellencamp, John	Cuttin' Heads	CD	Sony	SK-85098	U.S.A.	2001	6.99
Mellencamp, John	Dance Naked	CD	Mercury	522-428-2	U.S.A.	1994	5.99
Mellencamp, John	Human Wheels	CD	Mercury	314-518-088-2	U.S.A.	1993	6.99
Mellencamp, John	John Cougar	CD	Riva	814-995-2	U.S.A.	1979	10.99
Mellencamp, John	John Mellencamp	CD	Columbia	CK-69602	U.S.A.	1998	6.99
Mellencamp, John	Mr. Happy Go Lucky	CD	Mercury	314-532-896-2	U.S.A.	1996	6.99

M

Artist	Title	Format	Label	Catalog No	Country	Released	Value
Mellencamp, John	Nothin' Matters And What If It Did	CD	Riva	814-994-2	U.S.A.	1980	10.99
Mellencamp, John	Radio's Greatest Hits (Promo)	CD	Mercury	SACD-718	U.S.A.	1993	39.99
Mellencamp, John	Rough Harvest	CD	Mercury	314-558-355-2	U.S.A.	1999	8.99
Mellencamp, John	Scarecrow (MFSL Gold Cd)	CD	Mobile Fidelity	UDCD-604	U.S.A.	1985	19.99
Mellencamp, John	The Best That I Could Do	CD	Mercury	P2-36738	U.S.A.	1997	7.99
Mellencamp, John	The Kid Inside	CD	Original Masters	510	U.S.A.	1998	8.99
Mellencamp, John	The Lonesome Jubilee (MFSL Gold Cd)	CD	Mobile Fidelity	UDCD-634	U.S.A.	1987	24.99
Mellencamp, John	Trouble No More	CD	ACK	90133	U.S.A.	2003	13.99
Mellencamp, John	Uh-Huh	CD	Mercury	814-450-2	U.S.A.	1983	10.99
Mellencamp, John	Whenever We Wanted	CD	Mercury	314-510151-2	U.S.A.	1991	8.99
Mellencamp, John	Your Life Is Now (Promo)	CD Single	Columbia	CSK-41476	U.S.A.	1998	6.99
Melton, Barry	Level With Me	CD	Line	RBCD-9.00373-0	Germany	1989	14.99
Melton, Barry	Songs Of The Next Great Depression	CD	One Way	OW-34506	U.S.A.	1981	8.99
Melton, Barry	Songs Of The Next Great Depression	CD	Line	RBCD-9.00297-0	Germany	1991	14.99
Melton, Barry/Levy/Dey Bros.	Melton, Levy And The Dey Brothers	CD	Acadia	ACA-8020	England	2001	11.99
Melvin, Harold/Blue Notes	Self Titled (1972 Album)	CD	Sony	SRCC-6326	Japan	1993	41.99
Melvin, Harold/Blue Notes	The Best Of...	CD	Epic	ZK-66338	U.S.A.	1995	8.99
Members	Going West	CD	Line	ALCD-9.00031-0	Germany	1989	10.99
Members	Going West	CD	Line	LICD-9.01341-0	Germany	1997	10.99
Memory Dean	Shake It Up	CD	Capricorn	314-534-660-2	U.S.A.	1997	5.99
Memphis Pilgrims/J Kaukonen	Mecca (W/Pete Sears)	CD	Relix	RRCD-2077	U.S.A.	1996	6.99
Memphis Slim/Matt Murphy	Live From Antone´s	CD	Line	ANCD-9.00450-0	Germany	1988	19.99
Men At Work	Brazil	CD	Columbia	CK-65732	U.S.A.	1998	6.99
Men At Work	Business As Usual + 4	CD	Sony	SK-86609	U.S.A.	2003	8.99
Men At Work	Cargo	CD	Sony	35-8P-16	Japan	1983	8.99
Men At Work	Cargo + 5	CD	Sony	SK-86608	U.S.A.	2003	8.99
Men At Work	Contraband - The Best Of...	CD	Columbia	CK-64791	U.S.A.	1996	8.99
Men At Work	Two Hearts	CD	Columbia	CDCBS-26492	England	1985	14.99
Men At Work/Colin Hay	Looking For Jack	CD	Columbia	CK-40611	U.S.A.	1987	24.99
Men At Work/Colin Hay	Topanga	CD	Line	LICD-9.01304-0	Germany	1995	10.99
Men Without Hats	Safety Dance UK-Remix	CD Single	EAMS	2305-2	Germany	1991	19.99
Mendes, Sergio	Brasil '86	CD	A&M	75021-5135-2	U.S.A.	1986	131.99
Menken, Alan/H. Ashman	Little Shop/Horrors (OST) Levi Stubbs	CD	Geffen	9-24125-2	U.S.A.	1986	11.99
Mennen	Back To The Real World + 2	CD	Victor Ent.	VICP-5845	Japan	1996	39.99
Merge	Self Titled	CD	BMG	BVCP-7330	Japan	1982	41.99
Merton Parkas	Complete Mod Collection	CD	Anagram	CDMGRAM-111	England	1997	14.99
Messina, Jim	Messina	CD	Warner Bros.	9-26557-2	U.S.A.	1981	8.99
Messina, Jim	Oasis	CD	Sony	SICP-8048	Japan	1979	20.99
Messina, Jim	One More Mile	CD	Warner Bros.	9-26560-2	U.S.A.	1983	8.99
Messina, Jim	Watching The River Run	CD	River North	51416-1175-2	U.S.A.	1996	8.99
Metallica	15 Pieces Of Live Sh*t (Promo)	2CD	Elektra	PRCD-8879-2	U.S.A.	1993	39.99
Metallica	And Justice For All	CD	Elektra	60812-2	U.S.A.	1988	8.99
Metallica	And Justice For All + 1	CD	Sony	25DP-5178	Japan	1989	29.99
Metallica	And Justice For All + 3 (W/Bonus Cd)	2CD	Phonogram	836-062-2	Australia	1994	49.99
Metallica	Die, Die My Darling	CD Single	Vertigo	562-233-2	Australia	1998	14.99
Metallica	Fuel (Disc 3)	CD Single	Vertigo	568-417-2	Germany	1998	15.99
Metallica	Garage Days Revisited (Rare L.E.)	CD	Mercury	888-788-2	Germany	1987	54.99
Metallica	Garage, Inc.	2CD	Elektra	62299-2	U.S.A.	1998	16.99
Metallica	Garage, Inc.	2CD	Elektra	62323-2	U.S.A.	1998	16.99
Metallica	Hero Of The Day	CD Single	Sony	SRCS-8253	Japan	1997	18.99
Metallica	Hero Of The Day (Part 1)	CD Single	Vertigo	578-575-2	Germany	1996	6.99
Metallica	Hero Of The Day (Part 2)	CD Single	Vertigo	578-577-2	England	1996	6.99
Metallica	Kill 'Em All	CD	Megaforce	MRI-CD-069	U.S.A.	1983	24.99
Metallica	Kill 'Em All (W/Am I Evil?/Blitzkrieg)	CD	Elektra	9-60766-2	U.S.A.	1983	29.99
Metallica	Kill 'Em All + 4 (W/Bonus Cd)	2CD	Phonogram	838-142-2	Australia	1998	49.99
Metallica	Live Sh*t: Binge & Purge (W/2 DVDs)	3CD	Elektra	62842-2	U.S.A.	2002	54.99
Metallica	Live Sh*t: Binge & Purge (W/3 Videos)	3CD	Elektra	61594-2	U.S.A.	1993	34.99
Metallica	Load	CD	Elektra	61923-2	U.S.A.	1996	8.99

M

Artist	Title	Format	Label	Catalog No	Country	Released	Value
Metallica	Mama Said	CD Single	Sony	SRCS-8135	Japan	1996	18.99
Metallica	Mandatory (Original Version/No "One")	CD	Elektra	PR8071-2	U.S.A.	1988	116.99
Metallica	Mandatory (Promo)	2CD	Elektra	PRCD-9927-2	U.S.A.	1997	36.99
Metallica	Master Of Puppets	CD	Elektra	60439-2	U.S.A.	1986	9.99
Metallica	Master Of Puppets (DCC Gold Cd)	CD	DCC	GZS-1133	U.S.A.	1986	39.99
Metallica	No Leaf Clover (Part 1)	CD Single	Vertigo	562-698-2	England	2000	9.99
Metallica	Nothing Else Matters	CD Single	Vertigo	562-572-2	Germany	1999	13.99
Metallica	One (3 " Cd/Red)	CD Single	Sony	10EP-3077	Japan	1988	164.99
Metallica	One (Ltd. Ed. Red Disc)	CD Single	Sony	23DP-5438	Japan	1989	59.99
Metallica	Reload	CD	Elektra	62126-2	U.S.A.	1997	8.99
Metallica	Reload + 4 (W/Bonus Cd)	2CD	Vertigo	535-409-2	Australia	1998	49.99
Metallica	Ride The Lightning	CD	Elektra	60396-2	U.S.A.	1984	9.99
Metallica	Ride The Lightning (DCC Gold Cd)	CD	DCC	GZS-1136	U.S.A.	1984	44.99
Metallica	S & M	2CD	Elektra	62463-2	U.S.A.	1999	12.99
Metallica	S & M (Clean)	2CD	Elektra	62504-2	U.S.A.	1999	11.99
Metallica	S & M Sampler (Promo)	CD	Elektra	PRCD-1429-2	U.S.A.	1999	17.99
Metallica	Self Titled	CD	Elektra	61113-2	U.S.A.	1990	9.99
Metallica	Self Titled + 1	CD	Sony	SRCS-5577	Japan	1991	27.99
Metallica	Self Titled + 4 (W/Bonus Cd)	2CD	Vertigo	510022-2	Australia	1998	49.99
Metallica	St. Anger (Clean/W/Bonus DVD)	2CD	Elektra	62879-2	U.S.A.	2003	14.99
Metallica	St. Anger (W/Bonus DVD)	2CD	Sony	SICP-373	Japan	1996	20.99
Metallica	St. Anger (W/Bonus DVD)	2CD	Elektra	62853-2	U.S.A.	2003	16.99
Metallica	Stone Cold Crazy (Rubiyat Rose DJ)	CD Single	Elektra	PRCD-8224-2	U.S.A.	1990	53.99
Metallica	The Black Album (Leather Sleeve)	CD	Vertigo	510-022-2	Germany	1991	73.99
Metallica	The Memory Remains (Cd 1)	CD Single	Vertigo	568-269-2	England	1997	10.99
Metallica	Turn The Page	CD Single	Vertigo	566-593-2	Germany	1998	11.99
Metallica	Until It Sleeps (Cd 1)	CD Single	Vertigo	578-145-2	Germany	1996	6.99
Metallica	Until It Sleeps (Cd 2)	CD Single	Vertigo	578-135-2	Germany	1996	6.99
Metallica	Whiskey In The Jar (Aussie 6-Track)	CD Single	Vertigo	566-965-2	Australia	1999	12.99
Metallica	Whiskey In The Jar (Disc 2)	CD Single	Vertigo	566-857-2	England	1999	10.99
Metro	Metro	CD	Line	TACD-9.00790-0	Germany	1989	10.99
Meyer, Ulf	Just Because	CD	Line	LICD-9.01282-0	Germany	1993	24.99
Michael, George	Greatest Hits (Promo)	CD	Sony	QY8P90075	Japan	1990	599.99
Michael, George	The Best Of (Promo Sampler)	CD	Epic	ESK-41661	U.S.A.	1998	34.99
Michaels, Gordon	Stargazer (W/Tony Levin)	CD	Pony Canyon	PCCY-10028	Japan	1979	24.99
Michaels, Lee	Absolute Lee	CD	One Way	OW-33647	U.S.A.	1996	19.99
Michaels, Lee	Barrel	CD	One Way	OW-33643	U.S.A.	1996	14.99
Michaels, Lee	Carnival Of Life	CD	One Way	OW-33640	U.S.A.	1996	14.99
Michaels, Lee	Fifth (W/Do You Know What..)	CD	One Way	OW-33644	U.S.A.	1996	49.99
Michaels, Lee	Hello: The Very Best Of	CD	Shout! Factory	DK-37485	U.S.A.	2004	11.99
Michaels, Lee	Live	CD	One Way	OW-33646	U.S.A.	1996	49.99
Michaels, Lee	Recital	CD	One Way	OW-33641	U.S.A.	1996	14.99
Michaels, Lee	Self Titled	CD	One Way	OW-33642	U.S.A.	1996	89.99
Michaels, Lee	Space & First Takes	CD	One Way	OW-33645	U.S.A.	1996	34.99
Michaels, Lee	The Best Of...	CD	One Way	OW-33648	U.S.A.	1997	24.99
Michaels, Lee	The Lee Michaels Collection + 4	CD	Rhino	R2-70374	U.S.A.	1992	24.99
Michelle Shocked	Deep Natural	2CD	Mighty Sound	8-20692-1001-2	U.S.A.	2002	12.99
Midler, Bette	The Rose	CD	Atlantic	82778-2	U.S.A.	1979	10.99
Midnight Oil	The Best Of The B-Sides (Promo)	CD	Columbia	CSK-3466	U.S.A.	1997	13.99
Midniters, Thee	Giant	CD	Marketing West	1002-C/WS-5,002	U.S.A.	1992	21.99
Midniters, Thee	Greatest	CD	Thump	206-579-089-2	U.S.A.	2002	14.99
Mighty Flyers	Undercover	CD	Line	STCD-9.00665-0	Germany	1988	14.99
Mighty Mighty Bosstones	Selections/Live In Middle East (Promo)	CD Single	Mercury	MECD-176	U.S.A.	1998	7.99
Mighty Mighty Bosstones	So Sad To Say	CD Single	Island	562-778-2	Australia	2000	10.99
Mighty Morphin P Rangers	TV Theme And Soundbites (Promo)	CD	Atlantic	PRCD-6019	U.S.A.	1994	5.99
Mike & The Mechanics	///Favourites///The Very Best Of///	CD	Virgin	7243-850639-2-3	Holland	2000	14.99
Mike & The Mechanics	A Time And Place	CD Single	Virgin	VSCDT-1351	England	1991	7.99
Mike & The Mechanics	Another Cup Of Coffee	CD Single	Virgin	7243-8-93100-2-3	England	1995	7.99

M

Artist	Title	Format	Label	Catalog No	Country	Released	Value
Mike & The Mechanics	Beggar On A Beach Of Gold	CD	Atlantic	82738-2	U.S.A.	1995	5.99
Mike & The Mechanics	Hits	CD	Virgin	72438-4144821	England	1996	10.99
Mike & The Mechanics	KBFH 10- 2 - 8, 1989	CD	King Biscuit	6M60100A	U.S.A.	1989	22.99
Mike & The Mechanics	KBFH 5/8 - 5/14 1995	CD	DIR Network	KB-95-20	U.S.A.	1995	22.99
Mike & The Mechanics	Living Years	CD	Atlantic	7-81923-2	U.S.A.	1988	6.99
Mike & The Mechanics	Mea Culpa And Other Songs... (Promo)	CD	Atlantic	PRCD-6052-2	U.S.A.	1995	10.99
Mike & The Mechanics	Mike + The Mechanics	CD	Atlantic	2-52496-2	Switzerlan	1985	9.99
Mike & The Mechanics	Mike And The Mechanics	CD	Virgin	7243-8-47671-2-9	EU	1999	8.99
Mike & The Mechanics	Nobody Knows (Promo)	CD Single	Atlantic	PR-2784-2	U.S.A.	1988	7.99
Mike & The Mechanics	Now That You've Gone	CD Single	Virgin	7243-8-95886-2	England	1995	5.99
Mike & The Mechanics	Off The Record # 95-17 April, 17, 1995	CD	Westwood 1	CO2MNO1XA	U.S.A.	1995	22.99
Mike & The Mechanics	Silent Running	CD Single	Virgin	7243-893566-2-5	England	1996	7.99
Mike & The Mechanics	Whenever I Stop	CD Single	Virgin	7243-8-96154-2-5	England	1999	7.99
Mike & The Mechanics	Word Of Mouth	CD	Atlantic	7-82233-2	U.S.A.	1991	6.99
Milano, Alyssa	Alyssa	CD	Pony Canyon	PCCY-00026	Japan	1989	28.99
Milano, Alyssa	Do You See Me? Box Set	CD	Pony Canyon	PCCY-00368	Japan	1992	34.99
Milano, Alyssa	Locked Inside A Dream Box Set	CD	Pony Canyon	PCCY-00204	Japan	1991	22.99
Milano, Alyssa	Look In My Heart	CD	Pony Canyon	D25Y-0273	Japan	1989	28.99
Milano, Alyssa	Look In My Heart + 1 (Gold Cd)	CD	Pony Canyon	D33Y-0356	Japan	1989	44.99
Milano, Alyssa	The Best In The World (Remix)	CD Single	Pony Canyon	PCCY-00059	Japan	1990	13.99
Miles, Buddy	Electric Church	CD	Line	LMCD-9.51169-Z	Germany	1992	19.99
Miles, Buddy	Them Changes	CD	Line	LMCD-9.51170-Z	Germany	1992	23.99
Miles, Buddy	Tribute To Jimi Hendrix	CD	Cas	CAS-70002-2	Germany	1996	6.99
Miles, Buddy	We Got To Live Together	CD	Line	LMCD-9.511671Z	Germany	1992	19.99
Miles, Buddy/Expresss	Expressway To Your Skull	CD	Line	LMCD-9.51168-Z	Germany	1992	19.99
Milira	Back Again!!!	CD	Motown	MOTD-6328	U.S.A.	1992	30.99
Milira	Self Titled	CD	Motown	MOTD-6297	U.S.A.	1989	29.99
Millenium	Hourglass	CD	Frontiers	FR-CD-066	Italy	2000	12.99
Miller, Brad	Power/Majesty - Vol. 1 (MFSL Gold)	CD	Mobile Fidelity	UDCD-504	U.S.A.	1978	91.99
Miller, Brad	Power/Majesty - Vol. 2 (MFSL Silver)	CD	Mobile Fidelity	MFCD-812	U.S.A.	1984	39.99
Miller, Steve	Abracadabra	CD	Eagle	EAMCD044	EC	1998	10.99
Miller, Steve	Anthology	CD	Capitol	7-94488-2	U.S.A.	1990	7.99
Miller, Steve	Book Of Dreams	CD	Eagle	EAMCD042	EC	1998	10.99
Miller, Steve	Book Of Dreams (DCC Gold Cd)	CD	DCC	GZS-1077	U.S.A.	1995	39.99
Miller, Steve	Born 2B Blue	CD	Capitol	7-48303-2	U.S.A.	1988	7.99
Miller, Steve	Box Set Sampler (Promo)	CD	Capitol	DPRO-79817	U.S.A.	1994	19.99
Miller, Steve	Brave New World	CD	Capitol	7-91246-2	U.S.A.	1989	10.99
Miller, Steve	Children Of The Future	CD	Capitol	7-91245-2	U.S.A.	1989	10.99
Miller, Steve	Fly Like An Eagle (DCC Gold Cd)	CD	DCC	GZS-1033	U.S.A.	1993	32.99
Miller, Steve	Greatest Hits	CD	Eagle	559-240-2	England	1998	10.99
Miller, Steve	Greatest Hits (DCC Gold Cd)	CD	DCC	GZS-1103	U.S.A.	1997	39.99
Miller, Steve	Italian X Rays	CD	Capitol	7-94447-2	U.S.A.	1990	5.99
Miller, Steve	Living In The 20th Century	CD	Capitol	7-46326-2	U.S.A.	1986	5.99
Miller, Steve	Number 5	CD	Capitol	7243-8-29686-2-7	U.S.A.	1990	10.99
Miller, Steve	Sailor	CD	Capitol	7-94449-2	U.S.A.	1990	10.99
Miller, Steve	Steve Miller Band Live!	CD	Eagle	8573804872	Australia	1998	11.99
Miller, Steve	The Joker (JVCXR Audiophile)	CD	JVC	JVCXR-0043-2	U.S.A.	1973	18.99
Miller, Steve	Wide River	CD	Polydor	314-519-441-2	U.S.A.	1993	7.99
Miller, Steve	Your Saving Grace	CD	Capitol	7-94448-2	U.S.A.	1990	49.99
Miller, Steve/Band	Box Set	3CD	Capitol	0777-7-89826-2-3	U.S.A.	1994	24.99
Miller, Steve/Band	KBFH (Ltd. Numbered)	2CD	King Biscuit	7930188002-2	U.S.A.	2002	23.99
Mills, Russell	Pearl + Umbra	CD	Instinct	INS-501-2	U.S.A.	2000	10.99
Mills, Russell/Undark	Em:t3396 (Brian Eno, David Sylvian)	CD	Em:t	EM:T3396	England	1996	29.99
Mills, Russell/Undark	Undark (U2/David Sylvian)	CD	Instinct	INS-526-2	U.S.A.	2000	29.99
Mills, Stephanie	For The First Time	CD	Motown	MOTD-5475	U.S.A.	1976	24.99
Milsap, Ronnie	Keyed Up	CD	RCA	5993-2-R	U.S.A.	1983	104.99
Milsap, Ronnie	No Gettin' Over Me	CD	RCA	PCD1-4060	U.S.A.	1989	126.99
Milsap, Ronnie	One More Try For Love	CD	RCA	PCD1-5016	U.S.A.	1983	119.99

M

Artist	Title	Format	Label	Catalog No	Country	Released	Value
Minogue, Kylie	An Interview With (Promo)	CD	BMG	KM002	EU	1997	207.99
Minogue, Kylie	B Language - Sunday Telegraph DJ	CD	Sunday Telegraph	KYLIENEWS	Australia	2004	17.99
Minogue, Kylie	Better Devil You Know (W/2 Prints)	CD Single	Alfa	ALCB-121	Japan	1990	44.99
Minogue, Kylie	Better The Devil You Know	CD Single	PWL	9031-71673-2	Germany	1990	28.99
Minogue, Kylie	Body Language (11 Tracks)	CD	EMI	GCDA-658	China	2003	39.99
Minogue, Kylie	Body Language (12 Tracks)	CD	EMI	7243-595758-27	Taiwan	2003	36.99
Minogue, Kylie	Body Language (12 Tracks)	CD	EMI	7243-595645-2-4	England	2003	16.99
Minogue, Kylie	Body Language (13 Tracks)	CD	Festival	337562	Australia	2003	24.99
Minogue, Kylie	Body Language (14 Trk)	CD	Toshiba-EMI	TOCP-66260	Japan	2003	59.99
Minogue, Kylie	Body Language (16 Tracks)	CD	Capitol	7243-5-95758-2-7	U.S.A.	2003	24.99
Minogue, Kylie	Body Language (Promo)	CD	EMI	BODYLANG01	England	2003	34.99
Minogue, Kylie	Body Language Interview (Promo)	CD	Parlophone	MININT02	England	2003	44.99
Minogue, Kylie	Breathe	CD Single	Deconstruction	570142	England	1998	12.99
Minogue, Kylie	Breathe (Promo)	CD Single	Deconstruction	BREATHE02	England	1998	16.99
Minogue, Kylie	Butterfly Remixes	CD	Blue Plate	B2-001	U.S.A.	2002	134.99
Minogue, Kylie	Can't Get You Out ... (18 Track/Promo)	CD	Toshiba-EMI	PCD-2580	Japan	2002	29.99
Minogue, Kylie	Can't Get You Out.. (2 Track/Promo)	CD Single	Toshiba-EMI	PCD-2579	Japan	2002	189.99
Minogue, Kylie	Can't Get You Out.. (Promo)	CD Single	EMI	200-1429	Mexico	2001	24.99
Minogue, Kylie	Can't Get You Out... (Promo)	CD Single	Capitol	DPRO-16905	U.S.A.	2001	29.99
Minogue, Kylie	Can't Get You Out... (Promo)	CD Single	EMI	000885-2	Brazil	2002	149.99
Minogue, Kylie	Can't Get You.. Remixes (Promo)	CD	Parlophone	KYLIE-6TRACKS	England	2001	59.99
Minogue, Kylie	Can't Get You... (Cd 1)	CD Single	Mushroom	020542	Australia	2001	8.99
Minogue, Kylie	Can't Get You... (DJ/Black Die Cut Slv)	CD Single	FMR	OUTTA1	Australia	2001	74.99
Minogue, Kylie	Can't Get You...(Promo)	CD Single	Parlophone	CDRDJ6562	England	2001	12.99
Minogue, Kylie	Celebration	CD Single	PWL	PWCD257	England	1992	14.99
Minogue, Kylie	Come Into My World	CD Single	Parlophone	7243-551879-2-5	France	2002	12.99
Minogue, Kylie	Come Into My World (Promo)	CD Single	EMI	CDRDJ-6590	England	2002	12.99
Minogue, Kylie	Come Into My World (Promo)	CD Single	Festival	WORLD1	Australia	2002	54.99
Minogue, Kylie	Come Into My World (Promo)	CD Single	Capitol	DPRO-17566	U.S.A.	2002	29.99
Minogue, Kylie	Confide In Me	CD Single	Mushroom	D11815	Australia	1994	24.99
Minogue, Kylie	Confide In Me	CD Single	RCA	21229982	Germany	1994	19.99
Minogue, Kylie	Confide In Me (Cd 1)	CD Single	Deconstruction	74321-22747-2	England	1994	19.99
Minogue, Kylie	Did It Again	CD Single	Deconstruction	543942	England	1997	31.99
Minogue, Kylie	Did It Again	CD Single	Deconstruction	74321-53570-2	England	1997	14.99
Minogue, Kylie	Did It Again (Promo)	CD Single	Deconstruction	DID1	England	1997	14.99
Minogue, Kylie	Enjoy Yourself	CD	Mushroom	MUSH32209.2	Australia	1992	11.99
Minogue, Kylie	Enjoy Yourself (W/Box/2 Stkrs/6 Cards)	CD	PWL	29B2-77	Japan	1989	74.99
Minogue, Kylie	Enjoy Yourself (W/Poster)	CD	PWL	HFCD9	England	1989	54.99
Minogue, Kylie	Feel The Fever (Promo/Interview)	CD	Parlophone	FEVER03	England	2001	54.99
Minogue, Kylie	Fever (12 Tracks W/ 7 Trk. Bonus Cd)	2CD	EMI	7243-54322-2-8	Taiwan	2002	44.99
Minogue, Kylie	Fever (12 Tracks)	CD	Parlophone	7243-535804-2	England	2001	11.99
Minogue, Kylie	Fever (12 Tracks) + 7 (W/Bonus Cd)	2CD	Parlophone	7243-543222-2-8	Hong Kong	2002	34.99
Minogue, Kylie	Fever (12 Tracks) + 7 (W/Bonus Cd)	2CD	EMI	5432222	Mexico	2002	29.99
Minogue, Kylie	Fever (12 Tracks) + 7 (W/Bonus Cd)	2CD	EMI	5432222	England	2002	21.99
Minogue, Kylie	Fever (12 Tracks) + 7 (W/Bonus Cd)	2CD	EMI	5432222	Brazil	2002	37.99
Minogue, Kylie	Fever (12 Tracks) + 7 (W/Bonus Cd)	2CD	EMI	7243-535804-2-1	Columbia	2002	29.99
Minogue, Kylie	Fever (12 Tracks) + 9 (W/Bonus Cd)	2CD	EMI	7243-539136-0-1	Korea	2002	37.99
Minogue, Kylie	Fever (13 Tracks)	CD	Mushroom	MUSH33464.2	Australia	2001	21.99
Minogue, Kylie	Fever (14 Tracks)	CD	Toshiba-EMI	TOCP-65873	Japan	2001	44.99
Minogue, Kylie	Fever (14 Tracks/2 Initial Press)	CD	Capitol	CDP-3767020	U.S.A.	2001	24.99
Minogue, Kylie	Fever (18 Tracks)	CD	Toshiba-EMI	TOCP-65974	Japan	2002	54.99
Minogue, Kylie	Fever (29 Tracks) W/Bonus Cd	2CD	Toshiba-EMI	TOCP-66130/1	Japan	2002	49.99
Minogue, Kylie	Fever (DJ/Misprinted Track Listing)	CD	Parlophone	FEVER02	England	2001	64.99
Minogue, Kylie	Fever (Promo)	CD	Capitol	CDP37670	U.S.A.	2001	28.99
Minogue, Kylie	Fever (Promo/Black Die Cut Sleeve)	CD Single	FMR	FEVER1	Australia	2002	114.99
Minogue, Kylie	Finer Feeling	CD Single	Alfa	ALCB503	Japan	1992	34.99
Minogue, Kylie	Finer Feelings	CD Single	PWL	PWCD227	England	1992	22.99
Minogue, Kylie	Finer Feelings	CD Single	Mushroom	D11180	Australia	1992	36.99

M

Artist	Title	Format	Label	Catalog No	Country	Released	Value
Minogue, Kylie	Give Me Just A Little More Time	CD Single	PWL	9031763872	Germany	1992	14.99
Minogue, Kylie	Give Me Just A Little More Time	CD Single	PWL	PWCD212	England	1992	21.99
Minogue, Kylie	Got To Be Certain (3")	CD Single	PWL	8.20900	Germany	1988	49.99
Minogue, Kylie	Got To Be Certain (3")	CD Single	Columbia	CBS652868-3	France	1988	74.99
Minogue, Kylie	Grandes Exitos (Minogue Spelled Wrong	CD	BMG	060424	Venezuela	2002	69.99
Minogue, Kylie	Greatest Hits	2CD	Mushroom	MUSH32217.2	Australia	1998	24.99
Minogue, Kylie	Greatest Hits	CD	PWL	4509-90574-2	Germany	1992	29.99
Minogue, Kylie	Greatest Hits	CD	Alfa	ALCB648	Japan	1992	64.99
Minogue, Kylie	Greatest Hits	CD	Mushroom	TVD93366	Australia	1992	74.99
Minogue, Kylie	Greatest Hits (33 Tracks)	2CD	Jive	9224682	England	2002	18.99
Minogue, Kylie	Greatest Hits (35 Tracks)	2CD	BMG Victor	BVC2-34005/6	Japan	2003	59.99
Minogue, Kylie	Greatest Hits (W/75 Minute Megamix)	2CD	Mushroom	MUSH33065.2	Australia	1997	22.99
Minogue, Kylie	Greatest Hits '87 - '97	2CD	PWL	82876539672	Singapore	2003	29.99
Minogue, Kylie	Greatest Hits '87 - '97	2CD	PWL	82876539672	Taiwan	2003	41.99
Minogue, Kylie	Greatest Hits '87 - '97	2CD	Festival	337492	Australia	2003	34.99
Minogue, Kylie	Greatest Hits '87 - '97 (W/Frangrance)	2CD	PWL	82876539672	Malaysia	2003	39.99
Minogue, Kylie	Greatest Remix Hits Volume 1	2CD	Mushroom	MUSH32213.2	Australia	1998	27.99
Minogue, Kylie	Greatest Remix Hits Volume 2	2CD	Mushroom	MUSH32214.2	Australia	1998	27.99
Minogue, Kylie	Greatest Remix Hits Volume 3	2CD	Mushroom	MUSH33046.2	Australia	1998	24.99
Minogue, Kylie	Greatest Remix Hits Volume 4	2CD	Mushroom	MUSH33104.2	Australia	1998	24.99
Minogue, Kylie	Hand On Your Heart (2 Trk W/Sticker)	CD Single	Alfa	09B3-44	Japan	1989	22.99
Minogue, Kylie	Hand On Your Heart (3 Tracks)	CD Single	Alfa	11B3-45	Japan	1989	34.99
Minogue, Kylie	Hand On Your Heart (3")	CD Single	Columbia	6549643	Netherland	1989	59.99
Minogue, Kylie	Hand On Your Heart (3")	CD Single	PWL	246935-2XS	Germany	1989	34.99
Minogue, Kylie	Head Mix (Promo)	CD	Capitol	20933-1	U.S.A.	2001	324.99
Minogue, Kylie	Hits (16 Tracks)	CD	Deconstruction	74321785342	England	2000	11.99
Minogue, Kylie	Hits (16 Tracks)	CD	Festival	333212	Australia	2000	29.99
Minogue, Kylie	Hits + (14 Tracks)	CD	Deconstruction	07822-10604-2	U.S.A.	2000	21.99
Minogue, Kylie	Hits + (14 Tracks)	CD	BMG	HYO2101	China	2000	41.99
Minogue, Kylie	Hits + (16 Tracks)	CD	BMG	74321-80275-2	Taiwan	2000	34.99
Minogue, Kylie	I Should Be So Lucky (3")	CD Single	Columbia	651489	France	1988	424.99
Minogue, Kylie	Impossible Princess (12 Track)	CD	Mushroom	33069.2	Australia	1997	29.99
Minogue, Kylie	Impossible Princess (13 Tracks)	CD	BMG Victor	BVCM-37437	Japan	2003	44.99
Minogue, Kylie	Impossible Princess (DJ/Withdrawn)	CD	BMG	KYLIE1	England	1997	149.99
Minogue, Kylie	Impossible Princess 24 Trk (Bonus Cd)	2CD	BMG	82876-511152(-)	England	2003	21.99
Minogue, Kylie	Impossible Princess 24 Trk (Bonus Cd)	2CD	BMG	82876-51115-2	Taiwan	2003	39.99
Minogue, Kylie	Impossible Princess Sampler (Promo)	CD	Mushroom	KYLIE-1	Australia	1997	49.99
Minogue, Kylie	Impossible Remixes	2CD	Mushroom	MUSH33129.2	Australia	1998	29.99
Minogue, Kylie	In Your Eyes	CD Single	Parlophone	5505952	England	2002	9.99
Minogue, Kylie	In Your Eyes (Cd 2)	CD Single	Mushroom	020682	Australia	2002	36.99
Minogue, Kylie	In Your Eyes (Promo)	CD Single	EMI	2001452CD	Mexico	2001	29.99
Minogue, Kylie	In Your Eyes (Promo)	CD Single	Parlophone	CDRDJ6569	England	2002	12.99
Minogue, Kylie	In Your Eyes (Promo)	CD Single	EMI	0009052	Brazil	2002	38.99
Minogue, Kylie	Interview - Light Years (Promo)	CD	Parlophone	MIN-INT-001	England	2000	79.99
Minogue, Kylie	Intimate & Live	2CD	Tricycle	TNCP-17~8	Japan	1999	67.99
Minogue, Kylie	Intimate & Live	2CD	Mushroom	MUSH33183.2	Australia	1998	26.99
Minogue, Kylie	Kylie's Remixes 1	CD	Alfa	25B2-20	Japan	1988	49.99
Minogue, Kylie	Kylie's Remixes 2 (W/2 Postcards)	CD	Alfa	ALCB-564	Japan	1992	49.99
Minogue, Kylie	Kylie's Remixes, Vol. 1	CD	Mushroom	D19756	Australia	1993	17.99
Minogue, Kylie	Kylie's Remixes, Vol. 2	CD	Mushroom	MUSH32212.2	Australia	1992	24.99
Minogue, Kylie	Let's Get To It	CD	Warner Bros.	9031757662	Korea	1991	29.99
Minogue, Kylie	Let's Get To It	CD	Mushroom	MUSH32216.2	England	1991	21.99
Minogue, Kylie	Let's Get To It + 3 (W/Bonus 3" Cd)	CD	Alfa	ALCB-406	Japan	1991	89.99
Minogue, Kylie	Light Years (14 Tracks)	CD	Mushroom	MUSH33283.2	Australia	2000	21.99
Minogue, Kylie	Light Years (14 Tracks)	CD	Parlophone	7243-528400-2-1	Taiwan	2000	38.99
Minogue, Kylie	Light Years (15 Track)	CD	EMI	5284562	Argentina	2000	44.99
Minogue, Kylie	Light Years (15 Tracks)	CD	Toshiba-EMI	TOCP-65488	Japan	2000	59.99
Minogue, Kylie	Light Years (15 Tracks)	CD	Parlophone	5284002	England	2000	16.99

M

Artist	Title	Format	Label	Catalog No	Country	Released	Value
Minogue, Kylie	Light Years (15 Tracks)	CD	Toshiba-EMI	TOCP-53339	Japan	2003	47.99
Minogue, Kylie	Light Years (16 Tracks)	CD	Parlophone	5284572	Germany	2000	34.99
Minogue, Kylie	Light Years (23 Tracks) (Bonus Cd)	2CD	EMI	7243-532129-2-6	Taiwan	2000	44.99
Minogue, Kylie	Light Years (Tri Fold Envelope Pk/DJ)	CD	Parlophone	LIGHT001	England	2000	74.99
Minogue, Kylie	Love At First Sight	CD Single	EMI	5513962	France	2002	9.99
Minogue, Kylie	Love At First Sight	CD Single	EMI	5511122	France	2002	9.99
Minogue, Kylie	Love At First Sight	CD Single	Mushroom	020942	Australia	2002	17.99
Minogue, Kylie	Love At First Sight	CD Single	Capitol	DPRO-16930-2	U.S.A.	2002	29.99
Minogue, Kylie	Love At First Sight (Promo)	CD Single	Parlophone	200-1484	Mexico	2002	29.99
Minogue, Kylie	Love At First Sight (Promo)	CD Single	FMR	LAFS1	Australia	2002	54.99
Minogue, Kylie	Love At First Sight (Promo)	CD Single	Capitol	DPRO17420	U.S.A.	2002	47.99
Minogue, Kylie	Love At First Sight (Promo)	CD Single	EMI	CDRDJ-6577	England	2002	12.99
Minogue, Kylie	Mixes	2CD	Deconstruction	74321-58715-2	England	1998	19.99
Minogue, Kylie	Never Too Late	CD Single	PWL	PWCD45	England	1989	29.99
Minogue, Kylie	Never Too Late (3")	CD Single	Columbia	6556173	France	1989	59.99
Minogue, Kylie	Never Too Late (3")	CD	PWL	246561-2XS	Germany	1989	29.99
Minogue, Kylie	Never Too Late (3")	CD Single	Columbia	655617-1	France	1989	46.99
Minogue, Kylie	Non Stop History + 1	CD	PWL	HFCD31	England	1994	24.99
Minogue, Kylie	Non Stop History + 1	CD	Mushroom	MUSH32208.2	Australia	1994	24.99
Minogue, Kylie	On A Night Like This (Cd 2)	CD	EMI	889310	Taiwan	2000	24.99
Minogue, Kylie	On A Night Like This (Promo)	CD Single	Parlophone	CDMINDJ002	England	2000	12.99
Minogue, Kylie	On A Night Like This (Promo)	CD Single	Mushroom	THIS1	Australia	2001	54.99
Minogue, Kylie	Please Stay (Cd 1)	CD Single	Parlophone	CDRS6551	England	2000	12.99
Minogue, Kylie	Please Stay (Promo)	CD Single	Parlophone	CDRDJ6551	England	2000	37.99
Minogue, Kylie	Please Stay (Promo)	CD Single	Parlophone	CDRDJ6551	England	2000	12.99
Minogue, Kylie	Red Blooded Woman	CD Single	Mushroom	021742	Australia	2004	17.99
Minogue, Kylie	Red Blooded Woman	CD Single	EMI	7243 54828423	Sweden	2003	9.99
Minogue, Kylie	Red Blooded Woman (Promo)	CD Single	Parlophone	CDMINDJ007	England	2003	12.99
Minogue, Kylie	Red Blooded Woman (Promo)	CD Single	Capitol	7087-6184300-2	U.S.A.	2004	17.99
Minogue, Kylie	Rhythm Of Love	CD	Mushroom	MUSH32215.2	Australia	1990	28.99
Minogue, Kylie	Rhythm Of Love	CD	Alfa	ALCB-173	Japan	1990	39.99
Minogue, Kylie	Rhythm Of Love (Promo)	CD	PWL	Y12-22	Japan	1990	124.99
Minogue, Kylie	Santa Baby (Promo)	CD Single	Parlophone	CDRDJX6551	England	2000	36.99
Minogue, Kylie	Secret	CD	EMI	KYLIESAMPLER	Taiwan	2004	149.99
Minogue, Kylie	Self Titled	CD	BMG Victor	BVCM-37436	Japan	2003	44.99
Minogue, Kylie	Self Titled	CD	Deconstruction	74321-22749-2	Taiwan	1994	44.99
Minogue, Kylie	Self Titled	CD	BMG Victor	BVCP-7460	Japan	1994	34.99
Minogue, Kylie	Self Titled	CD	Deconstruction	227492	England	1994	16.99
Minogue, Kylie	Self Titled (24 Track) W/Bonus Cd	2CD	BMG	82876-510982(-)	England	2003	15.99
Minogue, Kylie	Self Titled (25 Tracks)	2CD	BMG	82876-51098-2	Taiwan	2003	39.99
Minogue, Kylie	Self Titled (Holographic/4 Cards)	CD	BMG Victor	BVCP-6068	Japan	1997	62.99
Minogue, Kylie	Shocked (W/2 Postcards)	CD Single	Alfa	ALCB-296	Japan	1991	29.99
Minogue, Kylie	Slow	CD Single	Mushroom	021645	Australia	2003	21.99
Minogue, Kylie	Slow	CD Single	Toshiba-EMI	TOCP-40168	Japan	2003	29.99
Minogue, Kylie	Slow	CD Single	Mushroom	021642	Australia	2003	9.99
Minogue, Kylie	Slow	CD Single	Parlophone	7243-553363-0-9	Taiwan	2003	19.99
Minogue, Kylie	Slow (Black Fold Out Promo)	CD Single	EMI	CDMINDJ006	England	2003	38.99
Minogue, Kylie	Slow (Pock It !) Available 14 Days	CD Single	EMI	5534722	England	2003	24.99
Minogue, Kylie	Slow (Promo)	CD Single	EMI	CDP-2001574	Mexico	2003	24.99
Minogue, Kylie	Slow (Promo)	CD Single	Capitol	DPRO-18244	U.S.A.	2003	24.99
Minogue, Kylie	Slow (Promo)	CD Single	Parlophone	CDSP261	England	2003	19.99
Minogue, Kylie	Soft & Gentle	CD Single	EMI	CDLIC139	England	1998	17.99
Minogue, Kylie	Some Kind Of Bliss	CD Single	Deconstruction	74321-51725-2	England	1997	12.99
Minogue, Kylie	Some Kind Of Bliss	CD Single	Mushroom	MUSH01695.2	Australia	1997	29.99
Minogue, Kylie	Some Kind Of Bliss	CD Single	BMG Victor	BVCP-8885	Japan	1997	24.99
Minogue, Kylie	Some Kind Of Bliss	CD Single	BMG	74321-51726-2	England	1997	36.99
Minogue, Kylie	Some Kind Of Bliss	CD Single	BMG	74321-51725-2	Taiwan	1997	44.99
Minogue, Kylie	Special Sample (Promo)	CD	Alfa	Y12-40	Japan	1992	199.99

M

Artist	Title	Format	Label	Catalog No	Country	Released	Value
Minogue, Kylie	Spinning Around (Cd 1)	CD Single	Parlophone	CDRS6542	England	2000	9.99
Minogue, Kylie	Step Back In Time (3")	CD Single	Columbia	656493-1	Netherland	1990	46.99
Minogue, Kylie	Tears On My Pillow (3")	CD Single	PWL	171000-2LC	Germany	1990	19.99
Minogue, Kylie	The Locomotion (3")	CD Single	PWL	2477152	Germany	1988	89.99
Minogue, Kylie	The Locomotion (3")	CD Single	Alfa	10SR-34	Japan	1988	74.99
Minogue, Kylie	The Month (Sunday Times Promo)	CD	Sunday Times	PROMO-CD-ROM	England	2003	9.99
Minogue, Kylie	What Do I Have To Do	CD Single	PWL	PWCD72	England	1990	29.99
Minogue, Kylie	What Kind Of Fool	CD Single	Alfa	ALCB-613	Japan	1992	39.99
Minogue, Kylie	What Kind Of Fool	CD Single	PWL	PWCD241	England	1992	19.99
Minogue, Kylie	Where Is The Feeling (Promo)	CD Single	Deconstruction	PDTD-1101	Japan	1994	429.99
Minogue, Kylie	Where Is The Feeling (Promo)	CD Single	Deconstruction	PDTD-1101	Japan	1994	399.99
Minogue, Kylie	Word Is Out	CD Single	PWL	PWCD204	England	1991	29.99
Minogue, Kylie	Wouldn't Change A Thing (3")	CD Single	Warner Bros.	246763-2XS	Germany	1989	21.99
Minogue, Kylie	Your Disco Needs You	CD Single	Festival	020262	Australia	2001	21.99
Minogue, Kylie	Your Disco Needs You (Cd 1)	CD Single	EMI	8899162	Germany	2001	11.99
Minogue, Kylie	Your Disco Needs You (Cd 2)	CD Single	EMI	020262	Germany	2001	11.99
Minogue, Kylie/10 Postcards	Fever (12 Tracks) + 7 (W/Bonus Cd)	2CD	Parlophone	EKPD-1027	Korea	2002	59.99
Minogue, Kylie/Compilation	Confide In Me (Deconstruction)	CD	BMG	74321-89576-2	England	2001	11.99
Minogue, Kylie/Compilation	Confide In Me (Deconstruction)	CD	BMG	74321-89576-2	Taiwan	2001	44.99
Minogue, Kylie/Del. 1st Day	Best Of 1987-1992 (W/Bonus DVD)	2CD	Marais Prod	MPCD-23021	France	2003	99.99
Minogue, Kylie/Interview	Fever (Promo/Cd Rom Bio/Photos)	CD	Parlophone	FEVER01	England	2001	99.99
Minogue, Kylie/K Washington	If You Were With Me Now	CD Single	PWL	PWCD208	England	1991	21.99
Minogue, Kylie/K Washington	If You Were With Me Now	CD Single	Mushroom	D11096	Australia	1992	36.99
Minogue, Kylie/K Washington	If You Were With Me Now	CD Single	PWL	9031-76002-2	Germany	1991	18.99
Minogue, Kylie/Moby	Love At First Sight/Extreme Ways (DJ)	CD	EMI	300702	Columbia	2002	54.99
Minogue, Kylie/Nick Cave	Where The Wild Roses Grow	CD Single	Mute	CDMUTE185E	England	1995	17.99
Minogue, Kylie/Nick Cave	Where The Wild Roses Grow	CD Single	Mute	74321-32934-2	France	1995	24.99
Minogue, Kylie/Nick Cave	Where The Wild Roses Grow (Promo)	CD Single	Reprise	PRO-CD-8038	U.S.A.	1995	21.99
Minogue, Kylie/Only 75 Copies	Take 40 Australia Salutes Kylie (Promo)	CD	Take 40	49459/100025	Australia	2002	133.99
Minogue, Kylie/Purple/Orange	Gr. Hits '87- '97 (Pink/Blue/Cd Wallet)	2CD	PWL	82876539672	Singapore	2003	44.99
Minogue, Kylie/R Williams	In Your Eyes/Mack The Knife (Robbie)	CD Single	EMI	CDDIF335	Argentina	2001	79.99
Minogue, Kylie/Target Promo	3 Trk (DJ) Live Came W/B Language	CD	Capitol	DPRO-18450-2	U.S.A.	2004	39.99
Minogue, Kylie/Various Artists	Kylie: A Tribute To	CD	Dressed To Kill	DOP192	England	1999	8.99
Minogue, Kylie/W/Poster	Wouldn't Change A Thing (W/Sticker)	CD Single	PWL	09B3-61	Japan	1989	34.99
Misfits	12 Hits From Hell (Recalled)	CD	Caroline	CAR-11207-2	U.S.A.	2002	249.99
Misfits	American Psycho (W/Poster)	CD	Geffen	25126-2	U.S.A.	1997	8.99
Misfits	Box Set Sampler Edition (Promo)	CD	Caroline	CAR-PRCD #17	U.S.A.	1996	19.99
Misfits	Collection II	CD	Caroline	CAR-7515-2	U.S.A.	1995	8.99
Misfits	Cuts From The Crypt	CD	Roadrunner	RRD-618467-2	U.S.A.	2001	8.99
Misfits	Earth A.D./Wolfsblood (W/Die Die..Single	CD	Plan 9	PL9-CD023	U.S.A.	1992	8.99
Misfits	Famous Monsters	CD	Roadrunner	RR-8658-2	U.S.A.	1999	8.99
Misfits	Legacy Of Brutality	CD	Plan 9	PL9-CD06	U.S.A.	1990	8.99
Misfits	Self Titled (Collection I)	CD	Plan 9	PL9-CD1	U.S.A.	1991	8.99
Misfits	Self Titled Coffin Box Set (W/Pin)	4CD	Caroline	CAR-7529-2	U.S.A.	1997	44.99
Misfits	Static Age	CD	Caroline	CAR-7520-2	U.S.A.	1997	8.99
Misfits	Walk Among Us	CD	Rhino	R2-79947	U.S.A.	2000	9.99
Missing Persons	Classic Masters	CD	Capitol	72435-38398-2	U.S.A.	2002	7.99
Missing Persons	Color In Your Life + 6	CD	One Way	OW-27880	U.S.A.	2000	8.99
Missing Persons	Lost Tracks	CD	One Way	OW-35189	U.S.A.	2002	8.99
Missing Persons	Rhyme & Reason + 6	CD	One Way	OW-27881	U.S.A.	2000	8.99
Missing Persons	Spring Session M + 2	CD	One Way	S21-18499	U.S.A.	1995	8.99
Missing Persons/Various Artist	Remixed Hits	CD	Cleopatra	CLP-0609-2	U.S.A.	1999	8.99
Mission In Burma	Catalog Sampler (Promo)	CD	Rykodisc	VRCD0339	U.S.A.	1997	16.99
Mitchell, Joni	Big Yellow Taxi	CD Single	Reprise	9-43600-2	U.S.A.	1995	10.99
Mitchell, Joni	Blue	CD	Reprise	2038-2	U.S.A.	1971	10.99
Mitchell, Joni	Blue (DCC Gold Cd)	CD	DCC	GZS-1132	U.S.A.	1997	43.99
Mitchell, Joni	Both Sides Now	CD	Reprise	9-47620-2	U.S.A.	2000	10.99
Mitchell, Joni	Chalk Mark In A Rain Storm	CD	Geffen	9-24172-2	U.S.A.	1988	8.99

M

Artist	Title	Format	Label	Catalog No	Country	Released	Value
Mitchell, Joni	Clouds	CD	Reprise	6341-2	U.S.A.	1969	11.99
Mitchell, Joni	Court And Spark	CD	Asylum	1001-2	U.S.A.	1974	8.99
Mitchell, Joni	Court And Spark (DCC Gold Cd)	CD	DCC	GZS-1025	U.S.A.	1992	79.99
Mitchell, Joni	Dog Eat Dog	CD	Geffen	GEFD-24074	U.S.A.	1985	9.99
Mitchell, Joni	Don Juan's Reckless Daughter	CD	Asylum	701-2	U.S.A.	1977	8.99
Mitchell, Joni	For The Roses	CD	Reprise	5057-2	U.S.A.	1972	10.99
Mitchell, Joni	Hejira	CD	Asylum	1087-2	U.S.A.	1976	12.99
Mitchell, Joni	Hissing Of Summer Lawns	CD	Asylum	1051-2	U.S.A.	1975	10.99
Mitchell, Joni	Hits	CD	Reprise	9-46326-2	U.S.A.	1996	8.99
Mitchell, Joni	Ladies Of The Canyon	CD	Reprise	6376-2	U.S.A.	1970	8.99
Mitchell, Joni	Miles Of Aisles	CD	Asylum	202-2	U.S.A.	1974	10.99
Mitchell, Joni	Mingus	CD	Asylum	505-2	U.S.A.	1978	14.99
Mitchell, Joni	Misses	CD	Reprise	9-46358-2	U.S.A.	1996	8.99
Mitchell, Joni	Night Ride Home (Deluxe)	CD	Geffen	GEFD-24388	U.S.A.	1991	34.99
Mitchell, Joni	Self Titled (AKA Song To A Seagull)	CD	Reprise	6293-2	U.S.A.	1968	9.99
Mitchell, Joni	Shadows And Light	2CD	East West	AMCY-2878-2	Japan	1998	34.99
Mitchell, Joni	Taming The Tiger	CD	Reprise	9-46451-2	U.S.A.	1998	12.99
Mitchell, Joni	Travelougue	2CD	Warner Bros.	9-47965-2	U.S.A.	2002	17.99
Mitchell, Joni	Turbulent Indigo	CD	Reprise	9-45786-2	U.S.A.	1994	10.99
Mitchell, Joni	Wild Things Run Fast (MFSL Gold Cd)	CD	Mobile Fidelity	UDCD-570	U.S.A.	1982	24.99
Mitchum, Robert	Calypso - Is Like So...	CD	Caroline	SCP-9701-2	U.S.A.	1995	19.99
Mizzy, Vic	Original Music From Addams Family	CD	RCA	07863-61057-2	U.S.A.	1991	18.99
Mizzy, Vic	The Ghost And Mr. Chicken (O.S.T.)	CD	Percepto	PERCEPTO-015	U.S.A.	2004	23.99
Mizzy, Vic	Vic Mizzy - Suites And Themes (Promo)	CD	Percepto	PERCEPTO-005	U.S.A.	2000	23.99
Mlimani Park Orchestra	Sikinde	CD	Line	MSCD-9.00902-0	Germany	1989	16.99
Moahni Moahna	Temple Of Life	CD	Victor Ent.	VICP-5520	Japan	1995	17.99
Moahni Moahna	Why	CD	Victor Ent.	VICP-5836	Japan	1997	17.99
Moby Grape	20 Granite Creek	CD	Line	LICD-9.00886-0	Germany	1990	29.99
Moby Grape	Live Grape	CD	Line	LICD-9.00335-0	Germany	1988	24.99
Moby Grape	Moby Grape	CD	San Francisco Soun	SFS-04805	U.S.A.	1967	14.99
Moby Grape	Vintage: Very Best Of	2CD	Columbia	C2K-53041	U.S.A.	1993	23.99
Moby Grape	Wow/Grape Jam	CD	San Francisco Soun	SFS-04801	U.S.A.	1991	17.99
Modern Jazz Quartet	Space	CD	EMI	7243-8-53816-2-1	England	1996	24.99
Modern Jazz Quartet	Under The Jasmin Tree	CD	EMI	0777-7-97582-2-7	U.S.A.	1993	15.99
Modern Lovers	And The Modern Lovers + 4	CD	Castle	CMRCD885	England	2003	12.99
Modern Lovers	Back In Your Life	CD	Wooded Hill	HILLCD-14	England	1997	29.99
Modern Lovers	Back In Your Life + 4	CD	Castle	CMRCD924	England	2004	12.99
Modern Lovers	Buzz Buzz Buzz	CD	Delta	47-038	England	2000	15.99
Modern Lovers	Home Of The Hits/Beserkley Story	2CD	Essential	ESDCD-786	England	1999	16.99
Modern Lovers	It's Time For	CD	Upside	UCD-60001-2	U.S.A.	1986	259.99
Modern Lovers	Jonathan Richman/Modern Lovers	CD	Beserkley	SOB-CD-0056	U.S.A.	1976	20.99
Modern Lovers	Jonathan Sings!	CD	Sire	9-45284-2	U.S.A.	1983	24.99
Modern Lovers	Live	CD	Line	BECD-9.00483-0	Germany	1987	12.99
Modern Lovers	Live	CD	Wooded Hill	HILLCD-15	England	1997	10.99
Modern Lovers	Live	CD	Castle	CMRCD923	England	2004	12.99
Modern Lovers	Live At The Longbranch Saloon	CD	New Rose	422439	France	1995	10.99
Modern Lovers	Mega Hits	CD	Beserkley	BZCD007	U.S.A.	1990	19.99
Modern Lovers	Precise Modern Lovers Order	CD	Rounder	CD-9042	U.S.A.	1994	19.99
Modern Lovers	Radio On	2CD	Snapper	SMD-CD-115	England	1997	19.99
Modern Lovers	Roadrunner (Best Of)	CD	Castle	SELCD-521	England	1998	12.99
Modern Lovers	Rock 'N Roll With The + 1	CD	Castle	CMRCD884	England	2003	12.99
Modern Lovers	Rock 'N' Roll With The Modern Lovers	CD	Beserkley	SOB-CD-0051	U.S.A.	1976	12.99
Modern Lovers	The Best Of	CD	Rhino	R2-75889	U.S.A.	1986	12.99
Modern Lovers	The Modern Lovers	CD	Line	BECD-9.00501-0	Germany	1987	20.99
Ardern Lovers	The Original Modern Lovers	CD	Line	LICD-9.00310-0	Germany	1988	12.99
Modern Lovers	The Original Modern Lovers	CD	Bomp	BCD-4021	U.S.A.	2000	11.99
Modern Lovers/Asa Brebner	Best No Money Can Buy	CD	Windjam	WJ-20120	U.S.A.	2001	11.99
Modern Lovers/Asa Brebner	Prayers Of A Snowball In Hell	CD	Ocean Music	OM-2008	U.S.A.	1996	6.99

Artist	Title	Format	Label	Catalog No	Country	Released	Value
Moebius, Dieter	Blotch	CD	Captain Trip	CTCD-220	Japan	2000	13.99
Moebius, Neumeier & Engler	Other Places	CD	Captain Trip	CTCD-044	Japan	1996	13.99
Moebius/Neumeier	Live In Japan	CD	Captain Trip	CTCD-425	Japan	2002	13.99
Mofungo	Work	CD	SST	SST-CD-740	U.S.A.	1989	9.99
Mohawk, Essra	Primordial Lovers MM (Ltd 2500)	CD	Rhino	RHM2-7720	U.S.A.	2000	22.99
Molly Hatchet	Beatin' The Odds	CD	Epic	EK-36572	U.S.A.	1990	11.99
Molly Hatchet	Cut To The Bone	CD	Sony	A-24186	U.S.A.	1995	7.99
Molly Hatchet	Devil's Canyon	CD	SPV	SPV23044352CD	Germany	1996	9.99
Molly Hatchet	Double Trouble Live	CD	Epic	EGK-40137	U.S.A.	1989	13.99
Molly Hatchet	Flirtin' With Disaster + 4	CD	Epic	EK-85385	U.S.A.	2001	10.99
Molly Hatchet	Greatest Hits + 3	CD	Epic	EK-85384	U.S.A.	2001	8.99
Molly Hatchet	KBFH - Greatest Hits Live	CD	King Biscuit	40001-2	Canada	2003	8.99
Molly Hatchet	Kingdom Of XII	CD	SPV	SPV08572062CD	Germany	2000	11.99
Molly Hatchet	Lightning Strikes Twice	CD	SPV	SPV07644342CD	Germany	1996	11.99
Molly Hatchet	Live/Agora Ballroom April 20, 1979	CD	Phoenix Gems	5002	U.S.A.	2000	13.99
Molly Hatchet	Locked And Loaded	CD	SPV	SPV08971342CD	Germany	2003	11.99
Molly Hatchet	No Guts... No Glory	CD	Epic	EK-38429	U.S.A.	1990	25.99
Molly Hatchet	Self Titled	CD	Epic	EK-35347	U.S.A.	1990	14.99
Molly Hatchet	Silent Reign Of Heroes	CD	SPV	SPV08529222CD	Germany	1998	8.99
Molly Hatchet	Super Hits	CD	Epic	EK-65271	U.S.A.	1998	9.99
Molly Hatchet	Take No Prisoners	CD	Epic	EK-37480	U.S.A.	1990	14.99
Molly Hatchet	The Deed Is Done	CD	Epic	EK-39621	U.S.A.	1990	12.99
Molly Hatchet	The Essential	CD	Epic	EK-87180	U.S.A.	2003	8.99
Momposina, Toto La	La Candela Viva	CD	Caroline	CAROL-2337-2	U.S.A.	1993	11.99
Monaco Blues Band	Black Out	CD	Line	STCD-9.00699-0	Germany	1988	24.99
Money Mark	Push The Button + 2	CD	Toy's Factory	TFCK-87949-50	Japan	1998	11.99
Money, Eddie	Can't Hold Back	CD	Columbia	CK-40096	U.S.A.	1986	7.99
Money, Eddie	Good As Gold	CD	Sony	A-28125	U.S.A.	1996	6.99
Money, Eddie	Life For The Taking	CD	Columbia	CK-35598	U.S.A.	1990	6.99
Money, Eddie	Love And Money	CD	Wolfgang	24744-2	U.S.A.	1995	6.99
Money, Eddie	No Control	CD	Columbia	CK-37960	U.S.A.	1990	6.99
Money, Eddie	Nothing To Lose	CD	Columbia	CK-44302	U.S.A.	1988	5.99
Money, Eddie	Playing For Keeps	CD	Columbia	CK-36514	U.S.A.	1990	38.99
Money, Eddie	Ready Eddie	CD	CMC INT.	06076-86271-2	U.S.A.	1999	4.99
Money, Eddie	Right Here	CD	Columbia	CK-46756	U.S.A.	1991	5.99
Money, Eddie	Self Titled	CD	Columbia	CK-66228	U.S.A.	1995	8.99
Money, Eddie	Shakin' With The Money Man	CD	CMC INT.	06076-86223-2	U.S.A.	1997	8.99
Money, Eddie	Super Hits	CD	Sony	SK-65274	U.S.A.	1997	5.99
Money, Eddie	The Best Of	CD	Columbia	CK-85731	U.S.A.	2001	8.99
Money, Eddie	The Essential	CD	Columbia	CK-89213	U.S.A.	2003	8.99
Money, Eddie	Then And Now (Live)	CD	Sanctuary	06076-86329-2	U.S.A.	2003	5.99
Money, Eddie	Unplug It In	CD	Columbia	CK-52909	U.S.A.	1992	7.99
Money, Eddie	Where's The Party?	CD	Columbia	CK-38862	U.S.A.	1990	44.99
Money, Eddie	You Can't Keep A Good...	CD	Connoisseur	VSOP-CD-336	England	2001	8.99
Money, Eddie/Ronnie Spector	Everybody Loves Christmas	CD Single	CMC INT.	06076-87241-2	U.S.A.	1997	14.99
Monkees	Anthology	2CD	Rhino	R2-75269	U.S.A.	1998	17.99
Monkees	Best Of (W/Bonus Karaoke Cd)	CD	Rhino	R2-73875	U.S.A.	2003	16.99
Monkees	Birds, The Bees And The Monkees + 5	CD	Rhino	R2-71794	U.S.A.	1994	8.99
Monkees	Changes	CD	Rhino	R2-71798	U.S.A.	1994	10.99
Monkees	Definitive Monkees (With Bonus Cd)	2CD	Warner Bros.	8573-86692-2	Germany	2001	14.99
Monkees	Greatest Hits	CD	Rhino	R2-72190	U.S.A.	1995	8.99
Monkees	Head + 6	CD	Rhino	R2-71295	U.S.A.	1994	9.99
Monkees	Headquarters + 6	CD	Rhino	R2-71792	U.S.A.	1995	8.99
Monkees	Headquarters Sessions (Ltd. 4500)	3CD	Rhino	RHM2-7715	U.S.A.	2000	206.99
Monkees	Instant Replay + 7	CD	Rhino	R2-71796	U.S.A.	1995	8.99
Monkees	Live 1967	CD	Rhino	R2-70139	U.S.A.	1987	8.99
Monkees	Missing Links Vol. 2	CD	Rhino	R2-70903	U.S.A.	1990	12.99
Monkees	Missing Links Vol. 3	CD	Rhino	R2-72153	U.S.A.	1996	12.99

M

Artist	Title	Format	Label	Catalog No	Country	Released	Value
Monkees	Missing Links Volume 1	CD	Rhino	R2-70150	U.S.A.	1988	12.99
Monkees	More Of The Monkees + 5	CD	Rhino	R2-71791	U.S.A.	1994	9.99
Monkees	Music Box (Box Set)	4CD	Rhino	R2-76706	U.S.A.	2001	39.99
Monkees	Pisces, Aquarius, Capricorn...+ 7	CD	Rhino	R2-71793	U.S.A.	1995	13.99
Monkees	Pool It	CD	Rhino	R2-72154	U.S.A.	1986	11.99
Monkees	Present + 5	CD	Rhino	R2-71797	U.S.A.	1995	9.99
Monkees	Sampler (Promo/Guitar Shaped)	CD	Rhino	PRCD-7080	U.S.A.	1994	29.99
Monkees	Summer 1967: Complete U.S. Concerts	4CD	Rhino	RHM2-7755	U.S.A.	2000	54.99
Monkees	The Essentials	CD	Rhino	R2-76057	U.S.A.	2002	8.99
Monkees	The Monkees + 3	CD	Rhino	R2-71790	U.S.A.	1994	8.99
Monkees	Then And Now	CD	Arista	A2CD-8432	U.S.A.	1986	8.99
Monkey See	Self Titled	CD	Teichiku	TKCF-45018	Japan	1997	22.99
Monks	Black Monk Time	CD	Repertoire	REP-4438-WP	Germany	2002	14.99
Monks	Black Monk Time +7	CD	Infinite Zero	43112	U.S.A.	1997	21.99
Monks	Five Upstart Americans + 2	CD	Captain Trip	CTCD-242	Japan	2000	14.99
Monks Of Doom	Forgery	CD	I.R.S.	0777-7-13163-2-6	U.S.A.	1992	17.99
Montand, Yves	Bravo A Yves Montand	CD	Columbia	WCK-90976	U.S.A.	1988	22.99
Montgomery, James/Band	Bring It On Home	CD	Conqueroot	1017	U.S.A.	2001	12.99
Montgomery, James/Band	First Time Out	CD	Capricorn	314-538-133-2	U.S.A.	1998	12.99
Montgomery, James/Band	The Oven Is On	CD	Tone-Cool	TC-1145	U.S.A.	1991	12.99
Montrose	Jump On It	CD	Wounded Bird	WOU-2963	U.S.A.	2002	8.99
Montrose	Jump On It	CD	Warner Bros.	WPCR-2562	Japan	1997	18.99
Montrose	Open Fire	CD	Wounded Bird	WOU-3134	U.S.A.	2002	8.99
Montrose	Open Fire	CD	Warner Bros.	WPCR-2563	Japan	1997	18.99
Montrose	Paper Money	CD	Warner Bros.	2-2823	U.S.A.	1990	7.99
Montrose	Paper Money	CD	Warner Bros.	WPCR-2560	Japan	1997	18.99
Montrose	Self Titled	CD	Warner Bros.	2-3106	U.S.A.	1990	12.99
Montrose	Self Titled	CD	Warner Bros.	WPCR-2559	Japan	1997	22.99
Montrose	The Very Best Of	CD	Rhino	R2-79982	U.S.A.	2000	11.99
Montrose	Warner Brothers Presents..	CD	Wounded Bird	WOU-2892	U.S.A.	2002	8.99
Montrose	Warner Brothers Presents...	CD	Warner Bros.	WPCR-2561	Japan	1997	18.99
Montrose, Ronnie	Bearings	CD	Alien Echo	ROMOCO-0-2001	U.S.A.	1999	29.99
Montrose, Ronnie	Diva Station	CD	Enigma	D2-73520-2	U.S.A.	1990	23.99
Montrose, Ronnie	Mean	CD	Pony Canyon	PCCY-00240	Japan	1991	49.99
Montrose, Ronnie	Mean	CD	Enigma	D2-73264-2	U.S.A.	1990	40.99
Montrose, Ronnie	Mr. Bones	CD	Sega	124145	U.S.A.	1996	23.99
Montrose, Ronnie	Music From Here	CD	Fearless Urge	FEAR201-RM-2	U.S.A.	1994	23.99
Montrose, Ronnie	Mutatis Mutandis	CD	I.R.S.	X2-13112	U.S.A.	1991	34.99
Montrose, Ronnie	Roll Over And Play Live!	CD	Alien Echo	ROMOCO-0-2000	U.S.A.	1999	29.99
Montrose, Ronnie	The Speed Of Sound	CD	Enigma	D2-73323-2	U.S.A.	1990	24.99
Montrose, Ronnie	Very Best Of	CD	Rhino	R2-79982	U.S.A.	2000	9.99
Monty Python	Always Look On The Bright Side..	CD Single	Virgin	PYTHD-1-664740	Germany	1991	7.99
Monty Python	Another Monty Python Box Set	3CD	Virgin	724357-933926	Holland	2002	22.99
Monty Python	Another Monty Python Record	CD	Virgin	CASCD-1049	England	1990	7.99
Monty Python	At The Movies Box Set	3CD	Virgin	724357-933827	Holland	2002	22.99
Monty Python	Contractual Obligation Album	CD	Arista	07822-18955-2	U.S.A.	1997	9.99
Monty Python	Contraptual Obligation ..(Charisma)	CD	Virgin	CASCD-1152	England	1990	7.99
Monty Python	Galaxy Song (Always '91/Xmas Song)	CD Single	Virgin	PYTHD2	England	1993	9.99
Monty Python	Holy Grail (O.S.T.)	CD	Virgin	CASCD-1103	England	1990	7.99
Monty Python	I Like Chinese	CD Single	Virgin	665260	Germany	1989	14.99
Monty Python	Instant CD Collection (W/Card)	6CD	Virgin	7243-8-39820-2-8	U.S.A.	1994	59.99
Monty Python	Instant Record Collection (Blue Bkg)	CD	Virgin	CASCD-1134	England	1990	11.99
Monty Python	Instant Record Collection (Brown Bkg)	CD	Arista	ARCD-8296	U.S.A.	1981	10.99
Monty Python	Live At City Center	CD	Arista	07822-18957-2	U.S.A.	1997	9.99
Monty Python	Live At Drury Lane	CD	Virgin	VVIPD-104	England	1989	7.99
Monty Python	Lust For Glory (DJ Cd Sampler Thingy)	CD	Virgin	DPRO-14236	U.S.A.	1994	14.99
Monty Python	M Python's Previous Record (Wh Bkg)	CD	Virgin	CASCD-1063	England	1990	7.99
Monty Python	Matching Tie And Handkerchief	CD	Arista	07822-18956-2	U.S.A.	1997	8.99

M

Artist	Title	Format	Label	Catalog No	Country	Released	Value
Monty Python	Matching Tie/Handkerchief (Wh Bkg)	CD	Virgin	CASCD-1080	England	1992	7.99
Monty Python	Monty Python And The Holy Grail	CD	Arista	ARCD-8958	U.S.A.	1997	8.99
Monty Python	Monty Python's Flying Circus (Foot/TV)	CD	BBC	BBC-CD-73	England	1973	49.99
Monty Python	Sings	CD	Virgin	MONT-D1	England	1989	7.99
Monty Python	The Complete A Poke In The Eye...	CD	Castle	ACSCD-020	England	1991	29.99
Monty Python	The Final Rip Off	2CD	Virgin	0777-7-86033-2-0	U.S.A.	1987	16.99
Monty Python	The Final Rip Off	2CD	Virgin	CD-MP-1	England	1987	17.99
Monty Python	The Meaning Of Life	CD	Virgin	7243-8-39859-2-0	England	1983	9.99
Monty Python	The Ultimate Monty Python Rip Off	CD	Virgin	CDV-2748	England	1994	11.99
Monty Python/Eric Idle	Eric Idle Sings Monty Python	CD	Restless	01877-73730-2	U.S.A.	2000	8.99
Monty Python/Eric Idle	Quite Remarkable Adv. Owl/Pussycat	CD	Dove	8154	U.S.A.	1997	12.99
Monty Python/Eric Idle	Rutland Isles	CD	Imusic	IMUCD-125	England	2003	8.99
Monty Python/Various Artists	The Best Comedy Album....	3CD	Virgin	7243-8-49758-2-1	England	2000	24.99
Moodswings	Moodfood (With Chrissie Hynde)	CD	Arista	18619-2	U.S.A.	1992	8.99
Moodswings	Pychedelicatessen	CD	Arista	07822-18785-2	U.S.A.	1997	8.99
Moodswings	Spiritual High (DJ Diff Vrsn Than Cd)	CD Single	Arista	ASCD-2458	U.S.A.	1992	12.99
Moody Blues	A Night At Red Rocks	2CD	Universal	04400-65275-2-9	U.S.A.	1993	15.99
Moody Blues	A Question Of... (MFSL Gold Cd)	CD	Mobile Fidelity	UDCD-737	U.S.A.	1970	44.99
Moody Blues	Caught Live +5	CD	PolyGram	820-161-2	England	1977	13.99
Moody Blues	Days Of Future Passed (MFSL Gold)	CD	Mobile Fidelity	UDCD-512	U.S.A.	1967	28.99
Moody Blues	Every Good Boy... (MFSL Gold)	CD	Mobile Fidelity	UDCD-643	U.S.A.	1971	38.99
Moody Blues	Hall Of Fame	CD	Ark 21	186-810-059-2	U.S.A.	2000	8.99
Moody Blues	Highlights From Time Traveller (Promo)	CD	Polydor	31452-5042-2	U.S.A.	1994	24.99
Moody Blues	I Know You're Out There...(CD Video)	CDV	Polydor	870-726-2	U.S.A.	1988	18.99
Moody Blues	In Search Of The Lost (MFSL Gold)	CD	Mobile Fidelity	UDCD-576	U.S.A.	1968	39.99
Moody Blues	Journey Into Amazing Caves	CD	Ark 21	186-810-065-2	U.S.A.	2001	10.99
Moody Blues	Journey Into Time	CD	PolyGram	844-047-2	Australia	1990	11.99
Moody Blues	Keys Of The Kingdom	CD	Polydor	849-433-2	U.S.A.	1991	13.99
Moody Blues	Long Distance Voyager (MFSL Gold)	CD	Mobile Fidelity	UDCD-700	U.S.A.	1981	51.99
Moody Blues	Octave	CD	London	820-329-2	U.S.A.	1978	10.99
Moody Blues	On The Threshold Of... (MFSL Gold)	CD	Mobile Fidelity	UDCD-612	U.S.A.	1969	19.99
Moody Blues	Say It With Love	CD Single	PolyGram	867-297-2	U.S.A.	1991	91.99
Moody Blues	Seventh Sojourn (MFSL Gold Cd)	CD	Mobile Fidelity	UDCD-718	U.S.A.	1972	53.99
Moody Blues	Strange Times + 2	CD	Polydor K.K.	POCP-7452	Japan	2000	29.99
Moody Blues	Sur la Mer	CD	Polydor	835-756-2	U.S.A.	1988	9.99
Moody Blues	The Best of The Moody Blues	CD	Polydor	314-535-800-2	U.S.A.	1996	10.99
Moody Blues	The Magnificent Moodies	CD	Repertoire	REP-4232-WY	Germany	1998	11.99
Moody Blues	The Moody Blues Anthology	2CD	Polydor	31456-5430-2	U.S.A.	1998	24.99
Moody Blues	The Other Side Of Life	CD	Polydor	829-179-2	U.S.A.	1986	9.99
Moody Blues	The Present	CD	PolyGram	810-119-2	Germany	1983	8.99
Moody Blues	This Is The Moody Blues	2CD	PolyGram	820-007-2	U.S.A.	1989	25.99
Moody Blues	Time Traveller Box Set	5CD	Polydor	31451-6436-2	U.S.A.	1991	39.99
Moody Blues	To Our Childrens... (MFSL Gold)	CD	Mobile Fidelity	UDCD-671	U.S.A.	1969	39.99
Moody Blues/Graeme Edge	Kick Off Your Muddy Boots + 1	CD	PolyGram	820-780-2	U.S.A.	1989	49.99
Moody Blues/Graeme Edge	Paradise Ballroom + 1	CD	Decca	820-781-2	Germany	1989	299.99
Moody Blues/John Lodge	Natural Avenue + 2	CD	Threshold	DIDX-031488	U.S.A.	1996	24.99
Moody Blues/Patrick Moraz	Out In The Sun (Played With Yes Also)	CD	Virgin	7243-8-39540-2-5	Holland	1977	13.99
Moody Blues/Patrick Moraz	The Story Of I (Played With Yes Also)	CD	Virgin	7243-8-39541-2-4	England	1976	13.99
Moody Blues/Ray Thomas	From Mighty Oaks	CD	PolyGram	820-782-2	U.S.A.	1989	59.99
Moody Blues/Ray Thomas	Hopes Wishes And Dreams	CD	Decca	820-783-2	Germany	1989	316.99
Moon, Keith/Who	Two Sides Of The Moon + 8	CD	Mausoleum	60038-2	U.S.A.	1975	9.99
Moore, Dudley	Songs Without Words	CD	GRP	GRD-9661	U.S.A.	1991	6.99
Moore, Dudley/Carol Stevens	That Satin Doll/Theme From Beyond...	CD	Collectables	COL-CD-6625	U.S.A.	2000	9.99
Moore, Gary	3 Originals	3CD	Castle	CLA-BX-904	EEC	1992	24.99
Moore, Gary	A Different Beat	CD	Victor Ent.	VICP-60921	Japan	1999	24.99
Moore, Gary	A Different Beat	CD	Raw Power	RAWCD-142	England	1999	13.99
Moore, Gary	A Portrait Of	CD	Castle	CHC-7082	Germany	1993	19.99
Moore, Gary	A Retrospective	CD	MCA	MCD-30461	Germany	1993	14.99

M

Artist	Title	Format	Label	Catalog No	Country	Released	Value
Moore, Gary	After Hours	CD	Virgin	CDV-2684	England	1992	8.99
Moore, Gary	After Hours	CD	EMI	786-269-2	Australia	1992	8.99
Moore, Gary	After Hours + 1	CD	Toshiba-EMI	TOCP-53270	Japan	2002	24.99
Moore, Gary	After Hours + 1	CD	Virgin	VJCP-28097	Japan	1992	15.99
Moore, Gary	After Hours + 4	CD	EMI	7243-5-83669-2-1	EU	2003	13.99
Moore, Gary	After Hours DJ Kit (Ppr Cvr/Pics/Fldr)	CD	Virgin	GMCDJ-1	England	1992	29.99
Moore, Gary	After Hours Preview (Promo)	CD	Virgin	VIR-PRO-2	Australia	1992	19.99
Moore, Gary	After Hours/Blues For Greeny	2CD	EMI	7243-5-92250 2-9	England	2003	19.99
Moore, Gary	After The War	CD	Virgin	CDV-2575	England	1989	10.99
Moore, Gary	After The War (3" CD W/Tin/Patch)	CD Single	Virgin	GMSCD-1	England	1989	14.99
Moore, Gary	After The War + 4	CD	Toshiba-EMI	TOCP-53268	Japan	2002	24.99
Moore, Gary	After The War + 4	CD	EMI	7243-5-83579-2	EU	2003	13.99
Moore, Gary	And Then The Man...	2CD	Accord	100101	France	1987	13.99
Moore, Gary	Back On The Streets	CD	Ariola	291.006	Germany	1992	8.99
Moore, Gary	Back On The Streets	CD	MCA Victor	MVCM-21033	Japan	1991	15.99
Moore, Gary	Back On The Streets	CD	MCA	MCD-01622	Germany	1978	8.99
Moore, Gary	Back On The Streets + 1	CD	Grand Slamm	SLAMCD-10	U.S.A.	1989	13.99
Moore, Gary	Back To The Blues	CD	Sanctuary	SANCD072	England	2001	8.99
Moore, Gary	Back To The Blues (DJ/Interview)	CD	Sanctuary	SANP3072	England	2001	11.99
Moore, Gary	Back To The Blues (DJ/Sampler)	CD	Sanctuary	SANP2072	England	2001	23.99
Moore, Gary	Back To The Blues + 2	CD	Victor Ent.	VICP-61331	Japan	2001	24.99
Moore, Gary	Back To The Streets: Rock Coll.	CD	EMI	7243-5-91089-2-6	EU	2003	13.99
Moore, Gary	Ballads & Blues 1982 - 1994	CD	Virgin	VJCP-25150	Japan	1994	15.99
Moore, Gary	Ballads & Blues 1982 - 1994	CD	Virgin	CDV-2768	England	1994	11.99
Moore, Gary	Best	CD	Victor Ent.	VICP-60253	Japan	1998	34.99
Moore, Gary	Blood Of Emeralds: Best + 11 (Bonus)	2CD	Virgin	CDMOORE-2	Sweden	1999	22.99
Moore, Gary	Blood Of Emeralds: Best Of Vol. 2	CD	Virgin	CDMOORE-2	Sweden	1999	14.99
Moore, Gary	Blues Alive	CD	Virgin	CDV-2716	England	1993	11.99
Moore, Gary	Blues Alive (Digipack/Limited)	CD	Virgin	CDVX-2716	England	1993	11.99
Moore, Gary	Blues Alive + 4 (W/3" Cd Single)	2CD	Virgin	VJCP-28164	Japan	1993	38.99
Moore, Gary	Blues And Moore	CD	Edel	EDL-2625-2	Germany	1992	12.99
Moore, Gary	Blues For Greeny	CD	Toshiba-EMI	TOCP-53272	Japan	2002	24.99
Moore, Gary	Blues For Greeny	CD	Virgin	CDV-2784	Holland	1995	11.99
Moore, Gary	Blues For Greeny (DJ/Sampler)	CD	Virgin	CDVDJ-2784	England	1995	10.99
Moore, Gary	Blues For Greeny (Promo Sampler)	CD	Virgin	CDVDJ-2784	England	1995	9.99
Moore, Gary	Blues For Greeny + 1	CD	Virgin	VJCP-25177	Japan	1995	15.99
Moore, Gary	Blues For Greeny + 2	CD	EMI	7243-5-83670-2-7	EU	2003	13.99
Moore, Gary	Blues For Greeny/After Hours	2CD	Virgin	581733-2	EU	2003	19.99
Moore, Gary	Castle Master Collection	CD	Castle	CMC-3001	Germany	1990	8.99
Moore, Gary	Corridors Of Power	CD	Relativity	88561-1003-2	U.S.A.	1982	11.99
Moore, Gary	Corridors Of Power	CD	Virgin	CDV-2245	England	1982	11.99
Moore, Gary	Corridors Of Power + 2	CD	Toshiba-EMI	TOCP-53262	Japan	2002	24.99
Moore, Gary	Corridors Of Power + 2	CD	EMI	7243-5-83574-2-4	EU	2003	13.99
Moore, Gary	Dark Days In Paradise	CD	Virgin	CDV-2826	England	1997	11.99
Moore, Gary	Dark Days In Paradise (DJ/Sampler)	CD	Virgin	CDVDJ-2826	England	1997	7.99
Moore, Gary	Dark Days In Paradise + 2	CD	Toshiba-EMI	TOCP-53273	Japan	2002	24.99
Moore, Gary	Dark Days In Paradise + 2	CD	EMI	7243-5-83671-2	EU	2003	13.99
Moore, Gary	Dbl Collection: Parisienne Walkways	2CD	Castle	CBC-8022-DX	Germany	1992	15.99
Moore, Gary	Desperado	CD	BMG	74321-46866-2	Germany	1997	10.99
Moore, Gary	Dirty Fingers	CD	Sanctuary	06076-81193-2	England	2002	13.99
Moore, Gary	Dirty Fingers	CD	Victor Ent.	VICP-2025	Japan	1990	15.99
Moore, Gary	Dirty Fingers	CD	Jet	JET-CD-007	England	1985	8.99
Moore, Gary	G-Force	CD	Victor Ent.	VICP-2024	Japan	1990	15.99
Moore, Gary	G-Force	CD	Sanctuary	06076-81192	England	2002	8.99
Moore, Gary	Greatest Hits	CD	Green Line	CDGLP-451	EEC	1990	11.99
Moore, Gary	Grinding Stone	CD	Sony	ESCA-5352	Japan	1991	15.99
Moore, Gary	Grinding Stone	CD	Columbia	467-449-2	England	1973	11.99
Moore, Gary	Hits And More	CD	Prima Musik	PMM-0563-2	Germany	1993	14.99

M

Artist	Title	Format	Label	Catalog No	Country	Released	Value
Moore, Gary	Ironstrike	CD	Avanti	ISTCD-003	U.S.A.	1989	14.99
Moore, Gary	Live At The Marquee	CD	Sanctuary	06076-81194	England	2002	13.99
Moore, Gary	Live At The Marquee	CD	Victor Ent.	VICP-2026	Japan	1990	15.99
Moore, Gary	Live At The Marquee	CD	Raw Power	RAWCD-034	France	1987	8.99
Moore, Gary	Milestones	2CD	Castle	MSSCD-107	England	1989	24.99
Moore, Gary	Night Riding	CD	Knight	KNCD-10014	England	1991	11.99
Moore, Gary	Nuclear Attack	CD	Spectrum	551-483-2	Germany	1995	8.99
Moore, Gary	Nuclear Attack: The Best Of	CD	Avenue	8.26227-ZR	Germany	1985	11.99
Moore, Gary	Out In The Fields: Best + 9 (W/Bonus)	2CD	Virgin	CDMOORE-1	Sweden	1998	21.99
Moore, Gary	Out In The Fields: Best + 9 (W/Bonus)	2CD	Virgin	VJCP 36078/79	Japan	1998	39.99
Moore, Gary	Out In The Fields: Best + 9 (W/Bonus)	2CD	Virgin	CDVX-2871	England	1998	21.99
Moore, Gary	Out In The Fields: Very Best Of	CD	Virgin	CDV-2871	EU	1998	11.99
Moore, Gary	Parisienne Walkways: Blues Coll.	CD	EMI	7243-5-91100-2-8	EU	2003	13.99
Moore, Gary	Ready For Love (3" CD/Box/Badge)	CD Single	Virgin	GMSCDX-2	England	1989	14.99
Moore, Gary	Rockin' Every Night	CD	Virgin	7-91258-2	U.S.A.	1986	8.99
Moore, Gary	Rockin' Every Night + 3	CD	Toshiba-EMI	TOCP-53263	Japan	2002	24.99
Moore, Gary	Rockin' Every Night + 3	CD	EMI	7243-5-83668-2-2	EU	2003	13.99
Moore, Gary	Rockin' Every Night/Live In Japan	CD	10 Records	XID-CD-1	England	1986	8.99
Moore, Gary	Run For Cover	CD	Relativity	88561-1004-2	U.S.A.	1985	11.99
Moore, Gary	Run For Cover + 1	CD	10 Records	DIXD-CD-16	Germany	1985	11.99
Moore, Gary	Run For Cover + 3	CD	Toshiba-EMI	TOCP-53266	Japan	2002	24.99
Moore, Gary	Run For Cover + 3	CD	EMI	7243-5-83577-2	EU	2003	13.99
Moore, Gary	Run For/Wild F/After (3 Pk Pic Cds)	3CD	Virgin	TPAK-18/354-350	England	1991	39.99
Moore, Gary	Run For/Wild F/After (Blue Box/3 Pic)	3CD	Virgin	787-8130-1	Holland	1991	24.99
Moore, Gary	Scars	CD	Sanctuary	06076-84564	England	2002	13.99
Moore, Gary	Scars	CD	Victor Ent.	VICP-61894	Japan	2002	15.99
Moore, Gary	Spanish Guitar: Best	CD	MCA Victor	MVCM-311	Japan	1992	29.99
Moore, Gary	Spotlight	CD	Sonet	SPCD-46	Sweden	1991	14.99
Moore, Gary	Still Got The Blues	CD	Virgin	CDV-2612	Germany	1990	8.99
Moore, Gary	Still Got The Blues (Pic Cd)	CD	Virgin	PCDV-2612	England	1990	14.99
Moore, Gary	Still Got The Blues + 5	CD	Toshiba-EMI	TOCP-53269	Japan	2002	24.99
Moore, Gary	Still Got The Blues + 5	CD	EMI	7243-5-83580-2-5	EU	2003	13.99
Moore, Gary	Still Got The Blues/After Hours	2CD	EMI	844-392-2	Australia	1997	19.99
Moore, Gary	Still Got The Blues/Blues Alive	2CD	EMI	7243-5-92077-2-8	England	2003	19.99
Moore, Gary	Streets And Walkways...	CD	Music Club	MCCD-272	England	1996	10.99
Moore, Gary	Telefonkarten Edition (W/Phonecard)	CD	Castle	SPC-9522-2	Germany	1994	14.99
Moore, Gary	That's Original	2CD	Castle	TFOCD2	England	1988	24.99
Moore, Gary	The Back To Black Collection	CD	Axe Killer	M/M-3063322	France	2000	14.99
Moore, Gary	The Collection	CD	Sanctuary	06076-81271-2	U.S.A.	2003	8.99
Moore, Gary	The Early Years	CD	WTG	NK-48779	U.S.A.	1991	8.99
Moore, Gary	The Essential (Ballads/Blues)	CD	EMI	07243-581431-2-6	EU	2003	13.99
Moore, Gary	The Greatest	CD	Toshiba-EMI	VJCP-51046	Japan	1998	28.99
Moore, Gary	Victims Of The Future	CD	10 Records	DIXCD-2	England	1983	11.99
Moore, Gary	Victims Of The Future + 1	CD	Mirage	88561-1005-2	U.S.A.	1984	11.99
Moore, Gary	Victims Of The Future + 3	CD	Toshiba-EMI	TOCP-53264	Japan	2002	24.99
Moore, Gary	Victims Of The Future + 3	CD	EMI	7243-5-83575-2-3	EU	2003	13.99
Moore, Gary	Walkways	CD	Spectrum	550-738-2	Germany	1994	8.99
Moore, Gary	We Want Moore!	CD	10 Records	GMDLCD-1	England	1984	13.99
Moore, Gary	We Want Moore! + 1	CD	Toshiba-EMI	TOCP-53265	Japan	2002	24.99
Moore, Gary	We Want Moore! + 1	CD	EMI	7243-5-83576-2-2	EU	2003	13.99
Moore, Gary	White Knuckles	CD	Victor Ent.	VICP-2027	Japan	1990	15.99
Moore, Gary	White Knuckles	CD	Raw Power	RAWCD-006	France	1985	11.99
Moore, Gary	Wild Frontier	CD	10 Records	DIXCD-56	England	1987	11.99
Moore, Gary	Wild Frontier (Pic Cd/Diff To 3 Pk Cd)	CD	10 Records	DIXPCD-56	England	1987	11.99
Moore, Gary	Wild Frontier + 2	CD	Virgin	VJCP-23130	Japan	1992	15.99
Moore, Gary	Wild Frontier + 3	CD	Toshiba-EMI	TOCP-53267	Japan	2002	24.99
Moore, Gary	Wild Frontier + 3	CD	EMI	7243-5-83578-2	EU	2003	13.99
Moore, Gary/Scars	Live At Monsters Of Rock	CD	Victor Ent.	VICP-62557	Japan	2003	24.99

M

Artist	Title	Format	Label	Catalog No	Country	Released	Value
Moore, Gary/Scars	Live At Monsters Of Rock	CD	Sanctuary	SANPR215	EU	2003	13.99
Moore, Gary/Scars	Live At Monsters Of Rock	CD	Sanctuary	06076-84642-2	U.S.A.	2003	8.99
Moore, Gary/Skid Row	34 Hours	CD	Sony	ESCA-5533	Japan	1992	24.99
Moore, Gary/Skid Row	34 Hours	CD	Columbia	480525-2	England	1995	8.99
Moore, Gary/Skid Row	34 Hours + 2	CD	Repertoire	REP-4968-WZ	Germany	2001	11.99
Moore, Gary/Skid Row	Skid	CD	Sony	ESCA-5534	Japan	1992	27.99
Moore, Gary/Skid Row	Skid	CD	Columbia	477360-2	England	1994	8.99
Moore, Ian	Modernday Folklore	CD	Capricorn	9-42038-2	U.S.A.	1995	7.99
Moore, Ian	Self Titled	CD	Capricorn	9-42018-2	U.S.A.	1993	7.99
Moore, Rick	Slow Burnin' Fire	CD	Line	LICD-9.01331-0	Germany	1998	21.99
Moore, Rick/Mr. Lucky	Satisfied	CD	Line	LICD—9.01364-0	Germany	2000	21.99
Moore, Vinnie	Mind's Eye	CD	Apollon	APCY-2008	Japan	1991	39.99
Moranis, Rick/Dave Thomas	Bob/Doug McKenzie - Grt White North	CD	Mercury	314-534-010-2	U.S.A.	1981	8.99
Moratti	Legends Of Tomorrow	CD	Bareknuckle	AVCB-66007	Japan	1997	29.99
Moraz, Patrick/Mainhorse	Mainhorse	CD	Free	FR-9902	Germany	1999	22.99
Moriah	Mirror Man	CD	BMI	MCD-1214	France	1992	65.99
Morissette, Alanis	Alanis	CD	MCA	MCAD-10253	Canada	1991	36.99
Morissette, Alanis	Now Is The Time	CD	MCA	MCAD-10731	Canada	1992	26.99
Morley, Angela/Art Garfunkel	Watership Down (O.S.T.)	CD	Pendulum	PEG022	U.S.A.	1998	64.99
Morning Dew	Definitive Collection: 1966 - 1969	CD	Collectables	COL-592	U.S.A.	1994	9.99
Morning Dew	Morning Dew W/K. Livgren Of Kansas	Mini Lp	Akarma	AK-195	Italy	2001	21.99
Morning Dew	Second Album	CD	Collectables	COL-655	U.S.A.	1995	9.99
Morning Wood	Self Titled	CD	Mercury	PHCR-1236	Japan	1994	20.99
Morningstar	Self Titled	CD	Sony	SRCS-9441	Japan	1978	21.99
Moroder, Giorgio	Best Of	CD	Repertoire	REP-4825-WG	Germany	2002	12.99
Moroder, Giorgio	From Here To Eternity	CD	Repertoire	REP-4759-WG	Germany	2002	12.99
Moroder, Giorgio/Joe Esposito	Solitary Men + 3	CD	Repertoire	REP-4949	Germany	2002	12.99
Morricone, Ennio	2 Mules/Sister Sara - Days Of Heaven	CD	Legend	CD16	Italy	1994	26.99
Morricone, Ennio	A Fistful Of Dollars (O.S.T.)	CD	Razor & Tie	7930182171-2	U.S.A.	1998	10.99
Morricone, Ennio	A Fistful Of Film Music	2CD	Rhino	R271858	U.S.A.	1995	14.99
Morricone, Ennio	An Ennio Morricone Anthology	CD	DRG	39208	Canada	1995	24.99
Morricone, Ennio	Cinema Paradiso (O.S.T.)	CD	DRG	CDSBL-12598	U.S.A.	1989	13.99
Morricone, Ennio	Giornata Nera Per L'ariete	CD	Point	PRCD-122	Italy	1996	17.99
Morricone, Ennio	Main Titles- Vol. 1	2CD	DRG	32920	Canada	1996	29.99
Morricone, Ennio	Red Sonja/Bloodline	CD	Varese	VCL-9001.6	U.S.A.	1990	179.99
Morricone, Ennio	The Good/The Bad/The Ugly (O.S.T.)	CD	EMI	7-48408-2	U.S.A.	1985	8.99
Morricone, Ennio	The Legendary Italian Westerns Vol. II	CD	RCA	9974-2-R	U.S.A.	1990	6.98
Morricone, Ennio/D Frontiere	Guns San Sebastian/Hang 'Em High	CD	Sony	AK-47705	U.S.A.	1991	54.99
Morricone, Ennio/V. Artists	(Ennio) Morricone RMX (Remixed)	CD	Reprise	2-86639	U.S.A.	2001	11.99
Morrill, Kent	Hard To Rock Alone	CD	Line	SUCD-9.00398-0	Germany	1987	6.99
Morris, John	The Producers (O.S.T.)	CD	Razor & Tie	RE-2147-2	U.S.A.	1997	14.99
Morris, John	Young Frankenstein (O.S.T.)	CD	One Way	MCAD-22192	U.S.A.	1975	11.99
Morrison, Dave	With Joe Soap	CD	Line	LICD-9.00717-0	Germany	1989	18.99
Morrison, Dave Band	Someone's In My Kitchen	CD	Line	LICD-9.00177-0	Germany	1988	6.99
Morrison, Van	A Night In San Francisco (Live)	2CD	Mercury	314-521-290-2	U.S.A.	1994	24.99
Morrison, Van	A Period Of Transition	CD	Polydor	31453-7457-2	U.S.A.	1977	9.99
Morrison, Van	A Sense Of Wonder	CD	Polydor	31453-7545-2	U.S.A.	1984	7.99
Morrison, Van	Astral Weeks	CD	Warner Bros.	1768-2	U.S.A.	1968	8.99
Morrison, Van	Avalon Sunset	CD	Mercury	839-262-2	U.S.A.	1993	9.99
Morrison, Van	Back On Top	CD	Point Blank	7243-8-47148-2-6	U.S.A.	1999	5.99
Morrison, Van	Beautiful Vision	CD	Polydor	537-542-2	Germany	1998	9.99
Morrison, Van	Best Of (Gold Cd)	CD	Polydor	841-970-2	Germany	1990	14.99
Morrison, Van	Best Of Van Morrison Vol. 1	CD	Mercury	841-970-2	U.S.A.	1998	10.99
Morrison, Van	Best Of Van Morrison, Vol. 2	CD	Mercury	314-517-760-2	U.S.A.	1993	8.99
Morrison, Van	Blowin' Your Mind (Sony Gold Cd)	CD	Epic	ZK-66220	U.S.A.	1995	19.99
Morrison, Van	Common One	CD	Polydor	537-541-2	U.S.A.	1998	8.99
Morrison, Van	Complete Bang Sessions	2CD	Purple Pyramid	CLP-1214	U.S.A.	2002	15.99
Morrison, Van	Days Like This	CD	Polydor	31452-7307-2	U.S.A.	1995	9.99

M

Artist	Title	Format	Label	Catalog No	Country	Released	Value
Morrison, Van	Down The Road	CD	Polydor	314-589-177-2	U.S.A.	2002	10.99
Morrison, Van	Enlightenment	CD	Mercury	847-100-2	U.S.A.	1993	7.99
Morrison, Van	Essential	CD	Purple Pyramid	CLP-1020-2	U.S.A.	2001	9.99
Morrison, Van	Hard Nose The Highway	CD	Polydor	31453-7452-2	U.S.A.	1973	8.99
Morrison, Van	His Band And The Street Choir	CD	Warner Bros.	1884-2	U.S.A.	1970	8.99
Morrison, Van	How Long Has This Been Going On	CD	Verve	314-529-136-2	U.S.A.	1996	11.99
Morrison, Van	Hymns To The Silence	2CD	Mercury	849-026-2	U.S.A.	1991	14.99
Morrison, Van	Inarticulate Speech Of The Heart	CD	Polydor	537-543-2	Germany	1998	8.99
Morrison, Van	Into The Music	CD	Polydor	537-540-2	Germany	1998	10.99
Morrison, Van	Irish Heartbeat	CD	Mercury	314-537-548-2	U.S.A.	1998	13.99
Morrison, Van	It's Too Late To Stop Now	2CD	Polydor	31453-7453-2	U.S.A.	1974	17.99
Morrison, Van	Live Grand Opera House Belfast	CD	Mercury	314-537-544-2	U.S.A.	1998	14.99
Morrison, Van	Millenium Collection	2CD	Millenium	20.4021-MI	Germany	1999	10.99
Morrison, Van	Moondance	CD	Warner Bros.	3103-2	U.S.A.	1970	8.99
Morrison, Van	No Guru, No Method, No Teacher	CD	Mercury	314-537-546-2	U.S.A.	1986	7.99
Morrison, Van	Poetic Champions Compose	CD	Mercury	314-537-547-2	U.S.A.	1998	13.99
Morrison, Van	Precious Time	CD Single	Pointblank	DPRO-13684	U.S.A.	1999	3.99
Morrison, Van	Saint Dominic's Preview	CD	Mercury	31453-7451-2	U.S.A.	1997	9.99
Morrison, Van	Selections/Philosophers Stone (Promo)	CD	Polydor	PRSAD-00659	U.S.A.	1996	8.99
Morrison, Van	Skiffle Sessions: Live In Belfast 1998	CD	Pointblank	48307	U.S.A.	2000	7.99
Morrison, Van	Super Hits	CD	Columbia	CK-65882	U.S.A.	1999	5.99
Morrison, Van	Tell Me....Songs Mose Allison	CD	Verve	314-533-203-2	U.S.A.	1996	11.99
Morrison, Van	The Healing Game	CD	Polydor	314-537-101-2	U.S.A.	1997	10.99
Morrison, Van	The Philosopher's Stone	2CD	Mercury	314-531-789-2	U.S.A.	1998	16.99
Morrison, Van	Too Long In Exile	CD	Mercury	314-519-219-2	U.S.A.	1993	8.99
Morrison, Van	Tupelo Honey	CD	Polydor	31453-7450-2	U.S.A.	1971	9.99
Morrison, Van	Veedon Fleece	CD	Polydor	31453-7456-2	U.S.A.	1974	10.99
Morrison, Van	Wavelength	CD	Polydor	31453-7458-2	U.S.A.	1978	10.99
Morrison, Van	You Win Again	CD	Virgin	7243-50258-2	U.S.A.	2000	7.99
Morrison, Van/L G Lewis	Let's Talk About Us	CD Single	Virgin	7243-8-97106-25	EU	2000	8.99
Morrissey	Alma Matters	CD Single	Mercury	314-574-757-2	U.S.A.	1997	4.99
Morrissey	Alma Matters (Promo)	CD Single	Mercury	MECP-274	U.S.A.	1997	7.99
Morrissey	Beethoven Was Deaf	CD	Parlophone	0777-7-89061-2-4	Holland	1993	9.99
Morrissey	Bona Drag	CD	Sire	9-26221-2	U.S.A.	1990	8.99
Morrissey	Boxers	CD Single	Parlophone	7243-8-81888-2-1	England	1995	7.99
Morrissey	Boxers	CD Single	Sire	9-41914-2	U.S.A.	1995	8.99
Morrissey	CD Singles '88-'91 Box Set	10 CD	EMI	7243-8-87293-2-1	England	2000	32.99
Morrissey	CD Singles '91-'95 Box Set	9 CD	EMI	7243-879745-2	England	2001	32.99
Morrissey	Certain People I Know	CD	EMI	8803652	Australia	1991	13.99
Morrissey	Dagenham Dave	CD Single	RCA	74321-29980-2	England	1995	4.99
Morrissey	Kill Uncle	CD	Sire	9-26514*2	U.S.A.	1991	8.99
Morrissey	Maladjusted	CD	Mercury	314-536-036-2	U.S.A.	1997	7.99
Morrissey	Morrissey At KROQ	CD Single	Sire	9-40184-2	U.S.A.	1991	9.99
Morrissey	Morrissey Sampler (Promo)	CD	Reprise	PRO-CD-9492-R	U.S.A.	1998	19.99
Morrissey	My Early Burglary Years	CD	Reprise	9-46874-2	U.S.A.	1998	9.99
Morrissey	My Love Life	CD Single	EMI	20-4483-2	England	1991	7.99
Morrissey	My Love Life	CD Single	Sire	9-40163-2	U.S.A.	1991	8.99
Morrissey	My Love Life E.P	CD Single	Toshiba-EMI	TOCP-6909	Japan	1991	13.99
Morrissey	November Spawned A Monster	CD Single	Sire	9-21529-2	U.S.A.	1990	4.99
Morrissey	November Spawned A Monster	CD Single	EMI	20-3734-2	England	1990	5.99
Morrissey	Now My Heart Is Full	CD Single	Sire	9-41700-2	U.S.A.	1994	5.99
Morrissey	Ouija Board, Ouija Board	CD Single	EMI	2036152	England	1989	8.99
Morrissey	Ouija Board, Ouija Board	CD Single	Sire	9-21424-2	U.S.A.	1989	8.99
Morrissey	Our Frank	CD Single	EMI	20-4155-2	England	1991	10.99
Morrissey	Rare Tracks	CD	Polygram K.K.	PHCR-4080	Japan	1998	21.99
Morrissey	Southpaw Grammar	CD	Reprise	9-45939-2	U.S.A.	1995	9.99
Morrissey	Sunny	CD Single	Parlophone	7243-8-82607-2-5	England	1994	5.99
Morrissey	That's Entertainment (Promo)	CD Single	EMI	CDSP156	Netherland	1997	136.99

M

Artist	Title	Format	Label	Catalog No	Country	Released	Value
Morrissey	The Boy Racer (CD 1)	CD Single	RCA	7432133294-2	England	1995	10.99
Morrissey	The Boy Racer (Promo)	CD Single	Reprise	PRO-CD-7789	U.S.A.	1995	10.99
Morrissey	The Loop (Les Inrockuptibles)	CD	EMI	SPCD-1598	France	1991	34.99
Morrissey	The Rare Tracks EP	CD Single	Polydor	PHCR-4080	Japan	1998	21.99
Morrissey	Under The Influence	CD	DMC	UTI-001-CD	England	2003	12.99
Morrissey	Vauxhall And I	CD	Sire	9-45451-2	U.S.A.	1994	7.99
Morrissey	Viva Hate	CD	EMI Odeon	CP32-5611	Japan	1988	14.99
Morrissey	Viva Hate + 8	CD	Parlophone	7243-8-56325-2-5	Holland	1997	11.99
Morrissey	We Hate It When Our Friends..	CD Single	Sire	9-40560-2	U.S.A.	1992	5.99
Morrissey	You Are The Quarry	CD	Attack	ATKCD001	England	2004	11.99
Morrissey	Your Arsenal	CD	Sire	9-26994-2	U.S.A.	1992	9.99
Morse, Steve	Coast To Coast	CD	MCA	MCAD-10565	U.S.A.	1992	8.99
Morse, Steve	High Tension Wires	CD	MCA	MCAD-6275	U.S.A.	1989	11.99
Morse, Steve	Major Impacts	CD	Magna Carta	MA-9042-2	U.S.A.	2000	9.99
Morse, Steve	Major Impacts, Vol. 2	CD	Magna Carta	MA-9070-2	U.S.A.	2004	9.99
Morse, Steve	Southern Steel	CD	MCA	MCAD-10112	U.S.A.	1991	8.99
Morse, Steve	Split Decision	CD	Magna Carta	MA-9058-2	U.S.A.	2002	10.99
Morse, Steve	Stand Up	CD	Wounded Bird	WOU-448	U.S.A.	2002	9.99
Morse, Steve	Stressfest	CD	High Street	72902-10345-2	U.S.A.	1996	7.99
Morse, Steve	Structual Damage	CD	High Street	72902-10332-2	U.S.A.	1995	7.99
Morse, Steve	The Introduction	CD	Elektra	9-60369-2	U.S.A.	1984	8.99
Morty And The Racing Cars	Love Blind	CD	Line	LICD-9.00066-0	Germany	1988	18.99
Moscow Chamber Orchestra	Kadans (MFSL Silver Cd)	CD	Mobile Fidelity	MFCD-916	U.S.A.	1987	19.99
Mose Jones	Mose Nose Knows!	CD	Line	LCCD-9.01269-0	Germany	1993	24.99
Mosley, Ian/Ben Castle	Postmankind	CD	Racket	RACKET-16	England	2001	14.99
Mossolov, Alexander	Sonaten/Turkmenische Nachte	CD	Line	CACD-9.00613-P	Germany	1991	12.99
Mother Gong	Every Witches Way	CD	Voiceprint	VP139CD	England	1993	21.99
Mother Gong	Eye	CD	Voiceprint	VP176CD	England	1994	10.99
Mother Gong	Fairy Tales	CD	Spalax	14813	France	1996	21.99
Mother Gong	Live 1991	CD	Mothermusic	MM-101	France	1991	27.99
Mother Gong	Magenta/She Made The World	CD	Voiceprint	VP134CD	England	1993	21.99
Mother Gong	Owl And The Tree	CD	Thunderbolt	CDTB-118	England	1996	11.99
Mother Gong	Owl In The Tree	CD	Voiceprint	VP278CD	England	2004	12.99
Mother Gong	The Best Of	CD	Blueprint	BP271CD	England	1998	18.99
Mother Gong	Tree In Fish	CD	Tapestry	76000-2	U.S.A.	1994	14.99
Mother Gong	Voiceprint Radio Sessions (Promo)	CD	Voiceprint	VPRO07CD	England	1994	15.99
Mother Gong	Wild Child	CD	Spalax	14521	France	1991	21.99
Mother Gong/Daevid Allen	Wild Child/Australia Aquaria/She	2CD	Alchemy	PILOT-72	England	2001	13.99
Mother Gong/G Smyth/Steffe	Glo - Even As We Are	CD	Gliss	CD002	England	1997	15.99
Mother Gong/Gilli Smyth	Mother	CD	Spalax	14818	France	1996	18.99
Mother Gong/Gilli Smyth	Politico-Historico-Spirito	CD	Voiceprint	VP185CD	England	1995	17.99
Mother Gong/Goddess Trance	Electric Shiatsu	CD	Voiceprint	VP205CD	England	2003	22.99
Mother Gong/Goddess Trance	Self Titled	CD	GAS	AGASCD-011	England	1996	22.99
Mother Love Bone	Apple + 2	CD	Lemon	CDLEM01	England	2003	18.99
Mother Love Bone	Self Titled	CD	Mercury	314-512-884-2	U.S.A.	1992	8.99
Mothersbaugh, Mark	Joyeux Mutato	CD	Rhino	R2-76667	U.S.A.	2000	19.99
Mothersbaugh, Mark	Muzik For Insomniaks Volume 1	CD	Enigma	7-73385-2	U.S.A.	1988	24.99
Mothersbaugh, Mark	Muzik For Insomniaks Volume 2	CD	Enigma	7-73366-2	U.S.A.	1988	24.99
Mothersbaugh, Mark	The Rugrats - Live Adventure	CD	Interscope	INTD-90190	U.S.A.	1998	6.99
Motley Crue	20th Century Masters: The Millennium	CD	Hip O	B000103402	U.S.A.	2003	8.99
Motley Crue	Afraid	CD Single	Elektra	AMCY-2079	Japan	1995	14.99
Motley Crue	Crucial Crue Sampler (Promo)	CD	Beyond	BYDJ-78032-2	U.S.A.	1999	8.99
Motley Crue	Decade Of Decadence (Crdbrd Slv)	CD	Elektra	WMC5-429	Japan	1991	53.99
Motley Crue	Decade Of Decadence '81 - '91	CD	Elektra	9-61204-2	U.S.A.	1991	9.99
Motley Crue	Dr. Feelgood (3 ")	CD Single	Warner Bros.	966-680-2	Germany	1989	12.99
Motley Crue	Dr. Feelgood + 6	CD	Hip O	067632	U.S.A.	2003	8.99
Motley Crue	Generation Swine	CD	Elektra	61901-2	U.S.A.	1997	6.99
Motley Crue	Generation Swine (Clean)	CD	Elektra	62066-2	U.S.A.	1997	6.99

Artist	Title	Format	Label	Catalog No	Country	Released	Value
Motley Crue	Generation Swine + 1	CD	East West	AMCY-2075	Japan	1997	19.99
Motley Crue	Generation Swine + 6	CD	Hip O	067634	U.S.A.	2003	9.99
Motley Crue	Girls, Girls, Girls + 5	CD	Hip O	067631	U.S.A.	2003	9.99
Motley Crue	Greatest Hits	CD	Hip O	067635	U.S.A.	2003	9.99
Motley Crue	Greatest Hits	CD	Polydor	POCP-7334	Japan	1998	24.99
Motley Crue	Live: Entertainment Or Death	2CD	Hip O	067638	U.S.A.	2003	11.99
Motley Crue	Live: Entertainment Or Death (Clean)	2CD	Hip O	067641	U.S.A.	2003	11.99
Motley Crue	Music to Crash Your Car To, Vol. 1	4CD	Hip O	B000146002	U.S.A.	2003	54.99
Motley Crue	New Tattoo + 3 (W/6 Trk Live CD)	2CD	Hip O	067644	U.S.A.	2003	15.99
Motley Crue	Quarternary	CD	Warner Bros.	WPCR-76	Japan	1994	19.99
Motley Crue	Quaternary + 4	CD	Warner Bros.	WPCR-76	Japan	1994	24.99
Motley Crue	Raw Tracks II (W/Tattoo Stickers)	CD	Warner Bros.	WPCP-3462	Japan	1990	24.99
Motley Crue	Raw Tracks, Vol. 1	CD	Warner Bros.	WPCP-3446	Japan	1988	24.99
Motley Crue	Self Titled + 1	CD	Warner Bros.	WPCP-5800	Japan	1994	17.99
Motley Crue	Self Titled + 1 (Ltd Package)	CD	Warner Bros.	WPZP-5800	Japan	1994	24.99
Motley Crue	Self Titled + 3 (W/O Vince Neil)	CD	Hip O	067633	U.S.A.	2003	9.99
Motley Crue	Shout At The Devil + 6	CD	Hip O	067629	U.S.A.	2003	9.99
Motley Crue	Supersonic And Demonic Relics + 1	CD	Polydor	POCP-9192	Japan	1999	24.99
Motley Crue	Supersonic And Demonic Relics + 2	CD	Hip O	067636	U.S.A.	2003	9.99
Motley Crue	Supersonic/Demonic Relics + 2(Clean)	CD	Hip O	067637	U.S.A.	2003	8.99
Motley Crue	Theatre Of Pain + 7	CD	Hip O	067630	U.S.A.	2003	9.99
Motley Crue	Too Fast For Love + 6	CD	Hip O	067628	U.S.A.	2003	15.99
Motley Crue/Vince Neil	Carved In Stone	CD	Beyond	398-578-125-2	U.S.A.	1995	7.99
Motley Crue/Vince Neil	Exposed	CD	Beyond	398-578-124-2	U.S.A.	1993	6.99
Motley Crue/Vince Neil	Live At The Whiskey - One Night Only	CD	Image	ID0075TN	U.S.A.	2003	11.99
Motor Boys Motor	Motor Boys Motor	CD	Line	ALCD-9.00043-0	Germany	1988	10.99
Motor Boys Motor	Motor Boys Motor	CD	Line	LICD-9.01348-0	Germany	1997	10.99
Motorhead	'92 Tour EP	CD	Epic	658809-2	Germany	1992	9.99
Motorhead	King Biscuit Flower Hour	CD	King Biscuit	70710-88029-2	U.S.A.	1997	6.99
Motorhead	March Or Die	CD	Epic	NK-48997	U.S.A.	1992	5.99
Motors	1	CD	Caroline	CAROL-1821-2	U.S.A.	1991	34.99
Motors	Airport-Motors' Greatest Hits	CD	Virgin	7243-8-39945-2-6	Germany	1995	12.99
Motors	Approved By The Motors + 2	CD	Disky	VI-646412	Holland	2001	12.99
Motors/Snakes	Happy & I Won't Love You ...	CD	Dischord	18	U.S.A.	1986	12.99
Mott	Drive On	CD	Columbia	487237-2	England	1975	17.99
Mott	Live - Over Here & Over There '75 - '76	2CD	Angel Air	SJPCD025	England	1999	17.99
Mott	Shouting And Pointing	CD	Columbia	489492-2	England	1976	17.99
Mott	The Gooseberry Sessions & Rarities	CD	Angel Air	SJPCD054	England	2000	21.99
Mott The Hoople	All The Way Live 1971/72	2CD	Nippon Crown	CRCL-4042-3	Japan	1999	21.99
Mott The Hoople	All The Young Dudes	CD	Columbia	491691-2	England	1972	11.99
Mott The Hoople	All The Young Dudes Anthology Box Set	3CD	Columbia	491-400-2	England	1998	103.99
Mott The Hoople	Backsliding Fearlessly: The Early Years	CD	Rhino	R2-71639	U.S.A.	1994	12.99
Mott The Hoople	Brain Capers + 2	CD	Angel Air	SJPCD160	England	2003	11.99
Mott The Hoople	Dudes	CD	Going For A Song	GFS065	U.S.A.	1999	15.99
Mott The Hoople	Friends And Relatives	2CD	Eagle	EDGCD-104	EC	1999	9.99
Mott The Hoople	Greatest Hits Live ! + 1 (Gold Cd)	CD	Purple Pyramid	CLP-0823-2	U.S.A.	2000	10.99
Mott The Hoople	Hoopling - Best Of Live	CD	Angel Air	SJPCD121	Austria	2002	11.99
Mott The Hoople	London To Memphis	CD	Sony	A-22677	U.S.A.	1992	5.99
Mott The Hoople	Mad Shadows + 2	CD	Angel Air	SJPCD158	England	2003	11.99
Mott The Hoople	Mott	CD	Sony	SRCS-9020	Japan	1996	24.99
Mott The Hoople	Mott The Hoople + 2	CD	Angel Air	SJPCD157	England	2003	11.99
Mott The Hoople	Mott The Hoople/Steve Hymas	CD	East World	EWO007CD	England	2001	11.99
Mott The Hoople	Original Mixed Up Kids	CD	Windsong	WINCD-084	England	1996	15.99
Mott The Hoople	Rock An Roll Queen	CD	Atlantic	7297-2	U.S.A.	1974	24.99
Mott The Hoople	Rock 'N' Roll Circus - Live	CD	Angel Air	SJPCD061	England	2000	17.99
Mott The Hoople	Super Hits	CD	Columbia	CK-65273	U.S.A.	1997	5.99
Mott The Hoople	The Ballad of Mott: A Retrospective	2CD	Columbia	C2K-46973	U.S.A.	1993	11.99
Mott The Hoople	The Best Of: The Island Years 69 - 72	CD	Spectrum	554-600-2	England	1990	10.99

M

Artist	Title	Format	Label	Catalog No	Country	Released	Value
Mott The Hoople	The Hoople	CD	Columbia	498248-2	England	1974	11.99
Mott The Hoople	Two Miles From Live Heaven	2CD	Captain Trip	CTCD-390/391	Japan	2000	19.99
Mott The Hoople	Two Miles From Live Heaven	2CD	Angel Air	SJPCD099	England	2001	17.99
Mott The Hoople	Wildlife + 2	CD	Angel Air	SJPCD159	England	2003	11.99
Mott/British Lions	Live & Rare	CD	Angel Air	SJPCCD044	England	1999	19.99
Mould, Bob	Bob Mould	CD	Rykodisc	RCD-10342	U.S.A.	1996	9.99
Mould, Bob	Last Dog And Pony Show (Bonus Cd)	2CD	Rykodisc	RCD-10443	U.S.A.	1998	7.99
Mounir, Mohammed	Mohamed Mounir	CD	Line	MSCD-9.00695-0	Germany	1989	22.99
Mountain	Avalanche	CD	Collectables	COL-CD-6871	U.S.A.	2002	11.99
Mountain	Best Of + 4	CD	Columbia	CK-61574	U.S.A.	2003	8.99
Mountain	Climbing !	CD	BGO	BGOCD112	England	1998	10.99
Mountain	Climbing ! + 1	CD	Columbia	CK-86577	U.S.A.	2003	10.99
Mountain	Flowers Of Evil	CD	Columbia	CK-52749	U.S.A.	1996	8.99
Mountain	Flowers Of Evil	CD	BGO	BGOCD113	England	1998	10.99
Mountain	Go For Your Life	CD	Sony	3067852	France	2001	14.99
Mountain	KBFH Presents Live	CD	King Biscuit	88047	Canada	2000	9.99
Mountain	Live: The Road Goes Ever On	CD	BGO	BGOCD111	England	1998	15.99
Mountain	Man's World	CD	Dream Catcher	CRIDE-12	England	1999	8.99
Mountain	Millenium Collection	2CD	Millenium	20.4030-MI	Germany	1999	10.99
Mountain	Mystic Fire	CD	Lightyear	54492-2	U.S.A.	2002	13.99
Mountain	Nantucket Sleighride	CD	BGO	BGOCD32	England	1994	10.99
Mountain	Nantucket Sleighride + 1	CD	Columbia	CK-86420	U.S.A.	2003	8.99
Mountain	On Top	CD	Columbia	A-22625	U.S.A.	1992	14.99
Mountain	Over The Top	2CD	Columbia	C2K-57167	U.S.A.	2001	18.99
Mountain	Super Hits	CD	Columbia	CK-65703	U.S.A.	1998	5.99
Mountain	Twin Peaks	CD	Columbia	CGK-32818	U.S.A.	1974	8.99
Mountain	Twin Peaks	CD	Columbia	472183-2	England	1974	8.99
Mountain/Felix Pappalardi	Don't Worry,Ma	CD	Prog. Line	PL-521	Australia	2001	10.99
Mountain/Leslie West	Alligator	CD	I.R.S.	X2-13016	U.S.A.	1989	16.99
Mountain/Leslie West	As Phat As It Gets	CD	Lightyear	54342-2	U.S.A.	1999	8.99
Mountain/Leslie West	Blood Of The Sun: 1969-1975	CD	Raven	RVCD-49	Australia	1996	13.99
Mountain/Leslie West	Blues To Die For	CD	Shrapnel	BB-2047-2	U.S.A.	2003	16.99
Mountain/Leslie West	Dodgin' The Dirt	CD	Shrapnel	BB-2015-2	U.S.A.	1993	10.99
Mountain/Leslie West	Leslie West Band/Great Fatsby	CD	TRC	TRC-34	Germany	2000	19.99
Mountain/Leslie West	Live !	CD	Shrapnel	BB-2013-2	U.S.A.	1993	12.99
Mountain/Leslie West	Mountain	CD	Columbia	CK-66439	U.S.A.	1996	9.99
Mountain/Leslie West	Mountain	CD	BGO	BGOCD479	England	2002	13.99
Mountain/Leslie West	Theme	CD	Passport	PBCD-6061	U.S.A.	1988	35.99
Mountain/Vagrants	Great Lost Vagrants Album	CD	Arista	ARCD-8459	U.S.A.	1987	15.99
Mountain/West, Bruce, Laing	Live 'N' Kickin'	CD	Columbia	472-960-2	Holland	1974	34.99
Mountain/West, Bruce, Laing	Whatever Turns You On	CD	Columbia	472-961-2	Holland	1973	34.99
Mountain/West, Bruce, Laing	Why Dontcha	CD	Columbia	CK-31929	U.S.A.	1973	8.99
Mouskouri, Nana	IL Meglio	CD	Morerecord	DV-5784	Italy	1994	106.99
Move	California Man	CD	EMI	7243-5-21215-2-6	EU	1999	11.99
Move	Looking On + 10	CD	Repertoire	REP-4692-WY	Germany	1998	13.99
Move	Message From the Country	CD	BGO	BGOCD238	England	1994	20.99
Move	'Shazam' + 9	CD	Repertoire	REP-4691-WY	Germany	1998	13.99
Move	Something Else From + 4	CD	Edsel	DIAB-8012	England	1999	13.99
Move	The BBC Sessions	CD	Strange Fruit	SFRSCD069	England	1998	14.99
Move	The Move + 16	CD	Repertoire	REP-4690-WY	Germany	1998	14.99
Moving Emotion/Tony Wilson	Moving Emotion/Tony Wilson	CD Single	Line	LICD-9.01177-E	Germany	1992	11.99
Moxy	Best Of: Self Destruction	CD	Unidisc Music	SPLK-7326	Canada	2003	12.99
Moxy	Best Of: Self Destruction	CD	Peacemaker	PACE-001	Canada	1994	8.99
Moxy	Greatest Hits	CD	Renaissance	RMED00184-2	U.S.A.	1997	14.99
Moxy	II	CD	Peacemaker	PACE-017	Canada	1994	8.99
Moxy	II	CD	Unidisc Music	AGEK-2242	Canada	2003	12.99
Moxy	Raw	CD	Bullseye	BLP-CD-4059	Canada	2002	12.99
Moxy	Ridin' High	CD	Unidisc Music	AGEK-2243	Canada	2003	12.99

M

SHOCK THE MONKEY

1   2   3   4   5   6   7   8

9   10   11   12   13   14   15   16

17   18   19   20   21   22   23   24

25   26   27   28   29   30   31   32

33   34   35   36   37   38   39   40

41   42   43   44   45   46   47   48

49   50   51   52   53   54   55   56

57   58   59   60   61   62   63   64

1   2   3   4   5   6   7   8

9   10   11   12   13   14   15   16

17   18   19   20   21   22   23   24

25   26   27   28   29   30   31   32

33   34   35   36   37   38   39   40

41   42   43   44   45   46   47   48

49   50   51   52   53   54   55   56

57   58   59   60   61   62   63   64

1
2
3
4
5
6
7
8
9
10
11
12
13
14
15
16
17
18
19
20
21
22
23
24
25
26
27
28
29
30
31
32
33
34
35
36
37
38
39
40
41
42
43
44
45
46
47
48
49
50
51
52
53
54
55
56
57
58
59
60
61
62
63
64

1
2
3
4
5
6
7
8
9
10
11
12
13
14
15
16
17
18
19
20
21
22
23
24
25
26
27
28
29
30
31
32
33
34
35
36
37
38
39
40
41
42
43
44
45
46
47
48
49
50
51
52
53
54
55
56
57
58
59
60
61
62
63

1

2

3

4

5

6

7

8

9

10

11

12

13

14

15

16

17

18

19

20

21

22

23

24

25

26

27

28

29

30

31

32

33

34

35

36

37

38

39

40

41

42

43

44

45

46

47

48

49

50

51

52

53

54

55

56

57

58

59

60

61

62

63

1

2

3

4

5

6

7

8

9

10

11

12

13

14

15

16

17

18

19

20

21

22

23

24

25

26

27

28

29

30

31

32

33

34

35

36

37

38

39

40

41

42

43

44

45

46

47

48

49

50

51

52

53

54

55

56

57

58

59

60

61

62

63

1

2

3

4

5

6

7

8

9

10

11

12

13

14

15

16

17

18

19

20

21

22

23

24

25

26

27

28

29

30

31

32

33

34

35

36

37

38

39

40

41

42

43

44

45

46

47

48

49

50

51

52

53

54

55

56

57

58

59

60

61

62

63

1

2

3

4

5

6

7

8

9

10

11

12

13

14

15

16

17

18

19

20

21

22

23

24

25

26

27

28

29

30

31

32

33

34

35

36

37

38

39

40

41

42

43

44

45

46

47

48

49

50

51

52

53

54

55

56

57

58

59

60

61

62

63

64

1   2   3   4   5   6   7   8
9   10   11   12   13   14   15   16
17   18   19   20   21   22   23   24
25   26   27   28   29   30   31   32
33   34   35   36   37   38   39   40
41   42   43   44   45   46   47   48
49   50   51   52   53   54   55   56
57   58   59   60   61   62   63   64

1
2
3
4
5
6
7
8
9
10
11
12
13
14
15
16
17
18
19
20
21
22
23
24
25
26
27
28
29
30
31
32
33
34
35
36
37
38
39
40
41
42
43
44
45
46
47
48
49
50
51
52
53
54
55
56
57
58
59
60
61
62
63
64

1   2   3   4   5   6   7   8

9   10   11   12   13   14   15   16

17   18   19   20   21   22   23   24

25   26   27   28   29   30   31   32

33   34   35   36   37   38   39   40

41   42   43   44   45   46   47   48

49   50   51   52   53   54   55   56

57   58   59   60   61   62   63   64

1   2   3   4   5   6   7   8

9   10   11   12   13   14   15   16

17   18   19   20   21   22   23   24

25   26   27   28   29   30   31   32

33   34   35   36   37   38   39   40

41   42   43   44   45   46   47   48

49   50   51   52   53   54   55   56

57   58   59   60   61   62   63   64

1   2   3   4   5   6   7   8

9   10   11   12   13   14   15   16

17   18   19   20   21   22   23   24

25   26   27   28   29   30   31   32

33   34   35   36   37   38   39   40

41   42   43   44   45   46   47   48

49   50   51   52   53   54   55   56

57   58   59   60   61   62   63   64

1

2

3

4

5

6

7

8

9

10

11

12

13

14

15

16

17

18

19

20

21

22

23

24

25

26

27

28

29

30

31

32

33

34

35

36

37

38

39

40

41

42

43

44

45

46

47

48

49

50

51

52

53

54

55

56

57

58

59

60

61

62

63

64

1

2

3

4

5

6

7

8

9

10

11

12

13

14

15

16

17

18

19

20

21

22

23

24

25

26

27

28

29

30

31

32

33

34

35

36

37

38

39

40

41

42

43

44

45

46

47

48

49

50

51

52

53

54

55

56

57

58

59

60

61

62

63

1

2

3

4

5

6

7

8

9

10

11

12

13

14

15

16

17

18

19

20

21

22

23

24

25

26

27

28

29

30

31

32

1   2   3   4   5   6   7   8

9   10   11   12   13   14   15   16

17   18   19   20   21   22   23   24

25   26   27   28   29   30   31   32

SPANK THE MONKEY

Page 266: 1) 10,000 Maniacs - In My Tribe With Peace Train **2)** 10cc - Original Soundtrack Japanese Mini LP CD **3)** Acoustic Aid With Live Justin Hayward and Live Jethro Tull **4)** Adam And The Ants - Dirk Wears White Socks **5)** The Adventure Club Sessions With Live XTC **6)** Aerosmith - Oh Yeah! Ultimate Hits - Japanese CD **7)** Aerosmith - Just Push Play - Japanese CD **8)** Aerosmith - Pump Limited Edition **9)** Alice And Chains - Music Bank Box Set **10)** Alice And Chains - The Nona Tapes EP **11)** The Wild Angels Soundtrack by Davie Allan And The Arrows **12)** The Allman Brothers Band - At Fillmore East MFSL CD **13)** Herb Alpert And The Tijuana Brass - Whipped Cream And Other Delights Japanese CD **14)** Ted Nugent And The Amboy Dukes - Journey To The Center Of The Mind **15)** Ambrosia - Self Titled Japanese CD **16)** Laurie Anderson - United States Live Box Set **17)** Jon Anderson - Best South America 1993 **18)** Animal Logic - Some Day We'll Understand - Promo Single **19)** Arzachel - Self Titled CD With Steve Hillage **20)** Association - Insight Out Japanese CD **21)** Anderson Bruford Wakeman Howe Picture Disc Promo CD (Comes In Blue Tray) **22)** The Iveys - Maybe Tomorrow Apple CD **23)** Badfinger - No Dice DCC Gold Apple CD **24)** Badfinger - Straight Up DCC Gold Apple CD **25)** Badger - One Live Japanese CD **26)** The Baker Gurvitz Army - Freedom CD/CD-Rom **27)** Ginger Baker - Do What you Like (Airforce LP's/Stratavarious) **28)** Long John Baldry - It Ain't Easy Produced By Rod Stewart and Elton John **29)** Bodacious D. F. - Self Titled With Marty Balin **30)** Marty Balin - Balince Best Of **31)** Peter Banks - Two Sides Of Peter Banks With John Wetton, Phil Collins and Steve Hackett **32)** Barbarella - Original Soundtrack by Bob Crewe **33)** Barbie - The Look (Rachel Sweet Sings) **34)** Pete Bardens - The Answer CD **35)** Pete Bardens - Self Titled CD **36)** Syd Barrett - The Madcap Laughs Japanese Mini LP CD **37)** Shirley Bassey - Bassey Sings Bond (Sings All James Bond Movie Title Theme Songs) **38)** Prince - Batman Soundtrack in a Tin Can **39)** Beach Boys - Special 14 Track CD Sampler Promo CD **40)** Beach Boys - The Pet Sounds Sessions Sampler Promo CD **41)** Beach Boys - Ten Years Of Harmony CD **42)** Beatles - Red And Blue CD Promo Sampler **43)** Beatles - Anthology 1 Promo Sampler CD **44)** Beatles - Anthology 2 Promo Sampler CD **45)** Beatles - Anthology 3 Promo Sampler CD **46)** Beatles - Abbey Road 1st Issue Release Japanese CD Front and Back **47)** Beatles - Anthology 2 CD-Rom Promo CD **48)** Beatles - The BBC Tapes - Original Masters Westwood One 6-CD Promo **49)** Beatles - Compact Disc EP Collection **50)** Beatles - CD Singles Collection **51)** Beatles - Complete Christmas Recordings Rarities Promo CD **52)** Beaver And Krause - Gandharva In A Wild Sanctuary **53)** Beck, Bogert And Appice - Live Japanese CD **54)** Jeff Beck And Jed Leiber - Frankie's House CD **55)** David Bedford - Rime Of The Ancient Mariner **56)** David Bedford - The Odyssey **57)** Chris Bell - I Am The Cosmos **58)** Chuck Berry - The Chess Box **59)** Elmer Bernstein - The Great Escape Original Soundtrack **60)** Flatt And Scruggs - The Beverly Hillbillies Soundtrack (Buddy Ebsen And Irene Ryan Sings) **61)** Black Sabbath - Under Wheels of Confusion CD Box Set **62)** Blind Melon - Soup Limited Edition Promo CD **63)** Blondie - Parallel Lines DCC Gold CD

Page 267: 1) Blood, Sweat And Tears - Self Titled MFSL Gold CD **2)** Michael Bloomfield - It's Not Killing Me Japanese CD **3)** Blue Cheer - Live And Unreleased '68/'74 Japanese CD **4)** Blue Cheer - Live And Unreleased Vol. 2 Japanese CD **5)** Blues Project - Anthology CD **6)** Blues Traveler - Straight On 'Till Morning Interview Disc Promo CD **7)** David Bowie - Bang Bang Promo CD **8)** David Bowie - BBC Classic Tracks Westwood One Promo CD **9)** David Bowie - BBC Sessions '69-'72 Sampler Promo CD (from recalled box set/some songs are alternate versions from the released version) **10)** David Bowie - Bowie At The BEEB Sampler Promo CD **11)** David Bowie - King Biscuit Flower Hour 2 CD April 10th-23rd 1989 **12)** David Bowie - The David Bowie Catalogue Promo CD **13)** David Bowie - Earthling In The City Promo CD **14)** David Bowie And Brian Eno - Rykodisc Promo Sampler CD **15)** David Bowie - Fame And Fashion RCA Greatest Hits CD **16)** David Bowie - Hours And Brilliant Minutes Promo CD **17)** David Bowie - World Premiere Weekend Interview Promo CD **18)** David Bowie - Live And Well.com Promo CD **19)** David Bowie - David Live Rykodisc CD **20)** David Bowie - Miracle Goodnight Promo CD **21)** David Bowie / The Nixons - On The Edge Westwood One Show #95-48 Promo CD **22)** David Bowie - Peter And The Wolf CD **23)** David Bowie - All Saints Promo 2 CD **24)** David Bowie - Santa Monica '72 Promo CD **25)** David Bowie - The Singles 1969-1993 3 CD with Little Drummer Boy Single **26)** David Bowie - High Tech Soul Sampler Promo CD **27)** David Bowie - Sound + Vision: The CD Press Release Promo CD **28)** David Bowie - Stage Rykodisc CD **29)** David Bowie/Tin Machine - II 4-track Album Sampler Promo CD **30)** David Bowie/Tin Machine - Radio Session CD **31)** David Bowie - Westwood One Show #99-23 Promo CD **32)** David Bowie - Westwood One Show #99-26 Promo CD **33)** Box Of Frogs - (2 'N 1 CD) Self Titled CD **34)** Bram Tchaikovsky - Strange Man Changed Man **35)** Brand X - X Trax **36)** Billy Bremner - Bash! CD **37)** Brimstone And Treacle - Original Soundtrack CD **38)** Bruford Levin Upper Extremities - Blue Nights Japanese CD **39)** Bryan Ferry - (As Time Goes By & Best Of Roxy Music) Promo Sampler **40)** Jeff Buckley - Live From The Bataclan **41)** Harold Budd - Fenceless Night Promo CD

Page 267 continued

42) Ex-Budgie - Budgie And Beyond CD **43)** Buggles - Adventures In Modern Recording Japanese CD **44)** Buggles - Age Of Plastic Japanese Mini LP CD **45)** Eric Burdon And The Animals - Love Is (with Andy Summers) **46)** James Burton - The Guitar Sounds Of James Burton **47)** Kate Bush - Kate Bush Live At Hammersmith Odeon CD/Video **48)** Byrds - Byrds 1990 Promo CD **49)** Byrds - Byrds 1990 Backpages Promo CD **50)** Byrds - Advanced Music Promo CD (Unreleased Track) **51)** Byrds - 3 Byrds Land In London (2-CD set) **52)** Byrds - Never Before CD **53)** John Cale - More Fragments Promo CD **54)** California Executives - Dancing and Romancing CD **55)** Robert Calvert - Captain Lockheed And The Starfighters CD **56)** Robert Calvert - Lucky Leif And The Longships CD **57)** Jim Capaldi - Short Cut Draw Blood **58)** Jim Carroll - I Write Your Name CD **59)** Jim Carroll - People who Died Promo CD **60)** Benjamin Orr/The Cars - The Lace CD **61)** The Cars - Door To Door CD **62)** The Cars - Self Titled DCC Gold CD **63)** Carlene Carter - Musical Shapes & Blue Nun (2 in 1 CD) **64)** Johnny Cash - Love God Murder Box Set

Page 268

1) Johnny Cash - Thirteen Promo CD **2)** Johnny Cash - The Solitary Man Interview With Tim Robbins Promo CD **3)** Fankhauser/Cassidy Band - Further On Up The Road CD **4)** Catapilla - Self Titled CD **5)** Cat Mother And The All Night Newsboys - Self Titled (Jimi Hendrix) CD **6)** Nick Cave - The Secret Life Of The Love Song & The Flesh Made Word (2 Lectures by Nick Cave) CD **7)** Harry Chapin - Tribute CD **8)** Cheap Trick - Woke Up With A Monster Promo Trick Box **9)** Cheech And Chong - Sleeping Beauty CD **10)** Chicago - Group Portrait Box Set CD **11)** Alex Chilton - 1970 **12)** Cinderella - Don't Know What You Got (Till It's Gone) CD Video **13)** John Cipollina - Raven CD **14)** Clannad - Family Tree Sampler Promo CD **15)** Eric Clapton - Box (1985 to 1994) Japanese CD **16)** Eric Clapton - Backless MFSL Gold CD **17)** Eric Clapton - Blues Sampler Promo CD **18)** Eric Clapton - Selections From Crossroads 2 Sampler Promo CD **19)** Eric Clapton/John Mayall - Blues Breakers Japanese Mini LP CD **20)** Eric Clapton - Selections From Rainbow Concert Promo CD **21)** John Cooper Clarke - Disguise In Love CD **22)** Clash - Rockers Galore Promo CD **23)** Billy Cobham - Spectrum (With Tommy Bolin) CD **24)** Leonard Cohen - More Fans Promo CD **25)** Colin Blunstone - Journey Japanese CD **26)** Judy Collins - Bread And Roses **27)** Phil Collins - Son Of Man Promo CD Single **28)** John Coltrane - Selections From Coltrane (The Classic Quartet - Complete Impulse! Studio Recordings Promo CD **29)** Concert For Bangla Desh (George Harrison, Ringo Starr, Bob Dylan) Apple CD **30)** Billion Dollar Babies/Alice Cooper - Complete Battle Axe CD **31)** Alice Cooper - Dragontown Limited Edition CD **32)** Alice Cooper - Easy Action CD **33)** Alice Cooper - Pretties For You CD **34)** Elvis Costello - Get Happy/Trust Promo with Button CD **35)** Elvis Costello - Almost Blue/Imperial Bedroom Promo with Button CD **36)** Elvis Costello - Punch The Clock/Goodbye Cruel World Promo with Button CD **37)** Elvis Costello/Burt Bacharach - Because It's A Lonely World Interview Promo CD **38)** Elvis Costello - Almost Blue/Imperial Bedroom Promo Sampler CD **39)** Elvis Costello - 2 1/2 Years CD Box Set **40)** Elvis Costello/Brodsky Quartet - Excerpts From The Juliet Letters Promo Sampler CD **41)** Elvis Costello - A Taste Of Extreme Honey Promo Sampler CD **42)** Elvis Costello - King Biscuit Flower Hour (May 27th-June 2nd 1991) Promo CD **43)** Elvis Costello - King Of America 2 CD Set **44)** Elvis Costello - Kojak Variety With 2 Bonus Tracks (limited to 200) **45)** Elvis Costello - Magic And Malice Promo Sampler CD **46)** Elvis Costello - Live At The El Macambo Promo CD **47)** Elvis Costello/Steve Nieve - Costello & Nieve Box Set CD **48)** Elvis Costello - Punch The World Promo Sampler CD **49)** Elvis Costello - Re-examine Promo Sampler CD **50)** Elvis Costello - Spike Advance CD **51)** Elvis Costello - Taking Liberties CD **52)** Elvis Costello - Undeniable Attraction(s) Promo Sampler CD **53)** Elvis Costello - Words And Music Promo CD **54)** Elvis Costello/Brodsky Quartet - Live At New York Town Hall Promo Sampler CD **55)** Elvis Costello - Overview Promo CD **56)** Cowsills - In Concert CD **57)** Cowsills - Self Titled CD **58)** Cranberries - Doors And Windows CD-Rom **59)** Johnny Crawford - The Best Of CD **60)** Crazy Horse - Crazy Moon (Lost 1978 Album) CD **61)** Papa John Creach - Self Titled CD (with Jefferson Airplane and Grateful Dead) **62)** Cream - Disraeli Gears MFSL Gold CD **63)** Cream - Fresh Cream DCC Gold CD **64)** Cream - Fresh Live Cream Video CD

Page 269

1) Creatures - A Beastiary Of CD **2)** Creedence Clearwater Revival - CCR Mix CD **3)** Creedence Clearwater Revival - Pendulum DCC Gold CD **4)** Marshall Crenshaw - Mary Jean & 9 Others CD **5)** Peter Criss - Self Titled Japan CD **6)** Critters - Anthology CD **7)** Crowded House - The Very Best Of 2-CD **8)** Cry Baby - Original Soundtrack **9)** Crosby, Stills & Nash - Allies CD **10)** Crosby, Stills & Nash - Boxed Set Promo Sampler CD **11)** Example of an early Cross CD (The first Warner Elektra Atlantic CDs looked like this for example: Yes, Genesis, and Queen) **12)** Billy Currie/Steve Howe - Transportation CD **13)** Tim Curry - The Best Of CD **14)** Dave Davies - AFL1-3603 Japanese CD

Page 270 continued

15) Dave Davies - AFL1-3603/Glamour On One CD **16)** Dave Davies - Unfinished Business Promo CD **17)** Jessie Ed Davis - Self Titled Japanese CD **18)** Jessie Ed Davis - Keep Me Comin' Japanese CD **19)** Jessie Ed Davis - Ululu Japanese CD **20)** Miles Davis - The Alternative Miles Davis Sampler CD **21)** DB's - Like This CD **22)** DB's - The Sound of Music CD **23)** Deaf School - 2nd Coming CD **24)** Deaf School - English Boys Working Girls Japanese CD **25)** Deaf School - 2nd Honeymoon Japanese CD **26)** Deaf School - Don't Stop The World Japanese CD **27)** Deep Purple - Fireball Limited Edition CD **28)** Deep Purple - Special Edition Gold CD **29)** Deep Purple - In Rock Limited Edition CD **30)** Deep Purple - Machine Head Limited Edition CD **31)** Delco - Music Sampler MFSL Promo CD

32) Sandy Denny/Strawbs - And The Stawbs CD **33)** Sandy Denny - Who Knows Where The Time Goes? CD Boxed Set **34)** Depeche Mode - Summer Tour '94 Promo CD Sampler **35)** Derek And The Dominos - Layla And Other Assorted Love Songs MFSL Gold CD (with Eric Clapton and Duane Allman) **36)** Mink DeVille - Sportin' Life CD **37)** Karla DeVito - Is This A Cool World Or What? CD **38)** Devo - Live Limited Numbered CD **39)** Devo - Oh, No! It's Devo CD **40)** Devo - Recombo DNA Limited Numbered CD **41)** Devo - Shout CD **41)** Dictators - Bloodbrothers CD **42)** Dictators - Manifest Destiny CD **43)** Dinosaurs - Self Titled CD (with John Cipollina) **44)** Dion/Fats Domino - Christmas In-Store Promo CD Sampler **45)** Dion - Yo Frankie Promo CD Sampler **46)** Disney - The Music Of Disney (A Legacy In Song) Boxed Set **47)** D.I.Y. - Promo CD Sampler **48)** Denny Doherty - Watcha Gonna Do Japanese CD **49)** Do They Know It's Christmas? Japanese CD Single (with Bob Geldolf and Others) **50)** Doors - Alive She Cried CD **51)** Doors - Best Of Limited Edition CD Set **52)** Doors - Selections From The Forthcoming Box Set Promo CD Sampler **53)** Doors - Boxed Set Advanced CD Promotional Copy **54)** Doors - Live At The Hollywood Bowl CD **55)** Doors - L.A. Woman DCC Gold CD **56)** Doors - Westwood One Show #00-28 Promo 2 CD **57)** Nick Drake - Fruit Tree CD Boxed Set **58)** Dream Academy - A Different Kind Of Weather Promo CD Picture Disc

59) Doctor Who - Variations On A Theme CD **60)** DTS - Digital Surround Compact Disc Sampler Vol. 2 Promo

61) Duran Duran - Essential Disc 2 Bonus CD **62)** Duran Duran - Essential Night Versions CD

Page 270

1) Bob Dylan - Good As I Been To You Promo CD Sampler **2)** Bob Dylan - Greatest Hits Vol. 3 2-CD (CDI) **3)** Bob Dylan - Le Sampler French CD Promo **4)** Bob Dylan - Live '96 Limited Numbered Promo CD **5)** Bob Dylan - Million Miles Promo CD Sampler **6)** Bob Dylan - The Bootleg Series, Vol. 1-3 Promo CD Sampler **7)** Bob Dylan - Self Titled (A Fool Such As I) CD **8)** Bob Dylan - Time Out Of Mind Promo CD Sampler **9)** Bob Dylan - Music And Words Promo CD Sampler **10)** Eagles - 1994 Tour Promo CD Sampler **11)** Earth, Wind & Fire - Expanded Editions Promo CD Sampler **12)** Elliot Easton/The Cars - Change No Change CD **13)** Eddie & The Cruisers/John Cafferty's Beaver Brown Band - Eddie & The Cruisers II (Eddie Lives!) Japanese CD **14)** Eire Apparent/Jimi Hendrix - Sun Rise CD **15)** Electric Flag - Live CD **16)** Electric Flag - The Trip Original Soundtrack CD **17)** Elf - Self Titled (with Ronnie James Dio) CD **18)** ELO - Out Of The Blue Millenium Mini LP CD **19)** ELO - Interview with Jeff Lynne Promo CD **20)** ELP - Selections From The Return Of The Manticore Boxed Set Promo Sampler CD **21)** ELP - Welcome Back My Friends To The Show That Never Ends Japanese Mini LP CD **22)** ELP - Works Vol. I Japanese Mini LP CD **23)** Keith Emerson - Night Hawks Original Soundtrack **24)** ELP - Live At The Isle Of Wight Festival 1970 CD **25)** England Dan & John Ford Coley - Dr. Heckle & Mr. Jive Japanese CD **26)** England Dan & John Ford Coley - Nights Are Forever Japanese CD **27)** Brian Eno - A Year Of Swollen Appendices CD **28)** Brian Eno - Civic Recovery Centre CD **29)** Brian Eno - Compact Forest Proposal CD **30)** Brian Eno - I Dormienti CD **31)** Brian Eno - Kite Stories CD **32)** Brian Eno - Lightness: Music For The Marble Palace CD **33)** Brian Eno/Peter Schwalm - Reigakusya Limited Edition Holographic CD **34)** Brian Eno - Nerve Net Promo CD Sampler **35)** Brian Eno - Sampler 1 & 2 Boxed Set Promo CD (no tray art) **36)** Brian Eno - Textures (Back & Front/Only Released to Libraries in England) CD **37)** Brian Eno - Music For White Cube CD **38)** Enya - The Frog Prince CD **39)** Essential Collections - Promo CD Sampler **40)** Everly Brothers - Best DCC Gold CD **41)** Donald Fagen - New Frontier CD Video **42)** Donald Fagen - Words And Music Promo CD **43)** Family - Music In A Doll's House & Family Entertainment Limited Edition Hardback Book CD **44)** Father And Sons - Self Titled (with Muddy Waters, Mike Bloomfield, Paul Butterfield & Buddy Miles) CD **45)** Bryan Ferry - The Archive & Live Collection CD **46)** Fillmore - Last Days (with Santana, Grateful Dead & Quicksilver Messenger Service) CD **47)** Wild Man Fischer - The Fischer King Limited Edition Boxed Set CD **48)** Flamin' Groovies - Jumpin' In The Night Japanese CD **49)** Flamin' Groovies - Now Japanese CD **50)** Flamin' Groovies - Still Shakin' CD **51)** Flash Fearless Vs. The Zorg Woman - Parts 5 & 6 (with Justin Hayward & Alice Cooper) CD **52)** Fleetwood Mac - Selections From The Chain Box Set Promo CD **53)** Fleetwood Mac - English Rose Japanese CD **54)** Fleetwood Mac - Tour '97 Promo CD Set **55)** Fleetwood Mac - The Chain CD Box Set

Page 270 continued

56) Flo & Eddie - The Best Of CD **57)** F M - Black Noise CD **58)** John Fogerty - Blue Moon Swamp Advanced Promo CD **59)** Ellen Foley - The Spirit Of St. Louis CD **60)** Frijid Pink - Hibernated Box Set CD **61)** Edgar Froese - Beyond The Storm CD **62)** Fugs - Songs From A Portable Forest CD **63)** Fugs - Electromagnetic Steamboat Limited Edition Numbered Boxed Set

Page 271

1) Future Perfect - Gryoscope Compilation CD **2)** Peter Gabriel - 3 Japanese Mini LP CD **3)** Peter Gabriel - Before Us A Brief History Promo CD Sampler **4)** Peter Gabriel - Digging In The Dirt Limited Edition CD Single **5)** Peter Gabriel - Steam Limited Edition House Shaped Box Single CD **6)** Peter Gabriel - Remasters Promo CD Sampler **7)** Peter Gabriel - Up (Advanced Promo CD with different tracks than the regular release/some added, some deleted) **8)** David Gates - First CD **9)** Genesis - Two Songs From The Longs w/Interview Promo CD **10)** Genesis - Three Sides Live (Paperlate Version) CD **11)** Genesis - Abacab (Signed by the Band) CD **12)** Genesis - Archive Vol. 1 Promo CD Sampler **13)** Genesis - Archive The Interviews CD **14)** Genesis - From Genesis To Revelation Limited Edition Gold CD (with 3 prints) **15)** Genesis - In The Studio (Abacab) Promo CD **16)** Genesis - Westwood One Show #00-35 2-CD **17)** Gentle Giant - In A Glass House Mini LP CD **18)** Gentle Giant - Under Construction Boxed Set **19)** Get Smart w/Don Adams and Barbara Feldon CD **20)** Dana Gillespie - Andy Warhol CD **21)** Allen Ginsberg/Paul McCartney - Ballad Of The Skeletons CD **22)** Roger Glover - Buttlefly Ball And The Grasshopper's Feast (with Deep Purple and Ronnie James Dio) CD **23)** Barry Goudreau/Boston - Self Titled CD **24)** Ron Grainer - The Prisoner Theme CD Single **25)** Grand Funk Railroad - Radio Promo Sampler CD **26)** Amy Grant - Lead Me On Signed Numbered Gold Disc **27)** Grateful Dead - Stayin' Alive Limited Promo German CD (Back & Front) **28)** Grateful Dead - Selections From The Arista Years Promo CD Sampler **29)** Grateful Dead - Without A Net Live Promo CD Sampler Clown Picture Discs **30)** Grateful Dead - Dick's Picks, Vol. 7-12, Promo CD Sampler **31)** Grateful Dead - Documentary Promo CD **32)** Grateful Dead - Steppin' Out With England '72 Promo CD Sampler **33)** Grateful Dead - For The Faithful... (Reckoning) CD **34)** Grateful Dead - Terrapin Station Boxed Set **35)** Grateful Dead - Dead In A Deck Promo Box w/Built to Last Picture CD & Grateful Dead Playing Cards **36)** Nick Gravenites/John Cipollina - Monkey Medicine CD **37)** Nick Gravenites - My Labors w/Michael Bloomfield **38)** Nick Gravenites - Bluestar CD **39)** Greenslade - Bedside Manners Are Extra CD **40)** Greenslade/Terry Pratchett - From The Discworld CD **41)** Greenslade/Patrick Woodroffe - Pentateuch Of The Cosmogony Limited Edition CD **42)** Green Hornet - Original Television Score Japanese Mini LP CD **43)** Peter Green - Me And The Devil Limited Edition Numbered 3-CD Box Set **44)** David Grisman - Hot Dawg MFSL Gold CD **45)** Grootna - Self Titled w/Marty Balin CD **46)** Gruppo Sportivo - Sucker Of The Century CD **47)** Gryphon - Red Queen To Gryphon 3/Raindance 2-on-1 CD **48)** GTO's - Permanent Damage w/Frank Zappa CD **49)** Gulliver's Travels - Self Titled w/Small Faces, Nice & The Lovin' Spoonful CD **50)** Steve Hackett/Quiet World - Steve's First Band Japanese Mini LP CD **51)** Bo Hansson - Lord Of The Rings CD **52)** Happy The Man - Retrospective CD **53)** Tim Hardin - 1 CD **54)** Tim Hardin - 2 CD **55)** Harley Davidson - Songs Deluxe Limited Edition Leather CD **56)** Eddie Harris - E.H. In The U.K. (with Yes, Jeff Beck, Stevie Winwood & Albert Lee)/Is It In (2-for-1) CD **57)** Richard Harris - The Webb Sessions '68-'69 CD **58)** Sugarcane Harris - Sugarcane w/Johnnie & Shuggie Otis CD **59)** George Harrison - All Things Must Pass Promo CD Sampler **60)** George Harrison - Cloud Nine Promo Picture Disc CD (with no front booklet) **61)** George Harrison - This Is Love Promo CD Single **62)** George Harrison - Best Of Dark Horse CD **63)** George Harrison - Wonderwall CD

Page 272

1) Mickey Hart & The Hartbeats - Heartbits CD **2)** Mickey Hart - Mystery Box Promo Advanced CD **3)** Mickey Hart/Henry Wolff/Nancy Hennings - Yamantaka CD **4)** Harvest Festival - Boxed Set **5)** Justin Hayward - Live In San Juan Capistrano **6)** Justin Hayward - Moving Mountains CD **7)** Jimi Hendrix - Band Of Gypsys/Are You Experienced/War Heroes/Hendrix In The West (Plus Collectors 16-page booklet) Limited Edition Boxed Set **8)** Jimi Hendrix - BBC Sessions Promo CD Sampler **9)** Jimi Hendrix - Boxed Set 8-Song Promo CD Sampler **10)** Jimi Hendrix - Concert CD **11)** Jimi Hendrix - Crash Landing CD **12)** Jimi Hendrix - Cry Of Love CD **13)** Jimi Hendrix - Day Tripper 3" CD Single (with unreleased tracks) **14)** Jimi Hendrix - Essential, Vol. One & Two 2-CD **15)** Jimi Hendrix - Live At The Fillmore East Promo CD Sampler **16)** Jimi Hendrix - Kiss The Sky CD **17)** Jimi Hendrix - Midnight Lightning Japanese CD **18)** Jimi Hendrix - Jimi Plays Monterey CD **19)** Jimi Hendrix - Radio One CD **20)** Jimi Hendrix - Electric Lady Land (rare nude cover fold-out version) **21)** Jimi Hendrix - Stages Boxed Set **22)** Jimi Hendrix - War Heroes CD **23)** Jimi Hendrix - Lifelines Boxed Set **24)** Jimi Hendrix - Live At Winterland + 3 Boxed Set w/t-shirt **25)** Don Henley - In The Studio End Of The Innocence Promo CD **26)** Don Henley - End Of The Innocence Limited Edition CD

Page 272 continued

27) Bernard Herrmann - The Day The Earth Stood Still CD (with extra tracks/came with Limited Laser Disc Boxed Set) 28) Bernard Herrmann - The Night Digger CD 29) Bernard Herrmann - (The Concert Suites/All The London Albums remastered/ Limited Edition) 30) Carolyn Hester - Self Tited (with Bob Dylan) 31) John Hiatt - Riding With The King MFSL Gold CD 32) John Hiatt - I'll Never Get Over You Japanese CD Single 33) John Hiatt - Walk On Promo Sampler CD 34) Dan Hicks - It Happened One Bite Japanese CD 35) Randy Holden/Blue Cheer - Guitar God Japanese CD 36) Music From Hollywood CD (with Bernard Herrmann, Franz Waxman and Max Steiner Live)

37) Mary Hopkin - Earth Song Apple CD 38) Mary Hopkin - Postcard Apple CD 39) Mary Hopkin - Those Were The Days Apple CD 40) Hot Tuna - Double Dose CD 41) Hot Tuna - Trimmed And Burning CD 42) Hot Tuna - Yellow Fever CD 43) Hourglass - Self Titled CD (with Duane and Gregg Allman) 44) Hourglass - Power Of Love (with Duane and Gregg Allman) 45) Humblebums - Self Titled CD (with Gerry Rafferty) 46) Humble Pie - Self Titled Japanese CD 47) Ides Of March - Vehicle CD 48) The Impacts - Wipe Out ! CD 49) Iron Butterfly - In-A- Gadda-Da-Vida MFSL Gold CD 50) It's A Beautiful Day - Greatest Hits (Limited Edition Picture) CD 51) Jackson Five - Soulsation ! Promo Boxed Set CD Sampler 52) Joe Jackson - Tucker Original Soundtrack CD 53) Joe Jackson - Will Power MFSL CD 54) Joe Jackson - Symphony No. 1 Advanced CD from BMG (different artwork from regular release) 55) Jade Warrior - At Peace CD 56) James Gang - Live In Concert MFSL Aluminum CD 57) Jean Michel Jarre - Oxygene MFSL Gold CD 58) Jars Of Clay - The White Elephant Sessions Promo CD 59) Jars Of Clay Platinum Limited Numbered Editon CD 60) Jefferson Airplane/Starship/Marty Balin - King Biscuit Flower Hour Airplane Chronicles September 11, 1989 Promo CD 61) Jefferson Airplane - Live 1967 (Promo Giveaway CD from Collector's Choice Music Label) 62) Jefferson Airplane - Live At The Monterey Festival CD 63) Jefferson Airplane - Loves You Boxed Set Promo Sampler CD

Page 273

1) Jefferson Airplane - We All Are One Italian Book (with a 3 song bonus CD) 2) Jefferson Starship - 10-31-00 B.B. King's Blues Club, New York City @ www.jeffersonstarshipf.com 3) Jefferson Starship - Blows Against The Empire (original version that was like the original album before Paul Kantner changed a song on the remastered version)

4) Jefferson Starship/Jefferson Airplane/Marty Balin - Starship Chronicles (same as the Airplane Chronicles version) King Biscuit Flower Hour 8/12 to 8/18, 1996 5) Jefferson Starship - Red Octopus DCC Gold CD 6) Garland Jeffreys - Escape Artist CD 7) Jellyfish - Comes Alive Promo CD 8) Jesus Christ Superstar/Andrew Lloyd Webber/Tim Rice - MCA Gold CD (with Ian Gillan of Deep Purple, Yvonne Elliman and Murray Head) 9) Antonio Carlos Jobim - The Man From Ipanema Boxed Set 10) Billy Joel - Words Without Music Promo Interview CD 11) Elton John - Madman Across The water Japanese Mini LP CD 12) Elton John - Westwood One Show # 01-15 April 14/15, 2001 13) Bruce Johnston/Beach Boys - Surfin' Pajama Party CD 14) Jon (Anderson of Yes) and Vangelis - Page Of Life German Version (with 4 different tracks than the American version but excluding Change We Must) 15) John Paul Jones/Diamanda Galas - The Sporting Life CD 16) John Paul Jones - Self Titled CD 17) John Paul Jones - Scream For Help Original Soundtrack Japanese CD (with Jimmy Page and Jon Anderson of Yes) 18) Janis Joplin - Farewell Song CD 19) Janis Joplin - In Concert CD 20) Janis Joplin - Janis CD Boxed Set 21) Judas Priest - Rocka Rolla (Winged Demon Cover Version) 22) Kaleidoscope - A Beacon From Mars CD 23) Kaleidoscope - Side Trips CD 24) Kama Sutra - Complete Kama Sutra Singles - Vol. 2 CD 25) Kama Sutra - Complete Kama Sutra Singles - Vol. 1 CD 26) Kansas/Morning Dew - Self Titled Mini LP CD (with Kerry Livgren) 27) Kansas/Steve Walsh - Schemer-Dreamer Japanese CD 28) Paul Kantner - A Guide Through The Chaos (Spoken Word) CD 29) Boris Karloff/Jean Arthur - Peter Pan (Original Broadway Cast) CD 30) Jorma Kaukonen/Tom Constanten - Embryonic Journey (Signed by each of them) CD 31) KBC Band - Self Titled CD (with Paul Kantner, Marty Balin, Jack Casady) 32) Keats - Self Titled (with Alan Parsons, Pete Bardens & Colin Blunstone) CD 33) Kentucky Colonels - Livin' In The Past (with Introduction by Jerry Garcia) CD 34) Greg Kihn - Again CD 35) Greg Kihn - RocKihnRoll CD 36) Carole King - Tapestry Revisited Limited Edition Tribute CD 37) King Crimson - Club CD #1, Live At The Marquee 1969 CD 38) King Crimson - Epitaph CD Boxed Set 39) King Crimson - Sometimes God Hides Promo CD 40) King Crimson - A Young Person's Guide To Japanese CD 41) King Crimson - Earthbound Japanese Mini LP CD 42) King Crimson - Epitaph Vol. 3 & 4, Japanese Mini LP CD 43) King Crimson - USA Japanese Mini LP CD 44) King Crimson/McDonald & Giles - Self Titled Japanese Mini LP CD 45) King Crimson/Daryl Hall - Sacred Songs (produced by Robert Fripp (first use of Frippertronics/basically a King Crimson Album with Daryl Hall singing) 46) Kingfish - Live 'N' Kickin' CD 47) Kingfish - Trident CD 48) Kinks - The Archway Tavern Collection Limited Edition Fan Club CD 49) Kinks - Selections From BBC Sessions Promo CD Sampler

Page 273 continued

50) Kinks - Borders Compilation Promo CD 51) Kinks - Velvel Promo Compilation Vol. 1 52) Kinks - Velvel Promo Compilation Vol. 2 53) Kinks - Velvel Promo Compilation Vol. 3 54) Kinks - Did Ya CD Single

55) Kinks - God Save The Kinks UK Promo Brown CD 56) Kinks - God Save The Kinks UK Promo Purple CD

57) Kinks - God Save The Kinks UK Promo White 2-CD 58) Kinks - Greatest Hits II, 1971-1975 Japanese CD

59) Kinks - Greatest Hits III, 1977-1984 Japanese CD 60) Kinks/Kast Off - Archway EP CD 61) Kinks - King Biscuit Flower Hour, Jan.29, 2001 Promo CD 62) Kinks/Michael Penn - King Biscuit Flower Hour, Oct. 22-28, 1990 Promo CD

63) Kinks - UK To The Bone CD 64) Kinks - Waterloo Sunset '94 EP CD Single

Page 274

1) Kinks - Westwood One, Show #95-26 Promo CD 2) Kiss - Guitar Case CD Box Set 3) Kiss/Lou Reed - The Elder Japanese Mini LP CD 4) Kiss - Killers CD 5) Kitaro - The Best Of Japanese CD 6) Kitaro - Twin Best Japanese CD

7) Klark Kent/Stewart Copeland - Kollected Works CD 8) Knebworth - Self Titled (with Eric Clapton, Paul McCartney, Pink Floyd) CD 9) Al Kooper - I Stand Alone Japanese CD 10) Al Kooper - Rare Special Advanced Promo CD 11) Al Kooper - What Do All These Recording Artists Have In Common??? Promo CD 12) Robby Krieger/The Doors - Self Titled MFSL Aluminum CD 13) Tuli Kupferberg - No Deposit, No Return CD 14) Daniel Lanois - Acadie CD 15) Last Emperor - Original Soundtrack (w/David Byrne & Ryuichi Sakamoto) CD 16) Timothy Leary - Beyond Life With CD (with different version of Legend Of A Mind/Timothy Leary's Alive by the Moody Blues)

17) Led Zeppelin - Profiled Promo CD 18) Led Zeppelin - The Girl I Love CD-Rom 19) Led Zeppelin - BBC Sessions CD Sampler (with medley of every Led Zeppelin song) 20) Led Zeppelin - Interview Disc 2003 (Promo CD for How The West Was Won) 21) Left Banke - Walk Away Renee/Pretty Ballerina CD 22) Legend - Original Soundtrack (with Jon Anderson of Yes and Bryan Ferry) CD 23) Tom Lehrer - Remains Of CD Boxed Set 24) John Lennon - Excerpts From First Lennon Boxed Set 25) John Lennon - Starting Over Promo CD 26) John Lennon/Yoko Ono - Two Virgins (Original CD Version) 27) Sean Lennon - Half Horse Half Musician Japanese CD 28) Jerry Lee Lewis - Complete Palomino Recordings CD 29) Liliput - Self Titled CD 30) Kerry Livgren/Kansas - Seeds Of Change CD

31) John Lodge - Natural Avenue CD (signed by John) 32) Jackie Lomax - Is This What You Want? Apple CD (with George Harrison, Paul McCartney, Ringo Starr) 33) Lord Of The Rings/Howard Shore - Fellowship Of The Ring Limited Edition CD

34) Lord Sutch & Heavy Friends - Self Titled CD (with Jimmy Page, John Bonham, Jeff Beck, Nicky Hopkins, Noel Redding)

35) Lord Sutch & Heavy Friends - Jack The Ripper CD (with Keith Moon, Ritchie Blackmore, Noel Redding & Matthew Fisher) 36) Lost Mixes - Self Titled CD (with Phil Collins, Yes, Mike & The Mechanics, Cars, ZZ Top, Doobie Brothers, Robert Plant, Foreigner & Fleetwood Mac) 37) Tina Louise/Gilligan's Island - It's Time For Fun CD 38) Love Spit Love - Self Titled with Bonus CD-Rom 39) Nick Lowe - Labour Of Lust CD (USA/different version from UK) 40) Nick Lowe - Pure Pop For Now People (USA/different version from UK/Jesus Of Cool) 41) Lulu - The Man Who Sold The World CD

42) Jeff Lynne/ELO - Armchair Theatre CD 43) Lynyrd Skynyrd - Old Time Greats CD 44) Mainhorse/Patrick Moraz - Self Titled CD 45) Malo - Celebration! CD Boxed Set 46) Mamas & Papas - Great Mamas & Papas Live! CD (John Phillips, MacKenzie Phillips, Denny Doherty, Spanky McFarlane) 47) Mandalaband - Eyes Of Wendor CD (with Barclay James Harvest, 10cc, Maddy Prior, Justin Hayward) 48) Mannix/Lalo Schifrin - Original Television Soundtrack CD 49) Ray Manzarek/The Doors - Myth And Reality (Spoken Word) CD 50) Maple Oak/Peter Quaife - Self Titled CD (Band that Pete went to after the Kinks)

51) Mark Almond - Last & Live CD 52) Jon Mark - Hot Night CD Single 53) Jon Mark - Hot Night CD 54) Jon Mark - Lady And The Artist CD 55) Mark Almond - Tuesday in New York CD 56) Bob Marley/Wailers - Songs Of Freedom CD Boxed Set 57) Bob Marley/Wailers - Catch A Fire Promo CD Sampler 58) Dave Mason - Some Assembly Required CD

59) Dave Mason - Alone Together MFSL Gold CD 60) Nick Mason/Fenn - Profiles CD 61) Nick Mason - Fictitious Sports CD 62) Will T. Massey - Self Titled CD (produced by Roy Bittan/sounds like Bruce Springsteen & John Cougar Mellencamp) 63) Matching Mole - Self Titled CD (w/Robert Wyatt) 64) Matthews Southern Comfort - Later That Same Year CD

Page 275

1) Maybe Baby/Paul McCartney - Original Soundtrack Promo CD 2) Mazzy Star - Fade Into You Limited Edition plus Live Tracks Promo CD 3) Paul McCartney - The Paul McCartney Collection UK Promo Sampler CD 4) Paul McCartney - Off The Ground The Complete Works 2-CD 5) Paul McCartney - Drivin' Rain Promo Sampler CD

6) Paul McCartney/Fireman - Rushes CD 7) Paul McCartney - Flowers In The Dirt Japanese 2-CD Set 8) Paul McCartney/Liverpool Sound Collage Self Titled CD 9) Paul McCartney - Rocks Promo CD 10) Paul McCartney - Wings Over America Japanese Mini LP 2-CD 11) Paul McCartney - Red Rose Speedway DCC Gold CD

Page 275 continued

12) Paul McCartney - Oobu Joobu Promo CD **13)** Paul McCartney/Thrillington - Thrillington (Ram Orchestrated) CD **14)** Country Joe McDonald - The Rag Baby EPs CD Boxed Set **15)** Country Joe McDonald - A Reflection On Changing Times CD Boxed Set **16)** Country Joe McDonald - Vietnam Experience CD **17)** Mike McGear/Paul McCartney - McGear Self Titled CD **18)** Christine McVie/Fleetwood Mac - Christine Perfect CD (Fleetwood Mac singer's first album) **19)** Meatloaf - Promo CD Sampler **20)** Meatloaf - Bat Out Of Hell 2 CD (Original 4-color picture disc version) **21)** Melanie - Candles In The Rain CD **22)** Melanie - Four Sides Of 2-CD **23)** Message To Love - The Isle Of Wight Music Festival 1970 CD (with Free, Jethro Tull, Jimi Hendrix, Joni Mitchell, Emerson, Lake & Palmer, The Doors, The Who, Moody Blues, Donovan, John Sebastian & Bob Dylan) **24)** Jim Messina - Messina CD

25) Metallica - Mandatory Metallica Promo 2-CD Set **26)** Metropolis - Original Soundtrack (with Jon Anderson of Yes) **27)** MGM - Soundtracks Promo 2-CD Set (Rykodisc reissues) **28)** George Michael - Ladies & Gentlemen The Best Of In-Store Promo Sampler CD **29)** Thee Midniters - Greatest Hits CD **30)** Midnight Oil - Best Of The B Sides Promo CD **31)** Mike & The Mechanics - King Biscuit Flower Hour Promo CD, May 8-14, 1995 **32)** Mike & The Mechanics - King Biscuit Flower Hour Promo CD, Oct. 2-8, 1989 **33)** Mike & The Mechanics - Westwood One Off The Record Special Promo CD, Show #95-17 **34)** Steve Miller - Book Of Dreams DCC Gold CD **35)** Steve Miller - Your Saving Grace CD **36)** Brad Miller - Power And The Majesty MFSL Aluminum CD **37)** Joni Mitchell - Night Ride Home Limited Edition CD **38)** Moby Grape - 20 Granite Creek CD **39)** Moby Grape - Self Titled CD

40) Moby Grape - Live Grape CD **41)** Modern Jazz Quartet - Under The Jasmin Tree Apple CD **42)** Modern Jazz Quartet - Space Apple CD **43)** Monterey International Pop Festival - June 16-18, 1967, Promo Sampler CD (with Interviews) **44)** Monterey International Pop Festival - June 16-18, 1967, CD Boxed Set (Large Version) **45)** Moody Blues/Graeme Edge - Kick Off Your Muddy Boots CD **46)** Moody Blues/Ray Thomas - Hopes, Wishes & Dreams CD **47)** Moody Blues/Ray Thomas - From Mighty Oaks CD (on the song Adam & I there is a momentary skip on all CDs)

48) Van Morrison - Selections From The Philosopher's Stone Promo CD **49)** Mark Mothersbaugh/Devo - Joyeux Mutato CD (Christmas) **50)** Motley Crue - Crucial Crue Sampler Promo CD **51)** Graham Nash - Innocent Eyes CD **52)** Neu! - Self Titled Promo CD Sampler **53)** Neverending Story/Klaus Doldinger - Die Unendliche Geschichte CD (German Version, Instrumental Songs Only) **54)** Newport Broadside - Self Titled CD (with Bob Dylan & Joan Baez) **55)** New Race - First And The Last CD (Radio Birdman, MC5, Stooges) **56)** New York Dolls/David Johansen/Syl Sylvain - Tokyo Dolls Live! Japanese Cd **57)** New York Dolls - Looking For A Kiss Japanese CD Video **58)** Nico - Chelsea Girls Japanese Mini LP CD (with Lou Reed and John Cale) **59)** Nine Inch Nails - Broken Cd (w/ 3 inch CD single) **60)** Nine Inch Nails - And All That Could Have Been Limited Edition 2-CD **61)** No New York - Self Titled Japanese CD (produced by Brian Eno, James Chance & Lydia Lunch) **62)** Mike Oldfield - Best Of Tubular Bells UK Promo CD **63)** Opal - Early Recordings CD **64)** Roy Orbison - I Drove All Night CD Single

Page 276

1) Osmonds - The Plan CD **2)** Other Ones - Self Titled CD (New Wave group) **3)** Jimmy Page - Death Wish II (Original Soundtrack CD) **4)** Jimmy Page/Robert Plant - A Songwriting Legacy Promo CD **5)** Jimmy Page/Robert Plant - Miller Promo CD (Page & Plant 1995 Tour) **6)** Larry Page/Kinks - Kinky Music CD **7)** Felix Pappalardi - Don't Worry, Ma CD **8)** Graham Parker - Vertigo CD (includes Live At The Marble Arch Promo) **9)** Alan Parsons - Freudiana CD **10)** Alan Parsons - I Robot MFSL CD (Laser Video Inc./1st Edition - No inserts) **11)** Alan Parsons - I Robot MFSL CD (Regular Version) **12)** Alan Parsons - I Robot CD (Classic DAD Version) **13)** Andy Partridge/XTC - Hello Club EP November 1994 CD (w/unreleased tracks) **14)** Passengers/U2 - Original Soundchat 1 Radio Documentary Promo 2-CD **15)** Pearl Jam - Alive Japanese CD **16)** Pearl Jam - Dissident Limited Edition CD Single

17) Dan Peek/America - Doer Of The Word Japanese CD **18)** David Peel - Have A Marijuana CD **19)** Pendragon - The Masquerade Overture 2-CD **20)** Performance - Original Soundtrack CD (with Mick Jagger & Randy Newman) **21)** Carl Perkins & Friends - A Rockabilly Session (with Eric Clapton, George Harrison, Ringo Starr & Dave Edmunds) **22)** Permanent Record - Original Soundtrack w/Lou Reed **23)** Tom Petty - Full Moon Fever MFSL Gold CD **24)** Tom Petty - Hard Promises MFSL Gold CD **25)** Tom Petty - Play Back Excerpts Vol. 2 CD Promo Sampler Boxed Set **26)** Tom Petty - Play Back Excerpts Vol. 1 CD Promo Sampler Boxed Set **27)** Tom Petty - Westwood One, Show #00-06, Feb. 5 & 6, 2000 Promo CD **28)** John Phillips/Merry Clayton - Brewster McCloud Original Soundtrack CD **29)** Michelle Phillips - Victim Of Romance Japanese CD **30)** Anthony Phillips/Genesis - Wise After The Event CD **31)** Photos - Self Titled CD (sounds like a cross between The Pretenders & The Ramones) **32)** Bobby Pickett - The Original Monster Mash CD **33)** PIL/Public Image Ltd. - Metal Box CD in a Tin Can **34)** Mike Pinder - Off The Shelf CD **35)** Mike Pinder - The Promise CD **36)** Pink Floyd - Atom Heart Mother MFSL Gold CD

Page 276continued

37) Pink Floyd - Dark Side Of The Moon MFSL Gold CD **38)** Pink Floyd - Echoes 8-track Promo Sampler CD
39) Pink Floyd - Meddle Japanese Mini LP CD **40)** Pink Floyd - Meddle MFSL Gold CD **41)** Pink Floyd - Piper At The
Gates of Dawn Boxed Set CD (Original Mono Version) **42)** Pink Floyd - Shine On Selected Tracks Promo CD Sampler **43)**
Pink Floyd - Is There Anybody Out There? Promo CD Sampler **44)** Pink Floyd - Westwood One, Show #01-17, April 28 &
29, 2001, Promo CD **45)** Wally Pleasant - Welcome To Pleasantville CD **46)** Poke In The Eye - The Complete A Poke In
The Eye With A Sharp Stick (Various Artists w/Monty Python) **47)** Police - Selections From Message In A Box Promo CD
Sampler **48)** Iggy Pop - Butt Town Demos, 1st Version **49)** Iggy Pop - Butt Town Demos, 2nd Version **50)** Iggy Pop/
Stooges - Fun House Boxed Set, Numbered Limited Edition **51)** Iggy Pop - King Biscuit Flower Hour, Sept. 15-21, 1997
Promo Cd **52)** Iggy Pop/Stooges - Raw Power (David Bowie produced version) **53)** Iggy Pop/Stooges - Raw Power (Iggy
Pop produced version) **54)** Pork Dukes - All The Filth CD **55)** Porky's Revenge - Original Soundtrack MFSL Aluminum CD
(w/George Harrison, Jeff Beck, Robert Plant, Phil Collins & Dave Edmunds) **56)** Andrew Powell/Alan Parsons - The
Philharmonia Orchestra Plays The Best Of Alan Parsons Project MFSL Aluminum CD **57)** Elvis Presley - Elvis Is Back! DCC
Gold CD **58)** Elvis Presley - Self Titled RCA Gold CD **59)** Billy Preston - Encouraging Words Apple CD **60)** Billy Preston -
That's The Way God Planned It Apple CD **61)** Pretenders - Don't Get Me Wrong Best Of (w/Cuban Slide EP) **62)** Pretend-
ers - Westwood One, Show #00-04,
Jan. 22-23, 2000 Promo 2-CD **63)** Pretty Things - Resurrection (SF Sorrow/Abbey Road 1998/David Gilmour)
64) Prisoner/Ron Gainer - Fab Featuring M.C. No. 9 CD Single

Page 277

1) Prisoner/Ron Gainer - File #1, 2 & 3 CDs **2)** Procol Harum - Broken Barricades Japanese Mini LP CD **3)** Procol Harum -
Broken Barricades MFSL Aluminum CD **4)** Procol Harum - Live Japanese Mini LP CD **5)** Mason Proffit - Come & Gone
CD **6)** Psychedelic Furs - Talk, Talk, Talk Advanced Promo CD **7)** Queen - Keep Yourself Alive Promo CD Single **8)** Queen
- Crown Jewels In-Store Play Promo CD Sampler **9)** Queen - Crown Jewels Boxed Set
10) Queen - Made In Heaven Promo CD (with Queen Symbols on Tray) **11)** Queen - A Night At The Opera - MFSL Gold
CD **12)** Quicksilver Messenger Service - The Ultimate Journey CD **13)** Robert Quine/Fred Maher - Self Titled CD **14)**
Radha Krsna Temple - Self Titled Apple CD **15)** Radio Birdman - Under The Ashes CD Boxed Set
16) Radiohead - Air Bag EP CD **17)** Radiohead - Creep Japanese CD Single **18)** Radiohead - Amnesiac Limited Edition Red
Hardback CD **19)** Radiohead - Pyramid Song Japanese CD Single **20)** Rain Parade - Perfume River Limited Edition Of
1,000 CD **21)** Real World Artists - Real World Promo CD Sampler **22)** Records - A Sunny Afternoon In Waterloo CD **23)**
Noel Redding/Band - The Missing Album CD **24)** Lou Reed - King Biscuit Flower Hour, Show #98-40, Sept. 28-Oct. 4,
1998 Promo CD **25)** Lou Reed - King Biscuit Flower Hour, Feb. 24-March 1, 1992 Promo CD **26)** Lou Reed - Power And
Glory Promo CD (with Live Tracks) **27)** Lou Reed - A Rock & Roll Life Promo 2-CD **28)** Remasterpieces - Atlantic Promo
CD Sampler **29)** R.E.M - Reckoning MFSL Gold CD **30)** R.E.M. - Green Limited Edition Hardback CD **31)** R.E.M. - Pop
Songs '89-'99 Promo CD **32)** R.E.M. - Tourfilm CD Video **33)** Renaissance - BBC Sessions CD **34)** Renaissance - Cam-
era, Camera CD **35)** Residents - Double Shot 3" CD Single **36)** Emitt Rhodes - Mirror Japanese CD **37)** Jonathan Richman
& The Modern Lovers - Self Titled CD
38) Risky Business - Original Soundtrack (with Tangerine Dream & Prince) **39)** Robbie Robertson/The Band - The Story Of
Storyville Promo CD **40)** Rockets/Crazy Horse - Self Titled CD **41)** Rockpile/Foghat - King Biscuit Flower Hour, Nov. 6,
2000 Promo CD **42)** Rocky Horror Picture Show - Rocky Horror Collection CD Boxed Set **43)** Rolling Stones - Remas-
tered Promo Gold CD **44)** Rolling Stones - Forty Licks Limited Edition CD Boxed Set **45)** Rolling Stones - Collector's
Edition Bonus CD **46)** Rolling Stones - Desert Island Survival Kit Promo CD **47)** Rolling Stones - Volumen 1 Promo Mexican
CD **48)** Rolling Stones - Volumen 2 Promo Mexican CD **49)** Rolling Stones - Say Ahhh! Promo CD **50)** Rolling Stones -
Voodoo Lounge Promo CD Sampler **51)** Roxy Music - King Biscuit Flower Hour, Sept. 14-20, 1998 Promo CD **52)**
Rubinoos - Back To The Drawing Board! CD **53)** Rubinoos - Paleophonic Bonus Disc Promo CD **54)** Runaways - Born To
Be Bad CD **55)** Runaways - Little Lost Girls CD **56)** Todd Rundgren - Somwhere/Anywhere? Japanese CD **57)** Todd
Rundgren - King Biscuit Flower Hour, Sept. 25, 2000 **58)** Todd Rundgren - Something/Anything? Japanese Mini LP CD **59)**
Todd Rundgren/Utopia - Oops! Wrong Planet MFSL Gold CD **60)** Todd Rundgren - A Wizard, A True Star Japanese Mini LP
CD **61)** Rush - Signals MFSL Gold CD **62)** Leon Russell - Self Titled DCC Gold CD **63)** Rutles - Rutles Highway Revisited
(Tribute Album with Tuli Kupferberg/The Fugs) **64)** Doug Sahm - Doug Sahm & Band (with Bob Dylan) Japanese CD

Page 278

1) Doug Sahm - Groovers Paradise (with Stu Cook & Doug Clifford/CCR) Japanese CD

Page 278 continued

2) Ed Sanders/The Fugs - American Bard CD **3)** Ed Sanders/The Fugs - Songs In Ancient Greek CD

4) Santana - Expanded Editions Promo CD Sampler **5)** Santana - S.F. Mission District Mini LP CD **6)** Boz Scaggs - Dig Limited Edition CD (with DVD) **7)** Boz Scaggs - Moments Japanese CD **8)** Seals & Crofts - Diamond Girl Japanese CD **9)** Dan Seals - Harbinger Japanese CD **10)** Dan Seals/England - Stones Japanese CD **11)** Dan Seals - Won't Be Blue Anymore Cd **12)** John Sebastian - Faithful Virtue: The Reprise Recordings Limited Numbered CD Boxed Set **13)** John Sebastian - John B. Sebastian (with Crosby, Stills & Nash) CD **14)** Secret Policeman's Other Ball - Self Titled (with Sting, Jeff Beck, Eric Clapton, Bob Geldof, Phil Collins & Donovan) **15)** The Seeds - Pushin' Too Hard/First CD **16)** Bob Seger - Mongrel CD **17)** Bob Seger - Turn The Page Promo CD (Back In '72 album version)

18) Bob Seger - Ramblin' Gamblin' Man CD **19)** Bob Seger - Seven CD **20)** Bob Seger - Smokin' O.P.'s CD

21) Ravi Shankar/Ali Akbar Khan - In Concert 1972 Apple 2-CD **22)** Del Shannon - Rock On CD **23)** Louie Shelton - {Hot & Spicy}(with Seals & Crofts first appearance since they broke up) **24)** Shock Treatment - Self Titled Original Soundtrack CD (sequel to Rocky Horror Picture Show) **25)** Gene Simmons/Kiss - Self Titled Japanese CD

26) Simon And Garfunkel - Old Friends Selections From Promo Sampler CD **27)** Paul Simon - Songs From The Capeman In-Store Promo Sampler CD **28)** Paul Simon - Greatest Hits Ect. (w/Stranded In A Limousine)

29) Paul Simon - Concert In The Park Promo CD Sampler **30)** Grace Slick/Great Society - Self Tited Collector's Item Cd (both Great Society Albums together on one cd) **31)** Grace Slick - Best Of (Shortened Budget Version)

32) Grace Slick - Best Of CD(Longer Version/Better) **33)** Small Faces - Odgen Nut Gone Flake Japanese Mini LP CD

34) Smashing Pumpkins - 1991 -1998 CD (Best Of) Promo CD **35)** Kendra Smith/Dream Syndicate/Opal - The Guild Of Temporal Adventures CD (w/fold out cardbord cover) **36)** Michael W. Smith - I Will Be Here For You Promo CD **37)** Michael W. Smith - Place In This World Promo (3 Remixes) CD **38)** Michael W. Smith - Kentucky Rose Promo CD **39)** Michael W. Smith - Picture Perfect (6 Remixes) Promo CD **40)** Michael W. Smith - All Access Promo CD (free with Worship Again) **41)** Michael W. Smith - Columbine (What Have We Learned?) Promo CD

42) Michael W. Smith - For You (5 Remixes) Promo CD **43)** Michael W. Smith - Somebody Love Me Promo CD

44) Patti Smith - The Patti Smith Masters CD Boxed Set **45)** Patti Smith - Patti Smith Promo CD Sampler

46) Smiths - Sheila Take A Bow CD **47)** Smiths - Stop Me CD **48)** Smothers Brothers - Aesop's Fables CD

49) Jill Sobule - Think Pink Promo CD (w/ Pink Case) **50)** Sonics - Full Force CD **51)** Sopwith Camel - The Miraculous Hump Returns From The Moon CD **52)** Phil Spector - Back To Mono (1958-1969) CD Boxed Set

53) Jon Spencer/Blues Explosion - Self Title Japanese CD **54)** Spiders From Mars - Self Titled CD **55)** Spirit - The Twelve Dreams Of Dr. Sardonicus MFSL Aluminum CD **56)** Spirit - The Mercury Years 2-CD

57) Spirit - The Adventures Of Kaptain Kopter And Commander Cassidy In Potatoland CD **58)** Spirit - Nature's Way CD Single **59)** Spitballs - Self Titled CD (Beserkley Various Artists) **60)** Spock's Beard - Snow Limited Hardback Cd Version

61) Spock's Beard - Snow Limited Edition 3 CD Version **62)** Bruce Springsteen - Born To Run Japanese Mini LP CD **63)** Bruce Springsteen - Before The Fame 2 CD (Recalled Early Springsteen) **64)** Bruce Springsteen Nebraska Japanese Mini LP CD

Page 279

1) Bruce Springsteen - Nebraska (Front And Back of the Promo w/ Extended My Father's House/Clocks in at 5 Minutes and 35 seconds/Regular Version is 5 Minutes and 4 seconds. However, the regular CD clocks in at 40 Minutes and 47 seconds for the whole CD and the rare version clocks in at 40 Minutes and 24 seconds. The way to know for sure that you have the rare version is there is <u>No</u> Made In The USA on the back of the case of the CD.)

2) Bruce Springsteen - Tracks Promo Sampler CD **3)** Spyro Gyra - Retrospective Limited Edition Numbered Promo CD **4)** Squeeze/Difford & Tilbrook - Self Titled CD **5)** Chris Stamey/Friends - Christmas Time CD **6)** Ringo Starr/All Starrs - Third All Starr Band, Vol. 1, Blockbuster CD **7)** Ringo Starr/All Starrs - And His All Starr Band Limited Edition w/Bonus CD **8)** Ringo Starr - You Never Know Curly Sue Promo CD **9)** Ringo Starr - Old Wave CD

10) Ringo Starr - Old Wave/Stop And Smell The Roses Promo CD Sampler (w/Unreleased Paul McCartney Track)

11) Ringo Starr - Stop And Smell The Roses CD **12)** Ringo Starr - Weight Of The World CD Single

13) Star Wars - A New Hope (Hear Star Wars The Way It Was Meant To Be Heard!) Promo CD Sampler

14) Steel Yard Blues - Original Soundtrack (with Nick Gravenites, Mike Bloomfield, Paul Butterfield & Maria Muldaur) Japanese CD **15)** Steely Dan - Remasters Promo CD Sampler **16)** Steely Dan - SFX Network Presents Steely Dan, Feb. 15-18, 2001 Promo CD **17)** Jim Steinman - Pandora's Box Original Sin (w/Ellen Foley) CD

18) Cat Stevens/Yusuf Islam - The Life Of The Last Prophet CD **19)** Rod Stewart - Storyteller CD Boxed Set

20) Al Stewart - Last Days Of The Century CD

Page 279 continued

21) Al Stewart - Year Of The Cat MFSL Aluminum CD (The song "If It Doesn't Come Naturally, Leave It" has a momentary skip on all copies of the CD) 22) Stiffs Live - Self Titled (with Elvis Costello, Nick Lowe, Wreckless Eric & Ian Dury) 23) Stephen Stills - Right By You CD 24) Stephen Stills - Illegal Stills CD 25) Sting - Peter And The Wolf CD 26) Sting - Nada Como El Sol (Spanish & Portuguese Selections of "Nothing Like The Sun") 27) Sly/Family Stone - A Whole New Thing Japanese CD 28) Stooges/Iggy Pop - Night Of Destruction Boxed Set 29) Stories - Self Titled CD 30) Strawberry Statement - Original Soundtrack CD (with Crosby, Stills, Nash & Young/Thunderclap Newman) 31) Stray Cats - Something Else Live Japanese CD 32) Streetband/Paul Young - Self Titled & London & Dilemma 2-CD 33) Styx - Man Of Miracles Japanese CD 34) Sugar - File Under Easy Listening Promotional CD File Boxed Set 35) Sun City - Artists United Against Apartheid CD (with Lou Reed, Peter Gabriel & Kate Bush)

36) Superstars In Concert/Prince's Trust - Self Titled CD (with Paul McCartney, Elton John, Ringo Starr, Eric Clapton, Tina Turner & Phil Collins) 37) Matthew Sweet - Blue Sky On Mars (Best Buy Bonus CD) 38) Matthew Sweet - Live From The Pit Global Satellite Network, May 26-June 2, 1997, Promo CD 39) Sweet Thursday - Self Titled CD (with Jon Mark & Nicky Hopkins) 40) Trapeze - Self Titled CD signed by the band 41) Bernie Taupin/Elton John/Farm Dogs - Immigrant Sons Advance CD (has different artwork than regular release) 42) John Tavener - The Whale Apple CD 43) James Taylor - Self Titled Apple CD 44) James Taylor - J.T. SACD 45) Terry & The Pirates - The Doubtful Handshake CD 46) Terry & The Pirates - Wind Dancer CD 47) B.J. Thomas - Greatest Hits Vol. 1 CD Signed by B.J. 48) Richard Thompson - Watching The Dark Promo CD Sampler 49) Richard Thompson - It (Selections from the You?Me?Us? Promo CD) 50) Billy Thorpe - Children Of The Sun CD 51) Three Dog Night - Harmony CD (Signed by the band) 52) Tiny Tim - God Bless Tiny Tim Japanese CD 53) Toad The Wet Sprocket - House Of Toad Promo CD (1989-1997) 54) Tool - Salival CD/DVD Boxed Set (with Clear Outside Slip-On Cover) 55) To Sir With Love - Original Soundtrack CD (with Lulu)

56) Pete Townshend - Interview With A Psychoderelict Promo CD 57) Pete Townshend - Live CDI 2-Video CD 58) Pete Townshend - Avatar CD Boxed Set (Mehar Baba Albums) 59) Pete Townshend - Live At The Fillmore 1996 Mini LP CD 60) Pete Townshend - The Lifehouse Chronicles Boxed Set 6-CDs 61) Pete Townshend - Psychoderelict (Censored & Uncensored Promo CD) 62) Pete Townshend - Scoop 3 Mini LP CD 63) Pete Townshend - Who Came First Limited Edition Hardback CD

Page 280

1) Pete Townshend - Windswept Pacific Promo 3-CD Boxed Set 2) Traffic - The Low Spark Of High Heeled Boys MFSL Gold CD 3) Traffic - Mr. Fantasy MFSL Gold CD 4) Doris Troy - Self Titled Apple CD 5) Maureen Tucker - Waiting For My Men CD (with Lou Reed, John Cale & Sterling Morrison) 6) Jethro Tull - Thick As A Brick MFSL Gold CD 7) Jethro Tull - Benefit Japanese Mini LP CD 8) Jethro Tull - The Ultimate Boxed Set (with Aqualung 25th Anniversary CD/Aqualung Picture Disc LP/25th Anniversary Video & signed sheet by Ian Anderson) 9) Jethro Tull - King Biscuit Flower Hour (March 19, 1989) Promo CD 10) Jethro Tull - Rocks On The Road CD Single 11) Jethro Tull - Stand Up MFSL Gold CD (with Pop-Up Booklet) 12) Jethro Tull - Living In The Past MFSL Gold 2-CD

13) Jethro Tull - Westwood One, Show #00-44, Oct. 28-29, 2000 Promo CD 14) Jethro Tull - A Gift Of Roses/Christmas Song 2000 Promo CD 15) Jethro Tull - Christmas Sampler Promo CD 16) Tina Turner - Private Dancer JVC XRCD 17) Tina Turner/Ike - River Deep Mountain High MFSL Aluminum CD 18) Dwight Twilley Band - Twilley Don't Mind CD 19) Twisted Sister - Big Hits & Nasty Cuts Best Of Japanese CD 20) Rob Tyner/MC5 - Blood Brothers CD 21) Rob Tyner/MC5 - It's Only Rock And Roll Promo CD 22) U2 - 7 Rare And Remixed Target CD

23) U2 - Westwood One - In Concert, Show #00-35, August 26-27, 2000 Promo 2-CD 24) U2 - Westwood One - In Concert, Show #98-15, April 6, 1998 Promo 2-CD 25) U2 - Westwood One - In Concert, Show #99-47, Nov. 20-21, 1999 Promo 2-CD 26) U2 - Unforgettable Fire MFSL Gold CD 27) UK - Danger Money CD 28) Tracey Ullman - You Broke My Heart In 17 Places CD 29) Tracey Ullman - You Caught Me Out CD 30) Tracey Ullman - Forever CD 31) Ultradisc II - Sampler MFSL Gold CD 32) Ultraman - Original Soundtrack Japanese CD Boxed Set 33) Undertones - On CD At Last! Promo CD Sampler 34) Urgh! - A Music War CD (with The Go-Go's, Police, XTC, Echo & The Bunnymen, Gary Numan, Devo, Dead Kennedys, The Cramps & Joan Jett & The Blackhearts) 35) Van Halen - Mini Best Japanese Isuzu CD 36) Stevie Ray Vaughn - Selections From SRV Promo CD Sampler 37) Velvet Underground - White Light White Heat Japanese Mini LP CD 38) Velvet Underground - Live 1969 Japanese Mini LP CD 39) Velvet Underground - Selections From Peel Slowly And See CD Boxed Set Promo Sampler 40) Velvet Underground - Live MCMXCIII (1993) Limited Edition CD (Black Vinyl with Peel Off Bananas) 41) Velvet Underground - And Nico Limited Edition Numbered CD (with Peel Off Banana) 42) Velvet Underground - The Peeling Of The Velvet Underground Greek Promo CD

Page 280 continued

43) Verve Pipe - Album Network Oct. 1-5, 1997 Promo 2-CD **44)** A Very Special Christmas - with Madonna, Eurythmics, Whitney Houston, Bon Jovi, U2, John Mellencamp & Sting **45)** Gene Vincent - Bird Doggin' The Complete Challenge Sessions CD **46)** Virtually Alternative - Album Network Promo CD (with XCT Live) **47)** Voiceprint - Voiceprint Newsprint Issue 5 Promo Sampler CD **48)** Oliver Wakeman/Clive Nolan - Hound Of The Baskervilles CD (with narration by Robert Powell) **49)** Rick Wakeman - Lisztomania Japanese CD **50)** Rick Wakeman/Wakeman with Wakeman - The Official Live Bootleg CD (Limited Edition Numbered Piano Shaped Box Set) **51)** Rick Wakeman - Rhapsodies Japanese CD **52)** Rick Wakeman - Treasure Chest Limited Edition Numbered CD Boxed Set **53)** Joe Walsh - Barnstorm MFSL Aluminum CD **54)** Jeff Wayne - War Of The Worlds 2-CD (with narration by Richard Burton/with Justin Hayward, David Essex & Phil Lynott) **55)** Roger Waters/Ron Geesin - Music For The Body CD

56) We Are The World - Self Titled CD (with Michael Jackson, Bruce Springsteen, Lionel Richie & Tina Turner)

57) Paul Weller - Heavy Soul Limited Edition CD (with 5 prints) **58)** Paul Westerberg - Suicaine Gratification Limited Edition CD Boxed Set **59)** What's Shakin' - Self Titled CD (with Lovin' Spoonful, Powerhouse with Eric Clapton & Stevie Winwood, Paul Butterfield Blues Band) **60)** Alan White - Ramshackled Japanese CD (with Jon Anderson of Yes) **61)** Who - 30th Anniversary Promo CD Sampler **62)** Who - 30 Years Of Maximum R&B Promo CD Sampler

63) Who - Rarities 1966-1972 Vol. 1 & 2, Japanese CD **64)** Who - BBC Sessions (with Bonus Best Buy CD)

Page 281

1) Who - Who's Last 2-CD Set **2)** Who - Live At Leed's Limited Numbered Edition Album Sized CD Boxed Set (with all inserts of original album) **3)** Who - Live At Leed's MFSL Gold CD **4)** Who - Quadrophenia MFSL Gold 2-CD

5) Who - Tommy CD (Ode with Ringo Starr, Merry Clayton & Rod Stewart) **6)** Who - Two's Missing CD

7) Who - Who's Next MFSL CD **8)** Wild Turkey - Battle Hymn CD **9)** John Williams - Indiana Jones And The Temple Of Doom Japanese CD **10)** Brian Wilson/Van Dyke Parks - Words And Music Promo CD **11)** Dennis Wilson/Beach Boys - Pacific Ocean Blue CD **12)** When The Wind Blows - Original Soundtrack (with David Bowie & Squeeze)

13) Wings/Paul McCartney - Hits & History Promo CD Sampler **14)** Winter Warnerland - Christmas CD (with George Harrison, Jessie Ed Davis & PeeWee Herman) **15)** Steve Winwood - Back In The High Life MFSL Gold CD

16) Stevie Wonder - At The Close Of A Century CD Boxed Set **17)** Woodstock - One and Two MFSL Limited Numbered Aluminum CD (without outer box) **18)** Woodstock - One and Two MFSL Limited Numbered Aluminum CD (with outer box)

19) Woodstock - CD Boxed Set (with Outtakes) **20)** Bruce Wooley/Camera Club/Buggles - English Garden CD **21)** Wreckless Eric/Le Beat Group Electrique - Self Titled CD **22)** Richard Wright/Pink Floyd - Wet Dream CD **23)** XTC - The Coat Of Many Cupboards Promo CD Sampler **24)** XTC - Dear God CD Single (with the Homo Safari Series) **25)** XTC - The Greatest Limited Edition Japanese CD (Rarities) **26)** XTC - King For A Day CD Single (with Crown Slipcase) **27)** XTC - The Loving 3" CD Single **28)** XTC - NAC Sampler Promo CD

29) XTC - Radios In Motion A History Of Promo CD Sampler **30)** XTC - Rag & Bone Buffet Promo CD Sampler

31) XTC - Senses Working Overtime 3" CD Single **32)** XTC - What Do You Call That Noise? Promo CD Sampler

33) Yardbirds - Little Games Sessions & More 2-CD **34)** Yes - The Best Of Yes 1970-1987 Japanese CD

35) Yes - Affirmative: The Yes Solo Family Album (with Track from Jon Anderson's Animation Album)

36) Yes - Fragile Japanese Mini LP CD **37)** Yes - Selections From Magnification & House Of Blues JVC DVD Audio CD **38)** Yes - King Biscuit Flower Hour, March 27-April 2, 2000 Promo CD **39)** Yes - Open Your Eyes Surround Sound CD **40)** Yes - New State Of Mind Promo CD **41)** Yes - YesSymphonic Promo CD **42)** Yes - Westwood One, Show #97-10, March 3, 1997 Promo CD **43)** Youngbloods - Ride The Wind CD **44)** Neil Young/Crazy Horse - The Complex Sessions CD **45)** Neil Young - Words And Music Promo CD **46)** Neil Young - Don't Spook The Horse Promo CD Sampler **47)** Frank Zappa - Apostrophe Rykodisc AU Gold CD **48)** Frank Zappa - Beat The Boots! CD Limited Edition Boxed Set, Vol. 1 **49)** Frank Zappa - Beat The Boots! CD Limited Edition Boxed Set, Vol. 2

50) Frank Zappa - Clean American Version Promo CD **51)** Frank Zappa - Dancin' Fool Japanese Promo Mini LP CD **52)** Frank Zappa - Ditties And Beer Promo CD **53)** Frank Zappa - Hot Rats Rykodisc Gold CD **54)** Frank Zappa - Kill Ugly Radio Promo CD **55)** Frank Zappa - Kill Ugly Radio Some More Promo CD **56)** Frank Zappa - Return Of The Son Of Kill Ugly Radio Promo CD **57)** Frank Zappa - Left Of The Dial Promo CD **58)** Frank Zappa - Half A Dozen Provocative Squats Promo CD **59)** Frank Zappa - Strictly Commercial Promo CD (with a Red Case) **60)** Zetospective - Dancing In The Face Of Adversity Promo 2-CD (with John Cale) **61)** Warren Zevon - Bad Luck Streak In Dancing School **62)** Led Zeppelin - The Complete Studio Recordings CD Boxed Set **63)** Jethro Tull - 25th Anniversary Cigar CD Boxed Set

Page 282 (Boxed Sets)

1) Aerosmith - Pandora's Box CD Boxed Set **2)** Asia - Quadra CD Boxed Set **3)** Joan Baez - Rare, Live & Classic CD Boxed Set **4)** Band - Across The Great Divide CD Boxed Set **5)** Syd Barrett - Crazy Diamond CD Boxed Set **6)** Jeff Beck - Self Titled CD Boxed Set **7)** Blue Thumb - All Day Thumbsucker Revisited CD Boxed Set (with Mark Almond & The Crusaders) **8)** Bonanza - Ponderosa Party Time! Various Artists CD Boxed Set (with Original Cast Members) **9)** James Brown - Star Time CD Boxed Set **10)** Byrds - Self Titled Black Box CD Boxed Set **11)** Harry Chapin - Story Of A Life CD Boxed Set **12)** Cher - Love Hurts Promo CD Wooden Box Set (with Tarot Cards) **13)** Joe Cocker - The Long Voyage Home CD Boxed Set **14)** Cream - Wheels Of Fire DCC Gold CD Boxed Set **15)** Doris Day - Pillow Talk CD Boxed Set **16)** Doris Day - It's Magic 1947-1950 CD Boxed Set **17)** Doris Day - Move Over Darling 1960-1967 CD Boxed Set **18)** Doris Day - Que Sera 1956-1959 CD Boxed Set **19)** Doris Day - Secret Love 1951-1955 CD Boxed Set **20)** Derek & The Dominos - The Layla Sessions 20th Anniversary Edition CD Boxed Set (with Outtakes) **21)** Disney - 75 Years Of Music & Memories CD Boxed Set **22)** ELP/Emerson, Lake & Palmer - Return Of The Manticore CD Boxed Set **23)** Fairport Convention - Unconventional CD Boxed Set **24)** Fleetwood Mac - Complete Blue Horizon Sessions 1967-1969 CD Boxed Set **25)** John Fogerty - Centerfield (with Zanz Cantz Danz/Recalled CD/later changed to Vanz Canz Danz). This picture was put here because I wanted to show the CD with the Original Longbox. **26)** Gong - Radio Gnome Trilogy CD Boxed Set **27)** Geri Halliwell/Spice Girls - Schizophonic Boxed Set (with CD, Keychain, Poster & Video) **28)** Humble Pie - The Immediate Years CD Boxed Set **29)** Jam - Direction, Reaction, Creation CD Boxed Set **30)** Jefferson Airplane - Loves You CD Boxed Set **31)** Jellyfish - Fan Club CD Boxed Set **32)** King Crimson - The Great Deceiver CD Boxed Set

Page 283 (Boxed Sets)

1) King Crimson - Thrak Limited Gold CD In Tin Case (this was put in boxed sets to show full effect) **2)** Megadeth - Cryptic Writings CD Special Limited Edition (with Blockbuster Bonus CD/Chaos Comic Book Trading Card) (this was put in boxed sets to show full effect) **3)** Steve Miller Band - Self Titled CD Boxed Set **4)** Monty Python's Flying Circus - The Instant Monty Python CD Collection Boxed Set **5)** Mott The Hoople - All The Young Dudes Anthology CD Boxed Set **6)** Bill Mumy/Lost In Space/Seduction Of The Innocent - The Golden Age CD (This was put in boxed sets to show full effect in plastic longbox) **7)** National Lampoon - The Best Of National Lampoon Radio Hour, Buy This Box Or We'll Shoot This Dog CD Boxed Set **8)** Bill Nelson - Noise Candy CD Boxed Set **9)** Randy Newman - Guilty: 30 Years Of Randy Newman CD Boxed Set **10)** PFM/Premiata Forneria Marconi - 10 Anni Live 1971-1981 Official Bootleg Series CD Boxed Set **11)** Pink Floyd - Shine On CD Boxed Set (with Bonus Digipack Early Singles, 8 Post Cards, 112-page Hardcover Book & Folded Cardboard Box) **12)** Police - Message In A Box CD Boxed Set **13)** Elvis Presley - The Complete 50's Masters CD Boxed Set (with stamps) **14)** Elvis Presley - The Other Sides Limited Edition Numbered CD Boxed Set **15)** Otis Redding - Otis! CD Boxed Set **16)** Roxy Music - The Thrill Of It All CD Boxed Set **17)** School House Rock! - Self Titled CD Boxed Set **18)** Spinners - Best Of The '70's & '80's CD Boxed Set (7 Albums) **19)** Squeeze - Six Of One Limited Edition Numbered CD Boxed Set **20)** Star Wars - Trilogy CD Boxed Set **21)** Steely Dan - Citizen Steely Dan 1972-1980 CD Boxed Set **22)** Max Steiner - Gone With The Wind CD Boxed Set **23)** Style Council - Complete Adventures Of Style Council CD Boxed Set **24)** Tangerine Dream - Tangents 1973-1983 CD Boxed Set **25)** Thin Lizzy - Vagabond Kings Warriors Angels CD Boxed Set **26)** T. Rex/Tyranosaurus Rex - Self Titled CD Boxed Set **27)** Jethro Tull - Twenty Years Of Jethro Tull CD Boxed Set **28)** Van Der Graaf Generator - The Box CD Boxed Set **29)** Velvet Underground - Final V.U. 1971-1973 Japanese CD Boxed Set (without Lou Reed) **30)** Who - Join Together CD Boxed Set **31)** Yes - Yes Years CD Boxed Set **32)** Zombies - Zombie Heaven CD Boxed Set

Artist	Title	Format	Label	Catalog No	Country	Released	Value
Moxy	Ridin' High	CD	Peacemaker	PACE-018	Canada	1994	8.99
Moxy	Self Titled	CD	Unidisc Music	AGEK-2241	Canada	2003	12.99
Moxy	Self Titled	CD	Peacemaker	PACE-016	Canada	1994	8.99
Moxy	Tribute To Buzz Sherman	CD	Unidisc Music	AGEK-2245	Canada	2003	12.99
Moxy	Under The Lights	CD	Unidisc Music	AGEK-2244	Canada	2003	12.99
Moxy	V	CD	Perris	PER5101-2	Canada	2000	8.99
Moxy	V + 1 (Live)	CD	Record Heaven	RHCD50	Sweden	2001	12.99
Moxy	V + 2 (Live)	CD	Bullseye	BLP-CD-4057	Canada	2002	12.99
Moxy/Leigh Ashford	Kinfolk	CD	Peacemaker	PACE-009	Canada	1994	14.99
Mozart	Mozart + 3	CD	Teichiku	TECX-25696	Japan	1994	13.99
Mozart, Wolfgang Amadeus	Die Gesamten Klaviersonaten (Teil 1)	CD	Line	CACD-9.00851-P	Germany	1990	12.99
Mozart, Wolfgang Amadeus	Die Gesamten Klaviersonaten (Teil 2)	CD	Line	CACD-9.00920-P	Germany	1990	12.99
Mozart, Wolfgang Amadeus	Die Gesamten Klaviersonaten (Teil 3)	CD	Line	CACD-9.00921-P	Germany	1990	12.99
Mozart, Wolfgang Amadeus	Die Gesamten Klaviersonaten (Tiel 4)	CD	Line	CACD-9.00922-P	Germany	1990	12.99
Mozart, Wolfgang Amadeus	Die Gesamten Klaviersonaten (Tiel 5)	CD	Line	CACD-9.00923-P	Germany	1990	12.99
Mr. Big	Japandemonium	CD	East West	AMCY-710	Japan	1994	21.99
Mr. Big	Live! Raw Like Sushi	CD Single	East West	AMCY-159	Japan	1990	21.99
Mrs Green	Mrs Green	CD	Line	BECD-9.00580-0	Germany	1988	12.99
Muldaur, Geoff	Blues Boy	CD	Rounder	11661-9635-2	U.S.A.	2001	8.99
Muldaur, Geoff	Password	CD	HighTone	HCD-8125	U.S.A.	2000	8.99
Muldaur, Geoff/Maria	Pottery Pie	CD	Warner Bros.	WPCP-3532	Japan	1987	99.99
Muldaur, Maria	Live In London	CD	Angel Air	SJPCD109	Austria	2002	9.99
Muldaur, Maria	Maria Muldaur	CD	Reprise	2148-2	U.S.A.	1973	11.99
Muldaur, Maria	Open Your Eyes (W/Stevie Wonder)	CD	Warner Bros.	WPCP-3630	Japan	1979	99.99
Muldaur, Maria	Richland Woman Blues + 2	CD	Pryaid	YDCD-0051	Japan	2001	24.99
Muldaur, Maria	Waitress In A Donut Shop	CD	Warner Bros.	WPCP-3627	Japan	1974	14.99
Muldaur, Maria	Waitress In A Donut Shop	CD	Reprise	2194-2	U.S.A.	1974	9.99
Mull, Martin	And His Fabulous Furniture...	CD	Capricorn	314-558-001-2	U.S.A.	1998	12.99
Mull, Martin	Mulling It Over... (Best Of)	CD	Razor & Tie	82178	U.S.A.	1998	12.99
Mulligan, Gerry/Ben Webster	Mulligan Meets Webster (MFSL Gold)	CD	Mobile Fidelity	UDCD-644	U.S.A.	1959	24.99
Mullins, Shawn	What Is Life (Promo)	CD	American	CSK-42386	U.S.A.	1999	7.99
Mumy, Bill/Lost In Space	Seduction Of Innocent/Golden Age	CD	Beat Bros.	BBRCD-6003	U.S.A.	1990	14.99
Mungo Jerry	Baby Jump	2CD	Essential	ESACD777	England	2000	17.99
Mungo Jerry	In The Summertime	CD	Castle	PIESD164	England	2000	8.99
Mungo Jerry	In The Summertime + 2	CD	Repertoire	REP-4177-WZ	Germany	1998	29.99
Mungo Jerry	Memoirs/Stockbroker (Electronically T)	CD	Repertoire	REP-4179-WZ	Germany	1991	29.99
Mungo Jerry	Self Titled	Mini Lp	Victor Ent.	VICP-62239	Japan	2003	44.99
Mungo Jerry	Self Titled/Electronically Tested	2CD	BGO	BGOCD286	England	1996	24.99
Mungo Jerry	The Best Of	CD	Music Club	MCCD-292	England	1998	7.99
Mungo Jerry	The Best Of	CD	Disky	SI-995442	Holland	2000	8.99
Mungo Jerry	The Early Years	CD	Dojo	EARLD3	England	1994	8.99
Mungo Jerry	The Very Best Of	CD	Sanctuary	06076-81171-2	U.S.A.	2002	8.99
Mungo Jerry	You Don't Have To Be.../Boot Power	2CD	BGO	BGOCD292	England	1996	24.99
Murray, Anne	Interview/Sampler (Promo)	CD	SBK	DPRO-04602	U.S.A.	1993	29.99
Muse	Muse EP (Ltd To 999)	CD Single	Dangerous	DREX-CDEP103	England	1998	335.99
Music Explosion	Anthology	CD	One Way	OW-18260	U.S.A.	1995	19.99
Music Explosion	Little Bit O' Soul	CD	Repertoire	REP-4576-WY	Germany	1995	24.99
Music Explosion	Little Bit O' Soul: The Best Of	CD	Sundazed	SC-11119	U.S.A.	2002	9.99
Music Machine	The Music Machine	CD	Repertoire	REP-4154-WZ	Germany	1991	24.99
Myrow, Fred/M Seagrave	Phantasm/+ 5 Phantasm II Trks (OST)	CD	Silva Screen	FILM-CD-071	England	1991	34.99
Mystery Romance	Human Sexuality	CD	Line	CUCD-9.00988-0	Germany	1990	6.99
Mystic Moods Orchestra	Another Stormy Night (MFSL Silve Cd)	CD	Mobile Fidelity	MFCD-821	U.S.A.	1983	79.99
Mystic Moods Orchestra	Nightide	CD	Capitol	66687	U.S.A.	1995	29.99
Mystic Moods Orchestra	One Stormy Night	CD	Capitol	66695	U.S.A.	1995	74.99
Mystic Moods Orchestra	Stormy Weekend	CD	Capitol	66695	U.S.A.	1995	44.99

Artist	Title	Format	Label	Catalog No	Country	Released	Value

N

Artist	Title	Format	Label	Catalog No	Country	Released	Value
Naess, Leona	I Tried To Rock You...	CD	MCA	088-112-699-2	U.S.A.	2001	7.99
Namba, Hiroyuki	Armitage III (O.S.T.)	CD	Pioneer	PICD-1002A	U.S.A.	1996	8.99
Nash, Graham	Earth & Sky	CD	Magic	1982202	France	2001	18.99
Nash, Graham	Innocent Eyes	CD	Atlantic	7-81633-2	U.S.A.	1986	14.99
Nash, Graham	Songs For Beginners	CD	Atlantic	7204-2	U.S.A.	1971	11.99
Nash, Graham	Songs For Survivors	CD	Artemis	751130-2	U.S.A.	2002	8.99
Nash, Graham	Wild Tales	CD	Atlantic	7288-2	U.S.A.	1973	9.99
National Health	Complete (All 3 Lps + 1)	2CD	East Side Digital	ESD-80402	U.S.A.	1990	42.99
National Health	D.S. Al Coda	CD	Voiceprint	VP129CD	England	1996	18.99
National Health	Missing Pieces	CD	Voiceprint	VP113CD	England	1996	18.99
National Health	Missing Pieces	CD	East Side Digital	ESD-81172	U.S.A.	1996	18.99
National Health	Of Queue And Cures	CD	Decal	CDLIK-70	England	1995	9.99
National Health	Playtime	CD	Cuneiform	CUNE-145	U.S.A.	2001	12.99
National Health	Self Titled	CD	Decal	CDLIK-66	England	1995	14.99
National Health/Alan Gowen	Before A Word... (W/ Richard Sinclair)	CD	Voiceprint	VP130CD	England	1996	22.99
National Health/Alan Gowen	Improvisations (W/Hugh Hopper)	CD	Voiceprint	VP186CD	England	1995	15.99
National Health/Alan Gowen	Two Rainbows Daily (W/Hugh Hopper)	CD	Cuneiform	RUNE-77	U.S.A.	1996	15.99
National Lampoon/V.A.	Buy This Box Set Or We'll Shoot...	3CD	Rhino	R2-72263	U.S.A.	1996	39.99
Nazareth	2 X S + 8	CD	Eagle	EAMCD141	Germany	2002	11.99
Nazareth	Back To The Trenches	2CD	Castle	CMEDD725	England	2003	15.99
Nazareth	BBC Radio One Live In Concert	CD	Windsong	WINCD005	England	1992	14.99
Nazareth	Boogaloo	CD	CMC Int.	06076-86263-2	U.S.A.	1999	7.99
Nazareth	Cinema + 4	CD	Eagle	EAMCD128	Germany	2001	11.99
Nazareth	Classics, Vol. 16	CD	A&M	75021-2514-2	U.S.A.	1991	6.99
Nazareth	Close Enough For Rock 'N' Roll	CD	A&M	75021-3109-2	U.S.A.	1976	7.99
Nazareth	Close Enough For Rock 'N' Roll + 7	CD	Eagle	EAMCD138	Germany	2002	11.99
Nazareth	Exercises + 4	CD	Eagle	EAMCD146	Germany	2002	11.99
Nazareth	Expect No Mercy	CD	A&M	75021-3343-2	U.S.A.	1977	8.99
Nazareth	Expect No Mercy + 7	CD	Eagle	EAMCD140	Germany	2002	11.99
Nazareth	From The Vaults	CD	Sequel	NEM-CD-639	England	1993	24.99
Nazareth	Greatest Hits	CD	A&M	314-540-513-2	U.S.A.	1996	6.99
Nazareth	Greatest Hits + 5	CD	Essential	ESMCD369	England	1996	11.99
Nazareth	Greatest Hits, Vol. 2	CD	Essential	ESMCD597	England	1999	13.99
Nazareth	Hair Of The Dog	CD	A&M	75021-3225-2	U.S.A.	1975	7.99
Nazareth	Hair Of The Dog + 6	CD	Eagle	EAMCD127	Germany	2001	11.99
Nazareth	Hair Of The Dog + 6	Mini Lp	Victor Ent.	VICP-61833	Japan	2002	29.99
Nazareth	Homecoming	CD	Eagle	EAMCD204	Germany	2002	8.99
Nazareth	Hot Tracks	CD	A&M	75021-3226-2	U.S.A.	1977	7.99
Nazareth	Live At The Beeb	2CD	Snapper	SMDCD272	England	2000	12.99
Nazareth	Loud 'N' Proud + 4	CD	Eagle	EAMCD133	Germany	2001	11.99
Nazareth	Love Hurts: The Rock Ballads	CD	Music Club	MCCD486	England	2002	8.99
Nazareth	Malice In Wonderland + 7	CD	Eagle	EAMCD136	Germany	2002	11.99
Nazareth	Move Me + 7	CD	Eagle	EAMCD149	Germany	2002	11.99
Nazareth	No Jive	CD	Griffin	55421-3932-2	U.S.A.	1991	7.99
Nazareth	No Jive +4	CD	Eagle	EAMCD148	Germany	2002	11.99
Nazareth	No Mean City + 5	CD	Eagle	EAMCD135	Germany	2002	11.99
Nazareth	Play 'N' The Game + 7	CD	Eagle	EAMCD139	Germany	2002	11.99
Nazareth	Rampant + 4	CD	Eagle	EAMCD134	Germany	2001	11.99
Nazareth	Razamanaz	CD	A&M	75021-3342-2	U.S.A.	1971	7.99
Nazareth	Razmanaz + 3	CD	Eagle	EAMCD132	Germany	2001	11.99
Nazareth	Self Titled	CD	A&M	75021-3169-2	U.S.A.	1972	7.99

Artist	Title	Format	Label	Catalog No	Country	Released	Value
Nazareth	Self Titled + 6	CD	Eagle	EAMCD145	England	2002	11.99
Nazareth	Snakes 'N' Ladders + 6	CD	Eagle	EAMCD143	Germany	2002	11.99
Nazareth	'Snaz	CD	A&M	75021-6703-2	U.S.A.	1981	10.99
Nazareth	'Snaz + 4 (W/Bonus Cd)	2CD	Eagle	EAMCD382	Germany	2001	22.99
Nazareth	Sound Elixir + 5	CD	Eagle	EAMCD147	Germany	2002	11.99
Nazareth	The Catch + 4	CD	Eagle	EAMCD142	Germany	2002	11.99
Nazareth	The Fool Circle + 7	CD	Eagle	EAMCD137	Germany	2002	11.99
Nazareth	Then And Now	CD	Sanctuary	06076-86328-2	U.S.A.	2002	8.99
Nazareth/Dan McCafferty	Into The Ride	CD	Eagle	EDMCD144	England	2002	11.99
Nazareth/Dan McCafferty	Self Titled	CD	Sequel	NEMCD-640	England	1994	11.99
Nazareth/Dan McCafferty	Self Titled + 7/Into The Ride + 2	2CD	Eagle	EDMCD144	Germany	2002	15.99
Nazareth/Manny Charlton	Drool	CD	Red Steel	RMCCD9210	U.S.A.	1999	10.99
Nazareth/Manny Charlton	Stonkin'	CD	Record Heaven	41	Sweden	2002	10.99
Negativeland	I Still Havn't Found....(Recalled U2 Cvr)	CD	SST	CD-272	U.S.A.	1991	99.99
Negron, Chuck/3 Dog Night	Am I Still In Your Heart	CD	Viceroy	VIC-8024-2	U.S.A.	1995	6.99
Negron, Chuck/3 Dog Night	Joy To The World	CD	Golden Arrow	0UF23<1005>	U.S.A.	1996	6.99
Neil, Vince	Carved In Stone +2	CD	Warner Bros.	WPCR-239	Japan	1995	19.99
Nektar	A Tab In The Ocean	CD	Bellaphon	289-09-002	Germany	1972	13.99
Nektar	Down To Earth	CD	Bellaphon	289-09-006	Germany	1974	13.99
Nektar	Greatest Hits Live	2CD	Classic Rock	CRP1010	England	2002	15.99
Nektar	Journey To The Centre Of The Eye	CD	Bellaphon	289-09-007	Germany	1971	13.99
Nektar	Live In New York	CD	Bellaphon	288-09-102	Germany	1991	12.99
Nektar	Magic Is A Child	CD	Bellaphon	289-09-005	Germany	1977	14.99
Nektar	Man In The Moon	CD	Voiceprint	VP259CD	Austria	2002	13.99
Nektar	More Live Nektar In New York	CD	Bellaphon	288-09-008	Germany	1991	12.99
Nektar	Nektar	CD	Bellaphon	288-09-001	Germany	1987	13.99
Nektar	Nektar - Highlights	2CD	Bellaphon	993-09-001	Germany	1987	14.99
Nektar	Recycled	CD	Bellaphon	289-09-003	Germany	1975	13.99
Nektar	Remember The Future + 2	CD	Bellaphon	9724426	Germany	2002	18.99
Nektar	Sounds Like This	CD	Bellaphon	290-09-003	Germany	1990	16.99
Nektar	Sunday Night At London Roundhouse	CD	Bellaphon	289-09-006	Germany	1974	12.99
Nektar	Sunday Night/London Roundhouse	2CD	Bellaphon	9724327	England	2002	24.99
Nektar	The Dream Nebula (1971 To 1975)	2CD	Purple Pyramid	CLP-0301-2	U.S.A.	1998	17.99
Nektar	The Prodigal Son	CD	Bellaphon	9729520	Germany	2001	11.99
Nektar	Unidentified Flying Abstract	CD	Bellaphon	9724525	England	2002	19.99
Nektar/Roye Albrighton	The Follies Of Rupert Treacle	CD	Voiceprint	VP260CD	Austria	2002	16.99
Nelson, Bill	Electricity Made Us Angels	CD	Populuxe	POPU003CD	EU	1995	14.99
Nelson, Bill	Noise Candy Box Set	6CD	Phantom	B00006SF98	England	2001	119.99
Nelson, Bill	Northern Dream	CD	Smiled	SM777CD	England	1971	14.99
Nelson, Bill	Quit Dreaming And Get on the Beam	CD	Enigma	7-73385-2	Canada	1989	25.99
Nelson, Bill	Sounding the Ritual Echo	CD	Enigma	7-73382-2	Canada	1989	29.99
Nelson, Bill	The Love That Whirls	CD	Cocteau	JCCD15	England	1982	29.99
Nelson, Bill	What Now, What Next?	2CD	Discipline Global	DGM9807	England	1998	32.99
Nelson, Rick	20th Century Masters: The Millennium	CD	MCA	314-113-016-2	U.S.A.	2003	8.99
Nelson, Rick	A Night To Remember	CD	Varese	302-061-045-2	U.S.A.	1999	8.99
Nelson, Rick	Album 7/Rick Sings Spirituals + 8	CD	Capitol	72435-32448	U.S.A.	2001	7.99
Nelson, Rick	Album Seven By Rick/It's Up To You	CD	BGO	BGOCD520	England	2001	17.99
Nelson, Rick	Am. Dream Box: Imperial/Verve '57-'62	6CD	Bear Family	BCD-16196	Germany	2001	159.99
Nelson, Rick	Another Side Of Rick/Perspective	CD	ACE	CDCHD-690	England	1998	14.99
Nelson, Rick	Best Always/Love And Kisses	CD	ACE	CDCHD669	England	1998	14.99
Nelson, Rick	Best Of The Latter Years: '63-'75	CD	ACE	CDCHD671	England	1997	14.99
Nelson, Rick	Bright Lights/Country Fever	CD	ACE	CDCHD-670	England	1998	16.99
Nelson, Rick	For Your Love/Sings For You	CD	ACE	CDCHD-667	England	1998	14.99
Nelson, Rick	From Chicago To LA	CD	Magnum	MACD-083	U.S.A.	2002	14.99
Nelson, Rick	Garden Party	CD	MCA	MCAD-31364	U.S.A.	1990	7.99
Nelson, Rick	Greatest Hits: Revisited (James Burton)	CD	Varese	302-061-163-2	U.S.A.	2001	8.99
Nelson, Rick	In Concert, The Troubadour 1969	CD	MCA	MCAD-25983	U.S.A.	1970	12.99
Nelson, Rick	Legacy Box Set	4CD	Capitol	72435-29521-2-0	U.S.A.	2000	58.99

Artist	Title	Format	Label	Catalog No	Country	Released	Value
Nelson, Rick	Live At The Aladdin	CD	Magnum	MACD-078	U.S.A.	1996	17.99
Nelson, Rick	Live, 1983-1985	CD	Rhino	R2-71114	U.S.A.	1989	9.99
Nelson, Rick	More Songs By Ricky/Rick Is 21 + 8	CD	Capitol	72435-32450	U.S.A.	2001	7.99
Nelson, Rick	More Songs By/Rick Is 21	CD	BGO	BGOCD521	England	2001	17.99
Nelson, Rick	Playing To Win + 6	CD	Capitol	72435-32453	U.S.A.	2001	7.99
Nelson, Rick	Rick Sings Nelson/Rudy The Fifth	CD	BGO	BGOCD441	England	1999	17.99
Nelson, Rick	Rick's Rarities 1964-1974	CD	ACE	CDCHD995	England	2004	14.99
Nelson, Rick	Ricky Sings Again/Songs By + 9	CD	Capitol	72435-32451	U.S.A.	2001	7.99
Nelson, Rick	Ricky/Ricky Nelson	CD	BGO	BGOCD440	England	1999	17.99
Nelson, Rick	Ricky/Ricky Nelson + 7	CD	Capitol	72435-32449	U.S.A.	2001	7.99
Nelson, Rick	Rockin' With Ricky	CD	ACE	CDCHD-85	England	1996	14.99
Nelson, Rick	Sings For You	CD	MCA	MCAD-31363	U.S.A.	1963	8.99
Nelson, Rick	Stay Young: The Epic Recordings	CD	Epic	EK-48920	U.S.A.	1993	11.99
Nelson, Rick	The Best Of	CD	Curb	D2-77484	U.S.A.	1991	7.99
Nelson, Rick	The Best Of Vol. 1	CD	EMI	E2-92771	U.S.A.	1991	8.99
Nelson, Rick	The Best Of Vol. 2	CD	EMI	E2-95219	U.S.A.	1991	8.99
Nelson, Rick	The EP Collection	CD	See For Miles	SEE-CD-483	England	1997	14.99
Nelson, Rick	Very Thought Of You/Spotlight On	CD	ACE	CDCHD668	England	1997	17.99
Nelson, Rick/Glen Campbell	Lost 60's Recordings (Seals/Crofts)	CD	Varese	302-066-447-2	U.S.A.	2003	13.99
Nelson, Rick/S. C. Band	And The Stone Canyon Band '69 -'76	CD	Edsel	EDCD-417	England	1995	22.99
Nelson, Rick/S. C. Band	And The Stone Canyon Band, Vol. 2	CD	Edsel	EDCD-521	England	1997	22.99
Nelson, Rick/S. C. Band	Garden Party/Windfall	CD	BGO	BGOCD333	England	2002	17.99
Nelson, Rick/S. C. Band	Rick Sings Nelson	CD	Line	LCCD-9.01271-0	Germany	1993	19.99
Nelson, Rick/S. C. Band	Rudy The Fifth	CD	Line	LCCD-9.01272-0	Germany	1993	19.99
Nelson, Rick/S. C. Band	Windfall	CD	Line	LCCD-9.01273-0	Germany	1993	19.99
Nenê	Milunano	CD	Line	BSCD-9.00738-0	Germany	1990	29.99
Nesmith, Michael	And The Hits Just Keep On Comin'	CD	Line	OLCD-9.51102-X	Germany	1991	15.99
Nesmith, Michael	And The Hits/Pretty Much Your...	CD	BMG	74321-773822	England	2000	15.99
Nesmith, Michael	From A Radio Engine...	CD	Line	OLCD-9.51142-Z	Germany	1992	12.99
Nesmith, Michael	Infinite Rider on the Big Dogma	CD	Line	OLCD-9.51143-Z	Germany	1992	15.99
Nesmith, Michael	Loose Salute	CD	Line	OLCD-9.51064-X	Germany	1991	19.99
Nesmith, Michael	Magnetic South	CD	Line	OLCD-9.51063-X	Germany	1991	11.99
Nesmith, Michael	Magnetic South/Loose Salute + 1	CD	BMG	74321-660442	England	1999	13.99
Nesmith, Michael	Nevada Fighter	CD	Line	OLCD-9.51065-X	Germany	1991	15.99
Nesmith, Michael	Nevada Fighter/Tantamount To... + 3	CD	BMG	74321-822352	England	2001	13.99
Nesmith, Michael	Pretty Much Your Standard...	CD	Line	OLCD-9.51103-X	Germany	1991	15.99
Nesmith, Michael	Silver Moon (Gold Cd)	CD	Audiophile Legends	102.821	Germany	2002	19.99
Nesmith, Michael	Tantamount To Treason Volume One	CD	Line	OLCD-9.51104-X	Germany	1991	15.99
Nesmith, Michael	The Garden	CD	Rio	RIOD-2001	U.S.A.	1994	7.99
Nesmith, Michael	The Older Stuff	CD	Line	OLCD-9.51225-Z	Germany	1992	12.99
Nesmith, Michael	The Prison	CD	Line	OLCD-9.51028-X	Germany	1991	12.99
Nesmith, Michael	The Prison	CD	Rio	RIOD2009	U.S.A.	1990	12.99
Nesmith, Michael	Tropical Campfire's	CD	Pacific Arts	PAAD-5000	U.S.A.	1992	8.99
Neu!	4	CD	Captain Trip	CTCD-020	Japan	1996	15.99
Neu!	Live '72	CD	Captain Trip	CTCD-045	Japan	1996	15.99
Neu!	Neu! (Promo Sampler)	CD	Astralwerks	ASW-69977-2	U.S.A.	1999	15.99
Neutral Spirits	Self Titled (Like The Doors)	CD	Gear Fab	GF-198	U.S.A.	2003	13.99
Neuwirth, Bob	99 Monkeys	CD	Koch	KOC-CD-8010	U.S.A.	1999	8.99
Neuwirth, Bob	Back To The Front	CD	Koch	KOC-CD-8009	U.S.A.	1998	8.99
Neuwirth, Bob	Havana Midnight	CD	Diesel Motor	1003	U.S.A.	1999	8.99
Neuwirth, Bob	Look Up	CD	Watermelon	1050	U.S.A.	1996	8.99
Neuwirth, Bob/Roger McGuinn	ST (Mama Cass/C Hillman/D Everly)	CD	Asylum	AMCY-2902	Japan	1999	29.99
Neuwirth, Bob/Roger McGuinn	ST (Mama Cass/C Hillman/D Everly)	CD	Water	WATER-109	U.S.A.	2003	12.99
Neville Brothers	Brother's Keeper (MFSL Gold Cd)	CD	Mobile Fidelity	UDCD-626	U.S.A.	1990	20.99
Neville Brothers	Fiyo On The Bayou (MFSL Gold Cd)	CD	Mobile Fidelity	UDCD-602	U.S.A.	1981	19.99
New England	Self Titled	CD	MCA	MVCM-346	Japan	1993	32.99
New Kids On The Block	Tour Souvenir Collection	CD	Sony	469282-2	Australia	1991	7.99
New Order	World (The Price Of Love) (Promo)	CD Single	Warner Bros.	PRO-CD-6276	U.S.A.	1993	10.99

N

Artist	Title	Format	Label	Catalog No	Country	Released	Value
New Race	Second Wave	CD	Revenge	MIG-29	France	1990	24.99
New Race	The First And The Last	CD	Line	LICD-9.00104-0	Germany	1987	17.99
New Riders/Purple Sage	Before Time Began	CD	Relix	RRCD-2024	U.S.A.	1986	10.99
New Riders/Purple Sage	Gypsy Cowboy/Adv. Of Panama Red	CD	BGO	BGOCD509	England	2000	17.99
New Riders/Purple Sage	Keep On Keepin' On	CD	MU	MCD-31109	U.S.A.	1989	7.99
New Riders/Purple Sage	Live	CD	Rhino	R2-71289	U.S.A.	1995	9.99
New Riders/Purple Sage	Marin County Line	CD	One Way	MCAD-22107	U.S.A.	1977	12.99
New Riders/Purple Sage	Midnight Moonlight	CD	Relix	RRCD2050	U.S.A.	1992	6.99
New Riders/Purple Sage	N.R.P.S./Powerglide	2CD	BGO	BGOCD551	England	2002	22.99
New Riders/Purple Sage	New Riders	CD	One Way	MCAD-22108	U.S.A.	1976	12.99
New Riders/Purple Sage	The Best Of The....	CD	Columbia	CK-34367	U.S.A.	1976	7.99
New Riders/Purple Sage	Wasted Tasters	CD	Raven	RVCD-36	Australia	1993	12.99
New Riders/Purple Sage	Who Are Those Guys	CD	One Way	MCAD-22109	U.S.A.	1977	12.99
New York Dolls	Archive Series	CD	Rialto	RMCD-238-Z	U.S.A.	2001	12.99
New York Dolls	Evil Dolls ~ New York Tapes 72 ~ 73	CD	Meldac	MECR-25025	Japan	1993	29.99
New York Dolls	From Paris With Love (L.U.V.)	CD	Red Star	SFTRI-682	U.S.A.	1998	10.99
New York Dolls	Glamorous Life Live	CD	DCC	EAZ-4022	U.S.A.	1999	8.99
New York Dolls	Hootchie Cootchie Dolls	CD	Solid	CDSOL-0016	Japan	1998	24.99
New York Dolls	Lipstick Killers (Mercer St. Sessions)	CD	ROIR	88561-5027-2	U.S.A.	1990	12.99
New York Dolls	Live NYC 1975 - Red Patent Leather	CD	Receiver	7-72596-2	England	1984	8.99
New York Dolls	Looking For A Kiss (CDV Video Single)	CDV	Pioneer	PIFP-1022	Japan	1990	19.99
New York Dolls	New York Dolls	CD	Mercury	832-752-2	U.S.A.	1973	8.99
New York Dolls	New York Tapes 72 - 73	CD	Skydog	62257.2	France	1993	11.99
New York Dolls	Paris' Burning	CD	Skydog	62-256-2	France	1993	11.99
New York Dolls	Paris Le Trash	CD	Triple X	51116-2	U.S.A.	1993	14.99
New York Dolls	Personality Crisis	CD Single	See For Miles	SEA-CD-3	England	1990	9.99
New York Dolls	Rock 'N' Roll	CD	Mercury	314-522-129-2	U.S.A.	1994	8.99
New York Dolls	Too Much Too Soon	CD	Mercury	834-230-2	U.S.A.	1974	11.99
New York Rock/Soul Revue	Live At The Beacon (Donald Fagen)	CD	Giant	9-24423-2	U.S.A.	1991	7.99
Newell, Martin	Let's Kiosk!	CD Single	Humbug	HUM1	England	1995	9.99
Newell, Martin	Radio Autumn Attic	CD	Cherry Red	CDMRED-206	England	2002	15.99
Newell, Martin	The Off White Album	CD	Humbug	BAH-25	England	1995	13.99
Newell, Martin	The Spirit Cage	CD	Cherry Red	CDMRED-176	England	2000	14.99
Newell, Martin	The Wayward Genius of Martin Newell	CD	Cherry Red	CDMRED-154	England	1999	14.99
Newell, Martin/Andy Partridge	The Greatest Living Englishman + 2	CD	Humbug	BAH-10	England	1993	8.99
Newhart, Bob	The Bob Newhart Anthology	2CD	Rhino	R2-76742	U.S.A.	2001	13.99
Newley, Anthony	The Best Of	CD	GNP	GNP-2243	U.S.A.	1995	7.99
Newley, Anthony/Bricusse	Willy Wonka & The Chocolate Factory	CD	Hip O	HIPD-40020	U.S.A.	1996	9.99
Newley, Anthony/L. Bricusse	The Roar Of The Greasepaint	CD	RCA	60351-RG	U.S.A.	1965	10.99
Newman, Randy	12 Songs	CD	Reprise	6373-2	U.S.A.	1988	7.99
Newman, Randy	Bad Love	CD	Dreamworks	50115	U.S.A.	1999	5.99
Newman, Randy	Born Again	CD	Reprise	3346-2	U.S.A.	1988	8.99
Newman, Randy	Faust + 20	2CD	Rhino	R2-73785	U.S.A.	2003	14.99
Newman, Randy	Faust: Words And Music	CD	Warner Bros.	PRO-CD-7775	U.S.A.	1994	9.99
Newman, Randy	Good Old Boys + 1	CD	Rhino	R2-78243	U.S.A.	2003	10.99
Newman, Randy	Guilty : 30 Years Box Set	4CD	Rhino	R2-75567	U.S.A.	1998	35.99
Newman, Randy	I Love L.A. (CDV)	CDV	Warner Bros.	925680-2	Germany	1983	35.99
Newman, Randy	Land Of Dreams	CD	Reprise	25773-2	U.S.A.	1988	11.99
Newman, Randy	Little Crinimals	CD	Reprise	3079-2	U.S.A.	1987	8.99
Newman, Randy	Lonely At The Top - The Best Of	CD	Warner Bros.	2292-41126-2	Germany	1987	9.99
Newman, Randy	Maverick (O.S.T.)	CD	Warner Bros.	45816-2	U.S.A.	1995	13.99
Newman, Randy	Parenthood (O.S.T.)	CD	Reprise	26001-2	U.S.A.	1989	18.99
Newman, Randy	Ragtime + 1 (O.S.T.)	CD	Rhino	R2-78245	U.S.A.	2002	10.99
Newman, Randy	Randy Newman	CD	Reprise	2-6286	U.S.A.	1968	13.99
Newman, Randy	Randy Newman Live	CD	Reprise	6459-2	U.S.A.	1995	8.99
Newman, Randy	Sail Away + 5	CD	Rhino	R2-78244	U.S.A.	2002	10.99
Newman, Randy	The Best Of	CD	Rhino	R2-74364	U.S.A.	2001	11.99
Newman, Randy	The Natural (O.S.T.)	CD	Warner Bros.	9-25116-2	U.S.A.	1984	14.99

N

Artist	Title	Format	Label	Catalog No	Country	Released	Value
Newman, Randy	The Paper (O.S.T.)	CD	Warner Bros.	45616-2	U.S.A.	1994	8.99
Newman, Randy	Trouble In Paradise	CD	Reprise	23755-2	U.S.A.	1988	13.99
Newton, Juice	Juice	CD	DCC	DRZ-152	U.S.A.	1997	47.99
Newton-John, Olivia	2	CD	Festival	336022	Australia	2002	10.99
Newton-John, Olivia	20th Century Masters: The Millennium	CD	Hip O	585412	U.S.A.	2002	8.99
Newton-John, Olivia	Back With A Heart	CD	MCA	70030	U.S.A.	1998	13.99
Newton-John, Olivia	Clearly Love	CD	Festival	D21037	Australia	1999	14.99
Newton-John, Olivia	Come On Over	CD	Festival	D21038	Australia	1999	14.99
Newton-John, Olivia	Country Girl	CD	EMI	494970	U.S.A.	1999	14.99
Newton-John, Olivia	Definitive Collection	CD	Universal	584279	U.S.A.	2002	8.99
Newton-John, Olivia	Don't Stop Believin'	CD	Festival	D21039	Australia	1999	14.99
Newton-John, Olivia	Gaia	CD	Festival	D21045	Australia	1999	14.99
Newton-John, Olivia	Grease (Dream Mix)	CD Single	Polydor	879 795-2	Germany	1991	30.99
Newton-John, Olivia	Greatest Hits, Vol. 1	CD	Festival	D21048	Australia	1999	18.99
Newton-John, Olivia	Greatest Hits, Vol. 2	CD	Festival	D21049	Australia	1999	18.99
Newton-John, Olivia	Greatest Hits, Vol. 3	CD	Festival	D21050	Australia	1999	18.99
Newton-John, Olivia	Have You Never Been Mellow + 1	CD	Festival	D21046	Australia	1999	17.99
Newton-John, Olivia	Highlights The Main Event (Live) + 3	CD	BMG	86487	U.S.A.	2001	8.99
Newton-John, Olivia	I Honestly Love You	CD Single	MCA	MCADS-72053	U.S.A.	1998	17.99
Newton-John, Olivia	If Not For You	CD	Festival	D19809	Australia	1998	14.99
Newton-John, Olivia	If You Love Me, Let Me Know	CD	MCA	MCAD-31018	U.S.A.	1974	44.99
Newton-John, Olivia	Let Me Be There	CD	Festival	D21035	Australia	1999	14.99
Newton-John, Olivia	Long Live Love	CD	Festival	D21036	Australia	1999	17.99
Newton-John, Olivia	Love Songs	CD	Festival	D26449	Australia	1999	10.99
Newton-John, Olivia	Magic: The Best Of (Grease Megamix)	CD	UTV	585233	England	2001	13.99
Newton-John, Olivia	Making A Good Thing Better	CD	Festival	D21040	Australia	1999	14.99
Newton-John, Olivia	Olivia	CD	Festival	D21034	Australia	1999	14.99
Newton-John, Olivia	Olivia Newton-John	2CD	Festival	D45377	Australia	1999	17.99
Newton-John, Olivia	One Woman's Live Journey + 1	CD	Festival	D32259	Australia	2000	16.99
Newton-John, Olivia	Physical	CD	Festival	D21042	Australia	1999	18.99
Newton-John, Olivia	Soul Kiss	CD	Festival	D21043	Australia	1999	18.99
Newton-John, Olivia	The Christmas Collection	CD	Hip O	314-585-413-2	U.S.A.	2001	8.99
Newton-John, Olivia	The Rumour + 1	CD	Festival	D21044	Australia	1999	14.99
Newton-John, Olivia	The Singles - Back To Basics	CD	Festival	D93361	Australia	1999	9.99
Newton-John, Olivia	Totally Hot	CD	Festival	D21041	Australia	1999	18.99
Newton-John, Olivia	Two Of A Kind	CD	Festival	D21047	Australia	2001	14.99
Newton-John, Olivia	Warm And Tender	CD	Festival	D19828	Australia	2001	17.99
Newton-John, Olivia	Warm And Tender (Promo/Box)	CD	Geffen	9-24257-2-DJ	U.S.A.	1989	71.99
Nice	All The Best	CD	Repertoire	REP-4822	Germany	2002	11.99
Nice	America: The BBC Sessions	CD	Receiver	RRCD-224	England	1996	8.99
Nice	Ars Longa Vita Brevis	CD	Line	IDCD-9.00224-0	Germany	1987	9.99
Nice	Ars Longa Vita Brevis + 1	CD	Repertoire	REP-4289-WY	Germany	1992	11.99
Nice	Ars Longa Vita Brevis + 7	2CD	Castle	CMQDD791	England	2003	15.99
Nice	BBC Sessions	2CD	Sanctuary	CMFCD457	U.S.A.	2002	15.99
Nice	Elegy + 6	CD	Virgin	CASCD-1030	England	1990	8.99
Nice	Five Bridges + 5	CD	Virgin	CASCD-1014	England	1990	8.99
Nice	Here Come The Nice - Immediate Anth.	3CD	Castle	CMETD-655-1-3	England	2000	21.99
Nice	Nice	CD	Line	INCD-9.00233-0	Germany	1987	9.99
Nice	The Immediate Collection	2CD	Recall	SMD-CD-203	England	1999	12.99
Nice	The Immediate Years Box Set	3CD	Charly	CDIMMBOX2	England	1995	15.99
Nice	The Nice	CD	Repertoire	REP-4290-WY	Germany	1992	11.99
Nice	The Nice + 5	CD	Castle	CMQDD792	England	2003	11.99
Nice	The Nice Collection	CD	Line	IDCD-9.00720-0	Germany	1989	9.99
Nice	The Swedish Radio Sessions	CD	Castle	CMRCD0349	England	2001	12.99
Nice	The Thoughts Of Emerlist Davjack	CD	Line	INCD-9.00228-0	Germany	1987	9.99
Nice	The Thoughts Of Emerlist Jack + 13	2CD	Castle	CMQDD790	England	2003	15.99
Nice	The Thoughts Of Emerlist Jack + 3	CD	Repertoire	REP-4238-WY	Germany	1992	11.99
Nichols, Nichelle/Star Trek	Down To Earth + 4	CD	Rev-Ola	CREV045	England	1997	11.99

Artist	Title	Format	Label	Catalog No	Country	Released	Value
Nichols, Nichelle/Star Trek	Out Of This World	CD	GNP	GNPD-2209	U.S.A.	1991	11.99
Nichts	Made In Eile	CD	Line	DKCD-9.00945-0	Germany	1990	24.99
Nickleback	Hesher	CD	Nick	NICK-505	Canada	1995	359.99
Nicks, Stevie	Bella Donna	CD	Modern	38139-2	U.S.A.	1981	9.99
Nicks, Stevie	Enchanted Box Set	3CD	Atlantic	83093-2	U.S.A.	1998	29.99
Nicks, Stevie	If You Ever Did Believe (Promo)	CD Single	Warner Bros.	PRO-CD-9500	U.S.A.	1998	13.99
Nicks, Stevie	Planets Of The Universe	CD Single	Reprise	9-42385-2	U.S.A.	2001	9.99
Nicks, Stevie	Rock A Little	CD	Modern	7-90479-2	U.S.A.	1985	8.99
Nicks, Stevie	Selections Enchanted Works (Promo)	CD	Atlantic	PRCD-8511	U.S.A.	1998	49.99
Nicks, Stevie	Street Angel	CD	Modern	92246-2	U.S.A.	1994	7.99
Nicks, Stevie	Street Angel + 2	CD	Toshiba-EMI	TOCP-3451	Japan	1994	20.99
Nicks, Stevie	The Divine	CD	EMI	724357626224	EU	2000	8.99
Nicks, Stevie	The Other Side Of The Mirror	CD	Atlantic	7-91245-2	U.S.A.	1989	8.99
Nicks, Stevie	The Wild Heart	CD	Modern	90084-2	U.S.A.	1983	9.99
Nicks, Stevie	Timespace - The Best Of	CD	Atlantic	7-91711-2	U.S.A.	1991	9.99
Nicks, Stevie	Trouble In Shangri-La	CD	Reprise	9-47372-2	U.S.A.	2001	7.99
Nico	Behind The Iron Curtain	CD	Line	5.00014	Germany	1988	49.99
Nico	Chelsea Girl	CD	Verve	835-209-2	U.S.A.	1967	11.99
Nico	Chelsea Girl	CD	Polydor K.K.	POCP-1846	Japan	1990	24.99
Nico	Chelsea Girl Live	CD	Cleopatra	CLP-0034-2	U.S.A.	1997	9.99
Nico	Classic Years	CD	Polygram	314-565-185-2	U.S.A.	1998	10.99
Nico	Desertshore	CD	Reprise	6424-2	U.S.A.	1970	13.99
Nico	Do Or Die! + 1 - The ROIR Sessions	CD	ROIR	RE117CD	France	1982	20.99
Nico	Drama Of Exile	CD	Cleopatra	CLP-1079-2	U.S.A.	1993	7.99
Nico	Drama Of Exile	CD	Line	LICD-9.00106-0	Germany	1987	12.99
Nico	Femme Fatale (2 Trks/Martin Hannett)	CD	Jungle	FREUD-CD-069	England	2002	16.99
Nico	Hanging Gardens	CD	Restless	7-72383-2	Canada	1990	10.99
Nico	Heroine + 2	CD	Anagram	CDM-GOTH-16	France	2002	21.99
Nico	Icon - (Rare And Unreleased)	CD	Cleopatra	CLP-9709-2	U.S.A.	1996	16.99
Nico	In Tokyo	CD	Solid	CDSOL-0010	Japan	1998	21.99
Nico	Innocent & Vain - An Introduction	CD	Polydor	589-421-2	EU	2002	13.99
Nico	Janitor Of Lunacy + 4	CD	Anagram	CDM- GOTH-7	England	2001	21.99
Nico	Live Heroes	CD	Aware-One	AWARE-385	U.S.A.	1986	10.99
Nico	Nico's Last Concert "Fata Morgana"	CD	SPV	084-96202	Germany	1994	18.99
Nico	The End...	CD	Island	314-518-892-2	U.S.A.	1974	13.99
Nico	The Marble Index + 2	CD	Elektra	74029-2	U.S.A.	1991	11.99
Nico	The Peel Sessions	CD	Strange Fruit	SFPS-064	Holland	1988	11.99
Nico/The Faction	Camera Obscura	CD	Beggars Banquet	BBL-63-CD	England	1988	10.99
Nico/Vs Trance Groove	Reich Der Traume	CD Single	Captain Trip	CTCD-239	Japan	1980	18.99
Niehaus, Lennie	Bridges Of Madison County (Promo)	CD	Warner Bros.	PRO-CD-8032	U.S.A.	1995	229.99
Nieve, Steve/Elvis Costello	Keyboard Jungle/Selections/Playboy	CD	Diablo	48142	England	1993	12.99
Nieve, Steve/Elvis Costello	Mumu	CD	Silvertone	9260192	Australia	2001	22.99
Night Ranger	20th Century Masters: The Millennium	CD	MCA	088-112-307-2	U.S.A.	2000	8.99
Night Ranger	7 Wishes	CD	MCA	MCAD-5593	U.S.A.	1985	14.99
Night Ranger	Big Life	CD	MCA	MCAD-5839	U.S.A.	1987	8.99
Night Ranger	Dawn Patrol	CD	MCA	MCAD-5460	U.S.A.	1982	12.99
Night Ranger	Feeding Off The Mojo	CD	Drive Ent.	DE2-46001	U.S.A.	1995	8.99
Night Ranger	Greatest Hits	CD	MCA	MCAD-42307	U.S.A.	1989	8.99
Night Ranger	Live In Japan	CD	MCA	MCAD-10024	U.S.A.	1990	11.99
Night Ranger	Man In Motion	CD	MCA	MCAD-6238	U.S.A.	1988	11.99
Night Ranger	Midnight Madness	CD	MCA	MCAD-31160	U.S.A.	1983	14.99
Night Ranger	Neverland + 1	CD	Zero	XRCN-1297	Japan	1997	8.99
Night Ranger	Rock In Japan Greatest Hits Live	CD	Dead Line	CLP-0616-2	U.S.A.	1999	15.99
Night Ranger	Seven + 1	CD	Zero	XRCN-2023	Japan	1998	10.99
Nighthawks	Jacks & Kings & Full House	CD	Line	LICD-9.00417-0	Germany	1987	24.99
Nighthawks	Open All Nite (MFSL Aluminum)	CD	Mobile Fidelity	MFCD-754	U.S.A.	1992	34.99
Nightnoise	A Different Shore	CD	Windham Hill	01934-11166-2	U.S.A.	1995	8.99
Nilsson, Harry	...That's The Way It Is	CD	BMG	74321-95911-2	Japan	2002	14.99

N

Artist	Title	Format	Label	Catalog No	Country	Released	Value
Nilsson, Harry	A Little Touch Of/In The Night & More	2CD	Camden	74321950272	England	2002	13.99
Nilsson, Harry	Aerial Pandemonium Ballet + 5	CD	Buddah	74465-99704-2	U.S.A.	2000	8.99
Nilsson, Harry	Duit On Mon Dei + 1	CD	BMG	74321-95909-2	Japan	2002	14.99
Nilsson, Harry	Greatest Hits	CD	RCA	07863-65107-2	U.S.A.	2002	8.99
Nilsson, Harry	Harry & Nilsson Sings Newman + 2	CD	BMG	74321-757442	England	2000	13.99
Nilsson, Harry	Knnillssonn + 1	CD	BMG	74321-95912-2	Japan	2002	14.99
Nilsson, Harry	Knnillssonn/That's The Way It Is	2CD	Camden	74321950262	England	2002	13.99
Nilsson, Harry	Nilsson '62 ~ The Debut Sessions	CD	RPM	RPM-804	England	1995	13.99
Nilsson, Harry	Nilsson Schmilsson (MFSL Gold Cd)	CD	Mobile Fidelity	UDCD-541	U.S.A.	1981	34.99
Nilsson, Harry	Nilsson Schmilsson (RCA Gold Cd)	CD	RCA	66599-2	U.S.A.	1981	35.99
Nilsson, Harry	Nilsson Schmilsson + 8	CD	BMG	74321-757452	England	2000	13.99
Nilsson, Harry	Pandemonium.../Aerial Ballet/Aerial + 4	2CD	BMG	74321-757422	England	2000	13.99
Nilsson, Harry	Pussy Cats + 4	CD	Buddah	74465-99615-2	U.S.A.	1999	11.99
Nilsson, Harry	Sandman	CD	BMG	74321-95910-2	Japan	2002	29.99
Nilsson, Harry	Sandman/Duit On Mon Dei	2CD	Camden	74321950242	England	2002	13.99
Nilsson, Harry	Skidoo/The Point! + 4	CD	BMG	74321-757432	England	2000	13.99
Nilsson, Harry	Son Of Schmilsson + 2	CD	BMG	74321-757462	England	2000	13.99
Nilsson, Harry	The Collection (Gold Cd)	CD	Audiophile Legends	APH-102.817	Germany	2001	14.99
Nilsson, Harry	The Harry Nilsson Anthology	2CD	RCA	66354-2	U.S.A.	1994	20.99
Nimoy, Leonard/Star Trek	Freaky Realistic	CD Single	Frealism	FRECD3	England	1993	15.99
Nimoy, Leonard/Star Trek	Highly Illogical	CD	Rev-Ola	CREV017CD	England	1993	8.99
Nimoy, Leonard/Star Trek	Music From Outer Space + 2	CD	Varese	VSD-5613	U.S.A.	1995	19.99
Nine Inch Nails	And All That Could... (Promo Sampler)	CD	Interscope	INTR-10675-2	U.S.A.	2002	12.99
Nine Inch Nails	And All That Could...(Leatherbound)	2CD	Nothing	0694931862	U.S.A.	2002	21.99
Nine Inch Nails	Deep (Tomb Raider) (Promo)	CD Single	Elektra	PRCD-1637-2	U.S.A.	2001	17.99
Nine Inch Nails	Disturbed (Interview)	CD	Disturbed	DIST001	England	1996	6.99
Nine Inch Nails	Halo 01 - Down In It	CD Single	TVT	2611-2	U.S.A.	1989	6.99
Nine Inch Nails	Halo 02 - Pretty Hate Machine	CD	TVT	2610-2	U.S.A.	1989	9.99
Nine Inch Nails	Halo 03 - Head Like A Hole	CD	TVT	TVT-2615-2	U.S.A.	1990	6.99
Nine Inch Nails	Halo 04 - Sin Long, Dub & Short	CD Single	TVT	TVT2617-2	U.S.A.	1989	7.99
Nine Inch Nails	Halo 05 - Broken	CD Single	TVT	7-92213-2	U.S.A.	1992	9.99
Nine Inch Nails	Halo 05 - Broken (3 " Single W/Halo 05)	CD	TVT	92213-22	U.S.A.	1992	19.99
Nine Inch Nails	Halo 06 - Fixed	CD Single	TVT	514-321-2	France	1992	9.99
Nine Inch Nails	Halo 07 - March Of The Pigs (Disc 1)	CD Single	TVT	854-001-2	England	1994	5.99
Nine Inch Nails	Halo 07 - March Of The Pigs (Disc 2)	CD Single	TVT	854-003-2	England	1994	5.99
Nine Inch Nails	Halo 08 - Closer (Further Away)	CD Single	TVT	854-059-2	England	1994	7.99
Nine Inch Nails	Halo 08 - The Downward Spiral	CD	TVT	7-92346-2	U.S.A.	1994	7.99
Nine Inch Nails	Halo 09 - Closer (Closer To God) # 2	CD Single	TVT	854-061-2	England	1994	7.99
Nine Inch Nails	Halo 10- Futher Down The Spiral	CD	TVT	INTDM-95811	U.S.A.	1995	7.99
Nine Inch Nails	Halo 11 - The Perfect Drug	CD Single	Interscope	INTDM-95007	U.S.A.	1997	7.99
Nine Inch Nails	Halo 13 - The Day The World Went...	CD Single	Interscope	INTDS-97026	U.S.A.	1999	5.99
Nine Inch Nails	Halo 15 - We're In This Together (Cd 2)	CD Single	Interscope	497-140-2	U.S.A.	1999	7.99
Nine Inch Nails	Halo 16 - Things Falling Apart	CD	Interscope	0694907442	U.S.A.	2000	6.99
Nine Inch Nails	Halo 17 - All That Could Have. (Disc 1)	CD	Interscope	0694931852	U.S.A.	2002	9.99
Nine Inch Nails	Halo 17 - Still (Disc 2)	CD	Nothing	0694931842	U.S.A.	2002	23.99
Nine Inch Nails	Piggy (Rick Rubin Remix)	CD Single	Nothing	PRCD-5923	U.S.A.	1994	36.99
Nine Inch Nails	Remixed	CD	Nothing	DPRO-01853-99	Germany	1995	34.99
Nine Inch Nails	We're In This Together (Promo)	CD Single	Interscope	INT5P-6687	U.S.A.	1999	11.99
Nine Inch Richards	Closer To Hogs (9 Inch Nails Takeoff)	CD Single	Shock	SHOCK-HA1008	Australia	1995	7.99
Nine Nine Nine	13th Floor Madness	CD	Line	ALCD-9.00073-0	Germany	1988	19.99
Nine Nine Nine	Concrete	CD	Line	ALCD-9.00017-0	Germany	1988	19.99
Nine Nine Nine	Concrete/13th Floor Madness	2CD	Line	LICD-9.21197-S	Germany	1995	24.99
Nine Nine Nine	The Albion Punk Years	CD	Line	LICD-9.01326-0	Germany	1996	19.99
Nirvana	Aneurysm (Promo)	CD Single	DGC	PRO-CD-1033	U.S.A.	1996	8.99
Nirvana	Bleach (Tupelo Cd)	CD	Sub Pop	TUPCD6	U.S.A.	1989	16.99
Nirvana	Come As You Are	CD Single	DGC	DGCDS-21707	U.S.A.	1992	6.99
Nirvana	From Muddy Banks Of Wishkah (Live)	CD	Geffen	25105-2	U.S.A.	1996	8.99
Nirvana	Heart Shaped Box	CD Single	Geffen	GED21849	France	1995	6.99

N

Artist	Title	Format	Label	Catalog No	Country	Released	Value
Nirvana	Hormoaning	CD	MCA Victor	MVCG-17002	Japan	1992	199.99
Nirvana	Hormoaning	CD	BMG	GEFD-21711	Australia	1992	72.99
Nirvana	In Utero (Clean Version)	CD	Geffen	24705-2	U.S.A.	1993	7.99
Nirvana	In Utero (MFSL Gold Cd)	CD	Mobile Fidelity	UDCD-690	U.S.A.	1997	39.99
Nirvana	In Utero (Test Press/Handwritten Text)	CD	DGC	DGCC/SD-24607	U.S.A.	1993	221.99
Nirvana	In Utero (UK)	CD	Geffen	24536-2	England	1998	9.99
Nirvana	Insecticide	CD	Geffen	24504-2	U.S.A.	1992	7.99
Nirvana	Lithium	CD Single	DGC	DGCDM-21815	U.S.A.	1995	6.99
Nirvana	Lithium (Live Promo)	CD Single	DGC	PRO-CD-4429	U.S.A.	1991	24.99
Nirvana	MTV Unplugged In New York (Live)	CD	Geffen	24727-2	U.S.A.	1994	8.99
Nirvana	Nevermind (MFSL Gold CD)	CD	Mobile Fidelity	UDCD-666	U.S.A.	1996	49.99
Nirvana	Nevermind: It's An Int. (DJ/5 Live)	CD	Geffen	PRO-CD-4382	U.S.A.	1992	95.99
Nirvana	Nirvana + 1 (Self Titled)	CD	Geffen	493523	Australia	2003	12.99
Nirvana	Pennyroyal Tea	CD Single	Geffen	GED-21907	Germany	1993	346.99
Nirvana	Singles	CD	MCA	24901	England	1998	24.99
Nirvana	Sliver Dive	CD Single	Tupelo	TUPCD-25	England	1993	30.99
Nirvana	Smells Like Teen Spirit	CD Single	DGC	DGCDS-21673	U.S.A.	1995	7.99
Nirvana/60's UK Band	All Of Us	CD	Edsel	EDCD-466	England	1996	10.99
Nirvana/60's UK Band	All Of Us + 4	CD	Universal	IMCD302	England	2003	13.99
Nirvana/60's UK Band	Black Flower	CD	Edsel	EDCD-378	England	1994	21.99
Nirvana/60's UK Band	Chemistry Box Set (W/To Markos III)	3CD	Edsel	FBOOK24	England	2003	51.99
Nirvana/60's UK Band	Local Anaesthetic	CD	Repertoire	REP-4109-WY	Germany	2002	16.99
Nirvana/60's UK Band	Orange And Blue	CD	Edsel	EDCD-485	England	1996	22.99
Nirvana/60's UK Band	Secret Theatre	CD	Edsel	EDCD-407	England	1995	16.99
Nirvana/60's UK Band	The Story Of Simon Simopath	CD	Edsel	EDCD-465	England	1996	10.99
Nirvana/60's UK Band	The Story Of Simon Simopath + 4	CD	Universal	IMCD301	England	2003	13.99
Nirvana/60's UK Band	To Markos III	CD	Universal	IMCD303	England	2003	22.99
Nirvana/60's UK Band	Travelling On A Cloud	CD	Polygram	510-974-2	England	1999	16.99
Nitty Gritty Dirt Band	Acoustic	CD	Liberty	C2-28169	U.S.A.	1994	8.99
Nitty Gritty Dirt Band	Alive/Rare Junk	CD	BGO	BGOCD245	England	1995	16.99
Nitty Gritty Dirt Band	All The Good Times	CD	BGO	BGOCD-93	England	1991	15.99
Nitty Gritty Dirt Band	Bang Bang Bang	CD	Dreamworks	0044-50125-2	U.S.A.	1999	7.99
Nitty Gritty Dirt Band	Dirt Band/An American Dream	CD	BGO	BGOCD455	England	1999	16.99
Nitty Gritty Dirt Band	Dirt, Silver & Gold	2CD	BGO	BGOCD592	England	2003	18.99
Nitty Gritty Dirt Band	Dream	CD	BGO	BGOCD311	England	1996	15.99
Nitty Gritty Dirt Band	Hold On	CD	Warner Bros.	25573-2	U.S.A.	1986	7.99
Nitty Gritty Dirt Band	Live Two Five	CD	Liberty	C2-93128	U.S.A.	1991	7.99
Nitty Gritty Dirt Band	More Great Dirt (Best, Vol. 2)	CD	Warner Bros.	25830-2	U.S.A.	1989	7.99
Nitty Gritty Dirt Band	Not Fade Away	CD	Liberty	C2-98564	U.S.A.	1992	8.99
Nitty Gritty Dirt Band	P D Fashion/Partners Brothers/Friends	CD	Wounded Bird	WOU-5113	U.S.A.	2004	11.99
Nitty Gritty Dirt Band	Pure Dirt	CD	BGO	BGOCD243	England	1996	15.99
Nitty Gritty Dirt Band	Ricochet	CD	BGO	BGOCD284	England	1996	15.99
Nitty Gritty Dirt Band	Stars & Stripes Forever	CD	Capitol	7243-8-33828-2	U.S.A.	1998	10.99
Nitty Gritty Dirt Band	Symphonion Dream	CD	Capitol	7243-5-80526-2	U.S.A.	2003	8.99
Nitty Gritty Dirt Band	The Christmas Album	CD	Rising Tide	53048	U.S.A.	1997	8.99
Nitty Gritty Dirt Band	The Rest Of The Dream	CD	MCA	MCAD-6407	U.S.A.	1990	7.99
Nitty Gritty Dirt Band	Twenty Years Of Dirt: The Best Of The	CD	Warner Bros.	25382-2	U.S.A.	1987	7.99
Nitty Gritty Dirt Band	Uncle Charlie & His Dog Teddy	CD	BGO	BGOCD22	England	1996	15.99
Nitty Gritty Dirt Band	Uncle Charlie & His Dog Teddy + 2	CD	Capitol	7243-5-41721-2	U.S.A.	2003	8.99
Nitty Gritty Dirt Band	Will the Circle Be Unbroken + 4	2CD	EMI	72435-35148-2-2	U.S.A.	2002	12.99
Nitty Gritty Dirt Band	Will The Circle Be Unbroken Vol. 2 (DJ)	CD	Universal	CD45-3011	U.S.A.	1989	9.99
Nitty Gritty Dirt Band	Will the Circle Be Unbroken, Vol. 2	CD	BGO	BGOCD400	England	2002	15.99
Nitty Gritty Dirt Band	Will the Circle Be Unbroken, Vol. 3	2CD	Capitol	7243-5-40177-2-0	U.S.A.	2002	12.99
Nitty Gritty Dirt Band	Will The Circle...Trilogy (5 CD/DVD)	6CD	Capitol	7243-5-91628-2	U.S.A.	2004	49.99
Nitty Gritty Dirt Band	Workin' Band	CD	Warner Bros.	25722-2	U.S.A.	1988	15.99
Nitzsche, Jack	3 Piece Suite: Reprise (1971-1973)	CD	Rhino	RHM2-7787	U.S.A.	2000	19.99
Nitzsche, Jack	Indian Runner (O.S.T.)	CD	Capitol	C2-96803	Canada	1991	18.99
Nitzsche, Jack	Revenge (O.S.T.)	CD	Silva Screen	FILMCD-065	U.S.A.	1990	15.99

N

Artist	Title	Format	Label	Catalog No	Country	Released	Value
Nitzsche, Jack	Starman (O.S.T.)	CD	Varese	VCD-47220	U.S.A.	1984	13.99
Nitzsche, Jack	The Lonely Surfer	CD	Collector's Choice	CCM-01952-RR	U.S.A.	2002	10.99
No Doubt	Live In Los Angeles Dec. 1995 (Promo)	CD	Universal	PRCD-6667	U.S.A.	1995	24.99
No Doubt/Blink-182	No Doubt/Blink-182 Best Buy (DJ/CD/DV	CD	Interscope	INTR-11159-9	U.S.A.	2004	5.99
Noble Rot	The Real Lust for Life	CD	Teichiku	TECX-25836	Japan	1994	29.99
Noble, Ike	Lonely People	CD	Line	TLCD-9.00353-0	Germany	1988	14.99
Nomi, Klaus	Encore!	CD	RCA	ND74421	Germany	1983	13.99
Nomi, Klaus	Klaus Nomi	CD	RCA	ND74420	Germany	1985	15.99
Nomi, Klaus	Simple Man	CD	RCA	ND74422	Germany	1982	14.99
Nomi, Klaus	The Collection	CD	RCA	ND-75004	Germany	1991	14.99
Norbert Und Die Feiglinge	Essen & Trinken	CD	Line	JPCD-9.01308-E	Germany	1995	11.99
Norbert Und Die Feiglinge	Frauen	CD Single	Line	JLCD-9.01316-0	Germany	1995	9.99
Norbert Und Die Feiglinge	Fussball	CD Single	Line	JLCD-9.01321-0	Germany	1995	9.99
Norbert Und Die Feiglinge	Herzblatt	CD	Line	LICD—9.01358-0	Germany	1998	11.99
Norbert Und Die Feiglinge	Herzblatt	CD Single	Line	JLCD-9.01360-0	Germany	1998	9.99
Norbert Und Die Feiglinge	Live	CD	Line	LICD—9.01350-0	Germany	1997	11.99
Norbert Und Die Feiglinge	Neue Deutsche Felle	CD	Line	LICD—9.01351-0	Germany	1997	11.99
Norbert Und Die Feiglinge	Norbert Und Die Feiglinge	CD	Line	LICD—9.01352-0	Germany	1997	11.99
Norbert Und Die Feiglinge	Rente	CD Single	Line	JLCD-9.01324-0	Germany	1996	9.99
Norbert Und Die Feiglinge	Todesanzeigen	CD	Line	LICD—9.01363-0	Germany	1998	11.99
Norbert Und Die Feiglinge	Weihnachten	CD Single	Line	JLCD-9.01336-0	Germany	1996	9.99
Norman, Monty	Dr. No (O.S.T.)	CD	EMI	7-96210-2	U.S.A.	1962	11.99
Notting Hillbillies/M Knopfler	Missing....Presumed Having..	CD	Warner Bros.	9-26147-2	U.S.A.	1990	8.99
Notting Hillbillies/M Knopfler	Will You Miss Me	CD Single	Vertigo	875643-2	England	1990	4.99
Notting Hillbillies/M Knopfler	Your Own Sweet Way	CD Single	Vertigo	NHBCD-1	England	1990	21.99
Nova, Aldo	A Portrait Of	CD	Epic	EK-48522	U.S.A.	1991	14.99
Nova, Aldo	Nova's Dream	CD	RCA	74321-41410-2	Canada	1996	14.99
Nova, Aldo	Self Titled	CD	Columbia	CK-37498	U.S.A.	1990	12.99
Nova, Aldo	Subject... Aldo Nova	CD	Columbia	CK-38721	U.S.A.	1990	14.99
Nova, Aldo	Twitch	CD	Columbia	CK-40001	U.S.A.	1990	11.99
Nova, Aldo/Jon Bon Jovi	Blood On The Bricks	CD	Polygram	848-513-2	U.S.A.	1991	11.99
NRBQ	All Hopped Up	CD	Line	MLCD-9.00225-L	Germany	1989	15.99
NRBQ	Grooves In Orbit	CD	Essential	ESM-CD-676	U.S.A.	1999	9.99
NRBQ	Kick Me Hard	CD	Line	MLCD-9.00265-L	Germany	1989	15.99
NRBQ	Lou And The Q	CD	Line	MLCD-9.00161-L	Germany	1989	15.99
NRBQ	Scraps	CD	Line	MLCD-9.00171-L	Germany	1989	15.99
NRBQ	Tapdancin' Bats	CD	Line	MLCD-9.00151-L	Germany	1989	15.99
NRBQ	Tiddly Winks	CD	Line	MLCD-9.00232-L	Germany	1989	15.99
NRBQ/John Sebastian	Live At The Wax Museum	CD	Dreamworks	YDCD-0100	Japan	2003	18.99
Nucleus	Elastic Rock	CD	Line	LMCD-9.00688-0	Germany	1990	19.99
Nucleus	Live In Bremen (1971)	2CD	Cuneiform	CUNE-173/4	U.S.A.	2003	16.99
Nucleus	Solar Plexus	CD	Line	LMCD-9.00743-0	Germany	1990	19.99
Nucleus	We'll Talk About It Later	CD	Line	LMCD-9.00729-0	Germany	1990	19.99
Nugent, Ted	Cat Scratch Fever + 2	CD	Epic	EK-65912	U.S.A.	1999	9.99
Nugent, Ted	Craveman	CD	Spitfire	SPT-15174-2	U.S.A.	2002	11.99
Nugent, Ted	Double Live Gonzo	2CD	Epic	E2K-35069	U.S.A.	1990	15.99
Nugent, Ted	Free-For-All + 3 (W/Meatloaf)	CD	Epic	EK-65913	U.S.A.	1999	9.99
Nugent, Ted	Full Bluntal Nugity	CD	Spitfire	SPT-15175-2	U.S.A.	2001	11.99
Nugent, Ted	Great Gonzos! The Best Of	CD	Epic	EK-65704	U.S.A.	1999	7.99
Nugent, Ted	If You Can't Lick 'Em... Lick 'Em	CD	Warner Bros.	32XD-939	Japan	1988	17.99
Nugent, Ted	If You Can't Lick 'Em...Lick 'Em	CD	Spitfire	SPT-15155-2	U.S.A.	2001	9.99
Nugent, Ted	Intensities In 10 Cities	CD	Epic	EK-37084	U.S.A.	1991	7.99
Nugent, Ted	Little Miss Dangerous	CD	Spitfire	SPT-15153-2	U.S.A.	2001	10.99
Nugent, Ted	Live At Hammersmith '79	CD	Epic	EK-64871	U.S.A.	1997	7.99
Nugent, Ted	Nugent	CD	Spitfire	SPT-15151-2	U.S.A.	2001	12.99
Nugent, Ted	Out Of Control	2CD	Epic	E2K-65425	U.S.A.	1998	16.99
Nugent, Ted	Penetrator	CD	Spitfire	SPT-15152-2	U.S.A.	2001	10.99
Nugent, Ted	Scream Dream	CD	Epic	EK-36404	U.S.A.	1990	11.99

N

Artist	Title	Format	Label	Catalog No	Country	Released	Value
Nugent, Ted	Self Titled + 4	CD	Epic	EK-65914	U.S.A.	1999	8.99
Nugent, Ted	Slightly Out Of Control	CD	Epic	ESK-5036	U.S.A.	1993	7.99
Nugent, Ted	Spirit Of The Wild	CD	Atlantic	9-82611-2	U.S.A.	1995	7.99
Nugent, Ted	State Of Shock	CD	Epic	EK-36000	U.S.A.	1990	11.99
Nugent, Ted	Super Hits	CD	Epic	EK-65400	U.S.A.	1998	5.99
Nugent, Ted	The Ultimate	2CD	Epic	E2K-86449	U.S.A.	2002	18.99
Nugent, Ted	Weekend Warriors	CD	Epic	EK-35551	U.S.A.	1990	13.99
Nugent, Ted/Amboy Dukes	Amboy Dukes (1st Lp)	CD	Repertoire	REP-4175-WZ	Germany	1991	20.99
Nugent, Ted/Amboy Dukes	Journey/Center Of The Mind + 1	CD	Repertoire	REP-4176-WZ	Germany	1991	20.99
Nugent, Ted/Amboy Dukes	Loaded For Bear: The Best Of	CD	Epic	ZK-66448	U.S.A.	1999	16.99
Nugent, Ted/Amboy Dukes	Marriage On The Rocks/Rock Bottom	CD	Line	LMCD-9.51164-Z	Germany	1992	24.99
Nugent, Ted/Amboy Dukes	Migration + 2	CD	Won-Sin	WS-885-674-2	Korea	2001	22.99
Nugent, Ted/Amboy Dukes	Survival Of The Fittest	CD	Line	LMCD-9.51165-Z	Germany	1992	24.99
Numan, Gary	'78 - '83 Best Of	2CD	Beggars Banquet	BEGA-150CD	England	1994	13.99
Numan, Gary	Anthology	DVD Aud	Silverline	288090	U.S.A.	2002	12.99
Numan, Gary	Archive	CD	Rialto	RMCD-205	U.S.A.	1996	9.99
Numan, Gary	Archive 2	CD	Rialto	RMCD-225	U.S.A.	1998	5.99
Numan, Gary	Asylum 1 (Box Set)	4CD	Alfa	ALCB-6-9	Japan	1990	49.99
Numan, Gary	Asylum 2 (Box Set)	4CD	Alfa	ALCB-10-13	Japan	1990	49.99
Numan, Gary	Asylum 3 (Box Set)	CD	Alfa	ALCB-31	Japan	1990	34.99
Numan, Gary	BBC in Concert: The Best of	CD	Varese	061064	U.S.A.	2000	8.99
Numan, Gary	Beserker + 4	CD	Cleopatra	CLP-0539-2	U.S.A.	1999	12.99
Numan, Gary	Black Heart	CD	Culture Press	P1004	England	1998	8.99
Numan, Gary	Cars (7 Remix Single)	CD Single	Beggars Banquet	BEG-264-CD	England	1993	18.99
Numan, Gary	Cars (Premier Mix)	CD Single	Polygram T.V.	576-273-2	England	1996	6.99
Numan, Gary	Collection	CD	Castle	229	England	1989	16.99
Numan, Gary	Dance + 5	CD	Beggars Banquet	BBL-28CD	England	1998	12.99
Numan, Gary	Dark Wonders: Best of	2CD	Recall	SMD-CD-372	England	2002	12.99
Numan, Gary	Disconnection	2CD	Sanctuary	81214	England	2002	16.99
Numan, Gary	Document Series Presents	CD	Connoisseur	VSOP-CD-113	England	1992	11.99
Numan, Gary	Down In The Park	CD	Sanctuary	80250	England	2001	9.99
Numan, Gary	Dream Corrosion (Live)	2CD	Eagle	1602	U.S.A.	2003	13.99
Numan, Gary	Exhibition (Different Tracks)	2CD	Vertigo	832-993-2	Canada	1987	52.99
Numan, Gary	Exhibition Tour 1987: Ghost	2CD	Numa	CLP-680-2	U.S.A.	1999	24.99
Numan, Gary	Exile + 1	CD	Cleopatra	CLP-0200-2	England	1999	9.99
Numan, Gary	Exile + 1	CD	Cleopatra	CLP-0200-2	U.S.A.	1998	7.99
Numan, Gary	Exposure: The Best of 1977-2002	CD	Universal	400008	England	2002	14.99
Numan, Gary	Here I Am	CD	Receiver	RRCD-186	England	1995	14.99
Numan, Gary	Human	2CD	Numa	1013	England	1995	24.99
Numan, Gary	Hybrid	CD	Artful	400003	England	2003	8.99
Numan, Gary	I, Assassin + 8	CD	Beggars Banquet	BBL-40CD	England	2002	12.99
Numan, Gary	Isolate: The Numa Years	CD	Numa	1008	England	1998	14.99
Numan, Gary	Live At Brixton	CD	Eagle	20001	U.S.A.	2003	14.99
Numan, Gary	Live Dark Light	2CD	Cleopatra	CLP-0334-2	U.S.A.	1998	12.99
Numan, Gary	Living Ornaments '79	2CD	Beggars Banquet	BEGA-155CD	England	2000	19.99
Numan, Gary	Living Ornaments '81	2CD	Beggars Banquet	BEGA-157-CD	England	1998	19.99
Numan, Gary	Machine + Soul + 7	CD	Cleopatra	CLP-0541-2	U.S.A.	1999	7.99
Numan, Gary	Metal Rhythm + 5	CD	EMI	22133	England	1999	10.99
Numan, Gary	My Dying Machine	CD	Receiver	RRCD-221	England	1999	8.99
Numan, Gary	New Anger	CD Single	Capitol	13005	U.S.A.	1990	22.99
Numan, Gary	New Dreams for Old: 1984-1998	CD	Spitfire	0522	U.S.A.	2000	8.99
Numan, Gary	Outland + 5	CD	EMI	21405	England	1999	9.99
Numan, Gary	Pure	CD	Spitfire	SPT-15088-2	U.S.A.	2001	12.99
Numan, Gary	Remodulate: The Numa Chronicles	2CD	Cleopatra	CLP-0335-2	England	1998	14.99
Numan, Gary	Replicas + 6	CD	Beggars Banquet	BBL-7CD	England	1998	12.99
Numan, Gary	Replicas/The Plan	2CD	Beggars Banquet	BEGA-152CD	England	1993	14.99
Numan, Gary	Sacrifice (Extended Mixes)	CD	Numa	1011	England	1994	8.99
Numan, Gary	Sacrifice + 4	CD	Cleopatra	CLP-0336-2	U.S.A.	1998	7.99

N

Artist	Title	Format	Label	Catalog No	Country	Released	Value
Numan, Gary	Selection	CD Single	Beggars Banquet	BBP-5CD	England	1989	10.99
Numan, Gary	Story So Far	3CD	Receiver	RRCD-221-223	England	1996	44.99
Numan, Gary	Strange Charm + 5	CD	Cleopatra	CLP-0534-2	U.S.A.	1999	8.99
Numan, Gary	Telekon + 5	CD	Beggars Banquet	BBL-19CD	England	1998	12.99
Numan, Gary	Telekon/I, Assassin	2CD	Beggars Banquet	BEGA-154CD	England	1993	14.99
Numan, Gary	The Best of Gary Numan: 1984-1992	CD	Emporio	666	England	1997	10.99
Numan, Gary	The Fury + 5	CD	Cleopatra	CLP-0389-2	England	1998	9.99
Numan, Gary	The Mix	CD	Cleopatra	CLP-0192-2	England	1998	14.99
Numan, Gary	The Other Side Of	CD	Receiver	RRCD-170	England	1992	10.99
Numan, Gary	The Plan	CD	Beggars Banquet	BBL-55CD	England	1999	18.99
Numan, Gary	The Pleasure Principle + 7	CD	Beggars Banquet	BBL-10-CD	U.S.A.	1998	12.99
Numan, Gary	The Pleasure Principle/Warriors	2CD	Beggars Banquet	BEGA-153CD	England	1993	14.99
Numan, Gary	The Radio One Recordings	CD	Strange Fruit	SFRSCD081	England	1999	14.99
Numan, Gary	The Skin Mechanic: Live	CD	EMI	21406	England	1999	8.99
Numan, Gary	The Sleeproom	CD	Receiver	RRCD-222	England	1999	7.99
Numan, Gary	Time To Die (Live)	CD	Receiver	RRCD-223	England	1999	14.99
Numan, Gary	Tubeway Army + 13	CD	Beggars Banquet	BBL-4CD	England	1998	12.99
Numan, Gary	Tubeway Army/Dance	CD	Beggars Banquet	BEGA-151CD	England	1993	18.99
Numan, Gary	Tubeway Army/Live At The Roxy	2CD	Beggars Banquet	BBL-4CD	England	1998	14.99
Numan, Gary	Tubeway Army: The Peel Sessions	CD	Strange Fruit	202	England	1989	15.99
Numan, Gary	Warriors + 6	CD	Beggars Banquet	BBL-47CD	England	2002	12.99
Numan, Gary	White Noise	2CD	Cleopatra	CLP-0030-2	U.S.A.	1998	14.99
Numan, Gary/Sharpe	Automatic	CD	Polydor	839-520-2	Germany	1989	14.99
Numan, Gary/Tubeway Army	Premier Hits (Remastered)	CD	Beggars Banquet	BBL-2007-CD	U.S.A.	1996	7.99
Numan, Gary/Tubeway Army	The Dramatis Project	CD	Dressed To Kill	457	England	2000	12.99
Nunn, Gary P.	Border States	CD	Line	SDCD-9.00576-0	Germany	1988	12.99
Nyro, Laura	An Evening With Live Japan 1994 + 5	CD	Universal	UICY-1139	Japan	2003	27.99
Nyro, Laura	Angel in the Dark	CD	Rounder	613176	U.S.A.	2002	7.99
Nyro, Laura	Christmas And The Beads Of Sweat	CD	Columbia	CK-30259	U.S.A.	1970	8.99
Nyro, Laura	Eli And The Thirteenth Confession + 3	CD	Columbia	CK-85763	U.S.A.	2002	13.99
Nyro, Laura	Live At The Bottom Line	CD	Pony Canyon	D25Y0344	Japan	1990	44.99
Nyro, Laura	Live At The Bottom Line	CD	A&M	14166-6430-2	U.S.A.	1989	29.99
Nyro, Laura	Live from Mountain Stage	CD	Blue Plate	403	U.S.A.	2000	13.99
Nyro, Laura	Live! The Loom's Desire	2CD	Rounder	613186	U.S.A.	2002	11.99
Nyro, Laura	Mother's Spiritual	CD	Line	CLCD-9.00924-0	Germany	1990	29.99
Nyro, Laura	Nested	CD	Sony	SRCS-6324	Japan	1993	209.99
Nyro, Laura	New York Tendaberry + 2	CD	Columbia	CK-85764	U.S.A.	2002	13.99
Nyro, Laura	Premium Best	CD	SME	SME-8823	Japan	1999	24.99
Nyro, Laura	Season of Lights... In Concert	CD	Sony	SRCS-6807	Japan	1999	33.99
Nyro, Laura	Smile	CD	Columbia	CK-33912	U.S.A.	1978	8.99
Nyro, Laura	Stoned Soul Picnic: The Best Of	2CD	Columbia	C2K-48880	U.S.A.	1997	12.99
Nyro, Laura	The First Songs	CD	Columbia	CK-31410	U.S.A.	1971	9.99
Nyro, Laura	Time And Love: The Essential Masters	CD	Columbia	CK-61567	U.S.A.	2000	8.99
Nyro, Laura	Walk the Dog & Light the Light	CD	Columbia	CK-52411	U.S.A.	1993	16.99
Nyro, Laura/Labelle	Gonna Take a Miracle + 4	CD	Columbia	CK-85764	U.S.A.	2002	8.99

O

Artist	Title	Format	Label	Catalog No	Country	Released	Value
O' Brien, Richard	Absolutely	CD	Medical	DOCTORCD1	England	1999	9.99
O' Brien, Richard	Brdwy Rocky Horror DJ CD Sampler	CD	RCA	CDJ-63814-2	U.S.A.	2001	9.99
O' Brien, Richard	Rocky Horror 25th Ann (Promo)	CD Single	Festival	ROCKY-1	Australia	2001	9.99
O' Brien, Richard	Rocky Horror Collection	5CD	Essential	ROK-CD-103	England	1997	34.99
O' Brien, Richard	Rocky Horror P. S. Aud Participation	2CD	Rhino	R2-71112	U.S.A.	1983	8.99
O' Brien, Richard	Rocky Horror P. S. Sing It!	CD	Rhino	R2-72178	U.S.A.	1995	8.99

Artist	Title	Format	Label	Catalog No	Country	Released	Value
O' Brien, Richard	Rocky Horror Picture S (20th An Gold)	CD	Rhino	R2-7159	U.S.A.	1995	14.99
O' Brien, Richard	Rocky Horror Picture S (Rarities Cd)	2CD	Essential	ESDCD-908	England	2000	14.99
O' Brien, Richard	Rocky Horror Picture Show (German)	CD	Multi Culture	MCRC0080597	Germany	1997	79.99
O' Brien, Richard	Rocky Horror Show (C. Lee/Brian May)	CD	Jay M W E	CDJAY-1299	England	1990	27.99
O' Brien, Richard	Rocky Horror Show (W/Gary Glitter)	CD	Stetson	SRCD6	England	1978	37.99
O' Brien, Richard	Shock Treatment (Rocky Horror 2)	CD	Rhino	R2-71678	U.S.A.	1981	24.99
O' Brien, Richard	The New Rocky Horror Show	CD	Columbia	472855-2	Australia	1992	24.99
O' Brien, Richard	The Rocky Horror Show	CD	Tring Int.	GRF231	EEC	1993	24.99
O' Ryan	Something Strong	CD	Zero	XRCN-1085	Japan	1991	19.99
O' Sullivan, Gilbert	20 Greatest Hits + 2	CD	Repertoire	REP-4260-WG	Germany	1992	24.99
O' Sullivan, Gilbert	A Stranger In My Own Backyard	CD	Polydor K.K.	KTCM-9004	Japan	1990	24.99
O' Sullivan, Gilbert	Back To Front	CD	Polydor K.K.	KTCM-9002	Japan	1990	24.99
O' Sullivan, Gilbert	Best Of	CD	Rhino	R2-70560	U.S.A.	1997	14.99
O' Sullivan, Gilbert	Best Of	CD	Rhino	R2-70560	U.S.A.	1991	12.99
O' Sullivan, Gilbert	Best Of	CD	Victor Ent.	VICP-61358	Japan	2001	29.99
O' Sullivan, Gilbert	Best Of	CD	Karussell	5191552	Australia	1992	14.99
O' Sullivan, Gilbert	By Larry	CD	Park	PRKCD-25	England	1994	29.99
O' Sullivan, Gilbert	Caricature Box Set (Best Of)	3CD	Rhino	RRH-77849-2	U.S.A.	2004	49.99
O' Sullivan, Gilbert	Every Song Has It's Play	CD	Park	PRKCD-30	England	1995	19.99
O' Sullivan, Gilbert	Every Song Has It's Play	CD	Polydor K.K.	KTCM-1016	Japan	1995	29.99
O' Sullivan, Gilbert	Greatest Hits	CD	BR Music	BRCD-46	England	1986	12.99
O' Sullivan, Gilbert	Greatest Hits	CD	Repertoire	REP-4260-WZ	Germany	1996	24.99
O' Sullivan, Gilbert	Happiness Is Me And You	CD	Ariola	74321-14052-2	Germany	1993	28.99
O' Sullivan, Gilbert	Himself	CD	Polydor K.K.	KTCM-9001	Japan	1990	22.99
O' Sullivan, Gilbert	I'm A Writer Not A Fighter	CD	Polydor K.K.	KTCM-9003	Japan	1990	22.99
O' Sullivan, Gilbert	In The Key Of G	CD	Festival	D30274	Australia	1990	14.99
O' Sullivan, Gilbert	In The Key Of G	CD	Toshiba-EMI	TOCP-6098	Japan	1990	29.99
O' Sullivan, Gilbert	Irlish	CD	Universal	0139422	Ireland	2000	19.99
O' Sullivan, Gilbert	Irlish	CD	Polydor K.K.	KTCM-1175	Japan	2000	29.99
O' Sullivan, Gilbert	Life & Rhymes	CD	Polydor K.K.	KTCR-1221	Japan	1992	54.99
O' Sullivan, Gilbert	Live In Japan	CD	Scana Norge	98085	Norway	1996	24.99
O' Sullivan, Gilbert	Nothing But The Best	CD	Nota Blu Musica	9409289	Italy	1994	30.99
O' Sullivan, Gilbert	Off Centre	CD	Polydor K.K.	KTCM-1107	Japan	1995	24.99
O' Sullivan, Gilbert	Original Collection 1971 - 1977	5CD	Polydor K.K.	KTCM9001/9005	Japan	1990	99.99
O' Sullivan, Gilbert	Piano Foreplay	CD	Victor Ent.	VICP-62326	Japan	2003	29.99
O' Sullivan, Gilbert	Rare Tracks	CD	Polydor K.K.	KTCR-1152	Japan	1992	22.99
O' Sullivan, Gilbert	Singer Sowing Machine	CD	Park	PRKCD-41	England	1997	19.99
O' Sullivan, Gilbert	Singer Sowing Machine	CD	Polydor K.K.	KTCM-1057	Japan	1997	29.99
O' Sullivan, Gilbert	Sounds Of The Loop	CD	Park	PRKCD-19	England	1993	19.99
O' Sullivan, Gilbert	Sounds Of The Loop	CD	Toshiba-EMI	TOCP-6897	Japan	1991	24.99
O' Sullivan, Gilbert	Southpaw	CD	Polydor K.K.	KTCM-9005	Japan	1990	25.99
O' Sullivan, Gilbert	The Greatest Hits	CD	Polydor K.K.	KTCM-1098	Japan	1998	29.99
O' Sullivan, Gilbert	The Little Album	CD	Polydor K.K.	KTCM-1222	Japan	1992	21.99
O' Sullivan, Gilbert	The Other Sides Of (B-Sides)	CD	Victor Ent.	VICP-62613	Japan	2004	34.99
O' Sullivan, Gilbert	The Very Best Of	CD	Pan Music	00.1101-PM	Israel	1995	14.99
O' Sullivan, Gilbert	Tomorrow Is Today - Live In Japan '93	CD	BR Music	BX-4232	England	1993	19.99
O' Sullivan, Gilbert	Tomorrow Is Today - Live In Japan '93	CD	Toshiba-EMI	TOCP-7843	Japan	1993	24.99
O' Sullivan, Gilbert	Twin Best	2CD	Victor Ent.	VICP-41173/74	Japan	2002	44.99
O' Sullivan, Gilbert	Unforgettable	CD	Castle	UNCD4	England	1987	12.99
Oak Ridge Boys	Bobbie Sue/Step on Out	CD	MCA	MCAD-5922	U.S.A.	1987	7.99
Oak Ridge Boys	Heartbeat	CD	MCA	MCAD-42036	U.S.A.	1987	6.99
Oak Ridge Boys	Room Service	CD	MCA	MCAD-31113	U.S.A.	1978	7.99
Oak Ridge Boys	Seasons	CD	MCA	MCAD-31124	U.S.A.	1986	6.99
Oasis	(What's The Story) Morning Glory?	CD	Epic	EK-67351	U.S.A.	1995	8.99
Oasis	Acquiesce (Promo Only 300)	CD Single	Creation	CCD-204P	England	1995	85.99
Oasis	Acquiesce (Promo)	CD Single	Sony	SAMPCM-603	England	1995	429.99
Oasis	Acquiesce/Interview (Promo)	CD	Epic	ESK-41571	U.S.A.	1998	29.99
Oasis	All Around The World	CD Single	Big Brother Ltd.	RKIDSCD-021	England	1998	8.99

O

Artist	Title	Format	Label	Catalog No	Country	Released	Value
Oasis	Be Here Now	CD	Epic	EK-68530	U.S.A.	1997	7.99
Oasis	Cast No Shadow (Promo/Less 100)	CD Single	Sony	SAMPCS-3707	Italy	1996	249.99
Oasis	Cum On Feel The Noize (Football DJ)	CD Single	Creation	CCD221	England	1995	133.99
Oasis	D' You Know What I Mean? (Promo)	CD Single	Epic	ESK-0979	U.S.A.	1997	6.99
Oasis	Definitely Maybe (W/Bonus Cd)	2CD	Epic	EK-66431	U.S.A.	1994	13.99
Oasis	Don't Go Away	CD Single	Epic	ESCA-6948	Japan	1998	24.99
Oasis	Don't Go Away (Promo)	CD Single	Epic	ESK-2591	U.S.A.	1997	12.99
Oasis	Don't Look Back In Anger	CD Single	Epic	34K-78356	U.S.A.	1996	7.99
Oasis	D'You Know What I Mean?	CD Single	Creation	CRESD-256	England	1997	8.99
Oasis	Familiar To Millions	2CD	Epic	E2K-85267	U.S.A.	2000	11.99
Oasis	Go Let It Out	CD Single	Sony	RKIDSCD-001	England	2000	4.99
Oasis	Heathen Chemistry	CD	Epic	EK-86586	U.S.A.	2002	8.99
Oasis	Heathen Chemistry (Numbered Promo)	CD	Sony	SAMPCM-115352	England	2002	54.99
Oasis	I Hope, I Think, I Know (Promo)	CD Single	Epic	SO-1	U.S.A.	1997	74.99
Oasis	Live Forever	CD Single	Creation	CRESD-185	England	1994	7.99
Oasis	Live Forever (Promo)	CD Single	Epic	ESK-6435	U.S.A.	1994	24.99
Oasis	Masterplan (Promo Sampler)	CD	Creation	CCD-241	England	1998	29.99
Oasis	Oasis WFM 96.9 Central (Promo)	CD	Epic	PRCD97162	Mexico	2000	99.99
Oasis	Roll With It	CD Single	Creation	CRESD-212	England	1995	6.99
Oasis	Some Might Say (Promo)	CD	Creation	CRESCD204	England	1995	8.99
Oasis	Stand By Me	CD Single	Creation	CRESD-278	England	1997	7.99
Oasis	Standing On The Shoulder Of Giants	CD	Epic	EK-63586	U.S.A.	2000	7.99
Oasis	Standing On The... (Promo)	CD	Big Brother	RKIDCD002P	England	2000	14.99
Oasis	Stop Crying Your Heart Out	CD Single	Big Brother	RKIDSCD-24	England	2002	6.99
Oasis	Sunday Times CD	CD	Big Brother	OASIS-25ST	England	2002	8.99
Oasis	Supersonic	CD Single	Sony	660317-1	Australia	1994	7.99
Oasis	Supersonic	CD Single	Creation	660317-2	Australia	1994	5.99
Oasis	The Hindu Times	CD Single	Big Brother	RKIDSCD-23	England	2002	5.99
Oasis	The Masterplan	CD	Epic	EK-69647	U.S.A.	1998	8.99
Oasis	What's The Story (Singles Cig. Box Set)	5CD	Sony	01-663707-14	England	1996	39.99
Oasis	Wonderwall	CD Single	Epic	49K-78204	U.S.A.	1995	7.99
Ocasek, Ric	Beatitude	CD	Geffen	GEFD-2022	U.S.A.	1982	7.99
Ocasek, Ric	Fireball Zone	CD	Reprise	9-26552-2	U.S.A.	1991	5.99
Ocasek, Ric	Quick Change World	CD	Reprise	9-45248-2	U.S.A.	1993	5.99
Ocasek, Ric	The Next Right Moment (Promo)	CD Single	Columbia	CSK-3462	U.S.A.	1997	10.99
Ocasek, Ric	This Side Of Paradise	CD	Geffen	9-24098-2	U.S.A.	1986	6.99
Ocasek, Ric	Troublizing	CD	Columbia	CK-67962	U.S.A.	1997	5.99
Ocean Colour Scene	Beside Ourselves	CD	MCA	MVCM-20072	Japan	1996	24.99
Ocean Colour Scene	Marchin' Already + 4	CD	MCA Victor	MVCE-24040	Japan	1997	29.99
Ocean Colour Scene	Mechanical Wonder (Special Edition)	CD	Universal	548-686-2	EU	2001	19.99
Ocean Colour Scene	Mechanical Wonder + 1	CD	Universal	UICI-2002	Japan	2001	29.99
Ocean Colour Scene	Moseley Shoals	CD	MCA	MCAD-11479	U.S.A.	1996	8.99
Ocean Colour Scene	Ocean Colour Scene (Orig. Label)	CD	Fontana	314-512-269-2	U.S.A.	1992	24.99
Ocean Colour Scene	One From The Modern	CD	Island	546-674-2	England	1999	10.99
Ocean Colour Scene	Songs For The Front Row- The Best Of	CD	Ark 21	186-810-077-2	U.S.A.	2001	8.99
Ocean Colour Scene	We Are The News	CD Single	MCA Victor	MVCE-18004	Japan	2000	22.99
Ocean Colour Scene	You've Got It Bad	CD Single	MCA	MCSTD-40036	England	1996	8.99
Ocean Colour Scene	You've Got It Bad	CD Single	MCA	MCADM-55217	U.S.A.	1996	3.99
Ocean Colour Scene	You've Got It Bad (Promo)	CD Single	MCA	MCA5P-3768	U.S.A.	1996	9.99
Ocean, Billy	Love Zone	CD	Jive	JRCD-8409	U.S.A.	1985	7.99
Ochs, Phil	20th Century Masters: The Millennium	CD	A&M	314-493-164-2	U.S.A.	2002	8.99
Ochs, Phil	A Toast To Those Who Are Gone	CD	Rhino	R2-70080	U.S.A.	1989	23.99
Ochs, Phil	All the News That's Fit to Sing	CD	Hannibal	4427	U.S.A.	1995	23.99
Ochs, Phil	American Troubadour	CD	A&M	728	U.S.A.	1997	33.99
Ochs, Phil	Farewells & Fantasies Box Set	3CD	Rhino	R2-73518	U.S.A.	1997	44.99
Ochs, Phil	Greatest Hits	CD	Edsel	EDCD-201	England	1994	33.99
Ochs, Phil	Gunfight At Carnegie Hall (MFSL Silver)	CD	Mobile Fidelity	MFCD-794	U.S.A.	1974	24.99
Ochs, Phil	I Ain't Marching Anymore	CD	Rykodisc	HNCD-4422	U.S.A.	1986	20.99

O

Artist	Title	Format	Label	Catalog No	Country	Released	Value
Ochs, Phil	In Concert	CD	Rhino	R2-73501	U.S.A.	1995	11.99
Ochs, Phil	Live At Newport	CD	Vanguard	77017	U.S.A.	1996	11.99
Ochs, Phil	Pleasures Of The Harbor	CD	Collector's Choice	137	U.S.A.	2000	8.99
Ochs, Phil	Rehearsals Retirement/Gunfight/C. H.	CD	Collector's Choice	150	U.S.A.	2000	8.99
Ochs, Phil	Tape From California	CD	Collector's Choice	138	U.S.A.	2000	8.99
Ochs, Phil	The Broadside Tapes 1 (Gold Cd)	CD	Folkways	CD-SF-40008	U.S.A.	1989	12.99
Ochs, Phil	The Early Years	CD	Vanguard	79566	U.S.A.	2000	9.99
Ochs, Phil	The War Is Over: The Best Of	CD	A&M	75021-5215-2	U.S.A.	1988	9.99
Ochs, Phil	There And Now: Live In Vancouver	CD	Rhino	R2-70778	U.S.A.	1990	12.99
Ochs, Phil	There But For Fortune	CD	Elektra	9-60832-2	U.S.A.	1989	9.99
O'Connor, Hazel	5 In The Morning	CD	Mystic	MYS-CD-122	England	1997	8.99
O'Connor, Hazel	Alive And Kicking (Live In L.A.)	CD	Nota Blu	9404207	England	1994	14.99
O'Connor, Hazel	Breaking Glass O.S.T.	CD	A&M	396943-2	Germany	1980	13.99
O'Connor, Hazel	Cover Plus	CD	Line	ALCD-9.00010-0	Germany	1987	14.99
O'Connor, Hazel	Cover Plus	CD	Freestyle	JHD056	England	1992	6.99
O'Connor, Hazel	Cover Plus/Sons And Lovers	2CD	Line	LICD-9.21196-S	Germany	1992	24.99
O'Connor, Hazel	Greatest Hits	CD	Success	22603CD	England	1992	9.99
O'Connor, Hazel	Hold On (Gold Cd)	CD	K Point	1821.1012-2	Czech	1994	14.99
O'Connor, Hazel	L. A. Confidential (Alive/Kicking In LA)	CD	Metrodome	METRO498	England	2001	14.99
O'Connor, Hazel	Live - Over The Moon	CD	Columbia	474867-2	Germany	1993	23.99
O'Connor, Hazel	My Friend Jack	CD Single	Columbia	659108-2	Germany	1993	7.99
O'Connor, Hazel	Refugees Of Love	CD Single	Columbia	660838-2	Germany	1994	7.99
O'Connor, Hazel	See The Writing On The Wall	CD	Line	ALCD-9.01291-0	Germany	1993	19.99
O'Connor, Hazel	Sons And Lovers	CD	Line	ALCD-9.00030-0	Germany	1987	14.99
O'Connor, Hazel	Time After Time	CD Single	Columbia	659536-2	Germany	1993	5.99
O'Connor, Hazel	To Be Freed	CD	Columbia	473687-2	Germany	1993	27.99
Oh's	Desire/Paint The Sky	CD	Line	BWCD-9.00600-0	Germany	1988	6.99
Oh's	Desire/Paint The Sky	CD	Line	LICD-9.01322-0	Germany	1996	6.99
Oingo Boingo	20th Century Masters - The Millennium C	CD	MCA	314-113-020-2	U.S.A.	2002	8.99
Oingo Boingo	Anthology	2CD	Hip O	069-490-494-2-3	U.S.A.	1999	19.99
Oingo Boingo	Best Of O' Boingo	CD	MCA	MCAD-10424	U.S.A.	1992	7.99
Oingo Boingo	Best Of: Skeletons In The Closet	CD	A&M	CD-5217	U.S.A.	1993	8.99
Oingo Boingo	Boingo	CD	Warner Bros.	24562-2	U.S.A.	1994	8.99
Oingo Boingo	Boi-ngo	CD	MCA	MCAD-5811	U.S.A.	1987	7.99
Oingo Boingo	Boingo Live	2CD	MCA	MCAD2-8030	U.S.A.	1988	18.99
Oingo Boingo	Dark At The End Of The Tunnel	CD	MCA	MCAD-6365	U.S.A.	1990	7.99
Oingo Boingo	Dead Man's Party	CD	MCA	MCAD-5665	U.S.A.	1985	7.99
Oingo Boingo	Farewell: Live Universal Ampitheater 19	2CD	A&M	314-540-504-2	U.S.A.	1996	18.99
Oingo Boingo	Good For The Soul	CD	A&M	CD-3252	U.S.A.	1983	24.99
Oingo Boingo	Nothing To Fear	CD	A&M	CD-3251	U.S.A.	1982	24.99
Oingo Boingo	Only A Lad	CD	A&M	CD-3250	U.S.A.	1981	8.99
Oldfield, Matt	My Own Advice	CD	To Music	TO2003CD	England	2002	18.99
Oldfield, Mike	A Virgin Compilation (Promo)	CD	Virgin	PRCD2113	U.S.A.	1987	39.99
Oldfield, Mike	Amarok	CD	Caroline	CAROL-49385-2	U.S.A.	2000	12.99
Oldfield, Mike	Amarok (Australian Gold CD)	CD	Virgin	CDVG-2640	Australia	1990	16.99
Oldfield, Mike	Best of Tubular Bells (Promo UK)	CD	Virgin	CDVDJ2936	England	2001	49.99
Oldfield, Mike	Boxed (Expanded)	3CD	Virgin	CDBOX-1	England	2002	26.99
Oldfield, Mike	Collection	2CD	Virgin	7243-8-12212-2-8	Holland	2002	24.99
Oldfield, Mike	Crises	CD	Caroline	CAROL-1850-2	U.S.A.	2000	12.99
Oldfield, Mike	Dicovery	CD	Caroline	CAROL-1851-2	U.S.A.	2000	12.99
Oldfield, Mike	Earth Moving	CD	Caroline	CAROL-49384-2	U.S.A.	2000	12.99
Oldfield, Mike	Earth Moving/Ommadawn/O Tubular B	3CD	Disky	HR-854582	Netherlands	1999	29.99
Oldfield, Mike	Elements	4CD	Virgin	7243-8-39089-2-9	England	1993	34.99
Oldfield, Mike	Elements Box Set	4CD	Virgin	7243-8-39089-2-9	England	1993	30.99
Oldfield, Mike	Exposed	2CD	Caroline	CAROL-1852-2	U.S.A.	2000	19.99
Oldfield, Mike	Far Above The Clouds (Cd1)	CD Single	Warner Bros.	3984269302	Germany	1999	9.99
Oldfield, Mike	Far Above The Clouds (Cd2)	CD Single	Warner Bros.	3984269312	Germany	1999	9.99
Oldfield, Mike	Five Miles Out	CD	Caroline	CAROL-1853-2	U.S.A.	2000	12.99

O

Artist	Title	Format	Label	Catalog No	Country	Released	Value
Oldfield, Mike	Five Miles Out/Crisis/Heaven's Open	3CD	Disky	HR-854592	Netherlands	1999	29.99
Oldfield, Mike	Guitars	CD	Warner Bros.	3984274012	Germany	1999	12.99
Oldfield, Mike	Heaven's Open	CD	Caroline	CAROL-49386-2	U.S.A.	2000	12.99
Oldfield, Mike	Hergest Ridge	CD	Caroline	CAROL-49368-2	U.S.A.	2000	12.99
Oldfield, Mike	Hibernaculum	CD Single	Warner Bros.	4509-98768-2	Germany	1994	9.99
Oldfield, Mike	Incantations	CD	Virgin	91270-2	England	1978	11.99
Oldfield, Mike	Incantations	CD	Caroline	CAROL-1854-2	U.S.A.	2000	12.99
Oldfield, Mike	Islands + 1	CD	Caroline	CAROL-49383-2	U.S.A.	1987	12.99
Oldfield, Mike	Let There Be Light	CD Single	Warner Bros.	0630-10804-2	Germany	1995	5.99
Oldfield, Mike	Let There Be Light (Holographic Cover)	CD Single	Warner Bros.	0630-10805-2	England	1995	14.99
Oldfield, Mike	Man In The Rain	CD Single	Warner Bros.	3984251842	Germany	1998	4.99
Oldfield, Mike	Music Wonderland	CD	Virgin	0777-7-86943-2	Netherlands	1980	19.99
Oldfield, Mike	Ommadawn	CD	Caroline	CAROL-1855-2	U.S.A.	2000	12.99
Oldfield, Mike	Platinum	CD	Caroline	CAROL-1856-2	U.S.A.	2000	12.99
Oldfield, Mike	Platinum/QE2/Five Miles Out	3CD	Caroline	TPAK-16	France	1994	29.99
Oldfield, Mike	QE2	CD	Caroline	CAROL-1857-2	U.S.A.	2000	12.99
Oldfield, Mike	Sentinel	CD Single	Warner Bros.	4509-91019-2	England	1992	13.99
Oldfield, Mike	Tattoo	CD Single	Warner Bros.	4509-91409-2	Germany	1992	7.99
Oldfield, Mike	Tattoo (Live At Edinburgh Castle EP)	CD Single	Warner Bros.	YZ708CDX	England	1992	7.99
Oldfield, Mike	The Bell	CD Single	Warner Bros.	4509-92261-2	England	1993	18.99
Oldfield, Mike	The Bell/Sentinel-Restructure	CD Single	Warner Music	9-40749-2	U.S.A.	1992	10.99
Oldfield, Mike	The Best Of Mike Oldfield: Elements	CD	Virgin	7243-8-39069-2-5	U.S.A.	1994	12.99
Oldfield, Mike	The Complete Mike Oldfield	2CD	Virgin	0777-7-86403-2-5	Holland	1985	16.99
Oldfield, Mike	The Essential - XXV	CD	Warner Bros.	3984-21218-2	Germany	1997	14.99
Oldfield, Mike	The Killing Fields	CD	Virgin	2-90591	England	1984	7.99
Oldfield, Mike	The Millennium Bell	CD	Warner Bros.	2-80885	Canada	1999	12.99
Oldfield, Mike	The Orchestral Tubular Bellls	CD	Disky	VI-863152	Netherlands	1975	9.99
Oldfield, Mike	The Songs Of Distant Earth	CD	Reprise	9-45933-2	U.S.A.	1994	10.99
Oldfield, Mike	Thou Art In Heaven	CD Single	Warner Bros.	48373-2	Germany	2002	6.99
Oldfield, Mike	To Be Free	CD Single	Warner Bros.	0927-467752	Germany	2002	9.99
Oldfield, Mike	Tr3s Lunas (Bonus Cd Rom)	2CD	Warner Bros.	2-45892	Spain	2002	11.99
Oldfield, Mike	Tubular Bells (Australia Gold Cd)	CD	Virgin	CDV2001	Australia	1973	104.99
Oldfield, Mike	Tubular Bells (SACD)	CD	Virgin	7243-8-50733-2-8	England	2001	24.99
Oldfield, Mike	Tubular Bells 2003 + 3 (Bonus DVD)	2CD	Warner Bros.	2-49921	Canada	2003	29.99
Oldfield, Mike	Tubular Bells II	CD	Reprise	9-45041-2	U.S.A.	1992	10.99
Oldfield, Mike	Tubular Bells III	CD	Warner Bros.	3984243492	Germany	1998	10.99
Oldfield, Mike	Voyager	CD	Warner Bros.	0630-15896-2	Germany	1997	12.99
Oldfield, Mike	Women Of Ireland (Cd 1)	CD Single	Warner Bros.	3984-21265-2	Germany	1997	9.99
Oldfield, Mike	Women Of Ireland [CD2]	CD Single	Warner Bros.	3984-20843-2	England	1997	9.99
Oldfield, Mike/Duo Sonare	Duo Sonare Play T Bells (Acoustic)	CD	MDG Scene	MDG-630-0628-2	Germany	1996	13.99
Oldfield, Mike/Sally	The Sallyangie - Children Of Sun + 6	2CD	Castle	CMDDD545	England	2002	14.99
Oldfield, Mike/Sally	The Sallyangie - Children Of The Sun	CD	Line	TACD-9.00586-0	Germany	1988	9.99
Oldfield, Sally	Anthology	CD	Castle	CLA-872-2	England	2000	15.99
Oldfield, Sally	Celebration	CD	Castle	CLA-6103-2	England	1986	38.99
Oldfield, Sally	Collection	CD	Castle	CLA-125-2	England	1986	10.99
Oldfield, Sally	Definitive Collection	2CD	Columbia	487421	Germany	1997	12.99
Oldfield, Sally	Easy	CD	Castle	CLACD-102	England	1986	15.99
Oldfield, Sally	Femme	CD	Sony	451034	Germany	2002	13.99
Oldfield, Sally	Flaming Star	CD	Eagle	70016	Germany	2001	9.99
Oldfield, Sally	Intincts	CD	Columbia	4630072	Germany	1988	38.99
Oldfield, Sally	Mirrors	2CD	Essential	ESACD872	England	2000	15.99
Oldfield, Sally	Morning Of My Life	2CD	Recall	SMD-CD-198	England	1998	24.99
Oldfield, Sally	Nightriding	CD	Castle	CLA-10021-2	England	1988	38.99
Oldfield, Sally	Playing The Flame	CD	Castle	CLACD-215	England	1990	34.99
Oldfield, Sally	Secret Songs	CD	MSM	10982	Germany	1996	38.99
Oldfield, Sally	Strange Day In Berlin	CD	Castle	CLA-216-2	England	1996	38.99
Oldfield, Sally	Three Rings	CD	MSM	95942	Germany	1994	9.99
Oldfield, Sally	Water Bearer	CD	Castle	CLACD-101	Sweden	1986	28.99

Artist	Title	Format	Label	Catalog No	Country	Released	Value
Oldfield, Terry	Across The Universe	CD	New World	NWCD-489	England	2000	7.99
Oldfield, Terry	All The Rivers Gold	CD	New World	NWCD-462	England	1999	7.99
Oldfield, Terry	Angel	CD	To Music	TO-2002	England	2002	15.99
Oldfield, Terry	Australia: Waking The Spirit + 1	CD	New World	NWCD-267	England	2002	17.99
Oldfield, Terry	Cascade	CD	New World	NWCD-140	England	1986	17.99
Oldfield, Terry	Earth Spirit	CD	New World	NWCD-413	England	1995	22.99
Oldfield, Terry	Icon	CD	New World	NWCD-291	England	1995	7.99
Oldfield, Terry	Illumination: A Celtic Blessing	CD	New World	NWCD-227	England	1992	13.99
Oldfield, Terry	In The Presence Of Light	CD	To Music	TO-2001	England	2001	18.99
Oldfield, Terry	Out Of The Depths	CD	New World	NWCD-252	England	1993	38.99
Oldfield, Terry	Reflections: The Best Of	CD	New World	NWCD-495	England	2000	13.99
Oldfield, Terry	Resonance	CD	New World	NWCD-170	England	1988	11.99
Oldfield, Terry	Reverence	CD	New World	NWCD-141	England	1986	11.99
Oldfield, Terry	Spiral Waves	CD	Voiceprint	VP117CD	England	1992	38.99
Oldfield, Terry	Spirit Of Africa	CD	New World	NWCD-242	England	1993	7.99
Oldfield, Terry	Spirit Of India	CD	New World	NWCD-426	England	1996	22.99
Oldfield, Terry	Spirit Of The Rainforest	CD	New World	NWCD-195	England	1990	8.99
Oldfield, Terry	Spirit Of The World	CD	New World	NWCD-482	England	2000	29.99
Oldfield, Terry	Spirit Of Tibet	CD	New World	NWCD-257	England	1994	13.99
Oldfield, Terry	Star Of Heaven	CD	New World	NWCD-184	England	1989	22.99
Oldfield, Terry	Turning Point	CD	New Earth	2106	England	2002	14.99
Oldfield, Terry	Zen: The Search For Enlightenment	CD	New World	NWCD-215	England	2001	21.99
Olson, Carla	Carla Olson	CD	Still Sane	089207	U.S.A.	1988	28.99
Olson, Carla	Honest as Daylight: The Best Of	CD	Houston Party	035	U.S.A.	2001	18.99
Olson, Carla	Reap The Whirlwind	CD	Watermelon	1026	U.S.A.	1994	7.99
Olson, Carla	Sweden USA	CD	Sound Carrier	2	U.S.A.	1988	12.99
Olson, Carla	Wave Of The Hand: The Best Of	CD	Watermelon	1046	U.S.A.	1995	12.99
Olson, Carla	Within An Ace	CD	Watermelon	1011	U.S.A.	1993	7.99
Olson, Carla/Gene Clark	So Rebellious A Lover	CD	Razor & Tie	RE-1992-2	U.S.A.	1987	25.99
Olson, Carla/Mick Taylor	Live	CD	Demon	197	England	1996	25.99
Olson, Carla/Mick Taylor	Live: Too Hot For Snakes	CD	Razor & Tie	RE-1987-2	U.S.A.	1990	17.99
Olson, Carla/Mick Taylor	The Ring Of Truth	CD	Evangeline	GEL-4024	England	2001	8.99
Olson, Carla/The Textones	Midnight Mission	CD	Acadia	ACA-8016	England	2002	9.99
Olsson, Nigel/Elton John	Move The Universe	CD	Sony	SRCS-352	Japan	2001	29.99
Olsson, Nigel/Elton John	Nigel (David Foster, Bruce Johnston)	CD	Sony	SRCS-6225	Japan	1979	24.99
Olsson, Nigel/Warpipes	Holes On The ... (Davy Johnstone)	CD	Artful	0-5109-17224-2-5	U.S.A.	1991	5.99
Omar & The Howlers	Big Leg Beat	CD	Line	STCD-9.00526-0	Germany	1987	16.99
O'Mara/Darling/Elgart	O'Mara/Darling/Elgart	CD	Line	COCD-9.00670-0	Germany	1988	12.99
OMD	Architecture And Morality + 7	CD	Virgin	82750	England	2003	23.99
OMD	Crush	CD	Disky	HR-87476-2	Netherlands	2000	10.99
OMD	Dazzle Ships	CD	Alliance	86090	England	1996	10.99
OMD	Junk Culture	CD	A&M	75021-3335-2	U.S.A.	1984	13.99
OMD	Liberator	CD	Virgin	88225	England	1993	9.99
OMD	Navigation: The OMD B-Sides	CD	EMI	810248	England	2001	10.99
OMD	O Manoeuvres In The Dark + 4	CD	Virgin	82748	England	2003	23.99
OMD	Organisation + 6	CD	Virgin	82749	England	2003	23.99
OMD	Sugar Tax	CD	Virgin	V2-86234	England	1991	6.99
OMD	The Best Of OMD	CD	Virgin	0777-7-86323-2-0	Holland	1988	10.99
OMD	The OMD Singles	CD	Virgin	7243-8-46520-2-9	U.S.A.	1998	7.99
OMD	The Pacific Age	CD	Virgin	86705	England	1998	9.99
OMD	The Peel Sessions: 1979-1983	CD	EMI	849068	England	2000	12.99
OMD	The Singles (W/Bonus Remixes Cd)	2CD	Virgin	46520B	England	1998	19.99
OMD	Universal	CD	EMI	41978	Germany	1999	8.99
Ongala, Remmy/Orchestra	Songs For The Poor Man	CD	Caroline	CAROL-2305-2	U.S.A.	1989	28.99
Only Ones	Alone In The Night	CD	Dojo	DOJO43	England	1994	14.99
Only Ones	Baby's Got A Gun	CD	Columbia	483662-2	England	1980	29.99
Only Ones	Darkness & Light (BBC Live)	2CD	HUX	HUX-030	England	2002	21.99
Only Ones	Even Serpents Shine	CD	Columbia	478503-2	England	1979	14.99

O

Artist	Title	Format	Label	Catalog No	Country	Released	Value
Only Ones	Live	CD	Demon	MAU-CD-603	England	1989	24.99
Only Ones	Live At The BBC	CD	Windsong	WINCD080	England	1996	28.99
Only Ones	Peel Sessions	CD	Strange Fruit	102	England	1995	13.99
Only Ones	Remains	CD	Anagram	CDM-GRAM-67	England	1993	12.99
Only Ones	Special View	CD	Epic	EK-36199	U.S.A.	1978	7.99
Only Ones	The Big Sleep	CD	Jungle	FREUD-CD-045	England	1993	12.99
Only Ones	The Immortal Story	CD	Columbia	471267-2	England	1992	12.99
Only Ones	The Only Ones	CD	Sony	ESCA-7732	Japan	1998	24.99
Only Ones/Peter Perret	Hearts On Fire (Live/The 1 + Video Cd)	2CD	Alchemy	PILOT-65	England	2000	14.99
Only Ones/Peter Perret	Live With The One	CD	Dwarf	VEN-004	England	1998	14.99
Ono, Yoko	A Story + 3	CD	Rykodisc	RCD-10420	U.S.A.	1997	8.99
Ono, Yoko	A Xmas Message From Yoko (Promo)	CD Single	Rykodisc	VROD-ONO	U.S.A.	1991	6.99
Ono, Yoko	Approximately Infinite Universe + 2	2CD	Rykodisc	RCD-10417/18	U.S.A.	1997	15.99
Ono, Yoko	Blueprint For A Sunrise	CD	Capitol	7243-5-36035-2-6	U.S.A.	2001	9.99
Ono, Yoko	Feeling The Space + 2	CD	Rykodisc	RCD-10419	U.S.A.	1997	8.99
Ono, Yoko	Fly + 2	2CD	Rykodisc	RCD-10415/16	U.S.A.	1997	14.99
Ono, Yoko	It's Alright (I See Rainbows) + 2	CD	Rykodisc	RCD-10422	U.S.A.	1997	8.99
Ono, Yoko	New York Rock (Promo)	CD	Capitol	7243-8-29843-2-0	U.S.A.	1995	8.99
Ono, Yoko	Onobox	6CD	Rykodisc	RCD-10224/29	U.S.A.	1992	84.99
Ono, Yoko	Open Your Box (Orange Factory Remix)	CD Single	Parlophone	7243-551058-2-0	England	2002	5.99
Ono, Yoko	Plastic Ono Band + 3	CD	Rykodisc	RCD-10414	U.S.A.	1997	10.99
Ono, Yoko	Season Of Glass + 2	CD	Rykodisc	RCD-10421	U.S.A.	1997	8.99
Ono, Yoko	Starpeace + 1	CD	Rykodisc	RCD-10423	U.S.A.	1997	8.99
Ono, Yoko	Walking On Thin Ice	CD Single	Twisted	7243-5-82669-2-4	U.S.A.	2003	5.99
Ono, Yoko	Walking On Thin Ice	CD Single	Capitol	82669	U.S.A.	2003	5.99
Ono, Yoko	Walking On Thin Ice (10 Mixes)	CD Single	Capitol	7243-5-85669-2	U.S.A.	2002	19.99
Ono, Yoko	Walking On Thin Ice (Promo)	CD Single	Parlophone	CDRDJ-6607.	England	2003	12.99
Ono, Yoko	Walking On Thin Ice: Best Of	CD	Rykodisc	VRCD-0230	U.S.A.	1992	8.99
Ono, Yoko	Walking On Thin.. (Pet Shop Boys) DJ	CD Single	Parlophone	CDRDJ 6607	England	2002	19.99
Ono, Yoko	Yin Yang	CD Single	Star 69	12502	U.S.A.	2002	5.99
Ono, Yoko/IMA	Rising	CD	Capitol	7243-8-35817-2-6	U.S.A.	1995	10.99
Ono, Yoko/IMA	Rising Mixes	CD	Capitol	7243-8-37268-0-6	U.S.A.	1996	10.99
Opal	Early Recordings + 1	CD	Rough Trade	ROUGH-US-53	U.S.A.	1989	59.99
Opal	Happy Nightmare Baby	CD	Victor Ent.	VDP-1320	Japan	1988	21.99
Opal	Happy Nightmare Baby	CD	SST	SST-CD-103	U.S.A.	1987	13.99
Opal/Southern Isolation	Southern Isolation	CD	Baphomet	SBTN6601-2	U.S.A.	2001	9.99
Orbison, Roy	A Black And White Night	CD	Orbison	ROBW7891-2J	U.S.A.	1999	10.99
Orbison, Roy	A Black And White Night (Gold Cd)	CD	Virgin	91295-2	U.S.A.	1989	34.99
Orbison, Roy	All Time Greatest Hits (DCC Gold Cd)	CD	DCC	GZS-1118	U.S.A.	1993	74.99
Orbison, Roy	Best Of The Sun Years	CD	Repertoire	REP-4807	Germany	2003	13.99
Orbison, Roy	Big Roy Orbison Singles Collection	CD	Monument	492743-2	England	2001	11.99
Orbison, Roy	Box Set	2CD	Orbison	11086	U.S.A.	1998	34.99
Orbison, Roy	California Blue 3 "	CD Single	Virgin	VSCD-1193	Austria	1989	12.99
Orbison, Roy	Communication... (MGM '65-'70)	CD	Raven	RVCD-6	Australia	1997	12.99
Orbison, Roy	Complete Sun Sessions	CD	Varese	302-066-233-2	U.S.A.	2001	9.99
Orbison, Roy	I Drove All Night (Nintendo Single)	CD Single	MCA	MCADS-54419	U.S.A.	1992	11.99
Orbison, Roy	In Dreams/Orbisongs	CD	Sony	474957-2	England	2002	10.99
Orbison, Roy	King Of Hearts	CD	Virgin	0777-7-86520-2-1	U.S.A.	1992	12.99
Orbison, Roy	Lonely And Blue (MFSL Gold)	CD	Mobile Fidelity	UDCD-758	U.S.A.	1961	39.99
Orbison, Roy	Lonely And Blue (Sony Gold Cd)	CD	Monument	JK-66219	U.S.A.	1960	19.99
Orbison, Roy	Mystery Girl (MFSL Gold Cd)	CD	Mobile Fidelity	UDCD-555	U.S.A.	1989	99.99
Orbison, Roy	Orbison (Box Set)	7CD	Bear Family	BCD-16423	Germany	2001	104.99
Orbison, Roy	RCA Sessions (W/Sonny James)	CD	Bear Family	BCD-15407	Germany	1987	16.99
Orbison, Roy	Sings Lonely and Blue/Crying	CD	Sony	474956-2	England	2002	10.99
Artison, Roy	The Anthology	CD	Orbison	ORB-3805-2	U.S.A.	1999	7.99
Orbison, Roy	The Fastest Guitar Alive	CD	Sony	SK-45405	U.S.A.	1991	31.99
Orbison, Roy	The Legendary Roy Orbison (Box Set)	4CD	Columbia	A4K-46809	U.S.A.	1991	24.99
Orbison, Roy	The Sun Years 1956-58	CD	Bear Family	BCD-15461	Germany	1989	23.99

O

Artist	Title	Format	Label	Catalog No	Country	Released	Value
Orbison, Roy	The Very Best Of Roy Orbison	CD	Virgin	7243-8-42350-2-4	U.S.A.	1996	9.99
Orphanage	By Time Alone + 5	CD	Avalon	MICY-1047	Japan	1998	22.99
Orr, Benjamin/The Cars	The Lace	CD	Elektra	9-60460-2	U.S.A.	1986	49.99
Orton, Beth	Best Bit EP	CD Single	Dedicated	61702-44020-2	U.S.A.	1998	7.99
Orton, Beth	Central Reservation + 4	CD	Heavenly	74321734792	Australia	1999	13.99
Orton, Beth	Daybreaker	CD	Astralwerks	7243-5-39918-2-1	U.S.A.	2002	9.99
Orton, Beth	She Cries Your Name	CD Single	Deconstruction	74321-409932	Australia	1996	5.99
Orton, Beth	Superpinkymandy	CD	Toshiba-EMI	TOCP-7984	Japan	2003	35.99
Orton, Beth	Trailer Park	CD	Dedicated	61702-44007-2	U.S.A.	1997	11.99
Orton, Beth/Spill	Don't Wanna Know... (William Orbit)	CD	Toshiba-EMI	VJCP-12008	Japan	1993	35.99
Oryema, Geoffrey	Night To Night	CD	Caroline	CAROL-2357-2	U.S.A.	1996	9.99
Osbourne, Ozzy	Bark at the Moon +1	CD	Epic	85429	U.S.A.	2002	8.99
Osbourne, Ozzy	Blizzard of Ozz + 1	CD	Epic	85247	U.S.A.	2002	8.99
Osbourne, Ozzy	Diary Madman/Bark Moon/Ultimate Sin	3CD	Sony	65612	U.S.A.	1998	20.99
Osbourne, Ozzy	Diary of a Madman +1	CD	Epic	85249	U.S.A.	2002	7.99
Osbourne, Ozzy	Down To Earth	CD	Epic	EK-63580	U.S.A.	2001	8.99
Osbourne, Ozzy	Down to Earth [Limited Edition]	CD	Epic	498474	U.S.A.	2001	9.99
Osbourne, Ozzy	Just Say Ozzy	CD	Epic	67242	U.S.A.	1995	8.99
Osbourne, Ozzy	Live at Budokan	CD	Epic	86525	U.S.A.	2002	5.99
Osbourne, Ozzy	Live at Budokan [Clean]	CD	Epic	86751	U.S.A.	2002	5.99
Osbourne, Ozzy	Mama, I'm Coming Home	CD Single	Sony	45K-74265	U.S.A.	1992	11.99
Osbourne, Ozzy	No More Tears +2	CD	Epic	85248	U.S.A.	2002	8.99
Osbourne, Ozzy	No More Tears Demo Sessions (Promo)	CD	Epic	ZSK-4643	U.S.A.	1991	149.99
Osbourne, Ozzy	No Rest for the Wicked +2	CD	Epic	85426	U.S.A.	2002	9.99
Osbourne, Ozzy	OzzFest, Vol. 1: Live	CD	Red Ant	7000	U.S.A.	1997	6.99
Osbourne, Ozzy	Ozzmosis + 1	CD	Sony	SRCS 7776	Japan	1995	19.99
Osbourne, Ozzy	Ozzmosis + 2	CD	Epic	86645	U.S.A.	2002	5.99
Osbourne, Ozzy	Ozzmosis Box Set (Promo Only 500)	2CD	Sony	XDCS-93189~90	Japan	1995	499.99
Osbourne, Ozzy	Randy Rhoads Tribute	CD	Sony	85444	U.S.A.	2002	7.99
Osbourne, Ozzy	See You On The Other Side + 2	CD	Sony	SRCS-7962	Japan	1996	34.99
Osbourne, Ozzy	Speak of the Devil	CD	Epic	67237	U.S.A.	1995	9.99
Osbourne, Ozzy	Ten Commandments	CD	Priority	CDL-57129	U.S.A.	1990	59.99
Osbourne, Ozzy	The Essential	2CD	Sony	86812	U.S.A.	2003	17.99
Osbourne, Ozzy	The Ozzman Cometh (W/Bonus Cd)	2CD	Epic	67980	U.S.A.	1997	19.99
Osbourne, Ozzy	The Ultimate Sin	CD	Sony	67239	U.S.A.	1995	9.99
Osibisa	African Dawn, African Flight	CD	Red Steel	RMCCD9226	England	2003	14.99
Osibisa	Aka Aka Kra	CD	Red Steel	RMCCD9218	England	2000	14.99
Osibisa	Black Magic Night (Live)	2CD	Sequel	NEECD-315	England	1999	14.99
Osibisa	Criss Cross Rhythms	CD	Point	2620042	Germany	1991	11.99
Osibisa	Happy Children	CD	One Way	OW-35164	U.S.A.	2000	10.99
Osibisa	Heads	CD	Line	LCCD-9.01268-0	Germany	1993	14.99
Osibisa	Live At Cropredy	CD	Red Steel	RMCCD9211	England	1999	14.99
Osibisa	Monsore	CD	AIM	AIM-1065-CD	Australia	1997	8.99
Osibisa	Mystic Energy	CD	Songhai Emp	SERCD001	U.S.A.	1980	8.99
Osibisa	Ojah Awake +3	CD	Red Steel	RMCCD9209	England	1999	14.99
Osibisa	Osibirock	CD	One Way	OW-35165	U.S.A.	2000	10.99
Osibisa	Osibisa	CD	Line	LCCD-9.01266-0	Germany	1992	14.99
Osibisa	Sunshine Day	CD Single	Red Steel	RMCCDS0001	U.S.A.	1995	4.99
Osibisa	Sunshine Day - The Pye/Bronze Anth.	2CD	Sequel	NEECD-313	England	1999	19.99
Osibisa	Superfly TNT	CD	Red Steel	RMCCD0196	England	1996	14.99
Osibisa	The Best Of	CD	Pegasus	PEG-CD-083	England	1997	11.99
Osibisa	The Warrior	CD	Point	2620052	Germany	1991	11.99
Osibisa	Unleashed: Live In India 1981	CD	Red Steel	RMCCD0200	England	1995	14.99
Osibisa	Urban Village	CD	Red Steel	RMCCD9228	England	2003	14.99
Osibisa	Very Best Of	CD	Red Steel	RMCCD0207	England	1995	14.99
Osibisa	Wango Wango	2CD	Snapper	SMDCD452	England	2004	12.99
Osibisa	Welcome Home	CD	Red Steel	RMCCD0208	England	1995	14.99
Osibisa	Woyaya	CD	Line	LCCD-9.01267-0	Germany	1993	14.99

O

Artist	Title	Format	Label	Catalog No	Country	Released	Value
Osmonds	20th Century Masters: The Millennium	CD	Universal	065000	U.S.A.	2002	7.99
Osmonds	Osmond Family Christmas	CD	Curb	D2-77513	U.S.A.	1991	12.99
Osmonds	Osmondmania! Osmond Family Gr. Hits	CD	Polydor	065634	U.S.A.	2003	7.99
Osmonds	The Plan	CD	Curb	D2-77956	U.S.A.	1973	15.99
Other Ones/Dead Related	The Strange Remain	2CD	Grateful Dead	GDCD-4062	U.S.A.	1999	11.99
Other Ones/Pop Group	Holiday	CD Single	Virgin	659-180-211	Germany	1987	19.99
Other Ones/Pop Group	Learning To Walk	CD	Virgin	CDV2569	Germany	1988	28.99
Other Ones/Pop Group	The Other Ones	CD	Virgin	CDV2404	England	1986	21.99
Otter, Anne Sofie Von	Home For Christmas	CD	Deutsche Gramm.	289-459-685-2	Germany	1999	24.99
Outland	Different Worlds + 1	CD	Avalon	MICP-10378	Japan	2003	20.99
Outlaws	Best Of: Green Grass And High Tides	CD	Arista	07822-18936-2	U.S.A.	1996	10.99
Outlaws	Diablo Canyon	CD	Shrapnel	SH-2017CD	U.S.A.	1994	12.99
Outlaws	Hittin' The Road Live	CD	Shrapnel	SH-2016CD	U.S.A.	1993	12.99
Outlaws	Hurry Sundown	CD	Coll Pipeline	TCP-016CD	U.S.A.	1994	7.99
Outlaws	Hurry Sundown	CD	Buddah	74465-99818-2	U.S.A.	2001	8.99
Outlaws	In The Eye Of Storm/Hurry Sundown	CD	Magic	3930327	France	2003	21.99
Outlaws	Lady In Waiting	CD	Buddah	74465-99817-2	U.S.A.	2001	8.99
Outlaws	Los Hombres Malo + 4	CD	Magic	3930368	France	2003	21.99
Outlaws	On The Run	CD	Raw Power	028	England	1986	24.99
Outlaws	Playin' To Win/Ghost Riders	2CD	Magic	3930261	France	2003	21.99
Outlaws	Self Titled	CD	Buddah	74465-99774-2	U.S.A.	2001	8.99
Outlaws	Self Titled/Lady In Waiting	CD	Magic	5213722	France	2003	21.99
Outlaws	Soldiers Of Fortune	CD	Pasha	32DP-625	Japan	1986	179.99
Outrage	Black Clouds	CD	Polydor	POCP-1156	Japan	1991	20.99
Outrage	Blind To Reality	CD	Polydor	POCP-1157	Japan	1991	20.99
Outrage	Days Of Rage (1986-1991)	CD	Polydor	POCP-7100	Japan	1995	20.99
Outrage	It's Packed	CD	East West	AMCM-4308-0	Japan	1997	28.99
Outrage	The Final Day	CD	Polydor	511868-2	Japan	1991	20.99
Outrage	The Great Blue	CD	Polydor	POCP-1158	Japan	1991	20.99
Outrage	The Great Blue	CD	Polydor	POCP-1035	Japan	1990	20.99
Outrage	Who We Are	CD	East West	AMCM-4281	Japan	1997	20.99
Ozric Tentacles	Vitamin Enhanced Ltd Box Set	6CD	Dovetail	DOVE-BOX-1	England	1993	64.99
Ozz	No Prisoners	CD	Line	URCD-9.00827-0	Germany	1989	29.99
Ozz 2	The Assassin	CD	Line	URCD-9.00822-0	Germany	1989	29.99

P

Artist	Title	Format	Label	Catalog No	Country	Released	Value
P (Johnny Depp/G Haynes)	P (Johnny Depp/Gibby Haynes)	CD	Capitol	32942	U.S.A.	1995	60.99
P.D.Q.-Bach	1712 Overture/Other Musical Assaults	CD	Telarc	80210	U.S.A.	1989	8.99
P.D.Q.-Bach	Addicted to P.D.Q. Bach...	CD	Vanguard	VMD-375	U.S.A.	1982	8.99
P.D.Q.-Bach	An Evening with PDQ Bach	CD	Vanguard	VMD-79195	U.S.A.	1990	8.99
P.D.Q.-Bach	Classical Talkity Talk Radio	CD	Telarc	80295	U.S.A.	1991	11.99
P.D.Q.-Bach	Ill-Conceived PDQ Bach Anthology	CD	Telarc	80520	U.S.A.	1998	11.99
P.D.Q.-Bach	Music for an Awful Lot of Winds	CD	Telarc	80307	U.S.A.	1992	11.99
P.D.Q.-Bach	Oedipus Tex & Other Choral Calamities	CD	Telarc	80239	U.S.A.	1990	11.99
P.D.Q.-Bach	The Intimate P.D.Q. Bach	CD	Vanguard	VMD-79335	U.S.A.	1974	8.99
P.D.Q.-Bach	The Short - Tempered Clavier...	CD	Telarc	CD-80390	U.S.A.	1995	11.99
P.D.Q.-Bach	Two Pianos Are Better Than One	CD	Telarc	80376	U.S.A.	1994	11.99
Pablo-Cruise	20th Century Masters: The Millennium	CD	A&M	314-493-017-2	U.S.A.	2001	13.99
Pablo-Cruise	A Place In The Sun	CD	A&M	75021-3236-2	U.S.A.	1977	11.99
Pablo-Cruise	A&M Gold Series	CD	Pony Canyon	D32Y-3058	Japan	1987	13.99
Pablo-Cruise	Classics, Vol. 26	CD	A&M	75021-2524-2	U.S.A.	1992	6.99
Pablo-Cruise	Lifeline	CD	Polydor K.K.	POCM-2006	Japan	1997	13.99
Pablo-Cruise	Part Of The Game	CD	Polydor K.K.	POCM-2009	Japan	1997	34.99

Artist	Title	Format	Label	Catalog No	Country	Released	Value
Pablo-Cruise	Reflector	CD	Polydor	POCM-2010	Japan	1995	45.99
Pablo-Cruise	Want You Tonight: Very Best Of	CD	Universal	490587	England	2000	9.99
Pablo-Cruise	Worlds Away	CD	A&M	75021-3198-2	U.S.A.	1978	10.99
Pack, David	Anywhere You Go	CD	Warner Bros.	WPCR-10509	Japan	1985	27.99
Page, Jimmy	Before The Balloon Went Up	2CD	Dressed To Kill	DRESS607	England	1998	10.99
Page, Jimmy	Death Wish II O.S.T.	CD	East West	AMCY-2745	Japan	1998	49.99
Page, Jimmy	Jimmy's Back Pages...The Early Years	CD	Sony	AK-52428	U.S.A.	1992	8.99
Page, Jimmy	Outrider	CD	Geffen	9-24188-2	U.S.A.	1988	8.99
Page, Jimmy	The Jimmy Page Collection	2CD	Dressed To Kill	ONEPAK542/3	England	2000	13.99
Page, Jimmy/Black Crowes	Live At The Greek + 2	2CD	Victor Ent.	VICP-61192~93	Japan	2000	19.99
Page, Jimmy/J. P. Jones	Lovin' Up A Storm	CD	Armoury	ARMCD017	Germany	2000	10.99
Page, Jimmy/Puff Daddy	Come With Me	CD Single	Epic	66026-2	Austria	1998	8.99
Page, Jimmy/Puff Daddy	Come With Me	CD Single	Epic	34K-78954	U.S.A.	1998	3.99
Page, Jimmy/R. Plant	A Songwriting Legacy (DJ/Miller/Reg)	CD	Atlantic	PRCD-6094/5-2	U.S.A.	1995	45.99
Page, Jimmy/R. Plant	Conversations With (No Quarter Promo)	CD	Atlantic	PRCD-5987-2	U.S.A.	1994	19.99
Page, Jimmy/R. Plant	Gallows Pole (Promo)	CD Single	Atlantic	PRCD-5921-2	U.S.A.	1994	28.99
Page, Jimmy/R. Plant	Most High (Single)	CD Single	Mercury	568-751-2	England	1998	5.99
Page, Jimmy/R. Plant	Most High Promo	CD Single	Atlantic	PRCD-8472	U.S.A.	1998	4.99
Page, Jimmy/R. Plant	No Quarter Unledded + 1	CD	Fontana	526-362-2	England	1984	19.99
Page, Jimmy/R. Plant	Sons Of Freedom (Promo)	CD Single	Atlantic	PRCD-8688	U.S.A.	1998	10.99
Page, Jimmy/R. Plant	Walking Into Clarksdale	CD	Mercury	83092-2	U.S.A.	1998	7.99
Page, Jimmy/R. Plant	Walking Into Clarksdale	CD	Mercury	558-025-2	Russia	1998	5.99
Page, Jimmy/R. Plant	When The World Was Young (Promo)	CD Single	Atlantic	PRCD-8726	U.S.A.	1994	10.99
Page, Jimmy/R. Plant	Wonderful One	CD Single	Atlantic	CD5-85591-2	U.S.A.	1994	7.99
Page, Jimmy/R. Plant	Wonderful One (Promo)	CD Single	Atlantic	PRCD-6119-2	U.S.A.	1994	14.99
Page, Jimmy/Roy Harper	Whatever Happened To Jugula	CD	Science Fiction	HUCD032	England	1999	13.99
Paice, Ashton, Lord	BBC Radio 1 Live in Concert	CD	Windsong	WINCD025	England	1992	15.99
Paice, Ashton, Lord	Malice In Wonderland	CD	Repertoire	REP-4568-WY	Germany	1995	19.99
Paice, Ashton, Lord	Malice In Wonderland + 8 (Special Ed)	CD	Purple	PUR-320	England	2001	29.99
Paladin	Charge !	2CD	Red Steel	RMCCD0202	England	1995	24.99
Pallas	Arrive Alive	CD	SPV	SPV08531652CD	Germany	2004	11.99
Pallas	Beat The Drum	CD	SPV	SPV08531482CD	Germany	2004	10.99
Pallas	The Blinding Darkness	2CD	SPV	08965562DCD	Germany	2003	14.99
Pallas	The Cross & The Crucible	CD	SPV	SPV08541522CD	Germany	2004	10.99
Pallas	The Cross & The Crucible (W/Booklet)	CD	SPV	SPV08741520CD	Germany	2004	20.99
Pallas	The Sentinel	CD	SPV	SPV08531992CD	Germany	2004	10.99
Pallas	The Wedge	CD	SPV	SPV08541152CD	Germany	2004	10.99
Palmer, Carl	Do Ya Wanna Play, Carl ?	2CD	Castle	CMEDD163	England	2001	19.99
Palmer, Carl	Working Live, Vol. 1	CD	Sanctuary	SANCD-172	England	2003	14.99
Palmer, Carl/ PM	1PM	CD	Voiceprint	MANTVP005CD	England	2000	14.99
Palmer, David/R.P.Orchestra	Orchestral Maneuvers (Pink Floyd)	CD	RCA	07863-57960-2	U.S.A.	1989	9.99
Palmer, Robert	20th Century Masters: The Mill. Coll.	CD	Island	314-546-556-2	U.S.A.	1999	8.99
Palmer, Robert	Addictions, Vol. 1	CD	Island	422-842-301-2	U.S.A.	1993	8.99
Palmer, Robert	Addictions, Vol. 2	CD	Island	314-510-345-2	U.S.A.	1992	7.99
Palmer, Robert	Best Of Both Worlds: Anthology '74-'01	2CD	Hip O	314-586-688-2	U.S.A.	2002	15.99
Palmer, Robert	Clues	CD	Island	422-842-353-2	U.S.A.	1986	8.99
Palmer, Robert	Don't Explain	CD	Cema	7243-4-98380-2	U.S.A.	1999	6.99
Palmer, Robert	Double Fun	CD	Island	422-842-592-2	U.S.A.	1978	15.99
Palmer, Robert	Drive	CD	Compendia	015095-4886-2-6	U.S.A.	2003	6.99
Palmer, Robert	Heavy Nova	CD	EMI	0777-7-48057-2-8	England	1988	7.99
Palmer, Robert	Honey	CD	EMI	7243-8-30301-2-5	England	1994	6.99
Palmer, Robert	Island Treasures	CD Single	Island	422-875-925-2	U.S.A.	1990	7.99
Palmer, Robert	Live At The Apollo	CD	Eagle	ER-20005-2	U.S.A.	2001	6.99
Palmer, Robert	Maybe It's Live	CD	Island	422-846-121-2	U.S.A.	2000	8.99
Palmer, Robert	Pressure Drop	CD	Island	422-842-594-2	U.S.A.	1975	25.99
Palmer, Robert	Pride	CD	Island	422-811-322-2	U.S.A.	1983	8.99
Palmer, Robert	Rhythm & Blues	CD	Pyramid	R2-75865	U.S.A.	1999	8.99
Palmer, Robert	Ridin' High	CD	Toshiba-EMI	TOCP-7438	Japan	1999	20.99

P

Artist	Title	Format	Label	Catalog No	Country	Released	Value
Palmer, Robert	Ridin' High	CD	EMI	0777-7-98923-2	U.S.A.	1992	6.99
Palmer, Robert	Riptide	CD	Island	422-826-463-2	U.S.A.	1985	6.99
Palmer, Robert	Riptide	CD	Polystar	P35D-20010	Japan	1985	14.99
Palmer, Robert	Secrets	CD	Island	422-842-354-2	U.S.A.	1979	19.99
Palmer, Robert	Sneakin' Sally Through The Alley	CD	Island	422-842-607-2	U.S.A.	1974	8.99
Palmer, Robert	Some People Can Do What They..	CD	Island	422-842-786-2	U.S.A.	1976	49.99
Palmer, Robert	Woke Up Laughing	CD	Blue Note	7243-4-93575-2-5	Holland	1998	6.99
Palmer, Robert/Vinegar Joe	Rock 'N Roll Gypsies	CD	Lemon	CDLEM15	England	2004	14.99
Palmer, Robert/Vinegar Joe	Six Star General	CD	Lemon	CDLEM03	England	2003	14.99
Pangea	Manchild	CD	Victor Ent.	VICP-60025	Japan	1997	29.99
Pantera	Best Of (W/Bonus DVD)	2CD	Rhino	R2-73932	U.S.A.	2003	20.99
Pantera	Cowboys From Hell	CD	Atlantic	91372-2	U.S.A.	1990	8.99
Pantera	Cowboys Hell/Vulgar Display/F Beyond	3CD	East West	7559-62483-2	U.S.A.	1993	29.99
Pantera	Far Beyond Driven	CD	East West	92302-2	U.S.A.	1994	8.99
Pantera	Off. Live: 100 Proof DJ Clean Sampler	CD	East West	PRCD-9890-2	U.S.A.	1997	10.99
Pantera	Official Live: 101 Proof W/Sticker	CD	East West	62068	U.S.A.	1997	8.99
Pantera	Reinventing The Steel	CD	East West	62451	U.S.A.	2000	7.99
Pantera	Reinventing The Steel + 7	2CD	Elektra	83011-2	U.S.A.	2001	34.99
Pantera	Reinventing The Steel (Clean)	CD	Elektra	62526	U.S.A.	2000	7.99
Pantera	Revolution Is My Name	CD	East West	AMCY-7261	Japan	2001	18.99
Pantera	Singles: 1991 - 1996	CD	Warner Bros.	7559-66013-2	Australia	1998	41.99
Pantera	The Great Southern Treandkill	CD	East West	61908	U.S.A.	1996	7.99
Pantera	The Great Southern Trendkill	2CD	Warner Bros.	7559-61998-2	Australia	2000	22.99
Pantera	Unofficial Hits (Promo)	CD	East West	PRCD-7374-2	U.S.A.	1998	15.99
Pantera	Vulgar Displays Of Power	CD	East West	91758-2	U.S.A.	1992	8.99
Pantera/Banned Cvr	Far Beyond Driven + 1	CD	East West	Pantera-1	Australia	1994	38.99
Papa John Creach	I'm The Fiddle Man	CD	One Way	30004	U.S.A.	1994	9.99
Papa John Creach	Papa Blues	CD	Bee Bump	BB-CD-03	U.S.A.	1992	10.99
Papa John Creach	Rock Father	CD	One Way	30005	U.S.A.	1994	9.99
Papa John Creach	S.T. (Jefferson Airplane/Grateful Dead)	CD	One Way	OW-34511	U.S.A.	1997	9.99
Papa John Creach	The Best Of	CD	Buddah	BDK-5707	U.S.A.	1994	14.99
Papa Wemba	Emotion	CD	Caroline	CAROL-2351-2	U.S.A.	1995	10.99
Papa Wemba	Molokai	CD	Caroline	CAR-2373-2	U.S.A.	1998	9.99
Paradis, Vanessa	Works (Promo)	CD	Polydor	DCI-3106	Japan	1992	153.99
Parker, Graham	12 Haunted Episodes	CD	Razor & Tie	RE-2817	U.S.A.	1995	7.99
Parker, Graham	Acid Bubblegum	CD	Razor & Tie	RT-2826-2	U.S.A.	1996	9.99
Parker, Graham	Another Grey Area + 1	CD	Razor & Tie	RE-1982	U.S.A.	1991	49.99
Parker, Graham	Big Man On Paper (Promo)	CD Single	RCA	9114-2-RDJ	U.S.A.	1989	8.99
Parker, Graham	Blue Highway (Live)	CD	Pilot	MCPILOT149	England	2003	11.99
Parker, Graham	Burning Questions	CD	Capitol	7-99003-2	U.S.A.	1992	6.99
Parker, Graham	Christmas Cracker	CD	Dakota Arts	DA40001-2	U.S.A.	1994	9.99
Parker, Graham	Deepcut To Nowhere	CD	Razor & Tie	7930182872-2	U.S.A.	2001	11.99
Parker, Graham	Everything Goes (Longer Version)	CD Single	RCA	9178-2-RDJ	U.S.A.	1990	5.99
Parker, Graham	Get Over It And Move On (Promo)	CD Single	Razor & Tie	RTS-728	U.S.A.	1996	8.99
Parker, Graham	GP + The Episodes - Live (Gold Cd)	CD	Razor & Tie	RTHCD-5051	U.S.A.	1996	8.99
Parker, Graham	Human Soul	CD	RCA	9876-2-R	U.S.A.	1989	6.99
Parker, Graham	King Biscuit Flower Hour Presents	CD	King Biscuit	KBF-CD-88060	U.S.A.	2001	10.99
Parker, Graham	Live Alone! Discovering Japan	CD	Demon	FIENDCD-735	England	1993	6.99
Parker, Graham	Live! Alone In America	CD	RCA	9673-2-R	U.S.A.	1989	8.99
Parker, Graham	No Holding Back Box Set	3CD	Demon	FBOOK15	England	1996	25.99
Parker, Graham	Passion Is No Ordinary Word	2CD	Rhino	R2-71425	U.S.A.	1993	25.99
Parker, Graham	Release Me (Promo)	CD Single	Capitol	DPRO-79390	U.S.A.	1992	5.99
Parker, Graham	Stiffs & Demons	CD	Music Club	MCCD-390	England	1999	11.99
Parker, Graham	Struck By Lightning	CD	RCA	3013-2-R	U.S.A.	1991	6.99
Parker, Graham	Temporary Beauty	CD	Camden	74321-487282	England	1997	9.99
Parker, Graham	The Best Of: 1988 - 1991	CD	RCA	07863-66097-2	U.S.A.	1992	7.99
Parker, Graham	The Mona Lisa's Sister	CD	Buddah	74465-99616-2	U.S.A.	1999	11.99
Parker, Graham	The Real Macaw + 1	CD	Razor & Tie	RE-1983	U.S.A.	1991	44.99

P

Artist	Title	Format	Label	Catalog No	Country	Released	Value
Parker, Graham	Ultimate Collection	CD	Hip-O	314-524-833-2	U.S.A.	2001	11.99
Parker, Graham/The Figgs	The Last Rock'N'Roll Tour	CD	Razor & Tie	RT-2827-2	U.S.A.	1997	8.99
Parker, Graham/The Rumour	BBC Live In Concert (1977 - 91)	CD	Windsong	WINCD083	England	1996	9.99
Parker, Graham/The Rumour	Frogs, Sprouts, Clogs & Krauts (No GP)	CD	Repertoire	REP-4219-WY	Germany	1994	14.99
Parker, Graham/The Rumour	Heat Treatment + 2	CD	Mercury	548-682-2	England	2001	15.99
Parker, Graham/The Rumour	Hold Back The Night	CD	Polygram	314-520-508-2	U.S.A.	1998	9.99
Parker, Graham/The Rumour	Howlin' Wind + 1	CD	Mercury	548-667-2	England	2001	15.99
Parker, Graham/The Rumour	Live On The Test (1977 - 78)	CD	Windsong	WHISCD002	England	1994	11.99
Parker, Graham/The Rumour	Not If It Pleases Me (2 BBC 1 Shows)	CD	HUX	HUX-003	England	1998	14.99
Parker, Graham/The Rumour	Not So Much A Rumour (No G Parker)	CD	Metro	METRCD043	England	2001	10.99
Parker, Graham/The Rumour	Purity Of Essence (No G Parker)	CD	Gadfly	227	U.S.A.	1997	11.99
Parker, Graham/The Rumour	Squeezing Out Sparks + 2	CD	Mercury	548-681-2	England	2001	17.99
Parker, Graham/The Rumour	Squeezing Out Sparks + Live Sparks	CD	Arista	07822-18939-2	U.S.A.	1996	8.99
Parker, Graham/The Rumour	Stick To Me	CD	Mercury	548-680-2	England	2001	14.99
Parker, Graham/The Rumour	That's When You... Acoustic Demos	2CD	Mercury	548-683-2	England	2001	24.99
Parker, Graham/The Rumour	The Best Of	CD	Vertigo	512-149-2	England	1992	14.99
Parker, Graham/The Rumour	The Parkerilla	CD	Mercury	842-263-2	U.S.A.	1978	12.99
Parker, Graham/The Rumour	The Up Escalator + 1	CD	Razor & Tie	RE-1980	U.S.A.	1991	9.99
Parker, Graham/The Rumour	The Up Escalator + 2	CD	Lemon	CDLEM13	England	2003	14.99
Parker, Graham/The Rumour	Vertigo (Live At The Marble Arch +)	2CD	Vertigo	534-100-2	England	1996	20.99
Parker, Graham/The Rumour	You Can't Be Too Strong - An Intro.	CD	Mercury	586-357-2	England	2001	12.99
Parker, Graham/The Shot	Steady Nerves	CD	Elektra	9-60388-2	U.S.A.	1985	28.99
Parker, Gregg	Black Dog	CD Single	Line	URCD-9.00849-E	Germany	1989	9.99
Parks, Van Dyke	A Sample Of The Genius Of (Promo)	CD	Rykodisc	VRCD-045234	England	1999	12.99
Parks, Van Dyke	Clang Of The Yankee Reaper	CD	Edsel	EDCD-213	England	1988	9.99
Parks, Van Dyke	Discover America	CD	Edsel	EDCD-210	England	1987	7.99
Parks, Van Dyke	Discover America	CD	Rykodisc	RCD-10453	U.S.A.	1999	12.99
Parks, Van Dyke	Idiosyncratic Path: The Best Of	CD	Diablo	DIAB807	England	1994	21.99
Parks, Van Dyke	Jump!	CD	Warner Bros.	9-23829-2	U.S.A.	1984	11.99
Parks, Van Dyke	Moonlighting	CD	Warner Bros.	9-46533-2	U.S.A.	1998	7.99
Parks, Van Dyke	Song Cycle	CD	Rykodisc	RCD-10452	U.S.A.	1999	10.99
Parks, Van Dyke	Tokyo Rose	CD	Warner Bros.	9-25968-2	U.S.A.	1989	6.99
Parks, Van Dyke/Jodie Foster	The Fisherman And His Wife	CD	Rabbit Ears	74041-70202-2	U.S.A.	1989	14.99
Parliament	Osmium + 3	CD	Vivid	VSCD-026	Japan	1971	29.99
Parr, John	Man With A Vision	CD	Blue Martin	BLM-330023-2	Switzerland	1992	12.99
Parr, John	Running The Endless Mile	CD	Atlantic	9-81689-2	U.S.A.	1986	19.99
Parr, John	Self Titled	CD	One Way	OW-35176	U.S.A.	2001	15.99
Parsons, Alan	Alan Parsons Live	CD	Connoisseur	VSOP-CD-262	England	1994	9.99
Parsons, Alan	Live	CD	RCA	09026-68229-2	U.S.A.	1995	8.99
Parsons, Alan	On Air + 1	2CD	Soundasia EX	XYCA-00031	Japan	1997	23.99
Parsons, Alan	Sound Check, Vol. 1 (MFSL Gold Cd)	CD	Mobile Fidelity	SPCD-015	U.S.A.	1994	54.99
Parsons, Alan	Sound Check, Vol. 2 (MFSL Gold Cd)	CD	Mobile Fidelity	SPCD-018	U.S.A.	1994	64.99
Parsons, Alan	The Time Machine + 1	CD	Artful	ARTFUL-CD-28	England	1999	14.99
Parsons, Alan	Try Anything Once (Gold Cd)	CD	Arista	17822-18744-2	U.S.A.	1993	44.99
Parsons, Alan	Try Anything Once (Jewelcase Version)	CD	Arista	07822-18741-2	U.S.A.	1993	8.99
Parsons, Alan/Andrew Powell	Ladyhawke + 9 (O.S.T.)	CD	GNP	GNPD-8042	U.S.A.	1985	9.99
Parsons, Alan/Andrew Powell	Play A Parsons Project (MFSL Silver)	CD	Mobile Fidelity	MFCD-806	U.S.A.	1983	149.99
Parsons, Alan/Eric Woolfson	Freudiana	CD	EMI	79-5415-2	England	1990	12.99
Parsons, Alan/Eric Woolfson	Freudiana (Sung In German)	CD	Electrola	1C568-7-96512-2	Germany	1990	69.99
Parsons, Alan/Keats	Keats	CD	Renaissance	RMED00111	U.S.A.	1996	10.99
Parsons, Alan/M.A.S.S.	Music Of The Alan Parsons Project	CD	Art & Music	CD-20.1691	EEC	1994	10.99
Parsons, Alan/Project	Ammonia Avenue	CD	Arista	ARCD-8204	U.S.A.	1984	8.99
Parsons, Alan/Project	Eve	CD	Arista	ARCD-8062	U.S.A.	1979	11.99
Parsons, Alan/Project	Eye In The Sky	CD	Arista	610-004-222	Germany	1983	9.99
Parsons, Alan/Project	Gaudi	CD	Arista	ARCD-8448	U.S.A.	1987	8.99
Parsons, Alan/Project	Gold Collection	2CD	Ariola	74321-54931-2	EU	1997	17.99
Parsons, Alan/Project	I Robot (Audiophile Cd)	CD	Classic	DAD-1035	U.S.A.	1977	34.99
Parsons, Alan/Project	I Robot (MFSL Silver Cd Reg Pressing)	CD	Mobile Fidelity	MFCD-804	U.S.A.	1977	59.99

P

Artist	Title	Format	Label	Catalog No	Country	Released	Value
Parsons, Alan/Project	I Robot (MFSL Silver/Laser Video Ed.)	CD	Mobile Fidelity	MFCD-804	U.S.A.	1977	119.99
Parsons, Alan/Project	Instrumental Works	CD	Arista	259-237-2	Germany	1988	13.99
Parsons, Alan/Project	Love Songs	CD	Arista	74321-91680-2	Holland	2002	11.99
Parsons, Alan/Project	Pyramid	CD	Arista	ARCD-8225	U.S.A.	1978	7.99
Parsons, Alan/Project	Stereotomy	CD	Arista	ARCD-8384	U.S.A.	1985	7.99
Parsons, Alan/Project	Tales Mystery/Imagination (MFSL Gold)	CD	Mobile Fidelity	UDCD-606	U.S.A.	1976	38.99
Parsons, Alan/Project	Tales Mystery/Imagination (O.Welles)	CD	Mercury	832-820-2	U.S.A.	1976	10.99
Parsons, Alan/Project	The Definitive Collection	2CD	Arista	07822-18962-2	U.S.A.	1997	16.99
Parsons, Alan/Project	Turn Of A Friendly Card	CD	Arista	ARCD-8226	U.S.A.	1980	14.99
Parsons, Alan/Project	Vulture Culture	CD	Arista	ARCD-8263	U.S.A.	1984	9.99
Parsons, Alan/Project	Works (Gold Cd)	2CD	Audiophile Legends	APH-102.881	Germany	1997	28.99
Parsons, Gram	Another Side Of This Life	CD	Sundazed	SC-11092	U.S.A.	2000	9.99
Parsons, Gram	Big Mouth Blues: A Conversation With	CD	Sierra	6024	U.S.A.	2002	8.99
Parsons, Gram	Cosmic American Music	CD	Sundown	77	England	1994	65.99
Parsons, Gram	G.P. / Grievous Angel	CD	Reprise	9-26108-2	U.S.A.	1973	13.99
Parsons, Gram	Sleepless Nights	CD	Polydor K.K.	POCM-2092	Japan	1998	34.99
Parsons, Gram	The Gram Parsons Anthology	2CD	Rhino	R2-76780	U.S.A.	2001	21.99
Parsons, Gram	Warm Evenings, Pale Mornings...	CD	Raven	RVCD-24	Australia	1991	16.99
Parsons, Gram/Fallen Angels	Live 1973 (Gold Cd)	CD	Sierra	SXCD-6002	U.S.A.	1996	13.99
Parsons, Gram/I.S.B.	Back At Home	CD	TKO Magnum	CDSD-086	England	2000	14.99
Parsons, Gram/I.S.B.	Safe At Home	CD	Shiloh	SCD4088	U.S.A.	1993	19.99
Parton, Dolly	9 To 5 And Odd Jobs	CD	RCA	07863-56337-2	U.S.A.	1994	11.99
Parton, Dolly	Rainbow	CD	Columbia	CK-40968	U.S.A.	1990	31.99
Partridge Family	A Christmas Card (S Jones, D Cassidy)	CD	Razor & Tie	RE-2006	U.S.A.	1992	13.99
Partridge Family	Crossword Puzzle	CD	Buddah	74465-99785-2	U.S.A.	2001	12.99
Partridge Family	Definitive Collection	CD	Arista	78560	U.S.A.	2001	12.99
Partridge Family	Greatest Hits	CD	Arista	ARCD-8604	U.S.A.	1989	10.99
Partridge Family	The Partridge Family Album	CD	Buddah	74465-99747-2	U.S.A.	2000	8.99
Partridge Family	The Partridge Family Notebook	CD	Buddah	74465-99748-2	U.S.A.	2000	12.99
Partridge Family	The Partridge Family Shopping Bag	CD	Buddah	74465-99784-2	U.S.A.	2001	6.99
Partridge Family	The Partridge Family Sound Magazine	CD	Buddah	74465-99749-2	U.S.A.	2000	11.99
Partridge Family	Up to Date	CD	Buddah	74465-99750-2	U.S.A.	2000	6.99
Pascoal, Hermeto	Brasil Universo	CD	Line	RICD-9.00523-0	Germany	1988	13.99
Pascoal, Hermeto	Lagoa Da Canoa	CD	Line	RICD-9.00520-0	Germany	1988	13.99
Passport/Klaus Doldinger	Balance Of Happiness	CD	Atlantic	7-82154-2	U.S.A.	1990	5.99
Pastorius, Jaco	Honestly: Solo Live	CD	Toy Factory	TFCK-87561	Japan	2000	27.99
Pastorius, Jaco	Invitation	CD	Warner Bros.	WPCP-4932	Japan	1983	36.99
Pastorius, Jaco	Invitation	CD	Warner Bros.	93624-7909-2	England	2002	8.99
Pastorius, Jaco	Jaco Pastorius + 2	CD	Epic	EK-64977	U.S.A.	2001	10.99
Pastorius, Jaco	Les Incontournables	CD	Warner Bros.	35880	France	2000	8.99
Pastorius, Jaco	Live in New York City, Vol. 2: Trio	CD	Big World	1002	U.S.A.	1991	12.99
Pastorius, Jaco	Live in New York City, Vol. 4: Trio 2	CD	Big World	1004	U.S.A.	1985	12.99
Pastorius, Jaco	Live in New York City, Vol. 5: Raca	CD	Big World	1005	U.S.A.	1985	12.99
Pastorius, Jaco	Live in New York City, Vol. 7: History	CD	Big World	1007	U.S.A.	1999	12.99
Pastorius, Jaco	Live New York City, Vol. 1: Punk Jazz	CD	Big World	1001	U.S.A.	1990	12.99
Pastorius, Jaco	Live New York City, Vol. 3: Pr. Land	CD	Big World	1003	U.S.A.	1991	12.99
Pastorius, Jaco	Live New York City, Vol. 6: Punk Jazz 2	CD	Big World	1006	U.S.A.	1999	12.99
Pastorius, Jaco	Punk Jazz: The Anthology	2CD	Rhino	R2-73779	U.S.A.	2003	24.99
Pastorius, Jaco	Rare Collection	CD	Polydor	1693	England	2000	14.99
Pastorius, Jaco	The Birthday Concert	CD	Warner Bros.	9-45290-2	U.S.A.	1995	11.99
Pastorius, Jaco	Twins I & II	2CD	Warner Bros.	WPCR-10609	Japan	1999	49.99
Pastorius, Jaco	Word of Mouth	CD	Warner Bros.	93624-8246-2	Germany	2002	12.99
Pastorius, Jaco/B M Trio	Standards Zone	CD	Rhino	R2-79335	U.S.A.	1990	26.99
Pastorius, Jaco/Bob Weir	Nightfood (Brian Melvin)	CD	Grateful Dead	GDCD-39022	U.S.A.	1988	9.99
Pastorius, Jaco/Brian Melvin	Jazz Street	CD	Timeless	CDSJP-258	Japan	1989	28.99
Pastorius, Jaco/Little Beaver	Party Down	CD	Columbia	CK-5432	U.S.A.	1993	8.99
Pastorius, Jaco/Pat Metheny	Jaco	CD	Improvising Artists	123846-2	Germany	1996	15.99
Patrol, Don	A Wire, A Deal And The Devil	CD	Record Station	STATCD-36	Germany	1992	55.99

P

Artist	Title	Format	Label	Catalog No	Country	Released	Value
Patrol, Don	Self Titled	CD	Record Station	STATCD-22	Germany	1990	65.99
Patto	Hold Your Fire (Ollie Halsall)	CD	Akarma	AK-190-CD	Italy	2002	15.99
Patto	Monkey's Bum (Ollie Halsall)	CD	Akarma	AK-201	Italy	2003	15.99
Patto	Roll 'Em, Smoke 'Em... (Ollie Halsall)	CD	Edsel	EDCD-510	England	1996	15.99
Patto	Self Titled (Ollie Halsall)	CD	Akarma	AK-185-CD	Italy	2002	15.99
Patto	Self Titled (Ollie Halsall)	CD	Repertoire	REP4446WP	Germany	2001	15.99
Paul Revere/The Raiders	A Christmas Past... And Present	CD	Columbia	CK-45310	U.S.A.	1969	10.99
Paul Revere/The Raiders	Alias Pink Fuzz + 6	CD	Repertoire	4962	Germany	2001	19.99
Paul Revere/The Raiders	Alias Pink Puzz + 4	CD	Sundazed	SC-6138	U.S.A.	2000	8.99
Paul Revere/The Raiders	Goin' to Memphis + 3	CD	Sundazed	SC-6136	U.S.A.	2000	8.99
Paul Revere/The Raiders	Greatest Hits	CD	Columbia	4625292	Australia	1990	8.99
Paul Revere/The Raiders	Greatest Hits + 4	CD	Columbia	CK-66009	U.S.A.	2000	8.99
Paul Revere/The Raiders	Greatest Hits Live	CD	Remember	RMB-75030	Belgium	1996	7.99
Paul Revere/The Raiders	Hard 'N' Heavy (With Marshmallow) + 4	CD	Sundazed	SC-6137	U.S.A.	2000	8.99
Paul Revere/The Raiders	Here They Come!	CD	Columbia	CK-9107	U.S.A.	1992	10.99
Paul Revere/The Raiders	Just Like Us! + 3	CD	Sundazed	SC-6127	U.S.A.	1998	8.99
Paul Revere/The Raiders	Legend of Paul Revere	2CD	Columbia	C2K-45311	U.S.A.	1990	15.99
Paul Revere/The Raiders	Midnight Rider + 4	CD	Sundazed	SC-6135	U.S.A.	2000	8.99
Paul Revere/The Raiders	Mojo Workout	2CD	Sundazed	SC-11097	U.S.A.	2000	18.99
Paul Revere/The Raiders	Revolution! + 3	CD	Sundazed	SC-6096	U.S.A.	1998	8.99
Paul Revere/The Raiders	Something Happening + 6	CD	Repertoire	4961	Germany	2001	19.99
Paul Revere/The Raiders	Something Happening +3	CD	Sundazed	SC-6097	U.S.A.	2000	8.99
Paul Revere/The Raiders	Super Hits	CD	Columbia	CK-66067	U.S.A.	2000	6.99
Paul Revere/The Raiders	The Essential Ride '63-'67	CD	Columbia	CK-48949	U.S.A.	1995	49.99
Paul Revere/The Raiders	The Spirit of '67 + 3	CD	Sundazed	SC-6095	U.S.A.	2000	8.99
Paul, Billy	Going East	CD	Sony	480865-2	Germany	1974	191.99
Paul, Lloyd	Crying At The Circus	CD	7 Records	769203	U.S.A.	1994	4.99
Pavement	Slanted/Enchanted Luxe/Reduxe +15	2CD	Matador	OLE-557-CD	U.S.A.	2002	20.99
Payne, Freda	Band Of Gold	CD	P-Vine	PCD-4960	Japan	1970	44.99
Payne, Freda	Christmas With Freda Payne	CD	Dove	DM-CA-8148-2	U.S.A.	1996	9.99
Payne, Freda	Reaching Out	CD	P-Vine	PCD-4962	Japan	1973	44.99
Payne, Freda	Unhooked Generation	2CD	Castle	CMDDD-341	England	2001	16.99
Peacock, Annette	Abstract Contact	CD	Ironic	IRONIC-5	U.S.A.	1988	24.99
Peacock, Annette	The Perfect Release	CD	Line	FECD-9.00484-0	Germany	1987	28.99
Peacock, Annette	X-Dreams	CD	Line	FECD-9.00490-0	Germany	1987	28.99
Pearl Jam	Alive	CD	Sony	SRCS-5884	Japan	1992	8.99
Pearl Jam	Alive	CD Single	Epic	657572-2	Austria	1991	6.99
Pearl Jam	Alive (Promo)	CD Single	Epic	ZSK-4041	U.S.A.	1991	34.99
Pearl Jam	Alive (Promo)	CD	Sony	ZSK-4041	U.S.A.	1991	95.99
Pearl Jam	Animal	CD Single	Epic	34K-77948	U.S.A.	1994	5.99
Pearl Jam	Animal	CD Single	Epic	660519-2	England	1994	15.99
Pearl Jam	Binaural (Fold Out Cover)	CD	Epic	EK-63665	U.S.A.	2000	7.99
Pearl Jam	Bootleg Series Promo Sampler	CD	Epic	ESK-16594-S1	U.S.A.	2001	18.99
Pearl Jam	Daughter	CD Single	Epic	34K-77938	U.S.A.	1993	4.99
Pearl Jam	Daughter (3" Cd)	CD	Sony	SRDS-8273	Japan	1993	22.99
Pearl Jam	Daughter (Promo)	CD Single	Epic	XPCD-351	England	1993	21.99
Pearl Jam	Dissident	CD Single	Epic	34K-77939	U.S.A.	1994	6.99
Pearl Jam	Dissident (Cover To Hold All 3 Live Cds)	CD Single	Epic	01-660291-19	Germany	1994	12.99
Pearl Jam	Even Flow	CD Single	Epic	34K-77934	U.S.A.	1992	7.99
Pearl Jam	Given To Fly	CD Single	Epic	34K-78797	U.S.A.	1997	6.99
Pearl Jam	Go	CD Single	Epic	659795-2	Austria	1993	7.99
Pearl Jam	Hail, Hail	CD Single	Sony	SRCS-8246	Japan	1997	12.99
Pearl Jam	Hail, Hail (Promo)	CD Single	Epic	PRCD-96828	Mexico	1997	23.99
Pearl Jam	Jeremy (Child With Gun Cover)	CD Single	Epic	658180-2	Austria	1992	10.99
Pearl Jam	Jeremy (Child With Gun Cover) Promo	CD Single	Epic	ZSK-4606	U.S.A.	1992	10.99
Pearl Jam	Jeremy (Rubberband Hand Cover)	CD Single	Epic	658180-2	Australia	1992	8.99
Pearl Jam	Last Kiss	CD Single	Epic	34K-79197	U.S.A.	1999	7.99
Pearl Jam	Light Years	CD Single	Epic	34K-79452	U.S.A.	2000	4.99

P

Artist	Title	Format	Label	Catalog No	Country	Released	Value
Pearl Jam	Live (Promo)	CD	Epic	ESK-16594-S1	U.S.A.	2000	24.99
Pearl Jam	Live On Two Legs (Fold Out Cover)	CD	Epic	EK-69752	U.S.A.	1998	9.99
Pearl Jam	No Code (Fold Open Cover)	CD	Epic	EK-67500	U.S.A.	1996	11.99
Pearl Jam	Not For You	CD Single	Epic	34K-77772	U.S.A.	1994	7.99
Pearl Jam	Nothing As It Seems	CD Single	Epic	34K-79416	U.S.A.	2000	4.99
Pearl Jam	Oceans	CD Single	Epic	658472-2	Austria	1992	6.99
Pearl Jam	Rearview Mirror (Promo)	CD Single	Sony	SAMP571	Australia	1994	76.99
Pearl Jam	Singles (Promo)	CD Single	Sony	XDCS-93300	Japan	1997	313.99
Pearl Jam	Spin The Black Circle	CD Single	Epic	34K-77771	U.S.A.	1994	4.99
Pearl Jam	State Of Love And Trust (DJ Only 250)	CD Single	Epic	XPCD-269	England	1992	82.99
Pearl Jam	Ten	CD	Epic	ZK-47857	U.S.A.	1991	7.99
Pearl Jam	Vitalogy (Leatherbound Look)	CD	Epic	EK-66900	U.S.A.	1994	7.99
Pearl Jam	Vs.	CD	Epic	ZK-53136	U.S.A.	1993	8.99
Pearl Jam	Wishlist	CD	Epic	34K-78896	U.S.A.	1998	6.99
Pearl Jam	Yield (Fold Out Cover)	CD	Epic	EK-68164	U.S.A.	1998	9.99
Pearl Jam	Yield Interview (Promo)	CD	Epic	CDNK-1349	Canada	1998	19.99
Pearl Jam/Neil Young	Merkinball	CD Single	Epic	34K-78199	U.S.A.	1995	11.99
Pearls Before Swine	When Jewels Were... Box (Ltd 2000)	4CD	Water	WATER-200	U.S.A.	2003	52.99
Pedersen, Herb	Southwest	CD	Line	CLCD-9.00929-0	Germany	1990	14.99
Peel, David/Apple Band	Bring Back The Beatles + 1	CD	Orange	ORANGE-6001	U.S.A.	1993	13.99
Peel, David/Apple Band	John Lennon For President + 1	CD	Orange	ORANGE-6002	U.S.A.	1980	13.99
Peel, David/Apple Band	The Battle For New York	CD	Halycon	64322-2	U.S.A.	1994	10.99
Peel, David/John/Yoko	Apple And Orange Recordings	16CD	Captain Trip	CTCD-320-335	Japan	2003	109.99
Peel, David/L East Side	And The Rest Is...Elektra Recordings	CD	Rhino	RHM2-7713	U.S.A.	2000	21.99
Peel, David/L East Side	The Pope Smokes Dope	CD	Globus	210289-2	U.S.A.	1999	13.99
Peel, David/Lower East Side	Have A Marijuana	CD	Line	LECD-9.51050-0	Germany	1991	17.99
Pendragon	1984-96 Overture	CD	Outer Music	OM-2011	U.S.A.	2001	13.99
Pendragon	9:15 Live	CD	Toff	PEND-3-CD	England	1990	13.99
Pendragon	Acoustically Challenged	CD	Metal Mind	PROGCD0085DG	Poland	2002	12.99
Pendragon	As Good As Gold	CD	Toff	MOB4CD	England	1996	13.99
Pendragon	Fallen Dreams + Angels	CD	Toff	MOB2CD	England	1994	13.99
Pendragon	Kowtow	CD	Toff	PEND-1-CD	England	1988	13.99
Pendragon	Live In Krakow 1996	CD	Toff	MOB5CD	England	1997	22.99
Pendragon	Not Of This World + 3	CD	Pony Canyon	PCCY-01502	Japan	2001	19.99
Pendragon	Once Upon A Time In England Vol 1	CD	Toff	MOB6CD	England	1999	11.99
Pendragon	Once Upon A Time In England Vol 2	CD	Toff	MOB7CD	England	1999	13.99
Pendragon	The History: 1984 - 2000	CD	Metal Mind	PROG-CD-0072-C	Poland	2000	11.99
Pendragon	The Jewel + 3	CD	Pony Canyon	PCCY-00654	Japan	1994	19.99
Pendragon	The Masquerade Overture	2CD	Toff	PEND7CD	England	1996	19.99
Pendragon	The Masquerade Overture + 1	CD	Toff	PEND7DP	England	1999	11.99
Pendragon	The Masquerade Overture + 3	CD	Pony Canyon	PCCY-00903	Japan	1996	19.99
Pendragon	The Rest Of Pendragon + 1	CD	Pony Canyon	PCCY-00657	Japan	1994	19.99
Pendragon	The Very, Very Bootleg	CD	Toff	MOB1CD	England	1993	11.99
Pendragon	The Window Of Life	CD	Toff	PEND6CD	England	1993	13.99
Pendragon	The World	CD	Toff	PEND5-CD	England	1991	10.99
Pendragon	Utrecht....The Final Frontier	CD	Toff	MOB3CD	England	1995	13.99
Penguin Cafe Orchestra	A Brief History	CD	EMI	812848	Holland	2002	9.99
Penguin Cafe Orchestra	A History Box Set	4CD	Virgin	7243-811482-2-8	Holland	2001	62.99
Penguin Cafe Orchestra	Broadcasting From Home	CD	Caroline	0777-7-87447-2-6	U.S.A.	1984	11.99
Penguin Cafe Orchestra	Concert Program	2CD	Windam Hill	01934-11169-2	U.S.A.	1995	19.99
Penguin Cafe Orchestra	E.P.	CD Single	Editions EG	EDSX-2	England	1987	29.99
Penguin Cafe Orchestra	Music From the Penguin Cafe	CD	Caroline	0777-7-87448-2-5	U.S.A.	1976	12.99
Penguin Cafe Orchestra	Oskar Und Leni	CD	Peregrina	50161	Holland	1999	15.99
Penguin Cafe Orchestra	Piano Music (Simon Jeffes)	CD	Zopf	ZOPFD003	England	2003	15.99
Penguin Cafe Orchestra	Preludes, Airs & Yodels	CD	Caroline	Carol-CD-1100-2	U.S.A.	1997	9.99
Penguin Cafe Orchestra	Self Titled	CD	Caroline	0777-7-87449-2-4	U.S.A.	1981	8.99
Penguin Cafe Orchestra	Signs Of Life	CD	Caroline	0777-7-8745-020	U.S.A.	1987	13.99
Penguin Cafe Orchestra	Single	CD Single	Editions EG	EDSX-2	England	1987	29.99

P

Artist	Title	Format	Label	Catalog No	Country	Released	Value
Penguin Cafe Orchestra	Union Café	CD	Zopf	WM332-852-498	France	2003	15.99
Penguin Cafe Orchestra	When In Rome	CD	Editions EG	0777-7-8745-129	U.S.A.	1988	13.99
Pentangle	A Maid That's Deep In Love	CD	Shanachie	79066	U.S.A.	1987	11.99
Pentangle	Basket Of Light	CD	Line	TACD-9.00555-0	Germany	1988	8.99
Pentangle	Basket Of Light + 4	DVD Aud	Silverline	288087	England	2002	14.99
Pentangle	Basket of Light + 4	CD	Castle	632	England	2000	12.99
Pentangle	Cruel Sister	CD	Castle	CMAR634	England	2000	10.99
Pentangle	Cruel Sister	CD	Line	TACD-9.00558-0	Germany	1988	8.99
Pentangle	Early Classics	CD	Shanachie	79078	U.S.A.	1992	12.99
Pentangle	Essential, Vol. 1	CD	Transatlantic	TRACD-602	England	1987	12.99
Pentangle	Essential, Vol. 2	CD	Transatlantic	TRACD-606	England	1987	12.99
Pentangle	Heritage	CD	EMI	576-287-2	Holland	2003	8.99
Pentangle	In The Round	CD	Varrick	0026	England	1990	12.99
Pentangle	Light Flight	2CD	Recall	SMD-CD-154	England	1997	14.99
Pentangle	Light Flight: The Anthology	2CD	Essential	ESACD-857	England	2000	17.99
Pentangle	Live At The BBC	CD	Strange Fruit	SFRSCD-046	England	1997	15.99
Pentangle	On Air	CD	Strange Fruit	SFRSCD-46	England	1997	14.99
Pentangle	One More Road	CD	SPV	SPV-084-92962	Germany	1993	11.99
Pentangle	Passe Avant	CD	Park	46	England	1999	9.99
Pentangle	People On The Highway (1968-71)	CD	Demon	FIENDCD12	England	1994	20.99
Pentangle	Reflection	CD	Line	TACD-9.00618-0	Germany	1988	28.99
Pentangle	So Early In The Spring	CD	Green Linnet	GLCD-3048	England	1990	14.99
Pentangle	Sweet Child	CD	Line	TACD-9.00552-0	Germany	1988	8.99
Pentangle	Sweet Child + 4	2CD	Castle	CMDDD132	England	2001	19.99
Pentangle	The Collection	CD	EMI	724357628723	Holland	2001	17.99
Pentangle	The Pentangle	CD	Line	TACD-9.00549-0	Germany	1988	8.99
Pentangle	The Pentangle + 7	CD	Castle	CMRCD131	England	2001	12.99
Pentangle	The Pentangle Family	2CD	Essential	ESACD931	England	2000	16.99
Pentangle	The/S Child/B Light/C Sister/Refl.	5CD	Line	PEN-5	Germany	1991	114.99
Pentangle	Think Of Tomorrow	CD	Green Linnet	GLCD-3057	U.S.A.	1991	10.99
People/Various Artists	Hold On To (Ian Anderson/Jack Bruce)	CD Single	BMG	74321-17585-2	Germany	1993	12.99
Perigeo	Abbiamo Tutti Un Blues Da Piangere	CD	Disconforme	74321676172	Andorra	1999	15.99
Perigeo	Azimut	CD	Disconforme	74321676162	Andorra	1999	15.99
Perigeo	Genealogia	CD	Disconforme	74321676182	Andorra	1999	15.99
Perkins, Carl	Back On Top (60's/70's)	4CD	Bear Family	BCD-16422	Germany	2000	80.99
Perkins, Carl	Best Of The Sun Years	CD	Repertoire	REP-4806	Germany	2003	15.99
Perkins, Carl	Country Boy's Dream: Dollie Masters	CD	Bear Family	BCD-15593	Germany	1994	15.99
Perkins, Carl	Original Sun Greatest Hits	CD	Rhino	R2-75890	U.S.A.	1990	4.99
Perkins, Carl	The Classic	5CD	Bear Family	BCD-15494	Germany	1986	80.99
Perkins, Carl	Up Through The Years '54-'57	CD	Bear Family	BCD-15246	Germany	1986	15.99
Perkins, Carl/Tribute	Go Cat Go! (W/Solo Beatles)	CD	Dinosaur	76401-84508-2	U.S.A.	1996	8.99
Perry, Joe/Project	Best Of : Music Still Does The Talking	CD	Raven	RVCD-90	Australia	1999	8.99
Perry, Joe/Project	I've Got the Rock'n'Rolls Again	CD	Columbia	CK-37364	U.S.A.	1981	11.99
Perry, Joe/Project	Let the Music Do the Talking	CD	Columbia	CK-36388	U.S.A.	1980	7.99
Perry, Joe/Project	Once a Rocker, Always a Rocker	CD	MCA	MCAD-11028	U.S.A.	1994	29.99
Perry, Linda/4 Non Blondes	In Flight	CD	Interscope	IND-90061	EC	1996	6.99
Pesci, Joe	Vincent Laguardia Gambini Sings...	CD	Columbia	CK-69518	U.S.A.	1998	11.99
Pet Shop Boys	A Red Letter Day	CD Single	Parlophone	CDRS-6452	England	1997	4.99
Pet Shop Boys	A Red Letter Day (Dbl. Slv.)	CD Single	Parlophone	CDR-6452	England	1997	13.99
Pet Shop Boys	Absolutely Fabulous	CD Single	EMI	724388142625	Australia	1994	13.99
Pet Shop Boys	Absolutely Fabulous	CD Single	Parlophone	7243-8-81535-2	Holland	1994	15.99
Pet Shop Boys	Absolutely Fabulous	CD Single	Parlophone	CDRS-6382	England	1994	13.99
Pet Shop Boys	Actually	CD Single	EMI	7-46972-2	Germany	1988	16.99
Pet Shop Boys	Actually	CD	Parlophone	CDPCSD-104	England	1987	13.99
Pet Shop Boys	Actually + 14/Further Listening	2CD	Parlophone	5305062	England	2001	11.99
Pet Shop Boys	Actually Special Edition	2CD	Parlophone	CDPCSDX-104	England	1988	34.99
Pet Shop Boys	Alternative	2CD	Parlophone	CDPCSDS-166	England	1995	12.99
Pet Shop Boys	Alternative (Limited Ed)	2CD	Parlophone	CDPCSD-166	England	1995	11.99

P

Artist	Title	Format	Label	Catalog No	Country	Released	Value
Pet Shop Boys	Alternative + 1	2CD	Toshiba-EMI	TOCP-8605/06	Japan	1995	24.99
Pet Shop Boys	Always On My Mind	CD Single	Parlophone	CDR-6171	England	1987	15.99
Pet Shop Boys	Always On My Mind (Promo)	CD Single	EMI	DPRO-04058	U.S.A.	1987	15.99
Pet Shop Boys	Aurally (Promo)	2CD	EMI	CDPSBDJ001	U.S.A.	1996	34.99
Pet Shop Boys	Before	CD Single	EMI	8-82834-2	Holland	1996	18.99
Pet Shop Boys	Before	CD Single	Atlantic	85489-2	U.S.A.	1997	9.99
Pet Shop Boys	Before (Cd 1)	CD Single	Parlophone	CDRS-6431	England	1996	4.99
Pet Shop Boys	Before (Cd 2)	CD Single	Parlophone	CDR 6431	England	1996	4.99
Pet Shop Boys	Before (Promo)	CD Single	Parlophone	CDRDJ6431	England	1996	8.99
Pet Shop Boys	Before 5 "	CDV	Atlantic	87049-2	U.S.A.	1996	7.99
Pet Shop Boys	Behavior + 3 (W/Bonus 3" Cd)	2CD	Toshiba-EMI	TOCP-6440	Japan	1990	28.99
Pet Shop Boys	Behaviour	CD	Parlophone	CDPCSD-113	England	1990	9.99
Pet Shop Boys	Behaviour (Promo)	CD	EMI	CDG0017	Australia	1990	34.99
Pet Shop Boys	Behaviour + 13/Further Listening	2CD	Parlophone	5305132	England	2001	17.99
Pet Shop Boys	Being Boring	CD Single	Parlophone	CDR-6275	England	1990	38.99
Pet Shop Boys	Being Remixed	CD Single	EMI	560-2041262	Germany	1990	40.99
Pet Shop Boys	Bilingual	CD	Parlophone	CDPCSD-170	England	1996	10.99
Pet Shop Boys	Bilingual (Cd 1)	CD Single	Parlophone	CDRS-6452	England	1996	7.99
Pet Shop Boys	Bilingual (Cd 2)	CD Single	Parlophone	CDRS-6452	England	1996	7.99
Pet Shop Boys	Bilingual (Spec. Ed)	2CD	Parlophone	CDPCSDX-170	England	1997	22.99
Pet Shop Boys	Bilingual (Special Editon) + 2	2CD	Toshiba-EMI	TOCP-50307/08	U.S.A.	1997	23.99
Pet Shop Boys	Bilingual + 15/Further Listening	CD	Parlophone	5305122	England	2001	18.99
Pet Shop Boys	Bilingual Interview (Promo)	CD	Parlophone	CDIN103	England	1996	45.99
Pet Shop Boys	Can You Forgive Her?	CD Single	EMI	8-80673-2	Holland	1993	4.99
Pet Shop Boys	Can You Forgive Her?	CD Single	Parlophone	CDRS-6348	England	1993	7.99
Pet Shop Boys	Can You Forgive Her? (Dbl. Slv.)	CD Single	Parlophone	CDR-6348	England	1993	12.99
Pet Shop Boys	D J Culture	CD Single	Parlophone	20-4549-2	Netherlands	1991	4.99
Pet Shop Boys	D J Culturemix	CD Single	EMI	20-4580-2	Germany	1991	22.99
Pet Shop Boys	Disco	CD	Parlophone	CDP-7464502	England	1986	9.99
Pet Shop Boys	Disco 2	CD	Parlophone	CDPCSD-159	England	1994	9.99
Pet Shop Boys	Disco 3	CD	Parlophone	5821402	England	2003	11.99
Pet Shop Boys	Discography	CD	Parlophone	CDPMTV-3	England	1991	8.99
Pet Shop Boys	Discography (Promo)	CD	Parlophone	CDPSBDJ1	England	1991	49.99
Pet Shop Boys	DJ Culture	CD Single	Parlophone	CDR-6301	England	1991	9.99
Pet Shop Boys	DJ Culturemix	CD Single	Parlophone	CDRX-6301	England	1991	13.99
Pet Shop Boys	Domino Dancing	CD Single	Parlophone	CDR-6190	England	1988	19.99
Pet Shop Boys	Essential	CD	Toshiba-EMI	TOCP-51059	Japan	1998	18.99
Pet Shop Boys	Go West	CD Single	Parlophone	CDR-6356	England	1993	5.99
Pet Shop Boys	Go West (Acetate)	CD Single	Toshiba-EMI	TOCP-8065	Japan	1993	104.99
Pet Shop Boys	Go West (Promo)	CD Single	EMI	E2-58084	U.S.A.	1993	11.99
Pet Shop Boys	Go West (Promo)	CD Single	EMI	DPRO-04619	U.S.A.	1993	11.99
Pet Shop Boys	Go West: The Remixes	CD Single	EMI	8-80910-2	Holland	1993	19.99
Pet Shop Boys	Heart	CD Single	Parlophone	CDR-6177	England	1988	12.99
Pet Shop Boys	Home And Dry	CD Single	EMI	7243-5-50531-2-1	Holland	2002	7.99
Pet Shop Boys	Home And Dry (Cd 1)	CD Single	Parlophone	CDRS-6572	England	2002	7.99
Pet Shop Boys	Home And Dry (Cd 2)	CD Single	Parlophone	CDR-6572	England	2002	7.99
Pet Shop Boys	Home And Dry (DVD)	CD Single	Parlophone	DVDR-6572	England	2002	8.99
Pet Shop Boys	Home And Dry (Promo)	CD Single	Parlophone	CDRDJ6572	England	2002	6.99
Pet Shop Boys	I Don't Know What You (Cd 1)	CD Single	Parlophone	CDRS-6523	England	1999	5.99
Pet Shop Boys	I Don't Know What You (Cd 2)	CD Single	Parlophone	CDR-6523	England	1999	5.99
Pet Shop Boys	I Don't Know What...	CD Single	EMI	24388-74790	Holland	1999	6.99
Pet Shop Boys	I Don't Know...	CD Single	Sire	35022-2	U.S.A.	2000	17.99
Pet Shop Boys	I Get Along (Cd 1)	CD Single	Parlophone	CDRS-6581	England	2002	7.99
Pet Shop Boys	I Get Along (Cd 2)	CD Single	Parlophone	CDR-6581	England	2002	7.99
Pet Shop Boys	I Get Along (DVD)	CD Single	Parlophone	DVDR-6581	England	2002	8.99
Pet Shop Boys	I Get Along (Promo)	CD Single	Parlophone	CDRDJ-6581	England	2002	10.99
Pet Shop Boys	I Wouldn't Normally Do..	CD Single	Parlophone	CDR-6370	England	1993	12.99
Pet Shop Boys	I Wouldn't Normally Do... (Promo)	CD Single	EMI	DPRO-19789	U.S.A.	1994	13.99

P

Artist	Title	Format	Label	Catalog No	Country	Released	Value
Pet Shop Boys	I Wouldn't Normally...	CD Single	EMI	8-81112-2	Holland	1993	8.99
Pet Shop Boys	I Wouldn't Normally... (Dbl. Slv)	CD Single	Parlophone	CDRS-6370	England	1993	12.99
Pet Shop Boys	In Depth (Promo W/Phonecard)	CD	Toshiba-EMI	SPCD-1071	Japan	1989	106.99
Pet Shop Boys	Introspective	CD	Parlophone	CDPCS-7325	England	1988	8.99
Pet Shop Boys	Introspective + 15/Further Listening	2CD	Parlophone	5305072	England	2001	15.99
Pet Shop Boys	It's A Sin	CD Single	Parlophone	CDR-6158	England	1987	26.99
Pet Shop Boys	It's Alright	CD Single	Parlophone	CDR-6220	England	1989	15.99
Pet Shop Boys	It's Alright (3")	CD Single	EMI	560-20-3450-3	Austria	1989	89.99
Pet Shop Boys	Jealousy (Cd 1)	CD Single	Parlophone	CDR-6283	England	1991	19.99
Pet Shop Boys	Jealousy (Cd 2) Digipack	CD Single	Parlophone	CDRS-6283	England	1991	20.99
Pet Shop Boys	Left To My Own Devices (Dbl. Slv.)	CD Single	Parlophone	CDR-6198	England	1988	13.99
Pet Shop Boys	Liberation (Cd 1)	CD Single	Parlophone	CDRS-6377	England	1994	7.99
Pet Shop Boys	Liberation (Cd 2)	CD Single	Parlophone	CDR-6377	England	1994	16.99
Pet Shop Boys	London (Promo)	CD Single	Parlophone	CDRDJX-6589	England	2000	13.99
Pet Shop Boys	Mini	CD Single	Toshiba-EMI	TOCP-61035	Japan	2000	37.99
Pet Shop Boys	New York City Boy	CD Single	Sire	350132	U.S.A.	1999	5.99
Pet Shop Boys	New York City Boy	CD Single	EMI	24388-77230	Holland	1999	5.99
Pet Shop Boys	New York City Boy (Cd 1)	CD Single	Parlophone	CDRS-6525	England	1999	5.99
Pet Shop Boys	New York City Boy (Cd 2)	CD Single	Parlophone	CDR-6525	England	1999	5.99
Pet Shop Boys	New York City Boy (Promo)	CD	EMI	CDRDJX-6525	England	1999	21.99
Pet Shop Boys	New York City Boy (Promo)	CD Single	Sire	PRO-74687-2	U.S.A.	1999	29.99
Pet Shop Boys	Nightlife	CD	Parlophone	5218572	England	1999	5.99
Pet Shop Boys	Nightlife (Limited Ed.)	CD	Parlophone	7243-523064-2-8	England	1999	13.99
Pet Shop Boys	Nightlife + 11	2CD	Sire	6-4344-35012-2	U.S.A.	1999	26.99
Pet Shop Boys	Originals Box Set	3CD	Parlophone	CDOMB-023	England	1997	25.99
Pet Shop Boys	Paninaro '95 (Cd 1)	CD Single	Parlophone	CDRS-6414	England	1995	8.99
Pet Shop Boys	Paninaro '95 (Cd 2)	CD Single	Parlophone	CDR-6414	England	1995	8.99
Pet Shop Boys	Paninaro '95 (Promo)	CD Single	Parlophone	CDRDJ-6414	England	1995	8.99
Pet Shop Boys	Paninaro '95 (Promo)	CD Single	EMI	E2-58369	U.S.A.	1995	11.99
Pet Shop Boys	Please	CD	Parlophone	CDPCS-7303	England	1986	12.99
Pet Shop Boys	Please + 13/Further Listening	2CD	Parlophone	5305042	England	2001	19.99
Pet Shop Boys	Promotion (Promo)	CD	Toshiba-EMI	PCD-0399	Japan	1993	153.62
Pet Shop Boys	Release	CD	Parlophone	5381502	England	2002	6.99
Pet Shop Boys	Release (Limited Ed)	CD	Parlophone	5385982	England	2002	16.99
Pet Shop Boys	Release (Promo)	CD	Parlophone	RELEASE01	England	2002	13.99
Pet Shop Boys	Release Special Ed. + 9	CD	EMI	724354148606	Hong Kong	2002	18.99
Pet Shop Boys	Rent	CD Single	Parlophone	CDR-6168	England	1987	15.99
Pet Shop Boys	Rent	CDV	EMI	TOFF-7504	Japan	1990	157.99
Pet Shop Boys	Sampler (Promo)	CD	Parlophone	PSB001	England	2001	29.99
Pet Shop Boys	Se A Vida É (Cd 1)	CD Single	Parlophone	CDR-6443	England	1996	4.99
Pet Shop Boys	Se A Vida É (Cd 2)	CD Single	Parlophone	CDRS-6443	England	1996	4.99
Pet Shop Boys	Self Titled (Promo)	CD	Toshiba-EMI	SPCD-1145	Japan	1990	184.99
Pet Shop Boys	Single (Cd 2)	CD Single	Parlophone	7243-8-83468-2-5	Holland	1992	4.99
Pet Shop Boys	So Hard	CD Single	Parlophone	CDR-6269	England	1990	10.99
Pet Shop Boys	So Hard	CD Single	Parlophone	20-4062-2	France	1990	16.99
Pet Shop Boys	So Hard	CD Single	EMI	560-20-4062-2	Germany	1990	15.99
Pet Shop Boys	So Hard	CD Single	EMI	E2-561-95	U.S.A.	1990	18.99
Pet Shop Boys	So Hard (KLF Vs Pet Shop Boys)	CD Single	EMI	20-4092-2	Germany	1990	38.99
Pet Shop Boys	Somewhere	CD Single	Toshiba-EMI	TOCP-40062	Japan	1997	37.99
Pet Shop Boys	Somewhere	CD Single	EMI	7243-8-84275-2-4	Holland	1997	8.99
Pet Shop Boys	Somewhere (Cd 1)	CD Single	Parlophone	CDRS-6470	England	1997	10.99
Pet Shop Boys	Somewhere (Cd 2)	CD Single	Parlophone	CDR-6470	England	1997	7.99
Pet Shop Boys	Somewhere (Promo)	CD Single	Parlophone	CDRDJ-6470	England	1996	19.99
Pet Shop Boys	Very	CD	Parlophone	CDPSCD-143	England	1993	38.99
Pet Shop Boys	Very (Limited Ed.)	CD	Parlophone	CDPSCD-143	England	1993	8.99
Pet Shop Boys	Very (Special Edition Orange)	CD	EMI	E2-89721	U.S.A.	1996	30.99
Pet Shop Boys	Very + 16/Further Listening	2CD	Parlophone	5305112	England	2001	14.99
Pet Shop Boys	Very + 6 Relentless	2CD	Parlophone	CDPCSDX-143	England	1993	28.99

P

Artist	Title	Format	Label	Catalog No	Country	Released	Value
Pet Shop Boys	Was It Worth It?	CD Single	Parlophone	CDR-6306	England	1991	7.99
Pet Shop Boys	Was It Worth It?	CD Single	EMI	E2-562-44	U.S.A.	1991	15.99
Pet Shop Boys	West End Girls	CD Single	ZYX	GDC-2020-8	Germany	1985	9.99
Pet Shop Boys	West End/Sunglasses/1 More Chance 3	CD Single	ZYX	8-5196	Austria	1986	12.99
Pet Shop Boys	What Have I Done To Deserve This?	CD Single	Parlophone	CDR-6166	England	1987	11.99
Pet Shop Boys	Where The Streets...	CD Single	EMI	560-20-4266-2	Holland	1991	15.99
Pet Shop Boys	Where The Streets...	CD Single	EMI	560-20-4254-2	Holland	1991	7.99
Pet Shop Boys	Where The Streets...	CD Single	EMI	E2-562-17	U.S.A.	1991	4.99
Pet Shop Boys	Where The Streets...(Can't Take...)	CD Single	Parlophone	CDR-6285	England	1991	19.99
Pet Shop Boys	Yesterday When I Was..	CD Single	EMI	8-81632-2	Holland	1994	5.99
Pet Shop Boys	Yesterday, When I Was Mad	CD Single	Parlophone	CDR-6386	England	1994	7.99
Pet Shop Boys	Yesterday, When... (Dbl. Slv)	CD Single	Parlophone	CDRS-6386	England	1994	13.99
Pet Shop Boys	You Only Love Me...	CD Single	EMI	7243-8-88172-2-6	Holland	2000	6.99
Pet Shop Boys	You Only Tell Me You (Cd 1)	CD Single	Parlophone	CDRS-6533	England	2000	6.99
Pet Shop Boys	You Only Tell Me You (Cd 2)	CD Single	Parlophone	CDR-6533	England	2000	6.99
Pet Shop Boys	You Only Tell Me You (Cd 3)	CD Single	Parlophone	CDRX-6533	England	2000	6.99
Pet Shop Boys	You Only Tell Me... (Promo)	CD Single	Parlophone	CDRDJ-6533	England	1999	18.99
Pet Shop Boys/P Rauhofer	Break 4 Love	CD Single	Star 69	STAR-CD12172	U.S.A.	2001	6.99
Peter & Gordon	A World Without.../I Don't Want to See..	CD	Collectables	2717	U.S.A.	1998	8.99
Peter & Gordon	All Time Greatest	CD	Madacy	57973	U.S.A.	1994	8.99
Peter & Gordon	All Time Greatest Hits Of	CD	Cema	57399	U.S.A.	1992	8.99
Peter & Gordon	Definitive Coll.: Knights in Rusty Armour 3CD	Collectables	0256	U.S.A.	2003	29.99
Peter & Gordon	EP Collection	CD	See For Miles	426	England	1995	28.99
Peter & Gordon	Greatest Hits	CD	Collectables	9644	U.S.A.	2003	8.99
Peter & Gordon	I Go to Pieces/True Love Ways	CD	Collectables	2715	U.S.A.	1998	8.99
Peter & Gordon	Original Hits	CD	Disky	DC-860922	Netherlands	1995	8.99
Peter & Gordon	Peter And Gordon (Mono/Stereo)	CD	EMI	7243-5-20189-2-5	EU	1999	13.99
Peter & Gordon	The Best Of	CD	Rhino	R2-70748	U.S.A.	1991	21.99
Peter & Gordon	The Ultimate	CD	Collector's Choice	189-2	U.S.A.	2001	9.99
Peter & Gordon	Ultimate Collection	CD	EMI	535931	Australia	2002	10.99
Peter & Gordon	Woman/Lady Godiva	CD	Collectables	2716	U.S.A.	1998	8.99
Peter & Gordon/Dave Clark 5	Dave Clark Five Vs. Peter & Gordon	CD	TF	R-280044	Japan	1987	14.99
Petra	Back To The Street	CD	Star Song	SSD-8073-2	U.S.A.	1990	12.99
Petra	Beat The System	CD	Star Song	SSD-8057-2	U.S.A.	1992	12.99
Petra	Beyond Belief	CD	Word	EK-48546	U.S.A.	1990	11.99
Petra	Captured In Time And Space	CD	Star Song	SSD-8065-2	U.S.A.	1989	11.99
Petra	Come And Join Us	CD	Word	EK-48801	U.S.A.	1992	11.99
Petra	Double Take	CD	Word	EK-69882	U.S.A.	1999	6.99
Petra	En Alabanza	CD	Word	0806-8-81565-2-7	U.S.A.	1992	8.99
Petra	God Fixation	CD	Word	EK-69150	U.S.A.	1998	6.99
Petra	Jekyll And Hyde	CD	Inpop	POD1267	U.S.A.	2003	14.99
Petra	More Power To Ya	CD	Star Song	SSD-8045-2	U.S.A.	1992	12.99
Petra	Never Say Die	CD	Star Song	SSD-8016-2	U.S.A.	1992	12.99
Petra	No Doubt	CD	Word	EK-67302	U.S.A.	1995	7.99
Petra	Not Of This World	CD	Star Song	SSD-8050-2	U.S.A.	1992	12.99
Petra	On Fire!	CD	Star Song	SSD-8106-2	U.S.A.	1990	11.99
Petra	Petra Means Rock	CD	Star Song	SSD-8138-2	U.S.A.	1989	8.99
Petra	Petra Praise Vol. 2: We Need Jesus	CD	Word	701-9929-605	U.S.A.	1992	9.99
Petra	Petrafied! The Very Best Of	CD	Star Song	SSD-8201-2	U.S.A.	1992	8.99
Petra	Petraphonics	CD	Star Song	SSD-8266-2	U.S.A.	1992	9.99
Petra	Power Praise	CD	Star Song	SSD-8285-2	U.S.A.	1993	8.99
Petra	Praise-The Rock Cries Out	CD	Word	EK-48862	U.S.A.	1992	9.99
Petra	Revival	CD	Inpop	71245	U.S.A.	2001	9.99
Petra	Rock Block	CD	Star Song	SSD-0058-2	U.S.A.	1995	8.99
Petra	Self Titled	CD	Word	EK-48802	U.S.A.	1992	10.99
Petra	Still Means War	CD	Word	0806-8-86229-2-3	U.S.A.	2002	8.99
Petra	The Early Years	CD	Star Song	SSD-0112-2	U.S.A.	1996	8.99
Petra	The Power Of Praise	CD	Word	0806-8-86253-2-0	U.S.A.	2003	8.99

P

Artist	Title	Format	Label	Catalog No	Country	Released	Value
Petra	This Means War!	CD	Star Song	SSD-8084-2	U.S.A.	1990	11.99
Petra	Unseen Power	CD	Word	EK-48859	U.S.A.	1991	8.99
Petra	Wake Up Call	CD	Word	EK-57606	U.S.A.	1993	7.99
Petra	War & Rememberance	CD	Star Song	SSD-8158-2	U.S.A.	1990	19.99
Petra	Washes Whiter Than	CD	Star Song	SSD-8014-2	U.S.A.	1992	12.99
Petty, Tom/Heartbreakers	A Higher Place	CD Single	Warner Bros.	18026	U.S.A.	1995	4.99
Petty, Tom/Heartbreakers	Anthology: Through the Years	2CD	MCA	170177	U.S.A.	2000	13.99
Petty, Tom/Heartbreakers	Damn The Torpedoes	CD	MCA	112399	U.S.A.	2001	6.99
Petty, Tom/Heartbreakers	Damn The Torpedoes (MFSL Gold Cd)	CD	Mobile Fidelity	UDCD-551	U.S.A.	1979	29.99
Petty, Tom/Heartbreakers	Damn Torpedoes/S Accents/Into Grt	3CD	MCA	380334	U.S.A.	1999	29.99
Petty, Tom/Heartbreakers	Echo	CD	Warner Bros.	9-47294-2	U.S.A.	1999	7.99
Petty, Tom/Heartbreakers	Free Girl Now (Promo)	CD Single	Warner Bros.	PRO-CD-9706-R	U.S.A.	1999	5.99
Petty, Tom/Heartbreakers	Full Moon Fever	CD	MCA	MCAD-6253	U.S.A.	1989	7.99
Petty, Tom/Heartbreakers	Full Moon Fever (MFSL Gold Cd)	CD	Mobile Fidelity	UDCD-735	U.S.A.	1989	44.99
Petty, Tom/Heartbreakers	Gone Gator Sampler (Promo)	CD	MCA	CD33-1478	U.S.A.	1991	7.99
Petty, Tom/Heartbreakers	Greatest Hits	CD	MCA	10813	U.S.A.	1993	9.99
Petty, Tom/Heartbreakers	Greatest Hits + 2	CD	MCA	10964	Germany	1993	11.99
Petty, Tom/Heartbreakers	Hard Promises	CD	MCA	112400	U.S.A.	2001	7.99
Petty, Tom/Heartbreakers	Hard Promises (MFSL Gold Cd)	CD	Mobile Fidelity	UDCD-565	U.S.A.	1981	26.99
Petty, Tom/Heartbreakers	Into The Great Wide Open	CD	MCA	MCAD-10317	U.S.A.	1991	7.99
Petty, Tom/Heartbreakers	It's Good To Be King	CD Single	Warner Bros.	17925	U.S.A.	1995	4.99
Petty, Tom/Heartbreakers	Learning To Fly (Promo)	CD	MCA	CD45-1482	U.S.A.	1991	18.99
Petty, Tom/Heartbreakers	Let Me Up (I've Had Enough)	CD	MCA	MCAD-5836	U.S.A.	1987	8.99
Petty, Tom/Heartbreakers	Live At The Olympic: Last DJ/More	CD	Warner Bros.	48434	Germany	2003	19.99
Petty, Tom/Heartbreakers	Long After Dark	CD	MCA	112446	U.S.A.	2001	7.99
Petty, Tom/Heartbreakers	Long After Dark (Diff. Cvr)	CD	Music For Pleasure	MFPCD-034	Australia	1982	10.99
Petty, Tom/Heartbreakers	Pack Up The Plantation Live!	CD	MCA	MCAD2-8021	U.S.A.	1986	7.99
Petty, Tom/Heartbreakers	Peace in L.A.	CD Single	MCA	MCAP54436	U.S.A.	1992	8.99
Petty, Tom/Heartbreakers	Playback Box Set	6CD	MCA	MCAD6-11375	U.S.A.	1995	29.99
Petty, Tom/Heartbreakers	Playback Excerpts # 1 Promo Box	CD	MCA	MCA3P-3604	U.S.A.	1995	24.99
Petty, Tom/Heartbreakers	Playback Excerpts # 2 Promo Box	CD	MCA	MCA3P-3624	U.S.A.	1995	24.99
Petty, Tom/Heartbreakers	Room At The Top	CD Single	Warner Bros.	9362-44662-2	Sweden	1999	5.99
Petty, Tom/Heartbreakers	Room At The Top (Promo)	CD Single	Warner Bros.	PRO-CD-9741	U.S.A.	1999	9.99
Petty, Tom/Heartbreakers	Room At The Top (Promo)	CD Single	Warner Bros.	PRO-CD-9703	U.S.A.	1999	9.99
Petty, Tom/Heartbreakers	Runnin' Down A Dream (Promo)	CD Single	MCA	OMCAT-1359	U.S.A.	1989	5.99
Petty, Tom/Heartbreakers	Self Titled	CD	MCA	MCAD-10135	U.S.A.	1991	8.99
Petty, Tom/Heartbreakers	She's The One Soundtrack	CD	Warner Bros.	9-46285-2	U.S.A.	1996	6.99
Petty, Tom/Heartbreakers	Southern Accents	CD	MCA	MCAD-5486	U.S.A.	1985	7.99
Petty, Tom/Heartbreakers	Swingin' (Promo)	CD Single	Warner Bros.	PRO-CD-9862	U.S.A.	1999	5.99
Petty, Tom/Heartbreakers	The Last DJ + Bonus DVD	2CD	Warner Bros.	9-48396-2	U.S.A.	2002	14.99
Petty, Tom/Heartbreakers	Walls	CD Single	Warner Bros.	17593	U.S.A.	1996	5.99
Petty, Tom/Heartbreakers	Walls (Promo)	CD Single	Warner Bros.	PRO-CD-8285	U.S.A.	1996	5.99
Petty, Tom/Heartbreakers	Walls (Promo)	CD Single	Warner Bros.	W0371CD	England	1996	5.99
Petty, Tom/Heartbreakers	Westwood 1 # 00-06, 2-5/6,1999	2CD	Westwood 1	CO0006A012800	U.S.A.	1999	39.99
Petty, Tom/Heartbreakers	Wildflowers	CD	MCA	45759	U.S.A.	1994	7.99
Petty, Tom/Heartbreakers	You Don't Know How.../Girls On LSD	CD Single	Warner Bros.	5439-18030-2	U.S.A.	1994	34.99
Petty, Tom/Heartbreakers	You're Gonna Get It	CD	MCA	MCAD-10134	U.S.A.	1991	7.99
Petty, Tom/Tribute	You Got Lucky	CD	Backyard	7239275450-2	U.S.A.	1994	4.99
PFM	10 Anni Live 1971-1981 Box Set	3CD	RTI	0217-2	Italy	1996	74.99
PFM	Chocolate Kings	CD	RCA	ND-71781	Italy	1975	14.99
PFM	Come Ti Va In Riva Alla Citta	CD	RCA	74321-100802	Italy	1981	14.99
PFM	Gli Anni Settanta	2CD	RCA	7474321602652-(2	Italy	2001	18.99
PFM	Jet Lag	CD	RCA	ND-75244	Italy	1977	14.99
PFM	Jet Lag (Gold Disc)	CD	RCA	74321-922862	Italy	2002	17.99
PFM	L'Isola Di Niente (Gold Cd)	CD	RCA	74321-896062	Italy	2001	17.99
PFM	Live In USA	CD	RCA	ND-71838	Italy	1988	14.99
PFM	Miss Baker	CD	Ricordi	74321441552	Italy	1996	19.99
PFM	Passpartú	CD	RCA	ND-75245	Italy	1978	14.99

P

Artist	Title	Format	Label	Catalog No	Country	Released	Value
PFM	Performance	CD	RCA	74321-100822	Italy	1980	14.99
PFM	Photos Of Ghosts	CD	Victor Ent.	VICP-60970	Japan	2000	24.99
PFM	Serendipity	CD	Sony	498901-2	Italy	2000	19.99
PFM	Story	CD	RCA	74321-21540-2	Italy	1995	14.99
PFM	Suonare Suonare	CD	RCA	74321-100812	Italy	1980	14.99
PFM	The World Became The World	CD	Victor Ent.	VICP-60971	Japan	2000	24.99
PFM/Gold CDs	Golden (Gold) (Storia/Amico/Ghosts)	3CD	RCA	CFD-01113	Italy	2001	44.99
P-Funk/George Clinton	Music/Motion Picture PCU	CD	Fox	10009-2	U.S.A.	1994	25.99
Phair, Liz	Exile in Guyville	CD	Matador	OLE-051-2	U.S.A.	1992	12.99
Phair, Liz	Juvenalia EP	CD Single	Matador	OLE-129-2	U.S.A.	1995	19.99
Phair, Liz	Self Titled	CD	Capitol	7243-5-22084-2-0	U.S.A.	2003	13.99
Phair, Liz	Supernova	CD Single	Matador	OLE-103-2	U.S.A.	1994	7.99
Phair, Liz	Whip-Smart	CD	Matador	92429-2	U.S.A.	1994	9.99
Phair, Liz	Whip-Smart	CD	MMG Inc.	AMCY-754	Japan	1994	11.99
Phair, Liz	Whitechocolatespaceegg	CD	Matador	7243-8-53554-2-4	U.S.A.	1998	8.99
Phantom Blue	Built To Perform	CD	Geffen	GEFD-24603	U.S.A.	1993	12.99
Phantom Blue	My Misery EP	CD Single	Roadrunner	RR-2379-3	Germany	1993	9.99
Phantom Blue	Self Titled	CD	Roadrunner	RR-9469-2	England	1989	33.99
Phantom Blue	Self Titled	CD	Shrapnel	SH-1043CD	U.S.A.	2000	20.99
Phenomena	Dream Runner	CD	Resurgent	4200	U.S.A.	1998	10.99
Phenomena	Phenomena (W/Bonus)	CD	Kiosk	CMP-62020	Germany	1996	19.99
Phenomena	Phenomena 1985-1996 X	CD	Parachute	CDAP005	England	1996	10.99
Phillips, Anthony	1984	CD	Virgin	CDOVD-321	Germany	1981	11.99
Phillips, Anthony	1984	CD	Virgin	VJCP-23048	Japan	1981	15.99
Phillips, Anthony	Anthology	CD	Blueprint	BP201CD	England	1995	12.99
Phillips, Anthony	Finger Painting- Missing Links Vol. 1	CD	Blueprint	BP209CD	Austria	1995	12.99
Phillips, Anthony	Gypsy Suite	CD	Blueprint	BP189CD	Austria	1994	12.99
Phillips, Anthony	Invisible Men + 4	CD	Blueprint	BP211CD	Austria	1990	13.99
Phillips, Anthony	Lyric Book W/Lyric Book	CD	Voiceprint	VP184CD	England	1995	23.99
Phillips, Anthony	Private Parts & Pieces IX: Dragonfly...	CD	Blueprint	BP229CD	Austria	1996	12.99
Phillips, Anthony	Private Parts & Pieces Part 3 - Antiques	CD	Blueprint	BP204CD	Austria	1981	12.99
Phillips, Anthony	Private Parts & Pieces VI Ivory Moon	CD	Blueprint	BP207CD	Austria	1994	12.99
Phillips, Anthony	Private Parts & Pieces VII: Slow Waves	CD	Blueprint	BP208CD	Austria	1994	12.99
Phillips, Anthony	Private Parts & Pieces Vol. VIII	CD	Blueprint	BP212CD	Austria	1992	12.99
Phillips, Anthony	Private Parts & Pieces, Part I + 1	CD	Blueprint	BP202CD	England	1995	12.99
Phillips, Anthony	Private Parts & Pieces, Part II + 1	CD	Blueprint	BP203CD	Austria	1995	12.99
Phillips, Anthony	Private Parts & Pieces, Part IV + 1	CD	Blueprint	BP205CD	Austria	1994	12.99
Phillips, Anthony	Private Parts And Pieces V	CD	Blueprint	BP206CD	Austria	1995	12.99
Phillips, Anthony	Sail The World	CD	Resurgence	RES102CD	Austria	1994	12.99
Phillips, Anthony	Sides	CD	Blueprint	BP210CD	Austria	1995	12.99
Phillips, Anthony	Slow Dance	CD	Blueprint	BP213CD	Austria	2002	12.99
Phillips, Anthony	Soft Vivace	CD	Astral	CD-1728	Spain	2002	15.99
Phillips, Anthony	Soiree Private Parts & Pieces X	CD	Blueprint	BP319CD	England	1999	12.99
Phillips, Anthony	Soundscapes	2CD	Snapper	997692	England	2003	16.99
Phillips, Anthony	The Archive Collection, Vol. 1	CD	Blueprint	BP279CD	EU	1998	12.99
Phillips, Anthony	The Archive Collection, Vol. 2	2CD	Blueprint	BP360CD	EU	2004	19.99
Phillips, Anthony	The Geese & The Ghost + 1	CD	Virgin	CDOVD-315	Germany	1990	15.99
Phillips, Anthony	The Living Room Concert (W/Lyric Bk)	CD	Blueprint	BP218CD	Austria	1995	49.99
Phillips, Anthony	The Skyroad- Missing Links Vol. 2	CD	Blueprint	BP329CD	England	2000	14.99
Phillips, Anthony	Wise After The Event + 1	CD	Virgin	CDOVD-322	England	1990	15.99
Phillips, Anthony /H.W.	Tarka	CD	Blueprint	BP219CD	Austria	1996	12.99
Phillips, Anthony/Cazenave	All Our Lives	2CD	Astral	CD-1725	Spain	2002	29.99
Phillips, Chynna	Naked And Sacred	CD	EMI	E2-35705	U.S.A.	1995	7.99
Phillips, Eddie	Riffmaster Of The Western World	CD	Line	OLCD-9.51029-X	Germany	1991	19.99
Phillips, John	John, The Wolf King Of LA	CD	Victor Ent.	UICY-3360	Japan	2002	25.99
Phillips, John	Phillips 66	CD	Eagle	WK-18854	U.S.A.	2001	8.99
Phillips, John/Bijou	Hawaii (Promo)	CD Single	Almo Sounds	AMS5P8066	U.S.A.	1998	5.99
Phillips, John/Bijou	I'd Rather Eat Glass	CD	Almo Sounds	AMSD-80022	U.S.A.	1999	5.99

P

Artist	Title	Format	Label	Catalog No	Country	Released	Value
Phillips, John/Bijou	When I Hated Him	CD Single	Almo Sounds	AMSD5-89015	U.S.A.	1999	4.99
Phillips, John/Rolling Stones	Pay Pack & Follow + 1 (W/R. Stones)	CD	Eagle	CTCR-14185	Japan	2001	29.99
Phillips, John/Rolling Stones	Pay Pack & Follow + 2 (Promo)	CD	Eagle	WK18475ADV	U.S.A.	2001	24.99
Phillips, Michelle	Victim Of Romance	CD	Victor Ent.	UICY-3364	Japan	2002	28.99
Phillips, Shawn	Another Contribution: An Anthology	CD	A&M	314-540-508-2	U.S.A.	1995	9.99
Phillips, Shawn	Best Of: The A & M Years	CD	A&M	314-540-016-2	U.S.A.	1992	11.99
Phillips, Shawn	Beyond Here Be Dragons	CD	Wounded Bird	WOU-4764	U.S.A.	2000	8.99
Phillips, Shawn	Bright White	CD	Wounded Bird	WOU-4402	U.S.A.	1999	8.99
Phillips, Shawn	Collaboration	CD	Wounded Bird	WOU-4324	U.S.A.	1999	8.99
Phillips, Shawn	Contribution	CD	Wounded Bird	WOU-4241	U.S.A.	1999	8.99
Phillips, Shawn	Do You Wonder ?	CD	Wounded Bird	WOU-4539	U.S.A.	1999	8.99
Phillips, Shawn	Faces	CD	A&M	75021-3135-2	U.S.A.	1990	28.99
Phillips, Shawn	Furthermore	CD	Wounded Bird	WOU-3662	U.S.A.	1999	8.99
Phillips, Shawn	I'm A Loner	CD	Wounded Bird	WOU-1748	U.S.A.	1999	8.99
Phillips, Shawn	No Category	CD	Fat Jack	2002	U.S.A.	2003	14.99
Phillips, Shawn	Second Contribution	CD	A&M	75021-3128-2	U.S.A.	1990	8.99
Phillips, Shawn	Shawn	CD	Wounded Bird	WOU-6006	U.S.A.	1999	8.99
Phillips, Shawn	Transcendence	CD	Wounded Bird	WOU-3028	U.S.A.	1999	8.99
Phillips, Shawn	Truth If It Kills	CD	Imagine	IMD2042	Canada	1997	7.99
Phillips, Simon	Out Of The Blue + 1	CD	Victor Ent.	VICP-60720	U.S.A.	1999	34.99
Phillips, Simon	Symbiosis	CD	Lipstick	LIP-8936-2	U.S.A.	1995	10.99
Phillips, Stu	Battlestar Galactica Box Set	4CD	Stu Phillips	SPCD-01/04	U.S.A.	1996	59.99
Phish	A Live One	2CD	Elektra	61777-2	U.S.A.	1995	8.99
Phish	A Picture Of Nectar	CD	Elektra	61274-2	U.S.A.	1991	8.99
Phish	A Sampler (Promo)	CD	Elektra	PRCD-8805-2	U.S.A.	1993	54.99
Phish	Billy Breathes	CD	Elektra	61971-2	U.S.A.	1996	6.99
Phish	Farmhouse	CD	Elektra	62521-2	U.S.A.	2000	9.99
Phish	Hampton Comes Alive	6CD	Elektra	62495-2	U.S.A.	1999	49.99
Phish	Hoist	CD	Elektra	61628-2	U.S.A.	1994	6.99
Phish	Junta + 3	2CD	Elektra	61413-2	U.S.A.	1988	11.99
Phish	Lawn Boy	CD	Elektra	61275-2	U.S.A.	1991	6.99
Phish	Live Phish, Vol. 1	2CD	Elektra	62702-2	U.S.A.	2001	12.99
Phish	Live Phish, Vol. 10	3CD	Elektra	62754-2	U.S.A.	2002	15.99
Phish	Live Phish, Vol. 11	3CD	Elektra	62755-2	U.S.A.	2002	15.99
Phish	Live Phish, Vol. 12	3CD	Elektra	62756-2	U.S.A.	2002	15.99
Phish	Live Phish, Vol. 13	4CD	Elektra	62806-2	U.S.A.	2002	18.99
Phish	Live Phish, Vol. 14	4CD	Elektra	62807-2	U.S.A.	2002	18.99
Phish	Live Phish, Vol. 15	4CD	Elektra	62808-2	U.S.A.	2002	18.99
Phish	Live Phish, Vol. 16	4CD	Elektra	62809-2	U.S.A.	2002	18.99
Phish	Live Phish, Vol. 17	3CD	Elektra	62868-2	U.S.A.	2003	15.99
Phish	Live Phish, Vol. 18	3CD	Elektra	62869-2	U.S.A.	2003	15.99
Phish	Live Phish, Vol. 19	2CD	Elektra	62870-2	U.S.A.	2003	12.99
Phish	Live Phish, Vol. 2	3CD	Elektra	62703-2	U.S.A.	2001	15.99
Phish	Live Phish, Vol. 20	2CD	Elektra	62871-2	U.S.A.	2003	12.99
Phish	Live Phish, Vol. 3	3CD	Elektra	62704-2	U.S.A.	2001	15.99
Phish	Live Phish, Vol. 4	3CD	Elektra	62705-2	U.S.A.	2001	15.99
Phish	Live Phish, Vol. 5	3CD	Elektra	62706-2	U.S.A.	2001	15.99
Phish	Live Phish, Vol. 6	3CD	Elektra	62708-2	U.S.A.	2001	15.99
Phish	Live Phish, Vol. 7	3CD	Elektra	62751-2	U.S.A.	2002	15.99
Phish	Live Phish, Vol. 8	2CD	Elektra	62752-2	U.S.A.	2002	12.99
Phish	Live Phish, Vol. 9	3CD	Elektra	62753-2	U.S.A.	2002	15.99
Phish	Rift	CD	Elektra	61433-2	U.S.A.	1993	6.99
Phish	Round Room	CD	Elektra	62850-2	U.S.A.	2002	8.99
Phish	Selections From Hampton Comes Alive (	CD	Elektra	PRCD-1427-2	U.S.A.	1999	14.99
Phish	Selections From Live Phish Vol. 7-12 (DJ	CD	Elektra	PRCD-1759-2)	U.S.A.	2002	8.99
Phish	Selections From Round Room (Promo)	CD	Elektra	PRCD-1850-2	U.S.A.	2002	8.99
Phish	Slip, Stitch & Pass	2CD	Elektra	62121-2	U.S.A.	1997	8.99
Phish	The Siket Disc	CD	Elektra	62598-2	U.S.A.	2000	7.99

P

Artist	Title	Format	Label	Catalog No	Country	Released	Value
Phish	The Story Of The Ghost	CD	Elektra	62297-2	U.S.A.	1998	6.99
Phish	The White Tape	CD	Phish Archives	1001	U.S.A.	1998	14.99
Phish	Undermind (W/Bonus DVD)	2CD	Elektra	62969-2	U.S.A.	2004	16.99
Phish/Mike Gordon	Inside In	CD	Rope A Dope	93185-2	U.S.A.	2003	7.99
Phish/Oysterhead	Grand Pecking Order	CD	Elektra	62677-2	U.S.A.	2001	7.99
Phish/Pork Tornado	Self Titled	CD	Rykodisc	RCD-10630	U.S.A.	2002	7.99
Phish/Trey Anastasio	One Man's Trash	CD	Phish Dry Goods	PHDG-47614-2	U.S.A.	2002	8.99
Phish/Trey Anastasio	Plasma	2CD	Elektra	62867-2	U.S.A.	2003	17.99
Phish/Trey Anastasio	Selections From His Forthcoming Lp (DJ)	CD	Elektra	PRCD-1765-2	U.S.A.	2002	8.99
Phish/Trey Anastasio	Self Titled	CD	Elektra	62749-2	U.S.A.	2002	8.99
Phish/Trey Anastasio	Sies De Mayo	CD	Elektra	62962-2	U.S.A.	2004	8.99
Phish/Trey Anastasio	Surrender To The Air	CD	Elektra	61905-2	U.S.A.	1996	7.99
Phish/Trey Anastasio	Trampled By Lambs...(W/Tom Marshall)	CD	Phish Dry Goods	PDG-1003-2	U.S.A.	2000	19.99
Photos/Wendy Wu	Photos (Sounds Like The Pretenders)	CD	Epic	491697-2	U.S.A.	1980	14.99
Pickett, Bobby/Crypt-Kickers	The Original Monster Mash	CD	Deram	844-147-2	U.S.A.	1991	28.99
Pied Pipers	Capitol Collector's Series (Best Of)	CD	Capitol	C2-95289	Canada	1992	58.99
PIL/Public Image Ltd	1st Issue/Flower Of R/Compact Disc	3CD	Virgin	TPAK-5	England	1990	24.99
PIL/Public Image Ltd	9	CD	Virgin	7-91062-2	U.S.A.	1989	7.99
PIL/Public Image Ltd	Compact Disc	CD	Virgin	CDV-2366	England	1986	5.99
PIL/Public Image Ltd	First Issue	CD	Virgin	CDV-2114	England	1986	19.99
PIL/Public Image Ltd	First Issue/Second Edition	2CD	Virgin	581-749-2	England	2003	23.99
PIL/Public Image Ltd	Flowers Of Romance	CD	Virgin	CDV-2189	England	1990	8.99
PIL/Public Image Ltd	Happy?	CD	Virgin	CDV2455	England	1987	5.99
PIL/Public Image Ltd	Live In Tokyo	CD	Virgin	0777-7874702-4	England	1986	13.99
PIL/Public Image Ltd	Metal Box W/Tin Can	CD	Virgin	0777-7-87473-2-1	England	1990	17.99
PIL/Public Image Ltd	Order Of Death (Blair Witch Mix)	CD Single	Chapter	CHA-0122	U.S.A.	1999	7.99
PIL/Public Image Ltd	Paris Au Printemps	CD	Virgin	CDV-2183	England	1990	8.99
PIL/Public Image Ltd	Plastic Box	4CD	Virgin	PILBOX-1	England	1999	32.99
PIL/Public Image Ltd	Second Edition	CD	Virgin	CDVD-2512	England	1986	8.99
PIL/Public Image Ltd	That What Is Not	CD	Virgin	2-91815	U.S.A.	1992	5.99
PIL/Public Image Ltd	The Greatest Hits So Far	CD	Virgin	2-91581	U.S.A.	1990	6.99
PIL/Public Image Ltd	This Is What You Want...This...	CD	Virgin	0777-7-87479-2-5	Holland	1984	13.99
Pinder, Mike	A People With One Heart	CD	One Step	OSR0435	U.S.A.	1996	15.99
Pinder, Mike	A Planet With One Mind	CD	One Step	OSR0434	U.S.A.	1995	15.99
Pinder, Mike	Among The Stars	CD	One Step	OSR0432	U.S.A.	1994	7.99
Pinder, Mike	Off The Shelf	CD	One Step	CD-5009	U.S.A.	1993	19.99
Pinder, Mike	The Promise + 2	CD	One Step	OSR0433	U.S.A.	1996	19.99
Pini, Mick 'Wildman'	Wildman	CD	Line	STCD-9.00846-0	Germany	1989	20.99
Pink Cream 69	36/140	CD Single	Sony	ESCA-5509	Japan	1991	9.99
Pink Cream 69	Change + 1	CD	Sony	ESCA-6184	Japan	1995	22.99
Pink Cream 69	Games People Play + 1	CD	Sony	ESCA-5754	Japan	1993	22.99
Pink Fairies	Do It	CD	Total Energy	NER-3017	England	1997	12.99
Pink Fairies	Golden Years 1969-1971	CD	Cleopatra	CLP-0188-2	England	1998	18.99
Pink Fairies	Kill 'Em & Eat 'Em	CD	Skyclad	53	England	1997	17.99
Pink Fairies	Kings Of Oblivion + 4	CD	Polydor	589-552-1	England	2002	16.99
Pink Fairies	Live Roundhouse/Prev Unrel./Do It	CD	Big Beat	CDWIKD-965	England	2002	12.99
Pink Fairies	Never Never Land + 4	CD	Polydor	589-550-2	England	2002	16.99
Pink Fairies	No Picture (W/Twink/Paul Rudolph)	CD	Captain Trip	CTCD-116	Japan	2000	15.99
Pink Fairies	Up the Pinks: Introduction	CD	Universal	589898	England	2003	12.99
Pink Fairies	What A Bunch Of Sweeties + 2	CD	Polydor	589-551-2	England	2002	16.99
Pink Fairies/A Colquhoun	Pick - Up The Phone America!	CD	Captain Trip	CTCD-292	Japan	1975	15.99
Pink Fairies/Hawk Fairies	Purple Haze (W/Nik Turner)	CD	Captain Trip	CTCD-117	Japan	2000	15.99
Pink Fairies/Twink	Lost Experimental Recordings: 1970	CD	Get Back	572	England	2000	11.99
Pink Fairies/Twink	Odds and Beginnings	CD	Captain Trip	CTCD-118	Japan	1975	15.99
Pink Fairies/Twink	The Never Never Land/Think Pink	CD	Get Back	599	England	2001	11.99
Pink Fairies/Twink	Think Pink	CD	Captain Trip	CTCD-115	Japan	1975	15.99
Pink Fairies/Twink	Think Pink	CD	Akarma	AK-64	Italy	2001	12.99
Pink Fairies/Warsaw Pact	Needle Time (Ltd 1000)	CD	Captain Trip	CTCD-238	Japan	1979	15.99

P

Artist	Title	Format	Label	Catalog No	Country	Released	Value
Pink Floyd	A Collection Of Great...	CD	Sony	28DP-5009	Japan	1991	27.99
Pink Floyd	A Great Collection Of Dance Songs	CD	Capitol	7243-5-26245-2-2	U.S.A.	2000	10.99
Pink Floyd	A Momentary Lapse Of Reason	CD	Columbia	CK-68518	U.S.A.	1997	8.99
Pink Floyd	A Saucerful Of Secrets	CD	Capitol	0777-7-46383-2-6	U.S.A.	1992	10.99
Pink Floyd	Animals	CD	Capitol	7243-8-29748-2-6	U.S.A.	2000	10.99
Pink Floyd	Another Brick Wall (Pt 2) 3"	CD Single	Columbia	38K-03118	U.S.A.	1988	29.99
Pink Floyd	Atom Heart Mother	CD	Capitol	0777-7-46381-2-8	U.S.A.	1994	10.99
Pink Floyd	Atom Heart Mother (MFSL Gold Cd)	CD	Mobile Fidelity	UDCD-595	U.S.A.	1970	49.99
Pink Floyd	Best Of Pink Floyd	CD	Creato	MDCD-1002	Japan	1988	29.99
Pink Floyd	Coming Back to Life (Promo)	CD Single	Columbia	CSK-7096	U.S.A.	1995	9.99
Pink Floyd	Dance Songs	CD	Columbia	CK-68520	U.S.A.	1997	7.99
Pink Floyd	Dark Side Moon (20th/Box W/Cards)	CD	EMI	0777-7-81479-2-3	England	1973	20.99
Pink Floyd	Dark Side Of The Moon	CD	EMI	8-29752-2	Argentina	1973	8.99
Pink Floyd	Dark Side Of The Moon	CD	EMI	CP35-3017	Japan	1973	24.99
Pink Floyd	Dark Side Of The Moon (30 Ann. Ed.)	CD	Capitol	7243-582136-2-1	U.S.A.	2003	13.99
Pink Floyd	Dark Side Of The Moon (Gold Cd)	CD	Toshiba-EMI	CP43-5771	Japan	1988	153.99
Pink Floyd	Dark Side Of The Moon (MFSL Gold)	CD	Mobile Fidelity	UDCD-517	U.S.A.	1973	44.99
Pink Floyd	Delicate Sound Of Thunder	2CD	Columbia	C2K-44484	U.S.A.	1988	12.99
Pink Floyd	Delicate Sound Thunder DJ Sampler	CD	Columbia	DISP-000031	U.S.A.	1988	34.99
Pink Floyd	Delicate Sound Thunder DJ Sampler	CD	Columbia	CSK-1375	U.S.A.	1988	34.99
Pink Floyd	Echoes - The Best Of	2CD	Capitol	7243-5-36111-2-5	U.S.A.	2001	15.99
Pink Floyd	Echoes 6 Track Promo Sampler	CD	EMI	CDLRL-054	U.S.A.	2001	24.99
Pink Floyd	Echoes 8 Track Sampler (Promo)	CD	Capitol	7087-6-15991-2-1	U.S.A.	2001	12.99
Pink Floyd	Echoes: The Best Of	2CD	EMI	7243-5-36111-2-5	Argentina	2001	11.99
Pink Floyd	Echoes: The Best Of (Gold Cd)	2CD	EMI	2CD/A278	Taiwan	2001	44.99
Pink Floyd	Echoes: The Best Of (Promo)	CD	EMI	PF1	Australia	2001	19.99
Pink Floyd	Final Cut	CD	Sony	SRCS-8488	Japan	1983	34.99
Pink Floyd	Full Of Secrets (Interview Cd)	CD	Holoview	3D-014	England	1990	7.99
Pink Floyd	High Hopes	CD Single	EMI	SPCD-1760	France	1994	39.99
Pink Floyd	High Hopes (Promo)	CD Single	Columbia	CSK-6440	U.S.A.	1994	6.99
Pink Floyd	Is Anyone Out There? (Ltd Ed)	2CD	Columbia	C2K-62058	U.S.A.	2000	39.99
Pink Floyd	Is There Anybody Out .. (Wall Live)	2CD	Columbia	C2K-62055	U.S.A.	2000	18.99
Pink Floyd	Is There Anybody Out There? (Promo)	CD	Columbia	CSK-12680	U.S.A.	2000	39.99
Pink Floyd	Keep Talking	CD Single	EMI	SPCD-1809	France	1994	25.99
Pink Floyd	Keep Talking (Promo)	CD Single	Columbia	CSK-6007	U.S.A.	1994	8.99
Pink Floyd	Keep Talking/Interviews (Promo)	CD	Columbia	CSK-6060	U.S.A.	1994	9.99
Pink Floyd	Learning To Fly	CD Single	EMI	CDEM26	England	1987	29.99
Pink Floyd	Learning to Fly (Promo)	CD Single	Columbia	CSK-2775	U.S.A.	1987	44.99
Pink Floyd	Learning to Fly (Promo)	CD Single	Columbia	SAMP-1167	U.S.A.	1987	44.99
Pink Floyd	London '66-'67 (With Bonus Cd Rom)	2CD	See For Miles	SFM-1967	England	1999	14.99
Pink Floyd	Lost For Words (Promo)	CD Single	Columbia	CSK-6228	U.S.A.	1994	34.99
Pink Floyd	Meddle	CD	Capitol	0777-7-46034-2-3	U.S.A.	1992	10.99
Pink Floyd	Meddle (MFSL Gold Cd)	CD	Mobile Fidelity	UDCD-518	U.S.A.	1971	37.99
Pink Floyd	Momentary Lapse - Off.Tour CD	CD	Columbia	CSK-1100	U.S.A.	1988	109.99
Pink Floyd	Money (Promo)	CD Single	EMI	CDEMDJ-620	Holland	2003	14.99
Pink Floyd	More	CD	Capitol	0777-7-46386-2-3	U.S.A.	1995	10.99
Pink Floyd	Obscured By Clouds	CD	Toshiba-EMI	EMI-CP32-5272	Japan	1972	21.99
Pink Floyd	Obscured By Clouds	CD	Capitol	0777-7-46385-2-4	U.S.A.	1995	10.99
Pink Floyd	On The Turning Away	CD Single	EMI	CDEM34	England	1997	24.99
Pink Floyd	On The Turning Away 3 "	CD Single	Sony	10EP-3005	Japan	1997	134.99
Pink Floyd	Pink Floyd * London * '66-'67	CD	See For Miles	SFMDP-3	England	1995	17.99
Pink Floyd	Pink Floyd Gift Set	4CD	Captiol	C2-91340	Canada	1993	39.99
Pink Floyd	Piper At The Gates Dawn (Mono)	CD	EMI	7243-8-59857-2-0	England	1997	99.99
Pink Floyd	Pulse (Deluxe Ed. W/Pulsating Light)	2CD	Columbia	C2K-67065	U.S.A.	1995	24.99
Pink Floyd	Relics	CD	Capitol	7243-8-35603-2-5	U.S.A.	1995	10.99
Pink Floyd	Run Like Hell / Comfortably Numb 3 "	CD Single	Columbia	13K-68657	U.S.A.	1988	29.99
Pink Floyd	Shine On - Selections From Box (DJ)	CD	Columbia	CSK-4848	U.S.A.	1992	11.99
Pink Floyd	Shine On Box Set (Singles Cd/Cards)	9CD	EMI	CXK-53180	England	1992	156.99

P

Artist	Title	Format	Label	Catalog No	Country	Released	Value
Pink Floyd	Shine On Sampler (Promo)	CD	EMI	SHINE-1	England	1992	14.99
Pink Floyd	Take It Back (Promo)	CD Single	Columbia	CSK-6069	U.S.A.	1994	14.99
Pink Floyd	Take It Back/Astronomy Dominie (live)	CD Single	Columbia	38K-77493	U.S.A.	1994	5.99
Pink Floyd	The Division Bell	CD	Columbia	CK-64200	U.S.A.	1994	8.99
Pink Floyd	The Final Cut	CD	Columbia	CK-68517	U.S.A.	1997	8.99
Pink Floyd	The First Three Singles (Mono)	CD Single	EMI	7243-8-59895-2-0	England	1997	11.99
Pink Floyd	The Piper At The Gates Of Dawn	CD	Capitol	0777-7-46384-2-5	U.S.A.	1994	10.99
Pink Floyd	The Wall	2CD	Sony	48DP5007-8	Japan	2001	59.99
Pink Floyd	The Wall	2CD	Capitol	7243-8-31243-2-9	U.S.A.	2000	15.99
Pink Floyd	The Wall (MFSL Gold Cd)	2CD	Columbia	UDCD-2-537	U.S.A.	1979	109.99
Pink Floyd	Tonite Let's All Make Love In London	CD	See For Miles	SEACD-4	England	1991	14.99
Pink Floyd	Ummagumma	2CD	Capitol	0777-7-46404-2-8	U.S.A.	1994	15.99
Pink Floyd	Us And Them, Symphonic Pink Floyd	CD	Point Music	446-623-2	U.S.A.	1995	5.99
Pink Floyd	Westwood 1 # 01-17, (4,28-29,01)	2CD	Westwood 1	CO0117A041801	U.S.A.	2001	149.99
Pink Floyd	What Do You Want From Me (live) DJ	CD Single	Columbia	CSK-7143	U.S.A.	1995	14.99
Pink Floyd	Wish You Were Here	CD	EMI	8-29750-2	Argentina	1975	8.99
Pink Floyd	Wish You Were Here	CD	Capitol	7243-8-29750-2-1	U.S.A.	2000	10.99
Pink Floyd	Wish You Were Here (Live)	CD Single	EMI	7243-8-82207-2-9	Holland	1995	7.99
Pink Floyd	Wish You Were Here (Sony Gold Cd)	CD	Columbia	CK-64405	U.S.A.	1975	84.99
Pink Floyd	Works	CD	Capitol	0777-7-46478-2-3	U.S.A.	1987	10.99
Pink Floyd/Friends	Interstellar Overdrive	CD	Power Sound 2001	PS-NEMS-1001-2	U.S.A.	1996	11.99
Pink Floyd/Mason & Fenn	Profiles	CD	Columbia	A-40142	U.S.A.	1985	14.99
Pink Floyd/Nick Mason	Nick Mason's Fictitious Sports	CD	Sony	WK-75070	U.S.A.	1981	14.99
Pink Floyd/Richard Wright	Broken China	CD	Guardian	7243-8-53645-2-5	U.S.A.	1996	10.99
Pink Floyd/Richard Wright	Wet Dream	CD	One Way	A-24090	U.S.A.	1978	29.99
Pink Floyd/Tribute	Tribute Angular: Signs Of Life	2CD	Musea	8224	England	2001	16.99
Pink Sapphire	From Me To You	CD	Hummingbird	HBCL-7045	Japan	1991	17.99
Pink Sapphire	Happy Together	CD	Hummingbird	HBCL-8001	Japan	1991	17.99
Pink Sapphire	P. S. I Love You	CD	Hummingbird	HBCL-7035	Japan	1990	17.99
Pinpoint	Third State	CD	Line	LICD-9.01338-0	Germany	1997	13.99
Pinpoint	Third State	CD	Line	ALCD-9.00223-0	Germany	1988	13.99
Pitton-Smith, Sir James	Lord Of Rings Trilogy Box (W/Poster)	3CD	Dressed To Kill	JRRT-755	England	2001	31.99
Pixies	14 Track Visa Promo	CD	4AD	VISA-3680	France	2000	104.99
Pixies	Alec Eiffel	CD Single	4AD	66444-2	U.S.A.	1992	8.99
Pixies	Death To The Pixies	2CD	Elektra	62118-2	U.S.A.	1997	13.99
Pixies	Death To The Pixies (Ltd Ed Box)	2CD	4AD	DADD7011CD	England	1997	61.99
Pixies	Dig For Fire (Promo)	CD Single	Elektra	PRCD8251-2	U.S.A.	1990	6.99
Pixies	Doolittle	CD	Elektra	9-60856-2	U.S.A.	1989	8.99
Pixies	Head On EP	CD	4AD	866-527-2	Canada	1991	17.99
Pixies	Monkey Gone to Heaven	CD Single	4AD	BAD-904CD	England	1989	17.99
Pixies	Monkey Gone To Heaven	CD Single	Elektra	9-66707-2	U.S.A.	1989	9.99
Pixies	Off You	CD Single	4AD	TAD2203	England	2002	6.99
Pixies	Planet Of Sound	CD Single	4AD	BAD-1003-CD	England	1991	9.99
Pixies	Surfer Rosa/Come On Pilgrim	CD	4AD	GAD-803-CD	England	1987	9.99
Pixies	Trompe Le Monde	CD	Elektra	9-61118-2	U.S.A.	1991	8.99
Pixies/Various Artists	Tribute To The Pixies	CD	Invisible	INV-179	Japan	2000	10.99
Plainsong	A To B	CD	Spin Along	SPACD002	England	2001	16.99
Plainsong	And That's That ('72 Shelved Music)	CD	Taxim	TX 2002-2-TA	U.S.A.	1992	19.99
Plainsong	Dark Side Of The Room	CD	Line	LICD-9.01247-0	Germany	1992	9.99
Plainsong	In Search Of Amelia Earhart	CD	Perfect Pitch	PP009	England	2002	16.99
Plainsong	Live In Austria	CD	Plainsong	PL0001	England	1997	16.99
Plainsong	New Place Now	CD	Blue Rose	BLUCD092	Germany	1999	16.99
Plainsong	On Air	CD	Strange Fruit	SFRSCD47	England	2001	15.99
Plainsong	Pangolins	CD	Blue Rose	BLUCD0299	Germany	2003	16.99
Plainsong	Sister Flute	CD	Line	LICD-9.01327-0	Germany	1996	19.99
Plainsong	Voices	CD Single	Line	TLCD-9.01296-0	Germany	1994	10.99
Plainsong	Voices Electric	CD	Line	LICD-9.01288-0	Germany	1994	9.99
Planer, Nigel/The Young Ones	Neil's Heavy Concept Album	CD	East West	4509-94852-2	England	1984	29.99

P

Artist	Title	Format	Label	Catalog No	Country	Released	Value
Planet P Project	Pink World	CD	MCA	MCAD-8019	U.S.A.	1984	20.99
Planet P Project	Self Titled	CD	Geffen	GEFD-4000	U.S.A.	1996	12.99
Plant, Robert	A Visit To Dreamland (Promo)	CD Single	Universal	20814-2	U.S.A.	2002	31.99
Plant, Robert	Calling To You	CD Single	Fontana	CDM-3	England	1993	14.99
Plant, Robert	Calling To You (Promo)	CD Single	Fontana	1734	France	1993	22.99
Plant, Robert	Dreamland + 5	2CD	Mercury	063-425-2	England	2002	15.99
Plant, Robert	Dreamland Interview Disc (Promo)	CD	Universal	DREAMINT1	England	2002	24.99
Plant, Robert	Fate Of Nations	CD	Atlantic	7-92264-2	U.S.A.	1993	7.99
Plant, Robert	Fate Of Nations Interview Cd (Promo)	CD	Fontana	FATEI - 1	Holland	1993	17.99
Plant, Robert	Heaven Knows (3")	CD Single	Atlantic	A9373CD	Austria	1988	16.99
Plant, Robert	Hurting Kind (I've Got My Eyes On You)	CD Single	Atlantic	7-96483-2	U.S.A.	1990	4.99
Plant, Robert	I Believe (Cd 2)	CD Single	Fontana	FATEX-2	England	1993	5.99
Plant, Robert	Manic Nirvana	CD	East West	AMCY-2743	Japan	1990	14.99
Plant, Robert	Manic Nirvana (Special Ed)	CD	Atlantic	7-91361-2	U.S.A.	1990	12.99
Plant, Robert	Morning Dew	CD Single	Mercury	582-958-2	EU	2002	5.99
Plant, Robert	Now and Zen	CD	Atlantic	7-90863-2	U.S.A.	1988	7.99
Plant, Robert	Principle Of Moments	CD	Atlantic	790-101-2	Germany	1983	7.99
Plant, Robert	Profiled (Promo)	CD	Atlantic	PRCD-3297-2	U.S.A.	1990	14.99
Plant, Robert	Ship Of Fools (W/Box)	CD Single	Warner Bros.	A9281CD	Germany	1988	24.99
Plant, Robert	The Hurting Kind	CD Single	Atlantic	96473-2	Germany	1990	10.99
Plant, Robert/Honeydrippers	Volume One	CD	Atlantic	7-90220-2	U.S.A.	1987	7.99
Plasmatics	Beyond The Valley Of 1984	CD	Plasmatics Media	102	U.S.A.	2000	10.99
Plasmatics	Coup De Grace	CD	Plasmatics Media	110	U.S.A.	2002	10.99
Plasmatics	Coup D'Etat + 1	CD	Razor & Tie	7930182215-2	U.S.A.	2000	10.99
Plasmatics	Final Days: Anthems For Apocalypse	CD	Plasmatics Media	108	U.S.A.	2002	10.99
Plasmatics	Kommander Of Kaos	CD	Plasmatics Media	104	U.S.A.	2000	10.99
Plasmatics	Maggots: The Record	CD	Plasmatics Media	105	U.S.A.	2001	10.99
Plasmatics	New Hope For T W/Metal Priestess	CD	Plasmatics Media	106	U.S.A.	2001	10.99
Plasmatics	New Hope For The Wretched + 3	CD	Repertoire	REP-4394-WY	Germany	1998	10.99
Plasmatics	New Hope For The Wretched + 7	CD	Cherry Red	CDMRED-204	England	2002	10.99
Plasmatics	Put Your Love In Me: Love Songs A	CD	Plasmatics Media	109	U.S.A.	2002	10.99
Plasmatics	W.O.W.	CD	Plasmatics Media	103	U.S.A.	2001	10.99
Plasmatics/Wendy O Williams	F*ck You And Loving It !! (Best Of)	CD	Plasmatics Media	101	U.S.A.	1999	10.99
Plasmatics/Wendy O Williams	Ultrafly/Homegirls - Deffest/Baddest	CD	Plasmatics Media	107	U.S.A.	2001	10.99
Plastic Bertrand	Ca Plane Pour Moi	CD	Repertoire	REP-4331-WG	Germany	1993	21.99
Plastic Bertrand	King Of The Divan: Best Of	CD	EMI	543-365-2	England	2003	10.99
Plastic Penny	2 Sides Of Penny	CD	Repertoire	REP-4368-WP	Germany	2002	15.99
Plastic Penny	Currency + 2	CD	Repertoire	REP-4369-WP	Germany	2002	15.99
Plastic Penny	The Best Of & Rarities	CD	Repertoire	REP-4766	Germany	2003	15.99
Player	Room With A View	CD	Victor Ent.	UICY-3345	Japan	1980	25.99
Pleasant, Wally	Hoedown	CD	Miranda	010500	Canada	1996	9.99
Pleasant, Wally	Houses Of The Holy Moly	CD	Miranda	HDCD-1105	Canada	1994	9.99
Pleasant, Wally	Songs About Stuff	CD	Miranda	6765-68-3032	Canada	1992	9.99
Pleasant, Wally	Wally World (Like Jonathan Richman)	CD	Miranda	6765-68-2913	Canada	1995	9.99
Pleasant, Wally	Welcome To Pleasantville	CD	Miranda	WP-91491	Canada	1993	9.99
Poco	20th Century Masters: The Millennium	CD	MCA	314-112-224-2	U.S.A.	2000	8.99
Poco	A Good Feelin' To Know	CD	Epic	EK-31601	U.S.A.	1989	6.99
Poco	Blue And Gray	CD	One Way	MCAD-22068	U.S.A.	1993	29.99
Poco	Cantamos	CD	Wounded Bird	WOU-3192	U.S.A.	2003	8.99
Poco	Cowboys & Englishmen	CD	One Way	MCAD-22067	U.S.A.	1993	29.99
Poco	Crazy Eyes	CD	Epic	EK-66968	U.S.A.	1995	6.99
Poco	Crazy Eyes (DTS)	CD	Sony	710215-4422-2-8	U.S.A.	1973	14.99
Poco	Deliverin'	CD	Epic	EK-30209	U.S.A.	1990	6.99
Poco	From The Inside	CD	Epic	EK-30753	U.S.A.	1991	6.99
Poco	From The Inside/A Good Feelin'	CD	BGO	BGOCD359	England	2002	12.99
Poco	Ghost Town/Inamorata	CD	Rhino	R2-72217	U.S.A.	1995	119.99
Poco	Head Over Heels	CD	MCA	MCAD-31327	U.S.A.	1975	6.99
Poco	Indian Summer	CD	MCA	MCAD-31353	U.S.A.	1977	10.99

P

Artist	Title	Format	Label	Catalog No	Country	Released	Value
Poco	Legacy	CD	BMG	75517-44954-2-7	U.S.A.	2001	6.99
Poco	Legend	CD	MCA	MCAD-31019	U.S.A.	1978	8.99
Poco	Legend (Gold Cd)	CD	MCA	MCAD-11206	U.S.A.	1978	28.99
Poco	Live	CD	One Way	MCAD-32337	U.S.A.	2000	6.99
Poco	Pickin' Up The Pieces + 1	CD	Epic	EK-66227	U.S.A.	1995	6.99
Poco	Rose Of Cimarron	CD	One Way	MCAD-22076	U.S.A.	2000	8.99
Poco	Running Horse	CD	Drifter's Church	3	U.S.A.	2003	9.99
Poco	Self Titled	CD	Epic	EK-26522	U.S.A.	1990	6.99
Poco	Seven	CD	Epic	EK-66985	U.S.A.	1995	6.99
Poco	The Forgotten Trail: (1969-1974)	2CD	Epic	E2K-46162	U.S.A.	1990	15.99
Poco	The Very Best Of	CD	BGO	BGOCD370	England	2002	12.99
Poco	Ultimate Collection	CD	Hip O	HIPCD-40136	U.S.A.	1998	8.99
Poco	Under The Gun	CD	MCA	MCAD-31334	U.S.A.	1980	8.99
Poco	Very Best Of	CD	Epic	EK-65731	U.S.A.	1999	10.99
Pogues	Rum, Sodomy And The Lash	CD	Warner Bros.	2292-44495-2	Germany	1985	16.99
Poindexter, Buster	Buster Goes Berserk	CD	RCA	9665-R	U.S.A.	1989	9.99
Poindexter, Buster	Buster Poindexter (David Johansen)	CD	RCA	6633-2-R	U.S.A.	1987	7.99
Poindexter, Buster	Buster's Happy Hour	CD	Rhino	R2-71680	U.S.A.	1994	7.99
Poindexter, Buster	Spanish Rocket Ship	CD	Island	314-524-414-2	U.S.A.	1997	8.99
Point Blank	Airplay	CD	MCA Victor	MVCM-353	Japan	2000	40.99
Point Blank	American Exce$$	CD	MCA Victor	MVCM-355	Japan	2000	40.99
Point Blank	On A Roll	CD	MCA Victor	MVCM-356	Japan	2000	40.99
Point Blank	The Hard Way	CD	MCA Victor	MVCM-354	Japan	2000	40.99
Poison	Crack A Smile... And More	CD	Captiol	7243-8-54363-9-2	U.S.A.	1996	9.99
Poison	Flesh & Blood	CD	Capitol	0777-7-91813-2-2	U.S.A.	1990	7.99
Poison	Greatest Hits 1986 - 1996 (W/DVD)	2CD	Capitol	7243-5-90434-0-1	U.S.A.	2003	19.99
Poison	Greatest Hits 1986-1996	CD	Captiol	7243-8-53375-2-9	U.S.A.	1996	9.99
Poison	Hollyweird	CD	Cyanide	CYND-6975-2	U.S.A.	2002	6.99
Poison	Look What The Cat Dragged In	CD	Capitol	0777-7-46735-2-5	U.S.A.	1986	8.99
Poison	Native Tongue	CD	Capitol	0777-7-98961-2-7	U.S.A.	1993	6.99
Poison	Open Up and Say...Ahh!	CD	Capitol	0777-7-48493-2-6	U.S.A.	1988	6.99
Poison	Power To The People	CD	Cyanide	CYND-6969-2	U.S.A.	2000	6.99
Poison	Rock Champions	CD	Capitol	7243-5-76273-2-0	England	2001	10.99
Poison	Swallow This Live + 4	CD	Capitol	0777-7-98038-2-8	U.S.A.	1991	9.99
Pokerface	Life's A Gamble + 2	CD	Teichiku	TKCF-45014	Japan	1996	35.99
Pokrovsky, Dmitri Ensemble	The Wild Field	CD	Caroline	CAROL-2316-2	U.S.A.	1991	7.99
Poledouris, Basil	Cherry 2000 (Ltd To 1500)	CD	Varese	VCL-8903.1	U.S.A.	1989	176.99
Poledouris, Basil	Flesh + Blood (O.S.T.)	CD	Varese	BCL-6002	U.S.A.	1992	32.99
Police	(Selections) Message In A Box (Promo)	CD	A&M	314-548-044-2	U.S.A.	1993	19.99
Police	Can't Stand Losing You - Live	CD Single	A&M	581-037-2	England	1995	5.99
Police	Don't Stand So...(Promo)	CD	A&M	CD-17435	U.S.A.	1986	39.99
Police	Every Breath You Take: The Classics	CD	A&M	31454-0380-2	U.S.A.	1995	7.99
Police	Ghost In The Machine	CD	A&M	75021-3730-2	U.S.A.	1995	8.99
Police	Greatest Hits	CD	A&M	540-030-2	England	1992	8.99
Police	Message In A Box: Comp Recordings	4CD	A&M	31454-0150-2	U.S.A.	1993	31.99
Police	Outlandos d'Amour	CD	A&M	75021-3311-2	U.S.A.	1995	7.99
Police	Regatta de Blanc	CD	A&M	75021-3312-2	U.S.A.	1995	7.99
Police	Roxanne '97	CD Single	Polydor	POCM-1240	Japan	1997	23.99
Police	Synchronicity	CD	A&M	75021-3735-2	U.S.A.	1995	8.99
Police	Synchronicity (MFSL Gold Cd)	CD	Mobile Fidelity	UDCD-511	U.S.A.	1983	24.99
Police	The Police Live	2CD	A&M	CD-0222	U.S.A.	1995	12.99
Police	Zenyatta Mondatta	CD	A&M	75021-3720-2	U.S.A.	1995	7.99
Police/Different Gear	When The World Is Running Down	CD Single	A&M	158-163-2	Australia	2000	12.99
Police/R. P. Orchestra	Arrested (The Police Orchestrated)	CD	Dunhill	DZS002	U.S.A.	1986	12.99
Police/Strontium 90	Police Academy (Pre - Police)	CD	Ark 21	61868-10003-2-7	U.S.A.	1997	12.99
Pontiac Brothers	1988Johnson	CD	Line	FBCD-9.00571-0	Germany	1988	6.99
Ponty, Jean-Luc/F Zappa	Ponty Plays Zappa : King Kong	CD	Blue Note	0777-7-89539-2-0	U.S.A.	1993	7.99
Pop, Iggy	American Caesar	CD	Virgin	7243-8-39002-2-0	U.S.A.	1993	6.99

P

Artist	Title	Format	Label	Catalog No	Country	Released	Value
Pop, Iggy	Avenue B	CD	Virgin	7087-6-14358-2-5	U.S.A.	1999	7.99
Pop, Iggy	Beat Em Up + 2	CD	Toshiba-EMI	VJCP-68313	Japan	2001	30.99
Pop, Iggy	Beside You	CD Single	Virgin	VUSCD77	England	1993	4.99
Pop, Iggy	Best Of Live	CD	MCA	784-021-2	Germany	1996	8.99
Pop, Iggy	Blah-Blah-Blah	CD	A&M	CD-5145	U.S.A.	1986	8.99
Pop, Iggy	Brick By Brick	CD	Virgin	V2-91381	U.S.A.	1990	6.99
Pop, Iggy	Butt Town (Demos/DJ/2 Atl. Covers)	CD	Virgin	PRCD-BUTT	U.S.A.	1990	24.99
Pop, Iggy	Corruption	CD	Virgin	724389624328	EU	1999	9.99
Pop, Iggy	Corruption (Promo)	CD	Virgin	DPRO-14351	U.S.A.	1999	5.99
Pop, Iggy	Extended Versions	CD	BMG	75517-46980-2	U.S.A.	2002	5.99
Pop, Iggy	Family Affair	CD Single	Skydog	62265-2	France	1995	14.99
Pop, Iggy	Heart Is Saved	CD	Virgin	7243-8-93405-2-5	Holland	1996	4.99
Pop, Iggy	Heart Is Saved (Promo)	CD Single	Virgin	DPRO-11084	U.S.A.	1999	5.99
Pop, Iggy	Heroin Hates You	CD	Other Peoples	OPM-2116	Canada	1997	10.99
Pop, Iggy	Hippodrome - Paris 77	CD	Revenge	MIG33/34	France	1990	14.99
Pop, Iggy	I Wanna Live (Promo)	CD	Virgin	IPCDJ96	England	1996	6.99
Pop, Iggy	Instinct	CD	A&M	CD-5198	U.S.A.	1988	4.99
Pop, Iggy	KBFH (9/15-9/21, 1997)	CD	DIR Network	COUXL01XE	U.S.A.	1997	24.99
Pop, Iggy	King Biscuit Flower Hour	CD	King Biscuit	70710-88033-2	U.S.A.	1997	9.99
Pop, Iggy	Live In NYC	CD	King Biscuit	70710-88055-2	U.S.A.	2000	9.99
Pop, Iggy	Live In The Cover-We Are Not Talking...	CD	Meldac	MECR-25020	Japan	1993	47.99
Pop, Iggy	Live Ritz N.C.Y. 86	2CD	Revenge	MIG-44	France	1992	14.99
Pop, Iggy	Livin' On The Edge Of The Night	CD Single	Virgin	VOZEPCD02	U.S.A.	1990	5.99
Pop, Iggy	Livin' On The Edge Of The Night	CD	Virgin	96497-2	U.S.A.	1990	5.99
Pop, Iggy	Living On The Edge... (3" Cd)	CD Single	Virgin	VUSCD-18	England	1990	10.99
Pop, Iggy	Lust For Life	CD Single	Virgin	7243-8-93844-2-0	Germany	1996	6.99
Pop, Iggy	Lust For Life	CD	Virgin	2-91343	U.S.A.	1990	7.99
Pop, Iggy	Lust For Life (Promo)	CD Single	Virgin	VUSCDJ-116	England	1996	10.99
Pop, Iggy	Masters Series	CD	Polygram	540-881-2	Germany	1998	9.99
Pop, Iggy	More Blah (Interview Cd)	CD	Holoview	3D-013	England	1990	5.99
Pop, Iggy	Naughty Little Doggie	CD	Virgin	7243-8-41327-2-9	U.S.A.	1996	7.99
Pop, Iggy	New Values + 2	CD	Buddah	74465-99662-2	U.S.A.	2000	8.99
Pop, Iggy	Night Of Iguana Box Set (Ltd./#)	4CD	Remedy	305-3862	France	1999	34.99
Pop, Iggy	Nude & Rude: The Best Of Iggy Pop	CD	Virgin	7243-8-42351-2	U.S.A.	1996	8.99
Pop, Iggy	Nuggets	2CD	Skydog	FREUD-CD-074	France	1999	18.99
Pop, Iggy	Party + 2	CD	Buddah	74465-99661-2	U.S.A.	2000	8.99
Pop, Iggy	Soldier + 2	CD	Buddah	74465-99660-2	U.S.A.	2000	8.99
Pop, Iggy	Some Weird Sin	CD Single	Revenge	CAX-9	France	1992	14.99
Pop, Iggy	The Heritage Collection	CD	Arista	07822-14612-2	U.S.A.	2000	9.99
Pop, Iggy	The Idiot	CD	Virgin	2-91342	U.S.A.	1990	8.99
Pop, Iggy	The Masters	CD	Eagle	EAB-CD-011	EC	1997	7.99
Pop, Iggy	The Passenger	CD Single	Virgin	7243-8-94921-2-5	England	1998	7.99
Pop, Iggy	TV Eye	CD	Virgin	7243-8-39628-2-2	U.S.A.	1978	8.99
Pop, Iggy	Wake Up Suckers !!!	CD	Skydog	SKY-62267-2	France	1995	14.99
Pop, Iggy	Wild America E.P.	CD	Virgin	7243-8-92106-2-0	England	1993	5.99
Pop, Iggy	Wild America: Rare Tracks (Japan)	CD	Toshiba-EMI	VJCP-20015	Japan	1994	21.99
Pop, Iggy	Wild Animal (Live 1977)	CD	Revenge	MIG-50/642050	France	1977	13.99
Pop, Iggy	Zombie Birdhouse (W/Bonus Cd)	2CD	Alchemy	PILOT-171	England	2003	15.99
Pop, Iggy/James Williamson	Kill City	CD	Line	LICD-9.00131-0	Germany	1987	21.99
Pop, Iggy/The Stooges	California Bleeding	CD	Bomp	BCD-4069	U.S.A.	1997	8.99
Pop, Iggy/The Stooges	Complete Fun House (Ltd. 3000)	7CD	Rhino	RHM2-7707	U.S.A.	2000	429.99
Pop, Iggy/The Stooges	Double Danger	2CD	Bomp	BCD-4076	U.S.A.	2000	12.99
Pop, Iggy/The Stooges	Fun House	CD	Elektra	74071-2	U.S.A.	1970	8.99
Pop, Iggy/The Stooges	Head On	2CD	Snapper	SMCD-142	England	1995	10.99
Pop, Iggy/The Stooges	I Got A Right	CD	Bomp	BCD139	U.S.A.	1977	8.99
Pop, Iggy/The Stooges	I'm Sick Of You	CD	Line	LICD-9.00093-0	Germany	1987	14.99
Pop, Iggy/The Stooges	I'm Sick Of You!	CD	Bomp	BCD113	U.S.A.	1977	9.99
Pop, Iggy/The Stooges	I'm Sick Of You/Kill City	2CD	Line	LICD-9.21175-S	Germany	1992	29.99

P

Artist	Title	Format	Label	Catalog No	Country	Released	Value
Pop, Iggy/The Stooges	Jesus Loves The Stooges	CD	Bomp	BCD114	U.S.A.	1977	7.99
Pop, Iggy/The Stooges	Live At The Whiskey-A-Go-Go	CD	Revenge	895104	France	1988	14.99
Pop, Iggy/The Stooges	Live In LA 73 + 1	CD	Snapper	155282	U.S.A.	1998	9.99
Pop, Iggy/The Stooges	Metallic K.O.	2CD	Skydog	FREUD-CD-70	France	1998	10.99
Pop, Iggy/The Stooges	Michigan Palace 10/6/73 (Live)	CD	Bomp	BCD-4079	U.S.A.	2000	8.99
Pop, Iggy/The Stooges	Night Destruction Lmtd Box Set (2,000)	6CD	Revenge	BOX-01/WM-375	France	1991	123.99
Pop, Iggy/The Stooges	Open Up & Bleed!	CD	Bomp	BCD-4051	U.S.A.	1995	5.99
Pop, Iggy/The Stooges	Raw Mixes Vol. 1 (1969) (Ltmd 1,000)	CD	Eagle	BM-002	France	1989	24.99
Pop, Iggy/The Stooges	Raw Mixes Vol. 2 (1970) (Lmtd 1,000)	CD	Eagle	BM-003	France	1989	24.99
Pop, Iggy/The Stooges	Raw Power (David Bowie Mix)	CD	Columbia	CK-32111	U.S.A.	1973	7.99
Pop, Iggy/The Stooges	Raw Power (Iggy Pop Mix)	CD	Columbia	CK-66229	U.S.A.	1997	9.99
Pop, Iggy/The Stooges	Rough Power	CD	Bomp	BCD4049	U.S.A.	1994	10.99
Pop, Iggy/The Stooges	Search And Destroy	CD	Curtiss	BM-004	France	1989	9.99
Pop, Iggy/The Stooges	Search Destroy (Out-Takes Gold Cd)	CD	Cleopatra	CLP-0556-2	U.S.A.	1999	8.99
Pop, Iggy/The Stooges	Studio Sessions	CD	Alchemy	PILOT-008	England	1996	15.99
Pop, Iggy/The Stooges	The Stooges	CD	Elektra	74051-2	U.S.A.	1987	10.99
Pop, Iggy/The Stooges	Wild Love	CD	Bomp	BCD-4083-2	U.S.A.	2001	8.99
Pop, Iggy/The Stooges	Year Of The Iguana	CD	Bomp	BCD4063	U.S.A.	1997	8.99
Popol Vuh	2 Orig. S.T. Werner Herzog's Nosferatu	CD	Gammarock	TIDE-9113-2	Austria	1992	38.99
Popol Vuh	Affenstunde	CD	Spalax	14205	France	1992	15.99
Popol Vuh	Agape - Agape.../Sei Still...	CD	Gammarock	TIDE-9128-2	Austria	1994	24.99
Popol Vuh	Agape-Agape/Love-Love	CD	Spalax	14-215	France	1992	15.99
Popol Vuh	Aguirre + 3	CD	Spalax	14974	France	1996	15.99
Popol Vuh	Bruder Des Schattens	CD	Spalax	14-208	France	1992	15.99
Popol Vuh	Coeur De Verre	CD	Spalax	14214	France	1992	15.99
Popol Vuh	Das Hohelied Salomos	CD	Spalax	14211	France	1992	15.99
Popol Vuh	Die Nacht Der Seele	CD	Spalax	14204	France	1992	15.99
Popol Vuh	Einsjaeger & Siebenjaeger	CD	Spalax	14218	France	1992	15.99
Popol Vuh	Einsjager.../ Lezte Tage...	CD	Gammarock	TIDE-9129-2	Austria	1994	24.99
Popol Vuh	Future Sound Experience	CD	Mystic	MYS-CD-151	England	1993	13.99
Popol Vuh	Hosianna Mantra	CD	Spalax	14209	France	1992	15.99
Popol Vuh	In Den Gärten Pharaos	CD	Spalax	14875	France	1994	15.99
Popol Vuh	Letzte Tage - Letzte Nachte	CD	Spalax	14-213	France	1992	15.99
Popol Vuh	Nicht Hoch Im Himmel	CD	Mystic	MYS-CD-121	England	1998	13.99
Popol Vuh	Perlenklänge - The Best Of	CD	ZYX	OHR-70027-2	Germany	1999	17.99
Popol Vuh	Seligpreisung	CD	ZYX	OHR-70025-2	Germany	1999	17.99
Popol Vuh	Shepherd's Symphony	CD	Mystic	MYS-CD-114	England	1997	13.99
Popol Vuh	Spirit Of Peace	CD	Spalax	14-216	France	1992	15.99
Popol Vuh	The Best Soundtracks/Werner Herzog Fi	CD	Gammarock	TIDE-9110-2	Austria	1994	38.99
Popol Vuh	Yoga	CD	Gammarock	TIDE-9119-2	Australia	1993	14.99
Poppy Family/Susan Jacks	Ghosts	CD	Sony	CPK-1455	Korea	1993	74.99
Poppy Family/Terry Jacks	Greatest Hits W/Susan Jacks	CD	A&M	0-7502-69998-2-9	Canada	1989	34.99
Porcupine Tree	Delerium Ep (Promo)	CD	Delerium	EP0016	England	2001	18.99
Porcupine Tree	In Absentia	CD	Lava	83604-2	U.S.A.	2002	13.99
Porcupine Tree	Metanoia	CD	Delerium	DELEC-CD079	England	2002	16.99
Porcupine Tree	On The Sunday Of Life	CD	Delerium	DELEC-CD-008	England	1997	22.99
Porcupine Tree	Radio Active (Promo/Only 500)	CD Single	Delerium	PROMO-CD1	England	1993	129.99
Porcupine Tree	Recordings (Ltd Numbered)	CD	Snapper	SMACD840	England	2001	59.99
Porcupine Tree	Sampler (Promo/Abstentia)	CD	Atlantic	STCD-300954-2	U.S.A.	2002	23.99
Porcupine Tree	Signify + 10 (W/Insignificance/Demos)	2CD	Delerium	DELEC-DCD-084	England	2003	29.99
Porcupine Tree	Stars Die (Delerium Years '91 -'97) (W/B	2CD	Kscope	SMADD851	EU	2002	24.99
Porcupine Tree	Stranger By The Minute	CD	Kscope	SMASCD107	England	1999	8.99
Porcupine Tree	The Sky Moves Sideways	CD	Delerium	DELEC-CD-028	England	1994	11.99
Porcupine Tree	Trains (Promo)	CD Single	Atlantic	PR03918	Germany	2002	85.99
Porcupine Tree	Up The Downstair	CD	Delerium	DELEC-CD-020	England	1993	18.99
Porcupine Tree	Voyage 34	CD	Delerium	DELECCDEP010	England	1992	77.99
Porcupine Tree	XM (Concert Edition/Only 1500)	CD	Lava	1.1	U.S.A.	2003	89.99
Pork Dukes	All The Filth!	CD	Vinyl Japan	ASKCD98	England	1999	14.99

P

Artist	Title	Format	Label	Catalog No	Country	Released	Value
Pork Dukes	Kum Kleen (DAMGOOD229CD)	CD	Damaged Goods	DAMGOOD229CD	England	2003	14.99
Pork Dukes	Squeal Meat Again	CD	Snail	DGU51	England	2002	14.99
Pork Dukes	Squeal Meat Again (T Press/Diff. Mix)	CD	Snail	DGU51	England	2002	29.99
Portman, Rachel/Brian May	Pinocchio (O.S.T.)	CD	London	452-740-2	U.S.A.	1996	16.99
Potter, Nic	Dreams In View 81-87	CD	Line	DACD-9.00637-0	Germany	1988	21.99
Potter, Nic	Dreams In View 81-87	CD	Line	LICD-9.01342-0	Germany	1997	21.99
Potter, Nic	Self Contained	CD	Line	DACD-9.00439-0	Germany	1987	28.99
Potter, Nic	The Blue Zone	CD	Line	DACD-9.00891-0	Germany	1989	21.99
Potter, Nic	The Blue Zone	CD	Line	LICD-9.01345-0	Germany	1997	21.99
Powell, Cozy	Dance With The Devil	CD Single	Old Gold	OG-6177	England	1992	22.99
Powell, Cozy	Drums Are Back (Jimmy Page/J Lord)	CD	Electrola	0777-79922-6-2	England	1992	24.99
Powell, Cozy	Especially For You	CD	Polydor	POCP-7326	Japan	1998	29.99
Powell, Cozy	Octopus	Mini Lp	Polydor	POCP-9169	Japan	1998	44.99
Powell, Cozy	Octopus	CD	Polydor	POCP-1813	Japan	1990	34.99
Powell, Cozy	Over The Top	CD	Polydor	POCP-1811	Japan	1990	34.99
Powell, Cozy	Sooner Or Later	CD	Elite	018-CDP	England	1991	34.99
Powell, Cozy	The Best Of	CD	Polydor	537-724-2	England	1997	8.99
Powell, Cozy	The Man In Black	CD Single	Old Gold	126236332	England	1992	22.99
Powell, Cozy	Tilt	CD	Polydor	POCP-1812	Japan	1990	34.99
Powell, Cozy/Bedlam	Anthology	2CD	Zoom Club	ZCRCD-19	England	1999	24.99
Powell, Cozy/Bedlam	Bedlam	CD	Zoom Club	ZCRCD-8	England	1998	15.99
Powell, Cozy/Big Bertha	Liv Ein Hamburg	2CD	Zoom Club	ZCRCD-17	England	1999	24.99
Powell, Cozy/Brian May	Drums Are.. (Jimmy Page/Jon Lord)	CD	Polydor	POCP-1205	Japan	1992	64.99
Powell, Cozy/Tribute	Cozy Powell Forever (Loudness/Sly)	CD	Electric Angel	EAR-001	Japan	1998	44.99
Power Station/Duran Duran	Living In Fear (W/ Robert Palmer)	CD	EMI	7243-8-53984-2-1	England	1996	8.99
Power Station/Duran Duran	Living In Fear + 2 (W/Robert Palmer)	CD	Toshiba-EMI	TOCP-50013	Japan	1997	24.99
Power Station/Duran Duran	Self Titled (W/Robert Palmer)	CD	Capitol	CDP-7-46127-2	Germany	1996	8.99
Power Station/Duran Duran	Self Titled (W/Robert Palmer)	CD	Toshiba-EMI	CP32-5075	Japan	1986	24.99
Praying Mantis	Demorabilia (W/ Photo Book)	2CD	Pony Canyon	PCCY-01342	Japan	1999	53.99
Praying Mantis	Only The Children Cry	CD Single	Pony Canyon	PCCY-00490	Japan	1993	14.99
Preisner, Zbigniew	Requiem For My Friend	CD	Line	LICD-9.01367-0	Germany	2001	13.99
Presley, Elvis	100 Super Rocks	4CD	RCA	VCD47146	Australia	1992	69.99
Presley, Elvis	100 Years From Now: Essential Vol. 4	CD	RCA	07863-66866-2	U.S.A.	1996	10.99
Presley, Elvis	15 Queens For A King	CD	RCA	ND-90047	Germany	1987	29.99
Presley, Elvis	16 Top Tracks	CD	RCA	BPCD-5020	Austria	1990	18.99
Presley, Elvis	18 Originale	CD	RCA	74321-20836-2	Germany	1994	21.99
Presley, Elvis	1987: Ten Years After	CD	RCA	8.11503	Japan	1987	44.99
Presley, Elvis	1999 World Tour (Some #rd/Some Not)	2CD	RCA	74321-64429-2	Australia	1998	20.99
Presley, Elvis	20th Anniversary 5 Single Set: Legend	5CD	RCA	159ECBOL-4A	U.S.A.	1997	19.99
Presley, Elvis	24 Karat Gold Hits ! (DCC Gold CD)	CD	DCC	GZS-117	U.S.A.	1997	49.99
Presley, Elvis	24 Karat Hits ! Sampler (Promo/Gold)	CD	DCC	GZS-1117	U.S.A.	1997	99.99
Presley, Elvis	2nd To None	CD	RCA	82876-55241-2	U.S.A.	2003	13.99
Presley, Elvis	30 # 1 Hits (Promo/Stern Magazine)	CD	BMG	74321-96306-2	Germany	2002	19.99
Presley, Elvis	30 # 1 Hits Sampler (Promo)	CD	BMG	74321-961332	EU	2002	34.99
Presley, Elvis	30 # 1 Sound Listening Sampler (DJ)	CD	BMG	RDJ-60593-2	U.S.A.	2002	74.99
Presley, Elvis	30 Suosituinta (Fan Club)	CD	RCA	74321506562	Finland	1997	54.99
Presley, Elvis	32 Film Hits	2CD	RCA	89388-2	Germany	1989	59.99
Presley, Elvis	32 Film Hits, Vol. 2	2CD	RCA	PD-89550-2	Germany	1991	59.99
Presley, Elvis	48 Original Hits (W/RCA Logo On Side)	3CD	RCA	74321-74591-2	Germany	2000	29.99
Presley, Elvis	50 Greatest Love Songs	2CD	RCA	07863-68026-2	U.S.A.	2001	21.99
Presley, Elvis	50 Worldwide Gold Hits, Vol. 1	2CD	RCA	07863-56401-2	U.S.A.	1996	24.99
Presley, Elvis	50 Years 50 Hits	CD	RCA	SVC2-0710-1/2	U.S.A.	1998	24.99
Presley, Elvis	50,000,000 Fans	CD	RCA	PCD1-5197	U.S.A.	1994	11.99
Presley, Elvis	50,000,000 Fans (Reprocessed Stereo)	CD	RCA	PCD1-2075	U.S.A.	1984	249.99
Presley, Elvis	50,000,000 Fans + 5	CD	RCA	07863-67463-2	U.S.A.	1997	11.99
Presley, Elvis	8 Songs Selected Swedish (Fan Club)	CD	RCA	74321-80250-2	Sweden	2000	24.99
Presley, Elvis	A Canadian Tribute (Ltd Release)	CD	RCA	74321-71337-2	U.S.A.	1999	28.99
Presley, Elvis	A Date With	CD	RCA	2011-2-R	U.S.A.	1996	11.99

P

Artist	Title	Format	Label	Catalog No	Country	Released	Value
Presley, Elvis	A Golden Celebration Box Set	4CD	RCA	07863-67456-2	U.S.A.	1998	46.99
Presley, Elvis	A Hundred Years From Now (DJ/200)	CD	RCA	RJC-66866-2	U.S.A.	1996	29.99
Presley, Elvis	A Legend	CD	RCA	ND-90025	Germany	1987	24.99
Presley, Elvis	A Legendary Performer, Vol. 1	CD	RCA	CAD1-2705	U.S.A.	1996	14.99
Presley, Elvis	A Legendary Performer, Vol. 2	CD	RCA	CAD1-2706	U.S.A.	1996	14.99
Presley, Elvis	A Mi Manera (Promo)	CD	BMG	AR-0002	Argentina	1999	69.99
Presley, Elvis	A Touch Of Platinum, Vol. 2	2CD	RCA	07863-67593-2	U.S.A.	1998	24.99
Presley, Elvis	A Valentine Gift For You	CD	RCA	07863-55353-2	U.S.A.	1997	12.99
Presley, Elvis	All The Best, Vol. 1	CD	RCA	BPCD-5039	Australia	1988	21.99
Presley, Elvis	All The Best, Vol. 1/2	2CD	RCA	74321-44630-2	Australia	1997	21.99
Presley, Elvis	All The Best, Vol. 2	CD	RCA	BPCD-5040	Australia	1988	21.99
Presley, Elvis	Alla En El Rancho Grande (Promo)	CD	BMG	E	Mexico	1998	64.99
Presley, Elvis	Almost In Love	CD	RCA	CAD1-2440	U.S.A.	1997	74.99
Presley, Elvis	Aloha From Hawaii + 5	CD	RCA	07863-67609-2	U.S.A.	1998	13.99
Presley, Elvis	Aloha From Hawaii Via Satellite	CD	RCA	07863-52642-2	U.S.A.	1994	17.99
Presley, Elvis	Always Elvis: The Dutch Album	CD	RCA	74321-48806-2	Netherlands	1997	20.99
Presley, Elvis	Always On My Mind	CD	RCA	74321-71038-2	France	1999	8.99
Presley, Elvis	Always On My Mind	CD	RCA	PCD1-5430	U.S.A.	1992	14.99
Presley, Elvis	Always On My Mind	CD Single	RCA	74321-48541-2	EU	1997	11.99
Presley, Elvis	Always On My Mind	CD Single	RCA	74321-50406-2	Netherlands	1997	8.99
Presley, Elvis	Always On My Mind (DJ/Unreleased)	CD Single	RCA	74321-50057-2	U.S.A.	1997	119.99
Presley, Elvis	Always On My Mind (Numbered Promo)	CD Single	RCA	ELVISDJ1/97	England	1997	109.99
Presley, Elvis	Always On My Mind: The Ultimate..	CD	RCA	74321-48984-2	EU	1997	16.99
Presley, Elvis	Amazing Grace: His Greatest..	2CD	RCA	07863-66421-2	U.S.A.	1994	26.99
Presley, Elvis	America The Beautiful	CD Single	RCA	74321-90402-2	EU	2001	8.99
Presley, Elvis	America The Beautiful (Different Cover)	CD Single	RCA	07863-60501-2	U.S.A.	2001	8.99
Presley, Elvis	An Afternoon In The Garden	CD	RCA	07863-66421-2	U.S.A.	1997	16.99
Presley, Elvis	Are You Lonesome Tonight?	4CD	RCA	74321447332	England	1997	39.99
Presley, Elvis	Are You Lonesome Tonight? (Promo)	CD Single	BMG	74321-84733-2	Netherlands	2001	24.99
Presley, Elvis	Are You Lonesome Tonight? (Promo)	CD Single	RCA	PRO-CD-4	Netherlands	1996	74.99
Presley, Elvis	Artist Of The Century Box Set	3CD	RCA	07863-67732-2	U.S.A.	1999	29.99
Presley, Elvis	As Recorded At Madison Square G.	CD	RCA	07863-54776-2	U.S.A.	1995	11.99
Presley, Elvis	At His Romantic Best (Avon)	CD	RCA	DPC1-0984	U.S.A.	1992	49.99
Presley, Elvis	Back In Memphis	CD	RCA	07863-61081-2	U.S.A.	1992	12.99
Presley, Elvis	Back To The 50's & 60's (Promo)	CD	BMG	160897	Netherlands	1997	59.99
Presley, Elvis	Best	CD	BMG Victor	BVCP-2618	Japan	1994	21.99
Presley, Elvis	Best Of Artist Of The Century	CD	RCA	07863-67910-2	U.S.A.	2000	11.99
Presley, Elvis	Best Of: RCA 100 Years Of Music	CD	RCA	07863-69384-2	U.S.A.	2001	21.99
Presley, Elvis	Blue Christmas	CD	RCA	07863-59800-2	U.S.A.	1995	13.99
Presley, Elvis	Blue Hawaii	CD	RCA	3683-2-R	U.S.A.	1995	14.99
Presley, Elvis	Blue Hawaii (20 Bit Remastered)	CD	BMG Victor	BVCP-7369	Japan	1995	13.99
Presley, Elvis	Blue Hawaii + 8	CD	RCA	07863-66959-2	U.S.A.	1997	13.99
Presley, Elvis	Blue Hawaii + 8 (Ltd Ed Hardback)	CD	RCA	07863-67469-2	U.S.A.	1997	21.99
Presley, Elvis	Blue Suede Box: Greatest Soundtracks	5CD	RCA	D-207350	U.S.A.	1997	99.99
Presley, Elvis	Blue Suede Shoes (Elvis Ballet)	2CD	RCA	07863-67458-2	U.S.A.	1997	44.99
Presley, Elvis	Blue Suede Shoes Collection Box	30CD	RCA	07863-68026-2	U.S.A.	2001	329.99
Presley, Elvis	Blue Suede Shoes: The Ult. + 2	CD	RCA	74321-55628-2	England	1998	16.99
Presley, Elvis	Bossa Nova Nena !! (Promo)	CD	BMG	I	Mexico	2000	64.99
Presley, Elvis	Burning Love	CD	RCA	07863-67742-2	U.S.A.	1999	11.99
Presley, Elvis	Burning Love	CD Single	RCA	74321-96824-2	Australia	2002	7.99
Presley, Elvis	Burning Love (Promo)	CD Single	BMG	74321-969122	Spain	2002	49.99
Presley, Elvis	Burning Love And Hits...	CD	RCA	CAD1-2595	U.S.A.	1991	14.99
Presley, Elvis	By Request	CD	RCA	R32P-1011	Japan	1986	39.99
Presley, Elvis	By Request Best 20	CD	BMG Victor	BVCP-2619	Japan	1994	21.99
Presley, Elvis	Can't Help... The Hollywood Hits	CD	RCA	07863-67873-2	U.S.A.	1999	17.99
Presley, Elvis	Christmas Classics	CD	RCA	9801-2-RRE	U.S.A.	1995	15.99
Presley, Elvis	Christmas Peace	2CD	RCA	82876-57111-2-8	U.S.A.	2003	19.99
Presley, Elvis	Classic Elvis	CD	RCA	74321-47682-2	Australia	1997	6.99

P

Artist	Title	Format	Label	Catalog No	Country	Released	Value
Presley, Elvis	Close Up Box Set	4CD	RCA	82876-50537-2	U.S.A.	2003	54.99
Presley, Elvis	Collector's Gold	3CD	RCA	3114-2-R	U.S.A.	1991	39.99
Presley, Elvis	Collector's Gold (Ltd Wooden Box)	3CD	RCA	3114-2-R	U.S.A.	1991	249.99
Presley, Elvis	Commemorative Juke B Series Vol. 1-5	5CD	RCA	8990(-4)-2-RH	U.S.A.	1989	149.99
Presley, Elvis	Complete 50's Masters Box (Stamps)	5CD	RCA	07863-66050-2	U.S.A.	1992	59.99
Presley, Elvis	Complete Single Collection (90 Pg Bk)	10 CD	BMG	DRF-7101/10	Japan	1999	449.99
Presley, Elvis	Cream Of The Catalouge (Promo)	CD	BMG	GILBEY-1	Australia	1996	599.99
Presley, Elvis	Crying In The Chapel	CD Single	RCA	74321-24524-2	Netherlands	1994	16.99
Presley, Elvis	Danske Single Hits	CD	RCA	PD-90551	Denmark	1990	29.99
Presley, Elvis	Devil In Disguise: Best Of Vol. 2 (Gold)	CD	Zounds	270002011	EU	2000	34.99
Presley, Elvis	Disco De Ouro	CD	RCA	74321-50730-2	Brazil	1997	39.99
Presley, Elvis	Don't Be Cruel	CD Single	RCA	74321-11061-2	Germany	1992	15.99
Presley, Elvis	Double Dynamite	CD	RCA	PDC2-1010	U.S.A.	1992	21.99
Presley, Elvis	Double Features Sampler (Fan Club)	CD	RCA	74321-85562-2	England	2001	39.99
Presley, Elvis	Easy Come, Easy Go/Speedway	CD	RCA	07863-66558-2	U.S.A.	1995	16.99
Presley, Elvis	Eaton King Of Rock 'N' Roll (Red/DJ)	CD	RCA	KCDP-51310	Canada	1995	89.99
Presley, Elvis	Elvis	CD	RCA	PCD1-5199	U.S.A.	1994	14.99
Presley, Elvis	Elvis !/King & His Movies (128 Pg Bk)	CD	RCA	DPC11624	U.S.A.	1997	29.99
Presley, Elvis	Elvis (Promo/30 # 1 Hits)	CD	BMG	CDX2582	Mexico	2002	19.99
Presley, Elvis	Elvis (RCA Gold Cd)	CD	RCA	07863-66659-2	U.S.A.	1995	31.99
Presley, Elvis	Elvis (Reprocessed Stereo)	CD	RCA	PCD1-1382	U.S.A.	1984	249.99
Presley, Elvis	Elvis (The Fool Lp)	CD	RCA	07863-50283-2	U.S.A.	1994	12.99
Presley, Elvis	Elvis (The Fool Lp) 20 Bit Remaster	CD	BMG Victor	BVCM-35033	Japan	1999	23.99
Presley, Elvis	Elvis + 8	CD	RCA	07863-67736-2	England	1999	11.99
Presley, Elvis	Elvis 2000 (Fan Club)	CD	RCA	74321-73825-2	Norway	1999	24.99
Presley, Elvis	Elvis 2000: The Best Of	2CD	RCA	74321-73748-2	Germany	2002	19.99
Presley, Elvis	Elvis 20th Ann. Blockbuster Sampler	CD	RCA	07863-67537-2	U.S.A.	1997	10.99
Presley, Elvis	Elvis 30 # 1 Hits	DVD Aud	RCA	07863-65053-9	U.S.A.	2002	24.99
Presley, Elvis	Elvis 30 # 1 Hits	CD	RCA	07863-68079-2	U.S.A.	2002	12.99
Presley, Elvis	Elvis 30 # 1 Hits Hardback Edition	2CD	RCA	82876-56402-2	U.S.A.	2003	23.99
Presley, Elvis	Elvis 30 # 1 Hits Sampler (Promo)	CD	RCA	RDJ-60619-2	U.S.A.	2002	49.99
Presley, Elvis	Elvis '56 (Collector's Ed)	CD	RCA	07863-66817-2	U.S.A.	1996	21.99
Presley, Elvis	Elvis Aaron Presley Box Set	4CD	RCA	07863-67455-2	U.S.A.	1998	47.99
Presley, Elvis	Elvis Aron Presley: Forever	CD	RCA	PDC2-1185	U.S.A.	1987	34.99
Presley, Elvis	Elvis Ballads: The Ultimate Coll.	CD	RCA	74321-68242-2	England	1999	14.99
Presley, Elvis	Elvis Blues: The Ultimate Coll.	CD	RCA	74321-76522-2	England	2000	14.99
Presley, Elvis	Elvis' Christmas Album	CD	BMG	74321-695762	EU	1999	14.99
Presley, Elvis	Elvis' Christmas Album	CD	RCA	PCD1-5486	U.S.A.	1994	21.99
Presley, Elvis	Elvis' Christmas Album	CD	RCA	CAD1-2428	U.S.A.	1995	12.99
Presley, Elvis	Elvis' Christmas Album (Orig. Cover)	CD	Rainbow	RXMCD-179	Australia	1990	49.99
Presley, Elvis	Elvis Country	CD	RCA	07863-66405-2	U.S.A.	1994	16.99
Presley, Elvis	Elvis Country: The Ultimate Coll.	CD	RCA	74321-68276-2	England	1999	14.99
Presley, Elvis	Elvis D. Feature: Speedway/Clambake	CD	RCA	PDC2-1250	U.S.A.	1989	29.99
Presley, Elvis	Elvis En Los '90s (Promo)	CD	RCA	BACK-CAT-2	Argentina	1994	649.99
Presley, Elvis	Elvis For Everyone !	CD	RCA	07863-53450-2	U.S.A.	1995	14.99
Presley, Elvis	Elvis Gospel 1957 - 1971	CD	RCA	9586-2-R	U.S.A.	1995	17.99
Presley, Elvis	Elvis Gospel: The Ultimate Coll.	CD	RCA	74321-76523-2	U.S.A.	2000	14.99
Presley, Elvis	Elvis In Concert	CD	RCA	07863-52587-2	U.S.A.	1992	19.99
Presley, Elvis	Elvis In Demand	CD	RCA	BPCD-5069	Australia	1989	69.99
Presley, Elvis	Elvis In Nashville	CD	RCA	8468-2-R	U.S.A.	1988	34.99
Presley, Elvis	Elvis Is Back !	CD	RCA	2231-2-R	U.S.A.	1996	12.99
Presley, Elvis	Elvis Is Back (DCC Gold) # Ed.	CD	DCC	GZS-1111	U.S.A.	1997	45.99
Presley, Elvis	Elvis La Pelvis (Promo)	CD	BMG	AR-0001	Argentina	1999	69.99
Presley, Elvis	Elvis Lovin' - The Ultimate Coll.	CD	RCA	74321-76520-2	England	2000	14.99
Presley, Elvis	Elvis Movies: The Ultimate Coll.	CD	RCA	74321-68241-2	England	1999	14.99
Presley, Elvis	Elvis Off Camera (Promo)	CD	BMG	74321-46658-2	Germany	1997	39.99
Presley, Elvis	Elvis Presley 1 (Laser 19)	CD	RCA	ND-90326	France	1989	19.99
Presley, Elvis	Elvis Presley 2 (Laser 20)	CD	RCA	ND-90327	France	1989	19.99

P

Artist	Title	Format	Label	Catalog No	Country	Released	Value
Presley, Elvis	Elvis Presley Interview Picture Disc	CD	Baktabak	CBAK-4007	England	1990	8.99
Presley, Elvis	Elvis Rockabilly: The Ultimate Coll.	CD	RCA	74321-76521-2	England	2000	14.99
Presley, Elvis	Elvis Rockin' The Ultimate Coll.	CD	RCA	74321-68240-2	England	1999	14.99
Presley, Elvis	Elvis The Exhibit (Promo)	CD	RCA	DPC-12260	U.S.A.	1998	449.99
Presley, Elvis	Elvis The King	CD	RCA	PD-90583	Germany	1993	16.99
Presley, Elvis	Elvis Uddrag Fra: Essential (Promo)	CD Single	BMG	ELVIS-DK.PRO	Denmark	1994	249.99
Presley, Elvis	Elvis: Legend Silver Ed (Same As Gold)	CD	RCA	PD-89000	Germany	1985	399.99
Presley, Elvis	Elvis: No 1 Hits (Same/Number One H)	CD	RCA	ND-90203	Germany	1987	24.99
Presley, Elvis	Elvis: The Legend (Numbered/Gold)	3CD	RCA	PD-8900	Germany	1984	849.99
Presley, Elvis	Essential 60's Masters (Promo)	CD	BMG	EP-0012	EU	1993	119.99
Presley, Elvis	Essential 60's Masters, Vol. 2	2CD	RCA	07863-66601-2	U.S.A.	1995	25.99
Presley, Elvis	Essential 70's Masters (W/Stamps)	5CD	RCA	07863-66670-2	U.S.A.	1995	69.99
Presley, Elvis	Essential Elvis: First Movies, Vol. 1	CD	RCA	6738-2-R	U.S.A.	1996	14.99
Presley, Elvis	Flaming S/Follow T D/Wild In Country	CD	RCA	07863-66557-2	U.S.A.	1995	16.99
Presley, Elvis	For Cd Fans Only (W/Book)	CD	BMG	DMC-12345	U.S.A.	1998	29.99
Presley, Elvis	For LP Fans Only	CD	RCA	1990-2-R	U.S.A.	1996	12.99
Presley, Elvis	For The Asking (The Lost Album)	CD	RCA	07863-61024-2	U.S.A.	1995	11.99
Presley, Elvis	Forever	2CD	RCA	ND-89004	Germany	1993	16.99
Presley, Elvis	Forever II	CD	RCA	PD-90680	Germany	1992	17.99
Presley, Elvis	Forever In Love	2CD	RCA	74321-49484-2	U.S.A.	1997	19.99
Presley, Elvis	Frankie & Johnny/Paradise H Style	CD	RCA	07863-66360-2	U.S.A.	1994	17.99
Presley, Elvis	From Elvis In Memphis	CD	RCA	07863-51456-2	U.S.A.	1997	11.99
Presley, Elvis	From Elvis In Memphis + 6	CD	RCA	07863-67932-2	U.S.A.	2000	11.99
Presley, Elvis	From Elvis Presley Boulevard	CD	RCA	1506-2-R	U.S.A.	1991	11.99
Presley, Elvis	From Memphis To Austria (Promo)	CD	BMG	47-6380	Germany	1994	349.99
Presley, Elvis	From Memphis To Venice (Promo)	CD	BMG	47-6380	Germany	1994	249.99
Presley, Elvis	From The Heart	CD	RCA	PD-90642	England	1992	17.99
Presley, Elvis	G.I. Blues	CD	RCA	3735-2-R	U.S.A.	1994	12.99
Presley, Elvis	G.I. Blues + 8	CD	RCA	07863-66960-2	U.S.A.	1997	13.99
Presley, Elvis	G.I. Blues + 8 (Ltd Ed Hardcover)	CD	RCA	07863-67460-2	U.S.A.	1997	21.99
Presley, Elvis	Gold Collection, Vol. 1	2CD	RCA	74321-7195-2	Germany	1993	24.99
Presley, Elvis	Gold Collection, Vol. 2	2CD	RCA	74321-7196-2	Germany	1993	24.99
Presley, Elvis	Gold Collection, Vol. 3	2CD	RCA	74321-7197-2	Germany	1993	24.99
Presley, Elvis	Gold Records, Vol. 4	CD	RCA	1297-2-R	U.S.A.	1994	12.99
Presley, Elvis	Gold Records, Vol. 4 + 6	CD	RCA	07863-67465-2	U.S.A.	1997	11.99
Presley, Elvis	Gold: The Very Best Of	2CD	RCA	74321-24974-2	Germany	1995	21.99
Presley, Elvis	Golden Records Vol 1 (Reproc. Stereo)	CD	RCA	PCD1-1707	U.S.A.	1984	154.99
Presley, Elvis	Golden Records, Vol. 1 (Rep. Stereo)	CD	RCA	PCD1-1707	U.S.A.	1994	249.99
Presley, Elvis	Golden Records, Vol. 1 + 6	CD	RCA	07863-67462-2	U.S.A.	1997	11.99
Presley, Elvis	Golden Records, Vol. 3	CD	RCA	2765-2-R	U.S.A.	1994	12.99
Presley, Elvis	Golden Records, Vol. 3 + 6	CD	RCA	07863-67464-2	U.S.A.	1997	11.99
Presley, Elvis	Golden Records, Vol. 5	CD	RCA	PCD1-4941	U.S.A.	1995	24.99
Presley, Elvis	Golden Records, Vol. 5 + 6	CD	RCA	07863-67466-2	U.S.A.	1997	11.99
Presley, Elvis	Good Luck Charm (Promo)	CD Single	BMG	74321-26645-2	Spain	1994	64.99
Presley, Elvis	Good Rockin' Tonight	2CD	RCA	SVC2-0824	U.S.A.	1988	74.99
Presley, Elvis	Good Rockin' Tonight: Best Of, Vol. 1	CD	RCA	CD-20026	Brazil	1989	24.99
Presley, Elvis	Good Rockin' Tonight: Best Of, Vol. 2	CD	RCA	CD-20027	Brazil	1989	24.99
Presley, Elvis	Good Rockin' Tonight: Best Of, Vol. 3	CD	RCA	74327-11719-2	Brazil	1992	19.99
Presley, Elvis	Good Rockin' Tonight: Best Of, Vol. 4	CD	RCA	74327-11720-2	Brazil	1992	19.99
Presley, Elvis	Good Times	CD	RCA	07863-50475-2	U.S.A.	1994	11.99
Presley, Elvis	Gospel Favorites	CD	RCA	74321-149122-2	Australia	1997	19.99
Presley, Elvis	Gospel Favorites: Take My Hand	CD	RCA	74321-70913-2	England	1999	10.99
Presley, Elvis	Gospel Treasury	2CD	RCA	DMC2-1427	U.S.A.	1996	19.99
Presley, Elvis	Gracia Divina (Fan Club)	CD	RCA	74321-46863-2	Argentina	1997	12.99
Presley, Elvis	Grandes Exitos Balades	CD	RCA	748211135929	Venezuela	2000	24.99
Presley, Elvis	Grandes Exitos, Vol. 2 Rock And Roll	CD	RCA	78636-7457-2	Venezuela	2001	24.99
Presley, Elvis	Great Country Songs	CD	RCA	07863-66880-2	U.S.A.	1996	16.99
Presley, Elvis	Great Performances	CD	RCA	PDC2-1258	U.S.A.	1994	17.99

P

Artist	Title	Format	Label	Catalog No	Country	Released	Value
Presley, Elvis	Greatest Hits (De 60 Storste Hits)	2CD	RCA	74321-84741-2-5	Denmark	2001	21.99
Presley, Elvis	Greatest Hits, Vol. 1	CD	RCA	BPCD-5083	Australia	1989	64.99
Presley, Elvis	Greatest Juke Box Hits	CD	RCA	07863-67565-2	U.S.A.	1997	14.99
Presley, Elvis	H. Hotel/Hound Dog/Other T. 10 Hits	CD	RCA	2079-2-R	U.S.A.	1996	13.99
Presley, Elvis	Harem Holiday/Girl Happy	CD	RCA	07863-66128-2	U.S.A.	1993	17.99
Presley, Elvis	He Touched Me	CD	RCA	07863-51923-2	U.S.A.	1992	14.99
Presley, Elvis	He Walks Beside Me	CD	RCA	07863-52772-2	Canada	1998	14.99
Presley, Elvis	Heart & Soul	CD	RCA	07863-66532-2	U.S.A.	1995	14.99
Presley, Elvis	Heartbreak Hotel	CD Single	RCA	07863-64475-2	U.S.A.	1996	10.99
Presley, Elvis	Het Mooiste Van Elvis Presley	CD	RCA	PD-74595	Netherlands	1990	21.99
Presley, Elvis	His 27 Best Songs	CD	RCA	SPCD-010787	Netherlands	1987	23.99
Presley, Elvis	His Hand In Mine (Elvis At Piano)	CD	RCA	ND-83935	Germany	1993	11.99
Presley, Elvis	His Hand In Mine (Elvis/Clouds)	CD	RCA	1319-2-R	U.S.A.	1996	14.99
Presley, Elvis	His Life And Music (W/176 Pg. Book)	4CD	RCA	7-20593-91112-4	U.S.A.	1994	99.99
Presley, Elvis	Hits Like Never Before: Essential Vol. 3	CD	RCA	2229-2-R	U.S.A.	1993	14.99
Presley, Elvis	How Great Thou Art	Mini Lp	BMG	BVCM-37092	Japan	1967	46.99
Presley, Elvis	How Great Thou Art	CD	RCA	3758-2-R	U.S.A.	1997	11.99
Presley, Elvis	Humo Selecterrt Meer Dan...	2CD	RCA	74321-80492-2	Belgium	2000	37.99
Presley, Elvis	I Mitti Musica	CD	RCA	74321-62629-2	Italy	1999	8.99
Presley, Elvis	I Wish You A Merry Christmas	CD	RCA	ND-89474	Germany	1990	29.99
Presley, Elvis	If Everyday Was Like Xmas	CD Single	RCA	74321-25214-2	Netherlands	1994	16.99
Presley, Elvis	If Everyday Was Like Xmas (Ltd Ed)	CD	RCA	07863-66482-2	U.S.A.	1994	24.99
Presley, Elvis	I'm 10,000 Years Old (Country)	CD	RCA	07863-66279-2	U.S.A.	1993	14.99
Presley, Elvis	I'm 10,000 Years Old (Country) + 6	CD	RCA	07863-67929-2	U.S.A.	2000	11.99
Presley, Elvis	In Person	CD	RCA	07863-53892-2	U.S.A.	1996	11.99
Presley, Elvis	In The 90's	CD	BMG	RCA-9028	Germany	1990	549.99
Presley, Elvis	It Happened W Fair/Fun Acapulco	CD	RCA	07863-66131-2	U.S.A.	1993	17.99
Presley, Elvis	It's Now Or Never (Gold Cd)	CD	Zounds	27220017	EU	1996	39.99
Presley, Elvis	Jailhouse Rock	CD	RCA	BPCD-5096	Australia	1990	14.99
Presley, Elvis	Jailhouse Rock	CD Single	RCA	74321-23813-2	Netherlands	1994	16.99
Presley, Elvis	Jailhouse Rock/Love Me Tender	CD	RCA	07863-67453-2	U.S.A.	1997	13.99
Presley, Elvis	Kid Galahad/Girls ! Girls ! Girls!	CD	RCA	07863-66130-2	U.S.A.	1993	24.99
Presley, Elvis	King Creole	CD	RCA	3733-2-R	U.S.A.	1991	12.99
Presley, Elvis	King Creole + 7	CD	RCA	07863-67454-2	U.S.A.	1997	13.99
Presley, Elvis	King Of Rock 'N' Roll Sampler (DJ)	CD	RCA	KCDP-51093	Canada	1992	59.99
Presley, Elvis	Kissin' Cousins/Clambake/Stay A Joe	CD	RCA	07863-66362-2	U.S.A.	1994	17.99
Presley, Elvis	L' Album Di	2CD	RCA	ND-89869	Italy	1988	34.99
Presley, Elvis	La Legende - 1954-57 - Romantique	CD	RCA	2868202	France	1998	19.99
Presley, Elvis	La Legende - 1956-57 - Rock 'N' Roll	CD	RCA	2868201	France	1997	19.99
Presley, Elvis	La Legende - 1973 - Aloha Hawaii Vol.1	CD	RCA	2868203	France	1998	19.99
Presley, Elvis	La Legende - Rock 'N' Roll	CD	RCA	2868401	France	1997	19.99
Presley, Elvis	La Voix Du Rock	2CD	RCA	74321-10343-2	France	1992	24.99
Presley, Elvis	La Voz Del Rock	CD	BMG	74321-130012	Spain	1992	59.99
Presley, Elvis	Latino ! (Fan Club)	CD	RCA	74321-49058-2	Argentina	1997	12.99
Presley, Elvis	Legendary	3CD	RCA	74321-78282-2	EU	2000	17.99
Presley, Elvis	L'Essentiel Elvis Presley	CD	RCA	74321-84484-2	France	2001	14.99
Presley, Elvis	Live A L/Charro/Change H/Trouble W	CD	RCA	07863-66559-2	U.S.A.	1995	16.99
Presley, Elvis	Live In Dallas, June 1975 (Fan Club)	CD	RCA	SPCD-230587	Netherlands	1987	34.99
Presley, Elvis	Live In Las Vegas	CD Single	RCA	PD-49178	Germany	1991	16.99
Presley, Elvis	Live In Las Vegas Box Set	4CD	RCA	07863-69354-2	U.S.A.	2001	44.99
Presley, Elvis	Live In Las Vegas Sampler (Promo)	CD	RCA	RDJ-68040-2	U.S.A.	2001	54.99
Presley, Elvis	Live In Las Vegas Sampler (Promo)	CD	RCA	74321-87482-2	England	2001	69.99
Presley, Elvis	Live Raw Early Recordings '55	CD	RCA	9210-2	U.S.A.	1997	16.99
Presley, Elvis	Love & Rock Songs	3CD	RCA	74321-70944-2	France	1999	59.99
Presley, Elvis	Love In Las Vegas/Roustabout	CD	RCA	07863-66129-2	U.S.A.	1993	17.99
Presley, Elvis	Love Letters (Promo)	CD Single	RCA	ELVIS-58	England	1993	194.99
Presley, Elvis	Love Letters From Elvis	CD	RCA	07863-54350-2	U.S.A.	1992	14.99
Presley, Elvis	Love Me Tender	CD	RCA	BPCD-5097	Australia	1989	14.99

P

Artist	Title	Format	Label	Catalog No	Country	Released	Value
Presley, Elvis	Love Me Tender	CD Single	RCA	07863-64885-2	U.S.A.	1997	12.99
Presley, Elvis	Love Me Tender Remix	CD Single	RCA	74321-16374-2	France	1993	8.99
Presley, Elvis	Love Me Tender: Romantic Elvis	CD	Ariola	353150	Germany	1987	20.99
Presley, Elvis	Love Songs	CD	RCA	74321-64791-2	England	1999	9.99
Presley, Elvis	Love Songs	CD	RCA	07863-67595-2	U.S.A.	1998	14.99
Presley, Elvis	Love Songs	CD	RCA	74321-12068-2	Germany	1993	34.99
Presley, Elvis	Loving You	CD	RCA	1515-2-R	U.S.A.	1991	12.99
Presley, Elvis	Loving You :10 Favorite Records/Cd	10 CD	RCA	ND-90542	Germany	1990	99.99
Presley, Elvis	Loving You + 8	CD	RCA	07863-67452-2	U.S.A.	1997	13.99
Presley, Elvis	Mahalo From Elvis	CD	RCA	CCD-7064	Canada	1991	29.99
Presley, Elvis	Mean Woman Blues	CD Single	RCA	PD-49474	Germany	1989	17.99
Presley, Elvis	Mega Elvis	CD	BMG Victor	BVCP-850	Japan	1995	19.99
Presley, Elvis	Memories Of Christmas	CD	RCA	4395-2-RRE	U.S.A.	1995	11.99
Presley, Elvis	Memories: The '68 Comeback Special	2CD	RCA	07863-67612-2	U.S.A.	1998	21.99
Presley, Elvis	Merry Christmas (Deleted In 1 Month)	CD	RCA	PCD1-5301	U.S.A.	1984	299.99
Presley, Elvis	Merry Christmas Baby	CD Single	RCA	PD-49149	Netherlands	1991	15.99
Presley, Elvis	Moody Blue	CD	RCA	2428-2-R	U.S.A.	1992	14.99
Presley, Elvis	Moody Blue (24 Bit Remastered)	Mini Lp	BMG Victor	BVCM-37102	Japan	2000	34.99
Presley, Elvis	Moody Blue (Promo)	CD Single	BMG	74321-512612	Belgium	1997	149.99
Presley, Elvis	Moody Blue + 9 - 1(No Let Me..)	CD	RCA	07863-67931-2	U.S.A.	2000	11.99
Presley, Elvis	My Happiness (Promo)	CD	RCA	2654-2-RDJ	U.S.A.	1990	69.99
Presley, Elvis	Mystery Train	CD Single	RCA	R10D-134	Japan	1989	26.99
Presley, Elvis	NBC TV Special + 8	CD	RCA	07863-61021-2	U.S.A.	1996	11.99
Presley, Elvis	Norske Favoritter	CD Single	BMG	ELVIS-PRO-1/96	Norway	1996	33.99
Presley, Elvis	Norske Hits	CD	RCA	74321-11974-2	Norway	1992	21.99
Presley, Elvis	Now	CD	RCA	07863-54671-2	U.S.A.	1993	16.99
Presley, Elvis	Off Camera (Promo)	CD	BMG	PROCD21029	Australia	1997	129.99
Presley, Elvis	On Stage (20 Bit Remastered)	CD	BMG Victor	BVCP-7366	Japan	1995	11.99
Presley, Elvis	On Stage + 6	CD	RCA	07863-67741-2	U.S.A.	1999	11.99
Presley, Elvis	On Stage February 1970	CD	RCA	07863-54362-2	U.S.A.	1995	13.99
Presley, Elvis	Original Hit Singles (3")	CD Single	RCA	PD-49467	Austria	1989	19.99
Presley, Elvis	Other Sides Of Box (Ltd/Numbered)	2CD	RCA	07863-66921-2	U.S.A.	1996	19.99
Presley, Elvis	Our Memories Of Elvis (Fan Club)	CD	RCA	SPCD-061188	Netherlands	1988	34.99
Presley, Elvis	Out Of The Box King/ Rock (Promo)	CD	RCA	RDJ-62328-2	U.S.A.	1992	64.99
Presley, Elvis	Out Of The Box: 6 From 60's (Promo)	CD	RCA	RDJ-62824-2	U.S.A.	1993	64.99
Presley, Elvis	Out Of The Box: Walk A Mile (Promo)	CD	RCA	RJC-66765-2	U.S.A.	1995	64.99
Presley, Elvis	Patriot (Limited Edition)	CD	RCA	SCD-4145	U.S.A.	2001	17.99
Presley, Elvis	Peace In The Valley: Complete Gospel	3CD	RCA	07863-67991-2	U.S.A.	2000	27.99
Presley, Elvis	Perfect For Parties (Promo)	CD	BMG	SPA-7-37	Germany	1993	449.99
Presley, Elvis	Platinum A Life In (No Fr Insert/Promo)	CD	RCA	RJC-67568-2	U.S.A.	1997	64.99
Presley, Elvis	Platinum A Life In Music (Promo)	CD	BMG	PROCD21031	Australia	1997	149.99
Presley, Elvis	Platinum A Life In Music Sampler (DJ)	CD Single	RCA	RDJ-67529-2	U.S.A.	1997	74.99
Presley, Elvis	Platinum A Life In Music Sampler (DJ)	CD	BMG	74321-492862	EU	1997	119.99
Presley, Elvis	Platinum Sampler (Promo)	CD	BMG	PLATINUM-001	Germany	1997	349.99
Presley, Elvis	Platinum: A Life In Music	4CD	RCA	07863-67469-2	U.S.A.	1997	49.99
Presley, Elvis	Portrait D' Une Legende, Vol. 1	CD	RCA	ND-90056	France	1987	17.99
Presley, Elvis	Portrait D' Une Legende, Vol. 2	CD	RCA	ND-90057	France	1987	17.99
Presley, Elvis	Pot Luck + 5	CD	RCA	07863-67739-2	U.S.A.	1999	11.99
Presley, Elvis	Pot Luck With Elvis	CD	RCA	2523-2-R	U.S.A.	1995	17.99
Presley, Elvis	Presley: The All Time Greatest Hits	2CD	RCA	ND-90100	Australia	1992	24.99
Presley, Elvis	Promised Land	CD	RCA	0873-2-R	U.S.A.	1995	12.99
Presley, Elvis	Promised Land + 8	CD	RCA	07863-67930-2	U.S.A.	2000	11.99
Presley, Elvis	Pure Gold	CD	RCA	07863-53732-2	U.S.A.	1996	13.99
Presley, Elvis	Pure Gold (Different Cover)	CD	Rainbow	RCD-113	Australia	1992	14.99
Arsley, Elvis	Radio Special The King Of Rock (DJ)	CD	RCA	RDJ-66121-2	U.S.A.	1992	79.99
Presley, Elvis	Rags To Riches (1st/0001-0999/DJ)	CD Single	RCA	EPFC001	England	1997	74.99
Presley, Elvis	Rags To Riches (2nd/1001-2000/DJ)	CD Single	RCA	EPFC001	England	1997	74.99
Presley, Elvis	Raised On Rock	CD	RCA	07863-50388-2	U.S.A.	1994	12.99

P

Artist	Title	Format	Label	Catalog No	Country	Released	Value
Presley, Elvis	Raised On Rock (20 Bit Remastered)	CD	BMG Victor	BVCM-35034	Japan	1999	23.99
Presley, Elvis	Rare Elvis	CD	RCA	PD-89003	Germany	1986	44.99
Presley, Elvis	RCA Victor 100 Anos	CD	RCA	74321-89763-2	Argentina	2001	24.99
Presley, Elvis	Reconsider Baby	CD	RCA	PCD1-5418	U.S.A.	1991	14.99
Presley, Elvis	Recorded Live On Stage Memphis	CD	RCA	07863-50606-2	U.S.A.	1994	11.99
Presley, Elvis	Remembering Elvis	CD	RCA	PDC2-1037	U.S.A.	1988	34.99
Presley, Elvis	Return Of The Rocker	CD	RCA	5600-2-R	U.S.A.	1990	27.99
Presley, Elvis	Rhythm & Country: Essential Vol. 5	CD	RCA	07863-67672-2	U.S.A.	1998	16.99
Presley, Elvis	Rock And Roll No. 2 (F Club/Book/Cd)	CD	BMG	74321-92723-2	France	2002	34.99
Presley, Elvis	Rock 'N' On, Vol. 1	CD	RCA	SPCD-1006	Australia	1989	27.99
Presley, Elvis	Rock 'N' On, Vol. 2	CD	RCA	SPCD-1008	Australia	1988	27.99
Presley, Elvis	Rocker	CD	RCA	PCD1-5182	U.S.A.	1996	14.99
Presley, Elvis	Romantique Elvis	CD	RCA	74321-15780-2	France	1993	21.99
Presley, Elvis	Roustabout	CD	RCA	BPCD-5084	Australia	1988	74.99
Presley, Elvis	RTL 4 Presenteert	CD	RCA	PS-CD-25	Netherlands	1991	11.99
Presley, Elvis	Rubberneckin' Remix	CD Single	RCA	82876-54341-2	U.S.A.	2003	5.99
Presley, Elvis	Selections Amazing Grace (Promo)	CD	BMG	74321-24079-2	Germany	1994	69.99
Presley, Elvis	Selections From Amazing Grace (DJ)	CD	RCA	RJC-66512-2	U.S.A.	1994	59.99
Presley, Elvis	Self Titled	CD	RCA	PCD1-5198	U.S.A.	1998	14.99
Presley, Elvis	Self Titled +6	CD	RCA	07863-67735-2	U.S.A.	1999	11.99
Presley, Elvis	Self Titled (Reprocessed Stereo)	CD	RCA	PCD1-1254	U.S.A.	1984	249.99
Presley, Elvis	Sentimental Me (Promo)	CD	RCA	74321-90770-2	Sweden	2001	109.99
Presley, Elvis	Separate Ways	CD	RCA	CCD-2611	Canada	1991	59.99
Presley, Elvis	Shake Rattle And Roll (DJ)	CD	RCA	6382-2-RDJ	U.S.A.	1992	149.99
Presley, Elvis	Shaped Cd 5 Single Wooden Box Set	5CD	Collectables	COL-CD-0801-5	U.S.A.	2000	99.99
Presley, Elvis	Silver Bells/Winter Wonderland (DJ)	CD Single	BMG	74321-551602	Belgium	1997	188.99
Presley, Elvis	Sings For Children And Grown Ups Too	CD	RCA	CAD1-2704	U.S.A.	1989	22.99
Presley, Elvis	Sings For Kids (Same As Grownups + 1	CD	RCA	75117-44867-2	U.S.A.	2002	11.99
Presley, Elvis	Sings Hits From His Movies Volume 1	CD	RCA	CAD1-2567	U.S.A.	1972	224.99
Presley, Elvis	Sings Leiber And Stoller	CD	RCA	3026-2-R	U.S.A.	1996	23.99
Presley, Elvis	Sings Wonderful World/Christmas	CD	RCA	4579-2-RRE	U.S.A.	1995	11.99
Presley, Elvis	Solid Gold	CD	RCA	CD-90434	Italy	1990	15.99
Presley, Elvis	Something For Everybody	CD	RCA	2370-2-R	U.S.A.	1994	17.99
Presley, Elvis	Something For Everybody + 4	CD	RCA	07863-67738-2	U.S.A.	1999	11.99
Presley, Elvis	South America Style (Promo)	CD	BMG	AR-0003	Argentina	2000	69.99
Presley, Elvis	Spinout/Double Trouble	CD	RCA	07863-66361-2	U.S.A.	1994	17.99
Presley, Elvis	Stereo '57: Essential Vol. 2	CD	RCA	9589-2-R	U.S.A.	1994	12.99
Presley, Elvis	Stranger In My Own... (Fan Club)	CD	RCA	74321-75372-2	Denmark	2000	24.99
Presley, Elvis	Stuck On You	CD Single	RCA	ND-49596	Germany	1987	19.99
Presley, Elvis	Such A Night: Essential Vol. 6	CD	RCA	07863-67840-2	U.S.A.	2000	11.99
Presley, Elvis	Sunrise	2CD	RCA	67675-2	U.S.A.	1999	19.99
Presley, Elvis	Suspicious Minds	2CD	RCA	07863-6767-2	U.S.A.	1999	21.99
Presley, Elvis	Suspicious Minds Live (Ltd/#rd)	CD Single	RCA	74321-85582-2	EU	2001	11.99
Presley, Elvis	Svenska Hits	CD	RCA	74321-24405-2	Sweden	1994	19.99
Presley, Elvis	Swedish Hit Colleciton Samper (DJ)	CD	BMG	BMGPROM-98	Sweden	2000	199.99
Presley, Elvis	Swedish Hit Collection	2CD	RCA	74321-79163-2	Sweden	2000	24.99
Presley, Elvis	Teddy Bear	CD Single	RCA	74321-25870-2	Netherlands	1995	16.99
Presley, Elvis	That's The Way It Is	CD	RCA	07863-54114-2	U.S.A.	1993	11.99
Presley, Elvis	That's The Way It Is (MFSL Gold Cd)	CD	Mobile Fidelity	UDCD-560	U.S.A.	1970	66.99
Presley, Elvis	That's The Way It Is Sampler (DJ)	CD	BMG	74321-76831-2	EU	2000	74.99
Presley, Elvis	That's The Way It Is: Special Edition	3CD	RCA	07863-67938-2	U.S.A.	2000	27.99
Presley, Elvis	The 50 Greatest Hits	2CD	RCA	74321-81102-2	England	2000	24.99
Presley, Elvis	The Alternate Aloha	CD	RCA	6985-2-R	U.S.A.	1996	14.99
Presley, Elvis	The Collection, Vol. 1	CD	RCA	74321-28988-2	Germany	1995	11.99
Presley, Elvis	The Collection, Vol. 2	CD	RCA	74321-33071-2	Germany	1996	11.99
Presley, Elvis	The Collection, Vol. 3	CD	RCA	74321-40053-2	Germany	1996	11.99
Presley, Elvis	The Collection, Vol. 4	CD	RCA	74321-42266-2	Germany	1997	11.99
Presley, Elvis	The Country Side Of	CD	RCA	74321-67553-2	Australia	1999	17.99

P

Artist	Title	Format	Label	Catalog No	Country	Released	Value
Presley, Elvis	The Country Side Of Elvis	2CD	RCA	07863-67990-2	U.S.A.	2001	19.99
Presley, Elvis	The Definitive Country Album	CD	RCA	ND-90417	Germany	1989	21.99
Presley, Elvis	The Definitive Film Album	CD	RCA	ND-90418	Germany	1989	21.99
Presley, Elvis	The Definitive Gospel Album	CD	RCA	ND-90416	Germany	1989	21.99
Presley, Elvis	The Definitive Love Album	CD	RCA	ND-90419	Germany	1989	21.99
Presley, Elvis	The Definitive Rock & Roll Album	CD	RCA	ND-90415	Germany	1989	21.99
Presley, Elvis	The Elvis Medley	CD	RCA	7-48211-13562-2	Mexico	1994	31.99
Presley, Elvis	The Essential 60's Masters (W/Stamps)	5CD	RCA	07863-66160-2	U.S.A.	1993	59.99
Presley, Elvis	The Essential Collection	CD	RCA	74321-22871-2	England	1995	21.99
Presley, Elvis	The Gift Box Set	2CD	RCA	74321-17160-2	Germany	1993	27.99
Presley, Elvis	The Great Performances	CD	RCA	2227-2-R	U.S.A.	1996	12.99
Presley, Elvis	The Heartbreaker	CD	BMG	S	Mexico	2000	64.99
Presley, Elvis	The Hits Of (Country Club)	CD	RCA	06192-18089-2	Canada	1994	21.99
Presley, Elvis	The Home Recordings	CD	RCA	07863-67676-2	U.S.A.	1999	11.99
Presley, Elvis	The Honeymoon Companion (DJ)	CD	RCA	RDJ-66124-2	U.S.A.	1992	114.99
Presley, Elvis	The King	CD	RCA	74321-14983-2	Italy	1993	15.99
Presley, Elvis	The Legend Lives On	5CD	BMG	V-86002-VK-3	Germany	1990	59.99
Presley, Elvis	The Legend Lives On	4CD	RCA	211911	U.S.A.	2001	59.99
Presley, Elvis	The Live Greatest Hits	CD	RCA	74321-84708-2	EU	2001	19.99
Presley, Elvis	The Live Greatest Hits (Promo)	CD	BMG	AR-0004	Argentina	2001	69.99
Presley, Elvis	The Memphis Record	CD	RCA	6221-2-R	U.S.A.	1991	17.99
Presley, Elvis	The Million Dollar Quartet	CD	RCA	2023-2-R	U.S.A.	1996	14.99
Presley, Elvis	The Movie Years (Promo)	CD	BMG	PROCD21104	Australia	1999	124.99
Presley, Elvis	The Number One Hits	CD	RCA	6382-2-R	U.S.A.	1991	12.99
Presley, Elvis	The Sun Collection	CD	RCA	ND-89107	Germany	1988	24.99
Presley, Elvis	The Sun Sessions CD	CD	RCA	6414-2-R	U.S.A.	1987	9.99
Presley, Elvis	The Sunday Times	CD	BMG	BMGSM62	England	2001	9.99
Presley, Elvis	The Top Ten Hits	2CD	RCA	07863-56383-2	U.S.A.	1996	26.99
Presley, Elvis	The Twelfth Of Never	CD Single	RCA	74321320122	EU	1995	8.99
Presley, Elvis	The Twelfth Of Never (Promo)	CD	BMG	74321-365702	Netherlands	1996	49.99
Presley, Elvis	The Very Best Of	CD	RCA	74321-44560-2	New Zeland	1997	9.99
Presley, Elvis	The Very Best Of Love	CD	RCA	EP2-5294	U.S.A.	2001	23.99
Presley, Elvis	Tigerman ('68 Comeback + 6)	CD	RCA	07863-67611-2	U.S.A.	1998	16.99
Presley, Elvis	Timeless Songs Sampler (Promo)	CD	RCA	KCDP-51321	Canada	1995	599.99
Presley, Elvis	Today	CD	RCA	07863-51039-2	U.S.A.	1992	11.99
Presley, Elvis	Today Tomorrow Forever Sampler (DJ)	CD	RCA	HEDJ-65121-2	U.S.A.	2002	114.99
Presley, Elvis	Today Tomorrow Forever Sampler (DJ)	CD	BMG	74321-95033-2	EU	2002	114.99
Presley, Elvis	Today, Tomorrow & Forever Box	4CD	RCA	07863-65115-2	EU	2002	61.99
Presley, Elvis	Tomorrow Is A Long Time	CD	RCA	07863-67740-2	U.S.A.	1999	16.99
Presley, Elvis	Tripack (That's T W/Forever/Vs. JXL)	3CD	RCA	07863-67593-2	Netherlands	2002	29.99
Presley, Elvis	Vino, Dinero Y Amor (Promo)	CD	BMG	L	Mexico	1998	64.99
Presley, Elvis	We Love Elvis	3CD	BMG Victor	RPOP-1003~5	Japan	1987	54.99
Presley, Elvis	We Love Elvis, Vol. 2	3CD	BMG Victor	B18D-41038~40	Japan	1989	49.99
Presley, Elvis	We Love Elvis, Vol. 3	3CD	BMG Victor	BVCP-8601~3	Japan	1995	34.99
Presley, Elvis	Welcome To My World	CD	RCA	07863-52274-2	U.S.A.	1997	13.99
Presley, Elvis	White Christmas	CD	RCA	07863-67959-2	U.S.A.	2000	11.99
Presley, Elvis	You Belong To My Heart (Promo)	CD	BMG	V	Mexico	2000	64.99
Presley, Elvis	You'll Never Walk Alone	CD	RCA	CAD1-2472	U.S.A.	1995	13.99
Presley, Elvis/10 Track	Artist Of The Century Sampler (DJ)	CD	BMG	74321-68133-2	EU	1999	199.99
Presley, Elvis/7 Track	Artist Of The Century Sampler (DJ)	CD	BMG	74321-61911-2	EU	1998	159.99
Presley, Elvis/Back Y Lighter	Out Of The Box: 6 From 60's (Promo)	CD	RCA	RDJ-62624-2	Canada	1993	69.99
Presley, Elvis/Black	Eaton King Of Rock 'N' Roll (Promo)	CD	BMG	KCDP-51096	Canada	1992	449.99
Presley, Elvis/Fan Club	Chante Mort Shuman/Doc Pomus	2CD	RCA	74321-74596-2	France	2000	39.99
Presley, Elvis/Fan Club	Chante Sid Tepper & Roy C. Bennett	2CD	RCA	74321-87105-2	France	2001	39.99
Presley, Elvis/James Burton	The Guitar Sounds Of James Burton	CD	A&M	540-553-2	Germany	1997	19.99
Presley, Elvis/Pin/Certificate	Film Can Set (W/Booklet/4 Photos)	4CD	RCA	07863-61835-2	U.S.A.	1993	69.99
Presley, Elvis/Ringo Starr	Don't Be Cruel (Promo)	CD Single	BMG Victor	PDTD-1051	Japan	1992	149.99
Presley, Elvis/Vs JXL	A Little Less Conversation	CD Single	RCA	07863-60555-2	U.S.A.	2002	7.99

P

Artist	Title	Format	Label	Catalog No	Country	Released	Value
Presley, Elvis/Vs JXL	A Little Less Conversation (Promo)	CD Single	BMG	74321-946422	Spain	2002	24.99
Presley, Elvis/Vs JXL	A Little Less Conversation (Promo)	CD Single	BMG	74321-943222	EU	2002	24.99
Presley, Elvis/W/8 Pg Booklet	The King Of Rock N' Roll Lives (DJ)	CD	RCA	RDJ-67983-2	U.S.A.	2000	34.99
Presley, Elvis/W/Flyer	Live In Las Vegas Sampler (Promo)	CD	BMG	74321-87482-2	EU	2001	69.99
Presley, Elvis/W/Press Kit	Elvis 30 # 1 Hits Sampler (Promo)	CD	RCA	RDJ-60593-2	U.S.A.	2002	89.99
Presley, Elvis/With Box	Today Tomorrow Forever (Free Cd)	CD	BMG	HEMJ-65123-2	U.S.A.	2002	74.99
Presley, Lisa Marie	To Whom It May Concern	CD	Capitol	7243-4-96668-0-1	U.S.A.	2003	10.99
Presley, Lisa Marie	To Whom It May Concern (DJ Sampler)	CD	Capitol	DPRO-7087-2	U.S.A.	2003	12.99
Preston, Billy	Encouraging Words + 3	CD	Capitol	0777-7-81279-2-5	U.S.A.	1993	26.99
Preston, Billy	That's The Way God Planned It + 3	CD	EMI	7975802	Germany	1991	26.99
Pretenders	Don't Get Me Wrong (W/Cuban Slide EP)	CD	Pickwick	4509-91885-2	England	1990	8.99
Pretenders	Get Close	CD	Sire	25488-2	U.S.A.	1986	6.99
Pretenders	Human	CD Single	Warner Bros.	WPCR-10394	Japan	1999	14.99
Pretenders	Human	CD Single	Warner Bros.	3984271512	England	1999	4.99
Pretenders	KBFH 10/5 To 10/11, 1998	CD	DIR Network	C169901XB	U.S.A.	1998	39.99
Pretenders	Kid	CD Single	Warner Bros.	0630-12161-2	England	1995	4.99
Pretenders	Last Of The Independents	CD	Sire	9-45572-2	U.S.A.	1994	7.99
Pretenders	Learning To Crawl	CD	Sire	9-23980-2	U.S.A.	1982	9.99
Pretenders	Loose Screw	CD	Artemis	751153-2	U.S.A.	2002	8.99
Pretenders	Loving You Is All I Know (Promo)	CD Single	Hollywood	PRCD-11030-2	U.S.A.	1999	7.99
Pretenders	Night In My Veins	CD Single	Sire	9-18163-2	U.S.A.	1994	5.99
Pretenders	Packed	CD	Sire	W2-26219	U.S.A.	1990	7.99
Pretenders	Popstar	CD Single	Warner Bros.	3984284352	England	1999	8.99
Pretenders	Pretenders	CD	Sire	6083-2	U.S.A.	1980	8.99
Pretenders	Pretenders II	CD	Sire	3572-2	U.S.A.	1981	9.99
Pretenders	The Isle Of View	CD	Warner Bros.	9-46085-2	U.S.A.	1995	8.99
Pretenders	The Singles	CD	Sire	9-25664-2	U.S.A.	1986	7.99
Pretenders	Viva El Amor	CD	Warner Bros.	9-47342-2	U.S.A.	1999	6.99
Pretenders	Westwood 1 #00-04, (1/22-23,00)	2CD	Westwood 1	CO0004A011100	U.S.A.	2000	49.99
Pretty Maids	Alive At Least	CD	XIII Bis	6403412	France	2003	20.99
Pretty Maids	Anything Worth Doing Is...	CD	Massacre	MASS-CD-0170	England	1998	14.99
Pretty Maids	Anything Worth Doing/Spooked	2CD	Massacre	MASS-CD-0355	England	2002	20.99
Pretty Maids	Carpe Diem	CD	Massacre	MASS-CD-0251	England	2000	11.99
Pretty Maids	Carpe Diem/First Cuts.. And Then	2CD	Massacre	MASS-CD-0379	England	2003	20.99
Pretty Maids	First Cuts... And Then Some	CD	Massacre	MASS-CD-0227	England	1999	14.99
Pretty Maids	Future World	CD	Sony	450-281-2	Sweden	1999	9.99
Pretty Maids	In Santa's Claws	CD Single	Sony	ESCA-5240	Japan	1990	15.99
Pretty Maids	Lethal Heroes	CD	Collectables	7405	U.S.A.	2003	8.99
Pretty Maids	Lethal Heroes/Jump The Gun	CD	Epic	466-365-2	Sweden	1990	11.99
Pretty Maids	Offside	CD Single	Columbia	472266-2	Japan	1992	17.99
Pretty Maids	Planet Panic	CD	Massacre	MASS-CD-0315	England	2002	11.99
Pretty Maids	Red, Hot And Heavy	CD	Epic	ESCA-5144	Japan	1984	15.99
Pretty Maids	Scream	CD	Massacre	MASS-CD-047	England	1995	12.99
Pretty Maids	Screamin' Live	CD	Massacre	MASS-CD-081	England	2003	14.99
Pretty Maids	Self Titled	CD	Epic	ESCA-5146	Japan	1984	20.99
Pretty Maids	Sin-Decade	CD	Columbia	47125-2	Germany	1992	14.99
Pretty Maids	Spooked + 2	CD	Epic	ESCA-6656	Japan	1997	30.99
Pretty Maids	Stripped	CD	Columbia	473964-2	Denmark	1993	15.99
Pretty Maids	The Best Of..Back To Back	CD	Epic	ESCA-7332	Japan	1998	29.99
Pretty Maids	The Best Of: Back To Back	CD	Massacre	MASS-CD-0169	England	1999	14.99
Pretty Things	Cross Talk (Gold Cd)	CD	Snapper	SDPCD-116	England	2000	18.99
Pretty Things	Electric Banana	CD	Repertoire	REP-4088-WZ	Germany	1991	14.99
Pretty Things	Emotions + 7	CD	Snapper	SMMCD-550	England	1998	9.99
Pretty Things	Emotions + 7 (Gold Cd)	CD	Snapper	SDPCD-111	England	2000	18.99
Pretty Things	Freeway Madness + 4 (Gold Cd)	CD	Snapper	SDPCD-117	England	2000	18.99
Pretty Things	Get A Buzz - The Best/Fontana Years	CD	Fontana	314-521-446-2	U.S.A.	1992	24.99
Pretty Things	Get The Picture?	CD	Snapper	SMMCD-549	England	1998	9.99
Pretty Things	Get The Picture? (Gold Cd)	CD	Snapper	SDPCD-114	England	2000	18.99

P

Artist	Title	Format	Label	Catalog No	Country	Released	Value
Pretty Things	Latest Writs - Greatest Hits	CD	Snapper	128232	U.S.A.	2000	14.99
Pretty Things	Live At The Heartbreak Hotel	CD	Line	LICD-9.00075-0	Germany	1988	28.99
Pretty Things	More Electric Banana	CD	Repertoire	REP-4089-WZ	Germany	1991	14.99
Pretty Things	Out Of The Island	CD	Inak	1726-2	Germany	1987	7.99
Pretty Things	Parachute + 6 (Gold Cd)	CD	Snapper	SDPCD-110	England	2000	18.99
Pretty Things	S.F. Sorrow + 4	CD	Snapper	155652	England	1998	9.99
Pretty Things	S.F. Sorrow + 4 (Gold Cd)	CD	Snapper	SDPCD-109	England	2000	18.99
Pretty Things	Savage Eye	CD	Snapper	155602	England	1998	9.99
Pretty Things	Savage Eye (Gold Cd)	CD	Snapper	SDPCD-113	England	2000	18.99
Pretty Things	Silk Torpedo + 2 (Gold Cd)	CD	Snapper	SDPCD-112	England	2000	18.99
Pretty Things	Singles A's & B's	3CD	Repertoire	REP-4937	Germany	2002	19.99
Pretty Things	The E.P. Collection Plus....	CD	See For Miles	SEECD-476	England	1997	31.99
Pretty Things	The Pretty Things	CD	Snapper	155482	England	1998	9.99
Pretty Things	The Pretty Things (Gold Cd)	CD	Snapper	SDPCD-115	England	1999	18.99
Pretty Things	The Pretty Things Collection	CD	Line	IMCD-9.00986-0	Germany	1990	28.99
Pretty Things	The Rhythm And Blues Years	2CD	Snapper	SMDCD343	England	2001	13.99
Pretty Things/Dave Gilmour	Resurrection (SF Sorrow Live 1998)	CD	Snapper	160042	England	1998	9.99
Price, Alan	A Price On His Head 1967-1970 + 11	CD	Repertoire	REP-4612-WY	U.S.A.	1996	14.99
Price, Alan	Alan Price Anthology	2CD	Recall	SMD-CD-204	England	1997	14.99
Price, Alan	Performing Price	CD	Edsel	EDCD-673	U.S.A.	2000	14.99
Price, Alan	Price To Play + 12	CD	Edsel	EDCD-628	U.S.A.	2000	11.99
Price, Alan	Rock And Roll Night/The Royal Court	CD	Edsel	EDCD-680	U.S.A.	2001	11.99
Price, Alan	The Price to Pay 1965-1967	CD	Repertoire	REP-4611-WY	Germany	1996	14.99
Price, Alan/Animals	O Lucky Man! (O.S.T.)	CD	Warner Bros.	2710-2	U.S.A.	1973	9.99
Price, Alan/Set	French 60's EP & Sp Collection	CD	Magic	525742	France	1996	20.99
Prince	1999	CD Single	Warner Bros.	7599-23822-2	Australia	1998	5.99
Prince	1999	CD	Warner Bros.	9-23720-2	U.S.A.	1983	10.99
Prince	Alphabet St. (3")	CD Single	Warner Bros.	920-930-2	Germany	1988	43.99
Prince	Around The World In A Day	CD	Warner Bros.	32XD-5	Japan	1985	59.99
Prince	Around The World In A Day (Large)	CD	Warner Bros.	9-25286-2	U.S.A.	1985	9.99
Prince	Batman O.S.T. (Black Tin)	CD	Warner Bros.	9-25978-2	U.S.A.	1989	11.99
Prince	Come (Promo)	CD Single	Warner Bros.	PRO-902	Germany	1994	13.99
Prince	Gold (Promo)	CD Single	Warner Bros.	WO325CDDJ	England	1995	23.99
Prince	Graffiti Bridge (Promo Pic Disc)	CD	Paisley Park	9-27493-2 DJ	U.S.A.	1990	27.99
Prince	I Wish U Heave (3")	CD Single	Warner Bros.	921-074-2	France	1988	78.99
Prince	Interactive (Windows/Mac)	CD Rom	Warner Bros.	2-12001	U.S.A.	1992	13.99
Prince	Lovesexy (Tracked Version)	CD	Warner Bros.	7599-25720-2	Germany	1988	29.99
Prince	My Name Was Prince (Promo)	CD	Warner Bros.	PCS-124	Japan	1993	1,249.99
Prince	One Nite Alone Live (W/Bonus Disc)	3CD	NPG	7-85337-70702-9	U.S.A.	2002	49.99
Prince	Prince Jazz Sampler (Promo)	CD	NPG	SCD-1001	U.S.A.	2002	109.99
Prince	Prince Live In Las Vegas (Promo)	CD	Hip O	B0000995-09	U.S.A.	2003	164.99
Prince	Purple Rain	CD	Warner Bros.	9-25110-2	U.S.A.	1984	8.99
Prince	Purple Rain (Gold Cd)	CD	Warner Bros.	43P2-0004	Japan	1984	161.99
Prince	Purple Rain (O.S.T.) (Disc German)	CD	Warner Bros.	38XP-88	Japan	1984	28.99
Prince	Rave Un2... (Promo Sampler CD)	CD	BMG	BMGPROM83	Sweden	1999	53.99
Prince	Scandalous Sex Suite	CD Single	Warner Bros.	WPCR-1515	Japan	1989	34.99
Prince	Self Titled (W/Pink Inlay Not Blue)	CD	Warner Bros.	7599-27402-2	Germany	1979	69.99
Prince	Sign 'O' the Times	2CD	Paisley Park	9-25577-2	U.S.A.	1987	11.99
Prince	The Best Of	CD	Warner Bros.	8122742722	France	2001	10.99
Prince	The Black Album (Recalled Version)	CD	Warner Bros.	2-45793	U.S.A.	1991	0,999.99
Prince	The Black Album (Regular Release)	CD	Warner Bros.	2-45793	U.S.A.	1994	12.99
Prince	The Crown Jewels (Promo)	CD	Warner Bros.	SAM-1037	Germany	1992	43.99
Prince	The Gold Experience	CD	Warner Bros.	45999-2	U.S.A.	1995	14.99
Prince	The Hits/The B-Sides	3CD	Warner Bros.	9-45440-2	U.S.A.	1993	26.99
Prince	The Vault... Old Friends 4 Sale	CD	Warner Bros.	WPCR-10553	Japan	1999	45.99
Prince	The Vault... Old Friends 4 Sale (DJ)	CD	Warner Bros.	2-47522-A	U.S.A.	1999	27.99
Prince	Undertaker (Playable/Most Destroyed)	CD	Cinram Inc.	930902H	U.S.A.	1993	297.99
Prince/N.P.G.	Exodus	CD Single	NPG	NPG-6103-2	Germany	1995	29.99

P

Artist	Title	Format	Label	Catalog No	Country	Released	Value
Prince/N.P.G.	Gold Nigga (W/Guess Who's Knocking)	CD	NPG	GN-1019-12	U.S.A.	1994	155.99
Prince/N.P.G.	Gold Nigga (W/Guess Who's Knocking)	CD	NPG	NPG-GN-1019-12	U.S.A.	1993	156.99
Prince/N.P.G.	Most Beautiful Girl/World (Promo)	CD Single	NPG	PRO-72516	U.S.A.	1994	43.99
Prince/N.P.G.	Thunder	CD	Warner Bros.	W0113CDDJ	England	1991	94.99
Prince/N.P.G.	Willing And Able (Promo)	CD Single	Warner Bros.	PRO-CD-5301	U.S.A.	1991	48.99
Prine, John	Aimless Love (MFSL Silver Cd)	CD	Mobile Fidelity	MFCD-856	U.S.A.	1989	61.99
Prior, Maddy/Tim Hart	Summer Solstice	CD	Mooncrest	CRESTCD-023	England	1996	8.99
Private Life	Self Titled	CD	Warner Bros.	32P2-2388	Japan	1988	20.99
Private Life	Shadows	CD	Warner Bros.	2-25803	U.S.A.	1987	14.99
Procol Harum	30th Anniversary Anthology	3CD	West Side	WESX-301/1-3	England	1997	24.99
Procol Harum	A & B - The Singles	3CD	Repertoire	REP-4971	Germany	2002	24.99
Procol Harum	A Salty Dog (MFSL Silver Cd)	CD	Mobile Fidelity	MFCD-823	U.S.A.	1969	38.99
Procol Harum	A Salty Dog... Plus + 5	CD	West Side	WESM-534	England	1999	14.99
Procol Harum	A Whiter Shade Of Pale + 4	CD	Repertoire	REP-4666-WY	Germany	1997	15.99
Procol Harum	Broken Barricades (MFSL Silver Cd)	CD	Mobile Fidelity	MFCD-846	U.S.A.	1969	44.99
Procol Harum	Broken Barricades + 3 (Ltd # Ed.)	CD	Repertoire	REP-4980	Germany	2002	22.99
Procol Harum	Classic Tracks & Rarities: An Anthology	2CD	Metro	METRDCD502	England	2002	8.99
Procol Harum	Exotic Birds And Fruit	CD	Repertoire	REP-4917	Germany	2000	15.99
Procol Harum	First Album +10 (Whiter Shade Pale)	CD	West Side	WESM-527	England	1998	14.99
Procol Harum	Grand Hotel + 2	CD	Repertoire	REP-4916	Germany	2000	15.99
Procol Harum	Greatest Hits	CD	A&M	32454-0523-2	U.S.A.	1995	8.99
Procol Harum	Home (MFSL Silver Cd)	CD	Mobile Fidelity	MFCD-793	U.S.A.	1970	29.99
Procol Harum	Home... Plus + 9	CD	West Side	WESM-535	England	1999	14.99
Procol Harum	In Concert/Edmonton Sym. Orch. + 1	CD	Repertoire	REP-4981	Germany	2002	15.99
Procol Harum	In Concert/Edmonton Symphony	CD	Chrysalis	32-1004-2	England	1972	12.99
Procol Harum	In Concert/Orchestra (MFSL Silver Cd)	CD	Mobile Fidelity	MFCD-788	U.S.A.	1972	49.99
Procol Harum	King Biscuit (97-12), 1997	CD	DIR Network	CONOCO2XD	U.S.A.	1997	39.99
Procol Harum	Pilgrim's Progress (Audio/Video)	2CD	Master Tone	MM5117	England	1995	29.99
Procol Harum	Procol Harum + 3/Shine On Brightly	2CD	BGO	BGOCD556	England	2002	16.99
Procol Harum	Procol's Ninth	CD	Repertoire	REP-4919	Germany	2000	15.99
Procol Harum	Return Prodigal Stranger: Int. (DJ)	CD	Zoo Ent.	ZP17044-2	U.S.A.	1991	21.99
Procol Harum	Shine On Brightly + 3	CD	Repertoire	REP-4667-WY	Germany	1997	15.99
Procol Harum	Shine On Brightly...Plus + 8	CD	West Side	WESM-533	England	1998	14.99
Procol Harum	Something Magic + 2	CD	Repertoire	REP-4918	Germany	2000	15.99
Procol Harum	The Long Goodbye (Symphonic)	CD	RCA	09026-68029-2	U.S.A.	1995	9.99
Procol Harum	The Prodigal Stranger (Leatherbound)	CD	Zoo Ent.	17733-1	U.S.A.	1991	29.99
Procol Harum/L John Death	Ain't Nothin To Get Excited About	CD	Repertoire	REP-4982	Germany	2002	18.99
Procol Harum/Matthew Fisher	Journey's End/I'll Be There	CD	BGO	BGOCD505	England	2000	16.99
Procol Harum/Matthew Fisher	Matthew Fisher/Strange Days	CD	BGO	BGOCD308	England	1996	16.99
Procol Harum/Mick Grabham	Mick The Lad + 4	CD	Angel Air	SJPCD012	England	1999	14.99
Product, Clive	Financial Suicide	CD	Line	UTCD-9.00813-L	Germany	1989	13.99
Professionals	I Didn't See It Coming +8	CD	EMI	7243-5-33588-2-2	England	2001	11.99
Professionals	Professionals (Unreleased Lp + Single)	CD	Virgin	7243-8-41012-2-0	England	1997	18.99
Prophet, Chuck	No Other Love	CD	New West	NW6039	U.S.A.	2002	5.99
Psychedelic Furs	Book Of Days	CD	Columbia	CK-45412	U.S.A.	1989	6.99
Psychedelic Furs	Forever Now + 6	CD	Columbia	CK-85916	U.S.A.	2002	8.99
Psychedelic Furs	Forever Now + 6 [Adv. Promo]	CD	Columbia	AK-85916-S1	U.S.A.	2002	11.99
Psychedelic Furs	Radio One Sessions	CD	Strange Fruit	SFRSCD003	England	1997	14.99
Psychedelic Furs	Should God Forget: A Retrospective	2CD	Columbia	C2K-65152	U.S.A.	1997	11.99
Psychedelic Furs	Talk Talk Talk + 3	CD	Columbia	CK-85917	U.S.A.	2002	9.99
Psychedelic Furs	Talk Talk Talk + 3 (Adv. Promo)	CD	Columbia	AK-85917-S1	U.S.A.	2002	11.99
Psychedelic Furs	The Psychedelic Furs + 4 (U.S. Cd)	CD	Columbia	CK-85918	U.S.A.	2002	9.99
Psychedelic Furs	The Psychedelic Furs + 2 (U.K. Cd)	CD	Columbia	493343-2	England	1980	10.99
Psychedelic Furs	The Psychedelic Furs + 4 (Adv. Promo)	CD	Columbia	AK-85918-S1	U.S.A.	2002	11.99
Psychedelic Furs	Until She Comes	CD Single	Columbia	44K-73855	U.S.A.	1991	5.99
Psychedelic Furs	World Outside	CD	Columbia	CK-47303	U.S.A.	1991	5.99
Psychic-TV	Mouth Of The Night + 1	CD	Vault	VAULT-23	England	1993	18.99
Psychic-TV	Splinter Test Box Set	3CD	PTV	SYARD2/3/6	France	1993	20.99

P

Artist	Title	Format	Label	Catalog No	Country	Released	Value
Puckett, Gary/Union Gap	Looking Glass	CD	Columbia	CK-48959	U.S.A.	1992	8.99
Puckett, Gary/Union Gap	Woman, Woman/Young Girl	CD	Collectables	COL-5826	U.S.A.	1997	14.99
Pure Food And Drug Act	Choice Cuts (W/H Mandel, Don Harris)	CD	Acadia	ACA-8033	England	2002	11.99
Pure Prairie League	Bustin' Out (W/Aime)	CD	RCA	4656-2-R	U.S.A.	1990	6.99
Pure Prairie League	Can't Hold Back	CD	One Way	OW-34525	U.S.A.	1998	9.99
Pure Prairie League	Concert Classics, Vol. 1	CD	Renaissance	RRCC-0701	U.S.A.	1999	10.99
Pure Prairie League	Firin' Up	CD	Mercury	514-686-2	U.S.A.	1995	27.99
Pure Prairie League	Greatest Hits	CD	RCA	07863-67821-2	U.S.A.	1999	8.99
Pure Prairie League	If The Shoe Fits	CD	RCA	1247-2-R	U.S.A.	1990	16.99
Pure Prairie League	Live!! Takin' the Stage	CD	RCA	2404-2-R	U.S.A.	1977	24.99
Pure Prairie League	Self Titled/If The Shoe Fits	CD	Renaissance	RMED00208	U.S.A.	1997	24.99
Pure Prairie League	Something In The Night	CD	Mercury	514-684-2	U.S.A.	1994	27.99
Pure Prairie League	Songs Of Pure Harmony (Live)	CD	Alchemy	PILOT-108	England	2001	11.99
Pure Prairie League	Two Lane Highway	CD	RCA	07863-53669-2-1	U.S.A.	1993	6.99

Q

Artist	Title	Format	Label	Catalog No	Country	Released	Value
Quartett/Brass	Culloo	CD	Line	COCD-9.00919-0	Germany	1989	12.99
Quartett/Brass	More Than Four	CD	Line	COCD-9.01068-0	Germany	1991	12.99
Quatermass	Self Titled + 2	CD	Repertoire	REP-4620-WZ	Germany	1998	17.99
Quatermass II	The Long Road + 1	CD	Angel Air	SJPCD033	England	1999	14.99
Quatermass II	The Long Road + 1	CD	Pony Canyon	PCCY-01156	Japan	1997	24.99
Quatro, Suzi	Annie Get Your Gun (Suzi Quatro)	CD	First Night	OCR-CD6024	England	1986	8.99
Quatro, Suzi	Best Of The 70's	CD	Disky	DC-990302	Netherlands	2000	8.99
Quatro, Suzi	Can The Can	CD	EMI	7243-8-52351-2-2	Australia	1973	10.99
Quatro, Suzi	Greatest Hits	CD	EMI	7243-4-99506-2-7	England	2000	8.99
Quatro, Suzi	Oh, Suzi Q	CD	Alfa	ALCB-658	Japan	1996	30.99
Quatro, Suzi	Original Hits	CD	Disky	BA-860112	Netherlands	1995	10.99
Quatro, Suzi	Self Titled	CD	Toshiba-EMI	CP21-6068	Japan	1990	23.99
Quatro, Suzi	Suzi Quatro/Quatro	CD	BGO	BGOCD499	England	2000	8.99
Quatro, Suzi	The Best Of	CD	Disky	DC-87000-2	Netherlands	1998	8.99
Quatro, Suzi	The Essential Suzi Quatro	2CD	EMI	7243-8-33346-2-9	Australia	1998	14.99
Quatro, Suzi	The Gold Collection	CD	Disky	DC-870002	Netherlands	1996	13.99
Quatro, Suzi	The Wild One: Classic Quatro	CD	Razor & Tie	2102	England	1996	11.99
Quatro, Suzi	Unreleased Emotion	CD	Connoisseur	VSOP-CD-260	England	1998	27.99
Quatro, Suzi	Wake Up Little Suzi	CD	Pure Gold	905115	England	2002	8.99
Quatro, Suzi	What Goes Around	CD Single	CMC Int.	356656	Germany	1995	5.99
Quatro, Suzi	What Goes Around	CD	EMI	823159	England	2003	8.99
Quatro, Suzi	What Goes Around (Live)	CD	CMC Int.	7243-5-21615-2-2	Germany	1995	8.99
Quatro, Suzi	Your Mama Won't/Aggro-Phobia	CD	BGO	BGOCD503	England	2000	8.99
Queen	25th Ann. Crown Jewels (DJ Sampler)	CD	Hollywood	HR-61265-2	U.S.A.	1992	24.99
Queen	A Day at the Races (MFSL Gold Cd)	CD	Mobile Fidelity	UDCD-668	U.S.A.	1976	24.99
Queen	A Day At The Races + 2	CD	Hollywood	HR-61035-2	U.S.A.	1991	9.99
Queen	A Kind Of Magic + 1	CD	Hollywood	HR-61152-2	U.S.A.	1986	10.99
Queen	A Night At The Opera (DCC Gold Cd)	CD	DCC	GZS-1144	U.S.A.	2000	33.99
Queen	A Night At The Opera (MFSL Gold Cd)	CD	Mobile Fidelity	UDCD-568	U.S.A.	1975	34.99
Queen	A Night At The Opera + 2	CD	Hollywood	HR-61065-2	U.S.A.	1991	14.99
Queen	Box Of Tricks (Patch/Pin/Video/Cd)	CD	Queen Prod.	CDQTEL-0001	England	1992	55.99
Queen	CD Single Box (3")	CD Single	EMI	TODP-2251-62	Japan	1991	186.99
Queen	Classic Queen	CD	Hollywood	HR-61311-2	U.S.A.	1992	7.99
Queen	Dragon Attack (Queen Tribute)	CD	De Rock	DERCD-091	U.S.A.	1997	10.99
Queen	Flash Gordon + 1	CD	Hollywood	HR-61203-2	U.S.A.	1991	12.99
Queen	Greatest Hits (OOP Artwork)	CD	Elektra	5E-564-2	U.S.A.	1983	29.99
Queen	Greatest Hits I/II	CD	Hollywood	HR-62042-2	U.S.A.	1994	19.99

Artist	Title	Format	Label	Catalog No	Country	Released	Value
Queen	Greatest Hits III	CD	Hollywood	HR-62250-2	U.S.A.	1999	7.99
Queen	Heaven For Everyone	CD Single	Parlophone	7243-8-82533-2-1	England	1995	6.99
Queen	Hot Space	CD	Hollywood	HR-61038-2	U.S.A.	1982	7.99
Queen	Innuendo	CD	Hollywood	HR-61020-2	U.S.A.	1991	6.99
Queen	Interviews And Press Conferences	CD	Hollywood	12-BR-83-CD	U.S.A.	1994	12.99
Queen	Jazz + 2	CD	Hollywood	HR-61062-2	U.S.A.	1991	11.99
Queen	Keep Yourself Alive (Promo)	CD Single	Hollywood	PRCD-11032-2	U.S.A.	1998	12.99
Queen	Live At Wembley '86	CD	Hollywood	HR-61104-2	U.S.A.	1992	8.99
Queen	Live Killers	2CD	Hollywood	HR-61066-2	U.S.A.	1991	19.99
Queen	Live Magic	CD	Hollywood	HR-61267-2	U.S.A.	1986	7.99
Queen	Made Heaven (Queen Sidebar/Case)	CD	Hollywood	HR-62017-2	U.S.A.	1995	24.99
Queen	News Of The World (MFSL Gold Cd)	CD	Mobile Fidelity	UDCD-588	U.S.A.	1977	24.99
Queen	News Of The World + 1	CD	Hollywood	HR-61037-2	U.S.A.	1991	14.99
Queen	Princes Of The Universe	CD Single	Hollywood	7243-8-88368-0-7	Holland	2000	11.99
Queen	Queen I + 3	CD	Hollywood	HR-61064-2	U.S.A.	1991	11.99
Queen	Queen II + 3	CD	Hollywood	HR-61232-2	U.S.A.	1991	11.99
Queen	Queen In Nuce	CD	Milestone	CD/MS-1001	Italy	1973	8.99
Queen	Queen Rocks	CD	Hollywood	HR-62132-2	U.S.A.	1997	6.99
Queen	Sheer Heart Attack + 1	CD	Hollywood	HR-61036-2	U.S.A.	1991	8.99
Queen	The Crown Jewels (25 Ann. Box Set)	8CD	Hollywood	HR-622002-ST01	U.S.A.	1998	59.99
Queen	The Game (MFSL Gold Cd)	CD	Hollywood	UDCD-610	U.S.A.	1980	19.99
Queen	The Game (Target Label)	CD	Elektra	5E-513-2	U.S.A.	1983	69.99
Queen	The Game + 1	CD	Hollywood	HR-61063-2	U.S.A.	1991	14.99
Queen	The Miracle	CD	Hollywood	HR-61234-2	U.S.A.	1989	6.99
Queen	The Queen Collection Box Set	3CD	Hollywood	HR-61407-2	U.S.A.	1992	19.99
Queen	The Works	CD	Hollywood	HR-61233-2	U.S.A.	1984	8.99
Queen	The Works (Orig Pink Pressing)	CD	Capitol	7-46016-2	U.S.A.	1984	18.99
Queen	These Are The Days Of ... (Promo)	CD Single	Hollywood	PRCD-10061-2	U.S.A.	1991	24.99
Queen	We Will Rock You	CD Single	Hollywood	HB-66573-2	U.S.A.	1991	4.99
Queen	Westwood 1 Show # 94-15 (4-4-94)	2CD	Westwood 1	HMUMO10100A	U.S.A.	1994	149.99
Queen /George Bush Sr.	We Are The Champions (Promo)	CD Single	Hollywood	PRCD-8347-2	U.S.A.	1991	17.99
Queen /No Copyright On CD	We Will Rock You (No C. Of Arms/CD)	CD Single	Parlophone	7243-5-52769-2-6	Germany	2003	79.99
Queen Latifa/C Richardson	Bringing Down The House (DJ Sampler)	CD Single	Hollywood	2061-64077-2	U.S.A.	2003	5.99
Queen/Vanguard	Flash (Remixes)	CD Single	Nebula	NEBCD041	England	2003	8.99
Queensryche	Classic Masters	CD	Capitol	7243-5-42674-2	U.S.A.	2003	8.99
Queensryche	Empire (Promo Ltd Ed.)	CD	EMI	CDP-7-92806-2	U.S.A.	1990	18.99
Queensryche	Empire + 3	CD	Capitol	7243-5-81070-2	U.S.A.	2003	9.99
Queensryche	Evolution Calling Sampler (Promo)	CD	Captiol	DPRO-04686	U.S.A.	1990	39.99
Queensryche	Greatest Hits	CD	Virgin	7243-8-49422-2-9	England	2000	9.99
Queensryche	Hear In The Now Frontier + 4	CD	Capitol	7243-5-80530-2	U.S.A.	2003	6.99
Queensryche	Hear In The Now Frontier +1	CD	Toshiba-EMI	TOCP-50160	Japan	1997	17.99
Queensryche	Live Evolution	2CD	Sanctuary	06076-84523-2	U.S.A.	2001	11.99
Queensryche	Live Evolution (Digipack)	2CD	Sanctuary	06076-84525-2	U.S.A.	2001	12.99
Queensryche	Operation Mindcrime	CD	Toshiba-EMI	CP32-5618	Japan	1988	29.99
Queensryche	Operation: Live Crime + 2	CD	Capitol	7243-5-34499-2	U.S.A.	2003	11.99
Queensryche	Operation: Mindcrime + 2	CD	Capitol	7243-5-81068-2	U.S.A.	2003	9.99
Queensryche	Promised Land + 4	CD	Capitol	7243-5-80529-2	U.S.A.	2003	7.99
Queensryche	Promised Land +2	CD	Toshiba-EMI	TOCP-8396	Japan	1994	17.99
Queensryche	Q2K	CD	Atlantic	7567-83225-2	U.S.A.	1999	8.99
Queensryche	Rage For Order	CD	Toshiba-EMI	CP32-5180	Japan	1986	29.99
Queensryche	Rage For Order (Charcoal Ring 2nd Ed)	CD	Toshiba-EMI	TOCP-7608	Japan	1993	24.99
Queensryche	Rage For Order + 4	CD	Capitol	7243-5-81069-2	U.S.A.	2003	10.99
Queensryche	Revolution Calling Box (EMI/W/Bonus)	9CD	Capitol	7243-5-84198-0	U.S.A.	2003	81.99
Queensryche	Road To The Promised Land (DJ)	CD	EMI	DPRO-19985	U.S.A.	1995	74.99
Queensryche	Self Titled + 10	CD	Capitol	7243-5-80528-2	U.S.A.	2003	12.99
Queensryche	The Warning + 3	CD	Capitol	7243-5-80527-2	U.S.A.	2003	12.99
Queensryche	Tribe	CD	Sanctuary	06076-84578-2	U.S.A.	2003	14.99
Quest	Natural Selection	CD	Line	COCD-9.00748-0	Germany	1989	11.99

Artist	Title	Format	Label	Catalog No	Country	Released	Value
Quicksilver M.S./Gary Duncan	Live at Fieldstone	CD	Captain Trip	CTCD-071	Japan	1998	18.99
Quicksilver M.S./Gary Duncan	Peace By Peace + 2	CD	Captain Trip	CTCD-094	Japan	1998	18.99
Quicksilver M.S./Gary Duncan	Shape Shifter	2CD	Captain Trip	CTCD-075/76	Japan	1998	18.99
Quicksilver Messenger Service	Anthology	CD	BGO	BGOCD270	England	1995	15.99
Quicksilver Messenger Service	Classic Masters	CD	Capitol	72435-36156-2-8	U.S.A.	2002	8.99
Quicksilver Messenger Service	Comin' Thru	CD	BGO	BGOCD88	England	1991	10.99
Quicksilver Messenger Service	Happy Trails	CD	BGO	BGOCD151	England	1992	10.99
Quicksilver Messenger Service	Just For Love	CD	BGO	BGOCD141	England	1992	10.99
Quicksilver Messenger Service	Lost Silver And Gold	2CD	Collector's Choice	CCM-109-2	U.S.A.	1999	18.99
Quicksilver Messenger Service	Quicksilver	CD	BGO	BGOCD217	England	1994	10.99
Quicksilver Messenger Service	Quicksilver Messenger Service (1st Lp)	CD	Edsel	EDCD-648	England	2000	13.99
Quicksilver Messenger Service	Shady Grove	CD	Edsel	EDCD-659	England	2000	16.99
Quicksilver Messenger Service	Solid Silver	CD	Edsel	EDCD-643	England	2000	10.99
Quicksilver Messenger Service	Sons Of Mercury	2CD	Rhino	R2-70747	U.S.A.	1991	24.99
Quicksilver Messenger Service	The Best Of	CD	Capitol	COL-57263	U.S.A.	1990	8.99
Quicksilver Messenger Service	Ultimate Journey	CD	See For Miles	SEE-CD-61	England	1993	13.99
Quicksilver Messenger Service	What About Me?	CD	BGO	BGOCD58	England	1990	10.99
Quiet Riot	Alive And Well	CD	Dead Line	CLP-0489-2	U.S.A.	1999	8.99
Quiet Riot	Collection	CD	Connoisseur	VSOP-CD-333	England	2001	9.99
Quiet Riot	Condition Critical	CD	Pasha	ZK-39516	U.S.A.	1990	12.99
Quiet Riot	Down To The Bone	CD	Kamikaze	KAM-1029	Canada	1995	14.99
Quiet Riot	Greatest Hits	CD	Epic	EK-64233	U.S.A.	1996	10.99
Quiet Riot	Guilty Pleasures	CD	Bodyguard	7	U.S.A.	2001	7.99
Quiet Riot	II	CD	Sony	25AP-1192	Japan	1979	35.99
Quiet Riot	Mental Health	CD	Pasha	ZK-38443	U.S.A.	1990	10.99
Quiet Riot	Mental Health	CD	Sony	25DP-5226	Japan	1988	14.99
Quiet Riot	Mental Health + 2	CD	Sony	SK-85779	U.S.A.	2001	9.99
Quiet Riot	QR	CD	Pasha	ZK-40981	U.S.A.	1988	13.99
Quiet Riot	QR	CD	Sony	25DP-5218	Japan	1988	24.99
Quiet Riot	QR III	CD	Pasha	ZK-40321	U.S.A.	1986	11.99
Quiet Riot	QR III	CD	Sony	32DP-469	Japan	1986	14.99
Quiet Riot	Self Titled	CD	Sony	25AP-880	Japan	1978	29.99
Quiet Riot	Terrified	CD	Moonstone	28096-3102-2	U.S.A.	1993	9.99
Quiet Riot	The Randy Rhoads Years	CD	Rhino	R2-71445	U.S.A.	1993	10.99
Quiet Riot	The Randy Rhodes Years	CD	MMG Inc.	AMCY-641	Japan	1994	14.99
Quiet Riot	Winner Takes All	CD	Columbia	A-21626	U.S.A.	1990	6.99
Quine, Robert/Fred Maher	Basic	CD	Virgin	7243-8-41887-2-6	England	1984	19.99

R

R

R.E.M.	20 Years Of (Cd-R Promo/White)	CD	Warner Bros.	PRO-CD-100596	U.S.A.	2001	174.99
R.E.M.	20 Years Of (Promo/Picture Front)	CD	Warner Bros.	PRO-CD-100596	U.S.A.	2001	74.99
R.E.M.	A Joyful Noise (Interview/Live)	2CD	Warner Bros.	PRO-CD-101236	U.S.A.	2003	74.99
R.E.M.	Acoustic Songs (Promo)	CD	Warner Bros.	PRO2002-2	France	1991	59.99
R.E.M.	All The Way To Reno	CD Single	Warner Bros.	9362-42395-2	Australia	2001	9.99
R.E.M.	All The Way To Reno	CD Single	Warner Bros.	WPCR-11012	Japan	2001	22.99
R.E.M.	All The Way To Reno	CD Single	Warner Bros.	W568CDX	England	2001	7.99
R.E.M.	All The Way To Reno (Promo)	CD Single	Warner Bros.	PRO2649	England	2001	11.99
R.E.M.	All The Way To Reno (Promo)	CD Single	Warner Bros.	PRO-CD-100702	U.S.A.	2001	11.99
R.E.M.	An A.O.R. Radio Staple (Promo)	CD	I.R.S.	IRSD-SEVEN	U.S.A.	1987	99.99
R.E.M.	At My Most Beautiful	CD Single	Warner Bros.	W477CD	England	1999	7.99
R.E.M.	At My Most Beautiful	CD Single	Warner Bros.	9362-44626-2	England	1998	5.99
R.E.M.	At My Most Beautiful (3")	CD Single	Warner Bros.	W477CDX	England	1998	8.99
R.E.M.	At My Most Beautiful (3")	CD Single	Warner Bros.	W477CDX	Japan	1998	6.99

Artist	Title	Format	Label	Catalog No	Country	Released	Value
R.E.M.	At My Most Beautiful (Promo)	CD Single	Warner Bros.	PRO-CD-9744	U.S.A.	1999	11.99
R.E.M.	At My Most Beautiful (Promo)	CD Single	Warner Bros.	W477CDDJ	England	1999	8.99
R.E.M.	Automatic For The People	CD	Warner Bros.	WPCP-4970	Japan	1992	26.99
R.E.M.	Automatic for the People	CD	Warner Bros.	9-45055-2	U.S.A.	1992	8.99
R.E.M.	Automatic For The....(Wooden Box)	CD	Warner Bros.	2451222	U.S.A.	1992	17.99
R.E.M.	Bad Day	CD Single	Warner Bros.	CD16533	Canada	2003	7.99
R.E.M.	Bad Day (CD 1)	CD Single	Warner Bros.	W624CD1	England	2003	6.99
R.E.M.	Bad Day (CD 2)	CD Single	Warner Bros.	W624CD2	England	2003	6.99
R.E.M.	Bad Day (Promo)	CD Single	Warner Bros.	PRO-CD-101174	U.S.A.	2003	11.99
R.E.M.	Bad Day (Promo)	CD Single	Warner Bros.	PRO4296	Germany	2003	11.99
R.E.M.	Bang & Blame	CD Single	Warner Bros.	W0275CD	England	1994	7.99
R.E.M.	Bang & Blame	CD Single	Warner Bros.	WPCR-2176	Japan	1993	18.99
R.E.M.	Bang & Blame	CD Single	Warner Bros.	9362-41857-2	Germany	1994	7.99
R.E.M.	Bang & Blame	CD Single	Warner Bros.	941857-2	U.S.A.	1994	10.99
R.E.M.	Bang & Blame	CD Single	Warner Bros.	9-41857-2	U.S.A.	1994	5.99
R.E.M.	Bang & Blame (Promo)	CD Single	Warner Bros.	WPCR-163	Japan	1994	18.99
R.E.M.	Bang & Blame (Promo)	CD Single	Warner Bros.	PRO-CD-7271-R	U.S.A.	1994	12.99
R.E.M.	Berry, Buck, Mills, Stipe (Promo)	CD	Warner Bros.	PCS105	Japan	1992	274.99
R.E.M.	Best Of: In Time 1986 - 2003	CD	Warner Bros.	9362-48381-2	England	2003	34.99
R.E.M.	Best Of: In Time 1986 - 2003	2CD	Warner Bros.	2-48550	U.S.A.	2003	34.99
R.E.M.	Best Of: In Time 1986 - 2003 (DJ)	CD	Warner Bros.	PRO4346	England	2003	21.99
R.E.M.	Best Of: In Time 1988-2003	2CD	Warner Bros.	WPCR-11701/2	Japan	2003	59.99
R.E.M.	Birth Of A Monster (Interview Disc)	CD	RPM	VP-001	England	1994	7.99
R.E.M.	Bittersweet Me	CD Single	Warner Bros.	WPCR-922	Japan	1996	21.99
R.E.M.	Bittersweet Me	CD Single	Warner Bros.	W0377CDX)	England	1996	7.99
R.E.M.	Bittersweet Me	CD Single	Warner Bros.	9-17490-2	U.S.A.	1996	4.99
R.E.M.	Bittersweet Me (Promo)	CD Single	Warner Bros.	PRO-CD-8462	U.S.A.	1996	9.99
R.E.M.	Bittersweet Me (Promo)	CD Single	Warner Bros.	PRCD430	Germany	1996	27.99
R.E.M.	Bittersweet Me (Promo)	CD Single	Warner Bros.	PRO2096	France	1996	29.99
R.E.M.	Bittersweet Me (Promo)	CD Single	Warner Bros.	W0377CDDJ	England	1996	14.99
R.E.M.	Bittersweet Me (Promo)	CD Single	Warner Bros.	PRO-CD-8476	U.S.A.	1996	7.99
R.E.M.	Close Up	CD	Baktabak	CBAK-4090	England	1995	5.99
R.E.M.	Crush With Eyeliner	CD Single	Warner Bros.	9-41904-2	U.S.A.	1994	5.99
R.E.M.	Crush With Eyeliner (Promo)	CD Single	Warner Bros.	W0281CDDJ	England	1995	21.99
R.E.M.	Crush With Eyeliner (Promo)	CD Single	Warner Bros.	PRO-CD-7781-R	U.S.A.	1995	9.99
R.E.M.	Crush With Eyeliner (Promo)	CD Single	Warner Bros.	PRO-CD-7455-R	U.S.A.	1995	9.99
R.E.M.	Daysleeper	CD Single	Warner Bros.	W0455CD	Germany	1998	5.99
R.E.M.	Daysleeper	CD Single	Warner Bros.	9-17129-2	U.S.A.	1998	9.99
R.E.M.	Daysleeper (Promo)	CD Single	Warner Bros.	PRO-CD-9486	U.S.A.	1998	9.99
R.E.M.	Daysleeper (Promo)	CD Single	Warner Bros.	PRO-00050	Germany	1998	5.99
R.E.M.	Daysleeper (Promo)	CD Single	Warner Bros.	PRO-CD-9482	U.S.A.	1998	7.99
R.E.M.	Dead Letter Office + 2	CD	I.R.S.	0777-7-13199-2-1	Holland	1993	12.99
R.E.M.	Document	CD	I.R.S.	32DP-842	Japan	1990	20.99
R.E.M.	Document + 6	CD	I.R.S.	0777-7-13200-2-6	England	1993	9.99
R.E.M.	Document/Life's Rich Pageant	2CD	EMI	5817792	England	2003	18.99
R.E.M.	Drive	CD Single	Warner Bros.	9362-40633-2	U.S.A.	1992	6.99
R.E.M.	Drive	CD Single	Warner Bros.	9362-40634-2	U.S.A.	1992	8.99
R.E.M.	Drive	CD Single	Warner Bros.	9-18729-2	U.S.A.	1992	9.99
R.E.M.	Drive (Promo)	CD Single	Warner Bros.	PRO-CD-5700	U.S.A.	1992	14.99
R.E.M.	E-Bow The Letter	CD Single	Warner Bros.	W0369CDX	England	1996	8.99
R.E.M.	E-Bow The Letter	CD Single	Warner Bros.	9362-43763-2	Germany	1996	8.99
R.E.M.	E-Bow The Letter	CD Single	Warner Bros.	9-17529-2	U.S.A.	1996	5.99
R.E.M.	E-Bow The Letter (Promo)	CD Single	Warner Bros.	PRO-CD-8400	U.S.A.	1996	12.99
R.E.M.	Electrolite	CD Single	Warner Bros.	WPCR-2182	Japan	1998	18.99
R.E.M.	Electrolite	CD Single	Larner Bros.	9-43810-2	U.S.A.	1997	4.99
R.E.M.	Electrolite (Promo)	CD Single	Warner Bros.	PRO-CD-8575	U.S.A.	1996	14.99
R.E.M.	Electrolite (Promo)	CD Single	Warner Bros.	W0383CDDJ	England	1996	7.99
R.E.M.	Eponymous	CD	Toshiba-EMI	TOCP-51082	Japan	1998	34.99

R

Artist	Title	Format	Label	Catalog No	Country	Released	Value
R.E.M.	Eponymous	CD	I.R.S.	466338-2	Austria	1988	9.99
R.E.M.	Everybody Hurts	CD Single	Warner Bros.	9362-40867-9	Germany	1993	15.99
R.E.M.	Everybody Hurts (CD 1)	CD Single	Warner Bros.	W0169CD1	England	1993	11.99
R.E.M.	Everybody Hurts (CD 1)	CD Single	Warner Bros.	9-40989-2	U.S.A.	1993	4.99
R.E.M.	Everybody Hurts (CD 2)	CD Single	Warner Bros.	W0169CD3	England	1993	11.99
R.E.M.	Everybody Hurts (CD 2)	CD Single	Warner Bros.	9-40992-2	U.S.A.	1993	4.99
R.E.M.	Everybody Hurts (Promo)	CD Single	Warner Bros.	PRO-CD-5900	U.S.A.	1993	22.99
R.E.M.	Fables Of The Reconstruction + 5	CD	I.R.S.	0777-7-13160-2-9	Holland	1992	12.99
R.E.M.	Fan Club Holiday Single	CD Single	Warner Bros.	ECD02	U.S.A.	2001	44.99
R.E.M.	Finest Worksong (End World/Time)	CD Single	I.R.S.	DIRM161	England	1988	62.99
R.E.M.	Get Up (Promo)	CD Single	Warner Bros.	PRO-CD-3716	U.S.A.	1988	34.99
R.E.M.	Green	CD	Warner Bros.	25P2-2389	Japan	1988	26.99
R.E.M.	Green (Promo Leatherbound)	CD	Warner Bros.	PRO-CD-3292	U.S.A.	1988	84.99
R.E.M.	Green/New Adventures In Hi-Fi	2CD	Warner Bros.	WE-872	France	1998	20.99
R.E.M.	Half A World Away	CD Single	Warner Bros.	PRO-CD-5798	U.S.A.	1992	37.99
R.E.M.	I Don't Sleep, I Dream (Promo)	CD Single	Warner Bros.	PRO-CD-7532-R	U.S.A.	1995	7.99
R.E.M.	I Took Your Name (Promo)	CD Single	Warner Bros.	PRO-CD-7894	U.S.A.	1995	24.99
R.E.M.	Ignoreland (Promo)	CD Single	Warner Bros.	PRO-CD-5844	U.S.A.	1992	22.99
R.E.M.	Ignoreland (Promo)	CD Single	Warner Bros.	PRO1650	Germany	1992	21.99
R.E.M.	I'll Take The Rain	CD	Warner Bros.	9362-42414-2	Germany	2001	8.99
R.E.M.	I'll Take The Rain (CD 1)	CD Single	Warner Bros.	W573CD	England	2001	11.99
R.E.M.	I'll Take The Rain (CD 2)	CD Single	Warner Bros.	W573CDX	England	2001	11.99
R.E.M.	I'll Take The Rain (Promo)	CD Single	Warner Bros.	PRO2802	England	2001	14.99
R.E.M.	I'll Take The Rain (Promo)	CD Single	Warner Bros.	PRO-2784	Germany	2001	14.99
R.E.M.	Imitation Of Life	CD Single	Warner Bros.	W559CD	England	2001	7.99
R.E.M.	Imitation Of Life	CD Single	Warner Bros.	WPCR11011	Japan	2001	21.99
R.E.M.	Imitation Of Life	CD Single	Warner Bros.	9362-44999-2	England	2001	4.99
R.E.M.	Imitation Of Life	CD Single	Warner Bros.	9-42363-2	U.S.A.	2001	3.99
R.E.M.	Imitation Of Life (Promo)	CD Single	Warner Bros.	PROCDR-100588	U.S.A.	2001	11.99
R.E.M.	Imitation Of Life (Promo)	CD Single	Warner Bros.	PRO-CD-100567	U.S.A.	2001	14.99
R.E.M.	Imitation Of Life (Promo)	CD Single	Warner Bros.	PRO2483	Germany	2001	12.99
R.E.M.	Imitation Of Life (Promo)	CD Single	Warner Bros.	CDWP056	Brazil	2001	47.99
R.E.M.	It's The End Of The World.... (CD 1)	CD Single	Warner Bros.	DIRM146	England	1987	16.99
R.E.M.	It's The End Of The World.... (CD 2)	CD Single	IRS	DIRMX-180	England	1987	19.99
R.E.M.	It's The End...(B/W Promo Sleeve)	CD Single	I.R.S.	DIRM-146	England	1987	57.99
R.E.M.	It's The End.....(Promo)	CD Single	I.R.S.	CD45-17476	U.S.A.	1987	24.99
R.E.M.	Lifes Rich Pageant + 6	CD	I.R.S.	0777-7-13201-2-5	Holland	1993	13.99
R.E.M.	Live For 99 X (Promo)	CD	Warner Bros.	PRO-CD-100721	U.S.A.	2001	149.99
R.E.M.	Losing My Religion	CD Single	Warner Bros.	W0015CD	England	1991	21.99
R.E.M.	Losing My Religion	CD Single	Warner Bros.	9362-40399-2	Holland	1991	16.99
R.E.M.	Losing My Religion	CD Single	Warner Bros.	9362-40037-2	Germany	1997	12.99
R.E.M.	Losing My Religion (Live Promo)	CD Single	Warner Bros.	PRO-CD-4881	U.S.A.	1991	21.99
R.E.M.	Losing My Religion (Promo)	CD Single	Warner Bros.	PRO-CD-4707	U.S.A.	1991	24.99
R.E.M.	Lotus	CD Single	Warner Bros.	9362-44601-2	England	1998	6.99
R.E.M.	Lotus (3")	CD Single	Warner Bros.	W466CDX	England	1998	9.99
R.E.M.	Lotus (Promo)	CD Single	Warner Bros.	PRO-CD-9575	U.S.A.	1998	12.99
R.E.M.	Lotus (Promo)	CD Single	Warner Bros.	PRO1118	England	1998	12.99
R.E.M.	Man On The Moon	CD Single	Warner Bros.	9362-40698-2	Germany	1992	4.99
R.E.M.	Man On The Moon (CD 1)	CD Single	Warner Bros.	W0143CD	England	1992	7.99
R.E.M.	Man On The Moon (CD 2)	CD Single	Warner Bros.	W0143CDX	England	1992	7.99
R.E.M.	Man On The Moon (Promo)	CD Single	Warner Bros.	PRO-CD-5894	U.S.A.	1992	12.99
R.E.M.	Man On The Moon (Promo)	CD Single	Warner Bros.	PRO-CD-5894	U.S.A.	1993	14.99
R.E.M.	Man On The Moon (Promo)	CD Single	Warner Bros.	PRO-CD-100021	U.S.A.	1992	31.99
R.E.M.	Monster	CD	Warner Bros.	9-45740-2	U.S.A.	1994	6.99
R.E.M.	Monster (Ltd Hardback Book/Cd)	CD	Labner Bros.	45763-2	U.S.A.	1994	29.99
R.E.M.	Monster (Promo)	CD-Rom	Warner Bros.	MAC-FORMAT	U.S.A.	1994	69.99
R.E.M.	Monster (Promo)	CD-Rom	Warner Bros.	WIN-FORMAT	U.S.A.	1994	39.99
R.E.M.	Monster (W/Sticker)	CD	Warner Bros.	WPCR-101	Japan	1994	32.99

Artist	Title	Format	Label	Catalog No	Country	Released	Value
R.E.M.	Monster/New Adventures In Hi-Fi	2CD	Warner Bros.	9362481242	Australia	2001	20.99
R.E.M.	Murmur (MFSL Gold Cd)	CD	Mobile Fidelity	UDCD-642	U.S.A.	1983	25.99
R.E.M.	Murmur + 4	CD	I.R.S.	0777-7-13158-2-4	Holland	1992	12.99
R.E.M.	Music Between Tours (Promo)	CD	Warner Bros.	PRO-986	Germany	1995	74.99
R.E.M.	Music From Tourfilm (Promo Gold)	CDV	Warner Bros.	PRO-CDV-4460	U.S.A.	1990	10.99
R.E.M.	Near Wild Heaven	CD Single	Warner Bros.	9362-40178-2	Germany	1991	8.99
R.E.M.	Near Wild Heaven	CD Single	Warner Bros.	W0055CDX	Germany	1991	14.99
R.E.M.	Near Wild Heaven (Promo)	CD Single	Warner Bros.	PRO-CD-5058	U.S.A.	1991	18.99
R.E.M.	New Adv. In Hi-Fi (Deluxe Ed.)	CD	Warner Bros.	9-46321-2	U.S.A.	1996	44.99
R.E.M.	New Adventures in Hi-Fi	CD	Warner Bros.	9-46320-2	U.S.A.	1996	8.99
R.E.M.	New Adventures In Hi-Fi	CD	Warner Bros.	WPCR-801	Japan	1996	44.99
R.E.M.	New Adventures In...(DJ Viewmaster)	CD	Warner Bros.	9-46320-1	U.S.A.	1996	34.99
R.E.M.	New Adventures...(Ltd Deluxe DJ Ed)	CD	Warner Bros.	2-46321-DJ	U.S.A.	1996	61.99
R.E.M.	Night Test Leper	CD Single	Warner Bros.	PRCD578	Germany	1996	64.99
R.E.M.	Nightswimming	CD Single	Warner Bros.	9362-40976-2	England	1993	7.99
R.E.M.	Nightswimming	CD Single	Warner Bros.	9362-40986-2	Germany	1993	7.99
R.E.M.	Nightswimming	CD Single	Warner Bros.	W0184CD	England	1993	7.99
R.E.M.	Not Bad For No Tour (Promo)	CD	Warner Bros.	PRO-CD-100727	U.S.A.	2001	31.99
R.E.M.	Orange Crush (3")	CD Single	Warner Bros.	W2960CD	Germany	1989	37.99
R.E.M.	Orange Crush (Promo)	CD Single	Warner Bros.	PRO-CD-3306	U.S.A.	1988	14.99
R.E.M.	Originals (Chronic/Murmur/Reckoning)	3CD	EMI	7243-8-35088-2-2	England	1995	24.99
R.E.M.	Out Of Time	CD	Warner Bros.	9-26496-2	U.S.A.	1991	8.99
R.E.M.	Out Of Time	CD	Warner Bros.	WPCP-4195	Japan	1991	24.99
R.E.M.	Out Of Time (Folio W/10 Postcards)	CD	Warner Bros.	926527-2	U.S.A.	1991	29.99
R.E.M.	Out Of Time/Warners 1 Coll (Bonus Cd)	2CD	Warner Bros.	26496-2	Singapore	2001	44.99
R.E.M.	Pop Song '89 (Promo)	CD Single	Warner Bros.	PRO-CD-3357	U.S.A.	1989	14.99
R.E.M.	Pop Songs 89-99 (Promo)	CD	Warner Bros.	SAM-00132	England	1998	39.99
R.E.M.	R.A.I.N.N. (PSA) Promo	CD	Atlantic	PRCD-6032-2	U.S.A.	1994	29.99
R.E.M.	R.E.M. In The Attic	CD	Capitol	72438-21684-2-3	U.S.A.	1997	14.99
R.E.M.	R.E.M.IX (Promo)	CD	Warner Bros.	PRO-CD-100885	U.S.A.	2002	29.99
R.E.M.	Radio Song	CD Single	Warner Bros.	9362-40251-2	U.S.A.	1991	7.99
R.E.M.	Radio Song	CD Single	Warner Bros.	9-40229-2	U.S.A.	1991	7.99
R.E.M.	Radio Song	CD Single	Warner Bros.	W0072CDX	England	1991	10.99
R.E.M.	Radio Song (Promo)	CD Single	Warner Bros.	PRO-CD-4808	U.S.A.	1991	11.99
R.E.M.	Reckoning (MFSL Gold Cd)	CD	Mobile Fidelity	UDCD-677	U.S.A.	1984	19.99
R.E.M.	Reckoning + 5	CD	I.R.S.	0777-7-13159-2-3	U.S.A.	1984	12.99
R.E.M.	Reveal	CD	Warner Bros.	9362-47946-2	England	2001	10.99
R.E.M.	Reveal	CD	Warner Bros.	WPCR-11010	Japan	2001	39.99
R.E.M.	Reveal	CDV	Warner Bros.	PROP05210	Germany	2001	22.99
R.E.M.	Reveal (Limited Edition Large Size)	CD	Warner Bros.	9-48078-2	U.S.A.	2001	12.99
R.E.M.	Sampler (Promo)	CD	Warner Bros.	PROCD6828-R	U.S.A.	1992	11.99
R.E.M.	Sampler/The Best Of R.E.M.	CD	I.R.S.	REM1	England	1992	114.99
R.E.M.	Shinny Happy People	CD Single	Warner Bros.	W0027CD	England	1991	11.99
R.E.M.	Shinny Happy People (Promo)	CD Single	Warner Bros.	PRO-CD-5060	U.S.A.	1991	38.99
R.E.M.	Shinny Happy People (Promo)	CD Single	Warner Bros.	PRO-CD-4888	U.S.A.	1991	12.99
R.E.M.	Shiny Chatty People	CD	Baktabak	CBAK-4041	England	1991	7.99
R.E.M.	Shiny Happy People	CD Single	Warner Bros.	9362-40079-2	Germany	1991	5.99
R.E.M.	Shiny Happy People	CD Single	Warner Bros.	9362-40078-2	Germany	1991	5.99
R.E.M.	Should We Talk About... (Promo)	CD	Warner Bros.	PRO-CD-3377	U.S.A.	1988	29.99
R.E.M.	Sidewinder (CD 1)	CD Single	Warner Bros.	W0152CD1	England	1993	8.99
R.E.M.	Sidewinder (Promo)	CD Single	Warner Bros.	PRO-2007-2	France	1992	46.99
R.E.M.	Sidewinder (Promo)	CD Single	Warner Bros.	PRO-CD-5903	U.S.A.	1993	14.99
R.E.M.	Singles Collected	CD	I.R.S.	7243-829642-2-3	Holland	1994	12.99
R.E.M.	Songs That Are Live (Promo)	CD Single	Warner Bros.	PRO-CD-7888	U.S.A.	1995	13.99
R.E.M.	Sponge (Promo)	CD Single	Columbia	CSK8219	U.S.A.	1996	19.99
R.E.M.	Stand (3" CD 1)	CD Single	Warner Bros.	W2833CDX	England	1989	59.99
R.E.M.	Stand (3" CD 2)	CD Single	Warner Bros.	W2833CD	England	1989	27.99
R.E.M.	Stand (3"/Maple Leaf Shaped)	CD Single	Warner Bros.	W7577CDX	England	1989	29.99

R

Artist	Title	Format	Label	Catalog No	Country	Released	Value
R.E.M.	Stand (Promo)	CD Single	Warner Bros.	PRO-CD-3353	U.S.A.	1989	14.99
R.E.M.	Strange Currencies	CD Single	Warner Bros.	9362-43513-2	England	1994	6.99
R.E.M.	Strange Currencies	CD Single	Warner Bros.	W0290CD	England	1995	7.99
R.E.M.	Strange Currencies	CD Single	Warner Bros.	WPCR-2178	Japan	1998	24.99
R.E.M.	Strange Currencies	CD Single	Warner Bros.	943513-2	U.S.A.	1994	10.99
R.E.M.	Strange Currencies	CD Single	Warner Bros.	9362-43513-2	Germany	1995	9.99
R.E.M.	Strange Currencies (Promo)	CD Single	Warner Bros.	PRO-6010	Germany	1995	24.99
R.E.M.	Strange Currencies (Promo)	CD Single	Warner Bros.	PRO-CD-7510	U.S.A.	1995	13.99
R.E.M.	Strange Currencies (Promo)	CD Single	Warner Bros.	W0290CD-DJ	England	1995	14.99
R.E.M.	Suspicion	CD Single	Warner Bros.	9362-44711-2	U.S.A.	1998	4.99
R.E.M.	Suspicion	CD Single	Warner Bros.	W488CD	England	1999	7.99
R.E.M.	Suspicion (3" Cd)	CD Single	Warner Bros.	0-5439-16940-9-6	Germany	1998	12.99
R.E.M.	Suspicion (3")	CD Single	Warner Bros.	W488CDX	Japan	1999	6.99
R.E.M.	Suspicion (Promo)	CD Single	Warner Bros.	W488CDDJ	England	1999	11.99
R.E.M.	Texarkana (Promo)	CD Single	Warner Bros.	PRO-CD-4826	U.S.A.	1991	29.99
R.E.M.	The Alternative Radio Sampler (DJ)	CD	Warner Bros.	CD-REM-92	England	1992	274.99
R.E.M.	The Automatic Box	4CD	Warner Bros.	9362-41268-2	Germany	1993	87.99
R.E.M.	The Best Of	CD	I.R.S.	DIRMH1	England	1991	11.99
R.E.M.	The Best Of: The IRS Years	CD	I.R.S.	7131282	France	1991	11.99
R.E.M.	The Great Beyond	CD Single	Warner Bros.	CD-44816	U.S.A.	1999	4.99
R.E.M.	The Great Beyond	CD Single	Warner Bros.	W516CD	England	1999	7.99
R.E.M.	The Great Beyond (Digipack Or Case)	CD Single	Warner Bros.	CD-44812	U.S.A.	1999	6.99
R.E.M.	The Great Beyond (Promo)	CD Single	Warner Bros.	PRO-CD-4218	U.S.A.	1999	14.99
R.E.M.	The Great Beyond (Promo)	CD Single	Warner Bros.	PRO-CD-4220-R	U.S.A.	1999	12.99
R.E.M.	The One I Love	CD Single	I.R.S.	2045372	Holland	1987	10.99
R.E.M.	The One I Love	CD Single	I.R.S.	DIRMX178	England	1988	26.99
R.E.M.	The One I Love	CD Single	I.R.S.	DIRM146	England	1987	44.99
R.E.M.	The R.E.M. Singles Collection	4CD	Warner Bros.	9362-40313-2	Germany	1991	87.99
R.E.M.	The R.E.M. Singles Collection	4CD	Warner Bros.	WPCP-4781~4	Japan	1992	129.99
R.E.M.	The Unauthorised Biography Of	CD	Chrome Dreams	ABCD-087	England	2001	7.99
R.E.M.	The Wake Up Bomb	CD Single	Warner Bros.	PRO-CD-8584	U.S.A.	1996	21.99
R.E.M.	This Book Is On	CD Single	Sonic Book	SIAE-SONIC.027	Italy	2001	19.99
R.E.M.	Tongue	CD Single	Warner Bros.	9362-43577-2	England	1995	5.99
R.E.M.	Tongue (Promo)	CD Single	Warner Bros.	SAM1504	England	1995	10.99
R.E.M.	Tongue (Promo)	CD Single	Warner Bros.	PRO-CD-7875-R	U.S.A.	1995	9.99
R.E.M.	Tongue (Promo)	CD Single	Warner Bros.	PRO-6053	Germany	1995	11.99
R.E.M.	Turn You Inside Out (Promo)	CD Single	Warner Bros.	PRO-CD-3446	U.S.A.	1988	24.99
R.E.M.	Up	CD	Warner Bros.	9-47112-2	U.S.A.	1999	8.99
R.E.M.	Up	CD Single	Warner Bros.	WPCR-2400	Japan	1998	34.99
R.E.M.	Up (Ltd 48 Page Book/Cd)	CD	Warner Bros.	9362-47151-2	U.S.A.	1998	24.99
R.E.M.	Up (Promo)	CD	Warner Bros.	WPCD-2400	Japan	1998	54.99
R.E.M.	Up (Promo)	CD	Warner Bros.	PROP00029	Germany	1998	34.99
R.E.M.	Up/New Adventures In Hi-Fi	2CD	Warner Bros.	936247832	Australia	2000	20.99
R.E.M.	Wake Up Bomb (Numbered Promo)	CD	Warner Bros.	PCS-231	Japan	1996	116.99
R.E.M.	What The Frequency...(Promo)	CD Single	Warner Bros.	PRO-CD-7155	U.S.A.	1994	9.99
R.E.M.	What's The Frequency Kenneth?	CD Single	Warner Bros.	9-41760-2	U.S.A.	1994	4.99
R.E.M.	What's The Frequency, Kenneth?	CD Single	Warner Bros.	9-18050-2	U.S.A.	1994	4.99
R.E.M.	What's The Frequency...	CD Single	Warner Bros.	WE739	England	1994	5.99
R.E.M.	What's The Frequency....	CD Single	Warner Bros.	W0265CD	England	1994	9.99
R.E.M./Hindu Love Gods	Self Titled (W/Warren Zevon)	CD	Giant	9-24406-2	U.S.A.	1990	34.99
R.E.M./Patti Smith	E-Bow The...(Promo/Also PRCD-3458)	CD Single	Warner Bros.	PRO6192	Germany	1996	9.99
R.E.M./Posies/Big Star	The Minus Five	CD	Hello Club	HEL-312-41	U.S.A.	1993	74.99
R.E.M./String Quartet	Tribute To R.E.M.	CD	Vitamin	CD-8517	U.S.A.	1999	4.99
Rabbitt, Eddie	Step By Step	CD	Liberty	C2-90531	Canada	1990	37.99
Rabbitt/John Bundrick	Boys Will Be Boys!	CD	Line	JECD-9.00859-0	Germany	1989	14.99
Rabbitt/John Bundrick	Dream Jungle (W/David Gilmour)	CD	Red Steel	RMCCD9221	England	1995	24.99
Rabbitt/John Bundrick	Run For Cover	CD	Red Steel	RMCCD0198	England	1995	24.99
Rabbitt/John Bundrick	Same Old Story	CD	Red Steel	RMCCD0183	England	1995	24.99

Artist	Title	Format	Label	Catalog No	Country	Released	Value
Rabbitt/John Bundrick	Tour Guide	CD	Red Steel	RMCCD0204	England	1995	24.99
Rabin, Trevor	90124	CD	Voiceprint	VP263CD	England	2003	12.99
Rabin, Trevor	Armageddon (O.S.T.)	CD	Columbia	CK-69689	U.S.A.	1998	9.99
Rabin, Trevor	Beginnings (Debut 1978 LP)	CD	Voiceprint	VP254CD	England	2002	12.99
Rabin, Trevor	Can't Look Away	CD	Elektra	9-60781-2	U.S.A.	1989	8.99
Rabin, Trevor	Deep Blue Sea (O.S.T.)	CD	Varese	VSD-6063	U.S.A.	1999	8.99
Rabin, Trevor	Enemy Of The State (O.S.T.)	CD	Hollywood	HR-62160-2	U.S.A.	1998	9.99
Rabin, Trevor	Face To Face	CD	One Way	OW-33659	U.S.A.	1980	10.99
Rabin, Trevor	Gone In 60 Seconds (O.S.T.)	CD	Varese	VSD-6182	U.S.A.	1999	11.99
Rabin, Trevor	Live In L.A.	CD	Voiceprint	VP256CD	England	2003	12.99
Rabin, Trevor	One (O.S.T.)	CD	Varese	VSD-6310	U.S.A.	2001	14.99
Rabin, Trevor	Trevor Rabin	CD	One Way	OW-33658	U.S.A.	1978	10.99
Rabin, Trevor	Wolf (Associate Prod By Ray Davies)	CD	One Way	OW-33660	U.S.A.	1981	10.99
Rabin, Trevor/Mark Macina	Con Air	CD	Hollywood	HR-62099-2	U.S.A.	1997	8.99
Radha Krsna Temple	The Radha Krsna Temple London + 1	CD	Capitol	0777-7-81255-2-5	U.S.A.	1993	15.99
Radio Birdman	Living Eyes (W/More Fun Ep Cd)	2CD	Citadel	CTCD551	Australia	2002	18.99
Radio Birdman	Radios Appear (Burn My Eye Ep Cd)	2CD	Citadel	CITCD-550	Australia	2002	18.99
Radio Birdman	Radios Appear (Overseas U.S. Version)	CD	Trafalgar	229255958-2	Australia	1988	29.99
Radio Birdman	Radios Apper With Burn My Eye EP	2CD	Red Eye	RED-CD-49	Australia	1995	22.99
Radio Birdman	Ritualism (Live Reunion)	CD	Citadel	CSR-001	Australia	1996	11.99
Radio Birdman	Ritualism Large Spec. Ed.	CD	Citadel	CSR-01	Australia	1996	29.99
Radio Birdman	The EP's	CD	Trafalgar	450990743-2	Australia	1992	24.99
Radio Birdman	The Essential Radio Birdman	CD	Sub Pop	SPCD-553	U.S.A.	2001	11.99
Radio Birdman	Under The Ashes	2CD	Trafalgar	255991-2	Australia	1988	46.99
Radiohead	Airbag / How Am I Drivin	CD	Capitol	7243-8-58701-2-5	U.S.A.	1998	39.99
Radiohead	Amnesiac (Leatherbound Bk Cd)	CD	Parlophone	7243-532767-2-0	Holland	2001	18.99
Radiohead	Amnesiac Sampler (Promo)	CD	EMI	AMNESIAC-01	England	2001	19.99
Radiohead	Bends (Plays Planet Telex/Destroyed)	CD Single	Parlophone	7243-8831155-6	England	1996	95.99
Radiohead	Bends + 2 (When I Like...DJ/Mistake)	CD	Toshiba-EMI	TOCP-8489	Japan	1995	154.99
Radiohead	College Karma EP (Promo)	CD	Capitol	7087-6-12073-2-3	U.S.A.	1997	18.99
Radiohead	Creep	CD Single	Toshiba-EMI	TOCP-8129	Japan	1993	17.99
Radiohead	Creep (Black Sessions/200/Promo)	CD Single	EMI	8806792	France	1993	224.99
Radiohead	Drill E.P. (Only 3000)	CD Single	EMI	CDR6312	England	1993	167.99
Radiohead	Fake Plastic Trees	CD Single	Capitol	7243-8-58424-2-9	U.S.A.	1995	28.99
Radiohead	I Might Be Wrong: Live (Fold Out Cvr)	CD	Capitol	7243-5-36616-2-5	U.S.A.	2001	9.99
Radiohead	Itch	CD	Toshiba-EMI	TOCP-8285	Japan	1994	28.99
Radiohead	Karma Police (Promo)	CD Single	Capitol	7087-6-12804-2-5	U.S.A.	1997	10.99
Radiohead	Kid A (Deluxe Ed. Cd)	CD	Capitol	7243-5-29684-2-8	U.S.A.	2000	14.99
Radiohead	Knives Out	CD Single	Capitol	7243-8-77668-0-8	U.S.A.	2001	8.99
Radiohead	Let Down (Promo)	CD Single	Toshiba-EMI	PCD-0849	Japan	1997	79.99
Radiohead	My Iron Lung	CD	Parlophone	7243-8-31478-2-3	Italy	1994	18.99
Radiohead	Not My Fault: Live KCRW (Promo)	CD	Capitol	7087-6-18082-2-3	U.S.A.	2003	124.99
Radiohead	OK Computer	CD	Captiol	7243-8-55229-2-5	U.S.A.	1997	10.99
Radiohead	Pablo Honey	CD	Capitol	0777-7-81409-2-4	U.S.A.	1993	8.99
Radiohead	Pyramid Song	CD Single	Toshiba-EMI	TOCP-61053	Japan	2001	23.99
Radiohead	Sampler 7 Titres (Promo)	CD	EMI	7243-527645-2-5	France	2003	87.99
Radiohead	Street Spirit (Fade Out) (Disc 2)	CD Single	Parlophone	7243-8-82522-2-5	England	1996	8.99
Radiohead	The Bends + 2	CD	Toshiba-EMI	TOCP-8489	Japan	1995	32.99
Radner, Gilda	Gilda Radner Live From New York	CD	Warner Bros.	9-45695-2	U.S.A.	1979	7.99
Rafferty, Gerry	Another World (W/Mark Knopfler)	CD	Pinnacle	HYP3218	England	2003	13.99
Rafferty, Gerry	Can I Have My Money Back?	CD	Line	TACD-9.00553-0	Germany	1988	14.99
Rafferty, Gerry	City to City (DCC Gold Cd)	CD	DCC	GZS-1075	U.S.A.	1995	59.99
Rafferty, Gerry	Hearts Run Dry	CD Single	Polydor	887-751-2	Germany	1988	12.99
Rafferty, Gerry	Night Owl	CD	EMI	CDP-7-46610-2	England	1979	39.99
Rafferty, Gerry	North And South	CD	Polydor	835-449-2	U.S.A.	1988	21.99
Rafferty, Gerry	On A Wing & A Prayer	CD	Polydor	517-238-2	Germany	1992	10.99
Rafferty, Gerry	Over My Head	CD	Polydor	523-599-2	Germany	1994	13.99
Rafferty, Gerry	Right Down The Line - The Best Of	CD	EMI	7-93264-2	U.S.A.	1989	9.99

R

Artist	Title	Format	Label	Catalog No	Country	Released	Value
Rafferty, Gerry	Shipyard Town	CD Single	Polydor	887-415-2	Germany	1988	12.99
Rafferty, Gerry	Sleepwalking (W/Red Box)	CD	EMI	724357608824	EU	2000	16.99
Rafferty, Gerry	The Very Best Of Gerry Rafferty	CD	Polygram T.V.	529-279-2	England	1995	19.99
Rain Parade	Emergency Third Rail../Explosions In...	CD	Restless	7-70019-2	U.S.A.	1984	12.99
Rain Parade	Perfume River (Live Ltd. 1,000)	CD	Rainfall	CLOUD006	England	2002	19.99
Rainbow	20th Century Masters: The Millennium	CD	Polydor	314-549-138-2	U.S.A.	2000	8.99
Rainbow	All Night Long: An Introduction	CD	Polydor	589-652-2	England	2002	11.99
Rainbow	Bent Out Of Shape	CD	Polydor	314-547-367-2	U.S.A.	1999	8.99
Rainbow	Bent Out Of Shape	CD	Polydor	547-367-2	Germany	1999	8.99
Rainbow	Best Of	CD	Polydor	800-074-2	Germany	1981	11.99
Rainbow	Catch The Rainbow - The Anth.	2CD	Polydor	065-538-2	EU	2003	19.99
Rainbow	Classic Rainbow	CD	Polydor	589-157-2	Holland	2001	10.99
Rainbow	Difficult To Cure	CD	Polydor	547-365-2	Germany	1999	8.99
Rainbow	Difficult To Cure	CD	Polydor	314-547-365-2	U.S.A.	1999	8.99
Rainbow	Down To Earth	CD	Polydor	547-364-2	Germany	1999	8.99
Rainbow	Down To Earth	CD	Polydor	314-547-364-2	U.S.A.	1999	8.99
Rainbow	Finyl Vinyl Live	CD	Polydor	P38P-20040	Japan	1987	19.99
Rainbow	Finyl Vinyl Live	2 Mini LP	Universal	UICY-9198/9	Japan	2001	29.99
Rainbow	Finyl Vinyl Live	CD	Polydor	827-987-2	U.S.A.	1986	8.99
Rainbow	Finyl Vinyl Live	CD	Polydor	547-368-2	Germany	1999	8.99
Rainbow	Live In Europe	CD	Mausoleum	60024	U.S.A.	1996	9.99
Rainbow	Live In Germany '76	CD	Spitfire	SPT-15074-2	U.S.A.	2001	8.99
Rainbow	Long Live Rock 'N Roll	Mini Lp	Universal	UICY-9193	Japan	2001	24.99
Rainbow	Long Live Rock 'N' Roll	CD	Polydor	547-363-2	Germany	1999	8.99
Rainbow	Long Live Rock 'N' Roll	CD	Polydor	314-547-363-2	U.S.A.	1999	8.99
Rainbow	On Stage	CD	Polydor	POCP-2291	Japan	1995	19.99
Rainbow	On Stage	CD	Polydor	547-362-2	Germany	1999	8.99
Rainbow	On Stage	CD	Polydor	314-547-362-2	U.S.A.	1999	8.99
Rainbow	Pot Of Gold	CD	Spectrum	544-651-2	England	2002	8.99
Rainbow	Rising	CD	Polydor	POCP-2290	Japan	1995	19.99
Rainbow	Rising	CD	Polydor	314-547-361-2	U.S.A.	1999	8.99
Rainbow	Rising	CD	Polydor	547-361-2	Germany	1999	8.99
Rainbow	Ritchie Blackmore's Rainbow	CD	Polydor	314-547-360-2	U.S.A.	1999	9.99
Rainbow	Ritchie Blackmore's Rainbow	CD	Polydor	547-360-2	Germany	1999	9.99
Rainbow	Ritchie Blackmore's Rainbow	CD	Polydor	POCP-2289	Japan	1999	24.99
Rainbow	Straight Between The Eyes	CD	Polydor	547-366-2	Germany	1999	8.99
Rainbow	Straight Between The Eyes	CD	Polydor	314-547-366-2	U.S.A.	1999	8.99
Rainbow	The Best Of	2CD	Polydor	800-074-2	Germany	1990	15.99
Rainbow	The Family Album	CD	Connoisseur	VSOP-CD-195	England	1994	8.99
Rainbow	The Very Best Of	CD	Polydor	P2 37687	Canada	1997	8.99
Rainbow	The Very Best Of	CD	Polydor	537-687-2	Germany	1997	9.99
Rainbow	The Very Best Of Rainbow	CD	Polydor	314-537-687-2	U.S.A.	1997	8.99
Rainbow/Don Airey	K.2	CD	MCA	MCD-15457	Germany	1988	28.99
Rainbow/Graham Bonnet	Here Comes The Night	CD	Griffin	GCD-113-2	U.S.A.	1993	19.99
Rainbow/Graham Bonnet	Line-Up	CD	Polygram	PHCR-4194	Japan	1994	34.99
Rainbow/Graham Bonnet	The Day I Went Mad	CD	Victor Ent.	VICP-60726	Japan	1999	29.99
Rainbow/Graham Bonnet	The Rock Singer's Anthology	CD	Vertigo	840-974-2	England	1990	34.99
Rainbow/Graham Bonnet	Underground	CD	Victor Ent.	VICP-60084	Japan	1997	29.99
Rainbow/Joe Lynn Turner	Brazen Abbot - Bad Religion	CD	Victor Ent.	VICP-60057	Japan	1997	15.99
Rainbow/Joe Lynn Turner	Brazen Abbot - Eye Of The Storm	CD	Victor Ent.	VICP-5757	Japan	1996	15.99
Rainbow/Joe Lynn Turner	Challenge Them All	CD Single	Pony Canyon	PCCY-001514	Japan	2001	11.99
Rainbow/Joe Lynn Turner	Holy Man	CD	Pony Canyon	PCCY-01463	Japan	2000	26.99
Rainbow/Joe Lynn Turner	Hurry Up And Wait	CD	MTM	99558	Germany	1999	12.99
Rainbow/Joe Lynn Turner	Hurry Up And Wait +1	CD	Pony Canyon	PCCY-01248	Japan	1998	29.99
Rainbow/Joe Lynn Turner	JLT	CD	MTM	68174	Germany	2003	12.99
Rainbow/Joe Lynn Turner	JLT	CD	Shrapnel	SH-1166CD	U.S.A.	2003	12.99
Rainbow/Joe Lynn Turner	JLT + 1	CD	Pony Canyon	PCCY-1651	Japan	2003	29.99
Rainbow/Joe Lynn Turner	Mother's Army - Fire On The Moon	CD	Victor Ent.	VICP-60350	Japan	1998	29.99

R

Artist	Title	Format	Label	Catalog No	Country	Released	Value
Rainbow/Joe Lynn Turner	Mother's Army - Fire On The Moon	CD	Victor Ent.	VICP-60350	Japan	1998	29.99
Rainbow/Joe Lynn Turner	Mother's Army - Planet Earth	CD	FEMS	APCY-8390	Japan	1997	29.99
Rainbow/Joe Lynn Turner	Mother's Army (Camine Appice)	CD	FEMS	APCY-8129	Japan	1993	39.99
Rainbow/Joe Lynn Turner	Nothing's Changed	CD	Pony Canyon	PCCY-00847	Japan	1995	29.99
Rainbow/Joe Lynn Turner	Nothing's Changed	CD	Music For Nations	CDMFN-189	England	1995	20.99
Rainbow/Joe Lynn Turner	Rescue You	CD	WEA	18P2-2766	Japan	1985	45.99
Rainbow/Joe Lynn Turner	Slam	CD	MTM	68138	Germany	2002	12.99
Rainbow/Joe Lynn Turner	Slam + 1	CD	Pony Canyon	PCCY-01522	Japan	2000	29.99
Rainbow/Joe Lynn Turner	Under Cover	CD	Shrapnel	SH-1112CD	U.S.A.	1997	12.99
Rainbow/Joe Lynn Turner	Under Cover + 1	CD	Pony Canyon	PCCY-01074	Japan	1997	29.99
Rainbow/Joe Lynn Turner	Under Cover Vol. 2	CD	Pony Canyon	PCCY-01354	Japan	1999	29.99
Rainbow/Joe Lynn Turner	Under Cover Vol. 2	CD	Shrapnel	SH-1129CD	U.S.A.	1999	12.99
Rainbow/Joe Lynn Turner	Waiting For A Girl Like You	CD Single	Pony Canyon	PCCY-01343	Japan	1999	12.99
Raincoats	Looking In The Shadows	CD	DGC	DGCD-24957	U.S.A.	1996	8.99
Raincoats	Moving	CD	Rough Trade	R3062	England	1993	21.99
Raincoats	Odyshape	CD	DGC	DGCD-24623	U.S.A.	1993	34.99
Raincoats	The Raincoats	CD	DGC	DGCD-24622	U.S.A.	1993	39.99
Raine, Nic	Bond Back In Action 1 (Red Case)	CD	Silva Screen	FILMCD-317	U.S.A.	1999	8.99
Raine, Nic	Bond Back In Action 2 (Gold Case)	CD	Silva Screen	SSD-1119	U.S.A.	2000	8.99
Rainer, Nic	The Essential James Bond	CD	Silva Screen	SSD-1034	U.S.A.	1994	8.99
Rainy Day	S.T. (Rain Parade/3 O'Clock/Opal)	CD	Rough Trade	ROUGHUS41CD	U.S.A.	1984	106.99
Raitt, Bonnie	Bonnie Raitt	CD	Rhino	R2-78377	U.S.A.	2001	8.99
Raitt, Bonnie	Fundamental	CD	Capitol	7243-8-56397-2	U.S.A.	1998	5.99
Raitt, Bonnie	Give It Up	CD	Rhino	R2-78378	U.S.A.	2002	8.99
Raitt, Bonnie	Glow	CD	Rhino	R2-78383	U.S.A.	2002	8.99
Raitt, Bonnie	Green Light	CD	Rhino	R2-78384	U.S.A.	2002	8.99
Raitt, Bonnie	Home Plate	CD	Rhino	R2-78381	U.S.A.	2002	8.99
Raitt, Bonnie	Longing In Their Hearts	CD	Capitol	0777-7-81427-2-0	U.S.A.	1994	6.99
Raitt, Bonnie	Luck Of The Draw	CD	Capitol	0777-7-96111-2	U.S.A.	1991	5.99
Raitt, Bonnie	Luck Of The Draw (DCC Gold Cd)	CD	DCC	GZS-1107	U.S.A.	1997	19.99
Raitt, Bonnie	Nick Of Time	CD	Capitol	0777-7-91268-2	U.S.A.	1992	5.99
Raitt, Bonnie	Nick Of Time (DCC Gold Cd)	CD	DCC	GZS-1099	U.S.A.	1996	29.99
Raitt, Bonnie	Nine Lives	CD	Rhino	R2-78385	U.S.A.	2001	8.99
Raitt, Bonnie	Road Tested	2CD	Capitol	7243-8-33705-2-8	U.S.A.	1995	12.99
Raitt, Bonnie	Silver Lining	CD	Capitol	7243-5-31816-2	U.S.A.	2002	5.99
Raitt, Bonnie	Streetlights	CD	Rhino	R2-78380	U.S.A.	2001	8.99
Raitt, Bonnie	Sweet Forgiveness	CD	Rhino	R2-78382	U.S.A.	2001	8.99
Raitt, Bonnie	Takin' My Time	CD	Rhino	R2-78379	U.S.A.	2002	8.99
Raitt, Bonnie	The Best Of: Capitol 1989-2003	CD	EMI	7243-5-82113-2-0	England	2003	11.99
Raitt, Bonnie	The Bonnie Raitt Collection	CD	Warner Bros.	7599-26242-2	U.S.A.	1990	8.99
Raitt, Bonnie	You Got It (Promo)	CD Single	Arista	ASCD2795	U.S.A.	1995	3.99
Ram Jam	The Very Best Of	CD	Epic	467506-2	Germany	1990	8.99
Ramases/10CC	Space Hymns (10CC Wrote/Played)	CD	Repertoire	REP-4108-WP	Germany	1991	26.99
Ramone, Dee Dee	Ain't It Fun	CD	Blackout	BLK-5008ECD	England	1997	12.99
Ramone, Dee Dee	Chinese Bitch	CD Single	Rough Trade	RTD-157.1756.3	England	1994	14.99
Ramone, Dee Dee	Greatest And Latest (Europe)	CD	Eagle	EDL-EAG-294-2	England	2000	8.99
Ramone, Dee Dee	Greatest And Latest + 1	CD	Toshiba-EMI	TOCP-65601	Japan	2000	29.99
Ramone, Dee Dee	Hop Around	CD	Other Peoples	OPM-1234	Canada	2000	9.99
Ramone, Dee Dee	Hop Around (Europe Version)	CD	Carazong	2000-006	England	2000	9.99
Ramone, Dee Dee	I Hate Freaks Like You	CD	Rough Trade	RTD-157.1757.1	England	1994	18.99
Ramone, Dee Dee	Live In N.Y.C. (W/Marky Ramone)	CD	G.B. Music	GB1004	U.S.A.	1999	19.99
Ramone, Dee Dee	W/Terrorgruppe (WR004/Red)	CD Single	Trash	T2001-CD009	Germany	2002	15.99
Ramone, Dee Dee	With Youth Gone Mad	CD	Trend	TIDCD-9	Netherlands	2003	19.99
Ramone, Dee Dee	Zonked!	CD	Other Peoples	OPM-2118	Canada	1997	11.99
Ramone, Dee Dee (King)	Standing In The Spotlight	CD	Sire	9-25884-2	U.S.A.	1989	19.99
Ramone, Joey	Christmas Spirit.. In My House	CD	Sanctuary	06076-84589-2	U.S.A.	2002	8.99
Ramone, Joey	Don't Worry About Me	CD	Sanctuary	06076-84542-2	U.S.A.	2002	8.99
Ramone, Joey	Don't Worry About Me	CD	Sanctuary	SANCD108	England	2002	13.99

R

Artist	Title	Format	Label	Catalog No	Country	Released	Value
Ramone, Joey	Don't Worry About Me	CD	Sanctuary	SANP1108	England	2002	14.99
Ramone, Joey	Don't Worry...(DJ/Alternate Art)	CD	Sanctuary	SANSP-84542-2	U.S.A.	2002	6.99
Ramone, Joey	Merry Xmas Baby (I Don't....)	CD Single	Sanctuary	06076-84541-2	U.S.A.	2001	6.99
Ramone, Joey	What A Wonderful World (DJ)	CD Single	Sanctuary	SANDJ-85523-2	U.S.A.	2001	6.99
Ramone, Joey	What A Wonderful World (DJ)	CD Single	Sanctuary	SANPR108	England	2002	11.99
Ramone, Joey/Sibling Rivalry	In A Family Way	CD	Alternative Tentacles	VIRUS-CD153	U.S.A.	1994	11.99
Ramone, Marky/The Intruders	Marky Ramone And The Intruders	CD	Thirsty Ear	THI-57032-2	U.S.A.	1997	6.99
Ramones	Acid Eaters	CD	Radioactive	RARD-10913	U.S.A.	1994	8.99
Ramones	All The Stuff (And More) - Vol. 1	CD	Sire	9-26220-2	U.S.A.	1990	9.99
Ramones	All The Stuff (And More) - Vol. II	CD	Sire	9-26618-2	U.S.A.	1991	9.99
Ramones	Animal Boy	CD	Warner Bros.	WPCR-3148	Japan	1990	13.99
Ramones	Anthology	CD	Rhino	R2-75817	U.S.A.	1999	20.99
Ramones	Best Of The Chrysalis Years	CD	Chrysalis	7243-5-38472-2-7	England	2002	8.99
Ramones	Chrysalis Years	3CD	Chrysalis	7243-5-41080-2-0	England	2002	29.99
Ramones	End Of The Century	CD	Warner Bros.	WPCP-3145	Japan	1990	19.99
Ramones	End Of The Century + 6	CD	Rhino	R2-78155	U.S.A.	2002	9.99
Ramones	Greatest Hits Live	CD	Radioactive	RARD-11459	U.S.A.	1996	6.99
Ramones	Halfway To Sanity	CD	Sire	9-25641-2	U.S.A.	1987	9.99
Ramones	¡Adios Amigos!	CD	Radioactive	RARD-11273	U.S.A.	1995	7.99
Ramones	It's Alive	CD	Sire	7599-26069-2	Germany	1978	9.99
Ramones	It's Alive	CD	Warner Bros.	WPCP-3502	Japan	1979	24.99
Ramones	Last Show All...(DJ/Outta/Diff Cover)	CD	Eagle	EAGO10P	England	1997	20.99
Ramones	Leathers From New York (Cd W/Book)	CD	Sonic Book	SONIC.008	Italy	1997	18.99
Ramones	Leave Home + 16	CD	Rhino	R2-74307	U.S.A.	2001	9.99
Ramones	Loco Live	CD	Warner Bros.	WPCP-4789	Japan	1992	19.99
Ramones	Loco Live (European Vrsn/Diff Tracks)	CD	Chrysalis	1901-3219012	England	1991	29.99
Ramones	Loco Live (U.S. Version)	CD	Sire	9-26650-2	U.S.A.	1992	8.99
Ramones	Mania	CD	Sire	9-25709-2	U.S.A.	1988	8.99
Ramones	Mondo Bizarro	CD	Radioactive	RARD-10615	U.S.A.	1992	8.99
Ramones	N.Y.C. 1978	CD	Alchemy	PILOT-79	England	2003	11.99
Ramones	Pleasant Dreams	CD	Warner Bros.	WPCR-3146	Japan	1990	19.99
Ramones	Pleasant Dreams + 7	CD	Rhino	R2-78156	U.S.A.	2002	9.99
Ramones	Pleasant Dreams + 7	CD	Warner Bros.	WPCR-11339	Japan	2003	24.99
Ramones	Poison Heart	CD Single	Chrysalis	0946-3-23917-2-8	England	1992	4.99
Ramones	Ramones + 8	CD	Rhino	R2-74306	U.S.A.	2001	9.99
Ramones	Road To Ruin + 5	CD	Rhino	R2-74308	U.S.A.	2001	9.99
Ramones	Rocket To Russia + 5	CD	Rhino	R2-74309	U.S.A.	2001	9.99
Ramones	Subterranean Jungle + 7	CD	Rhino	R2-78157	U.S.A.	2002	9.99
Ramones	Too Tough To Die + 12	CD	Rhino	R2-78158	U.S.A.	2002	9.99
Ramones	Too Tough To Die + 12	CD	Warner Bros.	WPCR-11341	Japan	2003	24.99
Ramones	We're Outta Here W/Video	CD	Radioactive	RARDG-11555	U.S.A.	1997	29.99
Ramones	We're Outta Here!	CD	Toshiba-EMI	TOCP-50387	Japan	1997	39.99
Ramones	We're Outta Here!	CD	Eagle	EDL-EAG007-2	England	1997	8.99
Ramones	You Don't Come Close	CD	Alchemy	PILOT-79	England	2000	11.99
Randy Pie	Highway Driver	CD	Repertoire	IMS-7016-WP	Germany	1995	34.99
Raphaels	Supernatural	CD	Track	TRK0005CD	England	2001	5.99
Rare Earth	Ecology	CD	Motown	MOTD-5202	U.S.A.	1991	24.99
Rare Earth	Ecology/Get Ready	CD	Motown	MOTD-8133	U.S.A.	1988	39.99
Rare Earth	Get Ready	CD	Motown	MOTD-5229	U.S.A.	1990	22.99
Rare Earth	In Concert	CD	Motown	MOTD-5443	U.S.A.	1971	59.99
Rare Earth	Ma	CD	Motown	530279	England	1994	16.99
Rare Earth	Made In Switzerland (Recorded Live)	CD	Line	LICD-9.00865-0	Germany	1989	17.99
Rascals	All I Really Need (3000) W/Posters	6CD	Rhino	RHM2-7804	U.S.A.	2002	90.99
Rascals	Peaceful World	CD	Sundazed	SC-6131	U.S.A.	1998	8.99
Rascals	The Island Of Real + 2	CD	Sundazed	SC-6131	U.S.A.	1998	10.99
Rascals/Felix Cavaliere	Castles In The Air	CD	Sony	ESCA-7871	Japan	1979	20.99
Rascals/Felix Cavaliere	Destiny	CD	Victor Ent.	VICP-60303	Japan	1975	23.99
Rascals/Felix Cavaliere	Dreams In Motion	CD	MCA	MCAD-11062	U.S.A.	1994	10.99

R

Artist	Title	Format	Label	Catalog No	Country	Released	Value
Rascals/Felix Cavaliere	Rascal Alone	CD	See For Miles	SEE-CD-232	England	1989	34.99
Rascals/The Young	Collections	CD	Warner Bros.	2-27618	U.S.A.	1967	11.99
Rascals/The Young	Groovin'	CD	Warner Bros.	2-27619	U.S.A.	1967	11.99
Rascals/The Young	Self Titled	CD	Warner Bros.	2-27617	U.S.A.	1966	11.99
Raspberries	Best	CD	Toshiba-EMI	TOCP-6362	Japan	1991	39.99
Raspberries	Capitol Collectors Series	CD	Capitol	7-92126-2	U.S.A.	1991	8.99
Raspberries	Fresh	CD	Toshiba-EMI	TOCP-6359	Japan	1991	34.99
Raspberries	Power Pop, Volume One	CD	RPM	RPM-162	England	1996	17.99
Raspberries	Power Pop, Volume Two	CD	RPM	RPM-163	England	1996	17.99
Raspberries	Self Titled	CD	Toshiba-EMI	TOCP-6358	Japan	1991	34.99
Raspberries	Side 3	CD	Toshiba-EMI	TOCP-6360	Japan	1991	34.99
Raspberries	Starting Over	CD	Toshiba-EMI	TOCP-6361	Japan	1991	40.99
Raspberries/Scott McCarl	Play On	CD	Titan	1426	U.S.A.	1997	15.99
Raspberries/Scott McCarl	Play On	CD	Thunderbird	CSA-109	England	1997	15.99
Ratt	Collage	CD	De Rock	DERCD-097	U.S.A.	1997	9.99
Ratt	Dancing Undercover	CD	Atlantic	7-81683-2	U.S.A.	1986	8.99
Ratt	Detonator	CD	Atlantic	A2-82127	U.S.A.	1990	7.99
Ratt	Detonator (Deluxe)	CD	Atlantic	AMZY-122	Japan	1990	28.99
Ratt	Essentials	CD	Rhino	R2-76053	U.S.A.	2002	8.99
Ratt	Infestation	CD	Portrait	VK-42815	U.S.A.	1999	8.99
Ratt	Invasion Of Your Privacy	CD	Atlantic	7-81257-2	U.S.A.	1985	8.99
Ratt	Out Of The Cellar	CD	Atlantic	7-80143-2	U.S.A.	1984	8.99
Ratt	Ratt And Roll 8191	CD	Atlantic	7-82260-2	U.S.A.	1991	8.99
Ratt	Reach For The Sky	CD	Atlantic	7-81929-2	U.S.A.	1988	8.99
Ratt	Self Titled	CD	Portrait	VK-69586	U.S.A.	1999	7.99
Ratt	Self Titled EP	CD	Atlantic	7-90245-2	U.S.A.	1983	7.99
Raven	All For One + 3	CD	Spitfire	SPT-15097-2	U.S.A.	2000	8.99
Raven	All For One + 5	CD	Sanctuary	06076-73009-2	U.S.A.	2002	8.99
Raven	All Systems Go! : The Neat Anthology	CD	Sanctuary	06076-73000-2	U.S.A.	2002	8.99
Raven	Architect Of Fear	CD	SPV	085-76282-CD	Germany	2003	9.99
Raven	Destroy All Monsters	CD	SPV	085-12132	Germany	1999	9.99
Raven	Everything Louder	CD	SPV	085-12162	Germany	1999	8.99
Raven	Glow	CD	SPV	085-12092	Germany	1999	9.99
Raven	Head's Up	CD	Victor Ent.	VICP-2065	Japan	1990	54.99
Raven	Life's A Bitch + 2	CD	Mayhem	9086-11143-2	U.S.A.	1998	8.99
Raven	Live At The Inferno	CD	SPV	210-18432	Holland	1999	9.99
Raven	Nothing Exceeds Like Excess	CD	Century Media	66043-2	England	2001	10.99
Raven	One For All	CD	Metal Blade	3984-14326-2	U.S.A.	2000	7.99
Raven	Raw Tracks	CD	Metal Blade	3984-14279-2	U.S.A.	1999	8.99
Raven	Rock Till You Drop + 8	CD	Sanctuary	06076-73007-2	U.S.A.	2002	8.99
Raven	Rock Until You Drop + 3	CD	Spitfire	SPT-15085-2	U.S.A.	2000	8.99
Raven	Stark Raven Mad: The Best Of	CD	Mayhem	9086-11136-2	U.S.A.	1998	8.99
Raven	Stay Hard + 2	CD	Mayhem	9086-11137-2	U.S.A.	1998	8.99
Raven	The Pack Is Back	CD	Mayhem	9086-11150-2	U.S.A.	1998	8.99
Raven	Wiped Out	CD	Spitfire	SPT-15086-2	U.S.A.	2000	8.99
Raven	Wiped Out + 3	CD	Pony Canyon	PCCY-01391	Japan	2000	24.99
Raven	Wiped Out + 4	CD	Sanctuary	06076-73008-2	U.S.A.	2002	8.99
Rave-Ups	Town & Country	CD	Line	WICD-9.00004-0	Germany	1988	17.99
Raw Material	Self Titled	CD	Akarma	AK-249	Italy	2003	12.99
Raw Material	Time Is...	CD	Repertoire	REP-4469-WWP	Germany	2002	11.99
Ray,Goodman & Brown	Self Titled	CD	Nippon Phonogram	PHCR-6077	Japan	1979	39.99
Raye, Julianna	Something Peculiar (Jeff Lynne Prod.)	CD	Reprise	9-45081-2	U.S.A.	1992	5.99
Real Kids	The New Rose Years	2CD	Last Call	3069852	France	2001	13.99
Records	A Sunny Afternoon In Waterloo	CD	Line	WFCD-9.00681-L	Germany	1989	28.99
Records	Paying For The Summer Of Love	CD	Angel Air	SJPCD078	Austria	2001	12.99
Records	Smashes, Crashes, And Near Misses	CD	Virgin	7243-8-40222-2-8	England	1988	15.99
Records	The Records/Shades In Bed	CD	On The Beach	FOAM-CD5	EU	2002	16.99
Records/Huw Gower	Ile de France (This Could Be Heaven)	CD	This Could Be	1	England	2000	14.99

R

Artist	Title	Format	Label	Catalog No	Country	Released	Value
Records/John Wicks	Rock 'Ola (No Will Burch)	CD	Rock Indiana	CINDI-069	Spain	1998	21.99
Records/Jude Cole	A View From 3rd Street	CD	Reprise	26164-2	U.S.A.	1990	9.99
Records/Jude Cole	AAA Sampler (Promo)	CD Single	Island	PRCD-70372-2	U.S.A.	1995	5.99
Records/Jude Cole	Baby It's Tonigh (2 Track/Promo)	CD Single	Reprise	PRO-CD-4007	U.S.A.	1990	18.99
Records/Jude Cole	Baby It's Tonight (1 Track/Promo)	CD Single	Reprise	PRO-CD-4013	U.S.A.	1990	16.99
Records/Jude Cole	Believe In You (Promo)	CD Single	Island	PRCD-70382-2	U.S.A.	1995	5.99
Records/Jude Cole	Compared To Nothing (Promo)	CD Single	Reprise	PRO-CD-4771	U.S.A.	1990	8.99
Records/Jude Cole	Falling Home	CD	Watertown	50815-2	U.S.A.	2000	11.99
Records/Jude Cole	House Full Of Seasons	CD Single	Reprise	PRO-CD-4495	U.S.A.	1990	9.99
Records/Jude Cole	I Don't Know Why I Act This Way	CD	Island	314-524-148-2	U.S.A.	1995	8.99
Records/Jude Cole	It Comes Around (Promo)	CD Single	Reprise	PRO-CD-5840	U.S.A.	1992	9.99
Records/Jude Cole	Just Another Night (Promo)	CD Single	Reprise	PRO-CD-6046	U.S.A.	1993	16.99
Records/Jude Cole	Self Titled	CD	Reprise	25553-2	U.S.A.	1987	92.99
Records/Jude Cole	Speed Of Life (Promo)	CD Single	Island	PRCD-7125-2	U.S.A.	1995	5.99
Records/Jude Cole	Start The Car	CD	Reprise	26898-2	U.S.A.	1992	11.99
Records/Jude Cole	Start The Car (Promo)	CD Single	Reprise	PRO-CD-5629	U.S.A.	1990	19.99
Records/Jude Cole	Tell The Truth (Promo)	CD Single	Reprise	PRO-CD-5842	U.S.A.	1992	7.99
Records/Jude Cole	Time For Letting Go (Promo)	CD Single	Reprise	PRO-CD-4337	U.S.A.	1990	19.99
Records/Jude Cole	You Were In My Heart (Promo)	CD Single	Reprise	PRO-CD-2864	U.S.A.	1987	10.99
Red Dawn	Never Say Surrender	CD	Toshiba-EMI	TOCP-7689	Japan	1993	25.99
Red Five	Flash	CD	Interscope	INTD-90057	U.S.A.	1996	4.99
Red Hot Chili Peppers	Blood Sugar Sex Magik	CD	Warner Bros.	26681-2	U.S.A.	1991	6.99
Red Hot Chili Peppers	By The Way	CD	Warner Bros.	9362-48140-2	U.S.A.	2002	5.99
Red Hot Chili Peppers	Californication	CD	Warner Bros.	9362-47386-2	U.S.A.	1999	5.99
Red Hot Chili Peppers	Freaky Styley + 4	CD	EMI	72435-40377-2-6	U.S.A.	2003	8.99
Red Hot Chili Peppers	Greatest Hits (Clean)	CD	Warner Bros.	9362-48654-2	U.S.A.	2003	7.99
Red Hot Chili Peppers	Greatest Hits (W/DVD)	2CD	Warner Bros.	9362-48596-2	U.S.A.	2003	24.99
Red Hot Chili Peppers	Limited Edition Hits (Promo)	CD	Warner Bros.	RHCP-2002	Canada	2002	52.99
Red Hot Chili Peppers	Live Rare Remix Box	3CD	Warner Bros.	9362-41405-2	Germany	1994	49.99
Red Hot Chili Peppers	Mothers Milk (MFSL Gold Cd)	CD	Mobile Fidelity	UDCD-683	U.S.A.	1989	18.99
Red Hot Chili Peppers	Mother's Milk + 6	CD	EMI	72435-40378-2-5	U.S.A.	2003	8.99
Red Hot Chili Peppers	One Hot Minute	CD Single	Warner Bros.	WO331CDX	Netherlands	1995	12.99
Red Hot Chili Peppers	One Hot Minute	CD	Warner Bros.	9362-45733-2	U.S.A.	1995	5.99
Red Hot Chili Peppers	Out In L.A.	CD	EMI	7243-8-29665-2-4	U.S.A.	1994	6.99
Red Hot Chili Peppers	Self Titled +5	CD	EMI	72435-40380-2-0	U.S.A.	2003	8.99
Red Hot Chili Peppers	Shallow Be Thy Grave	CD Single	Warner Bros.	9362437042	Australia	1996	9.99
Red Hot Chili Peppers	Taste The Pain	CD Single	EMI	E2-50285	U.S.A.	1989	5.99
Red Hot Chili Peppers	The Abbey Road E.P.	CD	EMI	0777-7-90869-2-4	Holland	1988	9.99
Red Hot Chili Peppers	The Chili Digi	CD Single	EMI	8803642	Australia	1992	16.99
Red Hot Chili Peppers	The Uplift Mofo Party Plan + 2	CD	EMI	72435-40379-2-4	U.S.A.	2003	8.99
Red Hot Chili Peppers	What Hits!?	CD	EMI	0777-7-94762-2-0	U.S.A.	1992	5.99
Red Krayola	God Bless The Red Krayola...	CD	Sunspots	SPOT-521-CD	Italy	2002	11.99
Redd Kross	Jimmie's Fantasy (W/Button)	CD Single	Phonogram	862-563-2	Australia	1993	14.99
Redding, Noel	The Missing Album (W/Dave Clarke)	CD	Griffin	GCD-371-2	U.S.A.	1995	10.99
Redding, Noel And Friends	Live From Bunkr	CD	Track	TRK1010CD	England	2001	12.99
Redding, Noel Band	Clonakilty Cowboys/Blowin'	CD	One Way	OW-71009	U.S.A.	2000	12.99
Redding, Noel/3:05 A.M.	On Tour	CD	Metrodome	MIDR0802	England	2001	9.99
Redding, Noel/Road	Seld Titled	CD	Akarma	AK-270-CD	Italy	2003	14.99
Redding, Otis	Dictionary Of Soul	CD	Atco	7-91707-2	U.S.A.	1966	4.99
Redding, Otis	Dictionary Of Soul	CD	Atlantic	20P2-2378	Japan	1991	19.99
Redding, Otis	Dock Of The Bay	CD	Atlantic	20P2-2362	Japan	1986	19.99
Redding, Otis	In Person At The Whisky A Go Go	CD	Rhino	8122-70380-2	U.S.A.	1992	8.99
Redding, Otis	Otis Blue (MFSL Gold Cd)	CD	Mobile Fidelity	UDCD-575	U.S.A.	1965	29.99
Redding, Otis	Otis! The Definitive Box Set	4CD	Rhino	R2-71439	U.S.A.	1993	53.99
Aredding, Otis	Pain In My Heart	CD	Atco	7-80253-2	U.S.A.	1965	8.99
Redding, Otis	The Dock Of The Bay	CD	Atco	7-80254-2	U.S.A.	1968	8.99
Redding, Otis	The Soul Album	CD	Atco	7-91705-2	U.S.A.	1966	7.99
Reddog	Reddog/Reincarnation	CD	Line	STCD-9.00659-0	Germany	1989	18.99

R

Artist	Title	Format	Label	Catalog No	Country	Released	Value
Reddy, Helen	Christmas	CD	EMI	72435-33838-2-4	U.S.A.	2000	8.99
Reddy, Helen	I Am Woman - Essential Collection	CD	Razor & Tie	7930182180-2	U.S.A.	1998	11.99
Red-Elvises/Brian Tyler	Six String Samurai (O.S.T.)	CD	Palm Pictures	PALMCD-2003-2	U.S.A.	1998	12.99
Reed, Dan/Network	Self Titled + 3	CD	Lemon	CDLEM05	England	2003	8.99
Reed, Lou	A Rock & Roll Life (Promo)	2CD	Sire	PRO-CD-3358	U.S.A.	1989	72.99
Reed, Lou	Adventurer (Promo)	CD Single	Sire	PRO-CD-8172	U.S.A.	1996	5.99
Reed, Lou	American Poet (Live 1972/The Tots)	CD	Alchemy	PILOT-83	England	2000	7.99
Reed, Lou	Animal Serenade	2CD	Sire	9362-48678-2-1	U.S.A.	2004	14.99
Reed, Lou	Berlin	CD	RCA	BG2-67489	U.S.A.	1998	8.99
Reed, Lou	Coney Island Baby	CD	RCA	0915-R	U.S.A.	1976	10.99
Reed, Lou	Different Times - Lou Reed in the 70s	CD	RCA	07863-66864-2	U.S.A.	1996	7.99
Reed, Lou	Ecstacy (Promo)	CD Single	Reprise	PRO-CD-100080	U.S.A.	2000	6.99
Reed, Lou	Ecstasy (Tour Ed. W/Perfect Night)	2CD	Reprise	9362479342	Australia	2000	27.99
Reed, Lou	Ecstasy (Adv. W/Diff. Cover)	CD	Warner Bros.	2-47425-AB	U.S.A.	2000	9.99
Reed, Lou	Growing Up In Public	CD	Buddah	74465-99658-2	U.S.A.	2000	9.99
Reed, Lou	Hooky Wooky	CD Single	Warner Bros.	9362-43665-2	Germany	1996	8.99
Reed, Lou	Hooky Wooky (Promo)	CD Single	Warner Bros.	PRO-CD-8083-R	U.S.A.	1996	6.99
Reed, Lou	KBFH February 24 - March 1, 1992	CD	DIR Network	H15E0100C	U.S.A.	1992	32.99
Reed, Lou	King Biscuit Sept 28 To March 4, 1998	CD	DIR Network	C165T01XA	U.S.A.	1998	32.99
Reed, Lou	Legendary	3CD	BMG	74321-94617-2-8	Australia	2002	20.99
Reed, Lou	Legendary Hearts	CD	BMG	ND-89843	England	1983	18.99
Reed, Lou	Live - Take No Prisoners	2CD	Arista	07822-10609-2	U.S.A.	2002	17.99
Reed, Lou	Live - Take No Prisoners	2CD	BMG	ND-90677-(2)	Germany	1992	17.99
Reed, Lou	Live In Concert (Same As Italy)	CD	BMG	74321-43157-2	U.S.A.	1999	9.99
Reed, Lou	Live In Italy (Italian Gold Cd)	CD	RCA	74321-862582	Italy	2001	16.99
Reed, Lou	Lou Reed	CD	BMG Victor	BVCP-2065	Japan	1992	24.99
Reed, Lou	Lou Reed	CD	RCA	74321-727122	Germany	2000	17.99
Reed, Lou	Lou Reed Live	CD	RCA	3752-2-R	U.S.A.	1975	12.99
Reed, Lou	Magic and Loss	CD	Sire	9-26662-2	U.S.A.	1992	5.99
Reed, Lou	Metal Machine Music	CD	Buddah	74465-99752-2	U.S.A.	2000	13.99
Reed, Lou	Mistrial	CD	RCA	PCD1-7190	U.S.A.	1986	13.99
Reed, Lou	Modern Dance	CD Single	Reprise	9362-24742-5-2	Germany	2000	6.99
Reed, Lou	New Sensations	CD	RCA	PCD1-4998	U.S.A.	1984	13.99
Reed, Lou	New York	CD	Sire	9-25829-2	U.S.A.	1989	6.99
Reed, Lou	NYC Man	2CD	RCA	82876-50564-2	U.S.A.	2003	12.99
Reed, Lou	Paranoia In The Key Of E (Promo)	CD Single	Warner Bros.	PCS-453	Japan	2000	29.99
Reed, Lou	Paranoia In The Key Of E (Promo)	CD Single	Warner Bros.	PR02019	Germany	2000	10.99
Reed, Lou	Perfect Day	CD	Camden	74321-523752	England	1997	6.99
Reed, Lou	Perfect Night Live In London	CD	Reprise	9-46917-2	U.S.A.	1998	7.99
Reed, Lou	Power And Glory (Unrel Live Promo)	CD Single	Sire	PRO-CD-5464	U.S.A.	1990	13.99
Reed, Lou	Rock And Roll Diary 1967-1980	CD	Arista	07822-18434-2	U.S.A.	1993	9.99
Reed, Lou	Rock And Roll Heart	CD	Buddah	74465-99657-2	U.S.A.	2000	10.99
Reed, Lou	Rock 'N' Roll Animal	CD	RCA	BG2-67948	U.S.A.	2000	9.99
Reed, Lou	Romeo And Juliette (Promo)	CD Single	Sire	PRO-CD-3619	U.S.A.	1989	13.99
Reed, Lou	Sally Can't Dance	CD	RCA	07863-69383-2	U.S.A.	2001	9.99
Reed, Lou	Selections/Thought Expressions (DJ)	CD	RCA	RDJ-62284-2	U.S.A.	1992	10.99
Reed, Lou	Set The Twilight Reeling (Purple Case)	CD	Warner Bros.	9-46159-2	U.S.A.	1996	7.99
Reed, Lou	Street Hassle	CD	Arista	07822-18499-2	U.S.A.	1978	13.99
Reed, Lou	The 1972 Interview	CD	Baktabak	CBAK4094	England	1996	10.99
Reed, Lou	The Bells	CD	Buddah	74465-99659-2	U.S.A.	2000	8.99
Reed, Lou	The Blue Mask	CD	RCA	07863-54221-2	U.S.A.	1999	9.99
Reed, Lou	The Definitive Collection	CD	Arista	07822-14610-2	U.S.A.	1999	9.99
Reed, Lou	The Essential	CD	RCA	74321-24797-2	Italy	1995	14.99
Reed, Lou	The Raven (Ltd Deluxe)	2CD	Warner Bros.	9362-48373-2-9	Germany	2003	19.99
Reed, Lou	The Very Best Of Lou Reed	CD	BMG	74321-660462	Germany	1999	9.99
Reed, Lou	The Wild Side	2CD	BMG	74321796002	Australia	2000	20.99
Reed, Lou	Transformer	CD	RCA	74321-601812	Australia	1998	9.99
Reed, Lou	Transformer (RCA Gold Cd)	CD	RCA	07863-66600-2	U.S.A.	1995	28.99

R

Artist	Title	Format	Label	Catalog No	Country	Released	Value
Reed, Lou	Transformer + 2	CD	RCA	07863-65132-2	U.S.A.	2002	9.99
Reed, Lou	Walk On The Wild Side - The Best Of	CD	RCA	3753-2-R	U.S.A.	1977	6.99
Reed, Lou	Walk On The Wild Side & Other Hits	CD	RCA	07863-52162-2	U.S.A.	1990	8.99
Reed, Lou	What's Good (Promo)	CD Single	Sire	PRO-CD-4988	U.S.A.	1992	10.99
Reed, Lou	Wild Child (1st Lp/Live RCA/PAIR Lps)	CD	RCA	PDC-2-1024	U.S.A.	1987	14.99
Reed, Lou/Gold Cds	Golden (Transformer/Berlin/Animal)	3CD	RCA	CFD-01115	Italy	2002	44.99
Reed, Lou/John Cale	Nobody But You	CD Single	Warner Bros.	7599-21555-2	Germany	1990	5.99
Reed, Lou/John Cale	Nobody But You (Promo)	CD Single	Reprise	PRO-CD-4056	U.S.A.	1990	6.99
Reed, Lou/John Cale	Songs For Drella	CD	Sire	9-26140-2	U.S.A.	1990	10.99
Reed, Lou/John Cale	Songs For Drella (Deluxe Edition)	CD	Reprise	9-26205-2	U.S.A.	1990	29.99
Reed, Lou/John Cale/Nico	Box (A Poet + 2/Bataclan '72/T-Shirt)	2CD	Alchemy	ABOX001	England	2003	44.99
Reed, Lou/Talking Heads	KBFH May 28 - June 3, 1990	CD	DIR Network	95L0100A	U.S.A.	1990	32.99
Reed, Lou/V St. James	Vanessa St. James - Sunday Morning	CD Single	Warner Bros.	5050466-9573-20	Germany	2003	6.99
Regenesis	Lamb For Supper - Live 2001	CD	Mystic	MYS-CD-149	England	2001	11.99
Reich, Steve	Music for 18 Musicians	CD	ECM	78118-21129-2	U.S.A.	1978	12.99
Reichel, Achim	Blues In Blond	CD	Line	DKCD-9.00974-0	Germany	1990	13.99
Reichel, Achim	Dat Shanty Alb´m	CD	Line	DKCD-9.01002-0	Germany	1989	13.99
Reichel, Achim	Klabautermann	CD	Line	DKCD-9.01006-0	Germany	1989	13.99
Reichel, Achim	Regenballade	CD	Line	DKCD-9.00985-0	Germany	1989	13.99
Reichel, Achim	Ungeschminkt	CD	Line	DKCD-9.01072-0	Germany	1991	13.99
Reid, Terry	Bang Bang You're Terry Reid	CD	BGO	BG0CD164	England	1996	13.99
Reid, Terry	Bang Bang, You're Terry Reid + 2	CD	Repertoire	REP-4862	Germany	2003	14.99
Reid, Terry	Fifth Of July	CD Single	Warner Bros.	YZ579CD	England	1991	10.99
Reid, Terry	River (W/David Lindley)	CD	Water	WATER-107	U.S.A.	2003	17.99
Reid, Terry	Rogue Waves	CD	BGO	BGOCD140	England	2002	14.99
Reid, Terry	Seed Of Memory (Prod By G Nash)	CD	Edsel	EDCD-425	England	1995	23.99
Reid, Terry	Self Titled	CD	BGO	BGOCD168	England	1996	20.99
Reid, Terry	Self Titled + 2	CD	Repertoire	REP-4861	Germany	2003	14.99
Reid, Terry	The Driver (Prod By Trevor Horn)	CD	Warner Bros.	9-26912-2	U.S.A.	1991	13.99
Reilly, Maggie	Echoes	CD	EMI	564-7-98836 2	England	1992	13.99
Reilly, Maggie	Elena	CD	EMI	7243-8-37563-2-2	Holland	1996	11.99
Reilly, Maggie	Elena (Deluxe Edition)	CD	EMI	7243-8-56815-3	Holland	1997	18.99
Reilly, Maggie	M.R All The Mixes	CD	EMI	7243-8-54988-2-4	Holland	1996	11.99
Reilly, Maggie	Midnight Sun	CD	EMI	7243-8-27351-2-0	Holland	1993	11.99
Reilly, Maggie	Starcrossed	CD	EMI	7243-5-25415-2-2	Holland	2000	11.99
Remains	A Session With The Remains	CD	Sundazed	SC-6069	U.S.A.	1996	8.99
Remo Four	Smile	CD	Line	SCCD-9.00196-0	Germany	1988	23.99
Remo Four	The Pye Singles	CD	Repertoire	REP-4186-WZ	Germany	1991	29.99
Remo Four/George Harrison	In The First Place (Wonderwall)	CD Single	Pilar	PILAR01CD	England	1999	14.99
Ren/Stimpy	Little Crock O' Christmas (DJ Interview)	CD	Epic	DISP-002158	U.S.A.	1993	11.99
Ren/Stimpy	Little Eediot (Promo Sampler)	CD	Nickelodeon	LXK-5473	U.S.A.	1993	29.99
Ren/Stimpy	You Eediot!	CD	Rhino	R2-75253	U.S.A.	1998	8.99
Renaissance	A Song For All Seasons	CD	Wounded Bird	WOU-6049	U.S.A.	2001	8.99
Renaissance	Archive Series	CD	Rialto	RMCD-227	U.S.A.	2001	12.99
Renaissance	Ashes Are Burning	CD	Repertoire	REP-4575-WY	Germany	1995	10.99
Renaissance	Azure D'Or	CD	Wounded Bird	WOU-6068	U.S.A.	2001	9.99
Renaissance	BBC Sessions	2CD	Wounded Bird	WOU-1001	U.S.A.	1999	19.99
Renaissance	Camera Camera	CD	HTD	HTD-CD-43	England	1995	10.99
Renaissance	Camera Camera	CD	Line	LICD-9.00042-0	Germany	1988	10.99
Renaissance	Can You Hear Me?	CD	Disky	SI-640432	Holland	2001	7.99
Renaissance	Da Capo	2CD	Repertoire	REP-4571-WL	Germany	1995	13.99
Renaissance	Day Of The Dreamer	CD	Mooncrest	CRESTCD-053	England	2000	10.99
Renaissance	First/Illusion	2CD	Line	LICD-9.21163-S	Germany	1992	19.99
Renaissance	Illusion	CD	Line	LICD-9.00425-0	Germany	1987	10.99
Renaissance	Illusion	CD	Repertoire	REP-4531-WY	Germany	1995	11.99
Renaissance	In The Beginning (Prologue/Ashes)	CD	Capitol	CDP-7-48451-2	U.S.A.	1988	39.99
Renaissance	In the Land of the Rising Sun	2CD	Toshiba-EMI	TOCP-66007-08	Japan	2002	44.99
Renaissance	Innocence	CD	Mooncrest	CRESTCD-033	England	1998	10.99

R

Artist	Title	Format	Label	Catalog No	Country	Released	Value
Renaissance	Innocents/Illusions (Self Titled/Illusion)	2CD	Castle	CMEDD-874	England	2004	15.99
Renaissance	King Biscuit Flower Hour Part 1	CD	King Biscuit	70710-88020-2	U.S.A.	1999	11.99
Renaissance	King Biscuit Flower Hour Part 2	CD	King Biscuit	70710-88026-2	U.S.A.	1997	11.99
Renaissance	Live And Direct	CD	Spiral	SCD-924	England	2002	12.99
Renaissance	Live At Carnegie Hall	2CD	Repertoire	REP-4506-WL	Germany	1994	13.99
Renaissance	Live At The Academy Of Music PA	CD	Mooncrest	CRESTCD-056	England	2000	11.99
Renaissance	Mother Russia	CD	Disky	SI-794142	Netherlands	2002	8.99
Renaissance	Nevada - Pictures In The Fire + 5	CD	Mooncrest	CRESTCD-054	England	2000	12.99
Renaissance	Novella	CD	Wounded Bird	WOU-6024	U.S.A.	2001	11.99
Renaissance	Ocean Gypsy	CD	Transatlantic	TRACD-307	England	1999	8.99
Renaissance	Prologue	CD	Repertoire	REP-4574-WY	Germany	1995	11.99
Renaissance	Renaissance + 2	CD	Repertoire	REP-4512-WY	Germany	1995	13.99
Renaissance	Renaissance's First Album	CD	Line	LICD-9.00421-0	Germany	1987	13.99
Renaissance	Scheherazade And Other Stories	CD	Repertoire	REP-4490-WY	Germany	1994	11.99
Renaissance	Songs For All Seasons	CD	Eagle	EDCMD-124	Germany	2002	10.99
Renaissance	Songs From The Renaissance Day	CD	Repertoire	REP-4672-WY	Germany	1997	10.99
Renaissance	Tales Of 1001 Nights - Volume 1	CD	Sire	9-26129-2	U.S.A.	1990	8.99
Renaissance	Tales Of 1001 Nights Volume 2	CD	Sire	9-26143-2	U.S.A.	1990	8.99
Renaissance	The Other Woman	CD	HTD	HTD-CD27	England	1995	8.99
Renaissance	The Other Woman	CD	Pony Canyon	PCCY-00751	Japan	1995	21.99
Renaissance	Time-Line	CD	Repertoire	REP-4655-WY	Germany	1997	11.99
Renaissance	Trip To The Fair	CD	Mooncrest	CRESTCD-034	England	1998	11.99
Renaissance	Turn Of The Cards	CD	Repertoire	REP-4491-WY	Germany	1994	10.99
Renaissance	Tuscany	CD	Toshiba-EMI	TOCP-65591	Japan	2000	34.99
Renaissance/Raphael Rudd	Awakening (W/Townshend/Haslam)	CD	Wedge	WM-80322	U.S.A.	1996	12.99
Renaissance/Raphael Rudd	Skydancer (W/Annie Haslam)	CD	Polystar	PSCW-1071	Japan	1991	39.99
Renaissance/Some #rd/Sign	The Scheherazade Musical (Promo)	CD	Scheherazade	SCH-CD001	England	1997	29.99
Renaissance/Stairway	Moonstone (W/McCarthy/Jane Relf)	CD	New World	NWCD-168	England	1988	13.99
Renaissance-Illusion	Through The Fire (Jane Relf)	CD	Spiral	SCD-923	England	2001	19.99
Renbourn, John	A Maid In Bedlam	CD	Line	TACD-9.00777-0	Germany	1989	15.99
Renbourn, John	A Maid In Bedlam	CD	Shanachie	SHANCD-79004	U.S.A.	1987	8.99
Renbourn, John	Another Monday	CD	Castle	CMRCD436	England	2002	8.99
Renbourn, John	BBC Live In Concert	CD	Varese	302-061-170-2	U.S.A.	2001	8.99
Renbourn, John	BBC Live In Concert	CD	Strange Fruit	SFRSCD076	England	1997	14.99
Renbourn, John	Collected	CD	Music Club	MCCD-388	U.S.A.	1999	8.99
Renbourn, John	Definitive Transatlantic Collection	CD	Essential	ESMCD569	England	1998	14.99
Renbourn, John	Faro Annie	CD	Castle	CMRCD534	England	2002	8.99
Renbourn, John	John Barleycorn	CD	Edsel	EDCD472	England	1996	18.99
Renbourn, John	Lady And The Unicorn/The Hermit	CD	Essential	ESMCD436	England	1996	14.99
Renbourn, John	Live In America	CD	Flying Fish	FF-70103	U.S.A.	1991	8.99
Renbourn, John	Lost Sessions	CD	Edsel	EDCD-490	England	1996	8.99
Renbourn, John	Self Titled + 3	CD	Castle	CMRCD359	England	2001	8.99
Renbourn, John	Self Titled/Another Monday	CD	Essential	ESMCD-408	England	1996	14.99
Renbourn, John	Sir John Alot.... + 3	CD	Castle	CMRCD597	England	2003	8.99
Renbourn, John	So Clear	2CD	Recall	SMDCD-152	England	2000	15.99
Renbourn, John	The Best Of - Goodbye Port Pie Hat	CD	Pulse	PLS-CD-147	England	1996	8.99
Renbourn, John	The Black Balloon	CD	Shanachie	SHANCD-97009	U.S.A.	1990	8.99
Renbourn, John	The Enchanted Garden	CD	Line	TACD-9.00781-0	Germany	1989	11.99
Renbourn, John	The Enchanted Garden	CD	Shanachie	SHANCD-79074	U.S.A.	1990	8.99
Renbourn, John	The Hermit	CD	Shanachie	SHANCD-97014	U.S.A.	1991	8.99
Renbourn, John	The Lady And The Unicorn + 1	CD	Castle	CMRCD625	U.S.A.	2003	8.99
Renbourn, John	The Mediaeval Almanac	CD	Demon	TRADEM-6	England	1989	18.99
Renbourn, John	The Nine Maidens	CD	Line	TACD-9.00783-0	Germany	1989	12.99
Renbourn, John	The Nine Maidens	CD	Flying Fish	FF-70378	U.S.A.	1995	8.99
Renbourn, John	The Ship Of Fools	CD	Flying Fish	FF-70466	U.S.A.	1995	8.99
Renbourn, John	The Three Kingdoms	CD	Shanachie	SHANCD-95006	U.S.A.	1990	18.99
Renbourn, John	There You Go + 2	CD	Big Beat	CDWIKD-186	England	1998	15.99
Renbourn, John	Transatlantic Anthology	2CD	Essential	ESACD858	England	2000	11.99

R

Artist	Title	Format	Label	Catalog No	Country	Released	Value
Renbourn, John	Traveler's Prayer	CD	Shanachie	SHANCD-78018	U.S.A.	1998	8.99
Renbourn, John	Under The Volcano	CD	Kicking Mule	KMCD3910	U.S.A.	1980	18.99
Renbourn, John/R Williamson	Wheel Of Fortune (W/Robin W)	CD	Flying Fish	FF-70626	U.S.A.	1994	8.99
Renbourn, John/S Grossman	Keeper Of The Vine: Best Of	CD	Shanachie	SHANCD-97028	U.S.A.	1999	8.99
Renbourn, John/S Grossman	Live (W/Stefan Grossman)	CD	Shanachie	SHANCD-95001	U.S.A.	1992	18.99
Renbourn, John/S Grossman	Snap A Little Owl	CD	Shanachie	SHANCD-97003	U.S.A.	1990	18.99
REO Speedwagon	2nd Decade Rock & Roll '81-'91	CD	Sony	ESCA 5466	Japan	1991	13.99
REO Speedwagon	2nd Decade Rock & Roll '81-'91	CD	Epic	EK-48527	U.S.A.	1991	6.99
REO Speedwagon	Building The Bridge	CD	Castle	119	U.S.A.	1996	7.99
REO Speedwagon	Decade of Rock & Roll '70-'80	2CD	Epic	E2K-36444	U.S.A.	1990	14.99
REO Speedwagon	Good Trouble	CD	Epic	EK-38100	U.S.A.	1990	13.99
REO Speedwagon	Hi Fidelity/You Can Tune/Live: You	3CD	Sony	85363	U.S.A.	2001	24.99
REO Speedwagon	Hi Infidelity	CD	Epic	EK-61614	U.S.A.	2000	12.99
REO Speedwagon	Hi Infidelity	CD	Sony	ESCA-7659	Japan	1997	13.99
REO Speedwagon	Hi Infidelity (Sony Gold Cd)	CD	Epic	EK-66233	U.S.A.	1981	53.99
REO Speedwagon	Keep On Rollin'	CD	Music Mill	MLI0071008	U.S.A.	2002	8.99
REO Speedwagon	Life As We Know It	CD	Epic	EK-40444	U.S.A.	1990	17.99
REO Speedwagon	Live: You Get What You Play	CD	Epic	EK-34494	U.S.A.	1990	14.99
REO Speedwagon	Lost In A Dream	CD	Epic	EK-32948	U.S.A.	1990	24.99
REO Speedwagon	Nine Lives	CD	Epic	EK-35988	U.S.A.	1990	13.99
REO Speedwagon	Only The Strong Survive	CD	Sony	A-32824	U.S.A.	1998	8.99
REO Speedwagon	R.E.O.	CD	Epic	EK-34143	U.S.A.	1990	13.99
REO Speedwagon	Ridin' The Storm Out	CD	Epic	EK-32378	U.S.A.	1990	12.99
REO Speedwagon	Self Titled	CD	Epic	982962	England	1971	129.99
REO Speedwagon	Simply The Best	CD	Sony	500733	England	2001	7.99
REO Speedwagon	T.W.O.	CD	Epic	EK-31745	U.S.A.	1989	13.99
REO Speedwagon	The Ballads + 3 (W/Bonus Cd)	2CD	Epic	EK-69425	U.S.A.	1999	13.99
REO Speedwagon	The Earth...	CD	Epic	EK-45246	U.S.A.	1990	5.99
REO Speedwagon	The Hits	CD	Epic	477149-2	Australia	1988	8.99
REO Speedwagon	This Time We Mean It	CD	Epic	EK-33338	U.S.A.	1990	68.99
REO Speedwagon	Wheels Are Turnin'	CD	Epic	EK-39593	U.S.A.	1990	9.99
REO Speedwagon	Wheels Are Turnin'	CD	Sony	32-8P-62	Japan	1984	13.99
REO Speedwagon	You Can Tune A Piano...	CD	Epic	EK-61613	U.S.A.	2000	8.99
Replacements	All For Nothing	2CD	Reprise	9-46807-2	U.S.A.	1997	19.99
Replacements	All Shook Down	CD	Sire	9-26298-2	U.S.A.	1990	6.99
Replacements	Don't Tell A Soul	CD	Sire	9-25831-2	U.S.A.	1989	7.99
Replacements	Hootenanny	CD	Twin Tone	TTR-8332-2	U.S.A.	1983	8.99
Replacements	Inconcerated Live (Promo)	CD	Sire	PRO-CD-3633	U.S.A.	1989	23.99
Replacements	Let It Be	CD	Restless	7-73761-2	U.S.A.	2002	9.99
Replacements	Pleased To Meet Me	CD	Sire	9-25557-2	U.S.A.	1987	7.99
Replacements	Sorry Ma, Forgot to Take Out...	CD	Twin Tone	TTR-8123-2	U.S.A.	1981	8.99
Replacements	Stink	CD	Twin Tone	TTR-8228-2	U.S.A.	1982	7.99
Replacements	Tim	CD	Sire	9-25330-2	U.S.A.	1985	7.99
Resende, Marcos	Nonchalance	CD	Line	BSCD-9.01098-0	Germany	1991	9.99
Residents	13th Ann Show Live In Holland	CD	Torso	CD018	Netherlands	1987	24.99
Residents	25 Years Of Eyeball Exellence	CD	Bomba	BOM-22058	Japan	1998	44.99
Residents	25th Anniversary Box Set	4CD	Quirk	6368213729	EEC	2003	124.99
Residents	Assorted Secrets (Numbered)	CD	Ralph	RA-08	U.S.A.	2000	99.99
Residents	Bad Day/Midway (Hybrid MAC/WIN)	CDR	Inscape	1-887428-03-8	U.S.A.	1995	79.99
Residents	Blow Off (Came W/Freak Show Hrdbk)	CD	Cryptic	SP02	U.S.A.	1992	49.99
Residents	Buckaroo Blues	CD	UWEB	UWEB-003	U.S.A.	1989	59.99
Residents	Commercial Album + 10	CD	East Side Digital	ESD-80202	U.S.A.	1988	18.99
Residents	Cube-E Live In Holland	CD	Enigma	7-72567-2	U.S.A.	1990	19.99
Residents	Daydream B-Liver	CD	UWEB	UWEB-005	U.S.A.	1991	34.99
Residents	Demons Dance Alone (Ltd 3000)	2CD	Euroralph	ER-033	Germany	2003	42.99
Residents	Diskomo + 3	CD	Torso	CD421	Netherlands	1990	22.99
Residents	Diskomo 2000	CD	East Side Digital	ESD-81512	U.S.A.	2000	5.99
Residents	Don't Be Cruel + 2	CD Single	Torso	CD166	Netherlands	1990	22.99

R

Artist	Title	Format	Label	Catalog No	Country	Released	Value
Residents	Dot . Com (Only 1200)	CD	Ralph	RA-09	U.S.A.	2000	99.99
Residents	Double Shot + 2 (3")	CD Single	Rykodisc	RCD3-1003	U.S.A.	1988	9.99
Residents	Duck Stab/Buster And Glen + 4	CD	East Side Digital	RESIDE-3	U.S.A.	1987	19.99
Residents	Eskimo + 4	CD	East Side Digital	RESIDE-2	U.S.A.	1987	19.99
Residents	Fingerprince + 4	CD	East Side Digital	RESIDE-4	U.S.A.	1987	22.99
Residents	Freak Show (Promo Hybrid MAC/WIN)	CDR	Voyager	CDRM-1255030	U.S.A.	1994	79.99
Residents	Freak Show (Promo/MAC)	CD-Rom	Euroralph	NONE	Denmark	1994	99.99
Residents	Freak Show + 1	CD	Euroralph	CD005	Denmark	1994	17.99
Residents	Freak Show 13th Ann Edition	2CD	Ralph	RA014	U.S.A.	2002	99.99
Residents	Freak Show Deluxe (Same + Cd-Rom)	CD	Euroralph	BOX002	Denmark	1994	39.99
Residents	George And James	2 Cd-Rom	Euroralph	NONE	Denmark	1993	99.99
Residents	George And James	CD	East Side Digital	ESD-81482	U.S.A.	2000	19.99
Residents	Gingerbread Man	CD	East Side Digital	ESD-80172	U.S.A.	1995	9.99
Residents	Gingerbread Man (Windows)	CD-Rom	Ion	40068	U.S.A.	1993	59.99
Residents	God In Three Persons	CD	East Side Digital	ESD-81502	U.S.A.	2000	12.99
Residents	God Three Persons (Vocal/No Vocal)	2CD	Euroralph	CD022	Denmark	2000	31.99
Residents	Have A Bad Day	CD	East Side Digital	ESD-81202	U.S.A.	1995	11.99
Residents	Heaven?	CD	Rykodisc	RCD-20012	U.S.A.	1986	14.99
Residents	Hell !	CD	Rykodisc	RCD-20013	U.S.A.	1986	15.99
Residents	Holy Kiss Of Flesh (3") Gatefold	CD Single	Rykodisc	RCD3-1007	U.S.A.	1988	9.99
Residents	Holy Kiss Of Flesh (3") Remixed	CD Single	Euroralph	SP04	Denmark	1993	14.99
Residents	Hunters	CD	Milan	73138-35701-2	U.S.A.	1995	9.99
Residents	Hunters (Diff Cvr/Räuber der Wildnis)	CD	Milan	74321-31169-2	Denmark	1995	16.99
Residents	I Hate Heaven (Promo/1500)	CD Single	Euroralph	CD-020	Denmark	1998	9.99
Residents	Icky Flix (O.S.T.)	CD	East Side Digital	ESD-81572	U.S.A.	2000	9.99
Residents	In Between Screams... (Only 1000)	CD	Ralph	NONE	U.S.A.	1999	26.99
Residents	Intermission	CD	East Side Digital	ESD-81312	U.S.A.	1998	18.99
Residents	Kaw-Liga (Prairie Mix) + 1 (3")	CD Single	Torso	CD322	Netherlands	1988	24.99
Residents	Kaw-Liga (The Housey Mix) + 1	CD Single	Torso	CD110	Netherlands	1989	17.99
Residents	Kettles Of Fish...	3CD	Euroralph	BOX-029	Denmark	2003	109.99
Residents	Land Of Mystery (Only 1300)	CD	Ralph	RA-005	U.S.A.	1999	42.99
Residents	Live At The Fillmore (Only 1200)	2CD	Ralph	NONE	U.S.A.	1998	116.99
Residents	Liver Music	CD	UWEB	UWEB-004	U.S.A.	1990	34.99
Residents	Louisiana's Lick (DJ/Gatefold/Poster)	CD	East Side Digital	ESDUNWAXED5	U.S.A.	1995	49.99
Residents	Mark Of The Mole + 5	CD	East Side Digital	ESD-80272	U.S.A.	1987	14.99
Residents	Meet The Residents + 4	CD	East Side Digital	ESD-80222	U.S.A.	1987	18.99
Residents	Not Available + 6	CD	East Side Digital	ESD-80192	U.S.A.	1987	14.99
Residents	Our Finest Flowers (5000/W/Note)	CD	East Side Digital	ESD-80782	U.S.A.	1992	15.99
Residents	Our Tired...	4CD	Euroralph	CD-017	Denmark	1997	114.99
Residents	Our Tired....	2CD	Rykodisc	RCD-10425	U.S.A.	1997	19.99
Residents	Petting Zoo	CD	East Side Digital	ESD-81662	U.S.A.	2002	8.99
Residents	Pollex Christi	CD	Ralph	RA001	U.S.A.	1997	99.99
Residents	Poor Kaw-Liga's Pain	CD Single	Euroralph	CD004	Denmark	1994	22.99
Residents	Prelude To "The Ted"	CD	Hello Club	HEL-38	U.S.A.	1993	42.99
Residents	Refused (Only 1333)	CD	Ralph	RA06	U.S.A.	1999	99.99
Residents	Residue Redux	CD	East Side Digital	ESD-81322	U.S.A.	1998	16.99
Residents	Roadworms: The Berlin Sessions	CD	East Side Digital	ESD-81532	U.S.A.	2000	14.99
Residents	Santa Dog '92	CD	UWEB	UWEB-009	U.S.A.	1992	34.99
Residents	Stars And Hank Forever + 1	CD	Torso	CD022	Netherlands	1986	22.99
Residents	Stranger Than Supper	CD	UWEB	USP-0012	U.S.A.	1990	34.99
Residents	The Big Bubble + 3	CD	East Side Digital	ESD-80342	U.S.A.	1989	14.99
Residents	The King And Eye	CD	Enigma	7-73547-2	U.S.A.	1989	24.99
Residents	The Mole Show Live At The Roxy	CD	Bomba	BOM-22062	Japan	1998	25.99
Residents	The Mole Show Live In Holland	CD	East Side Digital	ESD-80352	U.S.A.	1989	28.99
Aesidents	The Snakey Wake	CD	UWEB	UWEB-002	U.S.A.	1988	34.99
Residents	The Third Reich And Roll + 4	CD	East Side Digital	RESIDE-1	U.S.A.	1987	18.99
Residents	The Tunes Of Two Cities + 3	CD	East Side Digital	ESD-80282	U.S.A.	1988	18.99
Residents	U Willie/Guide Residents (W/Book)	CD	Ralph	RZ9302/RS9309	U.S.A.	1993	34.99

Artist	Title	Format	Label	Catalog No	Country	Released	Value
Residents	Whatever Happened To.. + 9	CD	East Side Digital	ESD-80592	U.S.A.	1991	17.99
Residents	Wormwood Live 1999 (Only 1200)	2CD	Ralph	RA-07	U.S.A.	1999	149.99
Residents	Wormwood: Curious... (W/Sticker)	CD	Euroralph	CD-019	Denmark	1998	14.99
Residents (CB/Eyebll/Skr/4 B)	Freak Show St (Cd/Lp/TShirt/Pstcrd)	CD	Euroralph	BOX001	Denmark	1994	99.99
Residents/ Bad Day CD-Rom	Graphical History Text (DJ Press Kit)	CDR	Euroralph	NONE	Denmark	1999	99.99
Residents/1000 (Promo)	For Elise (10 Min Longer Than Lp)	CD	Cryptic	CUBE-N-Y-E	U.S.A.	1990	99.99
Residents/500/Bubble Wrap	13th Ann (Live Japan Eyeball Show)	2CD	UWEB	UWEB-006/007	U.S.A.	1992	59.99
Residents/Combo Mechanico	High Horses (W/2 Raffle Tickets)	CD	Ralph	RA11	U.S.A.	2001	99.99
Residents/Hand #rd	Freak Show SE (W/Hrdbk/Only 1000)	2CD	Dark Horse	1-878574-32-9	U.S.A.	1991	49.99
Residents/No Lead Vocals	God In Three Persons Soundtrack	CD	Rykodisc	RCD-10045	U.S.A.	1988	9.99
Residents/Only 1003	Eat Exuding Oinks (Hand Numbered)	CD	Ralph	RA12	U.S.A.	2002	99.99
Residents/Only 3000	Demons Dance Alone (W/Bonus Cd)	2CD	East Side Digital	ESD-81672	U.S.A.	2002	69.99
Residents/Signed/U Willie	Santa Dog '88 (Green Or Yellow)	CD	UWEB	UWEB-001	U.S.A.	1988	34.99
Residents/W Cigar Box/1200	Roosevelt 2.0 (W/Abridged P Christi)	CD	Ralph	RA-010	U.S.A.	2000	99.99
Revell, Graeme	Crow: The City Of Angels (S.T./Promo)	CD	Hollywood	PRCD-62047-2	U.S.A.	1996	24.99
Rhinoceros	Better Times/Satin Chickens	CD	Collector´s Choice	CCM-386-2	U.S.A.	2003	9.99
Rhinoceros	Rhinoceros	CD	Collector´s Choice	CCM-284-2	U.S.A.	2002	8.99
Rhinoceros	Tiny Ghosts	CD	Rice Monster	RICEMOCD1	England	2003	19.99
Rhodes, Emitt	Daisy-Fresh...Best Of Dunhill Years	CD	Edsel	EDCD-569	England	1998	14.99
Rhodes, Emitt	Farewell To Paradise	CD	Victor Ent.	UICY-3376	Japan	2002	23.99
Rhodes, Emitt	Listen Listen The Best of Emitt Rhodes	CD	Varese	VSD-5591	U.S.A.	1995	9.99
Rhodes, Emitt	Mirror	CD	Victor Ent.	UICY-3375	Japan	2002	24.99
Rhodes, Emitt	Self Titled	CD	One Way	MCAD-22078	U.S.A.	1996	23.99
Rhodes, Emitt	Self Titled	CD	Victor Ent.	UICY-3321	Japan	2002	29.99
Rhodes, Emitt	The American Dream	CD	Victor Ent.	UICY-3322	Japan	2002	29.99
Rhodes, Emitt/M Go Round	You're A Very Lovely Woman (Live)	CD	Polydor	POCM-2015	Japan	1995	37.99
Rhodes, Emitt/M Go Round	You're A Very Lovely Woman/Live	CD	Pony Canyon	PCCY-10059	Japan	1996	39.99
Rich Kids	Ghosts Of Princes In Towers	CD	Dojo	CD-151	England	1993	13.99
Richard, Cliff	1950's	CD	EMI	7243-5-40061-2	England	2002	8.99
Richard, Cliff	1960's	CD	EMI	7243-4-97133-2-1	England	1998	8.99
Richard, Cliff	1960's/1970's/1980's Box Set	3CD	EMI	7243-4-98264-2-7	England	1998	24.99
Richard, Cliff	1970's	CD	EMI	7243-4-97134-2-0	U.S.A.	1998	8.99
Richard, Cliff	1980's	CD	EMI	7243-4-97135-2-9	England	1998	8.99
Richard, Cliff	1990's	CD	EMI	7243-5-40062-2	England	2001	8.99
Richard, Cliff	21 Today (Mono)	CD	EMI	495442-2	England	1998	14.99
Richard, Cliff	21 Today/32 Minutes/17 Seconds	CD	EMI	7243-5-34701-2	England	2001	11.99
Richard, Cliff	31st Of Febuary St./I'm Nearly Famous	2CD	EMI	0777-7-80491-2	England	1992	49.99
Richard, Cliff	32 Min/17 Sec/When/Spain (Stereo)	2CD	EMI	0777-7-80423-2	England	1992	49.99
Richard, Cliff	40 Golden Greats	2CD	EMI	CDS-7-92425-2	England	1989	20.99
Richard, Cliff	40th Anniversary Complete	5CD	EMI	493405-2	Australia	1998	44.99
Richard, Cliff	About That Man/His Land	2CD	EMI	0777-7-80482-2	England	1992	49.99
Richard, Cliff	Always Guaranteed + 8	CD	EMI	7243-5-83403-2-7	England	2004	11.99
Richard, Cliff	At The Movies	2CD	EMI	7243-8-52790-2	England	1996	12.99
Richard, Cliff	Carols	CD	Word	WRD-3034	England	1988	34.99
Richard, Cliff	Carols & Christmas Songs	CD	Alliance	ALD-025	England	1995	29.99
Richard, Cliff	Celebration	CD	EMI	CDP-791-370	England	1990	29.99
Richard, Cliff	Cliff + 16 (Mono/Stereo)	CD	EMI	495438-2	England	1998	14.99
Richard, Cliff	Cliff At Christmas	CD	EMI	7243-5-93498-2-4	England	2003	11.99
Richard, Cliff	Cliff In Japan (Live) /Two A Penny	2CD	EMI	0777-7-80441-2	England	1992	49.99
Richard, Cliff	Cliff Sings (M)/Me/My Shadows (St)	2CD	EMI	0777-7-80417-2-6	England	1992	49.99
Richard, Cliff	Cliff Sings + 16 (Mono/Stereo)	CD	EMI	495439-2	England	1998	14.99
Richard, Cliff	Cliff/Cliff Sings	CD	EMI	7243-5-34600-2	England	2001	11.99
Richard, Cliff	Don't Stop Me Now/Good News	2CD	EMI	0777-7-80438-2	England	1992	49.99
Richard, Cliff	Dressed For The Ocassion + 5	CD	EMI	7243-5-83404-2-6	England	2004	11.99
Richard, Cliff	Established 1958/Best Of Vol. 1	2CD	EMI	0777-7-80450-2	England	1992	49.99
Richard, Cliff	Every Face Tells A Story + 3	CD	EMI	7243-5-38370-2-0	England	2002	11.99
Richard, Cliff	Every Face Tells A Story/Small Corners	2CD	EMI	0777-7-80494-2	England	1992	49.99
Richard, Cliff	Finders Keepers/Cinderella	2CD	EMI	0777-7-80435-2	England	1992	49.99

R

Artist	Title	Format	Label	Catalog No	Country	Released	Value
Richard, Cliff	Green Light + 3	CD	EMI	7243-5-38369-2-4	England	2002	11.99
Richard, Cliff	Green Light/Thank You Very Much	2CD	EMI	0777-7-80496-2	England	1992	49.99
Richard, Cliff	Heathcliff Live	CD	EMI	7243-8-54768-2	England	1997	17.99
Richard, Cliff	Hymns And Inspirational Songs	CD	Alliance	ALD-022	England	1994	29.99
Richard, Cliff	I'm Nearly Famous + 5	CD	EMI	7243-5-33114-2-1	England	2001	11.99
Richard, Cliff	I'm No Hero + 2	CD	EMI	7243-5-33113-2-2	England	2001	11.99
Richard, Cliff	In Conversation	CD	Baktabak	CBAK-4085	England	1994	8.99
Richard, Cliff	It's A Small World	CD	Alliance	ALD-023	England	1994	29.99
Richard, Cliff	Listen To Cliff + 2 (Mono/2 Stereo)	CD	EMI	495441-2	England	1998	14.99
Richard, Cliff	Listen To Cliff/21 Today (Both Stereo)	2CD	EMI	0777-7-80420-2-6	England	1992	49.99
Richard, Cliff	Live & Guaranteed 1988	CD	EMI	7243-8-31697-2-6	England	1995	14.99
Richard, Cliff	Love Is Forever/Good News	CD	EMI	7243-5-41085-2	England	2002	11.99
Richard, Cliff	Love Is Forever/Kinda Latin (B Stereo)	2CD	EMI	0777-7-80432-2	England	1992	49.99
Richard, Cliff	Love Songs	CD	EMI	CDP-7-48049-2	England	1998	11.99
Richard, Cliff	Me & My Shadows/Listen To Cliff	CD	EMI	7243-5-34700-2	England	2001	11.99
Richard, Cliff	Me/My Shadows + 16 (Mono/Stereo)	CD	EMI	495440-2	England	1998	14.99
Richard, Cliff	My Songs	CD	EMI	7243-5-90965-2-0	England	2003	11.99
Richard, Cliff	Now You See Me.. Now You Don't + 3	CD	EMI	7243-5-38371-2-9	England	2002	11.99
Richard, Cliff	Private Collection (Video Cd)	CD	EMI	PMCD-491443-2	England	1988	10.99
Richard, Cliff	Real As I Wanna Be (Digipack Ltd.)	CD	EMI	7243-4-97951-2-9	England	1998	8.99
Richard, Cliff	Rock 'N' Roll Juvenile + 2	CD	EMI	7243-5-33115-2-0	England	2001	11.99
Richard, Cliff	Rock 'N' Roll Silver/Rock Connection	2CD	EMI	0777-7-80499-2	England	1992	49.99
Richard, Cliff	Rock On With	CD	Music For Pleasure	MFP-6005	England	1987	28.99
Richard, Cliff	Rockin' With	CD	EMI	7243-5-81703-2-0	England	2003	11.99
Richard, Cliff	Rockspel	CD	Kingsway	KMCD-2418	England	2002	11.99
Richard, Cliff	Self Titled (St)/When In Rome (Mono)	2CD	EMI	0777-7-80429-2	England	1992	49.99
Richard, Cliff	Self Titled/Don't Stop Me Now	CD	EMI	7243-5-41084-2	England	2002	11.99
Richard, Cliff	Silver + 3	CD	EMI	7243-5-38372-2-8	England	2002	11.99
Richard, Cliff	Sincerely/Cliff Live/Talk Of The Town	2CD	EMI	0777-7-80444-2	England	1992	49.99
Richard, Cliff	Sings The Standards	CD	EMI	7243-5-91059-2-5	England	2003	11.99
Richard, Cliff	Songs From Heathcliff	CD	EMI	7243-8-35762-2	England	1995	12.99
Richard, Cliff	Stronger + 5	CD	EMI	7243-5-83407-2-3	England	2004	11.99
Richard, Cliff	Take Me High/Help It Along	2CD	EMI	0777-7-80488-2	England	1992	49.99
Richard, Cliff	The Album	CD	EMI	0777-7-89114-2-5	England	1993	10.99
Richard, Cliff	The E.P. Collection	CD	See For Miles	SEE-CD-280	England	1989	28.99
Richard, Cliff	The Hit List	2CD	EMI	7243-8-30917-2-0	England	1994	24.99
Richard, Cliff	The Rock & Roll Years	CD	EMI	7243-8-59309-2-8	England	1997	13.99
Richard, Cliff	The Rock & Roll Years '58-'63 Box	4CD	EMI	7243-8-57881-2-3	England	1997	64.99
Richard, Cliff	The Rock Connection + 6	CD	EMI	7243-5-83416-2-1	England	2004	11.99
Richard, Cliff	The Singles Collection	6CD	EMI	7243-5-37551-2	England	2002	55.99
Richard, Cliff	The Whole Story - His Greatest Hits	2CD	EMI	7243-5-29322-2	England	2000	17.99
Richard, Cliff	The Winner	CD	Alliance	ALD-020	England	1995	29.99
Richard, Cliff	Together	CD	EMI	CDEMD-1028	England	1991	10.99
Richard, Cliff	Tracks 'N' Grooves/Best Of Vol. 2	2CD	EMI	0777-7-80485-2	England	1992	49.99
Richard, Cliff	Walking In The Light	CD	Alliance	ALD-024	England	1994	29.99
Richard, Cliff	Wanted	CD	Papillion	WANTED-1	England	2001	11.99
Richard, Cliff	When In Spain/Kinda Latin	CD	EMI	7243-5-41086-2	England	2002	11.99
Richard, Cliff	Wired For Sound + 2	CD	EMI	7243-5-33112-2-3	England	2001	11.99
Richard, Cliff	Wonderful Life/Aladdin (Both Stereo)	2CD	EMI	0777-7-80426-2	England	1992	49.99
Richard, Cliff/Program/Photos	Live At ABC Kingston 1962 Ltd. Ed.	CD	EMI	7243-5-37931-2-8	England	2002	29.99
Richard, Cliff/Shadows	Summer Holiday + 10	CD	EMI	7243-5-43995-2	England	2003	14.99
Richard, Cliff/Young Ones	The Young Ones	CD	Music For Pleasure	MFP-6020	England	1988	11.99
Richard, Zachary	High Time: Elektra Recordings (5000)	CD	Rhino	RHM2-7727	U.S.A.	2000	22.99
Richards, Keith	999	CD Single	Virgin	DPRO-12770	U.S.A.	1992	18.99
Richards, Keith	Eileen	CD Single	Virgin	V25H-12647	U.S.A.	1993	18.99
Richards, Keith	Eileen (Promo)	CD Single	Virgin	DPRO-12745	U.S.A.	1992	18.99
Richards, Keith	Eileen (Promo)	CD Single	Virgin	KRICH-1	England	1992	21.99
Richards, Keith	Main Offender	CD	Virgin	0777-7-86499-2-2	U.S.A.	1992	13.99

R

Artist	Title	Format	Label	Catalog No	Country	Released	Value
Richards, Keith	Take It So Hard (Promo)	CD Single	Virgin	PR-CD-2396	U.S.A.	1988	49.99
Richards, Keith	Talk Is Cheap (3/3" CD Singles)	3CD	Virgin	2-91047	England	1988	21.99
Richards, Keith	Talk Is Cheap (MFSL Gold Cd)	CD	Mobile Fidelity	UDCD-557	U.S.A.	1988	27.99
Richards, Keith	Wicked As It Seems (Promo)	CD Single	Virgin	DPRO-12715	U.S.A.	1992	18.99
Richards, Keith	Wicked As It Seems (Promo)	CD Single	Virgin	VUSCD-69	Denmark	1992	21.99
Richards, Keith	You Don't Move Me (Promo)	CD Single	Virgin	PR-CD-2557	U.S.A.	1988	14.99
Richards, Keith/X Winos	Live At The Hollywood Palladium	CD	Virgin	2-91808	U.S.A.	1991	6.99
Richards, Keith/X Winos	Live Palladium (W/Box/T-Shirt/Video)	CD	Virgin	VJCP-36032	Japan	1991	99.99
Richman, Jonathan	¡Jonathan, Te Vas A Emocionar!	CD	Rounder	CD-9040	U.S.A.	1994	10.99
Richman, Jonathan	A Plea For Tenderness	CD	Nectar Masters	NTMCD506	England	1995	10.99
Richman, Jonathan	Action Packed: The Best Of	CD	Rounder	1166-11596-2	U.S.A.	2002	11.99
Richman, Jonathan	And The Modern Lovers	CD	Rev-Ola	CREV008	England	1993	9.99
Richman, Jonathan	Back In Your Life	CD	Line	BECD-9.00466-0	Germany	1987	12.99
Richman, Jonathan	Having A Party With	CD	Rounder	CD-9026	U.S.A.	1991	10.99
Richman, Jonathan	Her Mystery Not Of High Heels...	CD	Vapor	9-48216-2	U.S.A.	2001	8.99
Richman, Jonathan	I, Jonathan	CD	Rounder	CD-9036	U.S.A.	1992	10.99
Richman, Jonathan	I'm So Confused	CD	Vapor	9-47086-2	U.S.A.	1998	8.99
Richman, Jonathan	Jonathan Goes Country	CD	Rounder	CD-9024	U.S.A.	1990	10.99
Richman, Jonathan	Jonathan Richman	CD	Rounder	RCD-9021	U.S.A.	1989	10.99
Richman, Jonathan	Jonathan Richman/Modern Lovers	CD	Line	BECD-9.00477-0	Germany	1987	12.99
Richman, Jonathan	Mega Hits	CD	Line	BECD-9.00496-0	Germany	1988	24.99
Richman, Jonathan	Modern Lover 88	CD	Rounder	RCD-9014	U.S.A.	1987	10.99
Richman, Jonathan	Rock 'N' Roll With The Modern Lovers	CD	Line	BECD-9.00488-0	Germany	1987	12.99
Richman, Jonathan	Rock 'N' Roll With The Modern Lovers	CD	Rev-Ola	CREV010	England	1993	9.99
Richman, Jonathan	Springtime In New York (Promo)	CD Single	Vapor	100844	U.S.A.	2001	6.99
Richman, Jonathan	Surrender To Jonathan	CD	Vapor	9-46296-2	U.S.A.	1996	8.99
Richman, Jonathan	The Modern Lovers	CD	Rev-Ola	CREV007	England	1993	9.99
Richman, Jonathan	You Must Ask The Heart	CD	Rounder	CD-9047	U.S.A.	1995	10.99
Richman, Jonathan/R Birds	Jonathan Jonathan	CD	Columbia	HVN-17CD	England	1992	24.99
Ridgway, Stan	Anatomy	CD	New West	NW6010	U.S.A.	1999	17.99
Ridgway, Stan	Big Heat + 6	CD	Capitol	13125	U.S.A.	1993	24.99
Ridgway, Stan	Black Diamond + 1	CD	New West	NW6034	U.S.A.	2002	17.99
Ridgway, Stan	Drywall Incident (O.S.T.)	CD	Birdcage	11016	Australia	1997	11.99
Ridgway, Stan	Drywall: Work The ...	CD	Capitol	28715	U.S.A.	1995	24.99
Ridgway, Stan	Film Songs	CD	Birdcage	15326	Australia	1997	11.99
Ridgway, Stan	Fly On The Wall (Int. And Music Promo)	CD	Geffen	PRO-CD-3508	U.S.A.	1989	19.99
Ridgway, Stan	Holiday In Dirt	CD	New West	NW6033	U.S.A.	2002	17.99
Ridgway, Stan	Mosquitoes	CD	Geffen	2-24216	U.S.A.	1989	8.99
Ridgway, Stan	Partyball	CD	Geffen	GEFD-24385	U.S.A.	1991	8.99
Ridgway, Stan	Songs That Made...Best Of	CD	I.R.S.	X2-13139	U.S.A.	1992	14.99
Ridgway, Stan	The Way I Feel Today	CD	Dis-Informatio	300-2	U.S.A.	1998	11.99
Ridgway, Stan/H Angels	Hecate's Angels (W/Stan's Wife/Stan)	CD	Birdcage	11010	Australia	1996	11.99
Ridley, Mike	Attitude Check	CD	R&A	10801-2	U.S.A.	1990	8.99
Riff Raff	Original Man	CD	Disconforme	DISC1953CD	Andorra	1999	10.99
Riff Raff	Outside Looking In	CD	Disconforme	DISC1951CD	Andorra	1999	14.99
Riff Raff	Self Tited	CD	Disconforme	DISC1952CD	Andorra	1999	10.99
RiffBurglars	Swag	CD	Line	INCD-9.00089-0	Germany	1987	24.99
Right Said Fred	I'm Too Sexy	CD Single	Charisma	96256-2	U.S.A.	1991	5.99
Righteous Brothers	Anthology 1962 - 1974	2CD	Rhino	R2-71488	U.S.A.	1989	99.99
Righteous Brothers	Reunion	CD	Curb	D2-77423	U.S.A.	1994	9.99
Righteous Brothers	The Very Best Of: Unchained Melody	CD	Verve	847-248-2	U.S.A.	1990	8.99
Riley, Terry	A Rainbow In Curved Air	CD	Columbia	MK-7315	U.S.A.	1969	8.99
Riley, Terry	Atlantis Nath (Ltd 1000 Signed)	CD	SRI Moonshine	SMM-001	U.S.A.	2002	34.99
Riley, Terry	Book Of Abbeyozzud	CD	New Albion	CDRILEYBOOK	U.S.A.	2000	17.99
Riley, Terry	Chanting The Light Foresight	CD	New Albion	CDRILEYCHAN	U.S.A.	1998	15.99
Riley, Terry	Descending Moonshine...	2CD	Kuckuck	KUCK-12047	Germany	1983	44.99
Riley, Terry	In C	CD	Wergo	WER-6650	Germany	2002	8.99
Riley, Terry	In C	CD	Columbia	94983-2	Germany	1968	8.99

R

Artist	Title	Format	Label	Catalog No	Country	Released	Value
Riley, Terry	In C	CD	Atma	22251	Canada	2001	8.99
Riley, Terry	In C (Mixed W/Brian Eno, Jon Hassell)	CD	Celestial Harmonies	13026-2	U.S.A.	1989	29.99
Riley, Terry	In C: 25th Anniversary Concert	CD	New Albion	CDRILEYIN-C	U.S.A.	1998	17.99
Riley, Terry	Keyboard Studies	CD	MDG Scene	MDG-1135	Germany	2002	19.99
Riley, Terry	Lisbon Concert	CD	New Albion	CDRILEYLISB	U.S.A.	1998	12.99
Riley, Terry	Music For A Gift	CD	Cortical Foundation	CORTI-01	U.S.A.	1998	13.99
Riley, Terry	Olson III	CD	Cortical Foundation	CDRILEYOLSO	U.S.A.	1999	12.99
Riley, Terry	Poppy Nogood...	CD	Cortical Foundation	CORTI-04	U.S.A.	1968	13.99
Riley, Terry	Reed Streams	CD	Cortical Foundation	CDRILEYREED	U.S.A.	1999	13.99
Riley, Terry	The Padova Concert	CD	Amiata	6-57711-0292-2-8	Italy	1992	8.99
Riley, Terry	With Pierre Marietan; Keyboard Studies	CD	Spalax	14542	France	1998	19.99
Riley, Terry	You're No Good	2CD	Cortical Foundation	CDRILEYYOUR	U.S.A.	2001	24.99
Riley, Terry	Zeitgeist Intuitive Leaps	CD	Work Music	WRK002-3	England	1994	24.99
Riley, Terry/Bang On A Can	In C	CD	Cantaloupe	21004	U.S.A.	2001	10.99
Riley, Terry/G Cheng-Cochran	Piano Music Of John Adam/Terry Riley	CD	Telarc	80513	Germany	1998	11.99
Rill, Markus/Gunslingers	Nowhere Beginns	CD	Line	LICD—9.01383-0	Germany	2001	18.99
Rimes, Leann	How Do I Live	CD Single	Curb	D2-73022	U.S.A.	1997	5.99
Riot	Angel Eyes	CD Single	Zero	XRCN-2018	Japan	1997	12.99
Riot	Born In America	CD	Metal Blade	3984-14234-2	U.S.A.	1999	8.99
Riot	Fire Down Under + 2	CD	Metal Blade	3984-14233-2	U.S.A.	1999	9.99
Riot	Inishmore	CD	Metal Blade	3984-14150-2	U.S.A.	1998	8.99
Riot	Live	CD	Metal Blade	3984-14011-2	U.S.A.	1993	12.99
Riot	Live In Japan	CD	Metal Blade	3984-14241-2	U.S.A.	1999	14.99
Riot	Narita	CD	Sony	CSCS-5023	Japan	1979	31.99
Riot	Night Breaker	CD	Metal Blade	3984-14239-2	U.S.A.	1999	9.99
Riot	Privilege Of Power	CD	Collectables	7448	U.S.A.	2003	8.99
Riot	Restless Breed	CD	Metal Blade	3984-14232-2	U.S.A.	1999	9.99
Riot	Riot In Japan - Live!!!	CD	Sony	SRCS-5810	Japan	1992	24.99
Riot	Rock City	CD	Sony	CSCS-5022	Japan	1977	24.99
Riot	Rock City	CD	Metal Blade	3984-14009-2	U.S.A.	1993	8.99
Riot	Shine On	CD	Zero	XRCN-2025	Japan	1998	9.99
Riot	Sons Of Society	CD	Metal Blade	3984-14249-2	U.S.A.	1999	8.99
Riot	The Brethren Of The Long House	CD	Metal Blade	3984-14240-2	U.S.A.	1999	14.99
Riot	The Privilege Of Power	CD	Sony	CSCS-5053	Japan	1990	17.99
Riot	Through The Storm	CD	Metal Blade	3984-14399-2	U.S.A.	2002	9.99
Riot	Through The Storm +1	CD	Toshiba-EMI	TOCP-67017	Japan	2000	24.99
Riot	Thundersteel	CD	Collectables	7404	U.S.A.	2001	12.99
Riot Squad/Graham Bonnett	Anytime (W/Mitch Mitchell)	CD	Repertoire	REP-4192-WZ	Germany	1991	11.99
Riot Squad/Graham Bonnett	Jump !	CD	Castle	CMRCD703	England	2003	11.99
Riperton, Minnie	Stay In Love	CD	Toshiba-EMI	TOCP-7736	Japan	1977	68.99
Rittenour, Lee	Rit	CD	Discovery	71013-2	U.S.A.	1995	54.99
Riverdogs/Vivian Campbell	Self Titled	CD	Epic	ZK-46021	U.S.A.	1990	11.99
Riverdogs/Vivian Campbell	Self Titled	CD	Sony	CSCS-5228	Japan	1990	12.99
Rivers, Bob	Best Of Twisted Tunes, Vol. 1	CD	Atlantic	83044-2	U.S.A.	1997	8.99
Rivers, Bob	Best Of Twisted Tunes, Vol. 2	CD	Atlantic	83045-2	U.S.A.	1997	8.99
Rivers, Bob	Chipmunks Roasting...	CD	Atlantic	83389-2	U.S.A.	2000	18.99
Rivers, Bob	More Twisted Christmas	CD	Atlantic	83043-2	U.S.A.	1997	24.99
Rivers, Bob	Take Baseball And Shove It (Promo)	CD Single	Atlantic	PRCD-5925	U.S.A.	1994	5.99
Rivers, Bob	Twisted Christmas	CD	Atlantic	90671-2	U.S.A.	1990	19.99
Rivers, Bob	Twisted Christmas Box Set	CD	Atlantic	82714-2	U.S.A.	1994	24.99
Rivers, Bob	Twisted Tunes	CD	Atlantic	82717-2	U.S.A.	1994	14.99
Rivers, Bob	White Trash Christmas	CD	Atlantic	83591-2	U.S.A.	2002	19.99
Rivers, Bob & Twisted Radio	I Am Santa Claus	CD	Atlantic	82548-2	U.S.A.	1993	14.99
Rivers, Johnny	At The Whisky A Go.../Here We Go..	CD	BGO	BGOCD241	England	1994	18.99
Rivers, Johnny	Changes/Rewind	CD	EMI	7-99900-2	U.S.A.	1992	43.99
Rivers, Johnny	Golden Hits + 12	CD	Magic	3930113	France	2001	20.99
Rivers, Johnny	In Action/Changes	CD	BGO	BGOCD355	England	1998	15.99
Rivers, Johnny	Last Boogie In Paris (Live)	CD	Varese	VSD-5580	U.S.A.	1995	24.99

R

Artist	Title	Format	Label	Catalog No	Country	Released	Value
Rivers, Johnny	Last Train To Memphis	CD	Soul City	SCRI-3009	U.S.A.	1998	11.99
Rivers, Johnny	Memphis Sun Recordings	CD	Soul City	SCRI-2008	U.S.A.	1991	9.99
Rivers, Johnny	Realization	CD	Soul City	SCRI-4010-2	U.S.A.	1998	9.99
Rivers, Johnny	Rewind/Realization	CD	BGO	BGOCD401	England	1998	15.99
Rivers, Johnny	Rocks The Folk/Meanwhile Back...	2CD	BGO	BGOCD299	England	1995	20.99
Rivers, Johnny	Slim Slo Slider/Home Grown	2CD	BGO	BGOCD453	England	1999	17.99
Rivers, Johnny	The Best Of Johnny Rivers	CD	EMI	8146102	Australia	1995	8.99
Rivers, Johnny	Totally Live At The Whisky A Go Go	CD	EMI	7243-8-32819-2-3	U.S.A.	1995	9.99
Robertson, Don	Dawn (Psychedelic)	CD	Akarma	AK-240-CD	Italy	2003	16.99
Robertson, Robbie	Contact From The Underworld...	CD	Capitol	7243-8-54243-2-8	U.S.A.	1998	8.99
Robertson, Robbie	In The Blood (Promo)	CD Single	Capitol	7087-6-12876-2-2	U.S.A.	1998	9.99
Robertson, Robbie	In The Blood (Promo)	CD Single	EMI	CDCLDJ	England	1998	18.99
Robertson, Robbie	Music For The Native Americans	CD	Capitol	7243-8-28295-2-2	U.S.A.	1994	11.99
Robertson, Robbie	Robbie Robertson (MFSL Gold Cd)	CD	Mobile Fidelity	UDCD-618	U.S.A.	1987	24.99
Robertson, Robbie	Storyville	CD	Geffen	GEFD-24303	U.S.A.	1991	8.99
Robertson, Robbie	The Story Of Storyville (Promo)	CD	Geffen	GEFD-91102	Canada	1991	13.99
Robinson, Chris	New Earth Mud (Advance Copy)	CD	Redline Ent.	ADC-2003	U.S.A.	2002	11.99
Robinson, Chris	New Earth Mud (W/Bonus DVD)	2CD	Redline Ent.	70009	U.S.A.	2002	9.99
Robinson, James/Change	Guilty	CD	Sony	32DP-853	Japan	1987	64.99
Robinson, Smokey/Miracles	The 35th Ann Collection Box Set	4CD	Motown	37463-6334-2	U.S.A.	1994	24.99
Robinson, Tom	2-4-6-8 Motorway (Gold Cd)	CD	K Point	1621.1006-2	Czech	1994	8.99
Robinson, Tom	Cabaret '79 Glad To Be Gay + 4	CD	Castaway Northwes	CNWVP003CD	U.S.A.	1997	14.99
Robinson, Tom	Glad To Be Gay	CD	Line	LICD-9.00261-0	Germany	1988	14.99
Robinson, Tom	Glad To Be Gay/Last Tango	2CD	Line	LICD-9.21215-S	Germany	1992	19.99
Robinson, Tom	Last Tango	CD	Line	LICD-9.00588-0	Germany	1989	14.99
Robinson, Tom	Last Tango/Midnight At The Fringe + 6	CD	Castaway Northwes	CNWVP002CD	Austria	1997	16.99
Robinson, Tom	Living In A Boom Time	CD	Kinetic	KRO-915	Canada	1992	14.99
Robinson, Tom	Love Over Rage	CD	Priority	P2-53913	U.S.A.	1994	7.99
Robinson, Tom	Loved By You (W/Glad To Be Gay '94)	CD Single	Cooking Vinyl	FRY-CD029	England	1994	8.99
Robinson, Tom	North By Northwest + 5	CD	Castaway Northwes	CNWVP004CD	Austria	1997	14.99
Robinson, Tom	Smelling Dogs	CD	Castaway Northwes	CNWVP013CD	England	2001	8.99
Robinson, Tom	Still Loving You + 5	CD	Castaway Northwes	CNWVP006CD	U.S.A.	1997	16.99
Robinson, Tom	War Baby + 8	CD	Castaway Northwes	CNWVP007CD	U.S.A.	1997	14.99
Robinson, Tom/Band	Power In The Darkness + Whole EP	CD	Razor & Tie	RE-2018	U.S.A.	1993	22.99
Robinson, Tom/Band	The Gold Collection	CD	EMI	7243-8-37231-2-6	England	1996	10.99
Robinson, Tom/Band	TRB Two	CD	Razor & Tie	RE-2019	U.S.A.	1993	8.99
Robinson, Tom/Cafe Society	Cafe Society Archives (Prod. By Kinks)	CD	Secret	001	Austria	1974	17.99
Robinson, Tom/Jakko Jakszyk	Blood Brother + 4	CD	Castaway Northwes	CNWVP-001CD	U.S.A.	1997	14.99
Robinson, Tom/Sector 27	Sector 27 Complete	CD	Castaway Northwes	CNWVP012CD	U.S.A.	2001	16.99
Roches, The	A Dove	CD	MCA	MCAD-10601	U.S.A.	1992	7.99
Roches, The	Another World	CD	Warner Bros.	25321-2	U.S.A.	1988	24.99
Roches, The	Can We Go Home Now?	CD	Rykodisc	RCD-10299	U.S.A.	1995	7.99
Roches, The	Collected Works Of The Roches	CD	Rhino	R2-73919	U.S.A.	2003	12.99
Roches, The	Keep On Doing	CD	Reprise	9-23725-2	U.S.A.	1987	7.99
Roches, The	No Trespassing	CD	Rhino	R2-70616	U.S.A.	1986	21.99
Roches, The	Nurds	CD	Warner Bros.	3475-2	U.S.A.	1988	9.99
Roches, The	Self Titled	CD	Warner Bros.	3298-2	U.S.A.	1987	9.99
Roches, The	Speak	CD	MCA	MCAD-6345	U.S.A.	1989	7.99
Roches, The	We Three Kings	CD	MCA	MCAD-10020	U.S.A.	1990	7.99
Roches, The	Will You Be My Friend?	CD	Liquid 8	12058	U.S.A.	2003	7.99
Rockets	Love Transfusion	CD	Line	LICD-9.00175-0	Germany	1988	22.99
Rockpile	Seconds Of Pleasure	CD	Line	LICD-9.00005-0	Germany	1987	8.99
Rockpile	Seconds Of Pleasure + 7	CD	Columbia	CK-63983	U.S.A.	2004	8.99
Rockpile/Foghat	King Biscuit Flower Hour 11/06/00	CD	King Biscuit	0240-2111-1063	U.S.A.	2000	39.99
Roden, Jess	Jess Roden & The Humans	CD	Line	LICD-9.01281-0	Germany	1995	19.99
Rodgers, Paul	Cut Loose	CD	Atlantic	80121-2	U.S.A.	1983	8.99
Rodgers, Paul	Electric	CD	CMC Int.	06076-86294-2	U.S.A.	2000	8.99
Rodgers, Paul	Listen	CD	Emanem	EMANEM-4078	England	2002	14.99

R

Artist	Title	Format	Label	Catalog No	Country	Released	Value
Rodgers, Paul	Live: Loreley Tapes	CD	SPV	085-44672	Germany	1997	12.99
Rodgers, Paul	Muddy Water Blues	CD	Victory	383-480-013-2	U.S.A.	1993	8.99
Rodgers, Paul	Muddy Waters Blues (DJ/Pick)	CD	Victory	SACD-679	U.S.A.	1993	49.99
Rodgers, Paul	Now & Live (Bonus Cd)	2CD	Velvel	VEL79790-2	U.S.A.	1997	10.99
Rodgers, Paul	Now + 1	CD	Victor Ent.	VICP-5815	Japan	1997	13.99
Rodgers, Paul	Saving Grace	CD Single	Velvel	VEL-CDPRO-009	U.S.A.	1997	7.99
Rodgers, Paul	Soul Of Love	CD Single	Velvel	VEL-CDPRO-003	U.S.A.	1997	7.99
Rodgers, Paul	The Chronicle	CD	Victor Ent.	VICP-5450	Japan	1998	31.99
Rodgers, Paul	The Hendrix Set EP	CD Single	Victory	383-480-014-2	U.S.A.	1993	24.99
Rodgers, Paul	Tribute To Muddy Waters	CD	Spitfire	SPT-15204-2	U.S.A.	1999	8.99
Rodgers/Hammerstein II	Sound Of Music (Gold CD W/Laser)	CD	Fox	4267-02	U.S.A.	1994	29.99
Roedelius	Jardin Au Fou + 6	CD	Captain Trip	CTCD-106	Japan	1979	14.99
Roedelius	Pink, Blue Amber	CD	Captain Trip	CTCD-040	Japan	2000	14.99
Roedelius	Selfportrait VII	CD	Captain Trip	CTCD-193	Japan	2000	14.99
Roedelius	Selfportrait VIII: Introspection	CD	Captain Trip	CTCD-421	Japan	2002	14.99
Roedelius /Schnitzler	Acon 2000/1 (Ltd 1000)	CD	Captain Trip	CTCD-297	Japan	2000	14.99
Rogers, Anthony	Identification	CD	Cavity	118AIC-0010	U.S.A.	1993	11.99
Rogers, D.J./E W Fire	Love Brought Me Back	CD	Sony	SRCS-6435	Japan	1978	34.99
Rogers, Kenny	I Prefer The Moonlight	CD	RCA	6484-2-R	U.S.A.	1987	5.99
Rogers, Kenny/First Edition	The Best Of	CD	Country Stars	CTS-55402	Germany	1989	12.99
Rogers, Kenny/First Edition	The Very Best Of	CD	Nippon Columbia	COCY-90039	Japan	1998	24.99
Rolling Stones	0ut Of Control	CD Single	Virgin	7243-8-95158-2-4	England	1998	14.99
Rolling Stones	12 X 5	CD	Polygram K.K.	POCD-1960	Japan	1997	34.99
Rolling Stones	12 X 5	CD	ABKCO	94022	U.S.A.	2002	11.99
Rolling Stones	12 X 5 (MFSL Cd)	CD	London	844-461-2	Germany	1984	14.99
Rolling Stones	40 Licks Sampler (Promo)	CD	Virgin	ROLLING #1	Spain	2002	43.99
Rolling Stones	ABKCO SACD Box Set	16 CD	ABKCO	06024-9814734	England	2003	459.99
Rolling Stones	Aftermath (MFSL Cd)	CD	London	820-050-2	France	1985	14.99
Rolling Stones	Aftermath (U.S.)	CD	ABKCO	94762	U.S.A.	2002	11.99
Rolling Stones	Aftermath [U.K.]	CD	ABKCO	94772	U.S.A.	2002	11.99
Rolling Stones	Almost Hear You Sigh (3")	CD Single	Sony	CSDS-8120	Japan	1990	15.99
Rolling Stones	Almost Hear You Sigh (3")	CD Single	Sony	655981-1	Netherlands	1990	34.99
Rolling Stones	Almost Hear You Sigh (3")	CD Single	Sony	655981-3	Netherlands	1990	34.99
Rolling Stones	Almost Hear You Sigh (Gold)	CD Single	Sony	656065-2	England	1990	13.99
Rolling Stones	Almost Hear You Sigh (Promo)	CD Single	Columbia	CSK-73093	U.S.A.	1989	35.99
Rolling Stones	Almost Hear You Sigh (W/Tin)	CD Single	Sony	656065-5	England	1990	49.99
Rolling Stones	Angie (3")	CD Single	Sony	656068-3	Netherlands	1990	54.99
Rolling Stones	Angie (3")	CD Single	Virgin	VJDP-10262	Japan	1991	19.99
Rolling Stones	Angie (3")	CD Single	Sony	656068-1	Netherlands	1990	54.99
Rolling Stones	Angie (Promo)	CD Single	Virgin	PCD-0862	Japan	1997	99.99
Rolling Stones	Another Side Of Steel Wheels	CD Single	Sony	CSCS-5116	Japan	1989	39.99
Rolling Stones	Anybody Seen My Baby	CD Single	Virgin	VSCDE-1653	Netherlands	1997	8.99
Rolling Stones	Anybody Seen My Baby	CD Single	Virgin	VSCDT-1653	England	1997	9.99
Rolling Stones	Anybody Seen My Baby (Promo)	CD Single	Virgin	VSCDJ-1653	England	1997	9.99
Rolling Stones	Anybody Seen My Baby (Promo)	CD Single	Virgin	VSCDXJ-1653	England	1997	12.99
Rolling Stones	Anybody Seen My Baby (Promo)	CD Single	Virgin	DPRO-12746	U.S.A.	1997	8.99
Rolling Stones	Anybody Seen My Baby?	CD Single	Virgin	7243-8-94597-2-2	England	1997	5.99
Rolling Stones	Beggars Banquet	CD	ABKCO	95392	U.S.A.	2002	11.99
Rolling Stones	Beggars Banquet	CD	Polygram K.K.	POCD-1969	Japan	1997	34.99
Rolling Stones	Beggars Banquet	CD	Polydor K.K.	P25L-25043	Japan	1991	44.99
Rolling Stones	Beggars Banquet (MFSL Cd)	CD	London	800-084-2	Germany	1984	14.99
Rolling Stones	Between The Buttons	CD	Polygram K.K.	POCD-1966	Japan	1997	34.99
Rolling Stones	Between The Buttons (MFSL Cd)	CD	London	820-138-2	Germany	1985	14.99
Rolling Stones	Between The Buttons (U.K.)	CD	ABKCO	95002	U.S.A.	2002	11.99
Rolling Stones	Between The Buttons (U.S.)	CD	ABKCO	94992	U.S.A.	2002	11.99
Rolling Stones	Big Hits: High Tide And Green Grass	CD	ABKCO	90012	U.S.A.	2002	11.99
Rolling Stones	Big Hits: High Tide And Green Grass	CD	Polygram K.K.	POCD-1964	Japan	1997	34.99
Rolling Stones	Black and Blue (Collector's Edition)	CD	Virgin	7243-8-39499-2-2	U.S.A.	1976	20.99

R

Artist	Title	Format	Label	Catalog No	Country	Released	Value
Rolling Stones	Bridges To Babylon (Promo/Slipcover)	CD	Virgin	CDVDJ2840	England	1997	44.99
Rolling Stones	Bridges To Babylon (W/Slipcase)	CD	Virgin	CDV-2840	Netherlands	1997	11.99
Rolling Stones	Bridges To Babylon (W/Slipcase)	CD	Virgin	CDVX-2840	England	1997	11.99
Rolling Stones	Bridges to Babylon With Slipcover	CD	Virgin	7243-8-44712-2-4	U.S.A.	1997	11.99
Rolling Stones	Coca-Cola Presenta - Vol 1 (Promo)	CD	Virgin	7243-4-83153-2-8	Mexico	1994	24.99
Rolling Stones	Coca-Cola Presenta - Vol 2 (Promo)	CD	Virgin	7243-4-83154-2-7	Mexico	1994	24.99
Rolling Stones	Collector's Edition (Bonus Cd/Box Set)	CD	Columbia	466918-2	Austria	1989	174.99
Rolling Stones	December's Children (And Everybody's)	CD	Polygram K.K.	POCD-1963	Japan	1997	34.99
Rolling Stones	December's Children (And Everybody's)	CD	ABKCO	94512	U.S.A.	2002	11.99
Rolling Stones	December's Children (MFSL Cd)	CD	London	820-135-2	Germany	1987	14.99
Rolling Stones	Desert Island Survival Kit (DJ Sampler)	CD	ABKCO	1848-2-PROMO	U.S.A.	1994	34.99
Rolling Stones	Dirty Work	CD	Sony	86321-2	Holland	1986	16.99
Rolling Stones	Dirty Work	CD	Virgin	7243-8-39648-2-6	U.S.A.	1986	9.99
Rolling Stones	Emotional Rescue (Collector's Edition)	CD	Virgin	7243-8-39501-2-6	U.S.A.	1980	14.99
Rolling Stones	England's Newest Hit Makers	CD	ABKCO	93752	U.S.A.	2002	11.99
Rolling Stones	Exile on Main Street (Collector's Edition)	CD	Virgin	7243-8-39503-2-4	U.S.A.	1972	14.99
Rolling Stones	Flip The Switch (Promo)	CD Single	Virgin	DPRO-12784	U.S.A.	1997	64.99
Rolling Stones	Flowers	CD	Polygram K.K.	POCD-1967	Japan	1997	34.99
Rolling Stones	Flowers	CD	ABKCO	95092	U.S.A.	2002	11.99
Rolling Stones	Flowers (MFSL Cd)	CD	London	820-139-2	Germany	1987	14.99
Rolling Stones	Forty Licks (Promo Sampler)	CD	Virgin	7087-6-17516-2-8	U.S.A.	2002	19.99
Rolling Stones	Forty Licks (Spec. Ed. Box Set)	2CD	Virgin	7243-8-13398-2-4	U.S.A.	2002	26.99
Rolling Stones	Forty Licks Sampler (Promo)	CD	Virgin	CDVDJ2964	England	2002	17.99
Rolling Stones	Four New Licks (Promo)	CD	Virgin	7087-6-17564-2-5	U.S.A.	2002	28.99
Rolling Stones	Get Yer Ya-Ya's Out (MFSL Cd)	CD	London	820-131-2	Germany	1987	14.99
Rolling Stones	Get Yer Ya-Ya's Out! [LIVE]	CD	ABKCO	90052	U.S.A.	2002	11.99
Rolling Stones	Get Yer Ya-Ya's Out! [LIVE]	CD	Polygram K.K.	POCD-1972	Japan	2002	34.99
Rolling Stones	Goats Head Soup (Collector's Edition)	CD	Virgin	7243-8-39498-2-3	U.S.A.	1973	14.99
Rolling Stones	Got Live If You Want It!	CD	Polygram K.K.	POCD-1965	Japan	1997	34.99
Rolling Stones	Got Live If You Want It!	CD	ABKCO	94932	U.S.A.	2002	11.99
Rolling Stones	Got Live If You Want It! (MFSL Cd)	CD	London	820-137-2	Germany	1987	14.99
Rolling Stones	Highwire	CD Single	Sony	656756-5	England	1991	12.99
Rolling Stones	Highwire	CD Single	Sony	656756-9	Netherlands	1991	35.99
Rolling Stones	Highwire	CD Single	Sony	656756-5	England	1991	9.99
Rolling Stones	Highwire (2 Tracks)	CD Single	Sony	656756-2	Australia	1991	64.99
Rolling Stones	Highwire (3 Tracks)	CD Single	Sony	656756-2	England	1991	5.99
Rolling Stones	Highwire (3")	CD Single	Sony	656756-1	Netherlands	1991	25.99
Rolling Stones	Highwire (3")	CD Single	Sony	CSDS-8184	Japan	1991	33.99
Rolling Stones	Highwire (Promo)	CD Single	Columbia	CSK-73742	U.S.A.	1991	14.99
Rolling Stones	Hot Rocks 1964 - 1971 # 1 (MFSL Cd)	CD	Polydor K.K.	P25L-25047	Japan	1985	29.99
Rolling Stones	Hot Rocks 1964 - 1971 # 2 (MFSL Cd)	CD	Polydor K.K.	P25L-25048	Japan	1985	29.99
Rolling Stones	Hot Rocks, 1964 - 1971	2CD	ABKCO	96672	U.S.A.	2002	21.99
Rolling Stones	Hot Rocks, 1964 - 1971 #1 (MFSL CD)	CD	London	820-141-2	France	1985	25.99
Rolling Stones	Hot Rocks, 1964 - 1971 #2 (MFSL CD)	CD	London	820-142-2	France	1985	25.99
Rolling Stones	I Can't Get No Satisfaction	CD Single	London	882-200-2	Netherlands	1990	29.99
Rolling Stones	I Go Wild	CD Single	Virgin	VSCDX-1539	England	1995	7.99
Rolling Stones	I Go Wild (3")	CD Single	Virgin	VJDP-10243	Japan	1994	17.99
Rolling Stones	I Go Wild (Promo)	CD Single	Virgin	DPRO-12709	U.S.A.	1995	12.99
Rolling Stones	I Go Wild (Promo)	CD Single	Virgin	VSCDJ-1539	England	1995	12.99
Rolling Stones	Interview (Promo)	CD	Sony	SAMP-CD-1408	England	1990	27.99
Rolling Stones	It's Only Rock 'N' Roll (Cd 1)	CD Single	Universal	1566012	England	1999	7.99
Rolling Stones	It's Only Rock 'N' Roll (Cd 2)	CD Single	Universal	1565982	England	1999	7.99
Rolling Stones	It's Only Rock 'n Roll (Coll.Edition)	CD	Virgin	7243-8-39500-2-7	U.S.A.	1974	18.99
Rolling Stones	Jump Back	CD	Virgin	VJCP-25155	Japan	1993	13.99
Arlling Stones	Jump Back (Picture Disc)	CD	Virgin	CDV-2726	Denmark	1993	15.99
Rolling Stones	Jump Back EP (Promo)	CD	Virgin	Stones-1	England	1993	39.99
Rolling Stones	Jump Back:The Best Of	CD	Virgin	7243-8-39321-2-2	Italy	1993	9.99
Rolling Stones	Let It Bleed	CD	ABKCO	90042	U.S.A.	2002	11.99

R

Artist	Title	Format	Label	Catalog No	Country	Released	Value
Rolling Stones	Let It Bleed	CD	Polygram K.K.	POCD-1971	Japan	2002	34.99
Rolling Stones	Let it Bleed (MFSL Cd)	CD	London	820-052-2	Germany	1986	14.99
Rolling Stones	Like A Rolling Stone	CD Single	Virgin	893237-2	Australia	1995	49.99
Rolling Stones	Like A Rolling Stone	CD Single	Virgin	7243-8-38523-2	U.S.A.	1995	4.99
Rolling Stones	Like A Rolling Stone	CD Single	Virgin	VSCDT-1562	Netherlands	1995	11.99
Rolling Stones	Like A Rolling Stone (Promo)	CD Single	Virgin	DPRO-11044	U.S.A.	1995	12.99
Rolling Stones	Like A Rolling Stone (Promo)	CD Single	Virgin	VSCDJ-1562	England	1995	24.99
Rolling Stones	Live At The Max (Promo CDV)	CDV	Polygram	SACD-1004	U.S.A.	1994	99.99
Rolling Stones	Love Is Strong	CD Single	Virgin	VSCDE-1503	Netherlands	1994	14.99
Rolling Stones	Love Is Strong	CD Single	Virgin	VSCDT-1503	Netherlands	1994	14.99
Rolling Stones	Love Is Strong	CD Single	Virgin	VSCDX-1503	England	1994	7.99
Rolling Stones	Love Is Strong	CD Single	Virgin	V25H-38446	U.S.A.	1994	9.99
Rolling Stones	Love Is Strong (3")	CD Single	Virgin	VJDP-10225	Japan	1994	34.99
Rolling Stones	Love Is Strong (Promo)	CD Single	Virgin	DPRO-14180	U.S.A.	1994	14.99
Rolling Stones	Love Is Strong (Promo)	CD Single	Virgin	DPRO-14155	U.S.A.	1994	21.99
Rolling Stones	Love You Live	2CD	Virgin	7243-8-45671-2-5	U.S.A.	1977	11.99
Rolling Stones	Made In The Shade	CD	Columbia	CK-40494	U.S.A.	1990	16.99
Rolling Stones	Made In The Shade	CD	Sony	450201-2	Netherlands	1990	16.99
Rolling Stones	Metamorphosis	CD	ABKCO	90062	U.S.A.	2002	11.99
Rolling Stones	Mixed Emotions (3")	CD Single	Sony	655193-3	Netherlands	1989	54.99
Rolling Stones	Mixed Emotions (W/Tin Can)	CD Single	Sony	655-214-2	England	1989	34.99
Rolling Stones	Mixed Emotions (W/Tin/Sticker)	CD Single	Sony	655193-5	England	1989	29.99
Rolling Stones	Mixed Emotions (Withdrawn 3")	CD Single	Sony	655193-2	Netherlands	1989	99.99
Rolling Stones	More Hot Rocks # 1 (MFSL Cd)	CD	London	820-515-2	Germany	1987	24.99
Rolling Stones	More Hot Rocks # 2 (MFSL Cd)	CD	London	820-516-2	Germany	1987	24.99
Rolling Stones	More Hot Rocks + 3	2CD	ABKCO	96262	U.S.A.	2002	21.99
Rolling Stones	No Security (2 Bonus Int. CDs)	3CD	Virgin	CDIVDJ-2880	England	1998	58.99
Rolling Stones	No Security (Live)	CD	Virgin	7243-8-46740-2-1	U.S.A.	1998	7.99
Rolling Stones	No Security (Promo Sampler)	CD	Virgin	CDVDJ-2880	England	1998	20.99
Rolling Stones	No. 2 (W/Sticker)	CD	Polygram K.K.	POCD-1913	Japan	1995	39.99
Rolling Stones	Out Of Control	CD Single	Virgin	7243-8-95801-2-3	England	1998	9.99
Rolling Stones	Out Of Our Heads	CD	Polygram K.K.	POCD-1962	Japan	1997	34.99
Rolling Stones	Out Of Our Heads (MFSL Cd)	CD	London	820-049-2	Germany	1965	14.99
Rolling Stones	Out Of Our Heads (U.K.)	CD	ABKCO	94302	U.S.A.	2002	11.99
Rolling Stones	Out Of Our Heads (U.S.)	CD	ABKCO	94292	U.S.A.	2002	11.99
Rolling Stones	Out Of Tears	CD Single	Virgin	VSCDE-1524	Netherlands	1994	8.99
Rolling Stones	Out Of Tears	CD Single	Virgin	V25H-38459	U.S.A.	1994	7.99
Rolling Stones	Out Of Tears	CD Single	Virgin	DPRO-14237	U.S.A.	1994	21.99
Rolling Stones	Out Of Tears	CD Single	Virgin	VSCDT-1524	England	1994	7.99
Rolling Stones	Out Of Tears (3")	CD Single	Virgin	VJDP-10240	Japan	1994	34.99
Rolling Stones	Out Of Tears (Tear Shaped)	CD Single	Virgin	VSCDX-1524	England	1994	21.99
Rolling Stones	Radio Sampler (Promo)	CD	Sony	RSCD-1	England	1990	94.99
Rolling Stones	Remastered Promo Gold Cd	CD	ABKCO	92152	U.S.A.	2002	119.99
Rolling Stones	Rewind	CD	Toshiba-EMI	CP35-5021	Japan	1984	28.99
Rolling Stones	Rewind	CD	Columbia	CK-40505	U.S.A.	1984	13.99
Rolling Stones	Rock And A Hard Place (3")	CD Single	Sony	655422-3	Austria	1989	49.99
Rolling Stones	Rock And A Hard Place (Promo)	CD Single	Columbia	CSK-73057	U.S.A.	1989	99.99
Rolling Stones	Rock And Roll Circus	CD	ABKCO	1268-2	U.S.A.	1995	8.99
Rolling Stones	Rolling Stones Singles Collection	CD	TF	T-1825	Japan	1988	44.99
Rolling Stones	Ruby Tuesday	CD Single	Sony	656892-2	England	1991	28.99
Rolling Stones	Ruby Tuesday	CD Single	Sony	656892-5	England	1991	19.99
Rolling Stones	Sad Sad Sad (3")	CD Single	Sony	656197-1	Netherlands	1990	24.99
Rolling Stones	Satanic Majesties Request (MFSL CD)	CD	London	820-129-2	Germany	1986	14.99
Rolling Stones	Say Ahhh! (Promo)	CD	Sony	SAMPCD-1347	Denmark	1989	74.99
Rolling Stones	Say Ahhh! (Promo)	CD	Columbia	CSK-1827	U.S.A.	1989	99.99
Rolling Stones	Sex Drive	CD Single	Sony	657334-2	Austria	1991	34.99
Rolling Stones	Sex Drive (Promo)	CD Single	Columbia	CSK-73789	U.S.A.	1991	21.99
Rolling Stones	Singles Collection - The London Years	3CD	ABKCO	92312	U.S.A.	2002	24.99

R

Artist	Title	Format	Label	Catalog No	Country	Released	Value
Rolling Stones	Singles Collection (Promo)	CD	ABKCO	121831	U.S.A.	1989	59.99
Rolling Stones	Singles Collection: London Yrs Box Set	3CD	ABKCO	1218-2	U.S.A.	1989	34.99
Rolling Stones	Some Girls (Collector's Edition)	CD	Virgin	7243-8-39505-2-2	U.S.A.	1978	14.99
Rolling Stones	Sparks Will Fly (Promo)	CD Single	Virgin	DPRO-12688	U.S.A.	1994	44.99
Rolling Stones	Star Box	CD	Sony	25DP-5500	Japan	1989	19.99
Rolling Stones	Steel Wheels	CD	Sony	465752-2	Austria	1989	14.99
Rolling Stones	Steel Wheels	CD	Virgin	CDV2742	England	1989	11.99
Rolling Stones	Steel Wheels	CD Single	Sony	465752-2	Denmark	1989	12.99
Rolling Stones	Steel Wheels	CD	Virgin	7243-8-39647-2-7	U.S.A.	1989	7.99
Rolling Stones	Sticky Fingers (Collector's Edition)	CD	Virgin	7243-8-39504-2-3	U.S.A.	1971	19.99
Rolling Stones	Still Life	CD	Virgin	72438-45674-2-2	U.S.A.	1982	10.99
Rolling Stones	Stones On Cd (Promo)	CD	Sony	SAMP-1103	Denmark	1986	199.99
Rolling Stones	Stripped	CD	Virgin	7243-8-41040-2-3	U.S.A.	1995	7.99
Rolling Stones	Sucking In The Seventies	CD	Sony	450205-2	Denmark	1986	29.99
Rolling Stones	Sympathy For The Devil (Promo/2trks)	CD Single	ABKCO	DEVIL96662RA	EU	2003	18.99
Rolling Stones	Sympathy For The Devil (Promo/3trks)	CD Single	ABKCO	DEVIL96662RB	EU	2003	19.99
Rolling Stones	Tattoo You (Collector's Edition)	CD	Virgin	7243-8-39502-2-5	U.S.A.	1981	14.99
Rolling Stones	Terrifying	CD Single	Sony	656122-5	England	1990	19.99
Rolling Stones	Terrifying (Promo)	CD Single	Columbia	CSK-1897	U.S.A.	1990	9.99
Rolling Stones	The Interview (Steel Wheels Promo)	CD	Columbia	CSK-1910	U.S.A.	1989	99.99
Rolling Stones	The Rolling Stones (MFSL Cd)	CD	London	820-047-2	Germany	1984	14.99
Rolling Stones	The Rolling Stones, Now!	CD	ABKCO	94202	U.S.A.	2002	11.99
Rolling Stones	The Rolling Stones, Now!	CD	Polygram K.K.	POCD-1961	Japan	1997	34.99
Rolling Stones	The Rolling Stones, Now! (MFSL Cd)	CD	London	820-133-2	Germany	1987	14.99
Rolling Stones	Their Satanic Majesties Request	CD	Polygram K.K.	POCD-1968	Japan	1997	34.99
Rolling Stones	Their Satanic Majesties Request	CD	ABKCO	90022	U.S.A.	2002	16.99
Rolling Stones	Through The Past...(Big Hits Vol. 2)	CD	Polygram K.K.	POCD-1970	Japan	2002	34.99
Rolling Stones	Through The Past....(Big Hits Vol. 2)	CD	ABKCO	90032	U.S.A.	2002	11.99
Rolling Stones	Time Is On My Side (3")	CD Single	London	PODD-1002	Japan	1990	54.99
Rolling Stones	Virgin Sampler Vol. 12	CD	Toshiba-EMI	PCD-0531	Japan	1995	156.99
Rolling Stones	Voodoo Lounge	CD	Virgin	7243-8-39782-2-9	U.S.A.	1994	7.99
Rolling Stones	Voodoo Lounge (DJ/Bklt/25 Cards)	CD	Virgin	VJCP-25130	Japan	1994	204.99
Rolling Stones	Voodoo Lounge- A Sampler (Promo)	CD	Virgin	DPRO—14158	U.S.A.	1994	39.99
Rolling Stones	Voodoo Lounge Cd-Rom	CD-Rom	Virgin	7-94546-09042-8	U.S.A.	1995	9.99
Rolling Stones	Welcome To Japan Sampler (Promo)	CD	Toshiba-EMI	PCD-2727	Japan	2003	1,299.99
Rolling Stones	Who Are The Stones? (Interview)	CD	Baktabak	CBAK-4008	England	1990	9.99
Rolling Stones	Wild Horses	CD Single	Virgin	7243-8-93402-2-8	Holland	1998	11.99
Rolling Stones	Wild Horses	CD Single	Virgin	VSCDT-1578	Netherlands	1996	7.99
Rolling Stones	Wild Horses	CD Single	Virgin	VSCDE-1578	Netherlands	1995	7.99
Rolling Stones	Wild Horses (Promo)	CD Single	Virgin	DPRO-11075	U.S.A.	1996	21.99
Rolling Stones	Wild Horses (Withdrawn/Promo)	CD Single	Virgin	VSCDJ-1578	England	1996	39.99
Rolling Stones	You Got Me Rocking	CD Single	Virgin	VSCDG-1518	England	1994	8.99
Rolling Stones	You Got Me Rocking	CD Single	Virgin	VSCDE-1518	Netherlands	1994	12.99
Rolling Stones	You Got Me Rocking	CD Single	Virgin	VJDP-10232	Japan	1994	21.99
Rolling Stones	You Got Me Rocking	CD Single	Virgin	VSCDJ-1518	England	1994	11.99
Rolling Stones	You Got Me Rocking (Perfecto/DJ)	CD Single	Virgin	DPRO-12702	U.S.A.	1994	12.99
Rolling Stones/Ry Cooder	Jamming With Edward	CD	Point Blank	7243-8-40403-2-1	U.S.A.	1972	8.99
Rolling Stones/Wanna Shorter	Undercover In The Night (1st Press)	CD	Toshiba-EMI	CP35-3087	Japan	1983	59.99
Rollins, Sonny	Saxophone Colossus (DCC Gold CD)	CD	DCC	GZS-1082	U.S.A.		29.99
Rollins, Sonny	Sound Of Sonny + 1 (DCC Gold Cd)	CD	DCC	GZS-1092	U.S.A.	1957	18.99
Rollins, Sonny/Quartet	Tenor Madness (Gold CD)	CD	DCC	GZS-1087	U.S.A.	1956	20.99
Ronettes	Early Years '61 - '62	CD	Rhino	R2-70524	U.S.A.	1991	9.99
Ronnie/Pomona Casuals	Everybody Jerk (With Arthur Lee)	CD	Del-Fi	DFCD-72112-2	U.S.A.	1995	9.99
Ronson, Mick	Don't Look Back	CD Single	Epic	660358-2	England	1994	13.99
Ronson, Mick	Hard Life	CD	Alchemy	167	England	2003	9.99
Ronson, Mick	Heaven And Hull	CD	Epic	EK-53796	U.S.A.	1994	7.99
Ronson, Mick	Indian Summer (Bonus Cd)	2CD	Alchemy	5038894001310	England	2000	8.99
Ronson, Mick	Just Like This (W/Bonus Cd)	CD	Alchemy	PILOT50	England	1999	24.99

R

Artist	Title	Format	Label	Catalog No	Country	Released	Value
Ronson, Mick	Main Man	2CD	Snapper	SMD-CD-119	England	1998	18.99
Ronson, Mick	Only After Dark (Slaughter + 3/Don't + 3)	2CD	Griffin	GCD-344-2	U.S.A.	1995	10.99
Ronson, Mick	Play Don't Worry + 9	CD	Snapper	155042	U.S.A.	1998	17.99
Ronson, Mick	Showtime	CD	Alchemy	PILOT-16	England	1999	10.99
Ronson, Mick	Slaughter On 10th Avenue + 4	CD	Snapper	155032	U.S.A.	1998	16.99
Ronson, Mick	The Mick Ronson Primer (Promo)	CD	Epic	ESK-6046	U.S.A.	1994	11.99
Ronson, Mick/Andi Sexgang	Arco Valley	CD	Dressed To Kill	METRO241	England	1999	8.99
Ronson, Mick/Various Artists	The Mick Ronson Memorial Concert	3CD	Alchemy	PILOT-94	England	2001	19.99
Ronstadt, Linda	A Merry Little Christmas	CD	Elektra	62572-2	U.S.A.	2000	10.99
Ronstadt, Linda	Box Set	3CD	Elektra	62472-2	U.S.A.	1999	49.99
Ronstadt, Linda	Box Set Sampler (Promo)	CD	Elektra	PRCD-1416-2	U.S.A.	1999	21.99
Ronstadt, Linda	Canciones de Mi Padre	CD	Asylum	60765-2	U.S.A.	1987	8.99
Ronstadt, Linda	Cry Like A Rainstorm...	CD	Asylum	60872-2	U.S.A.	1989	6.99
Ronstadt, Linda	Dedicated To The One I Love	CD	Elektra	61916-2	U.S.A.	1996	6.99
Ronstadt, Linda	Different Drum	CD	Toshiba-EMI	TOCP-7063	Japan	1995	29.99
Ronstadt, Linda	Different Drum	CD	Capitol	CDP-580131	U.S.A.	1974	28.99
Ronstadt, Linda	Don't Cry Now	CD	Asylum	2-5064	U.S.A.	1968	10.99
Ronstadt, Linda	Feels Like Home	CD	Elektra	61703-2	U.S.A.	1995	6.99
Ronstadt, Linda	Frenesi	CD	Elektra	61383-2	U.S.A.	1992	14.99
Ronstadt, Linda	Get Closer	CD	Asylum	60185-2	U.S.A.	1982	8.99
Ronstadt, Linda	Greatest Hits Volume 1 (DCC Gold Cd)	CD	DCC	GZS-1040	U.S.A.	1993	29.99
Ronstadt, Linda	Greatest Hits Volume 2 (DCC Gold Cd)	CD	DCC	GZS-1128	U.S.A.	1996	32.99
Ronstadt, Linda	Greatest Hits, Vol. 1	CD	Asylum	2-106	U.S.A.	1976	8.99
Ronstadt, Linda	Greatest Hits, Vol. 2	CD	Asylum	516-2	U.S.A.	1980	8.99
Ronstadt, Linda	Hand Sown...Home Grown	CD	Capitol	CDP-580125	U.S.A.	1969	41.99
Ronstadt, Linda	Hasten Down The Wind	CD	Asylum	1072-2	U.S.A.	1976	11.99
Ronstadt, Linda	Heart Like A Wheel	CD	Capitol	7-46073-2	U.S.A.	1974	6.99
Ronstadt, Linda	Linda Ronstadt	CD	Capitol	0777-7-80127-2-6	U.S.A.	1971	9.99
Ronstadt, Linda	Living In The U.S.A.	CD	Asylum	2-155	U.S.A.	1978	10.99
Ronstadt, Linda	Mad Love	CD	Asylum	2-510	U.S.A.	1980	10.99
Ronstadt, Linda	Mas Canciones	CD	Elektra	61239-2	U.S.A.	1990	8.99
Ronstadt, Linda	Prisoner In Disguise	CD	Asylum	1045-2	U.S.A.	1975	13.99
Ronstadt, Linda	Silk Purse	CD	Capitol	CDP-580126	U.S.A.	1970	32.99
Ronstadt, Linda	Simple Dreams	CD	Asylum	E2-104	U.S.A.	1977	8.99
Ronstadt, Linda	Stone Poneys	CD	Capitol	0777-7-80128-2-5	Holland	1995	47.99
Ronstadt, Linda	Stone Poneys - Evergreen, Vol. 2	CD	Capitol	0777-7-80129-2-4	U.S.A.	1967	23.99
Ronstadt, Linda	Stone Poneys And Friends, Vol. 3	CD	Capitol	0777-7-80130-2-0	U.S.A.	1967	23.99
Ronstadt, Linda	The Very Best Of	CD	Rhino	R2-76109	U.S.A.	2002	9.99
Ronstadt, Linda	Very Best Of + 4 (W/Outer Box)	CD	Elektra	812-73605-2	Taiwan	2002	19.99
Ronstadt, Linda	We Ran	CD	Elektra	62206-2	U.S.A.	1998	6.99
Ronstadt, Linda	Winter Light	CD	Elektra	61545-2	U.S.A.	1993	11.99
Ronstadt, Linda/E. Harris	Western Hall... (Emmylou Harris)	CD	Elektra	62408-2	U.S.A.	1999	10.99
Ronstadt, Linda/Nelson Riddle	For Sentimental Reasons	CD	Asylum	60474-2	U.S.A.	1986	10.99
Ronstadt, Linda/Nelson Riddle	Lush Life	CD	Asylum	60387-2	U.S.A.	1984	8.99
Ronstadt, Linda/Nelson Riddle	Round Midnight (3 Nelson Riddle Lps)	3CD	Asylum	60489-2	U.S.A.	1986	24.99
Ronstadt, Linda/Nelson Riddle	What's New	CD	Asylum	60260-2	U.S.A.	1983	9.99
Room Service	Self Titled (Unreleased Cd/Promo)	CD	East West	2-62053-P	England	1997	182.99
Rose Tattoo	25 To Life	2CD	SPV	08572092DCD	Germany	2000	17.99
Rose Tattoo	Angry Metal: 20 Great Tracks	CD	Repertoire	REP-4309-WG	Germany	2002	14.99
Rose Tattoo	Assault & Battery	CD	Repertoire	REP-4011-WZ	Germany	2002	11.99
Rose Tattoo	Never Too Old	2CD	Repertoire	REP-4601-WO	Germany	2002	16.99
Rose Tattoo	Nice Boys Don't Play Rock 'N' Roll + 1	CD	Festival	33557	Australia	2002	17.99
Rose Tattoo	Pain	CD	SPV	SPV08574212CD	Germany	2002	10.99
Rose Tattoo	Rock 'N' Roll Outlaw	CD	Repertoire	REP-4010-WZ	Germany	2002	11.99
Rose Tattoo	Scarred For Life	CD	Repertoire	REP-4049-WZ	Germany	2002	11.99
Rose Tattoo	Self Titled + 8	CD	Repertoire	REP-4103-WZ	Germany	2002	15.99
Rose Tattoo	Southern Stars	CD	Repertoire	REP-4050-WZ	Germany	2002	13.99
Rose Tattoo	The Best Of	CD	Dojo	DOJO-CD-126	England	1995	14.99

R

Artist	Title	Format	Label	Catalog No	Country	Released	Value
Rose, Doudou N'diaye	Djabote	CD	Caroline	CAROL-2340-2	U.S.A.	1992	10.99
Rosenbloom, David	Souls Of Chaos	CD	Line	COCD-9.00794-0	Germany	1990	4.99
Rosenman, Leonard	Beneath/Planet/Apes + 21 (Ltd 3,000)	CD	Film Score Monthly	FSM-VOL.3-NO.3	U.S.A.	1970	21.99
Rosenman, Leonard	Star Trek IV: The Voyage Home S.T.	CD	MCA	MCAD-6195	U.S.A.	1986	20.99
Rosenman, Leonard	The Lord Of The Rings + 4	CD	Intrada	FMT-8003D	U.S.A.	1991	15.99
Ross, Diana	14 Greatest Hits	CD	BMG Victor	R32M-1020	Japan	1986	14.99
Ross, Diana	A Very Special Season (Xmas)	CD	EMI	7243-8-31613-2-4	Holland	1994	13.99
Ross, Diana	All The Great Hits	CD	Motown	159638-2	U.S.A.	2000	8.99
Ross, Diana	All The Great Love Songs	CD	Motown	530-056-2	England	1984	17.99
Ross, Diana	Baby It's Me	CD	Motown	MOTD-5434	U.S.A.	1977	24.99
Ross, Diana	Chain Reaction	CD	Disky	DC-854682	Netherlands	1999	6.99
Ross, Diana	Chain Reaction	CD Single	EMI	880974-2	England	1993	12.99
Ross, Diana	Classic Diana Ross - Universal Masters	CD	Motown	159 959-2	England	2001	9.99
Ross, Diana	Diana Ross (1976)	CD	Motown	MOTD-5135	U.S.A.	1992	52.99
Ross, Diana	Diana Ross (1976)	CD	Polydor K.K.	POCT-1857	Japan	1976	34.99
Ross, Diana	Diana Ross Live	CD	Polydor K.K.	POCT-1902	Japan	1974	39.99
Ross, Diana	Eaten Alive	CD	Capitol	7-46184-2	England	1985	11.99
Ross, Diana	Eaten Alive	CD	RCA	PCD1-5422	U.S.A.	1985	18.99
Ross, Diana	Everday Is A New Day + 3	CD	Toshiba-EMI	TOCP-65206	Japan	1999	19.99
Ross, Diana	Every Day Is A New Day	CD	Motown	521-476-2	England	1999	8.99
Ross, Diana	Every Day Is A New Day	CD	Motown	314-549-522-2	U.S.A.	1999	6.99
Ross, Diana	Everything Is Everything	CD	Polydor K.K.	POCT-1901	Japan	1994	109.99
Ross, Diana	Everything Is Everything	CD	Motown	530-273-2	Germany	1994	106.99
Ross, Diana	Extended - The Remixes	CD Single	EMI	837725-2	England	2000	7.99
Ross, Diana	Forever Diana Box Set	4CD	Motown	3746363572	U.S.A.	1993	39.99
Ross, Diana	Goin' Back	CD Single	Toshiba-EMI	PCD2520	Japan	2001	71.99
Ross, Diana	Greatest Hits Live	CD	Toshiba-EMI	TOCP-5931	Japan	1989	12.99
Ross, Diana	If We Hold On Together	CD Single	Warner Bros.	23P4-2496	Japan	1990	12.99
Ross, Diana	In The Ones You Love	2CD	EMI	CDEM/S-45	England	1996	16.99
Ross, Diana	Lady Sings The Blues (O.S.T.)	CD	Motown	MOTD-758	U.S.A.	1972	11.99
Ross, Diana	Live At Caesar's Palace	CD	Motown	MOTD-5169	U.S.A.	1992	49.99
Ross, Diana	Live Stolen Moments + 1	CD	Toshiba-EMI	TOCP-7749	Japan	1993	14.99
Ross, Diana	Love & Life: The Very Best Of	2CD	EMI	535-862-2	England	2001	17.99
Ross, Diana	Love And Life - Very Best Of	CD	Toshiba-EMI	TOCP-65892/3	Japan	2001	31.99
Ross, Diana	Love And Life/Very Best Sampler (DJ)	CD	Toshiba-EMI	PCD-2511	Japan	2001	45.99
Ross, Diana	Love Child	CD	Polydor K.K.	POCT-9036	Japan	1997	28.99
Ross, Diana	Love From	CD	Disky	SI-794072	Netherlands	2002	12.99
Ross, Diana	Making Spirits Bright	CD	Hallmark	695XPR9726	U.S.A.	1994	13.99
Ross, Diana	Mohogany + 1	CD	Polygram	530-277-2	England	2000	13.99
Ross, Diana	One Woman	CD	EMI	CDONE 1	Holland	1993	12.99
Ross, Diana	Red Hot Rhythm And Blues	CD	RCA	6388-2-R	U.S.A.	1987	27.99
Ross, Diana	Ross	CD	Toshiba-EMI	TOCP-6345	Japan	1991	49.99
Ross, Diana	Ross	CD	RCA	PCD-14677	Japan	1983	69.99
Ross, Diana	Ross	CD	RCA	PCD1-4677	U.S.A.	1983	68.99
Ross, Diana	Self Titled (11 Tracks)	CD	Motown	B20D-61002	Japan	1970	14.99
Ross, Diana	Self Titled + 7	CD	Motown	440-016-816-2	U.S.A.	2002	8.99
Ross, Diana	Silk Electric	CD	RCA	4384-2-R	U.S.A.	1982	13.99
Ross, Diana	Someday We'll Be Together (Promo)	CD Single	Motown	374631157-2	U.S.A.	1994	35.99
Ross, Diana	Swept Away	CD	RCA	PCD1-5009	U.S.A.	1984	26.99
Ross, Diana	Swept Away	CD	RCA	PCD1-5009	U.S.A.	1984	34.99
Ross, Diana	Take Me Higher	CD Single	EMI	CDEM-388	England	1995	10.99
Ross, Diana	That's Why I Call You..	CD	Toshiba-EMI	TOCP-7093	Japan	1992	9.99
Ross, Diana	The Best Years Of My Life	CD Single	EMI	881213-2	England	1994	5.99
Ross, Diana	The Boss + 2	CD	Motown	314-549-524-2	U.S.A.	1999	11.99
Ross, Diana	The Greatest	CD	Toshiba-EMI	TOCP-51078	Japan	1998	23.99
Ross, Diana	The Magic Of	2CD	Motown	PSPCD-491	England	2001	17.99
Ross, Diana	The Motown Anthology	2CD	Motown	440-013-583-2	U.S.A.	2001	15.99
Ross, Diana	Touch Me In/Baby It's Me	CD	Motown	MOTD-8126	U.S.A.	1986	19.99

R

Artist	Title	Format	Label	Catalog No	Country	Released	Value
Ross, Diana	Upside Down Remix '93	CD Single	Motown	860087-2	Germany	1993	16.99
Ross, Diana	Very Best Of/Reach Out And Touch	CD	EMI	536-983-2	Netherlands	2001	11.99
Ross, Diana	Voces Legendarius	CD	Motown	CDBVL	Venezuela	2000	51.99
Ross, Diana	When You Dream	CD Single	Toshiba-EMI	TOCP-7526	Japan	1992	12.99
Ross, Diana	Why Do Fools Fall In Love	CD Single	EMI	881513-2	England	1994	5.99
Ross, Diana	Why Do Fools Fall In Love	CD	Capitol	7-46023-2	England	1981	9.99
Ross, Diana	Workin' Overtime	CD	Motown	MOTD-6274	U.S.A.	1989	8.99
Ross, Diana	Your Love	CD Single	EMI	881110-2	England	1993	5.99
Ross, Diana/Florence Ballard	The Supreme	CD	Spectrum	544-517-2	England	2001	9.99
Ross, Diana/Jackson 5	Diana! [Original TV Soundtrack]	CD	Motown	MOTD-5155	U.S.A.	1971	37.99
Ross, Diana/Marvin Gaye	Best Of M Gaye/TT/Diana And Marvin	CD	Motown	TCD08015TD	U.S.A.	1986	19.99
Ross, Diana/Marvin Gaye	Diana And Marvin	CD	Motown	012-157-173-2	U.S.A.	2001	12.99
Ross, Diana/Supremes	20th Century Masters: The Millennium	CD	Motown	012-159-185-2	U.S.A.	2000	8.99
Ross, Diana/Supremes	20th Century Masters: The Millennium	CD	Motown	012-157-929-2	U.S.A.	2000	8.99
Ross, Diana/Supremes	25th Anniversary	2CD	Motown	R28M-1003-04	Japan	1987	66.99
Ross, Diana/Supremes	25th Anniversary	2CD	Motown	MOTD2-5381	U.S.A.	1990	19.99
Ross, Diana/Supremes	40 Golden Motown Greats	2CD	Universal	530961-2	England	1998	22.99
Ross, Diana/Supremes	A Bit Of Liverpool/TCB	CD	Motown	159-618-2	England	2000	27.99
Ross, Diana/Supremes	A Go Go	CD	Motown	MOTD-5138	U.S.A.	1992	13.99
Ross, Diana/Supremes	A Little Bit Of Liverpool/TCB	CD	Motown	MOTD-8152	U.S.A.	1994	27.99
Ross, Diana/Supremes	Anthology	2CD	Motown	31453-0511-2	U.S.A.	1995	14.99
Ross, Diana/Supremes	At The Copa	CD	Motown	MOTD-5162	U.S.A.	1991	74.99
Ross, Diana/Supremes	Best Collection	CD	Universal	FPCT-41000	Japan	2002	24.99
Ross, Diana/Supremes	Complete	CD	F.L.C.	GBC-038	Japan	2001	24.99
Ross, Diana/Supremes	Do You Know Where...	CD	Polygram	EJS-4080	Japan	1997	24.99
Ross, Diana/Supremes	Floy Joy (No D Ross)	CD	Motown	MOTD-5441	U.S.A.	1972	58.99
Ross, Diana/Supremes	Graces: The Best Of	CD	Polygram K.K.	OCD-28001	Japan	1996	24.99
Ross, Diana/Supremes	Greatest Hits	CD	Daiichi Kikaku	OB-1042	Japan	1990	36.99
Ross, Diana/Supremes	Join The Temptations	CD	Polydor K.K.	POCT-1852	Japan	1968	39.99
Ross, Diana/Supremes	Join The Temptations/Together	CD	Motown	MOTD-8138	U.S.A.	1990	24.99
Ross, Diana/Supremes	Join The Temptations/Together	CD	Motown	159-507-2	England	2000	14.99
Ross, Diana/Supremes	Let The Sunshine In/Cream Of The	CD	Motown	159-588-2	England	2000	13.99
Ross, Diana/Supremes	Live At London's Talk Of The Town	CD	Motown	530-328-2	England	1994	13.99
Ross, Diana/Supremes	Lo Mejor	CD	Motown	7-31454-21332-5	Venezuela	2000	20.99
Ross, Diana/Supremes	Love Child/Supremes A Go-Go	CD	Motown	159-508-2	England	2000	25.99
Ross, Diana/Supremes	Merry Christmas + 2	CD	Motown	012-153-355-2	U.S.A.	1999	12.99
Ross, Diana/Supremes	More Hits/Sing Holland-Dozier-Holland	CD	Motown	159-589-2	England	2000	13.99
Ross, Diana/Supremes	Never Before Released Masters	CD	Motown	MOTD-9075	U.S.A.	1987	54.99
Ross, Diana/Supremes	New Ways But... (No Diana Ross)	CD	Motown	MOTD-5497	U.S.A.	1991	61.99
Ross, Diana/Supremes	Reflections	CD Single	Motown	ZD42876	Germany	1989	14.99
Ross, Diana/Supremes	Reflections + 2	CD	Motown	MOTD-5494	U.S.A.	1992	53.99
Ross, Diana/Supremes	Right On (No Diana Ross)	CD	Motown	MOTD-5442	U.S.A.	1970	74.99
Ross, Diana/Supremes	Sing Country And Western & Pop	CD	Motown	31453-0327-2	U.S.A.	1965	34.99
Ross, Diana/Supremes	Sing Country Western & Pop	CD	Motown	MOTD-5303	U.S.A.	1994	39.99
Ross, Diana/Supremes	Sings Rogers & Hart + 2	CD	Motown	440-016-817-2	U.S.A.	2002	13.99
Ross, Diana/Supremes	The Happening	CD Single	Motown	ZD45156	Germany	1991	14.99
Ross, Diana/Supremes	The Supremes Box Set	4CD	Motown	012-159-075-2	U.S.A.	2000	29.99
Ross, Diana/Supremes	The Supremes Limited Box Set	5CD	Motown	012-159-415-2	U.S.A.	2000	24.99
Ross, Diana/Supremes	Touch (No D Ross)	CD	Motown	MOTD-5447	U.S.A.	1971	53.99
Ross, Diana/Supremes	Universal Masters Collection	CD	Motown	542-133-2	England	1999	8.99
Ross, Diana/Supremes	We Remember Sam Cooke	CD	Motown	MOTD-5495	U.S.A.	1965	64.99
Ross, Diana/Supremes	Where Did Our /I Hear A Symphony	CD	Motown	159-509-2	England	2000	14.99
Ross, Diana/Supremes	With Love (From Us To You)	CD	Marginal	MAR-024	EEC	1995	39.99
Rossington Band, The	Love Your Man	CD	MCA	MCAD-42166	U.S.A.	1988	15.99
Rossington Collins Band	Anytime, Anyplace, Anywhere	CD	MCA	MCAD-31220	U.S.A.	1980	34.99
Rossington Collins Band	Anytime, Anyplace.../This Is The Way	2CD	BGO	BGOCD448	England	1999	14.99
Rossington Collins Band	This Is The Way	CD	MCA	MCAD-31323	U.S.A.	1982	34.99
Rossy	Island Of Ghosts	CD	Caroline	CAROL-2318-2	U.S.A.	1991	5.99

R

Artist	Title	Format	Label	Catalog No	Country	Released	Value
Roth, David Lee	A Little Ain't Enough	CD	Warner Bros.	2-26477	U.S.A.	1990	5.99
Roth, David Lee	Crazy From The Heart	CD	Warner Bros.	2-25222	U.S.A.	1985	10.99
Roth, David Lee	Diamond Dave	CD	Magna Carta	MA-9069-2	U.S.A.	2003	8.99
Roth, David Lee	DLR Band	CD	Wawazat	1217	U.S.A.	1998	8.99
Roth, David Lee	Dont Piss Me Off (Promo)	CD	Rhino	PRCD-7262	U.S.A.	1997	12.99
Roth, David Lee	Eat 'Em And Smile	CD	Warner Bros.	2-25470	U.S.A.	1986	7.99
Roth, David Lee	Just Like Paradise (3")	CD Single	Warner Bros.	W8119CD	Germany	1988	16.99
Roth, David Lee	Night Life (CD 2)	CD Single	Warner Bros.	WO249CD	England	1994	5.99
Roth, David Lee	Skyscraper	CD	Warner Bros.	2-25671	U.S.A.	1987	6.99
Roth, David Lee	The Best	CD	Rhino	R2-72988	U.S.A.	1997	11.99
Roth, David Lee	Your Filthy Little Mouth	CD	Reprise	45391-2	U.S.A.	1994	5.99
Roth, Uli Jon	Beyond The Astral Skies	CD	Toshiba-EMI	TOCP-8052	Japan	1993	39.99
Roth, Uli Jon	Earthquake	CD	Snapper	155802	England	2000	13.99
Roth, Uli Jon	Electric Sun	CD	Essential	ESDCD216	England	1994	18.99
Roth, Uli Jon	Fire Wind	CD	Snapper	155812	England	2000	13.99
Roth, Uli Jon	From Here To Eternity	3CD	Dressed To Kill	CLP0217-2	England	1998	18.99
Roth, Uli Jon	Live At Castle Donnington	2CD	SPV	SPV08974642CD	Germany	2002	17.99
Roth, Uli Jon	Metamorphosis	CD	Nippon Crown	CRCL-4819	Japan	2000	27.99
Roth, Uli Jon	Transcendal Sky Guitar	2CD	SPV	089-7203A	England	2000	21.99
Roth, Uli Jon	Transcendal Sky Guitar Vol. 1/2	2CD	Nippon Crown	CRCL-4760/1	Japan	2000	27.99
Roth, Uli Jon/Sky Of Avalon	Prologue To Symphonic Legends	CD	Zero	XRCN-1261	Japan	1996	19.99
Roth, Uli Jon/Tribute	Beyond Inspiration	CD	Lion Music	LMC078	Finland	2003	17.99
Rough Cutt	Live	CD	De Rock	DERCD-078	U.S.A.	1996	14.99
Rough Cutt	Self Titled (W/Paul Shortino)	CD	Warner Bros.	WPCP-4026	Japan	1990	29.99
Rough Cutt	Wants You!	CD	Warner Bros.	WPCP-4027	Japan	1991	41.99
Roulettes, The/Russ Ballard	Stakes And Chips + 8	CD	BGO	BGOCD130	England	1994	10.99
Roussel, Coco	Reaching Beyond	CD	Linden	LM-2006	U.S.A.	1992	14.99
Rowland, Bruce	Journey To The Center Of The Earth	CD	Varese	302-066-069-2	U.S.A.	1999	8.99
Rowland, Bruce	The Man From Snowy River (O.S.T.)	CD	Varese	VCD-47217	U.S.A.	1985	18.99
Roxy Music	Avalon	SACD	EMI	7243-5-83871-2-4	Germany	2003	24.99
Roxy Music	Avalon	CD	EMI	7243-8-47460-2-5	Germany	1999	8.99
Roxy Music	Best Of	SACD	EMI	7243-8-11268-2-0	Germany	2003	24.99
Roxy Music	Concert Classics	CD	Ranch Life	CRANCH-2	U.S.A.	1998	8.99
Roxy Music	Concerto (CDV)	2CD	Alchemy	PILOT-90	England	2001	15.99
Roxy Music	Country Life	CD	EMI	7243-8-47453-2-5	Germany	1999	8.99
Roxy Music	Country Life/Siren	2CD	EMI	7243-5-92251-2-8	Germany	2003	14.99
Roxy Music	Flesh And Blood	CD	EMI	7243-8-47459-2-9	Germany	1999	8.99
Roxy Music	For Your Pleasure	CD	EMI	7243-8-47449-2-2	Germany	1999	8.99
Roxy Music	Heart Still Beating	CD	EMI	7243-8-47461-2-4	Germany	1999	8.99
Roxy Music	King Biscuit August 14 - 20, 1998	CD	DIR Network	C15YPO1XC	U.S.A.	1998	79.99
Roxy Music	Ladytron (Live 1979)	CD	Superior	SU-29026	England	2002	13.99
Roxy Music	Live (2001)	2CD	Eagle	ER-20011-2	U.S.A.	2003	14.99
Roxy Music	Manisfesto	CD	EMI	7243-8-47458-2-0	Germany	1999	8.99
Roxy Music	Psalm (Audio/CDV)	2CD	Master Tone	MM5120	England	1995	19.99
Roxy Music	Reflections	2CD	Alchemy	PILOT-120	England	2002	14.99
Roxy Music	Self Title/For Your Pleasure	2CD	EMI	7243-5-81735-2-9	Germany	2003	14.99
Roxy Music	Self Titled	CD	EMI	7243-8-47447-2-4	Germany	1999	8.99
Roxy Music	Siren	CD	EMI	7243-8-47455-2-3	Germany	1999	8.99
Roxy Music	Stranded	CD	EMI	7243-8-47451-2-7	Germany	1999	8.99
Roxy Music	The Atlantic Years 1973-1980	CD	Atco	7-90122-2	U.S.A.	1987	8.99
Roxy Music	The Best Of Roxy Music	CD	Virgin	7243-8-10395-2-6	U.S.A.	2001	8.99
Roxy Music	The Early Years	CD	Caroline	7243-8-49440-2-6	U.S.A.	2000	8.99
Roxy Music	The Thrill Of It All Box Set	4CD	Virgin	7243-8-40970-2-8	England	1995	59.99
Roxy Music	Valentine (CDV)	CD	Alchemy	PILOT-51	England	2000	10.99
Roxy Music	Vintage (CDV)	CD	Alchemy	PILOT-74	England	2002	10.99
Roxy Music	Viva	CD	EMI	7243-8-47457-2-1	Germany	1999	8.99
Roxy Music/Bryan Ferry	Bryan Ferry/Roxy Music Sampler (DJ)	CD	Virgin	DPRO-14387	U.S.A.	1999	12.99
Roxy Music/Bryan Ferry	Street Life - Greatest Hits	CD	Reprise	9-25857-2	U.S.A.	1989	6.99

R

Artist	Title	Format	Label	Catalog No	Country	Released	Value
Roxy Music/Bryan Ferry	The Best Of Bryan Ferry + Roxy Music	CD	Virgin	7243-8-48173-2-9	U.S.A.	1999	8.99
Roxy Music/Bryan Ferry	The Ultimate Collection	CD	Editions EG	EGCTV-2	England	1988	10.99
Royal Guardsmen	Best Of	CD	DJ Specialist	7243-8-53027-2-5	U.S.A.	1998	7.99
Royal Guardsmen	Return Red Baron/Snoopy President	CD	Collectables	COL-2772	U.S.A.	2001	8.99
Royal Guardsmen	Royal Guardsmen Anthology	CD	One Way	S21-18147	U.S.A.	1995	17.99
Royal Guardsmen	Snoopy's Christmas	CD	Cema	2519	U.S.A.	1993	20.99
Royal Guardsmen	Vs. The Red Baron/& His Friends	CD	Collectables	COL-2771	U.S.A.	2001	8.99
Royal Philharmonic Orch	Symphonic Sounds - Beach Boys	CD	Intersound	9343	U.S.A.	1998	8.99
Rozsa, Miklos	Thief Of Bagdad / The Jungle Book	CD	Colosseum	CST-34.8044	England	1990	44.99
Rozsa, Miklos	Thief Of Bagdad/The Jungle Book	CD	Varese	VCD-47258	U.S.A.	1985	114.99
Rubinoos	Anthology (1977-1979)	CD	Essential	ESMCD-868	England	2000	14.99
Rubinoos	Back To The Drawing Board	CD	Line	BECD-9.00480-0	Germany	1987	28.99
Rubinoos	Basement Tapes	CD	One Way	OW-27733	U.S.A.	1981	14.99
Rubinoos	Basement Tapes Plus (3 ExtraTrks)	CD	Not Lame	NLA-005	U.S.A.	2000	11.99
Rubinoos	Crimes Against Music	CD	Air Mail	AIRCD-051	Japan	1998	27.99
Rubinoos	Crimes Against Nature	CD	Zip	ZIP012	U.S.A.	2002	9.99
Rubinoos	Garage Sale	CD	Big Deal	9012-2	U.S.A.	1994	14.99
Rubinoos	Garage Sale + 3	CD	Air Mail	AIRCD-041	Japan	1998	27.99
Rubinoos	Live In Japan	CD	Air Mail	AIRCD-055	Japan	2002	27.99
Rubinoos	Paleophonic + (I Day/That's Another)	CD	Air Mail	AIRCD-008	Japan	2000	27.99
Rubinoos	Paleophonic + Ind. Day, Crusin' Music	CD	Varese	302-066-133-2	U.S.A.	2000	7.99
Rubinoos	Paleophonic Bonus Cd (2 Unrel.)	CD Single	Varese	RUB-001	U.S.A.	2000	44.99
Rubinoos	The Basement Tapes + 3	CD	Air Mail	AIRCD-020	Japan	1998	27.99
Rubinoos	The Rubinoos	CD	Line	BECD-9.00474-0	Germany	1987	28.99
Rubinoos	The Rubinoos + 6	CD	Wooded Hill	HILLCD-20	England	1997	13.99
Rumplestiltskin	Black Magicians + 1	CD	Repertoire	REP-4211-WP	Germany	1992	49.99
Rumplestiltskin	Self Titled	CD	Repertoire	REP-4208-WP	Germany	1992	49.99
Runaways	And Now ...... The Runaways	CD	Anagram	CDM-GRAM-63	England	1993	14.99
Runaways	Born To Be Bad	CD	Marilyn	USMCD-1004	U.S.A.	1993	20.99
Runaways	Little Lost Girls	CD	Rhino	R2-70861	U.S.A.	1987	16.99
Runaways	Live In Japan	CD	Nippon Phonogram	PHCR-4175	Japan	1993	30.99
Runaways	Live In Japan	CD	Cherry Red	CDMRED-240	England	2003	16.99
Runaways	Neon Angels	CD	Mercury	838-583-2	U.S.A.	1992	16.99
Runaways	Queens Of Noise	CD	Polygram	PEG005	U.S.A.	1994	14.99
Runaways	Queens Of Noise	CD	Cherry Red	CDMRED-238	England	2003	16.99
Runaways	Self Titled	CD	Polygram	PEG004	U.S.A.	1994	14.99
Runaways	Self Titled	CD	Nippon Phonogram	PHCR-4174	Japan	1993	21.99
Runaways	Self Titled	CD	Cherry Red	CDMRED-237	England	2003	16.99
Runaways	The Best Of The Runaways	CD	Mercury	826-279-2	U.S.A.	1987	11.99
Runaways	Waitin' For The Night	CD	Cherry Red	CDMRED-241	England	2003	16.99
Rundgren, Todd	2nd Wind	CD	Warner Bros.	9-26478-2	U.S.A.	1991	5.99
Rundgren, Todd	A Cappella	CD	Rhino	R2-75761	U.S.A.	1985	11.99
Rundgren, Todd	A Cappella Tour	2CD	Nippon Crown	CRCL-7713/14	Japan	2001	32.99
Rundgren, Todd	A Wizard, A True Star	CD	Essential	ESM-CD-673	England	1999	11.99
Rundgren, Todd	An Elpee's Worth Of Productions + 4	CD	Rhino	R2-70519	U.S.A.	1992	12.99
Rundgren, Todd	Another Side Of Roxy	CD	Nippon Crown	CRCL-7715	Japan	2001	29.99
Rundgren, Todd	Back To The Bars	2CD	Essential	ESM-CD-704	England	1999	14.99
Rundgren, Todd	Best Of Todd Rundgren	CD	Victor Ent.	VICP-60254	Japan	1998	29.99
Rundgren, Todd	Best Of: I Saw The Light	CD	Essential	ESMCD-834	England	2000	11.99
Rundgren, Todd	Bootleg Series, Vol. 3 Nearly H. Tour	2CD	Castle	CMDDD716	England	1999	19.99
Rundgren, Todd	Bootleg Series: Vol. 1/Forum '94	2CD	Castle	CMEDD559	England	2002	19.99
Rundgren, Todd	Demos And Lost Albums	2CD	Nippon Crown	CRCL-7707/08	Japan	2003	38.99
Rundgren, Todd	Demos And Lost Albums	2CD	Nippon Crown	CRCL-7707/08	Japan	2001	32.99
Rundgren, Todd	Extended Versions	CD	BMG	75517-45783-2	U.S.A.	2001	5.99
Rundgren, Todd	Faithful	CD	Essential	ESM-CD-702	England	1999	11.99
Rundgren, Todd	Free Soul. The Classic Of	CD	Victor Ent.	VICP-60428	Japan	1998	32.99
Rundgren, Todd	Healing	CD	Essential	ESM-CD-705	England	1999	11.99
Rundgren, Todd	Hermit Of Mink Hollow	CD	Essential	ESM-CD-703	England	1999	11.99

R

Artist	Title	Format	Label	Catalog No	Country	Released	Value
Rundgren, Todd	Initiation	CD	Essential	ESM-CD-701	England	1999	11.99
Rundgren, Todd	King Biscuit Flower Hour 9/25/00	CD	DIR Network	0203-2143-3531	U.S.A.	2000	39.99
Rundgren, Todd	King Biscuit Live (Bonus CD Alone)	CD	King Biscuit	0036/0037	U.S.A.	2000	12.99
Rundgren, Todd	Liars	CD	Sanctuary	06076-86357-2	U.S.A.	2004	8.99
Rundgren, Todd	Live In Chicago '91	Mini Lp	Nippon Crown	CRCL-7704/5	Japan	1999	41.99
Rundgren, Todd	Live In N.Y.C. '78	Mini Lp	Nippon Crown	CRCL-7701	Japan	1999	41.99
Rundgren, Todd	Love Is The Answer	Mini Lp	Akarma	AK-214	Italy	2002	24.99
Rundgren, Todd	Nearly Human	CD	Warner Bros.	9-25881-2	U.S.A.	1989	12.99
Rundgren, Todd	No World Order Cd-Rom	CD-Rom	Elect. Arts	0-7845-0574-8	U.S.A.	1994	11.99
Rundgren, Todd	No World Order Lite	CD	Rhino	R2-71744	U.S.A.	1994	8.99
Rundgren, Todd	NWO (Version 1.01)	CD	Pony Canyon	PCCY-00457	Japan	1993	44.99
Rundgren, Todd	One Long Year	CD	Artemis	751-041-22	U.S.A.	2000	8.99
Rundgren, Todd	Parellel Lines (Promo)	CD Single	Warner Bros.	PRO-CD-3632	U.S.A.	1989	4.99
Rundgren, Todd	Reconstructed + 2	CD	Nippon Crown	CRCL-8850	Japan	2001	34.99
Rundgren, Todd	Re-Mixes	CD	Brilliant	BT-33099	Germany	2003	8.99
Rundgren, Todd	Runt	CD	Essential	ESM-CD-659	England	1999	11.99
Rundgren, Todd	Runt	CD	Pony Canyon	PCCY-00782	Japan	1995	13.99
Rundgren, Todd	Runt. The Ballad Of Todd Rundgren	CD	Essential	ESM-CD-660	England	1999	11.99
Rundgren, Todd	Singles	2CD	Victor Ent.	VICP-60269~70	Japan	1998	40.99
Rundgren, Todd	Something/Anything?	2CD	Essential	ESM-CD-672	England	1999	24.99
Rundgren, Todd	Something/Anything? (MFSL Gold Cd)	2CD	Mobile Fidelity	UDCD-2-591	U.S.A.	1972	62.99
Rundgren, Todd	Somewhere/Anywhere? (Unrel.Tracks)	CD	Victor Ent.	VICP-60492	Japan	2000	29.99
Rundgren, Todd	The Best Of: Go Ahead. Ignore Me	2CD	Essential	ESD-CD-650	England	1999	21.99
Rundgren, Todd	The Ever Popular Tortured Artist Effect	CD	Essential	ESM-CD-706	England	1999	11.99
Rundgren, Todd	Todd	CD	Essential	ESM-CD-674	England	1999	11.99
Rundgren, Todd	Todd Rundgren Live (With Bonus Cd)	2CD	King Biscuit	70710-88056-2	U.S.A.	2000	24.99
Rundgren, Todd	Todd Rundgren Vs. Utopia : Gr. Hits	2CD	Castle	CMDDD-262	England	2001	19.99
Rundgren, Todd	Up Against It	CD	Pony Canyon	PCCY-01121	Japan	1997	39.99
Rundgren, Todd	With A Twist...	CD	Guardian	7243-8-59866-2-8	U.S.A.	1997	5.99
Rundgren, Todd/Nazz	13th And Pine	CD	Distortions	OR1044	U.S.A.	1998	14.99
Rundgren, Todd/Nazz	From Philadelphia (Bonus Demos Disc)	CD	Air Mail	46234/2	Japan	2002	32.99
Rundgren, Todd/Nazz	Nazz	CD	Rhino	R2-70109	U.S.A.	1968	8.99
Rundgren, Todd/Nazz	Nazz III	CD	Rhino	R2-70111	U.S.A.	1970	11.99
Rundgren, Todd/Nazz	Nazz Nazz	CD	Rhino	R2-70110	U.S.A.	1969	14.99
Rundgren, Todd/Nazz	Nazz Vs. Toddzilla	CD	MA 4 Utopia	MARA02-1	U.S.A.	2002	14.99
Rundgren, Todd/Nazz	Open Our Eyes: The Anthology	2CD	Castle	CMEDD593	England	2003	15.99
Rundgren, Todd/Nazz	Todd Sings + 5	CD	Air Mail	AIRCD-042	Japan	2002	34.99
Rundgren, Todd/TR-i	No World Order	CD	Rhino	R2-71266	U.S.A.	1993	8.99
Rundgren, Todd/TR-i	No World Order + 1	CD	Pony Canyon	PCCY-00405	Japan	1993	32.99
Rundgren, Todd/TR-i	The Individualist	CD	Digital Ent.	DEE-6000	U.S.A.	1995	5.99
Rundgren, Todd/Tribute	Todd A True Star	CD	Pony Canyon	PCCA-01113	Japan	1997	29.99
Rundgren, Todd/Utopia	Adventures In Utopia	CD	Essential	ESM-CD-761	England	1999	11.99
Rundgren, Todd/Utopia	Another Live	CD	Essential	ESM-CD-756	England	1999	11.99
Rundgren, Todd/Utopia	Bootleg Series Vol. 2/KSAN 95FM '79	CD	Castle	CMRCD587	England	2002	11.99
Rundgren, Todd/Utopia	City In My Head	2CD	Essential	ESD-CD-732	England	1999	19.99
Rundgren, Todd/Utopia	Deface The Music	CD	Essential	ESM-CD-760	England	1999	11.99
Rundgren, Todd/Utopia	Deface The Music Tour	2CD	Nippon Crown	CRCL-7711/12	Japan	2001	32.99
Rundgren, Todd/Utopia	Live In Tokyo '79	Mini Lp	Nippon Crown	CRCL-7702/3	Japan	1999	44.99
Rundgren, Todd/Utopia	Oblivion Tour	CD	Nippon Crown	CRCL-7716	Japan	2001	29.99
Rundgren, Todd/Utopia	Oblivion, POV & Some Trivia	2CD	Rhino	R2-72287	U.S.A.	1996	29.99
Rundgren, Todd/Utopia	Oops! Wrong Planet	CD	Essential	ESM-CD-758	England	1999	11.99
Rundgren, Todd/Utopia	Oops! Wrong Planet (MFSL Gold Cd)	CD	Mobile Fidelity	UDCD-637	U.S.A.	1977	19.99
Rundgren, Todd/Utopia	Oops! Wrong Planet Tour	2CD	Nippon Crown	CRCL-7709/10	Japan	2001	32.99
Rundgren, Todd/Utopia	POV	CD	Passport	PBCD-6044	U.S.A.	1985	39.99
Rundgren, Todd/Utopia	Ra	CD	Essential	ESM-CD-757	England	1999	11.99
Rundgren, Todd/Utopia	Redux '92: Live In Japan	CD	Rhino	R2-71185	U.S.A.	1993	7.99
Rundgren, Todd/Utopia	Swing To The Right	CD	Essential	ESM-CD-759	England	1999	11.99
Rundgren, Todd/Utopia	Todd Rundgren's Utopia	CD	Essential	ESM-CD-755	England	1999	11.99

R

Artist	Title	Format	Label	Catalog No	Country	Released	Value
Rundgren, Todd/Utopia	Trivia	CD	Passport	PBCD-6053	U.S.A.	1986	39.99
Rundgren, Todd/Utopia	Utopia + 1	CD	Unidisc Music	AGEK-2050	Canada	1982	10.99
Running Man	Self Titled	CD	Repertoire	REP-4471-WP	Germany	2002	14.99
Rush	2112	CD	Sony	25-8P-5166	Japan	1988	19.99
Rush	2112	CD	East West	AMCY-2292	Japan	1997	21.99
Rush	2112	CD	MMG Inc.	AMCY-317	Japan	1991	19.99
Rush	2112	CD	Mercury	314-534-626-2	U.S.A.	1976	8.99
Rush	2112 (MFSL Gold Cd)	CD	Mobile Fidelity	UDCD-590	U.S.A.	1976	27.99
Rush	A Farewell To Kings	CD	East West	AMCY-2293	Japan	1997	21.99
Rush	A Farewell To Kings	CD	MMG Inc.	AMCY-319	Japan	1991	19.99
Rush	A Farewell To Kings	CD	Sony	25-8P-5167	Japan	1988	19.99
Rush	A Farewell To Kings	CD	Mercury	314-534-628-2	U.S.A.	1977	8.99
Rush	A Show Of Hands	CD	MMG Inc.	AMCY-295	Japan	1991	34.99
Rush	A Show Of Hands	CD	Mercury	314-534-637-2	U.S.A.	1988	8.99
Rush	A Show Of Hands	CD	Sony	25-8P-5162	Japan	1988	24.99
Rush	All The World's A Stage	CD	Mercury	314-534-627-2	U.S.A.	1976	8.99
Rush	All The World's A Stage	CD	MMG Inc.	AMCY-318	Japan	1991	27.99
Rush	Bravado (Promo)	CD Single	Atlantic	PRCD-4580-2	U.S.A.	1991	24.99
Rush	Caress Of Steel	CD	MMG Inc.	AMCY-316	Japan	1991	27.99
Rush	Caress Of Steel	CD	East West	AMCY-2291	Japan	1997	29.99
Rush	Caress Of Steel	CD	Mercury	314-534-625-2	U.S.A.	1975	8.99
Rush	Chronicles	2CD	Mercury	838-936-2	U.S.A.	1990	11.99
Rush	Chronicles	2CD	MMG Inc.	AMCY-327-8	Japan	1991	45.99
Rush	Closer To The Heart (Promo)	CD Single	Atlantic	PRCD-8804	U.S.A.	1999	9.99
Rush	Counterparts	CD	Atlantic	82528-2	U.S.A.	1993	7.99
Rush	Counterparts	CD	MMG Inc.	AMCY-608	Japan	1993	29.99
Rush	Different Stages (1st Pressing)	3CD	East West	AMCY-2891-3	Japan	1998	69.99
Rush	Different Stages (Promo/Different Cvr)	3CD	Anthem	AND3-1092	Canada	1998	20.99
Rush	Different Stages (Regular Pressing)	3CD	East West	AMCY-2891-3	Japan	1998	54.99
Rush	Different Stages Sampler (Promo)	CD	Atlantic	PRCD-8681	U.S.A.	1998	34.99
Rush	Different Stages Sampler (Promo)	CD	Anthem	PRCD-18	Canada	1998	24.99
Rush	Different Stages/Live (With Bonus Cd)	CD	Atlantic	83122-2	U.S.A.	1998	19.99
Rush	Double Agent (Promo)	CD Single	Atlantic	PRCD-5431-2	U.S.A.	1993	14.99
Rush	Dreamline (Promo)	CD Single	Anthem	PRO-8	Canada	1991	25.99
Rush	Dreamline (Promo)	CD Single	Atlantic	PRCD-4120-2	U.S.A.	1991	25.99
Rush	Driven (Promo)	CD Single	Atlantic	PRCD-8009	U.S.A.	1997	7.99
Rush	Exit Stage Left	CD	Sony	25-8P-5080	Japan	1988	29.99
Rush	Exit Stage Left	CD	MMG Inc.	AMCY-295	Japan	1991	34.99
Rush	Exit... Stage Left	CD	Mercury	314-534-632-2	U.S.A.	1981	8.99
Rush	Fly By Night	CD	MMG Inc.	AMCY-315	Japan	1991	27.99
Rush	Fly By Night	CD	East West	AMCY-2290	Japan	1997	29.99
Rush	Fly By Night	CD	Mercury	314-534-624-2	U.S.A.	1975	8.99
Rush	Ghost Of A Chance (Promo)	CD Single	Atlantic	PM-1119	Germany	1991	14.99
Rush	Ghost Of A Chance (Promo)	CD Single	Atlantic	PRCD-4458-2	U.S.A.	1991	24.99
Rush	Grace Under Pressure	CD	Mercury	314-534-634-2	U.S.A.	1984	8.99
Rush	Grace Under Pressure	CD	East West	AMCY-2298	Japan	1997	21.99
Rush	Grace Under Pressure	CD	Sony	35-8P-44	Japan	1985	19.99
Rush	Grace Under Pressure	CD	MMG Inc.	AMCY-292	Japan	1991	19.99
Rush	Grace Under Pressure	CD	Sony	25-8P-5077	Japan	1988	19.99
Rush	Half The World (Promo)	CD Single	Atlantic	PRCD-6930	U.S.A.	1996	24.99
Rush	Half The World (Promo/Very Limited)	CD Single	Anthem	PRCD-17	Canada	1997	31.99
Rush	Hemispheres	CD	Mercury	314-534-629-2	U.S.A.	1978	8.99
Rush	Hemispheres	CD	East West	AMCY-2294	Japan	1997	21.99
Rush	Hemispheres	CD	Sony	25-8P-5168	Japan	1988	19.99
Rush	Hemispheres	CD	MMG Inc.	AMCY-320	Japan	1991	19.99
Rush	Hold Your Fire	CD	MMG Inc.	AMCY-294	Japan	1991	19.99
Rush	Hold Your Fire	CD	Mercury	314-534-636-2	U.S.A.	1987	8.99
Rush	Hold Your Fire	CD	East West	AMCY-2300	Japan	1997	21.99

R

Artist	Title	Format	Label	Catalog No	Country	Released	Value
Rush	Hold Your Fire	CD	Sony	32-8P-288	Japan	1987	19.99
Rush	Hold Your Fire	CD	Sony	25-8P-5079	Japan	1988	19.99
Rush	In Rio	3CD	Atlantic	83672-2	U.S.A.	2003	16.99
Rush	In Rio	3CD	Warner Bros.	WPCR-11695	Japan	2003	49.99
Rush	Marathon (Promo/200)	CD Single	Anthem	PRO-1	Canada	1988	49.99
Rush	Moving Pictures	CD	Mercury	314-534-631-2	U.S.A.	1981	8.99
Rush	Moving Pictures	CD	Sony	25-8P-5076	Japan	1988	19.99
Rush	Moving Pictures	CD	MMG Inc.	AMCY-289	Japan	1991	19.99
Rush	Moving Pictures	CD	East West	AMCY-2296	Japan	1997	21.99
Rush	Moving Pictures (MFSL Gold Cd)	CD	Mobile Fidelity	UDCD-569	U.S.A.	1981	54.99
Rush	Nobody's Hero (Promo	CD Single	Atlantic	PRCD-5497-2	U.S.A.	1993	14.99
Rush	Nobody's Hero (Promo)	CD Single	Atlantic	PRCD-5430-2	U.S.A.	1993	14.99
Rush	Permanent Waves	CD	Mercury	314-534-630-2	U.S.A.	1980	8.99
Rush	Permanent Waves	CD	MMG Inc.	AMCY-288	Japan	1991	19.99
Rush	Permanent Waves	CD	East West	AMCY-2295	Japan	1997	21.99
Rush	Permanent Waves	CD	Sony	25-8P-5075	Japan	1988	19.99
Rush	Power Windows	CD	Sony	32-8P-101	Japan	1985	19.99
Rush	Power Windows	CD	MMG Inc.	AMCY-293	Japan	1991	19.99
Rush	Power Windows	CD	East West	AMCY-2299	Japan	1997	21.99
Rush	Power Windows	CD	Mercury	314-534-635-2	U.S.A.	1985	8.99
Rush	Power Windows	CD	Sony	25-8P-5078	Japan	1988	19.99
Rush	Presto	CD	MMG Inc.	AMCY-4	Japan	1989	29.99
Rush	Presto	CD	Atlantic	7-82040-2	U.S.A.	1989	8.99
Rush	Presto	CD	East West	AMCY-4	Japan	1989	29.99
Rush	Profiled! (Promo/Interview)	CD	Atlantic	PRCD-3200-2	U.S.A.	1989	25.99
Rush	Retrospective 1	CD	East West	AMCY-2287	Japan	1997	24.99
Rush	Retrospective 2	CD	East West	AMCY-2288	Japan	1997	24.99
Rush	Retrospective I (1974-1980)	CD	Mercury	314-534-909-2	U.S.A.	1997	10.99
Rush	Retrospective II (1981-1987)	CD	Mercury	314-534-910-2	U.S.A.	1997	8.99
Rush	Roll the Bones	CD	Atlantic	7-82293-2	U.S.A.	1991	8.99
Rush	Roll The Bones	CD	MMG Inc.	AMCY-286	Japan	1991	19.99
Rush	Roll The Bones	CD	Atlantic	7567-885900-2	Germany	1992	7.99
Rush	Roll The Bones (Promo)	CD Single	Anthem	PRO-9	Canada	1991	24.99
Rush	Roll The Bones (Promo)	CD Single	Atlantic	PM-1098	Germany	1991	14.99
Rush	Roll The Bones (Promo)	CD Single	Atlantic	PRCD-4260-2	U.S.A.	1991	34.99
Rush	Roll The Bones Radio Special (DJ)	CD	Anthem	PR-10	Canada	1991	74.99
Rush	Rush	CD	Mercury	314-534-623-2	U.S.A.	1974	8.99
Rush	Self Titled	CD	East West	AMCY-2289	Japan	1997	29.99
Rush	Show Don't Tell (Promo)	CD Single	Anthem	PRO-CD-3	Canada	1989	24.99
Rush	Show Don't Tell (Promo)	CD	Anthem	PRO-4	Canada	1989	24.99
Rush	Show Don't Tell (Promo)	CD Single	Atlantic	PR-3125-2	U.S.A.	1989	24.99
Rush	Show Don't Tell (Promo)	CD Single	Atlantic	PR-3082-2	U.S.A.	1989	34.99
Rush	Signals	CD	MMG Inc.	AMCY-291	Japan	1991	19.99
Rush	Signals	CD	East West	AMCY-2297	Japan	1997	21.99
Rush	Signals	CD	Sony	25-8P-5169	Japan	1988	19.99
Rush	Signals	CD	Mercury	314-534-633-2	U.S.A.	1982	8.99
Rush	Signals (MFSL Gold Cd)	CD	Mobile Fidelity	UDCD-614	U.S.A.	1982	29.99
Rush	Spirit Of Radio (B/W Or Color DJ)	CD Single	Atlantic	PRCD-8690	U.S.A.	1998	17.99
Rush	Stick It Out (Promo)	CD Single	Atlantic	PRCD-5314-2	U.S.A.	1993	14.99
Rush	Superconductor (Aborted/Promo)	CD Single	Anthem	PRO-7	Canada	1989	28.99
Rush	Superconductor (Promo)	CD Single	Atlantic	PRCD-3331-2	U.S.A.	1989	24.99
Rush	Sweet Miracle (Promo)	CD Single	Atlantic	PRCD-300930	U.S.A.	2002	8.99
Rush	Test For Echo	CD	Atlantic	82925-2	U.S.A.	1996	7.99
Rush	Test For Echo	CD	MMG Inc.	AMCY-995	Japan	1996	27.99
Arush	Test For Echo (Promo)	CD Single	Atlantic	PRCD-6885-2	U.S.A.	1996	14.99
Rush	Test For Echo (Promo)	CD Single	Atlantic	PRCD-6853-2	U.S.A.	1996	14.99
Rush	Test For Echo (Promo)	CD	Atlantic	PROP-197	England	1996	39.99
Rush	The Pass (Promo)	CD Single	Atlantic	PR-3175-2	U.S.A.	1989	24.99

Artist	Title	Format	Label	Catalog No	Country	Released	Value
Rush	The Pass (Promo)	CD Single	Atlantic	PR-3165-2	U.S.A.	1989	34.99
Rush	The Pass (Promo)	CD Single	Anthem	PRO-6	Canada	1989	24.99
Rush	The Pass (Promo)	CD Single	Anthem	PRO-5	Canada	1989	24.99
Rush	The Spirit Of Radio (W/Bonus Cd)	3CD	Warner Bros.	WPCR-11576/7	Japan	2003	44.99
Rush	Time Stand Still (Promo)	CD Single	Mercury	CDP-05	U.S.A.	1987	28.99
Rush	Vapor Trails	CD	Mercury	83531-2	U.S.A.	2002	8.99
Rush	Vapor Trails	CD	East West	AMCY-10015	Japan	2002	24.99
Rush	Virtuality (Promo)	CD Single	Atlantic	PRCD-8139	U.S.A.	1997	8.99
Rush /Cult	Tom Sawyer (Promo/2 Remixes)	CD Single	Dreamworks	PRO-CD-5101	U.S.A.	1998	16.99
Rush /Geddy Lee	Grace To Grace	CD Single	Atlantic	PRCD-300391	U.S.A.	2000	5.99
Rush /Geddy Lee	My Favorite Headache	CD	Atlantic	83384-2	U.S.A.	2000	7.99
Rush /Geddy Lee	My Favorite Headache	CD Single	Atlantic	PRCD-300343	U.S.A.	2000	5.99
Rush /Geddy Lee	Selections/My Favorite Headache (DJ)	CD	Atlantic	PRCD-300520	Canada	2000	12.99
Rush, Jennifer	Heart Over Mind	CD	Sony	32-8P-217	Japan	1987	18.99
Rush, Tom	At The Unicorn	CD	Night Light	DHS-58011	U.S.A.	1962	29.99
Rush, Tom	Blues Songs & Ballads (W/Got A Mind)	CD	Fantasy	FCD-24709-2	U.S.A.	1989	15.99
Rush, Tom	Late Night Radio	CD	Night Light	DHS-48011	U.S.A.	1984	29.99
Rush, Tom	Live At Symphony Hall	CD	Varese	305-056-222-2	U.S.A.	2001	8.99
Rush, Tom	Merrimack County/Ladies Love Outlaws	CD	BGO	BGOCD514	England	2001	22.99
Rush, Tom	New Year	CD	Night Light	DHS-28011	U.S.A.	1982	29.99
Rush, Tom	Self Titled	CD	Columbia	CK-9972	U.S.A.	1990	14.99
Rush, Tom	Self Titled (CBS)/Wrong End Of...	CD	BGO	BGOCD361	England	2000	22.99
Rush, Tom	Self Titled (Elektra)	CD	Collector's Choice	CCM-231-2	U.S.A.	2001	8.99
Rush, Tom	Take A Little Walk With Me	CD	Collector's Choice	CCM-230-2	U.S.A.	2001	8.99
Rush, Tom	The Circle Game	CD	Elektra	74018-2	U.S.A.	1968	8.99
Rush, Tom	Very Best Of: No Regrets	CD	Columbia	CK-65860	U.S.A.	1999	8.99
Russell, Brenda	Love Life	CD	Pony Canyon	D25Y-3301	Japan	1981	104.99
Russell, Leon	A Face In The Crowd	CD	Leon Russell	LRR0030011	U.S.A.	2001	8.99
Russell, Leon	Anything Can Happen	CD	Atlantic	91821-2	U.S.A.	1991	8.99
Russell, Leon	Asylum Choir II + 5	CD	DCC	SRZ-8014	U.S.A.	1990	10.99
Russell, Leon	Blues: Same Old Song	CD	Paradise Isl	1001	U.S.A.	1999	29.99
Russell, Leon	Carney	CD	DCC	SRZ-8006	U.S.A.	1989	10.99
Russell, Leon	Christmas Record (Promo)	CD Single	DCC	SRZ-PRO-002	U.S.A.	1989	34.99
Russell, Leon	Collection	CD	Castle	CCS313	England	1992	14.99
Russell, Leon	Delta Lady	CD	DCC	DRZ-918	U.S.A.	1991	8.99
Russell, Leon	Gimme Shelter (Best Of)	2CD	EMI	7243-8-52644-2-9	U.S.A.	1996	19.99
Russell, Leon	Guitar Blues	CD	Leon Russell	LRR0030010	U.S.A.	2001	12.99
Russell, Leon	Hank Wilson Vol. 2	CD	Leon Russell	LRR0030006	U.S.A.	2001	19.99
Russell, Leon	Hank Wilson Vol. 3: Legend...	CD	Ark 21	186-810-022-2	U.S.A.	1998	8.99
Russell, Leon	Hank Wilson Vol. 4	CD	Leon Russell	LRR0030012	U.S.A.	2001	19.99
Russell, Leon	Hank Wilson's Back + 2	CD	Capitol	7243-8-35537-2-3	U.S.A.	1995	10.99
Russell, Leon	Hymns Of Christmas	CD	Leon Russell	LRR0030014	U.S.A.	2001	12.99
Russell, Leon	Leon Live	2CD	Capitol	7243-8-38267-2-8	U.S.A.	1996	13.99
Russell, Leon	Leon Russell + 5 (DCC Gold Disc)	CD	DCC	GZS-1049	U.S.A.	1993	42.99
Russell, Leon	Live At Gilley's	CD	Atlantic	92903-2	U.S.A.	2000	7.99
Russell, Leon	Moonlight & Love Songs	CD	Leon Russell	LRR0030003	U.S.A.	2002	12.99
Russell, Leon	Retrospective	CD	Right Stuff	59785	U.S.A.	1997	9.99
Russell, Leon	Signature Songs	CD	Leon Russell	LRR0030008	U.S.A.	2001	29.99
Russell, Leon	Stop All That Jazz + 2	CD	DCC	SRZ-8011	U.S.A.	1990	10.99
Russell, Leon	Stop All That Jazz + 2	CD	Polystar	PSCW-1043	Japan	1991	20.99
Russell, Leon	The Best Of	CD	DCC	SRZ-8017	U.S.A.	1990	11.99
Russell, Leon	Will O' The Wisp	CD	DCC	7243-8-35539-2-1	U.S.A.	1995	10.99
Rutherford, Mike	Acting Very Strange	CD	Atlantic	80015-2	U.S.A.	1982	8.99
Rutherford, Mike	Smallcreep's Day	CD	Virgin	CASCD1149	U.S.A.	1989	14.99
Rutles	Achaeology	CD	Virgin	CDVUSX-119	England	1996	6.99
Rutles	Archaeology	CD	Virgin	7243-8-42200-2-0	U.S.A.	1996	7.99
Rutles	Archaeology + 4	CD	Virgin	VJCP-25277	Japan	1996	43.99
Rutles	Self Titled + 6	CD	Rhino	R2-75760	U.S.A.	1978	14.99

R

Artist	Title	Format	Label	Catalog No	Country	Released	Value
Rutles	Self Titled + 6	CD	MSI	MSIF-2083	Japan	1993	34.99
Rutles	Shangri-La	CD Single	Virgin	7243-8-93929-2-0	England	1996	4.99
Rutles	Shangri-La (Promo)	CD Single	Virgin	VUSCDJ-117	England	1996	14.99
Rutles/Eric Idle	Rutland Weekend Times + 2 (N Innes)	CD	MSI	MSI-10079	Japan	1995	114.99
Rutles/Neil Innes	Re-Cycled Vinyl Blues	CD	EMI	ASKCD125	England	1994	15.99
Rutles/Ollie Halsall	Caves	CD	Market Square	MSMCD103	England	1999	21.99
Ryder, Mitch	All Mitch Ryder Hits	CD	Sundazed	SC-6033	U.S.A.	1997	10.99
Ryder, Mitch	Detroit With	CD	MCA	MCAD-31129	U.S.A.	1971	24.99
Ryder, Mitch	Do You Feel Alright?	CD Single	Line	LICD-9.01218-E	Germany	1992	7.99
Ryder, Mitch	Get Out And Vote Live	CD	Total Energy	NER-3010	England	1997	24.99
Ryder, Mitch	Got Change For A Million?	CD	Line	LICD-9.00057-0	Germany	1987	21.99
Ryder, Mitch	How I Spent My Vacation	CD	Line	LICD-9.00047-0	Germany	1987	21.99
Ryder, Mitch	How I Spent My Vacation	CD	Line	LICD-9.01347-0	Germany	1997	21.99
Ryder, Mitch	How I Spent My/Naked But Not Dead	2CD	Line	LICD-9.21192-S	Germany	1992	32.99
Ryder, Mitch	In The China Shop	CD	Line	LICD-9.00181-0	Germany	1987	11.99
Ryder, Mitch	La Gash	CD	Line	LICD-9.01180-0	Germany	1992	7.99
Ryder, Mitch	Like A Rolling Stone	CD Single	Line	TLCD-9.01313-0	Germany	1995	7.99
Ryder, Mitch	Live At The Logo Hamburg	CD	Line	LICD-9.01306-0	Germany	1996	18.99
Ryder, Mitch	Live Talkies	CD	Line	LICD-9.00413-0	Germany	1987	8.99
Ryder, Mitch	Monkey Island	CD	Line	LICD-9.01332-0	Germany	1999	18.99
Ryder, Mitch	Naked But Not Dead	CD	Line	LICD-9.00052-0	Germany	1987	13.99
Ryder, Mitch	Naked But Not Dead	CD	Line	LICD-9.01340-0	Germany	1999	13.99
Ryder, Mitch	Never Kick A Sleeping Dog	CD	Line	LICD-9.00525-0	Germany	1987	32.99
Ryder, Mitch	Red Blood White Mink	CD	Line	LICD-9.00538-0	Germany	1988	12.99
Ryder, Mitch	Rev Up: The Best Of + 6	CD	Rhino	R2-70941	U.S.A.	1990	9.99
Ryder, Mitch	Rite Of Passage	CD	Line	LICD-9.01285-0	Germany	1994	7.99
Ryder, Mitch	See You Again	CD Single	Line	TLCD-9.01294-0	Germany	1994	7.99
Ryder, Mitch	Smart Ass	CD	Line	LICD-9.00065-0	Germany	1987	18.99
Ryder, Mitch	The Beautiful Toulang Sunset	CD	Line	LICD-9.01000-0	Germany	1990	12.99
Ryder, Mitch	The Detroit-Memphis Experiment	CD	Repertoire	REP-4117-WZ	Germany	1992	34.99
Ryder, Mitch/Detroit Wheels	Breakout...!!!	CD	Sundazed	SC-6008	U.S.A.	1993	8.99
Ryder, Mitch/Detroit Wheels	Sock It To Me ! + 3	CD	Sundazed	SC-6009	U.S.A.	1993	8.99
Ryder, Mitch/Detroit Wheels	Take A Ride + 1	CD	Sundazed	SC-6007	U.S.A.	1993	8.99

S

Artist	Title	Format	Label	Catalog No	Country	Released	Value
S.A.S. Band	Self Titled (Tull/Queen/Family/Fish)	CD	Bridge	BRG-CD-25	England	2000	22.99
S.A.S. Band/Roy Wood	Show (Leo Sayer/Richard O' Brien)	CD	Andrew Brel Music	ABMCD002	England	2001	39.99
S.O.S. Band, The	On The Rise	CD	Tabu	TBU-450165-2	Austria	1983	69.99
S.O.S. Band, The	Sands Of Time	CD	Tabu	TBU-460946-2	Austria	1986	72.99
S.O.S. Band, The	Take Your Time	CD	Columbia	CSCS-5007	Japan	1990	35.99
Sabri-Brothers	Ya Habib	CD	Caroline	CAROL-2311-2	U.S.A.	1990	9.99
Sacrifice	Total Steel	CD	Howling Bull	HBR-F0002	Japan	1990	84.99
Sadane, Marc/MTUME	Exciting	CD	Warner Bros.	WPCP-5164	Japan	1982	59.99
Sad-Cafe/Paul Young	Misplaced Ideals/Facades	2CD	Renaissance	RMED00196	U.S.A.	1998	12.99
Sad-Cafe/Paul Young	Saving Grace	2CD	Castle	CMDDD019	England	2000	13.99
Sad-Cafe/Paul Young	The Masters	CD	Eagle	EAB-CD-004	England	1997	9.99
Sad-Cafe/Paul Young	The Politics Of Existing	CD	Castle	CLACD272	England	1992	8.99
Sade	Diamond Life	CD	Epic	EK-85240	U.S.A.	1984	7.99
Sade	Diamond Life	CD	Epic	5005952000	England	1984	8.99
Sade	Interview Deluxe (Promo)	CD	Epic	ESK-4877	U.S.A.	1992	10.99
Sadista Sisters	The Sadista Sisters	CD	Line	TACD-9.00753-0	Germany	1989	19.99
Sadus	Swallowed In Black	CD	Roadrunner	RCD-9368	U.S.A.	1990	24.99
Safan, Craig	The Last Starfighter (O.S.T.)	CD	Intrada	MAF-7066	U.S.A.	1995	9.99

Artist	Title	Format	Label	Catalog No	Country	Released	Value
Saga	Beginner's Guide/Throwing Shapes + 1	CD	SPV	SPV07674912	Germany	2003	10.99
Saga	Behaviour + 1	CD	SPV	SPV07674362	Germany	2003	10.99
Saga	Detours	2CD	SPV	SPV08818002	Germany	1998	13.99
Saga	Full Circle	CD	SPV	SPV07621462	Germany	1999	10.99
Saga	Generation 13 + 1	CD	SPV	SPV07674922	Germany	2003	10.99
Saga	Heads Or Tails	CD	SPV	SPV07674392	Germany	2003	10.99
Saga	House Of Cards	CD	SPV	SPV07674392	Germany	2003	10.99
Saga	House Of Cards (Mini Hardback Book)	CD	SPV	SPV08872160	Germany	2001	19.99
Saga	Images At Twilight + 1	CD	SPV	SPV07674282	Germany	2002	10.99
Saga	In Transit	CD	SPV	SPV07674662	Germany	2003	10.99
Saga	Marathon	CD	SPV	SPV08574822	Germany	2003	10.99
Saga	Phase, Vol. 1	CD	SPV	SPV07674932	Germany	2003	10.99
Saga	Pleasure & The Pain + 1	CD	SPV	SPV07672882	Germany	2002	10.99
Saga	Security Of Illusion + 1	CD	SPV	SPV07674672	Germany	2003	10.99
Saga	Self Titled (W/Screensaver)	CD	SPV	SPV07674272	Germany	2002	10.99
Saga	Silent Knight (W/Bonus Cd Rom Video)	CD	SPV	SPV07674292	Germany	2003	14.99
Saga	Steel Umbrellas + 1	CD	SPV	SPV07674382	Germany	2003	10.99
Saga	The Saga Softworks	CD	SPV	SPV07674372	Germany	2003	10.99
Saga	Wildest Dreams	CD	Atlantic	81794-2	U.S.A.	1987	8.99
Saga	Worlds Apart (W/ Cd Rom Video)	CD	SPV	SPV07674682	Germany	2003	14.99
Sagal, Katey/Married W C	Well (W/Rita Coolidge/Jack White)	CD	Virgin	39543-2	U.S.A.	1994	29.99
Sagittarius/Gary Usher	Present Tense + 9	CD	Sundazed	SC-11053	U.S.A.	1997	9.99
Sagittarius/Gary Usher	The Blue Marble + 5	CD	Poptones	MC5036CD	England	2001	10.99
Sahm, Doug	Doug Sahm And Band (W/Bob Dylan)	CD	MMG Inc.	AMCY-46	Japan	1990	44.99
Sahm, Doug	Groovers Paradise	CD	Warner Bros.	WPCR-10655	Japan	2000	49.99
Sahm, Doug	S.D.Q.'98	CD	Watermelon	CD-11076	U.S.A.	1998	7.99
Sahm, Doug	The Atlantic Years (Limited 5000)	2CD	Rhino	RHM2-7845	U.S.A.	2004	44.99
Sahm, Doug	The Return Of Wayne Douglas	CD	Evangeline	GELM-4042	England	2000	9.99
Sahm, Doug/Fender/Tillman	Crazy Cajun's Cosmic Cowboys	CD	Edsel	EDCD-618	England	1999	13.99
Sahm, Doug/Friends	The Best Of (Atlantic Sessions)	CD	Rhino	R2-71032	U.S.A.	1992	11.99
Sahm, Doug/Garrett, Taylor	Live In Japan (MFSL Silver Cd)	CD	Mobile Fidelity	MFCD-757	U.S.A.	1991	24.99
Sahm, Doug/Sir Douglas B	Texas Tornado	CD	MMG Inc.	AMCY-47	Japan	1973	44.99
Sahm, Doug/Texas Tornados	Texas Tornadoes	CD	Reprise	9-26251-2	U.S.A.	1990	8.99
Sahm, Doug/TexasTornado	Texas Rock For Country Rollers	CD	Edsel	EDCD-535	England	1997	14.99
Sailor	Hideaway	CD	Epic	ESCA-7855	Japan	1978	20.99
Sailor	The Third Step	CD	Columbia	465582-2	Austria	1976	15.99
Saints	Wild About You 1976-1978	2CD	Raven	RVCD-107	Australia	2003	19.99
Sakamato, Ryuichi	Jungle Live Mix Untitled 01 (DJ/5000)	CD Single	Sony	SSK-5748	U.S.A.	1997	11.99
Sakamato, Ryuichi	Playing The Orchestra (DJ/W/Box)	CD	Virgin	9-91002-2	U.S.A.	1990	44.99
Sakamato, Ryuichi	Wuthering Heights (O.S.T.)	CD	Toshiba-EMI	TOCT-6691	Japan	2003	28.99
Sakamoto, Ryuichi/Iggy Pop	Risky (Promo)	CD Single	Columbia	PRO.414	England	1988	32.99
Sakamoto, Ryuichi	1996	CD	Milan	7313835759-2	U.S.A.	1996	16.99
Sakamoto, Ryuichi	Best Selection	CD	Alfa	32XA-52	Japan	1986	15.99
Sakamoto, Ryuichi	BTTB	CD	Sony	SK-89079	U.S.A.	1999	9.99
Sakamoto, Ryuichi	Cinemage	CD	Sony	SK-60780	U.S.A.	1999	7.99
Sakamoto, Ryuichi	Discord	CD	Sony	SK-60121	U.S.A.	1998	9.99
Sakamoto, Ryuichi	Heartbeat	CD	Virgin	7-86291-2-2	U.S.A.	1992	8.99
Sakamoto, Ryuichi	Neo Geo	CD	Epic	EK-40994	U.S.A.	1988	7.99
Sakamoto, Ryuichi	Sweet Revenge	CD	Elektra	61680-2	U.S.A.	1994	14.99
Sakamoto, Ryuichi	The Sheltering Sky (O.S.T.)	CD	Virgin	2-91597	U.S.A.	1990	17.99
Sakamoto, Ryuichi	Thousand Knives	CD	Nippon Columbia	COCA-9206	Japan	1991	18.99
Sakamoto, Ryuichi	Very Best Of Gut Years (With Inserts)	CD	For Life	FLCG-3035	Japan	1998	33.99
Sakamoto/David Byrne	The Last Emperor (O.S.T.)	CD	Virgin	7-90690-2	U.S.A.	1987	12.99
Sales, Soupy	Blaa-Oh Blaa-Oh: Reprise Recordings	CD	Rhino	RHM2-7747	U.S.A.	2000	16.99
Salonga, Lea	Lea Salonga	CD	Atlantic	82534-2	U.S.A.	1993	8.99
Salonga, Lea/Jonathan Pryce	Miss Saigon	2CD	Geffen	9-24271-2	U.S.A.	1990	22.99
Salonga, Lea/Jonathan Pryce	Selections From Miss Saigon (Promo)	CD	Geffen	PRO-CD-3974	U.S.A.	1990	19.99
Salter, Hans J.	Creature/ Blk Lagoon/I Shrinking Man	CD	Intrada	MAF-7054D	U.S.A.	1994	15.99

S

Artist	Title	Format	Label	Catalog No	Country	Released	Value
Salter, Hans J.	Music For Frankenstein	CD	Marco Polo	8.223477	Germany	1993	22.99
Sam The Sham/Pharaohs	The Best Of	CD	Rhino	R2-75329	U.S.A.	1998	11.99
Sambora, Richie	Undiscovered Soul +1	CD	Mercury	PHCR-1565	Japan	1997	19.99
Sandford/Townsend	Smoke From A Distant Fire	CD	Warner Bros.	WPCR-10755	Japan	1976	54.99
Sanguinetti, Alex	Akimbo	CD	Line	COCD-9.00795-0	Germany	1990	12.99
Santana	Abraxas (MFSL Gold Cd)	CD	Mobile Fidelity	UDCD-552	U.S.A.	1970	41.99
Santana	Abraxas + 3	CD	Columbia	CK-65490	U.S.A.	1998	8.99
Santana	Amigos	CD	Columbia	CK-33576	U.S.A.	1976	8.99
Santana	Beyond Appearances	CD	Columbia	CK-39527	U.S.A.	1985	8.99
Santana	Blues For Salvador	CD	Columbia	CK-40875	U.S.A.	1987	8.99
Santana	Borboletta	CD	Columbia	CK-33135	U.S.A.	1974	8.99
Santana	Caravanserai	CD	Columbia	CK-63595	U.S.A.	2003	8.99
Santana	Ceremony: Remixes & Rarities	CD	Arista	07822-58642-2	U.S.A.	2003	8.99
Santana	Classics	CD	Traditional Line	TL-1399	Germany	2002	8.99
Santana	Dance Rainbow Serpent Box Set	3CD	Columbia	C3K-64605	U.S.A.	1998	21.99
Santana	Definitive Collection (With Bonus Cd)	2CD	Sony	472641-9	Holland	1995	14.99
Santana	Evolution (Same As Historic Santana)	2CD	Thunderbolt	CDTB-502	England	1994	19.99
Santana	Festival	CD	Columbia	CK-34423	U.S.A.	1977	9.99
Santana	Freedom	CD	Columbia	CK-40272	U.S.A.	1987	7.99
Santana	Fried Neckbones And Home Fries	CD	Yeaah!	YEAAH004	England	2001	12.99
Santana	Havana Moon	CD	Columbia	CK-38642	U.S.A.	1983	7.99
Santana	Inner Secrets	CD	Columbia	CK-35600	U.S.A.	1978	7.99
Santana	Live At The Fillmore '68	2CD	Columbia	C2K-64860	U.S.A.	1997	10.99
Santana	Lotus	2CD	Columbia	C2K-46764	U.S.A.	1974	14.99
Santana	Marathon	CD	Columbia	CK-36154	U.S.A.	1979	10.99
Santana	Maria Maria	CD Single	Arista	07822-13774-2	U.S.A.	2000	3.99
Santana	Milagro	CD	Polydor	314-513-197-2	U.S.A.	1992	7.99
Santana	Moonflower + 3	2CD	Columbia	CK-63594	U.S.A.	2003	18.99
Santana	Mother Earth	Mini Lp	Akarma	AK-088	Italy	1999	14.99
Santana	Mother Earth Tour Cd (Promo)	CD	Columbia	CSK-2099	U.S.A.	1990	55.99
Santana	Oneness: Silver Dreams...	CD	Sony	487238-2	England	1998	10.99
Santana	S.F. Mission District (Mini Lp)	CD	Akarma	AK-068	U.S.A.	2000	16.99
Santana	Sacred Fire: Live South America	CD	Polydor	314-521-082-2	U.S.A.	1993	8.99
Santana	Sampler From The Serpent (Promo)	CD	Columbia	CSK-7217	U.S.A.	1995	8.99
Santana	Santana (Sony Gold Cd)	CD	Columbia	CK-64212	U.S.A.	1969	24.99
Santana	Santana + 3	CD	Columbia	CK-65489	U.S.A.	1998	8.99
Santana	Santana Exp. Editions DJ Sampler	CD	Columbia	CSK-5864-S2	U.S.A.	1998	14.99
Santana	Santana III + 3	CD	Columbia	CK65491	U.S.A.	1998	8.99
Santana	Shaman	CD	Arista	07822-14737-2	U.S.A.	2002	7.99
Santana	Shango	CD	Columbia	CK-38122	U.S.A.	1982	10.99
Santana	Smooth (W/Rob Thomas)	CD Single	Arista	07822-13718-2	U.S.A.	1999	3.99
Santana	Spirits Dancing In The Flesh	CD	Columbia	CK-46065	U.S.A.	1991	7.99
Santana	Supernatural	CD	Arista	07822-19080-2	U.S.A.	1999	7.99
Santana	Supernatural	CD	Arista	07822-19080-2	U.S.A.	1999	7.99
Santana	Swing Of Delight	CD	Columbia	CK-36590	U.S.A.	1980	8.99
Santana	The Best of Santana	CD	Columbia	CK-65561	U.S.A.	1998	8.99
Santana	The Best Of Santana Vol. 2	CD	Columbia	CK-85171	U.S.A.	2000	8.99
Santana	The Essential	2CD	Columbia	C2K-86698	U.S.A.	2002	14.99
Santana	The Very Best Of Santana	CD	Columbia	476763-2	Australia	1994	7.99
Santana	Ultimate Collection (Bonus Live Cd)	3CD	Sony	488544-2	Austria	1997	18.99
Santana	Viva Santana !	CD	Columbia	C2K-44344	U.S.A.	1988	13.99
Santana	Welcome + 1	CD	Columbia	CK-85944	U.S.A.	2003	8.99
Santana	Zebop !	CD	Columbia	CK-37158	U.S.A.	1981	7.99
Santana/Alice Coltrane	Illuminations	CD	Sony	483810-2	England	1998	8.99
Santana/Buddy Miles	Carlos Santana & Buddy Miles Live !	CD	Columbia	CK-66416	U.S.A.	1994	7.99
Santana/Greg Rollie	Roots	CD	33rd Street	3303	U.S.A.	2001	8.99
Santana/John McLaughlin	Love Devotion Surrender + 2	CD	Columbia	CK-63593	U.S.A.	2003	8.99
Santana/W/Jorge Of Malo	Santana Brothers	CD	Island	314-523-677-2	U.S.A.	1994	8.99

S

Artist	Title	Format	Label	Catalog No	Country	Released	Value
Santana/W/Jorge Of Malo	Viva Santana ! - Santana Brothers	CD	Spectrum	544-444-2	England	2000	8.99
Sargant Fury	Little Fish	CD	Warner Bros.	WMC5-604	Japan	1993	22.99
Sater, Almir	Instrumental	CD	Line	RICD-9.00575-0	Germany	1988	6.99
Satriani, Joe	An Anthology: The Electric	2CD	Epic	E2K-90717	U.S.A.	2003	19.99
Satriani, Joe	Crystal Planet	CD	Epic	EK-68018	U.S.A.	1997	7.99
Satriani, Joe	Crystal Planet + 1	CD	Sony	SRCS-8588	Japan	2000	21.99
Satriani, Joe	Dreaming # 11	CD	Epic	EK-68029	U.S.A.	1997	7.99
Satriani, Joe	Dreaming # 11	CD Single	Sony	SRCS-9290	Japan	1997	21.99
Satriani, Joe	Engines Of Creation	CD	Epic	EK-67860	U.S.A.	2000	7.99
Satriani, Joe	Engines Of Creation + 1	CD	Sony	SRCS-2234	Japan	2000	21.99
Satriani, Joe	Flying A Blue Dream	CD	Sony	CSCS-5029	Japan	1989	21.99
Satriani, Joe	Flying In A Blue Dream	CD	Epic	EK-68024	U.S.A.	1997	7.99
Satriani, Joe	G3 Live: Rockin' In The Free World	CD	Epic	EK-90856	U.S.A.	2004	11.99
Satriani, Joe	G3: Live In Concert (S Vai/E Johnson)	CD	Epic	EK-67920	U.S.A.	1997	7.99
Satriani, Joe	Live In San Francisco	2CD	Epic	E2K-85737	U.S.A.	2001	17.99
Satriani, Joe	Live In San Francisco	2CD	Sony	SRCS-2485/6	Japan	2000	32.99
Satriani, Joe	Not Of This Earth	CD	Sony	CSCS-5264	Japan	1986	21.99
Satriani, Joe	Not Of This Earth	CD	Epic	EK-68025	U.S.A.	1997	8.99
Satriani, Joe	Self Titled	CD	Epic	EK-68023	U.S.A.	1997	7.99
Satriani, Joe	Self Titled	CD	Relativity	88561-1500-4	U.S.A.	1995	8.99
Satriani, Joe	Self Titled	CD	Sony	SRCS-7823	Japan	1995	21.99
Satriani, Joe	Strange Beautiful Music	CD	Epic	EK-86294	U.S.A.	2002	11.99
Satriani, Joe	Strange Beautiful Music + 1	CD	Sony	EICP-107	Japan	2000	21.99
Satriani, Joe	Surfing With The Alien	CD	Epic	EK-63701	U.S.A.	1999	7.99
Satriani, Joe	Surfing With The Alien (MFSL Gold)	CD	Mobile Fidelity	UDCD-751	U.S.A.	1987	39.99
Satriani, Joe	The Extremist	CD	Epic	EK-68026	U.S.A.	1997	8.99
Satriani, Joe	The Extremist + 1	CD	Sony	SRCS-5940	Japan	1992	21.99
Satriani, Joe	Time Machine	2CD	Epic	E2K-68027	U.S.A.	1998	12.99
Satriani, Joe	Time Machine	2CD	Sony	SRCS-6857/8	Japan	1993	21.99
Saunders, Merl	Blues From The Rainforest	CD	Summertone	S2CD-01	U.S.A.	1990	7.99
Saunders, Merl	It's In The Air	CD	Summertone	7-29137-21632	U.S.A.	1993	9.99
Saunders, Merl/Jerry Garcia	Fire Up +	CD	Fantasy	FCD-7711	U.S.A.	1992	11.99
Saunders, Merl/Jerry Garcia	Keystone Encores	CD	Fantasy	FCD-7703-2	U.S.A.	1988	11.99
Saunders, Merl/Jerry Garcia	Live At Keystone, Vol. 2	CD	Fantasy	FCD-7702	U.S.A.	1988	11.99
Saunders, Merl/Jerry Garcia	Live At The Keystone, Vol 1 + 1	CD	Fantasy	FCD-7701	U.S.A.	1988	11.99
Savage Garden	Truly Madly Deeply - Ultra Rare Tracks	CD	Sony	SRCS-8535	Japan	1998	17.99
Savoy Brown	20th Century Masters: The Millennium	CD	Polydor	0422-882-939-2	U.S.A.	2002	8.99
Savoy Brown	A Step Further	CD	Deram	844-015-2	U.S.A.	1990	7.99
Savoy Brown	Archive Alive - Live Record Plant '75	CD	Archive	ACH-80014	U.S.A.	1998	8.99
Savoy Brown	Blue Matter	CD	Polygram	820-923-2	U.S.A.	1990	8.99
Savoy Brown	Boogie Brothers	CD	Deram	844-022-2	Germany	1991	12.99
Savoy Brown	Bring It Home	CD	Light Year	54213-2	U.S.A.	1997	7.99
Savoy Brown	Getting To The Point	CD	Rebound	520207	U.S.A.	1995	7.99
Savoy Brown	Hellbound Train	CD	Polygram	844-019-2	U.S.A.	1991	10.99
Savoy Brown	Hellbound Train Live: 1969-1972	2CD	Sanctuary	06076-81309-2	U.S.A.	2003	13.99
Savoy Brown	Jack The Toad	CD	Deram	844-021-2	Germany	1992	9.99
Savoy Brown	Jack The Toad Live: 1970-1972	CD	Mooncrest	CRESTCD-052	England	2000	12.99
Savoy Brown	Kings Of Boogie	CD	GNP	GNPD-2196	U.S.A.	1989	7.99
Savoy Brown	Let It Ride	CD	Roadhouse	74701-44001-2-8	U.S.A.	1990	8.99
Savoy Brown	Lion's Share	CD	Polygram	844-020-2	U.S.A.	1991	8.99
Savoy Brown	Live And Kickin'	CD	GNP	GNPD-2202	U.S.A.	1990	7.99
Savoy Brown	Live In Central Park	CD	Relix	RRCD-2014	U.S.A.	1994	8.99
Savoy Brown	Looking From The Outside	CD	Mooncrest	CRESTCD-051	England	2000	11.99
Savoy Brown	Looking In	CD	Polygram	844-017-2	U.S.A.	1990	8.99
Savoy Brown	Make Me Sweat	CD	GNP	GNPD-2193	U.S.A.	1988	8.99
Savoy Brown	Raw Live 'N Blue	2CD	Akarma	AK-165	Italy	2001	19.99
Savoy Brown	Raw Sienna	CD	Polygram	844-016-2	U.S.A.	1990	10.99
Savoy Brown	Rock 'N' Roll Warriors + 3	CD	Cleopatra	CLP-1246-2	U.S.A.	2002	8.99

S

Artist	Title	Format	Label	Catalog No	Country	Released	Value
Savoy Brown	Shake Down	CD	Deram	820-921-2	U.S.A.	1990	12.99
Savoy Brown	Skin 'N' Bone	CD	Deram	844-024-2	Germany	1992	24.99
Savoy Brown	Strange Dreams	CD	Blind Pig	BPCD-5082	U.S.A.	2003	7.99
Savoy Brown	Street Corner Talking	CD	Deram	844-018-2	U.S.A.	1990	7.99
Savoy Brown	The Blues Keep Me Holding On	CD	Light Year	54323-2	U.S.A.	1999	7.99
Savoy Brown	The Bottom Line Encore Collection	CD	Bottom Line	63440-47404-2	U.S.A.	1999	8.99
Savoy Brown	The Savoy Brown Collection	2CD	Polygram	844-328-2	U.S.A.	1993	24.99
Savoy Brown	Wire Fire	CD	Deram	844-023-2	Germany	1992	24.99
Saxon	A Collection Of Metal	CD	EMI	CDGOLD1055	England	1999	8.99
Saxon	BBC The Archives Series	CD	EMI	7243-4-97772-2-4	Germany	1999	12.99
Saxon	Collection	CD	Disky	DC-873472	Holland	1996	7.99
Saxon	Coming To The Rescue	2CD	Snapper	SMDCD389	England	2002	11.99
Saxon	Crusader	CD	EMI	7243-7-94954-2	England	1999	14.99
Saxon	Crusader +3	CD	Axe Killer	AXE3074312CD	France	2002	14.99
Saxon	Denim And Leather	CD	Disky	DC-867382	Holland	1996	8.99
Saxon	Denim And Leather	CD	EMI	7243-4-86738-2	England	1996	11.99
Saxon	Destiny + 3	CD	Axe Killer	AXE3063672CD	France	2001	18.99
Saxon	Diamonds And Nuggets + 5	CD	Angel Air	SJPCD070	England	2000	8.99
Saxon	Dogs Of War	CD	SPV	SPV08576012	Germany	1997	8.99
Saxon	Forever Free + 2	CD	SPV	SPV07674092	Germany	2002	9.99
Saxon	Greatest Hits Live !	CD	Castle	ESMCD132	England	1990	13.99
Saxon	Heavy Metal Thunder + 5 (WBonus Cd)	2CD	SPV	SPV08574482	Germany	2002	13.99
Saxon	Innocence Is No Excuse + 2	CD	Axe Killer	AXE3055522CD	France	2000	17.99
Saxon	Killing Ground	CD	SPV	SPV08572562	Germany	2002	8.99
Saxon	Live	CD	Arena Rock	1129	Sweden	2002	12.99
Saxon	Live At Donnington	CD	Angel Air	SJPCD045	France	2000	8.99
Saxon	Live In Nottingham	CD	Classic Rock	CRP1052	England	2003	12.99
Saxon	Live... In The Raw	CD	Zoom Club	ZCRCD43	England	2000	12.99
Saxon	Masters Of Rock	CD	EMI	7243-5-34695-2-8	England	2001	10.99
Saxon	Metalhead	CD	SPV	SPV08521502	Germany	1999	8.99
Saxon	Power And The Glory	CD	Axe Killer	AXE3046122CD	France	1999	12.99
Saxon	Power And The Glory	CD	EMI	7243-5-21303-2	England	1999	11.99
Saxon	Re: Landed	CD	Phoenix	PHMUKCD001	England	2001	11.99
Saxon	Rock Champions	CD	EMI	7243-5-76245-2-7	England	2001	10.99
Saxon	Rock 'N' Roll Gypsies + 2	CD	Connoisseur	VSOPCD352	England	2001	11.99
Saxon	Rock The Nations	CD	Griffin	GCD-552-2	U.S.A.	1995	16.99
Saxon	Self Titled	CD	EMI	7243-5-21295-2	U.S.A.	1999	11.99
Saxon	Solid Ball Of Rock + 2	CD	SPV	SPV07674082	Germany	2002	8.99
Saxon	Strong Arm Law/Denim Leather + 4	CD	Axe Killer	AXE305593CD	France	2000	28.99
Saxon	The Eagle Has Landed	CD	EMI	7243-5-21297-2	U.S.A.	1999	8.99
Saxon	The Eagle Has Landed - Live	CD	Toshiba-EMI	TOCP-8374	Japan	1982	19.99
Saxon	The Eagle Has Landed, Pt. 2	CD	SPV	SPV08521172	Germany	2001	8.99
Saxon	The Eagle Has Landed, Pt. 2	CD	CMC Int.	06076-86258-2	U.S.A.	1998	8.99
Saxon	Unleash The Beast	CD	CMC Int.	06076-86221-2	U.S.A.	1997	8.99
Saxon	Unleash The Beast + 1	CD	Avex Trax	AVCB-66016	Japan	1997	8.99
Saxon	Very Best Of Album Ever	CD	EMI	7243-5-39927-2-9	Holland	2002	10.99
Saxon	Wheels Of Steel	CD	EMI	0777-7-92116-2	U.S.A.	2000	13.99
Saxon	Wheels Of Steel + 6/Strong Arm + 5	2CD	EMI	7243-8-55209-2-1	England	1997	13.99
Scaggs, Boz	Boz Scaggs	CD	Atlantic	19166-2	U.S.A.	1978	17.99
Scaggs, Boz	Boz Scaggs & Band	CD	Columbia	CK-30796	U.S.A.	1971	44.99
Scaggs, Boz	Boz Scaggs & Band	CD	Sony	SRCS-9292	Japan	1994	49.99
Scaggs, Boz	Boz The Ballade	CD	Sony	SRCS-5684	Japan	1992	36.99
Scaggs, Boz	But Beautiful	CD	Gray Cat	GCD-4000-2	U.S.A.	2003	17.99
Scaggs, Boz	But Beautiful + 1	CD	Victor Ent.	VICP-62407	Japan	2003	29.99
Scaggs, Boz	Come On Home	CD	Virgin	7243-8-42984-2-5	U.S.A.	1997	8.99
Scaggs, Boz	Dig	CD	Virgin	7243-8-10635-2-1	U.S.A.	2001	5.99
Scaggs, Boz	Dig (Deluxe Leatherbound W/DVD)	2CD	Virgin	7087-6-16191-0-2	U.S.A.	2001	14.99
Scaggs, Boz	Down Two Then Left	CD	Columbia	CK-34729	U.S.A.	1977	8.99

S

Artist	Title	Format	Label	Catalog No	Country	Released	Value
Scaggs, Boz	Fade Into Light	CD	Virgin	VJCP-25260	Japan	1996	19.99
Scaggs, Boz	Fade Into Light	CD	Virgin	VJCP-25260	Japan	1996	33.99
Scaggs, Boz	Here's The Lowdown	CD	Collectables	COL-9347	U.S.A.	2003	7.99
Scaggs, Boz	Hits!	CD	Columbia	465042-2	Australia	1980	8.99
Scaggs, Boz	Middle Man	CD	Sony	SRCS-6223	Japan	1992	19.99
Scaggs, Boz	Middle Man	CD	Columbia	CK-65626	U.S.A.	1998	8.99
Scaggs, Boz	Moments	CD	Sony	25DP-5012	Japan	1970	49.99
Scaggs, Boz	Moments	CD	Columbia	CK-30454	U.S.A.	1990	44.99
Scaggs, Boz	My Time	CD	Columbia	CK-31384	U.S.A.	1972	44.99
Scaggs, Boz	My Time	CD	Sony	SRCS-6395	Japan	1988	23.99
Scaggs, Boz	My Time: Anthology	2CD	Columbia	C2K-65208	U.S.A.	1997	18.99
Scaggs, Boz	Other Roads	CD	Columbia	CK-40463	U.S.A.	1988	6.99
Scaggs, Boz	Silk Degrees	CD	Sony	35DP-20	Japan	1988	19.99
Scaggs, Boz	Silk Degrees (MFSL Gold Cd)	CD	Mobile Fidelity	UDCD-535	U.S.A.	1976	39.99
Scaggs, Boz	Silk Degrees (Sony Gold Cd)	CD	Columbia	CK-57205	U.S.A.	1976	24.99
Scaggs, Boz	Slow Dancer	CD	Columbia	CK-32760	U.S.A.	1977	8.99
Scaggs, Boz	Some Change	CD	Virgin	7243-8-39489-2-5	U.S.A.	1994	5.99
Scaggs, Boz	Star Box	CD	Sony	25DP-5202	Japan	1988	19.99
Scaggs, Boz	T-Bone Shuffle (Promo)	CD Single	Virgin	7087-6-12789-2-7	U.S.A.	1997	6.99
Scaggs, Boz	The Lost Concert	CD	Park South	75766-70582-2-5	U.S.A.	2001	9.99
Scandal	The Warrior Featuring Patty Smyth	CD	Columbia	CK-39173	U.S.A.	1984	11.99
Scandal/Patty Smyth	Greatest Hits	CD	Columbia	CK-65616	U.S.A.	1998	8.99
Scandal/Patty Smyth	Greatest Hits	CD	Sony	SRCS-8789	Japan	1998	39.99
Scandal/Patty Smyth	Isn't It Enough (Numbered Promo)	CD Single	Columbia	CSK-2744	U.S.A.	1987	14.99
Scandal/Patty Smyth	Look What Love Has Done (Promo)	CD Single	MCA	MCA5P-3238	U.S.A.	1994	12.99
Scandal/Patty Smyth	Never Enough	CD	Columbia	CK-40182	U.S.A.	1987	14.99
Scandal/Patty Smyth	Never Enough	CD	Sony	CSCS-6050	Japan	1987	34.99
Scandal/Patty Smyth	Scandalous (W/Scandal EP - 1)	CD	Sony	A-22626	U.S.A.	1995	7.99
Scandal/Patty Smyth	Self Titled	CD	MCA	MCAD-10633	U.S.A.	2003	5.99
Scandal/Patty Smyth	Sometimes Love... (3") W/Don Henley	CD	MCA	MVDM-28	Japan	1992	14.99
Scandal/Patty Smyth	Sometimes Love... (W/Don Henley)	CD Single	MCA	MCSTD1692	England	1992	8.99
Schenker, Michael/MSG	Adventures Of The Imagination	CD	Shrapnel	SH-1140CD	U.S.A.	2000	8.99
Schenker, Michael/MSG	Adventures Of The Imagination	CD	Steamhammer	CRCL-4745	Japan	2000	28.99
Schenker, Michael/MSG	Anthology	CD	Griffin	GCD-235-2	U.S.A.	1994	8.99
Schenker, Michael/MSG	Anthology	2CD	Toshiba-EMI	TOCP-53150/1	Japan	1991	74.99
Schenker, Michael/MSG	Arachnophobiac	CD	Mascot	M-7081	Netherlands	2003	9.99
Schenker, Michael/MSG	Aracnophobiac	CD	Avalon	MICP-10372	Japan	2003	24.99
Schenker, Michael/MSG	Armed And Ready (The Best Of)	CD	Music Club	MCCD-160	England	1994	14.99
Schenker, Michael/MSG	Assault Attack + 1	CD	Toshiba-EMI	TOCP-53142	Japan	1982	24.99
Schenker, Michael/MSG	Assault Attack/Rock Will Die	2CD	BGO	BGOCD321	England	1996	24.99
Schenker, Michael/MSG	Back To Attack Box Set	4CD	Zoom Club	ZCRCD96BOX	England	2003	54.99
Schenker, Michael/MSG	Back To Attack: Live	2CD	Zoom Club	ZCRCD80047	England	2003	17.99
Schenker, Michael/MSG	BBC Radio One Live In Concert	CD	Griffin	GCD-335-2	U.S.A.	1995	14.99
Schenker, Michael/MSG	Be Aware Of Scorpions	CD	SPV	085-72552-CD	Germany	2001	9.99
Schenker, Michael/MSG	Be Aware Of Scorpions + 1	CD	Steamhammer	CRCL-4792	Japan	2001	19.99
Schenker, Michael/MSG	Built To Destroy	CD	Toshiba-EMI	TOCP-6334	Japan	1983	14.99
Schenker, Michael/MSG	Built To Destroy	CD	Chrysalis	VK-41441	U.S.A.	1983	13.99
Schenker, Michael/MSG	Built To Destroy	CD	BGO	BGOCD344	England	1996	10.99
Schenker, Michael/MSG	Built To Destroy + 5	CD	Toshiba-EMI	TOCP-53143	Japan	1983	29.99
Schenker, Michael/MSG	Contraband - (Self Titled)	CD	Impact	IPTD-10247	U.S.A.	1991	9.99
Schenker, Michael/MSG	Dreams & Expressions	CD	Steamhammer	CRCL-4775	Japan	2000	9.99
Schenker, Michael/MSG	Essential	CD	Chrysalis	0946-3-21949-2-4	U.S.A.	1992	9.99
Schenker, Michael/MSG	Flying God	CD	Pony Canyon	PCCY-20005	Japan	2002	24.99
Schenker, Michael/MSG	Follow The Night (Promo)	CD Single	Capitol	DPRO-79281	U.S.A.	1988	7.99
Schenker, Michael/MSG	Forever And More	2CD	SPV	315-69402	Germany	2003	17.99
Schenker, Michael/MSG	Into The Arena 1972-1995 [Highlights]	2CD	Raven	RVCD-110	Australia	2000	16.99
Schenker, Michael/MSG	Lights Out	CD Single	Zoom Club	ZCRCD800464	England	2003	14.99
Schenker, Michael/MSG	M.S.G. + 1	CD	Toshiba-EMI	TOCP-53147	Japan	1991	20.99

S

Artist	Title	Format	Label	Catalog No	Country	Released	Value
Schenker, Michael/MSG	MS 2000: Dreams & Expressions	CD	Shrapnel	SH-1144CD	U.S.A.	2001	8.99
Schenker, Michael/MSG	MSG	CD	Toshiba-EMI	CP21-6053	Japan	1981	14.99
Schenker, Michael/MSG	MSG	CD	Impact	IPTD-10385	U.S.A.	1991	10.99
Schenker, Michael/MSG	MSG	CD	Toshiba-EMI	TOCP-53139	Japan	1981	20.99
Schenker, Michael/MSG	Nightmare The Acoustic M.S.G.	CD	Toshiba-EMI	TOCP-53148	Japan	1992	19.99
Schenker, Michael/MSG	One Night At Budokan	CD	BGO	BGOCD312	England	1996	10.99
Schenker, Michael/MSG	One Night In Budokan	2CD	Toshiba-EMI	TOCP-67243/4	Japan	1981	32.99
Schenker, Michael/MSG	Perfect Timing	CD	Capitol	CDP-7-46985-2	U.S.A.	1987	26.99
Schenker, Michael/MSG	Perfect Timing + 2 (McAuley/Schenker)	CD	Toshiba-EMI	TOCP-53145	Japan	1987	26.99
Schenker, Michael/MSG	Reactivate Live	4CD	Zoom Club	ZCRCD87BOX	England	2002	54.99
Schenker, Michael/MSG	Reactivate Live	2CD	Zoom Club	ZCRCD800465	England	2002	17.99
Schenker, Michael/MSG	Rock Will Never Die	CD	Chrysalis	CP32-5094	Japan	1984	15.99
Schenker, Michael/MSG	Rock Will Never Die + 6	CD	Toshiba-EMI	TOCP-53144	Japan	1984	22.99
Schenker, Michael/MSG	Save Yourself	CD	Capitol	CDP-7-92752-2	U.S.A.	1989	13.99
Schenker, Michael/MSG	Save Yourself + 3 (McAuley/Schenker)	CD	Toshiba-EMI	TOCP-53146	Japan	1989	23.99
Schenker, Michael/MSG	Self Titled	CD	Disky	90511	Netherlands	2000	8.99
Schenker, Michael/MSG	Self Titled	CD	Chrysalis	VK-41302	U.S.A.	1980	16.99
Schenker, Michael/MSG	Self Titled (U.K.)	CD	Chrysalis	CCD-1336	England	1981	16.99
Schenker, Michael/MSG	Self Titled/MSG	2CD	BGO	BGOCD316	England	1997	24.99
Schenker, Michael/MSG	Thank You	CD	SPV	085-72662-CD	Germany	2001	9.99
Schenker, Michael/MSG	Thank You	CD	Toshiba-EMI	TOCP-65245	Japan	1993	27.99
Schenker, Michael/MSG	Thank You With Orchestra	CD	Michael Schenker	71	U.S.A.	2000	16.99
Schenker, Michael/MSG	Thank You, Vol. 2	CD	Steamhammer	CRCL-4799	Japan	2000	29.99
Schenker, Michael/MSG	Thank You, Vol. 2	CD	SPV	085-72922-CD	Germany	2002	9.99
Schenker, Michael/MSG	Thank You, Vol. 3	CD	Shrapnel	SH-1158CD	U.S.A.	2002	9.99
Schenker, Michael/MSG	The Michael Schenker Group	CD	Toshiba-EMI	TOCP-53138	Japan	1980	29.99
Schenker, Michael/MSG	The Michael Schenker Story Live	2CD	Toshiba-EMI	TOCP-65243/4	Japan	1997	59.99
Schenker, Michael/MSG	The Michael Schenker Story Live	2CD	SPV	085-72672-CD	Germany	2001	14.99
Schenker, Michael/MSG	The Odd Trio	CD	Michael Schenker	5	U.S.A.	2001	16.99
Schenker, Michael/MSG	The Story Of	CD	Toshiba-EMI	TOCP-7917	Japan	1994	54.99
Schenker, Michael/MSG	The Unforgiven	CD	Steamhammer	CRCL-4720	Japan	1999	22.99
Schenker, Michael/MSG	The Unforgiven	CD	Shrapnel	SH-1126CD	U.S.A.	1999	9.99
Schenker, Michael/MSG	The Unforgiven World Tour: Live	2CD	Shrapnel	SH-1131CD	U.S.A.	1999	17.99
Schenker, Michael/MSG	Unplugged Live + 2	CD	Toshiba-EMI	TOCP-53149	Japan	1992	34.99
Schenker, Michael/MSG	Unplugged Live + 2 (Photo Bk/Sticker)	CD	Toshiba-EMI	TOCP-7396	Japan	1992	63.99
Schenker, Michael/MSG	Written In The Sand	CD	Z Records	JRCD-5167	Japan	1996	24.99
Schenker, Michael/MSG	Written In The Sand + 2	CD	Zero	XRCN-1283	Japan	1996	44.99
Schifrin, Lalo	Dirty Harry Anthology	CD	Aleph	003	Germany	1998	12.99
Schifrin, Lalo	Mannix + 1 (T.V./O.S.T.)	CD	Aleph	014	Germany	1999	12.99
Schifrin, Lalo/John E. Davis	Best Mission:Impossible Then/Now	CD	GNP	GNPD-8029	U.S.A.	1992	11.99
Schlong/Parody	Punk Side Story (West Side Story)	CD	Hopeless	HR602-2	U.S.A.	1994	5.99
Schmit, Timothy B.	Feed The Fire	CD	Lucan	2001	U.S.A.	2001	8.99
Schmit, Timothy B.	Feed The Fire + 1	CD	BMG Victor	BVCG-21020	Japan	2001	29.99
Schmit, Timothy B.	Playin' It Cool	CD	Wounded Bird	WOU-359	U.S.A.	2002	8.99
Schmit, Timothy B.	Playin' It Cool	CD	East West	AMCY-3012	Japan	1996	29.99
Schmit, Timothy B.	Tell Me The Truth	CD	MCA	MCAD-6420	U.S.A.	1990	35.99
Schmit, Timothy B.	Timothy B.	CD	MCA	MCAD-42049	U.S.A.	1987	35.99
Schmoelling, Johannes	Lieder Ohne Worte - Songs No Words	CD	Erdenklang	50802	Germany	1995	16.99
Schmoelling, Johannes	Recycle Or Die	CD	Viktoriapark	VP-03-3	Germany	2003	35.99
Schmoelling, Johannes	The Zoo Of Tranquility	CD	Erdenklang	81042	Germany	1998	18.99
Schmoelling, Johannes	The Zoo Of Tranquillity	CD	Theta	834-109-2	Germany	1988	18.99
Schmoelling, Johannes	White Out	CD	Polydor	843-395-2	Germany	1990	29.99
Schmoelling, Johannes	White Out + 2	CD	Viktoriapark	VP-00-1	Germany	2000	35.99
Schmoelling, Johannes	Wuivend Riet	CD	I.R.S.	971.160	Germany	1987	23.99
Schnabel, Arthur	Sonaten Fur Violine Und Klavier	CD	Line	CACD-9.00850-P	Germany	1990	12.99
Schneider, Fred/B-52's	Fred Schneider	CD	Warner Bros.	9-26592-2	U.S.A.	1991	4.99
Schneider, Fred/B-52's	Just Fred	CD	Reprise	9-46215-2	U.S.A.	1996	4.99
Schnitzler, Conrad	Blau + 6	CD	Captain Trip	CTCD-337	Japan	1974	16.99

S

Artist	Title	Format	Label	Catalog No	Country	Released	Value
Schon, Neal	Beyond The Thunder	CD	Higher Octave	77565B	U.S.A.	1995	8.99
Schon, Neal	Electric World	2CD	Higher Octave	77595	U.S.A.	1997	14.99
Schon, Neal	Late Night	CD	Columbia	CK-45106	U.S.A.	1989	8.99
Schon, Neal	Piranha Blues	CD	Blues Bureau	2041	U.S.A.	1999	13.99
Schon, Neal	Voice	CD	Higher Octave	7243-8-10418-2-6	Holland	2001	14.99
Schon, Neal/Jan Hammer	No More Lies (Untold P/Here To S)	CD	Razor & Tie	79301-82176-2	U.S.A.	1998	14.99
Schulze, Klaus	2001	CD	Brain	511-295-2	Germany	1991	18.99
Schulze, Klaus	Angst	CD	Thunderbolt	CDTB-027	England	1997	12.99
Schulze, Klaus	Are You Sequenced?	2CD	Warner Bros.	0630-16324-2	EU	1996	34.99
Schulze, Klaus	Audentity	2CD	Thunderbolt	CTTB-507	England	1996	24.99
Schulze, Klaus	Beyond Recall	CD	Caroline	CAROL-1873-2	U.S.A.	1991	9.99
Schulze, Klaus	Blackdance	CD	Brain	833-129-2	Germany	1992	11.99
Schulze, Klaus	Body Love Vol.2	CD	Brain	511-976-2	Germany	1992	11.99
Schulze, Klaus	Body Love, Vol. 1 (O.S.T.)	CD	Thunderbolt	CDTB-123	England	1996	11.99
Schulze, Klaus	Conquest Of Paradise	CD Single	ZYX	7481-8	Germany	1994	13.99
Schulze, Klaus	Contemporary Works 1	10 CD	Rainhorse	RHMR-200010	Germany	2000	149.99
Schulze, Klaus	Contemporary Works 2	5CD	Rainhorse	RHMR-200014	Germany	2004	74.99
Schulze, Klaus	Cyborg	2CD	Spalax	14922	France	1995	24.99
Schulze, Klaus	Das Wagner Desaster - Live	2CD	ZYX	90000-2	Germany	1994	24.99
Schulze, Klaus	Dig It	CD	Thunderbolt	CDTB-144	England	1994	8.99
Schulze, Klaus	Dosburg Online	CD	Warner Bros.	3984-20656-2	EU	1997	29.99
Schulze, Klaus	Dreams	CD	Thunderbolt	CDTB-039	England	1996	9.99
Schulze, Klaus	Dresden Performance	2CD	Caroline	CAROL-1865-2	U.S.A.	1991	18.99
Schulze, Klaus	Dune	CD	Thunderbolt	CDTB-145	England	1995	10.99
Schulze, Klaus	En=Trance	CD	Thunderbolt	CDTB-061	England	1996	11.99
Schulze, Klaus	Essential 72 - 93	2CD	Caroline	CAROL-1896-2	U.S.A.	1994	15.99
Schulze, Klaus	Goes Classic	CD	ZYX	20297-2	Germany	1994	11.99
Schulze, Klaus	Historic Edition Box Set (Only 2000)	10 CD	Manikin	KS 11-20	Germany	1995	149.99
Schulze, Klaus	History	CD	Brain	835-161-2	Germany	1988	19.99
Schulze, Klaus	In Blue	2CD	ZYX	90001-2	Germany	1995	24.99
Schulze, Klaus	Inter*Face	CD	Manikin	MRCD-7027	Germany	1995	12.99
Schulze, Klaus	Irrlicht	CD	Thunderbolt	CDTB-133	England	1996	9.99
Schulze, Klaus	Jubilee Edition Box Set (Only 1000)	25 CD	Manikin	KS 21-45	Germany	1997	799.99
Schulze, Klaus	Le Moulin De Daudet	CD	Virgin	395-942-2	France	1995	24.99
Schulze, Klaus	Live @ KlangArt 1	CD	Rainhorse	RHMR-200012	Germany	2001	24.99
Schulze, Klaus	Live @ KlangArt 2	CD	Rainhorse	RHMR-200013	Germany	2001	24.99
Schulze, Klaus	Live.... (1980)	2CD	Manikin	MRCD-7008	Germany	1995	24.99
Schulze, Klaus	Miditerranean Pads	CD	Thunderbolt	CDTB-081	England	1990	8.99
Schulze, Klaus	Mirage	CD	Thunderbolt	CDTB-033	England	1996	9.99
Schulze, Klaus	Moondawn	CD	Thunderbolt	CDTB-093	England	1991	9.99
Schulze, Klaus	Moondawn + 1 (The Original Master)	CD	Manikin	MRCD-7009	Germany	1995	11.99
Schulze, Klaus	Picture Music	CD	Thunderbolt	CDTB-098	England	1996	9.99
Schulze, Klaus	Royal Festival Hall, Vol. 1	CD	Caroline	CAROL-1879-2	U.S.A.	1993	9.99
Schulze, Klaus	Royal Festival Hall, Vol. 2	CD	Caroline	CAROL-1880-2	U.S.A.	1993	14.99
Schulze, Klaus	Schwarz Oder Weiss	CD	ZYX	20443-2	Germany	1998	15.99
Schulze, Klaus	Silver Edition Box Set (Only 2000)	10 CD	Manikin	KS 1-10	Germany	1993	149.99
Schulze, Klaus	The Dome Event: Cologne Cathedral	2CD	Caroline	CAROL-1881-2	England	1993	14.99
Schulze, Klaus	Timewind	CD	Brain	833-128-2	Germany	1992	10.99
Schulze, Klaus	Totentag	2CD	ZYX	81014-2	Germany	1994	34.99
Schulze, Klaus	Trancefer	CD	Thunderbolt	CDTB-146	England	1994	9.99
Schulze, Klaus	X	2CD	Thunderbolt	CDTB-501	England	1996	24.99
Schulze, Klaus	X Volume 2	CD	Thunderbolt	CDTB-201	England	2000	15.99
Schulze, Klaus/A. Grosser	Babel (W/Andreas Grosser)	CD	Virgin	CDVE5	England	1987	17.99
Schulze, Klaus/Rainer Bloss	Drive Inn	CD	Thunderbolt	CDTB-028	England	1996	11.99
Schulze, Klaus/Ultimate Editon	Box Set (Silver/Historic/Jubilee + 5 Cd)	50 CD	Série Poème	2000-1-50	Germany	2000	1,499.99
Schulze, Klaus/Wahnfried	Drums 'N' Balls (The Gancha Dub)	CD	Brain	539-653-2	Germany	1997	14.99
Schulze, Klaus/Wahnfried	Richard Wahnfried - Tonwelle + 2	CD	Innovative	IC-710.095	Germany	1990	12.99
Schulze, Klaus/Wahnfried	Richard Wahnfried - Miditation	CD	Innovative	IC-710. 096	Germany	1990	12.99

S

Artist	Title	Format	Label	Catalog No	Country	Released	Value
Schulze, Klaus/Wahnfried	Richard Wahnfried - Time Actor + 1	CD	Innovative	IC-710.094	Germany	1990	11.99
Schulze, Klaus/Wahnfried	Richard Wahnfried Plays Megatone	CD	Thunderbolt	CDTB-031	England	2000	12.99
Schulze, Klaus/Wahnfried	Trance-Appeal	CD	Brain	531-683-2	Germany	1996	14.99
Schulze, Klaus/Wahnfried	Trancelation	CD	ZYX	20296-2	Germany	1994	14.99
Scorpions	10 Light Years Away	CD Single	East West	3984-27550-2	Germany	1999	11.99
Scorpions	Acoustica	CD	East West	AMCE-7252	Japan	2001	32.99
Scorpions	Acoustica	CD	Warner Bros.	8573-88249-2	U.S.A.	2001	8.99
Scorpions	Action	CD	Karussell	511-014-2	Germany	1972	14.99
Scorpions	Alien Nation	CD Single	Mercury	862-673-2	Germany	1993	4.99
Scorpions	Alien Nation (Promo)	CD Single	Mercury	CDP-981	U.S.A.	1993	13.99
Scorpions	Animal Magnetism	CD	Toshiba-EMI	TOCP-53205	Japan	2000	32.99
Scorpions	Animal Magnetism	CD	Mercury	314-534-785-2	U.S.A.	1997	9.99
Scorpions	Animal Magnetism + 1	CD	Mercury	535-154-2	Germany	2002	12.99
Scorpions	Bad For Good: The Very Best Of	CD	Hip O	314-548-118-2	U.S.A.	2002	9.99
Scorpions	Best Of	CD	BMG	PCD1-3516	Canada	1984	8.99
Scorpions	Best Of	CD	BMG	ND74006	Germany	1984	8.99
Scorpions	Best Of	CD	EMI	497013-2	Australia	1999	10.99
Scorpions	Best Of Rocker 'N' Ballads	CD	Mercury	842-002-2	U.S.A.	1989	7.99
Scorpions	Best Of Volume 2	CD	BMG	BMGRD-Z123	Korea	1993	29.99
Scorpions	Best Of Volume 2	CD	BMG	07863-55085-2	Canada	1992	21.99
Scorpions	Big City Nights	CD	Universal	314-520-511-2	U.S.A.	1998	6.99
Scorpions	Big City Nights	CDV	Mercury	422-870-716-2	England	1988	21.99
Scorpions	Blackout	CD	Toshiba-EMI	TOCP-53206	Japan	2001	39.99
Scorpions	Blackout	CD	Mercury	PHCR-12505	Japan	1982	24.99
Scorpions	Blackout	CD	Mercury	314-534-786-2	U.S.A.	1997	9.99
Scorpions	Burner	CD	Universal	069-721-2	Switzerland	2002	12.99
Scorpions	Classic Bites	CD	Polygram	7314-586531-2	U.S.A.	2002	5.99
Scorpions	Crazy World	CD	Mercury	846-908-2	U.S.A.	1990	7.99
Scorpions	Crazy World	CD	Mercury	PHCR-1041	Japan	1990	24.99
Scorpions	Crazy World	CD	Mercury	846-908-2	U.S.A.	1990	7.99
Scorpions	Deadly Sting: Mercury Years (Clean)	CD	Mercury	314-536-285-2	U.S.A.	1997	8.99
Scorpions	Deadly Sting: The Mercury Years	2CD	Mercury	PHCR-4071/72	Japan	1997	42.99
Scorpions	Deadly Sting: The Mercury Years	CD	Mercury	314-534-344-2	U.S.A.	1997	9.99
Scorpions	Does Anybody Know	CD Single	East West	0630-15897-2	Germany	1996	3.99
Scorpions	Does Anybody Know (Promo)	CD Single	Atlantic	PRCD-6839	U.S.A.	1996	12.99
Scorpions	Don't Believe Her (3")	CD Single	Phonogram	PHDR-20	Japan	1991	34.99
Scorpions	Essential	CD	EMI	76648-20930-4	U.S.A.	2003	9.99
Scorpions	Essential	CD	EMI	583-219-2	England	2003	10.99
Scorpions	Eye II Eye	CD	East West	AMCE-7001	Japan	1999	29.99
Scorpions	Eye II Eye	CD	Koch	KOC-CD-8052	U.S.A.	1999	8.99
Scorpions	Eye II Eye	CD Single	East West	8573-80311-2	Germany	1999	5.99
Scorpions	Face The Heat	CD	Mercury	314-518-258-2	U.S.A.	1993	6.99
Scorpions	Face The Heat	CD	Mercury	518-280-2	Germany	1993	7.99
Scorpions	Face The Heat	CD	Mercury	314-518-258-2	Canada	1993	6.99
Scorpions	Fly To The Rainbow	CD	RCA	B2OD-41010	Japan	1997	22.99
Scorpions	Fly To The Rainbow	CD	BMG	ND70084	Germany	1983	9.99
Scorpions	Fly To The Rainbow	CD	RCA	5057-2-R	U.S.A.	1987	9.99
Scorpions	Gold Ballads	CD	EMI	0777-7-91015-2-8	Germany	2001	10.99
Scorpions	Here In My Heart	CD Single	EMI	7243-8-89141-0-9	England	2000	3.99
Scorpions	Hit Between The Eyes	CD Single	Mercury	866-621-2	Germany	1992	9.99
Scorpions	Holiday (Promo)	CD Single	Mercury	CDP-208	U.S.A.	1989	13.99
Scorpions	Holiday (Promo)	CD Single	East West	PR-02703	Germany	2001	18.99
Scorpions	Hot & Hard	CD	BMG	74321-15119-2	Germany	1993	15.99
Scorpions	Hot & Heavy	CD	RCA	07863-66194-2	U.S.A.	1993	11.99
Scorpions	Hot & Heavy	CD	BMG	07863-66194-2	Canada	1993	11.99
Scorpions	Hot & Slow	CD	RCA	ND-75029	Germany	1991	11.99
Scorpions	Hot & Slow	CD	RCA	07863-61074-2	U.S.A.	1991	11.99
Scorpions	Hot & Slow	CD	Mercury	07863-66194-2	Canada	1991	11.99

S

Artist	Title	Format	Label	Catalog No	Country	Released	Value
Scorpions	Hot & Slow: Best Masters	CD	BMG	07432-16151-2	Germany	1999	15.99
Scorpions	Hurricane 2000	CD Single	EMI	7243-8-88542-2-1	Netherlands	2000	5.99
Scorpions	Hurricane Rock	CD	Connoisseur	VSOP-CD-156	England	1990	9.99
Scorpions	I Can't Explain	CD Single	Mercury	876-191-2	U.S.A.	1989	6.99
Scorpions	I Can't Explain (Promo)	CD Single	Mercury	CDP-145	U.S.A.	1989	18.99
Scorpions	In Trance	CD	RCA	B20D-41011	Japan	1997	22.99
Scorpions	In Trance	CD	RCA	4128-2-R	U.S.A.	1991	9.99
Scorpions	In Trance	CD	BMG	ND-70028	Germany	1975	9.99
Scorpions	Live Bites	CD	Mercury	314-526-889-2	U.S.A.	1995	5.99
Scorpions	Live Bites	CD	Mercury	314-526-889-2	Canada	1995	5.99
Scorpions	Lonesome Crow	CD	Rhino	R2-70915	U.S.A.	1972	8.99
Scorpions	Lonesome Crow	CD	Hip O	825-739-2	U.S.A.	2002	9.99
Scorpions	Love At First Sting	CD	Toshiba-EMI	TOCP-53207	Japan	2002	32.99
Scorpions	Love At First Sting	CD	Mercury	314-534-787-2	U.S.A.	1997	8.99
Scorpions	Love Bites + 2	CD	Polygram	526-903-2	England	2002	10.99
Scorpions	Lovedrive	CD	Mercury	PHCR-12506	Japan	1979	24.99
Scorpions	Lovedrive	CD	Toshiba-EMI	TOCP-53204	Japan	2000	32.99
Scorpions	Lovedrive	CD	Mercury	314-534-784-2	U.S.A.	1997	9.99
Scorpions	Moment Of Glory	CD	Toshiba-EMI	TOCP-65484	Japan	2000	32.99
Scorpions	Moment Of Glory	CD	EMI	CDC-557019	U.S.A.	2000	9.99
Scorpions	Moment Of Glory (W/Cd-Rom)	2CD	EMI	7243-5-57020-2-9	EU	2000	44.99
Scorpions	No Pain No Gain (W/Ger Soccer Tm)	CD Single	Mercury	858-741-2	Germany	1994	12.99
Scorpions	Over The Top	CD Single	Mercury	MECP-257	U.S.A.	1997	14.99
Scorpions	Passion Rules The Heart	CD Single	EMI	5242-20-3207-2	England	1988	4.99
Scorpions	Pictured Life: All The Best	CD	BMG	74321-73842-2-7	Germany	2000	10.99
Scorpions	Pure Instinct	CD	East West	AMCE-950	Japan	1996	32.99
Scorpions	Pure Instinct	CD	Atlantic	82913-2	U.S.A.	1996	8.99
Scorpions	Pure Instinct (Clean)	CD	Atlantic	82935-2	U.S.A.	1996	7.99
Scorpions	Pure Instinct + 1	CD	Atlantic	AMCE-950	Japan	1996	19.99
Scorpions	Rhythm Of Love	CD Single	Toshiba-EMI	XP10-2014	Japan	1988	9.99
Scorpions	Savage Amusement	CD	Toshiba-EMI	TOCP-53209	Japan	2002	32.99
Scorpions	Savage Amusement	CD	Mercury	832-963-2	U.S.A.	1988	8.99
Scorpions	Savage Amusement	CD	EMI	564-7-46704 2	Germany	1988	8.99
Scorpions	Send Me An Angel	CD Single	Mercury	868-519-2	Germany	1990	4.99
Scorpions	Send Me An Angel	CD Single	Vertigo	VERCD-60	England	1990	4.99
Scorpions	Still Loving You	CD	Harvest	568-7-98732 2	Germany	1992	15.99
Scorpions	Still Loving You	CD	EMI	0777-7-98732-2-7	Germany	1992	15.99
Scorpions	Taken By Force	CD	Toshiba-EMI	TOCP-53202	Japan	2001	39.99
Scorpions	Taken By Force + 2	CD	Hip O	017900	U.S.A.	2002	9.99
Scorpions	Tease Me Please Me (3")	CD Single	Phonogram	PHDR-16	Japan	1991	32.99
Scorpions	The Millennium Collection	CD	Mercury	314-548-694-2	U.S.A.	2001	8.99
Scorpions	To Be No. 1	CD Single	East West	3984-26451-2	Germany	1999	6.99
Scorpions	To Be No. 1 (Promo)	CD Single	East West	PRO1189/1828	Germany	1999	17.99
Scorpions	Tokyo Tapes	CD	RCA	07863-53039-2	U.S.A.	1993	8.99
Scorpions	Tokyo Tapes	CD	Toshiba-EMI	TOCP-53203	Japan	2001	32.99
Scorpions	Tokyo Tapes (Long Version Fly..)	2CD	Hip O	017901	U.S.A.	2002	19.99
Scorpions	Under The Same Sun	CD Single	Phonogram	PHCR-8043	Japan	1993	14.99
Scorpions	Under The Same Sun (CD 1)	CD Single	Mercury	862-953-2	Germany	1993	5.99
Scorpions	Under The Same Sun (CD 2)	CD Single	Mercury	858-213-2	Germany	1993	5.99
Scorpions	Virgin Killer	CD	RCA	035627003127	Germany	1988	19.99
Scorpions	Virgin Killer (Withdrawn Cover)	CD	BMG	BVCP-7375	Japan	1976	24.99
Scorpions	When Love Kills Love	CD Single	East West	8573-87780-2	U.S.A.	2001	12.99
Scorpions	When You Came ...	CD Single	East West	AMCE-2136	Japan	1997	12.99
Scorpions	When You Came...	CD Single	East West	0630-16812-2	Germany	1996	7.99
Scorpions	Where The River Flows	CD Single	East West	0630-19682-2	Germany	1997	5.99
Scorpions	White Dove	CD Single	Mercury	856-575-2	Germany	1994	4.99
Scorpions	Wind Of Change	CD	Mercury	PHCR-2093	Japan	1991	14.99
Scorpions	Wind Of Change (3")	CD Single	Phonogram	PHDR-43	Japan	1991	44.99

S

Artist	Title	Format	Label	Catalog No	Country	Released	Value
Scorpions	Woman	CD Single	Mercury	858-489-2	Germany	1993	4.99
Scorpions	Woman (Promo)	CD Single	Mercury	CDP-1080	U.S.A.	1993	9.99
Scorpions	World Wide Live	CD	Toshiba-EMI	TOCP-53208	Japan	2002	32.99
Scorpions	World Wide Live	CD	Mercury	824-344-2	U.S.A.	1985	7.99
Scorpions	World Wide Live	CD	Mercury	314-534-788-2	U.S.A.	1997	9.99
Scorpions	You And I	CD Single	East West	0630-14523-2	Germany	1996	6.99
Scott, Marilyn	Without Warning	CD	Polydor K.K.	POCP-2041	Japan	1991	94.99
Scott, Tony	Astral Meditation/Voyage Into A Black...	2CD	Line	LICD-9.21328-0	Germany	1996	41.99
Scott, Tony	Dedications	CD	Line	COCD-9.0083-0	Germany	1989	19.99
Scott, Tony	Lush Life	2CD	Line	COCD-9.21156-S	Germany	1991	29.99
Scott, Tony	Lush Life - Vol. 1	CD	Line	COCD-9.00666-0	Germany	1989	19.99
Scott, Tony	Lush Life - Vol. 2	CD	Line	COCD-9.00667-0	Germany	1989	19.99
Scott, Tony	Voyage Into The Black Hole - Part 1	CD	Line	COCD-9.00590-0	Germany	1988	19.99
Scott, Tony	Voyage Into The Black Hole - Part 2	CD	Line	COCD-9.00591-0	Germany	1988	19.99
Scott, Tony	Voyage Into The Black Hole - Part 3	CD	Line	COCD-9.00592-0	Germany	1988	19.99
Scott/Raven	The Old Hood	CD	Line	YMCD-9.00768-0	Germany	1991	15.99
Scott-Heron, Gil	Free Will	CD	RCA	74321851612	France	2001	16.99
Scott-Heron, Gil	Ghetto Style	CD	Camden	74321-628062	Sweden	1998	13.99
Scott-Heron, Gil	Moving Target	CD	Arista	254-921	Germany	1992	16.99
Scott-Heron, Gil	Pieces Of A Man	CD	RCA	74321851632	France	2001	16.99
Scott-Heron, Gil	Reflections	CD	Arista	254-094	Germany	1992	16.99
Scott-Heron, Gil	Small Talk At 125th And Lenox	CD	RCA	74321851622	France	2001	16.99
Scott-Heron, Gil	The Best Of	CD	Arista	18306-2	U.S.A.	1984	13.99
Scott-Heron, Gil	The Mind Of	CD	TVT	TVT-4360-2	U.S.A.	2000	9.99
Scott-Heron, Gil/B. Jackson	From South Africa/South Carolina + 4	CD	TVT	TVT-4340-2	U.S.A.	1998	9.99
Scott-Heron, Gil/B. Jackson	Winter In America + 4	CD	TVT	TVT-4320-2	U.S.A.	1998	9.99
Screamin' Cheetah Wheelies	Big Wheel	CD	Capricorn	314-558-718-2	U.S.A.	1998	7.99
Screamin' Mother	Self Titled	CD	FEMS	APCY-8295	Japan	1995	28.99
Scruggs, Earl/Lester Flatt	Beverly Hillbillies (B. Ebsen/I. Ryan)	CD	Columbia	CK-57276	U.S.A.	1964	19.99
Scruggs, Earl/Various Artists	Earl Scruggs And Friends	CD	MCA	088-170-189-2	U.S.A.	2001	9.99
Sea Level	Ball Room	CD	BMG Victor	BVCA-2056	Japan	1992	61.99
Sea Level	Best Of	CD	Polydor	843-140-2	U.S.A.	1990	10.99
Sea Level	Cats On The Coast	CD	Capricorn	314-536-124-2	U.S.A.	1997	39.99
Sea Level	Long Walk On A Short Pier	CD	Capricorn	314-558-002-2	U.S.A.	1998	39.99
Sea Level	On The Edge	CD	Capricorn	314-558-382-2	U.S.A.	1998	39.99
Sea Level	Self Titled	CD	Capricorn	314-558-393-2	U.S.A.	1998	41.99
Seals And Crofts	Diamond Girl	CD	Warner Bros.	WPCP-4676	Japan	1991	174.99
Seals And Crofts	Greatest Hits	CD	Warner Bros.	3109-2	U.S.A.	1975	8.99
Seals And Crofts	Summer Breeze	CD	Warner Bros.	WPCP-4675	Japan	1991	64.99
Seals And Crofts	Summer Breeze	CD	Warner Bros.	7599-26744-2	U.S.A.	1995	8.99
Seals And Crofts/Dash Crofts	Today	CD	Light Year	54419-2	U.S.A.	2000	11.99
Seals And Crofts/L Shelton	{Hot & Spicy}	CD	Sin-Drome	SD-8929	U.S.A.	1998	16.99
Seals And Crofts/L Shelton	Guitar	CD	Light Year	54171-2	U.S.A.	1996	7.99
Seals And Crofts/L. Shelton	Urban Culture	CD	Light Year	54403-2	U.S.A.	2000	9.99
Seals, Dan	Best Of	CD	Curb	D2-77675	U.S.A.	1994	7.99
Seals, Dan	Certified Hits	CD	Capitol	7243-5-34450-2-7	U.S.A.	2001	5.99
Seals, Dan	Classics Collection Volume 1	CD	Capitol	7-95952-2	U.S.A.	1991	24.99
Seals, Dan	Classics Collection Volume 2	CD	Capitol	7-96384-2	U.S.A.	1992	24.99
Seals, Dan	Early Dan Seals	CD	Capitol	7-95561-2	U.S.A.	1991	11.99
Seals, Dan	Fired Up	CD	Warner Bros.	9-45628-2	U.S.A.	1994	6.99
Seals, Dan	Greatest Hits	CD	Capitol	7-95757-2	U.S.A.	1991	8.99
Seals, Dan	Harbinger	CD	East West	AMCY-6045	Japan	1999	64.99
Seals, Dan	In A Quiet Room	CD	Intersound	9153	U.S.A.	1995	8.99
Seals, Dan	In A Quiet Room II	CD	Tour Data	TDC0011	U.S.A.	1997	11.99
Seals, Dan	Make It Home (Prod By Louie Shelton)	CD	Light Year	54491-2	U.S.A.	2002	10.99
Seals, Dan	Montana Sky	CD	Capitol	KRB5423-2	U.S.A.	1999	5.99
Seals, Dan	My Baby's Got Good Timin'	CD	Capitol	S21-57078	U.S.A.	1994	14.99
Seals, Dan	On Arrival	CD	Capitol	7-91782-2	U.S.A.	1990	6.99

S

Artist	Title	Format	Label	Catalog No	Country	Released	Value
Seals, Dan	On The Front Line	CD	Captiol	7-46352-2	U.S.A.	1986	15.99
Seals, Dan	Rage On	CD	Capitol	CDP-546976	U.S.A.	1988	7.99
Seals, Dan	Rebel Heart	CD	Magic	5201242	France	1999	24.99
Seals, Dan	San Antone	CD	Magic	5213612	France	1999	24.99
Seals, Dan	Song Writer	CD	Liberty	7-98481-2	U.S.A.	1992	5.99
Seals, Dan	Stones	CD	East West	AMCY-6044	Japan	1999	44.99
Seals, Dan	The Best	CD	Capitol	7-48308-2	U.S.A.	1987	5.99
Seals, Dan	Walking The Wire	CD	Warner Bros.	9-26770-2	U.S.A.	1991	6.99
Seals, Dan	Won't Be Blue Anymore	CD	Captiol	7-46559-2	U.S.A.	1985	39.99
Seals, Dan/Southwest FOB	Smell Of Incense	CD	Blues Interactions	PCD-5177	Japan	1997	29.99
Seals, Dan/Southwest FOB	Smell Of Incense + 11	CD	Sundazed	SC-11060	U.S.A.	1998	10.99
Seals, Marvin	Melting Pot	CD	Rainman	RMCD114	U.S.A.	2004	9.99
Searchers	It's The/Take Me For... (MFSL Gold)	CD	Mobile Fidelity	UDCD-667	U.S.A.	1965	19.99
Searchers	Meet The/Sounds Like (MFSL Gold)	CD	Mobile Fidelity	UDCD-693	U.S.A.	1965	14.99
Seatrain	Self Titled (1st Lp)	CD	Edsel	EDCD-676	England	2000	11.99
Seatrain	Self Titled (2nd Lp)/Marblehead M	CD	BGO	BGOCD465	England	1999	10.99
Seatrain	Watch	CD	Line	LECD-9.00898-0	Germany	1990	12.99
Seatrain	Watch	CD	Wounded Bird	WOU-2692	U.S.A.	2003	8.99
Sebastian, John	Best Of John Sebastian	CD	Rhino	R2-70170	U.S.A.	1989	10.99
Sebastian, John	Faithful Virtue: The Reprise Recordings	3CD	Rhino	RHM2-7758	U.S.A.	2001	54.99
Sebastian, John	John B. Sebastian	CD	Line	LECD-9.00895-0	Germany	1990	34.99
Sebastian, John	King Biscuit Flower Hour	CD	King Biscuit	70710-88019-2	U.S.A.	1996	9.99
Sebastian, John	One Guy, One Guitar..(Tar Beach Live)	CD	HUX	HUX024	England	2001	12.99
Sebastian, John	Tar Beach	CD	Shanachie	8006	U.S.A.	1992	17.99
Sebastian, John	The Four Of Us	CD	Warner Bros.	WPCP-4387	Japan	1971	19.99
Sebastian, John	Welcome Back	CD	Warner Bros.	WPCP-4389	Japan	1976	19.99
Sebastian, John/J Band	Chasin' Gus' Ghost	CD	Hollywood	HR-62227-2	U.S.A.	1999	16.99
Sebastian, John/J-Band	I Want My Roots	CD	Music Masters	01612-65137-2	U.S.A.	1996	7.99
Seeds	A Web Of Sound	CD	Line	IMCD-9.00170-0	Germany	1988	18.99
Seeds	Evil Hoodoo	CD	Bam-Caruso	KIRI-082-CD	England	1988	34.99
Seeds	Future	CD	Line	IMCD-9.00173-0	Germany	1988	28.99
Seeds	Pushin' Too Hard/First	CD	Line	IMCD-9.00167-0	Germany	1988	47.99
Seeger, Pete	Bitter And The Sweet (MFSL Silver Cd)	CD	Mobile Fidelity	MFCD-873	U.S.A.	1962	34.99
Seeger, Pete	We Shall Overcome (All/Carnegie Hall)	2CD	Columbia	C2K-45312	U.S.A.	1989	24.99
Seger, Bob	Beautiful Loser	CD	Capitol	72438-19820-2-0	U.S.A.	1975	8.99
Seger, Bob	Greatest Hits	CD	Capitol	7243-8-30334-2-3	U.S.A.	1994	7.99
Seger, Bob	Seven	CD	Capitol	0777-7-81241-2-2	U.S.A.	1974	69.99
Seger, Bob	Smokin' O.P.'s	CD	Capitol	0777-7-99077-2-4	U.S.A.	1972	109.99
Seger, Bob/Silver Bullet Band	Against The Wind	CD	Capitol	7243-5-84316-2	U.S.A.	2003	8.99
Seger, Bob/Silver Bullet Band	Greatest Hits, Vol. 2	CD	Capitol	7243-85277-2-0	U.S.A.	2003	8.99
Seger, Bob/Silver Bullet Band	Hands In The Air (Promo)	CD Single	Capitol	DPRO-11178	U.S.A.	1995	5.99
Seger, Bob/Silver Bullet Band	It's A Mystery	CD	Capitol	0777-7-99774-2-0	U.S.A.	1995	7.99
Seger, Bob/Silver Bullet Band	Like A Rock	CD	Capitol	7-46195-2	U.S.A.	1986	7.99
Seger, Bob/Silver Bullet Band	Night Moves (DCC Gold Cd)	CD	DCC	GZS-1028	U.S.A.	1992	38.99
Seger, Bob/Silver Bullet Band	Nine Tonight	CD	Capitol	7-46086-2	U.S.A.	1981	8.99
Seger, Bob/Silver Bullet Band	The Distance	CD	Capitol	7-46005-2	U.S.A.	1982	7.99
Seger, Bob/Silver Bullet Band	The Fire Inside	CD	Capitol	7-91134-2	U.S.A.	1991	8.99
Seger, Bob/Silver Bullet Band	Turn The Page (Back '72 Version) (DJ)	CD Single	Capitol	DPRO-79562	U.S.A.	1995	24.99
Seger, Bob/System	Mongrel	CD	Capitol	0777-7-81240-2-3	U.S.A.	1970	69.99
Seger, Bob/System	Ramblin' Gamblin' Man	CD	Capitol	0777-7-96261-2-0	U.S.A.	1968	74.99
Selecter, The	Selected Selecter Selections	CD	Chrysalis	F2-21723	U.S.A.	1989	8.99
Sembello, Michael	Caravan Of Dreams	CD	Polydor	POCP-1252	Japan	1992	37.99
Senate	Sock It To Me One More Time	CD	Line	RTCD-9.01146-0	Germany	1992	4.99
Senise, Mauro	Mauro Senise	CD	Line	BSCD-9.00739-0	Germany	1990	13.99
Setzer, Brian	'68 Comback Special: Ignition	CD	Surfdog	SD-67124-2	U.S.A.	2001	8.99
Setzer, Brian	Live Nude Guitars	CD	EMI	546963	U.S.A.	1988	20.99
Setzer, Brian	Nitro Burnin' Funny Daddy	CD Single	Toy Factory	PRTF-903	Japan	2003	74.99
Setzer, Brian	Rockin' By Myself (Live)	CD	Toshiba-EMI	TOCP-7985	Japan	1993	47.99

S

Artist	Title	Format	Label	Catalog No	Country	Released	Value
Setzer, Brian	The Brian Setzer Collection '81-'88	CD	EMI	7243522538-2-1	U.S.A.	1999	8.99
Setzer, Brian	The Knife Feels Like Justice	CD	Razor & Tie	7930182190-2	U.S.A.	1999	8.99
Setzer, Brian/Orchestra	Guitar Slinger	CD	Interscope	INTD-90051	U.S.A.	1996	8.99
Setzer, Brian/Orchestra	Jump Jive An' Wail (Promo)	CD Single	Interscope	INT5P-6395	U.S.A.	1998	6.99
Setzer, Brian/Orchestra	The Dirty Boogie	CD	Interscope	INTD-90183	U.S.A.	1998	6.99
Setzer, Brian/Orchestra	VaVoom	CD	Interscope	0694907332	U.S.A.	2000	6.99
Sevag, Oystein	Close Your Eyes And See	CD	Windham Hill	01934-11126-2	U.S.A.	1993	9.99
Sevelle, Taja/Prince	Self Titled	CD	Paisley Park	25546-2	U.S.A.	1987	29.99
Seventh Wave	Psi-Fi	CD	Line	LICD-9.00408-0	Germany	1987	24.99
Seventh Wave	Things To Come	CD	Line	LICD-9.00401-0	Germany	1987	19.99
Sex Pistols	Anarchy In The U.K	CD Single	Virgin	7243-8-900412-0	England	1992	6.99
Sex Pistols	Chaos	CD	Restless	7-72922-2	Canada	1996	10.99
Sex Pistols	Filthy Lucre Live	CD	Virgin	7243-8-41926-2-4	U.S.A.	1996	7.99
Sex Pistols	God Save The Queen	CD Single	Virgin	7243-546483-2-8	England	2002	4.99
Sex Pistols	Jubilee + 3 Video	CD	Virgin	7243-8-12566-0-2	England	2002	9.99
Sex Pistols	Never Mind The Bollocks	CD	Toshiba-EMI	VJCP-23171	Japan	1993	29.99
Sex Pistols	Never Mind The Bollocks (W/Spunk)	2CD	Virgin	7243-8-41938-2-9	England	1996	14.99
Sex Pistols	Sex Pistols Self Titled Box Set	3CD	Virgin	7243-812567-2-5	England	2002	69.99
Sex Pistols	The Great Rock 'n' Roll Swindle	CD	Warner Bros.	9-45083-2	U.S.A.	1979	8.99
Sex Pistols/Steve Jones	Fire And Gasoline	CD	MCA	MCAD-6298	U.S.A.	1989	9.99
Sex Pistols/Steve Jones	Mercy	CD	MCA	MCAD-42006	U.S.A.	1987	7.99
Sha Na Na	34th And Vine	CD	Gold Castle	D2-71355	U.S.A.	1990	7.99
Sha Na Na	At The Hop (Audio/Video)	2CD	Master Tone	MM5121	England	1995	10.99
Sha Na Na	Best Of	CD	Ktel	80508-7-3061-2-6	U.S.A.	2003	8.99
Sha Na Na	From The Streets Of New York	CD	Buddah	BDK-2075	Germany	1994	12.99
Sha Na Na	Grease For Peace: The Best Of	CD	Buddah	74465-99842-2-8	U.S.A.	2000	8.99
Sha Na Na	Greatest Hits	CD	Madacy	056775416225	U.S.A.	1997	6.99
Sha Na Na	Greatest Hits	CD	Madacy	056775577223	U.S.A.	1992	7.99
Sha Na Na	Havin' An Oldies Party With	CD	Ktel	02277-5-0858-2-2	U.S.A.	1991	12.99
Sha Na Na	Heartbreak Hotel	CD	Richmond	MONDE-2354CD	England	1998	12.99
Sha Na Na	Hot Sox	CD	Buddah	BDKI-2600	Canada	2002	12.99
Sha Na Na	Hot Sox	CD	Buddah	BDK-2600	Germany	1994	12.99
Sha Na Na	Is Here To Stay	CD	Buddah	BDK-5692	Germany	1994	8.99
Sha Na Na	Is Here To Stay	CD	Buddah	BDKI-5692	Canada	2002	8.99
Sha Na Na	Live In Japan With Conny	CD	Nippon Columbia	COCC-14252	Japan	2000	49.99
Sha Na Na	Now	CD	Buddah	BDK-2605	Germany	1994	8.99
Sha Na Na	Now	CD	Buddah	BDKI-2605	Canada	2002	12.99
Sha Na Na	Rock 'N' Roll Dance Party	CD	Gold (Soh)	2101	U.S.A.	2003	12.99
Sha Na Na	Rock 'N' Roll/Here To Stay (Pair LP)	CD	RCA	SCD-4910	U.S.A.	1993	12.99
Sha Na Na	Rockin' Christmas	CD	Gold (Soh)	2105	U.S.A.	2002	12.99
Sha Na Na	Self Titled (1971 Lp)	CD	Buddah	BDKI-2304	Canada	2002	12.99
Sha Na Na	Self Titled (1971 Lp)	CD	Buddah	BDK-2034	Germany	1994	12.99
Sha Na Na	Sixteen Candles	CD	Richmond	MONDE-2347CD	England	1988	12.99
Sha Na Na	The Best Of	CD	Buddah	BDK-5703	Germany	1994	7.99
Sha Na Na	The Best Of	CD	Buddah	BDKI-5703	Canada	2002	8.99
Sha Na Na	The Best Of	CD	Buddah	74465-99842-2-8	England	2002	8.99
Sha Na Na	The Best Of (Pair LP)	CD	RCA	088826120126	U.S.A.	1990	12.99
Sha Na Na	The Night Is Still Young	CD	Buddah	BDK-2050	Germany	1994	12.99
Sha Na Na/Bobby Pickett	Cool Ghoul's Halloween Party Mix	CD	Ktel	02277-5-4045-2-4	U.S.A.	1998	7.99
Sha Na Na/Bobby Pickett	Halloween Oldies Party	CD	Madacy	056775035822	U.S.A.	1997	7.99
Sha Na Na/Henry Gross	I Keep On Rockin'	CD	Sonet	SNTCD-990	Sweden	1987	21.99
Sha Na Na/Henry Gross	I'm Hearing Things	CD	Zelda	ZR-1375	U.S.A.	2001	12.99
Sha Na Na/Henry Gross	Nothing But Dreams	CD	Zelda	ZR-1374	U.S.A.	1996	12.99
Sha Na Na/Henry Gross	One More Tomorrow: The Best Of	CD	Varese	VCD-5737	U.S.A.	1996	8.99
Sha Na Na/Henry Gross	Plug Me Into Something	CD	Pony Canyon	PCCY-10074	Japan	1975	119.99
Sha Na Na/Henry Gross	Release/Show Me To The Stage	CD	Chiswick	CDWIK104	England	1992	15.99
Sha Na Na/Henry Gross	She's My Baby	CD	Sonet	SNTCD-1008	Sweden	1989	21.99
Sha Na Na/Henry Gross	Yellow Lp/Plug Me Into Something	CD	Zelda	ZR-1376	U.S.A.	2002	12.99

S

Artist	Title	Format	Label	Catalog No	Country	Released	Value
Shack	Zilch (Arthur Lee/Love Backup Band)	CD	Ghetto	1L	England	1988	169.99
Shadows, The	20 Golden Greats	CD	EMI	7-46243-2	Holland	2000	11.99
Shadows, The	50 Golden Greats	2CD	EMI	7243-5-27586-2-3	England	2000	13.99
Shadows, The	A's B's & EP's	CD	EMI	7243-5-83110-2-0	England	2003	10.99
Shadows, The	At Abbey Road (23 Tracks)	CD	EMI	7243-8-23042-2-7	Holland	1998	11.99
Shadows, The	Best	CD	Music For Pleasure	6385	England	1998	14.99
Shadows, The	Best Of The	CD	Disky	DC-886862	Germany	1998	7.99
Shadows, The	Collection	2CD	EMI	7243-4-97411-2-6	Australia	1999	24.99
Shadows, The	Dance With The + 14 (Mono/Stereo)	CD	EMI	7243-4-99418-2-3	England	1999	10.99
Shadows, The	Dream Time	CD	Karussell	550-094-2	Germany	2000	7.99
Shadows, The	Favourite TV, Film & Show Tunes	CD	EMI	7243-5-20012-2-4	Australia	2000	14.99
Shadows, The	First 20 Years At The Top	3CD	EMI	7243-8-32167-2-7	England	2000	32.99
Shadows, The	From Hank, Bruce, Brian And John	CD	EMI	7243-4-99767-2-6	Holland	1999	11.99
Shadows, The	Golden Greats + 3	2CD	Toshiba-EMI	TOCP-65649~50	Japan	2000	42.99
Shadows, The	Good Vibrations Box Set	3CD	Disky	HR-853282	Germany	2000	14.99
Shadows, The	Guardian Angel + 8	CD	See For Miles	SEE-CD-679	England	1998	21.99
Shadows, The	Images	CD	Knight	KNCD-16014	England	1990	24.99
Shadows, The	In The Seventies	CD	EMI	7243-5-21729-2-4	England	1999	10.99
Shadows, The	Into The Light	4CD	EMI	7243-8-54749-2-7	England	1997	39.99
Shadows, The	Jigsaw + 14 (Mono/Stereo)	CD	EMI	7243-4-99770-2-0	England	1999	10.99
Shadows, The	Live Abbey Road/Liverpool Empire	CD	See For Miles	SEE-CD-732	England	2001	21.99
Shadows, The	Live At The Paris Olympia	2CD	Magic	3930235	France	2002	31.99
Shadows, The	Master Series	CD	Polydor	559-126-2	Holland	2000	12.99
Shadows, The	Moonlight Shadows	CD	Karussell	552-416-2	Germany	2000	7.99
Shadows, The	Out Of The Shadows + 13	CD	EMI	7243-4-99415-2-6	England	1999	10.99
Shadows, The	Rockin' With Curly Leads	CD	EMI	7243-5-20221-2-0	England	1999	10.99
Shadows, The	Self Titled (Columbia)	CD	EMI	7243-5-28239-2-5	England	2002	10.99
Shadows, The	Self Titled + 14 (Mono/Stereo)	CD	EMI	7243-4-98937-2-6	England	1999	10.99
Shadows, The	Shades Of Rock	CD	EMI	7243-5-20133-2-6	England	1999	10.99
Shadows, The	Shadow Music + 14	CD	Magic	7243-5-20109-2-9	France	1999	24.99
Shadows, The	Shadow Music/Shades Of Rock	CD	EMI	7-97933 2	England	1992	16.99
Shadows, The	Shadows Are Go !	CD	Scamp	SCP-9711-2	U.S.A.	1997	12.99
Shadows, The	Shadstrax	CD	See For Miles	SEE-CD-494	England	1998	20.99
Shadows, The	Simply Shadows	CD	Karussell	554-874-2	Germany	2001	7.99
Shadows, The	Single Collection	2CD	EMI	7243-8-33291-2-0	Holland	1997	24.99
Shadows, The	Sound Of The + 10 (Mono/Stereo)	CD	Magic	7243-4-99269-2-9	France	2000	24.99
Shadows, The	The Best Of	CD	Toshiba-EMI	TOCP-6381	Japan	1990	24.99
Shadows, The	The Best Of The	CD	Magic	3930082	France	2001	24.99
Shadows, The	The Best Of The	CD	Disky	DC-878662	Holland	1997	7.99
Shadows, The	The Complete Box Set	5CD	EMI	7243-496561-2-3	Australia	1999	54.99
Shadows, The	The E.P. Collection, Vol. 1	CD	See For Miles	SEE-CD-246	England	1996	27.99
Shadows, The	The E.P. Collection, Vol. 2	CD	See For Miles	SEE-CD-296	England	2000	27.99
Shadows, The	The E.P. Collection, Vol. 3	CD	See For Miles	SEE-CD-375	England	1993	27.99
Shadows, The	The Early Years: 1959-1966	6CD	EMI	0777-7-97171-2-5	England	1993	56.99
Shadows, The	The Final 60's	2CD	Magic	3930172	France	2002	31.99
Shadows, The	The Original Shadows	CD	Disky	TO-860132	Holland	1995	7.99
Shadows, The	The Shadows (Vocals)	CD	See For Miles	SEE-CD-475	England	1997	21.99
Shadows, The	The Shadows/Out Of The Shadows	CD	EMI	7-95732-2	England	2000	10.99
Shadows, The	The Story Of (W/Bonus Cd Rom)	2CD	EMI	724357610506	Holland	2000	19.99
Shadows, The	The Very Best Of	CD	EMI	7243-8-57467-2-7	England	2000	11.99
Shadows, The	With Strings Attached	CD	EMI	7243-5-26092-2-2	England	2000	10.99
Shadows, The/Alan Jones	A Shadow In Time	CD	VIP	VIPCD001	England	1996	12.99
Shadows, The/Brian Bennett	Collage	CD	C-Five	C5CD610	England	1995	10.99
Shadows, The/Brian Bennett	One Step Ahead	CD	C-Five	C5CD609	England	1995	10.99
Shadows, The/Brian Bennett	Ruth Rendell Mysteries, Vol. 2	CD	Polydor	847-524-2	England	1990	24.99
Shadows, The/Hank Marvin	All Alone With Friends	CD	Pickwick	PWKS-4070	England	1991	24.99
Shadows, The/Hank Marvin	Another Side Of	CD	Spectrum	554-515-2	England	1998	10.99
Shadows, The/Hank Marvin	At The Movies	CD	Universal	157057-2	England	2000	10.99

Artist	Title	Format	Label	Catalog No	Country	Released	Value
Shadows, The/Hank Marvin	Guitar Ballads	2CD	Metro	METRCD258	England	2004	14.99
Shadows, The/Hank Marvin	Guitar Legends	CD	EMI	7243-5-76433-2-0	Holland	2001	9.99
Shadows, The/Hank Marvin	Guitar Player	CD	EMI	7243-5-437019-2	Denmark	2002	10.99
Shadows, The/Hank Marvin	Guitar Syndicate	CD	See For Miles	SEE-CD-289	England	1990	28.99
Shadows, The/Hank Marvin	Handpicked	CD	Polydor	527-387-2	England	1995	10.99
Shadows, The/Hank Marvin	Hank Plays Cliff	CD	Metro	METRCD117	England	2003	10.99
Shadows, The/Hank Marvin	Hank Plays Holly	CD	Polydor	533-713-2	England	1996	10.99
Shadows, The/Hank Marvin	Hank Plays Live	CD	Polydor	537-428-2	England	1997	10.99
Shadows, The/Hank Marvin	Heartbeat	CD	Polydor	554-227-2	England	1997	10.99
Shadows, The/Hank Marvin	Into The Light	CD	Spectrum	517-148-2	England	1997	12.99
Shadows, The/Hank Marvin	Play Andrew Lloyd Webber/Tim Rice	CD	Polygram	539-479-2	England	1997	10.99
Shadows, The/Hank Marvin	Self Titled + 10	CD	EMI	7243-4-98208-2-1	England	1998	10.99
Shadows, The/Hank Marvin	Singles Collection	CD	Music Club	MCCD-452	England	2001	12.99
Shadows, The/Hank Marvin	Would You Belive It... Plus (20 Tracks)	CD	See For Miles	SEE-CD-210	England	1994	28.99
Shadows, The/Jet Harris	& Tony Meehan - The Best Of	CD	Spectrum	544-268-2	England	2000	9.99
Shadows, The/Jet Harris	Diamonds & Other Gems	CD	Deram	820-634-2	England	1988	12.99
Shadows, The/Jet Harris	Diamonds Are Trumps	CD	Solent	SLTD-116	England	2002	12.99
Shadows, The/Jet Harris	Inside Live HM Prison, Gloucester, '97	CD	Roller Coaster	RCCD-3010	England	2003	14.99
Shadows, The/Jet Harris	Tangent - Together (Studio Sessions)	CD	Zing	TAN-CD-003	England	1996	22.99
Shadows, The/Jet Harris	The Anniversary Album	CD	Q	CDMM-1038	England	1988	24.99
Shadows, The/Jet Harris	The Phoenix Rises	CD	Mustang	JET-001	England	2000	10.99
Shadows, The/Jet Harris	Two Of A Kind (W/Alan Jones)	CD	Zing	ZRCD-1213	England	1997	22.99
Shadows, The/John Farrar	Self Titled	CD	See For Miles	SEE-CD-484	England	1997	8.99
Shadows, The/Local Heroes	One Of Our Shadows Is Missing	CD	See For Miles	SEE-CD-500	England	1998	24.99
Shadows, The/Marvin/Welch	& Farrar - A Thousand Conversations	CD	Music For Pleasure	7243-8-59735-2-9	England	1997	10.99
Shadows, The/Marvin/Welch	& Farrar - Second Opinion Plus + 1	CD	See For Miles	SEE-CD-325	England	1991	29.99
Shadows, The/Marvin/Welch	& Farrar - Step From The Shadows	CD	See For Miles	SEE-CD-78	England	1998	29.99
Shadows, The/Marvin/Welch	Marvin, Welch & Farrar	CD	EMI	7243-5-76097-2-2	Netherlands	2000	10.99
Shadows, The/Marvin/Welch	Marvin, Welch & Farrar Plus + 3	CD	See For Miles	SEE-CD-324	England	1991	29.99
Shadows, The/Tribute	Twang !	CD	Pangaea	7243-8-33928-2	England	1996	11.99
Shankar, Ravi	Chants of India	CD	Angel	7243-8-55948-2-3	U.S.A.	1997	7.99
Shankar, Ravi/Ali A Khan	In Concert 1972	2CD	EMI	7243-8-53817-2-0	England	1996	119.99
Shannon, Del	1961-1990: A Complete Career Anth.	2CD	Raven	RVCD-51	Australia	1998	23.99
Shannon, Del	25 All-Time Greatest Hits	CD	Varese	302-066-270-2	U.S.A.	2001	8.99
Shannon, Del	Absolutely The Best	CD	Varese	302-061-099-2	U.S.A.	2001	8.99
Shannon, Del	Classic Masters	CD	Capitol	7243-5-43472-2	U.S.A.	2003	8.99
Shannon, Del	Drop Down And Get Me	CD	Line	INCD-9.00108-0	Germany	1990	10.99
Shannon, Del	Drop Down And Get Me + 2	CD	Varese	VCD-5927	U.S.A.	1998	8.99
Shannon, Del	EP Collection 1961-1965	CD	See For Miles	SEE-CD-677	England	1998	20.99
Shannon, Del	Further Adventures/Charles Westover	CD	BGO	BGOCD402	England	1998	18.99
Shannon, Del	Greatest Hits	CD	Line	BLCD-9.01031-L	Germany	1991	8.99
Shannon, Del	Hats Off To Larry	CD	Line	BLCD-9.00252-L	Germany	1989	10.99
Shannon, Del	I Go To Pieces	CD	Edsel	EDCD-174	England	1994	19.99
Shannon, Del	Little Town Flirt	CD	Line	BLCD-9.00333-L	Germany	1989	10.99
Shannon, Del	Little Town Flirt/Handy Man	CD	BGO	BGOCD388	England	1998	18.99
Shannon, Del	Live In England/And The Music....	CD	BGO	BGOCD280	England	1996	18.99
Shannon, Del	Rock On (W/Traveling Willburys)	CD	MCA	MCAD-10296	U.S.A.	1991	8.99
Shannon, Del	Runaway With/Hats Off To Del.. + 3	CD	BGO	BGOCD367	England	2002	18.99
Shannon, Del	Sings Hank Williams	CD	Line	BLCD-9.00760-L	Germany	1990	10.99
Shannon, Del	Sings Hank Williams/1661 Seconds	CD	BGO	BGOCD404	England	1998	18.99
Shannon, Del	The Best Of	CD	Repertoire	REP-4828-WG	Germany	2002	10.99
Shannon, Del	The Definitive Collection	2CD	Recall	SMD-CD-197	England	2000	12.99
Shannon, Del	The Del Shannon Collection	CD	Line	IMCD-9.00436-0	Germany	1988	8.99
Shannon, Del	The Story (W/Bonus Cd Rom)	2CD	EMI	7243-5-760170-2	England	2000	19.99
Shannon, Del	This Is My Bag/Total Commitment	CD	BGO	BGOCD307	England	1996	18.99
Sharks	Colour My Flesh (Not Phil Manzanera)	CD	Anagram	CD-GRAM-100	England	1996	8.99
Sharma, Pandit Shiv Kumar	Sampradaya	CD	Real World	72438-95617-2-2	U.S.A.	1999	12.99
Shatner, William/Star Trek	The Transformed Man	CD	Rev-Ola	CREV004CD	England	1992	20.99

S

Artist	Title	Format	Label	Catalog No	Country	Released	Value
Shaw, Sandie	Reviewing The Situation	CD	Line	OLCD-9.51160-X	Germany	1991	24.99
Sheep On Drugs	Double Trouble	CD	Caroline	INV057CD	U.S.A.	1996	6.99
Sheep On Drugs	From A To H And Back Again	CD	Island	162-448-007-2	U.S.A.	1994	7.99
Sheep On Drugs	Greatest Hits	CD	Island	162-888-006-2	U.S.A.	1993	6.99
Sheep On Drugs	Never Mind The Methadone	CD	Caroline	INV067CD	U.S.A.	1997	9.99
Sheep On Drugs	One For The Money	CD	Caroline	INV-061-CD	U.S.A.	1997	9.99
Sheep On Drugs	Two For The Show	CD	Caroline	INV123	U.S.A.	1998	9.99
Sheep On Drugs	Works Box Set	5CD	Underground	1075	U.S.A.	2002	34.99
Sheila-E	In Romance 1600	CD	Paisley Park	9-25317-2	Germany	1985	9.99
Sheila-E	Self Titled	CD	Paisley Park	25498-2	U.S.A.	1987	39.99
Sheila-E	Sex Cymbal	CD	Warner Bros.	26255-2	U.S.A.	1991	7.99
Sheila-E	Sex Cymbal (Promo/Can)	CD	Warner Bros.	26255-2-DJ	U.S.A.	1989	39.99
Sheila-E	The Glamorous Life	CD	Warner Bros.	25107-2	U.S.A.	1987	8.99
Sheila-E/The E.Train	Heaven	CD	Concord	4983	U.S.A.	2001	9.99
Sheila-E/The E.Train	The Writes Of Passage	CD	Concord	4934	U.S.A.	2000	9.99
Shelley, Pete	Heaven And The Sea	CD	Line	INCD-9.00234-0	Germany	1987	12.99
Shelley, Pete	Homosapein + 5	CD	Razor & Tie	RE-2126-2	U.S.A.	1995	18.99
Shelley, Pete	Homosapien + 6	CD	Grapevine	GRACD-201	England	1981	19.99
Shelley, Pete	The Best Of	CD	Toshiba-EMI	TOCP-64147	Japan	2003	24.99
Shelley, Pete	XL1 + 2	CD	Grapevine	GRACD-202	England	1983	19.99
ShelleyDevoto	Buzzkunst (P Shelley/H Devoto)	CD	Cooking Vinyl	COOK-CD-230	England	2002	9.99
Shepard, Vonda	A Very Ally Christmas	CD	Epic	BK-85196	U.S.A.	2000	8.99
Shepard, Vonda	Baby, Don't You Break.. (DJ)	CD Single	Jacket	JAC-PRO-3	U.S.A.	1999	6.99
Shepard, Vonda	By 7:30	CD	Jacket	JAC-222-2	U.S.A.	1999	6.99
Shepard, Vonda	Chinatown	CD	Navarre	JAC-3333	U.S.A.	2002	7.99
Shepard, Vonda	For Once In My Life	CD	Epic	5012832000	U.S.A.	2001	7.99
Shepard, Vonda	Heart Soul - New Songs/Ally McBeal	CD	Epic	BK-63915	U.S.A.	1999	6.99
Shepard, Vonda	It's Good, Eve	CD	Vesper Valley	VRA-85003	U.S.A.	1996	6.99
Shepard, Vonda	Searchin' My Soul (Promo)	CD	Vesper Valley	163931-2	U.S.A.	1992	5.99
Shepard, Vonda	Songs From Ally McBeal	CD	550 Music	BK-69365	U.S.A.	1998	6.99
Shepard, Vonda	The Radical Light	CD	Reprise	VRA-85005	U.S.A.	1992	6.99
Shepard, Vonda	Vonda Shepard	CD	Vesper Valley	VRA-85004	U.S.A.	1989	6.99
Shepherd, Kenny Wayne	Blue On Black	CD Single	Revolution	PRO-CD-8987	U.S.A.	1997	5.99
Shepherd, Kenny Wayne	Deja Voodoo (Promo)	CD Single	Giant	PRO-CD-7767	U.S.A.	1995	5.99
Shepherd, Kenny Wayne	Ledbetter Heights	CD	Giant	9-24621-2	U.S.A.	1995	6.99
Shepherd, Kenny Wayne	Live On	CD	Giant	9-24729-2	U.S.A.	1999	8.99
Shepherd, Kenny Wayne	The Spider And The Fly (Promo)	CD Single	Revolution	PRO-CD-8577-R	U.S.A.	1996	5.99
Shepherd, Kenny Wayne	Trouble Is...	CD	Giant	9-24689-2	U.S.A.	1997	8.99
Shepherd, Kenny Wayne	Was	CD Single	Giant	PRO-CD-100023	U.S.A.	2000	5.99
Sherman, Allan	The Best Of Allan Sherman	CD	Rhino	R2-75771	U.S.A.	1988	9.99
Sherman, Allan/Dr Demento	Spooky Tunes (My Son, The Vampire)	CD	Rhino	R2-71777	U.S.A.	1994	9.99
Sherman, Allan/Various Artists	That Was That Was The Week...	CD	Radiola	CDMR-1123	U.S.A.	1981	19.99
Sherman, Bobby	Bobby Sherman	CD	Ktel	3427-2	U.S.A.	1995	8.99
Sherman, Bobby	Getting Together	CD	Ktel	3431-2	U.S.A.	1995	8.99
Sherman, Bobby	Greatest Hits	CD	Ktel	3432-2	U.S.A.	1995	8.99
Sherman, Bobby	Here Comes Bobby	CD	Ktel	3428-2	Canada	1995	8.99
Sherman, Bobby	Here Comes Bobby/With Love, Bobby	CD	Collectables	COL-6858	U.S.A.	2001	9.99
Sherman, Bobby	My Christmas Wish	CD	KRB	KRB8063-2	U.S.A.	1998	9.99
Sherman, Bobby	Portrait Of Bobby	CD	Ktel	3430-2	U.S.A.	1995	8.99
Sherman, Bobby	Self Titled/Portrait Of	CD	Collectables	COL-6859	U.S.A.	2001	9.99
Sherman, Bobby	The Very Best Of	CD	Varese	302-066-131-2	U.S.A.	2000	8.99
Sherman, Bobby	With Love, Bobby	CD	Ktel	3429-2	U.S.A.	1995	8.99
Sherman, Theo	Champagne In The Starlight	CD	Line	RTCD-9.01151-0	Germany	1992	24.99
Sherman/Sherman	Chitty Chitty Bang Bang	CD	Rykodisc	RCD-10702	U.S.A.	1997	13.99
Sherman/Sherman	Chitty Chitty Bang Bang (Orig UK Cast)	CD	Mr Bang Bang	MRBB001	England	2002	11.99
Shire, David	Return To Oz (O.S.T.)	CD	Bay Cities	BCD-3001	U.S.A.	1985	45.99
Shire, David	The Taking Of Pelham One Two Three	CD	Retrograde	FSM-80123-2	England	1974	24.99
Shock	Pinultimate	CD	Bareknuckle	AVCB-66031	Japan	1998	29.99

S

Artist	Title	Format	Label	Catalog No	Country	Released	Value
Shocking Blue	20 Greatest Hits	CD	Repertoire	REP-4125-WZ	Germany	2002	12.99
Shocking Blue	At Home (W/Venus)	CD	Repertoire	REP-4041-WZ	Germany	2002	12.99
Shocking Blue	Dream On Dreamer/Good Times	CD	Repertoire	REP-4619-WZ	Germany	2002	12.99
Shocking Blue	In Pot/Attila	CD	Repertoire	REP-4610-WZ	Germany	2002	12.99
Shocking Blue	Scorpio's Dance	CD	Repertoire	REP-4086-WZ	Germany	2002	12.99
Shocking Blue	Singles A's & B's	2CD	Repertoire	REP-4639	Germany	2002	19.99
Shocking Blue	Third Album + 6	CD	Repertoire	REP-4317-WY	Germany	2002	12.99
Shoes	As Is (Limited Editon/Only 1311)	2CD	Black Vinyl	BV10596-2	U.S.A.	1996	69.99
Shoes	Best	CD	Black Vinyl	BV-9787	U.S.A.	1987	14.99
Shoes	Black Vinyl Shoes	CD	Black Vinyl	BV-10092-2	U.S.A.	1992	14.99
Shoes	Boomerang + 6 (Shoes On Ice)	CD	Black Vinyl	BV18190-2	U.S.A.	1990	14.99
Shoes	Fret Buzz	CD	Black Vinyl	BV-10495-2	U.S.A.	1995	14.99
Shoes	Present Tense/Tongue Twister	CD	Black Vinyl	BV-19888	U.S.A.	1988	14.99
Shoes	Propeller	CD	Black Vinyl	BV-10294-	U.S.A.	1994	14.99
Shoes	Silhouette	CD	Line	INCD-9.00110-0	Germany	1988	11.99
Shoes	Silhouette + 3	CD	Black Vinyl	BV15191-2	U.S.A.	1991	14.99
Shoes	Singles	CD	BR Music	BX-537-2	Holland	2000	11.99
Shoes	Stolen Wishes	CD	Black Vinyl	BV10189-2	U.S.A.	1989	14.99
Shoes	Tore A Hole	CD Single	Black Vinyl	BV10395-2	U.S.A.	1995	4.99
Shore, Howard	Lord Of The Rings - Fellowship/Ring	CD	Reprise	9-48110-2	U.S.A.	2001	9.99
Shore, Howard	Lord Rings Fellowship (Leatherbnd Ed.)	CD	Reprise	2-48328 (#2)	U.S.A.	2001	39.99
Shortlist	Funny Cider Sessions - 1981/1983	CD	Line	LICD—9.01357-0	Germany	1999	24.99
Shortlist	The Riffburglar Album	CD	Line	LICD-9.00064-0	Germany	1988	24.99
Shortlist	The Riffburglar Album/Swag	2CD	Line	LICD-9.21158-S	Germany	1992	29.99
Shostakovich/Prokofiev	Shostakovich/Prokofiev	CD	Line	CACD-9.00803-P	Germany	1990	12.99
Shout	Self Titled + 1	CD	Bareknuckle	AVCB-66017	Japan	1997	37.99
Shoveljerk	Swarm	CD	Capricorn	9-42051-2	U.S.A.	1996	4.99
Show-Ya	Backfire - Complete Best	CD	Toshiba-EMI	TOCT-6645	Japan	1992	24.99
Show-Ya	Hard Way (W/Photo Book)	CD	Toshiba-EMI	TOCT-5855	Japan	1990	39.99
Show-Ya	Hard Way Tour 1991	CD	Toshiba-EMI	TOCT-8411	Japan	1991	24.99
Show-Ya	Immigration	CD	Toshiba-EMI	TOCT-8405	Japan	1987	24.99
Show-Ya	Masquerade Show	CD	Toshiba-EMI	TOCT-8401	Japan	1985	24.99
Show-Ya	Outerlimits	CD	Toshiba-EMI	TOCT-8409	Japan	1989	24.99
Show-Ya	Queendom	CD	Toshiba-EMI	TOCT-8402	Japan	1986	24.99
Show-Ya	Touch The Sun	CD	Creedence	CCR-95515	Japan	1994	24.99
Show-Ya	Trade Last	CD	Toshiba-EMI	TOCT-8404	Japan	1987	24.99
Show-Ya	Turn Over	CD	Toshiba-EMI	TOCT-8406	Japan	1988	24.99
Show-Ya	Ways	CD	Toshiba-EMI	TOCT-8403	Japan	1986	24.99
Show-Ya	White	CD	Toshiba-EMI	TOCT-8408	Japan	1998	24.99
Shy	Brave The Storm + 6	CD	BMG	BVCP-7452	Japan	1996	37.99
Shy	Excess All Areas + 3	CD	BMG	BVCP-7453	Japan	1996	37.99
Shy	Welcome To The Madhouse	CD	Vertigo	PHCR-1267	Japan	1994	29.99
Siam	Prayer + 1	CD	Zero	XRCN-1253	Japan	1995	39.99
Sicroff, Elan	Journey to Inaccessible Places	CD	EG	EEGCD 45	England	1987	39.99
Siebel, Paul	Jack-Knife Gypsy	CD	Line	LECD-9.00951-0	Germany	1990	24.99
Siegel-Schwall Band	953 West	CD	Line	LICD-9.00282-0	Germany	1988	24.99
Siegel-Schwall Band	Live/The Last Summer	CD	Line	LICD-9.00284-0	Germany	1988	24.99
Siegel-Schwall Band	R.I.P. Siegel-Schwall	CD	Line	LICD-9.00289-0	Germany	1988	24.99
Siegel-Schwall Band	S.T./Sleepy Hollow	2CD	Line	LICD-9.21198-S	Germany	1992	34.99
Siegel-Schwall Band	Sleepy Hollow	CD	Line	LICD-9.00278-0	Germany	1988	24.99
Siegel-Schwall Band	The Siegel-Schwall Band	CD	Line	LICD-9.00274-0	Germany	1988	24.99
Sill, Judee	Heart Food	CD	East West	AMCY-6065	Japan	1999	24.99
Sill, Judee	Heart Food + 9 (Only 2500)	CD	Rhino	RHM2-7802	U.S.A.	2004	20.99
Sill, Judee	Judee Sill	CD	East West	AMCY-6064	Japan	1999	24.99
Sill, Judee	Self Titled + 10 (Only 2500)	CD	Rhino	RHM2-7836	U.S.A.	2004	20.99
Silver Metre	Silver Metre	CD	Akarma	AK-072	Italy	2002	13.99
Silverhead	Show Me Everything	CD	Captain Trip	CTCD-340	Japan	1974	15.99
Silverhead	Silverhead	CD	Line	LICD-9.00285-0	Germany	1987	16.99

S

Artist	Title	Format	Label	Catalog No	Country	Released	Value
Silverhead	Silverhead/16 And Savaged	2CD	Line	LICD-9.21174-S	Germany	1992	24.99
Silverhead	Sixteen And Savaged	CD	Line	LICD-9.00325-0	Germany	1987	16.99
Silvestri, Alan/Various Artists	Back To The Future III	CD	Soundtrack List.	SCLS-7001	Japan	1990	44.99
Simon And Garfunkel	Before The Fame (Rarities)	CD	Alchemy	PILOT-182	England	2003	11.99
Simon And Garfunkel	Bookends (MFSL Gold Cd)	CD	Mobile Fidelity	UDCD-732	U.S.A.	1968	26.99
Simon And Garfunkel	Bookends + 2	CD	Columbia	CK-66003	U.S.A.	2001	9.99
Simon And Garfunkel	Bridge Over Troubled Water (Gold Cd)	CD	Sony	SRCS-6768	Japan	1993	36.99
Simon And Garfunkel	Bridge Over Troubled Water + 2	CD	Columbia	CK-66004	U.S.A.	2001	9.99
Simon And Garfunkel	Bridge Troubled Water (Sony Gold Cd)	CD	Columbia	CK-64421	U.S.A.	1970	37.99
Simon And Garfunkel	Columbia Studio Recordings '64-70 Box	5CD	Columbia	C5K-63815	U.S.A.	2001	24.99
Simon And Garfunkel	Concert In Central Park/20 Grt. Hits	2CD	Warner Bros.	CDGEF007	Australia	1982	17.99
Simon And Garfunkel	Greatest Hits	CD	Columbia	CK-31350	U.S.A.	1972	5.99
Simon And Garfunkel	Live From New York City, 1967	CD	Columbia	CK-86754	U.S.A.	2002	8.99
Simon And Garfunkel	Old Friends Box Set	3CD	Columbia	C3K-64780	U.S.A.	1997	19.99
Simon And Garfunkel	Parsley, Sage, Rosemary & Thyme + 2	CD	Columbia	CK-66001	U.S.A.	2001	9.99
Simon And Garfunkel	Selections Old Friends Box Set (Promo)	CD	Columbia	CSK-2948-S1	U.S.A.	1997	14.99
Simon And Garfunkel	Sounds Of Silence + 3	CD	Columbia	CK-65998	U.S.A.	2001	9.99
Simon And Garfunkel	Tales From New York - Very Best Of	2CD	Columbia	496409-2	Australia	1999	19.99
Simon And Garfunkel	The Best Of Simon & Garfunkel	CD	Columbia	CK-66022	U.S.A.	1999	8.99
Simon And Garfunkel	The Best Of Simon & Garfunkel	CD	Sony	MHCP-153	Japan	2003	19.99
Simon And Garfunkel	The Concert In Central Park	CD	Warner Bros.	3654-2	U.S.A.	1982	8.99
Simon And Garfunkel	The Definitive Simon & Garfunkel	CD	Columbia	MOOD-CD21	England	1991	9.99
Simon And Garfunkel	The Essential	2CD	Columbia	C2K-90716	U.S.A.	2003	11.99
Simon And Garfunkel	The Essential + 7	2CD	Columbia	5134702000	Australia	2003	21.99
Simon And Garfunkel	Two Can Dream Alone (Tom/Jerry)	CD	Alchemy	PILOT-60	England	2000	13.99
Simon And Garfunkel	Wednesday Morning, 3 A.M. + 3	CD	Columbia	CK-65999	U.S.A.	2001	9.99
Simon, Carly	Another Passenger	CD	Elektra	2-1064	U.S.A.	1976	8.99
Simon, Carly	Anthology	2CD	Rhino	R2-78167	U.S.A.	2002	18.99
Simon, Carly	Anticipation	CD	Elektra	75016-2	U.S.A.	1971	8.99
Simon, Carly	Bells, Bears & Fishermen	CD	Bantam	35901	U.S.A.	1994	13.99
Simon, Carly	Boys In The Trees	CD	Elektra	2-128	U.S.A.	1978	7.99
Simon, Carly	Christmas Is Almost Here Again	CD	Warner Bros.	WPCR-11371	Japan	2002	24.99
Simon, Carly	Christmas Is Almost Here Again + 2	CD	Rhino	R2-73891	U.S.A.	2003	7.99
Simon, Carly	Clouds In My Coffee 1966-1996 Box	3CD	Arista	07822-18798-2	U.S.A.	1995	30.99
Simon, Carly	Come Upstairs	CD	Warner Bros.	7599-26355-2	U.S.A.	1996	8.99
Simon, Carly	Coming Around Again	CD	Arista	ARCD-8443	U.S.A.	1987	9.99
Simon, Carly	Film Noir	CD	Arista	07822-18984-2	U.S.A.	1997	6.99
Simon, Carly	Greatest Hits Live	CD	Arista	ARCD-8526	U.S.A.	1988	8.99
Simon, Carly	Have You Seen Me Lately ?	CD	Arista	ARCD-8650	U.S.A.	1990	7.99
Simon, Carly	Hello Big Man	CD	Warner Bros.	9-23886-2	U.S.A.	1983	28.99
Simon, Carly	Hotcakes	CD	Elektra	2-1002	U.S.A.	1974	8.99
Simon, Carly	Letters Never Sent	CD	Arista	07822-18752-2	U.S.A.	1992	6.99
Simon, Carly	My Romance	CD	Arista	ARCD-8582	U.S.A.	1990	7.99
Simon, Carly	Playing Possum	CD	Elektra	2-1033	U.S.A.	1975	8.99
Simon, Carly	Romulus Hunt: A Family Opera	CD	Angel	CDQ-54915	U.S.A.	1993	7.99
Simon, Carly	Self Titled	CD	Elektra	74082-2	U.S.A.	1971	8.99
Simon, Carly	Spoiled Girl	CD	Epic	EK-39970	U.S.A.	1985	6.99
Simon, Carly	Spy	CD	Warner Bros.	7559-60558-2	U.S.A.	1997	8.99
Simon, Carly	The Bedroom Tapes	CD	Arista	07822-14627-2	U.S.A.	2000	8.99
Simon, Carly	The Best Of	CD	Elektra	109-2	U.S.A.	1975	7.99
Simon, Carly	This Is My Life (O.S.T.)	CD	Qwest	26901-2	U.S.A.	1992	5.99
Simon, Carly	Torch	CD	Warner Bros.	7599-23592-2	U.S.A.	1987	8.99
Simon, Carly/Mick Jagger	No Secrets (W/Paul McCartney)	CD	Elektra	75049-2	U.S.A.	1972	9.99
Simon, Paul	1964-1993 Box Set	4CD	Warner Bros.	9-45394-2	U.S.A.	1993	24.99
Simon, Paul	Anthology	2CD	Warner Bros.	9362454082	Australia	1993	20.99
Simon, Paul	Collection - On My Way	2CD	Rhino	R2-73774	U.S.A.	2002	15.99
Simon, Paul	Concert In The Park	2CD	Warner Bros.	9-26737-2	U.S.A.	1991	19.99
Simon, Paul	Concert In The Park Sampler (Promo)	CD	Warner Bros.	PRO-CD-5220	U.S.A.	1990	14.99

S

Artist	Title	Format	Label	Catalog No	Country	Released	Value
Simon, Paul	Graceland	CD	Warner Bros.	9-46430-2	U.S.A.	1996	8.99
Simon, Paul	Greatest Hits, Etc. (Stranded Limo)	CD	Sony	32DP-371	Japan	1977	54.99
Simon, Paul	Greatest Hits, Etc. (Stranded Limo)	CD	Columbia	CK-35032	U.S.A.	1977	49.99
Simon, Paul	Hearts And Bones	CD	Warner Bros.	9-23942-2	U.S.A.	1983	6.99
Simon, Paul	Negotiations And Love Songs '71-'86	CD	Warner Bros.	9-25789-2	U.S.A.	1988	8.99
Simon, Paul	One-Trick Pony	CD	Warner Bros.	3472-2	U.S.A.	1980	8.99
Simon, Paul	Paul Simon	CD	Warner Bros.	9-25588-2	U.S.A.	1972	7.99
Simon, Paul	Rhythm Of The Saints	CD	Warner Bros.	9-26098-2	U.S.A.	1989	6.99
Simon, Paul	Rhythm Of The Saints (DJ/W/Box)	CD	Warner Bros.	9-26098-2-DJ	U.S.A.	1990	29.99
Simon, Paul	Songbook + 2 (Paul's 2nd LP 1965)	CD	Columbia	CK-90281	U.S.A.	2004	8.99
Simon, Paul	Songs From Capeman Sampler (DJ)	CD	Warner Bros.	PRO-CD-9106-R	U.S.A.	1997	10.99
Simon, Paul	Songs From The Capeman	CD	Warner Bros.	9-46814-2	U.S.A.	1997	6.99
Simon, Paul	Still Crazy After All These Years	CD	Warner Bros.	9-25591-2	U.S.A.	1975	8.99
Simon, Paul	There Goes Rhymin' Simon	CD	Warner Bros.	9-25589-2	U.S.A.	1973	7.99
Simon, Paul	You're The One	CD	Warner Bros.	9-47844-2	U.S.A.	2000	6.99
Simply Red	Greatest Hits	CD	East West	61993-2	U.S.A.	1996	4.99
Sinatra, Frank	Best Columbia Years 1943-1952	4CD	Columbia	C4K-64681	U.S.A.	1995	24.99
Sinatra, Frank	Capitol Years Box Set	21CD	Capitol	0724349898529	England	1998	499.99
Sinatra, Frank	Concepts Sampler (Promo)	CD	Capitol	70876-12177-2	U.S.A.	2001	13.99
Sinatra, Frank	Duets (DCC Gold Cd)	CD	DCC	GZS-1053	U.S.A.	1994	14.99
Sinatra, Frank	Duets 2 (DCC Gold Cd)	CD	DCC	GZS-1073	U.S.A.	1994	14.99
Sinatra, Frank	Francis Albert Sinatra/A C Jobim	CD	Reprise	9-46948-2	U.S.A.	1998	8.99
Sinatra, Frank	Frank Sintra Sings Cole Porter + 4	CD	Capitol	CDP-596611	U.S.A.	1991	8.99
Sinatra, Frank	In Concert '57 (DCC Gold Cd)	CD	DCC	ARZ-101-2	U.S.A.	1999	14.99
Sinatra, Frank	September Of My Years	CD	Reprise	9-46946-2	U.S.A.	1998	7.99
Sinatra, Frank	Songs Swingin' Lovers (MFSL Gold Cd)	CD	Mobile Fidelity	UDCD-538	U.S.A.	1955	91.99
Sinatra, Frank	The Capitol Years	3CD	Capitol	7-94317-2	U.S.A.	1990	23.99
Sinatra, Frank	The Reprise Collection Box Set	4CD	Warner Bros.	D-217009	U.S.A.	1990	34.99
Sinatra, Frank	The Voice (Gold Mastersound Cd)	CD	Columbia	CK-64368	U.S.A.	1994	16.99
Sinatra, Frank/Bing Crosby	The Best Of Bing And Frank (Xmas)	3CD	Eclipse	64916-2	U.S.A.	1994	14.99
Sinatra, Frank/Davis Jr./Martin	Summit In Concert (DCC Gold Cd)	CD	DCC	ARZ-102-2	U.S.A.	1999	29.99
Sinatra, Nancy	These Boots Are Made For Walkin' + 4	CD	Sundazed	SC-6052	U.S.A.	1995	9.99
Sinatra, Nancy	You Go Go Girl!	CD	Varese	302-066-059-2	U.S.A.	1999	8.99
Sinatra, Nancy/L Hazelwood	Fairy Tales And Fantasies	CD	Rhino	R1-70166	U.S.A.	1989	69.99
Sinclair/Sinclair	Destinations (Not Caravan Brothers)	CD	Line	RICD-9.00709-0	Germany	1988	7.99
Sinner	Comin' Out Fighting/Dangerous Charm	CD	Victor Ent.	VICP-60782	Japan	1999	41.99
Sinner	Danger Zone/Touch of Sin	CD	Victor Ent.	VICP-60780	Japan	1999	41.99
Sinner	Treasure (The Works 93-98)	CD	Zero	XRCN-10014	Japan	1998	29.99
Siouxsie/Banshees	A Kiss In The Dreamhouse	CD	Geffen	GEFD-24049	U.S.A.	1982	9.99
Siouxsie/Banshees	Best Of + 9	2CD	Polydor	065-150-2	England	2002	28.99
Siouxsie/Banshees	Hyaena	CD	Geffen	9-24030-2	U.S.A.	1984	9.99
Siouxsie/Banshees	Join Hands	CD	Geffen	GEFD-24047	U.S.A.	1983	9.99
Siouxsie/Banshees	Juju	CD	Geffen	GEFD-24050	U.S.A.	1981	9.99
Siouxsie/Banshees	Kaleidoscope	CD	Geffen	GEFD-24048	U.S.A.	1980	9.99
Siouxsie/Banshees	Kiss Them For Me	CD Single	Geffen	GEFDS-21650	U.S.A.	1993	6.99
Siouxsie/Banshees	Nocturne (With Robert Smith/Cure)	CD	Polydor	839-009-2	England	1983	11.99
Siouxsie/Banshees	O Baby Pt 2	CD Single	Polydor	853721-2	England	1994	4.99
Siouxsie/Banshees	O Baby Pt. 1	CD Single	Polydor	853719-2	England	1994	4.99
Siouxsie/Banshees	Once Upon A Time/The Singles	CD	Geffen	GEFD-24051	U.S.A.	1981	7.99
Siouxsie/Banshees	Peepshow	CD	Geffen	M2G-24205	U.S.A.	1988	9.99
Siouxsie/Banshees	Rapture (Promo Sampler)	CD	Geffen	PRO-CD-4710	U.S.A.	1994	11.99
Siouxsie/Banshees	Stargazer	CD	Polydor	SHECD2-3	England	1995	5.99
Siouxsie/Banshees	Superstition	CD	Geffen	GEFD-24387	U.S.A.	1991	8.99
Siouxsie/Banshees	The Peel Sessions	CD	Dutch East Indies	DEI8406-2	U.S.A.	1987	17.99
Siouxsie/Banshees	The Rapture	CD	Geffen	GEFD-24630	U.S.A.	1995	8.99
Siouxsie/Banshees	The Rapture - 4 Track Sampler (Promo)	CD	Polydor	RAPTURE1	England	1995	11.99
Siouxsie/Banshees	The Scream	CD	Geffen	GEFD-24046	U.S.A.	1978	9.99
Siouxsie/Banshees	Through The Looking Glass	CD	Geffen	M2G-24134	U.S.A.	1987	9.99

S

Artist	Title	Format	Label	Catalog No	Country	Released	Value
Siouxsie/Banshees	Tinderbox	CD	Geffen	9-24092-2	U.S.A.	1986	9.99
Siouxsie/Banshees	Twice Upon A Time - The Singles	CD	Geffen	GEFD-24482	U.S.A.	1992	7.99
Siouxsie/Morrissey	Interlude	CD Single	Parlophone	7243-8-81583-2-9	England	1994	14.99
Sir Douglas Quintet	Best Of Sir Douglas Quintet	CD	Sundazed	SC-123	U.S.A.	2000	8.99
Sir Douglas Quintet	Day Dreaming At Midnight	CD	Elektra	9-61474-2	U.S.A.	1994	7.99
Sir Douglas Quintet	Douglas Quinet+2=[Honkey Blues] + 3	CD	Acadia	ACA-8040	England	2002	10.99
Sir Douglas Quintet	Mendocino	CD	Neon	NE-34511	EC	1999	7.99
Sir Douglas Quintet	Mendocino + 6	CD	Acadia	ACA-8041	England	2002	10.99
Sir Douglas Quintet	She's About A Mover	CD	Edsel	NESTCD-918	England	1999	11.99
Sir Douglas Quintet	Sir Douglas Quintet Is Back	CD	Sundazed	SC-124	U.S.A.	2000	8.99
Sir Douglas Quintet	Texas Fever - Best Of	CD	AIM	AIM-2018-CD	Australia	2000	11.99
Sir Douglas Quintet	The Best Of (1968-75)	CD	Mercury	846-586-2	U.S.A.	1990	8.99
Sir Douglas Quintet	The Crazy Cajun Recordings	2CD	Edsel	MEDCD-599	England	1998	21.99
Sir Douglas Quintet	The Tracker + 10	CD	Edsel	DIAB-880	England	1998	9.99
Sir Douglas Quintet	Together After Five + 4	CD	Acadia	ACA-8042	England	2002	10.99
Sir Douglas Qunitet	1+1+1=4 & Return Doug Saldana + 4	CD	Raven	RVCD-147	Australia	2002	12.99
Sisterhood	A Lover's Concerto	CD Single	Line	PRCD-9.01242-E	Germany	1992	19.99
Sisters of Mercy	A Slight Case of Overbombing	CD	Elektra	9-61399-2	U.S.A.	1993	8.99
Sisters of Mercy	First And Last And Always	CD	Elektra	9-60405-2	U.S.A.	1985	7.99
Sisters of Mercy	Floodland	CD	Warner Bros.	9-60762-2	U.S.A.	1987	8.99
Sisters of Mercy	More	CD Single	Warner Bros.	9031-72693-2	Germany	1990	6.99
Sisters of Mercy	Some Girls Wander By Mistake	CD	Warner Bros.	CD-76476	England	1992	9.99
Sisters of Mercy	Temple Of Love	CD	Warner Bros.	9031-77384-2	England	1992	6.99
Sisters of Mercy	Vision Thing	CD	Elektra	9-61017-2	9-61017-2	1990	6.99
Skid Row	B-Side Ourselves	CD	Atlantic	82431-2	U.S.A.	1992	5.99
Skid Row	Forty Seasons: The Best Of Skid Row	CD	Atlantic	83103-2	U.S.A.	1998	9.99
Skid Row	Self Titled	CD	Atlantic	81936-2	U.S.A.	1989	10.99
Skid Row	Slave To The Grind	CD	Atlantic	82242-2	U.S.A.	1991	7.99
Skid Row	Slave To The Grind (Clean)	CD	Atlantic	82278-2	U.S.A.	1991	6.99
Skid Row	Subhuman Beings On Tour!!	CD	East West	7567-80630-2	Japan	1995	20.99
Skid Row	Subhuman Race	CD	Atlantic	82730-2	U.S.A.	1995	7.99
Skid Row	Thickskin	CD	Skid Row	SRR-19182-3	U.S.A.	2003	12.99
Skid Row/Prunella Scales	Dressing Up The Idiot + 2	CD	Warner Bros.	WPCR-1151	Japan	1997	23.99
Skids	Dunfermline - Best Of	CD	Virgin	2-90893	England	1987	7.99
Skin	Self Titled + 2	CD	Toshiba-EMI	TOCP-8187	Japan	1993	13.99
Skin Alley	Skin Tight	CD	Line	TACD-9.00754-0	Germany	1989	24.99
Skin Alley	Two Quid Deal?	CD	Line	TACD-9.00751-0	Germany	1989	24.99
Skinny Puppy	Selections From Brap (Promo)	CD	Nettwerk	NTCDPRO-9607	U.S.A.	1996	10.99
Sky Farmer	Amazing Grace	CD	Gear Fab	GF-191	U.S.A.	2002	11.99
Sky Kings	From Out Of The Blue	CD	Rhino	RHM2-7714	U.S.A.	1997	17.99
Skyy	Inner City	CD	Rams Horn	RHR-8022	EEC	1990	14.99
Slade	Alive Volume 2	CD	Polygram	849-179-2	England	1993	13.99
Slade	Crackers	CD	Castle	CCSCD-401	France	1994	17.99
Slade	Feel the Noize: The Very Best of Slade	CD	Polygram	537-105-2	England	1998	14.99
Slade	In Flame	CD	Polygram	849-182-2	U.S.A.	1999	13.99
Slade	Keep Your Hands Off My Power Supply	CD	Epic	ZK-39336	U.S.A.	1990	18.99
Slade	Merry Xmas Everybody '98 Remix	CD Single	Polygram	563-353-2	England	1998	6.99
Slade	Nobody's Fools	CD	Polygram	849-183-2	England	1993	13.99
Slade	Old New Borrowed And Blue	CD	Polygram	849-181-2	England	1998	13.99
Slade	Play It Loud	CD	Polygram	849-178-2	England	1993	14.99
Slade	Rogues Gallery	CD	Castle	CLACD-378	England	1985	14.99
Slade	Slade Alive!	CD	Polygram	841-114-2	England	1998	16.99
Slade	Slade On Stage	CD	Universal	547-413-2	England	2002	11.99
Slade	Sladest	CD	Polygram	837-103-2	England	1998	13.99
Slade	Slayed?	CD	Polygram	849-180-2	U.S.A.	1999	14.99
Slade	Slayed?	CD	Polydor K.K.	POCP-2174	Japan	1992	19.99
Slade	The Amazing Kamikaze Syndrome	CD	Castle	CLACD-381	France	1998	12.99
Slade	The Slade Collection 79-87	CD	Polygram	547-410-2	England	1999	9.99

S

Artist	Title	Format	Label	Catalog No	Country	Released	Value
Slade	The Slade Collection 81-87	CD	Castle	CCSCD372	France	1993	9.99
Slade	Till Deaf Do Us Part	CD	Universal	547-407-2	England	2002	10.99
Slade	Wall Of Hits	CD	Polygram	511-612-2	England	1993	9.99
Slade	We'll Bring The House Down	CD	Castle	CLACD-380	France	1981	10.99
Slade	Whatever Happened To Slade?	CD	Polygram	849-184-2	England	1993	13.99
Slade	You Boyz Make Big Noize	CD	Epic	ZK-40908	U.S.A.	1987	12.99
Slaughter	Fear No Evil + 1	CD	Victor Ent.	VICP-5538	Japan	1995	38.99
Slaughter	The Wild Life + 1 (W/Photo Book)	CD	Toshiba-EMI	TOCP-7094	Japan	1992	14.99
Slayer	Diabolus In Musica	CD	Universal	7314-586801-2	U.S.A.	2002	8.99
Slayer	Divine Intervention	CD	Universal	7314-586800-2	U.S.A.	2002	8.99
Slayer	G*d Hates Us All (W/Bonus DVD)	2CD	Universal	7314-586332-2	U.S.A.	2002	24.99
Slayer	Hell Awaits	CD	Metal Blade	3984-14031-2	U.S.A.	1994	8.99
Slayer	Live Undead	CD	Metal Blade	3984-14033-2	U.S.A.	1996	8.99
Slayer	Live: Decade Of Aggression	2CD	Universal	7314-586799-2	U.S.A.	2002	18.99
Slayer	Reign Of Blood	CD	Universal	7314-586796-2	U.S.A.	2002	8.99
Slayer	Seasons In The Abyss	CD	Polydor	PHCR-1042	Japan	1990	37.99
Slayer	Seasons In The Abyss	CD	Universal	7314-586798-2	U.S.A.	2002	8.99
Slayer	Show No Mercy	CD	Metal Blade	3984-14032-2	U.S.A.	1994	8.99
Slayer	Soundtrack To The Apocalypse Box	5CD	Universal	B000151902	U.S.A.	2003	89.99
Slayer	Soundtrack To The Apocalypse Box	4CD	American	B000163702	U.S.A.	2003	54.99
Slayer	South Of Heaven	CD	Universal	7314-586797-2	U.S.A.	2002	8.99
Slayer	Undisputed Attitude	CD	Universal	7314-586938-2	U.S.A.	2002	8.99
Slayton, Bobby	Raging Bully	CD	Miramar	09006-23106-2	U.S.A.	1998	7.99
Slick, Darby/Great Society	Sandoland - Self Titled	CD	Taxim	TX-2022-2-TA	U.S.A.	1995	12.99
Slick, Grace	Best Of (18 Trk Version)	CD	RCA	07863-67773-2	U.S.A.	1999	19.99
Slick, Grace	Dreams	CD	Si-Wan	SRMWP-1010	Korea	1998	20.99
Slick, Grace	Manhole	CD	Acadia	ACA-8015	England	2001	8.99
Slick, Grace	The Best Of	CD	RCA	75517-45742-2	U.S.A.	2000	7.99
Slick, Grace	The Best Of	CD	BMG	BVCM-31018	Japan	1999	29.99
Slick, Grace	Welcome To The Wrecking Ball	CD	Great Expectations	PIPCD029	France	1981	74.99
Slick, Grace/Great Society	Born To Be Burned	CD	Sundazed	SC-11027	U.S.A.	1995	10.99
Slick, Grace/Great Society	Collector's Item	CD	Columbia	CGK-30459	U.S.A.	1965	29.99
Slick, Grace/Great Society	Live At The Matrix	CD	Edsel	EDCD-280	England	1994	29.99
Slick, Grace/P. Kantner	Sunfighter	CD	RCA	07863-67421-2	U.S.A.	1997	11.99
Slick/Kantner/Freiberg	Baron Von Tollbooth/The Chrome Nun	CD	RCA	07863-67418-2	U.S.A.	1997	11.99
Slickee Boys	Here To Stay	CD	Line	LICD-9.00081-0	Germany	1988	24.99
Slim Tab Hunters	Rockin 'N Beatin'	CD	Line	GACD-9.00587-0	Germany	1988	19.99
Slipknot	Self Titled (W/Purity/F Limb Nursery)	CD	Roadrunner	403	U.S.A.	1999	28.99
Slits	Cut + 2	CD	Island	548186-2	England	2000	19.99
Slits	In The Beginning - A Live Anthology	CD	Jungle	FREUD-CD-057	England	1997	14.99
Slits	The Peel Sessions	CD	Strange Fruit	SFRSCD052	U.S.A.	1998	14.99
Sloan, P.F.	Child Of Our Times	CD	Varese	302-066-157-2	U.S.A.	2001	8.99
Small Faces	All Or Nothing	CD	Sony	AK-52427	U.S.A.	1992	8.99
Small Faces	Anthology 1965-1967	2CD	Deram	314-533-284-2	U.S.A.	1996	14.99
Small Faces	Boxed: The Definitive Anthology	2CD	Repertoire	REP-4429-WO	Germany	1995	19.99
Small Faces	Collections	CD	Line	IMCD-9.00657-0	Germany	1989	11.99
Small Faces	First Step (With Rod Stewart)	CD	Warner Bros.	1851-2	U.S.A.	1970	13.99
Small Faces	Greatest Hits	CD	Repertoire	REP-4597-WZ	Germany	1996	12.99
Small Faces	In Memoriam	Mini Lp	Victor Ent.	VICP-61243	Japan	2001	24.99
Small Faces	Nice (Audio/Visual)	2CD	Alchemy	PILOT-66	England	2000	10.99
Small Faces	Odds And Mods	CD	Fuel 2000	302-061-227-2	U.S.A.	2002	8.99
Small Faces	Ogden's Nut Gone Flake (Orig. Art)	CD	Essential	ESMCD-477	England	1997	8.99
Small Faces	Playmates	CD	Repertoire	REP-4267-WY	Germany	1996	34.99
Small Faces	Rarities	CD	Victor Ent.	VICP-61141	Japan	2000	29.99
Small Faces	Self Titled + 14	CD	Repertoire	REP-4173-WY	Germany	1992	12.99
Small Faces	Singles Collection	6CD	Essential	ESB-CD-725	England	1999	34.99
Small Faces	Small Faces + 24	2CD	Castle	CMDDD-553	England	2002	14.99
Small Faces	Small Faces + 5	CD	Essential	ESMCD-476	England	1997	8.99

S

Artist	Title	Format	Label	Catalog No	Country	Released	Value
Small Faces	The Autumn Stone + 3	CD	Essential	ESMCD-478	England	1997	8.99
Small Faces	The BBC Session	CD	Strange Fruit	SFRSCD089	England	2000	14.99
Small Faces	The Best Of Immediate	CD	Victor Ent.	VICP-61140	Japan	2000	24.99
Small Faces	The Darlings Of Wapping...	2CD	Sequel	NEECD-311	England	1999	12.99
Small Faces	The Immediate Anthology	CD	Charly	IMM-BOX1	England	1995	14.99
Small Faces	The Small Faces Collection	CD	Castle	CCSCD-108	France	1986	9.99
Small Faces/Mike D'Abo	Gulliver's Travels	CD	Castle	CMRCD-063	England	2001	17.99
Smashing Pumpkins	1991-1998 (Promo)	CD	Virgin	DPRO-14923	U.S.A.	1999	14.99
Smashing Pumpkins	Adore	CD	Virgin	7243-8-45879-2	U.S.A.	1998	8.99
Smashing Pumpkins	Aeroplane Flies High Sampler (DJ/12 Trk.	CD	Virgin	DPRO-11590	U.S.A.	1996	49.99
Smashing Pumpkins	Aeroplane Flies High Sampler (DJ/4 Trk.)	CD	Virgin	DPRO-11589	U.S.A.	1996	14.99
Smashing Pumpkins	Earphoria	CD	Virgin	7243-5-42706-2	U.S.A.	2002	8.99
Smashing Pumpkins	Earphoria (Promo)	CD	Virgin	DPRO-12694	U.S.A.	1994	14.99
Smashing Pumpkins	Gish	CD	Virgin	7243-8-39663-2	U.S.A.	1994	7.99
Smashing Pumpkins	MACHINA/The Machines of God	CD	Virgin	7243-8-48936-2	U.S.A.	2000	6.99
Smashing Pumpkins	Mellon Collie And The Infinite Sadness	2CD	Virgin	7243-8-40861-2	U.S.A.	1995	13.99
Smashing Pumpkins	Pisces Iscariot	CD	Virgin	7243-8-39834-2	U.S.A.	1994	5.99
Smashing Pumpkins	Rotten Apples: Gr. Hits + 16 (W/Bonus C	CD	Hut	CDHUTD70	England	2001	29.99
Smashing Pumpkins	Siamese Dream	CD	Virgin	0777-7-88267-2	U.S.A.	1993	6.99
Smashing Pumpkins	Siamese Dream Sampler (Promo)	CD	Hut	HUTSP1	England	1993	39.99
Smashing Pumpkins	The Aeroplane Flies High Box Set	5CD	Virgin	7243-8-38583-3	England	1995	39.99
Smashing Pumpkins	Zero	CD	Virgin	7243-8-38545-2	U.S.A.	2001	5.99
Smith	A Group Called Smith	CD	Varese	VSD-5489	U.S.A.	1994	73.99
Smith, Huey Piano	Twas The Night Before Christmas	CD	West Side	WESM-547	England	1998	7.99
Smith, Kendra	Five Ways Of Disappearing	CD	4AD	9-45853-2	U.S.A.	1995	6.99
Smith, Kendra	Guild Of Temporal Adventurers	CD	Fiasco	#831-052-001A	U.S.A.	1992	43.99
Smith, Mandy/Mandy	Positive Reaction + 5	CD	Warner Bros.	WPCR-313	Japan	1993	36.99
Smith, Michael W.	All Access Free W/Worship Again	CD	Reunion	6-02341-0019-5-3	U.S.A.	2002	12.99
Smith, Michael W.	Change Your World	CD	Geffen	GEFD-24491	U.S.A.	1992	6.99
Smith, Michael W.	Christmas	CD	RCA	07863-66169-2	U.S.A.	1989	8.99
Smith, Michael W.	Christmastime	CD	Reunion	02341-0015-2	U.S.A.	1998	8.99
Smith, Michael W.	Columbine - What Have We Learned? (D	CD	Reunion	23938-8	U.S.A.	1999	29.99
Smith, Michael W.	For You (Promo)	CD Single	Geffen	PRO-CD-4301	U.S.A.	1991	24.99
Smith, Michael W.	Freedom	CD	Reunion	CD-10002	U.S.A.	2000	8.99
Smith, Michael W.	Go West Young Man	CD	Reunion	7010063729	U.S.A.	1990	6.99
Smith, Michael W.	I 2 (Eye)	CD	Reunion	REND-24331	U.S.A.	1988	8.99
Smith, Michael W.	I Will Be Here For You (Promo)	CD Single	Geffen	PRO-CD-4445	U.S.A.	1992	24.99
Smith, Michael W.	I'll Lead You Home	CD	Reunion	701-0106-72X	U.S.A.	1995	8.99
Smith, Michael W.	Kentucky Rose (Promo)	CD Single	Reunion	MWS-10-1	U.S.A.	1993	24.99
Smith, Michael W.	Live The Life	CD Single	Reunion	83061-0185-2	U.S.A.	1997	5.99
Smith, Michael W.	Live The Life	CD	Reunion	CD10007	U.S.A.	1998	7.99
Smith, Michael W.	Love Me Good	CD Single	Reunion	02341-00102	U.S.A.	1998	5.99
Smith, Michael W.	Michael W. Smith 2	CD	Reunion	7010004722	U.S.A.	1984	8.99
Smith, Michael W.	Picture Perfect (Promo 3 Track)	CD Single	Reunion	RDJ-62554-2	U.S.A.	1993	24.99
Smith, Michael W.	Picture Perfect (Promo 6 Track)	CD Single	Geffen	PRO-CD-4452	U.S.A.	1992	24.99
Smith, Michael W.	Place In This World (3 Track Promo)	CD Single	Reunion	PRO-CD-4234	U.S.A.	1991	24.99
Smith, Michael W.	Project	CD	Reunion	701000272X	U.S.A.	1983	8.99
Smith, Michael W.	Somebody Love Me (Promo)	CD Single	Reunion	RDJ-62466-2	U.S.A.	1992	24.99
Smith, Michael W.	The Acoustic Set: A Live Recording	CD	Reunion	02341-011-8	U.S.A.	2000	24.99
Smith, Michael W.	The Big Picture	CD	Reunion	7-01-001027-7	U.S.A.	1986	8.99
Smith, Michael W.	The First Decade	CD	Reunion	701-0086-729	U.S.A.	1993	7.99
Smith, Michael W.	The Live Set	CD	Reunion	7010026726	U.S.A.	1987	8.99
Smith, Michael W.	The Second Decade '93 - '03	CD	Reunion	02341-0080-2	U.S.A.	2003	8.99
Smith, Michael W.	The Wonder Years Box Set	2CD	Reunion	7010085722	U.S.A.	1993	39.99
Smith, Michael W.	This Is Your Time	CD	Reunion	02341-0041-2	U.S.A.	1999	6.99
Smith, Michael W.	Worship	CD	Reunion	01241-49410-2	U.S.A.	2001	8.99
Smith, Michael W.	Worship + 2	CD	Reunion	02341-0025-2	U.S.A.	2001	8.99
Smith, Michael W./Paradigm	Ambient Tribute/Michael W. Smith	CD	Essential	CD70004	U.S.A.	1996	19.99

S

Artist	Title	Format	Label	Catalog No	Country	Released	Value
Smith, Michael W./R. Sterling	Michael W. Smith Coll. - Youth Choir	CD	Word	701-9255-590	U.S.A.	1991	19.99
Smith, Patti	1959 (Promo)	CD Single	Arista	ASCD-3446	U.S.A.	1997	14.99
Smith, Patti	CD Sampler (Promo)	CD	Arista	ASCD-9683	U.S.A.	1988	14.99
Smith, Patti	Dream Of Life + 2	CD	Arista	07822-18828-2	U.S.A.	1996	9.99
Smith, Patti	Easter + 1	CD	Arista	07822-18826-2	U.S.A.	1996	9.99
Smith, Patti	Glitter In Their Eyes (Promo)	CD Single	Arista	ARPCD-3813	U.S.A.	2000	7.99
Smith, Patti	Gone Again (Advance Cd)	CD	Arista	ARCD-8747	U.S.A.	1996	14.99
Smith, Patti	Gone Again (W/Bonus Tracks)	CD	BMG	07822-18747-2-4	England	1996	19.99
Smith, Patti	Gung Ho	CD	Arista	07822-14618-2	U.S.A.	2000	7.99
Smith, Patti	Horses + 1	CD	Arista	07822-18827-2-9	U.S.A.	1993	9.99
Smith, Patti	Land (1975-2002)	2CD	Arista	07822-14708-2	U.S.A.	2002	19.99
Smith, Patti	Masters: The Collected Works	6CD	Arista	07822-18933-2	U.S.A.	1996	74.99
Smith, Patti	Peace And Noise (Advance Cd)	CD	Arista	ARCD-8986	U.S.A.	1997	15.99
Smith, Patti	Peace And Noise + 3 (Bonus Tour EP)	2CD	BMG	07822-18986-2-1	Australia	1999	19.99
Smith, Patti	Radio Ethiopia + 1	CD	Arista	07822-18825-2	U.S.A.	1996	9.99
Smith, Patti	Summer Cannibals (Promo)	CD Single	Arista	ASCD-3008	U.S.A.	1996	5.99
Smith, Patti	The Patti Smith Masters (Promo)	CD	Arista	ASCD-3218	U.S.A.	1996	24.99
Smith, Patti	Trampin'	CD	Columbia	CK-90330	U.S.A.	2004	8.99
Smith, Patti	Wave + 2	CD	Arista	07822-18829-2	U.S.A.	1996	9.99
Smithereens	Green Thoughts	CD	Lemon	CDLEM09	England	2003	18.99
Smiths	An Extraordinary Ordinariness (Book)	CD Single	Sonic Book	SONIC.007	Italy	1997	21.99
Smiths	Best 1	CD	Sire	9-45042-2	U.S.A.	1992	6.99
Smiths	Best II	CD	Sire	9-45097-2	U.S.A.	1992	9.99
Smiths	Hatful Of Hollow	CD	Rough Trade	ROUGH-CD76	England	1984	11.99
Smiths	Headmaster Ritual (Withdrawn)	CD Single	Rough Trade	RTT215CD	England	1985	119.99
Smiths	How Soon Is Now? (Disc 1)	CD Single	Warner Bros.	4509-90627-2	England	1992	39.99
Smiths	How Soon Is Now? (Disc 2)	CD Single	Warner Bros.	4509-90628-2	England	1992	39.99
Smiths	Louder Than Bombs	CD	Sire	9-25569-2	U.S.A.	1987	9.99
Smiths	Meat is Murder	CD	Sire	9-25269-2	U.S.A.	1985	11.99
Smiths	Peel Session	CD	Dutch East Indies	DEI8302-2	England	1988	14.99
Smiths	Rank	CD	Sire	9-25786-2	U.S.A.	1988	5.99
Smiths	Sheila Take A Bow	CD	Line	LICD-9.00308-L	Germany	1987	34.99
Smiths	Singles	CD	Reprise	9-45932-2	U.S.A.	1995	9.99
Smiths	Stop Me	CD	Line	LICD-9.00440-J	Germany	1987	34.99
Smiths	Stop Me	CD Single	Rough Trade	VICP-2007	Japan	1990	79.99
Smiths	Stop Me If You've...	CD	Polydor	VDP-28025	Japan	1988	79.99
Smiths	Strangeways, Here We Come	CD	Victor Ent.	VDP-1278	Japan	1987	21.99
Smiths	Sweet And Tender Hooligan	CD Single	Reprise	9-43525-2	U.S.A.	1995	4.99
Smiths	The 12" Mixes	CD Single	Columbia	652973-2	Australia	1988	59.99
Smiths	The Queen Is Dead	CD	Victor Ent.	VICP-2004	Japan	1990	21.99
Smiths	The Smiths	CD	Victor Ent.	VICP-2001	Japan	1990	21.99
Smiths	The Very Best Of	CD	Warner Bros.	8573-88948-2	England	2001	11.99
Smiths	The World Won't Listen	CD	Victor Ent.	VICP-2005	Japan	1990	44.99
Smiths	This Charming Man	CD Single	Sire	9-40591-2	U.S.A.	1992	5.99
Smiths	This Charming Man (Disc 1)	CD Single	Warner Bros.	4509-90307-2	England	1992	39.99
Smiths	This Charming Man (Disc 2)	CD Single	Warner Bros.	4509-90308-2	England	1992	39.99
Smoke, The	High In A Room: The Anthology	2CD	Castle	CMEDD516	England	2002	19.99
Smoke, The	It's Smoke Time + 14	CD	Repertoire	REP-4348-WZ	Germany	2002	15.99
Smoke, The	Self Titled	CD	Gull	25114	England	1966	27.99
Smoke, The	Smoke This	CD	Ariola	63042	Germany	1997	9.99
Smoke, The	Sugarman: Best Of	CD	Repertoire	REP-4606-WY	Germany	2002	12.99
Smokin' Mojo Filters/P Weller	Come Together (Paul McCartney)	CD Single	Go! Discs Ltd.	GOD-CD-136	England	1995	7.99
Smothers Brothers	Aesop's Fables	CD	Music For Little	MLP-D2178	U.S.A.	1990	39.99
Smothers Brothers	Curb Your Tongue, Knave !	CD	Laugh.com	LGH1125	U.S.A.	2002	14.99
Smothers Brothers	Sibling Revelry - The Best Of	CD	Rhino	R2-75235	U.S.A.	1998	13.99
Snafu	All Funked Up	CD	Angel Air	SJPCD032	England	2000	14.99
Snafu	Self Titled	CD	Repertoire	REP-4391-WP	Germany	1998	14.99
Snafu	Self Titled/Situation Normal	2CD	Angel Air	SJPCD030	England	1998	24.99

S

Artist	Title	Format	Label	Catalog No	Country	Released	Value
Snafu	Situation Normal	CD	Repertoire	REP-4466-WY	Germany	2002	14.99
Snow, Mark	Truth And The Light: Music/X-Files	CD	Warner Bros.	9-46279-2	U.S.A.	1996	9.99
Snow, Phoebe	Self Titled + 7 (Gold Cd)	CD	DCC	GZS-1051	U.S.A.	1994	46.99
Sobule, Jill	Pink Pearl (Adv. Cd/Pink Promo Case)	CD	Beyond Music	BYADV-78068-2	U.S.A.	2000	9.99
Sobule, Jill	Things Here Are Different	CD	MCA	MCAD-6375	U.S.A.	1990	12.99
Soft Boys	1976 - 1981	2CD	Rykodisc	RCD-10234	U.S.A.	1993	19.99
Soft Boys	A Can Of Bees	CD	Rykodisc	RCD-20231	U.S.A.	1979	34.99
Soft Boys	Invisible Hits	CD	Rykodisc	RCD-20233	U.S.A.	1983	16.99
Soft Boys	Nextdoorland	CD	Matador	OLE-553-CD	U.S.A.	2002	9.99
Soft Boys	Raw Cuts	CD	Overground	OVER-05	England	1989	34.99
Soft Boys	Underwater Moonlight/And How It Got	2CD	Matador	OLE-500-2	U.S.A.	2001	17.99
Soft Cell	Cruelty Without Beauty + 3	2CD	Cooking Vinyl	SPART-116	England	2002	14.99
Soft Cell	Non Stop Ecstatic Dancing + 6	CD	Mercury	558-265-2	Germany	1998	12.99
Soft Cell	Non Stop Erotic Cabaret + 8	CD	Mercury	532595-2	Germany	1996	12.99
Soft Cell	Say Hello Wave Goodbye '91 (Cd 1)	CD Single	Mercury	868-101-2	England	1991	8.99
Soft Cell	Say Hello Wave Goodbye '91 (Cd2)	CD Single	Mercury	868-157-2	England	1991	8.99
Soft Cell	The Art Of Falling Apart + 4	CD	Mercury	558-266-2	England	1998	12.99
Soft Cell	This Last Night In Sodom + 6	CD	Mercury	558-267-2	Germany	1998	12.99
Soft Machine	BBC Radio 1 - Live In Concert	CD	Windsong	WINCD056	England	1994	19.99
Soft Machine	Bundles	CD	See For Miles	SEE-CD-283	England	1990	15.99
Soft Machine	Facelift	2CD	Voiceprint	VP233CD	England	2002	19.99
Soft Machine	Fourth/Fifth	CD	Columbia	493341-2	England	1999	9.99
Soft Machine	Jet Propelled Photographs	CD	Charly	CDGR-188	Germany	1997	8.99
Soft Machine	Land Of Cockayne	CD	One Way	S21-18936	U.S.A.	1996	12.99
Soft Machine	Live At The Paradiso	CD	Voiceprint	BP193CD	Austria	1995	19.99
Soft Machine	Six	CD	Columbia	494981-2	England	1973	8.99
Soft Machine	Six/Seven	CD	Edsel	EDCD740	England	2004	19.99
Soft Machine	Soft Machine (Live At Paradiso + 6)	CD	Movie Play Gold	MPG-74033	Portugal	1994	24.99
Soft Machine	Spaced	CD	Cuneiform	RUNE-90	U.S.A.	1996	11.99
Soft Machine	Third	CD	Columbia	471407-2	England	1970	8.99
Soft Machine	Volumes One & Two	CD	Big Beat	CDWIKD-920	England	1989	13.99
Solar Circus	Historical Retrospective	CD	Relix	RRCD2064	U.S.A.	1993	6.99
Solar Circus	Juggling Suns	CD	Relix	RRCD-2037	U.S.A.	1989	5.99
Solar Circus	Twlight Dance	CD	Relix	RRCD2047	U.S.A.	1992	5.99
Solid Gold Cadillac	Solid Gold Cadillac/Brain Damage	CD	BGO	BGOCD471	England	1999	14.99
Sonata Artica	Songs/Silence Live in Tokyo 2001 + 3	CD	Pony Canyon	PCKD-200092	Japan	2002	29.99
Sondheim, Stephen	A Funny Thing Happened...	CD	Rykodisc	RCD-10727	U.S.A.	1998	24.99
Sondheim, Stephen	A Little Night Music (W/Judi Dench)	CD	Tring Int.	TRING001	EEC	1995	154.99
Sonic Youth	Anagrama	CD Single	SYR	SYR-01-CD	U.S.A.	1997	7.99
Sonic Youth	Bad Moon Rising	CD	DGC	DGCD-24512	U.S.A.	1985	8.99
Sonic Youth	Dirty (W/Free 7" Single)	CD	Geffen	GEF-24493	Australia	1992	34.99
Sonic Youth	Goo (MFSL Gold Cd)	CD	Mobile Fidelity	UDCD-665	U.S.A.	1990	18.99
Sonic Youth	Goodbye 20th Century	2CD	SYR	SYR-4-CD	U.S.A.	1999	14.99
Sonic Youth	Hold That Tiger (Live)	CD	Goofin'	GOO-2	U.S.A.	1997	10.99
Sonic Youth	Invito Al Cielo	CD Single	SYR	SYR-3-CD	U.S.A.	1998	7.99
Sonic Youth	Made In USA (O.S.T.)	CD	Rhino	R2-71591	U.S.A.	1995	16.99
Sonic Youth	Silver Session (For Jason Knuth)	CD Single	SYR	SKR-1	U.S.A.	1998	7.99
Sonic Youth	Slaapkammers Met Slagroom	CD Single	SYR	SYR-2-CD	U.S.A.	1998	9.99
Sonic Youth/T Moore	Hurricane Floyd	CD	Sublingual	SUBLIN-007	U.S.A.	1999	9.99
Sonic Youth/T Moore	Piece For Jetson Dolma	CD	Victo	VICTO-045	Canada	1997	16.99
Sonic Youth/T Moore	Please Just Leave Me...	CD	Pure	PURE-37	U.S.A.	2001	9.99
Sonic Youth/T Moore/Cline	In-Store	CD	Father Yod	FYP-17	U.S.A.	2001	11.99
Sonic Youth/T Moore/Cline	Live At Easthampton Town Hall	CD	JMZ	JMZ-002	U.S.A.	2001	11.99
Sonic Youth/T Moore/Cline	Pillow Wand	CD	Little Brother	LB-011	U.S.A.	1997	11.99
Sonic Youth/T Moore/Fusinato	TM/MF	CD	Freeway Sound	FWS-002	Australia	2001	14.99
Sonic Youth/T Moore/Prati	3 Incredible Ideas	CD	Auditorium	AU-03	Italy	2001	19.99
Sonic Youth/T Moore/Prati	The Promise	CD	Materiali Sonori	MASO-90106	Italy	1999	13.99
Sonic Youth/T Moore/Renaldo	Fuck Shit Up	CD	Victo	VICTO-071	Canada	1993	16.99

S

Artist	Title	Format	Label	Catalog No	Country	Released	Value
Sonic Youth/T Moore/Sauter	Barefoot In The Head	CD	Forced Exposure	FE-015	U.S.A.	1990	12.99
Sonic Youth/T Moore/Surgal	Klangfarbenmelodie...	CD	Corpus Her	HERMES-011	New Zeland	1997	19.99
Sonic Youth/T Moore/Surgal	Not Me	CD Single	Fourth Dimension	FD-57-CD	England	1999	10.99
Sonic Youth/Y Eye	TV Shit	CD	Ecstatic Peace	E#38-CD	U.S.A.	1993	9.99
Sonics	Full Force!	CD	Line	EQCD-9.00387-0	Germany	1987	8.99
Sonics	Here Are The Sonics	CD	Norton	CNW-903	U.S.A.	1999	12.99
Sonics	Maintaining My Cool	CD	Jerden	JRCD-7001	U.S.A.	1991	11.99
Sonics	Psycho-Sonics	CD	Big Beat	CDWIKD-115	England	1993	12.99
Sons Of Angels	Thrill Of The Feel + 1	CD	Victor Ent.	VICP-61014	Japan	2000	49.99
Sordid Humor	Light Music For Dying People	CD	Capricorn	9-42031-2	U.S.A.	1994	5.99
Sorokas	Sorokas	CD	Line	TLCD-9.00516-0	Germany	1988	16.99
Soul Survival	Soul Sounds	CD	Line	RTCD-9.01145-0	Germany	1992	12.99
Soundgarden	Foreshocks (Promo Sampler)	CD	A&M	31454-8053-2	U.S.A.	1994	49.99
South, Joe	Anthology 1968 - 1975	CD	Universal	VSCD-1499	Japan	2000	31.99
South, Joe	Anthology: Mirror Of His Mind '68 -'75	CD	Raven	RVCD-94	Australia	2001	13.99
South, Joe	Classic Masters	CD	Capitol	7243-5-37469-2	U.S.A.	2002	8.99
South, Joe	Introspect	CD	Toshiba-EMI	TOCP-3501	Japan	1994	31.99
South, Joe	Introspect/Don't It Make You Want..	CD	Raven	RVCD-175	Australia	2003	13.99
South, Joe	The Best Of	CD	Koch	KOC-CD-8036	U.S.A.	1999	8.99
South, Joe	The Best Of	CD	Rhino	R21S-70994	U.S.A.	1992	19.99
Souther, J. D.	Black Rose	CD	Elektra	1059-2	U.S.A.	1976	13.99
Souther, J. D.	Home By Dawn	CD	Wounded Bird	WOU-5081	U.S.A.	2002	10.99
Souther, J. D.	John David Souther	CD	Elektra	5055-2	U.S.A.	1972	11.99
Souther, J. D.	You're Only Lonely	CD	Sony	SRCS-9236	Japan	1997	29.99
Souther, J.D.	You're Only Lonely	CD	Columbia	CK-36093	U.S.A.	1979	8.99
Souther, Richard	Cross Currents	CD	Narada	ND-63007	U.S.A.	1989	5.99
Souther,Hillman,Furay Band	The Souther - Hillman - Furay Band	CD	Elektra	7559-61164-2	Germany	1974	16.99
Souther-Hillman-Furay Band	The Souther - Hillman - Furay Band	CD	Line	LECD-9.51061-0	Germany	1991	16.99
Souther-Hillman-Furay Band	Trouble In Paradise	CD	Line	LECD-9.51052-0	Germany	1991	16.99
Southside-Johnny/A. Jukes	At Least We Got Shoes	CD	RCA Victor	R32P-1065	Japan	1986	44.99
Southside-Johnny/A. Jukes	Better Days	CD	Uni	IPTD-10445	U.S.A.	1991	6.99
Southside-Johnny/A. Jukes	Havin' A Party With Southside Johnny	CD	Epic	EK-36246	U.S.A.	1979	7.99
Southside-Johnny/A. Jukes	Live At The Bottom Line 1976	CD	Sony	ESCA-7595	Japan	1976	44.99
Southside-Johnny/A. Jukes	The Best Of	CD	Epic	EK-52733	U.S.A.	1992	9.99
Southside-Johnny/A. Jukes	The Jukes	CD	Mercury	834-347-2	U.S.A.	1979	14.99
Space Explosion/Faust	Self Titled + 1 (Cluster/Amon Duul)	CD	Captain Trip	CTCD-067	Japan	2000	19.99
Spandau Ballet	True	CD	Chrysalis	7243-5-37127-0-9	U.S.A.	2003	14.99
Spanky/Our Gang	Greatest Hits	CD	Mercury	314-546-332-2	U.S.A.	1999	8.99
Spanky/Our Gang	Like To Get To Know You	CD	Universal	VSCD-738	Japan	1999	31.99
Spanky/Our Gang	Spanky & Our Gang	CD	Universal	VSCD-737	Japan	1999	31.99
Spanky/Our Gang	Spanky And Our Gang	CD	Line	LMCD-9.51070-Z	Germany	1991	24.99
Spanky/Our Gang	Without Rhyme Or Reason	CD	Universal	VSCD-739	Japan	1999	31.99
Sparks	A Woofer In Tweeter's Clothing	CD	Repertoire	REP-4051-WZ	Germany	1991	12.99
Sparks	Amateur Hour (Audio/Live Video)	2CD	Master Tone	MM5125	England	1995	24.99
Sparks	Angst In My Pants	CD	Repertoire	REP-4760-WZ	Germany	2002	12.99
Sparks	Balls	CD	Oglio	OGL-89119-2	U.S.A.	2000	8.99
Sparks	Balls + 6 (W/ Bonus CD	2CD	Festival	33332	Australia	2000	27.99
Sparks	Big Beat + 2	CD	Island	IMCD201	England	1995	12.99
Sparks	Gratuitous Sax & Senseless Violins	CD	Logic	23267-2	U.S.A.	1995	8.99
Sparks	In Outer Space	CD	Repertoire	REP-4761-WZ	Germany	2002	12.99
Sparks	In The Swing	CD	Spectrum	550-065-2	England	1993	7.99
Sparks	Indiscreet + 3	CD	Island	IMCD200	England	1994	10.99
Sparks	Interior Design	CD	Thunderbolt	CDTB-141	England	1996	12.99
Sparks	Kimono My House + 2	CD	Island	IMCD198	England	1994	10.99
Sparks	Lil' Beethoven	CD	Palm Pictures	PALMCD-2126-2	U.S.A.	2003	8.99
Sparks	Music That You Can Dance To	CD	Curb	D2-77335	U.S.A.	1990	7.99
Sparks	No. 1 In Heaven	CD	Repertoire	REP-4768-WZ	Germany	1998	12.99
Sparks	Plagiarism	CD	Oglio	OGL-89109-2	U.S.A.	1998	8.99

S

Artist	Title	Format	Label	Catalog No	Country	Released	Value
Sparks	Profile: The Ultimate Sparks Coll.	2CD	Rhino	R2-70731	U.S.A.	1991	17.99
Sparks	Propoganda	CD	Polydor K.K.	PHCR-4829	Japan	1997	29.99
Sparks	Propoganda + 2	CD	Island	IMCD199	England	1994	12.99
Sparks	Pulling Rabbits Out Of A Hat	CD	Oglio	OGL-81604-2	U.S.A.	1998	8.99
Sparks	Self Titled	CD	Repertoire	REP-4052-WZ	Germany	1991	12.99
Sparks	Terminal Jive	CD	Repertoire	REP-4769-WZ	Germany	2002	12.99
Sparks	The 12" Mixes	CD	Oglio	OGL-81605-2	U.S.A.	1999	8.99
Sparks	The Best Of	CD	Repertoire	REP-4906	Germany	2003	12.99
Sparks	Whomp That Sucker	CD	Oglio	OGL-81601-2	U.S.A.	1998	8.99
Speak	Orizaba	CD	Capricorn	314-538-970-2	U.S.A.	1999	4.99
Speakman, D/Gong/P Atters	Psychic Atters - Mystic Minutes	CD	Captain Trip	CTCD-119	Japan	2000	16.99
Spear Of Destiny	Sod's Law	CD	Line	LICD-9.01250-0	Germany	1992	8.99
Spector, Phil/Various	A Christmas Gift For You	CD	Phil Spector	CD-4	U.S.A.	1989	28.99
Spector, Phil/Various	Back To Mono Box Set (W/Button)	4CD	ABKCO	7118-2	U.S.A.	1991	64.99
Spector, Phil/Various	Back To Mono Sampler (Promo)	CD	ABKCO	711831	U.S.A.	1991	32.99
Spector, Phil/Various	Christmas Gift For You (Promo)	CD Single	ABKCO	711832	U.S.A.	1992	10.99
Spector, Ronnie	Dangerous	CD	Raven	RVCD-48	Australia	1995	15.99
Spector, Ronnie	She Talks To Rainbows EP	CD Single	Kill Rock Stars	KRS348	U.S.A.	1999	7.99
Spector, Ronnie	Something's Gonna Happen	CD	Bad Girl Sounds	663609001023	U.S.A.	2003	9.99
Spector, Ronnie	Unfinished Business +1	CD	Lemon	CDLEM18	England	2004	14.99
Spedding, Chris	Backwood Progression + 2	CD	Repertoire	REP-4412-WY	Germany	2002	12.99
Spedding, Chris	Cafe Day Revisited	CD	Last Call	250075	France	2003	9.99
Spedding, Chris	Cafe Days (MFSL Silver Cd)	CD	Mobile Fidelity	MFCD-752	U.S.A.	1991	38.99
Spedding, Chris	Enemy Within + 2	CD	Repertoire	REP-4956-WY	Germany	2001	12.99
Spedding, Chris	Friday The 13th	CD	M.I.L.	9002	U.S.A.	1997	9.99
Spedding, Chris	Gesundheit	CD	Yeaah!	YEAAH019	England	2002	8.99
Spedding, Chris	Guitar Graffiti + 1	CD	Repertoire	REP-4945-WY	Germany	2002	12.99
Spedding, Chris	Hurt	CD	Repertoire	REP-4860-WY	Germany	2002	12.99
Spedding, Chris	I'm Not Like Everybody Else	CD	Repertoire	REP-4946-WY	Germany	2002	12.99
Spedding, Chris	Mean And Moody	CD	See For Miles	SEE-CD-372	England	1994	21.99
Spedding, Chris	One Step Ahead Of The Blues	CD	Last Call	307661	France	2003	9.99
Spedding, Chris	Self Titled + 3	CD	Repertoire	REP-4859-WY	Germany	2002	12.99
Spedding, Chris	The Only Lick I Know	CD	Repertoire	REP-4411-WY	Germany	2002	12.99
Spence, Alexander 'Skip'	Oar + 10	CD	Sundazed	SC-11075	U.S.A.	1999	18.99
Spence, Alexander 'Skip'	Various Artists - More Oar	CD	Birdman	BMR023CD	U.S.A.	1999	12.99
Spence, Joseph	Happy All The.. (Prod/P Rothchild)	CD	Water	WATER-110	U.S.A.	2003	12.99
Spencer, Jon Blues Exp.	Controversial Negro	CD	Toy's Factory	TFCK-87126	Japan	1998	22.99
Spencer, Jon Blues Exp.	Crypt Style	CD	1+2	CD-024	Japan	1991	22.99
Spencer, Jon Blues Exp.	Experimental Remixes	CD	Mute	MUTE-JSBX3-CD	England	1998	12.99
Spencer, Jon Blues Exp.	Extra-Acme	CD	Toy's Factory	TFCK-87169	Japan	1998	22.99
Spencer, Jon Blues Exp.	Heavy (Remix)	CD Single	Mute	MUTE-239-CD	England	1998	8.99
Spencer, Jon Blues Exp.	Plastic Fang	CD	Matador	OLE-542-CD	U.S.A.	2002	7.99
Spencer, Jon Blues Exp.	Plastic Fang (Candy Bag Version)	CD	Matador	OLE-666-CD	U.S.A.	2002	10.99
Spheeris, Jimmie	5 Song Sampler (Promo)	CD	Rain	4402-2	U.S.A.	2000	17.99
Spheeris, Jimmie	An Evening With	2CD	Rain	RR005	U.S.A.	1998	43.99
Spheeris, Jimmie	Isle Of View	CD	Rain	RR001	U.S.A.	1998	39.99
Spheeris, Jimmie	Ports Of The Heart	CD	Rain	RR004	U.S.A.	1999	38.99
Spheeris, Jimmie	Ports Of The Heart	CD	Sony	SICP-8025	Japan	1976	20.99
Spheeris, Jimmie	Spheeris	CD	Rain	RR006	U.S.A.	1998	38.99
Spheeris, Jimmie	The Dragon Is Dancing	CD	Rain	RR003	U.S.A.	1998	38.99
Spheeris, Jimmie	The Original Tap Dancing Kid	CD	Rain	RR002	U.S.A.	1998	38.99
Spiders From Mars/David Bowi	The Spiders From Mars (W/O David Bow	CD	Essential	ESMCD-894	England	2000	10.99
Spinal Tap	Bitch School	CD Single	MCA	MCSTD-1624	U.S.A.	1992	4.99
Spinal Tap	Break Like The Wind	CD	MCA	088-112-370-2	U.S.A.	2000	10.99
Spinal Tap	Spinal Tap + 2 (O.S.T.)	CD	Polydor	P2-49075	U.S.A.	2000	10.99
Spinal Tap	This Is + 2	CD	Polygram	314-549-075-2	U.S.A.	2000	10.99
Spiner, Brent/Star Trek	Ol' Yellow Eyes Is Back (Has S T Cast)	CD	Bay Cities	BCD-2004	U.S.A.	1991	49.99
Spinners	7 Original Lps On 4 Cds Box Set	4CD	Collectables	COL-CD-0085	U.S.A.	1998	39.99

S

Artist	Title	Format	Label	Catalog No	Country	Released	Value
Spirit	12 Dreams/Sardonicus (MFSL Silver)	CD	Mobile Fidelity	MFCD-800	U.S.A.	1972	39.99
Spirit	Chronicles 1967-1992	CD	Line	OLCD-9.91133-X	Germany	1991	12.99
Spirit	Chronicles 1967-1992	CD	DRG	DRG-22002	Canada	1991	12.99
Spirit	Clear Spirit + 4	CD	Epic	EK-65002	U.S.A.	1996	8.99
Spirit	Cosmic Smile	CD	Phoenix Gems	4002	U.S.A.	2002	9.99
Spirit	Feedback	CD	Epic	EPC-477941-2	Austria	1972	8.99
Spirit	I Got A Line On You	CD	Sony	A-24271	U.S.A.	1994	6.99
Spirit	Live At La Paloma	CD	Crew	CREW-22003	U.S.A.	1995	12.99
Spirit	Nature's Way (Interview/Promo)	CD	Crew	CREW-22002	U.S.A.	1991	24.99
Spirit	Nature's Way '92	CD Single	Line	LICD-9.01147-E	Germany	1992	13.99
Spirit	Potatoland	CD	Line	LICD-9.00092-0	Germany	1987	12.99
Spirit	Rapture In The Chambers	CD	I.R.S.	IRSD-82007	U.S.A.	1989	8.99
Spirit	Sea Of Dream	2CD	Acadia	ACAD-8017	England	2002	19.99
Spirit	Son Of Spirit	CD	Great Expectations	PIPCD-002	France	1983	21.99
Spirit	Spirit + 4	CD	Epic	EK-64965	U.S.A.	1996	8.99
Spirit	Spirit Of '76	2CD	BGO	BGOCD605	England	2003	15.99
Spirit	Tent Of Miracles	CD	Line	OLCD-9.91025-X	Germany	1991	12.99
Spirit	Tent Of Miracles	CD	DRG	DRG-22001	Canada	1990	12.99
Spirit	The Family That Plays Together + 6	CD	Epic	EK-65001	U.S.A.	1996	8.99
Spirit	The Mercury Years	2CD	Universal	534-602-2	U.S.A.	1997	14.99
Spirit	Twelve Dreams Of Dr. Sardonicus + 4	CD	Epic	EK-65003	U.S.A.	1996	8.99
Spirit Of John Morgan	Age Machine	CD	Repertoire	REP-4354-WP	Germany	2002	12.99
Spirit Of John Morgan	Self Titled	CD	Repertoire	REP-4351-WP	Germany	2002	12.99
Spirit Of The West	Labour Day	CD	Line	FBCD-9.00617-0	Germany	1988	3.99
Spirogyra	Bells Boots & Shambles	CD	Repertoire	REP-4137-WZ	Germany	2002	12.99
Spirogyra	Burn The Bridges: 1970 - 1971	CD	Repertoire	REP-4846-WZ	Germany	2002	12.99
Spirogyra	Old Boot Wine	CD	Repertoire	REP-4132-WZ	Germany	2002	12.99
Spirogyra	St. Radigans	CD	Repertoire	REP-4070-WZ	Germany	2002	12.99
Spirogyra	We Were A Happy Crew	CD	Mooncrest	CRESTCD-038	England	1999	13.99
Spitballs/Beserkley	The Spitballs (Label Supergroup)	CD	Line	BECD-9.00664-0	Germany	1988	34.99
Splender	Halfway Down the Sky	CD	Columbia	CK-69144	U.S.A.	1999	2.99
Split Enz	20th Century Masters: The Millennium	CD	Universal	314-981-771-2	England	2004	9.99
Split Enz	Anniversary	CD	Mushroom	939960-98010-28	Australia	1995	9.99
Split Enz	Beginning Of The Enz	CD	Mushroom	939760-32332-27	Australia	2003	9.99
Split Enz	Conflicting Emotions	CD	Mushroom	939760-32336-23	Australia	2003	9.99
Split Enz	Corroboree (Waiata)	CD	Mushroom	939760-32333-26	Australia	2003	9.99
Split Enz	Dizrythmia	CD	Mushroom	939760-32331-28	Australia	2003	9.99
Split Enz	Frenzy	CD	Mushroom	939760-32334-25	Australia	2003	9.99
Split Enz	Frenzy (USA Version/W/Luton Tapes)	CD	A&M	CD-3153	U.S.A.	1981	24.99
Split Enz	Gold Collection	CD	EMI	7243-8-21087-2	EEC	2000	8.99
Split Enz	History Never Repeats: 30th Ann. + 6	CD	Mushroom	939760-33619-20	Australia	2002	17.99
Split Enz	History Never Repeats: Best Of + 3	CD	EMI	7243-8-21087-2-6	England	1997	9.99
Split Enz	History Never Repeats: The Best Of	CD	A&M	75021-3289-2	U.S.A.	1987	5.99
Split Enz	Living Enz (Live)	2CD	Mushroom	939760-32328-24	Australia	2003	14.99
Split Enz	Mental Notes	CD	Mushroom	939760-32329-23	Australia	2003	9.99
Split Enz	Oddz And Enz	6CD	Mushroom	D80940	Australia	1992	79.99
Split Enz	Other Enz: Split Enz & Beyond Vol. 1	2CD	Raven	RVCD-100	Australia	1999	13.99
Split Enz	Rear Enz	6CD	Mushroom	D80946	Australia	1992	79.99
Split Enz	Second Thoughts	CD	Mushroom	939760-32330-29	Australia	2003	9.99
Split Enz	See Ya Round	CD	Mushroom	939760-32328-24	Australia	2003	9.99
Split Enz	Spellbound: The Very Best Of	2CD	Mushroom	MUSH33015-.2	Australia	1997	14.99
Split Enz	Stranger Than Fiction (Best Of)	CD	Disky	VI-882882	Holland	2004	7.99
Split Enz	Time And Tide	CD	Mushroom	939760-32335-24	Australia	2003	9.99
Split Enz	True Colours	CD	Mushroom	939760-32338-21	Australia	2003	11.99
Split Enz/Enzso	Enzso (Split Enz Tribute)	CD	Epic	EK-67877	U.S.A.	1996	22.99
Split Second, A	Neurobeat	CD	Line	TCCD-9.00424-0	Germany	1987	19.99
Spock's Beard	All On A Sunday	CD Single	SPV	05541623CDS	Germany	2001	6.99
Spock's Beard	Beware Of Darkness	CD	Giant Elec Pea	GEPCD-1018	EU	1996	12.99

S

Artist	Title	Format	Label	Catalog No	Country	Released	Value
Spock's Beard	Day For Night	CD	SPV	SPV08531392CD	Germany	1999	12.99
Spock's Beard	Day For Night + 1	CD	Avalon	MICP-10113	Japan	2000	27.99
Spock's Beard	Don't Try This At Home	CD	SPV	SPV08541162CD	Germany	2000	12.99
Spock's Beard	Don't Try This At Home Either	CD	Radient	RA-008	U.S.A.	2000	8.99
Spock's Beard	Feel Euphoria	CD	SPV	SPV08565772CD	Germany	2003	12.99
Spock's Beard	Feel Euphoria + 13 (W/Bonus Cd)	2CD	SPV	08765770DCD	Germany	2003	15.99
Spock's Beard	From The Vaults	CD	Radient	RA-005	U.S.A.	1998	14.99
Spock's Beard	Kindness Of Strangers + 1	CD	Victor Ent.	VICP-60234	Japan	1998	22.99
Spock's Beard	Live At The Whiskey/Nearfest	2CD	Radient	RA-007	U.S.A.	1999	17.99
Spock's Beard	Skin	CD Single	SPV	05531743CDS	Germany	2000	6.99
Spock's Beard	Snow	2CD	SPV	09265152DCD	Germany	2002	16.99
Spock's Beard	Snow (W/Bonus Cd)	3CD	SPV	09565150DCD	Germany	2002	39.99
Spock's Beard	The Beard Is Out There	CD	SPV	SPV07631372CD	Germany	2003	12.99
Spock's Beard	The Kindness Of Strangers	CD	Giant Elec Pea	GEPCD-1022	EU	1998	12.99
Spock's Beard	The Light	CD	Giant Elec Pea	GEPCD-1017	EU	1994	12.99
Spock's Beard	The Light - Artwork Collection	CD	SPV	SPV08728208CD	Germany	2004	13.99
Spock's Beard	The Official Bootleg	CD	Radient	RA-002	U.S.A.	1996	14.99
Spock's Beard	There And Here	2CD	Radient	RA-010	U.S.A.	2001	18.99
Spock's Beard	V	CD	Radient	3984-14335-2	U.S.A.	2000	8.99
Spock's Beard	V	CD	SPV	SPV08541232CD	Germany	2000	12.99
Spock's Beard	V + 1 (Digipack Case/Enhanced)	CD	SPV	SPV08741230CD	Germany	2000	22.99
Spooky Tooth	BBC Sessions	CD	Spitfire	SPT-13002-2	U.S.A.	1999	8.99
Spooky Tooth	Ceremony	CD	Edsel	EDCD-565	England	1998	14.99
Spooky Tooth	Comic Violence (Same As The Mirror)	CD	Dressed To Kill	384	England	2000	8.99
Spooky Tooth	Cross Purposes (No Gary Wright)	CD	A&M	314-161-445-2	U.S.A.	1999	5.99
Spooky Tooth	It's All About + 10	CD	Gone Beat	SP77009	Holland	1996	19.99
Spooky Tooth	Live In Europe	CD	Blues	BSTMCD002	England	1990	19.99
Spooky Tooth	Mirror	CD	Line	LICD-9.00090-0	Germany	1988	8.99
Spooky Tooth	Self Titled	CD	Griffin	GCD-223-2	U.S.A.	1994	8.99
Spooky Tooth	Spooky Two	CD	A&M	CD-3124	U.S.A.	1988	8.99
Spooky Tooth	That Was Only Yesterday: An Intro.	CD	A&M	314-541-049-2	U.S.A.	1999	11.99
Spooky Tooth	The Best Of	CD	Island	842-688-2	U.S.A.	1999	12.99
Spooky Tooth	The Last Puff	CD	Edsel	EDCD-468	England	1996	24.99
Spooky Tooth	Witness	CD	Progressive Line	PL-519	Australia	2000	14.99
Spooky Tooth	You Broke My Heart So...	CD	Progressive Line	PL-520	Australia	2000	14.99
Springfield, Dusty	A Brand New Me + 9	CD	Rhino	R2-71036	U.S.A.	1992	14.99
Springfield, Dusty	Dusty + 3	CD	Mercury	314-538-909-2	U.S.A.	1999	10.99
Springfield, Dusty	Dusty In Memphis + 8	CD	Mercury	063-297-2	EU	2002	10.99
Springfield, Dusty	Reputation	CD	Parlophone	79-4401-2	England	1990	8.99
Springfield, Dusty	Ultimate Collection	CD	Hip-O	314-585-634-2	U.S.A.	2001	8.99
Springfield, Rick	Rock Of Life	CD	RCA Victor	R32P-1140	Japan	1988	39.99
Springfield, Rick	Success Hasn't Spoiled Me Yet	CD	RCA	07863-54125-2	U.S.A.	1995	8.99
Springsteen, Bruce	18 Tracks	CD	Columbia	CK-69476	U.S.A.	1999	5.99
Springsteen, Bruce	2 Originals Box/Born To Run/Darkness	2CD	Columbia	480817-2	Australia	1995	18.99
Springsteen, Bruce	Before The Fame (Rare Withdrawn)	2CD	Pony Express	PER5899	U.S.A.	1999	24.99
Springsteen, Bruce	Blood Brothers (W/Video)	CD	Columbia	CSK-8879	U.S.A.	1996	17.99
Springsteen, Bruce	Born In The U.S.A.	CD	Columbia	CDCBS-86304	Australia	1984	13.99
Springsteen, Bruce	Born In The U.S.A.	CD	Sony	35DP-164	Japan	1988	24.99
Springsteen, Bruce	Born To Run (Sony Gold Cd)	CD	Columbia	CK-64406	U.S.A.	1975	44.99
Springsteen, Bruce	Chimes Of Freedom	CD Single	Columbia	CK-64969	U.S.A.	1988	8.99
Springsteen, Bruce	Darkness On The Edge Of Town	CD	Columbia	CDCBS-86061	Australia	1978	13.99
Springsteen, Bruce	Dead Man Walkin'	CD Single	Columbia	663190-2	Austria	1996	8.99
Springsteen, Bruce	Essential (W/Bonus CD)	3CD	Columbia	C2K-90773	U.S.A.	2003	20.99
Springsteen, Bruce	Greatest Hits	CD	Columbia	CK-67060	U.S.A.	1995	6.99
Springsteen, Bruce	Human Touch	CD	Columbia	CK-53000	U.S.A.	1992	5.99
Springsteen, Bruce	Hungry Heart	CD Single	Columbia	662315-2	Germany	1995	8.99
Springsteen, Bruce	In Concert/MTV Plugged	CD	Columbia	473860-2	Germany	1992	8.99
Springsteen, Bruce	Live 1975-1985 Box Set	3CD	Columbia	C3K-40558	U.S.A.	1992	19.99

S

Artist	Title	Format	Label	Catalog No	Country	Released	Value
Springsteen, Bruce	Live And Rare	CD	Columbia	SAMPCM 12867 2	Austria	2003	19.99
Springsteen, Bruce	Live Collection 1	CD Single	Sony	23DP-5248	Japan	1987	36.99
Springsteen, Bruce	Live In New York City	2CD	Columbia	C2K-85490	U.S.A.	2001	12.99
Springsteen, Bruce	Lonesome Day	CD Single	Columbia	673408-2	England	2002	8.99
Springsteen, Bruce	Lucky Town	CD	Columbia	CK-53001	U.S.A.	1992	5.99
Springsteen, Bruce	Missing	CD Single	Columbia	663508-2	Austria	1996	8.99
Springsteen, Bruce	My Hometown	CD Single	Columbia	38K-5728	U.S.A.	1988	11.99
Springsteen, Bruce	Nebraska/Tunnel (Grn Tint Cvr)/Ghost	3CD	Columbia	509646-2	Germany	2003	24.99
Springsteen, Bruce	One Step Up (3")	CD Single	Columbia	651442-2	England	1988	18.99
Springsteen, Bruce	One Step Up (3")	CD Single	Sony	10EP-3017	Japan	1988	52.99
Springsteen, Bruce	Promo Live In N.Y.C.	CD Single	Columbia	CSK-56656	U.S.A.	2000	29.99
Springsteen, Bruce	Roll Of The Dice	CD Single	Sony	SRCS-6599	Japan	1992	24.99
Springsteen, Bruce	Secret Garden	CD Single	Columbia	44K-77854	U.S.A.	1995	4.99
Springsteen, Bruce	Secret Garden	CD Single	Columbia	664324-5	Austria	1997	8.99
Springsteen, Bruce	Secret Garden	CD Single	Columbia	664324-2	Austria	1997	8.99
Springsteen, Bruce	Self Titled (Promo)	CD	Sony	XDDP-93084	Japan	1992	274.99
Springsteen, Bruce	Streets Of Philadelphia	CD Single	Columbia	44K-77383	U.S.A.	1994	5.99
Springsteen, Bruce	Telltales (Interview)	CD	ABCD	TELL-04	England	1988	11.99
Springsteen, Bruce	The Ghost Of Tom Joad	CD	Columbia	CK-67484	U.S.A.	1995	6.99
Springsteen, Bruce	The Rising (Leatherbound Ed.)	CD	Columbia	CK-86600	U.S.A.	2002	12.99
Springsteen, Bruce	Tougher Than The Rest (Promo/250)	CD	Columbia	BOSS1	Sweden	1992	227.99
Springsteen, Bruce	Tracks (Songs Book Bonus CD)	CD	Columbia	CSK-41555	U.S.A.	1998	12.99
Springsteen, Bruce	Tracks Box Set	4CD	Columbia	CXK-69475	U.S.A.	1998	24.99
Springsteen, Bruce	Tracks Sampler (Promo)	CD	Columbia	CSK-41561	U.S.A.	1999	12.99
Springsteen, Bruce	Tunnel Of Love	CD	Sony	25DP-5250	Japan	1987	24.99
Springsteen, Bruce	Tunnel Of Love	CD	Columbia	CK-40999	U.S.A.	1987	6.99
Springsteen, Bruce	Tunnel Of Love Express 1 (3")	CD Single	Sony	15EP-8009	Japan	1988	39.99
Springsteen, Bruce	Tunnel Of Love Express II (3")	CD Single	Sony	15EP-8010	Japan	1988	51.99
Springsteen, Bruce	Waitin' On A Sunny Day	CD Single	Columbia	673583-2	Australia	2003	5.99
Springsteen, Bruce/No UPC	Nebraska (Promo With Extended Song)	CD	Columbia	CK-38358	U.S.A.	1982	84.99
Springsteen, Bruce/P Scialfa	Patti Scialfa - Rumble Doll	CD	Columbia	XK-44223	U.S.A.	1993	6.99
Spyro-Gyra	20/20 (Holographic Cover)	CD	GRP	GRD-9867	U.S.A.	1997	8.99
Spyro-Gyra	Access All Areas	CD	Amherst	AMH-8007-2	U.S.A.	1984	9.99
Spyro-Gyra	Alternating Currents	CD	Amherst	AMH-8005-2	U.S.A.	1985	9.99
Spyro-Gyra	Breakout	CD	Amherst	AMH-8006-2	U.S.A.	1986	9.99
Spyro-Gyra	Carnaval	CD	Amherst	AMH-8003-2	U.S.A.	1980	9.99
Spyro-Gyra	Catching The Sun	CD	Amherst	AMH-8001-2	U.S.A.	1980	8.99
Spyro-Gyra	City Kids	CD	Amherst	AMH-8010-2	U.S.A.	1983	9.99
Spyro-Gyra	Collection	CD	GRP	GRD-9642	U.S.A.	1991	6.99
Spyro-Gyra	Dreams Beyond Control	CD	GRP	GRD-9714	U.S.A.	1993	5.99
Spyro-Gyra	Fast Forward	CD	GRP	GRD-9608	U.S.A.	1990	5.99
Spyro-Gyra	Freetime	CD	Amherst	AMH-8000-2	U.S.A.	1981	9.99
Spyro-Gyra	Got The Magic	CD	Windham Hill	01934-11439-2	U.S.A.	1999	5.99
Spyro-Gyra	Heart Of The Night	CD	GRP	GRD-9842	U.S.A.	1996	7.99
Spyro-Gyra	In Modern TImes	CD	Heads Up	HUCD-3061	U.S.A.	2001	5.99
Spyro-Gyra	Incognito	CD	Amherst	AMH-8004-2	U.S.A.	1982	9.99
Spyro-Gyra	Love & Other Obsessions	CD	GRP	GRD-9811	U.S.A.	1995	5.99
Spyro-Gyra	Morning Dance	CD	Amherst	AMH-8008-2	U.S.A.	1979	9.99
Spyro-Gyra	Point Of View	CD	MCA	MCAD-6309	U.S.A.	1989	6.99
Spyro-Gyra	Retrospective (Promo Ltd. 5000)	2CD	GRP	GRP3P-5267	U.S.A.	1997	24.99
Spyro-Gyra	Rites Of Summer	CD	MCA	MCAD-6235	U.S.A.	1988	5.99
Spyro-Gyra	Road Scholars	CD	GRP	GRD-9903	U.S.A.	1998	9.99
Spyro-Gyra	Road Scholars + 1	CD	Universal Victor	MVCJ-24015	Japan	1998	24.99
Spyro-Gyra	Spyro Gyra	CD	Amherst	AMH-8002-2	U.S.A.	1978	9.99
Spyro-Gyra	Stories Without Words	CD	Amherst	AMH8009-2	U.S.A.	1987	9.99
Spyro-Gyra	Three Wishes	CD	GRP	GRD-9674	U.S.A.	1992	5.99
Squeeze	20th Century Masters: The Millennium	CD	Universal	314-981-667-2	England	2004	9.99
Squeeze	A Round And A Bout	CD	I.R.S.	IRSD-82040	U.S.A.	1990	15.99

S

Artist	Title	Format	Label	Catalog No	Country	Released	Value
Squeeze	Annie Get Your Gun	CD Single	I.R.S.	IRSD-74007	U.S.A.	1990	7.99
Squeeze	Argybargy + 2	CD	A&M	540-803-2	England	1997	24.99
Squeeze	Babylon And On	CD	A&M	CD-5161	U.S.A.	1987	6.99
Squeeze	Big Squeeze: The Very Best Of	2CD	Universal	76648-898622	U.S.A.	2002	18.99
Squeeze	Classics, Vol. 25	CD	A&M	75021-2523-2	U.S.A.	1987	5.99
Squeeze	Cool For Cats + 2	CD	A&M	540-804-2	England	1997	24.99
Squeeze	Cosi Fan Tutti Frutti + 2	CD	A&M	540-802-2	England	1997	24.99
Squeeze	Domino	CD	Valley Ent.	VE-15046	U.S.A.	1999	8.99
Squeeze	Domino	CD	Toshiba-EMI	TOCP-65205	Japan	1999	18.99
Squeeze	East Side Story (MFSL Gold Cd)	CD	Mobile Fidelity	UDCD-739	U.S.A.	1981	24.99
Squeeze	East Side Story + 2	CD	A&M	540-805-2	England	1997	24.99
Squeeze	Electric Trains (Cd 1)	CD Single	A&M	581-269-2	England	1996	7.99
Squeeze	Electric Trains (Cd 2)	CD Single	A&M	581-271-2	England	1996	7.99
Squeeze	Frank	CD	A&M	CD-5278	U.S.A.	1989	6.99
Squeeze	Greatest Hits	CD	Uptown	08283971812	England	2001	8.99
Squeeze	Live at the Royal Albert Hall	CD	Polygram K.K.	POCM-1204	Japan	1997	15.99
Squeeze	Piccadilly Collection	CD	A&M	31454-0425-2	U.S.A.	1996	8.99
Squeeze	Play	CD	Reprise	9-26644-2	U.S.A.	1991	4.99
Squeeze	Play	CD	Warner Bros.	WPCP-4449	Japan	1991	25.99
Squeeze	Ridiculous	CD	Ark 21	61868-10051-2-4	U.S.A.	2000	5.99
Squeeze	Ridiculous	CD	I.R.S.	72438-38304-28	U.S.A.	1995	5.99
Squeeze	Ridiculous + 3	CD	Polydor K.K.	POCM-1149	Japan	1995	19.99
Squeeze	Singles - 45's And Under	CD	A&M	CD-3338	U.S.A.	1995	6.99
Squeeze	Six Of One Box Set	6CD	A&M	540801-2	England	1997	149.99
Squeeze	Some Fantastic Place	CD	A&M	31454-0140-2	U.S.A.	1993	4.99
Squeeze	Sweets From A Stranger + 2	CD	A&M	540-807-2	England	1997	24.99
Squeeze	This Summer	CD Single	A&M	581-191-2	England	1995	7.99
Squeeze	This Summer (Cd 1) (W/Box)	CD Single	A&M	581-837-2	England	1996	15.99
Squeeze	This Summer (Promo)	CD Single	I.R.S.	DPRO-10538	U.S.A.	1995	7.99
Squeeze	This Summer Remix (Cd 2)	CD Single	A&M	581-839-2	England	1996	7.99
Squeeze	Three From Babylon And On	CD Single	A&M	CD-17490	U.S.A.	1987	8.99
Squeeze	UK Squeeze + 2	CD	A&M	540-806-2	England	1997	24.99
Squeeze/Chris Difford	I Didn't Get Where I Am	CD	Adventure	ADVMCD1	England	2002	12.99
Squeeze/Chris Difford	No Show Jones (Promo)	CD Single	Adventure	ADVS3	England	2002	9.99
Squeeze/Difford/Tilbrook	Difford And Tilbrook	CD	A&M	CD-4985	U.S.A.	1984	66.99
Squeeze/Glenn Tilbrook	Parallel World	CD Single	Quixotic London	QUIXCD005	England	2001	7.99
Squeeze/Glenn Tilbrook	The Incomplete Glenn Tilbrook + 9	2CD	Quixotic London	QUIXCD007	England	2001	34.99
Squeeze/Glenn Tilbrook	This Is Where You Ain't	CD Single	Quixotic London	QUIXCD006	England	2000	7.99
Squier, Billy	16 Strokes: The Best Of	CD	Capitol	7243-8-31831-2-8	U.S.A.	1995	19.99
Squier, Billy	Classic Masters	CD	Capitol	7243-5-38331-2-1	U.S.A.	2002	8.99
Squier, Billy	Creatures Of Habit	CD	Capitol	C2-94303	Canada	1991	9.99
Squier, Billy	Emotions In Motion	CD	Capitol	C2-46480	Canada	1982	36.99
Squier, Billy	Enough Is Enough	CD	Capitol	CDP-7-46327-2	U.S.A.	1986	11.99
Squier, Billy	Extended Versions	CD	BMG	75517-46647-2	U.S.A.	2002	5.99
Squier, Billy	Happy Blue	CD	J-Bird	JBD-80256-2	U.S.A.	1998	7.99
Squier, Billy	King Biscuit Flower Hour Live	CD	King Biscuit	70710-88017-2	U.S.A.	1996	8.99
Squier, Billy	Reach For The Sky: The Anthology	2CD	Capitol	314-529-296-2	U.S.A.	1996	49.99
Squier, Billy	Tell The Truth	CD	Capitol	7-98690-2	U.S.A.	1993	5.99
Squire, Billy	Anthology	2CD	Polydor	POCP-7149/50	Japan	1996	39.99
Squire, Billy	Don't Say No	CD	Capitol	CDP-7-46479-2	U.S.A.	1981	6.99
Squire, Billy	Hear & Now	CD	Toshiba-EMI	CP32-5894	Japan	1990	17.99
Squire, Billy	Signs Of Life	CD	Capitol	C2-46481	Canada	1984	99.99
Squire, Billy	Tale Of The Tape	CD	Capitol	C2-48039	Canada	1980	60.99
Squire, Chris	Fish Out Of Water	CD	East West	AMCY-19	Japan	1990	37.99
Squire, Chris/Billy Sherwood	Conspiracy	CD	Purple Pyramid	CLP-0819-2	U.S.A.	2000	10.99
St. John, Kate	Indescribable Night	CD	Gyroscope	GYR-6612-2	U.S.A.	1995	19.99
St. John, Kate	Second Sight	CD	Thirsty Ear	THI-66034-2	U.S.A.	1997	19.99
St. Peters, Crispian	Anthology	CD	Repertoire	REP-4608-WY	Germany	2002	12.99

S

Artist	Title	Format	Label	Catalog No	Country	Released	Value
St. Peters, Crispian	Follow Me	CD	Repertoire	REP-4199-WZ	Germany	1991	12.99
St. Peters, Crispian	Follow Me	CD	Collectables	COL-5615	U.S.A.	2002	8.99
St. Peters, Crispian	The Pied Piper	CD	One Way	OW-31379	U.S.A.	1995	8.99
Stafford, Jim	Spiders And Snakes	CD	Polydor	833-073-2	Canada	1974	44.99
Stalk-Forrest Group	St. Cecilia: Elektra (Blue Oyster Cult)	CD	Rhino	RHM2-7716	U.S.A.	1970	19.99
Stalling, Carl/Bugs Bunny	Bugs Bunny On Broadway	CD	Warner Bros.	9-26494-2	U.S.A.	1990	8.99
Stalling, Carl/Bugs Bunny	The Carl Stalling Project: Vol. 2	CD	Warner Bros.	9-45430-2	U.S.A.	1995	11.99
Stalling. Carl/Bugs Bunny	Carl Stalling Project: Vol. 1	CD	Warner Bros.	W2-26027	U.S.A.	1990	14.99
Stallone, Frank/Sylvester	Self Titled	CD	Polydor	821-237-2	U.S.A.	1984	85.99
Stamey, Chris	Fireworks	CD	Rhino	R2-70766	U.S.A.	1991	4.99
Stamey, Chris	It's A Wonderful Life	CD	East Side Digital	ESD-80682	U.S.A.	1992	13.99
Stamey, Chris	It's Alright	CD	A&M	CD-5180	U.S.A.	1987	18.99
Stamey, Chris	Travels In The South	CD	Yep Roc	CD-YEP-2033	U.S.A.	2004	14.99
Stamey, Chris/Friends	Christmas Time	CD	East Side Digital	ESD-80812	U.S.A.	1993	17.99
Stamey, Chris/Kirk Ross	Robust Beauty Of Improper...	CD	East Side Digital	ESD-81052	U.S.A.	1993	11.99
Stampley, Joe/The Uniques	The Uniques Golden Hits	CD	Paula	CD-2208	U.S.A.	1990	14.99
Stanley, Michael	Coming Up For Air	CD	Intersound	9174	U.S.A.	1996	6.99
Stanley, Michael	The Ground	CD	Line Level	LIN-201	U.S.A.	2003	8.99
Stanley, Michael/Band	Cabin Fever	CD	Razor & Tie	RE-2000-2	U.S.A.	1992	44.99
Stanley, Michael/Band	Eighteen Down	CD	Razor & Tie	RE-2851-2	U.S.A.	2000	8.99
Stanley, Michael/Band	Friends And Legends	CD	Razor & Tie	RE-2026-2	U.S.A.	1993	64.99
Stanley, Michael/Band	Greatest Hits	CD	Razor & Tie	RE-2001-2	U.S.A.	1992	17.99
Stanley, Michael/Band	Heartland	CD	Razor & Tie	23939-2	U.S.A.	1990	8.99
Stanley, Michael/Band	Live At Tangiers	2CD	Razor & Tie	RE-2836-2	U.S.A.	1998	24.99
Stanley, Michael/Band	Michael Stanley/Band	CD	Razor & Tie	RE-2025-2	U.S.A.	1993	74.99
Stanley, Michael/Band	MSB	CD	Razor & Tie	RE-2004-2	U.S.A.	1992	48.99
Stanley, Michael/Band	Northcoast	CD	Razor & Tie	23940-2	U.S.A.	1992	19.99
Stanley, Michael/Band	Right Back at Ya' (1971-1983)	CD	Razor & Tie	23926-2	U.S.A.	1992	14.99
Stanley, Michael/Band	Stage Pass	CD	Columbia	CK-34661-2	U.S.A.	1991	8.99
Stanley, Michael/Band	You Break It, You Bought It	CD	Razor & Tie	RE-2035-2	U.S.A.	1990	19.99
Stanley, Michael/Band	You Can't Fight Fashion	CD	Razor & Tie	RE-2005-2	U.S.A.	1992	55.99
Stanley, Michael/Ghost Poets	Ghost Poets	CD	Razor & Tie	RE-2812-2	U.S.A.	1993	19.99
Starcastle	Chronos 1	CD	Sunsinger	8001	U.S.A.	2001	11.99
Starcastle	Citadel	CD	Renaissance	RMED00129	U.S.A.	1998	11.99
Starcastle	Concert Classics Vol. 5 - Live 1978	CD	Renaissance	RRCC00705	U.S.A.	1999	11.99
Starcastle	Fountains Of Light	CD	Renaissance	RMED00128	U.S.A.	1998	11.99
Starcastle	Fountains Of Light	CD	Sony	ESCA-7738	Japan	1998	34.99
Starcastle	Real To Reel	CD	Sony	ESCA-7740	Japan	1998	34.99
Starcastle	Shine On Brightly - Live 1979	CD	Alchemy	PILOT-111	England	2001	11.99
Starcastle	Starcastle	CD	Epic	EK-33914	U.S.A.	1976	11.99
Starpoint	Restless	CD	Elektra	9-60424-2	U.S.A.	1990	54.99
Starr, Ringo	4-Starr Collection (Promo)	CD	Rykodisc	VRCD-0264	U.S.A.	1995	13.99
Starr, Ringo	And His All Starr Band Tour 2003	CD	Koch	KOC-CD-9549	U.S.A.	2004	9.99
Starr, Ringo	Bad Boy	CD	Epic	EK-35378	U.S.A.	1978	6.99
Starr, Ringo	Beaucoups Of Blues + 1	CD	Capitol	7243-8-32675-2-1	U.S.A.	1995	12.99
Starr, Ringo	Blast From Your Past	CD	Capitol	7-4663-2	U.S.A.	1976	8.99
Starr, Ringo	Don't Go Where the Road Don't Go	CD Single	Private	74321-11369-2	Germany	1992	23.99
Starr, Ringo	Goodnight Vienna (Ext Six O'Clock)	CD	Capitol	0777-7-80378-2-8	U.S.A.	1993	8.99
Starr, Ringo	I Wanna Be Santa Claus	CD	Mercury	314-546-668-2	U.S.A.	1999	10.99
Starr, Ringo	La De Da	CD Single	Mercury	566-139-2	Germany	1998	8.99
Starr, Ringo	Live From Montreux	CD	Rykodisc	RCD-20264	U.S.A.	1993	14.99
Starr, Ringo	Never W/O You (Clapton/Gilmour/DJ)	CD Single	Koch	0147776KOCP	England	2003	29.99
Starr, Ringo	Old Wave + 1	CD	Capitol	7243-8-29675-2-1	U.S.A.	1994	50.99
Starr, Ringo	Ringo + 3 (DCC Gold Cd)	CD	DCC	GZS-1066	U.S.A.	1994	71.99
Atarr, Ringo	Ringo Rama (W/Bonus DVD)	2CD	Koch	KOC-CD-8429	U.S.A.	2003	14.99
Starr, Ringo	Ringo Rama Radio Hour (Live Track)	CD	Koch	KOC-SA-8429	U.S.A.	2003	118.99
Starr, Ringo	Ringo Starr And His All-Starr Band + 4	2CD	Rykodisc	RCD-10190	U.S.A.	1990	39.99
Starr, Ringo	Ringo Starr/Third All-Starr Band	CD	Blockbuster	4-00010-52451-8	U.S.A.	1997	8.99

Artist	Title	Format	Label	Catalog No	Country	Released	Value
Starr, Ringo	Ringo The 4th	CD	Atlantic	82416-2	U.S.A.	1992	6.99
Starr, Ringo	Sentimental Journey	CD	Capitol	0777-7-98615-2-1	U.S.A.	1995	10.99
Starr, Ringo	Starr Struck - Best of Ringo Starr Vol. 2	CD	Rhino	R2-70135	U.S.A.	1989	24.99
Starr, Ringo	Stop And Smell The Roses + 6	CD	Capitol	7243-8-29676-2-0	U.S.A.	1994	51.99
Starr, Ringo	The Anthology... So Far	3CD	Koch	KOC-CD-8312	U.S.A.	2001	24.99
Starr, Ringo	Vertical Man + 3 (Best Buy Bonus Cd)	2CD	Mercury	314-558-598-2	U.S.A.	1998	32.99
Starr, Ringo	VH1 Storytellers	CD	Mercury	314-538-118-2	U.S.A.	1998	7.99
Starr, Ringo	Weight Of The World (Promo)	CD Single	Private	PDJ-810003-2	U.S.A.	1992	19.99
Starr, Ringo	Weight of the World/Don't Be Cruel	CD Single	Private	01005-81003-2	U.S.A.	1992	9.99
Starr, Ringo	You Never Know (Promo)	CD Single	Giant	PRO-CD-5153	U.S.A.	1991	24.99
Starr, Ringo/Unreleased Paul	Old Wave/Stop Smell (DJ Sampler)	CD	Capitol	DPRO-66732	U.S.A.	1994	42.99
Starship	Knee Deep In The Hoopla	CD	RCA	PCD1-5488	U.S.A.	1985	5.99
Starship	Love Among The Cannibals	CD	RCA	9693-2-R	U.S.A.	1989	5.99
Starship	No Protection	CD	RCA	6413-2-G11	U.S.A.	1987	5.99
Starship	Starship's Gr Hits: 10 Yrs Of Change	CD	RCA	2423-2-R	U.S.A.	1991	5.99
Starship	We Built This City	CD	Camden	74321-511912	U.S.A.	1997	9.99
Starz	Attention Shoppers!	CD	Metal Blade	9-26570-2	U.S.A.	1991	21.99
Starz	Back In The Day '75/Early Days	CD	Drastic	DCC-0003-CD	U.S.A.	1992	21.99
Starz	Brightest Starz: Anthology	CD	Renaissance	RMED00146	U.S.A.	2000	19.99
Starz	Coliseum Rock	CD	Metal Blade	9-26571-2	U.S.A.	1991	44.99
Starz	Do It With The Lights On	CD	Drastic	DCC-0002-CD	U.S.A.	1992	21.99
Starz	Greatest Hits Live	CD	G.B. Music	GB1003	U.S.A.	1999	11.99
Starz	Live At El Mocambo (Live In Canada)	CD	Drastic	DCC-0008-CD	U.S.A.	1992	21.99
Starz	Live At The Agora, Cleveland, OH	2CD	Drastic	DCC-0012-CD	U.S.A.	1992	34.99
Starz	Live Fox Theatre St. Louis, MO	CD	Drastic	DCC-0006-CD	U.S.A.	1992	21.99
Starz	Live In Action	CD	Metal Blade	9-73430-2	U.S.A.	1989	15.99
Starz	Live In Charleston, W Virginia	CD	Drastic	DCC-0010-CD	U.S.A.	1992	21.99
Starz	Live In Cleveland, Ohio	CD	Drastic	DCC-0009-CD	U.S.A.	1992	21.99
Starz	Live In Dallas, Texas	CD	Drastic	DCC-0007-CD	U.S.A.	1992	21.99
Starz	Live In Louisville	2CD	Drastic	DCC-0005-CD	U.S.A.	2003	34.99
Starz	Live In Richmond, Virginia	CD	Drastic	DCC-0011-CD	U.S.A.	1992	21.99
Starz	Requiem	CD	Drastic	DCC-0001-CD	U.S.A.	1992	21.99
Starz	Self Titled	CD	Metal Blade	9-26558-2	U.S.A.	1991	21.99
Starz	Self Titled	CD	BGO	BGOCD621	England	2004	14.99
Starz	Violation	CD	Metal Blade	9-26559-2	U.S.A.	1991	21.99
Starz/Hellcats	Hellcats 1/P*ss Party Combo	CD	Drastic	DCC-0004-CD	U.S.A.	1992	21.99
Starz/Hellcats	Live At The Record Plant	CD	Drastic	DCC-0013-CD	U.S.A.	1992	21.99
Status Quo	Ain't Complaining	CD Single	Vertigo	QUOCD22	England	1988	22.99
Status Quo	Ain't Complaining (Video Single)	CDV	Vertigo	080-322-2	England	1988	57.99
Status-Quo	1+9+8+2	CD	Vertigo	800-035-2	England	1982	75.99
Status-Quo	12 Gold Bars	CD	Vertigo	PHCR-4215	Japan	1993	29.99
Status-Quo	12 Gold Bars	CD	Vertigo	800-062-2	England	1980	12.99
Status-Quo	12 Gold Bars, Vol. 2	CD	Vertigo	PHCR-4216	Japan	1993	29.99
Status-Quo	12 Gold Bars, Vol. 2	CD	Vertigo	822-985-2	England	1984	12.99
Status-Quo	A Few Bars More	CD	Vertigo	PHCR-4217	Japan	1993	29.99
Status-Quo	A Few Bars More	CD	Spectrum	550-002-2	England	1993	5.99
Status-Quo	Ain't Complaining	CD	Vertigo	834-604-2	England	1988	22.99
Status-Quo	B Sides & Rarities	CD	Castle	CCSCD-271	England	1990	17.99
Status-Quo	Back To Back	CD	Vertigo	814-662-2	England	1983	82.99
Status-Quo	Back To The Beginning	CD	Decal	CD-LIKD-81	England	1991	14.99
Status-Quo	Best Of	CD	Laserlight	21-294	Germany	1998	7.99
Status-Quo	Best of Status Quo 1968-1971	CD	Pickwick	PWKS-4080	England	1989	11.99
Status-Quo	Best of Status Quo 1972-1986	CD	Pickwick	PKWKS-4087-P	England	1989	11.99
Status-Quo	Best/Caroline	CD	Zounds	27200682-B	Germany	1996	6.99
Stat013-Quo	Castle Masters Collection	CD	Castle	CMC-3040	England	1991	14.99
Status-Quo	Dog Of Two Head + 5	CD	Essential	ESM-CD-626	England	1998	8.99
Status-Quo	Don't Stop	CD	TDK	TDCN-5597	Japan	1996	29.99
Status-Quo	Don't Stop (30th Anniversary)	CD	Universal	981-244-2	England	2003	8.99

S

Artist	Title	Format	Label	Catalog No	Country	Released	Value
Status-Quo	Great Box (12 Gold 1/2/N.E.C./Tokyo)	4CD	Nippon Phonogram	PHCR-3129~32	Japan	1991	199.99
Status-Quo	Greatest Hits	CD	Castle	TESSCD-010	Australia	1993	14.99
Status-Quo	Hello	CD	Vertigo	PHCR-2089	Japan	1973	29.99
Status-Quo	Hello	CD	Vertigo	848-172-2	England	1973	12.99
Status-Quo	Ice In The Sun	CD	Pickwick	PKD-3135	Australia	1991	8.99
Status-Quo	Ice In The Sun (Different Tracks)	CD	Pulse	PLS-CD-206	England	1997	8.99
Status-Quo	If You Can't Stand The Heat/1+9+8+2	CD	Vertigo	848-090-2	England	1991	11.99
Status-Quo	In The Army Now	CD	Vertigo	830-049-2	England	1986	11.99
Status-Quo	In The Army Now	CD	Vertigo	32PD-224	Japan	1986	29.99
Status-Quo	Introspective	CD	Baktabak	CINT-5003	England	1990	12.99
Status-Quo	It's Only Rock 'N' Roll	CD	Spectrum	550-190-2	England	1994	8.99
Status-Quo	Live	CD	Vertigo	510-669-2	England	1977	29.99
Status-Quo	Live Alive Quo	CD	Polydor	517-367-2	England	1992	10.99
Status-Quo	Live At The N.E.C.	CD	Vertigo	818-947-2	England	1982	12.99
Status-Quo	Ma Kelly's Greasy Spoon + 4	CD	Essential	ESM-CD-621	England	1998	10.99
Status-Quo	Ma Kelly's Greasy Spoonful Collection	CD	Victor Ent.	VICP-5578	Japan	1995	29.99
Status-Quo	Meilensteine Der Popmusik (Few Bars)	CD	Spectrum	550-002-2	Germany	1993	15.99
Status-Quo	Meilensteine Der Popmusik (It's Only R)	CD	Spectrum	550-190-2	Germany	1994	15.99
Status-Quo	Never Too Late	CD	Vertigo	800-053-2	England	1981	82.99
Status-Quo	Never Too Late/Back To Back	CD	Vertigo	848-088-2	England	1991	11.99
Status-Quo	On The Level	CD	Vertigo	842-101-2	England	1975	24.99
Status-Quo	On The Level (Different Sleeve)	CD	Vertigo	848-174-2	England	1975	11.99
Status-Quo	Original Recordings	CD	Castle	MAT-CD-291	England	1994	10.99
Status-Quo	Perfect Remedy	CD	Vertigo	842-098-2	England	1989	83.99
Status-Quo	Picturesque Matchstickable (Diff. Slv.)	CD	Victor Ent.	VICP-5376	Japan	1994	29.99
Status-Quo	Picturesque Matchstickable...+ 21	2CD	Castle	CMEDD718	England	2003	19.99
Status-Quo	Picturesque Matchstickable/Spare Prts	CD	PRT	25CP-62	Japan	1989	24.99
Status-Quo	Piledriver + 2	CD	Repertoire	REP-4119-WP	Germany	1990	12.99
Status-Quo	Quo/Blue For You	CD	Vertigo	848-089-2	England	1991	12.99
Status-Quo	Quotations Vol. 1 - The Beginning	CD	PRT	PRT-8.26699	England	1988	14.99
Status-Quo	Quotations Vol. 1/2	2CD	PRT	CBC-8014	England	1991	24.99
Status-Quo	Recollections	CD	Recollections	RECCD-001	England	1989	12.99
Status-Quo	Rock Giants	CD	Spectrum	554-107-2	Germany	1995	12.99
Status-Quo	Rock 'Til You Drop	CD	Vertigo	510-341-2	England	1991	8.99
Status-Quo	Rock 'Til You Drop	CD	Vertigo	PHCR-20	Japan	1991	29.99
Status-Quo	Rockin' All Over The World	CD	Vertigo	848-173-2	England	1977	8.99
Status-Quo	Rockin' Australia '97 (12 Gold Bars 1/2)	2CD	Mercury	534-713-2	Australia	1997	27.99
Status-Quo	Rocking All 0ver Years (Diff Trks/Slv)	CD	Vertigo	512-424-2	Italy	1992	29.99
Status-Quo	Rocking All Over The Years	CD	Vertigo	846-797-2	England	1990	19.99
Status-Quo	Rocking All Over The Years	CD	Vertigo	PHCR-1049	Japan	1990	29.99
Status-Quo	Roll Over Lay Down	CD	Vertigo	PHCR-1501	Japan	1996	29.99
Status-Quo	Self Titled (1984)	CD	Castle	MATCD291	England	1996	8.99
Status-Quo	Spare Parts + 5	CD	Essential	ESM-CD-625	England	1998	8.99
Status-Quo	Story Box Set	3CD	PRT	CD3PR-28	England	1990	11.99
Status-Quo	The Best Of: The Early Years	CD	PRT	CDNSP-7773	England	1985	7.99
Status-Quo	The Collection	CD	Castle	CCSCD-114	England	1987	7.99
Status-Quo	The Early Works	3CD	Castle	ESB-CD-136	England	1997	24.99
Status-Quo	The Early Years	CD	Dojo	EARLD-8	England	1992	8.99
Status-Quo	The Hitmachine	CD	Disky	DC-869802	Holland	1996	11.99
Status-Quo	The Other Side Of	CD	Connoisseur	VSOP-CD-213	England	1995	10.99
Status-Quo	The Other Side Of	CD	Connoisseur	VSOP-CD-213	England	1995	10.99
Status-Quo	The Singles Collection 1966-73	CD	Castle	CCS-CD-821	England	1998	12.99
Status-Quo	Thirsty Work	CD	Polydor K.K.	POCP-1485	Japan	1994	39.99
Status-Quo	Thirsty Work (Promo)	CD	Polydor	WORK-1CD	England	1994	9.99
Artus-Quo	To Be Or Not To Be	CD	Pickwick	PWKS-4051-P	England	1989	24.99
Status-Quo	Tokyo Quo	CD	Phonogram	PHCR-4171	Japan	1977	79.99
Status-Quo	Tune To The Music	CD	Ariola	291-008	England	1992	9.99
Status-Quo	Whatever You Want/Just Supposin'	CD	Vertigo	848-087-2	England	1991	184.99

S

Artist	Title	Format	Label	Catalog No	Country	Released	Value
Status-Quo	Whatever You Want: The Very Best Of	2CD	Polygram	553-507-2	England	1997	26.99
Status-Quo/Francis Rossi	Give Myself To You	CD Single	Virgin	VSCDT1594	England	1996	4.99
Status-Quo/Francis Rossi	King Of The Doghouse	CD	Virgin	CDV2809	England	1997	24.99
Status-Quo/John Du Cann	Nothing Better	CD	Repertoire	REP-4205-WY	Germany	1992	21.99
Stealers Wheel	Self Titled	CD	Lemon	CDLEM24	England	2004	11.99
Stealers Wheel	The Very Best Of	CD	Polygram	7314-5-40316-2-2	England	2001	8.99
Steam	Na Na Hey Hey Kiss Him Goodbye + 7	CD	Repertoire	REPUK1018	England	2003	14.99
Steamhammer	Junior's Wailing	CD	Repertoire	REP-4797-WY	Germany	2002	14.99
Steamhammer	MK II + 1	CD	Akarma	AK-243	Italy	2003	14.99
Steamhammer	MK II + 4	CD	Repertoire	REP-4236-WY	Germany	2002	14.99
Steamhammer	Mountains	CD	Akarma	AK-203	Italy	2003	14.99
Steamhammer	Mountains	CD	Repertoire	REP-4066-WY	Germany	2002	14.99
Steamhammer	Reflection	CD	Repertoire	REP-4871-WY	Germany	2002	14.99
Steamhammer	Reflection + 2	CD	Akarma	AK-234	Italy	2003	14.99
Steamhammer	Speech	CD	Repertoire	REP-4139-WY	Germany	2002	14.99
Steampacket	Steampacket/First R&B Festival	CD	Repertoire	RR-4090-WZ	Germany	1990	10.99
Steel Breeze	Cry Thunder	CD	Para-Sight	PSR-001-CD	U.S.A.	1989	234.99
Steel Breeze	Self	CD	Background	1	Germany	1997	21.99
Steele, Chrissy	Magnet To Steele	CD	Chrysalis	F2-21843	U.S.A.	1991	10.99
Steeler	Steeler (Yngwie Malmsteen/Ron Keel)	CD	Shrapnel	SH-1007CD	U.S.A.	1990	12.99
Steeleye-Span	A Parcel Of Rogues	CD	BGO	BGOCD323	England	1996	11.99
Steeleye-Span	A Rare Collection 1972-1996	CD	Raven	RVCD-90	Australia	1999	12.99
Steeleye-Span	A Stack Of	CD	Empirio	EMPRCD-668	England	1996	8.99
Steeleye-Span	All Around My Hat	CD	BGO	BGOCD158	England	1992	11.99
Steeleye-Span	Back In Line + 3	CD	Park	PRK-CD8	England	1991	11.99
Steeleye-Span	Bedlam Born	CD	Park	PRK-CD55	England	2000	9.99
Steeleye-Span	Below The Salt	CD	BGO	BGOCD324	England	1997	11.99
Steeleye-Span	Brass Monkey - Sound And Rumour	CD	Topic	TSCD501	England	1999	9.99
Steeleye-Span	Brass Monkey: Going & Staying	CD	Topic	TSCD531	England	2001	11.99
Steeleye-Span	Collected	CD	Music Club	MCCD-370	England	1998	7.99
Steeleye-Span	Commoners Crown	CD	BGO	BGOCD315	England	1996	12.99
Steeleye-Span	First Steps	CD	Talking Elephant	TECD-036	England	2001	11.99
Steeleye-Span	Gaudete	CD	Disky	SI-905073	Netherlands	2003	7.99
Steeleye-Span	Gone to Australia (On Tour 1975-1984)	CD	Raven	RVCD-123	Australia	2001	12.99
Steeleye-Span	Hark! The Village Wait	CD	Mooncrest	CRESTCD-003	England	1991	11.99
Steeleye-Span	Heritage (The Best Of - 1)	CD	EMI	7243-5-76301-2-2	Netherlands	2001	9.99
Steeleye-Span	Horkstow Grange	CD	Park	PRK-CD44	England	1998	9.99
Steeleye-Span	In Concert	CD	Park	PRK-CD27	England	1994	17.99
Steeleye-Span	Individually And Collectively	CD	Edsel	EDCD-634	England	2000	11.99
Steeleye-Span	Live At Last !	CD	BGO	BGOCD342	England	1997	12.99
Steeleye-Span	Marrowbones	2CD	Eagle	EDMCD123	England	2002	14.99
Steeleye-Span	Original Masters	2CD	BGO	BGOCD22	England	1997	15.99
Steeleye-Span	Please To See The King + 1	CD	Mooncrest	CRESTCD-005	England	1991	9.99
Steeleye-Span	Portfolio (4 Trks Less Than Lp)	CD	Shanachie	79071/2	U.S.A.	1989	9.99
Steeleye-Span	Present: The Very Best Of	2CD	Park	PRK-CD64	England	2002	21.99
Steeleye-Span	Rocket Cottage	CD	BGO	BGOCD318	England	1996	11.99
Steeleye-Span	Sails Of Silver + 3	CD	Park	PRK-CD40	England	1998	9.99
Steeleye-Span	Spanning The Years	2CD	Chrysalis	F2-32236	U.S.A.	1995	14.99
Steeleye-Span	Spanning The Years	2CD	EMI	7243-8-32236-2-6	England	1995	13.99
Steeleye-Span	Storm Force Ten	CD	BGO	BGOCD337	England	1997	12.99
Steeleye-Span	Tempted And Tried	CD	BGO	BGOCD537	England	2001	11.99
Steeleye-Span	Ten Man Mop	CD	Mooncrest	CRESTCD-009	England	1991	12.99
Steeleye-Span	The Best Of	CD	Chrysalis	CDP-32-1467-2	England	1984	8.99
Steeleye-Span	The Best Of	CD	EMI	7243-5-41355-2-1	England	2002	10.99
Steeleye-Span	The Best Of & The Rest Of	CD	Action Replay	CDAR-1012	England	1989	10.99
Steeleye-Span	The Collection	CD	Castle	CCSCD-292	England	1991	10.99
Steeleye-Span	The Early Years	CD	Connoisseur	VSOP-CD-132	England	1989	8.99
Steeleye-Span	The Hills Of Greenmore	2CD	Recall	SMD-CD-209	England	1998	15.99

S

Artist	Title	Format	Label	Catalog No	Country	Released	Value
Steeleye-Span	The Journey	2CD	Park	PRK-CD52	England	1999	17.99
Steeleye-Span	The King - The Best Of	CD	Mooncrest	CRESTCD-022	England	1996	8.99
Steeleye-Span	The Lark In The Morning: Early Years	2CD	Castle	CMDDD781	England	2003	12.99
Steeleye-Span	Time	CD	Park	PRK-CD34	England	1996	11.99
Steeleye-Span	Tonight's The Night... Live	CD	Shanachie	79080	U.S.A.	1991	8.99
Steeleye-Span/Bob Johnson	King Of Elfland's Daughter (P Knight)	CD	Edsel	EDCD342	Netherlands	1991	14.99
Steeleye-Span/Eliza Carthy	Angels & Cigarettes	CD	Warner Bros.	9362-47698 2	U.S.A.	2000	7.99
Steeleye-Span/Ian Anderson	Now We Are Six (W/David Bowie)	CD	BGO	BGOCD157	England	1992	12.99
Steeleye-Span/M Prior/J Tabor	Silly Sisters	CD	BGO	BGOCD214	England	1994	14.99
Steeleye-Span/M Prior/J Tabor	Silly Sisters - No More Time.. + 2	CD	Topic	TSCD450	England	1995	14.99
Steeleye-Span/M Prior/Kemp	Happy Families (W/ Rick Kemp)	CD	Park	PRK-CD4	England	1990	15.99
Steeleye-Span/M Prior/T Hart	Folk Songs Of Olde England, Vol. 1	CD	Mooncrest	CRESTCD-006	England	1991	12.99
Steeleye-Span/M Prior/T Hart	Folk Songs Of Olde England, Vol. 2	CD	Mooncrest	CRESTCD-010	England	1991	12.99
Steeleye-Span/M Prior/T Hart	Heritage (Folk Songs/Old Eng Comp)	CD	Disky	SI-905320	Netherlands	2003	7.99
Steeleye-Span/M Prior/T Hart	Heydays (F Songs Vol. 1/2/Summer S)	2CD	Castle	CMDDD809	England	2003	19.99
Steeleye-Span/M Prior/T Hart	Summer Solstice	CD	Mooncrest	CRESTCD-023	England	1996	12.99
Steeleye-Span/Maddy Prior	Arthur The King	CD	Park	PRK-CD58	England	2001	15.99
Steeleye-Span/Maddy Prior	Ballads & Candles	CD	Park	PRK-CD54	England	2000	15.99
Steeleye-Span/Maddy Prior	Bib & Tuck (W/ The Girls)	CD	Park	PRK-CD61	England	2002	15.99
Steeleye-Span/Maddy Prior	Carnival Band - Carols And Capers	CD	Park	PRK-CD9	England	1991	14.99
Steeleye-Span/Maddy Prior	Carnival Band - Carols At Christmas	CD	Park	PRK-CD45	England	1999	15.99
Steeleye-Span/Maddy Prior	Carnival Band - Gold F & Myrhh	CD	Park	PRK-CD59	England	2001	15.99
Steeleye-Span/Maddy Prior	Carnival Band - Hang Up Sorrow/Care	CD	Park	PRK-CD31	England	1996	15.99
Steeleye-Span/Maddy Prior	Carnival Band - I Saw Three Ships	CD Single	Park	PRK-CD16	England	1992	11.99
Steeleye-Span/Maddy Prior	Carnival Band - Sing Lustily...	CD	Saydisc	CD-SDL-383	England	1990	14.99
Steeleye-Span/Maddy Prior	Carnival Band - Tapestry Of Carols	CD	Saydisc	CD-SDL-366	England	1986	14.99
Steeleye-Span/Maddy Prior	Changing Winds	CD	BGO	BGOCD213	England	1992	12.99
Steeleye-Span/Maddy Prior	Flesh & Blood	CD	Park	PRK-CD38	England	1997	9.99
Steeleye-Span/Maddy Prior	Lionhearts	CD	Park	PRK-CD66	England	2003	15.99
Steeleye-Span/Maddy Prior	Memento - The Best Of	CD	Park	PRK-CD28	England	1995	9.99
Steeleye-Span/Maddy Prior	Ravenchild	CD	Park	PRK-CD49	England	1999	9.99
Steeleye-Span/Maddy Prior	Woman In The Wings	CD	BGO	BGOCD215	England	1994	12.99
Steeleye-Span/Maddy Prior	Year	CD	Park	PRK-CD20	England	1993	9.99
Steeleye-Span/Martin Carthy	A Collection	CD	Topic	TSCD750	England	1999	8.99
Steeleye-Span/Martin Carthy	Band Of Hope - Rhythms & Reds	CD	Music Club	MFCD-512	England	1994	8.99
Steeleye-Span/Martin Carthy	Because It's There	CD	Topic	TSCD389	England	1995	9.99
Steeleye-Span/Martin Carthy	Both Ears And The Tail (D Swarbrick)	CD	Atrax	ATRAX RECS 002	England	2000	14.99
Steeleye-Span/Martin Carthy	Brass Monkey - Going And Staying	CD	Topic	TSCD531	England	2001	11.99
Steeleye-Span/Martin Carthy	Brass Monkey - Live In Time/Space	CD	Weed	7905	EEC	2001	8.99
Steeleye-Span/Martin Carthy	Brass Monkey - So !	CD	Prestige	CDSGPO568	England	2000	14.99
Steeleye-Span/Martin Carthy	Brass Monkey: Sound & Rumour	CD	Topic	TSCD501	England	1998	12.99
Steeleye-Span/Martin Carthy	But Two Came By (W/D Swarbrick)	CD	Topic	TSCD343	England	1994	15.99
Steeleye-Span/Martin Carthy	Byker Hill (W/Dave Swarbrick)	CD	Topic	TSCD342	England	1994	15.99
Steeleye-Span/Martin Carthy	Crown Of Horn	CD	Topic	TSCD300	England	1995	12.99
Steeleye-Span/Martin Carthy	Landfall	CD	Topic	TSCD345	England	1996	11.99
Steeleye-Span/Martin Carthy	Life And Limb (W/D Swarbrick)	CD	Special Delivery	SPDCD-1030	England	1993	12.99
Steeleye-Span/Martin Carthy	Mrs Ackroyd - Yelp	CD	Mrs Ackroyd	DOG017	England	1997	19.99
Steeleye-Span/Martin Carthy	Mrs Ackroyd Band - Guns/Roses	CD	Mrs Ackroyd	DOG-010	England	1994	19.99
Steeleye-Span/Martin Carthy	Mrs Ackroyd Band /Oranges/Lemmings	CD	Mrs Ackroyd	DOG-007	England	1990	19.99
Steeleye-Span/Martin Carthy	Out Of The Cut	CD	Topic	TSCD426	England	1994	9.99
Steeleye-Span/Martin Carthy	Prince Heathen (W/ D Swarbrick)	CD	Topic	TSCD344	England	1994	10.99
Steeleye-Span/Martin Carthy	Rights Of Passage	CD	Topic	TSCD452	England	1995	9.99
Steeleye-Span/Martin Carthy	Rigs Of The Time: The Best Of	CD	Music Club	MCCD-145	England	1993	8.99
Steeleye-Span/Martin Carthy	Second Album (W/Dave Swarbrick)	CD	Topic	TSCD341	England	1993	15.99
Steeleye-Span/Martin Carthy	Selections (W/Dave Swarbrick)	CD	Edsel	EDCD682	England	2001	15.99
Steeleye-Span/Martin Carthy	Self Titled	CD	Topic	TSCD340	England	1993	9.99
Steeleye-Span/Martin Carthy	Shearwater	CD	Mooncrest	CRESTCD-008	England	1991	12.99
Steeleye-Span/Martin Carthy	Signs Of Life	CD	Topic	TSCD-503	England	1998	9.99

S

Artist	Title	Format	Label	Catalog No	Country	Released	Value
Steeleye-Span/Martin Carthy	Skin And Bone (W/ D Swarbrick)	CD	Topic	TSCD492	England	1992	12.99
Steeleye-Span/Martin Carthy	Sweet Wivelsfield	CD	Topic	TSCD418	England	1996	9.99
Steeleye-Span/Martin Carthy	The Carthy Chronicles Box Set	4CD	Free Reed	FRQCD-60	England	2001	58.99
Steeleye-Span/Martin Carthy	The Collection	CD	Green Linnet	GLCD-1136	U.S.A.	1993	8.99
Steeleye-Span/Martin Carthy	The Complete Brass Monkey	CD	Topic	TSCD467	England	1993	12.99
Steeleye-Span/Martin Carthy	The Definitive Collection	CD	Highpoint	HPO-6001	England	2003	8.99
Steeleye-Span/Martin Carthy	The Kershaw Sessions	CD	Strange Roots	ROOTCD002	England	1988	17.99
Steeleye-Span/Martin Carthy	Wood - Wilson- Carthy (Chris Wood)	CD	R.U.F.	RUFCD-05	England	1998	19.99
Steeleye-Span/Nigel Pegrum	Gnidrolog: Gnosis (W/Rick Kemp)	CD	Snails	GNCD-004-R	England	1999	20.99
Steeleye-Span/Nigel Pegrum	Gnidrolog: In Spite Of Harry's T + 4	CD	Audio Archives	AACD-031	England	1999	17.99
Steeleye-Span/Nigel Pegrum	Gnidrolog: Lady Lake	CD	Disques Rue B	GNCD-002-T	England	1999	19.99
Steeleye-Span/Nigel Pegrum	Gnidrolog: Live 1972 + 1	CD	Audio Archives	AACD-032	England	1999	16.99
Steeleye-Span/Rick Kemp	Backroom Boys/Girls: B Encounters	CD	Ariola	883-510-907	Germany	1997	8.99
Steeleye-Span/Rick Kemp	Escape	CD	Fellside	FECD114	England	1996	18.99
Steeleye-Span/Rick Kemp	Spies	CD	Fellside	FECD133	England	1998	18.99
Steeleye-Span/T/G Woods	In Concert	CD	Windsong	WINCD071	England	1995	15.99
Steeleye-Span/T/G Woods	Tender Hooks	CD	Cooking Vinyl	GUMBO-CD-019	England	2000	14.99
Steeleye-Span/T/G Woods	The Woods Band (Terry/Gay)	CD	Edsel	EDCD-687	England	2001	10.99
Steeleye-Span/Tim Hart	Nursery Rhyme/Drunken Sailor Lps - 2	CD	EMI	CDB-7-92187-2	England	1989	34.99
Steeleye-Span/Tim Hart	Self Titled	CD	BGO	BGOCD305	England	1996	18.99
Steely Dan	A Decade of Steely Dan	CD	MCA	MCAD-11553	U.S.A.	1985	5.99
Steely Dan	A Decade Steely Dan (MCA Gold Cd)	CD	MCA	MCAD-11214	U.S.A.	1985	18.99
Steely Dan	Aja	CD	MCA	088-112-056-2	U.S.A.	1999	7.99
Steely Dan	Aja (MFSL Gold Cd)	CD	Mobile Fidelity	UDCD-515	U.S.A.	1977	34.99
Steely Dan	Alive In America	CD	Giant	9-24634-2	U.S.A.	1995	5.99
Steely Dan	Alive In America Sampler (Promo)	CD	Giant	7706	U.S.A.	1995	19.99
Steely Dan	Best Selection	CD	Echo Industry	VC-3044	Japan	1988	24.99
Steely Dan	Can't Buy A Thrill	CD	MCA	088-111-886-2	U.S.A.	1998	7.99
Steely Dan	Citizen Steely Dan: 1972-1980 Box Set	4CD	MCA	MCAD-4-10981	U.S.A.	1993	29.99
Steely Dan	Countdown To Ecstasy	CD	MCA	088-111-887-2	U.S.A.	1998	7.99
Steely Dan	Everything Must Go (W/Bonus DVD)	2CD	Reprise	48490-2	U.S.A.	2003	12.99
Steely Dan	Gaucho	CD	MCA	088-112-055-2	U.S.A.	2000	8.99
Steely Dan	Gaucho (MFSL Gold Cd)	CD	Mobile Fidelity	UDCD-545	U.S.A.	1980	34.99
Steely Dan	Gold + 4 (Expanded Edition)	CD	MCA	MCAD-10387	U.S.A.	1991	5.99
Steely Dan	Katy Lied	CD	MCA	088-111-916-2	U.S.A.	1999	7.99
Steely Dan	One Hour Sale (Promo)	CD	Reprise	PRO-CD-101112	U.S.A.	2003	85.99
Steely Dan	Pretzel Logic	CD	MCA	088-111-917-2	U.S.A.	1999	7.99
Steely Dan	SFX Radio Concert Feb 15 -18, 2001	2CD	SFX Radio	P1707019611	U.S.A.	2001	74.99
Steely Dan	Showbiz Kids	2CD	MCA	088-112-407-2	U.S.A.	2000	15.99
Steely Dan	Steely Dan Coll. (Android Warehouse)	CD	Dressed To Kill	ONEPAK558	England	2000	11.99
Steely Dan	Steely Dan Promo Remaster Sampler	CD	MCA	CATRO2001-2	U.S.A.	2000	24.99
Steely Dan	The Royal Scam	CD	MCA	088-112-051-2	U.S.A.	1999	7.99
Steely Dan	The Very Best Of Steely Dan	2CD	MCA	MCLDD-19147	England	1985	12.99
Steely Dan	Two Against Nature	CD	Giant	9-24719-2	U.S.A.	2000	5.99
Steely Dan	Words + Music	CD	Giant	PRO-CD-100003	U.S.A.	2000	12.99
Steiner, Fred	Star Trek Vol 1 (Doomsday Machine)	CD	Varese	VSD-47235	U.S.A.	1986	15.99
Steiner, Fred	Star Trek Volume 2	CD	Varese	VSD-47240	U.S.A.	1986	15.99
Steiner, Max	Gone With Wind Deluxe Ed. Box Set	2CD	Rhino	R2-72269	U.S.A.	1996	24.99
Steinman, Jim	Bad For Good	CD	Epic	EK-36531	U.S.A.	1981	21.99
Steinman, Jim/Pandora´s Box	Original Sin (W/Ellen Foley)	CD	Virgin	CDV-2605	England	1989	24.99
Steppenwolf	16 Greatest Hits	CD	MCA	MCAD-37049	U.S.A.	1990	5.99
Steppenwolf	20th Century Masters: The Millennium	CD	MCA	088-111-954-2	U.S.A.	1999	8.99
Steppenwolf	7	CD	MCA	MCAD-1598	U.S.A.	1989	7.99
Steppenwolf	7	CD	Interscope	546-573-2	U.S.A.	2002	10.99
Steppenwolf	All Time Greatest Hits	CD	MCA	088-112-063-2	U.S.A.	1999	9.99
Steppenwolf	At Your Birthday Party	CD	MCA	MCAD-1668	U.S.A.	1989	7.99
Steppenwolf	At Your Birthday Party/7	2CD	BGO	BGOCD336	England	1996	16.99
Steppenwolf	Born To Be Wild: A Retrospective	2CD	MCA	MCAD2-10389	U.S.A.	1991	13.99

S

Artist	Title	Format	Label	Catalog No	Country	Released	Value
Steppenwolf	For Ladies Only	CD	MCA	MCAD-31354	U.S.A.	1990	9.99
Steppenwolf	For Ladies Only	CD	MCA Victor	MVCM-18507	Japan	1997	29.99
Steppenwolf	Hour Of The Wolf	CD	Sony	489439-2	Germany	1998	11.99
Steppenwolf	Live	CD	BGO	BGOCD412	England	1998	14.99
Steppenwolf	Monster	CD	BGO	BGOCD126	England	1991	14.99
Steppenwolf	Monster	CD	MCA	MCAD-31328	U.S.A.	1990	8.99
Steppenwolf	Night Riding	CD	Castle	KN10022	England	1992	24.99
Steppenwolf	Rise And Shine + 2	CD	I.R.S.	IRSD-82046	U.S.A.	1998	8.99
Steppenwolf	Self Titled	CD	MCA	MCAD-31020	U.S.A.	1990	7.99
Steppenwolf	Silver	2CD	Repertoire	REP-4640-WR	Germany	1997	16.99
Steppenwolf	Skullduggery	CD	Sony	489440-2	Germany	1998	11.99
Steppenwolf	Slow Flux	CD	Sony	489441-2	Germany	1998	11.99
Steppenwolf	Steppenwolf (MFSL Gold Cd)	CD	Mobile Fidelity	UDCD-714	U.S.A.	1968	54.99
Steppenwolf	Steppenwolf/The Second	2CD	BGO	BGOCD450	England	1999	16.99
Steppenwolf	The Collection	CD	Spectrum	13010	England	2003	10.99
Steppenwolf	The Second	CD	MCA	MCAD-31021	U.S.A.	1990	8.99
Steppenwolf	The Very Best Of	CD	Music Club	MCCD-263	England	2000	8.99
Steppenwolf	The Very Best Of ...	CD	Music Club	MCCD-263	England	1996	8.99
Steppenwolf	Universal Master Collection	CD	MCA	452-518-2	Holland	2001	10.99
Steppenwolf/Danny Johnson	Over Cloud Nine	CD	Rainman	RMCD115	U.S.A.	2003	14.99
Steppenwolf/John Kay	Feed The Fire	CD	CMC Int.	823909-2	England	1996	10.99
Steppenwolf/John Kay	Feed The Fire	CD	Winter Harvest	WH-3310-2	U.S.A.	1996	7.99
Steppenwolf/John Kay	Greatest Hits And More Live	2CD	Disky	DC-995462	Netherlands	2000	10.99
Steppenwolf/John Kay	Heretics & Privateers	CD	Cannonball	CBD-29119	U.S.A.	2001	11.99
Steppenwolf/John Kay	Live At 25	2CD	Rainman	RMCD118	U.S.A.	2003	16.99
Steppenwolf/John Kay	Lone Steppenwolf	CD	MCA	MCAD-31178	U.S.A.	1990	16.99
Steppenwolf/John Kay	Paradox	CD	EMI	7243-8-23908-2-4	England	1990	10.99
Steppenwolf/John Kay	Rock And Roll Rebels	CD	Qwil	NU-1563	U.S.A.	1987	28.99
Steppenwolf/John Kay	The Lost Heritage Tapes (1976)	CD	Macola	MAC-1201	U.S.A.	1997	13.99
Steppenwolf/John Kay	Wolftracks	CD	Nautilus	NR53	U.S.A.	1982	18.99
Steppenwolf/Sparrow	Collector's Item	CD	Repertoire	REP-4878	Germany	2001	22.99
Steppenwolf/Sparrow	Early Steppenwolf	CD	MCA	MCAD-31356	U.S.A.	1990	24.99
Steppenwolf/Sparrow	The Best Of (Tighten Up Your Wig)	CD	Columbia	CK-53044	U.S.A.	1993	15.99
Stevens, Cat	Buddha/Chocolate Box (Ltd. # Digipk)	CD	A&M	069-490-725-2	U.S.A.	2000	8.99
Stevens, Cat	Cat Stevens Box Set	4CD	A&M	314-585-285-2	U.S.A.	2001	38.99
Stevens, Cat	Catch Bull At Four (Ltd. # Digipack)	CD	A&M	069-490-723-2	U.S.A.	2000	8.99
Stevens, Cat	Early Tapes	CD	Karussell	550-108-2	EEC	1993	7.99
Stevens, Cat	Footsteps In The Dark: Gr Hits Vol. 2	CD	A&M	B0000269-02	U.S.A.	2003	8.99
Stevens, Cat	Foreigner (Ltd. # Digipack)	CD	A&M	069-490-724-2	U.S.A.	2000	8.99
Stevens, Cat	Greatest Hits (Ltd. # Digipack)	CD	A&M	314-542-962-2	U.S.A.	2000	8.99
Stevens, Cat	Matthew & Son	CD	Deram	820-560-2	England	1988	11.99
Stevens, Cat	Mona Bone Jakon (Ltd. # Digipack)	CD	A&M	069-490-672-2	U.S.A.	2000	8.99
Stevens, Cat	New Masters	CD	Deram	820-767-2	England	1989	9.99
Stevens, Cat	Remember	CD	Island	524-608-2	Germany	1999	9.99
Stevens, Cat	Tea For The Tillerman (Ltd. # Digipack)	CD	A&M	069-490-673-2	U.S.A.	2000	8.99
Stevens, Cat	Tea For The Tillerman (MFSL Gold Cd)	CD	Mobile Fidelity	UDCD-519	U.S.A.	1970	39.99
Stevens, Cat	Teaser And The Firecat (MFSL Gold)	CD	Mobile Fidelity	UDCD-649	U.S.A.	1970	23.99
Stevens, Cat	Teaser/The Firecat (Ltd. # Digipack)	CD	A&M	069-490-674-2	U.S.A.	2000	9.99
Stevens, Cat	The Very Best Of	CD	A&M	314-541-387-2	U.S.A.	2000	9.99
Stevens, Cat/Bub Roberts	A Tribute To Cat Stevens	CD	Master Tone	8020	U.S.A.	1997	7.99
Stevens, Cat/Three Box Set	Numbers/Izitso/Bk Earth (MFSL Gold)	3CD	Mobile Fidelity	UDCD-3-661	U.S.A.	1978	69.99
Stevens, Cat/Yusuf Islam	The Life Of Last Prophet (Bonus Cd)	2CD	Mountain Of Light	MOL-700001-CD3	U.S.A.	1995	44.99
Stevens, Corey	Blue Drop Of Rain	CD	Eureka	77053	U.S.A.	1995	7.99
Stevens, Corey	It's Over (Promo)	CD Single	Discovery	PRO-74559	U.S.A.	1996	4.99
Stevens, Corey	My Neighborhood (Promo)	CD Single	Discovery	PRO-74586	U.S.A.	1997	4.99
Stevens, Corey	One More Time (Promo)	CD Single	Discovery	PRO-74575	U.S.A.	1997	4.99
Stevens, Corey	Road To Zen	CD	Eureka	77061	U.S.A.	1997	7.99
Stevens, Ray	I Have Returned	CD	MCA	MCAD-31225	U.S.A.	1985	39.99

S

Artist	Title	Format	Label	Catalog No	Country	Released	Value
Stevens, Shakin'	Green Door (Basically Shaky Lp)	CD	Pickwick	PKD-3078	Australia	1981	158.99
Stevens, Shakin'	Merry Christmas Everyone	CD	Epic	469-260-2	England	1991	59.99
Stevens, Steve	Atomic Playboys	CD	Warner Bros.	9-25920-2	U.S.A.	1989	11.99
Stewart, Al	24 Carrots + 3	CD	Razor & Tie	RE-2008-2	U.S.A.	1980	39.99
Stewart, Al	24 Carrots + 5	CD	EMI	CDP-7-80024-2	U.S.A.	1980	49.99
Stewart, Al	An Acoustic Evening With	CD	EMI	7243-8-36973	Netherlands	1996	11.99
Stewart, Al	Best Al Stewart (Songs From Radio)	CD	Arista	ARCD-8433	U.S.A.	1992	6.99
Stewart, Al	Between The Wars	CD	Mesa	2-92558	U.S.A.	1995	44.99
Stewart, Al	Down In The Cellar	CD	EMI	7243-5-31426-2-9	Holland	2000	10.99
Stewart, Al	Famous Last Words	CD	Rhino	R2-79061	U.S.A.	1993	5.99
Stewart, Al	Last Days Of The Century	CD	Enigma	D2-73316	Canada	1988	8.99
Stewart, Al	Live At The Roxy, Los Angeles 1981	CD	EMI	7243-8-21687-2-0	England	1981	10.99
Stewart, Al	Modern Times + 3	CD	BGO	BGOCD156	England	2000	13.99
Stewart, Al	Orange	CD	Columbia	484441-2	England	1972	8.99
Stewart, Al	Past Present And Future	CD	Rhino	R2-71045	U.S.A.	1992	8.99
Stewart, Al	Rhymes In Rooms	CD	EMI	CDEMC-3613	England	1992	24.99
Stewart, Al	Russians And Americans + 6	CD	EMI	0777-7-89664-2-5	England	1993	49.99
Stewart, Al	Singer Songwriter	CD	EMI	724357640824	Holland	2001	8.99
Stewart, Al	The Best Of: Premium Gold Collection	CD	EMI	7243-8-53631-2-2	Germany	1996	10.99
Stewart, Al	The Very Best Al Stewart Album Ever	CD	EMI	7243-5-39150-2-5	Holland	2002	10.99
Stewart, Al	Time Passages	CD	Arista	ARCD-8342	U.S.A.	1978	5.99
Stewart, Al	Time Passages Live (Promo Lp + 1)	CD	BMG	75517-46956-2	U.S.A.	2002	5.99
Stewart, Al	To Whom It May Concern (1st 3 Lp's)	CD	EMI	7243-8-27709-2-3	England	1993	12.99
Stewart, Al	Year Of The Cat (MFSL Silver Cd)	CD	Mobile Fidelity	MFCD-803	U.S.A.	1976	215.99
Stewart, Al	Year Of The Cat + 3	CD	EMI	7243-5-35456-2-8	England	2001	9.99
Stewart, Dave	Greetings From The Gutter	CD	East West	61735-2	U.S.A.	1994	2.99
Stewart, Dave/Gaskin	As Far As The Dreams Can Go	CD	Line	BRCD-9.00894-0	Germany	1990	24.99
Stewart, Dave/Gaskin	Spin	CD	Line	BRCD-9.01140-0	Germany	1991	11.99
Stewart, Dave/Gaskin	The Big Idea	CD	Line	BRCD-9.00933-0	Germany	1990	11.99
Stewart, Dave/Gaskin	The Singles	CD	Line	BRCD-9.00890-0	Germany	1990	14.99
Stewart, Dave/Gaskin	Up From The Dark	CD	Rykodisc	RCD-10011	U.S.A.	1986	5.99
Stewart, Dave/Gaskin	Waking The Dog	CD Single	Line	LICD-9.01185-E	Germany	1992	19.99
Stewart, John	Blondes	CD	Line	LICD-9.00019-0	Germany	1990	14.99
Stewart, John	Blondes	CD	Line	LICD—9.01375-0	Germany	1990	14.99
Stewart, John	Bombs Away Dream Babies (W/Gold)	CD	Razor & Tie	RE-2034	U.S.A.	1979	69.99
Stewart, John	Lonesome Picker Rides Again	CD	Line	LECD-9.00948-0	Germany	1990	14.99
Stewart, John	Neon Beach	CD	Line	LICD-9.01001-0	Germany	1990	14.99
Stewart, John	Punch The Big Guy	CD	Line	LICD-9.00762-0	Germany	1990	14.99
Stewart, John	Sunstorm	CD	Line	LECD-9.00946-0	Germany	1990	14.99
Stewart, John	Trancas	CD	Line	LICD—9.01353-0	Germany	1984	14.99
Stewart, John	Trancas	CD	Line	LICD-9.00059-0	Germany	1987	14.99
Stewart, Rod	1964-1969	2CD	Alchemy	PILOT-44	England	1999	9.99
Stewart, Rod	A Night On The Town	CD	Warner Bros.	9362-47730-2	U.S.A.	2000	6.99
Stewart, Rod	A Reason To Believe (5 Mercury Lps)	3CD	Mercury	440-063-422-2	U.S.A.	2002	24.99
Stewart, Rod	A Spanner In The Works	CD	Warner Bros.	9362-45867-2	U.S.A.	1995	1.99
Stewart, Rod	Absolutely Live	CD	Warner Bros.	9-23743-2	U.S.A.	1982	6.99
Stewart, Rod	An Old Raincoat Won't...	CD	Repertoire	REP-4148-WP	Germany	1992	11.99
Stewart, Rod	As Time Goes By G A Songbook Vol. 2	CD	J Records	82876-55710-2	U.S.A.	2003	8.99
Stewart, Rod	Atlantic Crossing	CD	Warner Bros.	9362-47729-2	U.S.A.	2000	8.99
Stewart, Rod	Before The Fame	CD	Alchemy	PILOT-180	England	2003	8.99
Stewart, Rod	Blondes Have More Fun	CD	Warner Bros.	9362-47732-2	U.S.A.	2000	6.99
Stewart, Rod	Body Wishes	CD	Warner Bros.	7599-23877-2	U.S.A.	1984	10.99
Stewart, Rod	Camouflage	CD	Warner Bros.	9-25095-2	U.S.A.	1984	6.99
Stewart, Rod	Cigarettes And Alcohol (Promo)	CD Single	Warner Bros.	PRO-CD-9320	U.S.A.	1998	4.99
Stewart, Rod	Every Beat Of My Heart	CD	Warner Bros.	7599-25446 2	Germany	2000	9.99
Stewart, Rod	Every Picture Tells A Story	CD	Mercury	314-558-060-2	U.S.A.	1971	8.99
Stewart, Rod	Every Picture Tells Story (MFSL Gold)	CD	Mobile Fidelity	UDCD-532	U.S.A.	1971	28.99
Stewart, Rod	Faith Of The Heart	CD Single	Universal	UDS-56244	U.S.A.	1998	2.99

S

Artist	Title	Format	Label	Catalog No	Country	Released	Value
Stewart, Rod	Foolish Behaviour	CD	Warner Bros.	7599-27409-2	Germany	2002	24.99
Stewart, Rod	Foot Loose & Fancy Free	CD	Warner Bros.	9362-47731-2	U.S.A.	2000	7.99
Stewart, Rod	Gasoline Alley	CD	Mercury	314-558-059-2	U.S.A.	1970	8.99
Stewart, Rod	Gasoline Alley	CD	Repertoire	REP-4104-WP	Germany	1991	11.99
Stewart, Rod	Human	CD	Atlantic	7567-83411-2	U.S.A.	2000	2.99
Stewart, Rod	It Had to Be You....	CD	J Records	80813-20039-2	U.S.A.	2002	9.99
Stewart, Rod	Never A Dull Moment	CD	Mercury	314-558-061-2	U.S.A.	1972	8.99
Stewart, Rod	Ooh La La	CD Single	Warner Bros.	2-17195	U.S.A.	1998	1.99
Stewart, Rod	Out Of Order	CD	Warner Bros.	9-25684-2	U.S.A.	1988	4.99
Stewart, Rod	Self Titled	CD	Warner Bros.	9-25446-2	U.S.A.	1986	6.99
Stewart, Rod	Sing It Again Rod	CD	Mercury	314-558-062-2	Italy	1973	8.99
Stewart, Rod	Smiler	CD	Mercury	314-558-063-2	U.S.A.	1998	8.99
Stewart, Rod	Storyteller Box Set	4CD	Warner Bros.	9-25987-2	U.S.A.	1989	24.99
Stewart, Rod	The Best Of Rod Stewart	CD	Mercury	314-558-170-2	U.S.A.	1998	7.99
Stewart, Rod	The Best Of, Vol. 2	CD	Mercury	314-558-632-2	U.S.A.	1998	7.99
Stewart, Rod	The Mercury Anthology	2CD	Mercury	314-512-805-2	U.S.A.	1992	13.99
Stewart, Rod	The Rod Stewart Album	CD	Mercury	314-558-058-2	U.S.A.	1969	8.99
Stewart, Rod	Tonight I'm Yours	CD	Warner Bros.	9362-47717-2	U.S.A.	2000	7.99
Stewart, Rod	Unplugged... And Seated (Live)	CD	Warner Bros.	9-45289-2	U.S.A.	1993	7.99
Stewart, Rod	Vagabond Heart	CD	Warner Bros.	9-26300-2	U.S.A.	1991	6.99
Stewart, Rod	Very Best Of, Vol. 1	CD	Warner Bros.	08122-78328-2	U.S.A.	2001	7.99
Stewart, Rod	Very Best Of, Vol. 2	CD	Warner Bros.	08122-73911-2	U.S.A.	2003	7.99
Stewart, Rod	When We Were The New Boys	CD	Warner Bros.	9-46792-2	U.S.A.	1998	5.99
Stewky	Hello It's Crazy Me	CD	Stewky Music	TRBAZAAR.COM	U.S.A.	2000	8.99
Still Life	Self Titled	CD	Repertoire	REP-4198-WP	Germany	2002	14.99
Stills, Chris	100 Year Thing	CD	Atlantic	83022-2	U.S.A.	1998	2.99
Stills, Stephen	2	CD	Atlantic	7206-2	U.S.A.	1971	9.99
Stills, Stephen	Illegal Stills	CD	Columbia	CK-34148	U.S.A.	1976	7.99
Stills, Stephen	Right By You	CD	Atlantic	7-80177-2	U.S.A.	1984	34.99
Stills, Stephen	Stephen Stills	CD	Atlantic	82809-2	U.S.A.	1970	8.99
Stills, Stephen	Stephen Stills Live	CD	Atlantic	18156-2	U.S.A.	1975	8.99
Stills, Stephen	Stills	CD	Columbia	CK-33575	U.S.A.	1975	7.99
Stills, Stephen	Stills Alone	CD	Gold Hill	VR-3323	U.S.A.	1991	14.99
Stills, Stephen	Turnin' Back... (5 From Thoroughfare)	CD	Raven	RVCD-179	Australia	2003	13.99
Stills, Stephen/Manassas	Down The Road	CD	Atlantic	7250-2	U.S.A.	1973	14.99
Stills, Stephen/Manassas	Manassas	CD	Atlantic	82808-2	U.S.A.	1972	8.99
Stiltskin/Ray Wilson	The Mind's Eye (Genesis Singer)	CD	East West	61785-2	U.S.A.	1994	15.99
Sting	After The Rain Has Fallen	CD Single	A&M	497-326-2	England	1999	3.99
Sting	After The Rain Has Fallen	CD Single	A&M	497-325-2	England	1999	3.99
Sting	All This Time	CD-Rom	Starwave Corp.	70904-24	U.S.A.	1995	8.99
Sting	All This Time (3")	CD Single	Polydor	PCDY-10023	Japan	1991	20.99
Sting	At The Movies	CD	Polygram K.K.	POCM-1553	Japan	1997	21.99
Sting	Brand New Day	CD Single	A&M	497-152-2	England	1999	3.99
Sting	Brand New Day - The Remixes	CD	Victor Ent.	POCM-1300	Japan	2000	12.99
Sting	Brand New Day + 2	CD	Polydor K.K.	POCM-1281	Japan	1999	14.99
Sting	Brand New Day + 5	2CD	A&M	490-873-2	Germany	2000	16.99
Sting	Bring On The Night + 1	2CD	A&M	540-994-2	Germany	1998	13.99
Sting	Demolition Man	CD Single	A&M	31454-0162-2	U.S.A.	1993	3.99
Sting	Desert Rose	CD Single	A&M	069497212	Germany	1997	4.99
Sting	Dream Of Blue Turtles (MFSL Gold Cd)	CD	Mobile Fidelity	UDCD-528	U.S.A.	1985	29.99
Sting	Englishman In New York	CD Single	A&M	AMCD431	England	1988	21.99
Sting	Fields Of Gold	CD Single	A&M	580-303-2	England	1993	8.99
Sting	Fields Of Gold	CD Single	A&M	580-301-2	England	1993	8.99
Sting	Fields Of Gold	CD Single	A&M	314-580-259-2	U.S.A.	1993	8.99
Sting	Fields Of Gold (3")	CD Single	Polydor	PODM-1013	Japan	1993	27.99
Sting	Fields Of Gold: The Best Of	CD	A&M	31454-0269-2	U.S.A.	1994	7.99
Sting	If I Ever Lose My Faith In You	CD Single	A&M	580-175-2	England	1993	7.99
Sting	I'm So Happy I Can't Stop Crying	CD Single	A&M	314-581-983-2	U.S.A.	1996	7.99

S

Artist	Title	Format	Label	Catalog No	Country	Released	Value
Sting	Let Your Soul Be The Pilot (DJ)	CD Single	A&M	AMCDP-00164	U.S.A.	1996	14.99
Sting	Let Your Soul Be Your Pilot	CD Single	A&M	314-581-457-2	U.S.A.	1996	5.99
Sting	Let Your Soul Be Your Pilot	CD Single	A&M	314-581-456-2	U.S.A.	1996	4.99
Sting	Mercury Falling + 1	CD	A&M	540-998-2	Germany	1998	8.99
Sting	Nada Como El Sol (Nothing L/Spanish)	CD	A&M	CD-3295	U.S.A.	1988	8.99
Sting	Nothin' Bout Me	CD Single	A&M	580-529-2	England	1994	8.99
Sting	Nothing Like The Sun (MFSL Gold Cd)	CD	Mobile Fidelity	UDCD-546	U.S.A.	1987	28.99
Sting	Nothing Like The Sun + 1	CD	A&M	540-993-2	Germany	1998	8.99
Sting	Nuggets From Fields Of Gold (Promo)	CD	A&M	314-588-357-2	U.S.A.	1994	34.99
Sting	Send Your Love Remixes (Promo)	CD Single	A&M	STINGRX1	England	2003	179.99
Sting	Shape Of My Heart	CD Single	A&M	580-353-2	England	1993	7.99
Sting	Soul Cages (W/Orig. Fold Out Cover)	CD	A&M	75021-6405-2	U.S.A.	1991	19.99
Sting	Soul Cages + 1	CD	A&M	540-996-2	Germany	1998	8.99
Sting	Still Be Love In The World	CD	A&M	069408872	U.S.A.	2001	8.99
Sting	Ten Summoner's Tales Interview (DJ)	CD	A&M	314-548-029-2	U.S.A.	1993	18.99
Sting	Ten Summoners's Tales + 1	CD	A&M	540-997-2	Germany	1993	8.99
Sting	The Dream Of The Blue Turtles + 1	CD	A&M	540-992-2	Germany	1998	8.99
Sting	The Living Sea	CD	A&M	31454-0350-2	U.S.A.	1995	8.99
Sting	The Soul Cages	CD Single	A&M	390-759-2	Germany	1991	11.99
Sting	They Dance Alone	CD Single	A&M	390-325-2	Germany	1988	29.99
Sting	They Dance Alone (Promo)	CD Single	A&M	CD17613	U.S.A.	1987	4.99
Sting	This Cowboy Song	CD Single	A&M	580-957-2	England	1994	6.99
Sting	This Cowboy Song	CD Single	A&M	580-965-2	U.S.A.	1995	5.99
Sting	This Cowboy Song (3")	CD Single	Polydor	POCM-1095	Japan	1994	14.99
Sting	When We Dance	CD Single	A&M	580-859-2	England	1994	3.99
Sting	When We Dance	CD Single	A&M	580-861-2	England	1994	3.99
Sting	When We Dance	CD Single	A&M	580-847-2	Germany	1994	3.99
Sting	You Still Touch Me	CD Single	A&M	314-581-583-2	U.S.A.	1996	2.99
Sting/Eric Clapton	It's Probably Me	CD Single	A&M	AMCD883	England	1992	9.99
Sting/Gil Evans	Strange Fruit	CD Single	A&M	ITM-1499	England	1997	22.99
Sting/Police	The Very Best Of (24 Bit Gold)	CD	Universal	540-428-2	Malaysia	1997	29.99
Sting/Serge Prokofiev	Peter And The Wolf	CD	Polygram	429-396-2	U.S.A.	1990	13.99
Sting/The Chieftans	Mo Ghile Mear	CD Single	RCA	09026-68297-2	Germany	1995	13.99
Sting/The Police	Roxanne 97 - Puff Daddy Remix	CD Single	A&M	314-582-449-2	U.S.A.	1997	5.99
Sting/The Police	The Very Best Of Sting & The Police	CD	A&M	314-540-834-2	U.S.A.	1997	8.99
Sting/The Radioactors	Nuclear Waste	CD	Blueprint	BP181CD	Austria	1995	12.99
Sting/Various Artists	Brimstone & Treacle (O.S.T.)	CD	A&M	CD-3245	U.S.A.	1988	13.99
Sting/Various Artists	The Rainforest Foundation - Carnival!	CD	RCA	74321-44769-2	U.S.A.	1997	19.99
Stingl, Kiev	Teuflisch	CD	Line	DKCD-9.00999-0	Germany	1989	24.99
Stinson, Tommy/Bash & Pop	Friday Night Is Killing Me (Replacements)	CD	Sire	9-45133-2	U.S.A.	1992	10.99
Stoloff, Morris/George Duning	Picnic (O.S.T.)	CD	MCA	MCAD-31357	U.S.A.	1989	153.99
Stone Temple Pilots	Core	CD	Atlantic	82418-2	U.S.A.	1992	5.99
Stone Temple Pilots	Heaven & Hot Rods (Promo)	CD Single	Atlantic	PRCD-9159	U.S.A.	1999	4.99
Stone Temple Pilots	No. 4	CD	Atlantic	83255-2	U.S.A.	1999	5.99
Stone Temple Pilots	Purple	CD	Atlantic	82607-2	U.S.A.	1994	5.99
Stone Temple Pilots	Shangri-La Dee Da	CD	Atlantic	83449-2	U.S.A.	2001	5.99
Stone Temple Pilots	Thank You (Cd/DVD)	2CD	Atlantic	83682-2	U.S.A.	2003	24.99
Stone Temple Pilots	Tiny Music...Songs From the Vatican Gift	CD	Atlantic	82871-2	U.S.A.	1996	5.99
Stone Temple Pilots	Vasoline (Promo/Vaseline Pic)	CD Single	Atlantic	PRCD-5672-2	U.S.A.	1994	4.99
Stone, Carl	Carl Stone 1196	CD	Em:t	EM:T1196	England	1996	59.99
Stone, Sly	High On You	CD	Sony	ESCA-7581	Japan	1995	24.99
Stone, Sly	Precious Stone: In The Studio '63 - '65	CD	ACE	CDCHD539	England	1995	17.99
Stone, Sly	Who In The...: Warner Bros. Recordings	CD	Rhino	RHM2-7756	U.S.A.	2000	20.99
Stone, Sly/The Family Stone	A Whole New Thing + 1	CD	Epic	EK-66424	U.S.A.	1995	8.99
Stone, Sly/The Family Stone	Ain't But The One Way	CD	Warner Bros.	7599-23700-2	England	1996	10.99
Stone, Sly/The Family Stone	Anthology	CD	Epic	EGK-37071	U.S.A.	1990	7.99
Stone, Sly/The Family Stone	Back On The Right Track	CD	Warner Bros.	7599-26858-2	England	1996	10.99
Stone, Sly/The Family Stone	Back On The Right Track	CD	Warner Bros.	WPCP-4890	Japan	1992	24.99

S

Artist	Title	Format	Label	Catalog No	Country	Released	Value
Stone, Sly/The Family Stone	Back On The Right Track	CD	AIM	1072	Australia	2002	10.99
Stone, Sly/The Family Stone	Dance To The Music + 1	CD	Epic	EK-66427	U.S.A.	1995	8.99
Stone, Sly/The Family Stone	Fresh	CD	Epic	EK-32134	U.S.A.	1991	8.99
Stone, Sly/The Family Stone	Fresh (Withdrawn/Alt Takes)	CD	Epic	07464-321342	U.S.A.	1973	8.99
Stone, Sly/The Family Stone	Greatest Hits	CD	Epic	EK-30325	U.S.A.	1970	5.99
Stone, Sly/The Family Stone	Greatest Hits	CD	Epic	EK-30325	U.S.A.	1990	5.99
Stone, Sly/The Family Stone	Heard Missed Me, Well I'm Back	CD	Sony	ESCA-7582	Japan	1995	24.99
Stone, Sly/The Family Stone	Life + 1	CD	Epic	EK-66423	U.S.A.	1995	9.99
Stone, Sly/The Family Stone	Small Talk	CD	Sony	ESCA-5384	Japan	1991	24.99
Stone, Sly/The Family Stone	Stand !	CD	Epic	EK-64422	U.S.A.	1995	8.99
Stone, Sly/The Family Stone	Stand! (Sony Gold Cd)	CD	Columbia	CK-53410	U.S.A.	1969	41.99
Stone, Sly/The Family Stone	The Essential	2CD	Epic	E2K-86867	U.S.A.	2002	13.99
Stone, Sly/The Family Stone	There's A Riot Goin' On	CD	Epic	EK-30986	U.S.A.	1990	8.99
Stoneground	Bad Machines And Limousines	CD	Line	LICD-9.00612-L	Germany	1989	24.99
Stooges/Dark Carnival	Dark Carnival	CD	Zeus	59-CHEVY	Australia	1995	15.99
Stooges/Dark Carnival	Last Great Ride	CD	Sympathy For The	431	U.S.A.	1997	13.99
Stooges/Destroy All Monsters	1974 - 76 (Box Set)	3CD	Ecstatic Peace	47	U.S.A.	1995	59.99
Stooges/Destroy All Monsters	Bored	CD	Cherry Red	94	Germany	1999	11.99
Stooges/Destroy All Monsters	Silver Wedding Anniversary	CD	Sympathy For The	7-9027-6044-2-5	U.S.A.	1996	12.99
Stooges/Destroy All Monsters	Swamp Gas	CD	The End Is Near	TEIN-014	U.S.A.	2001	15.99
Stories	About Us	CD	Buddah	BDKI-2068	Canada	1994	22.99
Stories	Self Titled	CD	Buddah	BDKI-2051	Canada	1992	12.99
Stories	Traveling Underground	CD	One Way	OW-27735	U.S.A.	1993	14.99
Stories	Traveling Underground	CD	Buddah	BDKI-2078	Canada	1994	14.99
Stories	Walk Away From The Left Banke Plus	CD	See For Miles	SEECD-238	England	1989	24.99
Stories/Ian Lloyd	Planet X	CD	MVM	1997-01	U.S.A.	1997	34.99
Stormwind	Stargate + 2	CD	Dreamchaser	SCCD-7	Japan	1998	16.99
Story, Liz	17 Seconds To Anywhere	CD	Windham Hill	01934-11291-2	U.S.A.	1998	6.99
Story, Liz	Escape Of The Circus Ponies	CD	Windham Hill	WD-1099	U.S.A.	1990	7.99
Story, Liz	Liz Story With Joel DiBartolo	CD	Windam Hill	01934-11194-2	U.S.A.	1996	7.99
Story, Liz	My Foolish Heart	CD	Windham Hill	01934-11115-2	U.S.A.	1992	9.99
Story, Liz	Part Of Fortune	CD	RCA	3001-2-N	U.S.A.	1986	5.99
Story, Liz	Solid Colors	CD	Windham Hill	WD-1023	U.S.A.	1982	9.99
Story, Liz	Speechless	CD	RCA	3037-2-N	U.S.A.	1988	6.99
Story, Liz	The Gift	CD	Windham Hill	01934-11151-2	U.S.A.	1994	9.99
Story, Liz	Unaccountable Effect	CD	Windham Hill	WD-1034	U.S.A.	1985	9.99
Story, Liz	Welcome Home - The Best Of	CD	Windham Hill	01934-11619-2	U.S.A.	2001	9.99
Straight Eight	Shuffle 'N' Cut	CD	Line	TACD-9.00782-0	Germany	1989	24.99
Straight Eight	Straight To The Heart	CD	Line	TACD-9.00787-0	Germany	1989	29.99
Strange Advance	The Distance Between	CD	Line	CUCD-9.00983-0	Germany	1990	14.99
Stranger	Hit & Run	CD	Alfa	ALCB-3022	Japan	1994	60.99
Stranglers	10 + 8	CD	Epic	50997-504595-2-2	England	2001	10.99
Stranglers	5 Live 01	2CD	SPV	SPV08571052	Germany	2001	13.99
Stranglers	About Time	CD	When!	WENCD-001	England	1995	8.99
Stranglers	Access All Areas	CD	Stranglers Official	SOF001CD	England	1998	14.99
Stranglers	All Live And All Of The Night + 8	CD	Epic	50997-504594-2-3	England	2001	10.99
Stranglers	All Twelve Inches	CD	Epic	471416-2	Australia	1992	15.99
Stranglers	And Friends Live In Concert	CD	Castle	CMRCD454	England	2002	10.99
Stranglers	Apollo Revisited + 3 (Glasgow/11 23, 81	CD	Alchemy	PILOT-177	England	2003	14.99
Stranglers	At The BBC	CD	EMI	72434-97773-2-3	Holland	1998	12.99
Stranglers	Aural Sculpture + 8	CD	Epic	50997-504592-2-5	England	2001	10.99
Stranglers	Black And White + 6	CD	EMI	7243-5-34691-2-2	Holland	2001	10.99
Stranglers	Clubbed To Death (Mixes)	CD	Zoom Club	ZCRCD99	England	2002	19.99
Stranglers	Coup De Grace	CD	Eagle	EAGCD042	England	1998	8.99
Stranglers	Dreamtime+ 6	CD	Epic	50997-504593-2-4	England	2001	10.99
Stranglers	Feline (No Golden Brown) + 6	CD	Epic	50997-504591-2-6	England	2001	10.99
Stranglers	Friday The Thirteenth	CD	Eagle	EAGCD006	England	1997	8.99
Stranglers	In The Night	CD	Psycho	WOLCD-1030	England	1993	8.99

S

Artist	Title	Format	Label	Catalog No	Country	Released	Value
Stranglers	La Folie + 6	CD	EMI	7243-5-34688-2-8	Holland	2001	10.99
Stranglers	Laid Black	CD	Zenith	502780-600312-2	England	2002	14.99
Stranglers	Lies & Deception	2CD	Snapper	SMCD373	England	2002	11.99
Stranglers	Live At The Apollo	CD	Zenith	502780-600411-2	England	2003	14.99
Stranglers	Live Death/Night/Blood (Hope/Anchor)	CD	Castle	CMRCD455	England	2002	10.99
Stranglers	Live In London	CD	Rialto	RMCD-220	U.S.A.	1997	7.99
Stranglers	Live 'N Sleazy	2CD	Music Club	MCCD533	U.S.A.	2003	12.99
Stranglers	Live X-Cert + 7	CD	EMI	7243-5-34687-2-9	Holland	2001	10.99
Stranglers	Night Tracks	CD	Strange Fruit	SFNTCD020	England	1993	10.99
Stranglers	No More Heroes + 3	CD	EMI	7243-5-34407-2-5	England	2001	10.99
Stranglers	Norfolk Coast	CD	Liberty	72435-96951-2-9	England	2004	12.99
Stranglers	Peaches: The Very Best Of	CD	EMI	72435-40202-2-3	England	2002	10.99
Stranglers	Rattus Norvegicus + 4	CD	EMI	7243-5-34406-2-6	Holland	2001	10.99
Stranglers	Saturday Night, Sunday Morning (Hugh's	CD	Essential	ESMCD194	England	1993	29.99
Stranglers	Strangled From Birth And Beyond	CD	Stranglers Official	SOF002CD	England	1998	14.99
Stranglers	Stranglers Official Fan Club 1998	CD	Stranglers Official	SOF003CD	England	1998	14.99
Stranglers	Sweet Smell Of Success: Best Epic Yea	CD	Epic	50997-509826-2-4	England	2003	10.99
Stranglers	The Collection 1977-1982	CD	EMI	7-46066-2	England	1982	8.99
Stranglers	The Early Years 74-75-76	CD	Newspeak	SPEACK-CD-101	England	1994	10.99
Stranglers	The Gospel According To... + 3	CD	EMI	7243-5-34690-2-3	Holland	2001	10.99
Stranglers	The Hit Men	2CD	EMI	7243-8-55536-2-2	England	1997	16.99
Stranglers	The Men In Black + 3	CD	EMI	0777-7-90876-2-4	Holland	2000	10.99
Stranglers	The Old Testament Box Set	4CD	EMI	0777-7999242-3	France	1992	79.99
Stranglers	The Rarities	CD	EMI	72435-41079-2-4	England	2002	10.99
Stranglers	The Raven + 4	CD	EMI	7243-5-34689-2-7	Holland	2001	10.99
Stranglers	The Sessions	CD	Essential	ESSCD283	England	1995	8.99
Stranglers	The UA Singles '77 - '79	10 CD	EMI	72438-89172-2-3	England	2001	44.99
Stranglers	Written In Red	CD	When!	WENCD-009	England	1997	8.99
Stratos, Demetrio	Demetrio Stratos Boxset	5CD	Akarma	AK-1037-CD	Italy	2002	54.99
Stravinsky, Igor	Petruschka/Blaseroktett/Ragtime	CD	Line	CACD-9.00774-P	Germany	1990	12.99
Strawberry Alarm Clock	Anthology	CD	MCA	MCAD-22015	U.S.A.	1990	10.99
Strawberry Alarm Clock	Good Morning Starshine + 7	CD	MCA Victor	MVCE-22010	Japan	1997	29.99
Strawberry Alarm Clock	Good Morning Starshine/World In A ..	CD	Fat Chance	CRCD-1302	Germany	2004	19.99
Strawberry Alarm Clock	Incense & Peppermints	CD	One Way	MCAD-22083	U.S.A.	1993	10.99
Strawberry Alarm Clock	Incense And Peppermints + 1	CD	MCA Victor	MVCE-22007	Japan	1997	29.99
Strawberry Alarm Clock	Strawberries Mean Love	CD	Big Beat	CDWIKD-56	England	1992	12.99
Strawberry Alarm Clock	Wake Up.... It's Tomorrow + 2	CD	MCA Victor	MVCE-22008	Japan	1997	29.99
Strawberry Alarm Clock	World In A Sea Shell	CD	MCA Victor	MVCE-22009	Japan	1997	29.99
Strawbs	20th Century Masters: The Millennium	CD	A&M	6069-493-157-2-6	U.S.A.	2003	8.99
Strawbs	A Choice Selection Of	CD	A&M	CDMID-173	England	1992	8.99
Strawbs	Baroque & Roll	CD	Witchwood	WRC-CD-2004	England	2001	9.99
Strawbs	Blue Angel	CD	Witchwood	WMCD-2008	England	2003	8.99
Strawbs	Bursting At The Seams + 3	CD	A&M	540-936-2	Germany	1998	10.99
Strawbs	Concert Classics	CD	Renaissance	RRCC00706	U.S.A.	1999	8.99
Strawbs	Deadlines	CD	One Way	OW-34499	U.S.A.	1978	8.99
Strawbs	Deep Cuts/Burning For You	2CD	Witchwood	WCDCD-027	England	1996	24.99
Strawbs	Dragonfly	CD	Si Wan	SRMC-0083	Korea	1999	12.99
Strawbs	From The Witchwood + 1	CD	A&M	540-939-2	Germany	1998	10.99
Strawbs	Ghosts + 1	CD	A&M	540-937-2	Germany	1998	10.99
Strawbs	Grave New World + 2	CD	A&M	540-934-2	Germany	1998	10.99
Strawbs	Greatest Hits Live!	CD	Road Goes On	RGF-CD-015	England	1993	17.99
Strawbs	Halcyon Days (UK Version)	2CD	A&M	540-662-2	England	1997	20.99
Strawbs	Heartbreak Hill	CD	Road Goes On	RGF-024-CD	England	1996	8.99
Strawbs	Hero And Heroine + 2	CD	A&M	540-935-2	England	1998	10.99
Strawbs	Just A Collection Of Antiques..+ 3	CD	A&M	540-938-2	Germany	1998	10.99
Strawbs	Preserves Uncanned	2CD	Road Goes On	RGF-DCD003	England	2002	17.99
Strawbs	Ringing Down The Years/Don't Say...	2CD	Witchwood	WCDCD-039	England	1998	24.99
Strawbs	Self Titled	CD	Si Wan	SRMC-0088	Korea	2000	12.99

S

Artist	Title	Format	Label	Catalog No	Country	Released	Value
Strawbs	Strawberry Music Sampler No. 1	CD	Witchwood	WC-CD2002	England	2002	27.99
Strawbs	Strawbs In Concert	CD	Windsong	WINCD069	England	1995	15.99
Strawbs	Tears And Pain - An Introduction To	CD	Universal	493-369-2	England	2002	9.99
Strawbs	The Collection	CD	Spectrum	544-706-2	England	2002	8.99
Strawbs	The Complete	CD	Witchwood	WC-CD2001	England	2000	10.99
Strawbs	Very Best Of: Halcyon Days	2CD	A&M	31454-0951-2	U.S.A.	1998	20.99
Strawbs/Chas Cronk	Mystic Mountain Music	CD	Witchwood	MM-CD1	England	2002	10.99
Strawbs/Dave Cousins	Brian Willoughby - Old School Songs	CD	Witchwood	WMCD-2014	England	2003	14.99
Strawbs/Dave Cousins	Brian Willoughby - The Bridge	CD	Road Goes On	RGF-CD-020	England	1994	19.99
Strawbs/Dave Cousins	Two Weeks Last Summer	CD	Witchwood	SDRCD-010	England	2003	14.99
Strawbs/Dave Lambert	Fire - The Magic Shoemaker	CD	Castle	CMRCD-620	England	2002	12.99
Stray	Move It	CD	Line	TACD-9.00638-0	Germany	1988	13.99
Stray	Mudanzas	CD	Line	TACD-9.00635-0	Germany	1988	19.99
Stray	Saturday Morning Pictures	CD	Line	TACD-9.00632-0	Germany	1988	10.99
Stray	Stray	CD	Line	TACD-9.00626-0	Germany	1988	19.99
Stray	Suicide	CD	Line	TACD-9.00629-0	Germany	1988	19.99
Stray Cats	Blast Off	CD	EMI	7-91401-2	U.S.A.	1989	9.99
Stray Cats	Built For Speed	CD	EMI	7-46103-2	U.S.A.	1982	21.99
Stray Cats	Built For Speed	Mini Lp	BMG Victor	BVCM-37462	Japan	2004	29.99
Stray Cats	Choo Choo Hot Fish	CD	Jrs	35812-2	U.S.A.	1992	5.99
Stray Cats	Feline Frisky	2CD	Snapper	SMDCD-320	England	2001	12.99
Stray Cats	Gonna Ball	CD	Arista	400719-254019-8	Netherlands	1992	10.99
Stray Cats	Greatest Hits + 3	CD	Capitol	72435-21980-2-3	U.S.A.	2000	8.99
Stray Cats	Lonesome Tears	CD	Akarma	AK-230	Italy	2003	11.99
Stray Cats	Rant 'N' Rave With The	CD	Arista	400719-255677-9	Netherlands	1992	10.99
Stray Cats	Rock Therapy	CD	Toshiba-EMI	TOCP-53065	Japan	1986	20.99
Stray Cats	Runaway Boys	2CD	Snapper	SMD-CD-182	England	1997	12.99
Stray Cats	Runaway Boys: Retrospective '81 - '92	CD	EMI	553728	U.S.A.	1996	8.99
Stray Cats	Self Titled	CD	Arista	400719-253295-7	Netherlands	1990	10.99
Stray Cats	Something Else (Live)	CD	Receiver	RRCD184	England	1995	12.99
Stray Cats	Tear It Up (Live)	CD	Receiver	RRCD176	England	1997	12.99
Street, Andy	Music Inspried By Lord Of The Rings	CD	BCI Eclipse LLC	40126-2	Canada	2001	6.99
Streetband/Paul Young	Dilemma	CD	Line	TACD-9.00636-0	Germany	1988	24.99
Streetband/Paul Young	London	CD	Line	TACD-9.00630-0	Germany	1988	24.99
Streetband/Paul Young	London/Dilemma	2CD	Line	LICD-9.21216-S	Germany	1992	34.99
Strehli, Angela/Band	Soul Shake	CD	Line	ANCD-9.00451-0	Germany	1988	14.99
Streisand, Barbra	A Christmas Album	CD	Columbia	CK-9557	U.S.A.	1990	7.99
Streisand, Barbra	A Happening In Central Park	CD	Columbia	CK-9710	U.S.A.	1990	7.99
Streisand, Barbra	A Love Like Ours	CD	Columbia	CK-69601	U.S.A.	1999	6.99
Streisand, Barbra	A Star Is Born (W/Kris Kristofferson)	CD	Columbia	CK-86119	U.S.A.	2002	8.99
Streisand, Barbra	Album	CD	Columbia	7464-57374-2	U.S.A.	1993	8.99
Streisand, Barbra	And Other Musical Instruments	CD	Columbia	CK-32655	U.S.A.	1990	9.99
Streisand, Barbra	Back To Broadway	CD	Columbia	CK-44189	U.S.A.	1993	6.99
Streisand, Barbra	Barbra Joan Streisand	CD	Columbia	CK-30792	U.S.A.	1990	7.99
Streisand, Barbra	Butterfly	CD	Columbia	CK-33005	U.S.A.	1990	8.99
Streisand, Barbra	Christmas Memories	CD	Columbia	CK-85920	U.S.A.	2001	6.99
Streisand, Barbra	Classical Barbra	CD	Columbia	CK-33452	U.S.A.	1990	8.99
Streisand, Barbra	Color Me Barbra	CD	Columbia	CK-9278	U.S.A.	1990	7.99
Streisand, Barbra	Duets	CD	Columbia	CK-86126	U.S.A.	2002	9.99
Streisand, Barbra	Emotion	CD	Columbia	CK-39480	U.S.A.	1990	6.99
Streisand, Barbra	Greatest Hits	CD	Columbia	CK-9968	U.S.A.	1990	6.99
Streisand, Barbra	Greatest Hits, Vol. 2	CD	Columbia	CK-35679	U.S.A.	1993	6.99
Streisand, Barbra	Greatest Hits... And More	CD	Columbia	CK-45369	U.S.A.	1992	6.99
Streisand, Barbra	Guilty (W/Barry Gibb)	CD	Columbia	CK-36750	U.S.A.	1993	6.99
Streisand, Barbra	Higher Ground	CD	Columbia	CK-66181	U.S.A.	1997	6.99
Streisand, Barbra	Highlights From Just The Records	CD	Columbia	CK-52849	U.S.A.	1992	9.99
Streisand, Barbra	Je M'appelle Barbra	CD	Columbia	CK-9347	U.S.A.	1990	7.99
Streisand, Barbra	Just For The Record Box Set	4CD	Columbia	C4K-89077	U.S.A.	2003	19.99

S

Artist	Title	Format	Label	Catalog No	Country	Released	Value
Streisand, Barbra	Lazy Afternoon	CD	Columbia	CK-33815	U.S.A.	1990	7.99
Streisand, Barbra	Live Concert At The Forum	CD	Columbia	CK-31760	U.S.A.	1990	7.99
Streisand, Barbra	Memories	CD	Columbia	CK-37678	U.S.A.	1993	8.99
Streisand, Barbra	My Name Is Barbra	CD	Columbia	CK-9136	U.S.A.	1990	8.99
Streisand, Barbra	My Name Is Barbra 2	CD	Columbia	CK-9209	U.S.A.	1990	8.99
Streisand, Barbra	Nuts (O.S.T.)	CD	Columbia	CXK-40876	U.S.A.	1987	74.99
Streisand, Barbra	One Voice	CD	Columbia	CK-40788	U.S.A.	1993	6.99
Streisand, Barbra	People	CD	Columbia	CK-86103	U.S.A.	2002	8.99
Streisand, Barbra	Pins And Needles (Orig. Cast/Sings 6)	CD	Columbia	7464-57380-2	U.S.A.	1993	9.99
Streisand, Barbra	Simply Streisand	CD	Columbia	CK-9482	U.S.A.	1990	7.99
Streisand, Barbra	Sings Harold Arlen	CD	Columbia	7464-52722-2	U.S.A.	1993	9.99
Streisand, Barbra	Songbird	CD	Columbia	CK-35375	U.S.A.	1990	6.99
Streisand, Barbra	Stoney End	CD	Columbia	CK-30378	U.S.A.	1990	7.99
Streisand, Barbra	Streisand Superman	CD	Columbia	CK-34830	U.S.A.	1990	6.99
Streisand, Barbra	The Broadway Album	CD	Columbia	CK-85159	U.S.A.	2002	6.99
Streisand, Barbra	The Concert	2CD	Columbia	C2K-66109	U.S.A.	1994	15.99
Streisand, Barbra	The Concert (Highlights)	CD	Columbia	CK-67100	U.S.A.	1995	8.99
Streisand, Barbra	The Essential	2CD	Columbia	C2K-86123	U.S.A.	2002	14.99
Streisand, Barbra	The Mirror has Two Faces (O.S.T.)	CD	Columbia	CK-67887	U.S.A.	1996	6.99
Streisand, Barbra	The Movie Album	CD	Columbia	CK-89018	U.S.A.	2003	7.99
Streisand, Barbra	The Movie Album + 3 (W/Bonus DVD)	2CD	Columbia	CK-90742	U.S.A.	2003	24.99
Streisand, Barbra	The Second	CD	Columbia	7464-57378-2	U.S.A.	1993	8.99
Streisand, Barbra	The Way We Were	CD	Columbia	CK-85153	U.S.A.	2002	8.99
Streisand, Barbra	Third Album	CD	Columbia	7464-57379-2	U.S.A.	1993	8.99
Streisand, Barbra	Till I Loved You	CD	Columbia	CK-40880	U.S.A.	1993	7.99
Streisand, Barbra	Timeless - Live In Concert (Bonus Cd)	3CD	Columbia	C2K-61635	U.S.A.	2000	24.99
Streisand, Barbra	Wet	CD	Columbia	CK-36258	U.S.A.	1990	9.99
Streisand, Barbra	What About Today?	CD	Columbia	7464-47014-2	U.S.A.	1993	8.99
Streisand, Barbra	Yentl	CD	Columbia	CK-39152	U.S.A.	1990	9.99
Streisand, Barbra/B. Adams	I Finally Found Someone	CD Single	Columbia	38K-78480	U.S.A.	1996	5.99
Stretch	Elastique	CD	Repertoire	REP-4522-WY	Germany	2002	11.99
Stretch	Life Blood	CD	Repertoire	REP-4087-WZ	Germany	2002	11.99
Stretch	Story Of Elmer Gantry Box (36 Tracks)	2CD	Repertoire	REP-4602-WY	Germany	2002	17.99
Stretch	You Can't Beat Your Brain...	CD	Repertoire	REP-4200-WY	Germany	2002	11.99
Strife	Back To Thunder	CD	Line	LICD-9.00713-0	Germany	1988	24.99
String Driven Thing	Discotomy (SPM-WWR-CD-0038)	CD	World Wide	WWR-CD-0038	England	1992	22.99
String Driven Thing	Machine That...(SPM-WWR-CD-0026)	CD	World Wide	WWR-CD-0026	England	1991	18.99
String Driven Thing	S. T. (Charisma/SPM-WWR-CD-0027)	CD	World Wide	WWR-CD-0027	England	1992	20.99
String Driven Thing	Studio '72: Live Swiss '73/London '95	CD	Ozit	OZCD00022	England	2002	22.99
String Driven Thing	Suicide: Live In Berlin	CD	Ozit	OZCD00018	England	1997	22.99
String Driven Thing	The Early Years (Concord Lp + Demos)	CD	Green Tree	TRC-GTR-CD007	England	1993	22.99
String Driven Thing	The Machine That Cried	CD	Repertoire	REP-4207-WP	Germany	1991	20.99
String Driven Thing	The Machine That Cried + 3	CD	Ozit	OZCD-00021	England	1996	22.99
Strong, Barrett	Love Is You	CD	Line	TLCD-9.00369-0	Germany	1987	24.99
Strouse, Charles	Bye Bye Birdie (O.S.T.)	CD	RCA	1081-2-R	U.S.A.	1988	7.99
Strouse, Charles	Bye Bye Birdie (Orig. Broadway Cast)	CD	Columbia	CK-2025	U.S.A.	1988	8.99
Strummer, Joe	Earthquake Weather	CD	Epic	EK-45372	U.S.A.	1989	59.99
Strummer, Joe	Walker (O.S.T.)	CD	Virgin	7-90686-2	U.S.A.	1987	149.99
Strummer, Joe/Mescalero	Global A Go Go	CD	Hellcat	80440-2	U.S.A.	2001	10.99
Strummer, Joe/Mescalero	Rock Art & The X-Ray Style	CD	Hellcat	80424-2	U.S.A.	1999	10.99
Strummer, Joe/Mescalero	Steetcore + 4	CD	Epitaph	EICP-284	Japan	2003	29.99
Strummer, Joe/Mescalero	Streetcore	CD	Hellcat	80454-2	U.S.A.	2003	10.99
Stryper	7: Best Of Stryper	CD	Hollywood	HR-162391-2	U.S.A.	2003	8.99
Stryper	Against The Law	CD	Hollywood	HR-61187-2	U.S.A.	1990	11.99
Stryper	Can't Stop The Rock	CD	Hollywood	HR-61106-2	U.S.A.	1991	10.99
Stryper	In God We Trust	CD	Hollywood	HR-61186-2	U.S.A.	1988	11.99
Stryper	Soldiers Under Command	CD	Hollywood	HR-61184-2	U.S.A.	1985	14.99
Stryper	The Yellow And Black Attack	CD	Hollywood	HR-61183-2	U.S.A.	1984	17.99

S

Artist	Title	Format	Label	Catalog No	Country	Released	Value
Stryper	To Hell With The Devil	CD	Sony	32DP-579	Japan	1986	83.99
Stryper	To Hell With The Devil	CD	Hollywood	HR-61185-2	U.S.A.	1986	17.99
Stryper/King James	Self Titled (Robert Sweet/T Gaines)	CD	Star Song	SSD-1006-2	U.S.A.	1994	12.99
Stryper/King James	The Fall (No Sweet/Gaines)	CD	Viva	VIVAD160	Sweden	1997	16.99
Stryper/Michael Sweet	Real	CD	Benson	84418-4175-2	U.S.A.	1995	9.99
Stryper/Michael Sweet	Self Titled	CD	Benson	84418-2231-2	U.S.A.	1994	8.99
Stryper/Michael Sweet	Truth	CD	Restless	7-73706-2	U.S.A.	2000	14.99
Stryper/Michael Sweet	Truth + 2	CD	Restless	KICP-762	Japan	2001	19.99
Stryper/Michael Sweet	Truth Demos	CD	Michael Sweet	MSPCD77	U.S.A.	1998	24.99
Stryper/Michael Sweet	Unstryped: The Post-Stryper Sessions	CD	Perris	PER-07722	Canada	2000	12.99
Stryper/Robert Sweet	Love Trash	CD	World Gone Mad	WGM-777	U.S.A.	2000	8.99
Stryper/Sin Dizzy	He's Not Dead (Fox, Gaines)	CD	Perris	PER-0001-2	Canada	2000	18.99
STS 8 Mission	Blind + 2	CD	Teichiku	TECX-25678	Japan	1994	27.99
STS 8 Mission	Slippin' Into Fiction	CD	Teichiku	TECX-28168	Japan	1992	27.99
STS 8 Mission	The Mystery Of Time	CD	Teichiku	TECP-25491	Japan	1990	34.99
Stuermer, Daryl/Phil Collins	Another Side Of Genesis	CD	Urban Island	UIM0002	U.S.A.	2000	11.99
Stuermer, Daryl/Phil Collins	Live And Learn	CD	Urban Island	UIM0001	U.S.A.	1998	11.99
Stuermer, Daryl/Phil Collins	Steppin' Out	CD	GRP	GRP-9573	U.S.A.	1988	8.99
Stuermer, Daryl/Phil Collins	Waiting In The Wings	CD	Urban Island	56437-196222	U.S.A.	2001	11.99
Style Council	20th Century Masters: The Millennium	CD	Universal	314-589-097-2	U.S.A.	2003	8.99
Style Council	Best Of The (32 Bit Remaster)	CD	Universal	UICY-1076	Japan	2000	29.99
Style Council	Cafe Bleu	CD	Polydor	7314-557915-2-5	England	2000	9.99
Style Council	Cafe Blue - Style Council Cafe Best	CD	Universal	UICY-1123	Japan	2000	29.99
Style Council	Collection	CD	Polydor	7314-529483-2-8	England	1996	9.99
Style Council	Complete Adv. Box (W/Unreleased Lp)	5CD	Polydor	557-789-2	England	1998	59.99
Style Council	Confessions Of A Pop Group	CD	Polydor	7314-557916-2-4	England	2000	9.99
Style Council	Greatest Hits	CD	Polydor	7314-557900-2-3	England	2000	9.99
Style Council	Here's Some That Got Away	CD	Polydor	314-519-372-2	U.S.A.	1994	9.99
Style Council	Home And Abroad	CD	Polydor	829-143-2	U.S.A.	1993	16.99
Style Council	In Concert	CD	Polydor	7314-533143-2-0	England	1998	13.99
Style Council	Introducing	CD	Polydor	815-277-2	U.S.A.	1993	8.99
Style Council	Modernism: New Decade (Unrel. Lp)	Mini Lp	Universal	UICY-9099	Japan	2000	29.99
Style Council	On Film	CD	Polydor	06024-9813821-2	England	2003	9.99
Style Council	Our Favourite Shop	CD	Polydor	7314-559050-2-1	England	2000	9.99
Style Council	The Cost Of Loving	CD	Polydor	7314-557917-2-3	England	2000	9.99
Style Council	The Singular Adventures Of	CD	Polydor	837-896-2	U.S.A.	1989	9.99
Style Council	The Sound Of	CD	Polydor	04400-65643-2-6	England	2003	9.99
Style Council	The Ultimate Collection	3CD	Universal	06024-9813991-2	England	2004	24.99
Style Council/Dee C. Lee	Cajun Moon (3" Cd)	CD Single	Pony Canyon	PCDY-144	Japan	1997	14.99
Style Council/Dee C. Lee	Gift Compilation (W/Talbot & White)	CD	Pony Canyon	PCCR-00258	Japan	1996	44.99
Style Council/Dee C. Lee	Shrine	CD	Columbia	CD-CBS-26915	England	1986	44.99
Style Council/Dee C. Lee	Smiles	CD	Pony Canyon	PCCY-01223	Japan	1998	29.99
Style Council/Dee C. Lee	Thing Will Be Sweeter	CD	Pony Canyon	PCCY-00647	Japan	1995	34.99
Stylistics	A Special Style	CD	Nippon Columbia	33C38-7981	Japan	1986	93.99
Styx	21st Century Live	CD	CMC Int.	06076-86347-2	U.S.A.	2003	8.99
Styx	At the River's Edge: Live St. Louis	CD	CMC Int.	06076-86318-2	U.S.A.	2002	8.99
Styx	Best Of	CD	RCA	3116-2-R	U.S.A.	1977	5.99
Styx	Boat On A River	CD	A&M	396-959-2	Germany	1987	12.99
Styx	Brave New World	CD	CMC Int.	06076-86275-2	U.S.A.	1999	3.99
Styx	Caught In The Act: Live	CD	A&M	75021-6514-2	U.S.A.	1984	11.99
Styx	Classics Volume 15	CD	A&M	D-114822	U.S.A.	1987	5.99
Styx	Cornerstone	CD	A&M	CD-3239	U.S.A.	1979	8.99
Styx	Crystal Ball	CD	A&M	CD-3218	U.S.A.	1976	7.99
Styx	Cyclorama	CD	CMC Int.	06076-86337-2	U.S.A.	2003	8.99
Atyx	Edge Of The Century	CD	A&M	75021-5327-2	U.S.A.	1990	5.99
Styx	Equinox	CD	A&M	CD-3217	U.S.A.	1975	8.99
Styx	Extended Version	CD	CMC Int.	75517-45613-2	U.S.A.	2000	5.99
Styx	Greatest Hits Vol. 1	CD	A&M	CD-0387	U.S.A.	1995	9.99

S

Artist	Title	Format	Label	Catalog No	Country	Released	Value
Styx	Greatest Hits Vol. 2	CD	A&M	31454-0550-2	U.S.A.	1996	9.99
Styx	Kilroy Was Here	CD	A&M	CD-3734	U.S.A.	1983	8.99
Styx	Man Of Miracles	CD	BMG	BVCM-35028	Japan	1999	24.99
Styx	Man Of Miracles (Original RCA)	CD	RCA	3115-2-R	U.S.A.	1989	20.99
Styx	Paradise Theater	CD	A&M	CD-3240	U.S.A.	1980	5.99
Styx	Pieces Of Eight	CD	A&M	CD-3224	U.S.A.	1978	8.99
Styx	Return To Paradise	2CD	CMC Int.	06076-86212-2	U.S.A.	1997	11.99
Styx	Serpent Is Rising (Original RCA)	CD	RCA	0287-2R	U.S.A.	1989	44.99
Styx	Serpent Is Rising/Man Of Miracles	CD	One Way	OW-35144	U.S.A.	1999	24.99
Styx	Styx I	CD	One Way	OW-35130	U.S.A.	1972	11.99
Styx	Styx II	CD	RCA	3111-2-R	U.S.A.	1989	14.99
Styx	Styxworld Live 2001	CD	CMC Int.	06076-86311-2	U.S.A.	2001	5.99
Styx	The Best Of Styx (1973-1974)	CD	BMG	BVCM-31021	Japan	1999	24.99
Styx	The Grand Illusion	CD	A&M	CD-3223	U.S.A.	1977	5.99
Styx	The Serpent Is Rising	CD	BMG	74321-68410-2	Japan	1999	24.99
Styx	Yes I Can (Promo)	CD Single	CMC Int.	CMCDJ-87343-2	U.S.A.	2003	16.99
Styx/Reo Speedwagon	Arch Allies - Live At Riverport	CD	CMC Int.	06076-86299-2	U.S.A.	2000	14.99
Styx/Tommy Shaw	7 Deadly Zens	CD	CMC Int.	06076-86254-2	U.S.A.	1998	10.99
Styx/Tommy Shaw	7 Deadly Zens +1	CD	Victor Ent.	VICP-60407	Japan	1998	19.99
Styx/Tommy Shaw	Ambition	CD	Atlantic	81798-2	U.S.A.	1987	48.99
Styx/Tommy Shaw	Ambition	CD	Warner Bros.	32XD-859	Japan	1987	61.99
Styx/Tommy Shaw	Girls With Guns	CD	Spitfire	SPT-15119-2	U.S.A.	2000	59.99
Styx/Tommy Shaw	What If	CD	A&M	395097-2	Germany	1985	61.99
Sufaris, The	Fun City USA/Wipe Out	CD	Repertoire	REP-4118-WZ	Germany	1990	24.99
Sugar	Believe What You're Saying	CD	Rykodisc	RCD5-1039	U.S.A.	1994	4.99
Sugar	File Under Easy.. (CD W/File Case)	CD	Rykodisc	RCD-90300	U.S.A.	1994	34.99
Sugar	If I Can't Change Your Mind	CD Single	Rykodisc	RCD5-1031	U.S.A.	1992	4.99
Sugar	If I Can't Change Your Mind	CD	Creation	CRESCD-149L	England	1993	6.99
Sugar	If I Can't Change Your Mind	CD	Creation	CRESCD-149	England	1993	6.99
Sugar	Your Favorite Thing	CD Single	Rykodisc	RCD5-1038	U.S.A.	1994	4.99
Sugar	Your Favorite Thing (Promo)	CD Single	Rykodisc	VRCD-0300	U.S.A.	1994	9.99
Sugar-Blue	Blue Blazes	CD	Line	RRCD-9.01301-0	Germany	1994	8.99
Sugarcubes/Bjork	Here Today, Tomorrow Next Week!	CD	Elektra	60860-2	U.S.A.	1989	7.99
Sugarcubes/Bjork	It's-It	CD	Elektra	61426-2	U.S.A.	1992	8.99
Sugarcubes/Bjork	Life's Too Good	CD	Elektra	60801-2	U.S.A.	1988	7.99
Sugarcubes/Bjork	Stick Around for Joy	CD	Elektra	61123-2	U.S.A.	1992	7.99
Sugarcubes/Bjork	The Great Crossover Potential	CD	Elektra	62102-2	U.S.A.	1998	9.99
Sugarloaf	Don't Call Us, We'll Call You	CD	Repertoire	REP-4272-WP	Germany	2002	21.99
Sugarloaf	Self Titled/Sp. Earth (Minus A Few)	CD	Collectables	COL-5871	U.S.A.	1998	10.99
Sugarloaf	The Best Of	CD	Curb	D2-77597	U.S.A.	1992	7.99
Suggs/Madness	The Lone Ranger	CD	Warner Bros.	0630-12478-2	England	1995	8.99
Suggs/Madness	The Three Pyramids Club	CD	Warner Bros.	3984-23815-2	England	1998	8.99
Sullivan, Big Jim	Big Jim's Back	CD	Line	RTCD-9.01152-0	Germany	1992	22.99
Sullivan, Rocky	Internal Affairs	CD	Line	RBCD-9.00718-0	Germany	1989	12.99
Sulton, Kasim/Utopia	Quid Pro Quo	CD	Orchard	802365	U.S.A.	2002	10.99
Sulton, Kasim/Utopia	The Basement Tapes	CD	Slick Music	SM-003	U.S.A.	1998	10.99
Summer, Donna	Cats Without Claws (Cross Cd)	CD	Geffen	24040-2	U.S.A.	1984	37.99
Summer, Donna	State Of Independence	CD Single	Polygram	852-863-2	England	1996	5.99
Summers, Andy	A Windham Hill Retrospective	CD	Windham Hill	01934-11316-2	U.S.A.	1998	9.99
Summers, Andy	Charming Snakes	CD	Private Music	2069-2-P	U.S.A.	1990	29.99
Summers, Andy	Mysterious Barricades	CD	Private Music	2039-2-P	U.S.A.	1988	15.99
Summers, Andy	The Golden Wire	CD	Private Music	2048-2-P	U.S.A.	1989	12.99
Summers, Andy	The Last Dance Of Mr. X	CD	RCA	09026-68937-2	U.S.A.	1997	10.99
Summers, Andy	World Gone Strange	CD	Private Music	01005-82088-2	U.S.A.	1991	10.99
Summers, Andy	XYZ	CD	MCA	MCAD-42007	U.S.A.	1987	14.99
Summers, Andy/J. Etheridge	Invisible Threads	CD	Rhino	R2-79066	U.S.A.	1993	9.99
Summers, Andy/Robert Fripp	Bewitched	CD	A&M	CD-5011	U.S.A.	1984	14.99
Summers, Andy/Robert Fripp	Bewitched	Mini Lp	Universal	UICY-9241	Japan	2002	29.99

S

Artist	Title	Format	Label	Catalog No	Country	Released	Value
Summers, Andy/Robert Fripp	I Advance Masked	Mini Lp	Universal	UICY-9240	Japan	2002	29.99
Summers, Andy/Robert Fripp	I Advance Masked	CD	A&M	75021-4913-2	U.S.A.	1982	14.99
Summers, Andy/V. Biglione	Strings Of Desire	CD	RCA	09026-63326-2	U.S.A.	1998	14.99
Sunday All Over the World	Kneeling At The Shrine (Robert Fripp)	CD	Caroline	EG-2101-2	U.S.A.	1991	10.99
Super Mario/Kondo	Super Mario 64 (O.S.T.)	CD	Pony Canyon	PCCG-00357	Japan	1996	39.99
Super Mario/Kondo/Noriki	Super Mario World (O.S.T.)	2CD	Warner Bros.	WPCL-233~4	Japan	1991	154.99
Super Mario/Yoko Shimomura	Super Mario RPG	CD	NTT PUB	PSCN-5047~8	Japan	1995	181.99
Supertramp	Breakfast In America	CD	A&M	6069-493-349-2-5	U.S.A.	2002	8.99
Supertramp	Breakfast In America (MFSL Gold Cd)	CD	Mobile Fidelity	UDCD-534	U.S.A.	1979	54.99
Supertramp	Brother Where You Bound	CD	A&M	6069-493-354-2-7	U.S.A.	2002	8.99
Supertramp	Classics Volume 9	CD	A&M	75021-2507-2-7	U.S.A.	1990	5.99
Supertramp	Crime Of The Century	CD	A&M	6069-493-346-2-8	U.S.A.	2002	8.99
Supertramp	Crime Of The Century (MFSL Gold Cd)	CD	Mobile Fidelity	UDCD-505	U.S.A.	1974	34.99
Supertramp	Crisis? What Crisis	CD	A&M	6069-493-347-2-7	U.S.A.	2002	8.99
Supertramp	Even In The Quietest Moments	CD	A&M	6069-493-348-2-6	U.S.A.	2002	8.99
Supertramp	Famous Last Words	CD	A&M	6069-493-353-2-8	U.S.A.	2002	8.99
Supertramp	Free As A Bird	CD	A&M	6069-493-355-2-6	U.S.A.	2002	8.99
Supertramp	Indelibly Stamped	CD	Polygram	0828-393-129-2-9	Germany	1999	8.99
Supertramp	Is Everybody Listening ?	CD	Alchemy	PILOT-76	England	2001	11.99
Supertramp	It Was The Best Of Times	CD	EMI	7243-4-99389-2-2	Germany	1999	10.99
Supertramp	KBFH 5/10 To 5/16/99	CD	DIR Network	C1C6NO1XB	U.S.A.	1999	35.99
Supertramp	Paris	2CD	A&M	6069-493-350-2-1	U.S.A.	2002	16.99
Supertramp	Self Titled	CD	Polygram	0828-393-149-2-3	Germany	1999	8.99
Supertramp	Slow Motion	CD	Phantom	7243-5-38525-2-8	England	2003	5.99
Supertramp	Some Things Never Change	CD	Oxygen	6324-5-90002-2-7	U.S.A.	1997	5.99
Supertramp	The Very Best Of Supertramp Vol 1	CD	A&M	828-397-091-2	U.S.A.	1994	8.99
Supertramp	The Very Best Of Supertramp Vol. 2	CD	A&M	7314-540-047-2-5	Australia	1992	8.99
Supreme Beings Of Leisure	Divine Operating System	2CD	Palm Pictures	PALMCD-2087-2	U.S.A.	2002	19.99
Survivor	Caught In The Game	CD	Pony Canyon	PCCY-01369	Japan	1983	29.99
Survivor	Caught In The Game	CD	Volcano	61422-32188-2	U.S.A.	2001	10.99
Survivor	Empires	CD	Bareknuckle	AVCB-66078	Japan	1999	24.99
Survivor	Empires	CD	USG	USG-1032-2	U.S.A.	1999	13.99
Survivor	Eye Of The Tiger	CD	Volcano	61422-32011-2	U.S.A.	1999	10.99
Survivor	Greatest Hits	CD	Scotti Bros.	5217-2-SB	U.S.A.	1990	10.99
Survivor	Greatest Hits + 1	CD	Volcano	ZJCI-14040	Japan	2003	24.99
Survivor	Preminition	CD	Pony Canyon	D32Y0100	Japan	1985	29.99
Survivor	Preminition	CD	Volcano	61422-32187-2	U.S.A.	2001	10.99
Survivor	Prime Cuts: Classic Tracks	CD	Polygram	554-624-2	England	1999	8.99
Survivor	Self Titled	CD	Volcano	61422-32186-2	U.S.A.	2001	10.99
Survivor	Self Titled	CD	Pony Canyon	D32Y0099	Japan	1987	29.99
Survivor	Too Hot To Sleep	CD	Volcano	61422-32189-2	U.S.A.	2001	10.99
Survivor	Vital Signs	CD	Scotti Bros.	5215-2-SB	U.S.A.	1984	8.99
Survivor	When Seconds Count	CD	Scotti Bros.	ZK-40457	U.S.A.	1986	8.99
Swan, Billy	Billy Swan's Best	CD	Sony	AK-57913	U.S.A.	1993	8.99
Swan, Billy	Choice Cuts	CD	Sony	07989-28518-2	U.S.A.	1998	8.99
Swan, Billy	Choice Cuts Plus (6 Extra Tracks)	CD	Monument	497465-2	England	2000	10.99
Swan, Billy	Golden Classics	CD	Collectables	COL-5828	U.S.A.	1997	8.99
Swan, Billy	I Can Help/Rock 'N' Roll Moon	CD	See For Miles	SEE-CD-470	England	1997	14.99
Swan, Billy	Like Elvis Used To Do	CD	Koch	KOC-CD-8115	U.S.A.	2000	8.99
Swan, Billy	Self Titled/Four	CD	See For Miles	SEE-CD-471	England	1997	14.99
Swan, Billy	The Best Of	CD	Epic	EK-65218	U.S.A.	1998	8.99
Swan, Billy	The Best Of	CD	Sony	491449-2	England	2003	10.99
Swarbrick, Dave	50th Birthday Concert	CD	Cooking Vinyl	MASH-CD-001	England	1996	18.99
Swarbrick, Dave	Dave Swarbrick: Swarb! Box Set	4CD	Free Reed	FRQCD-45	England	2003	57.99
Swarbrick, Dave	English Fiddler	CD	Naxos World	76045-2	England	2003	9.99
Swarbrick, Dave	Flittin'	CD	Line	TACD-9.00789-0	Germany	1989	16.99
Swarbrick, Dave	Lift The Lid And Listen	CD	Storyville	1025702	Denmark	2003	12.99
Swarbrick, Dave	Live At Jackson Lane	CD	Gadfly	503	U.S.A.	1996	18.99

S

Artist	Title	Format	Label	Catalog No	Country	Released	Value
Swarbrick, Dave	Rags, Reels & Airs (W/M Carthy)	CD	Topic	TSCD517	England	1999	12.99
Swarbrick, Dave	Smiddyburn/Flittin'	CD	Essential	ESMCD-434	England	1996	11.99
Swarbrick, Dave	Smiddyburn/Flittin'	CD	Raven	RVCD-54	Australia	1996	11.99
Swarbrick, Dave	Swarbrick/Swarbrick 2	CD	Essential	ESMCD-355	England	1996	11.99
Swarbrick, Dave	The Ceilidh	CD	Storyville	1025703	Denmark	2003	12.99
Swarbrick, Dave/Simon Nicol	Close To The White Bear	CD	Woodworm	WRCD-028	England	1998	19.99
Sweet	2 Originals: Live At The Marquee/A	2CD	SPV	310-71270	Germany	2002	19.99
Sweet	A Cut Above The Rest	CD	Toshiba-EMI	TOCP-7520	Japan	1979	89.99
Sweet	Action	CD	BMG	74321-36448-2	Germany	1996	11.99
Sweet	Anthology	CD	Toshiba-EMI	TOCP-3422	Japan	1994	49.99
Sweet	Archive	CD	Rialto	RMCD-215	U.S.A.	1997	8.99
Sweet	Ballroom Blitz	CD Single	Capitol	7243-8-58609-2-8	U.S.A.	1997	5.99
Sweet	Ballroom Blitz 1973	CD	Dojo	DOJO89	England	1994	21.99
Sweet	Ballroom Blitz Live	CD	Castle	PIESD128	England	1999	8.99
Sweet	Ballroom Hitz: The Very Best Of Sweet	CD	Polygram	535-001-2	England	1996	11.99
Sweet	Best 37 Glamrock Songs	2CD	RCA	74321-62268-2	Holland	1998	21.99
Sweet	Biggest Hits	CD	RCA	74321-10630 2	Germany	1992	8.99
Sweet	Blockbuster Alternate Takes	CD	Cleopatra	CLP-0474-2	Holland	1999	8.99
Sweet	Chronology	CD	Delicious	DEL113	England	2002	19.99
Sweet	Cut Above The Rest	CD	Repertoire	REP-4202-WP	Germany	1992	11.99
Sweet	Desolation Boulevard	CD	Capitol	6324-2-74847-2	U.S.A.	2001	8.99
Sweet	Desolation Boulevard	CD	Capitol	CDP-7-48452-2	U.S.A.	1988	6.99
Sweet	Desolation Boulevard	CD	Castle	CLACD-170	France	1989	6.99
Sweet	Desolation Boulevard	CD	Capitol	C2-48452	Canada	1998	8.99
Sweet	Electric Landlady	CD	Receiver	RRCD-241	England	1997	8.99
Sweet	First Recordings 1968 - 1971	CD	Repertoire	REP-4140-WZ	Germany	2002	11.99
Sweet	Funny How Sweet Coco Can Be	CD	Ariola	290-856	Germany	1991	24.99
Sweet	Give Us A Wink + 2	CD	Capitol	74321-66011-2	England	1999	11.99
Sweet	Give Us A Wink + 4	CD	Repertoire	RR-4084-WZ	Germany	1990	11.99
Sweet	Glam Hit Box	3CD	Big Eye	BIG-4112-2	U.S.A.	2002	14.99
Sweet	Greatest Hits (Live 1973)	CD	Digimode Ent.	RM-1531	Denmark	1996	10.99
Sweet	Greatest Hits Remixed	CD	Cleopatra	CLP-0488-2	England	1999	8.99
Sweet	Hard Centres - The Rock Years	CD	Zebra	CDMZEB-II	England	1987	8.99
Sweet	Hit Singles - The Complete A & B Sides	2CD	Repertoire	REP-4591-WL	Germany	1995	11.99
Sweet	I Gradi Del Rock (Funny How...)	CD	RCA	74321-13526-2	Italy	1997	24.99
Sweet	Identity Crisis	CD	Repertoire	REP-4204-WP	Germany	1992	11.99
Sweet	Land Of Hope And Glory	CD	Receiver	RRCD-171	England	1993	8.99
Sweet	Les Genius Du Rock (Live For Today)	CD	Edition Atlas	RK-CD-497	France	1994	10.99
Sweet	Let's Go	CD	Empirio	EMPRCD-717	EU	1997	8.99
Sweet	Level Headed + 4	CD	Repertoire	REP-4234-WP	Germany	1991	11.99
Sweet	Live	CD	Master Tone	AB-3036	England	1995	8.99
Sweet	Live At The Marquee	CD	SPV	310-71270	Germany	2002	8.99
Sweet	Live At The Rainbow 1973	CD	Capitol	74321-69859-2	England	2000	14.99
Sweet	Live Breakdown	CD	Receiver	RRCD-189	England	1995	8.99
Sweet	Live For Today (Rare Versions/E D) + 1	CD	Trend	156.388	Austria	1993	10.99
Sweet	Live For Today (Rare Versions/Early D)	CD	Receiver	RRCD-175	England	1993	9.99
Sweet	Live For Today (Rare Versions/Early D)	CD	Teichiku	TECW-20412	Japan	1996	24.99
Sweet	Live In Japan (Rock & Roll Disgrace)	CD	Receiver	RRCD-169	England	1993	8.99
Sweet	Millennium Collection	2CD	Digimode Ent.	20.4037-MI	Germany	1999	14.99
Sweet	Off The Record + 2	CD	Capitol	74321-66010-2	England	1999	11.99
Sweet	Off The Record + 3	CD	Repertoire	RR-4085-WZ	Germany	1990	11.99
Sweet	Platinum Rare	CD	Repertoire	REP-4487-WP	Germany	1995	11.99
Sweet	Private Collection	CD	Receiver	RRCD-198	England	1995	8.99
Sweet	Rare Collection	CD	Teichiku	TECW-21886	Japan	1996	24.99
Sweet	Solid Gold Sweet	2CD	Recall	SMD-CD-208	England	1998	11.99
Sweet	Solid Gold: 15 Alternative Mixes	CD	Receiver	RRCD-214	England	1996	8.99
Sweet	Stairway To The Stars: Live And Rare	2CD	Castle	CMDDD521	England	2002	11.99
Sweet	Starke Zeiten	CD	Ariola	258-867	Germany	1988	24.99

S

Artist	Title	Format	Label	Catalog No	Country	Released	Value
Sweet	Sweet Fanny Adams + 2	CD	EMI	74321-66013-2	England	1999	9.99
Sweet	Sweet Originals	2CD	RCA	74321-62268-2	Germany	1998	24.99
Sweet	Sweetlife	CD	Delicious	DEL007	England	2002	19.99
Sweet	Teenage Rampage	2CD	Essential	ESACD800	England	1999	12.99
Sweet	The Best Of	CD	Capitol	C2-80324	Canada	1993	8.99
Sweet	The Collection	CD	Castle	CCSCD230	France	1989	7.99
Sweet	The Great Sweet Live	CD	Goldies	GLD-63192	Portugal	1995	7.99
Sweet	The Sweet (Bell LP) + 5	CD	Razor & Tie	82189	U.S.A.	1999	10.99
Sweet	The Sweet Collection	CD	BMG	74321-29275-2	Germany	1995	8.99
Sweet	The Sweet Featuring Andy Scott	CD	Maverick	1-1091	EEC	2000	8.99
Sweet	The Sweet Live!	CD	Starburst	CD-STB-8791	Australia	1993	8.99
Sweet	The Very Best Of	CD	CMC Int.	6006-6	Denmark	1996	8.99
Sweet	Waters Edge	CD	Repertoire	REP-4203-WP	Germany	1992	11.99
Sweet /Andy Scott	A	CD	AIM	AIM-1048	Australia	1993	10.99
Sweet /Andy Scott	A	CD	Jimco	JICK-89119	Japan	1993	24.99
Sweet /Andy Scott	A	CD	SPV	084-88832	Germany	1992	10.99
Sweet /Andy Scott	Alive And Giggin'	CD	Pseudonym	CDP-1027-DD	Holland	1995	27.99
Sweet /Andy Scott	Am I Ever Gonna...	CD Single	SPV	055-88963	Germany	1992	24.99
Sweet /Andy Scott	Glitz, Blitz And Hitz	CD	CNR Music	2002685	Holland	1996	18.99
Sweet /Andy Scott	Glitz, Blitz And Hitz	CD	Out Of Time	CD-EC5	England	1996	18.99
Sweet /Andy Scott	Hanover Sessions	4CD	Pseudonym	CDP-1028-DD	Holland	2003	59.99
Sweet /Andy Scott	Stand Up	CD Single	SPV	055-88843	Germany	1992	24.99
Sweet /Andy Scott	The Answer	CD	Pseudonym	CDP-1029-DD	Holland	1995	27.99
Sweet /Andy Scott	Thirty Years: The Solo Singles	CD	Repertoire	REP-4225-WY	Germany	1993	12.99
Sweet /Andy Scott	X-Ray Specs	CD Single	SPV	055-88583	Germany	1991	24.99
Sweet /Brian Connelly	Gold	CD	Gold	GOLD157	Holland	1997	7.99
Sweet /Brian Connelly	Greatest Hits	CD	Okido	OKR-11-8314-2	Holland	1997	8.99
Sweet /Brian Connelly	Greatest Hits	CD	Eclipse	64835-2	U.S.A.	1996	7.99
Sweet /Brian Connelly	Greatest Hits (Let's Go)	CD	Starlight	3885612	England	1998	8.99
Sweet /Brian Connelly	Take Away The Music	CD	Malibu	BFC-CD01	England	2002	14.99
Sweet /Brian Connelly	The Best Of Sweet (Success LP)	CD	Starling	CD043	Poland	1995	10.99
Sweet /Brian Connelly	The Sweet	CD	Legend	WZ-90053	EEC	1993	8.99
Sweet Thursday/Jon Mark	Sweet Thursday (Nicky Hopkins)	CD	Sony	A33504	U.S.A.	1998	9.99
Sweet, Matthew	100% Fun	CD	Zoo Ent.	72445-11081-2	U.S.A.	1995	7.99
Sweet, Matthew	Altered Beast	CD	Zoo Ent.	72445-11050-2	U.S.A.	1993	7.99
Sweet, Matthew	Blue Sky On Mars	CD	Zoo Ent.	61422-31130-2	U.S.A.	1997	7.99
Sweet, Matthew	Blue Sky On Mars Bonus Best Buy Cd	CD	Best Buy	61422-37223-2	U.S.A.	1997	11.99
Sweet, Matthew	Earth	CD	A&M	CD-5233	U.S.A.	1989	10.99
Sweet, Matthew	Girlfriend	CD Single	Zoo Ent.	72445-14042-2	U.S.A.	1991	4.99
Sweet, Matthew	Girlfriend	CD	Zoo Ent.	72445-11015-2	U.S.A.	1991	8.99
Sweet, Matthew	Goodfriend (DJ/Girlfriend Demos)	CD	Zoo Ent.	ZP17098-2	U.S.A.	1992	47.99
Sweet, Matthew	In Reverse + 4	CD	Zomba	9210012	Australia	1999	14.99
Sweet, Matthew	Inside	CD	Columbia	CK-40417	U.S.A.	1986	8.99
Sweet, Matthew	I've Been Waiting (Promo Anime Label)	CD Single	Zoo Ent.	ZP17070-2	U.S.A.	1992	11.99
Sweet, Matthew	Let Me Be The One (Promo)	CD Single	A&M	314-588-325-2	U.S.A.	1994	11.99
Sweet, Matthew	Live From The Pit (5,26 - 6,2,1997)	CD	G.S.Network	COPWR01XB	U.S.A.	1997	39.99
Sweet, Matthew	Self Titled (Japan Only)	CD	Avex	CTCR-16050	Japan	2003	24.99
Sweet, Matthew	Son Of Altered Beast	CD	Zoo Ent.	72445-11078-2	U.S.A.	1994	5.99
Sweet, Matthew	The Ugly Truth	CD Single	Zoo Ent.	72445-14096-2	U.S.A.	1993	7.99
Sweet, Matthew	Time Capsule	CD Single	Zoo Ent.	72445-14111-2	U.S.A.	1993	7.99
Sweet, Matthew	To Understand - Early Recordings Of	CD	Hip-O	314-556-222-2	U.S.A.	2002	8.99
Sweet, Matthew	Vertigo (Promo)	CD Single	A&M	CD-17706	U.S.A.	1989	11.99
Sweet, Matthew	We're The Same (Promo)	CD Single	Zoo Ent.	ZP17161-2	U.S.A.	1995	5.99
Sweet, Matthew	Where You Get Love (Promo)	CD Single	Zoo Ent.	ZP37217-2	U.S.A.	1997	6.99
Sweet, Rachel	B.A.B.Y The Best Of Rachel Sweet	CD	Metro	METRCD048	England	2001	9.99
Sweet, Rachel	Fool Around + 3 (Repertoire)	CD	Repertoire	REP-4218-WY	Germany	1991	16.99
Sweet, Rachel	Fool Around + 3 (Stiff)	CD	Stiff	STIFFCD-04	England	1993	16.99
Sweet, Rachel	Fool Around + 7: The Best Of	CD	Rhino	R2-70313	U.S.A.	1992	11.99

S

Artist	Title	Format	Label	Catalog No	Country	Released	Value
Sweet, Rachel	Protect The Innocent	CD	Stiff	STIFFCD-10	England	1993	104.99
Sweet, Rachel/Barbie	The Look (Rachel Sweet Sings)	CD	Rhino	R2-70797	U.S.A.	1990	44.99
Sweet, Rachel/Mark Shaiman	Stuart Saves His Family (Silver Bells)	CD	Milan	73138-35709-2	U.S.A.	1995	12.99
Sweet, Rachel/Various Artists	Cry-Baby - (O.S.T.) (3 Unrel. R. Sweet)	CD	MCA	MCAD-8038	U.S.A.	1990	11.99
Sweet, Rachel/Various Artists	Oldies But 80's (Voo Doo)	CD	Sony	AK-66396	U.S.A.	1994	11.99
Sweetwater	Cycles: Reprise Collection (Ltd 10,000)	CD	Rhino	RHM2-7702	U.S.A.	2000	24.99
Swim Two Birds	Not Serious	CD	Line	OLCD-9.51116-X	Germany	1991	6.99
Swing Set	The Soul Remains	CD	Line	LICD-9.01329-0	Germany	1996	5.99
Swinging Blue Jeans	25 Greatest Hits	CD	Music For Pleasure	7243-495483-2-9	England	1998	8.99
Swinging Blue Jeans	At Abbey Road	CD	EMI	7243-493327-2-0	England	1998	9.99
Swinging Blue Jeans	Best Of The 60's	CD	Disky	SI-250762	Holland	2000	8.99
Swinging Blue Jeans	Blue Jeans A' Swinging + 11	CD	Toshiba-EMI	TOCP-7549	Japan	1993	27.99
Swinging Blue Jeans	Blue Jeans A' Swinging + 12	CD	EMI	7243-856563-2-3	England	1997	15.99
Swinging Blue Jeans	Live In Cascade Beat-Club	CD	Repertoire	REP-4492-WY	Germany	1994	24.99
Swinging Blue Jeans	Live Shakin'	CD	Prestige	CDPT502	England	1999	11.99
Swinging Blue Jeans	The Best Of (Same As Lp)	CD	Toshiba-EMI	TOCP-6313	Japan	1990	27.99
Swinging Steaks	Southside Of The Sky	CD	Capricorn	9-42020-2	U.S.A.	1993	4.99
Sylvian, David	Alchemy: An Index... Special Edition	CD	Virgin	7243-591308-2-8	England	2003	11.99
Sylvian, David	Approaching Silence (W/Robert Fripp)	CD	Virgin	7243-848177-2-5	England	1999	9.99
Sylvian, David	Blemish	CD	Samadhi	8248774-001-2-7	England	2003	10.99
Sylvian, David	Blemish + 1	CD	Samadhi	PVCP-8775	Japan	2003	34.99
Sylvian, David	Brilliant Trees - Words With Shaman	CD	Caroline	CAROL-1812-2	U.S.A.	1984	7.99
Sylvian, David	Brilliant Trees Special Edition	CD	Virgin	7243-591307-2-9	England	2003	11.99
Sylvian, David	Camphor	CD	Virgin	7243-812197-2-0	England	2002	16.99
Sylvian, David	Camphor + 1	CD	Virgin	VJCP-68424	Japan	2002	34.99
Sylvian, David	Dead Bees On A Cake	CD	Virgin	7243-8-47071-2-5	U.S.A.	1999	9.99
Sylvian, David	Ember Glance Box (W/Book)	CD	Caroline	CAROL-1837-2	U.S.A.	1992	34.99
Sylvian, David	Everything And Nothing + 4 (Bonus Cd)	3CD	Virgin	72438-50195-2-4	England	2000	99.99
Sylvian, David	Flux + Mutability	CD	Virgin	0777-7-86694-2-5	England	1989	9.99
Sylvian, David	Gone To Earth	CD	Virgin	0777-7-86003-2-9	U.S.A.	1986	8.99
Sylvian, David	Gone To Earth + 7	2CD	Virgin	7243-591309-2-7	England	2003	18.99
Sylvian, David	Secrets Of Beehive Special Edition	CD	Virgin	7243-591310-2-3	England	2003	11.99
Sylvian, David	Secrets Of The Beehive	CD	Toshiba-EMI	TOCP-53040	Japan	1999	8.99
Sylvian, David	Songs From Dead Bees.. (Promo)	CD	Virgin	CDVDJ-2876	EU	1999	18.99
Sylvian, David/Holger Czukay	Plight & Preminition	CD	Virgin	CDVE11	England	1988	9.99
Sylvian, David/Ingrid Chavez	I Surrender (Cd # 2)	CD Single	EMI	7243-8-95632-21	EU	1999	7.99
Sylvian, David/R Sakamoto	Forbidden Colours (W/Ryuichi S)	CD Single	Virgin	VJCP-14025	Japan	1983	24.99
Sylvian, David/R Sakamoto	World Citizen (W/Ryuichi Sakamoto)	CD Single	Warner Bros.	WPCL-10043	Japan	2003	22.99
Sylvian, David/Robert Fripp	Damage (2 Track Promo)	CD Single	Virgin	DAMPRO-1	England	1994	11.99
Sylvian, David/Robert Fripp	Damage (Gold Cd With Bonus Single)	2CD	Virgin	7243-8-39905-2-8	Austria	1994	36.99
Sylvian, David/Robert Fripp	Damage 2001 Reissue	CD	Virgin	7243-8-11030-29	England	2001	8.99
Sylvian, David/Robert Fripp	Darshan	CD	Virgin	7243-8-39380(25)	Holland	1993	8.99
Sylvian, David/Robert Fripp	First Day + 1 (W/Photos/Outer Box)	CD	Virgin	CDVX-2712	England	1993	16.99
Sylvian, David/Robert Fripp	God's Monkey (Promo)	CD	Virgin	DPRO-12805	England	1993	99.99
Sylvian, David/Robert Fripp	Jean The Birdman (Cd 1)	CD Single	Virgin	VSCDG-1462	England	1993	14.99
Sylvian, David/Robert Fripp	Jean The Birdman (Cd 2)	CD Single	Virgin	VSCDT-1462	England	1993	14.99
Sylvian, David/Robert Fripp	The First Day	CD	Virgin	0777-7-88208-2-6	U.S.A.	1993	8.99
Sylvian, David/W/Book	Weatherbox (G Earth Instru Cd/Poster)	5CD	Virgin	DSCD1	England	1989	134.99
Syreeta	One To One	CD	Polydor K.K.	POCT-1921	Japan	1977	29.99
Syreeta	Stevie Wonder Presents	CD	Motown	530-401-2	England	1995	50.99
Syreeta	Syreeta	CD	Polydor K.K.	POCT-1920	Japan	1972	34.99
System, The	Pleasure Seekers	CD	East West	AMCY-6098	Japan	1985	45.99

S

Artist	Title	Format	Label	Catalog No	Country	Released	Value

T

Artist	Title	Format	Label	Catalog No	Country	Released	Value
T.Rex	20th Century Boy	CD	Relativity	88561-1147-2	U.S.A.	1992	7.99
T.Rex	20th Century Superstar Box Set	4CD	Universal	493-452-2	England	2002	64.99
T.Rex	25th Ann. Super Sampler (Tower)	CD	Teichiku	M/CD-30402	Japan	1997	134.99
T.Rex	4 Track Promo Sampler	CD	Edsel	MB-PROMO-1	England	1994	19.99
T.Rex	Bolan's Zip Gun + 21 (W/Bonus Cd)	2CD	Edsel	MEDCD-718	England	2002	18.99
T.Rex	Dandy In The Underworld + 5	CD	Polygram	314-534-360-2	U.S.A.	1997	9.99
T.Rex	Dandy In The... + 26 (W/Bonus Cd)	2CD	Edsel	MEDCD-720	England	2002	18.99
T.Rex	Dirtysweet, Vol. 1	CD	Edsel	FELD-1	England	1994	18.99
T.Rex	Dirtysweet, Vol. 2	CD	Edsel	FELD-2	England	1994	18.99
T.Rex	Electric Warrior +8	CD	A&M	493-113-2	EU	2001	7.99
T.Rex	Electric Warrior Sessions	CD	Purple Pyramid	CLP-0024-2	U.S.A.	1997	12.99
T.Rex	Futuristic Dragon + 23 (W/Bonus Cd)	2CD	Edsel	MEDCD-719	U.S.A.	2002	18.99
T.Rex	Great Hits 1972-1977 The A-Sides	CD	Polygram	314-534-361-2	U.S.A.	1997	7.99
T.Rex	Great Hits 1972-1977 The B-Sides	CD	Edsel	EDCD-402	England	1994	7.99
T.Rex	Live At The BBC	CD	Master Tone	8227	U.S.A.	1998	10.99
T.Rex	Maximum T. Rex	CD Single	Imperial	TECI-26	Japan	2002	21.99
T.Rex	Millennium Collection	2CD	Digimode Ent.	20.4026-MI	Germany	1999	17.99
T.Rex	Rabbit Fighter + 2	CD	Edsel	EDCD-403	England	1994	21.99
T.Rex	Self Titled (5th Album)	CD	A&M	A&M-10112	Germany	2002	11.99
T.Rex	Shadowhead	Mini Lp	Teichiku	TECI-24055	Japan	2001	39.99
T.Rex	Solid Gold: The Best Of	CD	Repertoire	REP-4800-WG	Germany	1999	14.99
T.Rex	Special Limited Editon (Silver)	CD	Teichiku	TECW-23559	Japan	1997	44.99
T.Rex	Special Sampler	CD	Teichiku	CD8-12-1	Japan	1989	29.99
T.Rex	Special Sampler (Promo)	CD	Teichiku	CD8-12-1	Japan	1989	59.99
T.Rex	T. Rex (Red Promo Sampler)	CD	Edsel	MARC20-50	England	1997	39.99
T.Rex	Tanx + 30 (W/Bonus Cd)	2CD	Edsel	MEDCD-716	England	2002	18.99
T.Rex	Tanx + 7	CD	Repertoire	REP-4892	Germany	2000	14.99
T.Rex	The Essential Collection Box Set	3CD	Relativity	88561-1063-2	U.S.A.	1991	29.99
T.Rex	The Singles A's & B's	2CD	Repertoire	REP-4993	Germany	2002	19.99
T.Rex	The Slider + 18 (W/Bonus Cd)	2CD	Edsel	MEDCD-715	England	2002	18.99
T.Rex	There Was A Time (Ltd 2000)	CD	Captain Trip	CTCD-346	Japan	1967	15.99
T.Rex	Zinc Alloy And The Hidden... + 5	CD	Polygram	314-534-357-2	U.S.A.	1997	9.99
T.Rex	Zinc Alloy And The.. + 29 (Xtra Cd)	2CD	Edsel	MEDCD-717	England	2002	18.99
T.Rex/Marc Bolan	20th Century Boy: Ultimate Collection	CD	Hip O	314-584-948-2	U.S.A.	2002	8.99
T.Rex/Marc Bolan	Essential Collection	2CD	Universal	493-432-2	England	2002	20.99
T.Rex/Marc Bolan	Marc - Songs/Granada TV Series	CD	Edsel	EDCD-545	England	1998	12.99
T.Rex/S P Took/Shagrat	Lone Star (W/Larry Wallis)	CD	Captain Trip	CTCD-312	Japan	1971	15.99
T.Rex/Tribute	Boogie With/Wizard + 19 (Bonus Cd)	2CD	Teichiku	M/CD-71003	Japan	1997	99.99
Tabor, June	A Cut Above	CD	Topic	TSCD410	England	1995	10.99
Tabor, June	A Quiet Eye	CD	Topic	TSCD510	England	2000	10.99
Tabor, June	Abyssinians	CD	Topic	TSCD432	England	1994	10.99
Tabor, June	Against The Streams	CD	Cooking Vinyl	COOKCD-071	England	1995	11.99
Tabor, June	Airs And Graces	CD	Topic	TSCD298	England	1995	10.99
Tabor, June	Aleyn	CD	Topic	TSCD490	England	1996	10.99
Tabor, June	Angel Tiger	CD	Cooking Vinyl	COOKCD-049	England	1997	11.99
Tabor, June	Anthology	CD	Music Club	MCCD-126	England	1993	10.99
Tabor, June	Aqaba	CD	Topic	TSCD449	England	1994	10.99
Tabor, June	Ashes And Diamonds	CD	Topic	TSCD360	England	1995	10.99
Tabor, June	Definitive Collection	CD	Highpoint	HPO-6003	England	2003	9.99
Tabor, June	Echo Of Hooves	CD	Topic	TSCD-543	England	2003	10.99
Tabor, June	On Air	CD	Strange Fruit	SFRSCD074	England	1998	14.99
Tabor, June	Rosa Mundi	CD	Topic	TSCD532	England	2001	10.99

Artist	Title	Format	Label	Catalog No	Country	Released	Value
Tabor, June	Some Other Time	CD	Hannibal	HNCD-1347	U.S.A.	1991	11.99
Tabor, June/Danny Thompson	Singing The Storm (S. Stevenson)	CD	Cooking Vinyl	COOKCD-102	England	1996	14.99
Tabor, June/Martin Simpson	A Cut Above	CD	Green Linnet	GLCD-3072	U.S.A.	1989	14.99
Tabor, June/Oyster Band	Freedom And Rain	CD	Cooking Vinyl	COOKCD-031	England	1990	13.99
Tabor, June/Oyster Band	Freedom And Rain	CD	Rykodisc	RCD-10194	U.S.A.	1990	13.99
Tabor, June/Oyster Band	Freedom Rain Tour '91 DJ Sampler	CD	Rykodisc	RCD-PRO-9012	U.S.A.	1991	24.99
Tai Phong	Last Flight	CD	Warner Bros.	WPCR-1718	Japan	1997	23.99
Tai Phong	Self Titled + 2	CD	Warner Bros.	WPCR-1716	Japan	1997	23.99
Tai Phong	Windows + 3	CD	Warner Bros.	WPCR-1717	Japan	1997	23.99
Talisman	Cats And Dogs	CD	Frontiers	FR-CD-146	Italy	2003	18.99
Talisman	Genesis	CD	Dino	DINCD-20	Sweden	1993	17.99
Talisman	Humanimal	CD	Polydor	523-329-2	England	1994	15.99
Talisman	Life	CD	Polydor	529-363-2	England	1995	15.99
Talisman	Self Titled	CD	Airplay	ARCD-5005	Sweden	1990	17.99
Talisman	Truth	CD	Frontiers	FR-CD-516	Italy	1999	19.99
Talking Heads	12 X 12 (Original Remixes)	CD	EMI	7243-5-21856-2-7	England	1999	14.99
Talking Heads	Blind	CD Single	Sire	CDEM-68	England	1988	4.99
Talking Heads	Blind	CD Single	Sire	PRO-CD-3022	U.S.A.	1988	4.99
Talking Heads	Fame (Naked/True St/Little Cr) Box	3CD	EMI	7243-8-31566-2-7	EEC	1994	49.99
Talking Heads	Fear Of Music	CD	Sire	6076-2	U.S.A.	1979	7.99
Talking Heads	Little Creatures	CD	Sire	9-25305-2	U.S.A.	1985	6.99
Talking Heads	More Songs About Buildings and Food	CD	Sire	6058-2	U.S.A.	1978	7.99
Talking Heads	Naked	CD	Sire	9-25654-2	U.S.A.	1988	5.99
Talking Heads	Once In A Lifetime Box Set (3 Cd/DVD)	4CD	Rhino	R2-73934	U.S.A.	2003	54.99
Talking Heads	Once In A Lifetime Liquid People Remix	CD	Warner Bros.	9362424072	Australia	2001	6.99
Talking Heads	Radio Head	CD Single	Sire	CDEM-1	England	1987	4.99
Talking Heads	Remain In Light	CD	Sire	6095-2	U.S.A.	1980	7.99
Talking Heads	Remixed	CD	EMI	7243-5-32569-2-0	England	1999	9.99
Talking Heads	Sand In The Vaseline	2CD	Sire	9-26760-2	U.S.A.	1992	14.99
Talking Heads	Speaking in Tongues	CD	Sire	9-23883-2	U.S.A.	1983	7.99
Talking Heads	Stop Making Sense + 7 (Spec New Ed)	CD	Sire	9-47489-2	U.S.A.	2002	8.99
Talking Heads	Talking Heads 77	CD	Sire	6036-2	U.S.A.	1977	7.99
Talking Heads	The Name Of This Band Is + 16	2CD	Rhino	R2-76489	U.S.A.	2004	15.99
Talking Heads	True Stories	CD	Warner Bros.	9-25512-2	U.S.A.	1986	6.99
Talking Heads/Heads	4 Song Sampler (Promo)	CD	MCA	MCA3P-3830	U.S.A.	1996	11.99
Talking Heads/Heads	Damage I've Done (Promo)	CD Single	MCA	MCA5P-3786	U.S.A.	1996	5.99
Talking Heads/Heads	Don't Take My Kindness ...	CD Single	MCA	MCSTD-48024	England	1996	5.99
Talking Heads/Heads	No Talking Just Head	CD	MCA	7674-11504-2	U.S.A.	1996	6.99
Talking Heads/Heads	No Talking Just Head (Advanced)	CD	MCA	MCA3P-90022	U.S.A.	1996	11.99
Ta-Mara/The Seen	Blueberry Gossip	CD	A&M	CD-5153	U.S.A.	1988	8.99
Ta-Mara/The Seen	Self Titled (Prince Related)	CD	Pony Canyon	D32Y-3017	Japan	1986	99.99
Tangerine Dream	220 Volt Live	CD	TDI	TDICD018	EU	1993	6.99
Tangerine Dream	67/90 (Only 400)	CD	Digital Matrix	DM-1108	Japan	1990	73.99
Tangerine Dream	Alpha Centauri + 1	CD	Castle	CMRCD566	England	2002	11.99
Tangerine Dream	Ambient Monkeys	CD	TDI	TDICD011	EU	1998	6.99
Tangerine Dream	Antique Dreams	CD	TDI	TDICD028	EU	2000	8.99
Tangerine Dream	Atem	CD	Castle	CMRCD495	England	2002	11.99
Tangerine Dream	Atlantic Bridges	CD	TDI	TDICD002	EU	2001	5.99
Tangerine Dream	Atlantic Walls	CD	TDI	TDICD003	EU	2001	6.99
Tangerine Dream	Book Of Dreams	2CD	Essential	EDFCD-353	England	1995	22.99
Tangerine Dream	Canyon Dreams (O.S.T.)	CD	TDI	TDICD021	England	2001	8.99
Tangerine Dream	Cat Scan (Promo)	CD Single	Private	2042-2-PP2	U.S.A.	1988	59.99
Tangerine Dream	Catch Me ... If You Can	CD	Edel	EDS-5413-2	Germany	1989	24.99
Tangerine Dream	Cyclone	CD	Virgin	7243-8-40251-2-0	England	1995	9.99
Tangerine Dream	Dead Solid Perfect	CD	Silva Screen	FILMCD-079	England	1989	12.99
Tangerine Dream	Deadly Care (O.S.T.)	CD	Silva Screen	FILMCD-121	England	1992	38.99
Tangerine Dream	Destination Berlin (O.S.T.)	CD	BMG	260-440	Canada	1989	13.99
Tangerine Dream	Dream Encores	CD	TDI	TDICD004	Germany	1998	8.99

T

Artist	Title	Format	Label	Catalog No	Country	Released	Value
Tangerine Dream	Dream Mixes	2CD	TDI	TDICD005	EU	2001	17.99
Tangerine Dream	Dream Mixes 2	CD	TDI	TDICD006	EU	2001	11.99
Tangerine Dream	Dream Mixes 3	CD	TDI	TDICD031	EU	2001	11.99
Tangerine Dream	Dream Mixes IV + 2 (W/Bonus Cd)	2CD	TDI	TDICD034	EU	2004	19.99
Tangerine Dream	Dream Music, Vol. 2	CD	Silva Screen	FILMCD-166	England	1995	16.99
Tangerine Dream	Dream Music: The Movie Music Of	CD	Silva Screen	FILMCD-125	England	1986	18.99
Tangerine Dream	Dream Sequence	2CD	Virgin	CDTDX-1	England	2000	24.99
Tangerine Dream	Dreamtime	CD Single	Miramar	MPCD-2805	U.S.A.	1993	38.99
Tangerine Dream	Electronic Mediation	CD	Castle	CMRCD565	England	2002	11.99
Tangerine Dream	Encore	CD	Virgin	7243-8-39443-2-3	England	1995	9.99
Tangerine Dream	Exit	CD	Virgin	7243-8-40519-2-1	England	1995	9.99
Tangerine Dream	Firestarter (O.S.T.)	CD	Varese	VSD-5251	U.S.A.	1993	24.99
Tangerine Dream	Flashpoint (O.S.T.)	CD	One Way	OW-18507	U.S.A.	1995	24.99
Tangerine Dream	Force Majeure	CD	Virgin	7243-8-40259-2-2	England	1995	9.99
Tangerine Dream	Goblin's Club	CD	Castle	CMACD556	England	2000	8.99
Tangerine Dream	Great Wall Of China	CD	TDI	TDICD022	EU	2001	8.99
Tangerine Dream	Green Desert	CD	Castle	CMRCD633	England	2003	11.99
Tangerine Dream	Heartbreakers (O.S.T.)	CD	Silva Screen	SIL-CD-1039	U.S.A.	1995	40.99
Tangerine Dream	Heartbreakers (O.S.T.)	CD	Silva Screen	SSD-1039	U.S.A.	1995	24.99
Tangerine Dream	Hollywood Years, Vol. 1	CD	TDI	TDICD007	EU	2001	8.99
Tangerine Dream	Hollywood Years, Vol. 2	CD	TDI	TDICD008	EU	2001	8.99
Tangerine Dream	Hyperborea	CD	Virgin	7243-8-39446-2-0	England	1995	9.99
Tangerine Dream	I-Box Set	6CD	TDI	TDICD030	EU	2001	62.99
Tangerine Dream	Inferno	CD	TDI	TDICD032	EU	2001	8.99
Tangerine Dream	Journey Through A Burning Brain Box	3CD	Castle	CMFTD525	England	2002	24.99
Tangerine Dream	Le Parc	CD	Castle	CMRCD634	England	2003	15.99
Tangerine Dream	Lily On The Beach	CD	Private Music	2057-2-P	U.S.A.	1989	16.99
Tangerine Dream	Live in Aachen, Germany	2CD	Boot Moon	001CD	EU	2004	18.99
Tangerine Dream	Live in Montreal, Canada	2CD	Boot Moon	002CD	EU	2004	18.99
Tangerine Dream	Live in Ottawa, 1986	2CD	Boot Moon	005CD	EU	2004	18.99
Tangerine Dream	Live in Paris, France	2CD	Boot Moon	003CD	EU	2004	18.99
Tangerine Dream	Live in Sydney, Australia	2CD	Boot Moon	004CD	EU	2004	18.99
Tangerine Dream	Live Miles	CD	Essential	ESMCD368	England	1996	8.99
Tangerine Dream	Logos Live	CD	Virgin	7243-8-39445-2-1	England	1995	9.99
Tangerine Dream	Marakesh (Promo)	CD Single	Private	2042-2-PP	U.S.A.	1988	59.99
Tangerine Dream	Mars Polaris	CD	TDI	TDICD016	EU	2001	7.99
Tangerine Dream	Melrose	CD	Private	261105	Holland	1990	7.99
Tangerine Dream	Melrose Yrs. (Optical/Lily/Melrose + 3)	3CD	TDI	TDICD033	EU	2003	15.99
Tangerine Dream	Miracle Mile (O.S.T.)	CD	BMG	260-016	Germany	1989	16.99
Tangerine Dream	Mota Atma	CD	TDI	TDP001CD	EU	2003	8.99
Tangerine Dream	Near Dark (O.S.T.)	CD	Silva Screen	FILMCD-026	England	1987	38.99
Tangerine Dream	Oasis (O.S.T.)	CD	TDI	7187-5-63009-2-2	Germany	2001	9.99
Tangerine Dream	Optical Race	CD	Private	259557	Holland	1989	7.99
Tangerine Dream	Optical Race (Promo)	CD Single	Private	662083	U.S.A.	1988	59.99
Tangerine Dream	Pergamon	CD	Essential	ESMCD413	England	1996	11.99
Tangerine Dream	Phaedra	CD	Virgin	7243-8-40062-2-8	England	1995	9.99
Tangerine Dream	Poland (All 4 Tracks)	CD	Castle	CMRCD641	England	2003	11.99
Tangerine Dream	Poland: The Warsaw Concert	2CD	Relativity	88561-8045-2	U.S.A.	1984	14.99
Tangerine Dream	Quinoa	CD	TDI	TDICD010	EU	2001	11.99
Tangerine Dream	Quinoa (Fan Club/2 Less Tracks)	CD	Volt	Volt 0001	Germany	1992	104.99
Tangerine Dream	Ricochet	CD	Virgin	7243-8-40064-2-6	England	1995	9.99
Tangerine Dream	Rockface	2CD	TDI	TDICD035	EU	2003	15.99
Tangerine Dream	Rockoon	CD	TDI	TDICD017	England	2001	7.99
Tangerine Dream	Rockoon (Red Or Purple)	CD	Essential	EMSCD403	England	1996	8.99
Tangerine Dream	Rubycon	SACD	Virgin	SACDV2025	England	2001	14.99
Tangerine Dream	Rubycon	CD	Virgin	7243-8-40063-2-7	England	1995	9.99
Tangerine Dream	Rubycon Revisited	CD	Evil Ear	001	Germany	1996	8.99
Tangerine Dream	Rumplestiltskin (W/Kathleen Turner)	CD	Rhino	R2-70458	U.S.A.	1992	34.99

T

Artist	Title	Format	Label	Catalog No	Country	Released	Value
Tangerine Dream	Self Title (Best Of)	CD	Disky	VI-873772	Holland	1996	8.99
Tangerine Dream	Self Titled (Best Of)	CD	Disky	V1-854382	Holland	1999	8.99
Tangerine Dream	Seven Letters From Tibet	CD	TDI	TDICD029	EU	2001	8.99
Tangerine Dream	Shy People (O.S.T)	CD	Silva Screen	FILMCD-027	England	1987	38.99
Tangerine Dream	Sohoman - Live In Sydney 1982	CD	TDI	TDICD014	Germany	1999	7.99
Tangerine Dream	Soundmill Navigator Live Phil. 76	CD	TDI	TDICD027	Germany	2000	22.99
Tangerine Dream	Stratosfear	CD	Virgin	7243-8-40065-2-5	England	1995	9.99
Tangerine Dream	Tangents (Promo Sampler)	CD	Virgin	DPRO-14221	U.S.A.	1994	18.99
Tangerine Dream	Tangents Box Set	5CD	Virgin	7243-8-39804-2-0	England	1994	34.99
Tangerine Dream	Tangents Box Set (Promo)	5CD	Virgin	BOXY4	England	1994	143.99
Tangerine Dream	Tango	2CD	TDI	TDICD026	EU	2001	12.99
Tangerine Dream	Tangram	CD	Virgin	7243-8-40263-2-5	England	1995	9.99
Tangerine Dream	The Analogue Space Years (Gold/W/Po	2CD	Purple Pyramid	CLP-0227-2	U.S.A.	1998	13.99
Tangerine Dream	The Best Of The Blue Years	CD	Castle	CCS-CD824	England	1998	11.99
Tangerine Dream	The Best Of The Pink Years	CD	Castle	CCS-CD815	England	1998	11.99
Tangerine Dream	The Collection	CD	Castle	CCSCD-161	England	1989	7.99
Tangerine Dream	The Dream Dice Box Set	13CD	TDI	TDICD001-012	Germany	1998	399.99
Tangerine Dream	The Dream Roots Collection	5CD	Essential	ESFCD420/5	England	1996	52.99
Tangerine Dream	The Keep (O.S.T.)	CD	Orange	ORCD-20011983	Canada	1983	34.99
Tangerine Dream	The Keep (O.S.T./Only 150)	CD	TDI	TDI010CD	EU	1997	104.99
Tangerine Dream	The Man Inside (O.S.T.)	CD	EMI	0-7777-95617-2-8	France	1991	22.99
Tangerine Dream	The Park Is Mine (O.S.T.)	CD	Silva Screen	FILMCD-080	England	1995	16.99
Tangerine Dream	The Private Music Of	CD	Private	01005-82105-2	Germany	1992	8.99
Tangerine Dream	Thief	CD	Virgin	7243-8-40520-2-7	U.S.A.	1995	13.99
Tangerine Dream	Thief (Expanded/15 Tracks)	CD	Orange	ORCD-20011981	Canada	1981	34.99
Tangerine Dream	Three O'Clock High (O.S.T.)	CD	Varese	VCD-47307	U.S.A.	1987	11.99
Tangerine Dream	Timesquare	CD	TDI	TDICD009	EU	1997	38.99
Tangerine Dream	Tournado	CD	TDI	TDICD011	Germany	2001	5.99
Tangerine Dream	Transsiberia	CD	TDI	TDICD012	EU	2001	8.99
Tangerine Dream	Turn Of The Tides + 1	CD	TDI	TDICD019	EU	2001	8.99
Tangerine Dream	Tyger	CD	Castle	CMRCD723	England	2003	11.99
Tangerine Dream	Tyranny Of Beauty	CD	TDI	TDICD020	EU	2001	6.99
Tangerine Dream	Tyranny Of Beauty (Promo Sampler)	CD	BMG	23056-2	Germany	1995	29.99
Tangerine Dream	Underwater Sunlight	CD	Castle	CMRCD654	England	2003	11.99
Tangerine Dream	Valentine Wheels	CD	TDI	TDICD013	EU	2001	8.99
Tangerine Dream	Vision Quest (O.S.T.)	CD	Geffen	9-24063-2	U.S.A.	1984	8.99
Tangerine Dream	Wavelength (O.S.T.)	CD	Varese	VCD-47223	U.S.A.	1988	24.99
Tangerine Dream	What A Blast: Architecture In Motion	CD	TDI	TDICD015	EU	1999	8.99
Tangerine Dream	White Eagle	CD	Virgin	7243-8-39444-2-2	England	1994	9.99
Tangerine Dream	Zeit	CD	Castle	CMRCD490	England	2003	11.99
Tangerine Dream	Zoning (O.S.T.)	CD	Repertoire	REP-4595-WY	Germany	1996	17.99
Tangerine Dream/V. A.	Risky Business (O.S.T.)	CD	Virgin	CDV-2302	U.S.A.	1985	18.99
Tarantino, Quentin/P Fiction	Pulp Fiction: Truth and Fiction	CD	MCA	MCA5P-3209	U.S.A.	1994	9.99
Tashian, Barry/Holly	Barry And Holly Tashian	CD	Line	SDCD-9.00640-0	Germany	1988	28.99
Tate, Tommy	The Tommy Tate Album	CD	Line	TLCD-9.00363-0	Germany	1988	32.99
Taupin, Bernie	He Who Rides The Tiger	CD	East West	AMCY-6147	Japan	2000	39.99
Taupin, Bernie/Farm Dogs	Immigrant Sons	CD	Sire	31014	U.S.A.	1998	4.99
Tavener, John	Celtic Requiem	CD	Capitol	CDP-7-82252-2	England	1993	83.99
Tavener, John	The Whale	CD	Captiol	0777-7-98497-2-7	U.S.A.	1992	27.99
Taylor, Alex	Dancing With The Devil	CD	Ichiban	ICH-9007-CD	U.S.A.	1994	24.99
Taylor, Alex	Dinnertime	CD	Capricorn	314-538-763-2	U.S.A.	1999	17.99
Taylor, Alex	Voodoo In Me	CD	Universe Prod.	CDSP-21309	U.S.A.	1990	8.99
Taylor, Andy/Duran Duran	Dangerous	CD	Pony Canyon	PCCY-10166	Japan	1990	28.99
Taylor, Andy/Duran Duran	Dangerous	CD	A&M	395-338-2	Germany	1990	14.99
Taylor, Andy/Duran Duran	Thunder	CD	MCA	MCAD-5837	U.S.A.	1987	19.99
Taylor, Andy/Duran Duran	Thunder	CD	MCA	32XD-547	Japan	1987	36.99
Taylor, Bobbie/Vancouvers	Self Titled (W/Tommy Chong)	CD	Motown	31453-0363-2	U.S.A.	1994	189.99
Taylor, Eddie	Still Not Ready For Eddie	CD	Line	ANCD-9.00452-0	Germany	1988	28.99

T

Artist	Title	Format	Label	Catalog No	Country	Released	Value
Taylor, James	Best Live	CD	Columbia	CK-66235	U.S.A.	1994	7.99
Taylor, James	Dad Loves His Work	CD	Columbia	CK-69803	U.S.A.	2000	8.99
Taylor, James	Dad Loves His Work (MFSL Gold Cd)	CD	Mobile Fidelity	UDCD-726	U.S.A.	1981	18.99
Taylor, James	Flag	CD	Columbia	CK-69802	U.S.A.	2000	8.99
Taylor, James	Gorilla	CD	Warner Bros.	7599-27293-2	U.S.A.	1990	8.99
Taylor, James	Greatest Hits	CD	Warner Bros.	2-3113	U.S.A.	1988	7.99
Taylor, James	Greatest Hits, Vol. 2	CD	Columbia	CK-85223	U.S.A.	2000	8.99
Taylor, James	Hourglass	CD	Columbia	CK-67912	U.S.A.	1997	7.99
Taylor, James	In The Pocket	CD	Warner Bros.	7599-27301-2	U.S.A.	1990	8.99
Taylor, James	James Taylor (Beatles Apple Cd)	CD	Capitol	7-97577-2	U.S.A.	1991	14.99
Taylor, James	JT	CD	Columbia	CK-69801	U.S.A.	2000	8.99
Taylor, James	JT (Sony Gold Cd)	CD	Columbia	CK-53787	U.S.A.	1977	29.99
Taylor, James	JT/Flag/Dad Loves His Work	3CD	Columbia	C3K-61422	U.S.A.	2000	21.99
Taylor, James	Live	2CD	Columbia	C2K-47056	U.S.A.	1993	12.99
Taylor, James	Mud Slide Slim	CD	Warner Bros.	256004	Australia	1971	14.99
Taylor, James	Mud Slide Slim	CD	Warner Bros.	2-2561	U.S.A.	1987	8.99
Taylor, James	N M Shine/N Die Young/That's W	3CD	Columbia	C3K-24641	U.S.A.	2000	21.99
Taylor, James	Never Die Young	CD	Columbia	CK-69805	U.S.A.	2000	8.99
Taylor, James	New Moon Shine	CD	Columbia	CK-46038	U.S.A.	1991	7.99
Taylor, James	October Road + 3 (W/Bonus Cd)	2CD	Columbia	CK-86695	U.S.A.	2002	14.99
Taylor, James	One Man Dog	CD	Warner Bros.	7599-25933-2	U.S.A.	1990	8.99
Taylor, James	Sweet Baby James	CD	Warner Bros.	2-1843	U.S.A.	1987	8.99
Taylor, James	That's Why I'm Here	CD	Columbia	CK-69804	U.S.A.	2000	8.99
Taylor, James	The Best Of	CD	Warner Bros.	08122-73837-2	U.S.A.	2003	9.99
Taylor, James	Walking Man	CD	Warner Bros.	7599-27285-2	U.S.A.	1990	7.99
Taylor, James/Orig. F Machine	Original Flying Machine 1967	CD	Gadfly	219	U.S.A.	1996	8.99
Taylor, John/Duran Duran	Feelings Are Good & Other Lies	CD	Revolver	REVXD215	England	1997	10.99
Taylor, John/Duran Duran	Feelings Are Good & Other Lies + 1	CD	Pony Canyon	PCCY-01063	Japan	1997	18.99
Taylor, Kate	Beautiful Road	CD	Front Door	333	U.S.A.	2003	8.99
Taylor, Kate	Sister Kate	CD	East West	AMCY-2588	Japan	1970	36.99
Taylor, Livingston	3-Way Mirror	CD	Epic	EK-57312	U.S.A.	1993	9.99
Taylor, Livingston	Bicycle	CD	Coconut Bay	COCO-147	U.S.A.	1996	10.99
Taylor, Livingston	Carolina Day: Collection (1970-1980)	CD	Razor & Tie	7930182161-2	U.S.A.	1998	9.99
Taylor, Livingston	Good Friends (Gold Cd)	CD	Chesky	JD-97	U.S.A.	1993	10.99
Taylor, Livingston	Ink	CD	Chesky	162	U.S.A.	1997	9.99
Taylor, Livingston	Ink +1	SACD	Chesky	253	U.S.A.	2003	14.99
Taylor, Livingston	Life Is Good	CD	Critique	90941-2	U.S.A.	1988	24.99
Taylor, Livingston	Our Turn To Dance	CD	Vanguard	VCD-79469	U.S.A.	1993	8.99
Taylor, Livingston	Over The Rainbow	CD	Capricorn	314-538-764-2	U.S.A.	1999	9.99
Taylor, Livingston	Self Titled	CD	Capricorn	314-538-132-2	U.S.A.	1997	9.99
Taylor, Mick	A Stones' Throw + 2	CD	Agent Con Sipio	AGCY-20001	Japan	1999	29.99
Taylor, Mick	Mick Taylor	CD	Columbia	CK-35076	U.S.A.	1995	7.99
Taylor, Mick	Stranger In This Town	CD	Maze	MCD1062	Canada	1990	24.99
Taylor, Mick/Miyuki	Mick & I	CD	Invoke	SB01	England	2001	12.99
Taylor, Roger	Electric Fire	CD	EMI	7243-4-96724-0-6	EU	1998	8.99
Taylor, Roger	Fun In Space	CD	Parlophone	7243-8-38201-2-2	England	1996	8.99
Taylor, Roger	Happiness?	CD	Parlophone	7243-8-30059-2-5	Germany	1994	11.99
Taylor, Roger	Happiness? +1	CD	Toshiba-EMI	TOCP-8290	Japan	1994	19.99
Taylor, Roger	Strange Frontier	CD	Parlophone	7243-8-38202-2-1	England	1996	8.99
Taylor, Roger/The Cross	The Cross + 1	CD	Virgin	VJD-32008	Japan	1988	37.99
Tea & Symphony	An Asylum For The Musically Insane	CD	Repertoire	REP-4559-WP	Germany	2003	13.99
Tears For Fears	Advice For The Young At Heart	CD Single	Polygram	875-145-2	U.S.A.	1990	8.99
Tears For Fears	Break It Down Again	CD Single	Mercury	862-331-2	France	1993	7.99
Tears For Fears	Elemental	CD Single	Mercury	858-499-2	U.S.A.	1994	7.99
Tears For Fears	God's Mistake	CD Single	Epic	34K-78064	U.S.A.	1995	14.99
Tears For Fears	Laid So Low (Tears Roll Down)	CD Single	Mercury	866-585-2	U.S.A.	1992	7.99
Tears For Fears	Raoul And The Kings Of Spain	CD	Epic	EK-67318	U.S.A.	1995	7.99
Tears For Fears	Saturnine Martial & Lunatic	CD	Mercury	528-114-2	Germany	1996	12.99

T

Artist	Title	Format	Label	Catalog No	Country	Released	Value
Tears For Fears	Seeds Of Love + 4	CD	Mercury	314-558-105-2	U.S.A.	2001	10.99
Tears For Fears	Songs Big Chair + 2 (MFSL Gold)	CD	Mobile Fidelity	UDCD-730	U.S.A.	1985	36.99
Tears For Fears	Songs From The Big Chair + 7	CD	Mercury	314-558-106-2	U.S.A.	1999	11.99
Tears For Fears	The Hurting + 4	CD	Mercury	314-558-104-2	U.S.A.	1999	10.99
Tears For Fears	Ultimate Collection (W/Bonus Cd)	3CD	Universal	98602-2	England	2003	24.99
Tears For Fears/Graduate	Acting My Age + 9	CD	Castle	CMRCD374	England	2001	13.99
Teaser	Self Titled	CD	Psuedonym	CDP-1045-DD	Holland	1997	14.99
Television	Adventure + 3	CD	Rhino	R2-73921	U.S.A.	2004	8.99
Television	Best Television And Tom Verlaine	CD	East West	AMCY-2562	Japan	1998	28.99
Television	Marquee Moon + 5	CD	Rhino	R2-73920	U.S.A.	2004	8.99
Television	Television	CD	Capitol	0777-7-98396-2-9	U.S.A.	1992	8.99
Television	The Blow Up	2CD	ROIR	RUSCD8249	U.S.A.	1999	14.99
Television Personalities	And Don't The Kids Just Love It	CD	Fire	REFIRE-CD7	England	1990	11.99
Television Personalities	And Don't The Kids...	CD	Fire	SFIRE002CD	England	2002	11.99
Television Personalities	Camping In France	CD	Zeit Dist.	OVER21CD	England	1991	17.99
Television Personalities	Closer To Gold	CD	Fire	FIRECD32	England	1996	11.99
Television Personalities	I Was A Mod...	CD	Zeit Dist.	OVER41CD	England	2002	17.99
Television Personalities	Mummy You're Not...	CD	Fire	SFIRE007CD	England	2002	11.99
Television Personalities	Painted Word	CD	Fire	SFIRE029CD	England	2002	11.99
Television Personalities	Part Time Punks: The Best Of	CD	Cherry Red	CDMRED152	England	2001	17.99
Television Personalities	Privilege	CD	Fire	SFIRE026CD	England	2003	11.99
Television Personalities	They Could Have Been Bigger...	CD	Fire	REFIRE-CD9	England	1990	11.99
Television Personalities	They Could Have...	CD	Fire	SFIRE014CD	England	2002	11.99
Temptations	A Song For You	CD	Motown	MOTD-5272	U.S.A.	1988	19.99
Temptations	A Song For You/Masterpiece	CD	Motown	1595102	England	2000	19.99
Temptations	Christmas Card	CD	Motown	MOTD-5251	U.S.A.	1990	6.99
Temptations	Cloud Nine/Puzzle People	CD	Motown	1594462	England	2000	14.99
Temptations	Emperors Of Soul Box Set	5CD	Motown	31453-0338-2	U.S.A.	1994	29.99
Temptations	Gettin' Ready	CD	Motown	MOTD-5373	U.S.A.	1989	7.99
Temptations	Give Love At Christmas	CD	Motown	MOTD-5279	U.S.A.	1990	8.99
Temptations	Live Copa/With Lot O' Soul	CD	Motown	ZD-72501	Germany	1968	22.99
Temptations	Live!	CD	Motown	MOTD-5499	U.S.A.	1992	14.99
Temptations	Meet The	CD	Motown	MOTD-5140	U.S.A.	1991	7.99
Temptations	Meet The/Sing Smokey	CD	Motown	1594432	England	2000	19.99
Temptations	My Girl	CD	Motown	5307592	England	2000	12.99
Temptations	Phoenix Rising	CD	Motown	530937	U.S.A.	1998	7.99
Temptations	To Be Continued	CD	Motown	MOTD-6207	U.S.A.	1990	7.99
Temptations	Together Again	CD	Motown	ZD-72616	Germany	1987	20.99
Temptations	Wish It Would Rain/In A Mellow Mood	CD	Motown	1595112	England	2000	12.99
Ten	1996- 1999	2CD	Mercury	PHCR-90035/6	Japan	1999	34.99
Ten	Fear The Force	CD Single	Mercury	PHCR-3082	Japan	1999	12.99
Ten	Name Of The Rose (Laminated Pass)	CD Single	Zero	XRCN-1291	Japan	1996	12.99
Ten	You're In My Heart	CD Single	Zero	XRCN-2015	Japan	1997	12.99
Ten Years After	A Space In Time	CD	BGO	BGOCD351	England	1997	14.99
Ten Years After	Alvin Lee & Company + 3	CD	Deram	820-566-2	England	1990	8.99
Ten Years After	Cricklewood Green + 2	CD	EMI	533-095-2	England	2002	12.99
Ten Years After	Live At The Fillmore East	2CD	Chrysalis	533-297-2	England	2001	17.99
Ten Years After	Recorded Live (11 Trks)	CD	BGO	BGOCD341	England	1997	14.99
Ten Years After	Recorded Live (13 Trks)	CD	Chrysalis	F2-21049	U.S.A.	1973	7.99
Ten Years After	Recorded Live (W/Hobbit) 14 Trks	2CD	EMI	576-205-2	England	2001	16.99
Ten Years After	Rock & Roll Music To The World	CD	BGO	BGOCD348	England	1997	14.99
Ten Years After	Self Titled + 6	CD	Deram	882-897-2	England	2002	12.99
Ten Years After	Ssssh	CD	CMK	7243-5-24828-2	U.S.A.	2001	12.99
Ten Years After	Sssh & Cricklewood Green (MFSL Gold)	CD	Mobile Fidelity	UDCD-687	U.S.A.	1970	31.99
Ten Years After	Stonedhenge + 4	CD	Deram	882-898-2	England	2002	12.99
Ten Years After	The Best Of	CD	Chrysalis	528-499-2	England	2000	11.99
Ten Years After	Undead + 4	CD	Deram	882-899-2	England	2002	12.99
Ten Years After	Watt	CD	Chrysalis	F2-21085	U.S.A.	1975	8.99

T

Artist	Title	Format	Label	Catalog No	Country	Released	Value
Tenacious D	Tenacious D	CD	Epic	EK-80234	U.S.A.	2001	8.99
Tenacious D	Tribute (Promo)	CD Single	Epic	ESK-56791	U.S.A.	2002	9.99
Tenacious D	Wonderboy	CD Single	Epic	673286-2	Australia	2001	4.99
Tenacious D	Wonderboy (Promo)	CD Single	Epic	ESK-24558	U.S.A.	2001	9.99
Tenpole Tudor	The Best Of	CD	Metro	METRCD49	England	2001	9.99
Terra Nova	Honesty	CD	King	K32Y-2191	Japan	1989	29.99
Terra Nova	Love Of My Life	CD Single	Victor Ent.	VICP-15077	Japan	1996	14.99
Terraplane	Black And White	CD	Sony	ESCA-7651	Japan	1985	24.99
Terraplane	Moving Target	CD	Sony	ESCA-7652	Japan	1987	24.99
Terrell, Tammi	Story Of (Only 500)	CD	Marginal	MAR-122	EEC	1996	24.99
Terry & The Pirates	Doubtful Handshake	CD	Line	LICD-9.00048-0	Germany	1988	28.99
Terry & The Pirates	Too Close For Comfort + 6	CD	Legend	LM-9014	France	1994	14.99
Terry & The Pirates	Wind Dancer	CD	Line	RBCD-9.00114-0	Germany	1991	28.99
Tesla	20th Century Masters: The Millennium	CD	Universal	490-779-2	U.S.A.	2001	9.99
Tesla	Bust A Nut	CD	Geffen	24713-2	U.S.A.	1994	7.99
Tesla	Five Man Acoustical Jam	CD	Geffen	9-24311-2	U.S.A.	1990	9.99
Tesla	Mechanical Resonance	CD	Geffen	M2G-24120	U.S.A.	1986	9.99
Tesla	Psychotic Supper	CD	Geffen	GEFD-24424	U.S.A.	1991	7.99
Tesla	Replugged Live	CD	Sanctuary	06076-84520-2	U.S.A.	2001	12.99
Tesla	The Great Radio Controversy	CD	Geffen	9-24224-2	U.S.A.	1989	7.99
Tesla	Time's Makin' Changes: The Best Of	CD	Geffen	24883-2	U.S.A.	1995	9.99
Texicans	The Texicans	CD	Line	LICD—9.01379-0	Germany	2001	10.99
The Q Tips/Paul Young	Live At Last!	CD	Line	OLCD-9.51159-X	Germany	1991	6.99
The Stills/Young Band	Long May You Run	CD	Reprise	2253-2	U.S.A.	1976	9.99
The Vision	10 Tracks Of Reggae & Dub Music	CD	Line	TCCD-9.00499-0	Germany	1987	12.99
The Vyllies	Sacred Games + 6	CD	Line	LICD-9.00316-0	Germany	1987	34.99
Theatre Of Hate	Revolution	CD	Line	LICD-9.00102-0	Germany	1988	12.99
Theatre Of Hate	Revolution	CD	Line	MLCD-9.01280-L	Germany	1992	12.99
Theatre Of Hate	Westworld	CD	Line	MLCD-9.01184-L	Germany	1993	12.99
Them/Van Morrison	The Story Of Them (1964-1966)	2CD	Deram	42284-4833-2	U.S.A.	1997	17.99
They Might Be Giants	Live!! New York City 10/14/94	CD	Elektra	PRCD-9083-2	U.S.A.	1994	53.99
Thievery Corporation	Sounds From Verve Hi Fi (Remixes)	CD	Verve	314-584-151-2	U.S.A.	2002	8.99
Thin Lizzy	Bad Reputation	CD	That	5322982	England	1993	8.99
Thin Lizzy	Black Rose	CD	Vertigo	830-392-2	England	1990	8.99
Thin Lizzy	Chinatown	CD	Vertigo	830-393-2	England	1993	8.99
Thin Lizzy	Fighting	CD	Vertigo	822-785-2	England	1990	8.99
Thin Lizzy	Great Box	4CD	Vertigo	PHCR-3113-16	Japan	1991	79.99
Thin Lizzy	Jail Break	CD	Vertigo	532-294-2	England	1996	12.99
Thin Lizzy	Johnny The Fox	CD	Vertigo	822-687-2	England	1990	8.99
Thin Lizzy	Life	2CD	Wounded Bird	WOU-3986	U.S.A.	2001	15.99
Thin Lizzy	Live And Dangerous	CD	Vertigo	838-030-2	England	1990	10.99
Thin Lizzy	Lizzy Killers	CD	Vertigo	800-060-2	England	1983	10.99
Thin Lizzy	New Day EP	CD	Decca	882-173-2	England	1989	22.99
Thin Lizzy	Nightlife	CD	Vertigo	842-433-2	England	1990	10.99
Thin Lizzy	Peel Sessions	CD	Strange Fruit	SFRSCD130	England	1995	39.99
Thin Lizzy	Remembering Part 1	CD	Rebound	520513	U.S.A.	1998	8.99
Thin Lizzy	Renegade	CD	Vertigo	842-435-2	England	1993	8.99
Thin Lizzy	Self Titled	CD	Decca	820-528-2	England	1990	10.99
Thin Lizzy	Shades Of A Blue Orphanage	CD	Decca	820-527-2	England	1988	10.99
Thin Lizzy	Thunder And Lightning	CD	Vertigo	810-490-2	England	1993	8.99
Thin Lizzy	Vagabonds Box Set	4CD	Mercury	556-495-2	England	2001	64.99
Thin Lizzy	Vagabonds Of The Western World	CD	Deram	820-969-2	England	1991	10.99
Thin Lizzy	Whiskey In The Jar EP	CD	Decca	882-167-2	England	1989	22.99
Thin Lizzy/John Sykes	20th Century	CD	Mercury	PHCR-1590	Japan	1997	16.99
Thin Lizzy/John Sykes	Best Of: Chapter One	CD	Mercury	PHCW-1074	Japan	2000	29.99
Thin Lizzy/John Sykes	Blue Murder (Nothin' But Trouble)	CD	Geffen	2-24419	U.S.A.	1994	9.99
Thin Lizzy/John Sykes	Blue Murder (Nothin' But Trouble) + 1	CD	Universal	UICY-3735	Japan	2002	22.99
Thin Lizzy/John Sykes	Blue Murder (Self Titled)	CD	Geffen	2-24212	U.S.A.	1989	15.99

T

Artist	Title	Format	Label	Catalog No	Country	Released	Value
Thin Lizzy/John Sykes	Blue Murder (Self Titled)	CD	Universal	UICY-3734	Japan	2002	22.99
Thin Lizzy/John Sykes	Chapter One	CD	Mercury	PHCR-82	Japan	1998	29.99
Thin Lizzy/John Sykes	Loveland	CD	Mercury	PHCR-1540	Japan	1997	19.99
Thin Lizzy/John Sykes	Nuclear Cowboy	CD	Mercury	PHCW-1063	Japan	2000	16.99
Thin Lizzy/John Sykes	Out Of My Tree	CD	Mercury	PHCR-1365	Japan	1995	19.99
Thin Lizzy/John Sykes	Please Don't Leave Me	CD	MCA	MVCM-309	Japan	1992	29.99
Thin Lizzy/Phil Lynott	Solo In Soho	CD	MSI	MSIG-0037	Japan	2003	21.99
Thin Lizzy/Phil Lynott	Solo In Soho	CD	Wounded Bird	WOU-3405	U.S.A.	2003	8.99
Thin Lizzy/Tribute	Blue Murder - Screaming Blue Murder	CD	RCA Victor	MVCG-149	Japan	1994	27.99
Third Ear Band	Abelard & Heloise	CD	Blueprint	BP310CD	England	2003	13.99
Third Ear Band	Alchemy	Mini Lp	Toshiba-EMI	TOCP-65786	Japan	2004	26.99
Third Ear Band	Brain Waves	CD	Materiali Sonori	MASO-90045	Italy	1993	8.99
Third Ear Band	Hymn To The Sphynx	2CD	Mooncrest	CRESTCD067	England	2001	13.99
Third Ear Band	Live	CD	Blueprint	BP157CD	England	2003	13.99
Third Ear Band	Live Ghosts	CD	Materiali Sonori	MASO-90004	Italy	1993	10.99
Third Ear Band	Magic Music	CD	Materiali Sonori	MASO-90016	Italy	1998	12.99
Third Ear Band	Music From Macbeth	CD	BGO	BGOCD61	England	1990	15.99
Third Ear Band	Music From Macbeth	Mini Lp	Toshiba-EMI	TOCP-65788	Japan	2004	26.99
Third Ear Band	New Age Magical Music	CD	Blueprint	BP257CD	England	2003	13.99
Third Ear Band	Self Titled	CD	BGO	BGOCD89	England	1990	15.99
Third Ear Band	Self Titled	Mini Lp	Toshiba-EMI	TOCP-65787	Japan	2004	26.99
Third Ear Band	Sonas From The Jukebox	CD	Blueprint	BP283CD	England	2003	13.99
This Mortal Coil	1983 - 1991 (Deleted/Day Of Release)	4CD	4AD	9-45135-2	U.S.A.	1993	84.99
This Mortal Coil	Box Set Sampler (Promo)	CD	4AD	PRO-CD-5876	U.S.A.	1993	16.99
Thomas, B. J.	Greatest Hits	CD	Rhino	R2-70752	U.S.A.	1990	10.99
Thomas, B. J.	Greatest Hits - Volume 1	CD	Varese	302-066-104-2	U.S.A.	2000	8.99
Thomas, B. J.	I Believe	CD	Warner Bros.	9-46475-2	U.S.A.	1995	8.99
Thomas, Guthrie	As Yet Untitled	CD	Line	SDCD-9.00908-0	Germany	1990	34.99
Thomas, Guthrie	Hobo Eagle Thief	CD	Line	SDCD-9.00915-0	Germany	1990	34.99
Thompson Twins	Here's To Future Days	CD	Arista	ARCD-8276	U.S.A.	1985	14.99
Thompson Twins	Into The Gap	CD	Arista	610-106-222	Germany	1984	26.99
Thompson Twins	Quick Step & Side Kick	CD	Arista	610-183-222	Germany	1983	26.99
Thompson Twins	Self Titled BMG Music Publishing DJ	CD	BMG	PUB039	England	2003	64.99
Thompson Twins	Side Kicks	CD	Arista	ARCD-8002	U.S.A.	1982	14.99
Thompson Twins	The Saint EP	CD	Warner Bros.	WPCP-4814	Japan	1992	14.99
Thompson, Chester	A Joyful Noise	CD	Camino	CAMCD16	England	1999	4.99
Thompson, Linda	Dreams Fly Away: A History Of	CD	Hannibal	HNCD1379	U.S.A.	1996	8.99
Thompson, Linda	Fashionably Late	CD	Topic	TSCD821	England	2002	11.99
Thompson, Linda	Give Me A Sad Song	CD	Fledg'ling	FLED-3020	England	2001	11.99
Thompson, Linda	One Clear Moment + 5 (Ltd 5000)	CD	Rhino	RHM2-7819	U.S.A.	2002	18.99
Thompson, Richard	1000 Years Of Popular Song	CD	Beeswing	BSW-003	England	2003	34.99
Thompson, Richard	Across A Crowded Room	CD	BGO	BGOCD139	England	2002	20.99
Thompson, Richard	Action Packed: Best Of Capitol	CD	Capitol	531-051-2	England	2001	9.99
Thompson, Richard	Amnesia	CD	Capitol	7-48845-2	U.S.A.	1988	9.99
Thompson, Richard	Big Chimney	CD Single	Hannibal	VHCD-1414	U.S.A.	1997	7.99
Thompson, Richard	Bug Music Sampler (Promo)	CD	Bug Music	PRCD-01	U.S.A.	1998	64.99
Thompson, Richard	Celtschmerz	CD	Flypaper	FLYCD-007	England	1998	13.99
Thompson, Richard	Crawl Back (Under My Stone) Promo	CD Single	Capitol	7087-6-13589-2-5	U.S.A.	1999	11.99
Thompson, Richard	Daring Adventures	CD	BGO	BGOCD138	England	2001	14.99
Thompson, Richard	Dark Hand Over... (Promo)	CD	Capitol	CDCLDJ-769	England	1996	7.99
Thompson, Richard	Ducknapped	CD	Beeswing	BWS-004	England	2003	34.99
Thompson, Richard	Easy There Steady Now (Promo)	CD	Capitol	DPRO-79364	U.S.A.	1994	9.99
Thompson, Richard	Guitar Vocal	CD	Hannibal	HNCD-4413	U.S.A.	1989	34.99
Thompson, Richard	Hands Of Kindness	CD	Hannibal	HNCD-1313	U.S.A.	1991	8.99
Thompson, Richard	Hard Cash (Various Artists)	CD	Special Delivery	SPDCD-1027	England	1990	19.99
Thompson, Richard	Henry The Human Fly	CD	Hannibal	HNCD-4405	U.S.A.	1991	34.99
Thompson, Richard	I Can't Wake Up... (Promo)	CD	Capitol	DPRO-79854	U.S.A.	1994	9.99
Thompson, Richard	I Feel So Good	CD Single	Capitol	C2-15728	Canada	1991	6.99

T

Artist	Title	Format	Label	Catalog No	Country	Released	Value
Thompson, Richard	I Feel So Good	CD Single	Capitol	CDCL-617	England	1991	8.99
Thompson, Richard	I Feel So Good (Promo)	CD Single	Capitol	DPRO-79730	U.S.A.	1991	9.99
Thompson, Richard	I Misunderstood (Promo)	CD Single	Capitol	DPRO-79967	U.S.A.	1991	11.99
Thompson, Richard	Industry	CD	Hannibal	HNCD-1414	U.S.A.	1997	10.99
Thompson, Richard	It (Promo Sampler)	CD	Capitol	DPRO-11214	U.S.A.	1996	12.99
Thompson, Richard	Live At Crawley 1993	CD	Flypaper	FLYCD-005	England	1995	13.99
Thompson, Richard	Live Mountain Stage (Promo)	CD	Capitol	7087-6-13857-2-4	U.S.A.	1999	12.99
Thompson, Richard	Mirror Blue	CD	Capitol	0777-7-81492-2	U.S.A.	1994	11.99
Thompson, Richard	Mock Tudor	CD	Capitol	7243-4-98860-2-5	U.S.A.	1999	8.99
Thompson, Richard	More Guitar (1985)	CD	Beeswing	BSW-002	England	2003	34.99
Thompson, Richard	Official Dutch Tour Single	CD Single	Capitol	7243-8-80275-2-6	Holland	1991	29.99
Thompson, Richard	Read About Love	CD Single	Capitol	CDCL-638	U.S.A.	1991	11.99
Thompson, Richard	Rumor And Sigh	CD	Capitol	7-95713-2	U.S.A.	1991	7.99
Thompson, Richard	Semi-Detached Mock Tudor	CD	Beeswing	BSW-001	England	2002	34.99
Thompson, Richard	She Said It...(1000 Copies)	CD Single	Cooking Vinyl	FRYCD155	England	2003	16.99
Thompson, Richard	Small Town Romance	CD	Hannibal	HNCD-1316	U.S.A.	1984	13.99
Thompson, Richard	Strict Tempo!	CD	Hannibal	HNCD-4409	U.S.A.	1993	17.99
Thompson, Richard	Sweet Talker (O.S.T.)	CD	Capitol	7-94490-2	U.S.A.	1992	12.99
Thompson, Richard	Teaches Traditional Guitar (W/Book)	CD	Homespun	HL00841083	U.S.A.	1996	16.99
Thompson, Richard	The Hannibal Sampler (Promo)	CD	Hannibal	VRCD-1303	U.S.A.	1991	73.99
Thompson, Richard	The Old Kit Bag	CD	Cooking Vinyl	COOKCD-251	England	2003	10.99
Thompson, Richard	The Old Kit Bag (W/Bonus Cd)	2CD	True North	TND-307	Canada	2003	14.99
Thompson, Richard	Turning Of The Tide (Promo)	CD Single	Capitol	DPRO-79388	U.S.A.	1988	9.99
Thompson, Richard	Two Letter Words	2CD	Flypaper	FLYCD-006	England	1997	19.99
Thompson, Richard	Ventura Show (Promo)	CD Single	Capitol	DPRO-79078	U.S.A.	1991	11.99
Thompson, Richard	Ventura Show (Promo)	CD Single	Capitol	SPRO-79105	U.S.A.	1991	11.99
Thompson, Richard	Watching the Dark (Best Of)	3CD	Hannibal	HNCD-5303	U.S.A.	1993	26.99
Thompson, Richard	Watching The Dark (Promo Sampler)	CD	Hannibal	VRCD-5303	U.S.A.	1993	11.99
Thompson, Richard	You? Me? Us?	2CD	Capitol	7243-8-33704-2-9	U.S.A.	1996	15.99
Thompson, Richard/Linda	First Light	CD	Hannibal	HNCD-4412	U.S.A.	1992	39.99
Thompson, Richard/Linda	Hokey Pokey	CD	Hannibal	HNCD-4408	U.S.A.	1991	32.99
Thompson, Richard/Linda	I Want To See...	CD	Hannibal	HNCD-4407	U.S.A.	1991	12.99
Thompson, Richard/Linda	Pour Down Like Silver	CD	Hannibal	HNCD-4404	U.S.A.	1991	35.99
Thompson, Richard/Linda	Shoot Out The Lights (Gold)	CD	Rykodisc	HNCD-81303	U.S.A.	1994	24.99
Thompson, Richard/Linda	Shoot Out The Lights + 1	CD	Hannibal	HNCD-1303	U.S.A.	1993	12.99
Thompson, Richard/Linda	Sunnyvista	CD	Hannibal	HNCD-4403	U.S.A.	1991	24.99
Thompson, Richard/Linda	The Best Of (Island Record Years)	CD	Island	314-542-456-2	U.S.A.	2000	9.99
Thornton, Billy Bob	Private Radio	CD	Lost Highway	088-170-236-2	U.S.A.	2001	4.99
Thornton, Billy Bob	Private Radio Sampler/Interview CD	CD	Lost Highway	MRNR-02143-2	U.S.A.	2001	8.99
Thorogood, George	And The Destroyers	CD	Rounder	CD-3013	U.S.A.	1986	22.99
Thorogood, George	Anthology	2CD	EMI	72435-27573-2-9	U.S.A.	2000	11.99
Thorogood, George	Bad To The Bone	CD	BGO	BGOCD94	England	2002	11.99
Thorogood, George	Boogie People	CD	EMI	7-92514-2	U.S.A.	1991	6.99
Thorogood, George	Boogie People	CD	BGO	BGOCD250	England	2002	11.99
Thorogood, George	Born To Be Bad	CD	EMI	546973	U.S.A.	1988	7.99
Thorogood, George	Born To Be Bad	CD	BGO	BGOCD224	England	2002	11.99
Thorogood, George	Haircut	CD	EMI	0777-7-89529-2-3	U.S.A.	1993	6.99
Thorogood, George	Haircut	CD	BGO	BGOCD573	England	2002	11.99
Thorogood, George	Half A Boy, Half A Man	CD	CMC Int.	06076-86270-2	U.S.A.	1999	8.99
Thorogood, George	Let's Work Together: Live	CD	BGO	BGOCD508	England	2002	11.99
Thorogood, George	Live	CD	EMI	7-46329-2	U.S.A.	1986	9.99
Thorogood, George	Live In '99	CD	CMC Int.	06076-86280-2	U.S.A.	1999	8.99
Thorogood, George	Live: Let's Work Together	CD	EMI	531948	U.S.A.	1995	4.99
Thorogood, George	Maverick	CD	EMI	7-46084-2	Australia	1985	9.99
Thorogood, George	Maverick	CD	BGO	BGOCD223	England	2002	11.99
Thorogood, George	More	CD	Rounder	CD-3045	U.S.A.	1986	22.99
Thorogood, George	Move It On Over	CD	Rounder	CD-3024	U.S.A.	1986	14.99
Thorogood, George	Nadine (Better Than The Rest)	CD	MCA	MCAD-20350	U.S.A.	1998	7.99

T

Artist	Title	Format	Label	Catalog No	Country	Released	Value
Thorogood, George	Ride 'Til I Die	CD	Eagle	ER-20007-2	U.S.A.	2003	7.99
Thorogood, George	Rockin' My Life Away	CD	EMI	7243-8-56220-2-1	U.S.A.	1997	4.99
Thorogood, George	The Baddest of George Thorogood	CD	EMI	E2-97718	U.S.A.	1992	8.99
Thorogood, George	The Usual (Promo Sampler)	CD	EMI	70876-12122-2-9	U.S.A.	1997	14.99
Thorogood, George	Who Do You Love?	CD	Rounder	RRCD11614	U.S.A.	2003	13.99
Thorpe, Billy	Children Of The Sun (Original Lp)	CD	Festival	D-19773	Australia	1993	10.99
Thorpe, Billy	It's All Happening	CD	Albert	465400-2	Australia	1981	14.99
Three Degrees	Best Of	CD	BMG	BVCM-37332	Japan	2002	35.99
Three Degrees	International	CD	Sony	SRCS-6492	Japan	1975	43.99
Three Dog Night	Captured Live At The Forum	CD	MCA	MCAD-31342	U.S.A.	1969	9.99
Three Dog Night	Celebrate: The Three Dog Night Story	2CD	MCA	MCAD2-10956	U.S.A.	1993	18.99
Three Dog Night	Cyan	CD	MCA	MCAD-31366	U.S.A.	1973	24.99
Three Dog Night	Hard Labor	CD	MCA	MCAD-31362	U.S.A.	1974	22.99
Three Dog Night	Harmony	CD	MCA	MCAD-31329	U.S.A.	1971	4.99
Three Dog Night	It Aint Easy	CD	MCA	MCAD-31047	U.S.A.	1970	10.99
Three Dog Night	Naturally	CD	MCA	MCAD-31355	U.S.A.	1970	4.99
Three Dog Night	One	CD	MCA	MCAD-31045	U.S.A.	1968	10.99
Three Dog Night	Seven Separate Fools	CD	MCA	MCAD-31339	U.S.A.	1972	7.99
Three Dog Night	Suitable For Framing	CD	MCA	MCAD-31046	U.S.A.	1969	10.99
Three Johns	Atom Drum Bop/The World By Storm	CD	Line	TRCD-9.00530-0	Germany	1988	28.99
Three Johns	The Death Of Everything	CD	Line	TCCD-9.00671-0	Germany	1988	10.99
Three Stooges	The Three Stooges	CD	MCA	MCAD-22184	U.S.A.	1995	8.99
Throbbing Gristle	20 Jazz Funk Greats	CD	Mute	MUTE-1095CD	England	1997	11.99
Throbbing Gristle	D.O.A. + 2	CD	Mute	MUTE-1094CD	England	1998	10.99
Throbbing Gristle	Final Musak	CD	Dressed To Kill	MIDRO849	England	2002	11.99
Throbbing Gristle	Greatest Hits	CD	Mute	MUTE-1001CD	England	1997	10.99
Throbbing Gristle	Heathen Earth + 2	CD	Mute	MUTE-1096CD	England	1990	9.99
Throbbing Gristle	Mission of Dead Souls + 2	CD	Mute	MUTE-1097CD	England	1991	10.99
Throbbing Gristle	One Hour Sample/TG 24 (Promo)	CD	Mute	PTG60CD	England	2002	39.99
Throbbing Gristle	Second Annual Report	CD	Mute	MUTE-1093CD	England	1991	12.99
Throbbing Gristle	TG 24	24CD	Mute	MUTE-9197	England	2003	229.99
Throwing Muses	Self Titled	CD	Nippon Columbia	33CY-1647	Japan	1987	92.99
Thunder	Backstreet Symphony + 10	2CD	Toshiba-EMI	TOCP-6729/30	Japan	1991	50.99
Thunder	Open the Window - Close the Door	CD	Victor Ent.	VICP-61069	Japan	2000	35.99
Thunderclap-Newman	Hollywood Dream + 6	CD	Polydor	833-794-2	England	1991	17.99
Thunderhead	Busted At The Border	CD	Victor Ent.	VICP-8035	Japan	1990	19.99
Thunderhead	Classic Killer Live!	CD	Victor Ent.	VICP-5380	Japan	1994	19.99
Thunderhead	Crime Pays	CD	Victor Ent.	VICP-5121	Japan	1991	19.99
Thunderhead	The Ballads	CD	Victor Ent.	VICP-5648	Japan	1995	19.99
Thunderhead	Were You Told the Truth About Hell?	CD	Victor Ent.	VICP-5565	Japan	1995	19.99
Thunders, Johnny	Endless Party	CD	Amsterdamned	70032-2	U.S.A.	2000	12.99
Thunders, Johnny	Have Faith	CD	Mutiny	60023-80005-2	U.S.A.	1996	8.99
Thunders, Johnny	Hollywood Babylon	CD	Captain Trip	CTCD-275	Japan	1987	15.99
Thunders, Johnny	Hurt Me	CD	Teichiku	TECP-25233	Japan	1990	22.99
Thunders, Johnny	Hurt Me More	CD	Solid	CDSOL-0013	Japan	1998	22.99
Thunders, Johnny	In Cold Blood	CD	Essential	ESM-CD-589	England	1997	13.99
Thunders, Johnny	Last Live In Japan Act. 1	CD	Solid	CDSOL-0011	Japan	1998	22.99
Thunders, Johnny	Last Live In Japan Act. 2	CD	Solid	CDSOL-0012	Japan	1998	22.99
Thunders, Johnny	Live & Wasted - Unplugged	CD	Receiver	RRCD-297-Z	England	2000	14.99
Thunders, Johnny	Que Sera Sera	CD	Jungle	FREUD-CD-049	Germany	1994	9.99
Thunders, Johnny	So Alone + 2	CD	Warner Bros.	WPCR-1817	Japan	1998	13.99
Thunders, Johnny	So Alone + 4	CD	Sire	9-26982-2	U.S.A.	1992	12.99
Thunders, Johnny	You Can't Put Your Arms... Box Set	3CD	Castle	CMETD-468	England	2002	16.99
Thunders, Johnny/H.B.	L.A.M.F. - The Lost '77 Mixes	CD	Jungle	FREUD-CD-044E	England	1994	21.99
Thunders, Johnny/H.B.	L.A.M.F. Revisited	CD	Receiver	RRCD-190	England	1994	14.99
Thunders, Johnny/H.B.	Live - Stations At The Cross Revisited	CD	Receiver	RRCD-188	England	1994	17.99
Thunders, Johnny/H.B.	Live At Max's Kansas City '79 + 4	CD	ROIR	RUSCD8219	U.S.A.	1995	10.99
Thunders, Johnny/H.B.	Thunderstorm In Detroit	CD	Captain Trip	CTCD-359	Japan	2001	15.99

T

Artist	Title	Format	Label	Catalog No	Country	Released	Value
Thunders, Johnny/H.B.	Vintage '77	CD Single	Jungle	JUNG5CD	England	1983	29.99
Thunders, Johnny/H.B.	What Goes Around...	CD	Bomp	BCD-4039	U.S.A.	1991	9.99
Thunders, Johnny/Heartbreake	D.T.K. - L.A.M.F.	CD	Jungle	CD-FREUD-4	England	1986	33.99
Thunders, Johnny/S. Sylvain	Live In Sweden 1984	2CD	Solid	CDSOL-0014/15	Japan	1998	64.99
Thunders, Johnny/S. Sylvain	Sad Vacation	2CD	Receiver	RRDCD-009-Z	England	1999	14.99
Thunders/Kramer	Gang War	CD	R.E.R. Ent.	RER-9001-2	U.S.A.	1995	14.99
Thurston, Bobby	Foolish Man	CD	Line	TLCD-9.00829-0	Germany	1989	41.99
Tiffany	Dreams Never Die (Pic Disc)	CD	MCA	MCD-10949	Philippines	1992	4.99
Tiffany	Hold An Old Friend's Hand CD	CD	Warner Bros.	25P2-2308	Japan	1988	29.99
Tiger	Tiger	CD	Line	RTCD-9.01153-0	Germany	1992	10.99
'Til Tuesday	Coming Up Close: A Retrospective	CD	Epic	EK-64944	U.S.A.	1996	8.99
'Til Tuesday	Everything's Different Now	CD	Epic	EK-44041	U.S.A.	1988	18.99
'Til Tuesday	Voices Carry	CD	Epic	EK-39458	U.S.A.	1990	19.99
'Til Tuesday	Welcome Home	CD	Epic	EK-40314	U.S.A.	1986	18.99
Tillery, Linda	Secrets	CD	Line	TLCD-9.00616-0	Germany	1988	28.99
Tillotson, Johnny	Greatest Hits	CD	Line	BLCD-9.01035-L	Germany	1991	10.99
Time/Morris Day	Daydreaming	CD	Warner Bros.	9-25651-2	U.S.A.	1987	26.99
Tiny Tim	God Bless Tiny Tim	CD	Warner Bros.	WPCR-1994	Japan	1998	39.99
Tiny Tim	Live! At The Royal Albert Hall (3500)	CD	Rhino	RHM2-7710	U.S.A.	2000	18.99
Tiny Tim/Brave Combo	Girl	CD	Rounder	CD-9050	U.S.A.	1996	7.99
Tiomkin, Dimitri	Giant	CD	Capitol	0777-7-92056-2-2	U.S.A.	1956	19.99
Tippett, Keith	Blueprint	CD	Voiceprint	VP146CD	England	2003	14.99
Tippett, Keith	Bristol Concert	CD	Whatever	WHAT-7CD	England	2003	14.99
Tippett, Keith	Dedicated To You, But You ...	CD	Disconforme	DISC1964CD	Andorra	1999	14.99
Tippett, Keith	Dedicated To You, But You ...	CD	Repertoire	REP-4449-WP	Germany	1994	14.99
Tippett, Keith	Dedicated To You, But You...	CD	Akarma	AK-227	Italy	2003	14.99
Tippett, Keith	Friday The 13th	CD	Voiceprint	VP-136-CD	England	2000	10.99
Tippett, Keith	Linuckea	CD	Future Music	FMR-70	England	2001	14.99
Tippett, Keith	Mujician I/2	CD	FMP	FMP-CD-095	Netherlands	1995	20.99
Tippett, Keith	Mujician III (August Air)	CD	FMP	FMP-CD-012	Netherlands	1987	19.99
Tippett, Keith	Une Croix Dans L'Ocean	CD	Victo	031	Canada	1995	16.99
Tippett, Keith	You Are Here... I Am There	CD	Disconforme	DISC1963CD	Andorra	1999	14.99
Tippett, Keith/Andy Sheppard	66 Shades Of Lipstick	CD	EG	EG-1590-2	EC	1990	8.99
Tippett, Keith/Centipede	Septober Energy	2CD	BGO	BGOCD485	England	2002	24.99
Tippett, Keith/Centipede	Septober Energy	CD	Disconforme	DISC1965CD	Andorra	1999	14.99
Tippett, Keith/Julie	Couple In Spirit	CD	EG	EEGCD 52	England	1988	24.99
Tippett, Keith/Julie	Couple In Spirit, Vol. 2	CD	La Cooka R	LCVP137CD	England	2001	14.99
Tippett, Keith/Mujician	Birdman	CD	Cuneiform	RUNE-82	U.S.A.	1996	12.99
Tippett, Keith/Mujician	Colours Fulfilled	CD	Cuneiform	RUNE-102	U.S.A.	1998	9.99
Tippett, Keith/Mujician	Poem About The Hero	CD	Cuneiform	RUNE-62	U.S.A.	1994	12.99
Tippett, Keith/Mujician	Spacetime	CD	Cuneiform	RUNE-162	U.S.A.	2002	9.99
Tippett, Keith/Mujician	The Journey	CD	Cuneiform	RUNE-42	U.S.A.	1992	12.99
Tippett, Keith/Ovary Lodge	Self Titled (Produced/Robert Fripp)	CD	Whatever	WHAT-4CD	England	2003	14.99
Tippetts, Julie	Shadow Puppeteer	CD	La Cooka R	LCVP101CD	England	2000	14.99
Tippetts, Julie/Driscoll	Sunset Glow	CD	Blueprint	BP317CD	England	1999	11.99
T N T	Daisy Jane	CD Single	Victor Ent.	VICP-15075	Japan	1997	6.99
T N T	Firefly	CD	Victor Ent.	VICP-5829	Japan	1997	24.99
T N T	Firefly & Live	CD	Shrapnel	SH-1109CD	U.S.A.	1997	8.99
T N T	Give Me A Sign	CD	MTM	0681-72	Germany	2003	9.99
T N T	Intuition	CD	Mercury	836-777-2	U.S.A.	1988	8.99
T N T	Intuition + 1	CD	Victor Ent.	VICP-60789	Japan	1999	20.99
T N T	Intuition + 1	CD	Nippon Phonogram	28PD-578	Japan	1989	18.99
T N T	Knights Of The New Thunder + 1	CD	Vertigo	818-865-2	Germany	1984	9.99
T N T	Realized Fantasies	CD	Atlantic	7-82266-2	U.S.A.	1992	10.99
T N T	Self Titled	CD	Vertigo	PHCR-4195	Japan	1994	21.99
T N T	Tell No Tales	CD	Mercury	830-979-2	U.S.A.	1987	8.99
T N T	The Big Bang Anthology	2CD	Spitfire	SPT-15037-2	U.S.A.	1999	19.99
T N T	Three Nights In Tokyo	CD	MMG Inc.	AMCY-490	Japan	1992	18.99

T

Artist	Title	Format	Label	Catalog No	Country	Released	Value
T N T	Till Next Time: The Best Of	CD	Mercury	PHCR-1427	Japan	1996	24.99
T N T	Transistor	CD	Spitfire	SPT-15036-2	U.S.A.	1999	10.99
Toad	B.U.F.O.	CD	Akarma	AK-268-CD	Italy	2003	14.99
Toad The Wet Sprocket	Acoustic Dance Party	CD Single	Columbia	44K-77727	U.S.A.	1994	16.99
Toad The Wet Sprocket	House Of Toad (Promo)	CD	Columbia	CSK-9989	U.S.A.	1997	6.99
Today/Teddy Riley	Self Titled	CD	Motown	MOTD-6261	U.S.A.	1988	44.99
Toe Fat	Self Titled	CD	Repertoire	REP-4416-WY	Germany	2002	14.99
Toe Fat	Self Titled/Two	CD	BGO	BGOCD278	England	2002	16.99
Toe Fat	Two	CD	Repertoire	REP-4417-WY	Germany	2002	14.99
Tokens	The Lion Sleeps Tonight (Wimoweh)	CD Single	RCA	07863-62955-2	U.S.A.	1994	5.99
Tom Tom Club	Boom Boom Chi Boom Boom	CD	Sire	9-25888-2	U.S.A.	1989	5.99
Tom Tom Club	Dark Sneak Love Action	CD	Sire	9-26951-2	U.S.A.	1992	5.99
Tom Tom Club	Sunshine And Ecstacy	CD Single	Sire	9-40444-2	U.S.A.	1992	5.99
Tom Tom Club	The Good The Bad And The Funky	CD	Rykodisc	RCD-10603	U.S.A.	2000	8.99
Tom Tom Club	Tom Tom Club	CD	Sire	3628-2	U.S.A.	1981	15.99
Tom Tom Club	You Sexy Thing	CD Single	Sire	9-40600-2	U.S.A.	1992	5.99
Tomlin, Lily	This Is A Recording	CD	Laugh.com	LGH1114	U.S.A.	2002	12.99
Tone Float	Musik Von Tone Float	CD	Captain Trip	CTCD-112	Japan	2000	14.99
Tool	In Store Sampler (Promo)	CD	Zoo	ZP17144	U.S.A.	1993	13.99
Tool	Salival (Box Set W/DVD)	CD	Volcano	61422-31159-2R	U.S.A.	2000	99.99
Tool	Selections From Aenima (Promo)	CD	Zoo	ZP17210-2	U.S.A.	1996	23.99
Tool	Self Titled (Promo)	CD	Volcano	VOL-32743-2	U.S.A.	2001	24.99
Torkanowsky, David	Steppin' Out	CD	Line	COCD-9.00900-0	Germany	1989	10.99
Torme, Bernie	White Trash Guitar + 4	CD	Retrowreck	RETRK105	England	1999	11.99
Torme, Bernie	Wild Irish + 4	CD	Retrowreck	RETRK103	England	1999	11.99
Torn, David	Best Laid Plans (W/Geoffrey Gordon)	CD	ECM	823-642-2	U.S.A.	1991	8.99
Torn, David	Cloud Above Mercury	CD	ECM	831-108-2	U.S.A.	1992	9.99
Torn, David	Door X	CD	Windam Hill	WD-1096	U.S.A.	1990	5.99
Torn, David	Tripping Over God	CD	CMP	CMP-CD-1007	U.S.A.	1995	8.99
Torn, David	What Means Solid, Traveller?	CD	CMP	CMP-CD-1012	U.S.A.	1996	8.99
Torn, David/Carter Burwell	Storyville (W/Geoffrey Gordon)	CD	Varese	VSD-5347	U.S.A.	1992	16.99
Torn, David/Elliot Sharp	GTR OBLQ (W/Vernon Reid)	CD	Knitting Factory	233	U.S.A.	1998	8.99
Tosh, Peter	Legalize It + 1	CD	Columbia	CK-65922	U.S.A.	1999	8.99
Toto	25th Anniversary: Live In Amsterdam	CD	Eagle	ER-20022-2	U.S.A.	2003	8.99
Toto	Absolutely Live	CD	Sony	474512-2	England	1999	10.99
Toto	Africa	2CD	Sony	511-309-2	Germany	2003	14.99
Toto	Circa 1980's	CD	Sony	SK-55045	U.S.A.	2003	7.99
Toto	Essential	CD	Sony	CK-90623	U.S.A.	2003	8.99
Toto	Fahrenheit	CD	Columbia	CK-40273	U.S.A.	1986	5.99
Toto	Greatest Hits	CD	Sony	485-500-2	Germany	1996	11.99
Toto	Greatest Hits.. And More	3CD	Sony	508-420-2	Austria	2002	21.99
Toto	Hold the Line: The Best Of	CD	Zounds	27000-20111	Germany	2001	11.99
Toto	Hydra	CD	Columbia	CK-36229	U.S.A.	1979	5.99
Toto	Isolation	CD	Columbia	CK-38962	U.S.A.	1984	7.99
Toto	IV	CD	Sony	CK-86544	U.S.A.	2002	12.99
Toto	Kingdom Of Desire	CD	Relativity	88561-1181-2	U.S.A.	1993	4.99
Toto	Livefields	CD	Sony	496204-2	England	1999	10.99
Toto	Love Songs	CD	Sony	SK-87114	U.S.A.	2003	7.99
Toto	Mindfields	CD	Sony	SK-69607	U.S.A.	1999	10.99
Toto	Mindfields (Diff Track Order)	CD	SME	SME-8888	Japan	1999	25.99
Toto	Past To Present 1977-1990	CD	Columbia	CK-45368	U.S.A.	1990	9.99
Toto	Past To Present 1977-1990	CD	Columbia	CSCS-5220	Japan	1990	44.99
Toto	Rock And Roll Band	CD	Columbia	CK-30866	U.S.A.	1999	6.99
Toto	Self Titled	CD	Columbia	CK-35317	U.S.A.	1978	6.99
Toto	Super Hits	CD	Columbia	CK-85347	U.S.A.	2001	5.99
Toto	Tambu	CD	Sony	SK-64957	U.S.A.	1995	6.99
Toto	The Seventh One	CD	Columbia	CK-40873	U.S.A.	1988	7.99
Toto	The Seventh One +1	CD	Sony	32DP-5001	Japan	1988	36.99

T

Artist	Title	Format	Label	Catalog No	Country	Released	Value
Toto	Through The Looking Glass	CD	CMC Int.	41457	U.S.A.	2002	8.99
Toto	Toto IV (MFSL Gold Cd)	CD	Mobile Fidelity	UDCD-747	U.S.A.	1982	32.99
Toto	Toto IV (Sony Gold Cd)	CD	Columbia	CK-64423	U.S.A.	1994	37.99
Toto	Toto XX: 1977-1997 (Reunion)	CD	Sony	SK-65832	U.S.A.	1998	8.99
Toto	Toto/Hydra/IV	3CD	Columbia	C3K-65394	U.S.A.	1997	24.99
Toto	Turn Back	CD	Columbia	CK-36813	U.S.A.	1981	7.99
Toto/Bobby Kimball	Rise Up	CD	Victor Ent.	VICP-5525	Japan	1994	22.99
Toto/Fergie Fredericksen	Equilibrium	CD	Avex	AVCB-66062	Japan	1999	19.99
Toto/John Warren	Private Motion	CD	Fun House	00GD-7101	Japan	1989	18.99
Toto/Joseph Williams	I Am Alive	CD	Kitty	KTCR-1803	Japan	1996	35.99
Toto/Joseph Williams	Self Titled + 2	CD	Cool Sound	COOL-007	Japan	1982	36.99
Toto/Joseph Williams	Three	CD	Kitty	KTCM-1064	Japan	1997	35.99
Toto/Steve Lukather	Candyman	CD	Sony	SRCS-7320	Japan	1994	14.99
Toto/Steve Lukather	Lukather	CD	Columbia	465657-2	Austria	1989	16.99
Toto/Steve Lukather	Lukather	CD	Sony	25D-5508	Japan	1988	16.99
Toto/Steve Lukather	Luke	CD	Miramar	09006-23098-2	U.S.A.	1997	9.99
Toto/Steve Lukather	No Substitutions: Live O (Larry Carlton)	CD	Victor Ent.	VICP-61240	Japan	2001	34.99
Toto/Steve Lukather	Santamental	CD	Bop City	1573	U.S.A.	2003	20.99
Touch	Complete Works (Diff Than Frontier)	2CD	Bareknuckle	AVCB-66041	Japan	1998	24.99
Touched By An Angel	The Album	CD	550 Music	BK-68971	U.S.A.	1998	8.99
Tour De Force	World On Fire	CD	FEMS	APCY-8283	Japan	1995	26.99
Tourists	Luminous Basement	CD	BMG	BVCM-7305	Japan	1997	34.99
Tourists	Should Have Been Greatest Hits	CD	Epic	EK-39318	U.S.A.	1984	11.99
Tower Of Power	Dinosaur Tracks (Ltd. 10000)	CD	Rhino	RHM2-7703	U.S.A.	2000	22.99
Townshend, Emma	Winterland (Pete's Daughter)	CD	East West	62174-2	U.S.A.	1998	4.99
Townshend, Pete	All The Best Cowboys..	CD	Atlantic	82812-2	U.S.A.	1982	7.99
Townshend, Pete	Another Scoop (Remastered)	Mini Lp	Eel Pie	EPR-007-1/2	England	2000	24.99
Townshend, Pete	Best Of Coolwalking...	CD	Atlantic	82712-2	U.S.A.	1996	11.99
Townshend, Pete	Deep End Live!	CD	Atlantic	7-90553-2	U.S.A.	1986	7.99
Townshend, Pete	Empty Glass (Atlantic Gold Cd)	CD	Atlantic	82544-2	U.S.A.	1993	74.99
Townshend, Pete	Interview With A Psychoderelict (DJ)	CD	Atlantic	PRCD-5161-2	U.S.A.	1993	24.99
Townshend, Pete	Lifehouse > Elements	CD	Red Line	70001	U.S.A.	2000	8.99
Townshend, Pete	Lifehouse Box Set (W/Book)	6CD	Eel Pie	EPR-002	England	2000	79.99
Townshend, Pete	Live - A Benefit For Maryville Academy	2CD	Platinum	9555	U.S.A.	1999	14.99
Townshend, Pete	Live - Sadler's Wells 2000	Mini Lp	Eel Pie	EPR-008-1/2	England	2000	49.99
Townshend, Pete	Live - The Empire 1998	Mini Lp	Eel Pie	EPR-009-1/2	England	2000	49.99
Townshend, Pete	Live > The Fillmore 1996	Mini Lp	Eel Pie	EPR-010-1/2	England	2000	49.99
Townshend, Pete	Live>La Jolla 2001 22/06/01	Mini Lp	Eel Pie	EPR-O14-1/2	England	2001	49.99
Townshend, Pete	Live>La Jolla 2001 23/06/01	Mini Lp	Eel Pie	EPR-O15-1/2	England	2001	49.99
Townshend, Pete	O' Parvardigar	CD Single	Eel Pie	EPR-012	England	2001	14.99
Townshend, Pete	Pete Townshend Live (Cdi Live)	2CD	Polygram	310690054-2	U.S.A.	1993	24.99
Townshend, Pete	Pete Townshend Live (DJ Cdi Sampler)	CD	Polygram	CDP-1102	U.S.A.	1993	14.99
Townshend, Pete	Psychoderelict	CD	Atlantic	7-82494-2	U.S.A.	1993	5.99
Townshend, Pete	Psychoderelict (Music Only)	CD	Atlantic	7-82535-2	U.S.A.	1993	8.99
Townshend, Pete	Scoop (Remastered)	Mini Lp	Eel Pie	EPR-006-1/2	England	2000	24.99
Townshend, Pete	Scoop 3	Mini Lp	Eel Pie	EPR-013-1/2	England	2001	49.99
Townshend, Pete	Scooped	2CD	Eel Pie	EPR016/7005-2	U.S.A.	2002	13.99
Townshend, Pete	The Iron Man	CD	Atlantic	A2-81996	U.S.A.	1989	5.99
Townshend, Pete	White City	CD	Atco	7-90473-2	U.S.A.	1985	8.99
Townshend, Pete	Who Came First + 6 (Deluxe Book Ed.)	CD	Rykodisc	RCD-90246	U.S.A.	1992	42.99
Townshend, Pete	Windswept Pacific DJ Box Set	3CD	Windswept Pacific	PTV1/2/3	U.S.A.	1993	99.99
Townshend, Pete/Promo	Psychoderelict (Censored/Music Only)	2CD	Atlantic	PRCD-5103-2	U.S.A.	1993	13.99
Townshend, Pete/R. Lane	Rough Mix	CD	Atco	7-90097-2	U.S.A.	1983	8.99
Townshend, Pete/R.Rudd	The Oceanic Concerts	CD	Rhino	R2-74289	U.S.A.	2001	6.99
Townshend, Pete/V.A.	Avatar (Meher Baba Ltd. Box Set)	4CD	Eel Pie	91129	England	1999	124.99
Townshend, Pete/V.A.	Jai Baba	CD	Eel Pie	EPR-011-1/2	England	2000	14.99
Toyah	Acoustic Album	CD	Qed	QED298	England	1998	8.99
Toyah	Anthem + 6 (Also Bonus Video)	CD	Connoisseur	EVSOP-CD-263	England	1999	15.99

T

Artist	Title	Format	Label	Catalog No	Country	Released	Value
Toyah	Best Of Toyah	CD	Connoisseur	CSAP-CD-115	England	1994	8.99
Toyah	Dreamchild	CD	SPV	96142	Germany	1999	9.99
Toyah	Looking Back (Best Of)	CD	Freestyle	JHD-139	England	1994	7.99
Toyah	Now & Then	CD Single	X-Ert	CDTOY2	England	1994	5.99
Toyah	Ophelia's Shadow	CD	Editions EG	EGCD-78	U.S.A.	1991	14.99
Toyah	Ophelia's Shadow	CD	Virgin	VJCP-28028	Japan	1991	14.99
Toyah	Phoenix + 1	CD	Receiver	RRCD235	England	1994	10.99
Toyah	Prostitute	CD	Vertical Species	VSR003CD	England	2003	12.99
Toyah	Sheep Farming.../The Blue Meaning	CD	Safari	VOORCD-4002	England	2002	19.99
Toyah	The Changeling (Bonus Tracks, Cdrom)	CD	Connoisseur	EVSOP-CD-264	England	1999	11.99
Toyah	Toyah! Live & More	CD	Connoisseur	CSAP-CD-125	England	1998	7.99
Toyah	Velvet Lined Shell	CD	Vertical Species	VSR001CD	England	2003	13.99
Traffic	Far From Home	CD	Virgin	7243-8-39490-2-1	U.S.A.	1994	7.99
Traffic	Feelin' Alright: The Best Of	CD	Island	314-542-272-2	U.S.A.	2000	8.99
Traffic	Heaven Is In Your Mind + 4	CD	Island	314-542-824-2	U.S.A.	2000	8.99
Traffic	Here Comes A Man	CD Single	Virgin	7243-8-92471-2-1	Holland	1994	4.99
Traffic	John Barleycorn Must Die + 2	CD	Island	314-548-541-2	U.S.A.	2001	9.99
Traffic	Last Exit	CD	Island	314-548-540-2	U.S.A.	2001	8.99
Traffic	Mr. Fantasy (MFSL Gold Cd)	CD	Mobile Fidelity	UDCD-572	U.S.A.	1968	24.99
Traffic	Mr. Fantasy + 5	CD	Island	314-542-823-2	U.S.A.	2000	9.99
Traffic	On The Road	CD	Island	7-90028-2	U.S.A.	1973	10.99
Traffic	Shoot Out At The ... (MFSL Gold Cd)	CD	Mobile Fidelity	UDCD-669	U.S.A.	1973	24.99
Traffic	Smiling Phases	2CD	Island	314-510-553-2	U.S.A.	1991	14.99
Traffic	The Collection	CD	Spectrum	544-558-2	England	2001	8.99
Traffic	The Low Spark Of ... (MFSL Gold Cd)	CD	Mobile Fidelity	UDCD-609	U.S.A.	1971	24.99
Traffic	The Low Spark Of High + 1	CD	Island	314-548-827-2	U.S.A.	2002	9.99
Traffic	Traffic (MFSL Gold Cd)	CD	Mobile Fidelity	UDCD-629	U.S.A.	1968	24.99
Traffic	Traffic + 3	CD	Island	314-542-852-2	U.S.A.	2001	9.99
Traffic	Welcome To The Canteen	CD	Island	314-548-847-2	U.S.A.	2002	7.99
Traffic	When The Eagle Flies	CD	Island	262-045	Germany	1974	7.99
Train	Self Titled (Longer 12 Trk/Diff Vrsn)	CD	Train	0001-2	U.S.A.	1996	103.99
Transatlantic	Bridge Across Forever	CD	Radient	3984-14382-2	U.S.A.	2001	14.99
Transatlantic	Live In America	2CD	Radient	RA-009	U.S.A.	2001	16.99
Transatlantic	SMPT:E	CD	Radient	3984-14290-2	U.S.A.	2000	21.99
Trapeze	High Flyers: The Best Of	CD	Threshold	820-957-2	U.S.A.	1995	22.99
Trapeze	Hold On	CD	Line	LICD-9.00485-0	Germany	1987	22.99
Trapeze	Hold On	CD	Purple Pyramid	CLP-329	U.S.A.	2002	10.99
Trapeze	Hot Wire	CD	One Way	OW-33649	U.S.A.	1996	23.99
Trapeze	Live At The Boat Club 1975	CD	Major League	MLP04CD	England	2004	15.99
Trapeze	Live In Texas	CD	Line	LICD-9.00494-0	Germany	1987	22.99
Trapeze	Live: Way Back To The Bone	CD	Receiver	RRCD-237	England	1998	19.99
Trapeze	Medusa	CD	Polygram	820-955-2	U.S.A.	1994	10.99
Trapeze	Trapeze	CD	Polygram	820-954-2	U.S.A.	1994	14.99
Trapeze	Welcome To The Real World	CD	Purple	PUR-301	England	1998	18.99
Trapeze	You Are The Music...We're..	CD	Polygram	820-956-2	U.S.A.	1994	14.99
Trapeze	You're The Music...	CD	Lemon	CDLEM04	England	2003	13.99
Trapeze/3 Live Albums	On The High Wire (Hold/Way/Dead)	2CD	Castle	CMDDD736	England	2003	15.99
Trashmen	Live Bird '65 - '67	CD	Sundazed	SC-11006	U.S.A.	1990	8.99
Trashmen	Surfin' Bird + 4	CD	Sundazed	SC-6064	U.S.A.	1995	8.99
Trashmen	The Great Lost Trashmen Album!	CD	Sundazed	SC-11007	U.S.A.	1990	8.99
Trashmen	The Trashmen: Bird Call ! (Box Set)	4CD	Sundazed	SC-11022	U.S.A.	1998	54.99
Trashmen	Tube City! The Best Of The Trashmen	CD	Sundazed	SC-11011	U.S.A.	1992	8.99
Trashmonk/Dream Academy	Mona Lisa Overdrive + 2	CD	Sony	ESCA-8337	Japan	2001	17.99
Trask, Stephen	Hedwig And The Angry Inch (O.S.T.)	CD	Hybrid	HY-20024-2	U.S.A.	2001	11.99
Trask, Stephen	Hedwig The Angry Inch (Orig. Cast)	CD	Atlantic	83160-2	U.S.A.	1999	11.99
Traveling Wilburys	Vol. 3 (Harrison, Dylan, Petty, Lynne)	CD	Warner Bros.	9-26324-2	U.S.A.	1990	14.99
Traveling Wilburys/Lynne	Vol. I (Harrison/Dylan/Petty/Orbison)	CD	Warner Bros.	9-25796-2	U.S.A.	1988	29.99
Travis	Flowers In The Window (Promo)	CD Single	Independiente	SAMPCS-10965-1	Austria	2001	5.99

T

Artist	Title	Format	Label	Catalog No	Country	Released	Value
Travis, Randy	Straight Talk With (Promo/Interview)	CD	Warner Bros.	PRO-CD-6363	U.S.A.	1993	11.99
Tree, Christopher	At Cathedral Of St. John The Divine	CD	Quakebasket	QB-015-CD	U.S.A.	2002	14.99
Tremeloes	African Lullaby	CD Single	Line	LICD-9.01204-E	Germany	1992	9.99
Tremeloes	All For One And One For All	CD	Line	LICD-9.01206-0	Germany	1992	34.99
Trettine, Caroline	Be A Devil	CD	Line	UTCD-9.00970-L	Germany	1990	26.99
Trichromes	Dice With The Universe	CD Single	33rd Street	3307	U.S.A.	2002	4.99
Trillion	Clear Approach	CD	Sony	ESCA-7715	Japan	1998	32.99
Trillion	Self Titled	CD	Sony	ESCA-7714	Japan	1998	23.99
Triumph	Allied Forces	CD	TRC	TRCD-6205	Canada	1995	9.99
Triumph	Allied Forces	CD	MCA	MCAD-5542	U.S.A.	1981	9.99
Triumph	Classics	CD	TRC	TRCD-6211	Canada	1995	6.99
Triumph	Classics	CD	MCA	MCAD-42283	U.S.A.	1990	6.99
Triumph	Edge Of Excess	CD	Victory	383-480-012-2	U.S.A.	1993	6.99
Triumph	In The Beginning (Self Titled)	CD	TRC	TRCD-6021	Canada	1995	8.99
Triumph	Just A Game	CD	MCA	MCAD-31118	U.S.A.	1979	8.99
Triumph	Just A Game	CD	TRC	TRCD-6203	Canada	1995	8.99
Triumph	KBFH Live In Concert	CD	King Biscuit	70710-88014-2	U.S.A.	1996	7.99
Triumph	Live At Festival Us	CD	TML	TML-79201	Canada	2003	11.99
Triumph	Never Surrender	CD	TRC	TRCD-6206	Canada	1995	8.99
Triumph	Never Surrender	CD	MCA	MCAD-31069	U.S.A.	1983	8.99
Triumph	Progressions Of Power	CD	TRC	TRCD-6204	Canada	1995	5.99
Triumph	Progressions Of Power	CD	MCA	MCAD-31088	U.S.A.	1979	5.99
Triumph	Rock 'N' Roll Machine	CD	MCA	MCAD-31119	U.S.A.	1979	8.99
Triumph	Rock 'N' Roll Machine	CD	TRC	TRCD-6202	Canada	1995	8.99
Triumph	Self Titled	CD	Attic	LAT-1012	Canada	1976	9.99
Triumph	Stages	CD	TRC	TRCD-6208	Canada	1995	8.99
Triumph	Surveillance	CD	MCA	MCAD-42083	U.S.A.	1987	8.99
Triumph	Surveillance	CD	TRC	TRCD-6210	Canada	1995	8.99
Triumph	The Sport Of Kings	CD	TRC	TRCD-6209	Canada	1995	7.99
Triumph	The Sport Of Kings	CD	MCA	MCAD-5786	U.S.A.	1985	7.99
Triumph	Thunder Seven	CD	TRC	TRCD-6207	Canada	1995	7.99
Triumph	Thunder Seven	CD	MCA	MCAD-39310	U.S.A.	1985	7.99
Triumvirat	A La Carte + 2	CD	EMI	7243-5-35171-2-0	Germany	2002	14.99
Triumvirat	Illusions On A Double Dimple + 4	CD	EMI	7243-5-35162-2-2	Germany	2002	14.99
Triumvirat	MediterraneanTales + 4	CD	EMI	7243-5-35161-2-3	Germany	2002	14.99
Triumvirat	Old Love Dies Hard + 1	CD	EMI	7243-5-35164-2-0	Germany	2002	14.99
Triumvirat	Pompeii + 1	CD	EMI	7243-5-35165-2-9	Germany	2002	14.99
Triumvirat	Russian Roulette	CD	EMI	7243-5-35166-2-8	Germany	2002	14.99
Triumvirat	Spartacus + 2	CD	EMI	7243-5-35163-2-1	Germany	2002	14.99
Triumvirat	Spartacus + 5 (Deluxe Edition)	CD	Friday	1002-2	England	2003	14.99
Troggs	Archeology (W/Troggs Tape DJ CD)	3CD	Fontana	5144232	England	1992	52.99
Troggs	Cellophane/Mixed Bag	CD	BGO	BGOCD343	England	1997	14.99
Troggs	From Nowhere/Trogglodynamite	CD	BGO	BGOCD340	England	1996	14.99
Troggs	The EP Collection	CD	See For Miles	SEECD-453	England	1996	9.99
Troggs/R.E.M.	Athens And Over	CD	Rhino	R2-71064	U.S.A.	1992	4.99
Troggs/R.E.M.	Don't You Know	CD Single	Essential	ESS-X-2014	England	1992	2.99
Trower, Robin	20th Century Blues	CD	Demon	FIENDCD753	England	1994	14.99
Trower, Robin	Anthology	CD	Connoisseur	VSOP-CD-197	England	1995	24.99
Trower, Robin	B.L.T./Truce	CD	BGO	BGOCD411	England	1998	12.99
Trower, Robin	Back It Up	CD	BGO	BGOCD426	England	1999	16.99
Trower, Robin	BBC Radio One Live	CD	Griffin	GCD-336-2	U.S.A.	1995	19.99
Trower, Robin	Beyond The Mist	CD	Passport	PBCD-6049	U.S.A.	1985	64.99
Trower, Robin	Bridge Of Sighs	CD	Capitol	72435-20811-2-7	U.S.A.	1999	12.99
Trower, Robin	Bridge Of Sighs (MFSL Gold Cd)	CD	Mobile Fidelity	UDCD-684	U.S.A.	1974	37.99
Trower, Robin	Caravans To Midnight/Victims Of Fury	CD	BGO	BGOCD352	England	1997	16.99
Trower, Robin	Collection	CD	Castle	CCSCD291	England	1992	12.99
Trower, Robin	Essential	CD	Chrysalis	F2-21853	U.S.A.	1991	12.99
Trower, Robin	For Earth Below/Live	CD	BGO	BGOCD347	England	1997	16.99

Artist	Title	Format	Label	Catalog No	Country	Released	Value
Trower, Robin	Go My Way	CD	Repertoire	REP-4921	Germany	2001	10.99
Trower, Robin	In The Line Of Fire	CD	Wounded Bird	WOU-2080	U.S.A.	2004	8.99
Trower, Robin	King Biscuit Flower Hour Live	CD	King Biscuit	70710-88012-2	U.S.A.	1996	8.99
Trower, Robin	Living Out Of Time	CD	V-12	788575010029	U.S.A.	2004	9.99
Trower, Robin	Long Misty Days/In City Dreams	CD	BGO	BGOCD349	England	1997	17.99
Trower, Robin	No Stopping Anytime	CD	Capitol	F2-21704	U.S.A.	1989	19.99
Trower, Robin	Passion	CD	GNP	GNPD-2187	U.S.A.	1987	15.99
Trower, Robin	Someday Blues	CD	Demon	FIENDCD931	England	1997	8.99
Trower, Robin	Speed Of Sound: The Best Of	CD	Fuel 2000	302-061-258-2	U.S.A.	2002	7.99
Trower, Robin	Take What You Need	CD	Wounded Bird	WOU-1838	U.S.A.	2004	8.99
Trower, Robin	This Was Now 1974-1998	CD	Demon	FIENDCD945	England	1999	11.99
Trower, Robin	Twice Removed From Yesterday	CD	Chrysalis	VK-41039	U.S.A.	1973	27.99
Trower, Robin	Twice Removed.../Bridge Of Sighs	CD	BGO	BGOCD339	England	1996	17.99
Troy, Doris	Doris Troy + 5	CD	Capitol	7-98701-2	U.S.A.	1992	24.99
True Believers	Hard Road	CD	Rykodisc	RCD-40287	U.S.A.	1994	9.99
Tubes	20th Century Masters: The Millennium	CD	A&M	314-490-766-2	U.S.A.	2000	8.99
Tubes	Genius Of America	CD	Popular	01624-12007-2	U.S.A.	1996	5.99
Tubes	Goin' Down	2CD	A&M	540-564-2	England	1996	99.99
Tubes	Infomercial: How To Become (BBC)	CD	HUX	HUX017	England	2000	14.99
Tubes	Love Bomb	CD	BGO	BGOCD188	England	1993	13.99
Tubes	Outside Inside	CD	BGO	BGOCD133	England	1998	14.99
Tubes	Remote Control	CD	A&M	CD-3242	U.S.A.	1979	33.99
Tubes	Self Titled	CD	A&M	CD-3161	U.S.A.	1988	20.99
Tubes	Self Titled (MFSL Silver Cd)	CD	Mobile Fidelity	MFCD-822	U.S.A.	1975	53.99
Tubes	T.R.A.S.H. (Rarities And Smash Hits)	CD	A&M	75021-3244-2	U.S.A.	1981	9.99
Tubes	The Best Of	CD	Alliance	C2-98359	U.S.A.	1992	6.99
Tubes	The Completion Backward Principle	CD	BGO	BGOCD100	England	1998	14.99
Tubes	What Do You Want...(Live)	CD	A&M	396-003-2	Germany	1978	14.99
Tubes	White Punks On Dope	CD	Acadia	ACA-8065	England	2004	9.99
Tubes	World Tour 2001	CD	Sanctuary	06076-86300-2	U.S.A.	2000	6.99
Tubes	Young And Rich	CD	A&M	CD-3222	U.S.A.	1988	63.99
Tubes	Young And Rich	CD	Pony Canyon	D18Y-4117	Japan	1989	64.99
Tubes/Fee Waybill	Don't Be Scared By These Hands	CD	West Coast	West-CD-11	Sweden	1996	19.99
Tubes/Fee Waybill	Read My Lips	CD	BGO	BGOCD283	England	1996	16.99
Tucker, Marshall/Band	A New Life	CD	Line	MLCD-9.00869-L	Germany	1989	12.99
Tucker, Marshall/Band	Carolina Dreams	CD	Line	MLCD-9.00899-L	Germany	1989	16.99
Tucker, Marshall/Band	Greatest Hits	CD	AJK Music	A-799-2	U.S.A.	1976	23.99
Tucker, Marshall/Band	Long Hard Ride	CD	Line	MLCD-9.00881-L	Germany	1989	13.99
Tucker, Marshall/Band	Searchin' For A Rainbow	CD	AJK Music	A-702-2	U.S.A.	1975	19.99
Tucker, Marshall/Band	Searchin' For A Rainbow	CD	Line	MLCD-9.00872-L	Germany	1989	13.99
Tucker, Marshall/Band	The Best Of The Capricorn Years	2CD	ERA	022775502725	U.S.A.	1994	51.99
Tucker, Marshall/Band	The Marshall Tucker Band	CD	Line	MLCD-9.00866-L	Germany	1989	12.99
Tucker, Marshall/Band	Together Forever	CD	Line	MLCD-9.00885-L	Germany	1989	13.99
Tucker, Marshall/Band	Troy Caldwell - Self Titled	CD	Cabin Fever	CFM9012	U.S.A.	1992	24.99
Tucker, Marshall/Band	Where We All Belong	CD	Line	MLCD-9.00875-L	Germany	1989	17.99
Tucker, Moe	Dogs Under Stress	CD	Sky	SKY-3103-2	Canada	1994	8.99
Tucker, Moe	Grl-Grup	CD	Lakeshore	LSD-CD2001	U.S.A.	1997	6.99
Tucker, Moe	I Spent A Week There The Other Night	CD	Sky	SKY-3104	Canada	1993	8.99
Tucker, Moe	I'm Sticking With You (J Richman)	CD Single	Lakeshore	LSD-CD-2002	U.S.A.	1997	10.99
Tucker, Moe	Life In Exile + 4 (MoeJadKateBarry EP)	CD	Rev-Ola	CREV-011CD	England	1993	14.99
Tucker, Moe	Life In Exile After Abdication	CD	50 Skidillion Watts	MOE7-2	Canada	1989	15.99
Tucker, Moe	Live In Seattle	CD	Captain Trip	CTCD-400	Japan	2002	18.99
Tucker, Moe	Oh No, The're Recording This Show	CD	New Rose	422418	France	1992	14.99
Tucker, Moe	Too Shy	CD Single	New Rose	NEW-152-CD	France	1992	9.99
Tucker, Moe	Wating For My Men	CD	Rokarola	7280850006	Germany	1998	19.99
Turner, Tina	Acid Queen + 3	CD	Razor & Tie	RE-1985-2	U.S.A.	1994	8.99
Turner, Tina	Break Every Rule	CD	Capitol	7243-8-19841-2	U.S.A.	2000	5.99
Turner, Tina	Collected Recordings - '60's To '90's	3CD	Capitol	7243-8-29724-2-6	U.S.A.	1994	24.99

Artist	Title	Format	Label	Catalog No	Country	Released	Value
Turner, Tina	Foreign Affair	CD	Capitol	0777-7-91873-2	U.S.A.	1989	6.99
Turner, Tina	Golden Eye	CD Single	Virgin	7243-8-38524-2-0	U.S.A.	1995	8.99
Turner, Tina	Hanes Special Edition (Promo)	CD Single	Virgin	DPRO-11544	U.S.A.	1996	4.99
Turner, Tina	Live In Europe	2CD	Capitol	0777-7-90126-2	U.S.A.	1988	10.99
Turner, Tina	Private Dancer + 2 (JVCXR Audiophile)	CD	Capitol	JVCXR-044-2	U.S.A.	1984	18.99
Turner, Tina	Private Dancer + 7	CD	Capitol	CDP-555833	U.S.A.	1997	11.99
Turner, Tina	Rough	CD	EMI	0777-7-95213-2-6	England	1995	8.99
Turner, Tina	Simply The Best (W/Bonus DVD)	2CD	Virgin	7243-5-90433-2-0	U.S.A.	2003	14.99
Turner, Tina	Sings Country (Same As Country Of)	CD	Hallmark	79351-53124-2-2	England	1999	6.99
Turner, Tina	Twenty Four Seven	CD	Virgin	7243-5-23180-2	U.S.A.	2000	5.99
Turner, Tina	What's Love Got... (O.S.T.)	CD	Capitol	0777-7-88189-2	U.S.A.	1988	8.99
Turner, Tina	Wildest Dreams	CD	Parlophone	7243-8-37684-2-4	Australia	1995	8.99
Turner, Tina	Wildest Dreams	CD	Virgin	7243-8-41920-2	U.S.A.	1996	5.99
Turner, Tina	Wildest Dreams (Bonus Cd)	CD	Parlophone	7243-4-95928-2-7	Australia	1996	19.99
Turner, Tina/Ike	Absolutely The Best	CD	Varese	VCD-1025	U.S.A.	1998	8.99
Turner, Tina/Ike	Bold Soul Sister: Best Of Blue Thumb	CD	Hip O	HIPD-40051	England	1997	8.99
Turner, Tina/Ike	Deliah's Power	CD	EMI	7243-576099-2-0	England	2001	10.99
Turner, Tina/Ike	Don't Play Me Cheap	CD	Collectables	COL-5763	U.S.A.	1997	8.99
Turner, Tina/Ike	Dynamite	CD	Collectables	COL-5298	U.S.A.	1994	8.99
Turner, Tina/Ike	Essential Collection	CD	Fuel 2000	302-061-396-2	U.S.A.	2004	8.99
Turner, Tina/Ike	Every Hit Single 1960- 1974	CD	AIM	2025	Australia	2001	10.99
Turner, Tina/Ike	Fool In Love	CD	King	1439	U.S.A.	1996	8.99
Turner, Tina/Ike	Funkier Than A Mosquito's Tweeter	CD	EMI	7243-5-37960-2-0	England	2002	10.99
Turner, Tina/Ike	Golden Classics	CD	Collectables	COL-5107	U.S.A.	1990	8.99
Turner, Tina/Ike	It's All Over	CD	Prestige	CDSGP058	England	1993	8.99
Turner, Tina/Ike	It's Gonna Work Out Fine	CD	Collectables	COL-5137	U.S.A.	1994	8.99
Turner, Tina/Ike	Kings Of Rhythm Band - Dance	CD	Collectables	COL-5759	U.S.A.	1996	8.99
Turner, Tina/Ike	Live 1964 And 1967	CD	P-Vine	PCD-3029	Japan	2003	18.99
Turner, Tina/Ike	Live In Paris	2CD	EMI	7243-576224-2-4	England	2001	18.99
Turner, Tina/Ike	Live! Ike & Tina Turner Show, Vols. 1-2	CD	One Way	OW-35168	U.S.A.	2000	8.99
Turner, Tina/Ike	Proud Mary: The Best Of	CD	EMI	E2-95846	U.S.A.	1991	8.99
Turner, Tina/Ike	River Deep Mountain High (Best Of)	CD	EMI	7243-486929-2-4	England	1996	8.99
Turner, Tina/Ike	River Deep Mountain High (Spector)	CD	A&M	0828-393179-2-4	England	2001	8.99
Turner, Tina/Ike	River Deep Mountain High (Spector)	CD	A&M	75021-3179-2	U.S.A.	1966	8.99
Turner, Tina/Ike	River Deep... (MFSL Silver)	CD	Mobile Fidelity	MFCD-849	U.S.A.	1966	132.99
Turner, Tina/Ike	Sexy-Seductive-Provocative	CD	Paula	PCD-9008	U.S.A.	1993	8.99
Turner, Tina/Ike	The Gospel According To	CD	Fuel 2000	302-061-181-2	U.S.A.	2002	8.99
Turner, Tina/Ike	The Ike & Tina Turner Revue Live	CD	Kent	CDKEND102	U.S.A.	1996	8.99
Turner, Tina/Ike	The Kent Years	CD	Kent	CDKEND182	U.S.A.	2002	8.99
Turner, Tina/Ike	The Seductive Provocative	CD	Paula	PCD-335	U.S.A.	1993	8.99
Turner, Tina/Ike	The Soul Of	CD	Collectables	COL-5297	U.S.A.	1994	8.99
Turner, Tina/Ike	The Soul Of	CD	P-Vine	PCD-3034	Japan	2003	18.99
Turner, Tina/Ike	The Very Best Of	CD	Prism	PLATCD507	England	2002	10.99
Turner, Tina/Ike	What You Hear Is What You Get	CD	EMI	7243-8-38309-2-3	England	1996	8.99
Turner, Tina/Ike	Workin' Together	CD	One Way	OW-33228	U.S.A.	2001	8.99
Turtles	Battle Of The Bands + 2	CD	Sundazed	SC-6038	U.S.A.	1994	8.99
Turtles	California Gold (Live)	CD	Laserlight	12-380	U.S.A.	1994	9.99
Turtles	Elenore + 8	CD	Repertoire	REP-4332-WY	Germany	1993	14.99
Turtles	Happy Together + 2	CD	Sundazed	SC-6037	U.S.A.	1994	8.99
Turtles	Happy Together + 9	CD	Repertoire	REP-4320-WY	Germany	1993	14.99
Turtles	It Ain't Me Babe (Stereo/Mono) + 2	CD	Repertoire	REP-4399-WY	Germany	1993	14.99
Turtles	It Ain't Me Babe + 3	CD	Sundazed	SC-6035	U.S.A.	1994	8.99
Turtles	The Best Of Volume 2 - Turtle Wax	CD	Rhino	R2-70159	U.S.A.	1988	8.99
Turtles	The Turtles 25 Classic Hits	CD	Repertoire	REP-4321-WG	Germany	1993	14.99
Artrles	The Turtles Anthology: Solid Zinc	2CD	Rhino	R2-78304	U.S.A.	2002	19.99
Turtles	Turtle Soup + 2	CD	Sundazed	SC-6086	U.S.A.	1994	8.99
Turtles	Turtle Soup +8	CD	Repertoire	REP-4398-WY	Germany	1993	14.99
Turtles	Turtles 20 Greatest Hits	CD	Rhino	RNCD-5160	U.S.A.	1984	8.99

T

Artist	Title	Format	Label	Catalog No	Country	Released	Value
Turtles	Wooden Head + 7	CD	Repertoire	REP-4400-WY	Germany	1993	14.99
Turtles	You Baby + 2	CD	Sundazed	SC-6036	U.S.A.	1994	8.99
Turtles	You Baby/Let Me Be (St/Mono) + 2	CD	Repertoire	REP-4401-WY	Germany	1993	14.99
Turtles/Crossfires	Out Of Control + 2	CD	Sundazed	SC-6062	U.S.A.	1995	8.99
Turtles/Flo & Eddie	Captured Live	CD	Rhino	R2-71153	U.S.A.	1992	12.99
Turtles/Flo & Eddie	Illegal, Immoral And Fattening	CD	One Way	A22673	U.S.A.	1992	11.99
Turtles/Flo & Eddie	Rock Steady With	CD	Epiphany	30006	U.S.A.	1998	9.99
Turtles/Flo & Eddie	The Best Of Flo & Eddie	CD	Rhino	R2-71097	U.S.A.	1987	14.99
Tush	Waiting For The Storm	CD	Zero	XRCN-1062	Japan	1992	28.99
Twain, Shania	Any Man Of Mine	CD Single	Mercury	MERCD433	England	1995	10.99
Twennynine/Lenny White	Best Of Friends	CD	Elektra	AMCY-2897	Japan	1979	94.99
Twilley, Dwight	Between the Cracks, Vol. 1	CD	Not Lame	NL-004	U.S.A.	1999	8.99
Twilley, Dwight	The Luck	CD	Big Oak Recordings	BORG001	U.S.A.	2001	8.99
Twilley, Dwight	Tulsa	CD	Copper	2252	U.S.A.	1999	8.99
Twilley, Dwight/Band	Rock Yourself	CD	Del Rack	DRZ-919	U.S.A.	1990	8.99
Twilley, Dwight/Band	Sincerely + 4	CD	DCC	SRZ-8002	U.S.A.	1990	29.99
Twilley, Dwight/Band	The Great Lost Twilley Band	CD	DCC	SRZ-8020	U.S.A.	1993	49.99
Twilley, Dwight/Band	Twilley Don't Mind + 1	CD	DCC	SRZ-8015	U.S.A.	1990	24.99
Twilley, Dwight/Band	XXI	CD	Right Stuff	7243-8-34569-2-7	U.S.A.	1996	8.99
Twisted Sister	Big Hits And Nasty Cuts	CD	East West	AMCY-2229	Japan	1997	24.99
Twisted Sister	Big Hits And Nasty Cuts: The Best Of	CD	Atlantic	82380-2	U.S.A.	1992	8.99
Twisted Sister	Club Daze Vol. I - Studio Sessions	CD	Spitfire	SPT-15023-2	U.S.A.	1999	10.99
Twisted Sister	Club Daze Vol. II - Never Say Never	CD	Spitfire	SPT-15059-2	U.S.A.	2001	10.99
Twisted Sister	Come Out & Play + 1	CD	Spitfire	SPT-15026-2	U.S.A.	1999	8.99
Twisted Sister	Live At Hammersmith	2CD	Spitfire	SPT-15078-2	U.S.A.	2001	8.99
Twisted Sister	Love Is For Suckers + 4	CD	Spitfire	SPT-15027-2	U.S.A.	1999	8.99
Twisted Sister	Noble Savage	2CD	Recall	SMD-CD-368	England	2002	12.99
Twisted Sister	Stay Hungry	CD	Atlantic	80156-2	U.S.A.	1984	8.99
Twisted Sister	The Essentials	CD	Rhino	R2-76078	U.S.A.	2002	8.99
Twisted Sister	Under The Blade	CD	Warner Bros.	18P2-2745	Japan	1985	24.99
Twisted Sister	Under The Blade + 1	CD	Spitfire	SPT-15024-2	U.S.A.	1999	9.99
Twisted Sister	You Can't Stop Rock & Roll + 3	CD	Spitfire	SPT-15025-2	U.S.A.	1999	8.99
Twisted Sister/Dee Snider	Never Let The ...	CD	Koch	KOC-CD-8058	U.S.A.	2000	12.99
Twisted Sister/Widowmaker	Blood & Bullets	CD	Esquire	74301-2	U.S.A.	1992	7.99
Twisted Sister/Widowmaker	Stand By For The Pain	CD	CMC Int.	06076-86903-2	U.S.A.	1998	6.99
Twisted Sister/Widowmaker	Stand By For The Pain	CD	Pony Canyon	PCCY-00732	Japan	1995	38.99
Tygers Of Pang Tang	Crazy Nights + 3	CD	Edgy	EDGY103	Austria	1997	14.99
Tygers Of Pang Tang	First Kill	CD	Castle	CLACD-258	France	1992	21.99
Tygers Of Pang Tang	Live At Nottingham Rock City	CD	Spitfire	SPT-15107-2	U.S.A.	2001	9.99
Tygers Of Pang Tang	Live At Wacken	CD	Spitfire	SPT-15149-2	U.S.A.	2001	9.99
Tygers Of Pang Tang	Live In The Roar	CD	Angel Air	SJPCD146	England	2003	14.99
Tygers Of Pang Tang	Singles	CD	MCA Victor	MVCM-318	Japan	1992	29.99
Tygers Of Pang Tang	Spellbound + 5	CD	Edgy	EDGY102	Austria	1997	14.99
Tygers Of Pang Tang	The Cage	CD	MCA Victor	MVCM-317	Japan	1992	29.99
Tygers Of Pang Tang	The Cage + 4	CD	Edgy	EDGY104	Austria	2001	14.99
Tygers Of Pang Tang	The Wreck-Age	CD	Spitfire	SPT-15106-2	U.S.A.	2001	9.99
Tygers Of Pang Tang	Wildcat + 8	CD	Edgy	EDGY101	Austria	2001	14.99
Tyla Gang	Moonproof	CD	Line	BECD-9.00150-0	Germany	1988	18.99
Tyla Gang	Yachtless	CD	Line	BECD-9.00503-0	Germany	1987	18.99
Tyla, Sean	Just Popped Out	CD	Line	LICD-9.00051-0	Germany	1989	18.99
Tyla, Sean	Redneck In Babylon	CD	Line	LICD-9.00011-0	Germany	1989	18.99
Tyla, Sean	Rhythm Of The Swing	CD	Line	INCD-9.00107-0	Germany	1989	18.99
Tyler, Bonnie	Best	CD	Sony	27200729-B	Holland	1997	10.99
Tyler, Bonnie	Faster Than The Speed Of Night	CD	Columbia	CK-38710	U.S.A.	1983	6.99
Tyler, Bonnie	Free Spirit	CD	Atlantic	82854-2	U.S.A.	1995	8.99
Tyler, Bonnie	Secret Dreams And Forbidden Fire	CD	Columbia	CK-40312	U.S.A.	1986	8.99
Tyler, Bonnie	The Definitive Collection (Bonus Cd)	CD	Sony	473522-9	Germany	1993	19.99
Tyner, Rob/MC5	Blood Brothers	CD	R&A	10601-2	U.S.A.	1990	15.99

T

Artist	Title	Format	Label	Catalog No	Country	Released	Value
Tyner, Rob/MC5	It's Only Rock And Roll	CD Single	RA	10621-2	U.S.A.	1990	15.99
Tyner, Rob/MC5	Rock And Roll People (Bonus Tracks)	CD	Captain Trip	CTCD-293	Japan	1977	15.99
Tyson, Ian	I Outgrew The Wagon	CD	Line	SDCD-9.00967-0	Germany	1990	15.99
Tyson, Sylvia	You Were On My Mind	CD	Line	SDCD-9.00964-0	Germany	1990	11.99

U

Artist	Title	Format	Label	Catalog No	Country	Released	Value
U.K.	Concert Classics - Vol 4 (Withdrawn)	CD	Renaissance	RRCC00704	U.S.A.	1999	9.99
U.K.	Danger Money	CD	Editions EG	EGCD-39	U.S.A.	1979	15.99
U.K.	Night After Night	CD	Editions EG	EGCD-42	U.S.A.	1979	14.99
U.K.	U.K.	CD	Editions EG	EGCD-35	U.S.A.	1978	8.99
U2	1990-2000 (Promo/500/17 (45's)/2 Cd)	CD	Universal	BXU213	England	2002	231.99
U2	3 Live Tracks Boston (Best Buy Promo)	CD Single	Interscope	INTR-10577-2	U.S.A.	2001	6.99
U2	Achtung Baby	CD	Nippon Phonogram	PHCR-704	Japan	1992	29.99
U2	Achtung Baby (Fold Out Cardboard)	CD	Island	314-510-490-2	U.S.A.	1991	7.99
U2	All That You ...(Promo/Interview)	CD	Island	U2INT900	Australia	2000	154.99
U2	All That You Can't Leave Behind + 1	2CD	Island	314-548-329-2	U.S.A.	2000	19.99
U2	All That You Can't Leave Behind + 1	CD	Island	548095-2	EU	2000	11.99
U2	Angel Of Harlem (3")	CD Single	Polystar	P10D-30007	Japan	1988	37.99
U2	Beautiful Day	CD Single	Victor Ent.	UICI-5002	Japan	2000	12.99
U2	Beautiful Day (Cd 2)	CD Single	Island	562-946-2	England	2000	4.99
U2	Beautiful Day (Promo)	CD Single	Island	CDP-679	Mexico	2000	19.99
U2	Beautiful Day (Promo)	CD Single	Island	BEAUTCD1	U.S.A.	2000	12.99
U2	Beautiful Day (Promo)	CD Single	Universal	MER00009	France	2000	107.99
U2	Best Of 1990 - 2000 & B Sides + DVD	2CD	Victor Ent.	UICI-9003	Japan	2002	29.99
U2	Best Of 1990 - 2000 (Promo Sampler)	CD	Island	PRCD7962-2	U.S.A.	2002	44.99
U2	Boy	CD	Island	7-90040-2	U.S.A.	1980	6.99
U2	Discotheque	CD Single	Polygram	854-775-2	Argentina	1996	19.99
U2	Discotheque	CD Single	Polygram K.K.	PHCR-8382	Japan	1997	12.99
U2	Discotheque	CD Single	Island	422-854-774-2	U.S.A.	1997	4.99
U2	Discotheque	CD Single	Island	422-854-789-2	U.S.A.	1997	4.99
U2	Discotheque (Promo)	CD Single	Island	DISCO-2	England	1997	29.99
U2	Discotheque (Promo)	CD Single	Island	854-877-2	Brazil	1997	106.99
U2	Discotheque (Promo)	CD Single	Island	DISCO-1	England	1997	8.99
U2	Electrical Storm	CD Single	Universal	063910-2	Argentina	2002	32.99
U2	Electrical Storm (Promo)	CD Single	Island	STORMCD01	England	2002	9.99
U2	Elevation	CD Single	Victor Ent.	UICI-5004	Japan	2002	12.99
U2	Elevation	CD Single	Island	588-669-2	Australia	2001	7.99
U2	Elevation (Promo Band Cover)	CD Single	Universal	ELECD2	England	2001	16.99
U2	Elevation (Promo)	CD Single	Interscope	10364-2	U.S.A.	2001	13.99
U2	Elevation (Tomb Raider Cvr Promo)	CD Single	Island	ELECD2	England	2001	15.99
U2	Elevation (Tomb Raider Promo Pic)	CD Single	Warner Bros.	7559-62669-2	Germany	2001	19.99
U2	Even Better Than...	CD Single	Island	422-866-977-2	Canada	1992	4.99
U2	Even Better Than... Remixes	CD Single	Island	422-864-281-2	U.S.A.	1992	4.99
U2	Excerpts/Rattle And Hum (Promo)	CD	Island	U2V7	England	1988	167.99
U2	Fly (Promo)	CD Single	Island	PRCD-6680-2	U.S.A.	1991	18.99
U2	Ground Beneath Her Feet (Promo)	CD Single	Interscope	GROUNDCD-1	England	2000	16.99
U2	Hasta La Vista Baby (Fan Club)	CD	Island	Hasta-CD-1	England	2000	59.99
U2	Hold Me, Thrill Me, Kiss Me, Kill Me	CD Single	Atlantic	PRCD-6237-2	U.S.A.	1995	8.99
U2	I Still Haven't Found...	CD Single	Island	664-987	Austria	1987	20.99
U2	If God Will Send His Angels (Promo)	CD Single	Island	CDP-762	Mexico	1998	89.99
U2	If God Will...(Promo)	CD Single	Island	ANGELCD-1	England	1997	14.99
U2	Last Night On Earth (Promo)	CD Single	Island	CDP-634-2	Mexico	1997	459.99
U2	Last Night On Earth (Promo)	CD Single	Island	PRCD-7517-2	U.S.A.	1997	14.99

U

Artist	Title	Format	Label	Catalog No	Country	Released	Value
U2	Last Night On Earth (Promo)	CD Single	Island	NIGHTCD1	England	1997	20.99
U2	Lemon	CD Single	Island	858-115-2	Australia	1993	25.99
U2	Lemon (Promo)	CD Single	Island	LEMCD1	England	1993	41.99
U2	Lemon (Promo)	CD Single	Island	PRCD-6800-2	U.S.A.	1993	85.99
U2	Melon (Fan Club)	CD	Island	MELONCD1	England	1995	34.99
U2	Million Dollar Hotel (Promo)	CD	Universal	MDHCD1	England	2000	39.99
U2	Mofo (Mexican Promo/Made In UK)	CD Single	Island	MOFOCD-1	Mexico	1997	349.99
U2	Mofo (Promo Acetate)	CD Single	Island	CIDRT684	Germany	1997	174.99
U2	Mofo Phunk Phorce (Promo)	CD Single	Island	MOFOCD2	England	1997	147.99
U2	Mysterious Ways (Promo)	CD Single	Island	U2-FREE	Japan	1991	129.99
U2	Mysterious Ways (Promo)	CD Single	Island	PRCD-6701-2	U.S.A.	1991	137.99
U2	New Year's Day	CD Single	Island	664-973-2	Austria	1983	9.99
U2	Numb (Promo)	CD Single	Island	PRCD-6785-2	U.S.A.	1993	121.99
U2	Numb (Promo)	CD Single	Island	PRCD-6795-2	U.S.A.	1993	122.99
U2	Numb (Promo)	CD Single	Island	NUMCD-1	England	1993	89.99
U2	October	CD	Island	7-90092-2	U.S.A.	1981	6.99
U2	One	CD Single	Island	422-866-533-2	U.S.A.	1992	4.99
U2	One (Promo)	CD Single	Island	PRCD-6706-2	U.S.A.	1991	23.99
U2	Please	CD Single	Island	572129-2	England	1997	7.99
U2	Please (Promo)	CD Single	Island	PLEASE-CD1	England	1997	19.99
U2	Pop + 1	CD	Polygram	PHCR-1835	Japan	1997	32.99
U2	Pop Muzik (Promo Only 250)	CD Single	Island	MUZIK-1	England	1997	51.99
U2	Previously	CD Single	Island	PRECD1	England	1996	24.99
U2	Previously (Promo)	CD	Island	PRCD-7335-2	U.S.A.	1996	21.99
U2	Pride (In The Name Of Love)	CD Single	Island	664-975	Austria	1984	26.99
U2	Rare And Remixed (Target Cd)	CD	Interscope	314-586-722-2	U.S.A.	2002	12.99
U2	Rattle And Hum	CD	Polystar	P24D-10054	Japan	1988	24.99
U2	Rattle And Hum	CD	Island	7-91003-2	U.S.A.	1988	8.99
U2	Staring At The Sun	CD Single	Island	854-973-2	England	1997	5.99
U2	Staring At The Sun	CD Single	Island	422-854-975-2	U.S.A.	1997	5.99
U2	Staring At The Sun (Promo)	CD Single	Island	PRCD-7445-2	U.S.A.	1997	14.99
U2	Staring At The Sun (Promo)	CD Single	Island	SUNCD-1	England	1997	16.99
U2	Stay (Faraway, So Close!) CD 1	CD Single	Island	858-077-2	England	1993	29.99
U2	Stay (Faraway, So Close!) CD2	CD Single	Island	858-079-2	England	1993	5.99
U2	Stay (Faraway, So Close)	CD Single	Island	422-858-097-2	Canada	1993	9.99
U2	Stay (Faraway, So Close) Promo	CD Single	Island	PRCD-6806-2	U.S.A.	1993	17.99
U2	Stay (Faraway, So Close) Promo	CD Single	Island	CIDDJ578	England	1993	34.99
U2	Stuck In A ... (Promo)	CD Single	Island	STUCKCD-1	England	2001	9.99
U2	Stuck In A Moment	CD Single	Island	572-806-2	Australia	2001	8.99
U2	Stuck In The (Canvas W/6 Postcards)	CD Single	Island	572-855-2	France	2001	39.99
U2	Summer Rain (Promo)	CD Single	Interscope	INTR-10220-2	U.S.A.	2000	9.99
U2	Sunday Bloody Sunday	CD Single	Island	664-971	Austria	1983	24.99
U2	Sweetest Thing	CD Single	Island	572-466-2	England	1998	5.99
U2	Sweetest Thing (3")	CD Single	Nippon Phonogram	PHDR-953	Japan	1998	19.99
U2	Sweetest Thing (Promo)	CD Single	Island	PRCD-7961-2	U.S.A.	1998	13.99
U2	Sweetest Thing (Promo)	CD Single	Island	SWEETCD1	England	1998	19.99
U2	Talk Pop (Promo Interview)	CD	Island	POP3	England	1997	24.99
U2	The Best Of 1980-1990	2CD	Island	314-524-612-2	U.S.A.	1998	16.99
U2	The Fly	CD Single	Island	422-868-885-2	U.S.A.	1991	5.99
U2	The Hands That Built America (Promo)	CD Single	Island	HANDSCD-1	England	2003	27.99
U2	The Joshua Tree (MFSL Gold Cd)	CD	Mobile Fidelity	UDCD-650	U.S.A.	1987	74.99
U2	The Unforgettable Fire	CD	Polystar	P35D-20002	Japan	1985	29.99
U2	The Unforgettable Fire	CD Single	Island	664-974	Austria	1985	24.99
U2	The Unforgettable Fire (MFSL Gold Cd)	CD	Mobile Fidelity	UDCD-624	U.S.A.	1984	28.99
U2	Theme From Mission Impossible	CD Single	Island	314-576-670-2	U.S.A.	1996	5.99
U2	U2 R.O.K.	CD Single	Island	664-972-2	Austria	1981	33.99
U2	U2-October 1991 (Promo Only 250)	CD Single	Island	U2-3	England	1991	359.99
U2	Under a Blood Red Sky	CD	Island	7-90127-2	U.S.A.	1983	8.99

U

Artist	Title	Format	Label	Catalog No	Country	Released	Value
U2	Walk On	CD Single	Island	588-846-2	England	2001	7.99
U2	Walk On	CD Single	Island	5889122	Australia	2001	7.99
U2	Walk On (Promo)	CD Single	Universal	WALKCD2	England	2001	24.99
U2	Walk On (Promo)	CD Single	Universal	WALKCD1	England	2001	19.99
U2	War (1st Pressing)	CD	Polystar	P35D-20008	Japan	1986	65.99
U2	War (MFSL Gold Cd)	CD	Mobile Fidelity	UDCD-571	U.S.A.	1983	24.99
U2	Westwood 1 # 00-35, (8,26-27-00)	2CD	Westwood 1	10035A081600	U.S.A.	2000	149.99
U2	Westwood 1 # 99-47 (11/20-21/99)	2CD	Westwood 1	19947A111099	U.S.A.	1999	149.99
U2	Westwood 1 Show # 98-15, (4,6,98)	2CD	Westwood 1	C125601XC	U.S.A.	1998	149.99
U2	WFM96.9 (Promo)	CD	Island	CDP-648	Mexico	1997	149.99
U2	Where The Streets... (Promo)	CD Single	Island	PR-2104-2	U.S.A.	1987	167.99
U2	Who's Gonna Ride...	CD Single	Island	422-864-521-2	U.S.A.	1992	4.99
U2	Who's Gonna Ride...	CD Single	Island	864-711-2	England	1992	29.99
U2	Who's Gonna Ride...	CD Single	Nippon Phonogram	PHCR-8706	Japan	1992	11.99
U2	Wide Awake In America	CD	Island	422-842-479-2	U.S.A.	1985	7.99
U2	With Or Without You (PAL/100 Only)	CDV	Island	IS319	England	1987	44.99
U2	Zooropa	CD	Nippon Phonogram	PHCR-1750	Japan	1993	24.99
U2	Zooropa	CD	Island	314-518-047-2	U.S.A.	1993	6.99
U2	Zooropa (Promo)	CD Single	Island	PRCD-6782-2	U.S.A.	1993	146.99
U2 /Promo	B Day (3") W/Folder/Airplane Tkt	CD Single	Universal	U21015	Taiwan	2000	241.99
U2/Passengers	Miss Sarajevo	CD Single	Island	854-481-2	England	1995	7.99
U2/Passengers	Miss Sarajevo (Promo)	CD Single	Polygram	CIDDJ-625	England	1995	24.99
U2/Passengers	Original Soundchat (Promo Interview)	2CD	Island	OST2	England	1995	69.99
U2/Passengers	Original Soundtracks 1	CD	Island	314-524-166-2	U.S.A.	1995	8.99
U2/Passengers	Passengers Orginal S.T. 1 (Promo)	CD	Island	PRCD-ML1	U.S.A.	1995	68.99
U2/Passengers	Your Blue Room (Promo)	CD Single	Island	OST3	England	1995	69.99
U2/The Edge	Captive (O.S.T.)	CD	Caroline	CAROL-1892-2	U.S.A.	1986	8.99
UB40	Tell Me Is It True (Promo)	CD Single	Virgin	DPRO-12258	U.S.A.	1997	5.99
UFO	Ain't Misbehavin'	CD	Metal Blade	7-73404-2	U.S.A.	1988	7.99
UFO	BBC Radio One Live In Concert	CD	Griffin	GCD-337-2	U.S.A.	1999	9.99
UFO	Covenant	CD	Shrapnel	SH-1142CD	U.S.A.	2000	16.99
UFO	Covenant	CD	Steamhammer	CRCL-4757	Japan	2000	24.99
UFO	Essential	CD	Toshiba-EMI	TOCP-3202	Japan	1994	11.99
UFO	Flying	CD	Line	GACD-9.00694-0	Germany	1988	10.99
UFO	Force It	CD	Toshiba-EMI	TOCP-53115	Japan	2000	24.99
UFO	Heaven's Gate (Live)	CD	Griffin	GCD-347-2	U.S.A.	1995	8.99
UFO	High Stakes	CD	Victor Ent.	VICP-5150	Japan	1992	29.99
UFO	High Stakes And Dangerous Men	CD	Essential	ESMCD-864	England	2000	11.99
UFO	In Session And Live In Concert	CD	Toshiba-EMI	TOCP-50764	Japan	1999	24.99
UFO	Lights Out	CD	Chrysalis	F2-21127	U.S.A.	1990	14.99
UFO	Lights Out + 1	CD	Toshiba-EMI	TOCP-53117	Japan	2000	28.99
UFO	Lights Out In Tokyo - Live	CD	Castle	ESSCD-191	England	1993	12.99
UFO	Live	CD	Line	GACD-9.00697-0	Germany	1988	10.99
UFO	Live	CD	Repertoire	REP-4698-WG	Germany	1999	11.99
UFO	Live In Texas	CD	Essential	ESMCD-862	England	2000	12.99
UFO	Making Contact	CD	Toshiba-EMI	TOCP-7205	Japan	1992	21.99
UFO	Making Contact +1	CD	Spitfire	SPT-15184-2	U.S.A.	2002	12.99
UFO	Making Contact + 1	CD	Toshiba-EMI	TOCP-53122	Japan	2000	34.99
UFO	Making Contact/Misdemeanour	2CD	BGO	BGOCD319	England	1996	17.99
UFO	Mechanix	CD	Spitfire	SPT-15180-2	U.S.A.	2002	12.99
UFO	Mechanix	CD	Toshiba-EMI	TOCP-53121	Japan	2000	19.99
UFO	Misdemeanor	CD	Toshiba-EMI	TOCP-7206	Japan	1992	20.99
UFO	Misdemeanor	CD	Toshiba-EMI	TOCP-53123	Japan	2000	24.99
UFO	No Heavy Petting	CD	BGO	BGOCD228	England	1998	17.99
UFO	No Heavy Petting	CD	Spitfire	SPT-15182-2	U.S.A.	2002	12.99
UFO	No Heavy Petting	CD	Toshiba-EMI	TOCP-53116	Japan	2000	29.99
UFO	No Heavy Petting	CD	Chrysalis	F2-21103	U.S.A.	1990	22.99
UFO	No Place To Run	CD	Toshiba-EMI	TOCP-7202	Japan	1992	30.99

U

Artist	Title	Format	Label	Catalog No	Country	Released	Value
UFO	No Place To Run	CD	Toshiba-EMI	TOCP-53119	Japan	2000	29.99
UFO	Obsession	CD	Toshiba-EMI	TOCP-53118	Japan	2000	24.99
UFO	Obsession	CD	Chrysalis	F2-21182	U.S.A.	1990	16.99
UFO	Obsession/No Place to Run	2CD	BGO	BGOCD229	England	1995	17.99
UFO	On With The Action	CD	Zoom Club	ZCRCD1	England	2000	15.99
UFO	Parker's Birthday	CD	Griffin	GCD-107-2	U.S.A.	1995	8.99
UFO	Phenomenon	CD	Chrysalis	F2-21059	U.S.A.	1990	14.99
UFO	Phenomenon	CD	Toshiba-EMI	TOCP-53114	Japan	2000	24.99
UFO	Phenomenon/Force It	2CD	BGO	BGOCD227	England	1995	17.99
UFO	Regenerator	CD	Zoom Club	ZCRCD80044	England	2001	15.99
UFO	Sharks	CD	Shrapnel	SH-1156-CD	U.S.A.	2001	8.99
UFO	Sharks + 3	CD	Victor Ent.	VICP-62034	Japan	2002	24.99
UFO	Space Metal	CD	Line	GACD-9.00704-0	Germany	1988	10.99
UFO	Strangers In The Night	CD	Capitol	F2-21209	U.S.A.	1990	14.99
UFO	Strangers In The Night + 2	CD	Toshiba-EMI	TOCP-65355	Japan	2000	40.99
UFO	The Best Of The Rest	CD	Chrysalis	F2-21644	U.S.A.	1988	9.99
UFO	The Decca Years	CD	Repertoire	REP-4311-WG	Germany	2002	12.99
UFO	The Early Years	CD	Castle	EARL9	England	1994	8.99
UFO	The Essential	CD	Chrysalis	F2-21888	U.S.A.	1992	9.99
UFO	The Wild, The Willing/The Innocent	CD	Toshiba-EMI	TOCP-7203	Japan	1992	25.99
UFO	The X - Factor: Out There And Back	2CD	Snapper	SMDCD-122	England	1998	17.99
UFO	Then & Now	CD	Sanctuary	06076-86330-2	U.S.A.	2003	8.99
UFO	Time To Rock: Best Of Singles A's/B's	CD	Repertoire	REP-4720-WG	Germany	2000	16.99
UFO	Twtwati	CD	Toshiba-EMI	TOCP-53200	Japan	2000	24.99
UFO	UFO 1	CD	Line	GACD-9.00691-0	Germany	1988	10.99
UFO	UFO 1	CD	Repertoire	REP-4742-WG	Germany	1999	11.99
UFO	Walk On Water	CD	CMC Int.	06076-86239-2	U.S.A.	1998	11.99
UFO	Walk On Water +3	CD	Zero	XRCN-1237	Japan	1995	17.99
UFO	Wild Willing & Innocent/Mechanix	2CD	BGO	BGOCD230	England	1995	18.99
UFO	Wild, The Willing/The Innocent + 1	CD	Toshiba-EMI	TOCP-53120	Japan	2000	31.99
Ugly Americans	Boom Boom Baby	CD	Capricorn	314-534-262-2	U.S.A.	1998	5.99
Ugly Americans	Stereophonic Spanish Fly	CD	Capricorn	314-532-458-2	U.S.A.	1996	5.99
UK Subs	Another Kind Of Blues	CD	Line	TCCD-9.00532-0	Germany	1988	10.99
UK Subs	Brand New Age	CD	Line	TCCD-9.00672-0	Germany	1988	14.99
UK Subs	Crash Course Live	CD	Line	TCCD-9.00675-0	Germany	1988	13.99
UK Subs	Diminished Responsibility	CD	Line	TCCD-9.00678-0	Germany	1988	16.99
UK Subs	Endangered Species	CD	Line	TCCD-9.00546-0	Germany	1988	11.99
Ullman, Tracey	Takes On The Hits	CD	Varese	302-066-376-2	U.S.A.	2002	11.99
Ullman, Tracey	The Best Of Tracey Ullman	CD	Repertoire	REP-4243-WG	Germany	1992	13.99
Ullman, Tracey	The Very Best Of	CD	Disky	DC-869772	Netherlands	1996	13.99
Ullman, Tracey	You Broke My Heart In 17 (Best Of)	CD	Rhino	R2-70292	U.S.A.	1992	27.99
Ullman, Tracey	You Caught Me Out + 6	CD	Repertoire	REP-4252-WY	Germany	1992	32.99
Ullman, Tracey/J L Ponty	Puss In Boots (Jean Luc Ponty)	CD	Rhino	R2-70456	U.S.A.	1991	8.99
Ulman, Tracey	You Broke My Heart In 17 Places + 5	CD	Repertoire	REP-4221-WY	Germany	1991	32.99
Ultimate Spinach	Box Set (S.T. + 2/Behold & See + 2/III)	3CD	Akarma	AK-121/3	Italy	2001	45.99
Ultravox	BBC Radio 1 Live In Concert	CD	Windsong	WINCD028	England	1992	14.99
Ultravox	Ha! Ha! Ha!	CD	Island	846-157-2	France	1977	14.99
Ultravox	I Am Alive	CD Single	DSB	DSB-3097-5	Germany	1992	5.99
Ultravox	Rage In Eden	CD	EMI	7243-857409-2-3	England	1997	8.99
Ultravox	Revelation	CD	DSB	DSB-3098-2	Germany	1993	6.99
Ultravox	Systems Of Romance	CD	Island	846-158-2	France	1978	14.99
Ultravox	Three Into One (Best Of Foxx)	CD	Polygram K.K.	PHCR-4827	Japan	1997	24.99
Ultravox	Ultravox!	CD	Island	846-159-2	France	1977	21.99
Ultravox	Vienna 92	CD Single	ZYX	6767-8	Germany	1992	5.99
Undertones	Best Of (Promo)	CD	Rykodisc	VRCD-0293	U.S.A.	1994	17.99
Undertones	Cher O'Bowlies	CD	EMI	7463652	England	1986	11.99
Undertones	Hypnotised + 5	CD	Rykodisc	RCD-10294	U.S.A.	1980	6.99
Undertones	Positive Touch + 4	CD	Rykodisc	RCD-10295	U.S.A.	1981	6.99

U

Artist	Title	Format	Label	Catalog No	Country	Released	Value
Undertones	The Undertones + 7	CD	Rykodisc	RCD-10293	U.S.A.	1979	15.99
Unicorn	Uphill All The Way	CD	Line	TACD-9.00745-0	Germany	1989	24.99
United States Of America	United States Of America (Joe Boyd)	CD	Edsel	EDCD-541	England	1997	17.99
Up All Night	Self Titled	CD	Alfa	ALCB-3065	Japan	1995	28.99
Urbanrobot	Voodoo Chile	CD Single	Line	URCD-9.00825-E	Germany	1989	9.99
Ure, Midge	Answers To Nothing	CD	Chrysalis	CCD-1649	England	1988	13.99
Ure, Midge	BBC Live In Concert	CD	Strange Fruit	SFRSCD086	England	1999	14.99
Ure, Midge	Breathe	CD Single	Arista	74321-37117-2	EC	1996	8.99
Ure, Midge	Cold, Cold Heart	CD Single	Arista	664-555	England	1991	6.99
Ure, Midge	Fields Of Fire	CD Single	Arista	7432158085-2	EU	1998	6.99
Ure, Midge	Guns And Arrows	CD Single	Arista	74321-140760-2	EC	1996	4.99
Ure, Midge	Let It Go?	CD Single	Arista	665-296	Germany	1992	6.99
Ure, Midge	Pure	CD	Arista	261-922	Germany	1991	4.99
Ure, Midge	The Gift	CD	EMI	7243-8-52963-2-1	England	1996	8.99
Ure, Midge	Very Best Of Midge Ure & Ultravox	CD	Chrysalis	0946-3-21995-2-2	U.S.A.	1993	7.99
Ure, Midge	Went To Coney Island On A...	CD	Evenmore	L00811-23-A	England	2000	15.99
Uriah Heep	20th Century Masters: The Millennium	CD	Mercury	314-586-363-2	U.S.A.	2001	8.99
Uriah Heep	A Time For Revlation Box Set	4CD	Essential	ESFCD-298	England	1996	99.99
Uriah Heep	Abominog + 4	CD	Sanctuary	06076-81122-2	U.S.A.	2001	10.99
Uriah Heep	Abominog + 4	CD	Essential	ESMCD-571	England	1997	10.99
Uriah Heep	Acoustically Driven	CD	Classic Rock	CRP0676	England	2002	13.99
Uriah Heep	Acoustically Driven (CD/DVD)	2CD	Classic Rock	CRP0991	England	2002	19.99
Uriah Heep	Across The Miles (Promo)	CD Single	Spitfire	CD-PRO-5032	U.S.A.	1998	19.99
Uriah Heep	Ballads	CD	Castle	CMRCD238	England	2001	11.99
Uriah Heep	Best Of Volume 2	CD	Essential	ESMCD-594	England	1998	7.99
Uriah Heep	Between Two Worlds	2CD	Snapper	SMDCD-386	England	2002	12.99
Uriah Heep	Blood On Stone: Anthology Vol. 2	2CD	Castle	CMEDD171	England	2001	17.99
Uriah Heep	Classic Heep: An Anthology	CD	Mercury	558-863-2	U.S.A.	1998	7.99
Uriah Heep	Come Away Melinda	CD Single	Classic Rock	CRL0692	England	2001	5.99
Uriah Heep	Conquest + 5	CD	Essential	ESMCD-570	England	1997	10.99
Uriah Heep	Demons And Wizards	CD	Mercury	812-297-2	U.S.A.	1972	8.99
Uriah Heep	Demons And Wizards + 5	CD	Castle	CMRCD672	England	2003	10.99
Uriah Heep	Different World + 2	CD	Essential	ESMCD-614	England	1998	10.99
Uriah Heep	Easy Livin'	2CD	Sanctuary	SANDD-189	England	2003	12.99
Uriah Heep	Electrically Driven	CD	Classic Rock	CRL0715	England	2001	14.99
Uriah Heep	Equator + 2	CD	Sony	493-339-2	England	1999	10.99
Uriah Heep	Fallen Angel + 4	CD	Sanctuary	06076-81123-2	U.S.A.	2001	10.99
Uriah Heep	Fallen Angel + 4	CD	Essential	ESMCD-561	England	1997	10.99
Uriah Heep	Firefly + 4	CD	Sanctuary	06076-81113-2	U.S.A.	2001	10.99
Uriah Heep	Firefly + 4	CD	Essential	ESMCD-559	England	1997	10.99
Uriah Heep	Firefly/Head First/Demons & Wizards	3CD	Castle	CLABX903	England	1992	29.99
Uriah Heep	Firefly/Innocent Victim/Fallen Angel	3CD	Essential	ESMBX-307	England	1998	29.99
Uriah Heep	Future Echoes Of The Past	2CD	Phantom	0605	England	2001	14.99
Uriah Heep	Greatest Hits	CD	Essential	ESMCD-418	England	1996	8.99
Uriah Heep	Head First + 3	CD	Essential	ESMCD-572	England	1997	10.99
Uriah Heep	Heartless Land (Promo)	CD Single	Eagle	EAGXS-056	Germany	1998	19.99
Uriah Heep	High And Mighty + 2	CD	Essential	ESMCD-468	England	1997	10.99
Uriah Heep	High And Mighty + 4	CD	Sanctuary	06076-81105-2	U.S.A.	2001	10.99
Uriah Heep	Innocent Victim + 2	CD	Sanctuary	06076-81114-2	England	2001	10.99
Uriah Heep	Innocent Victim + 2	CD	Essential	ESMCD-560	England	1997	10.99
Uriah Heep	King Biscuit Flower Hour Live	CD	King Biscuit	70710-88027-2	U.S.A.	1997	14.99
Uriah Heep	Lady In Black	CD Single	Classic Rock	CRL0720	England	2001	5.99
Uriah Heep	Live	CD	Mercury	822-790-2	U.S.A.	1973	8.99
Uriah Heep	Live (1973)	CD	Essential	ESMCD-320	England	1996	10.99
Uriah Heep	Live '73 (Expanded Deluxe Edition)	2CD	Castle	CMRCD772	England	2003	19.99
Uriah Heep	Live At Shepperton '74 + 3	CD	Essential	ESMCD-590	England	1999	6.99
Uriah Heep	Live In Europe '79 + 6	2CD	Sanctuary	06076-81115-2	U.S.A.	2001	14.99
Uriah Heep	Live In Moscow	CD	Castle	CLACD-276	England	1988	8.99

U

Artist	Title	Format	Label	Catalog No	Country	Released	Value
Uriah Heep	Live In Moscow + 2	CD	Sanctuary	06076-81124-2	U.S.A.	2001	10.99
Uriah Heep	Live In The U.S.A.	CD	Classic Rock	CRL1089	England	2003	14.99
Uriah Heep	Live In The U.S.A. (CD/DVD)	2CD	Classic Rock	CRL1164	England	2002	19.99
Uriah Heep	Look At Yourself	CD	Mercury	814-180-2	U.S.A.	1971	8.99
Uriah Heep	Look At Yourself + 7	CD	Castle	CMRCD671	England	2003	10.99
Uriah Heep	Look At Yourself/Very 'eavy	2CD	Castle	TFOCD7/1-2	England	1988	24.99
Uriah Heep	Raging Silence + 6	CD	Essential	ESMCD-612	England	1998	10.99
Uriah Heep	Rarities	CD	Castle	CMRCD237	England	2001	11.99
Uriah Heep	Remasters	2CD	Classic Rock	CRL0932	England	2002	12.99
Uriah Heep	Return To Fantasy + 4	CD	Sanctuary	06076-81104-2	U.S.A.	2001	10.99
Uriah Heep	Return To Fantasy + 4	CD	Essential	ESMCD-381	England	1996	10.99
Uriah Heep	Salisbury	CD	Mercury	811-389-2	U.S.A.	1970	8.99
Uriah Heep	Salisbury + 6	CD	Castle	CMRCD643	England	2003	10.99
Uriah Heep	Sea Of Light	CD	Spitfire	SPT-15033-2	U.S.A.	1998	10.99
Uriah Heep	Sea Of Light	CD	HTD	HTD-CD-33	England	1995	10.99
Uriah Heep	Sea Of Light/Spellbinder	2CD	SPV	310-21920	Germany	2000	14.99
Uriah Heep	Sea Of Light/Spellbinder	2CD	SPV	310-21920	Germany	2000	14.99
Uriah Heep	Self Titled (W/Birds Of Prey)	CD	Mercury	834-769-2	U.S.A.	1970	8.99
Uriah Heep	Sonic Origami	CD	Spitfire	SPT-15032-2	U.S.A.	1998	8.99
Uriah Heep	Sonic Origami	CD	Eagle	EADCD-043	England	1998	8.99
Uriah Heep	Spellbinder	CD	Spitfire	SPT-15034-2	U.S.A.	1999	8.99
Uriah Heep	Spellbinder	CD	SPV	085-76992-CD	Germany	1996	8.99
Uriah Heep	Spellbinder + 1	CD	Teichiku	TECW-25208	Japan	1996	24.99
Uriah Heep	Still 'eavy Still Proud + 3	CD	Essential	ESMCD-613	England	1998	9.99
Uriah Heep	Sweet Freedom + 3	CD	Essential	ESMCD-338	England	1996	10.99
Uriah Heep	The Collection	CD	Castle	PIESD-245	England	2000	7.99
Uriah Heep	The Landsdown Tapes	2CD	Castle	CMDDD441	England	2002	13.99
Uriah Heep	The Magician's Birthday	CD	Mercury	812-298-2	U.S.A.	1972	8.99
Uriah Heep	The Magician's Birthday + 2	CD	Essential	ESMCD-339	England	1996	10.99
Uriah Heep	The Magician's Birthday Party	CD	Classic Rock	CRL0933	England	2002	13.99
Uriah Heep	The Very Best Of	CD	Sanctuary	06076-81161-2	U.S.A.	2002	10.99
Uriah Heep	Travellers In Time: Anthology Vol. 1	2CD	Essential	ESDCD-818	England	2001	17.99
Uriah Heep	Two Sides Of (Electrically/Acoustically)	2CD	Classic Rock	CRL0731	England	2001	13.99
Uriah Heep	Very 'eavy...Very 'umble	CD	Griffin	GCD-105-2	U.S.A.	1995	8.99
Uriah Heep	Very 'eavy...Very 'umble + 8	CD	Castle	CMRCD642	England	2003	10.99
Uriah Heep	Very 'eavy/Salisbury/Look At Yourself	3CD	Castle	CBC-8039	Germany	1992	34.99
Uriah Heep	Very 'eavy/Salisbury/Look At Yourself	3CD	Essential	ESMBX-306	England	1998	39.99
Uriah Heep	Wonderland + 4	CD	Sanctuary	06076-81103-2	U.S.A.	2001	10.99
Uriah Heep	Wonderland + 4	CD	Essential	ESMCD-380	England	1996	10.99
Uriah Heep	You Can't Keep... Box Set	7 Mini Lp	Castle	CMXBX527	England	2002	49.99
Uriah Heep/David Byron	On The Rocks	CD	Repertoire	REP-4341-WY	Germany	1993	12.99
Uriah Heep/David Byron	Take No Prisoners	CD	Repertoire	REP-4283-WY	Germany	1998	12.99
Uriah Heep/Ken Hensley	Anthology	CD	Castle	569	U.S.A.	2000	12.99
Uriah Heep/Ken Hensley	Eager To Please	CD	Repertoire	REP-4342-WY	Germany	1998	12.99
Uriah Heep/Ken Hensley	Free Spirit	CD	Repertoire	REP-4343-WY	Germany	1998	12.99
Uriah Heep/Ken Hensley	From Time To Time	CD	Viceroy	VIC-6016-2	U.S.A.	1994	11.99
Uriah Heep/Ken Hensley	Glimpse Of Glory	CD	Mystic	MYS-CD-157	England	2003	10.99
Uriah Heep/Ken Hensley	Proud Words On A Dusty Shelf	CD	Repertoire	REP-4282-WY	Germany	1997	12.99
Uriah Heep/Ken Hensley	Running Blind	CD	Mystic	MYS-CD-153	England	2002	12.99
Uriah Heep/Ken Hensley	The Gods - Genesis	CD	Repertoire	REP-4418-WY	Germany	2002	14.99
Uriah Heep/Ken Hensley	The Gods - To Samuel A Son	CD	Repertoire	REP-4555-WY	Germany	2002	14.99
Uriah Heep/Metalium	Hero Nation Chapter Three	CD	Massacre	319	U.S.A.	2002	22.99
Usher, Gary	A Symphonic Salute To Brian Wilson	CD	Dreamsville	YDCD-0047	Japan	2001	31.99
Usher, Gary	Add Some Music to Your Day	CD	Poptones	MC5038CD	England	2001	12.99
Usher, Gary	Beyond a Shadow of Doubt + 9	CD	Dreamsville	YDCD-0054	Japan	2001	35.99
Usher, Gary/Richard Delvy	Hot Rod City + 8	CD	Sundazed	SC-11025	U.S.A.	1995	10.99

U

Artist	Title	Format	Label	Catalog No	Country	Released	Value

V

Artist	Title	Format	Label	Catalog No	Country	Released	Value
V2	Self Titled + 4	CD	Victor Ent.	VICP-60046	Japan	1997	39.99
Vagabond	A Huge Fan Of Life	CD	Victor Ent.	VICP-5608	Japan	1995	34.99
Vai, Steve	Alien Love Secrets	CD	Epic	EK-68031	U.S.A.	1997	8.99
Vai, Steve	Alive In An Ultraworld	2CD	Epic	E2K-85183	U.S.A.	2001	13.99
Vai, Steve	Fire Garden	CD	Epic	EK-67776	U.S.A.	1996	8.99
Vai, Steve	Flex-Able + 4	CD	Epic	EK-68033	U.S.A.	1997	9.99
Vai, Steve	Flex-Able Leftovers	CD	Epic	EK-69703	U.S.A.	1998	9.99
Vai, Steve	Infinite Steve Vai: An Anthology	2CD	Epic	E2K-90713	U.S.A.	2003	11.99
Vai, Steve	Mystery Tracks Archives, Vol. 3	CD	Favored Nations	FN2350-2	U.S.A.	2003	11.99
Vai, Steve	Passion And Warfare	CD	Epic	EK-68030	U.S.A.	1997	8.99
Vai, Steve	Sex & Religion	CD	Epic	EK-68032	U.S.A.	1997	8.99
Vai, Steve	Sex & Religion + 1	CD	Sony	SRCS-6796	Japan	1993	29.99
Vai, Steve	The 7th Song	CD	Epic	EK-85182	U.S.A.	2000	9.99
Vai, Steve	The Elusive Light and Sound, Vol. 1	CD	Favored Nations	FN2220-2	U.S.A.	2002	11.99
Vai, Steve	The Ultra Zone	CD	Epic	EK-69817	U.S.A.	1999	8.99
Vai, Steve	Ultra Zone + 1	CD	Sony	SRCS-8977	Japan	1999	29.99
Valensia/Valentine	Gaia (Holographic Cover)	CD	Mercury	PHCR-1253	Japan	1993	17.99
Valensia/Valentine	Kosmos Limited Edition	CD	Mercury	PHCR-1445	Japan	1996	18.99
Valensia/Valentine	V	CD	Polydor	POCP-7394	Japan	1991	17.99
Valensia/Valentine	VIII	CD	Mercury	PHCR-1631	Japan	1998	17.99
Valentine	4 United	CD	Polydor	POCP-7234	Japan	1997	17.99
Valentine	Believing Is Seeing	CD	Polydor	UICE-1003	Japan	2000	21.99
Valentine	Christmas In Heaven	CD Single	Polydor	POCP-7266	Japan	1997	23.99
Valentine	Hand In Hand	CD Single	Polydor	POCP-7031	Japan	1995	23.99
Valentine	I Believe In Music	CD Single	Polydor	POCP-7235	Japan	1997	23.99
Valentine	No Sugar Added	CD	Polydor	POCP-7322	Japan	1998	21.99
Valentine, Robby	Live & Demos	CD Single	Polydor	POCP-1460	Japan	1994	23.99
Valentine, Robby	Magic Infinity + 2	CD	Polydor	POCP-1418	Japan	1993	24.99
Valentine, Robby	Self Titled + 2	CD	Polydor	POCP-1417	Japan	1994	29.99
Valli, Frankie	Frankie Valli Solo	CD	Disky	DCD-5410	Netherlands	1995	29.99
Valli, Frankie/Four Seasons	The Very Best Of...	CD	Crimson	CRIMCD107	England	1998	11.99
Van Beethoven, Camper	II & III & Plus	CD	Line	FBCD-9.00320-0	Germany	1987	24.99
Van Beethoven, Camper	III	CD	Line	FBCD-9.00279-0	Germany	1987	19.99
Van Der Graaf Generator	Aerosol Grey Machine (W/Bonus)	CD	Fie!	FIE-9116	England	1997	10.99
Van Der Graaf Generator	An Introduction	CD	Virgin	7243-8-50390-2-7	England	2000	10.99
Van Der Graaf Generator	Curly's Airships (4 V D Graaf Members)	2CD	Masters Of Art	MASTER101	England	2000	24.99
Van Der Graaf Generator	David Jackson - Fractal Bridge	CD	Fie!	FIE-9113	England	1996	14.99
Van Der Graaf Generator	David Jackson - Tonewall Stands	CD	Voiceprint	VP104CD	England	1992	28.99
Van Der Graaf Generator	First Generation	CD	Virgin	0777-7-87546-2-6	England	1986	9.99
Van Der Graaf Generator	First Generation 1969 - 1971	CD	Virgin	COMCD2	England	1989	10.99
Van Der Graaf Generator	Godbluff	CD	Virgin	0777-7-87547-2-5	Holland	1975	9.99
Van Der Graaf Generator	H To He...	CD	Caroline	CAROL-1638-2	U.S.A.	1990	9.99
Van Der Graaf Generator	Hugh Banton Solo (Bach Goldberg Var)	CD	Fie!	FIE-9128	England	2002	14.99
Van Der Graaf Generator	Maida Vale: Radio One Sessions	CD	Strange Fruit	104	England	1995	9.99
Van Der Graaf Generator	Masters From The Vaults	CD	Classic Rock	CRL1116	England	2003	8.99
Van Der Graaf Generator	Now And Then	CD	Thunderbolt	CDTB-042	England	1996	12.99
Van Der Graaf Generator	Pawn Hearts	CD	Caroline	CAROL-1639-2	U.S.A.	1990	9.99
Van Der Graaf Generator	Second Generation 1975 - 1977	CD	Virgin	COMCD3	England	1989	12.99
Van Der Graaf Generator	Still Life	CD	Caroline	CAROL-1641-2	U.S.A.	1990	9.99
Van Der Graaf Generator	The Aerosol Grey Machine + 2	CD	Repertoire	REP-4647-WY	Germany	1997	10.99

Artist	Title	Format	Label	Catalog No	Country	Released	Value
Van Der Graaf Generator	The Box (Set)	4CD	Virgin	VDGGBOX1	France	2000	76.99
Van Der Graaf Generator	The Least We Can Do...	CD	Caroline	CAROL-1826-2	U.S.A.	1991	9.99
Van Der Graaf Generator	The Masters	CD	Eagle	EAB-CD-085	England	1998	9.99
Van Der Graaf Generator	The Quiet Zone/The Pleasure Dome	CD	Caroline	CAROL-1640-2	U.S.A.	1990	9.99
Van Der Graaf Generator	Time Vaults	CD	Spalax	14847	France	1996	12.99
Van Der Graaf Generator	Time Vaults	CD	Thunderbolt	CDTB-106	England	1985	12.99
Van Der Graaf Generator	Vital (Live)	CD	Caroline	CAROL-1636-2	U.S.A.	1990	9.99
Van Der Graaf Generator	World Record	CD	Virgin	0777-7-87555-2-4	Holland	1976	9.99
Van Halen	1984	CD	Warner Bros.	WPCR-10921	Japan	1984	22.99
Van Halen	1984	CD	Warner Bros.	9-47741-2	U.S.A.	2000	8.99
Van Halen	3	CD	Warner Bros.	WPCR-1600	Japan	1998	17.99
Van Halen	5150	CD	Warner Bros.	WPCR-1039	Japan	1986	22.99
Van Halen	5150	CD	Warner Bros.	9-25394-2	U.S.A.	1986	8.99
Van Halen	5150	CD	Warner Bros.	POP2-2619	Japan	1986	18.99
Van Halen	Amsterdam (Blue Tin Ltd)	CD Single	Warner Bros.	9362-43555-2	Germany	1995	11.99
Van Halen	Amsterdam (Promo)	CD Single	Warner Bros.	PRO-CD-7567-R	U.S.A.	1995	7.99
Van Halen	Balance	CD	Warner Bros.	9-45760-2	U.S.A.	1995	8.99
Van Halen	Balance + 1	CD	Warner Bros.	WPCR-110	Japan	1995	19.99
Van Halen	Best Of (Promo)	CD	Warner Bros.	2-46332-DJ	U.S.A.	1996	24.99
Van Halen	Best Of Volume 1	CD	Warner Bros.	9-46332-2	U.S.A.	1996	8.99
Van Halen	Best Of Volume One (W/Slipcase)	CD	Warner Bros.	0-93624-63322-8	Taiwan	2001	24.99
Van Halen	Best Of Volume One + 1	CD	Warner Bros.	WPCR-900	Japan	1996	24.99
Van Halen	Black And Blue (Promo)	CD Single	Warner Bros.	PRO-CD-3085	U.S.A.	1988	14.99
Van Halen	Can't Stop Lovin' You	CD Single	Warner Bros.	9362-43510-2	England	1995	7.99
Van Halen	Can't Stop Lovin' You (Black Tin)	CD Single	Warner Bros.	9362-43511-2	Germany	1995	11.99
Van Halen	Can't Stop Lovin' You (DJ/Remix)	CD Single	Warner Bros.	PRO-CD-7514-R	U.S.A.	1995	9.99
Van Halen	Can't Stop Loving You	CD Single	Warner Bros.	9-17909-2	U.S.A.	1995	5.99
Van Halen	Dirty Water Dog	CD Single	Warner Bros.	WPCR-2073	Japan	1998	14.99
Van Halen	Diver Down	CD	Warner Bros.	WPCR-10920	Japan	1982	22.99
Van Halen	Diver Down	CD	Warner Bros.	9-47718-2	U.S.A.	2000	8.99
Van Halen	Don't Tell Me	CD Single	Warner Bros.	9362-41919-2	Germany	1995	9.99
Van Halen	Don't Tell Me (Gold Tin)	CD Single	Warner Bros.	9362-41924-2	Germany	1995	11.99
Van Halen	Don't Tell Me (Promo)	CD Single	Warner Bros.	PRO-CD-7341	U.S.A.	1995	7.99
Van Halen	Dreams	CD Single	Warner Bros.	2-18592	U.S.A.	1993	7.99
Van Halen	Dreams (Promo)	CD Single	Warner Bros.	PRO-CD-6158	U.S.A.	1993	14.99
Van Halen	Fair Warning	CD	Warner Bros.	9-47740-2	U.S.A.	2000	8.99
Van Halen	Fair Warning	CD	Warner Bros.	WPCR-10919	Japan	1981	22.99
Van Halen	Feelin' (Promo)	CD Single	Warner Bros.	PRO-CD-7784-R	U.S.A.	1995	7.99
Van Halen	Feels So Good	CD Single	Warner Bros.	921-177-2	Germany	1989	22.99
Van Halen	Feels So Good (Promo)	CD Single	Warner Bros.	PRO-CD-3279	U.S.A.	1988	14.99
Van Halen	Feels So Good (Promo/Remix)	CD Single	Warner Bros.	PRO-CD-3422	U.S.A.	1988	14.99
Van Halen	Finish What You Started (DJ/Remix)	CD Single	Warner Bros.	PRO-CD-3240	U.S.A.	1988	14.99
Van Halen	For Unlawful Carnal Knowledge	CD	Warner Bros.	9-26594-2	U.S.A.	1991	8.99
Van Halen	Human Being (Promo)	CD Single	Warner Bros.	PRO-CD-8200	U.S.A.	1996	24.99
Van Halen	Human Being (Twister O.S.T. Single)	CD Single	Warner Bros.	WPCR-788	Japan	1996	15.99
Van Halen	II	CD	Warner Bros.	WPCR-10917	Japan	1979	22.99
Van Halen	III (Tin W/Babypack/11 Cards/Pick)	CD	Warner Bros.	9-46858-2	U.S.A.	1998	8.99
Van Halen	Jump (Tin Can/Stage Pass)	CD Single	Warner Bros.	9362-40796-2	Germany	1993	13.99
Van Halen	Live: Jump	CD Single	Warner Bros.	9362-40771-2	Germany	1993	13.99
Van Halen	Live: Right Here, Right Now	2CD	Warner Bros.	45198-2	U.S.A.	1993	10.99
Van Halen	Live: Right Here, Right Now	2CD	Warner Bros.	WPCR-2273/4	Japan	1993	34.99
Van Halen	Me Wise Magic	CD Single	Warner Bros.	9362-43795-2	Germany	1996	11.99
Van Halen	Me Wise Magic (Promo)	CD Single	Warner Bros.	PRO-CD-8474	U.S.A.	1996	10.99
Van Halen	Mini Best	CD Single	Warner Bros.	WPCR-1497	Japan	1997	13.99
Van Halen	Not Enough	CD Single	Larner Bros.	2-17810	U.S.A.	1995	6.99
Van Halen	Not Enough (Promo/Radio Remix)	CD Single	Warner Bros.	PRO-CD-7681	U.S.A.	1995	12.99
Van Halen	Not Enough (Promo/Soft Mix)	CD Single	Warner Bros.	PRO-CD-7838-R	U.S.A.	1995	12.99
Van Halen	OU812	CD	Warner Bros.	WPCR-2271	Japan	1988	22.99

V

Artist	Title	Format	Label	Catalog No	Country	Released	Value
Van Halen	OU812	CD	Warner Bros.	9-25732-2	U.S.A.	1988	8.99
Van Halen	Poundcake	CD Single	Warner Bros.	9362-40126-2	Germany	1991	8.99
Van Halen	Poundcake (3")	CD Single	Warner Bros.	WPDP-6283	Japan	1991	6.99
Van Halen	Poundcake (Promo)	CD Single	Warner Bros.	PRO-CD-4884	U.S.A.	1990	9.99
Van Halen	Right Now	CD Single	Warner Bros.	PRO-CD-5030	U.S.A.	1991	12.99
Van Halen	Runaround (Promo)	CD Single	Warner Bros.	PRO-CD-4922	U.S.A.	1990	12.99
Van Halen	Self Titled	CD	Warner Bros.	WPCR-10916	Japan	1978	22.99
Van Halen	Top Of The World	CD Single	Warner Bros.	9362-40243-2	Germany	1991	7.99
Van Halen	Top Of The World (Promo)	CD Single	Warner Bros.	PRO-CD-5027	U.S.A.	1990	14.99
Van Halen	Turns 15 (Promo)	CD	Warner Bros.	PRO-CD-6154	U.S.A.	1993	12.99
Van Halen	Van Halen	CD	Warner Bros.	9-47737-2	U.S.A.	2000	8.99
Van Halen	Van Halen (DCC Gold Cd)	CD	DCC	GZS-1129	U.S.A.	1994	37.99
Van Halen	Van Halen II	CD	Warner Bros.	9362477382	Australia	2000	8.99
Van Halen	Van Halen III	CD	Warner Bros.	9362-46662-2	U.S.A.	1998	8.99
Van Halen	When It's Love	CD Single	Warner Bros.	PRO-CD-3142	U.S.A.	1988	14.99
Van Halen	When It's Love	CD Single	Warner Bros.	921007-2	Germany	1988	22.99
Van Halen	Women And Children First	CD	Warner Bros.	9-47739-2	U.S.A.	2000	8.99
Van Halen	Women And Children First	CD	Warner Bros.	WPCR-10918	Japan	1980	22.99
Van Halen	Won't Get Fooled Again (Promo)	CD Single	Warner Bros.	PRO-CD-5961	U.S.A.	1993	14.99
Van Halen	Won't Get Fooled Again (Promo)	CD Single	Warner Bros.	PRO-CD-5961	U.S.A.	1993	26.99
Van Halen	You Really Got Me (3")	CD Single	Warner Bros.	WPDR-3085	Japan	1998	9.99
Van Zant, Johnny	Brickyard Road	CD	Atlantic	82110-2	U.S.A.	1990	7.99
Van Zant, Johnny	Collection	CD	Polydor	314-519-605-2	U.S.A.	1994	8.99
Van Zant, Johnny	KBFH Presents	CD	King Biscuit	70710-88028-2	U.S.A.	1997	8.99
Vandenburg	Alibi	CD	Wounded Bird	WOU-295	U.S.A.	2002	13.99
Vandenburg	Alibi	CD	East West	18P2-2769	Japan	1985	19.99
Vandenburg	Best Of	CD	Atco	7-90928-2	U.S.A.	1982	11.99
Vandenburg	Heading For A Storm	CD	Wounded Bird	WOU-9121	U.S.A.	2002	12.99
Vandenburg	Heading For A Storm	CD	East West	18P2-2768	Japan	1983	18.99
Vandenburg	Self Titled	CD	Wounded Bird	WOU-9005	U.S.A.	2002	14.99
Vandenburg	Self Titled	CD	East West	18P2-2767	Japan	1982	15.99
Vandenburg/Manic Eden	Self Titled + 1	CD	Victor Ent.	VICP-5361	Japan	1994	22.99
Vangelis	1492 Conquest Of Paradise	CD	Atlantic	7-82432-2	U.S.A.	1992	8.99
Vangelis	Albedo 0.39/Heaven And Hell	CD	RCA	74321-25954-2	EC	1995	17.99
Vangelis	Antarctica	CD	Polygram	815-732-2	U.S.A.	1983	7.99
Vangelis	Beaubourg	CD	BMG	BVCP-5027	Japan	1990	22.99
Vangelis	Best In Space	CD	RCA	74321-16170-2	England	1994	8.99
Vangelis	Blade Runner	CD	Atlantic	82623-2	U.S.A.	1994	7.99
Vangelis	Chariots Of Fire (MFSL Gold Cd)	CD	Mobile Fidelity	UDCD-622	U.S.A.	1981	29.99
Vangelis	China	CD	Polydor	813-653-2	U.S.A.	1983	6.99
Vangelis	Cosmos	2CD	Double Platinum	DBP-102029	Germany	2001	13.99
Vangelis	Direct	CD	Arista	ARCD-8545	U.S.A.	1988	6.99
Vangelis	El Greco	CD	Warner Bros.	83161-2	U.S.A.	1998	6.99
Vangelis	Gift	CD	Camden	74321-393372	EC	1996	8.99
Vangelis	Heaven And Hell	CD	BMG	BVCP-5024	Japan	1990	22.99
Vangelis	Ignacio	CD	Polygram	813-042-2	U.S.A.	1977	6.99
Vangelis	L'Apocalypse Des Animaux	CD	Polydor	831-503-2	U.S.A.	1973	9.99
Vangelis	Mask	CD	Polydor	825-245-2	Germany	1985	9.99
Vangelis	Mythodea	CD	Sony	SK-89191	U.S.A.	2001	6.99
Vangelis	Oceanic	CD	Atlantic	82953-2	U.S.A.	1996	8.99
Vangelis	Opera Sauvage	CD	Polydor	829-663-2-Y-1	U.S.A.	1979	7.99
Vangelis	Portraits	CD	Polydor	314-531-151-2	U.S.A.	1996	7.99
Vangelis	Reprise 1990 - 1999	CD	Atlantic	83308-2	U.S.A.	1999	6.99
Vangelis	See You Later	CD	Polydor	821-932-2	Sweden	1980	9.99
Vangelis	Soil Festivities	CD	Polydor	823-396-2	U.S.A.	1984	9.99
Vangelis	Space Themes	CD	RCA	74321-26459-2	Italy	1995	11.99
Vangelis	The Best Of Vangelis	CD	RCA	74321-13885-2	Germany	1978	8.99
Vangelis	The City	CD	Atlantic	7-82248-2	U.S.A.	1990	8.99

V

Artist	Title	Format	Label	Catalog No	Country	Released	Value
Vangelis	Themes	CD	Polydor	839-518-2	U.S.A.	1989	6.99
Vangelis	Voices	CD	Atlantic	82853-2	U.S.A.	1995	6.99
Vangelis/Irene Papas	Odes	CD	Polydor	833-864-2	England	1988	10.99
Vangelis/Neuronium	In London	CD Single	Chacra	CHACD-036	Canada	1992	7.99
Vanilla Fudge	Mystery	CD	Atlantic	7567-80805-2	Germany	1998	10.99
Vanilla Fudge	Near The Beginning	CD	Repertoire	REP-4127-WZ	Germany	1996	11.99
Vanilla Fudge	Near The Beginning + 3	CD	Sundazed	SC-6144	U.S.A.	1998	8.99
Vanilla Fudge	Psychedelic Sundae: The Best Of	CD	Rhino	R2-71154	U.S.A.	1993	7.99
Vanilla Fudge	Renaissance	CD	Repertoire	REP-4126-WZ	Germany	1996	11.99
Vanilla Fudge	Renaissance + 3	CD	Sundazed	SC-6143	U.S.A.	1998	8.99
Vanilla Fudge	Rock 'N' Roll	CD	Repertoire	REP-4168-WZ	Germany	1996	11.99
Vanilla Fudge	Rock 'N' Roll + 1	CD	Sundazed	SC-6145	U.S.A.	1998	8.99
Vanilla Fudge	Self Titled	CD	Rhino	33224	U.S.A.	1990	8.99
Vanilla Fudge	Self Titled + 2 (Hyperspace Records)	CD	East Rock	ERCD348	Korea	2002	15.99
Vanilla Fudge	The Beat Goes On	CD	Repertoire	REP-4261-WY	Germany	1996	11.99
Vanilla Fudge	The Beat Goes On + 2	CD	Sundazed	SC-6142	U.S.A.	1998	8.99
Vanilla Fudge	The Best Of Live	CD	Rhino	R2-70798	U.S.A.	1991	14.99
Vanilla Fudge	The Return	CD	Punahele	77625	U.S.A.	2002	8.99
Vanity 6	Self Titled (Prince Related)	CD	Warner Bros.	23716-2	U.S.A.	1982	78.99
Vanity Fare	The Sun the Wind and Other Things	CD	Collectables	COL-5614	U.S.A.	1995	9.99
Vanity Fare	The Sun the Wind and Other Things	CD	Repertoire	REP-4155-WZ	Germany	1991	14.99
Vanwarmer, Randy	American Morning	CD	Victor Ent.	VICP-67044	Japan	2000	26.99
Vanwarmer, Randy	Best Of	CD	Victor Ent.	VICP-60291	Japan	2000	32.99
Vanwarmer, Randy	Every Now And Then	CD	Etude	ETCD-190	U.S.A.	1996	24.99
Vanwarmer, Randy	I Am	CD	16th Avenue	D2-70553	U.S.A.	1990	39.99
Vanwarmer, Randy	Just When I Needed You Most: Best	CD	Essential	ESMCD689	England	1999	12.99
Vanwarmer, Randy	Sun, Moon And Stars	CD	Victor Ent.	VICP-96052	Japan	2000	34.99
Vanwarmer, Randy	The Things That You Dream	CD	Pony Canyon	PCCY-00740	Japan	1995	39.99
Vanwarmer, Randy	The Third Child	CD	Victor Ent.	VICP-5384	Japan	1994	39.99
Vanwarmer, Randy	The Vital Spark	CD	Alias	ALCD-194	England	1996	42.99
Vanwarmer, Randy	Warmer	CD	Victor Ent.	VICP-60299	Japan	2000	22.99
Vapors	Anthology	CD	One Way	S21-18332	U.S.A.	1995	7.99
Vapors	Turning Japanese-Best Of Vapor	CD	EMI	7243-8-53898-2-5	Holland	1996	8.99
Various Artists	1 Giant Leap (Robbie Williams/Stipe)	CD	Palm Pictures	PALMCD-2077-2	U.S.A.	2002	7.99
Various Artists	1 Step Up/2 Steps Back: Springsteen	2CD	Capitol	72438-59780-2-9	U.S.A.	1997	11.99
Various Artists	10 Out Of 10 Tower Cd	CD	Real World	7087-6-14340-2-6	U.S.A.	1999	7.99
Various Artists	100 Tears : A Tribute To The Cure	CD	Cleopatra	CLP-0001-2	U.S.A.	1997	19.99
Various Artists	100% Handmade Music Volume II	CD	Acoustic Disc	ACDS-16	U.S.A.	1995	24.99
Various Artists	15th Ann. Rocky H Picture Show Box	4CD	Rhino	R-71011	U.S.A.	1990	23.99
Various Artists	1969 (O.S.T.)	CD	Polydor	837-362-2	U.S.A.	1988	24.99
Various Artists	1st Edition - Audion Sampler (Jem/DJ)	CD	Audion	SYNCD-105	U.S.A.	1986	12.99
Various Artists	20 Xmas Stars II (America, M Blues)	CD	Kid's Records	CMND-0148	U.S.A.	2000	9.99
Various Artists	2002 Toyota Camray (Promo Cd)	CD	Disc Marketing	6-43027-8002-2-4	U.S.A.	2002	5.99
Various Artists	20th Cent. Blues: Songs/Noel Coward	CD	Kala	4601	Canada	1998	11.99
Various Artists	20th Cent. Fox - Music/Golden Age	CD	Varese	VSD-5937	U.S.A.	1998	9.99
Various Artists	24 K Gold Sampler (RCA Promo)	CD	RCA	RJC-66713-2	U.S.A.	1995	119.99
Various Artists	24 Karat Gold Disc Sampler	CD	DCC	GZS-PRO-1	U.S.A.	1993	94.99
Various Artists	45's On CD - Volume III ('66-'69)	CD	Mercury	D-100029	U.S.A.	1988	8.99
Various Artists	A Cole Porter Songbook	CD	Concord	JAZ45122	U.S.A.	1997	9.99
Various Artists	A Flock Of Seagulls Gr. Hits Remixed	CD	Cleopatra	CLP-0697-2	U.S.A.	1999	8.99
Various Artists	A Future To This Life - Robocop	CD	Rhino	R2-71888	U.S.A.	1994	8.99
Various Artists	A Rock 'N' Roll Christmas (Bob Seger)	CD	Polygram	314-520-244-2	U.S.A.	1994	7.99
Various Artists	A Soulful Christmas (Borders)	CD	Rhino	R2-72212	U.S.A.	1995	7.99
Various Artists	A Special Acousic Christmas	CD	Lost Highway	B000103802	U.S.A.	2003	8.99
Various Artists	A To Z Of British TV Themes - Vol. 1	CD	Play It Again	PLAY-004	England	1992	49.99
Various Artists	A To Z Of British TV Themes - Vol. 2	CD	Play It Again	PLAY-006	England	1994	49.99
Various Artists	A To Z Of British TV Themes - Vol. 3	CD	Play It Again	PLAY-010	England	1996	19.99
Various Artists	A To Z Of British TV Themes - Vol. 4	CD	Play It Again	PLAY-009	England	1998	19.99

V

Artist	Title	Format	Label	Catalog No	Country	Released	Value
Various Artists	A Tribute To Brian Eno (Brand X)	CD	Cleopatra	CLP-0016-2	U.S.A.	1999	11.99
Various Artists	A TV Christmas Dinner (TV Actors)	CD	Laserlight	12-956	U.S.A.	1997	8.99
Various Artists	A Very Brady Sequel (O.S.T.)	CD	Angel	7243-8-53048-2-8	U.S.A.	1995	5.99
Various Artists	A Very Special Christmas 5	CD	A&M	069-493-138-2-1	U.S.A.	2001	9.99
Various Artists	A Very Special Christmas (MFSL Gold)	CD	Mobile Fidelity	UDCD-508	U.S.A.	1987	110.99
Various Artists	A Very Special Christmas 1	CD	A&M	CD-3911	U.S.A.	1990	7.99
Various Artists	A Very Special Christmas 2	CD	A&M	31454-0003-2	U.S.A.	1992	7.99
Various Artists	A Very Special Christmas 3	CD	A&M	31454-0764-2	U.S.A.	1997	7.99
Various Artists	A Very Special Christmas Live	CD	A&M	069-490-484-2	U.S.A.	1999	7.99
Various Artists	A Walton's Christmas	CD	Page	707220	U.S.A.	1999	8.99
Various Artists	A Window On The Real World (Promo)	CD	Virgin	70876-13271-2-0	U.S.A.	1999	8.99
Various Artists	A Winter's Solstice	CD	Windham Hill	WD-1045	U.S.A.	1985	7.99
Various Artists	A Winter's Solstice II	CD	Windham Hill	WD-1077	U.S.A.	1988	7.99
Various Artists	A Winter's Solstice III	CD	Windam Hill	WD-1098	U.S.A.	1990	7.99
Various Artists	A Winter's Solstice IV	CD	Windham Hill	01934-11134-2	U.S.A.	1993	7.99
Various Artists	A Winter's Solstice V	CD	Windam Hill	01934-11174-2	U.S.A.	1995	7.99
Various Artists	A&M Records Christmas Sampler	CD	A&M	315-480-482-2	U.S.A.	1993	14.99
Various Artists	About Last Night [O.S.T.]	CD	EMI	7-46560-2	U.S.A.	1986	8.99
Various Artists	Absolute Beginners O.S.T.	CD	Virgin	CDV-2386	England	1986	9.99
Various Artists	Acoustic (Radiohead/Paul Weller)	2CD	Echo	ECV21	England	2002	14.99
Various Artists	Acoustic Aid - Unplugged	CD	Oxymoron	KOME-98.5	U.S.A.	1992	55.99
Various Artists	Adios Amigo: (Arthur Alexander)	CD	Razor & Tie	RT-2814	U.S.A.	1994	14.99
Various Artists	Adults Only Vol. 1 (Music For Porn)	CD	Trojan	CDTRL-305	England	1992	9.99
Various Artists	Adults Only Vol. 2 (Music For Porn)	CD	Trojan	CDTRL-308	England	1992	9.99
Various Artists	Adv. Club S (DJ Unrel. XTC Jellyfish)	CD	Adventure Club	ACS001	U.S.A.	1993	24.99
Various Artists	After the Hurricane (MFSL Gold Cd)	CD	Mobile Fidelity	UDCD-529	U.S.A.	1989	206.99
Various Artists	Ain't No Bologna (Am. Gram. Promo)	CD	American	AGCD200	U.S.A.	1991	8.99
Various Artists	Ain't Nuthin But A She Thing	CD	London	422-828-674-2	U.S.A.	1995	7.99
Various Artists	Album Network's Virtually Alt. (DJ)	CD	Album Network	B#0328-8	U.S.A.	1994	12.99
Various Artists	All Tomrrow's Parties 1.0 (V.U. Tribute)	CD	ATP	ATPRCD1	England	2001	12.99
Various Artists	Amateur (O.S.T. W/Liz Phair)	CD	Matador	92500-2	U.S.A.	1995	6.99
Various Artists	America: A Tribute To Heroes	2CD	Columbia	0694931882	U.S.A.	2001	12.99
Various Artists	American Graffiti (OST Pic Cd W/Vid)	CD	Universal	3133-1-1	U.S.A.	1998	15.99
Various Artists	American Psycho (John Cale)	CD	Koch	KOC-CD-8077	U.S.A.	2000	7.99
Various Artists	Amongst Friends [O.S.T.] Mick Jones	CD	Atlantic	7-82530-2	U.S.A.	1993	5.99
Various Artists	Animal House (O.S.T. Pic Cd W/Video)	CD	Universal	3158-2-1	U.S.A.	1998	15.99
Various Artists	Another Christmas Gift From Line - 1987	CD	Line	LICD-9.00500-G	Germany	1987	39.99
Various Artists	Another Day In Paradise (O.S.T.)	CD	V2	63881-27040-2	U.S.A.	1998	14.99
Various Artists	Antones - 10th Anniversary Live	CD	Line	ANCD-9.00446-0	Germany	1988	39.99
Various Artists	As Seen On TV	CD	UTV	314-556-568-2	U.S.A.	2001	8.99
Various Artists	Atco Records 52 (W/David Gray)	CD	Atco	07863-68102-2-5	U.S.A.	2002	8.99
Various Artists	Atlantic/Atco Remasters (Promo)	CD	Atlantic	PRCD-4233-2	U.S.A.	1991	13.99
Various Artists	Austin Powers - Spy Who.... (O.S.T.)	CD	Maverick	9-47348-2	U.S.A.	1999	8.99
Various Artists	Austin Powers In Goldmember	CD	Maverick	9-48310-2	U.S.A.	2002	8.99
Various Artists	Austin Powers: International Man...	CD	Hollywood	HR-62112-2	U.S.A.	1997	8.99
Various Artists	Babdorb.com (W/2 Unrel. Orb)	2CD	Shanachie	SHI-4001	U.S.A.	2002	15.99
Various Artists	Back To Mine New Order	CD	DMC	BACKCD11	England	2001	9.99
Various Artists	Back To The Beach (O.S.T.)	CD	Columbia	CK-40892	U.S.A.	1987	48.99
Various Artists	Bah! Humbug! (Portsmouth Sinfonia)	CD	Laserlight	12-777	U.S.A.	1996	28.99
Various Artists	Basquiat - Original Soundtrack	CD	Island	314-524-260-2	U.S.A.	1996	8.99
Various Artists	Bat Head Soup (Ozzy Tribute)	CD	Toshiba-EMI	TOCP-65443	Japan	2000	24.99
Various Artists	Bay Blues Live (Jefferson Airplane)	CD	Arti Faxt	ART-12011	U.S.A.	1997	14.99
Various Artists	Bearsville Anthology	2CD	Essential	ESA-CD-927	England	2000	19.99
Various Artists	Bearsville Sampler	CD	Essential	ESM-CD-691	England	1999	19.99
Various Artists	Beauty/The Beast: Of Love And Hope	CD	Capitol	CDP-7-91583-2	U.S.A.	1989	34.99
Various Artists	Before The Fall — The Peel Sessions	CD	Strange Fruit	SFRSCD203	England	1991	49.99
Various Artists	Beserkley Chartbusters - Vol. 1	CD	Line	BECD-9.00489-0	Germany	1987	29.99
Various Artists	Beserkley Chartbusters, Vol. 1	CD	Rev-Ola	CREV010	England	1993	14.99

V

Artist	Title	Format	Label	Catalog No	Country	Released	Value
Various Artists	Best J Bond 30th Ann. (Bonus Cd)	2CD	EMI	0777-7-98560-2-2	U.S.A.	1992	27.99
Various Artists	Best Of Blackberry Way - Mini Hits 2	CD	Line	LICD-9.01310-0	Germany	1996	12.99
Various Artists	Best Of Blackberry Way - Mini Hits 2	CD	Line	BWCD-9.00531-0	Germany	1988	12.99
Various Artists	Best Of British Virgin Promo	CD	Virgin	CATF-05036-2	U.S.A.	2002	9.99
Various Artists	Best Of Godzilla 1954 -1975	CD	GNP	GNPD-8055	U.S.A.	1998	11.99
Various Artists	Best Of Godzilla 1984 - 1995	CD	GNP	GNPD-8056	U.S.A.	1998	17.99
Various Artists	Best Of King Biscuit, Vol. 1	CD	Sandstone	D233005-2	U.S.A.	1991	12.99
Various Artists	Best Of King Biscuit, Vol. 2	CD	Sandstone	D233006-2	U.S.A.	1991	12.99
Various Artists	Best Of King Biscuit, Vol. 3	CD	Sandstone	D233007-2	U.S.A.	1991	12.99
Various Artists	Best Of King Biscuit, Vol. 4	CD	Sandstone	D233008-2	U.S.A.	1991	12.99
Various Artists	Best Of Mountain Stage - Volume 1	CD	Blue Plate	BPM-001CD	U.S.A.	1991	13.99
Various Artists	Best Of Mountain Stage - Volume 3	CD	Blue Plate	BPM-003CD	U.S.A.	1991	13.99
Various Artists	Best Of Mountain Stage - Volume 4	CD	Blue Plate	BPM-004CD	U.S.A.	1993	13.99
Various Artists	Best Of Mountain Stage - Volume 7	CD	Blue Plate	BPM007CD	U.S.A.	1999	13.99
Various Artists	Best Of Mountain Stage - Volume 8	CD	Blue Plate	BPM-008CD	U.S.A.	1999	13.99
Various Artists	Best Of Princes Trust Concerts	3CD	L&D	LBSCD-011	England	1996	74.99
Various Artists	Beyond The Valley Of The Dolls (OST)	CD	Harkit	HRKCD8032	England	2003	24.99
Various Artists	Big Lebowski (O.S.T.)	CD	Mercury	MEAD-148	U.S.A.	1997	10.99
Various Artists	Bill And Ted's Bogus Journey	CD	MMG Inc.	AMCY-274	Japan	1991	12.99
Various Artists	Blaxploitation	2CD	Global TV	RADCD43	England	1996	14.99
Various Artists	Blaxploitation: The Sequel	2CD	Global TV	RADCD54	England	1997	14.99
Various Artists	Blues Anytime - Vol. 1 & 2	CD	Line	IDCD-9.00679-0	Germany	1988	24.99
Various Artists	Blues Anytime - Vol. 3 & 4	CD	Line	IDCD-9.00680-0	Germany	1988	24.99
Various Artists	Bob Dylan The 30th Ann Concert	CD	Columbia	C2K-53230	U.S.A.	1993	14.99
Various Artists	Bonanza Box Set (Michael Landon)	4CD	Bear Family	BCD-15684-DI	Germany	1993	56.99
Various Artists	Brace Yourself! - (Otis Blackwell)	CD	Shanachie	5702	U.S.A.	1994	24.99
Various Artists	Breakin' (O.S.T.)	CD	Polygram	821-919-2	Germany	1984	103.99
Various Artists	Breakin' 2: Electric Boogaloo (O.S.T.)	CD	Polydor	823-696-2	Germany	1985	94.99
Various Artists	Brewster McCloud OST (John Phillips)	CD	Chapter III Classics	CHA-1004-2	U.S.A.	2000	13.99
Various Artists	Bright Lights, Big City (O.S.T.)	CD	Warner Bros.	9-25688-2	U.S.A.	1988	7.99
Various Artists	Bring It On Home Vol. I	CD	Columbia	JK-52997	U.S.A.	1994	10.99
Various Artists	Bringing It All Back Home Vol. 1	CD	Valley Ent.	VE-15011	U.S.A.	2000	5.99
Various Artists	Bringing It All Back Home Vol. 2	CD	Valley Ent.	VE-15012	U.S.A.	1999	5.99
Various Artists	Bringing It All Back Home Vol. 3	CD	Valley Ent.	VE-15013	U.S.A.	2000	5.99
Various Artists	British Rock Symphony (Alice Cooper)	CD	Point Music	314-538-006-2	U.S.A.	1999	8.99
Various Artists	Bull Durham (O.S.T.)	CD	Capitol	7-90586-2	U.S.A.	1988	83.99
Various Artists	Bummed Out Christmas	CD	Rhino	R2-70912	U.S.A.	1989	8.99
Various Artists	Buster (O.S.T.)	CD	Atlantic	7-81905-2	U.S.A.	1988	7.99
Various Artists	Bye Bye, Love (Dave Edmunds Unrel.)	CD	Giant	9-24609-2	U.S.A.	1993	8.99
Various Artists	California Jam 2 Live	CD	Columbia	CK-35389	U.S.A.	1995	24.99
Various Artists	Can't Hardly Wait (O.S.T.)	CD	Elektra	62201-2	U.S.A.	1998	5.99
Various Artists	Canterbury Tales (R. Wyatt/J Hendrix)	3CD	Eagle	EEECD006	Germany	2000	24.99
Various Artists	Casablanca Records - Greatest Hits	CD	Polygram	P2-26253	U.S.A.	1996	8.99
Various Artists	Cash Cow: The Best Of Giorno Poetry	CD	ESD	80712	U.S.A.	1993	28.99
Various Artists	Cat People: A Tribute To Cat Stevens	CD	Dressed To Kill	METRO444	England	2000	7.99
Various Artists	CBGB's And The Birth Of U.S.Punk	CD	Ocho	OCHOCD013	England	2002	11.99
Various Artists	Celebration: The Big Sur Folk Festival	CD	Essential	ESMCD-871	England	2000	14.99
Various Artists	Century 21 Gold Disc # 119 (Promo)	CD	Century 21	01S0200	U.S.A.	1987	16.99
Various Artists	Century 21 Gold Disc # 128 (Promo)	CD	Century 21	01W0A00A	U.S.A.	1987	16.99
Various Artists	Century 21 Gold Disc # 553 (Promo)	CD	Century 21	4UX0100A	U.S.A.	1987	16.99
Various Artists	Century 21 Hit Disc # 771B (Promo)	CD	Century 21	4AK0100A	U.S.A.	1989	16.99
Various Artists	Chef Aid: The South Park Album	CD	Columbia	CK-69631	U.S.A.	1998	6.99
Various Artists	Chef/Friends: Songs/South Park (DJ)	CD	Columbia	CSK-41670	U.S.A.	1998	11.99
Various Artists	Christmas Sampler (Promo W/Roches)	CD	MCA	CD33-1167	U.S.A.	1990	5.99
Various Artists	Chronicles Sampler (Polygram Promo)	2CD	Polygram	SACD-934	U.S.A.	1994	14.99
Various Artists	City Of Angels O.S.T.	CD	Warner Bros.	9-46867-2	U.S.A.	1998	8.99
Various Artists	Class Of '55 Memphis...	CD	Polygram	830-002-2-M-1	U.S.A.	1986	11.99
Various Artists	Classic Masters Series One (Promo)	CD	Captiol	70876-12179-2-6	U.S.A.	2001	7.99

Artist	Title	Format	Label	Catalog No	Country	Released	Value
Various Artists	Classical Sampler (MFSL Gold Cd)	CD	Mobile Fidelity	UDCD-CS-1	U.S.A.	1987	167.99
Various Artists	Close Encounters/Third Kind (O.S.T.)	CD	Arista	07822-19004-2	U.S.A.	1998	8.99
Various Artists	CMC Presents In Concert (Yes, Styx)	CD	CMC Int.	06076-86235-2	U.S.A.	1998	8.99
Various Artists	CMP Collection 1996 (Jack Bruce)	CD	CMP	CMP-CD-5005	U.S.A.	1996	8.99
Various Artists	Cocteau Twins/Pixies Sampler (Promo)	CD	4AD	4AD-US-2003	U.S.A.	2003	23.99
Various Artists	Cole Porter - Grt American Composers	2CD	Columbia	C21/2-7926	U.S.A.	1989	10.99
Various Artists	Color Of Money - (O.S.T. W/D Henley)	CD	MCA	MCAD-6189	U.S.A.	1986	8.99
Various Artists	Columbia Rec Radio Hour, Volume 1	CD	Columbia	CK-66466	U.S.A.	1994	8.99
Various Artists	Columbia Rec Radio Hour, Volume 2	CD	Columbia	CK-67498	U.S.A.	1996	8.99
Various Artists	Complete Buddah Chart Singles Vol. 1	CD	BMG	75517-49516-2	U.S.A.	1996	12.99
Various Artists	Complete Buddah Chart Singles Vol. 2	CD	BMG	75517-49517-2	U.S.A.	1996	12.99
Various Artists	Complete Kama Sutra Singles Vol. 1	CD	BMG	75517-49518-2	U.S.A.	1996	12.99
Various Artists	Complete Kama Sutra Singles Vol. 2	CD	BMG	75517-49519-2	U.S.A.	1996	12.99
Various Artists	Concert /Rock & Roll Hall Fame	2CD	Columbia	C2K-67477	U.S.A.	1996	14.99
Various Artists	Country Bears - (O.S.T.)	CD	Walt Disney	60774-7	U.S.A.	2002	8.99
Various Artists	Crazy Rock (Joe Piscopo)	CD	Sony	A-22154	U.S.A.	1991	5.99
Various Artists	Creature/Black Lagoon (And Other....	CD	Monstrous Movie	MMM-1952	U.S.A.	2000	14.99
Various Artists	Cupid's Revenge	CD	Continuum	COND-19502	U.S.A.	1994	8.99
Various Artists	Dance Music Set Free - Edition 2	CD	Line	TLCD-9.00527-0	Germany	1988	12.99
Various Artists	Days Of Thunder (O.S.T.)	CD	Geffen	9-24294-D2	U.S.A.	1990	7.99
Various Artists	Dead Man Walking	CD	Columbia	CK-67522	U.S.A.	1995	9.99
Various Artists	Dead Parrot Society	CD	Rhino	R2-71049	U.S.A.	1993	8.99
Various Artists	Decade Of Music (Billboard/Promo)	CD	Sony	A-23565	U.S.A.	1992	10.99
Various Artists	Delco Electronics Music... (MFSL)	CD	Mobile Fidelity	SPCD-8	U.S.A.	1987	24.99
Various Artists	Deluxe Edition Sampler (Best Buy DJ)	CD	Universal	CATF-05125-2	U.S.A.	2004	8.99
Various Artists	Der Samper 40	CD	Line	LICD-9.00810-J	Germany	1989	13.99
Various Artists	Der Sampler 26	CD	Line	LICD-9.00346-J	Germany	1987	13.99
Various Artists	Der Sampler 27	CD	Line	LICD-9.00347-J	Germany	1988	13.99
Various Artists	Der Sampler 28	CD	Line	LICD-9.00348-J	Germany	1988	13.99
Various Artists	Der Sampler 29	CD	Line	LICD-9.00349-J	Germany	1988	13.99
Various Artists	Der Sampler 30	CD	Line	LICD-9.00350-J	Germany	1988	13.99
Various Artists	Der Sampler 31	CD	Line	LICD-9.00621-J	Germany	1989	13.99
Various Artists	Der Sampler 32	CD	Line	LICD-9.00622-J	Germany	1989	13.99
Various Artists	Der Sampler 33	CD	Line	LICD-9.00623-J	Germany	1989	13.99
Various Artists	Der Sampler 34	CD	Line	LICD-9.00624-J	Germany	1989	13.99
Various Artists	Der Sampler 35	CD	Line	LICD-9.00625-J	Germany	1989	13.99
Various Artists	Der Sampler 36	CD	Line	LICD-9.00806-J	Germany	1989	13.99
Various Artists	Der Sampler 37	CD	Line	LICD-9.00807-J	Germany	1989	13.99
Various Artists	Der Sampler 38	CD	Line	LICD-9.00808-J	Germany	1989	13.99
Various Artists	Der Sampler 39	CD	Line	LICD-9.00809-J	Germany	1989	13.99
Various Artists	Derek Lawrence Sessions - Take 1	CD	Line	LICD-9.01118-0	Germany	1991	18.99
Various Artists	Derek Lawrence Sessions - Take 2	CD	Line	LICD-9.01119-0	Germany	1991	18.99
Various Artists	Detroit Rock City (O.S.T.)	CD	Mercury	314-546-389-2	U.S.A.	1999	8.99
Various Artists	Diana Princess/Wales (Promo)	CD	Columbia	CSK-3795	U.S.A.	1997	14.99
Various Artists	Dirty Dancing Live In Concert	CD	RCA	9660-2-R	U.S.A.	1989	8.99
Various Artists	DIY (Promo Sampler)	CD	Rhino	PRO2-90134	U.S.A.	1993	14.99
Various Artists	Dogs In Space (OST) Eno, Iggy, INXS	CD	Mercury	832-748-2	Germany	1986	79.99
Various Artists	Don't Tell Mom/Babysitter's Dead (ST)	CD	Giant	9-24428-2	U.S.A.	1991	8.99
Various Artists	Dr. Demento Christmas Novelty CD	CD	Rhino	R2-75755	U.S.A.	1989	12.99
Various Artists	Dr. Martens: Capitol Records Promo	CD	Capitol	7087-6-11279-2-8	U.S.A.	1996	7.99
Various Artists	Dr. Martens: Shoe Pie (4AD Promo)	CD	4AD	01970011	U.S.A.	1997	8.99
Various Artists	Dracula - Hammer Horror	CD	Silva Screen	SSD-1026	U.S.A.	1993	9.99
Various Artists	Dreaming/Wh Xmas (Simon/Garfunkel)	CD	Sony	A-15438	U.S.A.	1992	24.99
Various Artists	Drum - South African Jazz And Jive	CD	Line	MSCD-9.01092-0	Germany	1991	24.99
Various Artists	DTS Multichannel CD Sampler, Vol. 2	CD	Digital Surround	162751-05	U.S.A.	2002	29.99
Various Artists	Earth Day '96 (Neil Young)	CD	HMV	EARTH1996	Canada	1996	12.99
Various Artists	Earthquake Album (Live Prog Benefit)	CD	Tring Int.	ANT010	EEC	1996	8.99
Various Artists	Earthrise (All Star Benefit Song)	CD	Rhino	R2-71830	U.S.A.	1994	8.99

V

Artist	Title	Format	Label	Catalog No	Country	Released	Value
Various Artists	Easy Rider + 19 (O.S.T.)	2CD	Hip O	B0002115-02	U.S.A.	2004	16.99
Various Artists	Easy Rider O.S.T.	CD	MCA	088-119-153-2	U.S.A.	2000	8.99
Various Artists	Electric Dreams (O.S.T.)	CD	Virgin	077778646624	Holland	1984	14.99
Various Artists	Electronic Toys (Early Electro Pop)	CD	Captain Trip	CTCD-274	Japan	1960	14.99
Various Artists	Electronic Tribute To Led Zeppelin	CD	Vitamin	CD-8649	U.S.A.	2002	9.99
Various Artists	Encino Man (OST) Queen/Cheap Trick	CD	Hollywood	HR-61330-2	U.S.A.	1992	9.99
Various Artists	Encomium Tribute Led Zeppelin (Adv)	CD	Atlantic	PRCD-6132	U.S.A.	1995	44.99
Various Artists	Epic (In Store Play Sampler) Promo	CD	Epic	ESK-56866	U.S.A.	2002	5.99
Various Artists	Eternity II - A Romantic Collection	CD	Real Music	RM3223	U.S.A.	1997	4.99
Various Artists	Even Santa Gets The Blues (B B King)	CD	Virgin	7243-8-40654-2-3	U.S.A.	1995	29.99
Various Artists	Farm Aid: Volume One Live	2CD	Redline Ent.	01241-41478-2	U.S.A.	2000	8.99
Various Artists	Fast Times At Ridgemont High (O.S.T.)	CD	Elektra	60158-2	U.S.A.	1982	7.99
Various Artists	Fillmore - The Last Days	2CD	Epic	Z2K-31390	U.S.A.	1972	19.99
Various Artists	Films Of Ron Howard	CD	Milan	73138-35800-2	U.S.A.	1997	24.99
Various Artists	Fire & Skill: The Songs Of The Jam	CD	Epic	EK-62215	U.S.A.	1999	8.99
Various Artists	FMQB - CD Sampler Vol.5/#1 (May '96)	CD	FMQB	FMQBMR51	U.S.A.	1996	9.99
Various Artists	Folkways: Tribute Guthrie/Leadbelly	CD	Columbia	CK-44034	U.S.A.	1988	34.99
Various Artists	For Our Children Too!	CD	Rhino	R2-72494	U.S.A.	1996	8.99
Various Artists	For The Love Of Harry (Nilsson)	CD	Music Masters	13254	U.S.A.	1995	8.99
Various Artists	For The Love Of Todd (Rundgren)	CD	Third Lock	TLRCD004	U.S.A.	1995	12.99
Various Artists	Frat Rock	CD	Rhino	RNCD-75778	U.S.A.	1987	8.99
Various Artists	Freddy's Dead - The Final Nightmare	CD	Warner Bros.	9-26726-2	U.S.A.	1991	8.99
Various Artists	Friends (O.S.T.)	CD	Reprise	9-46008-2	U.S.A.	1994	7.99
Various Artists	Fritz The Cat/Heavy Traffic (O.S.T.)	CD	Fantasy	FCD-24745-2	Germany	1996	10.99
Various Artists	Funky Alternatives Volume One & Two	CD	Line	TCCD-9.00578-0	Germany	1988	12.99
Various Artists	Furthur	CD	Hybrid	HY20012	U.S.A.	1996	7.99
Various Artists	Furthur More	CD	Hybrid	HY-20003	U.S.A.	1997	7.99
Various Artists	Future Perfect (3 Unrel Brian Eno)	CD	Gyroscope	GYR-6609-2	U.S.A.	1994	7.99
Various Artists	Gathering On The Mountian	CD	Relix	RRCD2099	U.S.A.	1999	8.99
Various Artists	Ghostbusters II (O.S.T.)	CD	MCA	MCAD-6306	U.S.A.	1989	8.99
Various Artists	Girls Just Want To Have Fun (O.S.T.)	CD	Polygram	824-510-2	U.S.A.	1985	47.99
Various Artists	Give The People What We Want	CD	Sub Pop	SPCD575	U.S.A.	2001	9.99
Various Artists	Glam Mania (T. Rex, Slade)	CD	Crimson	CRIMIDCD32	England	1997	8.99
Various Artists	Glory Of Gershwin	CD	Mercury	314-526-091-2	U.S.A.	1994	10.99
Various Artists	Godzilla (O.S.T.) Wallflowers	CD	Epic	EK-69338	U.S.A.	1998	8.99
Various Artists	Godzilla Songbook	CD	Vap Inc.	VPCD-81381	Japan	2001	32.99
Various Artists	Godzilla Vs. Mothra	CD	Toshiba-EMI	TYCY-5348	Japan	1993	35.99
Various Artists	Golden Throats 1	CD	Rhino	R2-70187	U.S.A.	1988	12.99
Various Artists	Golden Throats 2	CD	Rhino	R2-71007	U.S.A.	1991	12.99
Various Artists	Golden Throats 3 - Sweethearts..	CD	Rhino	R2-71867	U.S.A.	1995	9.99
Various Artists	Golden Throats 4 (Beatles Songs)	CD	Rhino	R2-72593	U.S.A.	1997	19.99
Various Artists	Good Rockin' Tonight Sun Records + 1	CD	Warner Bros.	WPCR-11170	Japan	2001	39.99
Various Artists	Grace Of My Heart (O.S.T.)	CD	MCA	MCAD-11510	U.S.A.	1997	8.99
Various Artists	Grease (O.N. John, J. Travolta)	CD	Polygram K.K.	POCP-2632	Japan	1998	24.99
Various Artists	Grease (O.S.T. Pic Cd W/Video)	CD	Polydor	PRSAD00620	U.S.A.	1998	15.99
Various Artists	Grease + 12 (O.S.T./W Bonus CD)	2CD	Polydor	80001011-02	U.S.A.	2003	16.99
Various Artists	Gremlins (O.S.T.)	CD	Geffen	24044-2	Germany	1993	39.99
Various Artists	Grok This! Defacing Todd Rundgren	CD	Medicine Park	MP101	U.S.A.	1998	8.99
Various Artists	Guitar Speak	CD	I.R.S.	IRSD-42240	U.S.A.	1988	19.99
Various Artists	Guitar Speak III	CD	I.R.S.	CCSCD-373	EEC	1991	29.99
Various Artists	Guitar Workshop	CD	Line	TACD-9.00669-0	Germany	1988	14.99
Various Artists	Haight Ashbury 60's (Airplane, Dead)	CD-Rom	Rockument	ROO1	U.S.A.	1995	9.99
Various Artists	Happy Anniversary, Charlie Brown!	CD	GRP	GRD-9596	U.S.A.	1989	8.99
Various Artists	Happy Together: White Whale Best Of	CD	Varese	VSD-6035	U.S.A.	2002	8.99
Various Artists	Harley: Road Songs (Leather CD Pouch)	2CD	Capitol	T2-3132	U.S.A.	1994	24.99
Various Artists	HDCD Sampler (Promo)	CD	Ref Rec	RR-S3CD	U.S.A.	1992	18.99
Various Artists	Headtravel: Exploring Electronic Music...	CD	Man Made	MAN-50000-2	U.S.A.	1995	14.99
Various Artists	Hear 'N Aid (Rush/Kiss/Dio)	CD	Polygram	PHCR-4218	Japan	1986	24.99

Artist	Title	Format	Label	Catalog No	Country	Released	Value
Various Artists	Help - Charity Project Children Bosnia	CD	Go Discs Ltd.	422-828-682-2	U.S.A.	1995	12.99
Various Artists	Hempilation II: Freetheweed	CD	Capricorn	314-538-240-2	U.S.A.	1998	9.99
Various Artists	Hempilation: Freedom Is...	CD	Capricorn	314-532-551-2	U.S.A.	1996	9.99
Various Artists	Here We Go 'Round (Traffic)	CD	Rykodisc	RCD-10717	U.S.A.	1998	8.99
Various Artists	Higgeldy - Piggledy Punk Rock Vol. 1	CD	Line	DICD-9.51056-L	Germany	1991	24.99
Various Artists	Highlander: The Original Scores (All 3)	CD	Edel	0028892EDL	Germany	1995	12.99
Various Artists	Highway 61 (O.S.T.) Nash The Slash	CD	Intrepid	N21S-0009	Canada	1992	10.99
Various Artists	Holiday Greetings/Geffen Records	CD	Geffen	PRO-CD-4363	U.S.A.	1991	54.99
Various Artists	Hollow Reed (P Weller I Shall Be..)	CD	RCA	09026-68630-2	U.S.A.	1996	9.99
Various Artists	Home Alive - The Art Of Self Defense	2CD	Epic	E2K-67486	U.S.A.	1996	14.99
Various Artists	Honor Them All	CD	Windham Hill	01934-11339-2	U.S.A.	1998	7.99
Various Artists	Hope Floats (O.S.T.) Bob Seger	CD	Capitol	7243-4-93402-2-0	U.S.A.	1998	14.99
Various Artists	House Of America	CD	Premier Soundtracks	7243-8-21793-2-0	England	1997	7.99
Various Artists	I Guess We Didn't Save The Lp	3CD	Rhino	PRO-90045-A/B/C	U.S.A.	1990	34.99
Various Artists	I Shot Andy Warhol (O.S.T.)	CD	Tag	92690-2	U.S.A.	1996	5.99
Various Artists	IASCA/MFSL Cert. Test Compact Disc	CD	Mobile Fidelity	SPCD-7	U.S.A.	1987	341.99
Various Artists	If A Tree Falls (Dan Fogelberg)	CD	Rhino	R2-72495	U.S.A.	1996	4.99
Various Artists	If It Ain't Stiff A Stiff Records Collection	CD	Metro	METRCD65	U.S.A.	2001	11.99
Various Artists	I'm Your Fan - Songs/Leonard Cohen	CD	Atlantic	7-82349-2	U.S.A.	1991	14.99
Various Artists	Immediate Single Collection - Vol. 1	CD	Line	INCD-9.00565-0	Germany	1988	11.99
Various Artists	Immediate Single Collection - Vol. 2	CD	Line	IDCD-9.00566-0	Germany	1988	11.99
Various Artists	Immediate Single Collection - Vol. 3	CD	Line	INCD-9.00567-0	Germany	1988	11.99
Various Artists	Immediate Single Collection - Vol. 4	CD	Line	INCD-9.00568-0	Germany	1988	11.99
Various Artists	Immediate Single Collection - Vol. 5	CD	Line	INCD-9.00569-0	Germany	1988	11.99
Various Artists	Immediate Singles Collection - Vol. 1	CD	Sony	AK-47351	U.S.A.	1991	14.99
Various Artists	Immediate Singles Collection - Vol. 2	CD	Sony	AK-46994	U.S.A.	1991	14.99
Various Artists	Immediate Singles Collection - Vol. 3	CD	Sony	AK-47892	U.S.A.	1991	14.99
Various Artists	In A Field Of Their Own:Glastonbury '92	2CD	NME	GLASTON1DCD	England	1992	34.99
Various Artists	In Their Own Words - Volume 1	CD	Razor & Tie	RT-2813	U.S.A.	1994	11.99
Various Artists	In Their Own Words - Volume 2	CD	Razor & Tie	RT-2824	U.S.A.	1996	11.99
Various Artists	Inner Flame: Rainer Ptacek Tribute	CD	Atlantic	83008-2	U.S.A.	1997	8.99
Various Artists	Invictus Chartbusters	CD	Sequel	NEMCD-986	England	1999	8.99
Various Artists	It Ain't Me Babe, Songs Of Bob Dylan	CD	Castle	CMRCD-261	England	2001	11.99
Various Artists	James Bond - 13 Original Themes	CD	Liberty	7-46079-2	U.S.A.	1983	8.99
Various Artists	Jazz Sampler (MFSL Gold Promo)	CD	Mobile Fidelity	JS-1	U.S.A.	1987	208.99
Various Artists	Jenny McCarthy's Surfin' Safari	CD	I.D.	INTD-90072	U.S.A.	1996	5.99
Various Artists	Jerry Maguire (O.S.T.) (Dylan Alt. Take)	CD	Epic	EK-67910	U.S.A.	1996	8.99
Various Artists	Jesus Christ Superstar (Orig L Cast) Gol	2CD	MCA	MCAD2-10950	U.S.A.	1996	44.99
Various Artists	Johnny Cash Gunter Gabriel & Andere	CD	Bear Family	BCD-16601-AR	Germany	2002	9.99
Various Artists	Josh's Blair Witch Mix	CD	Chapter	CHA-0120	U.S.A.	1999	5.99
Various Artists	Joyride	CD	4AD	9-46825-2	U.S.A.	1997	13.99
Various Artists	Just In Time For Xmas (Squeeze/Db's)	CD	I.R.S.	X2-13052	U.S.A.	1990	16.99
Various Artists	Just Say Mao (L Reed/Strawman Live)	CD	Sire	9-25947-2	U.S.A.	1989	6.99
Various Artists	Just Say Noel (Aimee Mann, XTC)	CD	Geffen	GEFD-25107	U.S.A.	1996	6.99
Various Artists	Kermit Unpigged	CD	BMG	78400-15004-2	U.S.A.	1994	21.99
Various Artists	KFOG Live From Archives 6	CD	KFOG Radio	ARCH6-2	U.S.A.	1999	29.99
Various Artists	KFOG Live From The Archives 7	CD	KFOG Radio	ARCH7-2	U.S.A.	2000	29.99
Various Artists	Kiss My Ass- Classic Kiss Regrooved	CD	Mercury	314-522-123-2	U.S.A.	1994	6.99
Various Artists	Knebworth '90	2CD	Polydor	847-042-2	U.S.A.	1990	17.99
Various Artists	Knights Of The Blues Table	CD	Viceroy	54189-2	U.S.A.	1997	14.99
Various Artists	Lampoon's Animal House (O.S.T.)	CD	MCA	MCADE-11808	U.S.A.	1998	7.99
Various Artists	Legacy Rock Experience (Promo)	CD	Columbia	JSK-8789	U.S.A.	1996	12.99
Various Artists	Legally Blonde (O.S.T.)	CD	A&M	069493078-2	U.S.A.	2001	6.99
Various Artists	Legendary Horror Films (Universal)	CD	Disconforme	SFCD33566	Italy	2002	8.99
Various Artists	Let The Music...(Aerosmith Tribute)	CD	Video Arts	VACM-1176	Japan	2001	29.99
Various Artists	Lilith Fair '99 - New Music Sampler (DJ)	CD	Arista	ARCD-9088	U.S.A.	1999	7.99
Various Artists	Liner - New Tracks 2	CD	Line	LICD-9.01300-E	Germany	1994	12.99
Various Artists	Liner - New Tracks 3	CD	Line	LICD-9.01320-E	Germany	1996	12.99

V

Artist	Title	Format	Label	Catalog No	Country	Released	Value
Various Artists	Liquid Sky (O.S.T.)	CD	Varese	VCD-47181	U.S.A.	1983	65.99
Various Artists	Little Guitars (Tribute Van Halen)	CD	Toshiba-EMI	TOCP-65353	Japan	2000	24.99
Various Artists	Little Guitars (Tribute Van Halen)	CD	Eagle	EAGCD113	U.S.A.	2000	8.99
Various Artists	Live From 6a: Conan O'Brien	CD	Mercury	314-536-324-2	U.S.A.	1997	7.99
Various Artists	Live From The River Music Hall Vol. 1	CD	Eastern Front	EFR-CD-114	U.S.A.	1998	17.99
Various Artists	Live Mountain Stage Vol. 8 (G. Parker)	CD	Blue Plate	BPM-008CD	U.S.A.	1999	13.99
Various Artists	Live On Letterman	CD	Reprise	9-46827-2	U.S.A.	1997	7.99
Various Artists	London R&B Sess. Live Hope/Anchor	CD	Line	ALCD-9.00135-0	Germany	1988	12.99
Various Artists	Long Journey Home (E. Costello)	CD	Unisphere	09026-68963-2	U.S.A.	1998	5.99
Various Artists	Lost Highway O.S.T.	CD	Interscope	INTD-90090	U.S.A.	1996	7.99
Various Artists	Lost In The Stars - Music/Kurt Weill	CD	A&M	CD-5104	U.S.A.	1985	14.99
Various Artists	Lost Mixes (Yes, Mike/Mechanics)	CD	Warner Bros.	OPCD-1659	U.S.A.	1994	24.99
Various Artists	Loud, Fast & Out Of Control (Promo)	CD	Rhino	PRCD-7451	U.S.A.	1999	61.99
Various Artists	Macross Plus Song Collection	CD	Victor Ent.	VICL-41084	Japan	1999	24.99
Various Artists	Mad About You (O.S.T.)	CD	Atlantic	82983-2	U.S.A.	1997	6.99
Various Artists	Magnolia O.S.T.	CD	Reprise	9-47583-2	U.S.A.	1999	6.99
Various Artists	Manchester - So Much (Peel Sessions)	CD	Strange Fruit	SFRCD-202	England	1990	37.99
Various Artists	Married To The Mob (O.S.T./Eno)	CD	Reprise	25763-2	U.S.A.	1988	44.99
Various Artists	Mastersound Sampler (Promo/Gold)	CD	Columbia	CSK-4757	U.S.A.	1992	54.99
Various Artists	Maybe Baby (DJ/Unrel. McCartney)	CD	Virgin	CDVDJ2916	England	2000	29.99
Various Artists	Medium Rare (DJ/Unrel. J. Cale Live)	CD	Rykodisc	VRCD-0001	U.S.A.	1993	18.99
Various Artists	Meet Me On The Other Side	CD	Medicine Park	MP102	U.S.A.	1999	8.99
Various Artists	Message To Love/Isle Wight Festival 197	2CD	Video Arts	VACM-1016/7	Japan	1995	44.99
Various Artists	Metal 1 - Volume 1	CD	Victor Ent.	VICP-23111	Japan	1994	44.99
Various Artists	Metal 1 - Volume 2	CD	Victor Ent.	VICP-23156	Japan	1995	44.99
Various Artists	Metal Monday - Volume 1	CD	Line	MMCD-9.01244-0	Germany	1992	23.99
Various Artists	Metallica Assault (Tribute)	CD	Eagle	EAGCD129	U.S.A.	2000	8.99
Various Artists	Metallica Assault (Tribute)	CD	Video Arts	VACM-1164	Japan	2000	24.99
Various Artists	Miami Vice (O.S.T.)	CD	MCA	MCAD-6150	U.S.A.	1985	10.99
Various Artists	Miami Vice II (O.S.T.)	CD	MCA	MCAD-6192	U.S.A.	1986	10.99
Various Artists	Million Dollar Hotel (Bono, U2, Eno)	CD	Interscope	3145423952	U.S.A.	2000	7.99
Various Artists	Miniatures (XTC, Robert Wyatt, Fripp)	CD	Blueprint	BP159CD	Austria	1994	11.99
Various Artists	Miss Congeniality	CD	TVT	6940-2	U.S.A.	2000	8.99
Various Artists	Mission Impossible	CD Single	Island	314-576-671-2	U.S.A.	1996	10.99
Various Artists	Modern Rock Live (B Traveler, Jewel)	2CD	Sony	DIDX-038914	U.S.A.	1996	57.99
Various Artists	Monterey Int. Pop Festival Box (Large)	4CD	Rhino	R2-70596	U.S.A.	1992	46.99
Various Artists	Moody Guitars	CD	Line	VVCD-9.01123-L	Germany	1991	24.99
Various Artists	Moonlighting (T.V. Soundtrack)	CD	MCA	MCAD-6214	U.S.A.	1984	8.99
Various Artists	More Music From Valley Girl (O.S.T.)	CD	Rhino	R2-71879	U.S.A.	1994	32.99
Various Artists	Motels, Fixx, Berlin-Greatest Hits Live	CD	Rainman	RMCD113	U.S.A.	2003	12.99
Various Artists	Mother & Child	CD	I.R.S.	7243-8-35173-2-9	U.S.A.	1995	11.99
Various Artists	Mother 2 (Earthbound 2) O.S.T.	CD Single	Sony	SRCL-3024	Japan	1994	54.99
Various Artists	Mott The Hoople Family Album	CD	Connoisseur	VSOP-CD283	England	2000	8.99
Various Artists	Moulin Rouge (O.S.T.)	CD	Interscope	06949-3035-2	U.S.A.	2001	8.99
Various Artists	Mountain Stage Sampler (Promo)	CD	Blue Plate	BPM-SAM-1	U.S.A.	1994	14.99
Various Artists	MTV 120 Minutes Live	CD	Atlantic	83052-2	U.S.A.	1998	7.99
Various Artists	Muppet Treasure Island (O.S.T.)	CD	Angel	7243-8-37159-2-3	U.S.A.	1996	23.99
Various Artists	Music From Spider-Man (Holographic)	CD	Columbia	CK-86402	U.S.A.	2002	7.99
Various Artists	Music From The Motion Picture Heat	CD	Warner Bros.	9-46144-2	U.S.A.	1995	8.99
Various Artists	Music Hollywood + 6 (Live Herrmann)	CD	Columbia	CK-66691	U.S.A.	1995	10.99
Various Artists	Music Too Good For Words	CD	I.R.S.	IRSD-39099	U.S.A.	1988	8.99
Various Artists	Music Too Good For Words, Two	CD	I.R.S.	IRSD-39112	U.S.A.	1988	8.99
Various Artists	Musn't Grumble (Marriott Mem. Concert)	CD	Sanctuary	SANCD-112	England	2002	19.99
Various Artists	Mystery Men (O.S.T.)	CD	Interscope	INTD-90345	U.S.A.	1999	8.99
Various Artists	Narada Sampler #1	CD	Narada	ND-31007	U.S.A.	1985	8.99
Various Artists	National Lampoon Senior Trip	CD	Capricorn	9-42050-2	U.S.A.	1995	7.99
Various Artists	Natural Born Killers (O.S.T.) T Reznor	CD	Interscope	92460-2	U.S.A.	1994	7.99
Various Artists	Never Mind Pistols Here's ...(W/Book)	CD	Dressed To Kill	METRO730	England	2001	8.99

Artist	Title	Format	Label	Catalog No	Country	Released	Value
Various Artists	New Orleans Music : New Music Jazz	CD	Line	COCD-9.00917-0	Germany	1990	24.99
Various Artists	New Orleans Music : Vocal Jazz	CD	Line	COCD-9.00918-0	Germany	1990	24.99
Various Artists	New Orleans Music: Jump Jazz	CD	Line	COCD-9.00916-0	Germany	1990	24.99
Various Artists	Newport Broadside (Bob Dylan)	CD	Vanguard	662127	France	1992	13.99
Various Artists	Night And Day - Cole Porter Songbook	CD	Verve	847-202-2	U.S.A.	1990	8.99
Various Artists	Night Of The Guitar (W/Steve Howe)	CD	I.R.S.	IRSD-83000	U.S.A.	1989	24.99
Various Artists	Nipper's #1 Hits 1956 -1986 (RCA)	CD	RCA	9902-2-R	U.S.A.	1989	8.99
Various Artists	No Boundaries (Pearl Jam - Last Kiss)	CD	Epic	EK-63653	Mexico	1999	8.99
Various Artists	No New York (Produced By Brian Eno)	CD	Polygram K.K.	ONCO-002	Japan	1978	44.99
Various Artists	No Nukes (B Springsteen Live 1979)	2CD	Asylum	60592-2	U.S.A.	1997	19.99
Various Artists	Noites Cariocas Choro All Stars Live	CD	Line	BSCD-9.00771-0	Germany	1990	24.99
Various Artists	Not Fade Away (Buddy Holly)	CD	Decca	DRND-11260	U.S.A.	1996	5.99
Various Artists	Nothing In Common (O.S.T.)	CD	Arista	ARCD-8438	U.S.A.	1986	7.99
Various Artists	Nuggets Selections From (Promo)	CD	Rhino	PRCD-7296	U.S.A.	1998	24.99
Various Artists	Nuggets Vol. 1 Box Set	4CD	Rhino	R2-75466	U.S.A.	1998	44.99
Various Artists	Nuns On The Run	CD	Mercury	846-043-2	U.S.A.	1990	21.99
Various Artists	On A Starry Night	CD	Windam Hill	01934-11213-2	U.S.A.	1997	5.99
Various Artists	One Hit Wonders	CD	Polygram	314-520-272-2	U.S.A.	1993	29.99
Various Artists	One Voice (With Amy Grant)	CD	MCA	MCAD-11403	U.S.A.	1996	5.99
Various Artists	Orange County (O.S.T.) W/Bonus Cd	2CD	Columbia	CK-85933	U.S.A.	2001	14.99
Various Artists	Out On The Rolling Sea (V. D. Parks)	CD	Green Linnet	GLCD-3095	U.S.A.	1994	14.99
Various Artists	Over The Top (O.S.T.)	CD	Columbia	CK-40655	U.S.A.	1987	11.99
Various Artists	Part 1-Gathering On The Mountain	CD	Relix	RRCD2103	U.S.A.	2000	8.99
Various Artists	Part 2-Gathering On The Mountain	CD	Relix	RRCD2104	U.S.A.	2000	8.99
Various Artists	Part 3-Gathering On The Mountain	CD	Relix	RRCD2105	U.S.A.	2000	8.99
Various Artists	Party At Palace (McCartney, Clapton)	CD	Virgin	7243-8-12833-2-5	U.S.A.	2002	9.99
Various Artists	Passion - Sources	CD	Real World	01704-62301-2-4	U.S.A.	1989	11.99
Various Artists	Peace Together (U2 With Lou Reed)	CD	Island	74321-15538-2	Germany	1998	9.99
Various Artists	Peaceful Christmas	CD	Regency	V20019	U.S.A.	1993	8.99
Various Artists	Perfect Day (Reed, Bono)	CD Single	Chrysalis	7243-8-84934-2-0	England	1997	7.99
Various Artists	Permanent Record (OST) L Reed Unrel	CD	Epic	EK-70879	U.S.A.	1988	44.99
Various Artists	Peter And The Wolf (Eno, Phil Collins)	CD	Viceroy	VIC-6006-2	U.S.A.	1993	19.99
Various Artists	Phantom Of The Opera/The Mummy	CD	Disconforme	SFRCD33562	Italy	2002	9.99
Various Artists	Pickin' On Clapton	CD	CMH	CD-8514	U.S.A.	1999	5.99
Various Artists	Pickin' On CSNY	CD	CMH	CD-8511	U.S.A.	2000	5.99
Various Artists	Pickin' On Grateful Dead ...Tribute	3CD	CMH	CD-1791	U.S.A.	2001	14.99
Various Artists	Pickin' On Jerry Garcia	CD	CMH	CD-8603	U.S.A.	2001	5.99
Various Artists	Pickin' On The Allman Brothers	CD	CMH	CD-8538	U.S.A.	2000	5.99
Various Artists	Pickin' On The Eagles - A Tribute	CD	CMH	CD-8505	U.S.A.	1999	5.99
Various Artists	Pickin' On The Rolling Stones	CD	CMH	CD-8537	U.S.A.	2000	5.99
Various Artists	Pickin' On Zeppelin - A Tribute	CD	CMH	CD-8544	U.S.A.	2000	5.99
Various Artists	Pink Cadillac (O.S.T.)	CD	Warner Bros.	9-25922-2	U.S.A.	1989	6.99
Various Artists	Pink Flamingos 25th Ann. (O.S.T.)	CD	Hip O	HIPD-40058	U.S.A.	1997	11.99
Various Artists	Piss And Vinegar (Graham Parker)	CD	Buy Or Die	BOD96035	U.S.A.	1996	8.99
Various Artists	Planes, Trains And Automobiles (OST)	CD	MCA	MCAD-6223	U.S.A.	1987	39.99
Various Artists	Planes, Trains And Automobiles (OST)	CD	Warner Bros.	32XD-926	Japan	1987	54.99
Various Artists	Platinum Girl - A Tribute To Blondie	CD	Cleopatra	CLP-0784-2	U.S.A.	2000	6.99
Various Artists	Plus From Us	CD	Caroline	CAROL-2327-2	U.S.A.	1993	11.99
Various Artists	Poems/E A Poe (I Pop, Ed Sanders)	CD	Mercury	314-536-480-2	U.S.A.	1997	8.99
Various Artists	Polar Shift (Unreleased Steve Howe)	CD	Private	2083-2-P	U.S.A.	1991	7.99
Various Artists	Porky's Revenge	CD	Mobile Fidelity	MFCD-797	U.S.A.	1985	69.99
Various Artists	Porn To Rock (Porn Stars Sing)	CD	Captain Trip	CTCD-395	Japan	2000	22.99
Various Artists	Practical Magic (O.S.T. Stevie Nicks)	CD	Warner Bros.	9-47140-2	U.S.A.	1998	12.99
Various Artists	Pret-A-Porter	CD	Sony	CK-66791	U.S.A.	1994	6.99
Various Artists	Pret-A-Porter (O.S.T.)	CD	Sony	SRCS-7532	Japan	1994	24.99
Various Artists	Pretty In Pink (O.S.T.)	CD	A&M	CD-3293	U.S.A.	1986	8.99
Various Artists	Pretty In Pink (O.S.T.)	CD	Pony Canyon	D32Y-3078	Japan	1987	14.99
Various Artists	Progfest 2000 (Spock's Beard)	CD	Musea	FGBG-4379.AR	France	2001	29.99

Artist	Title	Format	Label	Catalog No	Country	Released	Value
Various Artists	Psycho - Horror And Fantasy At Movies	CD	Silva Screen	SILVAD-3003	England	1992	8.99
Various Artists	Pulp Fiction (O.S.T.)	CD	MCA	MCAD-11103	U.S.A.	1994	6.99
Various Artists	Punk Lost & Found	CD	Shanachie	5705	U.S.A.	1996	14.99
Various Artists	Radio 4 You Replugged	CD	Line	LICD-9.01286-L	Germany	1993	14.99
Various Artists	Rare Rock Tracks (Epic Unrel. Tracks)	CD	Columbia	JSK-42604	U.S.A.	1999	8.99
Various Artists	Rat Race (O.S.T.)	CD	Beyond	398-578-209-2	U.S.A.	2001	5.99
Various Artists	Real World Sampler (Promo)	CD	Virgin	7243-8-44597-4-2	England	1996	8.99
Various Artists	Red Hot + Blue (MFSL Gold Cd)	CD	Mobile Fidelity	UDCD-542	U.S.A.	1990	59.99
Various Artists	Red Hot + Country (CSN/J Browne)	CD	Mercury	P2-22639	U.S.A.	1994	7.99
Various Artists	Red Hot + Dance (EMF Brian Eno Mix)	CD	Columbia	CK-52826	U.S.A.	1992	5.99
Various Artists	Red Hot + Rio	CD	Verve	P2-33183	U.S.A.	1996	5.99
Various Artists	Red Hot + Riot (Fela Tribute)	CD	MCA	088-113-075-2	U.S.A.	2002	10.99
Various Artists	Red Hot And Rhapsody	CD	Antilles	314-557-788-2	U.S.A.	1998	10.99
Various Artists	Redbeard's All Access (Greg Lake Live)	CD	KTXQ	Q-102	U.S.A.	1993	29.99
Various Artists	Relix Mag 20th Ann. Show (Ltd. Ed.)	CD	Relix	RBRS0005	U.S.A.	1993	7.99
Various Artists	Relix Sampler # 1	CD	Relix	RRCD-2015	U.S.A.	1989	8.99
Various Artists	Relix Sampler #2	CD	Relix	RRCD-2038	U.S.A.	1989	8.99
Various Artists	Relix: Music For The Mind	CD	Relix	RRCD-2043	U.S.A.	1990	4.99
Various Artists	Relix's Best Of Truck Driving Songs	CD	Relix	RRCD2083	U.S.A.	1997	7.99
Various Artists	Remasterpieces (Yes, Genesis Promo)	CD	Atlantic	PRCD-6012-2	U.S.A.	1994	9.99
Various Artists	Renaissance Records Sampler (Promo)	CD	Renaissance	RMED-00200	U.S.A.	1997	14.99
Various Artists	Renaissance Records Winter (Promo)	CD	Renaissance	RMED-00100	U.S.A.	1996	14.99
Various Artists	Repo Man (O.S.T.)	CD	MCA	MCAD-39019	U.S.A.	1984	11.99
Various Artists	Return Grievous Angel (G.Parsons)	CD	Almo Sounds	AMSD-80024	U.S.A.	1999	10.99
Various Artists	Revealing Songs Of Yes - A Tribute	CD	Purple Pyramid	CLP-1143-2	U.S.A.	2001	8.99
Various Artists	Revealing Songs Of Yes: A Tribute	CD	Store For Music	SFMMCD013	England	2001	8.99
Various Artists	Revenge The Nerds (Unrel Rubinoos)	CD	Rock 'N' Roll	72392-75539-2	U.S.A.	1984	10.99
Various Artists	Rob Zombie's Halloween Hootenanny	CD	DGC	DGCD-25214	U.S.A.	1998	8.99
Various Artists	Robotech - Perfect Collection	2CD	Harmony Gold	7-39991-93112-2	Canada	2004	49.99
Various Artists	Rock & Roll /Lowell George Tribute	CD	CMC Int.	06076-86242-2	U.S.A.	1997	14.99
Various Artists	Rock Aid Armenia (Yes, ELP, Rush)	CD	BMG	BVCZ-3	Japan	1990	21.99
Various Artists	Rock Goes To The Movies/In Dreams	CD	Sony	A-22837	U.S.A.	1992	17.99
Various Artists	Rock 'N' Roll High School	CD	Sire	6070-2	U.S.A.	1979	8.99
Various Artists	Rocketown Records 5 Years	CD	Rocketown	0806-8-86193-2-9	U.S.A.	2001	5.99
Various Artists	Rockfile - Volume 11	CD	Line	BLCD-9.00852-L	Germany	1989	17.99
Various Artists	Rockfile - Volume 12	CD	Line	BLCD-9.00853-L	Germany	1989	17.99
Various Artists	Rockfile - Volume 13	CD	Line	BLCD-9.00854-L	Germany	1989	17.99
Various Artists	Rockfile - Volume 14	CD	Line	BLCD-9.00855-L	Germany	1989	17.99
Various Artists	Rockfile - Volume 15	CD	Line	BLCD-9.00856-L	Germany	1989	17.99
Various Artists	Rockfile - Volume 16	CD	Line	BLCD-9.00876-L	Germany	1989	17.99
Various Artists	Rockfile - Volume 17	CD	Line	BLCD-9.00877-L	Germany	1989	17.99
Various Artists	Rockfile - Volume 18	CD	Line	BLCD-9.00878-L	Germany	1989	17.99
Various Artists	Rockfile - Volume 19	CD	Line	BLCD-9.00879-L	Germany	1989	17.99
Various Artists	Rockfile - Volume 20	CD	Line	BLCD-9.00880-L	Germany	1989	17.99
Various Artists	Rockfile - Volume 21	CD	Line	BLCD-9.00903-L	Germany	1990	24.99
Various Artists	Rockfile - Volume 22	CD	Line	BLCD-9.00904-L	Germany	1990	24.99
Various Artists	Rockfile - Volume 23	CD	Line	BLCD-9.00905-L	Germany	1990	24.99
Various Artists	Rockfile - Volume 24	CD	Line	BLCD-9.00906-L	Germany	1990	24.99
Various Artists	Rockfile - Volume 25	CD	Line	BLCD-9.00907-L	Germany	1990	24.99
Various Artists	Rockfile - Volume 26	CD	Line	BLCD-9.00936-L	Germany	1990	24.99
Various Artists	Rockfile - Volume 27	CD	Line	BLCD-9.00937-L	Germany	1990	24.99
Various Artists	Rockfile - Volume 28	CD	Line	BLCD-9.00938-L	Germany	1990	24.99
Various Artists	Rockfile - Volume 29	CD	Line	BLCD-9.00939-L	Germany	1990	24.99
Various Artists	Rockfile - Volume 30	CD	Line	BLCD-9.00940-L	Germany	1990	24.99
Various Artists	Rockfile - Volume 36	CD	Line	BLCD-9.00976-L	Germany	1990	24.99
Various Artists	Rockfile - Volume 37	CD	Line	BLCD-9.00977-L	Germany	1990	24.99
Various Artists	Rockfile - Volume 38	CD	Line	BLCD-9.00978-L	Germany	1990	24.99
Various Artists	Rockfile - Volume 39	CD	Line	BLCD-9.00979-L	Germany	1990	24.99

V

Artist	Title	Format	Label	Catalog No	Country	Released	Value
Various Artists	Rockfile - Volume 40	CD	Line	BLCD-9.00980-L	Germany	1990	24.99
Various Artists	Rockfile - Volume 41	CD	Line	BLCD-9.00992-L	Germany	1991	24.99
Various Artists	Rockfile - Volume 42	CD	Line	BLCD-9.00995-L	Germany	1991	24.99
Various Artists	Rockfile - Volume 43	CD	Line	BLCD-9.00993-L	Germany	1991	24.99
Various Artists	Rockfile - Volume 44	CD	Line	BLCD-9.00994-L	Germany	1991	24.99
Various Artists	Rockfile - Volume 45	CD	Line	BLCD-9.00995-L	Germany	1991	24.99
Various Artists	Rockfile - Volume 46	CD	Line	BLCD-9.01016-L	Germany	1991	24.99
Various Artists	Rockfile - Volume 47	CD	Line	BLCD-9.01017-L	Germany	1991	24.99
Various Artists	Rockfile - Volume 48	CD	Line	BLCD-9.01018-L	Germany	1991	24.99
Various Artists	Rockfile - Volume 49	CD	Line	BLCD-9.01019-L	Germany	1991	24.99
Various Artists	Rockfile - Volume 50	CD	Line	BLCD-9.01020-L	Germany	1991	24.99
Various Artists	Rockfile Volume 1	CD	Line	BLCD-9.00731-L	Germany	1989	17.99
Various Artists	Rockfile Volume 10	CD	Line	BLCD-9.00767-L	Germany	1989	17.99
Various Artists	Rockfile Volume 2	CD	Line	BLCD-9.00732-L	Germany	1989	17.99
Various Artists	Rockfile Volume 3	CD	Line	BLCD-9.00733-L	Germany	1989	17.99
Various Artists	Rockfile Volume 31	CD	Line	BLCD-9.00956-L	Germany	1990	24.99
Various Artists	Rockfile Volume 32	CD	Line	BLCD-9.00957-L	Germany	1990	24.99
Various Artists	Rockfile Volume 33	CD	Line	BLCD-9.00958-L	Germany	1990	24.99
Various Artists	Rockfile Volume 34	CD	Line	BLCD-9.00959-L	Germany	1990	24.99
Various Artists	Rockfile Volume 35	CD	Line	BLCD-9.00960-L	Germany	1990	24.99
Various Artists	Rockfile Volume 4	CD	Line	BLCD-9.00734-L	Germany	1989	17.99
Various Artists	Rockfile Volume 5	CD	Line	BLCD-9.00735-L	Germany	1989	17.99
Various Artists	Rockfile Volume 6	CD	Line	BLCD-9.00763-L	Germany	1989	17.99
Various Artists	Rockfile Volume 7	CD	Line	BLCD-9.00764-L	Germany	1989	17.99
Various Artists	Rockfile Volume 8	CD	Line	BLCD-9.00765-L	Germany	1989	17.99
Various Artists	Rockfile Volume 9	CD	Line	BLCD-9.00766-L	Germany	1989	17.99
Various Artists	Rodgers & Hammerstein Songbook	CD	Sony	SK-53331	U.S.A.	1993	8.99
Various Artists	Rough Trade Shops Electronic 01	2CD	Rough Trade	CDSTUMM203	England	2002	22.99
Various Artists	Rubaiyat - Elektra's 40th Anniversary	2CD	Elektra	9-60940-2	U.S.A.	1990	12.99
Various Artists	Rubaiyat: Elektra's 40th Ann (DJ)	4CD	Elektra	PRCD-8208-2	U.S.A.	1990	69.99
Various Artists	Rudolph Frosty/Friends Xmas Songs	CD	Sony	LK-67766	U.S.A.	1997	8.99
Various Artists	Runaway Bride (O.S.T.)	CD	Columbia	CK-69923	U.S.A.	1999	7.99
Various Artists	S Night Fever (O.S.T.) (MFSL Gold)	CD	Mobile Fidelity	UDCD-716	U.S.A.	1977	49.99
Various Artists	S R 35th Master Sound Sampler (Gold)	CD	Columbia	CSK-5033	U.S.A.	1993	54.99
Various Artists	Sabrina The Teenage Witch (O.S.T.)	CD	Geffen	GEFD-25220	U.S.A.	1998	4.99
Various Artists	San Francisco Live (Jefferson Airplane)	CD	Arti Faxt	ART-12010	U.S.A.	1997	14.99
Various Artists	Saturday Morning Cartoons' Gr Hits	CD	MCA	MCAD-11348	U.S.A.	1995	8.99
Various Artists	Saturday Night Fever Soundtrack	CD	Polydor	P2-25389	U.S.A.	1995	8.99
Various Artists	Saturday Night Live Vol. 1	CD	Dreamworks	0044-50205-2	U.S.A.	1999	9.99
Various Artists	School House Rock! Rocks	CD	Lava Records	92681-2	U.S.A.	1996	7.99
Various Artists	Schoolhouse Rock Box Set	4CD	Rhino	R2-72455	U.S.A.	1996	32.99
Various Artists	Scooby-Doo's Snack Tracks	CD	Rhino	R2-75505	U.S.A.	1998	10.99
Various Artists	Searching For Jimi Hendrix (Tribute)	CD	Right Stuff	72438-59782-2-7	U.S.A.	1999	7.99
Various Artists	Select Trax Vol. 10; Sweet Taste Xmas	CD	Southwest Wholesal	ST010	U.S.A.	1996	12.99
Various Artists	Selections From The Prince Of Egypt	CD	Dreamworks	DRMDM-58011	U.S.A.	1998	3.99
Various Artists	September Songs: Music Of Kurt Weill	CD	Sony	SK-63046	U.S.A.	1997	9.99
Various Artists	Sgt. Pepper's Lonely Hearts....O.S.T.)	2CD	Polydor	314-557-076-2	U.S.A.	1978	14.99
Various Artists	Shag	CD	Sire	9-25800-2	U.S.A.	1989	9.99
Various Artists	Shake Compilation - Shake To Date	CD	Line	ALCD-9.00255-0	Germany	1988	13.99
Various Artists	She Rock	CD	Razor & Tie	7930189025-2	U.S.A.	1999	5.99
Various Artists	Short Cuts (O.S.T.) Elvis Costello Unrel	CD	Imago	72787-21014-2	U.S.A.	1993	6.99
Various Artists	Slipped Disc (Crystal Pepsi/Promo)	CD	Cema	S21-17499	U.S.A.	1993	14.99
Various Artists	Slippery Ballerina (M. Tucker, W. Eric)	CD	Casino	CAS-3018	U.S.A.	1999	9.99
Various Artists	SNL Live Vol. 2 (N Young, Pretenders)	CD	Dreamworks	0044-50206-2	U.S.A.	1999	9.99
Various Artists	Snoopy!!!	CD	DRG	6103	U.S.A.	1976	11.99
Various Artists	Some Kind Of Wonderful (O.S.T.)	CD	BGO	BGOCD178	England	1993	11.99
Various Artists	Some Sides Of Line - 20th Anniversary	CD	Line	LICD—9.01356-0	Germany	1998	10.99
Various Artists	Some Songs/Kill Rock Stars Singles	CD	Kill Rock Stars	KRS-276	U.S.A.	2002	24.99

V

Artist	Title	Format	Label	Catalog No	Country	Released	Value
Various Artists	Someone Left... (Jimmy Webb Songs)	CD	Polygram	555-430-2	England	1998	12.99
Various Artists	Sometimes God Smiles (Promo)	CD	Discipline Global	DGM9808	U.S.A.	1998	6.99
Various Artists	Songs From Sacred Napkin (Promo)	CD	Rykodisc	RCD-PRO-9001	U.S.A.	1990	4.99
Various Artists	Songs From The Cool World	CD	Warner Bros.	9-45009-2	U.S.A.	1992	11.99
Various Artists	Songs Of Jimmie Rodgers - A Tribute	CD	Sony	CK-67676	U.S.A.	1996	8.99
Various Artists	Songs Of Pete Seeger Vol. 1	2CD	Appleseed	1024	U.S.A.	1998	13.99
Various Artists	Songs Of Pete Seeger Vol. 2	CD	Appleseed	APR-CD-1055	U.S.A.	2001	8.99
Various Artists	Soul Man (O.S.T.) Lou Reed Unrel	CD	A&M	CD-3903	U.S.A.	1986	18.99
Various Artists	Sound Of Soul - The Timeless Soul	CD	Line	TLCD-9.00475-0	Germany	1987	12.99
Various Artists	Sounds Of Astralwerks: 2002 (Promo)	CD	Astralwerks	7243-8-13056-0-7	U.S.A.	2002	14.99
Various Artists	Sounds Of Womadelaide 2001	CD	Womad In The Park	WAZ001	Australia	2001	14.99
Various Artists	South Park: Bigger, Longer & Uncut	CD	Atlantic	83199-2	U.S.A.	1999	8.99
Various Artists	Space Ghost's Musical Bar-B-Que	CD	Rhino	R2-72876	U.S.A.	1997	6.99
Various Artists	Spider-Man : Rock Refl./Super-Hero	CD	Windthrop	WIN-1003-2	U.S.A.	2000	14.99
Various Artists	Spy Mag. Presents: Spy Music Vol.1	CD	Rhino	R2-71749	U.S.A.	1994	14.99
Various Artists	Spy Mag. Presents: Spy Music Vol.2	CD	Rhino	R2-71750	U.S.A.	1996	12.99
Various Artists	Spy Mag. Presents: Spy Music Vol.3	CD	Rhino	R2-71751	U.S.A.	1994	12.99
Various Artists	Star Trek Sound Effects	CD	GNP	GNPD-8010	U.S.A.	1988	8.99
Various Artists	Starbucks Celebrates World of Music	CD	Real World	RW552	U.S.A.	1999	7.99
Various Artists	Steel Magnolias (O.S.T.)	CD	Polydor	341-582-2	U.S.A.	1989	141.99
Various Artists	Steelyard Blues	CD	Warner Bros.	WPCR-10716	Japan	2000	24.99
Various Artists	Stolen Roses - Songs Of Grateful Dead	CD	Grateful Dead	GDCD-4073	U.S.A.	2000	7.99
Various Artists	Stone Cold Queen (Tribute)	CD	Video Arts	VACM-1173	Japan	2001	29.99
Various Artists	Stone Free: A Tribute To Jimi Hendrix	CD	Reprise	9-45438-2	U.S.A.	1993	7.99
Various Artists	Stoned Immaculate - Music The Doors	CD	Elektra	62475-2	U.S.A.	2000	6.99
Various Artists	Straight To Hell	CD	Repertoire	REP-4224-WY	Germany	1991	34.99
Various Artists	Sullivan Years - Best/Broadway Vol. 1	2CD	TVT	TVT-9436-2	U.S.A.	1992	17.99
Various Artists	Sullivan Years - Best/Broadway Vol. 2	2CD	TVT	TVT-9440/1	U.S.A.	1993	17.99
Various Artists	Sullivan Years - Rodgers/Hammerstein	2CD	TVT	TVT-9443/4	U.S.A.	1993	17.99
Various Artists	Sun City + 1 (Artists Un. Ag. Apartheid)	CD	Razor & Tie	RE-2007	U.S.A.	1993	43.99
Various Artists	Superfoxy	CD	Line	YMCD-9.00932-L	Germany	1990	24.99
Various Artists	Supernatural Fairy Tales (Sampler DJ)	CD	Rhino	PRCD-7195	U.S.A.	1996	19.99
Various Artists	Supernatural Fairy Tales Box Set	5CD	Rhino	R2-72451	U.S.A.	1996	79.99
Various Artists	Survival (Unreleased Anthony Phillips)	2CD	Virgin	7243-8-44631-2-0	England	1997	24.99
Various Artists	Sweet Charity - Original Cast	CD	Columbia	CK-2900	U.S.A.	1966	8.99
Various Artists	Sweet Relief, Benefit Victoria Williams	CD	Columbia	OK-57134	U.S.A.	1993	5.99
Various Artists	T.V. Family Christmas	CD	Scotti Bros.	75271-2	U.S.A.	1992	24.99
Various Artists	Tales From Yesterday	CD	Magna Carta	MA-9003-2	U.S.A.	1995	12.99
Various Artists	Tame Yourself	CD	Rhino	R2-70772	U.S.A.	1991	8.99
Various Artists	Tanzania Dance Bands - Volume 2	CD	Line	MSCD-9.01117-0	Germany	1991	24.99
Various Artists	Teacher (OST/Ian Hunter/38 Special)	CD	Toshiba-EMI	TOCP-8394	Japan	1984	59.99
Various Artists	Teacher (OST/Ian Hunter/38 Special)	CD	Capitol	CDP-7460622	U.S.A.	1984	49.99
Various Artists	Tee Vee Toons: The Commercials	CD	TVT	TVT-1400-CD	U.S.A.	1989	8.99
Various Artists	Teen Wolf (O.S.T.)	CD	Metronome	829-029-2	Germany	1985	309.00
Various Artists	Television's Gr. Hits, Vol. 1	CD	TVT	TVT1100-CD	U.S.A.	1986	15.99
Various Artists	Television's Gr. Hits, Vol. 2	CD	TVT	TVT-1200-CD	U.S.A.	1986	15.99
Various Artists	Television's Gr. Hits, Vol. 3	CD	TVT	TVT1300-CD	U.S.A.	1987	15.99
Various Artists	Television's Greatest Hits Sampler (DJ)	CD	TVT	TVT-1905-2P	U.S.A.	1996	14.99
Various Artists	Tender Voices (E Burdon, R Stewart)	CD	Line	VVCD-9.01115-L	Germany	1991	24.99
Various Artists	That '70s Album (Rockin')	CD	Volcano	61422-31155-2	U.S.A.	1990	7.99
Various Artists	That 70's Show Presents Jammin'	CD	Volcano	61422-31156-2-7	U.S.A.	1999	7.99
Various Artists	That's Rio Brazil Sound	CD	Line	RICD-9.00873-E	Germany	1989	24.99
Various Artists	That's Core Jazz - Volume 1	CD	Line	COCD-9.00868-0	Germany	1989	24.99
Various Artists	That's Core Jazz - Volume 2	CD	Line	COCD-9.01125-E	Germany	1991	24.99
Various Artists	That's Line - 6	CD	Line	LICD-9.01106-J	Germany	1991	24.99
Various Artists	That's Line 1	CD	Line	LICD-9.00841-J	Germany	1990	24.99
Various Artists	That's Line 2	CD	Line	LICD-9.00842-J	Germany	1990	24.99
Various Artists	That's Line 3	CD	Line	LICD-9.00843-J	Germany	1990	24.99

V

Artist	Title	Format	Label	Catalog No	Country	Released	Value
Various Artists	That's Line 4	CD	Line	LICD-9.00844-J	Germany	1991	24.99
Various Artists	That's Line 5	CD	Line	LICD-9.00845-J	Germany	1991	24.99
Various Artists	That's Sawdust Country - Vol. 1	CD	Line	SDCD-9.00711-E	Germany	1990	24.99
Various Artists	That's Timeless Soul - Vol. 1	CD	Line	TLCD-9.00422-0	Germany	1988	12.99
Various Artists	The 60's (O.S.T.)	CD	Mercury	MEAD-178	U.S.A.	1999	34.99
Various Artists	The 7 Inch Wonders of the World	CD	SST	SST-CD-070	U.S.A.	1986	24.99
Various Artists	The 70's (O.S.T.)	CD	Island	314-542-473-2	U.S.A.	2000	29.99
Various Artists	The Apple E.P. (Apple Shaped)	CD	Capitol	1991	England	1991	25.99
Various Artists	The Arista Masters (Promo)	CD	Arista	ASCD-3248	U.S.A.	1996	8.99
Various Artists	The Basketball Diaries	CD	Island	314-524-093-2	U.S.A.	1995	8.99
Various Artists	The Best Of American Music... (Promo)	CD	Magic	1982282	France	2001	17.99
Various Artists	The Best of Bond... James Bond	CD	Capitol	72435-22607-2-0	U.S.A.	1999	8.99
Various Artists	The Best Of Louie Louie	CD	Rhino	R2-70605	U.S.A.	1988	19.99
Various Artists	The Best Of Star Trek Soundtracks	CD	RCA	74321-65245-2-5	England	1999	8.99
Various Artists	The Best Of Star Trek, Vol. 2	CD	GNP	GNPD-8051	U.S.A.	1996	12.99
Various Artists	The Best Of Star Trek-30th Ann.	CD	GNP	GNPD-8053	U.S.A.	1996	12.99
Various Artists	The Brady Bunch Movie (O.S.T.)	CD	Milan	73138-35698-2	U.S.A.	1995	6.99
Various Artists	The Breakfast Club (O.S.T.)	CD	A&M	CD-509994	U.S.A.	1985	8.99
Various Artists	The Breakfast Club (O.S.T.)	CD	Pony Canyon	D32Y-3548	Japan	1985	14.99
Various Artists	The Bridge School Concerts Vol. One	CD	Reprise	9-46824-2	U.S.A.	1997	7.99
Various Artists	The Brill Building Sound Box Set	4CD	Ktel	5025-2	U.S.A.	1993	54.99
Various Artists	The Cobra Records Story	2CD	Capricorn	9-42012-2	U.S.A.	1993	34.99
Various Artists	The Color Purple (O.S.T.)	2CD	Warner Bros.	9-25389-2	U.S.A.	1985	74.99
Various Artists	The Concert For New York	2CD	Columbia	C2K-86270	U.S.A.	2001	11.99
Various Artists	The Crow (O.S.T.)	CD	Atlantic	82519-2	U.S.A.	1994	8.99
Various Artists	The Cutting Edge (O.S.T.)	CD	Rykodisc	RCD-10738	U.S.A.	1998	56.99
Various Artists	The Dukes Of Hazzard + 1 (O.S.T.)	CD	Scotti Bros.	72392-75522-2	U.S.A.	1982	8.99
Various Artists	The End Of Violence (O.S.T.)	CD	Outpost	OPRD-30008	U.S.A.	1997	8.99
Various Artists	The Essential Collections (Promo)	CD	Columbia	JSK-59598	U.S.A.	2003	8.99
Various Artists	The Finest Of Hard Rock, Vol. 4	2CD	Ktel	330199-2	Switzerland	1994	14.99
Various Artists	The Finest Of Hard-Rock - Vol. 1	2CD	K-Tel	330083-2	Switzerland	1994	14.99
Various Artists	The Fire/Fury Records Story	2CD	Capricorn	9-42009-2	U.S.A.	1993	34.99
Various Artists	The Harder They Come Deluxe Ed.	2CD	Hip O	069495-2	U.S.A.	2003	16.99
Various Artists	The Honky Tonk Demos (Dire Straits)	CD	Line	LICD-9.01067-0	Germany	1991	39.99
Various Artists	The Ice Storm	CD	Velvel	VEL-79713	U.S.A.	1997	7.99
Various Artists	The Island Story 1962-1987	2CD	Island	7-90684-2	U.S.A.	1987	13.99
Various Artists	The Jewel/Paula Records Story	2CD	Capricorn	9-42012-2	U.S.A.	1993	34.99
Various Artists	The Joe Meek Story - Volume 1	CD	Line	TRCD-9.01081-0	Germany	1991	20.99
Various Artists	The Joe Meek Story - Volume 2	CD	Line	TRCD-9.01082-0	Germany	1992	20.99
Various Artists	The July 1995 Guide	CD	Warner Bros.	RBO-3181	U.S.A.	1995	3.99
Various Artists	The Lost Boys (O.S.T.) Lou Gramm	CD	Atlantic	7-81767-2	U.S.A.	1987	5.99
Various Artists	The Monster Mash Rock 'N' Roll Party	CD	Retro	NOV10022	Canada	1998	8.99
Various Artists	The Monterey Pop Sampler (Promo)	CD	Rhino	PRO2-90130	U.S.A.	1992	109.99
Various Artists	The Muppet Movie (O.S.T.)	CD	BMG	7-4860-30019-2	U.S.A.	1993	44.99
Various Artists	The Music From U.N.C.L.E.	CD	Razor & Tie	RE-2133-2	U.S.A.	1997	10.99
Various Artists	The On-U Sound Celebration	CD	Line	TCCD-9.00662-0	Germany	1988	14.99
Various Artists	The Other Sister (O.S.T.)	CD	Hollywood	HR-62180-2	U.S.A.	1999	8.99
Various Artists	The Pallbearer (O.S.T.)	CD	Hollywood	HR-62058-2	U.S.A.	1996	7.99
Various Artists	The Prince Of Egypt Sampler (Promo)	CD	Dreamworks	PRO-CD-5129	U.S.A.	1998	6.99
Various Artists	The Prince's Trust Collection (Best Of)	CD	Telstar	TCD-2275	England	1986	8.99
Various Artists	The R&R Sound of Detroit	CD	Line	TLCD-9.00582-0	Germany	1988	12.99
Various Artists	The Ray Davies Songbook	CD	Connoisseur	VSOP-CD-244	England	1997	9.99
Various Artists	The Rugrats Movie (O.S.T.)	CD	Interscope	INTDE-90181	U.S.A.	1998	4.99
Various Artists	The Scepter Records Story	3CD	Capricorn	9-42003-2	U.S.A.	1992	49.99
Various Artists	The Secret Policeman's Other Ball	CD	Rhino	R2-71048	U.S.A.	1992	39.99
Various Artists	The Secret Policeman's Third Ball	CD	Virgin	CDV2458	England	1987	10.99
Various Artists	The Sopranos (O.S.T.)	CD	Columbia	497460-2	Australia	1999	8.99
Various Artists	The Sound Of Alabama Vol. 1	CD	Line	TLCD-9.00411-0	Germany	1988	12.99

V

Artist	Title	Format	Label	Catalog No	Country	Released	Value
Various Artists	The Sound Of St. Louis - Vol. 1	CD	Line	TLCD-9.00367-0	Germany	1988	8.99
Various Artists	The Specialist (The Remixes)	CD	Epic	EK-66661	U.S.A.	1994	6.99
Various Artists	The Sting (O.S.T. Pic Cd W/Video)	CD	Universal	3184-1-1	U.S.A.	2002	15.99
Various Artists	The Strawberry Statement O.S.T.	CD	Sony	AK-52419	U.S.A.	1992	34.99
Various Artists	The Sullivan Years - British Invasion	CD	TVT	TVT-9428-2	U.S.A.	1990	8.99
Various Artists	The Sullivan Years : Rock Classics	CD	TVT	TVT-9430-2	U.S.A.	1991	13.99
Various Artists	The Sullivan Years: Sixties Rock	CD	TVT	TVT-9426-2	U.S.A.	1991	13.99
Various Artists	The Sullivan Years: The Mod Sound	CD	TVT	TVT-9429-2	U.S.A.	1991	8.99
Various Artists	The Swingtime Records Story	2CD	Capricorn	9-42024-2	U.S.A.	1994	34.99
Various Artists	The Twilight Zone (O.S.T.)	CD	Warner Bros.	599-23887-2-6	EEC	2002	15.99
Various Artists	The Ultimate Star Trek	CD	Varese	302-066-163-2	U.S.A.	2000	8.99
Various Artists	The Unplugged Collection Volume One	CD	Warner Bros.	9-45774-2	U.S.A.	1994	6.99
Various Artists	The Warriors (O.S.T.)	CD	Spectrum	551-161-2	Canada	1999	9.99
Various Artists	The Wizard Of Oz (O.S.T.)	CD	Rhino	R2-71999	U.S.A.	1995	8.99
Various Artists	The Wraith - (Interceptor) O.S.T.	CD	Scotti Bros.	847-312-2	Germany	1985	106.99
Various Artists	The X-Files: Songs In The Key Of X	CD	Warner Bros.	9-46079-2	U.S.A.	1996	6.99
Various Artists	The X-Files: The Album	CD	Elektra	62200-2	U.S.A.	1998	6.99
Various Artists	Thelma & Louise	CD	MCA	MCAD-10239	U.S.A.	1991	5.99
Various Artists	Themes From Classic Science Fiction...	CD	Varese	VSD-5407	U.S.A.	1993	8.99
Various Artists	Then Sings... (Gospel Sampler)	CD	Mobile Fidelity	GS-1	U.S.A.	1982	119.99
Various Artists	There's Something About Mary	CD	Capitol	7243-4-95737-2-7	U.S.A.	1998	7.99
Various Artists	They Shall Not Pass (Sisters Of Mercy)	CD	Abstract	AABT-400CD	France	1988	19.99
Various Artists	This Is Jazz (Columbia/Epic Promo)	CD	Columbia	CSK-41096	U.S.A.	1998	7.99
Various Artists	This Is Where I Belong	CD	Rykodisc	RCD-10621	U.S.A.	2002	8.99
Various Artists	Tibetan Freedom Concert	3CD	Capitol	7243-8-59110-2-6	U.S.A.	1997	14.99
Various Artists	Time Will Show Wiser (Gene Clark)	CD	Triad	TRICD-001	England	1989	28.99
Various Artists	Timeless: Hank Williams Tribute	CD	Lost Highway	088-170-239-2	U.S.A.	2001	7.99
Various Artists	TM Century Gold Disc # 405 (Promo)	CD	TM Century	930227F	U.S.A.	1987	13.99
Various Artists	TM Century Gold Disc # 510 (Promo)	CD	TM Century	921012C	U.S.A.	1987	13.99
Various Artists	TM Century Gold Disc # 568 (Promo)	CD	TM Century	930323I	U.S.A.	1987	13.99
Various Artists	TM Century Gold Disc #10 (Promo)	CD	TM Century	930147B	U.S.A.	1987	13.99
Various Artists	Todd (Rundgren)/A True Star	CD	Pony Canyon	PCCA-01113	Japan	1997	24.99
Various Artists	Together For The Children Of Bosnia	CD	London	452-100-2	U.S.A.	1996	10.99
Various Artists	Toon Tunes (Cartoon Theme Songs)	CD	Rhino	R2-72752	U.S.A.	1997	8.99
Various Artists	Torch Song Trilogy (O.S.T)	CD	Polygram	837785-2	U.S.A.	1988	7.99
Various Artists	Touched By An Angel: Xmas Album	CD	Epic	BK-69710-2	U.S.A.	1999	5.99
Various Artists	Trainspotting #2 (O.S.T. DJ Cd) (I Pop)	CD	Capitol	7243-8-21686-2-1	U.S.A.	1997	8.99
Various Artists	Transatlantic (The Label) Story Box Set	3CD	Essential	ESF-CD-654	England	1998	29.99
Various Artists	Tribute To Jeff (Porcaro Of Toto)	CD	Zebra	ZD-44005-2	U.S.A.	1997	28.99
Various Artists	Tribute To Jerry Garcia	CD	Relix	RBRS0009	U.S.A.	1997	11.99
Various Artists	Tribute to Patti Smith	CD	Doppelganger	DOP50	England	1997	9.99
Various Artists	Tribute To Steve Goodman	2CD	Mobile Fidelity	MFCD-2-854	U.S.A.	1988	69.99
Various Artists	Tribute: Hank Marvin/Shadows	CD	Pangaea	7243-8-33928-2-7	U.S.A.	1996	8.99
Various Artists	Tributo A The Cure - Por Que No..	CD	Warner Bros.	28265-2	U.S.A.	1999	19.99
Various Artists	Tromeo & Juliet	CD	Oglio	OGL-89103-2	U.S.A.	1997	9.99
Various Artists	TV's Gr. Hits, Vol. 5 (Holographic)	CD	TVT	TVT-1700-CD	U.S.A.	1996	15.99
Various Artists	TV's Gr. Hits, Vol. 6 (Holographic)	CD	TVT	TVT-1800-CD	U.S.A.	1996	15.99
Various Artists	TV's Gr. Hits, Vol. 7 (Holographic)	CD	TVT	TVT-1900-CD	U.S.A.	1996	15.99
Various Artists	Twilight Zone Original TV Scores	5CD	Soundtrack Listeners	SLCS-7080-84	Japan	1991	164.99
Various Artists	Ultimate Dirty Dancing OST (26 Songs)	CD	RCA	82876-57718-2	U.S.A.	2003	11.99
Various Artists	Ultradisc II Sampler (MFSL Gold Cd)	CD	Mobile Fidelity	SPCD-016	U.S.A.	1987	29.99
Various Artists	Ultraman Complete Song Collection	5CD	Columbia	COCX-30717-21	Japan	1999	99.99
Various Artists	Under The Covers (Story Of Lp Covers)	CD-Rom	Graphix Zone	76917-31075-1-9	U.S.A.	1996	8.99
Various Artists	Undercover - Songs/Lou Reed (Promo)	CD	Warner Bros.	PRO-CD-8052	U.S.A.	1996	20.99
Various Artists	Unelectric (Townshend/Rundgren)	CD	Warner Bros.	JCD-3138	U.S.A.	1995	12.99
Various Artists	United States Of Poetry (Jim Carroll)	CD	Mercury	314-532-139-2	U.S.A.	1996	5.99
Various Artists	Until The End Of The World	CD	Warner Bros.	9-26707-2	U.S.A.	1991	8.99
Various Artists	Up, Up & Away (Songs/Jimmy Webb)	CD	Sequel	NEMCD-410	England	1999	9.99

V

Artist	Title	Format	Label	Catalog No	Country	Released	Value
Various Artists	URGH! A Music War (Live XTC/Police)	CD	A&M	CD-6019	U.S.A.	1981	89.99
Various Artists	Valley Girl (O.S.T.) Josie Cotton	CD	Rhino	R2-71590	U.S.A.	1994	8.99
Various Artists	Velvet Goldmine (O.S.T.)	CD	Polygram	314-556-035-2	U.S.A.	1998	8.99
Various Artists	VH1 Behind The Music (Target)	CD	Warner Bros.	27779	U.S.A.	1999	6.99
Various Artists	VH1 Storytellers	CD	Interscope	0694905112	U.S.A.	2000	7.99
Various Artists	VH1's The Big 80's - Christmas	CD	Rhino	R2-74381	U.S.A.	2001	8.99
Various Artists	Voiceprint Sampler 2003	CD	Voiceprint	VP2003CD	England	2003	14.99
Various Artists	Voices Of The Real World	CD	Real World	12438-48119-2-1	U.S.A.	2000	7.99
Various Artists	Voices That Care	CD	Giant	9-40054-2	U.S.A.	1991	20.99
Various Artists	Vol. 1-Then & Now	CD	San Francisco Soun	SFS-03931	U.S.A.	1994	14.99
Various Artists	Vol. 2-Then & Now	CD	San Francisco Soun	SFS-03932	U.S.A.	1994	14.99
Various Artists	Volume Nine (Paul Weller)	CD	RTM	9VCD9	England	1994	8.99
Various Artists	Volunteer Jam Vol. 1 (Capricorn Live)	CD	Capricorn	BLH-9704-2	U.S.A.	1999	7.99
Various Artists	We Are Family	CD Single	Tommy Boy	TBCD2331	U.S.A.	2001	8.99
Various Artists	We Are The World - USA For Africa	CD	Polygram	824-822-2	U.S.A.	1985	53.99
Various Artists	We Will Fall: The Iggy Pop Tribute	CD	Royalty	RTY106	U.S.A.	1997	5.99
Various Artists	Weltmusik	CD	Line	MSCD-9.00700-0	Germany	1989	14.99
Various Artists	We're All Normal - Love/A Lee Tribute	CD	Alias	A-058	U.S.A.	1994	24.99
Various Artists	West Side Story (Sony Gold Cd)	CD	Columbia	CK-53152	U.S.A.	1993	14.99
Various Artists	What's Shakin (E Capton/Powerhouse)	CD	Elektra	9-61343-2	U.S.A.	1993	24.99
Various Artists	What's Up Matador	2CD	Matador	OLE-163-2	U.S.A.	1997	8.99
Various Artists	When Pigs Fly - Songs You Never ...	CD	A2X	XEMU-1011	U.S.A.	2002	12.99
Various Artists	When Saturday Comes (O.S.T.)	CD	Polygram	532-307-2	England	1996	8.99
Various Artists	When The Wind Blows (O.S.T.)	CD	Virgin	0777-7-86706-2-9	Holland	1986	8.99
Various Artists	White Album - Windham Hill Collection	CD	Windam Hill	D120272	U.S.A.	1997	7.99
Various Artists	White Men Can't Jump (DJ/Sampler)	CD Single	EMI	DPRO-04883	U.S.A.	1992	12.99
Various Artists	White Nights (O.S.T.)	CD	Atlantic	7-81273-2	U.S.A.	1985	7.99
Various Artists	Whole Lotta Lava	CD	Sony	AK-53922	U.S.A.	1993	6.99
Various Artists	Wild At Heart (O.S.T.)	CD	Polydor	845-098-2	U.S.A.	1990	6.99
Various Artists	Windham Hill - The Impressionists	CD	Windham Hill	WD-2047	U.S.A.	1992	8.99
Various Artists	Windham Hill Holiday DJ Sampler 2000	CD	Windham Hill	WDJ-11575-2	U.S.A.	2000	8.99
Various Artists	Winter Wonderland (Jesse Ed Davis)	CD	Warner Bros.	PR0-CD-3328	U.S.A.	1988	74.99
Various Artists	Winters Of Discontent - Peel Sessions	CD	Strange Fruit	SFRSCD204	England	1991	34.99
Various Artists	Wir Können Auch Anders	CD	Line	CICD-9.01284-0	Germany	1993	12.99
Various Artists	Wizard Of Oz (1998 Cast Recording)	CD	TVT	TVT-1020-2	U.S.A.	1998	11.99
Various Artists	Wizard Of Oz (Story/Songs Of) Pop Up	CD	Rhino	R2-75516	U.S.A.	1998	10.99
Various Artists	Wizard Of Oz Deluxe Edition Box Set	2CD	Rhino	R2-71964	U.S.A.	1995	29.99
Various Artists	WLIR-Kives Unplugged	CD	Resturant	1003-2	U.S.A.	1997	14.99
Various Artists	Wolfrider's Reflections: Songs/Elfquest	CD	Warp Graphics	WG-101	U.S.A.	1992	11.99
Various Artists	Women Live From Mountain Stage	CD	Blue Plate	BPM-308CD	U.S.A.	1997	13.99
Various Artists	Woodstock (MFSL Silver/W/Program)	4CD	Mobile Fidelity	MFCD-4-816	U.S.A.	1971	249.99
Various Artists	Woodstock (The Best Of)	CD	Atlantic	82618-2	U.S.A.	1994	8.99
Various Artists	Woodstock 94	2CD	A&M	31454-0289-2	U.S.A.	1994	13.99
Various Artists	Woodstock '94 Sampler (Promo)	CD	A&M	314-588-372-2	U.S.A.	1994	19.99
Various Artists	Woodstock '99	2CD	Epic	E2K-63770	U.S.A.	1999	13.99
Various Artists	Woodstock Diary	CD	Atlantic	82634-2	U.S.A.	1994	9.99
Various Artists	Woodstock- Unreleased Tracks (DJ)	CD	Atlantic	PRCD-5826	U.S.A.	1994	19.99
Various Artists	Woodstock: 3 Days Peace/Music Box Se	4CD	Atlantic	82636-2	U.S.A.	1994	29.99
Various Artists	Xanadu	CD	Jet	465054-2	Australia	1980	8.99
Various Artists	X-Files: Songs In Key Of X (Adv.)	CD	Warner Bros.	2-46079-A	U.S.A.	1996	12.99
Various Artists	X-Sampler (Virgin Promo Sampler)	CD	Virgin	VVSAM1	England	1991	5.99
Various Artists	Y Tu Mama Tambien (Eno, Zappa)	CD	Zomba	61422-32191-2	U.S.A.	2001	14.99
Various Artists	Young Einstein (O.S.T.)	CD	A&M	CD-3929	U.S.A.	1989	16.99
Various Artists	You're A Good Man, Charlie Brown	CD	RCA	09026-63384-2	U.S.A.	1999	12.99
Various Artists	Zabriskie Point (O.S.T.)	CD	Rhino	R2-72462	U.S.A.	1970	24.99
Various Artists	Zetrospective (Unrel. John Cale On Cd)	CD	Island	846-225-2	England	1989	34.99
Various Artists (Alex Chilton)	Line Xmas Excursions	CD Single	Line	LICD-9.01135-E	Germany	1991	34.99
Various Artists (Big Star)	Slow Dancin' - Line's Gr. Dance Songs	CD	Line	VVCD-9.01111-L	Germany	1991	17.99

Artist	Title	Format	Label	Catalog No	Country	Released	Value
Various Artists (Jethro Tull)	25 Very Rare Masters From The Sixties	CD	Line	LICD-9.01333-0	Germany	1996	20.99
Various Artists (Jethro Tull)	Derek Lawrence Sessions - Take 3	CD	Line	LICD-9.01120-0	Germany	1992	18.99
Various Artists (Jethro Tull)	The Derek Lawrence Story - Sampler	CD Single	Line	LICD-9.01138-E	Germany	1991	22.99
Various Artists (Line)	Liner - New Tracks 1	CD	Line	LICD-9.01220-E	Germany	1992	12.99
Various Artists (Mickey Jupp)	Pop Patterns - Line's Greatest Popsters	CD	Line	VVCD-9.01126-L	Germany	1991	9.99
Various Artists (Roy Harper)	Acoustic Affairs - Line's Gr. Unplugged	CD	Line	VVCD-9.01127-L	Germany	1991	17.99
Various Artists (The Nice)	Copycats - Line's Greatest Dylans	CD	Line	VVCD-9.01128-L	Germany	1991	17.99
Various Artists /Jobim	Wave - A C Jobim Songbook	CD	Polygram	314-535-528-2	U.S.A.	1996	7.99
Various Artists/4AD	Liliput (W/Large Book)	2CD	4AD	LILIPUT-1/2	U.S.A.	1992	129.99
Various Artists/Annie Haslam	Poetry In Motion (Justin Hayward)	CD	Eagle	EAMCD89	U.S.A.	1990	14.99
Various Artists/Anthony Phillips	Intergalactic Touring Band (A. Haslam)	CD	Voiceprint	VP251CD	England	2003	11.99
Various Artists/B. Springsteen	Uncut - Born To Run 2003 - Vol One	CD	Uncut	UNCUT-2003-04A	U.S.A.	2003	7.99
Various Artists/B. Springsteen	Uncut - Born To Run 2003 - Vol Two	CD	Uncut	UNCUT-2003-04B	U.S.A.	2003	7.99
Various Artists/Band Aid	Do They Know It's Christmas?	CD	Nippon Phonogram	PHDR-902	Japan	1992	99.99
Various Artists/Barbara Eden	I Dream Of Jeannie (Dot Lp/H V PTA)	CD	Recrash	RR-6733	U.S.A.	2000	24.99
Various Artists/Beach Boys	Making God Smile (B Boys Tribute)	CD	Silent Planet	SPRO94	U.S.A.	2002	8.99
Various Artists/Bee Gees	Melody (O.S.T.) W/CSNY	CD	Polydor	POCP-2007	Japan	1971	26.99
Various Artists/Beserkley	Beserk Times - Live Over Germany	CD	Line	BECD-9.00512-0	Germany	1988	24.99
Various Artists/Best Of	Rough Trade Shops Rock'N' Roll 01	2CD	Mute	STUMM-212	England	2002	18.99
Various Artists/Billy Joel	Thanks For You 25th/Sony (Scaggs)	CD	Sony	25DP-5200	Japan	1988	32.99
Various Artists/Bonanza	Christmas On The Ponderosa	CD	BMG	7-5517-56732-2-2	U.S.A.	2000	6.99
Various Artists/Brian Eno	Glam Bam Thank You Ma'am (L Reed)	CD	Buddah	74465-99617-2	U.S.A.	1999	8.99
Various Artists/Carole King	Tapestry Revisited (Leatherbound Ed.)	CD	Lava	02604-2	U.S.A.	1995	13.99
Various Artists/Carpenters	If I Were A Carpenter (Tribute)	CD	A&M	31454-0258-2	U.S.A.	1994	8.99
Various Artists/Chuck Berry	Chuck B. Covered - Tribute	CD	Hip O	HIPD-40076	England	1998	8.99
Various Artists/Clash	Burning London: Tribute (Adv. Cd)	CD	Sony	AEK-69106-S1	U.S.A.	1999	12.99
Various Artists/Curtis Mayfield	A Tribute To Curtis Mayfield	CD	Warner Bros.	9-45500-2	U.S.A.	1993	7.99
Various Artists/David Bowie	Uncut - Starman (Bowie Tribute)	CD	Uncut	UNCUT-2003-03	U.S.A.	2003	7.99
Various Artists/DGM	Sometimes God Hides (K Crimson DJ)	CD	Discipline Global	DGM-PRO1	U.S.A.	1996	6.99
Various Artists/DGM	Sometimes God Smiles (K Crimson DJ)	CD	Discipline Global	DGMSAM2	U.S.A.	1998	6.99
Various Artists/Dion/F Domino	Christmas In-Store Promo Sampler	CD	Right Stuff	DPRO-66733	U.S.A.	1994	22.99
Various Artists/Dury, Ian	Brand New Boots And Panties	CD	Gold Circle	GC-50012-2	U.S.A.	2001	9.99
Various Artists/E Broughton	Wit Sind (Caravan) Live 90's Best Vol.2	CD	Captain Trip	CTCD-214	Japan	1997	15.99
Various Artists/Ellen Foley	Shelter (The Cryer/Ford Musical)	CD	Original Cast	OC-9785	England	2000	13.99
Various Artists/Elvis Costello	A&M Records Convention Relief	CD	A&M	314-548-057-2	U.S.A.	1994	29.99
Various Artists/Fleetwood Mac	Legacy: Tribute/ Rumours	CD	Atlantic	83054-2	U.S.A.	1998	6.99
Various Artists/G. Harrison	Romanian Angel Appeal (Bob Dylan)	CD	Warner Bros.	9-26280-2	U.S.A.	1990	6.99
Various Artists/Godzilla	Howl (Grunts/Growls/Toho Monsters)	CD	Sony	SRCL-2531	Japan	1992	36.99
Various Artists/Gong	Wir Sind Kinder Live 90's Vol. 1 (Faust)	CD	Captain Trip	CTCD-157	Japan	1997	15.99
Various Artists/Grateful Dead	Deadicated (Tribute) E. Costello	CD	Arista	ARCD-8669	U.S.A.	1991	8.99
Various Artists/Grateful Dead	Dedicated (Limited Edition Promo)	CD	Arista	ARCD-8669	U.S.A.	1991	35.99
Various Artists/Grateful Dead	Pickin' On The G Dead ... A Tribute	CD	CMH	CD-8022	U.S.A.	1997	5.99
Various Artists/GratefulDead	Stayin' Alive (Limited # Sampler)	CD	Line	GDCD-9.00750-E	Germany	1989	199.99
Various Artists/Gravenites	Mill Valley Bunch (Bloomfield/Dryden)	Mini Lp	Comet	UV-087	Italy	2003	34.99
Various Artists/H Faltermeyer	Thief Of Hearts (O.S.T.)	CD	Polygram	822-942-2	Germany	1984	28.99
Various Artists/Hanna-Barbera	Pic-A-Nic Basket Of Cartoon Classics	4CD	Rhino	R2-72290	U.S.A.	1996	54.99
Various Artists/Harvest	Harvest Festival Box Set	5CD	EMI	7243-5-21198-2-0	England	1999	57.99
Various Artists/Hello Club	Hello Club 1993 Sampler	CD	Hello Club	HEL-S	U.S.A.	1993	49.99
Various Artists/Hello Club	Hello Club 1994 Sampler	CD	Hello Club	HEL-1994	U.S.A.	1994	49.99
Various Artists/Hole/Iggy Pop	Gold Dust Woman EP	CD Single	Polydor	575-373-2	Australia	1996	5.99
Various Artists/Jeff Lynne	Lynne Me Your Ears Tribute	2CD	Not Lame	NL-070	U.S.A.	2001	24.99
Various Artists/Jimmy Rogers	Blues (Led Zep, Clapton, Stones, Stills)	CD	Atlantic	83148-2	U.S.A.	1999	9.99
Various Artists/Jobim	A Twist Of Jobim	CD	Verve	314-533-893-2	U.S.A.	1997	7.99
Various Artists/Jobim	Girl/Ipanema - A. C. Jobim Songbook	CD	Polygram	314-525-472-2	U.S.A.	1995	7.99
Various Artists/John Barry	The Golden Child (O.S.T.)	CD	Toshiba-EMI	CP32-5343	Japan	1986	63.99
Various Artists/John Cale	KCRW Rare On Air - Live Volume 1	CD	Mammouth	MR0074-2	U.S.A.	1994	24.99
Various Artists/John Peel	The John Peel Sessions	CD	Dutch East Indies	DEI8601-2	U.S.A.	1990	13.99
Various Artists/Jon Anderson	Metropolis (O.S.T.)	CD	Columbia	CK-39526	U.S.A.	1984	15.99

Artist	Title	Format	Label	Catalog No	Country	Released	Value
Various Artists/Jon Anderson	Metropolis (O.S.T.)	CD	Sony	25DP-5391	Japan	1984	24.99
Various Artists/Kids Orchestra	Langley Schools Music Project (Rock)	CD	Bar None	AHAON-122	U.S.A.	2001	10.99
Various Artists/King Biscuit	Best Of The Best/ 25 Years Of Rock	CD	King Biscuit	KBF-88044	U.S.A.	1998	12.99
Various Artists/King Biscuit	Show That Never Ends: Progressive M	CD	BMG	1231745	U.S.A.	1998	12.99
Various Artists/L A Workshop	Norwegian Wood (Beatles Tribute)	CD	Nippon Columbia	CA-72725	Japan	1988	29.99
Various Artists/Leiber-Stoller	The Daisy/Tiger Records Story	CD	Sundazed	SC-11080	U.S.A.	2003	8.99
Various Artists/Man	Christmas At The Patti (Dave Edmunds)	CD	Voiceprint	PNTVP110CD	England	1999	11.99
Various Artists/Mike/Mech	Rude Awakening (O.S.T.)	CD	Elektra	9-60873-2	U.S.A.	1989	14.99
Various Artists/Moody Blues	Gloryland - World Cup USA '94	CD	Mercury	PHCR-1259	Japan	1994	12.99
Various Artists/Movie Themes	Pimps, Players & Private Eyes	CD	Sire	9-26624-2	U.S.A.	1991	14.99
Various Artists/Movie Trailers	Monster Rock 'N' Roll..(Songs/Trailers)	CD	DCC	DZS-050	U.S.A.	1990	10.99
Various Artists/N Order Unrel	Manchester United.... (Promo)	CD	Virgin	VTCD350	England	2002	29.99
Various Artists/Narada	Forever Wild	2CD	Narada	ND-63926	U.S.A.	1996	9.99
Various Artists/Narada	Narada Decade: The Ann. Collection	2CD	Narada	ND-63911	U.S.A.	1993	9.99
Various Artists/Narada	Wisdom Of The Wood	CD	Narada	ND-61029	U.S.A.	1991	9.99
Various Artists/Nick Lowe	Stiffs Live (E Costello, Wreckless Eric)	CD	Demon	MAUCD621	England	1992	19.99
Various Artists/P Holsapple	Best Of Mountain Stage - Volume 5	CD	Blue Plate	BPM-005CD	U.S.A.	1993	13.99
Various Artists/Peter Yarrow	You Are What You... (OST/Butterfield)	CD	Sony	SRCS-8522	Japan	1997	32.99
Various Artists/Phil Collins	Porky's Revenge + 2 (George Harrison)	CD	Columbia	CK-90875	U.S.A.	2004	8.99
Various Artists/Phil Collins	Urban Renewal (2001)	CD	Warner Bros.	8573-87637-2	Germany	2001	8.99
Various Artists/Pomus, Doc	Till The Night Be Gone	CD	Rhino	R2-71878	U.S.A.	1995	12.99
Various Artists/Prince	Minneapolis Funk (USA 12" Version)	CD	Warner Bros.	8-09274-82382-3	France	2000	34.99
Various Artists/R Thompson	The World Is A Wonderful Place	CD	Green Linnet	GLCD-3086	U.S.A.	1993	19.99
Various Artists/R Wakeman	Music For The 3rd Millennium (1,000)	CD	AMP	AMP-CD039	England	1999	20.99
Various Artists/R. Thompson	Beat The Retreat (Cardboard Version)	CD	Capitol	0777-7-95929-2-0	U.S.A.	1994	14.99
Various Artists/R.E.M.	Best Of Mountain Stage - Volume 2	CD	Blue Plate	BPM-002CD	U.S.A.	1991	13.99
Various Artists/R.E.M.	Best Of Mountain Stage - Volume 6	CD	Blue Plate	BPM-006CD	U.S.A.	1999	13.99
Various Artists/Randy Newma	Cats Don't Dance (O.S.T.)	CD	Polygram	534-655-2	U.S.A.	1997	17.99
Various Artists/Roger Daltrey	Wizard Of Oz (Dreams Come True)	CD	Rhino	R2-72405	U.S.A.	1996	9.99
Various Artists/Roger McGuinn	Rare Surf Vol. 5: Capitol Masters 1	CD	Captain Trip	CTCD-255	Japan	1965	23.99
Various Artists/Roger Waters	Sony M Multichannel SACD Sampler	CD	Sony	4-237-607-01	U.S.A.	2001	29.99
Various Artists/Ron Geesin	Electric Toys (Early Electro Pop)	CD	Captain Trip	CTCD-392	Japan	1970	15.99
Various Artists/Roxy Music	More For Your Pleasure Tribute	CD	Dressed To Kill	DOP-126	England	1999	7.99
Various Artists/Rubinoos Live	Beserkely Chartbusters (Live Over Ger.)	2CD	Essential	ESA-CD-870	England	2000	15.99
Various Artists/Saxon	Demons (O.S.T.) W/Rick Springfield	CD	Victor Ent.	VDP-1087	Japan	1986	203.99
Various Artists/Shatner/Nimoy	Spaced Out (H Illogical, Bilbo Baggins)	CD	Universal	MCLD-19361	England	1997	12.99
Various Artists/Sky Saxon	Yahowha Collection: God And Hair	13CD	Captain Trip	CTCD-130-142	Japan	2000	144.99
Various Artists/Star Trek	Star Trek: The Astral Symphony	CD	Milan	262-832	France	1991	14.99
Various Artists/Steve Miller	Revolution (O.S.T.) Quicksilver M S	CD	Rykodisc	RCD-10710	U.S.A.	1997	14.99
Various Artists/Stiff	The Stiff Records Box Set	4CD	Demon	R2-71062	U.S.A.	1992	49.99
Various Artists/The Who	Who Covers Who - A Tribute	CD	Cargo	CMD-011	U.S.A.	1994	9.99
Various Artists/Tori Amos	FM 101.9 Live/Music Hall Vol 1	CD	KSCA	KSCA-01-2	U.S.A.	1995	14.99
Various Artists/Tribute	Badlands/Springsteen's Nebraska	CD	Sub Pop	SPCD-525	U.S.A.	2000	8.99
Various Artists/Tuli Of Fugs	Rutles Highway Revisited	CD	Shimmy Disc	CSU1-285	U.S.A.	1990	27.99
Various Artists/Uncut	Instant Karma 2002 [Lennon Tribute]	CD	Uncut Magazine	UNCUT-2002-11	England	2002	7.99
Various Artists/Unrel Yes Edit	Beyond Artists (2 Unrel Live Blondie)	CD	Beyond	39-7091-119	U.S.A.	1999	13.99
Various Artists/Yoko Ono	Every Man Has A Woman (E. Costello)	CD	Polydor	P2-23490	U.S.A.	1984	44.99
Vaughan Brothers	Family Style	CD	Epic	ZK-46225	U.S.A.	1990	9.99
Vaughan, Stevie Ray	Blues At Sunrise	CD	Epic	EK-63842	U.S.A.	2000	8.99
Vaughan, Stevie Ray	Couldn't Stand The Weather +5	CD	Epic	EK-65871	U.S.A.	1999	8.99
Vaughan, Stevie Ray	Couldn't Stand The.. (Sony Gold)	CD	Epic	EK-64425	U.S.A.	1984	24.99
Vaughan, Stevie Ray	Greatest Hits	CD	Epic	EK-66217	U.S.A.	1995	8.99
Vaughan, Stevie Ray	In Step + 5	CD	Epic	EK-65874	U.S.A.	1999	8.99
Vaughan, Stevie Ray	In The Beginning	CD	Epic	EK-53168	U.S.A.	1992	9.99
Vaughan, Stevie Ray	Live Alive	CD	Epic	EGK-40511	U.S.A.	1986	8.99
Vaughan, Stevie Ray	Live at Carnegie Hall	CD	Epic	EK-68163	U.S.A.	1997	8.99
Vaughan, Stevie Ray	Live At Montreux 1982 & 1985	2CD	Epic	E2K-86151	U.S.A.	2001	14.99
Vaughan, Stevie Ray	Real Deal Sampler (Promo)	CD	Epic	ESK-41913	U.S.A.	1999	14.99

V

Artist	Title	Format	Label	Catalog No	Country	Released	Value
Vaughan, Stevie Ray	Soul To Soul + 3	CD	Epic	EK-65872	U.S.A.	1999	8.99
Vaughan, Stevie Ray	SRV Box (Promo Sampler)	CD	Epic	ESK-16355-S1	U.S.A.	2000	15.99
Vaughan, Stevie Ray	SRV Box Set	4CD	Epic	E4K-65714	U.S.A.	2000	29.99
Vaughan, Stevie Ray	Texas Flood + 5	CD	Epic	EK-65870	U.S.A.	1999	8.99
Vaughan, Stevie Ray	The Real Deal: Greatest Hits Vol. 2	CD	Epic	EK-65873	U.S.A.	1999	8.99
Vaughan, Stevie Ray	The Sky Is Crying	CD	Epic	EK-47390	U.S.A.	1991	8.99
Vaughan, Stevie Ray	The Sky Is Crying (MFSL Gold Cd)	CD	Mobile Fidelity	UDCD-723	U.S.A.	1991	54.99
Vaughan, Stevie Ray/A. King	In Session (Live With Albert King)	CD	Stax	SCD-7501-2	U.S.A.	1999	8.99
Vega, Suzanne	99.9 Degrees F	CD	A&M	314-540-005-2	U.S.A.	1992	5.99
Vega, Suzanne	Best Of: Tried And True	CD	A&M	314-540-945-2	U.S.A.	1999	8.99
Vega, Suzanne	Days Of Open Hand	CD	A&M	75021-5293-2	U.S.A.	1990	6.99
Vega, Suzanne	Nine Objects Of Desire	CD	A&M	314-540-583-2	U.S.A.	1996	5.99
Vega, Suzanne	Retropective: The Best Of	CD	A&M	6069-493670-2	U.S.A.	2003	8.99
Vega, Suzanne	Retrospective: The Best Of + 8	2CD	A&M	602498088845	England	2003	24.99
Vega, Suzanne	Self Titled	CD	A&M	75021-5072-2	U.S.A.	1990	5.99
Vega, Suzanne	Self Titled (Gold Cd)	CD	Pony Canyon	D33Y-3397	Japan	1989	74.99
Vega, Suzanne	Sessions At West 54th	CD Single	Polydor	POCM-9031	Japan	1997	22.99
Vega, Suzanne	Solitude Standing	CD	A&M	75021-5136-2	U.S.A.	1990	5.99
Vega, Suzanne	Songs In Red & Gray	CD	A&M	6069-493111-2	U.S.A.	2001	8.99
Vega, Suzanne	The Best Of: Tried And True + 6	2CD	A&M	490-718-2	EU	2000	24.99
Velvet Opera	Elmer Gantry's Velvet Opera	CD	Repertoire	REP-4495-WP	Germany	2002	14.99
Velvet Opera	Ride A Hustler's Dream + 2	CD	Repertoire	REP-4531-WP	Germany	2002	14.99
Velvet Underground	1965 - 1970 (W/96 Page Book)	CD	Sonic Book	SCONC-029	Italy	2003	16.99
Velvet Underground	And Nico (Peelable Banana Cd Box)	CD	Verve	823-290-2	Germany	1967	49.99
Velvet Underground	Another View	CD	Polygram	829-405-2	U.S.A.	1986	8.99
Velvet Underground	Best Of Lou Reed/Velvet Underground	CD	Global	RADCD21	England	1995	14.99
Velvet Underground	Bootleg Series Vol. 1	3CD	Polydor	314-589-067-2	U.S.A.	2001	24.99
Velvet Underground	Chronicles	CD	Mercury	849-318-2	Australia	1991	19.99
Velvet Underground	Final V.U. 1971-73 Box Set (No Reed)	4CD	Captain Trip	CTCD-350-353	Japan	2001	54.99
Velvet Underground	Live At Max's Kansas City	CD	Atlantic	9500-2	U.S.A.	1972	9.99
Velvet Underground	Live MCMXCIII (1 Cd Version)	CD	Sire Records	9-45465-2	U.S.A.	1993	6.99
Velvet Underground	Live MCMXCIII (2 Cd Version)	2CD	Sire	9-45464-2	U.S.A.	1993	10.99
Velvet Underground	Live MCMXCIII (Deluxe Black Ed.)	CD	Sire	9-45434-2	U.S.A.	1993	39.99
Velvet Underground	Loaded (Original Lp Version)	CD	Warner Bros.	9-27613-2	U.S.A.	1970	8.99
Velvet Underground	Loaded (With Bonus Cd) (Holographic)	CD	Rhino	R2-75263	U.S.A.	1997	16.99
Velvet Underground	Peel Slowly And See Box Set	5CD	Polydor	315-427-887-2	U.S.A.	1995	34.99
Velvet Underground	Ride Into The Sun (Promo)	CD Single	Polydor	4066	France	1995	29.99
Velvet Underground	Rock & Roll: An Introduction To	CD	Polydor	549-690-2	England	2001	8.99
Velvet Underground	Selections/Peel Slowly And See (DJ)	CD	Polydor	PRSAD-00040	U.S.A.	1995	19.99
Velvet Underground	Sweet Jane (Promo)	CD Single	Sire	PRCD-7	Germany	1993	19.99
Velvet Underground	Sweet Jane/Beginning To See.. (DJ)	CD Single	Warner Bros.	PRO-CD-6623	U.S.A.	1990	24.99
Velvet Underground	The Best Of	CD	Polygram	841-164-2	U.S.A.	1989	7.99
Velvet Underground	The Peeling Of Velvet Underground	CD	Verve	156-939-2	Israel	2000	34.99
Velvet Underground	Velvet Life (3" Cd W/Book)	CD	Sonic Book	SCONC-010	Italy	1997	19.99
Velvet Underground	Velvet Underground & Nico	CD	Polydor	314-531-250-2	U.S.A.	1996	7.99
Velvet Underground	Velvet Underground (3rd)	CD	Polydor	314-531-252-2	U.S.A.	1996	7.99
Velvet Underground	Velvet Underground Live 1969 Vol. 1	CD	Mercury	834-823-2	U.S.A.	1988	7.99
Velvet Underground	Velvet Underground Live 1969 Vol. 2	CD	Mercury	834-824-2	U.S.A.	1988	7.99
Velvet Underground	Velvet Underground/Nico (MFSL Gold)	CD	Mobile Fidelity	UDCD-695	U.S.A.	1967	24.99
Velvet Underground	Velvet Underground/Nico + 20/Deluxe	2CD	Polydor	314-589-588-2	U.S.A.	2002	12.99
Velvet Underground	Venus In Furs	CD Single	Sire	9362-41400-2	Germany	1994	9.99
Velvet Underground	VU	CD	Polygram	823-721-2	U.S.A.	1985	9.99
Velvet Underground	What Goes On Box Set	3CD	Raven	RVCD-28	Australia	1993	54.99
Velvet Underground	White Light/W Heat (MFSL Gold Cd)	CD	Mobile Fidelity	UDCD-724	U.S.A.	1968	24.99
Velvet Underground	White Light/White Heat	CD	Polydor	314-531-251-2	U.S.A.	1996	7.99
Velvet Underground/ Ltd 3000	Le Bataclan '72 + 2 (Reed/Cale/Nico)	CD	Alchemy	PILOT193	England	2003	29.99
Velvet Underground/A Maclise	Astral Collapse	CD	Quakebasket	QB-016-CD	U.S.A.	2003	12.99
Velvet Underground/A Maclise	Brain Damage in Oklahoma City	CD	Siltbreeze	SILT-081	U.S.A.	1968	12.99

V

Artist	Title	Format	Label	Catalog No	Country	Released	Value
Velvet Underground/A Maclise	Invasion of the Thunderbolt Pagoda	CD	Siltbreeze	SILT-078	U.S.A.	1968	12.99
Velvet Underground/A Maclise	The Cloud Doctrine (W/John Cale)	2CD	Sub Rosa	SR-182-CD	Belgium	2003	15.99
Velvet Underground/D. Yule	Live In Seattle	CD	Captain Trip	CTCD-401	Japan	2000	21.99
Velvet Underground/Tribute	15 Minutes (W/Nirvana)	CD	Imaginary	ILLCD-047P	England	1994	99.99
Velvet Underground/Tribute	Heaven And Hell (Same As 15 Min.)	CD	Communion	20	U.S.A.	1990	99.99
Ventures	'93 Live In Japan	CD	Toshiba-EMI	TOCP-8105	Japan	1993	28.99
Ventures	Acoustic Rock	CD	M&I	MYCV30047	Japan	2000	23.99
Ventures	EP Collection Box Set	4CD	Toshiba-EMI	TOCP-8291-94	Japan	1994	154.99
Ventures	In Space	CD	Toshiba-EMI	TOCP-6389	Japan	1990	12.99
Ventures	Live Box, VOL. 2	4CD	Toshiba-EMI	TOCP-7149-52	Japan	1992	153.99
Ventures	Live In Japan '65 (Complete)	CD	Toshiba-EMI	TOCP-3386	Japan	1998	24.99
Ventures	Play Telstar	CD	Toshiba-EMI	CP21-6022	Japan	1990	14.99
Ventures	Radical Guitars	CD	Iloki	1006	U.S.A.	1997	49.99
Ventures	Say Yes	CD	Toshiba-EMI	TOCP-7154	Japan	1992	33.99
Ventures	Super Now	CD	Toshiba-EMI	TOCP-51002	Japan	1997	18.99
Ventures	Tele Ventures - Perf. Great TV Themes	CD	EMI	553738	U.S.A.	1996	8.99
Ventures	Walk-Don't Run—The Best Of	CD	EMI	7-93451-2	U.S.A.	1990	7.99
Ventures/Barry McGee	Born In Lousiana	CD	Bad News	BNCY-28	Japan	1997	24.99
Ventures/Nokie Edwards	1999 Plugged And Unplugged	CD	King	KICP-701	Japan	1999	69.99
Ventures/Nokie Edwards	The Great World Hits	CD	King	292A82	Japan	1989	27.99
Ventures/Nokie Edwards	Vol. 2 - The Greatest Hits	CD	King	KICS-7	Japan	1990	31.99
Vera, Billy/The Beaters	By Request (Same As Alfa Records Lp)	CD	Rhino	R2-70858	U.S.A.	1986	16.99
Vera, Billy/The Beaters	Retro Nuevo	CD	Capitol	7-46948-2	U.S.A.	1988	7.99
Verlaine, Tom	Dreamtime + 2	CD	Infinite Zero	9-14508-2	U.S.A.	1994	29.99
Verlaine, Tom	Flash Light	CD	I.R.S.	IRSD-42050	U.S.A.	1987	8.99
Verlaine, Tom	Kaleidoscopin'	CD Single	Fontana	875-043-2	England	1990	15.99
Verlaine, Tom	Self Titled	CD	Warner Bros.	WPCP-4161	Japan	1979	18.99
Verlaine, Tom	Self Titled (Right Mix Version)	CD	Collector's Choice	CCM-316-2	U.S.A.	2003	9.99
Verlaine, Tom	The Miller's Tale: A Tom Verlaine Anth.	2CD	Virgin	7243-8-41650-2-4	U.S.A.	1996	24.99
Verlaine, Tom	The Wonder	CD	Fontana	842-420 -2	England	1990	19.99
Verlaine, Tom	The Wonder	CD	Nippon Phonogram	PPD-1137	Japan	1990	24.99
Verlaine, Tom	Warm And Cool	CD	Rough Trade	R2882	England	1992	29.99
Verlaine, Tom/Matrix # Z11571	S. T. (Wr. Mix/No Mngmt Details Back)	CD	Collector's Choice	CCM-316-2	U.S.A.	2002	134.99
Veronique/R Carpenter	Self Titled	CD	A&M	CD-9154	Canada	1989	78.99
Verve	Bitter Sweet Symphony (Cd 1)	CD Single	Virgin	7243-8-94359-2-4	England	1998	5.99
Verve	The Drugs Don't Work	CD Single	Virgin	7243-8-94536-2-1	England	1997	3.99
Verve	This Is Music (Radio Promo)	CD Single	Virgin	DPRO-11041	U.S.A.	1995	17.99
Verve-Pipe	Album Network (Oct 1 - 5 , 1997) DJ	2CD	RCA	IFPI-L792	U.S.A.	1997	94.99
Vicious Rumors	Cyberchrist	CD	Victor Ent.	VICP-60373	Japan	1998	20.99
Vicious Rumors	Something's Burning	CD	Alfa	ALCB-3136	Japan	1996	18.99
Victor, David	Proof Through The Night	CD	Bareknuckle	AVCB-66065	Japan	1999	29.99
Vigilantes Of Love	Blister Soul	CD	Capricorn	9-42042-2	U.S.A.	1995	5.99
Vigilantes Of Love	Slow Dark Train	CD	Capricorn	314-534-509-2	U.S.A.	1997	5.99
Vincent, Gene	And The Blue Caps + 5	CD	Capitol	72435-40684-2-3	U.S.A.	2002	9.99
Vincent, Gene	Bluejean Bop !/And His Blue Caps	CD	Collectables	COL-2712	U.S.A.	1998	8.99
Vincent, Gene	Bluejean Bop + 6	CD	Capitol	72435-40685-2-2	U.S.A.	2002	9.99
Vincent, Gene	Complete Challenge Sessions	CD	Magnum	CDMF-109	England	2002	14.99
Vincent, Gene	Rocks !/A Date With	CD	Collectables	COL-2712	U.S.A.	1998	8.99
Vincent, Gene	Sounds Like/Crazy Times	CD	Collectables	COL-2720	U.S.A.	1998	8.99
Vincent, Gene	The Ep Collection, Vol. 2	CD	See For Miles	SEE-CD-492	England	1998	15.99
Vincent, Gene	The Ep Collecton, Vol. 1	CD	See For Miles	SEE-CD-253	England	1996	15.99
Vincent, Vinnie/Invasion	All Systems Go	CD	Chrysalis	VK-41626	U.S.A.	1988	21.99
Vincent, Vinnie/Invasion	Euphoria	CD	Metaluna	MR-001	U.S.A.	1996	21.99
Vincent, Vinnie/Invasion	Self Titled	CD	Toshiba-EMI	TOCP-7972	Japan	1986	21.99
Visage	Best Of : Fade To Grey	CD	Polydor	314-521-053-2	U.S.A.	1993	8.99
Visage	The Anvil	CD	One Way	OW-34518	U.S.A.	1997	10.99
Visage	The Damned Don't Cry	CD	Spectrum	544-381-2	England	2000	8.99
Visage	Visage	CD	One Way	OW-34519	U.S.A.	1997	8.99

V

Artist	Title	Format	Label	Catalog No	Country	Released	Value
Vitale, Joe	Plantation Harbor	CD	Wounded Bird	WOU-529	U.S.A.	2002	8.99
Vitale, Joe	Roller Coaster Weekend	CD	Wounded Bird	WOU-8114	U.S.A.	2002	8.99
Vixen	How Much Love	CD Single	EMI	DPRO-0454	U.S.A.	1990	19.99
Vixen	Rev It Up	CD	EMI	D-154615	U.S.A.	1990	9.99
Vixen	Self Titled	CD	EMI	CDP-7-46991-2	U.S.A.	1988	13.99
Vixen	Tangerine	CD	CMC Int.	06076-86246-2	U.S.A.	1998	10.99
Vixen	The Best Of: Full Throttle	CD	Razor & Tie	7930182188-2	U.S.A.	1999	10.99
Voice Of The Beehive	Sex & Misery (Andy Partridge Song)	CD	Discovery	77036	U.S.A.	1995	8.99
Voivod	Angel Rat	CD	MCA	MCAD-10293	U.S.A.	1991	7.99
Voivod	Best Of	CD	Noise	74081	U.S.A.	2003	8.99
Voivod	Dimension Hatross	CD	Noise	74076	U.S.A.	1999	9.99
Voivod	Killing Technology	CD	Noise	74077	U.S.A.	1998	10.99
Voivod	Kronic	CD	Hypnotic	1065	U.S.A.	2000	11.99
Voivod	Lives	CD	Metal Blade	3984-14338-2	U.S.A.	2000	11.99
Voivod	Negatron	CD	Hypnotic	1040	U.S.A.	2000	7.99
Voivod	Negatron (Enhanced)	CD	Pet Rock	60019	U.S.A.	1995	8.99
Voivod	Nothingface	CD	MCA	MCAD-6326	U.S.A.	1989	13.99
Voivod	Phobos	CD	Hypnotic	1057	U.S.A.	1998	9.99
Voivod	Rrroooaaarrr!	CD	Noise	74079	U.S.A.	1998	13.99
Voivod	Self Titled	CD	Chophouse	44015	U.S.A.	2003	7.99
Voivod	The Outer Limits	CD	MCA	MCAD-10701	U.S.A.	1993	7.99
Voivod	War And Pain	CD	Metal Blade	3984-14049-2	U.S.A.	1994	8.99
Von Groove	Mission Man	CD	Bareknuckle	AVCB-66002	Japan	1997	29.99

W

Artist	Title	Format	Label	Catalog No	Country	Released	Value
W.A.S.P.	Animal F*ck Like A Beast	CD	Enigma	7-72512-2	U.S.A.	1990	8.99
W.A.S.P.	Double Live Assassins	2CD	CMC Int.	06076-86237-2	U.S.A.	1998	10.99
W.A.S.P.	Double Live Assassins (W/Crdbrd Slv)	2CD	Snapper	SAP-CD-901	England	1998	13.99
W.A.S.P.	Dying For The World (Promo)	CD	Metal-Is	MISPR022	England	2002	22.99
W.A.S.P.	Dying For The World + 1	CD	Metal Is	06076-85232-2	U.S.A.	2002	11.99
W.A.S.P.	Dying For The World + 3	CD	Victor Ent.	VICP-61939	Japan	2002	34.99
W.A.S.P.	First Blood...Last Cuts	CD	Capitol	0777-7-80517-2-5	U.S.A.	1994	19.99
W.A.S.P.	First Blood...Last Cuts (W/Box)	CD	Toshiba-EMI	TOCP-8072	Japan	1993	34.99
W.A.S.P.	Helldorado	CD	CMC Int.	06076-86269-2	U.S.A.	1999	9.99
W.A.S.P.	Helldorado (W/3-D Card)	CD	Snapper	SMA-CD-818	England	1999	11.99
W.A.S.P.	Helldorado + 2	CD	Victor Ent.	VICP-60666	Japan	1999	25.99
W.A.S.P.	Inside The Electric Circus + 2	CD	Snapper	SMM-CD-505	England	1997	8.99
W.A.S.P.	Kill, F*ck, Die (Ltd Ed. Flip Pack)	CD	Castle	RAWCD114	England	1997	12.99
W.A.S.P.	Last C + 7/S.T. + 3/Headless + 6 Box	3CD	Snapper	SMDCD6106	England	2000	29.99
W.A.S.P.	Live Animal	CD	Enigma	7-72235-2	Canada	1990	9.99
W.A.S.P.	Live...In The Raw + 4	CD	Snapper	SMM-CD-506	England	1997	8.99
W.A.S.P.	Self Titled (1984) + 2	CD	Snapper	SMM-CD-501	England	1997	8.99
W.A.S.P.	Self Titled (1984)+ 2/Last Command+ 7	2CD	Snapper	SMDCD391	England	2002	14.99
W.A.S.P.	Still Not Black Enough + 3	CD	Castle	120-2	England	1996	8.99
W.A.S.P.	Still Not Black Enough +1	CD	Victor Ent.	VICP-5560	Japan	1995	19.99
W.A.S.P.	The Best Of The Best	CD	Snapper	636551182522	U.S.A.	2000	8.99
W.A.S.P.	The Crimson Idol	2CD	Snapper	0636551414524	U.S.A.	1998	12.99
W.A.S.P.	The Crimson Idol (DJ/Sampler)	CD	Toshiba-EMI	TOCP-6705	Japan	1992	34.99
W.A.S.P.	The Crimson Idol + 13	2CD	Recall	SMD-CD-145	England	1998	14.99
W.A.S.P.	The Crismon Idol	2CD	Victor Ent.	VICP-60334/5	Japan	1992	44.99
W.A.S.P.	The Headless Children + 6	CD	Snapper	SMM-CD-509	England	1998	8.99
W.A.S.P.	The Last Command + 7	CD	Snapper	SMM-CD-502	England	1997	8.99
W.A.S.P.	The Sting (DJ/Plastic Slv/Inlay)	CD	Snapper	SMA-CD-836	England	2000	22.99

W

Artist	Title	Format	Label	Catalog No	Country	Released	Value
W.A.S.P.	The Sting (W/Crdbrd Slv)	CD	Snapper	SMA-CD-836	England	2000	11.99
W.A.S.P.	Unholy Terror	CD	Metal-Is	06076-85204-2	U.S.A.	2001	11.99
W.A.S.P.	Unholy Terror (DJ/Plastic Slv/Inlay)	CD	Metal-Is	MISPR005	England	2001	22.99
Wainwright III, Louden	The Atlantic Recordings (Ltd 5000)	CD	Rhino	RHM2-7709	U.S.A.	2000	24.99
Waite, John	Figure In A Landscape	CD	Gold Circle	GC-10005-2	U.S.A.	2001	7.99
Waite, John	Ignition	CD	Chrysalis	VK-41376	U.S.A.	1982	23.99
Waite, John	Ignition/No Brakes	CD	One Way	OW-34551	U.S.A.	2001	9.99
Waite, John	King Biscuit Flower Hour Live	CD	King Biscuit	70710-88051-2	U.S.A.	1999	8.99
Waite, John	Live & Rare Tracks	CD	One Way	OW-34558	U.S.A.	2001	9.99
Waite, John	Mask Of Smiles	CD	EMI	CDP-7-46167-2	U.S.A.	1985	34.99
Waite, John	Mask Of Smiles/Rover's Return	CD	One Way	OW-34230	U.S.A.	2001	9.99
Waite, John	No Brakes	CD	EMI	CDP-7-46078-2	U.S.A.	1984	14.99
Waite, John	Rover's Return	CD	EMI	CDP-7-46332-2	U.S.A.	1987	8.99
Waite, John	Temple Bar	CD	Imago	72787-21033-2	U.S.A.	1995	9.99
Waite, John	The Complete Vol. 1: Falling ...	CD	EMI	7243-8-54241-2	U.S.A.	1996	8.99
Waite, John	The Essential	CD	Chrysalis	F2-21864	U.S.A.	1992	8.99
Waite, John	When You Were Mine	CD	Mercury	314-536-207-2	U.S.A.	1999	9.99
Waits, Tom	Alice	CD	Epitaph	86632-2	U.S.A.	2002	6.99
Waits, Tom	Anthology Of	CD	Asylum	9-60416-2	U.S.A.	1985	8.99
Waits, Tom	Beautiful Maladies: The Island Years	CD	Island	314-524519-2	U.S.A.	1998	8.99
Waits, Tom	Big Time	CD	Island	422-842470-2	U.S.A.	1988	7.99
Waits, Tom	Blood Money	CD	Epitaph	86629-2	U.S.A.	2002	7.99
Waits, Tom	Blue Valentine	CD	Elektra	2-162	U.S.A.	1990	7.99
Waits, Tom	Bone Machine	CD	Island	314-512580-2	U.S.A.	1992	7.99
Waits, Tom	Closing Time	CD	Asylum	2-5061	U.S.A.	1990	8.99
Waits, Tom	Dime Store Novels, Vol. 1	CD	Alchemy	PILOT-82	England	2001	11.99
Waits, Tom	Foreign Affairs	CD	Asylum	2-1117	U.S.A.	1990	7.99
Waits, Tom	Frank's Wild Years	CD	Island	422-842357-2	U.S.A.	1987	8.99
Waits, Tom	Heart Attack And Vine	CD	Asylum	2-295	U.S.A.	1990	8.99
Waits, Tom	Mule Variations	CD	Epitaph	86547-2	U.S.A.	1999	7.99
Waits, Tom	Night On Earth	CD	Island	314-510725-2	U.S.A.	1992	24.99
Waits, Tom	Nighthawks At The Diner	CD	Asylum	2-2008	U.S.A.	1990	7.99
Waits, Tom	Rain Dogs	CD	Island	422-826382-2	U.S.A.	1985	5.99
Waits, Tom	Small Change	CD	Asylum	1078-2	U.S.A.	1990	7.99
Waits, Tom	Swordfishtrombones	CD	Island	422-842469-2	U.S.A.	1983	5.99
Waits, Tom	The Asylum Years	CD	Asylum	9-60494-2	U.S.A.	1986	8.99
Waits, Tom	The Black Rider	CD	Island	314-518559-2	U.S.A.	1993	7.99
Waits, Tom	The Early Years, Vol. 1	CD	Rhino	R2-70557	U.S.A.	1993	14.99
Waits, Tom	The Early Years, Vol. 2	CD	Rhino	R2-71089	U.S.A.	1993	14.99
Waits, Tom	The Heart Of Saturday Night	CD	Asylum	2-1015	U.S.A.	1990	7.99
Waits, Tom	Used Songs (1973-1980)	CD	Rhino	R2-78351	U.S.A.	2001	8.99
Waits, Tom/Crystal Gayle	One From The Heart	CD	Columbia	CK-37703	U.S.A.	1990	8.99
Wakefield	The Lost Warthog Tapes	CD	Gear Fab	GF-193	U.S.A.	2003	8.99
Wakeman, Adam	100 Years Overtime	CD	President	RWCD-26	England	1994	11.99
Wakeman, Adam	Neurasthenia	CD	Voiceprint	ATTCD001	England	2003	16.99
Wakeman, Adam	Real World Trilogy	3CD	President	RWCD-31	England	1997	36.99
Wakeman, Adam	Soliloquy	CD	President	RWCD-15	England	1993	11.99
Wakeman, Oliver	Heaven's Isle	CD	Verglas	VGCD0015	England	1999	20.99
Wakeman, Oliver/Clive Nolan	Jabberwocky	CD	Verglas	VGCD014	England	1999	20.99
Wakeman, Oliver/Clive Nolan	The Hound of the Baskervilles	CD	Verglas	VGCD022	England	2002	20.99
Wakeman, Oliver/Steve Howe	The 3 Ages Of Magick	CD	Resurgence	RES144CD	England	2001	16.99
Wakeman, Rick	1984 (Jon Anderson Vocal)	CD	Griffin	GCDWR-160-2	U.S.A.	1994	8.99
Wakeman, Rick	2000 A.D. Into The Future	CD	President	RWCD-21	England	1993	15.99
Wakeman, Rick	A Quate Mane - Atomic Gilda Remix	CD Single	M P	MPRCD-031	England	1999	7.99
Wakeman, Rick	African Bach	CD	President	RWCD-20	England	1993	11.99
Wakeman, Rick	Almost Live In Europe	CD	Store For Music	SFMCD014	England	2001	7.99
Wakeman, Rick	Aspirant Sunrise	CD	President	RWCD-17	England	1993	14.99
Wakeman, Rick	Aspirant Sunset	CD	President	RWCD-18	England	1993	14.99

W

Artist	Title	Format	Label	Catalog No	Country	Released	Value
Wakeman, Rick	Aspirant Sunshadows	CD	President	RWCD-19	England	1993	14.99
Wakeman, Rick	Can You Hear Me?	CD	Hope	HOPEVP107CD	England	2001	8.99
Wakeman, Rick	Christmas Variations	CD	Hope	HRH-CD006	England	1997	14.99
Wakeman, Rick	Chronicle Of Man	CD	President	RWCD-34	England	2000	14.99
Wakeman, Rick	Cirque Surreal	CD	Magnum	MACD-075	U.S.A.	1996	17.99
Wakeman, Rick	Classic Tracks	CD	Store For Music	SFMCD003	England	2001	10.99
Wakeman, Rick	Cost Of Living	CD	Griffin	GCDWR-159-2	Canada	1994	14.99
Wakeman, Rick	Country Airs	CD	President	RWCD-10	England	1992	20.99
Wakeman, Rick	Crimes Of Passion + 1	CD	President	RWCD(P)-3	England	1993	16.99
Wakeman, Rick	Criminal Record	Mini Lp	Universal	UICY-9301	Japan	2003	26.99
Wakeman, Rick	Criminal Record	CD	Pony Canyon	D32Y-3127	Japan	1988	24.99
Wakeman, Rick	Def. Music (Tales/Future & Past + 1)	CD	Store For Music	SFMCD010	England	2001	17.99
Wakeman, Rick	Fields Of Green	CD	Griffin	GCD-581-2	U.S.A.	1996	8.99
Wakeman, Rick	Greatest Hits	2CD	Herald	HER-007	U.S.A.	1994	14.99
Wakeman, Rick	Heritage Suite	CD	President	RWCD-16	England	1993	11.99
Wakeman, Rick	Journey Centre Earth (20 Bt/Orig Bklt)	Mini Lp	Universal	UICY-9262	Japan	2003	26.99
Wakeman, Rick	Journey To The Centre... (MFSL Gold)	CD	Mobile Fidelity	UDCD-633	U.S.A.	1974	23.99
Wakeman, Rick	Journey To The Centre... (MFSL Silver)	CD	Mobile Fidelity	MFCD-848	U.S.A.	1974	19.99
Wakeman, Rick	King Arthur (20 Bit Rem/Orig. Booklet)	Mini Lp	Universal	UICY-9263	Japan	2003	26.99
Wakeman, Rick	King Biscuit Flower Hour Live	CD	King Biscuit	70710-88009-2	U.S.A.	1995	7.99
Wakeman, Rick	Light Up The Sky	CD Single	President	WAKEY-4	England	1994	7.99
Wakeman, Rick	Lisztomania (O.S.T.)	Mini Lp	Universal	UICY-9294	Japan	2003	26.99
Wakeman, Rick	Lisztomania (O.S.T.)	CD	Polydor K.K.	POCM-1913	Japan	1993	24.99
Wakeman, Rick	Live (Same As Live In Nottingham)	CD	Voiceprint	VP250CD	England	2002	8.99
Wakeman, Rick	Live At Hammersmith	CD	President	RW-CD-2	England	1985	7.99
Wakeman, Rick	Live In Nottingham	CD	Classic Rock	CRP-1050-2	England	2002	8.99
Wakeman, Rick	Master Series	CD	Polygram	540-894-2	Germany	1998	8.99
Wakeman, Rick	Morning Has B (Kevinmayhewltd.com)	CD	Kevin Mayhew	149005	U.S.A.	2000	14.99
Wakeman, Rick	Night Airs	CD	President	RWCD-9	England	1990	7.99
Wakeman, Rick	No Earthly Connection	Mini Lp	Universal	UICY-9295	Japan	2003	26.99
Wakeman, Rick	Orisons	CD	Hope	HOPEVP105CD	England	2001	11.99
Wakeman, Rick	Out Here (Promo)	CD	Music Fusion	RICKPROMO1	England	2003	8.99
Wakeman, Rick	Out Of The Blue (South America 2001)	CD	Music Fusion	MFCD-005	England	2002	8.99
Wakeman, Rick	Out There	CD	Music Fusion	MFW-6093X	England	2003	10.99
Wakeman, Rick	Phantom Power	CD	President	RWCD-35	England	2001	14.99
Wakeman, Rick	Piano Vibrations (Rick's 1st Lp) Covers	CD	Voiceprint	VP249CD	England	2003	8.99
Wakeman, Rick	Prayers	CD	Myrrh	MYRCD-1296	England	1993	10.99
Wakeman, Rick	Preludes To A Century	CD	President	RWCD-33	England	2000	14.99
Wakeman, Rick	Recollections - The Very Best Of	CD	A&M	069-490-774-2	U.S.A.	2000	8.99
Wakeman, Rick	Return To The Center Of The Earth	CD	EMI	7243-5-56763-2-0	U.S.A.	1999	11.99
Wakeman, Rick	Rhapsodies	2CD	Canyon	D50Y3128	Japan	1986	312.99
Wakeman, Rick	Rock N' Roll Prophet Plus 4	CD	President	RWCD-12	England	1993	12.99
Wakeman, Rick	Sea Airs	CD	President	RWCD-8	England	1988	13.99
Wakeman, Rick	Selections Journey Center Earth Inst.	CD	Griffin	GCD-779-2	U.S.A.	1998	8.99
Wakeman, Rick	Silent Nights	CD	President	RWCD1	England	1994	7.99
Wakeman, Rick	Simply Acoustic	CD	Hope	HOPEVP101CD	England	2001	8.99
Wakeman, Rick	Six Wives (20 Bit Remastered)	Mini Lp	Universal	UICY-9261	Japan	2003	26.99
Wakeman, Rick	Softsword: King John/ Magna Charter	CD	President	RWCD-24	England	1994	15.99
Wakeman, Rick	Songs Of Middle Earth	CD	BMG	75517-47503-2	U.S.A.	2002	9.99
Wakeman, Rick	Special Sampler (Promo)	CD	Jimco	JSP-0001	Japan	1991	149.99
Wakeman, Rick	Stella Bianca Alla.. (Black Nights + 4)	CD	M P	MPRCD-027	England	1999	18.99
Wakeman, Rick	Tales Of Future And Past	2CD	Purple Pyramid	CLP-1034-2	U.S.A.	2001	11.99
Wakeman, Rick	The Art In Music Trilogy	3CD	Music Fusion	MFACD002	England	1997	28.99
Wakeman, Rick	The Caped Collection	2CD	Snapper	SMD-CD-314	England	2000	14.99
Wakeman, Rick	The Classical Connection	CD	President	RWCD-13	England	1993	7.99
Wakeman, Rick	The Classical Connection 2	CD	President	RWCD-14	England	1993	7.99
Wakeman, Rick	The Family Album	CD	President	RWCD4	England	1987	7.99
Wakeman, Rick	The Masters (Gold Cd)	2CD	Purple Pyramid	CLP-0565-2	U.S.A.	1999	13.99

Artist	Title	Format	Label	Catalog No	Country	Released	Value
Wakeman, Rick	The Natural World Trilogy	3CD	Music Fusion	MFACD001	England	1997	28.99
Wakeman, Rick	The New Gospels	2CD	Hope	HOPEVP103CD	England	2001	16.99
Wakeman, Rick	The Piano Album	CD	Castle	CMRCD-180	England	2001	15.99
Wakeman, Rick	The Piano Tour Live	2CD	Hope	HOPEVP102CD	England	2001	14.99
Wakeman, Rick	The Private Collection	CD	President	RWCD-23	England	1994	32.99
Wakeman, Rick	The Seven Wonders Of The World	CD	President	RWCD-27	England	1995	7.99
Wakeman, Rick	The Word & The Gospels	2CD	BMO	BMO002/3	England	1986	17.99
Wakeman, Rick	The Word And Music	CD	Hope	HOPEVP104CD	England	2001	13.99
Wakeman, Rick	The Yes Piano Vibrations	CD	Classic Rock	CRP-1014	England	2002	19.99
Wakeman, Rick	Themes	CD	President	RWCD-32	England	1998	11.99
Wakeman, Rick	Time Machine	CD	President	RWCD7	England	1988	14.99
Wakeman, Rick	Treasure Chest Box Set 1,000	8CD	Voiceprint	VPTCCD1/8	England	2002	119.99
Wakeman, Rick	Tribute	CD	Movie Play	MPRCD-037	Italy	2001	10.99
Wakeman, Rick	Two Sides Of Yes - Volume 1	CD	Legends	CRL0857	England	2002	11.99
Wakeman, Rick	Two Sides Of Yes - Volume 2	CD	Legends	CRP0952	England	2002	11.99
Wakeman, Rick	Visions (Same As Visions Of Paradise)	CD	President	RWCD-28	England	1995	14.99
Wakeman, Rick	Voyage: The Very Best Of	2CD	A&M	540-567-2	Germany	1996	21.99
Wakeman, Rick	W/ W Piano Shaped Box (Ltd 1,000)	CD	Griffin	GCDRW-156-2	U.S.A.	1994	69.99
Wakeman, Rick	Welcome A Star	CD Single	Hope	HRHS-001	England	1995	8.99
Wakeman, Rick	White Rock (O.S.T.)	Mini Lp	Universal	UICY-9296	Japan	2003	26.99
Wakeman, Rick	White Rock II	CD	Musea	MFCD004	England	1999	8.99
Wakeman, Rick	Wizard And The Forest Of All Dreams	CD	Music Fusion	MFCD6092X	England	2002	29.99
Wakeman, Rick/Adam	No Expense Spared	CD	President	RWCD-22	England	1993	11.99
Wakeman, Rick/Adam	Romance Of The Victorian Age	CD	President	RWCD-25	England	1994	16.99
Wakeman, Rick/Adam	Tapestries	CD	President	RWCD-29	England	1996	11.99
Wakeman, Rick/Adam	Vignettes	CD	President	RWCD30	England	1996	16.99
Wakeman, Rick/Adam	Wakeman W/Wakeman: Off. Bootleg	2CD	Griffin	GCDRW-156-2	Canada	1994	12.99
Wakeman, Rick/Adam	Wakeman With Wakeman	2CD	President	RWCD-11	England	1993	12.99
Wakeman, Rick/D. Cousins	Hummingbird	CD	Witchwood	WMCD-2007	England	2002	14.99
Wakeman, Rick/E. Rock E.	Live On The Test	CD	Windsong	WHISCD-007	England	1994	20.99
Wakeman, Rick/M Fasciano	Black Knights At The Court Of...	CD	West Coast Prod.	WCPCD-1009	EEC	1994	26.99
Wakeman, Rick/N Wisdom	Norman Wisdom - A World Of	CD	Ambient	AIOM5CD	England	1991	29.99
Wakeman, Rick/R. Ramedios	A Suite Of Gods	CD	President	RWCD-5	England	1988	12.99
Wakeman, Rick/T Fernadez	Zodiaque	CD	President	RWCD-6	England	1988	17.99
Walden, Nara Michael	Looking At You, Looking At Me	CD	Atlantic	AMCY-6097	Japan	1983	51.99
Walden, W.G. Snuffy	The Stand (O.S.T.)	CD	Varese	VSD-5496	U.S.A.	1994	8.99
Walker Brothers	The Collection	CD	Line	IMCD-9.00714-0	Germany	1989	4.99
Walker, Butch	Left Of Self Centered	CD	Arista	07822-14743-2	U.S.A.	2002	6.99
Walker, Jerry Jeff	Bein' Free	CD	Line	LECD-9.00934-0	Germany	1990	13.99
Walker, Jerry Jeff	Five Years Gone	CD	Line	LECD-9.00952-0	Germany	1990	13.99
Walker, Jerry Jeff	Gypsy Songman	CD	Line	SDCD-9.00419-0	Germany	1987	13.99
Walker, Les	Whatever Mood You're In	CD	Line	RTCD-9.01178-0	Germany	1992	4.99
Walking Wounded	New West	CD	Line	FBCD-9.00386-0	Germany	1987	10.99
Wall Of Voodoo	Call of the West	CD	I.R.S.	CD-70026	U.S.A.	1987	12.99
Wall Of Voodoo	Dark Continent	CD	I.R.S.	CD-70022	U.S.A.	1990	34.99
Wall Of Voodoo	Happy Planet	CD	I.R.S.	IRSD-5997	U.S.A.	1987	24.99
Wall Of Voodoo	Index Masters	CD	Restless	7-70111-2	U.S.A.	1993	34.99
Wall Of Voodoo	Mexican Radio (3")	CD Single	I.R.S.	CC-31020	U.S.A.	1989	26.99
Wall Of Voodoo	Seven Days In Sammystown	CD	I.R.S.	IRSD-5662	U.S.A.	1989	44.99
Wall Of Voodoo	Ugly Americans...	CD	I.R.S.	IRSD-42140	U.S.A.	1988	54.99
Wallflowers	Letters From the Wasteland (Promo)	CD Single	Interscope	INTR-10401-2	U.S.A.	2001	5.99
Wallflowers	One Headlight (Promo)	CD Single	Interscope	INT5P-6072	U.S.A.	1996	5.99
Walsh, Joe	Barnstorm	CD	MCA	MVCM-8001	Japan	1972	24.99
Walsh, Joe	Barnstorm (MFSL Silver Cd)	CD	Mobile Fidelity	MFCD-777	U.S.A.	1972	39.99
Walsh, Joe	But Seriously,Folks	CD	Elektra	6E-141	U.S.A.	1978	8.99
Walsh, Joe	Got Any Gum?	CD	Warner Bros.	9-25606-2	U.S.A.	1987	28.99
Walsh, Joe	Greatest Hits: Little Did He Know	CD	MCA	MCAD-11679	U.S.A.	1997	10.99
Walsh, Joe	Look What I Did! - Joe Walsh Anth.	CD	MCA	MCAD2-11233	U.S.A.	1995	20.99

W

Artist	Title	Format	Label	Catalog No	Country	Released	Value
Walsh, Joe	Ordinary Average Guy	CD	Epic	ZK-47384	U.S.A.	1991	6.99
Walsh, Joe	So What	CD	MCA	MCAD-10761	U.S.A.	1974	15.99
Walsh, Joe	Songs For A Dying Planet	CD	Epic	ZK-48916	U.S.A.	1992	6.99
Walsh, Joe	The Confessor	CD	Warner Bros.	9-25281-2	U.S.A.	1985	8.99
Walsh, Joe	The Smoker You... (MCA Gold Cd)	CD	MCA	MCAD-11170	U.S.A.	1973	63.99
Walsh, Joe	There Goes The Neighborhood	CD	Elektra	5E-523-2	U.S.A.	1981	6.99
Walsh, Joe	You Bought It You Name It	CD	Wounded Bird	WOU-3884	U.S.A.	2002	8.99
Walsh, Joe	You Can't Argue With A Sick Mind	CD	MCA	MCAD-31120	U.S.A.	1976	6.99
Walton, Joice	Downsville Girl	CD	Line	LICD-9.01303-0	Germany	1994	5.99
War	All Day Music (Gold Disc)	CD	Avenue	ASR-10605-2	U.S.A.	1995	12.99
War	Anthology 1970-1974	2CD	Avenue	R2-71774	U.S.A.	1994	18.99
War	Colleccion Latina	CD	Avenue	R2-72866	U.S.A.	1997	6.99
War	Deliver The Word (Gold Disc)	CD	Avenue	ASR-10607-2	U.S.A.	1995	12.99
War	Greatest Hits (Gold Disc)	CD	Avenue	ASR-10601-2	U.S.A.	1995	12.99
War	Grooves/Mess. Gr. Hits + 8 (Xtra Cd)	2CD	Avenue	R2-75903	U.S.A.	1998	16.99
War	Platinum Jazz (Gold Disc)	CD	Avenue	ASR-10606-2	U.S.A.	1995	12.99
War	The Very Best Of	2CD	Rhino	R2-73995	U.S.A.	2003	19.99
War	The World Is A Ghetto (Gold Disc)	CD	Avenue	ASR-10603-2	U.S.A.	1995	12.99
War	War Live	2CD	Rhino	R2-71052	U.S.A.	1992	13.99
War	Why Can't We Be Friends? (Gold Disc)	CD	Avenue	ASR-10602-2	U.S.A.	1995	12.99
Ward, Anita	Ring My Bell	CD Single	Line	TLCD-9.00882-E	Germany	1989	6.99
Ward, Anita	The Anita Ward Album/Ring My Bell	CD	Line	TLCD-9.00404-0	Germany	1987	28.99
Ware, Leon	Velvet Nights	CD	Century	CECC-00395	Japan	1987	72.99
Warhorse	Outbreak Of Hostilities	CD	Thunderbolt	CDTB-104	England	2002	12.99
Warhorse/Ashley Holt	Red Sea + 6 (W/Nick Simper)	CD	Angel Air	SJPCD-035	England	1999	12.99
Warhorse/Ashley Holt	Self Titled	CD	Repertoire	REP-4055-WP	Germany	1990	14.99
Warhorse/Ashley Holt	Self Titled + 5 (W/Nick Simper)	CD	Angel Air	SJPCD034	England	1999	12.99
Warlock	Burning The Witches	CD	Mercury	830-902-2	Germany	1984	12.99
Warlock	Hellbound	CD	Vertigo	824-660-2-Q	Germany	1985	13.99
Warlock	Triumph And Agony	CD	Mercury	832-804-2	Germany	1987	14.99
Warlock	True As Steel	CD	Mercury	830-237-2	Germany	1986	14.99
Warlord	Deliver Us	CD	FEMS	APCY-8179	Japan	1993	92.99
Warnes, Jennifer	Famous Blue Raincoat (Gold)	CD	Rock The House	RTHCD-5052	U.S.A.	1990	63.99
Warnes, Jennifer	Famous Blue Raincoat (L Cohen Songs)	CD	Private	PVT2092	U.S.A.	1991	8.99
Warnes, Jennifer	First We Take Manhatten	CD	Zounds	2700020109	Germany	2001	8.99
Warnes, Jennifer	First We Take Manhatten (Promo)	CD Single	RCA	JW1	Germany	1987	8.99
Warnes, Jennifer	First We Take/I've Had/Up Where (3")	CD Single	A&M	CY37581	U.S.A.	1988	49.99
Warnes, Jennifer	Just Jennifer	CD	Deram	820-989-2	Germany	1992	34.99
Warnes, Jennifer	Love Lifts Us Up: A Collection 1969-198	CD	Raven	RVCD-185	Australia	2004	15.99
Warnes, Jennifer	Rock You Gently	CD Single	Arista	665391	Germany	1992	8.99
Warnes, Jennifer	Shot Through The Heart	CD	BMG	74321-19737-2-4	Germany	1994	8.99
Warnes, Jennifer	The Best Of	CD	Arista	ARCD-8348	U.S.A.	1990	8.99
Warnes, Jennifer	The Hunter	CD	Private	4007192-61974-0	Germany	1992	8.99
Warnes, Jennifer	The Very Best Of	CD	BMG Victor	BVC2-37003	Japan	2000	29.99
Warnes, Jennifer	The Well (W/V D Parks/Arlo Guthrie)	CD	Sin-Drome	8960	U.S.A.	2001	12.99
Warnes, Jennifer/Bill Medley	I've Had The Time Of My Life	CD Single	RCA	PD49626	England	1987	8.99
Warrant	'86 - '97 Live	CD	CMC Int.	06076-86218-2	U.S.A.	1997	8.99
Warrant	Belly To Belly, Vol. 1	CD	CMC Int.	06076-86200-2	U.S.A.	1996	4.99
Warrant	Cherry Pie	CD	Columbia	CK-46929	U.S.A.	1990	9.99
Warrant	Cherry Pie (No Ode To Tipper Gore)	CD	Columbia	CK-46929	U.S.A.	1990	14.99
Warrant	Dirty Rotten Filthy Stinking Rich	CD	Columbia	CK-44383	U.S.A.	1988	7.99
Warrant	Dog Eat Dog	CD	Columbia	CK-52584	U.S.A.	1990	7.99
Warrant	Greatest And Latest	CD	Dead Line	CLP-0694-2	U.S.A.	1999	8.99
Warrant	Rocking Tall	CD	Sony	A-28127	U.S.A.	1996	7.99
Warrant	The Best Of	CD	Sony	SK-64775	U.S.A.	1996	8.99
Warrant	Ultraphobic	CD	CMC Int.	CMC-7203-2	U.S.A.	1995	8.99
Warrant	Under The Influence	CD	Perris	PER-00842	Canada	2001	9.99
Warren, Leslie Ann	Cinderella - (1965 T.V. Cast)	CD	Sony	SK-53528	U.S.A.	1993	12.99

W

Artist	Title	Format	Label	Catalog No	Country	Released	Value
Warrior	Ancient Future	CD	Metal Blade	3984-14175-2	U.S.A.	1998	9.99
Warrior	Code Of Life	CD	Nuclear Blast	6601	U.S.A.	2001	13.99
Warrior	Fighting For The Earth	CD	Metal Blade	9-26531-2	U.S.A.	1991	30.99
Warwick, Dionne	Aquarela Do Brasil	CD	Arista	07822-18777-2	U.S.A.	1994	5.99
Warwick, Dionne	Definitive Collection	CD	Arista	ARCD-9050	U.S.A.	1999	8.99
Warwick, Dionne	Dionne (Produced By Barry Manilow)	CD	Arista	75517-45601-2	U.S.A.	1979	7.99
Warwick, Dionne	Her Classic Songs, Vol 1	CD	Curb	D2-77878	U.S.A.	1997	7.99
Warwick, Dionne	Here I Am/Here Where There Is Love	CD	Sequel	NEM-CD-760	England	1995	12.99
Warwick, Dionne	Hot! Live And Otherwise	CD	BMG Victor	A32D-3	Japan	1981	59.99
Warwick, Dionne	Hot, Live & Otherwise	CD	Arista	A2CD-8111	U.S.A.	1980	121.99
Warwick, Dionne	How Many Times....	CD	Nippon Columbia	32RD-71	Japan	1983	104.99
Warwick, Dionne	I Say A Little Prayer	CD	Curb	D2-77894	U.S.A.	1997	7.99
Warwick, Dionne	Make Way For...\The Sensitive Sound Of	CD	Sequel	NEM-CD-760	England	1995	12.99
Warwick, Dionne	No Night So Long	CD	Nippon Phonogram	32RD-70	Japan	1980	173.99
Warwick, Dionne	Presenting\Anyone Who Had A Heart	CD	Sequel	NEM-CD-760	England	1995	12.99
Warwick, Dionne	Sings Cole Porter	CD	Arista	ARCD-8573	U.S.A.	1990	5.99
Warwick, Dionne	Sings Dionne	CD	River North	51416-1431-2	U.S.A.	1998	5.99
Warwick, Dionne	Soulful	CD	Disky	DCD-5401	Netherlands	1994	29.99
Warwick, Dionne	The Windows Of The World	CD	Disky	DCD-5400	Netherlands	1994	29.99
Was Not Was/ S P Atkinson	Don't Walk Away (W/Don And David)	CD	Fontana	842-684-2	Germany	1982	44.99
Washington Jr., Grover	Reed Seed	CD	Motown	3746352362	U.S.A.	1979	68.99
Wasserman, Rob	Duets (Lou Reed, Rickie Lee Jones)	CD	MCA	MCAD-42131	U.S.A.	1988	13.99
Wasserman, Rob	Trios (MFSL Gold Cd)	CD	Mobile Fidelity	UDCD-752	U.S.A.	1994	23.99
Wasserman, Rob/Lou Reed	Trios (E Costello, N Young, B Wilson)	CD	GRP	MCG-4021	U.S.A.	1994	8.99
Waters, Muddy	Fathers/Sons (Bloomfield, Butterfield)	CD	Chess	CHD-92522	U.S.A.	1989	14.99
Waters, Muddy	Folk Singer + 2 (MFSL Gold Cd)	CD	Mobile Fidelity	UDCD-593	U.S.A.	1964	35.99
Waters, Muddy	Martin Scorsese Presents	CD	Universal	B000482-02	U.S.A.	2003	8.99
Waters, Muddy	Muddy Mississippi Waters Live + 11	2CD	Epic	E2K-86559	U.S.A.	2003	16.99
Waters, Muddy	The London Muddy Waters Sessions	CD	MCA	CHD-9298	U.S.A.	1989	8.99
Waters, Muddy/J. Winter	Hard Again + 1	CD	Epic	EK-86817	U.S.A.	2004	8.99
Waters, Muddy/J. Winter	I'm Ready	CD	Blue Sky	ZK-34928	U.S.A.	1978	8.99
Waters, Roger	Amused To Death (Sony Gold Cd)	CD	Columbia	CK-53196	U.S.A.	1992	51.99
Waters, Roger	Bravery Being Out Of Range (Promo)	CD Single	Columbia	CSK-4830	U.S.A.	1992	34.99
Waters, Roger	Flickering Flame - Solo Years Vol. 1	CD	Columbia	5079062000	Australia	2002	9.99
Waters, Roger	In the Flesh (SACD)	CD	Columbia	C2S-85235	U.S.A.	2001	14.99
Waters, Roger	In The Flesh Live	2CD	Sony	SRCS-2393-4	Japan	2000	23.99
Waters, Roger	In the Flesh Live	2CD	Columbia	C2K-85235	U.S.A.	2000	13.99
Waters, Roger	Radio K.A.O.S.	CD	Columbia	CK-40795	U.S.A.	1987	9.99
Waters, Roger	The Pros And Cons Of Hitch Hiking	CD	Columbia	CK-39290	U.S.A.	1984	11.99
Waters, Roger	The Tide Is Turning	CD Single	Mercury	CD-EM-37	England	1987	46.99
Waters, Roger	The Tide Is Turning (Promo)	CD Single	Mercury	CDP-367	U.S.A.	1990	7.99
Waters, Roger	The Wall - Berlin '90 Promo	CD	Columbia	CSK-2126	U.S.A.	1990	13.99
Waters, Roger	The Wall - Live In Berlin (Remaster)	2CD	Mercury	B0000752-02	U.S.A.	2003	14.99
Waters, Roger	The Wall Live In Berlin	2CD	Mercury	846-611-2	U.S.A.	1990	7.99
Waters, Roger	The Wall: Live In Berlin (Promo)	CD	Mercury	CDP-318	U.S.A.	1990	14.99
Waters, Roger	Three Wishes (Promo)	CD Single	Columbia	CSK-4941	U.S.A.	1992	15.99
Waters, Roger	What God Wants, Part I (Promo)	CD Single	Columbia	CSK-4607	U.S.A.	1992	19.99
Waters, Roger	What God Wants, Part I (Single)	CD Single	Columbia	658139-5	England	1992	8.99
Waters, Roger/Cyndi Lauper	Another Brick in the Wall (Part 2)	CD Single	Mercury	CDP-342	U.S.A.	1990	9.99
Waters, Roger/Ron Geesin	Music From The Body	CD	Restless	7-72395-2	Canada	1990	7.99
Watersons	For Pence And Spicy Ale + 7	CD	Topic	TSCD462	England	1993	11.99
Watersons	Frost And Fire + 7	CD	Topic	TSCD136	England	1990	11.99
Watersons	Green Fields + 3	CD	Topic	TSCD500	England	1998	11.99
Watersons	Mighty River Of A Song (4 CD/DVD)	5CD	Topic	TSFCD4002	England	2004	44.99
Watersons	Reflections	3CD	Topic	TSBX1002	England	1998	34.99
Watersons	Sound, Sound Your Instruments...	CD	Topic	TSCD346	England	1996	11.99
Watersons	The Definitive Collection	CD	Highpoint	HPO-6004	England	2003	11.99
Watersons	The Early Days	CD	Topic	TSCD472	England	1994	11.99

W

Artist	Title	Format	Label	Catalog No	Country	Released	Value
Watersons	Yorkshire Garland	CD	Topic	TSCD167	England	1992	11.99
Watersons/Blue Murder	No One Stands Alone	CD	Topic	TSCD537	England	2002	11.99
Watersons/Lal/Mike	Bright Phoebus	CD	Leader	LESCD 2076	England	2000	19.99
Watersons/Lal/Mike	Shining Bright	CD	Topic	TSCD519	England	2002	12.99
Watersons/Lal/Norma	A True Hearted Girl	CD	Topic	TSCD507	England	1999	11.99
Watersons/Lal/Oliver Knight	A Bed Of Roses	CD	Topic	TSCD505	England	1999	11.99
Watersons/Lal/Oliver Knight	Once In A Blue Moon	CD	Topic	TSCD478	England	1996	11.99
Watersons/Martin Carthy	Waterson: Carthy	CD	Topic	TSCD475	England	1994	11.99
Watersons/Martin Carthy	Waterson: Carthy - A Dark Light	CD	Topic	TSCD536	England	2002	11.99
Watersons/Martin Carthy	Waterson: Carthy - Broken Ground	CD	Topic	TSCD509	England	1999	11.99
Watersons/Martin Carthy	Waterson: Carthy - Common Tongue	CD	Topic	TSCD488	England	1996	11.99
Watersons/Mike	Mike Waterson + 2	CD	Topic	TSCD516	England	1999	11.99
Watersons/Norma	Bright Shiny Morning	CD	Topic	TSCD520	England	2000	11.99
Watersons/Norma	Norma Waterson (Richard Thompson)	CD	Hannibal	HNCD-1393	England	1996	10.99
Watersons/Norma	The Very Thought Of You	CD	Hannibal	HNCD-1430	U.S.A.	1999	10.99
Watersons/Oliver Knight	Mysterious Day	CD	Topic	TSCD528	England	2002	11.99
Watkins, Kit	A Different View	CD	Linden	LM-2003	U.S.A.	1991	16.99
Watkins, Kit	Ambient Realms (Loops For Acid)	CD	Sonic Foundry	55065	U.S.A.	2000	24.99
Watkins, Kit	Azure	CD	Linden	LM-2017	U.S.A.	1994	16.99
Watkins, Kit	Beauty Drifting	CD	Linden	LM-2024	U.S.A.	1996	16.99
Watkins, Kit	Circle	CD	Linden	LM-2009	U.S.A.	1993	16.99
Watkins, Kit	Early Solo Works 1980-82	CD	Linden	LM-2001	U.S.A.	1991	16.99
Watkins, Kit	Holographic Tapestries	CD	One Way	OW-35163	U.S.A.	2000	8.99
Watkins, Kit	Kinetic Vapors	CD	Linden	LM-2014	U.S.A.	1993	16.99
Watkins, Kit	Labyrinth	CD	One Way	OW-35160	U.S.A.	2000	8.99
Watkins, Kit	Sampler	CD	Linden	LM-2004	U.S.A.	1991	19.99
Watkins, Kit	Sunstruck	CD	One Way	OW-35161	U.S.A.	2000	8.99
Watkins, Kit	The Unseen	CD	MP3.com	33914	U.S.A.	2000	16.99
Watkins, Kit	Thought Tones Vol. 1	CD	Linden	LM-2002	U.S.A.	1991	16.99
Watkins, Kit	Thought Tones Volume 2	CD	Linden	LM-2005	U.S.A.	1992	16.99
Watkins, Kit	Wet, Dark, And Low	CD	One Way	OW-35162	U.S.A.	2000	8.99
Watkins, Kit/Coco Roussel	In Time	CD	Linden	LM-2016	U.S.A.	1994	16.99
Watley, Jody	Affection + 2	CD	Victor Ent.	MVCM-539	Japan	1995	34.99
Watson, Russell	Encore	CD	Decca	470-300-2	England	2001	9.99
Watts, Charlie/Rolling Stones	From One Charlie Box Set (W/Book)	CD	Continuum	19104-2	England	1991	34.99
Watts, Charlie/Rolling Stones	I've Got A Crush On You (Promo)	CD Single	Virgin	CWCDJ96	France	1996	35.99
Watts, Charlie/Rolling Stones	Long Ago & Far Away	CD	Point Blank	7243-841695-2-7	U.S.A.	1996	6.99
Watts, Charlie/Rolling Stones	Warm & Tender	CD	Continuum	19310-2	U.S.A.	1993	7.99
Waxman, Franz	Frankesntein/Bride Of Frankenstein + 1	CD	Disconforme	SFCD33554	Italy	2000	17.99
Waxman, Franz	The Bride Of Frankenstein	CD	Silva Screen	SSD-1028	U.S.A.	1993	19.99
Wayne, Jeff	Eve Of War (Ben Liebrand Remix)	CD Single	Columbia	655126-6	England	1989	16.99
Wayne, Jeff	War Of The Worlds (Justin Hayward)	2CD	Columbia	CDX-96000	England	1995	34.99
Wayne, Jeff	War Of The Worlds Cd-Rom	CD-Rom	GT	7427-251513-0-7	U.S.A.	1998	25.99
Wayne, Jeff/Anthony Hopkins	Spartacus (W/Catherine Zeta - Jones)	2CD	Sony	472030-2	England	1992	28.99
Wayne, Jeff/Promo	War Of The Worlds - The New Files	CD Single	Columbia	X-FILE-CD	U.S.A.	1995	21.99
Webb, Jack	Just The Tracks Ma'am: Warner Bros.	CD	Rhino	RHM2-7711	U.S.A.	2000	19.99
Webb, Jimmy	Angel Heart	CD	Columbia	CK-66654	U.S.A.	1982	13.99
Webb, Jimmy	Angel Heart	CD	Sony	SRCS-6153	Japan	1991	18.99
Webb, Jimmy	Archive	CD	Warner Bros.	9548-32063-2	Germany	1993	18.99
Webb, Jimmy	El Mirage	CD	East West	AMCY-2768	Japan	1998	18.99
Webb, Jimmy	Jim Webb Sings Jim Webb	CD	Epic	ESCA-7574	Japan	1995	29.99
Webb, Jimmy	Land's End	CD	East West	AMCY-2767	Japan	1998	55.99
Webb, Jimmy	Letters	CD	Warner Bros.	WPCR-10305	Japan	1999	29.99
Webb, Jimmy	Suspending Disbelief	CD	Elektra	9-61506-2	U.S.A.	1993	5.99
Webb, Jimmy	Ten Easy Pieces	CD	Guardian	7243-8-52826-2-1	U.S.A.	1996	14.99
Webb, Jimmy	Words And Music	CD	Warner Bros.	WPCR-10304	Japan	1999	29.99
Webber, Andrew Lloyd	Phantom Of The Opera	CD	Pony Canyon	D50H0009	Japan	1988	253.99
Weddings, Parties, Anything	No Show Without Punch	CD	Line	UTCD-9.00811-L	Germany	1989	24.99

W

Artist	Title	Format	Label	Catalog No	Country	Released	Value
Ween	From Record Quebec by Ween (DJ)	CD	Sanctuary	SANDJ-85562-2	U.S.A.	2003	16.99
Ween	Live at Stubb's 7/2000	3CD	Chocodog	1004	U.S.A.	2002	54.99
Ween	Pink Triangle	CD	DGC	PRO-CD-1102	U.S.A.	1996	67.99
Weiland, Scott	12 Bar Blues	CD	Atlantic	83084-2	U.S.A.	1997	5.99
Weiland, Scott	Barbarella (Promo)	CD Single	Atlantic	PRCD-8452	U.S.A.	1998	7.99
Weiland, Scott	Lady, Your Roof Brings Me Down (DJ)	CD Single	Atlantic	PRCD-8325-2	U.S.A.	1997	7.99
Weiland, Scott	Opposite Octave Reaction (Promo)	CD Single	Atlantic	PRCD-8566	U.S.A.	1998	5.99
Weir, Bob	Ace	CD	Grateful Dead	GDCD4004	U.S.A.	1988	9.99
Weir, Bob	Ace (Line Version)	CD	Line	GDCD-9.00649-0	Germany	1989	9.99
Weir, Bob	Bobby & The Midnights	CD	Arista	ARCD-8558	U.S.A.	1981	8.99
Weir, Bob	Weir Here (Best Of)	2CD	Hybrid	HY—20332	U.S.A.	2004	16.99
Weir, Bob/Ratdog	Evening Moods	CD	Grateful Dead	GDCD-4072	U.S.A.	2000	9.99
Weir/Wasserman	Live	CD	Grateful Dead	GDCD-4053	U.S.A.	1997	9.99
Weisberg, Tim	4	CD	A&M	CD-3121	U.S.A.	1988	9.99
Weisberg, Tim	High Risk	CD	Cypress	14166-0101-2	U.S.A.	1991	19.99
Weisberg, Tim	Naked Eyes	CD	Fahrenheit	781619-3451-2	U.S.A.	1994	7.99
Weisberg, Tim	Outrageous Temptations	CD	Cypress	14166-0123-2	U.S.A.	1989	34.99
Weisberg, Tim	The Best Of: Smile	CD	A&M	75021-3261-2	U.S.A.	1979	34.99
Weisberg, Tim	Time Traveler: Three Decade Journey	CD	Fahrenheit	781619-2006-2	U.S.A.	1999	8.99
Weisberg, Tim	Undercover	CD	Fahrenheit	781619-9602-2	U.S.A.	1996	6.99
Welch, Bob	French Kiss (Special Edition Boxed)	CD	EMI	7243-576247-2-5	EU	2000	14.99
Welch, Bob	French Kiss/Three Hearts	CD	Edsel	EDCD-548	U.S.A.	1998	16.99
Welch, Bob	Looks At Bop	CD	Orchard	ORCD2528-2	U.S.A.	2000	11.99
Welch, Bob	Man Overboard / The Other One	CD	Edsel	EDCD-539	U.S.A.	1998	16.99
Welch, Bob	The Best Of Bob Welch + 2	CD	Rhino	R2-70597	U.S.A.	1991	8.99
Weller, Paul	A Heavy Soul Ep	CD Single	Polydor K.K.	POCP-7260	Japan	1997	20.99
Weller, Paul	Above The Clouds (Promo)	CD Single	Go! Discs Ltd.	GOD-CD-91	England	1992	34.99
Weller, Paul	Days of Speed + 1	CD	Sony	EICP-13	Japan	2001	20.99
Weller, Paul	Heavy Soul (Deluxe Ed. W/Cards)	CD	Go! Discs Ltd.	524-417-2	England	1997	20.99
Weller, Paul	Heavy Soul (Promo Sampler)	CD	Island	HEAVY-CD1	England	1997	11.99
Weller, Paul	Heavy Soul + 1	CD	Polygram K.K.	POCP-7250	Japan	1997	29.99
Weller, Paul	Heliocentric + 2	CD	Polydor K.K.	POCP-7470	Japan	2000	20.99
Weller, Paul	He's The Keeper	CD Single	Island	562655-2	England	2000	6.99
Weller, Paul	Illumination + 2	CD	Sony	EICP-132	Japan	2002	34.99
Weller, Paul	Illumination + DVD (PAL)	CD	Sony	5094899000	England	2002	14.99
Weller, Paul	It's Written In The Stars (Cd1)	CD Single	Independiente	ISOM-63MS	England	2002	8.99
Weller, Paul	It's Written In The Stars (Cd2)	CD Single	Independiente	ISOM-63SMS	England	2002	8.99
Weller, Paul	Kings Road Sampler (DJ/350)	CD	Go! Discs Ltd.	KINGS-1	England	1997	103.99
Weller, Paul	Live Wood	CD	Island	828561-2	Germany	1994	10.99
Weller, Paul	Live Wood + 2	CD	Pony Canyon	POCY-00601	Japan	1994	17.99
Weller, Paul	Modern Classics (Bonus Cd)	2CD	Island	524-558-2	England	1998	17.99
Weller, Paul	Modern Classics + 2	CD	Polydor K.K.	POCP-7337	Japan	1998	20.99
Weller, Paul	More Wood (Little Splinters)	CD	Pony Canyon	PCCY-00509	Japan	1993	35.99
Weller, Paul	Self Titled + 1	CD	Pony Canyon	POCY-00337	Japan	1992	19.99
Weller, Paul	Sexy Sadie (Promo/Numbered)	CD Single	Universal	PN-PCD2	England	2003	34.99
Weller, Paul	Stanley Road	CD	Pony Canyon	POCY-00747	Japan	1995	19.99
Weller, Paul	Sunflower (Promo)	CD Single	Go! Discs Ltd.	GOD-CD-102	England	1997	17.99
Weller, Paul	Sweet Pea, My Sweet Pea	CD Single	Victor Ent.	VICI-5001	Japan	2000	10.99
Weller, Paul	The Weaver EP (Promo)	CD Single	Go! Discs Ltd.	GOD-CD-107	England	1993	19.99
Weller, Paul	Wild Wood	CD	Pony Canyon	POCY-00455	Japan	1993	19.99
Weller, Paul	Wild Wood	CD Single	Go Discs Ltd.	857-2792	England	1993	5.99
Weller, Paul	Wild Wood (Promo)	CD Single	Go! Discs Ltd.	GOD-CD-104	England	1993	23.99
Weller, Paul	Wild Wood + 3 (Bonus Cd)	2CD	Go Discs Ltd.	828-513-2	U.S.A.	1994	24.99
Weller, Paul/Dee C. Lee	Things Will Be Sweeter	CD	Pony Canyon	POCY-00647	Japan	1995	13.99
Weller, Paul/Indian Vibes	Remixes	CD	Toshiba-EMI	VJCP-15003	Japan	1994	17.99
Weller, Paul/Movement	Into Tomorrow	CD Single	Freedom High	FHPC-1	England	1991	48.99
Weller, Paul/Slam Slam	Free Your Feelings (Dee C. Lee)	CD	MCA	MCAD10147	U.S.A.	1991	14.99
Weller, Paul/Tracie	Far From The Hurting Kind	CD	Polystar	PSCR-5483	Japan	1996	39.99

W

Artist	Title	Format	Label	Catalog No	Country	Released	Value
Welles, Orson	The Very Best Of	CD	Stardust	CLP-1077-2	U.S.A.	2001	8.99
Wendy & Lisa	Always In My Dreams	CD	Sony	A-27988	U.S.A.	2000	7.99
Wendy & Lisa	Are You My Baby	CD	Disky	VI-86881	Netherlands	1996	12.99
Wendy & Lisa	Eroica	CD	Atlantic	91378-2	U.S.A.	1990	18.99
Wendy & Lisa	Eroica (Promo Sampler)	CD	Virgin	WALCD1	England	1990	12.99
Wendy & Lisa	Fruit At The Bottom	CD	Columbia	CK-44341	U.S.A.	1989	10.99
Wendy & Lisa	Lolly Lolly	CD Single	Virgin	662-118-2	England	1989	24.99
Wendy & Lisa	Satisfaction	CD Single	Virgin	VSCD-1194	England	1989	12.99
Wendy & Lisa	Self Titled	CD	Columbia	CK-40862	U.S.A.	1987	9.99
Wendy & Lisa	Strung Out	CD Single	Virgin	VSCDT1272	England	1990	7.99
Wendy & Lisa	Waterfall (3")	CD Single	Virgin	VSCD-1223	England	1989	12.99
West Coast All Stars	Naturally	CD	Hori Pro	CM9001	Japan	1998	29.99
West Coast Pop Art Exp Band	Part One + 2 (Not The Same As Vol. 1)	CD	Sundazed	SC-6173	U.S.A.	2001	7.99
West Coast Pop Art Exp Band	Vol. 3 + 2	CD	Sundazed	SC-6175	U.S.A.	2001	8.99
West Coast Pop Art Exp Band	Volume 2 + 2	CD	Sundazed	SC-6174	U.S.A.	2001	8.99
West Coast Pop Art Exp Band	Volume One + 8	CD	Sundazed	SC-11047	U.S.A.	1997	7.99
Westbrook, Kate	Good-Bye Peter Lorre	CD	Line	FECD-9.51060-0	Germany	1991	13.99
Westbrook, Mike	For The Record	CD	Line	TACD-9.00785-0	Germany	1989	24.99
Westbrook, Mike	Love/Dream And Variations	CD	Line	TACD-9.00788-0	Germany	1989	24.99
Westbrook, Mike	Pierides	CD	Line	COCD-9.00377-0	Germany	1987	24.99
Westerberg, Paul	14 Songs	CD	Sire	9-45255-2	U.S.A.	1993	7.99
Westerberg, Paul	14 Songs (Promo CD/Book Limited Ed)	CD	Reprise	9-45335-2	U.S.A.	1993	19.99
Westerberg, Paul	Come Feel Me Tremble	CD	TVT	TVT-3872-2	U.S.A.	2003	12.99
Westerberg, Paul	Dyslexic Heart	CD Single	Epic	659125-1	Australia	1993	13.99
Westerberg, Paul	Eventually	CD	Reprise	9-46176-2	U.S.A.	1996	6.99
Westerberg, Paul	Mono (Grandpa Boy)	CD	Vagrant	VR368	U.S.A.	2002	11.99
Westerberg, Paul	Stereo/Mono	2CD	Vagrant	VR369	U.S.A.	2002	19.99
Westerberg, Paul	Suicaine Gratification	CD	Capitol	7243-8-59004-2-6	U.S.A.	1999	9.99
Westerberg, Paul	Suicaine Gratification (Del. Box Set)	CD	Capitol	7243-4-98939-2-4	U.S.A.	1999	24.99
Westerberg, Paul	World Class Fad	CD Single	Reprise	9362-40948-2	England	1993	9.99
Westerberg, Paul/Grandpaboy	Grandpaboy EP	CD	Sound Proof	MCD-1315	U.S.A.	1997	14.99
Wet Willie	Dixie Rock	CD	Capricorn	314-538-135-2	U.S.A.	1998	26.99
Wet Willie	Drippin' Wet ! - Live	CD	Capricorn	314-558-003-2	U.S.A.	1998	21.99
Wet Willie	Keep On Smilin'	CD	Capricorn	314-536-134-2	U.S.A.	1997	29.99
Wet Willie	Mannorisms	CD	Wounded Bird	WOU-4983	U.S.A.	2003	8.99
Wet Willie	Self Titled	CD	Capricorn	314-558-383-2	U.S.A.	1998	26.99
Wet Willie	The Wetter The Better	CD	Capricorn	314-538-654-2	U.S.A.	1999	12.99
Wet Willie	Wet Willie II	CD	Capricorn	314-558-394-2	U.S.A.	1998	26.99
Wet Willie/Jimmy Hall	Rendevouz With The Blues	CD	Capricorn	314-532-460-2	U.S.A.	1996	29.99
Wetherwax, Michael	Cage (O.S.T.)	CD	AJK Music	A-468-2	U.S.A.	1989	9.99
Wetton, John	Akustika-Live in Amerika	CD	Blueprint	BP226CD	Austria	1995	13.99
Wetton, John	Arkangel + 1	CD	Pony Canyon	POCY-01109	Japan	1997	13.99
Wetton, John	Arkangel + 2	CD	Eagle	EAGCD020	EC	1998	9.99
Wetton, John	Battle Lines (Voice Mail + 1)	CD	Blueprint	BP240CD	Austria	1996	10.99
Wetton, John	Caught In A Crossfire + 2	CD	Avalon	MICP-10162	Japan	1999	17.99
Wetton, John	Chasing The Deer	CD	Pony Canyon	POCY-00701	Japan	1995	17.99
Wetton, John	Chasing The Deer	CD	Blueprint	CP282CD	EU	1998	10.99
Wetton, John	Chasing The Dragon	CD	Blueprint	BP227CD	Austria	1994	11.99
Wetton, John	Hazy Monet - Live In New York	CD	Blueprint	BP296CD	Austria	1997	10.99
Wetton, John	King's Road 1972-1980	CD	Editions EG	EGCD-70	U.S.A.	1987	14.99
Wetton, John	Live At The Sun Plaza Tokyo 1999	2CD	Blueprint	BP335CD	England	2000	19.99
Wetton, John	Nomansland - Live In Poland	CD	Giant Elec Pea	GEPCD-1025	EU	1999	16.99
Wetton, John	Rock Of Faith	CD	Giant Elec Pea	GEPCD-1033	EU	2003	14.99
Wetton, John	Rock Of Faith + 2	CD	Avalon	MICP-10347	Japan	2003	17.99
Wetton, John	Sinister	CD	Giant Elec Pea	GEPCD-1029	EU	2001	16.99
Wetton, John	Sub Rosa 1998	CD	Blueprint	BP314CD	EU	1998	9.99
Wetton, John	Voice Mail	CD	Pony Canyon	PCCY-00573	Japan	1994	10.99
Wetton, John/G. Downes	John Wetton/Geoffrey Downes	CD	Stallion	STALL103CD	England	2001	12.99

W

Artist	Title	Format	Label	Catalog No	Country	Released	Value
Wetton, John/Ken Hensley	More Than Conquerors	CD	Classic Rock	CRL0884	England	2002	14.99
Wetton, John/Ken Hensley	One Way Or Another	CD	Classic Rock	CRL0883	England	2002	14.99
Wetton, John/Mogul Trash	Self Titled (W/J Litherland/Colosseum)	CD	Disconforme	DISC1929CD	Andorra	1999	14.99
Wetton/Manzanera	One World	CD	Blueprint	BP241CD	Austria	1987	12.99
White Lion	Big Game	CD	Atlantic	7-81969-2	U.S.A.	1989	7.99
White Lion	Fight To Survive	CD	Grand Slamm	SLAMCD-1	U.S.A.	1985	24.99
White Lion	Mane Attraction	CD	Atlantic	7-82193-2	U.S.A.	1991	7.99
White Lion	Pride	CD	Atlantic	7-81768-2	U.S.A.	1987	8.99
White Lion	The Best Of	CD	Atlantic	7-82425-2	U.S.A.	1992	7.99
White Sister	Fashion By Passion	CD	FM	WKFM-XD-76	England	1986	16.99
White Sister	Self Titled	CD	Toshiba-EMI	TOCP-8102	Japan	1984	34.99
White Tiger	Raw	CD	M.I.L.	5100	U.S.A.	1999	27.99
White Tiger	Self Titled + 1	CD	E.M.C.	EMC-3653	U.S.A.	1999	27.99
White Tiger/Mark St. John	Magic Bullet Theory	CD	Loch Ness M.	LNMRCD-1003	U.S.A.	2002	9.99
White Tiger/Mark St. John	Project	CD	Loch Ness M.	LNMRCD-1002	U.S.A.	1999	9.99
White Witch	A Spiritual Gathering	CD	Capricorn	314-546-220-2	U.S.A.	1999	38.99
White Witch	Self Titled	CD	Capricorn	314-538-734-2	U.S.A.	1999	54.99
White Wolf	Endangered Species	CD	BMG	BVCP-7455	Japan	1996	24.99
White Wolf	Standing Alone	CD	BMG	BVCP-7454	Japan	1996	36.99
White, Alan/Jon Anderson	Ramshackled	CD	East West	AMCY-23	Japan	1990	54.99
White, Barry	Barry & Glodean	CD	Priority	P2-53687	U.S.A.	1981	49.99
White, Barry	Beware	CD	Southbound	CDSEWM-074	England	1993	53.99
White, Barry	Can't Get Enough	CD	Mercury	314-532-165-2	U.S.A.	1974	9.99
White, Barry	I've Got So Much To Give	CD	Mercury	814-836-2	U.S.A.	1973	53.99
White, Barry	Just Another Way To Say I Love You	CD	Mercury	314-532-166-2	U.S.A.	1975	9.99
White, Barry	Just For You Box Set	3CD	Mercury	314-514-143-2	U.S.A.	1992	24.99
White, Barry	Stone Gon'	CD	Mercury	836-516-2	U.S.A.	1973	9.99
White, Barry	Together Brothers (O.S.T.)	CD	Mercury	314-546-217-2	U.S.A.	1999	9.99
White, Barry/Love U. Orch.	He's All I Got	CD	Priority	08724-87083-2-5	U.S.A.	1992	19.99
White, Barry/Love U. Orch.	In Heat	CD	Mercury	636252-2	Germany	2003	7.99
White, Barry/Love U. Orch.	Rhapsody In White	CD	Mercury	314-558-201-2	U.S.A.	1974	9.99
White, Barry/Love U. Orch.	Self Titled	CD	MCA Victor	MVCM-442	Japan	1993	36.99
White, Barry/Love U. Orch.	The Best Of	CD	Mercury	314-526-945-2	U.S.A.	1995	7.99
White, Barry/Love U. Orch.	White Gold	CD	Mercury	314-546-218-2	U.S.A.	1999	7.99
White, Lynn	Love And Happiness	CD	Line	TLCD-9.00581-0	Germany	1988	29.99
White, Lynn	Success	CD	Line	TLCD-9.00361-0	Germany	1988	29.99
White, Rev. Billy C.	Pianist Envy	CD	Hightone	HCD-8051	U.S.A.	1994	7.99
Whitesnake	1978-1982 (Boxed Set)	4CD	Polydor	POCP-2221/4	Japan	1992	89.99
Whitesnake	1987 Versions	CD	Sony	23DP-5233	Japan	1987	24.99
Whitesnake	20th Century Masters: The Millennium	CD	Geffen	314-490-657-2	U.S.A.	2000	5.99
Whitesnake	Come An' Get It	CD	Geffen	9-24167-2	U.S.A.	1990	11.99
Whitesnake	Come An' Get It	Mini Lp	Polydor	POCP-9219	Japan	1999	24.99
Whitesnake	Come And Get It	CD	Universal	UICY-3725	Japan	2000	24.99
Whitesnake	Come And Get It	CD	Polydor	POCP-1824	Japan	1990	22.99
Whitesnake	Give Me All Your Love	CD Single	EMI	CDEM-23	England	1987	4.99
Whitesnake	Give Me All Your Love (3")	CD Single	Sony	10EP-3007	Japan	1987	14.99
Whitesnake	Greatest Hits	CD	Geffen	GEFD-24620	U.S.A.	1994	6.99
Whitesnake	Greatest Hits (Geffen Years)	CD	Sony	SRCS-7440	Japan	1994	17.99
Whitesnake	Here I Go Again	2CD	Universal	493-402-2	U.S.A.	2002	12.99
Whitesnake	Live At Hammersmith	Mini Lp	Polydor	POCP-9216	Japan	1999	24.99
Whitesnake	Live At Hammersmith	CD	Universal	UICY-3722	Japan	2000	24.99
Whitesnake	Live At Hammersmith	CD	Polydor	POCP-1821	Japan	1990	22.99
Whitesnake	Live In The Heart Of The City	CD	Polydor	POCP-1823	Japan	1990	22.99
Whitesnake	Live In The Heart Of The City	Mini Lp	Polydor	POCP-9218	Japan	1999	24.99
Whitesnake	Live In The Heart Of The City	CD	Universal	UICY-3724	Japan	2000	24.99
Whitesnake	Live In The Heart Of The City	CD	Geffen	9-24168-2	U.S.A.	1990	13.99
Whitesnake	Live In The Heart Of The City + 2	2CD	EMI	592-181-2	England	2003	13.99
Whitesnake	Love Hunter	Mini Lp	Polydor	POCP-9215	Japan	1999	24.99

W

Artist	Title	Format	Label	Catalog No	Country	Released	Value
Whitesnake	Love Hunter	CD	Universal	UICY-3721	Japan	2000	24.99
Whitesnake	Love Hunter	CD	Polydor	POCP-1820	Japan	1990	22.99
Whitesnake	Love Hunter	CD	Geffen	9-24176-2	U.S.A.	1990	15.99
Whitesnake	Ready An' Willing	CD	EMI	0777-7-52054-2-8	England	1978	14.99
Whitesnake	Ready An' Willing	Mini Lp	Polydor	POCP-9217	Japan	1999	24.99
Whitesnake	Ready An' Willing	CD	Polydor	POCP-1822	Japan	1990	22.99
Whitesnake	Ready An' Willing	CD	Universal	UICY-3723	Japan	2000	24.99
Whitesnake	Restless Heart + 3 (W/Cardboard Slv)	CD	Toshiba-EMI	TOCP-50090	Japan	1997	23.99
Whitesnake	Restless Heart Sampler (Promo)	CD	Toshiba-EMI	PCD-0825	Japan	1997	14.99
Whitesnake	Saints And Sinners	CD	Geffen	9-24173-2	U.S.A.	1990	9.99
Whitesnake	Saints And Sinners	Mini Lp	Polydor	POCP-9220	Japan	1999	24.99
Whitesnake	Saints And Sinners	CD	Universal	UICY-3726	Japan	2000	24.99
Whitesnake	Saints And Sinners	CD	Polydor	POCP-1825	Japan	1990	22.99
Whitesnake	Self Titled	CD	Geffen	9-24099-2	U.S.A.	1987	8.99
Whitesnake	Self Titled + 2	CD	EMI	CDP-7-46702-2	England	1987	10.99
Whitesnake	Slide It In	CD	Geffen	4018-2	U.S.A.	1990	9.99
Whitesnake	Slide It In (U.S. Remix)	CD	Sony	23DP-5232	Japan	1984	25.99
Whitesnake	Slide It In (UK Remix)	CD	Sony	32AP-2681	Japan	1984	25.99
Whitesnake	Slip Of The Tongue	CD	Geffen	9-24249-2	U.S.A.	1989	5.99
Whitesnake	Slip Of The Tongue	CD	Sony	CSCS-5001	Japan	1989	13.99
Whitesnake	Snakebite	CD	Geffen	9-24174-2	U.S.A.	1996	8.99
Whitesnake	Starkers In Tokyo	CD	Toshiba-EMI	TOCP-50314	Japan	1997	13.99
Whitesnake	The Best	CD	Polydor	POCP-1543	Japan	1991	22.99
Whitesnake	The Best	CD	Universal	UICY-2580	Japan	2000	24.99
Whitesnake	The Silver Anniversary Collection	2CD	EMI	581-694-2	Germany	2003	15.99
Whitesnake	Trouble	CD	Polydor	POCP-1819	Japan	1990	13.99
Whitesnake	Trouble	Mini Lp	Polydor	POCP-9214	Japan	1999	24.99
Whitesnake	Trouble	CD	Geffen	9-24175-2	U.S.A.	1990	18.99
Whitesnake/Bernie Marsden	And About Time, Too! + 3	CD	Purple	PUR-313	England	2001	17.99
Whitesnake/Bernie Marsden	Look At Me Now + 3	CD	Purple	PUR-314	England	2001	17.99
Whitesnake/Company Snakes	Burst The Bubble	CD	SPV	093-7-2682	Germany	2002	9.99
Whitesnake/Company Snakes	Here They Go Again: Live	CD	SPV	085-72112	Germany	2001	9.99
Whitesnake/David Coverdale	Greatest Hits	CD	Teichiku	TECX-20922	Japan	1995	11.99
Whitesnake/David Coverdale	Into The Light	CD	EMI	7243-5-28123-2-4	England	2000	10.99
Whitesnake/David Coverdale	Into The Light	CD	Toshiba-EMI	TOCP-65475	Japan	2000	19.99
Whitesnake/David Coverdale	Into The Light	CD	EMI	7243-8-23788-2-2	Holland	1997	9.99
Whitesnake/David Coverdale	Love Is Blind	CD Single	Toshiba-EMI	TOCP-40143	Japan	2000	26.99
Whitesnake/David Coverdale	Northwinds + 2	CD	Spitfire	SPT-15076-2	U.S.A.	2000	9.99
Whitesnake/David Coverdale	White Snake & Northwinds	CD	Teichiku	TECP-40813-4	Japan	1978	22.99
Whitesnake/David Coverdale	White Snake + 2	CD	Spitfire	SPT-15075-2	U.S.A.	2000	9.99
Whitesnake/David Coverdale	Whitesnake & Northwinds + 4	CD	Purple	PUR-340D	England	2003	17.99
Whitesnake/Doug Aldrich	Alter Ego	CD	Z Records	ZR1997057	England	2001	17.99
Whitesnake/Doug Aldrich	Bad Moon Rising - Blood On Streets	CD Single	Pony Canyon	PCCY-00425	Japan	1993	18.99
Whitesnake/Doug Aldrich	Bad Moon Rising - Flames On Moon	CD	Pony Canyon	PCCY-01412	Japan	1999	20.99
Whitesnake/Doug Aldrich	Bad Moon Rising - Full Moon Fever	CD Single	Pony Canyon	PCCY-00203	Japan	1991	20.99
Whitesnake/Doug Aldrich	Bad Moon Rising Self Titled	CD	Pony Canyon	PCCY-00202	Japan	1991	20.99
Whitesnake/Doug Aldrich	BMR (Opium M) No Holy War/TBOMD	CD	Avalanche	AVR-0034	U.S.A.	1996	11.99
Whitesnake/Doug Aldrich	BMR (Opium Music...) Minus Free	CD	Seagull	SICD-9611	Germany	1996	17.99
Whitesnake/Doug Aldrich	Burning Rain (Pleasure To Burn)	CD	Z Records	ZR1997042	England	2001	9.99
Whitesnake/Doug Aldrich	Burning Rain (Pleasure To Burn)	CD	Pony Canyon	PCCY-01475	Japan	2000	29.99
Whitesnake/Doug Aldrich	Burning Rain (Self Titled)	CD	Pony Canyon	PCCY-01353	Japan	1999	29.99
Whitesnake/Doug Aldrich	Burning Rain (Self Titled)	CD	Z Records	ZR1997041	England	2000	9.99
Whitesnake/Doug Aldrich	Electrovision	CD	Pony Canyon	PCCY-01128	Japan	1997	26.99
Whitesnake/Doug Aldrich	Highcentered	CD	Avalanche	AVR0028	U.S.A.	1996	19.99
Whitesnake/Doug Aldrich	Highcentered	CD	Pony Canyon	PCCY-541	Japan	1994	26.99
Whitesnake/Doug Aldrich	Lion - Dangerous Attraction	CD	Pony Canyon	PCCY-00542	Japan	1994	29.99
Whitesnake/Doug Aldrich	Lion - Trouble In Angel City	CD	Grand Slamm	SLAMCD-5	U.S.A.	1989	11.99
Whitesnake/Empire	Hypnotica	CD	Lion Music	LMC2110	Finland	2002	15.99

W

Artist	Title	Format	Label	Catalog No	Country	Released	Value
Whitesnake/Empire	Trading Souls	CD	Lion Music	LMC74	Finland	2003	19.99
Whitesnake/Snakes	Marsden/Moody Live In Europe	CD	Pony Canyon	PCCY-01318	Japan	1998	43.99
Whitesnake/Snakes	Once Bitten...+ 2	CD	Pony Canyon	PCCY-01271	Japan	1998	36.99
Whitesnake/Young & Moody	Young & Moody + 3	CD	Repertoire	RR-4633-WY	England	1996	14.99
Whitesnake/Young & Moody	Young & Moody/Nearest Hits Album	CD	Buried Tr.	TROV1	England	1992	12.99
White-Stripes	White Blood Cells (W/Bonus DVD)	CD	Sympathy For The	63881-27154-2RE	U.S.A.	2001	14.99
Who	20th Century Masters: The Millennium	CD	MCA	088-111-951-2	U.S.A.	1999	6.99
Who	30 Years Of Maximum R&B DJ Sampler	CD	MCA	MCA3P-3082	U.S.A.	1994	26.99
Who	30 Yrs. Of Maximum R & B Box Set	4CD	MCA	MCAD4-11020	U.S.A.	1994	24.99
Who	30th Anniversary Sampler (Promo)	CD	MCA	MCA3P-2592	U.S.A.	1993	22.99
Who	A Quick One + 10	CD	MCA	MCAD-11267	U.S.A.	1995	9.99
Who	Face Dances + 5	CD	MCA	MCAD-11634	U.S.A.	1997	8.99
Who	Hooligans	2CD	MCA	MCAD2-12001	U.S.A.	1981	24.99
Who	It's Hard + 4	CD	MCA	MCAD-11635	U.S.A.	1997	8.99
Who	Join Together Box Set	2CD	MCA	MCAD2-19501	U.S.A.	1990	14.99
Who	Live At Leeds	CD	MCA	MCAD-11215	U.S.A.	1995	8.99
Who	Live At Leeds (MFSL Gold Cd)	CD	Mobile Fidelity	UDCD-755	U.S.A.	1970	38.99
Who	Live At Leeds + 19 Deluxe Edition	2CD	MCA	088-112-618-2	U.S.A.	2001	16.99
Who	Live At The Isle Of Wight Festival 1970	2CD	Columbia	C2K-65084	U.S.A.	1996	19.99
Who	Live Leeds Box (Full Lp Size Inserts)	CD	MCA	MCAD-11230	U.S.A.	1998	49.99
Who	Live The Blues To The Bush/1999	2CD	Music Maker	293149L	U.S.A.	2000	29.99
Who	Magic Bus The Who On Tour	CD	MCA	MCAD-31333	U.S.A.	1968	7.99
Who	Meaty Beaty Big and Bouncy	CD	MCA	MCAD-37001	U.S.A.	1985	7.99
Who	My Generation	CD Single	Polydor	854-637-2	Germany	1996	5.99
Who	My Generation - The Very Best	CD	MCA	MCAD-11462	U.S.A.	1996	11.99
Who	My Generation + 17 (Deluxe Edition)	2CD	MCA	088-112-926-2	U.S.A.	2002	17.99
Who	Odds And Sods + 12	CD	MCA	MCAD-11718	U.S.A.	1998	9.99
Who	Quadrophenia	2CD	MCA	MCAD2-11463	U.S.A.	1996	15.99
Who	Quadrophenia (MFSL Gold Cd))	2CD	Mobile Fidelity	UDCD-2-550	U.S.A.	1973	92.99
Who	Rarities Vol. 1 / Vol 2 (1966 - 1972)	CD	Polydor K.K.	POCP-2350	Japan	1994	21.99
Who	Royal Albert (11, 22, 2000) Bonus Cd	3CD	SPV	093-7-4882	U.S.A.	2003	16.99
Who	Sell Out + 10	CD	MCA	MCAD-11268	U.S.A.	1995	6.99
Who	Sings My Generation	CD	MCA	MCAD-31330	U.S.A.	1966	7.99
Who	Talkin' 'Bout Their Generation	CD	Baktabak	CBAK-4067	England	1993	8.99
Who	The BBC Sessions + 7 (Bonus Disc)	CD	Polydor	088-111-960-2	U.S.A.	1999	30.99
Who	The Kids Are Alright (O.S.T.)	CD	MCA	314-543-694-2	U.S.A.	2001	8.99
Who	The Singles	CD	Polydor K.K.	POCP-2351	Japan	1994	26.99
Who	The Ultimate Collection (W/Bonus Cd)	2CD	MCA	088-112-877-2	U.S.A.	2002	18.99
Who	The Who By Numbers + 3	CD	MCA	MCAD-11493	U.S.A.	1996	8.99
Who	The Who Collection	CD	Polydor	IMCD4/1	England	1985	5.99
Who	Tommy	CD	MCA	MCAD-11417	U.S.A.	1996	8.99
Who	Tommy (MFSL Gold Cd)	CD	Mobile Fidelity	UDCD-533	U.S.A.	1969	28.99
Who	Tommy + 17 (Deluxe Edition)	2CD	MCA	B0001386-36	U.S.A.	2003	16.99
Who	Tommy Interactive Adv.	CD-Rom	Interplay	BS-C95-263-0	U.S.A.	1999	29.99
Who	Two's Missing	CD	MCA	MCAD-31222	U.S.A.	1987	49.99
Who	Who Are You (MFSL Gold Disc)	CD	Mobile Fidelity	UDCD-561	U.S.A.	1978	43.99
Who	Who Are You + 4	CD	MCA	MCAD-11492	U.S.A.	1996	8.99
Who	Who's Better, Who's Best	CD	MCA	MCAD-8031	U.S.A.	1988	8.99
Who	Who's Last (Live)	2CD	MCA	MCAD2-8018	U.S.A.	1984	21.99
Who	Who's Missing	CD	MCA	MCAD-31221	U.S.A.	1985	9.99
Who	Who's Next (MCA Gold Cd)	CD	MCA	MCAD-11312	U.S.A.	1971	23.99
Who	Who's Next (MFSL Gold Cd)	CD	Mobile Fidelity	UDCD-754	U.S.A.	1971	143.99
Who	Who's Next + 20 (Deluxe Edition)	2CD	MCA	088-113-056-2	U.S.A.	2003	16.99
Who	Who's Next + 7	CD	MCA	MCAD-11269	U.S.A.	1996	9.99
Who/London Philharmonic	Who's Serious	CD	BMG	09026-63111-2	U.S.A.	1998	7.99
Who/London Symphony Orch.	Tommy (Pinball Eyes Cover) R Stewart	CD	Rhino	R2-71113	U.S.A.	1972	59.99
Who/Original Cast	The Who's Tommy	2CD	RCA	BG2-61874	U.S.A.	1993	11.99
Who/Various Artists	Quadrophenia (O.S.T.)	2CD	Polydor K.K.	P48P-25060/1	Japan	1979	21.99

W

Artist	Title	Format	Label	Catalog No	Country	Released	Value
Who/Various Artists	Quadrophenia (O.S.T.)	CD	Polydor	314-543-691-2	U.S.A.	2000	8.99
Who/Various Artists	Tommy (O.S.T.)	2CD	Polydor	422-841-121-2	U.S.A.	2000	19.99
Whodini	Escape	CD	Avex Trax	AVCZ-95071	Japan	1984	116.99
Why Store	The Why Store	CD	Line	LICD-9.01370-0	Germany	2000	7.99
Widespread Panic	Ain't Life Grand	CD	Capricorn	9-42027-2	U.S.A.	1994	8.99
Widespread Panic	Another Joyous Occasion	CD	Widespread Panic	12	U.S.A.	2000	8.99
Widespread Panic	Ball	CD	Sanctuary	06076-84604-2	U.S.A.	2003	8.99
Widespread Panic	Bombs And Butterflies	CD	Capricorn	314-534-396-2	U.S.A.	1997	8.99
Widespread Panic	Don't Tell The Band (W/Bonus Cd)	CD	Sanctuary	06076-84507-2	U.S.A.	2001	9.99
Widespread Panic	Don't Tell The Band Bonus Ep	CD	Sanctuary	D6076845072VA	U.S.A.	2001	6.99
Widespread Panic	Everyday	CD	Capricorn	9-42013-2	U.S.A.	1993	9.99
Widespread Panic	Light Fuse Get Away	2CD	Capricorn	314-558-145-2	U.S.A.	1998	14.99
Widespread Panic	Live Backyard Austin, TX (Bonus DVD)	2CD	Sanctuary	06076-86350-2	U.S.A.	2003	12.99
Widespread Panic	Live In The Classic City	3CD	Sanctuary	06076-84552-2	U.S.A.	2002	16.99
Widespread Panic	Panic In The Streets (W/Bonus Cd)	2CD	Volcano	828765372022	U.S.A.	2003	12.99
Widespread Panic	Selections Live In The Classic City (DJ)	CD	Sanctuary	SANSP-84552-2	U.S.A.	2002	9.99
Widespread Panic	Space Rangler	CD	Capricorn	9-42001-2	U.S.A.	1992	8.99
Widespread Panic	'Til The Medicine Takes	CD	Capricorn	314-546-203-2	U.S.A.	1999	8.99
Widespread Panic	Widespread Panic	CD	Capricorn	9-40001-2	U.S.A.	1991	7.99
Widowmaker/Ariel Bender	Straightfaced Fighters	2CD	Castle	CMDDD586	England	2002	18.99
Widowmaker/Ariel Bender	Too Late To Cry	CD	Line	JECD-9.00867-0	Germany	1989	30.99
Widowmaker/Ariel Bender	Widowmaker	CD	Line	JECD-9.00858-0	Germany	1989	26.99
Wiedlin, Jane	Fur	CD	EMI	0777-748683-2-7	U.S.A.	1988	10.99
Wiedlin, Jane	Jane Wiedlin	CD	I.R.S.	IRSD-5638	U.S.A.	1985	24.99
Wiedlin, Jane	Kissproof World	CD	Painful Discs	PD-001	U.S.A.	2000	7.99
Wiedlin, Jane	Tangled	CD	EMI	7-90741-2	U.S.A.	1990	24.99
Wiedlin, Jane	The Very Best Of Jane Wiedlin	CD	EMI	0777-7-89663-2-6	U.S.A.	1993	31.99
Wiedlin, Jane	World On Fire - The Mixes (Promo)	CD Single	EMI	DPRO-4575	U.S.A.	1990	21.99
Wilburn Brothers	The Hits Of The	CD	Edsel	EDCD-540	England	1998	38.99
Wild Boyz/Glam Band	Unleashed !	CD	Polaris	PRI-2311-1	Canada	1991	34.99
Wild Turkey	Battle Hymn	CD	Edsel	EDCD-333	England	1991	17.99
Wild Turkey	Live In Edinburgh	CD	Audio Archives	AACD-043	England	2001	13.99
Wild Turkey	Stealer Of Years	CD	Transatlantic	TRACD-314	England	1999	7.99
Wild Turkey	Turkey + 3	CD	Progressive Line	PL-541	Australia	2001	13.99
Wilde, Kim	You Keep Me Hangin' On (Remixes)	CD Single	Warner Bros.	28XD-840	Japan	1987	40.99
Williams Jr., Hank	The Pressure Is On	CD	Curb	D2-77727	U.S.A.	1981	4.99
Williams Sr., Hank	The Original (Promo/Timeless)	CD	Lost Highway	02162	U.S.A.	2002	43.99
Williams, Andy	47 Classic Tracks Box Set (4 Lps)	2CD	Collectables	COL-0030	U.S.A.	1979	33.99
Williams, Deniece	Niecy	CD	Sony	SRCS-6485	Japan	1982	104.99
Williams, Deniece	Songbird	CD	Sony	SRCS-6432	Japan	1977	279.99
Williams, Deniece	When Love Comes Calling	CD	Sony	SRCS-6433	Japan	1979	19.99
Williams, Jerry Lynn/N Hopkins	Peacemaker (W/Clapton/S R Vaughn)	CD	Urge	URGE-333	U.S.A.	1996	7.99
Williams, John	Close Encounters Third Kind (O.S.T.)	CD	Varese	VSD-5275	U.S.A.	1977	12.99
Williams, John	Empire Of The Sun (O.S.T.)	CD	Warner Bros.	9-25668-2	U.S.A.	1987	9.99
Williams, John	Empire Strikes + 11 (Holographic)	2CD	RCA	09026-68747-2	U.S.A.	1997	19.99
Williams, John	Empire Strikes Back Special Edition	CD Single	RCA	09026-68821-2	U.S.A.	1997	6.99
Williams, John	Harry Potter/Sorcerer's... (Spec 1st Ed)	CD	Warner Bros.	83491-2	U.S.A.	2001	15.99
Williams, John	Harry Potter/The Sorcerer's... (Cd Rom)	2CD	Warner Bros.	7567-93086-2	Australia	2001	10.99
Williams, John	Hear Star Wars The Way It... (Promo)	CD	RCA	RCDJ-68795-2	U.S.A.	1997	12.99
Williams, John	Indiana Jones/Temple Of Doom (O.S.T.)	CD	Polydor K.K.	POCP-2014	U.S.A.	1984	49.99
Williams, John	Jaws 2 (O.S.T.)	CD	Varese	VSD-5328	U.S.A.	1978	53.99
Williams, John	Raiders Of The Lost Ark + 12 (O.S.T.)	CD	DCC	DZS-090	U.S.A.	1995	39.99
Williams, John	Return Of The Jedi - Special Edition	CD Single	RCA	09026-68974-2	U.S.A.	1997	6.99
Williams, John	Schindler's List (O.S.T.)	CD	MCA	MCAD-10969	U.S.A.	1993	9.99
Williams, John	Seven Years In Tibet (O.S.T.)	CD	Sony	SK-60271	U.S.A.	1997	8.99
Williams, John	Star Wars A New Hope - Spec Edition	CD Single	RCA	09026-68973-2	U.S.A.	1997	6.99
Williams, John	Star Wars Episode I: Ult Ed. (65 Trks.)	2CD	Sony	S2K-89460	U.S.A.	2000	15.99
Williams, John	Star Wars New Hope + 7 (Holographic)	2CD	RCA	09026-68746-2	U.S.A.	1997	15.99

W

Artist	Title	Format	Label	Catalog No	Country	Released	Value
Williams, John	Star Wars Ret. Jedi + 25 (Holographic)	2CD	RCA	09026-68748-2	U.S.A.	1997	15.99
Williams, John	Star Wars Trilogy Box Set	4CD	20th Century Fox	07822-11012-2	U.S.A.	1993	29.99
Williams, John	Star Wars: Phantom Menace (17 Trks)	CD	Sony	SK-61816	U.S.A.	1999	8.99
Williams, John	The Accidental Tourist	CD	Warner Bros.	25846-2	U.S.A.	1989	72.99
Williams, John	The Poseidon Adventure (Only 3000)	CD	Film Score Monthly	VOL.1 NO.2	U.S.A.	1998	58.99
Williams, John	The Star Wars Trilogy	CD	Sony	SK-45947	U.S.A.	1990	7.99
Williams, Lucinda	Car Wheels On A Gravel Road	CD	Mercury	314-558-338-2	U.S.A.	1998	10.99
Williams, Lucinda	Essence	CD	Lost Highway	088-170-197-2	U.S.A.	2001	8.99
Williams, Lucinda	Lucinda Williams + 6	CD	Koch	KOC-CD-8005	U.S.A.	1998	12.99
Williams, Lucinda	Passionate Kisses	CD Single	Rough Trade	ROUGH-US-66CD	U.S.A.	1989	8.99
Williams, Lucinda	Ramblin'	CD	Folkways	CD-SF-40042	U.S.A.	1991	8.99
Williams, Lucinda	Sweet Old World	CD	Elektra	61351-2	U.S.A.	1992	10.99
Williams, Mason	Mason Williams Phonograph Record	CD	Warner Bros.	2-1729	U.S.A.	1990	9.99
Williams, Mason	Music 1968-1971	CD	Vanguard	VCD-137/38	U.S.A.	1992	8.99
Williams, Patrick	Threshold	CD	Soundwings	SWD2107	U.S.A.	1988	53.99
Williams, Paul	A&M Greatest Hits	CD	Polydor K.K.	POCM-1536	Japan	1997	24.99
Williams, Paul	Back To Love Again	CD	Pioneer	PICP-1132	Japan	1997	24.99
Williams, Paul	Bugsy Malone (O.S.T.)	Mini Lp	Universal	UICY-9186	Japan	1976	24.99
Williams, Paul	Here Comes Inspiration	CD	Pony Canyon	PCCY-10187	Japan	1991	59.99
Williams, Paul	Just An Old Fashioned Love Song	Mini Lp	Universal	UICY-9185	Japan	1971	24.99
Williams, Paul	Life Goes On	CD	Polydor K.K.	POCM-2024	Japan	1995	35.99
Williams, Paul	No Ordinary Fool	CD	Polydor K.K.	POCM-2027	Japan	1975	59.99
Williams, Paul	Phantom Of The Paradise (O.S.T.)	CD	A&M	CD-69831	Canada	1974	19.99
Williams, Paul	Someday Man	Mini Lp	Warner Bros.	WPCR-11465	Japan	1970	24.99
Williams, Paul/Friends	In Memory Of Robert Johnson	CD	Line	LICD-9.00300-0	Germany	1989	14.99
Williams, Robbie	Angels	CD	Chrysalis	7243-8-84983-2-6	England	1997	8.99
Williams, Robbie	Angels	CD Single	Toshiba-EMI	TOCP-50609	Japan	1998	24.99
Williams, Robbie	Angels (Ltd W/3 Postcards)	CD Single	Chrysalis	CDCHSS5072	England	1997	23.99
Williams, Robbie	Angels (Promo)	CD Single	Chrysalis	CDCHSDJ-5072	England	1997	10.99
Williams, Robbie	Escapology	CD	Virgin	7243-5-81777-2-5	U.S.A.	2003	9.99
Williams, Robbie	Escapology (Promo)	CD	Virgin	RWESCDJ001	England	2002	12.99
Williams, Robbie	Escapology Ltd Box Set	CD	Chrysalis	724358057928	Taiwan	2002	35.99
Williams, Robbie	Escapology Sampler (Promo)	CD	Virgin	177110	U.S.A.	2003	14.99
Williams, Robbie	Eternity (Promo Embossed)	CD Single	Chrysalis	CDHSDJ5126	England	2001	17.99
Williams, Robbie	Eternity/The Road To Mandalay	CD Single	Chrysalis	7243-8-79538-2-6	England	2001	7.99
Williams, Robbie	I've Been Expecting You + 2	CD	Toshiba-EMI	TOCP-50717	Japan	1998	22.99
Williams, Robbie	Let Love Be Your (Promo Embossed)	CD Single	Chrysalis	CDHSDJ5124	England	2001	10.99
Williams, Robbie	Let Love Be Your Energy	CD Single	Chrysalis	7243-8-79170-0-2	Holland	2001	8.99
Williams, Robbie	Let Me Entertain You	CD Single	Chrysalis	85984-2-2	Germany	1988	10.99
Williams, Robbie	Let Me Entertain You	CD Single	Chrysalis	CDCHSS-5080	England	1998	6.99
Williams, Robbie	Life Thru A Lens	CD	Chrysalis	7243-8-21313-2-8	Holland	1997	10.99
Williams, Robbie	Life Thru A Lens + 2	CD	Toshiba-EMI	TOCP-50094	Japan	1997	14.99
Williams, Robbie	Millennium (Disc 2)	CD Single	Chrysalis	7243-8-86091-2-8	England	1998	7.99
Williams, Robbie	Millennium (Promo)	CD Single	Chrysalis	CDCHSDJ-5099	England	1998	14.99
Williams, Robbie	Millennium CD 1 (W/3 Postcards)	CD Single	Chrysalis	CDCHSS5099	England	1998	9.99
Williams, Robbie	Mr. Bojangles	CD Single	Chrysalis	7243-550651-2-4	Italy	2002	18.99
Williams, Robbie	No Regrets (Ltd Edition)	CD Single	Chrysalis	7243-8-86419-2-0	England	1998	9.99
Williams, Robbie	No Regrets (Ltd Edition)	CD Single	Chrysalis	CDCHSS5100	England	1998	10.99
Williams, Robbie	No Regrets/Antmusic	CD Single	Chrysalis	7243-8-86419-2-0	England	1998	10.99
Williams, Robbie	Old Before I Die	CD Single	Chrysalis	83846-2-9	Germany	1997	9.99
Williams, Robbie	Old Before I Die	CD Single	Chrysalis	7243-8-83822-2-9	Italy	1997	10.99
Williams, Robbie	Rock DJ	CD Single	Chrysalis	7243-889210-2-2	EU	2000	9.99
Williams, Robbie	She's The One	CD Single	EMI	7243-8-87938-0-3	France	1999	6.99
Williams, Robbie	She's The One	CD Single	Chrysalis	7243-8-87914-0-3	England	1999	10.99
Williams, Robbie	She's The One (Promo)	CD Single	Chrysalis	CDCHSDJ-5112	England	1999	20.99
Williams, Robbie	Supreme (Cd 1)	CD Single	Chrysalis	7243-8-89790-0-9	EU	2000	5.99
Williams, Robbie	Supreme (Cd 2)	CD Single	Chrysalis	7243-8-89781-2-5	England	2000	7.99
Williams, Robbie	Swing When You're Winning + 6 VCD	2CD	Chrysalis	7243-536826-2-0	England	2001	24.99

W

Artist	Title	Format	Label	Catalog No	Country	Released	Value
Williams, Robbie	The Ego Has Landed	CD	Capitol	7243-4-97726-2-5	U.S.A.	1998	6.99
Williams, Robbie/K. Minogue	Kids	CD Single	Chrysalis	7243-8-89441-0-6	England	2000	9.99
Williams, Robbie/K. Minogue	Kids	CD Single	Chrysalis	7243-8-89441-2-0	England	2000	9.99
Williams, Robbie/K. Minogue	Kids (Cd 2)	CD Single	EMI	88944106	Taiwan	2000	24.99
Williams, Robbie/K. Minogue	Kids (Promo)	CD Single	Chrysalis	CDCHSDJ5119	England	2000	17.99
Williams, Robbie/N. Kidman	Somethin' Stupid	CD Single	Chrysalis	7243-550317-0-9	England	2001	10.99
Williams, Robin	Reality...What A Concept	CD	Laugh.com	LGH-1104	U.S.A.	2002	11.99
Willis, Kelly	Bang Bang	CD	MCA	MCAD-10141	U.S.A.	1991	8.99
Willis, Kelly	What I Deserve	CD	Rykodisc	RCD-10458	U.S.A.	1999	6.99
Wilson Phillips	Greatest Hits	CD	SBK	72435-22085-2-4	U.S.A.	2000	8.99
Wilson Phillips	Shadow And Light	CD	SBK	CDP-98924	U.S.A.	1992	6.99
Wilson Phillips	Wilson Phillips	CD	SBK	CDP-93745	U.S.A.	1990	8.99
Wilson Phillips	You're In Love (Promo)	CD Single	SBK	DPRO-19729-W	U.S.A.	1991	11.99
Wilson, Brian	(Leatherbound Promo W/Lithograph)	CD	Sire	PRO-CD-3176	U.S.A.	1988	84.99
Wilson, Brian	Brian Wilson + 14 (Deluxe)	CD	Rhino	R2-79960	U.S.A.	2000	9.99
Wilson, Brian	Gettin' In Over My Head	CD	Rhino	R2-76471	U.S.A.	2004	8.99
Wilson, Brian	I Just Wasn't Made...(Promo Interview)	CD	MCA	MCA5P-3575	U.S.A.	1995	29.99
Wilson, Brian	I Just Wasn't Meant For These Times	CD	MCA	MCAD-11270	U.S.A.	1995	8.99
Wilson, Brian	Imagination	CD	Giant	9-24703-2	U.S.A.	1998	7.99
Wilson, Brian	Imagination (Dj/Advance/Diff. Artwork)	CD	Giant	2-24703-AB	U.S.A.	1998	21.99
Wilson, Brian	Imagination (W/ Best Buy Int. Cd)	2CD	Giant	2-24703-2	U.S.A.	1998	69.99
Wilson, Brian	Imagination + 1	CD	BMG	BVCG706	Japan	1999	32.99
Wilson, Brian	Live At The Roxy Theatre + 5	2CD	Brimel	SANDD107	U.S.A.	2002	19.99
Wilson, Brian	Love And Mercy	CD Single	Sire	921-032-2	Germany	1988	7.99
Wilson, Brian	Pet Sounds Live + 2	CD	Toshiba-EMI	TOCP-66088	Japan	2002	32.99
Wilson, Brian	Your Imagination	CD Single	Giant	2-17216	U.S.A.	1998	4.99
Wilson, Brian/Van D Parks	Words + Music (Promo)	CD	Warner Bros.	PRO-CD-8029	U.S.A.	1994	29.99
Wilson, Brian/Van D Parks	Orange Crate Art	CD	Warner Bros.	9-45427-2	U.S.A.	1995	6.99
Wilson, Carl	Long Promised Road (Promo)	CD	Capitol	DPRO12138	U.S.A.	1999	124.99
Wilson, Carl	Self Titled	CD	Sony	SRCS-6102	Japan	1981	162.99
Wilson, Carl	Youngblood	CD	Sony	SRCS-6103	Japan	1984	193.99
Wilson, Carnie & Wendy	Hey Santa!	CD	SBK	K2-27113	U.S.A.	1993	7.99
Wilson, Dennis	Pacific Ocean Blue	CD	Epic	ZK-34354	U.S.A.	1977	74.99
Wilson, Murry/Brian's Dad	The Many Moods Of Murry Wilson	CD	Toshiba-EMI	TOCP-66037	Japan	2002	29.99
Wilson, Nancy/Heart	Live At McCabe's Guitar Shop	CD	Epic	EK-69837	U.S.A.	1999	8.99
Wilson, Nancy/Jazz	What's New	CD	Toshiba-EMI	CP38-3010	Japan	1982	54.99
Wilson, Ray/Genesis	Change + 3	CD	Inside Out	6-93723-00262-0	Germany	2003	14.99
Wilson, Tony	Do Your Own Thing	CD	Line	RTCD-9.01183-0	Germany	1992	18.99
Wilson, Tony	Walking The Highwire	CD	Line	LICD-9.01222-0	Germany	1992	14.99
Wind In The Willows/Blondie	Self Titled (W/Blondie)	CD	Edsel	EDCD-642	England	2000	14.99
Windham Hell	Reflective Depths Imbibe	CD	Moribund	DEAD-22-CD	U.S.A.	2002	14.99
Windham Hell	South Facing Epitaph	CD	Moribund	DEAD-07-CD	U.S.A.	1994	14.99
Windham Hell	Window Of Souls	CD	Moribund	DEAD-13-CD	U.S.A.	1996	14.99
Winningham, Mare/Actress	Lonesomers	CD	Razor & Tie	82837-2	U.S.A.	1998	11.99
Winningham, Mare/Actress	What Might Be	CD	Bay Cities	BCD-2007	U.S.A.	1992	28.99
Winston, George	All the Seasons of George Winston	CD	Windham Hill	01934-11266-2	U.S.A.	1998	8.99
Winston, George	December - 20th Anniversary Edition	CD	Windham Hill	01934-11611-2	U.S.A.	2001	8.99
Winston, George	Forest	CD	Windham Hill	01934-11157-2	U.S.A.	1994	8.99
Winston, George	Selections By George Winston	CD	Windham Hill	WD-96-23	U.S.A.	1996	7.99
Winston, George/Vince Guaral	Linus & Lucy	CD	Windham Hill	01934-11184-2R	U.S.A.	1996	10.99
Winstone, Norma	Edge Of Time	CD	Disconforme	DISC1962CD	Italy	2000	9.99
Winter, Edgar	Collection	CD	Rhino	R2-70895	U.S.A.	1986	8.99
Winter, Edgar	Entrance	CD	Epic	EK-48536	U.S.A.	1970	9.99
Winter, Edgar	I'm Not A Kid Anymore	CD	Thunderbolt	CDTB-156	England	1996	8.99
Winter, Edgar	Jasmine Nightdreams	CD	Sony	SICP-8009	Japan	2002	24.99
Winter, Edgar	Jasmine Nightdreams (DTS)	CD	Sony	710215-4420-2-0	U.S.A.	2002	14.99
Winter, Edgar	Mission Earth	CD	Rhino	R2-70709	U.S.A.	1989	8.99
Winter, Edgar	Roadwork	CD	Epic	EGK-91249	U.S.A.	1972	7.99

W

Artist	Title	Format	Label	Catalog No	Country	Released	Value
Winter, Edgar	Shock Treatment	CD	Epic	EK-32461	U.S.A.	1974	24.99
Winter, Edgar	The Best Of	CD	Epic	467507-2	Germany	1990	8.99
Winter, Edgar	The Best Of	CD	Epic	EK-85927	U.S.A.	2002	8.99
Winter, Edgar	The Edgar Winter Album	CD	Sony	SICP-8011	Japan	2002	25.99
Winter, Edgar	White Trash (MFSL Gold Cd)	CD	Mobile Fidelity	UDCD-715	U.S.A.	1971	21.99
Winter, Edgar/Group	They Only Come Out At Night	CD	Epic	EK-31584	U.S.A.	1972	6.99
Winter, Edgar/Leon Russell	The Real Deal (Montrose/Derringer)	CD	Thunderbolt	CDTB-182	England	2002	8.99
Winter, Edgar/Rick Derringer	Live In Japan	CD	Thunderbolt	CDTB-134	England	2002	14.99
Winter, Edgar/Rick Derringer	Live In Japan + 2	CD	Teichiku	TECP-28255	Japan	1990	19.99
Winter, Edgar/W/Johnny	Winter Blues (L Russell/R Derringer)	CD	Pyramid	R2-75808	U.S.A.	1999	8.99
Winter, Edgar/White Trash	Recycled	CD	Sony	SICP-8010	Japan	2002	25.99
Winter, Johnny	38 32 20 Blues	CD	Go	7243-564021-2-6	England	2002	6.99
Winter, Johnny	3rd Degree	CD	Alligator	ALCD-4748	U.S.A.	1990	8.99
Winter, Johnny	A Lone Star Kind Of A Day	CD	Relix	RRCD-2042	U.S.A.	1990	8.99
Winter, Johnny	A Rock & Roll Collection	2CD	Columbia	C2K-46985	U.S.A.	1994	12.99
Winter, Johnny	A Stranger In Your Eyes	CD	Spalax	14601	France	1968	15.99
Winter, Johnny	And...../Live	CD	BGO	BGOCD610	England	2004	15.99
Winter, Johnny	Best Of	CD	Columbia	CK-85926	U.S.A.	2002	8.99
Winter, Johnny	Birds Can't Row Boats (Rarities)	CD	Relix	RRCD-2034	U.S.A.	1988	28.99
Winter, Johnny	Black Cat Bone - El. Bluesman Vol. 2	CD	Thunderbolt	CDTB-193	England	1999	8.99
Winter, Johnny	Blues In A Box	3CD	M.I.L.	9901	U.S.A.	1998	19.99
Winter, Johnny	Captured Live!	CD	Blue Sky	ZK-33944	U.S.A.	1976	8.99
Winter, Johnny	Deluxe Edition	CD	Alligator	ALCD-5609	U.S.A.	2001	7.99
Winter, Johnny	Ease My Pain	CD	Sundazed	SC-6071	U.S.A.	1997	8.99
Winter, Johnny	Electric Blues Man	2CD	Thunderbolt	CDTB-509	England	1999	24.99
Winter, Johnny	Guitar Slinger	CD	Alligator	ALCD-4735	U.S.A.	1984	8.99
Winter, Johnny	Hey, Where's Your Brother?	CD	Capitol	0777-7-86512-2	U.S.A.	1992	8.99
Winter, Johnny	Jack Daniels Kind Of Day	CD	Thunderbolt	CDTB-142	England	1996	24.99
Winter, Johnny	Johnny Winter + 5	CD	Columbia	CK-85734	U.S.A.	2004	8.99
Winter, Johnny	Let Me In	CD	Capitol	0777-7-86244-2	U.S.A.	1991	7.99
Winter, Johnny	Liberty Hall Sessions (W/J Reed)	CD	Thunderbolt	CDTB-175	England	2002	11.99
Winter, Johnny	Live At The Texas Opry House	CD	Thunderbolt	CDTB-185	England	2002	11.99
Winter, Johnny	Live In Houston Busted In Austin	CD	Thunderbolt	CDTB-100	England	1996	34.99
Winter, Johnny	Live In NYC 1997	CD	Virgin	7243-8-45527-2	U.S.A.	1998	8.99
Winter, Johnny	Live Johnny Winter And	CD	Columbia	CK-30475	U.S.A.	1971	11.99
Winter, Johnny	Livin' In The Blues	CD	Sundazed	SC-6070	U.S.A.	1997	8.99
Winter, Johnny	Lone Star Shootout	CD	Fuel 2000	302-061-160-2	U.S.A.	2001	8.99
Winter, Johnny	No Time To Live	CD	Thunderbolt	CDTB-136	England	2002	11.99
Winter, Johnny	Nothin' But The Blues	CD	Blue Sky	ZK-34813	U.S.A.	1990	8.99
Winter, Johnny	Original Winter: The Sixties Sessions	CD	Thunderbolt	CDTB-218	England	2001	11.99
Winter, Johnny	Progressive Blues Experiment	CD	Magic	5244222	France	1999	15.99
Winter, Johnny	Raised On Rock	CD	Prestige	CDSGP0306	U.S.A.	2002	6.99
Winter, Johnny	Raw To The Bone	CD	Thunderbolt	CDTB-126	England	2002	8.99
Winter, Johnny	Saints & Sinners	CD	Columbia	CK-66420	U.S.A.	1996	8.99
Winter, Johnny	Scorchin' Blues	CD	Blue Sky	ZK-52466	U.S.A.	1992	6.99
Winter, Johnny	Second Winter	CD	Columbia	CK-9947	U.S.A.	1969	7.99
Winter, Johnny	Second Winter (MFSL Gold Cd)	CD	Mobile Fidelity	UDCD-753	U.S.A.	1969	28.99
Winter, Johnny	Serious Business	CD	Alligator	ALCD-4742	U.S.A.	1985	8.99
Winter, Johnny	Still Alive And Well + 2	CD	Columbia	CK-66421	U.S.A.	1994	9.99
Winter, Johnny	Still Alive And Well/Captured Live !	CD	BGO	BGOCD478	England	2002	15.99
Winter, Johnny	Suicide Won't.. - El. Bluesman Vol. 1	CD	Thunderbolt	CDTB-192	U.S.A.	1998	8.99
Winter, Johnny	Texas Blues	2CD	Snapper	SMD-CD-185	England	1998	12.99
Winter, Johnny	The Return Of Johnny Guitar	CD	Music Club	MCCD-270	U.S.A.	2000	8.99
Winter, Johnny	The Winter Of '88	CD	MCA	MCAD-42241	U.S.A.	1988	12.99
Artist, Johnny	Walking By Myself	CD	Relix	RRCD-2048	U.S.A.	1992	8.99
Winter, Johnny	White Heat (W/J Reed/W Dixon)	CD	M.I.L.	3031	U.S.A.	1997	8.99
Winter, Johnny	White Hot & Blue	CD	Tristar	35276	England	1995	28.99
Winter, Johnny	White Hot Blues	CD	Columbia	CK-65213	U.S.A.	1997	9.99

W

Artist	Title	Format	Label	Catalog No	Country	Released	Value
Winter, Johnny	White Lightning (Live Dallas)	CD	Thunderbolt	CDTB-149	U.S.A.	1996	8.99
Winter, Johnny	Winter Essentials 1960-1967	CD	Fuel 2000	302-061-309-2	U.S.A.	2003	8.99
Winter, Johnny	Winter Heat	CD	M.I.L.	3037	U.S.A.	1998	8.99
Winter, Johnny/Calvin Johnson	Blues To The Bone	CD	Relix	RRCD-2054	U.S.A.	1995	7.99
Winter, Johnny/Uncle J Turner	Back In Beaumont (Uncle J Turner)	CD	Thunderbolt	CDTB-77	England	1997	11.99
Winters, Jonathan	Peter And The Wolf (Winters Narrates)	CD	Angel	7243-8-49918-2	U.S.A.	1989	27.99
Winters, Jonathan	Stuff'N Nonsense	CD	Laugh.com	LGH-1059	U.S.A.	2001	8.99
Winters, Jonathan	Wonderful World Of	CD	Laugh.com	LGH-1103	U.S.A.	2002	8.99
Winwood, Steve	20th Century Masters: The Millennium	CD	Island	314-564-791-2	U.S.A.	1999	8.99
Winwood, Steve	About Time	CD	Wincraft	880047-0001-2	U.S.A.	2003	8.99
Winwood, Steve	About Time + 3	2CD	Sanctuary	SANDD130	England	2004	24.99
Winwood, Steve	Arc Of A Diver (MFSL Gold Cd)	CD	Mobile Fidelity	UDCD-579	U.S.A.	1980	24.99
Winwood, Steve	Arc Of The Diver	CD	Island	842-365-2	U.S.A.	1990	7.99
Winwood, Steve	Back In The High Life	CD	Island	830-148-2	U.S.A.	1986	6.99
Winwood, Steve	Back In The High Life (MFSL Gold Cd)	CD	Mobile Fidelity	UDCD-611	U.S.A.	1986	24.99
Winwood, Steve	Chronicles	CD	Island	842-364-2	U.S.A.	1993	6.99
Winwood, Steve	Junction Seven	CD	Virgin	7243-8-44059-2	U.S.A.	1997	6.99
Winwood, Steve	Keep On Running	CD	Island	848-745-2	Germany	1996	14.99
Winwood, Steve	Refugees Of The Heart	CD	Virgin	2-91405	U.S.A.	1990	6.99
Winwood, Steve	Roll With It	CD	Atlantic	90946-2	U.S.A.	1990	7.99
Winwood, Steve	Steve Winwood	CD	Island	842-774-2	U.S.A.	1990	7.99
Winwood, Steve	Steve Winwood (MFSL Gold Cd)	CD	Mobile Fidelity	UDCD-691	U.S.A.	1977	19.99
Winwood, Steve	Talking Back To Night (MFSL Gold)	CD	Mobile Fidelity	UDCD-674	U.S.A.	1982	24.99
Winwood, Steve	Talking Back To The Night	CD	Island	842-366-4	U.S.A.	1990	6.99
Winwood, Steve	The Finer Things Box Set	4CD	Island	314-516-860-2	U.S.A.	1995	39.99
Wirtschaftswunver	Salmobray	CD	Line	DKCD-9.51053-0	Germany	1991	29.99
Wishbone Ash	Almighty Blues	CD	Classic Rock	CRL1139	England	2003	12.99
Wishbone Ash	Archive Series	CD	Rialto	RMCD-224	U.S.A.	1998	9.99
Wishbone Ash	Argus + 3	CD	MCA	088-112-816-2	U.S.A.	2002	8.99
Wishbone Ash	Bare Bones	CD	Sanctuary	06076-81131-2	U.S.A.	2002	8.99
Wishbone Ash	BBC Radio One Live	CD	Griffin	GCD-338-2	U.S.A.	1995	9.99
Wishbone Ash	BBC Radio One Live	CD	Windsong	WINCD004	England	1992	14.99
Wishbone Ash	Bona Fide	CD	Talking Elephant	TECD040	England	2002	9.99
Wishbone Ash	Classic Ash	CD	MCA	MCAD-10578	Germany	1977	9.99
Wishbone Ash	Distillation	3CD	Repertoire	REP-4649-CX	Germany	1998	44.99
Wishbone Ash	Four	CD	MCA	MCAD-10350	U.S.A.	1991	9.99
Wishbone Ash	Front Page News	CD	MCA	MCAD-11027	U.S.A.	1994	9.99
Wishbone Ash	Here To Hear	CD	I.R.S.	IRSD-82006	U.S.A.	1990	8.99
Wishbone Ash	Illuminations	CD	HTD	HTD-CD-67	England	1996	11.99
Wishbone Ash	In Concert (W/Bonus DVD)	2CD	Classic Rock	CRL1016	England	2002	15.99
Wishbone Ash	Just Testing	CD	MCA	MCLD19375	England	1997	11.99
Wishbone Ash	Live At The BBC	CD	Band Of Joy	BOJCD-012	England	1996	14.99
Wishbone Ash	Live Dates	2 Mini LP	Universal	UICY-2384/5	Japan	2000	49.99
Wishbone Ash	Live Dates	2CD	BGO	BGOCD293	England	2002	11.99
Wishbone Ash	Live Dates	2CD	MCA	MCAD2-10396	U.S.A.	1991	11.99
Wishbone Ash	Live Dates 3	CD	Eagle	EAMCD325	England	2001	11.99
Wishbone Ash	Live In Bristol	CD	Classic Rock	CRL1045	England	2003	12.99
Wishbone Ash	Live In Chicago	CD	Permanent	PERM-CD-6	England	1992	8.99
Wishbone Ash	Live In Geneva	CD	Pavement	76962-32255-2-7	U.S.A.	1997	8.99
Wishbone Ash	Live In Windy City	CD	Angel Air	SJPCD112	England	2002	11.99
Wishbone Ash	Live: Time Line	CD	Receiver	RRCD-216	England	1997	8.99
Wishbone Ash	Living Proof - Live In Chicago	CD	Griffin	GCD-247-2	U.S.A.	1994	7.99
Wishbone Ash	Locked In	CD	Repertoire	REP-4557-WY	Germany	2002	11.99
Wishbone Ash	Lost Cause In Paradise	CD	Yeaah!	YEAAH036	England	2002	8.99
Wishbone Ash	Mother Of Pearl: Live	CD	Culture Press	P1002	England	1998	12.99
Wishbone Ash	New England	CD	MCA	MCAD-2238	Germany	1993	9.99
Wishbone Ash	New England/Front Page News	CD	BGO	BGOCD405	England	2002	15.99
Wishbone Ash	No Smoke Without Fire	CD	MCA	MCLD-19374	England	1997	11.99

Artist	Title	Format	Label	Catalog No	Country	Released	Value
Wishbone Ash	Noveau Calls	CD	I.R.S.	IRSD-42101	U.S.A.	1990	9.99
Wishbone Ash	Number The Brave	Mini Lp	Universal	UICY-9092	Japan	2000	24.99
Wishbone Ash	On Air	CD	Strange Fruit	SFRSCD021	England	1997	14.99
Wishbone Ash	Pilgrimage	CD	MCA	MCAD-10233	U.S.A.	1991	9.99
Wishbone Ash	Psychic Terrorism	CD	Resurgent	4580	U.S.A.	2000	11.99
Wishbone Ash	Raw To The Bone	CD	Castle	CLACD-390	England	1993	12.99
Wishbone Ash	Self Titled	CD	BGO	BGOCD234	England	2002	12.99
Wishbone Ash	Self Titled	CD	MCA	MCAD-10661	U.S.A.	1991	8.99
Wishbone Ash	Strange Affair	CD	Talking Elephant	TECD048	England	2003	12.99
Wishbone Ash	Take 2 (Argus/Pilgrimage)	2CD	MCA	MCD-33003	EC	1995	15.99
Wishbone Ash	The Best Of	CD	MCA	MCAD-11620	U.S.A.	1997	8.99
Wishbone Ash	The King Will Come: Live	CD	Receiver	RRCD-276	England	1999	8.99
Wishbone Ash	There's The Rub	CD	MCA	MCAD-10448	U.S.A.	1991	9.99
Wishbone Ash	There's The Rub/Locked In	CD	MCA	MCLD-19249	England	1997	15.99
Wishbone Ash	Time Was: Wishbone Ash Collection	2CD	MCA	MCAD2-10765	U.S.A.	1993	15.99
Wishbone Ash	Trance Visionary (W/Bonus CD)	2CD	Resurgence	RES140CD	England	1999	14.99
Wishbone Ash	Twin Barrels Burning	CD	Castle	CLACD-389	EEC	1993	12.99
Wishbone Ash	Twin Barrels Burning	CD	Griffin	GCD-171-2	U.S.A.	1995	12.99
Wishbone Ash	Warriors	2CD	Recall	SMDCD483	England	2004	11.99
Wishbone Ash/Martin Turner	Walking The Reeperbahn	CD	Blueprint	BP298CD	England	1999	14.99
Wishbone Ash/Tony Kishmam	Catch 22	CD	Pure	003642560-2	U.S.A.	1997	10.99
Witch-Doctors	Witchdoctors A Go-Go	CD	Dionysus	ID-123326	U.S.A.	1994	8.99
Witchery	Dead, Hot, and Ready + 7	CD	Toy's Factory	TFCK-87202	Japan	1999	39.99
Witness	Witness (W/Neal Schon)	CD	Arista	ARCD12-8491	U.S.A.	1988	20.99
Witt, Joachim	M Rchenblau	CD	Line	DKCD-9.00997-0	Germany	1989	29.99
Wobble, Jah	30 Hertz Collection	CD	Meta	58137-00062	U.S.A.	2000	7.99
Wobble, Jah	30 Hertz Collection (Diff Tracks/USA)	2CD	Eagle	EDMCD-107	England	2000	14.99
Wobble, Jah	Amor	CD Single	Island	CIDX-IS-602	England	1994	4.99
Wobble, Jah	Early Yrs (Bedroom Album/Tradewinds)	2CD	30 Hertz	30HZCD-15	England	2001	16.99
Wobble, Jah	Fly	CD	30 Hertz	30HZCD-19	England	2003	14.99
Wobble, Jah	Fureur (Fury) + 3 (Molam Dub Lp)	CD	East West	B00008RUTN	Canada	2003	12.99
Wobble, Jah	Heaven And Earth	CD	Island	CID-8044	England	1995	14.99
Wobble, Jah	I Offer You Everything	CD Single	30 Hertz	30HZCD-6	England	1998	9.99
Wobble, Jah	Magical Thought	CD Single	30 Hertz	30HZCD-4	England	1997	23.99
Wobble, Jah	Mount Zion	CD Single	30 Hertz	30HZCD-7	England	1998	5.99
Wobble, Jah	Psalms	CD	Southern	18522-2	Belgium	1994	16.99
Wobble, Jah	Requiem	CD	30 Hertz	30HZCD-2	England	1997	14.99
Wobble, Jah	The Inspiration Of William Blake	CD	30 Hertz	30HZCD-13	England	1996	13.99
Wobble, Jah	The Legend Lives On: In Betrayal + 7	CD	Virgin	CDV-2158	England	1994	9.99
Wobble, Jah	The Light Programme	CD	30 Hertz	30HZCD-3	England	1997	14.99
Wobble, Jah	Umbra Sumus	CD	30 Hertz	30HZCD-5	England	1998	13.99
Wobble, Jah/Bill Laswell	A Dub Transmission	CD	Palm Pictures	PALMCD-2073-2	U.S.A.	2001	12.99
Wobble, Jah/Bill Laswell	Reconstructions/V (Axiom/5 Remixes)	CD	Palm Pictures	AXIOM-2093	U.S.A.	2003	12.99
Wobble, Jah/Deep Space	Beach Fervour Spare	CD	30 Hertz	30HZCD-11	England	2000	16.99
Wobble, Jah/Deep Space	Deep Space	CD	30 Hertz	30HZCD-9	England	1999	12.99
Wobble, Jah/Deep Space	Five Beats	CD	30 Hertz	30HZCD-20	England	2003	17.99
Wobble, Jah/Deep Space	Largely Live In Hartlepool/Manchester	2CD	30 Hertz	30HZCD-16	England	2001	17.99
Wobble, Jah/Evan Parker	Passage To Hades	CD	30 Hertz	30HZCD-14	England	2001	14.99
Wobble, Jah/Holger Czukay	Full Circle (W/Jaki Liebezeit)	CD	Caroline	CAROL-1876-2	U.S.A.	1992	11.99
Wobble, Jah/I Of Heart	Amor	CD Single	Island	CID-IS-602	England	1994	7.99
Wobble, Jah/I Of Heart	Becoming More Like God	CD Single	Island	CID-571	England	1994	9.99
Wobble, Jah/I Of Heart	Bomba	CD Single	Boys Own	BOICD-2	England	1990	14.99
Wobble, Jah/I Of Heart	English Roots Music	CD	30 Hertz	30HZCD-21	England	2003	11.99
Wobble, Jah/I Of Heart	Erzulie	CD Single	Oval	102-CD	England	1991	8.99
Wobble, Jah/I Of Heart	Full Moon Over Shopping Mall	CD	30 Hertz	30HZCD-10	England	2000	14.99
Wobble, Jah/I Of Heart	Molam Dub	CD	30 Hertz	30HZCD-12	England	2000	16.99
Wobble, Jah/I Of Heart	Rising Above Bedlam	CD	Atlantic	82386-2	U.S.A.	1992	11.99
Wobble, Jah/I Of Heart	Take Me To God	CD	Island	CID-8017	England	1994	14.99

W

Artist	Title	Format	Label	Catalog No	Country	Released	Value
Wobble, Jah/I Of Heart	The Celtic Poets	CD	30 Hertz	30HZCD-1	England	1998	16.99
Wobble, Jah/I Of Heart	The Sun Does Rise	CD Single	Island	CID-587	England	1994	4.99
Wobble, Jah/I Of Heart	The Sun Does Rise (#rd Cardboard)	CD Single	Island	CIDX-587	England	1994	12.99
Wobble, Jah/I Of Heart	The Ungodly Kingdom EP	CD Single	Oval	107-CD	England	1992	8.99
Wobble, Jah/I Of Heart	Visions Of You	CD Single	Oval	103-CD	England	1992	8.99
Wobble, Jah/I Of Heart	Without Judgement + 5	CD	Restless	7-72750-2	U.S.A.	1993	11.99
Wobble, Jah/Solaris	Live In Concert (W/Laswell/Budd)	CD	30 Hertz	30HZCD-18	England	2002	14.99
Wobble, Jah/T Of Sound	Shout At The Devil	CD	30 Hertz	30HZCD-17	England	2002	16.99
Wobble, Jah/Zi Lan Liao	Five Tone Dragon	CD	30 Hertz	30HZCD-8	England	1998	14.99
Womack, Bobby	Across 110th Street (O.S.T.)	CD	Rykodisc	RCD-10706	U.S.A.	1997	6.99
Womack, Lee Ann	I Hope You Dance	CD	MCA	088-170-099-2	U.S.A.	2000	7.99
Womack, Lee Ann	I Hope You Dance (W/Book)	CD	MCA	088-170-181-2	U.S.A.	2000	10.99
Wonder, Stevie	At The Close of a Century	4CD	Mowtown	012-153-992-2	U.S.A.	1999	44.99
Wonder, Stevie	Characters	CD	Motown	MCD06248MD	U.S.A.	1987	7.99
Wonder, Stevie	Down To Earth	CD	Polydor K.K.	POCT-1803	Japan	1966	29.99
Wonder, Stevie	Down To Earth/I Was Made To...	CD	Tamla	TCDO8053TD	U.S.A.	1995	34.99
Wonder, Stevie	Eivets Rednow (S Wonder Backwards)	CD	Polydor K.K.	POCT-5510	Japan	1995	49.99
Wonder, Stevie	Eivets Rednow (S Wonder Backwards)	CD	Motown	31453-0549-2	U.S.A.	1995	42.99
Wonder, Stevie	Fulfillingness First Finale (Ltd. Digipack)	CD	Motown	012-157-581-2	U.S.A.	2000	8.99
Wonder, Stevie	Greatest Hits Vol. 2	CD	Motown	3746303132	U.S.A.	1971	9.99
Wonder, Stevie	Hotter Than July (Ltd. Digipack)	CD	Motown	012-157-583-2	U.S.A.	2000	8.99
Wonder, Stevie	In Square Circle	CD	Motown	3746361342	U.S.A.	1985	7.99
Wonder, Stevie	Innervisions (Ltd Digipack)	CD	Motown	012-157-580-2	U.S.A.	2000	8.99
Wonder, Stevie	Innervisions (MFSL Gold Cd)	CD	Mobile Fidelity	UDCD-554	U.S.A.	1973	44.99
Wonder, Stevie	Love Songs	CD	Motown	9050MD	U.S.A.	1985	7.99
Wonder, Stevie	Music Of My Mind (Ltd. Digipack)	CD	Motown	012-157-578-2	U.S.A.	2000	8.99
Wonder, Stevie	My Cherie Amour/Signed Sealed...	CD	Motown	MOTD-8106	U.S.A.	1969	24.99
Wonder, Stevie	Natural Wonder	2CD	Motown	MOTD-0546	U.S.A.	1995	6.99
Wonder, Stevie	Original Musiquarium 1 (Ltd. Digipack)	2CD	Motown	012-159-741-2	U.S.A.	2000	22.99
Wonder, Stevie	Someday At Christmas	CD	Motown	3746352552	U.S.A.	1967	7.99
Wonder, Stevie	Song Review - A Grts Hits Collection	CD	Motown	31453-0767-2	U.S.A.	1996	13.99
Wonder, Stevie	Songs Key Of Life (Ltd Digipack)	2CD	Motown	012-157-582-2	U.S.A.	2000	22.99
Wonder, Stevie	Talking Book (Ltd. Digipack)	CD	Motown	012-157-579-2	U.S.A.	2000	8.99
Wonder, Stevie	The Ballad Collection	2CD	Universal	UICT-9001/2	Japan	2000	13.99
Wonder, Stevie	The Jazz Soul Of Little Stevie	CD	Motown	37463-5219-2	U.S.A.	1992	75.99
Wonder, Stevie	The Secret Life Of Plants	2CD	Motown	530-106-2	Germany	1996	34.99
Wonder, Stevie	The Woman In Red	CD	Motown	3746361082	U.S.A.	1984	8.99
Wonder, Stevie	Tribute To Uncle Ray	CD	Motown	530-449-2	England	1995	126.99
Wonder, Stevie	Uptight	CD	Motown	MOTD-5183	U.S.A.	1995	13.99
Wonder, Stevie	Where I'm Coming From	CD	Motown	530-223-2	England	1995	7.99
Wonder, Stevie	With A Song In My Heart	CD	Motown	MOTD-5150	U.S.A.	1992	29.99
Wondermints	Bali	CD	Sanctuary	SANCD001	England	1998	10.99
Wondermints	Cellophane EP	CD	Sony	ESCA-8012	Japan	1999	19.99
Wondermints	Mind If We Make Love To You	CD	Image Ent.	ID2976WM	U.S.A.	2002	8.99
Wondermints	Wonderful World Of Wondermints	CD	Castle	CMRCD027	England	1996	9.99
Wondermints	Wondermints	CD	Castle	CMRCD026	England	1996	9.99
Wood, Ron	1,2,3,4	CD	Sony	23DP-5589	Japan	1981	49.99
Wood, Ron	Gimme Some Neck	CD	Columbia	CK-35702	U.S.A.	1979	8.99
Wood, Ron	I've Got My Own Album To Do	CD	Warner Bros.	9-45692-2	U.S.A.	1974	11.99
Wood, Ron	Josephine (Promo)	CD Single	Continuum	13210-2	U.S.A.	1992	18.99
Wood, Ron	Not For Beginners	CD	SPV	085-72762-CD	Germany	2001	11.99
Wood, Ron	Now Look	CD	Warner Bros.	9-45693-2	U.S.A.	1975	8.99
Wood, Ron	Show Me	CD Single	Continuum	12210-2	U.S.A.	1992	4.99
Wood, Ron	Slide On Live	CD	Continuum	19309-2	U.S.A.	1993	7.99
Wood, Ron	Stay With Me	CD Single	Continuum	12309-2	U.S.A.	1993	9.99
Wood, Roy	Boulders	CD	BGO	BGOCD219	England	1996	14.99
Wood, Roy	Exotic Mixture: The Best Of	2CD	Repertoire	REP-4744	Germany	1999	17.99
Wood, Roy	Introducing Eddy & The Falcons + 5	CD	Edsel	EDCD-1624	England	1999	16.99

W

Artist	Title	Format	Label	Catalog No	Country	Released	Value
Wood, Roy	Mustard (Line Version)	CD	Line	JECD-9.00864-0	Germany	1989	12.99
Wood, Roy	Mustard... Plus + 7	CD	Edsel	EDCD-625	England	1999	16.99
Wood, Roy	Outstanding Performer	CD	Castle	CMQCD447	England	2003	14.99
Wood, Roy	Starting Up	CD	Castle	CMRCD208	England	2001	8.99
Wood, Roy	Very Best Of: Through The Years	CD	EMI	7243-8-54202-2-1	England	1996	8.99
Wood, Roy	Wizzard Brew	CD	EMI	7243-521205-2-9	England	1999	11.99
Woodmansey, Woody	Woody Woodmansey's U-Boat	CD	Castle	CMAR714	England	2001	8.99
Woods	It's Like This	CD	Line	DECD-9.00318-0	Germany	1987	28.99
Woodward, Edward	Dracula (Spoken Word)	CD	Dove Audio	08312<1005>	U.S.A.	1992	14.99
Woolley, Bruce/C. Club	English Garden	CD	Epic	494978-2	England	1979	14.99
Wraith	Riot	CD	Neat Metal	NM007	France	2001	14.99
Wraith	Schizophrenia	CD	Neat Metal	NM014	France	2001	14.99
Wrathchild	Delerium	CD	Heavy Metal	HMR-XD-137	England	1989	20.99
Wrathchild	Stakk Attakk	CD	Heavy Metal	HMR-PD-18	England	1984	22.99
Wrathchild	The Biz Suxx, But We Don't Care	CD	Heavy Metal	HMR-XD-116	England	1988	11.99
Wrathchild America	3-D	CD	Atlantic	9-82186-2	U.S.A.	1991	8.99
Wrathchild America	Climbin' The Walls	CD	Atlantic	7-81889-2	U.S.A.	1989	22.99
Wray, Link	Born To Be Wild (Live)	CD	Line	LICD-9.00690-0	Germany	1989	17.99
Wray, Link	Bullshot	CD	Line	LICD-9.00142-0	Germany	1988	18.99
Wray, Link	Live At The Paradiso	CD	Line	LICD-9.00217-0	Germany	1988	24.99
Wreckless Eric	Almost A Jubilee (BBC 1977 - 2002)	CD	HUX	HUX-039	England	2003	11.99
Wreckless Eric	At The Shop!	CD	New Rose	NR-715	France	1990	34.99
Wreckless-Eric	Big Smash + 8	CD	Stiff	STIFFCD-13	Holland	1993	23.99
Wreckless-Eric	Greatest Stiffs	CD	Metro	METRCD044	England	2001	9.99
Wreckless-Eric	Le Beat Group Electrique	CD	New Rose	ROSE-179-CD	France	1989	19.99
Wreckless-Eric	The Donovan Of Trash	CD	Sympathy For The	33-1/3-RIP	Canada	1993	10.99
Wreckless-Eric	Wreckless Eric + 2	CD	Stiff	STIFFCD-02	Holland	1993	19.99
Wreckless-Eric/Clay Harper	East Of Easter	CD	Casino	ALT-3115-2	U.S.A.	1997	4.99
Wreckless-Eric/Eric Goulden	Karaoke	CD	Silo	SILOCD12	France	1997	19.99
Wreckless-Eric/Hitsville H B	Hitsville House Band /12 O'Clock...	CD	Casino Int.	CAS-3008	U.S.A.	1994	11.99
Wreckless-Eric/Len Bright	Len Bright Combo (2 Lps On One)	CD	Southern Domestic	SND-001	England	2003	16.99
Wright, Gary	Dream Weaver	CD Single	Reprise	9362-40495-2	Germany	1992	7.99
Wright, Gary	Extraction	CD	Repertoire	REPUK1011	Germany	1971	18.99
Wright, Gary	First Signs Of Life	CD	Triloka	7211-2	U.S.A.	1995	7.99
Wright, Gary	The Dream Weaver	CD	Warner Bros.	2868-2	U.S.A.	1975	7.99
Wright, Gary	The Right Place	CD	Warner Bros.	WPCP-5099	Japan	1996	20.99
Wright, Gary	Who I Am	CD	Cypress	YD-0111	U.S.A.	1988	13.99
Wright, Luther/The Wrongs	Rebuild The Wall (P Floyd Bluegrass)	CD	Universal	4400161102	Canada	2002	8.99
Wright, Tim/Little Brother	Survival	CD	Line	LICD-9.01221-0	Germany	1992	6.99
Writing On The Wall	The Power Of The Picts	CD	Repertoire	REP-4854	Germany	2002	13.99
Wyatt, Robert	A Short Break	CD	Blueprint	BP108CD	England	1996	8.99
Wyatt, Robert	Boxerpts	CD	Hannibal	VHNCD1440	U.S.A.	1999	9.99
Wyatt, Robert	Compilation (Nothing Can/Rottenhat)	CD	Rhino	R2-79459	U.S.A.	1990	19.99
Wyatt, Robert	Cuckooland	CD	Hannibal	HNCD1468	U.S.A.	2003	8.99
Wyatt, Robert	Dondestan	CD	Rhino	R2-79469	U.S.A.	1991	9.99
Wyatt, Robert	Dondestan (Revisited)	CD	Thirsty Ear	THI-57057-2	U.S.A.	1998	8.99
Wyatt, Robert	End Of An Ear	CD	Sony	50997-493342-29	Holland	1999	11.99
Wyatt, Robert	Ep's	5CD	Hannibal	HNCD-1440	U.S.A.	1999	42.99
Wyatt, Robert	Flotsam Jetsam	2CD	Rough Trade	R-3112	England	1995	44.99
Wyatt, Robert	Going Back A Bit (A Little History Of)	2CD	Virgin	CDVDM-9031	England	1994	39.99
Wyatt, Robert	Mid-Eighties	CD	Rhino	R2-79488	U.S.A.	1993	8.99
Wyatt, Robert	Nothing Can Stop Us	CD	Thirsty Ear	THI-57050-2	U.S.A.	1998	10.99
Wyatt, Robert	Old Rottenhat	CD	Thirsty Ear	THI-57051-2	U.S.A.	1998	11.99
Wyatt, Robert	Rock Bottom	CD	Thirsty Ear	THI-57015-2	U.S.A.	1998	11.99
Wyatt, Robert	Ruth Is Stranger Than Richard	CD	Thirsty Ear	THI-57044-2	U.S.A.	1998	11.99
Wyatt, Robert	Shleep	CD	Thirsty Ear	THI-57040.2	U.S.A.	1997	8.99
Wyatt, Robert	Solar Flares Burn For You	CD	Cuneiform	RUNE-175	U.S.A.	2003	11.99
Wyatt, Robert	The Animals Film	CD	Rough Trade	R-3172	England	2000	24.99

W

Artist	Title	Format	Label	Catalog No	Country	Released	Value
Wyatt, Robert	The Peel Sessions	CD	Strange Fruit	WMD672005	France	1992	14.99
Wyatt, Robert/Tribute	Soup Songs (W/Phil Manzanera)	2CD	Jazzprint	JPCD-101	England	2000	21.99
Wyatt, Robert/Various Artists	M W Pour Robert Wyatt	CD	In Poly Sons	IPS0401	France	2002	19.99
Wyatt, Robert/Walter Prati	Robert's Dr. - 3 Var/Duchess W/ Book	CD	Sonic Book	SONIC.028	Italy	2002	21.99
Wyman, Bill	Compendium (First 3 LPs + 8)	2CD	Koch	KOC-CD-8056	U.S.A.	2001	16.99
Wyman, Bill	Monkey Grip	CD	Polydor	PSCR-5413	Japan	1995	18.99
Wyman, Bill	Monkey Grip	CD	Sequel	NEMCD846	England	1998	10.99
Wyman, Bill	Self Titled	CD	Sequel	NEMCD848	England	1998	10.99
Wyman, Bill	Stone Alone	CD	Sequel	NEMCD847	England	1998	10.99
Wyman, Bill	Stuff	CD	Victor Ent.	VICP-5202	Japan	1992	24.99
Wyman, Bill/Rhythm Kings	Anyway The Wind Blows + 2	CD	Velvel	63467-79768-2	U.S.A.	1999	10.99
Wyman, Bill/Rhythm Kings	Double Bill (George Harrison)	2CD	Ripple	BTFLYCD-015	England	2001	19.99
Wyman, Bill/Rhythm Kings	Groovin' (Ltd Ed. Numbered)	CD Single	Ripple	BTFLYS-003	England	2000	5.99
Wyman, Bill/Rhythm Kings	Struttin' Our Stuff	CD	Velvel	VEL-79708-2	U.S.A.	1998	7.99
Wyman, Bill/Rhythm Kings	Wyman's Rythm Kings Sampler (DJ)	CD	Koch	KOC-SA-8286	U.S.A.	2001	19.99
Wyman, Bill/Various Artists	Willie/Poor Boys - Tear It Up (Brooker)	CD	Blind Pig	BPCD-5012	U.S.A.	1994	8.99
Wyman, Bill/Various Artists	Willie/Poor Boys (Watts, Page/Rogers)	CD	Passport	PCD-6047	U.S.A.	1984	20.99
Wyman, Bill/Various Artists	Willie/Poor Boys (Watts, Page/Rogers)	CD	Blind Pig	BPCD-5009	U.S.A.	1985	8.99
Wynn, Steve	Static Transmission + 8 (1st 1000)	2CD	DBK Works	DBK-105-CD	U.S.A.	2003	14.99

X

Artist	Title	Format	Label	Catalog No	Country	Released	Value
X-Ray Spex	Conscious Consumer	CD	Receiver	RRCD-205	England	1995	10.99
X-Ray Spex	Germ Free Adolescents	CD	Caroline	CAROL-1813-2	U.S.A.	1991	13.99
X-Ray Spex	Live At The Roxy Club	CD	Receiver	RRCD140	England	2001	10.99
X-Ray Spex	Obsessed With You	CD	Receiver	RRCD-145	England	1991	10.99
X-Ray Spex	The Anthology	2CD	Castle	CMDDD369	England	2001	15.99
XTC	Apple Venus Volume 1	CD	TVT	TVT-3250-2	U.S.A.	1999	8.99
XTC	Apple Venus, Volume 1 (Intrumental)	CD	Pony Canyon	PCCY-01612	Japan	2002	31.99
XTC	Ballad Of Peter Pumpkinhead (CD 2)	CD Single	Virgin	665-418	England	1992	5.99
XTC	Ballad Of Peter Pumpkinhead (Promo)	CD Single	Geffen	GEFDM-21813	U.S.A.	1992	8.99
XTC	Ballad Of Peter Pumpkinhead [CD 1]	CD Single	Geffen	21813-2	U.S.A.	1991	4.99
XTC	Ballad Of Peter Pumpkinhead [CD 3]	CD Single	Virgin	VSCDG-1415	England	1992	6.99
XTC	Beeswax (Some B-Sides 1977 - 1982)	CD	Virgin	VJCP-23145	Japan	1992	34.99
XTC	Black Sea + 3	CD	Virgin	724385063626	England	2001	11.99
XTC	Coat Many Cupboards (Sampler Promo)	CD	Caroline	CAR-69995	England	2001	14.99
XTC	Coat of Many Cupboards Box Set	4CD	Virgin	7243-8-11900-2-9	Holland	2002	49.99
XTC	Compact XTC - The Singles 1978-85	CD	Virgin	0777-7-86476-2-1	England	1985	13.99
XTC	Dear God (All Of Homo Safari Series)	CD Single	Virgin	CDEP-3	England	1987	23.99
XTC	Dear Madame Barnum (Promo)	CD Single	Geffen	PRO-CD-4447	U.S.A.	1992	12.99
XTC	Demo Tracks	CD Single	Virgin	VJCP-14044	Japan	1992	18.99
XTC	Disappointed	CD Single	Virgin	VOZCD-142	Australia	1992	9.99
XTC	Disappointed [CD 1]	CD Single	Virgin	VSCDG-1404	England	1992	6.99
XTC	Disappointed [CD 2]	CD Single	Virgin	VSCDG-1412	England	1992	6.99
XTC	Drums And Wireless	CD	Nighttracks	CDNT008	England	1994	9.99
XTC	Drums And Wires + 3	CD	Virgin	724385065323	England	2001	11.99
XTC	Easter Theatre	CD Single	Cooking Vinyl	FRY-CD-080	England	1999	4.99
XTC	English Settlement (Full Lp)	CD	Virgin	724385066023	England	2001	13.99
XTC	Exp.Together (Dub Go 2/Drums/Wires)	CD	Virgin	260-944-217	England	1990	13.99
XTC	Fossil Fuel - 1977-92 (Limited Metal)	CD	Virgin	74328-421282-7	England	1996	49.99
XTC	Go 2 + 1	CD	Virgin	724385066627	England	2001	11.99
XTC	Homespun	2CD	Pony Canyon	PCCY-01415	Japan	1999	35.99
XTC	I'd Like That	CD Single	Cooking Vinyl	FRY-CD-083	England	1998	6.99
XTC	I'm The Man Who ...(Plastic Cvr.)	CD Single	Idea	FRYCD-095	England	2000	4.99

X

Artist	Title	Format	Label	Catalog No	Country	Released	Value
XTC	I'm The Man Who Murdered Love	CD Single	Idea	1DCA6365	U.S.A.	2000	5.99
XTC	King For A Day (3 ") Crown Shpd Cvr	CD Single	Virgin	VSCD-1177	England	1989	21.99
XTC	King For A Day (CD 2)	CD Single	Geffen	21236-2	U.S.A.	1989	6.99
XTC	King For A Day (Promo)	CD Single	Geffen	PRO-CD-3522	U.S.A.	1989	14.99
XTC	King for a Day [CD 1]	CD Single	Virgin	DIDX005188	England	1989	6.99
XTC	Mayor of Simpleton [3 " CD]	CD Single	Virgin	CSIG000224	England	1989	12.99
XTC	Mummer + 6	CD	Virgin	724385067228	England	2001	11.99
XTC	NAC (Nonesuch Sampler)	CD	Geffen	PRO-CD-4398	U.S.A.	1992	14.99
XTC	Nonsuch	CD	Virgin	724385067822	England	2001	11.99
XTC	Nonsuch (Gold Embossed/Pic Disc)	CD	Virgin	CDV-2699	England	1992	24.99
XTC	One Of The Millions	CD Single	Geffen	27552-2	U.S.A.	1989	14.99
XTC	Oranges & Lemons	CD	Virgin	724385068324	England	2001	11.99
XTC	Oranges & Lemons (MFSL Gold Cd)	CD	Mobile Fidelity	UDCD-682	U.S.A.	1989	17.99
XTC	Oranges/Lemons (3 (3") Cd DJ Box)	3CD	Virgin	CDVT-2581	England	1989	11.99
XTC	Radios In Motion (Promo Sampler)	CD	Geffen	PRO-CD-4397	U.S.A.	1992	9.99
XTC	Rag & Bone Buffet	CD	Geffen	GEFD-24417	U.S.A.	1990	11.99
XTC	Rag And Bone... (Promo Sampler)	CD	Geffen	PRO-CD-4251	U.S.A.	1990	14.99
XTC	Senses Working Overtime (3" Cd)	CD Single	Virgin	CDT-9	England	1982	18.52
XTC	Skylarking (MFSL Gold W/No Mermaid S)	CD	Mobile Fidelity	UDCD-615	U.S.A.	1986	26.99
XTC	Skylarking (With Mermaid Smiled)	CD	Virgin	724385069024	England	2001	11.99
XTC	The Big Express + 3	CD	Virgin	724385069222	England	2001	11.99
XTC	The Greatest	CD	Virgin	VJCP-51047	Japan	1998	34.99
XTC	The Loving (3" CD)	CD Single	Virgin	VSCD-1201	England	1989	13.99
XTC	This Is Not... (Nonesuch DJ Sampler)	CD	Geffen	PRO-CD-4396	U.S.A.	1992	10.99
XTC	Transistor Blast - Best Of BBC Sessions	4CD	TVT	TVT-3240	U.S.A.	1998	30.99
XTC	Upsy Daisy Assortment (Advance)	CD	Virgin	GEFD-A-25137	U.S.A.	1997	9.99
XTC	Wasp Star (Apple Venus Vol. 2)	CD	TVT	TVT-3260-2	U.S.A.	2000	8.99
XTC	Wasp Star (Apple Venus, Pt. 2) Inst.	CD	Pony Canyon	PCCY-01613	Japan	2002	20.99
XTC	Waxworks (Some Singles 1977-1982)	CD	Geffen	GEFD-4037	U.S.A.	1982	8.99
XTC	What Do You... (Transistor Blast/DJ)	CD	TVT	TVT-3245-2P	U.S.A.	1998	15.99
XTC	White Music + 7	CD	Virgin	724385069123	England	2001	11.99
XTC	XTC: BBC Radio 1 Live In Concert	CD	Windsong	WINCD026	England	1992	9.99
XTC/Andy Partridge	Fuzzy Warbles Volume 1	CD	Ape House	APE-CD-001	England	2002	20.99
XTC/Andy Partridge	Fuzzy Warbles Volume 2	CD	Ape House	APE-CD-002	England	2002	20.99
XTC/Andy Partridge	Fuzzy Warbles Volume 3	CD	Ape House	APECD-003	England	2003	20.99
XTC/Andy Partridge	Fuzzy Warbles Volume 4	CD	Ape House	APECD-004	England	2003	20.99
XTC/Andy Partridge	Hello Recording Club CD Nov. 1994	CD	Hello	HEL-411	U.S.A.	1994	130.99
XTC/Andy Partridge	Orpheus/Lowdown (Ltd Ed/W/P Blegvad)	CD	Ape House	APECD-005	England	2003	24.99
XTC/Andy Partridge	Orpheus/Lowdown (W/Peter Blegvad)	CD	Pony Canyon	PCCY-01676	Japan	2003	21.99
XTC/Andy Partridge	Through The Hill (H Budd/Gold Band)	CD	Gyroscope	GYR-6608-2	U.S.A.	1994	8.99
XTC/Andy Partridge	Through The Hill + 2 (H Budd)	CD	Polydor	POCP-1431	Japan	1994	15.99
XTC/Dukes Of Stratosphear	Chips From The Chocolate Fireball	CD	Virgin	7243850673229	England	2001	11.99
XTC/Star Park	The School Guide To XTC (W/Book)	CD	Sonic Book	SONIC.021	Italy	1999	21.99
XTC/Various Artists	A Testimonial Dinner - The Songs	CD	Thirsty Ear	THI-57019.2	U.S.A.	1995	7.99
XTC/Various Artists	Music Inspired/Avengers (Partridge Son	CD	Big Ear	EAZ-4013	U.S.A.	1998	7.99

Y

Artist	Title	Format	Label	Catalog No	Country	Released	Value
Y & T	BBC Live In Concert	CD	Varese	302-061-069-2	U.S.A.	2000	8.99
Y & T	Best Of '81 To '85	CD	A&M	75021-5309 2	U.S.A.	1990	11.99
Y & T	Black Tiger	CD	Polydor	POCM-1984	Japan	1982	39.99
Y & T	Contagious	CD	Geffen	9-24142-2	U.S.A.	1987	16.99
Y & T	Down For The Count	CD	Polydor	POCM-1987	Japan	1985	25.99
Y & T	Earthshaker	CD	Polydor	POCM-1983	Japan	1981	34.99

Artist	Title	Format	Label	Catalog No	Country	Released	Value
Y & T	Earthshaker	CD	A&M	CD-3736	U.S.A.	1981	19.99
Y & T	Endangered Species	CD	Music For N	CDMFN-229	England	1997	8.99
Y & T	Endangered Species + 1	CD	Bareknuckle	AVCB-66025	Japan	1997	24.99
Y & T	In Rock We Trust	CD	Polydor	POCM-1986	Japan	1984	24.99
Y & T	Live Friday Rock Show/BBC Live	CD	Strange Fruit	SFRSCD-071	England	1998	15.99
Y & T	Mean Streak	CD	Polydor	POCM-1985	Japan	1983	31.99
Y & T	Musically Incorrect	CD	Varese	VSD-1014	U.S.A.	1998	11.99
Y & T	Open Fire (Live)	CD	Polydor	POCM-1988	Japan	1985	59.99
Y & T	Struck Down	CD	Mondo	MRC-10020	U.S.A.	1978	26.99
Y & T	Ten	CD	Geffen	9-24283-2	U.S.A.	1990	16.99
Y & T	Ultimate Collection	CD	Hip O	069-490-889-2	U.S.A.	2001	12.99
Y & T	Unearthed Vol. 1	CD	Meanstreak	MMCO3101	U.S.A.	2003	14.99
Y & T	Yesterday And Today	CD	Mondo	MRC-10010	U.S.A.	1976	24.99
Y & T	Yesterday And Today Live	CD	Metal Blade	9-26572-2	U.S.A.	1991	9.99
Yamamoto, Kenji	Dragonball Z (O.S.T.)	CD	Nippon Columbia	COCC-13062	Japan	1995	8.99
Yamashirogumi, Geinoh	Akira (O.S.T.)	CD	JVC	JMI-1001	U.S.A.	1990	6.99
Yancey, Erika	Ericka	CD	RCA	07863-67470-2	U.S.A.	1997	197.99
Yankovic, Weird Al	Running With Scissors	CD	Volcano	61422-32118-2	U.S.A.	1999	11.99
Yankovic, Weird Al	UHF - Soundtrack And Other Stuff	CD	Scotti Bros.	ZK-45265	U.S.A.	1989	8.99
Yankovic, Weird Al/W. Carlos	Peter The Wolf/Carnival Animals Pt. 2	CD	Columbia	MK 44567	U.S.A.	1988	54.99
Yanni	Chameleon Days	CD	Private Music	2043-2-P	U.S.A.	1988	6.99
Yanni	Dare To Dream	CD	Private Music	01005-82096-2	U.S.A.	1992	6.99
Yanni	Devotion - The Best Of	CD	Windham Hill	01005-82153-2	U.S.A.	1997	8.99
Yanni	Heart Of Midnight	CD	Silva Screen	SSD-1050	U.S.A.	1992	6.99
Yanni	I Love You Perfect	CD	Silva Screen	SSD-1015	U.S.A.	1993	6.99
Yanni	If I Could Tell You	CD	Virgin	7243-8-49893-2-3	U.S.A.	2000	7.99
Yanni	In Celebration of Life	CD	Private Music	01005-82093-2	U.S.A.	1991	6.99
Yanni	In My Time	CD	Private Music	01005-82106-2	U.S.A.	1993	6.99
Yanni	In The Mirror	CD	Private Music	0100582150-2	U.S.A.	1997	6.99
Yanni	Keys To Imagination	CD	Private Music	2008-2-P	U.S.A.	1986	10.99
Yanni	Live At The Acropolis	CD	Private Music	01005-82116-2	U.S.A.	1993	6.99
Yanni	Love Songs	CD	Private Music	01005-82167-2	U.S.A.	1999	6.99
Yanni	Optimystique	CD	Private Music	2052-2-P	U.S.A.	1989	6.99
Yanni	Out Of Silence	CD	Private Music	2024-2-P	U.S.A.	1987	6.99
Yanni	Port Of Mystery	CD	Windham Hill	01934-11241-2	U.S.A.	1997	5.99
Yanni	Reflections Of Passion	CD	Private Music	2067-2-P	U.S.A.	1992	6.99
Yanni	Steal The Sky	CD	Rhino	R2-75668	U.S.A.	1999	13.99
Yanni	The Very Best Of Yanni	CD	Private Music	0193411568-2	U.S.A.	2000	8.99
Yanni	Tribute	CD	Virgin	7243-8-44981-2-2	U.S.A.	1997	6.99
Yanni	Winter Light	CD	Private Music	01005-82176-2	U.S.A.	1999	6.99
Yardbirds	25 Greatest Hits	CD	Repertoire	REP-4258-WG	Germany	1992	11.99
Yardbirds	BBC Sessions	CD	Warner Bros.	9-46694-2	U.S.A.	1997	6.99
Yardbirds	Birdland	CD	Favored Nations	FN2280	U.S.A.	2003	8.99
Yardbirds	Birdland (Advance Cd/Diff Back)	CD	Favored Nations	FN2280-A	U.S.A.	2003	12.99
Yardbirds	Collection	CD	Castle	CCSCD-141	England	1987	14.99
Yardbirds	Cumular Limit	CD	Alchemy	PILOT-24	England	2000	24.99
Yardbirds	Five Live Yardbirds (Speed Corrected)	CD	Rhino	R2-70189	U.S.A.	1988	7.99
Yardbirds	Five Live Yardbirds + 8	CD	Repertoire	REP-4775-WY	Germany	1999	14.99
Yardbirds	For Your Love + 13	CD	Repertoire	REP-4757-WY	Germany	1999	14.99
Yardbirds	Greatest Hits, Volume One (1964-1966)	CD	Rhino	RNCD-75895	U.S.A.	1986	12.99
Yardbirds	Having A Rave Up + 11	CD	Repertoire	REP-4758-WY	Germany	1999	14.99
Yardbirds	Little Games Sessions & More	2CD	EMI	0777-7-98213-2-7	U.S.A.	1992	17.99
Yardbirds	Live Featuring Jimmy Page (Recalled)	CD	Mooreland Street	MS-33068-2	U.S.A.	2000	169.99
Yardbirds	Please Don't Tell Me...(Promo)	CD Single	Favored Nations	FN2281-P	England	2003	7.99
Yardbirds	Roger The E./Over Under ...+ 10	CD	Repertoire	REP-4681-WP	Germany	1998	14.99
Yardbirds	Roger The Engineer + 4	CD	Line	IMCD-9.00137-0	Germany	1986	9.99
Yardbirds	Shapes Of Things	4CD	Decal	CD-LIK-BOX-1	EEC	1991	39.99
Yardbirds	Shapes Of Things Box Set	4CD	Alfa	ALCB-527-528	Japan	1994	99.99

Y

Artist	Title	Format	Label	Catalog No	Country	Released	Value
Yardbirds	Smokestack Lightning	2CD	Sony	A2K-48655	U.S.A.	1991	15.99
Yardbirds	Special Digest (Promo)	CD	Alfa	Y12-53	Japan	1991	149.99
Yardbirds	The BBC Sessions	CD	Repertoire	REP-4777-WY	Germany	1999	13.99
Yardbirds	Train Kept A-Rollin Box (T-Shirt/Button)	4CD	Charly	CD-LIK-BOX-3	England	1993	54.99
Yardbirds	Ultimate!	2CD	Rhino	R2-79825	U.S.A.	2001	14.99
Yardbirds	Vol. 2 Blues, Backtracks	2CD	Sony	A2K-48658	U.S.A.	1991	15.99
Yardbirds	Where The Action Is (BBC Sess. +8)	2CD	Alchemy	PILOT-10	England	1997	39.99
Yardbirds	Yardbirds W/Sonny Boy Williamson + 7	CD	Repertoire	REP-4776-WY	Germany	1999	14.99
Yearwood, Trisha	How Do I Live (Without You)	CD Single	MCA	MCADS-72015	U.S.A.	1997	5.99
Yello	One Second	CD	Polygram	832-675-2	U.S.A.	1987	11.99
Yello	Solid Pleasure	CD	Vertigo	VERT-83392	Germany	2002	8.99
Yes	9012 Live - The Solos	CD	MMG Inc.	AMCY-375	Japan	1985	24.99
Yes	9012Live The Solos	CD	East West	AMCY-4043	Japan	1996	39.99
Yes	America (Promo)	CD Single	CMC Int.	CMC-DJ-87203-2	U.S.A.	1996	11.99
Yes	BBC Sessions 1969-1970 (Gold Cd)	2CD	Purple Pyramid	CLP-0246-2	U.S.A.	1998	14.99
Yes	Close To The Edge + 4	CD	Rhino	R2-73790	U.S.A.	2003	9.99
Yes	Evening Of Yes Music Plus (DJ)	CD	Herald	HER-PRO-2	U.S.A.	1994	20.99
Yes	Extended Versions	CD	BMG	75517-45919-2	U.S.A.	2002	5.99
Yes	Fragile (Atlantic Gold Cd)	CD	Atlantic	82524-2	U.S.A.	1993	74.99
Yes	Fragile + 2	CD	Rhino	R2-73789	U.S.A.	2003	9.99
Yes	Highlights - The Very Best Of Yes	CD	Atlantic	7-82517-2	U.S.A.	1993	6.99
Yes	In A Word Box Set	5CD	Rhino	R2-78186	U.S.A.	2002	34.99
Yes	Keys To Ascension - Live (Gold Cd)	2CD	CMC Int.	0607686208-2	U.S.A.	1996	20.99
Yes	Keys To Ascension 2 (Gold Cd)	2CD	Purple Pyramid	CLP-0159-2	U.S.A.	1997	20.99
Yes	Keystudio (Keys Ascension Studio)	CD	Castle	CMRCD177	England	2001	11.99
Yes	King Biscuit # 00-14, 3-27- 4/2/00	CD	DIR Network	YL939BO271374	U.S.A.	2000	69.99
Yes	Lightning Strikes (Promo)	CD Single	Beyond	BYDJ-78060-2	U.S.A.	1999	11.99
Yes	Magnification (Best Buy Bonus Cd)	2CD	Beyond	398-578-203-2	U.S.A.	2001	28.99
Yes	Magnification (Blk Ltd. Ed/Bonus Cd)	2CD	Eagle	EGDLT-189	U.S.A.	2002	28.99
Yes	Magnification (Borders Bonus Cd)	2CD	Beyond	398-578-203-2	U.S.A.	2001	28.99
Yes	Magnification (FYE Bonus Cd)	2CD	Beyond	398-578-203-2	U.S.A.	2001	28.99
Yes	Magnification/House Of Blues JVC DJ	DVD Aud	Beyond	YESDVDA	U.S.A.	2000	99.99
Yes	New State Of Mind (Promo)	CD Single	Beyond	BYCD226	U.S.A.	1997	22.99
Yes	Open Your Eyes (Promo)	CD Single	Beyond	2690-2	U.S.A.	1997	12.99
Yes	Open Your Eyes (Promo)	CD	Festival	PRD98/02	Australia	1997	17.99
Yes	Open Your Eyes (W/Yes Sticker)	CD	Victor Ent.	VICP-60215	Japan	1997	29.99
Yes	Open Your.. (Ltd Ed Surround Sound)	CD	Beyond	BYCD3075	U.S.A.	1997	32.99
Yes	Selections From... In A Word (Promo)	CD	Rhino	PRCD-400059	U.S.A.	2002	10.99
Yes	Self Titled	CD	East West	AMCY-4025	Japan	1969	19.99
Yes	Special Digest (Promo)	CD	Atco	ASCD-26	Japan	1991	142.99
Yes	State Of Play (Promo)	CD Single	Victory	CDP-1244	U.S.A.	1994	12.99
Yes	Talk + 1	CD	Spitfire	SPT-15209-2	U.S.A.	1994	10.99
Yes	That, That Is (Promo)	CD Single	CMC Int.	CMC-DJ-87207-2	U.S.A.	1996	11.99
Yes	The Best Of Yes - 1970 -1987	CD	East West	AMCY-6051	Japan	1999	34.99
Yes	The Ladder (Limited Tour Edition)	2CD	Eagle	EAGTE088	England	1999	24.99
Yes	The Story Of (Promo)	CD	Atco	PSCD-5	Japan	1987	106.99
Yes	The Ultimate Yes + 5 (W/Bonus CD)	3CD	Rhino	R2-78042	U.S.A.	2004	14.99
Yes	The Yes Album	CD	East West	AMCY-362	Japan	1971	15.99
Yes	The Yes Story (Gold CD)	2CD	Dejavu Retro	R2CD-42-55	Germany	2003	13.99
Yes	Time And A Word+ 4	CD	Rhino	R2-73787	U.S.A.	2003	9.99
Yes	Union + 1	CD	Arista	261-558	Germany	1991	10.99
Yes	Westwood 1 Show # 97-10, 3 - 3 - 97	2CD	Westwood 1	COMN201XA	U.S.A.	1997	149.99
Yes	Yes + 6	CD	Rhino	R2-73786	U.S.A.	2003	9.99
Yes	Yes Active (Talk Video Exp.)	CD-Rom	Compton's New	0-4544506562-7	U.S.A.	1994	20.99
Yes	Yes Album + 3	CD	Rhino	R2-73788	U.S.A.	2003	10.99
Yes	Yes Years Box Set (Promo)	4CD	Atlantic	PRCD-4019-2	U.S.A.	1991	199.99
Yes	Yesstory	2CD	Atco	7-92202-2	U.S.A.	1992	10.99
Yes	YesSymphonic Tour	CD Single	Yes LLC	YES-78204-2	U.S.A.	2001	24.99

Artist	Title	Format	Label	Catalog No	Country	Released	Value
Yes	Yes-Today	2CD	Snapper	SMDCD375	England	2002	12.99
Yes	Yesyears Box Set	4CD	Atco	7-91644-2	U.S.A.	1991	24.99
Yes	Yesyears Promo Cd Single Box	CD	Atco	PRCD-4009-2	U.S.A.	1991	14.99
Yes/A.B.W.H.	A.B.W.H. (Bl. Tray Gold Pic Label Cd)	CD	Arista	ARCD85-90126	U.S.A.	1989	29.99
Yes/A.B.W.H.	An Evening Of Yes Music Plus	2CD	Fragile	CDFRL002	EEC	1993	28.99
Yes/A.B.W.H.	Evening Of Yes Music Plus (Gold Cd)	2CD	Herald	HER-006	U.S.A.	1994	30.99
Yes/A.B.W.H.	Evening Yes Music Plus Sampler (DJ)	CD	Herald	HER-PRO-1	U.S.A.	1994	34.99
Yes/Anderson, Wakeman, H.	Original Members Of Yes	CD	KRB	KRB8117-2	U.S.A.	2001	8.99
Yes/Badger	Fierce Rock 'N Roll (Tony Kaye LP)	CD	Bagagaboo	J281	Canada	1989	13.99
Yes/Badger	One Live Badger (Tony Kaye Lp)	CD	East West	AMCY-593	Japan	1993	28.99
Yes/Badger	One Live Badger (Tony Kaye Lp)	CD	Repertoire	REP-4373-WY	Germany	1993	14.99
Yes/Badger	White Lady (Tony Kaye LP)	CD	Epic	EICP-7077	Japan	2001	24.99
Yes/Empire	Mark I (Peter Banks Lp)	CD	One Way	OW-31443	U.S.A.	1995	9.99
Yes/Empire	Mark II (Peter Banks Lp)	CD	One Way	OW-32650	U.S.A.	1996	9.99
Yes/Empire	Mark III (Peter Banks Lp)	CD	One Way	OW-32179	U.S.A.	1996	9.99
Yes/Esquire	Coming Home + 2 (Chris Squire's Son)	CD	Renaissance	RMED00185	U.S.A.	1997	8.99
Yes/Esquire	Esquire (Chris Squire's Son)	CD	Renaissance	RMED00117	U.S.A.	1987	8.99
Yes/Flash	Flash (Peter Banks Lp)	CD	One Way	S21-17796	U.S.A.	1993	14.99
Yes/Flash	In The Can (P Banks/Tony Kaye Lp)	CD	One Way	S21-56841	U.S.A.	1993	13.99
Yes/Flash	Out Of Our Hands (Peter Banks Lp)	CD	One Way	S21-17414	U.S.A.	1993	13.99
Yes/Flash	Psychosync (Peter Banks Lp)	CD	Blueprint	BP242CD	EU	1997	15.99
Yes/Igor Khoroshev	Piano Works	CD	IK	7101	U.S.A.	1999	14.99
Yes/London Philharmonic	Symphonic Music Of Yes	CD	RCA	09026-61938-2	U.S.A.	1993	12.99
Yes/London Philharmonic	Symphonic Music Of Yes	CD	BMG	BVCF-1516	Japan	1993	12.99
Yes/Peter Banks	Can I Play You Somethng?	CD	Blueprint	BP301CD	England	1999	13.99
Yes/Peter Banks	Instinct	CD	Wildcat	WLD-9205	U.S.A.	1994	6.99
Yes/Peter Banks	Self-Contained	CD	One Way	OW-30339	U.S.A.	1995	7.99
Yes/Peter Banks	Two Sides Of (Wetton/Collins/Hackett)	CD	One Way	S21-18009	U.S.A.	1994	34.99
Yes/The Verge	Yes Remixes (W/Slipcase)	CD	Rhino	R2-73872	U.S.A.	2003	8.99
Yes/Various Artists	Affirmative: The Yes Solo Family Album	CD	Connoisseur	VSOP-CD-190	England	1993	14.99
Yes/Various Artists	Friends And Relatives	2CD	Purple Pyramid	CLP-0337-2	U.S.A.	1998	7.99
YMO/R Sakamoto	BMG	CD	Restless	7-72703-2	Canada	1981	13.99
YMO/R Sakamoto	Complete Service	2CD	Alfa	ALCA-9055/6	Japan	1999	28.99
YMO/R Sakamoto	Service	CD	Restless	7-72706-2	Canada	1983	13.99
YMO/R Sakamoto	Technodon	CD	Toshiba-EMI	TOCT-24245	Japan	1993	34.99
YMO/R Sakamoto	UCYMO (3D Ltd Cover)	2CD	SME	MHCL-295-6	Japan	2003	51.99
Yogi, Maharishi Mahesh	Maharishi Mahesh Yogi	CD	BGO	BGOCD331	England	1999	14.99
Youlden, Chris	Second Sight	CD	Line	LICD-9.01027-0	Germany	1991	14.99
Youlden, Chris	Soulmate	CD Single	Line	LICD-9.01199-0	Germany	1992	7.99
Young Fresh Fellows	Includes A Helmet	CD	Line	UTCD-9.00987-L	Germany	1990	15.99
Young Gods	Young Gods	CD	Line	TCCD-9.00455-0	Germany	1987	19.99
Young, James	Out On A Day Pass	CD	Line	FBCD-9.00551-0	Germany	1988	13.99
Young, James	Out On A Day Pass	CD	Absolute	ABSCD-102	U.S.A.	1993	13.99
Young, James/Jan Hammer	City Slicker	CD	Absolute	ABSCD-101	U.S.A.	1985	14.99
Young, La Monte	Just Stompin' Live....	CD	Rhino	R2-79487	U.S.A.	1993	49.99
Young, La Monte	The Second Dream...	CD	Rhino	R2-79467	U.S.A.	1990	99.99
Young, La Monte	The Well - Tuned Piano	CD	Rhino	R2-79452	U.S.A.	1992	49.99
Young, Neil	After The Gold Rush	CD	Reprise	2283-2	U.S.A.	1970	8.99
Young, Neil	After The Goldrush	CD	Warner Bros.	WPCR-2529	Japan	1997	24.99
Young, Neil	Are You Passionate?	CD	Reprise	9-48111-2	U.S.A.	2002	7.99
Young, Neil	Comes A Time	CD	Reprise	2266-2	U.S.A.	1978	8.99
Young, Neil	Dead Man O.S.T. (Advanced Promo)	CD	Vapor	VAPOR-46171	U.S.A.	1996	10.99
Young, Neil	Decade	2CD	Reprise	2257-2	U.S.A.	1977	14.99
Young, Neil	Eldorado	CD	Warner Bros.	20P2-2651	Japan	1989	50.99
Young, Neil	Everybody Knows This Is Nowhere	CD	Reprise	2282-2	U.S.A.	1969	8.99
Young, Neil	Everybody's Rockin'	CD	Geffen	069-490-706-2	U.S.A.	2000	8.99
Young, Neil	Freedom	CD	Reprise	9-25899-2	U.S.A.	1989	7.99
Young, Neil	Freedom (Promo Picture Disc)	CD	Reprise	9-25899-2	U.S.A.	1989	9.99

Y

Artist	Title	Format	Label	Catalog No	Country	Released	Value
Young, Neil	Harvest	CD	Reprise	2277-2	U.S.A.	1972	8.99
Young, Neil	Harvest	CD	Warner Bros.	WPCR-2530	Japan	1997	24.99
Young, Neil	Harvest	DVD Aud	Reprise	9-48100-9	U.S.A.	2002	14.99
Young, Neil	Harvest Moon	CD	Reprise	9-45057-2	U.S.A.	1992	8.99
Young, Neil	Harvest Moon	CD	Warner Bros.	WPCP-4992	Japan	1992	10.99
Young, Neil	Landing On Water	CD	Geffen	9-24109-2	U.S.A.	1986	8.99
Young, Neil	Life	CD	Geffen	9-24154-2	U.S.A.	1987	8.99
Young, Neil	Lucky Thirteen	CD	Geffen	GEFCD-24452	U.S.A.	1993	6.99
Young, Neil	Mirrorball (Cardboard Version)	CD	Reprise	9-45934-2	U.S.A.	1995	15.99
Young, Neil	Mystery Train	CD	Polydor	9493014	Germany	2001	6.99
Young, Neil	Neil Young	CD	Reprise	6317-2	U.S.A.	1969	8.99
Young, Neil	Neil Young Unplugged	CD	Reprise	9-45310-2	U.S.A.	1993	8.99
Young, Neil	No More (Promo)	CD Single	Reprise	PRO-CD-3864	U.S.A.	1989	9.99
Young, Neil	Old Ways (MFSL Gold Cd)	CD	Mobile Fidelity	UDCD-663	U.S.A.	1985	23.99
Young, Neil	Ragged Glory	CD	Reprise	9-26315-2	U.S.A.	1990	8.99
Young, Neil	Road Rock - Friends & Relatives	CD	Reprise	9-48036-2	U.S.A.	2000	8.99
Young, Neil	Silver & Gold	CD	Reprise	9-47305-2	U.S.A.	2000	7.99
Young, Neil	Silver And Gold (Deluxe Ltd Ed.)	CD	Reprise	9-47742-2	U.S.A.	2000	24.99
Young, Neil	The Needle And The Damage Done	CD Single	Reprise	9362-40958-2	Germany	1993	7.99
Young, Neil	Trans	CD	Geffen	GED-2018	Germany	2002	14.99
Young, Neil	Words And Music	CD	Reprise	PRO-CD-100173	U.S.A.	2000	10.99
Young, Neil	Zuma	CD	Reprise	2242-2	U.S.A.	1975	8.99
Young, Neil/Bluenotes	This Note's For You	CD	Reprise	9-25719-2	U.S.A.	1988	6.99
Young, Neil/Bluenotes	This Note's For You (Promo)	CD Single	Reprise	PRO-CD-3091	U.S.A.	1988	14.99
Young, Neil/Crazy Horse	Arc	CD	Reprise	9-26746-2	U.S.A.	1991	10.99
Young, Neil/Crazy Horse	Big Time	CD Single	Reprise	936-243-731-2	Germany	1996	5.99
Young, Neil/Crazy Horse	Broken Arrow (Cardboard Cover)	CD	Reprise	9-46291-2	U.S.A.	1996	6.99
Young, Neil/Crazy Horse	Complex Sessions	CD Single	Reprise	PRO-CD-7342	U.S.A.	1994	29.99
Young, Neil/Crazy Horse	Don't Spook The Horse (DJ Sampler)	CD	Reprise	C2-121544-01	U.S.A.	1997	17.99
Young, Neil/Crazy Horse	Live Rust	CD	Reprise	2296-2	U.S.A.	1979	8.99
Young, Neil/Crazy Horse	Mansion On The Hill	CD	Reprise	9-21759-2	U.S.A.	1990	7.99
Young, Neil/Crazy Horse	Rust Never Sleeps	CD	Reprise	2295-2	U.S.A.	1979	8.99
Young, Neil/Crazy Horse	Sleeps With Angels	CD	Reprise	9-45749-2	U.S.A.	1994	6.99
Young, Neil/Crazy Horse	Weld	2CD	Reprise	9-26627-2	U.S.A.	1991	10.99
Young, Neil/Crazy Horse	Year Of The Horse	2CD	Reprise	9-46652-2	U.S.A.	1997	13.99
Young, Paul	Oh, Girl (Promo)	CD	Columbia	CSK-73377	U.S.A.	1990	5.99
Young, Paul	The Secret Of Association	CD	Columbia	CK-39957	U.S.A.	1985	4.99
Young, Steve	To Satisfy You	CD	Line	SDCD-9.00143-0	Germany	1989	24.99
Young, Victor	Around The World In 80 Days (O.S.T.)	CD	MCA	MCAD-31134	U.S.A.	1958	8.99
Youngbloods	Earth Music	CD	Edsel	EDCD-274	England	1994	13.99
Youngbloods	Elephant Mountain	CD	Line	LECD-9.01021-0	Germany	1990	13.99
Youngbloods	Elephant Mountain (MFSL Silver Cd)	CD	Mobile Fidelity	MFCD-792	U.S.A.	1969	56.99
Youngbloods	Get Together/Elephant Mountain	CD	One Way	OW-34535	U.S.A.	1999	16.99
Youngbloods	Ride The Wind	CD	Line	LECD-9.01021	Germany	1990	13.99
Youngbloods	Rock Festival	CD	Line	LECD-9.01012-0	Germany	1990	13.99
Youngbloods	Self Titled	CD	Edsel	EDCD-271	England	1994	13.99

Z

Artist	Title	Format	Label	Catalog No	Country	Released	Value
Zappa, Dweezil	Automatic	CD	Favored Nations	FN2050-2	U.S.A.	2000	13.99
Zappa, Dweezil	Confessions	CD	Barking Pumpkin	D2-74232	U.S.A.	1991	13.99
Zappa, Dweezil	Havin' A Bad Day	CD	Rykodisc	RCD-10057	U.S.A.	1990	15.99
Zappa, Dweezil	My Guitar Wants To Kill Your Mama	CD	Chrysalis	VK-41633	U.S.A.	1988	14.99
Zappa, Dweezil	Vanity Cd	CD	Barking Pumpkin	BPCD-666	U.S.A.	1992	19.99

Artist	Title	Format	Label	Catalog No	Country	Released	Value
Zappa, Dweezil/Ahmet	Music For Pets (Promo)	CD	Zappa	UMRK-6970P-3	U.S.A.	1995	10.99
Zappa, Dweezil/Ahmet	Shampoohorn - Z	CD	Barking Pumpkin	BPCD-71706	U.S.A.	1994	18.99
Zappa, Frank	200 Motels + 5	2CD	Rykodisc	RCD-10513/14	U.S.A.	1997	23.99
Zappa, Frank	Absolutely Free	CD	Rykodisc	RCD-10502	U.S.A.	1995	8.99
Zappa, Frank	Ahead Of Their Time	CD	Rykodisc	RCD-10559	U.S.A.	1995	7.99
Zappa, Frank	Apostrophe	CD	Rykodisc	RCD-10519	U.S.A.	1995	8.99
Zappa, Frank	Apostrophe (Rykodisc Gold Cd)	CD	Rykodisc	RCD-80519	U.S.A.	1995	28.99
Zappa, Frank	Apostrophe/O Sensation (Remixed)	CD	Rykodisc	RCD-40025	U.S.A.	1986	17.99
Zappa, Frank	Baby Snakes	CD	Rykodisc	RCD-10539	U.S.A.	1995	10.99
Zappa, Frank	Beat Boots Box 1 (W/T-Shirt & Button)	9CD	Rhino	R-70907	U.S.A.	1991	249.99
Zappa, Frank	Beat The Boots Box 2 (W/Beret & Pin)	8CD	Rhino	R-70372	U.S.A.	1992	249.99
Zappa, Frank	Boulez Conducts Zappa/P Stranger	CD	Rykodisc	RCD-10542	U.S.A.	1995	8.99
Zappa, Frank	Broadway The Hard Way	CD	Rykodisc	RCD-10552	U.S.A.	1995	9.99
Zappa, Frank	Burnt Weeny Sandwich	CD	Rykodisc	RCD-10509	U.S.A.	1995	12.99
Zappa, Frank	Cheap Thrills	CD	Rykodisc	RCD-10579	U.S.A.	1998	6.99
Zappa, Frank	Chunga's Revenge	CD	Rykodisc	RCD-10511	U.S.A.	1995	10.99
Zappa, Frank	Civilization Phaze III - Act 1 (Hrdbk Cvr)	2CD	Barking Pumpkin	UMRK-01	U.S.A.	1994	34.99
Zappa, Frank	Clean American Version (In-Store CD)	CD	Rykodisc	VRCD-0501	U.S.A.	1995	9.99
Zappa, Frank	Cruising With Ruben & The Jets	CD	Rykodisc	RCD-10505	U.S.A.	1995	11.99
Zappa, Frank	Cucamonga	CD	Del-Fi	71261	U.S.A.	1998	6.99
Zappa, Frank	Dancin' Fool (Promo Mini Lp)	CD Single	Video Arts	SVAM-0065	Japan	2002	85.99
Zappa, Frank	Ditties And Beer (Promo)	CD	Rykodisc	ZAP-2	England	1993	26.99
Zappa, Frank	Does Humor Belong in Music?	CD	Rykodisc	RCD-10548	U.S.A.	1995	8.99
Zappa, Frank	Everything Is Healing Nicely	CD	UMRK	03	U.S.A.	1999	59.99
Zappa, Frank	Fillmore East: June 1971	CD	Rykodisc	RCD-10512	U.S.A.	1995	10.99
Zappa, Frank	For Collectors Only	CD	Disky	DC-905010	Netherlands	2003	7.99
Zappa, Frank	Francesco Zappa	CD	Rykodisc	RCD-10546	U.S.A.	1995	8.99
Zappa, Frank	Frank Zappa Meets The Mothers...	CD	Rykodisc	RCD-10547	U.S.A.	1995	9.99
Zappa, Frank	Freak Out!	CD	Rykodisc	RCD-10501	U.S.A.	1995	9.99
Zappa, Frank	FZ: OZ	CD	Vaulternative	VAULT-1	U.S.A.	2002	59.99
Zappa, Frank	Guitar	2CD	Rykodisc	RCD-10550/51	U.S.A.	1995	24.99
Zappa, Frank	Half A Dozen Provocative Squats (DJ)	CD	Rykodisc	VRCD-0513/14	U.S.A.	1997	12.99
Zappa, Frank	Halloween	DVD Aud	Vaulternative	1101	U.S.A.	2003	17.99
Zappa, Frank	Have I Offended Someone?	CD	Rykodisc	RCD-10577	U.S.A.	1997	9.99
Zappa, Frank	Hot Rats	CD	Rykodisc	RCD-10508	U.S.A.	1995	10.99
Zappa, Frank	Hot Rats (Rykodisc Gold Cd)	CD	Rykodisc	RCD-10066	U.S.A.	1987	121.99
Zappa, Frank	Jazz From Hell	CD	Rykodisc	RCD-10549	U.S.A.	1995	9.99
Zappa, Frank	Jazz from Hell	CD	Rykodisc	RCD-10549	U.S.A.	1995	9.99
Zappa, Frank	Joe's Garage: Acts 1-3	2CD	Rykodisc	RCD-10530/31	U.S.A.	1995	16.99
Zappa, Frank	Just Another Band From L.A.	CD	Rykodisc	RCD-10515	U.S.A.	1995	14.99
Zappa, Frank	Kill Ugly Radio (Promo)	CD	Rykodisc	VRCD-0502	U.S.A.	1995	29.99
Zappa, Frank	Kill Ugly Radio Some More (Promo)	CD	Rykodisc	VRCD-0503	U.S.A.	1995	29.99
Zappa, Frank	Läther	3CD	Rykodisc	RCD-10574/76	U.S.A.	1996	19.99
Zappa, Frank	Left Of The Dial (Promo)	CD	Rykodisc	VRCD-0505	U.S.A.	1996	12.99
Zappa, Frank	London Symphony Orchestra, Vols. 1/2	2CD	Rykodisc	RCD-10540/41	U.S.A.	1987	12.99
Zappa, Frank	Lumpy Gravy	CD	Rykodisc	RCD-10504	U.S.A.	1995	8.99
Zappa, Frank	Make A Jazz Noise	2CD	Rykodisc	RCD-10555/56	U.S.A.	1995	18.99
Zappa, Frank	Mystery Disc	CD	Rykodisc	RCD-10580	U.S.A.	1998	9.99
Zappa, Frank	No Commercial Potential (Promo)	CD	Rykodisc	ZAP-1	England	1993	24.99
Zappa, Frank	One Size Fits All	CD	Rykodisc	RCD-10521	U.S.A.	1995	9.99
Zappa, Frank	One Size Fits All (Rykodisc Gold Cd)	CD	Rykodisc	RCD-80521	U.S.A.	1995	34.99
Zappa, Frank	Orchestral Favorites	CD	Rykodisc	RCD-10529	U.S.A.	1995	8.99
Zappa, Frank	Over-Nite Sensation	CD	Rykodisc	RCD-10518	U.S.A.	1995	8.99
Zappa, Frank	Peaches En Regalia 3 "	CD Single	Rykodisc	RCD3-1001	U.S.A.	1985	7.99
Zappa, Frank	Playground Psychotics	2CD	Rykodisc	RCD-10557/58	U.S.A.	1995	21.99
Zappa, Frank	Rare Meat	CD	Del-Fi	70010-2	U.S.A.	1994	8.99
Zappa, Frank	Return Of Son Of Kill Ugly Radio (DJ)	CD	Rykodisc	VRCD-0504	U.S.A.	1996	29.99
Zappa, Frank	Roxy & Elsewhere	CD	Rykodisc	RCD-10520	U.S.A.	1995	8.99

Z

Artist	Title	Format	Label	Catalog No	Country	Released	Value
Zappa, Frank	Sexual Harassment in the Workplace 3 "	CD Single	Rykodisc	RCD3-1010	U.S.A.	1988	7.99
Zappa, Frank	Sheik Yerbouti	CD	Rykodisc	RCD-10528	U.S.A.	1995	9.99
Zappa, Frank	Ship Arriving Too Late...	CD	Rykodisc	RCD-10537	U.S.A.	1995	8.99
Zappa, Frank	Shut Up 'N Play Yer Guitar [Complete]	3CD	Rykodisc	RCD-10533/34/35	U.S.A.	1995	19.99
Zappa, Frank	Sleep Dirt	CD	Rykodisc	RCD-10527	U.S.A.	1995	9.99
Zappa, Frank	Son of Cheap Thrills	CD	Rykodisc	RCD-10581	U.S.A.	1999	6.99
Zappa, Frank	Stricly Genteel	CD	Rykodisc	RCD-10578	U.S.A.	1997	10.99
Zappa, Frank	Strictly Commercial	CD	Rykodisc	RCD-40500	U.S.A.	1995	10.99
Zappa, Frank	Strictly Commercial (Red Case)	CD	Rykodisc	VRCD-10500	Canada	1995	34.99
Zappa, Frank	Studio Tan	CD	Rykodisc	RCD-10526	U.S.A.	1995	8.99
Zappa, Frank	The Best Band You Never...	2CD	Rykodisc	RCD-10553/54	U.S.A.	1995	14.99
Zappa, Frank	The Grand Wazoo	CD	Rykodisc	RCD-10517	U.S.A.	1995	9.99
Zappa, Frank	The Interviews Volume 2	CD	Baktabak	CBAK4074	England	1996	9.99
Zappa, Frank	The Lost Episodes	CD	Rykodisc	RCD-40573	U.S.A.	1996	6.99
Zappa, Frank	The Man From Utopia	CD	Rykodisc	RCD-10538	U.S.A.	1995	8.99
Zappa, Frank	The Yellow Shark	CD	Rykodisc	RCD-10560	U.S.A.	1995	14.99
Zappa, Frank	Them or Us	CD	Rykodisc	RCD-10543	U.S.A.	1995	9.99
Zappa, Frank	Thing-Fish	2CD	Rykodisc	RCD-10544/45	U.S.A.	1995	23.99
Zappa, Frank	Threesome No. 1 Box Set	3CD	Rykodisc	RCD-40582	U.S.A.	2002	24.99
Zappa, Frank	Threesome No. 2 Box Set	3CD	Rykodisc	RCD-40583	U.S.A.	2002	24.99
Zappa, Frank	Tinsel Town Rebellion	CD	Rykodisc	RCD-10532	U.S.A.	1995	10.99
Zappa, Frank	Uncle Meat	2CD	Rykodisc	RCD-10506/07	U.S.A.	1995	17.99
Zappa, Frank	Waka/Jawaka	CD	Rykodisc	RCD-10516	U.S.A.	1995	8.99
Zappa, Frank	Weasels Ripped My Flesh	CD	Rykodisc	RCD-10510	U.S.A.	1995	8.99
Zappa, Frank	We're Only In It For The Money	CD	Rykodisc	RCD-10503	U.S.A.	1995	11.99
Zappa, Frank	We're Only In/Lumpy Gravy (Remixed)	CD	Rykodisc	RCD-40024	U.S.A.	1986	12.99
Zappa, Frank	You Are What You Is	CD	Rykodisc	RCD-10536	U.S.A.	1995	13.99
Zappa, Frank	You Cant Do That... Vol. 5	CD	Rykodisc	RCD-10569-/70	U.S.A.	1995	14.99
Zappa, Frank	You Can't Do That... Vol. 1	2CD	Rykodisc	RCD-10561/62	U.S.A.	1995	14.99
Zappa, Frank	You Can't Do That... Vol. 6	2CD	Rykodisc	RCD-10571/72	U.S.A.	1995	14.99
Zappa, Frank	You Can't Do That..., Vol. 2	2CD	Rykodisc	RCD-10563/64	U.S.A.	1995	14.99
Zappa, Frank	You Can't Do That..., Vol. 3	2CD	Rykodisc	RCD-10565/66	U.S.A.	1995	14.99
Zappa, Frank	You Can't Do That..., Vol. 4	2CD	Rykodisc	RCD-10567/68	U.S.A.	1995	14.99
Zappa, Frank	Zappa in New York	2CD	Rykodisc	RCD-10524/25	U.S.A.	1995	14.99
Zappa, Frank	Zappa Picks [Jonathan Fishman/Phish]	CD	Rykodisc	RCD-10584	U.S.A.	2002	7.99
Zappa, Frank	Zappa Picks [Larry LaLonde/Primus)	CD	Rykodisc	RCD-10585	U.S.A.	2002	6.99
Zappa, Frank	Zappa Plays Zappa: A Tribute	CD	UMRK	02	U.S.A.	1996	29.99
Zappa, Frank	Zomby Woof	CD Single	Rykodisc	RCD3-1011	U.S.A.	1988	12.99
Zappa, Frank	Zoot Allures	CD	Rykodisc	RCD-10523	U.S.A.	1995	9.99
Zappa, Frank/Atsushi Yanaka	Tokyo Ska Paradise Orch Meets	CD	Video Arts	VACK-1179	Japan	2001	24.99
Zappa, Frank/Bossini	Prophetic Attitude	CD	L 'Empreinte Digitale	13071	Canada	1997	24.99
Zappa, Frank/C. Beefheart	Bongo Fury	CD	Rykodisc	RCD-10522	U.S.A.	1995	9.99
Zappa, Frank/Ed Palermo	E P Big Band Plays F Zappa	CD	Astor Place	4005	U.S.A.	1997	54.99
Zappa, Frank/GTO's	Permanent Damage	CD	Enigma	7-73397-2	U.S.A.	1989	60.99
Zappa, Frank/Persuasions	Frankly A Cappella	CD	Rhino	R2-79832	U.S.A.	2000	9.99
Zappa, Frank/Tribute	Zappa's Universe	CD	Polygram	314-513-575-2	U.S.A.	1993	8.99
Zappa/MGM Soundtracks	Sneak Preview, Volume 1 (Promo)	2CD	Rykodisc	VRCD-0700	U.S.A.	1997	19.99
Zappa/Pamela Des Barres	I'm With The Band	CD	Warner Bros.	2-523539	U.S.A.	1995	13.99
Zappa/Wild Man Fischer	The Fischer King	2CD	Rhino	RHM2-7701	U.S.A.	1999	54.99
Zazou, Hector	Sahara Blue (2 Withdrwn Sylvian Trks)	CD	Tristar	WK-57779	U.S.A.	1992	66.99
Zazou, Hector	Sahara Blue (2 Withdrwn Sylvian Trks)	CD	Made To Measure	MTM32	England	1992	66.99
Zazou, Hector	Sahara Blue (2 Withdrwn Sylvian Trks)	CD	Ariola	74321-11208-2	Germany	1992	66.99
Zazou, Hector	Songs From The Cold Seas	CD	Columbia	CK-67068	U.S.A.	1994	8.99
Zazou, Hector/John Cale	The Long Voyages (7 Remix Version)	CD Single	Columbia	COL-661201-5	France	1995	24.99
Zazou, Hector/John Cale	The Long Voyages [3 Remix Version]	CD Single	Columbia	COL-661201-2	France	1995	10.99
Zebra	3.V	CD	Atlantic	7-81692-2	U.S.A.	1986	13.99
Zebra	IV	CD	Frontiers	FR-CD-158	Italy	2003	15.99
Zebra	KBFH Presents Zebra Live	CD	King Biscuit	70710-88052-2	U.S.A.	1999	10.99

Z

Artist	Title	Format	Label	Catalog No	Country	Released	Value
Zebra	Live	CD	Atlantic	7-82094-2	U.S.A.	1990	11.99
Zebra	No Tellin' Lies	CD	Atlantic	7-80159-2	U.S.A.	1984	21.99
Zebra	No Tellin' Lies/3.V	CD	One Way	OW-35172	U.S.A.	2001	8.99
Zebra	Self Titled	CD	Atlantic	7-80054-2	U.S.A.	1983	12.99
Zebra	The Best Of: In Black And White	CD	Mayhem	9086-11133-2	U.S.A.	1998	12.99
Zeno	Listen To The Heart + 3	CD	Toshiba-EMI	TOCP-67247	Japan	2000	34.99
Zeno	Listen To The Light + 3	CD	MTM	199654	Germany	1999	14.99
Zeno	On The Road	CD	Play	10009	U.S.A.	2003	7.99
Zeno	Self Titled	CD	Toshiba-EMI	TOCP-67245	Japan	2000	33.99
Zeno	Zenology	CD	Zero	XRCN-1226	Japan	1995	13.99
Zeno	Zenology + 4	CD	Toshiba-EMI	TOCP-67246	Japan	2000	34.99
Zephyr	Going Back To Colorado	CD	Warner Bros.	1897-2	U.S.A.	1971	13.99
Zephyr	Going Back To Colorado	CD	Warner Bros.	WPCR-32	Japan	1994	24.99
Zephyr	Sunset Ride	CD	One Way	OW-35170	U.S.A.	2000	13.99
Zephyr	Zephyr	CD	BGO	BGOCD41	England	1990	10.99
Zephyr	Zephyr Live	CD	Tommy Bolin	TBACD-6	England	1997	13.99
Zero	Chance In A Million	CD	Whirled	WRR-1960	U.S.A.	1994	5.99
Zero	Here Goes Nothin' (MFSL Silver Cd)	CD	Mobile Fidelity	MFCD-778	U.S.A.	1987	41.99
Zero	Nothin' Goes Here (MFSL Silver Cd)	CD	Mobile Fidelity	MFCD-784	U.S.A.	1990	34.99
Zero	Nothin' Lasts Forever	CD	Pop Mafia	PMR90017	U.S.A.	1998	5.99
Zero	Zero	CD	Pop Mafia	PM010	U.S.A.	1997	5.99
Zevon, Warren	A Quiet Normal Life: The Best Of	CD	Asylum	60503-2	U.S.A.	1986	7.99
Zevon, Warren	Bad Luck Streak In Dancing School	CD	Elektra	7559-60561-2	Germany	1980	8.99
Zevon, Warren	Excitable Boy	CD	Asylum	118-2	U.S.A.	1978	9.99
Zevon, Warren	Genius: The Best Of	CD	Rhino	R2-73771	U.S.A.	2002	9.99
Zevon, Warren	I'll Sleep When I'm Dead	2CD	Rhino	R2-73510	U.S.A.	1996	24.99
Zevon, Warren	Learning to Flinch [Felt/Metal Edition]	CD	Giant	24496-2	U.S.A.	1993	22.99
Zevon, Warren	Life'll Kill Ya	CD	Artemis	751003	U.S.A.	2000	11.99
Zevon, Warren	Mr. Bad Example	CD	Giant	24431-2	U.S.A.	1991	39.99
Zevon, Warren	Mutineer	CD	Giant	24618-2	U.S.A.	1995	11.99
Zevon, Warren	My Ride's Here	CD	Artemis	751124	U.S.A.	2002	12.99
Zevon, Warren	Self Titled	CD	Asylum	1060	U.S.A.	1976	8.99
Zevon, Warren	Sentimental Hygiene + 2	CD	Capitol	7-80621-2	U.S.A.	2003	9.99
Zevon, Warren	The First Sessions + 2	CD	Varese	066438	U.S.A.	2003	9.99
Zevon, Warren	Transverse City + 1	CD	Capitol	7-80620-2	U.S.A.	2003	8.99
Zevon, Warren	Wanted Dead Or Alive	CD	One Way	72438-19048-24	U.S.A.	1996	10.99
Zevon, Warren	Wanted Dead or Alive/A Leaf in ..	CD	Capitol	7-80741-2	U.S.A.	2003	10.99
Zombie, Rob	American Made Music to Strip By	CD	Interscope	490349	U.S.A.	1999	7.99
Zombie, Rob	American Made Music to Strip.. [Clean]	CD	Interscope	490499	U.S.A.	1999	7.99
Zombie, Rob	Hellbilly Deluxe	CD	Geffen	25212	U.S.A.	1998	8.99
Zombie, Rob	Hellbilly Deluxe [Clean]	CD	Geffen	25305	U.S.A.	1998	8.99
Zombie, Rob	Living Dead Girl	CD Single	Geffen	GED-22377	EU	1999	5.99
Zombie, Rob	The Sinister Urge [Clean]	CD	Universal	493162	U.S.A.	2001	8.99
Zombie, Rob	The Sinister Urge [W/Bonus CD]	2CD	Universal	493210	U.S.A.	2001	14.99
Zombies	Begin Here	CD	Line	BACD-9.00837-L	Germany	1989	19.99
Zombies	Begin Here + 17	CD	Repertoire	REP-4939	Germany	2001	14.99
Zombies	EP Collection	CD	See For Miles	SEECD-358	England	1992	13.99
Zombies	Live On The BBC	CD	Victor Ent.	VICP-61638	Japan	2001	24.99
Zombies	Odessey And Oracle + 16	CD	Repertoire	REP-4940	Germany	2001	13.99
Zombies	Singles A's & B's	2CD	Repertoire	REP-4985	Germany	2002	14.99
Zombies	The Zombies Collection Vol.1	CD	Line	IMCD-9.00692-0	Germany	1989	19.99
Zombies	Zombie Heaven (Promo Sampler)	CD	Big Beat	ZOMPROM-1	England	1997	24.99
Zombies	Zombie Heaven Box Set	4CD	Big Beat	ZOMBOX-7	England	1997	44.99
Zombies	Zombies Collection Vol.2	CD	Line	IMCD-9.00693-0	Germany	1989	19.99
Zombies/Colin Blunstone	Some Years: It's The Time Of	CD	Epic	EK-66449	U.S.A.	1995	19.99
Zonazul	Zonazul	CD	Line	RICD-9.00836-0	Germany	1989	14.99
Zoo, The	Shakin' The Cage	CD	Capricorn	9-42004-2	U.S.A.	1992	4.99
Zoppi	One Sun (Promo)	CD Single	MCA	MCAR-25026-2	U.S.A.	2000	5.99

Z

Artist	Title	Format	Label	Catalog No	Country	Released	Value
ZZ Top	Afterburner	CD	Warner Bros.	25342-2	U.S.A.	1985	7.99
ZZ Top	Antenna	CD	RCA	66317	U.S.A.	1994	7.99
ZZ Top	Antenna (Promo Sampler)	CD	RCA	RDJ-62732-2	U.S.A.	1990	18.99
ZZ Top	Deguello	CD	Warner Bros.	3361-2	U.S.A.	1987	8.99
ZZ Top	Double Back/Back To The Future III	CD Single	Warner Bros.	7599-21561-2	France	1990	10.99
ZZ Top	El Loco	CD	Warner Bros.	3593-2	U.S.A.	1987	8.99
ZZ Top	Eliminator	CD	Warner Bros.	23774-2	Australia	1983	7.99
ZZ Top	Fandango	CD	Warner Bros.	256604	Australia	1975	8.99
ZZ Top	First Album	CD	Warner Bros.	3268-2	U.S.A.	1987	8.99
ZZ Top	Greatest Hits	CD	Warner Bros.	26846-2	U.S.A.	1992	8.99
ZZ Top	Mescalero	CD	RCA	51168	U.S.A.	2003	8.99
ZZ Top	One Foot In The Blues	CD	Warner Bros.	45815-2	U.S.A.	1994	9.99
ZZ Top	Recycler	CD	Warner Bros.	26265-2	U.S.A.	1990	6.99
ZZ Top	Recycler (Limited Edition/Metal)	CD	Warner Bros.	9-26458-2	U.S.A.	1990	34.99
ZZ Top	Rhythmeen	CD	RCA	66956	U.S.A.	1996	7.99
ZZ Top	Rio Grande Mud	CD	Warner Bros.	3269-2	U.S.A.	1987	8.99
ZZ Top	Six Pack	3CD	Warner Bros.	25661-2	U.S.A.	1987	22.99
ZZ Top	Tejas	CD	Warner Bros.	3272-2	U.S.A.	1987	7.99
ZZ Top	The Best Of	CD	Warner Bros.	3273-2	U.S.A.	1984	9.99
ZZ Top	Tres Hombres	CD	Warner Bros.	3270-2	U.S.A.	1987	9.99
ZZ Top	XXX	CD	RCA	67850	U.S.A.	1999	8.99
Zzebra	Panic	CD	Disconforme	DISC1955CD	Andorra	1999	12.99
Zzebra	Self Titled	CD	Disconforme	DISC1954CD	Andorra	1999	12.99
Zzebra	Take It Or Leave It	CD	Disconforme	DISC1956CD	Andorra	1999	12.99

Z

THE END
OF THE BIG MONKEY

DO YOU WANT A MONKEY ON YOUR BACK?

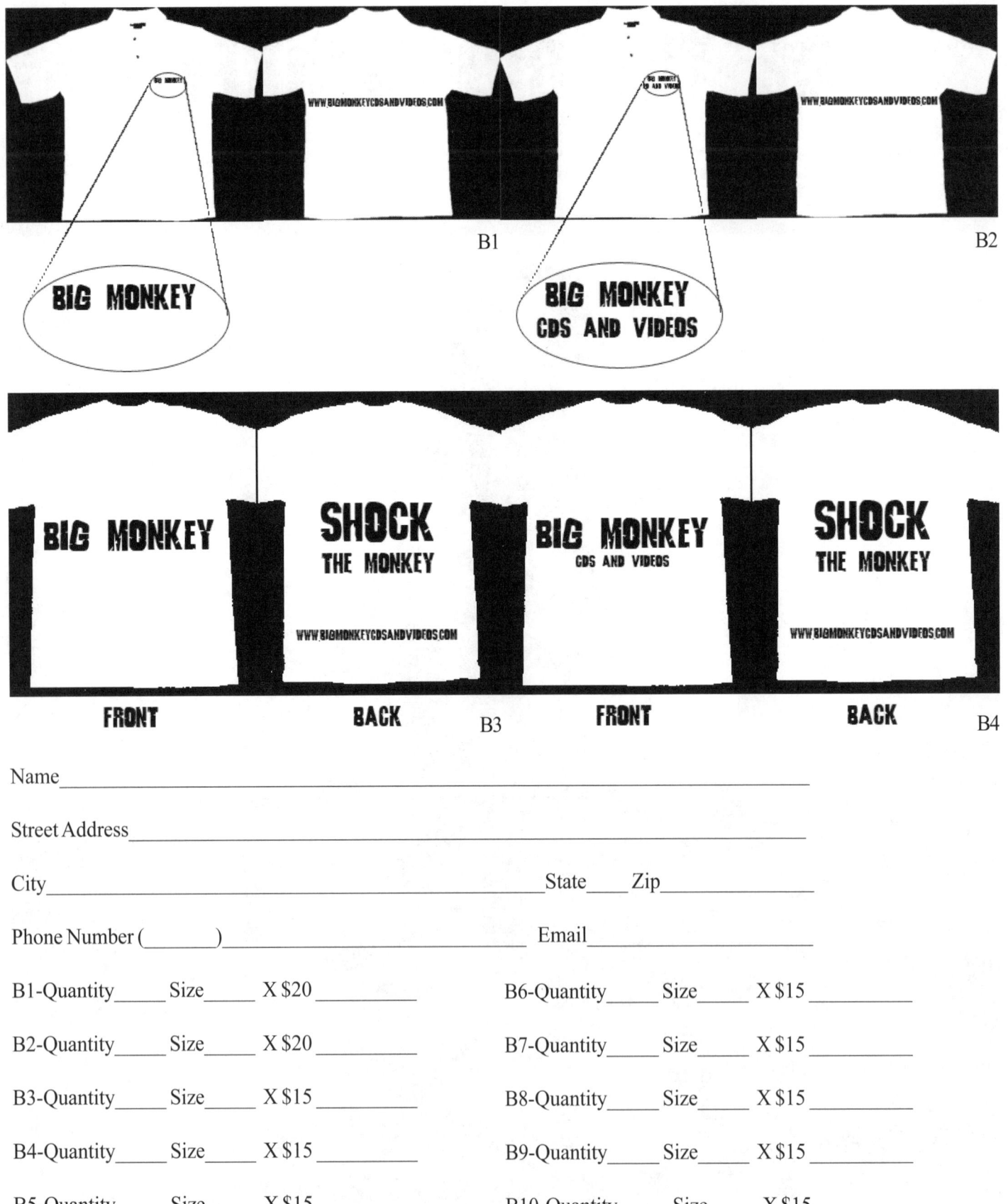

B1

B2

BIG MONKEY

BIG MONKEY
CDS AND VIDEOS

BIG MONKEY   SHOCK
                  THE MONKEY

                  WWW.BIGMONKEYCDSANDVIDEOS.COM

BIG MONKEY   SHOCK
CDS AND VIDEOS   THE MONKEY

                  WWW.BIGMONKEYCDSANDVIDEOS.COM

FRONT   BACK   B3   FRONT   BACK   B4

Name_____

Street Address_____

City_____ State____ Zip_____

Phone Number (_____)_____ Email_____

B1-Quantity_____ Size_____ X $20 _____   B6-Quantity_____ Size_____ X $15 _____

B2-Quantity_____ Size_____ X $20 _____   B7-Quantity_____ Size_____ X $15 _____

B3-Quantity_____ Size_____ X $15 _____   B8-Quantity_____ Size_____ X $15 _____

B4-Quantity_____ Size_____ X $15 _____   B9-Quantity_____ Size_____ X $15 _____

B5-Quantity_____ Size_____ X $15 _____   B10-Quantity_____ Size_____ X $15 _____

DO YOU WANT A MONKEY ON YOUR BACK?

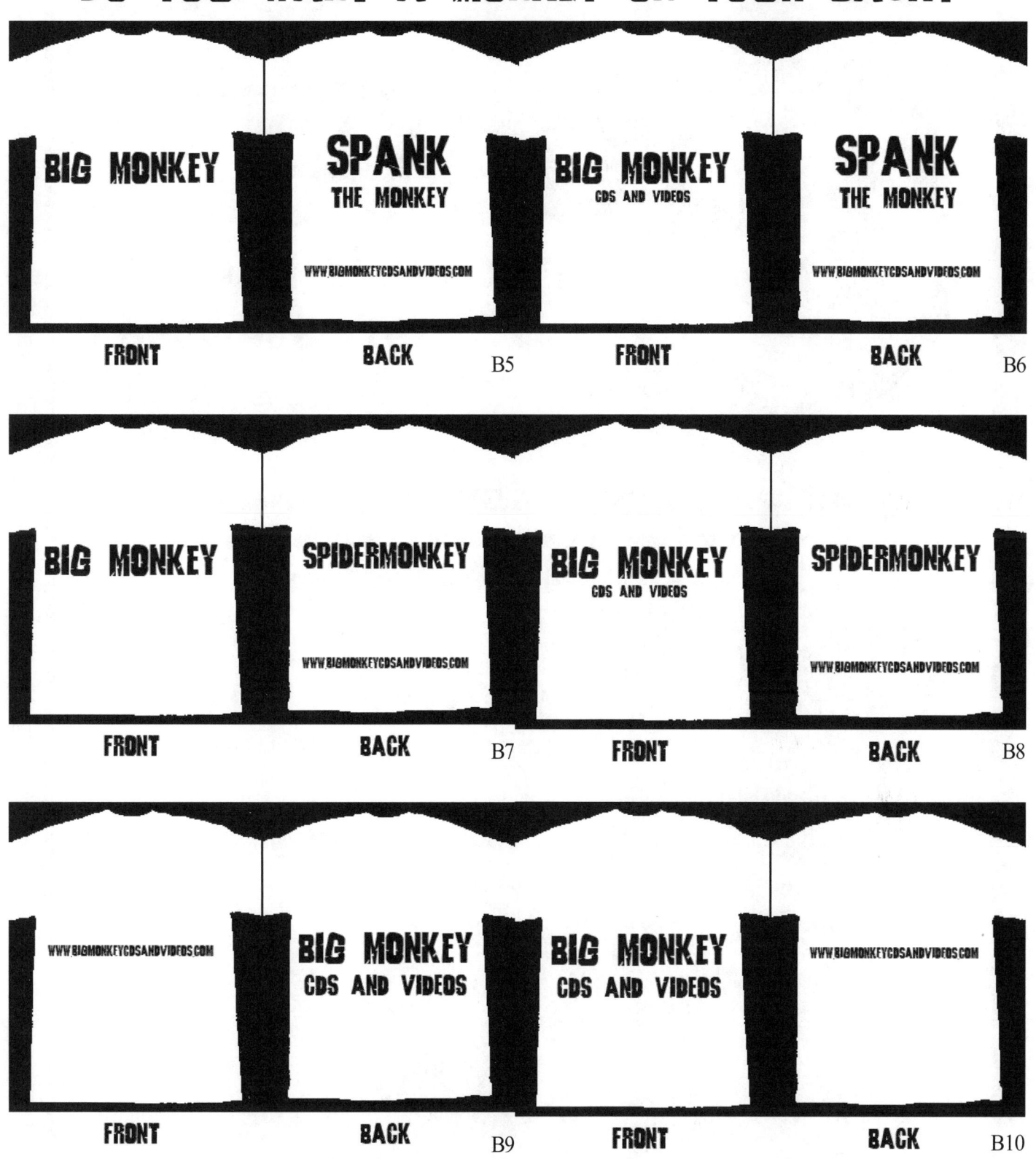

For Mail Orders: Richard A. Colon
3730 Fairfiled Ave. #173
Shreveport, LA 71104

Or Visit: www.bigmonkeycdsandvideos.com
My user ID on eBay is: bigmonkeycdsandvideos